THE FAR EAST AND AUSTRALASIA

1976-77

THE FAR EAST AND AUSTRALASIA

1976–77

A Survey and Directory of Asia and the Pacific

LONDON
EUROPA PUBLICATIONS LIMITED
18 BEDFORD SQUARE WC1B 3JN

Eighth Edition 1976-77

ISBN 0 900 36295 2

Library of Congress Catalog Card Number 74 - 417170

AUSTRALIA AND NEW ZEALAND
James Bennett (Collaroy) Pty. Ltd., Collaroy, N.S.W., Australia

INDIA
UBS Publishers Distributors Pvt. Ltd.,
P.O.B. 1882, 5 Ansari Road, Daryaganj, Delhi 6

JAPAN
Maruzen Co. Ltd., Tokyo

Printed and bound in England by
STAPLES PRINTERS LIMITED
at The Stanhope Press, Rochester, Kent.

Foreword

THE FAR EAST AND AUSTRALASIA is an annual reference book on the countries of Asia, including the Soviet Union in Asia, from Afghanistan eastwards, Australia and New Zealand and the Pacific Islands.

The first part of the book deals with topics relevant to the entire area, such as development problems, trade, commodities and religion, and contains a guide to the major international organizations concerned with the area.

Information on individual countries is given within sections on the major regions of the area: South Asia, South-East Asia, East Asia, Australasia and the Pacific Islands. Each major section has an introductory essay on the regional geography, politics and economy. The essays, by acknowledged experts on the area, present a range of different points of view on the controversial issues involved in Asia and the Pacific. For each country or territory there are essays on its geography, history and economy, a statistical survey and detailed information on its major political, economic and commercial institutions. All information has been revised from authoritative sources, in the country concerned wherever possible.

A general reference section, including biographies of prominent and distinguished personalities in the area, appears after the information on individual countries.

August 1976

Acknowledgements

The co-operation, interest and advice of all the authors who have contributed to this volume have been invaluable and greatly appreciated. We are also, of course, greatly in the debt of innumerable organizations connected with the Asian and Pacific region, especially the national statistical and information offices, whose co-operation in providing information we gratefully acknowledge. We are also indebted to the International Institute for Strategic Studies, 18 Adam Street, London, WC2N 6AL, for the use of defence statistics from *The Military Balance*.

We must also acknowledge our debt to other publications. The following, in particular, have been of immense value in providing regular coverage of the affairs of the Asian and Pacific region: *Asia Research Bulletin*, Singapore; *The Far Eastern Economic Review*, Hong Kong; *The Economist*, London; *IMF Survey*, Washington; and *Keesing's Contemporary Archives*, Keynsham. We are also indebted to the editors of *Business International*, New York, and *The President*, Tokyo, for their assistance in compiling information on the principal industrial companies operating in the region; to Mr. David Goodman, of the Contemporary China Institute, London, for biographies of prominent people in the People's Republic of China; and to Dr. Werner Klatt, O.B.E., for compiling the estimates in the statistical survey of the People's Republic of China.

Contents

General Introduction

Regional Organizations

Australasia

The Pacific Islands

Other Reference Material

Maps

Index of Territories

Contributors

Bryant J. Allen, Department of Geography, University of Papua New Guinea
(Introduction to Pacific Islands, p. 1089.)

John Bastin, Reader, History of South-East Asia, S.O.A.S., University of London.
(History of Brunei, p. 391.)

Charles Bawden, Professor of Mongolian, S.O.A.S., University of London.
(Physical and Social Geography, History and Economic Survey of Mongolia, pp. 934, 935, 938.)

Iain Buchanan, Lecturer in Geography, University of Leicester, England.
(South Asia—Physical, Social and Economic Geography, p. 133, South-East Asia—Physical, Social and Economic Geography, p. 365, Economic Survey of Indonesia, p. 454.)

Keith Buchanan, Professor Emeritus, Victoria University of Wellington, Wellington, New Zealand; Canadian Commonwealth Fellow and Visiting Professor, McGill University, Montreal.
(Asia and the Pacific, p. 3, Population in Asia, p. 29, East Asia—Physical, Social and Economic Geography, p. 681.)

T. M. Burley, Operations Officer, Asian Development Bank, Manila, Philippines.
(History and Economic Survey of Brunei, p. 391, Economic Survey of North Korea, p. 881, South Korea, p. 884, The Philippines, p. 560.)

Malcolm Caldwell, Lecturer in South-East Asian Economic History, S.O.A.S., University of London.
(Economic Survey of Malaysia, p. 518.)

Renato Constantino.
(History of the Philippines, p. 552.)

B. H. Farmer, Director, Centre of South Asian Studies, Cambridge, England.
(Physical and Social Geography of Bangladesh, p. 177, Bhutan, p. 220, India, p. 207, Maldives, p. 274, Nepal, p. 277, Pakistan, p. 293, Sri Lanka, p. 331.)

C. A. Fisher, Professor of Geography, S.O.A.S., University of London.
(Physical and Social Geography of Brunei, p. 391, Burma, p. 400, Cambodia, p. 427, Indonesia, p. 446, Laos, p. 492, Malaysia, p. 509, Philippines, p. 551, Singapore, p. 588, Thailand, p. 615, Viet-Nam, p. 643.)

W. B. Fisher, Professor of Geography, University of Durham, England.
(Physical and Social Geography of Afghanistan, p. 150.)

C. P. FitzGerald, Emeritus Professor, A.N.U., Canberra.
(History of China, p. 704, Taiwan, p. 714.)

Michael Freeberne, Lecturer in Geography, S.O.A.S., University of London.
(Physical and Social Geography of China, p. 701, Hong Kong, p. 774.)

M. P. Gopalan, Press Foundation of Asia, Manila.
(Economic Survey of Hong Kong, p. 778.)

Alec Gordon, Visiting Lecturer in Economics, University of Papua New Guinea.
(Economic Survey of Burma, p. 409, Viet-Nam, p. 652.)

J. M. Gullick, former Malaysian Civil Servant.
(History of Malaysia, p. 510.)

H. A. de S. Gunasekera, Secretary, Ministry of Planning and Economic Affairs, Sri Lanka.
(Economic Survey of Sri Lanka, p. 338.)

Mahmud Husain, Vice-Chancellor, University of Karachi, Pakistan.
(History of Pakistan, p. 294.)

P. H. M. Jones, *Far Eastern Economic Review*, Hong Kong.
(Economic Survey of south Viet-Nam, p. 656.)

Hisao Kanamori, President, Japan Economic Research Center (Nihon Keizai Kenkyu Center), Tokyo, Japan.
(Economic Survey of Japan, p. 810.)

Frank King, Professor of economic history and Director, Centre of Asian Studies, University of Hong Kong.
(History and Economic Survey of Macao, pp. 925, 926.)

E. Stuart Kirby, Professor of Economics, Asian Institute of Technology, Bangkok, Thailand.
(The Soviet Far East and Eastern Siberia, p. 957.)

Werner Klatt, O.B.E., Fellow, St. Antony's College, Oxford (retd.); former economic adviser to the Foreign Office, London.
(Agrarian Issues in Asia, p. 53, Economic Survey and Statistical Survey of People's Republic of China, pp. 716, 734.)

Michael Leifer, Department of International Relations, The London School of Economics and Political Science, University of London.
(History and Economic Survey of Cambodia, pp. 427, 431.)

David Lim, formerly of the Economic Research Centre, University of Singapore.
(Economic Survey of Singapore, p. 592.)

A. E. McQueen, Deputy Director of Economic Planning, New Zealand Government Railways.
(Australasia—Social and Economic Geography, p. 985, Physical and Social Geography of Australia, p. 991, New Zealand, p. 1049.)

Norman Miners, lecturer in political science, University of Hong Kong.
(History of Hong Kong, p. 775.)

Helen Moody, formerly with Institute of Development Studies, University of Sussex.
(Aid and Investment, p. 70.)

Ramon H. Myers, Curator, East Asian Collection, Hoover Institute, Stanford, Calif., U.S.A.
(Economic Survey of China (Taiwan), p. 729.)

Andrew C. Nahm, Director, Center for Korean Studies, Western Michigan University, Kalamazoo, U.S.A.
(History of Korea, p. 867.)

Geoffrey Parrinder, Professor of the Comparative Study of Religions, University of London.
(The Religions of Asia, p. 41).

M. Ruth H. Pfanner, Ford Foundation, Bangkok, Thailand.
(Economic Survey of Burma, p. 409.)

Jan M. Pluvier, Institute for Modern Asiatic History, Amsterdam.
(History of Indonesia, p. 448.)

Kevin Rafferty, former correspondent, *Financial Times*, London; editor *Business Times*, Kuala Lumpur, Malaysia.
(History and Economic Survey of Afghanistan, pp. 153, 158, Economic Survey of Bangladesh, p. 181, of Pakistan, p. 302.)

Peter Robb, Lecturer in History, S.O.A.S., University of London.
(History of Bangladesh, p. 181, of India, p. 210.)

J. W. Rowe, Professor of Economics, Massey University, New Zealand.
(Economic Survey of New Zealand, p. 1055.)

A. J. K. Sanders, Secretary, Anglo-Mongolian Society, London.
(Statistical Survey of Mongolia, p. 942.)

John Sargent, Lecturer in Geography, S.O.A.S., University of London.
(Physical and Social Geography of Japan, p. 799, Korea, p. 866.)

Kingsley M. de Silva, Professor of Ceylon history, University of Ceylon.
(History of Sri Lanka, p. 332.)

Josef Silverstein, Professor of Political Science, Rutgers University, U.S.A.
(History of Burma, p. 402.)

C. G. F. Simkin, Professor of Economics, University of Sydney, N.S.W., Australia.
(Asia's Trade, p. 81, Economic Survey of Australia, p. 1000.)

E. H. S. Simmonds, Professor of Thai Languages and Literatures, S.O.A.S., University of London.
(History and Economic Survey of Laos, pp. 492, 497.)

Paul Sithi-Amnuai, Vice-President, Bangkok Bank Ltd., Bangkok, Thailand.
(Economic Survey of Thailand, p. 620.)

Ralph Smith, Lecturer, History of South-East Asia, S.O.A.S., University of London.
(History of Viet-Nam, p. 644.)

Philip A. Snow, Bursar, Rugby School, England.
(Bibliography of the Pacific Territories, p. 1149, Pacific biographies.)

Richard Storry, Fellow, St. Antony's College, Oxford.
(History of Japan, p. 801.)

E. J. Tapp, Associate Professor of History, University of New England, Australia.
(History of Australia, p. 993, New Zealand, p. 1051.)

George Thomson, Professor of Government, Nanyang University, Singapore.
(History of Singapore, p. 588.)

Lt.-Col. G. E. Wheeler, former Director, Central Asian Research Centre, London.
(Soviet Central Asia, p. 957.)

Dick Wilson, Financial Editor, Straits Times Press, Singapore; formerly Editor, *Far Eastern Economic Review*, Hong Kong.
(Development Problems of Asia, p. 61, Economic Survey of India, p. 218.)

David K. Wyatt, Professor of South-East Asian History, Cornell University, U.S.A.
(History of Thailand, p. 616.)

Calendar of Events

1975

SEPTEMBER

1 *Papua New Guinea:* the island of Bougainville unilaterally declared independence as the Republic of the North Solomons.

2 *Sri Lanka:* three ministers from the Lanka Sama Samaja Party were dismissed from the United Front Government by the Prime Minister, leaving only the Sri Lanka Freedom Party and the Communist Party represented in the Government.

9–28 *Cambodia:* Prince Norodom Sihanouk returned from exile in Peking for the first time since his overthrow in 1970.

16 *Papua New Guinea:* gained its independence from Australia.

17 *Sri Lanka:* there was a major cabinet re-organization.

21 *Malaysia:* the Sultan of Kelantan, Tuanku Yahya Putra, was installed as the sixth Yang di-Pertuan Agong (Supreme Head of State) for a five-year term.

22 *South Viet-Nam:* the new piastre was introduced at a rate of one to 500 old piastres.

24 *SEATO:* it was decided at a meeting of the Ministerial Council to phase out the organization over the following two years.

27 *Malaysia:* the link between the Malaysian ringgit and the U.S. dollar was ended.

OCTOBER

1 *Gilbert and Ellice Islands:* the British colony was divided into two separate territories: the Gilbert Islands and Tuvalu, formerly the Ellice Islands.

24 *India:* four soldiers were killed in the most serious border incident with China for some years.

31 *Sabah:* Tun Mustapha, the Chief Minister, resigned.
Thailand and Cambodia: diplomatic relations were established between the two countries.

NOVEMBER

1 *Sabah:* Syed Kuruak took over as Chief Minister.

3 *Bangladesh:* the deputy Chief of Army Staff, Brigadier Khalid Musharaf, staged a bloodless coup.

7 *Bangladesh:* Khalid Musharaf was killed in a counter coup led by Major-General Ziaur Rahman, Chief of Army Staff. Power passed to the chiefs of staff of the three armed services.
India: the Supreme Court reversed the decision of the Allahabad High Court taken in June that Indira Gandhi was guilty of malpractice in the 1971 elections and was banned for six years from standing for elective office.

11 *Australia:* the Governor-General, Sir John Kerr, dismissed the Labor Government under Gough Whitlam when the Senate's continuing refusal to pass money supply bills had created a constitutional impasse. A caretaker government under the Liberal leader, Malcolm Fraser, held office until elections in December.

15–21 *Viet-Nam:* in talks between delegations from North and South Viet-Nam, it was decided to hold elections for a joint National Assembly in the first half of 1976.

20 *Laos and Thailand:* the border was closed and the Thai ambassador recalled after 3 days of heavy border clashes.

25/26 *Laos:* the coalition government was dissolved.

28 *East Timor:* the communist Revolutionary Front for the Independence of East Timor (Fretilin) party unilaterally declared independence for East Timor from Portugal.

29 *New Zealand:* in the general election, the Labour Party, which had been in office since 1972, lost to the National Party.

30 *Laos:* the King abdicated.

30 *India:* presidential rule was imposed on the state of Uttar Pradesh.

DECEMBER

1–2 *Laos:* the country was declared a republic.

7 *East Timor:* Indonesian forces invaded.

8 *Indonesia:* Portugal broke diplomatic relations with Indonesia over the invasion of East Timor.

12 *East Timor:* the UN General Assembly called on Indonesia to withdraw forces from East Timor.

13 *Australia:* in the general election the Liberal party won a substantial majority of seats in the House of Representatives and a majority in the Senate and formed a coalition government with the National (Country) Party.

17 *East Timor:* a pro-Indonesian government was formed with a view to integration with Indonesia.

19 *Republic of Korea:* the Prime Minister Kim Jong Pil and his cabinet resigned. Choi Kya Hah became the new Prime Minister and 8 new ministers were included in his cabinet.
India: the ruling Congress Party annual conference agreed to postpone for a year elections to the Lok Sabha due in early 1976.

31 *Macao:* the Portuguese military presence was ended after 400 years, with the withdrawal of the last forces.

1976

JANUARY

1 *Thailand and Laos:* the border was re-opened.

2 *Solomon Islands:* internal self-government was instituted in the British protectorate.

5 *Cambodia:* a new constitution came into force, naming the country Democratic Cambodia.

8 *China:* Premier Chou En-lai died.

9 *India:* freedom of speech and six other fundamental rights were suspended.

14 *Malaysia:* the Prime Minister, Tun Abdul Razak, died.

15 *Malaysia:* Hussein Onn was sworn in as the new Prime Minister.

22 *India:* presidential rule in the state of Uttar Pradesh was lifted.

28 *Papua New Guinea:* a truce with the Bouganville secessionists was called.

31 *India:* presidential rule was imposed in the state of Tamil Nadu.

FEBRUARY

7 *China:* it was officially confirmed that Hua Kuo-feng, a Deputy Premier and Minister of Public Security, had been appointed acting Premier following the death of Chou En-lai.

10 *Macao:* a new constitution came into force giving internal autonomy in administrative, economic and financial affairs.

12 *China:* posters denouncing Vice-Premier Teng Hsiao-p'ing, who had been expected to succeed Chou En-lai, appeared in Peking.

23–24 *ASEAN:* a summit meeting in Bali, Indonesia, agreed a Treaty of Amity and Co-operation and the establishment of a secretariat for the Association.

27 *Thailand:* an attempted military coup was foiled.

28 *Thailand:* the Socialist Party leader, Boonsanong Punyodyana, was assassinated.

MARCH

5 *Indonesia:* presidential elections to be held in March 1978 were announced.

12 *India:* President's rule was imposed on the state of Gujarat, the only remaining state not controlled by the Congress Party.

20 *Cambodia:* elections were held for a new 250-member People's Representative Assembly.
Australia: in state elections in Victoria the Liberal government was returned for its eighth term with an increased majority.

24 *North Mariana Islands:* U.S. President Ford signed legislation to give the islands Commonwealth status with the U.S.A. when the trusteeship agreement expired.

27 *Philippines:* chiefs of staff of all the armed services were replaced.

31 *Singapore:* the British military presence was ended with withdrawal of the remaining forces.

APRIL

4 *Cambodia:* the Cabinet accepted Prince Sihanouk's resignation as Head of State.

4 *Thailand:* in elections for the House of Representatives the Democratic Party won a majority over the incumbent Social Action Party.

7 *China:* Teng Hsiao-p'ing was dismissed from all his party and government posts; Hua Kuo-feng was confirmed as Premier and first Vice-Chairman of the Communist Party by the Politburo.

13 *Cambodia:* the Cabinet resigned and a new government headed by Tol Saut was appointed.

14 *Sabah:* general elections were held and Tun Mohamed Fuad Stephens was sworn in next day as Chief Minister.

25 *Viet-Nam:* voting for a new National Assembly for the unified country began.

30 *Democratic People's Republic of Korea:* Kim Il resigned as Prime Minister for reasons of health and was succeeded by Park Sung Chul.

MAY

6 *Malaysia and Cambodia:* diplomatic relations were established between the two countries.

11 *Australia:* in state elections in New South Wales the Labor Party won by a narrow majority over the Liberal Party who had been in office for 10 years.

14 *India and Pakistan:* agreement was made to restore diplomatic relations broken off in December 1971 over the secession of East Pakistan as Bangladesh.

30 *India:* the Congress Party approved Indira Gandhi's proposal to change the constitution.

31 *East Timor:* a newly-convened "People's Representative Council" approved integration with Indonesia.

JUNE

2 *Philippines:* diplomatic relations with the U.S.S.R. were established.

6 *Sabah:* Tun Mohamed Fuad Stephens, new Chief Minister, and four ministers were killed in an air crash.

9 *Taiwan:* there was a major cabinet reshuffle.

15 *Laos:* a new currency, the liberation kip, was introduced.
China: it was officially announced that Mao Tse-tung would no longer receive distinguished foreign visitors.

18 *Pakistan and India:* an agreement was signed on the restoration of air links and overflights between the two countries.

21 *India and Pakistan:* ambassadors between the two countries were named.

24 *Viet-Nam:* the first session of the joint National Assembly opened.
Philippines: Manila was officially designated as the capital city again, instead of Quezon City.

27 *India:* the state of emergency had been in force for a year.

JULY

2 *Viet-Nam:* the National Assembly proclaimed the country re-unified as the Socialist Republic of Viet-Nam, with its capital at Hanoi.

3 *Viet-Nam:* the government of the re-unified country was announced.

17 *East Timor:* East Timor was formally integrated as the 27th province of Indonesia, although Portugal had not formally ceded its sovereignty.

27 *Japan:* former Prime Minister Kakuei Tanaka was arrested on charges of accepting bribes from a U.S. aerospace corporation in a major scandal.

28 *China:* a severe earthquake in Tangshan in Hopei province virtually destroyed the city with enormous loss of life.

AUGUST

1 *Japan and Cambodia:* diplomatic relations were established between the two countries.

6 *Thailand and Viet-Nam:* the two countries agreed to re-establish diplomatic relations.
Japan: reparation payments to countries occupied during World War II were completed.

16 *Sri Lanka:* the fifth summit conference of non-aligned nations opened in Colombo.

18 *Australia:* a severe anti-inflation budget was presented.

20 *Viet-Nam:* the re-united country formally applied for United Nations membership.

26 *Bangladesh:* a United Nations hearing of Bangladesh's dispute with India over the diversion of the River Ganges waters by India began.

28 *Republic of Korea:* opposition leader Kim Dae Jung and former President Yun Po were sentenced to 8 years' jail.

30 *Cambodia and Thailand:* the two countries agreed to open their common border for trade.

SEPTEMBER

1 *India:* Opposition members walked out of the Lok Sabha in protest against a Bill to change the country's constitution.

9 *People's Republic of China:* Mao Tse-tung, Chairman of the Chinese Communist Party and founder of the People's Republic of China, died.

15 *Japan:* the cabinet resigned.

16 *Japan:* the Prime Minister, Takeo Miki, reshuffled the cabinet, making few changes in the cabinet which had resigned.

Abbreviations

A.A.S.A.	Associate of the Australian Society of Accountants
A.B.	Bachelor of Arts
A.B.C.	Australian Broadcasting Commission
A.C.	Companion of the Order of Australia
Acad.	Academy
Act.	Acting
A.C.T.	Australian Capital Territory
ADB	Asian Development Bank
A.D.C.	Aide-de-camp
Adm.	Admiral
Admin.	Administration, Administrative, Administrator
Af.	Afghani
A.F.C.	Air Force Cross
A.F.I.A.	Associate of the Federal Institute of Accountants (Australia)
a.i.	ad interim
A.I.C.C.	All-India Congress Committee
AID	Agency for International Development (U.S.A.)
A.I.F.	Australian Imperial Forces
A.I.R.	All-India Radio
Alt.	Alternate
A.M.	Master of Arts; Member of the Order of Australia
Amb.	Ambassador
A.M.N.Z.I.E.	Associate Member New Zealand Institute of Engineers
Anon.	Anonymous
ANU	Australian National University
ANZAC	Australian and New Zealand Army Corps
A.N.Z.I.C.	Associate New Zealand Institute of Chemists
ANZUS	Australia, New Zealand and the United States
A.O.	Officer of the Order of Australia
A.P.	Andhra Pradesh
approx.	approximately
Apptd.	appointed
A.R.	Autonomous Region
ASEAN	Association of South-East Asian Nations
ASPAC	Asian and Pacific Council
Asscn.	Association
Assoc.	Associate, Associated
A.S.S.R.	Autonomous Soviet Socialist Republic (U.S.S.R.)
Asst.	assistant
Aug.	August
Aust.	Australia
b.	born
B.A.	Bachelor of Arts
B.Admin.	Bachelor of Administration
B.Agr.	Bachelor of Agriculture
B.A.Sc.	Bachelor of Applied Sciences
B.B.A.	Bachelor of Business Administration
B.B.C.	British Broadcasting Corporation
B.Ch., B.Chir.	Bachelor of Surgery
B.C.L.	Bachelor of Civil Law; Bachelor of Canon Law
B.Comm.	Bachelor of Commerce
B.D.	Bachelor of Divinity
Bd.	Board
Bd., Blvd., Bld.	Boulevard
B.E.	Bachelor of Engineering; Bachelor of Education
B.Ec.	Bachelor of Economics
B.E.E.	Bachelor of Electrical Engineering
B.E.M.	British Empire Medal
B.L.	Bachelor of Law
Bldg.	Building
B.Litt.	Bachelor of Letters
B.L.S.	Bachelor of Library Sciences
B.Mus.	Bachelor of Music
B.O.C.	British Oxygen Company Ltd.
B.P.	British Petroleum; Boîte Postale (Post-box)
B.Paed.	Bachelor of Pædiatrics
Brig.	Brigadier
B.S.	Bachelor of Surgery
B.S., B.Sc.	Bachelor of Science
B.S.A.	Bachelor of Scientific Agriculture
C.	Centigrade
C.A.	Chartered Accountant
Cabt.	Cabinet
Cal.	Calcutta
Cantt.	Cantonment
cap.	capital
Capt.	Captain
C.B.	Companion of the (Order of the) Bath
C.B.E.	Commander of the (Order of the) British Empire
C.C.P.	Chinese Communist Party
C.C.P.C.C.	Chinese Communist Party Central Committee
C.D.F.C.	Commonwealth Development Finance Company Ltd.
C.E.	Civil Engineer
Cen.	Central
CENTO	Central Treaty Organization
C.F.P.	Communauté française du pacifique
C.H.	Companion of Honour
Chair.	Chairman
Chap.	Chapter
Ch.B.	Bachelor of Surgery
Ch.M.	Master of Surgery
C.I.E.	Companion of (the Order of) the Indian Empire
Cie.	Company
c.i.f.	Cost, insurance and freight
circ.	circulation
C.-in-C.	Commander-in-Chief
cm.	centimetre(s)
C.M.	Master in Surgery
Cmdre.	Commodore
CMEA	Council for Mutual Economic Aid (COMECON)
C.M.G.	Companion of (the Order of) St. Michael and St. George
CNRRA	Chinese National Relief and Rehabilitation Administration
Co.	Company; County
C.O.	Commanding Officer
Col.	Colonel
Coll.	College
Com.	Commercial
COMECON	*see* CMEA
Comm.	Commission
Commdr.	Commander
Commr.	Commissioner
Conf.	Conference
Co-op.	Co-operative
Corpn.	Corporation
Corr.	Corresponding
Corresp.	Correspondent; Corresponding

C.P. .. .. Communist Party
C.P.I. .. .. Communist Party of India
Cpl. .. .. Corporal
C.P.O. .. .. Central Post Office
C.P.P.C.C. .. Chinese People's Political Consultative Conference
C.P.S.U. .. Communist Party of the Soviet Union
C.S.C. .. .. Conspicuous Service Cross
C.S.I. .. .. Companion of (the Order of) the Star of India
C.S.I.R.O. .. Commonwealth Scientific and Industrial Research Organization
C.St.J. .. Commander of (the Order of) St. John of Jerusalem
Cttee. .. .. Committee
C.V.O. .. .. Commander of the (Royal) Victorian Order

D.Agr. .. .. Doctor of Agriculture
D.B. .. .. Bachelor of Divinity
D.B.E. .. .. Dame Commander of (the Order of) the British Empire
D.C.L. .. .. Doctor of Civil Law
D.D., D.Dr. .. Doctor of Divinity
D. de l'Univ. .. Docteur de l'Université
D.D.S. .. .. Doctor of Dental Surgery
D.D.Sc. .. .. Doctor of Dental Science (Melbourne)
Dec. .. .. December
D.Econ. .. Doctor of Economics
Del. .. .. Delegate, Delegation
D. en D. .. Docteur en Droit (Doctor of Law)
D. en Fil. y Let. Doctor of Philosophy and Letters
D.Eng. .. .. Doctor of Engineering
Dem. .. .. Democratic
dep. .. .. deposit(s)
Dept. .. .. Department
D.F.A. .. .. Diploma of Fine Arts
D.F.C. .. .. Distinguished Flying Cross
Dip.N.Z.L.S. Diploma of the New Zealand Library Society
Dipl. .. .. Diploma
Dir. .. .. Director
Div. .. .. Divisional
D.K. .. .. Derjat Kerabat (Malaya)
D.L. .. .. Doctor of Laws
D.Lit(t). Doctor of Letters; Doctor of Literature
D.Met. .. .. Diploma of Meteorology
D.Mus. .. .. Doctor of Music
D.Phil. .. .. Doctor of Philosophy
D.Phil.Nat. .. Doctor of Natural Philosophy
D.P.M. .. .. Dato Paduka Makhota (Most Honourable Order of the Crown)
D.P.R. .. .. Democratic People's Republic
Dr. .. .. Doctor
Dr.Jur. .. .. Doctor of Laws
D.R.V.N. .. Democratic Republic of Viet-Nam
D.S.C. .. .. Distinguished Service Cross
D.Sc. .. .. Doctor of Science
D.S.O. .. .. Distinguished Service Order
D.T.M. .. .. Diploma of Tropical Medicine
D.T.M. and H. Diploma of Tropical Medicine and Hygiene
D.V.M. .. .. Doctor of Veterinary Medicine
D.V.Sc. .. Doctor of Veterinary Science

E. .. .. East, Eastern, Evening, Embassy
ECAFE .. Economic Commission for Asia and the Far East (UN) (*see* ESCAP)
Econ. .. .. Economist, Economics
ECOSOC .. Economic and Social Council (UN)
E.D. .. .. Doctor of Engineering
Ed. .. .. Editor
ed. .. .. educated
Ed.B. .. .. Bachelor of Education
Ed.M. .. .. Master of Education
Edn. .. .. Edition
EEC .. .. European Economic Community
EFTA .. European Free Trade Association
Elec. .. .. Electrical
Eng. .. .. Engineer, Engineering
Eng.D. .. .. Doctor of Engineering
EPTA .. .. Expanded Programme of Technical Assistance (UN)
Esc. .. .. Escudos
ESCAP .. .. Economic and Social Commission for Asia and the Pacific UN
Esq. .. .. Esquire
est. .. .. established; estimate
Ext. .. .. External, Externas

f. .. .. founded
F. .. .. Fahrenheit
F.A.A. .. .. Fellow Australian Academy of Sciences
F.A.C.E. .. Fellow of the Australian College of Education
F.A.I.A.S. .. Fellow of the Australian Institute of Agricultural Science
F.A.I.I. .. Fellow of the Australian Insurance Institute
F.A.I.M. .. Fellow of the Australian Institute of Management
F.A.M.S. .. Fellow Indian Academy of Medical Sciences
FAO .. Food and Agriculture Organization
F.A.S.A. .. Fellow of the Australian Society of Accountants
F.C.O. .. .. Foreign and Commonwealth Office
Feb. .. .. February
Fed. .. .. Federation, Federal
FIDES .. .. Fonds d'Investissement pour le Développement Economique et Social (Investment Fund for Economic and Social Development)
FIDOM .. Fonds d'Investissement des Départements d'Outre-Mer (Investment Fund of the Overseas Territories)
Fin. .. .. Financial
F.N.I. .. .. Fellow of the National Institute of Sciences of India
F.N.Z.I. .. Fellow of the New Zealand Institute
f.o.b. .. .. free on board
F.P.A.N.Z. .. Fellow, Public Accountant, New Zealand
F.R.A.C.I. .. Fellow of the Royal Australian Chemical Institute
F.R.A.C.P. .. Fellow Royal Australasian College of Physicians
F.R.A.C.S. .. Fellow of the Royal Australasian College of Surgeons
F.R.A.I.A. .. Fellow of the Royal Australian Institute of Architects
F.R.A.S. .. Fellow of the Royal Astronomical Society; Fellow of the Royal Asiatic Society
Fri. .. .. Friday
F.R.Met.Soc. .. Fellow of the Royal Meteorological Society
F.R.M.S. .. Fellow of the Royal Microscopical Society
F.R.S. .. .. Fellow of the Royal Society
F.R.S.A. .. Fellow of the Royal Society of Arts

F.R.S.N.Z.	Fellow of the Royal Society of New Zealand
F.S.S.	Fellow of the Royal Statistical Society
ft.	feet
FUNC/K	Front uni national du Kampuchea (United National Front of Cambodia)
F.Z.S.	Fellow of the Zoological Society
GATT	General Agreement on Tariffs and Trade
G.B.E.	Knight (or Dame) Grand Cross of (the Order of) the British Empire
G.C.	George Cross
G.C.B.	Knight Grand Cross of (the Order of) the Bath
G.C.I.E.	(Knight) Grand Commander of the Indian Empire
G.C.M.G.	Knight Grand Cross of (the Order of) St. Michael and St. George
G.C.S.I.	Knight Grand Commander of the Star of India
G.C.V.O.	Knight Grand Cross of the (Royal) Victorian Order
G.D.P.	Gross Domestic Product
Gen.	General
G.M.B.E.	Grand Master of the Order of the British Empire
G.N.P.	Gross National Product
Gov.	Governor
Govt.	Government
G.P.O.	General Post Office
Grp. Capt.	Group Captain
GRUNC/K	Gouvernement royal d'union nationale du Kampuchea (Royal Government of National Union of Cambodia)
ha.	hectare(s)
h.c.	honoris causa
H.C.	High Commission(er)
H.E.	His Eminence; His (or Her) Excellency
H.H.	His (or Her) Highness
H.I.H.	His (or Her) Imperial Highness
hl.	hectolitre(s)
H.M.	His (or Her) Majesty
Hon.	Honorary
H.Pk.	Hilali-i-Pakistan
H.Q.	Headquarters
H.R.H.	His (or Her) Royal Highness
H.S.H.	His (or Her) Serene Highness
Hum.D.	Doctor of Humanities
IAEA	International Atomic Energy Agency
IAS	Indian Administrative Service
IBRD	International Bank for Reconstruction and Development (World Bank)
ICAO	International Civil Aviation Organization
ICC	International Control Commission
ICFTU	International Confederation of Free Trade Unions
ICOM	International Council of Museums
I.C.S.	Indian Civil Service
IDA	International Development Association
I.E.S.	Indian Educational Service
IFC	International Finance Corporation
I.F.S.	Indian Forest Service
IGC	International Geophysical Committee
ILO	International Labour Organization
IMCO	Inter-Governmental Maritime Consultative Organization
IMF	International Monetary Fund
I.M.S.	Indian Medical Service

Inc.	Incorporated
Ind.	India; Independent
Ing.	Engineer
Insp.	Inspector
Inst.	Institute
Int., Internat.	International
IPU	Interparliamentary Union
Ir.	Engineer
Is.	Island(s)
I.S.E.	Indian Service of Engineers
ITU.	International Telecommunications Union
Jan.	January
J.C.D.	Dr. Canon Law
J.D.	Doctor of Jurisprudence
Jnr., Jr.	Junior
J.P.	Justice of the Peace
Jt.	Joint
J.S.D.	Doctor of Juristic Science
J.U.D.	Doctor of Canon or Civil Law
K.B.E.	Knight Commander of (the Order of) the British Empire
K.C.B.	Knight Commander of (the Order of) the Bath
K.C.I.E.	Knight Commander of (the Order of) the Indian Empire
K.C.M.G.	Knight Commander of (the Order of) St. Michael and St. George
K.C.S.I.	Knight Commander of the Star of India
K.C.V.O.	Knight Commander of the Royal Victorian Order
kg.	kilogramme(s)
K.G.	Knight of (the Order of) the Garter
K.K.	Kaien Kaisha (Limited Company) (Japan)
K.L.M.	Koninklijke Luchtvaart Maatschappij N.V. (Royal Dutch Airlines)
km.	kilometre(s)
K.M.N.	Kesatria Mangku Negara (Malaysian decoration)
K.St.J.	Knight of (the Order of) St. John
K.T.	Knight of (the Order of) the Thistle
Kt.	Knight
kW.	kilowatt(s)
kWh.	kilowatt hours
Lib.Dip.	Librarian Diploma
Libr.	Librarian
Lic.	Licenciado (Licenciate of law)
L.H.D.	Doctor of Literature
Litt.D.	Doctor of Letters
LL.B.	Bachelor of Laws
LL.D.	Doctor of Laws
LL.M.	Master of Laws
LN	League of Nations
L.R.C.P.	Licentiate of the Royal College of Physicians
Lt., Lieut.	Lieutenant
Ltd.	Limited
m.	million
M.A.	Master of Arts
M.Agr.Sc.	Master of Agricultural Science
Maj.	Major
Man.	Manager; Managing
MAPHILINDO	Malaya, Philippines, Indonesia
M.Arch.	Master of Architecture
M.B.	Bachelor of Medicine
M.B.E.	Member of (the Order of) the British Empire

M.C. .. .. Military Cross
M.Ch. .. .. Master of Surgery
M.Com. .. Master of Commerce
M.D. .. .. Doctor of Medicine
M.D.S. .. .. Master of Dental Surgery
M.Ec. .. .. Master of Economics
Med. .. .. Medical
mem. .. .. member
Mfg. .. .. Manufacturing
Mgr. .. .. Monsignor, Monseigneur
M.H.A. .. Member of the House of Assembly
M.I.E.Aust. .. Member of the Institution of Engineers of Australia
Mil. .. .. Military
M.L. .. .. Master of Laws
M.L.A. .. .. Member of the Legislative Assembly
M.L.C. .. .. Member of the Legislative Council
M.M. .. .. Military Medal
M.P. .. .. Member of Parliament; Madhya Pradesh
M.P.H. .. .. Master of Public Health
M.Pharm. .. Master of Pharmacy
M.R.C.P. .. Member of the Royal College of Physicians
M.R.C.S. .. Member of the Royal College of Surgeons
M.R.C.V.S. .. Member of the Royal College of Veterinary Surgeons
M.R.S.H. .. Member of the Royal Society for the Promotion of Health
M.R.S.L. .. Member of the Royal Society of Literature
M.S. .. .. Master of Science; Master of Surgery
M.Sc. .. .. Master of Science
M.Sc.Tech. .. Master of Technical Science
MSS. .. .. Manuscripts
Mt. .. .. Mount, Mountain
M.Th. .. .. Master of Theology
M.V.O. .. .. Member of the Royal Victorian Order
MW. .. .. Megawatt(s)
MWh. .. .. Megawatt hour(s)

N. .. .. North, Northern
Nat. .. .. National
N.D.Y.L. .. National Democratic Youth League
N.E.F.A. .. North-East Frontier Agency
N.F. .. .. Nouveau Franc (New Franc)
NLF .. .. National Liberation Front (of South Viet-Nam)
Nov. .. .. November
N.P.C. .. .. National People's Congress
N.R. .. .. Nepalese Rupee(s)
N.S.W. .. .. New South Wales
N.T. .. .. New Taiwan
N.V. .. .. Naamloze Vennootschap (Limited Company)
N.W.F.P. .. North-West Frontier Province
N.Y. .. .. New York
N.Y.C. .. .. New York City
N.Z. .. .. New Zealand

O.B.E. .. .. Officer of the Order of the British Empire
O.C. .. .. Officer Commanding
Oct. .. .. October
O.D.I. .. .. Overseas Development Institute
OECD .. .. Organisation for Economic Co-operation and Development
O.F.M. .. .. Order of Friars Minor
O.M. .. .. Member of the Order of Merit
O.P. .. .. Order of Preachers (Dominicans)
Oper. .. .. operations
Org. .. .. Organization, organizing
O.S.B. .. .. Order of St. Benedict
p.a. .. .. per annum
P.A.F. .. .. Philippines Air Force
P.A.L. .. .. Philippines Air Lines, Inc.
Pan Am .. Pan American World Airways, Inc.
Parl. .. .. Parliament, Parliamentary
P.C. .. .. Privy Counsellor
Perm. .. .. Permanent
Phar.D. .. Doctor of Pharmacy
Ph.D. .. .. Doctor of Philosophy
Ph.L. .. .. Licentiate of Philosophy
P.L.A. .. .. People's Liberation Army (China)
P.M.N. .. .. Panglima Mangku Negara (Malaysia)
P.N. .. .. Pakistan Navy
P.N.G. .. .. Papua New Guinea
P.N.I. .. .. Partai Nasional Indonesia
P.O. .. .. Post Office
P.O.B. .. .. Post Office Box
Pol., Polit. .. Political
P.R. .. .. People's Republic; Public Relations
Pref. .. .. Prefecture
Pres. .. .. President
PRG .. .. Provisional Revolutionary Government (of South Viet-Nam)
Prof. .. .. Professor
Propr. .. .. Proprietor
Prov. .. .. Province
PTT .. .. Post, Telegraphs, Telephones
Pty. .. .. Proprietary
p.u. .. .. paid up
publ. .. .. publication

Qld. .. .. Queensland
Q.C. .. .. Queen's Counsel

R.A.A.F. .. Royal Australian Air Force
R.A.F. .. .. Royal Air Force
R.A.N. .. .. Royal Australian Navy
Ref. .. .. Reference
Rep., rep. .. Republican, representative
Repub. .. Republic
Res. .. .. Reserve(s)
Rev. .. .. Reverend
R.I. .. .. Royal Institute
RMB .. .. Renminbi ("People's Currency" in China)
R.N. .. .. Royal Navy
R.N.Z.A.F. .. Royal New Zealand Air Force
Rps. .. .. Rupiahs
Rs. .. .. Rupees
R.S.F.S.R. .. Russian Soviet Federative Socialist Republic
Rt. .. .. Right
R.T.A. .. .. Royal Thai Army

S .. .. South, Southern
S.A. .. .. South Africa
S.B. .. .. Bachelor of Science
Sc.D. .. .. Doctor of Science
Sdn. Bhd. .. Sendirian Berhad (Limited Company) (Malaysia)
SEATO .. .. South-East Asia Treaty Organization
Sec. .. .. Secretary
Secr. .. .. Secretariat
Sept. .. .. September
SICT .. .. Standard International Trade Classification
Sir J. J. .. Sir Jamsetjee Jeejeebhoy
S.J. .. .. Society of Jesus (Jesuits)
S.J.D. .. .. Doctor of Juristic Science
S.M. .. .. Master of Science

S.M.R. .. Standard Malaysian Rubber Scheme
S.O.A.S. .. School of Oriental and African Studies, University of London
Soc. .. .. Society
SPC .. .. South Pacific Commission
S.Pk. .. .. Sitara-e-Pakistan
sq. .. .. square
S.S.R. .. .. Soviet Socialist Republic
S.T.D. .. .. Sacrae Theologiæ Doctor (Doctor of Sacred Theology)
Supt. .. .. Superintendent

T. .. .. Tasmania
TAB .. .. Technical Assistance Board (UN)
T.A.C. .. .. Technical Assistance Committee
TASS .. .. Telegrafnoye Agenstvo Sovietskogo Soiuza (Soviet News Agency)
T.D. .. .. Territorial Decoration
Techn., tech. .. technical
Th.D. .. .. Doctor of Theology
Th.L. .. .. Theological Licentiate
Th.M. .. .. Master of Theology
Tk. .. .. Taka
trans. .. .. translator, translated
Treas. .. .. Treasurer
T.U. .. .. Trade Union
T.U.C. .. .. Trades Union Congress
T.W.A. .. Trans World Airlines, Inc.

U.K. .. .. United Kingdom
UN .. .. United Nations
UNCDF .. United Nations Capital Development Fund
UNCTAD .. United Nations Conference on Trade and Development
UNCURK .. United Nations Commission for the Unification and Rehabilitation of Korea
UNDP .. .. United Nations Development Programme
UNEF .. United Nations Emergency Force
UNESCO .. United Nations Educational, Scientific and Cultural Organization
UNHCR .. United Nations High Commission for Refugees
UNICEF .. United Nations Children's Fund
UNIDO .. United Nations Industrial Development Organization
UNKRA .. United Nations Korean Reconstruction Agency
Univ. .. .. University
UNMOGIP .. United Nations Military Observer Group for India and Pakistan
UNROB .. United Nations Relief Office, Bangladesh
UNROD .. United Nations Relief Operation, Dacca.
UNRRA .. United Nations Relief and Rehabilitation Administration
UNRWA .. United Nations Relief and Works Agency
U.P. .. .. United Press; Uttar Pradesh
UPU .. .. Universal Postal Union
U.S.(A.) .. United States (of America)
U.S.S.R. .. Union of Soviet Socialist Republics

V. .. .. Victoria
V.C. .. .. Victoria Cross
V.D. .. .. Volunteer Officers' Decoration; Victorian Decoration
Ven. .. .. Venerable

W. .. .. West, Western
W.A. .. .. Western Australia
Wash. .. .. Washington
WFTU .. .. World Federation of Trade Unions
WHO .. .. World Health Organization
WMO .. .. World Meteorological Organization

Y.M.C.A. .. Young Men's Christian Association
Y.W.C.A. .. Young Women's Christian Association

LATE INFORMATION

BANGLADESH

Defence

(*September* 1976)

Chief of Air Staff: Air Commodore A. G. MAHMOOD (acting).

A. G. Mahmood replaces M. G. Tawab, who was killed in air crash September 1st, 1976.

JAPAN

Cabinet change

(*September 15th*, 1976)

Minister of Foreign Affairs: ZENTARO KOSAKA.

MONGOLIA

Cabinet change

(*August 8th*, 1976)

Minister of Foreign Affairs: MANGALYN DUGERSUREN.

NEPAL

Cabinet change

(*September* 1976)

Minister for Law, Justice and Communications: RABINDRA NATH SHARMA.

Minister for Health: BITAMBAR THOJ KHATI.

State Minister for Home and Panchayat Affairs: DELLI SHER RAI.

General Introduction

Asia and the Pacific

Keith Buchanan

PERSPECTIVES

Perspective: Centre and Periphery

In earlier editions of this essay we stressed the global changes which followed the Second World War, changes which manifested themselves in the emergence of the Asian nations from the old forms of colonialism; in their growing political influence both individually and collectively through the UN; and in their growing technological competence which finds expression in the industrial and military fields. We stressed that these changes took on a special significance because of the size of Monsoon Asia's population—some 2,250 million people, increasing at rates varying from 1.8 per cent per annum to 3.5 per cent, so that their numbers may double by the end of the century. We quoted Owen Lattimore's view that "we have now crossed over into a period in which things happening in Asia, opinions formed in Asia and decisions made in Asia will largely determine the course of events everywhere in the world".

Since these views were originally expressed, two major sets of developments have asserted themselves with increasing emphasis. The first is the crisis which has caught up the "overdeveloped" societies of the White North. This is seen largely in economic terms but, as the economist Robert Heilbroner reminds us, it is a more complex and deeply-rooted phenomenon which is disturbingly reminiscent of the disintegration of the Roman Empire. To quote Heilbroner: "Then, as now, we find order giving way to disorder; self-confidence to self-doubt; moral certitude to moral disquiet. There are resemblances in the breakdown of cumbersome economic systems, in the intransigence of privileged minorities." And, exploring the analogy further, he asks whether the great corporations and ministries are our latifundia, the U.S.S.R. our Byzantium, China and North Viet-Nam our Goths and Visigoths.*

The second development is the virtually complete failure of Western-inspired policies in the dependent zone of "peripheral capitalisms" which extends from the Pacific westwards to take in the entirety of "Free Asia" (and much of Africa and Latin America). It is a failure—epitomized by the Indochina War—to impose by military means the political will of the West. It is a failure—epitomized by South Asia's growing hunger—of Western policies of "aid" and "development". It is a failure—demonstrated by the "run-away" population growth in South Asia—of Western programmes of birth control. And, because the advice and policies "sold" by the West to many Asian nations have not succeeded in arresting what Heilbroner terms "the descent into hell" of these nations, it has been impossible to halt the rise of régimes whose authoritarianism is diametrically opposed to those democratic ideals professed by the West. Or, perhaps, a cynic might observe, the rise of such régimes, which ensure a semblance of stability, is not unwelcome to those groups whose major concern is with unimpeded access to the resources, and especially the cheap labour resources, of the Periphery.

But the perspectives in which these comments are made are long-term perspectives, encompassing the lifetimes of our children and our grandchildren. In the short-term perspective it may be that the picture can be interpreted otherwise. For in spite of its policy of decolonization, in spite of its military defeats, the Centre, by the weaving of the "new and subtler webs" of neocolonial dependency, maintains control of the economic resources of much of the Periphery. Its peoples represent 29 per cent of the world's population; they use up 80 per cent of the world's resources.

Perhaps, then, the failure of the Centre in its Asian periphery is a moral failure and, as we know, morality and economics are not to be mixed. . . . Or is the over-consumption at the Centre a factor contributing not only to the dehumanization and impoverishment of the Periphery but also to the economic and cultural disintegration of the Centre itself?

A Two-Tier World

We live—in spite of "development decades" and the declamations of politicians—in a two-tier world. The "two tiers" are readily recognizable: the U.S.A. had a *per caput* national income of over $4,200 in 1970; India had a *per caput* income less than one-fortieth of this. The U.S.A. spends annually some $20,000 million in advertising (designed to create a demand for trivial and socially irrelevant goods); this is twice the Indonesian G.N.P. and about one-third of the Indian G.N.P. Americans, it is estimated, spend some $3,000 million per year on their pets; this is twice the G.N.P. of Sri Lanka and over half the G.N.P. of Malaysia. The peoples of the affluent nations of the Centre face "a crisis of overeating" (it is estimated that one-third of the population of the U.S.A. is overweight); the peoples of South Asia live on the knife-edge of starvation. "Mountains" of unmarketable beef pose an agricultural problem to the technocrats of the Centre; the children in many parts of Asia (and in Africa and Latin America too) grow up physically and mentally stunted as a result of chronic protein deficiency.

The poverty of the nations of Asia, of the Periphery as a whole, and the wealth of the Centre are not simply coincidences; rather are they structurally related. In the words of Professor Peter Townsend, "the poverty of deprived *nations* is comprehensible only if we attribute it substantially to the existence of a system of international social stratification, a hierarchy of societies with vastly different resources in which the

* Robert Heilbroner, *Learning to Live with the Future* in Observer Review, Dec. 29th, 1974.

wealth of some is linked historically and contemporaneously to the poverty of others".* Or, as André Gunder Frank puts it more bluntly: "development generates underdevelopment"; the wealth of Europe and the poverty of Asia are sides of the same coin. Moreover, the available evidence suggests that the yawning gulf in living levels which today separates the peoples of Europe and Asia is, historically speaking, of relatively recent origin, and that as late as the eighteenth century the lot of a European peasant differed little from that of his Asian counterpart.

Now, the same processes of "development" which created the wide gap in living levels between the nations of the Centre and the dependent territories of the Periphery, such as the countries of Monsoon Asia, gave rise to an increasing divergence at both regional and social levels *within* the dependent territories. The regional gap is represented in Asia by the uneven development within the former Dutch East Indies, within former French Indochina, within Malaya, or even within a country never formally colonized such as Thailand or China. The social gap is illustrated by the extreme concentration of wealth and economic power in the hands of a tiny élite group: in the Philippines, for example, it is estimated that 90 per cent of the country's wealth is controlled by less than 10 per cent of the population (representing some 50 families); in Pakistan 80 per cent of all bank funds and 87 per cent of all insurance funds are controlled by 20 families. . . . And at the other extreme are the scores of millions in city and country who are unemployed, the hundreds of millions who are underemployed, the uncounted millions for whom life is little but a nightmare of chronic hunger and disease, all those for whom the future is, in Myrdal's words, a prospect of "utter and increasing impoverishment".

Can we, Robert S. McNamara asks, "imagine any human order surviving with so gross a mass of misery piling up at its base?"

Social and Ecological Dimensions of Development

For perhaps a dozen generations the economies of Asia have been warped by "association with the mercantile and colonialist nations"; for perhaps a generation the élites of Asia and the various international development agencies have attempted to solve the condition resulting from this warping, the condition known as "underdevelopment", through techniques of development drawn from the unique historical experience of the developed nations of the Centre.

That the successes achieved should have been limited and patchy is scarcely surprising. There is, for example, little agreement as to just what is meant by "development". That it is not simply synonymous with "economic growth" is underlined by the numerous examples (e.g. Pakistan, Thailand, the Philippines) of "growth without development"; a rapid growth in G.N.P. is, as Pakistan illustrated, perfectly compatible with sharp increases in unemployment and growing regional and social disparities. That "development" implies progress towards the "high mass-consumption societies" of the Rostow *schema* is still assumed by many who should know better. The realities of the population/resource equation, however, suggest, as Robert Heilbroner has emphasized, that "the process of industrial growth will become increasingly difficult to sustain because of resource limitations and increasingly dangerous because of pollution problems"; there is no prospect that the brief affluence the Centre has enjoyed will endure, even less that it can be "transplanted" by development techniques to the nations of the Periphery. Indeed, there are those who argue, as does Denis Goulet, that the only possible future is one of austerity, with "voluntary austerity" (based on the elimination of superfluous consumption) in the overdeveloped nations matching the "imposed austerity" of the poor nations. Demographic conditions, too, make any re-enactment of the Centre's development experience improbable. In many nations of the Periphery growth rates are twice those experienced by the nations of the Centre during their phase of economic take-off; the rural economy is overcrowded and the economic structures of the cities (lacking the developed secondary sectors characteristic of the nineteenth-century Western city) are unable to absorb more than a small proportion of the great flood of urban migrants.

Models of development based on the experience of the developed nations of the Centre are thus largely irrelevant in an Asian context. It is not therefore surprising that the most effective and realistic development programmes have been those of the East Asian socialist states which have rejected both Western and Soviet models of development in favour of models developed out of the historical experience of the East Asian peoples and more firmly rooted in the ecological conditions of East Asia. Even the most cursory examination of the human and physical ecology of the Monsoon lands will emphasize that development planners, like military men, confront a highly specialized and diversified environment and that if this is ignored no amount of money, manpower or material equipment will achieve a breakthrough.

The Environments of Monsoon Asia

The civilizations of Asia are both vegetable and vegetarian, relying on human and animal muscle for power and concerned with the production of food crops, with livestock products playing a very restricted role in the economy. Because of the intense, almost garden-type of cultivation and because of the importance of irrigation in maximizing yields and stabilizing output, Asian civilizations are typically lowland civilizations, seeking out what Joseph Spencer terms "the moist aquatic fringes" of the continent—the coastal lowlands and the great river valleys which probe deep into the heart of the continent and the occasional alluvial-floored lake basins. In such environments irrigated cropping provides very high

* In *The Concept of Poverty* ed. Peter Townsend (London 1970). In the same essay he observes "In many important respects it would be fair to conclude that the structure of underdevelopment has been created by centuries of association with the mercantile and colonialist nations".

calorie outputs per unit area in the shape of grain or root crops; the nearby seas or rivers or even the flooded paddy fields provide protein in the shape of crops of fish. In contrast to the developed societies of the Centre, based on profligate use of non-renewable resources, the traditional societies of Asia base their life on the use of resources that, wisely managed, are being constantly renewed.

Monsoon Asia offers three major types of environment to man: the uplands of its interior; the island-dotted shallow seas of its margining continental shelf; and, between uplands and seas, an irregular girdle of largely alluvial lowlands.

The uplands comprise the worn-down remains of old and resistant massifs, such as the Deccan of south India or the uplands of south China, or great uplifted blocks such as that of Tibet. They also include gigantic loops of younger and more elevated fold mountains such as those which form the Himalayas and the discontinuous belt of uplands which extends south from Japan through the Philippine-Indonesian arcs to New Zealand and the fold mountains which are crumpled against the eastern edge of the Australian block. Such uplands in Asia have been largely negative areas in the past, offering, in their specialized "ecological niches", refuge areas for a diversity of tribal peoples. Today, they play a different role, for the older rocks contain metallic minerals while the younger fold mountains and basins contain important reserves of oil and natural gas.

The shallow fringing seas of Monsoon Asia have throughout history played an important role in uniting the various sectors of the Asian fringe; in addition, and especially in South-East Asia, they have constituted habitats for specialized human groups such as the Orang Laut or "Sea Gypsies" of the Malay world. Their major importance to the traditional societies has always been as a source of protein. Today, the greater part of the protein intake of Japan, South Korea and South-East Asia is derived from fish and the protein potential of the marine and freshwater environments of South-East Asia alone is estimated at 70 million tons annually. Increasingly, however, the Asian continental shelf environment is emerging as a major source of petroleum. The Chinese continental shelf, extending from the Yellow Sea south to the Paracel Islands, appears to have large reserves; most of the South-East Asian continental shelf has already been allocated to oil companies; and Indonesia has moved into the top rank of oil producers.

"Mountain, sea and *sawah*"—these constitute, as we have seen, the major types of Asian environment, and of these the most important, in terms of population-carrying capacity, is the *sawah* or irrigated lowland environment. These lowlands comprise the Indus-Ganges crescent of North India; the river basins of mainland South-East Asia and the lowlands of Indonesia; the Hwang-ho, Yangtse Kiang and Si Kiang valleys of China; and the discontinuous fringe of lowlands in Korea and Japan. All are protected by high mountains or sea; all are irrigable and comparatively fertile. And within each of them plant and animal life—including human life—is dominated by the seasonal rhythm of the monsoon. Favoured by soils that, if not always fertile, are easy-working, they are scarcely true "regions of increment"—regions where no major problems of food-getting are experienced. Rainfall variability is great and may lead to crop failure and the threat of famine for tens of millions; river regimes are erratic and flooding is as important as drought in producing hunger. Biological conditions pose other difficulties for there are few regions in the world where the biological environment is as hostile. The Asian peasant—and perhaps four out of every five Asians are peasants—has long been caught in the same vicious circle as the African: disease → inefficient farming → malnutrition → heightened susceptibility to disease. . . . And yet none of these environmental problems is insuperable for, as the Chinese experiment shows, given the appropriate social and political conditions, man can reshape both his physical and his biological environment—by water storage schemes and irrigation, by soil improvement and afforestation and by eliminating many of the diseases which kill or ravage their human hosts.

The Human Ecology of Monsoon Asia

The most basic of all statistics for a peasant society —the man/cultivated land ratio—is given for each major statistical "region" of the Asian-Pacific world in the table below.

For Europe, by comparison, the cultivated land per head amounts to 0.31 ha., for North America 1.03 ha. The "nutrient density" levels in Asia are thus generally

POPULATION AND CULTIVATED LAND

	Population (million)	Cultivated Land (million ha.)	Land per Head (ha.)
South Asia	716	197	0.27
China	760	111	0.15
East and South-East Asia	317	72	0.22
Other Asian centrally planned economies	36	5	0.13
Oceania	15	45	3.0

Source: Ceres Nov./Dec. 1974.

high and this is underlined by the fact that China's nutrient density is seven times that of North America and twenty times that of Oceania. The second basic aspect is that these high densities in Asia are the result of the concentration of population in certain ecologically favoured areas (i.e. areas suited to intensive garden-style farming); in China, for example, the cultivated area represents only slightly over one-ninth of the area of the country and is concentrated on the level loess plains of the northwest and the alluvial flats of the great river basins. Each of these concentrations of population can be broken down into an infinite number of villages, tiny social and economic "cells"; it is this cell-like structure which gives the rural civilizations of Asia their strength and their resilience. The technologically more "sophisticated" nations of the Centre are, in contrast, much more rigid, depending on complex transport and power networks and constant transfusions of energy and raw materials. The Indochinese Wars have indicated the tremendous survival capacity of these Asian peasant societies in the face of the massed conventional weaponry of the most powerful nation on earth.

We have spoken of "Asian peasant societies" and have indicated some points of contrast with the societies of the Centre. Nevertheless, it is important that, while emphasizing this contrast, we do not lose sight of the fact that the adjective "Asian", like the adjective "European", can become a meaningless abstraction, glossing over the infinite diversity of the Asian world itself. A diversity of physical or racial types, from the dwarf negro of the southern forests to the tall fair-skinned Pakistani; a linguistic diversity—over two hundred language groups in India alone—and a diversity of scripts; a diversity of faiths, including some half dozen major religions and a great profusion of numerically less important faiths; a diversity of economic conditions ranging from the "institutionalized anarchy" of Laos to the austere planned economies of the Asian communist countries.

But it is a patterned diversity. The hundreds of thousands of "cells" which make up Asian society show a close clustering in the ecologically-favoured areas, separated by a thin scattering of less-developed cells in the intervening upland areas. If we extend the biological metaphor, we may regard some of these cell-aggregations, these closely-linked village and urban communities which make up the "high civilizations" of Asia, as among the oldest living organisms on earth—and this millennial quality they owe in part to their fine adjustment to their environmental settings.

In the west, in the valleys of the Indus and Ganges, the Indian culture world is derived from the Indus Valley Civilization which flourished in the middle of the third millennium B.C.; from this evolved the civilization termed by Sir Mortimer Wheeler the Ganges Civilization and which reached the southern tip of the subcontinent in the first century A.D. In eastern Asia, the basin of the Hwang-ho, an area of loess and loess-derived alluvium, was supporting a dense village-dwelling population by 2500 B.C. By 1500 B.C. the developed Bronze Age Civilization of the Shang was flourishing in the middle Hwang-ho region and by 221 B.C. Shih Huang-ti unified the empire with the use of iron weapons; established with the Great Wall a clear defensive line against the tribes of the steppes; and then deployed his armies southwards to incorporate the largely Tai-inhabited regions of central and south China into the Ch'in empire. And by consolidating the state organization and laying the foundations of a tightly-knit bureaucratic system he contributed to determining the specific character of the Chinese culture-world for the next two millennia. And, a wedge separating the Indian and Chinese culture-worlds, the frayed-out upland mass of South-East Asia, with its high mountain chains, its giant river valleys and its fringing island-garlanded seas, contains also wide alluvial lowlands. These isolated lowlands—those of the Irrawaddy, the Menam, the lower Mekong and the Red River—served as cradle areas for the Burmese, Thai, Khmer and Vietnamese civilizations. These, together with the Malay civilization which developed around the seas of the "South-East Asian Mediterranean" (influenced by Hinduism, Islamized, then peripherally influenced by Catholicism), made up what we may term the "South-East Asian culture-world".

And to these three major culture-worlds we may add the "derived civilizations" (or "moonlight civilizations" as de Riencourt terms them) which developed on the narrow coast plains of Korea and Japan. Their early cultures "reflected" the light of the Chinese culture and their subsequent development was strongly influenced by China.

An Ecological Framework for Development

Each of these major cultures had as a core area a lowland, usually alluvial, environment. From these lowland cores these "high civilizations" spread on to the fringing uplands, displacing or absorbing with varying degrees of success the tribal groups who occupied the agriculturally less attractive hill regions. Today, each of these culture-worlds shows a duality—"moist" alluvial environments contrast with "dry" upland environments; the "high civilizations" of the dominant groups contrast with the "tribal cultures" (often highly sophisticated in their organization and adjustment to the environment) of the upland margins.

These five major culture-worlds, each exhibiting what we may term a lowland and an upland "facies", may be regarded as the basic ecological regions of Monsoon Asia. Within them, the relationship between man and land, between the various cultures and the ecological niches in which they have developed—these are the product of an immensely long history during which the various human groups have, hesitantly at first, but then with increasing assurance, explored the varied environments of the Monsoon Lands and their potential. Explored them—and also transformed them, so that today in the most anciently and closely settled regions the term "natural environment" has little meaning; rather are we dealing, as in the areas of intensive rice-growing, with man-made environments.

Man, through his remodelling of the physical face of the earth by terracing, through his maintenance by irrigation of artificial soil-water conditions, through the manuring and the cultivation which over long centuries have transformed the very soil itself, is part of a closely-knit ecological complex. And, as the wide contrasts in levels of irrigation technology between the peoples of East and South-East Asia show, the "cultural" components in this complex are as significant as the "physical" components. Indeed, as Pierre Gourou has suggested, commenting on the thinly settled character of China's uplands, the culture of a people may be regarded as a prism through which the influence of that people impinges on the environment and through which they in turn receive the influences of the environment. . . .

Today, with the advantages of hindsight, we can see that one of the most important reasons for the limited success of post-independence development planning in non-Communist Asia was the neglect of these ecological realities. Development techniques which appear to have succeeded in the advanced nations of the Centre were transplanted indiscriminately into totally different ecological contexts. Not surprisingly, these "allegedly universalist solutions" didn't work but it was not until the Second Decade of Development was well advanced that the planners began to accept the idea that development, if it is to be meaningful, must be firmly rooted in the human and physical ecology of Asia; it must, in short, be what Ignacy Sachs has termed "ecodevelopment".

Ecodevelopment, in Sachs' definition, "is a style of development that, in each ecoregion, calls for specific solutions to the particular problems of the region in the light of cultural as well as ecological data and long term as well as immediate needs. Accordingly, it operates with criteria of progress that are related to each particular case, and adaptation to the environment, as postulated by the anthropologists, plays an important part." And as to the role of aid and of foreign models, Sachs comments: "Instead of placing too much emphasis on external aid, it (i.e. ecodevelopment) relies on the capabilities of human societies to identify their problems and devise their own original solutions to them, though drawing on the experience of others." Chinese development techniques, with their emphasis on self-reliance, decentralization and the potential of the masses, come close to this ideal.

With such an approach the solutions to the problems of food, shelter, and industrialization take on a different form from that we are accustomed to discern, given our "universalist and diffusionist philosophy of development". The universalist views implicit in the Green Revolution, for example, are rejected in favour of a greater emphasis on the specific potentialities of each ecoregion with regard to food production and a greater use of that "practical science of primitive peoples and peasants whose richness and accuracy are constantly surprising anthropologists and ethnobotanists". Indeed, only an overweening scientific arrogance could, as the world confronts an "energy crisis", explain the attempts to replace highly efficient local farming systems by so-called "developed systems" characterized by minimal efficiency in terms of energy conversion.* Perhaps, too, in a world in which the question of non-renewable resources asserts itself as the Achilles heel of all development, those ecoregions of Asia, dominated by what Pierre Gourou terms "vegetable civilizations", offer, with careful management and exploitation of the tropical vegetation formations and water bodies, an inexhaustible source of industrial raw materials for the building and chemical industries. But again this is impossible without a rejection of external-derived concepts, in this case the idea firmly rooted in European culture that forest clearing and progress are synonymous.

As for shelter, in 1950 India, for example, was short of 2.8 million housing units; by 1960, 9.3 million; by 1970, before the "energy crisis", 12.0 million. In part, this is due to increasing population, but also to the impossibility of rehousing along standards derived from those of the Centre. A fixation on a "misunderstood modernity" has led to the large-scale discarding (at least in the cities of Asia) of traditional housing styles well adapted to the ecosystems. But the use of building materials of local origin, whether bamboo, *attap* or mud, makes possible a range of housing styles far more suited to the Asian environment than imported styles using concrete, corrugated iron and aluminium. Moreover, the energy input represented by these traditional building styles is a fraction of that needed for imported modern building styles†—and few Asian countries will be able to afford to disregard this aspect. The possibilities of using an "ecological" approach even in the field of urban planning are illustrated by the New Bombay Plan; this is for a city of 2 million inhabitants, whose housing will be built on very small plots from local materials by the families concerned, and which will be knit together by a system of rapid public transport.

And, a final major development issue: in regions like Asia characterized by high population densities, where labour is one of the cheapest production factors, surely the emphasis on capital-intensive industry is ecologically ridiculous? Does not the Chinese pattern of dispersed labour-intensive industries integrated with city-based capital-intensive industries represent a style of development far more relevant to the needs of Asia—because more attuned to ecological realities—than any imported development "model"?

The Irrelevance of Alien Development Models

By the middle of the 1970s the carefully cultivated myths about political and economic progress were wearing distinctly thin and the realities of Asia, the

* Oriental wet-rice cultivation is "the most productive, by far, of any farm system"; measured in energy terms its output is 40 times the input. By comparison, Richard Merrill quotes a figure of 2.6 for the energy output/energy input ratio of California rice production, of 0.77 for raw vegetables and 1.36 for all raw crops. Western farming is increasingly a gigantic "energy sink".

† In the U.K. the energy-cost of constructing a rammed earth, steel and glass dwelling is estimated at one-eleventh the energy-cost of constructing a conventional brick, concrete and steel house.

often harsh realities, could no longer be disregarded. And perhaps the dominating reality is that conventional, which means "alien", development models had done little to solve any of the major issues confronting the peoples and the nations of Asia. Which, it may be remarked in parentheses, is scarcely to be wondered at, since the economic theories on which such "models" were based were proving a less than adequate guide to economists and politicians attempting to cope with the crisis in the countries of the Centre.

In Asia, as in the remainder of the Periphery, economic development had failed to narrow the gap in living levels between the peoples of the Periphery and of the Centre. In many Asian nations, moreover, the gap between a small and privileged predatory élite and the impoverished masses widened; frequently, as in the case of areas afflicted with the Green Revolution, this widening gap is a direct result of "development". Ambitious schemes of financial aid have too often had the strange effect of enriching small élite groups, of benefiting donor nations more than receiving nations, of increasing the dependence of the nations of the Periphery; it is for these reasons that Mahbub ul Haq can say that "the developing world would have been better off" if it had not received the aid it got in recent years. Policies of population restriction, peddled by politicians and economists of the White North as an answer to the problem of poverty, have manifestly failed (Taiwan and South Korea are cited as "success stories" but this ignores the level of foreign aid which makes them quite atypical cases); the labour force of the next fifteen years is already born and these youngsters constitute the core of the so-called "population problem". Policies of industrialization have not only been irrelevant because of their capital-intensive character but also because of their concentration on consumer goods, rather than on the producer goods most Asian nations need to develop a self-sustaining economy. Moreover, many "major" industrial projects represent mere assemblage plants, established to take advantage of the miserably low wage rates in some Asian countries. And the impact of the failure of the Centre's ambitious schemes of "economic development" to arrest the process of subjective (and objective) pauperization in Asia has been enhanced by the agonizingly protracted failure of the most powerful and wealthy nation of the Centre to impose on South-East Asia a military solution to what are essentially political and economic problems.

The results of the failure of the orthodox development policies of the Centre to arrest what Robert Heilbroner terms "the descent into hell" of much of the Periphery have been two-fold. First, as James P. Grant of the Overseas Development Council has pointed out, the increasing crisis of under-employment and unemployment, coinciding with the emergence of China from the haze of travesties and plain lies about its social and economic achievements, seems to have enhanced "the attractiveness of the Maoist model to many in the developing countries"; at the very least it has made it clear that there *are* alternatives to orthodox development strategies—and that some of the alternatives *can* work. Secondly, in those Asian countries where a strong left-wing movement capable of mounting alternative development strategies has not yet emerged, we are witnessing a shift from the forms of democratic government towards army-based "praetorian" régimes. Such régimes may, indeed, be congenial to some outside governments—but the logic of their policies is too often such as to intensify and prolong underdevelopment. Which means that increasingly the contrast is not that between "Free World" Asia and socialist Asia but that between the military authoritarianisms and the socialist societies. The contrast is described by Barang: "According to the best informed, it seems that the armed forces (of the Asian socialist countries) play the role assigned them by the civil authorities, while being collaborating parties in the political process, according to a dialectic relationship without an equivalent in the capitalist world (and, for this reason, often denied by Western observers). By contrast, in non-socialist Asia, the guns have far too often tended to command the parties—or to suppress them. This is certainly no accident."

THE SOCIAL AND ECONOMIC PATTERNS OF ASIA AND THE PACIFIC

Crowded Lands and Empty Lands

One of the most striking contrasts between the countries of the Far East and of Australasia is the contrast in population density. The overall density for those Asian countries with which we are concerned in this volume is 75 per sq. km.; this is approximately three times the world average and is over thirty times the density for Australasia. It is the awareness, perhaps subconscious, of these great disparities, of this juxtaposition of crowded Asian countrysides and almost empty lands of recent European settlement in the South-West Pacific, that has in part helped shape Australasian attitudes to Asia and especially to Asian immigration. Figures for the nutrient density (i.e. density per sq. km. of crop land) show that the crop land of humid Asia is supporting a density of population twice as great as the world average and about ten times the density for Australasia (the exclusion of pasture lands in the calculation of this ratio exaggerates the real densities in Australia and New Zealand). India has a nutrient density of 350 people per sq. km., over most of South-East Asia the density is 350-400, in China it is double this, and in Indonesia and Japan the density is respectively four and almost six times as great as that of India. There are thus major contrasts in population pressure between the various sectors of the region and these contrasts are exaggerated by economic structures for, to use a very simple simile, an undiversified economy (i.e. that of Indonesia) is rather like a single-storey house—it soon gets crowded; economic diversification, which opens up new sectors of the economy (or adds more storeys to the house), makes it possible to accommodate a much larger population and at a higher level of living. Japan is an excellent example of this for here the development of manufacturing and of service industries makes it possible to sustain at a relatively high level of living a population whose nutrient density is many times that of the economically less diversified countries of South-East Asia.

This contrast between crowded lands and empty lands is found also within the territory of most of the nations of the Asian-Pacific world. In Australasia the densely-settled south-east and east form a narrow fringe on an almost empty continental interior; in New Zealand the North Island—and especially the Auckland and Wellington regions—dominates the population map while in both the North and South Islands great stretches of upland country have negligible densities of population. Contrasts of this sort are, however, most marked in Asia. In China nine-tenths of the population live on one-sixth the area of the country; in the Indian sub-continent almost half the population lives on slightly over one-fifth of the area; in mainland and insular South-East Asia the upland regions (such as the Annamite Cordillera) or the forested interiors (as in Borneo) are virtually empty, while the lowlands and the great alluvial plains may support over one thousand people per sq. km. This contrast between thinly peopled uplands (occupied by primitive shifting cultivators) and closely settled lowlands (occupied by peoples belonging to the "high cultures" of Asia) is rooted in the cultural history of the region. Over the whole of Monsoon Asia—and especially in Eastern Asia—peasant culture is based on intensive, almost garden-style, cultivation of grains and vegetables. For countless generations man has assessed the environment in terms of this culture, choosing those types of land lending themselves to intensive use and rejecting or by-passing other environments. Lacking techniques of upland farming and livestock rearing (e.g. the mixed farming of Western Europe) he has avoided the upland areas or has used them destructively as a source of firewood or constructional timber. And, because of this "cultural bias", once population pressure became unbearable it was relieved not by colonization of adjoining uplands but by the seeking out and occupation of neighbouring river basins and alluvial plains. Asia, "over-populated" Asia, still awaits the agricultural revolution, involving the development of new pasture strains and of upland livestock rearing and the extension of commercial tree crops, which will make possible the redistribution of population over the empty lands of the mountains and the interiors.

City and Countryside

The Australasian sector of the Asian-Pacific world—and, because of its longer period of modern economic development, Japan—contrast strikingly with the remainder of the region in degree and character of urbanization. Australia and New Zealand, with four-fifths of their populations classed as urban, are almost as heavily urbanized as the United Kingdom; in Japan almost three-quarters of the population is urban, approximately the same proportion as in France. By contrast, in the rest of Monsoon Asia the percentage of population classed as urban nowhere exceeds 30 (Philippines 29.9, South Korea 28.6) and in most countries the proportion is 20 per cent or below (India 21 per cent, China 23 per cent, South-East Asia about the same). As for the city-dwelling population (defined as those dwelling in agglomerations of 100,000 people or more), the proportion in most Asian countries except Japan and South Korea appears to be less than one-tenth of the total. The percentages may be low; the absolute figures are, however, very large, the urban population of China, as an example, being over 50 million in 1953.

Because the rate of total population growth is high the pace of urbanization in Asia is very rapid; in the 1940s and 1950s it was of the order of 4.7 per cent p.a., as compared with the rate of 2.1 per cent experienced in Western Europe during its period of most rapid urbanization in the late nineteenth century. The annual growth rate of individual Asian cities has been even higher: for Jakarta between 1955 and 1959 it was 11 per cent, for Kuala Lumpur between 1947 and 1970 it was 7 per cent. And, looking to the future, many Asian cities can be expected to double their population in the next 15–20 years; indeed, Kingsley Davis has estimated that metropolitan Calcutta's population may increase fivefold by the end of the century, to reach 36 million.

It is worth stressing the rapid pace of this urbanization and the role of the Third World city as both a cause and an effect of continued underdevelopment and poverty.

The number of people in many of the great cities of Asia now doubles in ten years or less. Much of this increase is taking place in the shantytowns, the *bidonvilles*, on the periphery of the great metropolitan agglomerations; in these population may double in five to seven years. Penetrating along waterways and rail lines in Jakarta, fingering deep towards the modern business core of Calcutta, girdling Ho Chi Minh City (formerly Saigon), with a noose of festering slums, the squatter community is emerging as the dominant form of urban reality in this last third of the twentieth century. These squatter settlements are, in the words of Götz Hagmüller, "a sombre tribute to human ingenuity in the face of privation". They are, moreover, and as he so rightly stresses, "the most viable shelter for their inhabitants in economic terms"—though this fact is largely ignored by governments whose resources are inadequate to provide more than a pathetic fraction of the houses needed and whose "low-cost" housing schemes combine drabness and the promise of early squalor with a complete absence of that community sense which pervades many squatter settlements. And we should not lose sight of the political implications of this pseudo-urbanization, for behind the feelings of despair and individual helplessness these disinherited and uprooted squatter masses conceal a major potential for social upheaval and revolutionary change. This is because they nourish hopes of a better life, because by their very existence the slum and squatter communities are successfully "challenging a cherished symbol: the sanctity of property rights and the civil order on which it stands". As Erich H. Jacoby sees it, the landless semi-urbanized peasants of the cities and the landless of the rural areas will come together within organized peasant and worker movements and thus: "the semi-urbanized peasants in the large cities of South Asia and Latin America will come to function as a gigantic pressure group for *agrarian* changes within the very precincts of political power" (emphasis added KB).

The role of the Third World—and South Asian—city as "a cause and effect of continued under-development and poverty" derives in part from the colonial origin of many of Asia's great cities. Colonialism, it is now increasingly recognized, was little concerned with the economic development of the colonized countries. The cities in Asia which it created were economically related much less to the needs of their own hinterland than to the needs of the wider world economy. Indeed, to quote Hagmüller again, the city "may be seen as a link in the chain of a worldwide urban system of exploitation, *a vehicle for the transfer of material, physical and spiritual energy* from rural to metropolitan areas, from poor to rich nations, from the Third World countries to the post-industrialized countries" (emphasis in original). Such a transfer, a "transfer without transformation", contributes little to the economic development of the country concerned. Moreover, the bigger the city, the greater the scale of this transfer, this flow—and the stronger the "pull" on migrants from the countryside and the greater the retardation of real economic development.

Urban economic structures are warped. The secondary industries which made possible the growth of the great cities of the Western world are poorly developed for what little capital there is finds more profitable outlets for investment in the service industries or in construction; unemployment rates in the urban centres of South-East Asia are estimated at 15–25 per cent and the vast array of petty and unskilled operations conceals a high proportion of underemployed whose contribution to the economy of the city or nation is marginal. There is a "tertiary involution" of labour no less than of capital for, "while urban labour potential increases, many workers fail to find employment, not only in industry—which is lacking or underdeveloped—but also in the organized service sector". The level of life of this "pseudotertiary" sector—or, as Hagmüller so aptly describes it, this "hand-to-mouth sector", stands in sharp contrast to that of the elite groups—the white collar bureaucrats, the technicians, the doctors. The metropolitan concentration of these elite groups illustrates that, in a free enterprise system, skills, like capital, flow into those sectors and those areas where remuneration is highest—and not necessarily where the need is greatest. . . . The countryside thus remains starved of capital and of medical, technical and other desperately needed skills and thus continues to stagnate. The urban areas have to provide the basic social services—schools, housing, hospitals (all often needlessly extravagant)—demanded by this proliferating élite. And these needlessly heavy social costs of urbanization are a heavy drain on the scarce investment funds of many Asian nations and so help to prolong, even, aggravate, the condition of under-development.

That some direction of man-power, and especially skilled man-power, is essential to overcome some of the problems of urbanization in Asia comes up inevitably against the argument that this is an intolerable encroachment on freedom. And yet, as Javier Prats Llauradó insists: "Complete freedom of employment of graduates may be logical and democratic in a country which can afford it, but we may well ask why a poor country, which finds that the expropriation of land and the strict planning of the means of production are normal courses to follow, should leave the hiring of its best trained men to liberal free play". This is a question which it is increasingly urgent for the Asian nations to confront.

The relationships between city and countryside and the whole process of urbanization are quite different in the socialist states of East Asia. The differences are most clearly illustrated by the People's Republic of China. Industrialization has been on a large scale and an apparently successful attempt has been made to disperse new development. Medium and small cities have a sizeable industrial component while the development of industry at the commune level has diffused sophisticated industries deep into the countryside. Such dispersed industrialization, combined with the modernization and intensification of agriculture, has made it possible not only to control the "blind migration" of peasants towards the cities but also to absorb in the rural sector most of the continuing increase in the labour force. That labour and skills, like all other resources of a developing nation, must be directed to the regions or sectors where the social needs are greatest, is a fundamental tenet of Chinese development planning. And that such a direction is not regarded as a constraint is due partly to the Chinese policy of reducing the differentials between town and country, between mental work and manual work, but above all to the substitution of moral for material incentives in the field of economic development. Which suggests that the negative, anti-developmental, role of the city commented on above can be overcome only by a fundamental re-structuring of society as a whole. . . .

Economies and Semi-Economies

There are major contrasts between Australasia/Japan and the great majority of the countries of Asia in the levels of their economy and, closely linked with this, the character of their economic structure. The levels of economic development are indicated crudely by the *per caput* G.N.P., measured in U.S. $. For much of Asia this is of the order of $100; for Japan $2,300; for Australia and New Zealand it is higher than the Japanese figure. Other indices, such as steel or energy consumption, show this same cleavage. Even more striking are the contrasts in economic structure or, to be more precise, in the degree of integration of the national economy. Australia, New Zealand and Japan possess developed and closely articulated economies similar to those of the developed nations of the Atlantic world; all sectors of the economy are "meshed" into a smoothly working economic machine. By contrast, the economies of the majority of Asian countries are "disarticulated" economies, economies in which the subsistence farming sector, the export-oriented sector (whether based on agriculture, mining or manufacturing) and the urban sector are only linked in the most tenuous way. Indeed, the modern sector—the sector dominated by the great firms and by the cities—is tied in more closely to the economy of overseas countries than to the economy of the rural hinterland. This *disarticulation* is in part a legacy of colonial days and results from the *domination* of outside forces (the former metropolitan government, the great trading, mining or industrial groups); this domination has created a *dependent* economy, or a semi-economy, little related to the needs of an independent nation. One of the major problems facing national planners is the need to overcome this disarticulation, to integrate the modern sectors of the economy with the traditional agricultural sector. Without such an integration the modern sector tends to develop at a disproportionate rate and at the expense of the well-being of the country as a whole (*cp.* the almost cancerous growth of the great cities referred to above), the rural areas stagnate and a dangerously explosive economic and political situation results. And without such an integration, without the creation of a smooth-functioning economy under national control and embracing the entirety of the state area, real development is impossible.

As a result of external domination the economy of most Asian countries is warped and vulnerable. The warping resulted from their historical role as sources of raw materials and as markets for the industries of the metropolitan countries of Western Europe. They still depend heavily on the export of primary produce; the proportions range from 56 per cent in the case of India to 100 per cent in the case of South Viet-Nam and Cambodia. Only Japan (8 per cent) is an exception; Australia (84 per cent) and New Zealand (93 per cent) show in this respect strong similarities with their Asian neighbours. This heavy dependence on primary products at a time when the price levels for these products are subject to unpredictable fluctuations, with a general downward trend, results in a high degree of economic vulnerability; long-term planning is virtually impossible in such an economic climate. And where the range of primary products exported is limited (as in the case of New Zealand, heavily dependent on livestock products, or Malaysia, heavily dependent on tin and rubber) this vulnerability is increased.

A Generation of Development

It is now over thirty years since the end of the Second World War and many of the nations of Asia have experienced two decades of independence. It is appropriate here to attempt to evaluate what has happened and to spell out more fully the human implications of the economic processes described above.

One of the most striking aspects of the last two or three years is the questioning not merely of orthodox "development" strategies but of the whole development process itself. This scepticism regarding the relevance of much of the conventional wisdom in this field can only be welcomed; it is important enough to merit a separate section (*see below:* "Time to Stand Development Theory on its Head"). The disappointments of the so-called "Decade of Development" certainly contributed to the growth of a new realism; as the decade drew to a close it was realized, to quote Professor Denis Goulet, that "the world is perhaps no closer to a victory over misery than before. Indeed, for most of the world's people development remains a distant dream if not a nightmare." As for those developed societies where the conventional indices such as G.N.P. or per capita income *had* increased, economists such as E. J. Mishan underlined the impossibility of infinite growth in a finite world, stressed the human and economic costs of a good deal of recent development and, along with American economists such as Lekachman, stressed the uselessness of G.N.P. as an index of economic (or human) well-being. It remained for Richard Wilkinson to challenge the cultural arrogance with which the "developed" societies sell their version of "development" to the rest of humanity and to advance the thesis that, measured in terms of labour input or energy input, the "developed" industrial societies are markedly less efficient than more "backward" ones. He stresses—something of major importance when we confront the issue of Asian development—that many of the things conventionally regarded as indices of development and progress represent mere attempts to compensate for those things lost with the decay of traditional society, and he comes to the conclusion that "the experience of none of the developed countries suggests that future development will of itself eliminate poverty, reduce slums or cope with any of our social problems". But we will return to these basic questions in the next section; for the moment we will confine ourselves to the orthodox interpretation of economic realities.

The broad economic picture since the Second World War certainly indicates that, in "Free Asia", there has been a continuing shift from agricultural to non-agricultural employment. That this sectoral change has been "basically a shift from rural to urban poverty, rather than a fundamental improvement in productivity and welfare over the whole economy" is borne out by the cautious comments of various UN reports. For perhaps 70 per cent of the population of "Free Asia" there seems to have been no major improvement in living standards; diets are no better than in the 1930s and housing remains wretched, with a great gap separating the few rich from the innumerable poor. Population growth cancels out economic advancement for, given existing socio-political conditions, the mass of labour, instead of being (as in China or, an earlier date, Japan) a factor for progress, is one of the main obstacles to progress. In spite of a policy aimed at economic independence, dependence on outside goods and technology has increased, for industrialization based on consumer goods and a policy of import substitution has led to a heavy demand for foreign-manufactured capital equipment and for outside technology. The fact that much of this consumer goods industry is in the hands of branches of foreign firms and that foreign aid and investment ties these countries into the economies of the advanced metropolitan countries has aggravated the dependent status referred to in the preceding section. Moreover the consumer industries are oriented not to the needs of the peasantry or the urban masses but to the needs of a relatively small élite group. The growth of these industries is often cited as evidence that the Asian nations are reaching the point of economic "take-off"; this overlooks that once demand has been met it will be impossible to sustain existing growth rates, for the commodities being produced are irrelevant to the well-being of the peasantry or the urban masses and the purchasing power of these groups in any case is at present insignificant. Not only are such capital-intensive industries imperfectly integrated with the labour-intensive craft industries or with agriculture but the rising capital/labour ratio and rising productivity associated with their development has led to the emergence of a small economically-favoured sector in the population of the great cities. The relative well-being of this privileged group stands in sharp contrast to the great mass of those in the craft and service sectors, including the messenger boys, bar girls, hawkers, cab-drivers and servants who live in the slums and the shanty towns.

Economically, then, Asian society has become increasingly polarized as the growth within the modern enclave sector has given rise to widening economic—and hence social—disparities and to the threat of increasingly social conflict as an increasing sector of the population sees ever more clearly that the escape from poverty—and the initiation of real nation-wide development—is impossible within the existing class structure. The condition of Free Asia a quarter of a century after the end of the Second World War has been meticulously explored by Gunnar Myrdal in his monumental *Asian Drama*; in Myrdal's words: "The plight of the masses of people in the underdeveloped economies of South Asia would be serious enough if income were evenly distributed. . . . The high degree of inequality means that the vast majority in each nation are forced to eke out an existence on annual incomes well below the already quite inadequate national average. Regardless of the crudity of the empirical evidence . . . it cannot and in fact does not conceal the reality of massive poverty."

It may well be interjected that economic statistics suggest an imposing pace of development and thus belie the above picture. But, given the emphasis on "the development of Asian economies rather than on the development of Asia's peoples", an imposing statistical façade may, and often does, conceal the reality of continuing underdevelopment, of deteriorating conditions for the great mass of the people. And not only does this façade conceal widening social disparities, it may also conceal widening regional disparities which may jeopardize the political stability, even the very existence, of some of the tenuously surviving new nation states of Asia. In India the G.N.P. increased by some 50 per cent in the 1960s yet a recent study shows that 40–50 per cent of the total population has a *per capita* income below the official poverty line where malnutrition begins; moreover, the *per capita* income of this group has declined while the average *per capita* income has been increasing. In the Philippines the G.N.P. grew at a rate of some 7 per cent per annum during the 1960s but regional inequalities between Luzon and Mindanao widened, and this was an important fact in the revolt in the southern Philippines. In Pakistan a sustained growth rate of 6 per cent per annum during the 1960s was accompanied by increasing unemployment, by a drop of one-third in real wages in the industrial sector and by a doubling of the *per capita* income disparity between East and West Pakistan. And, as Mahbub ul Haq comments: "in 1968, while the international world was still applauding Pakistan as a model of development, the system exploded"—and economic factors no less than political factors contributed to this explosion.

The patterns of development in Japan and the socialist countries have been different from those in the rest of Monsoon Asia. There is a dynamic lacking in other countries; at the same time few countries appear more widely different than a G.N.P.-maximizing Japan and a welfare-maximizing China. Japan, whose economy has benefited from both the Korean and Vietnam wars, today has the world's third largest G.N.P. Her development has been based on expanding markets in South and South-East Asia (partly a result of Dulles' strategy of using Japan to counter communist trade efforts in the region), and on the resources of South-East Asia and Australasia (in 1970, 40 per cent of Japan's iron ore imports came from Australia). The thrust of Japanese development since 1945 has increasingly integrated the less developed economies of the Western Pacific, from Australasia to South Korea, into the highly industrialized economy of Japan and there are many who see the country as the leader of some future Asian-Pacific Defence and Development Community.

The last year or so has, however, seen the emergence of three factors which may blunt this economic thrust. Firstly, Australia's increasing reluctance to become simply a source of raw materials for Japan, and especially as far as minerals are concerned (New Zealand's Government, by contrast, is still open-mouthed at the "Japanese miracle"). Secondly, there is at least the beginning of criticism of the negative aspects of Japanese economic expansion in South-East Asia. Foreign investors, says N. S. Setiawan, "use Indonesia purely as a market and do not help develop real industries"; he goes on to emphasise that what Indonesia needs is "not just assemblying workshops such as Toyota and other companies have built". Thirdly, it is belatedly realized, and even in Japanese official circles, that the ecological and human costs of the country's economic "miracle" had been somehow overlooked. But by 1972 the Japanese *Environmental White Paper* admitted: "The environmental problem now seems to be approaching a point of explosion. Degradation of the environment represents a real threat to each citizen of the nation and *enormous losses to the nation as a whole* . . ." (my italics). A "miracle of economic development" that results in "enormous losses to the nation as a whole" is a strange phenomenon. And yet some Japanese writers, such as Jun Ui, claim that it is precisely the fact that Japanese manufacturers ignored the (costly) need for anti-pollution measures that gave them a critically important "edge" over their competitors.

The pattern of development and the goals of development have been rather different in the East Asian socialist countries and especially in the Chinese People's Republic. Technological progress has been steady and indeed has surprised many outside observers. Using the conventional yardstick of per capita G.N.P. and relying on "establishment" estimates the growth rate of China's economy since 1949 is estimated variously at between 1 per cent and 4 per cent annually. More recently, Curtis Ullerich has suggested the real size of China's G.N.P. (at 1952 prices) "as most certainly being somewhere between $170 and 190 billion"; this would imply an annual growth rate of "well over 10 per cent", producing a fivefold increase in per capita G.N.P. in 20 years. At the same time, Ullerich stresses that China is far less preoccupied with maximizing G.N.P. than is the West; rather is the emphasis on minimizing social inequalities and thus improving the overall quality of life of the Chinese people. Given this emphasis, given the size of China's internal market and given her broad resource base the outward thrust in search of markets and raw materials which is typical of an expanding capitalist economy such as that of Japan has been lacking; China's development has been largely "inner-directed". Moreover, however impressive the growth rate, since the Cultural Revolution Maoist economic development has not merely played down the importance of expanding production as a virtual end in itself but has deliberately and positively emphasized economic development as a factor in helping to create "the new socialist man". As noted below this involves a policy of "building on the worst" which is diametrically opposed to the capitalist tendency to "build on the best" (i.e. the most immediately profitable). Chinese planners seem determined to pursue this policy of "transforming man" even if, *over the short term*, it means a lower rate of economic growth. *Over the long term* they believe that the sense of selflessness and purpose inculcated in the "new man" will release a huge reservoir of enthusiasm, energy, and creativity and that this will make it possible to push socialist construction to even higher levels. The cumulative testimony of a wide range of Western businessmen and of economists, such as Galbraith, who have visited China in the last year or so suggests that this indeed has taken place, that, in Curtis Ullerich's words: "China seems to have found the key to accelerated development and to the problem of surmounting material backwardness within humanly acceptable time spans". If this is the case, the significance of Chinese technological achievements in the nuclear field is dwarfed by the long-term significance of what the Chinese term "the spiritual atom bomb" of Maoist thought. And the challenge of this new society, with its rejections of old priorities and old motivations and its emphasis on "men" rather than "things", will not be confined to Japan or China's other Asian neighbours. Indeed, in a world in which ecological degradation and pollution seem inseparable from economic development the success of the Chinese in diffusing throughout their countryside an efficient low-impact technology and their virtual elimination of "waste" in certain industrial and urban contexts are achievements from which even the most "developed" societies might learn.

Time to Stand Development Theory on its Head

That India, "the forward bastion of free enterprise in Asia", a state which up to 1969 had received £5,350 million of foreign economic assistance, should in the mid-1970s be still plagued by chronic food shortages, by a growing polarization between rich and poor, and a steady drift toward dictatorship suggests that the time has arrived for a reassessment of the whole concept of development in Asia (perhaps, too, in the advanced societies).

In its simplest form "development" is regarded as progress along a road leading from lesser development to greater; "progress" is conveniently, if unrealistically, measured by various technological indices such as steel production or energy consumption or by that "lunatic index of economic well-being"—the G.N.P. The more G.N.P. the better—or so the conventional wisdom goes. That "development" or "economic growth" may create as much illfare as welfare, that it may lead to widening social and regional disparities and to large-scale cultural liquidation was overlooked. Today, however, conditions in Asia and the rest of the Third World demonstrate that, in the words of Mahbub ul Haq, " a high growth rate has been, and is, no guarantee against worsening poverty and economic explosions"; that, in the words of two other scientists: "increasing *per capita* G.N.P. is consistent with diminishing social welfare, or, at least, with mounting social dissatisfaction".

Such conditions suggest that Asian planners—and their mentors in the White North—should reject the accepted yet manifestly inaccurate concept that development is something that can be measured by some sort of index of physical output and rather regard it, as many French experts do, as a process leading to "the development of all men and of the whole man". This means rejecting the processes of maximizing G.N.P. for such processes lead to what has been termed "growth without development", the condition in which, behind the statistical facade of a steadily rising G.N.P., social and economic disparities between classes and regions grow progressively wider. The gap in levels of living and welfare between the White North (the Centre) and the Third World (the Periphery) increases as, and this has been demonstrated by André Gunder Frank, development at the Centre creates underdevelopment at the Periphery. And within areas of dependent development in the Third World economic processes create this same Centre/Periphery phenomenon on a smaller scale, e.g. the widening gap between Bangkok and Northeast Thailand, between the west coast of Malaysia and the northeast, between Luzon and Mindanao, between the Jakarta area and densely populated Central Java.* One of the questions which hangs like a sword over the future of Asia is: how long will so many scores of millions tolerate "development policies" which shunt them on to one side as simply irrelevant, which deny them any meaningful participation in the shaping of their lives?.

The alternative has been set out by Mahbub ul Haq, Senior Economic Adviser to the World Bank: "the problem of development must be defined as a selective attack on the worst forms of poverty . . . We were taught to take care of our G.N.P. as this will take care of poverty. Let us reverse this and take care of poverty as this will take care of the G.N.P. In other words, let us worry about the *content* of the G.N.P even more than its rate of increase". And he adds, "employment should become a primary objective of planning" (*see "The Danger Point"* below). The country whose economic achievements are most relevant to the other countries of Asia is, he suggests, China which has achieved "full employment and equitable income distribution at a relatively low level of *per capita* income". The time has come to discard the usual rhetoric of the China-watchers and to undertake a full and objective analysis of China's *experience*. Asians, he suggests—and he speaks as an *Asian* expert—have had their fill of "tired old trade-offs and crooked-looking production functions", of old ideas polished-up and old theories dusted-off. They—and perhaps many non-Asians too—realize it is time to "take a fresh look at the entire theory and practice of development".

The Danger Point

In the first paragraph of this Introduction we spoke of the attitudes and viewpoints of Asian peoples. It is these hundreds of millions of peasants and proletarians, and not the politicians now holding the stage, who will define Asian realities in the last quarter of the twentieth century—and for proletarians no less than peasants the dominant reality is likely to be a revolutionary reality.

In the overdeveloped society of Japan the pace of economic development has led to pollution on a scale sufficient to provoke a widespread and increasingly radical revolt among the citizenry. Says a Japanese newspaper: "many of the citizens' movements against pollution are started by concerned people who do not subscribe to membership in any political party . . . Once these independent movements start growing, they can absorb a variety of people full of energies. These . . . become a militant and visible part of the movement, displaying an immense force and often go beyond the expectations of the leaders of the movements themselves. This . . . seems to suggest that in today's society opportunities are ripe for violent and rebellious acts to take place". The Japanese *Environmental White Paper* says the country is approaching "a point of explosion"—but this is a socio-political as well as an ecological explosion. . . .

Japan, however, is exceptional and throughout the Third World (and in most of the non-socialist countries of Asia) "the danger point", as W. H. Pawley has stressed, lies in the problem of employment, in what an American expert has called "the global job crisis". This arises from the fact that the economies of "Free Asia" are at present quite unable to provide employment for more than a fraction of the total labour force, that population growth means an increase in the labour force of countries where unemployment levels often exceed those of the West during the Great Depression and where underemployment levels (converted to an "unemployment equivalent") may attain 50 per cent of the labour force. Pawley sums up the situation in the Third World thus: "Un- and underemployment, arising basically from the enormous imbalance between human numbers needing work and the amount of capital available to employ them, and accentuated every year by an influx which far exceeds the outflow at the other end—this problem of employment and not the technical ability to produce food—represents the danger point in 90–100 countries comprising 70 per cent of the world's population". And included in this 90–100 countries are most of the nations of non-socialist Asia. Family limitation is no answer to this problem for, as Pierre Pradervand has shown, even the most sophisticated contraceptive programmes are unlikely to affect the size of the labour supply for a generation; and Asia—or the Third World—cannot afford to wait that long. Orthodox development plans with their *capital-intensive* industry (and increasingly capital-intensive agriculture) merely aggravate the problem; what is needed, as Oshima stresses, are new and more *labour-intensive* technologies in industry and agriculture. And such a radically new strategy means, as is made clear by Mahbub ul Haq, that employment should become a primary objective of planning, that the pool of labour should be treated as given, and that "it must be combined with the existing capital stock irrespective of how low the productivity of labour or capital may be".

The Algerian planner A. Remili has stressed that an examination of "the economy of waste" is fundamental to an understanding of poverty. Such an examination would draw attention to the immense waste of precious human resources resulting from unemployment and underemployment in Asia; this may conservatively be estimated at 200,000 million manhours yearly in non-socialist Asia. This waste is one of the major causes of poverty; as the example of "overpopulated" China shows, this tremendous potential wealth can be mobilized and this mobilization can be a powerful means of breaking the poverty barrier and, perhaps even more important, of making possible not only "the development of all men" but also "the development of the whole man".

And, it may be observed, the wastage of human resources in Asia today is not only humanly indefensible; it also contributes to the instability of many Asian societies. The "intolerable economic and social

---

* According to N. S. Setiawan (*see* Bibliography) 263 of the foreign investments in Indonesia in 1972 were in Jakarta, 15 in Central Java.

conditions" involved, may well, as Pawley suggests, "lead to such a degree of social upheaval that political and administrative systems break down . . . In this event," he adds, "we can forget about economic and social progress".

That we need a new perspective on the human aspects of Asian development can no longer be doubted; that the relevance of China's experience in confronting the critical issues of unemployment and under-employment will be heeded is more doubtful. But one thing is certain—and that is that, as peasants and proletarians rediscover the idea of the system of power, the truth that suffering is *caused*—Asian governments and their Western and Soviet mentors can no longer peddle "development" policies that, in their obsession with production, have forgotten that development is *for* people . . . for, as the Chinese say, "Of all things in the world, people are the most precious".

Men, Machines and Politics

Perhaps this "new perspective on development in Asia" can be found in the concept of an "intermediate technology".

Asia, we have underlined, is a poor continent. It is unlikely ever to attain the ephemeral affluence at the moment being enjoyed by the developed nations of the Centre. And, given this reality, the words of Gandhi have an immediate relevance: the poor of the world cannot be helped by mass production, only *by production by the masses*. And of production by the masses E. F. Schumacher has written: "The system . . . mobilizes the priceless resources which are possessed by all human beings, their clever brains and skilful hands, *and supports them with first-class tools*. . . . The technology of *production by the masses*, making use of the best of modern knowledge and experience, is conducive to decentralization, compatible with the laws of ecology, gentle in its use of scarce resources, and designed to serve the human person instead of making him the servant of machines."

Such a viewpoint is still dismissed by many technocrats, for whom "development" is synonymous with "progress" as defined by the economists, the specialists, of the Western or Soviet blocs. But as Mrs. Gandhi comments: "To most people, progress has become synonymous with imitation of Western models but wherever we have followed models from the industrial society and have been insensitive to our own circumstances the results have not been happy. The time has come for us to think deeply about the kind of progress we want." And this thinking has to overcome the intellectual blindness that fails to realize the achievements of peripheral countries such as India in the days before steel, electricity, concrete and the other "inputs" associated with modern high-impact technologies; it has to recognize that, if it costs £2,000 (say) to create a work place in modern industry, the capital required to accommodate the annual population increase of even one country such as India exceeds by far the total net inflow of capital into the whole of the Periphery; above all it has to recognize, as E. F. Schumacher stresses, that "the primary consideration (of development) cannot be to maximize output per man; it must be to maximize work opportunities for the unemployed and the underemployed. For a poor man the chance to work is the greatest of all needs, and even poorly paid and relatively unproductive work is better than idleness."

Such a "self-help technology, or democratic or people's technology" can, as the examples of the East Asian socialist régimes demonstrate, be diffused swiftly. It is "gentle in its use of scarce resources"and can utilize resources too limited to be attractive to large scale technology, and because of this ease in dispersal and because it does not demand the capital-inputs demanded by large scale technology it does not contribute to the wide social or regional differences associated with most other types of technology. And since it is a technology within the reach of each small community it does not contain the danger that it will, like many technical processes, become a means whereby a class or an individual can dominate others. "There should", said Gandhi, "be no place for machines that concentrate power in a few hands and turn the masses into mere machine minders. . . ."

The advantages of an "intermediate technology" in a context such as that of Monsoon Asia are obviously impressive and the last two decades of development in the socialist states of East Asia have demonstrated how skilled planning can integrate such a technology with, on one hand, the most sophisticated modern technology and, on the other, with traditional or "peasant" crafts. The Chinese experience, however, has underlined clearly one thing—and that is the importance of political and social re-structuring as a prerequisite for the successful introduction of new technologies. For control over technology is a means whereby social and political control can be strengthened in an area such as Monsoon Asia. This, indeed, is recognized by overseas interests and local élite groups—and it is only when the economic and political hold of such groups is broken that significant technological change becomes possible. In David Dickson's words: "Intermediate technology is ideally suited to policies that stress the importance of self-help, being based on the general concept of 'development from below'. Yet the implementation of these policies, and the social structures that they imply, is a political task."

Of Desperation and Despots . . .

Yet, in truth, the difficulties of breaking with the "transferred wisdom" of the former colonial powers have proved insuperable outside those nations which have carried through a revolutionary transformation of society. The links between local élite groups and outside interests have been too strong, and because present development patterns offer little hope to the masses, because the gap between rich and poor widens, there develops a socially and politically explosive situation. The answer to mass desperation has been a proliferation of despotisms as the dominant group has recourse to increasingly authoritarian measures to maintain stability. Civilian régimes become overtly (South Korea) or covertly (Singapore) military in character and in the final stages the military takes over; since 1960, says Marcel Barang in *Le Monde Diplomatique*, there have been some forty coups in Asia.

Perhaps there is no inherent reason why authoritarian régimes in Asia should have proved incapable of surmounting the problem of creating real economic development; indeed, many writers see no possibility of even developed societies confronting the problems of the future without a strong measure of authoritarianism. And elsewhere in the countries of the Periphery military régimes, or military-backed régimes, have shown that they possess the ability to break through some of the "blockages" which arrest the development process, even of initiating the beginnings of development on a broad front. During the immediate post-colonial period in Asia this was particularly the case: the army was a revolutionary force, contributing to the disintegration of outdated structures; it was a stabilizing force; it was a force of modernization, supporting the aspirations of the middle class and the demands of the masses for social change; above all, its ranks contained a high proportion of those possessing administrative or technological competence in many Asian countries.

But during the last fifteen to twenty years the Cold War has drawn in most of the nations of Asia. The confrontation between the U.S.A. and the U.S.S.R. meant that the tensions and the frustrations resulting from increasing subjective (and objective) pauperization in the nations of Asia tended to be interpreted rather as manifestations of the devious designs of countries such as China or the U.S.S.R. on the independence of such "free world" nations; such designs could, so the conventional wisdom ran, be thwarted by building up the local military by sale or donations of equipment, by training an officer élite in the U.S.A. and by linking the various countries in regional military pacts. The effect of this containment policy has been set out by Marcel Barang: "The establishment of a security girdle around the socialist world proceeded of necessity by the reinforcement of existing local armies or by the creation of new indigenous forces to serve in the anti-communist struggle. Financing Taiwan, rearming and setting Japan on its feet, the United States undertook to contain China with strong régimes: South Korea, Indochina, Thailand, Pakistan, Indonesia. . . . Throughout the whole of the region there flowed in not only arms and military material but also civil aid, then investments: Asia, a battlefield, is also an immense market and the source of a virtually unlimited pillage."

Such a policy provided the setting for the militarization of Asian life, a militarization which converted the police into a para-military organization; this trend reaches its logical outcome in Indonesia where for the last three years the police forces have been integrated with the Ministry of Defence. There is, it is true, a variety of militarist régimes, ranging from the "khaki socialism" of Burma to the hard-line dictatorship of Park in Korea, from the "new order" of the Indonesian generals to the "new society" of the Philippines. Nevertheless, in many parts of Asia we are confronted with armies which occupy their own countries, with armies which, from Pakistan to Burma and Indonesia, increasingly extend their control of the major sectors of the economy, which are deeply caught up in a mesh of corruption (an Indonesian bureaucrat has estimated that 30 per cent of his country's G.N.P. is lost through corruption). But, whatever their origin, however heavy a burden they may be on the state's resources (42 per cent of Singapore's government revenues in 1972–73 were swallowed up by defence and the maintenance of "internal security"), however potent an anti-developmental force they may be, they are able to count on increasing outside support because of their role in maintaining the internal security necessary for effective exploitation of "free Asia's" biggest resource—its labour force. The relationship between outside interests and the increasing militarization of so many Asian states has been summarized by Barang: "Given the perfecting and exorbitant cost of modern arms, and given, too, a process of economic expansion focused not simply on raw materials but which tends towards the multiplication of the branches of firms seeking cheap labour, the military régimes often take on a technocratic character which they lacked twenty years ago. Much more powerful than formerly, better armed, more 'modern', more solidly rooted in socio-economic realities, they are less vulnerable to drastic *coups*. . . ." At the same time, the type of exploitative "development" with which these régimes have become accomplices creates major contradictions. And of these perhaps the greatest is the fact that behind the "economic miracles" associated with the rapid expansion of labour-intensive light industries such as textiles and electronics the reality of poverty deepens, the vulnerability of the economy is increased—and the road to real and autonomous development is closed off. Which, coupled with an inflation rate of 25 per cent, explains the growing social and political tensions from Seoul to Singapore. . . . The close interlocking of internal and external interests is thus first shaping, then perpetuating, social and political structures which, for the mass of people in non-socialist Asia, can only mean a deepening crisis of underdevelopment, an acceleration of the "descent into hell. . . ." Autonomous development, the beginning of an immensely painful ascent from dehumanizing poverty, these things are possible only to societies which have literally fought their way out of the global economic system dominated by, and manipulated by, the Centre. The Chinese experience is convincing; that this lesson has not passed unobserved is indicated clearly by the recent history of the Indochinese lands.

THE ASIAN-PACIFIC LANDS AND THE WORLD

Dependency—Old and New

Many years ago, speaking of South-East Asia, Owen Lattimore observed: "People live out their lives in a geographical setting most of the components of which appear to be relatively stable; but everything that the people do within the setting alters the relationship of the components, and when the impact of other peoples from the outside is added, the changing of relationships becomes more complicated.

Our own age has contributed the most potent of all agencies of change: relentless acceleration of the speed of movement, both economic and military."* It is the aim of this section to describe in general terms the economic and military impact of outside peoples on the Asian/Pacific world and to indicate something of the character of the new Asia that is emerging.

After the Second World War the structures of formal European colonialism in Asia were swept away. Some cultural and commercial ties persisted, as in the case of Britain and India or France and Cambodia, but these were overshadowed by new alignments and new regional groupings developed in response to American involvement in the region or in response to the increasing commercial penetration by a resurgent Japan. The old polarization of trade on the metropolitan country has, in the case of former European colonies, largely disappeared and the trade of the Asian countries has become increasingly polarized on the U.S.A. and Japan. The former dominates the trading pattern of those countries with whom she has strong military ties (South Korea, Japan, the Philippines, formerly South Viet-Nam), has replaced Britain in the commercial hegemony of South Asia and is now moving into what was one of Britain's last economic preserves, the Australasian world. Japan's trade with, and investment in, the underdeveloped Asian/Pacific nations has transformed the pattern of investments in the region; in 1975 she was the leading investor in Thailand and South Korea and ranked second in Taiwan, Indonesia and the Philippines.

The result is a new pattern of dependence. This is most clearly illustrated by some of the South-East and East Asian nations; by 1970, 70 per cent of the exports of South Korea, 79 per cent of the exports of the Philippines and 55 per cent of Taiwan's exports went to Japan and the United States. In return, these two countries accounted for 68 per cent of South Korea's imports, 69 per cent of Taiwan's, 57 per cent of the Philippines' and 51 per cent of Thailand's. This increasing dependence on the United States and Japan is documented for selected Asian nations in Table 1.

This pattern of dependence, which binds the Asian nations to the U.S.A. and Japan, is strengthened by the flow of foreign investments. The story of postwar foreign investment in Asia, it has been said, is the progressive advance of U.S. and Japanese capital. U.S. direct investment in underdeveloped Asian countries trebled during the 1960s, when it was growing at a rate of 18 per cent annually, compared with a rate of 11 per cent in all underdeveloped countries. By 1975 the book value of U.S. direct investments in the underdeveloped countries of Asia was U.S. $4,000 million; her investments in the developed Pacific nations included $2,700 million in Japan, $3,700 million in Australia (1971) and $24,100 million in Canada (1971). Japanese investments rose from $760 million in 1971 to $1,770 million in 1973; by 1975 Japan was the leading investor in Thailand and South Korea and ranked second in Indonesia, the Philippines and Taiwan.

Table 1

PERCENTAGE OF AVERAGE TRADE DEPENDENCE OF SELECTED ASIAN NATIONS ON THE U.S.A. AND JAPAN

	1957–59	1969–71
HONG KONG		
Imports . . .	23.5	37.0
Exports . . .	17.5	41.0
INDONESIA		
Imports . . .	29.0	48.0
Exports . . .	19.5	46.5
SOUTH KOREA		
Imports . . .	58.0	68.0
Exports . . .	73.0	73.5
MALAYSIA		
Imports . . .	10.5	24.5
Exports . . .	22.5	29.0
PHILIPPINES		
Imports . . .	61.5	57.0
Exports . . .	74.0	79.0
THAILAND		
Imports . . .	40.0	52.5
Exports . . .	30.5	37.5
TAIWAN		
Imports . . .	75.0	67.5
Exports . . .	45.0	55.0

Source: Donald Sherk, quoted in *Bulletin of Concerned Asian Scholars* (*BCAS*), April-June 1975.

These developments reflect the sharpened awareness of the economic potential of the Asian-Pacific region on the part of the business community and the politicians. In December 1972 *Business International* commented: "Asia/Pacific leads in profit potential . . . . Data on the earnings ratios of U.S. firms with direct investments in the Far East . . . show an average annual return of 12.9 per cent for 1965–69, compared to worldwide average annual return of 10.7 per cent . . . The Far East return (in manufacturing) is 16.3 per cent, compared to 9.18 per cent for the world as a whole . . . The figures for 1969 show that U.S. investments in the Far East return 17.2 per cent (and in Japan 22.2 per cent) compared to 12 per cent in Europe and 8.6 per cent in Canada." Such statistics help us to understand more clearly the comment by Kenneth Rush, U.S. Deputy Secretary of State, that: "Our trade with Asia now equals 85 per cent of our trade with Western Europe and is growing more rapidly" or that of William Overholt, made later in 1974 that: "In the 1970s and 1980s the Pacific Basin is likely to emerge as the centre of world economic dynamism and growth."

The significance of the Asian region to U.S. business is indicated by Table 2 overleaf.

* *Geographical Journal*, Dec. 1967

Table 2

SALES BY MAJORITY-OWNED AFFILIATES OF U.S. COMPANIES IN ASIA—1966–72

(million $)

	All Industries	Petroleum	Manu-facturing
1966 . .	5,374	2,779	1,616
1968 . .	7,102	3,445	2,495
1970 . .	9,488	4,354	3,398
1972 . .	16,365	7,667	5,029

Source: Survey of Current Business quoted in *BCAS* April-June 1975.

Sales thus increased some three and a half times and some 46 per cent of the sales were to Japan. But the pattern of expansion shows some significant contrasts between various countries; sales to India, for example, were up by only 14 per cent while sales to Indonesia increased almost fivefold. These latter, as in other East Asian countries, are closely connected with the expansion of the manufacturing and petroleum industries.

Of Export Platforms, Continental Shelves and Ocean Deeps . . .

By the late 1960s five nations accounted for more than half the world export of manufactured goods from the underdeveloped nations of the Periphery to the developed societies of the Centre. Hong Kong ranked first, India second, Taiwan third and South Korea sixth. This rapid expansion of manufacturing industry in Hong Kong, South Korea and Taiwan is largely "the result of new investment and production by and for global enterprises with products exported to the metropolitan countries. There is minimal impetus to the kind of balanced growth that could benefit the masses of Asia's rural poor".*

This investment and this expansion of manufacturing industry in Asia is best understood against the background of the global strategies of the multinational corporations seeking to exploit the two major assets of the Asian/Pacific world: its abundant, expanding and cheap labour and the energy resources and potential resources of metallic minerals of the Pacific and its margins.

This policy has been forced on the U.S. corporations by the increasing encroachment of foreign firms in the U.S. home markets. These firms are mainly Japanese. Low consumption levels and thus low wages in Japan gave them a marked advantage over the U.S. producer; they possessed moreover a high level of productivity due, ironically, to the licensing of U.S. know-how and, as a consequence, they were able to undersell U.S. firms in the latter's home market. The reaction of U.S. business has been to attempt to recapture the market by cutting production costs. This has meant the creation in low-wage areas of the world of what Furtado has termed "export platforms" where a wide range of electronic and other consumer goods could be produced by U.S. firms employing local labour and shipped back to the U.S. at competitive prices. In the words of Barnet and Müller: "Production of the traditional industrial goods that have been the mainstay of the U.S. economy is being transferred from $4-an-hour factories in New England to 30 cents-an-hour factories in the 'export platforms' of Hong Kong and Taiwan".† The striking contrasts in hourly wages for comparable task and skill levels between the U.S.A. and selected Asian countries are illustrated by table 3 (data from Barnet & Müller):

Table 3

DIFFERENTIAL HOURLY WAGE RATES IN SELECTED INDUSTRIES

(rates in $ U.S.)

Consumer electronic products:			
Hong Kong	0.27	U.S.A.	3.13
Taiwan	0.14	U.S.A.	2.56
Office-Machine parts			
Hong Kong	0.30	U.S.A.	2.92
Taiwan	0.38	U.S.A.	3.67
Semiconductors			
Korea	0.33	U.S.A.	3.32
Singapore	0.29	U.S.A.	3.36

Source: Global Reach, p. 127.

Given such contrasts it is scarcely surprising that as early as the end of 1970 over a quarter of the labour force of U.S. global firms was outside the territory of the U.S.A., that with increasing production of cars and electronic equipment and clothes and furniture by branches of U.S. firms in the "export platforms" of Asia and other parts of the Periphery‡ the U.S.A. becomes "increasingly dependent on exports of agricultural products and timber to maintain its balance of payments and increasingly dependent on imports of finished goods to maintain its standard of living".§

The big Japanese firms have been following a similar pattern of dispersal, partly to overcome the pollution problem but chiefly to take advantage of cheap and high quality labour in the free export zones of Singapore, South Korea (Masan) and Taiwan (Kaohsiung). These overseas activities, based on non-unionized labour, have effectively been used as safety valves during the last two years' recession in Japan; in Masan, for example, *Asahi Shimbun* reported that eight Japanese factories had ceased operations by January 1975 and "more were planning to pack up".

It is clear from this that the remarkable increase in the export of light manufactures from some South-East and East Asian countries can scarcely be regarded as indicating the beginning of self-sustaining

* Mark Selden "American Global Enterprise and Asia" in *BCAS* April-June 1975 p. 27.

† Richard J. Barnet and Ronald E. Müller, *Global Reach*, p. 216.

‡ Bulova now assembles Swiss-made watches in American Samoa for import into the U.S.A. The tariff savings more than offset the costs of a 21,000 mile airlift: Barnet and Müller, p. 305.

§ Barnet and Müller, p. 216.

economic growth. Rather does industrial development of the type discussed perpetuate the old pattern of dependence with decision-making confined to the head office of the company, whether in the U.S.A. or Japan. The decision of National Semiconductor to scale down operations in Singapore in order to take advantage of lower Malaysian wage rates by opening a factory in Malacca (1974) illustrates the ephemeral character of some recent "development" in Asia and the continuing vulnerability of such "development" to outside decision-making.

One major factor, then, attracting investment into the Asian/Pacific world has been the cheap labour resources of the region; the most striking result of this investment is the "export platform" style of economy. A second and locally more potent factor is the energy resources of the Asian continental shelf and the metallic minerals of the Pacific margins and the ocean floor. The oil and natural gas resources are associated with the belt of young fold mountains which girdle East and South-East Asia and with the basins of sedimentary rocks which occur in e.g. Sinkiang, Szechwan and North-East China. These oil and gas-bearing deposits, however, extend far beyond the swamps and the narrow coast plains of the Asian margin on to the shallow continental shelf which sweeps in a great arc from the coast of Korea, through the China Sea towards the waters of the South-East Asian Mediterranean. Two technological developments contributed to the realization of the region's offshore oil potential: the computer which has been described as "the oil man's compass"* and which made possible swift and sophisticated analysis of geophysical data and the offshore drilling rig (developed in the Gulf of Mexico in 1948 and first used in South-East Asia in 1958). A third invention, that of the cryogenic tanker, made possible the transport of the gas which had long bedevilled Asian oil exploitation; what had been a troublesome side-product became a major economic asset so that Michael Morrow can write: "A gas bonanza is now technically possible."

But real development of South-East Asia's oil depended not merely on new technology but also on a favourable investment climate. This was achieved with the U.S.-supported Suharto coup in 1965. Following this and the liquidation of the Indonesian Communist Party, following the consolidation of Lee Kuan Yew and Marcos and the putting down of the left-oriented rebellions in Malaya, Kalimantan (Borneo) and Brunei, U.S. firms began to invest heavily in South-East Asian oil development. A Chase Manhattan Bank study estimated that between 1970 and 1985 $65,000 million would be invested by the oil industry in the Pacific Basin region; another estimate projected investments of $10 million in natural gas resources alone by 1980. And in the last two or three years the increasing pressure of the Arab oil-producing nations on the great oil companies increased the companies' interest in South-East Asian oil, for increased South-East Asian production would give the companies a powerful lever in their negotiations with Middle Eastern governments.†

Meanwhile, the reported size of China's reserves (300,000 million barrels compared with 356,000 million for the Middle East), the as yet unmeasured potential of the basin of the East China Sea, and the emergence of Japan as the world's largest oil importer introduce a new element into the relationship of the four super-powers of the Pacific Basin: China, Japan, the U.S.A. and the U.S.S.R.

The metallic mineral wealth of the Basin includes important resources of strategic metals: the nickel of New Caledonia, for example, and the copper of the newly developed mines in Bougainville and in West Irian. In the most recent period increasing interest has been aroused by the ferromanganese deposits of the Pacific Ocean floor. These deposits consist of "manganese nodules, lumps the size of potatoes that carpet the world's oceans far from land and as much as 20,000 feet beneath the water's suface. They are extremely rich in nickel, cobalt, copper and manganese, some of the minerals most important to industrial society".‡ And as far as is known, the area most thickly strewn with these deposits is the central Pacific floor between 40°N and 40°S.

That the technology for deep sea mining exists is suggested by the work of Global Marine and the achievements of its vessel *Glomar Challenger*. Global Marine works in co-operation with Lockheed while two other U.S. companies, Kennecott Copper and Tenneco, have the expertise to start ocean mining. The latter company, in association with three Japanese trading firms and subsidiaries of U.S. Steel and Union Minière, has already filed a detailed claim to a mine site on the Pacific floor. Newman states that "at least 100 companies around the world, thirty-three in Japan alone, have gone into the ocean mining business."§ These developments, and they are little more than the tip of an iceberg so far, sharply underline the importance of the Pacific basin in the world struggle for resources. They underline, too, the importance of the current (March 1976) UN Law of the Sea Conference, for the bloc of 105 developing nations are adamantly opposed to any use of the deep seabed for private corporate gain; rather do they "see the ocean floor as the perfect laboratory to nurture their concept of a 'new economic order'". In this they are likely to be opposed by the developed nations who see in ocean mining a means of breaking the increasingly tight hold the countries of the

* Michael Morrow, "The Politics of Southeast Asia Oil" in *Bulletin of Concerned Asian Scholars*, April-June 1975, p. 34.

† Considerations of profits worked in the same direction. In Morrow's words: "December 1974 Persian Gulf producers limited the international oil companies to $0.34 gross income from sale of a barrel of Abu Dhabi crude. . . . At the same time, under Indonesia's production-sharing contract, oil companies were grossing about $6.17 on a $12.60 barrel of Indonesian crude".

‡ Barry Newman, "Behind the Glomar Sub Hunt" in *The Nation* (N.Y.) Oct. 11th, 1975, p. 330. Contains a useful map showing the world distribution of these deposits.

§ *ibid.*

Periphery are beginning to exercise over their raw materials by developing an independent source of minerals. The significance of the issue to the U.S.A. has been stated by Barry Newman: "At the moment, this country imports 82 per cent of its nickel, 82 per cent of its manganese, 77 per cent of its cobalt and 4.6 per cent of its copper. With an ocean-mining industry to by-pass foreign sources, the United States would be importing only 23 per cent of its manganese by 1990 . . . and imports of nickel, cobalt and copper would be cut to zero".*

Whether developed by global corporations or by some form of international agency, ocean mining in the Pacific and its margin may revolutionize the economy of many Pacific nations within the next decade. Its impact will be particularly great on the otherwise resource-poor island nations, expecially if the concept of a 200 mile economic zone becomes a reality. And the development of the mining of strategic metals will further enhance the geopolitical importance of a region which in the last decade has emerged as a key area in the energy politics of the globe.

The Geopolitics of the Pacific: Old Wine in New Bottles

These economic factors have played an important role in shaping U.S. policies in the Asian/Pacific world for there are those who see in this region the newest "heartland of the world". Such a view is held by Rocco M. Paone, professor of foreign affairs at the U.S. Naval Academy at Annapolis: "The Western portion of the Indian Ocean heartland includes much of the untapped mineral, agricultural and forest resources of some of the most fertile regions of Africa . . . Along the northwestern border is concentrated about 60 per cent of the world's oil reserves. The northern portion of this heartland includes the manpower resources of India and on its eastern and southeastern areas are located the enormous riches of the East Indies and the rapidly developing continent of Australia†". Whoever controls this heartland, Paone argues, can be dominant in shaping world politics.

America's Indochina wars demonstrated that any attempt to control the Asian/Pacific heartland by ground forces was doomed to failure and today, with U.S. ground forces maintaining a precarious toe hold only in South Korea, a new and more flexible policy of control has emerged. This "blue-water policy" involves the pulling back of U.S. forces to a girdle of island bases stretching from Japan through the Marianas southwards to Australia and westwards to Diego Garcia; the recognition that in Admiral Zumwalt's words: "future U.S. involvement overseas will call first for the high-technology, capital-intensive services—our naval forces—to support the indigenous armies of threatened allies"; finally, a more sophisticated combination of military and economic strategies to secure control over the region's resources and to safeguard and expand the field for U.S. trade and investment.

Such a policy implies a growing emphasis on naval power and in January 1972 the U.S. Pacific Command was given operational jurisdiction over the Indian Ocean and its margins; this marks the emergence of the navy as the main arm of U.S. power in the Asian/Pacific region. U.S. troops withdrawn from mainland Asia are being relocated in island bases; the Third Marine Division was moved to Okinawa and many of the Air Force units pulled out of Thailand have been moved to Clark Air Base in the Philippines. Naval forces have been built up and U.S. and Soviet warships have been regularly deployed in the Indian Ocean; the great naval base at Subic Bay near Manila now services three times the number of warships it did in 1964 and houses a stockpile of ammunition six times that of a decade ago. Meanwhile, along the whole front of the Western Pacific a closely-knit pattern of bases has emerged. Yokosuka is "home port" for the flagship of the Seventh Fleet and the carrier USS *Midway*; Okinawa (under Japanese administration) has become the most important logistical base for the U.S. Army in Asia; Micronesia houses a SAC B52 base and a Polaris missile submarine base; facilities on the Indian Ocean island of Diego Garcia are being expanded; new bases are being constructed and existing ones enlarged in Australia (where U.S. uncertainty regarding the future of her bases may have been a factor contributing to Premier Whitlam's fall‡). The thinking behind this new pattern was set out in 1974 by Admiral Thomas H. Moorer: "U.S. general-purpose forces are deployed to the Western Pacific to deter aggression and to reassure our allies, particularly Korea and Japan, of our continuing interest and ability to play a major stabilizing role in the area. These forward deployed forces would be crucial in a major conflict, serve as a deterrent to regional escalation of local confrontation, and demonstrate our resolve to remain a Pacific power". And the mechanics of this "offshore strategy" were clearly demonstrated by the *Mayaguez* "affair" in 1975.

The new strategy (which suggests that even the traumatic experience of the Indochinese War has not greatly deflected U.S. policy-makers) means that CINCPAC is today responsible for maintaining U.S. interests in an area totalling 94 million square miles, or some two-fifths of the total area of the globe. Such a task has meant a renewed U.S. emphasis on links with her traditional Pacific allies: Japan, Taiwan, the Philippines, Australia and New Zealand. Japan, says Michael Klare, is already responsible for the defence of U.S. bases in Japan and Okinawa and participates in the provision of an air defence network covering South Korea as well as Japan; she is expected to take over many of the high-technology tasks performed by

* Barry Newman *loc. cit.*, p. 331.

† *Military Review*, Dec. 1970 quoted by Michael Klare "The Nixon-Kissinger Doctrine and America's Pacific Basin Strategy" in *BCAS*, April-June 1975.

‡ See Malcolm Salmon "La CIA, le gouverneur et les intérêts de l'Amérique" in *Le Monde Diplomatique*, Feb. 1976, p. 32.

U.S. forces, including anti-submarine warfare.* And, at the other end of the Pacific, Australia has purchased from the U.S. a squadron of 3-PC "Orion" aircraft to patrol the Indian Ocean and Australian bases seem likely to take over the function of Thai bases (e.g. Utapao) being phased out as a result of the Bangkok government's new attitude.

Japan is clearly the linch-pin of this whole strategy. Indeed, as early as 1954 a memorandum submitted to the U.S. Secretary of Defense by the Joint Chiefs of Staff stated clearly that "Orientation of Japan toward the West is the keystone of United States policy in the Far East"; that the loss of South-East Asia would "drive Japan into an accommodation with the Communist Bloc", and that the integration of China's military potential with the industrial capacity of Japan and the resources of South-East Asia would threaten not only the entire Western Pacific but also South Asia and the Middle East.† America's ruinous South-East Asia policy can be regarded as, in part at least, a policy designed to keep open the markets and the resources of South-East Asia for Japan within a Free World structure; this would have the double advantage of diverting the Japanese export drive from the U.S.A. and of linking the future of Japan with the survival of the capitalist system and of America's client regimes in Asia. However, while Japan has long enjoyed a privileged position in America's geopolitical designs in the Asian/Pacific world, it has nonetheless been a subordinate one, one which leaves the country dependent on U.S.-controlled supplies of resources. Yet the inevitable thrust of Japan is towards a more self-reliant role in Pacific affairs and above all towards greater economic independence (her attempted oil-deals with China illustrate this trend and the difficulties to be surmounted)‡. This will bring her increasingly into conflict with the United States' efforts to shape the development of the Asian/Pacific world along lines congenial to U.S. business interests. The contradiction within America's Asian/Pacific strategy is thus basic: Japan's participation is essential and increased Japanese participation can only strengthen the country militarily and economically yet, as Klare points out: "the United States cannot help to build a stronger Japan without at the same time generating pressures for greater Japanese autonomy in economic and military affairs and thus increased dissension and competition within the Pacific Basin system as a whole."§

* This section draws heavily on Michael Klare's study in the *Bulletin of Concerned Asian Scholars*, April-June 1975. A useful summary of this will be found in Klare's article "A New Strategy for the Pacific" in *The Nation* (N.Y.), May 31st, 1975.

† *The Pentagon Papers* (Gravel Edition, Boston, 1971), vol. 1, p. 450.

‡ In late February 1976 China informed Japan that crude oil exports to Japan would be cut from 400,000 tons per month to 200,000 tons. China is also reported to have made the decision to export oil to Japan through the American major oil companies.

§ *The Nation*, May 31st, 1975.

Reference was made above to the sophisticated blending of military and economic strategies designed to advance the interests and safeguard the position of the U.S.A. and the West as a whole in the Asian/Pacific world. This blending is admirably illustrated by the massive support given by the White North to what is termed the modernization of the region's economies, a process which increases, is designed to increase, the dependence of the Asian/Pacific nations on the "director societies" of the North.

The strategic potential of the whole development process was stated by the later Secretary of Defense James R. Schlesinger as early as 1963: "the United States has failed to take advantage of the power potential implicit in aid and trade through its failure to develop concepts and mechanisms of deterrence in ways akin to what has been done in the military field . . . No system of deterrence can exclusively stress the carrot and ignore the stick".‖ The use of the military "stick" has been illustrated in Indochina; it is costly, alienates world opinion and unpredictable in its results. Economic pressures and sanctions are far more discreet and effective but can be used only against nations whose development process and whose economy are dependent on the advanced nations for markets or for capital or technology; a largely self-sufficient economy such as that of China or Viet-Nam is impervious to economic pressures.

Modernization along Western capital-intensive lines, involving industrialization and infrastructural development, increases the degree of dependence and thus the vulnerability of a nation to outside pressure. Industrialization and agricultural modernization lead to an increasing dependence on imported petroleum; capital-intensive industrialization leads to an increasing dependence on imported technology;¶ agricultural specialization for a cash market leads to a growing dependence on imported foodstuffs (and fertilizers). And at a period when the U.S. Secretary of Agriculture asserts bluntly "Food is a weapon"** the combination of heavy dependence on grain imports and rising populations makes the countries of Southern Asia particularly vulnerable to outside pressure; this vulnerability was, indeed, demonstrated a decade ago when the price of U.S. food aid to India was the

‖ "Strategic Leverage from Aid and Trade" in *National Security*, ed. by David M. Abshire and Richard V. Allen (N.Y. 1963), cited by Michael Klare *op. cit.*

¶ Technology, says Denis Goulet, is "the cutting edge of the policy used by the industrially advanced societies to domesticate Third World development". "Exporting Technology to the Third World" *Perspectives* (Cambridge, Mass.), Vol. II, No. 1 (1973).

** A CIA study underlines the leverage the U.S.A. might gain from the use of food as a foreign policy weapon: "As custodian of the bulk of the world's exportable grain, the U.S. might regain the primacy in world affairs it held in the immediate post-World War II era." Quoted in *The Profits of Doom* (War on Want, London, 1976). The CIA's assessment of the potential impact of long-range weather changes on the food situation in Monsoon Asia and on the "leverage" which the U.S.A. might have under these conditions is referred to in "La C.I.A. et l'arme alimentaire" in *Le Monde Diplomatique*, Sept. 1975, p. 13.

opening up of the fertilizer sector of Indian industry to U.S. business.

This growing technological and foodstuffs dependence, coupled with the increasing burden of foreign debts* incurred as a result of extravagant and unrealistic development programmes, seems inseparable from the use of alien development models. At the very least it poses uncomfortable queries as to why the nations of Free Asia are encouraged to persist in their Gadarene course.

"The Dissolving View . . ."

The last ten years in the Asian/Pacific region have been "years of the dissolving view", years during which old landmarks have disappeared and the shape of things to come is uncertain. Some of this change is the result of largely indigenous developments such as the steady evolution of the Chinese economy, the building in Cambodia of an austere peasant socialism or the centrifugal tendencies of minority-dominated regions within many states of South-East and South Asia. Others reflect the impact on the region of crises or shifts in policy external to the region; these include the so-called "energy crisis", the international currency crisis due to lack of confidence in both the pound sterling and the dollar, and the increasing trade rivalry within the capitalist bloc. But perhaps most important of all has been the emergence of a new and more complex world in which the strategic balance is no longer determined by the U.S.A. and U.S.S.R. alone but by the relationships between five key world power centres: China, Japan, Western Europe, the Soviet Union and the United States. And the last decade has witnessed, too, the emergence of new regional power centres; the classic example is, perhaps, Brazil but in Asia countries such as Iran, India, possibly the new Viet-Nam fall in this category.

The dominating reality of the Asian/Pacific world is clearly that of China. Over a decade ago General de Gaulle said of Asia: "On this continent there can be no peace, nor any war imaginable without Chinese being involved." He saw in the opening of official relations between France and the People's Republic of China a contribution "to the attenuation, already started, of the contrasts and the dramatic oppositions of the camps which divide the universe". This diplomatic impact of China has been—and will continue to be—great, but in a world in which the affluent nations have not yet solved the problem of humanizing technology, and the impoverished nations the problem of lifting the burden of a dehumanizing poverty, the social and economic achievements of the Chinese carry an impact even greater than their diplomatic achievements. They are confronting many of the basic problems confronting the rest of mankind—the relationship between man and machine, between town and country, between capital-intensive and labour-intensive production, as well as basic problems of population planning and education—and they appear to be achieving a high degree of success. J. K. Galbraith reminds us: "The Chinese economy isn't the American or European future. But it is the Chinese future. And let there be no doubt: for the Chinese it works."† Perhaps the most important aspect is that the Chinese have demonstrated that there *are* alternatives to Western capitalism or Soviet communism and that the success of any alternative depends on its fitness for the environment. Galbraith comments that the Chinese economic system is "better adapted to its particular circumstance" than, say, the socialist-cum-communist states of the West. Such a quality of adaptation implies a strong awareness of ecological realities (including a strong sense of history) and perhaps the most important lesson of China to the other developing nations is this need for any successful development programme to be firmly rooted in environmental and historical realities. The relevance of Sachs' comments on "ecodevelopment" is obvious in this context.

Traditional Japan has been regarded by many as the supreme example of a society infused by a profound ecological awareness; in Ian McHarg's words: "In that culture there was sustained an agriculture at once incredibly productive and beautiful, testimony to an astonishing acuity to nature."‡ Today, Japan is the classic example in Asia, if not the world, of a country whose very existence is imperilled by the neglect of ecological principles. Pollution-related diseases, the probable diversion of one-sixth of the country's limited cropland to industry by 1985, the wiping out by pollution of almost one-half of the country's fishing grounds—these are the results of an "economic miracle" much of whose seeming success was achieved by ignoring the most basic measures needed to ensure the well-being of the people and the health of their environment. Ecologically Japan has become, as one expert puts it, "an octopus which eats its own legs"—and under such conditions it becomes increasingly difficult to predict Japan's future.

China shows a high degree of self-sufficiency in industrial raw materials; Japan, by contrast, is heavily and increasingly dependent on imports. The economy is one depending on a rapid rate of turnover (it operates with less than three weeks' supply of major raw materials) and, indeed, as Jon Halliday terms it, it is a "bicycle economy; if it slows down, it is in danger of toppling over and crashing". This vulnerability was dramatically demonstrated by the "oil crisis". Between 1960 and 1971 the percentage of Japan's energy output derived from oil had doubled; almost all the oil was imported and two-thirds came from the giant U.S. and Anglo-Dutch companies. In 1974 the cost of Japan's oil imports rose by some $7,000 million and the economic growth rate had to be slashed to 2½ per cent per annum. This sort of vulnerability is essential to bear in mind in any assessment of Japan's military potential. Japan cer-

* Between 1968 and 1973 the national debts of the Asian nations to foreign countries increased by 108.9 per cent; see *Ceres*, Jan./Feb. 1976, pp. 22–23.

† *Observer Review*, July 1st, 1973.

‡ Ian McHarg, *Design with Nature* (New York, 1971), p. 27.

tainly has ambitions—in 1970 Nakasone emphasized that Japan's growing interests and assets in South-East Asia would necessitate military power to defend them—and the Third, Fourth and Fifth Defence Plans have each involved a doubling of expenditure over their predecessors. But the "oil crisis" demonstrated the flimsy basis on which these ambitions rest and, as Halliday has emphasized: "The oil experience has been repeated in other fields. Virtually everywhere that Japan has envisaged trying to break away from the United States, it has rapidly been brought to heel." And in the purely economic field recent years have seen a sharpening conflict between a recession-haunted America and the resurgent Asian nation whose economy she had done so much to rebuild. Again, Japan proved unequal to the conflict and had to give way to the pressure to accept "voluntary export quotas".

Southern Asia has been plagued by the gap between food needs and food output, by the destructive impact of an imported technology, by the increasing dependence of the region on outside aid which has resulted in a distortion of planning priorities, by growing unemployment and underemployment (which means an increasing wastage of human resources), and by a growing fragmentation along ethnic, including tribal, lines. That, in spite of the optimistic claims of the politicians, the countries of Southern Asia have not yet begun to overcome the food crisis has been demonstrated by the famines in India and Bangladesh during recent years. The hope of the Green Revolution has "withered"; even in districts where it achieved some measure of "success" it resulted in a growing polarization of society and in deteriorating living levels for the lower classes. The whole question of "ecological viability" is posed; is an agricultural system, based on high inputs of fertilizer and pesticides and dependent on irrigation pumps and tractors, really viable at a time of rapidly expanding energy costs? More critical, can a new technology be grafted on to an unchanged social base* without tearing society apart?

No less important has been the Indian experience of foreign "aid". Successive governments have become increasingly "hooked on" to massive injections of funds. During the period of the Third Plan alone these have totalled $6,000 million. The price of this "aid" has been a growing control over the direction and scope of economic development by outside groups such as the IMF. The original socialist content of Indian planning has been progressively reduced in favour of development strategies favouring the private—and especially the foreign—investor. And the pervasive influence of an outside group—in this case the World Bank—on the socio-economic development of the country has been well summarized by Cheryl Payer: "The Bank's agricultural programme aims at the creation of a stratum of prosperous capitalist farmers and encourages the use of expensive commercial inputs such as fertilizers; it has exerted specific pressure . . . for favourable conditions for foreign investment in India's fertilizer industry; it is a vigorous advocate of birth control; and it continues to press for further import liberalization and the relaxation or elimination of most domestic controls as well." As Cheryl Payer observes, ironically, "The type of planning which the World Bank advice favours is hardly that which the Indians embarked on in the early 1950s." And this, indeed, is true not only of Southern Asia but of most of the Periphery.

By 1975 the impact of foreign-guided "development" was creating a desperate situation. India's internal situation was such that police violence and imprisonment without trial were becoming fashionable, if last-ditch, answers to the chronic economic unrest and outbreaks of hopeless violence which were born of continuing and worsening poverty. And with the collapse of State government, direct rule from New Delhi was increasing. External adventures provided some distraction from internal problems. The "liberation" of East Pakistan created a joint Indian-Soviet client-state and widened the horizon for Indian merchants and entrepreneurs. But even without the ineptitude of Sheikh Mujibur Rahman's administration it becomes increasingly clear that Bangladesh is a political entity of dubious viability. Its population of 74 million may reach anything between 150 and 230 million by the end of the century; unemployment, according to what is termed a "reasonable expectation", will remain constant at 30 per cent; moreover, even with a drastic reduction in fertility, the urban population is expected to grow to over 55 million by the end of the century. A recent U.N. report states: "The investment in urban infrastructure and in industrial and commercial enterprises to absorb this population in productive employment is staggering. There is a possibility of a large, chronically unemployed urban proletariat, which will pose problems of law and order and political stability unmatched by anything this country has seen in the past." To an India unable to feed its own people or to maintain internal order, and confronted by a continuing flow of hungry refugees over the border into West Bengal, the acquisition of such a client-state seems a dubious gain. So, too, does India's takeover of Sikkim or her virtual entry into the "nuclear club".

The "crisis of Bangladesh" has its roots partly in Bengali nationalism and this catches up West Bengal as strongly as East Bengal (or Bangladesh). Here, in this north-eastern sector of the subcontinent, the inevitable conflict between the politics of liberal reform and rural revolution in a poverty-stricken and long-neglected agrarian region will be played out—and it is a conflict which will become increasingly caught up with the great power rivalries in this part of Asia. But Bengali nationalism is not an isolated example of the emergent nationalisms of Asia. Pakistan is faced with potentially similar fissiparous tendencies on her western fringes and it may be that, as some have argued, the whole of the subcontinent will shatter into a mosaic of ethnic units. Which implies that the fragile unity imposed by Western arms and Western administration was merely a

* Cheryl Payer notes that Cuba and North Viet-Nam have been the most successful adopters of the "Green Revolution" improved seeds.

passing phase, that alien patterns of government are no less irrelevant to South Asia's needs than alien development models.

This imposition of alien models is part of an attempt, to use Michael Hudson's phrase, "to domesticate the Third World". Today this failure of Western technology is clear for all to see in South-East Asia. The biggest failure is the attempt of America and her allies to "domesticate" the Indochinese peoples. The scale of this failure, following on the earlier failure to domesticate the Chinese and Korean revolutions, is evident from the fact that, after a U.S. expenditure in Viet-Nam estimated at $330,000 million, left-wing régimes today hold the whole east flank of continental Asia from the Amur bend (some 53°N) to within 8° of the equator.

And elsewhere in South-East Asia—in Thailand, Malaysia, the Philippines—America's military and political failure is forcing a rethinking of future policies. Yet a rethinking which confines itself to such matters as military bases, military alliances, external policies, is assuredly only the beginning and of no value at all unless it be extended to the examination of internal policies and development strategies. No secure future can be built on a policy which achieves the outward semblance of growth by allowing (or, as in the case of Singapore, encouraging) foreign capital to maximize profits by exploiting the low wage levels characteristic of "underdeveloped" societies. No country can build a viable future by allowing itself to be turned, as is the case of Indonesia, into a source of cheap raw materials for the developed societies, particularly when these materials are non-renewable or exploited (as are the forest resources) under conditions which prevent their renewal. No country can base its future on expensive "miracles" of technology grafted on an unchanged social base, a reality brutally illustrated by the Green Revolution in Java where, in the words of Richard W. Franke, the optimistic plans and programmes of the technocrats, the military rulers and the big landowners "have created only increased human suffering and promise more of the same".*

It is in the unwillingness of many South-East Asian governments to examine their internal policies, especially as far as minority groups and other politically or economically marginal groups are concerned, that we must seek the explanation for the unrest which, in spite of two decades of counter-insurgent efforts, continues to simmer throughout the region. In the Philippines the Marcos government has been unable to crush the Moslem Revolutionary Forces in the south or the rebel movements in Central Luzon and the Sulu Archipelago. In Burma guerrilla forces belonging to various minority tribes are reportedly in control of much of the mountainous northern border zone. In Malaysia remnants of the Malayan Peoples Liberation Army continue to defy government efforts to dislodge them from their bases along the Thai border. And in Thailand, in spite of a U.S.-inspired counter-insurgent programme,† guerrilla forces in the northern hills and in the Muslim south are growing at a steady 10–20 per cent a year. South-East Asia is thus bordered by a zone of smouldering unrest and the longer the causes of this unrest are neglected, the longer the local governments pin their faith on a military solution, the greater is the likelihood that the pattern of events in South Viet-Nam will be repeated; already, indeed, the situation in the southern Philippines is regarded by some as a replica of Viet-Nam in the early stages of the war. Almost a decade ago the present writer saw South-East Asia's future in the following terms: "Looking to the future, the trend towards more radical types of political and economic structure may be expected to continue. This will not be because of propaganda or subversion but because the "liberal"—or free enterprise—alternative not only fails to 'deliver the goods' in a Third World context but also because it fails to create a decent society; in other words, it not only fails to create the conditions in which men may *have* more but also the conditions in which they may *be* more. This prospect of a leftward shift is one which many in the West regard with fear and suspicion; indeed, at the moment a bloody and ruinous war is being fought to arrest this trend in South Viet-Nam. Yet even a perfunctory—but objective—examination of conditions in South-East Asia or other parts of the Third World, will drive home the fact that for these countries *there is no other solution* to the gigantic problems that face them; that, for the peoples of South-East Asia, the examples of China, of North Viet-Nam and above all North Korea provide an object lesson whose significance is becoming increasingly obvious—and relevant. If this is true, then many of the existing South-East Asian régimes may prove to be transitional phenomena, whose continuing existence is made possible only by massive external support which maintains the régimes in power without at the same time solving the economic problems which beset them. And with mounting population pressure these problems grow inexorably more acute."‡ This vision was not received charitably in the West—but subsequent events have served to vindicate the essential accuracy of this prognosis.

Events in Asia certainly contributed, if only marginally, to the Labour Parties' successes in Australia and New Zealand in late 1972. In both cases, political change reflected apprehension over domestic developments and the effects of Britain's entry into the European Economic Community on the two countries' high living standards. But equally important was the disenchantment with the traditional politics of what had long been regarded as ultra-loyal, and white, Pacific appendages of Britain. The two countries turned inwards and this growing preoccupation with domestic affairs was clearly reflected by the strong reaction of the voters when, in 1975, the

* Richard W. Franke, "Miracle Seeds and Shattered Dreams in Java" in *Natural History*, Vol. 83, No. 1, Jan. 1974, p. 88.

† Over U.S. $600 million have been spent by the U.S. to upgrade the counter-insurgent capacity of the Thai armed forces.

‡ Keith Buchanan, *The Southeast Asian World* (London, 1967), p. 158.

left-wing governments, having failed to cope with such internal problems as inflation and law and order, were replaced by strongly right-wing administrations. In their relationships with the nations of Asia both left-wing and right-wing administrations have moved towards a clearer recognition of Asian realities. Both countries have recognized the People's Republic of China, both appear to have abandoned the clichés of the "Yellow peril" type and to see Asians as neighbours with whom new patterns of co-existence within the Western Pacific must be worked out.

Perhaps these new attitudes to Asia are neither dramatic nor unexpected; certainly they reflect policies of response rather than of initiative and equally certainly the guiding hand is still basically that of the United States. This is most clearly evident in Australia where Malcolm Fraser's Liberal-National-Country coalition is committed to a more definite pro-American policy. The new government has, for example, called for a strengthening of the U.S. position in the Indian Ocean, something equally to be desired in the eyes of the New Zealand government, by expanding facilities at Diego Garcia and has offered the new $50 million naval base at Cockburn Sound in Western Australia as a support base. This support of the U.S. anti-Soviet build-up is linked with the intention and desire to maintain close relations with the People's Republic of China. China, it is to be noted, has taken favourable note of Australia's defence policy and a Hsinhua news bulletin on January 1st, 1976, detailed Australia's expenditure of $62.5 million on new weapons system and echoed Mr. Fraser's words that "Australia would play its part" in the defence against the Soviet military build-up.*

In the economic field there is little doubt that the future of both countries will be closely linked to the growing demands for raw materials, minerals, agricultural products and forestry products, needed by the industrializing nations of East Asia and especially by Japan. But the full development of such a trade is obviously going to depend on a sharp reduction in the existing wealth differentials between the peoples of Asia and those of Australasia. Equally important, it will depend upon the extent to which the peoples of Australasia are prepared to allow their countries to be exploited for irreplaceable raw materials whose export for overseas processing means, in the long term, the export of those resources needed for future industrialization and, in the short term, the export of jobs desperately needed locally.

The early seventies were a particularly dramatic period for all the Asian and South Pacific nations. For all its eventfulness, however, it has provided more questions than answers in the realm of political and economic change—and precisely because these questions are of momentous importance the answers to them will involve still more profound and critical changes in the region. Will Japan make a sustained bid for economic—if not political and military—hegemony over non-socialist East and South-East Asia? Will she, as some observers predict, remilitarize to the point of acquiring nuclear weapons? Will the United States compete or co-operate with such expansion, or complement it by consolidating her position around the Indian Ocean? If neocolonization is to be pursued along these lines, however, how will such a policy be reconciled with *rapprochement* with China? Indeed, does the "new China policy" represent a real departure from past policies? If so, what will be the Soviet Union's reaction—both to China and the two major capitalist powers in the region? And finally, what will be the popular reaction in the "Third World" countries—from Pakistan through Indonesia to South Korea—on whose lands power politics will be played out? These countries of the Periphery contain one thousand million people, mostly poor, mostly peasants, and there is clear evidence—in Indochina, India, Bangladesh, Indonesia and elsewhere—that the play of power politics is inseparable from the politics of peasant revolt. In this respect, the next decade promises to be no less painful than the last.

* *New Asia News* (Tokyo), Jan. 30th, 1976.

BIBLIOGRAPHY

GLOBAL PERSPECTIVES

ALBERTINI, J. M. Les mécanismes du sous-développement (Paris, 1967).

AMIN, SAMIR. "Accumulation and Development: A Theoretical Model" in *Review of African Political Economy* No. 1, 1974.

BAIROCH, PAUL. Diagnostic de l'évolution économique du Tiers-Monde 1900–1966 (Paris, 1967).

BARAN, PAUL A. The Political Economy of Growth (New York, 2nd edn., 1962).

BARNET, R. J. & MÜLLER, R. E. Global Reach: The Power of the Multinational Corporations (New York, 1974).

BENOT, YVES. Qu'est-ce que le développement? (Paris 1973).

BUCHANAN, KEITH. "Profiles of the Third World" and "The Third World and Beyond" in *Developing the Underdeveloped Countries*, ed. Alan B. Mountjoy (London, 1971), pp. 17–51.

The Geography of Empire (Nottingham, 1972).

COOMBS, PHILIP H. "Education on a treadmill" in *Ceres* (UN) May/June 1971.

CRITCHFIELD, RICHARD. The Golden Bowl Be Broken: Peasant Life in Four Cultures (Bloomington and London, 1973).

DICKSON, DAVID. Alternative Technology and the Politics of Technical Change (London, 1974).

DUMONT, RENÉ. Lands Alive (London and New York, 1965).

Types of Rural Economy (London, 1957).

Utopia or Else (London, 1974).

La croissance . . . de la famine! (Paris, 1975).

DUMONT, RENÉ, and ROSIER, BERNARD. The Hungry Future (London and New York, 1968).

FANON, FRANTZ. The Wretched of the Earth (translated by C. Farrington) (London, 1965).

FOSSAERT, ROBERT. L'avenir du capitalisme (Paris, 1961).

GOULET, DENIS. "The Disappointing Decade of Development" in *The Center Magazine* Sept. 1969.

GOULET, DENIS & HUDSON, MICHAEL. The Myth of Aid: the Hidden Agenda of the Development Reports (New York, 1971).

GRIFFIN, KEITH. The Green Revolution: an Economic Analysis (UNRISD, Geneva, 1972).

HAGMÜLLER, GÖTZ. "A noose around the city" in *Ceres* Nov/Dec 1970.

HEILBRONER, ROBERT. The Great Ascent (New York and Evanston, 1963).

An Inquiry into the Human Prospect (London, 1975).

HENSMAN, C. R. From Gandhi to Guevara (London, 1969).

Rich Against Poor: The Reality of Aid (London, 1971).

HOROWITZ, DAVID. "Sometime in the seventies a zero hour will strike" in *Ceres* March/April 1969.

JACOBY, ERICH H. "The coming backlash of semi-urbanization" in *Ceres* Nov/Dec 1970.

Man and Land: The Fundamental Issue in Development (London, 1971).

JALÉE, PIERRE. The Third World in the World Economy (London, 1969).

JOLLY, RICHARD et al., eds. Third World Employment (Harmondsworth, 1973).

JULIEN, CLAUDE. Suicide of the Democracies (London, 1975).

MAGDOFF, HARRY. The Age of Imperialism (New York, 1969).

MERRILL, RICHARD. "Towards a Self-sustaining Agriculture" in *Journal of the New Alchemists* No. 2 (Woods Hole, Mass., 1974).

MYRDAL, GUNNAR. Economic Theory and Under-developed Regions (London and New York, 1963).

PAWLEY, W. H. "In the year 2070" in *Ceres* July/Aug 1971.

PAYER, CHERYL. The Debt Trap: The IMF and the Third World (Harmondsworth, 1974).

RAPOPORT, AMOS. "The Ecology of Housing" in *Ecologist* January 1973.

SACHS, IGNACY. "Ecodevelopment" in *Ceres* Nov./Dec. 1974.

SAMPEDRO, JOSÉ LUIS. Decisive Forces in World Economics (London, 1967).

SCHUMACHER, E. F. Small is Beautiful (London, 1973).

STAVRIANOS, L. S. The Promise of the Coming Dark Ages (San Francisco, 1976).

UL HAQ, MAHBUB. "Employment in the 1970s: A New Perspective" in *International Development Review* Vol. XIII, No. 4, 1971.

WERTHEIM, W. F. Evolution and Revolution (Harmondsworth, 1974).

WILKINSON, RICHARD G. Poverty and Progress (London, 1973).

WOLF, ERIC. Peasant Wars of the Twentieth Century (London, 1971).

THE ASIAN WORLD

BARANG, MARCEL, *et al.* "Les militaires et le pouvoir . . . dans l'Asie des confrontations" in *Le Monde Diplomatique* February 1975.

BELL, PETER & RESNICK, STEPHEN. "The Contradictions of Post-war development in Southeast Asia" in *Journal of Contemporary Asia* Vol. 1, No. 1, 1970.

BHAGAVAN, M. R., *et al.* The Death of the Green Revolution (Haslemere Group, London, 1973).

BHATTACHARYA, DEBESH. "A Critical Survey of Indian Planning and its Achievements" in *Journal of Contemporary Asia* Vol. 3, No. 2, 1973.

BUCHA, M. J. B. "Growthmanship is not Sufficient: It Leaves the Poor Behind" in *Ceres* Jan./Feb. 1974.

BUCHANAN, KEITH. Out of Asia (Sydney, 1968).

CHOMSKY, NOAM. American Power and the New Mandarins (Harmondsworth, 1969).
At War with Asia (New York, 1970).

EDWARDES, M. Asia in the Balance (Harmondsworth, 1962).
Asia in the European Age (London, 1961).

FRANKE, RICHARD W. "Miracle Seeds and Shattered Dreams in Java" in *Natural History* Vol. 83, No. 1, January 1974.
"Solution to the Asian Food Crisis: "Green Revolution" or Social Revolution" in *Bulletin of Concerned Asian Scholars* (*BCAS*), Nov./Dec. 1974, pp. 2–13.

FRIEDMAN, EDWARD & SELDEN, MARK. (eds) America's Asia: Dissenting essays on Asian-American Relations (New York, 1971).

GALTUNG, JOHAN. "Technology and Dependence" in *Ceres* Sept./Oct. 1974.

GOUGH, KATHLEEN & SHARMA, H. P. (eds). Imperialism & Revolution in South Asia (New York & London, 1973).

GROUSSET, RENÉ. The Sum of History (translated by A. and H. Temple Patterson) (London, 1951).

GURLEY, JOHN G. "Capitalist & Maoist Economic Development" in *Bulletin of Concerned Asian Scholars* (San Francisco) April–July 1970.

HALLIDAY, JON. A Political History of Japanese Capitalism (New York, 1975).

HALLIDAY, JON & MCCORMACK, GAVAN. Japanese Imperialism Today (Harmondsworth, 1973).

HARRIS, MARVIN. "How Green the Revolution" in *Natural History* Vol. 81, No. 6, June/July 1972.
"The Withering Green Revolution" in *Natural History* Vol. 82, No. 3, March 1973.

HARRIS, R. Independence and After (Oxford University Press, London, 1962).

HOWELL, LEON, and MORROW, MICHAEL. Asia, OIL Politics and the Energy Crisis (IDOC/North America, New York, 1974).

KLARE, MICHAEL. "The Nixon-Kissinger Doctrine and America's Pacific Basin Strategy" in *BCAS* April–June 1975, pp. 3–14.
"Les alliances américaines en Asie" in *Le Monde Diplomatique* September 1975.

MACEWAN, ARTHUR. "Contradictions in Capitalist Development: The Case of Pakistan" in *Review of Radical Political Economics* Spring 1971.

MARCH, ANDREW L. The Idea of China (New York, 1974).

MCGEE, T. G. The Southeast Asian City (London, 1967).

MAMDANI, MAHMOOD. The Myth of Population Control (New York & London, 1972).

MENDE, T. Southeast Asia between Two Worlds (London, 1955).

MONDE DIPLOMATIQUE, LE. "Japon: le temps des choix" December 1975.

MORROW, MICHAEL. "The Politics of Southeast Asian Oil" in *BCAS* April–June 1975, pp. 34–43.

MYRDAL, GUNNAR. Asian Drama: an Inquiry into the Poverty of Nations (Harmondsworth, 1968).

OMVEDT, GALE. "Agrarian Crisis in India" in *BCAS* Nov.–Dec. 1974, pp. 17–23.

OSHIMA, HARRY T. "The time to change to labour-intensive policies is now" in *Ceres* Nov./Dec. 1970.

PALMER, INGRID. Science and Agricultural Production (UNRISD, Geneva, 1972).

PANIKKAR, K. M. Asia and Western Dominance (London, 1953).

PELZER, K. Pioneer Settlement in the Asiatic Tropics (New York, 1945).

PONS, PHILIPPE. "Le nouveau pari économique du Japon" in *Le Monde Diplomatique* September 1975.

RAM, HOHAN. "La nouvelle course aux armaments stratégiques dans l'océan Indién" in *Le Monde Diplomatique* September 1975.

REDDY, AMULYA KUMARN. "The Trojan Horse" in *Ceres*, March/April 1976.

RISKIN, CARL. "Maoism & Motivation: Work Incentives in China" in *Bulletin of Concerned Asian Scholars* (San Francisco) July 1973.

ROBBINS, J. Too Many Asians (New York, 1959).

ROMEIN, JAN. The Asian Century (London and Berkeley, 1962).

SASAO HISASHI. "Japanese Industries: Recession and Beyond" in *AMPO* (Tokyo) Oct.–Dec. 1975, pp. 2–7.

SCHUMACHER, E. F. "Asia Undermined" in *Resurgence*, July/Aug. 1976.

SELDEN, MARK (ed.). Remaking Asia: Essays on the American Uses of Power (New York, 1974).
"American Global Enterprise in Asia" in *BCAS* April–June 1975, pp. 15–33.

SETIAWAN, N. S. "The Industries We Need" in *Nusantara* June 15, 1973 (trans. in U.S. Embassy (Jakarta) Translation Unit Press Review June 15, 1973).

SPENCER, J. E. Asia East by South (New York and London, Rev. edn., 1971).

STAVIS, BEN. "China's Green Revolution" in *Monthly Review* (New York) October 1974.

STEADMAN, JOHN M. The Myth of Asia (London, 1970).

SUN TZE. "Indonesia's PERTAMINA and the Politics of Dependence" in *AMPO* (Tokyo) July–Sept. 1975, pp. 93–97.

UI, JUN (ed). Polluted Japan (Tokyo 1972).

UNESCO. Leadership and Authority, edited by G. Wijeyewardene (Singapore, 1968).

Social Change and Economic Development, edited by Jean Meynaud (Paris, 1963).

UNITED NATIONS. The Asian Population Conference 1963 (New York, 1964).

Economic and Social Commission for Asia and the Pacific (yearly reports).

WEISSKOPF, THOMAS E. "Dependence and Imperialism in India" in *Review of Radical Political Economics* Spring 1973.

WILEY, PETER. Vietnam and the Pacific Rim Strategy (San Fransisco, 1969).

THE PACIFIC WORLD

BROWN, LAURA, and COHEN, WALTER. "Hawaii Faces the Pacific" in *Pacific Research and World Empire Telegram* Vol. VI, No. 1, 1974.

FURNAS, J. C. Anatomy of Paradise (London, 1950).

GALE, ROGER. "Securing Micronesia . . . for the Pentagon" in *AMPO* (Tokyo) July–Sept. 1975, pp. 62–67.

GALLATIN INTERNATIONAL BUSINESS SERVICE. *The Pacific-Asia World* (New York, 1967).

HORNE, DONALD. The Lucky Country (Harmondsworth, 1964).

LEE, GEORGE. "Hawaii and the Pacific Community in the Year 2000" in *Hawaii Pono Journal* Vol. 1, No. 1, November 1970.

OLIVER, DOUGLAS L. The Pacific Islands (New York, 1961).

PRICE, A. G. The Western Invasions of the Pacific and its Continents (Oxford, 1963).

ROSE, A. JAMES. Dilemmas Down Under (New York and London, 1966).

STANFORD RESEARCH INSTITUTE. Trade and Development in the Pacific Area (S.R.I., California, 1967).

STANNER, W. E. H. The South Seas in Transition (Sydney and London, 1953).

WENKAM, ROBERT. The Great Pacific Rip-off: Corporate Rape in the Far East (Chicago, 1974).

Population in Asia

Keith Buchanan

THE SHADOW OF MALTHUS

It has become increasingly fashionable to explain the underdevelopment of Asia, as of the Third World generally, in terms of "overpopulation". The peoples of Asia are, it is implied, breeding beyond the capacity of the land to support them. This simplistic explanation of Asian poverty echoes the ideas of the Rev. Thomas Malthus; "economic take-off", it is implied, will be attained only when the Asian countries begin to curtail their rate of population growth. However, as this chapter will attempt to show, demographic realities in Asia are a good deal more complex. Indeed, the failure of so many Asian nations to arrest the deterioration in living levels for the mass of their citizens must be attributed to the failure of their planners and their foreign advisors to appreciate that social and economic progress is a prerequisite for, rather than a consequence of, population planning. Population growth rates in Asia *are* high—but it is sometimes forgotten that man is born not merely with a belly to fill but also with hands capable of acquiring all the skills needed to get food and clothing and shelter and with a brain beside whose creative subtlety the most complex electronic gadgetry is of small account. And today in Asia the major human divide is that which separates those states (such as China or North Korea) which are engaged in realizing this human potential and those which see man solely as a "labour input", a producer of G.N.P. and a creator of profits.

Monsoon Asia's population of 2,000 million in the mid-1970s is about equal to that of the world in 1939; by the end of this century it will have increased by 75 per cent to 3,500 million, 56 per cent of the world total. But before we examine this "population explosion", its cause and its implications, the reader may wish to consult the statistical tables on pp. 37-39.

WHY THE "POPULATION EXPLOSION"?

The conventional wisdom attributes the "population explosion" in the nations of the Periphery to the fact that these countries had acquired (or been given) modern techniques of death control without the modern techniques of birth control which are today part of the social pattern of the more affluent societies. Such an incomplete transfer of the technology of the demographic revolution resulted inevitably in a very rapid rate of population growth as a result of the widening divergence between a continuing high birth rate and a rapidly declining death rate. And the explanation for the latter was the continuing improvement in public health measures and, above all, the eradication of endemic and epidemic diseases.

Such an explanation is neat and tidy and can be used to explain the nineteenth-century population growth in Europe as well as the twentieth-century growth in the countries of Asia. Yet it is by no means without its critics. Brown and Wray have recently stressed that there is little evidence to support any causal relationship between public health measures and population increases. The decline in death rates in eighteenth-century England occurred without any major "breakthrough" in medical technology. The classic example of Ceylon, where the eradication of malaria is frequently linked with a dramatic decline in the death rate and an increase in population, is questioned by Brown and Wray, who state, "falling death rates in Ceylon go back as far as 1905 and show an accelerated downward trend in the 1940s, completely independent of malaria eradication programmes". They point out that the global attack on malaria began in the 1950s, *after* death rates began falling globally; that as far as antibiotics are concerned there is "no causal relationship between the development of antibiotics and lower mortality".

The chief factor in the decline of mortality rates is, they find, improved nutrition; this, to achieve its maximum impact, must be associated with educational improvement, community development, social reform and educational expansion. "Over and over in a given population", they write, "we find that when death rates start to decline and the number of people increases, there has been a change in the quality and availability of food." And in this context it should be stressed that half of the world's 60 million deaths occur among children under five years of age and that half of these—or 15 million deaths—are due to a combination of malnutrition and infection; the potential demographic impact of improved food levels is obvious. This might lead, it could be argued, to rapid population increases which would wipe out any nutritional improvement. In fact, this does not appear to happen—and it does not happen because "as mortality rates decline, parents respond by having fewer children". Convergent with this is the dictum of Dr. Harold Taylor of the Population Council, that "parents will not stop having children until they believe that those they already have are going to survive". These considerations are, we shall see, of primary importance when considering the demographic future of Asia.

"THE MENACE OF OVERPOPULATION"

The "population crisis" has become one of the fashionable issues of our time, an issue in which idealism and cynicism, ethnocentrism and altruism, myth and reality are closely interwoven. And it is an issue most clearly illustrated by the lands of Monsoon Asia, not merely because here is over one-half of humanity, but because Asia has long been regarded as the cradle of teeming hordes (who in popular mythology possess a peculiar predilection for lands other than their own) and Perils, Yellow or Brown of skin. But a full understanding of the population issue demands that we see the Asian world in its broadest context, as part of the Third World or the Periphery, because relations between Centre and Periphery have played an important role in the emergence of the issue.

The crusade against the "menace of population" contains a motley assemblage in its ranks: an American scientist who conjures up the phrase "people pollution"; a celebrated English novelist who thinks there are already too many people in the world; a Nobel Prize winner who sees overpopulation creating stresses under which "it may become impracticable to regard all human life as sacred"; a former U.S. Secretary of Defence who, after attempts at depopulating Indochina, becomes President of the World Bank and finds the world's population growth "horrific".... And, in the background, the powerful organizations, with lavish private backing, trying to sell the idea that birth control, and birth control alone, may be the swiftest solution to the problems facing world society. The idea that "Whatever your cause, it's a lost one unless we control population"; that "The surging growth of population is basically responsible for the pollution of our environment"; that without population control "the resulting human misery and social tensions will inevitably lead to chaos and strife—to revolutions and wars . . ."; that "U.S. aid (is) nullified by the population explosion". And the citizens of the richest and best-fed nation on earth, a nation which has had to withdraw from a bloody war against Asian peasants, are solemnly told that "Hungry Nations Imperil the Peace of the World".

These statements are cited, not to pour scorn on the idea that there is such a thing as a "population problem". There is, throughout the Periphery and especially in the non-socialist Asian nations, a very real and growing problem of unemployment and underemployment. Moreover, if present trends continue, many Asian countries will have to fashion entirely new life patterns if the potentially disruptive effects of increasingly high population densities are to be avoided. The statements are cited as examples of the way in which population growth can be, and is, used to provide a superficially credible explanation of problems which may have little relationship to population growth, however "explosive". It is a production-obsessed and profit-hungry industrial system geared to the creation of unnecessary "wants" and not population growth which is responsible for growing pollution. Aid programmes for Asia are "nullified", not by the "population explosion", but by the continent's reactionary social and economic structures, structures propped up, incidentally, by those very outside groups most vocal about Asia's "population problem". It was, as is now clear from the Pentagon Papers, the global interests of the U.S.A. and not the supposed hunger of people in the densely-settled lowlands of Indochina that caused the protracted agony of the Viet-Nam War or the civil war in Cambodia.

AN ALTERNATIVE VISION

Perhaps there is an alternative interpretation, a more realistic interpretation, of the issues posed by the "population explosion". But before proceeding to this analysis we should stress four general points:

First, the conventional picture of the population problem, for all its emphasis on the qualities of scientific objectivity,* is at best an incomplete, at the worst a deliberately slanted, picture. That it is the burden of resource consumption *per capita* and not the mere mass of population as such that is critical is ignored—yet unless consumption is taken into account the very different significance of numerically similar population increases in different societies cannot be appreciated. And, in a continent such as Asia, the almost total emphasis on the population/food equation to the exclusion of the employment problem is equally misleading; expansion of job opportunities in Asia will be much more difficult than expansion of food output since it depends on major structural change.

Second, discussion of population growth and birth control tends to emphasize the global picture and to overlook the strong regional and social contrasts in the demographic situation. Many parts of the Periphery—including many Asian countries—need more, not fewer, people for the effective development of their economies; in the words of Yves Benot: "Many of today's underdeveloped countries could well show up as underpopulated if they were to experience the same development process as that experienced by nineteenth-century Europe." And even in the densely peopled areas of non-socialist Asia the economic structure of society is such that the typical peasant holding depends for its viability on the operator having a large family; such, too, that in the absence of Western-style social security systems, an ageing couple can find shelter and security only among their children. . . . In these circumstances, as several non-Western experts have stressed, there is little motivation for working class families to accept any limitation of births—for the Europocentric vision of the birth control salesmen just doesn't make sense in an Asian environment.

Third, while the terms "birth control" and "family planning" tend to be used interchangeably, it is important to distinguish clearly between the two. Family planning is an educational process in which the couple take control, as thinking human beings, of their own lives and those of their children. Birth control is essentially a technology which is "administered" to selected groups. And, as Pradervand has insisted, "these two visions derive from two different visions of the process of development, even of man himself".

Fourth, and most important of all, there is little evidence that conventional birth-control policies can achieve any solution even to the problem as seen by the population control enthusiasts themselves. Their

* So frequently reiterated that we are reminded of Emerson's remark: "The louder he talked of his honour, the faster we counted our spoons."

basic assumption, that economic development will follow population control (as President L. B. Johnson put it: "less than $5 invested in population control is worth $100 invested in economic growth") simply cannot be proved, for in no country of the non-socialist periphery have birth control programmes succeeded; the oft-cited examples of South Korea or Taiwan are, because of the massive aid they have received, quite atypical. There is no consistent relationship between low rates of population growth and high rates of economic growth.

Moreover, if we accept the judgement that the most critical problem facing Asia and other regions of the Periphery is the problem of employment, even the most sophisticated programme of population control can bring no alleviation of the problem before the end of this century. For, as Pradervand shows, 5–6 years must be allowed for the establishment of a programme, 7–8 years for it to be widely adopted—then 15 years will elapse before contraception has any significant impact on the labour market. And he concludes: "Contraception cannot therefore have any short-term impact on the most urgent economic problem of the Third World."

RESOURCES FOR ASIA'S MILLIONS

In spite of the strident headlines of the neo-Malthusians, we have to underline that even by the end of the century, when Asia's 2,250 million inhabitants have become 3,500 million, the Monsoon Lands will still be a fair way removed from any real congestion. Indeed, these 2,250 million people, if packed rather less closely than on London's Underground at rush hours, could be accommodated in a twenty kilometre square. . . . The main problem is not space—but the capacity of the earth, of the Asian lands in particular, to feed man and supply the fibres, the timbers, the metals and the fuels needed to sustain his economic systems. And considering the limitations to expanding food production we have to pose the question: are the limitations posed by the environment or are they man-made? That they are largely the result of what Josué de Castro terms "the inhuman condition of our civilization" is illustrated by Bangladesh which, says W. H. Pawley "could grow three crops a year if several hundreds of millions of dollars could be found for flood control and irrigation. The amount is small* in relation to the cost of landing a man on the moon . . . , not to speak of the vaster sums spent on armaments."

Asia's food potential has to be seen within the context of the earth's total potentially cultivable area. One of the latest estimates of this is that made by Walter H. Pawley, Director of the Policy Advisory Bureau in FAO. Given two major technical breakthroughs—the development of techniques of permanent cropping on humid tropical soils and of cheap techniques of desalination of sea water and its distribution for irrigation—he estimates the potentially cultivable area of the world "at 12 thousand million crop hectares, or considerably more than ten times the crop hectares presently harvested". And looking towards the 36,000 million people who, given existing trends, will occupy the globe by 2070, he comments: "I would not at all exclude the possibility that the land resources of our earth could supply sustenance for 36 thousand million people 100 years from now and feed them well, and furthermore without recourse to synthetic foods."

Food, then, need not be the limiting factor to the growth of world population that it is sometimes claimed to be. This is not to deny the reality of large scale undernutrition and malnutrition over much of the Periphery, of savage and murderous famines such as have been experienced recently in parts of India and Indonesia. But such conditions are a result of the economic structuring of global society;† new structures, as the example of China shows, can cope with the famines which conventional wisdom regards as symptomatic of "overpopulation" and create conditions for the sustained expansion of crop output and employment in the rural areas. It is only by such restructuring, which wipes out the "get-rich-quick industry of the few" which, as de Castro observes, is at the same time "the industry of hunger for the many", that the food-producing potential of which Pawley speaks can be realized. The struggles of the Chinese, the Koreans and the Indochinese peoples, the emerging struggles in other parts of the Monsoon Lands, represent the first steps in such a restructuring.

When the relationship between population and non-renewable minerals and mineral fuels is examined, the inadequacy of such simplistic ratios as population to area (which still obsess the textbook-producers and the experts) is clear. *What is critically relevant are the consumption levels of various groups.* Wayne H. Davis contrasts the ecological impact of the average Indian with that of the average American; on the basis of ecological impact and resource depletion he estimates that the population growth of the U.S.A. is "10 times as serious as that of India". The uneven impact on resources is indicated by the estimate that the U.S.A. alone, whose population is a mere 6 per cent of the world's total, is consuming some 50–60 per cent of the world's non-renewable resources; by the fact that Asia, excluding Japan, "where nearly one-half the world population resides, consumes energy . . . at a rate equivalent to burning slightly over 100 lb. of coal per year. This is about the amount that is consumed in the United States per person in two days."‡ Lauchlin Currie has emphasized the importance of consumption levels in any discussion of population

* And could be reduced to a fraction of the suggested amount if Bangladesh were capable of following the Chinese example and mobilizing its wasted manpower for large-scale schemes of flood control and irrigation. But Bangladesh is part of the Free World and its people enjoy the freedom to starve or drown.

† For a non-Asian illustration *see* Claude Meillassoux "Development or Exploitation: is the Sahel Famine Good Business?" in *Review of African Political Economy*, Vol. 1, No. 1, 1974.

‡ Harrison Brown, *The Challenge of Man's Future* (New York, 1956), p. 161.

issues. Says Currie: "Children of the wealthy probably impose a more severe drain on the resources of the community than those of the poor, precisely because their standards of consumption and education are so much higher. . . . To an economist the fact that they can pay for this additional consumption is irrelevant. From the point of view of the real income of the society . . . such increased consumption by the wealthy means less saving by them, less consumption goods for the poor, and, ultimately, less future production. The burden imposed by the well-to-do, in real economic terms, is not measured by their income but by their consumption." Currie, of course, is concerned with individual families within one nation but his remarks may be extended to the relations between nations at the international level. For central to the whole problem of population and resources (and thus to the whole "population problem") is the affluence of the White North (or Centre) which rests on prodigal use of the resources of the entire globe. This relationship between the plundering of the resources of the Periphery for the benefit of the Centre and the population issue has been emphasized by Pierre Pradervand, who sees "a growing structural opposition between the developed nations' 'Babylonian' consumption level and the Third World"; who emphasizes, more explicitly, that "unless they restrain levels of consumption it is fallacious and hypocritical on the part of the industrialized nations to recommend birth control to the nations of the Third World."

Perhaps it may appear that the charge of "prodigality" is slenderly based. But for every Asian to enjoy an American level of affluence would call for an annual production of 30,000 million tons of iron ore, 500 million tons of lead, 350 million tons of zinc—in other words, between 100 and 200 times the present world production of these minerals. We may wonder whether restriction of consumption and the restriction of the number of consumers in the Periphery are essential prerequisites for the affluence of the societies of the Centre. And if we find it hard to accept the view that the availability of mineral resources is a major limiting factor to population growth, it is because the apparent inadequacy of basic minerals is a structural problem caused by the reckless squandering of world resources by a handful of nations. The adoption of a "steady-state economy"* by the developed nations would totally alter this aspect of the "population problem".

If the problem of food supply is not as insuperable as often implied; if the problem of metals and fuels is due to their monopolization by a small group of powerful nations which leads to apparent scarcities; it is nevertheless true that rapid population growth within existing socio-political structures does pose a problem to the nations of non-socialist Asia. And this problem arises from the fact that the economies of the area are unable to provide employment for more than a fraction of the total labour force, and that population growth means an increase in the labour force of countries where unemployment levels often exceed those of the West during the Great Depression and where 50 per cent of the labour force may be underemployed. Pawley sums up the situation in the Periphery thus: "Un- and under-employment, arising basically from the enormous imbalance between human numbers needing work and the amount of capital available needed to employ them, and accentuated every year by an influx which far exceeds the outflow at the other end—this problem of employment and not the technical ability to produce food—represents the danger point in 90–100 countries comprising 70 per cent of the world's population." Now, we have already seen that, because of various time-lags, even the most sophisticated programme of birth control cannot significantly affect the size of the labour force before the end of the century. Under these circumstances the strident and fashionable campaign for massive birth control programmes as an answer to the problems of poverty and underemployment in Asia can only be regarded as naive or, since those who peddle it are no fools, as concealing deeper and more devious motives.

The Algerian planner A. Remili has reminded us that, if we would understand that world poverty which is so conveniently explained away as due to "overpopulation", we must concern ourselves with the "economy of waste". Such an examination would draw attention to the immense wastage of precious human resources resulting from unemployment and underemployment in Asia. Conservatively this may be estimated at some 200,000 million man-hours yearly; it is one of the major causes of Asian poverty. That such a wastage results not from populations "breeding like rabbits" but from the distortion of economic structures imposed by capitalism is demonstrated by the People's Republic of China, a country which, in 1949, exhibited all the most horrendous symptoms of overpopulation but which, a decade later, was facing an actual shortage of labour.

MISERY, MARGINALIZATION AND MOTIVATION

The simplistic and static analyses of Asia's "population problems", of the "population problems" of the rest of the Periphery and of the "lower classes" in the developed societies† have one thing in common—their lack of human awareness or of simple humanity. Yet without such awareness and humanity it is not easy to understand the dynamics of population growth in Asia.

Brown and Wray spell out for us some of these human realities—and these explain not only the high rates of growth but also the opposition to birth

* On this *see* Howard T. Odum, "Energy, Ecology and Economics" in *Ambio* (Stockholm), Vol. II, No. 6.

† Yves Benot draws attention to the fact that there are, within the Western nations, the same relations of exploitation between the capitalist élite in power—*the Centre*—and the dominated strata—*the Periphery*—as between the rich nations of *the Centre* and the poor nations of *the Periphery*.

control planners. And perhaps if we could bring ourselves to realize that the peoples of Asia are not so very different from us in the West, that in their societies, too, children "are also desired for themselves"—not simply because they play an economic role or represent security in old age—we might find "Asian population dynamics" rather less of a mystery. . . . As Brown and Wray emphasize: "Parents are not enthusiastic about family planning in the presence of high infant and childhood mortality rates. Family planning implies that planning will be successful and parents should be able to plan that their existing children will survive to adulthood." A high infantile mortality rate, a childhood menaced by killing or deforming disease, the ever-present menace of famine —all these result in a situation (is it indeed so surprising?) in which parents "will not stop having children until they believe that those they already have are going to survive". So the evidence from Bangladesh shows "a direct relationship between the death of a child and the probability of a birth in the family during the subsequent year". In the Philippines "total fertility is lower in couples who have lost no children; it is also lower in communities where mortality rates are lower". And this pattern is repeated in Egypt, where "a mother who has lost at least one child will desire a larger number of surviving children and will actually have more births than women in the community who have lost no children". This is one dimension of the human situation which we must comprehend if we seek an understanding of the failure of Western schemes of birth control to have any significant impact on the population growth rates of Asia.

The second dimension derives from the human reactions to the process termed by Samir Amin "marginalization". This marginalization is the result of the warping of the economic structure which global capitalism, with its emphasis on the international division of labour, produces in its dependent territories. Its manifestations are, in Samir Amin's words, "the proletarianization of small agricultural producers and cottage industry workers, rural semi-proletarianization and impoverishment without proletarianization of peasants organized in village communities, urbanization and massive increase of urban unemployment and underemployment. . . ." And this impoverishment is of critical importance in any analysis of demographic problems—for under conditions of massive and increasing underemployment and impoverishment a large family represents the only form of social and economic security; in Samir Amin's words: "There is thus *no motivation* for working class families to accept the proposed limitation of births; quite the contrary."

Such a conclusion—that marginalization and poverty are of critical importance in explaining the large families and rapid population growth of many Third World countries—is diametrically opposed to the conventional wisdom of the birth-control lobbyists; in their teachings poverty is not the *cause*, but the *consequence*, of large families. . . . The demographic variable, it is implied, is an independent variable, an unreal line of reasoning whose attractiveness lies in the fact that by arguing thus the pressing need for a radical restructuring of world society may be bypassed or at least deferred. The unreality of the conventional wisdom of the White North is best illustrated by India, whose peasant masses have been the target of a largely U.S.-planned birth-control propaganda campaign which, for gimmickry, bizarreness and unintended humour, as well as scale, is probably without a parallel in the whole of the Periphery; comments Claire Sterling, there is "an army of 'motivators', paid to recruit 'acceptors' who are in turn paid for being sterilized, and along with 'that' are 16,000 specially trained doctors, 5,000 rural family planning centres and 25,000 sub-centres, 800 mobile units for sterilization operations and insertions of the loop, a new state factory capable of turning out 144 million Nirodh condoms a year, and a capillary distribution network whereby major private industries deliver these contraceptives free of charge to the remotest of hamlets along with tea, cigarettes, batteries and soap. . . ." Zalin B. Grant reports that in 1967 AID began shipment of nearly 200 million condoms to India, the first batch (a reflection of America's "archaic domestic inhibitions") being stamped "Sold for the Prevention of Disease". Grant continues: "Besides exposing a few U.S. hypocrisies, India's need for condoms created rather strange ideological bedfellows. A U.S.-financed condom factory—India's first—recently opened in the Communist-run state of Kerala. The state's family-planning minister is a Catholic-Marxist. (In Nepal, U.S. condoms are distributed through a Russian-built cigarette factory.)" Even the elephants are recruited for this elephantinely subtle attempt to change the most basic and intimate values of Indian society and, on the advice of a Ford Foundation consultant, an elephant was purchased as a mobile bill-board; the unfortunate animal was, in Grant's words, "plastered with birth control posters and sentenced, like a pachyderm Sisyphus, to spend her life trudging to Indian villages with the message. . . ." Meanwhile, the rate of growth of India's population rose from 21.64 per cent over the decade 1951–61 to 24.66 per cent over the decade 1961–71, suggesting that, whatever the combination of dollars, Madison Avenue sales gimmicks and computer-based and foundation-funded expertise might accomplish back in the United States, it was sadly inadequate when applied to the "problems" of Asian societies. And it is inadequate because it neglects the human realities of these societies, because it proceeds on the tacit assumption that all that is needed to change society—and the behaviour patterns of the individuals and families making up that society—is a massive input of the White North's technology. And such an assumption is possible only to groups who have a mechanistic concept of man "as a robot which specialists in the social sciences can manipulate at their will".

"THE WORLDS OF DIFFERENT PEOPLES HAVE DIFFERENT SHAPES . . ."

The Khanna Project, a million-dollar pilot project in the field of birth control in the Punjab, brings us face-to-face with the human realities and demographic implications of "marginalization". Financed chiefly by the Rockefeller Foundation and the Indian Government, it also provides a picture of the élitism and the Western-oriented value-systems of the social engineers who—from Rostow and Huntington to the directors of the Rockefeller or Ford Foundations, from the academic experts of our western universities to the western-trained field workers on whom they must rely—are trying to "domesticate the Third World". It also demonstrates the total inability of the neo-Malthusians to comprehend the true nature of the reality they are trying to transform.

We are fortunate in having an Asian analysis of this project—that by Mahmood Mamdani—an analysis which spells out clearly the political motivations behind many projects of this type devised, so we are assured, to "aid" the peoples of the Periphery. Mamdani sees, perhaps more clearly than would be possible to a European, the implicit belief running through the whole project—that by reducing population growth structural change in society may be avoided. He spells out the strange misconception that plagued the directors of the Khanna Project—that "overpopulation is a malady of society" (rather than a symptom of a much deeper malady) and shows how "the perception of overpopulation as a disease became an analytic tool for misunderstanding". He comments, ironically, on the dogged belief of those who directed this programme that "the behaviour of the population, given the environment and its constraints, is not rational; it is thus susceptible to 'education' ", and on how, as the failure of the programme became evident to all, its directors remained convinced that the fundamental problem lay not in the programme but in the villagers' "mistaken" perceptions of reality. To this very day, indeed, these villagers, and hundreds of millions like them, have not even begun to understand what the American experts kept telling them—that they are poor because they have large families; they *know*, as did their ancestors before them and as Mamdani demonstrates so convincingly, that *the reality is that the way to solve the poverty problem was by having large families*. . . . What the villagers never understood was why all these experts were in their villages, and so many dollars were being spent, to prevent births when "surely everybody knows that children are a necessity of life".

The area in which the Khanna Project was undertaken is typical of much of the Periphery. Farm labour is, overall, underemployed; on the other hand, there is considerable unemployment for half the year with a labour shortage for the remainder. Given the level of technology, the key element in the economy was labour and a large family was an economic necessity. In the words of a Jat farmer: "Without sons, there is no living off the land. The more sons you have, the less labour you need to hire and the more savings you can have." This attitude is corroborated by the village blacksmith: "(to the problem of poverty) there is only one way out. And that is to have enough sons. Don't smile. If I have sons they will work outside, labour even as animals do; but save . . . A rich man invests in his machines. We must invest in our children. It's that simple"; and by the village potter, who introduces another important factor favouring large families—the desperate quest for security in old age: "You think I am poor because I have too many children. (He laughs.) If I didn't have my sons, I wouldn't have half the prosperity I do. And God knows what would happen to me and their mother when we are too old to work and earn." This truth was stressed some years back by May and Heer in their computer analysis of son survivorship; in India, they showed, for a man to be certain of having a son living when he attained the age of 65 a family of five children was necessary. As is so often the case, the "irrational" attitudes of the illiterate marginal masses of Asia are in fact more rational than the counsels urged on them by the experts of the White North.

Walter Goldschmidt has said, "the worlds of different peoples have different shapes"—but because of our arrogant belief that technology has given us a monopoly of truth we do not perceive these "different shapes" nor do we recognize the cohesion and the logic behind these alternative worlds perceived by the peoples of the Periphery.*

INTERLUDE: OF HUMAN VALUES . . .

We have commented earlier on the confusion in much of the anti-natalist literature between "birth control" and "family planning"; to this Pradervand adds the conceptual confusion between the motivation for family planning and the provision of contraceptive services. We have stressed earlier that the adoption of family planning is an educational process, both for the couple and for the society as a whole. The majority of birth control programmes which the experts and the bureaucrats of the North are seeking to foist on the peoples of Asia are above all technological in their content; age-old social and human realities are ignored and the solution to the "people problem" becomes simply a matter of devising increasingly effective methods of birth control and administering them to the masses.

The horrifying naivety of such an attitude has been spelled out by Pierre Pradervand: "One is somewhat shaken to see folk such as the population officer of USAID pushing prostaglandine as *the* solution to the demographic problem . . . one is shocked by the naivety and lack of sensitivity of such an attitude: is it really believed that, when women can have an abortion just as if they were brushing their teeth, this will have no important cultural, sociological, psychological and spiritual repercussions? From what con-

* Though Heinrich von Loesch, drawing on the ideas of John Pitchford, suggests "that optimal paths of development leading through a period of overpopulation are imaginable. Overpopulation helps to collect a sizable capital stock before subsequent population reduction optimizes the population size in relation to the capital stock, i.e. improves the standard of living. Maybe we should more calmly face an extended period of world overpopulation, and concentrate our efforts now on a subsequent reduction in world population size, from which our grandchildren might be the first to benefit."

cept of man can such an approach spring? These are absolutely vital questions which it is imperative that the countries of the Third World solve before technocratic 'civilization' erodes their cultural bases." Remili also emphasizes the destructive impact of birth control programmes which are formulated simply in technological terms and superimposed on an unchanged traditional society. He comments: "It is by action at all the levels of social reality, by the radical transformation of society and of morals that it is possible to speed up a little the abandonment of behaviour patterns which are as intimate and as rooted in the deepest levels of human existence as procreative patterns." And Han Suyin sees in contraception as such something which, in the capitalist world at least, is bound up with exploitation and the class struggle.

It is these negative aspects of birth control which distinguish it most clearly from family planning. The latter, says Samir Amin, "can be an effective means of liberating women in all societies, developed as underdeveloped". But it can be effective only if society has undergone radical change. Few couples are likely to plan their families unless there is some possibility of being able to plan their whole life—and this depends on a stable income and security of employment, upon the existence of a reasonably developed medical infrastructure and of a system of social security for the aged, upon education and a high degree of feminine emancipation. It is for this reason that anti-natalist programmes have little chance of success except in countries which are approaching or have reached the stage of economic "take-off" and which have transformed the traditional pattern of social and economic relations. And of this the best example is the People's Republic of China, where an integrated policy of total development, involving education, politicization, the development of welfare and social security services, the emancipation of women, and a wholesale restructuring of the economy provided the basis for the most dramatic confrontation of the problems posed by a seemingly runaway increase in the population. Given security and faith in, and control of, their future (which economic development in China provided for the Chinese masses) men and women will begin planning the size of their family; where these things are lacking the most lavishly funded programmes of contraception are worthless. The examples of China and India offer proof, on a subcontinental scale, of this truth; it is disastrous for much of the population of Asia that those experts from the North, or those local élites trained in the North, are unlikely to heed the lessons China has to offer in the demographic field.

BEHIND THE PAINTED VEIL

The American geographer Wilbur Zelinsky states: "We do not yet have enough facts, historical models or general theory concerning the demography and population geography of the underdeveloped lands to describe, evaluate, and interpret their population/resource problems at all adequately, to predict the future course of these problems, or to prescribe infallible solutions". Yet, in spite of the ignorance prevailing in this field, "infallible solutions" are not only being propounded but administered to the peoples of Asia, of the Periphery as a whole. Under these circumstances it is pertinent to pose the old question: *cui bono?*—who is going to benefit from this selling of panaceas whose benefits are at the best dubious, at the worst demonstrably non-existent?

Certainly, as Weissman points out, "this sudden interest of the world's rich in the world's poor" is something that "makes good dollars and cents". Equally certainly this new concern is not simply with crude and immediate profits; rather is it more accurately to be interpreted as part of a more sophisticated long-term strategy designed to safeguard the position and the power of the developed nations of the Centre. And in this strategy the critical elements are, as suggested earlier, access to raw materials; the preservation of the global *status quo*; and the countering of the threat to White dominance posed by the rapid growth of non-white populations. Population control directed towards the masses of the Periphery and the "socially handicapped groups" (e.g. ethnic minorities) in the advanced societies provides an answer to each of these problems.

The Ford Foundation-sponsored organization *Resources for the Future* pointed out that for the "less-developed" nations "a sustained increase in living levels can by no means be guaranteed with the assurance it can be for the United States and other more advanced industrial countries". What is discreetly veiled is that the continuing progress of the developed nations of the Centre depends on the availability of "surpluses" from the nations of the Periphery and that these would vanish if economic stagnation in the Periphery ended and/or existing rates of population growth continue;* that the uncertainty regarding the future development of the Periphery arises from the assumption that the siphoning of resources from Periphery to Centre will continue without interruption. Pierre Pradervand, we have seen, speaks of the "growing structural opposition between the Babylonian consumption of the developed nations and the Third World", and it can be argued that the Centre's birth control schemes are designed, in part at least, to attenuate this "opposition".

An even stronger element, hidden behind "the painted veil" of supposedly humanitarian population policies, appears to be the determination to counter any possible shift in the balance of world power which might result from continuing rapid population growth in Asia and other countries of the Periphery. Michael Hudson, speaking of the World Bank and of U.S. policy in general, comments: "The Bank's neo-Malthusianism and its endorsement of the political

* If the population of the Indian subcontinent, *given no increase whatever*, were to consume copper at the same *per capita* rate as did that of the U.S. in the 1960s it would consume 450 million tons in the coming century. This is ten times U.S. consumption between 1860 and 1960. *See* S. R. Eyre, "Man the Pest: the Dim Chance of Survival" in *The New York Review*, Nov. 18, 1971, p. 22.

and economic *status quo* . . . is part of a general strategy to freeze today's balance of power among all nations, as well as among the political parties within these nations, so as to maintain American hegemony and that of its political allies in the backward countries. Whether or not this is or is not a conscious plan, the fact remains that Mr. McNamara has enunciated that (1) *population growth under existing institutional constraints implies political change,* and (2) the present socio-economic institutions have not significantly evolved, and will not significantly evolve, at the hands of the present governments, so that (3) further population growth implies a change of government, probably to the benefit of parties less closely associated with the United States" (emphasis added, K.B.). The proposal to curtail population growth, Hudson argues, does not serve the needs of the backward nations but rather the political interest of the aid-donor nations, specifically the U.S.A., in maintaining an unsatisfactory *status quo.* Josué de Castro (a former director of FAO) is even more forthright, speaking of the pill as "North America's best guarantee of continuing a dominant minority. . . ."

The third element behind contemporary neo-Malthusianism is hinted at in the above paragraphs—and that is that the rapidly increasing populations of coloured people in Asia and the other countries of the Periphery or among ethnic minorities contain a menace to the white man's domination at global or national levels. The words of the nineteenth century French politician Faguet, "the yellow and black perils will smother our race and destroy our civilization"* live on in the subconscious of the West; the testing of new contraceptive techniques among ethnic minorities or coloured groups, the "administering" to them of birth control programmes, seem to many observers in the nations of the Periphery convincing evidence of this fear.

BEYOND THE TECHNOLOGICAL FIX . . .

What is becoming increasingly evident to the masses of the Periphery, which is demonstrated by Mamdani's analysis of the Khanna Project, is that the ambitious programmes of population control sponsored by the White North are scarcely the innocuous and disinterested projects their promoters would have us believe and that, even if the programmes are taken at face value—as designed to lift the burden of poverty from "the damned of the earth"—they are almost worthless.

This is not to deny that over the long term population growth does present problems. Clearly, over a perspective of, say, the next hundred years it does, though McNamara is horrified at the prospect of a Third World population of 14,000 million by 2040, while W. H. Pawley can envisage a population "about 50 times the present level 100 years from now". What we should stress is that rapid population growth is "essentially a secondary effect of backwardness rather than the primary cause" and that "population control without fundamental social reform does nothing in itself to tackle the related underlying causes of poverty". And what is increasingly clear is that the so-called "population problem" just cannot be solved by somehow tacking a programme of birth control on to an unchanged rural society. Once a certain threshold of social and economic security has been reached, once a certain level of medical and educational progress has been achieved, and the equality of sexes becomes a reality, people will begin to plan their families. And they will do this not because they have been bribed, bullied or cajoled into this by foreign experts or foundations but because they will know they no longer have to bring into the world five or six children in order to provide them with security in old age, because they will realize a planned family offers many human advantages to both children and parents. And to those who claim this is impossible we would point to the remarkable achievements of the Chinese people (once cited as the most dreadful example of "overpopulation") in bringing about an almost sensational decline in the rate of population growth. This success is largely ignored by the experts of the White North and it is ignored because what the Chinese achieved was possible only after an overturning of the old society, after the creation of new socio-economic structures and after withdrawal from the White-dominated global system. The long-drawn-out agony of Indochina serves to indicate the tenacity with which this truth will be resisted . . . yet with every month that passes, with every increment to the swarming masses of jobless or underemployed, with every famine that erupts in Africa, India or Indonesia, the bankruptcy of "orthodox" population and development policies becomes clearer and the relevance of China's experience more insistent.

* Quoted in Jacques Barzun, *Race: A Study in Superstition* (Harper Torchbook, N.Y., 1965), p. 233.

STATISTICS

Table 1

POPULATION IN THE ASIAN-PACIFIC REGION

Sub-Region	Mid-1975 Population (millions)	Annual % Rate of Growth 1970–75	Crude Birth Rate ('000) 1970–75	Crude Death Rate ('000) 1970–75
East Asia	1,006	1.65	26.2	9.8
China (incl. Taiwan)	839	1.66	26.9	10.3
Japan	111	1.26	19.2	6.6
Other	56	2.15	30.2	8.7
South Asia	1,250	2.53	41.9	16.7
Eastern	324	2.70	42.4	17.1
Middle	838	2.44	41.7	17.0
Australia & New Zealand	17	1.83	21.2	8.1
North America	237	0.90	16.5	9.3
Europe (excl. U.S.S.R.)	473	0.56	16.1	10.6

Source: UN Population Division, Doc. ESA/P/WP.55 (May 1975).

Figures are population projections, based on "medium variant" assumptions, as assessed in 1973.

The pattern is dominated by the population clusters of Mainland East Asia, the Indian subcontinent and South-East Asia; these contain 55 per cent of the world's people.

Note that growth rates are markedly lower in East Asia than in South Asia. Note, too, that the high rate of growth in the population of South Asia is in spite of a death rate about 70 per cent higher than that of East Asia. Crude birth rates in most of South Asia (around 40/000) are still considerably lower than those in Bangladesh or some countries in Africa and Latin America, where the rates are close to, or even exceed, 50 per 1,000.

Table 2

RURAL AND PEASANT POPULATION, 1960

	% Dependent on Agriculture		% Rural	
World	57		67	
East Asia	69		77	
China (incl. Taiwan)		76		82
Japan		33		57
Middle South Asia	74		83	
India		74		82
Pakistan		76		88
South-East Asia	75		82	
Oceania	25		34	
Australia		11		19
New Zealand		15		27

Source: UN Population Division, Doc. ESA/P/WP.57 (Sept. 1975).

Note that as of 1960 some four-fifths of Monsoon Asia's population was rural and almost three-quarters dependent on agriculture. Moreover, even if the estimates of the shift towards an urban/industrial way of life should prove correct (something the present writer doubts . . .), the proportion of the population of countries such as India and China classified as rural will be as high as two-thirds even by the end of the century; for countries such as Viet-Nam and Indonesia it will be as high as seven-tenths and in Bangladesh almost nine-tenths. These proportions are, obviously, to be related to a greatly increased total population in the countries of Monsoon Asia; what this means in absolute figures is indicated by Table 5.

Table 3
ESTIMATED POPULATION GROWTH, 1950–2000
(millions)

	1950		1975		2000*	
WORLD	2,501		3,967		6,253	
EAST ASIA	675		1,006		1,369	
China (incl. Taiwan)		558		839		1,148
Japan		84		111		133
MIDDLE SOUTH ASIA	475		838		1,501	
India		353		613		1,059
Pakistan		36		71		147
SOUTH-EAST ASIA	173		324		592	
OCEANIA	13		21		33	
Australia		8		14		20
New Zealand		2		3		4

* Medium variant.

Source: UN Population Division, Doc. ESA/P/WP.55 (May 1975).

UN projections suggest that the world's population will increase by 150 per cent between 1950 and 2000. The various regions of Asia show sharply contrasting trends. Thus, while the population of East Asia is expected to double its 1950 total by the year 2000 (and that of Japan to increase by less than 60 per cent), the population of Middle South Asia is expected to increase by 215 per cent, that of South-East Asia by 240 per cent and that of Pakistan by over 300 per cent. The overall population density of Middle South Asia is, it may be stressed, already 50 per cent higher than that of East Asia, and in detail India's is over twice that of China. Given present population densities and projected growth rates it is clear that the main "crisis area" lies in South Asia. Here the sort of restructuring of the society and the economy which has permitted East Asia to confront its problem of population growth has scarcely begun.

Table 4
URBANIZATION, 1950–2000

	% OF POPULATION URBANIZED						URBAN POPULATION (millions)			
	1950		1975		2000		1950		2000	
WORLD	29		39		50		715		3,103	
EAST ASIA	17		31		43		111		591	
China (incl. Taiwan)		11		23		36		62		414
Japan		50		75		87		42		116
MIDDLE SOUTH ASIA	16		21		32		74		481	
India		17		21		32		60		342
Pakistan		15		27		42		6		62
SOUTH-EAST ASIA	13		22		35		23		207	
OCEANIA	64		72		78		8		26	
Australia		80		86		92		7		19
New Zealand		72		83		91		1		4

Source: UN Population Division, Doc. ESA/P/WP.54 (April 1975).

While the urban sector in Japan, as that in Australia and New Zealand, is expected to amount to some nine-tenths of the total population by the end of the century, the urbanized sector in many Asian countries will still not greatly exceed one-third to two-fifths of the total population.

Population estimates suggest that by the year 2000 the urban population of Monsoon Asia will be about 1,200 million and the number of cities with a population exceeding one million will have increased from 100 in 1975 to 238.

Table 5

ESTIMATED RURAL POPULATIONS, 1950–2000

(millions)

	1950	1975	2000
World	1,787	2,410	3,150
East Asia	563	697	778
China (incl. Tawian)	496	642	734
Japan	42	28	17
Middle South Asia	401	661	1,019
India	293	481	717
Pakistan	31	52	85
South-East Asia	150	252	385
Oceania	4	6	7
Australia	2	2	2
New Zealand	0.5	0.5	0.4

Source: UN Population Division, Doc. ESA/P/WP.54 (April 1975).

During the second half of this century the heart of the population problem is represented by the growth of the rural populations of Asia. This table gives estimates for the rural populations of major regions after allowance has been made for the shifts of population to the cities summarized in Table 4. These estimates suggest the size of the employment problem facing parts of rural Asia. Note that, while the world's rural population is expected to increase by 70 per cent between 1950 and 2000, the rural population of India, Pakistan and South-East Asia is expected to rise by 150 per cent. China's rural population may increase by some 50 per cent but that of the developed nations (Japan, Australia and New Zealand) will decline.

BIBLIOGRAPHY

AMIN, SAMIR. "Accumulation and Development: A Theoretical Model" in *Review of African Political Economy* Vol. 1, No. 1, Aug.–Nov. 1974.

BENOT, YVES. Qu'est-ce que le développement (Paris, 1974).

BARCLAY, WILLIAM, *et al.* "Population Control in the Third World" in *NACLA Newsletter* (Berkeley), Dec. 1970.

BIRD, KAI. "Sterilization in India: Indira Gandhi Uses Force" in *The Nation* (New York), June 19th, 1976.

BROWN, ROY E., and WRAY, JOE D. "The Starving Roots of Population Growth" in *Natural History* Vol. 83, No. 1, Jan. 1974.

DE CASTRO, J. Le livre noir de la faim (Paris, 1962).

CURRIE, LAUCHLIN. "The Tangled Crisis: Economics and Population" in *Population Bulletin* April 1967.

DAVIS, WAYNE H. "Overpopulated America" in *The New Republic* (Washington) Jan. 10, 1970.

DUMONT, RENÉ, and ROSIER, BERNARD. The Hungry Future (London, 1969).

ENKE, STEPHEN. Economics for Development (London 1964). Especially Section 4.

FAO, *Ceres* Nov./Dec. 1973: Special issue devoted to population problems (contains articles by Ester Boserup, René Dumont, Colin Clark and Pierre Pradervand).

GOULET, DENIS, and HUDSON, MICHAEL. The Myth of Aid: The Hidden Agenda of the Development Reports (New York, 1971).

GRANT, ZALIN B. "The Ford Condom in India's Future" in *The New Republic* Sept. 13, 1969.

HARVEY, DAVID. "Population, Resources and the Ideology of Science" forthcoming in *Economic Geography* (Worcester, Mass.).

IRFED. *Développement et civilisations* No. 47–48 (special number on population and development: contains articles by Samir Amin, René Dumont, Pierre Pradervand, A. Remili and Han Suyin).

JALÉE, P. The Pillage of the Third World (New York, 1969).

JOHNSON, STANLEY. Life Without Birth (London, 1970).

JOLLY, RICHARD *et al.* (ed.) Third World Employment (Harmondsworth, 1973).

KATO, HIDETOSHI. "A View of Densely Populated Societies" translated in "The Wheel Extended" *Toyota Quarterly Review* April 1, 1972.

VON LOESCH, HEINRICH. "The Capillarity Process" in *Ceres* Sept./Oct. 1974.

MCNAMARA, ROBERT. Interview with, in *The Observer* Oct. 3, 1971.

MAMDANI, MAHMOOD. The Myth of Population Control (New York and London, 1972).

MEISTER, ALBERT. "The urbanization crisis of rural man" in *Ceres*, Nov./Dec. 1970.

MEHTA, M. M. "Wanted: 200 million new jobs by 1980" in *Ceres* Sept./Oct. 1972.

OMRAN, ABDEL R. "The Demographic Jigsaw" in *Ceres* July–Aug. 1974.

PAWLEY, W. H. "In the Year 2070" in *Ceres* July/Aug. 1971.

POSINSKY, S. H. "Overpopulation?" in *American Anthropologist* Vol. 74, October 1972, pp. 1321–1323 (especially bibliography).

PRADERVAND, PIERRE. "Les pays nantis et la limitation des naissances . . ." in *Développement et civilisations* No. 39–40, Mar.–June 1970.

RIDGEWAY, JAMES. The Politics of Ecology (New York, 1971). Especially Ch. 6.

SINGH, NARENDRA. "Overpopulation is no excuse" in *Ceres* May/June 1976.

STERLING, CLAIRE. "India's Birth Control Progress" in *The Washington Post* Sept. 30, 1970.

WATTENBERG, BEN. "The Nonsense Explosion" in *The New Republic* April 4 and 11, 1970.

WEISSMAN, STEVE. "Why the Population Bomb is a Rockefeller Baby" in *Ramparts* (Berkeley) May 1970.

WRAY, JOE D. "Birth Planning in China" excerpt from article in *People* (International Planned Parenthood Federation) Vol. 1, No. 4, 1974, reprinted in Technology for Development (London, VCOAD, 1975).

ZELINSKY, WILBUR. "The Geographer and his Crowding World" in *Revista Geografiea* (Rio de Janeiro) No. 65, Dec. 1966.

The Religions of Asia

Geoffrey Parrinder

Islam

Islam means "submission" or surrender to God, and a Muslim, from the same root, is a surrendered man. This faith was taught by Muhammad but Muslims object to being called Muhammadan or Mahometan, because they do not worship the founder of their religion. Although a late starter among the world's great religions, Islam is a universal faith with some 500 million followers in Asia and Africa.

HISTORY

Muhammad lived from A.D. 570–632 in Arabia, which was largely pagan and polytheistic with small communities of Jews and Christians. The town of Mecca was already a sacred place and it was part of the religious genius of Muhammad to purge some of its holy sites of idolatrous associations and incorporate them into the new religion, particularly the Ka'ba shrine, a cube-like sanctuary in the middle of Mecca. Jewish and Christian figures were also honoured by Muhammad, especially Abraham, Moses and Jesus, and many of their stories occur in the sacred book, the Koran. But the central themes of Muhammad's teaching came in his own experience: the unity of God, his word to man, the judgement of unbelievers and paradise for the righteous. From 610 onwards Muhammad received divine visions and messages and preached a monotheistic faith, but most of the leaders of Mecca rejected it and in 622 Muhammad migrated to Medina 200 miles to the north. This "migration" (*Hijra* or *Hegira*) was later taken as the beginning of the Muslim era from which its calendar is dated. In Medina, Muhammad became leader of a community and after successful battles against the Meccans he eventually ruled over most of Arabia, and returned to Mecca in triumph in 630, cleansing the Ka'ba of idols but going back to Medina where he died two years later.

Muhammad was followed by Caliphs (*Khalifas*, "successors") who greatly extended the rule of Islam. Under Abu Bakr the Arab armies conquered Babylon, and under 'Umar (Omar) Syria, Palestine and Egypt fell to their rule. Jerusalem and Alexandria surrendered, led by their Christian patriarchs who were glad to be rid of Byzantine Greek overlords. Arab rule was not unduly oppressive, allowing the survival of Christian communities to this day in Syrian, Coptic, Greek and other churches. Arab armies slowly pressed on into North Africa, crossed into Spain in 711, and were only repelled from central France by Charles Martel in 732 at the Battle of Poitiers. To the east the second Persian empire fell to the Arabs, who entered northern India in 705 and sent embassies as far as China. As the Arab empire settled down it absorbed eastern and western cultures and produced its own contributions; Greek philosophy, mathematics and medicine were preserved by the Arabs during the Dark Ages of Europe.

The Arab empire dominated the Near and Middle East, from Spain to central Asia, and the caliphate came to be located in Baghdad till its fall to the Mongols in 1258. After the capture of Constantinople (Istanbul) the caliph lived there till his office was abolished by the Turkish Government in 1924. In modern times the Turkish empire broke up into independent nation states and Turkey itself became westernized and secularized, a tendency which has operated in varying degrees in many Islamic countries.

BELIEF AND PRACTICE

There are Five Pillars of practical religion in Islam:

The first is the Witness that "there is no god but God" (*Allah*) and that "Muhammad is the Apostle of God". This confession is called from the minaret or a mosque by a *muezzin* ("crier") at the times of daily prayer. It stresses the unity and omnipotence of God, but it does not necessarily make Muslims into fatalists, an attitude which may derive as much from social as from theological reasons;

The second Pillar is Prayer which is to be said five times a day, turning towards the Ka'ba shrine in Mecca. Muslims unroll prayer mats and pray in a *mosque* (a "place of prostration"), at home, or wherever they are, bowing and prostrating to God and reciting set verses from the Koran in Arabic. On Fridays there is congregational worship in central mosques attended by men but not normally by women, in which worship includes the formal prayers and usually a short sermon;

No collection of money is made in the mosque but the third Pillar is Almsgiving which provides for the sick and poor in lands where there are few social services;

The fourth Pillar is Fasting from food and drink, which is obligatory on all healthy adults during the hours of daylight for the whole of the ninth month, Ramadan. The sick, pregnant women, travellers and children are exempt, but adults should fast when restored to normal life. Some modern states extend exemption to students, soldiers and factory workers, and it is said that the true fast is from sin. Since the Islamic year is lunar, the date of Ramadan gets a little earlier each year compared with the solar calendar and in northern countries in summer fasting is a considerable trial. The fast ends with one of the two great Muslim festivals, *Id al Fitr* or *Little Bairam*.

The fifth Pillar is Pilgrimage (*hajj*) to Mecca which is incumbent at least once in a lifetime on every Muslim, who may then take the title *Hajji*. About a million pilgrims go every year to Mecca, which is the holy city forbidden to all but Muslims, and some take months or years to perform the ambition of a lifetime, travelling by air, sea, lorry or on foot. The pilgrimage is in the twelfth month and must be performed in simple dress donned at ten miles distance from Mecca, women being veiled from head to foot. The central ritual entails going round the Ka'ba seven times, kissing a Black Stone in its walls, and visiting hills outside Mecca where sheep and other animals are sacrificed. At the same time Muslims all over the world sacrifice sheep and this makes the chief festival, *Id al Kabir*, *Qurban* or *Bairam*. This ceremony unites all Muslims and is popularly linked with Abraham's sacrifice of a sheep in place of his son. The birthday of the Prophet is another popular modern anniversary.

The Holy War (*Jihad*) was the means of the unparalleled spread of Islam in the first centuries, but despite pressures it has not been elevated into a Pillar of religion and today theologians interpret the Jihad as war against sin in the soul.

The Koran (*Qur'an*, "recitation" or "reading") is regarded as the very Word of God and not to be subjected to criticism. The Koran is about as long as the New Testament, in 114 chapters (*suras*) of uneven length, the longest ones coming first after the opening chapter. The Opening (*Fatiha*) is repeated twice at least at all times of daily prayer, preceded by the ascription "in the name of God, the Merciful, the Compassionate". Two short chapters at the end are also used in prayers, and instructed and pious Muslims may repeat other chapters, always in Arabic. Modern translations of the Koran are now allowed for private use and there have always been many commentaries. The chief message of the Koran is the majesty of God, his oneness, demand for human obedience and coming judgement. The later and longer chapters include much family and social legislation, for marriage, divorce, personal and communal behaviour.

The Koran is not the only authority for Muslims, but it is supplemented by masses of Traditions (*Hadith*) which include sayings attributed to the Prophet and his companions, and doctrine and morals are further interpreted by Comparison and Consent. Four law schools arose which apply Islamic law (*shari'a*) to all activities of life. In Asia the two principal law schools are the *Hanafi* in central Asia and the Indian sub-continent, and the *Shafi'i* in the East Indies. In modern times interpretation of law ranges between conservative rigorism and modernism; many of the Traditions are questioned but the Koran remains sacrosanct.

The Islamic community (*umma*) is the basis of the brotherhood of Islam, which from the early centuries aimed at making this religion international and above tribal rivalries. This is still the ideal, though the rise of nationalism has brought divisive interests into the Muslim world.

SECTS AND MYSTICS

The great majority, probably over 80 per cent, of Muslims are *Sunni*, followers of "the path", custom or tradition. They accept the first four caliphs (Abu Bakr, 'Umar, 'Uthman, 'Ali) as "rightly guided", receive six authentic books of Traditions, and belong to one of the four schools of law. Other Muslims claim to follow true tradition but differ on its interpretation.

Shi'a Muslims

The major division came early. The Shi'a or "followers" of 'Ali believed that as cousin and son-in-law of Muhammad, 'Ali should have been his first successor. When at last his turn came there was a division and another caliph was set up in Damascus. The Shi'a became linked with patriotism in Iraq which objected to rule from Syria, and Husain, a son of 'Ali, went to found a kingdom in Iraq but was intercepted by rival troops and slain at Karbala. Husain became the great Shi'a martyr, the anniversary of whose death in Muharram, the first month of the year, is the occasion for days of mourning and long Passion Plays in Shi'a towns. At the climax of the play Husain receives the key of intercession from Gabriel and promises paradise to all who call upon him.

The basic Shi'a beliefs are the same as those of the Sunni but 'Ali is added after Muhammad in the confession of faith. Their most distinctive doctrine is that of the *Imam*, spiritual "leader", which was used in preference to caliph for the head of state. Most Shi'a are Twelvers, recognizing twelve Imams, of whom the last disappeared in A.D. 878, but it is believed that he will return again as the *Mahdi* ("guided one") to put down evil and restore righteousness on earth. In 1502, Shi'ism became the established religion of Iran and it is strongest there and in Iraq and north India.

Isma'ilis

Some of the Shi'a are Isma'ilis, believing that it was the seventh Imam, Isma'il, who was the last when he disappeared in 765, hence they are also called Seveners. There were political as well as religious reasons for the schism and while the Fatimid dynasty in Egypt imposed it, elsewhere the movement was persecuted as dangerous. There are mystical beliefs in the "light" of the Imam, eternal and ever-present, and various grades of initiation into mysteries. There are small groups of Isma'ilis in Afghanistan and Turkestan, and larger ones in Pakistan, Bangladesh and India. Offshoots are most of the Khojas whose leader is the Aga Khan. These Isma'ili Khojas are found in Bombay, Gujarat, Sind, East Africa, and other Indian and neighbouring towns. They number over 200,000, in active and educated communities, noted for social works.

Ahmadiyya Movement

At Qadian in India and Lahore in Pakistan are centres of a modern movement called Ahmadiyya, after Ghulam Ahmad of the Punjab who, from 1890, was set forth as the expected Mahdi, Messiah and Avatar. After struggles and divisions the Ahmadiyya have published many books in English, sent missionaries to Africa, and propounded teachings most of which are orthodox Islam but with some modern polemics.

Sufis

Sufi mystics have been found in all branches of Islam from the early days, so called from the woollen (*suf*) robes which they wore, like Christian monks. In face of orthodox formalism and deism, the Sufis taught the love of God and sometimes this became almost pantheism or identity with God. The Sufis came to be accepted, partly through the efforts of the Persian philosopher Ghazali, himself a mystic. Many popular shrines are tombs of holy men or shaikhs, where relics are revered and votive gifts are placed.

DISTRIBUTION

Islam is the state religion of Afghanistan, where most of the population are Sunni Muslims, and of Pakistan, one of the largest Muslim societies, estimated at 97.1 per cent of the population. In Bangladesh at the 1974 census over 85 per cent, 60.6 million, were Muslims and according to the 1971 census in India there were 61.4 million Indian Muslims. Indonesia is predominantly Muslim with 94 per cent of the population, over 112 million, adherents at the 1971 census. Islam is the state religion in Malaysia, followed by most Malays. There are Muslim minorities in Sri Lanka, Burma, Thailand and the Philippines and in Soviet Central Asia and China there are some large Muslim communities.

Hinduism

Hinduism is the name given by Europeans to the major religion of India, estimated to have 453 million adherents in the 1971 Census.

HISTORY

The name is derived from India and the river Indus in the north-west. Here flourished an extensive city culture from about 2,500 to 1,500 B.C., contemporary with ancient Mesopotamia and Egypt. These cities were destroyed by invading Aryans but remains indicate that Indus Valley religion included worship of a Mother Goddess and a Lord of Yogis and animals like Shiva, a great god today. A caste system arose from conquest and colour at the head of which were the Brahmin priests who imposed their religion.

The Brahmins compiled the most ancient religious texts, the *Vedas* ("knowledge"), in four collections, though these were not written down for many centuries but passed on orally. The history of Hinduism is scanty, with no historical founder and no organized church, but development can be traced in religious texts. The Vedas are hymns to many gods of heaven and earth, and they portray a relatively simple religion in some ways like that of the Homeric Greeks who were also Aryans. The Vedic hymns were probably compiled between 1500 and 800 B.C. but their use was restricted to the upper castes, and today they are used only by priests and at marriage and funeral ceremonies. They were followed by the *Upanishads* ("sitting-down-near", teaching sessions), dialogues of which the chief were compiled between 800 and 300 B.C. The Upanishads are called *Vedanta* ("end of the Vedas") though this term is also used for some later philosophies. They discuss philosophical questions, like those which Greek thinkers considered a little later: the origins of the world and man, the nature of divinity and the human soul, death and immortality, self-discipline and devotion.

From this time onwards arose masses of religious works which became the chief inspiration of most Hindus. Two great epic poems, the *Mahabharata*, "great India" story, and the *Ramayana*, "the story of Rama", include myth, history, theology and ethics. The personal gods of the Vedas reappear but with many others, no doubt from the Indus Valley and indigenous sources. A creating deity Brahma plays a small part, but Shiva, Vishnu and the Goddess come from now on to be the major deities of Hinduism. Vishnu, a minor Vedic god, became important through his *Avatars* ("descents"), visible embodiments on earth in animal and human form. The two chief human Avatars were Rama and Krishna, the latter a dark god of herdsmen, a warrior king, and a lover of the soul. A small section of the Great Epic is the *Bhagavad-Gita*, "the Song of the Lord" Krishna, the most popular of all Indian scriptures, which gives the teaching of the god Krishna on reincarnation, salvation, deity and devotion. Stories of Krishna and other gods continued in the *Puranas*, "ancient tales", composed down to the Middle Ages. Many mediaeval Indian poets also produced popular songs in praise of Krishna, Rama, Shiva and the Goddess, and devotional groups flourished especially in Bengal and southern India.

In modern times external influences and internal pressures brought reforms of Hinduism. Muslim invasions began in the eighth century but became most potent under the rule of the Mughals from the sixteenth to the nineteenth centuries. Christian missions and European trade developed especially in the nineteenth and twentieth centuries. Both Islam and Christianity criticized Hinduism for polytheism and idolatry, and practices such as suttee (widow-burning). Modern Hinduism is often presented as "eternal truth", including all that is best from other faiths but with its special emphasis either in pantheism or devotion.

BELIEFS

Belief in the indestructibility of the soul is basic to Hinduism, it is both pre-existence and post-existence. Transmigration from one life to another, or reincarnation, is universally held, but the endless births and deaths are a harsh cycle from which ways of salvation are offered, through knowledge, works or devotion. The next life is conditioned by *Karma*, "works" or the entail of works. This explains the inequalities and sufferings of life, to those who accept it in faith, but it does not necessarily lead to fatalism. Karma can be improved by good actions and the next rebirth be to a higher level. But those who do wrong may descend to the animal level or even lower, hence there is a great respect for animal life and many Hindus are vegetarians.

From early times Indians have practised self-discipline and there are many holy men, sadhus, swamis, and the like. *Yoga* is a general name for both discipline and union, related to the English "yoke". It may consist in forms of physical exercise and control, in Hatha ("force") Yoga. Some adepts claim super-natural powers, like levitation. Most practitioners engage in breath-control and sit in cross-legged postures. Raja ("royal") Yoga proceeds to mastery of mind, concentration or emptying of thought, and attainment of supreme knowledge or bliss.

The Caste System

The caste system greatly developed over the centuries. In theory there are four basic castes: Brahmin priests, Raja rulers and warriors, Vaishya artisan merchants, and Shudra servants. The first three are "twice born" through initiation with sacred threads at adolescence. But the castes have been expanded with many local and occupational castes, said to number over 3,000, with further sub-castes, and below these are millions of outcastes who perform the most menial tasks. Caste distinctions are rigid in theory, and Brahmins in particular are offended by any contact with low castes; eating between castes is prohibited. Many occupational and guild distinctions remain but modern conditions, liberal laws and closer communications, are breaking down exclusiveness. Communal quarrels arise between castes and religions, particularly in anything that touches the sacredness of the cow.

TEMPLES AND WORSHIP

India is a land of magnificent architectural monuments, most of them religious. The temples have small inner sanctuaries surrounded by large open paved courtyards, tanks for ritual washing, and walls with stone gates and towers. Temple worship is performed by priests without much lay assistance, but people visit the courtyards for quiet prayer and meditation.

Modern temples are less impressive but there are countless little shrines by the wayside or in the middle of streets, at which people stop to place gifts and pray. Hindu homes have rooms or corners for images and devotion, where flowers are placed and incense burns. Worship is performed at home and there is no sabbath or regular obligation to visit temples, though for festivals and annual events great crowds assemble there, when images are carried in procession in chariots or on elephants.

There are countless holy places, from the Himalayas in the north to the extreme southern capes, and pilgrimages are made to seven chief sites. The holiest place of all is Benares (Varanasi) on the middle Ganges, where steps (*ghats*) lead down from temples into the sacred river in which people wash and pray. "Burning ghats" are reserved for cremation, the normal lot of the Hindu dead. Benares is full of holy men, dressed in yellow robes or smeared with ashes, begging and awaiting death in the sacred city. Great assemblies are held here and at other places every few years, at which millions of people gather to bathe in the river.

There are many Hindu festivals and all deities have sacred days. *Holi* in the spring is an ancient fertility feast when coloured water is squirted on participants and the praises of Krishna and his loves are chanted. *Dashara* or *Dassehra* in the autumn is marked by carnival figures of the hero Rama and his demon enemy Ravana, the latter being packed with crackers which are set alight at the end. *Divali* in November is a feast of lights for the gracious goddess Lakshmi, consort of Vishnu, when lamps welcome the patroness of wealth, business and learning. In other popular feasts the god of fortune, Ganesha, son of Shiva, is carried in the form of images of pink elephants, or Shiva the lord both of Yoga and the dance is depicted as the dancing god within a flaming circle, often represented in bronze images.

ORGANIZATION AND DISTRIBUTION

There is little widespread organization in Hindu religion. The followers of Shiva, Vishnu and the Mother are joined in their own cult sympathy, and sometimes divided between cults in antagonism. There are centres of learning and worship, but many local differences of practice. Monasteries and retreat houses (*ashrams*) cater for cults and societies, but no large-scale monastic organization compares with those of Buddhism and Christianity. Many Hindu holy men are solitaries and may be seen sitting alone or living in secluded places with a few disciples.

In modern times the Brahmo and Arya Samaj have organized themselves, and also significant is the Ramakrishna Mission. Taking its name from a nineteenth-century holy man of Bengal, Shri Ramakrishna, and directed by his disciple Swami Vivekananda, the Mission initiated religious, educational and social works and undertakes much literary propaganda. From its centre in Calcutta the Ramakrishna Mission has established branches throughout India and in Europe and America, and by using English as well as Indian languages it is one of the most effective propagandists of Vedantic pantheism. From Pondicherry, south of Madras, the Aurobindo Ashram also engages in meditation, education, industrial work, and literary propaganda, and there are many smaller similar agencies.

Hinduism is virtually confined to the peoples of the Indian sub-continent, though it is practised also in Bali and by peoples of Indian origin in Sri Lanka. It has commonly been said that a Hindu is one born into a caste and who accepts the Vedic scriptures, and therefore it is an ethnic and not a missionary religion. But in past centuries Hinduism spread as far away as Bali and Cambodia, and today some of its missionaries choose Europe and America as their fields.

Other Indian Religions

PARSIS

An ancient religion which in origins was akin to that of the Aryan Indians was practised by related peoples in Iran, but it survives today mainly in small communities in India. The Parsis (Persians) migrated to India from the ninth century onwards under pressure from Muslim invaders and settled chiefly in the region of Bombay, though there are groups elsewhere in India and East Africa, numbering in all about 120,000. The prophetic reformer of the religion was Zoroaster (Zarathushtra), generally dated 630–553 B.C. He taught faith in one God, *Ahura Mazda* ("Lord Wisdom"), who was goodness opposed to the spirit of evil, *Ahriman*. In hymns, *Gathas*, attributed to him, Zoroaster told of visions of the heavenly court to which he was summoned and received the doctrines and duties which would reform his country's religion. He was not successful at first but after some ten years he did better in Bactria to the east of Persia, and after years of preaching Zoroaster was killed in a struggle with opposing priests. His religion slowly developed, led by priests called *Magi*, and in the early Christian centuries it became the state religion of Iran until the Muslim invasion.

Belief and Practice

The basic Parsi scriptures are the *Avesta*, which include hymns and ritual and practical regulations and are still recited in ancient Persian. Belief in the opposition of the good and evil spirits has caused this religion to be called dualistic, but Parsis claim that the dualism is temporary since at the end Ahura Mazda will triumph. There is a strong moral emphasis and its followers call it the Religion of the Good Life; by virtuous conduct and moderation men help God to overcome evil. Ahura Mazda is the supreme God but there are other angelic and demonic spirits; especially important is Mithra or Meher, a god of the old Iranian religion who now becomes the judge of death. Belief in life after death is strong in Zoroastrianism and probably influenced Judaism and Christianity with its ideas of angels and demons, the end of the world, judgement and eternal life. It is believed that departed souls have their deeds weighed in scales and then cross a narrow bridge to paradise; the evil fall into a purgatory but eventually all are saved.

Parsi temples contain no images but sacred fire always burns there, fed by sandalwood, and so they are called "fire temples" by other Indians. The dead are disposed of in "towers of silence" where vultures destroy the flesh, which must not defile the earth or fire. Some of these towers are outside Bombay, though closed to the public, but elsewhere Parsi dead are buried in lead coffins. There have been reforms in modern times and religious instruction is given in new expositions of the faith. Parsi priests wear white robes and old Parsis have traditional dress with hard hats and robes, but many Parsis wear modern European or Indian dress. As a small ingrown community the Parsis are highly educated and in trade and public service they play a role out of all proportion to their size. Women are emancipated, enter temples equally with men, and take part in educational and public affairs.

JAINS

The Jains are an Indian religious community numbering 2.6 million at the 1971 census. It is possible that the religion existed in India before the arrival of the Aryan invaders about 1,500 B.C., since its beliefs in reincarnation and types of asceticism seem to have been non-Aryan. The Jains say that their religion is eternal and is renewed in successive ages by *Jinas* ("conquerors"), of whom there have been twenty-four at long intervals in the present world eon. The last Jina was given the title of Mahavira ("great man") and lived in the sixth century B.C., a little before Gautama Buddha whose life was similar in some ways. After the death of his parents Mahavira left his wife and family (though one sect says he was celibate) and went about naked begging alms and seeking enlightenment. He achieved this after thirteen years and became a Jina and omniscient. He is said to have had great success, with a community of 50,000 monks and nuns and many lay followers. Mahavira died in the lower Ganges valley, entering *Nirvana*, the "blowing out" of desire and life.

Belief and Practice

Jains do not believe in a creator God, since the world is eternal, and they have been called atheistic. But the twenty-four Jinas are objects of worship and some Hindu gods also figure in their temple imagery. Jains believe in the eternity of countless souls, which are immersed in matter and evil, but by renunciation of desire they can rise to Nirvana at the ceiling of the universe. Monks are the nearest to salvation and sectarian differences divide the "white-clad" monks in robes from the "sky-clad" who are naked. The best known Jain doctrine is "non-violence" or harmlessness. All life is sacred, and this belief involves vegetarianism and abstention from taking any life by hunting, farming or fishing. Monks sweep the ground in their path to avoid treading on insects, filter their drink, and wear cloths before their mouths to keep out insects. In modern times Jain stress on non-violence has inspired reformers, like the Hindu Gandhi.

Despite ascetic practices and absence of deity, the Jains have built some of the most splendid temples in India through the patronage of rich followers. The main anniversary is at the end of August when wrongs are confessed, fasting practised, and the birthday of Mahavira is celebrated. The Hindu feast of Divali is also popular and the goddess Lakshmi is invoked for success. Being excluded from many occupations that involve taking or endangering life, the Jains have prospered in commerce and are influential in public affairs. Some modern Jains try to adapt asceticism to current conditions, but monks continue on the hard way to Nirvana.

SIKHS

The Sikhs are one of the largest Indian religious minorities with 10.3 million followers at the 1971 census, the men easily recognizable by turbans and beards. The Sikh religion is relatively modern and developed from Hindu devotional movements with some influence from Islam.

Mediaeval Hindu poets sang the praises of Krishna and Rama, the Avatars of Vishnu, and in the fifteenth century Kabir concentrated on Rama as the sole deity. Kabir was a Muslim weaver of Benares but trained by a Hindu teacher, and he taught that there is one God behind the many names of Allah, Rama and Krishna. Kabir composed and sang poems denouncing priests and scriptures and he suffered persecution, though at his death both Hindus and Muslims claimed him for their own and rival shrines commemorate him. The followers of the path of Kabir, *Kabir-panthis*, number about a million, chiefly in north-central India.

A little later in the Punjab lived Nanak (1469–1538) who founded the Sikhs. He was a Hindu who also sought the unity of God and had a vision in which he was told to teach faith in God as the True Name. He travelled widely but was most successful in the Punjab where groups of *Sikhs* ("disciples") followed him. Nanak was the great *Guru* ("teacher") and though he was followed by nine other Gurus they were regarded as essentially identical with Guru Nanak. The Sikhs suffered persecution from the Muslims and the tenth Guru, Govind Singh, founded an inner militant society, Khalsa, with initiation by a sword and adding the name Singh ("lion") to all initiates. Members of the Khalsa have five marks: beard and hair uncut (hence the turban), wearing shorts, steel comb in hair, steel bangle on the right wrist, and steel dagger at the side. With this militant force the Sikhs won independence in the Punjab till British rule came. But at the partition of India in 1947 the line between India and Pakistan ran right through the Punjab and the Sikhs rose to assert their independence. They were expelled from Pakistan and had to accept a place in the Indian state, though constant moves have been made towards fuller autonomy, with leaders fasting to gain their end.

Belief and Practice

Sikhs believe in one God, with Guru Nanak his perfect teacher, and their temples have no images. Their scriptures, the *Adi Granth* ("first book"), contain poems by Kabir and Hindu and Muslim composers, as well as by Guru Nanak and other Gurus. It is an anthology of lofty religious verse which is chanted daily, in the Punjabi language, by Sikhs in public and private devotion.

Sikh temples are usually white buildings with golden domes, and alongside is a tank or small lake for ritual washing. The Adi Granth scriptures are carried into the temple at dawn and chanted by relays of readers till night, when the book is returned to a treasury. The principal shrine is the Golden Temple at Amritsar, the most sacred Sikh town and centre of administration. Beside the temple are free hostels and kitchens for the community and for visitors of any race or religion. Sikhs are found in many Indian cities, as well as in Africa and Europe, but their strength remains in the Punjab.

Buddhism

Buddhism arose in India though it has almost disappeared there, and its great successes as a missionary religion have been in South-East and East Asia, to which it took Indian thought and culture.

HISTORY

The founder was named Siddhartha but is more generally known by the family name of Gautama (the Sanskrit form; Gotama in Pali), or from his clan Shakyamuni, "the sage of the Shakyas". The dates commonly accepted for Gautama by Western scholars are 563–483 B.C., though Chinese Buddhists put them hundreds of years earlier. Primary evidence is scanty and begins with inscriptions made by the emperor Asoka from about 260 B.C.

Gautama was born in Kapilavastu in north-central India, near Nepal, of a local king and into the warrior caste rather than the priestly Brahmin. From many legends it is clear that his parents were married, the birth was not virginal, and the boy grew up in relative seclusion but was married and had a son. Riding outside the palace at the age of twenty-nine Gautama saw four signs: an old man, a sick man, a corpse and an ascetic. These showed him the suffering of the world, and the calm of leaving it, and led to his great renunciation. He left his wife and child by night, and for years tried various teachers and ways towards enlightenment but without success. Finally, near Gaya on a tributary of the Ganges, Gautama sat under a tree called the Bo or Bodhi-tree, the "tree of enlightenment", and waited for light to come. After a day and a night knowledge came; he understood the rising and passing away of beings, the cause of suffering, the end of rebirth and the way to Nirvana. Now he was a Buddha, an "enlightened one", and went to preach his doctrine in a park to the north of the holy city of Benares.

The Buddha was followed at first by small groups of monks and laymen but soon became successful, especially in middle India where the town of Rajagriha (modern Rajgir) was a centre for the religion. For some 40 years the Buddha went about teaching, retiring to monastic buildings during the rains. The monastic Order (*Sangha*) was the centre of activity, and after some hesitation orders of nuns were formed as well. Finally, the Buddha died after eating tainted pork and was cremated, tradition saying that his relics were divided between eight regions.

At the Buddha's death 500 monks met in a cave and the chief disciple, Ananda, recited the *Vinaya*, the monkish rules that form the first part of the Buddhist scriptures. The Buddha himself and his followers came into conflict with Brahmin priests, Jains, Yoga teachers and others, and taught that the way of the Buddha was best. They rejected the Hindu scriptures and were regarded as heretics. There was also some caste rivalry and possibly Buddhism inherited both some of the communal differences and the religious beliefs of the ancient Indus Valley cultures.

A great impulse to the spread of Buddhism was given by Asoka in the third century B.C., who turned from martial conquests to the peaceful way of Buddhism, inscribing decrees ordering faith and morality, restoring Buddhist sacred sites, and sending missionaries to Ceylon and elsewhere. Buddhism became the dominant religion of South-East Asia, despite some remains of ancient animism. In the first Christian century Buddhist monks took scriptures, images and relics to China, and in the sixth century to Japan, in both countries mingling with local religions which retained much of their appeal. In the land of its origin Buddhism flourished for over a thousand years, but finally almost died out in India under pressure from reviving Hindu devotional cults and destruction of temples and monasteries by invading Muslims. Recently there has been some Buddhist success among the Indian outcastes.

BELIEFS

The Buddha taught *Dharma* (or *Dhamma*) which is law, virtue, right, religion or truth, and this is expounded as the Middle Way between the extremes of sensuality and asceticism. At his enlightenment Gautama saw the solution of the suffering that had troubled him and enunciated it in the Four Noble Truths. These are: the universal fact of suffering, the cause of suffering which is craving or desire, the cessation of suffering by ending craving, and the method of cessation by the Noble Eightfold Path. This Path is a way of discipline in eight steps, each of which is called Right. They fall into three groups, the first beginning the path in Right View and Resolve. Then come practical activity in Right Speech, Action and Livelihood. Finally, there are higher spiritual states: Right Effort, Concentration and Contemplation.

This is a scheme of moral and spiritual improvement without reference to the Hindu gods. Some of them appear in Buddhist legend but always subservient to the Buddha. The Hindu teaching of the impersonal divine Brahman seems to have been unknown to the Buddha and his system has been called atheistic or agnostic. But in fact the Buddha himself is the supreme and omniscient teacher and object of adoration. A Buddhist does not save himself, but he relies on the teaching of experts and the celestial Buddha.

The Buddha also criticized the Hindu doctrine of the soul, which he declared could not be identified with any of the bodily elements. At death the five constituents of the body dissolved and were not passed on to another life. Yet Buddhism held firmly to the Indian belief in rebirth, and the cycle of existence was caused by desire from which one could escape only by following the path of the Buddha. The link between one life and another was *Karma*, the entail of deeds which determined a higher or lower destiny in the next life. To get free from this round of existence was the supreme goal, the indescribable *Nirvana* (*Nibbana*), blowing out desire and life.

Northern Buddhism

These are the basic beliefs of southern Buddhists, but in the north further doctrines developed in which multitudes of celestial beings offered gracious help to mankind. Southern Buddhists believe that there have been several Buddhas in the past and there will be some in the future, the next one, Maitreya, being a fat jolly figure bringing fortune. But in the present long world eon there is only one Buddha, the supreme Gautama. In northern Buddhism not only are thousands of Buddhas accepted now but there are countless *Bodhisattvas* ("beings of enlightenment"), who have deferred their own salvation until all beings are saved. This led to a universalism and a religion of faith and grace which was able to absorb many Chinese and other deities in the guise of Bodhisattvas. The Chinese Kwanyin (Japanese Kwannon) is the "lady of compassion", not a goddess but a Bodhisattva, a kindly giver of children and a saviour who immediately hears the cries of all suppliants. In Tibet the Dalai Lama is the incarnation of this Bodhisattva, not of Gautama.

More abstruse philosophical doctrines were also taught in northern Buddhism: the three bodies of the Buddha, and an idealistic doctrine of the Void in which Buddhas and believers are merged in a neutral monism somewhat like the Hindu Brahman. There were links with Chinese Taoism in this pantheism, and later Zen Buddhism emerged from the fusion of ideas. On the popular level Pure Land Buddhism offered the hope of a Western paradise where another Buddha, Amida, called men to himself.

SCHOOLS AND ORGANIZATION

The southern Buddhists call themselves *Theravada*, followers of the "tradition of the elders". They are found in Sri Lanka, Burma, Thailand, Laos and Cambodia, where their graceful buildings, dagobas, pagodas or wats, decorate towns and countryside. Here relics are enshrined, innumerable Buddha images sit in various postures, and worshippers go to meditate. Traditional education was in the monasteries which are still strong. Yellow-robed monks go on begging-rounds every morning, and scholars study the scriptures, the *Tripitaka* ("three baskets"). There are minor sects but general uniformity of belief and practice.

The northern Buddhists are *Mahayana*, followers of the "great Vehicle" to salvation, as against the others whom they call *Hinayana*, of the "small Vehicle". In Tibet Mahayana Buddhism has traditionally been the state religion, incorporating some beliefs of a primitive Bon religion whose gods are taken as guardians of Buddhism. There are two chief schools of monks, the Yellow Hats being reformed and dominant, and the Red Hats of an earlier tradition. The chief monks are Lamas, of whom the chief is the Dalai Lama who lived in the Potala palace in Lhasa. In 1959 he fled from the Chinese to India and lives there in exile. Despite oppression, Buddhism remains the religion of the Tibetan people.

Buddhism in China and Japan

Buddhism was at first opposed in China, since it withdrew young men from active life into monasteries and its teaching seemed to be contrary to the popular cults of the ancestors. But despite some fierce persecutions Buddhism became part of Chinese life and exercised a great influence not only on religion but on culture and the arts. Confucian scholars criticized the use of relics but popular devotion cherished them, and Buddhist monks became particularly active in reciting texts at funerals and memorial services. Chinese Buddhism evolved the popular *Pure Land* sects, the meditative *Ch'an*, and the scholarly and tolerant *Tien-Tai*. Under Communism Buddhist activity has been severely restricted and many monasteries have been closed or converted into schools and barracks. But there has also been extensive restoration of Buddhist centres in the interests of antiquarian study and the preservation of monuments of national culture, in famous cave-temples and grottoes in Shansi, Honan and Sinkiang. A strictly controlled Chinese Buddhist Association was founded in 1953, and with the suppression of the monastic order the future of Buddhism in China depends upon the ability of its lay followers to adapt themselves to modern conditions.

In Japan Buddhism appealed to both leaders and people. In the sixth century A.D. it came first from Korea and then from China, and brought with it writing and Chinese culture. Buddhism soon gained a firm footing in Japan under the regent Prince Shotoku, who was regarded as an incarnation of the Bodhisattva Kwannon. Buddhism came to terms with the ancient Japanese Shinto religion by declaring that the Shinto gods were manifestations of Buddha originals. When the colossal bronze Buddha at Nara was begun the emperor received the blessing of the chief Shinto deity. A synthesis called Dual (*Ryobu*) Shinto was formed in which Buddhists controlled all but the most important Shinto shrines. This lasted over a thousand years, till the Shinto revival in 1868 when Ryobu Shinto was abolished. Buddhism came under attack for a time, but it had entered too deeply into Japanese life and its contribution to thought and the arts could not be hidden.

Japanese Buddhism adopted Chinese schools: Pure Land as *Jodo*, and Tien-Tai as *Tendai*. The school of Nichiren opposed the emotional cults by claiming to return to the original teaching of the Buddha, but he was still the glorified Shakyamuni sitting on a Vulture Peak in the Himalayas. Chinese Ch'an became known to a wider world through Japanese *Zen* (both based on an Indian word for "meditation"). It stressed the search for enlightenment in daily work and so encouraged many arts. It also became popular with the military, the Samurai warriors, in Zen teaching of judo, archery and swordsmanship. Zen teachers are critical of some traditional texts, but they use basic ones in meditation techniques and they have monasteries where Zen is taught. Zen monks are the only ones in Japan who continue the daily begging round.

Japanese Buddhism has developed congregational worship more than other parts of the Buddhist world, and there are great temples with lavish ritual services. There are modern sectarian movements which show the influence of Shinto naturalism and sometimes of Christianity. From Japan Buddhist missions have gone to the Pacific islands, especially Hawaii, and the western parts of the U.S.A.

Organization

The different Buddhist schools have loose organization. Traditionally monasteries have been the centres of doctrine and discipline, and their chief abbots are the religious authorities; in centralized systems such as Tibet the Dalai Lama and the Panchen Lama disputed the supremacy. Monks and nuns are, of course, celibate, but where there are large numbers of priests, as in Japan, they are usually married. Since the days of Asoka, laymen have been encouraged to attend the monasteries at weekly or fortnightly special days, and many go there also for meditation during the rainy season.

Other East Asian Religions

CONFUCIANISM

It has been debated whether Confucianism was a religion, but what has been known in the West under this title was a compound of ancient Chinese popular cults, ancestral worship, state ritual and moral precepts. Alongside and often mingling with this Confucianism were also indigenous Taoism and imported Buddhism, which together have been called the Three Religions or rather Three Ways of China, since none of them was an exclusive system.

K'ung-fu-tse or Master K'ung, latinized as Confucius, lived in the state of Lu in north China, 551–478 B.C. Of humble rank and largely self-educated he became a teacher asking questions and giving maxims, like a Chinese Socrates, rather than a systematic philosopher. Some of his pupils came to occupy high office, but although in later life Confucius toured the country looking for a state which would put his ideas into practice, he was unsuccessful. It is said, on dubious grounds, that he then compiled the Chinese Classics: the *Book of History*, the *Book of Odes* and the *Book of Changes*, and also the *Annals of Lu*. Confucius was not a founder of a religion, though he criticized some forms of ritual. His thoughts are found in a small book called *Analects* (*Lun Yu*) and they emphasize the importance of propriety (*li*) in personal and social conduct. Filial piety and correct observance of ancestral cults are commended, and the duties of rulers to subjects as well as servants to masters. His personal religious attitude appears in the sense of Heaven (*T'ien*) inspiring him, judging his acts and hearing prayer.

About a hundred years later his most famous follower, Mencius, praised Confucius as the greatest of all sages and he was more successful in advising rulers to follow just and peaceful ways. The cult of Confucius grew slowly: by the second century B.C. Chinese emperors adapted his teachings to their purposes, and in A.D. 59 sacrifice was ordered to Confucius in every school. He was called "the Teacher of ten thousand generations", but he was not deified and Confucian halls were different from the temples of other religions, with memorial tablets instead of images. The scholars (mandarins) were concerned with the preservation of the teachings of Confucius and until this century examinations for public service were in the Confucian classics.

The popular religion of China was a worship of nature and hero gods, similar to those of India or ancient Greece. In the villages the gods of earth were the most important for work, and the god of the hearth dominated homes. "Wall and moat" gods protected towns, and storm and disease spirits were propitiated at need. The local cults were idealized in great state functions when the emperor sacrificed to heaven on the marble terraces of the Temple of Heaven in Peking, or paid homage to the agricultural gods at a great altar of Land and Grain. The emperor ploughed the first furrow in spring and cut the first corn in summer, as a model for the country.

Cults of the ancestors were highly developed in China, though it has been claimed that they were filial piety and not religious worship. Great expense was made at funerals and incense burnt daily before the tablets of the recently dead. Later the tablets were removed to ancestral halls, with the tablet of the family founder on the highest shelf. At the winter solstice sacrifices were offered and food eaten communally, while in the Festival of Hungry Souls lighted paper boats are sent sailing down rivers to help the dead in their journey to the afterworld.

In modern times many of the old temples and images of village and town gods have been destroyed, but ancestral ceremonies are still widely observed. Confucius has been attacked as a feudalist but also honoured as the greatest national teacher. In 1961 his tomb was redecorated but Red Guards ransacked it in 1967. Yet Confucianism has not been classified as a religion and remains as an invisible force in which some of the old attitudes continue in new guise.

TAOISM

Taoism is China's indigenous nature and personal religion and inspires much of its culture and philosophy. The word Tao (pronounced *dow*) is a path or way, regarded as the true principle of life and the universe. There is a Tao of heaven, a Tao of earth and a Tao of man which is harmony with these. In Confucian writings Tao is moral and practical, but in Taoism it is mystical and universal.

Lao Tse is a legendary figure who is said to have lived just before Confucius and rebuked him, but this reflects later controversy. Lao Tse is said to have written the *Tao Te Ching*, the classic of "the Way and its Power", in 81 chapters. This is a charming and profound work, perhaps written in the third century B.C. by an anonymous quietist. Tao is here called indefinable and eternal, it cannot be grasped, but by quietness its influence extends over the 10,000 material things. This is a nature mysticism, in which a favourite symbol is water which passively overcomes everything. Formal morality is opposed by "actionless activity", and militarism is strongly repudiated.

Two centuries later this quietism was taken further by Chuang Tse who taught that men should live according to nature, and practise a kind of Yoga or "sitting in forgetfulness". The *Yang* and *Yin*, positive and negative principles of nature, are seen in heaven and earth, light and dark, male and female, and are symbolized in the circle with two pear-shaped halves that appears in much oriental decoration. Taoists began the search for supernatural powers which would come by living naturally, controlling breathing, eating uncooked food and walking through fire. Anchorites lived in the country drinking dew, and expeditions set out for the Isles of the Blest whose inhabitants were supposed to be immortal. The unfortunate associations with magic led Taoism into superstition, and the close link of its priests with the people brought many temples of earth and city gods under their care.

When Buddhism arrived in China it was both opposed and imitated by the indigenous religions. Taoist temples and images multiplied, and rituals for helping the living and the dead developed from Buddhist examples. Lao Tse received the title of "Emperor of Mysterious Origin" and other gods were added to form a pantheon which had huge and often frightening images, while heavens and hells dazzled the pious. More philosophical was the mingling of Taoism and Buddhism in the Ch'an (Zen) sect which sought enlightenment by the way of nature. In the arts Taoism had great influence by applying the principle of "seeing without looking" to painting and writing.

Nowadays attack on superstitions has led to the outward decline of Taoism, except in Hong Kong, Taiwan and Malaysia. In China the association of Taoism with secret societies made it the potent force in revolts like the Boxer Rising in 1900, and the Pervading-Unity Tao society which was crushed only in the 1950s. A governmental Chinese Taoist Association was established in 1957, later than societies controlling other religions. But the spirit of Taoism remains as a pervading influence in Chinese life, appealing to the traditional love of nature, reflecting scepticism towards doctrinaire programmes and military excesses, and cultivating physical and spiritual health.

SHINTO

When Buddhist monks arrived in Japan in the sixth century A.D. they called the religion of the country *Shen-Tao*, the "Way of the Gods", contrasted with the Way of the Buddha. There was no writing, and the monks wrote down the Chronicles of Japan (*Nihongi*) which give Shinto mythology and traditional stories of the country.

It is said that in the beginning heaven and earth were not yet separated into *Yo* and *In*, like the Chinese Yang and Yin. Then appeared the chief deity, the sun goddess Amaterasu. Her brother the storm god, Susanowo, made Amaterasu hide in the cave of heaven till she was induced to emerge by other deities, a myth explaining light and dark, summer and winter, and eclipses. Later Amaterasu sent her grandson

Ninigi to rule the earth and marry the goddess of Mount Fuji, and they were the ancestors of the first emperor of Japan, Jimmu Tenno. Thus, the royal family claimed descent from the supreme deity, while other notables took various gods as their ancestors.

There are countless Shinto deities, associated with mountains and earth, rain and wind, sea and harbours, food and fertility. One of the most popular is Inari the rice god who is represented by the fox and has many images in this form. Japanese love of nature appears in pilgrimages which are made to sacred mountains, and in the location of their temples. Traditionally Shinto temples were small wooden buildings, based on ancient patterns which are constantly renewed, situated in large parks with fountains and decorative rocks, but many smaller shrines are by the wayside or in towns.

When Buddhism came Dual Shinto was formed and many temples came under Buddhist control, being embellished with images and ritual. After the first contact with Europeans Japan was closed to the West from the seventeenth century to 1868 and the country was ruled by feudal dictators (Shoguns). But Shinto revival gathered strength and was associated with the emperor as the descendant of Amaterasu. In 1868 the emperor Meiji was restored to effective power and State Shinto was established. Adoration of the emperor grew and reverence to the imperial portrait was imposed in all public life and in schools, even those of Buddhists and Christians. For a time it was said that Shinto was a world religion, since the emperor was child of the sun. This emperor-centred Shinto was not traditional though it inspired fanatical patriotism, and in 1946 the emperor repudiated "the fictitious idea that the emperor is manifest god".

The State Shinto shrines were disestablished in 1947 and had to rely on public support. But some great national shrines, like that of Amaterasu at Ise, have remained important and are attended on occasions of national significance. The ordinary Shinto shrines are directed by bodies of priests who perform the rituals, and lay people attend to offer prayers and recite texts. The quietness and beauty of the surroundings add to their attraction, but some of the smaller shrines are deserted. In Japanese homes there are shelves for Shinto or Buddhist symbols, at which incense, leaves and water are regularly offered.

Sect Shinto

After the establishment of State Shinto it was seen that distinction would have to be made for popular modern movements which were called Sect Shinto. Some of the new sects are Buddhist, and others centre round mountain pilgrimages, but the most notable are communities in which healing by faith is important. They are like societies or churches, with known founders, and relatively monotheistic. "The Teaching of Golden Light" (*Konko-kyo*) was founded in the last century by Kawade Bunjiro who said that the god of golden metal possessed him and was the sole deity. Though a Shinto priest Bunjiro denounced narrow patriotism and taught the need for sincere rather than ritual prayer. About the same time a woman, Miki Nakayama, founded "the Teaching of Heavenly Wisdom" (*Tenri-kyo*). She practised healing by faith and encouraged her followers to work communally at building temples, schools and houses. A new city of Tenri has been built round a sanctuary where it is believed that a new age will soon begin. This is the richest and largest religious organization, with more than 2 million followers and thousands of missionary teachers.

In 1930 the "Creative-Value Study Society" (*Sokagakkai*) arose from the militant Nichiren sect of Japanese Buddhism. Suppressed during the war it has strong support among the working classes and is militantly political, with a political party (*Komeito*) which has members in the Japanese Diet.

Christianity in Asia and the Pacific

Christianity began as an Asian religion, and although its chief expansion was to the West yet it has remained in minorities in the Near East and has spread in missions to most Asian countries. The Syrian Orthodox Church in India claims to have been founded by the Apostle Thomas and there is evidence of its existence at least from the fifth century. The rites and traditions are derived from the Jacobite Church of Syria, which separated from other Orthodox churches after the Council of Chalcedon in 451. These Indian churches are divided into Orthodox Syrian and Mar Thoma Syrian, and a further section has been in communion with Rome since the seventeenth century as one of its Uniate churches. These Syrian Christians are found almost exclusively in Malabar, Travancore and Cochin, and number over a million. Other Christian communities all over India are the result of modern Western missions and have 12 million adherents, of whom more than half are Roman Catholics. In Pakistan there are a million Christians.

Burma and Sri Lanka have each about a million Christians, the latter being largely Roman Catholic and strong among the mixed Ceylonese peoples. In Indonesia there are over 6 million Christians, mostly Protestant, and about 2 million each in Viet-Nam and Korea. Japan has a profusion of Christian sects, with over a million members. Christianity has had a long and chequered history in China. Nestorian missionaries were active there from the seventh century to the ninth, Jesuits and others from the sixteenth, and there were many missions in modern times. The last censuses gave over 3 million Chinese Christians, but all foreign missionaries have been expelled, most churches closed, and 1967 was said to be the first year this century when no Easter services were held in public in China.

The Philippines is the one Christian nation in Asia, with 30 million Roman Catholics and 4 million Protestants. The first missionaries arrived in the sixteenth century and mass movements led to the formal Christianization of the whole population within a century, with the non-Christian culture largely replaced by that of the Spanish missionaries.

In Oceania both missions to indigenous populations and the influx of many Europeans, especially in Australia and New Zealand, led to the dominance of Christianity. Most of the Maoris, Fijians, Samoans and Tongans were converted from the nineteenth century onwards, but there are smaller numbers of Christians in New Guinea and Papua. For Oceania, including Australia and New Zealand, the latest estimates give nearly 10 million Protestants and 4 million Roman Catholics.

BIBLIOGRAPHY

GENERAL

NOSS, J. B. Man's Religions (New York, 4th edn., 1968).

PARRINDER, E. G. (Editor). Man and his Gods (London, 1971).

RINGGREN, H., and STRÖM, A. V. Religions of Mankind (Stockholm and Edinburgh, 1964, 1967).

ISLAM

ARBERRY, A. J. The Koran Interpreted (Oxford, 1965).

FISHER, H. J. Ahmadiyya (Oxford, 1963).

GABRIELI, F. Muhammad and the Conquests of Islam (London, 1968).

GUILLAUME, A. Islam (Harmondsworth and Baltimore, 1954).

HAMIDULLAH, M. Le Prophète de l'Islam (Paris, 1959).

LEWIS, B. The Arabs in History (London and New York, 1950).

SMITH, M. The Way of the Mystics (London, 1956).

SMITH, W. C. Islam in Modern History (Princeton, London, 1957).

WATT, W. M. Muhammad, Prophet and Statesman (Oxford and New York, 1961).

HINDUISM

BASHAM, A. L. The Wonder that was India (London, 1954).

DE BARY, W. T. (ed.). Sources of Indian Tradition (New York and London, 1958).

HUTTON, J. H. Caste in India (Bombay, 3rd edn., 1961).

RADHAKRISHNAN, S. The Hindu View of Life (London and New York).

SEN, K. M. Hinduism (Harmondsworth and Baltimore).

THOMAS, P. Hindu Religion, Customs and Manners (Bombay, 3rd edn., 1956).

WOOD, E. YOGA (Harmondsworth and Baltimore, 1959).

ZAEHNER, R. C. Hinduism (Oxford and New York, 1962).
Hindu Scriptures (London and New York, 1965).

PARSIS

DUCHESNE-GUILLEMIN, J. Zoroastre (Paris, 1948).
The Hymns of Zarathustra (London, 1952).

MASANI, R. P. The Religion of the Good Life (London and New York, 2nd edn., 1954).

ZAEHNER, R. C. The Teachings of the Magi (London and New York, 1975).

JAINS

GUÉRINOT, A. La Religion Djaïna (Paris, 1926).

JAINI, J. Outlines of Jainism (Cambridge, 1940).

SCHUBRING, W. The Doctrine of the Jains (Banaras, 1962).

SIKHS

ARCHER, J. C. The Sikhs (Princeton, 1946).

MCLEOD, W. H. Gurū Nānak and the Sikh Religion (Oxford, 1968).

SINGH, T. (Editor). Selections from the Sacred Writings of the Sikhs (London, 1960).

SINGH. T. Sikhism (Bombay, 2nd edn., 1951).

VAUDEVILLE, C. Kabīr (Oxford, 1974).

BUDDHISM

CONZE, E. Buddhist Thought in India (London, 1962).
Buddhist Scriptures (Harmondsworth and Baltimore, 1959).

ELIOT, C. Hinduism and Buddhism (London, 1921).

HOFFMAN, H. The Religions of Tibet (London and Münich, 1956).

LAMOTTE, E. Histoire du Bouddhisme indien (Louvain, 1958).

MORGAN, K. (Editor). The Path of Buddha (New York, 1956).

PERCHERON, M. Buddha and Buddhism (London, New York and Paris, 1957).

THOMAS, E. J. The Life of Buddha (London, 3rd edn., 1952).
The History of Buddhist Thought (London, 2nd edn., 1953).

CONFUCIANISM AND TAOISM

CHAN, WING-TSIT. Religious Trends in Modern China (New York, 1953).

CREEL, H. G. Confucius, the Man and the Myth (New York and London, 1951).

DE BARRY, W. T. (ed.). Sources of Chinese Tradition (New York and London, 1960).

FUNG YU-LAN. A Short History of Chinese Philosophy (New York, 1958).

HUGHES, E. R. Religion in China (London, 1950).
Chinese Philosophy in Classical Times (London, 1942).

MASPERO, H. Les religions chinoises (Paris, 1950).
Le Taoïsme (Paris, 1950).

WALEY, A. (Translator). The Analects of Confucius (London, 4th edn., 1956).

WALEY, A. Three Ways of Thought in Ancient China (London, 1953).
The Way and its Power (London, 3rd edn., 1949).

WELCH, H. The Parting of the Way (London, 1957).

SHINTO

ANESAKI, M. History of Japanese Religion (London, 1930).

BELLAH, R. N. Tokugawa Religion (Glencoe, Illinois, 1957).

HAMMER, R. Japan's Religious Ferment (London and New York, 1961).

HERBERT, J. Shinto (London, 1967).

TSUNODA, R. (Editor). Sources of Japanese Tradition (New York and London, 1958).

VAN STRAELEN, H. The Religion of Divine Wisdom (Tokyo, 1954).

CHRISTIANITY

BROWN, L. W. The Indian Christians of St. Thomas (Cambridge, 1956).

COXILL, H. W. (Editor). World Christian Handbook (London, 1972).

CROSS, F. L. (Editor). The Oxford Dictionary of the Christian Church (Oxford, 2nd edn., 1958).

NEILL, S. A. History of Christian Missions (Harmondsworth, 1964).

Agrarian Issues in Asia

W. Klatt

Following the distressingly poor record of farm production and food consumption in 1974, 1975 brought an unexpected recovery. Tentative estimates suggest an unusually high average increase of almost 8 per cent in the production of crops throughout the non-communist parts of the Asian continent. A new record was reached in most major food and non-food items. The improvement was more modest in the livestock sector which, in any event, tends to react to favourable crops with a certain time lag.

The position is less certain as far as the communist parts of Asia are concerned. Their performance is of necessity influenced decisively by the record of the People's Republic of China. As it continues to release only a bare minimum of statistical information, the estimates of the Food and Agriculture Organization of the UN for communist countries in Asia and thus for the continent as a whole are at best tentative. Comparison between preliminary totals for 1971–1975 and totals for 1961–1965 is revealing. In the non-communist parts of Asia, both crop and livestock production increased at an average annual rate of between 2.6 and 2.7 per cent, and thus only slightly faster than the population. On the face of it, the communist countries did better, but the possibility of exaggerated estimates cannot be ruled out. Throughout Asia, the record of cereals, which hold a dominant position in both farm output and food consumption, is close to the overall average, and this means that the basic ingredient of the Asian diet continues to be in short supply, even if a good harvest gives a temporary respite. The preference given to cereals has been to some extent at the expense of other crops, and of legumes (pulses) in particular. On the other hand, sugar and vegetable oils have done a good deal better than cereals. These foodstuffs, like meat and dairy products, are of course marked by high elasticities of demand. Whilst they are beyond the means of large numbers of consumers, they are increasingly being sought after by the wealthy sections of urban and rural communities.

Notwithstanding the temporary reprieve of 1975, throughout most parts of Asia the long-term situation remains serious, since the population continues to increase at high rates. This trend annuls most of the progress made in overall agricultural and industrial production, since this has to be shared by rapidly growing numbers of producers and consumers. In this situation, the search for new employment opportunities rivals the need to increase the supply of daily requirements. Agricultural and agrarian matters thus continue to be vital aspects of the Asian scene.

During the first two decades after 1945, industrial development ranked high in the minds of political leaders, social engineers and economic planners. By comparison, agriculture was at a disadvantage, at best taken for granted, at times even thought to be largely expendable as a relic of the past. Yet, in the area reaching from the Khyber Pass to the China Sea the village still provides—as it has always done—work and livelihood for the bulk of the population. Almost everywhere outside Japan, the only fully industrialized country in Asia, the rural population accounts for at least two-thirds of the total, and over half the working population is usually engaged in agriculture. Well over half the average family budget is spent on food, and well over one-third of the gross domestic product is contributed by the agricultural sector. Thus food and farming are among the most important, though often neglected, aspects of life in Asia. This fact has found general recognition only fairly recently, after a series of disappointments which, in the 1950s, set back the seemingly promising process of development. The setbacks led to a re-thinking of the role of agriculture and a reconsideration of priorities. As a result, almost everywhere in Asia a good deal of attention is given nowadays to agrarian issues.

The pursuit of agriculture does not differ, in principle, from other human occupations. Yet agriculture has certain characteristics which are absent from the environment of other occupations. Farming, unlike industry or commerce, has to take account of space and weather as limiting factors. For these, if for no other reasons, agriculture rarely gives as high a return per unit of labour as is the case in industry where work is usually done in a strictly confined space and uninhibited by the hazards of nature. In order to compensate for the disadvantages caused by these constraints, it is sometimes necessary to give assistance to the farming community from public funds so as to keep the gap between urban and rural incomes from widening too sharply. However, the more the agricultural sector is able to expand in step with overall national development, the more it is possible to dispense with support operations of this kind.

Seasonal fluctuations are the cultivator's greatest curse. Indeed, the most significant effect of the weather is that which causes seasonal variations in agricultural output, labour requirement and farm income. In general, industry and commerce have nothing like these seasonal variations to contend with. In consequence, the farm industry is perpetually saddled with under-utilized or over-extended human and material capacities. Surplus and scarcity of labour can thus exist side by side within one and the same rural community. The amount of labour readily available for transfer to other occupations is rarely as large as the uninitiated like to believe. Unplanned internal migration can thus harm the agricultural sector without necessarily aiding the process of industrialization.

The art of farming lies in reducing, if not overcoming altogether, the effects of the impediments created by space and nature. There are, in principle,

Table 1
FARM AND FOOD PRODUCTION IN ASIA, 1971–75
(1961–65 = 100)

	1971	1972	1973	1974	1975	Average 1971–75	Average increase 1961–65 to 1971–75 (% per annum)
Non-Communist Countries							
Food production:							
Total . . .	125	121	132	129	139	128	2.5
Per capita . . .	102	97	103	98	103	101	0.1
Agricultural production:							
Total . . .	125	122	133	129	139	130	2.7
Per capita . . .	102	97	103	98	103	101	0.1
Crop production:							
Total . . .	126	121	132	128	138	129	2.6
Per capita . . .	103	97	103	97	103	101	0.1
Livestock production:							
Total . . .	123	127	132	136	139	131	2.7
Per capita . . .	101	102	103	103	103	102	0.2
Communist Countries							
Food production:							
Total . . .	125	124	130	133	136	130	2.7
Per capita . . .	109	106	109	110	111	109	0.9
Agricultural production:							
Total . . .	126	124	131	134	137	130	2.7
Per capita . . .	110	107	111	111	112	110	1.0
Crop production:							
Total . . .	128	125	133	136	140	132	2.8
Per capita . . .	112	107	112	113	114	112	1.1
Livestock production:							
Total . . .	120	124	127	129	132	126	2.3
Per capita . . .	105	106	107	107	107	106	0.6

Source: FAO, *Monthly Bulletin of Agricultural Economics and Statistics*, Vol. 24, No. 11, November 1975.

no bounds to the possibilites of doing so, though pre-industrial societies are restricted in their choices. Change of crop rotation, multi-cropping with the aid of plants of different genetic characteristics, water control and chemical compounds are some of the technical devices which come to mind. All of them can help in levelling the seasonal fluctuations in the use of labour and material resources. The same is true of certain farm machines, though they have to be applied with discretion if they are not to displace farm labour before alternative employment is found outside the rural sector.

Owing to the constraints caused by distance and space, economies of scale are far less significant within farming than outside it. Unlike, say, industrial manufacturing, agriculture is largely a two-dimensional affair, though with growing intensification the deep layers of the soil are mobilized, as they are in deep mining operations. The handicaps caused by the two-dimensional nature of farming can be partly overcome by the use of chemical fertilizers or by machines which open up the deep layers of the soil. One of the chief advantages of the new techniques applied in the so-called "green revolution" lies in the fact that it is based on biological and chemical techniques rather than the use of products of the engineering industry. It thus has the virtue of providing farm inputs which are divisible and thus neutral to economies of scale. This means that they can be applied on small and large farms with equal benefit. Where, however, governments subsidize the domestic price of farm products and the import price of tractors, harvesters and the like, far from creating additional need for labour, the new technology displaces farm workers.

Another important factor which operates in the countryside needs to be mentioned. In agriculture, unlike industry, the producer, besides being a consumer of his own product, can—in principle—also be a processor of intermediate and finished products,

Table 2

ASIAN AGRICULTURAL INDICATORS, 1970–73

Countries	Population Growth 1965–71 % p.a.	Life Expectancy 1970 years	G.N.P. 1970 $ *per capita*	Man/Land Ratio 1970 per ha.	Agricultural Population 1970 % of total	Agricultural Production 1970 % G.D.P	Food Production 1952–72 % p.a.	Food Consumption 1970 calories a day	Food Consumption 1970 protein grammes a day
South Asia:									
Pakistan . .	2.9	51	130	4.6	70	37	3.0	2,280	59
Bangladesh . .	2.6	48	70	8.2	70	55	1.6	1,860	39
India . .	2.2	41	110	3.4	68	45	2.4	2,060	53
Sri Lanka . .	2.3	65	100	6.3	52	33	3.6	2,240	50
South-East Asia									
Malaysia (West)	2.8	65	400	1.8	56	32	5.2	2,400	52
Thailand . .	3.1	56	210	3.1	76	32	5.3	2,330	52
Indonesia .	2.0	47	80	3.8	68	47	2.0	1,920	43
Philippines .	3.1	51	240	4.5	69	30	3.2	1,920	45
Far East:									
Taiwan . . .	2.6	68	430	10.0	44	19	4.6	2,675	69
China . . .	1.8	50	160*	7.7	66	27	2.3*	2,370*	63*
Japan . . .	1.1	73	2,130	18.5	21	7	4.3	2,470	76
Asian Developing Countries Total (excl. China and Japan) . .	2.6	50	265	4.5	67	40	3.5	2,050	52

* Probably overstated.

Sources: UN Demographic Yearbook 1973; *World Bank Atlas 1973*; FAO, *Monthly Bulletin of Agricultural Economics and Statistics*, Vol. 23, No. 9, September 1974; *Taiwan Statistical Data Book*, Economic Planning Council, Taipei, 1974.

which he, again, may either consume or sell. He is therefore able to select and alter his pattern of production, utilization and marketing to an extent normally not open to the industrial manager and worker, who are usually engaged in producing a more limited range of products and who are rarely at the same time producers, salesmen and consumers of their own output. This range of choice is restricted, however, where the landowner lays down his tenants' pattern of production and utilization. By virtue of the choice left to the producer, agriculture is far less easily controlled by government than is industry. Being, moreover, practised by millions of individuals, farming resists planning to the extent of being unplannable—an understandable reason for the antagonistic attitude of autocratic and centralistic régimes towards the countryside.

As a factor of production, land is in a category all by itself. Unlike other resources, it is practically indestructible, but at the same time it is available only within the limits prescribed by natural conditions. Even in countries which are densely populated, land which can be irrigated is scarce and expensive. Of course, conditions vary enormously. Almost one-quarter of the area of South-East Asia is still farmed in hills and jungles by the "cut and burn" technique of shifting cultivation—a form of rotation of fields instead of crops as practised in areas of settled farming. At the other end of the scale, the rubber and tea plantations of, for instance, Malaya and Sri Lanka, often operating under foreign management and with foreign labour, are so commercialized as to be outside the nexus of farming in its narrow sense. They are not the prime problem areas of Asia; these are found where subsistence farming prevails, i.e. where less than 0.5 of an acre (0.2 hectare) of irrigated land, yielding one crop or less than 250 kilos (550 lbs.) of grain a year, or no more than 2,000 calories a day, is available per head of population. This situation exists over wide areas of Asia.

High birth and low mortality rates aggravate the situation. Unless a steady annual growth rate of 3 per cent can be achieved in agriculture, average *per capita* farm incomes and food supplies remain stagnant. As to employment, in spite of large investment in industry only a small proportion of the natural increase in population is absorbed outside the rural areas. In fact, they harbour more people today than 25 years ago, and in the next two decades the farm population of Asia (outside China) is likely to increase by another 300 million or by 50 per cent. As growing numbers of young people cease to die in infancy and old people live longer, sons have to wait longer before taking over the family homestead. This is one of the factors which contributes to tension in the villages and to unplanned migration to urban areas.

Where land is scarce, it provides its owner with economic wealth, social status and political power. Those who have access to land, labour, capital and know-how frequently combine the functions of landlord, merchant and money-lender. Small cultivators, share croppers and farm labourers are highly dependent on these influential men. In this situation, polarization is a common feature of village society in Asia. The gaps between the well-to-do and the poor widen where policies designed to blunt the edges of conflict are limited to technological and economic projects whilst social and political issues are deferred or shelved.

The role which the farming industry fulfils in developing countries is manifold. Apart from providing a place of work and a source of income for the bulk of the country's working population, it supplies the foodstuffs needed by both rural and urban consumers and also some raw materials and men required in industry. Food and farming serve, moreover, as the chief sources of government revenue, usually collected in the form of indirect taxes or export levies. They thus provide some of the financial resources required for essential capital investment in the public sector. At the same time, the rent paid by tenants, in so far as it does not finance landowners' consumption, finds its way into private investment in industry and commerce. The financial and material requirements of the State tend to increase greatly in the course of modernization. Unless others pay for it in the form of foreign aid, the growth of farm production is a prerequisite of general expansion. If the capital needed for development is extracted from a more or less stagnant agricultural sector, the cost of industrialization and modernization becomes excessively high in human and material terms. A prosperous and expanding farm sector can reduce this cost significantly. There is thus every reason to give farming matters a place of high priority in the planning of development.

This is, in fact, increasingly recognized throughout Asia. The time when unlimited trust was placed in the transforming powers of industrialization has gone. Neither infrastructure nor resource endowment justified such optimism. Nowadays more balanced approaches are being made. In the industrial sphere, for some time past annual rates of growth have ranged from 6.5 to 8.5 per cent in South and South-East Asia. They would have been more effective, had they been accompanied by high rates of farm production, by low rates of population growth, and by equal rates of distribution of benefits between groups of widely different wealth and income. In fact, agricultural output did not grow enough in the last decade to surpass significantly the rate at which the population of Asia increased. When the gaps between the growth rates of industrial and non-industrial output, and between farm production and food requirements had become too glaring to be neglected any longer, efforts were made to improve the performance of agriculture. The response was unexpectedly great and speedy. By now, one-third of the acreage which is planted with wheat on the Indian sub-continent and one-sixth of the area growing paddy (rice) in South and South East Asia benefit from the newly developed high-yielding varieties, largely planted under conditions of regulated irrigation, substantial fertilizer application and improved crop cultivation.

Much has been written about the "miracles" of the so-called "green revolution". Without wishing to denigrate the achievements of some devoted teams of plant breeders and agronomists, the orders of magnitude are such as to indicate a partial success only. Some areas in South-East Asia, such as Thailand, and some parts of the human diet, such as plant protein, have hardly been affected so far. The new technology has not yet been applied to millets, oilseeds and pulses or to commercial crops, such as sugar cane and cotton. More important still, its benefits have accrued largely from ready access to land, labour, capital and know-how. Thus the marginal cultivator and small tenant has hardly been touched and the landless labourer, a restive element in some Asian societies today, has been largely by-passed by the new technology. The process of development followed fairly closely the historically familiar pattern, favouring the haves to the disadvantage of the have-nots, whose position has hardly improved and has thus, by comparison, deteriorated.

No disagreeable consequences would have to be expected from such disparities, were it not for the fact that in the twentieth century—unlike the nineteenth—the citizen who feels neglected considers himself entitled to make his grievances heard publicly. Even if, in the narrow confines of the village community, he hesitates to do so on his own, urban intellectuals are nowadays readily at hand to act on behalf of the underprivileged and to provide political leadership. The social disparities caused by the scarcity of land have by now reached explosive proportions in some parts of Asia. The reasons for discontent in the rural areas are self-evident. In the villages of the Philippines, one-seventh of the farm families, covered by a survey carried out some years ago, earned between them only 3 per cent of all rural incomes. In Pakistan over half the farm population has less than one-tenth of the cultivated area at its disposal. In Bangladesh four-fifths of the landholdings have to make do with two-fifths of the farm area. In India, half the landholders farmed less than one-tenth of the land at the time of the 1970-1971 census.

At the other end of the social scale there is a high degree of concentration of land in the hands of a small number of farmers. If statistics of ownership rather than management existed, the concentration of land in the hands of a few landowners would be even more striking. To make matters worse, smallholders have to share their crops, to an even greater extent than large farmers, with their work, milk and meat animals. Also small holdings frequently serve as the homestead of at least two families. This is clearly revealed by an Indian survey of conditions in farms of different sizes. Last, but not least, tenants invariably have to pay half—or more than half—of their crop at harvest time to the owner of the land. Thus, risks taken by tenants in the interest of farm improvement, double, unless the owner of the land shares in the cost of the input—and this he rarely does. Tenancy thus operates as a disincentive in any programme designed to raise crop yields.

The political parties in power, which are almost always identified with the interests of the landed gentry, are invariably short of remedies in this situation. In case of public disturbances they tend to have recourse to police action rather than political solutions. This reaction may well suffice in an emergency, but it rarely provides a remedy in the long run. On the other hand, the supporters of the concept of "peaceful coexistence" and of co-operation with the "progressive" forces of the national bourgeoisie have little to offer either. Thus it falls largely upon the followers of the concept of "guerrilla warfare", directed from the rural areas against the urban centres of the political establishment, to formulate the demands of the underprivileged groups in the villages and to identify themselves politically with their grievances.

The list of incidents of unrest in rural areas is long indeed. To give only one instance, a report of the Indian Ministry of Home Affairs on the causes and nature of current agrarian tensions, issued in New Delhi in 1970, recorded forcible occupation of land in recent years in almost every State of the Indian Union. The report attributed these disturbances to the widening gap between relatively affluent farmers and the large body of small landholders and landless agricultural labourers in the villages of India. Similar examples could be given from almost every other rural area in Asia.

Leaving aside instances dating back to colonial times, the disturbances which have occurred since the end of the last war in almost every case can be traced to the activities of former anti-Japanese freedom fighters who were originally trained by Allied Commanders in the art of jungle warfare against the Japanese invaders. It speaks for the determination of these men and their followers that a quarter of a century later they still apply their war-time techniques to their struggle against established authority. In their efforts to defeat their enemies in Europe and Asia, Britain, France and the Netherlands had no alternative to accepting left-wing overtures wherever they were made. Yet, with hindsight one may well attribute many of Asia's present troubles to that fateful decision to accept the co-operation with basically antagonistic forces. Had the preparations for granting independence to Asian colonial territories been sufficiently far advanced to permit Allied co-operation with the leaders of the nationalist movements rather than with their communist adversaries, Asia might well be in better shape than it is today.

Since the end of the second world war, armed guerrillas have used what chances they have had in various parts of Asia. The simultaneous outbreak of disturbances in areas as far apart as Andhra (India), Burma, Malaya, Indonesia and Central Luzon (Philippines) in 1948 appears to have been more than a mere coincidence. In fact, there is sufficient evidence to suggest that, following the foundation of the Cominform in the autumn of 1947 and the subsequent Asian Youth Conference in Calcutta early in 1948, agreement in principle was reached on the timing and the character of the various insurrections. The militant actions which followed the Cominform guidelines of national liberation movements directed against the ruling classes of capitalist colonial powers were as inappropriate in South and South-East Asia in the 1940s as communist activities had been in Shanghai and elsewhere in China in the late 1920s. A change in strategy and tactics clearly became necessary. The defeat of the Kuomintang on the mainland of China by Mao Tse-tung presented itself as an alternative to those of Asia's intellectuals who had suspected since the early days of the Comintern that the Soviet pattern might not be applicable in the agrarian communities of Asia.

Even before the Sino-Soviet dispute came into the open, some Asian revolutionary cadres sensed that they were facing the choice between two revolutionary alternatives—an entirely novel and disturbing experience. It happened to coincide with a choice being presented to them between parliamentary co-operation on the domestic front with the "progressive" elements of the Parties in power and fighting them to the finish, by extra-parliamentary means if necessary. To left-wing cadres, operating in the conditions prevailing in Asia's backward agrarian communities, the lessons of the Chinese model appeared increasingly more relevant than earlier revolutions. The classical communist concept about the role of the industrial proletariat in the revolutionary class struggle became less relevant as it emerged that, in spite of fervent attempts at industrialization, the agrarian character of Asian society remained almost unchanged. Since Mao had won the revolution by conquering the cities from the periphery of the countryside, this strategy clearly commended itself also in the case of other, predominantly agrarian communities on the continent of Asia. In consequence, the village poor—to use the appropriate communist idiom—became one of the chief targets of political agitation, indoctrination and organization.

Although the insurrections which have occurred in Asia since the end of the second world war differ sufficiently not to fit a strictly uniform pattern, they tend to have certain features in common. On the whole, the revolutionary groups which instigate and lead the insurrections, operate in country districts inhabited by ethnic, communal or linguistic minorities, frequently located in border areas between States which have different forms of government and state security. Invariably in the areas chosen land is scarce, the incidence of tenure is high and the cultivators are poor. Often a political reservoir in the form of organized labour is close at hand, as in adjacent sugar, tea or rubber plantations.

The strategy applied by the insurgents is generally modelled on that used by Mao at the time when he had to rely exclusively on the co-operation—willing or otherwise—of the Chinese villager. Reform of land tenure, tax relief and distribution of landlords' property without compensation are always given the highest priority in the political propaganda disseminated among the villagers. Occasional reference is made to setting up, in the future, mutual aid teams or producers' co-operatives, but collectives and communes are not mentioned at this stage as the ultimate forms of organization. The revolutionary cadres often live for long periods under primitive conditions among the villagers, who are otherwise hardly visited by any outsiders. Rarely do the revolutionary cadres feel any inhibition about raiding a wealthy village or looting a landlords' farmhouse. Sometimes this is found to happen more than once during or after the main harvest season. Agitation meetings are held among the most dissatisfied sections of the village community. Acts of terror are directed chiefly against local representatives of the central and provincial government authorites. After open clashes weapons of foreign origin are usually found. On the mainland of Asia many of these have been carried, often by members of hill tribes, across national borders. This has been going on since the early 1950s, and any visit to villages in border areas provides new evidence of this kind.

The revolutionary cadres are usually also well-equipped with means of communication which allow them at short notice to advance from, or to retreat into, neighbouring jungles or swamps as the situation may require. So as to cause a maximum of confusion, they frequently change the names of their organizations, operate through front organizations and use the techniques of conspiracy and deception. As the initiative rests with the insurgents most of the time, they usually hold down police and military forces up to ten times their own number. In none of the territories in which they have been active since the end of the second world war have they been routed completely, though they have had to lie low for long periods of time in most of their areas of operation.

In Malaya, a small revolutionary force, which survived the "emergency" of the 1950s by withdrawing into the jungle on the Thai side of the border, continues to run sorties into Malay territory from time to time. Other groups operate in Sarawak and North Kalimantan. In neighbouring Thailand, members of the Thai Peoples' Liberation Armed Forces co-operate with the remnants of the Malayan Peoples' Liberation Army. In the north of the country, members of the hill tribes (Meo and Yao) are the principal recruits of the guerrilla forces. In the north east they work mainly among the ethnic Lao minority. In the central plain, north of Bangkok, where tenant farming is steadily displacing owner-cultivators, the Farmers' Liberation Association, a communist front organization, is operating illegally among tenants and small cultivators. In Burma, both the white flag and the red flag communists, as they are commonly called, have been operating for many years from the jungle, which they only leave for the open country when they have to replenish their meagre stocks. Successive Burmese governments have claimed more than once to have routed the dacoits, as the insurgents are usually called, but time and again these have reappeared in various parts of Northern, Eastern and Central Burma.

In the Philippines, even during the war the insurgents (Huks) directed their guerrilla activities less against the Japanese than against landowners whom they accused of collaborating with the enemy. The owners of landed property have remained their prime target to this day, particularly in the provinces of Papanga and Tarlac (Central Luzon), where they are closely associated with the interests of the sugar industry. The economic and social conditions under which small tenants and workers on the sugar estates live are such as to have given a Maoist group under José M. Sison a new opportunity to gain influence in Central Luzon. Maoists under Commander Dante, a guerrilla leader, have also become an important factor lately among the Huks. The fact that President Marcos felt it necessary in September, 1972, to declare a state of emergency and to promise, against the traditional opposition of the sugar lobby, sweeping reforms of land tenure conditions is a measure of the seriousness of the situation. In Indonesia, where D. N. Aidit saw the task of the Communist Party in essence as creating the preconditions of an agrarian revolution, the abortive *coup* of 1965 precipitated the fall of President Sukarno and the end of operations in the villages by groups of insurgents. Those who survived the upheaval of 1965 have tried to regroup and to devise a new strategy, but so far rural unrest has been kept under control by General Suharto's military regime.

On the Indian sub-continent, strategically the most important part of Asia, the rural situation deserves special attention. In India, Pakistan, Bangladesh and Sri Lanka (Ceylon), well over 100 million cultivators and their families eke out a precarious existence in some 800,000 villages, many of which have not yet been touched by modern ways of life—except the country bus and the transistor radio, both powerful tools in the hands of radicals set on disrupting the unstable balance of an outdated system of social and economic relations.

In India, where for many years the Communist Party followed Moscow's directives most faithfully, the controversy over collaborating with the "progressive" forces of the Congress Party, the open doctrinal conflict between the Soviet Union and China, and China's attacks in the area of the North East Frontier Agency and in the Ladakh region of Kashmir proved too great a strain on the Party's unity. In 1964 the split between the right-wing CPI and a left-wing, Marxist faction, forming the CPI(M), became effective. Soon thereafter a further split was caused when a group on the extreme left of the CPI(M)led an armed insurrection of cultivators in the rural Naxalbari sub-division (Darjeeling District) of West Bengal. The area of disturbances lies near the border of Bangladesh and Nepal and close to the sensitive frontiers of Tibet and Bhutan where the People's Republic of China has political and strategic interests. After the CPI(M) had expelled the "Naxalites" in 1967, the Marxist-Leninist CPI(M-L) emerged in 1969. Since the landslide victory of the Indian Congress Party (R) in the mid-term elections of 1971, in which the electorate rejected left-wing as well as right-wing radicalism, the "Naxalites" have been greatly weakened as a political force. Most of their leaders are in prison and incidents of rural unrest have become less frequent than in the past. In Sri Lanka and Bangladesh, the groups of the Left have also suffered temporary setbacks. In India, Indira Gandhi who, after the elections of 1971, placed agrarian matters at the head of her reform programme, did not gain the political support needed for its implementation. Jayaprakash Narayan became the symbol of the opposition on the Left and on the Right, most prominently in his native Bihar, where social contrasts are particularly stark. In June 1975 Indira Gandhi's Government proclaimed a national emergency under the Maintenance of Internal Security Act of 1971 and ordered the arrest of many members of the opposition. Once again, agrarian measures, such as the alleviation of small cultivators' debts, the guarantee of minimum wages for farm workers and the abolition of bonded labour, ranked prominently in the Government's Twenty-point reform programme announced in July 1975. Its implementation, like similar efforts in the past, seems in doubt as long as the power structure remains unchanged. The position is no better in the two successor states of Pakistan, where in 1972 President Bhutto and the late Sheikh Mujib respectively announced drastic agrarian reforms, without being able to implement them. The picture which emerges is one of violence to promote change being face to face with violence to forestall it. The margin left for conciliation is narrow and it is shrinking.

To counter situations of rural unrest effective reforms have to be introduced. These are bound to encroach upon the economic gains, social status and political power of those who are at present the main beneficiaries of the *status quo* and thus its staunchest defenders.

The need for institutional changes is nonetheless urgent. To limit farm improvements to the "gentleman farmer" or "kulak"—as the beneficiaries of the "green revolution" are sometimes called—is likely to lead to social disparities and thus in turn to political discontent. This trend can be arrested only if technological devices are disseminated widely and their application is guaranteed as a result of institutional adjustments which lead to the participation, on a large scale, of small tenant cultivators and landless labourers—the most vulnerable groups in the villages of Asia. The statistical records, for example those of Thailand, show beyond any reasonable doubt that the smaller the farm, the higher the yield—provided that owner-occupancy or security of tenure make the cultivator's efforts worthwhile. Distributive measures are no substitute for participation in the process of production and in the benefits derived from it. Even those with no access to land can share in rearing pigs (in non-Muslim countries) and in producing poultry and eggs—provided that Governments support the dispersal, rather than the concentration, of this type of animal husbandry. Small tenants can participate in these developments, provided they are given statutory security of tenure at more reasonable rents than those generally in operation at present. Landless labourers need not be excluded from this kind of agricultural planning either. They can participate, in particular if progressive land taxes are raised locally and are used locally, for example, in public works programmes designed to create badly needed rural feeder roads, feeder canals and feeder communications with local markets. Finally the hill tribes can be trained if they are given the opportunity to participate in the assembly, and eventually in the production, of light-weight, but high-value industrial products, such as watches and transistor equipment.

There are hardly any limits to the opportunities of improving the lot of the rural dwellers in Asia, provided traditional patterns are moulded to meet modern requirements. Changes of this kind presuppose, however, flexible adjustments in the power structure as it exists in most Asian rural communities today. If roadblocks are put in the path of evolutionary change, it is difficult to see how explosions of a revolutionary character can be avoided or be contained when they occur.

The 1974 World Food Conference limited its efforts to remedial short-term measures in the international sphere and to proposals for the technical improvement of food production and distribution at national levels. By comparison, social and political matters were either treated in a cursory manner or ignored altogether. This may be expected of a gathering of the kind organized under the auspices of the United Nations. However, there is little virtue in avoiding some of the most crucial issues which will have to be faced in the future. If Asia's agrarian malaise is to be treated in an effective manner, a more comprehensive knowledge of the rural body politic is required than the practitioners of agricultural development usually have at their command. Programmes designed to replace rather than to accompany overdue institutional changes are bound to disappoint. The concept of technical and economic innovations as substitutes for social and political change has no longer sufficient credibility to satisfy the growing numbers of dispossessed and disenchanted. Asia's rural and urban dwellers alike have discovered that increasingly a high incidence of dispersal of operating units goes together with a great deal of concentration of economic prosperity as well as social status and political power. They have begun to challenge this pattern which will have to be changed if the aim of increased production matched by equitable distribution is to be put into effect. Firm security of tenure, transfer of land from large-scale owners to operators, accompanied by a just agricultural tax system, an effective public works programme and genuine institutions of local government, could go a long way towards creating the preconditions for the implementation of the dual programme of economic growth and welfare, which most of Asia's ruling élites profess to favour. A policy of this kind could spare Asia's communities the most costly alternative of revolutionary change.

BIBLIOGRAPHY

BOSERUP, E. The Conditions of Agricultural Growth (London, 1965).

BROWN, J. R., and LIN S. (eds.). Land Reform in Developing Countries (Hartford, Conn., 1968).

BROWN, L. R. Seeds of Change. Overseas Development Council (New York, 1970).

BUNTING, A. H. Change in Agriculture (London, 1970).

CARRERE, H. D'ENCHAUSSE, and SCHRAM, S. R. Marxism and Asia (London, 1969).

CLARK, C., and HASWELL, M. The Economics of Subsistence Agriculture (London, 1966).

DUCKHAM, A. N., and MASEFIELD, G. B. Farming Systems of the World (London, 1971).

EICHER, C., and WITT, L. (eds.). Agriculture in Economic Development (New York, 1964).

FROELICH, W. (ed.). Land Tenure, Industrialisation and Social Stability (Milwaukee, Wis., 1961).

GOUROU. P. The Tropical World (London, 1953).

GRIGG, D. The Harsh Lands (London, 1970).

JACOBY, E. H. Man and Land (London, 1971).

KLATT, W. "Matters of Food and Farming in Asia" in *Food Policy*, Vol. 1, No. 2, February 1976.
"Asia After The World Food Conference" in *International Affairs*, Vol. 51, No. 3. July 1975.
"Reflections on Agricultural Modernisation in Asia" in *Pacific Affairs*, Vol. 46, No. 4, Winter 1973–74.

LEAGANS, J. P., and LOOMIS C. P. (eds.). Behavioral Change in Agriculture (Ithaca, New York, 1971).

LEHMANN, D. (ed.). Agrarian Reform and Agrarian Reformism (London, 1974).

MASEFIELD, G. B. A. Handbook of Tropical Agriculture (Oxford, 1949).

MELLOR, J. W. The Economics of Agricultural Development (Ithaca, New York, 1966).

MOSHER, A. T. Creating a Progressive Rural Structure. Agricultural Development Council (New York, 1969).

PARSONS, K. H., and PENN, H. J. (eds.). Land Tenure (Madison, Wis., 1956).

SCALAPINO, R. A. (ed.). The Communist Revolution in Asia (Englewood Cliffs, New Jersey, 1969).

SCHULTZ, T. W. Transforming Traditional Agriculture (New Haven, 1964).

SOUTHWORTH, H. M., and JOHNSTON, B. F. (eds.). Agricultural Development and Economic Growth (Ithaca, New York, 1967).

TAI, H. C. Land Reform and Politics (Berkeley, Calif., 1974).

THORBECKE, E. (ed.). The Role of Agriculture in Economic Development (New York, 1969).

TUMA, E. H. Twenty-six Centuries of Agrarian Reform (Berkeley, Calif., 1965).

WALTON, K. The Arid Zones (London, 1969).

WARRINER, D. Land Reform in Principle and Practice (Oxford, 1969).

WEITZ, R. From Peasant to Farmer (New York, 1971).

WARTHON, C. R. (ed.). Subsistence Agriculture and Economic Development (Chicago, 1969).

WOODRUFF, M., BROWN, J. R., and LIN, S. (eds.). Land Taxation, Land Tenure and Land Reform in Developing Countries (Hartford, Conn., 1967).

WRIGLEY, G. Tropical Agriculture (London, 1969).

American Association for the Advancement of Science, Food: Politics, Economics, Nutrition and Research (Washington, 1975).

Asian Development Bank, Asian Agricultural Survey. 2 vols. (Manila, 1968).

Asian Development Bank, Regional Seminar on Agriculture (Manila, 1969).

FAO, World Land Reform Conference. Country Papers (Rome, 1966).

FAO, The State of Food and Agriculture 1973 (Rome, 1973).

Ford Foundation, India's Food Crisis and Steps to meet it (New Delhi, 1959).

Rockefeller Foundation, A Partnership to Improve Food Production in India (New York, 1969).

U.S. President's Advisory Committee, The World Food Problem. 3 vols. (Washington, 1967).

Development Problems of Asia

Dick Wilson

When Gunnar Myrdal, the Swedish statesman-economist, published in 1968 his long-awaited book on Asian economic development problems, he called it *Asian Drama: An Inquiry into the Poverty of Nations*. The drama, he explained, lay in the "inner conflicts operating on people's minds; between their high-pitched aspirations and the bitter experience of a harsh reality; between the desire for change and improvement and mental reservations and inhibitions about accepting the consequences and paying the price." Such conflicts, of course, are part of human history all over the world, but never have they raged with such intensity and force as in the Asia of our day.

Like the countries of Africa and Latin America and of the Arab world, Asia—with one significant exception—is part of the developing, or under-developed world. Like theirs its economic life is backward, old-fashioned and inefficient, characterized by subsistence farming and a virtual absence of modern manufacturing industry. Many of its people are not yet touched by the money system, and live by barter and exchange.

But Asia is also the Cinderella of the developing world, of what in contemporary United Nations jargon is called "the South" (in contradistinction to the economically advanced and industrialized countries of Europe, North America and Japan—"the North"). The obstacles to modernization are measurably greater than in Africa, whose past is more easily overcome, or than in Latin America, where large-scale Europeanization has quickened the pace of innovation. In most of the Asian countries the pattern of society is near-feudal. The typical peasant, who accounts for a good 70 or 80 per cent of the total population, is ignorant, superstitious, apathetic and sceptical of the possibility of re-ordering his environment.

Only after the Second World War, in the late 1940s, was any concerted effort made to overcome these handicaps and to set in train a process of purposive social and economic change, and three decades are not enough to register convincing results. Thus, Myrdal, concerned to examine why the gap between the North and the South—the advanced and the less-developed—is actually growing wider rather than narrowing, chose to analyse Asia because Asia constituted the worst case in the development tragedy. To give it a very rough measure, the developing countries of Asia, with more than half the world's population, enjoy only about one-tenth of the world's wealth and production, and this share is dwindling rather than expanding. Their average annual income per head stands at a derisory £60, compared with £80 in Africa, £220 in Latin America and £350 in the world as a whole.

The Example of Japan

One country stands, however, as a symbol of hope. Japan celebrated in 1968 the centenary of the so-called Meiji Restoration which inaugurated that country's first deliberate attempt to modernize itself along Western lines. The ground which Japan has traversed over those hundred years, even including the bitter set-backs of the Second World War period, is such that the Japanese economy now ranks third in the whole world after the American and the Soviet, having overtaken the British and German in terms of Gross National Product within the past few years. Japan is twice as populous as Britain or West Germany, and so she ranks about twentieth in the world league for income per head or living standards, but she disposes of more wealth and goods than any single West European country.

Since Japan is an Asian nation, and one which stubbornly refused to deal with the Europeans for two decisive centuries prior to 1868, this achievement gives vicarious pleasure, and ground for hope, in other Asian countries. Recent research in Japan tends to suggest that conditions there in the early nineteenth century were such as to render the development of a modern form of capitalism inevitable, and scholars are less and less willing to equate the economic situation of Japan in the mid-nineteenth century with that of India or China today.

Nevertheless, Japan's success in economic modernization gives encouragement to those who yearn for a similar break-through in the other Asian countries, just as the Japanese military defeat of Tsarist Russia more than seventy years ago stirred the political ambitions of other Asians impatient with the European imperialist yoke. It also means that the development problem of contemporary Asia has to be discussed to the exclusion of Japan, and most of the remarks that follow are concerned with Asia minus Japan.

AGRICULTURE

The central issue in the Asian development drama is that of agriculture, the traditional source of livelihood of the population and still for most countries the largest single source of wealth. The methods by which rice, wheat and other crops are grown by peasants in most parts of Asia are extraordinarily old-fashioned. Jawaharlal Nehru, the late Prime Minister of India, used to express his shame and astonishment that so many Indian peasants still used the plough that had been developed in Vedic times more than three thousand years ago. Irrigation systems had been developed in many Asian civilizations (an outstanding example may be found near the ruins of Angkor Wat in Cambodia), but in many Asian villages chemical fertilizer, modern machines and the development of better strains of seeds were introduced only within the past ten years.

During the first half of the twentieth century Indian production of foodgrains expanded by an annual average of about 0.5 per cent, and this was probably typical of other countries too. From the early 1950s the tempo of improvement has quickened. The United Nations statistical indices show an improvement of some 40 per cent during the decade 1955–65. But the tempo tended to fluctuate badly, and fell to only 3 per cent a year during the 1960s. The common experience of the Asian governments was that their initial efforts to boost farm output paid off so handsomely that they became complacent, unaware that the annual increases in the harvests of the 1950s were more the result of the return to peace-time conditions after the Second World War (and, in China's and India's case, after the additional turmoil of civil war and partition) than of any encouragement by the government.

Once the crop results had more or less regained their pre-war levels (and this was effected, on the whole, during the decade of the 1950s), it became apparent that more costly inputs would be needed to maintain the momentum. In the 1960s the UN estimated the average annual growth in foodgrain harvests in Asia at a mere 2.6 per cent, and as late as 1967 it was still possible for the President of the Asian Development Bank to argue that Asian food production in the preceding twelve months was rather less than the pre-war level. The technological advances of the so-called "green revolution" have quickened the tempo in the early 1970s.

In conditions where weather can cause the loss of tens of millions of tons of rice or wheat in a single country, trends are difficult to establish over a short number of years. These crops require the application of water, neither too much nor too little, at certain stages of their growth. If the rains come too early or too late, if they continue too long or are unusually heavy, then crops can either shrivel into the ground or be washed out of the fields. Drought and flood are the twin terrors of the Asian farmer, and only a well-planned, sustained and expensive programme of water conservancy (strengthening river banks, reafforestation to prevent soil erosion, measures against silting, systems of irrigation and drainage canals) can provide some protection against them.

China suffered three consecutive years of bad weather in 1959–61, as a result of which many people died of malnutrition and others survived on bark, grass and insects. Under the relatively efficient administration of the Communists few people actually starved, but the big Yellow River flood in northern China at the end of the Second World War took almost a million lives, and the Bengal famine in the early 1940s cost about 3 million lives. There have been cases of actual starvation in Bihar as recently as 1966, and desperate food shortages have occurred during the 1960s in some parts of Indonesia.

Reform of Land Tenure

Land reform is one improvement which virtually all Asian governments have tried to make. It has both political and economic implications. Japan's post-war "miracle" owes much to the American-imposed land reform of the occupation years. Taiwan has completed a most successful "Land to the Tiller" programme. In India the process of land redistribution has been somewhat slow, in the Philippines and elsewhere even slower. In China, North Viet-Nam, North Korea and Mongolia the reform was followed by co-operativization and collectivization. China introduced the so-called People's Commune in 1958 as the ultimate model for socialist agriculture and rural life in an Asian context, but the model has not so far been followed elsewhere.

The consequences of collectivization are still disputed by scholars: it allows public works (notably irrigation) to be carried out on a scale impossible for the owners of small holdings, yet it would appear also to diminish the incentives for the more enterprising peasants to produce more. The whole question of the lengths to which collective ownership should be pushed in China's villages was central to the conflict within the country's Communist leadership that became bound up with the Cultural Revolution of 1966–69. In India politicians and planners are, at least in private, resigned to a situation where improvements in agriculture are bound, on the whole, to benefit the already better-off peasants rather than the worse-off, and this ultimately will pose a political problem.

Improvements in Agricultural Yield

Meanwhile technical reforms are being carried out throughout the continent. Only a third of Asia's land area is arable, but in most countries it has been found possible to extend the acreage sown to crops by a small proportion, and also to increase the extent of double-cropping (even, in some well-endowed areas, treble-cropping) on the same piece of soil. But the most important contribution to bigger harvests has been to increase the yield of each acre. This is done by providing four new inputs: chemical fertilizer, artificial water supply, new and better strains of seeds and improved machinery with electrification.

Only from the mid-1960s did China and India seriously promote chemical fertilizer, which is expensive. The Japanese farmer applies as much chemical fertilizer to his land as the West European, but the Indian or Chinese farmer has at best one-eighth of that amount, acre for acre. Irrigation is gradually spreading, but still less than a third of Asia's farmlands are irrigated. Mechanization is nowadays less popular with planners because it is so costly, and the one thing that almost all Asian farmlands do not lack is adequate man-power. At the moment it is the new seeds that are attracting the limelight. After years of laboratory work, new hybrid strains of rice and wheat have been developed which happily combine the qualities of the highest-yielding types in the world with the essential characteristics of the local type. To take one example, dwarf varieties of wheat are now spreading which make the crops less vulnerable to wind and rain. But the benefits of the "green revolution" seemed to stabilize by the mid-1970s, ruling out the hope of continuing the momentum it had seemed to build up at the beginning.

Asia's Trade in Agricultural Produce

Meanwhile, Asia continues to be a large food importer. India in recent years has been importing about nine million tons a year, China five. Asia is importing more than 20 million tons of wheat annually, and since 1964 has become a net importer of rice in spite of producing 60 per cent of the world crop. Most of this wheat and rice is shipped from North and South America and from Australia, and a large proportion of it has been supplied free or with liberal repayment terms under American aid. But India is having to pay the equivalent of half of her total export earnings, China and Pakistan a quarter of theirs, merely to acquire food for consumption, and this is obviously unsatisfactory when the long-term need is for machinery and industrial materials to speed Asian development. Only from about 1971, did the "green revolution" begin to change this picture. Average calorie intake in Asia is thought to be around 2,050 per day, substantially less than the minimum requirement suggested by the United Nations.

Agricultural problems embrace more than food-grains. Cash crops of various kinds, ranging from tea and sugar to vegetable oils and rubber, are also extremely important to the Asian economies. These (and minerals) were the original cause of Europe's attraction to the Orient, and their commercial development, even in some cases introduction from other continents, was often the work of Europeans over the past century or so. Most Asian countries are still dependent on primary commodities for their export earnings: Ceylon relies on tea, rubber and coconuts for 90 per cent of her export earnings, Malaysia on tin and rubber for 60 per cent of hers. Unfortunately for them the modern international trading system ensures that the price for such commodities (which are often perishable, with little margin for improvement and increasingly easily substituted by synthetic materials of various kinds) tends always to fall, while the price of the manufactured goods which Asia buys from the West in return for her commodities tends constantly to rise.

The stabilization of commodity prices has proved an elusive goal of Asian and other under-developed countries. Agriculture in Asia is so old-fashioned that European and American farmers are proving competitive (in spite of higher labour costs) in a number of products formerly the preserve of tropical producers—soya beans and rice, for instance. Asia's share in world exports of crude materials of all kinds slumped by a third in the decade 1955–65, a recent UN survey found, and this loss is compounded by the discrimination which many Western countries operate in favour of their own farmers.

Thailand provides an example of a country which has rather successfully diversified its agricultural exports to become less dependent on a few crops. But, as a recent United Nations *Survey* of Asia remarked, "Economic development is, after all, difficult enough without having to be burdened by the additional task of developing new export products while more traditional outputs are available but either hampered in their access to foreign markets or subjected to sharp declines in value . . .". In Malaysia the fall in the world rubber price (by 20 U.S. cents a pound) over twelve months has recently caused a loss of some £50 million in export earnings—and every time this kind of thing happens, the government has to make further slashing cuts in the country's development programme.

INDUSTRY

It is in this context that the urgency of industrialization in Asia must be seen. Only by developing modern industry can Asian countries hope to become really independent of the West, able to meet their own capital development needs and psychologically secure. The roots of modern industry, in fact, go a long way back in both India and China. Jamsetji Tata opened his pioneering cotton mill in Nagpur on the same day in 1877 on which Queen Victoria was declared Empress of India, while Dwarkanath Tagore, the poet Rabindranath's grandfather, bought India's largest coal mine in 1836. Steel has been made in Bihar, in eastern India, and in Manchuria, in northeastern China, since the early years of this century. But these early enterprises were small and isolated, and it was only in the post-war period that comprehensive industrialization schemes were pursued.

In the past two decades very long strides have been made. According to UN figures, industrial output in Asia increased almost tenfold during those twenty years, and if only heavy industry is included the rise was even greater. Average annual industrial growth in the developing countries of Asia during the 1960s was about 8 per cent, which means that industry has been expanding more than twice as fast as the other sectors of the economy. In the 1970s so far the figure has been 12 per cent for East and South-East Asia, 4 per cent for South Asia. Steel output, in terms of ingots and metal for casting, stood at little more than 10 million tons ten years ago, but has now reached some 20 million tons (Japan's production is currently around 120 million tons a year, more than either Britain or Germany, and this is left out of the calculation).

Machinery manufacture has grown tremendously, and both India and China are now able to export complete industrial plant. Both have a well-developed nuclear energy industry, which in China's case has allowed the explosion of an H-bomb several years after political disagreements had caused the departure of the Soviet scientists advising her. India has also conducted an independent peaceful nuclear explosion, although she has also utilized American, Canadian and European atomic technology. The Chinese have boasted of having developed by their own techniques and without the aid of foreign advisers a 12,000-ton hydraulic free forging press, 10,000-ton ocean vessels, large electron microscopes, transistorized electronic computers and complete sets of automated metallurgical and chemical industrial equipment.

India is about in the same class, but has in most cases leant on foreign expertise and help. The first giant steel works to be put up in India under public ownership were largely the creation of their British, German and Soviet designers, but subsequent ones will be entirely Indian-designed and Indian-built.

Both countries aim eventually at complete self-reliance but the Indians have preferred to keep open the short-cuts which foreign help can provide. No country in Asia has yet been able to produce jet aircraft or large ships (except Japan, which is not merely the world's biggest shipbuilder but is responsible for more than half of current world production of ships).

Priorities in Industrial Development

Most of the developing countries of Asia emphasized heavy industry in the early days of their post-war industrialization programmes. Both China and India chose to follow the Soviet model in this matter, allocating more investment funds to the steel mills, power generation, chemicals and the engineering industries than to either agriculture (which was more or less left to take care of itself) or light industry (which was felt to be of secondary importance, catering chiefly for the consumer market and contributing little to the country's industrial potential).

Within a decade, however, the planners in both Peking and New Delhi were having second thoughts about this. It was gradually realized that agricultural development would require more funds if it were to proceed towards food self-sufficiency, and also that light industry provided the household consumer goods which farmers needed and which constituted an important incentive for their work. Both agriculture and light industry also accounted for the greater part of most Asian export earnings, so essential for the purchase in turn of foreign food, fertilizer and capital equipment. By the mid-1960s a better balance between these various sectors in the economy was being achieved.

Controversy continued to rage, however, about the relationship between state activity and private enterprise in industry. With the exception of the Communist countries, notably China, where private enterprise had been eliminated or suffocated by the mid-1950s, Asian industrial ownership and management has all along been shared between government and private entrepreneur. Asian nationalism tended to be suspicious of its native capitalists, who symbolized for the most part an almost "unpatriotic" collaboration with Western or foreign interests. Thus, Chiang Kai-shek, pillar of the Asian right wing, once declared that China should control private capital "in order to prevent the capitalistic control of the people's livelihood . . . National industries must be created". Mr. Nehru was a notable advocate of the public sector, and his daughter, Prime Minister Indira Gandhi, has recently reduced yet further the role of the private sector in India. The greatest success in the development of efficient industries outside of Japan, though on a somewhat small scale, has nevertheless been in Hong Kong, Taiwan and South Korea.

FINANCE

The speed at which Asian agriculture and industry can be developed depends, of course, to a very large extent on the amount of funds available. This in turn is primarily dictated by the domestic savings and taxes of each country itself; given the low standard of living, the margin for capital accumulation is naturally small.

Domestic Savings

Most Asian governments derive only about one-fifth of their revenues from direct taxation such as income tax. Unlike the typical Western government, they depend much more on customs duties and other indirect taxes. The tendency is for them to find it increasingly hard to obtain compulsory savings through taxation.

The improvement of agricultural yields has primarily benefited the peasant or the farmer, who is better equipped than the city dweller to avoid taxation. Some of the Indian states are abolishing land revenue at a time when the planners in the centre are desperately calling for more funds to be raised from the land. It is politically impossible, given the democratic structure, for any Indian government to impose an agricultural income tax, and even in China, where more authoritarian methods are accepted, the central government cannot get what it wants from the localities. As the political balance of power shifts in favour of the rural *vis-à-vis* the urban population throughout developing Asia, the prospect for centrally organized savings diminishes.

The Indian economic development plan for the year 1967/68 envisaged a slump in the rate of domestic savings from the 9 per cent of the two previous years to only 6.5 per cent, but its authors commented that this trend was "inconsistent with the accepted long-term goal of self-reliance at an adequate rate of growth. For this goal would require a saving rate of close to 20 per cent of national income." The problem is even tougher in a country such as Indonesia where inflation caused consumer prices to rise by 600 per cent in both 1965 and 1966, and where the new regime has only recently been able to bring it under control.

Income from Abroad

Assistance is sought from outside, in three principal forms: aid, export earnings and foreign investment. Asia is an important beneficiary of the West's economic aid programmes, currently receiving between 45 per cent and 50 per cent of the total annually disbursed. A similar proportion of the Communist countries' aid (including China's) goes to the developing nations of Asia. The most recent OECD calculation is that official net flows (bilateral and multilateral, i.e. including loans from the World Bank and other international institutions) from the West to Asia averaged $4,664 million a year from 1970–73, and over the preceding decade the flow was maintained at an average of just under $3,000 million. Cumulative aid offers to Asia from the Soviet bloc to the beginning of 1971 have been calculated at just over $4,500 million.

But the climate for aid is worsening with the diminution of the cold war rivalry between the U.S.A. and the U.S.S.R., the political disenchantment of the "North" with the politics of the "South", and the resentment in the North over the South's success in raising prices through cartels for its oil and raw materials. Corruption in high places is extensive in Asia, and the priority of the public welfare is not always recognized. The Indo-Pakistan war of 1965, which wasted a good deal of aid resources that had been supplied to these two relatively go-ahead members of the Asian South, was closely followed by the exposure of the extravagances of the Sukarno government in Indonesia. Corruption and graft tarnish the image of Asian development, a spectacular case being that of the Thai dictator, Marshal Sarit, who amassed at least £12 million during his period as Prime Minister in 1958–63.

The upshot was that aid ceased to expand and it became more difficult for Western governments to get Treasury allocations for it (the American Congress was a notable rebel against more ambitious foreign aid programmes). It was made clear to the Asians that foreign aid could not be relied upon for ever. In fact, no one ever intended it to be permanent. Taiwan provides a remarkable case-study of a developing economy which has now, after enormous annual handouts from the U.S., become self-generating in its growth. But countries such as India will require aid for another decade if the economic "take-off" is to be attained as quickly as possible.

Another problem over aid relates to its servicing. To the extent that most aid is in the form of loans (and some donors include in their "aid" private investment for which the remittance of profits and dividends in foreign exchange must be conceded), the burden of debt service has now reached alarming proportions. India has to earmark almost one quarter of its entire export earnings to this, Pakistan one-fifth. The capacity of such countries to borrow further is in question, and this alone would seem enough to ensure the de-emphasis of aid as an agent of development. In any event it is recognized that foreign aid contributes only a small fraction of the total funds devoted to Asian development, the vastly greater part coming from the people's own savings and taxes.

There is also the psychological aspect of aid. Some people are encouraged by foreign interest, others become more inert. The Chinese, who have not only forsworn foreign aid since 1960 but have in any case disbursed abroad more aid than they ever received themselves from the Soviet Union, are fierce advocates of total self-reliance. "The people must not look outward, extend their hands and depend upon others", said one of their spokesmen a year or two ago. One of the most difficult dilemmas is whether—and to what extent—to meet emergency demands for food relief when Asian crops fail. The Americans feel obliged for humanitarian reasons to respond fully to such calls, but they also know that their generosity could be fatally weakening the necessary resolve which the Asians themselves must form if they are to solve their own food problem.

Foreign private investment remains a relatively small item in the total financial picture. Most Asian governments tend to regulate private investment too closely for Western businessmen's comfort, and the opportunities are probably greater elsewhere—within the West itself. Nevertheless, an influential place is occupied in India and in most of the other developing countries of Asia by Western firms, usually operating in association with local capital and working under some difficulty. Their role in the transmission of techniques, both managerial and technological, is particularly appreciated. Pioneer industries in many newly industrializing countries are favoured by tax holidays, tariff protection and other privileges: Malaysia, Thailand and Singapore are especially noted for this.

The only way in which a country can earn its own foreign exchange is by exporting, and increasing attention is now being paid to this. Unfortunately, as has been seen, the traditional primary commodities in which Asia is so rich are tending to fall in price. High hopes are therefore placed on the export potential of new light industry, especially textiles, plastic ware and light machinery including electrical appliances and radios. But another difficulty has been encountered here, namely that the rich industrialized markets are reluctant to allow unlimited entry of cheap manufactures. This is partly because of competition with domestic industry, partly out of defence considerations (if the U.S. became totally dependent on Asia for all its garments and cloth, it would be disabled from clothing its armed forces in the event of war).

Nevertheless, the most enterprising of the Asian developers have gained substantial shares of the American and West European markets in these items in spite of the latter's attempts to regulate them, notably under the long-term cotton textile export agreement negotiated at Geneva in 1962 and again in 1973. The effect of the Geneva pact, which originally applied only to cotton textiles but is now being extended to cover synthetic fibre products from Asia, was to freeze the situation more or less as it stood in 1962, to the benefit of Hong Kong and the few others who had pioneered the road and to the disadvantage of the new entrants who would have liked to challenge them later in the 1960s. But so far the experiment of internationally regulating the import of low-cost manufactures from Asia has been confined to textiles—although most advanced markets also impose unilateral quotas on household goods, toys, radios and the like when they come from low-wage countries in Asia and elsewhere.

POPULATION

All of Asia's development problems are compounded by the population explosion. The various national censuses taken in 1960 and 1961 showed for the first time beyond doubt that the population growth in many countries of Asia (including India and Pakistan, which between them contain almost one-fifth of humanity) then stood at an annual rate of some 2.5 per cent, almost half as much again as had been supposed earlier. The results of the censuses, and their comparison with the previous decennial censuses (which had been the first since before the war), were fully reviewed at the Asian Population Conference in New Delhi in 1963, and it is from that relatively recent date that the full meaning of the explosion sank in.

The reasons for the increase are clear: in many parts of Asia the death rate was halved during the 1950s by the inexorable advance of public health, medicine and hygiene. But there is not yet a corresponding fall in the birth rate, since this is a product not merely of medical progress but of changes in social attitude and economic environment. Asians are, if anything, less troubled than Westerners by religious objections to birth control. But their tradition attaches supreme importance to the family as a social unit and channel of social forces. The Indian or Chinese peasant still feels that there is a premium on having a large family, especially of sons, since they alone can ensure their parents' comfortable old age and provide the hands necessary to swell the family's fortunes. Neither the authoritarian Chinese Communists nor the Nehruvian gradualists of India have been able seriously to impinge on these sentiments except among the intellectuals and urban dwellers who are the more direct heirs to Westernization.

Contraception is still an uncertain process, and one requiring a fairly costly investment in terms of propaganda, instruction and materials. The Indian Government allotted a paltry U.S. $1.3 million to family planning in its first Five-Year Plan in the early 1950s: the Fourth Plan, just finished, devoted U.S. $200 million and that is still only scratching at the surface of the problem. Abortion was the principal factor in Japan's success in reducing its population growth from 2 per cent to 1 per cent a year during the past two or three decades, but it is both costly and distasteful. India is emphasizing sterilization as a partial answer, and a Minister of Family Planning was himself voluntarily sterilized after his third child. But the consensus is that it will take another decade or more for any results of present family planning campaigns to be seen in a lower birth rate, and that the population explosion will go on for another generation or so.

Implications of the Population Explosion

Asia is thus certain, barring full-scale war or pestilence, to increase its numbers by half over the next twenty-five years from the present 2,250 million to around 3,650 million in 2000: the question really is whether it can provide enough food for them all. Looked at in historical perspective, it must be conceded that what is now happening is nothing more than the restoration of the pre-Industrial Revolution balance between the continents or civilizations. Asia probably accounted for two-thirds of mankind at the time of the Napoleonic Wars, but the population explosion in nineteenth-century Europe has reduced that proportion to something like 57 per cent. Now the boot is on the other foot, and Asia's share by the end of this century will most likely be 62 per cent or a little more. It would be irrational for Europeans or Americans to object to such a redress, so to speak, although many Asian nationalists still think as the *Guardian* newspaper of Rangoon did in June 1961 when it editorialized:

> Behind all the talk about population pressure and the need for control in Asia is the fear and bad conscience that one day soon enough masses of Asians will erupt and inundate with fire and sword the prosperous areas of the world in sole occupation by the European races. . . . Any lecture about population pressures appears unreal.

Luckily the main stream of Asian thought now accepts the need for limitation. A recent conference (the Asian Conference on Children and Youth in National Planning and Development, held in Bangkok in 1967) concluded: "In effect, population growth is endangering the quality of mankind, as a large part of national resources must be devoted to simply maintaining existing levels of living, leaving few resources available for improving those levels." In a reasonably good year of normal weather the typical Asian economy can these days expand by some 5 per cent, but half of that painfully gained advance must be written off from the start because of the 2.5 per cent growth in population. To put it another way, if the Indian population had remained stable since the country's independence in 1947, the gain in *per capita* annual income since then would now be four times what it actually is. Even the anti-Malthusian Chinese Communists now concede that birth control will promote economic development.

It will also help to alleviate what is going to be Asia's single most distressing problem over the coming decades, namely how to provide gainful employment for the vast numbers of school-leavers now entering the adult labour market (the age structure of Asia is such that every other Asian is under 21!). The Indian Fourth Plan, for instance, envisaged the creation of 19 million new wage-earning jobs during the five years 1969–73, but it also envisaged 23 million new entrants to the labour market. The work force in developing Asia will expand by 56 per cent during the two decades 1960–80, according to the report of the Asian Conference on Industrialization (1965), creating a need for 336 million new jobs! Even in authoritarian China the Communists find it difficult to get school-leavers to work on the land. Education has in the past been a passport to white-collar work, and it is typical of most Asian societies for manual work to be despised. Hence, the Chinese Communist insistence on everyone doing a stint of manual work every year no matter how high they stand in the hierarchy, and Mao's preference for part-time schools which pay their own way from their own part-time production.

EDUCATION

Indeed, it is now fairly widely recognized in Asia that modernization is not merely a matter of juggling with the economic structure and putting in new investments. The main burden of Professor Myrdal's masterpiece, *Asian Drama*, was the importance of changing the social structure, social attitudes and traditional values if a modern type of economic development was to succeed. It is little use creating a few ultra-modern steel mills about the Indian countryside if in their shadow you can still see peasants resisting new methods of cultivation, refusing to limit their families and faithfully observing the traditional Hindu taboos against the slaughter of useless cows.

Educational reform—what the economists call the human factor—is fundamental to everything else.

Probably some 60 per cent of Asia's school-age children are currently attending school of some kind between the ages of 5 and 14 (another 10 per cent of them are sent out to work and the rest stay at home to help informally at household tasks). The Asian governments agreed at a UNESCO Conference in Karachi in 1960 that they would aim to achieve seven years of compulsory free primary education by 1980. But even this modest programme is extremely costly and is held up by a shortage of trained teachers.

The number of schoolchildren in the Indian state of Orissa has more than quadrupled in ten years: one can imagine the strain thus placed on buildings, staff and teaching materials. Teachers are badly paid in most Asian countries, and in India it is common for them to strike for salary increases. Asian Ministers of Education agreed at Tokyo in 1962 that they should spend between 4 per cent and 5 per cent of their countries' Gross National Product on education, but the actual performance falls short of this by about half. Average government spending is an annual $2 a head, compared with $70 in Britain.

Illiteracy thus remains an important problem in Asia, where only one in three persons can read and write. In Nepal the ratio is only one in twenty. Illiteracy tends to be self-perpetuating in a society such as India where the education system discriminates against women: 80 per cent of Indian mothers are reckoned to be illiterate and thus unable to teach their children.

Changes in the traditional curriculum are also badly needed, especially in the interests of vocational relevancy and the acquisition of a more rational and scientific outlook. In Ceylon it was recently found that 85 per cent of schoolchildren preferred arts to science, and that education actually increases unemployment because school-leavers refuse to take up any kind of manual work. The spectre of the "educated unemployed", whom education has left unfitted for the social needs of the present-day, is well known from Shanghai to Bombay. Asia is not lacking in scientific talent, and has produced many Nobel Prizewinners in scientific subjects. The Chinese nuclear programme is evidence of what can be done when it is considered important enough, and when political priorities are accorded to it. But the diffusion of science down to the schools leaves much to be desired.

PLANNING

These, then, are the principal problems that beset the modernization drive in Asia. How has the development strategy itself developed over these past two decades or so? It goes without saying that the concept of central planning is now broadly accepted. When India. China and Pakistan inaugurated their first Five-Year Plans in 1951, 1953 and 1955 respectively, Asia demonstrated its preference for planning (only colonial Hong Kong has maintained an unfashionable *laissez-faire* policy towards its economy, and with some success, but then its challenge was a small one by comparison with India or China).

Not that the plans have kept out of trouble. China's Second Plan was thrown out almost before it began, in favour of the ill-fated *Great Leap Forward*, and the Third Plan had to be delayed for three years because of the economic set-backs that followed. India's Fourth Plan was also delayed by three years because of the stagnation which crop failures and the war with Pakistan caused. Both India and China were in the later 1960s working in practice on annual rather than quinquennial plans because of the uncertainties that surrounded their immediate economic future.

Chinese and Indian Planning

The idea of planning remains, however, a fixed part of the Asian scene. Its content has altered as experience gradually revealed the deficiencies of the so-called Mahalanobis model (in India) or Soviet pattern (in China), both of which placed great stress on heavy industrialization requiring an extremely high rate of savings or else a massive inflow of foreign aid. Both the Chinese and the Indians have now learned that there is a political limit to the forcing upwards of savings in a poor economy, that there is also a limit to aid hand-outs in a growingly sceptical world, and that a balance between agriculture, heavy industry and light industry is an important condition of steady growth.

The Chinese, surprisingly, have shown themselves to be the more temperamental developers. In 1958 they plunged with little preparation into an entirely new and imaginative policy, the *Great Leap Forward*. By mobilizing man-power as never before, by decentralizing planning and by stirring the whole nation into a frenzy of hard work they managed to double their growth rate from about 6 per cent to 12 per cent, but the tempo could not be maintained and the economy then went into a recession which lasted for several years. Tremendous resources were wasted, for example, in the campaign to construct backyard steel furnaces in every village. Yet the Leap contained some features that made sense for Chinese conditions, and there was never any question of China going back to the Soviet model again. Similarly, the stress on heavy industry in the Indian Plans changed during the Third Plan period.

The Indian Plans have gained world-wide fame as models of a distinctively Indian reconciliation between three often conflicting goals—a high rate of economic growth, greater social justice and democratic freedom. The text of the first Five-Year Plan is required reading for officials and economists throughout the third world. But a change is discernible after two decades' experience. After repeated pressure from the growing Indian business community and from external advisers (notably the American Government, source of most of India's foreign aid, and the World Bank) the Indian Government began after Nehru's death to liberalize the controls through which it had enforced planning in the past. Particularly from 1966 onwards the greater freedom extended to entrepreneurs and industrialists, together with the growing orientation towards the rural sector, meant that the central planners' control over the rate of saving was weakened. Some observers questioned whether India had not in effect rejected the bold long-term planning which had brought its economic development thus far, while others rejoiced at the release of private energies to take up the torch from the bureaucracy. Only time will tell which is right. Meanwhile, Mrs. Gandhi's nationalization of the major Indian banks and of the import of raw materials in 1969 helped to restore the balance in favour of the planners.

The case of India is worth dwelling further on, if only because it is both the largest and the worst (i.e. the most difficult development challenge) in Asia. The Indians hoped to double the *per capita* income of their people over a generation, or 25 years. This would entail an annual *per capita* income growth of about 3 per cent, which in turn, given the population explosion, means an overall economic growth rate of between 5 per cent and 5.5 per cent. If this could have been maintained, by 1976, after five Five-Year Plans, the average Indian could hope to enjoy the far from princely annual income of £50.

Even this modest goal has proved, however, over-ambitious. After three Plans costing an aggregate of £16,000 million in new investment, the *per capita* income has risen (at constant prices) by only 2 per cent a year. The average Indian income fell short of the £50 target in the mid-1970s by a considerable margin. Most of the other developing countries of Asia have done a little better than India, but the Asian average is brought near the Indian performance because of the huge Indian population.

Economic Performance Throughout the Region

In Asia as a whole (always, of course, excepting Japan) the economic growth rate during the 1950s and 1960s has been about 4 per cent a year. This covers a very uneven record, both in time and in space; income per head has actually fallen in some countries in some years, in Ceylon, for instance, in 1967 and in India between 1964 and 1967. The UN's *Economic Survey of Asia and the Far East 1972* indicated a growth rate in developing Asia in 1960–70 of only 4.9 per cent or 2.2 per cent per head of population. One feature of the 1960s was the relatively faster growth of the smaller countries of East and South-East Asia which started their serious planning later than India or China but from a higher base in terms of the then existing living standards and natural resources. The only countries in developing Asia to maintain a growth rate higher than 5 per cent a year during the 1960s were Malaysia, Taiwan, South Korea, Thailand, the Philippines and Pakistan.

Americans have been quick to point to the fact that these are, on the whole, the countries which have followed a more liberal policy towards private enterprise, both domestic and foreign, and have avoided unnecessary controls. The laggards until now have been Indonesia (rich in natural resources but slow to discipline itself to the long-term development tasks) and India (which has the most efficient and experienced planning mechanism, but working from the lowest possible base in terms of social immobility and economic backwardness).

As for the so-called economic development "race" between India and China, the two contenders for giant power status on the Asian mainland, conclusive comparisons are made impossible by the unreliability of our knowledge of Chinese performance. All that can safely be said is that the Indian tortoise has not, in fact, so far compared unfavourably with the Chinese hare, but that the revolutionary base for future modernization is probably better secured in China than in India. Both countries' real annual growth since 1949 has averaged between 3 and 4 per cent only. Outside observers used to deplore the excesses of the Chinese Communists at home, but it is now being realized that rapid modernization does seem to require changes in social attitudes which only a forceful overthrow of vested interests can decisively accelerate.

The oil price rise in 1973–74 hit Asia very badly indeed, with an extra oil bill for the region of $4,000 million to $5,000 million in 1974 alone, while the inflation rate in Asia reached 31 per cent in 1974, according to the UN's *Economic Survey of Asia and the Pacific* 1974. The survey was pessimistic about the region's food, population and balance of payments problems.

INTERNATIONAL ORGANIZATIONS

Luckily the Asian countries are not alone in facing their modernization challenge. Many international forums and frameworks have been provided for their co-operation and mutual encouragement. Outstanding among these are the Colombo Plan, a largely British initiative which pioneered the concept of long-term planning, and ESCAP, the United Nations Regional Economic and Social Commission for Asia and the Pacific. ESCAP offers a permanent secretariat in Bangkok dealing with all problems of development affecting the area. Its annual conference provides a sounding-board for the region's economic preoccupations, and its research studies have been found invaluable. Recently it has fathered two vigorous children in the Asian Institute for Economic Development and Planning and the Asian Development Bank. It is extremely proud of its achievement in gaining the co-operation of the four countries which share the Mekong River (Laos, Thailand, Cambodia and Viet-Nam, a quartet which is far from harmonious politically) in an ambitious multi-national project to harness the river's energies for the common good.

But when all this has been said, ESCAP remains a creature of its governments and a prisoner of the UN bureaucratic style. Its role was inhibited in the earlier years by the presence as full members of such non-Asian states as the United Kingdom, France, the Netherlands and the U.S.A., and it has not been able to achieve the authority of its sister organizations in Africa and Latin America, largely because of the unusual heterogeneity of the area it has to cover.

Asian voices were prominent in the four full-scale UNCTAD conferences held since 1964, although there has been widespread disappointment over the failure of the UN in general to carry through the goals of the First Development Decade (the 1960s) and of UNCTAD in particular to gain the agreement of both North and South for the international measures necessary to quicken the development tempo in Asia and elsewhere. The Second Development Decade (the 1970s) was intended to continue the campaign, with a target of 6 per cent annual growth for all developing countries.

More recently there have entered on the scene for the first time exclusively Asian organizations or groupings devoted in whole or in part to these problems. After a number of false starts the South-East Asian countries have settled down to a grouping of their own called ASEAN (Association of South-East Asian Nations) which has taken the first steps towards regional economic co-operation, notably in such fields as communications and transport. An Asian Coconut Community was formed in 1968 and there is an Association of Natural Rubber Producing Countries in which Malaysia takes an energetic lead to stabilize prices at a reasonably high level. Preliminary work has been done on some kind of free trade area and a regional payments union, but political trust between ASEAN members is still fragile and the atmosphere can be guessed from the fact that none of them is willing to merge its national airline into a regional enterprise.

JAPAN AND AUSTRALIA

Japan has an important role to play in the coming years, not merely as an example of what can be achieved in the Asian context, but as the second biggest donor of aid to the region after the U.S.A. and as the only great industrialized power to have an unreservedly vital stake in the stability and progress of the area. Britain is withdrawing from Asia, the U.S.A. could always retreat in an access of isolationism, but, as one of her Foreign Ministers used often to remark, Japan cannot move to the other side of the Pacific. Until now Japan has left the initiative in Asian affairs to the U.S.A.

But gradually the Japanese have begun to accustom themselves to taking a more active role. Regular Asian conferences are now held at the Ministerial level, under Japanese sponsorship, to promote co-operation in various economic matters. Indonesia, whose economic waywardness had become the despair of most Western governments, is now widely seen as a "Japanese responsibility" in the sense that Japan, of all Western donors, is expected to take the most active interest in its progress. Asians remember with indignation the Greater East Asia Co-prosperity Sphere of an earlier generation, and the Japanese are still not fully trusted or liked. But they are bound to play an increasingly helpful part in the region's affairs, even though they failed to sponsor a "Marshall-Aid type" rehabilitation and development programme for Asia after the Viet-Nam War.

Finally, there are the Anglo-Saxons of the region, Australia and New Zealand. Accorded the compliment a few years ago of admission to the inner circle of "regional", as distinct from "non-regional" members of ESCAP, these two nations enjoy an unusual goodwill in Asia proper. Sometimes their representatives try to argue that they too are developing countries, at least in the sense that they are thirsty for capital and largely dependent upon primary commodities rather than manufacturing.

Since their standard of living exceeds that of many European countries, however, such claims are not seriously received, although the recent policy of negotiating long-term contracts for the export of large quantities of the newly-discovered iron and other minerals in Western Australia to feed the steel mills of Japan has evoked serious domestic criticism on the ground that Australia should insist on processing the ores herself and not allow herself to become a mere "quarry for the Japanese".

As Britain carries through her gradual withdrawal from South-East Asia, and as the spectre of American isolationism is raised from time to time, the Australians and New Zealanders are aware that their self-interest lies in forging ever closer links with their Asian neighbours, not only the immediately contiguous Indonesia but the mainland states as well. It is likely that in the years to come they will be more and more seen as belonging to the Asian region.

BIBLIOGRAPHY

LEHMANN, DAVID (ed.). Agrarian Reform and Agrarian Reformism (London, 1974).

MYRDAL, GUNNAR. Asian Drama, An Inquiry into the Poverty of Nations (New York and London, 1968).

WILSON, DICK. Asia Awakes (London and New York, 1970).

The Colombo Plan, 22nd Annual Report (Columbo, 1976).

Far Eastern Economic Review, Asia 1976 Yearbook, (Hong Kong, 1976).

Journal of Development Planning No. 7, Economic Cooperation among Member Countries of the Association of South-East Asian Nations (New York, 1974).

UN, Economic Survey of Asia and the Pacific (Bangkok and New York, 1976).

Aid and Investment

Helen Moody

ASIA: THE CHALLENGING ARENA

A third of the world's population live in the less developed countries (LDCs) of southern and eastern Asia*, and much of this vast population suffers from poverty on a scale unknown elsewhere in the world. This is especially true of the South Asian sub-continent, where the combination of very high population levels and growth rates, lack of natural resources, and propensity to natural disaster, enlarges the problems of development beyond those experienced in many other parts of the third world.

In the 1950s and 1960s two factors brought Asia into prominence in the pattern of international relations. First, the extent of its poverty, and secondly, it became an arena for ideological conflict between the three main power blocs. In the conflicts between North and South Korea, in Indochina, between India and Pakistan, and East and West Pakistan, the great powers have played a direct or indirect role.

The main challenge of economic development is in Asia, and that challenge presents itself in the unstable context of political confrontation. The developed countries' stake in Asia, whether seen in political or strategic terms, or in the light of concern for the welfare of its poverty-stricken people, is enormous.

In the past, the developed world's direct economic and political interest in Asia was reflected in the colonization of much of the area. The colonies provided the West with resources such as rubber, tea, cotton and jute. Today it is mineral resources which are the main commodities of international exploitation, and with a few exceptions, such as Malaysia and Indonesia, the countries of Asia are relatively poor in mineral resources, especially oil. This lack of resources has been reflected in the pattern of foreign investment (*see* section on Private Investment).

Since the significance of Asia's poverty far outweighs the significance of such natural resources as it possesses, it is not surprising that official economic aid has figured far more prominently than private investment in the flow of capital from the advanced countries. In 1970–73, official aid accounted for 81 per cent of the capital flow to Asia from the developed countries in the Organization for Economic Co-operation and Development (OECD), and the multilateral aid agencies, the other 19 per cent consisting of private investment and private export credits. For all LDCs taken together, official aid accounted for only 42 per cent of total resource flows. However, this pattern is now changing, as private investment in Asia increases and real aid flows decline. In 1974 official aid to Asia accounted for only 70 per cent of total capital flows.

Yet even in official aid the sheer size of Asia has created a challenge which the advanced countries find daunting. Although the area absorbs about half of all official aid from OECD countries, in relation to the size of population, aid to Asia has in recent years been about three-quarters of the world average. This can be partly accounted for by the fact that other countries, notably in Africa, have closer links with one or two major sources of aid, but more conspicuously it is a function of size, for heavily populated countries tend to receive less aid *per capita* than countries with small populations. Within the area, for instance, the small territories of the Pacific region receive nearly thirteen times the world average of aid *per capita*.

In terms of aid, the needs of the South Asian sub-continent overshadow the rest of Asia, just as Asia overshadows the rest of the world. India and Pakistan were the first countries to attain their independence in the post-war dismantlement of empires. India was the first of the less developed countries to be the object of a concentrated international exercise aimed at promoting development, the India Consortium. Theories of development, at the levels both of scholarship and of applied policy, tend to be conditioned by reference to India's experience, and to a lesser extent Pakistan's.

For that reason, a separate section is devoted here to the case of the South Asian sub-continent. For Asia as a whole, however, the most conspicuous conditioning factor in the pattern of aid has been, not the challenge of development, but rather the strategic requirements of the main power blocs.

History of Aid to Asia

Until the establishment of the India Consortium in 1958, the link between aid and strategic interests was generally accepted as a natural one, so that countries which received aid in the early 1950s did so for strategic reasons. From 1948–52 the U.S.A. was preoccupied with European reconstruction under the Marshall Plan, and aid committed to Asia amounted to less than U.S. $800 million, nearly half of which was for Taiwan, for obvious strategic reasons. With the freezing of the Cold War in Europe, Asia became the next field for rivalry between the U.S.A. and the Soviet Union. Extensive U.S. involvement in eastern Asia began with the Korean War, and several Asian countries began to receive aid in large quantities from the U.S.A., and a few in lesser quantities from the Soviet Union, reaching a peak in 1954 and 1955.

A second phase began around 1958, a new peak being accounted for largely by commitments to India and Pakistan. With the establishment of the United

* Except where otherwise stated, Asia is used here to refer to South, South-East and East Asia, excluding China, Japan, North Korea and North Viet-Nam. Australasia refers to the less developed territories of the Pacific, i.e. excluding Australia and New Zealand.

States Agency for International Development in 1961, U.S. aid programmes for a time became more consciously geared to development objectives. At the same time, largely as a result of the establishment of the India and Pakistan consortia, other OECD countries became more deeply involved in aid programmes in the area. Whereas in 1960 only $360 million or 19 per cent of all aid to Asia was contributed by countries other than the U.S.A., by 1967 their share in absolute terms had more than trebled, to $1,124 million or 35 per cent of the total. The inauguration in 1960 of the "Development Decade", and the growing commitment by western countries and international agencies to assisting the "Third World" to meet the challenge of development accelerated this trend for a time.

Yet, despite this lip-service to the challenge of poverty and aid for development, in Asia, more clearly than elsewhere, it is possible to distinguish clearly between countries that have received aid primarily for strategic reasons and countries which have received aid in the broader context of commercial relations and the promotion of economic development.

Table 1 shows the principal recipients of aid from Western donors. South Korea and South Viet-Nam (and Taiwan in the early 1960s) are examples of countries which received aid largely for strategic reasons, and India the most striking example of a country receiving aid for development reasons. Those countries which received aid for non-economic reasons usually received larger quantities of assistance, with a higher proportion of grants, and for a wider range of purposes.

Table 1 also shows that most aid to Asia comes from bilateral sources, but a clue to the character of aid to different countries can be obtained in the figures for multilateral aid. Multilateral agencies account for 26 per cent of aid to India and 16 per cent of aid to Pakistan, which is an indication of the extent to which aid to these countries is the outcome of a general international concern, rather than any specific national interest, whereas those countries, e.g. South Korea, South Viet-Nam and Laos, which received aid for more strategic reasons, were aided negligibly by multilateral agencies.

The initial concentration on the developmental objectives of aid was relatively short-lived. The

Table 1

Net receipts by Asian recipients* of bilateral Official Development Assistance† from OECD member countries and resources at concessional terms from multilateral agencies‡ 1969–74.

	1969 & 1970		1971 & 1972		1973 & 1974		1969–74
	Bi-lateral ($ U.S. million)	Multi-lateral ($ U.S. million)	Bi-lateral ($ U.S. million)	Multi-lateral ($ U.S. million)	Bi-lateral ($ U.S. million)	Multi-lateral ($ U.S. million)	Average§ *per capita* ($ U.S.)
India . . .	1,506	219	1,292	314	1,059	825	1·5
Pakistan	675	72	635	81	492	146	5·5
Bangladesh .			208	24	649	253	
Indonesia	765	28	995	90	1,054	184	4·3
South Korea	596	16	657	33	483	52	9·6
Laos . . .	134	2	136	2	130	2	22·7
Philippines .	117	8	220	13	346	22	3·1
Thailand	133	9	105	10	118	10	1·8
South Viet-Nam	897	4	1,026	5	1,114	3	26·7
Papua New Guinea	264	2	329	9	450	7	70·4
Others	704	76	994	100	1,493	113	—
TOTAL . . .	5,837	436	6,597	681	7,388	1,617	
WORLD TOTAL .	11,277	1,564	12,943	2,108	15,365	3,614	

* South, South-East and East Asia, and Oceania, excluding Australia, China, Japan, New Zealand, North Korea and North Viet-Nam.

† Official Development Assistance (ODA) is all flows to LDCs which: (*a*) are administered with the promotion of economic development and welfare as its main objective; (*b*) are concessional in character, and contain a grant element of at least 25 per cent.

‡ I.D.A., agencies of the UN family and the European Development Fund.

§ Based on UN 1972 mid-year estimates.

Source: Development Co-operation, Efforts and Policies of the Members of the Development Assistance Committee, 1973, 1974 and 1975 Reviews, OECD, 1973, 1974 *and* 1975.

combination of specific Asian events and a growing disillusionment among donors and recipients as to the effects of aid programmes (see below) meant that by the mid-1960s the developmental impetus of aid programmes was fading.

The difficulties experienced by India in achieving its Third Five Year Plan, followed by the 1965 war with Pakistan, led to the growing disillusionment, and the trend was accelerated by the increasing military commitment of the U.S.A. in Viet-Nam, which turned attention back to earlier strategic perspectives. The war in Indochina made it difficult to plan long term development in the region (and also brought dollars to some countries, notably Thailand and South Korea, in such large quantities that official aid became less significant).

What started under President Johnson's administration as annoyance with the behaviour of the recipients of U.S. aid developed, under President Nixon's administration, into a more general loss of interest in aid as a major instrument of policy. From 1966 onwards, the advocates of aid in the U.S. were increasingly on the defensive. In an attempt to sustain the credibility of aid, they shifted their case. The emphasis was no longer on the challenge of development, the long-term needs of the world's poorer countries, but on what had already been achieved, the "success stories", the places where U.S. aid, administered in large doses during an earlier period when the climate for aid had been more favourable, had yielded observable results. India and Pakistan ceded pride of place in the propaganda of U.S. aid to Taiwan and South Korea.

These success stories can be explained largely by the large quantities of assistance received, often with a high proportion of grants, given primarily for non-economic reasons. But large quantities of aid received for strategic purposes have not necessarily contributed to a real alleviation of poverty amongst those sections of the population in greatest need, or to a more equitable distribution of income, and success has tended to be measured simply in terms of crude economic growth. (For further discussion, see section below on the Aid Relationship).

The loss of impetus in aid programmes was not universal. In some Western countries support for aid remained relatively strong, and their programmes continued to expand. Among Asia's principal Western sources of aid, only the U.S.A., Australia, Canada and Japan have attached a high priority to Asia in the distribution of their aid. The reasons differ. In the case of the U.S.A., the concentration is the result of a strategic commitment in East Asia together with a more general commitment in India and Pakistan. Australia is heavily committed in Papua New Guinea, while Canada has always concentrated its aid on the South Asian sub-continent.

Since the mid-1960s Japan has become an important supplier of foreign capital to Asia. In 1973 89 per cent of its overseas development aid (ODA) went to Asia, mostly South-East Asia. The Asian aid programme grew from its reparation payments after World War II and was based on Japan's general foreign policy aim of establishing its Asian identity, and the economic aim of expanding trade relations. However, this outflow does not indicate any great altruism. Only a very small percentage of its total outflow has been ODA, (15 per cent in 1973), and a higher than average proportion has been private investment and export credits on hard commercial terms. Most of this aid has been for specific projects, and directed towards industry and trade development, very little going to social infrastructure and welfare projects. Furthermore, the impact of the oil crisis on Japan's balance of payments and the slowing of its rapid economic growth has retarded Japan's aid performance in recent years. After a record total outflow (i.e. including private flows) of about $5,500 million in 1973, net flows to developing countries fell in 1974 to less than $3,000 million. Japan's foreign investment, and therefore its foreign aid programme, has shown a marked decline, and also a reallocation, particularly towards Latin America, so that Asian countries are likely to attract less Japanese resources in the future.

The expansion in the 1960s in the aid programmes of the smaller donors, such as Sweden and Canada, which were anxious to identify a role for themselves separate from that of the major donors, gave developing countries in Asia some opportunity to exploit the differences between the aid programmes of individual donors. The smaller donors, which have relatively little interest in the maintenance of spheres of influence, have been for the most part inclined to give Asia the priority that would seem appropriate in relation to its poverty and the size of its population. But the decline of U.S. participation in what had once been known as the "common aid effort" meant that the notion of a world-wide programme of action was now difficult to sustain.

In the late 1960s and early 1970s, as donors became more sceptical of aid programmes and increasingly disillusioned, so their economic self-interest became a more important consideration in their aid allocations. Aid tended to be given to those countries which provided raw materials to the donor countries, and potential markets for their goods, and which were hospitable to Western private investment.

Countries such as Malaysia and Indonesia acquired the status which Taiwan and South Korea had held in the mid-1960s, with the added advantage, for aid agencies, that aid to these countries could be defended at home in terms of a commercial interest in large potential markets. This was particularly true of the expanding Japanese aid programme in Asia.

Although in the early 1970s there seemed to be the likelihood of some reorientation of aid programmes, back to real development objectives, with an emphasis on aiding the very poorest communities (*see* section on The Aid Relationship), by 1973 and 1974 the international aid situation seemed to reach a turning point. There was a growing feeling that after years of development effort, little progress had been achieved, and in 1974 ODA represented only 0.35 per cent of the total GNP of Development Assistance

Committee (DAC) members, which was well below the target of 0.7 per cent to which donor countries had earlier subscribed, and even below their 1960 performance.

Then, upon this scene of disillusionment and belt-tightening came the oil crisis and subsequent world-wide inflation and recession, affecting both developed and developing countries. This at first served to accelerate the tendency to reduce aid programmes; then the World Bank and other international bodies pointed out that many LDCs would be the most seriously affected countries by the quadrupling of oil prices, combined with a crisis in world foodgrain supplies. Therefore a number of international initiatives were taken to help the most seriously affected developing countries with the additional problems they faced. The UN identified a list of most seriously affected countries, and some additional emergency aid has been committed by DAC members to these countries, while the UN has established an Emergency Fund to help them meet the higher oil and commodity prices. Asian countries included on this list are India, Pakistan, Bangladesh, Sri Lanka and Laos. In addition, the International Monetary Fund (IMF) made arrangements in 1974 to borrow about 3,000 million dollars under the newly created Oil Facility to help both developed and developing countries finance their increased oil import bills.

Since the oil price rise there has been a big increase in lending to LDCs from the oil-producing countries. The Organisation of Petroleum Exporting Countries (OPEC) concessionary aid commitments in 1974 were $5,300 million, and actual concessionary transfers were $2,200 million (source: DAC). Additional resources were also channelled to LDCs through the IMF and World Bank on non-concessional terms. OPEC assistance, however, is characterized by a marked geographical concentration. In 1974 almost two-thirds of its bilateral commitments went to Arab countries, and 90 per cent to Arab and other Muslim countries. Concentration is on Egypt, Syria and Jordan. In Asia Pakistan was the principal beneficiary of OPEC aid, with India, Bangladesh and Sri Lanka also receiving some assistance.

So far we have not discussed the assistance received by Asian countries from the Soviet Union, other East European countries, and China. Detailed figures on aid from the centrally planned economies are not included, because of the difficulty in obtaining compatible and current figures. The principal Asian recipient of Soviet aid is Viet-Nam, but India, Bangladesh and Pakistan have also received assistance. In 1973 India received a large food aid loan of 2 million tons of wheat from the U.S.S.R., and Bangladesh received a commitment of $28 million, and Pakistan of $210 million. Bangladesh also received some emergency assistance from other East European countries, which have also aided Burma, Nepal and Sri Lanka. In the Sukarno era Indonesia received substantial quantities of assistance from the U.S.S.R., but following the assumption of power by the Suharto regime this programme was suspended. Recently, however, there have been signs that the Soviet Union has joined the large number of Western donors now assisting Indonesia. The U.S.S.R. it to finance most of the expected $100 million cost of two dams and hydro-electric stations in Indonesia, one of the few big aid programmes from the U.S.S.R. to South-East Asia in recent years.

China's aid programme, which started in 1953, was originally limited to communist countries, and particularly aimed at reconstruction in North Korea and North Viet-Nam. The first non-communist countries to receive Chinese aid, amounting to about $50 million, were Cambodia, Indonesia and Nepal in 1956. After that, Chinese assistance dropped sharply until the early 1960s, but disbursements rose considerably in the late 1960s and early 1970s. Viet-Nam remains the principal Asian recipient, but Laos, Pakistan and Sri Lanka have also received some commitments in the 1970s. About half China's aid is project assistance, the rest going towards budget support, relief, and to adjust trade deficits with China. Chinese aid has been on generous financial terms, in the form of long-term interest-free loans, with grant elements usually varying between 75 and 85 per cent.

The Aid Relationship

To understand the growing disillusionment and scepticism on the part of both aid donors and recipients, we must look briefly at some of the issues in the aid relationship.

Aid has rarely been given for solely humanitarian and altruistic reasons. We have seen that aid programmes in Asia expanded initially under the impetus of strategic considerations. Although later they came to be oriented more towards development objectives, all aid programmes have taken into account the self-interest of donors. Where there have not been direct political strings involved, aid programmes have usually taken account of the donor's economic interests, to a greater or lesser degree, as well as the developmental objectives of the assistance.

Thus a major consideration has been the donor's own balance of payments position, and for this reason aid has been increasingly given in the form of loans rather than grants. While the assistance given to Eastern Asia for strategic purposes in the early 1960s was largely in the form of grants, later there was a general trend to move from grants to loans. By 1965 the loan element in bilateral aid to Asia and Australasia had risen to 42 per cent, compared with less than 10 per cent in the early 1950s. This set a pattern of aid giving which was later to give rise to the large debt burden of many developing countries, which has become a major concern for both donors and recipients. As the percentage of loans increased, so did the stringency of the terms on which aid was lent. European and Japanese loans bore interest at nearly commercial rates, and as U.S. aid increased, so did the interest rate on its loans, from 0.75 per cent to 2.5 per cent.

The advent of additional sources of aid enhanced the flow, but it also multiplied the problems. As well as the change from grants to loans and the increasing interest rates, the real cost to recipients of these loans was raised still further by the increasing frequency with which donors, in order to promote their commercial interests, tied their loans to their own goods and services, and to specific projects. By tying loans to goods and services they not only increased the cost of aid by denying recipients access to cheaper suppliers, but they have also contributed to the distortion of many of the economies of LDCs, by encouraging the use of inappropriate technology, and in turn made a considerable contribution to the unemployment problem in LDCs, which has been a major cause of concern in recent years.

As aid agencies became more sceptical of the results they were achieving they became more selective, in terms both of the countries they aided and of the activities they were prepared to finance. There was a shift away from general support for a development plan towards aid for specific projects, and there was increasing urgency in the demand for quick and visible results. This further aided the distortion of many recipient economies by the concentration on large-scale, visible projects, usually benefiting the more urban, industrialized sections of the population. It also meant that such results were more likely to be achieved in countries which were already relatively developed, or which had exploitable natural resources, or which were pursuing policies that were aiming at a rapid increase in output, without much concern for more fundamental changes in the structure of society or for the distribution of the benefits of development.

An early manifestation of this approach was the aid donors' support for the industrialization policies of Pakistan. These policies failed to improve the distribution of income, especially between East and West Pakistan, and the subsequent break-up of Pakistan threw some doubt on the desirability of the policies pursued in Pakistan in the 1960s. It is possible to see some analogies between the policies pursued in Indonesia in the 1970s and those in Pakistan in the 1960s. In Indonesia, as previously in Pakistan, there is serious unemployment and income maldistribution existing side by side with accelerating economic growth and increased foreign exchange earnings, largely as the result of the income from oil exploration and extraction. Yet, because of this growth, and because of the wealth of Indonesia's resources, aid money is flowing into Indonesia, with little heed to the likely long-term consequences of the country's particular economic policies.

Thus the growing strain in the relations between Asian countries and their sources of aid from the mid-1960s on was not just the result of specific Asian events, but also a reflection of a worldwide deterioration in the climate for aid. Throughout the world there was a growing scepticism on the part of the providers of aid and a growing frustration on the side of the recipients.

For a time, disillusionment with dependence on external assistance led to a certain consolidation of Asian relationships. A conspicuous initiative was the creation, in 1966, of the Asian Development Bank (ADB), but its dependence on external funds, especially Japanese, has prevented it from becoming an operational focus of Asian co-operative relationships. In the early 1970s its pace of lending increased substantially, and in 1974 the Asian Development Fund was established as a vehicle for the Bank's concessional lending. But the rate of disbursement has lagged behind loan commitments, and the Bank, because of the insufficiency of its soft resources, continues to direct most of its lending towards the more prosperous countries, and for commercially viable projects. Thus South Korea and the Philippines, followed by Pakistan and Malaysia, have been the major beneficiaries of ADB loans.

We have said that in the early 1970s, before the oil crisis, there was some evidence that the attitude of aid givers was undergoing another change, exhibiting a concern to identify the results of aid in terms of relief of poverty, rather than crude measures of economic growth.

Among the developing countries of Asia, there were three main reactions to this new approach. There were some countries, notably India, in which the policy-makers were by now so bored or disillusioned with aid that this latest quirk in the donors' fancy passed almost unnoticed. At the other extreme, a few countries, notably Indonesia, took their cue, as Pakistan had done in the 1960s, and presented policies and programmes designed to meet the new fashion. But in these and most other countries there were some administrators who understood what had happened, and who had realized that aid had become a marginal resource, to be used selectively for a few specific tasks within their general policy frameworks.

In any case, this new direction was quickly overshadowed by the economic crisis, which brought in a new set of considerations. Further, major concern now centred on the enormous debt burden of the developing countries, for the debt problem was accentuated by the energy crisis and the consequent inflation, so that this problem has come increasingly to dominate international discussion on aid and development. At the end of 1973 the LDC's outstanding debt (including undisbursed*) exceeded $118,893 million. This debt problem stems from the accumulation of external borrowing by the LDCs. Not all of it results from concessional aid, but 37 per cent of the total disbursed debt is bilateral debt resulting from ODA loans by DAC countries. Table 2 shows the relatively high percentage of debt resulting from official bilateral and multilateral aid, and indicates that for most of these Asian countries only a relatively small percentage is due to suppliers' credit, bank and other commercial borrowing.

The large outstanding debt of many countries, resulting now in annual debt service payments which in some cases exceed current aid inflows, is thus a major international concern. The case for aid of course should rest on a country's poverty rather than its indebtedness, and the limited amount of concessional aid that is available should not be used to help

* i.e. debt on loans committed, but not yet disbursed.

Table 2

External Public debt (including undisbursed) Outstanding of Selected Asians Countries, as of December 31st 1973.

(U.S. $ millions)

	Total	Bilateral Official	Multi-lateral
Indonesia	6,616·4	5,008·3	626·9
South Korea	4,413·1	1,974·0	736·8
Malaysia	1,119·6	301·0	498·7
Philippines	1,376·2	616·3	478·9
Bangladesh	835·5	347·7	259·1
India	12,365·8	8,535·0	3,387·3
Pakistan	5,151·2	3,594·9	947·6

Source: World Bank, *Annual Report 1975*, p. 92.

the more prosperous countries with their indebtedness. But for the poorer LDCs, experiencing debt problems, of which India is the outstanding example, the debt problem is an indication of the need for increased concessional flows, including debt relief.

India and Pakistan

In the early 1950s India, with only marginal resort to aid, embarked on a prolonged effort to promote planned development, in accordance with the "socialist" principles prescribed in its constitution. India's effort was widely admired, but the extent to which this effort called for help from the advanced countries was not perceived until 1957, when a foreign exchange crisis forced the government to seek international assistance from the countries which were its principal short-term creditors. The consolidation and refinancing arrangements which resulted led to the establishment of what became known as the India consortium.

When the India consortium was established it was not envisaged as a long-term operation. At independence, India had inherited large sterling balances accumulated during the Second World War. It was able to finance the comparatively small foreign exchange cost of the First Five-Year Plan (1951–56) by drawing on reserves, through normal commercial channels, and from its export earnings in the boom which followed the outbreak of the Korean War.

The second Five-Year Plan (1956–61) was a more ambitious exercise, which included a rapid building-up of Indian heavy industry, especially the steel industry. Three steel mills were to be built, one at Bhilai, by the U.S.S.R., one at Rourkela by the Germans, and one at Durgapur, by the British. It was intended that the construction of these plants should be phased, but varying delays in negotiations resulted in their being started more or less at the same time.

In 1957–58, the second year of the plan, India ran into a foreign exchange crisis, as a result of which it had to seek help from the governments of its main creditors. Temporary alleviation was arranged, and in August 1958, the World Bank convened a meeting attended by Canada, the Federal Republic of Germany, Japan, the U.K. and the U.S.A. for further discussions on India's foreign exchange situation. That meeting, convened on an ad hoc basis, subsequently came to be considered the first meeting of the India Consortium.

By the third meeting of the group, in September 1960, it was already taking a more long-term view, as it turned to consideration of India's requirements in the period of the third Five-Year Plan (1961–66). Gradually a procedure was evolved, under which the group held two meetings a year, one to review progress, and another to offer "pledges", or provisional offers, of aid. These pledges were then the subject of detailed negotiation, commitment, and ultimately disbursement.

The Pakistan Consortium, established in 1960, took more or less the same form as the India Consortium. Indeed, the main reason for establishing it was to avoid the appearance of discriminating in India's favour. Although the new regime of President Ayub Khan was bringing some sort of order to Pakistan's economy, it was generally thought that Pakistan's economic prospects were dim, when compared with India's.

By the middle of Pakistan's second Five-Year Plan (1960–65), the country's apparent economic performance had improved dramatically, and interest in the consortium quickened. As a result, aid to Pakistan during the period of the second plan increased at an annual rate of nearly 30 per cent.

In both countries, technical assistance has been relatively unimportant, but they have received large quantities of American surplus commodities under PL 480*. From 1956 to 1962 India received (excluding gifts) under PL 480 about 65 million tons of U.S. farm products, valued at about $4,800 million. The amounts actually disbursed from all OECD sources and multilateral agencies up until 1970 are shown in Table 3.

It will be seen that India, with nearly five times the population of Pakistan, received approximately two and a half times as much aid. During the period of the second plan, Pakistan's industrial output doubled, and this rapid increase is generally attributed in large measure to the fact that aid *per capita* to Pakistan was twice as large as aid to India.

The early 1960s saw the rapid evolution of the two consortia, so that aid was flowing fairly smoothly to the two countries and in increasing quantities. But by 1964 it was clear that India's Third Five-Year Plan was in trouble, and that India was getting into grave economic difficulty.

* *PL* 480. Under Public Law 480, enacted in 1954, the U.S.A. provides commodities drawn from its agricultural surpluses. The bulk of PL 480 shipments are sold to the recipient for local currencies. A small proportion of the proceeds is reserved for U.S. overseas expenditure and for loans to American and other foreign private investors, but the larger part is made available in grants and loans to the recipient country. Since 1966, the U.S.A. has made a growing proportion of PL 480 loans repayable in dollars. The programme has also been known as "Food for Peace" and "Food for Freedom".

Table 3

Official aid to India and Pakistan (disbursements*) from OECD members and multilateral agencies, *1960–70*.†
(U.S. $ million)

	India			Pakistan		
	Bilateral	Multilateral	Total	Bilateral	Multilateral	Total
1960 . . .	736	45	781	254	8	262
1961 . . .	620	43	663	252	14	266
1962 . . .	667	61	728	378	15	393
1963 . . .	903	70	973	483	22	505
1964 . . .	1,113	88	1,201	494	24	518
1965 . . .	1,083	204	1,287	454	69	523
1966 . . .	1,082	144	1,226	342	70	412
1967 . . .	1,143	207	1,350	426	107	533
1968 . . .	908	96	1,004	397	98	495
1969 . . .	718	125	843	300	73	373
1970 . . .	749	56	805	385	80	465
Total . .	9,722	1,139	10,861	4,165	580	4,745

*** Official grants and loans, and gifts in kind, net of amortization and of contributions to multilateral agencies by India and Pakistan though figures include some Indus Basin disbursements.**

† N.B. These figures are not compatible with those in Table 1.

Source: DAC Statistics.

Then in 1965, Pakistan's growing friendliness with China, and the outbreak of hostilities over Kashmir, led to the suspension of American aid. In a deteriorating international climate for aid, the war was taken as evidence of the developing countries' "irresponsibility".

For a time the consortia did not meet, and when they were reconvened, the cumulative effect of the war, the failure of India's Third Plan, and poor harvests in both countries following the failure of the monsoon in two successive years, had sufficiently undermined the donors' confidence that a return to the old procedures was impossible. The character of consortium meetings changed. The abandonment of formal pledging, with published figures, took the emphasis away from the flow of aid, leaving both consortia rather less certain of their *raison d'être*. With the discipline of formal pledging procedures removed, the effectiveness of the consortium as a fund-raising mechanism declined, as can be seen from the later disbursement figures in Table 3. The U.S. aid programme never recovered its former position as the solid centre of the western aid effort in South Asia. Total disbursements to South Asia, measured in current prices, fell by nearly 20 per cent between 1965 and 1969, and in terms of the net transfer of resources (i.e. minus repayments) the 1969 level was nearly 40 per cent less than that of 1965. In real terms the difference would be even greater.

The aid requirements in India's fourth Plan, which came into effect in April 1969, were in the order of $5,000 million, an average of $1,000 million a year. Against this, aid commitments for the years 1969–70 and 1970–71 totalled $1,655.87 million, with some donors exhibiting a desire to go back to the old emphasis on project lending.

Later, in 1971, following the clash between East and West Pakistan, resulting in the formation of Bangladesh, the tide turned temporarily in India's favour, the collapse of Pakistan putting India's political process into relatively favourable light. However, India's relations with the U.S.A., due to America's pro-Pakistan stance, remained cool, leading to a reluctance by India to ask for further PL 480 assistance.

The victory of the Indian National Congress in the Indian elections of 1971 brought about a revival of interest in the remarkable survival of Indian democracy. For the year beginning April 1973 the consortium members agreed on a target of $700 million for non-project assistance, including debt relief, and $500 million project assistance.

But "later" was too late. It might have been possible for the Government of India to exploit its position, by playing some sort of diplomatic game of persuasion, but it had played that game once, in 1966, and lost, and it was not going to try again. India's major concern now is not aid as such, but to secure an adequate net flow of resources in the face of a mounting debt-service burden. While there had been a positive net aid in the 1960s, by the 1970s the balance was falling rapidly. Total external debt outstanding at the end of 1973 stood at $12,365.8 million, and the ratio of debt-service to export earnings was over 30 per cent. Although India received over $400 million in debt relief from 1966–67 to 1970–71, even on the most optimistic of assumptions it was clear that the amount of aid would be no more than sufficient to enable India to scrape through. The lesson drawn by India's planners was that never again could they be, or should they be, as dependent on aid as they had been in the 1960s.

Yet, while declaring its intention, in the preparatory document for the Fifth Plan, of reducing the net flow of aid to zero by 1980, India has, despite its wariness of aid, been forced into a new reliance on it, due largely to the effect of petroleum price increases. The relatively buoyant economic trends of South-East Asia in the early 1970s contrasted sharply with events in much of South Asia, and for the Indian subcontinent, where the economic base is so small relative to energy needs, the impact of the new oil prices has been disastrous. All countries except Nepal were placed on the UN's list of countries most seriously affected by the economic events of the early 1970s.

India, which is relatively highly industrialized, and whose agricultural sector requires large quantities of chemical fertilizer, has had an enormously increased import bill. Poor monsoons affecting the harvest in 1972 and again in 1975 has meant that India, with Bangladesh, Pakistan and Sri Lanka, has had to make large food purchases. India's foreign exchange reserves have been left barely adequate to meet emergencies. At the same time, world demand for India's (and Bangladesh's and Sri Lanka's) main traditional exports, tea and jute, has been depressed for more than a decade. India has received some assistance from OPEC countries, and by 1975 had received commitments of $835 million from Iran and $110 million from Iraq, although disbursement of these amounts has been rather slow. In late 1975 India also sought to borrow an initial $200 million from IMF's newly established oil facility fund.

The June 1975 Declaration of Emergency by Indira Gandhi had a considerable impact on India's foreign relations. The Soviet reaction was to strengthen its already strong ties with India and to back the State of Emergency, while there was little official reaction from Western countries, although the move was extremely unpopular with the Western press. Although the cancellation of President Ford's visit to India in late 1975 was an indication of disapproval, the Declaration of Emergency as yet seems to have had little effect on India's aid relations.

The Soviet Union, although not a member of the India Consortium, began increasing economic, technical and military aid to India in the mid-1950s, but in the mid-1960s maintained as neutral a position as possible between India and Pakistan in order to limit China's growing influence in Pakistan. During the events of 1971 the U.S.S.R.'s support for India was clearly indicated and, although U.S. aid to India far outweighs Soviet aid, in trade, the Soviet Union has become India's second most important export market.

After the events of 1971 Pakistan, too, faced a rising debt problem, and in April 1971 sought a major postponement of its repayments. But foreign assistance to Pakistan in the early 1970s failed to reach the estimated and desired level. Partially this was due to the realization by the donors that past aid policies had, by mainly assisting development in West Pakistan, exacerbated the differences between East and West Pakistan that had led to the war, and partially it was a result of reaction to that war. But Pakistan has been a major beneficiary of OPEC aid, because of its traditional close religious links with the Persian Gulf countries.

Bangladesh

Although the Bengali opponents of Ayub Khan and Yahya Khan claimed that foreign aid served West Pakistan's interests, the development strategy of Bangladesh has, since its inception, relied heavily on foreign aid for its fulfilment.

The needs of reconstruction after the war of 1971 awakened in donors a particular motivation for aid: the single perception of immediate and desperate need. The urgent need to relieve the plight of the refugees in India and the distress of the people in Bangladesh resulted in a mammoth international relief operation. By the end of 1974 about $2,000 million* in aid had been committed, a considerable quantity of which was food aid for immediate famine relief. India initially contributed the bulk of assistance, followed by the U.S.A. and considerable assistance from the Soviet Union. By the middle of 1974 dependence on foreign aid for development expenditure had increased from a projected 66 per cent to 75 per cent. Yet there were signs that this "emergency" aid was drying up, and foreign exchange reserves were very low. Then the floods of August 1974 led to a new inflow of relief aid, and Bangladesh sought $317.5 million in foreign exchange to meet the immediate needs of flood and food relief.

While the need for aid in Bangladesh was obvious, the response to it has been overcast by doubt about the effects of past aid. Many economists in the Bangladesh government were aware of the pitfalls of aid but the overwhelming need meant that they were prepared to try again. But the attempt has not been without a price. While vast amounts of much needed assistance were received, and there was much honest and humanitarian relief work done in Bangladesh, aid there has also provided a source of much corruption, and has led to allegations of misappropriation and personal fortune making. Then in November 1974 Bangladesh agreed, after more than two years of resistance, to the formation of a multilateral consortium. Having previously wished to avoid what it considered a greater exercise of foreign economic leverage through a consortium approach, the 1974 floods and consequent foreign exchange crisis, food shortages and famine, forced Bangladesh to concede to donor terms. Through the consortium Bangladesh obtained commitments for over $1,000 million for 1975, but in return had to make concessions to the IMF request for a stabilization programme.

Bangladesh has also received some assistance from the oil producing countries, through both bilateral aid and the IMF oil facility. In early 1975 the United

* There is considerable variation in the estimated amounts of aid committed to or received by Bangladesh. Some estimate total commitments to be as high as $3,500 million. Table 1 indicates that the amount received from DAC sources only by the end of 1974 was just over $1,000 million. It can be assumed that commitments from all sources are considerably higher, and may well be over $2,000 million.

Arab Emirates offered Bangladesh a package of "soft" loans, project assistance, and oil. Of the $70 million loan offered, $50 million is to be unrestricted balance of payments support and plans have been drawn up for collaboration on cement and fertilizer factories to be built in Bangladesh.

The future of Bangladesh's aid programme, in the light of the August 1975 coup, and the changing international aid climate, remains a question mark, along with that of the rest of Asia.

The future of aid to Asia

Doubts about the future of foreign aid, scepticism of donors, and cynicism of recipients, dominate the international aid situation in the mid-1970s.

In Asia, as elsewhere, there are many administrators who would like to be able to disregard aid. But the continuation of great poverty in some countries, compounded by the energy crisis, the debt problem, and the needs of reconstruction in many parts of Asia, means that while the prospects of aid to Asia are not auspicious, the desire for aid, and the need for it, have not disappeared. There are few developing countries in Asia which would not take the necessary steps to get considerably more aid, in the hope of achieving more development, if only they could find it.

In Indo-China the need for reconstruction is clear, but the extent of Western preparation to assist in that process, or the desire to seek it, is as yet uncertain. Resources will be needed, but will the regimes be prepared to pay the price of renewed foreign intervention? In Bangladesh the need for reconstruction continues, but how long will the western powers continue to assist that effort with high levels of assistance?

In Indonesia foreign powers are competing to gain access to the country's mineral resources, and this is reflected in Indonesia's current sizable aid receipts. How long will it be before donors match their words with their actions, and ensure that their aid programmes really concentrate on, and their benefits really reach, the poorest populations, and don't simply help the rich get richer? In India, more than anywhere, aid administrators are aware of the pitfalls of aid and the need to rely on it only as a marginal resource. While it is unlikely that India will figure largely in the evolution of future aid programmes, its debt burden and the economic setbacks that resulted from the oil crisis means it will be some time before India can finally manage without the Western aid donors, or before the donors should abandon India.

Foreign Private Investment

There is some connection between the evolution of attitudes to aid in Asia and attitudes to foreign private investment. In the aftermath of independence, the bulk of foreign investment was in plantations and commerce. This preponderance was generally unacceptable to newly independent countries, and for several years foreign investment was regarded at best as an irrelevance, a remnant of imperial rule which would, in the nature of things, decline. By far the largest investor in Asia was the United Kingdom.

In the late 1950s some developed countries began to pursue investment opportunities in developing countries. This was particularly true of the U.S.A., the Federal Republic of Germany and Japan, countries which were also prominent in the rapid expansion of aid. From about 1966, the deteriorating climate for official aid led some developing countries to reconsider private investment as a possible alternative, or at least as another means of promoting development. Attitudes towards foreign private investment have continued to vary between countries and over time.

Experience of aid had taught the developing countries of Asia the need to be selective in private investment as well as aid. In some countries, with India as a notable example, the need for some foreign investment in some sectors was admitted, but this admission was made so reluctantly, and so hedged with restrictions, that there has been comparatively little large-scale investment.

In fact throughout the 1960s Asia was a relatively insignificant recipient of foreign private investment. This was largely due to the lack of natural resources in that area, and partially due to the negative attitude of the Asian countries themselves in that period. At the end of 1967, according to an OECD estimate, the value of accumulated foreign investments in developing countries was approximately $35,000 million (DAC *Annual Review*, 1973). Approximately 14 per cent of this was in developing countries of Asia and Australasia (excluding the Middle East). Investment in Asia ($5,000 million) was less than in Africa ($6,600 million), and less than a third of investment in Latin America and the Caribbean ($18,000 million). Something approaching half the accumulated foreign investment in Asia were British. The next largest investor was the U.S.A., with approximately a third. But in the newer sectors Japan and the Federal Republic of Germany were rapidly becoming significant.

But in the late 1960s and early 1970s Asia received an increasing amount of investment. In 1973 the stock of direct investments in Asia had risen to $10,500 million, or 18 per cent of the total ($58,200 million) foreign investment in developing countries (DAC *Annual Review*, 1975).

Table 4 shows this increasing investment and the change in the sectoral distribution of it.

The rather small proportion of foreign investment in the petroleum industry from 1965 to 1968, and the very small proportion in mining, are partially explained by the relative absence of foreign capital in India's petroleum and iron ore industries, and by the fact that Indonesia's potential resources had not yet been fully exploited. The large proportion of foreign investment in other industries consists largely of British plantation interests in South Asia and West Malaysia.

By the late 1960s and early 1970s there had been an increase in investment in all sectors, and direct investment flows were fast catching up with those in Latin America. This increase is partially accounted for by the increase in petroleum mining in Indonesia and

Table 4

Sectoral distribution of total DAC direct investment in Asia and Australasia, 1965–72; annual average flows. (U.S. $ million)

	Petroleum*	Mining	Manufacturing	Other	Total
1965 and 1966:					
Asia and Australasia	62	28	129	117	336
World Total	751	223	945	588	2,507
1967 and 1968:					
Asia and Australasia	92	37	185	99	413
World Total	734	305	942	530	2,511
1969 and 1970:					
Asia and Australasia	155	104	147	68	474
World Total	1,240	138	1,133	547	3,058
1971 and 1972:					
Asia and Australasia	567	125	363	236	1,291
World Total	1,382	267	1,572	1,029	4,250

* Including natural gas.

Source: Development Co-operation, Efforts and Policies of the Members of the Development Assistance Committee, 1973 Review, OECD, 1973.

Malaysia, but also by the growing investment throughout Asia in industries involving the processing of labour intensive components, for example, electronics.

Malaysia is still a major recipient of British private investment, and has been active in recent years in encouraging the expansion of private investment. Similarly Indonesia, where, according to Indonesian figures, the inflow of foreign capital increased from $17 million in 1969 to $137 million in 1970.

The overall increase can also be accounted for by the more favourable climate for such investment prevalent in much of Asia in the early 1970s. Recently there has been an expansion of new forms of private investment, such as joint ventures. In the oil sector, the more traditional concessional agreements are gradually being replaced by production sharing agreements, a development which has allowed the co-operation of foreign capital in countries not otherwise willing to accept direct foreign investment in the traditional form, for example, India and Burma. But the increase can be accounted for mainly by the expansion of Japanese private investment, especially in South-East Asia. Japanese private investments rose from $204 million in 1972 to $1,301 million in 1973. In 1972–73 Japan invested about $320 million in Indonesia, $259 million in South Korea, and $93 million in Malaysia. 1973 was marked by the establishment of many textile and electronic joint ventures by Japanese producers in many Asian countries.

This increase in Japanese investment in Asia has been accompanied by a growing resentment within the Asian countries at the unwillingness of the Japanese companies to take local aspirations and interests into account. In 1974, when the Japanese Prime Minister, Tanaka, toured South-East Asia, he was met in almost every country he visited by large and vocal demonstrations and press comment against Japanese investment policies. In fact, as we have seen, 1974 saw a marked fall in Japanese private investment and aid, and there was an almost complete absence of the establishment of new joint ventures.

The varying investment climate, between countries and over time, has been due to the considerable controversy that exists over the advantages and disadvantages of foreign private investment. Some of the arguments for and against it closely parallel those surrounding aid programmes.

The supporters of private investment claim that it represents an important source of capital and technology, that it may lead to domestic production of goods that would otherwise have to be imported, or to increased exports, and that it provides improved management, so that it makes a major contribution to the development process. The critics of private investment on the other hand argue that it has worsened income distribution between the rich and the poor, both within and between countries, that it has often resulted in transfers of inappropriate technology, or that there is a tendency for foreign investors to import plant and equipment which may be available locally, and that it takes no account of local conditions in a way that will maximize their contribution to the welfare of LDCs.

Host countries are often particularly concerned over the question of the degree to which foreign private investment affects their sovereignty or control over their natural resources and economic activities. They thus seek increasing control, including the right to nationalization and compensation in accord with their own national legislation, and especially the right of supervision of multinational corporations, whose use of transfer pricing as a means of tax evasion is believed to be common, and increasing bargaining power over the flow of direct investments and foreign ownership in their countries so as to enhance their own returns.

The effect of foreign private investment on the balance of payments of the developing countries has long been a subject of controversy. Yet it is clear that foreign investors take more out of a country in terms of profits than they put in in terms of new capital. But this does not necessarily mean that the investment is not beneficial for the host country, for the benefits of foreign investment should be judged not by its contribution to the balance of payments, but by its overall contribution to economic development. But the assessment of the value of such investment to the recipient country in developmental terms is not simple. There is truth on both sides, but the balance of evidence is sufficiently unfavourable, especially in countries suffering from severe unemployment or maldistribution of income, for a cautious attitude to foreign investment to be understandable.

BIBLIOGRAPHY

BRECHER, IRVING and ABBAS, S. A. Foreign Aid and Industrial Development in Pakistan (Cambridge University Press, 1972).

CEYLON, MINISTRY OF FINANCE. External economic assistance: a review from 1950–64, by Dr. N. M. Perera (Colombo: Ec. Aff. Div., Gen. Treasury, 1964).

COLOMBO PLAN BUREAU. Technical Co-operation under the Colombo Plan (annual).

ELDRIDGE, P. L. The Politics of Foreign Aid in India (Weidenfeld and Nicolson, London, 1969).

INDIA, MINISTRY OF FINANCE. External assistance (Delhi, Govt. of India Press, annual). Report of the committee on utilization of external assistance 1964 (Delhi, Govt. of India Press, 1964).

INTERNATIONAL BANK FOR RECONSTRUCTION AND DEVELOPMENT. The World Bank Group in Asia (Washington, June 1967).

JACOBY, NEIL H. A.I.D. Discussion Paper No. 11: (Taiwan): an evaluation of U.S. economic aid to Free China, 1951–65 (Bureau for the Far East Agency for International Development, Washington, 1966).

KIDRON, MICHAEL. Foreign investments in India (Oxford Univ. Press, 1965).

MASON, EDWARD S. Economic development in India and Pakistan: Occasional papers in International Affairs No. 13 (Harvard Univ. Center for International Affairs, 1966).

PAKISTAN, GOVERNMENT. Summary descriptions of projects for the Pakistan Consortium (Karachi, Govt. Print Office, annual).

ORGANIZATION FOR ECONOMIC CO-OPERATION AND DEVELOPMENT. Aid to agriculture in developing countries (OECD, Paris, 1968).

Development Co-operation efforts and policies of the members of the Development Assistance Committee (annual).

Resources for the developing world (the flow of financial resources to less-developed countries 1962–68) (OECD, Paris, 1970).

Geographical distribution of financial flows to less developed countries (disbursements) 1960–64 (OECD, Paris, 1966).

Geographical distribution of financial flows to less developed countries (disbursements) 1965 (OECD, Paris, 1967).

Geographical distribution of financial flows to less-developed countries (disbursements) 1966–67 (OECD, Paris, 1970).

ONSLOW, CRANLEY. Asian Economic Development (London, Trinity Press, 1965).

PEARSON, LESTER B. (*et al.*). Partners in Development, Report of the Commission on International Development (Praeger, N.Y., 1969).

RANIS, GUSTAV. U.S. Aid Policies in Asia; in papers and proceedings of a conference held by the Japan Economic Research Center in January 1968 (Japan Economic Research Center, February 1968).

RAO, V. K. R. V., and NARAIN, DHARM. Foreign aid and India's economic development (London, Asia Publishing House, 1964).

REDDAWAY, W. B. Effects of U.K. direct investment overseas: an interim report; Univ. of Cambridge, Department of Applied Economics Occasional papers 12 (Cambridge Univ. Press, 1967).

UN ECONOMIC COMMISSION FOR ASIA AND THE FAR EAST. Industrial Developments in Asia and the Far East; 4 vols. (UN, New York, 1966).

WHITE, JOHN. Pledged to Development: a study of international consortia and the strategy of aid (Overseas Development Institute, London, 1967).

Japanese Aid (Overseas Development Institute, London, 1964).

Regional Development Banks (espec. Chap. 2. "The Asian Development Bank") (Overseas Development Institute, London, 1970).

ZINKIN, MAURICE and WARD, BARBARA. Why Help India? (Pergamon Press, London, 1963).

Asia's Trade

C. G. F. Simkin

GROWTH IN THE 1960s

(*see* Table 1)

The 1960s was a most favourable decade for world trade. It grew by 10 per cent a year in U.S. dollar value and, reflecting the comparatively mild inflation of the decade, by no less than 9 per cent a year in volume. Asia's overall share of this rapidly expanding trade was also steady at about 11 per cent of world exports and 12 per cent of world imports; the difference was mainly due to foreign aid or capital inflows. Nor, despite formerly influential arguments by such economists as Myrdal and Prebisch, was there any marked shift in the terms of trade between manufactures and primary commodities. For developed countries the annual average improvement in the terms of trade was only 0.5 per cent and this was at the expense of oil exporting countries, whose terms of trade declined by 2 per cent a year during the 1960s. For other developing countries terms of trade also improved but by only 0.5 per cent a year.*

The overall figures conceal important differences between East, South-East and South Asia. East Asia's share of world trade doubled in the 1960s to reach 9 per cent, South-East Asia's share fell from 3.5 to 2 per cent, and South Asia's share fell from 2 to 1 per cent. These figures apply to non-communist countries, but the share of trade for communist Asian countries, excluding trade with one another, also declined from 1.5 per cent of the world total in 1960 to less than 1 per cent in 1970.

The expanding trade of East Asia was dominated by the remarkable economic resurgence of Japan, whose share of world trade doubled to reach 6.5 per cent, about the same as for the United Kingdom. South Korea, Taiwan and Hong Kong, which became, increasingly, subsidiary manufacturing areas for Japan, the United States and Western Europe, about trebled their combined share of both world exports and world imports. In 1970 they accounted for over 2.5 per cent of world trade, although their exports were then only three-quarters of their imports because of aid, capital flows, or invisible trade transactions.

In South-East Asia, the two countries which did relatively best during the 1960s were the Philippines and Thailand, whose combined exports almost doubled in value. Those of Indonesia, Malaysia, and Singapore fell from 2.5 to 1.3 per cent of world exports. South Viet-Nam, Cambodia, and Laos never had more than 0.2 per cent of world exports and, as they became ravaged by war, their combined exports fell from $157 million in 1960 to only $50 million in 1970. Burma's exports also suffered, for different reasons, falling from $226 million to $108 million.

India, of course, dominates the trade of South Asia but its share of world trade halved to become only 0.7 per cent in 1970. The main reason was a relative decline in net aid flows because India's exports rose in value from $1,300 million in 1960 to $2,000 million in 1970, while its imports actually fell from $2,300 million to $2,100 million. Pakistan, including Bangladesh in the 1960s, on the other hand, raised exports from $400 million to $800 million, more rapidly than India, and almost doubled imports to $1,100 million. Sri Lanka was less fortunate: its exports declined, even absolutely, as did its imports. The small landlocked countries, Afghanistan and Nepal, however, became more involved in trade so that their exports almost doubled from a low combined level of $70 million in 1960.

There was little growth in the combined exports of communist Asian countries—China, Mongolia, North Korea and North Viet-Nam—to the rest of the world, but their combined imports rose by about one-third to $3,000 million in 1970. At this level they exceeded corresponding exports by over a quarter, largely because of Soviet and East European aid to North Viet-Nam or, in lesser degree, to Mongolia and North Korea.

CHANGES IN 1970–1975

From 1970 to 1973 there was a strong worldwide boom corresponding to a surge in the annual growth rate of industrial production in advanced countries from 2 to 10 per cent. The volume of world trade increased by two-fifths over its 1969 level, reaching an annual growth rate of 12 per cent. The boom, however, was associated with a price explosion which raised the value of world exports from $246,000 million in 1969 to $525,000 million in 1973, when their prices rose by 24 per cent. In the following year, prices rose still more rapidly by 39 per cent, but the boom was then collapsing. The volume of world exports increased by a more normal 5 per cent in 1974 and fell by 6 per cent in 1975. Their value, after increasing by 46 per cent in 1974, rose by only 4 per cent in 1975.

The big price increase of 1973, and the lesser increases of preceding years, went with rising wages in advanced countries and booming demands for primary products. Towards the end of that year the OPEC cartel quadrupled the price of oil, and improved their terms of trade by 128 per cent in 1974. Industrial countries' terms of trade deteriorated by 12 per cent. Continuing price increases for other primary products improved the terms of trade for non-oil developing countries during 1973 by 6 per cent, but in 1974 they deteriorated by 4 per cent.

All this put severe strain on the mechanism of international payments. In 1974, industrial countries' previous current surplus of $11,000 million changed to a deficit of $10,000 million, and non-oil developing

* International Monetary Fund, *Annual Report*, 1974, p. 19.

countries' deficit of $6,000 million increased to one of $22,000 million. The current account surplus of major oil exporting countries jumped from $6,000 million to $70,000 million, but they lessened strain on other countries by investing abroad something like $34,000 million. During 1975, however, oil prices remained steady, and the trade surplus of oil exporters dropped from $100,000 million to $65,000 million. This change was matched by a fall in the trade deficit of advanced countries from $67,000 million to $37,000 million, but that of non-oil developing countries worsened from $35,000 million to $45,000 million.

The oil crisis and the onset of world recession dramatically broke Japan's long run of exceptional economic growth. This highly industrialized country was a pace-setter during the boom, and its exports more than trebled in value between 1969 and 1974, reaching $56,000 million or 6.6 per cent of the world total. Its imports, however, rose even more rapidly, from 5.8 per cent to 7.3 per cent of world imports, and led to a current account deficit of $4,700 million in 1974. That large deficit coincided with the oil crisis, to which Japan was peculiarly vulnerable as oil was about a fifth of its imports before the OPEC price increase; after it, they reached 34 per cent of imports. The onset of world recession reduced the growth of Japan's real exports from an average rate of 12 per cent for 1970–74, and one of 17 per cent in 1974, to less than 1 per cent in 1975. In that year, the value of merchandise exports did not increase, and that of imports actually fell to reduce the trade deficit from $6,500 million to $2,000 million, or only 4 per cent of merchandise exports.

The small rapidly industrializing countries of East Asia also continued rapid growth up to 1974. Their combined exports rose from $4,800 million in 1970 to $16,000 million in 1974, and their combined imports from $6,400 million to $20,600 million. They, too, were badly affected by leaping oil prices, as mineral fuels were 4.3 per cent of their imports in 1973 but 10.2 per cent in 1974. Taiwan, which had achieved small trade surpluses in 1970 and 1971, and substantial trade surpluses averaging nearly $700 million in the next two years, was plunged into a deficit of $825 million in 1974, equal to a seventh of its exports. But in 1975 this deficit was reduced to $657 million.

South-East Asia's exports quadrupled between 1970 and 1974 to reach $24,000 million or 2.8 per cent of the world total. Imports trebled and almost equalled exports in 1974. But rates of increase were uneven between countries. Indonesia, mainly because of expanding oil output and the 1974 price jump, increased its export receipts from $1,100 million to $7,400 million. Singapore, emulating the industrial development of East Asia, quadrupled its domestic exports and trebled its entrepôt trade. Thailand, gaining from good harvests and rising prices for rice, rubber and tin, also trebled export receipts. For Malaysia and the Philippines the increase was about 150 per cent. South Viet-Nam rather surprisingly increased the value of its exports from $11 million in 1970 to $78 million in 1974, but they sufficed for only a tenth of its imports. Mainly because of an expansion of timber production, Laos raised its exports by half over this period to reach a fifth of imports. Cambodia's exports fell from $39 million in 1970 to $7 million in 1972, and thereafter ceased.

India's exports and imports both doubled in value between 1970 and 1974 but, largely because of oil, its trade balance swung from a modest surplus of $2.2 million in 1972 to a deficit of $1,120 million in 1974. Pakistan trebled its export receipts and achieved an even balance of trade in 1972 and 1973, but in 1974 it had a deficit of $619 million, equal to a third of export receipts. Bangladesh's export receipts, gaining from high prices for jute, rose from $260 million to $358 million in 1973 when they covered two-fifths of imports; but in 1974 export receipts fell a little and imports rose by a quarter. Sri Lanka's export receipts, stationary from 1969 to 1973, increased from $390 million to $521 million in 1974 and imports rose from $423 million to $691 million. Between 1970 and 1974, Afghanistan's exports almost trebled and its imports only doubled; but up to 1973, Nepal's exports were stationary and its imports rose by a sixth. Altogether South Asia's share of world exports declined from 1.0 to 0.6 per cent over these four years and its share of world imports fell from 1.2 to 0.8 per cent.

The share of communist Asian countries also declined from 0.9 per cent of world trade in 1970. By far the greater part of this trade is conducted by China, whose exports rose from $2,100 million in 1970 to $6,300 million in 1974. Most of China's trade has come to be conducted with non-communist countries, and they supplied 87 per cent of its imports during 1974. Japan was the leading partner with 24 per cent of China's total trade, followed by the United States and Hong Kong with shares of 8 and 7 per cent. The Soviet Union's share had shrunk to little more than 2 per cent.

COMPOSITION OF TRADE

Rapid growth of East Asian trade went with marked changes in the commodity composition of exports and, to a lesser extent, in that of its imports (*see* Table 1). As Japan became a major, fully-fledged industrial power, heavy manufactures increased as a proportion of exports from 27 per cent in 1960 to 53 per cent in 1974, and light manufactures declined from 62 to 43 per cent. (At the same time, food and materials declined from 10 to 4 per cent.) Iron and steel, ships, motor vehicles, machines, and electronic products became the country's leading exports, and it was moving to leadership as both a producer and exporter of a wide range of "high-technology" products.

This shift helped smaller East Asian countries to develop labour-intensive industries and become exporters of light industrial goods. Hong Kong, threatened, after China became communist, by loss of the entrepôt trade upon which it had so long depended, built up manufacturing, at first through refugees from Shanghai and other industrial areas of China. By 1960 domestic exports had become three times as large as re-exports, light manufactures are now more than four-fifths of domestic exports, and

Table 1

ASIAN TRADE, 1960–74

	Japan			Other East Asia*			South-East Asia*			South Asia		
	1960	1970	1974	1960	1970	1974	1960	1970	1974	1960	1970	1974
Exports† (U.S. $ million)	4,058	19,318	55,596	886	4,777	15,953	4,600	6,270	24,182	2,179	3,209	6,195
Percentage of world trade	3.2	6.2	6.6	0.6	1.6	1.9	3.6	2.0	2.8	1.7	1.0	0.7
Imports†	4,495	18,881	62,075	1,667	6,417	20,576	4,553	7,990	23,944	3,519	3,769	8,944
Percentage of world trade	3.3	5.8	7.3	1.3	2.0	2.4	3.4	2.4	2.8	2.6	1.2	1.1
Composition of Exports (per cent):												
Food and materials (SITC 0, 1, 2, 4)	10.1	5.5	3.5	28.6	13.9	13.0	78.4	65.0	55.0‡	65.4	56.0	51.6
Mineral fuels (SITC 3)	0.4	0.2	0.5	0.8	0.5	0.8	8.9	15.5	20.6‡	0.8	1.0	0.9
Light manufactures (SITC 6, 8, 9)	62.1	47.1	43.2	62.8	70.3	64.9	9.9	14.2	16.4‡	32.5	38.2	43.0
Heavy manufactures (SITC 5, 7)	27.4	47.2	52.8	7.8	15.3	21.3	2.8	5.3	8.0‡	1.3	4.8	4.4
Composition of Imports (per cent)												
Food and materials (SITC 0, 1, 2, 4)	61.2	49.0	36.2	36.1	30.9	32.3	35.4	21.6	22.1‡	33.2	31.6	33.0
Mineral fuels (SITC 3)	16.5	20.7	40.1	4.9	4.7	10.2	9.4	10.4	10.0‡	7.5	7.4	14.5
Light manufactures (SITC 6, 8, 9)	7.1	13.7	12.5	34.2	30.9	21.4	31.4	29.5	31.2‡	24.3	24.3	20.1
Heavy manufactures (SITC 5, 7)	15.2	16.6	11.2	24.8	33.5	36.1	23.8	38.5	36.7‡	35.0	36.7	32.4
Direction of Exports (per cent) to/from												
Japan				13.0	13.1	16.6	11.0	22.3	30.5	5.1	10.5	10.6
Other Asia	36.3	31.4	24.9	33.7	18.2	18.0	38.4	31.3	29.7	20.1	22.3	24.4
U.S.A.	27.3	31.1	33.6	16.7	38.8	32.1	15.4	17.1	18.6	13.4	12.2	12.1
Western Europe	11.9	15.1	15.9	18.0	18.2	19.4	22.0	17.5	14.1	37.7	26.7	28.2
Eastern Europe	1.6	2.5	2.8	—	—	—	3.8	3.6	2.0	6.4	17.5	12.9
Oceania	4.5	4.2	4.8	3.9	3.3	4.4	3.5	2.8	3.1	4.9	2.8	3.7
Rest of world	18.4	15.7	18.0	14.7	8.4	9.5	5.9	5.4	2.0	12.4	8.0	8.1
Direction of Imports (per cent) from/to												
Japan				20.5	33.6	30.4	13.9	24.6	22.8	6.7	7.3	9.7
Other Asia	30.9	29.7	47.2	28.3	23.5	27.3	43.6	27.2	37.4	20.4	15.9	29.4
U.S.A.	34.6	29.5	20.4	23.0	20.7	20.9	13.6	15.6	17.3	22.6	25.2	17.2
Western Europe	8.8	10.4	8.6	21.2	15.6	12.6	24.5	20.7	14.4	39.8	24.7	23.2
Eastern Europe	1.4	3.7	3.4	—	0.3	—	0.8	2.2	0.9	4.2	12.2	8.7
Oceania	9.0	9.6	7.9	2.4	2.4	2.4	2.8	4.5	4.2	4.9	2.7	3.2
Rest of world	15.3	17.1	12.5	4.6	3.9	6.4	0.8	5.2	3.0	1.4	12.0	8.6

* Excludes communist countries. † Includes trade with communist countries. ‡ 1973, excluding Cambodia and South Viet-Nam.

Sources: Various issues of the following UN publications: *Yearbook of International Trade Statistics*; *Monthly Bulletin of Statistics*; IMF, *International Financial Statistics*; IMF, *Direction of Trade.*

heavy manufactures over one-seventh. But the official classification of machinery includes radios and similar electronic products, which form the bulk of Hong Kong's "heavy" industrial exports.

South Korea and Taiwan followed the same development, helped by Japanese, American and European firms, which placed orders for both finished products and components of a labour-intensive kind, and established branch factories in the two countries. In 1960 they had been exporters mainly of primary products, and exports covered only a tenth of South Korea's imports or little more than a half of Taiwan's. By 1973, however, South Korea's exports were three-quarters of its imports, and Taiwan had achieved a large trading surplus. Light manufactures, in 1974, had become 68 per cent of South Korea's exports and 58 per cent of Taiwan's. "Heavy" manufactures, again mainly electronic goods, were 17 per cent of exports in South Korea and 27 per cent in Taiwan. Textiles, including clothing, were the biggest category of their exports, about 33 per cent for South Korea and 28 per cent for Taiwan. Plywood and other timber products were also important, being 5 per cent of South Korea's exports and 10 per cent of Taiwan's.

It is remarkable that, by 1973, Hong Kong, South Korea and Taiwan were all exporting a bigger value of domestic manufactures than much larger India, notwithstanding India's long lead as an industrial exporter. Their combined manufactured exports even reached a quarter of Japan's total, and far exceeded that of all South-East Asian countries together.

Partly because of these changes, Japan's imports of light manufactures rose from 7 per cent of its total imports in 1960 to 13 per cent in 1974. Its imports of mineral fuels rose from 17 to 40 per cent, not enough to offset a fall in food and materials from 61 to 36 per cent, but enough to raise primary products to 76 per cent of Japan's total imports.

Industrialization raised the proportion of heavy manufactures in imports from 34 to 36 per cent for South Korea, and from 38 to 46 per cent for Taiwan. Mineral fuels became 9 per cent of South Korea's import in 1973 but 15 per cent in 1974. Even in 1974, they were only 6 per cent for Taiwan which was efficiently tapping its own small resources of oil and natural gas. Taiwan also reduced dependence on imports of food and materials which have fallen to a quarter of its imports, and in which soya beans and raw cotton bulk large. For South Korea the corresponding proportion is a third.

There has been little change in the composition of South-East Asia's exports, which are very largely primary products. Food and materials still comprise at least three-quarters of exports for Malaysia, the Philippines, Thailand and South Viet-Nam; for Burma, Cambodia and Laos, the proportion exceeds 90 per cent. It has fallen to 30 per cent for Indonesia only because the proportion of oil has risen from 26 per cent in 1960 to 49 per cent in 1973 and 70 per cent in 1974.

The Philippines and Singapore, however, have succeeded in developing exports of manufactures. These constitute 16 per cent of the Philippines' exports, and in Singapore now exceed re-exports. Thailand appears, on the official classification of manufactured exports, to have raised these to 25 per cent of total exports, and Malaysia to 28 per cent. But the classification includes the important export of tin metal and, if this is excluded, the proportion would fall to 19 per cent for Thailand and to 13 per cent for Malaysia.

Greater changes have occurred on the side of imports. If manufactures still make only a modest contribution to South-East Asian exports, they have replaced a good many imports in domestic markets. Between 1960 and 1974, light manufactures declined from 29 to 23 per cent of imports in the Philippines, from 43 to 23 per cent in Thailand, and from 55 to 42 per cent in Burma. They fell from 46 to 33 per cent in Indonesia up to 1973, but in the following year rose to 45 per cent as high oil prices led there to something like a consumer boom. The proportion rose in Singapore, but only because of entrepôt trade.

Heavy manufactures, correspondingly, have become the largest category of imports; 46 per cent in Indonesia, through mining and other developments, over 40 to 46 per cent in the Philippines, Thailand and Burma, and 33 per cent in Singapore. Mineral fuels have also risen relatively to other imports; in 1973 they were generally over an eighth of the total except in Brunei, Burma and Indonesia, all themselves oil producers, and in Malaysia where the proportion was 7 per cent. These proportions about doubled in 1974 with the steep rise of oil prices.

Food and materials, mainly because of agricultural developments associated with the Green Revolution, have fallen from 25 to 9 per cent of total imports in Indonesia, and from 46 to 27 per cent in Malaysia. They have also fallen from 57 to 18 per cent in Singapore, as the above two countries became more self-sufficient in rice, and from 17 to 4 per cent in Burma. In the Philippines, however, the cradle of the Green Revolution, food and materials were still nearly 15 per cent of total imports in 1974, and it was a net importer of rice.

In South Asia, food and materials have dropped from two-thirds to half total exports. For Afghanistan they were 75 per cent in 1973, and natural gas, all sent to the U.S.S.R., accounted for another 13 per cent. Nepal's proportion was also high at 86 per cent in 1970, and jute goods comprised the great remainder of its exports. The proportion was lower at 44 per cent in 1974 in Bangladesh, whose exports comprise jute and leather goods. India had about the same proportion, and Pakistan a lower one of 39 per cent.

India raised the proportion of manufactured exports from 46 per cent in 1960 to 52 per cent in 1974/75 and, rather strikingly, the proportion of heavy manufactures from less than 2 to 12 per cent. Textiles still comprised 18 per cent, and leather goods 4 per cent. There is a wide variety of other light manufactures, and a similar variety of primary products, including, besides the major item of tea, coffee, sugar, oil cakes, cashew nuts, tobacco, pepper, hides and skins, wool, manganese and iron ore. Most of the iron ore goes to Japan and now accounts for 5 per cent of total exports.

Imports of food and materials increased from 34 per cent of India's imports in 1960 to 26 per cent in 1974/75, reflecting improvements in rice and wheat production. This proportion fell from a third to a quarter for Nepal, and for Afghanistan the proportion doubled to about a third. In Sri Lanka it rose from 41 to 46 per cent. After the loss of Bangladesh, the proportion for Pakistan became 32 per cent, and for Bangladesh has been over half.

In spite of a substantial contribution from its own oil fields, the proportion of mineral fuels in India's imports rose from 6 per cent in 1960 to 19 per cent in 1973, and then to 26 per cent in 1974/75. Natural gas fields enabled Pakistan to reduce its corresponding proportion from 12 to 8 per cent, but in 1973/74 this rose to 18 per cent. The proportion had been fairly stable, at modest levels, in Afghanistan, Nepal and Sri Lanka; but in 1974 it rose from 11 to 20 per cent in Sri Lanka, and Nepal's oil imports probably increased in value by half.

Import substituting industrialization between 1960 and 1973 reduced the proportion of light manufactures in imports from 63 to 33 per cent in Afghanistan and from 30 to 17 per cent in Sri Lanka. But for Pakistan the proportion was steady at about 22 per cent, and in India, after rising from 22 per cent in 1960 to 27 per cent in 1972, it fell to 10 per cent in the crisis year 1973 and was only 18 per cent in 1974/75.

Imports of heavy manufactures between 1960 and 1973 remained a fairly stable proportion of imports for India and Pakistan at about a third of the total. This proportion rose in Afghanistan to a sixth, and in Sri Lanka was steady at about a fifth. In Nepal there was an apparent relative increase from 7 per cent in 1960 to 15 per cent in 1971.

DIRECTION OF TRADE

Japan, more than any other country, is the pivot of trade for East and South-East Asia. Indonesia, with the increasing exploitation of its oil and timber resources, sent more than half its exports to Japan in 1973, and drew a third of its imports from that country. The Philippines. South Korea and Thailand sent over one-quarter of their exports to Japan, as did South Viet-Nam in 1972, and drew between one-quarter and one-half of their imports from it. Taiwan drew about one-third of its imports from Japan and relied upon it for about one-seventh of its exports. Malaysia, Singapore and Hong Kong each drew about a fifth of their imports from Japan, and supplied it with 7 to 17 per cent of their exports. For South-East Asia as a whole the export proportion, in 1974, was 31 per cent and the import proportion 23 per cent as compared with 11 and 14 per cent in 1960, or with 22 and 25 per cent in 1970. Japan, too, as was mentioned above, is the biggest single trading partner for China.

The United States has taken a fairly steady proportion of Japan's exports, at about a quarter, and its share of Japan's imports has declined from a third to a fifth. Its share of Hong Kong's imports has been steady at around an eighth, but its share of the Colony's exports has fallen from a fifth to a little over a quarter. However, it has become an increasingly important market for the industrial outputs of South Korea and Taiwan although, with reduction of aid, a relatively decreasing source of their imports. Its share of Taiwan's exports rose from 12 to 40 per cent between 1960 and 1970, and that of South Korea's exports from 12 to 47 per cent; but in 1974 this latter share fell back to 34 per cent mainly because of market difficulties for South Korea's textile industries. The United States now provides a quarter of Taiwan's and a third of South Korea's imports.

It is as important a trading partner for the Philippines as for Taiwan, taking more than a third of exports and providing more than a quarter of imports. For other South-East Asian countries its export proportion ranges from 14 per cent for Singapore, to 8 per cent for Thailand and Laos. The import proportion was as high as 47 per cent for South Viet-Nam, because of that country's dependence on U.S. aid, but otherwise ranges from 16 per cent for Indonesia, to 10 per cent for Malaysia, except that for Burma it is as low as 2 per cent.

Hong Kong and Singapore, partly because of their distinctive entrepôt trade, find other Asian markets together more important than either Japan or the United States. Hong Kong, in 1974, sent 22 per cent of its exports to these other Asian countries and obtained 41 per cent of its imports from them; for Singapore the proportions were 41 per cent of exports and 49 per cent of imports. Burma and Thailand, which send much rice to food-deficient countries, derived two to three-fifths or more of their export receipts from Other Asia; Burma drew 37 per cent of imports from Other Asia and Thailand 25 per cent. Malaysia is also highly dependent on inter-Asian trade, which accounts for a third of both its exports and imports.

Western Europe has become a somewhat more important trading partner for East Asia, and a less important one for South-East Asia. In 1974 it took 13 to 16 per cent of exports from Japan, South Korea and Taiwan. Corresponding import proportions, in 1974, were 9 per cent for Japan, 6 per cent for South Korea, 15 per cent for Taiwan, and 18 per cent for Hong Kong.

There have been similar import proportions for South-East Asian countries: 11 to 16 per cent for the Philippines, Singapore, Laos, and South Viet-Nam, and 22 to 25 per cent for the other countries, although for Cambodia it was as high as 39 per cent in 1970. Export proportions, between 1960 and 1974, fell from 22 to 5 per cent in Indonesia (again because of its rapidly increasing trade in petroleum and timber), from 31 to 25 per cent in Malaysia, from 22 to 15 per cent in Singapore, and from 19 to 14 per cent in the Philippines. They rose, however, from 14 to 18 per cent in Thailand and from 19 to 25 per cent in Burma.

Eastern Europe has little part in the trade of East or South-East Asia although, in 1974, it took 5 per cent of Malaysia's exports and supplied 8 per cent of Burma's imports. The position is different in South Asia: the U.S.S.R. takes 30 per cent of Afghanistan's exports and, together with other East European countries, 17 per cent of India's exports and 5 per cent of Sri Lanka's. In 1970 it took 12 per cent of Pakistan's exports but only 5 per cent in 1974. Owing to substantial aid from Eastern Europe, the import proportions are lower notwithstanding bilateral agreements which regulate this trade. In 1974, this proportion was 12 per cent for India, 4 per cent for both Pakistan and Sri Lanka and 2 per cent for Afghanistan.

Western Europe, however, is still the major market for South Asia's exports, taking between 27 and 40 per cent of those from Afghanistan, Bangladesh, India, Pakistan and Sri Lanka. It also supplied between 21 and 29 per cent of their imports in 1974.

These import proportions are higher than those for the United States, except in the case of Bangladesh which drew 29 per cent of its imports from this country in 1974. But corresponding proportions for Afghanistan, Nepal and Sri Lanka were below 6 per cent; for India the proportion was 15 per cent and for Pakistan 23 per cent. Export proportions were also low, the highest being 14 per cent for India and 25 per cent for Bangladesh.

A good deal of South Asian trade is intra-continental, and could be higher but for acute political divisions. India is by far the most important foreign market for Nepal, and supplies more than half of its imports. About an eighth of Afghanistan's trade is also with India, and another tenth with Pakistan. Much of Bangladesh's trade was directed to India following its separation from Pakistan; in 1972 about two-thirds of its recorded imports came from India, and India took three-fifths of its recorded exports. (There is a considerable smuggling trade). But in 1974 India supplied only 9 per cent of Bangladesh's imports and took 11 per cent of its exports.

Not much trade is conducted between South Asia and East of South-East Asia. Japan, in 1974, took 13 per cent of India's and 6 per cent of Pakistan's exports, mainly cotton, jute and iron ore, but only 5 per cent of Sri Lanka's and Bangladesh's exports, and negligible proportions for other South Asian countries. It supplied 38 per cent of imports to Afghanistan and Nepal, and 9 to 10 per cent to India, Pakistan, Bangladesh and Sri Lanka. Relatively small amounts of textiles, raw cotton, tea and spices go from South Asia to most South-East Asian countries, and Burma sends rice to India, Bangladesh and Sri Lanka.

CURRENT PROBLEMS

Most Asian countries have had serious problems over their balances of payments because of food

Table 2

DEVELOPING ASIAN COUNTRIES: EXTERNAL ACCOUNT DATA, 1974–75

(U.S. $ million)

	Merchandise Exports		Merchandise Import Surplus		Foreign Exchange Reserves	Petroleum Imports	Fertilizer Imports	Food Grain Imports
	1974	1975	1974	1975	Dec. 1975	1974	1974	1974
South Korea	4,461	4,885	2,383	−1,212*	1,542	1,020	118	517
Taiwan	5,526	5,302	1,457	657	1,074	851	39	498
Hong Kong	5,959	6,334	809	433	1,078†	419	2	221
Philippines	2,671	2,275	765	1,608	1,289	653	84	155
Indonesia	7,426	6,259	−3,584	−1,374‡	577	183	227	390
Malaysia	4,233	3,825	−78	−279	1,321	396	64	240
Singapore	5,811	5,376	2,569	2,757	2,913	2,007	63	160
Burma	188	175‡	−41	−55‡	116	n.a.	2	1
Thailand	2,466	2,373	579	702	1,605	694	84	22
Laos	10	n.a.	42	n.a.	n.a.	8	n.a.	15
Cambodia	19	n.a.	258	n.a.	n.a.	51	1	269
South Viet-Nam	77	n.a.	887	n.a.	201†	132	62	222
Afghanistan	229	214‡	−3	n.a.	71	9	18	9
Pakistan	1,113	1,049	619	1,102	311	157	37	133
Bangladesh	347	326	749	943	130	62	53	196
India	3,926	4,299	1,120	1,903	841	1,481	490	637
Sri Lanka	523	531*	170	174*	45	143	36	261

* Projection based on 11 months. † Total reserves, March 1975. ‡ Projection based on three-quarters.

Sources: United Nations Publications: IMF, *International Financial Statistics*, June 1976, *Direction of Trade*, various issues. FAO, *Trade Yearbook, 1974*. Asian Development Bank, *Key Indicators*, Oct. 1975.

shortages, disturbing changes in world prices, and difficulties connected with foreign aid.

During 1972–73 food became scarcer, and desperately scarce in large parts of South Asia. Agricultural output fell between 1970 and 1972 by 20 per cent in Bangladesh, 8 per cent in India, and 5 per cent in Burma and Sri Lanka; it declined by 6 per cent in Pakistan during 1971 and recovered little during 1972, and in Nepal it declined by 3 per cent in 1972. Thailand, the largest rice exporter in the region, also had a 4 per cent fall of agricultural output in 1972, and there were smaller falls in the Philippines, Indonesia and South Viet-Nam.

This situation led to high imports of food grains in developing Asian countries, $3,000 million in 1973 and $3,900 million in 1974, when they reached 7 per cent of total imports. But most of the increased value of food imports came from higher prices; that of rice rose from $147 a ton in 1972 to $350 in 1973 and to $542 in 1974. The strain was made worse by the damage from increasing warfare to agricultural production in Cambodia and South Viet-Nam, formerly rice exporters but requiring, in 1973 and 1974, average combined grain imports of $382 million, as compared with $627 for India, $128 for Pakistan and $185 for Bangladesh. South Korea also required heavy grain imports in these two years, as did the Philippines.

Then, in 1974, the price of petroleum rose from $3.29 per barrel to $11.58. Very soon the price of nitrogeneous fertilizers also trebled, and they had represented about half the quite inadequate average use of 8 kilogrammes of fertilizers per hectare in South and South-East Asian countries. In 1973, these countries spent $605 million on imported fertilizers, but in 1974 $1,220 million; in terms of volume imports were down by about a third, with unfortunate consequences for Asian agriculture. Only oil-rich Indonesia could afford to import more fertilizer.

In 1973 oil accounted for 18 per cent of imports in Japan, 10 to 15 per cent in the Philippines, Singapore, Thailand, India and Nepal, 5 to 10 per cent in South Korea, Hong Kong, Malaysia, Afghanistan, Pakistan and Sri Lanka and for about 3 per cent in Taiwan and Bangladesh. The price of oil more than trebled in 1974, severely straining their balances of payments. For some countries the strain was eased by substantial new OPEC aid, totalling $1,577 million to Asia between January 1973 and June 1975. South Korea, Bangladesh and Sri Lanka were thus able to maintain their oil imports at something near the 1973 volume. So, without such aid, were Hong Kong, Singapore and Thailand; and Taiwan was able to double the volume of its relatively small oil import. But Pakistan and India, the major recipients of OPEC aid, had to cut the volume of their oil imports by more than a third; as had, for different reasons, Cambodia and South Viet-Nam.

A more serious effect of the higher oil prices and the associated collapse of the world boom was on the terms of trade for Asian countries. Those for East Asian countries, whose exports are predominantly manufactures, declined by about a quarter over 1974 and 1975. Japan's current balance of payments changed from a record surplus of $6,600 million in 1972 to a deficit of $4,700 million in 1974, although this was eliminated in 1975 by a 13 per cent reduction in its volume of imports, including those from Asian countries. Between 1972 and 1974 South Korea's current balance changed from a small deficit of $370 million to one of $2,027 million, and Taiwan's from a surplus of $512 million to a deficit of $1,115 million. There was no improvement in South Korea's deficit in 1975, but for Taiwan a considerable improvement as its deficit for the first three-quarters of 1975 was $408 million.

Exporters of primary products, other than Indonesia, fared worse, but somewhat unevenly because of different movements in world prices. Between 1970 and 1974 import prices doubled for developing Asian countries as a whole. Export prices for vegetable oils, rice and sugar about trebled. Those for cotton, rubber, timber and tin about doubled. But those for jute and tea increased by only a third. In 1975 export prices fell, except for jute and petroleum, by half for vegetable oils, by a third for rubber and sugar, by a fifth for cotton and timber, and by a sixth for tea. Before the end of 1975 the price of jute also began to fall, that of oil had become steady.

Notwithstanding the boom in commodity prices during 1974, terms of trade were less favourable in that year for most Asian countries than they had been in 1970. The striking exception was Indonesia where oil helped its terms of trade to improve from 100 to over 200. They had also improved for Thailand from 100 in 1970 to 121 in 1973, because of the world shortage of grains, but they fell back to 101 in 1974 and were only 92 in the first quarter of 1975. For Burma the grain shortage also meant an improvement in the terms of trade, to 117 in 1974. Pakistan and India had gained, in 1972, from higher prices for cotton and jute, which improved their terms of trade by about a tenth; but after that India's terms of trade worsened by more than a quarter, although Pakistan's improved slightly in 1974. Sri Lanka's terms of trade continuously worsened after 1970 and, by 1974, had fallen to 69. Bangladesh, in the single year 1974, had a deterioration of more than a third. The Philippines had improving terms of trade up to 1974 but they began to decline markedly in 1975. Malaysia's terms of trade had fluctuated, but declined by 5 per cent in 1974 from a level which was itself 13 per cent below the 1970 level.

There was, of course, an associated worsening of balances of trade. Between 1973 and 1975, the Philippines' small export surplus changed to a large import surplus of $1,608 million; Singapore's import surplus doubled to $2,757 million, and Thailand's almost doubled to $876 million. The situation was worse in South Asia. There Pakistan's import surplus rose from $20 million to $1,102 million, Bangladesh's from $518 million to $888 million, India's from $293 million to $1,903 million, and Sri Lanka's from $33 million to $174 million. And Indonesia's export surplus, which had reached $3,584 million in 1974, fell to $1,374 million in 1975. Only Burma seemed to have had improvement in this respect as its small export surplus rose from $25 million in 1973 to $55 million in 1975.

Asian countries had obvious need for greater foreign aid. This had been about $4,200 million in 1971, of which official aid came to $3,700 million, private export credits to $377 million, and loans raised in world capital markets to $38 million. During 1972 the total declined a little in money terms and fell by a tenth in real terms, mainly because official aid to India dropped from $986 million to $582 million and that to Pakistan from $456 million to $262 million, although aid to Bangladesh rose from $15 million to $207 million. There was a big increase of aid in 1973, from $4,100 million to $7,000 million but by only a third in real terms. Much of this increase was associated with three disaster areas; Bangladesh and South Viet-Nam received $437 million each, and Cambodia $142 million. India's official aid receipts increased to only $687 million, and Pakistan's fell to $189 million. Some of the increase, moreover, was associated with private aid. Export credits, halved in the previous year, now fully recovered, the countries most affected by this change being Indonesia, South Korea and Thailand. Loans raised on world markets more than trebled to reach $933 million, the major borrowers being Indonesia, the Philippines, South Korea and Hong Kong.

Aid slowed down again in 1974, increasing to only $8,300 million and falling by a tenth in real terms, in spite of much greater aid for India ($1,009 million), Pakistan ($412 million), South Viet-Nam ($673 million), Cambodia ($307 million) and Taiwan ($353 million). But aid to Bangladesh increased by only a tenth in 1974, while Asian import prices increased by nearly a half, and smaller money flows of official aid went to Taiwan, South Korea, Hong Kong, the Philippines, Indonesia, Singapore, Thailand, Laos, Burma, Afghanistan and Nepal. Taiwan, South Korea, Hong Kong, the Philippines and Malaysia were all substantial borrowers in world capital markets during 1974, and Indonesia raised $992 million in such markets during the first half of 1975. OPEC aid has already been mentioned; in 1974 it amounted to a tenth of all official aid to Asian countries.

There were hopeful signs of improvement after the dismal events of 1973 and 1974. The major one was a recovery of food production in Asia, perhaps by 5 per cent in 1975, and the 1975/76 rice harvest was a good one. Thailand was trying to dispose of a big export surplus, and the Philippines had more than regained self-sufficiency in rice. India's wheat crop was also good.

Oil prices seemed to have stabilized, and some Asian countries reduced their dependence on imported oil. India's domestic output had been stationary at just over 7,000 million metric tons, but in 1975, its first offshore oil field, the Bombay High, began to produce oil. In Burma output increased by a seventh, and new discoveries were being made. Malaysia increased its output by a tenth, and Thailand had made offshore discoveries of natural gas. The most important oil development was in China, which has now become a larger producer than Indonesia through additions to the output of the Taching field from offshore sites in the Yellow Sea; by 1980, it has been estimated, China could supply Indonesia's present export to Japan.

There is hope, too, of both a marked slackening of world inflation and a recovery of demand for Asian exports. Lesser inflation would mean a reduction in the rise of Asian import prices; taking the Philippines as an example, import prices rose by only 8 per cent in 1975 as compared with 74 per cent in the previous year. Recession in the industrial countries seems to have ended. According to OECD forecasts real GNP may rise, during 1976, by 6 per cent in the United States, by 4 per cent in Japan and by 2 per cent in Western Europe. In April 1976 world prices for food were 5 per cent higher, on an annual basis, those for fibres were 10 per cent higher, and those for metals 8 per cent higher.

Some hope, moreover, was entertained that the fourth UNCTAD conference at Nairobi in May 1976 would lead to an easing of the debt service burden which presses heavily on some Asian countries. In 1972, the ratio of debt service to exports of goods and services was 24 per cent in India, 17 per cent in Pakistan and Burma and 14 per cent in Sri Lanka and South Korea; in 1974 it was 18 per cent for Afghanistan and over 6 per cent for Bangladesh. The hope was that creditor countries would agree to a substantial reduction of official debts owed by developing countries.

Major Commodities of Asia and the Pacific

Rice

Rice is the staple food of all the countries of Monsoon Asia and 90 per cent of the total world acreage under rice lies within the area. The predominance of rice as a food crop is based on its ability to give yields very high in nutritional value and frequently to produce satisfactory yields where no other crop will grow, e.g. in coastal marshes.

Most of the areas in South and South-East Asia where rice is grown have high population density and low income *per capita*. The crop in about 80 per cent of these areas depends on rainfall for its source of water and as such faces the uncertainties of droughts and floods. In addition, there are problems of pests, diseases and unsuitable soils. These have kept average rice yields very low: 1.5 to 1.8 tons per hectare as compared with more than 5.5 tons per hectare in Australia, Japan, Spain and U.S.A.

Because of the supreme importance of rice as a food for half the world's population (only 5 per cent enters into international trade), and because of the crop's traditional—though declining—role as a foreign exchange earner for the governments of many developing countries, much effort has been devoted to increasing output.

VARIETIES

Wet rice cultivation is typically associated with the alluvial lowlands of Monsoon Asia, since the best natural conditions for this type of agriculture are obtained there, but rice tolerates a wide range of geographic, climatic and ecological conditions and can be adapted to various locations including non-submerged land, where upland rice is grown. All varieties of rice can be classified into two main groups: *indica* and *japonica*. (There is also an intermediate or *java* type, cultivated in parts of Indonesia). The *indica* group, prevalent in tropical Asia, and covering a very high proportion of the total rice area of Asia, has been associated with a very low yield and primitive production techniques. The *japonica* type, which predominates in Taiwan, Korea and Japan, is very responsive to natural and artificial fertilizers and also to the longer hours of sunshine enjoyed in these areas.

Improved Strains

The main reason for the low rice yields in these areas was due to the lack of proper varieties. The conventional varieties were tall and leafy and lodged when subjected to improved agronomic practices and high rates of nitrogenous fertilizers. The International Rice Research Institute has developed a series of stiff-stemmed, semi-dwarf varieties with upright leaves that respond positively to high rates of fertilizers and other improved cultural practices. Similar varieties have also been developed in several other tropical and subtropical countries. These commonly yield 5.0 to 8.0 tons of paddy rice per hectare. Most of the newly developed varieties are also resistant to common pests, diseases and some of the soil problems. Scientists at IRRI, as well as in various countries are in the process of developing varieties that will also have tolerance to drought, flood, deep water and sub-optimum temperatures. Farmers growing these varieties face less risk of crop-failures and are therefore more prone to invest in other production inputs. Both improved varieties and improved agronomic practices are essential for a sustained increase in production.

PRODUCTION AND TRADE

The 1975/76 world rice crop was the third record in succession, estimated at 347 million metric tons, up 6 per cent from the previous season. The gain was attributed to an excellent summer monsoon, coupled with several years of attractive prices and some increased use of high-yielding varieties.

The outstanding crop resulted in exportable supplies of 8.5 to 9.0 million tons. Imports, however, may fall below recent levels to little more than 7 million tons as a result of good harvests and above-normal stocks in many importing countries.

Nearly half the increased production occurred in chronically deficit India, where an almost faultless monsoon boosted production at least 9 million tons above the poor crop of 1974/75. Major increases have also been registered in neighbouring supplier countries such as Pakistan, Burma, and Thailand. In Thailand, for example, production was expected to exceed 15 million tons, up nearly 4 per cent from the 1974 crop. Thai export offerings were considered uncompetitive during much of 1975, and 500,000 tons of unsold old-crop rice have been carried into 1976. This, combined with the new-crop surplus, put Thai export availabilities at nearly 2 million tons.

Burma carried old-crop rice into 1976 and, with anticipated new supplies, may be able to export as much as 500,000 tons, the highest level for 4 years. About a third of this is expected to go to Sri Lanka. Burmese rice exports in 1975 were estimated at 370,000 tons, up 86 per cent from the previous year's.

Pakistan's 1975/76 crop was nearly 7 per cent above the previous year's. The exportable surplus is put at 900,000 tons (including 200,000 unsold from the 1974 crop).

Although Thailand and Burma have traditionally been two of Asia's main suppliers, Pakistan and the People's Republic of China are increasingly the dominant forces in world rice trade.

The People's Republic of China became Asia's leading supplier in 1973, when other Asian exporters reduced offerings, and has maintained that position ever since. However, its exports in 1976 may decline to perhaps 1.2 million tons from an estimated 1.5 million in 1975 as the world market becomes increasingly competitive.

In most other exporting countries, supplies also appear larger than in 1975. North Korea is reported to have at least 200,000 tons available for shipment.

Indonesian production continued to grow steadily as more area came under high-yielding varieties, double-cropping increases, and marshlands were drained for rice cultivation. The 1975 crop was about 24 million tons (16.3 million, milled) 5 per cent above 1974's.

South Korea's 1976 rice policy seems somewhat contradictory. Although the 1975 crop appeared significantly damaged by a late-season attack of brown planthoppers, the Government has put production at 6.48 million tons, up 5 per cent from the 1974 record. With heavy stocks (800,000 tons) in hand, Korea claimed rice self-sufficiency, in early 1976 in spite of a continuing policy prohibiting the serving of rice in restaurants on two days a week and specifying the mixing of barley with rice to extend Government rice supplies.

Sri Lanka continued to fill most of its rice deficit under a longstanding rice/rubber barter arrangement with the People's Republic of China. Although the 1975 season was one of the driest on record, prospects for the 1976 crop (harvested in February-March, July-August) improved as the drought ended and new Government policies encouraged increased production. Imports were expected to decline by 25 per cent to about 300,000 tons in 1976.

In Bangladesh, as in India, a favourable 1975 monsoon led to expanded output and the likelihood of significant gains in per capita consumption of rice. Production in 1975/76 is estimated at 18.5 million tons, up 8 per cent from that of a year earlier. Though there are reports of inadequate storage facilities and some spoilage, "surpluses" in Bangladesh tend to be short lived. Barring new problems with port congestions, imports are likely to remain near 1975 levels.

The Philippines appeared to be self-sufficient in rice for the first time since 1971 in early 1976. The 1975 crop was untouched by typhoons, and production for 1975/76 was estimated at nearly 6 million tons, up almost 6 per cent from that of 1974/75, exceeding consumption needs by about 100,000 tons (milled), permitting some build up of stock. Officials say they do not intend to buy any rice in 1976.

The end of war in Indochina will probably result in the re-emergence of the area as a major source of export supplies. Although availabilities will probably not return to pre-World War II levels, 500,000 tons could well be offered from this region by 1980. Limited quantities of Viet-Nam-origin rice have already been exported, although most observers believe that the country does not yet have a rice surplus.

The situation in Cambodia was apparently less favourable in early 1976. There were reports that much of the country suffered acute hunger during the latter stages of the war and immediately after. There was evidence that the monsoon may not have been as generous in Cambodia's main rice-growing regions as it was over most of the rest of Asia. The possibility of Cambodia offeing rice before 1977 must, therefore, be considered unlikely. However, when both Cambodia and Viet-Nam are able to overcome the effects of war, most observers expect them to alter the Asian supply picture sharply.

In South Asia, both Pakistan and India are showing increased interest in the foreign exchange potential of larger exports to the Middle East. This is indicated by both more aggressive marketing, and by strong research efforts to develop highyielding basmati-type varieties. In addition, Pakistan is expected to build a dozen new mills and storage facilities this year to boost the quality of its often-criticized coarse-rice offerings.

STATISTICS

PADDY PRODUCTION

('000 metric tons)

	1971	1972	1973	1974	1975†
FAR EAST					
Bangladesh	14,896	15,134	19,356	17,222	19,000
Burma	8,175	7,361	8,559	8,446	8,720
Cambodia	2,732	2,138	953	635	n.a.
China, People's Republic*	106,001	102,000	109,000	112,025	113,000
India	64,603	58,868	65,613	61,500	70,500
Indonesia	20,064	18,031	21,900	22,800	23,100
Japan	14,152	15,391	15,717	15,902	17,000
Korea, Democratic People's Republic*	2,800	3,000	3,300	3,500	n.a.
Korea, Republic	5,560	5,504	5,858	6,182	6,485
Laos	812	817	883	900	n.a.
Malaysia	1,806	1,826	1,969	2,053	2,200
Nepal	2,680	2,010	2,402*	2,200	2,500
Pakistan	3,393	3,495	3,578	3,277	3,800
Philippines	5,100	4,414	5,594	5,660	6,380
Sri Lanka	1,397	1,313	1,313	1,875	1,105
Taiwan	3,031	3,197	2,954	3,250	n.a.
Thailand	14,201	11,669	13,934	12,982	15,000
Viet-Nam, Democratic Republic*	3,900	4,400	4,100	4,200	n.a.
Viet-Nam, Republic	6,324	6,348	7,025	7,200	7,400
TOTAL (incl. others)	281,856	266,995	294,404	292,115	n.a.
OCEANIA	319	268	328	429	n.a.
WORLD TOTAL	309,616	294,384	323,507	323,347	342,845

* Estimates. † Preliminary.

Source: FAO, *Production Yearbook 1974* and *Rice Trade Intelligence, Dec. 1975; BAEcon Statistics Division (Philippines); Bank of Thailand Monthly Bulletin May 1975.*

EXPORTS

('000 metric tons, milled equivalent)

	1970	1971	1972	1973	1974
FAR EAST					
Burma	667	831	511	133	214
Cambodia	178	32	18	—	—
China (incl. Taiwan)*	1,830	2,158	2,316	3,449	3,005
Korea, Democratic People's Republic†	89	103	100	102	250
Nepal	247	228	195	228	58
Pakistan	482	182	198	789	597
Singapore	47	47	71	44	15
Thailand	1,064	1,576	2,119	849	1,124
Viet-Nam, Democratic Republic*	18	20	20	20	20
Australia	129	102	179	157	137
WORLD TOTAL	8,824	9,319	9,464	9,265	8,854

*FAO estimates. † Unofficial figure.

Source: FAO *Trade Yearbook 1974.*

IMPORTS
('000 metric tons, milled equivalent)

	1971	1972	1973	1974
FAR EAST				
Hong Kong	371	458	426	333
India	540	326	264	59*
Indonesia	508	734	1,657	1,151
Japan	13	3	24	63
Korea, Republic	1,007	750	335	360
Malaysia	251	230	310	362
Pakistan	—	60	—	—
Philippines	370	445	312	169
Singapore	306	377	239	163
Sri Lanka	339	266	344	297
Viet-Nam, South	137	272	270	306
WORLD TOTAL	9,189	9,185	9,687	8,713

* FAO estimates.

Source: FAO *Trade Yearbook 1974*; RCA and National Gram's Authority (Philippines).

Tea

Tea is a beverage made from the dried young leaves and unopened leaf-buds of the tea plant, an evergreen shrub or small tree (*Camellia sinensis*). Black and green tea are the most common finished products. The former accounts for the bulk of the world's supply and is associated with machine manufacture and generally the plantation system, which guarantees an adequate supply of leaf to the factory. The latter, mainly produced in China and Japan, is to a great extent produced by peasants, and much of it is consumed locally. India, Bangladesh and Sri Lanka (Ceylon) between them account for about two-thirds of total world output of tea, with China, Indonesia, Japan and Taiwan as other main Asian producers. A number of factors determine the flavour and quality of the finished product: climate, soil, age of leaf, time of harvest, and, particularly, method of preparation. Black, green and oolong tea can all be produced through different processes from leaves of the same plant, though each region generally concentrates on one type.

VARIETIES

Two main groups can be recognized: the China and the Assam. The former group consists of slow-growing dwarf trees, giving lowish yields but resistant to unfavourable weather conditions, while the latter group comprises trees which grow taller and more quickly and respond favourably to tropical conditions. Although tea will grow almost anywhere where it is warm and wet and with a high humidity, the temperature level is the crucial factor in deciding the size and quality of the crop since some varieties under certain conditions will flush all the year round while others will not.

PRODUCTION AND TRADE

World production of tea in 1973 reached an all-time record of 1,570,000 metric tons. Production in 1974 was about the same as that of 1973 owing mainly to droughts in East Africa and Sri Lanka. As demand for tea did not slacken, prices increased during 1974 by an average of over 30 per cent, reaching 50 per cent in Calcutta.

Exports from all producers reached 688,700 tons in 1973, of which 526,275 tons were from Asian producers, with Sri Lanka accounting for 205,515 tons. The country redirected its exports from the United Kingdom and the U.S.A. to Pakistan and some near east countries such as Egypt, Libya and Saudi Arabia. The U.S.S.R. and Poland greatly reduced their imports from Sri Lanka. Tea imports continued to decline in developed western countries but this was more than matched by larger purchases of the U.S.S.R. and near eastern countries and by increasing domestic demand in India. The figure for imports in the Far East continued to be larger than that before 1971, mainly due to Pakistan, which formerly drawing its supplies from Bangladesh, became an importer.

PROSPECTS

According to the FAO *Monthly Bulletin of Agricultural Economics and Statistics* (Feb. 1975), "shortage and high costs of fertilizers and the continual increases in prices of all inputs may be a curb on the expansion of tea production in the next few years".

At the Symposium on International Tea Market Expansion held in London in December 1974, it was agreed that a central body needed to be set up to explore new markets for expanding the world tea trade.

STATISTICS

AREA PLANTED
(hectares)

	1969	1970	1971	1972	1973	1974
Bangledesh†	42,667	42,637	42,928	42,649	42,866	42,603
China, People's Republic*	n.a.	n.a.	303,000	317,500	328,000	n.a.
India	354,133	356,516	358,675	360,126	361,533	n.a.
Indonesia	62,471	62,407	65,477	62,124	6,1800	61,100
Japan	49,700	51,600	53,900	55,500	57,200	58,400
Malaysia	2,999	2,978	2,968	2,986	2,977	2,925*
Papua New Guinea	2,271	2,957	3,353	3,766	3,706	n.a.
Sri Lanka	241,401	241,799	241,667	241,858	242,302	242,191
Taiwan	35,685	34,400	34,200	33,500	33,000	33,000
Viet-Nam, South	8,270	8,215	8,460	7,960	7,360	7,500

* Estimate. † Figures for 1969 apply in Pakistan.

PRODUCTION
(made tea, in metric tons)

	1970	1971	1972	1973	1974	1975
Bangladesh‡	31,381	12,449	23,836	27,550	32,159	29,343*
China, People's Republic§	n.a.	259,984	291,229	307,000	n.a.	n.a.
India	418,517	435,468	455,996	471,952	492,116*	489,393*
Indonesia	44,048	48,207	49,777	54,546*	50,230	n.a.
Japan	91,198	92,911	94,832	100,968	95,238	105,448
Malaysia	3,381	3,325	3,364	3,462	3,237†	2,991*
Papua New Guinea	971	1,402	2,689	3,577	n.a.	n.a.
Sri Lanka	212,210	217,773	213,475	211,271	204,038	213,679
Taiwan†	27,648	26,924	26,229	28,639	24,173	26,092
Viet-Nam, South	5,545	5,800	5,100	6,250	6,000*	6,000

* Estimates. † Figures for "crude" tea. ‡ Figures for 1970–71 apply to Pakistan. § FAO estimates.

EXPORTS
(metric tons)

	1970	1971	1972	1973	1974	1975
Bangladesh	—	—	13,186	20,311	21,167	24,104
China*	30,000	41,000	42,000	34,000	50,000	53,000
India	200,155	204,388	209,814	188,192	205,909	219,709
Indonesia	36,897	40,202	38,529	35,576	50,230	45,961
Japan	1,498	1,424	1,883	2,170	1,833	2,210
Malaysia	976	810	n.a.	n.a.	n.a.	n.a.
Papua New Guinea	1,169	1,803	2,792	3,965	4,431	n.a.
Sri Lanka	208,277	200,798	190,088	205,515	185,066	212,433
Taiwan	20,389	22,807	21,301	21,114	17,219	20,116
Viet-Nam, Democratic Republic*	1,680	1,650	1,750	1,590	2,210	n.a.
Viet-Nam, South	109	134	601	n.a.	n.a.	n.a.

* Estimates.

Source: International Tea Committee, *Annual Bulletin of Statistics.*

Rubber

Of a total world production of 3.3 million metric tons of natural rubber, Asian countries produced all but 253,500 tons in 1975. The principal producers are Malaysia, Indonesia, Thailand, Sri Lanka and India. For several of these countries rubber is the most important export commodity. Outrivalling natural rubber, synthetic rubber production stood at about 6.5 million tons in 1975, of which 789,000 tons were produced in Japan, 37,500 tons in Australia and 23,000 tons in India. The Association of Natural Rubber Producing Countries was set up in October 1970 in Kuala Lumpur where it was agreed to establish a joint regional marketing system to co-ordinate the production and marketing of natural rubber, to promote technical co-operation and the stabilization of prices. ANRPC members in mid-1976 were: Sri Lanka, India, South Viet-Nam, Thailand, Malaysia, Indonesia, Singapore and Papua New Guinea.

CULTIVATION

Rubber cultivation is suited both to estate and smallholder methods of farming, giving regular year-round employment, but being adaptable to irregular activity without harm to the trees. Nevertheless, it is the estates which have pioneered both the development of cultivation techniques and the improvement of the clones, or selected strains. In general plantation methods are now much more efficient, productivity being often as much as three times that of smallholdings on a per acre basis. But because of much denser planting—up to 400 trees to the acre as against an average of 120 per acre on estates—the productivity of smallholdings was, until the beginning of this decade, equal to that of estates. However, only by replanting with selected strains and rationalizing production and processing can smallholders hope to remain competitive.

DEVELOPMENT

A major development of post-war years has been the development of selected clones (strains) of high yield, particularly in Malaya and Indonesia. These may either be planted as seedlings, or propagated by grafting on to seedlings of ordinary trees (root stock) and planted out subsequently. The necessity for extensive replanting as the first generation of rubber plants came to an end of production throughout South-East Asia has made possible the replacement of old stock with new clonal material of better quality. In Malaysia, particularly, standards of production have risen remarkably and some estates claim a potential productive capacity of 3,000 lb./acre against 300–400 lb./acre from smallholdings or from estates planted with unselected trees. In 1965, technical specifications for the grading of rubber (SMR) were made official and supplementing this standardization is a Plasticity Retention Index under which rubber is classified into one of three ranges. Thus, natural rubber has responded to the challenge of synthetics by improving its competitive position as an industrial product, graded to the various requirements of industrial customers. For this reason, and because of the likelihood of rising costs of the oil-derivatives (styrene and butadiene) from which synthetics are made, natural rubber will probably hold its own in world markets; but it is likely that smallholders, even with their lower overheads, will not be able to continue to profit from rubber unless (as has now begun to happen in Malaysia) they adopt the selected strains, and centralize their processing facilities on a co-operative basis.

STATISTICS

WORLD PRODUCTION AND CONSUMPTION OF RUBBER
('000 metric tons)

	1970	1971	1972	1973	1974	1975
Production of natural rubber . .	3,102.5	3,085.0	3,125.5	3,512.5	3,447.5	3,292.5
Production of synthetic rubber .	5,875.0	6,147.5	6,630	7,505	7,390	6,507.5
TOTAL PRODUCTION .	8,977.5	9,232.5	9,755	11,017.5	10,837.5	9,800
Consumption of natural rubber .	2,992.5	3,095	3,235	3,410	3,520	2,355
Consumption of synthetic rubber .	5,625	6,130	6,605	7,317.5	7,265	6,600
TOTAL CONSUMPTION . .	8,617.5	9,225	9,840	10,727.5	10,785	9,955

Source: International Rubber Study Group, *Rubber Statistical Bulletin.*

PRODUCTION OF NATURAL RUBBER
(metric tons)

	1971	1972	1973	1974	1975
Malaysia	1,318,518	1,304,147	1,542,323	1,549,293	1,477,582
West Malaysia	1,270,436	1,258,149	1,465,162	1,485,115	1,416,560
Estates	661,573	659,334	673,643	684,146	599,055
Smallholdings	608,863	598,815	791,519	800,969	817,505
East Malaysia	48,082†	146,168†	77,161†	64,178†	61,022†
Indonesia	819,311	773,655	885,802	854,964	825,000
Estates	238,742	214,048	223,129	248,401	n.a.
Smallholdings	580,569	559,607	662,673	606,563	n.a.
Thailand‡	316,323	336,919	381,954	379,188	348,737
Sri Lanka	141,409	140,371	154,675	132,008	148,751
Viet-Nam	34,533	20,294	20,619	21,979	15,000*
Cambodia	1,147	15,312	16,500*	17,750*	10,000*
India	98,884	109,137	123,232	128,351	136,019
Africa§	203,750	208,500	224,500	232,750	208,500
Brazil	24,231	25,818	23,402	18,606	19,348
Others*	55,500	64,500	75,000	91,000	101,500
TOTAL*	3,085,000	3,125,000	3,512,500	3,447,500	3,292,500

* Estimated. † Net exports. ‡ Exports plus consumption.
§ Estimated exports plus consumption.

Source: International Rubber Study Group, *Rubber Statistical Bulletin.*

EXPORTS OF NATURAL RUBBER TO MAJOR CONSUMING COUNTRIES, 1975
('000 metric tons)

	U.S.A.	U.S.S.R.	West Germany	Japan	U.K.	China	France	Total*
West Malaysia and Singapore	363·7	144·1	139·3	65·0	133·2	140·5	100·3	1,904·1
Indonesia	198·6	430	42·5	17·6	7·4	0·4	11·9	788·3
Sri Lanka	5·4	9·2	9·1	0·9	20	91·6	2·2	140·9
Thailand	29·4	3·4	4·3	188·6	0·5	1·1	1·2	334·7
Viet-Nam†	0·1	—	2·6	1·3	—	—	11·7	23·0
Cambodia‡	5·6	—	3·0	2·3	5·7	—	16·2	47·7

* Including others. † 1974 only. ‡ 1969 only.

Source: International Rubber Study Group, *Rubber Statistical Bulletin.*

EXPORTS OF BLOCK NATURAL RUBBER
(metric tons)

	1972	1973	1974	1975
Malaysia	280,127	376,096	404,905	433,005
Singapore	87,052	105,389	n.a.	n.a.
Indonesia	291,727	360,725	381,931	401,306

Source: International Rubber Study Group, *Rubber Statistical Bulletin.*

Tin

MINE PRODUCTION

World* production of tin-in-concentrates (tin metal content of tin concentrates) in 1975 was 172,600 metric tons as against 180,500 tons in 1974. The 4.4 per cent fall in production was partly due to export control affecting most producers, which has been in force since April 1975. Thailand and Malaysia showed falls of nearly 4,000 tons each against their 1974 output levels. In the case of Thailand, however, unreported tin production is believed to be responsible for the lower 1975 figure.

SMELTER PRODUCTION

World* production of primary tin metal showed a steadier movement, falling by only 2.3 per cent to 174,900 tons from 179,100 tons in 1974, compared with mine production. Of the major tin producers of South-East Asia, only Indonesia showed an improvement on its 1974 production level. Towards the end of 1975 there was a significant expansion in Indonesia's smelter capacity. Thailand showed the largest fall, of 3,200 tons, in smelter production, probably due to smaller amounts of concentrates reaching its smelters, followed by Australia (1,400 tons) and Malaysia (1,300 tons).

* World totals of production and consumption generally exclude the People's Republic of China, the German Democratic Republic, Mongolia, North Korea and the U.S.S.R.

CONSUMPTION

The serious slump in economic activity throughout the industrialized world affected the consumption of primary tin metal estimated at 171,100 tons, a fall of 14 per cent. Consumption in the Far East and Australasia was 40,383 tons in 1975 compared with 47,393 tons in 1974. The most significant fall in 1975 was one of 5,700 tons for Japan.

PRICES

A depressing factor in the market on 1975 was the increased exports of tin from the People's Republic of China, which were estimated to have increased from approximately 10,000 tons per year in 1973 and 1974 to approximately 14,500 tons in 1975. In January 1975 the International Tin Council (ITC) raised the floor and the ceiling prices for tin to M$900 per pikul and M$1,100 per pikul, an upward adjustment of M$50 per pikul in each case which was considered necessary in view of increased cost of production but the new range quickly required intervention by the Buffer Stock Manager as the price was almost continuously in the lower sector (M$900–M$980). The 1975 average price for Penang Straits Tin, ex-works, was M$963.79 per pikul, well below the previous year's high average figure of M$1,136.63 per pikul.

STATISTICS

PRODUCTION OF TIN-IN-CONCENTRATES
(metric tons)

	1972	1973	1974	1975
Burma	500*	580*	600*	600*
Indonesia	21,766	22,492	25,630	24,391
Japan	873	811	550	645
Laos	787	748	612	522
Malaysia	76,830	72,260	68,122	68,364
Thailand	22,072	20,921	20,339	16,406
Korea, Republic	76*	63*	24*	24*
TOTAL ASIA	122,900	117,880	115,880	110,950
Australia	11,997	10,801	10,114	9,231
TOTAL WORLD	194,300	184,000	180,500	172,600

* Estimate.

Note: Total figures for Asia are rounded off to the nearest 10 tons.

PRODUCTION OF PRIMARY TIN-METAL
(metric tons)

	1972	1973	1974	1975
Indonesia	12,010	14,632	15,065	17,826
Japan	1,349	1,438	1,327	1,219
Malaysia	91,001	82,468	84,394	83,070
Thailand	22,281	22,927	19,827	16,630
TOTAL ASIA	126,640	121,470	120,610	118,750
Australia	7,027	6,904	6,714	5,254
TOTAL WORLD	190,000	184,700	179,100	174,900

CONSUMPTION OF PRIMARY TIN-METAL
(metric tons)

	1972	1973	1974	1975
India*	3,000	4,600	3,000	2,850
Indonesia	300*	406	335	500
Japan	32,341	38,676	33,817	28,088
Korea, Republic	538	948	643*	560
Malaysia	183	224	249	260
Pakistan*	360	360	360	360
Philippines*	650	800	950	960
Taiwan*	520	430	480	480
Thailand	340	330	322	252
Other Asia	2,260	2,580	2,580	2,580
TOTAL ASIA	40,490	49,350	42,740	36,890
Australia	3,465	4,273	4,293	3,133
New Zealand*	360	360	360	360
TOTAL WORLD	191,500	213,400	199,000	171,100

* Estimates.

Note: Total figures for Asia are rounded to the nearest 10 tons.

Source: International Tin Council, *Statistical Bulletin.*

Petroleum

Excluding the Soviet Union, Indonesia is by far the largest crude oil producer and exporter in Asia. Brunei is a much less important exporter, while Burma is approximately self-sufficient. The other Asian and Pacific producers, China, India, Pakistan, Japan and Australia, mostly have to rely on substantial oil imports to satisfy their requirements. A boom is taking place in South-East Asian oil, and is described fully in the *Introduction to Physical, Social and Economic Geography of South-East Asia* pp. 383-384.

Crude oil is transferred from its source by pipeline and/or tanker to the refinery, which is likely to be situated in a consuming country: hence Singapore, Malaysia, India, Japan and Australia all refine large proportions of imported crude.

The main stages in the refining process are: gas separation, which is mostly completed before the crude oil actually reaches the refinery; distillation, carried out in a fractionating tower, where the oil is heated and the resulting vapours cooled to different temperatures to separate out diesel oils, kerosene, gasoline and gases; conversion processes, for example, "cracking", which by chemical change breaks down heavier hydrocarbons into the lighter gasoline; extraction processes, for separating special products like wax or toluene; and special treatments, to remove unwanted impurities.

STATISTICS

PETROLEUM PRODUCTION IN THE FAR EAST AND AUSTRALASIA

('000 metric tons, including natural gas liquids)

	1971	1972	1973	1974	1974 '000 Barrels Per Day	1975*	1975 '000 Barrels Per Day
Australia	14,870	15,040	18,990	17,900	358	21,600	452
Brunei/Sarawak	9,510	13,210	15,360	13,400	268	13,620	288
Burma	920	970	1,000	1,000	20	1,020	21
China	25,500	30,090	50,000	65,000	1,300	76,000	1,500
India	6,850	7,360	7,360	7,300	146	8,060	164
Indonesia	44,290	53,850	66,730	71,500	1,430	65,320	1,315
Japan	760	720	700	700	14	610	12
Pakistan	450	420	430	400	8	342	7
TOTAL (including New Zealand, Taiwan and Thailand)	103,370	121,930	160,840	177,480	3,550	186,757	3,763

* Preliminary.

REFINERY CAPACITY

('000 metric tons)

	1971	1972	1973	1974	1975*
Australia	30,850	32,050	30,530	32,950	33,650
Bangladesh	1,500	1,500	1,500	1,500	1,500
Burma	1,255	1,255	1,225	1,300	1,300
India	22,020	22,020	23,220	26,220	26,220
Indonesia	21,310	21,310	21,310	21,310	21,020
Japan	179,195	207,785	227,960	245,710	270,950
Korea, Republic	10,500	19,000	19,000	19,000	19,000
Malaysia	3,200	3,200	3,200	3,200	6,200
New Zealand	2,700	2,700	2,700	2,700	2,700
Pakistan	3,350	3,350	3,350	3,350	3,500
Philippines	9,750	12,850	13,350	13,350	13,350
Sarawak	3,000	3,000	3,000	3,000	1,000
Singapore	18,300	24,150	36,750	42,250	45,750
Sri Lanka	2,000	2,000	2,000	2,000	2,000
Taiwan	5,750	11,000	11,000	15,000	15,000
Thailand	4,650	7,800	7,810	7,810	7,810
China*	28,000	34,000	43,000	43,000	51,000

Estimates. *

Source: Institute of Petroleum, London.

We acknowledge with many thanks the assistance of the following bodies in the preparation of these articles: the International Rice Research Institute, the International Tea Committee, the Natural Rubber Producers' Research Association, the International Rubber Study Group, the International Tin Council and the Institute of Petroleum.

REGIONAL ORGANIZATIONS

The United Nations in Asia and the Pacific

ECONOMIC AND SOCIAL COMMISSION FOR ASIA AND THE PACIFIC—ESCAP

Sala Santitham, Bangkok, Thailand
Telephone: 813544

Founded in 1947 to encourage the economic and social development of Asia and the Far East. The title ESCAP, which replaced ECAFE, was adopted after a re-organization in 1974.

MEMBERS

Afghanistan
Australia
Bangladesh
Bhutan
Burma
Cambodia
China, People's Republic
France
India
Indonesia
Iran
Japan
Korea, Republic
Laos
Malaysia
Mongolia
Nauru
Nepal
Netherlands
New Zealand
Pakistan
Philippines
Singapore
Sri Lanka
Thailand
Tonga
U.S.S.R.
United Kingdom
U.S.A.
Viet-Nam, South
Western Samoa

ASSOCIATE MEMBERS

Brunei
Cook Islands
Fiji
Gilbert Islands
Hong Kong
Papua New Guinea
Solomon Islands
Trust Territory of the Pacific Islands
Tuvalu

ORGANIZATION

(as of April 1976)

The work of the Commission is conducted through its annual sessions and, under the direction which it gives in its new conference structure, through the meetings of its main committees, *ad hoc* conferences and *ad hoc* working groups of government officials or experts. Other activity includes field missions, training courses and seminars. Technical assistance is provided for governments, while the secretariat continually provides its services at headquarters in Bangkok.

The nine main legislative committees are:

Agricultural development;
Development planning;
Industry, housing and technology;
Natural resources;
Population;
Social development;
Statistics;
Trade;
Transport and communications.

A Staff Service on Shipping and Ports is maintained at the Secretariat; its work will be taken over by a new wing of the Committee on Transport and Communications.

Executive Secretary: J. B. P. Maramis (Indonesia).

Deputy Executive Secretary: Princy H. Siriwardene (Sri Lanka).

FUNCTIONS

ESCAP's three fields of activity are as follows: promoting regional co-operation on social and economic problems, with increasing attention to sub-regional approaches as well as assistance to individual governments in planning and carrying out balanced development programmes. The emphasis is on activities which aim to increase food production, reduce mass poverty, and reduce population pressures and unemployment in Asia; and together with a new emphasis on agricultural problems, more attention is being paid to the application of science and technology to development.

Another new priority is the direct involvement of society at all levels, and of women especially, in the process of development.

Although ESCAP does not itself distribute capital aid, it has helped to set up and attract funds for regional and sub-regional projects that, in turn, provide development assistance. It is also increasingly becoming the executing agency for regional projects.

ANNUAL SESSIONS

At its yearly sessions the Commission examines the region's problems, reviews progress, sets new goals and priorities and may launch new projects.

32nd Session, Bangkok, March-April 1976: established guidelines under policy changes announced at the 1974 session.

The main emphasis has been on mutual self-help amongst developing countries and on self-reliance of the region. The Commission called for action to increase the members' share in world shipping (3 per cent in 1976); for special measures for land-locked and island countries; and for greater co-operation with the World Food Council.

Next session: Bangkok, March or April 1977.

NEW INSTITUTIONS

An intergovernmental council is to be set up in 1977 for the four regional training institutions (ACDA, ACTRSWD, Asian Development Institute and Asian Statistical Institute below); it will be assisted by a co-ordinating committee of technical staff, while an expert advisory committee will serve each institution, all to be set up in 1976.

A regional centre in Iran will provide research and training facilities for women; and a regional centre for the transfer of technology is to be established in India.

The constitution of a new organization, the Asia-Pacific Telecommunity, was opened for signature in April 1976. Its headquarters are expected to be in Bangkok. It will be directed by a General Assembly (first session in August 1977) and a management committee. It will create telecommunication networks linking the countries of the region, and will also serve as a forum for technical questions. The founding agreement had been signed by 15 countries in April 1976.

BUDGET

For 1974–75, ESCAP's budget was about U.S.$11 million. This sum formed part of the regular United Nations budget in the economic and social fields. The regular budget was supplemented in 1975 by U.S.$6.7 million from various technical assistance sources. Extra-budgetary aid is provided by an increasing number of ESCAP countries and some others; at the same time, further sums are being sought to permit expanded activity.

Regional advisers and supporting personnel are paid from technical assistance funds. In addition, a UN Development Advisory Team (UNDAT) whose work is co-ordinated by UN Headquarters, in close consultation with ESCAP, is stationed in Fiji to serve the South Pacific area.

REGIONAL PROJECTS

Set up by ESCAP or with its aid.

Asian Centre for Development Administration (ACDA): 3, Jalan Spooner, Kuala Lumpur, Malaysia; f. 1973 to assist countries of the region to speed their advancement from the planning stage to implementation of projects by means of development management training, problem-solving research and consultancy services. Dir. S. Mahadeva.

Asian Centre for Training and Research in Social Welfare and Development (ACTRSWD): c/o UNDP, P.O.B. 1864, Manila, Philippines; opened February 1976; to assist member governments in formulating and carrying out a new strategy designed for the particular needs for social welfare in the region; to encourage self-dependence in spite of poverty.

Asian Clearing Union (ACU): c/o Bank Markazi, Tehran, Iran; f. 1974 to provide clearing arrangements to save foreign exchange and promote the use of domestic currencies in trade transactions among developing countries; part of ESCAP's Asian trade expansion programme; the Bank Markazi, Tehran, is the Union's agent; mems.: Bangladesh, India, Iran, Nepal, Pakistan, Sri Lanka; Chair. H. E. Tennekoon, Governor, Central Bank of Ceylon, Sri Lanka.

Asian Coconut Community: P.O.B. 343, Jakarta, Indonesia; f. 1969 to promote, co-ordinate, and harmonize all activities of the coconut industry towards better production, processing, marketing and research; mems.: India, Indonesia, Malaysia, the Philippines, Sri Lanka and Thailand; Dir. Godofredo P. Reyes, Jr.

Asian Development Bank; *see* page 108.

Asian Development Institute: P.O.B. 2–136, Sri Ayudhya Road, Bangkok, Thailand; f. 1964 as a regional staff college to raise the technical competence of development planners and administrators through training, research and advisory services; Dir. Dr. Vinyu Vichit-Vadakan.

Asian Free Trade Zone: f. 1975; provides for the reduction and eventual elimination of tariff and non-tariff barriers in trade; co-operation in commodities, industrial and other goods; and preferences for the least developed countries. Bangladesh ratified the agreement in February 1976; it is to come into force after ratification by three signatories; mems.: Bangladesh, India, Republic of Korea, Laos, Pakistan, the Philippines, Sri Lanka, Thailand; part of ESCAP's trade liberalization programme.

Asian Highway Network Project: Asian Highway Transport Technical Bureau, ESCAP Secretariat, Sala Santitham, Bangkok; f. 1959 to form a network of over 60,000 kilometres in 15 Asian countries; more than four-fifths of the network is open to motor vehicles in all weather; Officer-in-Charge S. Masood Husain.

Asian Statistical Institute: Economic Co-operation Centre Bldg. Annexe, 42 Honmuracho, Ichigaya, Shinjuku-ku, Tokyo, Japan; f. 1970; trains professional statisticians; prepares teaching materials, provides facilities for special studies and research of a statistical nature, assists in the development of statistical education and training at all levels in national and sub-regional centres. Dir. A. G. Miller (Australia).

Committee for Co-ordination of Investigations of the Lower Mekong Basin (Mekong Committee): *see* page 121.

Committee for Co-ordination of Joint Prospecting for Mineral Resources in Asian Offshore Areas (CCOP/East Asia): The White Inn, No. 41, Sukhumvit Soi 4, Bangkok, Thailand; f. 1966 to reduce the cost of advanced mineral surveying and prospecting to member nations by a co-ordinated regional approach involving the pooling of expertise and resources such as ships, aircraft and expensive scientific equipment; works in partnership with developed nations which have provided geologists and geophysicists as technical advisors; has received aid from UNDP and other sources since 1972; mems.: Cambodia, Indonesia, Japan, the Republic of Korea, Malaysia, the Philippines, Singapore, Thailand and South Viet-Nam. Project Manager/Co-ordinator Dr. C. Y. Li.

Committee for Co-ordination of Joint Prospecting for Mineral Resources in the South Pacific Area (CCOP/SOPAC): c/o Mineral Resources Division, Private Mailbag, G.P.O., Suva, Fiji; has received support from UNDP since 1974; mems.: Cook Islands, Fiji, New Zealand, Papua New Guinea, Solomon Islands, Tonga and Western Samoa; Head of Office Dr. L. W. KROENKE, UNDP Marine Geologist.

Pepper Community: c/o ESCAP, Sala Santitham, Bangkok, Thailand; f. 1972 for joint action among world producing countries on the standards, supplies, marketing and promotion of pepper; the three members supply 80 per cent of world exports in pepper; next session: India, February or March 1977; mems.: India, Indonesia and Malaysia; Dir. LAKSHMI NARAIN SAKLANI (India).

Regional Mineral Resources Development Centre: temporary address: c/o ESCAP, Sala Santitham, Bangkok, Thailand; f. 1974 to achieve rapid discovery and use of the region's deposits of minerals, and to make use of research capacity; the centre was expected to move to the Mining and Metallurgical Research Centre, Directorate of Mines, Bandung, Indonesia.

Typhoon Committee: Secretariat, Water Bureau, Quezon City Development Bank, Quezon City, Philippines: f. 1968, an intergovernmental committee to mitigate typhoon damage through improved hydrological and meteorological observation, and telecommunication facilities. It also aims at establishing pilot flood forecasting and warning systems in river basins prone to flooding; and to initiate and promote complementary preventive and protective measures. Mems.: Cambodia, Hong Kong, Japan, Republic of Korea, Laos, The Philippines and Thailand; Chief of Typhoon Committee Secretariat Dr. S. N. SEN.

PUBLICATIONS

Economic and Social Survey for Asia and the Pacific.
Economic Bulletin for Asia and the Pacific.
Asian Industrial Development News.
Small Industry Bulletin.
Electric Power in Asia and the Far East.
Water Resources Journal.
Oil and Natural Gas Map of Asia.
Mineral Distribution.
Asian Population Programme News
Asia Population Studies Series.
Social Work Education and Development Newsletter.
Statistical Yearbook for Asia and the Pacific.
Quarterly Bulletin of Statistics for Asia and the Pacific.
Statistical Indicators in ESCAP Countries.
Foreign Trade Statistics of Asia and the Pacific.
Regional Economic Co-operation Series.
Transport and Communication Bulletin for Asia and the Pacific.

THE TRUSTEESHIP COUNCIL

The Trusteeship Council has supervised United Nations' Trust Territories through the administering authorities to promote the political, economic, social and educational advancement of the inhabitants towards self-government or independence.

MEMBERS

The Council consists of member states administering Trust Territories, permanent members of the Security Council which do not administer Trust Territories, and enough other non-administering countries elected by the Assembly for three-year terms to ensure that the membership is equally divided between administering and non-administering members.

Administering Country:
United States

Other Countries:
China, People's Republic
France
U.S.S.R.
United Kingdom

ORGANIZATION

The Council meets once a year, generally in June. Each member has one vote, and decisions are made by a simple majority of the members present and voting. A new President is elected at the beginning of the Council's regular session each year.

The only territory remaining under United Nations trusteeship is the Trust Territory of the Pacific Islands (Micronesia). This has been designated a strategic area, and the supervisory functions of the United Nations are, in its case, exercised by the Trusteeship Council under the authority of the Security Council.

A UN mission visited the Trust Territory in April-May 1976 to investigate local attitudes to the future status of the territory.

INTERNATIONAL BANK FOR RECONSTRUCTION AND DEVELOPMENT
INTERNATIONAL DEVELOPMENT ASSOCIATION

1818 H Street, N.W., Washington, D.C. 20433, U.S.A.

The World Bank was established in 1945. It aims to assist the economic development of member nations by making loans, in cases where private capital is not available on reasonable terms, to finance productive investments. Loans are made either direct to member governments, or to private enterprises with the guarantee of their governments. The International Development Association began operations in 1960. Affiliated to the World Bank, it advances capital on more flexible terms to developing countries.

President and Chairman of Executive Directors: Robert S. McNamara (U.S.A.).
Regional Vice-President, East Asia and the Pacific: Bernard Bell (U.S.A.).
Regional Vice-President, South Asia: Ernest Stern (U.S.A.).

LOANS TO COUNTRIES IN ASIA AND THE PACIFIC
(approved in fiscal year July 74-June 75).

	IBRD Loans		IDA Credits	
	Project	$'000	Project	$'000
Bangladesh . .			Third import programme	75,000
			Ashuganj fertilizer	33,000
			Population project	15,000
			Barisal irrigation	27,000
			Forestry	24,000
Burma			Telecommunications	21,000
India . . .	Fertilizer co-operative	109,000	Industrial imports	200,000
	Industrial finance co.	100,000	Rajasthan irrigation	83,000
			Sindhri fertilizer	91,000
			Agriculture	35,000
			Rajasthan dairy development	27,700
			Madhya Pradesh dairying	16,400
			Godavari river barrage	45,000
			Drought prone areas	35,000
			Agricultural refinancing	75,000
			West Bengal agriculture	34,000
			Chambal area devt.	24,000
Indonesia . .	Jakarta urban development	25,000		
	Water supplies	14,500		
	Development finance	50,000		
	Industry	115,000		
	Irrigation	65,000		
	Agricultural research	21,500		
	Power	41,000		
Korea, Republic .	Urbanization	15,000		
	Development finance co.	60,000		
	Programme loan	100,000		
	Education	22,000		
	Railways	100,000		
Malaysia . .	National electricity board	45,000		
	Land settlement	36,000		
	Agriculture	28,500		
Pakistan . .	Gas pipeline co.	60,000		
Philippines . .	National power corpn.	61,000		
	Population	25,000		
	Shipping	20,000		
	Development finance	30,000		
	Irrigation	17,000		
	Rural development	25,000		
	Industry	30,000		
Sri Lanka . . .			Dairy development	9,000
			Programme credit	15,000
			Development finance co.	4,500
Western Samoa . .			Highways	4,400

INTERNATIONAL FINANCE CORPORATION—IFC

1818 H Street, N.W., Washington, D.C. 20433, U.S.A.

Founded in 1956 as an affiliate of the World Bank to encourage the growth of productive private enterprise in its developing member countries.

President: ROBERT S. MCNAMARA (U.S.A.).
Executive Vice-President: LADISLAUS VON HOFFMAN (Federal Republic of Germany).
Director of Investments, Asia: JUDHVIR PARMAR (India).

INVESTMENTS IN THE FAR EAST AND AUSTRALASIA
(year ending June 30th, 1976)

	Company	Sector	Total Project Investment ($'000)	IFC Investment ($'000)
India	Mahindra Ugine Steel Co. Ltd.	Steel	40,310	9,500
Indonesia	P.T. Semen Cibinong	Cement	29,900	6,500
	P.T. Kamaltex	Textiles	7,300	3,000
Korea, Republic	Gold Star Co. Ltd.	Electronics	27,200	17,300
Nepal	Scaltee Hotel Ltd.	Tourism	7,350	3,182
Pakistan	Pakistan Industrial Credit and Investment Corpn. Ltd.	(third commitment)	34	34
Philippines	Philippine Polyamide Industrial Corpn.	Nylon filament	21,300	7,000
	RFM Corpn.	Food processing	4,000	1,200
	Maria Cristina Chemical Industries Inc.	Ferroalloys	4,700	2,000

REGIONAL OFFICES OF UN BODIES

FOOD AND AGRICULTURE ORGANIZATION—FAO

Rome, Italy

Regional Office for Asia and the Far East: Maliwan Mansion, Phra Atit Rd., Bangkok 2, Thailand.

INTERNATIONAL CIVIL AVIATION ORGANIZATION—ICAO

Montreal, Canada

Regional Office for Far East and Pacific: Sala Santitham, Rajadamnoen Ave., P.O.B. 614, Bangkok, Thailand.

INTERNATIONAL LABOUR ORGANISATION—ILO

Geneva, Switzerland

Regional Office for Asia: P.O.B. 1759, Bangkok, Thailand.

UNITED NATIONS CHILDREN'S FUND—UNICEF

New York, U.S.A.

Office of the Director for East Asia and Pakistan: (excluding South Central Asia) P.O.B. 2-154, Bangkok, Thailand.

Office of the Director for South Central Asia: 11 Jor Bagh, New Delhi 110003, India.

UNITED NATIONS EDUCATIONAL, SCIENTIFIC AND CULTURAL ORGANIZATION—UNESCO

Paris, France

Regional Centre for Science and Technology in South Asia: 40B Lodi Estate, New Delhi 5, India.

Regional Centre for Science and Technology for South-East Asia: Jalan Thamrin 14, Tromol Pos 273/JKT, Jakarta, Indonesia.

Regional Office for Education in Asia: Darakarn Building, 920 Sukhumvit Rd., P.O.B. 1425, Bangkok 11, Thailand.

UNITED NATIONS UNIVERSITY

Headquarters: 29th Floor, Toho Seimei Building, 15-1 Shibuya 2-chome, Shibuya-ku, Tokyo 150, Japan.

WORLD HEALTH ORGANIZATION—WHO

Geneva, Switzerland

Regional Office for South-East Asia: World Health House, Indraprastha Estate, Ring Rd., New Delhi 1, India.

Regional Office for the Western Pacific: P.O.B. 2932, 12115 Manila, Philippines.

WORLD METEOROLOGICAL ORGANIZATION—WMO

Geneva, Switzerland

WMO Regional Associations: Asia, South-West Pacific.

UN INFORMATION CENTRES

Afghanistan: Shah Mahmoud Ghazi Watt, P.O.B. 5, Kabul.

Australia: 20 Bridge St., Sydney; P.O.B. R. 226, Royal Exchange Sydney 2000 (also covers Fiji and New Zealand).

Burma: 132 University Ave., Rangoon.

India: 55 Lodi Estate, New Delhi-110003 (also covers Bhutan).

Japan: Shin Ohtemachi Bldg., Room 450, 2–1 Ohtemachi 2-chome, Chiyoda-ku, Tokyo.

Nepal: Lainchaur, Lazimpat, P.O.B. 107, Kathmandu.

Pakistan: Bungalow No. 24, Ramna 6/3, 88th Street, P.O.B. 1107, Islamabad.

Papua New Guinea: Granville House, 3rd Floor, Cuthbertson St., P.O.B. 472, Port Moresby (also covers Solomon Islands).

Philippines: Metropolitan Bank Bldg., 6813 Ayala Ave., Makati, Rizal, P.O.B. 2149, Manila.

Sri Lanka: 204 Buller's Rd., P.O.B. 1505, Colombo 7.

Thailand: Sala Santitham, Bangkok (also covers Cambodia, Laos, Malaysia, Singapore and Viet-Nam).

Anzus Treaty

Department of Foreign Affairs, Canberra, A.C.T. 2600, Australia

The ANZUS Security Treaty was signed in San Francisco in 1951 to co-ordinate defence as the first step to a more comprehensive system of regional security in the Pacific. This system was developed further in 1954 by the South-East Asia Collective Defence Treaty (the Manila Treaty).

MEMBERS

Australia New Zealand U.S.A.

ORGANIZATION

ANZUS COUNCIL

The ANZUS Council is the main consultative organ of the ANZUS Pact, consisting of the Foreign Ministers, or their deputies, of the three signatory powers. Meetings are generally held once a year, in one of the three capitals. The 25th meeting was to be held in Australia during 1976. Official talks, and other forms of practical co-operation, are held more frequently.

The organization has no permanent staff or secretariat, and costs are borne by the government in whose territory the meeting is held.

The instruments of ratification are deposited with the Government of Australia in Canberra.

MILITARY REPRESENTATIVES

The Council meetings are attended also by a military officer representing each country. These officers also meet separately, and it is their function to advise the Council on military co-operation.

SECURITY TREATY

The treaty itself is brief, containing only 11 articles. Like the NATO treaty upon which it was based, the ANZUS treaty is largely a declaratory, constitutional document which is not drafted in precise and detailed legal terms.

In the words of the preamble to the treaty, the purposes of the signatory powers are: "to strengthen the fabric of peace in the Pacific Area"; "to declare publicly and formally their sense of unity, so that no potential aggressor could be under the illusion that any of them stand alone in the Pacific Area"; "to co-ordinate further their efforts for collective defence for the preservation of peace and security pending the development of a more comprehensive system of regional security in the Pacific Area".

The Parties to the treaty undertake to "consult together whenever in the opinion of any of them, the territorial integrity, political independence or security of any of the parties is threatened in the Pacific" (Article 3). Each Party is bound to act to meet the common danger according to its constitutional processes, since each Party recognizes that an armed attack on any of the Parties would be dangerous to its own peace and safety (Article 4).

An armed attack in the terms of the treaty includes an armed attack on the metropolitan territory of any of the Parties, or on the island territories under its jurisdiction in the Pacific, or on its armed forces, public vessels or aircraft in the Pacific.

Any armed attack and all measures taken as a result thereof shall be immediately reported to the Security Council of the UN. These measures are to be terminated when the Security Council has taken the measures necessary to restore and maintain international peace and security (Article 4).

Asian Development Bank—ADB

2330 Roxas Boulevard, Pasay City, Philippines (P.O.B. 789, Manila 2800).

Telephone: 80-72-51/61; 80-65-11/29; 80-26-31/69.

Sponsored by the UN Economic and Social Commission for Asia and the Pacific (ESCAP), the Bank commenced operations in December 1966. Members: 28 countries within the ESCAP region and 14 other countries.

ORGANIZATION

BOARD OF GOVERNORS

All powers of the Bank are vested in the Board which may delegate its powers to the Board of Directors except in such matters as admission of new members, changes in the Bank's authorized capital stock, election of Directors and President, amendment of the Charter. One Governor and one Alternate Governor appointed by each member country. The Board meets at least once a year.

BOARD OF DIRECTORS

Responsible for general direction of operations and exercises all powers delegated by the Board of Governors. Composed of twelve Directors elected by the Board of Governors, eight representing member countries within the ESCAP region and four representing the rest of the member countries. Each Director serves for two years and may be re-elected. The President of the Bank, though not a Director, is Chairman of the Board.

Chairman of Board of Directors and President: TAROICHI YOSHIDA (Japan).

Vice-President: C. S. KRISHNA MOORTHI (India).

ADMINISTRATION

Departments: Operations, Projects (I and II), Administration, Controller's, Treasurer's.

Offices: Secretary, General Counsel, Economic, Internal Auditor and Information.

Secretary: DOUGLAS C. GUNESEKERA (Sri Lanka).

General Counsel: GRAEME F. REA (New Zealand).

AIMS

To foster economic growth and co-operation in the region and to accelerate the economic progress of the developing countries of the region, either collectively or individually, by:

Promoting investment of public and private capital for development purposes in the ESCAP region.

Utilizing the available resources for financing development, giving priority to those regional, sub-regional and national projects and programmes which will contribute most effectively to the harmonious economic growth of the region as a whole, and having special regard to the needs of the smaller and less developed member countries.

Meeting requests from members in the region to assist in the co-ordination of development policies and plans with a view to achieving better utilization of their resources, making their economies more complementary, and promoting the orderly development of their foreign trade, in particular, intra-regional trade.

Providing technical assistance for the preparation, financing and execution of development projects and programmes, including the formulation of specific project proposals; providing technical assistance also on the functioning of existing institutions or the creation of new institutions, on a national or regional basis, in such fields as agriculture, industry and public administration.

Co-operating with UN, its subsidiary agencies and other international organizations concerned with the investment of development funds in the region.

FINANCIAL STRUCTURE

Capital: As of December 31st, 1975, the ADB has an authorized capital of U.S. $3,676.35 million, of which $3,201.54 million has been subscribed. Of the amount subscribed $1,055.64 million is "paid-in" capital and $2,145.90 million remains "callable" capital as a credit backing for the bank's obligations. The "paid-in" capital is payable in instalments by members, 46.25 per cent in gold or convertible currencies and 53.75 per cent in the currency of the member. As of December 31st 1974, all the instalments due, totalling $959.62 million, had been paid except for $0.25 million due from Cambodia.

These totals include a capital increase approved in 1971, and special increases in the capital stock by three members in 1975.

Ordinary Funds: Composed mainly of subscribed capital and borrowings. Ordinary Fund operations are mainly direct loans to governments, national development banks, public and private entities, international agencies, for particular development projects in such fields as industry, agriculture, power, transport and communications. Subscriptions to ordinary capital stock as at December 31st, 1975, are as follows:

	SUBSCRIPTIONS (million U.S. $)
Asia and the Pacific:	
Afghanistan	14.42
Australia	256.35
Bangladesh	45.24
Burma	24.13
Cambodia	10.56
China (Taiwan)	48.25
Fiji	3.01
Gilbert Islands	0.18
Hong Kong	24.13
India	280.48
Indonesia	241.27
Japan	603.17
Korea, Republic	223.17
Laos	1.27
Malaysia	120.63
Nepal	6.51
New Zealand	68.04
Pakistan	96.51
Papua New Guinea	4.16
Philippines	105.56
Singapore	15.08
Solomon Islands	0.30
Sri Lanka	25.69
Thailand	60.32
Tonga	0.18
Viet-Nam, South	36.19
Western Samoa	0.07
	2,314.88
Other Countries:	
Austria	15.08
Belgium	15.08
Canada	75.40
Denmark	15.08
Finland	6.03
France	75.40
Germany, Federal Republic	102.54
Italy	60.32
Netherlands	33.17
Norway	15.08
Sweden	6.03
Switzerland	15.08
United Kingdom	90.48
U.S.A.	361.90
	886.67
TOTAL	3,201.54

Special Funds: In 1972 the Bank established Special Funds for concessional lending with contributions from member countries and from its own resources. Contributions up to the end of 1975 amounted to $56.14 million.

These consist of the Technical Assistance Special Fund and the Multi-Purpose Special Fund.

Asian Development Fund: Established in June 1974 as the new facility for concessional lending. This will replace the Special Funds. Contributions up to the end of 1975:

	CONTRIBUTIONS (million U.S. $)
Australia	22.80
Belgium	6.86
Canada	9.70
Denmark	6.22
Finland	3.60
Germany, Federal Republic	56.52
Japan	314.82
Netherlands	17.15
New Zealand	5.14
Norway	3.88
Switzerland	7.63
United Kingdom	35.54
U.S.A.	100.00
TOTAL	589.87
Set-aside resources	57.43
Supplementary resources:	
Italy	1.50
GRAND TOTAL	648.81

The total of the Special Funds and the Asian Development Fund is therefore $704.95 million which is available for concessional lending operations.

ACTIVITIES

(Cumulative totals to end of 1975)

228 projects in 21 countries have been assisted in 221 loans, 177 of which were for projects in progress at the end of 1975. These consisted of 105 ordinary loans and 72 Special Funds loans.

LOANS

	Projects	Amount (U.S. $ million)
Agriculture	46	346.89
Agro-industry	18	241.97
Industry	40	576.97
Public utilities	72	907.57
Transport and telecommunications	48	491.57
Education	4	27.60
Total	228	2,583.57

REGIONAL ACTIVITIES

	Projects	Amount (U.S. $)
Agriculture	9	1,971,000
Development financing institutions	6	299,450
Electric power	1	—*
Industry	3	280,000
Transport and communications	5	3,145,000
Others	8	536,000
Total	32	6,231,450

* Assistance in mobilizing funds from other sources, and in implementing the project.

Twenty-two technical assistance projects were completed in 1975, bringing the total number of completed projects to 102.

TECHNICAL ASSISTANCE

	Projects	Amount (U.S. $ million)
Agriculture	66	10.43
Agro-industry	9	0.69
Industry	18	1.64
Public utilities	29	6.98
Transport and telecommunications	26	4.53
Education	2	0.19
Others	6	0.85
Total	156	25.32

LOANS BY COUNTRY

(U.S. $ million)

	Ordinary Capital Resources	Special Funds Resources
Afghanistan	—	34.05
Bangladesh	11.40	125.38
Burma	6.60	60.20
Cambodia	—	1.67
China (Taiwan)	99.99	
Fiji	6.70	6.70
Hong Kong	41.50	
Indonesia	153.93	113.28
Korea, Republic	433.60	3.70
Laos	—	11.69
Malaysia	248.56	3.30
Nepal	2.00	55.54
Pakistan	235.17	100.05
Papua New Guinea	—	14.30
Philippines	332.65	15.30
Singapore	101.38	3.00
Sri Lanka	14.13	56.71
Thailand	233.20	8.10
Tonga	—	1.30
Viet-Nam, South	3.93	40.67
Western Samoa	—	10.59
Total	1,924.74*	658.83

* Excluding three loans totalling $1,350,000 approved but incorporated in subsequent loans.

LOANS APPROVED IN 1975
(U.S. $ million)

		Ordinary Capital	Special Funds	Total Project Costs
Bangladesh	Ashuganj fertilizer	—	30.00	249.40
	Agricultural credit	—	9.43	13.50
	Greater Dacca gas distribution	—	12.20	26.90
Burma	Jute mill	—	25.30	43.30
	Power transmission (supplementary)	—	6.10	10.60*
Hong Kong	Sha Tin sewage treatment	20.00	—	61.50
Indonesia	Java fisheries development	13.20	—	21.30
	Gohor Lama palm oil processing	11.30	—	15.60
	Karangsambung multi-purpose	2.90	—	5.40
	Garung hydro-electric	19.80	—	31.90
	Teluk Lada area development (phase I)	12.20	—	21.60
	Surabaya Institute of Technology	14.50	—	25.20
	Belawan and Surabaya ports (phase I)	4.35	—	6.50
Korea, Republic	Samrangjin pumped storage	1.00	—	1.80
	Machine manufacturing	17.50	—	29.90
	Road improvement	43.00	—	89.30
	Korea Development Bank (fourth)	40.00	—	—
Malaysia	Tenom Pangi power	1.20	—	1.40
	Third Sarawak electricity supply	22.70	—	31.50
	Jerangau-Jabor development road	23.70	—	42.20
Nepal	Jute development (supplementary)	—	0.53	0.60*
	Tribhuvan international airport	—	10.00	12.80
	Gandak-Hetauda power (supplementary)	—	2.50	3.90*
	Second power	—	3.80	5.40
Pakistan	Gas turbine generation	—	22.00	30.90
	Mirpur Mathelo fertilizer	38.00	12.00	196.40
	Industrial Development Bank of Pakistan (third)	25.00	—	—
Philippines	First and second Mindanao power (supplementary)	22.70	—	74.80*
	Pulangui river irrigation	13.50	—	23.90
	Mindanao secondary and feeder roads	0.50	—	1.30
	Laguna de Bay development	27.50	—	45.20
	Development Bank of the Philippines	25.00	—	—
	Provincial cities water supply	16.80	—	35.60
Sri Lanka	Urea fertilizer	—	30.00	152.00
Thailand	Mae Moh power (supplementary)	15.00	—	32.20*
	Second Mae Moh power	22.70	—	34.50
	Industrial Finance Corporation of Thailand (third)	20.00	—	—
	Fisheries development	20.00	—	40.90
Western Samoa	Development Bank of Western Samoa	—	1.00	—
	Power (supplementary)	—	1.40	1.80*
	Total	494.05	166.26	1,421.00

*** Only additional costs are indicated for supplementary loans.**

TECHNICAL ASSISTANCE APPROVED IN 1975
(U.S. $'000s)

		Preparation of Projects	Advisory and Operational
Afghanistan	Kama Irrigation and power	185.00	—
	Seeds	49.00	—
Bangladesh	Agricultural credit	48.50	—
	Serajgonj integrated rural development	325.00	—
	Agricultural credit*	—	350.00
	Greater Dacca gas distribution*	—	200.00
Burma	Forest industries	98.00	—
	Sedawgyi multi-purpose	49.00	—
Indonesia	South East Sulawesi transmigration and development†‡	495.60	—
	Smallholder development*	161.00	—
	Karangsambung multi-purpose*	100.00	—
	Bandung urban development and sanitation†‡	1,163.00	—
	Belewan and Surabaya ports (phase 1)*	100.00	—
Korea, Republic	Samrangjin pumped storage*	100.00	—
	Nakdong river basin development†	300.00	—
Laos	Tha Ngon agricultural development (supplementary)	—	57.00
	Reconstruction and development programming†	—	320.00
Nepal	Dhangarhi groundwater development	200.00	—
	Jute development*	—	90.00
	Tribhuvan international airport*†‡	—	250.00
	Second power*	—	230.00
Pakistan	Industrial development Bank of Pakistan*	—	150.00
Papua New Guinea	East Sepik agricultural development	300.00	—
Philippines	Pulangui river irrigation*	100.00	—
	Luzon roads feasibility study†	310.00	—
	Mindanao secondary and feeder roads*	100.00	—
	Laguna de Bay development*	100.00	—
Western Samoa	Development Bank of Western Samoa*	—	90.00
	Power (supplementary)*	—	14.50
	Total	4,284.10	1,751.50

* Approved in conjunction with a loan.
† To be financed by UNDP, with the Bank acting as Executing Agency.
‡ Actual financing by UNDP for those projects may be different from the figures indicated above, as a result of the financial review of UNDP's programme resources currently being carried out.

REGIONAL ACTIVITIES

(Total committed up to end of 1975: $5,541,450)

Asian agricultural survey and updating work
Regional conferences of development banks of Asia
Southeast Asian regional transport survey
Regional seminar on agriculture
Contribution to Asian vegetable research and development centre (Taipeh)
Study of South-east Asia's economy in the 1970s
Law Association for Asia
Western Pacific credit and security research project
Evaluation study of Nong Khai/Vientiane bridge
Contribution to Asian industrial survey
Coconut industry study
Panel meeting on development bank training facilities
Study of Asian Institute for Economic Development and Planning
Contributions to feasibility study training courses of Asian Productivity Organization
Workshop on irrigation water management
Strait of Malacca ferry service
Nam Ngum hydropower project
Regional Workshop on small and medium industry project development
ESCAP regional commodity balance sheets project
South-east Asian Agency for Regional Transport and Communications Development
Regional programme on development banking
International Rice Research Institute
Outreach programmes in vegetable research in Republic of Korea, Philippines and Thailand.
Seminar on harbour management and planning.
Fish market study

Association of South East Asian Nations—ASEAN

c/o ASEAN National Secretariat, Ministry of Foreign Affairs, Saranrom Palace, Bangkok, Thailand.

Established August 1967 at Bangkok, Thailand, to accelerate economic progress and to increase the stability of the South-East Asian region.

MEMBERS

Indonesia | Philippines | Thailand
Malaysia | Singapore

ORGANIZATION

MINISTERIAL CONFERENCE

Composed of the Foreign Ministers of member states; meets annually in each member country in turn.

STANDING COMMITTEE

Meets once a month between Ministerial meetings for consultations, at present in Singapore.

SECRETARIAT

A common secretariat is to be established in Jakarta, Indonesia.

Secretary-General: Gen. HARTONO REKSO DHARSONO (Indonesia).

PERMANENT COMMITTEES

Committee on Food and Agriculture: Kuala Lumpur, Malaysia.
Committee on Shipping: Jakarta, Indonesia.
Committee on Communications and Air Traffic Services: Manila, Philippines.
Committee on Civil Air Transport: Bangkok, Thailand.
Committee on Commerce and Industry: Singapore.
Committee on Transport and Telecommunications: Manila, Philippines.
Committee on Science and Technology: Jakarta, Indonesia.
Committee on Mass Media: Manila, Philippines.
Committee on Finance: Manila, Philippines.
Committee on Tourism: Kuala Lumpur, Malaysia.
Committee on Socio-Cultural Activities: Manila, Philippines.

SPECIAL COMMITTEES

Special Co-ordinating Committee of ASEAN Nations: Bangkok, Thailand.
ASEAN Brussels Committee (ABC): Brussels, Belgium.
ASEAN Co-ordinating Committee for Reconstruction and Rehabilitation of Indochina States (ACCRRIS): Kuala Lumpur, Malaysia.
Special Committee of the ASEAN Central Banks and Monetary Authorities: Bangkok, Thailand.
ASEAN Geneva Committee: Geneva, Switzerland.
Committee to establish a forum for parliamentary discussions between member states.

AIMS

To accelerate the economic growth, social progress and cultural development in the region through joint endeavours in the spirit of equality and partnership in order to strengthen the foundation for a prosperous and peaceful community of South-East Asian nations.

To promote regional peace and stability through abiding respect for justice and the rule of law in the relationship among countries of the region and adherence to the principles of the United Nations Charter.

To promote active collaboration and mutual assistance on matters of common interest in the economic, social, cultural, technical, scientific and administrative fields.

To provide assistance to each other in the form of training and research facilities in the educational, professional, technical and administrative spheres.

To collaborate more effectively for the greater utilization of their agriculture and industries, the expansion of their trade, including the study of the problems of international commodity trade, the improvement of their transportation and communication facilities and the raising of the living standards of their people.

To promote South-East Asian studies.

To maintain close and beneficial co-operation with existing international and regional organizations with similar aims and purposes, and explore all avenues for even closer co-operation among themselves.

ACTIVITIES

Economic co-operation and development. The ASEAN Geneva Committee was formed in March 1973 to assist member countries in their participation in the Multilateral Trade Negotiations at the GATT Secretariat.

A Joint Study Group was set up by ASEAN and the EEC in May 1975 to meet in Brussels twice a year. This group is to discuss possibilities for economic co-operation between the regions.

The ASEAN Confederation of Chambers of Commerce and Industry was formed in 1972. President: Tunku RAZALEIGH HAMZAH (Malaysia).

Joint research and technology. Experts from member countries have drawn up joint programmes to investigate problems of food technology.

Education. Exchanges of teachers and students are arranged, and facilities for teaching the languages, history and geography of member countries are increased. ASEAN scholarships are awarded.

Communications. The Malaysian and Thai national airlines have pooled some of their services. Telecommunications networks in the region have been improved.

Tourism. Visits of up to 7 days may be made to other member countries without a visa; tourists may also obtain ASEAN Common Collective Travel Documents for package tours and may use these in lieu of a passport within the member countries.

Cultural exchanges. Tours by theatrical and dance groups, holding of art exhibitions and exchange of radio and television programmes, films and visual aids. Cultural exchanges and social workers' exchange programmes are also arranged.

MINISTERIAL CONFERENCES

The ninth annual session was held in Manila, the Philippines in June 1976.

MEETING OF HEADS OF STATE AND GOVERNMENT

Denpasar, Bali, Indonesia, February 1976; agreed that joint ventures would be established producing urea, superphosphates, potash, petrochemicals, steel, soda ash, newsprint and rubber products.

Two major documents were signed:

Treaty of Amity and Co-operation, laying down principles of mutual respect for the independence and sovereignty of all nations; non-interference in the internal affairs of one another; settlement of disputes by peaceful means; and effective co-operation among the five countries.

Differences would be settled through direct negotiations, and to facilitate this the five nations would constitute a High Council comprising a representative with the rank of Minister from each. Decisions of the Council must be unanimous.

Declaration of Concord, giving guidelines for action in economic, social and cultural relations. This included co-operation in the pursuit of political stability in the region; the members would give priority to the supply of one another's needs for commodities, particularly food and energy, in any emergency. This last aim would be approached by forming industrial projects in common.

The long-term objective of a preferential trade arrangement was acknowledged; the first priority in trade, however, was to develop joint action in the international markets.

The declaration called for assistance between member states in the event of a natural disaster.

MEETING OF ECONOMY MINISTERS

Kuala Lumpur, March 1976; agreed to set up four medium-sized industries requiring feasibility surveys to be conducted by Indonesia and Malaysia for urea, by the Philippines for superphosphates, by Singapore for diesel engines and by Thailand for soda ash. Equity participation would be open to the member states, and the products would be granted regional trade preferences.

The Colombo Plan for Co-operative Economic Development in South and South-East Asia

12 Melbourne Avenue, P.O. Box 596, Colombo 4, Sri Lanka

Set up in 1950 in the framework of the Commonwealth and subsequently joined by South-East Asian countries, Japan and the U.S.A.

MEMBERS

Within the Area

Afghanistan
Bangladesh
Bhutan
Burma
Cambodia
Fiji
India
Indonesia
Iran
Korea, Republic
Laos
Malaysia
Maldives
Nepal
Pakistan
Papua New Guinea
Philippines
Singapore
Sri Lanka
Thailand
Viet-Nam, South

Outside the Area

Australia
Canada
Japan
New Zealand
United Kingdom
U.S.A.

OBSERVERS (1975)

United Nations Development Programme (UNDP)
Economic and Social Commission for Asia and the Pacific (ESCAP)
International Labour Organisation (ILO)
Commonwealth Secretariat
Asian Development Bank (ADB)
United Nations Fund for Population Activities (UNFPA)
European Economic Community (EEC)
Food and Agriculture Organization (FAO)
United Nations Educational, Scientific and Cultural Organization (UNESCO)
Federal Republic of Germany
Iraq

ORGANIZATION

THE CONSULTATIVE COMMITTEE

The Consultative Committee is the highest deliberative body of the Colombo Plan and consists of Ministers, representing the member governments, who meet annually. Their meeting is preceded by a meeting of senior officials who are directly concerned with the operation of the Plan for their various countries. The officials work on a number of committees and identify the most important issues for discussion by the Ministers. Each year one of the committees discusses a special topic selected the previous year. The work of the committees is reported to the Ministers for ratification.

The Consultative Committee meets in a different member country each year. All members take part on equal terms and the meetings are attended by representatives of the Observers (above) and the Colombo Plan Bureau as a participating body.

Information Officers' Meetings are held every alternate year as part of the session of the Consultative Committee.

THE COUNCIL FOR TECHNICAL CO-OPERATION IN SOUTH AND SOUTH-EAST ASIA

President: Adlinsjah Jenie (Indonesia).

The Colombo Plan Council for Technical Co-operation, which holds sessions in Colombo several times a year, is a forum for consultation on the general principles within which Technical Co-operation operates, subject to the general direction of the Consultative Committee. It serves as a co-ordinating and receiving body. It has also been charged by the Consultative Committee with the responsibilities of carrying out information activities on the Colombo Plan as a whole. It is composed of representatives of member governments, who are generally their diplomatic representatives in Colombo, but at times representatives are sent for that purpose. The executive arm of the Council is the Colombo Plan Bureau.

THE COLOMBO PLAN BUREAU

Director: LEONORE E. T. STORAR (U.K.).

Adviser on Intra-Regional Training: Dr. AMINUL HUQ (Bangladesh).

Principal Information Officer: P. R. CHONA (India).

FUNCTIONS

1. Maintains a record of technical assistance given and received under the Colombo Plan together with statistics on costs.
2. Prepares periodic progress reports on the scheme and on the Colombo Plan at such intervals as the Council may require.
3. Circulates among member countries notification of training facilities and experts available within the region.
4. Promotes knowledge of the Colombo Plan and support for its aims in member countries and elsewhere through publications and mass media material.
5. Maintains the Drug Advisory Programme (*see* below).
6. Assists host countries in the administration of Consultative Committee meetings, and other member countries in such other matters as may be requested.
7. Represents the Colombo Plan at meetings where its representation is required.

ACTIVITIES

TECHNICAL CO-OPERATION

By the supply of experts and the provision of technical training to trainees and students from South and South-East Asia and the supply of special equipment for training and research.

From 1950 to December 1974, 105,880 trainees and **students had received technical training and 27,027 experts and equipment to the value of $675.1 million had been provided.**

During 1974, 10,011 trainees and students received train**ing; 3,110 experts were sent out; value of equipment supplied was $42.7 million; total value of co-operation activities from the inception of the Plan to December 1974 was over $2,324.5 million, spent in the proportion of 18 per cent on trainees and students, 51 per cent on experts and 31 per cent on technical equipment.**

Of the 10,011 training places provided in 1974, Japan is the major donor country, providing 3,673 places, i.e. 37 per cent of the total. The United Kingdom (2,117) is the second largest donor, closely followed by Australia (1,686) and the United States (1,678).

Indonesia was the largest recipient of training and student awards during 1974 with 1,278 awards, followed by India (893), Thailand (884) and South Viet-Nam (883).

Of the 3,110 experts provided in 1974, Japan is the major donor country, providing 1,578 assignments i.e. 51 per cent of the total. Australia (911) is the second largest donor followed by the United Kingdom (291) and the United States (278).

Papua New Guinea was the largest recipient of experts (588) during 1974 followed by Indonesia (467), the Philippines (405) and Thailand (269).

DRUG ADVISORY PROGRAMME

Began in 1973, aiming to eliminate the causes and ameliorate the effects of drug abuse in member states. The programme acts as a supplement to national campaigns and is co-ordinated with the work of UN and other agencies concerned with drug problems. It has an advisory role and does not conduct any campaign operations.

Seminars have been held in member countries, aiming to inform governments and the public and to help organize remedial measures. Assistance is given in training narcotics officials by means of exchanges, fellowships, study, training and observation. Bilateral and multilateral talks among member countries are held.

Member countries are helped in establishing central narcotics control offices or boards, revising legislation on narcotics, improving law enforcement and in improving public understanding of these matters by the use of mass media, workshops and seminars.

Drug Adviser: PIO A. ABARRO (Philippines).

STAFF COLLEGE FOR TECHNICIAN TRAINING

Established in Singapore in 1974 as the first multilateral project of the Colombo Plan. All 27 member governments contribute to its operating costs.

The College is administered by a Governing Board consisting of a representative from each member government, the Director of the College and the Director of the Colombo Plan Bureau.

The main functions of the College are:

(i) to undertake programmes in the development of staff and in the training of staff for technician education;

(ii) to conduct study conferences and courses in technician education for senior administrators;

(iii) to undertake research in any special problems in the training of technicians in the region;

(iv) to give advice and other facilities for training of technicians within and outside the region.

Chairman of the Governing Board: J. P. TRIPP (U.K.).

Director: Dr. L. S. CHANDRAKANT (India).

TECHNICAL AID
(U.S. $'000)

Receiving Country	1974				
	Trainees	Experts	Equipment	Other	Total
Afghanistan	1,545.6	3,446.6	663.5	494.2	6,149.9
Australia	0.3	3.3		—	3.6
Bangladesh	1,399.7	728.0	117.5	2,616.9	4,862.1
Bhutan	148.4	26.3	40.8	15.1	230.6
Brunei	5.4	109.0	—	14.3	128.7
Burma	1,212.1	1,666.5	368.8	362.3	3,609.7
Cambodia	647.7	66.4	15.3	181.1	910.5
Fiji	424.2	3,806.1	42.3	641.3	4,913.9
India	2,884.4	2,519.8	780.4	477.1	6,661.7
Indonesia	6,602.0	6,918.2	8,028.3	3,680.7	25,229.2
Iran	1,139.7	955.5	560.4	140.6	2,796.2
Korea, Republic	2,323.8	845.0	1,134.0	261.1	4,563.9
Laos	1,333.0	7,885.3	10,044.6	694.2	19,957.1
Malaysia	3,358.6	2,809.8	958.1	2,439.1	9,565.6
Maldives	120.8	10.9		79.8	211.5
Nepal	1,398.2	2,059.2	801.8	936.6	5,195.8
Pakistan	1,254.6	928.3	203.8	597.4	2,984.1
Papua New Guinea	2,141.7	104,877.9	—	81.1	107,100.7
Philippines	2,260.9	3,782.4	675.5	1,364.1	8,082.9
Singapore	1,944.5	1,175.5	75.2	360.4	3,554.6
Sri Lanka	1,754.8	517.0	398.1	311.3	2,981.2
Thailand	3,203.8	2,727.8	972.2	2,267.5	9,171.3
Viet-Nam, South	5,487.9	13,118.1	16,788.0	289.6	35,684.6
Entire Area	2,571.8	470.9	62.5	367.4	3,472.6
Total	45,164.0	161,453.8	42,731.1	18,671.2	268,020.1

FLOW OF FUNDS FROM COLOMBO PLAN DONOR COUNTRIES
(Total Net Official Disbursements, in $ U.S. million)

	1973						
	Australia	Canada	Japan	New Zealand	United Kingdom	U.S.A.	Total
Afghanistan	0.72	—	0.90	0.01	0.43	33.00	35.06
Bangladesh	4.35	45.0	28.97	0.76	6.54	135.00	220.62
Bhutan	0.26	—	0.09	0.03	—	—	0.38
Burma	1.50	0.383	56.27	0.06	0.81	—	59.02
Cambodia	2.10	0.0984	10.82	0.41	0.62	125.00	139.05
Fiji	2.93	—	0.02	1.39	8.25	1.00	13.59
India	2.32	74.0	68.98	0.22	88.94	84.00	318.46
Indonesia	28.65	21.7	142.86	2.19	19.52	158.00	372.92
Iran	0.22	—	−0.47	—	0.42	−15.00	−14.81
Korea, Republic	0.89	—	156.64	0.27	0.62	91.00	249.42
Laos	2.30	0.245	5.42	0.19	2.17	54.00	64.32
Malaysia	6.00	—	15.45	1.00	8.72	3.00	34.17
Maldives	0.14	—	0.01	0.03	0.24	—	0.42
Nepal	0.62	—	1.25	0.02	5.42	10.00	17.31
Pakistan	2.74	21.9	14.28	0.15	10.77	120.00	169.84
Papua New Guinea	210.96	—	0.19	—	0.02	—	202.17
Philippines	1.54	—	141.58	0.43	0.33	64.00	207.88
Singapore	1.54	0.620	3.51	0.26	16.73	—	22.66
Sri Lanka	2.52	5.6	3.82	0.04	3.95	9.00	24.93
Thailand	5.27	0.423	17.63	1.02	2.84	24.00	51.18
Viet-Nam, South	7.94	1.0	17.99	0.95	0.40	403.00	431.28
Regional and General	—	—	—	0.38	2.38	—	2.76
Total	276.51	170.96	686.21	9.81	180.12	1,299.00	2,622.61

Source: Annual Reports of the Colombo Plan and Individual Contributions Chapters.

BILATERAL CAPITAL AND TECHNICAL AID IN 1974

	$ Million
Australia	378.1
Canada	232.2
Japan	n.a.
New Zealand	13.4
United Kingdom	230.0
U.S.A.	1,524.0
Total	2,377.7

FINANCE

Contributions to cover expenses are normally equal from member governments; temporarily governments with a GNP of less than U.S. $1,000 million a year contribute at half the normal rate.

PUBLICATIONS

The Colombo Plan Newsletter (monthly).

Annual Report of the Consultative Committee.

Annual Report of the Council for Technical Co-operation.

This is the Colombo Plan.

A Compendium of Some Major Colombo Plan Assisted Projects in South and South-East Asia (rev. edition 1976).

Agriculture in the Colombo Plan Region.

New Dimensions of International Technical Co-operation (Singapore 1974).

Development Aid—Contributions of Major Donors (Second edition 1975).

New Directions in Vocational Guidance (Philippines 1974, Pakistan 1976).

Intra-regional Technician Training (Sixth Colloquium, 1975).

Narcotics and Drug Abuse Problems (Sri Lanka 1973).

Drug Abuse Prevention Education (Philippines 1974).

Prevention and Control of Drug Abuse (Pakistan 1975).

Indus Waters Treaty

A Treaty governing the use of the Indus Basin waters, signed September 1960.

SIGNATORIES

India **Pakistan**

International Bank for Reconstruction and Development (World Bank)

THE INDUS BASIN

Some 50 million people depend for their livelihood upon the six rivers of the Indus Basin flowing from the Himalayas to Pakistan and the Arabian Sea. These rivers are the Indus itself, the Jhelum, the Chenab, the Ravi, the Sutlej and the Beas. Before 1947, the rivers fed the irrigation canals of the Punjab in undivided India. At the transfer of power in 1947, most of the irrigated area became part of Pakistan although some canals and headworks went to India. Since 1951 the World Bank had been trying to settle differences between India and Pakistan over the division of river water and these attempts came to fruition in the Indus Waters Treaty in 1960. Under the Treaty the waters of the three eastern rivers, the Ravi, Beas and Sutlej were allocated to India and the waters of the three western rivers, the Indus, the Jhelum and the Chenab to Pakistan. Storage and irrigation works to the value of over U.S. $1,200 million have been constructed.

INDUS COMMISSION

Indian Commissioner: B. S. Bansal.
Pakistan Commissioner: S. Habib-ur-Rahman.

The two-man Commission is responsible for establishing and maintaining co-operative arrangements for the implementation of the Indus Water Treaty, and for promoting co-operation between the parties in the development of the waters of the rivers. The Commission reports at least once a year to member governments. First Meeting March 1961.

DEVELOPMENT FUNDS

Simultaneously with the signing of the Treaty, an international financial agreement was executed by the Governments of Australia, Canada, Federal Republic of Germany, New Zealand, Pakistan, United Kingdom, United States and by the IBRD. This agreement created the Indus Basin Development Fund to finance the construction of irrigation and other works in Pakistan.

In April 1964 a Supplemental Agreement came into force, providing for a further $315 million in foreign exchange. The aggregate resources of the Fund in foreign exchange and in Pakistani rupees amount to the equivalent of $1,600 million.

The Indus Basin Development Fund also financed a study, completed in 1967, of the water and power resources of West Pakistan to provide the Pakistan Government with a basis for development planning.

In May 1968, an agreement was executed by the Governments of Canada, France, Italy, Pakistan, the United Kingdom, the United States and the IBRD creating the Tarbela Development Fund to finance the construction of a dam on the Indus River at Tarbela.

Administration

The Indus Basin and Tarbela Development Funds are administered by the IBRD.

INDUS BASIN DEVELOPMENT FUND

System of Works

The following major operations have been undertaken by Pakistan and financed from the Indus Basin Development Fund:

1. Construction of the Mangla Dam on the Jhelum River. This Dam was inaugurated in November 1967.
2. Development of 3 million kW. of hydroelectric potential in West Pakistan.
3. Construction of six new barrages.
4. Construction or re-modelling of eight link canals. The first link canal system, joining the Chenab and Sutlej Rivers, was completed in March 1965.

The Indus Basin Development Fund Agreement, as supplemented in 1964, provided for the following contributions:

Grants

Australia	£A11,634,643
Canada	Canadian $38,910,794
Germany, Federal Republic	DM206,400,000
India*	£62,060,000
New Zealand	£NZ1,503,434
United Kingdom	£34,838,571
U.S.A.	U.S. $295,590,000

* *See* also Article 5 of Indus Water Treaty.

Loans

IBRD (World Bank)	U.S. $ 80,000,000
IDA (International Development Association)	U.S. $ 58,540,000
U.S.A.	U.S. $121,220,000

The United States has also contributed U.S. $235,000,000 in Pakistan rupees. Pakistan is providing £440,000 and the remainder of the local currency required.

TARBELA DEVELOPMENT FUND

The construction of the Tarbela Dam was undertaken by Pakistan and financed by the Tarbela Development Fund which will receive the balance of the Indus Basin Development Fund available after the other works have been completed and the following contributions by the parties to the Tarbela Development Fund Agreement:

Canada	Canadian $5,000,000
France	150,000,000 francs
Italy	25,000,000,000 Lire
United Kingdom	£10,000,000
U.S.A.	U.S. $50,000,000
IBRD	U.S. $25,000,000

Pakistan is to provide the Tarbela Development Fund with rupees for the required local expenditure. The Canadian, U.K. and U.S. contributions can be used only for expenditures in those countries. The contributions of the U.S. and the IBRD are residual.

Further special contributions were made in August 1975 to help finance the cost of repairs and additional works at the dam, which was seriously damaged in 1974. These consisted of the following credits, expressed in U.S. dollar equivalents.

Australia	$1,300,000
Germany, Federal Republic	$6,300,000
Italy	$10,000,000
United Kingdom	$6,000,000
U.S.A.	$10,000,000
IDA	$8,000,000

In addition Canada has agreed to release the balance of its contribution to the 1968 Fund; the total amount provided was $41,600,000.

INDUS WATERS TREATY

1. The Preamble recognizes the need to fix and delimit the rights and obligations of the Governments of India and of Pakistan concerning the use of the waters of the Indus river system.
2. Allots the waters of the three eastern rivers to India with certain minor exceptions. The transition period will be 10 years.
3. The waters of the three western rivers are allotted to Pakistan with certain stated exceptions.
4. Pakistan undertakes to construct a system of works.
5. India is to contribute to the Indus Basin Development Fund £62.06 million in 10 equal yearly instalments.
6. Both countries recognize their "Common interest in the optimum development of the rivers, and, to that end, they declare their intention to co-operate, by mutual agreement, to the fullest possible extent".
7. The Treaty sets up a permanent Indus Commission consisting of two persons, one appointed by each of the two Governments. The functions of the Commission will be "to establish and maintain co-operative arrangements between the parties in the development of the waters of the rivers".
8. Where differences cannot be settled by agreement between the Commissioners the Treaty establishes machinery for resort to a Neutral Expert (who is to be a highly qualified engineer) for a final decision on technical questions.
9. Differences which cannot be settled by the Neutral Expert will be treated as disputes, and failing resolution by agreement between the two Governments will be referred to a Court of Arbitration.
10. The Treaty has eight annexures. The principal matters covered in these annexures are:
    (a) Agricultural use by Pakistan of water from the tributaries of the Ravi river.
    (b) Agricultural use by India of water from the western rivers.
    (c) The use of the water of the western rivers by India for the generation of hydroelectric power.
    (d) The storage of water by India on the western rivers.
    (e) The questions which may be referred to a Neutral Expert.
    (f) The appointment and procedure of a Court of Arbitration.
    (g) Transitional arrangements relating to the supply of water to Pakistan during the transition period.
11. The Treaty came into force on January 12th, 1961, on the exchange of ratification.

Mekong River Development Project

c/o ESCAP, Sala Santitham, Bangkok, Thailand

To develop the water resources of the Lower Mekong Basin, including mainstream and tributaries, for hydry-electric power, irrigation, navigation, fisheries, flood control and other purposes.

MEMBERS

Cambodia   Laos   Thailand   South Viet-Nam

CO-OPERATING COUNTRIES

Australia
Austria
Belgium
Canada
Denmark
Egypt
Finland
France
Federal Republic of Germany
Hong Kong
India
Indonesia
Iran
Israel
Italy
Japan
Netherlands
New Zealand
Norway
Pakistan
Philippines
Sweden
Switzerland
United Kingdom
U.S.A.

CO-ORDINATION COMMITTEE

Committee for Co-ordination of Investigations of the Lower Mekong Basin: meets three or more times annually, chairmanship rotating between the four member (riparian) states (1976, Thailand).

Chairman: Dr. BOONROD BINSON (Thailand).

ADVISORY BOARD

Composed of members of outstanding international reputation to advise the Committee on technical, financial, economic and other matters; Chair. (1975): Dr. V. H. UMBRICHT (Switzerland).

EXECUTIVE AGENT

Responsible for day-to-day management and co-ordination between sessions of the Committee. Assisted by a staff provided by the riparian member countries and the United Nations (ESCAP and UNDP).

Executive Agent: W. J. VAN DER OORD.

MAIN ACTIVITIES

Data Collection

In such fields as hydrology, meteorology, mapping and levelling, agriculture and industry. An indicative development plan for the water resources of the Basin was published in 1972.

Mainstream Projects

Feasibility reports have been completed for the Pa Mong project by the U.S.A. and for the Sambor project by Japan. A project on the Tonle Sap is also being investigated.

Two bridges across the Mekong are planned, at My Thuan in the Viet-Nam delta, and between Laos and Thailand in the area of Vientiane and Nong Khai.

Tributary Projects

Thirteen dams have been built on tributaries of the Mekong, mostly with bilateral help from the donor countries.

The Committee has undertaken three multilateral schemes: these are the two phases of the Nam Ngum project in Laos, the first of which was completed in 1971; and the Prek Thnot project in Cambodia, on which work remained suspended since 1975. The second phase of the Nam Ngum project, to provide 80 MW of hydro-electric power, is scheduled for completion in 1978.

The total hydro-electric generating capacity of the dams in 1976 is approximately 150 megawatts, and irrigation is provided for a total of nearly 300,000 hectares.

Agricultural Projects

Pre-investment preparation for 10 pioneer agricultural projects has been completed for the committee by the World Bank, FAO and the Asian Development Bank, with mutilateral financial support.

Three pioneer projects and part of another have been started; the total current financial commitment for these is $17 million.

The Committee also sponsors eight experimental and demonstration farms in the basin.

Navigation Improvement

Hydrographic surveys, rock-blasting, channel marking and dredging, improvement in cargo-handling facilities and craft construction.

Other Projects

Experimental farms, mineral surveys, fisheries and forestry, power market surveys, economic studies and professional training.

FINANCE

CONTRIBUTIONS

(Total contributions or pledged at end of 1975, in U.S. $'000 equivalent).

Australia	6,181
Austria	111
Belgium	651
Canada	9,304
Denmark	1,228
Egypt	5
Finland	10
France	12,922
Germany, Federal Republic	31,277
Hong Kong	20
India	975
Indonesia	30
Iran	353
Israel	1,194
Italy	1,062
Japan	34,837
Netherlands	15,908
New Zealand	1,837
Norway	10
Pakistan	250
Philippines	431
Sweden	20
Switzerland	962
United Kingdom	3,464
U.S.A.	45,645
SUB-TOTAL	168,687

Cambodia	14,405
Laos	6,002
Thailand	112,092
Viet-Nam, South	16,270
SUB-TOTAL	148,769
UN and UN agencies	24,339
Asian Development Bank	7,850
IBRD	3,450
Foundations and others	1,110
SUB-TOTAL	36,749
GRAND TOTAL	354,205

South Pacific Commission

Post Box D5, Nouméa, New Caledonia

The Commission's purpose is to promote the economic and social welfare and advancement of the peoples of the South Pacific region. The region contains approximately 4½ million people, scattered over some 30 million square kilometres.

MEMBERS AND THEIR TERRITORIES

Australia:
Norfolk Island

Fiji

France:
French Polynesia
New Caledonia
Wallis and Futuna Islands
*New Hebrides

Nauru

New Zealand:
Cook Islands
Niue
Tokelau Islands

Papua New Guinea

United Kingdom:
Gilbert Islands
Pitcairn Island
Solomon Islands
Tuvalu
*New Hebrides

U.S.A.:
American Samoa
Guam
Trust territory of the Pacific Islands

Western Samoa

Associate: **Tonga.**

*** The New Hebrides is a Condominium jointly administered by France and the United Kingdom.**

ORGANIZATION

SOUTH PACIFIC CONFERENCE

The Conference is held annually and since 1974 combines the former South Pacific Conference, attended by delegates from the countries and territories within the Commission's area of action, and the former Commission Session, attended by representatives of the participating governments. Each government and territorial administration has the right to send a representative and alternates to the Conference, and each representative (or in his absence an alternate) has the right to cast one vote on behalf of the government or territorial administration which he represents.

The Conference examines and adopts the Commission's work programme and budget for the coming year, and discusses any other matters within the competence of the Commission.

The fifteenth meeting of the Conference took place in Nauru, in September and October 1975.

Planning and Evaluation Committee: meets in April or May each year to evaluate the preceding year's work programme, and to draft the programme and budget for the coming year; it decides on two themes of regional interest to be discussed by the Conference.

Committee of Representatives of Participating Governments: approves the Commission's administrative budget, and nominates the Commission's principal officers.

SECRETARIAT

The Secretariat was reorganized in 1967 to provide a Programme Research and Evaluation Council, which has a supervisory and advisory role and is responsible for the administration of projects of the Commission's Work Programme.

COUNCIL MEMBERS

(1976)

Secretary-General: Dr. M. SALATO.
Programme Director (Health): Dr. G. LOISON (France).
Programme Director (Social): Dr. F. MAHONY (U.S.A.).
Programme Director (Economic): Dr. G. MOTHA (Australia).

FIFTEENTH CONFERENCE

The 15th South Pacific Conference gave priority to work in the following fields during 1975:

Health programme

Special projects on nutrition, dengue fever and fish poisoning; training courses on dental and paradental diseases, epidemiology and mental health; regional seminars on cancer and primary prevention of psychiatric disorders; the provision of epidemiological and health information services.

Social development programme

A regional media centre; a regional English language teaching centre; youth leader training; community education training centre; a regional conference of Directors of Education; training courses on census methods and audio-visual methods and techniques; work on development and conservation of culture; production of audio-visual materials; tape exchange; population monographs.

Economic development programme

Special projects on inshore and outer reef fisheries, vegetable production, cattle under coconuts, veterinary pathology laboratory; regional meeting on soil science and land use, statistics and fisheries; training courses on vegetable and tuber crops, weed control in vegetables, pig and poultry production, food crops, nutrition and home economics and statistics; expert committee on tropical skipjack.

General

Special project on conservation of nature and natural resources, short-term specialist services, study visits and assistance to applied research in the fields of health and economic and social development; funds for regional travel by students; grant-in-aid towards South Pacific arts festival.

AIMS

Each territory has its own programme of economic and social development. The Commission assists these programmes by bringing people together for discussion and study, by research into some of the problems common to the region, by providing expert advice and assitance and by disseminating technical information.

ACTIVITIES

The Commission is engaged in a number of special projects of interest to the region as a whole. It also organizes technical meetings, conferences, seminars and training courses. It finances research and study visits, and collects, prepares and distributes information. The work of the Commission is in three main fields:

Health: public health; environmental health and sanitation, including the recycling of waste matters; health education; epidemiology; nutrition; mental health; dental health; research and training.

Social Development: language-teaching, including production of language-teaching materials; audio-visual aids; educational broadcasting; urban re-organization and rural development; community education for women; out-of-school youth education; conservation and enhancement of culture; population and demography.

Economic Development: improvement in plant and animal production; plant and animal quarantine and protection; agricultural extension; inshore and outer reef fisheries; economic affairs; statistics; research and training.

BUDGET

(1976)

Estimated Revenue	$A
Contributions of Participating Governments	2,443,825
Grants from Territories	25,444
Other Sources	33,684
Total	2,502,953

Estimated Expenditure	$A
Administration	362,181
Work Programme and Services	2,140,772
Total	2,502,953

PUBLICATIONS

South Pacific Bulletin, Annual Reports, Reports of SPC Technical Meetings, South Pacific Conference Proceedings, Statistical Bulletins, South Pacific Commission Technical Papers, Information Documents, Handbooks and Information Circulars and Newsletters in fields of health, economic and social development.

Other Regional Organizations

These organizations are arranged under the following sub-headings:

- Agriculture, Forestry and Fisheries
- Aid and Development
- The Arts
- Documentation
- Economics and Finance
- Education
- Government and Politics
- Labour
- Law
- Medicine
- Planning and Housing
- Press, Radio and Telecommunications
- Religion
- Science
- Tourism
- Trade and Industry
- Transport
- Women's Associations

AGRICULTURE, FORESTRY AND FISHERIES

Food and Agricultural Organization of the United Nations (FAO) Regional Office for Asia and The Far East: Maliwan Mansion, Phra Atit Road, Bangkok 2, Thailand; f. 1945; functions through a variety of Commissions and Councils (*see* below); *Regional Representative:* Dr. D. L. UMALI.

Asia and Far East Commission on Agricultural Statistics: c/o FAO Regional Office, Maliwan Mansion, Phra Atit Rd., Bangkok, Thailand; f. 1966; to review the state of food and agricultural statistics in the region and to advise member countries on the development and standardization of agricultural statistics. Mems.: 18 regional and non-regional countries. Sixth Session Manila, the Philippines, March 1976.

Chair. for 6th Session Dr. T. A. MIJARES; Tech. Sec. H. K. OH. Publs. *Periodic Report* and *Periodic Progress Report of the 1970 Census of Agriculture*, each published three times a year.

Asia-Pacific Forestry Commission: c/o FAO Regional Office, Maliwan Mansion, Phra Atit Rd., Bangkok 2, Thailand; f. 1949. Aims: to co-ordinate national forest policies; to exchange information and to make recommendations. Mems.: 17 regional and 3 non-regional countries.

Sec. J. TURBANG.

FAO Regional Commission on Agricultural Extension for Asia and the Far East: c/o FAO Regional Office, Maliwan Mansion, Phra Atit Rd., Bangkok 2, Thailand; f. 1966 to study and report on questions relating to the development of agricultural extension within the region with particular emphasis on rice production.

FAO Regional Commission on Farm Management for Asia and the Far East: c/o FAO Regional Office, Maliwan Mansion, Phra Atit Rd., Bangkok, Thailand; f. 1966 to stimulate and co-ordinate farm management research and extension activities and to serve as a clearing-house for the exchange of information and experience among the member countries in the region.

Indo-Pacific Fisheries Council: c/o FAO Regional Office, Maliwan Mansion, Phra Atit Rd., Bangkok 2, Thailand; f. 1948 to develop fisheries, encourage and co-ordinate research, disseminate information, recommend projects to governments, propose standards in technique and nomenclature. Seventeenth session and Symposium, Colombo, Sri Lanka, Oct.-Nov. 1976. Mems.: eighteen countries.

Regional Sec. D. D. TAPIADOR (FAO). Publs. *Proceedings, Regional Studies.*

International Rice Commission: c/o FAO Regional Office, Maliwan Mansion, Phra Atit Rd., Bangkok, Thailand; f. 1948 to promote national and international action on production, conservation, distribution and consumption of rice, except matters relating to international trade. Mems.: 41 countries.

Plant Protection Committee for the South East Asia and Pacific Region: c/o FAO Regional Office, Maliwan Mansion, Phra Atit Rd., Bangkok-2, Thailand; f. 1956 to act as an advisory body on the Plant Protection Agreement for the South-East Asia and Pacific Region. Eleventh session, 1978. Mems.: 20 countries.

Chair. J. D. MORSCHEL; Exec. Sec. D. B. REDDY. Publs. *Quarterly Newsletter*, *Reports of Biennial Meetings*, Technical Documents, Information Letters, Consultant Reports and ad-hoc Expert Panel Reports.

International Crops Research Institute for the Semi-Arid Tropics (ICRISAT): 1-11-256 Begumpet, Hyderabad, India; f. 1972 as world centre for genetic improvement of sorghum, pearl millet, pigeonpea, chickpea and groundnut and for development of improved farming systems for the world's semi-arid tropics; research covers all physical and socio-economic aspects of improving the entire system of agriculture on unirrigated land.

Dir. RALPH CUMMINGS (U.S.A.).

International Rice Research Institute: P.O.B. 933, Manila, Philippines; f. 1960; conducts basic research on the rice plant and its cultural management with the objective of increasing the quantity and quality of rice available for human consumption; disseminates results of research and plant materials; operates a training programme for rice scientists, maintains an information centre on rice research, holds periodic conferences and symposia.

Dir.-Gen. NYLE C. BRADY. Publs. *Annual Report*, *Technical Bulletins*, *Technical Papers*, *The IRRI Reporter*, *Research Highlights*, *International Bibliography of Rice Research.*

AID AND DEVELOPMENT

Afro-Asian Rural Reconstruction Organization (AARRO): C-117/118 Defence Colony, New Delhi 110024, India; f. 1962 to reconstruct the economy of the rural peoples of Africa and Asia, and to explore opportunities collectively for co-ordinated efforts to promote welfare and eliminate thirst, hunger, disease and poverty among rural people; Sixth General Conference February 1978, Cairo; mems. 12 African and 13 Asian countries including one national co-operative organization.

Pres. The Philippines; Sec.-Gen. SAAD MOHAMMED OSMAN (Egypt); Dir. M. R. KAUSHAL (India). Publ. *Rural Reconstruction* (quarterly).

Foundation for the Peoples of the South Pacific (FSP): 158 West 57th Street, New York, N.Y. 10019, U.S.A.; f. 1965 to research and implement a programme of development related to basic needs as perceived by the indigenous people, encouraging self-help. Regional Secretaries at Sydney, Australia; Geneva, Switzerland; Honolulu, Hawaii, U.S.A.; and Saipan, Trust Territory of the Pacific Islands.

Pres. ELIZABETH SILVERSTEIN; Exec. Dir. STANLIE W. HOSIE (U.S.A.).

THE ARTS

Afro-Asian Writers' Permanent Bureau: 104 Kasr El-Aini St., Cairo, Egypt; f. 1958 by Afro-Asian People's Solidarity Organization. Mems.: 78 writers' organizations.

Sec.-Gen. YOUSSEF EL-SEBAI (Egypt). Publ. *Afro-Asian Literature Series, Lotus* (quarterly).

DOCUMENTATION

South-East Asian Regional Branch of the International Council on Archives (SARBICA): f. July 1968 Kuala Lumpur conference with grant from UNESCO; Indonesia, Malaysia, Philippines, Singapore, Thailand, South Viet-Nam, Cambodia, Laos.

Chair. Mrs. HEDWIG ANUAR (Singapore); Sec.-Gen. JOHN DAVIES (Malaysia). Publs. *Journal of the South-East Asian Archives* (annually), *Southeast Asia Microfilms Newsletter* (twice a year).

ECONOMICS AND FINANCE

Afro-Asian Organization for Economic Co-operation: AFRASEC Special P.O. Bag, Chamber of Commerce Bldg., Midan Al-Falaki, Bab el Louk, Cairo, A.R.E.; f. 1958 to speed up industrialization and implement exchanges in commercial, financial and technical fields. Mems.: Central Chambers of Commerce in 45 countries.

Pres. ZAKAREYA TEWFIK; Sec.-Gen. AHMED FARID MOSTAFA. Publ. *Afro-Asian Economic Review.*

Institute of Economic Growth, Asian Research Centre: University Enclave, New Delhi 7, India; f. 1967 to bring the resources of social science to bear upon the solution of problems connected with social and economic development in South and South-East Asia; specialized library and documentation services; biennial training programme in sociology of development.

Dir. of Institute Prof. P. B. DESAI; Head of Centre Dr. T. N. MADAN. Publs. *Asian Social Science Bibliography* (annual), *Contributions to Indian Sociology* (N.S.) (annual), *Studies in Asian Social Development* (every two years).

Pacific Basin Economic Council: Associated Chambers of Manufactures of Australia, Industry House, Barton, Canberra, Australia; f. 1967 as Pacific Basin Economic Co-operation Council, present name adopted 1971; the Council is a businessmen's organization composed of the representatives of business circles of Australia, Canada, Japan, New Zealand and the U.S.A., and special participants from developing countries; the Council aims to co-operate with governments and international institutions in the economic development of the Pacific Area. The Council's activities are the promotion of economic collaboration among the member countries and co-operation with the developing countries in their effort to achieve self-sustaining economic growth. Ninth meeting, Vancouver, Canada, 1976.

Chair. Sir JAMES VERNON, C.B.E.; Exec. Dir.-Gen. W. J. HENDERSON.

EDUCATION

Asia Foundation: 550 Kearny St., San Fransisco, Calif. 94108, U.S.A.; to strengthen Asian educational, cultural and civic activities with American assistance; provides grants to educational, cultural, social and other projects. Representatives in 14 Asian countries.

Chair. RUSSELL G. SMITH; Pres. HAYDN WILLIAMS; Sec. TURNER H. MCBAINE. Publs. *The Asian Student* (fortnightly), *Program Quarterly, President's Review* (annual), *Orientation Handbook* (annual).

Asian Institute of Technology: P.O.B. 2754, Bangkok, Thailand; f. 1959 by SEATO; became independent 1967; four different postgraduate degrees are offered in 14 academic areas, which are mainly engineering. Student enrolment for 1974–75 was 360, from 22 nations; there are about 70 teachers from 18 nations. Supported largely by overseas governments, foundations and business organizations.

Pres. Dr. MILTON E. BENDER, Jr.

Association of Southeast Asian Institutions of Higher Learning (ASAIHL): Secretariat, Ratasastra Building, Chulalongkorn University, Henri Dunant Street, Bangkok 5, Thailand; f. 1956; to promote the economic, cultural and social welfare of the people of South-East Asia by means of educational co-operation and research programmes. Mems.: 49 university institutions.

Pres. Prof. MAHAR MARDJONO (Indonesia); Exec. Sec. Prof. Dr. PRACHOOM CHOMCHAI. Publs. *Newsletter, Handbook of Southeast Asian Institutions of Higher Learning* (annual) Reports.

South-East Asian Ministers of Education Organisation (SEAMEO): c/o SEAMES, Darakarn Bldg., 920 Sukhumvit Rd., Bangkok 11, Thailand; f. 1965. Objects: to promote co-operation among the South-East Asian nations through education, science and culture, and to advance the mutual knowledge and understanding of the peoples in South-East Asia. SEAMEO has a permanent secretariat (SEAMES) and regional project centres in Bogor (Indonesia), Singapore, Penang (Malaysia), Los Baños and Manila (Philippines) and Bangkok (Thailand). Mems.: Cambodia, Indonesia, Laos, Malaysia, the Philippines, Singapore, South Viet-Nam and Thailand. Assoc. Mems.: Australia, France, New Zealand.

Pres. Hon. CHAI YONG YII (Singapore); Dir. Dr. VITALIO BERNARDINO. Publs. Centres publish academic journals, reports of conferences and seminars, brochures, monthly or quarterly newsletters and occasional publications; SEAMES publishes reports of conferences and seminars, brochures and a quarterly.

GOVERNMENT AND POLITICS

Afro-Asian Peoples' Solidarity Organization (AAPSO): 89 Abdel Aziz Al Saoud St., Manial, Cairo; f. 1957 as the Organization for Afro-Asian Peoples' Solidarity; acts as a permanent liaison body between the peoples of Africa and Asia and aims to ensure their economic, social and cultural development. Board of Secretaries is composed of 17 members from Algeria, Angola, Egypt, Guinea, India, Iraq, Japan, Palestine Liberation Organization, Somalia, South Africa (African

National Congress), South Viet-Nam, Tanzania, U.S.S.R., People's Democratic Republic of Yemen, Zambia. Mems.: 75 national committees and affiliated organizations.

Pres. and Sec.-Gen. YOUSSEF EL-SEBAI (Egypt). Publs. *Solidarity* (monthly), *Afro-Asian Publications* (73 published).

Asian and Pacific Council (ASPAC): f. 1966; meetings of Foreign Ministers of the nine member states were held annually until 1972. A regional community was envisaged, in political, economic, cultural and social fields.

The Standing Committee, which was composed of ambassadors, decided to suspend further meetings of the Council in June 1973. Mems.: Australia, Japan, Republic of Korea, New Zealand, Philippines, Taiwan, Thailand, South Viet-Nam. Five regional projects were set up under ASPAC, of which three (in Australia, Japan and Thailand) had ceased operations by March 1975. The remaining projects are:

Cultural and Social Centre: Seoul, Republic of Korea; opened 1968.

Food and Fertilizer Technology Centre: 116 Huai Ning Street, Taipei, Taiwan; Dir. S. C. CHANG.

Eastern Regional Organization for Public Administration (EROPA): Rizal Hall, Padre Faura St., P.O. Box 474, Manila, Philippines; f. 1958 to promote regional co-operation in improving knowledge, systems and practices of governmental administration, to help accelerate economic and social development; organizes regional conferences, seminars, special studies, surveys and training programmes. There are four technical centres covering Research and Training, Local Government, Organization and Management and Land Reform. Mems.: 11 countries, 55 organizations, 148 individuals.

Chair. Gov. HIROSHI MIYAZAWA (Japan); Sec.-Gen. Dean CARLOS P. RAMOS (Philippines). Publs. *EROPA Review* (bi-annual), *EROPA Bulletin* (quarterly), occasional books.

South East Asia Treaty Organization—SEATO: P.O.B. 517, Bangkok, Thailand; f. 1954 by the eight signatories of the South-East Asia Collective Defence Treaty and the Pacific Charter; Pakistan withdrew in 1968; France withdrew from military activities in 1974; a defensive alliance with programmes for health, development and education in the Philippines and Thailand, and activities to counteract subversion. The ministerial Council decided in September 1975 to disband the organization over two years. Foreign Ministers will continue to meet once a year for informal discussion. Mems.: Australia, France, New Zealand, Philippines, Thailand, United Kingdom, U.S.A.

Sec.-Gen. SUNTHORN HONGLADAROM (Thailand).

South Pacific Forum: f. 1971; latest meeting March 1976, Rotorua, New Zealand, at which a resolution favoured the exclusion from the region of land-based nuclear weapons. Mems.: Australia, Cook Islands, Fiji, Nauru, New Zealand, Niue Island, Papua New Guinea, Tonga, Western Samoa.

World Anti-Communist League (WACL): Freedom Centre, San 5-1 Chang Chung-Dong, Chung-Ku, C.P.O. Box 7173, Seoul, Republic of Korea; f. 1954 as the Asian People's Anti-Communist League. Ninth General Conf. May 1976, Seoul, Korea. Mems.: 5 regional organizations, 69 countries and territories, 9 int. orgs.; 17 orgs. are assoc. mems.

Hon. Chair. Dr. KU CHENG-KANG (Taiwan); Sec.-Gen. Dr. WOO JAE-SUNG (Republic of Korea). Publs. *WACL Bulletin* (quarterly), *WACL Newsletter* (monthly).

LABOUR

Brotherhood of Asian Trade Unionists (BATU): P.O.B. 163, Manila, Philippines; f. 1963 as the regional body in Asia of the World Confederation of Labour, to develop mutual co-operation among Asian Trade Unionists through exchanges of information, conferences, and educational activities; 5 million mems. and 34 delegates from 9 countries.

Pres. JUAN C. TAN (Pres. Federation of Free Workers, the Philippines). Publs. *The Asian Worker* (quarterly), and workers education pamphlets and training manuals.

International Confederation of Free Trade Unions—Asian Regional Organization (ICFTU—ARO): P-20 Green Park Extension, New Delhi 16, India; f. 1951. Mems.: 21 million in 28 organizations in 18 countries.

Pres. Dr. P. P. NARAYANAN; Asian Regional Sec. V. S. MATHUR. Publs. *Asian Labour* (monthly), *Asian Trade Union Information Service* (fortnightly).

LAW

Asian-African Legal Consultative Committee: 20 Ring Rd., Lajpat Nagar IV, New Delhi 24, India; f. 1956. Aims: places the Committee's views on legal issues before the International Law Commission of the United Nations; considers legal problems referred to it by member countries; acts as an advisory body of legal experts to the member countries and provides for an exchange of views and information on other legal matters of common concern. Reconstituted 1957 to enable participation by African countries. Seventeenth session, Kuala Lumpur, Malaysia, 1976. Mems.: 31 countries.

Pres. Dr. E. KAZEMI (Iran); Sec.-Gen. B. SEN (India).

Law Association for Asia and the Western Pacific (Lawasia): c/o Japanese Institute of International Business Law, Inc., 3-18-6, Hachobori, Chuo-ku, Tokyo 104; f. 1966 to promote the administration of justice, the protection of human rights and the maintenance of the rule of law within the region, to advance the standard of legal education, to promote uniformity within the region in appropriate fields of law and to advance the interests of the legal profession. Fourth Conference: September 1975, Tokyo. Mems.: 55 asscns. in 21 countries; 2,500 individual mems.

Pres. TAKEO SUZUKI (Japan). Publs. *Lawasia* (journal, twice a year), proceedings of conference, research reports.

MEDICINE

Asia Pacific Academy of Ophthalmology: 1013 Bishop St., Honolulu, Hawaii, U.S.A.

Pres. Dr. AKIRA NAKAJIMA (Japan); Sec.-Gen. Dr. W. J. HOLMES.

Asian Pacific League of Physical Medicine and Rehabilitation (*Ligue de Médicine Physique et de Réadaptation de l'Asie et du Pacifique*): c/o P. L. Colville, 28 Collins Street, Melbourne 3000, Australia.

Asian-Pacific Dental Federation: c/o P.O.B. 234, Greenhills Post Office, Rizal, Philippines; f. 1955 to establish closer relationship among dental associations in Asian and Pacific countries and to encourage research, with particular emphasis on dental health in rural areas. Mems.: 12 national associations. Eighth congress: the Philippines, 1977.

Pres. G. RIZALI NOOR (Indonesia); Sec.-Gen. Dr. ROBERT Y. NORTON (Australia). Publ. *APDF APRO Newsletter*.

Federation of Asian Pharmaceutical Associations (FAPA): Hizon Bldg., 29 Quezon Blvd., Quezon City, Philippines; f. 1964; aims to develop pharmacy as a profession and as an applied science; membership comprises national pharmaceutical associations in the following countries: Australia, India, Indonesia, Israel, Hong Kong, Japan, Republic of Korea, Malaysia, Pakistan, the Philippines, Singapore, South Viet-Nam, Taiwan, Thailand.

Pres. Dr. MORIZO ISHIDATE (Japan); Sec.-Gen. Prof. EMILIO D. ESPINOSA (Philippines). Publ. *Journal* (yearly).

Pan-Pacific Surgical Association: Room 236, Alexander Young Building, Honolulu, Hawaii 96813, U.S.A.; f. 1929 to bring together surgeons to exchange scientific knowledge relating to surgery and medicine. Mems.: 2,700 regular, associate and senior mems. from 44 countries. Thirteenth congress: Honolulu, February 1975; fourteenth congress 1978.

Sec.-Gen. DONALD A. JONES, M.D.; Chair. of the Board JOHN R. WATSON, M.D., F.R.C.S.(E) (Hawaii).

PLANNING AND HOUSING

Afro-Asian Housing Organization (AAHO): 28 Rameses St., Cairo, Egypt; f. 1965 to promote co-operation between African and Asian countries in housing, reconstruction, physical planning and related matters.

Sec.-Gen. ABDEL HAMID EL ZANFALY (Egypt).

Eastern Regional Organization for Planning and Housing: 4A Ring Rd., Indraprastha Estate, New Delhi-1, India; f. 1958 to promote and co-ordinate the study and practice of housing and regional town and country planning. Fifth congress, March 1975, Manila, the Philippines. Mems.: 72 organizations and 145 individuals in 13 countries; regional offices at Tokyo, Bandung and Kuala Lumpur.

Pres. Prof. CESAR H. CONCIO; Sec.-Gen. C. S. CHANDRASEKHARA. Publs. *EAROPH News and Notes* (monthly), *Town and Country Planning* (bibliography), conference reports.

International Planned Parenthood Federation: East and South-East Asia and Oceania Region, 246 Jalan Ampang, Kuala Lumpur 16-03, Malaysia; work in a wide variety of aspects of family planning.

Regional Exec. Dir. SYED ADAM AL-JA'FRI. Publs. *Concern* (newsletter, quarterly) and occasional library bulletins and monographs.

PRESS, RADIO AND TELECOMMUNICATIONS

Asian Broadcasting Union: Headquarters: NHK Broadcasting Centre, 2-2-1 Jinnan, Shibuya-ku, Tokyo 150, Japan; f. 1964 to assist in the development of radio and television in the Asian/Pacific area, particularly in its use for educational purposes. Twelfth General Assembly, November 1975, Adelaide, Australia. Mems.: 64 mems. in 46 countries.

Pres. T. S. DUCKMANTON (Australia); Sec.-Gen. Sir CHARLES MOSES, C.B.E. (Box 4103, G.P.O., Sydney, Australia); Hon. Deputy Sec.-Gen. ICHIRO MATSUI (Japan). Publs. *ABU Newsletter* (monthly in English), *ABU Technical Review* (bi-monthly in English).

Asian-Oceanic Postal Union: Room 312, Post Office, Building, Manila D-406, Philippines; f. 1962; to extend, facilitate and improve the postal relations between the member countries and to promote co-operation in the field of postal services. Mems.: Australia, China (Taiwan), Indonesia, Japan, Republic of Korea, Laos, New Zealand, Philippines, Thailand.

Acting Dir. FELIZARDO R. TANABE; Exec. Officer GODOFREDO B. SEÑIRES. Publ. *AOPU Annual Report;* AOPU Exchange Programme of Postal Officials.

Organization of Asian News Agencies: c/o Antara News Agency, 53 Jalan Antara, Jakarta, Indonesia; f. 1961; a UNESCO sponsored organization for the purposes of co-operation on professional matters and mutual exchange of news, features, etc., among the national news agencies of Asia. Mems.: ANTARA, AP of Pakistan, BERNAMA, Central News Agency, HAPDONG, Orient Press, Philippine News Agency, Press Trust of India, United News of India, Viet-Nam Press, CESMOS Economic News Agency.

Pres. Maj.-Gen. HARSONO (Indonesia); Sec.-Gen. MOH. NAHAR (Indonesia).

Press Foundation of Asia: P.O.B. 1843, Manila, Philippines; f. 1967; an independent, non-profit-making organization governed by its newspaper members; acts as a professional forum for about 300 newspapers in Asia; aims to reduce cost of newspapers to potential readers, to improve editorial and management techniques through research and training programmes and to encourage the growth of the Asian press. Mems.: 300 newspapers.

Chair. KIM SANG MAN (Repub. of Korea); Chief Exec. AMITABHA CHOWDHURY (India); Publs. *Media* (monthly), *Asian Press and Media Directory* (annual), *Data for Decision* (weekly).

RELIGION

Christian Conference in Asia: 480 Lorong 2, Toa Payoh, Singapore 12; f. 1959 under title East Asia Christian Conference; structure rearranged and title changed to CCA at 5th Assembly, Singapore, 1973. Aims: to promote co-operation and joint study into matters of common concern among the Churches of the region and to encourage interaction with other regional Conferences and the World Council of Churches. Mems.: National Christian Councils (16) and Churches (79) in 17 countries as follows: Australia, Bangladesh, Burma, Hong Kong, India, Indonesia, Japan, Republic of Korea, Laos, Malaysia, New Zealand, Pakistan, Philippines, Singapore, Sri Lanka, Taiwan, and Thailand.

Pres. Dr. T. B. SIMATUPANG (Indonesia), Rev. Dr. WON YANG KANG (Repub. of Korea), Mrs. JURGETTE HONCULADA (Philippines), Bishop J. V. SAMUEL (Pakistan). Publs. *CCA Directory* (annual), *CCA News* (monthly) and various others.

World Fellowship of Buddhists: 33 Sukhumvit Rd., Bangkok 11, Thailand; f. 1950 to promote among members strict observance and practice of the teachings of the Buddha; to secure unity, solidarity and brotherhood among Buddhists; to promote the sublime doctrine of the Buddha; to organize and carry out activities in the field of social, educational, cultural and other humanitarian services; to work for securing peace, harmony among men and happiness for all beings and to collaborate with other organizations working to the same ends. Eleventh General Congress, November 1975. Regional centres in 34 countries.

Pres. H.S.H. Princess POON PISMAI DISKUL; Hon. Gen. Sec. AIEM SANGKHAVASI; Hon. Treas. Miss AMPHAI YAEMGESORN. Publ. *WFB Review* (bi-monthly).

SCIENCE

Pacific Science Association: Bishop Museum, P.O.B. 6037, Honolulu, Hawaii 96818; f. 1920 to promote co-operation in the study of scientific problems relating to the Pacific region, more particularly those affecting the prosperity and well-being of Pacific peoples; sponsors Pacific Science Congresses and Inter-Congresses. Next (fourteenth) Congress, Novosibirsk, U.S.S.R., August 1979; third Inter-Congress, Indonesia, 1977. Mems.: institutional representatives from 51 areas, scientific societies, individual and corporate mems.

Pres. Dr. A. P. KAPITSA (U.S.S.R.); Sec. BRENDA BISHOP. Publs. *Information Bulletin* (six issues a year).

TOURISM

East Asia Travel Association: c/o Japan National Tourist Organization, 2-13 Yurakucho, Chiyoda-ku, Tokyo, Japan; f. 1966 to promote tourism in the East Asian region, encourage and facilitate the flow of tourists to that region from other parts of the world, and to develop regional tourist industries by close collaboration among members. Ninth General Meeting, May 1975, Singapore. Mems.: 8 national tourist organizations, 7 airlines and 3 travel agent associations.

Pres. JOSÉ S. CLEMENTE; Sec.-Gen. KENJI SAKUMA (Japan).

Pacific Area Travel Association (PATA): 228 Grant Ave., San Francisco, Calif. 94108; f. 1952 for the promotion of travel to and between the countries and islands of the Pacific. Twenty-first conference, Kuala Lumpur, 1972. Mems.: 1,202 in 47 countries.

Exec. Vice-Pres. F. MARVIN PLAKE. Publ. *Pacific Travel News*.

South Asia Travel Commission: New Delhi, India; permanent secretariat set up March 1969; charged with examination of the question of reducing air fares, introduction of concessional arrangements and encouragement of more liberal air charter policies; mems. Afghanistan, Sri Lanka, India, Iran, Mongolia, Nepal, Pakistan.

TRADE AND INDUSTRY

Asian Productivity Organization: Aoyama Dai-ichi Mansions, 4-14 Akasaka, 8-chome, Minato-ku, Tokyo, Japan; f. 1961 to strengthen the productivity movement in the Asian region and disseminate technical knowledge. Mems. 14 countries.

Sec.-Gen. MORISABURO SEKI. Publs. *A.P.O. News* (monthly), various technical titles.

Association of Natural Rubber Producing Countries (ANRPC): Natural Rubber Bldg., 266 Jalan Ampang, Kuala Lumpur, Malaysia; f. 1970; the association aims to bring about co-ordination in the production and marketing of natural rubber, to promote technical co-operation amongst members and to bring about fair and stable prices for natural rubber. Structure: Annual Assembly, Executive Committee, Committee of Experts, Secretariat. A joint regional marketing system for natural rubber has been agreed in principle. Seminars and meetings on technical and statistical subjects are held. Mems.: India, Indonesia, Malaysia, Papau New Guinea, Singapore, Sri Lanka and Thailand.

Sec.-Gen. Dr. MOELJONO PARTOSOEDARSO (Indonesia). Publs. reports of meetings, technical papers, *Quarterly Statistical Bulletins*.

Commission on Asian and Far Eastern Affairs of the International Chamber of Commerce: c/o The Board of Trade, 150 Rajbopit Rd.. Bangkok, Thailand; f. 1952 to act as spokesman of businessmen of Asia and the Pacific region. Meets every two years; Twenty-fourth session Colombo, Sri-Lanka, December 1976. Mems.: ICC National Committees in 12 countries and associate mems. without voting rights in 6 countries.

Chair. S. AMBALAVANER; Exec. Sec. A. C. POULIER.

Confederation of Asian Chambers of Commerce and Industry: c/o Australian Chamber of Commerce, Commerce House, Barton, Canberra, A.C.T. 2600, Australia; f. 1966; composed of the national chambers of commerce and industry covering Asia and Australasia; 11 full and 10 affiliate mems.

Pres. F. R. G. STRICKLAND (Australia); Sec.-Gen. R. PELHAM THORMAN (Australia).

International Co-operative Alliance: Regional Office and Education Centre for South-East Asia: 43 Friends' Colony (East), New Delhi 110014, India; f. 1960; promotes economic relations and encourages technical assistance among the national co-operative movements; represents the ICA in other regional forums; holds courses, seminars and conferences. Mems.: 14 countries.

Regional Dir. P. E. WEERAMAN; Dir. (Education) J. M. RANA. Publs. *ICA Regional Bulletin* (quarterly), *ICA Trade News* (monthly), *Documentation Bulletin for S.E. Asia* (quarterly), *Annotated Bibl. of Lit. on Co-operative Mvt. in S.E. Asia* (half-yearly supplement).

International Rubber Study Group: Brettenham House, 5–6 Lancaster Place, London, WC2E 7ET; founded to provide a forum for the discussion of problems affecting rubber and to provide statistical and other general information on rubber. 31 member countries.

Sec.-Gen. Dr. L. BATEMAN. Publs. *Rubber Statistical Bulletin*, *International Rubber Digest* (monthly).

International Tea Committee: Sir John Lyon House, 5 High Timber St., Upper Thames St., London, EC4V 3NH; f. 1933 to administer the International Tea Agreement. Now serves as a statistical and information centre. Mems.: Sri Lanka, Kenya, India, Indonesia, Malawi, Mozambique, Bangladesh, Tanzania, Uganda.

Chair. A. D. McLEOD; Sec. Mrs. E. E. E. MOOIJEN. Publs. *Bulletin of Statistics* (annual), *Statistical Summary* (monthly).

International Tin Council: Haymarket House, 1 Oxendon Street, London SE1Y 4EQ, England; f. 1956; operates the Fourth International Tin Agreement, which is intended to regulate the international tin market by the prevention of excessive fluctuation in prices, the alleviation of difficulties arising from maladjustment between demand and supply and the ensuring of an adequate supply of tin at reasonable prices at all times. Maximum and minimum prices are laid down and all producing countries must contribute to a buffer stock of tin, which is controlled by a manager in accordance with the provision of the agreement. The Council meets at least four times a year. Mems. in the Far East and Australasia: Australia, India, Indonesia, Japan, Republic of Korea, Malaysia, Thailand. First Council operative 1956–61; Second Council 1961–66; Third Council 1966–71; Fourth Council from July 1st, 1971.

Exec. Chair. H. W. Allen; Buffer Stock Man. P. A. A. de Koning; Sec. N. L. Phelps; Publs. *Statistical Bulletin* (monthly), *Statistical Year Books*, conference reports, market reports, *Tin Statistics 1963–1973, Tin Prices 1956–1973, 1973, 1974, Annual Reports.*

South-East Asia Iron and Steel Institute: Box 1818, Maxwell Road Post Office, Singapore 1; f. 1970 to encourage regional co-operation, provide advisory services and an exchange of information, especially statistics; to promote standardization of steel products and their uses; to undertake training programmes. Holds symposia; organizes a development programme of training technical staff. Mems.: Australia, China (Taiwan), Indonesia, Japan, Malaysia, Philippines, Singapore, Thailand and 26 countries outside the region.

Sec.-Gen. E. Yoshitake. Publs. *SEAISI Quarterly*, monthly bulletin.

TRANSPORT

Orient Airlines Association: Manila; f. 1967; enables members to exchange information .nd plan the development of the industry within the region by means of research, technical and marketing committees. Mems.: Air Viet-Nam, Cathay Pacific Airways Ltd., China Air Lines, Garuda Indonesian Airways, Japan Air Lines, Korean Air Lines, Malaysian Airline System, Philippine Airlines, Qantas Airways Ltd., Singapore Airlines and Thai Airways International.

Sec.-Gen. Capt. S. Quimbo.

WOMEN'S ASSOCIATIONS

Federation of Asian Women's Associations (FAWA): NFWC Bldg., 962 Escoda St., Ermita, Manila, Philippines; f. 1959 to promote better understanding and co-operation among the women of Asia, to enhance the role of Asian women in the economic, cultural, social and spiritual development of the Asian region and to increase their participation in world affairs, to make possible the access of all Asian women to educational and cultural activities, to promote human welfare and to defend human rights. Mems.: 415,000.

Pres. Mary S. Lee (Republic of Korea); Sec. Mrs. Nicolasa J. Tria Tirona (Philippines). Publ. *FAWA News Bulletin* (every three months).

Pan-Pacific and South East Asia Women's Association (PPSEAWA): 9407 109th Drive, Sun City, Arizona 85351, U.S.A.; f. 1928 (Hawaii) to strengthen the bonds of peace by fostering better understanding and friendship among women of all Pacific and South-East Asia areas, and to promote co-operation among women of these regions for the study and improvement of social conditions; international projects include a PPSEAWA Scholarship Fund and Education Aids Abroad; international conference, June 1975, Seoul; affiliated countries include American Samoa, Australia, Cook Island, Fiji, India, Japan, Republic of Korea, Malaysia, Mexico, New Zealand, Papua New Guinea, Philippines, Taiwan, Thailand and the U.S.A.; also has consultative status with UN and UNESCO.

Pres. (1975–78) Dr. Grace Stuart Nutley (U.S.A.). Publs. Conference Reports.

South Asia

SOUTH ASIA
Scale 1:17,000,000 approx.
ONE INCH TO 260 MILES
0 Miles 260 390
Towns over 1 million people
" over 100,000 people
Boundaries - international
- provincial etc.
Oil pipeline
Railways
Roads
track
Canal
Airports
Sand desert
Marsh
Salt pan
Ice cap
Feet
16,000
10,000
6,000
3,000
1,500
1,000
600
300
Sea Level
Land Depression
AFGHANISTAN
PAKISTAN
BALUCHISTAN
INDIA
(BHARAT)
NEPAL
BHUTAN
BANGLADESH
BURMA
TIBET
CHINA
SRI LANKA
(CEYLON)
ASSAM
SHAN STATES
Arabian Sea
Bay of Bengal
INDIAN OCEAN
Andaman Sea
Tropic of Cancer
Himalaya Range
Thar Desert
Vindhya Range
Satpura Range
Western Ghats
Eastern Ghats
Deccan
Karachi
Hyderabad
Quetta
Lahore
Amritsar
Multan
Delhi
Agra
Bombay
Poona
Ahmadabad
Calcutta
Howrah
Madras
Bangalore
Mysore
Colombo
Dacca
Rangoon
Mandalay
Lhasa
Kathmandu
Everest
29,028
100 fathoms
Andaman Islands
(India)
Nicobar Islands
(India)
Laccadive Islands
(India)

South Asia

Iain Buchanan

(with a contribution by KEITH BUCHANAN)

PERSPECTIVE

A glance at the world population map reveals four major concentrations of population: Europe, the eastern United States, China-Japan and India-Pakistan. Almost one-fifth of the human race lives in the Indo-Pakistan sub-continent, on a land area which represents one thirty-third of the world's land surface. The aggregate population is over 750 million; this is approximately one-third the total for Asia and over three times that of the U.S.A.

The average density of population is not abnormally high; in pre-war days it was, in round figures, 100 per square kilometre which was about the average for Europe. But, as elsewhere in Asia, there are wide contrasts in density between the various parts of the sub-continent, contrasts rooted strongly in the geographical environment. The Northern Plains and the Coastlands, with fertile level land and abundant water, contain two-thirds of the sub-continent's population on one-third of the area. The upland area of the Indian Plateau has only modest soil and water resources and, containing approximately one-third of the sub-continent's area, supports most of the remaining third of the population. And the desert areas of the north-west and the Highland Rim, one-third of the area, have a negligible population.

A population locally closely clustered on the earth—and a population still dominantly rural in character. Recent decades have witnessed a steady process of urbanization and the sub-continent contains as many cities and large towns as North America but eight out of every ten people still dwell in villages or small towns.

The human complexity of the sub-continent is as great as that of any major world region. Five major race types may be distinguished. Four major language families, comprising 179 languages, subdivided into 544 dialects, are spoken by its peoples. Religious groupings are as numerous, are more complex, and more important politically. Two-thirds of the population are Hindus—but Hinduism is not homogeneous and its adherents may be grouped into Vaishnavas, Sivaites and Saktas and these in turn may be subdivided into more than a hundred sects. The adherents of Islam are divided, as elsewhere, into Sunnite and Shi'ite groups. Tribal religions are as numerous as the tribes themselves. In addition, there are numerous varieties of Christians; two sects of Parsis; two sects of Buddhists; innumerable subdivisions of the Sikh community. . . . And the Hindu group, moreover, is divided socially into four major caste groups, or Varnas, and these are subdivided into about 3,000 castes, which in turn are broken down into some tens of thousands of subcastes. The traditional "human fabric" of the sub-continent is thus one of extreme variety; recent economic development, by increasing the gradients of wealth and poverty, by superimposing thereon the new social and physical elements of modern urban-industrial society, has added yet further to this variety.

ENVIRONMENTAL DIVERSITY

The sub-continent has an area of slightly over 4 million sq. km. (*cp.* North America 18 million sq. km., Europe 5 million sq. km.) and is sharply framed by the sea to the south, and by the wall of the Himalayas, backed by the Tibetan Plateau, to the north. It has always been most vulnerable to the invader in the north-west and it has been through the passes of this thinly-peopled and permeable sector of the frontier that invaders, from the earliest Indo-Aryans to the Muslim invaders, have poured southeastwards into the fertile northern plains. Only with the beginning of what K. M. Panikkar terms the "Vasco da Gama stage" of Asian history did this change and European sea-control begin to expose the sub-continent to a threat from a new quarter—from an immensely long sea-coast which was margined by some of the major population concentrations of the region. It was from this direction that the European powers—France, Portugal, England—began their penetration of India; the problem of the North-West Frontier was inherited by England, it is true, but the subsequent colonial period saw an increasing external orientation of trade and contacts and though the administrative centre of the Indian Empire might be Delhi, well inland and well placed to pull together the disparate parts of the new empire, it was on the coastal margins that the pace of city growth was greatest and the major commercial metropolises (Karachi, Bombay, Madras, Calcutta, Dacca) emerged.

At the level of generalization involved in an essay of this length the physical elements in the environment may be described as showing a triple arrangement—whether of structural features, climate, vegetation or soils.

The structure of the sub-continent is dominated by the triangular massif of central and south India; this presents a steep face to the west (Western Ghats) and is tilted gently to the east. Its northern edge is represented by the Aravalli Range, curving round northwestwards to the vicinity of Delhi. The massif consists of ancient crystalline rocks and it contains the major mineral deposits of the sub-continent; these include not only a wide range of metallic minerals but also extensive coal deposits. It is fringed by alluvial coast plains, wide in the east and broadening out in the deltas of the great east-flowing rivers, narrower and less continuous in the west. The second major structural element is the northern fold belt of the Himalayas, a series of parallel ridges crumpled against the edge of the Tibetan mass and forming a great arc some 1,500 miles from the Indus in the west to the Brahmaputra in the east. This arc is flanked to the east and west by rather similar folded belts—the curving line of the Arakan Yoma extending from Assam to southern Burma and the Sulaiman and the Kirthar Ranges to the west. Between the crystalline block of the Deccan and the close-packed folds of the Himalayas is the third element in the sub-continent's structure—the immense down-warped trough of the Indus and Ganges. This, with an area of 300,000 square miles and an average width of about 200 miles, is the biggest alluvial lowland in the world, and it plays a decisive role in the population geography and agriculture of the sub-continent.

The Indo-Pakistan region is dominated by the monsoon—whose vagaries introduce a major hazard into agricultural planning—and is often thought of in terms of a wet tropical climate. It is true that parts of Assam are among the wettest places on earth but it should also be stressed that vast areas are arid or semi-arid and that over wide areas there is a clearly defined and cooler winter which excludes such areas from the category of true tropical climates. Forty-four per cent of the sub-continent, mainly in the north-west, is, in fact, either arid or semi-arid; humid tropical climates without a significant cool season occupy slightly over one-quarter of the region and humid mesothermal climates (i.e. climates where the winter temperature drops to below 18°C.) occupy the same proportion of the sub-continent. The vegetation, much altered by man and by his grazing animals, follows closely the climatic pattern; thorn scrub or a scanty desert vegetation dominates the hills and deserts of the north-west, evergreen broad-leaved forest is dominant in the high rainfall areas of the Western Ghats, of Ceylon and of Bengal, and most of the Deccan and its foothills is dominated by tropical deciduous forest degenerating into thicket (jungle) as a result of man's cutting, felling or firing. The same human impact, extending over countless generations, has also ravaged the more fragile of the soils. The soil pattern shows the same triple arrangement; in terms of agriculture and human geography it is dominated by the alluvial soils of the northern lowlands and coastal margins; these support half of the total population. Over wide areas, however, the soils are lateritic or true laterites—poor soils whose nutrients have been removed by millennia of leaching under conditions of seasonally heavy rainfall and high temperatures. The third soil type—the so-called "regur" type—is a dark heavy soil with, in spite of its colour, a low humus content. It is well developed on the basalt outflows of the north-west Deccan where it is the typical cotton-growing soil but it is found elsewhere on a wide variety of parent materials.

This summary inventory reveals the limitations—and some of the potentials—of the environmental base on which the nations of South Asia must build their economies. It is an inventory which suggests that only by careful budgeting, i.e. long-term and effective planning, can the shadow of poverty be lifted from the one-fifth of the human race who live in these marginal monsoonal lands of South Asia.

HUMAN DIVERSITY

Physical characteristics

The people of the sub-continent show a wide diversity of physical types. Skin colour ranges from the almost black skin of some south Indian groups to the so-called wheaten colour, identical with that of the Spaniard or Italian, typical of the higher castes of northern India; hair and eyes are generally dark, but blue eyes and auburn hair occur in the north-west; head-form is generally long but pockets of broad-headed people occur along the coast and in the north-east.

Language

The earliest languages spoken in India appear to have belonged to the Austro-Asiatic group; their spread was linked with the spread of a rudimentary agriculture and a megolithic culture. The speakers of these languages were driven by more powerful later groups into the remoter recesses of the Indian peninsula and are today represented by the tribal peoples of the north-east Deccan. They were succeeded by Dravidian-speaking peoples who began advancing into the sub-continent some five millennia ago. Today the Dravidian languages are typical of much of southern peninsular India; they may be subdivided into the Andhra and Tamil groups. Telugu, spoken by 38 million people, is the only representative of the first group; the Tamil group includes Tamil (31 million), Kannada (17 million) and Malayalam (17 million). The northern Deccan and much of the great lowland of Northern India is dominated by languages of the Indo-Aryan group, brought in by two waves of invaders, and falling into an Outer (earlier) zone and an Inner zone. This group is the most important of the sub-continent's language groups; to it belong such major languages as Hindi (133 million), Bengali (34 million), Bihari, Marathi and Punjabi. Finally, in the north-east, the Tibeto-Chinese languages overlap into India though they are spoken by less than one per cent of the sub-continent's population. The linguistic fragmentation of the area has impeded unification; the attempt to make Hindi written in the Devanagari script the official language of the Indian Union has, in recent years, provoked a strong reaction from non-Hindi speakers. This threatens to pull apart the country by creating linguistic states which are virtually "sub-nations" (such as Tamil Nadu) and which might in time strive towards full independence.

Religion

Even more important than these racial and linguistic differences has been the cleavage of the sub-continent along religious or communal lines; it was along these latter dividing lines that the partition of the area into the two political units of India and Pakistan took place in 1947. Three major religious groupings may be distinguished: the Hindus, the Muslims and the adherents of the tribal religions; to these we may add small minority groups such as the Christians, Jains, Sikhs, Buddhists and Parsis.

The Hindus number 453 million, nine-tenths of these being concentrated into a compact bloc of

Hindu-majority areas stretching through central and south India. In pre-partition days this Hindu-majority area contained almost two-thirds of the sub-continent's area and almost three-quarters of its population. Hinduism and its associated social system have been described as one of the most enduring organisms ever devised by humanity. It has produced leaders in almost every field of human activity; it has inspired great works of art; above all, it has extended its influence to every area of India and gives a spiritual and emotional unity to two-thirds of the continent. The caste system which is an integral part of traditional Hinduism has been a source of both strength and weakness. On the positive side, the individual castes perform charitable functions and, like the mediaeval guilds, form self-governing and self-ordering communities, with influence extending over wide areas. On the negative side, they split India into several thousand water-tight communities; this "atomization" of Indian society has facilitated conquest by outsiders and hinders the development of any real national consciousness.

Islam did not become a factor of major importance in the sub-continent until the twelfth century; today its adherents total over a hundred million. Geographically, the most distinctive feature is the subdivision of the Muslim community into two blocks of unequal area but approximately equal population in the north-west (now Pakistan) and the north-east (now Bangladesh). In pre-partition days, within the area where Muslims formed a distinct majority were to be found three-fifths of the total Muslim population; the remainder were scattered as minority groups in the north and central sectors of the Hindu bloc.

The partition of the area into the political units of the Islamic Republic of Pakistan and the Indian Union in 1947 was followed by large-scale redistribution of population which had the effect of considerably reducing the size of the religious minorities in the communal blocs described above. As a result of the emigration of some 5 million Hindus and Sikhs and of the immigration of 6 million Muslims the proportion of Muslims in West Pakistan rose from 79 per cent (1941) to 97 per cent; in East Pakistan the emigration of Hindus raised the Muslim majority from 71 per cent to 85 per cent in Bangladesh in 1974. In India 83 per cent of the population was Hindu, 11 per cent Muslim and 6 per cent other groups (Christians, Sikhs, etc.) at the 1971 census.

Sri Lanka's population adds to this diversity. Seventy per cent are Sinhalese, of Aryan descent, linguistically related to the Bengalis, mainly Buddhist—but maintaining a kind of caste system—and broadly divided into Kandyan and Lowland Sinhalese. Almost 18 per cent are Tamils, mainly Hindu, and themselves divided into various "Ceylon" Tamils and more recently arrived "Indian" Tamils. The rest of the island's population consists of minorities such as the Muslim Moors (5 per cent), Burghers (Christian Eurasians), and Malays.

POPULATION: DISTRIBUTION AND CHANGE

The general distribution of population in the subcontinent is summarized below:

Estimated Population Density in 1975

	Persons per sq. km. of:	
	Total area	Cropland*
Bangladesh	545	870
Bhutan	25	379
India	189	381
Nepal	88	631
Pakistan	84	370
Sri Lanka	216	751
Asia	81	480
World	30	280

* Includes inedible crops.

Nearly one-half of the sub-continent's population dwells in the northern plains formed by the rivers Indus, Ganges and Brahmaputra; these make up 22 per cent of the land area and have an average density of over 250 per sq. km., rising to over 400 in the eastern delta region. Only one other region in the world—the Yangtze lowland of China—has a comparable area and density of population. A second major zone of population concentration comprises the coastal lowlands; with 12 per cent of the sub-continent's area they contain 20 per cent of the population. The uplands of the Indian Plateau are approximately equal in area and population to Eastern Europe. They contain some 28 per cent of the population with an average density of approximately 60 per sq. km.; this average is, however, much higher in the alluvial valleys and in the north-east where mineral wealth has encouraged industrialization and the concentration of population. The margining uplands of the Himalayas and the deserts of the north-west show the lowest densities and contain less than 6 per cent of the sub-continent's population. Since over four-fifths of the population is agricultural the heaviest concentrations of population show a close correlation with the major areas of good farmland. A density of 100 per square kilometre was about the pre-war average for the sub-continent and about the upper limit of dense rural settlement in Europe. Areas with densities below this figure comprise in general the areas of poorer land; they support a population approximately equivalent to that of Africa south of the Sahara—on one-tenth the area.

Urbanization

The urban sector forms a world apart and possesses a significance out of all proportion to its size for it contains the majority of those with political and economic abilities (and power) and an awareness of new ideas and new techniques. It is a sizeable sector, in terms of absolute population, and a sector that is growing rapidly; the 40 million or so urban dwellers of pre-war days has increased over the last generation to close on 120 million. The general picture is summarized below:

Urban Population, about 1970

	Per cent Urban	Per cent in Cities of 100,000 or more
India	20	9.0
Nepal	4	1.4
Pakistan/Bangladesh	14	10.5
Sri Lanka	22	7.5
England and Wales	79.4	42.0

The relatively slow pace of rural development, or actual stagnation in some areas, together with the imagined or real opportunities of the great cities, have, as in the majority of under-developed countries, encouraged a strong flow of migration to the urban areas. City populations, with the exception of Colombo, have thus grown at a much faster rate than the total population; to take but two examples, the annual growth rate of Karachi is twice that of Pakistan as a whole and that of Delhi almost 2.5 times the Indian average. This increasing concentration in the cities is accompanied not only by a growing income differential between the rural and the urban worker (urban family incomes appear to be from two to four times as high as rural family incomes) but also by a widening differential between rich and poor *within* the cities. It is these processes that are in part responsible for the social and political instability which has become almost endemic in contemporary South Asia.

Rate of Population Increase

The 750 million or so people of the sub-continent seem likely to increase by at least 75 per cent between 1975 and 2000. Growth rates in the nineteenth century were erratic but during the present century increasingly effective health measures led to a steady drop in the death rate. However, since the region was an economically dependent region there was little attempt to achieve a diversified economy which, by raising living levels, *might* have contributed to a decline in fertility. The region remained dominantly rural, dominantly illiterate and dominantly poor and it preserved the high birth rate associated with these conditions. The result has been a rapid expansion of population (India 2.5 per cent per annum). The basic problem of the whole region, as indeed of Asia as a whole, is that of absorbing the massive increase in the labour force resulting from this population explosion. When we bear in mind the data presented to the 1954 meeting of the Colombo Plan Consultative Committee that in India the one-tenth of the farmers who were fortunate enough to have irrigated land were idle for about three months of the year and that the remaining nine-tenths had no work on their land for nine to ten months every year, the dimensions of the problem, the tragic waste of human resources, can be appreciated. And the belief that a "crash" programme of family planning offers any solution is disposed of by the United Nations *Report on the Family Planning Programme in India*. This forecasts that, *even with a rapid decline in fertility*, the population of India in 1985 will be around 650 million; this is because the size of the younger age-groups is now so large that even with smaller families the absolute growth rates will continue very high. The predicted growth rate is 2.7 per cent, higher than the present growth rate and twice the rate of the period 1930–50. Population control thus offers no short-term solution and the only policy with any hope of absorbing population growth and providing a stable base for industrialization is an accelerated programme of rural development.

POINT OF DEPARTURE: THE SUB-CONTINENT ON THE EVE OF INDEPENDENCE

The point of departure for the nations which today divide the Indo-Pakistan sub-continent may be best understood if we sketch in, in impressionistic fashion, the main elements in the economic pattern of the sub-continent before partition. At the top was a small class, perhaps one million strong, consisting of wealthy landowners and others living on their private incomes; below, a small middle class, some 15 million strong, consisting of clerks, teachers, small businessmen, traders and the like; at the base, the masses who could be subdivided into two major groups, first, some 70 million peasant cultivators, secondly, workers in all other categories—agricultural labourers, general labourers, handicraft and industrial workers—totalling some 65 million.

Agriculture was the basis of the social and economic structure, supporting two-thirds of the working population. Those in agriculture, totalling somewhat over 100 million, comprised approximately half a million landed magnates, many of whom owned vast estates containing hundreds of villages; secondly, a class about one million strong owning substantial farms (30 acres or more in size); thirdly, some 70 million peasant farmers, one-half of whom farmed holdings of less than five acres; lastly, some 32 million agricultural labourers, two-thirds of whom were totally landless.

The industrial structure of the sub-continent showed clearly the impact of its development as a dependent area. British policy had been to develop the region as a source of industrial raw materials and as a market for the manufactured exports of the metropolitan country. This was facilitated by the creation in the late nineteenth century of an extensive rail network which enabled British manufactures to penetrate to all corners of India and made possible large-scale exports of raw materials. By 1900 the region was an important source of cereals, textile raw materials, tea and oil seeds; it was a large-scale importer of manufactured goods including textiles, iron and steel products and machinery. And the character of development is indicated by an estimate that in 1911 97 per cent of the British capital invested in the sub-continent was devoted to purposes auxiliary to the commercial penetration of the local market and in no way connected with industry. The First World War initiated a measure of industrialization; however, the system of Imperial Preference established in 1927 gave British manufactures an advantage over both Indian and non-British manufactures and, by giving comparable advantages to imports of Indian raw materials into Britain, gave an institutional form to the dependent and tributary status of the Indian economy *vis-à-vis* that of the metropolitan power.

The result of this, combined with the impact of the Great Depression, is seen in the figures for factory employment: over the seventeen years from 1897 to 1914 these increased by 530,000 but over the similar period from 1922 to 1939 they rose by only 390,000. When war broke out in 1939 India had no production of machinery, of non-ferrous metals, nor the basic industrial chemicals; her steel industry supplied only one-half of the country's limited requirements; although the world's largest producer of hides, she was almost entirely dependent on imported industrial leathers. And, given the steady increase in population, the slow expansion of factory industry and the decline of the handicraft sector, the agricultural sector was inevitably called on to absorb an ever-increasing labour force; in pre-independence days the sub-continent was one of the few major regions of the world where the agrarian population was increasing in both absolute and relative terms.

The overall result was a poverty of an intensity unknown in the West, an intensity, indeed, with few parallels even in the under-developed world. Almost one-fifth of the human race dwelled in the sub-continent; of these, in pre-war days three-fifths were either poorly nourished or very poorly nourished; in Bengal, which may be taken as typical of the closely-settled areas, the peasants were, to quote the Director of Public Health, "taking to a diet on which even rats could not live for more than five weeks". And how finely-poised was the balance between life and death from starvation was driven home by the disastrous Bengal famine of 1943.

The new nations which emerged in the sub-continent—India, Pakistan, Ceylon—thus inherited from the colonial era a truncated and dependent economy and a backward rural economy shadowed by the ever-present menace of famine; for the 400 million people of the sub-continent these conditions represented the point of departure from which they were to begin their journey as independent nations. Yet—and this is important to stress—these countries are not lacking in resources. Even a summary inventory of the sub-continent's resources shows the region to be well-endowed with the basic raw materials for heavy industry. It has one of the largest high-grade iron ore fields in the world; the reserves of this field are equivalent to three-quarters of the United States reserves but have a higher iron content (64 per cent). It possesses virtually unlimited manganese resources, large reserves of chromite and copper and of light metal ores such as bauxite and magnesite. It has coal reserves estimated at between 70,000 and 80,000 million tons; of this, 13,000 million tons is of good quality and easily workable. Hydroelectric resources are estimated at 27 million horse-power, of which only a fraction is used. Agricultural resources are no less impressive. The region has a virtual monopoly of jute, is one of the world's leading cotton producers and an important producer of wool, silk and hemp. Oil seeds of various types represent another important group of industrial crops and the region is the leading producer (outside the Communist bloc) of sugar, tobacco, hides and skins. Above all, the sub-continent has a vast population with a heritage of skilled craftsmanship which goes back to the days when Indian textiles were the height of European fashion and Indian steel was used to forge the famous blades of Damascus. This population tends to be regarded as a problem; however, as René Dumont has observed, properly mobilized and with adequate incentives (not necessarily material) it can be converted into a major factor for progress. Herein lies the greatest challenge faced by the developing nations of the region.

PATTERNS OF DEVELOPMENT

With the coming of independence what had been the British Indian Empire was fragmented; Burma, administered separately since 1935, became independent and the remainder of the Indian mainland split into the dominantly Hindu Indian Union and the Islamic Republic of Pakistan, consisting of an Eastern and a Western sector separated by over 1,000 miles of Indian territory. And, as the "steel frame" represented by the colonial government and, above all, the army (recruited mainly in the north, in the Punjab, the United Provinces and the border regions of the Himalayas) was removed, strong regional, parochial and linguistic rivalries asserted themselves, illustrated by the communal strife in Ceylon and by the drive for linguistic states (achieved in 1956) in the Indian Union. A new phase in what W. A. Wilcox has termed "the dialectic between unity and fragmentation" had begun—and this fragmentation of peoples and kingdoms, which throughout history had left the peoples of the sub-continent powerless in the face of invaders, threatened to render them powerless in the struggle against a poverty which knew no national or ethnic frontiers.

The situation in 1975, that is, after 25 years of independence and planned development, is summarized in the table on page 138.

The detailed economic evolution of the South Asian countries is discussed within the separate country surveys (*below*); here attention is confined to some of the major themes common to the area as a whole.

The most striking features are the low levels of agricultural progress and income as suggested by per capita G.N.P. By contrast, China had an average foodgrain production increase of 2.5 per cent over the same period and has a G.N.P. per capita of between two and four times the South Asian level; income levels are one to two per cent those of most Western countries, and lower than most other Asian countries; besides, the rough average conceals major disparities

Selected Economic and Social Indices, 1970–75

Annual average percentage growth in:	SRI LANKA	INDIA	PAKISTAN	BANGLADESH
Population	2.1	2.5	2.5	3.0
Grain production . . .	−0.2*	0.9	0.8	−2.0
Industrial production . . .	4.5	4.0	4.6	−4.0
Index of agricultural productivity (units) 1968–72†.	5.3	3.9	4.2	
Inhabitants per doctor	6,151	4,500	16,240	11,000
GNP/cap US $ (1975) . .	120	85	120	60
Annual growth in GNP/cap (%)	0.5	0.8	1.8	−2.5

* 1969–70 to 1973–74. † A unit represents production of 1 million calories/male worker in agriculture.

within a population. Growth rates are below those of population increase and, except for Bangladesh, the distortion of development priorities towards industrialization is clear: in India, for example, the manufacturing sector employs 18 per cent of the labour force, contributes over 22 per cent of G.N.P., and receives some 27.5 per cent of development spending, while agriculture, with 68 per cent of the labour force, contributes 44 per cent of G.N.P. and receives 21 per cent of development spending. Within agriculture, there is a further distortion towards emphasizing industrial cash crops at the expense of food crops: between 1969–70 and 1973–74, the area under foodgrains increased by 2 per cent, and production by 4 per cent; while the area under cotton, jute, and tea decreased by one per cent and production increased by 428 per cent—suggesting that expansion of acreage as much as improved farm techniques and management and high levels of farm investment in a few favoured areas (such as the Punjab) accounted for the marginal increase in foodgrains, while high levels of farm management and investment more than quadrupled cash crop production. Paul Bairoch's index of agricultural productivity enables us to assess the situation; on his scale the "minimum physiological threshold", which makes adjustment for a non-agricultural sector and various types of loss, is 3.8 units; the level at which a country is potentially beyond the famine risk he places at 4.9 units per active male worker in agriculture. Pakistan, Bangladesh and India are below this "famine threshold"; his data suggests that this is no temporary feature but the result of a long-term decline in agricultural productivity (India 1909–14 5.4 units, 1968–72 3.9 units). Physical factors—an uncertain monsoonal climate, soils of limited fertility, human and plant diseases—are certainly partly responsible—but only partly, for far more important have been the structural or social factors; as René Dumont observes: "a diseased society means diseased land". And the social factors which, in Southern Asia, are responsible for the lagging tempo of rural development are many: excessive concentration of land in the hands of a land-owning group which uses its political power to block the taxation and land redistribution which might provide some finance for development; the gap, as in India, between legislation and practice; the domination of the countryside by a rural *élite* of landowners who are often moneylenders too; the failure, in spite of the community development schemes and the like, to produce the rural leaders on whom real development in the countryside depends. Given these things, technical progress (in the shape of water-storage and irrigation schemes, increased use of fertilizers and better seeds) remains slow and agriculture remains the Achilles' heel of South Asian development. And this is so not only because, as Bairoch has demonstrated and as the experience of eighteenth- and nineteenth-century Europe shows, the attainment of a certain level of agricultural productivity is an essential prerequisite for an industrial revolution but also because the growth of population is such that it is quite impossible in the foreseeable future to absorb the likely increase of population into modern industry; only by intensified rural development (following a variant perhaps of the Chinese pattern) can this increase be absorbed.

Widening Disparities—and Revolutionary Potential—in the Countryside

One of the salient features of the last generation has been the fact that, despite legislation, socio-economic disparities have widened in the countryside. In Bangladesh, India and Pakistan increasing concentration of land ownership has been accompanied by a sharp rise in the size of the landless labourer group. Only in Sri Lanka does there appear to have been any marginal redistribution of wealth away from the rich—in 1973, according to official figures, the middle 40 per cent of the population received 32 per cent of all income (compared to 25.9 per cent in 1963), while the poorest 30 per cent received 9.4 per cent (compared to 7.4 per cent in 1963)—however, the island's landless labourers, and especially plantation workers, have seen a decline in relative and real incomes.

The situation in India is more serious. Indian rural society is made up of some half a million villages, seven-tenths of which have a population of less than 500. Holdings of under 5 acres make up three-quarters of the total number of holdings, but contain less than one-sixth of the country's cultivated land; conversely, large holdings (over 10 acres) represent one-seventh of all holdings but contain almost two-thirds of the cropland. Indian agriculture is becoming increasingly polarized between, on the one hand, capitalist and market-orientated large farms and, on the other, small holdings characterized by low productivity, underemployment and indebtedness—the latter forcing the smallholder to lease or sell part of his land. Indeed, it is the bankruptcy of the smallholder which provides the basis for the growth of the large units by providing the latter with labour and land; by the same token, landlessness among small farmers increases.

Between 1951 and 1964, according to official Indian figures, the percentage of agricultural households owning no land increased from 50 per cent to 61 per cent, with a consequent increase in the proportion of landless labourers; during the decade 1961–71, the number of cultivators declined by 22 per cent, and at present landless labourers comprise between 30 and 50 per cent of the population in most States.

In Bangladesh the situation is similar. Although concentration of land ownership was less marked in the 1950s compared with India, landlessness has increased dramatically since the early 1960s: between 1961 and 1974, the proportion of landless cultivators rose from 17.5 per cent to an estimated 40 per cent, a proportion which certainly increased during 1974/75.

In Pakistan, too, the proportion of landless peasants and agricultural labourers has increased sharply since the mid-1960s. According to the Pakistan Planning Commission, some 4 million farmers are likely to be evicted between 1970 and 1985 as Pakistan's agriculture develops along more mechanized lines.

The élite groups of the region—from urban middle classes to rural landowners—are economically more powerful, politically more entrenched, and generally freer than ever before to circumvent legislation designed to redistribute wealth and achieve greater social equity; as a corollary to this, corruption is rampant throughout the body politic, feeding the economic crisis, and in turn nurtured by it. This is evident in India, where the wealthier vested interests—*kulak* farmers, marketing middlemen, financiers, and administrators—operate a highly lucrative "parallel economy" funded by "black", or untaxed, money (reliably estimated to be at least equal in amount to tax-accountable funds in the economy); in this way scarce resources such as restricted imports, expensive gold, fertilizers, and foodgrain are manipulated, contracts and favours are bought, and land speculation goes unfettered. That little farm income is taxed, that tax evasion is virtually uncontrolled, that smuggling, hoarding and profiteering are endemic, and that administrative corruption is an undisputed part of Indian economic and political life, mean almost unrestricted growth of such a "parallel economy", pervading all aspects of the wider economy, increasing the concentration of wealth, and aggravating current difficulties. Corruption and economic crisis interact upon one another—economic distress, for example, has led to widespread collapse of routine administration (according to Bihar's Chief Minister, for example, 75 per cent of the State's food inspectors are corrupt), and administrative collapse merely deepens economic distress. "Black" money and electoral politics are profitably combined, gold smuggling involves billions of rupees (according to one source, Rs. 9,000 million in the Dubai market alone), and private manipulation of the foodgrain trade is so effectively organized—from big farmer to urban retailer—that no Central Government procurement scheme can operate. In this latter respect, the takeover of the wheat trade in 1973 was abandoned within a year; in a situation where the wholesale price of wheat had doubled between 1971 and 1974, and the retail price had risen by two or three times that rate, there was no possibility of the administration curbing private hoarding and profiteering. In West Bengal alone, well over Rs. 1,000 million of "black" money entered the foodgrain trade between 1973 and 1974—with far higher sums invested in the richer grain-producing States. Such abuses are not isolated cases—they pervade India's economic and political structure, and their very pervasiveness marks the end of India's 24-year-long experiment in moderate "State capitalist" planning.

As landowning, business and bureaucratic élites entrenched themselves in power, and as the economies they controlled continued to fracture under the pressures of rapid population growth, sluggish and distorted economic growth and mismanagement, discontent amongst the poor became increasingly articulate. During the 1960s and early 1970s, the myth of rural India's "political passivity" disintegrated—as a clear relationship emerged between economic dispossession and class-based, left-wing political militancy. Increasingly the spearhead of, and the organizing force behind, peasant militancy is represented by the "rebel Left Communists"; the political philosophy of this group includes peasant-based guerrilla warfare (e.g. the Naxalbari revolt in May 1967), the rejection of parliamentary democracy (which distinguishes them from the "orthodox" Communist groups), and an analysis which sees the Congress Government as a captive of imperialism ruling a neo-colonial state. Given the growing weight of rural and urban poverty, and the evident failure of past policies to create either a meaningful level of social justice or a workable framework for thoroughgoing economic development, the future is likely to see a steady increase in the influence of the "rebel" group and a growing interest in the relevance of the Chinese model of agrarian reform to the problems of the Indian countryside. This, in theory, would be the first stage of a programme aimed at extending the struggle from the countryside to the cities, and ultimately linking peasants, mill workers, workers in transport and semi-processing industries, and the unemployed in a common front.

In the 1960s, peasant resistance to *kulak* control expressed itself in numerous—but often self-defeating—acts of open protest (such as the strike of landless labourers in East Thanjavur in 1968), as well as in the formation of revolutionary groups such as the Naxalites. Then, in the early 1970s, other militant left-wing groups emerged, espousing the rights of the dispossessed—the urban workers, landless labourers and small farmers, exploited tribal minorities, and low caste Indians: the Dalit Panthers, the Hawkers' Sena, and the Adivasi Movement are notable examples. As the economic situation worsened during 1973 and 1974, widespread violence erupted and major strikes occurred (notably the 1974 Railway Strike): in Gujarat, after two months of mass demonstrations, the State Assembly was dissolved in March 1974; in Bihar, after 60,000 troops and police were sent in to quell a spate of riots and demonstrations—35 State Ministers were sacked. Among the militant left-wing groups that have emerged over the past five years—some on the basis of communal or minority group support—an explicit policy line is the uniting of *all* dispossessed groups, urban and rural, in a common front.

Thus, in the midst of gathering economic chaos and political instability, the shape of militant opposition to the establishment in India and Bangladesh is becoming clearer. And as this political polarization develops, the institutions of parliamentary democracy are giving way to a strict, increasingly right-wing authoritarianism. In Bangladesh, Mujib Rahman's assumption of Presidential power in early 1975, following the declaration of a State of Emergency, was a logical outcome of three years of economic crisis and political violence. In India, too, similar conditions may be seen to justify a similar formalizing of élite control. Already, India has seen the creation of what some call a "Police Raj": the Central and State Police Forces have been vastly expanded, new internal security units and para-military groups have been formed, and the Centre's police expenditure has increased 52 times since 1951 to the 1974–75 allocation of Rs. 1,564 million. Together with a police expenditure by State Governments of nearly Rs. 3,000 million in 1974–75, India now spends more on internal security than she spends on either planned irrigation and flood control or medicine and public health—despite the worst famine conditions for over thirty years, and diseases of epidemic proportions.

One may question whether or not India's, or Bangladesh's, short-term economic future will show slight improvement—what is beyond question is the inevitability of a radical restructuring of economic life, a transformation which, if it is to overcome the chronic sickness of the economy, must be nothing short of revolutionary. Equally, one may speculate on the manner of achieving such a revolutionary change in South Asia: the traditional ambivalence and the slow slide into anarchy will prevail for a while, to be followed—perhaps inevitably—by a period of right-wing authoritarianism; but it is still too early to judge whether India's ultimate fate will be shaped by agrarian revolution along some variant of the Chinese line, or by urban-based revolution along the more "orthodox" Soviet line. Both elements of the Indian Left have growing disaffection to draw upon, both are in the ascendancy, and yet both are still relatively immature. That Bangladesh will ultimately move towards agrarian revolution is perhaps more certain—but the gestation period of such revolution will be long and painful. It is, perhaps, dangerous to be too doctrinaire in mapping the direction of such long-term trends.

The "Green Revolution" and Rural Development

One catalyst in this process of widening disparities has been the "Green Revolution", begun in 1965 with the introduction of American-sponsored Higher-Yielding Varieties (HYV) of wheat and rice. Yet the "Green Revolution" itself merely accentuated a trend towards the expansion of capitalist farming—based on the planting of Locally Improved Varieties of grain (notably CO-25 and ADT-27 rice)—which involved increased consolidation of large-scale holdings, greater use of capital-intensive methods, increasing eviction of small-scale peasants and their conversion to either wage-labourers or rural-urban migrants, and a widening disparity between areas of higher productivity (such as the wheat areas of the Punjab and Haryana states, and pockets of rice cultivation in Tamil Nadu and Andhra Pradesh) and the bulk of India's farmland—unirrigated, long neglected, and dependent upon the vagaries of the monsoon. Haryana, a model "Green Revolution" state and location of the capital, New Delhi, stands in marked contrast to such food-deficit and famine-struck states as Assam, Bihar or West Bengal. With a population of 11 million, Haryana spends 15 times more on irrigation than does Assam (population 16 million); its *per capita* income is almost 10 times that of West Bengal (population 50 million). Similarly in Pakistan, where agricultural output doubled between 1960 and 1970, the impact of the "Green Revolution" has been overwhelmingly located in the Punjab—especially in the already wealthy Canal Colony districts. Reflecting the massive polarization of wealth between Pakistan's provinces and between rich and poor classes of landholder, 80 per cent of the tractors and 95 per cent of the tube-wells responsible for the higher yields are in the Punjab, and 80 per cent of the Punjab's tube-wells were sunk by cultivators with holdings of over 10 hectares.

In the wider context of rural development in South Asia, the eight-year experience of the "Green Revolution" poses a vital question: can such technological solutions work as an alternative to thorough-going economic and social reform? To obtain higher yields, the use of HYV grains presently depends upon well-irrigated land, large holdings, a high capital input (mechanical aids, irrigation facilities, fuel oil, fertilizers, pesticides and so on as a package), and large-scale credit. Thus, such agricultural "improvement" is confined to the already wealthy minority of land-owners—in India, the top 14 per cent of rural households who manage 66 per cent of the total cropped area. Indeed, the very conception of planning in South Asia restricts any wider rural development. For agriculture has, since the inception of planning in India, Pakistan, and Sri Lanka, been given meagre attention by planners, reflecting an inherent bias towards urban and heavy industrial development (in India, public expenditure on agricultural development declined from 36 per cent during the First Plan to 21 per cent during the Fourth Plan). Agriculture-related industries have failed to keep pace with agricultural needs—Indian fertilizer production, for example, has been at 50 per cent installed capacity since 1970, and in 1973 India was short of a million tons of fertilizer (calculated at existing levels of consumption—which, even for traditional seed varieties, is 5 per cent that needed for optimal use). Despite well-developed nuclear know-how, Indian industry has yet to produce enough drilling gear for such a basic need as a tube-well.

Furthermore, essential rural infrastructure has been neglected. In India, for example, only 3 per cent of known water resources have been developed (a fact dramatized during the 1972 famine in Maharashtra, where—in 26 years of independence—the proportion of irrigated crops had risen from 6 per cent to only 7.5 per cent, and where the State spent twice as much on relief projects during two years as it spent on irrigation projects in 20 years). On the other hand, while the Ministry of Power and Irrigation has emphasized power projects and irrigation works in the more productive crop regions, there has been relatively little attention paid to the vital need for flood control measures: in the 20 years up to 1974, the national flood control programme cost Rs. 3,470 million—or as much as was spent on nuclear projects between 1970 and 1974. In pre-1972 Pakistan, large-scale irrigation work was almost wholly concentrated in the already better-off Western wing—yet despite this, the long neglect of a serious deforestation problem was a major contributing factor to the recent floods in both Pakistan and Bangladesh. Such flooding was aggravated, in Bangladesh, by the construction during the past 20 years of roads and railways across traditional flow channels, and by a long-standing neglect of regular dredging and digging out of canals; in addition, despite twelve major floods since 1954, no comprehensive programme of flood control has yet been implemented.

For the past two decades, South Asia has lacked any meaningful land reform; existing land reform legislation has long been side-stepped with ease by local administrations and the wealthy; and recent reform measures (such as the "land ceiling" legislation in India and Sri Lanka in 1972) have been seriously diluted by vested land-owning interests in political power, and rarely backed by credit and other support facilities which could make reform an effective instrument of social justice. And as the concentration of ownership increases, as rents rise from the "official" 40–45 per cent to nearer 70 per cent, as credit availability to the small farmers evaporates under increasing interest rates and indebtedness, and as the large farmer expands his investment, his productivity, and his control of the market and local government apparatus, so too does the proportion of dispossessed small farmers increase. Indeed, as we have seen, this process of widening disparities is not new—but the increase in the percentage of agricultural households without land, and the consequent increase in the proportion of landless labourers, have accelerated markedly over the past ten years as a result of both agricultural rationalization and famine. In Bangladesh, the problem of growing landlessness arising from application of "Green Revolution" principles to farming lay at the heart of a sharp debate over agricultural strategy during 1972—but the Government silenced its critics and proceeded to encourage capital-intensive farming, based on HYV grains, by expanding its Integrated Rural Development Programme.

As rural change in South Asia proceeds in this fashion, the extent of poverty—both rural and urban—is bound to increase. According to Professor P. Bardhan, the percentage of people below the poverty line in rural India rose from 38 per cent in 1961 to 53 per cent in 1968 (taking a conservative estimate of Rs. 15 *per capita* per month—at 1960–61 prices—as the minimum standard of living in a rural area); over the same period, according to the economist P. D. Ojha, the percentage of the rural population affected by serious malnutrition rose from 52 per cent to 70 per cent. The Bangladesh Planning Commission, in 1972, described conditions in virtually identical terms; while in 1974, according to the Bangladesh Economic Association, 46 million people (mainly landless and small farmers) out of a population of 74 million lived below the poverty line, unable to afford a minimum diet of 2,100 calories a day. In 1970, before widespread famine affected the country, Bangladesh had an estimated rural unemployment rate of 32 per cent—and an urban unemployment rate, depending on the town, of between 20 and 48 per cent. Clearly, the conditions that give rise to such levels of unemployment also seriously undermine the purchasing power of those lucky enough to earn—thus, for agricultural labourers in Bangladesh real income—at 1966 prices—has declined sharply from 852 taka to 580 taka per annum between 1964 and 1973.

Throughout South Asia, very low levels of disposable income—especially rural incomes, which for most of the population are declining in real terms and relative to urban incomes—are a reflection of governmental failure to tackle the problems of an increasingly inequitable agrarian structure, involving excessive rents, widespread usury, perpetual indebtedness of small farmers, increasing eviction and landlessness, deepening poverty and increasing rural-urban migration.

Thus, agricultural "rationalization"—as exemplified by the "Green Revolution"—is advancing as a phenomenon seemingly unrelated to fundamental rural improvement, reflecting the planners' failure to confront the obvious institutional obstacles to full mobilization of the region's ample—but either abused or underutilized—resources of land, labour, capital and skills. Certainly, mechanization is no solution to the problems of an overpopulated agricultural system—given the vast pool of un- and under-employed labour; neither is the transformation of small-holders into wage-labourers—when wage levels are rapidly outstripped by rising prices, when demand for agricultural labour is declining or at best stagnant, and when industry cannot absorb even 10 per cent of the existing urban unemployed, let alone rural-urban migrants.

In India, the myth of the "Green Revolution" had faded by 1973—it had not secured a really productive agricultural system beyond the Punjab and pockets of three other States, it was well beyond the means of the vast majority of farmers, it had aggravated the most fundamental problem of unemployment, widened socio-economic and regional disparities, and created an unreal and short-lived complacency.

As a solution to India's food problem, the "Green Revolution" was defeated as much by its internal (and alien) logic as by the multitude of institutional obstacles to rural change it either avoided or aggravated. Above all, the success of such a strategy presupposed the existence of an economic and socio-political structure which simply was not there—not in government or political will, not in land tenure conditions, not in marketing system, and not in social or economic organization as a whole. Lacking the context necessary to give it direction, the experiment failed. The ultimate irony, perhaps, was the massive increases in prices of imported oil, petrochemicals and non-petrochemical fertilizers—the very commodities upon which the "Green Revolution" depended; India was thus faced, in 1974, with the realization that her food supply was more firmly mortgaged to expensive imports than foreign grain purchases suggested—yet, out of this realization might come a reappraisal of the inherent productivity of India's own resources. Meanwhile, the heyday of the "Green Revolution" must be seen for what it was—a brief interlude between famines.

1972-75: The Famine Years

During the past three years, ample evidence has accumulated to show that large parts of South Asia have been suffering from severe famine. Since 1972, at least 2 million people have died as a direct result of starvation; but taking into account deaths caused by malnutrition, undernourishment, and diseases encouraged by such conditions, the toll of what the French agronomist René Dumont has described as potentially "the worst famine in the history of the world" could well exceed 4 million. The scale of the disaster, and the increasingly defeatist response to these problems in the West (expressed in the growing demand for stringent population control policies, and a *triage* approach to poor countries) make it imperative to question the very basis upon which agricultural development has been occurring in South Asia over the past quarter century.

There is no doubt that agricultural production has failed to keep pace with population growth. In India, between 1970–71 and 1973–74, production of foodgrains (including rice, wheat, millets, and gram) fell from 108.4 million metric tons to 107 million metric tons—that is, from a daily *per capita* production of 19.4 oz. to just below 18 oz.; in Bangladesh, foodgrain production fell from 12.14 million metric tons in 1969–70 to 11.18 million metric tons in 1973–74—a drop in daily *per capita* production from 16.5 oz. to 14.5 oz. Thus, foodgrain production declined both absolutely and in *per capita* terms.

However, three essential qualifications must be made to such figures. Firstly, they refer to gross *production*, not availability or consumption: even accounting for imports, the retention of seed grain, hoarding, and wastage in storage and distribution mean that *net consumption* levels are far lower—in India around 15 oz. *per capita*, in Bangladesh around 12 oz. *per capita*.

Secondly, such average figures ignore the *quality* of foodgrains, in particular the proportion of key protein crops (pulses) to total foodgrains. In all South Asian countries, the protein and vitamin content of crop production has consistently declined over the past decade, partly because of the increasing poverty of peasant producers, partly because of the high price of staple wheat and rice, and partly because of official neglect of diversification (one aspect of this being the policy of encouraging cultivation of high-yielding staples). Thus, in India, while total foodgrain production increased between 1963 and 1973, total pulse production dropped from 11.44 million metric tons to 11 million metric tons (equivalent to a drop in daily *per capita* production of 25 per cent—from 2.43 oz. to 1.8 oz.); in Sri Lanka, where the production of higher-protein crops such as green gram, sorghum, and soybeans has recently increased, total production of the basic *dhal* (or lentils) was still a bare 987 cwt. in 1973. Overall, during the period 1970–74, *per capita* productivity in South Asian agriculture declined (despite the "Green Revolution"), and the average diet declined in both quantitative and qualitative terms. For most of the region's population, the normal diet is grossly deficient in proteins generally, in vitamins A, B and C, and in the basic minerals such as calcium, phosphorus and iron. As a result of declining *per capita* consumption of meat, milk, pulses and vegetables, these deficiencies have worsened; susceptibility to disease has thus increased, infant mortality rates have increased, congenital malformities are more prevalent, and the efficiency of labour is lower. The food problem, therefore, is not simply the need for *more* food—it is also the need for *better* food. In this respect, the failure of South Asian agriculture has been dual: starch production declined, and famine ensued; protein production fell at an even faster rate, and already severe malnutrition intensified.

A third qualification which must be made in dealing with average production or consumption figures is that such figures conceal wide variations between areas and between groups of the population—variations which reflect regional differences in agricultural productivity, differences in living standards, the functioning of the foodgrain market, and so on. Given the grossly disparate economic structure in South Asia, this consideration is crucial. In terms of food availability there is a vast difference between a jealously administered food surplus State and a poorer, food deficit State; equally, there is no comparison between a New Delhi businessman's family and a Bihari agricultural labourer's family. For the grain market operates on the principle of greatest profit, not on that of greatest need—thus grain goes to areas of greatest purchasing power, and in areas of least purchasing power prices are determined by a commodity's scarcity value. It is not surprising, then, that an estimated 2 million tons of grain were smuggled from Bangladesh into India during 1973–74; or that it was officially estimated in late 1974 that over 15 million of West Bengal's 50 million people were living on less than one meal a day—for in West Bengal, with high rates of unemployment and landlessness, wage rates for agricultural labourers ranged from Rs. 2 to Rs. 2.50 a day, while the price of rice was over Rs. 3.30 a kilo. Similar deprivation prevailed in northern Bangladesh as the price of rice reached a peak of 400 taka per *maund* (approx. 50p a kilo.) in October 1974, or ten times its 1970 price, with no compensating increase in wages. In such famine-stricken districts as Rangpur and Sylhet, the luckier inhabitants existed on 6–7 oz. of food a day—while in Rangpur district alone, during 1974, deaths from starvation approached 100,000.

South Asia's poor food production record during the first half of the 1970s was certainly due, in part, to the succession of droughts and flooding (most serious in the States of Maharashtra, Orissa, Bihar, Assam, and West Bengal, and over much of Bangladesh). But far more significant in the long run has been the failure to prevent or at least mollify such natural disasters, and minimize their effects. In this respect, official neglect of basic agricultural development since the inception of planning, the collapse of the marketing system, and the abortive emergency relief measures taken—all compounded by administrative incompetence and rampant corruption—contrast dramatically with the Chinese approach to the succession of natural disasters and agricultural failures between 1959 and 1961.

The widespread drought and flooding which afflicted much of South Asia between 1972 and 1975 highlighted the many weaknesses inherent in the rural situation: the neglect of infrastructural development since independence, for example, and the absence of effective land reform. The State and Central administrations showed themselves unable to cope with major natural disasters.

While grain output increased during 1974/75 in India, it decreased in Bangladesh and Pakistan. Continuing food imports, high import prices for both oil and fertilizers, and increasing foreign debt and balance of payments problems indicate little amelioration of conditions in the region. In N.E. India and Bangladesh, famine remained a problem throughout 1975.

Foreign Aid and Development

In such a situation, the role of foreign aid in a country's development process is clearly of great importance. Since independence, South Asia—and especially India and Pakistan—has been heavily dependent upon foreign aid for economic, social, and military development. Between 1951 and 1974, India received nearly U.S. $20,000 million, of which 85 per cent came from the Aid-India consortium; during the same period, Pakistan received some U.S. $8,000 million—of which 86 per cent came from the West and Japan. Together with this financial aid has gone extensive technical aid, particularly from the West (but increasingly, in the case of India, from the U.S.S.R.): in the case of Pakistan, for example, development programmes since the mid-1950s have been drafted largely by economists supplied by Harvard's Development Advisory Service.

However, the long-term utility of such aid, in terms of advancing broadly-based and equitable national development, is being increasingly questioned. Foreign aid has certainly allowed India and Pakistan to spend heavily on non-productive military expansion, but it would seem to have other, more fundamental, disadvantages. It has, for example, made the pattern of economic development heavily dependent upon external policy pressures—pressures determined by the donors' (including, increasingly, the Soviet Union's) strategic political and economic interests in the region. Thus, domestic policy has been deflected from any sustained and radical programmes of socio-economic and political change—targets are safely set in terms of quantitative growth, rather than the far more important qualitative development of backward and distorted economic structures. To a large extent, government is carried out by "client-elites", reluctant to compromise either their own vested interests or foreign interests in the status quo—in this respect, Indian nationalization measures have been greatly diluted by the country's dependence upon foreign aid and private investment.

Reflecting such dependence, development is strongly guided by Western conceptions of what is "desirable" policy. Thus, there is a tendency to measure progress in terms of the rate of growth of G.N.P., rather than the content of G.N.P. In agriculture, many elements of the "new strategy" of rural development—especially the "Green Revolution"—have been directly inspired and promoted by the United States, with foreign aid to agriculture concentrated in such projects. Again, foreign aid tends to favour programmes of birth control as opposed to programmes of job creation as a solution to "overpopulation" and unemployment, and a related preference is that for large-scale capital-intensive projects as opposed to labour-intensive development in both agriculture and industry. Such predilections mean, first, that aided development has little qualitative impact on grass-roots problems amongst the peasantry and the mass of unemployed and underemployed in general, and second, that such development merely accentuates socio-economic and regional disparities—for example, at least 75 per cent of all foreign aid to Pakistan, before 1972, was spent in the Western Wing, and a large proportion of this went into three projects (construction of the national capital at Islamabad and the Mangla and Tarbela dams). Foreign aid tends to concentrate on existing foci of development and domestic political power, and in areas particularly attractive to foreign private investment—hence the neglect, until recently, of Bangladesh, of Sri Lanka during the phase of nationalization, and the continuing neglect of Central India.

One indication of the way in which a high level of foreign aid leads to strong economic and political dependence on the part of the recipient country can be seen in the amount and role of counterpart funds controlled by Western governments. Particularly in India, donor countries have come to control extremely large proportions of local currency, giving them immense influence in internal economic, fiscal, and social policy. For example, through its PL 480 programme the United States had accumulated holdings of nearly Rs. 24,000 million in India—a sum equivalent to over 50 per cent of total currency in circulation in 1972. Such funds are used to finance foreign enterprises, establish educational and research institutions, publish books, disseminate propaganda, and exert control over domestic policy to ensure its general compatibility with the donor countries' interests. In 1974, however, a large proportion of these funds reverted to India.

Some argue that foreign aid has tended to discourage whole-hearted domestic development by its very availability. Access to PL 480 aid, for example, may have blunted India's fight for agricultural self-sufficiency during the 1950s and 1960s. But, clearly, simple availability of foreign aid is only one factor impeding progress towards agricultural self-sufficiency in South Asia. Conditions governing the use of aid, for example, usually work against thoroughgoing agrarian reform; in addition, the quality of national economic policies—with or without aid—often leave much to be desired. Illustrating this latter point, Sri Lanka's large import of such basic foodstuffs as potatoes, onions, chillies, and rice (of which 30 per cent of national needs must be imported), reflects a serious neglect of comprehensive rural development by consecutive governments—at least until 1972, when the United Front government restricted food imports and free rations, and launched an extensive, if not radical, land reform programme.

A frequent criticism of foreign aid is that it is heavily "tied" to purchases of goods from donor countries, thus limiting a government's ability to purchase needed goods, at competitive prices, on the free market, and maintain supplies of spare parts. Often, "tied" purchases are made at prices well above the world market level—with the donor benefiting far more than the recipient. For India, in 1970–71, over 75 per cent of all aid came in the form of tied loans—compared to about 48 per cent during the period of the First Plan. This increase in the proportion of tied loans applies to all South Asian countries, who are having to bear the extra charges (shipping, insurance, loss of foreign exchange) such aid involves. The real value of aid—even if its gross value rises—is steadily declining.

Finally, as the table on p. 145 indicates, foreign aid not only restricts available domestic capital (as in the case of counterpart funds), it also constitutes a serious—and growing—drain on foreign exchange which could be used as a buffer against vagaries in the world primary commodity market and continually rising prices for manufactured goods imports, and to import needed goods at free market prices—thus helping to reduce persistent trade deficits. India, Pakistan, Bangladesh, and Sri Lanka have a combined external debt of nearly U.S. $16,000 million, and the repayment of foreign loans accounts for between 23 per cent (India) and 50 per cent (Sri Lanka) of export earnings. However, such a calculation ignores the region's terms of trade: all countries are significant oil and fertilizer importers, and all but Pakistan are major food importers—thus, with rises in import prices, India's 1972–73 trade surplus had become, in 1974–75, a deficit of 10,450 million rupees. As the table indicates, the proportion of annual aid to India effectively cancelled by debt servicing rose from 27.8 per cent in 1967–68 to 63.4 per cent in 1973–74; because of higher loan charges, aid was in effect becoming more expensive. Although total annual foreign aid *declined* by almost 30 per cent over the six years, the total annual debt service *increased* by nearly 60 per cent. In the region as a whole, as all countries had to increase borrowing after 1971, the debt burden will rise steeply during the later 1970s.

Clearly, there is need for a thorough reappraisal of the role of foreign aid in the development of such countries as India and Pakistan. But, inevitably, such a reappraisal presupposes a change of attitude to overall foreign involvement in the Third World. In South Asia, the increasing competition between the Soviet Union and the United States for strategic political advantage and economic influence is intensifying foreign involvement in the region's domestic affairs. A concomitant of this is greater dependence upon foreign interests, and this in turn is merely helping to perpetuate political and economic structures which—over a quarter of a century—have shown themselves incapable of improving the quality of life for the vast majority of the region's population.

The Problems of Industrialization

It is against this background that we should set the problems of industrialization faced by South Asia. The manufacturing economy is dualistic: a modern sector of capital-intensive industries and labour-intensive industries on the one hand, and a mass of small-scale, labour-intensive, industries catering mainly for a poor local market on the other. The former, employing some 10 per cent of the labour force, accounts for most manufacturing output by value; the latter is far less productive and profitable. One grows increasingly capital-intensive, although in some activities profitably uses cheap labour, and export-oriented; the other grows more labour-intensive and less productive within a small local market. Effective development, as opposed to quantitative growth, might involve rationalizing and enlarging the labour-intensive sector, dispersing its activities from main urban areas. But in practice industrialization means development of the large, capital-intensive, export-oriented, and urban-located unit. Given the kind of industrial structure outlined

The Cost of Foreign Aid to India, 1967–74
(Rs. million)

	(1) Export Earnings	(2) External Assistance	(3) Debt Service	(3) as a Percentage of (1)	(3) as a Percentage of (2)
1967–68 . . .	11,928	11,956	3,330	27.8	27.8
1970–71 . . .	15,352	7,914	4,500	29.3	56.8
1971–72 . . .	16,545	9,636	4,750	27.8	49.3
1972–73 . . .	19,545	7,297	4,880	25.0	66.9
1973–74 . . .	24,110	8,607	5,426	22.6	63.4

above, the common view that modern industrial development can solve the problem of population growth needs careful examination. To set this idea into its correct perspective one has only to relate the cost of creating one job in modern industry to the annual increment of population. Accepting the very low figure of $3,500 for the first and multiplying by the present population increase of 19 million annually, the cost of a policy of industrialization which would absorb existing population growth works out at $66,500 million yearly; this sum represents over ten times present net Western aid (public and private) to the whole of the underdeveloped world. Ambitious plans for industrialization, often aid-financed, are increasing industrial output by four to five per cent yearly, but these programmes face the problems of low home purchasing power and increasing export-orientation, coupled with foreign control. Moreover, the rate of growth is quite inadequate to absorb the swelling army of unemployed; to take the example of India, at the end of the Second Five-Year Plan there were some 8.8 million unemployed while the Third Five-Year Plan aimed at providing some 14 million jobs over a period when 17 million new entrants came on to the labour market—making a backlog, at the end of the Plan period, of 12 million unemployed. At the end of the 1974–75 Annual Plan (the Fifth Plan is in abeyance), there were an estimated 35 million unemployed, including some 3.3 million "educated unemployed"—a problem illustrated by the high job-vacancy/applicant ratio in the tertiary sector (about 1:400). This, however, takes no account of the permanently under-employed or irregularly employed—some estimates put the number of workers unemployed or without a regular job at around 150 million in India alone. A measure of under-employment can be found in Battacharya's observation that, as early as 1951, some 30 per cent of the rural labour force could be withdrawn from agriculture (with no significant reorganization of farming) without any drop in total output; by 1970, this proportion of "disguised unemployed" had risen to between 35 per cent and 40 per cent. This steady process of "developing backwards" emphasizes the need for a drastic change in economic policies and for a concentration on labour-intensive rather than capital-intensive development—and this applies to all of South Asia.

Two other aspects of industrialization are important: first, the dependent quality of the industrial economies now emerging; second, the role played by industry in accentuating rather than narrowing the wide socio-economic and regional disparities in the area. Industrialization is dependent in that it has been heavily underpinned by external aid (the contrast with China, whose industrialization has been financed with its own resources, is striking); such aid, as we have seen, involves a heavy repayment burden, and may also involve deflection of the original planning policies through the unwillingness of Western donors to channel aid to the public sector, without considerable control over investment. As a result, the Indian private sector has been expanding more rapidly than the public sector since the mid-1950s and so too has foreign control of Indian industry. Notably, such control is not only Western: according to Tarun Roy, in 1972 the Soviet Union controlled 80 per cent of India's electricity generating equipment industries, 80 per cent of oil extraction, 34 per cent of oil refineries, 80 per cent of heavy engineering industries, 30 per cent of iron and steel industries, 60 per cent of electrical equipment industries and 25 per cent of power industries. Increasingly, the West and the Soviet Union are competing for economic and political influence in India; and, in the industrial sector, the mechanics of foreign control applied by both blocs are increasingly similar.

Direct foreign control by majority investment is only one form of control: in large sections of Indian industry, it is possible for foreign companies—through collaboration agreements for technical know-how, marketing facilities, and patent and licensing agreements—not only to control an industry and its role in the local economy, but also to remit to their home offices vast amounts in the form of profits, dividends, royalties, and head office expenses. Certainly, the significance of the process whereby foreign companies, with very low actual investment in South Asia, get their branded goods made in the area and market them at high profits, cannot be underestimated in any consideration of capital flow. For example, one large British company in India—manufacturing a wide range of popular non-durable consumer goods—made a repatriated profit of Rs. 800,000 in 1970 on an original investment of only Rs. 15,000.

In terms of finance and organization South Asia has remained a dependent area: in recent years American and Soviet technological dominance and increasing reliance on foreign "aid" and capital investment have stifled the Indian industrialist class which was emerging in late colonial times; the "national bourgeoisie" so vital in Western economic development no longer exists as an independent group in South Asia. Instead—in India, Pakistan, and Sri Lanka—domestic industrial enterprise is largely represented by a small group of monopoly capitalists (such as the Tatas and Birlas in India, and members of the Halai Memon and Dawoodi Bohra immigrant groups in Pakistan) whose role is complementary to foreign investment, and whose concentration of control in industry tends to divert the potential investment of the middle classes into hoarding, real estate, and conspicuous consumption. Thus, the structure of "dependent capitalism" in South Asia is such that the pattern of industrial development is distorted—by the operation of foreign aid, foreign private investment, highly concentrated domestic monopoly investment, and diffuse middle-class investment—to form an industrial sector which is insecurely based, lacks internal integration and effective overall management, and lacks any close integration with the rest of the national economy. In addition, South Asian industrial economies are strongly localized in a few centres such as the Karachi, Bombay, and Calcutta regions, and have long developed at the expense of agriculture, with only minimal "spread" or "feedback" effects—beyond gross inflation of the urban tertiary sector and intensification of a labour-displacing, capitalist agricultural system in a few favoured niches of the subcontinent. Superimposed on a traditional pattern of great human diversity, these regional economic inequalities increasingly aggravate the tensions and antagonisms which arise from this diversity. Recent unrest in Sri Lanka highlights a situation where industrialization is strongly localized and wealth is concentrated in very few hands, where unemployment stands at some 15 per cent, and where an ethnic division of labour and communal suspicions are increased by uneven development. Gunnar Myrdal states that income per head in West Pakistan in 1958 was some 30 per cent of that in East Pakistan and suggests that concentration of economic development in West Pakistan during the First Five-Year Plan widened this gap; in 1964, per caput incomes were 363 rupees for the West and 273 for the East. Between 1960 and 1970 the annual rate of growth of income in West Pakistan was 6.2 per cent, while it was only 4.2 per cent in the East. Thus, by 1970, the West's per caput income was 61 per cent higher than that of the East: the income gap doubled in percentage terms, and increased even more in absolute terms. And the degree of personal concentration of wealth and power is suggested by the control exerted over Pakistan's economy by the country's so-called "20 families" (belonging to West Indian minority groups—members of which migrated to Pakistan with Partition in 1947): in 1970, the "20 families" controlled 66 per cent of Pakistan's industrial capital, 80 per cent of bank funds, and 97 per cent of insurance funds. Such concentration of control not only impeded the development of pre-1972 Pakistan, but—in particular—exacerbated the East-West disparity (as these families reside, and concentrated investment, in what was until 1971 West Pakistan).

In all South Asia regional differences in the pace of industrialization (dominantly urban-based) seem to be leading to widening regional and urban/rural income differentials. The general pattern seems to be one of stagnating or declining rural incomes and rising levels of income among industrial producers and trading groups. The experience of India and Sri Lanka illustrates the process of widening income differentials between the rural sector and the industrializing urban sector: in India, the average living standard in rural areas has declined from 27 per cent of the average urban living standard in 1951–52 to 17 per cent in 1972–73; in Sri Lanka, using 1952 wage levels as a base of 100, average industrial wage rates increased to 120 by 1972, while average agricultural wage rates decreased to 97.

TOWARDS AN ASIAN DEVELOPMENT MODEL

The countries of South Asia face the problem of narrowing both the gap in living levels between themselves and the developed nations and the differential in rates of development between themselves and their East Asian neighbours. Equally important is the need to bridge the widening gap between a limited number of "poles of development" and the rest of their territory, between the relative affluence of a small proportion of their citizens and the impoverishment of the great mass of their population. These disparities are, in part at least, the result of recent economic development and they threaten to create in the region a pre-revolutionary situation of the type that has emerged in other parts of the Third World.

In assessing the relevance of various "models of development" to the countries of the region we do well to bear in mind the specific features of the region's contemporary geography, features which pose problems very different to those faced by a developing Europe two centuries ago. Europe, it is often overlooked, carried through its industrial revolution *after* it had successfully transformed its agricultural system; the rate of population growth was low (about 0.5 per cent yearly) and its colonial territories offered both markets and sources of raw materials. South Asia, by contrast, faces the problem of carrying through simultaneously an agricultural revolution, an industrial revolution, and a social revolution; it has to do this at a time when its population growth rates are running at very high levels and its countries possess no colonies but have to fit themselves into a world whose resources and markets are dominated by the advanced industrial nations. Under such conditions, the European model of development, often considered the answer to the needs of the developing countries, is largely irrelevant; in the words of Gunnar Myrdal:

> "All the under-developed countries are now starting out on a line of economic policy which has no close historical precedent in any advanced country."

This, however, is not yet recognized widely and in the meantime economic development policies are modelled closely on those of the Western "liberal" economy (with an appropriate indigenous facade) and are heavily dependent on foreign aid. And that such an approach simply does not deliver the goods is underlined by Paul Bairoch who estimates that, at the 1953–1965 pace of development, it will take the Third World as a whole 110 years to reach the *present* level of development of the West, that for non-communist Asia the gap is of the order of 150 years. It is also underlined by the growing indebtedness of the region.

The region's large and growing population is conventionally regarded as a problem; it is also, as René Dumont pointed out fifteen years ago, a major asset. In Dumont's words:

> "Monsoon Asia's greatest source of wealth is her huge population. The main cause of her backwardness is the inefficient employment of this labour force. . . . Even without modern equipment, the resumption of certain types of work by the peasants during the seasons of under-employment on the land would represent a net gain and a productive exploitation of a natural source of wealth."

The huge dimensions of this pool of under-utilized labour can be estimated approximately by taking the number of farm families in the area (*ca.* 75 million) and multiplying by the total of days in the agricultural year when the farmer is unemployed. Assuming 90 days a year for the latter we arrive at a total of 6,750 *million man-days;* this represents the wastage of energy and skills for family heads only and is a heavy under-estimate if we take as our base the Colombo Plan Consultative Committee's estimate of idle time in India (9–10 months yearly on unirrigated land). The mobilization of these resources of labour, the rational use of the region's land resources (developments which depend on structural change—which means political change—in the countryside), these developments are the essential preliminaries to the introduction of improved and more intensive techniques. Once the infrastructure for development, in the shape of water-storage and irrigation systems, terracing, roading and the like, has been created by the peasant, then, and only then, does it become possible and profitable to employ fertilizers, improved seed varieties and more intensive rotations. Such an intensified agriculture is essential for a sound policy of industrialization for which it would provide food, raw material and markets; such a policy of "labour-investment" makes possible the creation of a network of labour-intensive rural industries which would complement the capital-intensive industries of the modern sector. And such an intensification of agriculture and development of rural industries would make it possible to narrow the disparities between countryside and city commented on above.

The Future

For two decades the nations of South Asia have been striving to reach the point of "economic take-off" by following modified versions of the liberal development *schema*. Plans have been based on the concept that increases in income should be directed into the hands of a small elite, on the assumption that this will lead to a high rate of saving, which the elite will invest, thus increasing the country's productive assets and providing a basis for economic growth. Such a process increases inequalities within South Asian societies, it is recognized, but these very inequalities will yield more economic growth—which in turn will raise the living standards of all classes. "Concentration of income", according to the economist Gustav Papanek in his study of Pakistan, "contributes to the growth of the economy and real improvement of the lower income groups only because inequalities in income result substantially in increased savings and not in consumption."

However, evidence from India and Pakistan supports only part of this thesis: economic growth, in quantitative terms, has been achieved; but not the qualitative development of sound social and economic structures capable of mobilizing available resources (especially labour) and ensuring increasing standards of living throughout the population. Further, the growth achieved has not necessarily been achieved through a high rate of domestic saving for investment.

The experience of Pakistan shows that the investment pattern of the "entrepreneurial elite" is hardly productive—during the Second Plan (1961–66), according to Richard Nations, "no more than 26 per cent and perhaps as little as 10.5 per cent of domestic resources found their way into productive non-agricultural investment". Illustrating this, a study of Dacca in the mid-1960s showed that 42.5 per cent of urban personal savings were spent on gold ornaments, consumer durables, and housing. In India, net investment as a percentage of National Income rose from 5.5 per cent in 1950–51 to 11 per cent in 1972–73, while domestic saving as a percentage of National Income rose from 5.5 per cent to 9.9 per cent over the same period. Thus, the domestic savings rate has long been less than the investment rate, and—as Battacharya points out—"foreign aid was expected to bridge the investment-savings gap that exists in the economy, and has been relied upon to do so". One problem in mobilizing savings is the very concentration of control and ownership itself—a concentration which, as already pointed out, diverts potential investment of the middle classes into non-productive channels.

As for the distribution of the benefits of increased economic growth, some measure can be found in comparing official figures for the growth of industrial company profits and changes in factory wage levels over the period 1950–66: while company profits rose, on average, by over 300 per cent during the period, real wages for unskilled labour showed little improvement during 1951–64, declined substantially in 1964, and continued to decline during 1965 and 1966.

All evidence points to a growth in G.N.P. per capita, except in 1972 and 1973; increasing capitalization per worker (and a concomitant decline in industry's—and agriculture's—capacity to absorb more labour) together with growing concentration of production in larger, more capital-intensive units; increasing affluence amongst a small minority—an index of which can be found in the sales of luxury items in India (such as cars, air-conditioners, and refrigerators), which showed a three-fold increase in 1957 and a seven-fold increase in 1968; and finally decreasing or stagnant wage rates amongst the lower paid, the people most affected by rapidly increasing inflation, particularly in prices of basic foodstuffs such as sugar, bajra grain, juwar, and rice (in Pakistan, over the two years 1971 and 1972, wholesale prices of these commodities rose by between 100 per cent and 150 per cent). Production in large-scale manufacturing certainly increased and so too did agricultural production on large-holdings using HYV and LIV grains and capital-intensive methods. In addition, indices of social welfare and education have shown improvement. But whatever statistical measures one uses, the averages conceal the fundamental facts that the gap between the rich and poor is widening, and that the poor are growing poorer, in the countries of South Asia.

The mounting tensions in the region suggest that a re-examination of the prevailing growth model is long overdue, that economic policies which accord yet further advantages to the already advantaged groups, whether landlords or industrial entrepreneurs, contribute powerfully to dividing yet further societies already fragmented by religion, caste, disparities in economic power and in uneven access to political power. In the absence of basic change in the political and social structures, the injection of aid and the introduction of new technologies may, indeed, result in an increase in the G.N.P., but the gains accrue to a very small elite group; the great mass of the population remains at a wretched level of existence, though increasingly alive to what it sees as the injustices of the present social system.

Real development in South Asia is no nearer than it was twenty years ago. With some 50 million unemployed, the region must somehow absorb a population increase of over 200 million in the next decade. The events of the past three years merely underscore the basic issue which confronts all the free enterprise countries of Asia: can any underdeveloped country, whose politicians, in Gunnar Myrdal's words, "are reluctant to enact reforms that would effectively curb the power and affluence of the upper class", attain any degree of modernization or reach the "point of take-off" without passing through a revolutionary upheaval? Given the view of many that the lot of India's masses is still pitiful, that "India is nearer communism today than when aid gathered momentum" and that most of the underdeveloped countries are relatively poorer than before the "Decade of Development" began, is the belief expressed by President Eisenhower in 1958 that large-scale foreign aid will raise levels of living, "defeat the spread of communism" and narrow the gap between the rich and the poor nations any longer tenable? Can the level of capital accumulation necessary for development be achieved by a policy of deliberately favouring a small and wealthy elite group, coupled with a policy of polite persuasion of landlords and richer peasants or are more radical and authoritarian measures necessary? Can any country afford to waste its most abundant and precious resource—its people—on the scale that India and Pakistan do, or should not Myrdal's remarks about agriculture—that the aim of planning should be "to raise labour utilization and to do so while the labour force is increasing rapidly"—apply to all sectors of the economy? And, ultimately, when the level of living rises so slowly, when the majority live close to the very margin of survival, do individual liberties really have so much value? These are the issues today posed in South Asia and with each year that passes they become more acute—and the development policies of Meiji Japan and Communist China more relevant.

Authoritarianism and Development in South Asia

With the events in Bangladesh between Sheikh Mujib's assumption of Presidential rule and the installation in November 1975 of Major-General Ziaur Rahman's martial law government, and the consolidation of emergency rule in India after June 1975, South Asia's political and economic development reached a notable but predictable watershed. Amidst growing anarchy, the pretence of democracy was abandoned first by Bangladesh and then by India and authoritarianism was imposed in an attempt to retrieve a measure of stability. Sheikh Mujib's civil dictatorship was replaced, within eight months, by a military one; after a year of the Emergency, India still had a civilian regime.

The key question is: will such authoritarian rule reverse or aggravate a state of chronic economic crisis? A number of trends are apparent: first, the crucial area of rural development has not been significantly affected; second, despite nationalization measures taken over the past three years in India, Bangladesh, Pakistan, and Sri Lanka, there has been little change, except in Sri Lanka, in the effective pattern of ownership and control of agriculture and industry; third, despite such pronouncements as Mrs. Gandhi's "Twenty Points Programme", effective economic priorities remain little changed: industrial development rather than integral rural reform is emphasized (as indicated by India's 1976/77 budget, which allocated over 20 per cent of development funds to the steel and power industries and just 8.8 per cent to irrigation and flood control); finally, there has been only marginal impact on corruption.

BIBLIOGRAPHY

ANDRUS, J. R., and MOHAMMED, A. F. The Economy of Pakistan (London, 1958).

BAIROCH, P. The Economic Development of the Third World Since 1900 (London, 1975).

BARDHAN, P. Poverty in Rural India in the Sixties in *Economic and Political Weekly*, 1973 (Bombay).

BATTACHARYA, DEBESH. A Critical Survey of Indian Planning and its Achievements in *Journal of Contemporary Asia*, Vol. 3, No. 2, 1973.

BETTELHEIM, CHARLES. India Independent (London, 1968).

BIARDEAU, MADELEINE. India (London, 1960).

BOSE, S. R., The Trend of Real Income of the Rural Poor in *Pakistan Development Review* 1968.

BOWRING, P., and LIFSCHULTZ, L. India: Farmers Await an Emergency Transfusion in *Far Eastern Economic Review*, Oct. 24th, 1975.

DAVIS, KINGSLEY. The Populations of India and Pakistan (Princeton, 1957).

DUBE, S. C. India's Changing Villages (London, 1958).

DUMONT, RENÉ. Lands Alive (London and New York, 1965).

ETIENNE, GILBERT. Indian Agriculture—or the Art of the Possible (translated by Megan Mothersole; Berkeley, 1968).

FARMER, B. H. Ceylon—A Divided Nation (London, 1963).

GAVI, PHILIPPE, Eruption in India in *Ramparts* April 1970.

GOUGH, KATHLEEN, and SHARMA, HARI P. Imperialism and Revolution in South Asia (New York and London, 1973).

GRIFFIN, KEITH B. Financing Development Areas in Pakistan in *Pakistan Development Review*, Winter 1965.

GUPTA, S. C. New Trends of Growth, in *Seminar* (New Delhi, No. 38).

HAQ, MAHBUB UL. Employment in the 1970s—A New Perspective in *International Development Review*, Vol. XIII, No. 4, 1971.

IYER, RAGHVACHAN (Editor). South Asian Affairs (St. Antony's Papers No. 8; London, 1966).

KAPP, K. W. Hindu Culture, Economic Development and Economic Planning in India (Bombay, 1963).

KARAN, P. P., and JENKINS, W. M. The Himalayan Kingdoms (London and New York, 1963).

KHAN, A. R., What has been Happening to real Wages in Pakistan? in *Pakistan Development Review* 1967.

LIFSCHULTZ L. The Subsontinent's Nightmare *and* Bangladesh: A State of Siege, in *Far Eastern Economic Review*, August 30th, 1974.

MAJUMDAR, D. N. Races and Cultures of India (Bombay, 1944, 1958).

MALENBAUM, W. Prospects for Indian Development (London, 1962).

MAMDANI, MAHMOOD. The Myth of Population Control (London, 1972).

MICHEL, A. A. The Indus Rivers (New Haven and London, 1967).

NAIR, KUSUM. Blossoms in the Dust (London, 1961).

PAPANEK, GUSTAV F. Pakistan's Development, Social Goals and Private Incentives (Cambridge, Mass., 1967).

PRADERVAND, P., Les pays nantis et la limitation des naissances dans le Tiers Monde in *Développement et civilisations* March–June 1970.

REED, W. E. Areal Interaction in India (Chicago, 1967).

RUDRA, ASHOK. The Green and Greedy Revolution, in *South Asian Review* July 1971.

SEGAL, RONALD. The Crisis of India (Harmondsworth, 1965).

SIDDIQUI, KALIM. Conflict, Crisis, and War in Pakistan (London, 1972).

SPATE, O. H. K., and LEARMONTH, A. T. A. India and Pakistan (London, 1967).

WILCOX, WAYNE A. India, Pakistan and the Rise of China (New York, 1964).

ZACHARIAH, K. C. A Historical Study of Internal Migration in the Indian Subcontinent 1901–31 (London, 1964).

Afghanistan

PHYSICAL AND SOCIAL GEOGRAPHY

W. B. Fisher

Occupying an area of approximately 250,000 square miles (estimates range between 240,000 and 270,000 square miles) Afghanistan has the shape of a very irregular oval with its major axis running N.E.-S.W. and extending over roughly 700 miles, and the minor axis at right angles to this, covering about 350 miles. The country is in the main a highland mass lying mostly at an altitude of 4,000 ft. (1,200 metres) or more, but it presents a highly variable pattern of extremely high and irregular mountain ridges, some of which exceed 20,000 ft. (6,000 metres); ravines and broader valleys, parts of which are very fertile; and an outer expanse of undulating plateau, wide river basins, and lake sumps.

Politically, Afghanistan has two frontiers of major length: one on the north with the Turkmen, Uzbek and Tadzhik Republics of the U.S.S.R., the other (on the south and east) with Pakistan.

This frontier follows what was once termed the Durand Line (after the representative of British India, Sir Mortimer Durand, who negotiated it in 1893 with the Ruler of Afghanistan). So long as the British occupied India, it was generally accepted as forming the Indo-Afghan frontier, but in 1947 with the recognition of Pakistan as a successor to the British, the Afghan government recalled that for much of the eighteenth century, Peshawar and other parts of the Indus Valley had formed part of a larger Afghan state, and were moreover occupied largely by Pashtuns, who are of closely similar ethnic character to many Afghans. Accordingly, the Durand Line frontier was denounced by Afghanistan, and claims were made that the territories as far as the line of the Indus, including Chitral, Swat, and Peshawar, and continuing as far as the Pashtun areas of the North-west Frontier Province and Baluchistan, ought to be recognized as an autonomous state, "Pashtunistan". This remains a topic of dispute between Afghanistan and Pakistan.

There are shorter but no less significant frontiers on the west with Iran, and on the north-east with Kashmir and with China. This last was fully agreed only in 1963, and the precise location of others in the south and west has not been fully delimited: an indication of the extreme difficulties of terrain, and an explanation of the uncertainty regarding the actual area of Afghanistan. It is noteworthy that, in order to erect a "buffer" between the then competing empires of Russia and India, under the Durand treaty of 1893 the Wakhan district, a narrow strip of land 200 miles long and under 10 miles wide in its narrowest part, was attached to Afghanistan. This strip controls the Baroghil pass over the Pamir, and avoids having a Soviet-Indian frontier.

PHYSICAL FEATURES

The main topographical feature of Afghanistan is a complex of irregular highlands that is relatively broad and low in the west, and very much higher and also narrower towards the east. In this eastern part the mountains form a group of well-defined chains that are known by the general name of the Hindu Kush (Hindu destroyer), and are linked further eastward first to the Pamirs and then to the main Himalaya system. The Eastern Hindu Kush ranges form the southern defining limit of the Wakhan strip whilst a short distance to the north and east, a small but high ridge, the Little Pamir, forms the topographic link between the Hindu Kush and the main Pamir. From maximum heights of 20,000–24,000 ft. (6,000–7,000 metres) the peaks decline in altitude westwards, attaining 15,000–20,000 ft. (4,500–6,000 metres) in the zone close to Kabul. Further west still, the ridges are no more than 12,000–15,000 ft. (3,500–4,500 metres) and in the extreme west they open out rather like the digits of a hand, with the much lower Parapamisus ridges (proto-Pamir) forming the last member of the mountain complex. The various ridges are distinguished by separate names. The Hindu Kush, which has a general altitude of about 15,000 ft. (4,000 metres) with peaks 7,000–10,000 ft. higher still, is however narrow, and crossable by quite a number of passes, some of which are indirect and snow-bound for much of the year.

In geological structure, Afghanistan has close affinities both to Iran further west, and, as has just been stated, to the massive Himalayan system further east. Development of present-day land-forms has been greatly influenced by the existence of several large, stable masses of ancient rocks, which have acted as cores around which rock series of younger age first developed and were then closely wrapped as fold structures. Most important of these ancient massifs, or "shield" areas so far as Afghanistan is concerned, is the plateau of the Deccan, the effect of which was to "bunch" a series of tight folds in a double loop or garland on its northern side. In this way can be explained the existence of the "knot" or "bunch" of fold structures lying partly in Afghanistan, and comprising the Pamir which forms the eastern limb and the Hindu Kush that makes up the western segment of the "garland". The abrupt change of direction and swinging of the fold structures from an east-west to, in some places, a north-south direction are a direct result of the presence of the resistant mass of the Deccan. The fold ranges themselves are composed in part of sediments mainly laid down under water, and include limestones with some sandstones, and are of Cretaceous and later age, Eocene especially. Extensive heat and pressure in some regions have metamorphosed original series into schists and gneiss; and there has been much shattering and cracking of the rock generally, with the consequent development of fault-lines and overthrust zones. A further feature in much of Afghanistan has been a good deal of differential earth movement, uptilting, downwarping and local adjustment which make the region particularly susceptible to earth tremors, which occur frequently, usually on a small scale. Occasionally, however, a major disaster occurs, the latest being in the Uzbek Republic of the U.S.S.R., just north of Afghanistan, in 1976.

As a consequence of frequent crustal disturbance, the rise of magma from the earth's interior has produced lava-flows, and minor volcanos. Most of these are in a stage of old age—being merely fissures from which emanate gas, steam and mud flows; and the presence of soft volcanic debris adds considerably in places to soil fertility.

As far as river drainage is concerned, Afghanistan forms a major watershed, from which rivers flow outward. The Amu Darya (Oxus) rises on the north side of the Hindu Kush and flows northwestwards into the U.S.S.R. Here, away from the mountains the presence of loess (a yellowish soil of high fertility) in small pockets offers scope for agriculture. The Hari Rud rises a short distance only from the Amu Darya, but flows westward through Herat to terminate in a salt, closed basin on the Iranian frontier. From the south and west of the Hindu Kush flow a number of streams that become tributaries of the Indus; and in the extreme south-west the Helmand river flows through to end like the Hari Rud in a closed basin that is partly within Iranian territory. The Helmand basin is of interest in that because of a curious balance in water-level at its lowest part, the river here reverses its flow seasonally, and remains for much of its length non-brackish instead of becoming progressively more saline, as is normal when there is no outlet to the sea. The Helmand basin thus offers distinct potential for agricultural improvement, and in fact schemes for irrigation are in process of development. But political difficulties (part of the lower basin is Iranian territory) and remoteness are inhibiting factors.

The areas of lower, and in the main more densely peopled areas occur either as a series of peripheral zones to north and south, or as a series of interior valleys and basins between the main mountain ridges of the centre. Largest of these areas is the piedmont lying on the northern flanks of the mountains, and dropping northwards in altitude to merge into the steppelands of Soviet Central Asia. This is Bactria, a region of, in places, light yellowish loessic soils. An interior situation, shut off from the sea by mountains means that rainfall is deficient, and falls mainly over the mountains. Streams fed partly by mountain snow-melt straggle across the plain, to lose themselves in the sand, feed salt swamps, or in a few cases, join others to form larger rivers such as the Hari Rud. Much of Bactria thus consists of semi or full desert with sheets of sand and gravel in many places, with, nearer the mountains, outwash of larger, coarser scree. Given stable political conditions this area with its areas of highly fertile loess soils and moderate water supplies offers much scope for economic development. For long inhabited by pastoral nomads, and disputed politically between various claimants: Afghan, Iranian and Soviet, this northern zone is now developing rapidly with irrigated cotton growing as a main element. Links with the U.S.S.R. are considerable, and the two chief towns of Herat in the west and Mazar-i-Sharif in the north have grown considerably in size over the past few years.

On the south, towards the east, is the Kabul basin, which is a relatively flat zone hemmed in closely by steep mountain ridges. Some distance away to the north-west, and reachable through two major passes is the narrower Vale of Bamian; whilst south-east of Kabul occurs another fertile lowland zone around Jellalabad. Here lower elevation and southerly situation produce warmer conditions, especially in winter, as compared with most of the rest of Afghanistan.

In the south-west, extending through Ghazni as far as Kandahar, there is another series of cultivated zones; but the extent of this piedmont area is much smaller than the corresponding one we have just described as Bactria. To the west, aridity, the price of declining altitude, increases, so the lowland passes into the desert areas of Registan and the Dasht-i-Mayo. Registan has seasonal flushes of grass, which support relatively large numbers of pastoral nomads, who, however, are becoming increasingly settled following irrigation development on the Helmand and Arghandab rivers.

Two other regional units may be mentioned. South of the Parapamisus and Kuh-i-Baba mountain ranges are a number of parallel but lower massifs, with narrow valleys between. Here because of altitude there is relatively abundant rainfall, but owing to topography, the region is one of remoteness and difficulty. This is the Hazarat, so called from the name of the Hazara inhabitants; and it still remains despite a central position one of the least known and visited parts of the country. Another equally remote highland, this time located north-east of Kabul, is Nuristan, again high and mountainous, but well-wooded in places, and supporting a small population of cultivators and pastoralists who use the summer pastures of the high hills, and move to lower levels in winter.

CLIMATE

Climatically, Afghanistan demonstrates a very clear relationship with Iran and the Middle East, rather than with Monsoon Asia, in that it has an almost arid summer, a small amount of rainfall which is largely confined to the winter season, and considerable seasonal variation in temperature. The monsoonal condition of heavy summer rainfall does not occur, despite Afghanistan's nearness to India. Annual rainfall ranges from 4-6 in. (10-15 cm.) in the drier, lower areas of the west and north, to 10-15 in. (25-40 cm.) in the east; and on the highest mountains there is more still. Kabul, with an average of 13 in. per annum, is typical of conditions in the east, and Herat with 5 in. typical of the west. Almost all this falls in the period December to April, though there can be a very occasional downpour at other times, even in summer, when a rare damp monsoonal current penetrates from the Indian lowlands. Temperatures are best described as extreme. In July, the lowlands experience temperatures of 110°F., (43°C.) with 120° not uncommon—this is true of Jellalabad on the edge of the Indus lowlands. But the effects of altitude are important, and Kabul, at an elevation of 6,000 ft. does not often experience temperatures of over 100°F. (38°C.). Winter cold can be bitter, with minima of –10° to –15°F. (–22° to –26°C.) on the higher plateau areas; and as a result there are heavy blizzards in many mountain areas. The January mean at Kabul is 25°F. (–4°C.). Generally speaking, a seasonal temperature range of 80-100°F. is characteristic of many areas (cf. 26°F. for London). A further difficulty is the prevalence of strong winds, especially in the west, where a persistent and regular wind blows almost daily from June to September and affects especially the Sistan area of the lower Helmand basin, where it is known as the *Wind of 120 Days.*

With highly varied topography and climate, Afghanistan has a wide range of plant life—a good deal of which is not yet fully recorded. Conditions range from Arctic and Alpine type flora on the highest parts to salt-tolerant arid zone species in the deserts. Woodland occurs in a few areas, but much has been used for fuel in a country that has cold winters.

PEOPLE AND ACTIVITIES

The considerable variation in the types of terrain, and the considerable obstacles imposed by high mountains and deserts, have given rise to marked ethnic and cultural differences, so that heterogeneity in human populations is most characteristic. The Pashtuns live mainly in the centre, south and east of the country, and are probably numerically the largest group. The Ghilzais, also of the areas adjacent to Pakistan, are thought to be of Turkish origin, like the Uzbeks who live in the north, mainly in the Amu Darya lowlands. Another important element are the Tadzhiks or Parziwans who are of Persian origin, and in the opinion of some represent the earliest inhabitants of the country. Other groups, such as the Hazara (who are reputed to have come in as followers of Ghenghis Khan), and the Chahar Aimak may have Mongol ancestry, but they now speak Persian and the Hazara are Shi'a Muslims. In the north-east, the presence of fair-haired groups has suggested connection with Europe. Another possibly indigenous group of long-standing, is the Nuristani or Kafirs, now small in number. Most Afghans (the Hazara and Qizilbash of Kabul excepted) are Sunni.

For long a difficult topography, extreme climate with a generally deficient rainfall, and political instability inhibited economic progress. Small communities lived by cultivation where water and soil were available, and there were relatively numerous pastoralists, mostly nomads, who formed an important section of the community. Even today, it is estimated that about 15 per cent of the population is nomadic, and tribal organization is strong.

Two major handicaps, arising directly from its geography, have long been the fragmented nature of the settlement pattern and the difficulties of physical communications between the various communities. Scale of production and size of markets have consequently been very limited: local standards often prevail and the central government does not find it easy to develop full control. So inherently strong is this fact of regional subdivision and diversity that the improvement of infrastructure (roads, airfields, radio and telephonic communication), undertaken with vigour over the past few years, has largely resulted in the intensification of regionalism.

In common with other countries of south-west Asia, Afghanistan experienced severe drought between 1968–72: this is thought to have been due to a major cyclical climatic shift that is traceable over a very wide area of the Northern Hemisphere. The economic consequences of this drought have been considerable, though varied regionally within Afghanistan, not only for the 80 per cent or so of the population who still live directly by agriculture, but, as well, through restriction on water supplies for developing manufacturing and other activities.

Because of Afghanistan's former location as a buffer between Russia and British India, railways approached from various sides, but none actually penetrated the country, and so Afghanistan is one of the few parts of the world still to be totally without railways. During 1975 possibilities of constructing a railway with Indian assistance were discussed. The plan is to link Kabul, Kandahar, Herat and Islamqala (on the Iranian frontier) with a line that would be 1,000 miles in length and cost £500 million. A possible extension from Kabul to Zahidan in Iran and the Pakistan border is also under consideration. The narrowness (despite the great height) of the mountain barrier as compared with the Himalayas, has made Afghanistan a traditional routeway between north and south, and at present, helped by various foreign agencies and governments, there is a programme for considerable road improvement and development. Given the difficulties of terrain, Afghanistan now possesses a reasonably good road system, with some very good sections. Air transport is also an increasingly important factor. Better accessibility has also resulted in the growth of a small, but far from insignificant tourist traffic.

HISTORY

Kevin Rafferty

Afghanistan was never a colony in the sense of being ruled by a Western colonial power, but its present-day boundaries were imposed upon it by the Great Powers of this and the last century. It is a historic land, variously described as the "crossroads of the world" or "cockpit of Asia", but sorting out that history offers difficulties.

There is the problem first of all of working out what is or was Afghanistan. That is a much more difficult task than to do a similar exercise for, say, Thailand. The word "Afghanistan" means "the country of the Afghans", that is Pathans or Pushtuns. But in its modern sense, the country has existed only since 1747, though the name "Afghanistan" first appears in the tenth century referring to a land to the east of the present country and bounded by the Indus. Much more rewarding is to consider Afghanistan as the country of the Hindu Kush. In that sense, it links the West with the east of both India and China; it offers a back door to the Soviet Union. Countless merchants and invaders have criss-crossed Afghanistan throughout history using the Oxus River (now called Amu Darya) and going through the narrow Hindu Kush passes and defiles. The famous "Silk Route" passed through the Hindu Kush when the caravan trail was already old. Alexander the Great went that way; so did merchants with indigo and Chinese silk; so did nomads from the Steppes, Buddhist monks, Moghuls, and the often hard-pressed armies of the British Raj.

EARLY HISTORY

Considering the great waves of human history that have flowed over what is known today as Afghanistan, it is surprising that they left so little permanent trace behind. This makes piecing together the rich history of the area an exceedingly tricky task. Persians, Greeks, Indians, Chinese, Huns, Mongols, Moghuls and finally Europeans, pagans, Buddhists, Hindus, Muslims and Christians, believers in the power of one God, of many, and of none, all swept over Afghanistan and conquered and finally fell to local tribes who were themselves migrants in the stream of history. By the time of the tenth century A.D., conquerors, makers of dynasties, unmakers of dynasties, all come and go with frequent clash of battle.

The first mention in history of the area now covered by Afghanistan comes in about the sixth century B.C. when Darius I was on the throne of Persia. Modern Afghanistan was probably divided into three or four Achaemenian Satraps. The chances are that Bactria included the plain of Oxus, that Arachosia included Qandahar and Aria, the valleys around Herat. Another area, Drangiana, possibly included parts of south-west Afghanistan, and the regions of Sindhu and Ghandara were almost certainly present day Sind and the North West Frontier (with possibly the part of the Punjab) of Pakistan. Confirmation of some of these facts comes from Herodotus.

However, modern archaeological finds have led experts to conjecture that some Afghan cities may have pre-dated even the Persians. These include Balkh, the centre of Bactria. Because of its position as a water source on good natural routes it may have been an important place as early as the third Millenium when the lapis lazuli trade to Mesopotamia was just starting.

Afghanistan remained in Persian hands until Darius III was defeated by Alexander in the fourth century B.C. Alexander spent some years pacifying Afghanistan and setting up five cities including Qandahar, then called Alexandria. Modern Qandahar derives its name from the Arabic form of Alexander, Iskander. When Alexander died, his empire was split. Seleucus, one of Alexander's generals, took the eastern Satraps including the greater part of Afghanistan but since his centre of power lay to the west, he could not prevent the eastern areas of Afghanistan coming under control of the empire of Chandragupta Maurya from India. Some confirmation of Indian sway is provided by discovery of two so-called Asoka edicts near Qandahar.

In the end, Asia swallowed the Greeks. Only in Bactria did they flourish until the middle of the second century B.C. when nomads defeated them. By that time internal quarrels and the rise of a strong Parthia had weakened Bactria. However, some Greek rulers clung on in the more accessible areas and Greek influences lingered till the Christian era.

By the middle of the second century, three barbarian nomadic groups appear, the Hsiung-nu Huns, the Yuĕh-chi, and the Saka. The Hsiung-nu defeated the Yuĕh-chi and forced them to flee to the Afghanistan area. The Sakai settled around the Hindu Kush towards India. The history at this point is uncertain but eventually the Kushans, the dominant tribe in the Yuĕh-chi confederacy, established a kingdom which at its height stretched from Bactria to the frontiers of China and down to Mathura in India. Peshawar, present day capital of Pakistan's North West Frontier Province, was the centre of the Kushan Empire. They fostered the arts and Buddhism, and developed the famous silk route through to China. But the Kushan Empire did not survive long and began to decline in the middle of the third century. Once again, the cockpit of Asia was plunged into confusion with much to-ing and fro-ing and the frequent clash of arms.

There were Kushan princes still ruling in various provinces. There were Sassanids, or Sassanians, challenging from Iran. There was a threatening Turco-Mongol confederacy. One Mongol group called Hephatalites (or White Huns) dominated for about a century and were particularly punishing of Buddhism. Then the Turks, allied to the Sassanids, smashed the Hephatalites and took over the area until the Chinese arrived in 658 A.D. But Chinese rule was shortlived because Arab armies had already reached the borders of Afghanistan.

The Arabs already had possession of Herat and Balkh by the time the Chinese gained control of eastern Afghanistan. The Turks and the Chinese successively weakened each other so that there was no outside resistance to the Arabs. Even so it took a long time before the whole of Afghanistan to the Hindu Kush came under the sway of Islam. Parts of the east were not converted until the ninth century and the centre until the eleventh.

Again the area of Afghanistan went through a succession of changing dynasties as the Caliphate weakened and various men claiming nominal allegiance to the Caliph were able to carve out a kingdom for themselves. There were Tahirids followed by Safarids and Samanids; under the last Bokhara, Balkh and Samarkand enjoyed golden days. The next empire was that of Mahmud of Ghazni. He came to power in 998 A.D., brought all Afghanistan under his rule, conquered the Punjab as far as Multan, and conducted seventeen annual raids into India in which he exacted vast treasures. His court was a glorious one and included such people as Firdausi the poet and Albiruni the polymath. But the Ghaznavid Empire also proved the corrupting influence of power and the instability of dynastic rule. It had been founded by Mahmud's grandfather when he, a former Turkish slave, Alptigin, displaced the local ruler of Ghazni. The Ghaznavid empire crumbled because Mahmud's successors did not have his brilliance. The Ghaznavids themselves came under pressure of the Seljuks, a tribe of the Ghuzz who seized Khorassan. But it was another group, the Ghorids, who moved in 1152 and sacked Ghazni.

The Ghorids came from the obscure hill country up the Hari Rud from Herat, an area which had remained isolated and extremely poor. The Ghorid empire was also shortlived. Ala-ud-din Husayn had been responsible for sacking Ghazni. But he was driven out by the Seljuks. Then his nephews Mu'izzud-din (Mohammad of Ghor) and Ghiyas-ud-Din drove to Ghazni again and carved out a shortlived empire reaching from Herat to Ajmer in India. The Ghorids have extra importance because their general Qutub-ud-din Rybik became Sultan of Delhi when the Indian possession became cut off from those near the Hindu Kush. The Qutub-Minar in Delhi is named after him.

No sooner had Mohammad of Ghor died than the empire fell apart before the armies of Sultan Ala-ud-din Mohammad, known as the Khwarezm Shah. For a brief time his dynasty had an empire starting from Chinese Turkestan and this time extending westward to the borders of Iraq. He was able to mount an invasion of Baghdad early in the thirteenth century. However, he had hardly reached his destination when he learnt that his dominion was being threatened by yet another invasion, this time from the Mongol Genghis Khan. Genghis Khan had consolidated his grip on Mongolia by 1206 and then started looking around for fresh fields to conquer. By 1216, he had extended his rule to the Sinkiang Province of present day China, bordering on the Karakorams and the Hindu Kush mountains, and started to come south. Mohammad of Khwarezm had 400,000 cavalry under his command but did not consider this enough to face Genghis Khan's hordes who by this time had seized parts of Trans-Oxiana and were spreading destruction and death before them. He turned and retreated to the Caspian. Only his son, Jalal-ud-din, was prepared to face the Mongols and using Ghazni as his headquarters, he did manage to inflict two defeats. Genghis Khan himself turned to give siege to Bamiyan (the historic Buddhist city which today has the largest Buddha in the world, a 175-ft. high statue carved out of the rock). In the siege Genghis Khan's grandson was killed and that so infuriated the Mongol that he laid Bamiyam utterly waste. By 1222 the whole of Afghanistan was in Genghis Khan's hands and was made to pay dreadfully for its resistance.

More than a century passed before a coherent administration was put together again. When the legendary Kublai Khan came to the throne, Afghanistan suffered badly again because two of its local rulers took sides, one for Kublai Khan and one against him.

Genghis Khan's empire once more proved to be a personal one. It did not long survive his death in 1227 and fell quickly into a series of petty kingdoms. Then Timur the Lame (Tamurlane) in the 14th century put the pieces and the armies together and repeated some of Genghis Khan's Mongol devastations. However, his successors, the Timurites, based on Herat, brought an era of peace and stability and patronage of learning and the arts.

This rule, once more, was shortlived. War and warring was never far from the Hindu Kush. The Uzbecs, a Turkic people, entered Herat in 1507 and drove out Babur, a direct descendant of Genghis Khan and Timur. Babur fell back on Kabul from which he was to found the great Moghul empire. From his Kabul base, he took Qandahar before turning towards India. Having defeated the last of the Lodi Afghan kings of India at Panipat, north of Delhi, he transferred the capital to Agra. However, he did not forget Kabul and when he died in 1530, his body was returned there.

The shifting of Babur's base to Agra stretched Moghul rule in Afghanistan and they had to yield areas to the Safavids of Persia. Qandahar was disputed between the two. The early 18th century offered the Pathans their first taste of power. For a brief while, when Ghilzai Mir Wais revolted against the declining Safarids, they ruled even Persia itself. But then the Persians hit back. In 1736 Nadir Kuli Khan, a brigand, proclaimed himself as Nadir Shah, ruler of Persia. He extended his rule through Afghanistan and went on to sack Delhi and carry away the famous peacock throne and Koh-i-Noor diamond. But once again that empire did not survive its founder.

THE COMING OF MODERN AFGHANISTAN

Nadir Shah was obviously impressed by the Pathans and placed them in high positions in his empire. This gave them a chance in the confusion surrounding the assassination of Nadir Shah in 1747. They seized it. An Afghan chief of the Sadozai clan, Ahmed Khan Abduli, took a contingent of some several thousand Afghans and was elected king in Qandahar with the title Dur-i-duran (pearl of the age) from which the dynastic name Durrani was derived. He built up his rule in the area now known as Afghanistan and was also able to exact tribute from the adjoining areas of Kashmir, Sind and Baluchistan. When he died, he was succeeded by his son Timur who moved the capital from Qandahar to Kabul. On Timur's death it seemed once again that another empire would break into fragments. He left 20 sons who squabbled for the throne, lost territory in the north to the Uzbecs, and other parts to other feuding families. The Sadozans sought alliance with the Barakzais (Mohammedzais) another powerful clan, betrayed them, and were driven to Herat by the Barakzais. At this point, Afghan rule really looked in disarray with Sikhs attacking from the east and the Persians grumbling in the west.

In Ghazni, Dost Mohammad, the youngest of the Barakzai brothers had come to the fore. He went on to take Kabul, thus inviting the attention of the British who were inevitably concerned about Afghanistan which they regarded as the key to India. They distrusted Dost Mohammad, tried to replace him by the Sadozai, Shah Shuja, and involved themselves in the bitter first Afghan war. Only after the disastrous retreat from Kabul and massacre in 1842 did the British realize the error of their ways. They allowed Dost Mohammad to go back and take the throne, Shah Shuja having been killed by his own people as the British left.

Dost Mohammad ruled Afghanistan for 20 years and won the title of Amir-i-Kabir (the Great Amir). He named his third son Sher Ali to succeed him. Sher Ali spent the first few years establishing himself over his brothers. Then in the late 1870s he upset the British when he received a Russian mission in Kabul but refused to welcome a British one on the same terms. This led to the second British-Afghan War from 1878–81 in which the British captured Jalalabad and Qandahar. Sher Ali fled and died leaving his son as regent. Yaqub in 1879 agreed to receive a British embassy at Kabul and to conduct his foreign policy with the "wishes and advice of the British Government".

However, in September 1879, the British envoy and his companion were murdered in Kabul, so British forces again occupied Kabul, exiled Yaqub and in 1880 recognized a grandson of Dost Mohammad, Abdurrahman Khan, as Amir of Kabul. Just as they prepared to leave the capital, they learnt that a British force in Meilwand near Qandahar had been wiped out, so once again they returned with a vengeance and seized Qandahar. This intervention ceased in 1881, when a change of government in London led to the abandoning of the "forward policy". Abdurrahman remained on the throne where he organized the Government despotically, converted the Kafir areas by force, and renamed them Nuristan, and agreed to the Durand line effectively establishing the modern-day boundary between British India and Afghanistan. The British had taken the Khyber Pass as part of the spoils of the Second Afghan war. In October 1901, Abdurrahman died and was succeeded by his eldest son Habibullah Khan.

MODERN AFGHANISTAN

It is worth considering what kind of country Emir Abdurrahman took over. His boundaries were fixed for him by the Great Powers of British India and Imperial Russia. The Afghanistan he tried to wield into shape was by no means a nation state in the European sense of the term. It contained large numbers of people who did not speak the same language. Most Afghans owed their first loyalties to their tribe which had its own much longer and more personal history. Moreover, tribal groupings often spilled over to the neighbouring countries. Even the majority Pathan tribes straddled Afghanistan and British India. There were Baluch in Afghanistan whose cousins and nearest kinfolk were in Iran or British India. There were Turkomen, Uzbecs, Tajiks, Kirghiz, the majority of whom were in Imperial Russian territory but who also had large numbers in modern Afghanistan.

In terms of language, Afghanistan was—and is—a living tower of Babel. Its Indo-European languages include Pushtu, Dari (the Afghan Farsi), the language of the Tajiks, Farsiwan, the Hezaras, Qizilbash and Aimaq, as well as Nuristani, Dardic and Pamir dialects. That is not all. The Mongolian peoples speak Uralic-Altaic languages of which the subgroups include Kirghizi and the tongue of the Uzbecs. Moreover the Brahui tribes speak a totally different language, a Dravidian one which is akin to those of South India.

Although its external boundaries were fixed by outsiders who wanted Afghanistan as a buffer state, the internal power of the emir was by no means secure. The tribal leaders were conscious that they had started Afghanistan and the Durrani dynasty by electing the first ruler so as the better to protect their territory against outsiders. The emir had to ponder how far the tribal elders would let his writ run.

Emir Abdurrahman solved all of these problems by a rough policy, a sort of imperialism from within. He built up a strong army led by Ghulam-Harda Charkhi and was not afraid to conduct more than a dozen major campaigns which he called "civil wars". He eliminated tribal leaders who opposed him, confiscated their weapons, levelled their forts, and, if necessary, held their sons hostage to prevent their fathers waging war again. He pushed the administration into rural areas and tried to make officials loyal to him.

He did not forget the influence of the religious leaders. He made the mullahs take tests in religious knowledge to prove their claims. The number of

Islamic religious leaders dwindled. The emir did not live to have to face the repercussions of this brutal policy which, for example, produced a concentration of religious power in the hands of a smaller number of mullahs.

He also provided for his succession by naming his son Habibullah. The transition was smooth. There was no civil war and Habibullah began the arduous journey to the modern world by opening schools, factories and building roads and encouraging a weekly paper written in Persian. In foreign affairs Habibullah observed a careful neutrality. But there was evidence that Emir Abdurrahman had simply squashed the opposition but not extinguished it. This flared up when Habibullah was assassinated in 1919 near Jalalabad.

For a while there was turmoil in Afghanistan, which was settled when Habibullah's third son, Amanullah Khan, won himself the succession largely by seizing the treasury. He immediately declared Afghanistan to be completely independent in both internal and external affairs, a pronouncement which led to the third war between Afghanistan and Britain. The fighting was inconclusive but did lead to a peace in which the independence of Afghanistan was recognized and diplomatic relations opened with both Britain and the Soviet Union.

The new King Amanullah was an unusual man who persisted in his radicalism even when he had power. He tried to push through a series of reforms including the unveiling of women; the removal of parents' rights to betroth their children; the dismissal of government officials who wanted to have more than one wife; the curbing of the rights of the religious leaders and the introduction of secular laws in preference to the Islamic Shariah. In all this he showed a dashing sense of action and awareness of how to bring Afghanistan into the modern world; it was accompanied by an unmatched political naiveté in thinking that this was the way to do it. He learned that he could not ride roughshod over both vested tribal and Islamic chieftains. In the end the tribal and religious leaders ganged up against him and again Afghanistan was plunged into civil war. In January 1929, Kabul was seized by Baccha-i-Saqao, a brigand, and Amanullah abdicated. He tried to come back, failed, and left for exile in Italy. The Baccha held Kabul for a nine-month reign of terror before being driven off by Amanullah's cousin, Mohammad Nadir Khan, a former war minister, and his brothers. In the general assembly held soon afterwards, Nadir Khan was elected king as Nadir Shah. He tried to consolidate the country, but he was assassinated in November 1933.

Surprisingly the changeover proved easy and Nadir's son, Mohammad Zahir, took over as king at the age of 19.

The long reign of Zahir Shah was marked throughout by its caution. For the first 20 years he was strongly under the influence of his three uncles, Hashim Khan, Shah Mahmud and Shah Wali Khan. They had shown remarkable forbearance in allowing Zahir to come to the throne in the first place. However, the arrangement not to squabble for the throne was helpful to them because with King Zahir there, he reigned while they ruled.

In 1953 Mohammad Daoud Khan, a cousin of the king, challenged the surviving and ageing uncles, Shah Mahmud and Shah Wali Khan, who allowed him to become Prime Minister although they were uneasy and distrusted his zeal. The main impact of the new prime minister was one of vigour in starting a series of five year economic plans. The price, said critics, was in bringing the cold war in economic terms to Afghanistan. He did this by playing off America and the Soviet Union to obtain aid.

In 1956 Sardar Daoud obtained the approval of the Loya Jirga (tribal council) to accept military aid from the Soviet Union. He was able to do this only by claiming that Washington had refused a request for military assistance. The request had been made by the pre-Daoud Government and had carried strings that Afghanistan must have a security guarantee of its border. Washington had pointed to the huge undefended frontier with the Soviet Union and said that such a guarantee would be meaningless, so Moscow gave military aid and came to provide the backbone of Afghanistan's forces.

Prime Minister Daoud also pressed the Pashtunistan issue against Pakistan and used this way of getting popular support and clearing the hurdles in the way of popular acceptance of Soviet aid. Though Afghanistan had accepted the Durand line as the border with British India, it had not accepted that Pakistan, with its own Pathans of the North West Frontier, should inherit the same border. Diplomatic relations with Pakistan were broken in 1961.

Sardar Daoud was able to use the military assistance to modernize the army and thus once more strengthen the hold of the army and the Government over the country as a whole.

For all this spirit of modernization, which included allowing women to drop their veils, Sardar Daoud presented no plans to take Afghanistan towards democracy. Such moves only came with his resignation in 1963.

The new Prime Minister, Doctor Yusuf, was the first not to be a member of the royal family. Not only that but he was also not a Pathan. The first thing his Government did was to present a new democratic constitution designed by a group of young intellectuals. The constitution combined Islamic religious and political ideas with institutions familiar to the west. It was intended to bring about popular participation in politics both locally and nationally. Unfortunately this included a rigid separation of the powers and allowed parliament constantly to snipe at the executive. This might not have been too bad if Afghanistan had not been ruled under an autocratic thumb so long that there were many grievances to air. Even this might not have been so bad had the king followed up his promise to allow political parties. But right to the end of his regime the parties, which might also have helped channel the hot steam of debate especially if they had a chance of power, were not allowed to. So instead of being a focus for regulating and producing a consensus from the diverse elements of Afghan society, the parliament proved a battleground for the Government and the tribes.

Afghanistan had a succession of well-meaning prime ministers, but their achievements amounted to little and were not able to make much dent in Afghanistan's problems though relations were restored with Pakistan in 1965. The country remained backward with 85 per cent of its people excluded both from politics and the modern economy; at the same time an increasing restless elite was created in Kabul which included a number of the younger educated men in the country who had to see illiterate elected leaders squabbling in parliament while the government machine floundered through a corrupt slow-moving bureaucracy. The time was ripe for change and Daoud moved back in again.

COUP AGAINST KING ZAHIR

On July 17th, 1973, King Zahir was in Italy when he learnt he had been deposed by a *coup d'état* in which his cousin and brother-in-law, Sardar Mohammad Daoud was the best known figure. Sardar Daoud took office as Head of State, Prime Minister, Foreign Minister and Minister of Defence. The Monarchy was abolished, so was the 1964 constitution, and Afghanistan was declared a Republic.

Even today, it is not clear who engineered the coup. Its supporters included young Moscow-trained officers of middle and junior rank. The evidence now seems to be that President Daoud was brought into its planning late on, and was expected to be rather more of a figurehead than he has proved. In the early days of the coup, a lot was heard of the "central committee" running Afghanistan, but recently President Daoud has made all the running and has been able to replace his more left-wing ministers. There is rarely a mention of the central committee.

There is no evidence that Moscow was directly involved in the coup though it has been a major benefactor. It is the supplier of most of Afghanistan's military equipment and responsible in large measure for training Kabul's force. However, it would be unfair to describe President Daoud as being in Moscow's pocket. He has striven to retain a balance and to be friendly to all countries. Some observers think he would like to loosen the Soviet strings, for example, by sending some of his officers to Britain for training, but he is constrained by his shortage of funds.

As to the whys and wherefores of the coup of 1973, it was clearly a "palace revolution". There is no doubt that there were many critics of the Government of King Zahir but these were probably irrelevant to events except in ensuring that there was not much opposition to the palace plotters. King Zahir's Government had become overwhelmed by its own hesitations and lack of decisiveness and this lack of progress made for acceptance of the new regime. Sardar Daoud was able to say at his first news conference, "I can safely say that this was in every sense of the word a bloodless coup. It not only enjoyed the co-operation of the army but also the support of all the people particularly the intellectuals and the youths." When necessary reforms fail to be introduced in the normal manner, then the resort to revolutionary action must take place.

But the new rulers have been slow to implement any large scale reforms. The most noticeable change when Daoud came to power was the raising of the temperature with Pakistan over the issue of Pashtunistan. There were hostile broadcasts from both Kabul radio and from Pakistan which were stilled only in 1976 when Pakistan's Prime Minister, Mr. Bhutto, went to Kabul. The question of Pashtunistan and alleged Afghan support for the National Awami Party in Pakistan had figured largely in what amounted to a treason trial in Pakistan in 1975 and 1976. But for all its lack of obvious energy on questions of social reform and after all its leader is now elderly, the Daoud Government began to push the economy of Afghanistan along at a better pace and appeared firmly in the saddle.

AFGHANISTAN AND THE SOVIET UNION

In the last century British secret agents played "the Great Game" over the Roof of the World in the Karakorams and the Hindu Kush to try to prevent the Soviet Union from gaining a stranglehold on Afghanistan. British lives were lost in three bloody Afghan wars to secure influence over Afghanistan, which was seen as the key to India and the world beyond. Palmerston wrote: "A Russian force in occupation of Afghanistan might not be able to march on to Calcutta, but you will find in such case a very restless spirit displayed by the Burmese, the Nepalese and by all the uncorporated states scattered about the surface of our Indian possession."

Today it would be wrong to say that the Kremlin controlled Kabul. President Daoud is too independent a spirit to allow that. Yet it clearly exercises what Curzon called the Power of Menace over Afghanistan to a degree which would have made the one-time British rulers of the Indian subcontinent exceedingly alarmed. The armed forces of Afghanistan are trained, equipped and supplied by the Soviet Union. Presumably their members include senior officers who owe some special loyalty to Moscow. The Soviet Union has financed much of Afghanistan's aid and industrial projects and has advisers keeping watch in Kabul. There is no sign that it is preparing or prepared to move in to take active control of Afghanistan, or that it would like to assume the obligations that such an active role would imply. But clearly Kabul today would be hard-pressed to carry out a policy directly against the wishes and interests of Moscow.

So why are the alarm bells not ringing in the West? One reason is undoubtedly that Afghanistan is no longer the only key to India and the east. Both communications and armed forces are much more mobile than they used to be. In addition, the Soviet Union has more direct ways of ensuring its influence in India and its policy is unsuccessful there.

Some people—like the Pakistanis—remain highly suspicious and distrust Soviet intentions. They say Moscow is anxious to gain its own warm water port. If Pakistan were broken up, say, through the Pashtunistan issue, then it and Karachi on the Arabian Sea would be there for the taking. However, the Kremlin's aims are probably nothing like as clear cut as that. Soviet ambitions have been historically centred on the Middle East or Constantinople rather than India. Secondly, the Soviet time scale is probably different and the perspective is more likely to be 50 or 100 years rather than immediate, in which case the Kremlin probably sees no reason to draw international attention to itself by provoking action by using Afghanistan. One senior British official, Giles Bullard, writing in an unofficial capacity, likened the Soviet action to that of an elephant leaning on a wall. The elephant was not too keen to be seen pushing but if there were any cracks on the wall, then he would discover them and the bits would not fall on him.

ECONOMIC SURVEY

Kevin Rafferty

The greatest problem of trying to present an accurate economic profile of Afghanistan is that it is a backward, underdeveloped country where correct information is hard to come by. Only 10 per cent of the people can read or write. (All figures must be subject to scepticism because there has never been a proper census of population.) Some economic statistics are published but they tend to be at best out of date and even then not very reliable. And since more than 80 per cent of the people of Afghanistan are rural and nomadic, scattered in remote villages dotted over the predominantly mountain and desert countryside, it is doubtful how much they are affected by government or anyone else's Western-style "guesstimates" of what is their economic performance.

Assessment of Gross National Product (G.N.P.), for example, illustrates the difficulties. The Government estimated G.N.P. for 1971–72* at 89,500 million afghanis. The official exchange rate is Afs. 45 to the dollar so that would mean total G.N.P. of $2,000 million or about $110 a head, which may have risen to $115 a head given real growth of 3 per cent in 1973–74 and 4 per cent in subsequent years. However, the problems of making dollar conversions are complicated because there is a free market rate which was about Afs. 56 to $1 in early 1975 and 52 at the end. And not everyone would accept the Afghanistan figures. By their own methods of calculations, American sources assessed G.N.P. for 1974 at U.S.$1,500 million or $80–85 a head. Afghanistan's population would usually be estimated at the end of 1975 to be about 19 million and to be growing at slightly more than 2 per cent a year. This is based on official estimates that it increased from 14.5 to 18.3 million between 1963 and 1973. But since there has been no complete census, and official guesses are based on crude and partial returns, the figures must be regarded with some circumspection.

Since the mid-1960s Afghanistan's economy has been rather stagnant, though it seems to have been improving since President Daoud took over in 1973. Most experts consider that the rate of growth of G.N.P. has been between 2 and 3 per cent a year, and probably fell below the growth rate in population in the late 1960s and early 1970s. Since President Daoud's Government took over in 1973, it has raised growth targets to 4 per cent a year for 1974–75 and 1975–76 and these may well have been met, given that the new Government has managed more economic cohesion. Equally important, after a disastrous drought at the start of the 1970s, agricultural production has picked up in the last two years. However, suffice it to say that Afghanistan is one of the poorest and most disadvantaged countries in the world. It is on the United Nation's official list as one of the least developed countries in the world, and it suffers the additional handicap of being landlocked.

THE START OF ECONOMIC PLANNING

Before the 1930s Afghanistan was still in the Middle Ages as far as economic development was concerned. The great armies and trade caravans of ancient times had struggled over it, but modern development had ignored it because with the coming of sea power from the fifteenth century onwards there were less arduous ways to India and China than through Afghanistan and the cold, high, dangerous Hindu Kush passes. Even the railway age bypassed Afghanistan. Only in 1932 when the Banke Millie Afghan (National Bank) was established was there a start to modern economic development. Before that the only modern features were the Government's workshops in Kabul chiefly intended to attend to the needs of the army, and one small hydro-electric station. The formation of the bank gave an impetus to the foundation of private companies. These were mainly dealing in trade for karakul and lamb skins and wool, but textile and sugar companies were also set up. However, progress was slow and even at the end of the Second World War, internal trade was carried by caravan and inter-city roads were not paved. Only about 20,000 kilowatts of power was produced and few consumer goods were made locally.

* The Afghanistan year runs from March 21st to March 20th of the following year.

In 1946, the new Prime Minister, Shah Mahmud Khan, started what he wanted to develop as an ambitious economic development programme using Afghanistan's agricultural exports as its base. But he failed for lack of finance. He hoped to get U.S. money as the backbone of the $100 million foreign component of the $450 million plan to develop industry, extend hydro-electricity and irrigation programmes, introduce better education and health care. After negotiations the U.S. Export-Import Bank was prepared to lend $21 million for three dams and followed it up by another $18.5 million loan for similar work.

The next attempt to start economic planning came when Mohammad Daoud took over as Prime Minister in 1953. Again, he ran into problems in finding foreign finance, and Washington refused to lend general support to the first five-year plan which got under way in 1957. It was ready only to provide money for individual projects. However, the Prime Minister, Daoud, neatly sidestepped that problem by improving relations with the Soviet Union and delicately playing off the U.S.S.R. and the U.S.A. so that the U.S.A. closely followed and almost matched Soviet aid to Afghanistan. Moscow was prepared to underwrite a general five-year exercise. In all, between 1957 and 1972 the Soviet Union offered more than $900 million to support the plans or nearly 60 per cent of foreign aid, although some Western experts say that the sums promised were larger than the money handed over. The U.S. came closely second though it generally offered better terms for its aid.

The first three plans (from 1957 to 1961 for the first; 1962 to 1967 for the second; 1968 to 1972 for the third) cannot really be described as an attempt to control the whole economy, though the Government described the economy as its "guided economy" and later "mixed guided economy". The plans offered a series of projects basically to improve the infrastructure and bring Afghanistan at least closer to the twentieth century.

The first plan set the pattern by putting great emphasis on communications, particularly road building and the establishment of air links both national and international. In addition, 32 industrial projects were listed for starting, though not all were started. The achievements of the first plan were patchy. Its great merits were the attempt to get planned economy development started at all, to tap external sources of finance, and at the same time to realize the need for internal finance. The great drawback was that the daring in planning was not matched by daring or so much success in implementation.

By the time of the second plan, the difficulties of the planning were beginning to be apparent, at least to outsiders. Proper cost-benefit studies were neglected, and the impact of projects on income and job opportunities was virtually ignored. The second plan also attempted to expand the role of the public sector because private industry was not big enough to undertake developments in power, gas, supply and making of cement, chemicals, and other important capital intensive industry. One problem which was not properly examined beforehand was where to find competent operators and managers to run the plants.

At the dawn of the third plan, the Government reviewed the achievements and the lessons of the first two plans and emphasized the need to turn to more quickly yielding projects. However, in practice Afghanistan discovered that the ability to switch was more difficult than stating the intentions to switch.

For all this, 16 years of planning and public investment of Afs. 53,000 million produced an impressive list of achievements. Before planning started there were no paved roads in Afghanistan, few permanent bridges and air transport was almost non-existent. At the end of the third plan the country had 2,780 kilometres of paved roads and two international and 29 local airports. Dams and bridges were constructed. Registration of motor vehicles in Kabul went up from 16,000 in 1962 to 52,000 in 1971. Nor was this all. In industry, production of cotton cloth went up by four times to 62 million metres, cement making was started, and output of the soap, sugar and coal industries went up by between 100 and 300 per cent. Electricity production rose to 422.6 million kilowatt hours, or by nearly nine times. Natural gas production was started and reached 2,635 million cubic metres annually, much of which is exported to the Soviet Union. Shoe production was started. There were big achievements in education where the number of schools rose from 804 to nearly 4,000, teachers from 4,000 to 20,000, and students from 125,000 to 700,000. Industrial employment rose from 18,000 in 1962 to nearly 27,000 in 1971. More than 60 private enterprise industries were set up employing nearly 5,000 people.

The fourth plan was published in 1973 and looked again to Soviet help as its mainstay but the planning procedure was disrupted by the coup and actual planning has been on an annual basis. However, early in 1975 the Soviet Union agreed to make funds available for the five-year term. The aim was that the Soviet Union would help build an oil refinery, a chemical fertilizer factory as well as help in geological prospecting. More money will be spent on irrigation in the north of Afghanistan and the produce grown this way will in turn be exported to the Soviet Union. The World Bank, the U.S.A. and the Federal Republic of Germany are again major donors, and the People's Republic of China last year provided $55 million though Peking has recently complained that President Daoud is under Moscow's thumb.

THE ECONOMY IN THE MID-1970s

Agriculture

Agriculture is the most important contributor to Afghanistan's economy today, providing half the national income and four-fifths of the country's exports. Of the total land area of nearly 65 million hectares, 14 million hectares are considered cultivable and about 8 million are being cultivated. Irrigation is a major problem and of the 6 million irrigable hectares only 60 per cent are irrigated. The impact of lack of water was shown sharply in 1971 when there was severe drought as a result of which the production of wheat, the main crop, dropped from nearly 2.5 million tons to below 2 million tons and millions of important livestock were slaughtered. It took two years for the crops to recover but 1974–75 production of wheat was up to 2.7 million tons, and in the 1975–76 year ending in March 1976 it is estimated to have risen to 2.9 million tons. These are considerable rises, amounting to 10 per cent in the latest year, and should allow Afghanistan to recover its ability to feed itself which was lost in the later years of the rule of King Zahir Shah when food production was rising at an annual 1.5 per cent only, or less than the rise in population growth each year.

Equally impressive was the rise in cotton production in 1975–76 from 149,000 tons to 180,000. In the past one of the problems was that wheat and cotton tended to be competitive for the use of land. Part of the increase of the wheat production can be attributed to better weather, but other reasons are increased use of new seeds and of fertilizers, of which consumption rose from 44,000 tons in 1973–74 to 70,000 tons in 1975–76. Over the past two years, cotton production has gone up by 75 per cent, a vast improvement, especially since it had been in the doldrums since 1963 when it had topped 100,000 tons.

Other food crops are officially estimated to have kept up or slightly improved their production. Fruit rose from 865,000 tons to 880,000 tons and sugar beet from 67,000 to 105,000 tons; the latter increase will mean a saving on sugar imports from the Soviet Union and West Germany. Smaller grain crops remained about steady in the 1974–75 year, the last one for which figures have been given: barley was 360,000 tons; maize 760,000; and rice 420,000 tons. There were important advances in smaller sectors, of 67 per cent in silk production, 26 per cent in the breeding of chickens and 8 per cent in pasteurized milk.

The severe drought of 1970 and 1971 is estimated to have cost between 30 per cent and 50 per cent of Afghanistan's livestock which in 1970 were estimated at 6.5 million karakul sheep, 15 million ordinary sheep, 3.7 million cattle, 3.2 million goats and 500,000 horses. By 1975 they were estimated to have increased to the 1970 levels.

Industry

Although its series of economic plans set up modern industry and took Afghanistan out of the handicraft age, the contribution of industry to the gross domestic product is small, less than 10 per cent. Handicrafts, especially carpet making and weaving, still contribute more to G.D.P. than modern industry. Industrial employment has hardly changed since 1971 when it was estimated that 27,000 people were employed out of the total working population of about 4 million. Even the oldest established and largest industry, cotton textiles, is not able yet to produce enough cloth—output was 87,000 metres in 1974–75—to satisfy domestic demand. Cement production has begun to pick up again, and rose to 146,000 tons in 1974–75, having dropped to 73,000 tons in 1971 from a 1966 peak of 174,000 tons, after a decline in construction. The Government has shown its anxiety to get new industries going. In 1972 it established an Industrial Development Bank. And in the 1975–76 year several other industrial plans were announced.

These include plans for new factories including a nail-making factory, textiles mills, a plastic bag works, anti-freeze plant, a raisin sorting operation and two liquorice extraction plants, all of which will be in the private sector. Plans for the public sector include ventures for metal tools, woollen goods, leather works and an engraving plant for making ornaments from such local precious stones as lapis lazuli. In an agreement with Federal Germany it was announced in January 1976 that an $8 million woollen mill is to be built at Qandahar with Iranian credit. It will have a capacity of 200,000 metres of high quality cashmere, 200,000 metres of other cloth and 300 tons of thread for carpet weaving. It will employ 1,700 men.

Mining

Afghanistan has extensive mining resources of coal, salt, chrome, iron ore, silver, gold, fluorite, talc, mica, copper and lapis lazuli, but the country's problems of access and transport have posed questions about whether it is worth mining them. The most successful find has been of natural gas, most of which is piped to the Soviet Union in payment for imports and debts. Production may get up to 4,000 million cubic metres a year soon, compared to 2,700 million in 1975–76. However, unless new gas finds are made the existing fields may be exhausted some time before the turn of the century. Other minerals have been more disappointing. Coal production reached a peak of 164,000 tons in 1970–71 and lapis lazuli has varied between 5 and 10 tons a year. Chrome and salt are also mined.

Iron ore reserves at Hajigak in Bamiyan province with millions of tons of high-grade ore are the most promising of recent discoveries. The only snag is that although the ore would fetch a good price, that would not be sufficient to offset the high costs of exporting it from remote Afghanistan which has no sea-port of its own, nor even rail lines. Some commentators cherish dreams of using the iron with the natural gas to make steel, but for the moment such are pipe-dreams. However, the Daoud Government has turned its mind seriously to an investigation of which of Afghanistan's rich mineral resources may be worth further exploitation. It hopes to start production of barite, talc and mica soon.

Trade

As regards trade, the Government figures show the unreliability of the official statistics. For example, original figures for the 1974–75 year suggested that Afghanistan had a trade deficit of more than $40 million; but upon revision this turned out to be a small trade surplus. Exports are worth about $200 million a year at the current rate, and the main items are fresh fruit and vegetables which go to Pakistan and India, natural gas to the Soviet Union, karakul which goes to the fur markets of Europe, carpets and rugs, raw cotton and dried fruit and nuts, which are just beginning to make inroads into the developed country markets.

Imports include machinery, petroleum oil, pharmaceuticals, textiles and other consumer goods. Afghanistan is in the happy position, practically unique to the poor non-oil-producing countries, in that its oil-producing neighbours, Iran and the Soviet Union, have allowed it oil at cheap prices.

Exports in the last year have shown a slow growth, rising by an estimated 3 per cent in the first half of 1975–76. For the declines in earnings, karakul and carpets were mainly to blame. Import payments have jumped sharply, so that Afghanistan will most likely have a trade gap of perhaps $10 million or more in the 1975–76 year and will have to draw down its reserves which had been built up to nearly $120 million in mid-1975, because of good trade results and a heavier aid inflow.

Afghanistan's main trading partner is the Soviet Union, which provides more than a quarter of imports and takes nearly 30 per cent of the country's exports. India takes another 20 per cent of Afghan goods, although that figure has recently fluctuated, and the U.K. takes about 16 per cent. Japan is the second largest import supplier with about 15 per cent and the U.S. comes third with 10 per cent. Afghanistan has been able to maintain large imports with the help of foreign aid, but this has recently begun to cause strains on foreign exchange because of heavy repayments and Kabul has had to ask for debt rescheduling. In an attempt to get round trade problems caused by Afghanistan's lack of a sea-port, a London firm in 1976 began a weekly rail container service to Kabul via Eastern Europe. This 40-day service will be faster than the sea route via Karachi and less cumbersome than the overland route where customs have to be cleared at the border.

Money and Finance

The slow growth of the economy has created difficulties in raising the Government's internal revenues. Half of the ordinary revenues come from indirect taxes. The next largest contributors are public enterprises (13 per cent) and natural gas revenues (12.5 per cent). Only 10 per cent of the revenues comes from direct taxes. In 1972–73 domestic revenues totalled Afs. 5,872 million, which showed only a slight rise from the Afs. 5,702 million of two years previously. Administration and defence was the biggest spender, accounting for nearly 38 per cent of expenditure. Social Services took 20 per cent.

In 1975 the Government decreed that all banks in Afghanistan had been nationalized in an attempt to bring about a more organized banking system. The move was directed at the Banke Millie Afghan, as the other banks were already under government control. The chief bank is the Da Afghanistan Bank, the central bank which also does commercial business. Money supply has expanded in recent years by between 10 and 15 per cent. In December 1972 money supply was Afs. 8,789 million; in 1973, Afs. 9,663 million; and in 1974, Afs. 11,092 million.

Tourism

In recent years tourism has been an important contributor to Afghanistan's earnings, raising up to $10 million a year from visitors who numbered between 90,000 and 100,000 a year. The peak was 113,000 in 1971. At one time Afghanistan had the reputation of being a "hippy paradise" particularly because drugs could be obtained cheaply locally and are freely used locally. But this has been curbed and embassies will refuse to grant visas to people who look as if they cannot support themselves. But so far Afghanistan's location off the main air routes of the world and its poor hotel facilities (apart from two international hotels in Kabul) has meant that it has not been able to tap the lucrative Western package holiday market. Its main tourist visitors are travellers going overland to or from Pakistan and India.

THE ECONOMY AND SOCIAL BENEFITS

Since planning in Afghanistan started nearly 20 years ago it has produced some splendid achievements. Schools have been built, factories opened, roads laid and they are there to see as impressive monuments to all the official zeal.

The achievements most obvious to the foreigner are probably the roads built with Soviet and American help. Before the planning started, it could take days along dirt tracks even to travel between the most important cities. Now it is possible to go through Afghanistan from end to end in about two days. The country has 1,550 miles of modern paved roads. The most magnificent is the highway between Kabul and Shir Khan on the Soviet border in the north which crosses the Hindu Kush through the two-mile Salang tunnel and shortens the distance between Kabul and the rich north by 120 miles. Another road links the capital with Peshawar (Pakistan) in the east, and stretches to Qandahar to the south and on to Herat near the border with Iran, so that the route which Alexander the Great took is now completely paved and open to use by buses and lorries. Airports have also been opened in Kabul and Qandahar for international travel. Afghanistan has its own airlines, Ariana for international flights, and Bakhtar for domestic ones.

However, for all this, the question can still be asked as to whether the best use has been made of the plan money and the foreign aid. Afghanistan has a population of about 19 million. The major towns are Kabul, the capital, with 500,000 people, Qandahar which has 136,000 people in the main wool and fruit-producing area, and Herat with 106,000 people in the west. More than 30 per cent of the first three plan expenditures went to building the giant highways, but what use are such roads in helping the local people living in scattered rural areas to get their crops to market? Or to bring them in to modern life, especially when bus services are few and vehicles ancient? Although 85 per cent of the people of Afghanistan are living in rural areas, and although their agriculture contributes 50 per cent to G.N.P. and 90 per cent of foreign exchange earnings, a much smaller proportion of the plan expenditure went to help agriculture or livestock and very little of the money going in those directions went to the smaller farmers For example, of the Afs. 12,500 million spent on the agricultural sector, half went merely to two huge irrigation projects. More attention to feeder roads to the markets or to local irrigation might have reaped better benefits, raised foodgrain production higher than the 1.5 per cent annual increase in the ten years to 1962, and done much to bring the poorer people closer to the market economy.

Another crying need of Afghanistan is for labour-creating projects. The labour force has increased by about 100,000 a year, but very few of these new entrants have been able to find jobs.

Yet another problem has been the lack of ability to see a project through to its conclusion, a fact which was not helped by the long gestation period of many plan ventures. Even the schemes which have been finished under aid were often poorly assessed in advance, a fact which Afghanistan is finding out today. Qandahar airport, costing $15 million (an American project) has proved to be the whitest of white elephants as there is hardly enough international air traffic even for Kabul. The Balkh textile mill (French aid) was more costly than it should have been, and the Mazar-i-Sharif fertilizer factory (Soviet aid) was based on outdated technology. Factories in the public sector have generally operated below capacity because of inadequate supplies or poor machinery or the inability to plan maintenance.

In the last few years there have been some notable improvements. Agricultural production has gone up, thanks to better weather, improved seeds and more application of fertilizer. Afghanistan has shown that it still offers plenty of grounds for hope and progress in agriculture. Its cotton has proved competitive in world markets. Its fresh fruit could be exported right round the Gulf area, and dried fruit like raisins could have world-wide markets.

In the industrial sphere the authorities have made determined efforts to promote new industries, particularly those based on local products and ones which will generate jobs quickly. This must have been occasioned by the fact that even the select Kabul élite were having difficulty finding jobs. However, there is a long way to go before enough jobs are created to absorb the net addition to the labour force.

Another problem is administration and training, a greatly neglected area of the Plan era. Without improvement, Afghanistan will continue to need foreign experts and advice even in the most basic areas, and the civil service machine will continue to be cumbersome, not to say bumbling—which only makes the development tasks further on the road slower and more difficult.

Beyond all these are the socio-economic questions. Afghanistan is largely tribal and 2.8 million of its people are nomadic. The problem of development is made more difficult in a society like this. On top are language barriers.

The pattern of society in Afghanistan is remarkably static. Though there is some marginal movement, the tendency is for a son to follow in his father's ploughprints. Outside the cities, the chances are that he will not have any schooling and will not have any adolescence and hardly any childhood. As soon as he is big enough to walk and talk, a son can be usefully employed looking after sheep or other animals.

To make any breakthrough the authorities would have somehow to penetrate the traditional hostility to government. Officials are usually met by a "mud curtain" of the village because of the suspicion—justifiable in the past—that the officials have come to extract something from the village.

There is also the problem of the role of women. In 1959, Prime Minister Daoud passed a law saying that women no longer had to veil themselves. But the status of women has hardly changed much. When a boy is born, he is greeted with bonfires and pistol shots signifying rejoicing, that another man, a warrior, has entered the world. The father sees him as another defender of the family honour; the mother feels that her position is more secure in the family. But when a girl comes into the world, the reaction is more likely to be one of shame. Educational opportunities for girls have increased, though of the roll of 720,000 pupils in all educational institutions in 1970, only 96,000 were girls. In village schools, there were only 13,000 girls. Of an estimated 100,000 Afghan women who have finished some kind of schooling only about 5,000 are employed, mainly in the professions and the majority of these in teaching. There are hardly any women in industry—because of the high unemployment rate.

STATISTICAL SURVEY

AREA AND POPULATION

Total Area	Estimated Mid-Year Population				Density (per sq. km.)
	1970	1971	1972	1973	1973
250,000 sq. miles (647,497 sq. km.)	17,087,278	17,480,280	17,882,326	18,293,841	28.2

Note: Population estimates are derived by assuming a steady rate of growth from 1965, when the country's population was conjectured. Some authorities believe that the official estimates overstate the size of the population.

Ethnic Groups (1963)

Pashtuns or Pathans	Tadzhiks	Uzbeks	Hazarahs	Nomads
8,800,000	4,300,000	800,000	444,000	650,000

PROVINCES*
(1970)

	Area (sq. km.)	Population	Density (per sq. km.)	Capital (with population)
Uruzgan	34,000	513,100	15.1	Tareenkoot (48,200)
Badghis	24,700	329,500	13.3	Qala-i-nau (78,400)
Bamian	19,200	356,200	18.5	Bamian (46,200)
Badakhshan	42,600	354,600	8.3	Faizabad (64,700)
Baghlan	18,600	641,800	34.5	Baghlan (103,600)
Balkh	15,100	364,100	24.1	Mazar-i-Sharif (44,500)
Parwan	5,600	913,300	163.0	Charikar (93,800)
Paktia	17,600	859,100	48.8	Gardiz (40,300)
Takhar	11,800	508,800	43.1	Taluqan (68,600)
Jawzjan	24,700	442,100	17.9	Sheberghan (56,500)
Zabul	20,000	368,600	18.4	Qalat (51,200)
Samangan	16,000	213,400	13.3	Uiback (39,500)
Ghazni	31,400	1,136,400	36.1	Ghazni (44,700)
Ghour	35,100	333,000	9.5	Cheghcheran (62,700)
Fariab	22,900	447,500	19.5	Maimana (57,100)
Farah	57,800	323,500	5.6	Farah (29,600)
Kunduz	7,400	417,400	56.4	Kunduz (82,500)
Qandahar	45,100	763,100	16.9	Qandahar (130,800)
Kabul	4,500	1,330,100	295.7	Kabul (513,000)
Kapisa	5,800	354,900	78.4	Mahmoodraqi (72,700)
Kunarha	10,300	339,300	32.9	Asadabad (28,900)
Laghman	9,100	229,100	25.2	Meterlam (74,700)
Logar	4,500	318,300	70.7	Pulialam (27,500)
Nangarhar	7,600	842,100	110.8	Jelalabad (50,400)
Neemroze	50,000	125,400	2.5	Zarunj (17,400)
Wardak	10,300	427,900	41.5	Maidan (55,900)
Herat	41,500	706,100	17.0	Herat (73,700)
Helmand	59,700	325,800	5.5	Bost (29,200)
Total	652,900†	14,284,500	21.9	

* Population figures refer to settled inhabitants only, excluding kuchies (nomads), estimated at 2,801,800 for the whole country in 1970.

† Other sources give the total area as 250,000 square miles (647,497 sq. km.).

Source: Department of Statistics, Ministry of Planning, *Statistical Pocket-Book of Afghanistan.*

PRINCIPAL CITIES
(estimated population at July 1st, 1973)

Kabul (capital)	534,350	Herat	108,750
Qandahar	140,024	Tagab	106,777
Baghlan	110,874	Charikar	100,443

Source: Central Statistics Office, Prime Ministry, Kabul.

Births and Deaths: Average annual birth rate 49.8 per 1,000; death rate 26.4 per 1,000 (UN estimates for 1965–70).

EMPLOYMENT*

	1971/72	1972/73
Agriculture	3,120,000	3,200,000
Manufacturing (incl. Handicrafts)	280,000	300,000
Construction and Mining	110,000	120,000
Transport and Communications	30,000	30,000
Other Production Industries	330,000	350,000
Education and Health Services	30,000	40,000
Government Institutions	70,000	70,000
Commerce	110,000	110,000
Unknown	110,000	110,000
TOTAL LABOUR FORCE	4,190,000	4,330,000

*Excluding kuchies (nomads).

Source: Central Statistics Office, Prime Ministry, Kabul.

Total economically active population (1970): 6,000,000, including 4,890,000 in agriculture (ILO and FAO estimates).

AGRICULTURE

LAND USE, 1968
('000 hectares)

Arable Land	7,844
Permanent Crops	136
Permanent Meadows and Pastures	6,020
Forest Land	2,000
Other Areas	48,750
TOTAL	64,750

Source: FAO, *Production Yearbook 1974.*

PRINCIPAL CROPS
(twelve months ending March 20th)

	AREA ('000 hectares)			PRODUCTION ('000 metric tons)		
	1971/72	1972/73	1973/74	1971/72	1972/73	1973/74
Wheat	2,350	2,891.1	2,236	1,915	2,450	2,270
Maize	500	460	470	670	720	760
Rice (paddy)	200	210	210	350	400	420
Barley	315	320	322	355	350	360
Cotton	54	51.6	74.8	63	58	105
Sugar beet	4.4	4.6	5.3	60	63	63.6
Sugar cane	2.5	0.5	0.7	50	17.3	22.2
Vegetables	91	92	92	725	658	680
Fruits	136	136.5	136.7	650	820	840

Source: Central Statistics Office, Prime Ministry, Kabul.

1974/75 ('000 metric tons): Wheat 2,275, Maize 770, Rice 420, Barley 380.

LIVESTOCK

('000)

	1970–71	1971–72*	1972–73*	1973–74*
Cattle	3,700	3,600	3,500	3,550
Sheep†	22,900	23,000	23,644	n.a.
Goats	3,300	2,100	2,200	2,300
Horses	370*	360	385	411
Asses	1,275*	1,200	1,225	1,251
Mules	30*	25	27	28
Buffaloes	35*	32	32	33
Camels	300	300	300	300

* FAO estimate. † Including Karakul sheep, numbering 6.8 million in 1971.

Source: FAO, *Production Yearbook 1974*.

LIVESTOCK PRODUCTS

('000 metric tons—FAO estimates)

	1971	1972	1973	1974
Beef and Veal	40	41	41	42
Mutton and Lamb	} 106	90	92	93
Goats' Meat		16	16	16
Poultry Meat	n.a.	6	6	6
Edible Offals	29.8	30.1	30.6	31.1
Cows' Milk	258	276	294	310
Sheep's Milk	162	194	202	208
Goats' Milk	40	42	44	46
Buffaloes' Milk	2	2	3	3
Hen Eggs	9.0	9.9	10.3	10.8
Wool: Greasy	n.a.	22.4	23.1	24.0
Clean	12.1	12.3	12.7	13.2

Source: FAO, *Production Yearbook 1974*.

FORESTRY

('000 cubic metres)

	Roundwood Removals			Sawnwood Production		
	1971*	1972*	1973	1971*	1972*	1973*
Coniferous (soft wood)	2,340	2,404	2,465	345	305	360
Broadleaved (hard wood)	4,260	4,280	4,355	60	55	50
Total	6,600	6,684	6,820	405	360	410

* FAO estimates.

Source: FAO, *Yearbook of Forest Products 1973*.

Inland Fishing (1964–73): Total catch 1,500 metric tons each year (FAO estimate).

INDUSTRIAL AND MINERAL PRODUCTION

(Twelve months ending March 20th)

		1971/72	1972/73	1973/74	1974/75
Ginned Cotton	'000 tons	16.8	15.3	25.0	32.6
Cotton Fabrics	million metres	61.8	60.2	61.3	68.1
Woollen Fabrics	'000 metres	284.0	273.0	133.4	133.6
Rayon Fabrics	,, ,,	10,547.0	14,787.0	29,887.0	20,865.0
Cement	'000 tons	73.0	90.6	135.0	144.2
Electricity	million kWh	422.6	486.9	525.4	527.2
Wheat Flour	'000 tons	92.3	63.0	48.0	49.4
Sugar	,, ,,	8.5	7.1	7.4	8.9
Vegetable Oil	,, ,,	4.0	3.9	4.2	6.3
Coal	,, ,,	135.0	70.9	116.3	186.8
Natural Gas	million cu. metres	2,635.4	2,849.4	2,735.0	2,946.0

Sources: Department of Statistics, Kabul, *Survey of Progress 1971–72*, and Central Statistics Office, Prime Ministry, Kabul.

FINANCE

100 puls (puli) = 2 krans = 1 afghani.

Coins: 25 and 50 puls; 1, 2 and 5 afghanis.

Notes: 10, 20, 50, 100, 500 and 1,000 afghanis.

Exchange rates (April 1976): £1 sterling = 82.8 afghanis (official rate) or 104.9 afghanis (free rate):

U.S. $1 = 45.00 afghanis (official rate) or 57.00 afghanis (free rate).

1,000 afghanis = £9.53 = $17.54 (free rates).

Note: Multiple exchange rates were in operation before March 1963. Between 1956 and 1963 the official base rate was U.S. $1 = 20.00 afghanis. Since March 1963 there has been a single official rate of $1 = 45.00 afghanis. In terms of sterling, the official exchange rate was £1 = 108.00 afghanis from November 1967 to August 1971; and £1 = 117.26 afghanis from December 1971 to June 1972. Some trade takes place at the official rate; some at rates determined by discounts or premiums; and some at free market rates, which fluctuate widely.

BUDGET

(million afghanis, twelve months ending September 21st)

Revenue	1972/73	1973/74	1974/75*
Direct Taxes	573	818	1,022
Indirect Taxes	2,939	3,540	6,035
Revenue from monopolies and other enterprises	928	736	447
Natural Gas Revenue	727	690	1,175
Revenue from other property and services	708	872	1,043
Other Revenue	246	364	530
Total Revenue	6,121	7,020	10,252

Expenditure	1972/73	1973/74	1974/75*
Administration	517	540	444
Defence, Security	1,731	1,885	2,030
Social Services	1,230	1,412	1,439
Economic Services	442	448	456
Total Ministries	3,900	4,285	4,369
Foreign Debt Service	1,035	1,411	1,840
Subsidies (exchange etc.)	721	835	1,341
Total Ordinary	5,650	6,531	7,550
Development Budget	2,387	1,986	2,250

* Estimates.

Source: Statistical Information about Afghanistan 1350–1352, Department of Statistics, Office of the Prime Minister, Kabul.

GOLD RESERVES

Bank of Afghanistan

('000 U.S. dollars at March 21st)

1972	35,920
1973	39,350
1974	39,350
1975	40,940

Source: IMF, *International Financial Statistics.*

CURRENCY IN CIRCULATION

(million afghanis at March 21st)

1972	6,785
1973	8,180
1974	9,057
1975	10,038

December 21st, 1975: 11,515 million afghanis.

Source: IMF, *International Financial Statistics.*

COST OF LIVING

(Twelve months ending March 20th. Base: 1961/62=100)

	1969/70	1970/71	1971/72	1972/73	1973/74	1974/75
All Items	208	265	313	267	246	280
Cereals	219	318	401	307	233	278
Meat	215	223	204	245	311	356
Fruits	235	215	228	261	351	372
Vegetables	242	248	241	218	294	282
Other Food Articles	146	147	162	203	206	213
Non-Food Items	115	117	120	123	133	144

Source: Central Statistics Office, Prime Ministry, Kabul.

NATIONAL ACCOUNTS

(million afghanis, at 1965 market prices)

	1967	1968	1969
Agriculture, Forestry and Fishing	28,300	29,050	29,117
Mining	280	540	700
Manufacturing	5,707	5,777	6,200
Construction	860	900	990
Transportation, Communication, Utilities	1,481	1,630	1,820
Wholesale and Retail Trade*	7,122	7,350	7,650
Ownership of Dwellings	4,673	4,800	4,900
Public Administration and Defence	2,890	3,150	3,528
Other services	2,174	2,200	2,300
Net Domestic Product	53,487	55,397	57,205

* Including storage, hotels and restaurants.

Source: United Nations, *Quarterly Bulletin of Statistics for Asia and the Pacific,* March 1974.

BALANCE OF PAYMENTS

(U.S. $ million, twelve months ending March 20th)

	1971/72	1972/73
Merchandise trade:		
Exports	95.9	121.0
Imports	−125.1	−138.0
Trade balance	− 29.2	− 17.0
Adjustment between customs and exchange records	5.7	− 6.4
Adjusted trade balance	− 23.5	− 23.4
Tourism*	6.4	6.9
Project assistance (services component)	− 6.0	− 7.2
Foreign grants and loans	49.8	55.7
Foreign debt service	− 28.1	− 29.5
Net residual transactions (including errors and omissions)	12.5	− 4.6
Allocation of IMF Special Drawing Rights	4.3	—
BALANCE (net monetary movements)	+ 15.4	− 2.2

* Provisional figures.

Sources: Bank of Afghanistan; Ministries of Finance, Commerce and Planning, Kabul.

FOREIGN AID

(U.S. $ million, twelve months ending March 20th)

SOURCE	1971/72	1972/73	1973/74
Import of commodities aid	22.9	26.1	8.0
Other grants	11.3	5.9	7.3
Foreign project and non-project loans	47.2	40.1	53.2
TOTAL	81.4	72.1	68.5

Source: Central Statistics Office, Prime Ministry, Kabul.

EXTERNAL TRADE

(million afghanis, twelve months ending March 20th)

	1968–69	1969–70	1970–71	1971–72	1972–73	1973–74
Imports*	9,267	9,410	6,271	14,155	12,645	n.a.
Exports	5,348	6,180	7,160	8,427	10,046	9,556

*Including imports under commodity loans and grants from foreign countries and international organizations. In recent years the value of these imports (in million afghanis) was: 4,383.5 in 1968–69; 3,940.1 in 1969–70.

PRINCIPAL COMMODITIES

IMPORTS (U.S. $'000)	1972/73	1973/74
Commercial Imports:		
Sugar	9,597.8	13,071
Tea	9,603.7	10,143
Other food products	1,962.6	2,472
Petroleum products	6,518.3	8,387
Medicinal products	5,048.5	4,982
Chemical products	3,567.3	5,838
Rubber tyres and tubes	8,334.9	11,611
Textiles	8,930.5	13,241
Non-metallic minerals	11,744.3	18,744
Metals and metal manufactures	3,332.4	5,434
Machinery	4,330.8	6,668
Motor vehicles	4,383.1	5,262
Other transportation equipment	4,202.3	4,238
TOTAL (incl. others)	96,219.4	127,558
Non-project Loan and Grant Financed Imports:		
Wheat	19,135.3	10,292
Petroleum products	2,940.0	2,721
Chemical fertilizers	5,607.8	16,801
TOTAL (incl. others)	31,795.8	55,293 (combined)
Project Loan and Grant Financed Imports	29,083.4	
TOTAL	157,098.6	182,851

EXPORTS (million afghanis)	1972/73	1973/74
Casings	151.3	92.2
Fresh fruits	847.4	1,272.1
Dried fruits and nuts	2,522.9	2,869.8
Apricot kernels	122.5	135.4
Hides and skins	252.9	339.9
Karakul skins	1,269.8	960.5
Oil seeds	197.1	214.3
Wool and other fine animal hair	476.5	343.5
Raw cotton	910.2	429.6
Natural gums	192.9	147.8
Medicinal herbs	63.2	147.8
Natural gas	1,378.7	1,110.4
Carpets and rugs	877.2	889.2
Fur coats	405.1	117.1
TOTAL (incl. others)	10,045.6	9,556.3

PRINCIPAL TRADING PARTNERS

IMPORTS (U.S. $'000)	1972/73	1973/74
Czechoslovakia	534.9	727
Germany, Fed. Republic	14,254.4	11,165
India	11,730.9	18,885
Japan	24,187.1	31,704
Pakistan	6,348.8	5,465
U.S.S.R.	39,043.9	38,321
United Kingdom	5,654.4	7,689
U.S.A.	16,475.8	21,954
TOTAL (incl. others)	157,098.6	182,851

EXPORTS (million afghanis)	1970/71	1971/72	1972/73
Czechoslovakia	49.9	111.8	226.5
Germany, Fed. Republic	366.9	730.2	614.7
India	1,134.2	401.0	2,446.1
Lebanon	125.2	456.4	293.8
Netherlands	114.3	297.9	52.4
Pakistan	512.7	439.3	428.1
Switzerland	329.5	392.2	391.9
U.S.S.R.	2,752.6	3,256.1	2,929.5
United Kingdom	1,155.1	1,670.7	1,610.7
U.S.A.	212.6	182.1	200.0
TOTAL (incl. others)	7,160.1	8,427.2	10,045.6

Source: Various Afghan government and USAID documents.

TOURISM

International Tourist Arrivals by Country

	1970	1971	1972	1973	1974
Australia	2,072	2,703	2,614	2,974	3,349
France	6,536	8,130	7,649	6,442	8,541
Germany, Federal Republic	5,472	7,524	7,020	7,516	7,157
India	1,881	1,533	2,231	3,619	n.a.
Pakistan	51,250	51,792	49,121	28,470	26,864
United Kingdom	9,309	10,117	9,067	8,875	10,112
U.S.A.	9,572	11,965	11,630	12,769	10,369
Others	14,141	19,345	20,906	20,997	29,830
Total	100,233	113,109	110,238	91,662	96,222

Receipts from Tourism: U.S. $4.3 million in 1969; $7.8 million in 1970; $11 million in 1971.

Source: Central Statistics Office, Prime Ministry, Kabul.

TRANSPORT

CIVIL AVIATION

(twelve months ending March 20th)

	1970/71	1971/72	1972/73	1973/74
Kilometres flown ('000)	3,022	4,032	3,604	3,595
Passengers carried	69,132	74,236	81,669	80,317
Passenger-km. ('000)	200,621	202,620	203,300	198,000
Freight ton-km. ('000)	8,587	9,974	15,107	16,100
Cargo	8,349	9,676	14,744	14,900
Free luggage	138	148	163	1,000
Mail	100	150	200	200

Source: Central Statistics Office, Prime Ministry, Kabul.

ROAD TRAFFIC

Motor Vehicles in Use.

	1971/72	1972/73	1973/74
Passenger cars	15,486	18,791	20,257
Commercial vehicles	9,600	6,603	7,483

Source: Central Statistics Office, Prime Ministry, Kabul.

COMMUNICATIONS MEDIA

Telephones in use: 20,492 in 1973/74.

Radio sets in use: 450,000 in 1973.

Daily newspapers: 18 in 1970 (total circulation: 101,000 .

EDUCATION

(1973/74)

	Institutions	Pupils
Primary Schools	1,345	482,194
Village Schools	1,882	139,728
Middle Schools	517	108,795
Lycées	197	51,663
Commercial, Agricultural and Technical Schools	14	4,444
Teacher Training Colleges	10	5,086
Religious Schools	13	4,165
Universities and Higher Institutes	13	8,011

Note: Teachers in all institutions totalled 18,158 in 1970.

Source: Central Statistics Office, Prime Ministry, Kabul.

THE CONSTITUTION

After a republic was established by military coup in July 1973, a special ordinance abolished most of the 1964 Constitution. A new Constitution was drafted which was still being studied by a 20-member commission in 1976.

THE GOVERNMENT

HEAD OF STATE

Lt.-Gen. MOHAMMAD DAOUD.

CABINET

(*August* 1976)

Head of State, Prime Minister, Minister of Foreign Affairs, Minister of National Defence: Lt.-Gen. MOHAMMAD DAOUD.

First Deputy Prime Minister: Dr. MOHAMMAD HASSAN SHARQ.

Second Deputy Prime Minister, Minister of Finance: SAID ABDUL ELLAH.

Minister of Justice: Dr. ABDUL MAJID.

Minister of the Interior: ABDUL QADEER.

Minister of Education: ABDUL QAYEUM.

Minister of Frontier Affairs: FAIZ MOHAMMAD.

Minister of Mines and Industries: ABDUL TAWAB ASSEFI.

Minister of Communications: ABDUL KARIM ATTAYEE.

Minister of Public Health: Dr. ABDULLAH OMAR.

Minister of Culture and Information: Dr. ABDUR RAHIM NEVIN.

Minister of Agriculture: AZIZULLAH WASEFI.

Minister of Planning: ALI AHMED KHURAM.

Minister of Commerce: MOHAMMAD KHAN JALALAR.

Minister of Public Works: GHAUSUDDIN FAYEQ.

PARLIAMENT

Prior to the *coup* of July 17th, 1973, the Shura (Parliament) consisted of the Meshrano Jirgah (House of Elders) and the Wolesi Jirgah (House of the People). The Shura was dissolved on July 28th, 1973.

POLITICAL PARTIES

No political parties had been officially authorized before the *coup* of July 17th, 1973.

DIPLOMATIC REPRESENTATION

EMBASSIES ACCREDITED TO AFGHANISTAN

(Kabul unless otherwise stated)

(E) Embassy.

Algeria: New Delhi, India.

Argentina: Teheran, Iran (E).

Australia: Islamabad, Pakistan (E).

Austria: Zarghouna Wat (E); *Chargé d'affaires a.i.:* Dr. R. F. KREUTEL.

Bahrain: Teheran, Iran.

Bangladesh: Wazir Akbar Khan Mena (E); *Chargé d'Affaires:* NOORUDDIN AHMED.

Belgium: Teheran, Iran (E).

Brazil: Teheran, Iran (E).

Bulgaria: Wazir Akbar Khan Mena (E); *Ambassador:* STOYAN RADOSLAVOV.

Burma: New Delhi, India (E).

Canada: Islamabad, Pakistan (E).

Chile: Washington, D.C., U.S.A.

China, People's Republic: Shah Mahmoud Ghazi Wat (E); *Ambassador:* KAN YEH-TAO.

Czechoslovakia: Taimani Wat, Kale Fatullah (E); *Ambassador:* KARMELITA ZDENEK.

Denmark: Teheran, Iran (E).

Egypt: Wazir Akbar Khan Mena (E); *Ambassador:* AHMAD MUHAMMAD ABU ZAID.

Finland: Moscow, U.S.S.R. (E).

France: Nedjat Wat (E); *Ambassador:* GEORGE PERRUCHE.

German Democratic Republic: Teheran, Iran (E).

Germany, Federal Republic: Wazir Akbar Khan Mena (E); *Ambassador:* Dr. J. HOFFMAN.

Ghana: New Delhi, India (E).

Greece: Teheran, Iran (E).

Hungary: Teheran, Iran (E).

India: Malalai Wat (E): *Ambassador:* RAM PRATRAP SINGH.

Indonesia: Wazir Akbar Khan Mena (E); *Ambassador:* ABDUL HABIR.

Iran: Malekyar Wat (E); *Ambassador:* HUSSEIN DAOUDI.

Iraq: Malalai Wat, Shar-e-Nau (E); *Ambassador:* N. A. KADER HADISSI.

Italy: Khwaja Abdullah Ansari Wat (E); *Ambassador:* VALERIO BRIGANTI COLONNA ANGELINI.

Japan: Wazir Akbar Khan Mena (E); *Ambassador:* JUNJI YAMADA.

Jordan: Teheran, Iran (E).

Korea, Democratic People's Republic: Wazir Akbar Khan Mena (E); *Chargé d'Affaires:* KIM BONG JE.

Korea, Republic: Wazir Akbar Khan Mena; *Ambassador:* MEUNG JUN CHOI.

Kuwait: Teheran, Iran (E).

Lebanon: Teheran, Iran (E).

Libya: Wazir Akbar Khan Mena; *Ambassador:* AL HADI OMAR ELHERIK.

Malaysia: Teheran, Iran (E).

Mexico: New Delhi, India (E).

Mongolia: Moscow, U.S.S.R. (E).

Morocco: Teheran, Iran (E).

Nepal: New Delhi, India (E).

Netherlands: Teheran, Iran (E).

Norway: Teheran, Iran (E).

Pakistan: Zarghouna Wat (E); *Ambassador:* ALI ARSHED.

Philippines: New Delhi, India (E).

Poland: Guzargah Wat (E); *Ambassador:* BOGUSLAW PASZEK.

Qatar: Teheran, Iran (E).

Romania: Teheran, Iran (E).

Saudi Arabia: Wazir Akbar Khan Mena (E); *Ambassador:* HOSSEIN DAOUD FATTANI.

Senegal: Teheran, Iran (E).

Spain: Teheran, Iran (E).

Sri Lanka: New Delhi, India (E).

Sudan: New Delhi, India (E).

Sweden: Teheran, Iran (E).

Switzerland: Teheran, Iran (E).

Syria: New Delhi, India (E).

Thailand: New Delhi, India (E).

Turkey: Shah Mahmoud Ghazi Wat (E); *Ambassador:* (vacant).

U.S.S.R.: Dar-ul-Aman Wat (E); *Ambassador:* M. POZANOV.

United Kingdom: Karte Parwan (E); *Ambassador:* K. R. CROOK.

U.S.A.: Khwaja Abdullah Ansari Wat (E); *Ambassador:* T. ELLIOT.

Viet-Nam, Democratic Republic: Moscow, U.S.S.R. (E).

Yugoslavia: Wazir Akbar Khan Mena (E); *Ambassador:* BORISLAV SAMONIKOV.

Afghanistan also has diplomatic relations with Cuba, Tunisia and the United Arab Emirates.

JUDICIAL SYSTEM

Prior to the *coup* of July 17th, 1973, the judiciary of Afghanistan consisted of the Supreme Court, the highest judicial authority, three High Courts, a Court of Appeal, 28 Provincial Courts, 216 Primary Courts and a number of Special Courts. On July 28th, 1973, the powers of the Supreme Court, which include administrative powers within the framework of the judicial organization, were transferred to a council set up within the Ministry of Justice.

RELIGION

The official religion of Afghanistan is Islam. The great majority are Muslims of the Sunni (Hanafi) sect, and the remainder belong to the Shi'a sect. A minority of Hindus and Sikhs are living in different parts of the country.

THE PRESS

PRINCIPAL DAILIES

Anis (*Friendship*): Kabul; f. 1927; evening; Independent; news and literary articles: Persian and Pashtu; circ. 25,000; Editor-in-Chief IBRAHIM ABBASSI.

Badakshan: Faizabad; f. 1945; Persian and Pashtu.

Bedar: Mazar-i-Sharif; f. 1920; Persian and Pashtu; circ. 1,500.

Daiwan: Sheberghan.

Ettifaqi-Islam: Herat; f. 1920; Persian and Pashtu; circ. 1,500.

Ettehadi-Baghlan: Baghlan; f. 1921; Persian and Pashtu.

Helmand: Bost; f. 1953; twice weekly; Pashtu.

Hewad: Kabul; f. 1949; Pashtu; Editor MIR SAID BARIMAN; circ. 5,000.

Jamhouryat (*Republic*): Kabul; f. 1973; official organ; Dari and Pashtu; Editor-in-Chief Dr. ASIF SOHAIL; circ. *c.* 50,000.

Kabul Times: Kabul; f. 1962; English; circ. 5,000; Editor N. M. RAHIMI.

Nangarhar: Jalabad; f. 1918; Persian and Pashtu; circ. 1,500.

Seistan: Farah; f. 1947; twice weekly.

Tulu-i-Afghan: Kandahar; f. 1924; Pashtu; circ. 1,500.

Wolanga: Gardiz; f. 1941; Pashtu; circ. 1,000.

PERIODICALS

Adab: Kabul; f. 1953; organ of the Faculty of Literature Univ. of Kabul.

Afghan Journal of Public Health: Institute of Public Health, Ansari Wat, Kabul; 2 per month; Editor A. SATAR AHMADI, M.D.

Afghan Tebbi Mojalla: Faculty of Medicine, Kabul University; monthly.

Afghanistan: Kabul; 1946; quarterly; English and French; historical and cultural; Historical Society of Afghanistan, Kabul.

Akhbare Erfani: Ministry of Education, Kabul; f. 1952; fortnightly.

Aryana: Kabul; f. 1943; quarterly (Pashtu and Dari); cultural and historical; produced by the Historical Society of Afghanistan.

Badany Rauzana: Department of Physical Education, Kabul University; quarterly.

Eqtesad: Afghan Chamber of Commerce and Industry, Darul Aman Watt, Kabul; monthly; Editor PAINDA MOHAMMED MOHEBZADA.

Hawa: Afghan Air Authority, Kabul; f. 1957.

Irfan: Ministry of Education, Kabul; f. 1923; monthly; Persian.

Jamhouryat: Kabul; every two months; Editor MOHAMMED ASSEF SOHIL.

Kabul: Pashtu Tolana, Kabul; f. 1931; 2 per month; Pashtu; literature, history, social sciences; Editor MOHAMMED MOHEM PATWAL.

Kabul Pohantoon: Kabul University; monthly.

Karhana: Kabul; f. 1955; monthly; produced by the Ministry of Agriculture; circ. 2,500; Editor M. Y. AINA.

Kocheniano Zhaqh: Ministry of Education, Kabul; f. 1957; monthly.

Mairmun: Kabul; f. 1955; Persian and Pashtu; produced by the Women's Welfare Association.

Pamir: Kabul; f. 1951; organ of the Municipality; fortnightly.

Pashtun Zhaqh: Ansari Wat, Kabul; f. 1940; programmes of broadcasts; issued by Kabul Radio; 2 per month.

Sera Miasht: Red Crescent Society, Kabul; f. 1958.

Talim wa Tarbia: Kabul; f. 1954; monthly; published by Institute of Education.

Urdu: Kabul; f. 1922; monthly; military journal; issued by the Ministry of National Defence.

Zhwandoon: Kabul; Persian; illustrated; Editor NAJEEBULLAH RAHEQ; circ. 10,000.

Zeru: Pashtu Tolana, Kabul; f. 1949; weekly.

NEWS AGENCIES

Bakhtar News Agency: Kabul; f. 1939; Pres. MOHAMMED KAZIM AHANG.

FOREIGN BUREAUX

The following Foreign Agencies are represented in Kabul: Agence France-Presse (AFP), Deutsche Presse-Agentur (DPA), and Tass.

PRESS ASSOCIATION

Journalists' Association: c/o Department of Press and Information, Sanaii Wat, Kabul.

PUBLISHERS

Afghan Book: P.O.B. 206, Kabul; f. 1969 by Kabir A. Ahang; books on various subjects, translations of foreign works on Afghanistan, books in English on Afghanistan and Dari language textbooks for foreigners; Man. Dir. JAMILA AHANG.

Afghanistan Publicity Department: c/o Kabul Times, Kabul; publicity materials; answers enquiries about Afghanistan.

Book Publishing Institute: Kabul; f. 1966 by co-operation of the Government Press, Bakhtar News Agency and leading newspapers.

Book Publishing Institute: Herat; f. 1970 by co-operation of Government Press and citizens of Herat; books on literature, history and religion.

Book Publishing Institute: Qandahar; f. 1970 by citizens of Qandahar, supervised by Government Press; mainly books in Pashtu language.

Educational Publications: Ministry of Education, Kabul; text-books for primary and secondary schools in the Pashtu and Dari languages; also two monthly magazines, one in Pashtu and the other in Dari.

Government Press: Kabul; f. 1870 under supervision of the Ministry of Information and Culture; four daily newspapers in Kabul, one in English; weekly, fortnightly and monthly magazines, one of them in English; books on Afghan history and literature, as well as textbooks for the Ministry of Education; thirteen daily newspapers in thirteen provincial centres and one journal and also magazines in three provincial centres.

Historical Society of Afghanistan: Kabul; f. 1931; mainly historical and cultural works and two quarterly magazines: *Afghanistan* (English and French), *Aryana* (Dari and Pashtu); Head Dr. M. YAKUB WAHIDI.

Institute of Geography: Faculty of Letters, Kabul University; geographical and related works.

Kabul University Press: Kabul; publishes textbooks for Kabul and Nangarhar Universities, College Journals, etc.

Pashto Tolana: Kabul; f. 1937 by the Department of Press and Information; research works on Pashtu language.

RADIO

Radio Afghanistan: P.O.B. 544, Kabul; Acting Pres. and Head of Broadcasting S. Y. WASEEQ; the Afghan Broadcasting station is under the supervision of the Ministry of Information; Home service in Dari, Pashtu and Balochi; Foreign service in Urdu, Arabic, English, Russian, German, Dari and Pashtu.

Number of radio receivers: 906,037 in 1976.

A television service is planned for the end of 1977.

FINANCE

(cap.=capital; p.u.=paid up; res.=reserves; m.=million; Afs.=Afghanis.)

BANKING

In June 1975 all banks were nationalized.

CENTRAL BANK

Da Afghanistan Bank: Ibne Sina Wat, Kabul; f. 1939; the central bank; main functions: banknote issue, foreign exchange control and operations, credit extensions to banks and leading enterprises and companies, government and private depository, government fiscal agency; 63 local brs.; cap. Afs. 480m.; dep. 8,915m. (August 1974); Gov. MOHAMMED HAKIM (acting).

Overseas Corporations:

The Trading Company of Afghanistan Inc.: 122–126 West 30th St., New York, N.Y. 10001, U.S.A.

The Trading Company of Afghanistan Ltd.: Riverbank House, 67 Upper Thames St., London, EC4V 3AH, England.

Agricultural Development Bank of Afghanistan; P.O.B. 414, Kabul; f. 1955; makes available credits for farmers, co-operatives and agro-business; aid provided by IBRD and UNDP; auth. share cap. Afs. 1 billion; Pres. A. AFZAL; Gen. Man. G. GRAESEL.

Banke Millie Afghan (*Afghan National Bank*): Head Office: Jada Ibn Sina, Kabul; f. 1932; brs. throughout Afghanistan and in Pakistan; London Office: (as Afghan National Bank Ltd.) 22 Finsbury Square, E.C.2; offices in New York and Hamburg; cap. Afs. 500m.; dep. 1,284m. (March 1975); Pres. M. JAFAR MOKHTARZADA.

Export Promotion Bank of Afghanistan: Pres. Prof. Dr. ZABIOULLAH ELTEZAM.

Industrial Development Bank of Afghanistan: P.O.B. 14, Kabul; f. 1973; provides financing for industrial development; cap. and dep. Afs. 500m.; Pres. Dr. NOUR ALI; Gen. Man. CLAUDE BLANCHI.

There are no foreign banks operating in Afghanistan.

Mortgage and Construction Bank: 2 Jade' Maiwand, Kabul; f. 1955 to provide short and long term building loans; cap. Afs. 60m.; Pres. ESMATOLLAH ENAYAT SERAJ.

Pashtany Tejaraty Bank (*Afghan Commercial Bank*): Mohammad Jan Khan Wat, Kabul; f. 1954 to provide long- and short-term credits, forwarding facilities, opening letters of credit, purchase and sale of foreign exchange, transfer of capital, issuing travellers' cheques; cap. p.u. Afs. 250m.; total resources Afs. 3,244m. (March 1975); Pres. GUL AHMAD NOOR; 18 brs. in Afghanistan and abroad.

There are no foreign banks in Afghanistan.

INSURANCE

Afghan Insurance Co.: P.O.B. 329, 26 Mohd. Jan Khan Wat, Kabul; f. March 1964; marine, aviation, fire, motor and accident insurance; cap. p.u. Afs. 15m.; Pres. ABDUL RASHID; Gen. Man. N. H. SIMONDS.

One foreign insurance company operates in the country: *Ingosstrakh* (Soviet National Company).

There is one national insurance company:

TRADE AND INDUSTRY

CHAMBER OF COMMERCE

Afghan Chamber of Commerce and Industry: Darulaman Wat, Kabul; Pres. Dr. MOHAMMAD AKBAR OMER.

TRADING CORPORATIONS

Qandahar Woollen Factory: Qandahar; formed for the export of wool.

Pashtoon Food Processors Inc.: P.O.B. 3025, Kabul; f. 1946; processes and exports Red Afghan raisins; 64 mems.; Pres. A. MOOSA.

Textile Company: P.O.B. 267, Kabul; manufactures rayon, nylon, silk and other synthetic fibres.

Herat Pistachio Company: Herat; formed for the export of pistachio nuts.

Balkh Union: export and import agency handling exports of wool, hides and karakul.

Wool Company: deals with wool exports.

Afghan Carpet Exporters Guild: Charrahi, Anssari Shah-i-naw, Kabul; f. 1966; exports traditional hand-knotted carpets and rugs; Pres. K. M. NASSERI; Vice-Pres. HAJI-MOHD TAHER NADERI.

Office S. M. Azam Azimi: P.O.B. 498, Kabul; f. 1972; carries out import-export transactions.

TRADE UNIONS

There are no trade unions in Afghanistan.

TRANSPORT

RAILWAYS

There are plans to build a railway system by 1983.

ROADS

Ministry of Communication and Ministry of Public Works: Kabul; in 1971 there were about 6,000 km. of all-weather tarmac and gravel roads. All-weather highways now link Kabul with Qandahar and Herat in the south and west, Jelalabad in the east and Mazar-i-Sharif and the Oxus in the north. Road development continues with the aid of Soviet and American loans.

Afghan Motor Service and Parts Co.: Zendabanon Workshops, P.O.B. 86, Kabul; passenger services in Kabul; long-distance freight and passenger services from Kabul to most parts of the country; trucking services in all towns; Pres. HAFIZULLAH RAHIMI; Vice-Pres. KHAWJA MOENODDIN.

A trolley-bus network is being built in Kabul.

INLAND WATERWAYS

River ports on the Oxus are linked by road to Kabul.

CIVIL AVIATION

Civil Aviation Authority: Ansari Wat, Kabul; Pres. SULTAN MAHMOUD GHAZI.

There are modern international terminals at Kabul and Qandahar.

NATIONAL AIRLINE

Ariana Afghan Airlines Co. Ltd.: P.O.B. 76, Ansari Wat, Kabul; f. 1955; international services to Amritsar, Beirut, Damascus, Frankfurt, Istanbul, London, New Delhi, Paris, Rome, Tashkent, and Teheran; Pres. AMINULLAH NAJIB; 1 Boeing 720B, 2 727-100C.

The following airlines also operate service to Afghanistan: Aeroflot, IAC, Iran Air, TMA (cargo).

Bakhtar Afghan Airlines: Ansari Wat, P.O.B. 3058, Kabul; f. 1968; internal services between Kabul and 17 regional locations; Pres. A. A. ETEMADI; Dir. of Operations Capt. R. NAWROZ.

TOURISM

Afghan Tourist Organization: Salang Wat, Kabul; f. 1958; Pres. M. O. SERADJ; Vice-Pres. R. A. SULTANI. Publishes monthly Afghan Travel News (in English) and a quarterly Statistical bulletin.

Afghan Tour: Kabul; official travel agency; Gen. Man. R. A. SULTANI.

ATOMIC ENERGY

Atomic Energy Commission: Faculty of Science, Kabul University, Kabul; Pres. of Commission and Dean of Faculty Dr. F. M. RAOUFY.

DEFENCE

Armed Forces: (1976) Total strength 88,000; army 80,000; air force 8,000; reserves total 162,000 and para-military forces comprise 25,000 gendarmes; military service lasting two years is compulsory for every able-bodied man.

Equipment: The army's equipment and training are very largely provided by the Soviet Union. The air force has 160 Russian-built combat aircraft.

Defence Expenditure: Estimated defence expenditure in 1973–74 was 2,022 million afghanis (U.S. $45 million).

EDUCATION

The traditional system of education in Afghanistan was religious instruction in Madrasas, or Mosque schools. These centres are still active, but a modern educational system has been built up over the past sixty-five years.

Since 1933 primary, middle and secondary schools have been opened all over the country. The development of education since 1961 has been rapid especially at the primary level where enrolment has risen from 231,000 to 621,922 by 1973. In 1973 there were 3,227 primary and village schools. By 1973 the number of middle schools had risen to 517, and the number of lycées had risen to 197.

In 1974 a programme of educational reform was introduced to encourage the expansion of technical education and practical training schemes (especially in agriculture) designed to meet the country's development needs.

Teacher training began on an organized scale in the early 1950s. The University of Kabul was founded in 1932 when the Faculty of Medicine was established. It now has 11 Faculties. In 1972 a second university was founded in Jelalabad, Nangarhar province; again the nucleus was provided by a Medical Faculty.

Progress is also being made in women's education, and girls' schools are now found in all major cities.

UNIVERSITIES

Kabul University: Kabul; 1,027 teachers, 8,994 students.

University of Nangarhar: Jelalabad; 61 teachers, 410 students.

BIBLIOGRAPHY

GENERAL

AFGHAN TRANSPORT & TRAVEL SERVICE. Afghanistan—Ancient Land with Modern Ways (London, 1961).

CAROE, OLAF. The Pathans.

GRASSMUCK, GEORGE, and ADAMEC, LUDWIG (editors). Afghanistan: Some new approaches (Center for Near Eastern and North African Studies, University of Michigan, 1969).

GREGORIAN, VARTAN. The Emergence of Modern Afghanistan (Stanford University Press, Stanford, 1969).

GRIFFITHS, JOHN C. Afghanistan (Pall Mall Press, London, 1967).

KESSEL, FLINKER and KLIMBURG. Afghanistan (photographs, 1959).

KING, PETER. Afghanistan, Cockpit in Asia (Bles, London, 1966, Taplinger, N.Y., 1967).

KLIMBURG, M. Afghanistan (Austrian UNESCO Commission, Vienna, 1966).

SHALISI, PRITA K. Here and There in Afghanistan.

WATKINS, MARY B. Afghanistan, an Outline (New York, 1962).

Afghanistan, Land in Transition (Van Nostrand, Princeton, N.J., 1963).

WILBER, DONALD N. Afghanistan (New Haven, Conn., 1956).

Annotated Bibliography of Afghanistan (New Haven, Conn., 1962).

TOPOGRAPHY AND TRAVELS

BURNES, Sir ALEXANDER. Cabool (John Murray, London, 1842).

BYRON, ROBERT. Road to Oxiana.

ELPHINSTONE, M. An Account of the Kingdom of Caubul and its Dependencies in Persia, Tartary and India (John Murray, London, 1815).

FERRIER, J. P. Caravan Journeys.

HAHN, H. Die Stadt Kabul und ihr Umland (2 vols., Bonn, 1964–65).

HAMILTON, ANGUS. Afghanistan (Heinemann, London, 1906).

HUMLUM, J. La Géographie de l'Afghanistan (Gyldendal, Copenhagen, 1959).

MASSON, CHARLES. Narrative of various journeys in Baluchistan, Afghanistan and the Punjab (Bentley, London, 1842).

MOHUN LAL. Journal.

WOLFE, N. H. Herat (Afghan Tourist Organization, Kabul, 1966).

WOOD, JOHN. A Personal Narrative of a Journey to the Source of the River Oxus by the Route of Indus, Kabul and Badakshan (John Murray, London, 1841).

HISTORY

ADAMEC, LUDWIG W. Afghanistan 1900–1923 (University of California, Berkeley, 1967).

Afghanistan's Foreign Affairs to the Mid-Twentieth Century (University of Arizona Press, Tucson, 1974).

BOSWORTH, C. E. The Ghaznavids (Edinburgh University Press, 1963).

CAMBRIDGE HISTORY OF INDIA, Vols. I, III, IV, V, VI.

DOLLOT, RENÉ. Afghanistan (Payot, Paris, 1937).

DUPREE, LOUIS, and LINNET, ALBERT (Editors). Afghanistan in the 1970s (Praeger, New York, 1974 and Pall Mall Press, London).

FLETCHER, ARNOLD. Afghanistan, Highway of Conquest (Cornell and Oxford University Presses, 1965).

FRASER-TYTLER, Sir W. KERR. Afghanistan (Oxford University Press, 1950, 3rd edn., 1967).

GOVERNMENT OF INDIA. The Third Afghan War, 1919 (Calcutta, 1926).

GREGORIAN, VARTAN. The Emergence of Modern Afghanistan—Politics of Reform and Modernization 1880–1946 (Stanford University Press, 1970).

GROUSSET. L'Empire des Steppes.

KHAN, M. M. S. M., Editor. The Life of Abdur Rahman, Amir of Afghanistan (John Murray, London, 1900).

KOHZAD, A. A. Men and Events (Government Printing House, Kabul).

MACRORY, PATRICK. Signal Catastrophe (Hodder & Stoughton, London, 1966).

MASSON, V. M., and ROMODIN, V. A. Istoriya Afghanistana (Akad. Nauk, Moscow, 1964–65).

MOHUN LAL. Life of the Amir Dost Mohammed Khan of Kabul (Longmans, London, 1846).

NORRIS, J. A. The First Afghan War, 1838–42 (Cambridge University Press, 1967).

SYKES, Sir PERCY. A History of Afghanistan (Macmillan, London, 1940).

TATE, G. P. The Kingdom of Afghanistan (London, 1911).

ECONOMY

ASIAN CONFERENCE ON INDUSTRIALIZATION. Industrial Development: Asia and the Far East (Report of Manila Conference, 1965, published by ECAFE, Bangkok).

MALEKYAR, ABDUL WAHED. Die Verkehrsentwicklung in Afghanistan (Cologne, 1966).

RHEIN, E. and GHAUSSY, A. GHANIE. Die wirtschaftliche Entwicklung Afghanistans, 1880-1965 (C. W. Leske Verlag, Hamburg 1966).

Bangladesh

PHYSICAL AND SOCIAL GEOGRAPHY

B. H. Farmer

Bangladesh covers 55,598 square miles (143,998 square kilometres). It straddles the Tropic of Cancer, extending between 21° 5′ and 26° 40′ North latitude, and between 88° 5′ and 92° 50′ East longitude. It is almost surrounded by India, except for a short southeastern frontier with Burma and a southern, deltaic coast fronting the Bay of Bengal.

From the passing of the British Empire in India on August 15th, 1947, until the end of the Indo-Pakistan war of December 1971, what was to become Bangladesh was the eastern wing of Pakistan: that is, East Pakistan or East Bengal. At the conclusion of the war, Bangladesh became an independent country.

PHYSICAL FEATURES

Almost all of Bangladesh is a plain, largely made up of the still-growing, annually-flooded Ganges-Brahmaputra delta, together with a tongue of similar wet plain running up the Surma River between the Assam Plateau and the Lushai Hills (both in India; though Bangladesh includes a very small portion of lower foothills country which, on the Assam boundary, includes some tea plantations). As in West Bengal (India), belts of older and less fertile alluvium lend some little diversity to the plains: notably in the regions known as Barind and the Madhupur Jungle Tract. To the east of the delta lie the Chittagong Hill Tracts, an area of steep, roughly parallel ranges largely covered with thick jungle, much of it bamboo.

For the most part, however, Bangladesh is deltaic, and its rural people have evolved a remarkable semi-aquatic life style adapted to deep flooding in the monsoon: for instance, by constructing earthen plinths fifteen or more feet high to raise their houses above flood-level (or so they hope) and by sowing varieties of rice which will grow in deep water.

CLIMATE

The climate of Bangladesh, like that of India, is dominated by the seasonally-reversing monsoons. There is, however, no real cool season like that of northern India. In the capital, Dacca, for example, the average January temperature is 67°F, and the average July temperature 84°F. The "summer", if it can be called such, is remarkably equable: the average monthly temperature is 84°F. from May right through to September. The "winter" is dry, and crops (in the absence of irrigation or of water-holding depressions, where winter rice can be grown) have to depend on moisture remaining in the soil from the monsoon. There are pre-monsoon rains in April and May, but it is the south-west monsoon that brings heavy rain in earnest: 75 per cent of Dacca's annual average total of 74 inches arrives between June and September. Bangladesh has, in fact, a typical humid tropical monsoon climate. But it is a climate subject to violence from time to time, for example when a tropical cyclone sweeps in, charged with energy and with water vapour and accompanied by high winds, and devastates low-lying areas in the coastal parts of the delta. Such "extreme natural events" tend to bring high seas and flooding with salt water, so that there is damage to the soil as well as terrible loss of life and of crops.

SOILS

Much of Bangladesh has relatively good, young alluvial soils, many of them benefiting from renewal by flooding. There is, however, more local variation than might at first sight be expected: for example, areas of sandy soils on the one hand, and of swamp soils on the other, to say nothing of Barind and the Madhupur Jungle Tract. The Chittagong Hills have, as might be expected, poor skeletal soils.

MINERALS AND POWER

Bangladesh is not rich in mineral resources. There is some lignite and peat near Sylhet, Mymensingh and Faridpur, but they are water-logged, difficult to dry and of inferior quality. Coal has been found at workable depth in the Bogra District. Perhaps the most significant find, however, is that of natural gas mainly in the Sylhet District: already this supplies fertilizer plants and a cement factory. There is a sizeable hydro-electric plant in the Chittagong Hill Tracts.

POPULATION

Bangladesh had an estimated population of 76.8 million in July 1975, an average density of about 1,380 per square mile. Apart from territories less than 500 square miles in area, Bangladesh is the most densely populated country in the world, despite its overwhelmingly rural and agricultural nature.

Even then average densities are misleading: the density of population is lower than the average in such areas as Barind and the Madhupur Jungle Tract, and higher than the very high average in other areas, notably those along the lower Padma and Meghna Rivers.

Bangladesh has one rapidly-growing conurbation, that around the capital, Dacca, with a population of 1.3 million, including suburbs, in 1974.

ETHNIC GROUPS

Most of the inhabitants of Bangladesh are short, dark people with subdued Mongolian features; but there are rather different tribal groups in the Chittagong Hill Tracts. Bengali is the principal language (as it is in Indian West Bengal); some tribal peoples retain their own languages.

HISTORY

Peter Robb

The existence of Bangladesh is the result of a number of historical accidents. There has not been, from time immemorial, a Bangla nation. The concept of the nation, in its modern exclusive sense, is new to the sub-continent. Yet Bangladesh does have roots in the past: in the distinctions between the Bengali region and the rest of South Asia, and in the divisions between Bengali Muslims and Hindus, between East and West Bengal. The distinct character of Bengal has truly ancient origins; the separate identity of the Muslims is a more recent phenomenon.

During the period of British rule about two-thirds of the population of the eastern divisions (Rajshahi, Dacca and Chittagong) were Muslim. The number of Muslims in Bengal was probably due to the activities of Muslim saints in the thirteenth century, before the thorough establishment there of Brahminical Hinduism; and this helped determine the character of Islam in this region. The Mughal administration and even more that of the Nawab of Bengal after the Mughal decline in the eighteenth century, was carried on except at the highest levels largely by Hindu intermediaries. Although a Muslim elite was drawn to Bengal from North India and further afield, and though it was estimated in 1901 that as many as one-sixth of Bengali Muslims may have had foreign blood, the bulk of the Muslim population remained what it had been in the thirteenth century: poor, almost wholly rural, strongly influenced by Hindu custom. The use of *sunni* law was notable in Bengal under British rule, and knowledge of Persian and the influence of Islam had spread even to the Hindu elite; but the poor agriculturists, though notionally Muslim, were as distant from Islamic culture as from their rulers, and continued in some cases even the worship of local Hindu gods.

BRITISH RULE

The establishment of British rule quickened the decline of the Muslim ruling classes. Muslim *faujdars* (district officials) were replaced by Europeans, and, though the progressive centralization of revenue administration deprived mainly Hindu officials, it also diverted income from Muslims. Only in the judicial service did Muslims continue to thrive, until the 1830s and the abolition of the use of Persian; elsewhere, with the frank Europeanization adopted after the 1790s, Muslims found only minor administrative careers open to them. The Muslim rulers had not engaged in trade, and thus were denied the benefits which some Indians were able to find under the British; nor had they been much involved as revenue farmers or *zamindars*, and thus did not become English-style landlords with the permanent settlement of the revenue in 1793.

The bulk of the Muslim population was not immediately affected by the coming of the British. But gradually, during the early nineteenth century, their position declined. The tendency of the permanent settlement and of the initially high level of taxation was to depress the status of the peasantry until increasing numbers became landless labourers. The competition of British manufactures and the demand for raw materials transformed the economy into one subservient to that of Britain; the Muslim weavers of Dacca were particularly badly affected. Dacca's population is estimated to have dropped dramatically in thirty years from 1801, probably by more than half. In the later nineteenth century, with the growth of Calcutta and of road and rail networks which ignored the old centres up-river, and under an administration that was overstretched and ill-informed about local conditions, East Bengal became increasingly a backwater.

There was some reaction to these changes. The Fara'idi movement led by Hajji Shariat-Allah (1781–1840) and his son, Didu Miyan, embodied both religious and economic responses: it preached the strict adherence to Quranic duties and abandonment of Hindu practices, but also opposition to Hindu landlords. Thus among possible reactions to the West, for Muslims as for Hindus, were attempts to purify and standardize religion. Though the Fara'idi movement went underground and dwindled in importance, the impulse it represented was taken up elsewhere during the nineteenth century. By the end of the nineteenth century, Muslims were under-represented in the administration and hardly represented at all in the boards and committees of local self-government. (In 1886 Muslims held less than 13 per cent of executive and just over 3 per cent of judicial posts, with over 31 per cent of the population.) There was a competitive system of appointment; thus Muslim failure was blamed on their reluctance to take up Western education: certainly in 1871/72 they made up only a little more than 14 per cent of school and college-goers in Bengal. The proportion was to increase (23 per cent in 1881/82) and, thanks largely to the formation of Dacca University, numbers were to go on rising even after the proportion began to drop again in the 1920s; but it is clear that there were fewer among Bengali Muslims ready to groom themselves as minor officials for the British than there were among Hindus, where some had traditional callings as writers and administrators.

In the early twentieth century, then, the mass of the Muslim population had interests which could be seen as distinct from those of the Hindus; and, though the Western-educated Muslim elite had more in common with their Hindu colleagues than with their co-religionists, it was easy for them to feel at a disadvantage. The next step was for them to begin to consider the Muslim masses as their community. The British helped by treating Muslims as a separate political interest at least from the late nineteenth century; the Muslim elite could use the size of the

Muslim population as an argument for a greater share of offices and privileges.

The Muslim elite began obviously to diverge from the Hindu early in the twentieth century. The partition of Bengal (allegedly for administrative reasons) in 1905 created a controversy in which some Muslims were to be found on both sides; but the anti-partition agitation proved rather aggressively Hindu, and, even more important, the experience between 1905 and 1911 (when the partition was annulled) revealed to East Bengalis the advantages of a separate administration centred on Dacca. The concession of separate electorates for Muslims in 1909, 1919 and 1935 encouraged the development of separate political organizations; while a long series of communal riots hardened attitudes between the rank and file of the communities. The more conscious each became of the unique features of his religion the more likely friction became; and the more local administration passed into Indian hands, the more this friction could be expressed in political terms by such measures as, for example, regulations by municipal authorities for or against cow-killing. During this century, moreover, changes in the constitution, including after 1920 limited but in relative terms enormous expansions of the elective principle, sent the Muslim élite politicians in search of a constituency; thus they began to bridge the gap between them and the depressed mass of their co-religionists, reaching at least to the higher sections of the Muslim peasantry, often in the context of an appeal to their religion.

Even so, for a long time, the political élites of both communities continued to meet at several points, and in Bengal it seemed that regional feeling was on the whole more potent than communal passions. Bengal Muslims as well as Hindus reacted to the fact that Bengal, which in the nineteenth century, for the first time, had been central to a great empire, had become once more peripheral with the development of the initially Bombay-dominated Indian National Congress and the moving of the imperial capital from Calcutta to Delhi.

The strategies of those Muslims who feared Hindu dominance shifted during the twentieth century from reliance on the British to reliance on Islamic power outside India, to reliance on the strength of the Muslim-majority provinces inside India. But the fears were naturally most powerful in minority provinces. In the late 1930s the growth area of the Muslim League was the United Provinces. Thus in the 1937 elections in Bengal Fazlul Huq's Krishak Proja Samiti was overwhelmingly successful and the Muslim League won only 39 of 119 Muslim seats. Fazlul Huq defied the central organization under Jinnah, and the local League as well, until he was eventually forced to resign in 1943 and a League ministry was formed under Khwaja Nazim al-din. The experience of power in the 1940s repeated for many middle-class Muslims the lesson learnt by an earlier generation after 1905, and persuaded them of the possible advantages of Pakistan. Fazlul Huq did not campaign against this in 1945–46. The conversion to Pakistan in Bengal was, therefore, sudden and late. Even then it is probably true that Bengali Muslims endorsed the separation of the whole of Bengal from India and not the "moth-eaten" Pakistan they received in 1947.

PARTITION OF PAKISTAN FROM INDIA

East Pakistan, with an area of 55,000 square miles and a population of about 40 million, was one of five provinces of Pakistan, the four western ones together numbering about 35 million. The remaining Hindu minority of about 13 per cent was mainly agricultural. East Pakistan faced economic difficulties because partition meant the loss of the Calcutta jute mills and market. At the same time it was attached to a country a thousand miles away, of Muslims, but ones radically different in race, language and temperament. Because of the recruiting policy of the British since 1857, predominantly from the so-called loyal and martial races of the north-west, East Pakistanis had little part in the army, which was to become the most important organ of the Pakistan state. There was also an influx of West Pakistani (mainly Punjabi) officials, merchants and entrepreneurs. In March 1948 M. A. Jinnah declared Urdu Pakistan's official language. In East Pakistan, however, less than one per cent had Urdu as their mother tongue; 7½ per cent did in West Pakistan, and Punjabis and Sindhis, though they might not speak it at home, nonetheless identified with it. There ensued an agitation whose significance Jinnah did not live to realize; fed by other Bengali discontents, it helped create the conviction that East Pakistan was a colony of the West. Demonstrations turned to riots; in February 1952 demonstrating students were shot, February 21st thereafter becoming a "Martyrs' Day". In March 1954 the Muslim League party was routed in the provincial elections, retaining only 9 of 309 seats in the provincial assembly. The Pakistan government then admitted Bengali as joint official language with Urdu, but soon afterwards Fazlul Huq's ministry was dismissed on the charge of separatism and direct rule by the Centre imposed. In October 1955 Pakistan was reorganized into two wings, east and west, making East Pakistan a nominally equal partner with the West, with equal representation in the central legislative assembly.

DISPUTE AND WAR BETWEEN EAST AND WEST PAKISTAN

Many observers thought that East Pakistan should now be satisfied. But the composition of those involved in politics in East Pakistan was changing. Language among Bengal Muslims had long been something of a class matter, the more aristocratic and "Islamic" having adopted Urdu. What was happening now, however, was the growth in education and ambition among classes of younger middle-class Bengali-speakers, who felt they were still denied effective participation in the army, in commerce, and in the ruling circles of Pakistan; they became convinced that the West was determined to exploit the resources of the East while denying it its share of central power. Their suspicion deepened with the failure to hold elections under the new constitution, the advent of

General Ayub Khan's military government, and his dismissal of his popular first governor of East Pakistan, General Azam Khan. Ayub's "Basic Democracy" reduced the electorate to 40,000, and made the local assembly into a puppet body. On the re-election of Field Marshal Ayub Khan as President in 1965, it was held that the defeat of Fatima Jinnah in the East had been engineered. In the Indo-Kashmir war of September 1965 East Pakistan was denuded of troops for Kashmir and dependent on China for protection from India.

The leader of the malcontents was Sheikh Mujibur Rahman. First active in support of the language movement and imprisoned when the Huq ministry was dismissed in 1954, he stood for the limitation of the central authority to defence and foreign affairs and the retention by each wing of its own resources. This radical form of autonomy became the creed of Mujib's party, the Awami League. Ayub expressed the view that this demand was tantamount to secession. Mujib was imprisoned in 1966 and detained on various charges.

He was released in February 1969 with the fall of Ayub; President Yahya Khan announced elections, which were eventually held in December 1970 after being postponed because of the great flood of the previous month. The devastation and the West's alleged negligence in sending relief was used by the Awami League to foster the sense of injury against the West. The result was a sweeping victory for the Awami League, which secured 288 of 300 seats in the Provincial Assembly and 160 of the 162 seats allotted to East Pakistan in the National Assembly with a total of 303 elective seats. Mujib therefore commanded a majority in the National Assembly and should have become Prime Minister of Pakistan.

This Yahya Khan could not accept, and the Awami League remained adamant for their radical form of autonomy. In March negotiations broke down and on March 10th the League forced the issue with a de facto seizure of power after a general strike of police and administration. On March 26th the independence of Bangladesh was proclaimed. The step was more extreme than the League's power justified. Undoubtedly it was encouraged by the sympathy of India, and by hopes of Indian support.

CREATION OF BANGLADESH

The West Pakistani army began a vigorous repression of the Awami League's rebellion. Refugees flooded into India, and India, making no attempt to close its borders, began worldwide propaganda about the resultant difficulties. The problem soon reached such proportions that India had little choice but to intervene. On December 4th the Indian army invaded in support of the *Mukhti Bahini* (freedom fighters) and other irregular Bengali groups operating inside East Pakistan. The campaign was brief and successful, and Pakistan's forces surrendered on December 16th. Bangladesh's independence became a reality.

The new country gained prompt international recognition, but was beset by enormous difficulties. There were delicate diplomatic issues to be resolved, and a pressing need for international aid. The loss of professionals through the murder of Bengalis and the removal of Punjabis and Sindhis led to serious manning problems in commerce and the public services. A problem of order was exacerbated by the failure of armed cadres to disband completely, and by campaigns against Biharis: as Urdu-speakers, the Biharis' loyalty was held to be suspect. The change of regime made no contribution to the region's economic problems, and the participation of India raised the spectre of another colonialism to replace those of the past.

The first signs, however, were encouraging. Sheikh Mujib was released by Pakistan and returned in January 1972. Following India's example and renouncing the Pakistani idea of the Islamic state, Bangladesh was declared secular and given a parliamentary constitution. Mujib was the first Prime Minister and was confirmed with a sweeping majority in March 1973. The Indo-Pakistan agreement of August that year provided for a three-way repatriation of prisoners of war. On February 22nd, 1974, Pakistan finally recognized Bangladesh. In April, Bangladesh signed an agreement abandoning the trial of Pakistani prisoners accused of war crimes. The exchange of prisoners was completed, but a visit to Bangladesh by President Bhutto in June did not resolve the questions of the transfer of Biharis and the division of assets held by undivided Pakistan.

Gradually matters worsened again. Political stability was threatened by opposition groups which resorted to terrorism and included both political extremes: on the one hand, the National Socialist party and the right-wing Muslim groups which had opposed secession; on the other, the pro-Chinese wing of the National Awami party and a number of Maoist groups which co-operated with Indian Naxalite groups from West Bengal. In October 1973 the Awami League formed an alliance with the Communist party and the pro-Soviet wing of the National Awami party with a joint policy of suppressing terrorism. A militia, the *Rakkhi Bahini*, was formed to assist the police. The situation was aggravated by disastrous floods in July and August 1974 which damaged the crops and led to widespread famine. At the end of December the Government declared a state of emergency and all fundamental rights guaranteed by the constitution were suspended. Four weeks later, the Bangladesh Parliament adopted a constitution Bill which replaced the parliamentary by a presidential form of government and provided for the introduction of a one-party system. Mujib became president for a second time, assuming absolute powers, and created the Bangladesh *Krishak-Sramik* (Peasants and Workers) Awami League, excluding all other parties from government.

Serious criticism of Mujib had begun to be heard. His government had seemed unable to cope with the severe economic and political strains of recent months: in some areas the price of rice had risen by 400 per cent since 1971 and there were allegations of high-level corruption. Mujib's anti-corruption drives, it was said, had not touched his close associates and relations involved in questionable deals. His popularity, abroad to some extent as well as in Bangladesh, remained even after his assumption of absolute power at the end of 1974.

On August 15th, 1975, however, there was an anti-Mujib coup led by a group of discontented young army majors who assassinated Mujib and his family and put Mushtaq Ahmed, the former Commerce Minister, in power. The army majors themselves went into residence in the President's palace, remaining involved to the extent of promoting their supporters in the armed services. This was to prove dangerous; but for the moment the accession of Mushtaq continued the dominance of the Awami League, of which he had long been an important leader. Soon further signs of strain appeared, and on November 2nd, 1975, the expected counter-coup took place. In a period of confusion a former Prime Minister and several other prominent figures were murdered in jail, and General Khalid Musharaf, a pro-Mujib figure, came briefly to power. Major Dalim and the other authors of the August coup were exiled. Musharaf's control was incomplete, however, and after a day's serious fighting in the Dacca cantonment he and many of his supporters were killed. Mushtaq resigned as President in favour of the Chief Justice of the Supreme Court, Abusadat Mohammad Sayem, who was sworn in as President on November 6th. Power was assumed by the three service chiefs jointly, as Deputy Martial Law Administrators; but Major-Gen. Ziaur Rahman, Chief of Army Staff, who had led the overthrow of Khalid Musharaf after being at one stage his prisoner, has taken precedence over his colleagues, Mosharraf Hossain Khan, Chief of Naval Staff, and M. G. Tawab, then Chief of Air Staff. The new government, like that of Mushtaq Ahmed, has retained for the country the name of People's Republic of Bangladesh and endorsed the democratic, secular ideals favoured by Mujib and India. Gen. Zia has promised an early return to representative government. But there has been a major constitutional change nonetheless: the supremacy of the army, with a non-political President, has ended rule by the Awami League.

The future is uncertain. Though Mujib as father of the nation is thus replaced by "Major Zia" (as he was known in the liberation war), remnants of the *Rakkhi Bahini* still evidently revere his name. Civil unrest continues, apparently in several places but notably in Mymensingh where "Tiger" Siddiqi, an appointee of Mujib, has resisted his replacement by the new government.

Bangladesh's foreign policy since Mujib's death had been characterized by growing animosity towards India: India's role in the "liberation war" is apparently being written out of history. Several contentious issues, including the alleged diversion of the Ganges' water-flow by India's Farakka barrage, the killing of the Indian High Commissioner, and some rumours of communal disturbances against Hindus in Bangladesh, have been raised on both sides, and Bangladesh has sought or threatened to seek international support for its position. It has earnestly been seeking new allies, especially in the Islamic world; but its major continuing need is still for foreign aid. Most major powers, including the U.S.S.R. and the People's Republic of China, have participated in aid programmes, but the aid hoped for as a result of the resumption of relations with Pakistan has not been forthcoming, although trade agreements have led, for example, to the purchase of jute on favourable terms.

ECONOMIC SURVEY

Kevin Rafferty

Bangladesh gained its independence in 1971, as almost the poorest country in the world. The devastation at independence, followed by turmoil, drought and floods in the next few years, made it one of the poorest of the poor nations of the world. Then in 1975 came a gleam of hope. For the first time for years, the weather was kindly, the crops were good, prices fell, industry began to pick up and, under the new government inspired by the military, discipline was re-asserted and law and order improved.

For all this, Bangladesh will remain for years to come among the poorest countries in the world. Its land area is small and population in 1975 reached 77 million, making it the eighth most populous country in the world. Bangladesh has more people per square mile, 1,380, than any other country, apart from city states such as Hong Kong and Singapore. If account is taken of all the river areas, population density would be 2,500 per square mile. That alone would be bad enough, but Bangladesh is also poor. With its degree of poverty, figures become academic because their translation in hard currency turns on unreliable or unrealistic exchange rate valuations. Annual *per capita* income in Bangladesh is certainly below $75. The Government in 1972 said that half the population had a deficiency in calorie intake, and more than 80 per cent a deficiency in vitamins. Consumption of rice and wheat declined in absolute quantity in the 1960s. Cloth consumption allows for a single simple loin cloth per person per year. About 20 per cent of the people are literate. Bangladesh has fewer than 20,000 private cars, only 6,000 buses, 50,000 telephones, 300,000 radios, and 10,000 televisions. Such statistics also illustrate that a few Bengalis do enjoy a privileged life and that the lot of the ordinary man is worse than even the humble average quoted.

But, more than that, Bangladesh has few resources with which it can begin to build prosperity. The population is increasing at more than 2 per cent a year so that by the turn of the century it is expected to be about 150 million. Moreover, Bangladesh is dependent on jute for between 80 and 90 per cent of its export earnings, and jute is in constant decline on the world markets.

None of this is to say that there is no future for Bangladesh. Indeed, in 1975/76 there were reasons for hope. However, even if the brightest, wildest ideas were seized upon and worked, and even if everything (including the weather) was favourable for Bangladesh, its struggle would be uphill for a long time. The topography hardly helps. Bangladesh is flat apart from tiny strips of hills, is criss-crossed by constant rivers and by two huge rivers, the Ganga (Ganges) and the Brahmaputra. It is vulnerable to flood and drought and prone to cyclones.

In 1976, a major dispute arose with India. The Dacca Government claimed that Indian withdrawal of waters through the Farakka Barrage built across the River Ganga just before it enters Bangladesh to flush the River Hooghly and free Calcutta Port from silting was highly damaging to Bangladesh during the lean season. In the middle of the lean season the flow of water from the river decreased so drastically that it had serious effects on irrigation projects, navigation and industry. Talks to try to solve disputes had not produced agreements by June 1976.

ECONOMIC HISTORY TO BEFORE INDEPENDENCE

The area which is today Bangladesh used to be the rural hinterland of Calcutta in the days of British India. Long before that, the land had been renowned for its spices, for soil fertility, and the fine quality Dacca muslin. With the coming of the British and the creation of Calcutta as the great port and industrial centre of India, Eastern Bengal began to suffer as the most able people drifted towards the opportunities of the metropolis, and the new industries sprang up in and around it. By the time of partition in 1947, East Bengal was the richest jute-growing area in the world, but had very little industry of its own. All but a few jute-processing mills were in and around Calcutta. At partition, it was decided that Calcutta should go to India, leaving East Pakistan without a large town of its own.

The new Pakistan was split into two and separated by 1,000 miles of India. East Pakistan contained 55 per cent of the population, but the capital was in the west. West Pakistanis dominated Pakistan: they composed the majority of the senior civil servants and, more important, from 1958 (when General Ayub Khan became President) only a few of the army generals were Bengalis and then none of the senior ones. The war and struggle with India for Kashmir only concentrated more attention by the West Pakistani rulers on the needs of West Pakistan.

East Pakistan was neglected. The Government of Pakistan did encourage the building of jute mills but few other industries were established. However, for the first 20 years, Pakistan relied on jute earnings which were the most important supplier of foreign exchange for all Pakistan, on which industry, chiefly in the west, could be built up. The West received the major share of Plan development spending and the West, comparatively, grew more affluent. In the 1950s the West was 20 per cent richer; by 1960 it was 30 per cent; by 1970 per capita income in West Pakistan was probably twice that of the East.

By the time of the independence war in 1971, economists from the East pointed bitterly to the disparities of resources between the two wings of Pakistan. They claimed that, allowing for the overvalue of the Pakistan rupee, actions of successive Governments based in the West had resulted in the transfer of resources from West to East Pakistan of 30,000 million rupees. This would be $3,000 million given a rate of 10 rupees to one U.S. dollar. The official rate was 4.76 rupees to the dollar, but the complaint of the Bengalis was that the true rate was 10 rupees per dollar and East Pakistan's jute exports were contributing enormously to Pakistan but the province was not getting a fair share of either internal resources or foreign assistance.

THE ECONOMY AFTER INDEPENDENCE

When independence came late in 1971, Bangladesh, desperately poor, was ill-suited to face the difficult economic climate of the 1970s. It had to recover from the devastation of the liberation struggle when millions of refugees had fled to India: homes had been destroyed, livestock killed and much of the (albeit poor) infrastructure destroyed. It had a lack of experience in bureaucratic and economic management and administration which had been run for so long from the west. For the first year, it received massive funds from the United Nations relief operation and from friendly countries, such as India, and generous ones such as the United States. In subsequent years, Bangladesh was hit first by drought and then by floods which reduced harvests and meant that the country was having to import nearly 2 million tons of food per year, a sixth of its needs. Given the soaring world prices of food grains, this was a heavy drain on Bangladesh's funds and the cost of food imports alone was more than Bangladesh was earning for all its exports.

Then there were the political ramifications. Sheikh Mujibur Rahman, the new leader of the country, had little experience in administration. The new rulers dedicated the country to socialism and quickly nationalized the jute mills, textile factories and most of the other major industries. The Biharis, Urdu-speaking Muslims who migrated from Bihar and Uttar Pradesh to East Pakistan after Partition, were excluded from the economy because many of them had sided with the Pakistan forces during the liberation struggle. Yet they had industrial skills and experience and their exclusion put a greater strain on the economy.

The inexperience of labour was matched by the inexperience of management and exacerbated by the extravagant and unrealistic promises of socialism. Industry's contribution to gross domestic product was small, about 8 per cent, but one of the industries was jute manufacturing, providing a major part of foreign exchange reserves.

Then there was political manipulation. Large-scale smuggling, backed by prominent people, increased prices and caused uncertainty over food supplies. Prices of essential commodities rose by up to 300 per cent. The long-maintained refusal to devalue the taka, the Bangladesh currency fixed at independence at par with the Indian rupee, meant that jute prices were kept far too high on world markets to be competitive while the benefit was not felt in lower import prices which were kept high by scarcities and bureaucracy.

Sheikh Mujib had gathered into his planning commission the most talented economists of Bangladesh, probably a team unparallelled in the world. They produced an eminently sensible five-year plan, hoping to produce real growth of 5.5 per cent a year until 1977/78. The plan concentrated on the simple but essential things, like rural development and food production, and was surprisingly honest about Bangladesh's shortcomings; but its targets were hopelessly optimistic and the "bench-mark" output was well above the actual economic performance in 1972/73, the opening year of the plan. But even if the plan had been fulfilled in all its details, the state of Bangladesh can be seen from some of the plans per capita targets. Rice consumption per day in 1977/78 would be 15.61 ounces, compared with 15.41 in 1969/70 and 12.91 in 1972/73; sugar consumption per year in 1977/78 would be 4.48 lb., compared with 4.22 in 1969/70 and 3.0 in 1972/73; textiles consumption in 1977/78 would be 8.14 yards per year compared with 7.5 in 1969/70 and 4.96 in 1972/73; tea consumption in 1977/78 would be 0.22 lb. per year compared with 0.14 in 1969/70 and 0.16 in 1972/73; consumption of electricity in 1977/78 would be 3.56 kWh per year compared with 1.63 in 1969/70 and 1.64 in 1972/73; consumption of gas in 1977/78 would be 21.37 cubic feet per year compared with 5.27 in 1969/70 and 4.93 in 1972/73.

For all their economic competence, however, the planning commission had great difficulty in implementing their programme: they antagonized many of the bureaucrats and were also outsiders to the political process and often did not know how to obtain political approval for policies. Sheikh Mujibur Rahman was so much pre-eminent that even trivial matters were referred to him.

Given all the natural calamities and the poor political performance, Bangladesh got nowhere near its aims. When Sheikh Mujib was killed in 1975, the country was still poorer than it had been in 1969/70, its last "normal" year as part of Pakistan, yet the population had increased by 10 million since then.

That is not wholly to condemn the economic performance of Sheikh Mujibur Rahman's Bangladesh. In many ways, his was an inexperienced regime feeling its way but its failures were magnified by the political squabbling and by a distinct shift in the world economic climate against Bangladesh. In fact, towards the end of his rule, stimulated by the International Monetary Fund, Sheikh Mujibur Rahman had begun to preside over a more disciplined economy. He finally devalued the taka and curbed the growth of money supply. Credit for such successes has fallen to his successors.

THE ECONOMY IN 1975/76

The new military leader, General Ziaur Rahman, has a team of economic and professional experts led by Dr. M. N. Huda, Kazi Anwarul Haque, Professor Abul Fazal and Dr. Md. Abdur Rashid. General Zia retains the important portfolios of Finance, Home Affairs and Information. The new Government takes a more favourable attitude to private enterprise while making it plain that the key industries, jute, sugar, and cotton textiles, will remain in the public sector. Even after some small industries are sold, the public sector will still run 75 per cent of industry. The Government has said it is going to pay compensation for industries nationalized, both domestic and foreign (though not industries run by Pakistanis which are classified as abandoned properties). It has reduced the number of ministries and divisions from 43 to 36 and has set up a national economic council with an executive committee to try to ensure that decisions are taken and implemented quickly.

In terms of performance, 1975/76 was Bangladesh's best year. Foodgrain production rose by 17 per cent. Gross domestic product (G.D.P.) rose in real terms by about 12 per cent and, in constant 1972/73 prices, rose to more than G.D.P. for 1969/70. In *per capita* terms it is still below 1969/70. Prices fell by about 10 per cent in 1975 compared with a rise of 80 per cent in 1974. Large-scale smuggling has been almost eliminated.

One thing which might upset progress would be instability, if the promised return to political activities in August 1976 and the general elections in February 1977 lead to squabbling and chaos.

AGRICULTURE

Agriculture is the most important sector of the Bangladesh economy. It accounts for nearly 60 per cent of G.D.P. and employs 80 per cent of the people. Rice is the main food crop and production of milled rice in 1975/76 reached nearly 13 million tons, a record. The main crop is harvested from October onwards after the monsoon and in 1975/76 yielded about 7 million tons (milled). Two other rice crops are grown: one dependent on irrigation and harvested in spring, yielded 2.7 million tons in 1975/76, and the summer crop reached more than 3 million tons; all crops were higher than usual. A smaller amount of wheat is grown, 270,000 tons in the 1975/76 year. Ten per cent of production goes to waste or to provide seed. Even with this amount of food grain available, Bangladesh had to import 1.5 million tons of grain. Allowing for all grains, *per capita* food grain consumption is only 16 ounces per day and, unlike many other countries, grain is practically the only source of food. Fish consumption, for example, is only 4 lb. per person each year. (The proviso has to be made that all production figures must be treated with scepticism. Foreign experts sometimes deride official methods of calculating harvests; no one can be quite sure of the population size. What can be said with certainty is that the ordinary Bengali gets little enough to eat.)

Yields of food grain have traditionally been low, averaging about 12.5 maunds per acre (1 maund = 82.27 lb.). The highest yields have been obtained from the spring crop, in which new seeds have been used most successfully, and yields of up to 24 maunds per acre have been realized there. However, in international rice trials in 1975 and 1976 local Bangladesh varieties of new seed took the first three places. In these trials the winning grain achieved yields of between 70 and 80 maunds per acre. Bangladesh's combined rice crops occupy 24.2 million acres, which is more than the total cultivated land of 22 million acres.

There is evidence lately of a drift of people from the countryside to the towns. One problem typical of the subcontinent is that farms are small and landholdings liable to be fragmented. This creates inefficiencies in production and means that economies of scale often cannot be realized. In time of hardship it means that a farmer may sell his land to stay alive, and there is evidence that this happened in 1973 and 1974, increasing the number of landless to possibly 40 per cent of the population, adding to the pressure of migration to the towns in the hope of at least ration shop food prices.

JUTE

Jute is the main non-food crop and the cash crop of Bangladesh. It was traditionally sown on 2.5 million acres yielding up to 7 million bales (1 bale is 400 lb.). About half the crop is exported as raw jute and the rest processed in Bangladesh for export as jute goods. Immediately after independence, the area of jute sown fell sharply to 1.5 million acres as better prices could be obtained from planting rice. As a result, production dropped to 4 million bales in 1974/75, though it recovered to 4.5 million bales in 1975/76. One good sign reported in 1975/76 was a marginal increase in the yield of the jute crop. Using traditional methods, jute has yielded 3 bales per acre, but on selected land with new seeds yield of 5 bales are possible, and 4.5 bales per acre have been achieved in actual cultivation. The Government is helping the farmers to buy the new seeds and giving technical assistance.

INDUSTRY

Industry is small in Bangladesh and contributes less than 10 per cent to G.D.P. It is dominated by jute processing which contributes a third of the value added by all manufacturing. Cotton textiles and cigarettes come next. The performance of industry since independence has been disappointing and up to 1974/75, only cotton and sugar had surpassed the 1969/70 performance in terms of output. Overall industrial production in 1974/75 was 90 per cent of that in 1969/70. Industries have had problems with inefficient production, poor quality management and distorted pricing policies, with goods sometimes sold at prices below their cost of production. The capacity utilization rate has been poor. The nationalized Jute Industries Corporation, in particular, has made big losses which have been a considerable drain on the Government budget.

MINING

Mining so far has not been very important in Bangladesh because the country has few proven mineral resources apart from natural gas. Reserves of gas are estimated at several million million cubic feet and the country is hoping to use them for setting up fertilizer plants and eventually for a petrochemical complex. In 1975 Bangladesh made contracts with six foreign companies for offshore oil exploration in the Bay of Bengal. The geological structures are believed to be good and some oil finds have been reported, though not yet in commercial quantities.

The only other mineral resources are coal of which large reserves of 700 million tons have been discovered, though the quality of the coal is low grade.

TRADE

Jute is all-important as far as the trading account is concerned. Bangladesh receives 85 per cent of its export earnings from the commodity. Total exports in 1975/76 were expected to be about $350 million (virtually the same as in each of the previous two years), of which raw jute and jute goods will contribute $285 million, an increase of $50 million. The only other important exports commodities are tea, earning about $25 million per year, and leather, worth a similar amount. Because the land is low-lying, Bangladesh tea is not of a high grade, but its strong liquor and dust quality is useful for blending and giving body to mass market tea. With the increase in the world market price of tea, the commodity has been one of the few successes since independence. After a year or so at very low levels, annual tea production has recovered to 70 million lb., as much as it reached in the best Pakistan times. Before the middle of 1975, Bangladesh raw jute was being offered at £200 per ton and having difficulty in finding sales. By the end of the year devaluation allowed a reduction in price to £155 per ton. The effect was seen immediately. In the eleven months before devaluation, sales of raw jute averaged 68,500 bales (worth just under £2 million) per month; after devaluation, the monthly average was 268,000 bales (value £6.3 million).

Jute goods have also suffered both because of internal and external factors. Internally, the labour unions whose leaders were close to the Awami League caused endless problems; moreover management was inexperienced and unequal to the difficulties after nationalization. Externally, the world recession led to a sharp drop in demand for prime products such as carpet backing. And, all the time, jute is under serious threat from synthetic substitutes.

In 1976, Bangladesh jute had a slight edge in price over the synthetics affected by successive oil price rises. But, according to all international studies, prospects for jute are gloomy except in the poorer and developing countries where the market is smaller and growth likely to be slower. If jute is to survive it needs a more vigorous marketing policy and more reliable production and delivery in which costs will be kept down to keep jute goods ahead.

It has been suggested that Bangladesh should stop growing jute and use the land for food grains to remove the need for food imports: in 1975/76 food imports alone came to about $360 million or more than the total value of Bangladesh's exports. However, it is doubtful whether all the land under jute could be turned over to grain, and jute is more durable to flood conditions which often hit Bangladesh. Total imports in 1975/76 fell slightly to about $1,300 million, or $100 million less than in 1974/75. Of the rest of the import bill, $150 million is accounted for by petroleum and petroleum products, $60 million by cotton, $60 million by fertilizers, $40 million by edible oil and $10 million by cement. Imports of capital goods were valued at $155 million in 1975/76.

All this means that, for the foreseeable future, Bangladesh needs more than $1,000 million per year in aid simply to keep the economy turning over at a low level. The aid donors have suggested that minor exports like handicrafts and fish products should be promoted, but these are not likely to have any immediate effect on the trade gap. Import substitutes could be considered and might be a better proposition when the fertilizer plant gets into production. Donors also suggest export promotion to improve the chances of Bangladesh goods in international markets, but in this Bangladesh comes against entrenched interests in the developed countries. Even jute goods are subject to quotas in the European Community because continental European jute makers have been concerned to protect a few thousand jobs, although the life of their jute industries is not expected to go beyond a decade.

Industry, trade and everyone will be hampered for years by Bangladesh's poor communications. Because of the countless rivers, it can take a day to travel from Dacca to Chittagong, the main port 200 miles away. For the first two years after independence, Chittagong and the other port, Khulna, were badly congested, but conditions had improved considerably by 1975/76.

GOVERNMENT FINANCIAL AND ECONOMIC POLICY

In 1975 and 1976 the Bangladesh Government has tightened its economic policy. The measures started in April 1975, under Sheikh Mujibur Rahman, when the money supply was reduced by 22 per cent. In May 1975 the Government devalued the taka, changing the exchange rate against the pound sterling from 18.97 to 30.00 (in 1976 the currency was re-valued against the falling pound, to 28.10 on April 30th and to 26.70 on June 7th). Along with these measures, the Government undertook to abstain from deficit financing, to fix a ceiling on credit and to improve its tax efforts. The price of rationed rice was increased by 50 per cent and that of wheat by 40 per cent.

As a result of all these policies, an annual increase of money supply of 30 per cent and an inflation rate of 50 per cent have been checked: in 1975/76 retail prices fell by about 10 per cent. A reform programme has started, thanks largely to the good harvest. Hoarding and smuggling have been cut.

Official revenue collections improved by more than 50 per cent in 1974/75 and the Government has kept its promise to the International Monetary Fund (IMF) to avoid deficit financing. The priorities of the latest annual development plan won praise from the World Bank. It stresses investment in agricultural production as the main effort. But domestic resource mobilization is expected to cause problems in the future. The tax base is very narrow, with a tax ratio of about 6 per cent of G.D.P., so there is little response to changes in income. The major revenue earners are custom duties, sales taxes and excise duties, all of which depend heavily on imports. A possible solution is to increase the range of indirect taxes because excise duty comes from only a few products, like cigarettes, cement, petroleum products, gas and sugar. As for direct taxes, the most important potential source of revenue would be to tax the agricultural sector but at the moment there would be enormous administrative difficulties about this, not to speak of the political problems which have deterred many of the national governments of South Asia from introducing a direct agricultural income tax.

DEVELOPMENT

In *per capita* terms, Bangladesh has still not returned to the levels of "prosperity" of Pakistan days in spite of a better harvest. Tackling the development problem is a longer way off. It is difficult to describe Bangladesh's real poverty to people used to Western comforts. Dacca, the capital, is a city which has few of the graces of a capital. Its population has expanded from about 100,000 in 1947 to about 2 million in 1976. Unemployment is a problem and the pressure on the land in the villages has led to a constant influx of people from the countryside. In 1975 the Government of Sheikh Mujib took the desperate measure of forcing thousands of people out of their shacks on the airport road in Dacca and dumping them several miles outside the city. The measure only temporarily stemmed the drift to Dacca. The shanty colonies have begun to spring up again.

If progress has to be made, the Government has to tackle the immense poverty, underemployment and unemployment in the rural areas. Food is always a problem, nutrition is even more so. Proper irrigation is a key, ensuring better crop yields and therefore economic development; although Bangladesh has so much water, only 2 million acres have ensured irrigation supplies. Work is not always available to the young. Although more than 50 per cent of children enrol for school, regular schooling is foreign to perhaps the majority of children. Health care is rudimentary.

One international expert wrote graphically: "Per capita income is only a proxy for many different kinds of deprivation. More than half of all families are below the acceptable calorific intake, while more than two-thirds are deficient in proteins and vitamins. Houses are single rooms . . . and have no water or electricity. Less than 20 per cent of the population are literate. Estimates of unemployment and under-employment range from one-quarter to one-third of the labour force. About one in every four live-born children dies before their fifth birthday. The expectation of life of 48 years contrasts with 70 years in developed countries. In addition to all these indicators, the special disabilities faced by women in Bangladesh substantially reduce the quality of life."

However, in the last year, for perhaps the first time, the Government has tried to tackle the development problem. One of the brightest civil servants opted to move from the President's secretariat to take the responsibility for family planning. And the Government is also promoting a self-help programme in the villages. Its outline has been much criticized by some foreign experts but at least it is a first attempt to deal with the most pressing problems. In some villages where pilot efforts have been made there have been some outstanding successes. Food production has increased by the application of basic husbandry techniques. Village ponds have been cleaned and filled with fish to provide another source of food and even a better one of much needed protein. Local schools have been started and health and nutrition improved, but such villages are only a few of the 60,000 villages of Bangladesh.

STATISTICAL SURVEY

AREA AND POPULATION

Area	Population			
	Feb. 1st, 1961 (Census)	July 1st, 1970 (estimate)†	March 1st, 1974 (Census)‡	July 1st, 1975 (estimate)
55,598 sq. miles*	50,853,721	60,675,000	71,316,517	76,820,000

* 143,998 sq. km.

† Excluding adjustment for underenumeration at the 1961 census. According to the Pakistan Planning Commission (PPC), the census result understated the total population (in both wings of pre-1971 Pakistan) by about 8.3 per cent. The PPC estimated the population of East Pakistan (now Bangladesh) to be 64 million at January 1st, 1968.

‡ Probably understated by about 3 million.

DIVISIONS* (1961 Census)

Chittagong	13,629,650
Dacca	15,293,596
Khulna	10,066,900
Rajshahi	11,850,089
Total	50,840,235

* Excluding aliens, who numbered 13,486 at the time of the census.

CHIEF TOWNS

	1961 Census	1974 Census
Dacca (capital)	556,712	1,319,970
Chittagong	364,205	458,000
Khulna	127,970	436,000
Narayanganj	162,054	176,899

Births and Deaths: Average annual birth rate 49.7 per 1,000; death rate 21.6 per 1,000 (UN estimate for 1965–70).

Employment: (1974 census, provisional): Total economically active population 25,181,328 (males 18,740,364; females 6,440,964), excluding adjustment for under-enumeration. About 20 million are active in agriculture.

AGRICULTURE

LAND USE, 1971/72

(million acres)

Total area	35.3
Forests	5.5
Not available for cultivation	6.6
Other uncultivated land	0.7
Total non-agricultural area	12.8
Fallow land	2.1
Net sown area	20.4
Total cultivated area	22.5
Sown more than once	8.7
Total cropped area	29.1
Multi-cropping index	129

PRINCIPAL CROPS

(Twelve months ending June 30th)

	Area (million acres)	Yield (tons per acre)	Production (million tons)		
	1969/70	1969/70	1969/70	1972/73	1973/74
Rice (milled)	25.50	0.46	11.62	9.93	11.72
Wheat	0.30	0.35	0.10	0.09	0.11
Sugar cane	0.40	18.50	7.40	5.32	6.34
Potatoes	0.21	4.05	0.85	0.75	0.72
Sweet potatoes	0.18	4.65	0.84	0.68	0.63
Pulses	0.90	0.32	0.29	0.22	0.21
Oilseeds	0.85	0.45	0.38	0.32	0.30
Jute	2.45	0.54	1.32	1.17	0.97

1974/75: Production of milled rice 11.1 million tons.

LIVESTOCK

(FAO estimates, October to September)

	1969/70	1970/71	1971/72	1972/73	1973/74
Cattle	26,800,000	26,000,000	25,500,000	26,000,000	26,709,000
Buffaloes	n.a.	650,000	630,000	650,000	674,000
Sheep	720,000	700,000	680,000	700,000	727,000
Goats	n.a.	11,300,000	11,000,000	11,500,000	11,938,000
Horses	45,000	45,000	45,000	43,000	43,000
Chickens	27,010,000	27,820,000	28,500,000	29,000,000	29,717.000
Ducks	4,700,000	4,850,000	5,000,000	5,200,000	5,337,000

1974/75 (FAO estimates): 27,418,000 cattle; 753,000 sheep.

Source: FAO, mainly *Production Yearbook*.

LIVESTOCK PRODUCTS
(FAO estimates, metric tons)

	1971	1972	1973	1974
Beef and veal	157,000	147,000	151,000	155,000
Buffalo meat		3,000	4,000	4,000
Mutton and lamb	47,000	2,000	2,000	2,000
Goats' meat		44,000	46,000	48,000
Poultry meat	30,000	31,000	32,000	32,000
Edible offals	40,626	39,100	40,466	41,681
Cows' milk	700,000	688,000	700,000	713,000
Buffalo milk	100,000	100,000	105,000	106,000
Sheep's milk	13,000	13,000	13,000	13,000
Goats' milk	495,000	484,000	506,000	526,000
Butter	n.a.	8,288	8,567	8,713
Cheese	n.a.	9,061	9,365	9,524
Hen eggs	22,145	22,848	23,310	23,868
Other poultry eggs	10,913	11,250	11,700	12,007
Wool: greasy	900	900	900	900
clean	540	540	540	540
Cattle hides	90,800	90,000	91,000	93,366
Buffalo hides	2,700	2,730	2,820	2,910
Goat skins	10,600	10,400	10,800	11,213

1975 (FAO estimates, metric tons): Meat 250,000; Cows' milk 725,000; Buffalo milk 107,000; Sheep's milk 14,000; Goats' milk 546,000.

Source: FAO, *Production Yearbook.*

FORESTRY

ROUNDWOOD REMOVALS
(FAO estimates, '000 cubic metres)

	Coniferous (soft wood)		Broadleaved (hard wood)		Total	
	1971	1972	1971	1972	1971	1972
Sawlogs, veneer logs and logs for sleepers	20	20	800	830	820	850
Pitprops (mine timber)	—	—	—	—	—	—
Pulpwood	—	—	65	60	65	60
Other industrial wood	15	15	245	255	260	270
Total Industrial Wood	35	35	1,110	1,145	1,145	1,180
Fuel wood	450	500	8,850	9,100	9,300	9,600
Total Removals	485	535	9,960	10,245	10,445	10,780

Source: FAO, *Yearbook of Forest Products.*

SAWNWOOD PRODUCTION
('000 cubic metres)

	1971	1972
Coniferous sawnwood (incl. boxboards)	10*	10*
Broadleaved sawnwood (incl. boxboards)	385	400
	395	410
Railway sleepers	15*	15*
Total	410	425

* FAO estimate.

Source: FAO, *Yearbook of Forest Products.*

FISHING

('000 metric tons)

	1965	1966	1967	1968	1969	1970
Inland waters	218.7	218.7	220.2	221.0	229.5	211.9
Indian Ocean	40.0	40.0	44.9	45.4	47.8	35.3
TOTAL CATCH	258.7	258.7	265.1	266.4	277.3	247.2

Source: FAO, *Yearbook of Fishery Statistics.*

INDUSTRY

SELECTED PRODUCTS

(Public sector only, July 1st to June 30th)

		1969/70	1972/73	1973/74	1974/75
Jute textiles	'000 tons	560	446	500	444
Hessian	" "	228	155	172	146
Sacking	" "	279	210	227	228
Carpet backing	" "	33	54	66	40
Others	" "	20	27	35	30
Cotton cloth	million yards	60	58	79	86
Cotton yarn	million lb.	106	81	96	101
Newsprint	'000 tons	36	28	26	29
Other paper	" "	31	21	24	25
Cement	" "	53	32	53	143
Steel ingots	" "	54	68	74	76
Re-rolled steel products	" "	99	119	128	150
Petroleum products	" "	853	776	323	761
Urea fertilizer	" "	96	211	279	69
Ammonium sulphate	" "	4.7	6.0	10.3	4.9
Chemicals	" "	8.5	5.3	5.7	7.0
Soaps	" "	8.7	8.0	10.4	5.9
Refined sugar	" "	93	19	88	98
Footwear	'000 dozen	586	448	391	280
Wine and spirits	'000 galls.	813	n.a.	614	700
Tea*	million lb.	67	53	61	66
Edible oil and vegetable ghee	'000 tons	19.1	14.1	18.4	15.4
Cigarettes	'000 million	1.9	1.1	1.1	1.8

* Including production in the private sector.

Source: Nationalized Industries Division, Public Sector Corporations, Planning Commission and Bureau of Statistics.

FINANCE

100 paisa = 1 taka.

Coins: 1, 2, 5, 10, 25 and 50 paisa.

Notes: 1, 5, 10 and 100 taka.

Exchange rates (June 1976): £1 sterling = 26.70 taka; U.S. $1 = 15.05 taka.

100 taka = £3.745 = $6.644.

Note: The taka was introduced in January 1972, replacing the Pakistan rupee. At the same time the currency was devalued by 34.6 per cent, so that the taka would be at par with the Indian rupee. Until May 1975 the link with India was retained and Bangladesh maintained an official exchange rate against sterling at a mid-point of £1 = 18.9677 taka. Before the "floating" of the pound in June 1972 this was equivalent to a rate of U.S. $1 = 7.279 taka. In May 1975 the currency was devalued by 36.8 per cent against sterling, the new exchange rate being £1 = 30.00 taka. This remained in effect until April 1976, when a new rate of £1 = 28.10 taka was introduced. In June 1976 this was adjusted to £1 = 26.70 taka. The average market rate of taka per U.S. dollar was: 7.595 in 1972; 7.742 in 1973; 8.113 in 1974; and 12.019 in 1975.

CURRENT BUDGET
(million taka, July 1st to June 30th)

REVENUE	1973/74	1974/75*	1975/76†
Custom duties	1,187	1,400	2,400
Import licence tax‡	—	340	—
Excise duties	836	1,440	1,550
Sales tax	434	580	1,050
Stamps	112	120	120
Motor vehicle taxes	17	12	12
Entertainment taxes	25	55	55
Income taxes	332	451	651
Land revenue	55	55	55
Other taxes and duties	93	89	72
Interest receipts	107	321	637
Railways	309	408	439
Other revenue	432	684	513
TOTAL	3,939	5,955	7,554

EXPENDITURE	1973/74	1974/75*	1975/76†
General administration	863	894	738
Justice and police	495	656	724
Defence	421	711	752
Scientific departments	29	33	39
Education	649	825	897
Health	153	200	258
Social welfare	19	24	27
Agriculture	97	115	121
Manufacturing and construction	110	109	138
Transport and communication	164	158	164
Debt service	183	269	389
Food subsidy	963	916	1,006
Railways	279	402	439
Contingency	—	—	300
TOTAL	4,425	5,311	5,992

* Revised budget. † Budget estimate. ‡ Tax imposed in June 1974 and abolished in May 1975.

Source: Ministry of Finance.

PUBLIC SECTOR DEVELOPMENT EXPENDITURES

(estimates, million taka)

	1974/75	1975/76
Agriculture	639	1,150
Rural development	285	480
Water and flood control	860	1,360
Industry	650	1,360
Power, scientific research and natural resources	712	1,510
Transport	812	1,250
Communication	186	345
Physical planning and housing	340	660
Education and training	288	450
Health	218	330
Population planning	77	250
Social welfare	20	40
Manpower and employment	13	30
Cyclone reconstruction	150	285
TOTAL DEVELOPMENT EXPENDITURE	5,250	9,500

Source: Ministry of Finance.

FOREIGN AID

(U.S. $ million, July 1st to June 30th)

DONOR	1972/73
Canada	34
India	16
Japan	12
Netherlands/Belgium	6
Sweden	7
U.S.S.R.	34
United Kingdom	15
U.S.A.	56
TOTAL	180

1973/1974: Total Aid disbursed $400 million.

COST OF LIVING

(Middle class families in Dacca, 1969/70=100)

	1972/73	1973/74	Dec. 1974	Dec. 1975
Food	185	263	529	398
Fuel and lighting	192	250	370	351
Housing and household requisites	132	161	199	403
Clothing and footwear	229	355	418	386
Miscellaneous	179	236	339	354
All items	182	253	430	386

Source: Bangladesh Bureau of Statistics.

NATIONAL ACCOUNTS

GROSS DOMESTIC PRODUCT AT CONSTANT FACTOR COST

(provisional estimates, million taka at 1972/73 prices)

	1969/70	1974/75
Agriculture	31,836	29,701
Industry	4,281	3,735
Construction	2,377	1,756
Power and gas	124	265
Transport services	2,399	2,615
Trade services	3,864	3,924
Housing services	2,293	2,494
Public administration	1,263	2,462
Banking and insurance	258	349
Professional and other services	3,138	3,297
TOTAL	51,833	50,598

Source: Planning Commission.

BALANCE OF PAYMENTS

(U.S. $ million)

	1973	1974
Merchandise exports f.o.b.	357.9	348.0
Merchandise imports f.o.b.	−789.7	−989.4
TRADE BALANCE	−431.8	−641.4
Exports of services	65.1	78.1
Imports of services	−142.8	−178.8
BALANCE ON GOODS AND SERVICES	−509.5	−742.1
Unrequited transfers (net)	273.9	267.2
BALANCE ON CURRENT ACCOUNT	−235.5	−475.0
Long-term capital (net)	115.1	380.1
Short-term capital (net)	−0.3	−2.5
Net errors and omissions	−10.5	−14.9
TOTAL (net monetary movements)	−131.2	−112.3

Source: IMF, *International Financial Statistics.*

EXTERNAL TRADE

(million taka)

	1969/70*	1972	1973	1973/74*
Imports	3,480.0	1,460.0	5,039.5	5,013.0
Exports	2,593.5	2,273.2	2,525.2	2,769.0

COMMODITIES

Imports	1972	1973	1973/74*
Foodstuffs	205.3	1,423.2	1,386.4
Raw materials	491.0	1,275.0	1,383.3
Manufactured goods	433.6	1,810.7	1,928.9
Others	330.1	530.6	314.4
Total	1,460.0	5,039.5	5,013.0

Exports	1972	1973	1973/74*
Raw jute	859.9	896.0	910.9
Jute textiles	1,201.6	1,319.7	1,530.6
Tea	44.7	81.2	99.3
Others	167.0	228.3	228.2
Total	2,273.2	2,525.2	2,769.0

* Twelve months from July 1st to June 30th.

JUTE EXPORTS

('000 long tons)

	1969/70	1970/71	1971/72	1972/73
Raw Jute	636	396	180	n.a.
Jute Products	495	488	280	333

TRANSPORT

RAILWAYS

(July 1st to June 30th)

	1968/69	1969/70	1970/71	1971/72	1972/73
Passenger-kilometres (million)	3,549	3,317	2,095	n.a.	2,815
Freight: net ton-km. (million)	1,185	1,568	1,038	n.a.	891

Source: United Nations, *Statistical Yearbook*.

ROAD MOTOR VEHICLES

(number in use)

	1971	1972
Passenger Cars	63,600	66,700
Commercial Vehicles	22,000	23,300

INTERNATIONAL SEA-BORNE SHIPPING
(Twelve months ending June 30th)

	1969	1971	1972
Vessels ('000 net reg. tons):			
Entered	3,687	1,294	3,089
Cleared	4,475	1,045	3,173
Goods Loaded ('000 long tons)	1,087	825	275
Chalna	844	n.a.	n.a.
Chittagong	243	n.a.	n.a.
Goods Unloaded ('000 long tons)	3,901	3,501	2,141
Chalna	852	n.a.	n.a.
Chittagong	3,049	n.a.	n.a.

EDUCATION
(1972 estimate)

	Number	Students
Primary Schools	36,000†	5,500,000*
High Schools		1,030,000
Technical Colleges and Institutes	296†	176,000
Universities	6	16,466

* 1968. † March 1973.

THE CONSTITUTION

(Promulgated November 1972; amended 1973, 1974, 1975)

SUMMARY

Fundamental Principles of State Policy

The Constitution is based on the fundamental principles of the State, namely nationalism, socialism, democracy and secularism. It aims to establish a society free from exploitation in which the rule of law, fundamental human rights and freedoms, justice and equality are to be secured for all citizens. A socialist economic system is to be established to ensure the attainment of a just and egalitarian society through state and co-operative ownership as well as private ownership within limits prescribed by law. A universal, free and compulsory system of education shall be established.

Fundamental Rights

All citizens are equal before the law and have a right to its protection. Arbitrary arrest or detention, discrimination based on race, age, sex, birth, caste or religion and forced labour are prohibited. Subject to law, public order and morality, every citizen has freedom of movement, of assembly and of association. Freedom of conscience, of speech, of the Press and of religious worship are guaranteed.

GOVERNMENT

The President

The President is the constitutional Head of State and is elected for a term of five years. He is eligible for re-election. The supreme control of the armed forces is vested in the President. He appoints the Vice-President, the Prime Minister and other Ministers as well as the Chief Justice and other judges.

The Executive

Executive authority shall rest in the President and shall be exercised by him either directly or through officers subordinate to him in accordance with the constitution.

There shall be a Council of Ministers to aid and advise the President. All ministers shall hold office during the pleasure of the President.

The Legislature

Parliament (*Jatiya Sangsad*) consists of a unicameral legislature. It comprises 300 members and, for ten years, an additional 15 women members. Members of Parliament, other than 15 women members, are directly elected on the basis of universal adult franchise from single territorial constituences. Persons aged 18 and over are entitled to vote. The parliamentary term lasts for five years unless sooner dissolved by the President. War can be declared only with the assent of Parliament. In the case of actual or imminent invasion, the President may take whatever action he may consider appropriate.

THE JUDICIARY

The Judiciary comprises a Supreme Court with High Court and an Appelate Division. The Supreme Court consists of a Chief Justice and such other judges as may be appointed by the President. The High Court division has such original appelate and other jurisdiction and powers as are conferred on it by the Constitution and by other law. The Appelate division has jurisdiction to determine appeals from decisions of the High Court division. Subordinate courts, in addition to the Supreme Court, have been established by law.

Elections

An Election Commission supervises elections for the Presidency and for Parliament, delimits constituencies and prepares electoral rolls. It consists of a Chief Election Commissioner and other Commissioners as may be appointed by the President. The Election Commission is independent in the exercise of its functions. Subject to the Constitution, Parliament may make provision as to elections where necessary.

Note: A state of emergency was proclaimed in December 1974 and fundamental constitutional rights such as freedom of speech and of associations were suspended. Martial law was imposed in August 1975 and parliament was dissolved in November 1975.

THE GOVERNMENT

HEAD OF STATE

President, Chief Martial Law Administrator, in charge of President's Secretariat and Cabinet Secretariat, Minister of Defence, Law, Parliamentary Affairs and Foreign Affairs: Justice ABUSADAT MOHAMMAD SAYEM.

Special Assistant to President: Justice A. SATTAR.

ADVISORY COUNCIL

(*July* 1976)

Deputy Chief Martial Law Administrator, Minister of Finance, Home Affairs, Information and Broadcasting: Maj.-Gen. ZIAUR RAHMAN.

Deputy Chief Martial Law Administrator, Minister of Communications, Flood Control, Water Resources and Power: Rear-Admiral MOSHARRAF HOSSAIN KHAN.

Deputy Chief Martial Law Administrator, Minister of Petroleum and Food: Air Vice-Marshal MUHAMMAD KHADEMUL BASHAR.

Minister of Education: Prof. ABUL FAZAL.

Minister of Agriculture: A HUQ.

Minister of Jute, Land Administration, Local Government, Rural Development and Co-operatives: KAZI ANWARUL HAQUE.

Minister of Public Works and Urban Development: Dr. MD. ABDUR RASHID.

Minister of Planning and Commerce: Dr. MIRZA NURUL HUDA.

Minister of Health, Population Control and Labour: Dr. MOHAMMAD IBRAHIM.

Minister of Relief and Rehabilitation: BENITA ROY.

Minister of Industries: A. K. M. HAFIZUDDIN.

DEFENCE

Chief of Army Staff: Maj.-Gen. ZIAUR RAHMAN.

Chief of Naval Staff: Rear-Admiral MOSHARRAFF HOSSAIN KHAN.

Chief of Air Staff: Air Vice-Marshal MUHAMMAD KHADEMUL BASHAR.

POLITICAL PARTIES

In August 1975 President Mushtaq Ahmed banned all political parties and disbanded the Bangladesh Awami League. Normal political activities were to be resumed in August 1976.

DIPLOMATIC REPRESENTATION

HIGH COMMISSIONS AND EMBASSIES ACCREDITED TO BANGLADESH

(Dacca, unless otherwise stated)

Afghanistan: House 161, Road 13/2, Dhanmandi; *Chargé d'Affaires:* FASSIHUDDIN ZIA.

Algeria: Hanoi, Viet-Nam.

Argentina: Hotel Intercontinental, Room 703 & 934; *Chargé d'Affaires:* NICOLAS ADRIAN SONSCHEIN.

Australia: Hotel Purbani, 9th Floor; *High Commissioner:* P. J. FLOOD.

Austria: New Delhi, India.

Belgium: Plot 40, Rd. 21, Block B, Banani; *Ambassador:* MARCEL VAN ROEY.

Bhutan: New Delhi, India.

Bulgaria: House 12, Rd. 127, Gulshan Model Town; *Ambassador:* DIMO KAMBOUROV.

Burma: Plot 38, Rd. 11, Banani; *Ambassador:* THIRI PYANCHI SITHU U MAUNG MAUNG.

Canada: House 69, Rd. 3, Dhanmandi R/A; *High Commissioner:* J. S. GODSELL.

China, People's Republic: Plot NE(L)6, Rd. 83, Gulshan; *Ambassador:* CHUANG YEN.

Cuba: New Delhi, India.

Czechoslovakia: House CWS/A-12, 71 Gulshan Ave., Gulshan Model Town; *Ambassador:* ADOLF PANZ.

Denmark: House NW(K) 21, Rd. 55, Gulshan; *Ambassador:* HENNING HALCK.

Egypt: House NE(N)-9, Rd. 90, Gulshan; *Ambassador:* MOHAMMAD WAFAA HEGAZI.

Finland: New Delhi, India.

France: Hotel Purbani, 9th Floor; *Ambassador:* ROBERT DUVAUCHELLE.

Gabon: Paris, France.

German Democratic Republic: 32/34, Rd. 74, Gulshan Model Town; *Ambassador:* WOLFGANG BAYERLACHER.

Germany, Federal Republic: House Kalpana 7, Green Rd., Dhanmandi R/A; *Ambassador:* Dr. W. A. RITTER.

Ghana: New Delhi, India.

Greece: New Delhi, India.

Hungary: House 10, Rd. 9, Gulshan Model Town; *Ambassador:* LAJOS BOZI.

India: House 120, Rd. 2, Dhanmandi R/A; *High Commissioner:* SAMAR SEN.

Indonesia: CWS(A) 10, 75 Gulshan Ave., Rd. 30; *Ambassador:* EFFENDI NUR.

Iran: House CWS-77B, Rd. 24, Gulshan; *Ambassador:* KIUMARS VAZEEN.

Iraq: House 64, Gulshan Ave.; *Chargé d'Affaires:* Dr. SAAD AL-KHAFAGI.

Italy: 18/A New Eskaton Rd.; *Ambassador:* LUDOVICO BARATTIERI DI SAN PIETRO.

Japan: 1 Shantinagar; *Ambassador:* ICHIRO YOSHIOKA.

Korea, Democratic People's Republic: Road 115, House CEN(H) 38, Gulshan Model Town; *Ambassador:* YU SONG JIN.

Korea, Republic: House 533, Rd. 8, Dhanmandi; *Chargé d'Affaires:* HAE HON JONG.

Kuwait: House 143-B, Rd. 5, Dhanmandi; *Ambassador:* SAUD ABDUL AZEEZ AL-HUMAIDHI.

Libya: House CWN(C)-4, Gulshan Ave.; *Ambassador:* ALI HUSSEIN ALGHADAMSI.

Malaysia: House 14, Rd. 113, Gulshan; *High Commissioner:* ISMAIL AMBIA.

Mauritius: New Delhi, India.

Mongolia: New Delhi, India.

Nepal: House 17, Rd. 59, Gulshan Model Town; *Ambassador:* HARKA BAHADUR THAPA.

Netherlands: House 17, Rd. 59; *Ambassador:* Dr. F. VAN DONGEN.

New Zealand: New Delhi, India.

Norway: New Delhi, India.

Pakistan: Hotel Purbani, Room 816; *Ambassador:* MOHAMMED KHURSHID.

Poland: House CWN/B-21, Rd. 44, Gulshan; *Ambassador:* Dr. STANISŁAW GUGALA.

Romania: 126 Gulshan Ave., Rd. 111; *Ambassador:* IOSIF CHIVU.

Saudi Arabia: *Ambassador:* (vacant).

Singapore: New Delhi, India.

Spain: New Delhi, India.

Sweden: 73 Gulshan Ave., Gulshan Model Town; *Ambassador:* LENNARD FINNMARK.

Switzerland: House 47, Rd. 41, Gulshan Model Town; *Ambassador:* ETIENNE SUTER.

Thailand: 138 Gulshan Ave.; *Ambassador:* SURACHIT KHANITHANON.

U.S.S.R.: NE(J) 9, Rd. 79, Gulshan; *Ambassador:* V.P. STEPANOV.

United Kingdom: DIT Bldg. Annexe; *High Commissioner:* BARRY SMALLMAN.

U.S.A.: Adamjee Court, Motijheel; *Ambassador:* DAVID E. BOSTER.

Vatican City: House NW(K) 9, Rd. 50, Gulshan; *Ambassador:* Most Rev. EDWARD CASSIDY.

Viet-Nam: New Delhi, India.

Yugoslavia: House 14, Rd. 9, Gulshan Model Town; *Ambassador:* Dr. DEJAN KOSTIC.

Bangladesh also has diplomatic relations with Barbados, Brazil, Iceland, Lebanon, Luxembourg, Mexico, Oman, the Philippines, Portugal, Sudan, Tunisia, the United Arab Emirates and the People's Democratic Republic of Yemen.

JUDICIAL SYSTEM

Chief Justice of Bangladesh: Justice SYED A. B. MAHMUD HOSSAIN.

Note: See also under the Constitution.

RELIGION

According to preliminary results of the 1974 census, over 85 per cent of the population are Muslims, the rest are caste Hindus, scheduled castes, Buddhists, Christians and tribals.

Complete freedom of religious worship is guaranteed under the Constitution (q.v.).

CHURCH OF BANGLADESH

The Bishop of Dacca: Rt. Rev. J. D. BLAIR.

ROMAN CATHOLIC CHURCH

Archbishop of Dacca: Most Rev. THEOTONIUS AMAL GANGULY, C.S.C., Archbishop's House, Dacca 2.

THE PRESS

PRINCIPAL DAILIES

BENGALI

Azad: 27A Dhakeswari Rd., Dacca; f. 1936; Editor ZAINUL ANAM KHAN; circ. 30,000.

Dainik Azadi: Anderkilla, Chittagong; f. 1960; Editor MOHAMMAD KHALED; circ. 10,000.

Dainik Bangla: 1 D.I.T. Ave., Dacca; f. 1964; Editor NURUL ISLAM PATWARI; circ. 40,000.

Ittefaq: 1 Ram Krishna Mission Rd., Dacca 3; f. 1955; Editor ANWAR HOSSAIN; circ. 130,000.

Sanghad: 263 Bangshal Rd., Dacca 1; f. 1950; AHMADUL KABIR; circ. 10,000.

ENGLISH

Bangladesh Observer: Observer House, 33 Toynbee Circular Rd., Dacca 2; f. 1948; Editor OBAIDUL HAQ; circ. 30,000–45,000.

Bangladesh Times: 81 Motijheel Rd., Dacca; f. 1974; Editor ENAYETULLAH KHAN; circ. 20,000.

People's View: 129 Panchlaish Residential Area, Chittagong; Editor NURUL ISLAM; circ. 5,000.

PERIODICALS

(Dacca unless otherwise stated)

BENGALI

Ahmadfi: 4 Bakshibazar; fortnightly; Editor MOHD FAZLUL KARIM MOLLAH.

Arafat: 86 Qazi Alauddin Rd., weekly; Editor M. A. BARI.

Begum: 66 Lyall St., women's weekly; Editor NURJAHAN BEGUM; circ. 15,000.

Bichitra: 1 D.I.T. Ave.; f. 1972; weekly; Editor NURUL ISLAM PATWARI; circ. 30,000.

Chitrali: film weekly; Editor SYED MOHAMMAD PARVEZ; circ. 60,000.

Purbani: film weekly; Editor SHAHADAT HOSSAIN; circ. 60,000.

Saogat: 66 Lyall St.; monthly; Editor M. NASIRUDDIN.

ENGLISH

Bangladesh Gazette: weekly; government publication.

Bulletin of Statistics: monthly.

Financial Times: monthly.

Holiday: 40/1 Naya Pattan, 2; f. 1965; Editor FAZAL M. KAMAL.

New Economic Times: weekly.

Saturday Post: weekly; Editor HABIBUL BASHAR.

NEWS AGENCIES

Bangladesh Sangbad Sangasta (*Bangladesh News Agency*): Dacca.

Eastern News Agency (E.N.A.): Dacca.

PUBLISHERS

Adeylebros & Co.: 60 Patuatuly, Dacca 1.

Anwari Publications: 5/1 Simson Rd., Dacca 1.

Banga Sahitya Bhavan: 144 Government New Market, Dacca-5; f. 1950; school and college textbooks, general literature, etc.; Chief Editors A.-H. HASHEM KHAN, A. MASUD KHAN.

Biswakosh: 316 Government New Market, Dacca.

Boighar: 149 Government New Market, Dacca.

Chalantika: 177 Government New Market, Dacca.

Continental Publications: 18-19, Dhanmandi Hawkers Market, Dacca 5; f. 1957; publishers, importers and distributors of scientific and technical books; Chief Exec. M. A. NOOR.

Crescent Publishers: 77 Patuatuly, Dacca 1.

Kitabistan: 3 Liaquat Ave., Dacca.

Lekha Prokashani: 18 Pyaridas Rd., Dacca 1.

Mowla Bros.: Bangla Bazar, Dacca 1.

Mullick Bros.: 3/1 Bangla Bazar, Dacca; textbooks and schoolbooks.

Oxford University Press: P.O.B. 88, 114 Motijheel C.A., Dacca; f. 1952; academic and educational; Man. M. ISLAM.

Pak Kitab Ghar: 39 Patuatuly, Dacca.

Paramount Book Corporation: Ashraf Chamber, 66 Bangabandhu Ave., Dacca 2; Administrator D. H. KHONDKER.

PUBLISHERS ASSOCIATION

The Bangladesh Publishers and Booksellers Association: 3rd Floor, 3/12 Liaquat Ave., Dacca 1; Sec. Z. I. KHAN.

RADIO AND TELEVISION

RADIO

Radio Bangladesh: 28A Rd. 2, Dhanmondi Residential Area, Dacca 5; f. 1971; 6 regional stations broadcast 88 hours on week-days, 92 hours on Sundays; external service broadcasts 11 programmes daily in 8 languages; Dir.-Gen. M. YAHIA KHAN.

There are five main stations in addition to Dacca: Rajshahi, Chittagong, Sylhet, Rangpur, Khulna.

TELEVISION

Bangladesh Television (BTV): Television Bhavan, P.O.B. 456, Rampura, Dacca; f. 1964, under state control since 1971; daily broadcasts from Dacca Station of 4½ hours; experimental transmissions at Natore Station; stations under construction at Chittagong, Sylhet and Jessore; Dir.-Gen. AMIR-UZ-ZAMAN KHAN.

FINANCE

BANKING

Central Bank

Bangladesh Bank: Motijheel Commercial Area, Dacca 2; f. 1972; Gov. A. A. K. H. Ahmed.

COMMERCIAL BANKS

In 1972 all 12 commercial banks were nationalized and six incorporated banks established:

Agrani Bank: 9 Dilkusha Commercial Area, Dacca 2; 289 brs.; cap. 30m. taka, res. 10.5m. taka (1973); Chair./ Man. Dir. M. Fazlur Rahman.

Janata Bank: 1 Dilkusha Commercial Area, Dacca 2; 310 brs.; cap. 30m. taka, res. 25m. taka (1974); Man. Dir. Mushfeq-us-Saleheen.

Pubali Bank: 24-25 Dilkusha Commercial Area, Dacca 2; 173 brs.; cap. p.u. 20m. taka, dep. 162m. taka (Dec. 1974); Man. Dir. M. Khaled.

Rupali Bank: 34 Dilkusha Commercial Area, Dacca 2; 213 brs.; cap. 30m. taka, res. 3.6m. taka (1973); Man. Dir. Abdul Wahed.

Sonali Bank: Motijheel Commercial Area, Dacca 2; 360 brs.; cap. 30m. taka, dep. 2,102m. taka (1973); Man. Dir. K. A. Rashid.

Uttara Bank: 42 Dilkusha Commercial Area, Dacca 2; 72 brs.; cap. 20m. taka, dep. 718m. taka (1973); Man. Dir. Ruhul Amin.

Foreign Banks

American Express International Banking Corpn.: Dacca, Chittagong.

Chartered Bank: Dacca, Chittagong.

Grindlays Bank: Dacca (4 brs.), Chittagong, Khulna.

United Bank of India: Barisal, Bogra, Brahmanbaria, Chandpur.

DEVELOPMENT FINANCE ORGANIZATIONS

House Building Finance Corporation: HBFC Bldg., 22 Purana Paltan, Dacca 2; f. 1952; provides credit facilities at low interest for house-building; cap. authorized 100m. taka (subscribed by the Bangladesh Government) credit facilities exist in 129 towns and villages, 4 zonal offices and 10 regional offices; Dir. K. M. E. Subhan.

Bangladesh Agricultural Bank: 84 Motijheel Commercial Area, Dacca 2; Man. Dir. Hemayetuddin Ahmed.

Bangladesh Industrial Bank: 4-6 Floor, Agrani Bank Building, Motijheel Commercial Area; Dir. A. H. M. Kamaluddin.

Bangladesh Shilpa Rin Sangstha: 1-2 Floor, Agrani Bank Building, Motijheel Commercial Area, Dacca 2; Man. Dir. A. N. M. Sulaiman.

Bangladesh Small Scale Industries Corporation: 137 Motijheel Commercial Area, Dacca 2; Chair. and Man. Dir. M. Ayubur Rahman.

INSURANCE

The Bangladesh Government in August 1972 set up a National Insurance Corporation together with four subsidiary corporations (*see* below) to regulate all national and foreign general and life insurance companies.

Only two nationalized insurance companies are now operating:

Shadharan Bima: Motijheel Commercial Area, Dacca; government-owned.

Jiban Bima: Motijheel Commercial Area, Dacca; government-owned.

Foreign Insurance Companies

Guardian Assurance Group: Ispahani Building, 14/15 Motijheel, P.O.B. 42, Dacca 2; Man. M. M. Z. Mogri.

Royal Insurance Co. Ltd.: 47 Motijheel, Dacca 2; Branch Sec. M. A. Shah; agent for *London & Lancashire Insurance Co. Ltd.*

Queensland Insurance Co. Ltd.: Adamjee Court, Motijheel, Dacca 2; Branch Sec. N. Palmer.

American International Underwriters Insurance Co. Ltd.: American Life Building, 18/20 Motijheel, Dacca 2; Man. S. K. Hussein; agent for *New Hampshire Insurance Co. Ltd.*

Norwich Union Fire Insurance Society Ltd.: 10K Motijheel, Dacca 2; Man. M. G. Kebria; agent for *Scottish Union and Maritime Insurance Cos Ltd.*

Home Insurance Co. Ltd.: 31 Banglabandhu Ave., Dacca; Man. G. Falleiro.

South British Insurance Co. Ltd.: c/o Finlay House, Agrabad, Chittagong; Man. B. M. Kadwani.

TRADE AND INDUSTRY

In 1972 the Government took over all cotton, jute and other major industrial enterprises and the tea estates. Management Boards are appointed by the Government.

GOVERNMENT SPONSORED ORGANIZATIONS

Bangladesh Engineering and Shipbuilding Corporation: Shilpa Bhaban, 4th Floor, Motijheel Commercial Area, Dacca; Chair. A. S. Noor Mohammad.

Bangladesh Fertilizer, Chemical and Pharmaceutical Corporation: Shilpa Bhaban, 2nd Floor, Motijheel Commercial Area, Dacca; Chair. Mofizur Rahman.

Bangladesh Fisheries Development Corporation: 24/25 Dilkhusha Commercial Area, Dacca 2; f. 1964; Chair. A. Latif.

Bangladesh Food and Allied Industries Corporation: Amin Court, 4th Floor, Motijheel Commercial Area, Dacca; f. 1972; Chair. Mohammad Ali.

Bangladesh Forest Industries Development Corporation: 28 Banglabandhu Ave., Dacca; Chair. Brig. (Rtd.) M. R. Majumdar.

Bangladesh Oil and Gas Corporation: 122/124 Motijheel Commercial Area, Chamber Building, Dacca.; Chair. Dr. Habibur Rahman.

Bangladesh Paper and Board Corporation: Shilpa Bhaban, 3rd Floor, Motijheel Commercial Area, Dacca 2; f. 1972; Chair. Mofizur Rahman.

Bangladesh Steel Mills Corporation: Jiban Bima Bhaban, 24 Motijheel Commercial Area, Dacca; Chair. A. S. Noor Mohammad.

Bangladesh Sugar Mills Corporation: Shilpa Bhaban, 6th Floor, Motijheel Commercial Area, Dacca; Chair. Mohammad Ali.

Bangladesh Tanneries Corporation: 74 Dilkhusha Commercial Area, Dacca; Chair. Mofizur Rahman.

Bangladesh Textile Industries Corporation: Shadaran Bima Bhaban, 33 Dilkhusha Commercial Area, Dacca; f. 1972; Chair. A. T. M. Shamsul Huq.

Trading Corporation of Bangladesh: R.B.F.C. Bldg., 22 Purana Paltan, Dacca 2; f. 1972; Chair. A. K. M. HEDAYETUL HUQ.

Export Promotion Bureau: 122-124 Motijheel Commercial Area, Dacca 2; f. 1972; under the Ministry of Commerce and Foreign Trade; regional offices in Chittagong, Khulna and Rajshahi; Dir.-Gen. M. MOKAMMEL HUQ.

Planning Commission: Planning Commission Secretariat, Eden Bldgs., Dacca; f.1 972; responsible for all aspects of economic planning and development including the preparation of the Five Year Plans and annual development programmes (in conjunction with appropriate government ministries), promotion of savings and investment, compilation of statistics and evaluation of development schemes and projects; Chair. (vacant).

CHAMBERS OF COMMERCE

Agrabad Chamber of Commerce and Industry: P.O.B. 70, Chamber Building, Bangabandhu Rd., Chittagong; Pres. M. A. ANWAR.

Bogra Chamber of Commerce and Industry: Jhawtala Rd., Bogra; Pres. AMJAD HOSSAIN TAJMA.

Chittagong Chamber of Commerce and Industry: Chamber House, Agrabad Commercial Area, Chittagong; f. 1963; 2,319 mems.; Pres. A. M. ZAHIRUDDIN KHAN.

Dacca Chamber of Commerce and Industry: 65–66 Motijheel Commercial Area, Dacca 2; f. 1960; 680 mems.; Pres. K. A. SATTAR.

Khulna Chamber of Commerce and Industry: 49 Haji Ali Rd., Khulna; f. 1934; Pres. H. R. KHONDKER.

Narayanganj Chamber of Commerce and Industry: Chamber Building (2nd Floor), 122-124 Motijheel C.A., Dacca; Narayanganj Office: 137 Bangabandhu Sharak; Pres. RASHID AHMED.

Rajshahi Chamber of Commerce and Industry: P.O. Ghoramara, Rajshahi; f. 1960; 48 mems.

Sylhet Chamber of Commerce and Industry: Lal Digirpar, Sylhet.

TRADE ASSOCIATIONS

Bangladesh Jute Association: 937 Bangabandhu Rd., Narayanganj; Chair. M. S. ALI.

Bangladesh Jute Export Corporation: 14 Topkhana Road, Dacca-2; f. 1972; Chair. BADRUDDIN AHMED.

Bangladesh Tea Board: 111/113 Motijheel Commercial Area, Dacca 2; Chair. JAMSHED ALI.

CO-OPERATIVE

Chattagram Bahini Kalyan Shamabaya Samity Ltd.: 70 Agrabad Commercial Area, Osman Court, Chittagong; f. 1972.

MAJOR INDUSTRIAL COMPANIES

Ashuganj Fertilizer and Chemical Co. Ltd.: Ellal Chamber, 11 Motijheel Commercial Area, Dacca 2; urea and ammonia fertilizer producers.

Jute Trading Corporation Ltd.: Agrami Bank Bldg., Motijheel C/A, Dacca 2; f. 1967; raw jute; Dir. BADRUDDIN AHMAD.

Karim Jute Mills Ltd.: Karim Chambers, 99 Motijheel Commercial Area, Dacca; jute products; Dir. ABDUL GHANI AHMED; 3,200 employees.

Pharmapak Laboratories Ltd.: 26 Tejgaon Industrial Area, Dacca; pharmaceuticals; Man. Dir. ABDUS SATTAR.

Other industries presently in operation include the Bangladesh metal tools and machinery complex at Dacca, an oil refinery at Chittagong, natural gas plants at Sylhet and Titas, Chattack, Rashidpur, Kailash Tila, Haluganj and Ashuganj, a cement factory at Chattack, the Khulna shipyard, as well as petrochemical and pharmaceutical plants at Fenchuganj and Ghorasal.

TRANSPORT

RAILWAYS

Railway Division, Ministry of Communication.

The Bangladesh Railway Board was dissolved in 1973 and the Railway Division in the Ministry of Communication established for policy-making and government control of the railway system. The railway system consists of 1,786 route miles.

ROADS

There are approximately 2,340 miles of surfaced roads and about 1,014 miles of unsurfaced roads; 425 miles of road are under construction.

Bangladesh Road Transport Corporation: D.I.T. Ave., Dacca; land transportation services.

INLAND WATERWAYS

In Bangladesh there are some 5,000 miles of navigable waterways on which are located the main river ports of Dacca, Narayanganj, Chandpur, Barisal and Khulna. A river steamer service connects these ports several times a week.

Bangladesh Inland Water Transport Corporation: 6 Dilkusha Commercial Area, Dacca 2; water transportation services.

SHIPPING

The chief ports are Chittagong and Chalna. Vessels of up to 575 ft. in overall length can be manoeuvred on the Karnaphuli river. A modern seaport is being developed at Mangla.

Bangladesh Shipping Corporation: 28/1 Toynbee Circular Rd., Motijheel Commercial Area, P.O.B. 53, Dacca-2; f. 1972; maritime shipping line; Chair. and Man. Dir. Capt. Q. A. B. M. RAHMAN.

Bangladesh Steam Navigation Co. Ltd.: Batali Hills, Chittagong; coastal services; Chair. A. K. KHAN; Man. Dir. A. M. Z. KHAN.

Chittagong Port Trust: Saltgola, Chittagong; provides bunkering and lighterage facilities as well as provisions and drinking water supplies.

CIVIL AVIATION

Dacca and Chittagong are international airports. There are also airports at all major towns.

Biman (*Bangladesh Airlines*): Biman Bhaban, Motijheel Commercial Area, Dacca 2; f. 1972; fleet of 8 Fokker Friendships and 2 Boeing 707s. Domestic service covers all major towns; flights to Calcutta and Kathmandu; international services from Dacca to Bangkok, Dubai and London.

DEFENCE

Armed Forces (1975): Total strength 36,000; army 30,000; navy 500; air force 5,500; military service is voluntary.

Equipment: The army has 5 infantry brigades, one tank regiment, 3 artillery regiments. The air force has 14 combat aircraft, 7 Russian and 7 American (little equipment is operational).

Defence Expenditure: The defence budget for 1975/76 is 752 million taka.

EDUCATION

In 1972 the Government set up an Education Commission with the aim of effecting radical reforms in the system of education. The main purpose of the reforms will be to help meet the manpower needs of the country by stressing primary, technical and vocational education.

The administration and organization of the educational system in Bangladesh, run by both public and private enterprise, is the responsibility of the Department of Education. Education is not compulsory but the Government provides free primary education for five years. Secondary schools and colleges in the private sector vastly outnumbered Government institutions: in 1975 Government high schools comprised 3 per cent of the country's total, whilst only 34 colleges, out of a total of 626, were Government-owned.

UNIVERSITIES

Bangladesh Agricultural University: Mymensingh; 277 teachers, 2,600 students.

Bangladesh University of Engineering and Technology: Ramna, Dacca; 209 teachers, 1,737 students.

University of Chittagong: University Post Office, Chittagong; 204 teachers, 2,705 students.

University of Dacca: Ramna, Dacca; 722 teachers, 12,879 students.

Jahangirnagar University: Savar, Dacca; 96 teachers, 689 students.

University of Rajshahi: Rajshahi; 312 teachers; 7,382 students.

BIBLIOGRAPHY

AHMAD, NAFIS. An Economic Geography of East Pakistan (OUP, London, 2nd edn., 1968).

AYOOB, MOHAMMED, *et al.* Bangla Desh: A Struggle for Nationhood (Vikas Publications, Delhi-Bombay-London, 1970).

HAFEEZ, ZAIDI S. M. The Village Culture in Transition: a Study of East Pakistan Rural Society (Honolulu: East-West Center Press, 1971).

KHAN, AZIZUR RAHMAN. The Economy of Bangladesh (London, 1972).

LOSHAK, DAVID. Pakistan Crisis (Heinemann, London, 1972).

NAVLAKHA, SUREN. "Emergence of Bangladesh" in *Studies in Asian Social Development* No. 2 (Vikas Publishing House, Delhi-Bombay, 1974).

RAPER, ARTHUR F. Rural Development in Action (Cornell University Press, Ithaka-London, 1970).

ROBINSON, E. A., and GRIFFIN, KEITH (Editors). The Economic Development of Bangladesh within a Socialist Framework (Macmillan, London, 1974).

SIDDIQUI, KALIM. Conflict, Crisis and War in Pakistan (Macmillan, London, 1972).

SOBHAN, REHMAN. Basic Democracies Works Programme and Rural Development in East Pakistan (Bureau of Economic Research, Dacca, 1968).

[*See also Pakistan.*]

Bhutan

PHYSICAL AND SOCIAL GEOGRAPHY

B. H. Farmer

Bhutan is situated between the high Himalayas and the Ganges Plains, between India and China's Tibetan territory. It extends approximately from 26° 45′ to 28° 20′ north latitude, and from 88° 50′ to 92° 05′ east longitude, covering 46,800 square kilometres (18,000 square miles).

PHYSICAL FEATURES

Bhutan's physiography is similar to that of Nepal, the Terai belt being known here, as in nearby Bengal and Assam, as the Duars. From them the outermost ranges rise abruptly; then range piles upon range till, as in Nepal the snow-capped ranges are reached. There are a series of striking transverse gorges, useful as gateways.

CLIMATE

It is difficult to be precise in the absence of reliable data. Darjeeling, at 2,250 metres (7,376 ft.) between Nepal and Bhutan, moves from 4.4°C (40°F) (mean January) to 17°C (62°F) (mean July); and receives 305 cm. (123 inches) of rainfall in an average year, over 255 cm. (100 inches) between June and September).

SOILS AND NATURAL RESOURCES

There is little reliable scientific information on soils. In the Himalayas natural soils are likely to be thin, skeletal and poor (though improved by terracing), better soils being confined to valley bottoms and the Duars.

Vegetation (and the widespread clearing thereof) shows similarities with eastern Nepal.

Bhutan has not revealed mineral deposits of any importance, though there is a proposal to mine coal in the south-east of the kingdom.

POPULATION AND ETHNIC GROUPS

Bhutan's first census was conducted in November and December 1969. It revealed a total population of 1,034,774. This population is unevenly distributed, being densest along valleys in the Duars.

In Bhutan the Bhutias seem to be the indigenous people, but there have been many contacts with Tibet, and there are numerous Nepalese settlers in the Duars.

HISTORY

the late Dorothy Woodman

(Revised by the Editor)

Bhutan's high valleys lying between the foothills of Assam and West Bengal to the south and the Tibetan plateau to the north have made this the most isolated of all Himalayan countries, and her history the least recorded. The larger monasteries and forts were built in the sixteenth century and there is evidence, mainly in manuscripts found in Tibetan monasteries, of an earlier period. The first King—he was called the Dharma Raja—was a lama, Sheptoon La-Pha, and he gave the country some political entity in the seventeenth century. His successor, Doopgein Sheptoon, appointed governors of territories (penlops) and governors of forts (jungpens) to administer the country. The third Dharma Raja, probably influenced by Tibet, conceived the idea of separating temporal and spiritual authority. Henceforth, until the present century, the Dharma Raja fulfilled only a spiritual role and appointed a dewan, later to be known as the Deb Raja, to exercise temporal rule.

The country, divided among a number of warring chieftains, acquired importance in 1771 when the Court of Directors of the East India Company suggested that the exploration of Assam and Bhutan might disclose fresh channels for British trade. The Collectors of Rangpur and Cooch Behar were instructed to ascertain the prospects of Bhutan as a market for British goods and, later, as a through route to Lhasa. A number of Missions followed, the most famous of which was led by Bogle. They were rebuffed by the Bhutanese who had their own less organized methods of barter in the Duars. In 1775 the Bengal Government ordered Mr. Purling to secure the possession of all cultivated tracts extending to the foothills and to consider the hills as the frontier. When Assam was occupied in 1826, after the first Anglo-Burmese war, the frontier with Bhutan became a more serious affair. More Missions were sent to Bhutan. They became increasingly unwelcome and Bhutanese officials responded to British arrogance with crude behaviour. The Eden Mission of 1864 was a complete failure which led to the annexation of the Bengal Duars and the Anglo-Bhutanese war. The British had vastly superior military organization and military forces and it was only the extremely difficult mountainous country which made them decide not to annex Bhutan. By the Treaty signed at Sinchula Pass near the Indian border in 1865 Bhutan agreed to the formal cession of the Duars to British India in return for an annual subsidy to be paid from the revenues of the ceded territory. This comprised an area of rich lands 215 miles in length with an average of about 22 miles in width. In 1910, a new Anglo-Bhutanese Treaty was signed which placed all foreign relations under the supervision of the Indian government. This right passed to India in 1949 with the signing of the Treaty of Friendship between Bhutan and India.

The winds of change began to affect Bhutan during the 1960s, when the King and his officials obtained from India a greater measure of independence. They gained Indian agreement to have their country marked as a separate entity on Indian maps and in 1969, the Tsongdu (National Advisory Council) adopted a resolution calling for entry to the UN. Bhutan was formally admitted to membership of the United Nations on September 21st, 1971. At the same time they recognize the help which India has contributed towards their communications, without which little progress can be made. Jeepable roads now link the valleys of Paro, Thimphu and Tashigong with the plains of Bengal and Assam such that Bhutan now has a network of roads totalling over 1,000 kilometres and the first airfield was inaugurated in March 1968 by Mr. Morarji Desai, India's Deputy Prime Minister.

In 1969 the monarchy became dependent on popular assent, the Tsongdu having voted on an amendment to the Constitution initiated in 1968 by King Jigme Dorji Wangchuk. The Monarch must now seek a vote of confidence every three years, a member can bring a vote of no-confidence at any time, and all adults over seventeen now have the vote. Lamas still play an important role in every part of life, and are as influential as they were in the lives of the Tibetan people in pre-communist days.

On July 21st, 1972, the 43-year-old King Jigme Dorji Wangchuk, who was noted for his reforming zeal and his insistence on the sovereignty of Bhutan, died and was succeeded by the 17-year-old Crown Prince Jigme Singhye Wangchuk. The new King was educated in Bhutan and England and when proclaimed Crown Prince was made Chairman of the Planning Commission. On August 20th King Singhye at a press conference stated that he wished to strengthen friendship with India further, that the Indo-Bhutanese Treaty did not need any review and acknowledged the contribution that Indian technical assistance was playing. (Apart from 400 development experts some 1,000 Indians are assisting in the country's administration.)

In September 1974, after the virtual annexation of Sikkim by India, the Bhutan Government announced that it did not wish to replace its present Indian advisers when their term expires. However, during a four-day visit to Delhi in December 1974, the King stressed that Bhutan will continue to maintain close co-ordination with India in matters of foreign policy and expressed satisfaction with the existing defence and security arrangements.

ECONOMIC SURVEY

In Bhutan, as in the other Himalayan kingdoms, real or suspected needs of strategy have provided a catalyst for the predominantly agrarian economy, for social services and for education. Bhutan's third Five-Year Plan (1972–76) involves expenditure totalling Rs. 355 million of which 93 per cent is being provided by India. The first bank was opened in Phuntsholing at the end of 1968 and a new branch is being built at Thimphu. Bhutan will now print its own money instead of using Indian rupees.

This gentle edging into the modern world of a people who are 95 per cent illiterate will inevitably lead to the growth of national consciousness, of a demand for greater expression of opinion in internal, as well as in external, affairs. Ten years ago there were only 36 primary schools with some 2,500 pupils. By 1973 these figures had increased to over 100 and to more than 16,000 respectively. Moreover a university college is being built at Thimphu during the third Five-Year Plan. In 1972 development projects under construction included a woodwork centre at Paro, weaving centres at Tashigong, Tongsa, Mongar and Thimphu, a bamboo work centre at Shemgong and a nut and bolts factory at Samchi. The principal towns have electricity while the total generated exceeds 1,500 kilowatts and is likely to be doubled during the Third Plan. Internal administration is extending with the growth of communications between high, isolated valleys.

Under Indian sponsorship, Bhutan is now a full member of the Colombo Plan and in 1972 became a member of ECAFE (now ESCAP).

STATISTICAL SURVEY

Area: 18,000 sq. miles (6,000 sq. miles of forests).

Population: 1,034,774 (Census of November-December 1969). Mid-1974: 1,145,000 (UN estimate).

AGRICULTURE

PRINCIPAL CROPS
(FAO estimates, '000 metric tons)

	1972	1973	1974
Rice (paddy)	256	262	268
Wheat	56	58	59
Maize	51	52	54
Barley	7	7	7
Buckwheat	4	4	4
Millet	4	4	4
Mustard seed	2.0	2.1	2.1
Potatoes	30	32	34
Other roots and tubers	5	5	5
Pulses	2	2	2
Tobacco	0.7	0.7	0.7
Jute	4.4	4.6	4.8

Source: FAO, *Production Yearbook 1974.*

Cardamom: 300 metric tons (estimate) in 1971.

LIVESTOCK
(unofficial estimates, '000 head)

	1972*	1973*	1974
Cattle	184	187	191
Pigs	52	53	54
Sheep	37	37	38
Goats	20	20	20
Buffaloes	4	4	4
Horses	17	18	18
Asses	15	16	16*
Mules	7	7	7*
Poultry	94	96	98

* FAO estimates.

Source: FAO, *Production Yearbook 1974.*

Cows' Milk: 11,000 metric tons per year (FAO estimate.)

FINANCE

Bhutanese and Indian currency are both legal tender.
Bhutanese currency: 100 chetrums = 1 ngultrum (Nu).
Coins: 5, 10, 20, 25 chetrums, 1 ngultrum.
Notes: 1, 5 and 10 ngultrums.
Indian currency: 100 paisa = 1 rupee.
Coins: 1, 2, 3, 5, 10, 20, 25 and 50 paisa; 1 rupee.
Notes: 1, 2, 5, 10, 20, 100, 1,000, 5,000 and 10,000 rupees.

Exchange rates (June 1976): 1 ngultrum = 1 rupee; £1 sterling = 16.275 ngultrums of rupees; U.S. $1 = 9.174 ngultrums or rupees.
100 ngultrums or Indian rupees = £6.14 = $10.90.

Note: Since April 1974 Bhutan has issued its own currency, the ngultrum, which is at par with the Indian rupee and circulates with it inside the country. For details of previous changes in the exchange rate, *see* the chapter on India.

BUDGET

Revenue: 1971-72: Rs. 27.5 million; 1972-73: (n.a.).

Expenditure: 1971-72: Rs. 69.1 million; 1972-73: Rs. 71.1 million (proposed); roads, primary education, court and government expenses, construction works and establishment. Privy Purses for Royalty, and expenditure on monasteries, have been settled and curtailed.

OUTLAY BY SECTOR
(Rs. '000)

	1971–72	1972–73 (proposed)
Agricultural Co-operatives	15,780	15,580
Power	5,300	6,250
Industry and Mining	3,000	7,700
Transport and Communications	18,450	15,250
Medical and Social Services	20,930	19,950
Other Sectors	5,600	6,870

DEVELOPMENT PLANS

First Five-Year Plan
(1961–66)

Expenditure: Rs. 106 million.

Second Five-Year Plan
(1966–71)

Expenditure: Rs. 200 million.

(*a*) Micro hydro-electric projects; two have been completed at Thimphu and Paro, and a third is under construction at Wangdiphodrang.
(*b*) Industrial surveys.
(*c*) Horticulture.

Third Five-Year Plan
(1971-76)

Proposed Expenditure: Rs. 350 million.
Note: India is to provide Rs. 330 million.

AID

Up to February 1972 India gave Rs. 351 million to Bhutan in the form of financial aid. Subsidies have also been granted to the value of Rs. 763.7 million to finance projects such as road and bridge construction, an airfield, geological, power and transport surveys and the cost of services.

TRADE

All external trade is with India. The main exports are timber, fruit and coal, while textiles and light equipment are imported. Other export commodities include Bhutan Distillery products such as rum, gin, whisky and liquors; Fruit Preservation Factory products such as orange and pineapple juices, jams and marmalades.

EDUCATION
(1973)

Primary Schools	100
High Schools	2
Public Schools	2
Teachers' Training School	1
Agricultural Colleges	3
Junior Technical School	1
Pupils	16,000

THE GOVERNMENT

Head of State: His Majesty Druk Gyalpo JIGME SINGHYE WANGCHUK (succeeded July 1972).

Royal Advisory Council: Established 1965 and composed of eight members, one representing H.M. the King, two representing the Lamas and five regional representatives of the people.

COUNCIL OF MINISTERS
(*July* 1976)

Minister of Trade, Industry and Forests: H.R.H. NAMGYAL WANGCHUK.

Home Minister: LYONPO TAMJI JAGAR.

Finance Minister: LYONPO CHOGYAL.

Minister of Foreign Affairs: LYONPO DAWA TSERING.

Minister of Communications: LYONPO SANGYE PENJOR.

(*Note:* The last-named also acts as Bhutan's Permanent Representative at the United Nations).

NATIONAL ASSEMBLY

A National Assembly (*Tsongdu*) was established in 1953. The Assembly has a three-year term and meets twice yearly in spring and autumn. Present strength is 150 members, of whom 110 are indirectly elected by village headmen. Ten seats are reserved for the monastery (*see* Religion below) and the remainder are occupied by officials, the ministers, their deputies and the 4 chief justice members of the National Assembly. The Assembly enacts laws, advises on constitutional and political matters and debates all important issues. Both the Royal Advisory Council and the Council of Ministers are responsible to it.

The country was formerly an Absolute Monarchy but H.M. the late King, Jigme Dorji Wangchuk, voluntarily surrendered the absolute powers of the Monarchy to establish a new political system described as "Democratic Monarchy". During 1969 Assembly sessions, the Assembly was made a sovereign body under the following provisions:

1. The right of veto by the King was removed.
2. Full freedom of speech is guaranteed.
3. Power to remove the King at any time by a two-thirds majority vote.
4. A vote of confidence in the King is to be taken every three years and requires a two-thirds majority. In the event of a no-confidence vote, the King is to abdicate but the Wangchuk Dynasty is always to provide the ruler in order of succession.
5. The Assembly has the right to appoint and remove ministers.

The system of government is unusual since power is in effect shared between the monarch, the executive and legislative branches and with the *Jey Khempo* or monastic head of Bhutan's 6,000 Lamas.

LOCAL ADMINISTRATION

Provinces: There are eight Provinces each ruled by a Dzongda (District Officer).

Regions: The revenue is collected by the village headmen and remitted to the District Headquarters.

POLITICAL PARTIES

There are no political parties in Bhutan.

DIPLOMATIC REPRESENTATION

Bangladesh: New Delhi, India.

India: Lungtenzempa, Thimphu; *Representative:* I. B. KHOSLA.

JUDICIAL SYSTEM

Bhutan has a Civil and a Criminal Code.

High Court: Established February 1968 to review Appeals from Lower Courts; 6 Judges.

Appeal Court: The Supreme Court of Appeal is H.M. the King.

Magistrates Courts: All cases are heard by Local Magistrates. Appeals are made to the High Court.

RELIGION

Religion: The population practises a Tibetan form of Buddhism of the Mahayana branch. The sect of Buddhism supported by the dominant race (Bhutias) is the Dukpa (Red-Cap) Sect of Lamaism. Monasteries are numerous. The chief monastery is situated at Tashichho Dzong and contains 1,000 Lamas. There are some 6,000 Lamas in all headed by a monastic head (*Jey Khempo*).

THE PRESS

Kuensel: Weekly government newspaper; in English, Dzongkha and Nepalese.

FINANCE

BANKING

Bank of Bhutan: Head Office at Phuntsholing; brs. at Thimphu, Samdrup Jongkhar and Gaylegphug; f. May 1968 under Royal Charter to provide banking facilities throughout the kingdom of Bhutan. An agreement between the Royal Government of Bhutan and the State Bank of India was concluded in early 1972 under which the State Bank of India became a 40 per cent shareholder of the Bank of Bhutan as from March 1st, 1972; auth. cap. Rs. 5m. and cap. p.u. Rs. 2.5m. (in Indian Rupees and Bhutanese currency in fully paid shares of Rs. 1,000 each). Branches to be opened at Samchi, Chimakothi, Tashigang and Chirang. Board of Directors (comprising 4 Directors, including the Chairman, nominated by the Royal Govt. of Bhutan and 3 Directors, including the Managing Director, nominated by the State Bank of India). Directors nominated by the Bhutan Govt.: H.R.H. ASHI DECHHEN WANGMO WANGCHUCK (Representative of His Majesty in the Ministry of Development), H.R.H. NAMGYAL WANGCHUCK (Minister of Trade, Industry & Forests), DASHO TSHEWANG PENJORE (Royal Advisory Councillor). Directors nominated by the State Bank of India: M. MANDAL, P. K. SEN; Chair. LYONPO CHOGYAL (Minister of Finance, Bhutan); Man. Dir. H. C. VISHNOI (State Bank of India).

INSURANCE

Royal Insurance Corporation of Bhutan: Chair. H.R.H. ASHI SONAM CHHODEN WANGCHUCK; Man. Dir. DASHO UGEN DORJI.

TRANSPORT

ROADS AND TRACKS

Main roads connect India with Western, Central and Eastern Bhutan. They are all fair weather metalled roads. A 90-km. road, completed in 1969, links the east-west road to Thimphu and Paro; also extends to the Ha Valley. A 480-km. east-west lateral road now links Paro and Tashigang. Northern Bhutan has only mule tracks. In 1972 motorable roads totalled 368 kilometres.

Ponies and mules are still the chief means of transport on the rough mountain tracks.

State Transport Department: Phuntsholing; f. 1962; operates a fleet of 31 buses and 52 lorries (1972).

TOURISM

An hotel is planned in Thimphu. Tourists stay in government-run guest houses. Bhutan became more accessible to tourists in 1974 when facilities were improved and the Department of Tourism began arranging package tours.

CIVIL AVIATION

Bhutan's first airport was opened at Paro in March 1968. It is served by DC-3s of Jamair, an Indian airline operating weekly flights from Hashimara (West Bengal) to Paro.

DEFENCE

The 5,000 strong Royal Bhutanese army is under the direct command of the King. Training facilities are provided by an Indian Military Training Team. No reference is made in the Indo-Bhutan Treaty to any aid by India for the defence of Bhutan, but when the Prime Minister of India visited Bhutan in November 1958 he declared that any act of aggression against Bhutan would be regarded as an act of aggression against India.

EDUCATION

In 1968 the first students—18 boys—completed the eleven-year course of free government education. Some of the schools are co-educational and run along the lines of an American private school but using a British syllabus. There are no mission or private schools, all schools in Bhutan being subsidized by the Government. More than 500 Bhutanese students are receiving higher education in India on Indian Government scholarships. Bhutanese students are also receiving higher education and training in various technical fields in Australia, Japan, New Zealand, Singapore and the U.K. There are five main linguistic groups in Bhutan but Dzongkha, spoken in western Bhutan, has been designated the official language. The provision of Bhutanese textbooks is a problem since written languages use Tibetan script.

INDO-BHUTAN TREATY

The political status of Bhutan depends largely on the Treaty of Friendship with India signed on August 8th, 1949.

Treaty of Friendship between the Government of India and the Government of Bhutan.

Article 1 There shall be perpetual peace and friendship between the Government of India and the Government of Bhutan.

Article 2 The Government of India undertakes to exercise no interference in the internal administration of Bhutan. On its part the Government of Bhutan agrees to be guided by the advice of the Government of India in regard to its external relations.

Article 3 In place of the compensation granted to the Government of Bhutan under Article 4 of the Treaty of Sinchula and enhanced by the treaty of the eighth day of January 1910 and the temporary subsidy of Rupees one lakh per annum granted in 1942, the Government of India agrees to make an annual payment of Rupees five lakhs to the Government of Bhutan. And it is further hereby agreed that the said annual payment shall be made on the tenth day of January every year, the first payment being made on the tenth day of January 1950. This payment shall continue so long as this treaty remains a force and its terms are duly observed.

Article 4 Further to make the friendship existing and continuing between the said governments, the Government of India shall, within one year from the date of signature of this treaty, return to the Government of Bhutan about thirty-two square miles of territory in the area known as Dewangiri. The Government of India shall appoint a competent officer or officers to mark out the area so returned to the Government of Bhutan.

Article 5 There shall, as heretofore, be free trade and commerce between the Government of India and of the Government of Bhutan; and the Government of India agrees to grant to the Government of Bhutan every facility for the carriage, by land and water, of its produce throughout the territory of the Government of India, including the right to use such forest roads as may be specified by mutual agreement from time to time.

Article 6 The Government of India agrees that the Government of Bhutan shall be free to import with the assistance and approval of the Government of India, from or through India into Bhutan, whatever arms, ammunition, machinery, warlike materials or stores may be required or desired for the strength and welfare of Bhutan and that this arrangement shall hold good for all time as long as the Government of India is satisfied that the intentions of the Government of Bhutan are friendly and that there is no danger to the Government of India from such importations. The Government of Bhutan, on the other hand, agrees that there shall be no export of such arms, ammunition, etc., across the frontier of Bhutan either by the Government of Bhutan or by private individuals.

Article 7 The Government of India and the Government of Bhutan agree that Bhutanese subjects residing in Indian territories shall have equal justice with Indian subjects and that Indian subjects residing in Bhutan shall have equal justice with the subjects of the Government of Bhutan.

Article 8 (1) The Government of India shall, on demand being duly made by the Government of Bhutan, take proceedings in accordance with the provisions of Indian Extradition Act, 1903 (of which a copy shall be furnished to the Government of Bhutan), for the surrender of all Bhutanese subjects accused of any of the crimes specified in the first schedule of the said Act who may take refuge in Indian territory.

(2) The Government of Bhutan shall, on requisition being duly made by the Government of India, or by any officer authorized by the Government of India in this behalf, surrender any Indian subjects, or subjects of a foreign power, whose extradition may be required in pursuance of any agreement or arrangements made by the Government of India with the said power, accused of any of the crimes specified in the first schedule of Act XV of 1903, who may take refuge in the territory under the jurisdiction of the Government of Bhutan and also any Bhutanese subjects who, after committing any of the crimes referred to in Indian territory shall flee into Bhutan, on such evidence of their guilt being produced as that satisfy the local court of the district in which the offence may have been committed.

Article 9 Any differences and disputes arising in the application or interpretation of this treaty shall in the first instance be settled by negotiation. If within three months of the start of negotiations no settlement is arrived at, then the matter shall be referred to the Arbitration of three arbitrators, who shall be nationals of either India or Bhutan, chosen in the following manner:

(i) one person nominated by the Government of India;
(ii) one person nominated by the Government of Bhutan;
(iii) a Judge of the Federal court or of a High Court of India, to be chosen by the Government of Bhutan, who shall be Chairman.

The judgement of this tribunal shall be final and executed without delay by either party.

Article 10 This treaty shall continue in force in perpetuity unless terminated or modified by mutual consent.

BIBLIOGRAPHY

BHUTAN

CHAKRAVARTI, P. C. India's China Policy (Indiana University Press, Bloomington, 1962).

GORDON, EUGENE. Nepal, Sikkim and Bhutan (Oak Tree Press, London, 1972).

HAAB, ARMIN, and VELLIS, NINON. Bhutan-Fürstenstaat am Götterthron (Mohn. Gütersloh, 1961).

HERMANNS, Father MATTHIAS. The Indo-Tibetans (Fernandes, Bombay, 1954).

KARAN, P. P. Bhutan: A Physical and Cultural Geography (University of Kentucky Press, Lexington, 1967).

KARAN, P. P., and JENKINS, W. M. The Himalayan Kingdoms: Bhutan, Sikkim and Nepal (Van Nostrand, Princeton, 1963).

KUHN, DELIA, and KUHN, FERDINAND. Borderlands (Knopf, New York, 1962).

LAMB, ALISTAIR. The China-India Border: The Origins of the Disputed Boundaries (Chatham House Essays, Oxford University Press, London, 1946).

Asian Frontiers: Studies in a Continuing Problem (Pall Mall Press, London, 1968).

LEIFER, M. Himalaya: Mountains of Destiny (Galley Press, London, 1962).

MEHRA, PARSHOTAM. The Younghusband Expedition. An Interpretation (Asia Publishing House, 1968).

NEBESKY-WOJKOWITZ, RENE VON. Where the Mountains are Gods (Weidenfeld and Nicolson, London, 1956).

PALLIS, MARCO. The Way and the Mountains (Owen, London, 1961).

RUSTOMJI, N. K. Enchanted Frontiers: Sikkim, Bhutan and India's North-Eastern borderlands (O.U.P., London, 1970).

SNELLGROVE, DAVID L. Himalayan Pilgrimage (Bruno Cassirer, Oxford, 1961).

The Sino-Indian Boundary Question (Foreign Language Press, Peking, 1962).

WHITE, CLAUDE. Sikkim and Bhutan: Twenty-One Years on the North-East frontier, 1887–1908 (Arnold, London, 1909).

WOODMAN, DOROTHY. Himalayan Frontiers: a political review of British, Chinese, Indian and Russian rivalries (Barrie and Jenkins, London, 1969).

India

PHYSICAL AND SOCIAL GEOGRAPHY

B. H. Farmer

India is one of the largest countries in the world, with an area of 3,287,590 square kilometres (1,269,000 square miles), including the Indian portion of Jammu and Kashmir, which is disputed between India and Pakistan. India stretches from 8° to 33° 15′ North latitude, and from 68° 5′ to 97° 25′ East longitude. Its northern frontiers are with Tibet (ruled by the People's Republic of China), Nepal and Bhutan. Its great southern peninsula stretches far down into the tropical waters of the Indian Ocean. On the north-west it bounds Pakistan; on the north-east, it borders on Burma. Bangladesh is surrounded on all sides but the south by Indian territory.

PHYSICAL FEATURES

India has three well-marked and, indeed, obvious relief regions: the Himalayan system in the north, the plateaux of the peninsula and, in between, the great plains of the Indus and Ganges basins.

The Himalayan system, between the Tibetan Plateau and the Indo-Gangetic Plains, is made up of complex ranges arranged more or less in parallel, but in places combining and then dividing again, in others (particularly in the highest places) taking on the apparent form of a series of peaks divided by deep gorges rather than that of a range. The Great Himalaya is, in general, just such an array of giant peaks, mostly over 6,100 metres (20,000 ft.) in height, covered by perpetual snows, and nurturing great glaciers which in turn feed the rivers flowing to the Indus, Ganges and Brahmaputra. The southernmost range of the system, the Siwaliks, presents a wall-like margin to the plains; while in the extreme north-east the whole system bends very sharply on crossing the Brahmaputra and forms the wild, forest-clad country of the Naga and other hills on the marches of Burma.

Peninsular India, the "Deccan" or South Country, begins at another, but more broken wall, that fringes the plains to the south, and stretches away to Kanyakumari (Cape Comorin) the southernmost extremity of India. The whole peninsula is built, fundamentally, of ancient and largely (though not entirely) crystalline rocks which have been worn down through long geological ages and now form a series of plateaux, mostly sloping eastward and drained by great rivers, like the Mahanadi, Krishna (Kistna) and Godavari, flowing to the Bay of Bengal. Where plateaux end abruptly their edges present, from the lower plains or plateaux below, the appearance of mountain ranges. This feature is most evident in the Western Ghats, the great scarp overlooking the narrow western coastal plain. Two rivers, the Narmada (Narbada) and Tapti, flow east. Between them, and on east into the jungle country of Chota Nagpur, lies wild hilly territory that has done much to isolate the southern Deccan form the plains through long periods of Indian history. The Garo and Khasi Hills of Meghalaya form a detached piece of plateau country.

In places there are variants on the ancient crystalline-rock plateau theme. Thus, in the northeastern Deccan narrow, down-faulted basins preserve the most important of India's coal measures; while inland of Bombay, and covering most of the State of Maharashtra, great basalt flows have given rise to distinctive countryside with broad open valleys floored by fertile (though difficult) "black cotton soils" separated by flat-topped hills.

The west coast is fringed by a narrow alluvial plain. That on the east coast is generally wider, especially where it broadens out into the highly productive deltas of the great east-flowing rivers.

The Indo-Gangetic Plain, between the Siwaliks and the northernmost plateau-edges of the Deccan, is one of the really great plains of the world. Consisting entirely of alluvium, it presents an appearance of monotonous flatness from the air or, indeed, to the uninitiate traveller on land. In fact, however, its general flatness conceals a great deal of variety. The fine muds and clays of the Ganges-Brahmaputra delta contrast, for instance, with the sands of the Rajasthan Desert at the western extremity of the Indian portion of the plains. Almost everywhere, too, there is a contrast of floodplains (along the rivers) and naturally dry belts, often of older alluvium, well above the reach of even the highest floods.

CLIMATE

"As is well known, the climate of India is dominated by the monsoon; that is, by the seasonal reversal of wind which brings a seasonal change from dry weather to wet." Simple statements like this, though true in a very broad sense, take no account of a great deal of local variation and complexity—not surprising features of a country like India with a vast size and extremely varied relief. Thus, in north India at any rate, there are not two seasons, but three. A "cool season" lasts from December to February, and brings average temperatures of 50–60°F. to Delhi and the Punjab, but with a high diurnal range (from as high as 80°F. by day to freezing point or below at night); and, although this is the season of the "dry" north-east monsoon, depressions from the north-west may bring rain to the Punjab and, indeed, farther down the plains to the east. In the "hot season" of the north, temperatures rise till, in May, the average is 90°–95°F. (as high as 120°F. by day). and rain is very rare. With the "burst" of the monsoon in June and July, temperatures fall and the rains begin, to last till September or October.

In the Ganges delta, to take another regional example, the "cool season" is less cool than in Delhi (67°F. average for January in Calcutta), the hot season less hot (86°F. May average), and the rains much heavier—there is hardly a year in which Calcutta's streets do not suffer serious flooding at least once. The "hot season" is, moreover, punctuated by "mango showers", which are even more significant in Assam.

In the peninsula, the coolness of the "cool season" tends to be diminished as one goes south, as does the striking heat of the "hot season", partly because in places like Bombay temperatures are never as high as in, say, Delhi, partly because, in the far south it is always hot, except where temperatures are mitigated by altitude. In Tamil Nadu, for example, average monthly temperatures vary only from 76°F. in January to 90°F. in May and June. In the peninsula, too, the south-west monsoon brings particularly heavy rains to the westward-facing scarps of the Western Ghats, which receives 200 to 250 cm. (80 to 100 in.) in four months. The dry season also decreases southward till in Kerala, in the far south-west, it lasts for only a month or two. In Tamil Nadu, there is an almost complete reversal of the normal monsoonal rainfall regime: the heaviest rains fall in what, in the north, is the dry season (October to January, inclusive) and the south-west monsoon period is relatively dry (principally because the State lies in the lee of the Western Ghats).

The theme of contrast in Indian climate is best expressed by drawing attention to the tremendous difference between, on the one hand, the deserts of Rajasthan and the rather less dry sands of Ramanathapuram (Ramnad), in southeastern Tamil Nadu, and, on the other, verdant landscapes of the north-eastern Deccan and of Kerala. Sometimes these contrasts are to be seen during a very short journey, such as that from Trivandrum, the capital of Kerala, to Kanyakumari (Cape Comorin) and on into Tamil Nadu.

There is another dominant theme in Indian climate —violence: violent rains and floods when the monsoon bursts, violent rain almost whenever rain falls (so that rapid run-off and soil erosion are almost omnipresent hazards), violent heat and violent wind at least seasonally; and violent fluctuations between wet years and dry years, and between good years and bad years (for extreme climatic variability also characterizes much of India, especially the semi-arid regions). Agriculture in many parts of India is indeed a perpetual gamble with the weather.

SOILS

India unfortunately lacks a good modern soil map compiled on a uniform and scientific basis. Certain general statements, however, may be made. Thus the soils of the Himalayan mountains and plateaux are generally thin, skeletal and infertile, except in intermont basins or in areas of artificial terracing, and therefore artificial depth and fertility. The soils of the peninsula are also generally poor, though for a different reason—that in general they have been derived from long years of weathering from unpromising crystalline rocks. There are, however, noteworthy exceptions—particularly the rich alluvia, with a generally high potential for improvement by means of fertilizers, to be found in the east coast deltas of the Mahanadi, Godavari, Krishna (Kistna) and Kaveri (Cauvery), and the *regur* (black cotton soils) of the basalt areas of Maharashtra. The latter are naturally of quite high fertility and retain moisture (an important property in a monsoon climate especially in the axis of semi-aridity that runs east of the Ghats through Poona) but are sticky, erodible and hard to cultivate when wet, and also difficult to irrigate satisfactorily.

The soils of the plains are, by nature, generally much more fertile than those of the Himalayas or of the Deccan, though this does not apply to the sandier soils that are to be found (for example) in the Rajasthan Desert, or to the leached soils of old alluvial terraces like those on the western margins of the Bengal delta. But infertility has tended to creep in as a result of human occupancy. This is partly, and very widely, a matter of long continued cultivation without adequate manuring, partly a matter of salinity and alkalinity induced by a causal chain that stretches from canal irrigation through rising water-tables to the capillary ascent of salts to the surface. The problem of salinity particularly afflicts the fields of Uttar Pradesh.

VEGETATION

The tremendous variations in rainfall, not to say temperature and relief to be met in India mean that there must have been, far back in time, very wide variations in natural vegetation. These probably ranged from near-desert or even complete desert (in Rajasthan); through thorn scrub (in semi-arid regions like the western Maharashtran Deccan) and tropical dry deciduous forest (in slightly wetter areas lying along a broad crescentic belt from the middle Ganges plains to Hyderabad and Madras) and tropical moist deciduous forest (in the north-east Deccan); to tropical wet evergreen forest, approaching rain forest (along the Western Ghats and in Kerala). There must also have been a complete altitudinal gradation from plains vegetation through deciduous and coniferous forests to montane vegetation in the Himalayas.

But over much of India the hand of man has lain heavily on the vegetation. Little natural vegetation of any sort survives in the plains or in the east and west coast deltas and coastal strips, except in rare groves; or, for that matter, over much of Tamil Nadu or the plateau areas of Maharashtra (apart from the still-forested eastern districts of the latter State). In all these regions, and many more, the landscape is dominated not by natural vegetation but by arable cultivation. Even in apparently uncultivated areas the natural vegetation has been modified out of all recognition. It may well be that much of the Rajasthan Desert is man-made or, at any rate, degraded by man. The savanna-like jungles of parts of central India have developed from denser forest formations by the action of man and his animals. Even the pleasant forests of the north-east Deccan, dominated by *sal* (*Shorea robusta*, a useful timber tree), are often, if not generally, derived from more heterogeneous forests by the action of fire. Not surprisingly, India's forest resources, though not by any means inconsiderable, do not by any means match her needs.

MINERALS

India possesses some of the largest and richest reserves of iron ore in the world. These occur particularly in the north-east Deccan, in the States of Bihar, Orissa and the western part of West Bengal. Other deposits occur farther afield—for example, round Salem, in Tamil Nadu; in Karnataka; and in Goa. Altogether it has been estimated that India has reserves of no less than 22,000 million tons of iron ore. This is ample to supply the country's present industrial needs and to allow of exports to such countries as Japan.

Unfortunately, resources of coal, particularly of coking coal, are much more meagre, though by no means negligible (perhaps 80,000 million tons of poor and medium coals but only 2,500 million tons of coking coals). Some 95 per cent of Indian production, and nearly all of the coking coal, comes from seams in the down-faulted basins in the north-east Deccan to which reference has already been made. It will be appreciated that the bulk of the iron ore reserves are in the same region: this is India's good fortune so long as reserves of coking coal last. Elsewhere, there is a little coal in Assam and lignite in Rajasthan and Tamil Nadu.

Oil and natural gas resources so far known include those of Assam, Gujarat and the sea-floor off Bombay. But India is unlikely ever to be a major producer of oil or gas.

India is rich in the non-ferrous minerals used in alloys, notably in manganese (of which India in most years is the second or third most important producer in the world: ores are found widely-distributed in the Deccan). Other important non-ferrous metals are much more scarce, though some lead is mined in Bihar and some copper in the north-east Deccan. About 75 per cent of the world's mica comes from India, notably from Bihar, Tamil Nadu and Rajasthan.

There is no shortage of building-stone or of the raw materials for the cement industry.

POPULATION

India's population at mid-1975 was estimated to be 598,100,000 (including the disputed territory of Jammu and Kashmir). The rate of increase between 1961 and 1971 was about 2.6 per cent per annum, considerably higher than the prevailing rate in the past. By any standards, large areas of India are now over-populated; economic development is a constant race against population increase; and the control of future growth has become a burning issue and, indeed, a matter of official government policy.

There are great variations in population density in the Indian countryside. There are very high densities of rural population in the rice-growing areas of the lower Ganges plain and in the Bengal delta; in parts of Assam; in parts of the eastern peninsular deltas and around Madras; in Kerala; and in the coastal plains stretching from south of Bombay north into Gujarat. Less spectacular, but still high densities are to be found in the upper Ganges plains and in the Punjab, in Assam, and in Tamil Nadu generally. At the other extreme, low densities occur in the Himalayas and Rajasthan Desert (not surprisingly), in the jungle-covered hills and plateaux of the northeastern Deccan (though these have been invaded by mining, by the iron and steel industry, and by agricultural colonists, refugees from Bangladesh); in inland Gujarat and Saurashtra; and in the marchland-hills that stretch from west to east in the region of the Narmada and Tapti.

India also has its great and growing urban concentrations, especially in and around Bombay, Calcutta and Madras.

ETHNIC GROUPS

The peoples of India are extremely varied in composition. It is not particularly profitable to attempt to divide them into "racial" groups distinguished by physical characteristics (though it may be of interest that representatives of what are often held to be primitive stocks may be met, especially among jungle tribes). It is more profitable to consider the linguistic divisions of the Indian people, particularly since these in large measure form the basis for the current division of the federal Union into States. The languages of north India are of the Indo-Aryan family, the most important member of which is Hindi, the language particularly of Uttar Pradesh and Haryana (now separated by an inter-State boundary from the Punjabi-speaking area to the west). Other members of the family (whose corresponding linguistic States will be readily identified) are Rajasthani, Bihari, Bengali, Oriya and Marathi. In south India the languages are of a quite different family, the Dravidian; and include Tamil (in Tamil Nadu), Malayalam (in Kerala), Telugu (in Andhra Pradesh), and Kannada (in Karnataka). There are also many tribal languages in the jungle areas and Tibetan languages in the Himalayas.

As is well known, Indian society is also divided into castes, each of which is endogamous and into one of which a man or woman enters irrevocably at birth. Status and, to some extent, occupation are still largely determined by caste, and caste considerations enter largely into politics; though the scene is a rapidly shifting one in many regions.

Religion is in India both a divisive and a cohesive force. Communal friction and disharmony are often largely a matter of religion, especially as between Hindus and Muslims in north India. But most of India's peoples, apart from certain tribal groups, are united to a greater or lesser extent by cultural traits and the consciousness of a common heritage, and these derive in very large measure from age-old Hinduism.

HISTORY

Peter Robb*

Hindu India

A mature Indian civilization began, so far as our present knowledge goes, about the middle of the third millenium B.C. About that time, amidst the cultures of the Baluch hills, based on villages of mud brick houses, apparently stable communities occupying sites of not more than two acres, a radically different culture arose in the Indus valley. The sophisticated trading cities which developed are known as the Indus valley or Harappa culture. This civilization extended from Indian Punjab to the Arabian Sea, Gujarat and the Gulf of Cambay. The cities were laid out in grid patterns with efficient drainage systems, writing was practised in a script as yet undeciphered, and trade was carried on by sea with the Sumerians of ancient Iraq. Little is known of their religion, but it may be that this culture provided some of the groundwork of later Hindu civilization. The culture lasted about a thousand years, showing remarkable physical and apparently administrative continuity, until it was suddenly overthrown, probably by the non-urban illiterate Aryan tribes of the Vedic period.

A pastoral people with aristocratic organization, the Aryans spread in migratory waves over Sind and the Punjab, tending their cattle. They also composed hymns to the nature deities, later written down as the *Rg Veda*. These include the beginnings of philosophic reflection and rituals. The people were evidently vigorous and they, or those who followed them, moved on into the Ganges valley. Eventually there arose agriculture and cities, and there was a gradual mixing with the original inhabitants. The Aryans are the first of many invaders from the northwest who (until modern times) have partly been absorbed and partly added to the polyglot nature of Indian society. The special and lasting contribution of the Aryans, however, was that out of a gradual coalescing of tribes into kingdoms, and a diversification of pastoral into specialist occupations, there came eventually a hardening of social divisions into the four classes of priest, warrior, farmer and serf. Racial integration deepened as the tribes continued their move east as far as Bengal. The pastoralists of the Punjab had now become agriculturists, centred on cities with palaces and temples of wood. Even in the early period, before they began to build in brick or stone, the tribes seem to have had skilled bronze smiths. They drove chariots to battle (and must have had the supply of artisans which this required); they had begun to include in their pantheon gods connected with earlier tradition; and they were developing the caste system. The Indo-Aryans had become Hindus. Their heartland remained in the Doab.

India enters the historical period about 600 B.C. There were two major movements at this time. The clash of cults produced a series of universal religions, and organized kingdoms began to develop into empires. In reaction to the ritualism and spell-making of the Brahmins there appeared many protesting sects, from which Jainism and the religion of Gautama the Buddha have survived. Hinduism in response itself underwent radical changes which produced a higher religion.

At the time of the Buddha, Bimbisara had began to consolidate his kingdom, Magadha, an area formerly on the periphery of Aryan influence, to the east of Kasi (Varanasi). After about 494 B.C., Magadha emerged as the first major power of India; it lasted about 150 years, and its territories, in the 4th century B.C., included the Ganges basin and much of the rest of North India. The brief invasion of the northwest by Alexander between about 327 and 325 B.C., provided an opportunity for Candragupta Maurya to overthrow the last of the Magadhan Nandas, and to establish the greatest of the ancient Indian empires, the Mauryan. This empire developed a sophisticated administrative structure and provided a degree of unity to much of North India. Candragupta's grandson, the greatest of the Mauryans (273-232 B.C.), left the earliest contemporary records of significance, which show his rule as humane internally and non-aggressive externally, clearly influenced by Buddhism. Some of the features of a certain strand of Hinduism: non-violence, vegetarianism, pilgrimages, were evident in this period.

Within fifty years of Asoka's death the empire collapsed. For a time by the Sungas of Malwa ruled not a centralized state but, setting the pattern of the future, a loose confederacy of semi-autonomous peoples. The northwest experienced a series of invasions. Meanwhile other kingdoms rose and fell in Orissa, Gujarat and Malwa and in the south.

Out of this confusion, in 320 A.D., arose the second of the great empires: that of the Guptas. In the time of Candra Gupta II the Guptas became the paramount power of India, their realm stretching from the Bay of Bengal to the Gulf of Cambay and far into the north-west. It is generally agreed that ancient India attained its apogee under the Guptas with an efficient bureaucracy. Indian literature reached its peak with the poet Kalidas; art, science, philosophy and law all flourished. It was an age of achievement and consolidation.

Towards the end of the fifth century the White Huns and associated tribes descended on north India, destroying the Gupta empire and all political unity. From this period come many of the customs of Hindus which, in a later age, reformers sought to eradicate, such as *sati* (widow-burning) and tantric practices. Power became localized again.

Muslim India

In the late twelfth century armies of Turkish slaves and Afghan chieftains spilled over into the Ganges valley. Subsequently cut off from Central

* This article is in part a revision of an earlier version by Percival Spear.

Asia by the Mongols, these people were reinforced by some Muslim refugees and mixed with local populations; they set up a military empire, the Delhi sultanate, which came to control, briefly in the fourteenth century, a vast area extending to the Hindu empire of Vijayanagar in the far south. It was succeeded by regional sultanates after the sack of Delhi by Timur (Tamerlane) at the end of the century, until, in the fifteenth, the Lodi Afghans restored Delhi's authority over most of north India. They fell in turn in 1526 to the Mughal ruler of Kabul, Babur, whose successors extended enormously the territory over which they had control. Through a complex system of indirect rule, utilizing existing administrations and officials as much as possible Mughal authority was maintained with a minimum of imperial officials. Thus too the influence of Mughal culture came to be supreme in the Hindu as well as the Muslim elite.

The empire collapsed during the eighteenth century as cohesive forces were weakened. Aurangzib became embroiled in a major war in the Deccan. The situation worsened after his death in 1707, with the sack of Delhi by the Persian ruler, Nadir Shah, in 1739, and with the subsequent establishment of Afghan power in the northwest under Ahmad Shah Abdali. Aurangzib's successors eventually became pensioners of first the Marathas (strong again under Brahmin leadership) and then the British; former Mughal governors, or non-Mughals such as Europeans, Marathas, and the Sikhs under Ranjit Singh, established independent centres of power. Thus the third great Indian empire went the way of its predecessors; like them it left a cultural and political legacy which was obscured but not lost.

British Rule

The British East India Company came to India in Mughal times to trade. In the eighteenth century, however, from insignificant and peripheral trading posts, they began to accumulate territory and then, in Bengal after 1765, to administer one of the Mughal provinces. Later they expanded their territories further to protect those they had already, and then to reach "natural" frontiers taking on the Marathas and later the Sikhs. By the mid-nineteenth century they ruled most of India directly, and all of it was under their ultimate control: theirs was the first empire to achieve this completeness.

But, ignorant of Indian conditions as they were, they had no choice but to follow Mughal precedent and operate a system of indirect administration. Of course, as their power grew, they had to take positive steps to evolve an administrative structure, but government except at the highest levels always remained in Indian hands, and the European ideas that were introduced were always limited in their application by Indian realities. Inevitably, however, British rule tended to strengthen those institutions for which the British found a use, and to innovate (deliberately or unwittingly) in the areas of life in which their influence was greatest, most notably in introducing the Western exclusive notions of both property and sovereignty, and later, Western concepts of the rule of law, legal equality, progress, social justice, nationalism, and representative democracy. That so much remained unchanged, does not alter the fact that much also was transformed.

The need for the co-operation of Indians, not only in the traditional roles of prince and *zamindar*, but also in a modern-style bureaucracy, encouraged deliberate attempts to educate Indians in English so that they could provide the minor officials without whom government as the British conceived it could not function. Moreover, the size and complexity of India meant that the government there, though subordinate to Parliament, had to have independent power to make laws, under the Crown (after 1859) as under the Company.

Some of the British at first thought it their mission to "bring light" to India. Never wholeheartedly part of British policy, such interference came to be especially suspect after the revolt of 1857–58, which temporarily removed British rule from much of north India (though not Punjab), and was interpreted as a conservative reaction to British missionary activities, land revenue policies, and annexation of the last major independent centre of Mughal culture, Awadh (Oudh). In the later nineteenth century *laissez-faire* became the justification for policies, just as utilitarianism had been earlier; but in practice this did not prevent government involvement in economic development, famine relief, tenancy relations, and even social reform. Thus, just as the early revenue settlements and the development of commercial agriculture had subtly distorted the shape of rural society, so after the 1860s the increasingly centralized administration, the long continuation of peace, and the building of telegraphs, railways and canals left their mark on India. India became a market and a source of raw materials rather than a producer of finished goods, and many former centres found themselves without a role in the new economic system; later agricultural production seems to have increased, and the pressure of population to have been offset, until the end of the century, by the growth of the coastal and railway cities and the enlargement of the cultivated area, and yet rising prices seem to have strained the relationships of rural society, and the right to partition and transfer property rights to have disturbed the operation of rural credit, so that in the balance sheet of benefit and loss from British rule some areas and classes fared much worse than others.

From the first there were reactions to the changes and the most important in the long term were on the periphery of Indian society. In the towns the British impact created new classes: those engaged in Western-style commerce, those in government service, and those in professions such as law and medicine and teaching. These people had a number of shared interests which superseded, at least on occasions, caste and communal differences and they found they had much more in common (chiefly the wish for better conditions and opportunities under the British for improvements in municipal administration and for changes in the policy of the central government) with similar people throughout India. If the British did not create Indian unity, then certainly, for these people, they made it necessary. After 1885, with the consolidation of administration at Calcutta, and the development of the press and communications, members of the Western-educated elites began to come together in an annual alliance called the Indian National Congress.

Among parallel elite groups there were social and religious reactions as well. British rule, being non-Islamic, posed a special problem for orthodox Muslims, and, while most adapted themselves, a few took the logical step of regarding India as *dar-al harb* (land of war). Among Hindus, Rammohan Roy's *Brahmo Samaj* (1830) was followed by various movements for social reform, or to achieve the benefits of Western ethics and education without the risks of religious contamination. After 1875 some Muslims followed suit in Sayyid Ahmad Khan's Aligarh movement. In the twentieth century such developments came to involve wider ranges of people. From the late nineteenth century traditional society and religion had turned increasingly back on itself. Lower classes of Muslims came to share a religious training at newly-founded seminaries or to come under the influence of their products; a Hindu revival was marked by renewed interest in popular festivals.

In the nineteenth century the spokesmen to whom the central government listened most easily, for all the careful rapport in the districts between officials and traditional power networks, were naturally those who spoke their language both literally (in English) and metaphorically (in the appeal to a British liberal rhetoric). It was enough for such Indians in their annual Congress debates, that they should stand for India because of their class and education. With successive constitutional changes, however, they began to need wider support, and to justify their role through their popularity, not their talents. Inevitably they came into contact with the popular religious movements. These were new men, even though in many ways they did closely resemble the stalwarts of the Congress (Gokhale, Mehta, Naoroji) in their background and hopes for India, because of their standing with the mainstream of Indian society and the methods of permanent concerted agitation which they were thus able to employ. Such men were succeeded in the twentieth century by Gandhi, who, with a total rethinking of the organization and approach of the Congress, marked also the advent of new regions and levels of politics on the national scene to replace the long dominance of Bombay.

After 1857 the British had shown their determination to hold on to power, by recruiting for the Indian army only from "loyal" classes, by reserving the higher reaches of administration for Europeans, and by demonstrating in a number of other ways that India was a subject empire. But they needed the collaboration of Indians, not least the Western-educated classes, and later their consent to help overcome financial difficulties. Thus they had at least to listen to educated opinion. They were led, thereby, after 1885 to introduce local self-government (with powers to raise local revenue); in 1892, indirectly, and again in 1909 to the concession of the elective principle in choosing who were to advise, though not control, the executive through the legislative councils; and finally between 1915 and 1919 to an even more important breakthrough, public admission that they would have to transfer power (not sovereignty) to Indian hands. In the 1920s and 1930s this promise, by affecting a wide range of policies and because of the radical transformation in Indian politics, was translated into an expectation that the British would relinquish sovereignty as well. The problem then was how to resolve that regional, communal and constitutional disunity which earlier had been seen as justifying the retention of a British ringmaster.

The Indian princes, semi-autonomous rulers of areas vast and small, were a problem that was not so much solved as shelved. The unrepresentative character of the Indian political elite was an argument canvassed by conservatives but not something that could be much diminished while the British continued to fashion a Western-style constitution which emphasized the politician's talents. It was the Muslim problem which had to be solved. Muslims were not one community; but in north India during the late nineteenth century the Urdu-speaking elite began to divide along religious lines, for reasons of linguistic, social and religious competition, while in the twentieth century Muslims increasingly gained at least the semblance of unity among themselves and entered politics as a community even when co-operating with the largely Hindu Congress because of separate Muslims electorates (1909) and through Muslim issues in political agitations. During the last thirty years of British rule, the Congress conducted campaigns (1919–22, 1929–32, 1942) under the leadership of Mohandas Gandhi, using his method of peaceful non-co-operation or civil disobedience (*satyagraha*), though often based locally on local issues and less peaceful methods. In between these campaigns, the Congress participated in the constitution, under dyarchy (the partial transfer of responsibility to Indians, 1919) and provincial self-government (1935). Both the agitation and the politics required mobilization of support, and, especially at local levels, tended to use religious appeals and organization. Thus, though it rested on fundamental differences between the two religions in doctrine and custom, the Muslim sense of danger from the Hindu majority grew as the prospect of majority rule came closer, and this sense was transmitted from the political classes who hoped to inherit British power through the *ulama* to the population at large. The sense was not helped by the Congress insistence, in spite of its definite discipline and programme, that it was an alternative government to the British, and thus superior in status to other political associations; the fact that the dangers were real, at least at the street level, was shown in many savage communal riots, which though due to faults on both sides were obviously more alarming for the community in a minority. In the 1940s, Muslim demands hardened, after the resignation of Congress ministries and its subsequent outlawing because of Gandhi's "Quit India" campaign. The British began to treat the Muslim League, which had at last consolidated its all-India status, as an equal with the Congress. After the war the British believed they could hold India only by force, and they had lost the will for this. Thus, after 1945, the British wanted to go, and when the Muslim League under Jinnah stood in their way, the British Prime Minister, Clement Attlee, and the last Viceroy, the Earl Mountbatten, cut the knot and partitioned the country. The majority Muslim areas, never wholeheartedly behind the League, found themselves yoked, for a time, as a new country: Pakistan.

Independent India

India became an independent Dominion on August 15th, 1947. The new Prime Minister, Jawaharlal Nehru, promised that it now would "awake to life and freedom". His administration, however, was marked by continuity as well as change.

The immediate task was to restore the authority of the government following a rising tide of panic and massacre as refugees fled from one part to the other of divided Punjab. Millions were uprooted and hundreds of thousands killed as the Boundary Force set up by Mountbatten proved wholly inadequate to its task. Both the migration and the enormous death toll have left permanent marks on India and Pakistan, but in the short term order was restored quite quickly. To do so, however, took the life of Gandhi who had rushed to Delhi to try to stop the communal violence, and was assassinated in January 1948 by a Hindu extremist who seems to have considered him too conciliatory to the Muslims. As Nehru told the nation "the light has gone out"; but the shock of Gandhi's death restored it, at least for a time, by discrediting communalists.

It was necessary also to unify the country. When the British left there were 362 princely states, varying enormously in size and population. The British had absolved them from their allegiance to the Crown, but apparently left uncertain their future and even the basis on which a decision about their future would be taken, whether, for example, it should be by the rulers or the governments or the people. But, although in theory a state could opt for independence, or for union with either India or Pakistan, in practice the withdrawal of British suzerainty made the first option difficult (if not impossible) while the second was a real choice only for those states adjacent to the borders between the two new countries. By independence day all but four had acceded to one or the other; and during 1948 the Home Minister, Vallabhbhai Patel, aided by V. P. Menon, bullied and cajoled those which had joined India into being absorbed into the new states of the Indian federation.

Of the princely states which were still aloof, two had Muslim rulers but largely Hindu populations. The ruler of the first, Junagadh (on the Kathiawar coast), finally opted for Pakistan. There were disturbances, Indian troops marched in, and, the prince having fled to Pakistan, the state was united with India after a plebiscite. The Nizam of Hyderabad, the second of these mainly Hindu states and the largest princely domain of British India, had hoped for independence, but this depended (as the state was landlocked) on Indian goodwill, which was not forthcoming. Eventually after an extremist group had taken power in the state, it was invaded by Indian forces and taken into the Indian union. (At the same time Kalat was absorbed by Pakistan).

Kashmir, with its predominantly Muslim population and Hindu ruler, also had remained undecided, until October 1947 when Pathan tribesmen from Pakistan invaded in support of an internal rising. The Maharaja was promptly persuaded to opt for India, whose troops retained for him Jammu (with its Hindu-Sikh majority) and the Vale. A "popular" government was installed under Sheikh Abdullah, with a promise of a plebescite to follow. Later, when the Sheikh quarrelled with the raja, and began to speak of independence, the idea of a plebiscite was dropped, and the Sheikh was removed and imprisoned without trial. India has regarded the state as part of India since 1954 (when the Kashmir assembly proclaimed that it had joined the union) and, although the dispute with Pakistan continues, the border now seems bound to harden more or less along the truce lines arranged by the United Nations after the brief war of 1948, thus leaving most of the territory with India, but with Pakistan the areas overrun in 1947.

Unity was maintained within India firstly through the constitution, which established the union as a secular parliamentary democracy on the Western model, with a federal structure but a strong centre. Jawaharlal Nehru's own wishes were closely reflected in the shape of the administration, though he recognized that, as a whole, the document might cause difficulties in future. In January 1950 India became a republic with a President as its constitutional head, but recognizing the British sovereign as Head of the Commonwealth. There are two Houses of Parliament, the Lok Sabha (House of the People) and the Rajya Sabha (Council of States), the former elected by adult suffrage, the latter representing states' interest. The executive, a Cabinet under a Prime Minister, is responsible to the Lok Sabha; and thus India followed the British model. In other respects, however, the example of the U.S.A. was followed: the Supreme Court is empowered to decide constitutional questions, including those relating to the declaration of fundamental rights which the constitution contains. The diversity of India and a fear of "Balkanization" were reflected, however, in the distribution of functions. The centre controls defence, foreign affairs, railways, ports and currency, and is vested with residuary powers; also, in listed subjects, it can override the states, while the President's emergency powers allow, for example, the suspension of a state government and the imposition of President's rule.

Indian unity was threatened further by reorganization of the former British provinces along linguistic lines. What was conceded to Andhra in 1952–53 was refused to Bombay until 1960 (when Gujarat and Maharashtra were separated) and to Punjab until

1966 (when Haryana was formed out of "Hindu" Pubjab). Nehru had opposed linguistic states but it seems that the limited and gradual responses by the centre to some extent defused separatist tendencies, and that secession can be avoided in spite of the linguistic divisions as long as local interests are served by the union.

The role of English as an official language (scheduled to end in 1965) has been championed by non-Hindi speakers, especially in Tamil Nadu, as a means of preventing Hindi dominance of the civil service and central institutions. Nehru again proved accommodating and promised vernacular examinations for the services and the continuing use of English, thus ensuring that any move to Hindi would be gradual and that Hindi enthusiasts would have to be restrained in the interests of non-Hindi speakers.

The supremacy of the Congress was ensured by the resolution of internal struggles in favour of Nehru, and by campaigns outside it against communalist and communist parties. Through the election of P. N. Tandon as Congress President against the Prime Minister's wishes, Vallabhbhai Patel sought, it seems, to limit his old rival's power and the accretion of influence by the office of Prime Minister, though probably not actually to displace Nehru himself. With Patel's death, and by gathering support in Tandon's Working Committee, Nehru was able to outflank this movement and became undisputed dictator of his party. He had to pay the price, if such he saw it, of working with rightists in his Cabinet and the Congress.

From 1951 until the Chinese invasion in 1962 Nehru reigned supreme. Parallel to the assertion of his personal will came the securing of Congress dominance. The assassination of Gandhi provided the occasion for an outright attack on communalist parties (as well as communalists with Congress) who had been encouraged by the war with Pakistan and the influx of Hindi refugees. The issue was further defused by the Nehru-Liaquat pact in 1950, temporarily settling the relations between the two countries. At the first general election in 1951–52 communist parties fared badly and Congress scored an overwhelming victory.

Against communists, too, Nehru waged a constant campaign, especially in Andhra and Kerala. He was successful largely through tireless electioneering, though once, under the influence of his daughter, Indira Gandhi (as Congress President), he intervened in Kerala to remove a Communist Government.

The very success of Nehru's Congress posed a problem, however. In British times Congress repeatedly had been faced with the incompatibility of its twin roles as disciplined political movement committed to a definite programme, and as alternative government containing a variety of points of view. In so far as Congress became the inevitable party of government after independence, it was bound to attract the ambitious and thus to find it difficult to evolve a consistent ideology: a compendium of more or less diverse interests could not also be a unified force for, say, socialism. For there did not evolve after independence, any more than before, a fully democratic structure with a credible alternative party or parties of government. This lack resulted partly from deliberate Congress policy, partly from the wide slice of the political sphere encompassed by the Congress, as a result of its history as the central nationalist movement, and partly from the divisions among opposition groups. Potential or long-standing opposition leaders have been able to take office at times under the Congress while permanent opposition groupings of any size have proved elusive. Socialists, for example, originating in the Congress Socialist Party (1934), formed the Socialist Party in 1948, which evolved into the PSP in 1952. But in 1955 Rammanohar Lohia and others split from their colleagues over the police firing under a PSP government in Kerala, and over possible co-operation with the Congress. Ever since only short-term periods of unity have been possible. The leaders, Lohia, Jayaprakash Narayan, Asok Mehta, J. B. Kripalani and so on, have tended to be individualists rather than organization-men. Thus the pre-eminence of Congress during the independence struggle has been modified and preserved.

There was broad continuity too, under Nehru, in the personnel of government. In spite of a certain shift in legislative and party membership towards agricultural classes and peasant castes, the beneficiaries have tended to be those already dominant socially or economically: individuals whose ability and resources brought them to the top proved mostly to be members of dominant landholding castes. The monopoly of politics by an English-speaking professional elite, whose talents fitted them to negotiate with the British, may have continued slowly to be weakened as it began to be with the advent of popular agitation in the 1920s; but independence and democracy have also further emphasized the resilience of customary power structures which had operated all along beside the British-inspired politicians. Thus caste, for example, has accommodated itself to democracy though the meaning of both has been subtly changed in the process. Even the communist government in Kerala seems to have been largely upper class (though supported in factories and villages) and by no means immune from opportunists or free from self-seeking and corruption.

Change did not spread either to the bureaucracy, widely regarded as being inefficient and corrupt. Nehru opted for continuity among the administrators, partly through necessity, for the Congress cadres could not replace the bureaucracy the British had built. At the highest levels, it is true, political leaders displaced the administrator-rulers, often not receiving the advice of civil servants except on the bare question of legality.

The political office-holders have combined bureaucratic and political functions. At lower levels, however, the executive functions of the higher civil servant remained, as for example in the district officer as the fount of authority in the locality. The advent of *panchayati raj* and the involvement of local elected agencies in development programmes after 1959 represented a contrary trend, but the bureaucrats have mostly reasserted their role. *Panchayati raj* has become, rather, a means of extending state and national political allegiances and networks to lower levels.

Independence did change the priorities of government, even when policies continued existing trends. Thus Nehru continued the social reforming tendencies which resulted from Western influence in British days, but with a determination impossible for alien rulers. He insisted on the secular nature of India's government, on equality before the law: untouchability was formally abolished under the constitution and on the passage of Acts providing, among other things, for divorce, monogamy, and equal rights of inheritance for women. Though he had to draw on his personal prestige to secure this major achievement, it is safe to say that he would not have insisted if there had not been a sufficient body of opinion in favour of the changes, and if it had not been politically safe. (In 1951 he agreed to drop the Hindu Code Bill.) On the other hand it is also true that this favourable opinion is largely limited to sections of the middle classes, and that change, for example in the position of women, has not been rapid. Under Nehru too, education was greatly expanded, but (repeating the mistake of the British) most notably at university and higher technical levels, and in towns; in the countryside the literacy rate is still very low, about one in four.

The diversion of resources to development was the other major area of change within continuity. The creation of the National Planning Commission in 1950 was followed by three Five-Year Plans. The first, aimed specially at agricultural production, was considered a great success, production increasing, it was claimed, by 25 per cent and national income by 18 per cent. Along with this went the great Damodar power and irrigation project and the commencement of the Hirakud dam: Nehru's main remedy was industrialization. The Second Plan was more ambitious. The cost was nearly double the First Plan, some £6,000 million in all, including three new steel plants, sponsored respectively by the United Kingdom, the Federal Republic of Germany and the U.S.S.R. The Third Plan (1961–66) was still more ambitious, calling for an outlay of nearly £8,000 million, of which external aid was to provide £2,500 million. It ran into serious difficulties, and the revised Fourth Plan (1969–74) was seriously affected by the Indo-Pakistan war and a cut-off in U.S. aid. Yet the steel, aluminium and cement industries have greatly expanded, while the machine tool, diesel, steam and electric engine, automobile and fertilizer industries have been virtually created *de novo*. Industrial production expanded 50 per cent in eight years (1951–59).

What was new and remarkable in these programmes was the conscious attempt to plan a mixed economy as a weapon against poverty. What was unfortunate perhaps was the perpetuation of the British emphasis on large-scale projects and imported remedies, and the neglect of agriculture in favour of heavy industry. Under the Second Plan only four per cent was spent on rural development, while spectacular projects were favoured by both India and the donor countries, for reasons of national pride and administrative convenience. In spite of the "green revolution" in wheat, food production lagged behind industrial growth.

Nor has growth resulted in a fundamental redistribution of wealth. There was an attack on the great estate-holders of northern India, but, though the estates were divided, the great volume of landless labourers was little diminished. The abolition of landlordism and more recently princely purses has affected the families at the very highest levels; but the undoubted benefits of economic development since independence have been absorbed almost exclusively by middle groups or minorities of rich peasants, while the inhabitants of India's innumerable villages are, if anything, poorer then before. This, more than corruption or bureaucracy, seems to be the stumbling block in such programmes as the one for family planning. The enormous disparity between rich and poor has not been reduced.

During these years Nehru conducted foreign affairs with little interference. He began with the support of nationalist forces in Indonesia, mainland S.E. Asia and elsewhere. Acutely aware of East-West tension, and of the dangers of an atomic war in the post-war years he declared the policy of non-involvement, and strove to build up a third force of uncommitted nations. This led him to welcome the Communist rise to power in China in 1949 and brought him to the Bandung conference of Afro-Asian states in 1955.

This was the zenith of Nehru's international influence and from this moment his star seemed to decline. He was forthright in condemning Britain and France over Suez in 1956 but offended Indian right-wing opinion by being less clear on the U.S.S.R. in Hungary. In 1959 the Chinese decision to rule instead of control Tibet, followed by the Dalai Lama's flight to India, put him under further pressure from right-wing opinion and embroiled him with China itself. It gradually became clear that China did not regard its border with India as settled, and, partly under pressure from public opinion and the army, Nehru agreed to a policy of asserting Indian presence up to the border it claimed. The dispute became serious with the discovery of a Chinese road across the desolate Aksi Chin plateau in northeast Kashmir. Nehru made some war-like speeches, and the Indians engaged in minor skirmishes. Suddenly, in 1962, the Chinese advanced in full force against apparently unprepared Indian positions, overran them, continued rapidly on into India, and then withdrew to their earlier positions. Thus Nehru's plan for an unaligned bloc headed by India in close friendship with China was finally destroyed, and the way was open for even closer ties with the Soviet Union. India's remaining credit as a peace-maker was undermined with the occupation of Goa, Nehru having finally abandoned, under heavy internal pressure, the unpromising negotiations with Portugal to have the territory accede to India without force.

The Period Since Nehru

The last eighteen months of his life saw an ageing Nehru much criticized for defects in his policies. Population growth had balanced increased national production, military costs against Pakistan and China inhibited plans for a further constructive effort, and orthodox inertia at home obstructed projects which it feared to oppose. There were grave doubts, however, about what would happen after Nehru was dead. No-one had been groomed to take his place. In the event, the transition was smooth, and the succession passed to Lal Bahadur Shastri, not the most able nor the closest to Nehru among the outgoing Cabinet, but something of a consensus figure. Before he had fully found his feet he was faced with a national crisis over the proclamation of Hindi as the national language in January 1965. There followed the Rann of Kutch incident with Pakistan in April and the three-weeks war with Pakistan in September. His stature grew with this last event. He died, however, in January 1966, after going to Tashkent to meet President Ayub Khan and the Soviet Premier Kosygin. His successor was Nehru's daughter, Indira Gandhi, who, with the kingmaker Kamaraj in the background and the existing Congress team except for Morarji Desai, ruled the country until the General Election of 1967. The austere Morarji Desai went out because he would be Prime Minister or nothing. The General Election proved to be something of a political watershed, for in ended the nearly general domination of the Congress both at the Centre and in the States. It retained power at Delhi with a much reduced majority. Indira Gandhi continued as Prime Minister but was now strengthened by a deal with Morarji Desai who became Deputy Premier and Finance Minister. In the States the Congress was less fortunate. In Madras (subsequently re-named Tamil Nadu) the separatist D.M.K. took power and in Kerala Communist rule was restored. Elsewhere anti-Congress ministeries were set up in several States. Most of the anti-Congress coalitions proved so unstable that mid-term elections were held in a broad band of States from Haryana to West Bengal. In West Bengal the swing to the left continued and the local Congress was routed but elsewhere instability continued. The chief beneficiaries of these Congress losses were the left-wing pro-Communist groups and the Hindu nationalist party, the Jan Sangh.

In Bengal political anarchy reigned. Leaders and supporters on all sides became embroiled in campaigns of violence; revolutionary terrorists, the Naxalites, murdered landowners and political leaders in the countryside and also in Calcutta itself. To cope with this menace, Indira Gandhi's government armed itself in 1971 with special powers.

The Congress managers had supported Indira Gandhi as another consensus figure, and had no intention of reducing their influence in her favour, or condoning any substantial change in the Congress programme. The events of 1967, however, had shaken their credibility, and shown to many, including Mrs. Gandhi, that the Congress needed a new image and revitalized organization if it was to remain in power. It was not in Mrs. Gandhi's personal style, either, to leave the initiative in the hands of others. The crisis was precipitated by the death of the respecte President Zakir Husain in May 1969. The Presidenc possessed considerable reserve powers which woul place in it a key position in the event, as then seeme quite possible, of the next general election failing t give the Congress an overall majority. The right-win had already secured the election of the rightis Siddavvanahali Nijalingappa as President of th Congress, and they now adopted over the head of Mrs Gandhi, the rightist K. C. Reddy as the Congres presidential candidate. She retorted by implementin the long-standing Congress promise to nationalize th banks and by dismissing Mr. Desai from the Financ Ministry. She then supported the Vice-President, V. V Giri, a left-wing Congressman, for the Presidency. Hi success greatly strengthened her hand. In Novembe the Congress openly split, the Syndicate retaining th party organization and Mrs. Gandhi the popula support. There followed a year of uncertainty, Mrs Gandhi depending for a majority in the Lok Sabh on the left-wing group outside Congress. The Congres right wing on the other hand, looked increasingly fo support towards the Jan Sangh and Swatantra parties In September 1970, Congress success with Communis allies, in the Kerala elections, encouraged her t dissolve the Lok Sabha in December. The elections o February-March 1971 proved a notable success, bot for Mrs. Gandhi herself and her wing of the Congress She gained 350 out of 518 elective seats, an overal majority of 182 while the Congress (Opposition obtained 16 seats. Once again an effective oppositio had failed to emerge, largely because Mrs. Gandhi's Congress occupied the middle ground ideologicall and, by being in power, attracted recruits as th party of government. The opposition had no clea strategy. Congress (O) was left with little positiv policy; and the degree to which Mrs. Gandhi ha commandeered the territory of the socialists wa marked by their evident confusion about how t react to her: the PSP allied with Congress (R) but th Samyukta Socialist Party (SSP) with Congress (O) Jan Sangh and Swatantra, in both the Lok Sabha elections of 1971 and those in the United Province and Bihar in 1972. The difficulties of opposition wer revealed indeed in the odd bed-fellows chosen by th SSP in these elections and earlier in government i Bihar.

Hard on the election results came a fresh crisis Relations with Pakistan, never very cordial, had onl recently been strained by the hi-jacking of an India plane to Lahore and its destruction there. On Marc 25th, 1971, came the Pakistan government's actio in East Pakistan (now Bangladesh). India was face with an immense refugee problem: the Worl Bank estimated there were about 7,000,000 in August and nearly all of this burden was concentrated i West Bengal.

The first Indian reaction was to publicize th magnitude of a problem not of its making and to ask for help from the major powers and the United Nations. The next step was the conclusion in August 1971 of a treaty of friendship with the Soviet Union for 20 years. "Non-alignment" was specifically safeguarded and there was much about mutual co-operation, but the key lay in articles 8 and 9, in which the two countries promised mutual support short of force in the event of either country being attacked by a third party. India thus assured itself of non-interference from world powers and offset Chinese support for Pakistan. Substantial aid being withheld, India developed its third resource, support for the Bangladesh guerrilla forces. This went through three phases. It first sheltered them, then trained them and armed them, and finally gave them support along and across the border. Tension mounted until the Pakistan government commenced hostilities on December 6th with raids on Indian airfields in the west. The war lasted twelve days. India maintained its position in the west, but gained an unexpectedly rapid victory in the east. Pakistani forces surrendered on December 18th, and in all more than 90,000 prisoners were taken. United Nations action was blocked by the Soviet veto; China assisted Pakistan with little more than words; the United States showed its displeasure by sending warships but succeeded only in embittering its relations with India.

Indira Gandhi's personal position was now unassailable, and was further strengthened by the state elections in February-March 1972, which repeated the landslide victory of her Congress a year before. With Congress ministries in almost all states, Mrs. Gandhi was able to secure Chief Ministers who would carry out her policies. The return of the refugees, a vast operation, was completed by March 1972. Indian troops were withdrawn from Bangladesh. President Bhutto of Pakistan, though seeming to be realistic, faced a delicate situation, and yet in July 1972 he agreed with India to abandon the resort to force, to respect the Kashmir ceasefire line of December 1971, and to return to the international borders elsewhere. This agreement was ratified in August 1972. There was gradual progress also on the outstanding questions: the return of the Pakistani prisoners of war, the recognition of Bangladesh, the proposed "war trials", and the exchange of people between Pakistan and the new state in the east. On August 28th, 1973, a further agreement was signed, and three-way repatriation of prisoners began in September. Upon recognition by Pakistan in February 1974, Bangladesh agreed to abandon the proposed war trials. The exchange of prisoners was completed in May.

Soon, however, there appeared signs less encouraging for India. The explosion of its first nuclear device in May 1974 set back the improvement in relations with Pakistan, and resulted in much criticism of India throughout the world. Pakistan has made a more rapid political and military recovery than expected, and the fall of Mujib in Bangladesh (August 1975) has brought into the open several points of dispute with India, arising not so much out of substantive grievances as from fears of Indian dominance. The inclusion of Sikkim in the Indian Union (April 1975) soured relations with Nepal. India, apparently supreme in the subcontinent in 1971, has once again found its position threatened. Some of the early results of this shift, however, have promised a more pragmatic foreign policy. In mid-1976 agreement was reached with Pakistan on exchange of ambassadors and restoration of air links, and relations have improved with China to the point of an exchange of ambassadors.

Indira Gandhi's internal supremacy of 1971 also did not go unchallenged. A number of her measures were thwarted at first by the Supreme Court and, in the long term, economic disasters made it impossible for her to make much improvement in conditions, let alone carry out her promise to abolish poverty. During 1973 and 1974 unprecedented drought brought appalling famine to west and central India. Inflation, intensified by the worldwide oil crisis, seriously reduced the standard of living of the middle classes, and further reduced the circumstances of the urban poor. Riots broke out in a number of states, and in Gujarat street fighting forced the resignation of the state government and the imposition of President's rule. A strike of railway staff was suppressed by the army. In Bihar, the veteran socialist, Jayaprakash Narayan, headed a popular campaign against the local Congress government, alleging corruption, and during 1974 he sought allies outside Bihar and began also to attack the central government. His coalition lacked conviction in ideological terms, as it included parties both to the right and left of Congress, and this gave credibility to accusations that its only policy was to oppose Mrs. Gandhi. In May 1975 a version of the coalition, the Janata Front, contested and won the election in Gujarat which followed the ending of Presidents' rule; this reverse showed the degree to which economic and political difficulties since 1971 had dissolved support for Mrs. Gandhi's Congress.

In June 1975 the Allahabad High Court gave its judgement in a long-drawn out dispute, and found Mrs. Gandhi guilty of election malpractices (largely, though perhaps not entirely, of a technical nature). Immediately "spontaneous" demonstrations were organized in her support, while opposition groups demanded her resignation. The Supreme Court granted a stay of execution on the High Court order pending an appeal; but, unexpectedly, Mrs. Gandhi then had a state of emergency proclaimed and unknown numbers of her opponents arrested. The Houses of Parliament were recalled and, in the absence of non-government members (other than the CPI), rapidly approved constitutional amendments which removed from the jurisdiction of the courts, retrospectively, questions of the Prime Minister's election and the constitutionality of the emergency measures.

Mrs. Gandhi's motive for declaring the emergency is not yet clear. There were undoubtedly continuing prospects of a concerted campaign against her, and Jayaprakash Narayan was alleged to have called for non-co-operation by troops and government servants; yet the government justified itself in part by referring not to the immediate dangers but to the disturbances in Gujarat years before, riots in Bihar during 1974, and the assassination in January 1975 of L. N. Mishra, Minister of Railways. (There were also suggestions made, but no evidence given, of foreign backing for opposition groups.) Rumour has suggested that, among other things, Mrs. Gandhi found it necessary to consolidate her position within her own party; but an emergency would be an extreme step for such a purpose. Finally, there was much point in the argument that something was needed to overcome the inertia and corruption of the bureaucracy and to revitalize development programmes over which too much time had already been lost; but again a declaration of emergency would be an unorthodox means of achieving this end.

Whatever the motive, it is clear that Mrs. Gandhi is now securely in power for the foreseeable future. Opposition within India has been silenced where it has not been imprisoned. Precensorship of the press was lifted in September 1975, but the threat of reprisals remains to keep the newspapers in check. In January 1976 the only effective state opposition, that of the separatist D.M.K. in Tamil Nadu, was removed (after a long press campaign) by the imposition of President's rule; and the Janata Front in Gujarat was replaced in March 1976 by President's rule, despite its relative insignificance as effective opposition.

There have been some undoubted gains under the emergency. Aspects of administration have improved; and the economy, helped also by the excellent monsoon in 1975, has benefited to the extent of a decrease in retail prices at a time of worldwide inflation. On the other hand, the recent events also represent a definite shift in the balance of the constitution. In August 1975 the Law Minister, Hari Ramachandra Gokhale, declared in the Lok Sabha that it was a "very ridiculous position" that the Prime Minister, the "undisputed national leader", supported as she was by the vast majority in her constituency, should have her election subject to judicial scrutiny. Clearly this doctrine (popularity placing a leader above the law), and the constitutional amendments which have backed it up, represent a considerable extension in the authority of the Prime Minister and, indirectly, the Congress. For the Congress in the long term it will exacerbate the problem of being the consensus party; already it has found it necessary to close its membership against the opportunists who rushed to join after the emergency was declared. The very success of the economic programme also has its dangers. The effects of shock tactics such as these are not likely to be long-lived; on the other hand, whereas an emergency for immediate political dangers may be lifted soon after that danger has passed, an emergency justified by its economic benefits, designed to remove India's poverty, will have no such natural end.

ECONOMIC SURVEY

Dick Wilson

India is the fifth largest country in the world by area and the second most populous. But it is only the tenth country ranked by wealth and production, with a Gross National Product of U.S. $66,000 million in 1974–75. Its inhabitants' average *per capita* income is among the lowest in the world: India is not even among the first hundred countries ranked by income per head. But since about 1950 the government has undertaken for the first time in the country's history an organized economic development programme, one of the earliest and best-conceived in the entire developing world of Asia, Africa and Latin America.

RESOURCES

The riches of Hindustan which attracted the merchants of the East India Company in earlier centuries proved ultimately disappointing, and when the British left India in 1947 the general opinion was that the country was poor in soils and mineral deposits. Since then more prospecting has been carried out and the mineral picture has become brighter. When the FAO and UNESCO published in 1968 their new world soil map, it revealed that Indian soils enjoyed a higher natural fertility than had been supposed, and that about a third of the nation's land area was potentially good crop land.

Mineral Resources

"Except in the case of minerals such as iron ore, aluminium ore, titanium ore, manganese and rare metals, mica and a few other minerals," Dr. D. N. Wadia admits in *The Gazeteer of India*, the country's resources in "economic minerals and the non-ferrous metals are . . . limited". The Himalayan region remains largely unexplored geologically, and the northern plains are devoid of minerals. But the two eastern States of Bihar and Orissa are extremely rich in iron, manganese and other ores, besides possessing three-quarters of India's coal reserves. They have thus become the principal industrial centre of the country. The iron reserves in these two States are calculated at over 8,000 million metric tons, and half of the world's best mica comes from the Bihar mines. Madhya Pradesh, Andhra and Tamil Nadu also enjoy good iron and manganese reserves, Mysore yields gold and Kerala in the south possesses rich heavy-mineral sands yielding ilmenite, monazite, zircon and other strategic minerals. Oil is so far chiefly found in Assam and Gujarat.

India's total coal reserves have been estimated at 80,000 million metric tons, and iron at 21,600 million—about a quarter of the world's total. The manganese deposits of about 160 million metric tons are the third largest in the world. High-grade reserves of bauxite are said to total 94 million metric tons. But India is relatively handicapped in copper, zinc, lead, tin and nickel, all extremely important industrial minerals, and rock phosphate and sulphur for the chemical fertilizer industry has still to be imported.

The potential oil-bearing area is claimed to be about 400,000 square miles. Throughput of the Indian oil refineries currently reaches some 23 million tons a year of which some 9 million tons are produced domestically, the rest imported.

The full programme of prospecting has only just begun, however, and it would be rash to come to any final conclusions about India's mineral potential until it is completed.

Human Resources

In 1966 the Indian population was unofficially estimated to have passed the 500 million mark: in 1975 the population exceeded 600 million, with the current annual growth rate put at 2.5 per cent. There have been three national censuses since the Second World War. That of 1951 showed a total population of 361 million, and at that time, in the absence of completely comparable data for earlier years, it was assumed that the rate of increase was about 1.5 per cent a year. But the 1961 census total was 439 million, which meant an average annual increase in the intervening decade of 2.2 per cent. This brought it home to India's leaders that the population expansion was hindering their economic development plans. As the *Draft Outline of the Fourth Five-Year Plan* put it in 1966, "Under Indian conditions, the quest for equality and dignity of man requires as its base both a high rate of economic growth and a low rate of population increase".

The reason for the quickening of population growth lies in the medical revolution. Public health campaigns against malaria and other diseases, as well as the general advance in hygiene and immunization, have caused the death rate to fall dramatically, from 31 per thousand in the 1930s to 23 per thousand in the 1950s and 16 per thousand today. But the birth rate is slower to decline. From 45 per thousand in the 1930s it has now been reduced to only 35. The average natural increase rate over the first fifteen years of planned development in India, from 1951 to 1965, was 2.5 per cent. The life expectancy at birth had risen to 50 by 1968, and the density of population per square kilometre stood at 156 in 1967. The age structure of the population at the 1961 census showed that 41 per cent of the total population were under fifteen years of age, and 15 per cent were under five.

Family planning was adopted as an official policy in 1952, but little cash investment was directed towards its promotion in the First Five-Year Plan. Only in the Third Plan, beginning in 1961, was it stated that "the objective of stabilizing the growth of population over a reasonable period must be at the very centre of planned development". The investment for family planning was Rs. 260 million in the Third Plan; in the Draft Fifth Plan this was raised to Rs. 5,600 million. But implementation of population control policies is a State subject, not a central one. In 1970 there were over 31,000 full-time regular Government centres throughout India giving advice and treatment on birth control. By early 1970 more than 7.2 million people had been sterilized and 3.9 million IUDs inserted. Some States have introduced welfare disincentives for parents having more than three children and legislation compelling sterilization after a certain number of children was introduced in some states in 1976.

The authorities claim that preliminary studies suggest the beginning in some areas of a decline in birth rate. The goal is to bring it down from its present 3.6 per cent to 2.5 per cent over the next seven years or so.

The Labour Force

The 1961 census showed that of the 439 million population, 250 million were not at work; of the rest, 100 million were cultivators, 32 million agricultural labourers, 12 million worked in household industry, 8 million in manufacturing industry, 7 million in trade and commerce and 30 million in other occupations. Some 82 per cent of the total population was rural, 18 per cent lived in towns and cities. Despite the gradual increase in urban and non-agricultural employment, India remains primarily an agricultural economy.

There is concern among the Indian leadership about the employment aspect of the population expansion. The Fourth Five-Year Plan, for example, envisaged the creation of 19 million new jobs but the entry of 23 million new entrants to the labour market. The government thus openly admits that it cannot keep up with the demand for employment, and this problem is likely to worsen in the next decade or two considering the large numbers of young people in the total population. In the decade 1966–75 more than 50 million people were added to the potential labour force, and over the fifteen-year period 1961–76 the total would be 70 million. Since urban pursuits and modern industry cannot possibly cope with such numbers, the Third and Fourth Plans emphasize expanded rural public works.

India's women are still considerably under-utilized in the economy. Of the 213 million women recorded in the 1961 census, over 70 per cent were not at work. Some 33 million were cultivators, 14 million agricultural labourers, 5 million worked in household industry, a million each in manufacturing industry and trade.

Average factory earnings were estimated in 1967 to be about Rs. 2,230 annually. Legislation assures a minimum wage, and the workers' earnings index reached 210 in 1964 (1947=100). Trade unionism is well developed in India. There are over 13,000 registered trade unions, claiming a total membership of more than 4½ million. The unions are, however, caught up in a bitter political conflict with each other and labour difficulties on this count have been legion at the modern factories recently erected. The central and State governments legislate for a complex structure of labour welfare and labour-management relations provisions. The *gherao*, by which management is physically trapped in its offices until labour demands are met, has now become a common instrument of union tactics in Indian industry.

AGRICULTURE

Agriculture ceased to account for more than half of India's national income in about 1966, but it still represents almost half and is the biggest single contributor. Some 70 per cent of the population depend on the land for their living, and agriculture provides not only the bulk of the nation's food but also raw materials for the cotton textile, jute, sugar and other industries. It provides a large proportion of India's exports.

India is the largest producer in the world of groundnuts, jute, rapeseed, sesame seed and tea, and has a virtual monopoly of lac production. It is the second biggest producer of rice and castor beans.

Of India's total geographical area of 327 million hectares (807 million acres), just over 40 per cent is cultivated, but since a small portion is sown more than once in a year the total cropped area is calculated at 156 million hectares. Cereals take up the greater part of the sown area, occupying 95 million hectares in 1972 (of which 32 million rice), with pulses taking a further 22 million, cotton 7.5 million and oilseeds 11 million. There are two crop seasons known as *kharif* (rice, maize, cotton etc.) and *rabi* (wheat, barley, gram etc.). India also possesses extensive plantations producing tea, rubber and coffee, employing about 1.2 million people. They are mainly in the northeastern hill districts and along the south-west coast.

Foodgrain production in 1975/76 was a record 114 million tons, compared with 101 and 105 million tons in the two previous years. Because of the failure of food production to keep pace with the population growth, India is obliged to import cereals. In 1972 imports had been reduced from 7.5 million tons in the mid-1960s to half a million tons, but in 1974/75 they exceeded 5 million tons again, the momentum of the foodgrain production campaign having slipped. The Food Corporation of India was set up in 1965 to organize food procurement and distribution. Andhra Pradesh, Madhya Pradesh, Maharashtra, Orissa, Punjab and Tamil Nadu normally have surplus of food. Kerala, Bengal and others are normally in deficit and depend on the central government for their supplies.

Government Agricultural Policy

Land tenure has been a preoccupation of the government since independence, at which time about two-fifths of the land was in some form of intermediate tenure. Since then some 20 million tenants have been given their own land, and legislation has been passed strengthening cultivators' security of tenure, reducing their rents and in some cases giving them legal ownership. But it is still estimated that about 1 per cent of the rural population owns 20 per cent of the land, and the land reform campaign is not regarded as completed. Efforts have been made to promote co-operative farming, but with little success.

Apart from the reform of the land tenure system, the main official effort in Indian agriculture in the past two decades has been to improve yields. Some progress has been made in extending the sown area and the incidence of multiple-cropping (which now covers some 15 per cent of the sown area). But by far the most important factor in increasing overall production, both of foodgrains and of the important cash crops, is the artificial boosting of yields per acre.

Irrigation is one part of this, but does not yet cover more than one-fifth of the sown area. In any case the water that has been provided is more in the way of drought prevention than of supplies plentiful enough to enable the plants to derive the full benefit of artificial fertilization. It was only relatively recently that the government awoke to the importance of chemical fertilizer in boosting food output. The supply available to Indian farmers, either from local production or import, has risen from a mere 700,000 metric tons in 1965 to 2.8 million in the year 1973–74. From about 1968 the widespread benefits of new hybrid seed strains of rice and wheat began to be felt, the product of painstaking research, largely American-financed, going back many years.

Since 1960 the Ford Foundation has helped to run Intensive Agricultural District Programmes, sometimes known as "package programmes", in selected high-yielding areas, to show how an adequate input of water supply, fertilizer, new seeds and other aids could dramatically increase yields. Each year the area under these programmes has expanded.

INDUSTRY AND POWER

The history of organized industry in India can be traced back for more than a century, to the establishment in the 1850s of the cotton textile industry in Bombay. Jute manufacture in Bengal and coal mining were also among the pioneers, and Jamsetji Tata launched the first modern steel mill in the early years of this century. Some degree of protection was given to industry by the British imperial government in the 1920s, but a full-scale concerted effort to develop industry on a nation-wide basis had to wait until the 1950s.

In the First and Second Five-Year Plan period, 1951-61, the growth and diversification of industry were remarkable. Three new steel works, each with a million tons capacity, were set up in the public sector with British, Soviet and West German help at Durgapur, Bhilai and Rourkela respectively. The two large existing mills in the private sector were expanded, and in 1976 Indian steel production had reached the 5 million tons annual level. A contract was signed with the U.S.S.R. (after American interests had withdrawn from the project) for another large steel complex being constructed at Bokaro.

The foundations were also laid in the 1950s of heavy electrical and heavy machine tools industries, heavy machine building and other branches of heavy engineering, and the production of machinery for the manufacture of cement and paper also began for the first time. The manufacture of such basic chemicals as caustic soda, soda ash, sulphuric acid and fertilizer was expanded, and such new chemical products as urea, ammonium phosphate, penicillin, synthetic fibres, industrial explosives and polyethylene were produced.

Output also increased substantially in such industries as bicycles, sewing machines, telephones, electrical goods, textile and sugar machinery. New skills were learnt by the workers and a large and growing class of industrial managers came into being. Organized industrial production almost doubled in those ten years to 1961, while new industrial townships and new factory districts in the environs of all the main cities sprang up.

The power industry also advanced very fast in the 1950s. Aggregate installed capacity was under a million kW. in 1945, yet by March 1972 it had reached 17 million kW. Electricity generated in the year 1971–72 totalled 64,600 million kWh. Both steam-powered and diesel-powered plant have expanded, but the growth was the most outstanding in the hydro-electric field. Some of the dams constructed for this purpose are among the largest in the world. It was estimated that by March 1970 some one in eight of India's towns and villages had been electrified.

Nuclear power is expected to play a growing role in future. Experimental reactors, a plutonium plant, a thorium plant, a uranium metal plant and a heavy water reconcentration plant are all in operation at the Badha Atomic Research Centre at Trombay, near Bombay, on a budget of about £12 million a year. On the basis of the work done here, with and without foreign technical help. India joined the nuclear "club" in May 1974 with an underground explosion. Meanwhile the first nuclear power station has been erected at Tarapur, another is going up at Rana Pratap Sagar in Rajasthan, and a third is planned at Kalpakkam in Tamil Nadu.

Mention should also be made of the light industrial sector. Textiles, for example, have provided an important—though stagnant—source of export earnings, and almost all daily needs and household goods are produced widely by private concerns.

The Structure of Industry

The question of the relationship between publicly owned and privately owned industry has been controversial throughout all this development. The Congress Party's famous 1947 Industrial Policy Resolution, as amended in 1956, reserved a sizeable part of heavy industry for the exclusive operation of the state—including all defence and nuclear installations, new ventures in heavy industry and utilities, mining (including oil), aircraft manufacture and aviation. Only as late as 1962, under heavy pressure from the World Bank and India's foreign aid donors, was the so-called "escape clause" invoked to allow private enterprise into oil refining, on the argument that the state was unable to put up the new capacity required and that if private interests were willing they should be allowed to go ahead. Later the reluctance of the Indian government to allow the Bokaro steel mill to be in the private sector or to let American corporations into the chemical fertilizer field in a big way became an issue in the deterioration of Indian-American relations in the late 1960s. Concessions were, however, made from about 1966 onwards which allowed foreign private interests to operate in such fields as the Indian fertilizer industry with some assurances of profitability. In view of the enormous financial losses incurred by so many of the state-owned industries, the feeling in Indian business circles is that private industry is likely to challenge the public sector much more strongly in the years to come. But Mrs. Gandhi's nationalization of the Indian banks in the middle of 1969 and all insurance firms in May 1971, seemed to presage a further government effort to curb the private sector, especially the power of the big family concerns typified by the Birla empire. A new industrial licensing policy announced in February 1970 had the effect of favouring smaller entrepreneurs over the big "dynasties" in certain industries.

THE TRANSPORT SYSTEM

India's domestic trade is probably worth some Rs. 700,000 million, maybe more, and it is carried by rail, river, coastal shipping and road—in that order. With 60,149 route kilometres in 1972/73, the Indian railway system is the second largest single network in the world. It is also the biggest nationalized undertaking in India. Minerals, coal and food-grains are mostly transported by rail.

The inland navigable waters extend to 8,000 k.m

In 1974 the Indian fleet totalled 3,090,000 g.r.t., the second largest in Asia. The major ports are Bombay, Calcutta, Cochin, Kandla, Madras, Mangalore, Marmagao, Pradip, Tuticorin and Visakhapatnam.

Aviation services are well developed in India. Scheduled services in 1973 exceeded 73 million kilometres. The Indian Airlines Corporation handles domestic flights and also serves India's immediate neighbours, while the Air India Corporation serves more than 20 countries throughout the world. Both are state-owned, after nationalization of private firms, and are efficiently run. In 1973/74 there were 133,700 kilometres of surfaced and metalled roads and 695,000 kilometres of other roads.

The road system is not good by comparison with rail. A National Highways system between the state capital, major ports and highway systems of neighbouring countries exceeded over 28,820 kilometres in 1973. The registered number of motor vehicles on the road, including motor cycles, was only 1.8 million in 1972. There is some manufacture of motor cars and lorries, but still in rather small numbers for the population.

Tourism

Tourism is a neglected industry and an under-utilized source of foreign exchange earnings in India. The number of foreign tourist visitors in 1974 was 423,000—far below the number attracted to, say, Hong Kong or Japan. Lack of sufficient modern hotel, transport and other facilities was the main handicap, but the new concentration on foreign exchange-earning on the part of government and plans for further public investment in the tourist industry suggest that an expansion is round the corner. India has much to offer in terms of scenery and exoticism, and could rival Africa for big game hunting.

FINANCE

The most important revenue sources available to the central Government are customs and excise duties, corporation and income tax, debt services and profits of the Reserve Bank.

The revenues allowed to the States under the Indian Constitution are the States' own taxes and duties, together with a share of the taxes levied centrally (11,982.1 million rupees in 1974/75) and grants from the centre. In the central budget for 1974/75 about 17 per cent of gross revenues went to the states leaving a net revenue for the centre of 56,408.6 million rupees. The total resources transferred from the centre to the State governments, including loans, reached Rs. 27,470 million in the 1972/73 Budget. Well over half of the State revenues derive from taxation, chiefly land revenues, sales tax, State excise duties, registration and stamp duties (all levied by the States) and shares of central taxes and duties. Agricultural taxation is a State subject, and in 1967 the State Chief Ministers rejected the centre's proposal to tax farming incomes; indeed, some States have abolished or reduced their land tax.

The largest item of expenditure in the central budget is defence, which took about 30 per cent (16,797.3 million rupees in 1974/75) followed by development at 20 per cent (11,073.4 million rupees) and debt servicing at 16.5 per cent (9,751.3 million rupees).

The 1976/77 central budget was a record expansionary one of 130,000 million rupees. Defence spending was 25,400 million rupees and development spending was increased by 31 per cent to 78,000 million rupees.

The estimated public debt outstanding by the Government of India in March 1971 was Rs. 144,200 million, of which Rs. 77,610 million was internally raised and Rs. 66,590 million externally (the shares of which as of 1968 were from the U.S.A. Rs. 27,000 million, World Bank and International Development Association Rs. 8,000 million, Britain Rs. 5,000 million, U.S.S.R. Rs. 4,000 million and others Rs. 10,000 million). The consolidated public debt of the State governments totalled Rs. 54,000 million in March 1966.

The potential of raising further internal revenue seems limited. It is usually estimated that Indians are hoarding gold worth about £1,500 million in all, but attempts to get this into state hands have failed. The government has issued gold bonds, but with little success. Since the State governments are so reluctant to tax their own farmers, the central exchequer has nowhere else to go.

Prices and Banking

Prices have tended to rise fairly steadily since the early 1960s. The wholesale price index for all commodities, based on 1961/62=100, stood at 317 at the end of 1974. The consumer price index for industrial workers, again for all items, reached 331 by November 1974 (1960=100). After two years of inflation in excess of 20 per cent, prices fell by about 3 per cent in 1975/76. The money supply stood at Rs. 87,590 million in January 1973. The rupee's link with sterling was ended in September 1975, when it was pegged to a "basket" of currencies.

Banking has become very active and widespread. At the end of September 1974 there were 14,000 state-owned and 17,000 private bank branch offices. The 14 largest domestic banks were nationalized in July 1969 as part of an attempt to assert Congress as a radical party and win the 1972 elections. Life insurance had been nationalized in 1956.

Bank deposits and currency in circulation in March 1975 were 116,160 million rupees and 65,820 million rupees respectively.

DEVELOPMENT OF THE ECONOMY

Under British rule little consistent and serious attention was given to economic development. In 1934 M. Visvesvarya published a book entitled *Planned Economy for India* which offered a draft ten-year plan. The Indian National Congress began studying the subject in 1938, and the Government set up a Department of Planning and Development in 1944. Three war-time plans suggested by groups outside the government helped to establish a climate favourable to planning after the war: these were the Bombay Plan of a group of industrialists, the People's Plan prepared by M. N. Roy for a trade union group, and the Gandhian Plan drafted by S. N. Agarwal.

In March 1950 the Planning Commission was established to prepare a plan for "the most effective and balanced utilization of the country's resources". This almost coincided with the Commonwealth Conference later in 1950, which called for economic planning in the Asian Commonwealth countries under what became known as the Colombo Plan.

First Five-Year Plan

The First Plan was submitted to Parliament in December 1952, and covered the period 1951–52 to 1955–56. Its objective was to initiate a process of development which "will raise living standards and open out to the people new opportunities for a richer and more varied life". Economic planning, it stated, was to be viewed "as an integral part of a wider process aiming not merely at the development of resources in a narrow technical sense, but at the development of human faculties and the building up of an institutional framework adequate to the needs and aspirations of the people". The late Jawaharlal Nehru, then Prime Minister, was not merely the Chairman of the Planning Commission (among his many other posts) but took a personally active part and lead in its discussions and decisions. The First and subsequent Plans bore the marks of his literary style, his compassion and his predilection for the Soviet model of rapid industrialization and modernization. He was no collectivist, indeed he preferred the co-operative idea as a solution for Indian agricultural organization, but he did favour strong state controls over private enterprise. In this respect he reflected the intellectual opinion of the Indian nationalists of his generation. Under Nehru's leadership the First

Plan acquired a world-wide reputation as a unique attempt to reconcile the three different objectives of economic development, social welfare and political democracy.

The emphasis in the First Plan was on infrastructure—agriculture, irrigation, power and transport. It also devoted much attention to the basic social and institutional groundwork for economic development. The stated aim was to double per capita income (and raise consumption standards by 70 per cent) over a 25-year period (i.e. one generation or five five-year plans). Within the currency of the First Plan, national income was to be expanded by 11 per cent, and the rate of saving from 5 per cent of national income to 6.75 per cent. State expenditure of Rs. 19,600 million was planned, of which 27 per cent would go to transport and communications, 31 per cent to agriculture, irrigation and community development, only 4 per cent to industry and mining. About 90 per cent of the funds would come from internal resources, only 10 per cent in the form of external assistance. In the early years of her planning, India had the advantage of sterling balances accumulated during the Second World War; it was only in the second half of the 1950s that she began to feel the draught of foreign exchange shortages.

The Second Five-Year Plan

But the First Plan was more a document on paper, an earnest of intentions, than a blueprint for action. For one thing it was approved only half-way through the period it was meant to cover. For another thing, the statistics and administration necessary for the operation were largely lacking. It was the Second Plan, covering the period 1956–57 to 1960–61, which really took the country firmly into the business of economic development. The Second Plan carried further the basic infrastructural reforms of the First Plan, but added a new emphasis on heavy industry, seen to be the hard core of future development which could not be undertaken so early by the private sector. The Second Plan placed before the nation the goal of "a socialistic pattern of society", meaning not merely an enhanced national income but also "greater equality in incomes and wealth". It defined the key role of the public sector, which for the first time was to invest more funds than the private entrepreneurs themselves. The long-term target of doubling national income was brought forward by 3 years (i.e. it was to be achieved over 22 years).

The Plan envisaged the spending of Rs. 46,000 million, or two and a half times the level of its predecessor. A similar proportion was to go to transport and communications (28 per cent), but the allocation to agriculture, irrigation and community development was proportionately reduced (to 20 per cent) and that to industry and mining greatly enlarged (to 20 per cent). Because of the increased spending, only three-quarters of the funds were to come from domestic resources, and foreign assistance was relied on for 24 per cent. Even the 76 per cent of Plan spending which would come from internal resources was dependent on the imposition of heavier taxation. Deficit financing to the extent of Rs. 9,500 million was also part of the Second Plan.

The actual out-turn of the two plans taken together was not unpromising. National income was expanded by an annual average of 4 per cent during the decade, although population growth meant that the per capita income grew by the far slower rate of just under 2 per cent a year. The overall increase in national income in the ten-year period was 42 per cent. Industrial production went up much faster, almost doubling in the decade, the annual average growth being 9 per cent. As we have seen, three new giant public steel mills were constructed during the Second Plan period and the foundations laid of other branches of heavy industry. But there were disappointments, too. The fluctuating performance of agriculture, so dependent on the uncertain monsoon, made planning difficult. The growing foreign exchange shortage, caused by the stagnation of exports and the run-down of the war-time balances, began to put the squeeze on imports of machinery and materials needed for Plan projects. There were severe administrative bottlenecks as the planning mechanism sought to operate for the first time over the whole country and in so many different fields of endeavour.

The Third Five-Year Plan

These difficulties caused the planners to introduce a note of greater realism in the Third Plan, covering the period 1961–62 to 1965–66. The target date for doubling national income was put back to its original term of 25 years. Two explicit long-term objectives were stated as the creation of non-agricultural employment for over 46 million people, reducing the proportion of the population dependent on the land from 70 per cent to 60 per cent, and the establishment of universal education up to the age of fourteen. During the Third Plan period the rate of investment was to be boosted from 11 per cent of national income to 14–15 per cent (meaning a net savings-income ratio of about 11.5 per cent). A new theme of the Third Plan was self-sufficiency in agriculture and self-reliance in industrialization within ten years, and independence from foreign aid within fifteen years. During the five-year currency of the Plan, national income was to be raised by 30 per cent, per capita income by 17 per cent to the Rs. 385 level.

Towards these goals an expenditure of Rs. 75,000 million by the government was envisaged, or 63 per cent more than in the preceding Plan. The proportion allocated to transport and communications was only 20 per cent (below the First and Second Plan). Industry and mining received 20 per cent as before, but agriculture, irrigation and community development were given an increased proportion of 23 per cent. The proportion to be derived from foreign aid rose to 33 per cent, or Rs. 25,000 million, and deficit financing would be allowed to the extent of Rs. 12,000 million. In fact the public sector outlay proved bigger than was planned, the out-turn being Rs. 86,300 million. Since private investors put in an estimated Rs. 41,000 million during the quinquennium, the overall investment was of the order of Rs. 120,000 million.

The results of the Third Plan were nevertheless most disappointing. This was partly because of external accidents such as the fighting with Chinese forces on the Himalayan border in 1962 and the outbreak of war with Pakistan over Kashmir in the Plan's final year. Defence spending began to eat heavily into development funds. The weather also played havoc with the crops, especially in the final year of the quinquennium. There was a sharp increase in prices, too. The actual rate of economic growth was a mere half of the annual 5 per cent target, and the only saving grace was the substantial boost in industrial capacity.

India's economic performance during the first fifteen years of planning was thus below the target set by Nehru and his planners when they began, although it was still very much better than ever before. The growth in national income represented an annual average of 3.75 per cent, and the growth in per capita income was less than half that: 1.75 per cent. At that rate, if India can do no better in future, a doubling of *per capita* income would take nearer 40 than 25 years, But the measurement of progress by growth of income is misleading, since much of the investment that has been made has gone into infrastructure for future income that has not yet borne its full fruit. Thus, during the first Three Plans, although *per capita* income rose by only 30 per cent, installed electrical power was quadrupled. As the *Fourth Five-Year Plan Draft Outline* claimed, "During the past fifteen years, a stagnant economy has been set stirring and moving, a traditional society is getting modern and mobile."

The Delayed Fourth Plan

The drafting of the Fourth Plan, which ought to have covered the period 1966–67 to 1970–71, was delayed by the set-backs of 1965 and 1966, war with Pakistan, the suspension of American aid and disastrous drought leading to crop failure. Only in August 1966 was a *Draft Outline* published. This drew the lessons from the debacle. The objectives were listed as follows: (a) to boost exports and substitute domestic production for imports, (b) to check inflation and avoid deficit financing, (c) to maximize agricultural production, (d) to give priority in industry to those sectors contributing towards agriculture, such as fertilizer, pumps and farm implements, (e) to give attention to light industry in order to provide consumer goods for the farmers to buy, (f) to economize on expensive new development projects and concentrate on completing those already begun, and (g) to promote family planning more earnestly.

The targets were a 48 per cent growth in national income to Rs. 2,950 million (at 1965–66 prices), a foodgrain harvest by the end of the quinquennium of 120 million tons, a 31 per cent expansion of agricultural output and a 68 per cent expansion in industry (89 per cent in steel). The base year of 1965–66 was, of course, a very poor one, and if the targets are compared with the year *before*, which was not so bad, then the annual growth in national income during the Fourth Plan comes to 5.5 per cent, that in *per capita* income 3 per cent (to Rs. 532).

The *Draft Outline* proposed investment in the public sector of Rs. 160,000 million (85,000 million by the centre, 74,000 million by the States), and Rs. 77,000 million in the private sector, to make an aggregate of Rs. 237,000 million. In 1969 these figures were raised to Rs. 243,980 million, of which only Rs. 143,980 million public and as much as Rs. 100,000 million private. The revised Plan assumed Rs. 40,300 million of foreign aid (the equivalent of £580 million a year), representing 28 per cent of public sector investment, 17 per cent of public-plus-private investment during the quinquennium. Some 25 per cent of the outlay was allocated to industry and mining, 21 per cent to agriculture, irrigation and community development, 19 per cent to transport and communications.

In the end the Fourth Plan was postponed by three years. The announcement was made at the end of 1967 that it would begin in 1969–70, and meanwhile three annual plans governed the intervening period.

The revised Fourth Plan published in May 1970 proposed to spend £13,820 million in the 1969–74 quinquennium, for a 5½ per cent average annual growth rate and a target of halving foreign aid. But the plan had to be reshaped because of the interruption of the Bangladesh war in 1971, and the consequent cut-off of American aid. Growth in 1970–71 was only 4.6 per cent, and in the two succeeding years less than 2 per cent.

The Fifth Five-Year Plan

The Fifth Plan (1974–79) stated as its aims the removal of poverty and the attainment of economic self-reliance free from foreign aid. The target was to spend Rs. 476,000 million in investment (Rs. 451,000 million from domestic savings and Rs. 24,000 million in foreign aid) to achieve an average growth of 5.5 per cent during the quinquennium. The Plan started out under the cloud of the sudden setback of quadrupled oil import prices during 1974, was invalidated almost as soon as it was published. A revised plan, with lower targets and expenditure increased to 510,000 million rupees, was expected to be presented during 1976. During 1975/76 economic growth in real terms was between 5 and 6 per cent.

Between 1965 and 1973 India's average annual growth in G.N.P. per head was estimated by the World Bank at 1.5 per cent, with population growing at 2.3 per cent. The 1972 G.N.P. was estimated at Rs. 465,000 million (U.S. $61,940 million) and the G.N.P. per head at Rs 825 ($110).

FOREIGN TRADE AND BALANCE OF PAYMENTS

India's foreign trade reached a level of Rs. 88,000 million in 1975–76, but there are doubts about the potential growth of her exports and, as a consequence, about her capacity to import more in future. Indeed trade began to level off in 1968 for the first time in many years, and then the near-trebling of the oil import bill in 1973–74 dealt a further blow to the trade balance.

Exports remained virtually stagnant during the 1950s, and India's share in world exports dropped from over 2 per cent in 1950 to under 1 per cent in 1965. There was heavy reliance on three traditional export lines—tea, cotton textiles and jute manufactures—which together were earning between 40 per cent and 50 per cent of the total export cheque during the 1960s. New items were becoming better established during the 1960s, however, notably iron ore, sugar, steel goods, handloom fabrics and engineering goods. India's sales to the U.S.A. and to the Soviet Union and Eastern Europe expanded during the 1960s, while exports to Western Europe declined.

In June 1966 the rupee was devalued by 36 per cent, the new rate of exchange being 7.50 to the U.S. $ and roughly 18 to the pound sterling. One purpose of this controversial measure was to shake exports out of their rut, it being freely admitted that the old exchange rate made the new manufactured goods which India was seeking to sell abroad relatively uncompetitive. But at the same time that the rupee was devalued, various incentives and subsidies previously attaching to exports were abolished, and export duties were imposed on the traditional export lines for which the new exchange rate was unlikely to increase world demand. Exports in 1975/76 rose by 15 per cent to 38,000 million rupees.

India is nevertheless exporting a growing quantity of the products of her newer industries, and it is these which have the growth potential (her exports of cotton textiles to the U.S.A., Britain and other important markets are restricted under quota arrangements with those Governments). Recent orders include ones for railway wagons and locomotives to the U.S.S.R. and South Korea, refrigerators to Italy, U.S.S.R. and Iran, telecommunications equipment to African countries, electrical transmission lines to the U.S.A., motor cars and diesel engines. Engineering exports in 1973–74 reached the value of Rs. 2,000 million.

Imports into India reached the annual level of Rs. 7,200 million in the First Plan, Rs. 9,800 million in the Second and Rs. 12,300 million in the Third; the Fourth Draft Outline proposed Rs. 15,300 million. The main items which have increased substantially in recent years are chemical fertilizer, cereals (until 1972), machinery, cotton, oil products, chemicals and steel. Out of a total import bill of between U.S. $2,700 million and $3,000 million, India's spending on foreign food and fertilizer rose from $660 million in 1964–65 to $770 million in the following year and $950 million in 1966–67 (declining in the following years). Raw cotton and jute were responsible for just over $100 million in each of those years. Machinery and transport equipment accounted for over $1,000 million in 1964–65 and 1965–66, but fell to $760 million in 1966–67 and further in 1967–68. This trend partly reflects India's growing capacity to provide her own machinery for industrial expansion, but it is also an indicator of the damage done by the 1965–67 crisis to the development effort. In post-devaluation rupee terms, imports rose to 48,680 million rupees in 1974/75, with oil accounting for nearly a quarter.

In 1974/75 the U.S.S.R., the U.S.A. and the United Kingdom were India's principal overseas markets, and the U.S.A., Iran, Japan, the U.S.S.R. and the Federal Republic of Germany its principal suppliers. A complex structure of trade agreements has been built up with the U.S.S.R. and Eastern European countries, many of which are now investing capital funds in Indian industry as well as buying from India the cheap consumer goods for which they used formerly to depend on China. A State Trading Corporation was established in 1956 to deal with Soviet bloc trade and to fill in the gaps which private trading had left. It specializes in barter and link arrangements. All foreign trade, and especially imports, are subject to strict Government control licensing.

As has been seen, the trade balance is normally in India's disfavour: the deficit was 4,200 million rupees in 1973/74 and a record 12,000 million rupees for 1975/76. This gap was filled by foreign aid.

FOREIGN ECONOMIC AID

Up to March 1973, approximately £6,850 million in foreign economic assistance had been disbursed to India, and some 60 per cent of this derived directly from the U.S.A. The gross aid flow in 1971–72 was £515 million, and in 1972–73 it was put at £390 million. But debt servicing now amounts to more than Rs. 6,000 million a year, so the net flow is much smaller.

When her First Plan began India had the advantage of possessing sizeable sterling balances in London, the outcome of her Second World War procurements. These cushioned her against foreign exchange deficits and enabled her to import more development material from abroad than she was actually able to afford from export or other earnings at the time. By the mid-1950s, however, this cushion had disappeared and India found herself in the position of either having to slow down her development programmes drastically or else to rely on large amounts of foreign aid. As a leading advocate of non-alignment who had frequently clashed with Mr. John Foster Dulles, Nehru could well have been rebuffed by the only foreign aid donor with resources large enough to meet India's needs, namely the U.S.A. But in fact Washington did come to the rescue, and the Indian economy enjoyed the distinction of becoming the first one to be underwritten by both the Soviets and the Americans. On the Western side, aid to India became institutionalized through the so-called Consortium or Aid-India Club organized by the World Bank in 1958, comprising ten Western donors (for further details, *see* chapter on *Aid and Investment*).

Much of the aid comes in the form of foodgrains, and most of that under the American PL 480 provisions which carry very easy terms. Of the gross aid flow to India from all sources during the Third Plan period of £2,150 million, some 30 per cent came in the form of food and debt servicing took another

19 per cent, leaving only half for real development purposes).

The flow of aid was badly interrupted by the war over Kashmir in 1965, which happened by bad luck to coincide with a period of balance of payments difficulties on the side of the U.S.A. and Britain. In any event the climate of opinion in the West was turning gradually against aid, and the Indian aid programme never fully recovered. The Indian nuclear explosion of 1974 did not help to restore aid donors' confidence and U.S. aid was cut off for a time. Foreign aid for 1974/75 totalled 4,800 million rupees. The 1975/76 budget provided for 13,400 million rupees in external assistance.

The Indian goal to become independent of foreign aid by 1978–79 was abandoned in 1975 because of higher oil prices. India receives economic aid from almost every donor in the world, the chief sources being, apart from the World Bank and the International Development Association and other international agencies, the U.S.A., the United Kingdom, Canada, Japan, Federal Republic of Germany, France, Italy, Holland, Belgium, Austria and the Soviet Union.

CONCLUSION

Of the many paradoxes which characterize the Indian economy, one of the most striking is that India is at one and the same time one of the best administered and yet also one of the poorest and slowest-moving of all the economies of the Third World. There is more experience and less waste of aid than almost anywhere else in the South, and India's needs are better accepted. There is widespread goodwill towards Indian development. And yet the performance to date has been disappointing, at least to those foreigners who had hoped for a faster timetable.

Another paradox is that although the India of Nehru, at least, was foremost in internationalism, her size is so great that she is bound to seek virtual self-sufficiency in material things. India thus on the one hand supports the demand of the rubber-growing developing countries for commodity price stabilization and better assurance of markets, yet on the other hand feels obliged to launch a synthetic rubber industry of her own to meet her own industrial and technical ambitions. This potential near-sufficiency explains the relative smallness of India's foreign trade.

So far the conflicting goals of the Nehru vision—democracy, fast progress and equality—have managed uncomfortably to co-exist in the changes that have been set afoot in this society of 600 million people. But it is doubtful if they can remain in harness much longer. A choice has increasingly to be made between welfare (which means essentially consumption now) or growth (which means more cake to share out in the future): it is in the nature of democracy to prefer the former to the latter, since the short term always looms largest, especially to people who have never known prosperity.

On the other hand it could be argued that what happens in Delhi, what the politicians and scholars and administrators do, is becoming less and less consequential in an economy which is proliferating progress through thousands of rural and urban entrepreneurs. The planners have seen to it that Indian industry now has a good start (and is currently working far below capacity, so that further advances are possible without more investment), and the hybrid seed researchers have seen to it that the go-ahead farmers in favoured areas (perhaps one in three) can now see success within their grasp. Whatever further mistakes are made in New Delhi, and however ungenerous the foreign aid donors are in the 1970s, it would seem that nothing can stop the ferment of change which is the guarantee of India's economic advance.

STATISTICAL SURVEY

AREA AND POPULATION*

Area	Census Population				Estimated Population (mid-year)		Density (per sq. km.)
	March 1st, 1961	April 1st, 1971§					
		Males	Females	Total	1974	1975	1975
3,287,590 sq. km.†	439,234,771‡	284,044,814	264,109,755	548,154,569	586,266,000	598,100,000	181.9

* Including Sikkim (incorporated into India on April 26th, 1975) and the Indian-held part of Jammu and Kashmir.

† 1,269,346 sq. miles.

‡ Including an estimate of 626,667 for the former Portuguese territories of Goa, Daman and Diu, incorporated into India in December 1961.

§ Figures exclude adjustment for undernumeration, estimated at 1.67 per cent.

STATES AND TERRITORIES

States	Capitals	Area (sq. kilometres)	Population (1971 Census)
Andhra Pradesh	Hyderabad	276,754	43,502,708
Assam*	Dispur	78,523	14,957,542
Bihar	Patna	173,876	56,353,369
Gujarat	Gandhinagar	195,984	26,697,475
Haryana	Chandigarh‡	44,222	10,036,808
Himachal Pradesh	Simla	55,673	3,460,434
Jammu and Kashmir†	Srinagar	138,995	4,616,632
Karnataka	Bangalore	191,773	29,299,014
Kerala	Trivandrum	38,864	21,347,375
Madhya Pradesh	Bhopal	442,841	41,654,119
Maharashtra	Bombay	307,762	50,412,235
Manipur	Imphal	22,356	1,072,753
Meghalaya	Shillong	22,489	1,011,699
Nagaland	Kohima	16,527	516,449
Orissa	Bhubaneswar	155,842	21,944,615
Punjab	Chandigarh‡	50,362	13,551,060
Rajasthan	Jaipur	342,214	25,765,806
Sikkim	Gangtok	7,107	204,760
Tamil Nadu	Madras	130,069	41,199,168
Tripura	Agartala	10,477	1,556,342
Uttar Pradesh	Lucknow	294,413	88,341,144
West Bengal	Calcutta	87,853	44,312,011
Territories	Chief Towns		
Andaman and Nicobar Islands	Port Blair	8,293	115,133
Arunachal Pradesh	Itanagar	83,578	467,511
Chandigarh	Chandigarh	114	257,251
Dadra and Nagar Haveli	Silvassa	491	74,170
Delhi	Delhi	1,485	4,065,698
Goa, Daman and Diu	Panaji	3,813	857,771
Lakshadweep	Kavaratti	32	31,810
Mizoram*	Aizawl	21,087	n.a.
Pondicherry	Pondicherry	480	471,707

* Population figures for Assam include those for Mizoram.

† Figures refer only to the Indian-held part of the territory. The total area of Jammu and Kashmir is 222,802 square kilometres.

‡ Chandigarh forms a separate Union Territory, not within Haryana or Punjab.

PRINCIPAL TOWNS
(population at 1971 census*)

Town	Population	Town	Population	Town	Population
New Delhi (capital)	301,801	Agra	591,917	Gwalior	384,772
Bombay	5,970,575	Varanasi (Banaras)	583,856	Hubli-Dharwar	379,166
Delhi	3,287,883	Madurai	549,114	Coimbatore	365,368
Calcutta	3,148,746	Indore	543,381	Mysore	355,685
Madras	2,469,449	Allahabad	490,622	Visakhapatnam	352,504
Hyderabad	1,607,396	Patna	473,001	Jamshedpur	341,576
Ahmedabad	1,585,544	Surat	471,656	Kozhikode (Calicut)	333,979
Bangalore	1,540,741	Vadodara (Baroda)	466,696	Jodhpur	317,612
Kanpur (Cawnpore)	1,154,388	Cochin	439,066	Vijayawada (Vijayavada)	317,258
Nagpur	866,076	Jabalpur (Jubbulpore)	426,224	Salem	308,716
Pune (Poona)	856,105	Trivandrum	409,672	Trichurapalli (Tiruchirapalli)	307,400
Lucknow	749,239	Amritsar	407,628	Rajkot	300,612
Howrah	737,877	Srinagar	403,413		
Jaipur (Jeypore)	615,258	Sholapur	398,361		
		Ludhiana	397,850		

* Figures refer to the city proper in each case. For urban agglomerations, the following populations were recorded: Delhi 3,647,023 (incl. New Delhi); Calcutta and South Suburban 7,031,382 (incl. Howrah); Madras 3,169,930; Hyderabad 1,796,339; Ahmedabad 1,741,522; Bangalore 1,653,779; Kanpur 1,275,242; Nagpur 930,459; Pune 1,135,034; Lucknow 813,982; Jaipur 636,768; Agra 634,622; Varanasi 606,721; Madurai 711,501; Indore 560,936; Allahabad 513,036; Patna 491,217; Surat 493,001; Vadodara 467,487; Jabalpur 534,845.

BIRTH AND DEATH RATES

	Birth Rate (per 1,000)	Death Rate (per 1,000) (years)	Life Expectancy at Birth	Growth Rate (%)
1951–61	41.7	22.8	41.2	21.64
1961–71	n.a.	14.0	52.6	24.66

ECONOMICALLY ACTIVE POPULATION*
(1971 census)

	Males	Females	Total
Agriculture, hunting, forestry and fishing	104,119,100	25,843,900	129,963,000
Mining and quarrying	798,700	124,100	922,800
Manufacturing (incl. repair services)	14,871,700	2,195,800	17,067,500
Electricity, gas and water supply	522,800	9,600	532,400
Construction	2,011,800	203,500	2,215,300
Trade, restaurants and hotels	8,230,200	518,100	8,748,300
Transport, storage and communications	4,255,300	145,900	4,401,200
Finance, insurance, property and business services	1,251,800	38,100	1,289,900
Community, social and personal services (excl. repair services)	11,985,700	2,032,200	14,017,900
Other activities (not adequately described)	1,028,000	187,100	1,215,100
Total	149,075,136	31,298,263	180,373,399

* Excluding Sikkim and a part of the North East Frontier Agency. Figures exclude persons who were unemployed or seeking work for the first time. Distribution by economic activity is based on a 1 per cent sample tabulation of census returns.

AGRICULTURE

LAND USE*

('000 hectares)

	1971/72	1972/73
Arable Land†	160,800	161,590
Under Permanent Crops	4,350	4,620
Permanent Meadows and Pastures	13,080	12,870
Forest Land	65,710	67,450
Other Areas	62,280	59,620
TOTAL	306,220	306,150

* Reported area only. Total area (excl. Sikkim) was 328,048,000 hectares, including the Indian-held part of Kashmir-Jammu.

† Net area sown plus fallow lands.

PRINCIPAL CROPS

(April 1st to March 31st)

	AREA ('000 hectares)			PRODUCTION ('000 metric tons)		
	1971/72	1972/73	1973/74	1971/72	1972/73	1973/74
Rice (milled)	37,758	36,688	38,011	43,068	39,245	43,742
Sorghum (Jowar)	16,777	15,513	16,964	7,722	6,968	8,992
Cat-tail millet (Bajra)	11,773	11,817	13,646	5,319	3,929	7,086
Maize	5,668	5,838	6,021	5,101	6,388	5,643
Finger millet (Ragi)	2,425	2,329	2,392	2,208	1,923	2,131
Small millets	4,477	4,265	4,532	1,669	1,552	1,864
Wheat	19,139	19,463	19,057	26,410	24,735	22,073
Barley	2,455	2,449	2,625	2,577	2,379	2,327
Total cereals	100,472	98,362	103,247	94,074	87,119	93,857
Chick-peas (Gram)	7,912	6,967	7,691	5,081	4,537	4,006
Pigeon peas (Tur)	2,346	2,424	2,576	1,683	1,928	1,364
Dry beans, dry peas, lentils and other pulses	11,893	11,524	12,614	4,330	3,442	4,384
Total food grains	122,623	119,277	126,128	105,168	97,026	103,611
Groundnuts	7,510	6,990	6,900	6,181	4,092	5,799
Sesame seed	2,392	2,288	2,358	449	385	486
Rapeseed and mustard	3,614	3,319	3,428	1,433	1,808	1,692
Linseed	2,064	1,726	1,876	529	428	471
Castor beans	453	426	529	154	145	235
Total oil seeds	16,033	14,749	15,091	8,746	6,858	8,682
Cotton (lint)	7,800	7,679	7,601	6,564	5,417	5,819
Jute	815	700	793	5,684	4,978	6,220
Kenaf (Mesta)	296	293	370	1,150	1,112	1,456
Tea	357	359	361	435	456	472
Gur	2,390	2,452	2,722	11,626	12,763	14,046
Sugar cane	2,390	2,452	2,722	113,570	124,867	137,833
Tobacco	458	445	447	419	364	441
Potatoes	492	505	533	4,826	4,451	4,626
Chillies (dry)	753	682	732	494	412	488

Source: Directorate of Economics and Statistics, Ministry of Agriculture and Irrigation, Department of Agriculture, New Delhi, India.

LIVESTOCK

(FAO estimates, '000 head)

	1972	1973	1974
Cattle	178,865	179,400	179,900
Sheep	40,395	40,200	40,000
Goats	68,024	68,500	69,000
Pigs	6,456	6,700	6,900
Horses	966	930	900
Asses	980	980	980
Mules	90	92	95
Buffaloes	57,941	59,000	60,000
Camels	1,126	1,130	1,130
Poultry	117,500	117,705	117,910

Source: FAO, *Production Yearbook 1974.*

MILK PRODUCTION, 1973/74

(metric tons)

Cows' Milk	9,744,000
Buffaloes' Milk	12,760,000
Goats' Milk	696,000

Source: Ministry of Agriculture and Irrigation, Government of India, 1975.

OTHER LIVESTOCK PRODUCTS

(FAO estimates, metric tons)

	1972	1973	1974
Beef and Veal	68,000	70,000	71,000
Buffalo Meat	114,000	116,000	116,000
Mutton and Lamb	114,000	116,000	117,000
Goats' Meat	263,000	268,000	268,000
Pig Meat	52,000	53,000	54,000
Poultry Meat	90,000	95,000	100,000
Other Meat	80,000	84,000	87,000
Edible Offals	97,630	99,353	99,876
Tallow	33,000	33,100	33,200
Butter and Ghee	438,000	438,300	438,600
Hen Eggs	80,000	81,000	81,200
Wool: Greasy	35,500	35,700	36,100
Clean	22,200	22,200	22,400
Cattle Hides (fresh)	428,000	438,000	440,000
Buffalo Hides (fresh)	294,000	300,000	306,999
Sheep Skins (fresh)	32,400	33,300	34,194
Goat Skins (fresh)	65,340	66,600	67,588

Source: FAO, *Production Yearbook 1974.*

FORESTRY

ROUNDWOOD REMOVALS

(FAO estimates, '000 cubic metres)

	Coniferous (soft wood)		Broadleaved (hard wood)		Total	
	1971	1972	1971	1972	1971	1972
Sawlogs, veneer logs and logs for sleepers	1,215	1,260	5,200	5,370	6,415	6,630
Pitprops (mine timber)	—	—	1,110	1,150	1,110	1,150
Pulpwood	30	50	350	530	380	580
Other industrial wood	70	70	2,130	2,180	2,200	2,250
Total Industrial Wood	1,315	1,380	8,790	9,230	10,105	10,610
Fuel wood	3,100	3,200	100,400	102,800	103,500	106,000
Total	4,415	4,580	109,910	112,030	113,605	116,610

Source: FAO, *Yearbook of Forest Products.*

SAWNWOOD PRODUCTION

('000 cubic metres)

	1967	1968	1969	1970*	1971*	1972*
Coniferous sawnwood (incl. boxboards)	575	600	625	650	675	700
Broadleaved sawnwood (incl. boxboards)	1,725	1,800	1,875	1,950	2,025	2,100
	2,300	2,400	2,500	2,600	2,700	2,800
Railway sleepers	237	187	184	196	200	200
Total	2,537	2,587	2,684	2,796	2,900	3,000

* FAO estimate.

Source: FAO, *Yearbook of Forest Products.*

FISHING

('000 metric tons, live weight)

	1968	1969*	1970	1971	1972	1973
Indian Ocean:						
Bombay duck	82.4	76.3	78.4	71.5	51.5	140.0
Marine catfishes	23.7	26.8	50.6	48.9	41.2	47.4
Ponyfishes (Slipmouths)	36.5	44.1	49.4	32.7	32.6	31.8
Indian oil-sardine (Sardinelle)	301.4	174.2	226.0	209.3	125.4	72.7
Shortbodied mackerel and Indian mackerel	20.8	91.8	139.2	204.6	121.2	69.9
Other marine fishes	334.2	384.5	408.3	434.5	427.3	631.0
Total Sea Fish	799.0	797.7	951.9	1,001.5	799.2	992.8
Shrimps and prawns	99.8	107.6	121.7	148.8	159.7	207.7
Other marine animals	5.1	6.5	12.0	11.1	12.6	9.9
Total Sea Catch	903.9	911.8	1,085.6	1,161.4	971.5	1,210.4
Inland waters:						
Freshwater fishes	621.7	693.2	670.5	690.2	665.8	747.6
Total Catch	1,525.6	1,605.0	1,756.1	1,851.6	1,637.3	1,958.0

* Provisional figures. Revised total (in '000 metric tons) is 1,606.8.

Source: FAO, *Yearbook of Fishery Statistics.*

1974 ('000 metric tons): Total catch 2,255.3.

MINING

		1970	1971	1972	1973
Hard Coal	'000 metric tons	73,698	71,499	74,766	77,077
Lignite	,, ,, ,,	3,544.6	3,660	3,067	3,305
Iron Ore: gross weight	,, ,, ,,	31,366	34,310	35,476	35,401
metal content	,, ,, ,,	19,654	21,543	22,221	22,175
Bauxite	,, ,, ,,	1,374	1,517	1,684	1,285
Chalk	,, ,, ,,	48	48.8	60.1	64.7
Clay	,, ,, ,,	1,315	1,489	1,610	n.a.
Dolomite	,, ,, ,,	1,134.9	1,320	1,348	1,431
Gypsum	,, ,, ,,	915	1,088	1,105	880.8
Limestone	,, ,, ,,	23,843	25,079	25,946	24,259
Manganese Ore: gross weight	,, ,, ,,	1,665.2	1,841	1,643	1,461
metal content	,, ,, ,,	632.1	680.8	614.3	542.5
Crude Petroleum	,, ,, ,,	6,809	7,185	7,373	7,197
Salt (unrefined)	,, ,, ,,	5,588	5,426	6,521	6,864
Asbestos	metric tons	11,000	13,581	12,359	11,838
Chromium Ore: gross weight	,, ,,	270,879	273,060	294,500	287,216
metal content	,, ,,	135,241	137,518	139,718	145,056
Copper Ore*	,, ,,	10,256	12,000	14,624	17,335
Corundum	,, ,,	412	318	} 3,626	265
Garnet (abrasive)	,, ,,	986	1,391		2,760
Kyanite	,, ,,	119,043	63,382	67,897	53,941
Lead Concentrates*	,, ,,	2,499	3,035	3,719	6,776
Magnesite (crude)	,, ,,	354,291	295,604	250,931	193,266
Mica (crude)†	,, ,,	21,894	19,775	18,956	18,630
Phosphate Rock: Apatite	,, ,,	15,997	11,307	} 229,000	145,000
Phosphorite	,, ,,	156,353	232,170		
Pyrites (unroasted)	,, ,,	26,400	40,886	30,723	41,507
Sillimanite	,, ,,	4,489	4,326	4,046	3,086
Steatite	,, ,,	159,000	177,000	211,000	207,000
Tungsten Concentrates*	,, ,,	23	19	21	17
Zinc Concentrates*	,, ,,	8,246	8,403	9,483	13,190
Gold*	kilogrammes	3,241	3,656	3,290	2,946
Silver*	,,	1,540	3,773	4,427	4,254
Diamonds: industrial	'000 metric carats	4	4	4	4
gem	,, ,, ,,	16	15	16	17
Emeralds	,, ,, ,,	11.6	22.5	21.4	3.4
Natural Gas	million cubic metres	488	560	693	682

* Figures refer to the metal content of ores and concentrates.
† Exports, including scrap and splittings.

Sources: The Times of India Directory and Yearbook 1976; United Nations, *The Growth of World Industry*.

1974 ('000 metric tons): Hard coal 83,240, Lignite 3,010, Iron ore 34,240 (gross weight), Bauxite 1,072, Crude petroleum 7,490, Copper 28.1 (metal content), Lead concentrates 8.4 (metal content), Zinc concentrates 16.6 (metal content), Natural gas 720 million cubic metres.

INDUSTRY

		1971	1972	1973
Refined Sugar*	'000 metric tons	3,381	3,840	n.a.
Cotton Cloth	million metres	7,356	8,024	7,833
Jute Manufactures†	'000 metric tons	1,087	1,116	1,032
Paper and Paper Board	,, ,, ,,	785	804	768
Sulphuric Acid	,, ,, ,,	1,021	1,308	1,320
Soda Ash	,, ,, ,,	479	486	470
Fertilizers	,, ,, ,,	847	1,034	1,046
Petroleum Products	,, ,, ,,	18,104	18,276	19,116
Cement	,, ,, ,,	14,932	15,756	15,006
Pig Iron	,, ,, ,,	6,740	7,183	7,341
Finished Steel	,, ,, ,,	4,676	4,852	4,788
Aluminium	metric tons	176,118	179,100	154,332
Diesel Engines (stationary)	number	83,846	72,672	137,196
Sewing Machines	,,	328,850	312,000	264,000
Radio Receivers	,,	1,944,000	1,920,000	1,656,000
Electric Fans	,,	1,944,000	2,520,000	2,076,000
Passenger Cars and Jeeps	,,	50,292	52,632	55,248
Passenger Buses and Trucks	,,	37,452	33,924	36,336
Motor Cycles and Scooters	,,	106,944	111,900	126,888
Bicycles	,,	1,929,600	2,224,000	2,544,000

* Figures relate to crop year (beginning November) and are in respect of cane sugar only.

† Figures refer to production by members of the Indian Jute Mills Association and one non-member.

Source: Central Statistical Organization, *Monthly Abstract of Statistics.*

FINANCE

100 paisa (singular, paise) = 1 Indian rupee.
Coins: 1, 2, 3, 5, 10, 20, 25 and 50 paisa; 1 rupee.
Notes: 1, 2, 5, 10, 20, 100, 1,000, 5,000 and 10,000 rupees.
Exchange rates (June 1976): £1 sterling = 16.275 rupees; U.S. $1 = 9.174 rupees.
100 Indian rupees = £6.14 = $10.90.

Note: Between September 1949 and June 1966 the Indian rupee had a par value of 21 U.S. cents (U.S. $1 = 4.7619 rupees). From June 1966 to December 1971 the exchange rate was $1 = 7.50 rupees (1 rupee = 13.33 U.S. cents). In terms of sterling, the rate between November 1967 and August 1971 was £1 = 18.00 rupees. In December 1971 a new central exchange rate of £1 = 18.9677 rupees was established. Until the "floating" of the pound in June 1972 this was equivalent to a rate of U.S. $1 = 7.279 rupees. Until September 1975 the Indian authorities maintained the exchange rate against sterling, thus allowing the rupee to "float" in relation to other currencies. Since September 1975 the rupee has been pegged to a "basket" of currencies of India's principal trading partners. The average market rates (rupees per U.S. dollar) were: 7.594 in 1972; 7.742 in 1973; 8.102 in 1974; 8.376 in 1975.

BUDGET

(million rupees, April 1st to March 31st)

Revenue	1973/74	1974/75
Customs	9,742.0	9,360.5
Union excise duties	26,338.4	30,449.1
Corporation tax	6,270.0	6,610.0
Income tax	6,730.0	7,090.0
Other taxes	1,439.5	1,477.5
Interest receipts	7,858.8	8,621.6
Dividends and profits	1,830.9	1,909.2
Other receipts	2,555.6	2,872.8
Gross current revenue	62,765.2	68,390.7
Less states' share of taxes	−11,735.7	−11,982.1
Net current revenue	51,029.5	56,408.6
Capital accounts receipts	26,860.0	30,990.0
Total	77,889.5	87,398.6

Expenditure	1973/74	1974/75
Interest payments	8,974.8	9,751.3
Administrative services	3,353.7	3,890.9
Defence	15,511.3	16,797.3
Other general services	1,678.4	2,022.2
Social and community services	3,243.8	4,508.1
Economic services	6,600.8	6,035.6
Aid and contributions	11,184.7	11,073.4
Total current expenditure	49,547.5	54,078.8
Capital expenditure	34,840.0	34,570.0
Total	84,387.5	88,648.8

Currency in circulation: 65,820 million rupees (February 1976).

INTERNATIONAL RESERVES
(U.S. $ million at December 31st)

	1967	1968	1969	1970	1971	1972	1973	1974	1975
Gold	243	243	243	243	264	264	293	298	284
IMF Special Drawing Rights	—	—	—	44	161	268	296	294	248
Reserve position in IMF	—	—	—	21	83	83	92	—	—
Foreign exchange	419	439	683	698	699	566	461	733	841
TOTAL	662	682	926	1,006	1,206	1,180	1,142	1,325	1,373

Source: IMF, *International Financial Statistics.*

BALANCE OF PAYMENTS
(million Special Drawing Rights)

	1971			1972		
	Credit	Debit	Net	Credit	Debit	Net
Merchandise						
Exports (f.o.b.)	1,967	—	1,967	2,202	—	2,202
Imports (mainly c.i.f.)	—	2,605	−2,605	—	2,379	−2,379
TRADE BALANCE	—	638	− 638	—	177	− 177
Non-monetary gold	n.a.	n.a.	n.a.	n.a.	n.a.	n.a.
Merchandise freight	78	16	62	87	18	69
Insurance on merchandise	10	—	10	12	—	12
Other transportation	66	79	− 13	60	67	− 7
Travel	40	24	16	44	26	18
Investment income	47	349	− 302	41	326	− 281
Other government services	42	34	8	36	28	8
Non-merchandise insurance	6	22	− 16	9	18	− 9
Other private services	62	98	− 36	65	98	− 33
TOTAL GOODS AND SERVICES	2,318	3,227	− 909	2,556	2,960	− 404
Unrequited Transfers:						
Private	209	17	192	206	13	193
Colombo Plan	38	—	38	7		7
U.S. Government	29	—	29	95		95
Other government transfers	17	8	9	1	35	− 34
TOTAL CURRENT ACCOUNT	2,611	3,252	− 641	2,865	3,008	− 143
Private long-term capital	47	69	− 22	62	64	− 2
Private short-term capital (net)	—	3	− 3	—	1	− 1
Local government capital (net)	—	1	− 1	—	1	− 1
Central government capital	1,032	239	793	628	348	280
Deposit money banks	8	7	1	18	17	1
Reserve Bank (net liabilities)	—	11	− 11	—	19	− 19
TOTAL CAPITAL ACCOUNT (net)	757	—	757	258	—	258
Net errors and omissions	—	94	− 94	—	234	− 234
Allocation of SDRs	101	—	101	100	—	100
BALANCE (net monetary movements)	123	—	123	—	19	− 19

Source: International Monetary Fund, *Balance of Payments Yearbook.*

EXTERNAL TRADE
(million rupees, April 1st to March 31st)

	1969/70	1970/71	1971/72	1972/73	1973/74	1974/75
Imports	15,821	16,342	18,245	18,674	29,554	44,681
Exports	14,087	15,244	16,032	19,644	25,183	32,986

COMMODITIES

Imports (c.i.f.)	1973/74	1974/75
Food	5,471	8,550
Cereals	4,731	7,638
Beverages and Tobacco	4	10
Crude Materials, Inedible	1,842	2,189
Textile Fibres	928	664
Minerals, excl. Fuels and Precious Stones	299	638
Mineral Fuels and Lubricants	5,606	11,570
Animal and Vegetable Oils and Fats	649	349
Chemicals	3,575	7,119
Fertilizers, Manufactured	1,628	4,252
Basic Manufactures	5,393	7,631
Iron and Steel	2,495	4,173
Copper	708	730
Metal Manufactures	219	273
Machinery and Transport Equipment	6,516	6,698
Non-Electrical Machinery	4,266	3,968
Power-generating Machinery, non-electrical	479	452
Metal-working Machinery	239	304
Industrial Machinery and Parts	3,285	3,072
Electrical Machinery	1,300	1,501
Transport Equipment	950	1,229
Miscellaneous Manufactured Articles	417	456
Other Items	81	41
Total	29,554	44,681*

Exports	1973/74	1974/75
Food	6,788	10,134
Tea	1,460	2,240
Beverages and Tobacco	710	823
Crude Materials, Inedible	3,623	4,312
Metal Ores and Scrap	1,560	1,967
Cotton Fibres	367	171
Mineral Fuels and Lubricants	154	204
Animal and Vegetable Oils and Fats	321	344
Chemicals	582	1,037
Basic Manufactures	9,989	11,565
Leather and Leather Goods	1,722	1,449
Textile Yarns, Fabrics, etc.	5,677	6,198
Cotton Manufactures, excl. Yarn, Thread and Clothing	2,399	2,148
Jute Manufactures	2,257	2,929
Machinery and Transport Equipment	1,160	2,104
Miscellaneous Manufactured Articles	1,788	2,396
Other Items	68	67
Total	25,183	32,986

* Includes value of some articles which are under reference.

PRINCIPAL TRADING PARTNERS

Imports	1973/74	1974/75
Australia	438	1,185
Belgium	657	1,019
Burma	1	—
Canada	1,159	1,304
Czechoslovakia	267	333
France	703	812
German Democratic Republic	250	333
Germany, Federal Republic	2,058	3,069
Iran	2,676	4,727
Italy	494	784
Japan	2,595	4,535
Malaysia	321	112
Netherlands	566	476
Pakistan	—	—
Poland	462	929
Sri Lanka	9	2
Sweden	239	260
Switzerland	169	365
Thailand	18	23
U.S.S.R.	2,547	4,025
United Kingdom	2,522	2,134
United States	4,984	7,291
Yugoslavia	86	97

Exports (f.o.b.)	1973/74	1974/75
Australia	507	612
Belgium	444	518
Burma	15	46
Canada	310	440
Czechoslovakia	438	602
Egypt	149	524
France	486	839
German Democratic Republic	220	344
Germany, Federal Republic	864	1,050
Italy	693	521
Japan	3,585	2,949
Malaysia	246	281
Nepal	301	424
Netherlands	733	709
New Zealand	135	207
Pakistan	—	—
Poland	513	769
Sri Lanka	98	268
Sudan	186	665
U.S.S.R.	2,859	4,181
United Kingdom	2,627	3,063
United States	3,453	3,750
Yugoslavia	239	297

Source: Department of Commercial Intelligence and Statistics, Government of India, 1975.

TRANSPORT

RAILWAYS

(million)

	1970	1971	1972
Passengers	2,328.0	2,482.8	2,700.0
Passenger-kilometres	111,996	121,950	130,836
Freight (metric tons)	182.4	194.4	196.8
Freight tonne-kilometres	120,936	126,264	131,616

Source: Monthly Abstract of Statistics.

ROAD TRAFFIC

(Motor vehicles in use at December 31st)

	1969	1970	1971	1972
Private cars	570,148	588,837	619,826	646,463
Buses and coaches	85,692	91,283	98,122	102,690
Goods vehicles	305,218	318,915	333,333	346,020
Motor cycles and scooters	398,527	485,374	579,024	673,778

Source: International Road Federation, *World Road Statistics 1968-1972*, Geneva 1973.

INTERNATIONAL SEA-BORNE SHIPPING

(Twelve months ending March 31st)

	1971/72	1972/73	1973/74
Vessels* ('000 net reg. tons):			
Entered	17,818	17,336	19,471
Cleared	15,088	15,003	16,289
Freight† ('000 metric tons):			
Loaded	28,347	29,004	31,908
Unloaded	26,123	25,354	28,914

* Excluding minor and intermediate ports. † Including bunkers.

Source: United Nations, *Statistical Yearbook* and *Monthly Bulletin of Statistics*.

CIVIL AVIATION

('000)

	1971	1972	1973
Kilometres flown	59,340	66,800	73,200
Passenger kilometres	3,609,084	4,557,000	5,454,000
Freight tonne-kilometres	111,216	131,100	183,500
Mail tonne-kilometres	17,556	20,300	21,400

Source: United Nations, *Statistical Yearbook 1974*.

COMMUNICATIONS MEDIA
(1972)

Radios	12,772,000
Television sets	49,000
Telephones	1,396,000
Newspapers	4,923

Source: United Nations *Statistical Yearbook 1974.*

TOURISM
FOREIGN VISITORS

	1972	1973
Australia	9,315	13,070
Canada	9,360	11,741
France	17,998	28,009
Germany*	19,799	27,079
Italy	6,822	13,809
Japan	16,359	20,707
Switzerland	6,400	8,401
United Kingdom	50,864	58,723
U.S.A.	58,885	61,616
TOTAL (incl. all others)	342,950	409,895

* Figure includes visitors from both the German Democratic Republic and the Federal Republic of Germany.

Source: United Nations, *Statistical Yearbook, 1974.*

EDUCATION
(1970–71)*

	PUPILS†	TEACHERS
Primary: lower	63,100,000	1,026,152
upper	14,900,000	576,363
Secondary	8,400,000	523,341
Higher	2,540,000	119,000

* Academic year. † 1971–72.

Source: Central Statistical Organization, New Delhi; Department of Commercial Intelligence and Statistics, Calcutta.

THE CONSTITUTION

In June 1975, following the declaration of a state of emergency in India, the rights under articles 14, 19, 21 and 22 of the Constitution (which had guaranteed respectively: equality before the law; freedom of speech and expression, assembly and association rights, freedom of movement, property management and trade; protection of life and personal liberty; protection from arrest) were suspended and numerous amendments adopted, giving the Government greater powers with which to enforce and maintain the state of emergency. Natural rights were suspended and no court could enforce them; detainees under the Maintenance of Internal Security (Amendment) Bill 1975 could not be told the grounds of their detention, were forbidden bail and any claim to liberty through natural or common law; the proclamation of emergency was placed outside the jurisdiction of the courts, leaving no redress against misuse by the State of its powers even after the emergency; the President, Prime Minister and State governors were to be immune from criminal prosecution for life and from civil prosecution during their term of office.

The Constitution of India, adopted by the Constituent Assembly in November 1949, was inaugurated on January 26th, 1950, on which date India became a sovereign democratic republic.

The Constitution declares in the preamble that the People of India solemnly resolve to constitute a Sovereign Democratic Republic and to secure to all its citizens justice, liberty, equality and fraternity. There are 397 articles and 9 schedules, which form a comprehensive document. The Constitution is flexible in character, and a simple process of amendment has been adopted.

Union of States. The Union of India comprises 22 states and 9 Union Territories (1975). There are provisions for the formation and admission of new states.

The Constitution confers citizenship on a threefold basis of birth, descent, and residence. Provisions are made for refugees who have migrated from Pakistan and for persons of Indian origin residing abroad.

Fundamental Rights and Directive Principles. The rights of the citizen contained in Part III of the Constitution are declared fundamental and enforceable in law. "Untouchability" is abolished and its practice in any form is a punishable offence. The Directive Principles of State Policy provide a code intended to ensure promotion of the economic, social and educational welfare of the State in future legislation.

The President is the head of the Union, exercising all executive power on the advice of ministers responsible to

Parliament. He is elected by an electoral college consisting of elected members of both Houses of Parliament and the Legislatures of the States. The President holds office for a term of five years and is eligible for re-election. He may be impeached for violation of the Constitution. The Vice-President is the *ex-officio* Chairman of the Upper House and is elected by a joint sitting of both Houses of Parliament.

The Parliament of the Union consists of the President and two Houses: the Rajya Sabha (Upper House) and the Lok Sabha (House of the People). The Rajya Sabha consists of not more than 250 members, of whom 12 are nominated by the President. One-third of its members retire every two years. Elections are indirect, each state's legislative quota being elected by the members of the state's legislative assembly. The Lok Sabha consists of not more than 545 members elected by adult franchise; not more than 20 represent the Union Territories.

Government of the States. The governmental machinery of states closely resembles that of the Union. Each of these states has a governor at its head appointed by the President for a term of five years to exercise executive power on the advice of a Council of Ministers. The state's legislatures consist of the Governor and either one house (legislative assembly) or two houses (legislative assembly and legislative council). The term of the assembly is five years, but the council is not subject to dissolution.

Language. The Constitution provides that the official language of the Union shall be Hindi. (The English language will continue to be an associate language for many official purposes.)

Legislation—Federal System. The Constitution provides that bills, other than money bills, can be introduced in either House. To become law, they must be passed by both Houses and receive the assent of the President. In financial affairs, the authority of the Lower House is final. The various subjects of legislation are enumerated on three lists in the seventh schedule of the Constitution: the Union List, containing nearly 100 entries, including external affairs, defence, communications, and atomic energy; the State List, containing 65 entries, including local government, police, public health, education; and the Concurrent List, with over 40 entries, including criminal law, marriage and divorce, labour welfare. The Constitution vests residuary authority in the Centre. All matters not enumerated in the Concurrent or State Lists will be deemed to be included in the Union List, and in the event of conflict between Union and State Law on any subject enumerated in the Concurrent List the Union Law will prevail. In time of emergency Parliament may even exercise powers otherwise exclusively vested in the states. Under Article 356, "If the President on receipt of a report from the Government of a State or otherwise is satisfied that a situation has arisen in which the government of the State cannot be carried on in accordance with the provisions of this Constitution, the President may by Proclamation: (a) assume to himself all or any of the functions of the Government of the State and all or any of the powers of the Governor or any body or authority in the State other than the Legislature of the State; (b) declare that the powers of the Legislature of the State shall be exercisable by or under the authority of Parliament; (c) make such incidental provisions as appear to the President to be necessary": provided that none of the powers of a High Court be assumed by the President or suspended in any way. Unless such a Proclamation is approved by both Houses of Parliament, it ceases to operate after two months. A Proclamation so approved ceases to operate after six months, unless renewed by Parliament. Its renewal cannot be extended beyond a total period of three years. An independent judiciary exists to define and interpret the Constitution and to resolve constitutional disputes arising between states, or between a state and the Government of India.

Other Provisions of the Constitution deal with the administration of tribal areas, relations between the Union and States, inter-state trade and finance.

The Panchayat Raj scheme, which is designed to decentralize the powers of the Central and State Governments, has been extensively introduced. This scheme is based on the Panchayat (Village Council) and the Gram Sabha (Village Parliament) and envisages the gradual transference of local government from State to local authority. Revenue and internal security will remain State responsibilities at present.

THE GOVERNMENT

President: Fakhruddin Ali Ahmed.

Vice-President: Basappa Danappa Jatti.

THE CABINET

(*July* 1976)

Prime Minister, Minister of Planning, Atomic Energy, Electronics and Space: Indira Gandhi.

Minister of Finance: Chidambaram Subramaniam.

Minister of Defence: Bansi Lal.

Minister of Agriculture and Irrigation: Jagjivan Ram.

Minister of External Affairs: Yeshwantrao Balwantrao Chavan.

Minister of Law, Justice and Company Affairs: Hari Ramachandra Gokhale.

Minister of Home Affairs: Kasu Brahmananda Reddy.

Minister of Industry and Civil Supplies: Tonse Ananth Pai.

Minister of Railways: Kamlapati Tripathi.

Minister of Works, Housing and Parliamentary Affairs: Kotha Raghu Ramaiah.

Minister of Shipping and Transport: Dr. Gurdial Singh Dhillon.

Minister of Petroleum: Keshava Deva Malaviya.

Minister of Tourism and Civil Aviation: Raj Bahadur.

Minister of Health and Family Planning: Dr. Karan Singh.

Minister of Communications: Dr. Shanker Dayal Sharma.

Minister of Fertilizers and Chemicals: Prakash Chandra Sethi.

Minister without Portfolio: Syed Mir Qasim.

MINISTERS OF STATE

Commerce: D. P. CHATTOPADHYAYA.*

Law, Justice and Company Affairs: Dr. V. A. SAYED MOHAMMAD.

Planning: Dr. SANKAR GHOSE.

Revenue and Banking: PRANAB KUMAR MUKHERJEE.

Information and Broadcasting: VIDYA CHARAN SHUKLA.*

Supply and Rehabilitation: RAM NIWAS MIRDHA.

Petroleum and Chemicals and Defence Production: VITHAL GADGIL.*

Tourism and Civil Aviation: SURENDRA PAL SINGH.

Agriculture and Irrigation: ANNASEHEB P. SHINDE, SHAH NAWAZ KHAN.

Parliamentary Affairs, Home Affairs and Personnel: OM MEHTA.

Works and Housing: K. K. L. BHAGAT.

Health and Family Planning: CHAUDHURY RAM SEWAK.*

Railways: MOHD. SHAFI QURESHI.

Education, Social Welfare and Culture: Prof. S. NURUL HASAN.*

Energy and Parliamentary Assistant to the Prime Minister for the Departments of Atomic Energy, Electronic and. Space: KRISHNA CHANDRA PANT.

Industry and Civil Supplies: A. C. GEORGE, B. P. MAURYA, A. P. SHARMA.

Labour: K. V. RAGHUNATHA REDDY.*

Communications: (vacant).

External Affairs: (vacant).

Steel and Mines: CHANDRAJIT YADAV.

Shipping and Transport: HARIPRASAD MULSHANKAR TRIVEDI.

* In charge of Ministries or Departments.

PARLIAMENT

RAJYA SABHA

(Council of States)

Chairman: BASAPPA DANAPPA JATTI.

(*March* 1976)

PARTY	SEATS
Congress	164
Communist	11
Jana Sangh	8
Bharatiya Lok Dal (BLD)	7
Opposition Congress	5
Anna Dravida Munnetra Kazhagam	4
Communist (Marxist)	3
Muslim League	3
Dravida Munnetra Kazhagam (DMK)	2
Independents	17
Others	5
Nominated	8
Vacant	7
TOTAL	244

LOK SABHA

(House of the People)

Speaker: BALI RAM BHAGAT.

(*General election, March* 1971; *distribution of seats following by-elections*, 1973, 1974 and 1975.)

PARTY	SEATS
Congress	364
Jana Sangh	20
Congress (Opposition)	11
Swatantra	7
Socialist	5
Communist (Marxist)	25
Communist (CPI)	23
Dravida Munnetra Kazhagam (DMK)	19
Muslim League	3
Regional Parties	9
Independent	18
Others	17
Vacant	2
TOTAL	523*

* Excluding the Speaker who has no party affiliation.

STATES

The distribution of seats shown for the State legislatures refers to the situation after the elections held in February 1973, except in Manipur, Nagaland, Orissa and Uttar Pradesh, where elections were held in February 1974.

Congress	Indian National Congress (Ruling)
Congress (O)	Indian National Congress (Opposition)
Communist-CPI	Communist Party of India
Communist-Marxist	Communist Party of India (Marxist)

ANDHRA PRADESH

(Capital—Hyderabad)

Governor: R. D. BHANDARE.

Chief Minister: J. VENGAL RAO (Congress Party).

Legislative Assembly: 287 seats (Congress 216, Communist-CPI 8, Communist-Marxist 1, independents 18, others 39, vacant 5).

Legislative Council: 90 seats.

ASSAM

(Capital—Dispur)

Governor: LALLAN PRASAD SINGH.

Chief Minister: SARAT CHANDRA SINHA (Congress Party).

Legislative Assembly: 114 seats (Congress 94, Socialist 4, others 15, vacant 1).

BIHAR

(Capital—Patna)

Governor: Jagannath Kaushal.

Chief Minister: Dr. Jagannath Mishra (Congress Party).

Legislative Assembly: 318 seats (Congress 171, Communist-CPI 35, Congress (O) 27, Jana Sangh 24, Socialist 19, Swatantra 1, independents 15, others 24, vacant 2).

Legislative Council: 96 seats.

GUJARAT

(Capital—Gandhinagar)

Governor: Kambanthodath Kunhan Viswanathan.

Presidential rule was introduced in March 1976 and the Assembly suspended.

HARYANA

(Capital—Chandigarh)

Governor: R. S. Narula (acting).

Chief Minister: Banarasi Das Gupta (Congress Party).

Legislative Assembly: 81 Seats (Congress 52, Congress (O) 6, Jana Sangh 2, independents 11, others 10).

HIMACHAL PRADESH

(Capital—Simla)

Governor: Subramaniam Chakravarti.

Chief Minister: Dr. Yeshwant Singh Parmar (Congress Party).

Legislative Assembly: 68 seats (Congress 53, Jana Sangh 5, Communist-Marxist 1, independents 7, others 2).

JAMMU AND KASHMIR

(Capitals—Srinagar (Summer), Jammu (Winter))

Governor: Lakshmi Kant Jha.

Chief Minister: Sheikh Mohammed Abdullah.

Legislative Assembly: 75 seats (Congress 58, Jana Sangh 3, independents 9, others 5).

Legislative Council: 36 seats.

KARNATAKA

(Capital—Bangalore)

Governor: Uma Shankar Dikshit.

Chief Minister: Devaraj Urs (Congress Party).

Legislative Assembly: 216 seats (Congress 165, Congress (O) 24, Communist-CPI 3, Socialist 2, independents 21, other 1).

Legislative Council: 63 seats.

KERALA

(Capital—Trivandrum)

Governor: Niranjan Nath Wanchoo.

Chief Minister: Chelat Achutha Menon (Coalition Ministry; major partners: Congress Party, Communists-CPI, Muslim League).

Legislative Assembly: 133 seats (Congress 33, Communist-Marxist-Leninist 32, Communist-CPI 16, Kerala Congress 13, Muslim League 10, Socialist 8, Congress (O) 3, independent 1, others 16, vacant 1).

MADHYA PRADESH

(Capital—Bhopal)

Governor: Satya Narayan Sinha.

Chief Minister: Shyam Charan Shukla (Congress Party).

Legislative Assembly: 296 seats (Congress 226, Jana Sangh 43, Socialist 7, Communist-CPI 5, independents 12, vacant 3).

Legislative Council: Not yet formed.

MAHARASHTRA

(Capital—Bombay)

Governor: Ali Yavar Jung.

Chief Minister: Shankarrao Bhaorao Chavan (Congress Party).

Legislative Assembly: 270 seats (Congress 222, Jana Sangh 5, Communist-CPI 2, Communist-Marxist 11, independents 5, others 33, vacant 2).

Legislative Council: 78 seats.

MANIPUR

(Capital—Imphal)

Governor: Lallan Prasad Singh.

Chief Minister: Rajkumar Dorendra Singh (Congress Party).

Legislative Assembly: 60 seats (Manipur People's Party 20, Manipur Hills Union 12, Congress 13, Communist-CPI 6, Socialist 2, independents 5, Kuki National Assembly 2; the United Legislature Party was formed by the Manipur People's Party and the Manipur Hills Union).

MEGHALAYA

(Capital—Shillong)

Governor: Lallan Prasad Singh.

Chief Minister: Capt. Williamson Sangma (All Party Hill Leaders Conference.)

Legislative Assembly: 60 seats (All Party Hill Leaders Conference 37, Congress 8, independents 7, others 7, vacant 1).

NAGALAND

(Capital—Kohima)

Governor: Lallan Prasad Singh.

Presidential rule was introduced in March 1975.

ORISSA

(Capital—Bhubaneswar)

Governor: S. N. Shankar (acting).

Chief Minister: Mrs. Nandini Satpathy (Congress Party).

Legislative Assembly: 146 seats (Congress 69, Utkal Congress 35, Swatantra 21, Communist-CPI 7, Communist-Marxist 3, Socialist 2, independents 8, other 1).

PUNJAB

(Capital—Chandigarh)

Governor: Mahendra Mohan Chaudhury.

Chief Minister: Giani Zail Singh (Congress Party).

Legislative Assembly: 104 seats (Congress 68, Akali 25, Communist-CPI 10, Communist-Marxist 1).

RAJASTHAN

(Capital—Jaipur)

Governor: Dr. Jogendra Singh.

Chief Minister: Harideo Joshi (Congress Party).

Legislative Assembly: 184 seats, (Congress 144, Swatantra 11, Jana Sangh 7, Socialist 4, Communist-CPI 4, Congress (O) 1, independents 11, vacant 2).

SIKKIM

(Capital—Gangtok)

Governor: BIPIN BIHARI LAL.

Chief Minister: Kazi LHENDUP DORJI.

Legislative Assembly: 32 seats (Sikkim National Congress 32).

TAMIL NADU

(Capital—Madras)

Governor: MOHAN LAL SUKHADIA.

Presidential rule was introduced in January 1976.

TRIPURA

(Capital—Agartala)

Governor: LALLAN PRASAD SINGH.

Chief Minister: SUKHAMOY SEN GUPTA (Congress Party).

Legislative Assembly: 60 seats (Congress 41, Communist-Marxist 16, Communist-CPI 1, independents 2).

UTTAR PRADESH

(Capital—Lucknow)

Governor: Dr. MARRI CHANNA REDDY.

Chief Minister: NARAIN DUTT TIWARI (Congress Party).

Legislative Assembly: 425 seats (Congress 214, Bharatiya Kranti Dal 106, Jana Sangh 61, Communist—CPI 16, Congress (O) 10, Socialist 5, Communist-Marxist 2, Swatantra 1, Independents 5, others 3).

Legislative Council: 108 seats.

WEST BENGAL

(Capital—Calcutta)

Governor: ANTHONY LANCELOT DIAS.

Chief Minister: SIDDHARTHA SHANKAR RAY (Congress Party).

Legislative Assembly: 280 seats (Congress 216, Communist-CPI 36, Communist-Marxist 13, Congress (O) 2, independents 4, others 8, vacant 1).

UNION TERRITORIES

Andaman and Nicobar Islands (Headquarters—Port Blair): *Chief Commissioner:* S. M. KRISHNATRY.

Arunachal Pradesh (Capital—Indira Giri): *Chief Commissioner:* K. A. A. RAJA.

Chief Minister: PREM KHANDU THUNGON.

Assembly: introduced in 1975; 23 seats.

Chandigarh (Headquarters—Chandigarh): *Chief Commissioner:* N. P. MATHUR.

Dadra and Nagar Haveli (Headquarters—Silvassa): *Administrator:* K. G. BADLANI.

Delhi (Headquarters—Delhi): *Lieut.-Governor:* KRISHAN CHAND.

Goa, Daman and Diu (Capital—Panaji): *Lieut.-Governor:* S. K. BANERJI.

Chief Minister: SHASHIKALA G. KAKODKAR (Maharashtravadi Gomantak Party).

Legislature: 30 seats (Maharashtravadi Gomantak 18, United Goans (Sequiera Group) 10, Congress 1, independent 1).

Lakshadweep (Headquarters—Kavaratti): *Administrator:* M. C. VERMA.

Mizoram (Headquarters—Aizal): *Lieut.-Governor:* S. K. CHIBBER.

Chief Minister: L. CHALCHHUNGA (Mizo Union Party).

Assembly: 30 seats (Mizo Union 24, Congress 6).

Pondicherry (Capital—Pondicherry): *Lieut.-Governor:* CHEDDI LAL.

The Anna Dravidra Munnetra Kazhagam—Communist coalition Ministry resigned on March 27th, 1974. The Assembly was dissolved on March 28th, 1974.

POLITICAL PARTIES

The principal parties are:

Indian National Congress: 5 Dr. Rajendra Prasad Rd., New Delhi; was founded in 1885 by A. O. Hume, with the main object of creating national consciousness in India, and securing economic advance in the country. In 1907 Congress was split in two—the Extremists and the Moderates. In 1920, Mahatma Gandhi began to take a leading part in its activities and policies, and Congress soon became a mass organization fighting for complete independence. Before the 1967 elections a number of splinter groups broke away from Congress to form new parties. In 1969 Congress again split into two distinct organizations, with Mrs. Indira Gandhi's Government continuing in office with the support of the D.M.K. independent M.P.s and left-wing parties and the Indian National Congress (Opposition) forming as opposition party.

Aims: The well-being and advancement of the people and the establishment by peaceful means of a socialist, co-operative Commonwealth based on equality of opportunity and rights, aiming at world peace; the provision of basic needs and opportunities for culture; full employment in 10 years; Government control of large-scale industries and services; co-operative industry and agriculture; a neutral foreign policy.

President: D. K. BAROOAH.
Gen. Secretary: A. R. ATULAY.
Leader: Mrs. INDIRA GANDHI.

Indian National Congress (Organization): 7 Jantar Mantar Rd., New Delhi 110001; f. 1969; a break-away parliamentary group which became India's first recognized opposition party.

President: ASHOK MEHTA.

Chairman Parliamentary Group: MORARJI DESAI.

General Secretary: MANUBHAI PATEL.

Leader in Lok Sabha: S. N. MISHRA.

Leader in Rajya Sabha: M. S. GURUPADASWAMY.

Bharatiya Lok Dal (BLD): 1-2, Vithalbhai Patel House, Rafi Marg, New Delhi 110001; f. 1974 as a union of seven parties; the Swatantra Party, the Bharatiya Kranti Dal, the Uktal Congress, the Samyukta Socialist Party, and others. Aims to reverse the Congress Party's economic policy by giving first priority to agriculture, second priority to cottage and small-scale industries, and only third priority to heavy industries. It believes in the wide dispersal of ownership of property and of the means of production, and is opposed to concentration of economic power. Seeks the decentralization of power and policy-making.

President: CHARAN SINGH.

General Secretary: PILOO MODY, M.P. (detained June 1975).

Parl. Leader: RAJ NARAYAN.

Bharatiya Jana Sangh (*People's Party of India*): Vithalbhai Patel Bhavan, Rafi Marg, New Delhi. Believes in Integral Humanism as opposed to both Marxist economic interpretation of history and to capitalism. Pledged to check the spread of communism, stands for nationalism and democracy. Opposed to discrimination against, or in favour of, any section of the people on the basis of caste or creed. Upholds the right of all citizens to freedom of conscience and faith and the right to work. Against the establishment of a theocratic state and allows full freedom of modes of worship. Stands for co-partnership for labour in management and profits, Indianization of foreign-owned tea, drugs, soap, match, vegetable products, jute and cigarette industries and nationalization of foreign banks. Favours building up of an Indian nuclear deterrent and utilizing atomic power for speedy industrialization. Envisages foreign-aid-free Five-Year Plans and nationalization of foreign trade with communist countries. Stands for an independent foreign policy. Maintains that India should take lead in building the Indian Ocean Defence System with Afro-Asian Co-operation (excluding allies of great powers) and expand her navy.

President: L. K. ADVANI, M.P.

General Secretary: S. S. BHANDARI, M.P.

Parl. Leader: ATAL BIHARI VAJPAYEE, M.P.

Membership: 1,800,000.

Socialist Party: 16 Vithalbhai Patel House, Rafi Marg, New Delhi 110001; f. 1934. Aims to achieve, by democratic and peaceful means, a socialist society, free from social, political and economic exploitation of individual by individual and nation by nation. It seeks to organize, guide and lead peaceful revolutionary class struggles, mass movements and civil disobedience movement, to promote constructive efforts and secure political power by democratic means to eliminate injustices, social inequalities and feudal-capitalist exploitation.

Chairman: GEORGE FERNANDES.

General Secretary: S. MOHAN.

Parl. Leader: SAMAR GUHA.

The Communist Party of India: 7/4 A. Ali Rd., New Delhi.

Aims: The establishment of a socialist society led by the working class, and ultimately of a communist society.

Chairman: S. A. DANGE, M.P.

General Secretary: C. RAJESWARA RAO, M.P.

Membership: 406,322.

Communist Party of India (Marxist): 49 Lake Place, Calcutta 700029, West Bengal; f. 1946 as pro-Peking breakaway group of C.P.I., the Party declared its independence of Peking in 1968.

Chairman: A. K. G. OPALAN.

General Secretary: P. SUNDARAYYA.

Membership: 98,370 approx.

Dravida Munnetra Kazhagam (D.M.K.): Arivagam, Royapuram, Madras 600013; aims at full state autonomy for Tamil Nadu within the Union; regional languages as State languages; English as official language.

Leader: M. KARUNANIDHI.

Membership: over 200,000.

Shiromani Akali Dal: Amritsar; Sikh party; campaigns against Government interference in Sikh affairs and for greater power to individual states and allocation of heavy industry to Amritsar.

President: JATHEDAR MOHAN SINGH.

General Secretary: GIANI AJMER SINGH.

Peasants and Workers Party of India: Mahatma Phule Rd., Naigaum, Bombay 400014; to establish a People's Democracy; to nationalize all basic industries; industrialization; unitary state with provincial boundaries drawn on linguistic basis; Marxist.

General Secretary: DAJIBA DESAI.

Membership: about 10,000.

Akhil Bharat Hindu Mahasabha: Hindu Mahasabha Bhawan, Mandir Marg, New Delhi 1; aims: to establish a democratic Hindu state.

President: Prof. RAM SINGH.

Office Secretary: INDRA PRAKASH.

Membership: about 2 million.

All India Forward Block: 88 North Ave., New Delhi 110001; socialistic principles, including nationalization of key industries, land redistribution; advocates military action against Pakistan over Kashmir.

Chairman: HEMANTA KUMAR BOSE, M.L.A.

General Secretary: R. K. HALDULKAR.

Republican Party of India: Deeksha Bhoomi, Nagpur 440003, Maharashtra; main aims and objectives are to realize the aims and objects set out in the preamble to the Indian Constitution.

President: DADASAHEB GAIKWAD.

General Secretary: B. D. KHOBRAGADE.

DIPLOMATIC REPRESENTATION

EMBASSIES, HIGH COMMISSIONS AND LEGATION ACCREDITED TO INDIA

(HC) High Commission; (E) Embassy; (L) Legation.

Afghanistan: 9A Ring Rd., Lajpatnagar II (E); *Ambassador:* ABDURRAHMAN PAZHWAK (also accred. to Burma).

Algeria: 13 Sundar Nagar, New Delhi 110003 (E); *Chargé d'Affaires:* OMAR OUSSEDIK (also accred. to Malaysia).

Argentina: C27/28 South Extension Part II, New Delhi 110049 (E); *Ambassador:* FERNANDO MARÍA FERNANDES ESCALANTE (also accred. to Sri Lanka).

Australia: No. 1/50-G Shantipath, Chanakyapuri, New Delhi 110011 (HC); *High Commissioner:* PETER CAMPBELL JOHN CURTIS.

Austria: 18 Jor Bagh, New Delhi 110003 (E); *Ambassador:* Dr. WOLFGANG SCHALLENBERG (also accred. to Bangladesh and Sri Lanka).

Bangladesh: 56 Ring Rd., Lajpat Nagar (HC); *High Commissioner:* SAMSUR RAHMAN.

Belgium: 7 Golf Links, New Delhi 110003 (E); *Ambassador:* JEAN CHARLES SALMON.

Bhutan: Royal Bhutan Mission, 1/21 Shantiniketan, New Delhi 110021 (L); *Representative:* LYONPO SANGEY PENJORE (also accred. to Bangladesh).

Brazil: 8 Aurangzeb Rd., New Delhi 110011 (E); *Ambassador:* ROBERTO LUIZ ASSUMPÇÃO DE ARAUJO (also accred. to Sri Lanka).

Bulgaria: 198 Golf Links, New Delhi 110003 (E); *Ambassador:* STOYAN VLADIMIROV ZAIMOV.

Burma: Burma House, 3/50-F Nyaya Marg. Chanakyapuri, New Delhi 110021 (E); *Ambassador:* ZEYA KYAW HTIN UBA SHWE (also accred. to Afghanistan and Nepal).

Canada: 7/8 Shanti Path, Chanakyapuri, New Delhi 110021 (HC); *High Commissioner:* JOHN RYERSON MAYBEE.

Chile: 1/13 Shantiniketan, New Delhi 110021 (E); *Ambassador:* AUGUSTO MARAMBIO.

China, People's Republic: 50-D Shanti Path (E); *Ambassador:* CHEN CHAO-YUAN.

Colombia: 82D Malcha Marg, Chanakyapuri, New Delhi 110021 (E); *Ambassador:* F. N. DE BRIGARD.

Cuba: C-290 Defence Colony, New Delhi 110024 (E); *Ambassador:* Dr. JOSÉ LÓPEZ SÁNCHEZ (also accred. to Bangladesh and Sri Lanka).

Czechoslovakia: 50-M Niti Marg, Chanakyapuri, New Delhi 110021 (E); *Ambassador:* Dr. ZDENĚK TRHLIK (also accred. to Malaysia).

Denmark: 6 Golf Links Area, New Delhi 110003 (E); *Ambassador:* HENNING HALCK (also accred. to Bangladesh and Sri Lanka).

Ecuador: C-76 Paschim Marg, Vasant Vihar (E); *Chargé d'Affaires:* VINCENTE CRESPO ORDOÑEZ.

Egypt: 55-57 Sunder Nagar, New Delhi 110003 (E); *Ambassador:* ZAKARIA EL-ADLY IMAM.

Ethiopia: 29 Prithviraj Rd., New Delhi 110011 (E); *Ambassador:* G. MEKASHA.

Finland: 42 Golf Links, New Delhi 110003 (E); *Ambassador:* RIITTA ÖRÖ (also accred. to Bangladesh, Burma and Sri Lanka).

France: 2 Aurangzeb Rd., New Delhi 110011 (E); *Ambassador:* JEAN-CLAUDE WINCKLER.

Gabon: Paris, France (E).

German Democratic Republic: 2 Nyaya Marg, Chanakyapuri (E); *Ambassador:* WOLFGANG SCHÜSSLER (also accred. to Nepal).

Germany, Federal Republic: 6 Block 50G, Shanti Path, Chanakyapuri, New Delhi 110021 (E); *Ambassador:* GUNTHER DIEHL.

Ghana: 2 Golf Links, New Delhi 110003 (HC); *High Commissioner:* PAUL BOAKYE DUAH (also accred. to Afghanistan, Bangladesh and Sri Lanka).

Greece: 188 Jor Bagh, New Delhi 110003 (E); *Ambassador:* VASSILIOS VITSAXIS (also accred. to Bangladesh, Burma, Malaysia and Sri Lanka).

Guyana: 180 Jor Bagh, New Delhi 110003 (HC); *High Commissioner:* Sir EDWARD LUCKHOO.

Hungary: 15 Jor Bagh, New Delhi 110003 (E); *Ambassador:* Dr. FERENC TURI (also accred. to Burma, Singapore and Sri Lanka).

Indonesia: 50A Chanakyapuri, New Delhi 110021 (E); *Ambassador:* Lt.-Gen. SUGIHARTO.

Iran: 65 Golf Links, New Delhi 110003 (E); *Ambassador:* GHOLAM REZA TAJBAKSH (also accred. to Burma).

Iraq: 33 Golf Links, New Delhi 110003 (E); *Ambassador:* MOHAMMED SAYEED AL-SHHAF (also accred. to Burma).

Ireland: 13 Jor Bagh, New Delhi 110003 (E); *Ambassador:* DENIS HOLMES (also accred. to Malaysia).

Italy: 13 Golf Links, New Delhi 110003 (E); *Ambassador:* Dr. CARLO CALENDA.

Japan: Plot Nos. 4 and 5, Block 50G, Chanakyapuri, New Delhi 110021 (E); *Ambassador:* KINYA NIISEKI.

Jordan: 86 Malcha Marg, Chanakyapuri, New Delhi 110021 (E); *Ambassador:* ZUHAIR KHAIR (also accred. to Sri Lanka).

Kenya: E-27 Defence Colony, New Delhi 110024 (HC); *High Commissioner:* S. K. KIMALEL.

Korea, Democratic People's Republic: 11 Barakhamba Rd., New Delhi 110001 (E); *Ambassador:* YU SONG JIN.

Korea, Republic: Korea House, 5 Mansingh Rd., New Delhi 110001 (E); *Ambassador:* CHAN HUYAN PAR (also accred. to Afghanistan and Bangladesh).

Kuwait: 19 Friends Colony West, New Delhi 110014 (E); *Ambassador:* ESSA A. RAHMAN AL-ESSA (also accred. to Sri Lanka).

Laos: 4 Circular Rd., South Western Ext., Chanakyapuri, New Delhi 110021 (E); *Ambassador:* PHANGNA SOUK UPRAVAN (also accred. to Sri Lanka).

Lebanon: 3 Panch Sheel Marg, Chanakyapuri, New Delhi 110021 (E); *Ambassador:* MAHMOUD HAFEZ (also accred. to Sri Lanka).

Malaysia: 3 Link Rd., Jangpura, New Delhi 110014 (HC); *High Commissioner:* Tuan Haji ABDUL KHALID BIN AWANG OSMAN.

Mauritius: B/10 Malcha Marg, Chanakyapuri, New Delhi 110021 (HC); *High Commissioner:* RABINDRAH GHURBURRUN.

Mexico: 136 Golf Links, New Delhi 110003 (E); *Ambassador:* CARLOS GUTIÉRREZ-MACÍAS (also accred. to Afghanistan and Sri Lanka).

Mongolia: 34 Golf Links, New Delhi 110003 (E); *Ambassador:* BUYANTYN DASHTSEREN (also accred. to Bangladesh and Sri Lanka).

Morocco: 199 Jor Bagh, New Delhi 110003 (E); *Ambassador:* YOUNES NEKROUF.

Nepal: Barakhamba Rd., New Delhi 110001 (E); *Ambassador:* KRISHNA BOM MALLA (also accred. to Sri Lanka).

Netherlands: 6/50 F, Shanti Path (E); *Ambassador:* TJARK ASUEER MEURS (also accred. to Burma and Sri Lanka).

New Zealand: 39 Golf Links, New Delhi 110003 (HC); *High Commissioner:* Dr. C. C. AIKMAN (also accred. to Bangladesh and Sri Lanka).

Nigeria: 169/170 Jor Bagh, New Delhi 110003 (HC); *High Commissioner:* A. G. GOBIR (also accred. to Burma and Sri Lanka).

Norway: Kautilya Marg, Chanakyapuri, New Delhi 110021 (E); *Ambassador:* T. K. CHRISTIANSEN (also accred. to Bangladesh and Sri Lanka).

Oman: 22 Vasant Vihar, New Delhi 110001 (E); *Ambassador:* ALI MOHAMMED AL-JAMALI.

Pakistan: *Ambassador:* SYED FIDA HASSAN.

Papua New Guinea: *High Commissioner:* (to be announced).

Peru: D-290 Defence Colony, New Delhi 110024 (E); *Ambassador:* Dr. ALBERTO MACLEAN URZUA (also accred. to Iran).

Philippines: 50-N, Nyaya Marg, Chanakyapuri, New Delhi 110021 (E); *Ambassador:* ROMEO S. BUSUEGO (also accred. to Afghanistan).

Poland: 22 Golf Links, New Delhi 110003 (E); *Ambassador:* Gen. JAN CZAPLA.

Qatar: A-3 West End Colony (E); *Ambassador:* Dr. HASSAN ALU HUSSAIN AL NOAMAN.

Romania: 9 Tees January Marg, New Delhi 110011 (E); *Ambassador:* PETRE TANASIE (also accred. to Sri Lanka).

Saudi Arabia: 1 Eastern Ave., Maharani Bagh, New Delhi 110014 (E); *Ambassador:* Sheikh YUSUF AL-FOZAN.

Singapore: 48 Golf Links New Delhi 110003 (HC); *High Commissioner:* KENNETH MICHAEL BYRNE (also accred. to Bangladesh, Iran and Sri Lanka).

Spain: 12 Prithviraj Rd., New Delhi 110011 (E); *Ambassador:* D. L. M. C. MUÑOZ (also accred. to Bangladesh, Burma and Sri Lanka).

Sri Lanka: 27 Kautilya Marg, Chanakyapuri, New Delhi 110021 (HC); *High Commissioner:* JUSTIN SIRIWARDENE (also accred. to Afghanistan).

Sudan: 6 Jor Bagh, New Delhi 110003 (E); *Ambassador:* EL-AMIN EL-BESHIR (also accred. to Malaysia and Sri Lanka).

Sweden: Nyaya Marg, Chanakyapuri, New Delhi 110021 (E); *Ambassador:* LENARI FINNMARK (also accred. to Bangladesh and Sri Lanka).

Switzerland: Nyaya Marg, Chanakyapuri, New Delhi 110021 (E); *Ambassador:* ETIENNE SUTER.

Syria: 63 Sundar Nagar, New Delhi 110011 (E); *Ambassador:* RASLAN ALLOUSH (also accred. to Afghanistan).

Tanzania: E-106, Hill View, Greater Kailash, New Delhi 110048 (HC); *High Commissioner:* A. D. HASSAN.

Thailand: 56-N Nyaya Marg, Chanakyapuri, New Delhi 110021 (E); *Ambassador:* Dr. SULHATI CHUTHASMIT (also accred. to Afghanistan).

Trinidad and Tobago: 131 Jor Bagh, New Delhi 110003 (HC); *High Commissioner:* SOLOMON SATCUMAR LUTCHMAN (also accred. to Indonesia, Singapore and Sri Lanka).

Turkey: 27 Jor Bagh, New Delhi 110003 (E); *Ambassador:* GONDOGDU USTUN (also accred. to Burma and Sri Lanka).

Uganda: 172 Jor Bagh, New Delhi 110003 (HC); *High Commissioner:* Lt.-Col. M. E. OMBIA.

U.S.S.R.: Shanti Path, Chanakyapuri, New Delhi 110021 (E); *Ambassador:* VIKTOR F. MALTSHEV.

United Arab Emirates: 104 Malcha Marg, Chanakyapuri, New Delhi 110021 (E); *Ambassador:* MOHAMMED ISSA AL-ALI.

United Kingdom: Shanti Path, Chanakyapuri, New Delhi 110021 (HC); *High Commissioner:* Sir MICHAEL WALKER.

U.S.A.: Shanti Path, Chanakyapuri, New Delhi 110021 (E); *Ambassador:* WILLIAM SAXBE.

Uruguay: 70 Ring Rd., New Delhi 110024 (E); *Ambassador:* ALBERTO RODRIGUEZ.

Vatican: Niti Marg, Chanakyapuri (Apostolic Pronuncio), New Delhi 110021; *Nuncio:* Most Rev. LUCIANO STORERO.

Venezuela: N-114 Panchshila Park, New Delhi 110017 (E); *Ambassador:* TULIO CARDOZO FARIA.

Viet-Nam: 35 Prithvi raj Rd., New Delhi 110011 (E); *Ambassador:* CHU VAN BIEN (also accred. to Bangladesh).

Yemen, People's Democratic Republic: C-18 Friends Colony East, New Delhi 110014 (E); *Chargé d'Affaires:* ALI HUSSAIN MAZHAL.

Yugoslavia: 3/50G, Shanti Path, Chanakyapuri, New Delhi 110021 (E); *Ambassador:* ILIJA TOPALOSKI.

Zaire: 160 Jor Bagh, New Delhi 110003 (E); *Ambassador:* ILEKA MBOYO.

Monaco and San Marino are represented by Consuls-General.

India also has diplomatic relations with Barbados, Benin, Bolivia, Burundi, Cambodia, Cameroon, the Congo People's Republic, Costa Rica, Cyprus, the Dominican Republic, El Salvador, Fiji, the Gambia, Guinea, Haiti, Honduras, Iceland, the Ivory Coast, Jamaica, Lesotho, Liberia, Libya, Luxembourg, Madagascar, Malawi, Maldives, Mali, Malta, Mauritania, Mozambique, Nicaragua, Paraguay, Portugal, Rwanda, Senegal, Sierra Leone, Somalia, Swaziland, Togo, Tonga, Tunisia, the Upper Volta, Western Samoa, the Yemen Arab Republic and Zambia.

JUDICIAL SYSTEM

THE SUPREME COURT

The Supreme Court exercises exclusive jurisdiction in any dispute between the Union and the States (although there are certain restrictions where an acceding state is involved). It has appellate jurisdiction over any judgment, decree or order of the High Court where that Court certifies that either a substantial question of law or the interpretation of the Constitution is involved.

Provision is made for the appointment by the Chief Justice of India of judges of High Courts as *ad hoc* judges at sittings of the Supreme Court for specified periods, and for the attendance of retired judges at sittings of the Supreme Court. The Supreme Court has advisory jurisdiction in respect of questions which may be referred to it by the President for opinion. The Supreme Court is also empowered to hear appeals against a sentence of death passed by a State High Court, in reversal of an order of acquittal by a lower court, and in a case in which a High Court has granted a certificate of fitness.

The Supreme Court also hears appeals which are certified by High Courts to be fit for appeal, subject to rules made by the Court. Parliament may, by law, confer on the Supreme Court any further powers of appeal.

HIGH COURTS

The High Courts are the Courts of Appeal from the lower courts, and their decisions are final except in cases where appeal lies to the Supreme Court.

Trial by jury is the rule in original criminal cases before the High Court, but juries are not employed in civil suits.

LOWER COURTS

Provision is made in the Code for Criminal Procedure for the constitution of lower criminal courts called Courts of Session and Courts of Magistrates. The Courts of Session are competent to try all persons duly committed for trial, and inflict any punishment authorized by the law.

Appeals can be made from a single judge's decision in the High Court, sitting as a court of original criminal jurisdiction, to a bench of not less than two judges of the same Court sitting as a Court of Appeal. The President and the local government concerned exercise the prerogative of mercy.

The constitution of inferior civil courts is determined by regulations within each state.

SUPREME COURT

Chief Justice of India: The Hon. Justice A. N. RAY.

Judges of the Supreme Court: Hons. P. JAGAN MOHAN REDDY, D. G. PALEKAR, K. K. MATHEW, H. R. KHANNA, M. H. BEG, S. N. DWIVEDI, A. K. MUKHERJEA, Y. V. CHANDRACHUD, A. ALAGIRISWAMI, P. N. BHAGWATI, V. R. KRISHNA IYER, P. K. GOSWAMI, R. S. SARKARIA, N. L. UNTWALIA.

RELIGION

Number of adherents of the major Indian faiths:

Hinduism: According to the 1971 census Hindus form 82.72 per cent of the population (453.3 million).

Islam: Muslims are divided into two main sects, Shi'as and Sunnis. Most of the Indian Muslims are Sunnis. In 1971 the Muslim population numbered 61.4 million (11.21 per cent).

Buddhism: The Buddhists in Ladakh (Jammu and Kashmir) owe allegiance to the Dalai Lama. Head Lama of Ladakh: KAUSHAK SAKULA, Dalgate, Srinagar, Kashmir. In 1971 there were 3.81 million Buddhists in India (0.70 per cent of the population).

Sikhism: According to the 1971 census there were 10.3 million Sikhs in India (1.89 per cent of the population), the majority living in the Punjab.

Jainism: 2.6 million adherents (1971 census), 0.47 per cent of the population.

Zoroastrians: More than 120,000 Parsis practise the Zoroastrian religion.

Christians: There are 14.2 million Christians in India (1971 census), of whom more than half are Roman Catholics, the others being members of the ancient Syrian and the Protestant churches.

CHRISTIAN CHURCHES

THE ROMAN CATHOLIC CHURCH

Apostolic Pro-Nuncio to India: H.E. the Most Rev. LUCIANO STORERO, Apostolic Nunciature, Niti Marg, Chanakyapuri, New Delhi 110021.

The Church has 16 archdioceses, 58 suffragan dioceses and 2 prefectures apostolic for Catholics of the Latin rite. There are 3 archbishoprics, 8 suffragan bishoprics and 6 exarchates for the Oriental rite. Total number of Roman Catholics, 8,200,000.

THE CHURCH OF NORTH INDIA

Moderator: Rt. Rev. Dr. E. S. NASIR, Bishop's House, 1 Church Lane, New Delhi.

Total number of Anglican Christians: 2,690,500.

CHURCH OF SOUTH INDIA

Officer of the Synod: Moderator Rt. Rev. I. R. H. GNANADASAN, M.A., B.D.

There is a total congregation of about 1,376,824; publ. *The South India Churchman.* Office: C.S.I. Synod Secretariat, Cathedral, Madras 6.

National Christian Council of India: Christian Council Lodge, Nagpur-1, Maharashtra; Pres. Rt. Rev. P. MAR CHRYSOSTOM; Gen. Sec. M. A. Z. ROLSTON; publ. *National Christian Council Review.*

Federation of Evangelical Lutheran Churches in India: Ranchi, Bihar; Pres. Rt. Rev. R. B. MANIKAM; Sec. Dr. M. BAGE.

Mar Thoma Syrian Church of Malabar: Sabha Office, Tiruvalla-1, Kerala, 689101; Metropolitan Most Rev. Dr. JUHANON MAR THOMA; 420,000 mems.

Syrian Orthodox Church of the East: Catholicate Palace, Kottayam-4; Sec. Metropolitan DANIEL MAR PHILOXENUS.

United Church of North India and Pakistan: Church House, Mhow, M.P.; Sec. Rev. KENNETHYOHAN MASIH.

Other groups include Baptist and Methodist Churches.

THE PRESS

The Indian Press owes a large part of its development and present form to the traditions established at the time of the British raj. With the coming of independence the National Congress adopted a number of the press controls instituted by the colonial rulers. Far-reaching Press restrictions were enforced following the State of Emergency declared in June 1975, the most serious of which was the suspension of Article 19 of the Constitution, which guaranteed the right to freedom of speech and expression and empowered the central or state governments to impose restrictions through laws relating to libel, contempt of court or to matters liable to offend public morality or weaken the security of the state. The reporting of political debate in both Houses of Parliament was subsequently severely restricted.

Strict censorship was introduced in June 1975 and in November the Government announced plans to restructure the newspaper press. Legislation approved by Parliament in January and February 1976 gave the Government wide powers to prevent publication of material it considered objectionable.

The growth of a thriving Press has been made difficult by cultural barriers caused by religious, caste and language differences. Consequently the English Press, with its appeal to the educated middle-class urban readership throughout the state, has retained its dominance. Though there are more papers in Hindi, the total circulation of the English Press is the greater. The main Indian language dailies also appeal to the urban reader but by paying little attention to rural affairs they fail to cater for the increasingly literate provincial population who know no English. Most Indian papers have a relatively small circulation. Provincial papers frequently play upon religious or local sympathies to ensure their circulation.

Many papers, particularly the smaller ones, depend for news on government handouts and on the small number of news agencies, which results in a lack of variety in news content. Provincial papers which cannot afford agencies depend entirely on government handouts. All except the largest newspapers, which have their own correspondents, make use of agencies for foreign news.

The daily papers provide a relatively large proportion of domestic and international news particularly on politics; sports and finance receive good coverage. There is little sensationalism. Advertisements constitute on average 50 per cent of the contents of the larger papers. In contrast to the dailies the periodical press offers more articles of human interest, more coverage of local affairs and among periodicals the English sector plays a far less prominent role.

In 1974 there were 12,653 newspapers and periodicals with a combined circulation of about 300 million, of which 830 were dailies. English, Hindi and Tamil publications claim more than half (56 per cent) the total circulation in the country, selling 70 million, 60 million and 36 million copies respectively. Of the 12,653 newspapers, 7,926 or 62.6 per cent were under individual ownership, the central and state governments owned 443 or 3.5 per cent. Individual owners commanded a circulation of 38.8 per cent, public and private limited companies claimed a total circulation of 34.3 per cent.

The widest circulating and most influential newspapers are the metropolitan dailies in English which in 1972 totalled 73 with a combined circulation of 2.3 million, closely followed by 225 Hindi and 17 Bengali papers with circulation of 2.0 and 1.0 million respectively. A few papers are published simultaneously from several centres, notably the *Indian Express* in six cities, and the *Times of India*, the *Statesman* and the *Navbharat Times* at two each.

Among the most highly respected daily papers are the *Times of India* and the Hindi *Navbharat Times* (Bombay), the *Statesman* (Calcutta), the Bengali *Jugantar* (Calcutta), the *Hindu* (Madras), the *Hindustan Times* and the Hindi *Hindustan* (*New Delhi*).

In order of circulation the most popular dailies are: the *Indian Express*, the Malayam *Malayala Manorama*, the *Times of India*, the *Mathrubhumi*, the Bengali *Ananda Bazar Patrika*, the Hindi *Navbharat Times*, the *Hindu*, the *Statesman*, the *Dinamani*, the Hindi *Hindustan*, the *Hindustan Times*, the *Marathi Loksatta*, and the English *Tribune*.

The more popular weekly periodicals range from the cultural Tamil publications *Kumadam*, *Kalki* and *Anandavikatan* to the sensationalist English *Blitz*. *Filmfare*, *Sports and Pastime* and *Women's Own Weekly* are leading magazines, each catering for a particular readership. Among the largest monthly periodicals are the *Reader's Digest* and the Hindi religious publication *Kalyan*.

The most powerful groups own most of the large English dailies and frequently have considerable private commercial and industrial holdings. Three of the major groups are as follows:

Times of India Group (controlled by the JAIN and DALMIA families): includes the dailies, *Times of India*, the *Evening News of India* (Bombay), the Hindi *Navbharat Times*, the *Maharashtra Times* (Bombay), weeklies including the *Illustrated Weekly of India*, the Hindi *Dharmayug* and *Dinaman*, the fortnightly *Femina* and *Filmfare* and the Hindi monthly *Parag* and *Sarika*, etc.

Indian Express Group (controlled by the GOENKA family): the dailies, the *Indian Express*, the Marathi *Lokasatta*, the Tamil *Dinamani*, the Telugu *Andhra Prabha*, the Kannada *Kannada Prabha* and the English *Financial Express*, and the English weeklies *Everyman's*, the *Sunday Standard* and *Screen* and the Telugu *Andhra Prabha Illustrated Weekly*.

Hindustan Times Group (controlled by the BIRLA family): several dailies including the *Hindustan Times* (Delhi), the *Hindustan Times Evening News*, the *Hindustan Times Kanpur Supplement*, the *Leader* (Allahabad), the *Searchlight* (Patna), the Hindi *Hindustan* (Delhi) and *Bharat* (Allahabad), and the weekly *Overseas Hindustan Times*, *Eastern Economist*, the Hindi *Saptahik Hindustan* (Allahabad), the monthly Hindi *Nandan* (New Delhi) and *Pradeep* (Patna).

PRINCIPAL DAILIES

DELHI

Economic Times: Bahadur Shah Zafar Marg; f. 1961; published in Delhi from 1974; Editor Dr. D. K. RANGNEKAR; circ. (Bombay and New Delhi) 42,900.

Hindustan: P.B. 40, Connaught Circus; f. 1933; morning; Hindi; Editors G. N. SAHI and R. L. JOSHI; circ. 153,900.

Hindustan Times: Kasturba Gandhi Marg; f. 1923; morning; English; Nationalist; Editor HIRANMAY KARLEKAR; circ. 153,000.

Indian Express: P.O.B. 570, Mathura Rd.; f. 1932; morning; English; published simultaneously in Delhi, Madurai (Tamil Nadu), Madras (Tamil Nadu), Bangalore (Mysore), Vijayawada (Andhra Pradesh), Bombay (Maharashtra), Cochin (Kerala) and Ahmedabad (Gujarat); Editor-in-Chief S. MULGAOKAR; circ. (national) 400,300, (Delhi) 87,800.

Milap: 8A Bahadur Shah Zafar Marg; f. 1923; Urdu; Nationalist; Editor RANBIR SINGH; Man. T. R. KAPUR; also published from Jullundur and Hyderabad; circ. 55,840.

Motherland: Rani Jhansi Marg; f. 1971; English; Editor K. R. MALKANI; circ. 30,000.

Navbharat Times: 7 Bahadur Shah Zafar Marg; f. 1947; also published from Bombay; Hindi; Editor A. K. JAIN; circ. (national) 265,100; (Delhi) 198,300.

Patriot: P.B. 727, Link House, Bahadur Shah Zafar Marg; f. 1963; English; Editor P. VISWANATH; circ. 48,700.

Pratap: Pratap Bhawan, Bahadur Shah Zafar Marg; f. 1919; Urdu; Editor K. NARENDRA; circ. 30,000.

Statesman: Connaught Circus; f. 1875; English; Editor S. SAHAY; circ. 194,100.

Times of India: 7 Bahadur Shah Zafar Marg; f. 1838; English; published from Bombay, Delhi and Ahmedabad; Resident Editors GIRILAL JAIN, SHAM LAL; circ. (Delhi) 94,000.

Vir Arjun: Pratap Bhawan, Bahadur Shah Zafar Marg; f. 1954; Hindi; Editor K. NARENDRA; circ. 23,000.

ANDHRA PRADESH

Hyderabad

Andhra Bhoomi: 36 Sarojini Devi Rd., Secunderabad; f. 1960; Telugu; Editor GORA SHASTRI; circ. 15,800.

Andhra Janata: Lingampally, Hyderabad-27; f. 1955; Telugu; Editor P. N. RAO; circ. 5,300.

Deccan Chronicle: 36 Sarojini Devi Rd., Secunderabad; f. 1938; English; Man. Editor K. R. PATTABHIRAM; circ. 31,900.

Rehnuma-e-Deccan: Afzalgunj; f. 1949; morning; Urdu; Independent; Editor SYED VICARUDDIN; circ. 14,400.

Siasat Daily: f. 1949; morning; Urdu; Editor ABID ALI KHAN; circ. 9,900.

Vijayawada

Andhra Jyoti: P.O.B. 712; f. 1960; Telugu; Editor NARLA VENKATESWARA RAO; circ. 23,500.

Andhra Patrika: P.O.B. 534; f. 1914; Telugu; Editor S. RADHAKRISHNA; circ. 39,100.

Andhra Prabha: f. 1959; Telugu; Editor PANDITHARADHYULA NAGESWARA RAO; circ. 88,300 (Vijayawada edition), 28,700 (Bangalore edition).

Indian Express: George Oakes Building, Besant Rd., Gandhinagar 3; (*see also* under Delhi); circ. (Vijayawada, Bangalore, Madras, Cochin and Madurai) 204,600.

Assam

Assam Tribune: Tribune Buildings, Gauhati; f. 1938; English; Editor S. C. Kakati; circ. 24,900.

Dainik Assam (*Assam Tribune Gauhati*): f. 1965; Assamese; Editor K. N. Hazarika; circ. 21,700.

Bihar

Patna

Aryavarta: Mazharul Haque Path; f. 1940; Hindi; morning; Editor J. K. Mishra; circ. 78,700.

The Indian Nation: Mazharul Haque Path; f. 1930; morning; Editor Deena Nath Jha; circ. 52,900.

Pradeep: Buddha Marg; f. 1947; morning; Hindi; Editor R. Bhartiya; circ. 27,700.

Sada-E-Aam: Ashok Raj Path; f. 1942; Urdu; Editor S. R. Haider; circ. 8,100.

Sangam Daily: Lalazar Manzil, P.O.B. 26, Patna-4; f. 1953; Urdu; morning; Editor Ghulam Sarwar; circ. 14,287.

Searchlight: Buddha Marg; f. 1918; English; morning; Editor S. K. Rau; circ. 21,000.

Goa

Panaji

Gomantak: P.O.B. 41; f. 1962; Marathi; morning; Editor M. Gadkari; circ. 12,000.

Navhind Times: Rua Gracias; f. 1963; English; morning; Editor K. S. K. Menon; circ. 11,600.

Gujarat

Ahmedabad

Gujarat Samachar: Gujarat Samachar Bhavan; f. 1932; Gujarati; morning; Editor Shantilal A. Shah; circ. 99,000.

Indian Express: Janasatta Bldg., Mirzapur Rd.; English; *see* under Delhi; circ. (Ahmedabad) 17,800.

Sandesh: Sandesh Bldg., Cheekanta Rd.; f. 1923; Gujarati; Editor C. S. Patel; circ. 89,700.

Western Times: f. 1967; English; Editor Ramu Patel; circ. 14,500.

Jammu and Kashmir

Jammu

Kashmir Times: Residency Rd.; English; morning; Editor/Publisher V. Bhasin.

Karnataka

Bangalore

Deccan Herald: 16 Mahatma Gandhi Road; f. 1948. morning; English; Editor V. B. Menon; circ. 75,700.

Indian Express: 1 Queen's Rd.; *see* under Delhi; circ. (Bangalore, Madras, Madurai and Vijayawada) 204,600.

Kannada Prabha: 1 Queen's Rd.; Kannada; f. 1967; Editor K. S. Ramakrishna Murthy; circ. 47,000.

Kerala

Trivandrum

Kerala Kaumudi: P.B. 77, Pettah, Trivandrum; f. 1940; Malayalam and English; Editor K. Sukumaran; circ. 133,500.

Navakeralam: f. 1957; Malayalam; independent; Editor S. Sebastian; circ. 21,300.

Thaninram: f. 1964; Malayalam; Editor K. K. Nair; circ. 28,455.

Other Towns

Deepika: P.B. 7, Kottayam-I; f. 1887; Malayalam; independent; Chief Editor V. Z. Narively; circ. 47,828.

Express: P.B. 15, Trichur 680001; f. 1944; Editor K. Balakrishna; circ. 33,525.

Malayala Manorama: P.O.B. 26, K. K. Rd., Kottayam and Kozhikode; f. 1888; Malayalam; morning; Chief Editor K. M. Mathew; circ. 314,200. Also published from Calicut; circ. 101,676.

Mathrubhumi: P.B. No. 46, Robinson Rd., Kozhikode; f. 1923; Malayalam; Editor K. P. Kesava Menon; also published from Cochin; circ. 291,300.

Maharashtra

Bombay

Bombay Samachar: Red House, Sayed Abdulla Brelvi Rd., Fort; f. 1822; morning and Sunday weekly; Gujarati; political and commercial; Editors Mindo Desai (daily), Shantikumar J. Bhatt (Sunday); circ. 108,400 (daily), 122,100 (weekly).

The Economic Times: The Times of India Press, Dr. Dadabhoy Naoroji Rd., P.O.B. 213, Bombay-1; f. 1961; daily; English; Editor D. K. Rangnekar; circ. 46,000.

Evening News of India: Dr. Dadabhai Naoroji Rd.; f. 1923; evening; English; Editor Sham Lal; circ. 24,000.

The Financial Express: Express Towers, Nariman Point, I; f. 1961; daily; English; Editor V. K. Narasimhan circ. 20,000.

Free Press Bulletin: 21 Dalal St., Fort 1; f. 1947; English; evening; Editor C. S. Pandit; circ. 23,100.

Indian Express: Express Towers, Nariman Point, I; English; *see* under Delhi; circ. (Bombay and Ahmedabad) 109,700.

Jam-e-Jamshed: Ballard House, Mangalore St.; f. 1832; English and Gujarati; Chair. Rustom P. Marzban; Editor Adi Marzban; circ. 7,900, (Sunday) 11,800.

Janashakti: 21 Dalal St., Fort, 1; f. 1950; Gujarati; Independent Nationalist; Editor Harindra Dave; circ. 30,107.

Janmabhoomi: Janmabhoomi Bhavan, Ghoga St., Fort Bombay 400001; f. 1934; Gujarati; Propr. Saurashtra Trust; Editor J. M. Shukla; circ. 44,800.

Lokasatta: Newspaper House, Sassoon Dock, Colaba, 5; f. 1948; Marathi; Editor R. N. Late; circ. 129,400.

Maharashtra Times: The Times of India Press, Dr. Dadabhai Naoroji Rd.; f. 1962; Marathi; Editor G. S. Talwalkar; circ. 122,100.

Maratha: Lovegrove Rd., Worli, 18; f. 1956; Marathi; Editor Shirish Pai; circ. 47,000.

Navashakti: 21 Dalal St., Fort; f. 1932; Marathi; Editor-in-Chief P. V. Gadgil; circ. 46,000.

Navbharat Times: Dr. Dadabhai Naoroji Rd.; f. 1950; also published from New Delhi; Hindi; Editor A. K. Jain; circ. (Bombay) 67,000, (Delhi) 198,100.

Prajatantra: 211–219 Frere Rd., Fort, 1; f. 1954; evening; Gujarati; Editor Chamanlal V. Shah; circ. 23,457.

Sakal: Old Prabhadevi Rd.; f. 1970; daily and Sunday; Marathi; *see* under Poona.

Times of India: Dr. Dadabhai Naoroji Rd.; f. 1838; morning; English; published from Bombay, Delhi and Ahmedabad; Editor Sham Lal; circ. (Bombay and Ahmedabad) 199,400.

Nagpur

Hitavada: Wardha Rd.; f. 1911; morning; English; Editor G. T. Parande; circ. 11,300.

Maharashtra: Ogale Rd., Mahal; f. 1941; Marathi; Nationalist; Editor M. R. DANGRE; circ. 12.000.

Nagpur Times: 37 Farmland, Ramdaspeth; f. 1933; English; Editor A. G. SHEOREY; circ. 20,600 (Nagpur).

Nava Prabhat Hindi Daily: Kishore Bhavan Sitabuldi; f. 1947; Editor L. K. CHAURASIA; circ. 20,000.

Tarun Bharat: f. 1954; Marathi; Independent; Editor M. G. VAIDYA; circ. 45,200 (also published from Poona).

Pune (Poona)

Kesari: 568 Narayan Peth 30; f. 1881; Marathi; Editor J. S. TILAK; circ. 41,600.

Sakal: 595 Budhwar Peth, Poona 2; f. 1932; daily and Sunday; Marathi; Editor Shri S. G. MUNAGEKAR; Gen. Man. Lt.-Col. (retd.) V. V. JOSHI; circ. daily (Bombay and Pune) 96,300, Sunday 107,800.

PUNJAB

Aaj-Ki-Baat: Sadar Bazar, Gurgaon; Hindi; Editor V. P. AGRWAL.

Ajit: Nehru Garden Rd., Jullundur City; Punjabi; f. 1943; Editor S. S. HAMDARD; circ. 22,190.

Tribune: Chandigarh; f. 1881; English; Editor R. M. NAIR; circ. 118,600.

RAJASTHAN

Rajasthan Patrika: Gulab bagh, Jaipur 3; f. 1956; Editor K. C. KULISH; circ. 26,633.

Rashtradoot: H.O., P.O.B. 30, Sudharma, M.I. Rd., Jaipur 1; f. 1951; Hindi; Editor RAKESH SHARMA; circ. (Jaipur and Kota) 25,000.

TAMIL NADU

Madras

Andhra Patrika: 7 Thambu Chetty St.; f. 1914; evening; Telugu; Editor S. RADHA KRISHNA; circ. 53,200.

Daily Thanthi: 1 Rundalls Rd., Vepery, 600007; f. 1942; Tamil; Editor R. S. RATHNAM; circ. 263,500.

Hindu, The: 201A Mount Rd.; London Office: 2/3 Salisbury Court, Fleet St., E.C.4; f. 1878; morning; English; Independent; Man. Editor G. NARASIMHAN; Editor G. KASTURI; circ. 210,500.

Indian Express: Express Estates, Mount Rd. 2; *see* under Delhi; circ. (Madras, Madurai, Bangalore, Cochin and Vijayawada) 204,600.

Mail, The: Mail Buildings, Mount Rd.; London Office: 151 Fleet St., E.C.4; f. 1867; evening; English; Independent; Editor V. P. V. RAJAN; circ. 26,965.

Swadesamitran: Victory House, Mount Rd., 2; London Office: 2-3 Salisbury Court, E.C.4; f. 1880; evening; Tamil; Man. Editor C. R. RAMASWAMY; circ. 17,400.

Madurai

Dinamani: 137 Ramnad Rd. 9; f. 1951; morning; Tamil; Editor A. N. SIVRARAMAN; circ. (Madurai and Madras) 178,100.

Indian Express: 137 Ramnad Rd. 9; *see* under Delhi; circ. (Madurai, Madras, Bangalore, Cochin and Vijayawada) 204,600.

UTTAR PRADESH

Agra

Amar Ujala: City Station Rd., Agra 3, and 19 Civil Lines Bareilly; f. 1948 and 1969, respectively; Hindi; Edito D. L. AGRAWAL; circ. (Agra) 36,400, (Bareilly) 17,600

Sainik: Kaserat Bazar; f. 1925; Hindi; Editor S. P PATHAK; circ. 22,075.

Allahabad

Bharat: Leader Rd.; f. 1928; Hindi; Chief Editor Dr. M. D SHARMA; circ. 14,000.

Northern India Patrika: 10 Edmonstone Rd.; f. 1959 English; Chief Editor TUSHAR KANTI GHOSH; Gen Man. KALYAN DASGUPTA; Resident Editor S. K. BOSE circ. 38,400.

Kanpur

Daily Action: 2 Sarvodaya Nagar, P.O.B. 214; f. 1971 English; Man. Editor and Editor P. C. GUPTA; circ 12,800.

Daily Jagran: 2 Sarvodaya Nagar, P.O.B. 214; f. 1947 Hindi; Man. Editor P. C. GUPTA, Editor NARENDRA MOHAN; circ. 51,596.

Daily Veer Bharat: 48/15 Lathi Mohal, Kanpur 1; f. 1926 Hindi; Editor A. K. PANDEY; circ. 14,400.

Paigham: f. 1956; Urdu; Editor WAJIHUDDIN; circ. 10,562

Pratap: 22/120 Shri Ganesh Shankar Vidyarathi Rd.; f 1932; Hindi; Editor SURESH CHANDRA BHATTACHARYA circ. 18,340.

Lucknow

National Herald: published by Associated Journals Ltd., P.O.B. 122; f. 1938 Lucknow, 1968 Delhi; English; Editor M. CHALAPATHI RAU; circ. 45.000.

Pioneer, The: 20A Vidhan Sabha Marg; f. 1865; English; Editor S. N. GOSH; circ. 19,100.

Swantantra Bharat: f. 1947; Hindi; Editor ASHOK JI; circ 38,000.

Varanasi

Aj: Kabirchaura, P.O.B. 7; f. 1920; Hindi; Editor S. K GUPTA; circ. 37,700.

WEST BENGAL

Calcutta

Amrita Bazar Patrika: 14 Ananda Chatterji Lane; f. 1868; published at Calcutta; morning; English; Nationalist; Editor T. K. GHOSH; circ. 109,700.

Ananda Bazar Patrika: 6 Prafulla Sarkar St.; f. 1878; morning; Bengali; Editor A. K. SARKAR; circ. 279,900.

Dainik Basumati: 166 Bepin Behari Ganguly St.; f. 1921; Bengali; independent Nationalist; Editor KEDAR GHOSH; circ. 112,777.

Hindusthan Standard: 6 Prafulla Sarkar St.; f. 1937; English; Editor AVEEK SARKER; circ. 65,100.

Jugantar: 12 Ananda Chatterjee Lane; Bengali; f. 1937; Editor SOOKAMAL KANTI GHOSE; circ. 194,500.

Sanmarg: 160C Chittaranjan Avenue; f. 1948; Hindi; Nationalist; Editor P. A. MISHRA; circ. 28,600.

Statesman: Statesman House, 4 Chowringhee Square, also at Statesman House, New Delhi; f. 1875; morning; English; Independent; Editor S. NIHAL SINGH; circ. 183,900.

Vishwamitra: 12 Dalhousie Square East; f. 1916; morning; Hindi; commercial; Dir. B. C. AGARWAL; Editor KRISHAN CHANDRA AGRAWAL; circ. 63,200.

SELECTED PERIODICALS

DELHI (incl. NEW DELHI)

Africa Diary: F-15 Bhagat Singh Market; f. 1961; African news and current events, with Index; weekly; circulation in 75 countries; Editor HARI SHARAN CHHABRA.

African Recorder: 2 Gulmohay Park, P.O.B. 595, 1; f. 1962; fortnightly reference work on African affairs; Editor M. S. R. KHEMCHAND.

Akashvani: Mandi House, 1st Floor, New Delhi 110001, Post Bag 12; f. 1936; All India Radio programmes; Sunday; English; Hindi; Chief Editor G. C. CHUCKERVERTTY; circ. 8,000.

Asian Recorder: C-1/9 Tilak Marg, P.O.B. 595, 1; f. 1955; weekly reference work on Asian affairs; circ. in 70 countries; Editor M. HENRY SAMUEL.

Astana: 722 Jama Masjid; f. 1950; Urdu; monthly; religion and philosophy; Editor M. M. FARUQI; circ. 60,041.

Biswin Sadi: Daryaganj; f. 1937; monthly; Urdu; Editor K. GIRAMI; circ. 20,000.

Caravan: Jhandewalan Estate, Rani Jhansi Rd.; f. 1940; fortnightly; English; Editor VISHWA NATH; circ. 16,800.

Careers and Courses: 94 Baird Rd.; f. 1949; monthly; English; Editor A. C. GOYLE; circ. 44,300.

Career Digest: Shanker Market; f. 1964; English; monthly; Editor O. P. VERMA.

The Career Times: 5572, Gali 75, Regharpura; f. 1974; English; monthly; Editors D. R. B. L. SADANA, Prof. R. CHOPRA.

Champak: R.J. Rd., 110055; f. 1968; Hindi; fortnightly; circ. 37,042.

Competition Success Review: 48/4 East Patel Nagar; monthly; English; f. 1963; Editor S. KUMAR; circ. 10,008.

Dinaman: 10 Dariyaganj; f. 1965; Hindi news weekly; Editor RAGHUVIR SAHAY; circ. 43,300.

Diplomat's Directory, The: C-1/9 Tilak Marg; f. 1961; half-yearly journal for diplomats; Editor M. HENRY SAMUEL.

Eastern Economist: United Commercial Bank Building, Parliament St., P.O.B. 34; f. 1943; weekly; English; Editor V. BALASUBRAMANIAN; circ. 5,600.

Everyman's: Express Building; B.S. 2, Marg; f. 1973; weekly; English; Editor R. KRISHNA.

Filmi Duniya: 16 Darya Ganj, Delhi 6; f. 1958; monthly; Hindi; Editor NARENDRA KUMAR; circ. 85,000.

Foreign Affairs Report: Indian Council of World Affairs, Sapru House, Barakhamba Rd., New Delhi 110001; f. 1952; monthly; Editor Prof. M. S. RAJAN; circ. 2,000.

Income & Opportunity: 94 Baird Rd.; f. 1968; monthly; English; Editor KULDIP GOYLE; circ. 18,000.

India Quarterly: Indian Council of World Affairs, Sapru House, Barakhamba Rd.; f. 1945; quarterly; Man. Ed. Prof. M. S. RAJAN.

Indian and Foreign Review: Shastri Bhavan; f. 1963; fortnightly; review of political, socio-economic and cultural aspects of India and India in relation to the world; Chief Editor SHYAM RATNA GUPTA.

Indian Economic Diary: F-15 Bhagat Singh Market; f. 1970; weekly; Editor HARI SHARAN CHHABRA.

Indian Horizons: Azad Bhavan, Indraprastha Estate; f. 1951; quarterly; published by the Indian Council for Cultural Relations; Editor A. SRINIVASAN.

Indian Horticulture: India Council of Agricultural Research, Queen Victoria Rd.; f. 1956; quarterly; English; Editor K. B. NAIR; circ. 6,500.

Indian Observer: 26F Connaught Place; f. 1958; weekly; English; Editor DURLAB SINGH; circ. 66,733.

Indian Railways: P.O.B. 467, Ministry of Railways, Govt. of India; f. 1956; English; monthly; Editor P. U. C. CHOWDARY.; circ. 12,000.

Intensive Agriculture: Ministry of Food and Agriculture; f. 1955; monthly; English; Editor R. VERMA; circ. 45,000.

Jagat: 818 Kunde Walan, Ajmere Gate; f. 1958; monthly; Hindi; literary and cultural; Editor PREM CHAND VERMA; circ. 18,500.

Journal of Industry and Trade: Ministry of Foreign Trade; f. 1952; English; monthly; Dir. of Commercial Publicity V. C. TIWARI; circ. 6,590.

Kadambini: Connaught Circus; f. 1960; Hindi; monthly; Editor R. AWASTHI; circ. 41,080.

Krishak Samachar: A-1 Nizamuddin West; f. 1957; monthly; English, Hindi, Marathi; agriculture; Editor Dr. D. A. BHOLAY; circ. (English) 4,000, (Hindi) 4,000, (Marathi) 5,000.

Kurukshetra: Krishi Bhavan; fortnightly; English; Hindi; community development and village democracy; Editor P. SRINIVASAN; circ. 12,000.

Lalita: 92 Daryaganj; f. 1959; monthly; Hindi; Editor L. RANIGUPTA; circ. 20,000.

Link Indian News Magazine: Link House, Mathura Rd.; f. 1958; Independent; weekly; Chair. of the Editorial Board EDATATA NARAYANAN; Editor M. VENUGOPALA; circ. 11,000.

Nandan: Hindustan Times Press; f. 1963; monthly; Hindi; Editor J. PRAKSH BHARTI; circ. 111,447.

Nav Chitrapat: 92 Daryaganj; f. 1932; monthly; Hindi; Editor SATYENDRA SHYAM circ. 35,980.

New Age: 15 Kotla Rd., 1; f. 1953; organ of the Communist Party of India; weekly; English; Editor BHUPESH GUPTA, M.P.; circ. 15,684.

Organiser: 7E Rani Jhansi Marg, 55; f. 1947; weekly; English; Editor V. P. BHATIA; circ. 36,200.

Overseas Hindustan Times: Connaught Circus; f. 1950; English; weekly; Editor B. G. VERGHESE; circ. 3,182.

Panchjanya: Marina Bldg., Connaught Circus, New Delhi 1; f. 1947; weekly; Hindi; Gen. Man. JWALA PRASAD CHATURVEDI; Chief Editor K. R. MALKANI; circ. 47,380.

Parag: 10 Dariyaganj, Delhi 6; f. 1958; monthly; Hindi; Editor K. L. NANDAN; circ. 95,000.

Picture Parade: 5A/15 Ansari Rd., Darya Ganj; English; film monthly; Editor D. P. BERRY; circ. 10,000.

Picturegoer: 92 Daryaganj; f. 1940; monthly; English; Editor SATYENDRA SHYAM; circ. 5,000.

Priya: 92 Daryaganj; f. 1960; monthly; Hindi; Editor SATYENDRA SMYAM; circ. 25,000.

Punjabi Digest: Union Bank Bldg., Ajmalkhan Rd., P.O.B. 2549; f. 1971; literary, monthly; Gurmukhi; Chair. S. KAPUR SINGH, M.A., I.C.S.; Gen. Man. Sardar PARVESH BAHADUR SINGH; circ. 18,000.

Rang Bhumi: 5A/15 Ansari Rd., Darya Ganj; f. 1941; Hindi; films; Editor S. K. GUPTA; circ. 25,269.

Review: Bombay Life Bldg., Connaught Circus; f. 1928; monthly; English; Editor FRANK ANTHONY; circ. 7,880.

Sainik Samachar: AFO Mess, Dr. Rajendra Prasad Rd.; f. 1909; weekly; English, Hindi, Urdu, Tamil, Punjabi, Telugu, Marathi, Gorkhali, Malayalam editions; for the Indian Defence Forces; Principal Officers Lt.-Col. J. S. GULERIA and Dr. S. S. SHASHI.

Saptahik Hindustan: N-Block, Connaught Circus; f. 1950; weekly; Hindi; Editor M. S. JOSHI; circ. 89,300.

Sarita: Jhandewala Estate, Rani Jhansi Rd.; f. 1945; fortnightly; Hindi; Editor VISHWA NATH; circ. 85,600.

Shama: 13/14 Asaf Ali Rd., Ajmeri Gate; f. 1939; monthly; Urdu; Editor M. YUSUF DEHLVI; circ. 94,000.

Sher-i-Punjab: Union Bank Bldg., Ajmalkhan Rd.; P.O.B. 2549; f. 1911; weekly news magazine; Urdu; Chief Editor Sardar JANG BAHADUR SINGH; Man. Editor S. B. SINGH; circ. over 15,000.

Spokesman: 34 Theatre Communication Bldg., Connaught Place; f. 1951; weekly; English; Man. Editor GHANISHAM SINGH PASRICHA; circ. 10,600.

Sunday Standard: Bahadur Shah Zafar Marg; f. 1936; weekly; English; published simultaneously in Delhi, Madurai (Tamil Nadu), Madras (Tamil Nadu), Bangalore (Mysore), Vijayawada (Andhra Pradesh), Bombay (Maharashtra) and Ahmedabad (Gujarat); Editor-in-Chief S. MULGAOKAR; circ. (national) 485,600.

Sushama: 13/14 Asaf Ali Rd.; f. 1959; monthly; Hindi; Editor M. YUNUS DEHLVI; circ. 57,800.

Traveller in India: P.O.B. 2011, Delhi 6; f. 1957; monthly; English; transport and communication; Editor Director of Publications Division; circ. 20,000.

Vedic Light: Ram Lila Ground, Maharshi Dayanand Bhavan; f. 1967; monthly; journal for Vedic ideology; Editor OMPRAKASH TYAGI, M.P.

Vigyan Pragati: monthly; Hindi; scientific; Editor S. SHARMA; circ. 32,000.

Yojana: Planning Commission, Yojana Bhavan; f. 1957; fortnightly; English, Tamil, Bengali, Marathi, Gujarati, Assamese, Malayalam, Telugu and Hindi; Chief Editor S. SHRINIVASACHAR; circ. 37,000.

ANDHRA PRADESH

Hyderabad

Islamic Culture: P.O.B. 171; f. 1927; quarterly; English; Editor Dr. M. A. MUID KHAN; circ. 10,000.

Vijayawada

Sunday Standard: George Oakes Bldg., Besant Rd., Gandhinagar 3; *see* under Delhi; circ. (Vijayawada, Cochin, Bangalore, Madras and Madurai) 233,600.

BIHAR

Patna

Balak: P.O.B. 5, Govind Mitra Rd.; f. 1926; monthly; Hindi; for children; Man. Editor M. S. SINGH; circ. 10,600.

Bihar Herald: Kadamkuan, Patna 3; f. 1874; weekly; English; Editor ARUN ROY CHOUDHURY; circ. 8,000.

Bihar Information: P.R. D. Govt. of Bihar; f. 1952; weekly (also in Hindi, Urdu); Editor B. DWIVEDI.

Chunumunu: Naya Tola; f. 1950; monthly; Hindi; for children; Editor J. N. MISHRA; circ. 15,000.

Jyotsana: Rejendranagar; f. 1947; monthly; Hindi; Editor S. NARAYAN; circ. 16,000.

Spark: Patna-3; f. 1947; weekly; English; Editor G. S. DALMIA; circ. 9,000.

Yogi: Buddha Marg; f. 1934; weekly; Hindi; Editor B. S. VERMA; circ. 9,380.

GUJARAT

Ahmedabad

Akhand Anand: P.O.B. 50, Bhadra; f. 1947; monthly; Gujarati; Editor T. K. THAKKAR; circ. 49,900.

Aram: Sandesh Bhavan, Gheekanta; f. 1932; monthly; Gujarati; Editor C. S. PATEL; circ. 5,000.

Chitralok: Gujarat Samachar Bhavan, Khanpur, P.O.B. 254; f. 1952; weekly; Gujarati; films; Editor SHREYANS SHAH; circ. 24,000.

Stree: Sandesh Bhavan, Gheekanta, Ahmedabad; f. 1962 weekly; Gujarati; Editor Mrs. LILAVATI C. PATEL circ. 31,800.

Sunday Standard: Janasatta Karyalaya, Mirzapur Rd. weekly; English; circ. (Ahmedabad) 19,000.

Zagmag: Gujarat Samachar Bhavan, Khanpur; f. 1952 weekly; Gujarati; for children; Editor SHREYANS S SHAH; circ. 28,500.

KARNATAKA

Bangalore

Hosiery and Textile Journal: Kucba Rd., Mangatrai monthly; English and Urdu.

Mysindia: 38A Mahatma Gandhi Rd.; f. 1939; weekly English; news and current affairs; Editor D. N HOSALI; circ. 14,000.

Prajamata: North Anjaneya Temple Rd., Basavangudi f. 1931; weekly; Kannada; news and current affairs Chief Editor H. V. NAGARAJA RAO; circ. 86,200 (also published in Telugu).

Sunday Standard: 1 Queen's Rd.; *see* under Delhi; circ (Bangalore, Madurai, Madras, Cochin and Vijayawada) 233,400.

KERALA

Trivandrum

Janapatham: Government of Kerala; f. 1970; monthly, Malayalam; Editor M. DIVAKARAN; circ. 6,000.

Other Towns

Malayala Manorama: P.O.B. 26, Kottayam; f. 1956; weekly; Malayalam; Editor K. M. MATHEW; circ. 329,200.

Mathrubhumi Illustrated Weekly: Robinson Rd., Kozhikode (Calicut); f. 1932; weekly; Malayalam; Editor K. P. K. MENON; circ. 92,000.

MADHYA PRADESH

Krishak Jagat: P.O.B. 3, Bhopal-462-001; f. 1946; weekly; Hindi; also Marathi edition in Bombay; agriculture; Man. Editor S. C. GANGRADE; Chief Editor M. C. BONDRIYA; circ. 16,820.

MAHARASHTRA

Bombay

Asia Bulletin: c/o Asia Publishing House, Ballard Estate; f. 1954; monthly; English; publicity journal; Editor P. S. JAYASINGHE; circ. 24,546.

Beej: 62 Karwar St.; f. 1952; monthly; Gujarati; Editor Mrs. M. V. KOTAK; circ. 18,000.

Bharat Jyoti: 21 Dalal St., Fort, 1; f. 1938; weekly; English; Editor A. B. NAIR; circ. 66,400.

Bhavan's Journal: Bharatiya Vidya Bhavan, Chowpatty Rd.; f. 1954; fortnightly; English; Man. Editor J. H. DAVE; Editor S. RAMAKRISHNAN; circ. 32,800.

Blitz News Magazine: 17/17-H Cawasji Patel St., Fort; f. 1941; weekly, English, Hindi, Urdu and Marathi editions; Editor-in-Chief R. K. KARANJIA; circ. 251,400.

Business Digest of India: f. 1958; monthly; mid-year (annual) and special number; English; Editor S. A. THAKUR; circ. 10,000.

Chitralekha: Star Printery, 62 Karwar St.; f. 1950; weekly; Gujarati; Editors Mrs. M. V. KOTAK, H. L. MEHTA; circ. 150,000.

Commerce: Manek Mahal, 90 Veer Nariman Rd., Churchgate, 20; f. 1910; weekly; English; Editor VADILAL DAGLI; circ. 10,000.

Current: 15 Cawasji Patel St.; f. 1949; weekly; English; Editor A. SYED; circ. 37,918.

Dharmayug: Dadabhai Naoroji Rd.; weekly; Hindi; Editor D. V. BHARATI; circ. 214,300.

Eve's Weekly: Apollo St., Fort; Editor G. EWING; circ. 35,500.

Illustrated Weekly of India: Dr. Dadabhai Naoroji Rd.; f. 1929; weekly; English; Editor KHUSHWANT SINGH; circ. 288,168.

Imprint: Surya Mahal, 5 Burjorji Bharucha Marg, Bombay 400023; f. 1961; monthly; English; Editor R. V. PANDIT; circ. 25,000.

India Quarterly: c/o Asia Publishing House, Calicut St., Ballard Estate, 1; f. 1953; journal of the Indian Council of World Affairs; Editor S. L. POPLAI.

Indian and Eastern Engineer: Piramal Mansion, 235 Dadabhai Naoroji Rd.; f. 1858; monthly; English; Dir. and Editor MICK DE SOUZA; circ. 6,000.

Indian PEN: Theosophy Hall, 40 New Marine Lines, Bombay 400020; f. 1934; monthly; organ of Indian Centre of the International PEN; Editor SOPHIA WADIA.

Industrial India: 12 Rampart Row; f. 1960; monthly; English; official organ of the All-India Manufacturers' Asscn.

Industrial Times: f. 1958; fortnightly; English; Editor S. J. RELE; circ. 5,000.

Janmabhoomi Pravasi: Janmabhoomi Bhavan, Ghoga St., Fort, Bombay 400001; f. 1939; weekly; Gujarati; Editor J. M. SHUKLA; circ. 75,100 (incl. daily).

Jee: 62 Karwar St.; f. 1958; Gujarati; Editor Mrs. M. V. KOTAK; circ. 26,000.

Journal of the Indian Institute of Bankers: Apollo St.; f. 1930; quarterly; English; Editor VADILAL DAGLI; circ. 50,000.

Kaiser-i-Hind: Kaiser Chambers, Town Hall Rd., Fort; f. 1881; weekly; Anglo-Gujarati; National; Editor J. E. HEERJIBHEDIN; circ. 8,000.

Khadi Gramodyog: Irla Rd., Vile Parle; f. 1954; monthly; English; commerce and industry; Editor J. N. VERMA; circ. 8,100.

Mirror: Apollo St., Fort; f. 1961; monthly; English; Editor M. D. JAPETH; circ. 31,800.

Mother India: Sumati Publications Ltd.; f. 1935; monthly; English; Editor BABURAO PATEL; circ. 12,500.

Onlooker: 21 Dalal St., Fort; f. 1939; monthly; English; Editor F. N. KANGA; circ. 5,600.

People's Raj (*Lokrajya*): Directorate-General of Information and Public Relations, Sachivalaya, Bombay 400032; f. 1947; government activities and publicity; fortnightly; edition in Marathi, Urdu and English; circ. (all editions) 121,600.

Radio Times of India: 29 New Queen's Rd.; f. 1946; monthly; English; Editor D. D. LAKHANPAL; circ. 3,500.

Reader's Digest: Orient House, Mangalore St., Ballard Estate 1; f. 1954; monthly; English; Man. Dir. and Publisher T. PARAMESHWAR; Editor M. RANDOLPH; circ. 193,900.

Samarpan: Bharatiya Vidya Bhavan, Chaupatty; f. 1957; fortnightly; Gujarati; Editors H. DAVE, G. DESAI; circ.8,900.

Sarika: Times of India Building, Dadabhai Naoroji Rd.; London Office: 30A, District Rd., Sudbury, Wembley, Middx.; f. 1960; short story; monthly; Hindi; Editor KAMLESHWAR; circ. 33,700.

Screen: Express Towers, Nariman Point, Bombay 400021; f. 1951; film weekly; English; Editor S. S. PILLAI; circ. 110,000 (Bombay, Madras, New Delhi).

Star and Style: Bombay Samachar Marg; f. 1965; film and fashion fortnightly; English; Editor GULSHAN EWING; circ. 72,200.

Stardust: Agra Bldg., 2nd Floor, 119-121 Mahatma Gandhi Rd. 1; f. 1971; monthly; English; Editor NARI M. HIRA; circ. 120,000.

Sudha: Janmabhoomi Bhavan, Ghoga St., Fort; f. 1968; Women's weekly; Gujarati; Propr. SaurashtraTrust; Editor D. G. PATEL; circ. 12,000.

Sunday Lokasatta: Newspaper House, Sassoon Dock, Colaba 5; f. 1948; Marathi; Editor R. N. LATE; circ. 201,900.

Sunday Standard: Express Towers, Nariman Point; f. 1936; *see* under Delhi; circ. (Bombay) 129,000.

Urvashi: Lamington Rd.; f. 1959; weekly; Hindi; Editor R. R. K. NAHATA; circ. 17,822.

Vyapar: Janmabhoomi Bhavan, Ghoga St., Fort, Bombay 400001; f. 1949; financial journal; twice weekly; Gujarati; Editor S. J. VASANI; circ. 27,600.

Nagpur

All India Reporter: A.I.R. Ltd., P.O.B. 209, Congress Nagar, Nagpur 12; f. 1914; law journal; monthly; English; Chief Editor S. APPU RAO; circ. 30,000.

Criminal Law Journal: A.I.R. Ltd., P.O.B. 209, Congress Nagar, Nagpur 12; f. 1904; monthly; English; Editor S. APPU RAO; circ. 12,500.

Rekha: Chitar Oli Chowk, P.O.B. 373, Central Ave.; f. 1955; monthly; Hindi; Editor S. RANDIVE; circ. 20,300.

Pune (Poona)

Swaraj: Bombay Papers Ltd., 595 Budhwar Peth: f. 1936; weekly; Marathi; Man. Lt.-Col. V. V. JOSHI (Retd.); circ. 82,000.

RAJASTHAN

Dharti-Ke-Lal: P.O.B. 12, Kota; f. 1953; monthly; Hindi; agricultural; Editor BABU HINDU; circ. 33,927.

Rastravani: Shayam Sunder Bhargava Bldg., Jaipur Rd., Ajmer; f. 1951; weekly; Hindi; Editor K. BARNWALL; circ. 10,300.

TAMIL NADU

Madras

Ambili Ammavan: 2–3 Arcot Rd., Vadapalani; f. 1970; monthly; Malayalam; Editor Sri CHAKRAPANI; circ. 23,300.

Ambulimama: 2–3 Arcot Rd., Vadapalani; f. 1947; monthly; Tamil; Editor Sri CHAKRAPANI; circ. 55,000.

Ananda Vikatan: 151 Mount Rd.; f. 1924; weekly; Tamil; Editor S. BALSUBRAMANIAN; circ. 209,400.

Andhra Prabha Illustrated Weekly: Express Estates, Mount Rd., 600002; f. 1952; weekly; Telugu; Editor VIDVAN VISWAM; circ. 121,200.

Andhra Sachitra Varapatrika: 6 and 7 Thambu Chetty St.; f. 1908; weekly; Telugu; Chief Editor S. RADHAKRISHNA; circ. 66,100.

Antiseptic: 323/24 Thambu Chetty St.; f. 1904; monthly; English; Editor Dr. U. VASUDEVA RAU; circ. 14,500.

Bharatham: 2 R. K. Mutt Rd., Mylapore; f. 1959; weekly; Tamil; Editor P. S. RAJAGOPALAN; circ. 25,031.

Chandamama: 2–3 Arcot Rd., Vadapalani; f. 1947; children's monthly; editions in Hindi, English, Gujarati, Telugu, Kannada, Malayalam and Bengali; Editor CHAKRAPANI; combined circ. 415,500.

Chandoba: 2–3 Arcot Rd., Vadapalani; f. 1952; monthly; Marathi; Editor CHAKRAPANI; circ. 75,400.

Cinema Rangam: 65/5, Arcot Rd., 24; f. 1954; monthly; Telugu; films; Editor T. V. RAMANATH; circ. 21,600.

Dinamani Kadir: 137 Ramnad Rd. 9; Tamil; weekly; circ. 95,900.

Free India: 77 General Patters Rd., Mount Rd.; f. 1939; news and current affairs; weekly; English; Editor D. KRISHNAMURTHY; circ. 12,300.

Jahnamamu: 2–3 Arcot Rd., Vadapalani; f. 1972; monthly; Oriya; Editor Sri CHAKRAPANI; circ. 13,000.

Kalai: 193 Mount Rd.; f. 1958; monthly; Tamil; films; Editor A. SEENU; circ. 27,000.

Kalai Magal: P.O.B. 604, Madras 4; f. 1931; literary and cultural; monthly; Tamil; Man. Editor K. V. JAGANNATHAN, M.A.; circ. 44,500.

Kalki: 20 Dr. Guruswamy Mudaliar Rd., Chetput, Madras 31; f. 1941; literary and cultural; weekly; Tamil; Editor K. RAJENDRAN; circ. 166,500.

Kumudam: 83 Purasawalkam High Rd.; f. 1947; weekly; Tamil; Editor S. A. P. ANNAMALAI; circ. 427,700.

Malai Mani: 50 Edward Elliots Rd.; f. 1958; weekly; Tamil; Editor P. S. ELANGO; circ. 45,700.

My Magazine of India: 11 Barracks St., Seven Wells; f. 1929; monthly; English; Editor Miss V. SIVAGAMASUNDARI; circ. 14,320.

New Leader: 6 Armenian St.; f. 1887; weekly; English; Editor Rev. Fr. JAMES KOTTOOR; circ. 9,000.

Picturpost: 65/5 Arcot Rd., 24; f. 1943; monthly; English; films; Editor T. V. RAMANATH; circ. 50,000.

Puthumai: 101 Purusawalkam High Rd.; f. 1957; monthly; Tamil; Editor K. T. KOSALRAM; circ. 30,400.

Sunday Standard: Express Estates, Mount Rd. 2; *see* under Delhi; circ. (Vijayawada, Bangalore, Madras, Cochin and Madurai) 233,600.

Sunday Times: 69 Peters Rd.; f. 1956; weekly; English; Editor S. V. S. VINOD; circ. 48,400.

Swarajya: 20 Dr. Guruswamy Mudaliar Rd., Chetput; f 1956; English; weekly; Editor R. VENKATARAMAN; circ. 15,673.

Tamilnad Times: 105 C. N. Krishnaswamy Rd.; f. 1953; fortnightly; English; Editor M. RODGERS; circ. 30,341.

Thanga Thirai: 17 Whites Rd., Royapettah; f. 1960; fortnightly; Tamil; Editor A. RAMAMURTHI; circ. 30,000.

Thayaga Kural: 2-16 Mount Rd.; f. 1961; weekly; Tamil; Editor A. MA. SAMY; circ. 48,900.

Vani: f. 1949; fortnightly; Telugu; All India Radio journal; circ. 16,800.

Vanoli: f. 1939; fortnightly; Tamil; All India Radio journal; circ. 50,000.

Other Towns

Mathajothidam: 3 Arasamaram, Vellore; f. 1949; monthly; astrology; Tamil; Editor V. K. V. SUBRAMANYAM; circ. 27,300.

Sunday Standard: 137 Ramnad Rd., Madurai 9; *see* under Delhi; circ. (Madurai, Madras, Vijayawada and Bangalore) 233,600.

UTTAR PRADESH

Agra

Disha Bharati: Amar Ujala Bldg., City Station Rd., Agra 3; f. 1972; Hindi weekly; Editor: K. C. NIGAM; circ. 17,400.

Allahabad

Jasoosi Duniya: 5 Kolhan Tola St.; f. 1953; monthly; Urdu, Hindi; Editor S. ABBAS HUSAINY; circ. (both) 60,000.

Kahani: 5 Sardar Patel Marg; f. 1954; monthly; Hindi; Editor SRIPAT RAI; circ. 38,500.

Manmohan: Mitra Prakashan Ltd., 166 Muthiganj; f. 1949; children's monthly; Hindi; Editor S. V. A. MITRA; circ. 18,000.

Manohar Kahaniyan: Mitra Prakashan Ltd., 166 Muthiganj; f. 1940; monthly; Hindi; Editor A. MITRA; circ. 108,900.

Manorma: Mitra Prakashan Ltd., 166 Muthiganj; f. 1924; monthly; Hindi; Editor S. MITRA; circ. 44,200.

Maya: 166 Muthiganj; f. 1929; monthly; Hindi; Editors A. MITRA; circ. 47,900.

Saraswati: Indian Press (Publs.) Ltd., 36 Panna Lal Rd.; f. 1900; monthly; Hindi; Editor S. N. CHATURVEDI; circ. 5,400.

Kanpur

The Citizen: P.O.B. 188, Bhargova Estate; f. 1940; news and current affairs; weekly; English; Editor S. P. MEHRA; circ. 6,000.

Kanchan Prabha: 2 Sarvodaya Nagar, P.O.B. 214; f. 1974; Hindi; monthly; Man. Editor P. C. GUPTA; Editor Y. M. GUPTA; circ. 25,000.

Vyapar Sandesh: 26/104 Birhana Rd.; f. 1950; weekly; Hindi; gives latest market reports and rates of various commodities; Editor HARISHANKER SHARMA; circ. 14,000.

Lucknow

Gyan Bharati: B.N. Rd.; f. 1959; monthly; Hindi; Editor HARI KRISHNA; circ. 11,400.

Gyan Bharati Bal Pocket Books: B. N. Rd.; f. 1969; every two months; Hindi; Man. VIJAI SHARMA.

Janmat: Bhopal House, Lall Bagh, P.O.B. 123; f. 1954; Sunday; Bengali; Editor NARENDRA PANDE; circ. 5,800.

Jan Yug: 22 Kaiserbagh; f. 1942; weekly; Hindi; Editor RAMESH SINHA; circ. 13,300.

Panchajanya: G. B. Marg, Bans Mandi; f. 1948; weekly; Hindi; Editor D. N. MISHRA; circ. 31,000.

People (The): 10 Bhopal House, Lall Bagh; f. 1959; weekly; English; Editor N. L. GAUTAM; circ. 8,000.

Rashtra Dharma: P.O.B. 207, Dr. Raghubir Nagar; f. 1964; monthly; Hindi; Editor B. P. SHUKLA; Man. NAGESWAR SAHAI; circ. 10,000.

Other Towns

Current Events: 15 Rajpur Rd., Dehra Dun; f. 1955; monthly review of national and international affairs; English; Editor DEV DUTT; circ. 10,700.

Jeevan Shiksha: Sarvodaya Sahitya Prakashan, Chowk, Varanasi; f. 1957; monthly; Hindi; Editor TARUN BHAI; circ. 13,400.

Sudhanidhi: Dhancantari Karyalaya, Bijaigarh District, Aligarh; f. 1972; monthly; Hindi; Editor RAGHUBIR PRASAD TRIVEDI; circ. 10,000.

WEST BENGAL

Calcutta

Asian Books Newsletter: 55 Gariahat Rd., P.O.B. 10210; record of books in English published in Asia; monthly Editor Dr. K. K. ROY.

Assam Review and Tea News: 29 Waterloo St.; f. 1928; monthly; tea plantation industry; Editor J. N. BANERJEE; circ. 4,000.

Betar Jagat: All India Radio, Akashvani Bhawan, Eden Gardens; f. 1929; twice a month; Bengali; radio journal; Editor S. C. BASU; circ. about 60,000.

Bulletin of the Institution of Engineers (India): 8 Gokhale Rd.; f. 1920; monthly; Editor Col. B. T. NAGRANI; circ. 30,000.

Capital: 19 R. N. Mookerjee Rd.; f. 1888; weekly; English; leading financial weekly in India; Editor A. K. GANGULY; circ. 5,350.

Chitra Bharati: 3 Bysak Dighi Lane; f. 1955; weekly; Hindi; Editor M. P. PODDAR; circ. 47,400.

Desh: 6 Prafulla Sarkar St.; f. 1933; weekly; Bengali; Editor A. K. SARKAR; circ. 67,500.

Economic Studies: 2 Private Rd., Dum Dum, Calcutta 700009; f. 1960; monthly; English; Editor D. N. MUKHERJEE; circ. 10,000.

Fashion: 3 Bysak Dighi Lane, 7; f. 1961; monthly; Hindi; Editor M. P. PODDAR; circ. 20,000.

Indian Railway Gazette: 13 Ezra Mansions, P.O.B. 2361, 700001; Man. Editor R. L. SARAOGI; Editor L. K. PADMANABHAN; circ. 10,000.

Indian Medical Gazette: Block F, 105C New Alipore; f. 1961; monthly; English; Editor L. K. PANDEYA; circ. 23,212.

Indian Medical Review: 48B Sankaritola Street; f. 1953; monthly; English; Editor Dr. S. GHOSH; circ. 18,000.

Indian Trade Journal: Ministry of Commerce and Industry; f. 1906; weekly; English; circ. about 6,000.

Journal of the Indian Medical Association: 23 Samavaya Mansions, Corporation Place; f. 1930; twice monthly; English; Editor Dr. N. BANERJEE; circ. 30,000.

Journal of the Institution of Engineers (India): 8 Gokhale Rd.; f. 1920; monthly; English; Editor Col. B. T. NAGRANI; published in 8 parts, circ. of each part 17,000.

Journal of the Institution of Engineers (India) (Hindi Section): 8 Gokhale Rd.; f. 1920; 3 a year; Hindi; Editor Col. B. T. NAGRANI; circ. 10,000.

Modern Review: 77/2/1 Dharmtalla St.; f. 1907; monthly; English; independent; illustrated; socio-political; Editor ASHOKE CHATTERJEE; circ. 4,200.

Mohammadi: 49 Gardener Lane; f. 1904; weekly; Bengali; leading organ of the Muslims; Independent; Editor A. J. TARAFDAR.

Naba Kallol: 11 Jhamapooker Lane; f. 1960; monthly; Bengali; Editor S. C. MAZUMDAR; circ. 50,000.

Neetee: 4 Sukhlal Johari Lane; f. 1955; weekly; English; Editor M. P. PODDAR; circ. 25,000.

Screen: P-5, Kalakar St., Calcutta 70; f. 1960; weekly; Hindi; Editor M. P. PODDAR; circ. 35,000.

Soviet Desh: 1/1 Wood St., 16; f. 1960; fortnightly; Bengali, Oriya and Assamese; Editor G. L. KOLOKOLOV; circ. 57,100 (Bengali), 11,000 (Oriya), 11,500 (Assamese).

Statesman: Chowringhee Square; f. 1875; overseas weekly; English; Editor S. NIHAL SINGH.

Students' Journal of the Institution of Engineers (India): 8 Gokhale Rd.; f. 1920; quarterly; English; Editor Col. B. T. NAGRANI; circ. 40,000.

Suktara: 11 Jhamapooker Lane, 9; f. 1948; monthly; juvenile; Bengali; Editor M. MAJUMDAR; circ. 90,000.

Sunday Statesman: Chowringhee Square; weekly; Editor S. NIHAL SINGH.

NEWS AGENCIES

Samachar: 4 Parliament St., New Delhi 1; f. 1976 following merger of all Indian news agencies; independent; Chair. GOPALAN KASTURI.

FOREIGN BUREAUX

A.N.S.A.: D-31, South Extension Part 2, New Delhi 16; Chief Rep. UGO PUNTIERI.

Agence France-Presse: 11A Ratendone Rd., New Delhi 110001; Chief Rep. M. BIANCHI.

A.P.: 19 Narendra Place, Parliament St., New Delhi 110001; Chief MYRON BELKIND.

Middle East News: 1B-120 Laipatnager, New Delhi; Correspondent K. G. GANABATHY.

Reuters Ltd.: 27 Prithvi Raj Rd., New Delhi 110011; Chief Rep. G. I. RATZIN.

Tass News Agency: A-32 West End Colony, New Delhi 110023; Chief Rep. V. N. MATYASH.

United Press International: PTI Bldg., First Floor, Parliament St., New Delhi 110001; Chief Rep. JOSEPH L. GALLOWAY.

Other bureaux: Bangladesh Sangbad Sangstha; Czechoslovak News Agency; D.P.A. (Federal Republic of Germany); W.F.S. (London), etc.

CO-ORDINATING BODIES

Press Information Bureau: f. 1975 to co-ordinate press affairs with the government; represents newspaper management, journalistic profession, news agencies, Parliament; has power to examine journalists under oath and may censor objectionable material; Principal Information Officer (vacant).

Registrar of Newspapers for India: Shastri Bhavan, New Delhi 110001; f. 1956; a statutory body set up to collect statistics regarding the Press in India. It maintains a register of newspapers containing particulars about every newspaper published in India; Registrar N. SETHI.

The Press Council of India was disbanded in January 1976.

PRESS ASSOCIATIONS

All-India Newspaper Editors Conference: 50–51 Theatre Communication Bldg., Connaught Place, New Delhi 110001; Pres. B. N. AZAD; Sec.-Gen. VIRENDRA.

Indian and Eastern Newspaper Society: IENS Bldgs., Rafi Marg, New Delhi 110001; f. 1939; 301 mems.; Pres. A. G. SHEOREY; Sec. P. C. GANDHI; publs. *IENS Annual Press Handbook*; *Indian Press* (monthly).

Indian Federation of Working Journalists: Flat No. 29, New Central Mkt., Connaught Circus, New Delhi 110001; f. 1950; Pres. S. B. KOLPE; Sec.-Gen. T. R. RAMASWAMY; publ. *The Working Journalist* (monthly).

Indian Journalists Association: 1249-B Bowbazar St., Calcutta 700012; f. 1922; Pres. P. R. GANGULI.

Indian Languages Newspapers Association: Janmabhoomi Bhavan, Ghoga St., Fort, Bombay 400001; f. 1941; 315 mems.; Pres. A. R. BHAT; Sec. K. N. GOGATE; publ. *Language Press Bulletin* (non-political monthly).

Press Institute of India: Sapru House Annexe, Barakhamba Rd., New Delhi 110001; f. 1963; Dir. CHANCHAL SARKAR; Sec. G. PADMANABHAN; publ. *Vidura* (every 2 months) and special surveys; training courses.

PUBLISHERS

BOMBAY

George Allen & Unwin (India) Pvt. Ltd.: 103–105 Walchand Hirachand Marg, 400001; f. 1970; Man. Dir. D. R. BHAGI.

Allied Publishers Private Ltd.: 15 Graham Rd., Ballard Estate, 400001; f. 1934; economics, politics, history, philosophy; brs. at New Delhi, Calcutta, Madras, Bangalore; Chair. and Man. Dir. R. N. SACHDEV.

Asia Publishing House: Calicut St., Ballard Estate, Bombay 400038; f. 1942; humanities, social sciences, science and general; English and Indian languages.

Blackie and Son (India) Ltd.: Blackie House, 103–105 Walchand Hirachand Marg, P.B. 21, Bombay 400001; f. 1901; educational, scientific and technical, general and juvenile; brs. at Calcutta, Madras, New Delhi; Man. Dir. D. R. BHAGI.

Bombay Book Depot: Raja Ram Mohan Roy Marg, Girgaum 4; f. 1947; Partners S. BHATKAL, L. BHATKAL, P. N. KUMTNA, S. BHATKAL.

Hind Kitabs Ltd.: 32–34 Veer Nariman Rd., 400001.

International Book House Ltd.: 9 Ash Lane, M. Gandhi Rd.; general and educational books.

Jaico Publishing House: 125 Mahatma Gandhi Rd.; f. 1947; general paperbacks; import scientific, technical and educational books; Dirs. JAMAN SHAH, ASHWIN SHAH.

Kitab Mahal Publishers (Wholesale Division) Private Ltd.: Zero Rd. 56-A, Allahabad; high-class Hindi general and educational; Propr. S. M. AGARWAL.

Nirmala Sadanand Publishers: 35C Tardeo Rd., Bombay 400034 WB; f. 1967; Partners NIRMALA BHATKAL, MANMOHAN BHATKAL.

Orient Longman Ltd.: Nicol Rd., Ballard Estate, 400038.

Popular Book Depot, The: Abid House, Dr. Bhadkamkar Rd., 400007; f. 1924; Partners S. G. and R. G. BHATKAL.

Popular Prakashan Pvt. Ltd.: 35C Tardeo Rd., Bombay 400034; f. 1963; Dirs. S. G. and R. G. BHATKAL.

Prakashan Mandir: Dadysheth Agyary Lane 42; Propr. OMKAR KUMAR; importers and educational publishers.

Taraporevala, D. B., Sons and Co. (Private) Ltd.: 210 Dr. D. Naoroji Rd., Fort; f. 1864; general; Dir. M. J. TARAPOREVALA; Chief Executive R. J. TARAPOREVALA.

N. M. Tripathi (Private) Ltd.: Samaldas Gandhi Marg, 2; f. 1888; Chair. D. M. TRIVEDI; publishers and booksellers; law and rare books; Dir. and Gen. Man. A. S. PANDYA.

CALCUTTA

All-India Publishing Co. Ltd.: 30 Bidhan Sarani, 700006; f. 1920; Man. Dir. K. G. DAS, B.L.

Assam Review Publishing Co.: 29 Waterloo St., 700001; f. 1926; general; Man. J. N. BANNERJEE.

J. Bannerjee and Co:. 29 Joy Mitter St., 700005; f. 1891; statisticians and market reporters; Propr. B. CHATTERJEE; Man. B. S. BANERJEE.

Book Co. Ltd., The: 53 Harrison Rd., 700009; f. 1919; economics, politics, scientific, oriental, general and rare books; Dir. G. N. MITRA.

Britannia Publishers: 201 Harrison Rd., 700007; rare British, American and Continental publications.

British India Publishing Co.: Stephen House, Dalhousie Square, 700001; Manager A. BRIMS; Asst. Manager S. J. HONEYWELL.

Chuckerverty, Chatterjee and Co. Ltd.: 15 College Squar 7000012; Dir. BINODELAL CHAKRAVARTI.

David Maximillian and Co.: 12B Windsor House, Missio Row Extension, 700001; Propr. C. C. DAVID.

Eastern Law House Private Ltd.: 54 Ganesh Chund Ave., Calcutta 700013; f. 1918; legal, commercia accountancy and general; Man. Dir. B. C. DE; Dir ARUP K. DE, AJOY DE, ASOK DE.

Firma K. L. Mukhopadhyay: 257B B. B. GANGULY St f. 1950; Man. Dir. K. L. MUKHOPADHYAY.

Gurudas Chatterjee and Sons: Bidhan Sarani 203, 70000 Editor B. P. N. MUKHERJEE; general.

Ideal Publishers: 28/14 Station Rd., 700031; Propr. Mrs. I DAS; Manager U. DAS.

Intertrade Publications (India) Private Ltd.: 55 Gariaha Rd., P.O.B. 10210; f. 1954; economics and history Man. Dir. Dr. K. K. ROY.

Khadi Pradisthan: 15 College Square, 700012; Manage A. C. DAS GUPTA; Sec. H. P. DEVI.

Macmillan Company of India Ltd.: 2/10 Ansari Rd Daryaganj, Delhi 110006; Man. Dir. S. G. WASANI.

A. Mukherjee & Co. (P) Ltd.: 2 Bankim Chatterjee St 700012; f. 1940; educational and general; Man. Di AMIYA RANJAN MUKHERJEE.

New Era Publishing Co.: 31 Gauri Bari Lane, 700004 f. 1944; Propr. Dr. P. N. MITRA, M.A., B.L., D.S.((U.S.A.); Man. S. K. MITRA.

W. Newman and Co. Ltd.: 3 Old Court House St., 700001 f. 1854; general; Man. Dir. O. P. BHARGAVA.

Oriental Publishing Co.: 110 Arpuli Lane, 700012; f. 1910 Propr. D. N. BOSE; Man. D. P. BOSE.

Oxford and IBH Publishing Co.: Park Hotel Bldg., 17 Par St., 700016; science and technology; Mans. GULA PRIMLANI, MOHAN PRIMLANI.

Oxford Book and Stationery Co.: 17 Park St., 700016 f. 1921; Man. GULAB PRIMLANI.

Ray, Chaudhury and Co.: 119 Ashutosh Mukherjee Rd. 700025; Man. A. C. R. CHAUDHURY.

Renaissance Publishers Private Ltd.: 15 Bankim Chatterje St., 700012; philosophy; founder M. N. ROY.

M. C. Sarkar and Sons (Private) Ltd.: 14 Bankim Chatterje St., 700012; general.

Thacker's Press and Directories Ltd.: M.P. Works Privat Ltd., 6B Bentinck St., 1; London Agents: Keith & Slater Ltd., 24–27 High Holborn, W.C.1; referenc books.

DELHI and NEW DELHI

Amerind Publishing Co. (Pvt.) Ltd: 66 Janpath, New Delhi 110001; offices at Calcutta, Bombay and New York; Dirs. G. PRIMLANI, M. PRIMLANI.

Atma Ram and Sons: Kashmere Gate, Delhi 110006; brs Jaipur, Lucknow, Chandrigarh.

S. Chand and Co. (Pvt.) Ltd.: Ram Nagar, 110055; f. 1917 educational and general books in Hindi and English brs. in Jullundur, Lucknow, Bombay, Calcutta, Madras Hyderabad, Nagpur and Patna; Dirs. S. L. GUPTA R. K. GUPTA, RAVINIDRA K. GUPTA.

City Booksellers: Sohanganj St.; f. 1939; general; Propr. H CHANDRA.

Eurasia Publishing House (Private) Ltd.: Ram Nagar, New Delhi 110055; educational books in English and Hindi Dirs. S. L. GUPTA, R. K. GUPTA.

George G. Harrap and Co. Ltd.: c/o Oxford University Press, 2/11 Ansari Rd., Daryaganj, 110006; educational.

Hind Pocket Books Private Ltd.: G. T. Rd., Shahdara, Delhi, 110032; f. 1958; paperbacks in English, Hindi, Punjabi and Urdu; Man. Dir. DINANATH MALHOTRA; Sec. VISHWA NATH.

Indian University Publishers Ltd.: Kashmere Gate, 110006; f. 1950; technical and general in English, Hindi, Urdu and Punjabi; Man. C. B. MEDNN.

Khosla Publishing Co.: 3 Netaji Sukhas Marg, Daryaganj, P.O.B. 1389, Delhi 110006; f. 1901; directories; Partners K. R. and K. R. KHOSLA.

Motilal Banarsidas Ltd.: J. Nagar, 110007; f. 1903; Indological publishers; Prop. S. L. JAIN; brs. Patna, Varanasi.

Neel Kawal Prakashau: Raj Bhawan, 4/C Daryaganj; educational; Propr. S. K. AGGARWAL.

New Book Society of India: 6A, 53 W.E.A. Pusa Rd., 110005.

Orient Longmans Ltd.: 3–5 Asaf Ali Rd., 110001; Dir. and Sec. P. H. PATWARDHAN.

Oxford University Press: 2/11 Ansari Rd., Daryaganj, Delhi 110002; brs. at Bombay, Calcutta and Madras; Agents in India for Faber & Faber Ltd., University Tutorial Press Ltd., Monthly Review Press, New York, and the University Presses of Harvard, North Carolina, Stanford and Princeton; Gen. Man. C. H. LEWIS.

People's Publishing House Ltd.: Rani Jhansi Rd.; f. 1943; Gen. Man. N. PISHARODI.

Publications Division, The: Ministry of Information and Broadcasting, Government of India, Patiala House, New Delhi-1; art, literature, planning and development, general publications.

Rajkamal Prakashan (Private) Ltd.: 8 Faiz Bazar, 6; f. 1946; Hindi; literary books, quarterly journal of literary criticism, monthly trade journal.

Rajpal and Sons: Kashmere Gate, 110006; f. 1891; literary criticism, social and general, humanities, text books, juvenile literature; Hindi and English; Partners DINA NATH MOLHOTRA, VISHWA NATH; Exec. Dir. ISHWARCHANDRA KHANDELWAL.

Ranjit Printers and Publishers: 4872 Chandni Chowk, 6; f. 1949; historical, economical, political and general in Hindi and English; Man. Dirs. M. C. GUPTA and R. M. SHAHANI.

Roshan Book Depot: Nai Sarak; educational; Propr. G. DASS AGGARWAL.

Sahgal, N. D., and Sons: Dariba Kalan; f. 1917; politics, history, general knowledge, sport, fiction and children's books, in Hindi; Man. G. SAHGAL.

Shiksha Bharati: Dayanand Marg, Daryaganj, Delhi 110006; f. 1955; textbooks, popular science books and children's books in Hindi and English; Man. Partner SUDHIR MALHOTRA.

Technical and Commercial Book Co.: 75 Gokhale Market, Tis Hazari; f. 1913; Propr. B. R. MALHOTRA, B.A.; Man. D. N. MEHRA.

Vikas Publications: 5 Anasri Rd., D. Garj, 110006.

Yadav Prakahsan: Ajmeri Dwar; anatomy books, and charts in Hindi and English; Proprs. Y. N. and S. MITAL.

MADRAS

Higginbothams (Private) Ltd.: 165 Mount Rd., 2; branches at Bangalore, Ootacamund, Trivandrum, Coimbatore, Ernakulam, Mysore, Hyderabad and Madurai.

B. G. Paul and Co.: 4 Francis Joseph St.; f. 1923; general, educational and oriental; Man. K. NILAKANTAN.

Ranga Raju and Bros: Jagannadha Baugh, Saidapet; general; Propr. J. R. RANGA RAJU; Mans. J. P. RAJU, J. K. RAJU.

Srinivasa Varadachari and Co.: 2–16 Mount Rd.; f. 1879; educational; Propr. G. VENKATACHARI.

Thompson and Co. (Private) Ltd.: 33 Broadway, 1; general.

OTHER TOWNS

Balkrishna Book Co.: B-12A Niralanagar, Lucknow 7; f. 1944; general, scientific and Oriental; Propr. BALKRISHNA.

Banaras Book Corpn.: University Rd., Varanasi; educational; Dir. L. N. AGARWAL; Man. R. K. AGARWAL.

Catholic Press: Ranchi (Bihar); f. 1930; Dir. Rev. W. DELPUTTE, S.J.

Central Book Depot: 44 Johnston-gunj, Allahabad; Man. B. K. CHATTERJI.

P. C. Dwadash Shreni and Co. Ltd.: Barasani Bazaar, Aligarh; f. 1895; Dirs. H. C. and T. C. DWADASH SHRENI.

Garga Bros.: 1 Katra Rd., Allahabad; f. 1949; educational and reference; Partners R. N. GARGA, T. N. GARGA, P. N. GARGA, SANJAI GARGA.

Hindi Sahitya Sadan: Jahanabad P.O., Gaya; general; Proprs. R. PATHAK, K. N. SINHA; Man. N. K. PATHAK, M.I.S.A.

Hindusthan Publishing House: Shanti Bhawan, Nayagaon, Lucknow; Propr. A. KUMAR; Man. M. KUMAR.

Kitabistan: 30 Chak, Allahabad 211003.

Law Book Co.: Sardar Patel Marg, P.O.B. 4, Allahabad 1; f. 1929; legal books; Partners R. R. BAGGA, L. R. BAGGA, B. M. BAGGA, D. BAGGA.

Maheshanand and Sons: Bhaskar Bhavan, Ashoknagar, Lucknow; Man. SHIV PRASAD NAUTIYAL.

Narain Publishing House: Ajitmal, Etawah, Uttar Pradesh; f. 1941; publishers of illustrated *Hindi Who's Who*, directories and general; Propr. Mrs. LILA AGRAWAL.

National Academic Publishers: Ashok Raj Path, Patna 800006, Bihar; general, research and specialized publications on Bihar region; Dirs. B. K. SINHA, R. SINHA.

Navajivan Publishing House: P.O. Navajivan, Ahmedabad, 380014; f. 1919; Gandhian literature; Chair. MORARJI DESAI; Man. Trustee JITENDRA DESAI.

Pioneer Publishing Co.: Sardar Patel Marg, P.O.B. 4, Allahabad 1; f. 1972; law books; Partners J. N. BAGGA, Mrs. R. BAGGA, Mrs. S. BAGGA.

Ram Prasad and Sons: Hospital Rd., Agra 3; f. 1905; agricultural, arts, commerce, education, general, science, technical, economics, mathematics, sociology; Dirs. H. N., R. N., B. N. and Y. N. AGARWAL; Mans. S. N. AGARWAL and R. S. TANDON.

S. J. Singh and Co.: 51–52 Gwynne Rd., Lucknow; nature cure, health, general; Man. S. J. SINGH.

Standard Book Depot: Chowk, Kanpur; official agents for Govt. of U.P.; Propr. G. P. GARG; Man. B. N. AGARWAL.

United Publishers: 1 Katra Rd., Allahabad; f. 1964; reference and degree class publishers; Propr. Mrs. SHILA GARGA.

University Book Agency: 15B Elgin Rd., Allahabad; law; Partners S. D. KHANNA, L. KHANNA, N. KHANNA, K. KHANNA.

Upper India Publishing House Pvt. Ltd.: Aminabad, Lucknow; f. 1921; publishers of books in English and Hindi special subjects—Indian philosophy, history, religion, art and science; Man. Dir. S. BHARGAVA.

Uttarakhand Press: Bhaskar Bhavan, Ashoknagar, Lucknow.

RADIO AND TELEVISION

RADIO

All India Radio (AIR): Akashvani Bhavan, Parliament St., New Delhi 1; broadcasting in India is controlled by the Ministry of Information and Broadcasting. The service is financed from grants voted by Parliament annually; Dir.-Gen. P. C. CHATTERJI.

A comprehensive development plan has been evolved and there are now 73 broadcasting stations in the whole of India. There are at present regional stations operating from the following centres:

North: Delhi, Ajmer, Allahabad, Bhagalpur, Bhopal, Bikaner, Chandigarh, Gorakhpur, Gwalior, Indore, Jabalpur, Jaipur, Jodhpur, Jullundur, Kanpur, Lucknow, Mathura, Patna, Ranchi, Raipur, Rampur, Simla, Udaipur, Varanasi and Aligarh.

West: Bombay, Nagpur, Ahmedabad, Vadodara (Baroda), Pune (Poona), Rajkot, Bhuj, Parbhani, Sangli and Rajkot.

South: Madras, Tiruchi, Vijayawada, Trivandrum, Alleppey, Hyderabad, Trichur, Dhawar, Bangalore, Tirunelveli, Kozhikode (Calicut), Vishakhapatnam, Cuddapah, Bhadravathi, Pondicherry, Gulbarga and Coimbatore.

East: Calcutta, Cuttack, Gauhati, Kohima, Jaipur, Sambalpur, Siliguri, Port Blair, Imphal, Kurseong, Silchar, Agartala, Shillong, Aijal Tezu, Pasighat and Dibrugarh.

Radio Kashmir broadcasts from Srinagar, Jammu and Leh.

Broadcasting is particularly important in India owing to the difficulty of reaching the vast masses of the people by any medium other than the spoken word. To enable AIR to reach rural areas, listening is arranged by means of community sets installed for public use in a large number of villages.

AIR network is equipped with a total of 143 transmitters (medium and shortwave) and covers all the important linguistic areas in the country.

The News Services Division, centralized in New Delhi, is one of the largest news organizations in the world. In all, it broadcasts 240 daily news bulletins in 41 languages and in 34 local dialects, from Delhi in Home and External Services and from regional stations. The External Service transmits 61 news bulletins daily in 25 languages.

In 1975 there were 13,134,063 radio licences issued.

TELEVISION

Akashvani Doordarshan (*All India Radio-Television*): Television Centre, Akashwani Bhawan. Parliament St., New Delhi 110001; f. 1959; Dir. ROMESH CHANDER; programmes: 25½ hours weekly (15½ hours general service, 10 hours school service).

Bombay: began transmissions in 1972; comprises TV studio at Worli and relay transmitter at Sinhagarh, near Poona; broadcasts for 2½ hours in the evenings mainly in Hindi and Marathi.

Srinagar: commenced broadcasting three days a week from 1973 in Urdu and Kashmiri; Dir. SHAILENDRA SHANKAR.

Amritsar: began transmissions in 1973.

Jaipur: Expected to begin broadcasting by 1979.

Madras: Commissioned in 1975.

Lucknow: began broadcasting in 1975; a relay transmitter at Kanpur has extended the range of Lucknow's transmissions.

Calcutta: began transmitting in 1975 using relay stations at Durgapur, Asansol, Midnapur and Khargapur.

It has been forecast that most of the population will be covered by radio and television by 1979.

In 1975 314,155 television licences were issued.

FINANCE

(cap. = capital; p.u. = paid up; dep. = deposits; m. = million; Rs. = rupees; brs. = branches.)

BANKING

STATE BANKS

Reserve Bank of India: Mint Rd., Bombay 400001; f. 1935; nationalized 1949; sole right to issue notes; cap. Rs. 50m., dep. Rs. 35,035.9m. (August 1975); Gov. K. R. PURI; 12 brs.; publ. *Reserve Bank of India Bulletin* (monthly).

State Bank of India: New Administrative Bldg., Backbay Reclamation, Bombay 400020; f. 1955; cap. Rs. 56.3m., dep. Rs. 31,900m. (Dec. 1974); Chair. R. K. TALWAR; Man. Dir. T. R. VARADACHARY; Chief Man. Int. Div. K. K. BANERJI; 3,400 brs.

The State Bank of India has subsidiaries in Bikaner, Jaipur, Hyderabad, Indore, Mysore, Patiala, Saurashtra and Travancore. There are 28 state co-operative banks and 341 district co-operative banks.

India's 14 major commercial banks, listed below, were nationalized in 1970. They are managed by fifteen-member Boards of Directors (two directors to be appointed by the Central Government, one employee director, 1 representing employees who are not workmen, 1 representing depositors, three representing farmers, workers, artisans, etc.; five representing persons with special knowledge or experience, one Reserve Bank of India Official and one Government of India Official). The day-to-day administration of the bank is one of the chief functions of the government *Custodian* or Bank Chairman. The Department of Banking of the Ministry of Finance controls all banking operations.

Since nationalization, the number of bank branches has grown from 8,262 to 18,180 (July 1975) whilst deposits have increased from 46,000m. to Rs. 118,990m. (Dec. 1974).

Allahabad Bank Ltd.: 14 India Exchange Place, Calcutta 700001; f. 1865; cap. Rs. 10.5m., dep. Rs. 2,392.4 (Dec. 1974); Chair. and Man. Dir. S. D. VERMA; Gen. Man. A. GHOSH; 390 brs.

Bank of Baroda: 3 Walchand Hirachand Marg, Ballard Pier, Bombay 400038; f. 1908; cap. Rs. 25m., dep. Rs. 8,167.2m. (Dec. 1974); Chair. and Man. Dir. R. C. SHAH; 800 brs.

Bank of India: Express Towers, Nariman Point, Bombay 400021; f. 1906; cap. p.u. Rs. 40.5m., dep. Rs. 9,291.4m.

(Dec. 1974); Chair. and Man. Dir. JAGDISH N. SAXENA, 852 brs.

Bank of Maharashtra Ltd.: 1177 Budhwar Peth, P.O.B. 514, Pune (Poona) 2; f. 1935; cap. Rs. 15m., dep. Rs. 2,080.0m. (Dec. 1974); Chair. and Man. Dir. V. M. BHIDE; 428 brs.

Canara Bank Ltd.: P.O.B. 6648, 112 Jayachamarajendra Rd., Bangalore 560002, P.B. 6648; f. 1906; cap. Rs. 17.5m., dep. Rs. 5,486m. (Dec. 1974); Chair. and Man. Dir. C. E. KAMATH; Gen. Man. U. K. KINI; 813 brs.

Central Bank of India: Chander Mukhi, Narinam Point, Bombay 400001; f. 1911; cap. p.u. Rs. 47.5m., dep. Rs. 10,268m. (Dec. 1974); Chair. and Man. Dir. P. F. GUPTA; 1,219 brs.

Dena Bank: P.O.B. 41, 17 Horniman Circle, Bombay 400023; f. 1938; cap. p.u. Rs. 12.5m., dep. Rs. 302m. (Dec. 1974); Chair. and Man. Dir. R. A. GULMOHAMED; Gen. Man. H. K. SWALI; 590 brs.

Indian Bank: P.O.B. 1384, 17 North Beach Rd., Madras 600001; f. 1907; cap. p.u. Rs. 20m., dep. Rs. 2,795m. (Dec. 1974); Chair. and Man. Dir. G. LAKSHMINARAYANAN; Gen. Man. K. VENKATARAMA AYYER; 498 brs.

Indian Overseas Bank: 151 Mount Rd., Madras 600002; f. 1937; cap. p.u. Rs. 20m., dep. Rs. 2,492.6m. (Dec. 1974); Chair. A. M. KADHIRESEN; Gen. Man. B. K. VORA; 423 brs.

Punjab National Bank Ltd.: Tropical Bldgs., New Delhi; f. 1895; cap. p.u. Rs. 20m., dep. Rs. 8,400m. (Dec. 1974); Chair. and Man. Dir. T. H. TULI; Gen. Man. B. K. VORA; 1,100 brs.

Syndicate Bank: Bahadur Shah Zaffar Marg, New Delhi; f. 1925; cap. Rs. 14.2m., dep. Rs. 4,260.6m. (Dec. 1974); Chair. and Man. Dir. K. K. PAI; Gen. Man. H. N. RAO; 740 brs.

Union Bank of India: P.O.B. 3631, 66–80 Apollo St., Bombay 400001; f. 1919; cap. p.u. Rs. 12.5m., dep. Rs. 3,962.6m. (Dec. 1974); Chair. and Man. Dir. RAGH; Gen. Man. S. D. PARDIWALLA; 579 brs.

United Bank of India Ltd.: 16 Old Court House St., Calcutta 700001; f. 1950; cap. p.u. Rs. 26.9m., dep. Rs. 3,445.7m. (Dec. 1974); Chair. and Man. Dir. M. SEN SARMA; Gen. Man. P. K. SEN; 460 brs.

United Commercial Bank Ltd.: 10 Brabourne Rd., Calcutta 700001; London: 12 Nicholas Lane, E.C.4; f. 1943; cap. p.u. Rs. 28m., dep. Rs. 5,421m. (Dec. 1974); Chair. and Man. Dir. R. DESAI; Gen. Man. S. J. UTAMSINGH; 733 brs. and 6 overseas.

MAJOR PRIVATE BANKS

Andhra Bank Ltd.: Andhra Bank Bldg., P.O.B. 161, Sultan Bazar, Hyderabad; f. 1923; cap. Rs. 50m., dep. Rs. 1,415m. (Dec. 1974); Chair. K. K. NARAYAN; Gen. Man. M. V. SUBBA RAO; 347 brs.

Bank of Cochin Ltd.: Broadway, Ernakulam; f. 1928; cap. p.u. Rs. 475,672.5, res. Rs. 980,582; Chair. K. M. THARIYAN; Asst. Man. E. K. ANDREW, B.A., B.COM.; 55 brs.

Hindusthan Mercantile Bank Ltd.: 10 Clive Row, Calcutta; cap. p.u. Rs. 5m.; Chair. SETH MOHANLAL JALAN.

Mysore State Co-operative Apex Bank Ltd., The: 1 Pampamahakavi Rd., P.B. 654, Chamarajpet, Bangalore 18; f. 1915; cap. Rs. 28.7m., dep. Rs. 200m.; Pres. VEERASETHY CUSHANOOR; Man. Dir. H. K. CHINAIDAIAH.

Corporation Bank Ltd.: Mangaladevi Temple Rd., P.O.B. 88, Mangalore 1; f. 1905; cap. Rs. 3.7m.; dep. Rs. 50.3m.; Chair. M. R. KAMATH; 144 brs.

Karnataka Bank Ltd.: Dongerkery, Mangalore 3; cap. Rs. 2m.; dep. Rs. 27.8m.; Chair. K. S. ADIGA; 143 brs.

The New Bank of India Ltd.: Janpath, New Delhi 1; cap. Rs. 3.4m.; dep. Rs. 1,102m.; Chair. T. R. TULI; 176 brs.

The Oriental Bank of Commerce Ltd.: P.B. No. 329, E Block, Connaught Circus, New Delhi 1; cap. Rs. 1.7m.; dep. Rs. 57m.; Chair. R. P. OBEROI; 100 brs.

The Punjab and Sind Bank Ltd.: P.B. No. 27, H Block, Connaught Circus, New Delhi 1; cap. Rs. 2.2m.; dep. Rs. 993m.; Chair. S. INDERJIT SINGH; 280 brs.

The Sangli Bank Ltd.: P.O.B. 2, Rajwada Chowk, Sangli; cap. Rs. 2.9m.; dep. Rs. 30.9m.; Chair. K. D. CHUTTAR (acting); 76 brs.

United Western Bank Ltd.: P.O.B. 2, Chirmule Niketan, 143–146 Bhawani Peth, Satara City; cap. Rs. 2m.; dep. Rs. 28m.; Chair. V. S. DAMLE, 72 brs.

Vijaya Bank Ltd.: Bharatiya Vidya Bhavan Bldg., Race Course Rd., Bangalore 1; cap. Rs. 65.8m.; dep. Rs. 1,097m.; advances Rs. 628m.; Chair. M. SUNDER RAM SHETTY; 295 brs.

FOREIGN BANKS

Algemene Bank Nederland, N.V.: 32 Vijzelstraat, Amsterdam; 14 Veer Nariman Rd., Bombay 400001; Man. M. W. VAN HULZEN; in Calcutta, Man. H. L. L. M. VAN HAL; 3 brs.

Bank of America National Trust and Savings Association: Express Towers, Nariman Point, Bombay 400001; Asst. Man. L. SMITH; 3 brs.

Bank of Tokyo Ltd.: 6, 1-chome, Nihombashi Hongoku-cho, Chuo-ku, Tokyo, Japan; 2 Brabourne Rd., Calcutta 1; Gen. Man. S. MUTOLI; 3 brs.

Banque Nationale de Paris: 16 blvd. des Italiens, Paris 9; French Bank Bldg., P.O.B. 45, Homji St., Bombay 400007; Man. M. BIGOIN; 5 brs.

British Bank of the Middle East: 20 Abchurch Lane, London, EC4N 7AY; 314 Dr. Dadabhai Nar Rd., Fort, Bombay 400001; Man. F. J. ROBBINS.

Chartered Bank: 38 Bishopsgate, London, EC2N 4AH; Box 40, 4 Netaji Subhas Rd., Calcutta 700001; Amritsar, Bombay, Madras, New Delhi; Man. D. C. PORTER; 24 brs.

Citibank, N.A.: 399 Park Avenue, New York 10022, N.Y.; Bombay (3 offices): Air India Bldg., Nariman Point, Bombay 400001; Calcutta (2 offices), Madras (2 offices), New Delhi; Man. G. B. RICH; 8 brs.

Grindlays Bank Ltd.: 23 Fenchurch St., London, EC3M 3DD; Netaji Subhas Rd., Calcutta; Amritsar, Bangalore, Bombay (90 Mahatma Gandhi Rd.), Cochin, Darjeeling, Delhi, Madras, Simla, etc.; Gen. Man. K. WARNER; 56 brs.

Mercantile Bank Ltd.: 15 Gracechurch St., London, EC3N 0DU; f. 1853; brs.: Bombay: 52–60 M.G. Rd., 400023, Calcutta, Delhi, New Delhi, Madras and Visakhapatnam; Man. I. K. ALLEN; 20 brs.

Mitsui Bank Ltd.: 12 Yurakucho 1-chome, Chiyoda-ku, Tokyo; Bombay: 6 Wallace St., Bombay 400001; Gen. Man. SHOJI AYATA.

BANKING ORGANIZATIONS

Indian Banks' Association: Stadium House, 81–83 Veer Nariman Rd., Bombay 400020; 67 mems.; Chair. V. M. BHIDE; Sec. S. G. SHAH.

Indian Institute of Bankers: State Bank of India Bldg., Bombay Samachar St., Fort, Bombay 400001; Pres. K. R. PURI; Sec. S. N. SENGUPTA.

National Institute of Bank Management: 85 Nepean Sea Rd., Bombay 400006; Dir. N. C. MEHTA.

DEVELOPMENT FINANCE ORGANIZATIONS

Agricultural Finance Corpn. Ltd.: Dhanraj Mahal, Chatrapati Shivaji Marg, Bombay 400001; finances irrigation schemes and other projects, techno-economic and investment surveys and project analyses; Chair. V. M. BHIDE; Man. Dir. GHULAM GHOUSE.

Agricultural Refinance Corporation: Shree Niketan, Shivsagar Estate, Dr. A.B. Rd., Worli, Bombay 400018, f. 1963 to provide medium-term or long-term finance to schemes of agricultural development which cannot be satisfactorily financed by existing credit agencies; Chair. R. K. HAZARI; Man. Dir. M. A. CHIDAMBARAM.

Credit Guarantee Corporation of India Ltd.: Vidyut Bhavan, 3rd Floor, Pathakwadi, Bombay 400002; f. 1971; guarantees loans and other credit facilities extended by banks to small borrowers and co-operative societies; Chair. Dr. R. K. HAZARI; Man. Dir. M. J. AMBANI; Sec. M. SEQUEIRA.

Export Credit and Guarantee Corporation Ltd.: 10th floor, Express Towers, Nariman Point, Bombay 400001; f. 1956 to promote exports by providing a risk insurance cover to exporters against loss in export of goods and services and by offering guarantees to banks and financial institutions to enable exporters to obtain better facilities from them; Gen. Man. P. B. SATAGOPAN; Sec. N. CHANDRASEKHARAN.

Industrial Development Bank of India (IDBI): New India Centre, 17 Cooperage, P.O.B. 1241, Bombay 400039; f. 1964; wholly owned subsidiary of the Reserve Bank to co-ordinate and supplement other financial organizations and to finance and promote industrial development; regional offices at Calcutta, Madras, New Delhi and brs. in 12 states; authorized cap. Rs. 500m.; Chair. K. R. PURI; Board of Dirs. (*see* Reserve Bank of India); Gen. Man. C. S. VENKAT RAO.

Industrial Finance Corporation of India: Bank of Baroda Bldg., 16 Parliament St., P.O.B. 363, New Delhi 110001; 17 brs.; f. 1948 under the Industrial Finance Corporation Act to provide medium- and long-term finance to private and public limited companies and Co-operative Societies incorporated and registered in India, engaged in manufacture, preservation or processing of goods, shipping, mining, hotels and power generation and distribution. The Corporation promotes industrialization of less developed areas, and provides training in management techniques and development banking. IFC's activities are: (i) Granting of loans in rupees and foreign currencies; (ii) Subscribing to and underwriting of equity, preference and debenture issues of capital; (iii) Guaranteeing deferred payments for machinery imported or purchased within the country; cap. p.u. Rs. 100m.; Chair. BALDEV PASRICHA; Gen. Man. R. B. MATHUR.

Industrial Credit and Investment Corporation of India Ltd.: 163 Backbay Reclamation, Bombay 400020 BR; f. 1955 to assist private industrial enterprises by providing finance in both rupee and foreign currencies in the form of long- or medium-term loans or equity participations, sponsoring and underwriting new issues of shares and securities, guaranteeing loans from other private investment sources, furnishing managerial, technical and administrative advice to Indian industry; share cap. Rs. 125m.; res. Rs. 128m.; Chair. H. T. PAREKH.

In addition the Life Insurance Corporation of India and the Unit Trust of India provide loans for private development. There are also statutory finance corporations in each State.

STOCK EXCHANGES

Ahmedabad Share and Stock Brokers' Association: Manekchowk, Ahmedabad; f. 1894; 114 brs.; Pres. SHANTILAL KESHAVLAL SHAH; Sec. D. M. PANCHAL.

Bombay Stock Exchange: Dalal St., Bombay 400001; f. 1875; 504 mems.; Pres. JAYANT AMERCHAND; Chair. P. J. JEEJEEBHOY; Sec. A. J. SHAH.

Calcutta Stock Exchange Association Ltd.: 7 Lyons Range, Calcutta; f. 1908; 636 brs.; Pres. S. K. BAGLA; Sec. B. MAJUMDAR.

Delhi Stock Exchange Association Ltd.: 3 & 4/4B Asaf Ali Rd., New Delhi; f. 1947; 89 active brs.; Pres. HARBAN SINGH MEHTA; Exec. Dir. Col. H. C. VERMA.

Madras Stock Exchange Ltd.: Exchange Bldg., 16/17 Second Line Beach, Madras 600001; f. 1937; 33 mems.; Pres. K. KRISHNAMOORTHY; Exec. Dir. E. R. KRISHNAMURTI; Sec. Y. SUNDARA BABU.

INSURANCE

In January 1973 all Indian and foreign insurance companies were nationalized. The general insurance business in India is now transacted by only four companies, subsidiaries of the General Insurance Corporation of India.

General Insurance Corporation of India: Industrial Assurance Bldg., 4th floor, Churchgate, Bombay 400020; Chair. G. V. KAPADIA; Man. Dirs. K. P. MODI, M. K. VENKATESAN; the holding company; exercises supervision and control over the business transacted by the following subsidiaries:

- **National Insurance Company Ltd.:** 3 Middleton St., Calcutta 700016; Chair. and Man. Dir. S. C. CHATTERJEE.
- **New India Assurance Co. Ltd.:** New India Assurance Bldg., 87 Mahatma Gandhi Rd., Bombay 400001; Chair. and Man. Dir. V. C. VAIDYA.
- **Oriental Fire & General Insurance Co. Ltd.:** Jeevan Udyog, Asaf Ali Rd., New Delhi 110001; Chair. and Man. Dir. P. B. DASTUR.
- **United India Fire & General Insurance Co. Ltd.:** Dare House Extension, 4th Floor, 2/1 North Beach Rd., Madras 600001; Chair. and Man. Dir. B. B. SAWHNEY.

Life Insurance Corporation of India: Jeevan Bima Marg, Bombay 21; f. 1956; controls all life insurance business; Chair. Shri R. B. PRADHAN.

INSURANCE ASSOCIATION

Indian Insurance Companies' Association: Co-operative Insurance Bldg., Sir P. Mehta Rd., Fort, Bombay; f. 1928 to protect the interests of the insurance industry in India; 43 mems.

UNIT TRUST

Unit Trust of India: Bombay Life Bldg., 45 Veer Nariman Rd., Bombay 400023; f. 1964; controlled by the Reserve Bank of India; total assets Rs. 5,722m.; branches at New Delhi, Calcutta and Madras; Chair. of Trustees JAMES S. RAJ; Sec. V. V. ABHYANKAR.

TRADE AND INDUSTRY

TRADE ORGANIZATIONS

CHAMBERS OF COMMERCE

Chambers of Commerce have been established in almost all commercial and industrial centres. The following are among the most important.

Associated Chambers of Commerce and Industry of India: Allahabad Bank Bldg., 17 Parliament St., New Delhi; a central organization of Chambers; 12 Chambers of Commerce and Industry representing 1,500 companies throughout India; 180 associate mems.; Pres. N. S. BHAT.

Federation of Indian Chambers of Commerce and Industry: Federation House, Bazar Marg, New Delhi; 214 asscns. affiliated as ordinary mems, and 544 concerns as associate mems.; Pres. M. V. ARUNACHALAM; Sec.-Gen. G. L. BANSAL; publ. *Fortnightly Review*.

Indian National Committee of International Chamber of Commerce: Federation House, New Delhi 110001; f. 1928; organization mems. 44, associate mems. 165; Pres. A. K. JAIN; Sec.-Gen. G. L. BANSAL; Joint Sec.-Gen. P. CHENTSAL RAO.

Bengal Chamber of Commerce and Industry: 6 Netaji Subhas Rd., Calcutta; f. 1934; 203 mems.; Pres. A. L. MUDALIAR; Sec. M. GHOSE.

Bengal National Chamber of Commerce and Industry: P-11 Mission Row Extension, Calcutta; f. 1887; 265 mems. and 46 industrial and trading associations are affiliated, some having common working arrangements; Pres. S. B. DUTT; Sec. A. R. DUTTA GUPTA, M.A.

Bharat Chamber of Commerce: 195 Mahatma Gandhi Rd., Calcutta; f. 1900; 601 mems.; Pres. S. B. GOENKA; Sec. L. R. DASGUPTA.

Bihar Chamber of Commerce: Judges Court Rd., Patna 800001; f. 1926; 800 mems.; Pres. J. P. SAXENA.

Bombay Chamber of Commerce and Industry: Mackinnon Mackenzie Bldg., Ballard Estate, Bombay 1-BR; P.O.B. 473; f. 1836; 582 mems.; Pres. V. J. SHETH; Sec. B. P. GUNAJI.

Cocanada Chamber of Commerce: Commercial Rd., Kakinada 1 (Andhra Pradesh); f. 1868; 15 mem. firms; Chair. Sri. H. SITARAM; Sec. D. RADHAKRISHNA MURTY.

Gujarat Chamber of Commerce and Industry (*Gujarat Vepari Mahamandal*): Ranchhodlal Rd., P.O.B. 4045, Ahmedabad 380009; f. 1949; 4,256 mems.; Pres. INDRAVADAM PRANLAL SHAH.

Indian Chamber of Commerce: India Exchange, India Exchange Place, Calcutta 700001; f. 1923; 400 mems.; Pres. SANJOY SEN; Sec.-Gen. C. S. PANDE.

Indian Merchant's Chamber: 76 Veer Nariman Rd., Bombay 400020; f. 1907; Pres. G. PODAR; Sec. C. L. GHEEWAHA; publ. *Journal* (monthly).

Lahore Chamber of Commerce and Industry: P.O.B. 597, 11 Race Course Rd., Lahore; f. 1923; 3,000 mems.; Pres. M. AMIN AGHA; Sec. MIAN MAQBOOL AHMAD.

Madras Chamber of Commerce and Industry: Dare House Annexe, 3/4 Moore St., Madras 1; f. 1836; 143 mem. firms, 6 affiliated and 7 honorary; Chair. C. P. FEATHERSTONE; Sec. C. S. KRISHNASWAMI; M. M. MUTTIAH.

Maharashtra Chamber of Commerce: 12 Rampart Row, Fort, Bombay; f. 1927; over 1,500 mems.; Pres. S. M. RATHI; Sec. R. G. MOHADIKAR; publ. *Trade, Commerce and Industry Bulletin* (English).

Merchants' Chamber of Uttar Pradesh: 14/38 Civil Lines, Kanpur; f. 1932; 300 mems.; Pres. Dr. G. H. SINGHANIA; Sec. J. V. KRISHNAN.

Northern India Chamber of Commerce: Dehra Dun, Chandigarh, Punjab; f. 1912; 270 mems.; Pres. S. CHARANJIT SINGH; Hon. Sec. H. S. BALHAYA.

Oriental Chamber of Commerce: 6 Clive Row, Calcutta 1; f. 1932; 115 mems.; Pres. RUSI B. GIMI; Sec. M. S. SALEHJEE.

Punjab, Haryana and Delhi Chamber of Commerce and Industry: Phelps Bldg., 9A Connaught Place, P.B. 130, New Delhi 1; f. 1905; 303 mems.; Chair. B. D. KAPUR; Sec. M. L. NANDRAJOG.

Southern India Chamber of Commerce and Industry: Indian Chamber Bldgs., Esplanade, Madras 1; f. 1909; 1,000 mems.; Pres. K. S. G. HAJASHAREEFF; Sec. K. S. RAMANI.

United Chamber of Trade Asscn.: Katra Rathi Nai Sarak, Delhi; Pres. MA'HESHWAR DAYAL.

Upper India Chamber of Commerce: 14/69 Civil Lines, P.O.B. 63, Kanpur; f. 1888; 161 mems.; Pres. G. C. JAIN.

Uttar Pradesh Chamber of Commerce: 15/197 Civil Lines, Kanpur; f. 1914; 200 mems.; Pres. SARDAR INDERSINGH; Hon. Sec. B. K. SAKSENA.

FOREIGN TRADE CORPORATIONS

Export Credit and Guarantee Corporation Ltd.: Express Towers, 10th Floor, Nariman Point, Bombay 400001; f. 1964; to assist exporters by insuring risks involved in exports on credit terms and to supplement credit facilities by issuing guarantees, etc.; Chair. V. PAREKH; Sec. N. CHANDRASEKHRAN.

State Trading Corporation of India Ltd.: Chandralok, 36 Janpath, New Delhi 110001; f. 1956; Government undertaking dealing in exports and imports; brs. in Bombay, Calcutta, Madras, and in 19 overseas countries; Chair. V. V. PAREKH; Sec. Mrs. SURJEET.

The Minerals and Metals Trading Corporation of India Ltd.: Express Bldg., 9 and 10, Bahadur Shah Zaffar Marg, New Delhi 110001; f. 1963; export of iron and manganese ore, ferro-manganese, mica, coal and other minor minerals; import of steel, non-ferrous metals and other industrial raw materials, fertilizers and fertilizer raw materials, rough diamonds; auth. cap. Rs. 120m.; six regional offices in India and one in Japan; Chair. S. RAMACHANDRAN; Sec. O. P. GARG.

The Handicrafts and Handlooms Exports Corporation of India Ltd.: Lok Kalyan Bhavan, 11A Rouse Ave. Lane, New Delhi 110001; f. 1958; a subsidiary of State Trading Corpn. of India Ltd.; undertakes export of handicrafts, handloom goods and ready-to-wear clothes while promoting exports and trade development generally; Sona of India boutiques in New Delhi, New York, Paris, Tokyo and Nairobi and Carpet Warehousing Depot at Hamburg; auth. cap. Rs. 40m.; Chair. Mrs. PUPUL JAYAKAR; Sec. J. C. SARIN.

The Indian Motion Pictures Export Corporation Ltd.: 5th Floor, Shivsagar Estate, Dr. Annie Besant Rd., Worli, Bombay 400018; Chair. A. M. TARIQ; Man. Dir A. K. SUD.

The Trade Development Authority: P.O.B. 767, Bank of Baroda Bldg., 16 Parliament St., New Delhi 110001; f. 1971 to promote Indian exports; Exec. Dir. A. K. RAY.

INDUSTRIAL AND AGRICULTURAL ORGANIZATIONS

The following are the principal bodies in existence in 1976. *See* also "Major Industrial Companies".

GENERAL

Coal Mines Authority Ltd.: 15 Park Street, 3rd Floor, Calcutta 700016; Govt. of India holding co., responsible for planning and production of non-coking coal mines throughout India; Subsidiary: The National Coal Development Corpn. Ltd.; Chair. K. S. R. Chari.

Cotton Corporation of India Ltd.: Air India Bldg., 12th Floor, Nariman Point, Bombay 400021; f. 1970 to act as an agency in the public sector for the purchase, sale and distribution of home-produced cotton and controls the import of imported cotton; Chair. G. Ramanujam; Man. Dir. N. S. Kulkarni.

Fertilizer Corporation of India Ltd.: F43, South Extension, Part 1, Ring Rd., New Delhi 110049; f. 1961; six operating fertilizer factories, producing nitrogenous phosphatic and complex fertilizers; Chair. and Man Dir. K. C. Sharma.

Forest Development Corporation: Maharashtra; f. 1974 to undertake large-scale forest redevelopment to increase the income from timber and provide employment. In three years it expects to fell areas of uneconomic forest and plant them with teak.

Food Corporation of India: 16-20 Barakhamba Lane, New Delhi 110001; f. 1965 to undertake trading in food-grains on a commercial scale but within the framework of an overall government policy; to provide the farmer an assured price for his produce, supply food-grains to the consumer at reasonable prices; the Corporation purchases, stores, distributes and sells foodgrains and other foodstuffs and arranges imports (subject to the decision of the Government of India) and handling of foodgrains and fertilizers at the ports. It also distributes sugar throughout the country and has set up rice mills. Chair. R. N. Chopra; Man. Dir. N. Narasimha Rau.

Housing and Urban Development Corporation Ltd.: 12-A, Jamnagar House Hutments, New Delhi 110011; f. 1970; to finance and undertake housing and urban development programmes including the setting-up of satellite towns and building material industries; auth. cap. Rs. 100m.; Chair. Keshub Mahindra; Man. Dir. J. B. D'Souza.

Indian Dairy Corporation: Darpan Bldg., R. C. Dutt Rd., Vadodara 390005; objects: to promote dairying in India; to execute the UN World Food Programme "Operation Flood" which aims at improvement of milk marketing and dairy development by enabling the organized dairy sector to obtain a commanding share of the markets in Bombay, Calcutta, Delhi and Madras; acts as canalizing agency for the import and distribution of skim milk powder; Chair. Dr. V. Kurien; Man. Dir. A. K. Ray Chaudhuri.

Jute Corporation of India Ltd.: 1 Shakespeare Sarani, Calcutta 700016; f. 1971; Objects (i) to undertake price support operations in respect of raw jute; (ii) to ensure remunerative prices to producers through efficient marketing (iii) to operate a buffer stock to stabilize raw jute prices; (iv) to handle the import and export of raw jute; (v) to promote the export of jute goods; Chair. Dwaipayan Sen; Man. Dir. G. Ukil.

National Commission on Agriculture: Vigyan Bhavan Annexe, New Delhi; f. Aug. 1970 to examine the current progress of agriculture in India and to make recommendations for its improvement and modernization with a view to promoting the welfare and prosperity of the people; Chair. Shri N. R. Mirdha, M.P.

National Co-operative Development Corporation: 1C-56, South Extn. 11, New Delhi 110049; f. 1962 to plan and promote programmes for the production, processing, marketing, storage, export and import of agricultural produce and notified commodities through co-operative societies; Chair. Shri T. A. Pai, Minister of Industry and Civil Supplies; Man. Dir. Shri K. S. Bawa; publs. *Bulletin* (every 2 months), *Report* (annual).

National Industrial Development Corporation Ltd.: Chanakya Bhavan, N.D.M.C. Complex, Vinay Marg, P.O.B. 458, New Delhi 110021; f. 1954; auth. cap. Rs. 10m.; consultative engineering services to Central and State Governments, the UN and overseas investors; Chair. K. B. Rao; Man. Dir. R. K. Sethi; Sec. K. C. Bhalla.

National Mineral Development Corporation Ltd.: Mukarramjahi Rd., Hyderabad 500001; f. 1958; to exploit minerals in the public sector (excluding copper, coal, lignite oil and natural gas); may buy, take on lease or otherwise acquire mines for prospecting and developing; Chair. G. Ramanathan.

National Productivity Council: Lodi Rd., New Delhi; f. 1958 to increase productivity and to improve quality by improved techniques which aim at efficient and proper utilization of available resources of man-power, machines, materials, power and capital, raise the standard of living of the people, and improve the working conditions and welfare of labour; autonomous body representing national organizations of employers and labour, government ministries, professional organizations, Local Productivity Councils, small-scale industries and other interests; total mems.: 75.

National Research Development Corporation of India: 61 Ring Rd., Lajpat Nagar III, New Delhi 110024; f. 1953 to stimulate development and commercial exploitation of patents and inventions arising from national research; Chair. M. S. Pa; Man. Dir. Dr. C. V. S. Ratnam.

National Seeds Corporation Ltd.: Pusa, New Delhi; f. 1963 to improve and develop the seed industry in India; Chair. Dr. D. P. Singh; Man. Dir. N. S. Maini.

National Small Industries Corporation Ltd.: Near Industrial Estate, Okhla, New Delhi 110020; f. 1955 to aid, counsel, finance, protect and promote the interests of small industries; cap. auth. Rs. 35m., issued Rs. 35m., all shares held by the Government; Chair. K. N. Sapru.

Rehabilitation Industries Corporation Ltd.: 25 Free School St., Calcutta 700016; f. 1959 to create employment opportunities through industries for refugees from Pakistan, repatriates from Burma and Sri Lanka, and other persons of Indian extraction who have immigrated to India; Chair. D. K. Bose; Man. Dir. A. K. Ghosh, I.A.S.; Joint Man. Dir. and Sec. M. N. Chaudhuri, I.A.S.

State Farms Corporation of India Ltd.: Pusa, New Delhi; f. 1969 to administer the Central State Farms; activities include the production of quality seeds of high yielding varieties of wheat, paddy, maize, barja and jowar; advises on soil conservation, repair and servicing of tractors, consultancy services on farm mechanization; cap. Rs. 70m.; Chair. Dr. D. P. Singh; Gen. Man. Dr. K. S. Mann.

There are also industrial development corporations in the separate States. Organizations engaged in the financing of agricultural and industrial development are listed under *Finance*.

PRINCIPAL INDUSTRIAL ASSOCIATIONS

Ahmedabad Millowners' Association: Ranchhodlal Marg, Navrangpura, Ahmedabad 380009; f. 1891; Pres. Shri ROHITBHAI C. MEHTA; Sec. Shri R. M. DAVE.

Bombay Piece-Goods Merchants' Mahajan: Shaikh Memon St., Bombay 2; f. 1881; 1,884 mems.; Pres. N. L. SHAH; Vice-Pres. V. K. MEHTA; Sec. N. M. BORADIA.

Bombay Presidency Association: 107 M. Gandhi Rd., Fort, Bombay 1; f. 1886; Pres. NAUSHIR BHARUCHA; Hon. Secs. DARA VANIA, E. A. SETHNA.

Bombay Textile and Engineering Association: 343 opp. Railway Station, Grand Rd., Bombay; est. 1900; Pres. N. F. BHARUCHA; Hon. Sec. K. S. PUNEGAR.

Calcutta Baled Jute Association: 6 Netaji Subhas Rd., Calcutta 1; f. 1892; 58 mems.; Chair. S. C. BOTHRA; Sec. M. GHOSH.

Calcutta Flour Mills Association: 6 Netaji Subhas Rd., Calcutta 1; f. 1932; 25 mems.; Sec. M. GHOSE.

Calcutta Hydraulic Press Association: 6 Netaji Subhas Rd., Calcutta; f. 1903; 13 mems.; Chair. H. M. BENGANI; Sec. M. GHOSH.

Calcutta Trades Association: 18H Park St., Stephen Court, Calcutta 700016; f. 1830; Hon. Sec. S. K. MASKARA; Master N. K. JALAN.

East India Cotton Association Ltd.: Cotton Exchange, Marwari Bazar, Bombay 400002; f. 1921; 352 mems.; Pres. R. PURSHOTAMDAS; Sec. D. G. DAMLE; publ. *Indian Cotton Annual*.

Engineering Association of India: India Exchange, India Exchange Place, Calcutta; f. 1942; 15 affiliated asscns.; Pres. Shri STYA PAUL; Sec.-Gen. C. S. PANDE; Sec. Dr. R. D. VIDYARTHI.

Federation of Gujarat Mills and Industries: Federation Building, R. C. Dutt Rd., Vadodara (Baroda) 390005; f. 1918; 250 mems.; Pres. Shri B. M. PATEL; Sec. R. D. MUNSHI.

Grain, Rice and Oilseeds Merchants' Association: Grainseeds House, 72/80 Yusef Meheralli Rd., Bombay 400003; f. 1899; 700 mems.; Pres. DEVJI RATTANSEY; Sec. RASIKLAL J. BHATT, M.A.; publ. *Vanijya*.

Indian Chemical Manufacturers Association: India Exchange, Calcutta; f. 1938; 157 mems.; Pres. Shri B. HIMATSINGKA; Sec.-Gen. C. S. PANDE; publ. *Chemical Industry News* (monthly), and others.

Industries and Commerce Association: I.C.O. Association Rd., P.O.B. 70, Dhanbad (Dt. Dhanbad), Bihar; f. 1933; 50 mems.; Pres. P. K. AGRAWALA.

Indian Engineering Association: Royal Exchange, 6 Netaji Subhas Rd., Calcutta 1; f. 1895; 555 mems.; Pres. P. K. NANDA; Sec. M. GHOSH.

Indian Jute Mills Association: Royal Exchange, Calcutta 1; sponsors and operates export promotion, research and product development; regulates labour relations; Chair. B. G. BANGUR.

Indian Mining Association: 6 Netaji Subhas Rd., Calcutta 1; f. 1892; 50 mems.; Sec. K. MUKERJEE.

Indian Mining Federation: 135 Biplabi Rashbehari Basu Rd., Calcutta 700001; est. 1913; to aid and stimulate mining, particularly coal, and to protect the commercial interests; Chair. Shri SRIRAM GOENKA; Sec. Shri M. DAS.

Indian National Shipowners' Association: Scindia House, Ballard Estate, Bombay; f. 1930; 26 mems.; Pres. Capt. J. C. ANAND; Sec.-Gen. N. K. GOPALAN NAIR.

Indian Paper Mills Association: India Exchange, 8th Floor, India Exchange Place, Calcutta; f. 1939; 31 mems.; Sec. T. R. KRISHNASWAMI; Pres. S. N. DEY.

Indian Sugar Mills Association: India Exchange Bldg., Indian Exchange Place, Calcutta; est. 1932; 151 mems.; affiliated to the Indian Chamber of Commerce, Calcutta; Pres. M. PRASAD; Sec.-Gen. J. S. MEHTA.

Indian Tea Association: Royal Exchange, 6 Netaji Subhas Rd., Calcutta 7000001; f. 1881; 125 mems.; 245 tea estates; Chair. G. P. GOENKA; Sec. J. D'SOUZA.

Indian Tea Association (Assam Branch): Dikom P.O., Assam; f. 1899; 260 mems.; Sec. E. K. RAWSON-GARDINER.

Indian Tea Association (Surma Valley Branch): Silchar, Cachar, Assam; Chair. G. L. AGARWAL; Sec. M. K. CHAUDHURI.

Jute Balers' Association: 12 India Exchange Place, Calcutta 1; f. 1909; ordinary and Exchange mems. number over 500; represents all Indian Jute Balers; Chair. M. KALA; Sec. R. N. MOHNOT; publ. *The Jute Trade* (English, fortnightly).

Jute Development Office: 4 K. S. Roy Rd., Calcutta; f. 1966; Dir. Shri H. D. NAITHANI.

Master Stevedores' Association: Royal Exchange, Calcutta; f. 1934; 23 mems.; Pres. S. K. GORSIA; Sec. M. GHOSE.

Millowners' Association: Elphinstone Bldg., Veer Nariman Rd., Fort, Bombay; f. 1875; 110 mem. companies; Chair. R. N. MAFATLAL; Sec. R. L. N. VIJAYANAGAR.

Motor Merchants' Associations Ltd.: Sukh Sagar, 3rd Floor, Sandhurst Bridge, Bombay 400007.

Silk and Art Silk Mills' Association Ltd.: Resham Bhavan, 78 Veer Nariman Rd., Bombay 400020; f. 1939; 899 mems.; Chair. MAGANLAL H. DOSHI; Sec. R. K. BHATNAGAR.

Southern India Millowners' Association: Racecourse, Coimbatore 1, Tamil Nadu; f. 1933; 144 mems.; Chair. K. RAJAGOPAL; Sec. C. G. REDDI.

EMPLOYERS FEDERATIONS

Council of Indian Employers: Federation House, New Delhi; f. 1956; consists of:

- **All-India Organization of Employers:** Federation House, New Delhi 110001; f. 1932; mems. 39 industrial associations and 113 large industrial concerns; Pres. K. R. PODAR; Sec.-Gen. P. CHENTSAL RAO.
- **Employers' Federation of India:** Army and Navy Building, 148 Mahatma Gandhi Rd., Bombay; f. 1933; 220 mems.; Pres. N. H. TATA, N. M. VAKIL.

Employers' Association of Northern India: 14/69 Civil Lines, P.O.B. 344, Kanpur; f. 1937; 160 mems.; Chair. Dr. JAIPURIA; Sec. D. N. NIGAM.

Employers' Federation of Southern India: Dare House Annexe, 3/4 Moore St., P.O.B. 35, Madras 600001; 131 mem. firms; Chair. S. K. PARTHASARATHI; Sec. C. S. KRISHNASWAMI.

Bharat Krishak Samaj (*Farmers' Forum, India*): A-1 Nizamuddin West, New Delhi 110013; f. 1954 by the late Dr. Panjabrao Deshmukh; 1,014,000 mems.; national organization of farmers; Pres. Ex-Officio Union Minister for Agriculture; Chair. Shri R. SRINIVASAN; Sec.-Gen. Dr. D. A. BHOLAY; publ. *Krishak Samachar* (monthly, English, Hindi and Marathi); circ. 15,000.

TRADE UNIONS

Indian National Trade Union Congress—INTUC: 17 Janpath, New Delhi 110001; f. 1947; the largest and most representative T.U. organization in India; over 2,416 affiliated unions with a total membership of 2,428,012; affiliated to ICFTU; 20 state branches and 27 national industrial federations; Pres. B. C. BHAGAVATI; Gen. Sec. G. RAMANUJAM; Asst. Secs. R. L. THAKAR, H. D. MUKERJI; Treas. C. M. STEPHEN.

NATIONAL INDUSTRIAL FEDERATIONS

Indian National Cement Workers' Federation: Mazdoor Karyalaya, Congress House, Bombay 401004; Pres. H. N. TRIVEDI.

Indian National Chemical Workers' Federation: 'Tel Rasayan Bhavan, Tilak Rd., Dadar, Bombay; Pres. RAJA KULKARNI, M.P.

Indian National Defence Workers' Federation: 25/19, Karachi Khana, Kanpur; Pres. Dr. G. S. MELKOTE.

Indian National Electricity Workers' Federation: 19 Mazdoor Maidan, Power House, Jaipur 6; Pres. J. C. DIKSHIT, M.P.

Indian National Metal Workers' Federation: 15K Rd., Jamshedpur; Pres. Shri MICHAEL JOHN.

Indian National Mineworkers' Federation: 9 Lala Lajpatrai Sarani, Calcutta 700020; f. 1949; 200,000 mems. (est.) in 95 affiliated unions; Pres. KANTI MEHTA; Gen. Sec. S. DAS GUPTA.

Indian National Paper Mill Workers' Federation: Ballarpur, Distr. Chanda; Pres. G. SANJEEVA REDD; Gen. Sec. P. J. NAIR.

Indian National Plantation Workers' Federation: P.O.B. 13, Rehakari, Dibrugarh; 261,000 mems. (est.) in 24 affiliated unions; Pres. K. P. TRIPATHI; Gen. Sec. G. SARMAH.

Indian National Port and Dock Workers' Federation: Mazdoor Karyalaya, Congress House, Bombay 400004; f. 1954; Pres. H. N. TRIVEDI.

Indian National Press Workers' Federation: 19 Japling Rd., Lucknow.

Indian National Sugar Mills Workers' Federation: 19 Japling Rd., Lucknow; 50,000 mems. (est.).

Indian National Textile Workers' Federation: Mazdoor Manzil, G. D. Ambekar Marg, Parel, Bombay 400012; f. 1948; 371,084 mems.; Gen. Sec. A. T. BHOSALA.

Indian National Transport Workers' Federation: Ulubari, Gauhati 7; Gen. Sec. RAJA KULKARNI, M.P.

National Federation of Petroleum Workers: Tel-Rasayan Bhanuan, Tilak Rd., Dadar, Bombay 400014, f. 1959; 22,340 mems.; Pres. N. K. BHATT; Gen. Sec. RAJA KULKARNI.

All-India Trade Union Congress: 24 K. M. Munshi Lane, New Delhi 110001; f. 1920; affiliated to WFTU; 2,070,504 mems., 3,712 affiliated unions; 18 regional branches; Pres. Dr. RANEN SEN, M.P.; Vice-Pres. INDRAJIT GUPTA, M. S. KRISHNAN, M. ELIAS, B. D. JOSHI; Gen. Sec. S. A. DANGE; publ. *Trade Union Record* (English).

MAJOR AFFILIATED UNIONS

Annamalai Plantation Workers' Union: Valparai, Via Pollachi, Tamil Nadu; mems. over 21,000.

Zilla Cha Bagan Workers' Union: Malabar, Jalpaiguri, West Bengal; 21,000 mems.

United Trades Union Congress—UTUC: 249 Bepin Behai Ganguly St., Calcutta 700012; f. 1949; 387,097 mems. from 457 affiliated unions; Pres. N. SRIKANTAN NAIR Vice-Pres. T. CHAUDHURY, J. SETHI, S. BHATTACHARYA, S. V. R. ACHARYA, T. M. S. VAID; Gen.. Sec JATIN CHAKRAVORTY.

MAJOR AFFILIATED UNIONS

Bengal Provincial Chatkal Mazdoor Union: 64 Chittarajan Ave., Calcutta 12; textile workers; 28,33 mems.

All-India Farm Labour Union: c/o U.T.U.C., Jakkanpu New Area, Patna 1, Bihar; over 35,000 mems. (est.

Hind Mazdoor Sabha—HMS: Nagindas Chambers, 16 P. D'. Mello Rd., Bombay 40038; f. 1948; affiliated t ICFTU; mems. 1,144,164 from 525 affiliated unions; 1 regional brs.; Pres. A. SUBRAMANIAM; Gen. Se MAHESH DESAI; publ. *Hind Mazdoor.*

MAJOR AFFILIATED UNIONS

All-India Port and Dock Workers' Federation: Po Shramik Bhavan, 26 Dr. S. Basu Rd., Calcutt 700023; f. 1948; 175,000 mems.; 26 affiliated union Pres. S. R. KULKARNI; Gen. Sec. MAKHAN CHATTERJEE.

All India Khan Mazdoor (Mineworkers') Federation National House, 6 Tulloch Rd., Apollo Bunde Bombay 400039; f. 1962; mems. 210,000; Gen. Se Mahesh Desai.

Western Railway Employees' Union—WREU: Gra Rd. Station (East), Bombay 7; f. 1920; 65,00 mems.; Pres. Miss MANIBEN KARA; Gen. Sec. U. M PUROHIT; Joint Gen. Sec. JAGDISH AJMERA; Se K. C. TRIVEDI; publ. *Railway Sentinel.*

Calcutta Port Shramik Union: Port Shramik Bhava 26 Dr. Sudhir Basu Rd., Kidderpore, Calcutt 700023; mems. 31,286; Gen. Sec. MAKHAN CHATTERJEE.

HMS Steel Committee: Rourkela Mazdoor Sabha Bisra Rd., Rourkela 11, Dist. Sundergarh, Orissa mems. 42,000; Convener RAJKISHORE SAMANTRAI.

Confederation of Central Government Employees' Unions New Delhi; 700,000 mems. (est.); Gen. Sec. S. MADHUSUDAN.

AFFILIATED UNION

National Federation of Post, Telephone and Telegrap Employees—NFPTTE: 9 Pusa Rd., New Delh f. 1954; mems. 170,000 (est.); Gen. Sec. P. S. F ANJANEYALU.

National Federation of Indian Railwaymen—NFIR: 166/ Panchkuian Rd., New Delhi; f. 1953; mems. 348,00 (est.); Pres. A. P. SHARMA; Gen. Sec. KESHAV H KULKARNI.

AFFILIATED UNION

All-India Railwaymen's Federation—AIRF: 125E Baba Rd., New Delhi 1; f. 1924; 508,380 mems. (1973) Pres. GEORGE FERNANDES; Gen. Sec. PRIYA GUPTA publ. *Indian Railwaymen.*

All-India Bank Employees' Federation—AIBEF: 26/10 Birhana Rd., Kanpur 1; Gen. Sec. V. N. SEKHRI; pub *Bank Kramchari.*

All-India Defence Employees' Federation—AIDEF: Kirke Poona; 300,000 mems. (est.); Gen. Sec. S. M. JOSHI.

MAJOR INDUSTRIAL COMPANIES

GOVERNMENT INDUSTRIAL UNDERTAKINGS

The following are some of the more important industrial and commercial undertakings in which the government holds the majority of shares.

Bharat Electronics Ltd.: Jalahalli P.O., Bangalore 560013; f. 1954; cap. Rs. 100m.

Manufacture of electronic and radar equipment and electronic components.

Chair. and Man. Dir. Shri C. R. SUBRAMANIAN; employees: 16,000.

Bharat Refineries Ltd.: Bharat Bhavan, 4 & 6, Currimbhoy Road, Ballard Estate, Bombay 400 038.

Petroleum refining & marketing. Annual throughput about 3.75m. tonnes.

Chief Officials S. KRISHNASWAMI, J. B. MALIK; employees about 5,000.

Bokaro Steel Ltd.: Main Administrative Bldg., Bokaro Steel City; f. 1964; cap. Rs. 5,000m.

To manage the fourth steel plant in the public sector, under construction at Bokaro.

Chair. and Man. Dir. M. SONDHI; Sec. N. RATH.

Bharat Heavy Electricals Ltd.: 18–20 Kasturba Gandhi Marg, New Delhi 110001; f. 1964; cap. Rs. 1,300m.

Integrated world-wide service in power generation, transmission and utilization equipment, equipment for industries. Manufacturing divisions at Bhopal, Hardwar, Hyderabad, Jhansi and Tiruchirapalli.

Chair. V. KRISHNAMURTHY; Sec. M. NARAYANASWAMI.

Cement Corporation of India, Ltd.: Herald House, 5-A, Bahadur Shah Zafar Marg, New Delhi 1; f. 1965.

To install additional capacity for cement; cap. Rs. 300m.

Chair. and Man. Dir. Shri B. V. RAJU.

Fertilizer Corporation of India: F-43, South Extension Area, Part I, Ring Rd., New Delhi 110049; f. 1961; cap. Rs. 6,000m.

Manufactures fertilizers and many industrial products. Factories at Sindri (Bihar), Nangal (Punjab), Trombay (Maharashtra), Gorakhpur (Uttar Pradesh), Durgapur (West Bengal) and Namrup (Assam). Factories under construction at Barauni (Bihar), Namrup Expansion (Assam), Trombay Expansion (Maharashtra), Sindri Rationalization and Sindri Modernization (Bihar), Ramagundam (Andhra), Korba (Madhya Pradesh), Haldia (W. Bengal) and Talcher (Orissa).

Chair. and Man. Dir. K. C. SHARMA.

Hindustan Aeronautics Ltd.: Indian Express Bldg., P.B. 5150, Vidhana Veedhi, Bangalore, Karnataka; f. 1964.

Six divisions at Bangalore, Hyderabad, Kanpur, Korapur, Lucknow and Nasik.

Chair. Air Marshal O. P. MEHRA; Man. Dir. (Bangalore, Air Vice-Marshal A. S. RIKHY; employees: 36,000.

Hindustan Antibiotics Ltd.: Pune (Poona) 411018; f. 1954; cap. Rs. 35m.

Manufactures penicillin, streptomycin, and a number of antifungal antibiotics.

Man. Dir. C. N. CHARI; employees: 2,540.

Hindustan Shipyard Ltd.: Visakhapatnam 5, Andhra Pradesh; f. 1941; cap. Rs. 100m.

Shipbuilding and large-scale repair works. The shipyard has a training school which provides training in all the shipbuilding trades to apprentices.

Chair. and Man. Dir. Sri S. BALAKRISHNA SHETTY; employees: 5,348.

Indian Drugs and Pharmaceuticals Ltd.: N-12 & 13 South Extension, Part I, Ring Rd., New Delhi 100049; f. 1961; an undertaking of the Ministry of Petroleum and Chemicals; cap. Rs. 271.5m.

The corporation has three plants under its control: (i) an antibiotics research unit at Rishikesh, (ii) a synthetic drug project at Hyderabad and (iii) a surgical instruments plant at Madras.

Chair. and Man. Dir. L. K. BEHL; employees: over 8,000.

Indian Oil Corporation Ltd.: 254-C, Dr. Annie Besant Rd., Prabhadevi, Bombay 25; f. 1964.

The Refineries Division at New Delhi is responsible for the construction and management of the four government-owned refineries at Gauhati (Assam), Barauni (Bihar), Koyali (Gujarat) and Haldia (West Bengal). A fifth refinery at Mathura (Uttar Pradesh) is to become operational in 1980–81. The Pipelines Section of the Refineries and Pipeline Division, also in New Delhi, is responsible for the construction and operation of pipelines.

Chair. Shri C. R. DAS GUPTA.

National Mineral Development Corporation Ltd.: Mohan Singh Place, Irwin Rd., New Delhi 1; f. 1958.

The exploitation of minerals in the public sector, excluding coal, lignite, oil and natural gas; the acquisition of mines for prospecting and development and working them for producing minerals. Projects include iron ore at Kiriburu (Orissa), Bailadila (Madhya Pradesh, Dominalai and Kuremukh (Mysore) and diamonds at Panna (Madhya Pradesh).

National Organic Chemical Industries Ltd.: Mafatlal Centre, Nariman Point, Bombay 1; f. 1961; cap. p.u. Rs. 120m.

Manufactures and distributes petrochemicals; distribution of industrial and agricultural chemicals.

Man. Dirs. Dr. C. J. DADACHANJI, P. J. SCHOENMAKERS; employees: 1,055.

Oil India Ltd.: Duliajan P.O., Assam; f. 1959.

The Government of India and Burmah Oil Company Ltd. are equal shareholders. It has mining leases for the exploration and production of crude oil and natural gas in Nahorkatiya, Hugrijan, Moran and Dum Duma and a petroleum exploration licence in Arunachal Pradesh. It supplies crude oil to the two government-owned refineries at Barauni, Gauhati and Digboi. It is also engaged in the transport of oil and the sale of gas.

Chair. RAJA AJIT NARAYAN DEB; Man. Dir. Shri A. B. DAS GUPTA; employees: 3,848; publ. *O.I.L. News*, monthly; circ. 5,200.

PRIVATE COMPANIES

India's major industrial firms in the private sector arranged by total assets.

Tata Iron and Steel Co. Ltd.: Bombay House, 24 Homi Mody St., Fort, Bombay 400023; f. 1907; cap. Rs. 500m.

Manufacturer of 1.5m. tons p.a. of structurals, bars, rails, plates, sheets, strip, rolled rings, also tools, such as hoes, picks, beaters, etc.; by-products, such as coal tar, benzol, etc. Steel works at Jamshedpur (Bihar). One subsidiary company in India.

Chair. J. R. D. TATA; Vice-Chair. S. MOOLGAOKAR; employees: 55,000.

Indian Iron and Steel Co. Ltd.: 50 Chowringhee Rd., Calcutta 700071; f. 1918; cap. Rs. 276m.

Major establishments; iron and steel works at Burnpur and foundry at Kulti and the township of Burnpur and Kulti, West Bengal; ore mines (iron ore and manganese deposits) in Singhbhum district of Bihar; mining rights for phosphate rock and phosphate of lime near Ghatsila; collieries and coal lands at Ramnagore, Noonodih Jitpur and Chasnalla.

Chair. HITEN BHAYA.

Tata Engineering & Locomotive Co. Ltd.: Export Dept., Block A Shiv Sagar Estates, Annie Besant Rd., Worli, Bombay 400018; f. 1945; cap. Rs. 831.6m.

Manufactures and sells Tata Diesel truck and bus chassis, Tata P & H earth moving equipment, press tools and dies, special purpose machines. Factories at Jamshedpur and Poona. Turnover (1974–75): Rs. 2,200m.

Chair. S. MOOLGAOKAR; Vice-Chair. N. A. PALKHIWALA; employees: 25,000.

Associated Cement Companies Ltd.: Cement House, 121 Maharshi Karve Rd., Bombay 400020; f. 1936; cap. Rs. 300m.

Manufacture and sale of cement (15 cement works in 8 states), refractories (Katni), coal (Kotma and Nowrozabad), special products (Porbandar), engineering (Shahabad). Subsidiary: The Cement Marketing Company of India Ltd., Bombay.

Chair. N. A. PALKHIVALA; Man. Dir. P. K. MISTRY; employees: 32,000.

Scindia Steam Navigation Co. Ltd.: Scindia House, Dougall Rd., Ballard Estate, Bombay 1; f. 1919; cap. Rs. 135.3m.

Cargo and passenger services: India, Pakistan, U.K., Continent, Middle and Far East, Canada, Caribbean ports, U.S.S.R., U.S.A.; Eight subsidiaries at home and abroad.

Chair. K. M. D. THACKERSEY; employees: 2,666 (shore staff).

Delhi Cloth & General Mills Co. Ltd.: P.O.B. 1039, Bara Hindu Rao, Delhi 110006; f. 1889; cap. Rs. 196m.

Manufactures cotton and synthetic textiles, sulphuric acid, urea, PVC, caustic soda, alums, superphosphate, sugar, confectionery, alcohol, edible vegetable oils, calcium carbide, rayon type cord, electronic desk calculators, etc. (Delhi, Kota, Hissar, Dasna, Mawana and Daurala). One subsidiary company.

Man. Dirs. Dr. BHARAT RAM, Dr. CHARAT RAM; employees: 35,000.

India Tobacco Company Ltd., Virginia House, 37 Chowringhee, Calcutta 16, P.O.B. 89; f. 1910; cap. Rs. 250m.

Manufactures, distributes and sells many popular brands of cigarettes and smoking tobaccos. Factories at Monghyr (Bihar), Bangalore (Mysore), Saharanpur (U.P.), Kidderpore (West Bengal), Parel (Bombay).

Hindustan Aluminium Corporation Ltd.: Renukoot (District Mirzapur) U.P.; f. 1958; cap. Rs. 200m.

India's largest aluminium producity (capacity 95,000 tonnes per year). Produces alumina, aluminium and aluminium products and by-products.

Chair. G. D. BIRLA.

Premier Automobiles Ltd.: Construction House, Ballar Estate, Fort, Bombay 400001; f. 1944; cap. Rs. 74.8m.

Manufactures Premier Pioneer/Roadmaster commercia vehicles and President cars, and other engineerin items.

Chair. LALCHAND HIRACHAND; Dir. BHARAT G. DOSH employees: 10,089.

Tata Oil Mills Co. Ltd.: Bombay House, 24 Homi Mody St. Fort, Bombay 400023; f. 1917.

Manufactures edible oils, cosmetics, detergents an foods. Factories at Tatapuram (Kerala), Bombay Calcutta, Ghaziabad (Uttar Pradesh), Madras an Calicut.

Employees: 4,600.

Tata Power Co. Ltd.: Bombay House, 24 Homi Mody St. Fort, Bombay 1; f. 1919; cap. Rs. 75m.

Generates and distributes electricity in Bombay and th surrounding area.

Chair. N. H. TATA; Man. Dir. K. M. CHINNAPPA.

Hindustan Motors Ltd.: Birla Bldg., 9–1 R. N. Mukherje Rd., Calcutta 1; f. 1942; cap. Rs. 300m.

Manufactures cars, truck chassis, cranes, presse excavators, steel structurals, steel castings an forgings at factory at Hindmotor (Hooghly Distric and dumpers, crawler tractors, front end loaders a factory in Trivellore.

Chair. B. M. BIRLA.

Orient Paper Mills Ltd.: Brajrajnagar, near Jharsugud District Sambalpur, Orissa; f. 1936; cap. Rs. 100m.

The mills are situated at Brajrajnagar. A new mill a Amlai (Madhya Pradesh) is under construction.

Chair. G. P. BIRLA.

Indian Aluminium Co. Ltd.: 1 Middleton St., Calcutta 16 f. 1938; cap. Rs. 200m.

Owns and operates bauxite mines (Lohardaga, Biha 230,000 tonnes per year) (Chandgad, Maharashtra: 30 tonnes); alumina plants (Muri, Bihar: 72,000 tonne (Hirakud, Orissa: 21,000 tonnes) (Belgaum, Mysor 40,000 tonnes); sheet mills (Belur, West Bengal: 18,00 tonnes) (Taloja, Maharashtra—under construction 11,500 tonnes); Properzi plant (Alupuram, Keral 10,000 tonnes); foil plant (Kalwa, Maharashtra: 2,5 tonnes); powder and paste plant (Kalwa, Maharashtr 1,300 tonnes); extrusion plant (Alupuram, Keral 3,760 tonnes).

Chair. H. V. R. IENGAR; Man. Dir. J. B. LESLIE; Dir M. A. CHIDAMBARAM, P. C. GEORGE, D. D. MACKA Sir U. C. MAHATAB, K.C.I.E. (Maharajadhiraja BAHADU OF BURDWAN), A. H. J. MUIRHEAD, KESHUB MAHINDR S. K. MULLICK, T. D. SINHA; employees: 6,412.

Guest, Keen and Williams Ltd.: 97 Andul Rd., Howra 711103, West Bengal; f. 1931; cap. Rs. 100m.

Manufacture metal pressings, alloys and special stee industrial fasteners, automative forgings, electric stampings and laminations, strip wound cores. Factori in Howrah, Bombay and Bangalore.

Chair. K. C. MAITRA; Gen. Man. Dir. VINCENT EDKIN

Hindustan Lever Ltd.: Hindustan Lever House, 165/16 Backbay Reclamation, Bombay 400 020; f. 1933; ca employed Rs. 419m.

Manufacture and sale of washing products, toilet pr parations, edible fats, food products, animal an poultry feeds and chemicals. Factories in Bomba Calcutta, Shamnagar (West Bengal), Ghaziabad an

Etah (Uttar Pradesh) and Tiruchirapalli (Tamil Nadu). One subsidiary company and three trust companies for administering pensions, etc.

Chair. T. THOMAS; employees: 7,300.

Esso Standard Refining Company of India Ltd.: Administrative Building, Mahul, Bombay 74; f. 1952; cap. Rs. 30m.

Refinery at Trombay producing petrol, kerosene, diesel oils, fuel oils, solvents, LPG, asphalts. etc.

Chair. A. G. NEEF; Man. Dir. Dr. J. S. CAMA.

Dunlop India Ltd.: 57B Mirza Ghalib St., Calcutta 700016; f. 1926; cap. Rs. 107m.

Manufactures tyres and tubes for bicycles, automobiles, aircraft, earth-moving equipment, tractors, conveyor and transmission belting, hoses, Dunlopillo and metal products. Factories at Sahaganj (West Bengal) and Ambattur (Madras).

Man. Dir. R. G. S. NAIRN; employees: 10,170.

Voltas Ltd.: Volkart Building, 19 Graham Rd., Ballard Estate, Bombay, P.O.B. 900; f. 1954; cap. Rs. 62.3m.

An integrated marketing, engineering and manufacturing company with nine engineering and three marketing divisions maintaining country-wide selling and service organizations. Manufactures air-conditioning and refrigeration equipment, water coolers, core drills, diamond bits, water well drills, hoists, fork lift trucks, power capacitators and air pollution control equipment. Factory at Thana.

Man. Dir. A. H. TOBACCOWALA.

The Gwalior Rayon Silk Mfg. (Wvg.) Co. Ltd.: Birlagram, Nagda; f. 1947; cap. Rs. 963m.

Viscose staple fibre at Birlagram, Nagda (Madhya Pradesh) and Mavoor (Kerala). Dissolving pulp and paper at Mavoor (Kerala) and Harihar (Karnataka). Man-made fabrics at Birlanagar (Gwalior). Engineering division at Birlagram, Nagda (Madhya Pradesh), manufacturing rayon and allied chemical plant and machinery. Cotton textiles at Bhiwani (Haryana).

Chair. G. D. BIRLA; Pres. INDU H. PAREKH; employees: 15,000

The Great Eastern Shipping Co. Ltd.: Mercantile Bank Bldg., 60 Mahatma Gandhi Rd., Fort, Bombay 1; f. 1948; cap. Rs. 100m.

Shipowners and operators of owned and chartered ships; cargo service; liner service from Pacific coast of U.S.A. and Canada to India; worldwide tramp services; total freight and charter hire earnings about Rs. 126m. p.a.

Chair. A. H. BHIWANDIWALLA; employees about 1,500.

Union Carbide India Ltd.: Lakshmi Bldg., Sir Phirozshah Mehta Rd., Fort, Bombay 1; f. 1934; cap. Rs. 60m.

Manufactures all types of dry cells and batteries for radio and telecommunication purposes. Factories at Calcutta and Madras.

Subsidiary company: Metals and Ores Co.

Chair. KESHUB MAHINDRA; Man. Dir. J. W. L. RUSSELL.

Ahmedabad Electricity Company Ltd.: 83 Advent, General Bhonsle Marg, Backbay Reclamation, Bombay 400021; f. 1913; cap. Rs. 150m.

Generates and supplies electrical energy for Ahmedabad and suburbs.

Chief Exec. K. N. RAO.

Calico Dyeing and Printing Mills: Industrial Estates, Dr. Ambedkar Rd., Bombay 12; f. 1955; cap. Rs. 2.5m.

Processing, bleaching, dyeing, printing and finishing of all types of textiles.

Dirs. D. M. PAREKH, C. N. KOTHARY, H. N. KOTHARI, K. B. KAMDAR, P. U. MEHTA, N. S. PAREKH.

Indian Tube Company Ltd.: 43 Chowringhee Rd., Calcutta 16, P.O.B. 270; f. 1954; cap. Rs. 79.55m.

Manufactures steel tubes and cold rolled steel strips. Factory at Jamshedpur.

Chair. Sir JEHANGIR GHANDY, C.I.E.; Man. Dir. S. L. DASS.

Synthetics and Chemicals Ltd.: 7 Jamshedji Tata Rd., Churchgate Reclamation, Bombay 400 020; f. 1960; cap. Rs. 150m.

Manufactures synthetic rubber and latices. Factory at Bareilly.

Chair. TULSIDAS KILACHAND.

Century Spinning and Manufacturing Company Ltd.: Industry House, 159 Churchgate Reclamation, Bombay 1; f. 1897; cap. Rs. 100m.

Manufactures cotton and staple fibre yarn, organdie, mulls, voiles, shirtings, etc. Mill at Worli, (Bombay). Viscose Rayon Plant at Kalyan.

Chair. R. D. BIRLA.

Jessop & Co. Ltd.: 63 Netaji Subhas Rd., Calcutta 1; f. 1788; cap. Rs. 22.4m.

Manufacture of all types of rolling stock including electric multiple unit coaches, passenger coaches, structural and bridge steelwork, electric overhead travelling cranes, wharf cranes, diesel road rollers, sluice and crest gates, machine tools and heavy duty iron castings. Establishments: Dum Duma and Durgapur (all in West Bengal). Amount of output: Rs. 400m. annually.

Chair. and Man. Dir. R. J. SHANEY; employees 11,000.

Textile Machinery Corporation Ltd.: Belgharia, 24 Parganas, Calcutta; f. 1939; cap. Rs. 50m.

Manufactures textile machinery, rolling stock, boilers of all types, sugar mill machinery, steel and cast iron castings, machine tools, heavy, medium and light structurals and other engineering goods. Factory at Basudevpur (near Belgharia) and Agarpara.

Dirs. K. K. BIRLA, D. P. GOENKA, D. N. KAPUR, Dr. S. C. LAW, SUROTTAM P. HUTHEESING, G. R. PODAR, A. L. GOENKA.

Kesoram Industries and Cotton Mills Ltd.: 9/1 R. N. Mukherjee Rd., Calcutta 1; f. 1919; cap. Rs. 50m.

Manufactures cotton textiles and piece goods, rayon yarn, transparent paper, cellulose film, sulphuric acid, carbon disulphide, cast iron spun pipes and fittings, cement, refractories, etc.

Dirs. B. K. BIRLA, B. P. RAY, R. N. KHAITAN, R. K. BHUWALKA, P. D. HIMAT SINGKA, H. SOMANY, K. G. MAHESWARI.

The Bombay Dyeing & Manufacturing Co. Ltd.: Neville House, Ballard Estate, Bombay 1; f. 1879; cap. Rs. 100m.

Manufacturers and exporters of cotton yarn and textiles, and blends of cotton and synthetic fibres. Two mills and a processing works in Bombay.

Chair. NEVILLE N. WADIA; employees: 14,400.

Caltex Oil Refining (India) Ltd.: Caltex House, 8 Shoorji Vallabhdas Marg, Bombay 1, P.O.B. 155; f. 1955; cap. Rs. 60m.

Owns and operates petroleum refinery near Visakhapatnam (Andhra).

Chair. F. W. ZINGARO; Pres. V. P. RYAN; Man. Dir. F. H. LEVENHAGEN.

Rohtas Industries Ltd.: Dalmiangar, Shahabad District (Bihar), Railway Station, Dehri-on-Sone; f. 1933; cap. Rs. 150m.

Manufactures cement, paper, chemicals, asbestos cement sheets, vanaspati, vulcanized fibre, etc. Also has an electricity generating plant and workshop.

Chair. SHANTI PRASAD JAIN; Sec. P. R. KRISHNAMOORTHY.

Madura Mills Company Ltd.: New Jail Rd., P.O.B. 35, Madurai 625001; f. 1889; cap. Rs. 35m.

The mills are situated at Madurai, Tuticorin, Ambasamudram (Madras State) and at Serampore (West Bengal).

Chair. Rajah Sir M. A. MUTHIAH CHETTIAR.

Atul Products Ltd. (Gujarat): Arvind Asoka Aruna Mills Hospital Premises, Near Asoka Mills Ltd., Naroda Rd., Ahmedabad 380002; f. 1947; cap. Rs. 49m.

Manufacture dyes, chemicals, pesticides and pharmaceuticals. Factory at Atul.

Chair. KASTURBHAI LALBHAI; Man. Dirs. CHINUBHAI CHIMANBHAI, SIDDHARTH KASTURBHAI.

Larsen & Toubro Ltd.: L & T House, Narottam Morarji Marg, Ballard Estate, Bombay 400038; f. 1938; cap. Rs. 165m.

Manufacturers and suppliers of equipment to atomic energy, power, steel, cement, minerals and oil, chemical, food and pulp and paper industries, construction, earth moving, instruments and valves, and other industrial appliances and accessories, Four subsidiary companies.

Chair. H. HOLCK-LARSEN; Pres. N. M. DESAI; employees: 6,760.

Mahindra & Mahindra Ltd.: Gateway Bldg., Apollo Bunder, Bombay 400039; f. 1945; cap. Rs. 56.6m.

Manufactures "Jeep" range of vehicles, process control instruments, electronic equipment and components. Five subsidiaries and three associate companies in India.

Chair. and Exec. Dir. KESHUB MAHINDRA; Exec. Dirs. H. C. MAHINDRA, I. CHATTERJI, K. V. SARDESAI.

India Steamship Company Ltd.: India Steamship House, 21 Old Court House St., Calcutta 1, P.O.B. 2090; f. 1928; cap. Rs. 50m.

The company owns 22 cargo steamships and is engaged in carrying cargo between India, European ports and the United Kingdom.

Chair. K. K. BIRLA.

ACC-Vickers Babcock Ltd.: 18th Floor, Express Towers, Nariman Point, Bombay 1; f. 1959; cap. Rs. 100m.

Manufactures cement making machinery, mining equipment, boilers and pressure vessels. Factory at Durgapur.

Chair. S. MOOLGAOKAR.

Birla Jute Manufacturing Co. Ltd.: 15 India Exchange Place, Calcutta 1; f. 1919; cap. Rs. 60m.

Manufacture and sale of jute goods, calcium carbide, staple fibre yarn and cement, jute carpets and webbing. Major establishments: Birlapur (West Bengal), Satna (M.P.), Chittor (Rajasthan).

Subsidiary companies: India Linoleums Ltd., Assam Jute Supply Co. Ltd., Bharat Overseas Corporation.

Chief officials: Shri T. C. SABOO, Shri R. K. CHHAOCHHARIA, Shri R. L. THIRANI, Shri J. R. BIRLA, Shri S. N. PRASAD, Shri B. L. SHAH, Shri C. B. NEVATIA; employees: 744.

Andhra Valley Power Supply Company Ltd.: Bombay House, 24 Homi Mody St., Fort, Bombay; f. 1916; cap. Rs. 44m.

Generates and distributes electricity in Bombay and surrounding area.

Chair. N. H. TATA; Man. Dir. K. M. CHINNAPPA.

Jiyajeerao Cotton Mills Ltd.: Birlanagar, Gwalior; f. 1921 cap. Rs. 72m.

Manufactures variety of cloths and runs own powe house. Chemical plant at Porbandar producing soda ash and caustic soda.

Chair. M. P. BIRLA.

The Hindustan Construction Co. Ltd.: Construction House Ballard Estate, Bombay 1; f. 1926; cap. Rs. 27m.

Constructs concrete dams, railways and hydro tunnels railway and road bridges, earthwork, foundation work for power houses, buildings. docks, jetties. Establishments: Yamuna Hydel, Haldia Docks, Idikki and Cheruthoni, Sarada-Ghogra Barrages, Madras Ore Berth, Maneri Bhali Hydro-electric works. One subsidiary company.

Gen. Man. R. G. GANDHI; employees: 28,500.

Ashok Leyland Ltd.: Ennore, Madras; f. 1948; cap Rs. 100m.

The company manufactures about 7,000 chassis per annum.

Chair. S. RANGANATHAN; Deputy Chair. A. M. M. ARUNACHALAM, Man. Dir. R. J. HANCOCK.

The National Rayon Corporation Ltd.: Ewart House, Homi Mody St., Fort, Bombay 400023; f. 1946; cap. Rs. 57.4m.

Manufactures filament rayon, rayon tyre cord, tyre warp sheet, sulphuric acid, carbon-disulphide, caustic soda, chlorine, anhydrous sodium sulphate, hydrochloric acid, carbon tetrachloride, oleum, glauber salt and hydrogen gas. Factory at Mohone, Kalyan; six branches elsewhere in India. Ex-factory value of products (1974): Rs. 330.1m.

Chair. SHANTANU N. DESAI; employees: 7,800.

Siemens Engineering and Manufacturing Company of India Ltd.: G.P.O. Box 715, Calcutta.

India Cements Ltd.: Dhun Bldg., 175/1 Mount Rd., Madras 6000022; f. 1946; cap. Rs. 52m.

Manufacture cement, cement clinker, grinding media malleable cast iron material, etc. Factories at Sankarnagar (Tirunelveli District), Sankaridrug (Salem District).

Chair. R. RAMJEEDASS IYER; Man. Dir. K. S. NARAYANAN.

Indian Oxygen Ltd.: Oxygen House, P34 Taratala Rd. Calcutta 700053; f. 1935; cap. Rs. 61.6m.

Manufacturers and suppliers of industrial and medical gases; electrodes and other welding equipment including fluxes; cutting apparatus, medical and surgical equipment; installation of oxygen and other gas plants and high-pressure pipelines; liquid oxygen explosives. Factories and depots all over India; subsidiaries of BOC Ltd., London.

Man. Dir. K. D. MOORE; employees: 5,800.

The Alkali & Chemical Corporation of India Ltd.: 34, Chowringhee, Calcutta 16; f. 1937; cap. Rs. 46.5m.

Manufacturers of liquid chlorine, caustic soda, hydrochloric acid, paints, polythene, agricultural chemicals (Rishra, District Hooghly, West Bengal, Hyderabad, Andhra Pradesh).

Chair. DOUGLAS G. OWEN; Man. Dir. A. L. A. MUDALIAR; employees: 3,237

Philips India Ltd.: Philips House, 7 Justice Chandra Madhab Rd., Calcutta 700020; f. 1930; cap. Rs. 50m.

Manufactures lighting equipment and other radio and electronic goods. Factories at Calcutta, Poona and Kalwa.

Chair. and Man. Dir. J. G. C. VAN TILBURG.

TRANSPORT

RAILWAYS

Indian Government Administration (Railway Board): Rail Bhawan, Raisina Rd., New Delhi; Dir.-Gen. M. Srinivasan; Chair. G. P. Warrier.

The Indian Government exercises direct or indirect control over all railways in the Republic of India through the medium of the Railway Board.

State Railways

The railways have been grouped into nine zones:

Northern: Delhi; Gen. Man. V. P. Sawhney.

Western: Bombay; Gen. Man. A. K. Gupta.

Central: Bombay-VT; Gen. Man. B. D. Mehra.

Southern: Madras; Gen. Man. G. S. A. Saldhana.

Eastern: Calcutta; Gen. Man. E. J. Simoes.

South Eastern: Calcutta; Gen. Man. V. Ramanathan.

South Central: Secunderabad; Gen. Man. K. S. Rajan.

North Eastern: Gorakhpur; Gen. Man. S. C. Misra.

Northeast Frontier: Assam; Gen. Man. M. R. Reddy.

The total length of Indian railways in 1974 was 60,234 route kms. The total length of track was 104,770 km.

Note: An underground railway for Calcutta is scheduled for completion by 1979. It is expected to serve more than one million people and to total 17 km. in length.

ROADS

Ministry of Shipping and Transport (Roads Wing): Transport Bhavan No. 1, Parliament St., New Delhi 110001; in 1973-74 surfaced and metalled roads totalled 133,700 km., and other roads 695,000 km. India has a system of National Highways, with an aggregate length of about 28,819 km. in 1973 running through the length and breadth of the country, connecting the State capitals and major ports and linking with the highway systems of its neighbours. This system includes 55 highways and they constitute the main trunk roads of the country.

Central Road Transport Corporation Ltd.: 4 Fairlie Place, Calcutta 1; f. 1964 to supplement the transport capacity in the eastern sector of the country; Chair. S. K. Datta; Man. Dir. M. Yusuf Khan.

Border Roads Development Board: f. 1960 to accelerate the economic development of the North and Northeastern border areas; it has constructed 6,754 km. of new roads; improved 4,175 km. of existing roads and surfaced 7,591 km. (1974).

INLAND WATERWAYS

About 2,500 km. of rivers are navigable by mechanically propelled country vessels and 2,500 km. by large country boats. Services are mainly on the Ganga and Brahmaputra and their tributaries, the Godavari and Krishna.

Central Inland Water Transport Corpn. Ltd.: 4 Fairlie Place, Calcutta 1; f. 1967; main activities include shipbuilding and repairing; lighterage, river conservancy, bunkering; ship delivery; manning and operation of river craft; provision of ferry services and pleasure cruises; Chair. Cmdr. K. Chelliah; Man. Dir. M. Yusuf Khan.

East Bengal River Steam Service Ltd.: 87 Sovabazar St., Calcutta 5; f. 1906; Man. Dirs. K. D. Roy, B. K. Roy.

SHIPPING

India is the second largest ship-owning country in Asia. The shipping tonnage in 1974 was 3,090,000 g.r.t. There are 34 shipping companies in India. The major ports are Bombay, Calcutta, Cochin, Kandla, Madras, Mangalore, Marmagao, Pradip, Tuticorin and Visakahpatnam.

Bombay

Africana Company (Private) Ltd.: 289-93 Narshi Natha St., Bombay 400001; Chair. J. M. Kapadia.

American President Lines Ltd.: Forbes Bldg., Home St., Fort; agents for Royal Interocean Lines, Canadian City Line Ltd., Ellerman City Liners.

Bharat Line Ltd.: Bharat House, 104 Apollo St., Fort, 1; also at Calcutta, Bhavnagar and Madras.

Gill Amin Steamship Co. (Private) Ltd.: 15 Khorshed Bldg., Sir P.M. Rd. 1; services: Bombay–Karachi–Colombo–East and West Coast India–Burma.

Great Eastern Shipping Co. Ltd.: Mercantile Bank Bldg., 60 Mahatma Gandhi Rd., Bombay 400023; f. 1948; Chair. V. J. Sheth; Man. Dir. K. M. Sheth.

Lloyd Triestino: Neville House, Ballard Estate, P.O.B. 1080; also agents Anchor Line Ltd.

Mackinnon Mackenzie and Co. (Private) Ltd.: 4 Shoorji Vallabhdas Marg, Ballard Estate, Bombay; agents for Pan-ocean Shipping and Terminals Ltd.; P. & O. Lines; Waterman Line, Indoceanic Shipping Co. Ltd.; Nilhat Shipping Co. Ltd.; Stravelakis Bros. Ltd., Naess Shipping Co.; Bank Line Ltd.; Union Steam Ship Co. of New Zealand Ltd.; Global Bulk Transport, Inc.; National Bulk Carriers Inc.; Associated Bulk Carriers Inc.; Damodar Bulk Carriers (Goa) Ltd.; South India Shipping Corpn. Ltd.; Mauritius Steam Navigation Co. Ltd.; Apollo Shipping Co. Inc.; Netherlands Norness Shipping Co. Ltd.

Malabar Steamship Co. Ltd., The: 4th Floor, Express Towers, Nariman Point, 1; f. 1935; Chair. Pratapsingh Shoorji Vallabhdass, J.P.; Man. Dir. Dilip Shoorji.

Merchant Steam Navigation Co. (Private) Ltd.: 283-93 Narsi Natha St.

Mitsui OSK Lines Ltd.: Marshall's Bldg., 2nd Floor, Ballard Rd. 1.

Mogul Line Ltd.: 16 Bank St.; f. 1877; state-owned; Chair. Adm. S. M. Nanda; Man. Dir. J. G. Saggi.

Nedlloyd and Hoegh Lines: Patel-Volkart Ltd., 19 Graham Rd., Ballard Estate, 1.

NYK Line: c/o Indian Maritime Enterprises (Private) Ltd., 6th Floor, New Kamani Chambers, Mangalore St., Ballard Estate, 1.

Polish Ocean Lines: Bharat Insurance Bldg., 15A Horniman Circle, Bombay 1; Dir. J. Mondalski.

Scindia Steam Navigation Co. Ltd.: Scindia House, Narottam Morarjee Marg, Ballard Estate, 1; f. 1919; Chair. K. M. D. Thackersey; Dir.-in-Charge Mrs. Sumati Morarjee; also at Calcutta, Saurashtra and Mangalore ports.

Shipping Corporation of India Ltd.: Shipping House, 2229/232 Madame Cama Rd., Bombay 400021; f. 1961 as a government undertaking; fleet of 112 vessels, consisting of tankers, freighters, passenger-cum-cargo ships; operates bulk carriers; operates 27 services; Chair. and Man. Dir. Adm. S. M. Nanda.

South-East Asia Shipping Co. Ltd.: Himalaya House, Dr. Dadabhoy Naoroji Rd., Fort 1, Bombay 400001; f. 1948; Dirs. N. H. Dhunjibhoy, J. P. Bragg, D. H. Dhunjibhoy, Prof. M. S. Thacker, K. N. Dhunjibhoy.

United Liner Agencies of India (Private) Ltd.: Wavell House, Graham Rd., Ballard Estate, 1.

Yugoslav Line: Alice Bldg., Dadabhai Naoroji Rd.

CALCUTTA

American President Lines Ltd.: 3 Netaji Subhas Rd., 1.

Anchor Brocklebank Line: Agents Turner, Morrison & Co. Ltd., 6 Lyons Range, 1.

Anchor Line Ltd.: 4/5 Bankshall St., 1.

Asiatic Steam Navigation Co. Ltd.: 16 Strand Rd., 1.

Bharat Line Ltd.: 13 Brabourne Rd.

Brocklebanks' Cunard Service Agents: Mackinnon Mackenzie & Co. (P.) Ltd., 16 Strand Rd., Calcutta 1.

Central Gulf Steamship Corporation: 4 Clive Row, Calcutta.

Ellerman City Liners: Gladstone Lyall & Co. Ltd., 4 Fairlie Place.

Great Eastern Shipping Co. Ltd.: 5 Clive Row, P.B. 566.

Great India Steam Navigation Co. Ltd.: 8 Lyons Range.

India Shipping Co. Ltd.: 21 Old Court House St., P.O.B. 2090.

India Steamship Co. Ltd.: 21 Old Court House St., P.O.B 2090; Chair. K. K. BIRLA.

Indo-Burma Petroleum Co. Ltd.: Gillander House, Netaji Subhas Rd.; f. 1909; Man. Dir. S. B. BUDHIRAJA.

The Indo-China Steam Navigation Co. Ltd.: 4 Clive Row.

Jayanti Shipping Co. (Private) Ltd.: 4–5 Bankshall St.

Mackinnon Mackenzie & Co. (P) Ltd.: 16 Strand Rd., P.O.B. 163; agents for Union Steamship Co. (New Zealand) Ltd.

Malabar Steamship Co. Ltd.: 4 Lyons Range; f. 1935; Chair. PRATAP SINGH SHOORJI VALLABDASS, J.P.; Man. MULJI K. TANNA.

Mitsui OSK Lines Ltd.: Agents F. W. Heilgers & Co. (Private) Ltd., Shipping Dept. 1, India Exchange Place, 1, P.O.B. 185.

NYK Line: 2 Netaji Subhas Rd., 1; Agents James Finlay & Co. Ltd.

Patel-Volkart Ltd.: 5–7 Netaji Subhas Rd., P.O.B. 71, Calcutta 700001; Man. S. N. MIRCHANDANI.

Scindia Steam Navigation Co. Ltd.: 33 Netaji Subhas Rd.

MADRAS

American Mail Lines and American President Lines Ltd.: 6 Mysore Bank Bldg., PB, 37, Madras 600001.

Bharat Line Ltd.: 8 Second Line Beach; also in Bombay, Calcutta and Bhavnagar.

East Asiatic Co. (India) (Private) Ltd.: P.O.B. 146, Madras; also in Bombay, New Delhi and Calcutta.

Jugolinija: agents at Kakinda, Visakhapatnam and Tuticorin.

Messageries Maritimes Co.: 6–20 North Beach Rd. (P.O.B. 181).

Mitsui OSK Line: P.O.B. 63.

Southern Shipping Corporation (Private) Ltd.: 8 Second Line Beach, 1.

(Shipping companies are also represented at Aleppy, Calicut, Cochin, Kakinada, Pondicherry and Tuticorin).

CIVIL AVIATION

Air India: 218 Backbay Reclamation, Nariman Point, Bombay 400001; f. 1953; state corporation responsible for international flights; extensive services to 27 countries covering five continents; fleet of five Boeing 747 and nine Boeing 707; Chair. J. R. D. TATA; Man. Dir. K. K. UNNI.

Indian Airlines: Airlines House, 113 Gurudwara Rakab Ganj Rd., New Delhi; f. 1953; state corporation responsible for regional and domestic flights; services throughout India and to Burma, Sri Lanka, Bangladesh and Nepal; unduplicated route length; 39,171 km.; fleet of seven Boeing 737, nine Caravelles, sixteen HS-748, nine F-27, seven DC-3 and six Viscounts; Chair. and Man. Dir. Air Chief Marshal P. C. LAL.

The following airlines also serve India: Aeroflot, Air Ceylon, Air France, Alitalia, Ariana Afghan, British Airways, ČSA, EAA, EgyptAir, Ethiopian Airlines, Garuda, Gulf Aviation, Iran Air, Iraqi Airways, JAL, KLM, Kuwait Airways, Lufthansa, Pan American, Qantas, Royal Nepal, Sabena, Saudia, SAS, Singapore Airlines, Swissair, Syrian Arab, Thai International and TWA.

TOURISM

Department of Tourism of the Government of India: Ministry of Tourism and Civil Aviation, No. 1 Parliament St., Transport Bhawan, New Delhi; responsible for the formulation and administration of government policy for active promotion of tourist traffic to India, and for planning the organization and development of tourist facilities; regional offices at Delhi, Calcutta, Bombay and Madras; sub-offices at Agra, Aurangabad, Cochin, Jaipur, Jammu, Khajuraho, Varanasi; overseas offices at New York, San Francisco, Chicago, Toronto, London, Geneva, Frankfurt, Paris, Sydney, Brussels, Singapore, Mexico City, Stockholm, Milan, Tokyo, Rio de Janeiro and Vienna. Tourist Promotion Officers at Boston, Washington, Dallas, Miami, Seattle and Detroit.

India Tourism Development Corporation Ltd.: Jeevan Vihar, 3 Parliament St., New Delhi 110001; f. 1966 to promote tourism in India; runs hotels, motels, tourist transport services, duty free shops; production of tourist literature; Chair. and Man. Dir. M. S. SUNDARA.

CULTURAL ORGANIZATIONS

Lalit Kala Akademi (*National Academy of Art*): Rabindra Bhavan, New Delhi 110001; f. 1954; autonomous, government financed; sponsors national and international exhibitions; arranges seminars, lectures, films, etc.; Chair. K. J. KHANDALAVALA; publs. on ancient and modern Indian art; two journals *Lalit Kala* (ancient Indian art, annual), *Lalit Kala Contemporary* (modern art, half-yearly).

Sangeet Natak Akademi: National Academy of Dance, Drama and Music; Rabindra Bhavan, Feroze Shah Rd., New Delhi 110001; f. 1953; autonomous body responsible for promotion and organization of the arts; maintains Asavari, a gallery of musical instruments, Yavanika, a gallery of theatre arts and a listening room for research scholars; Chair. Smt. INDIRA GANDHI; Sec. Dr. SURASH AWASTHI; publs. *Sangeet Natak* (quarterly) and *News Bulletin* (every two months).

Indian Council for Cultural Relations: Azad Bhavan, Indraprastha Estate, New Delhi 110001; f. 1950 to strengthen cultural relations between India and other countries and to promote cultural exchanges.

THEATRE GROUPS

Bharatiya Natya Sangh: 34 New Central Market, New Delhi; Pres. Smt. KAMLADEVI CHATTOPADHYAYA.

Bohurupee: 11-A Nasiruddin Rd., Calcutta 17; Dir. Shri SOMBHU MITRA.

Children's Little Theatre: Aban Mahal, Gariahat Rd., Calcutta 19; f. 1951; Pres. Dr. BIBEK SEN GUPTA; Hon. Gen. Sec. Sri SAMAR CHATTERJEE; publ. *Rhythms & Rhymes*, quarterly.

Little Theatre Group: 6 Beadon St., Calcutta 6; Dir. Shri UPTAL DUTT.

Little Theatre Group: Flat 10, Shankar Market, Connaught Circus, New Delhi; Arts Dir. INDER DASS.

There are fourteen state Academies of Music, Dance and Drama; ten Colleges of Music, sixteen of Dance and Ballet and fourteen other Theatre Institutes, some of which have semi-professional companies.

ATOMIC ENERGY

Atomic Energy Commission: Chhatrapati Shivaji Maharaj Marg, Bombay 400001; organizes research on the release of atomic energy for peaceful purposes; Minister in Charge INDIRA GANDHI; Chair. and Sec. Dept. of Atomic Energy Dr. H. N. SETHNA.

Bhabha Atomic Research Centre (BARC): Trombay, Bombay 400085; f. 1957; national centre for research in and development of atomic energy for peaceful uses; 4 reactors: APSARA (1 MW, research and isotope production), CIRUS (40 MW, research, isotope production and materials testing), ZERLINA (Zero Energy Reactor for Lattice Investigations and New Assemblies); PURNIMA (Zero Energy Plutonium Oxide Fast Reactor); other facilities include a 5.5 MeV Van der Graaff accelerator, radio-chemistry and isotope laboratories, electronics prototype engineering laboratory, isotope production and processing unit, ISOMED —Sterilization Plant for Medical Products, pilot plants for production of heavy water, zirconium, titanium, etc., a Thorium plant, a Uranium metal plant, a fuel element fabrication facility, a fuel reprocessing plant, Food Irradiation and Processing Laboratory (FIPLY), gamma field and library and information services; research laboratories at Guaribidanur and Kashmir, Reactor Research Centre for Fast Reactor Development at Madras, Variable Energy Cyclotron at Calcutta; the centre successfully exploded an underground nuclear device in May 1974 at Pokaran, Rajasthan State; a fifth nuclear reactor R-5 (100 MW, plutonium production) is expected to go critical by 1978; Dir. Dr. RAJA RAMANNA.

Madras Atomic Power Project: Kalpakkam; will consist of two reactor units each of 235 MW capacity; unit I will go critical in mid-1977 and unit II in mid-1979.

Rajasthan Atomic Power Station: Consists of 2 units of 200 MWe each; first unit went critical in August 1972. The second unit will go critical in mid-1976.

Saha Institute of Nuclear Physics: 92 Acharya Prafulla Chandra Rd., Calcutta 700009; f. 1950; Dir. Prof. D. N. KUNDU.

Tarapur Atomic Power Station: Tarapur, Maharashtra; a 420 MW nuclear power station became operational in October 1969.

Tata Institute of Fundamental Research: Homi Bhabha Rd., Bombay 400005; f. 1945; fundamental research in nuclear science, theoretical physics, nuclear and solid state physics, solid state electronics, hydrology, cosmic rays and high energy physics, computer science and technology, molecular biology, radio astronomy, chemical physics and in mathematics; national research centre of the Government of India; Dir. B. V. SREEKANTAN.

Indian Space Research Organization (ISRO): F-Block, CBAB Complex, District Office Rd., Bangalore 560 009; f. 1969; scientific satellite launched in 1975 with Soviet aid; Chair. Prof. S. DHAWAN; Scientific Sec. Prof. P. D. BHAVSAR.

Indian National Committee for Space Research (INCOSPAR): c/o ISRO, F-Block, Cauvery Bhavan, District Office Rd., Bangalore 560009; f. 1962; Chair. Prof. S. DHAWAN; Sec. Prof. P. D. BHAVSAR.

In May 1974 India exploded its first nuclear device.

Institute of Nuclear Medicine and Allied Sciences: Probyn Rd., Delhi 110007; f. 1963; run by Research and Development Organization of the Ministry of Defence; carries out investigation into anaemia, Parkinson's disease, liver and kidney diseases, thyroid disorders; undertakes research in health physics, clinical biochemistry, radiation entomology and experimental medicine; also trains physicians and technicians in nuclear medicine; Dir. Col. S. K. MAZUMDAR, M.B., B.S., M.R.C.P.

In addition to Tarapur Atomic Power Station, already operating, two stations with two reactors of 200/235 MWe capacity each are under construction at Kota (Rajasthan) and Kalpakkam (Tamil Nadu). Another station at Narora (U.P.) will come into operation in 1981/2.

DEFENCE

Armed Forces: (1975) Total strength 956,000; army 826,000, navy 30,000, air force 100,000; there is also a Border Security Force of 100,000; military service is voluntary.

Equipment: In addition to its own *Vijayanta* tanks the army has British and Soviet tanks and British guns. The navy includes Soviet submarines and the air force includes British, French and Soviet planes.

Defence Budget: The defence budget for 1975–76 is Rs. 22,740m. (U.S. $2,660m.).

CHIEFS OF STAFF

Commander-in-Chief of the Army: Gen. TAPISHWAR NARAIN RAINA.

Commander-in-Chief of the Navy: Admiral JAL CURSETJI.

Commander-in-Chief of the Air Force: Air Marshal HRISHIKESH MOOLGAVKAR.

EDUCATION

Under the Constitution, education in India is primarily the responsibility of the individual State Governments, although the Government of India has several direct responsibilities, some specified in the Constitution, as for example, responsibility for the Central Universities, all higher institutions, promotion and propagation of Hindi, co-ordination and maintenance of higher education standards, scientific and technological research and welfare of Indian students abroad.

Education in India is administered at the centre by the Ministry of Education which is headed by a Union Minister of Education who is assisted by two Deputy Ministers. At State level, there is an Education Minister assisted by an Education Secretariat or in certain instances, by a Minister of State/Deputy Minister. Under the Five-Year Plan which began in 1969, priority has been given to an expansion in elementary and community education as well as in education for girls. Improvements are to be effected in teacher training and science education; standards are to be raised in postgraduate education and research; a reorganization of Polytechnic education and the development of Hindi and of textbook production are to take place. About Rs. 19,000 million was allocated for education in 1975. There are now facilities for free lower primary education in the age group 6–11 in all the States. Education in the upper primary stage is also free in twelve States.

Elementary Education: In lower primary classes (6–11 age-group) the total number of pupils increased from 48 million in 1965 to 64 million in 1975. Enrolment in higher primary classes (age-group 11–14) in 1975 was 15.2 million or 36 per cent of the age-group population. Similarly the number of primary schools has risen from about 387,963 in 1965 to 443,461 in 1975 and at the end of 1975 there were 1,230,470 teachers.

Basic Education: The notable characteristic of elementary education in India is the use of what is known as basic education. There is an activity-centred curriculum which correlates teaching with the physical and social environment of the child. Education is imparted through socially useful, productive activities such as spinning, weaving, gardening, leather work, book craft, domestic crafts, pottery, elementary engineering, etc. The emphasis at present is on introducing important features of basic education in non-basic schools. Basic education is the national pattern of all elementary education and all elementary schools will ultimately be brought over to the basic system. Twenty per cent already have, and the rest are gradually being converted under the "orientation" system which consists of programmes for teachers to reduce the differences between basic and non-basic education.

Secondary Education: Education at this level is provided for those at between the ages of 14 and 17. Many State Governments have taken steps to reorganize secondary schools, resulting in great expansion between 1965 and 1975. In 1975 there were 102,083 such schools with 8.2 million pupils and 741,240 teachers.

Most schools follow what is known as the "three language formula" which comprises teaching of: (1) the regional dialect, (2) Hindi, (3) English. Much emphasis is now also being laid on physical training, which has become a compulsory subject, particularly at secondary school level in conjunction with the programme of the National Fitness Corps.

Higher Education: The Universities are for the most part autonomous as regards administration. The Inter-University Board was founded in 1925 for the discussion of university problems. The University Grants Commission is responsible for the promotion and co-ordination of University Education and has the authority to make appropriate grants and to implement development schemes.

India had by 1975 a total of 120 universities, including 9 institutions with university status and some 8,000 university and affiliated colleges. There were 2.9 million students following courses of higher education and a total of 692,918 high and higher secondary school teachers in 1975.

Higher Technical Education: In 1975 there were 110 engineering and technology degree colleges with 21,235 students, and 43,380 students at diploma level.

Rural Higher Education: On the recommendation of the Rural Higher Education Committee, a National Council for higher education in rural areas was established in 1953 to advise the Government on all matters relating to the development of rural higher education. The Council has selected 14 institutions for development into rural institutes, some of which have already started functioning and their diplomas have been recognized.

Social Education: provides an educational base for community development programmes in the country, and includes eradication of illiteracy, education in citizenship, cultural and recreational activities and organization of youth and women's groups for community development.

Teachers' Training: There were 1,572 teacher training institutes in 1975. The percentage of trained teachers in primary, middle and high/higher secondary schools increased from 68.4, 74.6 and 67.9 in 1965 to 83.3, 85.3 and 79.2 in 1975 respectively.

UNIVERSITIES

Agra University: Agra 4, U.P.; 88,910 students.

University of Agricultural Sciences: Hebbal, Bangalore, Karnataka 560024; 150 teachers, 2,500 students.

Aligarh Muslim University: Aligarh, U.P.; 816 teachers, 9,555 students.

University of Allahabad: Allahabad 2, U.P.; 11,583 students.

Guru Nanak University of Amritsar: Amritsar, Punjab; 44,471 students.

Andhra University: Waltair, A.P.; 528 teachers, 76,489 students.

Andhra Pradesh Agricultural University: Rajendranagar, Hyderabad 500030, A.P.; 245 teachers, 2,036 students.

Annamalai University: Annamalainagar P.O., Tamil Nadu State; 306 teachers, 5,260 students.

Assam Agricultural University: Jorhat 4, Assam; 711 students.

Awadhesh Pratap Singh University: Rewa, M.P.; *c.* 17,500 students.

Banaras Hindu University: Varanasi 5, U.P.; 1,068 teachers, 14,000 students.

Bangalore University: Bangalore 1, Karnataka State; 1,960 teachers, 41,900 students.

The Maharaja Sayajirao University of Baroda: Vadodara (Baroda), Gujarat; 828 teachers, 17,936 students.

Berhampur University: Ganjam, Orissa; 46 teachers, 398 students.

Bhagalpur University: Bhagalpur, Bihar 812007; 1,569 teachers, 42,667 students.

Bhopal University: Habibganj, Bhopal 6; 612 teachers, 13,875 students.

University of Bihar: Sahnaya Bhavan, Muzaffarpur, Bihar; 54,971 students.

University of Bombay: Bombay 400032; 103,262 students.

University of Burdwan: Burdwan, West Bengal; 1,960 teachers, 60,577 students.

University of Calcutta: Calcutta, West Bengal 700032; 40 professors, 196,257 students.

University of Calicut: University P.O., Kerala; 72 teachers, 254 students.

University of Cochin: P.O. Tripunithura, Kerala; 618 students.

University of Delhi: Delhi 110007; 50 professors, 97,247 students.

Dibrugarh University: Rajabheta, Dibrugarh, Assam; 1,352 teachers, 25,302 students.

Gauhati University: Gauhati 14, Assam; 2,657 teachers, 59,866 students.

Gorakhpur University: Gorakhpur, U.P.; 206 teachers, 42,524 students.

Govind Ballabh Pant University of Agriculture and Technology: Nainital, U.P.; 306 teachers, 2,068 students.

Gujarat Ayurved University: Jamnagar, Gujarat; 2,599 students.

Gujarat University: Navrangpura, Ahmedabad 380009, Gujarat; 74,849 students in affiliated colleges.

Haryana Agricultural University: Hissar, Haryana; 1,115 students.

Himachal Pradesh University: Summer Hill, Simla 5,228 teachers, 4,230 students.

Indira Kala Sangeet University: Khairagarh, M.P.; 267 teachers, 5,400 students.

University of Indore: Indore 452001, M.P.; 817 teachers, 17,511 students.

Jabalpur University: Jabalpur, M.P.; 683 teachers, 18,345 students.

Jadavpur University: Calcutta 32; 474 teachers, 4,113 students.

Jamia Millia Islamia: New Delhi 110025; 201 teachers, 2,262 students.

University of Jammu: Canal Rd., Jammu; 10,332 students.

Jawaharlal Nehru Krishi Vishwa Vidyalala (Jawaharlal Nehru Agricultural University): Krishnagar, Jabalpur 4, M.P.

Jawaharlal Nehru University: New Delhi 57; 240 teachers, 2,084 students.

Jawaharlal Nehru Technological University: Hyderabad, A.P.

Jiwaji University: Vdihya Vihar, Gwalior 2, M.P.; 708 teachers, 33,931 students.

University of Jodhpur: Rajasthan; 571 teachers, 11,062 students.

Kalyani University: P.O. Kalyani Dt. Nadia, West Bengal; 1,964 students.

Kameshwara Singh Darbhagha Sanskrit University: Darbhagha, Bihar; 18,000 students.

Kanpur University: Kalyanpur, Kanpur 18; 129 teachers, 921 students.

Karnatak University: Dharwar, Mysore; 48,799 students

University of Kashmir: Hazratbal, Srinagar 6; 957 teachers, 13,475 students.

University of Kerala: Trivandrum, Kerala; 138,695 students.

Kurukshetra University: Kurukshetra, Punjab; 475 teachers, 5,362 students.

University of Lucknow: Badshaw Bagh, Lucknow, U.P.; 597 teachers, 26,186 students.

University of Madras: Chepauk, Triplicane P.O., Madras 600005, Tamil Nadu; 153,828 students.

Madurai University: Madurai 625021, Tamil Nadu; 65 teachers, 64,086 students.

Magadh University: Bodhgaya, Bihar; 64,838 students.

Marathwada University: Aurangabad (Deccan), Maharashtra; 2,001 teachers, 53,163 students.

Mahatma Phule Agricultural University: Maharashtra; 533 students.

Marathwada Agricultural University: Parbhani, Maharashtra.

Meerut University: Meerut, U.P.; 51,134 students.

Mithila University: Darbhanga, Bihar; 10,380 students.

University of Mysore: P.O.B. 14, Mysore 5; 95,154 students.

University of Nagpur: Nagpur, Maharashtra; 4,124 teachers, 98,328 students.

University of North Bengal: Raja Rammohanpur, Darjeeling, West Bengal; 16,812 students.

Orissa University of Agriculture and Technology: Bhubaneswar 3, District Puri, Orissa; 144 teachers, 1,313 students.

Osmania University: Hyderabad, 500007, A.P.; 54 professors, 62,061 students.

University of Patna: Patna 800005, Bihar; 12,605 students.

University of Poona: Ganeshkhind, Pune (Poona) 7; 96,768 students.

Punjab University: Chandigarh 14; 138,491 students (incl. affiliated colleges).

Punjab Agricultural University: Ludhiana, Punjab 141004.

Punjabi University: Patiala 4, Punjab; 25,000 students.

Rabindra Bharati University: Calcutta 700007; 214 teachers, 4,260 students.

University of Rajasthan: Gandhi Nagar, Jaipur 4; 509 teachers, 14,598 students.

Rajendra Agricultural University: Samastipur, Bihar.

Ranchi University: Ranchi-1, Bihar; 1,571 teachers, 41,087 students.

Ravishankar University: Raipur, M.P.; 26,343 students.

University of Roorkee: Roorkee, U.P.; 284 teachers, 1,926 students.

Sambalpur University: Sambalpur, Orissa; 1,035 teachers, 15,900 students.

Sadar Patel University: Vallabh Vidyanagar, Gujarat; 553 teachers, 14,850 students.

University of Saugar: Sagar, M.P.; 18,600 students.

Saurashtra University: Rajkot 1, Gujarat, 32,507 students.

Shivaji University: Vidyanagar, Kolhapur 4, Maharashtra 416004; 2,641 teachers, 77,954 students.

Shreemati Nathibai Damodar Thackersey Women's University: 1 Nathibal Thackersey Rd., Bombay 400020; 663 teachers, 20,534 students.

South Gujarat University: Surat, Gujarat; 985 teachers, 31,989 students.

Sri Venkateswara University: Tirupati, A.P.; 2,335 teachers, 22,820 students.

Tamil Nadu Agricultural University: P.O. Coimbatore 3, Tamil Nadu; 959 students.

University of Udaipur: Udaipur, Rajasthan; 396 teachers, 8,605 students.

Utkal University: Vani Vihar, Bhubaneswar 4; 1,673 teachers, 33,190 students.

Varanaseya-Sanskrit University: Varanasi 2, U.P.; 28,000 students (incl. affiliated colleges).

Vikram University: Ujjain, M.P.; 26,401 students.

Visva-Bharati: P.O. Santiniketan, District of Birbhum, West Bengal; 254 teachers, 1,366 students.

BIBLIOGRAPHY

GENERAL

BASHAM, A L. The Wonder that was India (Revised edn., Hawthorn, New York, 1963).

BOURKE-WHITE, M. Interview With India (Phoenix House, London, 1950).

GRIFFITHS, Sir PERCIVAL. Modern India (Ernest Benn, London, 4th edn., 1965).

JOHNSON, B. L. C. South Asia (Heinemann, London, 1969).

MOON, PENDEREL. Strangers in India (Faber and Faber, London, 1944).

O'MALLEY, L. S. S. Modern India and the West (Oxford University Press, London, 1941).

SINGH, R. L. (Editor). India: Regional Studies (for 21st Int. Geog. Congress by Indian Nat. Cttee. for Geog., Calcutta, 1968).

SPATE, O. H. K. and LEARMONTH, A. T. A. India and Pakistan (3rd edn., Methuen, London, 1967).

SPEAR, PERCIVAL. India, Pakistan and the West (Oxford University Press, London and New York, 3rd edn., 1958).

HISTORY AND POLITICS

AHMAD, AZIZ. Islamic Modernization in India and Pakistan 1857–1964 (Oxford University Press, London and New York, 1966).

AZAD, ABDUL KALAM. India Wins Freedom (Orient Longmans, Bombay, 1959).

AUSTIN, GRANVILLE. The Indian Constitution: Cornerstone of a Nation (Oxford University Press, London, 1966).

BHATKAL, RAMDAS G. (Editor). Political Alternatives in India (Popular Prakashan, Bombay, 1967).

BRASS, PAUL R. Language, Religion and Politics in North India (London, Cambridge University Press, 1975).

BRECHER, MICHAEL. Nehru: A Political Biography (Oxford University Press, London, 1959).

BROWN, W. NORMAN. The United States and India and Pakistan (Harvard University Press, Cambridge, Mass., 1953).

CHAVDA, V. K. India, Britain, Russia: A Study in British Opinion 1838–1878 (Sterling Publishers, Delhi; C. Hurst, London).

COUPLAND, R. India: a Re-statement (Oxford University Press, London, 1945).

CURRAN, J. A., Jr. Militant Hinduism in Indian Politics: A Story of the R.S.S. (Institute of Pacific Relations, New York, 1951).

DERRETT, J. DUNCAN M. Religion, Law and the State in India (Faber and Faber, London).

EDWARDES, MICHAEL. British India 1772–1947 (Sidgwick and Jackson, London, 1967).

ERDMAN, HOWARD L. The Swatantra Party and Indian Conservatism (Cambridge University Press, 1967).

GARRATT, G. T. (Editor). The Legacy of India (Oxford University Press, New York and London, 1937).

GLEDHILL, ALAN. The Republic of India: The Development of its Laws and Constitution (Stevens, London, 1952).

GRIFFITHS, Sir PERCIVAL. The British Impact on India (Macdonald, London, 1952).

GUPTA, K. The Hidden History of the Sino-Indian Frontier (Calcutta, Minerva Associates, 1974).

KARUNAKARAN, K. P. Continuity and Change in Indian Politics: a study of the Indian National Congress (People's Publishing House, New Delhi, 1964).

LAWRENCE, Sir WALTER. The India We Served (Cassell, London, 1928).

LUMBY, E. W. R. The Transfer of Power in India (Allen and Unwin, London, 1954).

MANSERGH, NICHOLA (Ed.). India: The Transfer of Power, 1942–47, 3 vols. (H.M.S.O., London, 1970–71).

MASANI, R. P. Britain in India (Oxford University Press, New York and Bombay, 1960).

MASON, PHILIP (Editor). India and Ceylon: Unity and Diversity (Oxford University Press, London, 1967).

MAXWELL, NEVILLE. India's China War (London, 1970).

MELLOR, ANDREW. India Since Partition (Turnstile Press, London, 1951).

MENON, V. P. The Integration of the Indian States (Orient Longmans, Bombay, 1956).

The Transfer of Power in India (Orient Longmans, Bombay, 1957).

MORAES, FRANK. India Today (The Macmillan Co., New York, 1960).

MUJEEB, M. The Indian Muslims (Allen and Unwin, London, 1967).

MUKHERJEE, S. N. Sir William Jones. British Attitudes to India in the Eighteenth Century (Cambridge University Press, 1967).

MURTY, K. SATCHIDANANDA (Editor). Readings in Indian History, Politics and Philosophy (Allen and Unwin, London).

OVERSTREET, G. D. and WINDMILLER, M. Communism in India (University of California Press, Berkeley, Calif., 1959).

PALMER, NORMAN D. The Indian Political System (Houghton Mifflin, Boston, 1962).

PANIKKAR, K. M. A Survey of Indian History (Asia Publishing House, Bombay, 1956).

PARK, RICHARD L. and TINKER, IRENE (Editors). Leadership and Political Institutions in India (Princeton University Press, New Jersey, 1959).

PHILIPS, C. H. Politics and Society in India (Praeger, New York, 1962).

PRASAD, BIMLA. The Origins of Indian Foreign Policy (Bookland, Calcutta, 1960).

PRASAD, RAJENDRA. India Divided (Hind Kitabs, Bombay, 1946).

SEAL, ANIL. The Emergence of Indian Nationalism (Cambridge University Press, 1967).

SHUKLA, SATYENDRA R. SIKKIM. The story of Integration (S. Chand & Co. (Pvt.) Ltd., New Delhi, 1976).

SMITH, D. E. India as a Secular State (Princeton University Press, New Jersey, 1963).

SMITH, D. E. (Editor). South Asian Politics and Religion (Princeton University Press, New Jersey).

SMITH, VINCENT A. The Oxford History of India (Clarendon Press, Oxford, 3rd edn., 1923).

SPEAR, PERCIVAL. India, A Modern History (University of Michigan Press, Ann Arbor, 1961).

TINKER, HUGH. Experiment with Freedom: India and Pakistan, 1947 (Oxford University Press, London, 1967).

India and Pakistan: A Political Analysis (Pall Mall Press, London, 2nd edn., 1967).

South Asia: A Short History (Pall Mall Press, London, 1966).

WEINER, MYRON (Editor). State Politics in India (Oxford University Press, London).

Party Politics in India: The Development of a Multi-Party System (Princeton University Press, New Jersey, 1957).

ZINKIN, TAYA. Challenges in India (Chatto and Windus, London, 1966).

SOCIAL LIFE

GANDHI, MOHANDAS K. Basic Education (Navajivan, Ahmedabad, 1951).

HAY, STEPHEN, WEILER, ROYAL and YARROW, ANDREW. Sources of Indian Tradition (Columbia University Press, New York, 1958).

HUSAIN, ABID. National Culture of India (Asia Publishing House, New York, 2nd edn., 1961).

HUTTON, J. H. Caste in India (Oxford University Press, London, 3rd edn., 1961).

KANUNGO, G. BEHARI. The Language Controversy in Indian Education (University of Chicago Press, Chicago, 1962).

LAMB, BEATRICE. India, a World in Transition (Praeger, New York, 1963).

MEHTA, G. L. Understanding India (Asia Publishing House, New York, 1962).

NARASIMHAN, V. A., *et al.* (Editors). The Languages of India (Varadachari, Madras, 1958).

NATARAJAN, S. A History of the Press in India (Asia Publishing House, Bombay, 1962).

RENOU, LOUIS. The Nature of Hinduism (Walker, New York, 1951).

ART AND CULTURE

AMBROSE, KAY. Classical Dances and Costumes of India (Black, London, 1950).

BOWERS, FAUBION. The Dance in India (Columbia University Press, New York, 1953).

BROWN, PERCY. Indian Architecture (Taraporevala, Bombay, 2 Vols., 1942).

COOMARASWAMY, ANANDA K. The Arts and Crafts of India and Ceylon (Foulis, London, 1913).

DUBOIS, JEAN ANTOINE. Hindu Manners, Customs and Ceremonies (Clarendon Press, Oxford, 3rd edn., 1906).

GANGOLY, O. C. Indian Architecture (Kutub, Bombay, 1946).

GOPAL, RAM and SEROZH, DADACHANJI. Indian Dancing (Phoenix House, London, 1951).

GUPTA, CHANDRA BHAN. Indian Theatre (Motilal Banar sidass, Benares, 1953).

KRAMRISCH, STELLA. The Art of India (Phaidon, New York 1954).

OMAN, JOHN CAMPBELL. The Brahmans, Theists and Muslims of India (Unwin, London, 2nd edn., 1907).

Cults, Customs and Superstitions of India (Unwin, London, 1908).

POPLEY, HERBERT A. The Music of India (Y.M.C.A. Calcutta, 2nd edn., 1950).

RAO, RAMACHANDRA. Modern Indian Painting (Rachana, Madras, 1953).

ZIMMER, HEINRICH. The Philosophies of India (Pantheon, New York, 1951).

ECONOMY

BASU, S. K. Studies in Economic Problems (Asia Publishing House, Bombay, 1965).

BAUER, P. T. Indian Economic Policy and Development (Allen and Unwin, London; Praeger, New York, 1961).

BHATT, V. V. Aspects of Economic Change and Policy in India, 1800–1960 (Allied Publishers, Bombay, 1962).

DUTT, R. C. Economic History of India (Publications Division, Delhi, 1960).

EPSTEIN, T. A. Economic Development and Social Change in South India (Oxford University Press, Bombay, 1962).

ETIENNE, GILBERT (translation by MOTHERSOLE, MEGAN). Studies in Indian Agriculture: the Art of the Possible (University of California Press, Berkeley, Calif., 1968).

FARMER, B. H. Agricultural Colonization in India since Independence (Oxford University Press, 1975).

GYAN, CHAND. The Socialist Transformation of the Indian Economy (Allen and Unwin, London, 1965).

HANSON, A. H. The Process of Planning: A Study of India's Five-Year Plans 1950–1964 (Oxford University Press, London, 1966).

KARNIK, V. B. Indian Trade Unions: A Survey (Manaktalas, Bombay, 1966).

MASON, EDWARD S. Economic Development in India and Pakistan: Occasional papers in International Affairs No. 13 (Harvard University Center for International Affairs, 1966).

RAO, V. K. R. V. and NARAIN, DHARM. Foreign Aid and India's Economic Development (Asia Publishing House, London, 1964).

ROSEN, G. Democracy and Economic Change in India (Cambridge University Press for University of California Press, 2nd. edn., 1967).

STREETEN, P. and LIPTON, M. (Editors). The Crisis of Indian Planning (Oxford University Press, London, 1968).

TURNER, R. (Editor). India's Urban Future (University of California Press, Berkeley and Los Angeles, Calif.; Cambridge University Press, London, 1962).

ZINKIN, MAURICE and WARD, BARBARA. Why Help India? (Pergamon Press, London, 1963).

Maldives

PHYSICAL AND SOCIAL GEOGRAPHY

B. H. Farmer

The Maldive Islands, long a British Protectorate, became an independent sultanate in 1965 and a republic in 1968. The name was changed in 1969 to the Republic of Maldives. They constitute a group of over 1,000 islands, strung out from north to south 400–500 miles south-west of Sri Lanka, and stretching from just north of the Equator to about 8° North latitude. Some 200 islands are inhabited; they support about 130,000 people of whom about a tenth live in the capital (Malé).

The Maldives rest on a submarine ridge, which may be volcanic in origin. They are grouped into nineteen atolls (rings of coral islands, each ring encircling a lagoon: the word *atoll* is itself, in fact, Maldivian). All of the islands are built entirely of coral, coral sand, and other coral detritus. The climate is similar to that of Colombo (see under *Sri Lanka*). Most of the islands are covered with coconut palms.

The Maldivians are thought to be of mixed descent, deriving from South Indians (Dravidians), Sinhalese and Arabs. They speak a language related to Sinhala, but are Muslim by religion.

HISTORY

It was in the twelfth century that the islanders adopted the Muslim religion, and the fourteenth century saw the first description of conditions there, recorded by Ibn Batutah, Arab traveller and historian. The ruler was a Sultan of the-ad-Din (Didi) dynasty. However, long before the extinction of the Sultanate in 1968, the Didi rank had been receding in importance in respect of the leadership of the country. The Portuguese, in their rapid and widespread colonization during the sixteenth century, established themselves on the islands in 1518, but stayed for only about ten years. In the seventeenth century the islands came under the protection of the Dutch rulers of Ceylon. When the British took possession of Ceylon in the late eighteenth century, they extended their protection to the Maldive Islands, and this was formally recorded in an agreement in 1887.

When Ceylon became independent in 1948, a new agreement provided that Britain should control the foreign affairs of the islands but should not interfere internally. The Sultan undertook to provide necessary facilities to British forces for the defence of the islands.

In 1956 the Maldivian and British governments agreed to the establishment of a Royal Air Force staging post on Gan, an island in the southernmost atoll, Addu. The Maldivian Government accorded free and unrestricted use by the United Kingdom Government of Gan Island and of 110 acres of Hittadu Island, for a radio station. Another agreement was signed in 1960, under which the Maldivian Government entrusted Gan and the demarcated area on Hittadu as a free gift to the United Kingdom, together with the free use of Addu lagoon and the adjacent territorial waters, for a period of thirty years—this period to be extendable by agreement. However, the British Government decided to close this base in 1975 and completed the evacuation of the Royal Air Force in March 1976.

Independence was achieved on July 26th, 1965. Maldives became a composite, sovereign and fully independent state, possessing all rights to conduct her own external relations with all other countries. Under the new agreement the British government retained those facilities in Addu Atoll accorded to them in 1960 for purposes of Commonwealth defence. The British Government also undertook to pay the Maldivian Government £100,000, with a further £750,000 spread over five years or more, for economic development. The Islands have been a member of the Colombo Plan since 1963 and of the United Nations since December 1965.

Constitutional Change, 1968

Maldives (as the island group is now designated) forms a completely Islamic state. An elected Sultan was head of state until 11 November 1968, when a republic was proclaimed. This constitutional change had been approved by nearly 81 per cent of those who voted in a referendum held throughout the islands in March 1968.

Under the pre-republican constitution, introduced in 1954 and amended in 1964 and 1967, the Sultan was elected for life by a special national convention. The entire administration of the state was carried out by the Prime Minister, assisted by his Cabinet. Members of the Cabinet were responsible to a *Majlis* of 54 members, eight of whom were nominated by the Sultan; the remainder were elected by adult suffrage in Malé and the nineteen atolls. The term of office for the Prime Minister and members of the Cabinet was the same as that of the *Majlis*—that is, five years; the Prime Minister was appointed by the Sultan on the recommendation of the *Majlis*.

The major provisions of the republican constitution are that executive power is vested in the President, the head of state, who is popularly elected every five years; he is assisted by a cabinet chosen by himself; cabinet ministers are individually responsible to the *Majlis*, elected every five years (further details are given below under *Constitution*).

In March 1975 the Prime Minister, Ahmed Zaki, was arrested and banished in a bloodless *coup* by President Amir Ibrahim Nasir who took over the duties of Prime Minister.

ECONOMIC SURVEY

Fishing

The economy of Maldives has a narrow base, being almost totally dependent on fisheries for its export earnings. Fishing is the basic industry; the male population of the islands engage themselves in this traditional daily occupation, and the catch mainly consists of bonito and tuna. This is cooked and cured and exported in a dried form, and known in the region as Maldive fish. This is the basic money-earner for the Maldivians, who find a ready market for it in Sri Lanka.

There are several thousand fishing boats built in the country out of coconut wood, each boat taking about a dozen fishermen. Using sails they go out to a distance of fifteen to twenty miles from the shores, depending on the prevailing winds and currents. Provided a good shoal is encountered, the daily catch per boat exceeds 500 and may be as much as 1,500. In mid-1975 the Government started mechanizing the local fishing vessels; diesel engines have been installed in more than a hundred sailing boats.

Other Economic Activities

The second largest commercial industry of the country is more an agricultural one—coconut, copra and coconut oil production. Although a major part of Maldivian daily diet comprises coconut, substantial quantities of copra are exported annually, particularly to the eastern ports of southern India.

The third principal occupation is coir yarn weaving, in which only women are engaged. In spite of several centuries of continued production of this commodity, the methods in use have not undergone much change; the women do the work in their own homes.

Collecting cowries is another occupation in which only women take part. Cowries and other varieties of shells are a natural product meant solely for export, and not generally used for any domestic purpose. Many varieties of shells in demand by collectors are found in Maldives, including some of the rarest in the world.

Mat weaving is another small-scale cottage industry, principally for women. Mats are woven out of a particular type of reed and then dried in the sun; most of the mat weaving is done in the three southernmost atolls of the archipelago. Beautiful colours are incorporated and some of the mats have commercial value abroad.

There is a small-scale cottage industry, which prevails throughout the islands, of applying lacquer as a design on vases and other containers. Finally, cadjan weaving is quite common in the islands; both men and women are engaged in this work. Cadjan is much in demand because of its value for roofing purposes, the heat of the tropical sun being reduced considerably by its use.

STATISTICAL SURVEY

Area: the archipelago consists of 19 atolls, comprising about 1,200 islands of which 203 are inhabited; the total area is 20,000 square miles, including lagoons. The land area is 298 square km. (115 square miles).

Population (1974): 128,697. The population of the capital, Malé, was 16,246.

Births and deaths (1975): 5,232 registered births; 1,539 registered deaths (including stillbirths).

Employment: Fishing, copra-production, and making coir yarn.

Agriculture: Coconut palms, papaya, screwpine, pomegranates, pineapples, some citrus fruit, plantains, breadfruit, sweet potatoes, millet, cassava, sorghum, maize, onions, chillies and yams.

Fishing: (1974): 92,517 cwt.

Currency: 100 larees=1 Maldivian rupee. Exchange rates (June 1976): £1 sterling=15.25 rupees; U.S. $1=8.60 rupees; 100 Maldivian rupees=£6.56=$11.63.

Budget: Government Expenditure (1975) 25,153,242 rupees.

Exports (1974—cwt.): dried fish 69,777; fresh fish 91,573; fresh white fish 944; other varieties of dried fish and fish products 6,865; cowries, redstones, tortoise shells 1,394. The total value of exports was Maldivian Rs. 15,566,723.

The entire output of Maldive fish is sold to the Sri Lanka Government and to the Marubeni Fishing Corporation of Japan.

Imports: Total value of imports (1975) 26,532,909 Maldivian rupees.

Transport: International shipping (metric tons): 2,133 loaded; 16,569 unloaded in 1975.

Communications (1975): radio licences issued 2,727.

Education (1975): Nursery: 16 teachers, 439 pupils; Primary and secondary: 60 teachers, 1,455 pupils.

THE CONSTITUTION

A referendum was held throughout Maldives in March 1968 to ascertain what form of government was desired by the Maldivians. Over 80 per cent of those who voted approved a proposal to establish a republic in place of the constitution of the Sultanate, which was introduced in 1954 and amended in June 1964 and July 1967. The Republic of Maldives was proclaimed on November 11th, 1968. The main provisions of the republican constitution are:

1. The Head of State is the President and he is vested with certain executive powers.

2. The President is elected by a popular vote every five years.
3. The President appoints a Cabinet.
4. The members of the Cabinet are individually responsible to the *Majlis*, or the elected legislature.
5. The powers of the President, the Cabinet and the legislature are laid down in the Constitution.

THE GOVERNMENT

(*July* 1976)

HEAD OF STATE

President and Prime Minister: AMIR IBRAHIM NASIR, N.G.I.V., R.B.K.

Vice-Presidents: ABDUL SATTAR FAMULADEIRI KILEGEFAN, AHMED HILMY FASHANA KILEGEFAN, IBRAHIM SHIHAB, ALI UMAR MANIKU, HASSAN ZAREER.

THE CABINET

Minister of Justice: MOOSA FATHHI.

Minister of Health: IBRAHIM RASHEED.

Minister of Public Safety: ABDUL HANNAN DOSHIMEINA KILEGEFAN.

Attorney-General: ADNAN HUSSAIN.

LEGISLATURE

MAJLIS

Comprises 48 members, of whom 8 are nominated by the President, 2 elected by the people of Malé and 2 elected from each of the 19 administrative districts.

Speaker: AHMED SHATHIR.

DIPLOMATIC REPRESENTATION

There are no resident diplomatic missions in Maldives. The following countries maintain diplomatic relations with the Republic of Maldives. In most cases the missions are in Sri Lanka: Australia, Burma, the People's Republic of China, Czechoslovakia, Egypt, France, the German Democratic Republic, the Federal Republic of Germany, Hungary, India, Indonesia, Iraq, Israel, Italy, Japan, the Democratic People's Republic of Korea, the Republic of Korea, Libya, Malaysia, Mexico, New Zealand, Pakistan, the Philippines, Singapore, Sri Lanka, the U.S.S.R., the United Kingdom, the U.S.A., Viet-Nam and Yugoslavia.

LAW AND RELIGION

The administration of justice is based on the Islamic Law of Shariat.

Islam is the State religion. The Maldivians are Sunni Muslims.

FINANCE

The State Bank of India and Habib Bank Ltd. have offices in Maldives.

TRANSPORT

SHIPPING

Powered vessels operate between Maldives and Sri Lanka at frequent intervals. They also call at other ports in India, Pakistan, Burma, Singapore and some Middle Eastern ports. Ships range from 800 to 3,000 tons.

CIVIL AVIATION

An airport is under construction on the island of Hululé, about a mile from the capital island, Malé.

Recently Maldives has established a state-owned airline, Air Maldives, and air transport, both for passenger and freight, is now conducted on a regular basis between Colombo and Malé. Air Ceylon and Air India flights also serve Maldives.

Nepal

PHYSICAL AND SOCIAL GEOGRAPHY

B. H. Farmer

Nepal is situated between the high Himalayas and the Ganges Plains, between India and China's Tibetan territory. It occupies about 139,860 square kilometres (54,000 square miles) and extends from 26° 20′ to 30° 10′ north latitude, and from 80° 15′ to 88° 15′ east longitude.

PHYSICAL FEATURES

Nepal's southernmost physical region is the Terai which, like the similar region in India, is a belt of low-lying plain, highly liable to flooding during the monsoon. North of it rise the Himalayas system. A series of transverse or more complex valleys break up the simple pattern of parallel ranges, and one of these, the Valley of Nepal, contains the capital, Kathmandu.

CLIMATE

It is difficult to be at all precise about the climate in the absence of accurate data. It would seem, however, that it exemplifies two main tendencies. In the first place, temperatures, for obvious reason, decrease as one moves from the Terai through the foothills and internal valleys to higher Himalayan ranges. At Kathmandu, 1,337 metres (4,388 ft.) above sea level, average monthly temperatures are 10°C. (50°F.) in January and 23°C. (73°F.) in May. In January the average daily maximum is 18°C. (65°F.) and the average minimum 2°C. (35°F.). In the highest Himalaya, of course, air temperatures are always below freezing point. In the second place, rainfall, other things being equal, tends to decrease from east to west, as it does, of course, in the Indian plains below. Eastern Nepal receives about 250 cm. (100 inches) per year; Kathmandu, 42 cm. (56 inches); and western Nepal about 100 cm. (40 inches).

SOILS AND NATURAL RESOURCES

There is little reliable scientific information on soils. As in corresponding parts of the Indian Himalaya, soils are likely to be skeletal, thin and poor on steep slopes (except where improved artificially under terraced cultivation); and better soils are probably confined to valley bottoms and interior basins, and to the Terai.

There has been a great deal of clearing for cultivation in the Terai, in interior valleys like the Valley of Nepal, and on lower hillsides. But over wide areas text-book examples of altitudinal zonation may be seen: tropical moist deciduous forests to 4,000 ft. (1,200 metres) or so; moist hill pine forests from 4,000 to 8,500 ft. (2,600 metres) or so; coniferous forests from 8,500 ft. to about 11,000 ft. (3,350 metres), alpine vegetation beginning at the latter altitude.

In Nepal, the only mineral so far discovered in significant quantities is mica, mined east of Kathmandu. There are local workings of lignite in the outermost range of mountains, and small deposits of copper, cobalt and iron ore. Raw materials exist for cement manufacture.

POPULATION AND ETHNIC GROUPS

At the census in June 1971 Nepal had a population of 11,556,000. At June 1974 the estimated population was 12,321,000. The population is unevenly distributed, with fairly dense clusters and ribbons along the valleys and in the Terai, a scatter of isolated upland settlements, and great empty spaces at high altitude.

In Nepal there are a number of tribes of Mongoloid appearance speaking Tibeto-Burman languages, for example Gurungs, Magars and Bhotiyas. There are also Gurkhas who claim Rajput origin, Newars in the Valley of Nepal and recent Indian immigrants in the Terai.

HISTORY

Geography has dictated the history of this independent State, 550 miles long and 100 miles broad, a rectangle lying slantwise across the Himalayas on the north-east frontier of India. It is the only practicable gateway from Tibet to the Indo-Gangetic plains, and a pattern of political non-alignment has been imposed by the fact that its borders are both with India and China.

The unification of such a country was clearly a problem. The inaccessibility of the country and its people retarded the development of a national unity which is still only a veneer in the more remote areas. The word *Nepal* appeared for the first time only in A.D. 879 and means the beginning of a new era. Although ancient Nepalese history is still only partially documented, it is assumed that from about the year 700 B.C. the Kirantis ruled. They are mentioned in Vedic literature and the Mahabharata. They are the ancestors of ancient Nepalese groups including the Newars, Rais, Limbus, Thamangs and Sunwars. During the rule of the Kirantis, Buddha was born in 560 B.C. in the small town of Lumbini in the Terai, near the Indian border. It is still a centre of pilgrimage for Buddhists all over the world, although the infiltration of Tantricism, Hinduism and Brahmanism has transformed both doctrine and practice. Between the ninth and the fourteenth century, the Valley, then, as now, the most important part of the country, was invaded from India until Jaya Sthithi Malla, a Southern Indian, began the Malla dynasty. Jaksha Malla, most able of the Malla Kings, extended his power far beyond the Nepal Valley. He divided his kingdom among his four heirs in 1488; Kathmandu, Bhatgaon, Patan and Banepa remained intact until the Gurkha conquest. The Gurkhas were originally a warlike tribe of the Rajput Kshatriyas who were driven out of India in 1303 by the Sultan, Alau-d-din. They escaped into the hills of central Nepal and gradually spread out into the region of Gorakhnath where they settled in about 1559. At this time the country was divided into small principalities and therefore vulnerable to the adventurous and energetic Gurkha, Prithvinarayan Shah.

The Gurkhas

Prithvinarayan Shah is the acknowledged maker of modern Nepal. Although he had no methodical education, he realized at an early age the wastage of family feuds and political rivalries between the rulers of Bhatgaon, Patan and Kathmandu. He conceived the idea of carving out a viable Kingdom in the Himalayas by conquering neighbouring territories. His idea was to conquer the valley of Nepal and from there to expand in all directions. The *Gorkha Vamsavali* describes in vivid detail how he ordered a general mobilization. By a series of campaigns ending in 1767 he was in control of the territories which today constitute Nepal. Just before his death in 1775, he was planning to annex Sikkim as he wanted to make his boundary continuous with Bhutan.

But Prithvinarayan Shah's contribution to the history of Nepal was not only that he gave it an entity but that he preserved it in its earliest days from the foreigner. He was excessively anti-foreign; he wanted to encourage the enterprise of all the castes and sects and he advised his countrymen to support native industries. His reign coincided with Britain's efforts to open up trade with Tibet and China. In his despatch of 16 March 1768, the Secretary to the Board of Directors of the East India Company instructed their representative in Calcutta "to obtain the best intelligence you can whether trade can be opened with Nepal and whether cloth and other European commodities may not find their way thence to Tibet, Lhasa and Western parts of China". The Gurkha King was adamant; he prohibited the entry of certain British traders to Kathmandu and advised the authorities in Lhasa not to be tempted by a British offer of establishing new relations between Bengal and Tibet. In short, had the Gurkha King been a less determined man, Nepal might well have become just another Princely State of British India. As it is the Shah dynasty which he founded remains to this day.

The central figure in Nepal during the vital years 1786-94 was Bahadur Shah. Like his Gurkha predecessors he was determined to extend the area of his country; his armies occupied states of the Baisis and Chaubisis and Kumaon and Garhwal in the west and Sikkim in the east. A portion of Tibetan Kachhar also was taken. His policy was even more vigorously pursued when his nephew, Rana Bahadur, then only 20, took over power in 1796. He outraged public sentiment by marrying a Brahmin girl, and subsequently the country fell apart into two warring families, the Pandes and Thapas. A revolt on the part of the Brahmins and hostile courtiers forced him to abdicate. When he regained the throne in 1804, he dismissed his Prime Minister, Damodar Pande, who had signed a treaty with the East India Company allowing it the right to appoint a British Resident in Nepal. He was succeeded by one of the most famous Prime Ministers in Nepalese history—Bhim Sen Thapa.

Bhim Sen Thapa continued an expansionist policy which brought him into conflict with British India, and, finally, to the Anglo-Nepalese war of 1814-16. He sued for peace in March 1816. Sir David Ochterlony, Britain's representative, replied: "You must take either a Resident or war", a phrase which long embittered the martial Nepalese. The Treaty of Segauli (4 March 1816) gave Britain the right to appoint a Resident and the cession of the hills of Kumaon, Garhwal, Nainital Simla, and a great portion of the Terai. She was also compelled to withdraw from Sikkim.

Rana Autocracy

Bhim Sen Thapa's authority remained virtually unchallenged until the young King Rajendra Vikram Shah came of age and decided to take control himself. Bhim Sen Thapa was dismissed in 1837 and imprisoned. He killed himself two years later. Out of the complete confusion, massacres and intrigues which followed, another outstanding figure emerged—Jung Bahadur Rana, and another chapter began in Nepalese history which lasted until 1950. He was astute and ruthless. He proclaimed himself Prime Minister and Commander-in-Chief of the Army. He assumed the title of Rana and, independently of the ruling Monarchy, distributed power among his own relations and made his own and their positions hereditary. He reversed the policy of his predecessors by allying himself with Britain and offering support in her war against the Sikhs. His strategic value was recognized when he visited Britain in 1848. And his offer to place troops at Her Majesty's disposal was redeemed at the time of the Indian Mutiny when he personally commanded a second army which besieged Lucknow. He substantially helped Lord Canning in his difficult task of suppressing it.

The Rana family now had a complete monopoly of power in every walk of life. From his birth a Rana could become a General or Colonel and from his fifteenth year he could pass as the Director of Education. The British encouraged the Ranas to follow an isolationist policy. The country remained backward industrially and intellectually. It was a recruiting ground for the British armies in which Gurkha regiments became famous for their toughness and loyalty. When the First World War started the British Government demanded and received permission for the free recruitment of Gurkha soldiers. Chandra Shamsher behaved like the ruler of a Princely State. He had his reward in 1923 when the Treaty of Segauli was revised. The Nepalese wanted an unequivocal declaration of their independence, but the British Government insisted on retaining those clauses which limited Nepal's external relations to those with Great Britain. A change in the designation of the British Resident was made; he was henceforth to be called officially *His Majesty's Minister Plenipotentiary and Envoy Extraordinary*. The King was now to be called *His Majesty* instead of *His Royal Highness*, and the Prime Minister, *His Highness the Maharajah of Nepal*. British titles were generously distributed on leading Ranas. An annual contribution of Rs.10 Lakhs was arranged to be remitted by the Indian Exchequer to the Nepalese ruler.

During Chandra Shamsher's reign (1901-29) the vexed question of Nepal's relations arose. The Treaty of 1792 had placed Nepal in an undefined position of satellite to China, and, until 1900, the Nepalese had sent a goodwill mission to Peking every twelfth year. In 1911, when the revolution in China confused international relations, the time came for the next mission. But when the Chinese High Commissioner at Lhasa raised the question of Nepal's vassalage under the old treaty, the Delhi authorities advised Chandra Shamsher to refuse to send it. By implication, Nepal unilaterally repudiated the 1792 Treaty.

In internal affairs, Chandra Shamsher made a small chink in Nepal's wall of isolation and there was some movement of social ideas. Under the enlightened world pressure, Chandra Shamsher abolished slavery in 1926, freeing some 60,000 people at a cost of Rs.37 Lakhs.

As long as British rulers remained in India, the Ranas felt secure. But the new ideas which swept India in the 1930s and were realized in 1947 influenced the 3 million Nepalese who lived in the frontier provinces of Bengal, Bihar and Uttar Pradesh and in turn spread into the Valley of Nepal. The enlightened policy of the British Labour Government from 1945–51 eliminated the need for strategic reserves such as Jung Bahadur had once provided to suppress the Indian Mutiny.

The King himself dramatically challenged the power of the Ranas in November 1950, refusing to sign death warrants of alleged plotters and taking political asylum in the Indian embassy.

In 1950 the Nepali National Congress was merged with the Nepali Democratic Congress, which had a similar programme, to form the Nepali Congress. The Nepali Congress, secretly helped by King Tribhuvan, went ahead with its plans to overthrow the Rana regime and armed struggle was now organized. All power was vested in the President, M. P. Koirala (half-brother of B. P. Koirala). The Chinese occupation of Tibet, beginning in October 1950, brought matters to a head, both for India and Nepal. The timing of King Tribhuvan's dramatic move in November was undoubtedly influenced by this development in Tibet. The Indian Government sent two planes to fetch him to Delhi. Local Nepalese greeted him enthusiastically. Along the border the insurgents struck, captured Nepal's second largest town, Birganj, and proclaimed a rival Government. In this trial of strength between the Nepali Congress and the Rana regime, the decisive factor was where did the army stand? It soon became clear that it was loyal to the regime. In these circumstances, some *modus vivendi* between the King, the Ranas and the Nepali Congress was necessary. Mr. Nehru and his colleagues stood firm on their support for the King, and the Nepalese Government finally accepted India's proposals on 7 January 1951. They provided for the return of the King to the throne, an amnesty for the insurgents if they laid down their arms, elections by 1952, and the formation of an interim Cabinet of 14 Ministers on the basis of parity between the Ranas and popular representatives. The Royal Family and the Nepali Congress leaders made a triumphal return to Kathmandu on 15 February 1951. Three days later the new Ministry was sworn in—it had been reduced from 14 to 10. Mohun Shumshere Jang Bahadur Rana was the Prime Minister and B. P. Koirala took the vital Home Ministry. It was the end of Ranarchy, and the beginning of an experiment in democracy.

Parliamentary Government

The experiment soon ran into difficulty. The Ranas fought a rear-guard action. They were not reconciled to the loss of their century-old absolute power. Nepali Congress leaders were divided and broke up into factions on a personal or an ideological basis, sometimes on both. King Tribhuvan declared a state of emergency in the country on 23 January 1952 and armed the Prime Minister with emergency powers. Extreme parties of Right and Left (the Rashtriya Mahasabha and the Communists) were declared illegal and political meetings banned indefinitely. Yet an Advisory Assembly of 40 people was set up and opened by the King on 4 July 1952. Its powers were limited; it could not discuss foreign policy, the King's personal behaviour and it could not pass a vote of no confidence in him. It lasted only two months; the King disagreed with his Ministers and they could not agree among themselves.

Once more King Tribhuvan tried to make an Advisory Assembly. It consisted of 112 members, but on its opening day—28 May 1954—the Nepali Congress boycotted it on the grounds that as the largest party it should have the right to form a government and command a majority in the Assembly. Internal rivalries, widespread corruption and nepotism combined to prevent the working of any Assembly. The Communists, working in front organizations since their party was illegal, made considerable headway especially among the younger generation of disillusioned intellectuals in Kathmandu.

Matters came to a head when King Tribhuvan died in March 1955. On his deathbed he dissolved the Royal Council of State and vested all Royal powers in the Crown Prince. The new King Mahendra Bir Birkram Shah Deva was tough, resolute, immensely hard-working and pragmatic. He made no pretence of believing in parliamentary democracy. In a National Day broadcast he said: "Some people say that democracy in Nepal is in its infancy. But infants do not indulge in corruption and bribery". He did not disguise his contempt for most politicians, but royal dictatorship, even of an energetic, intelligent and dedicated nationalist, did not give his country stability or prosperity.

On 17 December 1957 he announced that elections would be held in February 1959. They were held a week after the King had given Nepal her first Constitution providing for a Senate (mahasabha) consisting of 36 members of whom 18 would be elected by the Lower House and 18 nominated by the King, and a Lower House (Pratinidhi Sabha) which would consist of 109 members elected from single-member territorial constituencies. In a country where 96 per cent were illiterate, the elections were held with surprising success. People voted in some of the most remote areas, showing independence and responsibility. Most candidates gave priority to the abolition of the *Birta* system, by which landlords, mostly Ranas, held land tax-free; to the nationalization of the zamindari system; to irrigation; to co-operative farming; to cottage industries, and to government-supported medium industries. Most parties subscribed to this programme, though the Nepali Congress seemed the most likely to carry it out if elected. Its top echelons had subscribed to socialist ideas for many years.

This is clearly what was in the minds of the masses who gave the Nepali Congress 38 per cent of the total votes cast. This gave 74 seats in the Lower House out of the 109. On the right, the Gorkha Parishad won 19 seats or 17.1 per cent of the votes cast while the Communists won 4 seats, or 7.4 per cent. When the King appointed B. P. Koirala as Prime Minister and the first popularly elected Parliament of Nepal was opened in July 1959, it seemed as if the long road towards democracy was firmly routed. Yet the Constitution providing for a parliamentary government and civil rights left sovereignty in fact, not only in form, with the King. He could, for example, force the Prime Minister to resign; he could suspend the Cabinet and rule directly or with newly appointed ministers; he could prorogue Parliament or call for a special sitting; he had a veto over all legislation and constitutional amendments. This fundamental limitation of the democratic process at the core was a major cause of B. P. Koirala's frustration. Yet the overwhelming majority which his Party had secured was prepared to support him in his schemes for land reform. He gave greater security to tenants and redistributed some of the large estates owned by the Ranas. The Ranas themselves fought a rear-guard action which Koirala could still have won but for a growing tension between himself and the young King Mahendra. This clash of personalities, as in so many Asian countries where there is political awareness without corresponding administrative structure, gradually came to a head. On 15 December 1960, King Mahendra staged a *coup d'état*, and jailed B. P. Koirala and most of the top cadres of the Nepali Congress (they were released in October 1968). He dissolved parliament, suspended rights guaranteed by the constitution, substituting his own hand-picked council of ministers.

The Panchayat System

The royal *coup* demonstrated the loyalty of the army to King Mahendra, and this stable factor has remained true to this day. The King has worked immensely hard to build up a "partyless Panchayat democracy". He has a built-in disbelief in all party politics and politicians. His panchayat system, proclaimed in 1961 and promulgated under the Constitution the following year, is a five-tier administrative pyramid. At the apex is the King, who is not only Head of the State, but head of the Government with power to appoint and dismiss his own Ministers. That this panchayat system has come to stay in Nepal was clearly demonstrated in September 1967. The tenth session of the National Panchayat adopted a far-reaching programme based on a "Back to the Village" campaign, and a detailed scheme for panchayat administration. The decision of Nepali Congress leaders in May 1968 that they would co-operate with King Mahendra in the panchayat system led to the release of B. P. Koirala and his colleagues in October. Subsequently, in April 1969, 175 workers of the outlawed Nepali Congress Party, who had been in exile since the royal *coup* in 1960 and convicted *in absentia*, were released and allowed to return to civilian life. But not to party political life. The King and his Council of Ministers introduced well-known Royalist figures into the Cabinet and emphasized the fact that there could be no politics whatsoever except within the panchayat system. With the death early in 1972 of King Mahendra and the accession of his son, as King Birendra in February, liberal expectations were aroused regarding some relaxation of the late King's rather autocratic rule especially as King Birendra had been educated at Eton and Harvard.

This, together with grave food shortages brought about popular discontent which became vociferous when in March Surya Bahadur Thapa (a former Prime Minister) and Rishikesh Shaha (a former Foreign Minister) demanded that a parliamentary system be introduced, that the government be made responsible to the people, that the legislature be open both to the press and public and that the electoral system be broadened. The crisis deepened in June when twenty-six members of the National Panchayat tabled a vote of no confidence. Though it failed, discontent continued to rise unabated, and at a public meeting on August 12th, Mr. Thapa and several other members of the Panchayat accused the Government of failing to deal with the domestic problems of the country. The Government thereupon ordered the arrest of Mr. Thapa and a number of other political opponents. This led to scenes in the Panchayat, the suspension, for the session, of 12 members, and student strikes.

Relations with India had been uneasy ever since the suspension of parliamentary government in Nepal in 1960. The strategic importance of Nepal has, however, induced India to make efforts to remain on good terms with the kingdom.

Nepali determination to keep its giant neighbours, China and India, at an equal distance was reaffirmed by the new Prime Minister, Nagendra Prasad Rijal, appointed on July 16th, 1973, following the resignation of Kirtinidhi Bista.

King Birendra himself visited India in October

1973, spoke of the need for the two countries to reach a mutual understanding of each other's position and received assurances that India had no intention of encouraging anti-Nepali elements. During his visit, however, the brother of B.P. Koirala, the leader of the banned Nepali Congress, exiled in India, was shot dead in Bihar.

Anti-Indian feeling increased in Nepal during 1974, following India's annexation of Sikkim and the imposition of increasingly harsh trade terms by New Delhi. On the eve of King Birendra's coronation, in February 1975, New Delhi announced a tightening of security over the activities of the members of the banned Nepali Congress living in India. This gave rise to hopes of a thaw in the relations between the two countries.

The appearance of a number of pro-Delhi figures in the composition of the new Nepalese Government formed in May, reflects the desire to induce New Delhi to relax its hardline political and economic policies towards Nepal. On the other hand, it is likely that Nepal will attempt to forge closer links with the Soviet Union which, in view of India's hardline attitude, could prove an important factor for Nepal's political aspirations and economic programmes.

ECONOMIC SURVEY

The Nepalese economy has always been handicapped by the fact that the country is landlocked and that communications within the country itself are still in need of development. Until the 1950s there were virtually no roads at all. Since then, often with help from China or India, Nepal has begun to construct a network of roads and highways but the process is far from complete. Under the fourth Five-Year Development Plan (1970–75) the largest allocation went towards the improvement of communications.

This emphasis on infrastructure in the development strategy has, however, meant a relative lack of investment in direct production, with a consequent slow rate of growth. It is estimated by the IMF that in the 1960s G.D.P. increased in real terms by about 2 per cent per annum, about the same growth rate as that of the population. In 1973 official sources in Nepal put the annual growth rate at only 1 per cent.

Agriculture

Agriculture is the largest productive sector, employing about 90 per cent of the labour force. The principal crops are rice, maize, barley, millet, wheat, sugar-cane, tobacco, potatoes and oilseeds, but development has been slow owing to shortages of fertilizers, improved seed, irrigation and storage facilities and agricultural credit. Recent crops, moreover, have been disappointing and the Government has had to import grains. Steps are now being taken to develop agriculture with particular emphasis on irrigation. Improved techniques of land administration are being adopted, co-operatives are being established and the Agricultural Marketing Corporation is to undertake to purchase fertilizers, improve seeds, distribute food in areas of shortage, expand storage facilities and assist the Agricultural Development Bank in conducting credit and marketing operations with the co-operatives.

Trade

The landlocked nature of the country has also made it difficult for Nepal to diversify its foreign trade, 90 per cent of which is with India. Nepal exports mainly grains, jute and metal, papier-mâché, wood and cane products. In April 1973 the export bonus scheme was revised to give more incentive for the export of indigenous products. There had recently been some deflection of trade into re-exporting. Some problems of exporting had been alleviated by the second Trade and Transit Treaty, signed with India in August 1971, under which India provides road transport facilities, warehouse space at Calcutta and port facilities. Uncertainty in 1970 and the first part of 1971 over the signing of this treaty had adversely affected the economy, however, and the haul back has been slow.

The Budget for 1973–74 reflected the preoccupation with infrastructure, with about 75 per cent of expenditure allocated for development. Foreign aid has played a large part in financing development, with India, China and the U.S.A. as the largest contributors. The strategic situation of Nepal has resulted in an element of competition between these large powers over aid to the country. The Nepalese themselves, while accepting more assistance from India than from any other country, have tried to steer a neutral line between the communist and non-communist powers. Total foreign aid had, in fact, decreased from 352 million rupees in 1971–72 to 255 million rupees in 1973–74.

Nepal's official foreign exchange reserves have increased annually, based on the balance of payments position, which is marginally favourable, taking into account invisible earnings such as interest on short-term foreign investment, foreign cash grants and loans and the savings and pensions of Gurkha soldiers, which can make them relatively rich men in Nepalese terms. Holdings of Indian currency, to which much importance is attached, have, however, been falling, following the cessation of the export of grains to that country.

The prospect for the future holds out the hope that the growth rate of the economy will climb as the measures adopted under the infrastructure programme begin to take effect and reserves can be allocated to direct production and the improvement of marketing and credit institutions. A lesser emphasis on infrastructure is indicated in the ambitious fifth Five-Year Plan (1975–80) which allocates more reserves to agriculture and which commands an outlay of U.S. $1,150 million.

STATISTICAL SURVEY

AREA AND POPULATION

Area (sq. km.)	Population (1971 census)	
	Total	Kathmandu (capital)
141,577	11,555,983	353,756

Estimated Population: 12,321,000 (June 22nd, 1974).

ECONOMICALLY ACTIVE POPULATION
(1971 census)

	Males	Females	Total
Agriculture, hunting, forestry and fishing	3,187,307	1,392,245	4,579,552
Mining and quarrying	31	5	36
Manufacturing	45,391	6,511	51,902
Electricity, gas and water	1,570	26	1,596
Construction	4,876	140	5,016
Trade, restaurants and hotels	55,708	7,852	63,560
Transport, storage and communications	9,322	315	9,637
Financing, insurance, real estate and business services	3,331	135	3,466
Community, social and personal services	126,752	11,007	137,759
Total	3,434,288	1,418,236	4,852,524

AGRICULTURE

LAND USE
(sq. km.)

Total	Forest	Perpetual Snow	Cultivated	Reclaimable Waste	Unreclaimable Waste	Rivers, Roads, Towns
141,577	44,750	21,121	19,800	18,600	26,441	10,865

CROP AREA
(estimates—'000 hectares)

	Paddy Rice	Maize, Millet and Barley	Wheat	Oil Seeds	Tobacco	Jute	Sugar Cane	Potato
1973–74	1,227	605	274	114	5	33	16	53
1974–75	1,239	610	290	113	7	37	16	53

CROP PRODUCTION
('000 metric tons)

	1972/73	1973/74	1974/75
Paddy rice	2,010	2,416	2,453
Maize	822	814	827
Millet	159	167	168
Wheat	312	308	332
Oil seeds	60	65	65
Sugar cane	246	267	251
Tobacco	7	4	5
Jute	55	40	45
Potatoes	294	306	307

LIVESTOCK
(FAO estimates, '000 head)

	1971/72	1972/73	1973/74
Cattle	6,400	6,450	6,535
Buffaloes	3,692	3,762	3,831
Pigs	300	300	324
Sheep	2,220	2,250	2,266
Goats	2,300	2,300	2,348
Poultry	19,000	19,500	20,078

Source: FAO, *Production Yearbook 1974.*

LIVESTOCK PRODUCTS
(FAO estimates, '000 metric tons)

	1972	1973	1974
Beef and veal	4	4	4
Buffalo meat	16	16	16
Mutton and lamb	7	7	7
Goats' meat	10	10	10
Pig meat	5	5	5
Poultry meat	19	20	20
Edible offals	8.1	8.2	8.3
Cows' milk	193	208	210
Buffaloes' milk	420	430	439
Goats' milk	29	29	29
Butter and ghee	7.4	7.4	7.4
Cheese	71.9	77.1	77.3
Hen eggs	11.9	12.2	12.6
Wool (clean)	2.2	2.2	2.2

Source: FAO, *Production Yearbook 1974.*

FORESTRY

ROUNDWOOD REMOVALS
('000 cubic metres, excluding bark)

	Coniferous (soft wood)			Broadleaved (hard wood)			Total		
	1970	1971*	1972*	1970	1971	1972	1970	1971	1972
Industrial wood	20*	20	20	516	594	540	536	614	560
Fuel wood	95	100	100	8,300	8,400	8,600*	8,395	8,500	8,700*
Total	115	120	120	8,816	8,994	9,140	8,931	9,114	9,260

* FAO estimates.

1973: Coniferous industrial wood 32,000 cubic metres.

Source: FAO, *Yearbook of Forest Products.*

SAWNWOOD PRODUCTION

('000 cubic metres, including boxboards)

	1964	1965	1966	1967	1968	1969	1970	1971	1972*	1973*
Coniferous	13	6	7	7	7	10	10*	10*	10	10
Broadleaved	171	205	205	205	207	210	210	210	210	210
TOTAL	184	211	212	212	214	220	220	220	220	220

* FAO estimates.

Source: FAO, *Yearbook of Forest Products.*

Fishing: Total catch (in '000 metric tons) was 1.9 in 1970; 2.1 in 1971; 2.2 in 1972.

INDUSTRY

	1972/73	1973/74	1974/75
Jute (metric tons)	13,709	12,888	12,265
Sugar (metric tons)	10,627	14,197	11,926
Cigarettes ('000)	2,281,700	2,521,600	3,001,241
Matches (gross)	587,000	662,000	649,142
Synthetic textiles (metres)	499	—	—
Shoes (pairs)	79,394	82,494	355,717
Stainless Steel Utensils (metric tons)	245	209	156

FINANCE

100 paisa (pice) = 1 Nepalese rupee (NR).
Coins: 1, 2, 5, 10, 25 and 50 paisa; 1 rupee.
Notes: 1, 5, 10, 100, 500 and 1,000 rupees.

Exchange rates (June 1976): £1 sterling = 22.175 NR; U.S. $1 = 12.50 NR.
100 Nepalese rupees = £4.51 = $8.00.

Note: Between August 1958 and April 1960 the Nepalese rupee was valued at 14 U.S. cents (U.S. $1 = 7.143 rupees). In April 1960 the rupee was devalued by 6.25 per cent to 13.125 U.S. cents ($1 = 7.619 rupees) and this valuation remained in force until June 1966. From June 1966 to December 1967 the rupee's value was 13.13 U.S. cents ($1 = 7.616 rupees). Between December 1967 and February 1973 the exchange rate was $1 = 10.125 rupees (1 rupee = 9.8765 U.S. cents). From February 1973 to October 1975 the rate was $1 = 10.56 rupees (1 rupee = 9.47 U.S. cents). In October 1975 a new rate of $1 = 12.50 rupees (1 rupee = 8 U.S. cents) was introduced. In terms of sterling, the exchange rate was £1 = 21.333 rupees from April 1960 to June 1966; £1 = 21.325 rupees from June 1966 to November 1967; £1 = 24.30 rupees from December 1967 to August 1971; and £1 = 26.383 rupees from December 1971 to June 1972.

BUDGET ESTIMATES

(million NRs—Twelve months ending July 15th, 1975)

Revenue	
Land	95.0
Customs	327.1
Interest and Dividends	82.7
Excise	120.9
Income Tax	40.0
Other	342.8
TOTAL	1,008.5
Foreign Aid	270.2
External Loan	104.8
Internal Loan	100.0
Carry Balance (Surplus)	18.7
TOTAL	493.7
GRAND TOTAL	1,502.2

Expenditure	
REGULAR:	
Administration	182.8
Defence	97.3
Other	296.2
TOTAL	576.3
DEVELOPMENT:	
Industry and Commerce	84.0
Education	86.2
Agriculture	205.3
Health	54.0
Other	496.4
TOTAL	925.9
GRAND TOTAL	1,502.2

FOREIGN AID
('000 NRs)

	1973/74	1974/75*
India	112,700	133,948
China	34,300	44,000
United States	31,855	64,695
U.K.	19,576	16,526
Others	18,775	78,269
TOTAL	337,438	337,438

* Estimates.

FIFTH FIVE-YEAR PLAN (1975–80) PROPOSED EXPENDITURE
(million NRs)

	MINIMUM PROGRAMME	MAXIMUM PROGRAMME
Agriculture, land reform, irrigation, forestry and rehabilitation, etc.	3,167.0	3,970.8
Industry, commerce, electricity and mining	1,799.9	2,040.4
Transport and communication	2,527.1	3,385.4
Education, health, drinking water and other social services	1,703.0	2,007.4
TOTAL	9,197.0	11,404.0

INTERNATIONAL RESERVES
(U.S. $ million at December 31st)

	1968	1969	1970	1971	1972	1973	1974
Gold	9.7	8.2	5.1	5.3	5.1	5.5	5.6
IMF Special Drawing Rights	—	—	—	1.2	2.4	2.7	2.7
Reserve position in IMF	0.9	2.4	2.5	2.9	3.2	3.8	3.8
Foreign exchange	56.7	78.0	87.1	98.7	92.6	109.2	121.0
TOTAL	67.3	88.6	94.7	108.1	103.3	121.1	133.1

November 1975 (U.S. $ million): Foreign exchange 90.0; Total 101.6.

Source: IMF, *International Financial Statistics.*

MONEY SUPPLY*
(million NRs at July 15th)

	1969	1970	1971	1972	1973	1974	1975
Currency outside banks	470.2	531.4	577.3	602.3	695.9	878.6	916.5
Private sector deposits	102.1	93.4	52.7	64.3	82.4	106.6	75.2
Demand deposits	127.1	141.7	166.6	189.1	233.1	290.2	340.4
TOTAL MONEY	699.4	766.5	796.6	855.7	1,011.4	1,275.4	1,332.1

* Excluding Indian currency in circulation.

Source: IMF, *International Financial Statistics.*

COST OF LIVING
(Consumer price index for Kathmandu. Base: 1970=100)

	1967	1968	1969	1971	1972	1973	1974
Food	81.8	84.6	93.0	98.9	111.0	117.8	140.8
Fuel and light	102.3	93.8	102.3	101.7	107.2	116.9	124.4
Clothing	86.5	93.9	107.4	116.6	141.2	181.9	245.4
ALL ITEMS (excl. rent)	82.8	86.1	95.3	101.3	112.7	119.3	142.9

July 1975: Food 177.1; All items (excl. rent) 178.9.

Source: International Labour Office, mainly *Year Book of Labour Statistics.*

GROSS DOMESTIC PRODUCT

(million NRs at current factor cost, 12 months ending July 15th)

	1969/70	1970/71	1971/72	1972/73	1973/74
Agriculture, hunting, forestry and fishing	5,927	6,040	7,095	7,704	9,068
Mining and quarrying	4	1	2	3	3
Manufacturing (incl. cottage industries)	788	819	995	1,082	1,304
Electricity, gas and water	18	20	23	29	28
Construction	192	213	149	153	219
Wholesale and retail trade	363	372	381	390	399
Transport, storage and communications	192	234	285	347	422
Owner-occupied dwellings	729	745	762	779	1,685 (Owner-occupied dwellings to Other producers and services)
Finance, insurance and real estate services	128	139	145	163	
Public administration and defence	199	215	230	228	
Other producers and services*	256	279	332	382	
TOTAL	8,796	9,077	10,399	11,260	13,128

* Including hotels and restaurants, business services and community, social and personal services.

Source: United Nations, *Yearbook of National Accounts Statistics* and *Monthly Bulletin of Statistics.*

EXTERNAL TRADE

(Value in million NRs)

	1967/68	1968/69	1969/70	1970/71
Imports	478.6	747.7	884.6	699.0
Exports	392.9	572.0	489.2	400.6

COMMODITIES

(1970/71—million NRs)

	IMPORTS	EXPORTS
Food and Live Animals	133.0	264.2
Beverages and Tobacco	7.9	0.8
Raw Materials	29.0	80.3
Minerals and Fuels	71.7	—
Animal Fats, Vegetable Oils and Chemicals	6.9	0.9
TOTAL	248.5	346.2
Machinery and Transport Equipment	74.8	0.1
Other Manufactured Goods	267.0	46.3
Miscellaneous	108.7	8.0
TOTAL	450.5	54.4
GRAND TOTAL	699.0	400.6

TRANSPORT

ROAD TRAFFIC

(1972)

MOTOR CARS	COMMERCIAL PASSENGER VEHICLES	OTHER COMMERCIAL VEHICLES
11,131	396	1,546

CIVIL AVIATION

ROYAL NEPAL AIRLINES CORPORATION (1974/75)

Passengers	231,018
Freight (kg.)	19,423,000

TOURISM*

1970	45,970
1971	49,414
1972	52,930
1973	68,047
1974	77,000
1975	74,559

* Tourist arrivals.

EDUCATION
(1974/75*)

	Establishments	Teachers	Pupils
Primary	7,585	18,074	458,516
Secondary	1,761	7,749	216,309
Higher	80	1,499	23,404

* Including technical institutes.

Source: Research and Publicity Division, National Planning Commission Secretariat, HMG/Nepal.

THE CONSTITUTION

(*Promulgated December* 1962, *amended in* 1967 *and* 1975)

GOVERNMENT

The Constitution of Nepal comprises a constitutional monarchy with executive power vested in the King but ordinarily exercised on the recommendation of a Cabinet led by a Prime Minister, selected by the King from among the membership of the National Panchayat or Assembly. The Cabinet is responsible to the Panchayat but the King has power to grant or withhold assent to Bills at his discretion.

State Council

The Constitution also provides for a State Council which will declare upon the succession or appoint a Regency Council, besides giving advice to the King in times of emergency.

Legislature—Rashtriya Panchayat

The Rashtriya (National) Panchayat, which is at the apex of the party-less Panchayat system of democracy, is the supreme national unicameral legislature, comprising 135 members, 112 of whom are elected from among the members of the Anchal Sabhas (Zonal Councils), who in turn are elected from among the members of Zilla Sabhas (District Councils) who, again in turn, are elected from the Gaon Sabhas (Village Councils). In other words, membership of the Rashtriya Panchayat is based on the popular election of Local Panchayat (which is the basic unit of the four-tiered Panchayat System), from each of which members choose from among themselves representatives for District Panchayat. They may advance by similar stages to the zonal and then to the Rashtriya Panchayat. The remaining members are nominated by the Crown according to the Constitution.

The Rashtriya Panchayat is a perpetual body whose members are elected from Zonal Councils and serve a fixed term of four years. House proceedings are open to the public. A summary record of the proceedings of every meeting of the House or its committees is published.

Bills to the House to be presented by the Committees of the House, in consultation with Ministers. The annual budget is submitted to the House for consideration, deliberation and adoption. And in order that these legislative tasks be conducted with becoming dignity and efficiency, the members of the House fully enjoy the privilege of freedom from arrest for anything spoken in the House or the manner in which voting is exercised.

The Rashtriya Panchayat was formed on April 14th, 1963 (New Year's Day); and, constituted into the National Group, has been a member of the Inter-Parliamentary Union since September 1967.

CITIZEN'S RIGHTS AND DUTIES

Besides enumerating a number of fundamental rights, including the right against exile, the Constitution lays down a series of fundamental duties of the citizen.

AMENDMENTS

Amendments to the 1962 Constitution, adopted in 1967 and 1975 include the following: Prime Minister to be appointed by the King who may, if he wishes, consult the National Panchayat; Ministers to be collectively and individually responsible to the King; King to appoint directly the Zonal Commissioners who are to enjoy greater powers than the Chairmen of Zonal Panchayat Assemblies; Speaker of the House to be appointed by at least two-thirds of Rashtriya Panchayat; Associations for non-political purposes allowed but political parties continue to be banned; provision for appointment of an independent Election Commission; the country to be divided into four zones for electoral purposes, with elections for all elective bodies every four years on a rotational basis; elected members of National Panchayat can be recalled.

LAND REFORM

Under the Act, the Land Reform Programme has been implemented in phases. It was introduced for the first time in sixteen districts in 1964, in twenty-five districts in 1965, and it became applicable to all districts in 1966. Its basic objective is to develop the agricultural sector which may eventually foster the industrialization programme in the country. The important features of the programme are: fixation of a ceiling on land holdings; guarantee of tenancy rights; fixed rate of rent; provision of loans to peasants for agricultural purposes. The loan fund has been partly created by the compulsory saving scheme, which forms part of the land reform programme; compulsory saving is collected from both landowners and peasants at the ward level in each Village Panchayat.

THE GOVERNMENT

HEAD OF STATE

H.M. King Birendra Bir Bikram Shah Dev.

COUNCIL OF MINISTERS

(*July* 1976)

Prime Minister, Minister of Palace Affairs and Defence: Dr. Tulsi Giri.

Minister of Food, Agriculture and Irrigation and Land Reforms: Khadga Bahadur Singh.

Minister of Foreign Affairs: Krishna Raj Aryal.

Minister for Home and Panchayat Affairs: Bhoj Raj Ghimire.

Minister for Finance and General Administration: Dr. Bhekh Bahadur Thapa.

Minister for Law, Justice and Communications: Jo Mehar Shrestha.

State Minister for Water and Electricity: Harishchandr Mahat.

State Minister for Works and Transport: Balaram Ghar Magar.

State Minister for Forests and Health: Bhola Nath Jha

State Minister for Industry, Commerce and Education: D Harkha Bahadur Gurung.

NATIONAL PANCHAYAT

(National Assembly)

In December 1960 Parliament was dissolved. Political parties are banned under the Panchayat system, presided over by the King.

Chairman of the National Panchayat: (vacant).

"BACK TO THE VILLAGE" NATIONAL CAMPAIG

A constitutional body, formed in December 1975, wi responsibility for political affairs and the propagation Panchayat philosophy. All Cabinet members are e officio members of the Campaign.

Chairman: Khadga Bahadur Singh (Minister of Foo Agriculture and Irrigation and Land Reforms).

POLITICAL PARTIES

(All political parties were banned in December 1960).

Exiled members of the Nepali National Congress, led by former Prime Minister B. P. Koirala, are now based in New Delhi, India.

DIPLOMATIC REPRESENTATION

EMBASSIES IN KATHMANDU

Bangladesh: Krishna Kunji, Kamalpokhari; *Ambassador:* M. N. I. Choudhury.

Burma: Panipokhari; *Ambassador:* U Zahre Lian.

China, People's Republic: Toran Bhawan, Naksal; *Ambassador:* Tsao Chih.

Egypt: Ram Shah Path, P.O.B. 792; *Ambassador:* Anis Said Shenouda.

France: Lazimpat; *Ambassador:* Frédéric Max.

German Democratic Republic: *Ambassador:* Karl Gadow.

Germany, Federal Republic: Kanti Path; *Ambassador:* Eduard Mirow.

India: Lain Chaur; *Ambassador:* Maharajkrishna Rasgotra.

Israel: Lazimpat; *Ambassador:* Yair Aran.

Italy: Durbar Marg; *Ambassador:* Dr. Carlo Calenda.

Japan: Panipokhari; *Ambassador:* Seiken Sasaki.

Korea, Democratic People's Republic: Lainchaur; *Ambassador:* Choi uk Myong.

Korea, Republic: Keshar Mahal, Thamel; *Ambassad* Hong Soo-hui.

Pakistan: Panipokhari; *Ambassador:* Inayatullah.

Thailand: Thapathali; *Chargé d'Affiaires:* Charoon Sund rodyani.

U.S.S.R.: Dilli Bazar; *Ambassador:* Kamo B. Udumyan.

United Kingdom: Lain Chaur; *Ambassador:* Micha Scott.

U.S.A.: Panipokhari; *Ambassador:* William I. Cargo.

Nepal also has diplomatic relations with Afghanistan, Albania, Algeria, Argentina, Australia, Austria, Belgium, Bulgar Cambodia, Canada, Chile, Cuba, Czechoslovakia, Denmark, Ethiopia, Finland, Greece, Hungary, Indonesia, Iran, Ira Jordan, Kenya, Kuwait, Laos, Lebanon, Luxembourg, Malaysia, Mexico, Mongolia, Morocco, the Netherlands, New Zealar Nigeria, Norway, the Philippines, Poland, Romania, Singapore, Spain, Sri Lanka, Sudan, Sweden, Switzerland, Syr Tanzania, Turkey, Viet-Nam and Yugoslavia.

JUDICIAL SYSTEM

There is one Supreme Court, 15 Zonal and 75 District Courts. These have both civil and criminal jurisdiction.

The Supreme Court: The Constitution of Nepal provides for a Supreme Court which shall have a Chief Justice and not more than six other Justices unless otherwise specified by law. The Supreme Court is to hold appellate as well as original jurisdiction, and may function as a court of review. The Supreme Court protects the fundamental rights of the people and guarantees the Rule of Law.

Chief Justice: Hon. RATNA BAHADUR BISTA.

RELIGION

Over half the population are Hindus, which is the religion of the Royal Family. Most others are Buddhists. One per cent are Muslims.

BUDDHISM

Nepal Buddhist Association: Rev. AMRITANANDA, Ananda Kuti, Kathmandu.

Young Buddhist Council of Nepal: Rev. AMRITANANDA.

THE PRESS

Commoner: Naradevi, Kathmandu; English daily; Editor GOPAL DAS; circ. 7,000.

Gorkha Patra: Dharma Path, Kathmandu; Nepali daily; Editor GOPAL PRASAD BHATTARAI; circ. 25,000.

The Motherland: Kathmandu; English daily; Editor M. R. SHRESTHA; circ. 1,200.

Naya Samaj: Kathmandu; f. 1957; Nepali daily; Editor P. D. PANDEY; circ. 3,000.

Naya Sandesh: Kathmandu; Nepali and English; weekly; Editor RAMESH NATH PANDEY; circ. 2,200.

Nepal Bhasa Patrika: Bheda Singh, Kathmandu; Newari daily; Editor F. B. SINGH; circ. 800.

Nepal Samachar: Nepal Today Press, Kathmandu; Nepali daily; Editor S. N. SHARMA; circ. 900.

Nepal Times.

Nepali: Kathmandu; Hindi daily; Editor UMA KANT DAS; circ. 9,500.

Perspective: New Rd., Kathmandu; English weekly.

The Rising Nepal: Dharma Path, Kathmandu; f. 1965; English daily; Editor BARUN SHAMSHER RANA; circ. 20,000.

Royal Nepal Economist: 41/44 Tripureswar, Kathmandu; monthly in English and Nepali; Editor BHESH RAJ SHARMA; circ. 500.

Samaj: Dhobidhara, Kathmandu; Editor MANI RAJ UPADHYAYA; circ. 2,100.

Samaya: Ramashah Path, Kathmandu; Nepali daily; Editor MANIK LALL SHRESTH; circ. 30,000.

Sameeksha: Nepali weekly; Editor M. M. DIKSHIT; circ. over 4,000.

NEWS AGENCIES

Rastriya Sambad Samiti (R.S.S.): P.O.B. 220, Kathmandu; f. 1962; Chair. and Gen. Man. GOVINDA PRASAD PRADHAN.

FOREIGN BUREAUX

Agence France-Presse (*France*): G.P. Box 402, 6/126 Puranobhansor, Kathmandu; Man. KEDAR MAN SINGH.

Deutsche Presse-Agentur (*Federal Republic of Germany*): Kathmandu.

Tass (U.S.S.R.) is also represented.

Nepal Journalists Association (NJA): Kathmandu.

PUBLISHERS

Department of Publicity: Ministry of Communications, Kathmandu.

La Kaul Press: Palpa Tanben.

Mahabir Singh Chiniya Main: Makhan Tola, Kathmandu.

Mandas Sugatdas: Kamabachi, Kathmandu.

Ratna Pustak Bhandar: Bhotahitit Tola, Kathmandu.

Sajha Prakhashan: Kathmandu; f. 1966; educational and general; Chair. Shri KAMAL MANI DIXIT.

RADIO

Radio Nepal: Dept. of Broadcasting, His Majesty's Govt. of Nepal, P.O.B. 634, Singha Durdar, Kathmandu; f. 1951; broadcasts on short and medium wave in Nepali, Hindi, Newari and English. In 1971 there were about 60,000 receiving sets. Dir. Gen. R. R. POUDYAL.

There is no television.

FINANCE

(cap.=capital; p.u.=paid up; dep.=deposits; m.=millions; N.Rs=Nepali Rupees)

BANKING

Nepal Rastra Bank: Lalita Niwas, Baluwatar, Kathmandu; f. 1956; state bank of issue; cap. N.Rs. 10m.; dep. N.Rs. 705.7m. (December 1973); Gov. KUL SHEKHAR SHARMA.

Nepal Bank Ltd.: H.O. Dharmapath, Juddha Rd., Kathmandu; f. 1937; cap. p.u. N.Rs. 5m.; dep. N.Rs. 779m. (1975); Chair. HARIHAR JUNG THAPA; Gen. Man. ANANDA BHAKTA RAJBHANDARY; publ. *Nepal Bank Patrika* (ten a year).

Rastriya Banijya Bank (*National Commercial Bank*): Kathmandu; f. 1965; cap. p.u. N.Rs. 3m.; dep. N.Rs. 396m.; 50 branches; Gen. Man. B. M. SINGH.

Agricultural Development Bank: Dharmapath, Kathmandu; f. 1968; only statutory financial body providing credit to co-operatives, individuals and associations in agricultural development; receives deposits from individuals, co-operatives and other associations to generate savings in the agricultural sector; cap. p.u. N.Rs. 76.2m.; dep. N.Rs. 6.0m.; Chair. DIRGHA RAJ KOIRALA; Gen. Man. L. B. BISTO.

Agricultural Co-operative Societies also advance credit to members.

INSURANCE

There is one insurance company:

Rastriya Beema Sansthan (*National Insurance Corporation*): P.O.B. 527, Kathmandu, Nepal; f. December 1967; government undertaking; underwriting of life and general insurance business within and outside Nepal; cap. p.u. N.Rs. 2.4m.; Chair. N. K. ADHIKARY; Gen. Man. L. B. BISTA.

TRADE AND INDUSTRY

National Planning Commission: Kathmandu, Chair. The Prime Minister Rt. Hon. Nagendra Prasad Rijal; Vice-Chair. Hon. Dr. H. B. Gurung; Sec. G. B. N. Pradhan.

Federation of Nepalese Chambers of Commerce and Industry: Meera Home, Khichapokhari, P.O.B. 269, Kathmandu; f. January 1965; independent federation comprising 112 industrial and business organizations; represents members' interests and provides a variety of services; Pres. H. P. Giri; Vice-Pres. Krishna Man Sherchan; Sec.-Gen. Raj Bahadur Chipalu; publ. *Udyog Banijya Patrika* (fortnightly).

Nepal Chamber of Commerce: Nepal Bank Bldg. No. 2, P.O.B. 198, Kathmandu; f. 1952; non-profit making organization devoted to cause of industrial and commercial development in Nepal and to the service of its members; about 450 mems.; publs. *Chamber Patrika* (monthly, Nepalese), *Nepal Trade Directory*.

Agricultural Marketing Corporation: Teku, Kuleswar, P.O.B. 195, Kathmandu; f. June 1972; Functions: to procure and distribute inputs needed for agricultural development, namely chemical fertilizers, improved seeds, improved agricultural tools and implements, plant protection materials, etc.; all inputs are imported except improved seeds and small tools; cap. p.u. Rs. 10m.; mems. 262 retail dealers; Chair. Surendra Raj Sharma; Gen. Man. Sagar Bahadur Pradhan.

National Trading Ltd.: Teku, Kathmandu; f. 1962; government undertaking; imports and distributes construction materials, machinery, vehicles, consumer and luxury goods; handles clearing and forwarding of government consignments; exports Nepalese products, mainly timber, medicinal herbs, raw wool, hessian sacking, raw jute, handicrafts and curios; Exec. Chair. and Gen. Man. (vacant); publ. *Vyapar Patrika* (monthly trade journal) and other trade directories.

Nepal Industrial Development Corporation (NIDC): NIDC Bldg., P.B. No. 10, Kathmandu; f. 1959; state-owned, has shares in 15 industrial enterprises, offers financial and technical assistance to the private sector; cap. N.Rs. 250m.; Chair. Tej Bahadur Prasai; Gen. Man. R. P. Sharma; publs. *Industrial Digest* (annual), *Annual Report, Prospects of Industrial Investment in Nepal* and various brochures.

Nepal Resettlement Company: Kathmandu; f. 1963; government undertaking; engaged in resettling people from the densely-populated hill country to the western Terai plain.

Salt Trading Corporation Ltd.: Kalimati, Kathmandu; f. Sept. 1963 as a joint venture of the public and private sectors (30 and 70 per cent respectively) to manage the import and distribution of salt in Nepal; now also deals in sugar, edible oils and wheat flour throughout Nepal; Chair. A. M. Sherchan; Gen. Man. H. B. Malla.

TRADE UNION

Nepal Mazdoor Sangathan (*Nepal Labour Organization*): Central Office, Kathmandu; f. 1963; 14,000 mems.; Chair. M. K. Pokheral.

TRANSPORT

Ministry of Public Works, Transport and Health: Sec. Narayan Prasad Aryal.

ROADS

There are over 3,000 kilometres of roads, of which about 1,700 are metalled. About 2,000 kilometres were constructed during the last Three-Year and the third Five-Year Plan periods. There are short sections of motorable roads around Kathmandu and a mountain road, Tribhuwana Rajpath, links the capital with the Indian railhead at Raxual. The Siddhartha Highway, constructed with Indian assistance, was opened in 1972. It connects the Pokhara Valley in mid-west Nepal with Sonauli on the Indian border in Uttar Pradesh. A British-built section linking Butwal with Barghat and totalling 40 km. was opened in 1972. Mahendra Highway, formerly known as the East-West Highway, is under construction sector by sector. Its total length is estimated at 992 km. of which 655 km. had been completed in 1976. Construction of the 400 km. Pokhara-Surkhet road began in 1974.

RAILWAYS, ROPEWAYS AND CONTAINER TRANSPORT

Nepal Yatayat Samsthan (*The Transport Corporation of Nepal*): Responsible for the operation of road transport facilities, railways and ropeways.

A section of narrow-gauge railway 53 kilometres long links Jaya Nagar (India) with Janakpurdham and Bijalpura. A 42-kilometre ropeway links Hetauda and Kathmandu and can carry 25 tons of freight per hour throughout the year. Food grains, construction goods and heavy goods on this route are transported by this ropeway. A fleet of container trucks is being operated between Calcutta and Raxaul and other points in Nepal for transporting exports to, and imports from, third countries.

SHIPPING

Royal Nepal Shipping Corpn.: Kalimati, Kathmandu; f. 1971; became operational in May 1972; Man. Dir. Brig. Gen. R. S. Rana.

Royal Nepal Shipping Line: f. 1971; became operational in May 1972; Man. Dir. Dr. J. Jha.

CIVIL AVIATION

There are regular Boeing services to New Delhi, Calcutta, Patna and Bangkok (non-stop). RNAC plan to extend services to Hong Kong, Pakistan and Iran. Helicopter and charter services have been provided to the remote and higher mountain regions and larger towns.

Royal Nepal Airlines Corporation: RNAC Bldg., Kantipath, Kathmandu; f. 1958; fleet of 1 Boeing 727, 2 Avro HS-748, 4 DC-3, 5 Twin Otters, 2 Pilatus Porters, 2 Jet Ranger; Chair. B. B. Pradhan.

The following foreign airlines operate services to Nepal: Burma Airways, Indian Airlines Corporation, Thai International, Air-India, Pan American Airways, BOAC, Air France TWA, Lufthansa, SAS, Pakistan International Airways, KLM.

TOURISM

Department of Tourism: Ministry of Industry and Commerce, Basantpur, Kathmandu; Dir. M. Uprati.

Department of Information: Ministry of Communications, Ghantaghar, Kathmandu; Dir. Nagendra Sharma.

POWER

Nepal Electricity Corporation: Tundikhel, Kathmandu; f. 1962 to generate and distribute electricity in areas approved by H.M. Government; to develop electricity distribution with a view to fostering industrial development and economic welfare; Chair. KRISHNA RAJBHANDARI; Gen. Man. SHANKAR KRISHNA MALLA.

DEFENCE

Armed Forces (1975): 20,000 army; there is no air force; the 70-man Army Air Freight Dept. operates the aircraft.

Defence Budget (1973–74): Rs. 83.2 million (U.S. $8 million).

EDUCATION

Nepal presents a very varied educational picture, having six separate traditions of educational system. But the total picture is dominated by the fast expansion of teaching facilities since 1951. Whereas in 1950 the country had 321 primary schools with 8,050 students, in 1973-74 there were 7,585 primary schools with 392,229 pupils of which 15 per cent were girls, and 18,074 teachers. The number of secondary schools has grown considerably from two in 1950 to 1,761 in 1973. Since 1961, when there were 41,444 pupils, the number has grown to 216,309 in 1973-74.

The Ministry of Education supervises the finance, administration, staffing and inspection of government schools, and makes inspection of private schools receiving government subsidies. In other respects, private schools are autonomous. The National Educational Planning Commission recommends educational curricula, and in some cases these have been adopted by the private schools.

English schools were set up during the period of British influence in the nineteenth century, and give both primary and secondary education. These schools dominate secondary education. The government schools, which have expanded dramatically since 1951, give five years' free education, using Nepali as the medium of instruction. Vernacular schools give secular education to villagers in local dialects, while, in addition to Buddhist and Hindu religious establishments, there are a number of Basic schools, on the pattern set in India, which concentrate heavily on handicrafts and agriculture.

The oldest of the colleges of higher education in Nepal is Tri Chandra School in Kathmandu, set up in 1918, which gives four-year arts courses. The only other advanced college set up before the 1951 revolution is the Sanskrit College in Kathmandu, founded in 1948. By 1970 Nepal had forty-four institutes of higher learning, including the Tribhuvan University (founded 1959). The number of students enrolled in all higher institutions is 19,198 (1973-74). Apart from the single College of Education established in 1956 for the training of secondary school teachers and other educational personnel, there are also five Primary Teacher Training Centres at Birgunj, Kathmandu, Pokhara, Dharan and Palpa which organize various kinds of in-service training courses. Government expenditure on education has averaged about 8 per cent over the last ten years.

By the end of 1976 it is expected that 64 per cent of the school-age population will be receiving primary education, vocational education will be made available to 60 per cent of high school pupils and that those in receipt of higher education will be 19 per cent of secondary school enrolment. The teacher pupil ratio will be 30 : 1 at primary level, 25 : 1 at secondary level and 15 : 1 at high school level. Among other more important changes planned are research into better curricula, production and distribution of textbooks, more frequent examinations at higher education level and a more efficient administrative system.

UNIVERSITY

Tribhuvan University: Tripureswar, Kathmandu; 1,287 teachers, *c.* 17,451 students.

BIBLIOGRAPHY

BRAMER MIHALY, EUGENE. Foreign Aid and Politics in Nepal: A Case Study (Oxford University Press, 1965).

ELLIOT, J. H. Guide to Nepal (Newman, Calcutta, 1959).

ESKELUND, KARL. The Forgotten Valley (Alvin Redman, London, 1959).

GORDON, EUGENE. Nepal, Sikkim and Bhutan (Oak Tree Press, London, 1972).

HAGEN, TONI. Nepal—a Cultural and Physical Geography (University of Kentucky Press, 1960).

HAGEN, TONI, WAHLEN, F. T., and CORTI, W. R. Nepal: The Kingdom in the Himalayas (Kummerly and Frey, Berne, 1961).

HAMILTON, F. An Account of the Kingdom of Nepal (Constable, Edinburgh, 1819).

JAIN, GIRILAL. India Meets China in Nepal (Asia Publishing House, New York, 1959).

KARAN, P. P., and JENKINS, W. M. Nepal: A Cultural and Physical Geography (University of Kentucky Press, 1960).

The Himalayan Kingdoms: Bhutan, Sikkim and Nepal (Van Nostrand, Princeton, 1963).

KUMAR, SATISH. Rana Polity in Nepal: Origin and Growth (Asia Publishing House for the Indian School of International Studies, 1968).

LALL, DESAR. Lore and Legend of Nepal (Jagat Lall, Kathmandu, 1961).

LANDON, PERCIVAL. Nepal (Constable, London, 1928).

MIHALY, EUGENE B. Foreign Aid and Politics in Nepal (Oxford University Press for Royal Institute of International Affairs, London, 1965).

MORRIS, JOHN. A Winter in Nepal (Hart-Davis, London 1963).

NORTHEY, W. B. The Land of the Ghurkas: or the Himalayan Kingdom of Nepal (Heffer and Sons, Cambridge, 1937).

PANT, Y. P. Development of Nepal (Kitab Mahal, Allahabad, 1968).

PETECH, LUCIANO. Medieval History of Nepal (Istituto Italiano per il Medio ed Estremo Oriente, 1958).

REGMI, D. R. Ancient Nepal (Mukhopadhyay, Calcutta, 1960).

Modern Nepal: Rise and Growth in the Eighteenth Century (Mukhopadhyay, Calcutta, 1961).

ROSE, LEO E. Nepal: Strategy for Survival (California University Press, 1971).

SHRESTHA, B. P. An Introduction to Nepalese Economy (Nepal Press, Kathmandu, 1962).

SITWELL, SACHEVERELL. Great Temples of the East (Oblensky, New York, 1962).

SNELLGROVE, D. Himalayan Pilgrimage (Bruno Cassirer, Oxford, 1961).

TUCKER, FRANCIS. Gorkha: The Story of the Ghurkas of Nepal (Constable, London, 1957).

WHEELER, J. T. A Short History of the Frontier States of Afghanistan, Nepal and Burma (Colliers, New York, 1894).

WOODMAN, DOROTHY. Himalayan Frontiers: a political review of British, Chinese, Indian and Russian rivalries (Barrie and Jenkins, London, 1969).

WRIGHT, DANIEL (Editor). History of Nepal (Cambridge University Press, 1877).

Pakistan

PHYSICAL AND SOCIAL GEOGRAPHY

B. H. Farmer

Pakistan has an area of 803,943 square kilometres (310,403 square miles), excluding Jammu and Kashmir, which is disputed with India. It stretches between 23° 45′ and 36° 50′ North latitude and between 60° 55′ and 75° 30′ East longitude, and is bounded to the west, north-west and north by Iran and Afghanistan (a narrow panhandle in the high Pamirs separates it from direct contact with the U.S.S.R.), to the east and south-east by India and by Jammu and Kashmir, and to the south by the Arabian Sea.

Pakistan, like India, became independent on August 15th, 1947, and inherited, generally speaking, those contiguous districts of the former Indian Empire that had a Muslim majority. Its former eastern wing became the independent People's Republic of Bangladesh after the Indo-Pakistan war of December 1971. Pakistan shortly afterwards left the Commonwealth.

PHYSICAL FEATURES

Much of Pakistan is mountainous or, at any rate, highland. Its northernmost territories consist of the tangled mountains among which the western Himalayas run into the high Karakoram and Pamir ranges. From these the mighty River Indus breaks out through wild gorges to the plains. West of the Indus lies Chitral, a territory of hill ranges, deep gorges and high plateaux. South of this, on the Afghan border, structures are simpler, consisting essentially of a series of mountain arcs like the Safed Koh, Sulaiman and Kirthar Ranges, less complex in geological structure and lower in height than the Himalayas, Pamirs or Karakoram, breached by famous passes like the Khyber and Bolan, and enclosing belts of plateau country. Baluchistan, the westernmost part of West Pakistan's territory, is essentially a region of plateaux and ranges which run over the border into Iran.

Contrasting strongly with all this high and often mountainous terrain is the plain country to the south-east. Part of the great Indo-Gangetic Plain, this consists for the most part of the alluvium brought down by the Indus and its tributaries, of which by far the most important are the five rivers of the Punjab, the Jhelum, Chenab, Ravi, Beas and Sutlej (part of whose course lies, however, in Indian or Kashmiri territory). The southern part of the Indian border runs through the waterless wastes of the Thar Desert.

CLIMATE

The Pakistan plains, like those of northern India, have an annual cycle of three seasons. The "cool season" (December to February) has relatively low average temperatures (Lahore, 53°F. January) but warm days. Karachi, farther south and on the coast, is rather warmer (65°F. January average). This season is dry, apart from rain brought by northwesterly disturbances. The "hot season" (March to May) builds up to very high temperatures (Lahore, 89°F. May average, but up to 120°F. by day, and even hotter in that notorious hot-spot, Jacobabad; but rather cooler, 85°F. May average, in Karachi); this season is dry. From June to September the south-west monsoon brings more wind, lower temperatures, and rains that are everywhere relatively light (13.5 in. in four months at Lahore) and that fall off to little or nothing westward into Baluchistan and southward into Sind and the Thar Desert. Much of Pakistan would, in fact, be unproductive agriculturally if it were not for irrigation.

The mountains of Pakistan have a climatic regime modified by altitude and with a winter maximum of rainfall (such as it is) in the north-west; but, again, widely characterized by aridity.

SOILS

The soils of the plains of Pakistan, like those in similar physiographic circumstances in India, exhibit considerable variety. Those of the Thar desert tend to be poor and sandy, and there is a good deal of natural salinity in the more arid tracts, especially in Sind. More fertile alluvium follows the main rivers and also spreads more widely in the Punjab, but there is, again as in India, the danger of man-induced salinity and alkalinity with the spread of irrigation, and consequent rise in the water-table and capillary ascent of salts to the surface. Indeed, large areas of land have gone out of cultivation for just this reason.

The hill areas of Pakistan tend to have poor, skeletal mountain soils, though better conditions prevail in some intermont valleys.

VEGETATION

In the distant past, much of the plains area of Pakistan was probably covered with tropical thorn forest, degenerating into semi-desert or even true desert in the Thar. Similar dry types of vegetation may well have covered the western hills and plateaux, though there was dry evergreen forest on the Sulaiman and other relatively high ranges. The northern mountains, in Chitral and adjacent areas, showed a more complex altitudinal zonation, including pine forest.

Now, after centuries if not millennia of occupation by man and his animals, there is very little "natural" vegetation left, except for poor, semi-desert scrub in uncultivated portions of the plains of Pakistan (such as part of the Thal, between the Indus and Jhelum) and in Baluchistan; montane forests in parts of the western and northern hills (notably the Sulaimans). Even this surviving vegetation has been degraded by man: for instance, by the practice of pastoralism in Baluchistan and elsewhere in the western hills and plateaux.

Not surprisingly, Pakistan is desperately short of timber, and has actually planted irrigated forests, especially of shisham (*Dalbergia sissoo*) in the Thal and elsewhere.

MINERALS

Pakistan is not well endowed with mineral wealth. The only coal (mainly sub-bituminous and non-coking) is at Makerwal, west of the Indus in the old North-West Frontier Province, and round Quetta in Baluchistan. Production has now reached about a million tons annually, but imports are still necessary. Lignites are exploited near Peshawar. The only oilfield is a very small one, on the Potwar Plateau south of Rawalpindi; though a significant natural gas field, now supplying a string of power stations by pipeline, has been opened up at Sui. Iron ore deposits are very meagre, some of the better ones (e.g. those in Chitral) being almost inaccessible. Chromite alone amongst non-ferrous metal ores is mined in any quantity—near Hindubagh, Baluchistan. Salt, gypsum and magnesite are found, however, in the Salt Range.

POPULATION

The estimated mid-year population in 1975 was 70,260,000. Rapid population increase is a problem much as it is in India, and for similar reasons.

Pakistan has densities of over 750 per square mile in well-watered Districts like Lyallpur, but an overall average of only 226 per square mile (1975).

Pakistan also had sizeable conurbations in Karachi (3,469,000) and Lahore (2,148,000) at the 1972 census.

ETHNIC GROUPS

There are considerable contrasts of race within Pakistan. Tall, relatively fair and blue-eyed Pathans of the western hills contrast with darker, brown-eyed (though also often tall) "plainsmen"—itself a heterogeneous category.

Although the population of Pakistan is overwhelmingly Muslim, it is divided, not only by race but also by linguistic and by tribal differences. Punjabi, Baluchi and Pashtu (the language of the Pathans) are spoken. Tribal divisions are most noticeable in the western hills, but also affect the plains where there are Janglis (former lawless nomads, now largely cultivators), Thiringiuzars (camel-herders) and other "tribes".

HISTORY*

Mahmud Husain

(Revised by Sharif al Mujahid, 1976)

Pakistan as a separate political entity came into existence on August 15th, 1947. It was no doubt the result of the efforts of the Muslim people under the leadership of *Quaid-i-Azam* Muhammad Ali Jinnah. But the State of Pakistan was technically brought into being through an agreement amongst the three principal parties—the Indian National Congress, the Muslim League and the British Government. The June 3rd Plan embodied this agreement and the Indian Independence Act gave it constitutional and legal validity.

THE PROBLEMS OF PARTITION

From the very beginning, however, Pakistan suffered from certain handicaps and was faced with certain difficulties. Some of these were inherent in the situation while others were created by forces hostile to her very existence. The inherent difficulties were not only those with which any new state would normally be confronted but also those resulting from the fact that the entire machinery of Central Government was to be set up in a new capital; the services which were to administer the new state were themselves not compact and organic wholes but consisted of people belonging to different provinces of British India who had opted for Pakistan. The number of Muslims in the higher services was quite inadequate to run the state. This was particularly true of the Eastern wing which had hardly any senior civil servants to look after its affairs. Even the portion of the army which came to Pakistan did not consist of complete units but of officers and men who had opted for Pakistan, many of whom at the time of partition were either in India or abroad. Out of these elements the army of Pakistan had to be formed afresh. Moreover, two of the major provinces of Pakistan containing 80 per cent of her population, Bengal and Punjab, had themselves been divided and like the Centre, East Bengal also had to set up a new capital. As to political leadership, though the Muslim League had exercised unusual influence over the minds of the Muslims of the sub-continent before partition, it had not produced the kind of well-knit organization which

* Since 1947: for the pre-1947 period see *India: History*.

its chief rival the Indian National Congress had been able to do. It had undoubtedly in Muhammad Ali Jinnah a trusted and experienced leader but he died when Pakistan was only a year old and his chief lieutenant Liaquat Ali Khan was assassinated in 1951. No one of that eminence was then available to give a lead to the country. Also among the difficulties inherent in the situation was that Pakistan was split into two parts with a distance of over a thousand miles of Indian territory between them. Economically, Pakistan happened to be the very much less developed part of an under-developed sub-continent. She did possess certain agricultural assets, notably jute in the East and cotton in the West in addition to food crops in both the wings, but she had no industries worth the name. The Eastern wing was cut off from the jute mills of Calcutta and the Western from the textile mills of Ahmedabad and Bombay. The Eastern wing had also lost its natural port and commercial centre, Calcutta. To make things worse, Pakistan lacked both capital and the know-how for industrial development.

Indo-Pakistan Disputes

Other problems were the result of the Radcliffe Boundary Commission's award and the peculiar nature of Indo-Pakistan relations. The Kashmir question and the dispute over the canal waters were a corollary of the award. The State of Jammu and Kashmir had a large Muslim majority, was contiguous to Pakistan, and all its economic interests and communications linked it with Pakistan. But for the award which gave the Muslim majority district of Gurdaspur to India, India would not be geographically connected with it at all. However, India, through the Hindu Maharaja, secured its accession when he had already lost his hold over the State. Kashmir has since then poisoned the relations between India and Pakistan. The award also broke to pieces the irrigation system of the Punjab by awarding the headworks of the Punjab canals at Madhopur and Ferozepur to India. This gave India a weapon which she could and did use against Pakistan. As early as April 1948 water supply was cut off and Pakistan had to conclude an agreement under duress by which she surrendered essential riparian rights and agreed to make a payment to India for the use of water. Constant bickerings followed until the matter was taken up at an international level and an agreement arrived at through the good offices of, and a substantial loan from, the World Bank (*see* chapter *Indus Waters Treaty*).

India also withheld payment of Pakistan's share of the assets of the Reserve Bank of India. This led to a serious financial crisis in the very first year of Pakistan's existence. The state was on the verge of bankruptcy. It was only after Mahatma Gandhi's intervention that the Government of India released a portion of Pakistan's share of the assets.

Pakistan had also to face an unprecedented refugee problem. Massacres of the Muslims of East Punjab, Delhi and Rajputana, which had repercussions in West Punjab and North-West Frontier Province, resulted in the uprooting of millions of people in both countries. Pakistan in its nascent stage had to solve the problems arising out of the huge refugee influx.

POLITICAL AND CONSTITUTIONAL DEVELOPMENTS

Pakistan, which had become an independent Dominion under the Indian Independence Act 1947, was administered, to begin with, under the Government of India Act 1935, as adapted in Pakistan. Adaptation of the Act was natural in view of the new status. The position of the Governor-General himself had undergone a vital change in the sense that he was now the Governor-General of an independent Dominion. Moreover, under the Indian Independence Act a Constituent Assembly had been created which was very different from the Indian Legislative Assembly. Parliamentary government, which had existed in a rudimentary form in the provinces of India, was now implanted at the Centre as well as the provinces of Pakistan. The Indian Independence Act had abolished the special powers of the Governor-General which he had exercised ever since the time of Cornwallis (1786). Yet because of the unusual situation, the Governor-General was still armed with special powers to adapt the Government of India Act. Many arrangements which had yet to be made between the two Dominions consequent on partition and the new responsibility for the defence of the country made these powers necessary. But they were to be exercised by the Governor-General on the advice of the Cabinet. Hence these were essentially different from the powers of the Governor-General in the past.

The Constituent Assembly, to which power was transferred formally by Earl Mountbatten on August 15th, 1947, was a small house elected indirectly by the provincial legislatures on the basis of one member for a population of one million. It consisted of 69 members to begin with; soon, however, the number was raised to 79 of whom 44 represented East Bengal.

Quaid-i-Azam Muhammad Ali Jinnah was the first Governor-General. He derived his powers not so much from the office he held as from the position he occupied amongst the people. He was the father of the nation. His wishes were respected by everyone. He was also the President of the Constituent Assembly and kept one of the ministries—States and Frontier Regions—for himself. His presiding over the Cabinet meetings was considered natural by the people and ministers alike. It was only after his death (September 1948) that Prime Minister Liaquat Ali Khan came to occupy a predominant position in the government. Liaquat Ali Khan visualized for himself the chief role in government not as Governor-General but as Prime Minister. Khwaja Nazimuddin became Governor-General and played the role of a constitutional head of state.

The Drafting of a Constitution

Constitution-making was delayed in Pakistan for many reasons. Apart from the various problems confronted by Pakistan which demanded solution, a constitution incorporating the principles of Islam was something new and not easy to devise. The only notable steps towards constitution-making during the

Prime Ministership of Liaquat Ali Khan were the passing of the *Objectives Resolution* (1949) and the presentation of the *Interim Report of the Basiu Principles Committee* (1950).

By 1952, Liaquat Ali Khan had been assassinated and had been replaced by Khwaja Nazimuddin as Prime Minister, while Ghulam Muhammad had become Governor-General.

Taking advantage of discontent over food shortage the Governor-General dismissed Khwaja Nazimuddin's Cabinet in April 1953, even though it enjoyed the fullest confidence of the House. With the dismissal of this cabinet Pakistan entered an era of "Palace" intrigues. Muhammad Ali Bogra, Pakistan's Ambassador in Washington, was made Prime Minister. Renewed efforts were made towards constitution-making. This time the efforts were more successful. The question of representation between the Eastern and Western wings was settled by the Mohammad Ali Formula, under which the majority of the Lower House was to come from East Pakistan on the basis of population and of the Upper House from the four units of West Pakistan, but the number was fixed in such a way that in a joint session of the two Houses the members from each wing numbered 175 (East Pakistan 165 + 10, and West Pakistan 135 + 40). The two Houses were given equal powers and in case of conflict the joint House was to decide the issue. Another important provision in the formula was that if a bill was not supported by at least 30 per cent of the members from each wing it could not become law. Votes of confidence in the Government and the election of the President of Pakistan were also to be decided in joint session. On the basis of this formula a constitution was prepared. The Constituent Assembly also passed a measure curtailing the powers of the Governor-General. When this constitution was about to be passed the Constituent Assembly was dissolved by the Governor-General in October, 1954. Thus the several years' work of the Constituent Assembly was undone at one stroke, ostensibly because the Assembly was non-representative and because of undue delay in making the constitution, but in fact because the constitution curtailed the Governor-General's powers.

Ghulam Muhammad's idea was to present a constitution to his liking without bothering to create another Constituent Assembly. But the Federal Court, which declared valid Ghulam Muhammad's action in dissolving the Constituent Assembly, also declared that the constitution could be made only by the Constituent Assembly, which should be elected on the same basis as the first one, i.e. indirectly by the Provincial Legislatures. Now that the constitution of the Provincial Legislatures, the East Pakistan Assembly in particular, had undergone a radical change, the new Constituent Assembly was a very different body. Though the League was still the largest party in the new Assembly it did not have an overall majority (33 out of 80). The new Assembly had six parties represented, with none in the majority, compared with only two parties in the earlier Assembly.

The Constitutions of 1956 and 1962

Before taking up the work of writing the constitution the new Assembly turned towards the question of uniting all the provinces of West Pakistan into one single province. Zealously promoted by Ghulam Muhammad, it was particularly popular in the Punjab. In the smaller provinces where there was opposition to this idea, changes in the governments were brought about to facilitate its acceptance by the Provincial Assemblies. Having brought about the unity of West Pakistan the Assembly went ahead with the work of constitution-making. Finally in March 1956 the constitution was framed during the Prime Ministership of Chaudhri Muhammad Ali. The spade work done by the first Assembly proved extremely useful to the second. The constitution of 1956 provided for a federation of two provinces only, namely East and West Pakistan. It recognized the principle of parity of representation for the two provinces and provided for only one House. There were several Islamic provisions amongst the directive principles. The Head of the State was to be a Muslim and although Islam was not declared the State Religion, no law which went against the teachings of Islam was to be promulgated and the existing laws were to be brought into conformity with Islam. The rights of the non-Muslims were recognized and their personal laws were not to be interfered with. The question of joint versus separate electorates was put aside to be settled by the Legislatures. The Constitution of 1956 created a federation with a good deal of decentralization and established a parliamentary system of government. Urdu and Bengali were both recognized as state languages, though English was to be used for official purposes for a number of years. This constitution, however, was not given a fair trial. The services did not seem to be well inclined towards it and had ambitions of their own. Political parties being weak and not well organized, the services were able to assert themselves. Ghulam Muhammad and later his successor, Iskandar Mirza, did not believe in parliamentary government or any kind of democracy in Pakistan. And when the parliamentary system had become discredited—a situation to which he himself had so very largely contributed—Iskandar Mizra abrogated the Constitution (October 7th, 1958). Not being a popular leader he had realized that he had no chance of being elected as President under the Constitution of 1956. He now promulgated martial law under General Muhammad Ayub Khan, the then Commander-in-Chief. Parties were banned and the legislature was abolished.

A few days later (October 27th) General Muhammad Ayub Khan removed Iskandar Mirza, and himself became President. Martial law continued until in 1962 a new Constitution was promulgated, the most important feature of which was the institution of Basic Democracies. As local governmental institutions, Basic Democracies had indeed been in existence for some time. The Constitution provided for a presidential system of government and came closest to the French Constitution under General de Gaulle.

All executive power and a good deal of legislative

power was concentrated in the hands of the President and although he was elected for a term of five years, during the term he was practically irremovable. There was much more centralization of power than in the Constitution of 1956. The powers of the legislatures were limited, even in regard to finance. The system of election was indirect. The only election on a direct basis was provided at the lowest level when the Basic Democrats (40,000 in East Pakistan and 40,000 in West Pakistan, later raised to 60,000 each) were elected. All the councils at the *Tehsil*, district and division levels were indirectly elected, one after the other. For the election of the Provincial and Central Assemblies and the President, the entire body of Basic Democrats formed an Electoral College.

The Overthrow of Ayub Khan

In 1968 the regime had made the costly mistake of celebrating the tenth anniversary of President Ayub's seizure of power as the "Decade of Reforms". These celebrations were overdone and instead of popularizing the régime they created just the opposite effect and brought to the surface all the hitherto submerged opposition. What had been privately felt about corruption, nepotism and autocratic controls now began to be said in public. Religious elements and the students took the lead in anti-Ayub agitation. Disorders took place on a large scale and the urban workers and the peasantry, particularly in East Pakistan, became involved. What had seemed to be an extremely strong administrative structure appeared to crumble to pieces. President Ayub made concession after concession to public opinion and to the political parties and held a Round Table Conference with political leaders in February 1969, but all to no avail. Thus, when in March 1969 it became impossible to maintain law and order, he decided—or rather was forced—to quit and surrender power to his Commander-in-Chief, General Agha Muhammad Yahya Khan. Martial Law was once more proclaimed in Pakistan. The new President and Chief Martial Law Administrator, however, lost no time in announcing that general elections would be held in October 1970, later postponed to December 1970.

Thus the whole question of the constitution of Pakistan was once more re-opened. But certain important constitutional issues were settled by the President. Under one of his orders the new Assembly was to be elected on the basis not of parity but of the population of the various provinces, which meant that 56 per cent of seats were to go to East Pakistan. One Unit was dissolved and the provinces of the West Punjab, N.W.F.P., Sind (including Karachi) and Baluchistan actually started functioning separately from July 1970. Gone also was the system of Basic Democracy and the new constitution was to provide direct elections and a parliamentary system of government. The main issues that remained to be settled by the National Assembly were the extent of provincial autonomy in a federal set-up and the content of the Islamic element in the constitution.

However, following the postponement of the Constituent Assembly, events took a serious turn in the Eastern Wing. Internal turmoil, followed by India's invasion, resulted in the secession of the Eastern Wing of Pakistan as Bangladesh in December 1971. Military defeat thoroughly exposed and discredited the military dictatorship. Yahya Khan fell, and Zulfiqar Ali Bhutto, the founder and Chairman of the Pakistan People's Party, took over as President. Obviously it was in the most difficult circumstances that he had come to office. Immediately he had to deal with the aftermath of defeat. Even so the task of constitution-making was taken in hand.

The Constituent Assembly started meeting and a consensus was soon achieved among the leaders of all the parties represented in the Assembly (October 1972). A federal parliamentary system of government was agreed upon, with four units and two houses of legislature. The Prime Minister, answerable to the lower house, was to be the chief government executive, while the President elected by both houses voting together was visualized as a constitutional head. Quite a few subjects were assigned to the Federal Centre which would make it sufficiently effective, though considerable authority was still left in the hands of the four federal units. On the basis of the principles agreed upon the Constitution Committee of the Constituent Assembly prepared a draft for the consideration of the Assembly. Early in 1973 Pakistan at long last acquired a democratic constitution, framed by a directly elected assembly, which came into force on August 14th, 1973. At the inauguration of the Constitution the President, Zulfiqar Ali Bhutto, became the Prime Minister of Pakistan, since this office had now become the most important in the new set-up.

POLITICAL PARTIES

A few years before the partition of India the Muslim League, which had been founded in 1906, had become for all practical purposes the only party of the Muslims. To be sure, there were some nationalist Muslims in the Indian National Congress and certain Muslim organizations which as a rule co-operated with the Congress, but the influence of these organizations was in no way comparable to the influence which the League exercised over the Muslims. Among the Hindus also there were several parties, but the Indian National Congress was pre-eminent among them.

The Muslim League, however, was not a political party in the sense in which the term is ordinarily understood. It was more of a movement that had attracted people from various walks of life and represented different, even opposing, interests. That diverse elements should come under the banner of the League was a source of strength while the struggle for Pakistan lasted. Once, however, the goal was achieved, the presence of heterogeneous elements in the League became a cause of weakness. Earlier cohesion gave way to fissiparous tendencies. However, the achievement of Pakistan had given a tremendous prestige to the League and had been responsible for discrediting other parties which had opposed her creation. Only the Congress survived among the Hindus of East Bengal.

Thus in the first Constituent Assembly (1947–54) there were to begin with only two parties. Apart from the Muslim League Assembly Party there was a small opposition consisting of twelve Hindus belonging to the Congress. The League practically dictated terms. The absence of a strong opposition was, however, not a healthy phenomenon. When through secessions from the League itself new groups and parties were started, the League adopted an unreasonable attitude. Its highest leadership was not capable of distinguishing between opposition to a party and opposition to a state. Opposition to the League was considered opposition to Pakistan and those opposed to the League were termed enemies of Pakistan.

Gradually new parties arose in Pakistan, founded by men who were old Leaguers. Thus came into existence the Jinnah Muslim League of Mamdot in West Pakistan and the Awami Muslim League of Suhrawardy in East Bengal. Such was the charm of the name, that both these leaders called their organizations "Muslim League"; they had been Leaguers and their programmes were no different from the League's. A little afterwards, the two decided to amalgamate as the Jinnah Awami Muslim League. This League won nineteen seats in the Punjab elections in 1951. However, within a short time the two leaders parted company. Again the old nomenclature was revived, but after some time, under the pressure of Maulana Bhashani, the word "Muslim" was dropped from the Awami Muslim League. It opened its doors to non-Muslims and functioned under the joint leadership of Suhrawardy and Bhashani, one exercising considerable influence over the educated classes and the other over the peasantry. A secession within the Constituent Assembly brought into being the Azad Pakistan Party in the Punjab.

When in 1954 elections took place to the Provincial Assembly in East Bengal, the parties opposed to the League constituted a United Front. The component units of the Front were: the Awami League, the Krishak Proja, the Ganatantri Dal (or the Democratic Party) and the Nizam-i-Islam. The Pakistan National Congress was also closely allied with the United Front. The United Front evolved a programme consisting of twenty-one points with emphasis on Provincial Autonomy. It also demanded the dissolution of the First Constituent Assembly and the quashing of the *Basic Principles Committee Report*. United Front obtained 222 seats out of 309 while the League won only 9 seats.

No sooner were the elections over than a rift developed between the component elements, particularly between Fazlul Haq and the Awami League. Later when Suhrawardy joined the Central Government and advocated a pronounced pro-Western policy, Bhashani first challenged Suhrawardy within the party and when he could not carry the party with him, left it and formed his own National Awami Party (N.A.P.). In West Pakistan, though the League had won the Provincial Elections of 1951 in the Punjab (Liaquat Ali Khan was still alive), a number of small parties had become active, and these parties were greatly encouraged bv the League's débâcle in East Bengal in 1954. Apart from Mamdot's Jinnah Awami Muslim League and Mian Iftikharuddin's Azad Pakistan Party, Maulana Maududi's Jamaat-i-Islami also became quite active; it stood for an Islamic constitution and for the revival of Islamic values. It was a small party but it had a good organization and could count on a number of devoted and sincere workers. Also Allama Mashriqi's Islam League somewhat haphazardly appeared on the scene, only to go into oblivion again; it was banned early in 1958 after the murder of Dr. Khan Sahib. Other small groups, old and new, also began to show signs of life.

But any description of parties in Pakistan prior to 1958 would be incomplete without reference to a group of people known by the high-sounding name of the Republican Party. Since political parties were not well organized and their leadership since the death of Liaquat Ali Khan not very effective, ambitious civil servants could easily dominate the political scene in Pakistan. Several of them had been given political posts by Muhammad Ali Jinnah, Liaquat Ali Khan and Nazimuddin. They played one party against another and undermined their solidarity and thus were one of the chief factors in bringing about the instability over which they shed crocodile tears. In 1956, not content with playing one party against another, and one leader against another, they produced a party, a sort of "King's Friends", which was called the Republican Party and was placed under the leadership of Dr. Khan Sahib.

Actually a government of the Republican Party under the premiership of Firoz Khan Noon was in office when in October 1958 the army took over the government. The legislatures were dissolved and the parties were banned. Only shortly before President Ayub Khan promulgated a new constitution in 1962 were the parties allowed to function, though with certain restrictions. The first elections to the Basic Democracies had taken place in 1960, before the coming into force of the new constitution. At that time the Basic Democracies were viewed as instruments of local self-government only. Parties did not put up candidates—indeed parties were banned. It was these Basic Democracies which were said to have confirmed President Ayub in office. With the coming of the 1962 Constitution parties were revived.

The Revival of Parties

In the process of revival there occurred a schism in the Muslim League. The old guard of the League was opposed to President Ayub and the 1962 constitution while some of the Leaguers in the lower echelons had joined Ayub's presidential cabinet in June 1962. The latter ultimately chose Ayub Khan as the party chief, and their party came to be called Convention Muslim League. The original League party, which was revived through the convoking of the 1958 League council, came to be known as Council League and was led by Khwaja Nazimuddin, a veteran League leader and a former Governor-General and Prime Minister.

In Bengal there was a move not to revive parties at all but to fight unitedly for the restoration of democracy and against the Constitution of 1962. Thus had come into existence the N.D.F. (National Democratic

Front) with Nurul Amin, Ataur Rahman Khan, Hamidul Haq Choudhry and Abu Hussain Sarkar as leaders. But though the Front was never dissolved it lost much of its significance when several parties of East Bengal were revived, among them the Awami League, led by Sheikh Mujibur Rahman, the National Awami Party of Maulana Bhashani, and the Nizam-i-Islam.

When the time came for the election to the Basic Democracies in 1964 under the new Constitution, five opposition parties joined to form a Combined Opposition Party (C.O.P.) which included: (1) Council Muslim League, (2) the Awami League, (3) N.A.P., (4) the Nizam-i-Islam, (5) the Jamaat-i-Islami. The National Democratic Front gave its general support to them. Thus the election was fought between C.O.P. and the Convention Muslim League. The opposition presidential candidate, Miss Fatima Jinnah, made a great impression, but it was not to be expected that, under the then existing situation, she, or for that matter any person, could win against a candidate so powerfully entrenched as Field-Marshal Muhammad Ayub Khan. Her main contribution was that she demonstrated for the first time that the authority of Ayub Khan could be challenged.

A new party, the Pakistan People's Party, professing socialistic ideals, was formed in 1947 by Zulfiqar Ali Bhutto, who had been an enthusiastic supporter of President Ayub for eight years and served him as his minister. It is significant that, in spite of Leftists being more popular in East Pakistan, Bhutto's influence remained confined to West Pakistan. The N.A.P. was split, one section led by Wali Khan in East Pakistan and the other in the West; and in late 1968 certain non-political figures like Air Marshal Asghar Khan entered the political arena.

A few days before the fall of the Ayub regime in March 1969, Air Marshal Asghar Khan formed the Justice Party. However, because of the widespread belief that the profusion of parties in Pakistan militated against the restoration and successful working of democracy, attempts were made to bring about mergers. Several parties tried to come closer together in order to be able to work for the restoration of parliamentary democracy in the country. One of these efforts succeeded and several parties did join hands under the leadership of Nurul Amin. These parties included the Nizam-i-Islam, a section of the Awami League led by Nawabzada Nasrullah Khan, Asghar Khan's newly founded Justice Party and such remnants of the National Democratic Front as followed Nurul Amin. Collectively they came to be known as the National Democratic Party (N.D.P.).

Later Asghar Khan left the N.D.P. and founded the Tahrik-i-Istiqlal. Another Muslim League under Khan Abdul Qayyum Khan was also formed so that there were three Muslim Leagues, the Council Muslim League, the Convention Muslim League and Qayyum Khan's Muslim League.

Ulema or Muslim religious scholars have also been politically active. Not only the Jamaat-i-Islami but also the Jamiat-i-Ulama-i-Islam, were working for the establishment of the Islamic Order and against Socialism. Another organization of Sunni Ulama with more or less similar aims was formed to put up candidates in the elections. There was also a section of the Ulama (the Hazarvi Group) which had leanings towards Socialism and which worked in co-operation with the Pakistan People's Party during the elections.

In East Pakistan the party which made real headway was the Awami League under Mujibur Rahman. Bhashani had also a considerable following of his own particularly among the peasants.

Finally, one may point out a few general features of the parties. The parties in Pakistan are not like well-disciplined parties elsewhere. They have no democratic base; regular membership does not exist—it is mostly fictitious. There are working committees, organizing committees, co-ordination committees and conveners but they are seldom elected by the party membership at large. The party membership itself is indeterminate. Leaders are mostly self-appointed for all practical purposes. In Pakistan, therefore, it would be wrong be wrong to judge the influence of a party by its regular membership.

Most parties except the Muslim League were in effect regional or provincial parties. However, for a long time the Muslim League had been a house divided against itself and in any case had lost its glamour. The most popular party in West Pakistan was the Pakistan People's Party.

THE ELECTION AND AFTER

The first ever General Elections were held in December 1970. At the elections only two parties achieved overwhelming success, the Awami League in East Pakistan and the Pakistan People's Party in two of the largest provinces of West Pakistan—the Punjab and Sind. The Awami League had fought the elections on the basis of Six Points which were to ensure an extreme form of provincial autonomy and decentralization of authority.

The Awami League, having secured nearly all the seats from East Pakistan, obtained an absolute majority in the Central Legislature. In the normal course the largest party should have had the right to form the government but this would not be a workable proposition in Pakistan in view of the federal character of the state and the exclusively provincial character of the party concerned. The Awami League seemed to be inclined to coalesce with some of the smaller parties of West Pakistan. But the P.P.P. chief vehemently opposed the idea. He sought assurances on certain constitutional issues before the calling of the session of the National Assembly. As the P.P.P. was the second largest party in the Assembly, the President postponed the session to give an opportunity for arriving at a consensus on some of the remaining constitutional issues. Negotiations among the political parties *inter se* and between the President and the Awami League leader followed. It was during the period that these negotiations were on that the situation in East Pakistan took a new turn. The Awami

League, instead of making any concession on the Six Points, adopted a much more uncompromising stand and virtually advocated independence for East Pakistan, a very different proposition from the provincial autonomy on the basis of which elections had been won.

The administration of the province was paralysed and an intense hate campaign was launched against not only West Pakistan but also against all those inhabitants of East Pakistan itself whose mother-tongue was not Bengali. Finally on March 23rd, Pakistan Day, the Bangladesh flag was hoisted and the stage set for secession.

It was in these circumstances that the government decided to take action, claiming that it was necessary to put a stop to massacres and to save the integrity of the country. Mujib was arrested and brought over to West Pakistan.

When the Pakistan Army came into action, many Bengalis fled to India, some in sympathy with secession, others under duress or out of fear. The Karachi Government claimed that India was the base for Bengali insurgents' training and incursions into East Pakistan. There followed border clashes between Indian and Pakistani troops and finally, in December 1971, a regular invasion of East Pakistan by the Indian armed forces. However, the war did not remain confined to the East but spread to West Pakistan as well. It was a short but decisive war in which India achieved quick success, followed by surrender of Pakistan troops in the East, and a ceasefire in the West.

In the aftermath of the war, Bhutto's government embarked on the task of amending the constitution. The constitution proposed in 1972 seemed to have the support of all parties. In early 1973, however, opposition parties of the right and left formed a United Democratic Front to demand amendments which would create "a truly Islamic, democratic and federal constitution". Their fears that the constitution gave too much power to the Prime Minister and the central government were strengthened by events in Baluchistan where tribal fighting was followed, in February 1973, by the imposition of direct presidential rule and the taking of emergency powers. The amended constitution came into force in August 1973 with Bhutto as Prime Minister. The situation in Baluchistan remained grave and although the Government offered an amnesty for political opponents, fighting continued in the province. In addition, dissident movements became more active in the other provinces during 1974.

The National Awami Party was banned in February 1975 and many of its leading members were arrested, following the murder of the North-West Frontier Province's chief minister, Hayat Mohammed Sherpao. In the same month, despite the boycott of the opposition parties, the National Assembly adopted a constitution bill empowering the Government to extend the state of emergency beyond six months without parliamentary approval.

The Government's decision to ban the NAP was referred to the Supreme Court under the Political Parties Act of 1962. The Court's proceedings were boycotted by the NAP but the Court upheld the government's decision. Following the Court's ruling in October 1972, the Political Parties Act was amended in January 1976 to provide that any office bearer of a dissolved political party at the national and provincial level would be disqualified from being a member of Parliament or a provincial assembly and from being elected to them for a period of five years. Under this amendment, some 24 members who owed allegiance to the NAP before its dissolution would lose their seats in the national and provincial assemblies and the Senate.

Meanwhile, a new party, the National Democratic Party (NDP), was launched in November 1975, with Sher Baz Khan Mazari, leader of the Independent Group in the National Assembly, as leader. It claims the adherence of most of the former NAP leaders.

FOREIGN POLICY

The foreign policy of Pakistan has been conditioned very largely by Indo-Pakistan relations. This is not unexpected. When the idea of Pakistan was mooted, it evoked great hostility on the part of the Hindus of India irrespective of the party to which they belonged. And even when Pakistan was accepted by the Congress this acceptance was not genuine, as is evident from the resolution of the All India Congress Committee which approved the June 3rd plan: "Geography and the mountains and the seas fashioned India as she is and no human agency can change that shape .... Economic circumstances and the insistent demands of international affairs make the unity of India still more necessary. . . ." The Hindu Mahasabha Party was even more candid, saying: "India is one and indivisible and there will never be peace unless and until the separated areas are brought back into the Indian Union". Jawaharlal Nehru even after the partition said: "Both the dominions will unite into one country". Vallabhbhai Patel expressed "full hope and confidence that sooner or later we shall be again united in common allegiance to one country". According to Abul Kalam Azad, "Patel was convinced that the new State of Pakistan was not viable and could not last". It was not only in the beginning that such thoughts were expressed. They continued to be reiterated by Pandit Nehru and others. Keith Callard observed in 1959: "Many Indians feel that the creation of Pakistan was a tragic mistake which might still be corrected, at least so far as East Bengal is concerned".

Pakistan has thus been confronted from the very beginning with the problem of survival. India's territory and population are over four times those of Pakistan; her industrial potential is at least ten times as great and her armed forces, even before the massive military aid began to flow into India in the wake of the Indo-Chinese clashes of 1962, were three times those of Pakistan (the ratio of armed strength has been disturbed lately to the disadvantage of Pakistan). When one takes into account the fact that Pakistan was divided into two wings, one thousand miles apart, the ratio works further to the disadvantage of Pakistan. Pakistan, therefore, from Jinnah to Muhammad Ayub Khan made many attempts to come to some arrangement by which the two countries, instead of wasting their energies against one another, would come to some clear and friendly understanding and would settle the disputes by peaceful means. Jinnah spoke of a mutually evolved "Monroe Doctrine". Liaquat Ali Khan made a proposal for the settlement of disputes between the two countries by means of arbitration. Ayub Khan suggested an understanding on "common defence" to which Pandit Nehru's retort was "common defence against whom?". This was not long before the Indo-Chinese flare-up of 1962. Once Nehru threatened Pakistan with "other methods" and on another occasion he mooted loudly the idea of "police action" in East Pakistan.

Pakistan could not afford to belittle the importance of the anti-Pakistan feelings in India. She could not afford to consider the pronouncements of Indian leaders as empty threats, particularly because of her own relative weakness and because of India's record of settling territorial problems by the use of force in Kashmir, Jungadh, Hyderabad and Goa.

The basic difficulty in Indo-Pakistan relations seemed to be the very existence of Pakistan. Because of this basic difficulty the problems between the two countries remained unsolved. Among the causes which created estrangement, there was the position of minorities and the question of evacuee property. The Canal Water dispute and the dispute over some of the boundaries also proved difficult, but certain adjustments were made with regard to them. The construction of the Farakha Barrage in West Bengal was a comparatively recent step which had created dissatisfaction in Pakistan. Then there was the vital Kashmir question, to which a solution has not yet been found. Last but not least was the Bangladesh issue which attained such vast proportions, due to India's involvement. The result has been that there have been occasions when the two countries have fought local wars, as in Kashmir, and two fully-fledged wars in 1965 and 1971. Yet there are no two countries whose defence, security and prosperity more demand that they should be friends and allies. Instead of wasting their energies on armaments, they should devote themselves to the raising of the standard of living of the common man, for on that their future really depends.

Since the war of 1971 and its tragic outcome feeling has been growing in favour of an understanding with India on the basis of "live and let live", and ever since he took office as head of government, Mr. Bhutto has been advocating *rapprochement* with India. He achieved partial success in this policy in the shape of the Simla Agreement (July 1972), under which the withdrawal of Indian and Pakistani troops from occupied territory was mutually agreed upon. But the Simla Agreement has not had an altogether smooth passage, the withdrawal being held up for more than a year until another Indo-Pak agreement of August 1973 was concluded. The return of prisoners of war was completed in May 1974.

Linked with the problem of relations with India was the question of the recognition of Bangladesh. Pakistan's recognition of Bangladesh came in February 1974. Bhutto had insisted that Bangladesh give up plans for the trial of certain prisoners of war as a condition for normalizing relations. This was rejected by Sheikh Mujib, who also refused to attend the Islamic Summit Conference due to be held in Lahore in February 1974 and which would provide an opportunity to resolve the differences between the two countries. In an attempt to break the deadlock, a mission of foreign ministers of the Islamic countries was sent to Dacca. Finally, a few hours before the opening of the conference, Bhutto announced his decision to recognize Bangladesh. Relations between the two countries remained on the cool until the toppling of the Mujib regime in August 1975. Pakistan was the first country to recognize the new regime headed by Khondakar Mushtaq Ahmad, and also persuaded the West Asian Muslim countries to extend aid to Bangladesh. In the autumn of 1975 the two countries agreed to establish diplomatic relations, and the exchange of envoys took place in January 1976.

Relations with India, however, deteriorated further after the latter's nuclear test in May 1974. Further tension between the two countries was created in July as a result of alleged troop movements by India and Afghanistan on Pakistan's borders. Nevertheless, after assurances by India that the provisions of the Simla Agreement would be observed and that there would be no threat of the use of force in settling differences, an agreement was reached by both countries, in September, restoring communication and travel facilities which had been broken off at the time of the 1971 war. In January 1975, trade agreements and an agreement on the resumption of shipping services were also concluded. In May 1976 India and Pakistan agreed to exchange ambassadors in July, and in June agreement was reached on restoring severed air links.

Relations Beyond the Sub-Continent

Relations with India have largely influenced the relations of Pakistan with other nations. Pakistan felt at an early stage of her existence that the Commonwealth was not a particularly useful instrument for the resolution of her disputes with India. As to the two major blocs into which the world was divided, Pakistan, without allying herself definitely with one, was inclined towards the West for more than a decade of her existence. The United States being the most powerful nation in the Western Bloc, Pakistan tried to come closer to her, particularly from 1954 onwards when a Mutual Defence Assistance Agreement with the U.S. was concluded. In the same year she became a member of SEATO. In 1955 she joined the Baghdad Pact with the U.K., Turkey, Iraq and Iran. When Iraq left in 1958 this pact came to be known as CENTO. To reinforce CENTO a further bilateral agreement was concluded with the United States in 1959.

The annexation of Goa by India was a turning-point in the foreign policy of Pakistan. She started looking towards nations other than those belonging to the Western Bloc and she established closer relations with China. Pakistan received a bigger shock when, after the Indo-Chinese border skirmishes in 1962, the Western Powers, particularly the U.S.A., started giving massive military aid to India, thereby disturbing the entire balance of armed strength in the sub-continent. Pakistan tried further to develop relations with China and for the first time made serious efforts to bring about normalcy in her relations with the Soviet Union. This led to a deterioration in her relations with the United States and affected the economic and military aid which she had been receiving from that source. Closer relations with Turkey and Iran were developed and resulted in the establishment of RCD in 1964 (*see* Chapter *Regional Co-operation for Development*). The policy has paid dividends. When India and Pakistan were at war in 1965 and again during the East Pakistan crisis of 1971, China along with certain Muslim powers proved to be the only supporter of Pakistan.

The secession of East Pakistan and its aftermath created misgivings in Pakistan against both the U.S.A. and the U.S.S.R., the latter having openly sided with Bangladesh and India, while the former was believed to have done the same surreptitiously. Many people in West Pakistan believed that the U.K. was a centre of anti-Pakistan propaganda and in January 1972 Pakistan withdrew from the Commonwealth. Pakistan also severed diplomatic relations with several states which hastened to recognize Bangladesh, but relations were later restored. Recently, marked improvement has taken place in relations with the U.S.A.: the ban on arms sales to Pakistan was lifted after official visits by Bhutto in 1973 and 1975. Pakistan withdrew from SEATO in 1972, but has been attending CENTO ministerial council meetings since 1972.

With Afghanistan, Pakistan has had difficulties from the very beginning, the point at issue being "Pakhtunistan", which has been championed by Afghanistan but consistently regarded by Pakistan as an interference in her internal affairs. With the overthrow in July 1973 of King Zahir Shah and the establishment of a new regime in Afghanistan which revived the Afghan claims to the areas of Pakistan inhabited by Pathans, relations between both countries greatly deteriorated.

The foreign policy of Pakistan today is one of bilateralism, the aim being to reach an understanding with as many countries as possible, irrespective of their political systems.

ECONOMIC SURVEY

Kevin Rafferty

At independence in 1947, Muhammad Ali Jinnah, the country's founder and first Governor-General, was handed a "moth-eaten Pakistan". In 1971 even that Pakistan was torn apart and more than half its population detached to form the independent state of Bangladesh. Pakistan was thus cut off from its biggest foreign exchange earner, jute, and its industrialists lost a captive market of about 70 million people.

Yet in 1976 Pakistan was possibly in the best-favoured position of all the countries of the sub-continent. It was nearly self-sufficient in food production, and had important exports of rice and cotton textiles. It was the most manageable country politically because it is much smaller than India, with only four provinces against India's 22 states. Pakistan did not have the extreme pressure of population apparent in Bangladesh and India.

However, there were danger signs. The loss of Bangladesh cost Pakistan only 55,000 of its 365,000 square miles but its population has been increasing by 3 per cent each year. By the year 2000, at that rate, self-sufficiency would become a remoter possibility and so would all hopes of significant economic development. Talented people have already been leaving the country in their thousands. For all his political skills and attention to the problems of relations between the provinces, Zulfiqar Ali Bhutto, the Prime Minister, has not resolved the relationship between the provinces and the central Government in Islamabad, and he faces a conflict in Baluchistan with some tribal fighters. More damaging, Bhutto's preoccupation with political matters has led to a dangerous neglect of the economy. In 1976, in *per capita* terms, the output of Pakistan's economy was the same as in 1970.

HISTORY

At partition of India in 1947 Pakistan was inferior in every way to India. Moreover, the upheavals and bloodshed following the division of the Punjab and Bengal, and the award of part of each to India and Pakistan, brought a huge colony of displaced migrants from India to Pakistan. The division of the Punjab led to a dispute with India over vital irrigation water supplies and this was not settled until the early 1960s, and only then through the assistance of the World Bank and the promise of massive aid to allow Pakistan to build the Mangla and Tarbela dams. The manner of the 1947 partition and the war over Kashmir produced constant tensions between India and Pakistan, encouraging both countries to spend vast sums on defence which they could ill afford.

At partition, Pakistan was without a natural capital, without much industry to speak of, or experienced industrialists, and without a major port.

Pakistan was fortunate in its early years to have guaranteed foreign exchange earnings from jute, all of which came from East Pakistan and could be used to allow imports and the build-up of an infant industry, at least in basic goods like cotton textiles, food processing and engineering. During the 1960s

Ayub Khan gave both stable government and encouragement to private industry. Growth rates in West Pakistan were impressive: 10 per cent a year in industry and 5 per cent in agriculture. However, the gap between east and west grew, and so did the ill-feeling. This was particularly so after the cyclone in East Pakistan in November 1970, when possibly 500,000 Bengalis died and the rest felt neglected by the Islamabad rulers. So East Pakistan's voters overwhelmingly elected the Awami League, dedicated to more autonomy than the West was prepared to allow. A break was inevitable. The manner in which it came, with the Pakistan military unyielding to the end, meant that a gigantic military defeat was forced on Pakistan.

One inheritance of the years of Ayub Khan's rule was an administrative apparatus which strongly supported the *status quo*. Little was done to examine the underlying causes of poverty and lack of development, or to do anything about them. Banking and industrial assets became concentrated in the hands of a small number of businessmen. Some land reforms were introduced but the upper limit on land holdings remained high and the most stringent measures could be evaded. The measures had little impact on the problem of landlessness.

Zulfiqar Ali Bhutto took over as President of Pakistan after the fall of the military government in December 1971. He started by attacking the so-called "22 families" whom an eminent economist, Dr. Mahbub ul Haq, had accused of controlling two-thirds of Pakistan's industry and 80 per cent of its banking and insurance business.

Within a month of taking over and using his powers as a martial law President, Bhutto took over 11 groups of industries, including basic metals, heavy engineering, electrical goods, chemicals, electricity, gas, cement and the manufacturing and assembling of cars and tractors, installing new boards of directors to subject them to government control. Businessmen protested that the Government measure was equivalent to nationalization without compensation; eventually the taken-over industries were nationalized. Labour reforms (giving more rights to industrial workers), education reforms (extending free education for all to the matriculation level) and new land reforms were introduced. Economically, the effect was unsettling. Pakistan's economy began to run into problems. Savings and investment began to fall. Industrialists did not invest because they feared that new industries might be taken over.

Much more successful was devaluation of the Pakistani rupee from 4.76 per U.S. dollar to 11.0 per dollar in May 1972. That measure, which had been urged by the international monetary agencies for some time, replaced a complicated system of exchange rates in which bonus vouchers were issued for certain categories of exported goods and could then be used. The more realistic rate gave a great impetus to exports when the world was still moving through boom and there were great opportunities for Pakistan.

Pakistanis seized these opportunities. Exports of cotton and goods made of cotton increased substantially. Goods which would have been sold to the captive market of East Bengal found a good sale elsewhere for foreign currency. World foodgrain production in 1972 was poor and so Pakistan was able to sell rice, which would normally have gone to East Pakistan, on the international market. As a result, the value of Pakistan's exports increased from $698 million in 1972 to $958 million in 1973. Although imports rose even more, trade was almost balanced. However, as the world plunged into a recession in 1973, Pakistan's disabilities became obvious. In 1973 cotton and wheat were affected by flood. In 1974 there was drought and the prices of petroleum and other imports rose. In 1975 the world recession began to have a severe effect and the terms of trade deteriorated against Pakistan. Taking 1971 as 100, the terms of trade improved to 108 in 1972/73 and 122 in 1973/74, but then slumped in the next two years to 96 and 87. Export earnings remained fairly static ($1,105 million in 1974 and $1,005 million in 1975) while the cost of imports continued to rise, reaching $1,738 million in 1974 and $2,125 million in 1975.

As a result, the average Pakistani in 1976 was slightly worse off than in 1970. Using constant prices, gross domestic product (G.D.P.) *per capita* in the fiscal year 1974/75 was calculated at 1,431 rupees against 1,434 rupees in 1969/70. At 1975 prices consumption has increased because of government subsidies, particularly on food, but the price for this has been paid elsewhere by the economy. Investment and savings have both fallen and, from its good trading position in 1972 and 1973, Pakistan had a trade gap of more than $1,000 million each year in 1974/75 and 1975/76. Aid, both from the west and from Pakistan's Islamic friends in the Organization of Petroleum Exporting Countries (OPEC), has come to the rescue, but repayment of the loans may soon become a problem.

AGRICULTURE

Agriculture is still the most important contributor to Pakistan's economy, accounting for about 35 per cent of the nation's G.D.P. It is also responsible for the employment of 56 per cent of the labour force and directly and indirectly provides the majority of the country's exports. Because of unfavourable weather and other factors, agriculture has done badly since 1970. Having grown at an annual rate of 5 per cent between 1961 and 1970, the growth rates slumped to 0.3 per cent between 1971 and 1975, and in 1974/75 there was a 2 per cent decline in output. However, in 1975/76 there was an improvement, with growth of possibly as much as 4 per cent. Pakistani officials say that the increased output of all major crops apart from cotton is largely the result of government policy which is bringing vital changes in the infrastructure and the better availability of essential inputs like fertilizers. However, a major part is also attributable to the better rains in 1975 which came precisely at the right time for everything except cotton.

The most important crop is wheat, the production of which rose to 8 million tons in 1975/76, compared with about 7.5 million tons in each of the previous three years. That still leaves the country some way short of self-sufficiency, a goal which should have been within reach some years ago. But Pakistan is still importing about 1 million tons of wheat each year. In 1976/77 self-sufficiency may also elude Pakistan because of continuing faults in the giant Tarbela Dam, the largest earth-filled dam in the world, which should have been supplying Pakistan with about 7 million acre-feet of water per year for vital irrigation by 1976. Fertilizer and water are the key to better yields with the new varieties of seeds; it appears, however, that the "green revolution" in Pakistan has reached a critical point now that the easiest benefits have been obtained.

In terms of climate and irrigation facilities, Pakistan is similar to Egypt and the eastern Punjab of India, but it has done less well than either with its agricultural production. Yields for Pakistan's wheat are about 1,000 lb. per acre, compared with 2,000 lb. in the east Punjab and 2,600 lb. in Egypt. Pakistan's rice yield is just below that of the east Punjab but only half the 3,000 lb. per acre produced by Egypt, and far from the 4,800 lb. per acre produced in Japan, the world's most efficient rice producer. Pakistan's maize production is below 1,000 lb. per acre whereas the Indian Punjab's is just above that and Egypt's is 3,500. In production of cotton, Pakistan achieves only 40 per cent of Egyptian yields of 2,000 lb. per acre and once more falls below the standards set by the Punjab India, which produces 1,000 lb. per acre.

Pakistan's other major food crop is rice, much of which is exported, although sales of rice do not compensate for money spent on wheat imports. Production of milled rice in 1975/76 was 2.7 million tons, a rise of about 400,000 tons on the previous year. One of Pakistan's specialities is the production of aromatic *basmati* rice. Other food crops are maize, the production of which is nearly 1 million tons per year, and sugar cane (about 20 million tons per year).

The main non-food crop is cotton, production of which has traditionally been of the order of 4 million bales. In 1975/76, production fell to below 4 million bales because of weevils and heavy rains and floods which made replanting necessary in the Punjab. The loss of such a large part of the cotton crop will be a severe blow to Pakistan's export earnings.

Besides its crops, Pakistan has large herds of livestock. Taking five sheep or goats as equivalent to one head of cattle or one buffalo, Pakistan has about the same number of animals per person as the United States. Yet average production for each animal unit in Pakistan is only 10 per cent of the U.S. figure. The major reasons for this lack of productivity in Pakistan is inadequate cattle feed and poor management.

MINING AND POWER

Pakistan has a good range of minerals, including petroleum, natural gas, iron ore, uranium, chromite, gypsum and limestone. There may also be commercial deposits of copper, manganese, bauxite and phosphates. However, so far, mining has not yet been greatly developed in Pakistan apart from small oil fields and the gas pumped from Sui and Mari. Gas reserves are estimated at 17 million million cubic feet and the gas supplies both Karachi and Rawalpindi.

In the 1970s oil production met only about 11 per cent of Pakistan's needs, but the price rises of 1973 and 1974 have impelled new efforts for the search for more. The reasons why the other minerals, apart from chromite (exports of which go to the United States), have not been commercially developed are varied, ranging from the inaccessibility of some of the areas of Baluchistan to the heavy costs in infrastructure and expertise in setting up mining. For all its contacts with the West, Pakistan has never gone out of its way to seek foreign private investment.

Pakistan is also looking at hydro-electric power projects. The Tarbela Dam scheme, when it eventually comes on stream, will have a power capacity of 2,000 megawatts. In addition, the water from the mountains and hills of Pakistan-controlled Kashmir should be a source of hydro-electric power.

INDUSTRY

Industry in 1975/76 was expected to show 5 per cent growth after a poor year in 1974/75, when textiles especially were badly affected by the recession. Textiles, which form the bulk of manufacturing exports and are the mainstay of manufacturing industry, are still faring badly, hampered by restrictions imposed by the developed countries. Within the manufacturing sector, there are wide variations in the size of enterprises and the scale of their activities. They range from the large family concerns which have many interlinked interests and the big engineering works run by the Government to very small-scale factories and even individual workshops. One of the more important decisions of Bhutto's rule was to take the important industries involving large-scale investment into the public sector. During the 1970s that decision and the world recession have done much to create uncertainty. Private industrialists were frightened that Bhutto might be tempted to take over more industries and so they held back on investment, which fell from 2,221 million rupees in 1971/72 to 1,426 million rupees in 1974/75. Few of them regarded the President, now Prime Minister, as a socialist, but they thought that socialism might be an election winner. The industries taken over themselves have been troubled and only under the stricter financial regime of Rafi Raza, the Minister of Production, are they beginning to function efficiently. One problem was that the government's choice of the original industries taken over was decided as much by political considerations as by the needs of the coherent organization of industry.

In general, Pakistan's industry did not have the good start of Indian industry. The areas now comprising Pakistan were too much on the outer edges of the British Indian Empire and the great industries were run by Hindus. Pakistan has had some help from abroad. Contractors from the People's Republic of China built a heavy engineering complex near Tatila. A $200 million steel mill is being built near

Karachi by the U.S.S.R. and will be ready in the late 1970s, though many foreigners think that the steel mill project is too expensive. Industry is still unsophisticated. Textiles, for example, are concentrated at the cheaper end of the scale, largely turning out grey cloth. For all that, many economists have been impressed by the enterprise of Pakistanis.

That enterprise shows clearly in small-scale industries which have been much more successful than their larger counterparts, so much so that organizations such as the World Bank recommend that more encouragement should be given to smaller-scale industries. This sector has recorded some notable success stories, for example the sports goods industries around Sialkot, in the Punjab, and the carpet makers who have contributed greatly to Pakistan's export drive. Pakistan's trade is dependent for more than half its exports on two commodities, rice and cotton. In the 1975/76 fiscal year, out of total exports of $1,100 million, raw cotton exports were valued at $97 million, cotton yarn and cloth earned $300 million, and rice exports were $225 million. Because of the poor crop and recession, raw cotton exports fell from $158 million in 1974/75. Between 1972/73 and 1975/76 Pakistan's export earnings rose by 30 per cent but most of this can be attributed to a rise in price and, in terms of volume, exports failed to maintain the levels of 1972/73.

During those three years export prices of Pakistan goods rose, but import prices rose much more, and the almost balanced trade of 1972/73 was replaced by a deficit of more than $1,000 million two years later. Export earnings in 1975 covered less than half the cost of imports. If prices had remained constant in 1975, say officials, the trade gap would have been only $440 million. The main increases were in food imports, which reached $421 million in 1974/75 and were $300 million the following year, rising from only $167 million in 1972/73. Imports of petroleum oil and lubricants rose more startlingly, from $63 million in 1972/73 to $380 million in 1975/76. Imports of capital goods also rose sharply in price and their cost went up from $238 million in 1973 to more than $900 million in 1975/76.

Private business, especially textile mill owners, blame the Government for reacting too slowly and, for example, ignoring their advice to abolish duties. The Government has, however, tried hard to encourage the diversification of export markets. As a result, exports have become more widely distributed and in 1974/75 no country took more than 7 per cent of Pakistan's total exports. The United States is the largest supplier of imports to Pakistan, with 15 per cent, followed by Japan, the Federal Republic of Germany, and the United Kingdom. What has been especially marked has been the growth in trade with the Middle East. After the rise in oil prices imports from the Middle East cost $350 million in 1974/75. Pakistan's exports to the Middle East also rose to $300 million in 1974/75 from practically nothing in the mid-1960s, and there is evidence that the Middle East states have taken the place of East Pakistan (Bangladesh) for rice and some consumer food exports. Pakistan may be underdeveloped but in industrial skills production it is far ahead of the Middle East, even Iran.

FINANCE

The Government has managed to cover its successive enormous trade gaps by heavy borrowings from Western donors and OPEC countries. Immediately after the oil price rise, Pakistan's particular Islamic friendships with the Middle East nations meant that it was able to cover the vast trade gap more easily than had been expected. In 1973/74 Pakistan received more loans from OPEC ($610 million) than from Western aid donors ($539 million). However, assistance from the West continued to increase, to more than $700 million in 1975/76, while that from OPEC fell to $150 million. Moreover, from 1977, Pakistan will have to start repaying a $580 million Iranian loan. In the five years after 1977 debt repayment will become a major burden. Even in 1975/76, without debt relief of $182 million from the West, debts would have been 25 per cent of export earnings plus workers remittances, too heavy a burden to be sustained for long. Pakistan's total debts are huge, about $6,000 million or 55 per cent of the 1974/75 G.D.P. A number of OPEC loans are not on easy, soft terms. The Iranian loan, for example, though repayable with interest of only 2.5 per cent, has to be repaid in the five years from 1977.

Pakistan's budget is divided into two parts, the ordinary budget (of which more than 50 per cent is provided by custom and excise duties and only 9 per cent by non-tax revenue) and the development budget, which is heavily dependent on foreign aid and became completely so in 1974/75 because of the Government's huge commodity subsidies which made the current budget run into difficulty. Since then the Government has taken measures to cut the subsidies and has increased prices for water, fertilizers, power and public utilities to something more like economic levels. For this it won praise from agencies such as the World Bank, but subsidies continue to be high, totalling 2,500 million rupees in 1975/76 (a drop of 1,300 million rupees) or 2 per cent of G.D.P. More than 40 per cent of the ordinary budget goes on defence expenditure.

Pakistan's banks have a well organized structure with more than 3,000 branches throughout the country. Until 1974 the banks were largely controlled by the famous "22 families". Then they were nationalized and some mergers were made to provide five scheduled banks: the National Bank, Habib Bank, the United Bank, the Allied Bank of Pakistan and the Muslim Commercial Bank. In addition, there are other credit giving bodies like the Industrial Development Bank, The Pakistan Industrial Credit Corporation (which aids small and medium-sized businesses) and the Agricultural Development Bank.

One of the most important contributions to Pakistan's balance of payments is money sent home by Pakistanis who have gone abroad to seek their living. In the past, the United Kingdom was the most important source of these funds. But now there are Pakistanis working in Canada and the United States and all over the Middle East. Some of the smaller Gulf states, indeed, have more Pakistanis than local people. There are estimated to be 600,000 Pakistanis working abroad and in 1975 50,000 people emigrated. The Gulf states, in particular, have been a fruitful employment market because of the strange contrast whereby, thanks to oil earnings, the sheikhdoms have money but a shortage of skilled workers, while Pakistan has an abundance of workers with an industrial background and industrial skills but not enough jobs for them. How much money is coming through the migrants' channels is difficult to assess because whatever sums are recorded officially are undoubtedly an underestimate since more money comes in through informal ways. Most experts put the contribution of migrants to the Pakistani economy at about $300 million per year.

DEVELOPMENT

The rapid economic growth of the 1960s was accomplished without any major changes in the lives or prospects of the majority of Pakistanis. In spite of land reforms, the "ceiling" on land holdings remains high and the problem of landlessness has grown. In spite of Bhutto's promises, anything like socialism remains a long way off from real-life Pakistan today. Pakistan has a great deal of poverty but nothing as extreme as in Bangladesh or as concentrated as in the great metropolis areas of India.

The need for greater growth is pressing, however. The World Bank estimated that, unless there is an acceleration in development or a major change in Government policy, growth will average 4.7 per cent per year in the period to 1981. It will then be slightly lower because the immediate benefits of the Tarbela Dam will have been spent and the rate of agricultural growth, expected to be 3.5 per cent per year to 1981, will fall. From these projections, the annual growth rate of exports will be 5.5 per cent to 1981, falling to 3.2 per cent between 1982 and 1986. At these rates savings would average about 6 per cent each year, the rate to which they had fallen in 1974/75. In consequence, even in the fiscal year 1985/86, foreign capital would have to pay for 6 per cent of fixed investment. The balance of payments deficit on current account would continue to rise, reaching $1,300 million in 1981 and $2,400 million in 1985/86. Debt servicing will rise to 25 per cent of exports and remittances by 1986. The levels of foreign finance which were required to govern the deficit will probably be intolerably high, and to resort to the alternative of lowering imports will have repercussions which would lower the rate of growth.

But if the Government increases the annual growth rate to 6.4 per cent in the period to 1980/81 and thereafter to 6.7 per cent, the outlook would be considerably brighter. To do this, however, the annual growth of the agricultural sector would have to reach 4.5 per cent between 1975/76 and 1980/81 and to rise to 5.3 per cent thereafter. Manufacturing industry would have to grow by more than 8 per cent each year. Such high growth rates would allow exports to grow by 12 per cent per year in the first five years and then by 8 per cent per year in the following years, and savings to rise to 11 per cent of G.D.P. by 1980/81 and to 13 per cent by 1985/86. All this would allow the share of foreign capital in fixed investment to fall to 18 per cent by 1985/86. All of these factors would provide a major boost to the balance of payments and reduce the current account deficit from $1,200 million in 1974/75 to $900 million by 1980/81 and to under $450 million by 1985/86.

However, to accomplish such an improved performance requires much greater effort by the Government to lay the groundwork necessary for growth to flourish. This will be especially difficult in agriculture and would require at least a doubling in the rate of increase of fertilizer consumption, the provision of more tube-wells, better canal maintenance and improved credit and extension services to farmers.

The problems involved in modernizing Pakistan's agriculture are enormous. In spite of land reforms and rent reforms, 60 per cent of the country's farmers are tenants or partial tenants and mostly share-croppers. Under this system, the owner provides inputs, pays the taxes and water charges, and receives half of the output. Such a system does not provide sufficient incentive to the farmer to adopt new techniques. There is a good case for raising land taxes which at the moment amount to less than 2 per cent of total gross income. The Government took the first step towards improvement of the tax structure in November 1975, when it announced the restructuring of land taxes to make it more progressive. However, there is a problem in that agricultural taxes are so low. Something must also be done about the need for improved water control. Foreign experts have calculated that only a third of the water actually reaches the crops. This has two effects. The obvious one is that crops are denied water and yields are much lower than necessary. The other is that spilling the water leads to waterlogging and salinity. This is already apparent in a number of places.

In industry, it would be worth the Government's while to give greater encouragement to private industrialists working on a very small scale. Although small-scale industry provides only 20 per cent of the value added, it gives jobs to 85 per cent of the manufacturing labour force. Moreover, the investment for each additional job in small-scale industry is only 3,000 rupees, compared with 80,000 rupees in large-scale industry. And, on top of this, small-scale industry has done well at exporting in areas like carpets, surgical instruments and sporting goods, and foreign studies have shown that the small businessmen make as good as or better profit than larger concerns in spite of receiving fewer subsidies and facing more competition and higher interest rates.

Another vital problem facing Pakistan is to establish a proper balance between the provinces. The Punjab, which has more than half of Pakistan's population, is far ahead of, and far richer than, the other three, Sind, the North-West Frontier Province and Baluchistan. Bhutto has spent a lot of time in ensuring that his own Pakistan People's Party was master in each of the four provinces. This has set back development. The allocation of taxes on revenues between the provinces is another aspect of this relationship. There are signs now that Bhutto intends to do something about the question of development. Early in 1976 he abolished the *Sardari* system in Baluchistan, under which traditional tribal chiefs could levy their own taxes and keep their own jails. He also appointed Shahid Hussain, formerly with the World Bank, to be his economic adviser.

Whatever happens, Pakistan has an enormous population problem. Although it is impressive that Pakistan's workers and their skills are sought all over the Middle East, it should cause the Government to stop and think that its skilled men prefer (or need) to work outside the country. It should also be remembered that for every person who goes, there are many others who never have the chance or whose energies are completely untapped, and who remain underemployed, if they are employed, in the local villages. The U.S. AID Mission in Islamabad has great hopes for its "contraceptives inundation campaign", which is being introduced in Pakistan as a test-case.

STATISTICAL SURVEY

(figures relate to present-day Pakistan, excluding Bangladesh, except where otherwise stated).

AREA AND POPULATION*

Area	Census Population				Estimated Population (mid-year)		
	February 1st, 1961	September 16th, 1972					
		Male	Female	Total	1974	1975	1976
310,403 sq. miles†	42,978,261‡	34,417,000	30,475,000	64,892,000	68,214,000	70,260,000	72,368,000

* Excludes data for the disputed territory of Jammu and Kashmir. The Pakistan-held part of this region, known as Azad ("Free") Kashmir, has an area of 32,358 sq. miles and an estimated population of more than one million. Also excluded are Junagardh, Manavadar, Gilgit and Baltistan.

† 803,943 sq. kilometres.

‡ Excluding adjustment for underenumeration, estimated by the Pakistan Planning Commission to have been 8.3 per cent for the whole of Pakistan (including what is now Bangladesh).

Source: Planning Division.

ADMINISTRATIVE DIVISIONS

(estimated population at January 1st, 1975)

Provinces:	
Baluchistan	2,562,000
North-West Frontier Province	11,531,000
Punjab	39,961,000
Sind	14,924,000
Federal Capital Territory: Islamabad*	251,000
Total	69,229,000

* Includes centrally administered tribal areas.

Source: Ministry of Finance, Planning and Development.

POPULATION OF PRINCIPAL CITIES

	1961 Census	1972 Census		1961 Census	1972 Census
Islamabad (capital)	—	77,000	Peshawar	218,691	366,000
Karachi	1,912,598	3,469,000	Sialkot	164,346	212,000
Lahore	1,296,477	2,148,000	Sargodha	129,291	203,000
Lyallpur	425,248	820,000	Sukkur	103,216	156,000
Hyderabad	434,537	624,000	Quetta	106,633	159,000
Rawalpindi	340,175	615,000	Jhang	95,000	136,000
Multan	358,201	544,000	Bahawalpur	84,000	134,000
Gujranwala	196,154	366,000			

ECONOMICALLY ACTIVE POPULATION*
(labour force sample survey, January 1972)

Agriculture, hunting, forestry and fishing	10,515,285
Mining and quarrying	79,369
Manufacturing	2,222,111
Electricity, gas and water	65,096
Construction	610,374
Trade, restaurants and hotels	1,745,714
Transport, storage and communications	861,981
Finance, insurance, real estate and business services	149,638
Community, social and personal services	1,285,464
Other activities (not adequately described)	572,432
Total in Employment	18,107,464
Unemployed	373,766
Total Labour Force	18,481,230
Males	16,893,460
Females	1,587,770

* Persons aged 10 years and over, excluding institutional households.

Source: International Labour Office, *Year Book of Labour Statistics.*

AGRICULTURE

LAND USE 1972/73*
(million acres)

Reported area	131
Forests	5
Not available for cultivation	50
Other uncultivated land	28
Total Non-Agricultural Area	83
Fallow land	12
Net sown area	36
Total Cultivated Area	48
Sown more than once	6
Total Cropped Area	42
Irrigated area	31

* Total area (incl. unreported area) is 197 million acres.

PRINCIPAL CROPS

	Area ('000 acres)		Production ('000 long tons)			
	1973/74	1974/75	1971/72	1972/73	1973/74	1974/75
Rice (milled)	3,656	3,964	2,226	2,293	2,416	2,277
Wheat	15,105	14,549	6,782	7,325	7,508	7,460
Cat-tail millet (Bajra)	1,812	1,347	354	299	346	261
Sorghum (Jowar)	1,456	1,100	308	297	372	261
Maize	1,563	1,516	694	695	755	735
Barley	506	n.a.	102	107	137	n.a.
Chick-peas (Gram)	2,738	n.a.	503	544	601	n.a.
Mash	108	n.a.	20	17	22	n.a.
Masoor	238	n.a.	22	27	33	n.a.
Mung	169	n.a.	35	30	31	n.a.
Other pulses	715	n.a.	120	119	132	n.a.
Rape and mustard	1,330	n.a.	296	282	288	n.a.
Sesame	81	n.a.	13	10	12	n.a.
Cottonseed	4,559	5,019	1,393	1,381	1,296	1,248
Groundnuts	94	100	56	44	53	56
Cotton (lint)*	4,569	n.a.	3,979	3,947	3,704	3,567
Sugar cane	1,564	1,663	19,648	19,632	23,533	20,906
Tobacco†	115	n.a.	193	138	145	n.a.
Onions	58	n.a.	248	184	236	n.a.
Garlic	n.a.	n.a.	26	24	n.a.	n.a.
Chillies	79	n.a.	51	56	50	n.a.
Potatoes	58	n.a.	250	238	235	n.a.
Other vegetables	n.a.	n.a.	1,531	n.a.	n.a.	n.a.

1975/76: Wheat production 8,000,000 tons; rice (milled) 2,700,000 tons.

* Production in thousand bales. † Production in million lb.

Source: Ministry of Food, Agriculture and Underdeveloped Areas (Agricultural Wing), *Yearbook of Agricultural Statistics 1971–72*, Statistical Division (Ministry of Finance, Planning and Development), Planning Commission and other government sources.

LIVESTOCK
('000)

	1972	1973*	1974*
Cattle	12,600	12,869	13,154
Buffaloes	9,500	9,857	10,199
Sheep	16,720*	17,480	18,072
Goats	10,700	11,422	12,749
Chicken	23,600	27,500	30,800
Horses	410*	400	400
Asses	900*	900	900
Camels	850*	800	827

* FAO estimate.

Source: FAO, *Production Yearbook*, 1974.

LIVESTOCK PRODUCTS
(FAO estimates—'000 metric tons)

	1972	1973	1974
Beef and veal	128	131	133
Buffalo meat	49	50	51
Mutton and lamb	42	44	45
Goats' meat	35	37	40
Poultry meat	27	31	35
Other meat	10	10	10
Edible offals	43.7	45.1	46.4
Cows' milk	889	902	919
Buffaloes' milk	3,700	3,788	3,928
Sheep's milk	266	279	288
Goats' milk	409	437	490
Butter and ghee	188.7	193.2	200.3
Hen eggs	24.5	28.5	33.3
Wool (clean)	14.2	14.2	13.6

Source: FAO, *Production Yearbook*, 1974.

FORESTRY

ROUNDWOOD REMOVALS

(FAO estimates, '000 cubic metres)

	Coniferous (soft wood)			Broadleaved (hard wood)			Total		
	1972	1973	1974	1972	1973	1974	1972	1973	1974
Sawlogs, veneer logs and logs for sleepers	178	180	178	77	76	77	255	256	255
Other industrial wood	11	12	12	213	220	228	224	232	240
Fuel wood	400	410	423	7,545	7,793	8,045	7,945	8,203	8,468
Total	589	602	613	7,835	8,089	8,350	8,424	8,691	8,963

Source: FAO, *Yearbook of Forest Products.*

SAWNWOOD PRODUCTION

(FAO estimates, '000 cubic metres)

	1970	1971	1972	1973	1974
Coniferous sawnwood*	110	130	133	91	133
Broadleaved sawnwood*	15	10	10	—	10
	125	140	143	91	143
Railway sleepers	10	15	150	3	150
Total	135	155	293	94	293

* Including boxboards

Source: FAO, *Yearbook of Forest Products.*

FISHING

('000 metric tons)

	1967	1968	1969	1970	1971	1972	1973	1974	1975*
Inland waters	25.2	28.9	30.6	19.0	18.4	18.0	17.6	21.4	37.6
Indian Ocean	126.7	128.7	148.0	139.4	137.0	173.2	196.6	150.0	161.5
Total Catch	151.9	157.6	178.6	158.4	155.4	191.2	214.2	171.4	199.1

* Provisional.

Source: Pakistan Statistical Yearbook 1975.

MINING

(Years July to June)

	Production (tons)			
	1971/72	1972/73	1973/74	1974/75*
Chromite	33,169	17,840	13,187	9,263
Limestone	2,586,032	2,792,321	2,941,306	2,803,828
Gypsum	21,469	128,964	214,215	308,464
Fireclay	21,321	18,674	39,365	25,746
Silica sand	42,898	26,722	42,920	33,953
Celestite	254	112	155	578
Ochres	5,248	3,720	9,305	11,079
Iron ore	n.a.	n.a.	n.a.	n.a.
Rock salt	352,767	348,474	368,856	397,941
Coal ('000 metric tons)	1,251	1,160	n.a.	n.a.
Crude petroleum ('000 metric tons)	455	409	428*	n.a.
Natural gas (million cubic metres)	3,795	4,400	n.a.	n.a.

* Provisional.

Source: Government of Pakistan, Ministry of Finance, Planning and Economic Affairs, *Statistical Yearbook* 1975.

INDUSTRY

(Years July to June)

		1971/72	1972/73	1973/74	1974/75
Cotton Yarn	million lb.	740.1	829.2	836.6	774.6
Cotton Cloth	million yds.	751.3	704.0	708.2	664.8
Art Silk and Rayon Cloth	million sq. yds.	10.1	5.8	9.5	8.8
Sugar	'000 tons	369.1	426.2	598.4	495.5
Vegetable Ghee	,, ,,	158.9	184.3	220.9	267.1
Sea Salt	,, ,,	236.0	158.0	109.0	136.0
Cement	,, ,,	2,564.0	2,830.0	3,095.0	3,267.0
Urea	,, ,,	388.5	524.7	566.4	590.0
Superphosphate	,, ,,	27.0	45.0	22.3	31.2
Ammonium Sulphate	,, ,,	65.7	57.3	89.0	93.6
Sulphuric Acid	,, ,,	34.4	41.8	33.5	36.4
Soda Ash	,, ,,	75.6	73.1	79.9	75.9
Caustic Soda	,, ,,	33.8	34.8	36.9	36.2
Chlorine Gas	,, ,,	5.4	6.2	6.3	4.8
Cigarettes	million	21,772.0	27,623.0	27,477.0	26,804.0

Source: Government of Pakistan, Ministry of Finance, Planning and Economic Affairs, *Statistical Yearbook* 1975.

FINANCE

100 paisa = 1 Pakistani rupee.
Coins: 1, 2, 5, 10, 25 and 50 paisa; 1 rupee.
Notes: 1, 5, 10, 50 and 100 rupees.
Exchange rates (June 1976): £1 sterling = 17.62 rupees; U.S. $1 = 9.93 rupees.
100 Pakistani rupees = £5.68 = $10.07.

Note: From July 1955 to May 1972 the par value of the Pakistani rupee was 21 U.S. cents (U.S. $1 = 4.7619 rupees). Between May 1972 and February 1973 the central exchange rate was U.S. $1 = 11.00 rupees and the market rate $1 = 11.031 rupees. Since February 1973 the central rate has been $1 = 9.90 rupees and the market rate $1 = 9.931 rupees. In terms of sterling, the central exchange rate was £1 = 11.43 rupees from November 1967 to August 1971, and £1 = 12.41 rupees from December 1971 to May 1972.

CENTRAL GOVERNMENT BUDGET

(million rupees, July 1st to June 30th)

REVENUE	1972/73	1973/74*	1974/75*
Taxes on income:			
Personal	870.6	885.0	885.0
Corporation	250.1	265.0	265.0
Customs duties	2,643.9	3,907.0	5,937.6
Excise duties	2,265.1	2,765.7	3,000.0
General turnover tax	460.6	650.0	700.0
Other taxes	41.8	53.4	58.7
Other receipts	2,061.6	3,207.7	3,744.6
TOTAL	8,593.7	11,733.8	14,590.9

EXPENDITURE	1972/73	1973/74*	1974/75*
Interest on public debt	1,171.1	1,539.0	1,617.2
National defence	4,440.5	4,742.3	5,580.1
Education and health	94.5	257.1	507.2
Transfers to provinces and states:			
Taxes	873.6	882.0	1,254.6
Grants	50.3	253.7	304.0
Other current expenditure	2,182.3	5,341.3	5,941.7
Capital expenditure	1,794.0	2,398.7	3,585.8
Loans and advances to provinces and states (net)	1,356.0	1,549.1	2,069.0
Other loans and advances (net)	99.7	−32.2	92.2
TOTAL	12,062.0	16,931.0	20,951.8

* Estimates.

Source: United Nations, *Statistical Yearbook* 1974.

Foreign Aid (1973/74): Total disbursements U.S. $425 million.

COST OF LIVING

Consumer Price Index for industrial, commercial and government employees
(base: 1969/70=100)

	1971/72	1972/73	1973/74	1974/75
Food, beverages and tobacco	109.6	121.2	163.3	208.7
Clothing	109.3	121.7	176.0	219.4
Housing and household expenditure	110.2	115.6	142.1	178.5
Miscellaneous	116.0	125.7	146.5	186.1
ALL ITEMS	110.7	121.4	157.8	200.0

Source: Government of Pakistan, Ministry of Finance, Planning and Economic Affairs, *Statistical Yearbook*, 1975.

NATIONAL ACCOUNTS

(million rupees at current factor cost, July to June)

RESOURCES	1971/72	1972/73	1973/74	1974/75*
Agriculture, Fishing and Forestry	18,340	22,466	28,717	33,661
Mining, Quarrying and Manufacturing	7,825	9,728	12,747	17,412
Construction	1,763	2,298	3,114	4,750
Electricity, Gas, Water, Sanitation	823	955	1,217	1,340
Transport, Storage, Communications	3,233	4,260	5,565	7,200
Trade, Banking and Insurance	8,053	9,898	13,984	17,178
Ownership of Dwellings	1,913	2,237	2,868	3,588
Public Administration and Defence	3,445	4,430	5,140	6,816
Other Services	3,894	4,636	6,363	8,102
GROSS DOMESTIC PRODUCT	48,883	60,355	78,986	99,120
Net Factor Income from Abroad	99	463	617	897
GROSS NATIONAL PRODUCT	48,982	60,818	79,603	100,017

EXPENDITURE	1970/71	1971/72	1972/73	1973/74
Private Consumption	38,536	40,209	48,587	69,315
Government Consumption	5,270	6,310	7,563	8,555
Fixed Capital, Stock Changes	7,892	7,731	8,741	10,000
Foreign Trade (goods and services)	−1,401	−804	376	−4,455
Expenditure on Gross Domestic Product †	50,297	53,446	65,267	83,932
Net Factor Income from Abroad	−82	99	436	443
Expenditure on Gross National Product†	50,215	53,545	65,855	82,523
Indirect Taxes, net of Subsidies	−4,750	−4,563	−4,912	−4,946
GROSS NATIONAL PRODUCT AT FACTOR COST	45,465	48,982	60,818	79,603

* Provisional. † At market prices.

Source: Government of Pakistan, Ministry of Finance, Planning and Economic Affairs, *Statistical Yearbook*, 1974.

EXTERNAL TRADE

(million rupees, July 1st to June 30th)

	1970/71	1971/72	1972/73	1973/74	1974/75
Imports	3,602.4	3,495.3	8,398.3	13,569.6	20,924.9
Exports*	2,110.8	3,423.2	8,623.5	10,237.6	10,460.9

* Including re-exports.

Source: Government of Pakistan, Ministry of Finance, Planning and Economic Affairs, *Statistical Yearbook*, 1975.

COMMODITIES

('000 rupees)

IMPORTS	1971/72	1972/73	1973/74
Food			
Rice	20,996	23	19
Wheat	269,829	1,112,134	1,546,552
Sugar	26,578	428,503	126,218
Spices	17,053	44,098	45,532
Crude Materials inedible, excluding Fuels			
Raw and Waste Cotton	9,388	5,346	10,736
Raw Wool	23,707	69,536	38,369
Wood and Timber	58,467	74,195	58,601
Mineral Fuels, Lubricants and Related Materials			
Coal	4,194	6,747	9,980
Oil (Animal, Vegetable and Mineral)	385,576	946,164	2,378,955
Chemicals and Pharmaceuticals	175,952	375,502	535,795
Dyes and Colours	58,220	160,366	164,948
Manufactured Goods classified chiefly by material			
Paper, Pasteboard and Stationery	69,976	141,156	391,424
Rayon Yarn	7,514	21,061	168,237
Iron, Steel and Manufactures	438,953	876,430	1,109,779
Cutlery, Hardware and Tools	55,909	76,267	107,220
Non-ferrous Metals and Manufactures	59,085	155,345	309,923
Machinery and Transport Equipment			
Electrical goods	257,154	459,510	597,559
Machinery other than electric	594,254	738,943	1,196,233
Vehicles	197,197	482,779	1,077,719
Miscellaneous Manufactured Articles			
Building and Engineering Material	19,814	17,787	18,007

EXPORTS	1971/72	1972/73	1973/74
Food and Live Animals			
Fish (excl. Canned Fish)	96,746	192,477	179,846
Tea	—	—	44
Crude Materials inedible, excluding Fuels			
Raw Jute	49	—	114
Raw Cotton	954,747	1,166,975	376,112
Raw Wool	24,603	71,897	64,077
Raw Hides and Skins	19,601	16,896	23,545
Manufactured Goods classified chiefly by material			
Jute Manufactures	17,606	4,853	415
Cotton Twist and Yarns	605,630	1,974,288	1,865,417
Cotton Textiles	387,310	1,247,077	1,416,828

Source: Government of Pakistan, Ministry of Finance, Planning and Economic Affairs, *Statistical Bulletin*, 1974.

TRADING PARTNERS

('000 rupees)

	Imports			Exports		
	1971/72	1972/73	1973/74	1971/72	1972/73	1973/74
United Kingdom	353,331	683,270	950,153	259,853	630,170	686,640
U.S.A.	728,768	2,094,136	3,451,800	174,145	348,833	540,529
Japan	349,545	721,080	1,126,165	540,123	1,562,073	633,331
Germany, Federal Republic	343,971	748,683	1,050,671	105,279	305,850	463,454
Sri Lanka	109,432	298,146	355,955	65,298	205,262	128,436
Malaysia	15,635	58,140	91,100	23,826	56,486	53,132
Belgium and Luxembourg	41,259	105,793	257,486	28,430	76,887	143,649
France	76,260	112,852	342,486	62,152	183,372	266,048
Bahrain	2,112	1,815	7,628	28,725	25,224	101,438
Hong Kong	24,448	32,542	55,343	505,199	961,022	1,116,896
Australia	36,490	99,777	59,895	28,476	65,073	153,603
Italy	191,674	232,583	300,165	125,090	434,372	491,181
China, People's Republic	99,083	361,928	570,912	146,041	193,384	39,272

Source: Government of Pakistan, Ministry of Finance, Planning and Economic Affairs, *Statistical Bulletin*, 1974.

TRANSPORT

RAILWAYS

(July 1st to June 30th)

	1970/71	1971/72	1972/73	1973/74
Number of Passengers ('000)	126,037	124,207	135,175	140,652
Passenger-miles (million)	5,823	5,914	6,824	7,208
Freight ('000 tons)	12,341	12,599	12,317	11,009
Net Freight ton-miles (million)	4,581	4,722	5,112	4,491

Source: Ministry of Finance, Planning and Economic Affairs, *Statistical Yearbook*, 1974.

ROADS

	Passenger Cars	Motor Rickshaws	Taxis	Buses	Trucks	Total
1969	112,833	17,407	10,704	18,808	36,029	195,781
1970	141,263	19,438	12,786	21,600	42,003	237,573
1971	153,498	20,738	13,472	23,860	44,078	255,646
1972	156,571	21,485	14,010	26,583	45,842	264,491
1973	162,022	22,555	15,324	29,718	49,345	278,964

Source: Government of Pakistan, Ministry of Finance, Planning and Economic Affairs, *Statistical Bulletin*, 1974.

SHIPPING

	Vessels ('000 net registered tons)		Goods ('000 long tons)	
	Entered	Cleared	Loaded	Unloaded
1970–71	6,129	6,106	3,157	6,279
1971–72	5,872	5,701	3,010	6,296
1972–73	6,465	6,452	3,185	7,188
1973–74	6,650	6,600	3,045	7,440
1974–75	7,363	7,133	2,252	7,732

Source: Ministry of Finance, Planning and Economic Affairs, *Statistical Yearbook*, 1975.

CIVIL AVIATION

(domestic and international flights, July to June—'000)

	1970/71	1971/72	1972/73	1973/74	1974/75
Kilometres flown	29,081	23,627	21,651	23,545	28,183
Passenger-kilometres	1,953,108	1,478,630	1,303,342	1,584,930	2,224,090
Freight ton-kilometres	65,748	59,365	61,549	74,021	116,437
Mail ton-kilometres	6,779	8,069	6,237	4,788	4,804

Source: Government of Pakistan, Ministry of Finance, Planning and Economic Affairs, *Statistical Yearbook*, 1975.

TOURISM

	Tourist Arrivals
1970	122,097
1971	113,300
1972	100,963
1973	141,898
1974	152,200*

* Preliminary.

Source: Government of Pakistan, Ministry of Finance, Planning and Economic Affairs, *Statistical Bulletin*, 1974.

THE CONSTITUTION

The following proposals were unanimously adopted by leaders of all parliamentary parties, meeting in Islamabad under the Chairmanship of President Bhutto on October 20th, 1972. The new Constitution was adopted by the National Assembly on April 10th, 1973, and came into force on August 14th, 1973.

GOVERNMENT

In the Federal Parliamentary system the Head of the State is to be a constitutional President on whom the advice of the Prime Minister shall be binding in all respects. The Prime Minister, who is to be the chief executive, and his Cabinet shall be answerable to the Federal Legislature.

A constitutional amendment in February 1975 freed the government of the obligation to seek parliamentary approval to declare a state of emergency.

LEGISLATURE—NATIONAL ASSEMBLY AND SENATE*

The Federal Legislature shall comprise two houses—the lower house called the National Assembly with 200 members elected directly for a term of five years, on the basis of universal adult suffrage, and the upper house, called the Senate, of 63 members who serve for four years, half retiring every two years. Each Provincial Assembly is to elect 14 Senators. The tribal areas are to return five and the remaining two are to be elected from the Federal Capital Territory by members of the Provincial Assemblies. For a period of 10 years women are to get 10 seats in the National Assembly raising its strength to 210.

There shall be two sessions of the National Assembly and Senate each year, with not more than 120 days between the last sitting of a session and the first sitting of the next session.

The role of the Senate in an overwhelming majority of the subjects shall be merely advisory. Disagreeing with any legislation of the National Assembly, it shall have the right to send it back only once for reconsideration. In case of disagreement in other subjects, the Senate and National Assembly shall sit in a joint session to decide the matter by a simple majority.

An amendment to the Constitution shall require two-thirds majority in the National Assembly and its endorsement by a simple majority in the Senate. The members of the Senate may be taken in the Federal Cabinet provided their total number does not exceed 25 per cent of the total number of Central Ministers.

* Although the Constitution provides for a Senate of 63 members, the number in 1976 was still 45, the same as before the promulgation of the Constitution in 1973.

The stability of the parliamentary system is sought to be ensured through four main provisions. Firstly, the Prime Minister shall be elected by the National Assembly and the President must call on him to form a government. Secondly, any resolution calling for the removal of a Prime Minister shall have to name his successor in the same resolution which shall be adopted by not less than two-thirds of the total number of members of the lower house. The requirement of two-thirds majority is to remain in force for 15 years or three electoral terms whichever is more. Thirdly, the Prime Minister shall have the right to seek dissolution of the legislature at any time even during the pendency of a no-confidence motion. Fourthly, if a no-confidence motion is defeated, such a motion shall not come up before the house for the next six months.

All these provisions for stability shall apply *mutatis mutandis* to the Provincial Assemblies also.

PROVINCIAL GOVERNMENT

In the matter of relations between Federation and Provinces, Parliament shall have the power to make laws, including laws bearing on extra-territorial affairs, for the whole or any part of Pakistan, while a Provincial Assembly shall be empowered to make laws for that Province or any part of it. Matters in the Federal Legislative List shall be subject to the exclusive authority of Parliament, while Parliament and a Provincial Assembly shall have power to legislate with regard to matters referred to in the Concurrent Legislative List. Any matter not referred to in either list may be the subject of laws made by a Provincial Assembly alone, and not by Parliament, although the latter shall have exclusive power to legislate with regard to matters not referred to in either list for those areas in the Federation not included in any Province.

The executive authorities of every Province shall be required to ensure that their actions are in compliance with the Federal laws which apply in that Province. The Federation shall be required to consider the interests of each Province in the exercise of its authority in that Province. The Federation shall further be required to afford every Province protection from external aggression and internal disturbance, and to ensure that every Province is governed in accordance with the provisions of the Constitution.

To further safeguard the rights of the smaller provinces, a Council of Common Interests has been created. Comprising the Chief Ministers of the four provinces and four Central Ministers to decide upon specified matters of common interest, the Council is responsible to the Federal Legislature. The constitutional formula gives the net proceeds of excise duty and royalty on gas to the province concerned. The profits on hydro-electric power generated in each province shall go to that province.

THE GOVERNMENT

HEAD OF STATE

President: FAZAL ELAHI CHAUDHRY.

CABINET

(*July* 1976)

Prime Minister and Minister of Foreign Affairs, Defence and Atomic Energy: ZULFIQAR ALI BHUTTO.

Minister of the Interior, States and Frontier Regions: ABDUL QAIYUM KHAN.

Minister of Food and Agriculture, Co-operatives, Under-developed Areas and Land Reforms: Sheikh MOHAMMAD RASHID.

Minister of Education and Provincial Co-ordination: ABDUL HAFEEZ PIRZADA.

Minister of Social Welfare, Local Government and Rural Development: MALIK MERAJ KHALID.

Minister of Communications: MUMTAZ ALI BHUTTO.

Minister of Production: RAFI RAZA.

Minister of Religious Affairs, Minority Affairs and Overseas Pakistanis: MAULANA KAUSAR NIAZI.

Minister of Finance, Planning and Development: RANA MOHAMMAD HANIF KHAN.

Minister of Fuel, Power and Natural Resources: MOHAMMAD YUSUF KHATTAK.

Minister of Information and Broadcasting: MOHAMMAD HANIF KHAN.

Minister of Housing, Works and Urban Development: SYED NASIR ALI SHAH RIZVI.

Minister of Industries, Kashmir Affairs and Northern Affairs: SYED QAIM ALI SHAH JILLANI.

Minister of Law and Parliamentary Affairs: MALIK MOHAMMAD AKHTAR.

Minister of Labour, Manpower, Health and Population Planning: TAJ MOHAMMAD KHAN JAMALI.

Minister of Railways: HAFEEZULLAH CHEEMA.

Attorney-General: YAHYA BAKHTIAR.

Special Assistant for National Security: Gen. (Retd.) TIKKA KHAN.

Minister of Commerce and Tourism: MIR AFZAL KHAN.

Minister of State for Defence and Foreign Affairs: AZIZ AHMED.

FEDERAL LEGISLATURE

Under the 1973 Constitution the Federal Legislature comprises a lower house (the National Assembly) of 210 members (200 directly elected for five years plus 10 women members elected by the Assembly) and an upper house (The Senate) which has 63 members, of whom 56 are elected for a four-year term by the provincial assemblies.

NATIONAL ASSEMBLY

The Assembly comprises 210 members.

Speaker: SAHIBZADA FAROOQ ALI.

SENATE

In 1973, when the new Constitution came into effect, the Senate comprised 45 members. The Constitution provides for an increase to 63 members.

Chairman: HABIBULLAH KHAN.

POLITICAL PARTIES

Jamaat-i-Islami: Mansoorah, Multan Rd., Lahore; f. 1941; aims at the establishment of the Islamic state; Leader MIAN TUFAIL MUHAMMED.

Pakistan Democratic Party (P.D.P.): f. 1969; aims to uphold "democratic and Islamic values"; Sec.-Gen. Sheikh NASIM HASAN.

Pakistan Muslim League: Muslim League House, 33 Davis Rd., Lahore; Pres. PEER SAHIB PAGAROO; Sec.-Gen. MALIK MOHAMMAD QASIM.

Pakistan People's Party: f. Dec. 1967; party of the Government; Islamic socialism, democracy and an independent foreign policy; Chair. ZULFIQAR ALI BHUTTO; Sec.-Gen. MUBASHIR HASSAN.

National Awami Party: f. 1968; leftist; supports pro-Soviet line; Leader/Pres. KHAN ABDUL WALI KHAN. Banned in 1975.

PROVINCES

Pakistan comprises the four provinces of Sind, Baluchistan, Punjab and the North-West Frontier Province, plus the federal capital and "tribal areas" under federal administration.

Sind

Governor: DILAWAR KHAN.

Baluchistan

Governor: Mir AHMAD YAR KHAN, Khan of Kelat.

Governor's rule was imposed on December 31st, 1975, following the dismissal of the Baluchistan Ministry.

Punjab

Governor: MOHAMMAD ABBAS ABBASI.

North-West Frontier Province

Governor: Maj.-Gen. (Retd.) NASRULLAH KHAN BABAR.

DIPLOMATIC REPRESENTATION

EMBASSIES ACCREDITED TO PAKISTAN

(in Islamabad unless otherwise stated)

Afghanistan: 176, Shalimar 7/3; *Chargé d'Affaires:* Dr. RAHIM SHERZOY (also accred. to Thailand and Sri Lanka).

Albania: Cairo, Egypt.

Algeria: 72, St. 26, Shalimar F-6/2; *Chargé d'Affaires:* MOHAMED GHALIB NEDJARI.

Argentina: 7, St. 7, Shalimar 6/2; *Chargé d'Affaires:* Dr. MARIO IZAGUIRRE.

Australia: Diplomatic Enclave No. 2; *Ambassador:* J. D. PETHERBRIDGE (also accred. to Afghanistan).

Austria: 13, 1st St., Shalimar 6; *Ambassador:* Dr. ERNST JOSEF PLOIL.

Bangladesh: House 21, St. 88, G-6/3; *Ambassador:* ABDULLAH ZAHEERUDDIN.

Belgium: 40, St. 12, Shalimar 6; *Ambassador:* LEON OLIVIER.

Brazil: 194 Embassy Rd., Ramna 6/3; *Ambassador:* QUINTINO DESETA.

Bulgaria: Plot 29, St. 22, Shalimar 6/2; *Ambassador:* TOCHO TOCHEV.

Burma: 386, Shalimar 6/3; *Ambassador:* U TUN TIN (also accred. to Iran).

Canada: Diplomatic Enclave; *Ambassador:* K. W. MACLELLAN (also accred. to Afghanistan).

China, People's Republic: 23–24, Shalimar 6/4; *Ambassador:* LU WEI-CHAO.

Czechoslovakia: 25, Shalimar 6/2; *Ambassador:* VLADIMIR LUDVIK.

Denmark: Teheran, Iran.

Egypt: 449-F, St. 85, Ramna 6/4; *Ambassador:* OMRAN ABDEL SALAM EL-SHAFEI.

Finland: Ankara, Turkey.

France: 217-C, 54th St., Shalimar 7/4; *Ambassador:* POL LE GOURRIÉREC.

German Democratic Republic: Shalimar 6/3, St. 3 House 218; *Ambassador:* Dr. HANS MERITZKI.

Germany, Federal Republic: Ramna 5, Diplomatic Enclave; *Ambassador:* Dr. ULRICH SCHESKE.

Ghana: 4, St. 16, Shalimar 6/3; *Ambassador:* GORDON C. N. CUDJOE (also accred. to Iran).

Greece: Teheran, Iran.

Guinea: Peking, China.

Guyana: Washington, D.C., U.S.A.

Hungary: 164, Shalimar 6/3; *Ambassador:* KALMAN DOCZE.

India: *Ambassador:* KAYATYANI SHANKAR BAJPAI.

Indonesia: 171–172, Shalimar 6/3; *Ambassador:* RADEN MASIMAM ABIKUSNO.

Iran: 36–37 Attaturk Ave., Ramna 6; *Ambassador:* MANOUTCHEHR ZELLI (also accred. to Sri Lanka).

Iraq: 178, Ramna 6/3; *Ambassador:* ABDUL-MALIK SALIM AL-ZAIBAK (also accred. to Thailand.)

Italy: 448, Shalimar 6/3; *Ambassador:* Dr. OBERTO FABIANI.

Japan: Plot Nos. 53-70, Ramna 5/4; *Ambassador:* HIROSHI NEMOTO.

Jordan: 435, Ramna 6/4; *Ambassador:* Sheikh IBRAHIM AL-KATTAN (also accred. to Indonesia and Malaysia).

Korea, Democratic People's Republic: 9, 89th St., Ramna 6/3; *Ambassador:* (vacant).

Kuwait: 148-G, Attaturk Ave., Ramna 6/3; *Ambassador:* YOUSSEF ABDUL LATIF AL-ABDUL RAZZAQ.

Laos: Bangkok, Thailand.

Lebanon: Plot 26, St. 32, Shalimar 6/1; *Ambassador:* ABDUL RAHMAN ADRA (also accred. to Malaysia).

Libya: Plot 109-H, Ramna 6/3; *Ambassador:* S. M. TAYNAZ.

Malaysia: 7, St. 40, Shalimar 6; *Ambassador:* KAMARUDDIN MOHAMED ARIFF.

Mauritania: Peking, China.

Mauritius: 532-F, Ramna 6/4; *Ambassador:* AMEEN KASENALLY.

Mexico: Ankara, Turkey.

Mongolia: Peking, China.

Morocco: 206, Ramna 6/3; *Chargé d'Affaires a.i.:* ABDELLAH AIT EL-HADJ (also accred. to Malaysia).

Nepal: 506, 84th St., Attaturk Ave., Ramna 6/4; *Ambassador:* KHADGA MAN SINGH (also accred. to Turkey).

Netherlands: 5, 61st St., Shalimar 6/3; *Ambassador:* G. J. JONGEJANS.

Nigeria: 440, Shalimar 6/3; *Ambassador:* Alhaji ABDULKADIR DAFUWA GADAU.

Norway: Teheran, Iran.

Oman: 440 Bazar Rd., Ramna 6/4; *Ambassador:* SALIM MOHAMMAD AL-GHAYLANI.

Paraguay: Tokyo, Japan.

Philippines: 11, St. 26, Shalimar 6/2; *Ambassador:* (vacant).

Poland: 172, St. 88, Ramna 6/3; *Ambassador:* RYSZARD POSPIESZYNSKI.

Portugal: 130-H, Ramna 6/3, 90th St.; *Ambassador:* Dr. ANTÓNIO ALEXANDRE DA ROCHA.

Qatar: 201 Masjid Rd., Shalimar 6/4; *Ambassador:* MUBARAK NASSAR AL KUWARIT (also accred. to Malaysia).

Romania: 10, St. 90, Ramna 6/3; *Ambassador:* LUCIAN PETRESCU.

Saudi Arabia: Plot 436-F, Ramna 6/4; *Ambassador:* Sheikh RIYADH AL-KHATIB.

Senegal: Beirut, Lebanon.

Singapore: Cairo, Egypt.

Somalia: Jeddah, Saudi Arabia.

Spain: 180-G Attaturk Ave., Ramna 6/3; *Ambassador:* IGNACIO DE CASSO GARCIA.

Sri Lanka: 468-F, Ramna 6/4; *Ambassador:* Mrs. THEJA GUNAWARDHANA.

Sudan: 203, Ramna 6/3; *Ambassador:* SAYED AWAD GILKARIM FADLALLA (also accred. to Afghanistan).

Sweden: Diplomatic Enclave; *Ambassador:* RUNE NYSTROM.

Switzerland: 11, 84th St., Ramna 6; *Ambassador:* LUCIEN MOSSAZ.

Syria: 343, Shalimar 6/3; *Ambassador:* MOHAMMED SHABIR DREII.

Thailand: Diplomatic Enclave; *Ambassador:* WICHET SUTHAYAKHOM.

Turkey: 125-H, Ramna 6/3; *Ambassador:* ERDEM ERNER.

U.S.S.R.: Diplomatic Enclave, Ramna 4; *Ambassador:* S. A. AZIMOV.

United Arab Emirates: 228 Shalimar 6/3, 1st St.; *Ambassador:* RASHID SULTAN AL-MAKHAWI.

United Kingdom: Diplomatic Enclave, Ramna 5, P.O.B. 1122; *Ambassador:* J. C. W. BUSHELL.

U.S.A.: Diplomatic Enclave, Ramna 4; *Ambassador:* HENRY A. BYROADE.

Vatican City: 317, Shalimar 6/3, P.O.B. 1106 (Apostolic Nunciature); *Nuncio:* Mgr. JOSEPH UHAČ.

Viet-Nam: Peking, China.

Yugoslavia: 14, St. 87, Ramna 6/3; *Ambassador:* Dr. VIDO KNEZEVIC.

Pakistan also has diplomatic relations with Bahrain, Benin, Bolivia, Cameroon, the Central African Republic, Chad, Chile, Colombia, the Congo People's Republic, Costa Rica, Cuba, Cyprus, Ethiopia, the Gambia, Iceland, Ireland, the Ivory Coast, Jamaica, Kenya, the Republic of Korea, Liberia, Luxembourg, Madagascar, Maldives, Mali, Malta, Mozambique, New Zealand, Niger, Panama, Peru, Sierra Leone, Tanzania, Togo, Trinidad and Tobago, Tunisia, Uganda, the Upper Volta, Uruguay, Venezuela, the Yemen Arab Republic, the People's Democratic Republic of Yemen and Zambia.

JUDICIAL SYSTEM

SUPREME COURT

Rawalpindi

Chief Justice: Mr. Justice MUHAMMAD YAQUB ALI.

HIGH COURT OF LAHORE

Chief Justice: Mr. Justice SARDAR MOHAMMAD IQBAL.

HIGH COURTS OF SIND-BALUCHISTAN

Chief Justice: Mr. Justice ABDUL KADER SHAIKH.

HIGH COURT OF PESHAWAR

Chief Justice: Mr. Justice SYED GHULAM SAFDAR SHAH.

RELIGION

ISLAM

Islam is the state religion. Under the constitution of Pakistan the head of state must be a Muslim. Muslims made up 97.1 per cent of the population in 1961.

HINDUISM

Hindus make up 1.6 per cent of the population.

CHRISTIANITY

There is a small minority of Christians.

THE PRESS

Pakistan's press today is largely a remnant of the Muslim press that became prominent during the struggle for the national State (1940–47). The first Urdu-language newspaper, the daily *Urdu Akhbar*, was founded in 1836. After 1945, with the introduction of modern equipment, the more influential English newspapers, such as *Dawn* and *The Pakistan Times*, were firmly established, while several new Urdu newspapers, for example *Nawa-i-Waqt* and *Imroze*, became very popular.

In Pakistan there are 12 English dailies, 62 Urdu dailies and 10 in regional languages. In addition there are 230 weeklies and 16 bi-weeklies. These together with other publications number in all 1,222.

The Urdu press comprises 550 newspapers, with *Daily Jang, Mussawat, Imroze, Nawa-i-Waqt* and *Mashriq* being the most influential. The largest daily is *Daily Jang* (300,000 circ.). Though the English-language press reaches only 1 per cent of the population and totals 150 publications, it is influential in political, academic and professional circles.

PRINCIPAL DAILIES

RAWALPINDI

Daily Jang: P.O.B. 30, Gawal Mandi; Rawalpindi edn.; f. 1959; published simultaneously in Rawalpindi, Quetta and Karachi; Urdu; independent national; Editor-in-Chief Mir KHALIL-UR-RAHMAN; circ. (Rawalpindi) 65,000.

Daily Kohistan: Jamia Masjid Rd.; Urdu; published simultaneously in Lahore, Rawalpindi and Multan.

Daily Ta'Meer: Jamia Masjid Rd.; f. 1949; Urdu independent; Organizer S. M. AHSAN; Editor RIAZ HUMAYUN.

KARACHI

Aghaz: Preedy St., 11 Japan Mansion, Saddar, 2; Urdu; evening; Editor M. O. FARUQI.

Business Post: 4-5 Amil St., off Robson Rd., 1, f. 1963; morning; English; economic and business news; Editor AMEEN K. TAREEN.

Business Recorder: 531 Nazrul Islam Rd., 5; f. 1963; English; Editor M. A. ZUBERI.

Comment: 52 Ratan Talao, off Akhbar Rd.; f. 1952; evening; English; Editor H. M. ABBASI; circ. 2,000.

Daily Jang: editions in Karachi, Quetta, Rawalpindi and London; McLeod Rd., P.O.B. 52; f. 1937; morning and Sunday; Editor KHALIL-UR-RAHMAN; circ. 177,000(m); 220,000(s).

Daily Nai Roshni: Nai Roshni Bldg., Chundrigar Rd.; Urdu.

Daily News: Jang House, Chundrigar Rd.; f. 1962; evening; English; Editor WAJID SHAMSUL HASAN; circ. 42,000.

Dawn: Haroon House, Dr. Ziauddin Ahmed Rd., 4; f. 1942; English, Gujarati; Manager KHWAJA RAHMAN; Editors JAMIL ANSARI (English edn.), G. N. MANSURI (Gujarati edn.) circ. 60,000.

Evening Star: Haroon House, Dr. Ziauddin Ahmed Rd., 4; evening; English.

Hurriyat: Haroon House, Dr. Ziauddin Ahmed Rd.; daily; Urdu; Editor F. ZAIDA.

Leader: New Challi; daily; English; Editor S. AHMED.

Millat: 191 South Napier Rd.; f. 1946; Gujarati; Independent; circ. 9,400; Editor S. I. MATRI.

Morning News: Saifee House, Dr. Ziauddin Ahmed Rd.; f. 1942; published in Karachi, Rawalpindi and Lahore; English; Editor-in-Chief SULTAN AHMED.

Mussawat: off Frere Rd.; f. 1974; Urdu; Editor SHAUKAT SIDDIQUI.

Nauroze: McLeod Rd.; f. 1949; Urdu; Independent; Editor M. ASHRAF; circ. over 20,000.

Vatan: Haroon House, Dr. Ziauddin Ahmed Rd.; f. 1942; Gujarati; Editor M. J. M. NOOR; circ. 12,000.

LAHORE

Daily Business Report: 7A Nisbet Rd.; f. 1947; published simultaneously in Lahore and Lyallpur; Urdu; Editor CH. SHAH MOHAMMAD AZIZ.

Daily Rehbar: Urdu; Chief Editor MALIK MOHAMMAD HAYAT, T.K. *See* also Daily Rehbar, Bahawalpur.

Imroze: Rattan Chand Rd.; f. 1948; morning; Urdu; Editor Z. BABAR; circ. Lahore 48,000, Multan 17,000.

Mahgrabi Pakistan: Beadon Rd.; daily; Urdu; Editor M. SHAFAAT.

Mashriq Daily: 46 Nisbet Rd.; f. 1963; Urdu; simultaneous editions in Karachi, Lahore and Peshawar; Editor MAKIN AHSAN KALEEM; circ. 175,000.

Mujahid Daily: 4 McLeod Rd.; f. 1948; Urdu; Editor A'SI NIZAMI.

Nawa-i-Pakistan: Railway Rd.; f. 1948; Independent; Urdu; Editors MUJAHIDUL HUSAIN, MUHAMMED RAFIQUE.

Nawa-i-Waqt Daily: 4 Shahra-e-Fatima, Jinnah, Lahore; f. 1940; Urdu-English; simultaneous edition in Rawalpindi; Editor M. NIZAMI; circ. 300,000.

Pakistan Times: Rattan Chand Rd., P.O.B. 223; f. 1947; English; Liberal; Chief Editor K. M. ASAF; circ. 40,000.

Safeena: 78 Chamberlain Rd.; f. 1947; Urdu; Editor ALI SHAMSI; circ. 6,000.

OTHER TOWNS

Aftab: Hyderabad; Urdu; Editor R. A. AJMERI.

Al Falah: Chhoti Lal Kurti, P.O.B. 35, Peshawar Cantt.; f. 1939; Urdu and Pashtu; Editor S. ABDULLAH SHAH.

Al-Jamiat-e-Sarhad: Kocha Gilania Chakagali, Peshawar; f. 1941; Urdu-Pashtu; Editor S. M. HASSAN GILANI.

Daily Rehbar: Rehbar Office: Chah Fatehkhan, Bahawalpur; f. 1952; Urdu; Chief Editor MALIK MOHAMMAD HAYAT, T.K.; circ. 5,680. *See* also *Daily Rehbar*, Lahore (*above*).

Hilal-e-Pakistan: Haji Aminuddin Rd., P.O.B. 200, Hyderabad; f. 1946; Sindhi; Editor KARIM LOUTFI.

Indus Times: Indus Times Office, Hyderabad; English; Editor A. A. SINDHI.

Khyber Mail: 95A Saddar Rd., Peshawar; f. 1932; Independent; English; circ. 5,000; Editor ASKAR ALI SHAH.

Shahbaz: Kabuli Gate, Peshawar; f. 1947; Urdu and Pashtu; Editor A. KHATTAK; circ. 9,000.

Zamana: Jinnah Rd., Quetta; Urdu; Editor SYED FASIH IQBAL; circ. 85,000.

SELECTED WEEKLIES

Ajkal: Kabuli Gate, Peshawar; f. 1958; Urdu; Editor JAMIL AKHTAR.

Akhbar-e-Jehan: Jang House, Chundrigar Rd., Karachi; f. 1967; Urdu; independent national; illustrated family magazine; Editor-in-Chief Mir HABIB-UR-RAHMAN; circ. 70,000.

Al-Tahir Weekly: 25 Haroon Chambers, Altaf Hussain Rd., Karachi; f. 1956; Urdu; Editor SYED TAHIR HUSSAIN; circ. 10,000.

Al Wahdat: Peshawar; Urdu and Pashtu; Editor NURUL HAQ.

Amal: Aiwan-a-Abul Kaif, Abul Kaif Rd., Shah Qabool Colony, Peshawar; f. 1958; Urdu; Editor AQAI ABUL KAIF KAIFI SARHADDI.

Awam: Iftikhar Chambers, South Napier Rd., Karachi 2; f. 1958; Urdu; political; Editor ABDUR RAUF SIDDIQI; circ. 3,000.

Basant: Mutton Market, Rawalpindi; f. 1941; Urdu; Editor CH. HUKAM CHAND ANAND.

Chatan: 88 McLeod Rd., Lahore; f. 1948; Urdu; Editor AGHA SHORISH KASHMIRI.

Dastkari: 8 McLagan Rd., Shara-e-Quaid-e-Azam, Lahore; Urdu; women's; Editor Begum SHAFI AHMED.

Hilal: Hilal Rd., Rawalpindi; f. 1951; Urdu; Friday; Illustrated Services journal; Editor MUHAMMAD YUNUS; Business Man. A. GHAFOOR SIDDIQUI; circ. 25,000.

Illustrated Weekly of Pakistan: Haroon Chambers, South Napier Rd., P.O.B. 635, Karachi; f. 1948; Sundays; English; circ. 21,450; Editor AJMAL HUSAIN.

Insaf: P-929, Banni, Rawalpindi; f. 1955; Editor MIR ABDUL AZIZ.

Investor: 8 Muhamed Bldg., Bunder Rd., Karachi 1; f. 1955; English; Editor A. R. G. KHAN.

Karachi Commerce: P.O.B. No. 7442, 2/5 Akbar Rd., Karachi 3; f. 1947; English; Editor Z. I. ZOBAIRY; circ. 5,500.

Lahore: 113B Balwant Mansion, Beadon Rd., Lahore; f. 1952; Editor SAQIB ZIRAVEE; circ. 10,000.

Light: Ahmadiyya Building, Brandreth Bldg., Lahore 7; English; Editor MIRZA MUHAMMAD HUSSAIN.

Memaar-i-Nao: 39 K.M.C. Bldg., Leamarket, Karachi; Labour magazine; Urdu; Editor M. M. MUBASIR.

Naqid: Chughtai Manzil, Padshah Rd., Sadar-3, Karachi; f. 1955; Urdu; Editor BADAR CHUGHTAI.

Noor Jehan: 1 Koh-i-Noor Cinema Chambers, Marshal St., Karachi; f. 1948; circ. 16,000; film journal; Urdu: Editor N. S. CHAWLA.

Pak Kashmir: Pak Kashmir Office, Soikarur Chowk, Liaquat Rd., Rawalpindi; f. 1951; Urdu; Editor MUHAMMED FAYYAZ ABBAZI.

Parsi Sansar and Loke Sevak: Marston Rd., Karachi; f. 1909; English and Gujarati; Wed. and Sat.; Editor P. H. DASTUR.

Parwaz: Madina Office, Bahawalpur; Urdu; Editor MUSTAQ AHMED.

Pictorial: Jamia Masjid Rd., Rawalpindi; f. 1956; English; Editor MUHAMMAD SAFDAR.

Qalandar: Peshawar; Urdu; Editor R. U. K. SHERWANI.

Qindeel: 3A Shah Din Building, Shara-e-Quaid-e-Azam, Lahore; f. 1948; Urdu; Editor SHER MOHAMAD AKHTAR.

Quetta Times: Albert Press, Jinnah Rd., Quetta, Baluchistan; f. 1924; English; Editor S. RUSTOMJI; circ. 4,000.

Rahbar-e-Sarhad: Peshawar; f. 1956; Urdu; Editor M. SHABIR AHMAD.

Shahab-e-Saqib: Shahab Saqib Rd., Maulana St., Peshawar; f. 1950; Urdu; Editor S. M. RIZVI.

Statesman, The: 260-C Central Commercial Area P.E.C.H.S., Karachi 29; f. 1955; English; weekly; Editor MOHAMMAD OWAIS.

Sunday Post: 4 Amil St., off Robson Rd., Karachi 1; f. 1957; English; social and cultural magazine of general interest; Editor AMEEN TAREEN.

Tanvir: Bazar Qissa Khani, Peshawar; Independent; Urdu and Pashtu; Editor AMIR SIDDIQI.

Tarjaman-i-Sarhad: Peshawar; Urdu and Pashtu; Editor MALIK AMIR ALAM AWAN.

SELECTED PERIODICALS

(Karachi unless otherwise stated)

Afkar: Robson Rd.; f. 1945; Urdu; art, literature, films; monthly; Editor SAHBA LUCKNAVI.

Ahang: Pakistan Broadcasting Corpn., PBC Publications, Kassam Manzial, Randal Rd.; fortnightly; Urdu; Chief Editor SABIH MOHSIN.

Alam-i-Niswan: Peshawar Cantt., Peshawar; f. 1957; Urdu; monthly; Editor DOST MOHAMMAD FAKHRI.

Al-Ma'arif: Institute of Islamic Culture, Club Rd., Lahore; f. 1968; Urdu; monthly; Chief Editor Prof. M. SAEED SHEIKH; Editor S. H. RAZZAQI.

Criterion (*Journal of the Islamic Research Academy, Karachi*): 10/C/163, Federal "B" Area, Karachi 3805; literature, politics, religion; English; monthly; Editor KAUKAB SIDDIQUE.

Director: 42 Commercial Buildings, Shara-e-Quaid-e-Azam-Lahore; f. 1948; Urdu; monthly; films, literature and arts; circ. over 21,000; Editor M. FAZALHAQ.

Eastern Message: Pakistan Union Store, Jamia Masjid, Mipur Khas; f. 1959; English; quarterly; Editor Sultan AHMAD ANSARI.

Economic Observer: 827 Mohammadi House, McLeod Rd., P.O.B. 5202; f. 1948; fortnightly; English; circ. 4,000; Editor H. A. RAZI.

Economic Review: Al-Masiha, 3rd Floor, 47 Abdullah Haroon Rd., Karachi 3; f. 1969; monthly; Pakistan's economic development; Editor IQBAL HAIDARI; circ. 10,000.

Flyer International: Middle East House, Shahrah-e-Iraq, Karachi 1; aviation and tourism; Editor ASGHAR AHMAD.

Gul-o-Khar: 83 Shara-e-Quaid-e-Azam, P.O.B. 84, Lahore; f. 1949; films and literature; monthly; Urdu; Editor MUHAMMAD SADIQ.

Hamdard-i-Sehat: Institute of Health and Tibbi Research, Hamdard National Foundation, Hamdard, P.O. Nazimabad, Karachi 18; f. 1933; Urdu; monthly; Editor HAKIM MOHAMMED SAID.

The Herald: Haroon House, Dr. Ziauddin Ahmed Road, Karachi 4; f. 1970; monthly; English; Editor (vacant); circ. *c.* 10,000.

Industry and Trade Review: Inder St., Multan Rd., Lahore; f. 1959; English; monthly; Editor A. HAMID; circ. 6,200.

Islamic Studies: Islamic Research Institute, P.O.B. 1035, Islamabad; f. 1962; quarterly; Editor Dr. M. KHALID MASUD.

Izat Pakistan: Radio Pakistan, 71 Garden Rd.; fortnightly; Arabic.

Journal of the Pakistan Historical Society: 30 New Karachi Housing Society; f. 1950; English; quarterly; Editor Dr. MOINUL HAQUE.

Mah-i-Nau: P.O.B. 183; Pakistan Publications; f. 1948; illustrated, cultural monthly; Urdu; circ. 14,000; Editor MUHAMMED RAFIQ KHAWAR.

Makhzan: 2A Shah Din Bldg., Shara-e-Quaid-e-Azam, Lahore; f. 1906; monthly; Urdu; literary; Editor HAMID NIZAMI.

Medicus: Pakistan Chowk, Dr. Ziauddin Ahmed Rd., 1; f. 1950; English; medical journal; monthly; Editor M. S. QURESHI.

Muslim News (International): G.E.M. Chambers, Zaibunnisa St.; f. 1962; current affairs; monthly; Editor MEHDI ALI SIDDIQUI; circ. 10,000.

Pak Travel: 7A Nisbet Rd., Lahore; f. 1955; English; monthly; Editor MUZAFFAR ALI QURESHI.

Pakistan Calling: Pakistan Broadcasting Corpn., PBC Publications, Kassam Manzil, Randal Rd.; monthly; English, Urdu, Persian and Arabic; Chief Editor SABIH MOHSIN.

Pakistan Digest: 4 Amil St., Off Robson Rd., Karachi 1; f. 1974; monthly; English; Editor AMEEN TAREEN.

Pakistan Export Directory: Trade and Industry House, 14 West Wharf Rd., P.O.B. 4611; f. 1966; English; annually; Editor-in-Chief GHAZI NASEERUDDIN.

Pakistan Exports: Export Promotion Bureau; f. 1950; English; monthly; Editor MOHAMMAD HUSAIN.

Pakistan Horizon: Pakistan Institute of International Affairs, Strachan Rd.; f. 1948; international affairs; English; quarterly; Editor K. SARWAR HASAN; circ. 1,200.

Pakistan Journal of Scientific and Industrial Research: Pakistan Council of Scientific and Industrial Research, 39 Garden Rd., Karachi 0310; f. 1958; English; Chief Editor M. A. HALEEM; six times a year.

Pakistan Management Review: Pakistan Institute of Management, B.I.M., Shahrah Iran, Clifton, Karachi 6; f. 1960; English; quarterly; Editor HAFEEZ R. KHAN.

Pakistan Medical Forum: 15 Nadir House, I. I. Chundrigar Rd., Karachi 2; f. 1966; monthly; English; Man. Editor M. AHSON.

Pakistan Pictorial: P.O.B. 183, Karachi; f. 1948; English; all aspects of Pakistani life; non-political; published in seven languages including English, French, Urdu and Arabic; every two months; Editor S. AMJAD ALI; circ. 50,000.

Pakistan Press Directory: Chronicle Publications, Altaf Husain Rd.; P.O.B. 5257; annual.

Pakistan Review, The: Ferozsons Ltd., 60 Shara-e-Quaid-e-Azam, Lahore; f. 1953; English; monthly, political, cultural, social and economic affairs of Pakistan and the Islamic World; Editor-in-Chief Dr. A. WAHEED; Editor M. A. MAJEED.

Pakistan Textile Journal: 505 Qamar House, Bunder Rd.; f. 1950; monthly; English; Publisher-Editor MAZHAR YUSUF.

Pasban: Faiz Modh Rd., Quetta; Urdu; fortnightly; Editor MOLVI MOHD. ABDULLAH.

Perspective: P.O.B. 183, Sharah Iraq; f. 1948; English; monthly digest; Editor JALALUDDIN AHMAD; circ. 10,000.

Punjab Educational Journal: University Book Agency, Lahore; f. 1937; English; monthly.

Spem: Hamdard Waqf, Hamdard P.O.; f. 1959; English; quarterly; Editor HAKIM MOHAMMED SAID.

Statistical Bulletin: Statistical Div., I, S.M.C.H. Society; P.O.B. 7766; f. 1952; English; monthly.

Talimo Tarbiat: Ferozsons Ltd., 60 Shara-e-Quaid-e-Azam, Lahore; f. 1941; children's monthly; Urdu; Chief Editor A. HAMEED KHAN; circ. 31,000.

This Fortnight in Pakistan: 505 Qamar House, Bunder Rd.; f. 1965; Editor MAZHAR YUSUF and G. M. MEHKRI.

Trade and Industry: Trade and Industry House, 14 West Wharf Rd., P.O.B. 4611; f. 1957; English; monthly; Editor-in-Chief GHAZI NASEERUDDIN; Editor B. M. KUTTY.

Trade Chronicle: Altaf Husain Rd.; f. 1953; English; monthly; trade and economics; Editor ABDUL RAUF SIDDIQI; circ. 5,500.

Trade Journal: Aiwan-e-Tijarat, Nicol Rd.; f. 1961; official organ of the Chamber of Commerce and Industry; Editor SYED ALI BAQAR; circ. 3,000.

Vision: 1 Victoria Chamber, Victoria Rd.; monthly; English; Editor YUNUS M. SAID.

Voice of Islam: A.M. 20, off Frere Rd., Saddar; monthly; English; Editor MUMTAZ AHMAD; Man. M. W. GAZDAR.

West Pakistan: 21 Abbot Rd., Lahore; f. 1958; English; monthly; Editor SYED A. Z. ZAIN.

Woman's World: 43/4A P.E.C.H.S., Block 6; f. 1958; English; monthly; Editor Begum MUJEEB M. AKRAM.

Yaqeen International: Shahrah-e-Liaquat, Saddar, Karachi 3; f. 1952; English and Arabic; Islamic organ; Editor SAID UDDIN AHMAD.

FOREIGN BUREAUX

Associated Press of Pakistan: 12-H The Mall, Rawalpindi.

Reuters: No. 43, 27th Street, Shalimar 6, Islamabad.

UPI: Victoria Rd., at Randal Rd. (near Tram Godi); Chief SHIRIN MANZIL.

Antara News Agency, DPA and Tass also have offices in Pakistan.

PRESS ASSOCIATIONS

All Pakistan Newspapers Society: 3rd Floor, 32 Farid Chambers, Victoria Rd., Karachi-3; f. 1949; 76 mems.; Pres. M. H. HIDAYATULLAH; Hon. Sec. KAZI SAEED AKBAR.

PUBLISHERS

Amalgamated Press: Bazar Kathian, Sialkot City; printers of newspapers.

Barque and Co.: Barque Chambers, Barque Square, Ali Khan, Lahore; f. 1930; trade directories, Who's Who, periodicals; brs. in Karachi; Man. Dir. A. M. BARQUE.

The Book House: 8 Trust Bldg., Urdu Bazar, P.O.B. 734, Lahore.

Crescent Publications: Urdu Bazar, Lahore.

Din Muhammadi Press: McLeod Rd., Karachi; f. 1948; reference books; Man. Dir. KHAWAJA GHULAM HUSSAIN.

Director Magazine Book Depot: 42 Commercial Buildings, Shara-e-Quaid-e-Azam, Lahore.

Economic and Industrial Publications: Al-Masiha, 47 Abdullah Haroon Rd., Karachi 3; f. 1965; books on Pakistan's economic and industrial development and weekly investors' service on corporate companies in Pakistan.

Ferozsons Ltd.: Mr. Abdul Qayyum Khan, Peshawar; f. 1894; books, periodicals, maps, charts, stationery, etc.; Chair. Dr. A. WAHEED; Man. Dir. A. HAMEED KHAN.

Fine Art Printers: 46 Edwards Rd., Rawalpindi; f. 1928; Dirs. NAIEEM, SHAMEEM YAMIN.

Frontier Marketing Federation Ltd.: Sadar Rd., Peshawar Cantt.

Frontier Publishing Co.: Urdu Bazar, Lahore.

Government Publications: Manager of Publications, Central Publications Branch, Government of Pakistan, Block 44, Shahrah Iraq, Karachi.

International Printers: Dyal Singh Mansion, Shara-e-Quaid-e-Azam, Lahore; f. 1960; children's books; Principal Officials ZIA H. MIAN, T. M. MIAN.

Islami Kutub Khana: Sadar Bazar, Mianwali (Punjab).

Islamic Publications Ltd.: 13-E, Shah Alam Market, Lahore; Islamic literature in Urdu and English; Dir. AKHLAQ HUSSAIN.

Kitabistan Ltd.: f. 1950; Man. Dir. E. M. ABBASI.

Madni Publications: Darus Salam, Thatta (Sind).

Maktaba-e-Islamia: Chowk Bazar, Bahawalpur.

Mercantile Guardian Press and Publishers: 81–83 Shara-e-Quaid-e-Azam, Lahore; f. 1949; trade directories, etc.; Editor MAHMOOD AHMAD MIR.

Nairoshni: Nicol Road, Karachi 2.

Orientalia Publishers: Lahore; Islamic publications.

Pak Publishers: Urdu Bazar, Lahore.

Pakistan Publications: P.O.B. 183, Shahrah Iraq, Karachi 1; general interest and literary books and magazines about Pakistan in English, Urdu and Arabic, etc.

Pakistan Publishing Co. Ltd.: 56-N, Gulberg Industrial Colony, Lahore; f. 1932; textbooks; government printers; Man. Dir. S. M. SHAH.

Pakistan Publishing House: Victoria Chambers 2, A. Haroon Rd., Karachi; f. 1959; Dir. M. NOORANI, B.COM.

Peco Ltd.: P.O.B. 70, Lahore; f. 1936; Koran and Islamic literature; Man. Dir. JAMEEL MAZHAR.

Pioneer Book House: 1 Avan Lodge, Bunder Rd., P.O.B. 37, Karachi; periodicals, gazettes, maps and reference works in English, Urdu and other regional languages.

Publishers International: Bandukwala Building, 4 McLeod Road, Karachi; f. 1948; reference books, advertising; Man. Dir. KAMALUDDIN AHMAD.

Publishers United Ltd.: 176 Anarkali, Lahore; textbooks, technical, reference and general books.

Punjab Religious Books Society: Anarkali, Lahore 2; educational, religious, law and general; Chair. Rt. Rev. INAYAT MASIH, Bishop of Lahore; Gen. Man. Capt. H. C. RAE.

"Rast Guftar" Press: Bhawana Bazar, Lyallpur; f. 1889; Publishers and Printers; Man. and Propr. SHAMSHAR ALI BASKHSHI.

Shaikh Muhammad Ashraf: Kashmiri Bazar, Lahore; f. 1923; books on all aspects of Islam in English; Chief Ed. M. ASHRAF DARR; Man. S. A. HUSAIN SHAH.

Sindhi Adabi Board: Sind University Campus, Jamshoro, Hyderabad (Sind); f. 1951; history, literature, culture of Sind; translations into Sindhi, especially social sciences.

M. Siraj ud Din & Sons: Kashmiri Bazar, Lahore 8; f. 1905; religious books in many languages; Man. M. SIRAJ UD DIN.

Taj Company Ltd.: P.O.B. 530, Karachi; religious books; Gen. Man. KHALIL-UR-RAHMAN MUFTI.

Times Press: Mansfield St., Sadar, Karachi 3; f. 1948; books and periodicals; Man. Dir. SHUJAUDDIN.

Universal Publishing Co.: Urdu Bazar, Lahore.

PUBLISHERS' ASSOCIATION

Pakistan Publishers' and Booksellers' Association: Y.M.C.A. Bldg., Shara-e-Quaid-e-Azam, Lahore; Pres. CH. ABDUL HAMID; Sec. S. A. BUKHARI.

RADIO AND TELEVISION

RADIO

Pakistan Broadcasting Corpn.: 81A Satellite Town, Rawalpindi; f. 1972; Chair. SYED HAROON BOKHARI.

National broadcasting comprising seven stations: Rawalpindi-Islamabad, Karachi, Lahore, Multan, Peshawar, Hyderabad and Quetta. External services in 16 languages.

There were 1,630,000 radio receivers in use in 1971.

TELEVISION

Pakistan Television Corporation Ltd.: 1 Tulsa Rd., Lalazar Colony, P.O.B. 230, Rawalpindi, Punjab; f. 1967; Chair. SYED HAROON BOKHARI; Man. Dir. MASOOD NABI NOOR; Dir. (Programmes) AGHA NASIR.

Programmes daily 17.30–23.30 hours.

Extended transmissions on Saturdays.

In 1972 the number of television licences issued was 129,000.

FINANCE

(cap. = capital; p.u. = paid up; dep. = deposits; m. = million; Rs. = Rupees)

BANKING

In January 1974 all Pakistani banks were nationalized. Foreign banks were not affected, but were not permitted to open any new branches in Pakistan.

CENTRAL BANK

State Bank of Pakistan: Central Directorate, P.O.B. 4456, McLeod Rd., Karachi; f. 1948; controls and regulates currency and foreign exchange and has the sole right of note issue; cap. p.u. Rs. 30m.; dep. Rs. 5,881.6m. (June 30th, 1972); Gov. GHULAM ISHAQ KHAN; Deputy Gov. Dr. S. A. MEENAI.

Allied Bank of Pakistan Ltd.: Jubilee Insurance House, I. I. Chundrigar House, Karachi; f. 1974; cap. Rs. 5.4m.; dep. Rs. 338.8m. (Dec. 1970); Chair. FAROOQ A. SHEIKH; Pres. I. A. RIZVI.

Habib Bank Ltd.: Habib Bank Plaza, Karachi 21; f. 1941; cap. p.u. Rs. 90m.; res. Rs. 100m.; dep. Rs. 7,254m. (June 1974); over 1,250 branches throughout Pakistan and 55 overseas brs.; Pres. S. MUSTAFA ISMAIL; Chair./Man. Dir. RASHID D. HABIB.

Muslim Commercial Bank Ltd.: Adamjee House, I. I. Chundrigar Rd., Karachi; f. 1948; cap. p.u. Rs. 27.0m.; dep. Rs. 3,281m. (Dec. 1974); 825 branches in Pakistan; Chair. A. W. ADAMJEE; Pres. S. IRADAT HUSSIAN.

National Bank of Pakistan: I. I. Chundrigar Rd., Karachi; f. 1949; cap. p.u. Rs. 30m.; dep. Rs. 9,151m. (Dec. 1974); Pres. INAYAT ALI; Man. Dir. A. JAMIL NISHTAR.

Punjab National Bank: 5 Parliament St., New Delhi 110001; f. 1895; cap. 20m.; dep. 7,820.7m. (1973); 1,015 brs.; Gen. Man. SITA RAM MOHINDROO.

United Bank Ltd.: State Life Building No. 1, I. I. Chundrigar Rd., Karachi; f. 1959; cap. Rs. 58m.; dep. Rs. 8,510m. (Dec. 1975); Pres. M. A. K. YOUSUFI.

FOREIGN BANKS

Afghan National Bank (Pakistan) Ltd. (*Banke Millie Afghan*): Kabul; Karachi; Chair. ABDUL MADJID; Pres. A. GHANI GHAUSSY.

Algemene Bank Nederland, N.V.: Amsterdam; P.O.B. 4096, Mackinnon's Bldg., I. I. Chundrigar Rd., Karachi; Man. J. P. VAN HEUVEN.

Bank of America National Trust and Savings Association: 4th Floor, Jubilee Insurance House, I. I. Chundrigar Rd., Karachi; Vice-Pres. and Man. SHAFIQ AHMED.

Bank of India Ltd.: Bombay; Bunder Road, Karachi.

Bank of Tokyo Ltd.: Qamar House, M. A. Jinnah Rd., P.O.B. 4232, Karachi.

Chartered Bank: Lahore; Lyallpur; P.O.B. 4896, I. I. Chundrigar Rd., Karachi 2.

Citibank, N.A.: State Life Bldg., I. I. Chundrigar Rd., P.O.B. 4889; Karachi; br. in Lahore; Resident Vice-Pres. STEVEN H. CRABTREE.

European Asian Bank: P.O.B. 4925, State Life Bldg. 1A, I. I. Chundrigar Rd., Karachi; Man. J. E. C. HILDEBRANDT.

Grindlays Bank Ltd.: P.O.B. 5556, I. I. Chundrigar Rd., Karachi 2; 15 brs. in Karachi, Lahore, Rawalpindi, Islamabad, Peshawar, Quetta; Gen. Man. D. S. WHITTALL.

State Bank of India: Bombay; Karachi, Lahore.

Sumitomo Bank Ltd.: Tokyo; 111, Qamar House, Bunder Rd., Karachi 2.

United Commercial Bank Ltd.: Calcutta; Bunder Rd., P.O.B. 4811, Karachi.

CO-OPERATIVE BANKS

Co-operative Banks: 130 branches throughout Pakistan.

DEVELOPMENT FINANCE ORGANIZATIONS

Agricultural Development Bank of Pakistan: Shafi Court, Merewether Rd., Karachi; f. 1961; provides credit facilities to agriculturists and cottage industrialists in the rural areas and for allied objects; cap. authorized Rs. 200m.; total loans paid up (Sept. 1972) Rs. 1,536m.; Chair. RIAZUDDIN AHMED; Dep. Gen. Man. F. H. ABBASI; 11 regional offices and 89 field offices.

Industrial Development Bank of Pakistan: State Life Building No. 2, Wallace Rd., Karachi; f. 1961; provides credit facilities in Indian and foreign currencies for establishment of new industrial units and to meet needs of existing industrial enterprises; cap. p.u. Rs. 50m.; Man. Dir. NASIM AHMAD.

Investment Corporation of Pakistan: National Bank Bldg., I. I. Chundrigar Rd., P.O.B. 5410, Karachi 2; f. 1966 by the Government "to encourage and broaden the base of investments and to develop the capital market"; auth. cap. Rs. 200m., cap. p.u. Rs. 50m.; Chair. AKHTAR HUSAIN, Man. Dir. N. M. QURESHI.

National Investment (Unit) Trust: 6th Floor, National Bank Bldg., I. I. Chundrigar Rd., Karachi; mobilizes domestic savings to meet the requirements of growing economic development and enables investors to share in the industrial and economic prosperity of the country; assets total Rs. 625.8m.

Pakistan Industrial Credit and Investment Corporation Limited (P.I.C.I.C.): State Life Bldg. 1, I. I. Chundrigar Rd., Karachi 2; f. 1957 as an industrial development bank to provide financial assistance for the establishment of new industries and balancing/modernization of existing ones in the private sector; auth. cap Rs. 150m.; cap. p.u. Rs. 66.4m.; public joint stock company with 60 per cent and 40 per cent shareholdings of local and foreign investors respectively; Chair. N. M. UQUAILI; Man. Dir. (vacant); publ. *PICIC News* (quarterly).

STOCK EXCHANGE

Karachi Stock Exchange Ltd.: Stock Exchange Bldg., Kallian Rd., Karachi 2; f. 1947; 200 mems.; Pres. DARA F. DASTOOR.

INSURANCE

In 1972 all life insurance companies and the life departments of composite companies were nationalized and merged into State Life Insurance Corporation of Pakistan.

Department of Insurance: Block 66A, Shahrah-e-Iraq, Karachi; f. 1948; a government department attached to the Ministry of Commerce; regulates insurance business; Controller of Insurance A. M. KHALFE.

LIFE INSURANCE

State Life Insurance Corporation of Pakistan: State Life Insurance Bldg. No. 2, P.O.B. 5725, I. I. Chundrigar Rd., Karachi 2; f. 1972; Chair. D. M. QURAISHI.

Postal Life Insurance Organization: Tibet Centre, M. A. Jinnah Rd., Karachi; Dir. Gen. S. ATHAR MAHMUD.

GENERAL INSURANCE

Pakistan Insurance Corporation: Pakistan Insurance Building, M. A. Jinnah Rd., P.O.B. 4777, Karachi 2; f. 1953; reinsurance corporation handling all classes of insurance except life; majority of shares held by the government; Chair. M. YAKUB.

Central Insurance Co. Ltd.: Dawood Centre, P.O.B. 3988, Karachi 4; Chair. N. M. UQUAILI; Gen. Man. KHURSHID A. MINHAS.

Eastern General Insurance Co. Ltd.: Nadir House, I. I. Chundrigar Rd., Karachi; Chair. and Dir. HUSSAIN AFTAB.

Indus Assurance Co. Ltd.: Grindlays Bank Bldg., 3rd Floor, I. I. Chundrigar Rd., Karachi; Chair. A. H. MANGHI.

National Security Insurance Co. Ltd.: State Life Bldg. 2, 4th Floor, Wallace Rd., P.O.B. 5337, Karachi; Div. Man. MOHAMMAD MOIN.

Pakistan Guarantee Insurance Co. Ltd.: Serai Rd., P.O.B. 5436, Karachi 2; Gen. Man. FAZAL REHMAN.

Pioneer Insurance Co. Ltd.: 311–313 Qamar House, P.O.B. 5117, Karachi; Man. Dir. ABID ZUBERI.

Standard Insurance Co. Ltd.: 9th Floor, Mohammadi House, I. I. Chundrigar Rd., Karachi; Gen. Man. M. A. CHISTY.

Shalimar General Insurance Co. Ltd.: Nadir House, 3rd Floor, I. I. Chundrigar Rd., Karachi; Dir. A. R. NIZAMI.

Union Insurance Co. of Pakistan Ltd.: 9th Floor, Adamjee House, I. I. Chundrigar Rd., Karachi; Chair. MIAN MOHD AYUB.

United Insurance Co. of Pakistan Ltd.: Valika Chambers, Altaf Hussain Rd., Karachi 2; Chair. KAMRUDDIN VALIKA.

Universal Insurance Co. Ltd.: 63 The Mall, P.O.B. 539, Lahore; Chair. Lt.-Gen. M. HABIBULLAH KHAN.

Adamjee Insurance Co. Ltd.: Adamjee House, 6th Floor, I. I. Chundrigar Rd., P.O.B. 4850, Karachi; Man. Dir. D. W. PURNELL.

Alpha Insurance Co. Ltd.: State Life Bldg. No. 1-B, State Life Sq., off I. I. Chundrigar Rd., Karachi 2; f. 1951; Dir., Gen. Man. and Sec. V. C. GONSALVES.

Co-operative Insurance Society of Pakistan Ltd.: Co-operative Insurance Bldg., P.O.B. 147, The Mall, Lahore; Gen. Man. MAZHAR ALI KHAN.

Crescent Star Insurance Co. Ltd.: Nadir House, I. I. Chundrigar Rd., P. O. B. 4616, Karachi; Gen. Man. MUNIR AHMAD.

Eastern Federal Union Insurance Co. Ltd.: Qamar House, M. A. Jinnah Rd., P.O.B. 5005, Karachi-2; f. 1932; Chair. ROSHAN ALI BHIMJEE; Man. Dir. AZIM RAHIM.

Habib Insurance Co. Ltd.: P.O.B. 5217, Insurance House, No. 1 Habib Square, M. A. Jinnah Rd., Karachi; f. 1942; Chair. HUSEINALI A. JUMANI; Gen. Man. R. N. DUBASH.

International General Insurance Co. of Pakistan Ltd.: Finlay House, 1st Floor, I. I. Chundrigar Rd., Karachi 2; f. 1953; Gen. Man. and Sec. YUSUF J. HASWARY.

Khyber Insurance Co. Ltd.: 719-726 Muhammadi House, I. I. Chundrigar Rd., Karachi; Man. Dir. M. ZAFARUL AHSAN.

Mercantile Fire and General Insurance Co. of Pakistan Ltd.: 17 Chartered Bank Chambers, I. I. Chundrigar Rd., Karachi 2, f. 1958, Man. Dir. FAKHRUDDIN A. LOTIA.

Muslim Insurance Co. Ltd., The: Bank Square, The Mall, Lahore; f. 1934; brs. throughout Pakistan; Administrator TAHSIN AHMED.

New Jubilee Insurance Co. Ltd.: Jubilee Insurance House, I. I. Chundrigar Rd., P.O.B. 4795, Karachi; f. 1953; Man. Dir. S. C. SUBJALLY.

Pakistan General Insurance Co. Ltd.: P.O.B. 1364, Bank Square, Shahrah-e-Quaid-e-Azam, Lahore; f. 1948; Gen. Man. KHALID MASOOD KHAN LASHARIE; Chair. AMIR ABDULLAH KHAN.

The Pakistan Mutual Insurance Co. Ltd.: 17/B Shah Alam Market, Lahore; f. 1946; Chair. FATEH MOHD.

Premier Insurance Co. of Pakistan Ltd.: Premier Insurance Bldg., Wallace Rd., Karachi 2; f. 1952; Chair. M. M. BASHIR; Man. Dir. MAQBUL AHMED.

Sterling Insurance Co. Ltd.: 26 Balkishan Bldg., The Mall, Lahore, P.O.B. 119; f. 1949; Man. Dir. S. A. RAHIM.

INSURANCE ASSOCIATIONS

Insurance Association of Pakistan: Jamshed Katrak Chambers, Machi Miani, P.O.B. 4932, Karachi 2; f. 1948; membership comprises 40 companies (Pakistan and foreign) transacting general insurance business in Pakistan; issues tariffs and establishes rules for insurance in the country; brs. at Lahore; Chair. M. CHOUDHURY; Vice-Chair. SHARAFUL ISLAM KHAN; Sec. M. MAROOF.

Pakistan Insurance Institute: Adamjee Chambers, I. I. Chundrigar Rd., Karachi; f. 1951 to encourage insurance education; Sec. S. A. SHARFUDDIN.

TRADE AND INDUSTRY

GOVERNMENT-SPONSORED ORGANIZATIONS

Board of Industrial Management: N.S.C. Bldg., Moulvi Tamizuddin Rd., Karachi 2; f. 1972; responsible for supervising and co-ordinating the work of state-owned industrial enterprises; Chair. RAFI RAZA (Minister for Production, Town Planning and Industries); Vice-Chair. FEROZE QAISER (Special Assistant to Prime Minister for Economic Affairs). The Board has 60 state-owned enterprises under 10 corporations:

Federal Chemical and Ceramics Corporation Ltd.: Chair. MAHMOOD AHMAD.

Federal Light Engineering Corporation: Chair. M. AFZAL KHAN.

National Fertilizer Corporation: Chair. SYED BABAR ALI.

Pakistan Automobile Corporation: Chair. M. NASIM KHAN.

Pakistan Steel Mills Corporation Ltd.: 5th Floor, State Life Building 2, Wallace Rd., Karachi 4; f. 1968, responsible for establishment and operation of Karachi Steel Mills with an annual capacity of 1.1m. tons of finished steel products; Chair. A. R. FARIDI.

Pakistan Industrial Development Corporation (PIDC): PIDC House, Dr. Ziauddin Ahmad Rd., Karachi; f. 1962 by Act of Parliament; semi-autonomous; manufacturers of cement, fertilizers, machine tools, woollen and cotton textiles, carpets, chemicals; sugar, paper and heavy machinery; gas distributors; Chair. A. H. A. KAZI.

State Cement Corporation of Pakistan Ltd.: Chair. M. A. KHAN.

State Heavy Engineering and Machine Tool Corporation Ltd.: Chair. ABID HUSSAIN.

State Petroleum, Refining and Petro-Chemical Corporation: Chair. M. A. ALLAWALA.

National Design & Industrial Services Corporation: Chair. Dr. AHMED SHAH NAWAZ.

National Economic Council: supreme economic body with the President as Chairman. The Governors of the four Provinces, Deputy Chairman of Planning Commission, Chairman of Planning and Development Board of Government of Pakistan are its members.

Cotton Board: 3rd floor, Luxmi Bldg., M. A. Jinnah Rd., Karachi 2; f. 1950; Chair. ASHRAF W. TABANI; Sec. M. INAYAT.

Oil and Gas Development Corporation: 4th Floor, Central Hotel Bldg., Club Rd., Karachi 4; f. 1961; Man. Dir. Maj.-Gen. J. A. FARUQI; Sec. Lt.-Col. T. H. BASHIR.

Pakistan Industrial Technical Assistance Centre (PITAC): Ferozepur Rd., Lahore 16; f. 1962 by the Government to introduce modern industrial techniques by training and demonstration programmes; Chair. G. M. BAJWA; Gen. Man. MUSTAFA HASAN.

Trading Corporation of Pakistan: Karachi; f. July 1967; sole importer of country's total requirements in bulk ferrous and non-ferrous metals, edible oils and newsprint from world-wide sources and for guaranteed quality exports of miscellaneous commodities.

Sind Small Industries and Handicrafts Corporation (SICS): 310 A. M. Preedy St., Saddar, Karachi 3; Dir. ALI NAWAZ BOHIO.

Pakistan Water and Power Development Authority: WAPDA House, Shara-e-Quaid-e-Azam, Lahore; f. 1958; for development of irrigation, water supply and drainage, building of replacement works under the World Bank sponsored Indo-Pakistan Indus Basin Treaty; flood-control and watershed management; reclamation of waterlogged and saline lands; inland navigation; generation of hydroelectric and thermal power and its transmission and distribution; Chair. S. KHAN; publ. *Indus* (English, monthly), *Barqab* (Urdu, monthly), *Wapda Weekly, Annual Report* (English).

CHAMBERS OF COMMERCE

Federation of Pakistan Chambers of Commerce and Industry, The: Lalji Lakhmidas Building, Bellasis St., Karachi; f. 1950; 71 mems.; Pres. ABUR REHMAN HAJI HABIB; Sec.-Gen. TUFAIL AHMAD KHAN.

AFFILIATED CHAMBERS

Chamber of Commerce and Industry: Aiwan-e-Tijarat, P.O.B. 4158, Karachi 2; f. 1960; 3,767 mems.; Pres. G. R. ARSHAD; Sec. and Econ. Adviser AGHA M. GHOUSE.

Hyderabad Chamber of Commerce and Industry: 326 Quaid-e-Azam Rd., P.O.B. 99, Cantonment, Hyderabad; Pres. DOST MOHAMED; Sec. ABDUL SALIM.

Lahore Chamber of Commerce and Industry: P.O.B. 597, 11 Race Course Rd., Lahore; f. 1923; 3,000 mems.; Pres. A. AZIZ ZULFIKAR; Sec. MIAN MAQBOOL AHMAD.

Multan Chamber of Commerce and Industry: P.O.B. 90, Kutchery Rd., Multan; Pres. SHAIKH MAQBOOL AHMAD; Sec. A. D. MALIK.

Overseas Investors Chamber of Commerce and Industry: Chamber of Commerce Bldg., P.O.B. 4833, Talpur Rd., Karachi 2; 136 mems.; Pres. W. R. A. KIMBER; Sec. P. T. ENSOR, M.B.E.

Rawalpindi Chamber of Commerce and Industry: Chamber House, 108 Adamjee Rd., Rawalpindi; Pres. SH. ISHRAT ALI; Sec. MUSHTAQ AHMAD.

Sarhad Chamber of Commerce and Industry: Sarhad Chamber House, G.T. Rd., Panj Tirath, Peshawar; f. 1958; 400 mems., including three Trade Groups and one Town Association; Pres. HAJI ABDUL AZIZ SAVUL; Sec. AGHA MUHAMMAD.

Sukkur Chamber of Commerce and Industry: New Cloth Market, Sukkur; Pres. MUNAWWAR KHAN; Sec. MIRZA IQBAL BEG.

EMPLOYERS' AND TRADE ASSOCIATIONS

All-Pakistan Textile Mills Association: Muhammadi House, 3rd Floor, I. I. Chundrigar Rd., Karachi 2; Chair. HAMEED M. DADABHOY; Sec. S. M. USMAN.

The Karachi Cotton Association Ltd.: The Cotton Exchange, I. I Chundrigar Rd., Karachi; Chair. MAQBUL AHMAD; Sec. N. A. SYED.

Pakistan Banks' Association: National Bank of Pakistan Bldg., P.O.B. 4937, I. I. Chundrigar Rd., Karachi; Pres. JAMIL NISHTAR; Sec. SHEIKH LAL JANI.

Pakistan Cotton Ginners' Association: Bungalow 159, Block 'C', Unit 2, Shah Latifabad, Hyderabad; Chair. KH. MOHAMMAD MASUD; Sec. SYED ABBAS HUSSAIN.

Pakistan Film Producers' Association: Regal Cinema Bldg., Shahrah-e-Quaid-e-Azam, Lahore; Pres. NIAZI MALIK; Sec. SHAUKAT SHEIKH.

Pakistan Iron and Steel Merchants' Association: 2nd floor, Writers' Chambers, Dunolly Rd., Karachi; Pres. MAHER H. ALAVI; Sec. S. Z. ISLAM.

Pakistan Paint Manufacturers' Association: P.O.B. 3602, Block 14, Federal 'B' Area, Karachi 16; f. 1953; Chair. D. O. ANDERSON; Sec. ABDUR RAHMAN KHAN.

Pakistan Pharmaceutical Manufacturers' Association: 130–131 Hotel Metropole, Club Rd., Karachi; Chair. MUMTAZ A. SHEIKH; Sec. SYED ABBAS.

Pakistan Shipowners' Association: Ralli Bros. Bldg., Wood St., Karachi 2; Chair. A. D. AHMAD SQA; Sec. A. S. WAHEDNA.

Pakistan Silk and Rayon Mills' Association: 10 Bank House, 3 Habib Square, M. A. Jinnah Rd., Karachi 2; f. 1974; Chair. RAUF W. TABANI; Sec. M. H. K. BURNEY.

Pakistan Steel Re-rolling Mills' Association: Karachi Chambers, 6-Link McLeod Rd., Lahore; Chair. MOHAMMAD ASLAM; Sec. Sq. Ldr. KH. M. IKRAM.

Pakistan Sugar Mills' Association: 329 Alfalah Bldg., Shahrah-e-Quaid-e-Azam, Lahore; Chair. TAJ M. KHANZADA; Sec. ALI AHMED.

Pakistan Wool and Hair Merchants' Association: 27 Idris Chambers, Wood St., Karachi; Pres. SHEIKH SERAJ DIN.

TRADE UNIONS

Pakistan National Federation of Trade Unions: 406 Qamar House, M.A. Jinnah Rd., Karachi; f. 1962; 270 unions with total of 130,000 mems.; Pres. MOHAMED SHARIF; Sec.-Gen. RASHID MOHAMMAD; Publ. *PNFTU News*.

The principal affiliated Federations are:

All-Pakistan Railwaymen's Federation: 110 McLeod Rd., Lahore; f. 1948; 8 unions; 88,522 mems.; Pres MEHBOOB-UL-HAQ; Gen. Sec. CH. UMAR DIN.

Maghrabi Pakistan Khet Mazdoor Federation: Brandreth Rd., Lahore; f. 1954; plantation workers about 14,000 mems.

Pakistan Transport Workers' Federation: 110 McLeod Rd., Lahore; 17 unions; 92,512 mems.; Pres MEHBOOB-UL-HAQ; Gen. Sec. CH. UMAR DIN.

Sind Hari Federation (SHF): P.O. Umarkot, Sind; 1 unions; about 23,000 mems.; plantation workers Pres. A. G. SARHANDI; Sec.-Gen. L. H. PALLI.

Pakistan Mazdoor Federation: Landa Bazar, Lahore; f. 1951; 38 affiliated unions; 71,324 mems.; Pres. KHWAJ MOHAMMED HUSSAIN; Sec. MALIK FAZAL ILAHI QURBAN

United Trade Unions Federation of Pakistan: 1 Swam Narain Trust Bldg., Frere Rd., Karachi; 17 affiliate unions; about 15,000 mems.; Pres. MIRZA FAROOQ BE

MAJOR INDUSTRIAL COMPANIES

CEMENT

Gharibwal Cement Ltd.: Gharibwal District, Jhelum Head Office: 16 Shahreh Fatima Jinnah, Lahore management taken over by Government in 1972.

Pakistan Cement Industries: 65 Adanjee Rd., Rawalpin (Reg. Office); branches in Fareeqia, Hattar Distri and Hazara; management taken over by Governme in January 1972.

Zeal Pak Cement: P.O.B. 70, S.I.T.E. Hyderabad, Tan Mehd, Khan Rd.

Chemicals

sso (Pakistan) Fertilizer Co. Ltd.: Daharki District, Sukkur.

CI (Pakistan) Manufacturers Ltd.: 5 West Wharf Rd., P.O.B. 4731, Karachi-2.

Karnaphuli Rayon and Chemicals Ltd.: Chandraghona, Chittagong Hill Tracts; f. 1967; rayon filament yarn, cellophane; Chair. Mofitur Ranman.

Construction

Gammon Pakistan Ltd.: Gammon House, 400/2, Peshawar Rd., Rawalpindi; civil engineers and contractors; Dir. and Sec. S. M. Aslam.

Edible Oils

Burma Oil Mills Ltd.: V. M. Plaza, West Wharf Rd., Karachi.

Wazir Ali Industries: P.O.B. 7310, Kandawalla Bldg., M. A. Jinnah Rd., Karachi (Head Office); management taken over by the Government in 1973.

Electrical

Johnson and Phillips (Pakistan) Ltd.: C-10, S.I.T.E., Manghopir Rd., P.O.B. 3603, Karachi 16; Man. Dir. C. M. Meek.

Pakistan Cables Ltd.: Sind Industrial Trading Estate, Manghopir Rd., Karachi.

Engineering

National Motors Ltd.: Hab Chauki Rd., S.I.T.E., P.O.B. 2706, Karachi 28; State enterprise; manufactures trucks, assembles buses and land cruisers.

Pakistan Engineering Co. Ltd.: 6 Ganga Ram Trust Bldg., Shara-e-Quaid-e-Azam, Lahore; lathes, machine tools, diesel engines and other machinery; management taken over by Government in 1972.

Gas

Sui Gas Transmission Company Ltd.: State Life Bldg. 3, Dr. Ziauddin Ahmed Rd., P.O.B. 540, Karachi 4; natural gas transmission and pipeline construction.

Oil and Petroleum

Attock Oil Co. Ltd.: Rawalpindi; prospecting, drilling and refining.

Burma Eastern Ltd.: A-7, K.D.A. 1, Karachi.

National Refinery Ltd.: 4th Floor, Karim Chambers, Merewether Rd., P.O.B. 4557, Karachi 4; capacity of 14,000 BSD; kerosene, naphtha, diesel oil, jute batching oil, lubricating oil base stocks and asphalt.

Pakistan National Oils Ltd.: Karim Chambers, Merewether Rd., Karachi; import, storage, distribution and marketing of petroleum products and fertilizers; storage capacity 90,000 tons (1974); management taken over by Government in 1974; Man. Dir. M. A. Alvie.

Pakistan Oilfields Ltd.: Rawalpindi; prospecting, drilling and producing.

Pakistan Petroleum Ltd.: 4th Floor, P.I.D.C. House, Dr. Ziauddin Rd., Karachi; oil and gas; nationalized.

Pakistan Refinery Ltd.: Kerangi, Karachi.

Paper and Paper Board

Karnaphuli Paper Mills Ltd.

Packages Ltd.: 3rd Floor, Kandawala Bldg., M.A. Jinnah Rd., Karachi.

Pharmaceuticals

Glaxo Laboratories (Pakistan) Ltd.; N.P.T. House, I. I. Chundrigar Rd., Karachi (Head Office).

Steel

Beco Industries Ltd.: Badani Bagh, Lahore.

Metropolitan Steel Corporation Ltd.: Landhi Mills Area, Karachi; management taken over by Government in January 1972.

Sugar

Crescent Sugar Mills and Distillery Ltd.: Nishatabad, New Lahore Rd., Lyallpur.

Hyesons Sugar Mills Ltd.: Abdul Hye Chambers, P.O.B. 5246, Dockyard Rd., West Wharf, Karachi 2.

Premier Sugar Mills and Distillery Ltd.: Mardan, N.W.F.P.; Gen. Man. Abdul Qadar Khattak.

Tea

Lipton (Pakistan) Ltd.: West Wharf, Karachi.

Textiles

Burewala Textile Mills Ltd.: 403–405 Alfalah Bldg., Shahrah-e-Quaid-e-Azam, Lahore; Finance Man. and Sec. Mohammad Arif.

Colony Textile Mills: Ismailabad, Multan.

Husein Industries Ltd.: Jubilee Insurance House, 6th Floor, I. I. Chundrigar Rd., Karachi 2; Chair./Chief Exec. Latif E. Jamal.

Ravi Rayon Ltd.: 41-B/1 Empress Rd., opposite Shimla Pehari, Lahore; management taken over by Government in January 1972.

Tobacco

Khyber Tobacco Co. Ltd.: c/o Postmaster, Mardan.

Pakistan Tobacco Co. Ltd.: Mackinnons' Bldg., I. I. Chundrigar Rd., Karachi 2; cigarettes; Chair. K. Z. Hassan.

Premier Tobacco Industries Ltd.: Post Office, Maula Bux Colony, Jahangira Rd., District, Peshawar.

Vehicles

Atlas Autos Ltd.: F/36, Estate, Ave. S.I.T.E., P.O.B. 4429, Karachi.

Rana Tractor and Equipment: 5 Banduk Wala Bldg., I. I. Chundrigar Rd., Karachi; management taken over by Government in January 1972.

Miscellaneous

Adamjee Industries Ltd.: 5th Floor, Adamjee House, I. I. Chungrigar Rd., P.O.B. 4371, Karachi.

Haji Dossa Ltd.: 4th Floor, Jubilee Insurance House, I. I. Chundrigar Rd., Karachi 2.

Hyesons Group of Industries: Abdul Hye Chambers, Dockyard Rd., West Wharf, Karachi; G.I. pipes.

Kohinoor Industries: 25 West Wharf Rd., Karachi.

Pakistan Industries Ltd.: Jubilee Insurance House, McLeod Rd., Karachi; carpets, handicrafts, marble, onyx, etc.

TRANSPORT

RAILWAYS

Superintendent (General): Hamidullah Khan, Ministry of Railways, Islamabad.

Pakistan Railway Board: Chair: M. A. Aziz (Head Offices at Lahore).

The Pakistan rail system is state-owned and had 8,810 kilometres of track in 1975.

ROADS

The total of main roads in 1972 was 11,599 km., while secondary roads totalled 8,635 km.

Government assistance comes from the Road Fund, financed from a share of the excise and customs duty on sales of petrol and from development loans.

Sind Road Transport Corporation: 3-Modern Housing Society, Drigh Rd., Karachi-8; Chair. B. A. Khan, P.S.P.

Automobile Association of Pakistan, The: P.O.B. 76, 8H Multan Rd., Lahore; Chair. Nawabzada Syed Iqbal Hassan; Sec. Zia Ullah Shaikh, T.K.

Karachi Automobile Association: Standard Insurance House, I. I. Chundrigar Rd., Karachi 0226; f. 1958; Pres. (vacant); Sec.-Gen. Roshen Ali Bhimjee.

RIVERS, CANALS AND IRRIGATION

A score of large canals and hundreds of small ones criss-cross the territory of Pakistan watered by the rivers Sutlej, Ravi, Chenab, Jhelum, Indus and Swat. Many new canals and water works have been constructed.

In 1960 the Indus Basin Development Fund was established to finance irrigation in Pakistan and India. This project consists of two dams, six-barrages and eight link canals. The last stage of the scheme, the Tarbela dam, developed serious defects in its final stages of construction in 1975, with resultant huge losses.

SHIPPING

The chief port is Karachi. In 1974 the Government took control of maritime shipping companies.

National Shipping Corporation: NSC Bldg., Moulvi Tamizuddin Khan Rd., Karachi; f. 1963; 29 ships; cargo services to U.S.A., U.K., and Far East; five directors nominated by the Government, four elected by shareholders; Chair. Justice Amin Ahmed; Man. Dir. Commdr. Akhtar Hanif, P.N.

MAJOR SHIPPING COMPANIES

Pakistan Shipping Corporation: Old Ralli Brothers Building, Talpur Rd., P.O.B. 4959, Karachi; f. 1974 by the Government; Chair. R. Cowasjee; Man. Dir. M. S. Shaherwala. Manages and controls the following shipping companies:

Pan Islamic Steamship Co. Ltd.
Trans Oceanic Steamship Co. Ltd.
Chittagong Steamship Corporation Ltd.
Pakistan Shipping Line Ltd.
Crescent Shipping Lines Ltd.
Gulf Shipping Corporation Ltd.
United Oriental Steamship Co.
East and West Steamship Co. (1961).
Muhammadi Steamship Co. Ltd.

CIVIL AVIATION

The Department of Civil Aviation comes under the Ministry of Defence; Dir.-Gen. M. R. Rizvi.

Karachi is an international airport.

Pakistan International Airlines Corpn.: PIA Bldg., Karachi Airport; f. 1955; operates domestic services and international services to the Middle East, Far East, China, Sri Lanka, Tanzania, Libya, the U.S.A. and Europe; fleet of 2 Boeing 747s, 6 Boeing 707s, 4 720s, 8 F.27s, 3 DC-10; Chair. Air Marshal (retd.) M. Nur Khan; Man. Dir. Enver Jamall.

Foreign Airlines

The following foreign airlines are represented in Pakistan: Aeroflot, Air Ceylon, Air France, Alitalia, British Airways, East African Airlines, Garuda Indonesian Airways, Gulf Aviation, Iran Air, Iraqi Airways, JAL, KLM, Kuwait Airways, Lufthansa, Pan American, SAS, Saudi Arabia Airlines, Philippine Airlines, Royal Jordanian Airlines, Swissair, Syrian Arab Airlines, UTA.

TOURISM

Pakistan Tourism Development Corpn.: Hotel Metropole, Karachi 4; f. 1956; Dir.-Gen. Khwaja Masrur Husain, S.K.; brs. in Lahore, Peshawar, Rawalpindi, Kaptai, Gilgit, Quetta, Moenjodaro, Murree, Saidu Sharif and Abbottabad.

CULTURAL ORGANIZATIONS

Arts Council of Pakistan: Karachi; Exec. Dir. Irfan Husain; *Pakistan Arts Council*, Lahore: Pres. Justice S. A. Rahman; *Pakistan Arts Council*, Rawalpindi: Exec. Dir. Agha Babar.

ATOMIC ENERGY

Pakistan Atomic Energy Commission: responsible for organizing training and research centres in the field of nuclear science and technology and for installing and commissioning nuclear power and desalination plants; nuclear power plant at Karachi; Chair. Dr. MUNIR AHMAD KHAN; publ. *Nucleus* (quarterly).

Atomic Energy Minerals Centre: P.O.B. 658, Lahore; f. 1961; research and development in the nuclear minerals field; equipped with analytical, mineralogical, and mineral processing laboratories; Dir. M. ASLAM.

Atomic Energy Agricultural Research Centre: Tandojam; f. 1963; research in plant physiology, genetics, entomology, soil science; Dir. Dr. SHAUKAT AHMED.

Karachi Nuclear Power Station: equipped with a reactor of 137 MW (critical in 1971); fully operational 1972.

Pakistan Institute of Nuclear Science and Technology: Nilore, Rawalpindi; f. 1961; research; equipped with 5 MW swimming-pool-type reactor (critical 1966); Dir. Dr. ISHFAQ AHMAD.

Nuclear Institute for Agriculture and Biology: Lyallpur; f. 1972; research in plant breeding, entomology, soil sciences, plant physiology, microbiology and food preservation; Dir. Dr. M. NAQUI.

Atomic Energy Medical Centre, Karachi: Jinnah Postgraduate Medical Centre, Karachi 35; f. 1960; diagnosis and treatment of diseases using radioisotopes and radiation; Dir. Dr. R. A. KHAN.

Atomic Energy Medical Centre, Jamshoro: f. 1968; diagnosis and treatment of diseases using radioisotopes and radiation; Dir. Dr. MUNIR AHMAD SIDDIQUI.

Atomic Energy Medical Centre, Multan: Nishtar Medical College and Hospital, Multan; f. 1968; diagnosis and treatment of diseases using radioisotopes and radiation; Dir. Dr. N. KIZILBASH.

Atomic Energy Medical Centre, Lahore: f. 1963; diagnosis and treatment of diseases using radioisotopes and radiation; Dir. Dr. M. A. SHAHID.

Institute for Radiotherapy and Nuclear Medicine: Peshawar; f. 1973; diagnosis and treatment of diseases using radioisotopes and radiation; and research in cancerous and other diseases; Dir. Dr. GUL RAHMAN.

DEFENCE

Armed Forces: (1975) Total strength 392,000; army 365,000, navy 10,000, air force 17,000. Military service is selective and lasts for two years. In 1972 Pakistan withdrew from SEATO.

Equipment: The army has American and Soviet tanks, while the Air Force has American, French and Soviet planes. China has also supplied arms.

Defence Budget: The defence budget for 1975-76 is Rs. 7,020 million (U.S. $722 million).

CHIEFS OF STAFF

Chief of Staff, Army: General TIKKA KHAN.

Chief of Staff, Air Force: Air Marshal ZULFIQAR ALI KHAN.

Chief of Staff, Navy: Admiral MOHAMMED SHAREEF.

EDUCATION

Primary Schools: Universal and free primary education is a constitutional right. No fees are charged at primary schools run by the Government or local bodies, which run the majority of primary schools. Privately run educational institutions have been nationalized. There are also some fully independent institutions which meet their costs from donations and tuition fees. The syllabus contains reading, writing and arithmetic, social studies, elementary science, art work, crafts, manual labour and other activities that help to develop fundamental skills. Religion is compulsory at both primary and secondary level.

Secondary Education is a five year course commencing at the age of ten, and is sometimes divided into a three-year middle school course and a two-year high school course.

The new Education Policy (1972-80) envisages re-organization of secondary and intermediate education so as to promote the teaching of science and technology and to progressively integrate agro-technical education with general education.

UNIVERSITIES

University of Islamabad: University Campus, P.O.B. 1090, Islamabad; 122 teachers, 750 students.

University of the Punjab: Lahore; 289 professors, 5,901 students.

University of Sind: Jamshoro, Hyderabad; 390 teachers, 3,032 students.

Pakistan Agricultural University: Lyallpur; 360 teachers, 3,870 students.

Pakistan University of Engineering and Technology: Lahore; 138 teachers, 2,650 students.

University of Baluchistan: Sariab Rd., Quetta; 65 teachers, 589 students.

University of Karachi: University Campus, University Rd., Karachi 32; *c.* 350 teachers, *c.* 7,000 students.

University of Peshawar: Peshawar; 505 teachers, 8,756 students.

BIBLIOGRAPHY

GENERAL

AHMAD, KAZI S. A Geography of Pakistan (2nd edn., Oxford University Press, London, 1969).

DARLING, Sir MALCOLM. The Punjab Peasant in Prosperity and Debt (Oxford University Press, London, 1947).

FELDMAN, H. The Land and People of Pakistan (Black, "Land and Peoples Series", London, 1958).
Pakistan, An Introduction (Oxford University Press, London, 1960).

GHANI, A. R. Pakistan, a Select Bibliography (Lahore, 1959).

GLEDHILL, ALAN. Pakistan (Stevens, London, 1957).

IKRAM, S. M., and T. G. P. SPEAR. Cultural Heritage of Pakistan (Oxford University Press, London, 1956).

MAHAR, J. M. India and Pakistan, a Critical Bibliography (University of Arizona Press, Tucson, Ariz., 1964).

QURESHI, ISHTIAQ. The Pakistani Way of Life (Heinemann, "Way of Life Series", London, 1956).

SPATE, O. H. K., and LEARMONTH, A. T. A. India and Pakistan (3rd edn., Methuen, London, 1967).

STEPHENS, IAN. The Pakistanis. (Oxford University Press, London, 1967).

TINKER, HUGH. India and Pakistan: A Political Analysis (Pall Mall Press, London, 2nd revised edn., 1967).

WILBER, DONALD N. (Editor). Pakistan: Its People, Its Society, Its Culture (Human Relations Area Files Press, New York).

HISTORY AND POLITICS

AHMAD, AZIZ. Islamic Modernism in India and Pakistan (1857–1964) (Oxford University Press for Chatham House, London, 1967).

AHMED, H. Politics and People's Representation in Pakistan (Karachi, Ferozsons, 1972).

ALBIRUNI, A. H. Makers of Pakistan and Modern Muslim India (Ashraf, Lahore, 1950).

AMBEDKAR, B. R. Pakistan and the Partition of India (Thacker & Co., Bombay, 1946).

AYUB KHAN, MOHAMMAD. Friends not Masters: A Political Autobiography (Oxford University Press, London, 1967).

BHUTTO, Z. A. Foreign Policy of Pakistan (Karachi, Pakistan Institute of International Relations, 1964).
The Quest for Peace (Karachi, Pakistan Institute of International Relations, 1966).
The Myth of Independence (Karachi, Oxford University Press, 1969).

BINDER, LEONARD. Religion and Politics in Pakistan (University of California Press., Berkeley, Calif., 1961).

BOLITHO, HECTOR. Jinnah: Creator of Pakistan (John Murray, London, 1954).

CALLARD, KEITH. Pakistan, A Political Study (Allen & Unwin, London, 1957; Lawrence Verry, Mystic, Conn., 1965).
Foreign Policy of Pakistan (Institute of Pacific Relations, New York, 1959).

CHOUDHURY, G. W. Constitutional Development in Pakistan (Longmans, Lahore and London, 1959; Institute of Pacific Relations, New York, 1959).

CHOUDHURY, G. W., and PARVEZ HASAN. Pakistan's External Relations (Pakistan Institute of International Affairs, Karachi, 1958).

CONSTITUTION OF PAKISTAN. The Interim constitution of the Islamic Republic of Pakistan (Karachi, Man. of Publications, 1972).

FELDMAN, H. A. Constitution for Pakistan (Oxford University Press, London 1956).
Revolution in Pakistan: A Study of the Martial Lav Administration (Oxford University Press, Londo and New York, 1967).

JENNINGS, Sir IVOR. Constitutional Problems in Pakista (Oxford University Press, London, 1957).

MOHAMMAD ALI, CHAUDHRI. The Emergence of Pakista (Columbian University Press, New York, 1967).

MUJTABA, R. The Frontiers of Pakistan: a Study of Fron tier Problems in Pakistan's Foreign Policy (Karachi National Publishing House, 1971).

SAIYID, M. H. Mohammad Ali Jinnah (Ashraf, Lahore 1953).

SARWAR HASAN, K. Pakistan and the Commonwealt (Pakistan Institute of International Affairs, Karachi 1950).
The Strategic Interests of Pakistan (Pakistan Institut of International Affairs, Karachi, 1954).
Pakistan and the United Nations (Manhattan Publish ing Co., New York, 1960).

SAYEED, KHALID BIN. Pakistan, the Formative Phas (Pakistan Publishing House, Karachi, 1960).
The Political System of Pakistan (Allen & Unwin London, 1967).

SIDDIQI, ASLAM. Pakistan Seeks Security (Longmans Green & Co., Lahore, 1960).

SINGHAL, DAMODAR P. Pakistan (Prentice-Hall, Englewoo Cliffs, New Jersey, 1972).

SMITH, DONALD EUGENE (Editor). South Asian Politic and Religion (Princeton University Press, New Jersey 1968).

SPEAR, PERCIVAL. India, Pakistan and the West. (Oxfor University Press, London and New York, 3rd edn. 1958).

STEPHENS, IAN. Pakistan, 3rd edn. (Ernest Benn, London 1967).

SYMONDS, RICHARD. The Making of Pakistan (Faber an Faber, London, 1950).

TINKER, HUGH. Experiment with Freedom: India an Pakistan 1947 (Oxford University Press, London 1967).

ZIRING, LAWRENCE. The Ayub Khan era: politics in Pakis tan 1958–69 (New York, Syracuse University Press 1971).

ECONOMY

ANDRUS, J. R., and MOHAMMED, A. F. Trade, Finance an Development in Pakistan (Oxford University Press London, 1966).

GRIFFIN, KEITH and KHAN, AZIZUR RAHMAN. Growth an Inequality in Pakistan (Macmillan, St. Martin's Press London, 1972).

HAQ, MAHBUB UL. The Strategy of Economic Plannin (Oxford University Press, reprinted 1966).

JOSHI, P.C. "Land Reform and Agrarian Changes in India and Pakistan since 1947", in Dutta, Ratna and Joshi P.C., *Studies in Asian Social Development* No. (McGraw-Hill, Bombay-New Delhi, 1971).

LEWIS, STEPHEN R. Economic Policy and Industria Growth in Pakistan (Allen & Unwin, London, 1969).

MASON, E. S. Economic Development in India an Pakistan (Harvard University Center for Internationa Affairs, Cambridge, Mass., 1966).

PAPANEK, GUSTAV F. Pakistan's Development: Socia Goals and Private Incentives (Harvard Universit Press, Cambridge, Mass., and Oxford University Press London, 1967).

WATERSTON, ALBERT. Planning in Pakistan (Johns Hop kins, Baltimore, 1963).

Sri Lanka

PHYSICAL AND SOCIAL GEOGRAPHY

B. H. Farmer

Sri Lanka (formerly called Ceylon) consists of one large island and several smaller ones lying east of the southern tip of the Indian sub-continent. It has an area of 65,610 square kilometres (25,332 square miles.) The Bay of Bengal lies to its north and east and the Arabian Sea to its west. It is separated from India by the Gulf of Mannar and the Palk Strait, between which there lie, in very shallow water, the string of small islands known as "Adam's Bridge", linking Sri Lanka and India. Sri Lanka stretches from 5° 55′ to 9° 50′ north latitude and from 79° 40′ to 81° 55′ east longitude. Sri Lanka gained its independence on February 4th, 1948, under the familiar name "Ceylon". It took the ancient title Sri Lanka under a new constitution of May 22nd, 1972.

PHYSICAL FEATURES

Sri Lanka consists almost entirely of hard ancient crystalline rocks (though recent work has cast doubt on the age of some of them). Unaltered sedimentary rocks only occupy the Jaffna Peninsula (a raised coral reef) in the north and a strip down the north-west coast. Alluvial spreads follow the main rivers and also occupy infilled coastal lagoons, especially on the east coast.

The highest land in Sri Lanka occupies the south-centre, the "Up-country", and rises to over 1,500 metres (5,000 feet). The highest point is Pidurutalagala (2,524 metres or 8,280 feet). From the Up-country, the land falls by steps to a rolling coastal plain, narrow in the west and south-west, broadest in the north (though even there isolated hills rise above the general level). The rivers, apart from the longest, the Mahaweli Ganga (which has a complicated course), are generally short and run radially outwards from the Up-country.

CLIMATE

Sri Lanka has temperatures appropriate to its near-equatorial position, modified by altitude Up-country. In Colombo, at sea-level, mean monthly temperatures fluctuate only between 25°C. (77°F.) in January and 28°C. (82°F.) in May. At Nuwara Eliya, at 1,889 metres (6,199 feet), temperatures range between 14°C. (57°F.) in January and 16°C. (61°F.) in May.

A fundamental division in Sri Lanka, so far as rainfall and therefore agriculture are concerned, is that between the Wet and Dry Zones. The former occupies the southwestern sector of the island, and normally receives rain from both the south-west and north-east monsoons. Colombo, for example, has a mean annual rainfall of 236.5 cm. (93.1 inches): February, the driest month, receives 6.9 cm. (2.7 inches) and May, the wettest, 37.1 cm. (14.6 inches). The Dry Zone, covering the lowlands of the north and east and extending in modified form into the eastern Up-country, has a period of severe drought in the south-west monsoon and most of its rain from the north-east. Trincomalee, for example, with a mean annual rainfall of 164.8 cm. (64.9 inches), receives on average only 6.9 cm. (2.7 inches), 2.8 cm. (1.1 inches) and 5.1 cm. (2 inches) in May, June and July respectively (and mean *expectation* is less than the mean rainfall) but over 35.6 cm. (14 inches) in each of November and December. Commercial crops like tea and rubber are almost entirely confined to the Wet Zone.

SOILS AND NATURAL RESOURCES

Sri Lanka is fortunate to have a soil map based on modern scientific methods. The "red-yellow podzolic" soils of most of the Wet Zone and Up-country are not very fertile, but grow tree-crops and give a high response to fertilizers. Young soils are found on steeper slopes. Over a large part of the Dry Zone, especially the north-centre and south-east, "reddish-brown earths" require careful handling but are more fertile than is normal in the Tropics. In the Jaffna Peninsula soils are also, largely through human exertion, relatively fertile; but elsewhere in the Dry Zone, apart from alluvium, soils are generally infertile or difficult or both (although some can be improved).

The Wet Zone and wetter hills must once have been covered with wet evergreen forest akin to tropical rain forest, passing into drier forest on the lowland Dry Zone boundary, and into montane wet evergreen forest in the high hills. Most of this forest cover has disappeared with the advance of cultivation. A high proportion of the lowland Dry Zone is, however, still covered with dry mixed evergreen forest (producing valuable timbers such as ebony and satin-wood) which is probably secondary, the result of centuries of shifting cultivation. In the drier north-west and south-east this passes into thorn scrub; while in the eastern Dry Zone are patches of savanna-like grassland thought to be due to periodic burning.

Sri Lanka is poor in mineral wealth. There is no coal or oil; an estimated total of only 2.2 million tons of exploitable iron ore in scattered deposits; and virtually the only workable sources of non-ferrous metals are beach sands yielding ilmenite, rutile, monazite and zircon. Graphite and gem-stones are the most valuable mineral products of Sri Lanka at present. Salt is manufactured by the evaporation of sea water; and useful deposits of limestone and clay (for cement) and kaolin are beginning to be exploited.

POPULATION AND ETHNIC GROUPS

The population was estimated at 13,874,000 in July 1974. The crude birth-rate fell from 3.7 per cent in 1960 to 2.9 per cent in 1970. The population is very unevenly distributed. The Wet Zone and most of the Up-country have a dense rural population and also contain the principal conurbation (Colombo, population 563,705 in 1971) and a number of other towns, e.g. Kandy (91,942 in 1971). Much of the Dry Zone is still sparsely peopled, in spite of considerable colonization in the last thirty years or so.

Sri Lanka has a plural society. The majority group, the Sinhalese, speak a distinctive language related to the Indo-Aryan tongues of north India, and are mainly Buddhist. There are two groups of Tamils: "Ceylon Tamils", the descendants of Tamil-speaking groups who long ago migrated from South India, and "Indian Tamils", comparatively recent immigrants who came over to work on plantations, and their descendants: both are predominantly Hindu. There are also groups of Muslims (called "Moors") and Christians (drawn from the Sinhalese, Tamil and other communities).

HISTORY

Kingsley M. de Silva

Ancient Ceylon

Sri Lanka is a plural society whose roots go back more than 2,000 years. The Sinhalese and Tamils, the main component elements in Sri Lanka's plural society, have a common Indian origin but from two "racial" stocks, Aryan and Dravidian. Aryan settlement and colonization in the island began around 500 B.C. while Dravidian-Tamil settlements in Sri Lanka emerged a few centuries later.

The early settlements arose in the dry zone of Sri Lanka. The ancient Sinhalese developed a highly sophisticated irrigation system which became the basis of a thriving economy.. The introduction of Buddhism to the island around the third century B.C. had an impact on the people as decisive as the development of irrigation technology was in economic activity. Buddhism became the bedrock of the culture and civilization of the island, and the state religion. More importantly, the intimate connection between the land, the "race" and the Buddhist religion foreshadowed the intermingling of religion and national identity which has always had the most profound influence on the Sinhalese.

The ancient Sri Lankan kingdom had many of the attributes of a feudal polity. While the king was, in theory, an absolute ruler, custom and tradition acted as formidable constraints on his absolutism, and thus it was not a highly centralized autocratic state but one in which the balance of political forces incorporated a tolerance of centrifugalism.

The flourishing but highly vulnerable irrigation civilization of Sri Lanka's northern plain proved to be a tempting target for invasion from South India. The Sinhalese contributed to their own discomfiture by calling in Tamil assistance in settling disputed successions and dynastic squabbles. The tensions and conflicts between the Sinhalese and Tamils which emerged from this have been magnified far beyond the reality of historical fact. Folklore and mythology have fed the image of the Tamils as the implacable national enemy. This was especially so with regard to the collapse of Sri Lanka's hydraulic civilization in the thirteenth century A.D. Political instability within the Sinhalese kingdom was just as important a cause of its disintegration as Tamil invasion but it is the latter which is remembered as the crucial factor.

After the thirteenth century, with the establishment of a Tamil kingdom in the north of the island, there was, in fact, a geographical separation between the Sinhalese and the Tamils. The Sinhalese abandoned the north central plains and migrated to the hilly, wetter and forested south-west quarter of the island. Until the beginning of the twentieth century a vast forest belt lay between the two peoples. Not that they were totally isolated from each other; nor was there a break in the social and economic relations between them.

The beginnings of Western influence

Western influence emerged in the sixteenth century with the Portuguese intrusion into the affairs of the littoral. By 1600 they were well established, but within 60 years they were displaced by the Dutch, who in turn were dislodged by the British at the end of the eighteenth century. During this whole period, however, there were parts of the island under Sinhalese rule, most notably the Kandyan kingdom, the last of the independent Sinhalese states. There the traditional Sinhalese system prevailed in the administrative machinery, the social structure and the economy. The changes that took place in the littoral under the Portuguese and Dutch had little or no impact on the people of the Kandyan kingdom.

The fact that neither the Portuguese nor the Dutch were able to conquer the whole island was an important factor in the emergence, in the course of time, of a distinction among the Sinhalese themselves, between those of the south-west littoral, the low-country Sinhalese, and those of the Kandyan areas. This was based on custom and outlook fostered by colonial rule in the one instance and the absence of it in the other.

It was in these centuries that Christianity was introduced in all its sectarian variety by the Western powers. Under the Portuguese and the Dutch, converts to the official or orthodox version of Christianity came to be treated as a privileged group. Moreover, Roman Catholicism under the Portuguese and Calvinism under the Dutch were notable for their intolerance of the traditional faiths while under the Dutch the Roman Catholics too were under great pressure.

The impact of the Portuguese and the Dutch on the island's economy was more significant. By the fifteenth century cinnamon, which grew wild in the forests of the island's wet zone, had developed into one of the main exports of the island. The Portuguese and the Dutch monopolized the export trade in this valuable commodity, and the profits from it became the mainstay of the revenues they controlled in Sri Lanka. In the late eighteenth century the Dutch began to cultivate cinnamon in plantations. They also introduced other cash crops, such as coffee, sugar, cotton and tobacco, but these were comparatively minor products. It was under the British that the plantation system established itself as the most flourishing sector of the economy.

With the British conquest of the former Dutch possessions in Sri Lanka in 1795–96 the balance of power in the island shifted decisively against the Kandyans. By 1815 the British were masters of the Kandyan kingdom, and their control of it was effectively consolidated when they crushed the Kandyan rebellion of 1817–18. For the first time in several centuries the whole island was under the rule of one power. With the Colebrooke-Cameron reforms of 1832 a single administrative system was established for the island.

The consolidation of British rule

A period of experimentation in plantation crops began in the mid-1830s and within 15 years the success of one of these crops, coffee, radically transformed the economy of the island. When the coffee industry was mortally stricken by a leaf disease in the 1870s the plantation economy demonstrated a remarkable resilience and the three decades 1880 to 1910 saw a sustained growth in the plantation sector which matched, if it did not surpass, that achieved in the coffee era. It is in these years that the pattern was established of an overwhelming dominance in the island's economy of three major plantation crops: tea, rubber and coconuts. British interests were dominant in tea and strong in rubber, but much less so in coconuts; shipping, banks, insurance and the export-import trade were mainly if not entirely controlled by British commercial interests. Labour on the coffee plantations was predominantly (though not exclusively) immigrant Indian, largely seasonal migrants. But tea and, to a lesser extent, rubber required, unlike coffee, a permanent and resident supply of labour and, as a result, there developed a fundamental change in the character of immigrant Indian labour. With this Sri Lanka's Indian problem in its modern form had emerged.

One of the most far-reaching effects of the development of a capitalist economy on the foundation of plantation agriculture and trade was the growth of a new élite which was largely an indigenous capitalist class. The traditional élite, especially in the low-country, was absorbed into this expanding new élite. But they were soon left far behind in the two most important channels of mobility, the acquisition of a Western education and participation in capitalist enterprise. Elite status in fact became much less dependent on hereditary status and the holding of government office. The capitalist class was largely low-country Sinhalese with a sprinkling of Tamils and other minority groups. Kandyan representation in it was virtually non-existent.

Among the adverse effects of the growth of plantations was the lop-sided development of the economy, and the comparative neglect of traditional agriculture. This was despite the sustained, if not unbroken, effort made in the second half of the nineteenth century to rehabilitate the dry zone through a revival of the ancient irrigation works there.

In the 1830s and 1840s every sphere of activity, political, economic and social, had been affected by a passion for reform generated by Evangelicalism, in matters relating to religion and education, and by the secular "creed" of *laissez-faire*. But by the last quarter of the nineteenth century it was only in plantation enterprise that the old zest and energy was maintained, and the British administration had become much more sympathetic to the conservative forces in Sri Lanka society.

The first notable reversal of policy was with regard to Buddhism. The official attitude changed from neglect and studied indifference to one of according Buddhism a measure of judicious patronage and emphasizing the principle of the Government's neutrality in religious affairs. The change of attitude to the traditional élite was equally decisive: instead of a determined effort to reduce their powers and privileges there was now a policy of aristocratic resuscitation which continued into the first decade of the twentieth century. The motive in both instances was political, to build a counterweight to the more assertive sections of the élite who were seeking a share of political power in the colony.

The last three decades of the nineteenth century mark the first phase in the emergence of nationalism in Sri Lanka. While incipient nationalist sentiment was primarily religious in outlook and content, asserting the need for the primacy of Buddhist values and claiming that Buddhism was in danger, political overtones in it were visible from its inception, especially in the appeal to the native past as against a contemporary situation of foreign domination. The temperance movement, an integral part of the Buddhist revival in the first decade of the twentieth century, was an introduction, tentative but astutely restrained, to political activity and the rallying point of the recovery of national consciousness. But faith in the permanence of British control over the affairs of the island remained largely unshaken, and nobody in public life at the turn of the century could have imagined that Sri Lanka would be independent within 50 years.

Constitutional Reform and Transfer of Power

In the first two decades of the twentieth century the colonial authorities in the island successfully withstood the pressures of the élite for a share in the administration of the country. Neither the First World War, nor the perverse mishandling of the situation in the island in the wake of the Sinhalese-Muslim riots of 1915, led to a more pronounced radicalization of politics. The keynotes of the reform movement were restraint and moderation. The formation of the Ceylon National Congress in 1919 was evidence of the strength of these attitudes rather than of any notable departure from them.

The 1920s, on the other hand, were characterized by bolder initiatives in politics. In retrospect this decade marked the first phase in the transfer of power when the British began, for the first time, to contemplate the possibility, indeed the necessity, of sharing power on a formal basis with representatives of the indigenous population. There was at this time a significant heightening of working class activity and trade unionism which began to impinge on the political situation: the urban working class of Colombo and its suburbs was beginning to push its way into the political arena. Much more in the nature of an intractable problem was the breakdown of the comparative harmony of interests and outlook which had characterized relations between Sinhalese and Tamil politicians in the first two decades of the twentieth century. With the prospect of a transfer of a substantial measure of political power to the indigenous political leadership, minority groups led by the Tamils were increasingly anxious to protect their interests.

The constitutional reforms introduced in 1931 amounted to the first step towards self-government. Equally significant was the introduction of universal suffrage. It was the main determining factor in the re-emergence of "religious" nationalism, that is nationalism intertwined with Buddhist resurgence and its associated cultural heritage. Again, although the massive rural vote easily swamped the working class vote, universal suffrage strengthened the working class movement and opened the way for it to play an independent role in politics. By the early 1930s Marxists had established themselves in the leadership of the indigenous working class movement. On a different level universal suffrage was largely responsible for the broad impulse towards social welfare, especially in the years 1936–47. Among the most constructive achievements of this era was the purposeful programme of restoration of the irrigation schemes of the dry zone, and the settlement of colonists there, under the instigation of Stephen Senanayake, Minister of Agriculture and Lands for 15 years. The investment in education, health and food subsidies increased substantially, and this trend continued beyond 1947 to the detriment, it would seem, of economic growth.

The final phase in the transfer of power began under the leadership of Stephen Senanayake, the country's first Prime Minister, who was guided by a strong belief in ordered constitutional evolution to Dominion status on the analogy of constitutional development in the white dominions. In response to the agitation in Sri Lanka the British Government appointed the Soulbury Commission in 1944 to examine the constitutional problem there. The constitution that emerged from their deliberations was based substantially on one drafted for Senanayake in 1944 by his advisers. It gave the island internal self-government while retaining some Imperial safeguards in defence and external affairs, but Sri Lanka's leaders pressed, successfully, for the removal of these restrictions, and the island was granted independence, with Dominion status, on February 4th, 1948. The transfer of power was smooth and peaceful, a reflection of the moderate tone of the dominant strand of the country's nationalist movement. In general the situation in the country seemed to provide an impressive basis for a solid start in nation-building and national regeneration.

Independence and after, 1948-70

Stephen Senanayake understood the implications of the pluralism of Sri Lanka's society and his policies for the transfer of power and in the early years of independence were framed on that realistic basis. The Sri Lanka of Ceylon nationalism, of which he was the most influential advocate at the time of the transfer of power, emphasized the common interest of the island's ethnic and religious groups. It had as its basis the acceptance of the reality of a plural society, and sought the reconciliation of the legitimate interests of the majority and minority groups within the context of an all-island polity. This held out the prospect of peace and stability in the vital first phase of independence.

It was from the left that the main threat to the new government, and the balance of forces it sought to establish, was expected, but the Marxist parties were too divided by personality conflicts and ideological disputes to pose an effective challenge. Indeed, within a year of the grant of independence, Stephen Senanayake's United National Party (UNP) stabilized its position in the country and strengthened its hold on Parliament.

The first major challenge to the UNP-dominated Government emerged with Solomon Bandaranaike's formation of the Sri Lanka Freedom Party (SLFP) in September 1951, after he had crossed over to the opposition in July 1951. Its populist programme was directed at the large protest vote that went to the Marxist parties for want of a democratic alternative to the UNP, and at the rural areas which formed the basis of the UNP's hold on political power in the country.

Stephen Senanayake's death in March 1952 seemingly stabilized the equilibrium of political forces he had established. When, in May 1952, his son and successor as Prime Minister, Dudley Senanayake, won a massive electoral victory, the verdict of the electorate was in many ways an endorsement of the life's work of Stephen Senanayake. Nevertheless, by the mid-1950s the UNP's position in the country was being undermined, even though its hold on Parliament appeared to be as strong as ever. The economy was faltering, after a period of prosperity, and the attempt to reduce the budgetary allocation for food subsidies provoked violent opposition, organized by the left-wing parties, in August 1953. Besides, religious, cultural and linguistic issues were gathering momentum and developing into a force too powerful for the existing social and political set-up to accommodate or absorb. Neither the Government nor its left-wing critics showed much understanding of the sense of outrage and indignation of the Buddhists at what they regarded as the historic injustices suffered by their religion under Western rule. Bandaranaike successfully channelled this discontent into a massive campaign which swept the UNP out of office in 1956.

Bandaranaike's decisive victory was a significant point in Sri Lanka's history, heralding as it did the rejection of so much that had come to be accepted as part of the normal order of things in Sri Lanka. What it amounted to was a rejection of the concept of a Sri Lanka nationalism which Stephen Senanayake had striven to nurture, and the substitution of a more democratic and populist nationalism which was at the same time fundamentally divisive in its impact on the country because it was unabashedly Sinhalese and Buddhist in content.

Against the background of the worldwide celebration in 1956 of the 2500th anniversary of the death of the Buddha an intense religious fervour became the catalyst of a populist nationalism whose explosive effect was derived from its interconnection with language. Language became the basis of nationalism and Sinhala nationalism was consciously or unconsciously treated as being identical with Sri Lanka nationalism. And this the minorities, especially the Tamils, rejected. As a result 1956 saw the beginning of almost a decade of ethnic and linguistic tensions erupting occasionally into race riots and religious confrontation.

With the emergence of this linguistic nationalism there was increased pressure for the close association of the state with Buddhism, and a corresponding decline of Christian influence. On the whole Bandaranaike's Government was much more cautious in handling matters relating to the Christian minority than it was on the language issue. This was a matter of prudence and priorities. The language struggle took precedence over all else, and there was no desire to add to the problems of the Government by taking on an issue which was just as combustible.

Ideologically hazy and politically pragmatic, Bandaranaike's middle way offered people social change, social justice and economic independence from foreign powers. In the SLFP's populist programme the state's role in economic development was given great emphasis, and the pursuit of economic equality was a cardinal theme.

At the time of his assassination in September 1959, the culmination of a bitter struggle for power within his own party, Bandaranaike's hold on the electorate was not as strong as it had been in 1956–57. But his assassination dramatically changed the political situation and, after a few months of drift and regrouping, the SLFP emerged under the leadership of his widow, Sirimavo Bandaranaike, more powerful than ever before.

Unlike her husband, Sirimavo Bandaranaike was not reluctant to take on two inflammable issues at the same time. The pursuit of her husband's policy on language rights was accompanied by a determined bid to bring the schools under state control and to secularize education, antagonizing the Roman Catholics as decisively as her language policy alienated the Tamils.

A wide variety of economic enterprises, foreign and local, were nationalized. Socialism was viewed as a means of redressing the balance in favour of the Sinhalese-Buddhists and Sri Lanka nationals in a situation in which the island's trade was largely dominated by foreign capitalists and the minorities were disproportionately influential within the indigenous capitalist class. This extension of state control over trade and industry was justified on the grounds that it helped to curtail the influence of foreign interests and the minorities.

Two other events of significance during this period were the Bandaranaike-Shastri pact, and the establishment of a coalition government between the SLFP and the Trotskyist Lanka Sama Samaj Party (LSSP), both in 1964. The former laid the basis for an equitable settlement of Sri Lanka's Indian problem. Legislation introduced by Stephen Senanayake's Government in 1948 and 1949 had defined the right to Sri Lanka citizenship with elaborate care and rigidity, and eliminated the vast bulk of the Indians resident in Sri Lanka from the electoral registers, but while this had solved some problems it created a few and exacerbated others.

The coalition with the LSSP was designed to stabilize the Government by a shift to the left after the political turmoil of the early years of Mrs. Bandaranaike's regime which saw extended periods of rule under emergency powers in the wake of ethnic and religious confrontations, and an abortive plot by high-ranking police, military and naval officers to overthrow the Government. While the dominance of the SLFP in national politics had resulted in a corresponding decline in the electoral fortunes of the Marxist groups the *apertura a sinistra* was regarded as a necessity for keeping the UNP out of power. In joining the SLFP in a coalition, the LSSP came to accept the SLFP's stand on religion and they did so in order to protect their mass base. But the shift to the left, far from stabilizing the Government, had the immediate effect of causing a rift which precipitated its fall in December 1964, and contributed to its subsequent defeat in the general elections of March 1965.

Dudley Senanayake's UNP-dominated coalition enjoyed a five-year term of office. A resolute endeavour was made to maximize agricultural productivity, with self-sufficiency in food as the prime objective. The very considerable success achieved in this field gave the whole economy a boost. But, while its economic policies achieved substantial success, the Government's popularity was eroded by inflation and its conspicuous failure to solve the problem of educated unemployment. The rising expectations of an increasingly educated population had created an almost unmanageable problem for the Government. Sri Lanka, by now, was very much the example *par excellence* of population explosion.

Dudley Senanayake made ethnic and religious reconciliation the keynote of his policy. But his Government was placed on the defensive from the moment the Federal Party opted to join it in coalition. The opposition conducted a virulent campaign of ethnic hostility directed against these policies. The limits of a policy of ethnic and religious reconciliation were clearly demonstrated by his failure, in the face of this campaign, to implement some of the key legislative and administrative measures which would have made such a policy effective.

It was evident that the two Bandaranaikes between them had established a new equilibrium of forces within the country, and that their supporters and associates, the Marxists groups, as well as their opponents had to accommodate themselves to this. The primary feature of the new balance of forces was the acceptance of the predominance of the Sinhalese Buddhists within the Sri Lanka polity, and a sharp decline in status of the ethnic and religious minorities.

The United Front in Power, 1970-

The parties of Mrs. Bandaranaike's United Front (UF): the SLFP, the LSSP and the Communist Party (Moscow Wing), had, in their election campaign, given expression and leadership to the inchoate desires and feelings of the people and their expectations of a better life. Their election manifesto of 1970 held out the distinct assurance of purposeful, systematic and fundamental changes in every sphere of life.

The rhetorical flourishes indulged in during an acrimonious election campaign proved to be embarrassing when economic conditions showed no sign of improvement and the number of unemployed did not decrease. Confronted by precisely the combination of factors that had brought down its predecessor: unemployment, rising prices and scarcities of food items, the Government was floundering just as badly as Dudley Senanayake's Government.

More significantly the pace of change and reform in the first ten months (after June 1970) of the Government's tenure of office proved inadequate to satisfy the desires of the more militant and articulate young people whose political aspirations had been whetted by the zest with which they had worked to bring the Government to power. By the middle of March 1971 it was evident that the Government faced a deadly threat from the Janatha Vimukthi Peramuna (JVP), an ultra-left organization dominated by educated youths, unemployed or disadvantageously employed. The insurrection that broke out in April 1971 was not merely a stern warning to the political leadership of the UF but also a challenge to its credibility as a genuinely socialist government.

In the immediate sense the 1971 insurgency failed. The rebels were not the spearhead of a popular outburst against a tyrannical or repressive regime. Nor did they have the advantage of a dominating foreign presence against which they could have stirred up nationalist sentiment. There was no substantial support for them from either the rural areas or the urban working class. The rebellion was put down with considerable ruthlessness.

The insurrection of 1971 left an indelible mark on Sri Lanka, and the rebels, though defeated, partly shaped the future. It undoubtedly hastened the proceedings begun under the UF in 1970 for an autochthonous constitution for Sri Lanka; and it gave a tremendous impetus to the adoption of a series of radical economic and social changes, the most far-reaching of which was the Land Reform Law of 1972 and the nationalization of the plantations in 1975. During 1970–75 state control in trade and industry was accelerated and expanded to the point where the state had established a dominance of the commanding heights of the economy.

But the economic situation was growing rapidly worse. The UF Government had inherited a serious balance of payments problem and this was aggravated to a grave crisis, partly through the operation of external forces beyond its control. The crux of the problem is that the prices of the country's principal imports, but more particularly its food, rose to unprecedented heights, especially in 1973/74, while there has been no corresponding rise in the price of its exports. There was a sharp decline in the level of rice production in 1971 and 1972 from the record level of 75 per cent self-sufficiency which had been reached during the last year of the Senanayake Government's term of office in 1970. Although the position improved somewhat in 1974 and 1975 the 1970 level had not been regained in 1976.

The gravity of the economic crisis compelled the Government to take a critical look at food subsidies because they were absorbing too much foreign exchange. Trimming of food subsidies and cuts in welfare expenditure began in late 1971 and continued through 1973. A policy of domestic self-sufficiency in most food items and an emphasis on agricultural development were also forced upon the Government by the exchange crisis. The strategy of agricultural development and domestic self-sufficiency in rice was precisely the one preached for so long and practised with much greater sureness of touch by the Government's main challenger, the UNP. At the same time inflationary pressures have been greater than ever before, while the problem of unemployment is as serious as it ever was. As a result the Government has lost public support; its dismal record in by-elections to Parliament (by far the worst of any government since 1948) is evidence of this. By the middle of 1972 the UNP had recovered from its debacle at the polls in May 1970 and re-emerged as a viable democratic alternative to the current regime.

To save itself from further embarrassment the Government has tended to become increasingly authoritarian, eroding in the process many of the freedoms which had been taken for granted in Sri Lanka. No doubt this trend was originally an after-effect of the suppression of the rebellion in 1971. But it has been continued long after the rebels had been routed and the threat to state security had diminished substantially. Freedom of the press has been drastically curtailed. The Associated Newspapers of Ceylon, the main newspaper group in the island, has been brought under government control while the Independent Newspapers group, which had emerged as the main critic of the Government by 1973/74, has been closed since April 1974 under emergency regulations. With the passage of the *Interpretation Ordinance of 1972* and its subsequent amendment, the power of the courts to hear appeals against *mala fide* administrative decisions, and, with this, the only meaningful restraint against the misuse of administrative power for political purposes against opponents of the Government, has been eliminated. No local government elections have been held since March 1971. Severe restrictions have been imposed on the political activities of opposition parties, while the machinery of the state and administrative regulations have been used quite frequently for the harassment and intimidation of political opponents of the Government.

A new republican constitution was adopted in May 1972 on the initiative of the UF Government. It is an autochthonous constitution in which the National State Assembly (a unicameral legislature) is the supreme instrument of the state power of the republic. Thus one of its distinctive features is the absence of meaningful institutional or constitutional checks on executive power. While the new constitution is a notable landmark in the island's recent history, opposition parties have been antagonized by two issues stemming from its adoption. Firstly, the ruling coalition gave itself an extended term of two years (to May 1977) beyond the five years for which it was elected in May 1970. The opposition groups maintained that the Government had no legal or moral right to do so. Again, the adoption of a new constitution has been the critical starting point of a new phase in communal antagonism in the island especially as regards relations between the Sinhalese and the indigenous Tamils.

A by-product of the increasing alienation of the Tamils has been the conversion of a large section of the Tamils of the north to the idea of a separate Tamil state. The most militant agitators for separatism are the educated unemployed, now a substantial element in Tamil society. In 1974 Mrs. Bandaranaike negotiated the settlement, on a firm and amicable basis, of the vexed question of the status of the Indians in Sri Lanka. Nearly half a million of them would eventually be integrated into the Sri Lanka polity, and Sri Lanka citizenship will confer on them the political legitimacy which, as an ethnic group, they have not had since 1948. But relations between the Government and the leadership of the Ceylon Workers' Congress, the most powerful trade union cum political party of the Indians in Sri Lanka, have been as unfriendly as those with the leadership of the indigenous Tamils. As a result the Government has been oblivious to the plight of the plantation workers in the island who are, without a doubt, the most economically depressed group. While all sections of the population have felt the impact of the inflationary pressures of the 1970s, the effect of these on the plantation workers has been devastating: a precipitous decline from bare subsistence to grinding poverty.

There has been a marked improvement in relations between Buddhists and Roman Catholics in the 1970s. As against this, charges of favoured treatment of Muslims in the sphere of education have kindled anti-Muslim sentiment among the Sinhalese. There were sporadic Sinhalese-Muslim clashes in various parts of the island in 1974/75, with a dangerous confrontation at Gampola, near Kandy, in the last week of 1975. The clash that occurred in early 1976 at Puttalam, a Muslim stronghold in the north-west of the island, was the worst episode of communal violence since the Sinhalese-Tamil riots of the late 1950s.

This recrudescence of ethnic and religious tension seemed menacing enough on its own, but there were other events which made the last weeks of 1975 especially sombre for the Government. In October 1975 the political alliance between the SLFP and the LSSP which had lasted, in opposition and government, since 1964 came to an end. A rift within the ruling coalition became public knowledge in mid-August. A sharp difference of opinion over the mechanics of the nationalization of foreign-owned plantations in the island triggered off acrimonious bickering between these two major component units of the UF. All attempts to heal the rift proved futile, and the LSSP was expelled from the Government. One immediate effect was that the Government lost its most effective debaters as well as its two-thirds majority in the National State Assembly.

In these circumstances the Government would hardly have relished the vote of "no confidence" in the Prime Minister which was debated in the National State Assembly on December 23rd, 1975. The special significance of this debate lay in the nature of the charges levelled against the Prime Minister: she and her children were accused of acting in contravention of the Land Reform Law of 1972 in regard to a dozen or more land transactions. That the Government closed ranks and defeated the motion by a substantial margin hardly compensated for the damage it sustained by the fact that this was the first time in the parliamentary history of the country that accusations of this nature had been directed at a Prime Minister.

ECONOMIC SURVEY

H. A. de S. Gunasekera

GROSS NATIONAL PRODUCT

The Gross National Product of Sri Lanka in 1975 (at current factor cost prices) was estimated at 21,935 million rupees. The per capita national income was about 1,613 million rupees. Between 1959 and 1975 the sectoral composition of G.N.P. at constant (1959) factor cost prices showed a decline in the share of the agricultural sector from 39.1 per cent to 32.4 per cent. The manufacturing sector, on the other hand, increased its share from 11.6 per cent to 13.0 per cent. The share of all other sectors remained more or less constant during this period.

AGRICULTURE

Export Crops

About one-third of Sri Lanka's national income is derived from the cultivation, processing and export of three agricultural commodities—tea, rubber and coconuts. A substantial proportion of economic activity is indirectly sustained by export incomes. All these crops are grown largely in the Wet Zone of the island. Rubber and coconut both flourish mainly at low elevations, while the best tea is grown in the hill country at elevations of over 4,000 ft. above sea level. The bulk of the area under tea lies in the central hill district, although there is a considerable acreage of "low-grown" and "medium-grown" teas. Ceylon is the world's second largest producer of black tea.

In 1975 the estimated areas under two of the three main export crops were as follows: tea 597,691 acres and rubber 561,000 acres. According to 1965 figures coconut acreage stood at 1,152,428 acres. The bulk of the tea and rubber produced comes from estates of 100 acres and above, while coconut is largely a "smallholders" crop. In order to foster a healthy expansion of the tea and rubber industries, the Government operates a number of subsidy schemes which make payments to proprietors of tea and rubber lands who are prepared to replant with high-yielding strains of tea and rubber.

In addition to the three major export products there are a number of subsidiary crops such as arecanut (100,000 acres), cinnamon (33,000 acres), cocoa (26,000 acres) and citronella (34,700 acres). A substantial proportion of these products are also exported. Because of the overwhelming importance of the export industries in the economic activity of the country, conditions in Sri Lanka are extremely sensitive to the prices that her major exports fetch in world markets.

Rural Life

In 1970 about 50.8 per cent of the gainfully occupied population was in agriculture (including fishing, forestry and hunting). Agricultural production falls into two broad groups—estate agriculture, referred to above, and "domestic agriculture". Rather less than one-half of those employed in agriculture worked on the estates. This figure, however, does not give a true picture of the extent of the dependence of the population in domestic agriculture. For while the figures for the estates include all members of a family employed on them, the figures for the villages usually include only the head of the household. Domestic agriculture consists in the main of the cultivation of paddy lands. The estimated area under paddy in the Maha Season (1974/75) was 1,096,000 acres and the average yield per acre was about 46.2 bushels. In the Yala Season (1975) 623,000 acres were cultivated. Output during this season was seriously affected by severe drought condition. The Government has recently launched an intensive food drive in order to reduce the foreign exchange outlay on imports of rice. Besides increasing the area under cultivation, efforts are being made to increase the yields per acre through improved methods of cultivation and the use of high-yielding strains of seed-paddy.

Sri Lanka is predominantly a land of villages. No more than 22.36 per cent of the population can be classified as urban. The rapid growth of population and its concentration in the Wet Zone of the island has led to a pressure of population on the land. This pressure is evidenced both by the extremely small size of agricultural holdings and by the large number of landless people in the villages. Agricultural Colonization Schemes in the thinly populated parts of the island were initiated by the Government to relieve the pressure on land. Work on the Mahaveli Development Project which is proceeding smoothly will enable a significant transformation of the Dry Zone of Sri Lanka during the 1970s. In 1972 land reforms were undertaken and the ceiling on the holdings of agricultural land that may be owned by a family was fixed at 50 acres. The land reforms legislation, however, did not affect company-owned land. Land reform legislation passed in 1975 vested all company-owned land, both local and foreign, in the Land Reform Commission. The new measure adopted by the Government is expected to increase agricultural productivity and employment in the rural areas.

MINERAL AND POWER RESOURCES

No comprehensive geological survey of the island has yet been completed. There are no known deposits of petroleum or coal; scattered deposits of iron ore exist, as well as deposits of monazite and ilmenite sands. Some promising oil structures are currently being explored. The only mineral of commercial significance is graphite of which about 10,000 long tons are produced annually. The bulk of this is exported. In recent years the annual value of graphite exports has been 11 million rupees.

Although Sri Lanka is well known for her gems and precious stones there are no production figures available. The Government has recently set up two Corporations—the Graphite Corporation and the Gemming Corporation—to handle the graphite and gemming industries and maximize their foreign exchange earnings. A number of new incentives were offered to increase exports of gems and these have paid very rich dividends. In 1972 the value of gem exports was 15.9 million rupees, and the estimated value for 1973 was more than 150 million rupees.

Sri Lanka relies on the development of her water resources for her supplies of power. The present installed capacity amounts to about 359 megawatts of which 68 megawatts is thermal power. Energy from the Ukuwela project as well as the proposed Bowatenne project is estimated to be capable of meeting the island's requirements of power both for domestic and industrial purposes in the immediate future.

INDUSTRY

There has been a marked increase in Sri Lanka's industrial output in recent years. Manufacturing and handicrafts industry, which comprised barely 6 per cent of Gross National Product in 1958, accounted for nearly 15 per cent of Gross National Product in 1975. While successive governments since 1956 have been committed to policies of industrial development, recent industrial growth has been helped considerably by severe restriction, sometimes a total ban, of imports of manufactures—a policy necessitated by persistent deficits in the country's balance of payments.

The industrial structure is demarcated into the private sector and the public sector. The private sector covers a wide range of light consumer goods industries. The entry of new capital into this sector is regulated by the Government through the Approvals Division of the Ministry of Industries which grants "approvals" to industrial units on the basis of their economic feasibility and their capacity to save foreign exchange. The public sector industries are those which are undertaken by the state-sponsored Corporations. In 1975 there were 24 such Corporations engaged in the manufacture of the following products: cement, paper, ceramics, leather products, plywood, chemicals, mineral sands, hardboards, oil and fats, textiles, salt, hardware, tyres, steel, petroleum (refining) and fertilizers. These industries supply primarily the domestic market. However, vigorous efforts are being made to find export markets for the country's manufactured goods. Government policy on private foreign investment was spelled out in the White Paper on "Policy of the Government of Sri Lanka (Ceylon) on Private Foreign Investment". The Government welcomes foreign investments from any country in certain specified fields, and on terms which are considered appropriate in the context of the Government's general economic policies. A number of new projects where foreign investors are collaborating with the local industrialists and the State Sector have been approved, particularly in tourist development and in the fishing industry.

FOREIGN TRADE AND BALANCE OF PAYMENTS

The total value of exports (f.o.b.) in 1975 was 3,933 million rupees, and imports (c.i.f.) were valued at 5,251 million rupees: a trade deficit of 1,318 million rupees. Exports of tea, rubber and coconut continued to account for over 80 per cent of Sri Lanka's total exports of which tea alone accounted for 50 per cent in 1975. The main buyers of tea were the United Kingdom, Pakistan, the U.S.A., Iraq, Libya, Egypt, Australia and South Africa.

The People's Republic of China, the U.S.A. and the United Kingdom were the major buyers of rubber. The People's Republic of China is Sri Lanka's principal trading partner, followed by the United Kingdom. The importance of China in Sri Lanka's trade increased after the "Rice-Rubber Agreement" whereby Sri Lanka agreed to supply rubber in exchange for imports of rice. This agreement, originally negotiated in 1952, has been renewed from time to time since then.

Sri Lanka obtains somewhat over one-third of her imports from Commonwealth countries out of which the United Kingdom supplies about one-half. Approximately one-half of the value of imports consists of items in the "Food and Drink" category, and one-half are intermediate and investment goods. There has been a significant reduction in the imports of manufactured consumer goods owing to the Government's policy of encouraging import-substituting industries.

Balance of Payments

Despite the severely restrictive policy with regard to non-essential imports, the country has had persistent deficits in her balance of payments. A primary cause of this situation has been the continuing deterioration in her terms of trade. Since the mid-1960s the terms of trade have deteriorated by over 58 per cent. As a result, although there was an increase in the volume of exports, the country's capacity to pay for imports did not increase significantly.

In order to economize on the use of foreign exchange the Government continues to operate a rigid system of import control and exchange control. With a view to easing some of these controls a Foreign Exchange Entitlement Certificate (F.E.E.C.) Scheme was introduced in 1968. Under the scheme as it now operates, certain categories of goods can be imported under Licence and paid for through the purchase of foreign exchange at a premium of 65 per cent. At the same time, exchange earnings from non-traditional exports (that is, commodities other than tea, rubber and coconut products) as well as foreign exchange brought in by tourists can be converted into local currency at a premium rate of exchange.

The deficits in the balance of payments over the past years have been met by drawing on the country's foreign assets and by obtaining foreign aid under several commodity aid programmes and by drawings from the International Monetary Fund.

FINANCE

Banking

Currency is issued by the Central Bank of Ceylon which, in addition, is entrusted with the task of implementing a national monetary policy to secure both financial stability and economic growth. In 1972 the ceilings on commercial bank credit were lifted but credit for non-essential purposes continued to be restricted.

The two local banks, the Bank of Ceylon and the People's Bank, have a wide network of branches in Colombo and throughout the principal towns of the island. In 1975 the share of the Ceylonese banks in total deposits accounted for 85 per cent, whilst the British banks' share comprised 12 per cent. Indian and Pakistani banks held the balance of 3 per cent of the deposits.

Public Finance

The total revenue for the fiscal year 1975 is estimated at 5,086 million rupees and expenditure adjusted for anticipated under-expenditure is estimated at 7,483 million rupees, leaving a budget deficit of 2,397 million rupees. This deficit is to be bridged by domestic non-market borrowing of 1,231 million rupees and foreign finance of 1,080 million rupees. In the financial year 1976 a greater accent is placed on capital expenditure. Of a total net expenditure of 7,941 million rupees, net capital expenditure is estimated at 2,486 million rupees, slightly less than in the previous year. Net government revenue and net recurrent expenditure is estimated at 5,645 million rupees and 5,355 million rupees respectively, leaving a current account surplus of 290 million rupees. The overall budget deficit would be 2,298 million rupees. This deficit will be bridged by domestic non-bank borrowing of 1,300 million rupees, projects loans and grants of 250 million rupees and Commodity Aid counterpart funds of 750 million rupees.

The main sources of government revenue are import duties, income and profits taxes and business turnover taxes, export duties and excise duties, in that order of importance. A very important source of revenue in recent years has been the receipts from the sale of Foreign Exchange Entitlement Certificates which currently is charged at 65 per cent on most imports. The estimated revenue from this source for 1975 at 1,055 million rupees is approximately 20 per cent of revenue.

ECONOMIC DEVELOPMENT

In recent years, Sri Lanka has moved considerably in the direction of a "mixed economy" in which many spheres of activity are reserved for the Government sector. The bus service, the port, insurance, and the distribution of oil are all in the Government sector. This is in addition to the state-sponsored industrial corporations. A considerable proportion of imports, primarily of food and textiles, is handled by the Co-operative Wholesale Establishment and the Food Commissioner. A new company, Consolidated Exports, financed with Government and private capital, has been set up to function in competition with private firms in the export trade. The State Trading (General) Corporation was set up in 1971 to handle a wide range of imports.

Economic activity in Sri Lanka is severely constrained by balance of payments difficulties. The export earnings from the three main primary commodities have been static for a long period of time due to either price declines in the international markets or fall in domestic production or both. The Government has given high priority to the diversification of the export earnings to reduce the over-dependence on three commodities whose future prospects are not altogether very promising. The setting up of the Export Promotion Council is expected to guide the country in the future in evolving a unified export promotion policy which would before long generate a new non-traditional export-earning sector whilst at the same time helping the traditional sector to continue to play its vital role in earning foreign exchange.

In the Government's Five Year Plan (1972–76) considerable emphasis was placed on an import substitution programme. The ban on the import of certain food items created the right conditions for domestic production to expand very fast to meet the local needs. With a sustained effort in the next few years in paddy production, further savings on the import bill will help in easing the pressure on the balance of payments.

STATISTICAL SURVEY

AREA AND POPULATION

AREA (sq. km.)	POPULATION (Census of October 9th, 1971)					
	Total	RACES ('000)				
		Sinhalese	Ceylon Tamil	Indian Tamil	Ceylon Moors
65,610	12,711,143	9,147	1,416	1,195	824

Estimated Population: 13,874,000 (July 1st, 1974).

Towns (1971):* Colombo (capital) 562,160, Dehiwala-Mount Lavinia 154,785, Jaffna 107,663, Kandy 93,602, Galle 72,720.

* Provisional.

Births and Deaths (1972): 384,066 births registered (birth rate 29.5 per 1,000); 100,080 deaths registered (death rate 7.7 per 1,000).

ECONOMICALLY ACTIVE POPULATION

(1971 census, sample tabulation)

	MALES	FEMALES	TOTAL
Agriculture, hunting, forestry and fishing	1,319,219	504,741	1,823,960
Mining and quarrying	13,862	1,443	15,305
Manufacturing	247,084	100,333	347,417
Electricity, gas and water supply	9,194	248	9,442
Construction	111,210	1,204	112,414
Trade, restaurants and hotels	322,482	22,952	345,434
Transport, storage and communications	151,579	3,687	155,266
Finance, insurance, property and business services	24,409	1,938	26,347
Community, social and personal services	354,426	133,707	488,133
Other activities (not adequately described)	253,708	44,556	298,264
TOTAL IN EMPLOYMENT	2,807,173	814,809	3,621,982
Unemployed*	446,406	349,800	796,206
TOTAL	3,253,579	1,164,609	4,418,188

* Including persons seeking work for the first time.

AGRICULTURE

LAND USE, 1973

('000 hectares)

Arable Land	895
Under Permanent Crops	1,084
Permanent Meadows and Pastures*	439
Forest Land	2,899
Other Land	1,244
TOTAL	6,561

* Including scrub.

Source: FAO, *Production Yearbook 1974.*

PRINCIPAL CROPS

	AREA ('000 hectares)			PRODUCTION ('000 metric tons)		
	1972	1973	1974	1972	1973	1974
Rice (paddy)	543	571	638	1,313	1,313	1,875
Maize	20	29	31*	15	21	21*
Millet	23	32	22*	16	21	15*
Potatoes	3	4	3*	47	31	26*
Sweet potatoes	15	27	27*	56	91	95*
Cassava (manioc)	59	115	120*	318	616	600*
Dry beans	4*	5	5*	2	3	3*
Sesame seed	13.4	12.3	12.3*	6.7	6.9	7.3*
Coconuts	n.a.	n.a.	n.a.	2,104	1,374	1,350*
Copra	n.a.	n.a.	n.a.	295	95	109
Chillies	35	44	46*	32	40	42*
Onions	6	8	9	62	44	46
Sugar cane	3	4	16*	220*	194	272*
Cashew nuts	n.a.	n.a.	n.a.	0.3*	0.3*	0.3*
Coffee	4.9	5.9	6.0*	6.8	11.3	10.0*
Cocoa beans	19.7	19.3	19.3*	2	2	2
Tea	242	242	240*	213.5	211.3	201.0
Tobacco	14.*	14*	15.2*	9*	9*	9*
Natural rubber	n.a.	n.a.	n.a.	143.2	154.7	145*
Coir	n.a.	n.a.	n.a.	214.6*	142.5*	142.5*

* FAO estimate.

Source: FAO, *Production Yearbook 1974.*

LIVESTOCK
(year ending September 30th)

	1971/72	1972/73	1973/74*
Buffaloes	748,000	716,000	716,000
Cattle	1,617,000	1,673,000	1,673,000
Sheep	29,000	27,000	27,000
Goats	562,000	549,000	549,000
Pigs	102,000	112,000*	91,000
Chickens	7,227,000	7,528,000	8,000,000
Ducks	24,000	26,000	26,000

* FAO estimate.

Source: FAO, *Production Yearbook 1974.*

LIVESTOCK PRODUCTS
(metric tons)

	1972	1973	1974*
Beef and Veal	16,000	17,000	18,000
Buffalo Meat	5,000*	5,000*	5,000
Goats' Meat	1,000*	1,000*	1,000
Pig Meat	2,000*	2,000*	2,000
Poultry Meat	8,000*	8,000*	9,000
Cows' Milk	207,000	200,000	201,000
Buffaloes' Milk	56,000	44,000	45,000
Goats' Milk	5,000*	5,000*	5,000
Hen Eggs	26,672	25,506	26,200

* FAO estimate.

Source: FAO, *Production Yearbook 1974.*

FORESTRY

ROUNDWOOD REMOVALS

('000 cubic metres, all non-coniferous)

	1967	1968	1969	1970*	1971*	1972*	1973*
Sawlogs, veneer logs and logs for sleepers	325	340	345	360	370	380	504
Other industrial wood	350	360	365	375	385	395	400
Fuel wood	3,740	3,800	3,880	3,940	4,000	4,070	4,150
TOTAL	4,415	4,500	4,590	4,675	4,755	4,845	5,054

* FAO estimates.

Source: FAO, *Yearbook of Forest Products.*

SAWNWOOD PRODUCTION

('000 cubic metres, all non-coniferous)

	1967	1968	1969	1970*	1971*	1972*	1973*
Sawnwood (incl. boxboards)	135	140	145	150	155	160	160
Railway sleepers	14	15	15	15	15	15	15
TOTAL	149	155	160	165	170	175	175

* FAO estimates.

Source: FAO, *Yearbook of Forest Products.*

FISHING*

('000 metric tons)

	1968	1969	1970	1971	1972	1973	1974
Inland waters:							
Freshwater fishes	8.7	7.0	8.3	8.2	8.4	7.0	7.7
Indian Ocean:							
Marine fishes	134.0	121.7	85.7	73.3	89.0	89.9	96.9
Crustaceans and molluscs	3.0	6.0	4.1	3.7	4.5	3.8	6.1
TOTAL CATCH	143.7	134.7	98.1	85.2	101.9	100.7	110.7

* Excluding (*a*) quantities landed by Sri Lanka craft in foreign ports, and (*b*) quantities landed by foreign craft in Sri Lanka ports.

Source: FAO, *Yearbook of Fishery Statistics 1974.*

MINING

		1968	1969	1970	1971	1972	1973
Natural graphite	metric tons	10,802	11,418	9,787	7,510	7,140	7,170
Sand, silica and quartz	'000 metric tons	73	86	96	87	85	n.a.
Chalk	,, ,, ,,	59	104	126	n.a.	n.a.	n.a.
Salt (unrefined)	,, ,, ,,	101	114	65	65	156	n.a.

Source: United Nations, *The Growth of World Industry.*

INDUSTRY

		1969	1970	1971	1972
Beer	'000 hectolitres	83	89	45	87
Cigarettes	million	2,930	3,035	3,183	3,424
Cotton yarn	metric tons	2,316	1,837	2,919	4,886
Cotton fabrics	million metres	17	13	24	27
Cement	'000 metric tons	283	326	386	383
Raw sugar	,, ,, ,,	10.1	15.7	10.9	7.1

1973 ('000 metric tons): Cement 460, Raw sugar 10.

Sources: United Nations, *Statistical Yearbook* 1974; *The Growth of World Industry*; and *Statistical Yearbook for Asia and the Far East* 1973.

FINANCE

100 cents=1 Sri Lanka rupee.

Coins: 1, 2, 5, 10, 25 and 50 cents; 1 rupee.

Notes: 2, 5, 10, 50 and 100 rupees.

Exchange rates (June 1976): £1 sterling=15.25 rupees; U.S. $1=8.60 rupees.

100 Sri Lanka rupees=£6.56=$11.63.

Note: Between September 1949 and November 1967 the Ceylon (now Sri Lanka) rupee was valued at 21 U.S. cents (U.S. $1=4.7619 rupees). In November 1967 the rupee was devalued by 20 per cent to 16.8 U.S. cents ($1=5.9524 rupees) and this valuation remained in effect until August 1971 and from November 1971 to July 1972. In terms of sterling, the exchange rate was £1=14.286 rupees from November 1967 to November 1971; and £1=15.510 rupees from December 1971 to June 1972. From July 1972 to May 1976 the Sri Lanka authorities maintained an official exchange rate against sterling at a mid-point of £1=15.60 rupees, thus allowing the rupee's value to fluctuate against other currencies in line with sterling ("floating" since June 1972). In May 1976 the link with sterling was ended and the rupee's value has since been determined in relation to a weighted "basket" of currencies of Sri Lanka's trading partners. The average market rate (rupees per U.S. dollar) was: 6.4048 in 1973; 6.6485 in 1974; 7.0498 in 1975.

BUDGET
(million rupees)

Revenue	1974	1975*
General sales and turnover taxes	734.8	679.6
Selective sales taxes	749.6	831.2
Import levies	277.3	335.9
Export levies	660.1	429.9
Receipts from foreign exchange entitlement certificates	964.1	1,054.8
Income taxes	506.7	770.1
Gross receipts from government trading enterprises	434.1	454.0
Interest, profits and dividends	117.8	148.2
Sales and charges	147.0	96.9
Total (incl. others)	4,863.3	5,092.6

Expenditure	1974	1975*
Recurrent expenditure:	4,505.7	5,153.1
Defence and foreign affairs	292.3	328.7
Irrigation, power and highways	133.4	134.6
Education	606.0	681.8
Public administration and home affairs	346.2	408.3
Finance	884.2	1,004.0
Transport	230.8	248.0
Agriculture and lands	262.0	297.3
Posts and telecommunications	134.1	151.3
Health	297.3	338.1
Food, co-operatives and small industries	955.1	1,125.0
Capital expenditure:	1,277.0	1,960.3
Planning and economic affairs	177.2	126.4
Irrigation, power and highways	310.4	464.5
Industries and scientific affairs	70.8	272.2
Finance	131.4	76.0
Transport	49.7	199.8
Plantation industry	171.3	182.5
Agriculture and lands	100.6	145.4
Housing and construction	90.4	110.4
Sinking Fund contributions, repayments and payments to international organizations	375.7	437.7
Total	6,158.4	7,551.1

* Provisional.

Source: Central Bank of Ceylon, *Bulletin*, March 1976.

FOREIGN EXCHANGE RESERVES
(U.S. $ million at December 31st)

	1969	1970	1971	1972	1973	1974	1975
Central Bank	28	33	40	35	60	50	45
Government and Official	12	10	10	11	11	10	—
TOTAL	40	43	50	46	71	60	45

Source: IMF, *International Financial Statistics.*

CURRENCY IN CIRCULATION
(million rupees at December 31st)

1969	1,084
1970	935
1971	1,115
1972	1,202
1973	1,437
1974	1,539
1975	1,610

Source: IMF, *International Financial Statistics.*

COST OF LIVING
CONSUMER PRICE INDEX, COLOMBO
(base: 1970=100)

	1965	1966	1967	1968	1969	1971	1972	1973	1974
Food	78.6	79.9	82.5	88.7	93.7	101.9	108.0	121.7	138.9
Fuel and light	74.0	70.5	70.9	75.8	91.8	103.5	107.2	120.8	162.4
Clothing	92.3	85.4	85.0	87.5	95.3	105.6	119.1	135.5	149.0
Rent	92.5	92.5	92.5	92.5	98.8	100.0	100.0	100.0	100.0
ALL ITEMS	81.4	81.3	83.1	87.9	94.4	102.7	109.2	119.7	134.4

Source: International Labour Office, *Year Book of Labour Statistics.*

1975 average: Food 149.6; All items 143.5.

GROSS DOMESTIC PRODUCT BY ORIGIN
(million rupees at current prices)

	1971	1972*	1973*	1974*
Agriculture, hunting, forestry and fishing	3,857.2	4,119.0	5,025.6	8,356.4
Mining and quarrying	91.0	95.1	323.6	246.9
Manufacturing	1,480.1	1,727.8	2,017.0	2,474.8
Construction	751.1	711.1	802.1	1,011.3
Electricity, gas, water and sanitary services	38.5	36.2	39.5	34.3
Transport, storage and communications	1,203.8	1,333.4	1,525.0	1,683.4
Wholesale and retail trade	1,814.4	1,985.5	2,455.1	2,560.2
Banking, insurance and real estate	165.8	191.0	219.9	301.9
Ownership of dwellings	406.7	413.6	420.9	455.7
Public administration and defence	549.6	575.0	654.4	704.2
Other services	1,548.6	1,619.4	1,782.0	1,976.4
G.D.P. at Factor Cost	11,906.8	12,807.1	15,265.1	19,805.5
Net factor income from abroad	−121.0	−136.6	−110.6	−111.1
G.N.P. at Factor Cost	11,785.8	12,670.5	15,154.5	19,694.4
Indirect taxes, less subsidies	937.4	980.7	1,661.3	1,623.7
G.N.P. at Market Prices	12,723.2	13,651.2	16,815.8	21,318.1

* Provisional.

Source: Central Bank of Ceylon, *Annual Report 1974*.

BALANCE OF PAYMENTS 1974 (provisional)
(million rupees)

	Credit	Debit	Net
Goods and services:			
Merchandise trade f.o.b.	3,375.7	4,603.1	−1,227.4
Freight and merchandise insurance	13.1	20.2	−7.1
Other transport	159.8	46.1	113.7
Travel	8.7	7.1	1.6
Investment income	94.8	9.2	85.6
Government expenditure n.e.s.	33.0	24.6	8.4
Other services	107.1	120.2	−13.1
Total goods and services	3,820.3	4,971.3	−1,151.0
Transfer payments	308.4	56.0	252.4
Total current account	4,128.7	5,027.3	−898.6
Capital:			
Non-monetary sector:			
Direct investment	10.8	1.8	9.0
Other private long-term	1.2	2.5	−1.3
Other private short-term	—	15.0	−15.0
Central government	1,706.6	1,179.3	527.3
Monetary sector:			
Commercial banks—liabilities	—	—	—
Commercial banks—assets	—	97.2	97.2
Central bank—liabilities	178.6	—	178.6
Central bank—assets	60.4	—	60.4
Net IMF position	111.4	162.2	−50.8
Oil facility drawings	271.4	—	271.4
Special Drawing Rights	—	—	—
Total capital account	1,078.6	870.4	208.2
Errors and omissions	16.2	—	16.2

Source: Central Bank of Ceylon, *Annual Report 1974*.

EXTERNAL TRADE

(million rupees, excluding gold)

	1968	1969	1970	1971	1972	1973	1974	1975
Imports	2,173	2,543	2,313	1,986	2,064	2,715	4,554	5,251
Exports	2,035	1,916	2,021	1,946	1,939	2,617	3,447	3,923

Source: Central Bank of Ceylon, *Bulletin* and *Sri Lanka Customs Returns* 1975.

PRINCIPAL COMMODITIES

(million rupees)

Imports	1972	1973	1974
Rice	917	1,248	1,950
Flour	161	270	720
Milk and milk products	57	70	70
Meat, fish and eggs	83	52	50
Petroleum products	38	295	905
Fertilizers	63	111	221
Textiles (incl. clothing)	48	55	59
Medicinal and pharmaceutical products	41	36	44
Transport equipment	107	95	91
Machinery and equipment	181	224	186
Total (incl. others)	2,064	2,715	4,554

Exports	1972	1973	1974
Tea	1,162	1,261	1,360
Rubber	265	592	738
Coconut products	266	145	397
Precious and semi-precious stones	12	141	109
Other domestic exports	222*	349	846*
Total (incl. re-exports)	1,993*	2,596	3,449*

* Including the value of ships' bunkers.

Source: Statistical Abstract of Ceylon 1974.

PRINCIPAL COUNTRIES

('000 rupees)

	Imports		Exports	
	1974	1975	1974	1975
Australia	270,569	429,482	106,593	109,909
Belgium	35,190	16,566	28,800	12,962
Bulgaria	56,968	1,111	22,407	268
Burma	204,142	120,649	4,400	4,400
Canada	32,293	62,395	131,003	95,097
China, People's Republic	358,689	661,511	267,156	460,146
France	345,792	429,120	47,961	44,092
Germany, Federal Republic	199,355	252,047	196,700	118,217
India	218,950	149,898	4,645	2,129
Iran	172,941	217,730	74,597	116,519
Iraq	228,667	6,092	112,555	190,452
Italy	59,406	38,392	93,184	67,648
Japan	352,921	447,041	130,456	178,282
Korea, Republic	19,565	17,689	47,862	143,456
Kuwait	45,166	7,680	43,966	58,587
Netherlands	24,222	46,223	98,941	69,400
Pakistan	278,910	60	267,118	—
Saudi Arabia	446,984	636,595	61,672	94,211
Singapore	131,157	103,823	45,356	50,082
South Africa	49,460	30,557	110,330	120,624
U.S.S.R.	145,513	112,145	99,269	102,574
United Kingdom	170,345	223,482	353,683	311,144
U.S.A.	145,255	336,645	241,835	218,859
Total (incl. others)	4,554,000	5,251,000	3,447,000	3,922,936

Source: Sri Lanka Customs Returns 1975.

TOURISM

FOREIGN VISITORS

	1972	1973	1974	1975
Western Europe	33,877	50,704	56,309	60,660
Asia	14,156	16,510	15,619	23,779
North America	4,814	5,974	6,271	7,823
Eastern Europe	943	1,511	2,089	5,002
Australasia	1,403	1,809	2,502	3,638
Others	854	1,380	2,221	2,302
TOTAL	56,047	77,888	85,011	103,204

Source: Central Bank of Ceylon, *Bulletin*, March 1976.

Tourist expenditure ('000 rupees): 1969, 17,032; 1970, 21,503; 1971, 20,276.

TRANSPORT

RAILWAYS

('000)

	1971	1972	1973	1974
Passenger-kilometres	2,773,460	3,095,866	3,300,525	2,777,361
Freight ton-kilometres	327,850	333,748	321,082	310,234

Source: Central Bank of Ceylon, *Bulletin*, November 1975.

ROADS

VEHICLES REGISTERED

	1969	1970	1971	1972	1973
Cars	86,520	87,344	88,252	89,024	89,883
Motor-cycles	18,994	20,014	21,125	21,597	22,042
Buses	9,688	10,367	11,170	11,835	12,132
Goods Vehicles	31,197	32,952	33,692	33,996	34,396

Source: IRF, *World Road Statistics 1969-73.*

INTERNATIONAL SEA-BORNE SHIPPING

(Vessels: '000 net tons; Goods: '000 metric tons)

	1971	1972	1973	1974
Vessels:				
Entered	3,354	3,082	n.a.	n.a.
Cleared	2,632	2,823	n.a.	n.a.
Goods:				
Loaded	1,215	1,310	1,177	1,120
Unloaded	3,623	3,458	3,403	3,034

Source: United Nations, *Statistical Yearbook* and *Monthly Bulletin of Statistics.*

CIVIL AVIATION
(Air Ceylon domestic services)

	1971	1972	1973	1974
Kilometres flown ('000)	682	579	170	289
Passenger-kilometres ('000)	17,578	13,115	4,527	5,746
Cargo (ton-km.)	22,566	4,148	1,500	580

Source: Central Bank of Ceylon, *Bulletin*, November 1975.

EDUCATION
(1971)

	Schools	Pupils	Staff
Primary and Secondary	9,502	2,803,182	94,858
Teacher Training	27	7,239	562
Special	28	1,645	193

Sources (unless otherwise stated): Department of Census and Statistics, Colombo; Central Bank of Ceylon, Colombo (Foreign Aid Statistics).

THE CONSTITUTION

The Constitution of the new Republic of Sri Lanka (Ceylon) was adopted and enacted by the Constituent Assembly of the People of Sri Lanka on May 22nd, 1972.

The Constituent Assembly which was formed after the general elections in May 1970 drafted the new Constitution to make Ceylon a Unitary State known as the Republic of Sri Lanka where the sovereignty of the people is to be exercised through a National State Assembly of elected representatives of the people.

A summary of the main provisions of the new Constitution follows.

THE NATIONAL STATE ASSEMBLY

The Assembly consists of 157 representatives and exercises:

(*a*) the legislative power of the people;

(*b*) the executive power of the people, including the defence of Sri Lanka, through the President and Cabinet Ministers; and

(*c*) the judicial power of the people through Courts and other institutions created by law, except in the case of matters relating to its powers and privileges, wherein the judicial power of the people may be exercised directly by the National State Assembly.

The normal life of the Assembly is six years and there is universal suffrage for those over 18 years old.

EXECUTIVE GOVERNMENT

A cabinet of Ministers is vested with the direction and control of the government of the Republic and is collectively responsible to the National State Assembly and answerable to the National State Assembly on all matters for which they are responsible. The Prime Minister determines the number of Ministers and Ministries and the assignment of subjects and functions to Ministers. The Prime Minister and other Ministers of the Cabinet and Deputy Ministers are appointed by the President.

OTHER PROVISIONS

Buddhism: Buddhism has the foremost place among religions and it is the duty of the State to protect and foster Buddhism, at the same time allowing every citizen the freedom to adopt the religion of his choice.

Language: Sinhala is the official language and all laws shall be made or enacted in Sinhala. The use of Tamil, the language of the largest minority community, continues to be protected under the Tamil Language Act of 1958.

State Policy: The Republic is pledged to carry forward the progressive advancement towards the establishment in Sri Lanka of a socialist democracy.

President: The President of the Republic is the Head of State. He appoints the Prime Minister and the other Ministers.

Control of Finance: The National State Assembly has full control over public finance.

Creation of Courts: The National State Assembly may create and establish institutions for the administration of justice and the settlement of industrial and other disputes.

THE GOVERNMENT

President: WILLIAM GOPALLAWA, M.B.E.

THE CABINET

(*July* 1976)

Prime Minister and Minister of Defence, Foreign Affairs, Planning, Economic Affairs and Plan Implementation: SIRIMAVO RATWATTE DIAS BANDARNAIKE.

Minister of Irrigation, Power and Highways and Leader of the House: MAITHRIPALA SENANAYAKE.

Minister of Trade, Public Administration and Home Affairs: TIKIRI BANDA ILANGARATNE.

Minister of Education: DR. AL-HAJ BADIUDDIN MAHMUD.

Minister of Shipping, Aviation and Tourism: PUNCHI BANDAGUNATILAKA G. KALUGALLA.

Minister of Labour: MICHAEL PAUL DE ZOYSA SIRIWARDENA.

Minister of Industries and Scientific Affairs: TIKIRI BANDA SUBASINGHE.

Minister of Finance and Justice: FELIX REGINALD DIAS BANDARANAIKE.

Minister of Local Government: W. P. G. ARIYADASA.

Minister of Plantation Industry: RATNASIRI WICKRAMANAYAKE.

Minister of Agriculture and Lands: HECTOR SENERATH RAJAKARUNA BANDA KOBBEKADUWA.

Minister of Fisheries: S. D. R. JAYARATNE.

Minister of Housing and Construction: PIETER GERALD BARTHOLOMEUS KEUNEMAN.

Minister of Posts and Telecommunications: CHELLIAH KUMARASURIYAR.

Minister of Health: SIVA OBEYSEKERA.

Minister of Information and Broadcasting: RANAWAKEARACHIGE SOLMON PERERA.

Minister of Social Services: TIKIRI BANDA TENNAKOON.

Minister of Cultural Affairs: SEMAGE SALMAN KULATILEKE.

Minister of Parliamentary Affairs, Sports and Transport: KIRI BANDA RATNAYAKE.

Minister of Food, Co-operatives and Small Industries: S. K. K. SURIARACHCHI.

PARLIAMENT

NATIONAL STATE ASSEMBLY

Speaker: STANLEY TILAKARATNE.

GENERAL ELECTION, MAY 1970

	SEATS	VOTES
United National Party	17	1,879,996
Sri Lanka Freedom Party	90	1,817,349
Federal Party	13	245,747
Lanka Sama Samaja Party (Trotskyists)	19	443,224
Communist Party	6	169,149
Tamil Congress	3	115,557
Independents and Others	2	292,747

POLITICAL PARTIES

The main political parties are:

Sri Lanka Freedom Party: 301 Darley Rd., Colombo 10; f. 1951 by the former Premier, Solomon Bandaranaike; Socialist; stands for a neutralist foreign policy; nationalization of certain industries; Sinhala as the official language, with safeguards for minorities; Pres. Mrs. SIRIMAVO R. D. BANDARANAIKE.

United National Party: "Siri Kotha", Kollupituya, Colombo; Democratic Socialist party; aims at a neutralist foreign policy; Sinhala as the official language and State-aid to denominational schools; Pres. J. R. JAYEWARDENE; publ. *U.N.P. Journal* (weekly in Sinhala).

Federal Party: 16 Alfred House Gdns., Colombo 3; f. 1949; principal Tamil party; stands for a Federal constitution; Leader S. J. V. CHEQVANAYAKAM, Q.C.; Parliamentary Whip V. DHARMALINGAM, M.P.; Pres. A. AMIRTHALINGAM; Hoolai, Chulipuram; Hon. Sec. S. KATHIRAVELUPILLAI, M.P.

Lanka Sama Samaja Party (*Trotskyist Party*): f. 1935; stands for nationalization of foreign owned companies, opposed to communalism; Leader Dr. NANAYAKKARAPATHIRAGE M. PERERA; Sec. BERNARD SOYSAL; publs. *Sumasamajaya, Samadharmam* and *Samasamajist* (Trotskyist weeklies in Sinhala, Tamil and English respectively).

Mahajama Eksath Peramuna (*People's United Front*) 53, 2/7 Mansoor Bldg., Main St., Colombo 11; f. 1960 coalition 1965; left wing; strongly Sinhalese and Buddhist; scientific socialist; non-aligned; includes the former **Viplavakari Lanka Sama Samaja (VLSSP)**; 1,500 active mems.; 8,000 Youth Leaguers; Pres. DINESH GUNAWARDENE; Sec. SHANTHA LOKUPITIYA; publ. *Mahajana Eksath Peramuna* (weekly), *Pahara* (weekly)

Communist Party: 91 Cotta Rd., Colombo 8; f. 1943; pro Moscow; Chair. PIETER G. B. KEUNEMAN; National Organizer V. A. SAMARAWICKRAMA; 9,500 mems.; publs. *Maubima, Desabhimani, Forward* (weeklies in Sinhala, Tamil and English respectively), *Aththa* (Sinhala daily), *Nava Logaya* (Sinhala monthly).

Tamil Congress: strongly represented in northern and eastern Ceylon; Leader G. G. PONNAMBALAM.

DIPLOMATIC REPRESENTATION

HIGH COMMISSIONS, EMBASSIES AND LEGATION ACCREDITED TO SRI LANKA
(HC) High Commission; (E) Embassy; (L) Legation.

Afghanistan: Islamabad, Pakistan (E).

Argentina: New Delhi, India (E).

Australia: 3 Cambridge Place, Colombo 7 (HC); *High Commissioner:* A. H. BORTHWICK.

Austria: New Delhi, India (E).

Belgium: New Delhi, India (E).

Brazil: New Delhi, India (E).

Bulgaria: 22/1A Buller's Lane, Colombo 7 (E); *Ambassador:* STOJAN ZAIMOV.

Burma: 53 Rosmead Place, Colombo 7 (E); *Ambassador:* U MAHN THA MYAING.

Canada: 6 Gregory's Rd., Colombo 7 (HC); *High Commissioner:* Miss MARION ADAMS MACPHERSON.

China, People's Republic: 191 Dharmapala Mawatha, Colombo 7 (E); *Ambassador:* HUANG MING-TA.

Cuba: New Delhi, India (E).

Czechoslovakia: 47/47A Horton Place, Colombo 7 (E); *Ambassador:* FRANTIŠEK MALIK.

Denmark: New Delhi, India (E).

Egypt: 39 Dickman's Rd., Colombo 5 (E); *Ambassador:* MOHAMED ATEF EL NAWAWI.

Finland: New Delhi, India (E).

France: 89 Rosmead Place, Colombo 7 (E); *Ambassador:* PIERRE ANTHONIOSZ.

German Democratic Republic: 101 Rosmead Place, Colombo 7 (E); *Ambassador:* KRAFT BUMBEL (also accred. to Singapore).

Germany, Federal Republic: 16 Barnes Place, Colombo 7 (E); *Ambassador:* Dr. HILDEGUNDE FEILNER.

Ghana: New Delhi, India (HC).

Greece: New Delhi, India (E).

Guyana: New Delhi, India (HC).

Hungary: New Delhi, India (E).

India: 18-5/1 Sir Baron Jayatileke Mawatha, Colombo 1 (HC); *High Commissioner:* AVTAR SINGH.

Indonesia: 10 Independence Ave., Torrington Place, Colombo 7 (E); *Ambassador:* Mr. SOEKIRMAN.

Iran: Islamabad, Pakistan (E).

Iraq: 49 Dharmapala Mawatha, Colombo 3 (E); *Ambassador:* TOWFIQ ABDUL JABBAR MOHAMMAD SAID.

Italy: 586 Galle Rd., Colombo 3 (E); *Ambassador:* Dr. FABRIZIO FABBRICOTTI.

Japan: 20 Gregory's Rd., Colombo 7 (E); *Ambassador:* AKIRA YOSHIOKA.

Jordan: New Delhi, India (E).

Kenya: New Delhi, India (HC).

Korea, Democratic People's Republic: *Ambassador:* YU SONG JIN.

Korea, Republic: New Delhi, India (E).

Kuwait: New Delhi, India (E).

Laos: New Delhi, India (E).

Lebanon: New Delhi, India (E).

Malaysia: 63A Ward Place, Colombo 7 (HC); *High Commissioner:* MOHAMED MUSTAPHA BIN DATO MAHMUD.

Maldives: 25 Melbourne Ave., Colombo 4 (E); *Ambassador:* HUSSAIN ALI DIDI.

Mexico: New Delhi, India (E).

Mongolia: New Delhi, India (E).

Nepal: New Delhi, India (E).

Netherlands: New Delhi, India (E).

New Zealand: New Delhi, India (HC).

Nigeria: New Delhi, India (HC).

Norway: New Delhi, India (E).

Pakistan: 17 Sir Ernest de Silva Mawatha, Colombo 7 (E); *Ambassador:* ABDUR RAUF KHAN.

Philippines: 5 Torrington Place, Colombo 7 (E); *Ambassador:* LIBRADO D. CAYCO.

Poland: 48 Jawatte Rd., Colombo 5 (E); *Ambassador:* WIKTOR KINECKI.

Portugal: 20 Queen's Rd., Colombo 3 (L); *Chargé d'Affaires a.i.:* Dr. GIL FALDANHA.

Romania: New Delhi, India (E).

Singapore: New Delhi, India (HC).

Spain: New Delhi, India (E).

Sudan: New Delhi, India (E).

Sweden: New Delhi, India (E).

Switzerland: No. 7 Upper Chatham St., Colombo 1 (E); *Ambassador:* FRANÇOIS P. CHATELAIN.

Thailand: 10 Sir Ernest de Silva Mawatha, Colombo 7 (E); *Ambassador:* SUCHATI CHUTHASMIT.

Trinidad and Tobago: New Delhi, India (HC).

Turkey: New Delhi, India (E).

U.S.S.R.: 62 Sir Ernest de Silva Mawatha, Colombo 7 (E); *Ambassador:* RAFIK NISHANOV.

United Kingdom: Galle Rd., Kollupitiya, Colombo 3 (HC): *High Commissioner:* DAVID PASCOE AIERS (also accred. to Maldives).

U.S.A.: 44 Galle Rd., Colombo 3 (E); *Ambassador:* JOHN HATHAWAY REED (also accred. to Maldives).

Viet-Nam: New Delhi, India (E).

Yugoslavia: 32 Cambridge Place, Colombo 7 (E); *Ambassador:* SLOBADAN MARTINOVIC.

Sri Lanka also has diplomatic relations with Luxembourg and the Vatican City.

JUDICIAL SYSTEM

THE SUPREME COURT AND COURT OF CRIMINAL APPEAL OF SRI LANKA

Chief Justice: Hon. VICTOR TENNEKOON.

COURT OF APPEAL

Legislation to establish a Court of Appeal and abolish the right of appeal to the Privy Council in London was introduced in 1971 and passed in the following year, the Court holding its inaugural session on March 9th, 1972.

DISTRICT COURTS

There are twenty-eight District Courts in Sri Lanka. They have unlimited original civil jurisdiction and criminal jurisdiction in respect of all offences which are not within the exclusive jurisdiction of the Supreme Court. In the exercise of their criminal jurisdiction, District Courts try only cases committed to them for trial by Magistrates' Courts.

MAGISTRATES' COURTS

There are thirty-four Magistrates' Courts in Sri Lanka. A Magistrates' Court may not pass a sentence heavier than the following, except where an Ordinance has specially empowered it to do so:

(*a*) Imprisonment up to six months.
(*b*) Fine up to Rs.100.
(*c*) Whipping if the offender is under 16 years.

COURTS OF REQUESTS AND RURAL COURTS

There are thirty Courts of Requests in the island, and they have original civil jurisdiction in all actions in which the debt, damage or demand, or the value of land in dispute, does not exceed a stipulated amount. The courts, with the exception of the Colombo Court, are presided over by a District Judge or a Magistrate, who acts as Commissioner of Requests in addition to his duties as a District Judge or Magistrate. The Colombo Court is presided over by a separate Commissioner. There are forty-five Rural Courts in Sri Lanka.

CRIMINAL JUSTICE COMMISSIONS ACT

The Criminal Justice Commissions Act, passed in April 1972, set up a specially constituted Judicial Commission to try offences in connection with any rebellion, insurrection or any widespread breakdown of law and order, currency offences and sabotage of industrial plants.

CONSTITUTIONAL COURT

The new Constitution adopted in May 1972 provided for a Constitutional Court of five persons, appointed by the President, charged with ruling on the validity of legislation enacted within the National Assembly. Jurisdiction in these matters is now outside the sphere of ordinary courts.

RELIGION

BUDDHISM

Seventy-five per cent of the population are Theravada Buddhist. Buddhism was introduced into Ceylon in the third century B.C. by Arahan Mahinda, son of the Indian King Asoka. There are 12,000 Buddhist Bhikkhus (monks), living in 6,000 temples on the island.

Ceylon Regional Centre of the World Fellowship of Buddhists: 6 Paget Rd., Colombo 5; Sec. W. P. DALUWATTA.

Buddhist Congress: Pres. JINADASA SAMARAKKODI.

HINDUISM

The majority of the Tamil population are Hindus. The Hindu population numbers over two million.

ISLAM

The total Muslim population is over 600,000.

CHRISTIAN CHURCHES

CHURCH OF CEYLON

Bishop of Kurunagala: Rt. Rev. CYRIL LAKSHMAN WICKREMASINGHE; Bishop's House, Kandy Road, Kurunagala.

Bishop of Colombo: CYRIL ABEYNAYAKE; Bishop's House, Stewart Place, Colombo, 3.

METHODIST CHURCH IN SRI LANKA

President of Conference: Rev. G. DENZIL DE SILVA, B.D.

THE PRESBYTERY OF SRI LANKA

The Dutch Reformed Church in Sri Lanka.

Moderator: Rev. R. N. WIEMAN, B.D., M.TH.

CHURCH OF SOUTH INDIA

The Church of South India came into being in 1947 by a union of four Anglican Dioceses, four Methodist Districts and eight Councils of the South India United Church. About 5,000 members.

Bishop: Rt. Rev. D. J. AMBALAVNAR, B.A., B.D., M.TH., Jaffna Diocese, Vaddukoddai.

ROMAN CATHOLIC CHURCH

Archbishop: H.E. Cardinal THOMAS COORAY, O.M.I., B.A., PH.D., D.D., Metropolitan; Archbishop's House, Colombo 8. There are 11 Bishops.

THE PRESS

NEWSPAPERS

DAILIES

Newspapers are published in Sinhala, Tamil and English. There are three main newspaper publishing groups: Associated Newspapers of Ceylon Ltd., Independent Newspapers Ltd. and Times of Ceylon Ltd. In February 1973 legislation was passed setting up a Press Council of five members and imposing controls on newspapers, notably on the publication without official approval of Cabinet proceedings. In July 1973 ownership of Associated Newspapers was transferred by legislation, the Public Trustee acquiring 75 per cent of the shares for sale to the public, co-operative societies, trade unions, journalists and newspaper employees, but not to other newspaper groups.

Aththa: 95 Cotta Rd., Colombo 8; Sinhala; f. 1965; Communist; Editor B. A. SIRIWARDENE; circ. 41,000.

Ceylon Daily Mirror: c/o Times of Ceylon Ltd., 3 Bristol St., Colombo 1; f. 1961; English; published by the Times of Ceylon Ltd.; independent; Editor (Vacant); circ. 31,500; Sunday edition, *Sunday Mirror*.

Ceylon Daily News: Lake House, P.O.B. 248, Fort, Colombo; f. 1918; morning; published by the Associated Newspapers of Ceylon Ltd.; Editor S. TATHIRABITANA; circ. 67,537.

Ceylon Observer: Lake House, P.O.B. 248, Fort, Colombo; f. 1834; evening and weekly; published by the Associated Newspapers of Ceylon Ltd.; Editor W. LIONEL FERNANDO; circ. evening 8,151; weekly 83,632.

Dinamina: Lake House, P.O.B. 248; Fort, Colombo; f. 1909; morning; Sinhala; published by the Associated Newspapers of Ceylon Ltd.; Editor T. B. PERAMUNE TILLAKE; circ. 123,784.

Dinapathi: 5 Gunasena Mawatha, Colombo 12; Tamil; published by Independent Newspapers Ltd.; Editor S. T. SIVA NAYAGAM; circ. 34,400.

Eelanaadu: f. 1959; published by Eelanaadu Ltd.; Man. Editors K. P. HARAN; N. SABARATNAM.

Janadina: 47 Jayantha Weerasekera Mawatha, Colombo 10; Sinhala; published by Suriya Printers and Publishers Ltd.

Janata: Lake House, D. R. Wijiwardene Mawatha, Colombo; f. 1953; evening; Sinhala; published by the Associated Newspapers of Ceylon Ltd.; Editor D. F. KARIYAKARAWANA; circ. 37,908.

Lankadipa: Times of Ceylon Ltd., 3 Bristol St., Colombo 1; f. 1947; Sinhala; Editor D. H. ABEYSINGHE; circ. 510,000.

Mithran: 185 Grandpass Rd., Colombo 14; Tamil; published by Express Newspapers Ltd.; Editors K. V. S. VAS, K. SIVAPIRAGASAM.

Thinakaran: Lake House, Dr. Liipwarlene Nawzlta, Colombo; f. 1932; morning; Tamil; published by the Associated Newspapers of Ceylon Ltd.; Editor R. SIVAGURUNATHAN; circ. daily 35,081.

Virakesari: 185 Grandpass Rd., Colombo 14 (P.O.B. 160); f. 1930; morning; Tamil; Editor K. SIVAPRAGASAM; circ. 24,680.

SUNDAY PAPERS

Janasathiya: 47 Jayantha Weerasekara Mawatha, Colombo 10; Sinhala; published by Suriya Printers and Publishers Ltd.; Editor NIMAL HORANA.

Observer (*Magazine Edition*): f. 1923; Editor MERVYN DE SILVA (see *Ceylon Observer* above).

Shri Lankadipa: 3 Bristol St., Colombo; publ. by Times of Ceylon Ltd.; f. 1951; Sinhala; Editor D. H. ABEYSINGHE; circ. 120,000.

Silumina: Lake House, P.O.B. 248, Fort Colombo; f. 1930; Sinhala; Editor WIMALASIRI PERERA; circ. 366,000.

Sunday Times: P.O.B. 159, Colombo 1; f. 1923; independent; Editor H. E. R. ABAYASEKARA; circ. 36,000.

Thinakaran Vaara Manjari: Lake House, P.O.B. 1217, Fort, Colombo; f. 1948; Editor R. SIVAGURUNATHAN; circ. (Sunday edition) 39,247.

PERIODICALS

WEEKLIES

Ceylon Government Gazette: Government Press, P.O.B. 500, Colombo; f. 1802; official Government publication; circ. 54,364.

Ceylon News: Lake House, P.O.B. 248, Fort Colombo; f. 1938; articles from the *Ceylon Observer* and the *Ceylon Daily News*; published by the Associated Newspapers of Ceylon Ltd.

Chintamani: 5 Gunasena Mawatha, Colombo 12; Tamil; published by Independent Newspapers Ltd.; Editor S. T. SIVA NAYAGAM; circ. 55,700.

Desabhimani: 91 Cotta Rd., Colombo; Tamil; published by the Communist Party; Editor K. RAMANATHAN; circ. 10,000.

Forward: Colombo; English; Communist; circ. 9,000.

Gnanartha Pradipaya: Colombo Catholic Press, Colombo 8; Sinhala; National Catholic paper; Chief Editor HECTOR WELGAMPOLA; circ. 26,000.

Janawegaya: 29 Jayantha Weerasekera Ave., Colombo 10; f. 1973; Sinhala; political newspaper.

Maubima: 91 Cotta Road, Colombo; Sinhala; published by the Communist Party; circ. 18,000.

Mihira: Lake House, Fort, Colombo; Sinhala children's magazine.

Morning Star: American Ceylon Mission Press, Manipay; f. 1841; English and Tamil; Editors L. S. KULATHUNGAM (English), Rev. N. SUBRAMANIAM (Tamil).

Rasavahini: Bristol St., Colombo 1; Sinhala; published by the Times of Ceylon Ltd.; Editor D. H. ABEYSINGHE.

Riveirsa: 5 Gunasena Mawatha, Colombo 12; Sinhala; published by Independent Newspapers Ltd.; Editor G. LIYANAGE; circ. 170,000.

Samadharmam: 47 Driebergs Ave., Colombo 10; Tamil; organ of the Lanka Samaja Party, section of the Fourth International.

Sarasaviya: Lake House, P.O.B. 248, Fort, Colombo; f. 1963; Sinhalese; circ. 38,000.

Sathiaveda Pathukavalan: Jaffna; published by St. Joseph's Catholic Press; f. 1876; Tamil; Editor Rev. Fr. G. E. M. JOSEPH.

Sinhala Bauddhaya: Maha Bodhi Mandira, 13 Maligakanda Rd., Colombo 10; f. 1906; published by The Maha Bodi Society of Ceylon; Editor-in-Chief RAJA V. EKANAYAKA; circ. 25,000.

Siyarata: 532 Galle Road, Colombo 3; f. 1947; Sinhala organ of the United National Party.

Sutantiran: 194A Silversmith Street, Colombo; f. 1947 Tamil; Editor S. T. SIVANAYAGAM.

U.N.P. Journal: 532 Galle Rd., Colombo 3; English organ of the United National Party.

Vanitha Viththi: Times Building, Colombo; f. 1957; Sinhalese women's magazine; Editor M. DISANAYAKE; circ. 40,000.

Virakesari (*Weekly Illustrated edition*): 185 Grandpass Rd., Colombo 14 (P.O.B. 160); f. 1930; Editor K. V. S. VAS; circ. 25,110.

FORTNIGHTLIES, MONTHLIES, ETC.

Bosat, The: Vajirarama, Bambalapitiya, Colombo; f. 1937; Buddhist English monthly; Board of Editors Vens. NARADA, PIYADASSI and VINITA and J. S. GOMES.

Ceylon Business Express, The: 23 Canal Row, Colombo; f. 1940; policy to extol private enterprise and teach business efficiency; monthly; Editor D. J. S. PEIRIS.

Ceylon Causerie, The: Nadaraja Bldg., Galle Road, Colombo 3; f. 1929; illustrated monthly; English; Editor ALEXIS ROBERTS.

Ceylon Commerce: Ceylon National Chamber of Commerce, 2nd Floor YMBA Bldg., Main St., (P.O.B. 1375), Colombo 1; fortnightly.

Ceylon Estate News: Lochiel, Nalluruwa, Pandura.

Ceylon Journal of Adult Education: 1 Maliban Street, Colombo; published by Ceylon Literacy Campaign; Socialist; monthly; Editor T. P. ANERASINGHE, B.A., F.R.ECON.S.

Ceylon Law Recorder: Kotte; f. 1919; legal miscellany and law report of Ceylon; monthly; Editorial Board: N. E. WEERASOORIA, Q.C., W. S. WEERASOORIA, LL.B., PH.D.

Ceylon Teacher, The: 95 Main Street, Jaffna; monthly journal of the All-Ceylon Union of Teachers; Editor A. E. TAMBER, B.SC.

Ceylon Trade Journal: Department of Commerce, P.O. Box 1507, Colombo; f. 1935; published by the Department of Commerce, Colombo; monthly; Editor-in-Chief Dir. of Commerce.

Ceylon Woman: 5 Castle Terrace, Colombo 8; English; monthly; Editor SITA JAYAWARDANA.

Duthaya: Colombo Catholic Press, Colombo; monthly; Editor Rev. Fr. OSWALD GOMIS.

Financial Times, The: 323 Union Place, P.O.B. 330, Colombo 2; quarterly; commercial and economic affairs; Man. Editor CYRIL GARDINER; Deputy Editor J. A. ALOYSIUS; Business Man. P. M. ALOYSIUS.

Guvan Viduli Sangarawa: P.O.B. 574, Colombo; Sinhala; fortnightly; magazine of Sri Lanka Broadcasting Corporation.

Industrial Ceylon: Ceylon National Chamber of Industries, No. 2-1/12a, Bristol Bldg., Colombo 1; quarterly.

Janakavi: 47 Jayantha Weerasekera Mawatha, Colombo 10; Sinhala; fortnightly; Associated Editors WIMALAWEERA PERERA and NIMAL HORANA.

Navalokaya: Gampaha, W.P.; f. 1941; Sinhala; monthly; articles on literature, art, politics, education, science, etc.

Navayugaya: Lake House, D. R. Wijewardene Mawatha, Colombo; f. 1956; literary fortnightly; Sinhala; circ. 17,753.

Public Opinion: 723 Maradana Road, Colombo 10; monthly; Editor N. G. L. MARASINGHE.

Radio Times: P.O.B. 574, Colombo; English; fortnightly; magazine of Sri Lanka Broadcasting Corporation.

Rasavahini: 3 Bristol St., Colombo; f 1956; Sinhala; monthly; Editor M. DISANAYAKE.

Vanoli Mangari: P.O.B. 574, Colombo; Tamil; fortnightly; magazine of Sri Lanka Broadcasting Corporation.

QUARTERLIES, ETC.

Ceylon Journal of Medical Science: c/o The Librarian, University of Sri Lanka, Colombo Campus, P.O.B. 1698, Colombo 3.

Ceylon Journal of Science (*Biological Sciences*): f. 1924; twice yearly; published by the University of Sri Lanka, Peradeniya Campus; Gen. Editor Prof. H. CRUSZ.

Coconut Journal: Printing House, 16, 1/17 Baillie St., Colombo; f. 1956; quarterly; Editor VALENTINE S. PERERA.

Journal of the Ceylon Medical Association: 6 Wijerama Mawatha, Colombo 7; f. 1888; quarterly; Editors Prof. N. D. W. LIONEL, Dr. N. PARAMESHWARAN.

Symposium: 36 Vajira Road, Colombo; English; literature, art and films; quarterly; Editor W. B. C. SILVA.

Trade Directory for Ceylon and Overseas: Printing House, 16, 1/17 Baillie St., Colombo 1; f. 1958; quarterly; Editor VALENTINE S. PERERA.

Tropical Agriculturist, The: Agricultural Information Division, 102 Union Place, Colombo 2; f. 1881; research quarterly published by the Department of Agriculture; circ. 750.

PRESS AGENCIES

Press Trust of Ceylon: Negris Bldg., P.O.B. 131, Colombo 1; National Co-operative news agency of Sri Lanka; receives international and Asian news which is distributed to subscribers; Chair. A. K. PREMADASA; Sec. and Gen. Man. A. W. AMUNUGAMA.

FOREIGN BUREAUX

Reuters: P.O.B. 131, Negris Bldg., Colombo.

The following are also represented: Deutsche Presse-Agentur (DPA), Tass, United News of India, Press Trust of India, Hsinhua News Agency.

PUBLISHERS

Architecture and Arts Publication Co.: 75 Ward Place, Colombo 7.

Associated Newspapers of Ceylon Ltd.: (ANCL) Lak House, P.O.B. 248, Colombo; f. 1926; nationalized 1973; Chair. A. K. PREMADASA; Sec. S. R. A. DHARMARATNE.

W. E. Bastian and Co.: 23 Canal Row, Fort, Colombo 1; f. 1904; Man. Propr. W. D. E. BASTIAN.

H. W. Cave and Co. Ltd.: P.O.B. 25, Gaffoor Bldgs., Colombo 1; f. 1876; Dirs. C. J. S. FERNANDO, B. J. L. FERNANDO.

Christian Literature Society Book Shop; Front St., Colombo 11.

Colombo Catholic Press: 956, Gnanarathapradeepaya Mawatha, Borella, Colombo 8; f. 1865; liturgical books; publishers of *The Messenger*, *The Gnanarathapradeepaya*, *The Weekly;* Dir. Rev. Fr. F. MADIWELA.

Express Newspapers (Ceylon) Ltd.: 185 Grandpass Rd., Colombo 14; publishers of *Virakesari Daily*, *Virakesari Weekly*, *Mithran Daily*, *Mithran Weekly*; Chief Editor K. SIVAPIRAGASAM.

M. D. Gunasena and Co. Ltd.: 217 Olcott Mawata, Colombo 11; f. 1915; educational and general.

Hansa Publishers Ltd.: Hansa House, Clifford Ave., Colombo 3; general.

Independent Newspapers Ltd.: 5 Gunasena Mawatha, Colombo 12.

J. K. G. Jayawardena and Co.: B.T.S. Bldg., 203, 1/13 Olcott Mawatha, Colombo 11.

Karunaratne and Co.: 145 Olcott Mawatha, Colombo 11.

Lake House Printers and Publishers Ltd.: 41 W.A.D. Ramanayake Mawatha, P.O.B. 1458, Colombo 2; educational and general; Chair. R. S. WIJEWARDENE.

Printing House: 16, 1/17 Baillie St., Colombo 1; printers, publishers, booksellers, etc.; publishers of *Ceylon Who's Who* (annually), *Coconut Journal*, *Trade Directory for Ceylon and Overseas*, *Poultry Journal* (all quarterly); Editor VALENTINE S. PERERA.

Ratnakara Press Ltd.: 74 Dam St., Colombo 12.

Saman Publishers Ltd.: 49/16 Iceland Bldgs., Colombo 3.

Sandesa Ltd.: 44A Alfred House Gardens, Colombo 3; 185 Grandpass Rd., Colombo 14.

K. V. G. de Silva and Son (Colombo) Ltd.: 415 Galle Rd., Colombo 4; Chair. K. V. J. DE SILVA; Man. Dir. RAJAH WIJETUNGE.

Sri Lanka Publishing Co.: 209 Norris Rd., Colombo 11.

The Union Press: 169 Union Place, Colombo 2.

Union Printing Works: 210 Srimath Bennett Soysa Vidiya, Kandy; printers, publishers, bookbinders; Propr. Mrs. LEELAWATHIE GUNERATNE.

RADIO

National

Sri Lanka Broadcasting Corporation: Torrington Square; P.O.B. 574, Colombo 7; f. 1967; under Ministry of Information and Broadcasting; controls all broadcasting in Sri Lanka; 551 broadcasting hours a week, of which Sinhala National and Commercial 170 hours, Tamil National and Commercial All Asia 140 hours, Hindi All Asia Commercial 58 hours, English National and Commercial All Asia 160½ hours, Education Service 22½ hours; Chair. and Dir.-Gen. R. Tillekeratne.

Commercial

Sri Lanka Broadcasting Corporation: Torrington Square, P.O.B. 574, Colombo 7; *Domestic Services:* 191¼ hours (Sinhala 78¾ hours; Tamil 43¾ hours; English 68¾ hours); *Overseas Services:* 117 hours (Hindi 52 hours; English 46½ hours; Tamil 18½ hours); Chair. and Dir. Gen. R. Tillekeratne; Dir. English Services J. Barucha; Dir. Sinhala Services Thevis Guruge; Dir. Tamil Services K. S. Nadarajah.

In 1971 there were 500,000 radio licences.

There is no television in Sri Lanka.

FINANCE

(cap. p.u.=capital paid up; dep.=deposits; Rs.=rupees; m.=million).

BANKING

All domestic banks were nationalized in 1975.

Note: An export-import bank is to be set up to handle the financing of all foreign trade. It will be formed through an amalgamation of the foreign departments of the *People's Bank* and the *Central Bank of Ceylon* (*see* below) and is to be a wholly owned subsidiary of both banks.

Central Bank

Central Bank of Sri Lanka: P.O.B. 590, 34–36 Queens St., Colombo; f. 1950 by Act of Parliament; cap. Rs. 15m.; dep. 1,198m. (Dec. 1974); Gov. and Chair. of the Monetary Board H. E. Tennekoon; Sec. L. W. A. Weerasekera; publs. *Monthly Bulletin, Annual Report.*

National Banks

Bank of Ceylon: 41 Bristol St., Colombo; f. 1939; cap. p.u. Rs. 4.5m.; dep. Rs. 4.5m.; dep. Rs. 1,475m. (Dec. 1973); Chair. G. B. Wikramanayake; Gen. Man. M. Moheed.

Bank of Chettinad Ltd.: 256 Sea St., Pettah, Colombo; Man. P. M. Palaniappa Chettiar.

Commercial Bank of Ceylon Ltd.: P.O.B. 148, 57 Sir Baron Jayatilaka Mawatha, Colombo 1; f. 1969; cap. Rs. 5m., dep. Rs. 141,993m. (Dec. 1974); Chair. S. F. Amerasinghe.

People's Bank: G.C.S.U. Bldg., Sir Chittampalam Gardiner Mawatha, Colombo 2; f. 1961; provincial Co-operative banks taken over by People's Bank in 1975; cap. Rs. 6.7m.; Chair. Hector Abhayavardhana; Gen. Man. D. D. W. Kannangara.

State Development Banks

Agricultural and Industrial Credit Corpn. of Ceylon: P.O.B. 20,292 Galle Rd., Colombo 3; f. 1943; loan cap. Rs. 30m.; Chair. (vacant); Gen. Man. H. S. F. Goonewardena.

Ceylon State Mortgage Bank, The: 91 Horton Place, Colombo; f. 1931; Chair. (vacant); Gen. Man. H. B. Kapuwatte.

Development Finance Corpn. of Ceylon: 9 Horton Place, Colombo 7; f. 1955; Chair. W. Tennekoon; Gen. Man. S. Kanagaratnam.

Foreign Banks

Chartered Bank, The: 38 Bishopsgate, London, E.C.2; 17 Queen St., Colombo; f. 1853; Man. P. J. McNamara.

Grindlays Bank Ltd.: 23 Fenchurch St., London, EC3P 3ED; 37 York St., P.O.B. 112, Colombo 1; 142 Dam St., Colombo 12.

Hatton National Bank Ltd.: 16 Janadhipathi Mawatha, Fort, Colombo 1; cap. and dep. Rs. 292,563.3; Chair. E. J. Cooray; Gen. Man. M. Dharmaraja.

Habib Bank (Overseas) Ltd.: Karachi, Pakistan; Ceylon Office; 163 Keyzer St., Colombo (P.O.B. 1088).

Hongkong and Shanghai Banking Corporation: 24 Sir Baron Jayatilaka Mawatha, Fort, Colombo; Man. D. E. Steadman.

Indian Bank: P.O.B. 1384, Madras 1; P.O.B. 624, 48 Muldalige Mawatha, Colombo 1.

Indian Overseas Bank: Madras; 139 Main St., Overseas Bank Bldg., Pettah, Colombo 11.

State Bank of India: 16 Sir Baron Jayatilaka Mawatha, Fort, Colombo 1; Agent: E. R. A. da Cunha.

STOCK EXCHANGE

Colombo Brokers' Association, The: P.O.B. 101, Colombo; Produce and share brokers.

INSURANCE

Insurance Corporation of Ceylon: 267 Union Place, Colombo 2; f. 1961; Chair. H. J. Samarakkody.

Lloyds: London; Agents in Colombo: Aitken Spence & Co. Ltd., P.O.B. 5; Cable Address: "Aitken Colombo", Tel. 27861-7; Telex 1142.

TRADE AND INDUSTRY

CHAMBERS OF COMMERCE

Ceylon Chamber of Commerce: Lower Chatham St., Fort, Colombo (P.O.B. 274); est. 1839; incorp. 1895; Chair. V. L. Wirasinha; Sec. C. Dias.

Ceylon Moor Chamber of Commerce: 14 China St., Colombo 11; Pres. Sir Razik Fareed, O.B.E., M.P.; Admin. Sec. A. I. L. Marikar.

The National Chamber of Commerce of Sri Lanka: 2nd Floor, YMBA Bldg., Main St., Colombo 1, P.O.B. 1375; f. 1950; Pres. H. R. Fernando; Admin. Sec. T. Seneviratne; publ. *Ceylon Commerce.*

Sri Lanka National Council of the International Chamber of Commerce: 17 Alfred Place, Colombo 3; Chair. S. Ambalavanar; Hon. Sec. H. E. P. Cooray.

Indian Chamber of Commerce: 65 Bankshall St., Colombo 11.

Sinhala Chamber of Commerce: 203 1/12, Olcott Bldg., Olcott, Mawatha, Colombo 11; f. 1937; 2,500 mems.; Pres. K. A. G. PERERA; publ. *Sinhala Chamber of Commerce Bulletin* (monthly in Sinhala).

Subsidiary Organizations: Admin. Sec. RANJITH MENDIS.

Sinhala Development Fund: f. 1969.
Trade and Services Division.
Educational Division.
Building Development Corporation Ltd.: f. 1958 engaged in Trade and Industrial Engineering.

TRADE AND INDUSTRIAL ORGANIZATIONS

Industrial Development Board of Ceylon: No. 615 Galle Rd., Katubedda, Moratuwa; f. 1966 under Ministry of Industries and Scientific Affairs for the encouragement, promotion and development of the small-scale industries sector.

All Ceylon Small Industries Association: 146/4 First Cross St., Colombo 11.

All Ceylon Trade Chamber, The: 212/45, 1/3 Gas Works St., Colombo 11.

Ceylon Association of Manufacturers: c/o Ceylon Chamber of Commerce, P.O.B. 274, Colombo; f. 1955; Chair. R. N. HAPUGALLE; Sec. C. DIAS.

Ceylon Hardware Merchants Association: 449 Old Moor St., Colombo 12.

Ceylon Merchants' Chamber: De Mel Building, Chatham St., Colombo; f. 1926.

Ceylon National Chamber of Industries: 2-1-12A, Bristol Bldg., Colombo 1; f. 1960; 370 mems.; Chair. E. J. COORAY; Chief Exec. P. SANGARAPPILLAI. Publ. *Industrial Ceylon* (quarterly).

Sri Lanka Pharmaceutical Traders Association: P.O.B. 875, Colombo 12; Pres. J. CAMILLUS.

Ceylon Planters' Society, The: P.O.B. 46, Kandy; f. 1936; 1,247 mems.; Chair. W. A. DE SILVA; Sec. A. R. RAJENDRAM; 20 branch organizations; publ. *The Bulletin* (quarterly).

Sri Lanka Tea Board: P.O.B. 295, 574 Galle Rd., Colombo 3; f. 1976 to promote and expand tea consumption in world markets; Chair. AJIT GUNATILLEKE (Sec., Ministry of Plantation Industries).

Ceylon Textile Chamber: Australia Buildings, Colombo 1; f. 1942; 118 mems.; Chair. L. E. J. FERNANDO LAKRAJASINGHA, J.P.; Admin. Sec. LAMBERT DE SILVA.

Ceylonese Textile Traders' Association: 5, 2nd Cross Street, Colombo.

Chamber of Ceylonese Merchants by Descent: 146, 9/1 First Cross St., Colombo 11.

Coconut and General Products Exporters' Association: c/o The Ceylon Chamber of Commerce, P.O.B. 274, Colombo; Chair. W. KARUNARATNE; Sec. C. DIAS.

Coconut Marketing Board: 11 Duke St., Colombo 1; f. 1972; Board appointed under statute by Minister of Plantation Industry; Chair. Dr. S. TILAKARATNE; Gen. Man. S. GUNASEKERA.

Colombo Brokers' Association, The: P.O.B. 101, 59 Janadipathi Mawatha, Colombo 1; f. 1904.

Colombo Lighterage Co's Association: 140–142 Prince St., Fort, Colombo.

Colombo Rubber Traders' Association, The: P.O.B. 274, Colombo; f. 1918; Chair. P. A. SILVA; Sec. C. DIAS; The Secretary, Ceylon Chamber of Commerce (*ex-officio*).

Colombo Tea Traders' Association: P.O.B. 274, Colombo; f. 1894; Chair. R. WIJERATHE; Sec. C. DIAS.

Export Promotion Council of Ceylon: 5 Charlemont Rd., Colombo 6; f. 1960; commercial consultants and job placement bureau; publ. *Directory of Manufacturers and Industrialists* (annually).

Low-Country Products Association of Ceylon: 40 1/1 Upper Chatham St., Colombo 1; f. 1908; Chair. S. WILLIAM; Hon. Sec. M. H. G. A. BRITO-MUTUNAYAGAM; 130 mems.

Mercantile Chamber of Ceylon: 99-2/62 Gaffoor Building, 2nd Floor, Main St., Colombo 1; f. 1930; 350 mems.; Admin Sec., K. T. SHANMUGAM.

Sri Lanka Importers, Exporters and Manufacturers' Association: 26 Reclamation Rd., P.O.B. 1050, Colombo 11; f. 1955; Pres. (vacant); Hon. Gen. Sec. HERBERT R. PERERA, J.P.

Sri Lanka State Trading Corporation: Colombo; f. 1971; largest government import and export organization.

Tea Research Institute of Ceylon: St. Coombs, Talawakele; f. 1925 to research into all aspects of tea production and manufacture, and to provide and publish information derived from this research; 4 brs.; 60 research workers; Chair. D. S. JAYAWICKRAMA; Dir. M. A. V. DEVANATHAN.

THE CO-OPERATIVE MOVEMENT

The most important organizations on the consumer side are the Wholesale Stores Unions, which handle all foodstuffs and miscellaneous goods supplied by the Co-operative Wholesale Establishment, as well as running a large number of retail stores. The Co-operative Wholesale Establishment is at the head of the consumer co-operative movement. It was founded in 1943 and is administered by an autonomous Board of Directors.

EMPLOYERS' ORGANIZATIONS

Ceylon Estates Employers' Federation: 73/1 Kollupitiya Rd., Colombo 3 (P.O.B. 473); f. 1944; 338 mems.; Pres. S. M. DIAS; Sec. A. M. S. PERERA.

Planters' Association of Ceylon: Colombo; Chair. C. WIJENAIKE.

Employers' Federation of Ceylon: P.O.B. 858, 73/1 Kollupitiya Rd., Colombo 3; f. 1929; mem. International Organization of Employers; Chair. HENRY PIERIS; Sec. E. S. APPADURAI.

TRADE UNIONS

All Ceylon Federation of Free Trade Unions (ACFFTU): 94; 1/6 York Bldg., York St., Colombo 1; 6 affiliated unions, 65,000 mems.; Pres. W. K. WIJEMANNE; Gen. Sec. ANTONY LODWICK.

Ceylon Federation of Labour (CFL): No. 457 Union Place, Colombo 2; 15 affiliated unions; 300,000 mems.; Pres. Dr. N. M. PERERA; Gen. Sec. BATTY WEERAKOON.

Ceylon National Trade Union Confederation (CNTUC): 63, 1/7 Hidramani Bldg., Chatham St., Colombo 1; f. 1966; combined membership 457,000; Gen. Sec. V. ANNAMALAY.

Ceylon Trade Union Federation (CTUF): 123 Union Place, Colombo; f. 1941; 24 affiliated unions; 35,271 mems.; Sec.-Gen. N. SANMUGATHASAN.

Ceylon Workers' Congress (CWC): 72 Ananda Coomaraswamy Mawatha, Colombo 7; f. 1940; mainly plantation workers; 395,775 mems.; Pres. S. THONDAMAN; Sec. M. S. SELLASAMY; publs. *Congress News* (fortnightly in English), *Congress* (weekly in Tamil).

emocratic Workers' Congress (DWC): 14 Sunethra Lane, Thimbirigasyaya Rd., Colombo 5; f. 1956; 398,165 mems.; Pres. ABDUL AZIZ; Sec. V. P. GANESAN.

overnment Workers' Trade Union Federation (GWTUF): 22 affiliated unions; 100,000 mems.; controlled by the Lanka Sama Samaja Party.

ublic Service Workers' Trade Union Federation (PSWTUF): P.O.B. 500, Colombo; 100 affiliated unions; 100,000 mems.; Pres. J. A. K. PERERA; Gen. Sec. PIYADASA ADIPOLA.

ri Lanka Independent Trade Union Federation (SLITUF): 213 Dharmapala Mawatha, Colombo 7; f. 1960; 35 affiliated unions; 65,132 mems.; affiliated to Sri Lanka Freedom Party; Pres. HERBERT WICKRAMASINGHE; Gen. Sec. ANANDA DASSANAYAKE.

nion of Post and Telecommunication Officers: 11/4 Duke St., P.O.B. 15; Colombo 1; f. 1945; Pres. L. G. D. WICKREMASINGHE; Hon. Gen. Sec. U. L. BASIL DE SILVA; publ. *Postmark*.

MAJOR INDUSTRIAL COMPANIES

STATE CORPORATIONS

The following are government-sponsored, profit-making orporations:

eylon Cement Corporation: Independence Square, Colombo 7; factory at Kankesanturai and another at Puttalam; combined capacity of factories meets country's requirements and provides for export.

eylon Ceramics Corporation: Thumbowila, Piliyandala; factories at Piliyandala and Negombo; makes entire range of domestic crockery, sanitary ware, electrical porcelain, mosaic tiles, ultra-marine blue, scouring powder; refines its own kaolin and supplies refined kaolin to other industries; brick and tile factories at Bangademya, Anuradhapura, Weuda, Yatiyana, Odduchuddan, Irakkamam, Mahiyangana and Bollegala make roofing tiles, bricks, floor tiles, etc.

eylon Fertilizer Corporation: 35 W. A. D. Ramanayake Maw; factory at Ḥunupitiya.

eylon Fisheries Corporation: Rock House Lane, Mutwal, Colombo 15; f. 1964; main harbours at Mutwal and Galle; exports fish and fish products.

eylon Galvanising Industries Ltd.: Lady Catherine Estate Rd., P.O.B. 35, Ratmalana; f. 1967; cap. p.u. Rs. 3,750,000; manufactures galvanized steel sheets; Man. Dir. V. BALASUBRAMANIAM; Dir. K. SEIMIYA; 63 employees; Sales (1974) 7,538,762.

eylon Hotels Corporation: P.O.B. 259, 63 Janadhipathi Mawatha, Colombo 1; Chair. LLOYD WETTASINGHE; Gen. Man. N. SILVA.

eylon Leather Products Corporation: 141 Church Rd., Mattakkuliya, Colombo 15; manufacture and export of footwear, sports goods and leather goods; Chair. I. O. K. G. FERNANDO; Gen. Man. D. P. M. DAHANAYAKE.

eylon Mineral Sands Corporation: 167 Sri Vipulasena Mawatha, P.O.B. 1212, Colombo; ilmenite plant at Pulmoddai, rutile/zircon plant at China Bay.

eylon Oils and Fats Corporation: Seeduwa; f. 1958; manufacturers and exporters of mixed fatty acids, glycerine and compounded animal feeds.

eylon Petroleum Corporation: 113 Galle Rd., Colombo 3; terminal at Kolonnawa, Colombo; refinery at Sapugaskanda; controls **Colombo Gas**(1975); supplies gas for Government and private consumption; cap. (1975) £156,000.

Ceylon Plywoods Corporation: 420 Bauddhaloka Mawatha, Colombo 7; factory at Gintota, woodwork complex at Kosgama, timber extraction project at Kanneliya.

Ceylon Silks Ltd.: 50/22 Mayura Place, P.O.B. 132, Colombo 6; f. 1962; cap. Rs. 12m.; manufacture of rayon and synthetic textiles; Chair. G. CUMARANATUNGE; Consultant Adviser S. SANTANAM; 700 employees.

Ceylon State Hardware Corporation: 242 Havelock Rd., Colombo 5; factory at Yakkala, Cast Iron Foundry at Enderamulle.

Ceylon Steel Corporation: Office and works, Oruwala, Athurugiriya; f. 1961; steel rolling, manufacture of wire products, steel castings, machine tools, metallographic work and testing, etc.; cap. Rs. 121m.; Dirs. Prof. K. K. PERERA, Prof. S. TILAKERATNE, B. MANUKULASURIYA, Dr. J. S. GUNASEKERA, Prof. A. R. T. DE SILVA, L. N. DE L. BANDARANAIKE.

Ceylon Tea Export Corporation: f. 1971; handles exports to Communist countries.

Eastern Paper Mills Corporation: 356 Union Place, Colombo 2; paper boards, printing, pulp; Chair. K. C. THANGARAJAH; Gen. Man. A. B. PADMAPERUMA; factory at Valaichchenai.

Government of Sri Lanka (Ceylon) Successor to the Business Undertaking of British Ceylon Corporation Ltd.: P.O.B. 281, Colombo; soap, refined coconut oil, etc.

National Salt Corporation: 110 Sir James Peiris Mawata, Colombo 2; sea urns at Hambantotta and Mannar.

National Small Industries' Corporation: 181 Sir James Peiris Mawata, Colombo 2.

National Textile Corporation: 16 Gregory's Rd., Colombo 7; factories at Veyangoda, Thulhiriya and Pugoda.

Paranthan Chemicals Corporation: P.O.B. 1489, 29 Melbourne Ave., Colombo 4; factory at Paranthan.

Sri Lanka Sugar Corporation: 651 Elvitigala Mawatha, Colombo 5; factory at Galoya.

Sri Lanka Tyre Corporation: Nungamugoda, Kelaniya; factory at Kelaniya.

State Engineering Corporation: 120 W. A. D. Ramanayake Mawatha, Colombo 2.

State Fertilizer Manufacturing Corporation: 21 Anderson Rd., Colombo 5; f. 1966; Project Man. T. RODRIGO.

Sri Lanka State Flour Milling Corporation: 3-1/1 Station Rd., Colombo 3; mill at Mutuwal, Colombo 15.

United Motors Ltd.: P.O.B. 697, 100 Hyde Park Corner, Colombo 2; government acquired 1972; assembles motor vehicles, manufactures motor spares; Competent Authority L. C. WILLIAMS, B.E., F.I.E. (Ceylon), F.I.C.E.; Gen. Man. P. B. R. WICKREMASEKERA; 300 employees; Sales (1971–72) Rs. 15m.

A State Timber Corporation was inaugurated in 1968; functions include extraction of timber, saw milling, running of timber sales depots, exploration of possibilities of increased timber exploitation.

PRIVATE COMPANIES

The following are among the major private manufacturing companies in Ceylon, arranged in alphabetical order:

Aitken, Spence and Co. Ltd.: Lloyd's Bldgs., P.O.B. 5, Colombo; f. 1871; handles shipping, insurance, estate agency, travel and tourism, engineering, printing and carton manufacturing; Man. Dir. C. P. DE SILVA, B.SC. (Hons.), F.C.A.; 350 employees; Sales (1974) Rs. 10.2m.

Allied Industries Ltd.: Third Floor, Chartered Bank Bldg., Queen St., Colombo 1; coated stainless and carbon steel razor blades, paper clips, hair pins and clips; Chair. and Man. Dir. M. P. S. WIJAYAWARDENA.

Asbestos Cement Industries Ltd.: 175 Armour St., Colombo 12; cap. Rs. 7.5m.; asbestos cement products; Chair. T. C. A. DE SOYSA; Man. Dir. M. GANESAN.

Asian Electrical and Mineral Industries Ltd.: P.O.B. 1091, 411 Ferguson Rd., Colombo 15; f. 1969; manufactures Tungsram electric bulbs; Chair. RAY DE COSTA; Accountant/Chief Exec. D. E. G. ARULANANTHAM; 85 employees.

Associated Battery Manufactures (Ceylon) Ltd.: 481 Darley Rd., Colombo 10; f. 1960; manufactures batteries, battery components and antimonial lead; Chair. E. J. COORAY; 146 employees; Sales (1975) Rs. 14,830,000.

Associated Motorways Ltd.: 185 Union Place, Colombo 2; f. 1951; tyre rebuilding, rubber goods and rubber compounds; factories at Kalutara.

Browns Group Industries Ltd.: 481 Darley Rd., Colombo 10; air conditioners, ceiling fans, spring bed frames, agricultural trailers and implements, hardware, plastic goods, etc.

Ceylon Cold Stores Ltd.: P.O.B. 220, Colombo; manufacturers, wholesalers, retailers of food and beverages; exports sea food, spices, essential oils, fruit juices and processed meats.

Ceylon Cycle Industry Ltd.: Hokandara, Pannipitiya; bicycles.

Ceylon Pencil Company Ltd.: 94 Parakrama Rd., Peliyagoda; pencils and ball-point pens; Man. Dir. D. S. MADANAYAKE.

Ceylon Synthetic Textile Mills Ltd.: 752 Baseline Rd., Colombo 9; synthetic textiles, exports to Europe, Africa and Japan.

Contracts and Supplies Co.: P.O.B. 487, Colombo; f. 1960; importers of electrical and mechanical plant and equipment; engineers for water supply projects; 12 agencies; Man. Prop. R. CUMARASAMY; Imports Man. T. KANESHALINGAM; 72 employees; Sales (1972–73) Rs. 3.2m.

Contracts and Supplies (Mfg.) Ltd.: f. 1974; govt. approved manufacturers of CEYGMA water pumps; Man. Dir. R. CUMARASAMY; Exports Man. T. KANESHALINGAM; 90 employees; Sales (1974–75) Rs. 6.3m.

Glaxo Ceylon Ltd.: P.O.B. 1653, Colombo 1; infant milk foods and pharmaceuticals; Chair. G. ELLIS; Gen. Man. C. M. PIACHAUD.

Hayleys Ltd.: 400 Deans Rd., Colombo 10; f. 1952, originally Chas. P. Hayley and Co. f. 1878; handles the export of coir fibre and yarn, synthetic and natural fibre, twine, activated carbon, coconut shell charcoal; manufacture of agricultural and spraying equipment, formulation of crop protection and household chemicals; import of dyes and chemicals, veterinary preparations, engineering and office equipment; 10 subsidiaries; Man. Dirs. G. C. BOBBIESE, D. S. JAYASUNDERA, J. W. B. PERERA, E. S. R. DAVID; 2,000 employees; cap. p.u. (1976) Rs. 12m.

Hentley Garments Ltd.: 10 Old Airport Rd., Ratmalana; f. 1953; manufactures and exports clothes; Man. Dir. R. N. CHOKSY; Group Finance Man. V. SANGARAPILLAY; 1,085 employees.

H. Don Carolis & Sons Ltd. and **Parquet (Ceylon) Ltd.:** P.O.B. 48, Keyzer St., Colombo 11; f. 1860; exporters of wooden furniture, handicrafts and tea, and exporters of parquet flooring.

Hirdaramani Industries Ltd.: 65 Chatham St., Colombo clothing.

Indo-Ceylon Leather Company Ltd.: 80 Prince St., Colomb 2; tanners.

Jinasena Ltd.: P.O.B. 196, 4 Hunupitiya Rd., Colombo f. 1967, originally Jinasena and Co. f. 1905; manufactures agricultural machinery and surgical apparatu industrial agents; Man. Dir. T. N. JINASENA; Finan Dir. R. T. JINASENA; 200 employees; Sales (1974–7 Rs. 13m.

Lever Bros. (Ceylon) Ltd.: 258 Grandpass Rd., Colombo 1 f. 1938; soaps, cosmetics, toilet preparations, oils an fats; Chair. and Man. Dir. T. W. ELLIOTT.

Maliban Biscuit Manufacturers Ltd.: 389 Galle Rd Ratmalana.

Mercantile Motors and Industries Ltd.: 28 Sunethra De Rd., Kohuwela Nugegoda; f. 1969; automobile a general engineers, used car dealers; Chair. G. ONDAA JIE; Man. Dir. V. ONDAATJIE; 75 employees.

Modern Confectionery Works: P.O.B. 1100, 663 Prince Wales Ave., Colombo 14; f. 1945; Proprietor SELVAM KAGOO; Gen. Man. A. B. SUNDARARAJ KAGO

Nayagams Ltd.: Ragama Rd., Welisera, Ragama P.C f. 1959; manufactures electrical accessories, aluminiu and plastic goods; metallizing and printing on plastic Chair. and Man. Dir. S. M. NAYAGAM; Dir. and Facto Man. M. N. K. NAYAGAM; 200 employees; Sales (197 74) Rs. 2,200,000.

Reckitt and Colman of Ceylon Ltd.: Borupana Ferry Rd Ratmalana; f. 1962; manufactures pharmaceutical cosmetics and household products; Man. Dir. J. C. I DE MEL; 190 employees.

Richard Pieries and Co. Ltd.: 69 Hyde Park Corne Colombo 2; goods from rubber and latex foam, PV cloth.

Rio Paint Industries Ltd.: Main Rd., Attidiva, Dehiwal f. 1965; manufactures paint; Man. Dir. U. G. PERERA; Sales (1971–72) Rs. 500,000.

D. Samson Industries Ltd.: P.O.B. 46, Bataduwa, Gall f. 1962; manufactures and exports footwear, leath and travel goods; Chair. D. SAMSON RAJAPAKS Man. D. K. RAJAPAKSA; 300 employees.

Sri Lanka Distilleries Ltd.: Wadduwa; f. 1945; disti arrack, gin and rectified spirits; Man. Dir. M. V. E. COORAY; Sec. J. C. W. SILVA; 50 employees.

United Garments International Ltd.: 8 Old Airport Rd Ratmalana; manufactures and exports clothing; Ma Dir. W. SELLAMUTTU.

Usha Industries Ltd.: 68 Attidiya Rd., Ratmalana; f. 196 engaged in manufacture of sewing machines ar electric fans; Chair. Sir CYRIL DE ZOYSA; Man. Di K. W. G. ATUKORALE; 240 employees; Sales (1972–7 Rs. 6m.

Wellawatte Spinning and Weaving Mills: 324 Havelo Rd., Colombo 6; textiles.

TRANSPORT

RAILWAYS

Ceylon Government Railway: P.O.B. 355, Colombo 1 operates a network of about 1,396 km.; Gen. Ma V. T. NAVARATNE.

All railways are state-owned.

ROADS

Public Works Department: Ministry of Irrigation, Power, and Highways, Colombo; this Ministry maintains about 22,339 km. (1973) of roads. There is a national omnibus service with about 3,000 vehicles.

Ceylon Transport Board: 200 Kirula Rd., Colombo 5; f. 1957; nationalized organization reponsible for road passenger transport services; Chair. J. C. T. Kotalawala; Sec. Mahinda Elayaperuma; publs. *Transport News* and *Transport Management*.

SHIPPING

Colombo is one of the most important ports in the East and is situated at the junction of the main trade routes. The other main ports of Sri Lanka are Trincomalee, Galle and Jaffna. Trincomalee is the main port for shipping out tea.

Ceylon Association of Steamer Agents: 2nd Floor, Australia Bldg., York St., Colombo 1; f. 1966; primarily a consultative organization; represents members in dealings with Government Authorities; 30 mems.; Chair. M. L. D. Caspersz; Sec. B. C. Jayasuriya.

Port (Cargo) Corporation: P.O.B. 595, Church St., Colombo 1; f. 1958; responsible for all cargo handling operations in the Ports of Colombo, Galle and Trincomalee; Chair. and Chief Exec. S. M. B. Dolapihilla; Gen. Man. G. P. B. de Silva.

Shipping Companies

Ceylon Ocean Lines Ltd.: 99–2/4, 2/67 Gaffoor Buildings, P.O.B. 1276, Colombo 1; agents for Polish, Russian, East German, Romanian, Chinese and Bulgarian lines; also charter vessels; Chair. L. G. Gunasekara, b.a., ll.b.; Sec. N. N. Gunewardene.

Ceylon Shipping Corporation: No. 6 Sir Baron Jayatilleke Mawatha, Colombo 1; f. 1971 as government corporation; fleet of 9 vessels; Chair. P. B. Karandawala; Sec. M. Katugaha.

Ceylon Shipping Lines Ltd.: P.O.B. 891, Prince St., Colombo 1; controlling interest by State and the Ceylon Shipping Corporation Ltd.; Chair. T. C. A. de Soysa.

Eastern Star Lines Ltd.: 2nd Floor, National Bank Bldg., Fort, Colombo; services to Middle East, Persian Gulf and Indian coast; fleet of fourteen ships.

Messageries Maritimes Co.: 12 Sir Baron Jayatilleke Mawatha, Colombo; general representative for India, Pakistan, Sri Lanka, Indonesia and Burma.

INLAND WATERWAYS

There are 104 miles of canals open for traffic.

CIVIL AVIATION

The control of Civil Aviation is in the hands of the Department of Civil Aviation.

There are airports at Bandaranaike, Gal Oya, Jaffna, Batticaloa, Anuradhapura and Trincomalee.

Air Ceylon Ltd.: Lower Chatham St., P.O.B. 692, Colombo 1; f. 1947; operates daily internal services and international services between Colombo and Bombay, Madras, Tiruchirapalli, Karachi, London, Singapore, Kuala Lumpur, Bangkok, Paris, Malé, (Rep. Maldive); Chair. P. B. Kirandawala; Gen. Man. E. de S. Wickremaratane; fleet of one DC 8-50, one Trident 1E, two HS 748, one DC-3.

The following foreign airlines are represented in Colombo: Aeroflot, Air India, British Airways, Indian Airlines (IA), Pakistan International Airlines Corpn. (PIA), Singapore Airlines, Swissair, Maldivian Airways, KLM Royal Dutch Airlines.

Gal Oya, Jaffna, Batticaloa and Trincomalee are served by Air Ceylon; there is a domestic service from Bandaranaike to Jaffna and Tiruchirapalli, and from Colombo to Male (Maldives).

TOURISM

Ceylon Tourist Board: P.O.B. 1504, 25 Galle Face, Centre Rd., Colombo 3; f. 1966; Chair. Dharmasiri Senanayake; Dir. Publicity H. M. S. Samaranayake.

There were 39,654 tourists in 1971, 56,047 in 1972, 77,888 in 1973 and 85,011 in 1974.

CULTURAL ORGANIZATIONS

Department of Cultural Affairs: 135 Dharmapala Mawatha, Colombo 7; Dir. P. B. Weragoda.

National Theatre Trust: Department of Cultural Affairs, 135 Dharmapala Mawatha, Colombo 7; promotes development of theatre; Pres. P. H. Premawardhana; Sec. H. H. Bandara; publ. monthly bulletin of theatre news in Sinhalese.

Cultural Council of Sri Lanka: 135 Dharmapala Mawatha, Colombo 7; f. 1971; Admin. Trustee P. B. Weragoda.

DEFENCE

Armed Forces (1975): Total strength 13,600; army 8,900, navy 2,400, air force 2,300; there are also para-military forces of 16,300. Military service is voluntary.

Equipment: The army has some British armoured cars, the air force has Soviet and American planes, the navy has five Chinese gunboats.

Defence Budget: the defence budget for 1975 was Rs. 170.1m. (U.S. $24m.).

CHIEF OF STAFF

Commander-in-Chief of the Armed Forces: Maj.-Gen. D. S. Attygalle.

EDUCATION

The Department of Education in Sri Lanka was first established in 1869, so that Sri Lanka has already experienced a century of state-controlled education, but in recent years the policy and attitude of the Government towards education has undergone considerable changes. In a country where 62 per cent of the population are under 25 and 42 per cent are under 14, education is of extreme importance, and the role it plays in the future of the country cannot be over-estimated.

The formulation of educational policy is the responsibility of the Minister of Education who is assisted by his Permanent Secretary, the Director-General of Education, the central authority under legislation now in force. He in turn is assisted by an additional Permanent Secretary and three Deputy Directors-General each of whom is responsible for elementary, secondary and higher education respectively. The latter is also supervised and managed by the National Council of Higher Education established in 1966. The administration and management of the school system is divided into 15 regions each in charge of a Regional

Director. Government expenditure allocated to education at all levels has grown considerably over the last twenty years, from Rs. 120,012 million in 1952 to Rs. 657,900 by 1972. Enrolment at elementary (Level I) stage represented 89 per cent of the total population in the age range 5-11 and 33 per cent of these of school age (12-17) at secondary (Level II) stage in 1970.

Since 1947 education has been free and over 3 million children and students at present enjoy full-time education, and there are about 10,000 schools and 100,000 teachers. Ceylon has a literacy rate of 82 per cent.

School attendance is now compulsory between the ages of 5 and 13 and each year about 350,000 new children start school. Until recent years schools were streamed according to the language medium used, either Sinhala, Tamil or a small minority of English. Government policy has sought to abandon English progressively as the medium of instruction. In 1960 all denominational schools were taken over by state control.

Elementary Education (*Level* I)

This lasts seven years from 5 to 13. The first phase of Elementary Education is organized as Kindergarten classes; providing a balanced curriculum of subjects calculated to develop in particular the intellectual, social. physical, moral and practical aspects of the child's personality. Total enrolment in 1970 was 2,100,000 in 8,000 State schools with about 70,000 teachers.

Secondary Education (*Level* II)

The secondary course lasts for four years from 13 to 17. A new system of public examinations, the National Certificate of General Education (NCGE), came into effect in 1975 to replace the British examination system. A comprehensive post-primary education programme of four years (Grades VI–IX) open to everyone was set up, terminating ih the public examination for the NCGE at the end of Grade IX.

The NCGE will lay emphasis on practical subjects such as mathematics, science, health and physical education, social studies and pre-vocational studies. Admission to *Junior Technical Institutes* will be open to those with the NCGE and arrangements were being made by the Ministry of Education to organize vocational and technical courses after NCGE as well as for earlier school drop-outs. The Higher National Certificate of Education (HNCE), to be introduced in 1977, will be more employment-orientated. The *pre-university course* is being revised to benefit not merely the 10 per cent who enter university but also those who seek employment on terminating the course.

Technical and Vocational Education

Courses are provided, for which the entry requirement is six passes in the G.C.E. (or in the new NCGE), at technical institutes and colleges. Two-year full-time courses in engineering, industry, commerce and agriculture are available which may include a year of job experience. Vocational technical education to develop occupational skills begins after eight years of general education and includes two-year full-time craft or trade courses some of which may also be part-time. Total enrolment for all types of courses was about 7,600 in 1970.

Universities

The University of Sri Lanka has five campuses: at Colombo, Katubedda, Peradeniya, Vidyalankara and Vidyodaya. The yearly intake is about 5,000 and courses are offered in Arts, Sciences, Agriculture, Engineering, Medicine, Veterinary Science, Dentistry, Law and Education. The total number of students in 1973 was 14,735.

Teacher Training

Training courses normally last about two years. About 7,240 students were under training in 27 colleges in 1971.

Developments

The Government has appointed two committees to review general and technical education and higher education with a view to providing more nursery schools, increased school attendance, uniform curricula, the establishment of a University Grants Commission to replace the Council on Higher Education, a raising of general academic standards and the inauguration of three new universities in the North, South and East of Sri Lanka.

UNIVERSITIES

University of Sri Lanka, Colombo Campus: f. 1967; 395 teachers, 3,980 students.

University of Sri Lanka, Katubedda Campus: f. 1966; 320 teachers, *c.* 2,592 students.

University of Sri Lanka, Peradeniya Campus: f. 1942; 395 teachers, 4,650 students.

University of Sri Lanka, Vidyalankara Campus: f. 1959; 255 teachers including 74 part-time, 1,853 students.

University of Sri Lanka, Vidyodaya Campus: f. 1959; 142 teachers, 2,548 students.

BIBLIOGRAPHY

ARASARATNAM, S. Ceylon (Englewood Cliffs, N.J. Prentice-Hall, 1964).

COORAY, L. J. M. An Introduction to the Legal System of Ceylon (Lake House Investments Ltd., Colombo, 1972).
Reflections on the Constitution and the Constituent Assembly (Hansa Publishers, Colombo, 1971).

DE SILVA, COLVIN R. Ceylon Under the British (Colombo Apothecaries, 1950).

DE SILVA, K. M. (ed.). The University of Ceylon, *History of Ceylon*, Vol. 3 (Colombo, 1973).
(ed.). Sri Lanka, A Survey (London, 1976).

DEWARAJA, LORNA SRIMATHIE. A Study of the Political, Administrative and Social Structure of the Kandyan Kingdom of Ceylon (1707–1760) (Lake House Investments Ltd., Colombo, 1972).

FARMER, B. H. Pioneer Peasant Colonization in Ceylon: A Study in Asian Agrarian Problems (Oxford University Press, 1957).
Ceylon (in O. H. K. Spate and A. T. A. Learmonth, *India and Pakistan*, 3rd edn., Methuen, London, 1967).
Ceylon: a Divided Nation (Oxford University Press, 1963).

GOONEWARDENA, K. W. The Foundation of Dutch Power in Ceylon (1638–58) (Amsterdam, 1958).

JAYASURIYA, J. E. Education in Ceylon Before and After Independence 1939–1968 (Associated Educational Publishers, Colombo, 1969).

KANESHALINGAM, V. A Hundred Years of Local Government 1865–1965 (Modern Plastic Works, 154 Wolfendhal St., Colombo, 1972).

KEARNEY, R. N. Communalism and Language in the Politics of Ceylon (Duke University Press, Durham, N.C., 1967).
The Politics of Ceylon (Sri Lanka) (Cornell University Press, Ithaca and London, 1973).

LUDOWYK, E. F. C. The Story of Ceylon (Faber and Faber London, 1962).
The Modern History of Ceylon (London, 1965).

MARSHEL, H. Ceylon: A General Description of the Island and its Inhabitants (Tisara Prakasakayo, Dehiwala, 1969).

MENDIS, G. C. Early History of Ceylon, 4th edn. (Colombo, 1946).

MENDIS, V. L. B. The advent of the British to Ceylon 1762–1803 (Tisara Prakasakayo, Dehiwala, 1971).

NADESAN, S. Some Comments on the Constitution Assembly and the Draft Basic Resolutions (Lake House, Colombo, 1971).

NICHOLAS, C. W. and PARANAVITANA, S. A Concise History of Ceylon (Colombo, 1961).

PARANAVITANA, S. Art of the Ancient Sinhalese (Lake House Investments Ltd., Colombo, 1972).
History of Ceylon: Vol. 1 (Parts 1 and 2) (University of Ceylon, Colombo, 1959–1960).

RAGHAVAN, M. D. Tamil Culture in Ceylon (Kalai Nilayam Ltd., Colombo, 1972).

RAHULA, BHIKKHU. History of Buddhism in Ceylon: The Anuradhapura Period (Gunasena, Colombo, 1956).

REYNOLDS, C. H. B. (Editor). An Anthology of Sinhalese Literature up to 1815 (translated by W. G. Archer *et al*) (Allen and Unwin, London, 1971).

SARATHCHANDRA, Dr. E. R. Folk Drama of Ceylon (Cultural Department, Colombo, 1966).

WILSON, A. J. Politics in Sri Lanka 1947–1973 (Macmillan, London, Basingstoke, 1974).

WOODWARD, C. A. The Growth of a Party System in Ceylon (Brown University Press, Providence, Rhode Island, 1969).

WRIGGINS, W. HOWARD. Ceylon: Dilemmas of a New Nation (Princeton University Press, 1960).

South-East Asia

SOUTH-EAST ASIA
Scale 1 : 23,000,000 approx
ONE INCH TO 370 MILES
0 Miles 370 555
Towns over 1 million people
" over 100,000 people
Boundaries - international
- provincial etc.
Railways
projected
Roads
track
Airports
Canal
Marsh
Ice cap
Feet
16,000
10,000
6,000
3,000
1,500
1,000
600
300
Sea Level
Land Depression
BURMA
THAILAND
(Siam)
LAOS
CAMBODIA
VIETNAM
MALAYSIA
MALAYA
SARAWAK
SABAH
BRUNEI
INDONESIA
REP. OF THE PHILIPPINES
TAIWAN
(Rep. of China)
WEST IRIAN
South China Sea
Philippine Sea
Sulu Sea
Celebes Sea
Java Sea
Banda Sea
Molucca Sea
Seram Sea
Arafura Sea
Andaman Sea
Gulf of Siam
Gulf of Tonkin
Gulf of Martaban
Strait of Malacca
Strait of Makassar
Tropic of Cancer
Equator
100 fathoms
Rangoon
Mandalay
Bangkok
Phnom Penh
Saigon-Cholon
Hanoi
Haiphong
Vientiane
Canton
HONG KONG (Br.)
Victoria
Macao (Port.)
Taipeh
Kao-hsiung
Manila
Quezon City
Cebu
Davao
Kuala Lumpur
Singapore
Jakarta
Bandung
Semarang
Kunming
Kweiyang
Nanning
Changsha
Nanchang
Foochow
Amoy
Swatow
Hainan
Luzon
Mindanao
Borneo
(Kalimantan)
Sumatra
(Sumatera)
Celebes
(Sulawesi)
Moluccas
(Maluku)
Halmahera
Seram
Buru
Palawan
Mindoro
Samar
Leyte
Negros
Panay
Bohol
Mariana Is.
(U.S.Trust)
Guam
(U.S.)
Caroline Islands
(U. S. Trust)
Palau Is.
Kazan Is.
(Japan)
Ryukyu (Nansei) Islands
(Japan)
Okinawa
Naha
Paracel Is. (China)
Anambas Is. (Indon.)
Bunguran Is.(Indon.)
(Natuna)
Kuching
Pontianak
Banjarmasin
Balikpapan
Samarinda
Tarakan
Kota Kinabalu
Ujungpandang
(Makassar)
Manado
Ambon
Sorong
Sukarnapura
Merauke
Palembang
Medan
Padang
Jambi
Teluk Betung
George Town
Penang
Ipoh
Kuantan
Kota Bharu
Johore Bahru
Songkhla
(Singora)
Chiang Mai
Moulmein
Tavoy
Hue
Danang
Vinh
Zamboanga
Iloilo
Legaspi
Aparri
San Fernando
20°N
15°N
10°N
5°N
5°S
10°S

South-East Asia

Iain Buchanan

(with a contribution from KEITH BUCHANAN)

PERSPECTIVE

The South-East Asian world has an area of some 1.8 million square miles, almost evenly divided between the mainland and the fringing islands, and a population of over 300 million. This population is greater than that of the U.S.A. and its growth rate, and hence the area's *potential* population, is very much greater; United Nations estimates, indeed, suggest that by the end of the century South-East Asia may contain a total of some 590 million (almost one-tenth the population of the globe) as against 296 million in the U.S.A. *and* Canada. The area is important in terms of its resource endowment. It is a major source of tropical raw materials, not only foodstuffs but also industrial crops such as rubber and fibres, and it is the only major tropical area which enjoys a high degree of accessibility; this derives from its peninsular and island character and from the deep penetration of the interior by great rivers such as the Irrawaddy or Lower Mekong. It was this accessibility which explains the early integration of most of the area into the commercial, then colonial, empires of the Western European powers. The subsequent development of these colonial territories as dependent areas, whose economy was subservient to the needs of the highly developed economy of the metropolitan power, resulted in a warping and retardation of the South-East Asian economies and an impoverished and marginal quality of life for the great majority of South-East Asia's peoples.

The widespread poverty is indicated by levels of per capita income which in 1973 exceeded U.S. $500 only in Brunei and Singapore. Economic diversification is, with the exception of Malaysia, North Viet-Nam and the Philippines, still in its infancy. The agricultural sector is grossly inflated and polarized between inefficient production of food crops for local consumption and specialized production of export crops for the world market. The dangerously specialized—and hence vulnerable—character of these economies is emphasized by the dependence of their export trade on a very limited range of commodities: three primary products make up 75 per cent of the exports of Malaysia and Thailand. Modern industry is poorly developed; it employs fewer than 2 million people and, indeed, the tertiary or service sector employs 2.5 times as many people as secondary industry. And, as a consequence and a cause of poverty, social services are only now beginning to take shape: in 1950 only Thailand could show a literacy rate of over 50 per cent and as late as 1970 Laos had only 13 doctors and Indonesia a ratio of one doctor to 70,000 people (*cp.* U.S.A. 1:700). The major problems faced by the new states of South-East Asia arise from this fact of "under-development", from the disarticulation and domination of their economies which are legacies from the colonial period.

THE PHYSICAL SETTING

In broadest terms, the area can be described as the frayed-out ends of a great mountain system margined by, or occasionally diversified by, lowland areas. The upland areas include the remains of old massifs, with gently rolling topography, and zones of much younger fold mountains characterized by lofty mountains and steep slopes and diversified by active or extinct volcanic cones. These younger folds, interrupted by the sea, provide the backbone of the Indonesian and Philippine island groups, linking up with the great belt of fold mountains which rims the Western Pacific. The most striking and important of the lowland zones are the alluvial lowlands—those of the Irrawaddy, the Menam, the Mekong and the Red River and the coastal lowlands of the Indonesian islands. Except where swampy, these alluvial areas form a series of "favoured ecological niches"; in the past they were the cradle areas of some of the mainland peoples—the Burmese, the Thais, the Khmers and the Vietnamese—and today they are the most densely peopled zones since these are the zones most suited to irrigated rice cultivation. By contrast, the uplands, unsuited to intensive agriculture and often malarial, were avoided by the more advanced groups; today they are occupied by weaker and backward tribal peoples whose "slash-and-burn" agriculture imposes a low density of population.

The area experiences high temperatures most of the year and, except in "rain-shadow" areas such as central Burma or eastern Thailand, a generally high rainfall. The climax vegetation was originally forest but human interference has transformed the vegetation pattern. In the alluvial areas the natural vegetation of forest or swamp has been eliminated and replaced by a "man-made" vegetation of cultivated plants. Elsewhere, clearing for shifting cultivation has destroyed the forest vegetation and this has been replaced by a secondary vegetation of dense scrub or, in extreme cases, by open savanna grasslands. Today, as a consequence of these processes, the forest cover has become very patchy and there is great regional diversity of vegetation types. The high temperatures and high humidity which lead to a luxuriant vegetation contribute also to the luxuriance of the disease pattern. The population, especially the urban population, suffers from "social" diseases such as tuberculosis and the elimination of these is dependent on improved living conditions. The major endemic diseases are, however, the so-called "tropical diseases" such as malaria, various intestinal worm diseases, dysentery and scrub typhus. The vectors of these diseases, or the parasites themselves, have very definite ecological requirements so that the disease can frequently be controlled or eradicated by changing ecological conditions; this presupposes, however, both the technical know-how and a society organized in such a way that this knowledge can be applied. In the absence of such control, disease remains an important factor explaining the supposed lethargy and backwardness of many South-East Asian peoples.

THE PEOPLES OF SOUTH-EAST ASIA

The high degree of accessibility of the area, especially by water; its location between the two great culture-worlds of India and China; its "pioneer fringe" role in relation to the densely settled lands of eastern and southern Asia—all these things have encouraged what Dobby has described as "a constant convergence" of people on these south-eastern fringes of Asia. The result is a great diversity of peoples.

Many physical types are represented here: the negritoes of the island interiors, the slender brown-skinned Nesiots (akin to the Mediterranean race of Europe) whose distribution is from South China to the Indonesian islands, the broad-headed straight-haired Mongoloid peoples who spread southwards from China mingling with or displacing earlier peoples. Upon this racial diversity is superimposed a great diversity of linguistic groups. In the earliest period the mainland was dominated by peoples speaking languages of the Mon-Khmer group; the islands by peoples speaking Malayo-Polynesian languages. The linguistic homogeneity of the mainland was subsequently shattered by the irruption into the area of peoples speaking languages of the Sino-Tibetan group—Burmese, Thai, Vietnamese. These peoples pushed the earlier Mon-Khmer peoples into the forested uplands so that today, with the exception of Cambodia, all the major lowlands of mainland South-East Asia are dominated by people speaking languages of the Sino-Tibetan group; the peoples of the islands and peninsular Malaya remained, by contrast, solidly Malay in their speech, though many dialectal variations emerged.

A third element of diversity is in the field of religion. Hinduism and Buddhism were diffused widely throughout the region, including the islands, during the phase of Indianization in the early centuries of the Christian era. What may, for want of a better phrase, be described as the Chinese religion—an amalgam of animist, Taoist and Confucian ideas—spread south into the Vietnamese lands during the long period of Chinese control and left a lasting imprint on the social and political systems of this easternmost area. Islam reached the area in the Middle Ages. Its advance on the dominantly Buddhist mainland was confined to the Malay peninsula but it displaced Hinduism in the Indonesian islands (except Bali) and its advance into the northern Philippines was checked only by the Spaniards who had succeeded in establishing there an outpost of Spanish Catholicism. Both Buddhism and Islam (and the Catholicism which French missionaries brought to Viet-Nam) have shown themselves to be factors of considerable political importance in recent years, Buddhism as an element in the "Buddhist socialisms" of Burma and Cambodia, Islam as a component in Sukarno's "Marhaenism" or, in an extreme form, in movements such as Darul Islam.

Even before the European impact, then, the play of diverse influences on the area had resulted in a very complex human pattern. Generalizing, the high cultures of the area, those based on a sedentary rice-growing economy, were those of the great lowlands: the Burmese culture in the middle Irrawaddy lowland; the Thai culture in the plain of the Menam; the Khmer culture in the valley of the lower Mekong and the Vietnamese culture in the Red River valley; the Malay culture in the lowlands which border the South-East Asian Mediterranean. By contrast, the upland areas, including the tangled uplands and valleys of what is today Laos, were held by a diversity of tribal peoples, many of them speaking languages of the Mon-Khmer group, with rudimentary systems of social organization, and frequently dependent on a shifting cultivation and food-gathering economy. The attitude of these minority groups to their more advanced neighbours in the lowlands tended to be one of suspicion, even of hostility, and for long these upland areas constituted a sort of no-man's land beyond the effective control of any external group. Later, when the area was parcelled out between the European colonial powers, it was through these less closely settled areas that the frontiers were often drawn. This had two important consequences: first, that groups of culturally homogeneous people such as the Lao of the North or the Khmers of the Mekong delta were fragmented by the new frontiers; secondly, that each of the major political units of South-East Asia came to consist of a core region inhabited by the majority group and an upland periphery inhabited by minority peoples and very imperfectly integrated into the new states of which they were now citizens. Today, such minority groups make up more than 7 per cent of the population of Cambodia and Viet-Nam, about one-third of the population of Burma, and more than 50 per cent of the population of Laos. And to these groups must be added the later immigrants, especially Indian and Chinese, drawn into South-East Asia by the European economic development of the late nineteenth century. French plantation development in the Indochinese lands drew both Vietnamese and tribal peoples into the rubber-growing areas on the margins of the Annamite Cordillera; economic development drew Indian merchants and money-lenders into Burma and Chinese merchants into all the territories around the South China Sea; most striking of all, the development of tin and rubber in Malaya, based on Indian and Chinese indentured labour, created an entirely new ethnic situation in western Malaya, a situation in which the Malays found themselves outnumbered by these two immigrant groups. By contrast, away from these poles of development ethnic patterns underwent little change.

POPULATION: DISTRIBUTION AND TRENDS

One of the most striking features of the population of South-East Asia is its distribution patchiness. Java alone accounts for almost one-third of South-East Asia's population crowded on to less than one-thirtieth of the area's land surface; by contrast, 85 per cent is thinly settled with densities of under 50 per square km. and in six of the thirteen territories of South-East Asia the mean density is below this figure. This unevenness of distribution has been a feature from early times and is a reflection of the ecological needs of the dominant food crop—rice; the unevenness has nevertheless been increased by modern economic development, for improved agricultural services and new and better varieties of crops (as in Java) or improved techniques of flood control (as in Tonkin) made possible an increasing accumulation of population in the already closely-settled areas. Elsewhere, as in the western Malayan peninsula or in the uplands of South Viet-Nam, plantation development or mining development led to an increasing concentration of population in areas formerly only thinly peopled. It was in these areas, too, that the impact of improved health measures was most strongly felt, and these measures contributed to an increased rate of population growth. Today the extremes of density are represented by the crowded Red River lowland, where densities exceed 2,000 per square km., and the uplands of the Annamite Cordillera or parts of central Borneo, where densities drop below one-thousandth of this figure. These are crude densities; a more meaningful figure is provided by the *nutritional density* (i.e. density per unit-area of cultivated land): only in Cambodia does this drop below 300 per square km.; it is over 900 in Indonesia and over 1,000 in North Viet-Nam.

The population is growing rapidly (2.6 per cent per annum) and at a much faster rate than did the population of Europe during that continent's period of rapid population growth. Moreover, in contrast to Europe, South-East Asia's demographic revolution has not been accompanied by an economic revolution; there has been little real economic development to support the sudden increase in population. By 1980 South-East Asia will face the problem of accommodating physically and economically, in a region where the areas suited to the traditional rice economy are already densely populated and where the economy is still largely undiversified, an increase of over 150 million people. And since the majority of those who will enter the labour market in the next ten to fifteen years are already born, population planning is of only marginal relevance in confronting the immediate

Table 1

Crude Population Density and Nutritional Density, 1970

	Crude Density (per sq. km.)	Nutritional Density*
Brunei	21	450
Burma	41	314
Cambodia	39	250
Indonesia	81	960
Laos	13	502
Peninsular Malaysia	70	790
Sabah	9	580
Sarawak	8	600
Singapore	3,571	9,400
Philippines	123	514
Thailand	70	350
N. Viet-Nam	133	1,070
S. Viet-Nam	105	790

* Land planted with edible crops only.

problem; moreover, the number of potential parents already born is so large that, even if family size should fall, the absolute increment of population each year will continue to be very great. These considerations are of fundamental importance in relation to future economic planning in South-East Asia; they suggest that the optimum programme should be based not on the technologically complex and capital-intensive type of industrialization characteristic of the developed nations of the Western or Soviet blocs but rather on labour-intensive development of the type adopted by the Chinese. This high rate of population growth and the very high proportion of the population in the younger age groups (twice the figure for Western Europe) means that a very heavy burden of dependency is placed on the economy and on the shoulders of those in the working age-group. The provision of adequate schooling and technical training is a heavy burden in the countries of the West which possess the well-developed economic infrastructure on which all social services must depend; in South-East Asia such an economic infrastructure scarcely exists and the countries of the area are caught in a vicious circle in which poverty leads to inadequate schooling and poor

Table 2

Crude Birth Rates and Death Rates, Gross Reproduction Rates and Estimated Populations by 1980

	Birth Rate (per '000)	Death Rate (per '000)	Reproduction Rate	Estimated Population 1980 ('000)
Brunei	49	11	—	173
Burma	43	19	2.6	35,000
Cambodia	51	20	3.3	9,810
Indonesia	52	20	2.8	152,750
Laos	—	—	—	12,693
Sabah	53	7	3.4	826
Sarawak	54	5	3.4	1,379
Singapore	20	5	2.0	2,700
Philippines	49	18	3.5	55,267
Thailand	46	13	3.2	47,516
Viet-Nam	—	—	—	49,500

technical training facilities, and this in turn back to low productivity and poverty.

South-East Asia has a long tradition of urban life, reaching back to the trading cities and cult centres of pre-European days; the greater proportion of its population has, however, always been rural and village-dwelling. This situation has begun to change as a result of the increasing flow of migrants to the cities, and one of the most striking features of the post-independence period has been the almost mushroom growth of some of the great cities. The degree of urbanization varies; in Malaya about two-fifths of the population is urban, in the Philippines somewhat less than one-third, while in countries such as Cambodia and Thailand the proportion is much smaller and between one-eighth and one-tenth of the population is classed as urban (England and Wales over four-fifths). The pace of urbanization has accelerated greatly in recent years and in the case of the larger centres is well in excess of the rate of growth of the population as a whole; thus the population of Kuala Lumpur increased at the rate of 7 per cent per annum between 1947 and 1970, as against the national average of 3 per cent; that of Bangkok at a rate twice the average for Thailand as a whole between 1947 and 1960. Such growth rates give rise to a multitude of urban problems: housing and transportation difficulties, shortages of essential services such as water and sewerage, spiralling land prices and many social maladjustments. And the relative wealth of the cities attracts consumer-oriented industries and a disproportionate share of the country's professionally-trained personnel (in Bangkok the ratio of doctors to patients is ten times higher than the Thai average), leading to a widening gap between a stagnating or slowly developing countryside and the ostentatious and precariously-based wealth of a handful of cities. This growing divergence between the rural and urban sectors of society is an important factor making for instability; only by careful national planning and real rural development can the problem be tackled.

THE CONTOURS OF THE ECONOMY

The general features of these "under-developed" South-East Asian countries have already been indicated; let us delineate more clearly the contours of the economy.

In 1973 the estimated G.N.P. per head ranged from below $100 (in Burma, Cambodia and Laos) to more than $1,500 (in Brunei and Singapore); apart from Malaysia, no other South-East Asian country showed a figure above U.S. $300. That these figures are low by comparison with even the poorer countries of Europe needs no stressing; what can be stressed is that they are averages and conceal a distribution of wealth a good deal more uneven than would be the case in a developed country. The unevenness in the contribution of the three major sectors—the primary sector (agriculture, forestry, fishing and mining), the secondary sector (manufacturing industry), and the tertiary or service sector is indicated in table 4.

The primary sector is the largest employer of labour but its contribution to Gross Domestic Product is everywhere less than, or equivalent to, the contribution made by the service sector, a sector which is in a strict sense non-productive. Moreover, in few countries does industry contribute over 15 per cent of the Gross Domestic Product; in most countries the proportion is around one-eighth. And in all countries the tertiary sector's contribution to national wealth is much greater than the contribution of industry; in South Viet-Nam it is five times as great. Table 4 suggests a relatively inefficient agriculture (in Thailand the 78 per cent of the population employed in agriculture produces 35 per cent of the G.D.P.), yet this agriculture provides in some countries 80 per cent or more of the export earnings:

Table 3

Agricultural Products as percentage of Total Exports (by value)

	ALL CROPS	PLANTATION CROPS*
Indonesia	35	32
Malaysia	57	40
Philippines . . .	70	50
Thailand	71	24
S. Viet-Nam . . .	81	80

* Including smallholder production of plantation crops (e.g., rubber and sugar).

From this table another feature emerges—and that is the dominating role of plantation crops in the economies of some of the South-East Asian countries.

To the unevenness of income distribution and of the contribution of the three main sectors to the G.D.P. we can add a third feature—the uneven area distribution of various forms of economic activity, again more marked than in a developed economy. The tertiary sector is concentrated mainly in the capital cities, and the concentration of wealth and purchasing power in these urban areas tends to attract industrial development (largely geared to consumer industries). Greater Kuala Lumpur, for example, accounts for 44 per cent of production in manufacturing Peninsular Malaysia. The links between urban and rural development are slender; low agricultural productivity is a limiting factor as far as industry based on agricultural raw materials is concerned and the low purchasing power of the peasant masses means that, outside the towns, there is only a limited market for manufactured goods. And in the agricultural sector a high proportion of the income is derived from plantation crops produced, often by foreign companies, for overseas markets.

From this summary account it is apparent that one of the distinctive features of the economies of South-East Asia, as of many other Third World countries, is the phenomenon French economists have described as "disarticulation". The economy is not, as is the typical economy of a developed country, a smoothly running machine, all of whose components are closely intermeshed; rather does it consist of a series of more or less independent sectors: a traditional agricultural sector, largely folded in on itself, but including backward small-holding production of export crops; an enclave sector represented by foreign controlled extractive industries or plantations; and a largely tertiary urban sector, often parasitic and producing little. These elements are apparent in each South-East Asian country, and it is this disarticulation of the economy that is one of the chief causes of the area's backwardness; only by restructuring the economy as has been done in North Viet-Nam can the beginnings of progress be made.

The traditional agricultural sector has often remained isolated—and therefore largely self-sufficient in its economy—because of poor accessibility; examples of this are the north-east and north-west of Thailand, the north-east of Malaya, parts of Borneo and the larger Indonesian islands. These regions, and this applies even more to some of the minority areas in the uplands, are as yet only partially integrated into the national economy. The backwardness and low productivity of the rural sector is aggravated by another factor—that of domination. Land tenure systems make possible the domination of the peasantry by an often parasitic landlord group; lack of marketing systems exposes the peasant producer to economic domination by middle-man groups, ethnically alien as in the case of the Chinese merchants of Cambodia, Indonesia or Thailand, or the Indians of pre-independence Burma.

The enclave sector is represented by the mining industry, especially oil and tin, or by the modern plantation industry. The degree of integration of this sector into the national economy is often minimal; rather does the sector represent an extension of the economy of the developed countries and it is in the country where the operating firm is domiciled, rather than in the country where the mines or plantations are located, that the major economic decisions are taken. The sector thus has no internal dynamism and such conditions represent another form of domination, this time by outside nations. The rubber-growing areas of Malaya, or the Indochinese lands, are examples of this type of enclave; so, too, are the mining areas—the oilfields of Indonesia or the tin mining areas of Malaya.

The urban sector is also tied in less to the national economy than it is to that of the outside world. It is, as suggested earlier, a parasitic sector, consuming rather than producing, though there may be some preliminary processing of exports and consumer goods industries with a high imported content, e.g. assemblage of vehicles. It is in the major cities and especially the capital city that a high proportion of the country's administrative and commercial groups is concentrated, and the relatively high level of living of these groups creates a major demand for consumer goods, largely imported. Its economic life is nourished to a considerable extent by extraneous sources: by State expenditure which in South-East Asian countries such as Indonesia, Thailand and the Philippines is underpinned by foreign aid and customs revenues on imports often made possible by foreign aid. One result is a high level of indebtedness: the Philippines had a $4,000 million external debt and Indonesia one of nearly $16,000 million at the end of 1975. And the heavy dependence of many of these countries on external trade (exports represent between 15 per cent and 40 per cent of the G.N.P., as compared with between 7 and 10 per cent in the West at a comparable level of economic development) reinforces the external orientation of the urban sector and of those groups in urban society who live by trade.

The countries of South-East Asia thus are faced with the problem of achieving a political integration which will draw all groups, including minority groups, into the life of the nation; they face also the problem of overcoming the fragmentation of their economies (and their domination by outside groups), of re-structuring their economies and societies in such a way that development is no longer dependent on external conditions over which they have no control but on an internal dynamism in which all groups and sectors participate in a common development effort.

Table 4

Share of Major Sectors in National Economy (per cent), 1970

	PRIMARY		SECONDARY*		TERTIARY	
	(a)	(b)	(a)	(b)	(a)	(b)
Burma	68	40	8	15	24	45
Cambodia	78	41	4	15	16	39
Indonesia	65	54	8	10	24	35
West Malaysia	50	41	10	13	35	40
Philippines	65	33	9	16	23	33
Thailand	78	35	6	14	14	43
South Viet-Nam	60	32	4	10	33	54

Key: (*a*): percentage of total employment; (*b*): percentage of Gross Domestic Product

* Excluding construction.

THE PACE AND CHARACTER OF ECONOMIC PROGRESS

A rough indication of the pace of progress in the countries of South-East Asia is given in table 5; for comparison, the rate of population is added:

Table 5

	ANNUAL GROWTH RATE OF G.N.P.* per head, 1965–73 (%)	ANNUAL POPULATION GROWTH (%)
Brunei	3·7	3·8
Burma	0·7	2·2
Cambodia	−5·2	2·6
Indonesia	4·5	2·1
Laos	2·5	2·4
Malaysia	3·7	2·5
Philippines	2·6	3·0
Portuguese Timor	2·1	1·7
Singapore	9·4	1·8
Thailand	4·5	3·0
North Viet-Nam	−0·5	2·5
South Viet-Nam	−0·7	2·6

*At market prices.

It should be stressed that since the figure for the growth rate of G.N.P. lumps together agriculture, secondary industry and the service sector it gives at the best an imperfect index of real economic development. Thus, as shown above, the apparent growth rate for Thailand is relatively high but this is inflated by the expansion of the construction and financial sectors. By contrast, development of the manufacturing industries is more modest; it is partly the result of the operations of overseas companies and has not yet reached the point where the country is self-sufficient in textiles. And the continuing weakness of the agricultural sector (in a country which, according to some experts, has reached the point of "economic take-off") is underscored by the poverty and rural discontent in the east and north-east.

The general emphasis in industry in most South-East Asian countries is on the production of consumer goods (foodstuffs, textiles, paper and the like) and the output of capital goods or even machinery of all types remains limited; in the Philippines, one of the more "developed" nations of the region, for example, machinery and transport equipment together represent only one-tenth of the total industrial output. This general pattern is indicated in table 6; the developed economies of Japan and Australia are added for comparison.

Given such a situation, it is difficult to speak of any of the above South-East Asian countries as having reached the point of "economic take-off" for this latter must involve the production of a significant proportion of the producer goods, the capital equipment, on which future development and diversification depend. Table 6 suggests that most of the economies of the region are still dependent on the advanced nations of the Western or Soviet blocs for the machinery without which progress is impossible.

To this "structural warping" we must add another type of warping which has tended to be a concomitant of economic development along "free-enterprise" lines and that is the widening disparities between various social groups or various regions within the country. Economic development, unless carefully planned, may result in a growing concentration of wealth in the hands of a relatively small proportion of the population: Singapore, a servicing centre for Malaysia and Indonesia, has a per capita income three times that of Malaysia, sixteen times that of Indonesia—yet 50 per cent of Singapore's population earn per capita incomes which are less than one-fifth the national average; while in the Philippines the 4 per cent or so in the managerial and administrative groups have a median weekly income six times as high as the 61 per cent in the farming group. And the widening *regional* disparities created by development are well illustrated in the Philippines where the population of Manila has an average income two and a half times that for the country as a whole and four times that of Ilocos, Mountain Province or Visayas. Where such social or regional disparities in wealth occur in countries divided along ethnic lines (e.g. Malaya) or with strong regional or dialectal cleavages (e.g. Indonesia) their persistence, or aggravation, may result in an explosive political situation.

Table 6

Structure of Manufacturing: Contribution of Selected Industries

(%)

	FOOD, BEVERAGES, TOBACCO	TEXTILES, GARMENTS, LEATHER	MACHINERY, TRANSPORT EQUIPMENT
Burma	32.6	12.8	1.9
Indonesia	45·4	13·9	10.8
Peninsular Malaysia	25·4	2.1	6.0
Philippines	38.9	9.2	10.0
Singapore	24.1	3.8	12.5
Thailand	55·9	8.6	5.6
Japan	9.1	10.3	30.4
Australia	13.8	11.0	27.9

WIDENING INEQUALITIES IN SOUTH-EAST ASIA

Perhaps the most striking feature of development in South-East Asia since the early 1960s has been this growing polarization within the societies of the region. There has been a steadily increasing geographical polarization, with a widening of the disparities between the cities and the enclave economies on one hand and the rural hinterland on the other. There has been increasing social polarization as the gap between an affluent city-dwelling minority and the rural masses has widened. There has been growing cultural polarization between a largely western-educated, western-oriented elite and the largely illiterate, largely traditional masses.

Expressed in economic terms, the policies pursued by the free-enterprise nations of the region have not led to any effective mobilization of national resources which might wipe out underdevelopment. The opposite has been the case, for the policies followed have exaggerated the age-old contradiction between increasing wealth for a few and continuing poverty for the many. That this should be so, that there should have been no effective restructuring of society is largely due to the fact that decolonization left political power in the hands of elite groups shaped by western education and whose policies were constrained by continuing outside influences. The examples of Thailand, Indonesia and the Philippines illustrate the growing contradictions of development in South-East Asia.

In Thailand there have been impressive increases in the country's national income in the last decade but these have not been reflected in increases in rural incomes or in the generation of employment in Bangkok. Why this should be so can be seen from a comparison of growth rates in the various sectors (1966–1970):

	%
Construction	12.2
Banking, Insurance, Real Estate	19.2
Services	11.3
Manufacturing	11.7
Agriculture	3.9

As a Thai observer comments: "The recent increases in income have been too concentrated in Bangkok . . . and not enough has gone into the rural areas and provincial towns to increase the productive potential in agriculture and industry." According to a 1973 World Bank report, Thai agriculture is, at best, stagnant. Between 1962 and 1972, the Thai farmer's income remained stagnant, while the cost of living spiralled—thus, pressure on the farmer to invest has been pointless. Lacking storage facilities, he must sell rice in a buyer's market only to see its price soar due to the kind of large-scale hoarding that occurred in 1973.

In contrast to such rural stagnation, wealth has tended to accumulate in Bangkok which is becoming less part of Thailand and more an extension of the developed economies of the west, and the sharpening of regional inequalities between the capital and the impoverished interior, especially the north-east, threatens to undermine the cohesion of the Thai state. One factor in this kind of "polarizing" development is the increasing emphasis upon such marginally productive activities as tourism, which, before the end of the Indochina war, was expanding so fast that, by the end of the third Five-Year Plan (1976), it was expected to replace rice as Thailand's main export earner. A further uncertainty is introduced by the fact that much of the country's recent development has been dependent on U.S. funds disbursed as part of America's Indochina spending; according to one estimate "about half of the increase of the G.D.P. from 1965 to 1967 was attributable to military spending by the U.S. within Thailand"—between 1966 and 1971, direct and indirect U.S. military spending of about $1,750 million was equivalent to almost half the increase in Thailand's G.D.P. once more. Such spending has been an important factor in determining the type of "growth" in Bangkok, the emphasis upon military as opposed to agriculture-oriented infrastructure in the north, the pattern of "urbanization" in the north and east, and the high proportion of the labour force geared to servicing military bases (quite apart from its role in enriching the now-deposed military élite and increasingly alienating it from the rest of Thai society). In short, it has contributed more than any other factor to the polarization of Thai society and economy.

Indonesian development shows a similar polarization, accentuated after 1966 with the introduction of a "Western" model of development—opening the primary export sector to foreign private investment, and stressing self-sufficiency in rice through land improvement along the lines of the "Green Revolution", and consolidation of élite government. To tap Indonesia's vast resources of industrial raw materials, a massive foreign investment programme began in 1967, and in seven years new committed capital investment (including that in oil) rose from $200,000 to over $7,000 million. But this investment created little more than 200,000 jobs in a country with some 10 million unemployed, and the Government was called upon (so far with little results) to make greatly increased *pribumi*, or Indonesian, labour participation in foreign ventures mandatory. Meanwhile, the military-bureaucrat élite has prospered from close association with investment concentrated in the country's cities, mines, plantations and timber industries; it has formulated two Five-Year Plans—the first (1969–74) costing the equivalent of half of one year's national income and 66 per cent supported by foreign aid—to expedite "development"; and it has put the country still deeper into debt by borrowing over $16,500 million in ten years, on top of a $1,300 million foreign debt inherited from Sukarno—in 1973, 20 per cent of Indonesia's foreign exchange went to debt repayment.

By 1975, about 45 per cent of Indonesia's 8.7 million hectares of riceland had been improved—largely through BIMAS (mass guidance) and INMAS (mass intensification) schemes. But land *improvement* without land *reform* has not benefited the peasantry;

over 90 per cent of Javanese farmers still own less than 1 hectare of land, 50 per cent are landless, and tenants generally pay 60–70 per cent of their crop in rent, tax and debt repayment. Most peasants, despite near national self-sufficiency in rice, cannot achieve their own self-sufficiency. While retail prices have consistently and often rapidly risen, prices paid to producers have fallen in real terms. In the relationship between the present socio-economic structure and the play of market forces like prices, wages, and interest, the latter works in favour of those groups upon which the Government depends for support: rich landowners merely pass on their losses to those below them through larger exactions, while Indonesia's 2.5 million civil servants are entitled to various fringe benefits, often gain from two- or four-fold wage increases (as occurred in 1974) and can buy rice at 10–15 per cent of the retail price a labourer, hawker, or poor peasant must pay.

In the Philippines, a similar situation emerges. In 1974, over 1.7 million people (12 per cent of the labour force) were unemployed, and at least 5 million people underemployed; meanwhile, population grows at the rate of 3.5 per cent per annum and some 500,000 job-seekers enter the labour market annually. Since the mid-1960s increased agricultural specialization has been accompanied by a growing burden of tenancy and share-cropping for, though the contribution of agriculture to the economy has declined, the proportion of the labour force in agriculture (some 50 per cent) has not—despite the labour-displacing effect of the "Green Revolution"—and since 1963 little progress has been made towards implementing land reform measures on a scale which would significantly reduce the problems of tenancy, indebtedness, and maldistribution of rural wealth. By mid-1975 only 75,000 tenants out of 915,000 had been given preliminary titles under the 1972 land reforms. Thus, the peasant sector has been neglected, with agricultural development mainly in the plantation sector. Since 1970, for example, the rice acreage has been decreasing as more and more land is being planted with sugar; and since the early 1960s, the extension of the "Green Revolution"—with its consolidation of large-scale, capital-intensive, and monocultural "agribusinesses"—has had a clearly detrimental effect on the Filipino peasant rice economy. In the first place, the "Green Revolution" sharpened the polarization between rich and poor farmers; in the second place, as Marvin Harris points out in *Natural History* (June–July, 1972), it caused chaos in the local rice economy as a result of the inherent ecological weaknesses in its particular brand of farming. In 1969—when the Philippines finally achieved self-sufficiency in rice—President Marcos campaigned for re-election on the promise that the Republic would "never again" have to import rice: in 1971, the country was forced to import 500,000 tons of rice; since then, the annual shortfall in production has ranged from 500,000 tons to 1 million tons.

Postwar industrial development in the Philippines, relying on a policy of import substitution and occurring within the framework of the special relationship between the Republic and the United States, has been characterized by relatively rapid growth—but its efficiency, measured against world prices, is low, with minimal contribution to solving unemployment. Output is directed towards meeting the needs of wealthy urban consumers rather than the needs of the peasantry or of the export market, and there has long been an over-concentration of industrial development in the Manila area (80 per cent of total manufacturing).

It was thus inevitable that in recent years social and regional disparities should widen. The Filipino "system" encouraged this—a system built on economic and political nepotism, widespread corruption (which, according to Manila experts, consumes one-third of government revenue), and a system long sustained by heavy United States investment (some $2,000 million) and military and paramilitary involvement. It was this system that the nationalist Senator Benigno Aquino, writing in 1972, claimed had "built a self-perpetuating, lop-sided society of castes in which 1.5 per cent are privileged to enjoy the good life; the rest, the 75 per cent poor—even the 23.5 per cent middle-middle class—can barely make a living."

It was inevitable, too, that guerrilla activity would increase: in 1972, according to General Romeo Espino, the Armed Forces Chief of Staff, the "New Huk" field strength was equal to that of 1946—some 12,800 officers and men, with 8,850 fully armed. The guerrilla movements themselves claim fewer actual combatants, but a mass base which had increased to 400,000 supporters. In addition, there is increasing unrest amongst the Filipino middle classes, who see the concentration of economic and political power as detrimental to their interests. The Government's move towards strict authoritarianism in 1972, in the light of such factors, can be interpreted as an attempt to crush forcibly a growing left-wing movement and appease the strongly nationalistic middle classes, if possible, by policies which seem to offer the medium-scale entrepreneur greater scope for investment while encouraging foreign investment.

But the basic problems remain. In 1973, the Ranis Report on the Philippines' economy (commissioned by the I.L.O.) highlighted the growing polarization within Filipino society: "the past 20 years of unbalanced growth", involving highly localized and capital-intensive industrialization, concentration of ownership and control, a long-standing neglect of rural areas, and failure to implement an effective policy of job-creation, have created an "ultimately explosive" inequality in the distribution of wealth.

That these widening disparities are not inevitable consequences of development is suggested by the example of North Viet-Nam. Here, austere planning, involving the ploughing-back into development of almost two-fifths of national income, was (until the American bombing) making possible the emergence of a diversified economy. Two-fifths of the country's investment were going into the industrial sector and three-quarters of the investment in industry was in

the producer goods sector. And the danger of economic development creating regional disparities was, in part at least, being overcome by a policy of decentralization which aimed at developing "regional industry" (especially consumer goods) through the investment of human labour. This regional industry complemented the larger-scale units of the "centralized sector" so that the policy of industrial development was, like that of the People's Republic of China, one of "walking on two legs".

SOUTH-EAST ASIA'S POLITICAL GEOGRAPHY: SOME DOMINANT THEMES

After the Second World War the relatively simple political pattern of colonial days was replaced by a more complex pattern of a dozen separate national entities. These differed greatly in size and in population, in their resource endowment and, a legacy of the colonial period, in their economic orientation. Above all, they differ widely in their external alignment and the nature of their political system. In the early 1960s, some like Thailand, the Philippines and South Viet-Nam, were Western-aligned and formed part of a defence system designed to contain a hypothetical Chinese expansion; North Viet-Nam was part of the Communist world; Cambodia, Burma, to a lesser extent Indonesia were maintaining a precarious neutrality in the face of considerable external pressures; Laos was deeply split by Cold War rivalries. There was a similar diversity of political systems, ranging from the authoritarianism of Thailand or South Viet-Nam through the "Buddhist Socialisms" of Burma and Cambodia to the Communism of North Viet-Nam or the attempt at American-style democracy in the Philippines.

Yet beneath all these diversities the South-East Asian countries faced many common problems, and in their confrontation of these problems we can detect certain themes which give a unity to the area, indeed to the whole of the under-developed world. There is, first, the need to create workable institutional structures which will enable the nation to overcome the problem of ethnic fragmentation and to achieve effective mobilization of all the country's resources; here we must underline the contrast with Europe where economic development took place within existing societies which had been created over a long period of time—in South-East Asia such national societies scarcely exist. Secondly, and closely allied to this, is the search for national identity. These countries emerged from colonial status with no well-defined national territories but with boundaries which showed little regard for the ethnic or historical realities of the area. Under these circumstances, the "cult of the past", the turning back to history, myth and legend, becomes a means of creating a national consciousness; the glories of earlier periods provided an inspiration and a model for the society of today, as in pre-1970 Cambodia or in North Viet-Nam. A third theme is the tendency towards concentration of power in the hands of a strong ruler or a dominant or single political party. This is partly the result of the absence of any effective middle group and manifested itself in the organization of the state around a charismatic leader—a Sihanouk, a Sukarno, a Ho Chi Minh—who incarnated the successful struggle for independence, or single- or dominant-party governments which avoid the expensive and sometimes destructive dispersion of social and political energies associated in Asia with Western multi-party systems of government. A fourth theme was the need to bridge the gap between the masses and the small élite groups, to integrate the common man more effectively into the political life of the country. In states whose population is large or fragmented by geographical isolation or by linguistic barriers social, economic and political development depends on the encadrement and mobilization of the masses; the basis for such an encadrement has been provided by the dominant party or ideology organized around a charismatic leader: the Lao-Dong party and Ho Chi Minh in North Viet-Nam, Prince Sihanouk and the Khmers Rouges in Cambodia, the People's Action Party and Lee Kuan Yew in Singapore. Thus, in South-East Asia we have to concern ourselves not only with the political ideologies which are shaping the new nation-states but also with the personalities of the leaders who enshrine and interpret their ideologies.

Finally, we do well to bear in mind that the political geography of the countries of the Third World is being shaped not only by internal forces, resulting from the growing determination of their disinherited masses to create a decent, more human, life for themselves or, maybe, their children; it is also shaped by external forces striving to achieve a dominating position for themselves in this great belt of impoverished but resource-rich nations. The dramatic shifts in Indonesian and Indochinese politics must be seen against the background of this struggle between the United States and what is commonly termed "Communism" but which is rather a manifestation of revolutionary nationalism which rejects paternalism of all types, whether it be the paternalism of Washington or the paternalism of Moscow. The origins of the expanded Indochinese War must be sought in the determination of the U.S.A. to contain the spread of this Third World revolution and to prevent any rolling back of the frontiers of the "Free World" in an area which, to quote the President of the Bank of America (*California Business Magazine*, Sept.-Oct. 1968), is "rich in an immense variety of resources and potential capabilities . . . (in which) we would have giant, hungry new markets for our products and vast new profit potentials for our firms". It is unfortunate for the region that this U.S. pressure has progressively eliminated those governments which sought in a policy of non-alignment an escape fron the competing ambitions of the super-powers; that the "cold" war and the hot war consolidated the hold of military dictatorships in the region; that the "aid" schemes proffered by the developed nations have been more related to their own needs than to the needs of the populations "aided". And in Laos and South Viet-Nam, and more recently Cambodia, large-scale military intervention was creating precisely the political conditions the West sought to prevent—and was relentlessly destroying the social and economic fabric on which any government must ultimately rest.

INDOCHINA: THE ECOLOGY OF WAR

Both before and after the Viet-Nam "ceasefire" announced in January 1973, there was considerable discussion about the amount and nature of "reconstruction aid" to Indochina. The Nomura Research Institute of Japan estimated that Viet-Nam would need some $15,000 million, while Indochina as a whole would need $30,000 million. On the other hand, the Japanese Ministry of International Trade and Industry estimated in 1973 that Japan would be contributing $1,000 million annually to "reconstruction"; while the United States was expected to contribute a total of $7,600 million to the whole of Viet-Nam. The sums may appear small—when seen against the facts that, between 1965 and 1973, Japan's war-related trade amounted to over $6,500 million, and that the United States had—by 1973—spent some $250,000 million in fighting the Indochina War. Underlying the "aid" debate, there was intense competition between the United States and Japan for a firm economic stake in "reconstruction": aid was seen largely in terms of contracts for Western and Japanese corporations in the field of rebuilding infrastructure, factories, and urban facilities and—in South Viet-Nam—the extension of a "Green Revolution" package in agriculture, and the development of export-orientated consumer goods and assembly-line manufacturing, using one of the cheapest labour markets in East and South-East Asia (with wage levels one-third those of Singapore).

Whether or not such developments could absorb much more than a fraction of the massive pool of unemployed was seriously open to question. What was certain, however, was that any aid to South Viet-Nam, Laos, and Cambodia would need to be less for "reconstruction" than for a thorough reorganization of almost completely shattered economies and societies. The extent of the damage inflicted upon Indochina, especially over the past decade, is such that discussion of the amount of foreign aid is largely irrelevant.

Above all, it must be realized that the war in Indochina was the first war in history in which a sustained attempt had been made to manipulate—and completely transform—the entire physical and human environment of a country by means of modern, highly sophisticated technology. The natural vegetation cover, the rainfall régime, the soil pattern, the natural drainage pattern, the complex of animal life, and the complex of disease-bearing organisms were all—with varying degrees of success—manipulated to fight the enemy; and so too was the entire fabric of economic and social life of the population. The whole intricate physical and human ecology of large parts of South Viet-Nam, Laos, and Cambodia have been transformed—often irrevocably.

The war has been first and foremost an air war, in which bombing has played the major role. From 1965 to 1973, the United States dropped 7.5 million tons of bombs on Indochina—three and a half times the amount they dropped during the whole of the Second World War, and twelve times the Korean total. As a result, some 6,500 square miles of South Viet-Nam alone (about 10 per cent of the total area) have been converted into a totally infertile moonscape through craterization. In addition, by 1970, over 20 per cent of the total forested area, and 50 per cent of all cropland, had been sprayed with defoliant and crop-killing chemicals, and by 1973 some 700 square miles of land had been bulldozed clean of vegetation. Thus, by 1973, a further 20 per cent of South Viet-Nam's total land area had been virtually sterilized by defoliation, intensive crop-spraying, and bulldozing. In all, over 30 per cent of South Viet-Nam's area had been directly rendered infertile, largely by aerial war on the natural environment. Already, by 1969, according to Professor Arthur Westing, spraying had destroyed the equivalent of the country's timber needs up to the year 2000 (amounting to cash value, at 1969 prices, of over $600 million), as well as large areas of rubber plantations, and 200,000 acres of upland food-crop land. Westing underlined the significance of this by pointing out that in order to graduate from an underdeveloped to an "emerging" economy, South Viet-Nam's main hope must be in the production and export of its timber, rubber, and rice.

The severe loss of vegetation cover had two major, and inevitable, secondary effects: large-scale podsolization and laterization—the first a process whereby soil is bleached into an uncultivable sand, the second a process whereby iron compounds in the soil harden to the extent that soil becomes inert and completely impervious to all life-forming processes. Laterization, alone, has affected some 5,000 square miles of previously fertile soil in Cambodia and Laos, quite apart from its effect in Viet-Nam, while podsolization has set in over large areas of lowland Indochina—in the Quang Ngai and Quang Tri Provinces of Central Viet-Nam, for example, podsolization has occurred over more than 1,000 square miles of once fertile coastland which previously supported 900 people per square mile. As a result of the "secondary" effects of podsolization, laterization, spreading erosion, and uncontrolled run-off, the environment of a far larger area than that directly altered by aerial action has been seriously affected: for example, the 1970 floods in Central Viet-Nam were attributable largely to the heavy bombing and defoliation of the First Military Region, where the rivers have their sources; in 1969, an official report indicated the cost of the war on the South's economic infrastructure by estimating that it would take 15 years of day and night dredging to restore South Viet-Nam's internal waterways to their 1939 condition.

Quite apart from the long-term problems of "leaf abscission" and other after-effects of spraying on the existing vegetation, there is the serious problem of defoliant and crop-killing chemicals accumulating in the soil and water of both irrigated and non-irrigated lowlands in highly toxic quantities, poisoning the entire ecological cycle of plant growth and soil formation and the food-chain of human beings, animals (particularly bovines), and fish: according to scientists reporting to the American Association for the Advancement of Science, there is a proven relationship between the entry of defoliant chemicals into the food chain in Viet-Nam and a steady increase in the numbers of stillbirths, placental tumours, and child defects in the country since the mid-1960s.

Such elements of the legacy of war in Indochina are likely to endure for generations. According to Professor Westing, much of the forestland will never regenerate—the loss of leaf cover and consequent erosion have left large areas permanently barren or devoid of all but a useless bamboo or savannah-type vegetation. Of the 6,000-odd square miles of cropland sprayed between 1961 and 1970, a good proportion is back in cultivation—but over large areas the processes of laterization and podsolization have become irreversible, and remnants of toxic chemicals are still trapped in the waterways and soil of South Viet-Nam.

The direct effects upon the fabric of economic and social life in Indochina have been no less dramatic. South Viet-Nam has a traditionally village-based society, largely dependent upon small-holding wet-rice cultivation, with settlement determined by the presence of fertile and carefully irrigated soil and the location of ancestral land. What Professor Samuel Huntington has termed "forced-draft urbanization and modernization"—or the relocation of peasants from rural to urban areas, both as a result of bombing and to facilitate "free-fire zone" bombing in the countryside—has all but shattered traditional life. Between 1965 and 1973, the war in South Viet-Nam generated 6 million refugees, and the urban population increased from 15 per cent to 60 per cent of the total population, making South Viet-Nam one of the most heavily "urbanized" territories in Asia. Saigon, alone, grew from a city of 400,000 inhabitants to one of nearly four million.

By late 1972, 33 per cent of the Laotian population of 3 million were refugees, and by mid-1973 heavy and sustained bombing had generated at least 3 million refugees in Cambodia (45 per cent of the population). Such massive dislocation of settlement patterns—as well as the economic and social structure sustaining the Indochinese population—means, above all, serious distortion and regression of the entire development process. The economies of South Viet-Nam, Laos, and Cambodia are simply not geared to the demands of a large urban population; they have negligible secondary sectors (certainly in relation to available urban labour), severely damaged primary sectors (both in terms of food and industrial crops), and basic infrastructural facilities either devastated by war (as in the case of irrigation facilities, internal waterways, and marketing networks) or largely irrelevant to the needs of the immediate future (as in the case of the elaborate port facilities built by the U.S.A. in South Viet-Nam). By 1975 all countries were heavy importers of basic foodstuffs (according to the World Bank South Viet-Nam had to import at least 500,000 tons of rice in 1973, despite recent increases in the acreage of Higher-Yielding Variety, and Cambodia, whose rice acreage in 1974 was down to 45 per cent of the 1970 level, had turned from an exporter to a large-scale importer of rice within three years); all countries were heavily dependent upon foreign aid, which accounted for between 40 and 80 per cent of budgeted annual expenditure; all were importing beyond their means, and all were suffering from rampant inflation—which, combined with high unemployment and blatantly corrupt marketing arrangements, only widened the gap between the rich urban minority and the large majority of people near or below the poverty line. Here, one of the most pressing problems is that of a massive "tertiary involution" of the labour force, attendant on heavy rural-urban migration into towns whose economic structures are overwhelmingly geared to servicing and commerce and totally unable to offer productive employment to the large refugee population. As a consequence, petty tertiary occupations on the slenderest of profit margins proliferate—including touts, hawkers, beggars, and prostitutes. The process of "tertiary involution" has been aggravated by a large-scale foreign military presence, to which a good many "servicing" jobs owe their existence. The withdrawal of foreign military personnel from South Viet-Nam has already revealed the inherent instability of such an employment structure—one shared by Thailand, Cambodia, and Laos.

Thus, the economies and societies of South Viet-Nam, Cambodia, Laos, and—to a lesser extent—Thailand have been severely distorted by the Indochina War, so distorted that only a radical reorganization (rather than a piecemeal reconstruction) of the whole pattern of life can offer any likelihood of real progress. Such reorganization was clearly unattainable to the degree necessary while countries were still divided by war; thus the war's end has created the necessary conditions for effective internal development.

Certainly, the extent of devastation suffered by Viet-Nam over the past decade has been greater in the South than in the North. But since 1965, North Viet-Nam has been subject to some of the most intense bombing onslaughts in history—its heavy industrial capacity was destroyed, much of its infrastructure (including all major power facilities, railways, rail-yards, roads, and bridges) was under constant bombardment during the years of bombing, countless villages were obliterated, and—as the French geographer, Yves Lacoste, has shown—a serious attempt was made to undermine the entire irrigation system of the densely-populated Tonkin Delta (to an extent which would have proved catastrophic had the 1972 monsoon been heavier than usual). But the potential for economic disaster was far less than in the South, because of the quite different nature of economic and social organization. In particular, decentralization of the urban population, of industry, of economic and social services and of the administration, was accelerated; at the same time massive labour mobilization ensured that the farming economy—and the intricate irrigation system upon which it depended—survived the war. T. J. S. George, an editor of the *Far Eastern Economic Review*, points out that despite intensive bombing of urban areas, farmland, and economic infrastructure, the political organization and strength of nationalism in North Viet-Nam were decisive factors not only in planning elaborate defensive measures, but also in both reconstructing and rapidly *modernizing* the economy during and after the bombing. Infrastructural facilities were maintained and improved, industrial output was increased in various fields, both rice acreage and yields were increased, and large rebuilding schemes were quickly underway in urban areas.

As events during 1973 and 1974 demonstrated, foreign military intervention against indigenous forces in Indochina—despite a firepower ratio of almost 500 : 1—had gained no more than a decade of costly and pointless destruction. The victory of the National Liberation Front and the North Vietnamese in South Viet-Nam, the Khmer Rouge-led forces in Cambodia and the Pathet Lao in Laos, point to two significant facts: that the West has never really understood Indochina and its peoples and that it seriously underestimated the strength of an intensely nationalistic and well-disciplined peasant revolutionary movement.

INDOCHINA: PEACE AND PROSPECTS FOR DEVELOPMENT

By mid-1976, after more than a year of peace, the countries of Indochina, with a total population of about 57 million, had consolidated the bases of socialist reconstruction. The problems confronting the new governments of Viet-Nam, Cambodia and Laos are immense, and their solutions presuppose radical measures of reorganization and reconstruction. But solutions are neither uniform nor blindly doctrinaire: in each territory, specific historical, cultural, economic and social conditions must dictate a large measure of pragmatism. Above all, it must be recognized that all three countries have been severely affected by what was perhaps the most intense and violent war in history: in terms of its devastation of whole societies and economies, the Indochina War is unique. Never before has the materially overwhelming and technologically sophisticated military strength of a major industrial power systematically sought to destroy the very basis of economic, social and cultural life of poor and largely peasant countries in the manner attempted in Indochina. This attempt is now over, and the process of salvage and reconstruction must be determined—first and foremost—by the need to rebuild, almost from scratch, the agrarian basis of the economy, coupled with demolition of the artificial and grossly unproductive urban tertiary structures imposed during the war.

In Cambodia, there had long been a marked disparity between town and countryside. Indeed, the Cambodian economy was more thoroughly agrarian than that of any other South-East Asian country (with the possible exception of Laos), and the capital city represented little more than the home of the élite and a parasitic class of absentee landlords, moneylenders and traders. The seat of Khmer royalty, pre-1970 Phnom Penh, was also an enclave of Westernized metropolitanism and exploitative tertiary activities, distant from the Khmer peasantry and largely unproductive; it had little manufacturing, and the urban bourgeoisie was dependent either upon control of rural land, crops and marketing, or upon *compradore* business related to foreign firms, import-export trade and servicing. However, despite a poor social and economic infrastructure (in 1968, for example, the ratio of doctors to inhabitants was 1 : 15,000), there was no severe poverty—partly because there was little rural overcrowding, and partly because of a relatively benign land tenure system (although indebtedness was a problem). In 1970, Phnom Penh's one positive link with the countryside—the influence of Sihanouk's charismatic Royal Socialism—disappeared. The disparity between metropolis and countryside hardened into a complete contradiction.

The new Cambodian Government's policy represents more clearly than in any other territory the logic of successful peasant revolution against the parasitic dominance of city over countryside, and against a Western-backed, urban-oriented "client-élite". The evacuation of Phnom Penh in April 1975 was in keeping with this logic: it was not an instinctive reaction of antipathy or vengeance; indeed, it was—logistically—a rational move. Phnom Penh was not only a symbol of the long-standing control of Khmer agriculture by urban interests, or of five years of foreign control, oppression, and war; it was both artificial and redundant—a deformed outgrowth of alien culture, a city crammed with rural refugees who could not help themselves, be helped, or serve any useful function while there, a city that could not in any way support itself or be supported by a devastated countryside. A displaced rural population had to become rural again, resurrect its agricultural basis and resume farming as soon as possible. In addition, the nerve-centre of the old régime had to be rooted out before any new central administration could be installed. Decentralization was the obvious need: it would focus attention upon agriculture; it would also dissipate the influence of what had been a highly-centralized and almost wholly Phnom Penh-based régime, break the power of the *compradore* bourgeoisie, and eliminate the trappings of an alien culture.

The dissipation of Phnom Penh's strength, then, was an initial and essential move in the post-war reconstruction of Cambodia. So too was a rapid and forced revival of agricultural production. The area of cultivated land had fallen from 2.5 million hectares in 1969 to an estimated 800,000 hectares in 1974, and production had fallen over the same period from 3.8 million metric tons to about 950,000 metric tons, a fall in per capita production from 1.58 kilogrammes to about 0.37 kilogramme daily, marginally supplemented in later years by imports. In this respect, it is important to note that the most productive rice areas (Battambang, Kompong Thom, Prey Veng and the area south-west of the capital) were, in 1974, officially under Phnom Penh control. In addition, most rural infrastructure had been destroyed by 1975, as had nearly 40 per cent of all draught animals. Thus, even accounting for the inaccuracy of statistics in a divided country, the Khmer Rouge government faced a severe agricultural crisis and the threat of mass starvation when it assumed power in April 1975.

During the following year, all available labour was mobilized for rural work. The first planting, in April and May, was already late, and so speed was essential, with the "forced draft" nature of initial rural work dictated by sheer material necessity. But the Khmers Rouges faced another problem: unlike the Vietnamese peasantry, the Cambodians had not been politicized by 30 years of war: in the space of five years a conservative, Buddhist and relatively unhurried peasantry had been culturally uprooted and displaced, without developing any strong sense of revolutionary purpose. Thus, not only was the Government faced with a material production crisis, it was also faced with the problem of "radicalizing" a relatively unprepared peasantry to accept the rationale and the imperative of an all-out drive for speedy agricultural development and of mobilizing a sizeable urban population which had lost touch with the land. Disaffection was inevitable, in the process of telescoping a programme of radical agrarian change into little more than a year. Ultimately, the test of Cambodia's first years of revolution will be measured in terms of whether they laid the basis of a viable agricultural economy, provided sufficient food for the population, raised abysmally low living standards, and achieved real economic and political independence after a five-year-long war inspired and largely waged by foreigners.

Although there was major deprivation during the "first migration" from the towns in April-May 1975, planting resulted in a reportedly good November harvest; higher rice production has been accompanied by large-scale diversification into cash-cropping (rubber, sericulture, jute, cotton); and, with the help of imported Thai salt, the Tonle Sap fishing industry, which supplies a major part of Cambodian protein needs in the form of dried fish, was revived. From September 1975 a "second migration" involved the redeployment of much of the available labour force into areas previously neglected, to extend and intensify agricultural production. Throughout the year following the Khmer Rouge takeover, intensive infrastructural work concentrated on construction and rehabilitation of small-scale dams and windmills, digging and dredging irrigation canals, and reopening major roads and railways. By mid-July, Phnom Penh port had been dredged and all major roads were open; by the end of the year the Phnom Penh-Battambang railway had been repaired and reopened. A number of damaged power stations were operational, and several larger hydro-electric power schemes and dams (such as the Prek Thnot dam) were either fully repaired or near completion. However, emphasis remains on small and medium hydro-electricity and irrigation schemes, on a regional or provincial level.

Industrial rehabilitation has occurred on two fronts: the expansion of small-scale village projects and the reopening of a variety of larger industrial plants in Phnom Penh, indicating, among other things, that the city is being repopulated at least with workers, technical staff and civil servants. Although some doubt exists about the extent of industrialization (especially in view of the lack of raw materials and qualified staff) there is no doubt that textile production is well advanced, in keeping with the policy of self-sufficiency in clothing as well as food. At the level of social welfare, free schooling and medical care have been extended throughout the country, although the latter is hampered by a shortage of key medicines.

Foreign aid has been largely rejected (except for a reported $1,000 million grant from China) on the grounds that such aid compromises national independence. Thus, work in the first year of rehabilitation was almost entirely based on the principles of self-sufficiency. The basic unit of social and economic organization is the "production group" of about 10 families, with two elected leaders, within larger co-operative village units of 100–250 families, with a Khmer Rouge cadre to population ratio of about 1:100. Within such a structure, families are exhorted to emphasize poultry and livestock rearing and diversify cultivation, and labour is mobilized for infrastructural work, either in home localities or in neighbouring provinces.

In mid-1976 there was uncertainty about the leadership: until early 1976 the pro-Chinese Khieu Samphan and his associates seemed clearly in control, but it is claimed by some observers that, after the April 1976 meeting of the People's National Assembly, the "Stalinist" Ieng Sary and other pro-Hanoi and pro-Soviet officials gained the ascendant. This claimed shift of power, increased Soviet influence and the possible participation of Cambodia in the Hanoi-proposed Indochinese Summit meeting, aimed partly at establishing an "Indochinese federation", could jeopardize independent development in Cambodia and its policy of non-alignment with major power blocs, as well as change the significance of Indochina in regional politics.

In Cambodia, the events of April-May 1975, the bitter xenophobia of the early months of liberation, and the harsh remedy imposed by the new government can be understood only in relation to the five-year long trauma of a war that ravaged virtually the whole of Cambodia's economy and society, most of the rural infrastructure, and much of the crop-land. It was a war that was directed in part by proxy from Phnom Penh and in part directly from outside the country; and in establishing domestic and foreign policy priorities, the Khmer Rouge-led National United Front Government is understandably cautious of reliance either upon metropolitan-based administration or foreign aid—from whatever source.

In South Viet-Nam, the collapse of the Thieu regime was hastened to some extent by the U.S.A.'s earlier realization that victory was impossible. As in Cambodia and Laos, the U.S.A.'s retreat and the inherent corruption of its client-élites were both factors hastening the war's end. But the key factor was the ability of an indigenous revolutionary movement to sustain a long and bitter war of attrition within an environment it understood far better than did its adversaries. The National Liberation Front was thoroughly Vietnamese, and that was its decisive strength; although this very identity between the N.L.F. and the Vietnamese peasantry also, by definition, brought the United States' military and its allies into direct conflict with the bulk of the population—by trying to "clear the sea to isolate the fish" the United States literally had to scorch the countryside, and in doing so they entrenched their own (and Saigon's) isolation.

The 1973 Paris Agreements allowed the United States to extricate itself more speedily from an impossible situation, leaving the logic of "Vietnamization" to take its course. The N.L.F., together with North Vietnamese forces, confronted a Saigon army with little popular base and little will to fight. The latter's defeat was no surprise—what was surprising was their sudden and wholesale rout in March and April 1975. Certainly, few Western observers expected such an abrupt (and relatively peaceful) end to the war.

Long before the fall of Saigon, however, the N.L.F. had established secure liberated zones throughout South Viet-Nam, especially in the western uplands and the north; the level of organization in such zones was high—in liberated Quang Tri Province, for example, construction of a medical university was already under way in 1974; and cadres had long experience to draw upon—indeed, many had fought with the Viet-Minh in the 1950s. Thus, compared with Cambodia, South Viet-Nam possessed a more mature and better-trained body of revolutionary cadres, and far greater experience in the kind of social, economic and political development that would be necessary after the war. Besides, the Vietnamese were more politicized, and rural dwellers more receptive to the N.L.F. programme of change—after all, although negated by Ngo Dinh Diem, the Viet-Minh had already carried through large-scale land reform during the 1950s, affecting most of the South's arable land.

While the Revolutionary Government's first priority is to revive agriculture—resettling rural refugees, rebuilding villages and such infrastructural works as irrigation and drainage facilities, and bringing abandoned or bombed-out land back into cultivation—the authorities have an equally intractable problem in the administration and reform of major urban areas, especially Saigon-Cholon. Perhaps more than any other city in South-East Asia, Saigon has a foreign-oriented *compradore* economy with most of the occupied labour force employed in trade and services. Further, the city has for over a decade been the focal point of foreign military presence in Indochina, and its economy, society, culture and attitudes have been geared to accommodating and supplying this presence—in the process becoming deeply affected by the attendant cultural dislocation, extreme commercialization, *anomie* and corruption. Finally, for over two decades, Saigon has absorbed much of the human litter and degradation of war, and without doubt it now has the most diseased urban society in South-East Asia. The salvaging and transformation of Saigon is in some ways a far greater long-term challenge to the Revolutionary Government than rural development. The new authorities cannot apply the same logic to Saigon as was applied to Phnom Penh: not only is urban life a more integral part of Vietnamese society, it is also a problem area on a far greater scale.

While the N.L.F. proclaimed that its ultimate goal was socialism, the short-term programme was one of "advanced democracy": private business continued while State control over basic economic sectors increased and the banking system was restructured. Severe import restrictions were placed on non-essential goods and priority given to raw materials, machines and equipment for transport, industry and agriculture. Foreign investment was allowed "on the basis of mutual respect of independence" in industry and exploitation of natural resources, including offshore petroleum. An influx of administrative and technical personnel from the North brought needed help. From the outset, co-operation and integration with the North was an explicit part of policy-making: agriculture had top priority in the South (both food and cash crops like rubber), followed by medium-scale consumer industries, while the North would rely on heavy industry and mining. The pre-war complementality of the two would thus be re-established, with a more prosperous and steady unified market, and with direction firmly in the hands of the *Lao Dong* (Viet-Nam Workers') Party. In the South, rural development to attain self-sufficiency in food for all Viet-Nam within two or three years, the absorption of 2.5 million unemployed, and the "depopulation" of Saigon went hand in hand. It was estimated that rice land would absorb a million people, and more with reclamation: in the Mekong Delta alone there were 800,000 hectares of fallow land. Throughout 1975 virgin and fallow land was reclaimed in the "new economic zones", especially to the north and east of Saigon, with collective farms established to speed development, and provincial administrations providing transport, construction materials and four to six months' food rations to encourage migration from the towns. However, by May 1976 only 500,000 people had left Saigon. In existing ricelands there was no collective farm development, but land was redistributed from landlords to landless and families of dead N.L.F. soldiers and cadres, and rents lowered.

Developments in Viet-Nam since May 1975 must be seen in the context of the move towards complete reunification. While the country wss in many basic respects divided (for example, in economic system, in social and political attitudes and in administration), there was progressive reunification up to the declaration of formal reunification on June 24th, 1976. Both North and South were, throughout, under the direction of the one party (the *Lao Dong*) and maintained the one army; extensive movement of personnel, trade and mail between the two halves of Viet-Nam developed; moves were taken to integrate the education system, and the Saigon-Hanoi railway was rebuilt. In November 1975 Hanoi and Saigon announced preparations for "nationwide general elections to set up a national assembly and leading state organs for a reunited Viet-Nam". However, it was still underlined that, even after formal reunification and the enshrining of socialism as the state ideology, Viet-Nam would for some time comprise two zones, with two sets of policies, recognizing the advanced state of socialism in the North. Policy was considerably diluted for southern conditions: the "national democratic" revolution first had to be completed, with elimination of feudal land rights and the *compradore* economy, agricultural co-operation was being established only in the virgin "new economic zones", and capitalist and private ownership were tolerated and co-operated with.

However, each zone needed the other: rehabilitation of the South requires Northern aid and direction, and Northern development, especially under the 1976–80 development programme, requires the aid of southern agriculture and a technically advanced consumer industry. (The South is especially significant for the $12,000 million investment made by the U.S. in infrastructure, industry and capital-intensive agriculture). This, in the short term, is all the more important given the disappointing level of progress in the North during 1975 due to a combination of exceptionally bad weather, lack of labour and management initiative, post-war relaxation and the tendency towards adopting Soviet planning methods and priorities, which emphasize heavy industry and centralized economic control at the expense of agriculture and the small-scale village industry typical of much of the Northern economy.

Thus, under North Viet-Nam's 1973–76 Plan, which aimed at bringing the economy up to the 1965 level by 1975, targets were achieved in steel (176,000 tons), electric energy (from 505 million kWh in 1965 to 1,000 kWh) and coal (from 4 million tons in 1965 to 5 million tons). The rice harvest was the second best in 15 years although production per capita had dropped since 1965.

After a long period of "peaceful takeover" by the *Pathet Lao*, the Lao People's Democratic Republic was declared on December 1st, 1975, under the leadership of the Lao People's Revolutionary (Communist) Party. The new government is made up almost entirely of *Pathet Lao* veterans. The LPRP programme emphasizes austerity in food and clothing, politicization of those not already sympathetic with LPRP principles, self-sufficiency in food, and nationalism. But the programme does not involve tight discipline: a new, multi-tiered system of elected popular assemblies between the people and the national government has replaced the old system of government by appointment, and involves a form of guided democracy in combination with numerous mass organizations, including the *Pathet Lao* (the Party's military arm), which combines the duties of a fighting force, a production group working alongside the peasantry and a political unit which helps politicize the masses through study classes. There had been, by mid-1976, no land take-overs and no collectivization (preference is given to developing traditional Lao ideals of communal aid and mutual self-help), and care is taken to work within the precepts of Buddhism: indeed, the Buddhist Church regards Buddhism and the *Pathet Lao*'s conception of an egalitarian society as compatible. What is more, the *Pathet Lao* is the first ruling organization in Laos not drawn exclusively from lowland society: the two major tribal groups (the Meo and Lao Teng) are represented in the National Assembly Executive and at upper levels of the Army.

There has been no nationalization of existing industries; rather, some joint ventures (such as a Japanese-Laotian iron sheet factory) are encouraged, and this attitude has given Japanese investors, especially, hope that they can use Laos as an opening in Indochina for participation in wider ventures, such as hydro-electricity schemes, raw material exploitation, and development of road and rail links to the Vietnamese coast.

Nationalism is predominant in Laos, with a policy of equidistance between the U.S.S.R. and China, and a measured, pragmatic relationship with Viet-Nam and friendly relations with Cambodia (from whom it imported rice in late 1975 during the Thai blockade of the Mekong River).

Given recent changes in Cambodia, South Viet-Nam and Laos, the line of United States' influence has retreated south and east, towards Singapore and Indonesia. While economic penetration of Malaysia, Thailand and the Philippines will continue, there seems no doubt that these countries will increasingly disassociate themselves militarily from the United States, reach political accommodation with the new Indochina, and move economically and politically towards closer relations with China—retaining, nevertheless, a strongly anti-Communist position in domestic politics.

SOUTH-EAST ASIA: THE NEW GEOPOLITICAL PATTERN

With the establishment of Communist governments throughout Indochina, 1975 was perhaps the most decisive year for international relations in both South-East Asia and the Pacific region since the Geneva Agreements were signed in 1954. The United States' reappraisal of its role in the Western Pacific area was given a sharp jolt: by 1974 it was apparent that "Vietnamization", as a substitute for the commitment of U.S. troops to a ground war in Asia, was doomed to failure. But the speed and totality of the collapse of pro-Western regimes in Cambodia, South Viet-Nam and Laos came as a surprise, as did the manner of subsequent takeovers by Communist governments. In 1976 some 57 million South-East Asians had governments that the United States had spent nearly 30 years and some $400,000 million trying to pre-empt.

One aspect of the new order, then, is the effect upon American foreign policy. Changes in South-East Asia dictate a rethinking of military strategy, now that the southern flank of the U.S.A.'s Asian mainland presence has been decimated, not only by events in Indochina but also by Thailand's demand for a complete U.S. withdrawal from Thai soil, including the sophisticated communications system at Ramasun.

Further south, in Malaysia, Singapore, and Indonesia, the establishment of military bases is unlikely, despite Singapore's willingness to harbour and service U.S. warships and its planes and desire for the maintenance of an American military presence in the region.

But military affairs cannot be separated from economic ones. In so far as the U.S.A. has considerable economic interest in South-East Asia, which depends especially on a stable and pro-Western Indonesia, increasing emphasis is being placed on military aid to that country: in 1974 military grants and sales credits to Indonesia totalled $17.5 million; proposed grants and sales credits for 1976 total $42.5 million.

In addition to the strategic importance of Indonesia (and Singapore) to the United States, Thailand and the Philippines remain major points of a dual concern: for both a continuing military presence in South-East Asia and the preservation of friendly governments. While the Philippines has apparently demurred in favour of a continued (but renegotiated) U.S. military presence, despite the government's expressed concern over the "neutrality" of the country, Thailand confirmed in June 1976 that the U.S. withdrawal must be complete, except for the retention by the Thai government of "advisers".

Of great importance to the future geopolitical design of South-East Asia is the continuing instability within Thailand. There remains the danger of serious attempts by pro-American rightists and militarists to "destabilize" the shaky civilian coalition government of Seni Pramoj and allow for a right-wing military coup.

In July 1975 the *Far Eastern Economic Review* reported the existence of a "potentially powerful right-wing movement with an unusually sharp ideological character and mass appeal" comprising senior army officers, and supported by college lecturers, right-wing students, monks and businessmen. The movement charges that there is a left-wing threat to traditional institutions. Significantly, all senior army officers involved operate in fields where C.I.A. activity has been most important.

Some knowledge of the composition of the movement, its political outlook, and the nature of those sections of Thai society supporting it is of great importance in understanding the structure and possible future of internal Thai politics, and in understanding recent, present and future relations between Thailand, Laos, Cambodia, Malaysia, and China, the United States and the Soviet Union. One cannot appreciate Lao suspicions of Thailand, for example, without taking into account the many reports of right-wing provoked border disputes, incursions of Meo refugee mercenaries into north-west Laos, and attempts at counter-revolution in the Savannakhet area of southern Laos by Lao rightists operating from Thailand. Equally, it is hard to discount frequent and impartial reports of continued American involvement in right-wing "destabilization" activities within Thailand and across Thai borders—in addition to reports of increased Soviet activity in Thailand.

On the other hand, there is no doubt that left-wing and southern Muslim insurrection has increased in the country: 28 out of 71 provinces were under martial law in 1975, and 26.4 per cent of the 1975/76 budget went to defence and internal security (compared with 24.7 per cent on all economic development). Insurgency in the north and north-east assumes significance not only for the disaffection with Bangkok-oriented development that it represents, but also for the threat it poses to expanded mineral exploitation. Most tungsten and fluorspar (of which Thailand is in both cases, the second largest non-communist producer), as well as deposits of oil and other minerals, lie in the north and north-east.

In southern Thailand, communist and Muslim insurgency is being less vigorously tackled, and at the same time poses a threat to friendly relations with Malaysia as Bangkok uses the communists as a balancing power to the Muslim secessionists, and is therefore suspected by Malaysia of turning a blind eye to the presence of Malayan Communist Party forces, and in turn suspects Malaysia of sympathy for Thai Muslims. Relations between the two were strained when, in June 1976, Thailand ordered withdrawal of Malaysian troops stationed on Thai soil, following a Malaysian ground and air sweep into Thailand.

Whether or not Thailand's new right-of-centre coalition government will survive left, extreme right and militarist pressures is debateable. At present, the latter are in the ascendant, and any right-wing coup would have considerable impact upon the region—not least because Thailand's civilian governments under both Kukrit and Seni Pramoj have, since May 1975, made some attempt at accommodation with the countries of Indochina, and have succeeded in obtaining a major withdrawal of American military presence from the country. In both cases, the extreme right and the military have shown their hostility to the moves.

Since mid-1975 there has been considerable speculation over the emerging pattern of Indochinese geopolitics. As far as relations with other South-East Asian nations are concerned, a number of elements can be identified. Firstly, all Indochinese countries are too concerned with internal reconstruction to spend much effort "exporting" their revolutions. Verbal support for other liberation movements has been expressed, but material aid has been negligible. Secondly, it has generally been left to neighbouring countries to take the initiative in establishing diplomatic relations with Indochinese states, largely on the understanding that meaningful relations can exist only when former enemies indicate a willingness to respect the sovereignty of Indochinese territories as a basis for peaceful coexistence: alignments have been determined by the degree of hostility and wartime belligerence shown by South-East Asian governments towards Indochina. Thus, Thailand and Cambodia have both important trade links and full diplomatic relations: and of all ASEAN countries, only Malaysia, the most genuinely non-aligned nation in the Association, had (by June 1976) full diplomatic relations with Viet-Nam; Laos trades with Thailand but has no diplomatic relations, and Viet-Nam remains openly hostile to Thailand. Neither the Philippines nor Indonesia, whose governments were most active in supporting the U.S. role in Indochina, have diplomatic relations with Cambodia, Laos or Viet-Nam. Thirdly, while individual ASEAN states have been slow to find accommodation with a communist Indochina, for internal reasons and because of American influence on foreign policy, most have recognized the inevitability of coming to terms with the new South-East Asian order and are adjusting foreign policy accordingly, both by tacitly or openly recognizing the legitimacy of Indochinese governments, and by taking more positive steps towards consolidating ASEAN co-operation as a counterweight, especially against Viet-Nam, which is seen as a potentially dominant power in the region, supported by the Soviet Union. In this respect, ASEAN-Indochinese relations assume a wider strategic significance: some observers see China tacitly supporting ASEAN co-operation as a regional counter to Soviet influence, while Viet-Nam has consistently criticized members, especially Thailand, for forming a neocolonial alliance consistent with President Ford's Pacific Doctrine, representing not only neocolonial economic relations but a continuation of the U.S. military presence in South-East Asia.

However, as the Thai decision on complete American withdrawal indicates, there is disquiet, with the notable exceptions of Singapore and Indonesia, over U.S. military deployment in South-East Asia. But the question remains: will Soviet-American rivalry in the region polarize the alignments of South-East Asian nations or will some form of "zone of neutrality" emerge, along the lines long proposed by Malaysia?

Finally, there are signs that Indochinese states—at least Laos and Viet-Nam—are interested in more than mere trading relations in the economic field, and this may help to modify political strains. For example, both the Laotians and the Vietnamese (in the form of the South Vietnamese delegation) attended the April 1976 meeting of the Asian Development Bank, indicating a willingness to use loans from what had hitherto been considered an organ of "Western and Japanese neocolonialism"; in addition, there is the possibility of all Indochinese nations co-operating with Thailand to revive the Mekong River Scheme, now that the U.S.A. has abandoned the Mekong Committee; and, with Japan interested in expanding its investments in both Indochina and ASEAN (an interest reciprocated by Laos and Viet-Nam), it is possible that Japan may act as broker between the two regional groupings in stimulating the flow of aid, technology and resources.

Within Indochina, political developments are equally open to speculative interpretation. The simplistic view is that of a Moscow-dominated North Viet-Nam gradually gaining ascendancy, and thereby extending Soviet influence, over the whole of Indochina. A logical outcome of this would be the resurrection of the pan-Indochina Communist Party and the formation of an Indochinese Federation. While reports are conflicting, Laos has strenuously denied that "combatant solidarity" with North Viet-Nam has moved to the point where Laos is falling under Hanoi's dominance. Indeed, Laos maintains close relations with both Viet-Nam and Cambodia, and co-operates with both in economic affairs: landlocked, and deprived of a guaranteed outlet through Thailand, Laos uses Cambodia, and northern Viet-Nam, for the transit of goods. Economic links with Viet-Nam are growing, with the planned construction of new road and rail links to the east coast and a new port under Lao jurisdiction on Vietnamese soil, and the co-operative development of Laos' extensive reserves of timber, hydro-electricity, potash, anthracite and high-grade magnesite ore. But such links should not be interpreted as indicating North Vietnamese dominance, or increasing Soviet influence. Although Laos and Viet-Nam are in general agreement on Asian questions, except in respect of Cambodia, there has been a marked silence in the Laotian Government on controversial issues involving Moscow, Peking and Hanoi, and on the Soviet "Asian Collective Security" proposal. Laos has also maintained a careful policy in foreign affairs of equidistance between Moscow and Peking. Equally, Laotian support for Cambodia (in contrast with Viet-Nam's critical approach) reflects the Laotian concept of a strongly nationalistic socialism and is a support reciprocated by Cambodia, as the late-1975 despatch of 5,000 tons of rice to Laos, while it was under Thai blockade, symbolizes.

Recent interpretation of events in Cambodia, too, may suffer from the same neglect of the deep-seated significance of Khmer nationalism. Soviet or Vietnamese hegemony over Cambodia goes completely against the grain of the Cambodian revolutionary path, and against the grain of Khmer nationalism. This realignment of Cambodian politics can be predicated only on one major factor: the total collapse of the (so far) independent policy of achieving self-sufficiency through agrarian revolution. If the Cambodian experiment in fundamental revolution has failed, then so has the strength of Khmer nationalism and the attempt at retrieving Khmer independence.

Perhaps, too, there is an exaggeration of Hanoi's inclination for "imperialism" in the region, misconstruing necessary co-operation for the imposition of hegemony; and there is an undoubted lack of attention to one of the key reasons for the U.S. defeat in Viet-Nam: a strong Vietnamese nationalism.

ASEAN: PROGRESS AND PROSPECTS

Such conflicts of political interest in non-communist South-East Asia as that between Thailand and Malaysia are important in a wider context—that of the meaningful consolidation of regional co-operation withing the Association of South-East Asian Nations (ASEAN). Since its inception in 1967, ASEAN has been a largely ineffectual grouping of nations whose main common denominator was anti-communism. In so far as the original aims were basically economic and social, couched in vague terms of high principle, little concrete action resulted before 1976. ASEAN embraced countries of different levels of economic development, sharing some common interest in that they all depended on primary exports and had low levels of industrialization, a backward and over-populated peasant sector, a relatively poorly developed tertiary sector, and low average living standards, with the significant exception of Singapore. The Association embraced four major cultures, differing economic structures and different political systems, and contained a number of important political and/or economic conflicts; the Thai-Malaysian border dispute, the Malaysia-Singapore post-separation tensions, the mutual suspicions of the Singaporeans and the Indonesians, and the dispute centred on the Philippines' claim to Sabah. It hardly seemed a viable association.

In 1968 ASEAN commissioned a UN expert group to study the prospect of regional economic co-operation. The UN team's 1972 report suggested three separate but inter-related forms of co-operation for industrial development:

(a) *Selective trade liberalization*, item by item, to encourage increased specialization and exchange to be applied mainly in industries with underutilized capacity and an opportunity for profitable intra-ASEAN exchange. ASEAN members should substitute imports from other members for imports from non-member countries.

(b) *Complementarity agreements* in which private interests in individual industries or small groups of related industries, in the different countries, encouraged specialization of different countries on different products of the industry concerned. and their exchange—with assistance of tariffs and other incentives. This would affect a few larger enterprises producing a number of products or components which could be produced more efficiently and cheaply in larger volume with greater internal specialization.

(c) *Package deal agreements* negotiated between ASEAN countries for the establishment of new, large-scale projects, mainly in industries not yet in the region, and their allocation for a limited period to particular countries with tariff and other assistance. Studies were made of 13 package deals which could introduce new large-scale industries not established in ASEAN, and which depended for their viability upon access by a single large enterprise to an assured and preferential regional market.

A regional market would improve industrial efficiency, and joint action in the "package deal" industries could reduce the cost of investment by an estimated 30 per cent. Thus, ASEAN countries would be better able to serve their own markets, and their industries would be more competitive in world markets.

Recognizing one of the major objections to regional co-operation, that it encourages uneven development, the UN team stressed both complementarity and specialization of major products: for with simple relaxation of trade barriers, the industrially more advanced and efficient countries such as Singapore and Malaysia would benefit, while the less competitive economies, importing more, would suffer stagnant or shrinking economies.

Numerous other reservations existed. Singapore, with a relatively advanced industrial economy and low protective barriers, had reason to feel it might be held back through integration given the negotiating position of the larger, less developed, economies, with much higher tariff walls around their industrial sectors. On the other hand, such countries as Indonesia had strong feelings about Singapore's pre-eminence as both a financial and industrial centre, and a focus of Chinese business. At the same time, it was feared that regional co-operation would allow increased mobility and the migration of Chinese skill and capital to the country least hostile to them, a fear borne out by the large-scale movement of wealthy Indonesian Chinese and their money to Singapore after 1966, and a similar movement of wealthy and highly skilled Chinese from Malaysia after 1969.

A further problem was the often tenuous political relations between states. However, by 1976 most disputes causing political strain had been at least partially resolved, leaving the problem of some disagreement between political leaders dedicated to regional co-operation and national economic planners for whom regional co-operation is a side-issue. This problem arose partly out of the way in which ASEAN affairs were, until 1976, the province of foreign ministers. The Central Secretariat, which had been agreed upon in 1975, should bring economic planners together more firmly; in addition, the artificial separation between economic and political matters was finally dropped in 1976.

At the 1976 summit talks, and the following meeting of Economics and Planning Ministers, ASEAN achieved a more concrete foundation, if only that of a general compromise consensus, than it had ever possessed. But specific agreements along the lines of the 1972 UN Report were negligible, and where they were specific they remained tentative. On trade co-operation some items were noted for "future studies"; however, the Economics Ministers accepted rice and crude oil as priorities for preferential treatment (thus satisfying a basic Indonesian demand) with the qualification that priority of supply would be determined by a state of "critical shortage" and priority of purchase by a state of "glut", neither terms being defined. It was agreed that the guiding principle governing co-operation on commodities, especially on pricing, should be a spirit of assistance whereby member countries refrain from taking advantage of the adverse position faced by other members. It was also agreed that the list of priority commodities for preferential treatment might be expanded to include raw sugar, maize, fish, beef, vegetables, coconut and palm oil, logs and sawn timber, and clinker. There was also a resolving of outstanding issues holding up finalization of the international agreement on natural rubber price stabilization—a significant move, given the importance of rubber to Thailand, Malaysia and Indonesia (who together produce 86 per cent of world supply).

As for "package projects", five plants were formally designated "ASEAN industrial projects", eligible for preferential trading arrangements, and a group of experts was directed to examine the feasibility of "immediately establishing" plants to make urea in Indonesia and Malaysia, superphosphates in the Philippines, diesel engines in Singapore, and soda ash in Thailand. The projects were relatively small-scale, capable of establishment "within three years" without major capital outlay.

Thus, ASEAN deliberations in 1975 and 1976 had a rather bland, parochial quality. The common, and most severe problems of South-East Asian development lie in peasant agriculture: in exploitative agrarian relations, high rates of tenancy, indebtedness, landlessness, un- and under-employment, and inefficiency of non-viable, poorly capitalized, rented land holdings. With 70 per cent of the region's population thus affected to a greater or lesser degree, there is an acute need for regional co-operation over such questions as effective land reform, the creation of proper marketing and credit facilities, the productive mobilization of the region's 15 million unemployed and even greater number of underemployed, the development of effective and labour-absorbing forms of infrastructural schemes such as irrigation and roading, and rural health programmes—the decentralization of development, rather than its metropolitan concentration (the Philippines, for example, with 80 per cent of manufacturing concentrated in the Manila area, also has 37 per cent of its doctors and 46 per cent of its nurses serving that 10 per cent of the population living in Manila, leaving a nurse/population ratio in rural areas of 1 : 27,000).

In addition, ASEAN countries have to confront more decisively problems of trade and aid: besides rubber, they are in a leading position to press for price stabilization for tin (with Chinese support), coconut products, palm oil, tropical timber and, by co-operating as a group with other producers, other minor regional products such as pepper, sugar and various metallic minerals besides tin. Finally, with a total outstanding foreign debt of nearly $20,000 million, regional co-operation could lead to some modification of the problem of indebtedness and a concomitant harmonization of aid policy. But, in so far as ASEAN integration is heavily underwritten and encouraged by foreign interests, restricted by national jealousies, and given tenuous meaning as a counter to communism without attempting to solve the basic problems of development that foster communism, the Association of South-East Asian Nations seems destined for a narrow and ineffectual existence in the foreseeable future, certainly as far as the majority of its member countries' population is concerned.

OIL IN SOUTH-EAST ASIA

There is no doubt that substantial oil reserves lie in the continental shelf areas of the South China Sea, between the coasts of South Viet-Nam and those of southern Philippines and Sarawak—as well as in the Gulf of Thailand and the Java Sea. Equally, there is no doubt that oil was and is a major factor in United States' policy towards South-East Asia.

Given the estimate that half America's oil needs by 1985 would have to come from imports, or the estimate that by 1975 the United States would be importing some 450,000 barrels of oil a day from Asia, the significance of Asia's offshore oil potential becomes immediately apparent—particularly in view of the Middle Eastern situation. In any search for alternative sources of oil supply, however, the United States will find itself in competition with Japan, which is obtaining an increasing proportion of its oil needs from South-East Asia.

Burma and Indonesia have long made an important contribution to world oil output, but attention since 1960 focused on the shallow continental shelf extending from the coasts of Thailand in the west, through a great arc embracing Indonesian, Malaysian, Cambodian and Vietnamese waters towards Japan and Korea in the north-east. The waters of this continental shelf are shallow, and the rocks which underlie them appear to be similar to those yielding oil in the islands and on the mainland of South-East Asia.

By the early 1960s, according to Dr. Malcolm Caldwell, "the top people in America and elsewhere were already aware of the tremendous potential of the Indonesian and South-East Asian oil reserves".

The same month a largely unnoticed ECAFE committee, the "Committee for Co-ordination of Joint Prospecting . . . in Asian Offshore Areas", held its sixth session in Bangkok. This presented a summary of the aeromagnetic and marine survey work carried out under its auspices by scientists from Taiwan, Japan, the Republic of Korea, Malaysia, Thailand, South Viet-Nam, Indonesia, West Germany, the United Kingdom and the United States. The committee recommended that the order of priorities for future projects should be: (1) Zones 1, 2 and 3 in the Republic of Viet-Nam; (2) Malacca Straits; (3) Region II of the Philippines. By 1970 it appeared that the South-East Asian region is "one of the richest sources of oil ever discovered" and that "the shallow sea floor between Japan and Taiwan might contain one of the most prolific oil and gas reservoirs in the world".

Between 1955 and 1970, oil companies had already spent an estimated $20,000 million in oil exploration and development in East and South-East Asia. In 1970, David Rockefeller of the Chase Manhattan Bank estimated that by 1980 United States oil firms alone would spend $35,000 million developing the Asian-Western Pacific region. Between 1965 and 1970, approximately one million square miles of land and territorial continental shelf area (mainly in the region of Malaysia and Indonesia) had already been parcelled out as exploration blocks to United States, Japanese, Australian, Canadian, and French mining companies, with almost all the area and most of the companies involved in the oil search. Then in late 1970 the Saigon government divided its offshore waters into 18 blocks (later increased to 40) and passed a law governing the terms on which these concession areas were to be let—terms very low by world standards. By 1971 the whole South-East Asian region, except for Viet-Nam, had been parcelled out.

In 1972, Chase Manhattan Bank reported that total oil industry investment in Asia between 1970 and 1985 was expected to be about $65,000 million. Meanwhile, geological survey work had accelerated—over the continental shelf area, and within Thailand, Malaysia, and Indonesia—and further reserves were being discovered. In 1973, for example, it was announced that shale deposits in North Thailand's Tak Province contained a potential reserve of 2,000 to 3,000 million barrels of "sweet" (low sulphur) oil, and that bids for concessions would be invited before 1974. New strikes in Malaysia during 1973–74 promise to push Malaysia's oil production up five times to 500,000 barrels a day by 1978, while the extent of Indonesia's oil reserves are continually being revised upwards as a result of continuing geological surveys—in 1974 they were generally estimated at 15,000 million barrels, or 70 per cent of total known reserves in the Pacific area. According to Louis Kraar (*Fortune*, July 1973), "on the basis of recent finds and the quickening pace of exploration, General Sutowo (head of Indonesia's state oil corporation, Pertamina) predicts that the country will be able to pump three million barrels daily by 1980, or an amount as much as Kuwait produces today".

But perhaps the most remarkable discovery in the past two years was that of huge reserves of natural gas in the region. By 1973, estimates of oil industry expenditure in South-East Asia had risen again, with the projection that by 1980 around $10,000 million would be invested in natural gas development alone. The discovery of South-East Asia's natural gas potential was dramatic: in 1972, American sources estimated that there were only 34 gas fields with reserves of over 10,000,000 million cubic feet—20 in Russia, none in South-East Asia. Now it is accepted that there may be as many as five fields of this size in the region, all exporting by 1980.

Natural gas is a versatile, clean, cheap, and efficient fuel which for almost a century has been "burned off" simply because there was no means of transporting it over long distances. Now it can be transported to wherever it is needed as a result of recently developed liquefaction techniques and the construction of large Liquefied Natural Gas tankers. In 1972, natural gas supplied 20 per cent of the world's energy demand—largely in areas close to the source of supply— and even if this percentage is maintained, a spiralling world energy demand implies that the consumption, and especially the export, of natural gas will increase several times over the next decade.

Already, the Shell-Mitsubishi LNG project in Brunei is the largest in the world—by 1975, this plant was transporting over 280,000 million cubic feet of LNG to Japan annually. Similar projects are now being developed to tap vast reserves off Sumatra, Kalimantan, and Sarawak involving United States, Anglo-Dutch and Japanese investment in partnership with Pertamina and the Malaysian Government.

WORLD PERSPECTIVES OF SOUTH-EAST ASIAN OIL

The interest of Western and Japanese business in South-East Asian oil must be seen in the light of certain world trends: first, the rapidly rising demand for oil. World oil needs in 1968 were 40 million barrels a day; by 1980 it is estimated this will rise to 80 million.

Second, the steep rise in the United States demand for imported petroleum; according to the vice-chairman of Humble Oil, imports will make up 50 per cent of the United States oil supply by 1985 as against 35 per cent today; this will mean a daily import of 13 million barrels.

Third, the equally rapid rise in Japanese needs; these will amount to 12 million barrels daily by 1985 and Japanese Government policy aims at getting 30 per cent of this from Japanese controlled sources—which explains large-scale Japanese involvement in Asian-Australasian oil ventures.

Fourth, the increasingly successful pressure of Middle East/North African suppliers to boost their share of the oil wealth being extracted from their countries are moving towards "unilateral control over the pricing and taxation of all foreign oil production" and this will add billions of dollars to the oil bills of the West and Japan. There is thus a strong incentive to seek cheaper sources with more pliable client governments.

Fifth, and this is increasingly important as the awareness of the whole question of pollution grows—the South-East Asian oils have a very low sulphur content and, with the United States and Japan moving towards strict control of sulphur pollution, this characteristic becomes of major importance.

For the highly developed economies of the United States, of Western Europe and of Japan and for the developing Australasian economy the need for a dependable major source of cheap petroleum has never been greater. South-East Asia (and East Asia) offers such a source.

THE MINERAL BOOM, INDOCHINA, AND INDONESIA

The question which must be posed is whether the oil and other mineral potential of this region has been a major factor in the development of United States' strategy in South-East Asia. There is, it must be conceded, a remarkable coincidence between the events on the oil front summarized above and the careful fostering by the United States of the government of President Suharto in post-1965 Indonesia, its expansion of the Indochina War, and its military policy towards Thailand.

But the United States' defeat in Indochina has changed the whole picture of South-East Asian geopolitics—and in particular the West's ability to manipulate regional politics to accommodate its interest in local mineral extraction. The United States has abandoned its influence over offshore and onshore oil development in Indochina, and its interest in Thai oil development must be considered at risk as a result of Thailand's now seriously compromised political position.

Already in 1973, oil companies were reluctant to commit heavy investment to exploration and development around the South Vietnamese coast. During May and June, 1973, seven international oil companies and consortia made bids for drilling rights off the coast of South Viet-Nam—but against this must be weighed the fact that a further 20 companies invited to bid by the Saigon Government had not done so by the time tenders closed. Clearly, the political guarantees had been insufficient for large-scale oil investments in and around South Viet-Nam itself, and the fluidity of the Viet-Nam military situation was a major obstacle to such investment.

But what was more to the point, during the 1960s and up to 1973, was the confidence felt by large-scale mineral investors throughout South-East Asia as a whole in the ability of the United States to successfully maintain a "holding position" in Indochina and Thailand and guarantee political stability in the "Malay World". For the most lucrative area—in terms of raw materials—has never been primarily Indochina itself, but Indonesia.

Since the United States' support for France's effort in holding Indochina—by supplying 80 per cent of all funds needed for the war against the Viet-Minh—successive United States' governments have seen Indochina as a key part of the vital military rim needed for free access to the Malay World's vast store of industrial raw materials. In 1953, for example, President Eisenhower stressed the need to hold Indochina to preserve "the rich empire of Indonesia"; in 1967, after the main obstacle to foreign penetration fell with the overthrow of President Sukarno, Richard Nixon described Indonesia as "the greatest prize in the South-East Asian Area". After 1966, the growth of United States' (and increasingly, Japanese) investment in the country certainly bore out this assessment: in the last nine years, foreign investment in Indonesia has multiplied from a negligible few million dollars to over $7,000 million—overwhelmingly in oil, other minerals, and timber. In 1968, only a very small portion of Indonesia's resource potential had been investigated—according to government sources, some 3 per cent of exploitable area had been properly surveyed; by 1972, however, about 56 per cent of total land area had been geologically mapped and some 25 per cent of known mineral-bearing area had been intensively surveyed. While this remains a low figure, it clearly indicates both the intensity of exploratory work over the past few years, and the vast mineral potential yet to be realized.

We can judge the magnitude of the recent development of Indonesia's extractive export industries by the following examples: oil production increased from 170 million barrels in 1966 to nearly 504 million barrels in 1974 (over the same period estimates of Indonesia's share of world petroleum reserves have risen from 2 per cent to 3 per cent); between 1966 and 1974, tin production rose from 13,000 to 23,200 metric tons (with hopes for an increase to 28,000 tons by 1977, as a result of a United Nations survey of the islands of Bangka, Belitung, and Singkep concluded in 1973), nickel production rose from 117,400 to nearly one million metric tons, bauxite production rose from 701,000 to nearly 1.3 million metric tons—though production of bauxite, like that of tin, is restrained by the international quota system. Finally, of particular importance to Japan, the production of timber (in which one-third of all foreign capital outside the oil industry is invested) rose from 3.4 million cubic metres in 1966 to over 19 million cubic metres in 1973. In addition, there have been significant increases in the production of manganese, sulphur, gold, silver, and diamonds—all of which are at very early stages of development.

But perhaps one of the most significant developments was the start of copper exports in 1973 from Indonesia's first copper mine—a huge enterprise in West Irian owned by Freeport Sulphur, the first American corporation to commit investment to Indonesian mineral extraction following the passing of the 1967 Foreign Investment Law. By 1975, Freeport Sulphur had spent some $200 million on developing its West Irian mine, to tap the province's vast reserves of high-grade ore, including copper, gold and silver. In the Ertsberg Mountains region alone, the company has discovered some 33.5 million metric tons of such ore, and in 1974 production was 230,700 metric tons of 26 per cent pure copper concentrate.

THE MINERAL BOOM AND SINGAPORE: COLONIAL CITY OR CATALYST FOR DEVELOPMENT?

As a result of the mineral boom and rapidly increasing foreign investment in the region, Singapore has achieved a spectacular development over the past six years as the servicing centre of a new colonial-style economy in South-East Asia—a development both dramatic and symptomatic of a potentially explosive situation. For Singapore, with just over two million inhabitants, is extremely rich compared with its neighbours, has every conceivable facility for foreign "colonization" of the Malay World, and (with 76 per cent of its population Chinese) is ethnically distinct from its predominantly Malay hinterland. Singapore is the modern "colonial city" *par excellence*—interdependent with its hinterland, parasitic upon it, and alienated from it at one and the same time.

Largely because of this, Singapore's official statistics showing trade with the region are notoriously unreliable—trade figures for Indonesia are not published, and those for Malaysia and the Philippines are heavily underestimated. However, according to recent estimates (including those made by the Bank of America and the Indonesian authorities) it is almost certain that Singapore had a total trade of at least $7,000 million in 1972 (compared with an official $5,100 million), and that trade with Brunei, Malaysia, and Indonesia comprised between 35 and 40 per cent of the total—a proportion which in character was largely "colonial" (with the export of manufactured goods and the import of raw and semi-processed primary commodities predominating).

Besides its role in regional commodity trade, Singapore acts as a "sparking plug" for the Malay World's colonization in other ways. The city-state is a booming regional financial centre, especially in terms of its role as an Asian Dollar Market, mobilizing expatriate U.S. funds for regional investment. This market—like most other large-scale projects—has received strong backing from a government which sees Singapore as a "global city", a world financial, production, and business centre, and which views relations with the surrounding region and the Republic's role in foreign investment in this light. In 1968, Singapore's Asian Dollar fund stood at $33.2 million; by early 1976, it held nearly $13,000 million. Singapore's Asian Dollar market is now attracting funds from Europe for use in rapidly expanding economic activities in South-East Asia; in 1968, on the other hand, its funds were channelled instead to the Eurodollar Market. In addition, Singapore's role as a centre of commercial and merchant banking has greatly expanded: in 1963 there were 33 commercial banks in Singapore, and the first merchant bank appeared only in 1970; by late 1975 Singapore had 70 commercial banks (including 13 local banks) and 21 merchant banks. In all, 21 banks held "offshore" branch licences to take part in Asian Dollar and foreign exchange transactions.

Singapore is the largest oil-refining centre between the Middle East and Japan, with nine major refineries (five owned by Shell). At the end of 1973, Singapore's refinery complex had a capacity of over one million barrels per day—making Singapore the third largest refinery complex in the world, after Rotterdam and Houston. At present, the Republic refines mainly Middle Eastern crude for Japanese markets, but as Indonesian output increases and Japan's reliance on Indonesia grows, Singapore will inevitably process a greater proportion of oil from its immediate region.

Associated with its focal position in relation to the fast expanding mineral industry in and around Indonesia, Singapore has an increasingly sophisticated shipbuilding and repair industry (largely controlled by Japanese, U.S., and British capital).

With representatives of 30 major oil corporations based in Singapore, the Republic has attracted well over 250 oil-related companies. Many of these concerns, and others, are closely linked with the exploration and development of minerals other than oil. In addition, Singapore is the site of two geophysical computer centres as large and as sophisticated as any in the world.

Facilities such as these make Singapore a complete support base for the penetration of foreign capital and enterprise into the resource-rich hinterlands of Malaysia and Indonesia. For this role, Singapore's infrastructure—from financial to industrial—is so advanced it need fear little competition. (As an indication of this, the United States' trade centre was transferred from Bangkok to Singapore in 1973.) From such "head-link" activities, the Singapore Government and local businessmen have profited immensely—as evidenced by the increase of G.N.P. per capita from U.S. $620 in 1967 to $2,500 in 1975.

Domestic development in the city-state has, since 1967, been closely tuned to achieving the status of "global city", of "catalyst" for development in the entire Malay World, driven by a host of foreign investment incentives, draconian labour legislation, and a sophisticated system of state capitalism—with the Government not only developing economic infrastructure, but participating in the more profitable large private enterprises, and fostering a number of ambitious and profitable commercial enterprises of its own. The Government has developed one of the most sophisticated containerized ports in the world, established a number of large industrial estates in which foreign firms take full advantage of Singapore's rigidly-controlled cheap labour force and other incentives to export-oriented industries, and built up one of the materially most spectacular re-housing schemes in the non-Western world. Through numerous joint ventures, the Government has also gained a firm foothold in all of Singapore's main economic activities—including shipbuilding, oil refining, trade, tourism, and foreign investment financing.

By carefully marrying its own interests with local and foreign private interests, the Singapore Government has given the Republic the role and status of "global city". But in doing so, it is firmly held hostage by the system which created the port-city over 150 years ago—for Singapore is still very much a colonial style middle-man, prospering on the resources of its hinterland. Through the facilities it provides, foreign capital and enterprise penetrate the surrounding region in much the same way as they have done for over a century, extracting raw materials and paying the intermediary his commission. But now, Singapore's growth depends not only upon the flow of foreign capital and trade with its primary-producing hinterland, it also depends increasingly upon the inflow of Malaysian and Indonesian Chinese capital and enterprise, upon highly skilled immigrants from Malaysia, and upon cheap migrant labour (however, when large-scale retrenchments occur, as in 1974, it is the unskilled and semi-skilled Malaysian workers on short contracts who are immediately affected). Further, Singapore is now a large foreign investor in its own right in Malaysia and Indonesia and is increasingly trying to channel unwanted labour-intensive or pollution-intensive investment into these countries. Thus, a modern colonial relationship has consolidated between Singapore and its hinterland; and, as has traditionally been the case, this process has led to a rapidly widening disparity between city and countryside—between Singapore on the one hand and Indonesia and Malaysia on the other. In 1963, Singapore's per capita G.N.P. was six times that of Indonesia; in 1973, it was sixteen times greater.

But there is one significant difference now: while a colonial system persists in South-East Asia, while the component parts of this system are *economically* interdependent (at the same time as they are by definition economically disparate), these same basic components are politically independent. Now, the "global city" of Singapore—financial and industrial hub of South-East Asia, and on the threshold of becoming the world's third largest port and third largest oil refinery—is threatened by its own role, and alienated from its regional context economically, politically and culturally. Simply because its economy and society have developed strictly within the logic of a colonial system, Singapore's survival both as a colonial middle-man and an independent political entity is jeopardized. Particularly dangerous, in view of the long-held communal stereotypes in South-East Asia, is the manner in which the Singapore Government has presented the Republic's development as the result of a successful marriage between Western civilization and the Chinese capacity for enterprise, efficiency, and hard work.

The possibility of economic and communal jealousies in the region assuming the form of some kind of military confrontation seems to be taken seriously, whatever the debates over "regional co-operation". In 1975 Indonesia's armed forces amounted to 266,000 men, while Malaysia's accounted for a further 61,100. By comparison, Singapore, with an area barely a third the area of Greater London, and a population of some two million, had a total of 30,000 men in the armed forces, and a further 37,500 trained men in reserves and paramilitary units. While Malaysia spent an average of U.S. $29 per capita on defence in 1973 and Indonesia an average of less than $3, Singapore spent an average of $124. This is a significant sum, not only in comparison with the Malaysian and Indonesian figures, but also in comparison with Singapore's domestic per capita income figures—for $124 was equivalent to the annual per capita income of over 25 per cent of the Republic's population.

The relationship between Singapore, Malaysia, and Indonesia, then, exemplifies the growing disparity between city and countryside inherent in the operation of the economic system prevailing in South-East Asia. As the expansion of this new "colonialism" continues, so will the process of widening disparities—and it is in this context, perhaps, more than in any other, that we should view the future of Asia south of Indochina.

MANIFESTATIONS AND RESULTS OF THE MINERAL BOOM

In 1975 over 9,000 Americans were living in Singapore, about three times the number six years before; between 1965 and 1975, United States' investments in Singapore increased from $50 million to over $500 million; and the number of United States companies rose from 200 in 1968 to 450 in 1975. Between 1967 and 1975, Singapore changed dramatically from a rather stolid British outpost to the regional nerve-centre of a new, highly sophisticated, capital-rich, technology-intensive, and socially more profligate kind of foreign presence. Its role as colonial port-city swiftly gained a new face as major reserves of minerals, especially oil, were developed in and around Indonesia. Now, Singapore is the centre of a Texas-style oil rush which has already had a major impact on the economies and societies of South-East Asia.

Given the over-investment in luxury hotels apparent in many South-East Asian countries by 1969, the sudden influx of oilmen was a boon. But investment in hotel construction and luxury housing deflects funds from more critical sectors of local development. Indonesia, for example, has spent $5 million on an ultra-modern hospital for foreign guests at a time when the country's infant mortality rate is 125 per thousand and average life expectancy is 42 years, while public housing development—in such cities as Jakarta and Surabaya, blighted by huge and congested shanty slums and under pressure of ever-increasing rural-urban migration—accounts for a derisory fraction of municipal spending. Too often, the tendency is to hide, rather than clear, slums. The immediate short-term results of the oil boom are, then, the warping of economic and social development to meet the needs of a very small and transient group of foreign experts.

In January 1974 the Indonesian State Oil Corporation, Pertamina, renegotiated its original production-sharing agreements with oil companies (65 : 35 in favour of Pertamina, after subtracting 40 per cent for company production costs) to allow for a more favourable 85 : 15 sharing of production for that part of the price exceeding $5 a barrel. Companies can still subtract operating costs of 40 per cent before determining Pertamina's share (these are calculated at U.S. price levels and on the basis of the overseas level of living of U.S. oil personnel). Thus, their effective share is about 50 per cent.

It must be noted, however, that Indonesia's production-sharing contracts do not apply to Caltex, in its main producing areas, until 1983—and Caltex produces the bulk of Indonesian oil at present. One very attractive feature of Indonesian oil, therefore—apart from its high quality—is its profitability. As the company share of the late-1974 price of $12.60 a barrel was some $6.20, and as the real cost of producing oil in Indonesia is less than $1 a barrel, companies have greatly benefited from "global cartel-pricing". "Under the present circumstances," observes the *Far Eastern Economic Review* (Nov. 15th, 1974), "oil companies have every incentive to sell off as much Indonesian oil as they can: no other major producer offers them a better deal." As a result, the exploration boom accelerated, and the discovery rate rose accordingly. Exploration and development spending by oil companies in Indonesia rose from $78 million in 1969 to an estimated $690 million in 1975.

On the face of it, the investment laws governing oil profits appear relatively favourable to Thailand, Brunei, Indonesia and Malaysia (which has similar oil-sharing agreements to those of Indonesia). But ultimately most of the influence and profits accrue to the companies, which control not only exploration and development but also refining, shipping, distribution and trade in crude oil, refined fuel, and a wide range of petrochemicals (including many basic agrochemicals from fertilizers to pesticides). Thus, for example, the Indonesian state in reality becomes a junior partner of the oil companies and is bound to them by a strong mutuality of interests.

The terms under which the South-East Asian governments are prepared to allow exploitation of one of their most valuable resources are, by comparison with the terms negotiated by the Middle Eastern producers, generous in the extreme. Nevertheless, it may be argued, the exploitation of oil and other minerals cannot but give a major impetus to economic development in the region. After all, Malaysia is now self-sufficient in oil, and the value of Indonesian oil exports in 1975 was $4,933.1 million, compared with $1,600 million for 1973. But the question is not simply one of foreign exchange savings or the value of oil revenues—far more, the relevance of oil to producer countries is a question of the way in which development planning is structured to utilize most productively increased oil revenues.

For Indonesia, and other South-East Asian countries, the mineral boom may have little more effect than the opening of a Pandora's box. For development continues to be concentrated in a few capital-intensive enclaves, having negligible linkage with the rest of the economy. Infrastructural development is excessively geared to servicing these extractive enclaves, and what rural development there is tends to be modelled on "Green Revolution" principles which are largely irrelevant in countries where between 50 and 70 per cent of the population are poor small-holding peasants. Manufacturing development in the region has no doubt increased with the accelerated growth of mining industries, but the nature of this development in the secondary sector is such that it is not laying a firm basis for comprehensive indigenous industrialization in countries like Indonesia or Malaysia. As we have seen, industrial development tends to be heavily localized in a few favoured urban centres; a further characteristic is its excessive concentration on servicing an export-oriented extractive economy largely controlled by foreigners, and associated with this is the development of a range of foreign-owned export industries (especially assembly-line plants) which are only in the region because of the availability of very cheap labour and the existence of a host of investment incentives, particularly in the taxation field. Such manufacturing development is a spontaneous clutter rather than a planned basis for local industrialization, a hotch-potch of activities little related to the needs of overall economic development, having negligible spread effects, and certainly having very little linkage with the peasant agricultural economy. In the latter respect, one very important element is missing from the pattern of industrial development in South-East Asia (with the possible exception of Malaysia)—that is, the growth of rural-based industries. Indeed, many areas—such as Java—are seeing a sharp decline of rural industry in the face of competition from urban mass-production and imports.

Similarly, the Indonesian Government is making a major effort to encourage foreign investment into the development of large-scale, capital-intensive rice plantations outside Java as a more effective way of increasing food supply than reforming overpopulated, poverty-ridden Javanese agriculture: so far, at least seven schemes are being planned, involving between 80,000 and 100,000 hectares, capital expenditure of some $7,000 per hectare (compared to the $500–600 needed to prepare a normal wet rice field), and yields of 10 tons per hectare. Thus, it is hoped that during the Second Five Year Plan (1974–79) highly capitalized rice estate production will rise to a level which, if produced by Javanese smallholders, would actively involve some 3–4 million rural dwellers. An example of such a scheme is Pertamina's south Sumatran 20,000 hectare project, involving a capital outlay of $7,500 per hectare, and producing sufficient to feed Pertamina's local labour force, cover south Sumatra's rice deficit, and supply an export surplus. The labour-displacing character of this form of rural development is obvious but it is well in keeping with the logic of current economic planning, and in particular with the enclave-like nature of Indonesia's major industry—the oil industry.

Thus the process of industrialization and agricultural development is badly distorted; and the mineral boom, given the prevailing pattern of economic and political control (both local and foreign), is aggravating this distortion.

To the Indonesian Government, two of the country's most advertised attractions for foreign investment are its rich supply of resources and its abundance of cheap labour. The rest of South-East Asia shares these advantages. But while the abundance of resources (especially oil) may attract large-scale investment if political stability can be assured, this investment is, because of its capital-intensive nature, unlikely to make any significant impact on the employment problem. On the other hand, much of the labour-intensive manufacturing attracted to the region by the availability of cheap labour and generous fiscal incentives is of a notoriously footloose nature, with few linkages to other economic activities, and a tendency to employ the cheaper unskilled female labour; in such fields as electronics, toy production, garment making, and wig production, foreign firms often maintain factories for the duration of their concessionary tax holiday, employing unskilled labour for largely export production, and recouping their capital investment two or three times over, before relocating in a neighbouring tax jurisdiction. Such footloose tax-avoidance is common among firms investing in Indonesia, Singapore, Malaysia and Thailand.

Yet, clearly, some have benefited in Indonesia from oil development. As agent between the Government and foreign oil concerns, Pertamina handles 75 per cent of Indonesia's gross foreign exchange; as the base for a multiplicity of joint venture and subsidiary operations, many private and beyond government regulations, Pertamina also predominates in the development of Indonesia's "modern" home economy. Pertamina had a 1974/75 budget of $2,000 million (equivalent to over half the national budget), and net fixed assets of nearly $2,500 million. However, the company's over extension led to its virtual *débâcle* in 1975.

Meanwhile, given the steady increase of population, given that the number of those un- and under-employed may double within the next 30 years, the gap between the great mass of the population and those wealthy groups who will benefit from Asia's offshore oil boom grows wider. The prospects of real nation-wide development benefiting all classes are small; the shadow of increasing social tensions and ultimate internal armed conflict, falls across all of South-East Asia beyond Indochina.

Under these circumstances, South-East Asia's future may still partly be determined by the value the developed nations place on the region's energy resources and by the extent to which they are prepared to use military force to impose the stability needed to exploit these resources under conditions acceptable to the major oil companies. And in a world in which might, including economic might, is too often taken as synonymous for right, it is sobering to reflect that the 1974 *profits* of America's five main oil companies ($7,800 million) were equivalent to over 50 per cent of Indonesia's Gross National Product.

However, 1975 marked a development of perhaps greater long-term consequences for the whole South-East Asian region: by that year, the population of the region's Communist states had risen to 55 million, as Cambodia, South Viet-Nam and Laos fell decisively from Western control.

BIBLIOGRAPHY

GENERAL

BUTWELL, R. South-East Asia: Today and Tomorrow (New York, 1970).

CHEVERNY, J. Eloge du colonialisme (Julliard, Paris, 1961).

EVERS, HANS-DIETER (ed.). Modernization in South-East Asia (East Asian Social Science Monographs, Oxford University Press, 1973).

JACOBY, E. H. Agrarian Unrest in Southeast Asia (Asia Publishing House, Bombay, 2nd edn. 1961).

MENDE, T. South-East Asia Between Two Worlds (London, 1955).

OSBORNE, M., Region of Revolt: Focus on Southeast Asia. (Pergamon, 1970).

THOMPSON, V., & ADLOFF, R. Minority Problems in Southeast Asia (Stanford University Press, 1955).

UNESCO. Social Problems and Problems of Rural Development in South-East Asia (Paris, 1963).

WYATT, W. Southwards from China (London, 1952).

HISTORY

EDWARDES, M. Asia in the European Age (Thames and Hudson, London, 1961).

FIFIELD, R. H. The Diplomacy of Southeast Asia: 1945–1958 (Harper, New York, 1958).

FITZGERALD, C. P. Concise History of East Asia (Heinemann, London, 1967).

HALL, D. G. E. A History of South-East Asia (Macmillan, London, 2nd edition 1964).

HARRISON, B. South-East Asia: A Short History (Macmillan, London, 1963).

MATTHEW, H. G. (ed.). Asia in the Modern World (New York, 1963).

OSBORNE, MILTON. River Road to China: The Mekong Expedition, 1866–73 (Allen and Unwin, London, 1976).

PURCELL, V. The Revolution in South-East Asia (London, 1962).
South and East Asia since 1800 (Cambridge University Press, 1965).

SARKISYANZ, E. Südostasien seit 1945 (Munich, 1961).

TARLING, N. A Concise History of South-East Asia (Praeger, New York and Pall Mall Press, London, 1968).

ECONOMICS AND POLITICS

ALLEN, SIR RICHARD. A Short Introduction to the History and Politics of Southeast Asia (O.U.P. New York, 1970).

BRIMMELL, J. H. Communism in South-East Asia (Oxford University Press, London, 1958).

BUCHANAN, I. Singapore in South-East Asia (Bell, London, 1972).

CALDWELL, M. Indonesia (O.U.P. 1968).

CALDWELL, M. and TAN, L. Cambodia in the South-East Asian War (Monthly Review Press, 1973).

COWAN, C. D. (ed.). The Economic Development of South-East Asia (London, 1964).

GERASSI, J. North Vietnam: a Documentary (Bobbs-Merrill, New York, 1968).

HARRIS, R. Independence and After (Oxford University Press, London, 1962).

HOWELL, L., and MORROW, M. "The 'Invisible Gold' Hunt" in *Far Eastern Economic Review*, October 1st, 1973.

KHOI, LE THANH. L'économie de l'Asie du Sud-Est (Que Sais-je?, Paris, 1958).

KRAAR, L. "Oil and Nationalism Mix Beautifully in Indonesia" in *Fortune*, July 1973.

LÊ CHÂU. Le Viet-Nam socialiste: une économie de transition (Paris, 1966).
La revolution paysanne du sud Viet-Nam (Paris, 1966).

RANIS, G. Sharing in Development: A Programme of Employment, Equity and Growth in the Philippines (International Labour Organization, 1973).

SIEGEL, L. "ASEAN Integration" in *Pacific Research*, Nov.–Dec. 1973.

SILCOCK, T. H. The Commonwealth Economy in South-East Asia (Cambridge University Press, 1966).

UTRECHT, E. "Land Reform and Bimas in Indonesia" in *Journal of Contemporary Asia*, Vol. 3, No. 2, 1973.

WEISBERG, B. (ed.). Ecocide in Indochina (Harper and Row, 1971).

WIJEYEWARDENE, G. (ed.). Leadership and Authority (Singapore, 1968).

GEOGRAPHY AND CIVILIZATION

BUCHANAN, K. The Southeast Asian World (Bell, London, 1967).

CHALIAND, G. The Peasants of North Vietnam (Penguin Books 1969).

EAST, W. G., & SPATE, O. H. K. (eds.). The Changing Map of Asia (London, 4th edition 1961).

FISHER, C. A. South-East Asia (Methuen, London, 1964).

FITZGERALD, C. P. The Third China (Sydney, 1965).

GINSBURG, N. S. (ed.). The Pattern of Asia (Prentice Hall, Englewood Cliffs, New Jersey, 1960).

HALL, D. G. E. Atlas of South-East Asia (with Introduction) (London and New York, 1964).

LASKER, B. Peoples of South-East Asia (New York, 1944).

LE MAY, R. The Culture of South-East Asia (London, 1954).

MCGEE, T. G. The South-East Asian City (Bell, London, 1967).

RAWSON, P. Art of South-East Asia (Thames and Hudson, London, 1968).

SPENCER, J. E. Asia East by South (London and New York, revised edition 1971).

Brunei

PHYSICAL AND SOCIAL GEOGRAPHY

C. A. Fisher

Brunei covers 2,226 square miles (5,765 square kilometres) facing the South China Sea along the coast of northern Borneo. On its landward side it is both surrounded and split into two separate units by Sarawak but, unlike the latter, it does not form part of Malaysia.

PHYSICAL FEATURES AND CLIMATE

The greater part of Brunei's small territory consists of a low coastal plain, and only on its southern margins does it attain heights of over 1,000 feet (300 metres). Situated as it is, only 4°–5° N. of the equator, Brunei has a consistently hot and humid climate, with mean monthly temperatures around 80°F. (27°C.) and a heavy rainfall of over 100 inches (250 cm.), well distributed throughout the year. Except for those areas which have been cleared for permanent cultivation in the coastal zone, the country is covered by dense equatorial forest, though this has deteriorated in places as a result of shifting cultivation.

MINERALS

Apart from agricultural land adequate to feed its population and to produce a minute export of rubber, Brunei's natural resources consist exclusively of petroleum and natural gas from the Seria oilfield close to the Sarawak border and from the offshore field at South-West Ampa.

POPULATION

The estimated population in 1974 was 150,000, of which about 65 per cent were Brunei Malays and about 23 per cent Chinese, mainly in Bandar Seri Begawan and Seria. Bandar Seri Begawan, the capital, which occupies an impressive site overlooking the large natural inlet of Brunei Bay, had a population of 75,000 in 1976.

HISTORY

John Bastin

(Revised by T. M. Burley, 1975)

Brunei has long been a centre of human settlement although little is known about its early history. Chinese coins of the eighth century A.D. have been found at Kota Batu, two miles from Brunei Town, but these may have been introduced at a later period when Chinese trade with western Borneo was more extensively developed. Brunei is listed among the tributary states of the Hindu-Javanese empire of Majapahit in the second half of the fourteenth century but it soon afterwards became an independent sultanate. As the Brunei royal chronicles give only the names of rulers and not specific dates (the present ruler, Sultan Hassanal Bolkiah, is the twenty-ninth in the list), the date of the origin of the sultanate is uncertain. However, the Malay-Arabic inscription of the oldest tombstone at Brunei carries the equivalent Hijra date of A.D. 1432 so that by then at least Islam was already well established.

The first rulers of Brunei may not have been Malays, but Bisayas or Muruts, the designation *Malay* being applied to the peoples of western Borneo as they became Muslims. Islam only marginally affected the Kayans and Ibans but it made considerable progress among such peoples as the Melanaus whose chiefs were frequently replaced by Brunei princelings who married Melanau women. Together with the spread of Islam went a corresponding increase in Brunei's political power. By the sixteenth century the sultanate embraced most of the coastal regions of present-day Sarawak and Sabah. Tribute from the imperial domains was collected by Malays (and Arabs) settled at the mouths of the rivers.

The prosperity of the sultanate depended upon trade, a large part of which was carried on with Chinese merchants from the southern ports of China. In exchange for hornbill-ivory, bezoar stones, woods and edible birds'-nests, the Chinese brought silks, metals, stoneware and fine porcelains. The fact that large quantities of T'ang, Sung and Ming porcelain have been found attests to the extent and importance of the trade with China which continued until the late eighteenth century. Early European commercial contacts with Brunei, on the other hand, were minimal, and it was not until the arrival of James Brooke in Sarawak that Brunei was forced to adjust to the Western presence in South-East Asia.

The adjustment was often painful. In 1842, Sultan Omar Ali Saifuddin was obliged to appoint Brooke as Rajah of Sarawak, and four years later to cede the island of Labuan to Great Britain. Thereafter the sultanate was under growing pressure from the Brooke regime in the south and from American and European speculators in Sabah to cede more territory. The coast beyond Bintulu was in Brooke's hands by the 1860s, and during the following twenty-odd years the Sarawak frontier was advanced to include the Baram, Trusan and Limbang Rivers. During the same period (1877–78) the Brunei and Sulu rulers ceded 28,000 square miles of Sabah, from Gaya Bay to the Sibuco River, to agents of the embryo British North Borneo Company, formed in 1881. Sandwiched between the Company in the north and the Brooke state in the south, the former powerful sultanate of Brunei was reduced in size to a little more than 2,000 square miles, its Belait and Tutong districts being divided from Temburong by the lands of Sarawak. In 1888, Britain formally extended its protection over the sultanate, and in 1906 a British Resident (later High Commissioner) was appointed to the court of the ruler to advise on all matters of government except those relating to Islam and Malay custom.

Present Administrative and Political Structure

Brunei remains a self-governing sultanate. By the 1959 agreement Britain assumed responsibility for foreign relations and defence, leaving religion and social customs only in the Sultan's hands. In the same year a constitution established five councils to govern the state. These are the Privy Council, which is presided over by the Sultan and is concerned with amendments to the constitution and appointments to Malay customary posts; the executive Council of Ministers, which is also presided over by the Sultan and which is composed of the British High Commissioner, four unofficial members appointed by the Legislative Council, and six *ex-officio* members; the Legislative Council, which possesses general legislative powers, including finance, and is comprised of six *ex-officio* members, ten official and five unofficial members; the Religious Council, which advises the Sultan on all matters relating to Islam; and a Council of Succession. At a lower level there are four District Councils, the majority of whose members are elected by universal suffrage.

Under a new treaty signed on November 23rd, 1971, and presented to Parliament in April 1972, Britain, though continuing to assume responsibility for external affairs, will only advise on defence while leaving the Sultan in control of all internal matters.

Moves towards introducing more popular government were halted by a revolt in December 1962, led by A. M. Azahari and the People's Party, which was sparked off by the prospect of Brunei joining the new federation of Malaysia. Since then, the Brunei People's Independence Front has been vocal in demanding constitutional reform by the implementation of a full ministerial system and an elective Legislative Council as proposed in the White Paper of 1964; but the failure of the Front to win a majority of seats in the District Council elections in May 1968 suggests that there is no general dissatisfaction with the existing arrangements. In these elections the Independence Front, the only party to participate, lost in 15 of the 25 wards in which it was opposed by "royalist" independents, and finished with only 24 of the total of 55 District Council seats. The independents refused to exert any pressure on the 21-year-old Sultan Hassanal Bolkiah preparatory to his talks with the British Government in London late in 1968 over the future of Brunei. In view of the partial withdrawal of British forces "East of Suez" Britain's commitments under the 1959 agreement have been reduced.

ECONOMIC SURVEY

T. M. Burley

Brunei possesses an urban and industrial economy based on the exploitation of rich oil and gas resources. The 1974 population was estimated at 150,000, a density of 26 persons per square kilometre. Per capita income in 1973 was U.S. $1,370 but this almost certainly doubled in 1974 with the rapid increase in the price of oil. The 1974–78 Five-Year Plan calls for government investment of B$500 million. The plan stresses job opportunities through diversification: 10,000 new jobs are to be created. About 30 per cent of the population is in employment, half being government and public service workers.

The 1975 Investment Incentives Act exempts new investments from the 30 per cent tax charged on companies for periods of two to eight years depending on the size of the investment. Exemption from import duties on plans and machinery may also be given.

Agriculture

Brunei is dependent on imports for about 80 per cent of its food requirements, including the staple cereal, rice. Only 10 per cent of the land area is cultivated but much potential agricultural land lies undeveloped. Agricultural workers number only 1,000. Rice production is estimated at about 4,000 tons per annum, only 25 per cent of requirements. Rice, along with other cereals, livestock and livestock feeds, which together account for some two-thirds of imports, is a priority area for development. Attention is also being given to the production of coffee, coconuts, cocoa, sugar and tobacco and to increasing local production of fruits and vegetables.

Rubber is the leading export commodity: in 1974 some 500 tons were sold abroad: an estimated 27,000 acres (10,900 hectares) are under rubber, with some 3,000 acres (1,200 hectares) of high-yielding trees. However, the importance of rubber as a cash crop for up-river smallholders has declined in recent years, due to competitive wages paid by the Government for road-building and other public works.

Forestry is stressed in the 1974–78 Plan; approval has been given to Japanese contractors to construct a paper pulp mill at Kuala Lelait but in early 1976 none of the B$200 million investment had materilized.

The main protein ingredient in the Brunei diet is fish. But the livelihood of the approximately 800 fishermen was jeopardized by an invasion in March 1976 of poisonous algae, forcing the Government to ban sales of sea fish and shellfish.

Oil and natural gas

Brunei is one of the most important petroleum and gas producers in the Commonwealth. Early in 1975 the Government took a controlling interest in the Brunei Shell Petroleum Company, the only oil company operating in the country. Production in 1976 was around 200,000 barrels per day, output having been cut back due to the blow-out and loss of production at Champion Shoals. Some of the oil is refined locally but the bulk of it is pumped to Lutong and Miri in Sarawak.

In 1973 the Government obtained over B$300 million, or 80 per cent of its revenue, from petroleum-related revenues, but this soared to over B$900 million in 1974.

Production of natural gas in 1970 totalled 7,900 million cubic feet but output increased fivefold between 1973 and 1974: by the end of 1976, exports should be in the order of 775 million standard cubic feet per day. The natural gas liquefaction plant at Lumut, the largest in the world, cost U.S. $120 million and is designed to produce at its full capacity about 4 million tons of liquid gas per year. A contract has been signed to supply Japan with liquefied natural gas to the value of B$6,000 million over a 20-year period.

Infrastructure

Links with the outside world were greatly improved in 1975 with the establishment of the Royal Brunei Airlines. From an international standard airport at Bandar Seri Begawan, it operates to Singapore, Sabah and Hong Kong. The opening of the B$32 million port at Muara, able to handle 150,000 d.w.t. vessels, has prompted plans for a national shipping line. In 1974 there were about 150 vehicles per 1,000 persons, or a total of 22,272.

Foreign trade

Brunei achieved a trade surplus of B$529 million in 1973, with exports totalling B$852 million and imports amounting to B$323 million. For 1974 the comparable figures were much greater: B$1,902 million, B$2,353 million, and B$451 million. Major export markets were Japan, Sarawak, Taiwan and the Philippines, and imports were chiefly from Japan, the U.S.A. and Singapore. Machinery and transport equipment make up a third of Brunei's imports, with food and manufactured goods totalling another third.

The rising value of oil and gas exports has caused a substantial trade surplus since 1972. At mid-1975 foreign exchange reserves totalled almost B$2,000 million.

Finance

Government revenue in 1974 totalled B$975 million, almost treble the amount for 1973. Of the 1974 earnings, $686 million came from taxes (there is no personal income tax in Brunei and companies pay a flat 30 per cent tax on profits). As there are practically no industries apart from oil and natural gas, most of the $686 million will have been paid by Brunei Shell Petroleum and Brunei LNG, which exports liquefied gas to Japan. The effect of the rise in oil prices, which helped Brunei's oil revenue to jump to $1,970 million in 1974 from $762 million in 1973, is reflected in the fact that Brunei expected only $450 million from taxes when estimates were made at the end of 1973. Taxes for 1975 were expected to net a record $900 million.

Oil royalties and mining rents earned the state $216.9 million (compared with $62.9 million in 1973), although at the beginning of 1974 estimated earnings from this source were placed at $130 million. Oil royalties and mining rents for 1975 were provisionally estimated at $200 million, but the final figure could be well above this.

While revenue in 1974 set a record, expenditure rose modestly from $215 million to $273 million, giving the Government a surplus of $702 million, compared with $153 million in 1973. Expenditure in 1975 was expected to leap to $462 million, with $80 million of this going to the Development Fund. But this would still leave Brunei with a surplus of $711 million on the estimated revenue for the year, almost as much as the country's total investments at the beginning of 1974. Total investments at that time were $745 million, including $564 million in sterling assets and equities.

A price freeze was introduced in March 1974 to curb inflation. Despite higher prices, the greatly increased disposable incomes of the population has boosted consumer spending; initial data for 1975 suggests a near doubling in motor vehicle sales, for example. Paralleling these developments, interest rates have been progressively lowered to single figures.

STATISTICAL SURVEY

Area and Population: Area: 2,226 sq. miles (5,765 sq. km.); Population (1974 est.) 150,000 (Malays 65 per cent, Chinese 23 per cent, Indigenous 7 per cent. others 5 per cent); Bandar Seri Begawan (capital—1976 est.) 75,000.

BIRTHS, MARRIAGES AND DEATHS

	Live Births		Marriages		Deaths	
	Number	Rate (per 1,000)	Number	Rate (per 1,000)	Number	Rate (per 1,000)
1968	4,912	41.2	505	4.2	715	6.0
1969	4,614	37.0	605	4.9	691	5.5
1970	4,823	37.0	597	4.6	716	5.5
1971	5,181	38.4	646	4.8	801	5.9
1972	5,008	35.4	601	4.3	742	5.2
1973	5,034	34.7	846	5.8	701	4.8
1974	5,013	33.4	n.a.	n.a.	638	4.3

ECONOMICALLY ACTIVE POPULATION
(census of August 1971)

	Males	Females	Total
Agriculture, hunting, forestry and fishing	3,296	1,480	4,776
Mining and quarrying	2,720	195	2,915
Manufacturing	1,466	285	1,751
Electricity, gas and water	1,061	25	1,086
Construction	7,929	161	8,090
Trade, restaurants and hotels	3,332	857	4,189
Transport, storage and communications	2,034	93	2,127
Finance, insurance, property and business services	527	118	645
Community, social and personal services	11,146	3,217	14,363
Other activities (not adequately described)	51	19	70
Total in Employment	33,562	6,450	40,012
Unemployed	649	438	1,087
Total Labour Force	34,211	6,888	41,099

Source: International Labour Office, *Year Book of Labour Statistics.*

AGRICULTURE

LAND USE, 1971
('000 hectares)

Arable land	4
Land under permanent crops	9
Permanent meadows and pastures	6
Forest and woodlands	435
Other land	73
Inland water	50
Total	577

Source: FAO, *Production Yearbook.*

PRINCIPAL CROPS

(FAO estimates—'000 metric tons)

	1972	1973	1974
Rice (paddy)	5	6	6
Sweet potatoes	1	1	1
Cassava (Manioc)	3	3	3
Bananas	8	8	8
Natural rubber	0.1	0.4	0.5

LIVESTOCK

(FAO estimates—'000 head)

	1972	1973	1974
Cattle	3	3	3
Buffaloes	16	16	17
Pigs	14	14	14
Goats	1	1	1
Chickens	700	750	800
Ducks	38	40	42

LIVESTOCK PRODUCTS

(FAO estimates—metric tons)

	1972	1973	1974
Buffalo meat	1,000	1,000	1,000
Poultry meat	1,000	2,000	2,000
Edible offals	223	229	233
Hen eggs	1,110	1,215	1,280
Cattle hides (fresh)	6	6	6
Buffalo hides (fresh)	111	113	116

Source: FAO, *Production Yearbook 1974.*

MINING

('000 metric tons)

	1969	1970	1971	1972	1973
Crude petroleum	6,107	6,685	6,341	8,823	11,053
Natural gasoline	51	49	45	45	43
Natural gas*	191	224	220	453	n.a.
Sand, silica and quartz	28	175	309	n.a.	n.a.
Gravel and crushed stone	250	500	1,000	n.a.	n.a.

* Million cubic metres.

Source: United Nations, *The Growth of World Industry.*

INDUSTRY

('000 metric tons)

	1969	1970	1971	1972	1973
Motor spirit (petrol)	13	12	11	14	16
Naphthas	1	1	1	2	5
Distillate fuel oils	25	29	30	29	27
Liquefied petroleum gas from natural gas plants	2	2	17	15	n.a.
Electric energy*	126	138	150	192	200

* Million kWh.

Source: United Nations, *The Growth of World Industry.*

FINANCE

100 sen (cents) = 1 Brunei dollar (B$).

Coins: 1, 5, 10, 20 and 50 cents.

Notes: 1, 5, 10, 50 and 100 dollars.

Exchange rates (June 1976): B$1 = 1 Singapore dollar; £1 sterling = B$4.39; U.S. $1 = B$2.47.
B$100 = £22.78 = U.S. $40.41.

Note: The Brunei dollar (B$) was introduced in June 1967, replacing (at par) the Malayan dollar (M$). From September 1949 the Malayan dollar was valued at 2s. 4d. sterling (£1 = M$8.5714) or 32.667 U.S. cents (U.S. $1 = M$3.0612). This valuation in terms of U.S. currency remained in effect until August 1971. Between December 1971 and February 1973 the Brunei dollar was valued at 35.467 U.S. cents (U.S. $1 = B$2.8195). From February to June 1973 the Brunei dollar's value was 39.407 U.S. cents (U.S. $1 = B$2.5376). In terms of sterling, the exchange rate was £1 = B$7.347 from November 1967 to June 1972. The formal link with the Malaysian dollar, begun in June 1967, ended in May 1973 but the Brunei dollar remained tied to the Singapore dollar. Since June 1973 the Singapore dollar has been allowed to "float". The average market exchange rate (B$ per U.S. $) was: 2.809 in 1972; 2.444 in 1973; 2.437 in 1974; 2.371 in 1975.

BUDGET 1974
(B$'000—estimates)

Revenue	
Royalties (from oil)	130,000
Interest	32,000
Other	30,000
Total	192,000

Expenditure	
Royal Brunei Malay Regiment	59,254
Education	32,623
Public Works	21,866
Medical Services	12,797
Police	12,525
Other (including Development Fund)	52,000
Total	191,065

EXTERNAL TRADE
(B$ million)

	1966	1967	1968	1969	1970	1971	1972	1973	1974
Imports c.i.f.	150.0	130.9	206.6	218.7	256.1	456.5	300.2	323.2	450.9
Exports f.o.b.	225.5	248.3	281.4	270.1	282.2	310.7	497.4	852.1	2,388.3

PRINCIPAL COMMODITIES
(B$'000)

Imports	1971	1972	1973
Foodstuffs	37,466	43,145	51,800
Beverages and Tobacco	7,762	7,972	8,900
Crude minerals	6,624	7,646	4,300
Refined petroleum	4,603	5,209	6,900
Animal and vegetable oils	1,429	1,403	n.a.
Chemicals	17,667	17,981	23,000
Machinery and Transport Equipment	214,867	113,108	117,200
Manufactures	157,546	99,313	102,800
Miscellaneous	8,679	4,429	n.a.

Exports	1972*	1973*	1974*
Crude petroleum	462,054	762,000	1,970,000
Natural gas	1,952	46,500	291,000
Rubber	58	n.a	n.a.
Petroleum products	3,141	n.a.	n.a.
Total (incl. others)	469,691	830,720	2,353,000

* Figures are provisional. Revised totals (in B$'000) are: 497,379 in 1972; 852,056 in 1973; 2,388,313 in 1974.

PRINCIPAL COUNTRIES
(B$'000)

IMPORTS	1972	1973	1974
Australia	10,221	6,805	8,351
China, People's Republic	8,853	16,855	12,158
Germany, Fed. Republic	9,900	6,786	9,751
Japan	60,152	76,533	120,765
Netherlands	17,388	14,865	16,920
Singapore	45,458	50,064	67,071
United Kingdom	42,729	37,954	48,236
U.S.A.	57,413	51,114	90,215
TOTAL (incl. others)	300,206	323,229	450,897

EXPORTS	1972	1973	1974
Japan	258,816	647,288	1,868,311
Sarawak	56,412	84,181	169,099
Singapore	41,498	24,819	8,380
Taiwan	17,026	23,618	75,092
U.S.A.	41,444	50,786	122,346
TOTAL (incl. others)	497,379	852,056	2,388,313

Source: Statistics of External Trade—Brunei 1972–74.

Transport: *Road Transport:* (1972) Passenger cars 15,118, commercial vehicles 2,909, motor cycles and scooters 878; (1973) Passenger cars 16,992. *Shipping* (1973): Tonnage Entered 1,134,381. *Civil Aviation* (1973): Passengers embarked 63,882.

EDUCATION
(1973)

	SCHOOLS	PUPILS
Kindergarten	13	1,322
Primary	137	30,722
Secondary	26	12,479
Teacher Training	2	460
Vocational	2	206

In 1973 about 380 Brunei students were studying abroad.

Source (unless otherwise stated): *Commonwealth Fact Sheet, Brunei*, Commonwealth Institute, London.

THE CONSTITUTION

A new constitution was promulgated in September 1959. Under it sovereign authority is vested in the Sultan, who is to be assisted and advised by five Councils:

The Religious Council: In his capacity as head of the Islamic Faith, the Sultan is advised in all Islamic matters by the Religious Council, whose members are appointed by the Sultan.

The Privy Council: This Council, presided over by the Sultan, is to advise the Sultan on matters concerning the Royal prerogative of mercy, the amendment of the constitution and the conferment of ranks, titles and honours.

The Council of Ministers: Presided over by the Sultan, the Council of Ministers considers all executive matters as well as those raised by the Legislative Council. It is composed of 11 members, including the High Commissioner.

The Legislative Council: This council is presided over by a Speaker appointed by the Sultan. The Council introduces Bills, passes laws, exercises financial controls and scrutinizes government policies.

The Council of Succession: Subject to the Constitution this Council is to determine the succession to the throne should the need arise.

A Mentri Besar (Chief Minister) is responsible to the Sultan for the exercise of all executive authority. He is assisted by a State Secretary, an Attorney-General and a State Financial Officer.

The State is divided into four administrative districts, in each of which is a District Officer (Malay) responsible to the Mentri Besar.

Note: Parts of the constitution have been in abeyance since 1962.

THE GOVERNMENT

(*June* 1976)

The Sultan: H.H. MUDA HASSANAL BOLKIAH MU'IZZADDIN WADDAULAH (succeeded October 5th, 1967; crowned August 1st, 1968).

General Adviser to H.H. The Sultan: Pehin Dato ISA.

Mentri Besar: Pengiran DIPA NEGARA LAILA DI-RAJA Pengiran ABD. MOMIN bin Pengiran Haji ISMAIL.

State Secretary: Dato ABDUL AZIZ.

Acting State Financial Officer: H. C. WILLIAMS.

Attorney-General: Pehin Dato IDRIS TALOG DAVIES.

Head of Religious Affairs: Pehin Dato MOHD. ZAIN.

HIGH COMMISSIONER

The High Commissioner: Dato J. A. DAVIDSON.

POLITICAL PARTY

Barisan Kemerdeka'an Rakyat—BAKER (*Brunei People's Independence Front*): f. 1966; an amalgamation of all the former parties; Pres. ZAINAL ABIDIN PUTEH.

JUDICIAL SYSTEM

The judicial system was created by the Supreme Court Enactment, 1963, under which the Supreme Court consists of the High Court and the Court of Appeal. There are also Magistrates' Courts of First, Second and Third Class.

The Supreme Court: Consists of the Chief Justice and Commissioners of the Supreme Court appointed by the Sultan. The High Court has unlimited original jurisdiction in most civil matters and unlimited criminal jurisdiction.

Courts of Magistrates: There are Courts of Magistrates of the First, Second and Third Class. They have original jurisdiction in minor civil and criminal cases.

Courts of Kadhis: Deal solely with questions concerning Muslim religion, marriage and divorce. Appeals lie from these Courts to the Sultan in the Religious Council.

Chief Justice: GEOFFREY GOULD BRIGGS.

Chief Kadhi: Begawan Pehin Khatib Dato Seri UTAMA Haji METALI bin MAT YASSIN.

RELIGION

The official religion of Brunei is Islam, and His Highness the Sultan is head of the Islamic population. Muslims number about 60,000, most of them Malays. The Chinese population is either Buddhist, Confucianist, Taoist or Christian. Large numbers of the indigenous races are animists of various types. The remainder of the population are Roman Catholics, Anglicans or members of the American Methodist Church of Southern Asia.

ANGLICAN

Bishop of Kuching: The Rt. Rev. Datuk BASIL TEMENGONG, Bishop's House, P.O.B. 347, Kuching, Sarawak, Malaysia.

ROMAN CATHOLIC

Vicar Apostolic: The Rt. Rev. ANTHONY DENNIS GALVIN, O.B.E., Bishop's House, Miri, Sarawak, Malaysia.

THE PRESS

NEWSPAPERS

Borneo Bulletin: P.O.B. 69, Kuala Belait; f. 1953; Independent; English; weekly; Saturday; Man. and Man. Editor H. M. MABBETT; circ. 26,200.

Pelita Brunei: Dept. of Broadcasting and Information, Brunei; f. 1956; free newspaper in Romanized Malay, English and Chinese; weekly; circ. 20,000.

Salam: c/o Brunei Shell Petroleum Co. Ltd., Seria; f. 1953; free employee newspaper produced by the Brunei Shell Petroleum Co. Ltd.; English, Chinese and Romanized Malay in one edition; fortnightly; Friday; circ. 4,200.

PUBLISHERS

The Brunei Press: P.O.B. 69, Kuala Belait; incorp. 1959; Gen. Man. H. M. MABBETT.

The Star Press: Bandar Seri Begawan; f. 1963; Man. F. W. ZIMMERMANN.

RADIO AND TELEVISION

Radio and Television Brunei: Brunei; f. 1957; daily broadcasts in Malay, English, Chinese and local dialects; a new all-colour television service was opened in July 1975. Controller J. B. MILLAR; Assistant Controller MOHAMMED SALLEH ABDUL KADIR.

In 1973 there were 22,000 radio receivers.

FINANCE

BANKS

National Bank of Brunei Ltd.: P.O.B. 321, Bandar Seri Begawan; f. 1965; cap. B$45m., resources B$280m., dep. B$195m. (1974); Pres. Prince MOHAMMED BOLKIAH; Chair. B. H. KHOO; brs. in Seria, Kuala Belait, Tutong and Muara Port.

The Chartered Bank and Hong Kong and Shanghai Banking Corporation have branches in Brunei.

INSURANCE

A number of British insurance companies have agencies in Brunei.

TRADE AND INDUSTRY

Trade in Brunei is largely conducted by the agency houses, European and Chinese, and by Chinese merchants.

Brunei Shell Petroleum Co. Ltd.: Seria; the largest industrial concern in the State and the only oil company at present in production in Brunei; 50 per cent state holding; Chief Exec. J. CORDINGLEY; output (1974) 200,000 barrels per day.

Brunei Liquid Natural Gas Ltd.: Seria; natural gas production; owned 45 per cent Royal Dutch/Shell, 45 per cent Mitsubishi, 10 per cent Brunei Government; operate LNG plant at Lumut, the largest in the world, with a capacity of 5 million tons per year.

CHAMBER OF COMMERCE

Brunei State Chamber of Commerce: P.O.B. 2246, Bandar Seri Begawan; br. at Kuala Belait; 36 mems.

TRADE UNIONS

Brunei Oilfield Workers' Union: P.O.B. 175, Seria; f. 1961; 1,168 mems.; Pres. AHMAD TAMIN; Vice-Pres. IBRAHIM METUSSIN; Sec.-Gen. HUSSIN bin ISA; Treas. SANI BASRI.

Brunei Government Workers' Union: 2,691 mems.

Brunei Government Medical and Health Employees' Union: 334 mems.

Brunei Government Clerical and Peon Union: 180 mems.

TRANSPORT

RAILWAYS

There are no public railways in Brunei. The Brunei Shell Petroleum Company maintains an eight-mile section of light railway betewen Seria and Badas.

ROADS

There are some 370 kilometres of roads in Brunei and these are supplemented by 720 kilometres of district tracks. The main highway connects Bandar Seri Begawan, Tutong and Kuala Belait.

SHIPPING

Straits Steamship Co.: regular passenger and cargo services from Singapore, and non-scheduled services from Labuan and Bangkok.

Most sea traffic is handled by a deep-water port at Muara, 12 miles from the capital. The wharf at Bandar Seri Begawan itself is now used only for local vessels. There is a port at Kuala Belait and a tanker terminal at Seria handling shipments of crude oil. At Lumut there is a two-mile jetty for LNG carriers.

Rivers are the principal means of communication in the interior.

CIVIL AVIATION

There is an international airport at Bandar Seri Begawan. The Brunei Shell Petroleum Company operates a private airfield at Anduki.

Director of Civil Aviation: PETER HADFIELD; Department of Civil Aviation, State of Brunei.

Royal Brunei Airline: f. 1974; operates services to Hong Kong, Singapore, Kuching, Kotakinabalu, Bangkok and Manila; Chair. Pehin Dato ISA; 2 Boeing 737-200.

British Airways operate a weekly service between London and Brunei, Cathay Pacific Airways runs twice-weekly flights to Hong Kong, Malayasian Airline System operates a daily service to Malaysia, Thailand and Singapore, and Singapore Airlines operates a daily service to Singapore.

TOURISM

Brunei Tourist Association: P.O.B. 701, Bandar Seri Begawan; f. 1968; Chair. Dato R. D. Ross; Sec. VINCENT PANG.

DEFENCE

The Royal Brunei Malay Regiment numbered 1,550 men in 1972. Since 1971 the first line of defence is the responsibility of the Brunei Government, although the British Government is represented on the Brunei Defence Council and a Gurkha batallion of the British Army is stationed in Brunei. In 1975 Britain announced its intention of withdrawing the Gurkhas in the near future.

EDUCATION

In Brunei education is carried out in three different languages, Malay, English and Chinese, and schools are divided accordingly. There are also religious schools.

All Malay schools are government-administered and are in general co-educational. Primary schooling in the Malay schools lasts six years. Examinations at the end of the fourth year determine whether the pupils go on to prepare for entry to a government English medium or Malay medium secondary school, or to a religious school.

Secondary schooling lasts for seven years. After the third year promotion to the higher forms depends on examination performance. In 1973 there were 107 Malay schools with 21,027 pupils.

English medium schools are either government-administered or independent. Government English schools offer a three-year preparatory course for entry to English medium secondary schools. These prepare pupils for both Malay and English medium examinations. There were 12,370 pupils studying at 19 government English schools in 1973.

Chinese schools are not assisted by the government and cater for pupils at both primary and secondary levels. Religious schools are administered by the Religious Affairs Department. They take in pupils after the fourth year in Malay primary schools.

The only form of higher education offered in Brunei is teacher training. Students wishing to pursue other forms of higher education have to go abroad to continue their studies.

The state runs two teacher training institutions, one for religious teachers and one which caters for Malay and English schools.

BIBLIOGRAPHY

Brunei Annual Report, H.M.S.O., London.

See Malaysia.

Burma

PHYSICAL AND SOCIAL GEOGRAPHY

C. A. Fisher

Burma, which covers a total area of 261,218 square miles (676,552 square kilometres), lies to the east of India and Bangladesh and to the south-west of China, and has a long coastline facing the Bay of Bengal and the Andaman Sea. Much the greater part of its territory, between latitudes 28½° and 16° N., forms a compact unit surrounded on three sides by a great horseshoe of mountains and focusing on the triple river system of the Irrawaddy, Chindwin and Sittang. But in addition, Tenasserim, consisting of a narrow coastal zone backed by steep mountains, extends south from the Gulf of Martaban to Victoria Point only 10° N. of the equator.

PHYSICAL FEATURES

Structurally, Burma falls into three well-marked divisions, of which the first comprises the mid-Tertiary fold mountains of the west. These ranges, swinging in a great arc from the Hukwang valley to Cape Negrais, appear to represent a southward continuation of the eastern Himalayan series, though only after the latter has made a right-angled bend in the vicinity of the Tibeto-Burman border. From north to south these western ranges are known successively as the Patkai, Naga, and Chin Hills, and the Arakan Yoma, though the name hills is a singularly misleading designation for ranges whose summits exceed 12,000 ft. (3,650 metres) in the Patkai and 6,000 ft. to 8,000 ft. (1,800 to 2,400 metres) in the Chin and Naga sectors. Farther south, in the Arakan Yoma, the summit levels gradually decrease to between 3,000 ft. (900 metres) and 5,000 ft. (1,500 metres), but even there the mountains, consisting of a series of parallel serrated ridges, densely forested and fever-ridden, continue to provide a tremendous natural barrier between Burma and the Indian sub-continent, and even in British colonial times, when Burma formed part of the Indian Empire, the links between the two were almost exclusively by sea.

The second major structural unit consists of the eastern mountain systems, of Mesozoic or earlier origin, which, beginning as a continuation of the Yunnan plateau of China across the Burma border into the northeastern corner of Kachin State, extend thence through the Shan and Karenni plateaux into the more subdued but still rugged upland which forms the divide between Tenasserim and peninsular Thailand. In the far north, where this system adjoins the western mountain system, the general plateau level is of the order of 6,000 ft. (1,800 metres) with higher ridges frequently attaining 10,000 ft. (3,050 metres). The corresponding altitudes in the Shan area, however, are only about half as great, though here also the surface is severely dissected, with the main rivers, notably the great Salween, rushing southwards in deeply incised gorges.

In between the two main mountain systems described above lies the third major structural unit, namely the vast longitudinal trough of central Burma, formerly occupied by an arm of the early Tertiary sea, and now containing the great alluvial lowlands which form the cultural and economic heart of the country. Throughout the entire length of these lowlands the Irrawaddy provides the central artery, both of drainage and of communication. To the north it is paralleled by its largest tributary, the Chindwin, which joins it near the centre of the Dry Zone (*see below*) and farther south by the Sittang, which flows separately to the sea on the opposite side of the recent volcanic uplands of the Pegu Yoma. Central Burma is a zone of crustal instability; a severe earthquake in July 1975 caused extensive damage. Altogether, the Irrawaddy drains a total area of some 158,000 square miles (409,000 square kilometres), and its huge delta, originally covered with dense forest and swamp vegetation, has been cleared during the past hundred years to provide one of the greatest rice bowls of the world.

CLIMATE

Apart from the highest uplands in the far north of the country, the climate of practically the whole of Burma may be classified as tropical monsoonal, though important regional variations nevertheless occur within that overall category. In all parts of the country the main rains come during the period of the S.W. monsoon, i.e. between May and October inclusive, and those areas, notably Arakan and Tenasserim, which face the prevailing winds and are backed by steep and high ranges, receive some of the heaviest rainfall in the world, as, for example, Akyab, with an annual total of 204 in. (518 cm.), of which 196 in. (498 cm.) falls during the six months in question, and Amherst with 190 in. (483 cm.) of its 196 in. (498 cm.) also falling during the same period. Moreover, even the flat and low-lying Irrawaddy delta receives an annual rainfall of about 100 in. (250 cm.), again with some 95 per cent of it during the same half-year, and in all of these three areas mean annual temperatures are around 80°F. (27°C.), though the seasonal range varies from 12°F. (−11°C.) in Akyab to 6°F. (−14°C.) in Amherst.

However, over a considerable area in the interior of the central lowland, which constitutes a rain-shadow area relative to the S.W. monsoon, the total annual precipitation is less than 40 in. (100 cm.), and in some places even below 25 in. (64 cm.). And even though in this Dry Zone the seasonal incidence is essentially similar to that in the other areas already considered, the spectacular difference in total amount is reflected in a major change of vegetation from the prevailing heavy tropical monsoon forest elsewhere to a much more open cover and in places a mere thorny scrub. Moreover, the relative aridity is also responsible for a wider range of temperature, as is shown by Mandalay's 70°F. (21°C.) in January and 90°F. (32°C.) in April, immediately before the onset of the rains. Finally, in the eastern plateaux rainfall, though well above that of the Dry Zone, is nevertheless much less than along the western coastal margins, and this fact, combined with temperatures some 10° to 15F. (6° to 8°C.) below those of the torrid plains gives the Shan plateau the pleasantest climate of any part of the country.

NATURAL RESOURCES

Natural resources in Burma are closely related to the salient features of the country's physical geography. Thus, the greatest wealth of the humid mountain slopes lies in their timber, particularly teak; and while the young folded mountains of the west are not noted for mineral wealth, the older plateaux of the east have long been noted for a variety of metallic minerals, including the silver, lead and zinc of Bawdwin and the tungsten of Mawchi. Further south Tenasserim forms a minor part of the South-East Asian tin zone, though its resources in this respect are very small compared with those of Malaysia or even of Thailand. More important than any of these metals, or the sub-bituminous coal deposits at Kalewa, near the Chindwin/Myittha confluence, has been the petroleum which occurs in the Tertiary structures underlying the middle Irrawaddy lowlands. However, it must be stressed that even these are small by world standards, and that output, like that of the metallic minerals, has not yet regained the pre-war level.

It is in agricultural resources that Burma is potentially most richly endowed, and besides possessing in the delta an area capable of meeting local needs and providing a large surplus of rice for export, it also has in the Dry Zone a region well suited for the production of oil seeds and cotton, and in Tenasserim appropriate conditions for the cultivation of rubber.

POPULATION AND ETHNIC GROUPS

Burma's population was estimated at 31 million in 1975, a density of only 111 to the square mile, which is not merely far below that of India and China, but also well below the South-East Asian average of approximately 187. The greatest concentrations occur in the delta, and it is likewise in the lowlands, including also those of Arakan and Tenasserim, that the Burmese form the majority element in the population, while the uplands are more sparsely inhabited by a series of minority groups at varying levels of advancement. The Burmese, whose ancestors came from the Sino-Tibetan borders and eventually in early historical times supplanted all but a minor remnant of the earlier Mon population of lowland Burma, now form some 65 per cent of the total Burman population. A further 7–8 per cent consists of Shans, who are ethnic kinsfolk of the Thai and Lao, and, like the Burmese and the half-million Mons, follow the Theravada form of Buddhism.

Of the non-Buddhist indigenous groups, often referred to collectively as hill peoples, the Karens are the most numerous and indeed slightly outnumber the Shans. Their homeland occupies the uplands between the Shan plateau and Tenasserim, but many have migrated into the lowlands around Moulmein and to the Irrawaddy delta, and considerable numbers have discarded animism and adopted Christianity. Other upland peoples include the Kachins, Chins, Wa-Palaung, Lolo-Muhso and Nagas, who are still mostly animists and respectively form from 2.5 to 0.5 per cent of the total population.

Until recently Burma had a large Indian community, which before 1941 numbered over a million, but has since been successively reduced by repatriation so that today it is probably exceeded by the 372,000 Chinese. Largely because of its arrested economic development during the past two decades, Burma remains below the South-East Asian average in respect of urbanization, with Rangoon, its capital, totalling 3,186,886 inhabitants at the 1973 census and only nine other towns exceeding 100,000.

HISTORY

Josef Silverstein

History and geography have much in common in Burma. While the territory appears to form a land-bridge between India, China and South-East Asia, the land forms prove deceptive. The pattern of predominantly north-south rivers and valleys, enveloped by a crown of sharp and sometimes inhospitable hills and mountains, proved to be a strong barrier to those seeking easy access to the fertile land on the banks of its major rivers; one result of this was that the permanent population of Burma lived in relative isolation from its neighbours. Barriers, however, did not prevent contact with the outside; through wars, some trading and other means of contact, some migration and cultural exchange took place. The coastline also is deceiving. It too appears to beckon travellers and traders to its natural harbours at the mouths of its important rivers, but in fact the towns along the coast never became major or important centres of trade. For lying back and away from the main sea routes of the monsoon traders, commerce never developed and flourished.

Among the people who settled in Burma, a pattern of separation predominated. Despite the above-mentioned natural barriers, migration to the country via land is believed to be the main avenue of population movement. Little is known about the original settlers and early civilizations. The earliest known races who left traces of significant civilizations were the Pyus and Mons. Both lived in lower Burma along the banks or in the delta of the Irrawaddy River. Their successors were the Tibeto-Burman peoples, the ancestors of the contemporary Burmans. The Shan-Thai, who entered Burma somewhat later from Nanchao—an area which today is located in southern China—settled to the north and east of the Burmans in the hill areas of the country. Others, such as the Karens, Chins and Kachins entered at various times from the pre-Christian era to the late eighteenth century and also made their homes in the same area. Only the Karens moved gradually in large numbers to the plains area and settled among the Burmans and remnants of the ancient Mons. As a result of this migration pattern, together with the geographical features of Burma, most of the racial groups in Burma lived separated from each other. Each retained its own culture and identity. Only local warfare, intermarriage and intermingling among the racial groups living in close proximity provided for significant social and cultural exchange. No thoroughgoing assimilation took place and the peoples of Burma moved through the centuries living in partial isolation from each other and from their outside neighbours.

BURMA BEFORE BRITISH RULE

The Burmans, from the tenth century on, were the most numerous and, in terms of cultural, historical and political contribution to the varied heritage of Burma, were the most important group. Between their founding of the Pagan Dynasty in the eleventh century and the conquest of Burma in the nineteenth, the Burmans succeeded in unifying Burma under a single political authority on three separate and relatively short occasions.

The Pagan Dynasty lasted from the eleventh to the end of the thirteenth century. The Burman king Anahwrahta, the founder of the empire, succeeded in bringing the Mons under Burman rule and, more important, adopting Buddhism from them and propagating it throughout the developing empire. The Pagan Dynasty proved to be Burma's Golden Age, in which Indian-influenced culture—from written language to architectural development—flourished. The Mongol invaders in 1287 brought the period to an end when they sacked Pagan, drove the last kings from the city and destroyed the political and military power of the empire.

For the next two centuries, the Shans seemed on the verge of creating their own empire out of the remnants of the Pagan Dynasty. However, internal rivalries among the Shan princes prevented them from uniting and it was not until a new line of Burman kings arose (the Toungoo Dynasty) in the sixteenth century that Burma once again came under a single ruler. The Toungoo kings brought the Shans under permanent Burman rule and sought to increase the size of the empire at the expense of the neighbouring Thais. But continuous warfare weakened the power of the new line of kings and by the seventeenth century, the Toungoo Dynasty came to an end; Burma once again became the centre of quarrelling races, none strong enough to subdue and hold the rest.

Toward the end of the eighteenth century, Alaungpaya became the third Burman king to unite the country. Within a few years he not only conquered his indigenous rivals but in addition expanded the influence of his empire to the neighbouring areas of Assam, Manipur and Siam. During the era of this dynasty (the Konbaung) the Burmans repelled four invasion attempts by the Chinese. Early in the nineteenth century, rivalry with the British East India Company over border areas adjoining Burma and India—Arakan—and over influence in Assam and Manipur, brought the two powers into open warfare. Beginning in 1824, the Burmese and the British engaged in three wars, each ending in defeat for the former and the loss of territory and power. The third and final war in 1885–86 brought an end to Burman rule when the last king was captured and exiled.

Although the bare outline of history, suggested above, stresses the disunity among the peoples of Burma and the rise and fall of short-lived dynasties, there are other aspects of this history which suggest stability and continuity throughout this long period. The mass conversion of the Burmans and many of the minorities to Buddhism provided the basis for Burmese thought and values from the past to the present. The tradition of self-reliance among the peasantry, from the production of food and clothing to the education of the young, provides a picture of relative stability in the countryside, which stands in marked contrast to the rivalry and occasional chaos at the royal level. The self-contained racial groups husbanded their cultures and identities in the face of conquest and competition and emerged in the modern period as separate and distinct groups, which gave allegiance to rivals stronger than themselves, but little else. Finally, the general isolation of Burma from the outside world cut the country and its people off from the changes in other countries and left them unprepared for modifications in their social, economic and political institutions, which the British imposed on them.

BRITISH RULE

The development of colonial institutions and programmes was slow and pragmatic. Until the second Anglo-Burmese War in 1852, little was done in the two ceded territories—Arakan and Tenasserim—beyond the maintenance, as cheaply as possible, of law and order. Following that war and the acquisition of the rest of lower Burma, the British gave greater attention to making the area economically viable. Law and order in the countryside together with a policy of encouraging both indigenous and foreign peasants to clear and cultivate the land laid the foundation for Burma's development into the world's largest rice exporter. Economic transformation to a food-exporting nation brought with it the problems of foreign landowners, money lending, tenancy and land alienation. During this period, the British sought to use the existing system of local rule.

International rivalry in 1885 between France and Britain over the strategic area of upper, Burma, together with problems encountered by a British firm over its timber leases in upper Burma provided the basis for launching a third war against the Burmans. Meeting little or no opposition in capturing the king and occupying the territory, all of Burma came under British rule in 1886. The Shan princes generally accepted the changes and in turn were confirmed in their local authority. In time, the other minorities in the hill areas followed the Shans.

Between 1897 and 1942, British rule flowered and Burma underwent vast changes. Administratively, the first change occurred when the traditional system of local government was altered to make authority territorial, instead of personal, and the village headman replaced the local chieftain; the headmen became directly responsible to the district officer and a part of the central administrative hierarchy. Also about this time, the Chief Commissioner was raised to the office of Lieutenant-Governor and assisted by a council; Burma became a province of India. Reforms leading to self-government did not get under way until 1923, when a system of dyarchy was introduced and a partially elected legislative council was formed. In 1937 Burma was separated from India, received its own constitution, a fully elected legislature and a responsible cabinet. Four popular governments served until Burma was occupied by the Japanese in 1942. Although political instability and personal rivalries dominated Burma's political life during this period, the political élite learned the mechanics of parliamentary government. Through the period of reforms the hill areas were kept administratively separate from Burma proper with the result that uneven political development occurred in the two areas.

The administrative changes in Burma proper together with the development of Christian mission and Anglo-vernacular schools rendered invalid the traditional forms of education carried on by the Buddhist monks. The new indigenous élite and the recruits for the Western business firms were drawn from those who spoke English and had experienced Western-type education. The emergence of a commercial export economy, together with the development of an expansion of mineral and timber extractions complemented the administrative and educational changes and all contributed to undermining the traditions and customs of the people; social dislocation, instability, increased crime and the impoverishment of the peasantry resulted. In contrast, Rangoon grew to importance as a major port and commercial centre for foreign commercial interests. Among the hill peoples little or no change occurred and life among the various people in this area altered only slightly.

The Burman response to all these changes was to react politically. The first popular movement, the Young Men's Buddhist Association (YMBA), appeared before the First World War. Its main concern was religion not politics; however, following Britain's promise to India (given during the First World War) of eventual self-government, the YMBA was transformed to the General Council of Burmese Associations and the new organization headed the nascent nationalist movement. In 1920, the university students called a strike which won popular backing and thrust the students into national politics. Following the introduction of dyarchy, the GCBA split as its leaders contested with each other for seats in the legislative council and for followers. The key issue was whether to accept the reforms or fight for new ones.

In 1930, a new phase in Burmese politics developed. The impact of the world economic depression provoked a minority of rural Burmans to revert to superstition and challenge British rule in a hopeless gesture of revolt. The Saya San Revolt marked the first effort in the twentieth century to expel the British by force and violence. More important was the second movement. Drawn in the main from among the young intelligentsia and university students, who called themselves *Thakins* (masters), the movement sought to revive popular interest in the national language, traditions, identity and culture. It rejected the course of political development in progress and worked instead directly with peasant organizations, labour unions and youth. When the Second World War came to Burma, thirty of its leaders were in secret training for military activity, under the Japanese. From its ranks sprang the new generation of leaders who guided the nation through the war and to independence.

Burma in Transition (1942-48)

The invading Japanese Army scored rapid successes against the British defenders of Burma and within six months forced the Allied Forces out of Burma proper and parts of the hill areas. Accompanying the victorious Japanese were the new recruits and leaders of the Burmese Independence Army (BIA)—secretly created and trained by the Japanese before the war. Administration broke down inside Burma when the government and thousands of civil servants and Indians evacuated in the train of the defeated army. The BIA leaders expected to fill the administrative void and establish an independent Burma under their leadership; however, they found that the Japanese had other plans. Dr. Ba Maw, Burma's first Prime Minister in 1937, was called to head the administration and in 1943 was chosen to head the nominally independent Burma Government. Neither the Japanese nor the Burma Government under its control ever became popular with the people. Loss of the rice export market, shortages of consumer goods, brutal treatment by the Japanese and the hardships of war combined to prevent all efforts of the invaders to win local support.

The youthful leaders of the new Burma Army, together with their colleagues in government and outside, organized a resistance movement. Under the leadership of Aung San and in secret communication with the British in India, the Anti-Fascist People's Freedom League (AFPFL) rose in revolt in March 1945, and participated in the final stages of the Allied victory in Burma. When the Burma Government-in-exile returned in October 1945, it found a well-organized nationalist movement under strong leadership and equipped with goals and programmes confronting it. Until mid-1946, the Governor could make no headway with economic reconstruction due to his unwillingness to work with and through the AFPFL. A change in governors, a general strike and a change in policy in London broke the deadlock; in January 1947, Aung San and others travelled to London to discuss Burma's political future with the Prime Minister. Agreement was reached and the Burmese returned home to carry out the necessary steps to realize their goal of independence. Crucial to the success of their plans was the support of the hill peoples. This was secured and delegations from all the major ethnic groups participated in drafting the constitution.

Tragedy befell the nation on July 19th, 1947, when Aung San and six members of the Executive Council were assassinated. Quick work by the Governor, the success of Thakin Nu in stepping into Aung San's office and support from the AFPFL permitted Burma to complete all necessary steps in time to declare its independence outside the Commonwealth on January 4th, 1948. But, despite the happiness of the occasion, the facts of the economic destruction caused by the war, the discord within the governing party and the open competition with the communist parties of Burma suggested the dimensions of the problems lying ahead for Burma as a free and self-governing nation.

THE CONSTITUTIONAL PERIOD: 1948-62

The Union of Burma began its independent political life as a constitutional democracy. The fundamental law provided for an elected two-house legislature, a responsible prime minister and cabinet, and an independent judiciary. More important, however, was the manner in which it attempted to answer the ethnic question. In theory, a federal form of government was created with each of the states enjoying certain common powers, such as authority in local matters, education and taxation. Each state had an elected council and head. In practice, however, the federal structure was overlaid by strong central control. The Prime Minister had the final say in the selection of state heads, the allocation of central revenues for state use, and, through a variety of Burmanization policies, the central government tended to supersede the states and thereby nullify the constitutional guarantees of unity in diversity. Although certain states had the right of secession, none in fact ever attempted to employ it. From its infancy, the Union of Burma was plagued with political, social and economic problems which eventually led to an end of constitutional government.

When Burma became independent in 1948, the governing party was the AFPFL. Although it held an overwhelming majority of seats in Parliament and national support, it was faced with serious rivals, both in and out of Burma. Its major threat came from the communists who went into open revolt three months after independence. The People's Volunteer Organization (PVO), a mainstay in the AFPFL, split and a majority followed the communists. At the same time serious defections in the armed forces weakened it as the defender of the union. By 1949, the Karen National Defence Organization (KNDO) revolted over the failure of their people to receive the area and cultural protection they thought they deserved. Other ethnic groups also revolted. Despite the preponderance of opposition, the government did not collapse. It survived because the rebels fought each other as well as the government; the leadership of Nu united the people in support of the government and the armed forces ultimately reorganized and won control of the major portion of the countryside. By 1951, the worst of the rebellions was over and the government, while plagued with minor outbursts, could turn its attention to other matters.

During the 1950s, two elections were held. In both cases the AFPFL was the overwhelming victor. However, all was not right in the party, and in 1958 it split into two rival factions. To avoid open revolt, the Prime Minister invited the head of the army, General Ne Win, to form a caretaker government and prepare the country for new elections. Elections were held in 1960 and power returned to the victorious faction of the AFPFL which managed to win a complete victory at the polls. Nu once again became Prime Minister and he pledged his government to restore public confidence in democratic processes and bring racial harmony to the people. Internal troubles in his party together with increased demands by the Shans and Kachins for greater autonomy or even secession prohibited the government from attaining its goals; on March 2nd, 1962, the military, under the leadership of Ne Win, engineered a *coup*. All the members of the government were arrested along with the key leaders of the minorities. The constitution was set aside and the self-chosen Revolutionary Council began to rule by decree; thus ended Burma's experiment with constitutional government.

Burma's major social problem was how to bring unity to the diverse peoples living in the hills and on the plains. At the time of independence, the Burmans were the overwhelming majority among all the people; in addition they were the leaders of the independence movement. But Aung San and others saw the need for uniting all the people of Burma if independence was to be granted to an intact Burma. Their success resulted in the creation of the federal union described earlier. Following independence and the eruption of the several revolts, the loyalty of the hill minorities, especially the Shans, Kachins and Chins, made it possible for the new government to survive and eventually bring the dissidents under control. But while these minorities were supporting the government, others, especially the Karens and Mons, were not. The division among the minorities resulted in part from the constitution, which gave the hill peoples the states they desired and did not do the same for the others and in part from the fact that the minorities were divided physically and, at the time, had little communication and contact. In time, defections among the hill peoples took place as they felt the pressures of Burmanization upon their cultures and Burman influence in their local affairs. During the Caretaker Regime, dissidents among the Shans and Kachins went into open revolt and joined forces, in some areas, with the KNDO and the Communists. When elected government was restored in 1960, the divisions between the Burmans and the various minorities continued to widen. Finally, in 1962, the Prime Minister called a conference of all ethnic leaders to seek a solution to the problem of unity. No answer was found as the *coup* took place and nearly all the participants—especially those from the Shan State—were arrested. The constitutional era ended with this problem dominating all others.

From 1948 to 1962, the Burmese made several and varied attempts to cope with the economic problems of the nation. Little or no reconstruction was carried out after the Second World War mainly because the AFPFL leaders did not agree with the plans and priorities. Therefore, with independence, the people inherited an economy badly in need of capital and technical assistance, both to restore it to its pre-war status and then transform it to meet the needs of a nation desirous of transforming itself from a primary producing economy to one that was mixed. Under the original leaders of the AFPFL, socialism was seen as the best means of achieving this end. As a result a Two-Year Plan was drawn up, but never really implemented; the several revolts prevented any real effort to put it into effect. During the early 1950s, Western economists were brought in to develop a workable plan and time-table. A Seven-Year Plan was drawn up, but never really put into effect because the price of rice (the mainstay of the economy both before and after independence) fell and the necessary foreign exchange was not available. After some bitter experiences in state-trading on a type of barter arrangement to unload its rice surpluses, the Burmese in 1957 chose a new road to economic health. Under the leadership of Prime Minister Nu, the socialist goals were postponed and the nation called upon the private entrepreneur to step forward and play a role alongside government in restoring and transforming the economy. Following the restoration of elected government a new policy came into effect. Private enterprise was encouraged to enter into partnership with the government, and once its know-how had been passed along, to drop out. This policy never got very far in view of the *coup* and the different outlook of the military in economic matters.

Throughout the period of 1948–62, the economy languished while the population grew and popular expectation of improved conditions increased. Rice and extraction remained the basic means of earning foreign exchange. As a result, the economy was subject to the instability of world demand for its products. Little or no headway was made in developing an industrial sector or training personnel for manning it. By the time of the *coup*, Burma had experimented with several approaches to development—capitalism, socialism or mixed economy—but had not resolved the question of which was best for its needs.

The constitutional period was a time of troubles and experimentation; but the *coup* prevented the leaders and the people from benefiting from what they learned.

MILITARY RULE, 1962–74

During the greater part of the first decade of military rule (1962–72), the new leaders devoted themselves to demolishing and sweeping away the liberal constitutional system of their predecessors and replacing it with an arbitrary dictatorial system which sought to organize and maintain the support of the people. The "new order" was based on the rule of a few military senior officers, under the leadership of General Ne Win, and organized as the Revolutionary Council (RC). The ideas underlying the "new order" were incorporated in an ideological statement entitled the *Burmese Way to Socialism*, published in April 1962; it remained unchanged throughout the ten-year period, and it is the basis for many of the policies and much of the RC's programme. In form and theory, Burma is still a federal state; in actuality, the new leaders created a centralized bureaucracy which, for all practical purposes, treats the nation as a unitary state. A new hierarchy of Security and Administration Councils (SAC), composed of representatives of the army, the police and the civil service, form a network of administrative units which are linked together in a hierarchy with its apex in Rangoon and extend through the nation. To mobilize the people under its leadership, the RC created a new political party, the Burma Socialist Programme Party (BSPP) or *Lanzin* in July 1962. Building slowly, with emphasis upon loyalty, training and testing, the party finally emerged as a major organization of the military regime in 1971, when it called its first congress. With only 73,369 full members, of which 41,921 were drawn from the armed forces, the party was an *élite* group largely isolated from the civilian mass. At the Congress, General Ne Win was formally elected as its leader and a committee of 150 was chosen to assist the leader. The party identified its mission as twofold: to transform itself from a cadre to a mass party and replace centralism with democratic centralism; to aid in the transformation of the nation to a socialist democratic state under a new constitution. Its ideological basis remained the same as that of the Government, the *Burmese Way to Socialism*. The third new set of institutions created by the military to mobilize and involve the people was the establishment of a dual hierarchy of peasant and worker councils. Ultimately, it was planned that a single Peasants' and Workers' Council would bind the two hierarchies and together serve as a popular backdrop to the military government.

In July 1971, the military leaders announced plans to draw up a new constitution which would ensure that Burma's goal of becoming a socialist state would be realized.

To match the move toward constitutionalism, General Ne Win inaugurated several administrative changes in April 1972. He and twenty of his senior commanders retired from the Army and became civilian members of government. At the same time, the RC proclaimed the end of the Revolutionary Government and its replacement by the Government of the Union of Burma. U Ne Win became Prime Minister, nine of his retired officers, three active military senior officers and two civilians made up the first cabinet under this new order. Brigadier San Yu was promoted to General and took over command of the Army, became Deputy Prime Minister and Minister of Defence; he became the most powerful figure in the nation after U (formerly General) Ne Win. The intent of these changes was to restore the image of civilian rule and constitutional government. Also, to make the government more responsive to the people, the central administrative structure was overhauled. The number of Ministries was reduced from twenty-five to twenty, the Secretariat—a legacy of the colonial past—and the post of Secretary were abolished. The administrative hierarchy was also streamlined by reducing the levels, from the centre to the village, from five to four. The goal of this reform was to make the administration more responsive to the people.

Throughout the period of military rule, there was a remarkable stability in the nation's leadership. The Revolutionary Council came into existence in 1962 with a membership of 17 and was reorganized only once. The Council of Ministers—the Government of Burma—was also stable. During the 12 years of military rule, it was reorganized only twice. Compared with military rule in other nations, Burma's differed in one significant way—the military in Burma monopolized all power and in 12 years only three genuine civilians were given cabinet rank and only three in the final phase were admitted to membership in the highest level of government, the Revolutionary Council. This marked a significant difference between the Caretaker Government of Ne Win in 1958–60 and Military Rule from 1962 to 1974. In the earlier period, Ne Win drew upon highly qualified civilians to share power with members of the military both in making and implementing policy. The results then, unlike those achieved in the later period, were highly beneficial to the nation.

The leadership during the period of military rule was not only persistent but remarkably cohesive. There was one significant split only in the inner circle of *coup* leaders. In February 1963, Brigadier Aung Gyi resigned both his military commissions and his several offices over policy matters and ideology. Despite the social and economic consequences of military rule, the leaders remained firmly united and held the loyalty of their troops. General Ne Win was the dominant figure. Among those who enjoyed his confidence and played key roles in government and the military, General San Yu dominated all others. Until his retirement in mid-1969, Brigadier Tin Pe, a strong advocate of immediate and total socialism, enjoyed a special position in the ruling group. Initially, the military rulers were agreed upon maintaining their reputation as incorruptible servants of the people. Over the years, during this period, the reputations of all the ruling group were tarnished as the symbols of wealth and power—automobiles, quality of housing, special treatment, etc.—stood out in bold relief while the country sank into economic decay and poverty. Despite the General's exhortations to his fellow officers to be models for the people, the personal activity of the ruling group to further their own wealth and comfort did not split them apart.

Despite more than a decade of military rule, memories of popular government did not disappear. In an obvious bid for support and co-operation of the pre-*coup* political leaders, the RC on November 29th, 1968, established a committee of 33 former political leaders—called the Internal Unity Advisory Body—to advise it on ways and means of establishing national unity and to report by the end of May 1969. The committee interpreted its mandate liberally and presented a wide range of ideas and suggestions. U Nu, the former Prime Minister, called for the return of power to himself and the re-assembly of the last Parliament in order to effect a legal transfer of power to the General; only then could the basis be laid for the solution of the problem of national unity. Eighteen members of the committee combined to propose a return to constitutionalism and democratic socialism with proper protection for human social and political rights. A minority of eleven called for more not less socialism, the calling of a national unity congress and the partnership of political leftists and the military in a generally strengthened state. The work of the committee received wide publicity inside Burma; the General took no official note of it however, until November, when at a *Lanzin* national meeting, he dismissed or denounced most of the recommendations and called for national support of the programmes and policies of his government.

The awakening of the former political leaders did not end with the committee. U Nu, abroad in Europe and the U.S.A. denounced the Ne Win Government and called for its overthrow, either by persuasion or revolt. Following his trip, Nu and his supporters settled in Bangkok, Thailand where they continued to plan and organize, as well as publicize their efforts to topple the military government of Burma. In the Autumn of 1970 Nu reported agreement between himself and factions of dissidents from amongst the Shans, Karens and other indigenous minorities; in October 1970, U Nu and his supporters moved back to Burma and began their revolt. During the two years which followed, the movement was unable to penetrate deeply into Burma and its numbers remained small and it was unsuccessful in winning the support of any of the government forces or their commanders. Despite the backing of foreign oil interests, eager to support Nu in exchange for the right to explore Burma's coastline for oil deposits, the movement has proved to be no real match for the army of General Ne Win. In January 1972 U Nu resigned as President of the National United Liberation Front over the issue of the future of the federal state in Burma, and temporarily retired from politics.

A second source of opposition was the remnant of the Burma Communist Party. Despite internal dissention in 1967–68 over ideological issues, especially over how closely to adhere to the Cultural Revolution in China, and the murder of Than Tun and other key leaders, the BCP still remained a serious challenge to the military inside Burma. Despite the constant pressure the military sought to keep upon the Communists, they remained strong because of their ability to operate in the remote sections of the country and because they established strong links with the dissident minorities as well as with individual Burmese who sought political change. In order to weaken their foreign support, the Burmese Government in October 1970 re-established diplomatic relations with the People's Republic of China after three years of intensive propaganda warfare and occasional military clashes. Despite the willingness of the People's Republic to restore normal relations with the Burmese, it continued throughout the remainder of the period to give military aid and training to the Burma Communist Party, thus ensuring the permanence of this dissident force.

Political opposition emanated also from a third source, the indigenous minorities. The military rulers tried to bring about an end to their opposition in 1963, when they sought to negotiate directly with all factions. An amnesty was provided so that the leaders could come to Rangoon and hold face to face discussions. The discussions—in all cases except with a segment of the KNDO—broke down and rebellion was resumed. Until U Nu entered into agreement in 1970 with several minority groups, they had only the Burma Communist Party as their link with dissident Burmans. The resignation of Nu from the Liberation Front weakened the effort to weld together a solid opposition and at the end of military rule in 1974 the minorities were still in revolt, but their threat to Ne Win's government was no stronger than it had been at the beginning of military rule.

The reformation of values and attitudes among the people was a major concern of the Revolutionary Council. It sought to alter the character of the Burmese through educational reform; by training people for livelihood through more vocational and technical education. With all means of communications in government hands, the military rulers enjoyed a monopoly in this area. By concentrating on the school children, the leaders hoped to develop support for their government and ideology. In this way they hoped to develop among the rising generation new attitudes and loyalties, which in time would come to replace those of old.

Since becoming an independent nation in 1948, Burma has pursued a policy of non-alignment in world affairs. It supported the United Nations and contributed the third Secretary-General to that organization. Toward its immediate neighbours, India, Pakistan, China and Thailand, it has sought to maintain friendly relations with all. In 1960, it signed a boundary agreement and a treaty of friendship with the People's Republic of China. All remained constant under the military until 1967; in June a dispute arose with China over local Chinese demonstrations supporting the Cultural Revolution. Violence flared in Rangoon and Sino-Burmese relations deteriorated. China went so far as to give support to the Burmese communist insurgents, thus worsening an already difficult internal problem. The restoration of full diplomatic relations with China in 1970 permitted Burma to resume using the unexpended loans given to it a decade earlier; it was hoped that the resumption of diplomatic relations between the two nations also would see a lessening of aid to the Burma Communist Party; finally, it was hoped that the tensions between the two would be reduced. While the Burmese achieved the first goal, the other two were still unfulfilled at the time military rule ended. Throughout the period, Burma continued to have good relations with neighbours who had joined local regional organizations, but it did not alter its non-aligned policy and join any, despite an invitation from the Association for South-East Asian Nations (ASEAN) to do so.

Following the *coup* in 1963 the military began to bring the whole economy under its control and drive out all private interests. It began by nationalizing the banks and followed that by gradually taking over all trade and commerce and manufacturing; only agriculture and peasant land ownership remained in private hands, but the produce had to be sold to the government for distribution internally and for marketing abroad. All this was done in the name of the people by soldiers and state employees without business or trade experience. It succeeded in driving thousands of Indian merchants out of the country and caused the economy to stagnate, production to decline, distribution to break down and black markets and shortages to develop. From 1966 onward, the military oscillated between strict economic control and partial relaxation in the hope of encouraging the peasants to produce and deliver greater quantities of their product. But given the natural population increase and the state of the economy, the military never achieved the levels of production, distribution and exports in effect at the time they seized power.

Military rule ended formally on March 1st, 1974, but, as will be seen, the changes which followed really did not alter things veiy much.

THE SECOND CONSTITUTIONAL PERIOD

The new constitution of Burma differed widely from its predecessor. Although the state nominally is federal, in fact it is unitary. The five states and Burma proper have been replaced by seven states and seven divisions, all united in an administrative and political hierarchy. The new subdivisions were created out of Burma proper and all states and divisions are coequal. The structure of government is uniform throughout the union. It consists of four tiers; at the apex is the People's Assembly with popular representation from the entire nation. Each state or division has three levels of government—state or division People's Councils, township People's Councils and ward and village tract People's Councils. Each of these legislative bodies controls the executive and judicial branches at its level. Leadership under the new constitution is vested in the Council of State. This body of 28 members elected from the People's Assembly, chooses one of its members to be the Chairman; he in turn acts as President of the Socialist Republic. The Council acts in the absence of the People's Assembly and carries out other tasks assigned by the constitution. Administration at the national level is located in the Council of Ministers. This council too is elected from among the members of the People's Assembly. It chooses from among its members the Prime Minister, who also sits as the 29th member of the Council of State. The People's Assembly also chooses from among its members a Council of People's Justices, the highest judicial organ, a Council of People's Attorneys, whose job it is to protect the socialist system, the rights and privileges of the working people and advise the Councils of State and Ministers on legal matters. Finally, the constitution also provides for the creation of a Council of Inspectors—a variation of the old Chinese censorate. At all four levels of government, these councils are reproduced and bound together by the principle of democratic centralism. The people, in theory, remain in control by the right of recall. Real power in this system is vested in the Burma Socialist Programme Party. It is proclaimed as the only party in the nation and it is commanded to lead. As the author of the constitution, the only recognized party in the country, and as the chief agent for selecting candidates for elected office, it stands both inside and outside the formal structure of the state. Neither its constitution and rules nor its leaders and members are limited by the constitution. As the creation of the men who made the *coup* in 1962 and continue to lead in this second constitutional period, it does not effect a real change in leadership between the past and present period; despite the elaborate wording of the basic law, there are no real limits on the party and its leaders.

Following a rigid timetable, elections for all four tiers of government were held and the new constitution and the institutions it created came into existence on March 2nd, 1974. General Ne Win, now U Ne Win was elected as Chairman of the Council of State and therefore became the first president under the new basic law. Brigadier Sein Win, now U Sein Win became Prime Minister. General San Yu was chosen as Secretary of the Council of Ministers and is therefore, under the constitution, the legal successor to Ne Win. The other seats in the two Councils were filled with familiar military leaders from the immediate past. In all, 11 of the 29 members of the Council of Ministers were carried over from the previous Revolutionary Council. Following its organization, the People's Assembly adjourned, leaving the running of the state to the members of the two Councils and the hierarchies they commanded at all three subordinate levels of government.

Despite the return to constitutional government and elected leadership, the people were still plagued with the economic problems of the past. In June 1974, riots broke out over food shortages and maldistribution; 22 were reported killed and at least 60 injured. During the rainy season excessive flooding caused severe damage to the new crop and heralded another possible poor crop and further problems for the people. In December, following the return of U Thant's body to Burma for burial, riots developed after the students and Buddhist monks seized the body in order to give it a fitting burial—they complained that the Government was not going to give its most distinguished son proper respect and interment. The riots saw many killed and injured and the proclamation of martial law. While the immediate cause of this further unrest was the question of proper burial of U Thant, in fact, it was clearly associated with popular discontent over the continuing declining economic conditions in the country, growing corruption and ostentatious living among those in power and the inability to provide good government and social stability.

After further student riots in June 1975, the Government sent teams of ministers and deputy ministers to meet students and workers to demonstrate the Government's desire to learn from the people and, in turn, to reassure them that it intended to act upon their advice.

A government campaign against corruption and inefficiency in administration and state enterprises began: arrests and dismissals followed and continued throughout the year. The Government also launched a campaign against criminals and blackmarketeers, smugglers and heroin dealers.

Against this background, the Government made two important ministerial changes and added 17 deputy ministers. It sought to placate the people through larger expenditures for education and health, and the importation of consumer goods.

Unrest in Burma was not limited to students and workers; ethnic and political rebellion continued as it has since 1949.

The present Government continues the foreign policy of its predecessors. With a continued emphasis upon independence, non-alignment and friendship with all, especially its neighbours, the Government has sought to adapt to the political changes in the area while broadening its contacts with the states beyond. In May 1975, it established full diplomatic relations with the Government of North Viet-Nam and the Provisional Revolutionary Government in the South. It was receptive to Thailand's overtures for the improvement of relations between the two nations; Thailand said that it would no longer permit Burma rebels to operate against their homeland from Thai soil. Against this, the unilateral declaration by Burma of a 200-mile offshore exploration zone drew an immediate rejection from the Thai authorities who saw this as having an adverse effect upon the Thai fishing industry. Burma remained, as before, unwilling to join ASEAN.

Towards the nations beyond South-East Asia, Burma elevated its relations with the two Koreans to embassy level. It continued its good relations with Japan by accepting two large loans, one for commodity purchases and the second for use in the building of a new medical research centre. Toward the three great powers, the People's Republic of China, the U.S.S.R. and the U.S.A., it exchanged diplomatic visits and delegations. While Ne Win visited China, his Foreign Minister visited the U.S.A. and his Deputy Prime Minister went to the U.S.S.R.

In 1975 Burma continued as before with nearly the same men in power who were there under direct military rule. With no major changes in policies and programmes, the people continue to tolerate a regime which has not met their economic needs, has not given them real security and has not allowed them to try and solve their problems on their own. There is little likelihood that much will change or improve so long as the men in power continue as before.

ECONOMIC SURVEY

M. Ruth H. Pfanner

(Revised by ALEC GORDON and the Editor)

The Burmese economy has developed around its rich agricultural and forested lands and until 1964 was the world's largest rice exporter. Burma was heavily damaged during the Second World War and took many years to recover from its severe losses. Not until 1956 did Gross National Product reach its 1938/39 level. Total population was estimated at 31 million in 1975 and is increasing at about 2.4 per cent per year. Per capita G.N.P. was still 10 per cent below its pre-war level in 1963, when all original national accounts series were discontinued and replaced by new estimates of production. After that per capita output declined steadily until 1967/68, when it turned upwards. According to World Bank estimates, G.N.P. per head increased at an annual average of only 0.7 per cent between 1965 and 1973.

Since taking power in 1962 the military rulers have nationalized most important enterprises in all sectors of the country. Until recently internal sources were relied on for capital formation but since about 1972 increasing reliance has been placed on foreign aid and investment. Restrictions on domestic capitalists have also been eased somewhat.

Foreign trade has generally declined since the military takeover in 1962. Export earnings reached their highest level in 1963 but then slumped, mainly due to a sharp fall in rice exports. Because of the drop in export earnings, Burma also reduced its imports, despite the crippling effect of this on new investment projects and manufacturing industry dependent on imported raw materials.

Complete failure of the Government's rice procurement policy during and after the bumper 1973/74 crop year led to serious food shortages in towns. This provided a basis for widespread political and industrial unrest which was closely related to the riots in December 1974.

AGRICULTURE

Approximately 13 per cent of the total area of Burma is cultivated; another 11 per cent is unused but potentially productive land. The most productive areas lie in the deltas and along the valleys of the Irrawaddy and Sittang rivers, and the Arakan coast. Lack of irrigation retards agriculture in the Dry Zone, and Upper Burma and the Shan Hills Plateau are the least productive areas. Agriculture is characteristically extensive and per capita agricultural land of 0.8 of an acre (0.3 of a hectare) is high for the Far East.

Since the mid-1960s Burma met two basic problems with respect to agriculture, particularly rice. The first problem relates to a rising private domestic demand for rice and other agricultural products in spite of stagnating agricultural production. The demand for rice has been increasing at about 3 per cent annually since 1964–65, while paddy output has remained below the level of that year, leaving less exportable rice. Relative differences between rigid and lower official prices and those of private black market and international market have stimulated and sustained operations outside the official channels. The second is related to the deterioration of the international rice market following the apparent progress towards self-sufficiency by some developing countries, and the impact of concessionary rice sales by some developed states. A third problem appeared when shortages in Burma itself prevented the country from benefiting from the effects of poor Asian rice harvests in 1972 and 1973, and the cutbacks in American and Japanese output.

Rice

Paddy is by far the most important crop and accounts for about 50 per cent of total agricultural output. Production of paddy regained its pre-war level of 7.5 million tons only in 1962/63 but its pre-war acreage of 12.8 million acres was not reached again until 1974/75. Production in 1964/65 totalled 8.4 million tons, which was equalled only in 1973/74 and was almost reached again in 1974/75. In the intervening years production was well down. In 1975 after a good harvest, 9.08 million tons was produced, giving an estimated exportable surplus of 360,000 tons.

Whilst insurgent activity has undoubtedly restricted production in some areas the lack of incentive to farmers has been the main check on expansion. The government's buying monopoly has consistently offered low rice prices to farmers and moved the terms of trade to the great disadvantage of the countryside. Consequently the surplus available for export fell from one million tons in the 1960s. After the bad harvest of 1972–73 exports were suspended. Ironically, the bumper harvest of 1973–74 coincided with the breakdown of the government's rice procurement policy and the surplus for export was only about 200,000 tons, one-third of the target. Eventually, by the end of 1974 the Government was forced to alter its pricing policy in order to move rice into the towns and the export market. The procurement price was increased by 50 per cent to 900 kyats per 100 baskets (of 46 lb. each) and the above quota purchase price was raised 100 per cent to 1,200 kyats. In 1976 further increases in the procurement price of rice and other agricultural products were announced. The new prices mark a major change in economic policy although part of the farmers' gain may be eroded by rising prices in the manufactured goods which the farmers buy.

Some progress in growing high yielding rice strains has been made. These produced 1.5 million tons in 1974/75 or nearly 20 per cent of the total crop.

Other Crops

Other crops of minor importance are groundnuts, pulses and beans, cotton, sugar cane, chillies, jute, rubber, wheat and maize, Many of these crops, such as wheat, jute and groundnuts, have been encouraged in an effort to reduce imports or provide raw material for domestic industry.

Forestry

Burma's valuable forests occupy 67 per cent of its total area. All forest land is owned by the state and forest management has a long history. Since 1963 the State Timber Board has been handling all timber extraction, conversion and distribution. The most important timber is teak which has been a major export since the colonial period. Production in 1970–71 of 358,000 cubic tons of logs had not reached the pre-war level (1936–40) of 450,000 cubic tons. Other hardwoods such as pyinkado and in-kanyin have increased in importance and in 1968–69 production reached 981,000 cubic tons, double the pre-war output. Production of minor forest produce has been increasing steadily.

MINING

Although Burma is considered rich in minerals, output is well below the pre-war level. Petroleum and tin are the major mineral products but small quantities of tungsten, lead, zinc, antimony, silver and gold are also produced.

By early 1965 all the major mining enterprises had been nationalized. The Burmah Oil Company, now the People's Oil Industry, was nationalized with effect from January 1st, 1963. The Burma Corporation, in which the government previously participated on a joint venture basis for the development of tin, lead and zinc, was nationalized in January 1965 and is now known as the People's Bawdwin Industry. It is the only mining complex on a sustained basis.

Undoubtedly the most significant development for some time was the discovery in 1974 of a new oilfield at Letpando, 50 miles from the existing field at Chauk. Although small by international standards, its capacity of some 20,000 barrels per day is expected to double the total output of onshore wells in 1975, to 40,000 barrels per day when it goes into operation. Estimated domestic consumption in 1976 was about 23,000 barrels per day, so a modest export surplus will be available. In 1975 there was a total of 517 onshore wells producing about 21,000 barrels per day of crude oil. It is hoped that the completion of the pipeline building programme, to facilitate the transport of oil from the onshore wells to the coast, will enable Burma to increase its output and to start exporting oil by March 1977. Offshore exploration is underway and, if discoveries are made, the fields will be exploited in Indonesian fashion with the foreign companies acting as contractors for the national company.

INDUSTRY

Since the advent of military rule in 1962 the manufacturing sector, like the rest of the economy, has remained fairly static in relation to the rising population. The contribution of manufacturing to the gross domestic product reached 10.7 per cent in 1968/69 but fell to 8.4 per cent in 1973/74, when the sector employed 7.1 per cent of the total labour force. The majority of the value of industrial output was composed of the manufacture of food, beverages and tobacco, of which rice and rice products made up about 60 per cent. Other major industrial undertakings are the production of cooking oil, preserved fish and meat, cotton textiles and petroleum refining. Of less importance are the processing of other primary products, the production of cement, bricks, tiles, steel and consumer goods such as matches, textiles other than cotton, cigarettes and pharmaceuticals as well as brewing and distilling. In 1975 a loan was made from the Asian Development Bank for the establishment of a jute mill at Myaungmya, designed to make Burma self-sufficient in jute products at a total cost of U.S. $43.3 million.

State Intervention in Industry

In common with many developing countries the independent Government of Burma launched a programme of industrialization through the establishment of state manufacturing industries. In 1952 an Industrial Development Corporation was established and major enterprises set up under the government's industrial programme included a cotton spinning and weaving mill, a brick and tile factory, jute mill, steel rolling mill, three sugar mills, a brewery, cement and pharmaceutical plants and enterprises for tea packing and sericulture. Between 1952–53 and 1962–63 industrial production increased by 142 per cent.

The Revolutionary Council's policy had been for the state to expand its role in this sector and to take over large and medium-sized industries. On January 1st, 1971, the Government nationalized 69 medium-sized industrial establishments: 7 textiles, 45 foodstuff, 8 chemical, 3 metal, 1 engineering and five other factories. In 1970–71 there were 1,480 factories in the public sector and 80 others under construction. There were 15,346 private factories, of which 57 were governmentally-controlled. In 1969–70 about one-third of public enterprises employed more than 100 persons, whereas about three-quarters of private enterprises employed less than 10 persons and less than 1 per cent employed more than 100 persons.

DOMESTIC COMMERCE

Before independence (1948) British, Indians and Chinese dominated domestic trade. The Government has gradually increased its participation in this sector and squeezed the aliens out of the economy. Before 1964 this was effected mainly through the expansion of government importing agencies into the distribution of imported and domestic goods. In September 1963 the People's Stores Corporation, a centralized government distribution enterprise, was established to take over all existing government importing and distributing agencies and to draw up an overall scheme for the distribution of foreign and domestic goods. In 1964 all trading concerns in the country were nationalized. Shortages of consumer goods, particularly imported goods, developed and prices, which had fallen since 1961, started moving upwards. Consumer prices declined between 1968 and 1970, after which they rose again. Inflation sharply increased, reaching over 33 per cent in the year to August 1975.

POWER

The availability of cheap power is essential for industrial development. Though Burma has significant water-power potential present per capita power output is low for the Far East. Except for a few mines and industrial plants, power capacity is at present concentrated near Rangoon and owned by the government. Installed capacity for public use has been fairly constant since 1959, totalling 198,000 kW. in 1972. In December 1967 work began on the Mobye Dam in Kayah State which will boost the volume of water at the Lawpita hydroelectric power station. Three additional 28,000 kW. generators will be installed which will double the capacity of the plant.

TRANSPORT

Inland waterways, the Irrawaddy, Chindwin and the delta creeks, are the traditional arteries of Burmese commerce and the main roads and railways run north and south between the mountaines that separate the country from India and Thailand. The railways, domestic airways and the major inland water transport facilities are owned and operated by the Government and about one-third of the freight tonnage involved in the sea-borne trade of the country is carried by state-owned shipping under the management of the Burma Five Star Line Corporation.

Inland Transport

The railway network was 3,138 kilometres long in 1970, and the main route is from Rangoon to Mandalay. The bulk of goods traffic is transported by rail. Freight tonnage has been increasing slowly in recent years. The total number of passenger-kilometres increased from 1,541 million in 1962/63 to 3,073 million in 1972/73. These increases have been possible mainly because of the reduction of running times resulting from the dieselization of the railways.

Approximately 9.7 million passengers were carried by the vessels of the Inland Water Transport Board in 1972/73, an increase of 100 per cent since 1960/61. Freight carried also doubled during the same period to an estimated 1.9 million tons. During recent years the Board extended its service routes, enlarged its fleet and improved its maintenance facilities. Rail and water facilities are, however, still inadequate and considerable time is lost through breakdowns of obsolete equipment.

In 1970 Burma had 25,882 kilometres of roads, including 7,800 kilometres of paved roads. The number of registered passenger cars increased from about 18,400 in 1960 to 31,700 in 1973 and commercial vehicles rose from 18,500 to 34,300 over the same period. The increase in the number of road vehicles is very slow compared with that for Thailand. In 1963 the Road Transport Board was formed to nationalize gradually all passenger and freight road transport services.

Air Transport

The Burmese international airport is at Mingaladon (Rangoon) from which the Burma Airways Corporation (BAC, a government monopoly) operates an international network covering Calcutta, Kathmandu, Dacca, Bangkok and Hong Kong. Internally BAC serves 34 towns besides Rangoon. The airfields at Akyab and Moulmein have been expanded.

FOREIGN TRADE

Burma's export earnings reached a peak of 1,290 million kyats in 1963. Thereafter the value of exports declined and from 1967 to 1973 the annual total was between 500 and 660 million kyats, lower than in any year since 1947. The main reason for the decrease in earnings was a sharp fall in rice exports. In 1954 rice sales were valued at 952.7 million kyats, 80 per cent of total exports, but in 1973 rice exports earned only 87.8 million kyats (less than 14 per cent of the year's total). Export earnings increased to 954 million kyats in 1974 (when the export price of rice was triple that of 1973) and to 1,015 million kyats in 1975.

Burma's other principal source of foreign exchange is wood, especially teak. In 1954 teak exports earned 24 million kyats, only 2.0 per cent of the total for the year, but the figure rose to 232.2 million kyats in 1973 (36.3 per cent of total exports) and was virtually the same in 1974. Before the Second World War exports of petroleum and minerals were also of major importance but their place has now been taken by minor agricultural commodities such as pulses, oil cakes, raw rubber and cotton.

Until 1964, Burma was the world's largest rice exporter. The decline since 1961/62 has been attributed mainly to the effect on production of the low procurement prices paid by the Government and the inefficiency of the Government procurement system.

After a drastic decline of 47 per cent in rice exports between mid-1969 and mid-1971, the average export price of Burma rice reached a record low around mid-1971 and recovered by about 9 per cent in the remainder of 1971. In 1971 the average decline in price was 9 per cent compared with 32 per cent in 1970. Poor harvests drastically reduced export earnings in 1972, and in March 1973 rice exports had to be suspended altogether.

Since 1970 the value of timber exports has increased, and in 1973, with the drop in rice exports, teak was the largest single item in Burma's exports.

Burma exports mainly to food-deficit countries of the region, principally India and Sri Lanka. Exports to the European socialist countries increased steadily to 1963–64 and have since fallen off sharply. Since 1964 all foreign trade has been in the hands of the state, and trading policies have concentrated on bilateral trading agreements.

The country's main imports are textiles, machinery and transport equipment and the principal suppliers in 1974 were Japan, the People's Republic of China, Indonesia and the Federal Republic of Germany. In 1964/65 a 30 per cent increase in imports resulted in a large deficit of 334 million kyats. Drastic and indiscriminate cuts were made, customs duties increased and imports fell in 1966/67 to their lowest level for ten years. The trend was reversed in 1967/68 and with the fall in exports the trade gap widened. However by 1973 Burma once again had a foreign trade surplus In 1974 imports were valued at 614.6 million kyat and exports at 953.7 million kyats. The Governmen has been willing and able to control imports closel through the variation of customs duties, a licensin system and the expansion of state agencies into th sector.

RESERVES AND BALANCE OF PAYMENTS

The overall balance of payments deficit after 196 was financed through a reduction in gross reserves At the same time short-term external liabilitie were reduced by some 14 million dollars to 38 millior dollars at the end of 1971. It was also financed through a drawing of $5 million under the Compensatory Financing Decision of the International Monetary Fund In the process of using reserves, Burma sold $41 million of its gold. During 1971, Burma further drew $6.5 million from the International Monetary Fund to finance its large deficit in the foreign sector. Effective on December 27th, 1971, Burma established a central foreign exchange rate of 5.3487 kyats to $1 with wider margins, representing an 18 per cent devaluation from the initial par value expressed in terms of gold and an 11 per cent depreciation against the U.S. dollar. In February 1973 the kyat did not follow the dollar down but in January 1975 the currency was effectively devalued by over 20 per cent.

Burma's international reserves, worth U.S. $215 million at the end of 1964, fell below $100 million in 1970. After using almost all its gold holdings, the country's reserves were less than $50 million in January 1973. As a result of capital inflows, mainly foreign loans and credits, reserves again passed $200 million in August 1974. By February 1976 the figure had fallen to $130 million. The 1975/76 budget sombrely pointed out that foreign debts had soared to 2,763 million kyats ($550 million), of which $80 million were repayable in 1975/76.

ECONOMIC POLICY

Clear signs of a move away from economic autarchy are evident. Three decades of economic stagnation and agricultural decline were conceded in the 1974–75 budget when the new Minister for Planning and Finance, U Lwin, argued that in twelve years of army rule output had increased by 2.2 per cent per annum and population by 2.3 per cent. Increasing reliance on foreign finance is clear. No foreign aid or investment was envisaged in the 1966 Four-Year Plan. In the Second (1970) Plan $160 million in foreign aid was planned while, in the event, $700 million was offered and $500 million used. The "liberalization" of the Burmese socialist economy was further emphasized in 1976 with U Lwin's announcement of a new policy regarding state-owned corporations. In future they are to be run on a profit-making basis with incentive systems to improve productivity. State enterprises are to be financed by bank loans on a commercial basis.

Whether the policy change has come in time to avoid even further disruption of the economy and whether the change is in the right direction remains to be seen. But the increased growth rate of 6.1 per cent in net output reported for 1975/76 is a hopeful indicator. It seems that the policies of "Burmese Socialism" are on the way out. And the newly formed "Aid Burma" consortium of western creditors will undoubtedly take a leading role in outlining future national economic policy.

A New Direction

The year 1973 saw the initiation of a new economic policy, the main purpose of which was to strengthen external economic links. Burma joined the Asian Development Bank. Premier Ne Win's visits to several neighbouring countries even caused speculation that Burma might join ASEAN. By Burmese standards, the year was remarkable for the amount of foreign credits obtained. The IDA agreed to lend $33 million for the renovation of rail and river transport systems. Mitsui and Toyo are involved in a $22 million loan to construct a second oil refinery at Syrian, and a further $17 million is coming from Japan to finance purchases of supplies and equipment for Burmese government projects. Two fertilizer plants are being constructed with West German aid and improved relations with China have prompted the renewal of Chinese assistance in the construction of two cement works. Early in 1973, $13.5 million of Special Drawing Rights were secured from the IMF in order to underpin government plans to improve the balance of payments through diversifying and boosting agricultural exports. Whether this will redress the deficit in the short term remains to be seen. If it does not, further finance from the IMF may be conditional upon the Burmese Government's ability to gain the agreement of the IMF to its future domestic economic policies. In 1975 the Burmese Government continued to accept economic aid from abroad, with West Germany giving aid worth DM 75 million for expansion of the Bawdwin Mines. The Asian Development Bank made two loans: U.S. $25.3 million for the development of the jute industry and U.S. $6.1 million for a power transmission development project. Moreover, the Government may be weakening in its hostility towards domestic private capital. Privately owned rubber estates have been guaranteed immunity from nationalization for 30 years, and a list of over 200 manufacturing activities open to domestic private capital has been published by the authorities.

STATISTICAL SURVEY

AREA AND POPULATION

Area (square miles)				Population (1974 estimate—'000)			
Total	Shan States	Karen State	Kayah State	Total	Shan States	Karen State	Kayah State
261,218	60,155	11,731	4,529	30,170	3,178	856	127

1975: Estimated population 31 million.

PRINCIPAL TOWNS

(Census of March 31st, 1973)

Rangoon (capital)	3,186,886	Myingyan	220,129
Mandalay	417,266	Moulmein	202,967
Bassein	335,588	Prome	148,123
Henzada	283,658	Akyab	143,215
Pegu	254,761	Tavoy	101,536

EMPLOYMENT

(March 1975)

Total	Central and Local Government	Industry	Agriculture	Other Sectors
11,748,663	517,332	847,799	7,831,754	2,551,778

AGRICULTURE

PRINCIPAL CROPS

	AREA ('000 acres)			PRODUCTION ('000 metric tons)		
	1972/73	1973/74	1974/75*	1972/73	1973/74	1974/75*
Rice (paddy)	12,014	12,575	12,776	7,241	8,466	8,446
Wheat	137	156	167	26	24	41
Maize	235	219	223	55	61	59
Pulses	1,284	1,181	1,248	162	174	203
Groundnuts	1,563	1,638	1,671	377	405	459
Sesame seed	2,356	2,660	2,636	69	152	98
Cottonseed	} 532	527	538 {	28	24	} 45
Cotton (lint)				15	13	
Jute	288	291	166	88	78	39
Rubber	214	213	212	15	15	15
Sugar cane	292	235	227	2,000	1,661	1,185
Tobacco	161	108	127	56	42	59

* Provisional.

LIVESTOCK
('000 head)

	1971/72	1972/73	1973/74	1974/75*
Cattle	7,158	7,235	7,267	7,299
Buffaloes	1,643	1,601	1,646	1,690
Goats	570	766	732	699
Pigs	1,608	1,489	1,461	1,432
Chickens	15,840	16,068	15,682	15,296
Ducks	3,596	3,536	3,186	2,836

Sheep: 198,000 in 1972.

* Provisional.

LIVESTOCK PRODUCTS
(FAO estimates, '000 metric tons)

	1972	1973	1974
Beef and veal	69	74	75
Buffalo meat	14	15	15
Mutton and lamb	1	1	1
Goats' meat	3	3	3
Pig meat	57	70	73
Poultry meat	19	21	21
Edible offals	20.4	22.5	22.9
Cows' milk	325	327	330
Buffaloes' milk	32	34	35
Goats' milk	3	5	5
Butter and ghee	7.2	7.2	7.3
Cheese	20.4	20.5	20.7
Hen eggs	65.3	68.0	68.9
Other poultry eggs	13.0	13.5	13.9
Cattle hides	14.8	15.2	16.6
Buffalo hides	6.5	7.1	7.3

Source: FAO, *Production Yearbook 1974*.

FORESTRY

ROUNDWOOD REMOVALS

('000 cubic metres, all non-coniferous)

	1967	1968	1969	1970*	1971*	1972*	1973
Sawlogs, veneer logs and logs for sleepers	1,817	1,731	1,728	1,737	1,776	1,704	1,718
Other industrial wood	775	790	810	830	845	865	893
Fuel wood	12,180	12,460	12,740	13,230	18,081	18,377	18,559
TOTAL	14,772	14,981	15,278	15,797	20,702	20,946	21,170

* FAO estimates.

Source: FAO, *Yearbook of Forest Products*.

SAWNWOOD PRODUCTION

('000 cubic metres, all non-coniferous)

	1967	1968	1969	1970	1971	1972	1973
Sawnwood (incl. boxboards)	590	537	587	624	615	653	595
Railway sleepers	20	19	11	13	14	17	11
TOTAL	610	556	598	637	629	670	606

Source: FAO, *Yearbook of Forest Products*.

FISHING

('000 metric tons)

	1967	1968	1969	1970	1971	1972	1973	1974
Inland waters	108.1	112.4	115.3	121.0	122.9	124.2	125.3	126.2
Indian Ocean	272.6	283.7	298.6	311.4	319.8	329.1	338.1	307.6
TOTAL CATCH	380.7	396.1	413.9	432.4	442.7	453.3	463.4	433.8

Source: FAO, *Yearbook of Fishery Statistics 1974*.

MINING

		1970	1971	1972	1973
Hard coal	'000 metric tons	11	15	16	n.a.
Crude petroleum	,, ,, ,,	801	875	968	968
Lead-bearing ores	metric tons	4,485	7,505	6,255	n.a.
Zinc-bearing ores	,, ,,	3,733	3,648	3,575	n.a.
Tin-bearing ores	,, ,,	300	493	600	600
Tungsten-bearing ores	,, ,,	279	493	590	667
Silver-bearing ores*	,, ,,	19	21	19	26

* Refined silver.

Source: UN, *The Growth of World Industry 1973*.

INDUSTRY

		1970	1971	1972	1973
Salt, unrefined	'000 metric tons	157	186	210	170
Sugar, refined	" " "	49	51	61	67
Cigarettes	million	1,513	1,515	1,650	1,512
Cotton yarn*, pure	metric tons	6,135	6,193	6,317	7,469
Soap†	" "	6,899	8,692	13,219	n.a.
Cement	'000 metric tons	167	197	200	193
Motor gasoline	" " "	159	158	173	174
Kerosene	" " "	269	284	273	196

* Government factory production only.

† Government production only, twelve months ending September 30th of year stated.

Source: UN, *The Growth of World Industry 1973.*

FINANCE

100 pyas=1 kyat.

Coins: 1, 5, 10, 25 and 50 pyas.

Notes: 1, 5, 10, 20 and 25 kyats.

Exchange rates (June 1976): £1 sterling=11.84 kyats; U.S. $1=6.67 kyats.

100 kyats=£8.45=$14.98.

Note: Between September 1949 and August 1971 the kyat (known as the Burmese rupee before 1952) had a par value of 21 U.S. cents (U.S. $1=4.7619 kyats). From December 1971 to February 1973 the central exchange rate was $1=5.3487 kyats (1 kyat=18.696 U.S. cents). Between February 1973 and August 1974 the rate was $1=4.8138 kyats (1 kyat=20.773 U.S. cents). From August 1974 to January 1975 the currency was subject to "controlled floating". In January 1975 an exchange rate of $1=6.2391 kyats was established. Subsequently the exchange rate against the U.S. dollar has been adjusted from month to month. The average market rate (kyats per $) was: 5.454 in 1972; 4.907 in 1973; 4.858 in 1974; 6.454 in 1975. In terms of sterling, the value of the kyat between November 1967 and August 1971 was 1s. 9d. (8.75p), the exchange rate being £1=11.4286 kyats; from December 1971 to June 1972 the rate was £1=13.937 kyats.

BUDGET

(million kyats, April 1st to March 31st)

Receipts	1975/76
Revenue	1,664.2
Current account	12,665.7
Capital account	5.5
Debts	12.1
Loans and advances	91.9
Savings	33.0
Total	14,472.4

Expenditure	1975/76
Current expenditure	13,348.8
of which:	
Economic enterprises	5,167.4
Trade	4,760.5
Social welfare	856.9
National defence	787.2
Transport and communications	656.1
Construction	460.8
Administration	349.6
Capital account	1,511.0
of which:	
Mines	352.0
Industry	303.8
Transport and communications	189.8
Agriculture	142.1
Administration	124.9
Investments	29.9
Debts	417.8
Contributions	45.6
Loans and advances	124.2
Savings	44.0
Total	15,521.4

INTERNATIONAL RESERVES

(U.S. $ million at December 31st)

	1969	1970	1971	1972	1973	1974	1975
Gold	83.6	62.7	23.5	12.2	8.4	8.6	8.2
IMF Special Drawing Rights	—	—	—	6.1	11.7	11.7	9.4
Foreign exchange*	45.6	31.4	48.8	34.1	80.2	170.7	116.2
Total	129.2	94.1	72.3	52.4	100.3	191.0	133.8

* In February 1970 the Union Bank of Burma assumed control of the foreign assets of all banks and the small holdings of the insurance board.

Source: IMF, *International Financial Statistics.*

Currency in circulation (million kyats, September): 2,093.2 in 1971; 2,413.5 in 1972; 3,006.5 in August 1975.

COST OF LIVING

(Consumer Price Index for Rangoon. Base: 1970=100)

	1965	1966	1967	1968	1969	1971	1972	1973	1974
Food	81.6	112.0	110.9	113.6	107.9	102.4	114.8	150.0	187.4
Fuel and light	99.8	99.0	98.3	98.3	98.7	101.1	102.2	108.9	175.8
Clothing	77.6	88.1	99.2	113.3	94.7	102.3	100.0	108.1	132.7
Rent and repairs	93.0	98.3	96.6	102.3	100.3	104.0	90.1	102.0	124.8
All Items	83.5	106.4	103.9	110.1	104.3	102.2	109.9	135.8	172.4

August 1975: Food 274.7; All items 241.3.

Source: International Labour Office, mainly *Year Book of Labour Statistics.*

NATIONAL ACCOUNTS

(million kyats at current prices, 12 months ending September 30th)

Expenditure on the Gross Domestic Product

	1968/69	1969/70	1970/71	1971/72	1972/73	1973/74
Final consumption expenditure	8,846	9,168	9,474	9,712	10,547	13,378
Increase in stocks	194	293	175	133	156	293
Gross fixed capital formation	1,076	1,160	1,056	1,184	1,111	1,177
Total Domestic Expenditure	10,116	10,621	10,705	11,029	11,814	14,848
Exports of goods and services	552	535	584	664	625	984
Less Imports of goods and services	753	896	852	921	704	980
G.D.P. in Purchasers' Values	9,915	10,260	10,437	10,772	11,735	14,852

Cost-structure of the Gross Domestic Product

	1967/68	1968/69	1969/70	1970/71	1971/72	1972/73*
Compensation of employees	3,938	4,167	4,202	4,364	4,898	5,156
Operating surplus	3,867	4,131	4,373	4,334	4,031	4,761
Domestic Factor Incomes	7,805	8,298	8,575	8,698	8,929	9,917
Consumption of fixed capital	678	698	711	729	810	798
G.D.P. at Factor Cost	8,483	8,996	9,286	9,427	9,739	10,715
Indirect taxes, *less* subsidies	858	919	974	1,010	1,033	1,109
G.D.P. in Purchasers' Values	9,341	9,915	10,260	10,437	10,772	11,824

* Provisional figures. Revised total for G.D.P. is 11,735 million kyats.

GROSS DOMESTIC PRODUCT BY ECONOMIC ACTIVITY

	1970/71	1971/72	1972/73	1973/74
Agriculture (excl. livestock) and hunting	2,905	2,942	4,531	6,302
Forestry and logging	289	321		
Livestock and fishing	803	810		
Mining and quarrying	145	170	196	358
Manufacturing	1,082	1.083	1,049	1,247
Electricity	67	65	72	73
Construction	203	200	208	205
Wholesale and retail trade	2,595	2,712	2,972	3,919
Transport, storage and communications	631	640	621	604
Finance and insurance	129	169	2,086	2,144
Government services	838	903		
Other producers and services*	750	757		
TOTAL	10,437	10,772	11,735	14,852

* Including gas, water, hotels, restaurants, owner-occupied dwellings, real estate and business services, and community, social and personal services.

Source: United Nations, *Yearbook of National Accounts Statistics* and *Monthly Bulletin of Statistics.*

BALANCE OF PAYMENTS

(U.S. $ million)

	1971	1972	1973	1974
Merchandise exports f.o.b.	122.6	122.5	152.1	200.7
Merchandise imports f.o.b.	−141.4	−162.5	−206.8	−233.8
TRADE BALANCE	−18.8	−40.0	−54.7	−33.1
Exports of services	10.2	11.1	16.5	50.7
Imports of services	−52.8	−35.0	−38.9	−39.3
BALANCE ON GOODS AND SERVICES	−61.4	−63.9	−77.1	−21.7
Unrequited transfer (net)	18.7	18.4	17.6	14.5
BALANCE ON CURRENT ACCOUNT	−42.7	−45.6	−59.6	−7.1
Long-term capital (net)	5.3	12.1	63.7	40.2
Short-term capital (net)	−4.8	5.3	−1.2	26.7
Net errors and omissions	9.4	11.1	31.0	4.0
TOTAL (net monetary movements)	−32.8	−17.2	33.9	63.7
Allocation of SDRs	6.4	6.9	—	—
Changes in reserves, etc.	−26.4	−10.2	33.9	63.7

Source: IMF, *International Financial Statistics.*

EXTERNAL TRADE

(million kyats)

	1970	1971	1972	1973	1974	1975
Exports f.o.b.	515.8	609.6	654.7	627.5	953.7	1,015.2
Imports c.i.f.	807.0	933.3	866.6	522.2	614.6	n.a.

Source: UN Monthly Bulletin of Statistics, May 1976.

PRINCIPAL COMMODITIES
(million kyats)

Imports	1970/71	1971/72	1972/73*
Machinery and Transport Equipment	273.4	346.1	158.8
Base Metal Manufactures	117.4	107.8	74.0
Cotton Fabrics	42.4	39.6	15.9
Cotton Yarn	57.0	47.4	33.9
Milk and Milk Products	23.3	24.7	30.7
Pharmaceuticals	15.5	11.4	n.a.
Gunny Sacks	6.9	42.3	16.9
Paper	32.4	27.4	25.7
Refined Mineral Oil	15.9	12.9	20.5
Chemicals	29.5	25.5	23.0
Coal and Coke	18.1	13.8	13.7

* Provisional.

Exports	1970/71	1971/72	1972/73
Rice and Rice Products	286.2	287.5	116.8
Other Agricultural Products	104.0	152.5	160.0
Teak and Hardwood	140.0	149.1	194.7
Metals and Ores	26.4	34.0	34.8

PRINCIPAL COUNTRIES
(U.S. $ million)

Imports	1972	1973	1974
Bangladesh	4.9	9.8	14.6
China, People's Republic	13.4	22.7	33.3
France	1.5	4.2	13.3
Germany, Federal Republic	11.8	12.5	16.3
Indonesia	0.5	n.a.	19.8
Japan	36.8	54.3	68.6
Singapore	1.5	6.0	15.2
United Kingdom	9.1	9.3	11.3

Exports	1972	1973	1974
Bangladesh	7.3	14.7	22.0
Denmark	4.2	6.4	9.5
Hong Kong	3.5	7.2	13.3
Japan	14.6	41.2	27.8
Malaysia	3.0	4.6	13.6
Pakistan	2.2	5.1	9.0
Singapore	11.0	15.1	18.6
Sri Lanka	17.3	5.2	26.7
United Kingdom	12.4	13.4	8.7

Source: Direction of Trade INT/B 1974 *Annual* 1970–74.

TOURISM

	1971	1972	1973	1974*
Number of visitors	11,528	13,568	16,448	15,631

* Provisional.

TRANSPORT

ROAD TRAFFIC
('000)

	1969	1970	1971	1972	1973
Passenger cars	29.4	29.8	33.4	31.0	31.7
Commercial vehicles	30.0	31.0	32.3	33.4	34.3

RAILWAYS (Burma Railways Board)*
(million)

	1970–71	1971–72	1972–73	1973–74
Net ton-kilometres . .	67.4	63.7	49.8	34.5
Passenger-kilometres . .	204.6	225.0	256.1	246.3

* Twelve months beginning October 1st.

INLAND WATER TRANSPORT BOARD
(million)

	PASSENGERS	FREIGHT TONS
1971–72 . . .	9.8	2.2
1972–73 . . .	9.7	1.9
1974–75 . . .	10.0	1.9

INTERNATIONAL SEA-BORNE SHIPPING*
('000 metric tons)

	1970–71	1971–72	1972–73	1973–74
Freight loaded	1,031	1,265	985	650
Freight unloaded . . .	901	941	635	526

* Twelve months beginning October 1st.

Source: UN *Monthly Bulletin of Statistics.*

CIVIL AVIATION
(Burma Airways Corporation)

	PASSENGER MILES	FREIGHT ('000 tons)
1970–71 . . .	100,117	8.0
1971–72 . . .	113,866	7.4
1972–73 . . .	122,735	6.9

EDUCATION

(1974–75)†

	INSTITUTIONS	TEACHERS	PUPILS AND STUDENTS
Primary Schools	19,399	73,653	3,449,552
Middle Schools	1,202	17,967	762,871
High Schools	571	8,794	182,848
Vocational Schools*	27	618	5,319
Agricultural and Technical Institutes* .	5	165	2,292
Universities and Colleges	19	3,404	57,965

* 1969–70 figures. † Provisional.

THE CONSTITUTION

The constitution came into force in January 1974, following a national referendum held in December 1973. A summary of the main provisions follows.

Preamble: affirmation of the Burmese Way to Socialism.

Chapter I (*articles* 1–4) The State: definition and designation of Burma.

Chapter II (*articles* 5–27) Basic Principles: Burma a single-party state, power residing in the people; representation of the people; extent of state power.

Chapter III (*articles* 28–40) The State Structure: outline of central and local government.

Chapter IV (*articles* 41–63) The People's Assembly: elected directly by secret ballot; composition, conditions of office and powers.

Chapter V (*articles* 64–81) The Council of State: elected bv the Assembly; duties and rights of the Council.

Chapter VI (*articles* 82–94) The Council of Ministers: elected by the Assembly; tasks of the Council; responsibilities of Ministers.

Chapter VII (*articles* 95–110) The Council of People's Justices: elected by the Assembly; system of Bodies of Justices at central and local levels; basis on which justice to be administered; task of supervising all courts and judicial bodies.

Chapter VIII (*articles* 111–117) The Council of People's Attorneys: elected by the Assembly; duty to protect the rights of the people and report on the workings of the judicial system.

Chapter IX (*articles* 118–124) The Council of People's Inspectors: elected by the Assembly to inspect public undertakings.

Chapter X (*articles* 125–144) The People's Councils: Councils to be elected at every level of local and state government, headed by Executive Committees; duties of these.

Chapter XI (*articles* 145–172) Fundamental Rights and Duties of Citizens: qualification for citizenship; right to work, to recreation, to medical treatment and education; rights of women; right to vote, to freedom of expression, to participate in permitted political activity, to assembly, to reside, complain and sue; duty to protect the state, perform military service and pay taxes.

Chapter XII (*articles* 173–186) The Electoral System: aims; principle of direct election; constituency system; elegibility to stand for election; status of the Burma Socialist Programme Party; majority votes to count; conduct of elections.

Chapter XIII (*articles* 187–189) Recall, Resignation and Replacement: conditions under which a representative of the people may be replaced.

Chapter XIV (*articles* 190–193) The State Flag, the State Seal, the National Anthem and the State Capital.

Chapter XV (*article* 194) Amendments.

Chapter XVI (*articles* 195–209) General Provisions.

THE GOVERNMENT

(*May* 1976)

HEAD OF STATE

President: U NE WIN.

COUNCIL OF STATE

Chairman: U NE WIN.

Secretary: Gen. SAN YU.

Members:

U KYAW SOE
U KYAW ZAW
Col. KYAW WIN
U KHEN ZA MUNG
U KHIN MAUNG
U SOE HLAING
SAO OHN HNYA
U TIN THEIN
U TUN LIN
U DING RA TANG
U BA NYEIN
Col. MIN THEIN
Dr. MAUNG MAUNG
Dr. MAUNG LWIN
MAHN SAN MYAT SHWE
U HLA TUN PRU
Dr. HLA HAN
U THA DIN
U THAUNG KYI
Commdr. THAUNG TIN
Brig. THAUNG DAN
U THAN SEIN
U THAN SEIN (ARAKAN)
Dr. THEIN AUNG
THANKIN AUNG MIN
U SEIN WIN
U SAW ONN

COUNCIL OF MINISTERS

Prime Minister: U SEIN WIN.

Deputy Prime Minister and Minister for Planning and Finance: U LWIN.

Minister for Home and Religious Affairs: U KO KO.

Ministers for Industry: Col. TINT SWE, Col. MAUNG CHO.

Minister for Mines: U MAUNG MAUNG KHA.

Minister for Construction: U HTIN KYAW.

Minister for Transport and Communications: Col. SEIN LWIN.

Minister for Health: Col. KYI MAUNG.

Minister for Education: Dr. KHIN MAUNG WIN.

Minister for Defence: Maj.-Gen. KYAW HTIN

Minister for Agriculture and Forests: U YE GOUNG.

Minister for Trade: U HLA AYE.

Minister for Labour: U MAUNG MAUNG KHA.

Minister for Information: MAUNG LWIN.

Minister for Social Welfare: U VAN KULH.

Minister for Culture: U AYE MAUNG.

Minister for Foreign Affairs: U HLA PHONE.

Minister for Co-operatives: U TUN TIN.

PARLIAMENT

PYITHU HLUTTAW

Following national elections early in 1974, the first inaugural session of the Pyithu Hluttaw (People's Assembly) was convened on March 2nd, 1974. Sessions are presided over by the members of a panel of chairmen in rotation.

POLITICAL PARTY

Burma Socialist Programme Party (BSPP) (*Lanzin Party*): Rangoon; f. 1962; the only recognized political party; set up by the Revolutionary Council to implement its policies; consists of cadres as a nucleus for the new National Party; mems. 170,302 (full), 835,571 (candidate); publs. *Lanzin Thadin* (*Party News*) twice a month, *Party Affairs Journal* (monthly), *International Affairs Journal* (monthly); Chair. U NE WIN; Gen. Sec. Gen. SAN YU; Joint Gen. Sec. U THAUNG KYI.

DIPLOMATIC REPRESENTATION

EMBASSIES ACCREDITED TO BURMA

(Rangoon unless otherwise indicated)

Afghanistan: New Delhi, India.

Australia: 88 Strand Rd.; *Ambassador:* R. S. LAURIE

Austria: Bangkok, Thailand.

Bangladesh: 106–108 Rhyu St.; *Ambassador:* SAYYID ANWARAL KARIM (also accred. to Thailand).

Belgium: Bangkok, Thailand.

Bulgaria: Dacca, Bangladesh.

Canada: Kuala Lumpur, Malaysia.

China, People's Republic: 1 Pyidaungsu Rd.; *Ambassador:* YEH CHENG-CHANG.

Czechoslovakia: 326 Prome Rd.; *Ambassador:* LADISLAV JETMAR (also accred. to Singapore).

Denmark: Bangkok, Thailand.

Egypt: 81 Pyidaungsu Yeiktha Rd.; *Ambassador:* F. H. KAMEL.

Finland: Jakarta, Indonesia.

France: *Ambassador:* HUBERT YVER DE LA BRUCHOLLERIE.

German Democratic Republic: 17 University Ave.; *Ambassador:* SIEGFRIED KÜHNEL.

Germany, Federal Republic: 32 Natmauk Rd.; *Ambassador:* Dr. HANS FERDINAND LINSEER.

Greece: New Delhi, India.

Hungary: 84 Iaya Rd.; *Ambassador:* Dr. FERENC TURC.

India: 545–547 Merchant St.; *Ambassador:* N. P. ALEXANDER.

Indonesia: 100 (Ka) Pyidaungsu Yeiktha Rd.; *Ambassador:* SOERIA ATMADJA.

Iran: New Delhi, India.

Iraq: New Delhi, India.

Israel: 49 Prome Rd.; *Ambassador:* DAVID I. MARMOR.

Italy: 3 Lowis Rd.; *Chargé d'Affaires:* LUGII CORSI.

Japan: 100 Natmauk Rd.; *Ambassador:* TAKEO ARITA.

Korea, Democratic People's Republic: 30 Tank Rd.; *Ambassador:* MA JANG CHOL.

Korea, Republic: 591 Prome Rd.; *Ambassador:* JIN SANG AN.

Laos: Bangkok, Thailand.

Malaysia: 65 Windsor Rd.; *Ambassador:* MOHD. HUSSEIN KASIM.

Mongolia: Peking, People's Republic of China.

Nepal: 16 Nat. Mauk Yeiktha Rd.; *Ambassador:* BHARAT RAZ BHANDARY (also accred. to Laos, Malaysia and Singapore).

Netherlands: New Delhi, India.

Nigeria: New Delhi, India.

Norway: Bangkok, Thailand

Pakistan: 18 Windsor Rd.; *Ambassador:* HAFEEZ-UR RAHMAN.

Philippines: 11A Windemere Rd.; *Chargé d'Affaires:* Dr. JOSÉ V. DIZON.

Poland: Dacca, Bangladesh.

Romania: 71 Mission Rd.; *Chargé d'Affaires:* MIHAIL NICULESCU.

Spain: New Delhi, India.

Sri Lanka: 34 Fraser Rd.; *Ambassador:* H. R. PREMARATNE (also accred. to Laos).

Sweden: Bangkok, Thailand.

Switzerland: Bangkok, Thailand.

Thailand: 91 Prome Rd.; *Ambassador:* SRIONG TMANGRAKSAT.

Turkey: New Delhi, India.

U.S.S.R.: 52 Prome Rd.; *Ambassador:* ALEXEI I. ELIZAVETINE.

United Kingdom: 80 Strand Rd.; *Ambassador:* T. J. O'BRIEN.

U.S.A.: 581 Merchant St.; *Ambassador:* DAVID L. OSBORN.

Viet-Nam: 40 Komin Kochin Rd.; *Chargé d'Affaires:* VU XUAN ANG.

Yugoslavia: 39 Windsor Rd.; *Ambassador:* AZEM ZULFICARI (also accred. to Laos and Thailand).

Burma also has diplomatic relations with Algeria, Cambodia, New Zealand, Singapore and Zaire.

JUDICIAL SYSTEM

A new judicial structure was established in March 1974. Its highest organ, composed of members of the People's Assembly, is the Council of People's Justice. This Council, with three members of it selected for each occasion, serves as the central Court of Justice.

Chairman: U AUNG PE.

Below this Council are the state, divisional, township, ward and village tract courts formed with members of local People's Councils. Previous career judicial officials now serve as Law Officers at the new court.

RELIGION

Freedom of religious belief and practice is guaranteed for every citizen. About 75 per cent of the population are Buddhists.

Roman Catholic Bishop of Rangoon: Mgr. GABRIEL THOHEY, Archbishop's House, 289 Theinbyu St., Rangoon.

Episcopalian Bishop of Rangoon and Archbishop of Burma: Bishopscourt, 140 Pyidaungsu Yeiktha Rd., Dagon P.O., Rangoon.

THE PRESS

DAILIES

Botataung (*Vanguard Daily*): Rangoon; f. 1958; Burmese; nationalized; Editor U HTEIN LIN; circ. 4,500.

Guardian: 392 Merchant St., Rangoon; f. 1956; nationalized 1964; English; Editor-in-Chief U BA KYAW; circ. 15,000.

Hanthawaddy: 96 Aung San St., Mandalay; f. 1887; Burmese; nationalized 1969; Editor U WIN TIN; circ. 17,000.

Kyemon (*Mirror*): Rangoon; f. 1951; Burmese; nationalized. Editor U MYAT THU; circ. 51,000.

Loketha Pyithu Neizin (*Working People's Daily*): 212 Thien Byu St., Rangoon; f. 1963; Burmese and English; official newspaper; Chief Editor U HLA MYIANG; combined circ. 93,200.

Myanma Alin (*New Light of Burma*): 58 Komin Ko-chin Rd., Rangoon; f. 1914; Burmese; nationalized early 1969; Editor U SOE MAUNG; circ. 25,000.

Note: Daily newspaper readership in 1974 was estimated at 800,000.

WEEKLIES AND PERIODICALS

Gita Padetha: Rangoon; journal of Burma Music Council; circ. 10,000.

Guardian Magazine: 392 Merchant St., Rangoon; f. 1953; nationalized 1964; English literary magazine; monthly.

Myawaddy Magazine: 184 32nd St., Rangoon; f. 1952; Burmese; literary magazine; monthly.

Shu Ma Wa Magazine: 146 Western Wing, Bogyoke Market, Rangoon; Burmese; literary; monthly.

Thwe/Thauk Magazine: 185 48th St., Rangoon; f. 1946; Burmese; literary; monthly.

PRESS AGENCY

News Agency of Burma: 212 Theinbyu St., Rangoon f 1963; Government sponsored. Chief Editors U HLA TUN, U LUN AUNG.

FOREIGN BUREAUX

Agence France-Presse—AFP (*France*): 277 Bo Aung Gyaw St., Rangoon.

Agenzia Nazionale Stampa Associata—ANSA (*Italy*): Room 28, Bldg. 215, Yankim, Rangoon; Representative U TIN AYE.

Associated Press—AP (*U.S.A.*): 283 U Wisara Rd., Rangoon; Representative U SEIN WIN.

Hsinhua (*People's Republic of China*): 67 Prome Rd., Rangoon; Representative LI CHING-LIN.

Reuters: 162 Phayre St., Rangoon; Representative U ZAW MYINT THEIN.

Tass (*U.S.S.R.*): 30 (H) Inya Rd., Rangoon; Representative N. NOBOKOV.

United Press International—UPI (*U.S.A.*): 55 Kalagadan St., Rangoon; Representative U CHIT TUN.

PUBLISHERS

Hanthawaddy Press: Bo Aung Gyaw St. 157, Rangoon; f. 1889; general publisher of books and journals; Man. Editor U ZAW WIN.

Knowledge Publishing House: 130 Bogyoke St., Rangoon; publishers of travel, fiction, religious and political books and directories.

Kyipwaye Press: 84th St., Letsaigan, Mandalay; arts, travel, religion, fiction and children's books.

Myawaddy Press: 184 32nd St., Rangoon; journals and magazines; Exec. Officer U WINN MAUNG (MIN YU WEI).

Sarpay Beikman Management Board: 529 Merchant St., Rangoon; f. 1947; Burmese encyclopaedia, literature, fine arts and general; also translations; Chair. Lt.-Col. THURA TIN MAUNG (Deputy Information Minister); Vice-Chair. U SAW AUNG; Sec. U HTIN GYI.

Shumawa Press: 146 West Wing, Bogyoke Market, Rangoon; non-fiction of all kinds.

Shwepyidan Publishing House: 12 Haiaban St., Rangoon; philosophy, politics, law and religion.

Than Myit Baho Publishing House: Anawyatha Rd., Rangoon; scientific and technical.

Thu Dhama Wadi Press: 55-56 Maung Khine St., P.O.B. 419, Rangoon; f. 1903; Prop. U TIN HTOO; Man. U PAN MAUNG; religious books.

Trade Corporation for Printed Matter and Stationery: 550-552 Merchant St., Rangoon; books and periodicals on all subjects.

Universities Administration Office: Prome Rd., University Post Office, Rangoon; Chief Editor, Translations and Publications Dept. U WUN; Man. University Press U SOE MYINT.

ASSOCIATION

Burmese Publishers' Association: 146 Bogyoke Market, Rangoon; Pres. U ON PE.

RADIO

Burma Broadcasting Service: Prome Rd., Kamayut P.O.; Rangoon; f. 1946; broadcasts are made in Burmese, Shan, Karen, Chin, Kachin, Kayah and English; staff of 411; Dir.-Gen. U TIN MAUNG KYI; Dir. U KYAW NYEIN; Technical Dir. U WIN MG.

There were an estimated 627,000 radio receivers in 1974.

There is no television service in Burma.

FINANCE

All banks in Burma were nationalized in 1963 and amalgamated to form the People's Bank of the Union of Burma from November 1969. In April 1972 this was renamed the Union of Burma Bank.

Under a law of November 1975 there are four separate state-owned banks: the Union of Burma Bank, the Myanma Economic Bank, the Myanma Foreign Trade Bank and the Myanma Agricultural Bank each with its own management board. The Myanma Insurance Corporation is also to be established separately.

BANKING

(cap.=capital; dep.=deposits; p.u.=paid up; m.=million; Ks.=kyats.)

CENTRAL BANK

Union of Burma Bank: 24/26 Sule Pagoda Rd., Rangoon; f. 1976; cap. p.u. Ks. 200 m.; Chair. Dr. AYE HLAING; Advisor U TU MAUNG.

Myanma Economic Bank: 1/7 Latha St., Rangoon; cap. Ks. 80m. (1976); provides savings and credit facilities; Man. Dir. U AUNG SINT.

Myanma Foreign Trade Bank: 80-86 Barr St., Rangoon; cap. Ks. 30m. (1976); handles all foreign exchange and all international banking transactions; Man. Dir. U KO KO LAY; Gen. Man. U TIN U.

Myanma Agricultural Bank: 1/7 Latha St., Rangoon; Man. Dir. U BA SEIN.

INSURANCE

Myanma Insurance Corporation: 1 Maung Taulay St., Rangoon· Man. Dir. U KO KO GYI; Gen. Man. U SOE MYINT.

TRADE AND INDUSTRY

Socialist Economic Planning Committee: Rangoon; f. 1967; frames plans for a socialist economy; 10 mems.; Chair. U NE WIN; Vice-Chair. Gen. SAN YU.

GOVERNMENT CORPORATIONS

Agricultural Corporation: Rangoon.

Construction Corporation: Rangoon.

Industrial Planning Corporation: 192 Kaba-Aye Pagoda Rd., Rangoon; f. 1952.

Motion Picture Corporation: Shwedagon Pagoda Rd., Rangoon; import and distribution of foreign films.

Myanma Baw-dwin Corporation: Rangoon; nationalized Jan. 1965; development of tin, lead, zinc.

Myanma Export-Import Corporation: Rangoon; Chair. Lt.-Col. WIN PE.

Myanma Export-Import Corporation (Export Division): Rangoon; to control inter-governmental dealings in rice and other agricultural commodities.

Myanma Mineral Development Corporation: Rangoon; Dir.-Gen. UBA THAN HAQ.

Myanma Oil Corporation: 604 Merchant St., P.O.B. 1049, Rangoon; formerly Burmah Oil Company; nationalized Jan. 1963; Dir.-Gen. Maj. KYAW ZA.

Timber Corporation: Rangoon; f. 1948; extraction, processing, and main exporter of Burma teak and other timber.

CO-OPERATIVES

In 1970–71 the following co-operatives were formed: 60 township co-operatives, 18 agricultural producers co-operatives, 131 industrial co-operatives, 11 village co-operatives, 1,964 consumers' co-operatives and 703 co-operative credit societies.

WORKERS' AND PEASANTS' COUNCILS

Central People's Workers' Council: Rangoon; f. April 1968 to provide organization for self-government of workers; Chair. (vacant).

Central People's Peasants' Council: Rangoon; f. Feb. 1969; Chair. U THAUNG KYI; Sec. Lt.-Col. KYAW ZAW, B.A.F.

TRANSPORT

RAILWAYS

Burma Railways Board: Head Office: Bogyoke St., Rangoon, P.O.B. 118; government organization which manages State railways; railway mileage (1974) was 2,690 track miles; route mileage in 1974 totalled 1,949; Chair. U SEIN LWIN.

ROADS

The total length of all-weather motorable roads in Burma was over 13,512 miles in 1974.

Road Transport Corporation: Rangoon; f. 1963 to nationalize gradually all passenger and freight road transport; by 1970/71 operated 18 per cent of trucks and 30 per cent of passenger buses in Burma.

INLAND WATERWAYS

Inland Water Transport Corporation: 50 Phayre St., Rangoon; government-sponsored and non-profit-making. Its chief business is the conveyance of rice and rice products from the Irrawaddy Delta Stations, grains and pulses, oil cakes, wax and cotton bales from up-country and Central Burma to Rangoon for export. There is also a passenger steamer service, and fuel oils are carried in tankers. A modernization programme was announced in 1974, including a new dockyard and navigational channels in the Rangoon river. Chair. U HLA WIN; Gen. Man. U MAUNG MAUNG.

SHIPPING

Rangoon is the chief port. Vessels up to 15,000 tons can be accommodated.

Burma Port Corporation: P.O.B. 1, Pansodan St., Rangoon; Chair. U HLA MYINT; services: general port and harbour duties; fleet: 9 vessels totalling 4,700 tons gross and 20 smaller craft.

Burma Five Star Line Corporation: 132, 134, 136 Theinbyu Rd., Rangoon; f. 1959 by Defence Services Institute; 22 coastal and ocean-going steamers; Chair. U SEIN LWIN.

CIVIL AVIATION

Mingaladon Airport, near Rangoon, is equipped to international standards.

Burma Airways Corporation (BAC): 104 Strand Rd., Rangoon; f. 1948; internal network centred on Rangoon; services to 34 stations; external services to Bangkok, Calcutta, Katmandu, Hong Kong, Dacca (currently suspended), Phnom-Penh (currently suspended) and Singapore; operated by the Government; Man. Dir. (vacant); Operations Man. THAW NA; fleet of 1 Boeing 727, 2 F-28, 6 F-27, 6 DC-3.

The following foreign airlines are represented in Burma: Aeroflot, Air France, Air India, British Airways, CAAC (General Administration of Civil Aviation of China), Cathay Pacific Airways, Československé Aerolinie, IAC, Japan Air Lines, KLM, Lufthansa, Pan American, PIA, Polskie Linie Lotnicze, SAS, Thai Airways International.

ATOMIC ENERGY

Union of Burma Atomic Energy Centre: Kanbe Applied Research Institute, Yankin Post Office, Rangoon; f. 1955; departments of nuclear mineralogical research; nuclear research; radiation protection research; nucleonic instrumentation; Chair. Dr. MEHM THET SAN.

DEFENCE

Armed Forces: (1975) Total strength 167,000; army 153,000, navy 7,000, air force 7,000; para-military forces number 35,000.

Equipment: The army is mainly infantry, with American, British and Yugoslav light arms. There are also some British tanks and armoured cars. The navy is equipped with small craft (mainly gunboats). The air force has 11 combat aircraft and various transport planes and helicopters.

Defence Expenditure: Expenditure in 1972–73 was 545 million kyats (U.S. $101 million).

Chief of Staff of the Armed Forces: Maj.-Gen. KYAW HTIN.

EDUCATION

The organization and administration of education in the Union of Burma is the responsibility of the Ministry of Education. Three Directorates are in turn responsible to the Ministry for: (*a*) Basic education (primary, upper and lower secondary); (*b*) Technical and Vocational education; and (*c*) University Administration (including Higher Institutes). The main emphasis continues to be on primary education so that, for example, in 1969–70 86 per cent of all those receiving education were enrolled in State primary schools. Moreover, over the same period 65 per cent of State expenditure on education was allocated to this sector. Since 1962 considerable improvements in education have taken place. A Five-Year Education Plan (1965–70) was introduced which aimed to establish a network of primary schools throughout the country. Attendance, which lasts from the age of 5 to 9, is to be made compulsory by 1985–86. The study of science is being given priority in the school curriculum. Expansion of technical and vocational education at secondary (middle and high school) level and of education for the professions will, it is envisaged, be integrated with the requirements in the National Development Plans for skilled manpower.

Primary Schools

In 1974–75 the total enrolment in the State primary schools was 3,449,552 in 19,399 schools in which there were 73,653 teachers.

Lower Secondary (Middle) Schools

Education in lower secondary schools lasts four years from the age of 10 to 13 when pupils take the external government examination. In 1974–75 total enrolment at this level was 762,871 pupils in 1,202 schools in which there were 17,967 teachers.

Upper Secondary (High) Schools

These schools cater for those in the age range 14 to 19. In 1974–75 there were 182,848 pupils enrolled in 571 schools with 8,794 teachers.

Technical and Vocational

The total number of students attending full-time courses at technical schools, technical high schools and technical institutes was 3,341 in 1969–70. The number of those attending courses at agricultural colleges and high schools during the same period reached 945.

Teacher Training

Those attending courses at all levels in 1969–70 totalled 3,405.

Universities and Colleges

In 1974–75 there were 57,965 students attending 19 universities and colleges in which there were 3,404 teachers.

UNIVERSITIES

Arts and Science University, Mandalay: University Estate, Mandalay; *c.* 400 teachers, *c.* 7,000 students.

Arts and Science University, Rangoon: University Estate, Rangoon, University Post Office; *c.* 430 teachers, *c,* 7,000 students.

BIBLIOGRAPHY

GENERAL

CHHIBBER, H. L. The Physiography of Burma (Calcutta and London, 1933).

CHRISTIAN, J. LE ROY. Modern Burma (California University Press, Berkeley, 1942).

DONNISON, F. S. V. Burma (Benn, London, 1970).

HALL, D. G. E. Burma (Hutchinson, London, 2nd edition, 1956).

TINKER, H. The Union of Burma (Oxford University Press, London, 4th edition, 1967).

HISTORY

AUNG, MAUNG HTIN. A History of Burma (Columbia University Press, U.S.A., 1968).

CADY, J. F. A. History of Modern Burma (Cornell University Press, Ithaca, New York, 1958).

Thailand, Burma, Laos and Cambodia (Prentice-Hall Inc., Englewood Cliffs, New Jersey, U.S.A., 1966).

HALL, D. G. E. Early English Intercourse with Burma 1587–1743 (Frank Cass & Co., London, 1968).

HARVEY, G. E. History of Burma from the earliest times to the beginning of the English conquest (London, 1925).

British Rule in Burma (London, 1946).

MAW, BA. Breakthrough in Burma (Yale University Press, New Haven, 1968).

NU, THAKIN. Burma under the Japanese (Macmillan, London, 1954).

WOODMAN, D. The Making of Burma (Cresset Press, London, 1962).

A Narrative of the Mission to the Court of Ava in 1855, by Henry Yule; together with the Journal of Arthur Phayre, envoy to the Court of Ava; and additional illustrations by Colesworthy Grant and Linnaeus Tripe, with an Introduction by Hugh Tinker (facsimile reprint of Smith, older edn. of 1858) (Oxford University Press, Kuala Lumpur, London and New York, 1968).

ECONOMICS AND POLITICS

ANDRUS, J. R. Burmese Economic Life (Stanford University Press, Stanford, 1948).

COOKE, B. C. A. Burma, H.M.S.O. Overseas Economic Surveys (London, 1957).

DONNISON, P. S. V. Public Administration in Burma (London, 1953).

ECONOMIC SURVEY OF BURMA. Annual (Rangoon).

FURNIVALL, J. S. The Governance of Modern Burma (Institute of Pacific Relations, New York, 1960).

HAGEN, E. E. The Economic Development of Burma (Washington, 1956).

JOHNSTONE, W. C. Burma's Foreign Policy: a Study in Neutralism (Harvard University Press, Cambridge, Mass., 1963).

LEACH, E. R. Political Future of Burma (in *Futuribles*, ed. B. de Jouvenel, Geneva, 1963).

MAUNG, MAUNG. Burma's Constitution (Nijhoff, The Hague, 2nd edition, 1961).

MAUNG, MAUNG. Burma and General Ne Win (Asia Publishing House, London, 1969).

PYE, L. W. Politics, Personality, and Nation Building (Yale University Press, New Haven, 1962).

SIOK-HWA, CHENG. The Rice Industry of Burma, 1852–1940 (University of Malaya Press, Kuala Lumpur, and Oxford University Press, London, 1969).

SMITH, D. E. Religion and Politics in Burma (Princeton University Press, Princeton, 1965).

Cambodia

PHYSICAL AND SOCIAL GEOGRAPHY

C. A. Fisher

Cambodia occupies a relatively small and compact area of 181,035 square kilometres (69,898 square miles), between Thailand to the west, Laos to the north, and Viet-Nam to the east.

PHYSICAL FEATURES

Apart from the Cardamom and related mountains in the south which tend to shut it off from its short southern coastline, the greater part of the country consists of a shallow lacustrine basin, centred on Tonlé Sap ("the Great Lake") which was formerly much more extensive than it is today. This lowland drains eastwards, via the Tonlé Sap river, to the Mekong, which flows through the eastern part of the lowlands from north to south before swinging eastwards into Viet-Nam and so to the sea.

Throughout its course through Cambodia, the Mekong averages over a mile in width but is interrupted by serious rapids at Kratie, and by even more serious falls at Khone along the Laotian border. Moreover, its flow varies widely from season to season, and during the period of greatest volume between June and October, a substantial portion of its floodwaters is diverted up the Tonlé Sap river (whose flow is thus reversed) into the Great Lake itself, which comes to occupy an area at least twice as great as it does during the dry season in the early months of the year.

RESOURCES AND POPULATION

With relatively good alluvial soils, abundant irrigation water, and a tropical monsoon climate not marred by excessive rainfall, Cambodia has a considerable agricultural potential and could undoubtedly support both a wider area and a greater intensity of cultivation than it does at present. Moreover, the harnessing of its great hydro-electric potential, which under the projected Mekong scheme could go hand in hand with a more effective utilization of irrigation water, might also make a major contribution to future economic development.

Cambodia had an estimated 8,100,000 inhabitants and an average density of 45 per square kilometre in 1975. The capital city, Phnom-Penh, had a population of 450,000 in 1968, which was increased enormously in the early 1970s by refugees. In 1975 the majority of the urban population was evacuated to the countryside.

HISTORY

Michael Leifer

(with additional material by the Editor)

Modern Cambodia traces its origins to historical legend. It is told that an Indian Brahmin named Kaundinya arrived in the River Mekong delta and married Soma the daughter of the Naga (serpent deity) king known as the Lord of the Soil. Their physical union which symbolized the fertility of the kingdom was to enjoy a central place in Khmer cosmology. This legend derived from Indian cultural influences which took root in Indo-China at the beginning of the Christian era and gave rise there to distinctive political forms.

Pre-colonial History

The legend of political foundation relates more strictly to the Indianized predecessor of Kambuja (The Cambodian State) known as Fu-nan by its Chinese chroniclers. Fu-nan, the earliest of the great Indianized Kingdoms of Indochina is believed to have been established in the middle of the third century A.D. and located to the south-west of the delta of the River Mekong. It came to occupy a dominant position in the peninsula for five centuries although its immediate pre-Kambuja form, the State of Chen-la was to exist in partitioned condition, while its centre of political gravity moved northwards up the Mekong to the eastern end of the Cambodian plain. Khmer cultural and political traditions in the glorious Angkor period derive directly from the heritage of Fu-nan. For example, it was from Fu-nan that there originated the Indian cult of divine kingship in which the person of the monarch was associated with the unity and prosperity of the kingdom. The early kings of Kambuja looked to Fu-nan as the source of their ancestry and also as the fount of their claim to royal title.

The actual beginnings of the post-Fu-nan Cambodian state are somewhat clouded. Nonetheless, it is believed that in the seventh century during the Chen-la period the Shailendra dynasty of Java came to exercise some form of suzerainty. Jayavarman II who is known as the founder of the Khmer Kingdom and who claimed ties of ancestry from Fu-nan returned from exile or captivity in Java at the beginning of the ninth century. He achieved immediate political success after which he sought to legitimate his position through a cult practice which served similar purpose in a Java subject also to Indian influence. He arranged his enthronement as King at the hands of a Brahmin priest at a ceremony which was to symbolize the independence of his new founded kingdom from Javanese overlordship. This ceremony involved the establishment of a stone lingam (a phallic symbol in which the powers of the king were believed to reside) on a sacred mountain central in Hindu cosmology. He thus sponsored the cult of the deva-raja (God-king) which was to be an essential part of state organization during the triumphant period of Kambuja's existence. Jayavarman II who reigned from A.D. 802 to 850 established his capital north of the Great Lake close to the site where the complex of monumental temples were to rise over the next centuries. His dynasty saw the development of an advanced system of agricultural hydraulics which served the rice fields upon which the prosperity of the kingdom and the large population depended. A successor and distant relative, Indravarman (877–89), began the practice of temple building which demonstrated the architectural and artistic genius of the Khmers which reached its apogee with the wondrous Angkor Wat built by Suryavarman II in the early part of the twelfth century.

Following the death of Suryavarman II in approximately 1150, internal revolt and administrative neglect weakened the kingdom for a number of decades; in 1177 Angkor was invaded and sacked by the kingdom of Champa which lay to the east. In 1181, however, a fifty-year-old prince gained the throne and took the title Jayavarman VII. He extended the Khmer empire to an unprecedented dominion which ranged from the Annamite chain in the north to the Malay peninsula in the south. He also established a reputation as a builder of hospitals, hostels and roads and immortalized himself through the awe-inspiring Bayon, the centre-piece of his architectural legacy; the temple complex of Angkor Thom. But if his achievement was great, it lacked the artistic quality of the Angkor Wat period. He sustained Indian politico-religious forms but replaced Hindu deities with Mahayana Buddhism in a manner which continued to express the sacral qualities of the royal being. Under Jayavarman VII, Kambuja reached its political apogee; following his death in 1218 the empire went into progressive decline, never again to return to former glories.

The twelfth century had provided signs of strain within the Khmer empire. These signs were to become more evident in succeeding centuries. Territorial expansion and monumental construction works had placed an unbearable burden on a population increasingly alienated from the court religions. It was at this stage that the dependencies of empire not only began to loosen the bonds of Khmer dominion but also to intrude in the direction of the seat of the Khmer State. From about the middle of the thirteenth century the movement eastwards of Thai (Siamese) peoples began to erode the Khmer position. Between A.D. 1350 and 1430 there ensued a state of almost permanent war between the two peoples. This constant warring caused a diversion of labour from construction projects to military purposes and as a consequence temple building came to a halt, never to be resumed. The Thai brought with them a new religion, a Sinhalese reform of Theravada Buddhism which monks from Ceylon had taken initially to Burma at the end of the twelfth century. Its simple and austere message had a popular appeal which contrasted with the remote religion which underpinned state organization. This challenge to orthodoxy assisted the crumbling of the empire which was hastened by internal dissension and by the excessive burden of royal extravagance. The failure of the hydraulics system as a consequence of neglect and Thai depredations eventually made the capital site untenable and unsuitable for its purposes and in 1431 Angkor was abandoned to the Thai.

By 1434 the Court had re-established itself on the site of the modern capital of Cambodia, Phnom-Penh, where a replica of the cosmomagical temple mountain was constructed. During the reign of a king who called himself Suryavarman, the Cambodian state underwent a period of limited revival which was interrupted in 1473 by Siamese military success as a result of which the reigning monarch, the second son of Suryavarman was taken prisoner. However, a third son rallied the Khmers, ejected the invaders and ushered in a century in which intervention from the west was successfully resisted. The capital was then moved, first to Lovek, half-way between Phnom-Penh and the lower end of the Great Lake, and later on to Angkor itself. In 1593 the Siamese returned to the attack and probing as far as Lovek drove the royal family into exile in Laos. This invasion and defeat led to a period of internal disturbance marked by usurpation and assassination of monarchical incumbents. When a king was finally restored to the throne of Cambodia in 1603 it was through the good offices of Siam which released a captured prince to be crowned as a vassal.

In 1618 the capital site was again moved; this time to Oudong situated between Lovek and Phnom-Penh. Two years later Siamese suzerainty was removed as a result of a royal marriage with a daughter of the Nguyen dynasty of Annam (Viet-Nam). One important consequence of this union was an authorization by the Cambodian king, Jayajetta, for the Vietnamese to establish a custom-house at Prei Kor, the site of the modern city of Saigon. This concession was to facilitate extensive settlement by Vietnamese in the Mekong delta at Cambodian territorial expense.

In the early 1640s the Cambodian monarch, Chan the son of Jayajetta, converted to Islam and encouraged the settlement of Malay and Javanese migrants. In 1658 the apostate king was successfully challenged by an alliance of two of his brothers with Vietnamese support. The eighteenth century was to see a continuation of civil strife and both Siam and Annam took territorial advantage of Cambodia's debilitated state. At the end of the century, Cambodia was to lose its western provinces of Battambang and Siemreap. The king, Ang Eng, was even to be crowned in Bangkok. His son, Ang Chan, was enthroned in similar fashion but also paid tribute to the Vietnamese who had encroached throughout what was to become known as Cochinchina. By the beginning of the nineteenth century, Cambodia, territorially reduced, was wedged between competing neighbours who exercised a form of dual suzerainty.

The Colonial Period

In an attempt to halt the erosion of Cambodian territory by her neighbours, Ang Duong sought in 1854 to solicit French protection. This initiative failed because of French mishandling and Siamese obstruction. When, however, in June 1862 the Emperor of Annam ceded to France the three easterly provinces of what became known as the Colony of Cochinchina, the French sought to protect this acquisition by further expansion westward. In July 1863 the French Governor of Cochinchina, Admiral de la Grandière persuaded Ang Duong's son and successor, Norodom, to accept a protectorate which would permit France to control the external affairs of the country and to install a resident-general in the capital. Despite Siamese efforts to forestall formal ratification, the accord came into effect the following year. And in July 1864 the formal coronation of Norodom took place at Oudong with the crown, retrieved from Bangkok, being received from the hands of a French plenipotentiary. Siam, the former suzerain power, was to be appeased at this change of overlordship through a treaty of 1867 whereby France ceded formally on behalf of her ward the westerly provinces of Battambang, Siemreap and Sisiphon. However, the French were instrumental in restoring these territories to Cambodia in 1907.

In 1884 Cambodia entered into a second agreement with France which established a more complete imperial relationship and in 1887 the protectorate was amalgamated into the wider French *Union Indochinoise*. Colonial rule although somewhat harsh did not unduly dislocate the Cambodian state. The facade of monarchical authority was maintained although colonial control was exercised over the matter of royal succession. There were two significant but minor uprisings in the nineteenth century but little that might be regarded as a security problem. The elements of nationalist sentiment were not to be displayed until the 1930s. A major economic and social consequence of French rule was the way in which it facilitated the entry of Vietnamese either as labourers on the French established rubber plantations or in the lower echelons of the civil administration.

The fall of France in June 1940 made possible a revival of Siamese territorial ambitions. Under Japanese sponsorship the government in Bangkok reasserted a claim to the westerly provinces which had returned to Cambodia in 1907. After military clashes Japan intervened and forced an agreement in Thailand's favour signed in March 1941. The Japanese now enjoyed a dominant position in Indochina exploiting the peninsula for the prosecution of the war effort but leaving undisturbed the French administration. However, by the end of 1944 they became concerned over the allegiance of the French civic authorities and in March the following year moved with force to displace the colonial administration. On the twelfth of the month, King Norodom Sihanouk was persuaded to proclaim his country's independence.

The surrender of Japan in August 1945 and the return of the French in force soon after, saw a restoration of the colonial relationship. It saw also the arrest of Son Ngoc Thanh, the Japanese-sponsored Prime Minister, together with the emergence of a dissident anti-French resistance movement, the *Khmer Issarak*, formed in part of supporters of Thanh. The king sought initially to negotiate Cambodia's independence from France recognizing that his country was not in any position to wage armed struggle for this end. However, the limited political concessions that the French were willing to make compromised the position of the king who came under challenge for being too compliant. In 1946 the absolute monarchy had been abolished and in 1947 a constitution introduced which permitted popular political activity. And it was from the elected members of the National Assembly as well as the *Khmer Issarak* resistance, led by Thanh after his release in 1951, that the king encountered fierce criticism. In June 1952 in an attempt to ensure political stability and to accelerate progress towards independence he dismissed the National Assembly and assumed governmental powers for three years. In February the following year he set off on a diplomatic mission to try and force the hand of the French then facing serious difficulty in Viet-Nam and Laos. Through a series of public statements in Western capitals together with a venture into self-imposed exile in Bangkok, at a time when France was concerned about a popular drift away from the throne and towards the Cambodian associates of the communist-directed Viet-Minh, Sihanouk triumphed. His initiative at a propitious time led to French concessions and the declaration of Cambodian independence on November 9th, 1953. The following July at the Geneva Conference on Indochina this independence was accorded Great Power recognition.

Independent Cambodia

King Norodom Sihanouk had come to the throne in 1941 at the age of 19. He was not the son of the late king but owed his accession to the throne to a French-instituted method of selection. Under this arrangement Ang Duong's son had been succeeded by his brother. In 1941 the French returned to the senior branch of the royal family to suit their political purpose. It was believed that the young and inexperienced Prince Sihanouk would be a compliant monarch serving as an instrument of colonial rule. In practice Sihanouk was to become a national leader using his throne to great advantage. In 1955, however, Sihanouk's throne was to prove a serious obstacle to his personal exercise of political authority. Under the terms of the Geneva Agreements on Indochina of July 1954, Cambodia had pledged itself to a free and open political process to be demonstrated through elections to be conducted under the terms of the 1947 constitution. This constitution restricted the political role of the monarchy and there was every prospect that governmental office would be resumed by those politicians (from the Democratic Party) whom the king regarded as factious and self-seeking. In order to escape from the constricting cloak of the constitution under which he would reign more but rule less, Norodom Sihanouk announced his abdication from the throne in favour of his father, Norodom Suramarit. Now free, as Prince Sihanouk, to enter the political lists, the former king founded a political movement, the *Sangkum Reastr Niyum* (Popular Socialist Community), within which he sought to embody all streams of political opinion. *Sangkum* served as a popular national front based on coincident loyalty to Sihanouk and the nation. It trounced all opposition; in the elections of September 1955 *Sangkum* won every seat in the National Assembly. It repeated this performance in the three subsequent elections that were held. In April 1960 the death occurred of King Norodom Suramarit but a constitutional and political crisis was averted in June when Norodom Sihanouk became head of state without ascending to the lofty perch of the throne.

As head of state, Prince Sihanouk became literally the voice of Cambodia. He articulated its hopes and fears within the country and to the outside world. He ruled through a cabinet and parliament but never relinquished his recourse to popular appeal and sanction for his policies. He appeared a popular figure revered especially in the rural areas as the father figure of his country. However, his authority came under challenge from within the Cambodian elite, especially following the general elections of 1966. Increasing resentment of his personal political style and of his handling of the economy found expression in August 1969 with the assumption to office of an administration headed by the former Army Commander-in-Chief, Lt.-Gen. (later Marshal) Lon Nol. It was this administration which on March 18th, 1970, master-minded Sihanouk's removal from office as head of state through a unanimous decision of the country's legislature. At the time, Prince Sihanouk was out of the country, in Moscow, on the point of departing for a visit to the People's Republic of China. He continued his journey to Peking, where in May he established the Royal Government of National Union of Cambodia (GRUNC).

After going into exile, Prince Sihanouk and his supporters formed an alliance with their former enemies, a Marxist insurgent movement known as the *Khmers Rouges* ("Red Khmers"). These had been active opponents of Sihanouk since 1964 and launched an uprising against him in 1967. The insurgency spread to 11 of the 19 provinces by 1968 and the *Khmer Rouge* forces numbered about 3,000 by 1970. Following the Prince's overthrow, however, Sihanoukists and *Khmers Rouges* formed the National United Front of Cambodia (FUNC) in May 1970 and members of both groups participated in GRUNC. Their combined forces, supported by troops from North Viet-Nam and the National Liberation Front of South Viet-Nam, launched a civil war and quickly put the new regime of Lon Nol in jeopardy. North Vietnamese forces bore the brunt of the fighting in the early stages but most of them were withdrawn in 1972–73. As the Cambodian war progressed, the *Khmers Rouges* assumed a growing share of the military campaign against Lon Nol and their political influence in GRUNC increased correspondingly.

A precipitating circumstance of Sihanouk's deposition was the revealed presence in Cambodia of Vietnamese communist military formations using the sanctuary of the neutral country from which to prosecute the war in South Viet-Nam. It was during Prince Sihanouk's absence in Paris in March 1970 that inspired sackings of Vietnamese communist diplomatic missions occurred in Phnom-Penh. He refused to support the actions inspired by his government, which were portrayed as a protest against the Vietnamese communist presence, and the consequence was a series of bitter exchanges which culminated in his deposition. The sacking of the Vietnamese communist diplomatic missions was followed by a demand by the Cambodian Government that the Vietnamese communist military units leave the country. This Canute-like demand, however, caused the Vietnamese communists to move against the pitifully weak and ill-equipped Cambodian army. Towards the end of April 1970, the capital, Phnom-Penh, was in peril and only the military intervention of South Viet-Nam and the United States at the beginning of May checked the advance. Protracted conflict continued, however, and Cambodia succumbed to the brutalizing experience of Viet-Nam with the Government of Marshal Lon Nol under serious challenge by insurgent forces supporting the cause of Prince Sihanouk, in exile in Peking.

In October 1970 the name Cambodia was formally changed to the Khmer Republic, thus ending twenty-four years of constitutional monarchy.

In March 1972 Lon Nol declared himself President, an act approved by referendum in April. His governments were marked by factional conflict and their inability to deal with economic difficulties caused by the war. The January 1973 peace settlement for Viet-Nam did not have any effect in Cambodia as GRUNC refused all offers to negotiate. Lon Nol's Government was reduced to controlling urban enclaves in the face of *Khmer Rouge* assaults which just stopped short of overrunning the capital. From January 1975, however, by changing tactics aimed at cutting communications, and thus food and military supply, the defence perimeter of the capital, Phnom-Penh, was reduced progressively, sustained only by American airlift. On April 1st, President Lon Nol left Phnom-Penh en route for the United States, and on the 17th of that month the capital fell without resistance to the *Khmer Rouge* forces.

In the immediate wake of the *Khmer Rouge* military victory, GRUNC took control and the name of the country reverted to Cambodia (also referred to as Kampuchea). The country was subjected to a pre-arranged programme of radical social change in which members of the former governing class were either liquidated or directed into forced labour. The population at large was mobilized by coercion into the rural areas where they were put to work on a collectivist basis.

Prince Sihanouk was restored as Head of State, though he remained outside Cambodia until the end of 1975, except for a brief visit to the country in September. In December the third national congress of FUNC approved a draft constitution establishing a republican form of government. The constitution, promulgated in January 1976, officially named the country "Democratic Cambodia". Elections were held in March for a 250-member People's Representative Assembly, the seats being contested by 515 candidates of approved "revolutionary" standing. In April Prince Sihanouk resigned as Head of State and GRUNC was dissolved. The new Assembly chose Khieu Samphan, formerly the Minister of Defence, to be Head of State and appointed a new Council of Ministers in which the Prime Minister was Tol Saut (also written Pol Pot), reportedly the Secretary-General of the Cambodian Communist Party. The effect of the government changes was believed to be the elimination of the remaining Sihanoukists and their replacement by *Khmers Rouges*.

In its new constitution, Cambodia was described as neutral and non-aligned. However, in the first year of *Khmer Rouge* rule it became clear that a measure of alignment did exist and that relations with the People's Republic of China had a special importance. By contrast, tensions were evident with Cambodia's Vietnamese communist neighbours and armed clashes were reported along the common border.

ECONOMIC SURVEY

Michael Leifer

The Cambodian peace-time economy is based almost entirely on agriculture with a small industrial sector. The staple crop is rice which is grown on approximately 3,080,000 acres or 80 per cent of land suitable for cultivation. Although the lowland soil of the Khmer plain is not of remarkable fertility and restricts yield, seasonal flooding by the Mekong and Tonlé Sap makes possible wet-rice cultivation that suffices for the country's own needs and leaves a fluctuating but moderate surplus for export in normal circumstances. An abundance of fish from the many waterways and a supply of fresh vegetables provide in addition an ample subsistence diet for the predominantly rural population. There is little grinding poverty of the Indian variety; the average per capita income before 1970 was calculated at U.S. $130. There is moderate peasant indebtedness and an absence of acute land shortage; land holdings tend to be on an individual basis for the most part comprising less than twelve acres.

At the time of independence in 1953, Cambodia had an exceedingly small industrial base. There were a number of latex plants operated by French-controlled rubber companies together with a few factories which processed agricultural and forest products. Since then the scale of industrial enterprise has increased manifold as indicated by the production of 95 million kWh. of electricity in 1967. In principle, the aim of the Cambodian Government has been to eschew the grandiose in economic development and to concentrate on a limited range of enterprises to meet an increasing local demand and thus to save foreign exchange by reducing imports.

The programme of industrial development was initiated in the mid-1950s through the benefaction of the Chinese People's Republic. In June 1956 China granted Cambodia equipment valued at U.S. $22.4 million. This aid was allocated for the construction of a textile plant, a plywood factory, a cement factory and a paper mill. These concerns, which in some cases were completed with an additional infusion of Chinese aid, have had a chequered experience. Further agreements with China led to the completion of a second textile mill in 1967 and the construction of a glass plant. Of the other Communist countries Czechoslovakia has provided plants for tractor assembly and tyre production as well as a sugar refinery, all on a loan basis.

Prior to 1970, positive achievements were made in the development of infrastructure and social equipment. During the colonial period Cambodia was dependent on the River Mekong and the port of Saigon for her trading needs. The dependence on Saigon was reduced somewhat after the Second World War when the French developed Phnom-Penh as a port to receive ocean-going vessels. With independence, the Cambodian Government became only too painfully aware of the stranglehold that South Viet-Nam could exercise over the Mekong lifeline. Early in 1956 as a result of an intensification of bitterness between the two countries the Mekong was blocked temporarily; on a number of occasions since, convoys to Phnom-Penh have been seriously impeded despite the existence of Cambodian treaty rights to free passage. In order to circumvent this situation of dependence the Cambodian Government with major French assistance developed a port on the Gulf of Siam known as Sihanoukville (renamed Kompong-Som). This port was opened in 1960 in order to give Cambodia complete autonomy over its trade outlets. At the time that the construction of Sihanoukville began, the United States, for reasons of self-interest as well as benevolence, constructed a highway linking the port with the capital. In spite of serious erosion and subsidence along the road, due to the use of inappropriate materials, repair work kept the road functioning as a major artery. The Cambodians, however, with French and West German assistance have constructed a railway line from the port to Phnom-Penh to facilitate the speedy transportation of goods. In the development of social equipment, progress has been recorded in the building of schools, hospitals, clinics and dispensaries.

Cambodia has received project aid and loans from China, the Soviet Union, Yugoslavia, Czechoslovakia, France, West Germany, Japan and Australia. Foreign economic assistance has been, however, of moderate proportions and the Cambodian emphasis has been on self-help and project-sharing which has produced the French-sponsored oil refinery and truck assembly plant at Sihanoukville. Up to the end of 1963 the bulk of economic assistance came from the United States but in November of that year this was terminated at the insistence of the Cambodian Government. Between 1955 and 1962 economic and military assistance from the United States totalled more than U.S. $350 million. The bulk of this aid was not deployed in a way that its visible effect was easily demonstrated, much being allocated to public health, agricultural development and education. The cessation of this aid was to cause serious repercussions within the Cambodian economy and its effects are still being felt. At first the cessation of aid was softened by good harvests, French credits and borrowing from the Cambodian central bank. But from 1966 onwards serious financial difficulties arose from the government's inability to adjust expenditure to income. U.S. aid, particularly in the form of budgetary support and provision for the financing of the armed services enabled a level of expenditure and a style of urban living well beyond the real means of the country. Crop output in rice, cotton and jute together with smuggling was such that a budget deficit, though reduced in 1967 to 1,056 million riels through a cut in imports, remained a pressing problem. The state of world markets in primary products did not help Cambodia's trading and financial position. An additional difficulty which followed from government action in 1963 was the associated decision to nationalize the export and import trades. This move had the effect of freezing Chinese business interests and of inhibiting trade and commerce in general. However, another decision to nationalize banking had more successful consequences. Although foreign policy considerations inhibited Cambodia from participating in any of the recent attempts at regional co-operation in South-East Asia, she was involved in the attempt by the United Nations Economic Commission for Asia and the Far East to develop the water resources of the Lower Mekong basin. However an important project within Cambodia (the Prek Thnot tributary project) had hung fire because of Cambodian suspicions concerning the source of finance. In September 1968 at a meeting in Phnom-Penh, administrative arrangements for the Prek Thnot Power and Irrigation Development Project were agreed between ten donor countries, Cambodia and UN representatives. The outbreak of war, however, interrupted work on the project which was scheduled for completion in 1972.

The onset of war in Cambodia completely disrupted the economy. Military activity had a devastating effect on the latex plants and rubber production came to a virtual halt. In addition, the extent of Communist activity and the American bombing disrupted road and rail communications. In effect, the Khmer Republic reverted to a subsistence existence while public expenditure increased dramatically because the army grew from 35,000 to over 200,000 men. A resumption of U.S. economic and military aid served to assist with budgetary difficulties. The country remained on a war footing and, with much of its social and economic equipment destroyed and productive processes disrupted, became totally dependent on external financial assistance for its defence efforts. By April 1975, there was not a Cambodian economy, only the importation of foodstuffs financed by the United States Government.

With the assumption of *Khmer Rouge* control, the first priority was declared to be the restoration of the national economy. Partly to this end, the urban centres, including the capital, were cleared of their inhabitants who were driven into the rural areas to work on the land and in other tasks of economic reconstruction. The initial rigours of the collectivization of agriculture were sustained at human cost but a good first harvest and the virtual rehabilitation of Cambodia's small industrial sector, with Chinese technical assistance, placed the economy in a viable condition. It would appear that the objective of the new government is to make the economy more than just self-sufficient. In addition to the expansion of rice cultivation, by clearing new fields from brush and digging new irrigation channels, emphasis has been placed on cash crops such as cotton, rubber and timber.

STATISTICAL SURVEY

Note: Some of the statistics *below* represent only sectors of the economy controlled by the government of the former Khmer Republic. During the years 1970–75 no figures were available for areas controlled by the *Khmers Rouges*. No further statistics had been made available by the new regime at the time of going to press.

AREA AND POPULATION

Area	Population (1962 Census)					
	Total	Races				Phnom-Penh (capital)
		Khmer	Vietnamese	Chinese	Others	
181,035 sq. km *	5,728,771	5,334,000	218,000	163,000	14,000	393,995

* 69,898 square miles.

Estimated population: 6,701,000 at July 1st, 1969; 7,888,000 (UN estimate) at mid-1974; 7,735,279 (Government estimate) in 1976.

Other Towns: Battambang (38,800 in 1962), Kompong Chhnang, Kompong Cham, Kompong-Som (Sihanoukville).

Births and Deaths: Average annual birth rate 46.9 per 1,000; death rate 19.1 per 1,000 (UN estimates for 1965–70).

Employment (1970): Total economically active population 2,963,000, including 2,264,000 in agriculture (ILO and FAO estimates).

AGRICULTURE

LAND USE, 1971
('000 hectares)

Arable Land	1,769
Under Permanent Crops	67
Permanent Meadows and Pastures	580*
Forest Land	13,372*
Other Land	1,864
Total Land Area	17,652
Inland Water	452
Total	18,104

* 1967 figures.

Source: FAO, *Production Yearbook 1974.*

PRINCIPAL CROPS
('000 metric tons)

	Area ('000 hectares)			Production ('000 metric tons)		
	1972	1973	1974	1972	1973	1974
Maize	56	63	60*	80	73	70*
Rice (paddy)	1,548	737	681	1,927	1,050	635
Sugar cane	4	4	4*	235	220*	210*
Sweet potatoes	2	3	3*	20	20	21*
Cassava (Manioc)	2	3	3*	21	23	23*
Dry beans	29	30*	30*	18	18*	17*
Groundnuts (in shell)	14	13*	13*	14	13*	12*
Sesame seed	10	10	9*	6.6	6.5	6.0*
Coconuts	n.a.	n.a.	n.a.	43	43*	41*
Copra	n.a.	n.a.	n.a.	8.0*	8.0*	7.6*
Tobacco	14.1	7.5	7.3*	8.9	5.1	5.0*
Natural rubber	n.a.	n.a.	n.a.	15.3	16.5	16.3

* FAO estimates.

Source: FAO, *Production Yearbook 1974.*

LIVESTOCK
(FAO estimates—'000)

	1971/72	1972/73	1973/74
Cattle	2,100	2,000	1,800
Buffaloes	880	860	840
Pigs	1,000	1,050	950
Chickens	4,000	4,000	3,900
Ducks	2,000	1,950	1,920

Source: FAO, *Production Yearbook 1974.*

LIVESTOCK PRODUCTS
(FAO estimates, metric tons)

	1972	1973	1974
Beef and veal	19,000	17,000	17,000
Buffalo meat	5,000	5,000	5,000
Pig meat	33,000	32,000	30,000
Poultry meat	16,000	16,000	15,000
Edible offals	6,917	6,306	6,183
Cows' milk	18,000	19,000	19,000
Hen eggs	3,330	3,240	3,150
Duck eggs	2,350	2,250	2,200
Cattle hides	4,851	4,200	4,200

Source: FAO, *Production Yearbook 1974.*

FORESTRY

ROUNDWOOD REMOVALS
('000 cubic metres—FAO estimates)

	1970	1971	1972
Industrial wood	520	470	490
Fuelwood	3,550	3,660	3,780
TOTAL	4,070	4,130	4,270

Source: FAO, *Yearbook of Forest Products*

FISHING
('000 metric tons)

	1971	1972	1973
Inland waters	55.2	66.2	73.9
Pacific Ocean	22.0	21.0	10.8
TOTAL	77.2	87.2	84.7

Source: FAO, *Yearbook of Fishery Statistics 1973.*

MINING

		1969	1970	1971	1972	1973
Salt (unrefined)	'000 metric tons	98	52	42	36	31

INDUSTRY

SELECTED PRODUCTS

		1969	1970	1971	1972	1973
Distilled alcoholic beverages	'000 hectolitres	143	96	45	55	36
Beer	,, ,,	57	55	26	23	18
Soft drinks	,, ,,	248	98	25	25*	25*
Cigarettes	million	3,807	3,874	3,413	2,510	2,622
Cotton yarn (pure and mixed)	metric tons	1,139	1,171	1,068	1,094	415
Sawnwood[1]	'000 cubic metres	223	32	38	43	43
Bicycle tyres and tubes	'000	539	186	208	200*	200*
Rubber footwear	'000 pairs	2,760	2,230	1,292	1,000*	1,000*
Soap	metric tons	1,788	756	469	400*	400*
Naphtha	'000 metric tons	17	16	—	—	—
Motor spirit (petrol)	,, ,, ,,	44	41	5	—	—
Kerosene	,, ,, ,,	24	19	—	—	—
Jet fuel	,, ,, ,,	14	24	—	—	—
Distillate fuel oils	,, ,, ,,	146	111	11	—	—
Residual fuel oils	,, ,, ,,	132	76	14	—	—
Cement	,, ,, ,,	57	38	44	53	78
Electric energy[2]	million kWh.	128	133	148	166	150

Other products (1969): Jute bags 4.2 million; Paper 4,164 metric tons.

* Estimate. [1] FAO estimates for 1970–73. [2] Production by public utilities only.

FINANCE

100 sen=1 riel.

Coins: 10, 20 and 50 sen.

Notes: 1, 5, 10, 20, 50, 100 and 500 riels.

Exchange rates (April 1975): £1 sterling=3,945 riels; U.S. $1=1,675 riels.

10,000 riels=£2.535=$5.970.

Note: The riel was introduced in January 1955, replacing (at par) the Indo-Chinese piastre. From May 1953 the piastre's value was 10 old French francs. The initial exchange rate was thus U.S. $1=35 riels (1 riel=2.857 U.S. cents). Except for exchange transactions in U.S. dollars and sterling, the riel was linked to French currency, with a value of 10 French centimes after the introduction of the new French franc in January 1960. In August 1969 the multiple exchange rate system ended when the riel was devalued (in line with the French franc) to 16 milligrammes of gold, worth 1.8004 U.S. cents ($1=55.542 riels) until August 1971. In October 1971 the official rate became inoperative except for specified official transfers and a flexible "floating" rate was established, initially at $1=140 riels. Thus the riel's link to the French franc was effectively broken and the currency devalued. The "floating" rate was later adjusted upwards, reaching $1=120 riels in January 1972, but thereafter the currency was frequently devalued. The exchange rate was $1=187 riels at the end of 1972; and $1=275 riels at the end of 1973. In September 1974 the currency was devalued by 65 per cent, with the exchange rate altered from $1=420 riels to $1=1,200 riels. By the end of 1974 the rate was $1=1,650 riels. In terms of sterling, the exchange rate was £1=98 riels before November 1967; £1=84 riels from November 1967 to August 1969; and £1=133.30 riels from August 1969 to October 1971.

EXTERNAL TRADE

(million riels)

	1968	1969	1970	1971	1972	1973
Imports	4,043	4,234	3,010	4,346	6,263	14,200
Exports	3,098	2,729	2,165	825	634	2,733

COMMODITIES

(million riels)

IMPORTS	1972	1973
Agricultural and Food Products	3,461.0	7,720.6
Mineral Products	341.3	1,667.6
Textiles	781.7	1,814.2
Metals and Metal Manufactures	765.2	1,272.2
Pharmaceuticals	641.3	1,395.5
Chemicals	272.4	329.9
TOTAL (incl. others)	6,262.9	14,200.1

EXPORTS	1972	1973
Rice	99.1	14.0
Rubber	233.3	2,544.1
Haricot Beans	236.7	120.3
Sesamum	65.0	54.0
TOTAL (incl. others)	634.2	2,732.5

Source: Banque Nationale du Cambodge, *Bulletin Mensuel.*

PRINCIPAL TRADING PARTNERS*
(U.S. $'000)

Imports	1970	1971	1972	Exports	1970	1971	1972
Australia	n.a.	2,627	1,735	France	5,570	167	298
France	12,546	9,042	6,120	Hong Kong	5,480	1,124	1,347
Germany, Fed. Rep.	1,666	1,120	1,736	Italy	1,135	n.a.	3
Hong Kong	2,510	1,645	6,331	Japan	1,161	553	303
Japan	4,108	2,732	7,565	Netherlands	1,172	41	19
Singapore	3,794	4,120	2,261	Senegal	n.a.	1,653	n.a.
Switzerland	3,112	770	227	Singapore	1,970	789	749
Thailand	n.a.	n.a.	7,041	United Kingdom	1,432	43	46
United Kingdom	2,643	2,606	1,344	U.S.A.	1,030	38	122
U.S.A.	3,199	765	4,301	Viet-Nam, South	n.a.	n.a.	4,024
Total (incl. others)	41,927	28,056	42,599	Total (incl. others)	34,144	6,488	7,347

* Imports by country of production; exports by country of last consignment.

Source: United Nations, *Yearbook of International Trade Statistics*.

TRANSPORT

RAILWAY TRAFFIC

	1967	1968	1969	1970	1971	1972	1973
Passenger-kilometres (million)	143	173	170	109	91	56	54
Freight ton-kilometres (million)	66	70	78	83	10	10	10

ROAD TRAFFIC
(motor vehicles in use*)

	1965	1966	1967	1968	1969	1970	1971	1972
Passenger cars	18,100	19,300	21,700	23,100	24,500	25,900	26,400	27,200
Commercial vehicles†	9,800	10,300	10,600	10,700	10,900	11,000	11,100	11,100

* Including vehicles no longer in circulation. † Excluding tractors and semi-trailer combinations.

INTERNATIONAL SEA-BORNE SHIPPING
(freight traffic in '000 metric tons)

	Goods Loaded			Goods Unloaded		
	1971	1972	1973	1971	1972	1973
Phnom-Penh	95	34	29	308	416	420
Kompong-Som (Sihanoukville)	122	14	21	101	81	163
Total	217	48	50	409	497	583

CIVIL AVIATION
(scheduled services)

	1969	1970	1971	1972	1973
Kilometres flown ('000)	1,764	1,056	1,030	1,000	1,100
Passengers carried ('000)	100	41	107	112	140
Passenger-kilometres (million)	72.7	30.8	32.5	34	51
Freight ton-kilometres ('000)	500	400	658	700	500

COMMUNICATIONS MEDIA

	1968	1969	1970	1971	1972
Telephones in use	7,315	8,024	8,139	n.a.	9,196
Book titles published	185	n.a.	n.a.	n.a.	29
Radio receivers ('000)*	1,000	n.a.	1,025	1,050	1,100
Television receivers ('000)*	35	50	n.a.	n.a.	n.a.

* At December 31st.

EDUCATION

	Teachers		Students	
	1969	1971	1969	1971
Primary	23,964	18,444	989,464	484,088
Secondary: general	5,292	2,754	119,988	95,349
vocational	n.a.	n.a.	5,798	5,594
teacher-training	n.a.	n.a.	1,005	1,279
Higher	916*	1,263	6,154*	10,425

* 1970.

THE CONSTITUTION

A new constitution was approved on December 14th, 1975, by the third national congress of the National United Front of Cambodia. It was approved by the Royal Government of National Union on January 3rd, 1976, and promulgated two days later. The main provisions are summarized below.

Democratic Cambodia is an independent, united, peaceful and non-aligned democratic state. The constitution prohibits the establishment of foreign bases in Cambodia, and the state has the duty to protect the people from foreign aggression. Cambodia must struggle against all forms of aggression: intellectual, economic, military, social and diplomatic. It is a nation of workers and peasants and the means of production belong to the state and people.

Legislative authority rests with the Cambodian People's Representative Assembly, with 250 members elected by direct, universal suffrage for a five-year term. Seats are allocated on the following basis: 150 members represent peasants, 50 represent other working people and another 50 represent the armed forces. The Assembly elects the State Presidium (a President and two Vice-Presidents) and the Government. It also elects a Popular Tribunal which is to administer justice. The Assembly directs both domestic and foreign policy.

Unemployment does not exist and the standard of living of the people is guaranteed. The workers control the factories. Men and women have equal rights and are free to practise any religion which does not contribute to the destruction of the state.

THE GOVERNMENT

HEAD OF STATE

President of the State Presidium: Khieu Samphan.

CABINET

(*April* 1976)

President of the State Presidium: Khieu Samphan.

First Vice-President of the State Presidium: Sor Thon.

Second Vice-President of the State Presidium: Ngean Ros.

Prime Minister: Tol Saut.

Deputy Prime Minister and Minister of Foreign Affairs: Ieng Sary.

Deputy Prime Minister and Minister of National Defence: Son Sen.

Deputy Prime Minister and Minister of the Economy: Vorn Vet.

Minister of Information and Propaganda: Hu Nim.

Minister of Social Action: Ieng Thirith.

Minister of Culture and Education: Yun Yat.

Minister of Public Works: Toch Phoeun.

Minister of Health: Thioun Thioeun.

High Counsellor of the State Presidium: Pen Nouth.

PEOPLE'S REPRESENTATIVE ASSEMBLY

In national elections held on March 20th, 1976, 250 representatives were chosen out of 515 candidates for the Cambodian People's Representative Assembly.

President: NUON CHEA.

POLITICAL PARTY

Front uni national du Cambodge (FUNC): Phnom-Penh; f. 1970; Chair. PENN NOUTH.

DIPLOMATIC RELATIONS

By March 1976 the following countries had representatives in Phnom-Penh: Albania, the People's Republic of China, Cuba, the Democratic People's Republic of Korea, Laos, Viet-Nam and Yugoslavia.

By March 1976, in addition to the above, the following countries had recognized the new government: Afghanistan, Algeria, Australia, Bangladesh, Benin, Bulgaria, Burma, Burundi, Cameroon, Canada, the Central African Republic, Chad, the Congo People's Republic, Czechoslovakia, Denmark, Egypt, Equatorial Guinea, France, Gabon, the Gambia, the German Democratic Republic, Ghana, Guinea, Guinea-Bissau, Guyana, Hungary, India, Indonesia, Iran, Iraq, Italy, Japan, Jordan, Kuwait, Laos, Liberia, Libya, Madagascar, Malaysia, Mali, Malta, Mauritania, Mauritius, Mexico, Mongolia, Morocco, Nepal, New Zealand, Niger, Oman, Pakistan, Peru, the Philippines, Poland, Portugal, Qatar, Romania, Rwanda, Senegal, Sierra Leone, Singapore, Somalia, Sudan, Sweden, Syria, Tanzania, Thailand, Togo, Tunisia, Turkey, Uganda, the U.S.S.R., the United Arab Emirates, the United Kingdom, the Upper Volta, the Yemen Arab Republic, the People's Democratic Republic of Yemen, Zaire, Zambia.

JUDICIAL SYSTEM

Under the constitution of January 1976 justice is to be administered by a Popular Tribunal, elected by the People's Representative Assembly.

RELIGION

BUDDHISM

Before April 1975 the principal religion of Cambodia was Theravada Buddhism (Buddhism of the Little Vehicle), the sacred language of which is Pali. There were more than 2,500 monasteries throughout the land and nearly 20,000 Bonzes (Buddhist priests). However, reports indicate that since the change of regime religious practices are being discouraged.

Sangaraja of Cambodia: His Eminence HUOT TATH, Vat Unnalon, Phnom-Penh.

THE PRESS

Pa Idiwat (*Revolution*): Official journal.

RADIO

Radio Phnom-Penh: Phnom-Penh; f. 1975; official service.

FINANCE

No official information has been made available on financial organizations in Cambodia at the time of publication. However, it is reported that no currency is in circulation and a system of barter is in operation.

TRADE AND INDUSTRY

Under the constitution of January 1976 all means of production were nationalized but no detailed information on the organization of trade and industry has been announced.

TRANSPORT

Note: The following information applies to the situation before April 1975.

Railways: Gare Centrale de Phnom-Penh, Moha Vithei Pracheathippatay, Phnom-Penh. A line, built in 1930–32 and 1939–40 and totalling 385 km. in length, connects Phnom-Penh with the Thai border (at Poipet) via Battambang. Since June 1970, owing to war damage, only the Pursat-Poipet section (225 km). is open. Construction of a new line, 270 km. in length and linking Phnom-Penh with Kompong-Somville, via Takeo and Kampot, was started in 1960, opened in December 1969, has been closed since April 1970. Total length is about 1,370 km.

Roads: There are nearly 11,000 km. of motorable roads and tracks, of which about 2,000 km. are asphalted.

Waterways: The major routes are along the Mekong River, and up the Tonlé-Sap River into the Tonlé-Sap (Great Lake) covering in all about 1,400 km.

Civil Aviation: In January 1976 it was reported that air links had been established with Peking.

Shipping: The main port is Kompong-Som on the Gulf of Siam, which handles vessels up to 10,000 tons; the total of berths was raised to 10 in 1970 at a cost of U.S. $50m. Phnom-Penh, which lies some distance inland, can take steamers of up to 4,000 tons.

EDUCATION

Note: The information in this section applies to the situation before April 1975. No information on the structure of the educational system under the new regime is available at the time of publication and reports indicate that all formal schooling has been suspended.

In recent years the main aim of the Government in the field of education has been to combat illiteracy and to extend educational facilities to all parts of the country, including the more inaccessible mountain regions and the densely forested areas of the central provinces. Isolated border districts, such as Mondolkiri, Rattanakiri and Oddar Meanchey, where until recently no form of education was available, now have schools. In comparison with other countries at a similar stage of development, the illiteracy rate is low, particularly among men, nearly all of whom have attended religious schools for varying periods of time and have there learnt to read and write. Illiteracy, however, remains a problem, particularly among women in the more isolated areas. In 1964 a campaign against illiteracy was launched in which priests, soldiers, government officials, teachers and students participated; a permanent national committee was set up to direct the campaign and was aided by local provincial committees.

Today the majority of schools are state-controlled, the remainder being either private (357 schools in 1968) or run by religious orders. The development of education owes a great deal to the efforts of the population and of the religious orders. Since 1955, 90 per cent of the primary and secondary school building was carried out by the local population, who contributed either money, materials or labour. The State allocates 20–25 per cent of the total annual budget to education, but as a result of the participation of the people in educational development, the estimated provision of schools has been exceeded.

Primary Education

Education, as under the French system, starts at the age of six and the primary course lasts for six years. At the end of this an examination is held, after which about 50 per cent of children proceed to secondary education. In 1969–70 there were 959,123 children attending 4,525 primary schools. However, the war has seriously affected primary schooling, and in 1970–71 there were only 322,933 children attending 1,064 primary schools.

Secondary Education

In 1955 there were twelve secondary schools situated in the capital and the six main provincial towns of Battambang, Kompong Cham, Siemreap, Svay Rieng, Takeo and Kampot; total enrolment was then 5,300. Before the war there were 149 secondary schools and colleges open; in 1970–71 this number dropped to 83. Private secondary education is provided in 26 schools and 3 colleges. 75,619 pupils (of whom a third are girls) attend State secondary schools, and 3,857 attend private schools. The curriculum and the educational structure at the secondary level have been greatly modified in order to meet the needs of a developing industry and an expanded agricultural sector. Secondary education lasts seven years and is divided into two cycles: one of four and the second of three years, an examination, the "diplôme d'enseignement secondaire" is taken after four years. After this children specialize in technical education or continue an academic course for entry to a university. The "Baccalauréat" is taken in two parts at the end of a six-year course, and success in this enables the student to enter university.

Children enter secondary school at the age of twelve and for the first two years all children follow a common syllabus. Khmer is now the official language of instruction. For historical reasons, French has always been the first foreign language, but now there is a scheme to introduce English on a par with French.

Technical Education

There are now 107 technical schools and colleges, with a total of 8,201 students. There is a scheme to reorganize technical education into an independent, autonomous unit, which will speed up progress in this field.

Higher Education

In 1955 there were only two institutes of further education. The National Institute for Law, Politics and Economics (l'Institut National d'Etudes Juridiques, Economiques et Politiques) provided a practical course leading to a diploma and a course of higher studies leading to a degree in law. L'Ecole Royale de Médecine trained only health officers, and those wishing to train as doctors had to go to France. In 1957 the Institut National became the Faculté de Droit et des Sciences Economiques, and in 1960 the royal university was founded and incorporated the above faculty, as well as a faculty of Arts and Social Sciences and a Science faculty, which had been established in the previous year. In 1962 the Ecole Royale became the faculty of Medicine and Pharmacy. In 1959 the Buddhist University of Preah Sihanouk Reach was founded.

Because of the needs of the country for technicians, engineers and teachers—in particular for a rapidly expanding industrial sector and a modernizing agricultural sector—the Head of State encouraged the establishment of new universities, to be located not only in the capital but also in the provinces. In 1969–70 there was a total of 5,753 students attending the 5 universities in the Republic. Four of these have since had to close. Sixty per cent of university students are following scientific and technical courses. A new Teachers Training College attached to the University of Phnom-Penh has recently opened.

BIBLIOGRAPHY

ARMSTRONG, J. P. Sihanouk Speaks (New York, 1964).

BRIGGS, L. P. The Ancient Khmer Empire (Transactions of the American Philosophical Society, Philadelphia, 1951).

BRODRICK, A. H. Little Vehicle; Cambodia and Laos (London).

CADY, J. F. Thailand, Burma, Laos and Cambodia (Prentice-Hall Inc., Englewood Cliffs, New Jersey, 1966).

COEDES, G. Les Etats hindouisés d'Indochine et d'Indonésie (F. de Boccard, Paris, 1948).

COUR, CLAUDE-GILLES. Institutions Constitutionelles et Politique du Cambodge (Paris, 1965).

DELVERT, J. Le Paysan Cambodgien (Paris and the Hague, 1961).

FALL, B. Street Without Joy: Insurgency in Indo-China 1946–1963 (Pall Mall Press, London, 3rd revised ed. 1963).

FITZSIMMONS, T. (ed.). Cambodia, its People, its Society, its Culture (HRAF Press, New Haven, Conn., 2nd edn., 1959).

GROSLIER B. Angkor et le Cambodge au XVIe siècle (Paris, 1958).

HERTZ, M. F. A Short History of Cambodia from the days of Angkor to the Present (Stevens and Sons, London, 1958).

KIRK, DONALD. Wider War: The Struggle for Cambodia, Thailand and Laos (Praeger, N.Y., 1971).

LEIFER, M. Cambodia—The Search for Security (Pall Mall Press, London, 1967).

MACDONALD, M. Angkor (Cape, London, 1958).

MIGOT, A. Les Khmers (Paris, 1960).

PRESCHEZ, PHILIPPE. Essai sur la Démocratie au Cambodge (Paris, 1961).

SMITH, ROGER M. *Cambodia* in Governments and Politics of Southeast Asia, Edited by G. McT. Kahin (Ithaca, N.Y., 1964).
Cambodia's Foreign Policy (Ithaca, N.Y., 1965).

THIERRY, S. Les Khmers (Paris, 1964).

WILLMOTT, WILLIAM E. The Chinese in Cambodia (Vancouver, 1967).

See also Laos and Viet-Nam.

East Timor

Physical and Social Geography

East Timor is 14,925 sq. km. in area and occupies the eastern half of the island of Timor in the Malay Archipelago (East Indies). The western half of the island is Indonesian territory and constitutes part of the East Nusa Tenggara Province. In addition to the eastern half of Timor island, the territory also includes and enclave around Oé-Cusse (Ocussi Ambeno), on the north-west coast of the island, and the islands of Ataúro (Pulo Cambing) and Jaco (Pulo Jako). The territory is divided into the municipality of Dili, the capital, and eight circumscriptions.

Lying between 8° 15′ and 10° 30′ S. longitude and 123° 20′ and 127° 10′ E. latitude, the island of Timor is the southernmost part of an arc extending from the main Sunda (or Outer) chain of the Malay Archipelago, and its long axis runs roughly from west–south-west to east–north-east. Very irregular, rugged hills and mountains form the core of the island, which is split by a longitudinal series of depressions and by small, discontinuous plateaux. There are many old volcanoes but no evidence exists of any recent volcanic activity.

Some good soils have been formed from the older volcanic rock, but irrigation difficulties and other climatic factors severely inhibit agriculture. The south-east monsoon, blowing off the arid lands of Australia, brings a long dry season, and the wet season, during the West monsoon, is short and irregular. Within the island, great climatic variations are experienced due to relief. Vegetation is today characterized by tall-grass, low-tree savannas; these are undoubtedly man-made, and some traces remain of the original monsoon forests which yielded sandalwood, dye wood and wax and which attracted the early traders to the island. Palms predominate in the lowland savannas, but good grasslands are found at higher levels, although much of these have been ruined by the spread of scrubland.

The indigenous peoples are of mixed origin. The aboriginal population is now mainly found in the mountains and is composed basically of Melanesians, who probably resulted from the fusion of a basic Papuan stock with immigrant Asian elements. Evidence exists, also, of an Australoid strain. These peoples have been displaced from the more favoured areas by later Indonesian-Malay arrivals. There are communities of Chinese and other foreign Asians, who have gained control of a large proportion of the commerce conducted on the island. Animism is the predominant religion throughout Timor, but both Islam and Christianity have made some inroads.

History

The Portuguese began trading in Timor about 1520, principally for sandalwood, and they later established settlements and several ports on the island. They were forced to move to the north and east of the island by the Dutch. who had arrived in the early part of the eighteenth century and had established themselves at Kupana in the south-west. The division of the island between Portugal and the Netherlands was formalized in a treaty of 1859, though the boundaries were slightly modified in 1904. Portuguese Timor and Macao were administered as a single entity until 1896 when Portuguese Timor became a separate province. The eastern half remained a Portuguese overseas province when the Dutch recognized the western area as part of Indonesia in 1949.

The military coup in Portugal in April 1974 was followed by increased political activity in Portuguese Timor. In August 1975 the Democratic Union of Timor (UDT), since renamed the Anti-Communist Movement, demanded independence for Timor. UDT allied with the APODETI and Kota parties against the alleged threat of a Communist regime being established by the Revolutionary Front for the Independence of East Timor (Fretilin), and fighting broke out. The UDT forces were supported by the Indonesians. Gains on both sides were uneven, with Fretilin in control of Dili in mid-September. In the same month the Portuguese administration abandoned the capital and moved to the offshore island of Ataúro. A Portuguese attempt to arrange peace talks was rejected in October. The Indonesians intervened directly and by the beginning of December Indonesian troops contolled the capital.

Portuguese-Indonesian peace talks in Rome in November were unsuccessful, and diplomatic relations were suspended after Indonesian military involvement. Two meetings of the UN Security Council voted for immediate withdrawal of Indonesian troops.

Fretilin's unilateral declaration of independence in November was recognized in December by the People's Republic of China. In December the enclave of Ocussi Ambeno was declared part of Indonesian territory. In May 1976 the People's Representative Council of East Timor voted for integration with Indonesia. The United Nations did not recognize the composition of the Council as being representative, however, and by mid-1976 the Portuguese had not formally ceded the right to govern, although they had no remaining presence in the territory.

In July 1976, East Timor was proclaimed the 27th province of Indonesia, and a governor and deputy governor were appointed. Portugal appeared to have accepted the province's integration into Indonesia as a *fait accompli*.

Economy

The indigenous population of Timor has traditionally practised shifting cultivation, clearing land for cultivation by burning. The growing of coffee, cassava (manioc) and sugar cane began early in the 19th century and in the latter part rice, rubber, cinnamon and cocoa plantations were introduced.

Agriculture remains the mainstay of the economy, employing 90 per cent of the labour force and accounting for roughly 70 per cent of G.N.P. The principal crop is coffee, which provided nearly 88 per cent of export earnings in 1973. With the exception of coffee and the other main cash crop, copra, the economy is dominated by subsistence farming. Nevertheless the farmers are unable to provide adequate food for a population of nearly 640,000. The Two-Year Development Plan therefore lays emphasis on improving agricultural efficiency and diversification (2,400 contos are to be spent on arresting soil erosion). Attempts are being made to develop the rudimentary fishing industry on the north coast, and a potentially important livestock industry.

Industry is largely undeveloped and still organized on a local artisan basis. The existing industry is primarily concerned with bread production, wood preparation and furniture, alcohol and textiles. Projected industrial expansion is closely linked with ambitious plans for the development of infrastructure. The province already has an adequate 2,896 km. of roads but the Development Plan envisages spending 435,000 contos (72.8 per cent of the total) on roads, airport development and port improvements.

STATISTICAL SURVEY

AREA AND POPULATION

Area	Estimated Mid-Year Population		
	1970	1971	1972
14,925 sq. km.	610,541	621,767	636,553

	Births	Marriages	Deaths
1970	13,607	1,559	7,592
1971	12,764	1,369	5,350
1972	11,311	1,267	7,950
1973	10,012	1,058	5,846

AGRICULTURE

PRINCIPAL CROPS
(metric tons)

	1971	1972
Beans	3,027	7,762
Coffee	5,275	4,701
Copra	2,448	1,993
Groundnuts (unshelled)	885	488
Maize	11,428	8,730
Cassava (Manioc)	17,305	6,734
Rice	12,521	13,004
Rubber	1,003	121
Sweet potatoes	11,851	10,882
Tobacco	109	37

LIVESTOCK

	1970	1971	1972
Horses	114,152	119,441	119,786
Cattle	70,607	77,945	82,949
Buffaloes	125,148	134,747	132,988
Sheep	43,033	48,858	45,991
Goats	217,011	210,277	197,453
Pigs	224,268	235,237	216,662

INDUSTRY

		1971	1972	1973
Bread	metric tons	300.7	826	1,083
Vegetable oils	'000 litres	59.8	210	100
Brandy	,, ,,	67.0	60.5	85
Alcohol	,, ,,	4.8	6	2
Soap	metric tons	60.7	234.4	169
Electricity*	'000 kWh.	3,320	4,146	4,069

* Consumption.

FINANCE

100 centavos=1 Timor escudo; 1,000 escudos are known as a *conto*.

Coins: 10, 20 and 50 centavos; 1, 2½, 5 and 10 escudos.

Notes: 20, 50, 100, 500 and 1,000 escudos.

Exchange rates (June 1976): £1 sterling=55.30 escudos; U.S. $1=31.04 escudos.

1,000 Timor escudos=£18.08=$32.22.

Note: The Timor escudo is at par with the Portuguese escudo. Between September 1949 and August 1971 the exchange rate (par value) was U.S. $1=28.75 escudos (1 escudo=3.478 U.S. cents). From December 1971 to February 1973 the central exchange rate was $1=27.25 escudos. In terms of sterling, the exchange rate was £1=69.00 escudos from November 1967 to August 1971; and £1=71.006 escudos from December 1971 to June 1972. Since March 1973 the Portuguese escudo has been allowed to "float". The average market rate of exchange (escudos per U.S. dollar) was: 27.01 in 1972; 24.67 in 1973; 25.41 in 1974; 25.55 in 1975.

BUDGET
('000 escudos)

REVENUE	1974
Ordinary:	211,370
Direct taxes	44,696
Indirect taxes	36,440
Industries with special tributary conditions	21,000
Other taxes	35,536
Private domain, State firms and industries—participation in profits	8,173
Earnings from capital, shares and bonds of banks and companies	—
Reimbursements and restitutions	9,057
Consignments of receipts	56,468
Extraordinary:*	4,300
TOTAL*	215,670

EXPENDITURE	1974
Ordinary:	211,370
Provincial debt	2,546
Provincial government and national representation	2,326
Retirements, pensions, etc.	8,700
General administration and inspection	80,044
Treasury services	8,518
Justice services	2,102
Development sevices	53,106
National defence	5,914
Marine services	3,988
General charges	44,026
Previous periods	100
Extraordinary:*	4,300
TOTAL*	215,670

* Development Plan not included.

Portuguese Intermediate Development Plan, 1968–73: Investment in Portuguese Timor (1973) 187,745 contos.

CURRENCY IN CIRCULATION
('000 escudos at December 31st)

	1971	1972	1973	1974
Notes	111,923	136,422	150,322	188,861
Coins	15,134	18,789	20,095	22,431
TOTAL	127,057	155,211	170,417	211,292

EXTERNAL TRADE

('000 escudos)

	1970	1971	1972	1973	1974
Imports	207,119	207,685	200,211	251,643	309,981
Exports	95,773	130,517	140,551	161,783	139,512

PRINCIPAL COMMODITIES

('000 escudos)

Imports	1971	1972	1973	1974
Livestock and animal products	10,472	10,329	12,765	20,424
Vegetable products	9,558	12,388	25,854	20,327
Processed food, beverages and tobacco	39,984	30,115	46,458	43,189
Mineral products	23,314	18,269	23,893	35,088
Chemicals and allied products	13,091	15,954	20,803	21,642
Textiles and textile products	25,943	24,240	32,196	48,841
Base metals and products	19,472	23,281	20,891	29,067
Machines and apparatus; electrical material	21,940	20,204	16,474	43,965
Transport material	16,189	19,997	18,538	18,008

Exports	1971	1972	1973	1974
Coffee	117,927	132,633	145,931	136,618 (Coffee, Copra and Other vegetable products)
Copra	7,606	4,614	10,372	
Other vegetable products	2,184	1,801	1,279	
Fats and fatty oils, waxes, etc.	1,281	497	806	1,033
Processed food, beverages and tobacco	33	21	495	15
Plastic materials, rubber, etc.	1,009	391	569	1,611
Timber and timber products	—	—	1,685	9

PRINCIPAL COUNTRIES

('000 escudos)

Imports	1971	1972	1973	1974
Australia	27,605	32,478	35,341	35,670
China (Taiwan)	1,329	2,423	3,122	14,712
Hong Kong	7,848	7,524	9,914	14,429
Japan	20,574	18,530	18,392	21,275
Macao	23,341	16,776	26,952	31,511
Mozambique	23,435	17,654	22,275	15,752
Netherlands	5,840	4,833	6,560	5,747
Portugal	52,731	54,058	64,780	89,898
Singapore	27,491	28,122	38,331	60,652
United Kingdom	9,786	10,797	6,312	5,403

Exports	1971	1972	1973	1974
Belgium and Luxembourg	30,558	7,770	16,950	8,484
Denmark	23,451	23,402	23,862	8,190
Netherlands	20,481	29,723	29,140	7,557
Portugal	10,327	10,381	16,154	21,545
Singapore	10,632	6,914	16,000	61,944
U.S.A.	16,780	39,081	43,369	21,038

TRANSPORT

ROADS
(Vehicles in use)

	1971	1972
Passenger cars	707	820
Trucks and buses	427	477
Tractors	101	126
Motor cycles	839	1,022

SHIPPING

	1971	1972	1973
Vessels entered:			
Number	59	181	223
'000 gross reg. tons	119	140	164
Freight (metric tons):			
Unloaded	40	31	n.a.
Loaded	13	12	n.a.

CIVIL AVIATION

	1971	1972
Aircraft landed	1,477	1,736
Passengers:		
Disembarked	12,452	14,453
Embarked	11,950	13,785
Freight (kg.):		
Unloaded	76,725	76,241
Loaded	67,499	65,058
Mail (kg.):		
Unloaded	53,337	61,312
Loaded	19,228	21,642

TOURISM

	1971	1972
Arrivals	5,383	12,783

EDUCATION

(1971/72)

	Schools	Teachers	Students
Kindergarten	1	2	18
Primary	339	667	33,760
Secondary:			
High schools	1	14	197
Technical schools (commercial and industrial)	4	39	930
Other*	3	23	232

* Including two ecclesiastical schools and one teachers' training school.

Sources: Instituto Nacional de Estatística, Banco Nacional Ultramarino and Repartição Provincial dos Serviços de Estatística de Timor.

THE GOVERNMENT

Note: Portuguese government officials left the territory in December 1975, but by mid-1976 had not officially ceded the territory (*see* History, p. 440).

Governor: ARNALDO DOS REIS ARAÚJO.

POLITICAL PARTIES

PRINCIPAL PARTIES

Frente Revolucionária de Timor Leste Independente—FRETILIN (*Revolutionary Front for the Independence of Eastern Timor*): left-wing; advocates complete independence for eastern Timor; Pres. FRANCISCO XAVIER AMARAL; Vice-Pres. NICOLAU LOBATO; Sec.-Gen. ALARICO FERNANDES.

Movimento Anticomunista—MAC (*Anti-Communist Movement*): formerly União Democrática Timorense; previously favoured federation with Portugal, with a slow transition from the Portuguese rule, then supported integration with Indonesia; centre; allied with APODETI in Sept. 1975; Leader FRANCISCO LOPES DA CRUZ.

Associação Popular Democrática de Timor—APODETI (*Popular Democratic Association of Timor*): right-wing; advocates integration with Indonesia; Pres. ARNALDO DOS REIS ARAÚJO; Sec.-Gen. OSÓRIO SANCHES.

MINOR PARTIES

Kota: tribalist movement; in alliance with MAC and APODETI; Pres. JOSÉ MARTINS.

Partido Trabalhista (*Labour Party*): in alliance with MAC and APODETI.

Associação Popular Monarquica de Timor (*People's Monarchic Association of Timor*).

RELIGION

ROMAN CATHOLIC CHURCH

Suffragan See (attached to Metropolitan See of Goa): Dili; Rt. Rev. JOSÉ JOAQUIM RIBEIRO.

There are 3 parishes and 16 missions with a total personnel of 868; Roman Catholics number about 7,500.81

Note

The following sections on the Press, Radio, Finance, etc., refer to the situation before August 1975.

THE PRESS

Boletim Oficial: Dili; Government publication.

Voz de Timor: Dili; Dir. FRANCISCO LOPES DA CRUZ.

RADIO

Emissora de Radiodifusão de Timor: Dili; government station; programmes in Portuguese, Chinese and Tetum; Dir.-Gen. MARIANO LOPES DA CRUZ.

In 1974 there were 4,229 radio receivers.

There is no television in Timor.

FINANCE

ISSUING BANK

Banco Nacional Ultramarino: f. 1864; established in Timor 1911; (Head Office: Rua do Comércio 84, P.O.B. 2069, Lisbon 2).

INSURANCE

The following Portuguese insurance firms are represented in Portuguese Timor:

Companhia de Seguros Tagus, S.A.R.L.: Dili (Head Office: Rua do Comércio 40-64, Lisbon).

Companhia de Seguros Ultramarina, S.A.R.L.: agent in Dili; Sociedade Agrícola Pátria e Trabalho, Lda. (Head Office: Rua da Prata 108, Lisbon).

Companhia de Seguros O Alentejo, S.A.R.L.: Dili (Head Office: Praça dos Restauradores 47, Lisbon).

TRANSPORT

ROADS

There were 2,371 km. of roads in 1973, of which 687 km. were classified as first class, and 1,540 km. as seasonal tracks.

SHIPPING

Companhia Nacional de Navegação, S.A.R.L.: agent in Dili: Sociedade Agrícola Pátria e Trabalho, Lda. (Head Office: Rua do Comércio 85, Lisbon).

C.T.M.—Companhia Portuguesa de Transportes Maritimos, S.A.R.L.: agent in Dili: Sociedade Agrícole Pátria e Trabalho, Lda. (Head Office: Rua de S. Julião 63, Lisbon).

Royal Interocean Lines (*Heap Eng Moh Steamship Co. Pte. Ltd.*): agent in Dili: Banco Nacional Ultramarino.

CIVIL AVIATION

AOA Zamrud Aviation Corpn.: Djl. Merdeka III/I, Kupang; Agent JACK SINE.

Transportes Aéreos de Timor: Dili; f. 1946; services between Dili and Darwin, Dili and Kupang and domestic services within Timor; Gen. Man. Capt. ANTÓNIO RODRIGUES PEREIRA.

Trans-Australia Airlines: services between Baucau and Darwin.

Merpati Nusantara Airlines: services between Bali, Kupang and Dili.

Indonesia

PHYSICAL AND SOCIAL GEOGRAPHY

C. A. Fisher

Indonesia, which today comprises exactly the same area as the former Netherlands East Indies, lies along the equator between the southeastern tip of the Asian mainland and Australia. Along its western and southern coasts it abuts upon the Indian Ocean (which the former President Sukarno renamed the Indonesian Ocean); to the north it looks towards the Straits of Malacca and the South China Sea, and on the remote northern shore of West New Guinea (Irian Jaya) it has a direct frontage on to the Pacific Ocean.

With an overall distance of over 3,000 miles (4,800 km.) from east to west and 1,250 miles (2,000 km.) from north to south, Indonesia stretches over an area almost as big as Europe west of the U.S.S.R. However, since nearly four-fifths of the area between these outer extremities consist of sea, the total land surface of Indonesia amounts in fact, to 2,027,087 square kilometres (782,663 square miles), which makes it the fourteenth largest territorial unit in the world.

PHYSICAL FEATURES

This territory is divided between some 3,000 islands of very varied size and character. The largest exclusively Indonesian island is Sumatra, covering 541,174 square kilometres, though this is exceeded by the Indonesian two-thirds (550,848 square kilometres) of Borneo (Kalimantan). There are followed by the 412,781 square kilometres of Indonesian West New Guinea (Irian Jaya), then Celebes (Sulawesi) with 227,654 square kilometres and Java which, with the neighbouring island of Madura, totals 134,703 square kilometres and the remainder is made up by a series of much smaller islands comprising Bali and the Nusa Tenggara group, and the scattered and predominantly tiny Moluccas (Maluku) lying between Sulawesi and Irian Jaya.

These differences in size reflect fundamental differences in geological structure. All the large islands except Sulawesi stand on one of two great continental shelves, namely the Sunda Shelf, representing a prolongation of the Asian mainland though now largely covered by the shallow waters of the Malacca Straits, the Java Sea and the southernmost part of the South China Sea, and the Sahul Shelf which, beneath the similarly shallow Arafura Sea, links Irian with Australia. Geologically speaking, these two shelves represent ancient stable surfaces on the edges of which, as in Sumatra, Java and northeastern Kalimantan to the west, and Irian Jaya to the east, extensive folding has taken place in Tertiary and/or more recent times, as a result of compressional movements between the two. In all the above-mentioned islands, therefore, there are pronounced mountain ranges facing the deep seas along the outer edges of the shelves, and extensive lowland tracts, facing the shallow inner seas whose coastlines show all the characteristics of recent submergence. In contrast to these larger islands of western and eastern Indonesia, most of those lying between the two shelves, including Sulawesi as well as those of the Nusa Tenggara and Maluku groups, rise steeply from deep seas on all sides, and have only extremely narrow coastal plains.

Related to the recency of mountain building in most parts of the archipelago is the widespread vulcanity, much of it still in the active stage. Except in Kalimantan and Irian the culminating relief normally consists of volcanic cones, many of which exceed 3,000 metres in altitude, though the loftiest peaks of all are in fact the non-volcanic Punjak Jaya (5,000 metres) and Idenburg-top (4,800 metres) in the Snow Mountains of Irian Jaya.

However, although the most extensive lowlands occur along the eastern coast of Sumatra and the southern coasts of Kalimantan and Irian Jaya, the larger part of all three lowland areas consists of tidal swamp which, in its present state, is virtually useless for cultivation and, indeed, constitutes a major obstacle to the opening up of the better-drained areas further inland. While some parts of this tidal swamp are technically capable of being effectively drained and utilized, such reclamation has yet to be undertaken there. But it is far advanced in the narrower coastal lowlands of the smaller central island of Java, which moreover, in contrast to the larger outer islands, also contains many interior valleys of great natural fertility.

SOILS AND NATURAL RESOURCES

The much greater fertility of the soils of the eastern two-thirds of Java and nearby Bali, by comparison with nearly all the rest of Indonesia apart from a small part of interior and coastal northeastern Sumatra, arises from the neutral-basic character (as opposed to the prevailingly acidic composition elsewhere) of the volcanic ejecta from which they are derived. In the remaining nine-tenths or more of Indonesia, the soils—whether volcanically derived or not—are altogether poorer in quality than they are popularly assumed to be, and indeed are not noticeably better than in most other parts of the humid tropics.

As regards mineral wealth also, there has been a wholly unwarranted tendency to exaggerate the scale of Indonesia's resources. Apart from the considerable but not spectacular petroleum reserves, mostly in eastern Sumatra and parts of Kalimantan, which together yield between 1 and 2 per cent of total world production, and the more easily accessible but much less valuable tin deposits in the Sunda Shelf islands of Bangka, Belitung and Singkep, the repeated stories of great and widespread mineral wealth have never as yet led to any major production, although the known deposits of nickel, manganese, bauxite and low-grade iron may become economically significant in the future.

CLIMATE AND VEGETATION

Climatically the greater part of Indonesia may be described as maritime equatorial, with consistently high temperatures (except at higher altitudes) and heavy rainfall at all seasons, though in many parts of western Indonesia there are distinct peak periods of exceptionally heavy rain when either the north-east or the south-west monsoon winds are blowing onshore. However, the eastern half of Java, Bali, southern Sulawesi and Nusa Tenggara, which lie further to the south and nearer to the Australian desert, experience a clearly marked dry season during the period of the south-east monsoon (which changes direction to become the south-west monsoon over western Indonesia) between June–July and September–October. Thus, whereas in Pontianak, situated almost exactly on the equator on the west coast of Kalimantan, the monthly mean temperature varies only from 78°F. (25.6°C.) in December to 80°F. (26.7°C.) in July, and average monthly rainfall varies from 16 cm. (6.3 inches) in July to 40 cm. (15.7 inches) in December, out of a total annual rainfall of 320 cm. (126 inches), Surabaya in eastern Java, while showing even less variation in mean monthly temperature, which fluctuates between 79°F. (26.1°C.) and 80°F. (26.7°C.) throughout the year, has four months (December-March) each with over 24 cm. (9.4 inches) of rain, and four others (July-October) with less than 5 cm. (2 inches) each, out of an annual total of 173.5 cm. (68.3 inches).

While, therefore, nearly all of Indonesia in its natural state supported a very dense vegetation, though with significant variations in type as between tidal swamps, normal lowlands and lower slopes, and higher altitudes, the natural forest cover becomes progressively thinner as one goes eastwards from central Java to Timor, and over much of Nusa Tenggara the vegetation is better described as savanna.

POPULATION AND CULTURE

With an estimated population of 136 million in 1976, Indonesia ranks as the fifth most populous country in the world, after China, India, the U.S.S.R. and the U.S.A. So large a population spread over so vast and fragmented a territory presents a wide range of variation, notably in ethnic type, religion and language.

As a result of the combination of distinctly richer soils, less dense vegetation, a high proportion of lowland, an absence of extensive and unhealthy tidal swamp, and not least a central position within Indonesia as a whole, Java, together with the neighbouring islands of Madura and Bali, has in historic times proved to be by far the most favourable area to man. This situation is reflected, though in exaggerated form, in the astonishing fact that these three islands, which all told comprise less than one-thirteenth of the total area of Indonesia, contain almost two-thirds of its population. Thus, whereas the average density for Indonesia as a whole, according to the 1971 census, was 58 to the square kilometre, the corresponding figure for Java and Madura was 565 and for the rest of Indonesia 22.

Over the western two-thirds of Indonesia the predominant ethnic type is the so-called Deutero-Malay, basically southern Mongoloid in origin, to which belong virtually the entire indigenous populations of Java, Madura and Bali; the coastal peoples, together with many of the uplanders, of Sumatra; and most of the coastal inhabitants of Kalimantan, though the majority of the inland peoples of Kalimantan and of some parts of Sumatra are descendants of the earlier Proto-Malays. In the eastern third of the country the pattern is more complicated, with a preponderance of Proto-Malay, or mixed Proto-Malay, Melanesoid and in some cases also Australoid elements, in all but the coastal fringe, except in Irian Jaya whose indigenous population is predominantly Papuan. In the coastal areas of Sulawesi, Nusa Tenggara and Maluku the Deutero-Malay type is again evident, though in relation to the total population of these islands it forms a much smaller percentage than further west.

To a significant extent the main cultural divisions run parallel to the ethnic divisions already described. Thus the indigenous coastal peoples throughout western Indonesia are all Muslim with the solitary exception of the Balinese, who remain faithful to the Hinduism which formerly predominated over all the more advanced parts of western Indonesia. Nevertheless, although approximately 80 per cent of the total Indonesian population profess Islam, there are considerable variations in the degree of attachment to that religion as, for example, between the extremely staunch Acenese and Sundanese, of northern Sumatra and western Java respectively, the much laxer Sasaks of Lombok, the more typically orthodox coast Malays of eastern Sumatra and coastal Kalimantan, and the Javanese whose Islam is much modified by earlier Hindu survivals.

By contrast, most of the Proto-Malay peoples in the interiors of all these islands (except Java) are animists, though some have in recent times adopted Christianity. In the eastern third of the country the operative distinction lies between a much narrower Muslim coastal fringe and a predominantly animist interior, though in some of the islands the Muslim element is almost completely absent, and in several Christianity has made deep inroads.

Altogether some 25 different languages and 250 dialects have been recognized in Indonesia, and again the divisions tend to follow the basic ethnic divide between coastal and interior peoples in the several parts of the archipelago. However, since the achievement of independence great progress has been made in modernizing the old traders' *lingua franca*, often referred to as "market Malay", and propagating it as the national language, *Bahasa Indonesia*, in all parts of the country.

Besides the indigenous population, with whom the foregoing paragraphs are exclusively concerned, Indonesia contains one of the largest Chinese minorities in South-East Asia. This now numbers approximately 3 million (i.e. some 3 per cent of the total), and in addition there is a much smaller Arab community and a surviving remnant of the Eurasian minority which in late colonial times numbered some 200,000.

As elsewhere in South-East Asia these non-indigenous peoples are largely concentrated in the towns, of which, as is to be expected, all the largest are in Java. Besides Jakarta, the capital, whose population now exceeds 5 million (5,849,000 in 1971), Bandung (1,152,000 in 1971) and Surabaya and Semarang, likewise in Java, had totals respectively of 1,269,000 and 633,000 in 1971. Of the eighteen towns with populations between 180,000 and 620,000 in 1971 a further eight are in Java, but the list also includes Medan (620,000) and Palembang (614,000) in Sumatra, Ujungpandang (497,000) in Sulawesi, and Banjarmasin (277,000) in Kalimantan.

HISTORY

Jan M. Pluvier

EARLY HISTORY

Situated in an area through which important trade routes ran, the Indonesian island world could not fail to be affected by influences from outside. Around the beginning of the Christian era these influences came from India. During the so-called Hindu period two great Indonesian empires emerged: Srivijaya, with its centre in Sumatra and controlling the Malacca Straits (roughly A.D. 700–1200); and Majapahit, a Javanese state which from about A.D. 1300 held the greater part of the archipelago for a century and a half. A few remarks about the nature of these empires have to be made. First, their control over large territories, especially over those far away from the capital city, was very much indirect rule, with the real power in the hands of local princes—a situation which accounted for the strength of centrifugal forces whenever the power of the central government was on the wane. Secondly, the Indonesian states of the Hindu period were neither Indian colonies nor in any other way politically linked with India. India's expansion was exclusively cultural and its influence was confined to the higher strata of a society which continued to be essentially Indonesian in character. The "Hindu kingdoms" were Indonesian states in which the upper classes had, for several reasons, adopted elements of Indian civilization.

Somewhere between 1100 and 1300 another culture made its appearance in Indonesia. It came from India, too, but it was not indigenous there: Islam. Like Indian civilization it was adopted by the ruling classes in the Indonesian states, but unlike the Indian cultural elements of the previous millennium it also descended to the mass of the population. From the first Islamic centres in Malacca, Northern Sumatra (Achin) and East Java it spread over the entire archipelago, a process which lasted from roughly 1400 to 1900. In the structure of Indonesian society, however, this process of Islamization did not bring about any more essential changes than the process of Indianization had done. The village community, a social organization, living on *sawah* agriculture, based on communal labour and responsibility and economically self-sufficient, continued to be the fundamental unit of Indonesian society. Some industry and cattle breeding did exist and there were some signs of a monetary economy, but these were exceptions; in general there was neither production for a market nor profit-making. Socially and economically the villages had hardly any contacts with the outside world, the only link with which was provided by the authority of the princes or the local aristocratic classes. Towns were administrative and, seen from an economic point of view, almost entirely consumptive units.

European Influence

The third of the external influences which affected Indonesia—Europe—did not in any sense transform this basic structure of society, at least not until well into the nineteenth century. The Dutch traders who in 1602 joined forces in the United East Indian Company (V.O.C.)—the armed commercial organization with sovereign rights, which represented Holland in the archipelago for nearly two centuries—were a more powerful challenge to Indonesian society than Indian civilization and Islam had been in previous periods, but they, too, had to adapt themselves to the existing social structure. In the seventeenth century the Dutch establishments (Malacca, Batavia, Ambon) were mere enclaves in a huge territory where the power of the greater Indonesian kingdoms (Achin, Mataram, Bandjarmasin) was still predominant, and their trade and shipping constituted just one element, albeit an aggressive one, of the commercial intercourse in the area in which Chinese, Japanese, Siamese, Javanese, Indians and Arabs took part. A century later the situation had changed in that the Dutch company had monopolized the trade in the Moluccas, had guaranteed for itself a sort of unstable preponderance over Java and had conquered places like Padang and Makasar, but it was not yet an inter-insular power in the archipelago. Direct Dutch influence, in the territories which they controlled, did not, in general, go beyond the upper classes of native society; in fact, this society, not at all affected by the presence of the Europeans and hardly influenced by their power, went its natural course until the end of the eighteenth century.

DUTCH COLONIAL POLICY

At the time the Dutch state took over the possessions and assets of the company (1799), a change was taking place in the approach of the Dutch towards their overseas territories. The policy of passive adaptation to the feudal structure of society was abandoned. Stimulated by the industrial revolution and a sudden consciousness of European technical superiority, an urge to organize and regulate led to an active policy of penetrating deeper into the interior of Java. The main concern of the colonial politicians was to continue and to intensify the exploitation of the archipelago's material resources. That the first decades of the nineteenth century in Dutch colonial history became known as the "period of doubt" was the result not of any difference of opinion on this primary goal but of conflicting theories about the method which was most likely to guarantee the highest profits. During the British period, under Raffles' responsibility (1811–16), more liberal ideas had been introduced in Java, and after the Dutch had returned it seemed for a while that these new theories would win the day. They did not, however, for the leading colonial circles feared foreign competition and they were not convinced that private enterprise would be successful in speeding up production. The financial difficulties caused by the Java war—in which the Dutch reduced the entire island to submission, 1825–30—and the insufficient proceeds of the land-rent, led to a restoration of a system of forced labour and exploitation by the state.

During the period that the Culture System, introduced in 1830, was in force, the Dutch focussed their attention primarily on Java. After their return to Indonesia (1816) they controlled outside Java only the Moluccas and some points in Sumatra and the Celebes. By the Anglo-Dutch Treaty of 1824, in which they exchanged Malacca for Bencoolen, the archipelago, with the exception of Achin, was recognized as their sphere of influence, but they did not embark upon any comprehensive policy to impose their rule. They were definitely less aloof than the British were *vis-à-vis* Malaya during the same decades and they made their presence felt in large areas of Sumatra (particularly West Sumatra) and in Borneo (especially after the successful exploits of James Brooke in Sarawak), but on the whole their attitude towards the "Outer Islands", as the territories outside Java were referred to, was one of indifference.

This situation continued until the 1870s. By this time the industrial revolution had transformed the Netherlands into a more industrialized state and this economic change affected the Dutch approach to their overseas territories. Criticism of the Culture System on humanitarian grounds (*Multatuli*) coincided with criticism of the economic aspects of the system of state exploitation; and as the economically interested circles, which represented industrial capitalism, had become quite a powerful force in the Netherlands, their liberal tenets of free trade and private enterprise could not fail to carry the day. Indonesia had to supply the raw materials for industries in Holland, it had to become a market for Dutch industrial products and the opportunities it offered for capital investment had to be explored. In 1870 private enterprise was allowed to operate in the colony, where it found a rich field for its activities. The new liberal policy brought about a change of attitude towards the Outer Islands with their large natural resources. Between 1870 and 1910 the whole of Indonesia was brought under effective Dutch rule and, either by conquest (e.g. Achin War) or by treaty, incorporated into the Netherlands Indies, which was now given definite shape.

Social Policy

It was also during this period that the Indonesian social structure was most affected by influences from outside. Western penetration, which led to a direct confrontation between a capitalist economy with its dynamic and active elements on the one hand and the traditional pre-capitalist system on the other, in fact undermined the very foundations of the Indonesian native economy. The result was that while the Netherlands Indies, judged by its production capacity and its import and export figures, developed into one of the most prosperous European colonies in the world, the standard of living of the mass of the population steadily declined. An attempt to remedy this situation was undertaken during the first decades of the twentieth century. This so-called "Ethical Course", introduced in 1901, was a combination of free enterprise and a state-managed native welfare policy, which could boast of some substantial achievements. The magnitude of the problem, however, aggravated by the rapid growth of the population, seriously jeopardized the efforts to make amends for the neglect that in the past had characterized the official attitude in this field. Moreover, the ambiguous nature of Ethical colonial policy, which often forced the administration to choose between the conflicting interests of either Western enterprise or the Indonesian population, resulted in a failure to bring about any essential improvement. During the Trade Depression of the 1930s the government increased its regulatory and managerial powers in the economic sphere, but its primary goal in this was to prevent the success of Japanese competition and to carry European business safely through the economic disaster which hit Indonesia with unprecedented savagery, rather than to protect the Indonesian population. Ethical policy was never officially repealed, but in practice it ceased.

THE NATIONALIST MOVEMENT

In the political, as in the economic, sphere the 1930s showed a similar retrogression of Ethical principles. At the turn of the century Dutch colonial policy towards Indonesia was not unlike that of the British *vis-à-vis* India and in 1918 the People's Council was introduced as a representative body. In the same year the so-called "November Promises" referred to a future transfer of authority from Holland to the Indies and to constitutional reforms which would give the native population a greater share in administrative matters. From 1922, however, after the rise of the nationalist movement had caused fear in a great many Dutch hearts and the revolutionary high tide which had accompanied the end of the First World War had ebbed away, hardly anything was done in this respect: during the Trade Depression interference from The Hague was increasing instead of diminishing, while constitutional stagnation set in. In 1938 the government rejected an Indonesian proposal, the Soetardjo Petition, put forward in the People's Council in 1936, to convene a conference of representatives of the Netherlands and the Indies in order to discuss gradual reforms which, over a period of ten years or more if the conference should decide so, would lead to self-rule for Indonesia within the realm of the Kingdom of the Netherlands.

The nationalist movement, with its main centres in Java and West Sumatra, was originally moderate in nature, but during the First World War and under the influence of Marxist ideas, it took on a more radical appearance; the great Muslim association *Sarekat Islam*, founded in 1912, changed its policy from one of "collaboration with the administration for the well-being of the Indies" to one of opposition to the government and to "sinful" (i.e. non-native) capitalism. For some years some kind of co-operation between the Sarekat Islam and the Communist Party existed, but after the break of 1921 the Muslim party lost a good deal of its mass following, while the Communists had manoeuvred themselves into a rebellion (Java, 1926; Sumatra, 1927) which was suppressed and followed by a ban on Communism. The next stage of the development brought the genuine nationalists to the fore, genuine in the sense that they did not base their actions on any international ideal, such as Islam or Communism, but on pure Indonesian nationalism. The years between 1926 and 1934 were the years of Sukarno, Hatta and Sjahrir, characterized on the nationalist side by a policy of non-co-operation with the colonial authorities, and on the Dutch side by an intensification of political repression. Realizing that it was primarily the non-co-operative nationalist parties which were persecuted by the government, the nationalists changed tactics and dropped non-co-operation as a means of political struggle. Thus a process of reorientation began around 1934–35, giving the impression that the nationalist movement had returned to moderation—a false impression as the ultimate end of the struggle continued to be independence. The more moderate behaviour of nationalism induced the administration to relax its oppressive policy, though not, however, to change its course of withholding constitutional or political reforms. After Holland itself had become involved in the Second World War (1940) such reforms were not even taken into consideration, in spite of the nationalists' insistence on this as a pre-requisite for a closer co-operation between the Dutch and the Indonesians against a common enemy.

The Effect of Japanese Occupation

During the Japanese occupation (1942–45) the nationalist movement gained considerable strength. From its early beginnings Japanese policy, in Java at least, was directed to winning over the population with the help of those leaders who, because of their links with the masses, might be useful to this end. Some of the nationalist leaders were given official advisory posts in the Japanese-sponsored mass movements, but as they did not command a sufficiently large following among the population and as the Japanese fully realized that they collaborated only in order to prepare themselves for post-war contingencies it was not until late 1944 that the occupying authorities allowed them to obtain a more substantial share in political life. In the intervening years the Japanese accorded their favours to the aristocratic classes and, to a far greater extent, to Muslim religious leaders, the only group which held considerable influence over the population at grass-roots level.

The most important result of the Japanese occupation was the psychological effect of the sudden disappearance of the colonial regime, which, combined with the practical effect of Indonesians holding the administrative and technical positions formerly reserved for Europeans, gave fresh impetus to Indonesian self-confidence. The nationalist movement which arose after the war was, for the first time, a real mass movement, partly led by Islamic leaders whose influence had been greatly strengthened in comparison with the pre-war situation, partly by the nationalist politicians who had managed to win control over the quasi-political organizations as soon as the Japanese, in the last phase of the war, had committed themselves to the idea of granting independence to Indonesia.

The Revolutionary Years: 1945–49

The leadership of the nationalist movement was still essentially middle class, but during the revolution of August 1945, its hand was often forced by the younger generation which had developed new and radical ideals. Between the older nationalists and the young revolutionaries Sjahrir emerged as Prime Minister in November 1945, at the same time that Surabaya was the scene of stubborn Indonesian resistance against the British occupying forces. The clash between the middle-class leaders and the revolutionary young generation lasted until the attempted *coup d'état* of July 3rd, 1946, after which the country's leadership was certainly guaranteed to slide back into the hands of the old guard.

In the social field the Indonesian revolution was clearly characterized by the bourgeois nature of the leading *élite*; it was essentially a middle-class and primarily a nationalist, not in any sense a proletarian, revolution. The political leadership of this *élite* group was never endangered during the revolutionary years (1945–49), either by the small group around Sjahrir and Sjarifuddin (Prime Ministers 1945–47 and 1947–48 respectively) who advocated a parliamentary democracy along bourgeois lines, or by the Communists; the so-called Madiun affair of late 1948 did not constitute a serious challenge at all. Neither were the Dutch, after their return and their take-over of responsibility from the British occupying power in 1946, successful in creating a counterweight. Their so-called Malino-policy (1946–49) of setting up separate states as constituent parts of a projected United States of Indonesia was an attempt at isolating the revolutionary government of the Indonesian Republic as much as it was an attempt at a counter-revolution. It was based on the traditionally loyal aristocracy and the aristocracy's fear of the emerging middle-class nationalist leaders. In the end, however, it was not strong enough to counterbalance the influence of the latter.

INDEPENDENT INDONESIA

Negotiations between the Dutch and the government of the Indonesian Republic led to an initial agreement in November 1946, the Linggadjati Treaty, but misunderstandings over its interpretation and especially the Dutch insistence that the Republic give up its sovereign rights and incorporate itself in the United States of Indonesia during a transitional period under Dutch sovereignty, resulted in a break. In July 1947 full-scale fighting broke out, but under the auspices of the United Nations a truce was arranged in January 1948. New negotiations were unsuccessful; in a new military campaign the Dutch captured the entire republican government in December 1948, but facing hostile world opinion, intensifying guerrilla operations and distrust among the loyal politicians of the Malino states, they had to give in: on December 27th 1949, Indonesia became independent. It was a federal state—thus far the Dutch had been successful—but the United States of Indonesia did not survive the withdrawal of Dutch power for long. A strong unitarian movement, supported by republican leaders, swept the constituent states and the Malino authorities aside and in August 1950 Indonesia was proclaimed a unitary republic.

Parliamentary Democracy: 1949–57

After independence Indonesia faced many problems and, as these were emerging in a society which was politically far more articulate than in pre-war years, it also experienced greater difficulties in solving them than the colonial regime had done. No Indonesian government could afford to disregard public opinion and incur public discontent from which the opposition might make political capital. Any governmental system based on principles which for the most part are derived from abroad needs some time to mature. This is valid in almost any country; it was the more so in a nation which obtained its freedom after eight years of war and revolutionary turbulence. The coming of independence was accompanied by an upsurge of enthusiasm and a desire to build up a new state and society. At the same time, however, various dissonant forces were released once the only factor that had cemented them together had been eliminated. For one thing there was disappointment among the younger generation which had played a leading part in conducting the revolutionary struggle from the more dangerous outposts, and which now discovered that the country's leadership had slid back into the hands of the old-guard nationalists who were claiming superiority on the grounds of their experience and their better education.

Such a situation created problems which required a strong governmental structure and a sound party system. Neither of these conditions was met. Owing to lack of experts and competent civil servants after the dismissal of many Dutch and Eurasian officials, the administration functioned inefficiently and clumsily in the executive sphere as well as in the legislature. This last factor also accounted for the defects in the party system; capable and authoritative leaders were usually drawn into the higher ranks of the government and the civil service, leaving the parties under the command of second-rate people. Another factor was that most parties had come into being, and their leaders had begun their political careers, during the colonial period: their activities had been directed against the administration and after a national government had supplanted the foreign regime many parties still persisted in displaying an element of opposition and enmity towards all authority. As no party commanded an absolute majority in the legislature, all governments during the period of parliamentary democracy (1949–57) were coalition cabinets, none of them stable and none capable of finding either a common platform or a solution to any of the more pressing problems. Only in combating illiteracy did independent Indonesia achieve a great and most admirable success.

There were many fundamental problems with which the Indonesian governments had to cope. First the religious issue: whether or not Indonesia should be an Islamic state. The second problem concerned the integration of the army into the state and its position *vis-a-vis* the civilian government. On several occasions the downfall of a cabinet was caused by army interference and in many more cases the authority of the government and its appointees in the armed forces was openly defied by insurbordinate actions—a factor which greatly contributed to political instability. Thirdly there was the problem of regionalism which outwardly seemed to have been overcome in 1950, but which was definitely not extinct. The mood of dissatisfaction which crept into the regions outside Java was based not only on ethnological and cultural differences, but also, and primarily so, on economic considerations: income earned for Indonesia in Sumatra flowed to Java, a situation which confronted the government in Jakarta with an ugly and almost insoluble dilemma.

Guided Democracy: 1957–65

In 1957 parliamentary democracy gave way to a type of authoritarianism which was dubbed "guided democracy". In the course of a few years Sukarno, the leading architect of the new system, strengthened the executive power of the government, replaced the elected parliament by an appointed legislature and reintroduced the constitution of 1945. A badly organized revolt, in which supporters of parliamentary democracy, Sumatran separatists, Muslim fanatics and some sections of the army joined forces, broke out in 1958, but it was rapidly and efficiently suppressed and followed up with a ban, in 1960, on the Masjumi party and Sjahrir's socialist party.

During this period of "guided democracy", which lasted from 1957 until 1965, Sukarno was the central figure. He was able to demonstrate a mysterious mastery over the population, while at the same time he successfully played the two great contending power factions off against each other: on the one side the army, on the other the Communist Party which in the previous years had been capable both of emerging as the best organized political party and of capturing a large mass following.

In these days great emphasis was put on the unity of Indonesia, not only in a geographical sense—and directed against regional tendencies—but also in a national and social sense: hence Sukarno's insistence on close co-operation between all classes and sections of Indonesian society (*Nasakom*). In its foreign policy Indonesia, since independence a staunch advocate of "neutralism", followed an anti-Western course, as became evident in its actions against the Netherlands —which could be regarded as a completion of the nationalist revolution (the incorporation of Irian Jaya—West New Guinea—in 1963)—as well as by its opposition to "neo-colonialism": confrontation with Malaysia (1963–66).

This anti-Western course, the take-over of Dutch business firms, the inclusion of communism in the Nasakom-ideal and of some individual communists in the cabinet, contributed to give Indonesian policy a leftist image. In its essence it was not leftist, however. The opposition to imperialism and neo-colonialism served to arouse feelings of nationalist self-consciousness and to create a national consensus of opinion. Taking over foreign business was not the outcome of any socialist ideal, but part of a nationalist campaign. The Communist Party was not banned—in this Sukarno's government differed from traditional authoritarian systems—but it did not come any closer to the take-over which many observers seemed to fear. In the constitutional set-up of guided democracy there was no opportunity for the Communist Party, which in 1955 had polled 16.4 per cent of the votes, to show its strength in national elections; its growing influence among the masses, caused by the deteriorating economic situation, was most effectively counterbalanced by the increasing power of the army and by the government's policies which diverted the communists' activities from social to nationalist issues. In fact, guided democracy contributed to maintaining the social *status quo* in which Indonesia continued to be ruled by the middle-class *élite* which had captured the direction of political and economic affairs from the Japanese in 1945.

The New Order

The abortive coup by some army sections in October 1965 totally changed the situation. The military establishment used the event as an excuse to crack down on the communists, who were murdered by the thousands in the worst single massacre in South-East Asian history: in fact the entire left wing was eliminated. At the same time President Sukarno was deprived of his prerogatives. In March 1966 military commanders, led by General Suharto, assumed emergency powers. Gen. Suharto, appointed Chairman of the Presidium, used his new executive authority gradually to establish his "New Order". In February 1967 Sukarno handed over all power to Suharto. In March the People's Consultative Assembly removed the President from office and named Suharto acting President. He became Prime Minister in October 1967 and, after being elected by the Assembly, was inaugurated as President in March 1968.

The delicate balance of power on which Sukarno's authority had been based was completely destroyed. The armed forces became the most important power-factor, while the political parties were relegated to an even more inferior position than during "Guided Democracy". Even the Muslims, the staunchest allies of the army in the drive against the PKI and Sukarno, were not allowed to regain the political influence they commanded before the 1958 revolt. Yet, in spite of the changes, the coming to power of Suharto did not essentially alter the situation in which the middle class élite continued to rule the country. There was a change from a moderately right-wing authoritarian type of government to a harsh military dictatorship, but there was not, in fact, a switch from a really left-wing to a right-wing regime. The New Order represented a counter-revolution only in the sense that the social forces working towards improving the living conditions of the mass of the population were effectively blocked: the land-reform programme of 1960 was discontinued, peasants' associations and trade unions were banned.

Under the New Order the problems besetting the government were the same as before, and even more acute. There was no real solution to the economic difficulties although, with the help of Western countries and Japan, a programme of economic stabilization and rehabilitation was introduced in October 1966. The new regime offered better opportunities for foreign investment than the previous one and its general political orientation fitted in better with Western policy and strategy in South-East Asia. Up to mid-1975 Indonesia received nearly $5,000 million in loans from the so-called donor-countries (officially the Inter-Governmental Group for Indonesia, IGGI).

In spite of these huge financial injections, the Five-Year Plan introduced in April 1969 failed. By resorting to a tight-money policy as well as by allowing the importation of foreign goods, the Government's policy led to the ruin of Indonesian business firms. In 1968 a crash programme to improve rice production also failed: undue pressure was put on Javanese peasants to sell their crops at low prices and to buy expensive fertilizers imported by foreign (Swiss, West German) chemical industries. If anyone benefited from whatever economic improvements were made, it was certainly not the rural mass of the population, but a few categories of urban consumers: in order to satisfy their needs, to keep the towns quiet and to create the impression in the outside world that Indonesia was developing as a welfare state, the prices of rice and other necessities were artificially kept at a low level. In the countryside a scarcity of food occurred in 1973, not only, as usual, in the months immediately preceding the harvest, but also after it.

On the other hand the increasing dependence of Indonesia's economy on the West and Japan, endangered its freedom of economic and political action. Western and Japanese capital are heavily involved in exploiting Indonesia's natural resources, particularly oil, timber and fishing. In the two last-mentioned industries Indonesia has been forced to grant huge concessions, turning foreign capitalist activities into a campaign of depriving Indonesia as quickly as possible of its raw materials. Indonesia hardly benefited from foreign investments since the entrepreneurs were mostly interested in quick-yielding low-cost projects, and failed to make any tangible contribution to improving the country's production capacity.

Indonesia's dependence on the Western world also resulted in a new foreign policy. In 1966/67 the good relations with China were ended, and diplomatic relations with Malaysia re-established. The Suharto government still adhered formally to the principle of non-alignment and did not participate in any Western military alliance. However, it was a member of ASEAN which, although referring to Asian neutralism, fitted in with United States policy towards South-East Asia as formulated by President Nixon in 1969. In the early 1970s Indonesia had moved towards the West and this the more so when, in view of the débacle of U.S. policy in Indochina, insular South-East Asia was more and more regarded as the last American line of defence in the region.

In July 1971 general elections were held. A few political parties were allowed to participate, but some, particularly the Partai National Indonesia (PNI) and the new Muslim party, Partai Muslimin Indonesia (PMI), Masjumi's successor, were forced to accept leaders acceptable to the military establishment. The Government strongly supported the so-called *Sekber Golkar* (Secretariat of Functional Groups) which consequently won a handsome victory. In addition to the seats allotted to the armed forces the members of *Sekber Golkar* guaranteed the regime a comfortable parliamentary majority, and early in 1972 Suharto was re-elected. In January 1973 the political parties were forced to merge into two large organizations, one for the religious groups, and one for the secular parties. In fact the regime often declared itself against "politics": *Sekber Golkar* was described as a non-political body. In spite of the manoeuvres to increase the number of civilian cabinet ministers the regime remains predominantly military: the majority of local officials at all levels are military officers.

The New Order is far from widely accepted by the population. Any trace of resistance is brutally suppressed but, in spite of this, small guerrilla bands seem to be operating in Kalimantan and West Irian. In military circles discontent and personal rivalries manifest themselves; among Islamic leaders there is dissatisfaction over their minimal role in the political process, and in August 1973 there were riots when the government introduced a new marriage law. Students frequently demonstrated over corruption and rising prices. In January 1974 the outward stability of the regime was badly shaken by serious disturbances in Jakarta. Students played a major role in these, but they were probably manipulated by some elements within the military establishment who were displeased with their own position and with the government's policies.

In 1974 the increasing revenues from the oil industry caused a substantial improvement in Indonesia's balance of payments. Yet this did not produce any rise in the standard of living of the majority of the population. The Indonesian state itself failed to benefit either, due to the dubious financial activities of the state oil company. In early 1976, according to figures of Amnesty International, there were more than 100,000 political prisoners in prisons or concentration camps.

In 1975 Indonesia became involved in the independence movement in Portuguese Timor, the eastern part of the island of Timor, of which the rest was Indonesian territory, first supporting and later in the year intervening militarily on the side of the movements opposed to the establishment of a communist regime in the territory. In early 1976 the Portuguese administration had left, but not officially seceded the right to govern. In May 1976 the People's Representative Council of East Timor voted for integration with Indonesia. The United Nations declined to participate in a mission to establish the willingness of the East Timor people for integration as it had not observed the selection of the assembly members who voted for it. In July East Timor was integrated as the 27th province of Indonesia. Although not formally acknowledged by Portugal, integration appeared to have been accepted as a *fait accompli* by the Portuguese.

ECONOMIC SURVEY

Iain Buchanan

In terms of population, Indonesia is the fifth largest country in the world, with more than 130 million people in 1975. In terms of resources, it is one of the richest in the Third World, with sizeable oil and natural gas deposits and some of the richest timber stands in the world. Its position is economically and politically strategic, curving from the Indian Ocean, adjacent to the Malacca Straits and the South China Sea (Japan's main link with Europe and the Middle East), passing South Thailand, Malaysia, Singapore and the Philippines to the north and Australia to the south, to the Pacific Ocean and Micronesia. Yet Indonesia is one of the poorest countries in the world. In 1973 it had an average *per capita* income of U.S. $154, with the majority of the population living below this level, in a poor and overpopulated agricultural economy. The bulk of the population (66 per cent) is concentrated in the islands of Java and Madura (7 per cent of total area), and in Java, too, there is concentrated most of Indonesia's urban population, manufacturing and modern transport facilities, as well as some of the most productive agriculture and the bulk of the country's poorest peasantry.

It is against this background that the economic development of Indonesia since independence must be considered.

ECONOMIC TRENDS, 1950-65

During the Sukarno years Indonesia was inherently unstable economically, reflecting a combination of political obstacles to effective development. While Sukarno tried to develop an economy badly disrupted by the Second World War and the subsequent war with the Dutch, his policies were often counter-productive, over-compromising and sabotaged by the complex of vested interests in and around power. While a radical restructuring of the whole economic and political system was essential, it was also impossible, given the chronic antagonism between the nationalists, the Muslim establishment, communists and regional interests.

With an overwhelmingly agrarian economy, Indonesia's first priority was rural development. The agrarian structure was defective, and marked by high rates of tenancy, indebtedness, landlessness, under-employment and a majority of landholdings of unviable size (in 1955 the average holding in Java was officially 0.6 of a hectare, with over 50 per cent of the farming population in holdings of less than one hectare or half the size necessary for adequate family subsistence).

Reform was essential, but the two main reform laws, the 1960 Basic Agrarian Law and the 1960 Sharecroppers Act came too late, were too moderate, and were effectively sabotaged by a combination of landlord, orthodox Muslim and military interests. When the powerful Indonesian Communist Party, through its peasant associations, encouraged the peasantry to make their own unilateral land transfers, to enact legislation already on the books, those interests were directly threatened. When Sukarno took sweeping moves of nationalization against the Dutch, British, Americans and local Chinese, he was asserting an anti-imperialism that was a double-edged sword for Indonesians: first, the short-term advantages of using foreign investment as a means of gaining foreign exchange for development were lost, for Indonesia had neither the capital nor the expertise to develop effectively its own resources, and the institutional framework of a corrupt military, incompetent bureaucracy, and strongly capitalist

Table 1

Production of selected items, 1955–64

('000 metric tons)

	1955	1959	1964
Food crops:			
Rice (milled)	7,125	7,950	8,096
Maize	1,882	2,101	3,769
Cassava	9,380	11,923	12,223
Sweet potatoes	1,866	2,719	3,931
Groundnuts	216	255	261
Soybeans	345	431	392
	1954	**1958**	**1964**
Export products:			
Rubber	759.6	695.7	732
Copra (smallholder)	973.5	1,050.0	1,193
Palm oil (estate)	169.0	147.6	195
Tin concentrates	32.8	22.8	16.6
Crude petroleum	10,775	16,295	23,172

entrepreneurial èlite negated any possible benefits of economic independence; second, anti-Western moves alienated the Western-subsidized military establishment, the trader class and the large class of commercial croppers in Sumatra.

One result of this was deepening antagonism between Sumatra and other outer islands (which accounted for 85 per cent of all export income) on the one hand, and Java (whose imports of food, consumer goods, and capital equipment were subsidized by the outer islands' earnings) on the other. Sumatra, in particular, began direct trading with Malaysia and Singapore, thus depriving the central government of vital revenue. In this situation, corruption became endemic, and smuggling mushroomed and continued despite Confrontation with Malaysia and Singapore (1963–66). Hence trade figures are unreliable (since 1962, for example, Singapore, through which most of Indonesia's exports go, has refused to publish figures on trade with Indonesia).

Table 2

External trade

('000 million rupiahs)

	1955	1959	1964
Exports .	10,618	9,944	32,589
Imports .	6,888	5,228	27,973
Balance .	3,730 (35%)	4,716(47%)	4,616 (14%)

Export production is poorly reflected in trade figures, partly because of international price changes and partly because of smuggling of cash crop commodities. In 1950, 1955 and 1959, rubber and petroleum accounted for, respectively, 47 per cent and 17 per cent, 46 per cent and 23 per cent and 48 per cent and 27 per cent of the value of reported trade; tin moved from about 5 per cent to 6 per cent to 4 per cent. Thus, accounting for considerable rubber-smuggling from the mid-1950s onwards, over 80 per cent of the value of Indonesia's exports trade came from three commodities. As the figures show, Indonesia's trade balance deteriorated between 1955 and 1964. As for financial stability, between 1957 and 1965 the cost of living index (1957=100) rose by 19 per cent in 1959 and 594 per cent in 1965.

As table 1 shows, production during the decade 1954–1964 showed a sluggishness or decline for the most part: rubber production declined over the period by 3.6 per cent; smallholding copra production increased by 1.2 per cent per annum, estate palm oil production by 1.5 per cent per annum; tin production slumped by 50 per cent, and of the major export commodities only petroleum showed a significant increase in production (115 per cent). More significant, however, are the figures for food crop production. Rice production increased by 1.3 per cent per annum (almost 30 per cent of the rate of population increase). Taking into account seed retention and losses (about 6 per cent of production) and imports (6.31 million tons between 1958 and 1964), per capita annual consumption of rice declined from 91 kilogrammes in 1958 to 86 kilogrammes in 1964. However, aggregating rice and maize production (given the major boost to maize production which was part of Sukarno's policy), gross production *per capita* increased from 107 kilogrammes per annum in 1955 to 109 kilogrammes in 1959 to 111 kilogrammes in 1964 (with net consumption some 5 per cent less). By the mid-1960s, net food supplies available per capita (average 1964–66) were the second lowest in the world, and so too was average daily protein intake.

Thus, by 1965 the Indonesian economy was virtually stagnant, and had undergone little of the radical restructuring so necessary for development. The population remained amongst the poorest in the world (the average annual income per capita fell from $77 in 1960 to $69 in 1963). Wide disparities remained between a densely populated Java and the less densely populated outer islands, which provided most foreign exchange and subsidized development in Java. Infrastructural development had not brought transport facilities back to pre-war efficiency, despite considerable investment, and production suffered as a result of this and wider neglect. By 1966, Indonesia had incurred a foreign debt of $1,630 million ($854 million to the West and $775 million to the Eastern bloc) and the trading economy was bordering on chaos. What was more, little attempt had been made to exploit effectively large known reserves of timber and many basic minerals—commodities vital to the industrialized Western countries and Japan.

CONSOLIDATION OF THE "NEW ORDER"

After the 1965–66 crisis, the new Suharto administration began a change from a bureaucratic, badly-managed, centrally-controlled economy to a liberal market economy underpinned by State planning and foreign investment. The "New Order" openly reflected Western development concepts and strategies: Indonesia accepted the International Monetary Fund (IMF) stabilization programme; the new economic leaders were trained in the U.S.A.; Western aid resumed, channelled largely through the Intergovernmental Group for Indonesia (IGGI); food imports resumed from the West; and the 1967 Foreign Investment Law granted sweeping incentives to foreign investors.

The IMF stabilization model was followed closely. First, the government instituted anti-inflation measures including cuts in government spending and strict credit control. The 1967–72 period was marked by the achievement of a balanced budget by 1969, cuts in social expenditure (for example, free schooling was abolished), emphasis in government spending upon infrastructure, and tight credit control through high interest rates (in 1966, interest rates increased from 9 to 29 per cent per annum to 6 to 9 per cent per month for commercial bank lending, and 15 to 20 per cent per month on curb market lending: rates for 1967 and 1968 were, respectively, 3.5 per cent and 10 to 15 per cent per month, and 3.7 per cent and 8 per cent per month). Inflation dropped from 650 per cent in 1966, to 120 per cent in 1967, 85 per cent in 1968, and 10 per cent in 1969.

Secondly, the rupiah was devalued. The exchange rate moved from U.S. $1=Rs. 156 (1967) to $1=Rs. 325 (1969) then to $1=Rs. 415 (1971). At the same time, the complicated foreign exchange control was ended in 1970 after 30 years, by the merging of multiple exchange rates.

Thirdly, foreign investment was encouraged by the 1967 Foreign Investment Law. This encouraged investment outside transport, power, and telecommunications; but, even here, joint ventures were allowed, with the foreign investor having full powers to appoint managers and foreign personnel. Priority sectors for foreign capital included export-oriented industries, those using local raw materials, and manufacturing of basic consumer goods like food and clothing. Considerable incentives, including tax exemptions, were given to foreign investors. There was a guarantee of free profit repatriation and against state expropriation (although a general rider provided for eventual local participation, with no specific details announced).

Thus by 1970 a complete reversal of economic policy was accomplished within three years of the overthrow of Sukarno. The implications of this, and subsequent developments, are examined below.

Economic Planning: REPELITA I

In 1969, the First Five-Year Plan (*Repelita I*) began. Formulated by the National Planning Board (BAPPENAS) with American guidance, it was a modest plan involving expenditure equivalent to half a year's national income and 66 per cent underwritten by foreign aid (from 71 per cent IGGI aid in 1969 to 41.5 per cent in 1973/74). The plan had two objectives: the construction of an infrastructure to serve both foreign investment and agriculture (over 50 per cent of the Plan's budget went to infrastructural development) and modernization of the agricultural economy by irrigation rehabilitation and more especially the introduction of a "Green Revolution" strategy, using high-yielding varieties of rice, and increased use of fertilizer, pesticides and mechanical equipment, to achieve food self-sufficiency and lessen rural discontent. Agriculture, producing 55 per cent of the 1968 G.N.P., 60 per cent of exports, and involving 72 per cent of the population, was clearly a priority for planning.

Table 3

REPELITA I (1969–74)

('000 million rupiahs)

	'000 million rupiahs	%
Economic sector:	829	78.3
Agriculture and Irrigation	319	30.1
Industry and mining	130	12.3
Electricity	100	9.4
Communications and tourism	230	21.7
Villages	50	4.7
Social sector:	172	16.2
Health and family planning	42	4.0
Education and culture	95	9.0
Other social fields	35	3.3
General sector:	58	5.5
Defence and security	28	2.6
Miscellaneous	30	2.8
TOTAL	1,059*	100.0

* $3,851 million at the 1968 exchange rate ($1=275 rupiahs).

REPELITA II (1974–79)

	'000 million rupiahs	%
Economic sector:		
Agriculture and irrigation	1,001.6	19.1
Industry and mining	185.8	3.5
Electricity and power	387.8	7.4
Communications and tourism	831.7	15.8
Trade and co-operatives	37.9	0.7
Manpower and transmigration	69.7	1.3
Regional and local development	930.6	17.7
Social sector:		
Health, family planning and social welfare	192.1	3.7
Education, culture and religion	540.8	10.3
Housing and water supply	101.6	1.9
General sector:		
Defence and security	156.0	3.0
Scientific and technical research	101.3	1.9
State apparatus	123.0	2.3
Government capital participation	562.9	10.7
Information and communications	26.7	0.5
TOTAL	5,249.2†	100.0

† $12,650 million at 1973 exchange rate ($1=415 rps).

The plan called for an increase in rice area from 8.5 million hectares to 9.3 million by 1974 (largely by rebuilding delapidated irrigation systems) and the introduction of high-yielding varieties of rice into 4 million hectares of the planned 9.3 million by 1974 to achieve a 1974 production of 15.4 million tons of milled rice (33 per cent higher than 1968). Of the planned 319,000 million rupiahs allocated to agriculture, 74 per cent was for maintenance and construction of irrigation, 8.5 per cent for increasing rice production through the supply and distribution of seeds, fertilizers, mechanical inputs, credit, and technical services, 7.2 per cent was for improving estate cultivation, 3.1 per cent for forestry, and the remaining 7.2 per cent was for cultivation of secondary food crops, fisheries, poultry farming, cattle breeding, and dairying. Village development, in many ways complementary to the task of increasing production, absorbed 4.7 per cent of budgeted expenditure in addition to the 30 per cent allocated to agriculture and irrigation.

To extend the area under intensified cropping, the Government used the two key programmes of BIMAS (*Bimbingan Massa*, or Mass Guidance) and INMAS (*Intensifikasi Massa*, Mass Intensification). The first grew out of Sukarno's 1965 Mass Guidance for Self-sufficiency in Food Programme (*Bimbingan Masal*

Swasembada Bahan Makanan). In its revised form it is basically a programme to provide cheap credit from Bank Rakyat Indonesia (the State People's Bank) for essential inputs like fertilizers, pesticides and seeds. INMAS (also inspired in 1965) is geared to areas where farmers are financially more secure, and provides for the distribution of essential agricultural equipment. The two programmes are serviced within an organizational structure comprising the *Badan Usaha Unit Desa* (BUUD, or Hamlet Unit Enterprise Body) and the *Koperasi Usaha Unit Desa* (KUUD, or Hamlet Unit Enterprise Co-operative), and covering a BIMAS area of 600 to 1,000 hectares. The hamlet unit is the focal point for agricultural development, and the BUUD/KUUDs were designed to co-ordinate economic activities at this level, as well as to service the BIMAS/INMAS programmes. They have four functions: to provide credit from the State Bank, extension services, production needs such as fertilizers and seeds at fixed prices, and processing equipment (e.g., huskers and driers) to allow farmers to process their own grain and earn higher prices. The State Procurement Agency (BULOG) is responsible for collecting surplus grain through the BUUD/KUUDs, and stockpiling rice.

As for cash-cropping, forestry, fishing, poultry and livestock rearing, 17.5 per cent of agricultural spending, and 5.3 per cent of total plan spending, was allocated to rehabilitate and develop activities providing about 60 per cent of Indonesia's 1969 exports by value. All these sectors have been neglected: estate agriculture, small holding agriculture, fishing and forestry. Plans were to rationalize estate agriculture, concentrating on the more efficient: there was to be rehabilitation and expansion, technological improvement, better marketing and processing, and extension of credit to the better managed estates. However, little was said about small-holding cash-cropping, while forestry was to be left largely to foreign enterprise.

Besides irrigation, infrastructural development absorbed about 33 per cent of planned expenditure (road rehabilitation and electricity generation each took 9.4 per cent of the plan budget). A major obstacle to economic development had long been the weak infrastructure: 70 per cent of roads were virtually unfit for use, and two-thirds of railway motive power was over 40 years old; besides, infrastructural development had been very uneven, concentrating in Java and eastern Sumatra. To facilitate better marketing, and to allow expanded economic development throughout the archipelago, major infrastructural improvement was clearly essential.

As for industry, the Government saw previous nationalization and state intervention, foreign exchange restrictions, restrictions on imports of essential equipment, poor marketing and infrastructure, and inflation as contributing to industrial stagnation. Between 1966 and 1968, de-nationalization, encouragement of overseas investment, easing of foreign exchange restrictions, and a reduction in inflation were all expected to lead to industrial expansion. However, before the plan period, domestic manufacturing investment contracted. The plan was to boost industrialization, especially through foreign investment: hence the low proportion of planned spending on industry. The high profitability of manufacturing (because of low labour costs, generous fiscal incentives, and ample local raw materials) meant greater appeal to private capital, thus the government's planned 110,000 million rupiahs allocation was expected to be matched by private (largely foreign) investment of 140,500 million rupiahs. Five categories of industry were identified for special attention: agriculture-supporting industries, import-substituting industries, industries processing local raw materials, labour-intensive industries, and industries that induce regional development through their cumulative effect.

Specifically, fertilizer, cement and chemical industries would absorb 46 per cent of public plus private spending with emphasis on petrochemical complexes; for fertilizers and cement, especially, Indonesia was heavily dependent on imports. Other industries to be expanded were textiles (because the sector is labour-intensive and import-substituting), pulp and paper (linked to forestry), pharmaceutical industries, light and home industries, and metal, tool, and engineering industries.

Overall, productive capacity was to be raised by 90 per cent over the plan period. Near self-sufficiency was hoped for by 1974 in fertilizers (90 per cent imported), cement (50 per cent imported before a major construction boom), textiles (95 per cent imported) and pharmaceuticals (90 per cent imported), and petroleum and timber-based industries were expected to show dramatic increases in output, greatly reducing import-dependence in chemicals, plastics, synthetic fibres, processed timber, and paper.

Metal mining was to be left almost entirely to foreign investors, apart from some provision of infrastructure, operating within the scope of the 1967 Foreign Investment Law. Apart from oil and timber, metal extraction was a potentially highly profitable sector: besides established workings of tin and bauxite, and lesser workings of nickel and coal, Indonesia had considerable and relatively little developed reserves of nickel, copper, coal and precious metals. Foreign influence over the administration, and high costs of exploration, were both key factors in deciding government policy.

The greatest potential for mineral development was in oil and natural gas, especially offshore. Most production comes from the Caltex Sumatra fields, but apart from this there was little oil production (either offshore or onshore) in 1968. By 1970, however, over 30 oil companies had production-sharing agreements with the State oil company (PERTAMINA).

PERTAMINA was virtually autonomous from the National Planning Board (BAPPENAS), and was overseer of potentially the most profitable sector of the whole economy. In considering the evolution of the Indonesian economy after 1968, and in particular the significance of REPELITA I, the role of oil as a source of revenue, and of PERTAMINA as an entrepreneur, is of critical importance. By entering into production-sharing contracts with foreign oil companies, by controlling Indonesia's increasing oil revenues ($388 million in 1969 and $5,150 million in 1974), and by mortgaging this revenue to heavy foreign loans, PERTAMINA developed a "parallel economy" of its own with considerable influence in every sector and sub-sector of the national economy. Its management differed from that of BAPPENAS, its budget was separate (and at least half the value of the total national budget), and its priorities frequently did not coincide with those of the technocrats managing REPELITA I. Thus a clear distinction must be made, in terms of the structure of the "modern" Indonesian economy and in terms of development policy followed, between the economy of General Sutowo (PERTAMINA) and the economy of Dr. Widjojo (REPELITA).

During the five years up to 1974, then, PERTAMINA expanded its activities throughout the Indonesian economy at the same time as a semblance of planned economic development was being attempted under REPELITA I.

In assessing developments since 1969, it must be remembered that REPELITA was not a plan for thorough-going state-controlled economic change, setting imperative targets to be met. It was an indicative set of guidelines for government investment in agriculture, with the object of achieving self-sufficiency (at least in rice) and in infrastructural development necessary for foreign investment.

AGRICULTURE

Food crops

To assess progress in the agricultural sector since 1967, it is essential we recognize a number of key points.

Firstly, most of the 70 per cent of Indonesians living in rural areas work within a seriously defective agrarian structure. This is marked by a predominance of small, non-viable holdings; a marked disparity in land-ownership (60/70 per cent of land is owned by 10 to 20 per cent of rural families); a high degree of landlessness (40 to 45 per cent); a high degree of un- and under-employment, respectively about 18 per cent and 35 per cent; heavy indebtedness of over 60 per cent of Javanese peasants; a combination of high rents and high interest charges to local moneylenders, meaning that the renting small-holder retains little more than 30 per cent of his harvest. These features combine with inefficient marketing, credit and infrastructural facilities, and considerable administrative corruption. The result is a generally low-yielding agriculture marked by extensive poverty, malnutrition and inefficiency.

Secondly, there are marked regional disparities between areas within Java, and between Java and the outer islands.

Thirdly, non-agricultural activities are insufficiently developed to absorb much excess labour from the countryside. The decline of village industries as a result of urban industrialization, increasing capital-intensity in agriculture, and a high rate of population growth will increase un- and under-employment.

Fourthly, higher average production or productivity figures do not necessarily mean increasing returns to most farmers, and increasing and more widespread rural prosperity. A country may achieve self-sufficiency at a certain level of average production per capita without most of the population (especially rural) necessarily being individually self-sufficient.

Finally, while some areas of Java are overpopulated in terms of density (about 2,000 per square kilometre) the problem of Java's overpopulation is more correctly a problem of *under-employment*. This has

Table 4

Food and cash crop production 1968–74

(area in '000 hectares and production in '000 metric tons)

	1968		1970		1972		1974	
	Area	Production	Area	Production	Area	Production	Area	Production
Food crops:								
Rice (paddy) . . .	8,031	14,858	8,186	17,529	7,983	18,031	8,537	22,732
Maize . . .	3,220	3,166	3,018	2,888	2,160	2,254	2,648	3,240
Cassava . . .	1,503	11,356	1,434	10,451	1,418	10,042	1,400*	10,090*
Sweet potatoes . .	404	2,364	356	3,029	318	1,944	360*	2,250*
Groundnuts . . .	394	478	402	488	356	455	409	525
Soybeans . . .	677	420	684	488	685	518	753	550
Export crops:								
Sugar cane . . .	114	9,190	134	9,785	149	12,133	150*	13,500*
Tea	111	73	120	67	96	64	100*	67*
Coffee . . .	338	157	n.a.	185	388	189	390*	168*
Rubber . . .	n.a.	730	n.a.	811	n.a.	819	n.a.	985
Copra . . .	n.a.	629	n.a.	694	n.a.	820	n.a.	760*
Palm oil . . .	n.a.	188	n.a.	215	n.a.	269	n.a.	320*
Palm kernels . . .	n.a.	40	n.a.	48	n.a.	59	n.a.	67

* Estimates.

major relevance to policies of economic planning and population control in Indonesia.

In 1968, the gross production of milled rice was 11.66 million metric tons; by 1974/75, production had reached 15.4 million tons. The average annual increase in gross rice production had been 3.4 per cent between 1951 and 1971, production decreased by 3 per cent in 1972, and increased over the next three years by, respectively, 9 per cent, 3.5 per cent and 5.7 per cent. For 1975/76, a 4.8 per cent increase is expected bringing production up to 16.2 million tons.

Thus the quantitative target set under REPELITA I was achieved. But the 33 per cent increase was achieved by intensification of farming not by any major extension of cultivated land: planted rice area increased by only 469,000 hectares (5.8 per cent) between 1968 and 1974, compared with a planned 800,000 hectares.

The BIMAS intensification schemes were resumed in 1967, after two years lapse. They worked in conjunction with a number of multinational corporations (especially CIBA, Mitsubishi, Hoechst, and Agrarund Hydro-Teknik), with the government agreeing to pay $54 per hectare of riceland converted to "miracle rice". To this end, the companies subcontracted with local firms to provide most inputs of fertilizers, pesticides, and farm equipment; the government supplied HYV seeds, and the farmers their labour. Peasants were given loans through BIMAS agencies, to be repaid with a sixth of the harvest; this was to be collected by the army as a salary supplement for government employees.

By 1969, 20 per cent of riceland in Java was under contract to the multinational companies. But serious problems arose during the scheme: seed, fertilizers and pesticides never arrived; pesticides killed fish, a basic source of protein; farmers refused to repay loans; and armed compulsion was used to force peasant participation. Even in the best agricultural areas harvests were down from 2.5 tons per acre (1965) to 2 tons (1969), in many areas crops were largely lost because inputs never arrived, and some harvests were as low as 100 to 400 kilogrammes per acre. Peasants under-reported harvests to lower the rice levy, while local army officers over-estimated production to increase their share. The project continued into the 1970 dry season, and then ceased.

A new BIMAS was then introduced. Loans were granted directly to farmers by new village banks of the State Bank; supplies of fertilizer and pesticide at subsidized prices were made through the usual marketing channels instead of by direct government distribution, and farmers were given greater freedom to choose the mix of inputs they wished.

BIMAS went hand in hand with the INMAS scheme, and both worked at the hamlet level through the BUUD/KUUD scheme of co-operative development (*see* under Economic Planning). Since 1973 BUUDs and KUUDs have combined in many areas, and the BIMAS and INMAS programmes they service were officially estimated to have covered 4.8 million hectares by 1975. However, the effect of these schemes was not as widespread as this suggests as only 1.54 million hectares (18 per cent of riceland) was planted with HYV rice. Besides, there was a need for administrative reorganization, largely because of mismanagement and corruption in the distribution of BIMAS credit, especially for fertilizers. Another problem was the conflict between assuring a low rice price for the urban population and giving farmers a fair return. Subsidizing imported rice made it available at a third the international price (in 1974, $480 million were spent on rice subsidies) but the farm price was also kept down. To counter this, fertilizer subsidies were introduced, bringing the price down to 25 per cent of the world price but over 70 per cent of farmers still had no access to fertilizers, and also faced price rises of other commodities.

By holding down on-farm prices artificially, the government had not only dampened economic development, it penalized heavily the indebted peasant who had to sell or buy rice on the open market, at low selling prices and high buying prices. The rice subsidy freed 388,000 million rupiahs ($935 million) of urban expenditure for non-food consumer goods, but deprived growers of a potential income of 1,977,000 million rupiahs which could have been spent on industrial goods, including textiles. Further, the burden on the tenant and share-cropper farmer was increased by landowners and creditors passing down their losses in heavier exactions. In such a situation, BIMAS schemes had a detrimental effect on the small farmer: loans, and other facilities for increasing yields, were monopolized by larger farmers, and the smaller peasant's only incentive to grow more rice was the need to pay higher exactions, not to boost his real income.

In general, the government seemed more concerned with curbing inflation than ensuring a fair price to farmers. However, success in anti-inflationary policies led to a decision to raise the padi procurement price by 40 per cent in early 1975 and also to increase BIMAS credit per hectare by 29 per cent and the fertilizer price by 50 per cent. Although the fertilizer price increased proportionately more than the rice price, it was estimated that padi production costs would be lower than the sale price, giving a net gain of 11,180 rupiahs ($27) per ton of padi. It was hoped that the resulting increase in retail price would be neutralized by releases from BULOG stocks: but BULOG's influence is confined to main urban areas; elsewhere the price continued to rise. The small, indebted peasant, subject to such market conditions, fell deeper into debt.

Typically, a group of village landowners, government officers, and town employees control capital for poor farmers, and this capital forms loans against the future labour or crops of poor farmers at 30 to 40 per cent below the market wage for rural labour and the market price for rice. In such a situation, improved technology was considered ideal. It would (theoretically) raise food production and the standard of living, cut imports and food prices, and (by increasing his productivity) allow the smallholder to assert himself from lenders.

But the official loans and extension of technology did not reach the smallholder but accumulated amongst the wealthy, and smallholders and the landless have hardly participated at all in BIMAS programmes. Even in villages where ecological conditions were optimal for the success of HYV rice, and where class divisions were not as sharp as elsewhere, only 20 per cent of farm households were using loans in 1973 and in other villages the proportion was even lower.

The reason lay in the tenure system. With most farms well below viable size, and a high degree of landlessness, there is extreme concentration of land-ownership and debt-bondage—meaning that a few large landowners (owning over 10 hectares) use BIMAS credit, intensify production with low-wage labour under the *ijon kereja* system (work through debt bondage) over extensive areas, and thus control the bulk of the harvest at the same time as they increase it.

While the *ijon kereja* system is common, with many farmers preferring to use labour rather than capital-intensive measures the relationship between rich and poor in rural Java has gone beyond even increasing debt-bondage: in South Central Java, wealthy households use increased productivity to buy land of poorer peasants; in West Java, where disparities in land holdings are even more extreme, wealthier farmers buy Japanese rice-field tractors and home-milling equipment, and labour-saving harvesting equipment. In both cases, consolidation of the wealthy farmer's position leads to increasing rural-urban migration in an effort to escape deepening poverty: 130,000 migrants enter Jakarta annually, for example, despite a 1971 edict declaring it a "closed city".

Table 5

Rice intensification

(quintals/ha.)

	BIMAS Average	INMAS Average
1969 . .	38.14	36.28
1970 . .	44.98	41.92
1971 . .	44.23	39.45
1972 . .	49.38	43.45
1973 . .	51.26	45.56

Source: Buku Repelita II.

Table 6

Milled rice production

('000 metric tons)

	Gross	Net*
1968 . .	11,667	9,560
1969 . .	12,349	10,000
1970 . .	13,140	11,440
1971 . .	13,724	12,220
1972 . .	13,183	—
1973 . .	14,607	13,630
1974 . .	15,452	14,520
1975 . .	16,200	15,000†

* Allowing 6 per cent for seed and losses.

† Estimate.

Certainly, in terms of overall increased productivity, BIMAS has had notable results. Average productivity in areas affected by BIMAS/INMAS schemes is about twice that of ordinary fields.

But overall production figures are misleading. While gross rice production increased between 1968 and 1974 at an average annual rate of 5.4 per cent (about 2.3 per cent per capita), supplies are still low: average annual net rice availability per capita (including imports) rose from 87 kilogrammes per capita in 1968 to 124.8 kilogrammes per capita in 1974.

Further, this average conceals wide disparities between urban and rural dwellers and between social classes. Most rural dwellers exist on well below the average.

Another necessary qualification is that the increase in rice production was achieved partly by concentrating effort, irrigation facilities, and fertilizers to produce a second crop on land previously used for other crops. As a result, acreage and production of other food crops declined by 13 per cent and 9 per cent respectively. This qualitative change in farming had two main effects: first, with lower increases in production of higher protein staples like groundnuts and soybeans, and declines in production of sweet potatoes, cassava, and maize together with poor production of fish, animal meat, and milk (*see* Table 7) the average rural diet is far more starchy and less nutritious than it was in 1968; second, total staple food production per capita has declined, according to FAO estimates, from 167.4 kilogrammes to 162.1 kilogrammes between 1968 and 1973).

It would seem from the above that, although priority was given (at least theoretically) to agriculture in the 1969-74 plan, there was little qualitative improvement in rural conditions. Gross rice production increased, infrastructure such as irrigation works improved, and the area under HYV rice increased but the effects of these achievements were concentrated in a relatively small proportion of cropland and within a relatively small group of the population.

Cash crops

While data for cash crop production are less satisfactory than those for food production, available evidence suggests that progress has been variable especially in terms of the relative positions of estate and smallholder agriculture.

In 1969, estate and smallholder cash-cropping occupied about 35 per cent of arable area (over 6 million hectares) and provided 70 per cent of Indonesia's exports by value contributing such products as rubber, palm oil, tea, coffee, pepper, hard fibre, and copra. Coffee, tea and tobacco production went mainly to domestic consumption.

Of the 1969 rubber output of 738,000 metric tons, over 66 per cent came from smallholdings (rubber was then contributing over a quarter of all exports by value); smallholdings also accounted for 45 per cent of tea output, 25 per cent of sugar output, 80 per cent of tobacco, and almost all pepper, kapok, copra, coffee and spices (especially clove and nutmeg). Oil palm and sugar were predominantly estate crops.

Up to 1975, the most marked production increases have been in these two crops (refined estate sugar production, for example, rose from 550,000 tons in 1968 to nearly 1 million tons in 1974, but this was still below domestic demand), while production of palm oil and kernels increased by 70 per cent.

After a long period of virtual stagnation, rubber production increased by an average 5.2 per cent a year between 1970 and 1975. Although expansion of area accounted for part of this increase, most came from foreign and state plantations. Although smallholders account for over two-thirds of production, they were virtually ignored during REPELITA I. Of a total estimated smallholder area of 1.8 million hectares, only 20,000 hectares were replanted. In 1974, only 400,000 hectares were planted with trees at peak maturity and 100,000 hectares with high yielding trees. Trees over 25 years old covered more than 1 million hectares, and productivity was as low as 400 kilogrammes per hectare compared with 800 kilogrammes on foreign estates. Another 130,000 hectares is "sleeping area" (of remote or low-yielding trees tapped only when prices are high); thus, a short-term production increase is possible by tapping this area: in 1973, with the rise in world prices, smallholder output increased from 570,000 metric tons to 630,000 metric tons largely through exploiting the "sleeping area".

Increased productivity is impeded by the smallholder industry's structure. Rubber is a secondary crop for most farmers, who receive about 35 per cent of the final f.o.b. price. Although attempts have been made to establish co-operatives, these have largely failed for lack of official enthusiasm and capital.

Crops such as coconuts, coffee, spices, and kapok have equally suffered. Lack of official encouragement, poor infrastructural and marketing facilities, dispersal of production away from Java and throughout the archipelago or (as in the case of spices) concentration in distant, largely non-Malay, and neglected islands, and the relative insignificance of the crops as exports have all combined to weaken the small-holder cash crop sector.

Animal husbandry and fishing

The main sources of animal protein in rural Indonesia are fish, poultry and eggs. Beef products are more for urban consumption, and almost all high-grade meat is imported. Rural consumption of beef is limited by the need to maintain buffaloes as draft animals and cows as milk producers, but equally the difficulty of raising livestock for meat amongst smallholders is obvious (land is not available, and cattle-breeding is an expensive form of calorie production). Pork is produced and consumed entirely by the mainly urban

Table 7
Livestock products and fish
('000 metric tons)

	1968	1973
Beef, veal and buffalo meat*	155†	165
Mutton, lamb and goats' meat*	47†	36
Pig meat*	66†	89
Poultry meat*	61†	70
Cows' milk	34†	36†
Poultry eggs	126†	137
Fish (inland)	436.5	440.0
Fish (marine)	722.5	860.0

* Inspected production only, i.e. meat from animals slaughtered under government supervision.
† FAO estimate.

Chinese and the non-Malay population of eastern Indonesia.

After 1973 a more rapid growth in beef production is likely through expansion of large-scale ranching projects.

In 1971, the fishing industry contributed about 3.4 per cent of GNP and employed about 1.2 million people. Of an estimated total 1975 catch of 1.37 million tons, only 2 per cent was gained by modern methods, and a good proportion of the inland catch comes from irrigation canals, as a secondary activity to wet-rice farming; marine fishing is poorly developed, employing 850,000 fishermen and 245,000 vessels in 1975, and subject to increasing Japanese competition.

As so much fishing activity is part-time and linked to inland or coastal farming, estimates of either total number of people involved or total catch are bound to be vague. However, it is certain that fishing has a considerable potential for development: the potential sea catch alone is over 4.5 million tons. As fish is the basic source of animal protein in Indonesia, the need to realize this potential is clear.

MINING

Oil and natural gas

Oil deserves special attention for its decisive role in shaping the pattern and progress of Indonesian economic development, under the management of PERTAMINA, since 1968. Indonesia has 13,000 million barrels of estimated recoverable reserves of oil, and 34,700,000 million cubic feet of recoverable gas reserves. With a prospective area of 809,600 square kilometres on land, and 1,500,000 square kilometres offshore (to the 300 metre isobath), designated oil areas in Indonesia are ten times the size of the European North Sea area, with dozens of sedimentary basins not yet tested. At the end of 1975, Indonesia had 66 rigs working, 16 offshore and 50 onshore. While this was only a third of those operating in the boom period of 1973/74, the number was exceeded only by the United States, Canada and Mexico. With the most promising land and offshore area in South East Asia, Indonesia has seen the most comprehensive oil search in the region. In 1974 alone,

231 wells were drilled: 28 were oil producers, 18 gas producers, and 25 both oil and gas producers.

Exploration and development of oil and gas resources were accelerated after 1967: from $78 million in 1969, exploration and development expenditure rose to an estimated $690 million in 1975. Most of this activity involves United States investment: U.S. companies have over $2,400 million invested in Indonesian oil, and pump 90 per cent of all crude oil.

Between 1967 and 1974, crude oil production rose from 189 million barrels per year to 507 million, but dropped to 479.4 million in 1975/76. However, by March 1976 production had picked up to reach 1.5 million barrels per day for the first time.

In 1974, domestic consumption was 12 per cent of production (Japan took 62 per cent and the United States 26 per cent). On a per capita basis, Indonesia's oil consumption is 2 per cent that of the United States, but if the country accelerates industrialization fuel demand and depletion of reserves will increase. At the 1974/75 rate of extraction, the country had about 26 years' supply; if, as some planners hope, the rate doubles to nearer 3 million barrels per day by 1980, known reserves will be exhausted by 1990.

However, the companies that extract the oil (and their home governments) are reacting to growing "oil nationalism" in South East Asia by threatening a 33 per cent cut in exploration for new reserves. During 1975 and 1976, Indonesia increased its demands for a fairer part of company profit.

Except for Caltex, which gives the government a 60:40 profit split, most oil companies in Indonesia operate under the production-sharing formula introduced in 1966 by PERMINA, one of PERTAMINA's predecessors. This leaves ownership of the natural resources with the government, while the company acts as contractor and puts up necessary capital. Of oil and gas produced, 40 per cent is retained by the company as production costs, and the remainder is split between company and Government.

In April 1976 Caltex agreed to the government's demand for an extra $1 per barrel, leaving the company with $1.30, still higher than the average 50 cents per barrel in the Middle East. The government also hopes to gain an extra $2.50 from other companies—mainly from a cut in companies' cost deduction of 40 per cent of gross production.

Basically, the Government is willing to exchange lower oil exploration for higher revenue from production, sharing in companies dominating offshore activities, from which most future production increases will come.

The change in oil pricing must be seen in the light of a tight budgetary situation, and expenditure burdened by the PERTAMINA debt, preparations for the 1977 elections, increased military spending, a constantly rising development and administration bill, and movement from a year of a marked shortfall in projected revenue payments to a year of lower receipts (given sluggish oil production and exports).

In 1974/75 oil produced $2,600 million net in foreign exchange or 66 per cent of government revenue (compared with 10.5 per cent in 1967). 1975/76 oil revenues have been revised downwards by 24 per cent to about $3,000 million.

A balance needs to be established between a hasty recovery of oil production for immediate gain and slower recovery for long-term benefit. Insofar as oil revenues are not fundamentally affecting Indonesia's major development problems but, because of the institutional framework within which they are collected and used, actually exacerbating most of these problems, a proper utilization of oil revenue must wait on a thorough reappraisal of development priorities and structures. However, there exists the short-term problem of a desire to produce as much as possible to pay off PERTAMINA debts. Through the development and management of oil production in Indonesia, and overwhelming emphasis upon oil, there has been established a cumulative process of encouraging the development of a high-growth corporate machine, bringing about its own downfall by massive overspending and thereby encouraging further emphasis on short-term returns. Given the increase in debt servicing as a proportion of total export revenue from about 9 per cent in 1974/75 (the first year of REPELITA II) to 18.6 per cent in 1978/79, the question must be posed: is oil the basis of increasing self-reliance, as was assumed in 1974?

Other minerals

Mineral production outside the oil sector has developed considerably since 1967, with the exception

Table 8

Mineral production, 1955–74
(metric tons)

	1955	1959	1964	1967	1972	1973	1974
Tin	34,000	21,960	16,607	13,819	21,766	22,492	25,630
Bauxite	520,000	387,300	647,805	912,266	1,277,000	1,229,000	1,290,054
Nickel*	n.a.	n.a.	47,950	170,601	935,075	867,046	878,855
Coal	700,500	637,600	445,862	208,313	179,200	148,900	156,200
Copper	—	—	—	—	—	125,600†	230,700†

* Gross weight. The nickel content (in metric tons) was: 1,678 in 1964; 5,118 in 1967; 22,400 in 1972; 20,800 in 1973.
† 26 per cent concentrate.

of coal, which has shown a marked drop from its pre-war level of 2 million tons: while tin has yet to regain its 1954 peak output of 36,500 metric tons. The revival of bauxite production was already underway in the early 1960s, and the high post-1967 levels indicate a levelling off of production. The most dramatic increases have been in nickel and copper production.

All minerals are highly localized in production. Nickel is almost exclusively mined in Sulawesi. Indonesia has estimated reserves of over 40 million tons of nickel ore, sufficient, at 1974 extraction rates, for 47 years' production.

Copper is almost entirely produced in the Ertsberg Mountains area of Irian Jaya. The production company, Freeport Minerals, was the first investor to take advantage of the 1967 Foreign Investment Law, and embarked on a large-scale infrastructural development programme involving a 70-mile road, a new port, an airstrip and a power station. The 33.5 million tons of ore had a copper content of 3.5 per cent, together with small quantities of gold and silver, and its refined value was so high that Freeport earned enough in the first two years of production to recoup half the total financing of the project.

Bauxite is mined entirely on Bintan island, in the Riau archipelago, by ALCOA. However, ALCOA have confirmed a further major reserve of bauxite in West Kalimantan. At present 90 per cent of bauxite is exported to Japan.

Tin production comes from three mines on the islands, of Banka, Belitung, and Singkep, owned by the State Tin Corporation (P. N. Timah), with most production (about 16,000 tons) coming from Banka.

Coal production is undergoing major rehabilitation at its main producing region in South Sumatra. In 1975 Indonesia granted Royal Dutch Shell a concession area. With $7 million already spent in prospecting, the company has a proposed investment of $1,200 million for development over a 30-year period, to produce coal entirely for export. By the mid-1980s, it is expected that coal production will leap to 30 million metric tons per annum, becoming the second foreign exchange earner after oil. While recent figures on reserves are not available, a 1960 estimate put Indonesia's total reserves at 200 million tons of high grade coal, and 2,017 million tons of brown coal.

Forestry

Forests cover 120 million hectares, or two-thirds of the land area of Indonesia. While this is 35 per cent of all tropical forest reserves (comprising 70 per cent hardwood stands), only 24 million hectares are exploitable: protective forests, to regulate water supply and control floods, comprise 48 million hectares, forests which are suitable for conversion to farmland 18 million hectares, and damaged forests 30 million hectares. However, Indonesian forests contain the most extensive concentrations of tropical hardwoods in the world. A good site will produce 100 cubic metres per hectare of wood valued at $15 to $30 per cubic metre (f.o.b. 1969).

The timber industry is the fastest growing activity in Indonesia. Between 1963 and 1973 the output of logs for industrial use rose from 4 million cubic metres to an estimated 25 million cubic metres, a growth rate faster than the oil industry. Timber has become Indonesia's second largest source of export earnings, rising from 9.8 per cent of exports in 1970/71 to 19.9 per cent in 1973/74, but slumping to 8.8 per cent in 1974/75, as a result of recession in the industry. The export of logs and sawnwood rose from 3.4 million cubic metres in 1966 to 10.5 million in 1970, reaching a peak of 19.4 million cubic metres in 1973 and falling to 18.6 million in 1974/75. However, there are a number of major problems facing Indonesia's forestry economy. The first is robber-cutting: with over 120 million cubic metres of saleable timber extracted since 1966, over 3.0 million hectares of forest have been felled, including most of the best stands, with little regard for conservation. This exploitation reflects a lack of political control over private (and foreign) firms. With the most accessible and profitable stands gone, companies are driving further inland to less accessible and often more mixed stands, cutting indiscriminately to obtain valuable species as quickly as possible. The second problem is the high degree of speculation and therefore corruption involved in the industry. Thirdly, investors' excessive mechanization and employment of Filipino and Malaysian workers led to a relatively low creation of jobs for Indonesians and a banning of further foreign workers. Fourthly, there has been very little timber processing: although foreign concessionairies are expected to set up processing plants within three years of starting operations (leading to 60 per cent of log output being processed domestically within 10 years), few have done so: in 1973, 2 per cent of exports were of processed timber. The reasons are the high profitability of logging; the lack of infrastructure; the desire to keep processing in home countries; the difficulty of meeting international quality standards, due to shortage of skilled manpower and excessive bureaucracy: approval from eight ministries is needed for a new mill.

Government concern over the decline of productive area, the neglect of replanting, and company reluctance to "Indonesianize" led to a ban in 1974 on further concessions to foreigners (although domestic investment and sub-contracting to foreigners were still allowed). In 1975 the Government decreed that within 10 years of starting a logging project, indigenous Indonesian participation should be 51 per cent. However, with skilled Indonesian labour and capital scarce (51 per cent local participation involves tens of millions of dollars in many cases), together with a run-down of the best stands and ending of the five-year tax exemption for most companies, the industry is facing a difficult future: increased exploitative cutting, inefficiency and run-down are becoming characteristic.

Manufacturing

As a result of expansion in other sectors of the economy, notably mining and forestry, the proportion of GNP from manufacturing fell from 13.2 per cent in 1958 to 11.2 per cent in 1967 and 8.7 per cent in

1973. However, for all main products except cement the increase in output during REPELITA I far exceeded the overall 90 per cent increase in manufacturing output hoped for in 1969, although self-sufficiency is still remote (with some exceptions, such as rubber tyres and electronic components, the bulk of which are exported). In 1974/75, 1.5 million tons of cement were imported, 75 per cent of paper needs, 1 million tons of steel and steel products, 600,000 tons of urea, and about 30 per cent of textile requirements.

Table 9

Manufacturing production 1969–74

	1969/70	1974/75
Textiles (million metres)	450	900
Fertilizers ('000 tons urea)	84	200
Cement ('000 tons)	542	900
Paper ('000 tons)	15.8	47
Motor vehicles ('000 4-wheeled)	5	59
Steel ('000 tons)	—	309*

* Miscellaneous products.

A number of major manufacturing projects were either initiated or completed during the Plan period. These included two new fertilizer plants (one producing an estimated 350,000 tons of urea by 1976, the second expected to open in 1976), a major petrochemical complex in South Sumatra (which began producing polypropylene in early 1974), and expansion of the Krakatau Steel Company plant at Cilegon. All were major investments by PERTAMINA. Numerous other projects (including two floating fertilizer plants, a central oil terminal at Semangka in Java, and an oil refinery complex on Batam Island) were postponed as a result of the PERTAMINA cash crisis during 1975.

The government's industrialization policy has come under criticism on a number of points: through the generous incentive scheme for foreign investors, capital-intensive industries and foreign control have been encouraged, while labour-intensive industries have gone bankrupt and domestic capital has been pushed into smaller and less profitable industries; a sharp regional imbalance has developed with most approved foreign investment in manufacturing concentrating in Java (80 per cent of the total in Jakarta and West Java) and most domestic manufacturing investment following suit; and there was excessive dependence on PERTAMINA, allowing it free rein to channel oil earnings and foreign loans into whatever project its director, Gen. Ibnu Sutowo, agreed upon with President Suharto, and (through its pattern of investment) further aggravating the localized, capital-intensive nature of development.

As for the first point, "excessive foreign control" is a function of greater capital intensity of foreign manufacturing projects and larger individual projects compared with domestically financed projects: while total approved foreign investment in manufacturing between 1967 and 1975 was marginally smaller than its private domestic counterpart, it was concentrated in only 30 per cent of the number of projects put up by private domestic capital; as a result, there was greater capital-intensity (three times as much overall, five times as much in textiles) and greater economies of scale. Outside PERTAMINA, local investment was far more diffused and poorly organized than foreign.

Table 10

Approved foreign and domestic investments in manufacturing (1967–August 1974)

Total foreign (million $)	1,809.7
Number of foreign projects	446
Textiles (million $)	843.2
(projects)	68
Total domestic (million $)	2,041.9
Number of domestic projects	1,480
Textiles (million $)	833.9
(projects)	333
Capital intensity (million $ per project)	
Foreign (total)	4.1
Domestic (total)	1.4
Foreign (textiles)	12.4
Domestic (textiles)	2.5

Source: Investment Co-ordinating Board, Jakarta.

Labour displacement has certainly occurred as a result of modernization in the rubber processing, tobacco, and textile industries, and small-scale industries based on handicrafts, fisheries, food and drink, plastics, and chemicals have also suffered. An example of both labour displacement and the centripetal tendency in industrial development is the situation in southern Sulawesi where, between 1968 and 1972, the number of small industries decreased from 3,855 to 2,432 (a 37 per cent decrease in four years): the number of textile factories (based mainly on handloom production) declined from 974 to 111 and handicraft industries from 1,243 to 537.

The problem of job creation is highlighted by projections for the Second Five-Year Plan period: an estimated 2.62 million jobs, at the most, are expected to be created outside manufacturing leaving 3.4 million new entrants to the labour force to be absorbed by manufacturing. At a conservative estimate of $3,000 per worker for capital intensity, there would need to be a total investment in manufacturing of $10,200 million to absorb new entrants alone.

INFRASTRUCTURE

Transport

During REPELITA I, about 20 per cent of state spending ($770 million) was allocated to improvement of communications. Most of this went to improvements in Java, where, for example, all "highways" were asphalted and 90 per cent of provincial roads "improved". Overall, 60 per cent of all highways were asphalted and 50 per cent of all provincial roads improved.

In 1974, of 85,000 kilometres of roads, 21,000 kilometres were asphalted. Officially, 23 per cent of all roads were described as in "good condition", 26 per cent "fair", and 41 per cent "very bad". By the end of REPELITA II (1979), it is hoped, the proportions will be, respectively, 50 per cent, 41 per cent and 9 per cent. Of the 8,500 kilometres of railway track all is in Java and Sumatra: track and bridges are in poor condition and two-thirds of railway motive power is over 40 years old.

Indonesia's merchant fleet comprises 513 vessels, with a gross tonnage of 618,590 tons, and nine local shipping companies (including the state-owned Pelayaran Nasional Indonesia, or Pelni Lines, with 60 ships). However, in addition to this PERTAMINA operated 86 tankers, with a total capacity of 3 million deadweight tons (more tonnage than the Indonesian navy), at the end of 1974. There are eight ocean ports with a loading capacity of 40,000 metric tons per day. The two major ports, Tanjung Priok near Jakarta (5 million tons handled in 1973, accounting for 70 per cent of Indonesia's imports and a high proportion of exports) and Tanjung Perak near Surabaya (3.3 million tons), have both been modernized since 1970 with the aid of foreign loans. Inter-island communication is poorly developed, a serious deficiency for an archipelago nation the size of Indonesia.

In 1975, the main state airline, Garuda, operated 30 aircraft both domestically and internationally; Merpati, the second state airline, operates domestically and regionally. There are also about 45 private or semi-private airlines operating, some foreign-controlled and some involved primarily with mineral development, including Pelita, the PERTAMINA airline. With 41 fixed wing aircraft (including F.27s, F.28s, and a Boeing 707) and 82 helicopters, Pelita was the largest airline in Southeast Asia in terms of aircraft; however, in 1976 both Pelita and the PERTAMINA tanker fleet were heavily trimmed as part of efforts to overcome the state oil company's financial crisis.

Airports are small and geared to domestic use, with the exception of Jakarta's Halim airport, Medan in Sumatra, and Denpasar in Bali.

Power

In 1974 Indonesia had 205 electricity generating stations (public and private) with an installed capacity of 1,055 megawatts (1,000 megawatts in Java). This compared with 653 megawatts in 1966. Factories still rely largely on their own generators: only 20 per cent of electricity sold by the state company was for industrial use in 1974. Gas supply is limited to major towns; in 1974, total output was an estimated 70 million cubic metres. While Indonesia produced 156,200 tons of coal in 1974, coal imports are needed for gas production. Similarly, despite its position as an oil exporter, Indonesia must import certain grades of oil; refinery capacity is 400,000 barrels per day, from eight refineries, with domestic consumption absorbing an eighth of production (i.e., 190,000 barrels a day). Hydro-electric power provides 38.8 per cent of Indonesia's energy supply, diesel 26.3 per cent, gas 10.3 per cent and steam 24.5 per cent. In addition, and estimated 110 to 115 million cubic metres of fuel wood are used annually.

In 1975 the per capita consumption of electricity was still only 18 kilowatt hours, an extremely low figure compared with other poor Asian countries.

A major development of energy resources will result from the Japanese-financed Asahan project (combining an aluminium smelter and two hydro-electric power stations on the Asahan River in North-east Sumatra). This $1,000 million complex is the key Sumatran element in REPELITA II, and apart from its smelting activities it is expected to provide an hydro-electric power capacity of 604 megawatts by 1984.

TRADE

Indonesia's exports are dominated by oil, which has been the largest export earner since the early 1960s: in 1964, oil and oil derivatives accounted for 36.4 per cent of export earnings, compared with rubber's 32 per cent; by 1974/75 oil's share of export

Table 11

Exports of oil, timber, and rubber, by value (%).

	Rubber	Timber	Oil
1964 . . .	32.0	—	36.4
1970/71 . . .	24.6	9.8	37.3
1971/72 . . .	17.9	13.5	44.0
1972/73 . . .	10.6	12.8	51.4
1973/74 . . .	12.1	17.9	50.0
1974/75 . . .	5.9	8.8	71.0

value was 71 per cent. Because of increases in the oil price, export trade more than doubled in value between 1973/74 and 1974/75, from $3,210 million to $7,430 million. Over 95 per cent of Indonesia's exports are raw or semi-processed materials (apart from oil, timber and rubber, there is tin, bauxite, copper, palm oil, coffee and numerous smaller items such as spices).

Imports for 1974/75 were valued at $4,900 million, and consisted of unprocessed or semi-processed manufacturing and construction materials (chemicals, cement, yarn, iron ore, etc.), 45 per cent; consumer goods including food, 22 per cent; and capital goods such as machines, electrical and railway equipment, 33 per cent.

Indonesia's main trading partner is Japan (with 49 per cent of exports and 36 per cent of imports in 1973/74), followed by the United States (15 per cent of exports and 16 per cent of imports) and Singapore (11 per cent of exports and 6 per cent of imports). However, with increased Japanese purchases of Chinese oil, and decreased domestic demand for oil and timber in 1974/75, Japan accounted for a lower proportion of Indonesian exports that year. Further, accurate figures for Indonesia-Singapore trade are lacking—official data greatly underestimate the value of this trade. Besides official reticence over Singapore trade, there is considerable "unofficial" trade with Malaysia and the Philippines (including barter and smuggling). In 1974/75 Indonesia had a favourable balance of trade on visible account of over $1,500 million, due to high oil prices. In 1975/76, by contrast, imports were about $6,000 million, compared with estimated exports of only $4,843 million. By December 1974 Indonesia's foreign reserves stood at $1,500 million, but had dropped by September 1975 to $437 million because of the repayment of debts incurred by PERTAMINA.

PLANNING, FOREIGN AID AND FOREIGN INVESTMENT

REPELITA I was largely aid-financed with the 12-member Intergovernmental Group for Indonesia (IGGI), together with the International Monetary Fund (IMF), the World Bank and the Asian Development Bank (ADB) providing two-thirds of all funds. During the Plan period (1969–74) Indonesia obtained loans amounting to $3,422 million from the IGGI (compared with a total outlay in the Plan of $3,851 million). In addition, $800 million was borrowed from multilateral agencies over the same period. Planners had hoped that debt repayments would not exceed 5.6 per cent of exports during the Plan. Nevertheless, there was criticism by many, including influential generals, of over-reliance on foreign aid: the main complaint was that the IGGI consortium had appropriated the State's budgetary powers and had imposed a model of development which did not suit most Indonesians, and that aid was, in fact, a restraint on development. The development model Indonesia was following was undoubtedly Western-inspired and supported; through aid, control over planning was considerable.

However, overall aid to Indonesia is far more substantial than this, and the debt repayment burden is increasing rapidly. At the end of 1968 Indonesia's aid indebtedness was $3,133 million (IGGI $1,557.7 million, Soviet bloc and China $1,172.5 million). By the end of 1973 it stood at $7,000 million.

Circumstances began to change dramatically after the 1974/75 IGGI allocation of $900 million (up from $200 million in 1967/68). The 1975/76 official aid support amounted to $1,800 million (half from IGGI sources and half from non-IGGI sources such as the Middle East); 1976/77 aid requirements nearly doubled again, to $3,400 million (comprising $1,400 million concessional and semi-concessional finance, $1,000 million in export credits and $1,000 million in emergency finance to cover PERTAMINA overspending). By 1973 PERTAMINA's debt was being estimated at $10,000 million but few seemed to be convinced, and as late as 1976 observers were still giving estimates of around $3,000 million for the oil corporation's total debt. By mid-1976 PERTAMINA's total debt was confirmed as $10,000 million.

Although planners had hoped for a low debt charge on export revenue, debt repayment as a proportion of export earning will rise from 13.8 per cent in 1976 to 19.5 per cent in 1979 when the net transfer from abroad on aid account will be a mere $130 million (compared with $1,900 million in 1976). Not only is this a serious drain on foreign exchange reserves, it also has far-reaching implications for the funding and the efficacy of REPELITA II (1974–79). For example, while it was planned to reduce the foreign aid component of plan spending from 35 per cent in 1974/75 to 18 per cent in 1978/79, this now appears unrealistic.

It has been noted that REPELITA I was, to a large extent, a vehicle for creating a favourable infrastructural framework for foreign investment by freeing funds going to rice imports (through rural development) for other uses, and by investment in infrastructure needed to effectively develop manufacturing, forestry and mining.

An indication of this can be seen by combining foreign investment during the plan period with official spending: this shows that the spread of total investment bears no relation to that of government investment. By the end of the first plan, committed foreign investment in industry, mining (including oil) and forestry amounted to over $6,000 million; less $1,000 million as pre-Plan investment, this, combined with government investment, shows a total investment divided in terms of 60 per cent for industry, mining (including oil) and forestry, and

Table 12

Approved Foreign Investments by Sector and country of origin, 1967–August 1974*
(value in $ million, figures in brackets are number of projects)

	Agriculture and Forestry	Mining	Manufacturing				Hotels and Real Estate	Services	Total
			Textiles	Chemicals	Electronics	Others			
U.S.A.	42.5 (12)	602.9 (9)	21.7 (3)	17.8 (18)	18.6 (8)	89.0 (29)	47.3 (18)	13.3 (11)	851.3 (108)
Japan	93.5 (33)	76.0 (2)	516.5 (29)	31.0 (12)	9.5 (9)	234.5 (67)	62.1 (16)	16.3 (6)	1,038.9 (174)
Hong Kong	35.1 (14)	—	129.0 (19)	9.9 (9)	2.2 (2)	78.3 (42)	174.7 (21)	14.1 (9)	443.2 (116)
Singapore	13.6 (8)	—	1.5 (1)	6.7 (5)	3.1 (3)	52.1 (19)	48.7 (9)	—	126.1 (45)
Other Asia	379.3 (41)	2.1 (3)	52.3 (10)	17.6 (8)	1.4 (2)	33.2 (18)	9.9 (7)	5.5 (3)	501.3 (92)
W. Germany	—	—	—	11.5 (9)	8.0 (3)	142.6 (16)	—	—	162.1 (28)
Other Europe	57.0 (44)	7.0 (1)	113.7 (5)	29.9 (22)	13.5 (6)	66.7 (36)	57.1 (16)	16.1 (11)	360.8 (141)
Others	3.0 (2)	173.0 (5)	9.0 (1)	4.0 (6)	2.6 (2)	73.2 (27)	10.5 (6)	3.4 (6)	278.7 (55)
Total	624.0 (154)	861.0 (20)	843.7 (68)	128.4 (89)	58.9 (35)	769.6 (254)	410.3 (93)	68.7 (46)	3,764.6 (759)

* Excluding oil investment.

Source: Investment Co-ordination Board.

only 13 per cent for agriculture and irrigation. Even assuming a 40 per cent actual realization of committed foreign investment outside the oil industry (as some have claimed to be the case), there is a considerable distortion in overall investment priorities towards the three sectors of forestry, metal-mining and oil in the extractive export industries, and manufacturing. There are a number of significant implications of this pattern of investment. First it is, by definition, largely for foreign benefit. Given the generous provisions of the 1967 Foreign Investment Law, and the high profitability of mining, forestry, and the oil industry (40 per cent forestry in good years, 30 to 40 per cent mining) the most lucrative parts of the economy have been subject to high repatriation of capital and an accelerated rundown of resources which would be needed for any major domestic industrialisation. Second, it is for the most part capital intensive. For example, modern mining has a capital intensity of between $60,000 and $90,000 per worker. (Freeport Minerals' copper project in Irian Jaya employs 731 permanent workers for a $175 million investment and forestry has a capital-worker ratio of between $10,000 and $20,000). Investment in the modern extractive sector of the economy, then, does not make a marked contribution to job creation. However, manufacturing is more labour-intensive—but this raises a third problem. Virtually all manufacturing investment is in West Java, particularly around Jakarta, and thus the sectoral spread of investment is linked with a high concentration of manufacturing development (and proportionately high employment creation) within a small and well-serviced area of the archipelago. This metropolitan concentration of manufacturing reflects both gravitation of investment to the already most developed area in terms of infrastructure, business and administrative facilities, and readily available cheap labour, as well as a reluctance to decentralize to areas less well serviced and marked by lower standards of living. The process is circular: government policy is Java-centric, and so is investment not tied to a raw material; 60 per cent of jobs created by foreign investment are in Java, while development of the outer islands depends on capital-intensive "enclave" activities in the extractive sector.

Given Java's high rate of underemployment and unemployment, this might be a logical process. However, three factors limit local job creation: the high degree of capital intensity mentioned already; the concomitant decline of traditional occupations and local business with foreign investment in competitive modern industry; and, thirdly, the preference for foreign skilled workers such as Filipinos and non-Indonesian Malays in forestry and managerial staff in expatriate industries. If one assumes a maximum of one million jobs created by foreign investment, the annual rate of job creation since 1967 has been in the order of 120,000 per year, at most, in a job market increasing by over 1.2 million annually.

A final consideration relating to foreign investment is its concentration within a few non-traditional sectors: there is already the danger that the Indonesian economy may rely too heavily upon oil and timber, and localized industrialization, for development. Developments in food crop agriculture have been geared to "modernizing" rice production, at the expense of rural welfare, largely to cater for increased urban demand. Other food crops have been neglected, most cash crops, especially rubber, have also been neglected, and indigenous manufacturing and fisheries have suffered. Lack of infrastructural, technical, marketing and credit services are largely responsible for the low level of development, and the contraction, of the "traditional" economy and thus of "traditional" exports. Instead of diversifying, the economy is showing a serious tendency towards over-specialization.

FINANCE

After the removal of Sukarno from effective power in early 1966, the new administration introduced a strict policy of monetary stabilization (see the section on Consolidation of the "New Order") to curb inflation, increase export earnings, encourage saving and attract foreign investment. Inflation was brought down from 650 per cent in 1966 to 10 per cent in 1969, but in the process domestic investment was stifled through tight credit policies, and there was a marked increase in bankruptcies among local firms. With a more "open" economy than that before 1966, substantial support in stabilization efforts came from an increasing influx of foreign capital. During 1968/69, when the government began to take steps to prevent economic stagnation about 50 per cent of Indonesia's investments came from foreign capital.

However, easing of the 1966 and 1967 fiscal policies brought only temporary relief to domestic enterprise, which has continued to suffer from a poorly organized domestic banking system and an inadequate credit structure. The capitalist sector has been consistently critical of the planners for being too mindful of their IGGI, IMF and World Bank patrons, and for holding down domestic enterprise in favour of foreigners. For example, the easing of foreign exchange regulations in 1971 favoured foreign firms and local firms (often Chinese) with access to foreign capital (and therefore cheaper foreign loans), and neglected the smaller creditor. Similarly, State banks (which provide 80 per cent of all loans) tend to favour the larger indigenous Indonesian investor with collateral and the foreign investor. In 1974 only 11 per cent of credit from the State Bank was in the loans of up to 5 million rupiahs (U.S. $12,050) each granted to small businessmen.

The credit structure is inadequate both in the limited number of institutions able to extend credit and in the types of loan available. The State Bank dominates domestic credit, and local banks suffer from corruption. The government is trying to consolidate private commercial banks, reducing the number from 120 to 100 between September 1974 and April 1976. Of the 27 development banks (the Central Development Bank, Bapindo, and 26 provincial banks) little is known except that they are forbidden to operate on loan markets following PERTAMINA's financial crisis.

In 1972, a number of merchant banks, or "investment finance corporations", were set up to help broaden Indonesia's capital base: to help develop a stock exchange, foreign exchange market and money market, and provide other intermediary functions normally associated with merchant banks. The aim was to mobilize domestic savings (the official domestic savings rate is 4 per cent) and capital formation, and enable eventual local ownership of foreign-owned business, as called for in the first Five-Year Plan. But the scheme had limited success: few Indonesian companies are publicly traded, short-term credit extension made little progress, red tape and lack of domestic capital limited development of a local capital market, and the merchant banks can operate only in Jakarta.

The 11 foreign banks were originally allowed one branch and sub-branch in Jakarta, and their operations were thus confined. As most financing was of firms operating outside Jakarta, but with headquarters in the capital, this was no great obstacle. But since 1974, such financing was forbidden. Foreign bank advances must be syndicated with State or local private banks, with low lending ceilings imposed by the State Bank. This restricts the ability of local banks to service foreign investment. Besides, despite arrangements between foreign and local banks to overcome this problem, both banks are subject to the Ministry of Finance in identifying and financing projects for investment in the provinces.

The type of loans available are also inadequate for domestic enterprise. Basically, there are two forms: commercial loans up to one year and investment loans up to five years. Credit to local businessmen suffers from too low a ceiling and high interest rates. Special credit for small business is extended at 5 million rupiahs: this is both low, and subject to bureaucratic delays in extension (up to mid-1974, of 30,000 applications to Bank Indonesia, only 15 per cent to 20 per cent had been processed). Loans to local entrepreneurs of between 10,000 and 100,000 rupiahs ($24–$241) are similarly too small.

The tight credit controls imposed on all banks by the State Bank to limit inflation (caused, according to the Government, largely by the inflow of short term foreign capital) also tends to limit enterprise and production, especially amongst local entrepreneurs. With low lending ceilings and a standard 24 per cent interest on all loans (except for 12 per cent on investment loans of up to 5 years, with a 2 to 3 year grace period) high and quick returns are sought by businessmen, and small businessmen borrow at the risk of falling behind in debt repayments. BIMAS credit is an example of this: in 1973/74 there was a 25 per cent backlog in BIMAS repayments.

Thus, there is no effective intermediary economic infrastructure in the country to facilitate supplies of raw materials and semi-processed goods to local industrialists. As a result of an obsolete credit system, foreigners have moved into this intermediary hiatus: the Japanese, for example, offer "package deals" under which they supply raw materials, machinery, technology, marketing, consumption and financing.

The banking system in Indonesia is merely part of the larger state apparatus, tied up by bureaucratic inefficiency and subject to a philosophy of development which is little concerned with promoting small-scale enterprise or the principle of labour-intensive and decentralized investment.

The 1976/77 budget placed expenditure at $8,450 million: a 29 per cent increase over the previous budget (which in turn was 73 per cent higher than the 1974/75 budget). For the first time, development funds exceeded routine expenditure. The expenditure is divided as follows (in millions of $):

Table 13

Routine expenditure	
Salaries and pensions	1,550
Material costs	755
Regional subsidies	741
Debt servicing	432
Food imports	268
Other	104
TOTAL	3,850
Development expenditure	
Communications	1,000
Agriculture and irrigation	903
Electricity	507
Industry and mining	404
Education, culture, etc.	344
Defence and security	103
Other (incl. Pertamina)	1,339
TOTAL	4,600

The budget's funding is by indirect taxes (18.8 per cent); direct taxes (56.8 per cent), of which oil revenue is by far the largest item, planned to provide 47 per cent of budgeted revenue; personal taxes (2.3 per cent); foreign aid and export credits (20.1 per cent).

A continuing high reliance on the earnings of one commodity, a weak income tax system and relatively high indirect taxation indicate a tax system which, as a whole, is regressive, and unable to reduce disparities in the distribution of wealth and income. Measures to improve the tax system such as increased property tax, strengthened personal income tax collection and luxury taxes, have met strong opposition from the civilian and military élite.

THE DEBATE OVER DEVELOPMENT POLICY

The financial crisis which mounted during 1974 and 1975 as a result of PERTAMINA's massive $10,000 million borrowing, to finance what amounted to a "parallel economy" embracing every sector of the Indonesian economy, highlighted a debate over development policy which has been going on since the late 1960s.

Basically, there was a conflict of philosophy between the group of technocrats known as the "Berkeley Mafia", led by the chairman of BAPPENAS, Dr. Widjojo Nitisastro, and a powerful group of generals close to Suharto and including PERTAMINA's Sutowo and General Ali Murtopo, the director of the influential political planning organization, the Centre for Strategic and International Studies.

The BAPPENAS technocrats were, perhaps ironically, inclined towards a centralized form of policy-making, relying heavily upon the bureaucracy as a regulatory and implementing body and caught between domestic vested interests and the development philosophies of Western aid donors. Their approach to development was to combine capitalism with state regulation to ensure both economic growth and the stability needed for foreign investment and aid. Their problem was to accommodate the various interests of domestic capitalism, large and small, and to guarantee both them and foreign interests. Thus the controlling framework and bureaucracy were essential, but at the same time counter-productive for both local and foreign interests. It was a contradiction which had existed for years in Indonesia, and which was illustrated in one respect by the policy and implementation of "Indonesianization"—local capitalists wanted more indigenous participation in the economy, and the Government tried to make the bureaucracy ensure this at the same time as they tried to make the bureaucracy responsive to foreign investment needs. The contradiction was not helped by the fact that the bureaucracy was incompetent and heavily overmanned.

Sutowo chose not to work through or with the bureaucracy. His PERTAMINA empire epitomized indigenous state capitalism of the highest order. It was built up on the philosophy that all resources should go to "enlarging the cake": splitting it by emphasis on equality was "utopian" in a developing economy such as Indonesia's which, in Sutowo's view, could progress only through a process of industrialization akin to that of Meiji Japan; in any case, "the richer Indonesians are, the bigger their charity". It was the rate of increase in income, not the way this income was distributed, which was important.

Sutowo stressed that regulations alone do not bring capital: "even if there is an investment law, even if security and the economic situation are good, it is difficult to attract investors without a good infrastructure, . . . harbours, electricity, telecommunications. . ."

Sutowo, Murtopo and their supporters claimed that Indonesian technocrats confused modernization with Westernization; they wanted foreign capital, not tutelage, and to them the only way of cushioning the impact of foreign investment was to build a strong indigenous entrepreneurial élite, unfettered by a bureaucracy.

PERTAMINA's virtual collapse was both despite and because of its oil dependence and it indicated that, while Indonesia's domestic capitalism could, with an entrepreneur like Sutowo, reach dizzying proportions, such proportions simply did not square with the realities of Indonesia. They were macrocephalic, an anomaly, and their magnitude as well as the magnitude of PERTAMINA's collapse indicate that Indonesia is still a poor, underdeveloped and basically agricultural country for which rapid industrialization is an ill-chosen path.

STATISTICAL SURVEY

AREA

(sq. km.)

TOTAL	JAVA AND MADURA	SUMATRA	KALIMANTAN (Borneo)	SULAWESI (Celebes)	OTHER ISLANDS*
2,027,087	134,703	541,174	550,848	227,654	572,708

* Comprises Bali, Nusa Tenggara, Maluku and Irian Jaya.

POPULATION

(1971 Census—'000)

TOTAL	JAVA AND MADURA	SUMATRA	KALIMANTAN (Borneo)	SULAWESI (Celebes)	BALI	NUSA TENGGARA (Lesser Sunda Is.)	MALUKU (Moluccas)	IRIAN JAYA (West New Guinea)
119,232	76,103	20,813	5,152	8,535	2,120	4,559	995	955

Estimated population: 136 million (1976).

CHIEF TOWNS

POPULATION ('000)

	1961 Census	1971 Census		1961 Census	1971 Census
Jakarta (capital)	3,694	5,849	Malang	341	429
Surabaya	1,008	1,269	Yogjakarta	313	394
Bandung	973	1,152	Banjarmasin	214	277
Semarang	503	633	Pontianak	150	194
Medan	479	620	Tjirebon	158	187
Palembang	475	614	Padang	144	187
Ujungpandang (Makassar)	384	497	Bogor	154	183

Births and Deaths: Average annual birth rate 44.9 per 1,000; death rate 19.2 per 1,000 (UN estimates for 1965–70).

ECONOMICALLY ACTIVE POPULATION*

(1971 census, sample tabulation)

	Males	Females	Total
Agriculture, hunting, forestry and fishing	17,001,191	7,944,822	24,946,013
Mining and quarrying	86,224	5,911	92,135
Manufacturing	1,530,177	1,422,440	2,952,617
Electricity, gas and water	36,615	1,717	38,332
Construction	739,778	10,350	750,128
Trade, restaurants and hotels	2,352,996	1,799,371	4,152,367
Transport, storage and communications	914,536	17,715	932,251
Financing, insurance, real estate and business services	81,367	17,425	98,792
Community, social and personal services	2,903,951	1,076,351	3,980,302
Activities not adequately described	885,827	863,335	1,749,162
Total	26,532,662	13,159,437	39,692,099

* Excluding persons seeking work for the first time, numbering 407,971 (299,739 males, 108,232 females) at the time of the census.

AGRICULTURE

LAND USE, 1971

('000 hectares)

Arable and Under Permanent Crops	18,100
Permanent Meadows and Pastures	9,875
Forest Land	121,800
Other Land	31,360
Total Land Area	181,135
Inland Water	9,300
Total Area	190,435

PRINCIPAL CROPS

	Area ('000 ha.)			Production ('000 metric tons)		
	1972	1973	1974	1972	1973	1974
Rice (paddy)	7,983	8,383	8,537	18,031	21,500	22,732
Maize	2,160	3,288	2,648	2,254	3,690	3,240
Potatoes	34†	35†	37†	124	130†	138†
Sweet potatoes	318	350†	350†	2,066	2,180	2,180†
Cassava (manioc)	1,418	1,350†	1,350†	10,385	9,399	9,399†
Other roots and tubers	258†	266†	274†	1,300	1,330†	1,370†
Soybeans	685	751	753	518	529	550
Groundnuts (in shell)	356	407	409	470	505	525
Coconuts	n.a.	n.a.	n.a.	5,644*	5,377*	5,872*
Copra	n.a.	n.a.	n.a.	762	700†	720†
Palm kernels	n.a.	n.a.	n.a.	59	64	72
Palm oil	n.a.	n.a.	n.a.	269	289	334
Sugar cane	149	158	170†	12,133	10,680*	12,281*
Coffee	395	402	417†	179	163	182
Cocoa beans	4.9	5†	5.5	1.8	2	3.5
Tea	104	102	102†	59.9	66.3	64.6
Tobacco	175	172	172	n.a.	81	78
Kenaf (mesta)	6.7	7.4	7.4†	8.3	13.7	14.2
Natural rubber	n.a.	n.a.	n.a.	818.7	852.5	892.5

* Unofficial figure. † FAO estimate.

Source: FAO, *Production Yearbook 1974* and *Monthly Bulletin of Agricultural Economics and Statistics.*

LIVESTOCK

	1971-72	1972-73	1973-74
Cattle	6,260,000	6,682,000	6,687,000
Sheep	2,997,000	3,207,000	3,151,000
Goats	6,997,000	7,468,000	7,468,000*
Pigs	3,300,000	4,048,000	4,358,000
Horses	696,000	689,000	689,000*
Buffaloes	2,825,000	2,870,000	2,870,000*
Chickens	86,135,000	99,769,000	100,317,000*
Ducks	13,112,000	13,810,000	14,054,000*

* FAO estimates.

Source: FAO, mainly *Production Yearbook 1974.*

LIVESTOCK PRODUCTS
(metric tons)

	1972	1973	1974	1975
Beef and veal	132,000	135,000	135,000*	165,000* (Beef and veal and Buffalo meat)
Buffalo meat	34,000	30,000	30,000*	
Mutton and lamb	13,000	10,000	10,000*	39,000* (Mutton and lamb and Goats' meat)
Goats' meat	29,000	26,000	27,000*	
Pig meat	87,000	89,000	94,000*	94,000*
Poultry meat	70,000	70,000	78,000*	79,000*
Other meat	n.a.	13,000	12,000*	13,000*
Edible offals	51,633*	49,653*	49,991*	n.a.
Cows' milk	32,000	36,000*	43,000	43,000*
Hen eggs	53,000	61,800	62,300*	140,000* (Hen eggs and Other poultry eggs)
Other poultry eggs	72,000	75,400	77,000*	
Cattle hides	19,450*	19,875*	19,875*	n.a.
Buffalo hides	5,724*	5,049*	5,108*	n.a.
Sheep skins	2,760*	2,000*	2,067*	n.a.
Goat skins	5,760*	5,216*	5,349*	n.a.

Note: Figures for meat refer to inspected production only, i.e. from animals slaughtered under government supervision.

* FAO estimate.

Source: FAO, *Production Yearbook 1974* and *Monthly Bulletin of Agricultural Economics and Statistics.*

FORESTRY

ROUNDWOOD REMOVALS
('000 cubic metres, excluding bark)

	1967	1968	1969	1970	1971	1972	1973
Sawlogs, veneer logs and logs for sleepers:							
Coniferous	80	80	80	80	100	100	100*
Non-coniferous	4,800	5,500	7,000	10,700	13,705*	16,821*	25,197*
Pitprops (mine timber)		20	20	20*	20*	20*	20*
Pulpwood	42	25	19	20*	30*	40*	40*
Other industrial wood	1,665	1,714	1,815	1,865*	1,915*	1,965*	1,974
TOTAL INDUSTRIAL WOOD	6,587	7,339	8,934	12,685	15,770	18,946	27,331
Fuel wood	88,800	92,000	95,000	98,000*	100,000*	104,000*	107,000*
TOTAL	95,387	99,339	103,934	110,685	115,770	122,946	134,331
of which:							
Coniferous†	122	107	101	102	132	142	140*
Non-coniferous	95,265	99,232	103,833	110,583	115,638*	122,804*	134,191*

* FAO estimate.

† All industrial wood, including logs (*see* table), total pulpwood production and 2,000 cubic metres per year of other wood in 1968–72.

Source: FAO, *Yearbook of Forest Products.*

SAWNWOOD PRODUCTION
('000 cubic metres)

	1966	1967	1968	1969	1970*	1971*	1972*	1973*
Coniferous sawnwood†	16	16	20	20	20	20	20	20
Non-coniferous sawnwood†	1,765	1,765	1,662	1,662	1,662	1,662	1,662	1,662
Railway sleepers	15	19	19	19	19	24	24	11
TOTAL	1,796	1,800	1,701	1,701	1,701	1,706	1,706	1,693

* FAO estimates. † Including boxboards.

Source: FAO, *Yearbook of Forest Products.*

FISHING

('000 metric tons)

	1966	1967	1968	1969	1970	1971	1972	1973	1974
Inland waters	481.6	502.5	436.5	429.1	421.1	424.1	429.3	440.0	449.0
Indian Ocean	72.7	68.5	73.0	79.0	85.7	78.9	84.7	86.0	89.3
Pacific Ocean	647.5	609.4	649.5	706.3	721.7	741.5	753.8	774.0	803.6
TOTAL CATCH	1,201.8	1,180.4	1,159.0	1,214.4	1,228.5	1,244.5	1,267.8	1,300.0	1,341.9

Source: FAO, *Yearbook of Fishery Statistics 1974.*

MINING

		1972	1973	1974	1975
Coal	metric tons	179,248	148,855	156,153	206,388
Bauxite	,, ,,	1,276,578	1,229,375	1,290,054	922,556
Gold	kilogrammes	339.0	352.1	265.2	321.4
Silver	,,	8,683.9	8,832.0	6,464.6	4,758.4
Nickel (gross weight)*	metric tons	935,075	867,046	878,855	801,012
Tin	,, ,,	21,329	22,204	25,023	24,391
Crude petroleum	'000 barrels	394,806	489,012	501,838	477,127
Natural gas	'000 million cu. ft.	145,629	177,648	n.a.	n.a.

Source: Central Bureau of Statistics.

* The nickel content (in metric tons) was: 22,400 in 1972; 20,800 in 1973.

INDUSTRY

(Production in twelve months ending March 31st)

		1970–71	1971–72	1972–73†
Woven Textiles	million metres	598.4	732.0	852.0
Textile Yarn	'000 bales	217.0	239.0	287.0
Fertilizer	'000 tons	103.0	108.4	177.0
Cement	,, ,,	577.0	531.0	652.0
Paper	,, ,,	22.0	29.0	38.0
Glass	,, ,,	11.0	7.4	14.9
Tyres, Tubes	million	0.4	0.5	0.8
Batteries	'000 cases	56.0	72.0	72.0
Radio Sets	'000	393.0	416.0	700.0
Television Sets	,,	4.7	6.5	6.6
Motor Cars*	,,	2.9	16.6	23.0
Motor Cycles*	,,	31.0	50.0	100.0
Cigarettes	million	13.6	14.7	16.8
Matches	million boxes	322.0	348.0	475.0
Toothpaste	million tubes	25.2	26.0	30.0
Soap	'000 tons	132.2	132.4	132.0

* Assembled. † Preliminary figures.

Source: Central Bureau of Statistics.

FINANCE

100 sen = 1 rupiah (Rp.).
Coins: 1, 2, 5, 10, 25, 50 and 100 rupiahs.
Notes: 1, 2½, 5, 10, 25, 50, 100, 500, 1,000, 5,000 and 10,000 rupiahs.
Exchange rates (June 1976):
Exports: £1 sterling = 663.48 rupiahs; U.S. $1 = 374.00 rupiahs.
10,000 rupiahs = £15.07 = $26.74.
Imports: £1 = 736.21 rupiahs; U.S. $1 = 415.00 rupiahs.
10,000 rupiahs = £13.58 = $24.10.

Note: The new rupiah, equal to 1,000 old rupiahs, was introduced in December 1965. For converting the value of foreign trade transactions the average import rates (rupiahs per U.S. dollar) were: 78.0 in 1966; 153.7 in 1967; 300.1 in 1968; 326.0 in 1969; 365.0 in 1970; 393.4 in 1971. The present dollar-rupiah rates have been in force since August 1971. In terms of sterling, the exchange rates from December 1971 to June 1972 were £1 = 974.54 rupiahs (exports) and £1 = 1,081.37 rupiahs (imports).

BUDGET ESTIMATES

('000 million rupiahs—year ending March 31st)

Revenue	1975/76	1976/77
Direct Taxes	1,867.5	2,082.2
Income tax	52.4	81.5
Company tax	125.6	161.0
Oil companies tax	1,540.0	1,656.5
MPO	104.8	123.5
Ipeda	31.7	35.2
Other	13.0	24.5
Indirect Taxes	571.6	662.9
Sales tax (products)	109.9	151.7
Import duties	83.3	89.3
Excise	90.2	122.9
Sales tax (imports)	221.4	223.3
Export tax	31.7	36.3
Other oil receipts	13.1	17.7
Other	21.0	21.7
Non-tax Receipts	57.0	58.1
Total Domestic Revenue	2,496.1	2,803.2
Foreign Aid Receipts	238.6	717.4
Programme Aid	20.2	10.2
Project Aid and Export Credits	218.4	707.2
Total	2,734.7	3,520.6

Expenditure	1975/76	1976/77
Personnel Emoluments	602.4	644.8
Rice allowances	101.4	119.3
Salaries and pensions	418.7	438.0
Food allowances	42.2	45.7
Other remunerations	27.6	27.8
Missions abroad	12.5	14.0
Purchases of Goods	267.2	312.9
Domestic products	244.7	293.3
Foreign products	22.5	19.6
Regional Subsidies	279.3	307.0
Irian Jaya	19.7	19.7
Other regions	259.6	287.3
Debt Servicing	74.2	179.4
Domestic debts	2.5	7.2
Foreign debts	71.7	172.2
Other Ordinary Expenditure	243.2	156.2
Total Ordinary Budget	1,466.3	1,600.3
Rupiah Financing	1,050.0	1,213.1
Government savings	1,029.8	1,202.9
Programme Aid	20.2	10.2
Project Aid and Export Credits	218.4	707.2
Total Development Budget	1,288.4	1,920.3
Total	2,734.7	3,520.6

INTERNATIONAL RESERVES

(U.S. $ million at December 31st)

	1968	1969	1970	1971	1972	1973	1974	1975
Gold	4	4	4	2	2	2	2	2
IMF Special Drawing Rights	—	—	—	—	39	52	68	7
Reserve position in IMF	—	—	—	—	—	—	35	—
Foreign exchange	83	118	156	185	533	753	1,386	577
Total	86	122	160	187	574	807	1,492	586

Source: IMF, *International Financial Statistics.*

MONEY SUPPLY

('000 million rupiahs at December 31st)

	1968	1969	1970	1971	1972	1973	1974	1975
Currency outside banks	76.6	115.7	154.6	199.4	269.0	375.0	496.9	625.8

Source: IMF, *International Financial Statistics.*

COST OF LIVING

Consumer Price Index for Jakarta

(average of monthly figures. Base: 1970=100)

	1965	1966	1967	1968	1969	1971	1972	1973	1974
Food	1.2	13.2	37.1	88.8	91.5	102.6	113.2	162.4	229.4
Clothing	1.2	15.2	27.4	64.3	91.2	109.5	109.5	128.4	175.7
Rent, water, fuel and light	0.7	8.7	31.2	50.8	69.3	107.2	108.0	121.7	147.5
ALL ITEMS	1.1	12.5	33.6	75.8	89.0	104.3	111.1	145.6	204.8

1975: Food 276.5, All items 243.8.

Source: International Labour Office, mainly *Year Book of Labour Statistics.*

NATIONAL ACCOUNTS

Gross Domestic Product at constant 1960 market prices by Industrial Origin

('000 million rupiahs)

	1970	1971	1972	1973*
Agriculture, forestry, fishery	271	281	287	303
Mining and quarrying	32	34	41	50
Manufacturing	51	58	61	63
Electricity, gas and water supply	3	3	4	4
Construction	15	18	22	27
Wholesale and retail trade	100	108	124	138
Transport and communication	18	22	25	27
Banking and other finance	9	11	12	15
Ownership of dwellings	11	12	13	13
Public administration and defence	30	32	33	34
Services	31	32	32	33
GROSS DOMESTIC PRODUCT	571	611	654	707

* Preliminary figures.

FOREIGN AID

(1972–73)

	(million U.S.$)
U.S.A.	203.0
Japan	185.0
Germany, Federal Republic	46.9
U.K.	26.1
Australia	24.4
France	20.6
Canada	16.7
World Bank and Asian Development Bank	145.0
TOTAL (incl. others)	723.6

1975/76: Total $51,800 million.

EXTERNAL TRADE

(million U.S. $)

	1970	1971	1972	1973	1974	1975
Imports c.i.f.	1,001.5	1,102.8	1,561.7	2,346.6	3,841.9	4,769.8
Exports f.o.b.	1,108.1	1,233.6	1,777.7	3,210.8	7,426.3	7,102.5

PRINCIPAL COMMODITIES

(million U.S. $)

Imports	1971	1972	1973
Rice	19.9	49.7	82.2
Chemicals and pharmaceutical products	40.1	58.5	49.5
Fertilizers	23.5	44.1	61.6
Paints	3.5	22.5	31.4
Yarns	50.2	75.4	102.4
Textile fabrics	5.5	6.0	52.6
Cement	17.0	22.0	30.5
Reinforced concrete	14.1	12.8	80.5
Iron and steel bars, plates and pipes	66.7	98.8	163.3
Machines	181.7	243.0	526.6
Electro-motors and transformers	8.9	69.6	25.4
Railway equipment	79.5	100.0	199.0
Total (incl. others)	1,102.8	1,561.7	2,346.6

1974 (million U.S. $): Rice 374.2, Fertilizers 227.2, Iron and steel bars, plates and pipes 209.8, Cement 68.3, Total (incl. others) 3,841.9.

1975 (provisional): Rice 264.7, Fertilizers 381.9, Iron and steel bars, plates and pipes 310.2, Cement 72.7, Total (incl. others) 4,769.8.

Exports	1973	1974	1975*
Crustaceans and molluscs	59.4	n.a.	n.a.
Coffee	77.6	98.1	95.0
Tea	26.1	46.3	55.0
Pepper	28.9	24.3	25.9
Tobacco	39.7	35.5	25.7
Copra and copra cake	22.4	25.9	32.4
Rubber	391.4	479.2	370.0
Lumber	573.6	724.9	503.0
Palm oil	70.2	157.3	142.7
Tin	93.1	175.4	140.0
Crude oil	1,382.5	4,680.3	4,933.1
Petroleum products	226.2	531.1	378.3
Total (incl. others)	3,210.8	7,426.3	7,102.5

* Provisional.

PRINCIPAL COUNTRIES

(million U.S. $)

Imports	1971	1972	1973*
Australia	32.3	51.3	90.6
Belgium/Luxembourg	5.6	9.5	14.2
Canada	3.2	9.7	19.1
China, People's Republic	27.6	39.0	54.7
France	16.1	20.7	43.8
Germany, Fed. Republic	105.0	117.3	191.0
Hong Kong	17.3	25.0	53.0
Italy	7.0	15.1	25.9
Japan	360.9	531.8	734.1
Netherlands	51.1	66.8	86.5
Pakistan	14.2	20.3	34.0
Philippines	3.4	5.4	13.8
Singapore	70.0	102.0	134.4
Thailand	8.9	30.5	42.3
United Kingdom	46.4	63.7	101.2
U.S.A.	174.1	242.9	442.4
Total (incl. others)	1,102.8	1,561.7	2,346.6

1974 (U.S. $ million): Japan 1,139.2. Singapore 248.30.

1975 (U.S. $ million): Japan 1,477.4).

Exports	1971	1972	1973*
Australia	15.9	13.8	16.6
Belgium/Luxembourg	15.0	33.9	16.4
France	6.9	10.6	16.9
Germany, Fed. Republic	62.2	66.0	118.7
Hong Kong	11.1	13.0	14.0
Italy	9.2	24.6	38.6
Japan	550.4	901.8	1,707.4
Malaysia	31.1	30.6	34.3
Netherlands	71.1	78.1	100.9
Philippines	26.0	8.0	1.2
Singapore	160.8	133.7	341.0
U.S.S.R.	9.1	6.4	5.7
United Kingdom	11.9	23.5	32.1
U.S.A.	192.4	265.4	465.3
Total (incl. others)	1,233.6	1,777.7	3,210.8

Japan (U.S. $ million): 3,969.3 in 1974; 3,131.8 in 1975.

* Provisional.

TRANSPORT

RAILWAYS

	1971	1972	1973
Passenger kilometres (million)	3,623	3,352	2,725
Freight ton-kilometres (million)	949	1,038	1,068

Source: Department of Information, *Indonesian Handbook*, 1974.

ROADS—VEHICLES IN USE
(as at December 31st)

	1972	1973
Cars	277,210	307,739
Trucks	131,175	144,060
Buses	26,488	30,368
Motor Cycles	615,220	n.a.

INTERNATIONAL SEA-BORNE SHIPPING
('000 metric tons, excluding transit traffic and packing)

	1971	1972	1973	1974
Goods loaded*	43,693	60,077	70,977	72,646
Goods unloaded	4,327	6,234	8,940	8,714

* Including ships' stores and bunkers.

Source: UN *Monthly Bulletin of Statistics*.

CIVIL AVIATION
(scheduled services)

	1970	1971	1972	1973
Kilometres flown (million)	20.2	24.3	31.7	38.8
Passengers carried ('000)	826	994	1,287	1,695
Passenger-kilometres (million)	878	1,079	1,254	1,674
Freight ton-kilometres (million)	14.2	17.6	19.9	24.3
Mail ton-kilometres (million)	1.4	2.2	2.6	3.5

Source: UN *Statistical Yearbook 1974*.

COMMUNICATIONS MEDIA

(1974)

Radio Sets: 3,500,000.*

TV Sets: 236,828.

Newspaper Circulation: 1,800,000.

Telephones: 269,000 (1973).

* Estimate.

TOURISM

Visitors (1973): 309,675.

Receipts (1972): U.S. $47 million.

EDUCATION
(1972)

	SCHOOLS	TEACHERS	PUPILS AND STUDENTS
Basic	65,950	414,799	13,474,730
General	6,446	97,936	1,394,593
Teacher Education	499	8,668	95,053
Technological	1,163	25,955	285,786
Other Vocational	1,964	30,163	303,755

Source: Central Bureau of Statistics, *Statistik Indonesia 1973.*

Source (unless otherwise stated): Central Bureau of Statistics, *Indikator Ekonomi.*

THE CONSTITUTION

Indonesia has had three Constitutions, all provisional: August 1945, February 1950 and August 1950. In July 1959, th constitution of 1945 was re-enacted by Presidential decree:

GENERAL PRINCIPLES

The 1945 Constitution consists of 37 articles, 4 transitional clauses and 2 additional provisions, and is preceded by a preamble. The preamble contains an indictment of all forms of colonialism, an account of Indonesia's struggle for independence, the declaration of that independence and a statement of fundamental aims and principles. Indonesia's National Independence, according to the text of the preamble, has the state form of a Republic, with sovereignty residing in the People, and is based upon the *Pancasila:*

1. Belief in One Supreme God.
2. Just and Civilized Humanity.
3. Nationalism; the Unity of Indonesia.
4. Democracy; guided by the wisdom of unanimity arising from deliberations (*musjawarah*) and mutual assistance (*gotong royong*).
5. Social Justice; equality of political rights, equality of the rights of citizenship, social equality, cultural equality.

THE STATE ORGANS

Majelis Permusyawaratan Rakyat (*People's Consultative Assembly*)

Sovereignty is in the hands of the People and is exercised in full by the People's Consultative Assembly as the embodiment of the whole Indonesian People. The Consultative Assembly is the highest authority of the State, and is to be distinguished from the legislative body proper (Dewan Perwakilan Rakyat, *see below*) which is incorporated within the Consultative Assembly. The Consultative Assembly is composed of all members of the Dewan, augmented by delegates from the regions and representatives of the functional groups in society (farmers, workers, businessmen, the clergy, intelligentsia, armed forces, students, etc.). The Assembly sits at least once every five years, and its primary competence is to determine the Constitution and the broad lines of the policy of the State and the Government. It also elects the President and Vice-President, who are responsible for implementing that policy. All decisions are taken unanimously in keeping with the traditions of *musjawarah.*

Members are to be chosen by national elections. Follov ing the dissolution of the elected Assembly in 1960 ar pending general elections, the People's Consultativ Assembly (MPR) exercises the authority laid down in th 1945 Constitution.

The President

The highest executive of the Government, the Presiden holds office for a term of five years and may be re-electe As Mandatory of the MPR he must execute the policy the State according to the Decrees determined by th MPR during its Fourth General and Special Sessions. I conducting the administration of the State, authority an responsibility are concentrated in the President. Th Ministers of State are his assistants and are responsib only to him.

Dewan Perwakilan Rakyat—DPR (*House of Represent tives*)

The legislative branch of the State, the House Representatives, sits at least once a year. Every statu requires the approval of the DPR. Members of the Hou of Representatives have the right to submit draft bi which require ratification by the President, who h the right of veto. In times of emergency the Preside may enact ordinances which have the force of law, b such Ordinances must be ratified by the House of Repr sentatives during the following session or be revoked.

Dewan Pertimbangan Agung—DPA (*Supreme Adviso Council*)

The DPA is an advisory body assisting the Preside who chooses its members from political parties, function groups and groups of prominent persons.

Mahkamah Agung (*Supreme Court*)

The judicial branch of the State, the Supreme Court an the other courts of law are independen tof the Executive i exercising their judicial powers.

Badan Pemeriksa Keuangan (*State Comptrolling Body*)

Controls the accountability of public finance, enjoys i vestigatory powers and is independent of the Executiv Its findings are presented to the DPR.

THE GOVERNMENT

President: Gen. T. N. I. SUHARTO; inaugurated March 27th, 1968. Re-elected March 1973.

Vice-President: Sultan HAMENGKUBUWONO IX.

CABINET

(*May* 1976)

Minister of Defence and Security: Gen. MARADEN PANGGABEAN.

Minister of Foreign Affairs: H. ADAM MALIK.

Minister of Home Affairs: Lt.-Gen. AMIR MACHMUD.

Minister of Justice: Prof. Dr. M. KUSUMAADMADJA.

Minister of Information: Dr. KANGMAS MASHURI SALEH.

Minister of Education and Culture: Dr. SJARIF-THAYEB.

Minister of Religious Affairs: Prof. Dr. H. A. MUKTI ALI.

Minister of Social Affairs: H. M. S. MINTAREDJA.

Minister of Health: Prof. Dr. G. A. SIWABESSY.

Minister of Manpower, Transmigration and Co-operatives: Prof. Dr. SOEBROTO.

Minister of Trade: Drs. RADIUS PRAWIRO.

Minister of Finance: Prof. Dr. ALI WARDHANA.

Minister of Communications: Dr. EMIL SALIM.

Minister of Agriculture: Prof. THOJIB HADIWIDJAJA.

Minister of Industry: Lt.-Gen. MOHAMMAD JUSUF.

Minister of Mining Affairs: Prof. Dr. Ir. MOHAMMAD SADLI.

Minister of Public Works and Energy: Dr. Ir. SUTAMI.

Minister of State for Economic, Financial and Industrial Affairs: Prof. WIDJOJO NITISASTRO.

Minister of State for Public Welfare: Prof. SUNAWAR SUKOWATI.

Minister of State for Administrative Reforms: Dr. J. B. SUMARLIN.

Minister of State for Research: Prof. Dr. SOEMITRO DJOJOHADIKOETOEMO.

Minister of State for Administrative and Financial Affairs and State Secretary: Maj.-Gen. SUDHARMONO.

PARLIAMENT

HOUSE OF REPRESENTATIVES

(Dewan Perwakilan Rakyat—DPR)

In March 1960, a Presidential decree prorogued the elected Council of Representatives and replaced it by a nominated House of 283 members (increased to 460 in 1968). Elections were held in July 1971 when 53 million votes were cast representing a 79 per cent poll. Seats were distributed as shown below:

Speaker: Dr. IDHAM CHALID.

ELECTION
(July 3rd, 1971)

	SEATS
Government Functional Group (Sekber Golkar)	261
Armed Forces Functional Group	75
Partai Persatuan Pembangunan* comprising:	
NU Party (Muslim Scholars)	58
Parmusi Party (Muslim)	24
PSII Party (Muslim)	10
Perti Party (Muslim)	2
Partai Demokrasi Indonesia* comprising:	
PNI (Nationalist Party)	20
Parkindo (Christian Party)	7
Katholik (Catholic Party)	3
IPKI (Independence Upholders Party)	0
Murba (People's Party)	0
Women	—
Others	—
TOTAL	460

PEOPLE'S CONSULTATIVE ASSEMBLY

(Majelis Permusyawaratan Rakyat—MPR)

The Assembly, provided for under the 1945 Constitution, was most recently inaugurated in October 1972. It consists of the members of the House of Representatives and delegates of regional territories and of corporations and functional groups. It must meet at least once every five years. It is the highest authority in the State and appointed the President and Vice-President in March 1973, the former being responsible to the Assembly. Sixth session held in March 1973; total membership: 920.

Chairman: Dr. IDHAM CHALID.

Vice-Chairmen: Dr. SOEMISKUN; DOMOPRANOTO; J. NARO, S.H.; MOHD. ISANAENI.

	SEATS
Government Functional Group (Sekber Golkar)	392
Armed Forces Functional Group	230
Partai Persatuan Pembangunan* comprising:	
NU Party (Muslim Scholars)	78
Parmusi Party (Muslim)	27
PSII Party (Muslim)	13
Perti Party (Muslim)	3
Partai Demokrasi Indonesia* comprising:	
PNI (Nationalist Party)	27
Parkindo (Christian Party)	9
Katholik (Catholic Party)	4
IPKI (Independence Upholders Party)	1
Murba (People's Party)	1
Women	48
Others	87
TOTAL	920

* Formed January 1973.

POLITICAL PARTIES

A Presidential decree of January 1960 enables the President to dissolve any party whose membership does not cover a quarter of Indonesia, or whose policies are at variance with the aims of the State.

The following parties and groups participated in the general elections held in July 1971, though in January 1973 nine of them were involved in mergers from which two new parties, the *Partai Persatuan Pembangunan* and the *Partai Demokrasi Indonesia* were formed.

Partai Persatuan Pembangunan (*Development Unity Party*): f. 1973 as a result of the merger of four Islamic parties Pres. Dr. IDHAM CHALID.

Partai Demokrasi Indonesia (*Indonesian Democratic Party*): f. 1973 as a result of the merger of five nationalist and Christian parties; Gen. Chair. SANUSI HARDJADINATA.

Sekber Golkar (*Secretariat of Functional Groups*): f. 1964, reorganized 1971; a Government alliance of groups representing farmers, youth, veterans, co-operatives, entrepreneurs, women, labour; 392 seats in the MPR; Chair. Maj.-Gen. AMIR MURTONO.

DIPLOMATIC REPRESENTATION

EMBASSIES ACCREDITED TO INDONESIA

(Jakarta unless otherwise stated)

Afghanistan: 15 Jalan Tosari.

Algeria: 60 Jalan Cik Ditiro.

Argentina: 17 Jalan Panarukan.

Australia: 15 Jalan Thamrin, Gambir; *Ambassador:* R. A. WOOLCOTT.

Austria: 99 Jalan Hos. Cokroaminoto (also accred. to the Philippines).

Bangladesh: 7 Jalan Mendut; *Ambassador:* H. As. ATAUL KARIM.

Belgium: 4 Jl. Cicurug; *Ambassador:* J. LEBACQ.

Brazil: 38 Jalan Salemba Tengah.

Bulgaria: 34 Jalan Imam Bonjol; *Ambassador:* M. TODER-STOJONOV.

Burma: 109 Jalan Haji Agus Salim.

Canada: 6 Jalan Budi Kemuliaan; *Ambassador:* PETER JOHNSON.

Cuba: 57 Jalan Teuku Umar.

Czechoslovakia: 29 Jalan Prof. Mohd. Yamin.

Denmark: 34 Jalan Abdul Muis; *Ambassador:* CHRISTIAN KARSTEN (also accred. to the Philippines).

Egypt: 68 Jalan Teuku Umar.

Finland: 15 Jalan Dr. Kusurna Atmadja (also accred. to Burma and Malaysia).

France: 20 Jalan Moh. Thamrin; *Ambassador:* PIERRE GORCE.

German Democratic Republic: 74 Jalan Diponegoro.

Germany, Federal Republic: 1 Jalan M. H. Thamrin; *Ambassador:* Dr. KURT MÜLLER.

Hungary: 36 Jalan Diponegoro; *Ambassador:* IMRE URANOVIC (also accred. to Malaysia and New Zealand).

India: 44 Jalan Kebonsirih.

Iran: 2 Jalan Mangunsarkoro; *Ambassador:* MOHAMMAD ALI SHEKOHIYAN.

Iraq: 38 Jalan Teuku Umar (also accred. to Malaysia).

Italy: 47 Jalan Diponegoro.

Japan: 24 Jl. Thamrin; *Ambassador:* RYOZO SUNOBE.

Jordan: Islamabad, Pakistan.

Korea, Democratic People's Republic: 72/74 Jalan Teuku Umar; *Ambassador:* LI JANG HWA.

Korea, Republic: 13 Jalan Diponegoro; *Ambassador:* LEE CHAE-SOL.

Malaysia: 17 Jl. Imam Bonjol; *Ambassador:* Z. A. bin SULONG.

Mexico: 59 Jalan M. H. Thamrin (also accred. to Malaysia).

Netherlands: 18 Jl. Kebon Sirih; *Ambassador:* PAUL WILLEM JALINK.

New Zealand: 60 Jalan Prof. Mohd. Yamin; *Ambassador.* R. L. JERMYN.

Nigeria: Hotel Indonesia, Rooms 646 and 634.

Norway: 4 Jalan Padalarang; *Ambassador:* BJØRN I. KRISTVIK (also accred. to Malaysia).

Pakistan: 15 Jalan Teuku Umar; *Ambassador:* IQBAL HOSAIN.

Philippines: 8 Jalan Imam Bonjol.

Poland: 65 Jalan Diponegoro.

Romania: 45 Jalan Teuku Umar; *Ambassador:* THEODOR DITULESCU (also accred. to Malaysia and Singapore).

Saudi Arabia: 3 Jalan Imam Bonjol.

Singapore: 23 Jl. Proklamasi.

Spain: 7 Jalan Cianjur.

Sri Lanka: 45 Jl. Lembang (also accred. to Laos).

Sweden: 12 Jalan Taman Cut Mutiah.

Switzerland: 23 Jl. J. Laturharhary, S.H.; *Ambassador:* MAX FELLER.

Syria: 78 Jalan H. A. Salim (also accred. to Malaysia).

Thailand: 23 Jalan Diponegoro.

Trinidad and Tobago: New Delhi, India.

Turkey: 43 Jalan Imam Bonjol.

U.S.S.R.: 60 Jalan Imam Bonjol.

United Kingdom: 75 Jl. Thamrin; *Ambassador:* JOHN FORD.

U.S.A.: 5 Jalan Merdeka Selatan; *Ambassador:* DAVID D. NEWSON.

Vatican: 18 Jalan Merdeka Timur (Apostolic Nunciature).

Viet-Nam: 25 Jalan Teuku Umar.

Yugoslavia: 8 Jalan Diponegoro (also accred to Malaysia and Singapore).

Indonesia also has diplomatic relations with Ethiopia, Ghana, Greece, Kuwait, Laos, Lebanon, Liberia, Luxembourg, adagascar, Mali, Mongolia, Morocco, Nepal, Somalia, Sudan, Tanzania and Tunisia.

JUDICIAL SYSTEM

Supreme Court. The final court of appeal (cassation).

High Courts in Jakarta, Surabaya, Medan, Ujungpandang (Makassar), Banda Aceh, Bukit–Tinggi, Palembang, Bandung, Semarang, Banjarmasin, Menado, Den Pasar, Ambon and Jaya Pura deal with appeals from the District Courts.

District Courts deal with marriage, divorce and reconciliation.

Chief Justice: Prof. OEMAR-SENOADJI

There is one codified criminal law for the whole of Indonesia. Europeans are subject to the Code of Civil Law published in the State Gazette in 1847. For Indonesians the civil law is the uncodified customary law (*Hukum Adat*) which varies from region to region. Alien orientals (i.e. Arabs, Indians, etc.) and Chinese are subject to certain parts of the Code of Civil Law and the Code of Commerce. The work of codifying this law has started but in view of the great complexity and diversity of customary law it may be expected to take a considerable time to achieve.

RELIGION

The provisional 1971 Census figures gave the following percentage estimates:

	Per cent
Muslim	94
Christian	5
Hindu	} 1
Others	} 1

MUSLIM

Leader: IDHAM CHALID.

ROMAN CATHOLIC

Archbishop of Jakarta: Mgr. LEO SOEKOTO, S.J.

THE PRESS

PRINCIPAL DAILIES

Java

Angkatan Bersenjata: Jalan Asemka 29, Jakarta; official armed forces paper; Dir. Brig.-Gen. H. SUGANDHI; Editor Col. S. DJOJOPRANOTO; circ. 100,000.

Berita Yudha: Jl. Tanah Abang 11/35, Jakarta; official Army paper; Editor Brig.-Gen. M. NAWAWI ALIF; circ. 68,000.

Harian Umum Republic: Jl. Kepodang 20, Semarang; f. 1957; Publisher CHANDRA NAINGGOLAN; circ. 10,000.

Indonesian Daily News: Jalan Jend. Basuki Rachmat 52, Surabaya; f. 1957; English; Editor Hos. NURYAHYA; circ. 6,500.

Indonesian Observer: Jalan M. Sangadji 11, Jakarta; English; independent; Editors Mrs. HERAWATI DIAH, SUTOMO SATIMAN, TRIBUANA SAID, Mrs. D. HADMOKO SOEHOED; circ. 16,500.

Kedaulatan Rakyat: Jalan P. Mangkubumi 40-42, Yogjakarta; f. 1945; Indonesian; independent; Dir. SAMAWI; Editor M. WONOHITO; circ. 30,000.

Kompas: Pal Merah Selalatan 28, Jakarta Barat; Editor Drs. J. OETAMA; circ. 214,000.

Masa Kini: Jalan K.H.A. 121, Yogjakarta; f. 1966; Chief Editor H. ACHMAD BASUNI; circ. 25,000.

Merdeka: Jalan M. Sangaoji 11, Jakarta; f. 1945; Indonesian; independent; Editor-in-Chief B. M. DIAH; circ. 80,000.

Nasional: Beji 33, Yogjakarta; f. 1946; Indonesian; nationalist (PNI); Editor ISSUTHIAR; circ. 17,000.

Pelita: Jakarta; f. 1974; Indonesian.

Perwarta Surabaya: Petjinan Kulon 23, Surabaya, P.O.B. 85; f. 1905; Indonesian; Editors TJIOOK SEE TJIOE TAN, PHOA TJONG HWAY, S. RIDWAN, B. P. PARWAN; circ. 10,000.

Pikiran Rakyat: 133 Jalan Asia-Afrika, Bandung; f. 1950; independent; Editor SAKIT ALAMSJAH; circ. 42,000.

Sinar Harapan: Jl. Pintu Besar Selatan 93, Jakarta; f. 1961; independent; Editor SOEBAGYOPR; circ. 110,000.

Sipatahoenan: Jalan Dalem Kaum 42-44, Bandung; Sundanese; Editor Haji MUHAMMAD KENDANA; circ 7,000.

Suara Merdeka: Jl. Nerak 11, Semarang; f. 1950; Indonesian; Publisher Mr. HETAMI; Editor Mr. SOERWARNO; circ. 65,000.

Surabaya Post: Surabaya; independent; Prop. and Editor A. AZIZ; circ. 45,000.

Kalimantan (Borneo)

Indonesia Berjuang: Jalan Pangeran Samudra 71, Banjarmasin; f. 1946; Indonesian; Editor A. S. MUSAFFA SH; circ. 7,500.

Pembina: Samarinda; Indonesian.

Suara Kalimantan: Jalan Kalimantan 41, Banjarmasin; Indonesian; circ. 5,000.

Sumatra

Api Pancasila: Palembang; f. 1966; Editor T. S. LUBIS; circ. 7,500.

Haluan: Jalandamar 59 D-E, Padang; f. 1948; Editor-in-Chief CHAIRUL HARUN.

Harian Mertju Suar: Jl. Let. Kol. Martinus Lubis 48, Medan; f. 1966; Editor MAHJOEDANIL; circ. 15,000.

Medan Daily News: Jl. Sei Kera 37, Medan; f. 1969; English; Editor/Publisher H. A. DAHLAN; circ. 5,000

Mimbar Umum: Jalan Riau 79, Medan; f. 1947; Indonesian; independent; Editor ARIF LUBIS; circ. 50,000.

Suara Rakyat Semesta Palembang-Indonesia: Palembang; Indonesian; Editor DJADIL ABDULLAH; circ. 10,000.

Waspada: Jalan Suprapto/Katamso 1 and Pusat Pasar 126, Medan; Indonesian; f. 1947; Dir. Mrs. ANIIDRUS SAID; Editors ARSYAD YAHYA RITONGA, AMMARY IRABI; circ. 50,000 (daily); Sunday edition 50,000.

Sulawesi (Celebes)

Pedoman Rakyat: Jl. H. A. Mappanyukki 28, Ujungpandang (Makassar); independent; Editor M. BASIR; circ. 10,000.

Sultara: Jl. Korengkeng 34 Tilp 4563, 3773, Menado; f. 1968; Chief Editor V. R. MONTOLALU; circ. 6,000.

Bali

Harian Pagi Umum (*Bali Post*): Jl. Bisma 1, Den Pasar; f. 1948; circ. 10,000.

Suara Indonesia: Den Pasar; Indonesian.

Lombok

Lombok Baru: Ampenan; Indonesian.

Timor

Kupang: Indonesian.

PRINCIPAL WEEKLIES

Java

Berita Minggu: Jalan Pintu Besi 31, Jakarta; Indonesian; Editor MAWARDI RIVAL; circ. 10,000.

Business News: Jalan H. Abdul Muis 70, Jakarta; f. 1956; Indonesian and English; Chief Editor SANJOTO SASTROMIHARDJO; circ. 10,000.

Jakarta Weekly Mail: Jakarta; Indonesian.

Djojobojo: Pasar Besar Wetan 32, Surabaya; Indonesian.

Koran Minggu Pelopor Jogja: Jl. Jen. A. Yani 175A, Yogjakarta; f. 1966; Editor J. WIROSOEBROTO; circ. 7,500.

Lembaran Minggu: Jalan Asia-Afrika 133, Bandung; Indonesian.

Madjalah Merdeka: Jalan Hajam Wuruk 9; Indonesian.

Mangle: Jl. Lodaya 19, Bandung; f. 1957; Sundanese; circ. 30,000; Chief Editor R. H. UTON MUCHTAR.

New Standard: Jalan Hasanudin 48, Jakarta; English; Dir. S. H. NOTO; circ. 25,000.

Panjebar Semangat: Jalan Bubutan 87, Surabaya; f. 1933; Javanese; circ. 50,000.

Sapta Marga: Jalan Segara 5, Jakarta; Indonesian.

Selecta: Jakarta; illustrated; Editor SAMSUDIN; circ. 30,000.

Skrikandi: Jakarta; Editor Mrs. SOEDJONO; circ. 15,000.

Varia: Jakarta; illustrated; Editor R. ARIFIEN; circ. 40,000.

Wanita Nasional: Semarang: f. 1950; Indonesian; Editors Miss CHAFSAH AMIRIN, Miss SETIOWATI RAMELAN; circ. 10,000.

PRINCIPAL PERIODICALS

Al-Djami'ah: Institut Agama Islam Negeri, Demangan, Tromelpos 82, Yogjakarta; f. 1962; university journal of Islam; bi-monthly.

Angkasa: Jalan Tanah Abang Bukit 36, Jakarta; Indonesian Air Force magazine; Indonesian; monthly.

Bahasa dan Kesusasteraan: Jalan Diponegoro 82, P.O.B. 2625, Jakarta; f. 1967; linguistics and literature; bi-monthly; Dir. Mrs. RUDJIATI MULJADI.

Basis: P.O.B. 20, Yogjakarta; f. 1951; general Indonesian culture; monthly; Editor TH. GELDORP, S.J.; circ. 5,000.

Berita Negara: Jalan Pertjetakan Negara 21, Kotakpos 2111, Jakarta; f. 1960; official gazette; 3 times a week.

Bhayangkara: Jalan Veteran 34, Telukbetung, Lampung, Sumatra; f. 1967; three times weekly; Editor J. KOESRI.

Bina Pancasila: Jalan Dr. Wahidin 11/2, Jakarta; bi-weekly; Editor Dr. M. HOETAROEROEK; circ. 25,000.

Budaya: Jalan Faridan M. Noto 11, Yogjakarta; f. 1952; Indonesian culture; monthly.

Dunia Wanita: Jalan Pusat Pasar, P. 125, Medan; f. 1949; Indonesian; women; fortnightly; Chief Editor Mrs. ANIIDRUS SAID; circ. 10,000.

Economic Review of Indonesia: Ministry of Economic Affairs, Jalan Gajah Mada 8, Jakarta; f. 1947; English; quarterly.

Gajah Mada: Jalan Merapi 16, Yogjakarta; Indonesian; monthly.

Hemera Zoa (*Indonesian Journal of Animal Science*): Jalan Bubulak 32A, Bogor; f. 1886; bi-monthly; English, French, German.

Horison: Jalan Gajah 104, Jakarta; cultural; independent; Editor MOCHTAR LUBIS; circ. 10,000.

Idea: Fakultas Pertanian, Bogor; f. 1935; quarterly; English, Dutch.

Ilmu, Teknik dan Hidup: Jalan Sukabami 36, Jakarta; f. 1949; natural sciences; monthly; Indonesian.

Indonesia Magazine: Medan Merdeka Barat 28, Jakarta; monthly; Indonesian, English.

Indonesian Perspectives: Asean Publishing House, 128–130 Anson Rd., Singapore 2; trade, industry and tourism; monthly; English.

Intisari: Pal Merah Selatan 28, Jakarta Barat; monthly digest; Editor Drs. J. OETAMA; circ. (Oct. 1975) 130,500

Lembaga Penjelidikan Ekonomi dan Masyarakat Fakultas Ekonomi Universitas Indonesia: Jalan Salemba Raya 4, Jakarta; f. 1954; professional journal—economics and finance in Indonesia; Dir. S. B. JOEDONO; quarterly.

Majalah Ekonomis: Jalan Majapahit 1, Jakarta; monthly trade journal; Indonesian; Chief Editor S. ARIFIN HUTABARAT; circ. 10,000.

Majalah GPS Grafika: Jalan Sawah Besar 29, Jakarta; f. 1962; Indonesian; graphic arts; monthly.

Majalah Kedokteran Indonesia (*Journal of the Indonesian Medical Association*): Jalan Kesehatan 111/29, Jakarta 11/16; f. 1951; monthly; Indonesian, English; Editor Prof. Dr. BAHDER DJOHAN.

Mimbar Kabinet Pembangunan: Merdeka Baratag, Jakarta; f. 1966; monthly; Indonesian; published by Dept. of Information.

Mimbar Pembangunan: Merdeka Barat 9, Jakarta; f. 1968; Indonesian; monthly; published by Dept. of Information.

Mimbar Penerangan: Merdeka Barat 9, Jakarta; f. 1950; Indonesian; quarterly; published by Dept. of Information.

Nasional: Matraman Raya 50, Jakarta; f. 1948; Indonesian; Editor WIENAKTOE; circ. 20,000.

Penca: Jalan Gajah Mada 25, Jakarta; Indonesian; fortnightly.

Peraba: Bintaran Kidul 5, Yogjakarta; Indonesian and Javanese; Catholic; weekly.

Pertani: Perusahaan Pertanian Negara, Jalan Pasarminggu, Kalibata, Jakarta; f. 1963; Indonesian; agricultural; monthly; Pres./Dir. S. WARDOJO.

Publisistik: University of Jakarta; Jl. Gondangdia Lama 3, Jakarta; quarterly; Gen. Man. Drs. D. H. ASSEGAF, Man. Editor Drs. ALADDIN.

Purnama: Parapatan 34A, Jakarta; Indonesian; fortnightly; films.

Radjawali: Jalan Ir. H. Juanda 15, Jakarta; Indonesian; monthly; Civil Air Transport and Tourism; Dir. SALMAN HARDANI; Man. Editor MOERTHIKO.

Sinar Jaya: Jalan Sultan Aqung 67A, Jakarta; agricultural newspaper; bi-weekly; Chief Editor Ir. SURYONO PROJOPRANOTO.

Suara-Guru: Jalan Tanah-Abang III/24, Jakarta; f. 1958; Indonesian; teachers' magazine.

Surat Kabar Mingguan—Posminggu: Jalan Mataram 898, Semarang; Indonesian.

Yapenpa: Medan Merdeka Barat No. 9, Jakarta; Indonesian Overseas Feature Service; Foreign Languages Publishing Institute; magazines, booklets; twice a month; Exec. Man. Drs. T. ATMADI.

NEWS AGENCIES

Antara (*Indonesian National News Agency*): 53 Jalan Antara, Jakarta; f. 1937; 50 newspapers subscribe to the Agency (1974); 13 brs. in Indonesia, 3 abroad; connected with 22 foreign agencies; Gen. Man. HARSONO RENO UTOMO; Man. Dir. MOH. NAHAR; Editor-in-Chief Ch. R. PAKASI.

FOREIGN BUREAUX

Agence France-Presse (AFP): Jalan Indramaju 18, Jakarta.

Reuters: Jalan Autara 53, Jakarta.

DPA, Jiji Press, Kyodo News Service, Tass and UPI also have offices in Jakarta.

PRESS ASSOCIATIONS

Persatuan Wartawan Indonesia (*Journalists' Association of Indonesia*): Jalan Veteran 7-C, Jakarta; f. 1946; 3,000 mems.; Chair. ROSIHAN ANWAR, B. M. DIAH.

Persatuan Wartawan Tionghoa (*Chinese Journalists' Association*): 29 Pantjoran, Jakarta.

PUBLISHERS

Jakarta

BP Alda/Penca: 11A Jl. Tambak; f. 1973; general books; Man. RADIK UTOYO-SUDIRJO.

Balai Pustaka: 2 Jl. Dr. Wahidin; f. 1908; children's books, literary, scientific publications and periodicals; Pres. Drs. SOETOJO GONDO.

Bulan Bintang: 8 Jl. Kramat Kwitang I; f. 1954; religious, social science, natural and applied sciences, art; Man. AMELZ.

Dian Rakyat: 17 Jl. Ketapang Utara 1; f. 1963; textbooks; Man. SOFJAN ALISJAHBANA.

Djambatan: 152 Jl. Kramat Raya; f. 1958; children's books, textbooks, social sciences; Man. ROSWITHA PAMOENTJAK.

Dunia Pustaka Jaya: 31A Jl. Krmat II; f. 1971; fiction, essays, poetry and children's books; Man. AJIP ROSIDI.

Erlangga: Kramat 4/11; f. 1952; secondary school and university textbooks; Man. M. HUTAURUK, S.H.

Gramedia: 110 Jalan Gajah Mada; f. 1970; university textbooks, fiction and children's books; Man. P. K. OYONG, S.H.

Gunung Agung: 6 Jl. Kwitang, P.O.B. 145; f. 1950; children's books, textbooks, scientific publications; Pres. MASAGUNG.

BPK Gunung Mulia: 22 Jl. Kwitang; f. 1951; general books, children's books, religious books, home economics; Man. A. SIMANDJUNTAK.

Harapan Masa: 20 Jl. Karet Tengsin; f. 1952; textbooks, childrens' books, general books, Man. AMIN KROMOMIHARDJO.

Ichtiar: 6 Jl. Majapahit; f. 1959; textbooks, social science, natural and applied sciences, general books; Man. JOHN SEMERU.

Jaya Murni: 34 pav. Jl. Ir. H. Juanda; f. 1960; religious books and general books; Man. H. A. MALIK ISMAIL.

Kinta: 54A Jl. Cik Ditiro; f. 1950; textbooks, social science, general books; Man. RIVAI S. ATMADJA.

Mutiara: 36 Jl. Salemba Tengah; f. 1966; textbooks, religious books, social sciences, general books, ehildren's books; Man. H. OEMAR BAKRY DT. TAN-BESAR.

Pembangunan: 2 Jl. Raden Saleh; brs. in Bandung, Yogjakarta, Madiun and Surabaya; f. 1953; textbooks, children's books and scientific publications; Mans. SUMANTRI, SOEWONDO.

Pembimbing Masa: 69 Jl. Matraman Raya; f. 1964; textbooks, scientific publications, children's books and general books; Man. H. MACHMOED.

Pradnya Paramita: 8 Jl. Madiun; f. 1963; children's books, general books, educational and home economics; Man. SADONO DIBYOWIROYO SH.

Pustaka Antara: 28 Jl. Majapahit; f. 1952; textbooks, scientific publications, children's books and general books; Man. H. M. JOESOEF AHMAD.

Sinar Hudaya: 56A Jl. Senen Raya; f. 1967; religious books, textbooks, children's books and general books; Man. ADAM SALEH.

Soeroengan: 58 Jl. Pecenongan; f. 1950; textbooks and agriculture; Man. G. SILITONGA SH.

Tintamas Indonesia: 60 Jl. Kramat Raya; f. 1947; modern science and culture, especially Islamic works; Editor ALI AUDAH.

Widjaya: 48C Jl. Pecenongan; f. 1950; textbooks, children's books, religious and general books; Man. NAZAR YAHYA,

Yasaguna: 7 Gg. Batik—Jl. Bendungan Hilir; textbooks, agriculture and children's books; Man. HILMAN MADEWA.

Yayasan Penerbit Universitas Indonesia: 4 Jl. Raya Salemba; f. 1969; scientific publications; Man. Drs. SASANASURYA.

Bandung

Alumni: 11A Jalan Geusanulurn; f. 1969; university textbooks; Man. H. SOETARDJO.

Binacipta: 34 Jl. Cipunagara; f. 1967; textbooks, scientific publications, general books; Man. O. BARDIN.

Cerdas: 125 Jl. Palasari; f. 1961; general books; Man. H. ADANG AFFANDI.

Diponegoro: 36A Jl. Moh. Toha; f. 1967; religious books and general books; Man. A. DAHLAN.

Eresco: 11 Jl. Hasanudin; f. 1957; scientific publications and general books; Man. Mrs. P. ROCHMAT SOEMITRO.

Al Ma'Arif: 32-34 Jl. Tamblong; f. 1949; textbooks, religious books and general books; Man. H. M. BAHARTHAH.

Paramaartha: 440 Jl. Oto Iskandardinata; f. 1964; textbooks; Man. S. DARMOKO.

Pustaka Star: 46 Jl. Moh. Toha; f. 1957; textbooks; Man. H. USMAN ACHMAD.

Tarate: 26 Jalan Sumatera; f. 1955; primary and secondary school textbooks; Man. H. SOETARDJO.

Flores

Nusa Indah: 5 Jl. Katedral-Ende-Flores; f. 1973; religious and general books; Man. JOHANES MENJANG.

Kudus

Menara Kudus: 2 Jalan Menara; f. 1958; religious books (Moslem); Man. H. M. ZYAINURI NOOR.

Medan

Arta: 9 Jl. Jodipati; f. 1961; textbooks; Man. SOPAR SITUMORANG.

Damai: 93 Jl. Sei Deli; f. 1974; general books; Man. A. MURAD NASUTION.

Islamiyah: Jalan Dr. Sutomo P. 328–329; f. 1954; Man. H. Abd. DJALIL SIREGAR.

Maju: 341–342 Jl. Sutomo P.; f. 1950; textbooks, children's books and general books; Man. H. MOHD. ARBIE

Nurina: 69 Jl. Jend. A. Yani V; f. 1972; textbooks; Man. NAGA LUBIS.

Pustaka Andalas: 103 Jl. Sutomo; f. 1962; general books and children's books.

Pustaka Indonesia: 648 Jalan Dr. Sutomo; f. 1962; primary and secondary school textbooks; Man. H. SYAMSUDDIN M.

Surabaya

Assegaff: 136 Jl. Panggung; f. 1951; religious books, language books, lower school, textbooks; Man. HASAN ASSEGAFF.

Grip: 2 Jl. Kawung; f. 1968; textbooks and general books; Man. SURIPTO.

Jaya Baya: 2 (atas) Jl. Panghela, P.O.B. 250; f. 1945; textbooks; Man. TADJIB ERMADI.

Karunia: 18A Jl. Paneleh; f. 1971; textbooks and general books; Man. HASAN ABDAN.

Yogjakarta

Yayasan Kanisius: 24 Jl. P. Senopati; textbooks, religious books and general books.

Ujung Pandang

Bhakti Baru: 15 Jalan A. Yani; f. 1972; primary and secondary school textbooks; Man. M. ALWI HAMU.

PUBLISHERS' ASSOCIATION

IKAPI (*Association of Indonesian Book-Publishers*): Jalan Pengarengan 32, Jakarta-Pusat 111/4; f. 1950; 107 mems.; Pres. AJIP ROSIDI; Sec. ALI AMRAN.

RADIO AND TELEVISION

RADIO

Radio Republik Indonesia: R.R.I., Medan Merdeka Barat 4-5, Jakarta; f. 1945; 49 stations; Dirs. ABDUL HAMID (Dir.), M. AMINULLAH (Overseas Service), ATMOKO (Domestic Service), Ir. HENDRO SIDHARTO (Engineering), R. HUTAPEA (Administration), Drs. ANWAR RACHMAN (News Service); publ. *Media* (fortnightly).

In addition to national daily broadcasts in Indonesian, which include school and educational programmes, there are daily broadcasts overseas in Arabic, Chinese, English, French, Hindi, Malay and Urdu.

In 1974 there were an estimated 3,500,000 radio sets.

TELEVISION

Jajasan Televisi Republik Indonesia: Senayan, Jakarta; f. 1962; government controlled; Dir. M. N. SOEPOMO; publ. *Monitor TVRI*.

In 1974 there were 236,828 televisions in use.

FINANCE

(cap.=capital; dep.=deposits; p.u.=paid up; m.=million; amounts in rupiah.)

BANKING

The General Law on Banking, enacted in December 1967, remodelled the banking structure in Indonesia, which now comprises the following five categories of banks; Central Bank; General Banks; Savings Banks; Development Banks; Special Banks. Special Banks may be set up by the Government to provide banking facilities for specific sectors, e.g. agriculture, industry, communications; a Special Bank is planned to grant credit to farmers, retailers and other small businessmen.

In order to develop the country's capital market the Government, in mid-1973, issued licences for three new monetary institutions and seven investment banks. The three monetary institutions are to be: P.T. Merchant Investment Corporation (P.T. Merincorp), P.T. First Indonesian Finance and Investment Corporation (Ficorinvest) and P.T. Indonesian Investments International (Indovest).

The formerly integrated structure of the Central Bank, composed of five units, was replaced in January 1969 by a single Central Bank and six State banks.

Central Bank

Bank Indonesia: 2 Jalan M.H. Thamrin, Jakarta; f. 1828; nationalized 1951; promulgated the Central Bank in 1968; Gov. Rachmat Saleh.

State Banks

Bank Bumi Daya: Jl. Kebonsirith 66–70, P.O.B. 106, Jakarta; f. 1959; commercial foreign exchange bank; specializes in credits to the plantation and forestry sector; cap. p.u. 300m.; dep. 506,150m. (Dec. 1974); Pres. R. A. B. Massie, s.h.; 53 brs. in Indonesia; Overseas representative offices in Hong Kong and Amsterdam.

Bank Ekspor Impor Indonesia: Jl. Lapangan Setasiun 1, P.O.B. 32, Jakarta-Kota; specializes in credits for manufacture and export; cap. 200m.; dep. 63,802m. (March 1974); Pres. M. Djojomartono.

Bank Rakyat Indonesia: Jalan Veteran 8, P.O.B. 94 Jakarta; f. 1968; cap. 300m., dep. 143,966m. (March 1975); specializes in credits to co-operatives in agriculture and fisheries, in rural credit generally and international business; Pres. S. E. Permadi.

Bank Negara Indonesia 1946: 1 Jalan Lada, P.O.B. 1412/DAK, Jakarta-Kota; f. 1946; cap. Rp. 500m.; first and largest State-owned commercial bank; specializes in credits to the industrial sector as well as commercial transactions; Pres. Dir. R. Surjono Sastrahadikoesoemo; 238 domestic brs. and overseas brs. in Singapore, Hong Kong and Tokyo; Representative offices in London and New York; publ. *Tegas*.

Bank Tabungan Negara (*State Savings Bank*): Jalan Gajah Mada 1, Jakarta; cap. 100m.; specializes in promotion of savings among the general public; Dir. Kol. C. K. H. Soedjiwo, b.c. h.k.

Bank Dagang Negara (*State Commercial Bank*): Jalan M.H. Thamrin 5, P.O.B. 338 DKT, Jakarta; f. 1960; authorized State Foreign Exchange Bank; specializes in credits to the mining sector; cap. 250m.; dep. 237,796m. (Dec. 1974); Pres. Omar Abdalla.

Development Bank

Bank Pembangunan Indonesia (*Development Bank of Indonesia*): Gondangdia Lama 2–4, Jakarta; f. 1960; state bank; financial assistance to Government enterprises and privately-owned industrial and other productive enterprises; helps in development or establishment of new industries and other productive ventures, or expansion and modernization of existing enterprises; conducts feasibility studies of Government projects; auth. cap. 110m. Rupiah; cap. p.u. 60m. Rupiah; total financial resources 80,179m. Rupiah (Sept. 1974); cap. and dep. 26,264m. Rupiah (Sept. 1974); Pres. Kuntoadji.

FINANCE CORPORATIONS

P.T. Bahana Pembinaan Usaha Indonesia: Jalan Cik Tiro 25, Jakarta; f. 1973; cap. p.u. 2,500m.; Pres. Drs. Salamun, a.t.

P.T. Indonesian Development Finance Corporation: Jaya Bldg. Tk. 3, Jalan M. H. Thamrin, Jakarta; f. 1972; cap. p.u. 4,000m.; Pres. Drs. Soelakasono S. Mertokoesoemo.

P.T. Inter Pacific Financial Corporation: Nusantara Bldg. Tk. 4, Jakarta; f. 1973; cap. p.u. 300m.; Pres. R. H. Basoeni Ismail.

P.T. Multinational Finance Corporation: Bangkok Bank Bldg. Tk. 7, Jalan M. H. Thamrin 3, Jakarta; f. 1974; cap. p.u. 500m.; Pres. Soedono Salim.

P.T. Mutual International Finance Corporation: Nusantra Bldg. Tk. 17, Jakarta; f. 1973; cap. p.u. 300m.; Pres. Dr. Y. Panglakim.

P.T. Private Development Finance Company of Indonesia: Jalan Abdul Muis 60, Jakarta; f. 1973; cap. p.u. 37m.; Pres. Drs. Soediarso.

National Private Banks

There are 90 private commercial banks in Indonesia, consisting of 6 foreign exchange banks, 6 co-operative banks and 78 non-foreign exchange banks. The foreign exchange banks are: Bank Umum National, Bank Bali, Bank Dagang National, Panin Bank, Bank Pasifik and Bank Niaga.

Pan Indonesia (Panin) Bank: Jalan Pasar Pagi 24, Jakarta; Pres. Andi Gappa.

P.T. Bank Agung Asia: Jalan Pintu Besar Selatan 75, Jakarta; f. 1965; Pres. Djoni Polil.

P.T. Bank Amerta: 18 Jalan Kwitang, Jakarta; formerly Indonesian Banking Corpn.; Pres. Sadjito; Chair. B. P. H. Prabuningrat.

P.T. Bank Bali: 24 Jalan Pasar Pagi, Jakarta; f. 1954; foreign exchange bank; Chair. Jaja Ramli; Pres. G. Karjadi; Man. Dir. P. H. Sugiri.

P.T. Bank Buana Indonesia: 34-5 Jalan Asemka, Jakarta; f. 1956; cap. p.u. 1,100.1m.; brs. at Medan, Surabaya, Bandung and Semarang; Pres. B. P. H. Tjokrokoesoemo.

P.T. Bank Dagang Nasional Indonesia (*The Indonesian National Commercial Bank Ltd.*): 2 Jalan Balai Kota, Medan; f. 1945; foreign exchange bank; Pres. Paras Nasution.

P.T. Bank Niaga: Jalan Roa Malaka Selatan 5, Jakarta; Pres. Idham.

P.T. Bank Pasifik: Jalan Asemka 5, Jakarta; Pres. Sutanto Sugiarto.

P.T. Sejahteru Bank Umum: Jalan Tiang Bendera 15, Jakarta; f. 1972; Pres. Drs. Goesnar Djalil.

Bank Umum Nasional P.T.: Jl. Pintu Kecil 34, Jakarta; f. 1952; foreign exchange bank; cap. 1,500m., dep. 9,200m.; Man. Dirs. Kaharudin Ongko, M. Djailani, D. Soetanto, H. Chandra.

Banking Organization

Indonesian National Private Banks Association (*Perbankan Nasional Swasta—PERBANAS*):, Jalan Sindanglaja 1, Jakarta; f. 1952; 127 mems.; Sec.-Gen. O. P. Simorangkir; publ. *Keuangan dan Bank* (*Finance and Banking*) (quarterly).

Foreign Banks

The General Law on Banking permits foreign banks to operate in Indonesia under certain conditions. The following eleven foreign banks (*see* below) have been granted permission to resume operations for the first time since 1963.

Algemene Bank Nederland N.V.: Jalan Ir. H. Juanda 23, P.O.B. 2950, Jakarta; Man. M. W. van Hulzen.

American Express International Banking Corporation: Jl. Thamrin, Hotel Indonesia Bldg., P.O.B. 131/DKT, Jakarta; Vice-Pres. R. Roalsson.

Bangkok Bank Ltd.: Jalan M. H. Thamrin 3, Jakarta; br. at Jakarta-Kota; Man. and Asst. Vice-Pres. BOONCHARN TAYJASANANT.

Bank of America N.T. and S.A.: Jl. Medan Merdeka Utara 21, Jakarta; Man. R. L. HOUSER.

Bank of Tokyo: Jl. M. H. Thamrin 59, Wisma Nusantara Bldg., Jakarta; Man. K. ISHIDA.

Chartered Bank Ltd.: Jl. Abdul Muis 40, Jakarta; Man. M. K. BROWN.

The Chase Manhattan Bank, N.A.: New York; Jakarta Branch: Jalan Medan Merdeka Barat 6, P.O.B. 311; sub-br. at Jakarta-Kota; Vice-Pres. and Man. ADRIAN NOE.

Europaeisch-Asiatische Bank: 80 Jalan Imam Bondjol, Jakarta; Joint Mans. KLAUS KREMPEL, A. H. VAN LITH.

Citibank: Jalan M. H. Thamrin 55, and Jakarta-Kota br. at Jalan Hayam Wuruk 127; f. 1812; Resident Vice-Pres. J. L. WORTHINGTON; Vice-Pres. E. W. GLAZIER.

Hongkong and Shanghai Banking Corpn.: Jalan Gajah Mada 18, P.O.B. 2307, Jakarta; br. at Jalan Pintu Besar, Selatan 1098; Man. D. G. LACHLAN.

P.T. Bank Perdania: Jl. Raya Mangga Besar 7–9, Jakarta; Man. SHINJI SUZUKI.

STOCK EXCHANGE

Stock Exchange of Indonesia: c/o Perserikatan Perdagangan Uang dan Efek-Efek; P.O.B. 1224/Dak, Jakarta-Kota; f. 1952; 17 mems.; Chair. Drs. SOEKSMONO BESAR MARTOKOESOEMO; Sec. Drs. KHO HAN TIONG.

INSURANCE

Regulations have been introduced to limit the number of foreign companies licensed to operate to 12. In February 1974 a statement was issued by the Ministry of Finance emphasizing the need to form bigger units among the domestic companies, advising foreign companies to cooperate with domestic companies in joint ventures, and forbidding foreign investment in the life insurance sector. In November 1974 there were 56 general insurance companies consisting of 44 national companies, 12 foreign companies, 3 reinsurance companies, and 4 social insurance bodies.

Dewan Asuransi Indonesia (*Insurance Association of Indonesia*): Jalan Ir. H. Juanda 111/1A, Jakarta; Chair. B. B. A. WAHJDE; Sec. R. S. RAHARDJO.

Central Asia Insurance Co. Ltd.: 101 Jl. Pintu Besar Selatan (1st floor), Jakarta-Kota; f. 1958; general insurance; Dir. WARDOJO.

N.V. Pasti (N.V. Perusahaan Asuransi Timur): Jl. Jendral Basuki Rachmad 16, Malang, Java; f. 1956; Man. Dir. Prof. Dr. W. HARDIMAN SETIASARWANA.

Perurn A.K. Jasa Raharja: Perum Asuransi Kerugian, Jalan Kali Besar Timur 10, Jakarta-Kota; Man. MOCH SOEPRAPTO.

P.T. Asuransi Gajah Mada: Jl. Kali Besar Timur 4, Jakarta; f. 1953; general insurance; national company; Man. Dir. W. A. WOWOR.

P.T. Asuransi Indonesia-Amerika Basu: 143/22 Jalan Dr. Suharjo, Jakarto; f. 1975.

P.T. Asuransi Jasa Indonesia: Jl. Let. Jen. Haryono M.T., Kaveling 61, Jakarta; general insurance; national company; Pres. Maj.-Gen. of Police B. B. A. WAHJOE.

P.T. Asuransi Jiwasraya (*Jiwasaya Life Insurance Co. Ltd.*): 34 Jl. Ir. H. Juanda 34, P.O.B. 240, Jakarta; f. 1859; Pres. H. SJAFTARI; Sec. Dir. ABDULLAH.

P.T. Asuransi Republik: Jl. Abd. Muis 86, Jakarta; f. 1957; general insurance; Man. Dirs. B. NASUTION, NOEHAR, SUWITO REKSOATMOJO.

P.T. Lloyd Indonesia: Jalan Kepodang 12–14, Semarang; Man. EKA TJIPTA WIDJAJA.

P.T. Maskapai Asuransi Ampuh: Jl. Majapahit 24-26 Belakang, Jakarta; Dir. P. SULAIMAN.

P.T. Maskapai Asuransi Independent: P.T. Bank Buana Bldg. (2nd floor), 34/35 Jl. Asemka, Jakarta; f. 1957; general insurance; Dir. I. H. ADJIWIDJAYA; Man. M. D. WIDODO.

P.T. Maskapai Asuransi Indrapura: Gedung Jaya 2, Jl M. H. Thamrin, Jakarta; f. 1954; general insurance; Chair. HENRI GUNANTO, S.H.

P.T. Maskapai Asuransi Pancha: Jalan H. Agus Salim 27 A/B, Jakarta; f. 1957; general insurance; Man. John R. SIBIH.

P.T. Maskapai Asuransi Ramayana: Jalan Cengkeh 19H, Jakarta; f. 1956; general insurance; Dir. R. G. DOERIAT.

P.T. Maskapai Asuransi Waringin Lloyd: Jalan Kebon Sirih 13, Jakarta; Man. J. A. SUMENDAD.

P.T. Maskapai Asuransi Umum Wuwungan: Pintu Besar Utara 32, P.O.B. 1062, Jakarta; f. 1952; general insurance; national company; Dir. R. A. WUWUNGAN.

P.T. Maskapai Kebakaran Dan Umum Suntad (*Suntad Fire and General Insurance Co.*): 95B Jl. Tiang Bendera, Jakarta-Kota; f. 1964; Dir. R. SOEGIONO.

P.T. Maskapai Reasuransi Indonesia (*Reinsurance Company of Indonesia Ltd.*): 7-9 Jl. Veteran III, Jakarta; f. 1953; professional reinsurance; Man. Dir. Dr. T. S. T. GAUTAMA.

P.T. Perusahaan Asuransi Murni: Jl. Tiang Bendera 90, Jakarta; f. 1953; general insurance; Pres. A. HURSEPUNY.

P.T. Umum International Underwriters: 30 Jalan Salemba Raya, Jakarta; f. 1967; general insurance; Pres. WAHJOE, B.B.A.; Dir. Z. NASUTION.

Reasuransi Umum Indonesia P.T.: Jalan Salemba Raya 30, P.O.B. 2635, Jakarta IV/3; f. 1954; Man. SULAIMAN M. SUMITAKUSUMA.

Samarang Sea and Fire Insurance Co. Ltd.: Jl. Ir. H. Juanda 30, Jakarta; f. 1866; Mans. M. B. MURPHY and T. E. O'KEEFE.

Veritas Insurance Co. Ltd.: Kali Besar Timur 10, P.O.B 1338, Jakarta; f. 1878; Man. Dir. H. F. THENU.

TRADE AND INDUSTRY

National Development Planning Agency (BAPPENAS): 2 Taman Suropati, Jakarta; Chair. Prof. WIDJOJO NITISASTRO; Vice-Chair. J. B. SUMARLIN.

CHAMBER OF COMMERCE

Dewan Perniagaan dan Perusahaan—DPP (*Indonesian Chamber of Commerce and Industry*): 11 Jalan Merdeka Timur, Jakarta; Pres. M. SOEBCHAN Z. E.

TRADE ORGANIZATIONS

CAFI (*Commercial Advisory Foundation in Indonesia*): 9 Jl. Lombok, Jakarta; f. 1958; information services; Chair. Dr. R. Ng. S. SOSROHADIKUSUMO; Man. Dir. B. R. RANTI.

GINSI (*Importers' Association of Indonesia*): Wisma Nusantara Bldg., Jalan Mojopahit No. 1, Jakarta, P.O.B. 2744 Dkt.; f. 1956; mems.: 3,200 importers throughout Indonesia; Chair. B. R. MOTIK; Sec.-Gen. ZAINI NOORDIN.

Organisasi Exportir Hasilbumi Indonesia—OEHI (*Association of Exporters of Indonesian Produce*): Jl. Tjikini Raya 29, P.O.B. 13, Jakarta; f. 1946; 84 mems.; Chair. R. NG. S. SOSROHADIKOESOEMO.

Perkumpulan Koperasi Gabungan Pembelian Importir Indonesia G.A.—GAPINDO (*Indonesian Importers' Co-operative Union*): Kali Besar Timur 5-7, Jakarta.

Perserikatan Perdagangan Uang Efek-Efek (*Association of Money and Stockbrokers*): 3 Pintu Besar Utara, P.O.B. 1224/Dak, Jakarta-Kota; f. 1951; organizes the Stock Exchange; 37 mems. (15 banks and 3 brokers); Chair. Drs. SOEKSMONO BESAR MARTOKOESOEMO; Sec. Drs. KHO HAN TIONG; publ. *Daftuar Kurs Resmi* (Official List of Prices) (daily).

STATE TRADING ORGANIZATIONS

General Management Board of the State Trading Corporations (BPU-PNN): 94–96 Jalan Kramat Raya, CTC Bldg., Jakarta; f. 1961; Pres. Col. SUHARDIMAN; publ. *Majalah Perekonomian Nasional*.

P.N. Aneka Niaga: Jl. Kali Besar Timur IV/I, P.O.B. 1213 DAK, Jakarta-Kota; f. 1964; import and distribution of basic goods, bulb articles, sundries, provisions and drinks, and export of Indonesian produce.

P.N. Dharma Niaga Ltd.: Jalan Abdul Muis 6/8/10, Jakarta, P.O.B. 2028; f. 1964; import of technical articles, equipment and plant; factory representatives, repair and after sales service; export.

TRADE UNION ORGANIZATIONS

In 1973 there were 16 central trade unions in Indonesia, with a membership of 20,201,513. Not all trade unions belong to a central organization, some unions are affiliated to political parties, others are independent.

MAJOR INDUSTRIAL COMPANIES

The following is a selected list of some of the prominent companies in the more important industries currently operating in Indonesia. With a few exceptions, such as oil, rubber and tin, the industrial sector remains in its infancy and at present is composed of a very large number of small enterprises producing mainly consumer goods.

(All addresses in Jakarta except where otherwise stated.)

BICYCLE ASSEMBLY

P.T. Bina Logam: Bandengan Utara Waspada 46.

Firam I.N.I.: Jembatan Lima 48.

Bunda Safia: Comador Sudarso 347, Medan.

ENAMEL WARE

Sri Kentjana: Bandengan Utara 93.

P.T. Sedjati Ltd.: Jalan Pinangsia 14.

P.T. Sedjati: Jalan Pinangsia 14.

Java Enamel Factory: Orpa 50.

Indonesian Enamel Factory: Mampang Prapatan.

Pabriek Emaile Takari: Jalan Prof. Latumentan.

FOOD CANNING

Carlo Food Manufacturing Company: Jalan Garuda 36; f. 1954; division of P.T. Pido Trading Company; Pres. GOAN HOEY OEY; Man. Dir. WIRIA KARNADI.

Ong Tjay Bo: Muka Kampanan, Malang.

Jakti Products: Batu, Malang.

Canning Indonesian Products: Pelabuhan, Bali.

FOUNDRIES

P.T. Barata Metalworks and Engineering: Jl. Ngagel 109, Surabaya; f. 1971; Pres. I. SOESENO.

Indonesian Navy Dockyard: Tanjong Perak, Surabaya.

P.N. Kerata Api: Gereja Ajan, Bandung.

P.N. Tambang Timah Banka: Sungeiliat, Banka Island.

GLASS FACTORIES

Pabriek Gelas Tiong Hiem: Arabiki 18.

Pabriek Gelas Pasar Putih: Kartinin 56c.

IMPORTERS

P.T. Empat Tunggal Chakrawarti: Jalan K. H. Hasyim Asyhari S.; f. 1954.

STATE OIL CONCERN

P.N. Pertamina: 2-4-6 Perwira; Pres. and Chair. Maj.-Gen. PIET HARJONO.

PHARMACEUTICALS

Raja Pharma: Mojopahit 18.

P.T. Kimia Farma: (Production Unit) Jalan Veteran 9.

P.T. Bintang Tuju: Jalan Kretok.

Indonesian Drug House: P.O.B. 3339, Cikini Raya 88.

P.T. Nellco: Kebon Jeruk 18/6.

P.T. Bison: Jalan Kernenangan 1A.

P.T. Beta Pharma: Iskandar Dinata 72.

P.T. Tempo: Kebon Sirih 45.

P.T. Dupa: Jalan H.O.S. Tjokroaminoto 83; f. 1959; Dirs. Drs. E. LOOHO, Drs. J. MOKOGINTA.

P.T. Meda Pharma: Jen. Sudirman 276.

P.T. Kemboja: Jalan Kemboja 6.

Japhar Pharma: Jatipetamburan 11c/30.

P.T. Medi Pharma: Jen. Sudirman 276.

PAINT

P.T. Warna Agung (Patna Paint Factory): Gunung Sahari Ancol 3.

P.T. Indevitra: Jalan Darata 40.

Pabriek Tjat Indonesia: Jalan Darata 40.

P.N. Utama: Hajam Wuruk 127.

PAPER MILL

P.N. Letjes: Letjes, Propolinggo.

PLASTICS

Wellex Plastics Limited: Bandangan Utara 91.

Pabriek Plastik Dinar Unggul: Paal Merah 77.

P.T. Sinar Panah: Jalan Prof. Dr. Latumeten, Gg. Karung 39.

Pabriek Plastik Naga Sakhti: Bandangan Utara 52A.

Firma Radja Plastik: Jendral Urip Soemohardjobe, Solo.

Pabriek Plastik Mega: Raya Jembatan Lima 84.

Plastik Factory Dewi Mulia: Jalan Raya Barat 524, Bandung.

Kantjing Kimia Indonesian Industries: Jalan Jembatan Tiga 2; Pres. LIE ING FEN.

Golden Star Plastics Company: Jalan Bandangan Utara 2C.

Pioneer Plastics Limited: Jalan Bandangan Utara 43.

P.T. Cimone Jaya Chemical Industry: Cimone Km. 2, Tangerang.

RUBBER

Goodyear Tyre & Rubber Company: Jalan Pedjagalan, Bogor.

Indonesian Tyre & Rubber Works: Luar Desar Pantjorah, Pasar Minggu.

Java Rubber Industrie: Jalan Jakarta 12, Bandung.

Hevea Latex Rubber Works: Pekalangan, Tjeribon.

Perushaan Sepatu "Bata": Kali Bata.

TOOTH PASTE

Unilever Indonesia: Medan Merdeka Barat 1, P.O.B. 162; Chair. P. J. DE BEER.

The 999 Industries: Jalan Guntur 58.

P.T. Nusapharama: Jalan Mangga Dua 11/7.

TEXTILES

Wisma Usaha: Tjigarelang, Bandung.

Yo Kang Tek: Raya Barat 415, Bandung.

Ling Ling Weaving Mill: Raya Timur 268, Bandung.

Hoa An Weaving Mill: Kampung Malebar 215, Bandung.

P.T. Badan Tekstil Nasional: Oto Iskandar Dinata 79, Bandung.

TRANSPORT AND TOURISM

TRANSPORT

RAILWAYS

Perusahaan Jawatan Kereta Api (*State Railways*): Gereja 1, Bandung; seven regional offices; controls 7,246 km. (1973) of track, mainly on Java; Chief Dir. R. SOEMALI.

ROADS

Total length of roads in 1974 was about 85,000 km., of which about 21,000 km. were asphalted. In 1976 the Government initiated a five-year programme of highway and bridges construction totalling about 12,000 km. throughout the country.

MOTORISTS' ORGANIZATION

Notary Public: 8 Jl. Musium, Jakarta; Public Notary TAN THONG KIE.

SHIPPING

Indonesian Commercial Shipping Association: Chair. MOHAMMAD SAAD.

Pelayaran Nasional Indonesia—Pelni Lines: Jalan Patrice Lumumba, Jakarta; State-owned national shipping company; 60 ships.

Jakarta Lloyd P.N.: 28 Jl. Haji Angus Salim, Jakarta; f. 1950; services to U.S.A., Europe, Far East and Australia, twelve cargo vessels; Pres. and Dir. M. J. P. HAHIJARY.

P.N. Pertambangan Minyak Dan Gas Bumi Negara (PERTAMINA): 2–6 Jl. Perwira, P.O.B. 12, Jakarta; Pres./Man. Dir. PIET HARJONO; cargo and tanker service of state oil mining company; nine tankers etc.

P.T. Perusahaan Pelayaran Samudera—SAMUDERA INDONESIA: 43, Jl. Kali Besar Barat, Jakarta Kota; private company.

P.T. Trikora Lloyd: 1 Jl. Malaka, Jakarta-Kota, P.O.B. 1076/Dak.; f. 1964; Pres. Dir. S. BOEDIHARDJO.

P.T. Pelayaran Nusantara SRIWIJAYA RAYA: Jalan Tiang Bendera 52, Jakarta Barat; Dir. SJAHRUL GHOZI BAJUMI; interinsular cargo and passenger services; fleet of 4 cargo and 6 passenger-cargo vessels.

N.S.M. "Oceaan": 18 Jalan Gajah Mada, P.O.B. 289/JKT, Jakarta; regular services between Europe and Indonesia.

Blue Funnel Line: 18 Jalan Gajah Mada, P.O.B. 289/JKT, Jakarta; regular services between Indonesia, Europe and Australia.

Barber Blue Sea Line (BBS): 18 Jalan Gajah Mada, P.O.B. 289/JKT, Jakarta; regular services between the Far East and the U.S.A.

Ben Ocean: 18 Jalan Gajah Mada, P.O.B. 289/JKT, Jakarta; joint service of Ben Line, Blue Funnel. Glen Line and N.S.M. "Oceaan" to U.S.A. and Canada,

Thai Mercantile Marine Ltd.: agents: P. T. Samudera Indonesia, Kali Besar Barat 43, P.O.B. DAK/1244, Jakarta.

CIVIL AVIATION

P.T. Garuda Indonesian Airways: Jl. Ir. H. Juanda 15, Jakarta; f. 1950; operates domestic, regional and international services to Singapore, Kuala Lumpur, Bangkok, Bombay, Karachi, Athens, Rome, Frankfurt, Paris, Amsterdam, Hongkong, Tokyo, Sydney and Melbourne; 1975 fleet of 6 F27, 18 F28, 12 DC-9, 3 DC-8, 1 DC-10; Pres. Dr. WIWEKO SOEPONO.

Merpati Nusantara Airlines: Jl. Patrice Lumumba 2, Kemayoran, Jakarta; domestic and regional services; 3 Vanguard, 2 Viscount 800, 4 YS 11A, 2 Fokker F27-600, 2 HS 748, 4 DC-3, 7 Twin Otter; Pres. Vice-Marshal RAMU SAMARDI.

P.T. Bouraq Indonesian Airlines (BIA): 13 Jalan Kebon Sirih, Jakarta; f. 1970; private company; domestic services linking Jakarta with points in Kalimantan, Sulawesi and Tawau (Malaysia); 2 YS-11A, 3 HS 748, 3 DC-3; Pres. J. A. SUMENDAP.

Bali International Air Service: subsidiary of BIA; charter services; 2 Fokker F27, 1 Trislander, 4 BN-2A Islander; Gen. Man. Capt. SUJONO.

Mandala Airlines: Jalan Blora 23, Jakarta; f. 1969; domestic passenger services; 2 Viscount 800, 1 HS 748, Convair CV-600; Pres. Lt.-Gen. SOERJO.

P.T. Sempati Air Transport: Jalan Kartini Raya 55, Jakarta; f. 1968; subsidiary of P.T. Tri Usaha Bhakti; passenger and cargo services to Manila, Singapore and Kuala Lumpur; 3 Fokker F27, 1 DC-3; Chair. DOLF LATUMAHINA.

Seulawah Air Services Ltd.: 34 Jalan Malaku, Jakarta; f. 1968; domestic services; 1 Viscount 800, 2 Fokker F27, 1 DC-3; Chair. Lt.-Gen. R. SOERJO.

P.T. AOA Zamtud Aviation Corporation: f. 1969; Wisma Kartika Bldg., Jalan M. H. Thamrin, Jakarta; f. 1969; domestic services; 6 DC-3; Pres.-Dir. of Finance DJOEBER AFFANDI.

The following foreign airlines also serve Jakarta: Aeroflot, Air France, Air India, Alitalia, British Airways, Cathay Pacific Airways, Ceskoslovenske Aerolinie, Japan Air Lines (JAL), KLM, Lufthansa, MAS, Pan American, PIA, Qantas Airways, Scandinavian Airlines System (SAS), Swissair, Thai Airways International, EgyptAir, UTA.

TOURISM

Dewan Pariwisata Indonesia (*Indonesian Council for Tourism*): Jalan Diponergoro 25, Jakarta; f. 1957; private body to promote national and international tourism; Chair. (vacant); Vice-Chair. Sri BUDOYO.

ATOMIC ENERGY

National Atomic Energy Agency (*Badan Tenaga Atom Nasional*): Jalan Palatehan 1/26, Blok-K.V., Kebayoran Baru, Jakarta-Selatan; f. 1958; Dir.-Gen. Prof. Dr. A. BAIQUINI; publ. *Majalah Batan*.

DEFENCE

Armed Forces (1974): Total strength 270,000; army 200,000, navy 40,000, air force 30,000; military service is selective.

Equipment: The army has some British and Soviet equipment, while the navy and air force have Soviet and U.S. equipment. During 1975 Indonesia contracted agreements with the Netherlands, Spain and the U.S.A. providing a whole range of aircraft and an agreement with Australia provided patrol boats for the navy.

Defence Expenditure: Estimated defence spending for 1975/76 was U.S. $1,108 million.

Commander-in-Chief of the Armed Forces: Gen. M. PANGGABEAN.

CHIEFS OF STAFF

Army: Lt.-Gen. MAKMUN MUROD.

Navy: Admiral SUBIAKTO.

Air Force: Air Vice-Marshal S. BASARAN.

EDUCATION

Education is mainly controlled by the Department of Education and Culture under the Minister of Education and Culture but the Department of Religious Affairs also runs *Madasahs* (Islamic religious schools) at the primary level. General administration of the Department, including co-ordination and activities relating to staff assistance, is carried out by the Secretariat-General. Under the Minister three Directorates-General perform executive technical functions in the fields of in-school education, cultural education and sports, youth affairs and community education respectively. An Inspectorate-General assists the Minister and supervises other departmental organs while the Educational Development Office assists similarly in the field of research and planning.

The general pattern of education is as follows: elementary education starts from the age of 6 or 7 and lasts for six years. This is followed by three years of junior secondary school education and another three years of senior secondary school education. A further three years of academic level or five years of higher education may follow. Government expenditure in 1972–73 was 38,200 million Rupiah (4.86 per cent of the budget).

Primary Education

In the 1960s primary education grew considerably: by 1970, 12,805,000 pupils were enrolled compared with 7,970,000 in 1960. This represented 58.6 per cent of the school age population of 21,850,000 at this level. Though it represented a considerable achievement, it is to some extent offset by the fact that 65 per cent of pupils drop out of their last year of primary schooling. However, it is expected that eight years of compulsory education will be introduced by 1980.

Secondary Education

In the junior high schools 737,267 pupils were enrolled in 1970 which represented 7.1 per cent of the school age population of 10,350,000. At the senior high school level 5.2 per cent or 417,273 pupils out of a school age population of 8,050,000 were enrolled in 1970.

Technical and Vocational Education

This is the least developed aspect of the educational system but plans have been introduced to establish vocational subjects in the secondary schools. In 1972, there were 589,550 pupils at 3,127 technological and other vocational schools.

University Education

The total number of students attending courses in 1970 was 127,000 or 0.9 per cent of all those receiving education.

Further Developments

Since 1970 the State examinations have been gradually replaced by schools examinations. The Five-Year Educational Development Plan (1969/70-73/74) aimed to improve the curricula and teaching methods in both primary and secondary schools. New mathematics projects have been introduced and eight comprehensive schools were established on an experimental basis in 1972. The universities have been allocated increased funds to enable them to develop more rapidly.

UNIVERSITIES

STATE

Universitas Airlangga: Jalan Raya Dr. Sutomo 61, Surabaya, Java; 4,500 students.

Universitas Andalas: Jalan Jati 77, Padang, West Sumatra; 410 teachers, *c.* 3,000 students.

Institut Teknologi Bandung: Jalan Tamansari 64, Bandung, Java; *c.* 500 teachers, *c.* 6,400 students.

Institut Pertanian Bogor (*Bogor Agricultural University*): Jalan Oto Iskandardinata, Bogor; *c.* 430 teachers, *c.* 1,450 students.

Universitas Brawijaja: Jalan Guntur 1, Malang; *c.* 500 teachers, *c.* 4,250 students.

Universitas Cenderawasih: P.O.B. 120, Jajapura-Irain-Jaya Barat; *c.* 45 teachers, *c.* 600 students.

Universitas Diponegoro: Jalan Imam Barjo, S.H. 1, P.O.B. 270, Semarang; *c.* 830 teachers, *c.* 5,850 students.

Universitas Negeri Jambi: Jalan Merdeka 16, Jambi *c.* 50 teachers, *c.* 370 studnets.

Universitas Negeri Jember: Jalan Panglima Besar Sudirman, Jember; *c.* 700 teachers, *c.* 2,500 students.

Universitas Negeri Jendral Soedirman: Jalan Pengadilan 1, Purwokerto; 150 teachers, 1,200 students.

Universitas Gajah Mada: Bulaksumur, Yogjakarta; 860 teachers, 14,200 students.

Universitas Hasanuddin: Jalan Mesjid Raya, Ujungpandang (Makassar); *c.* 825 teachers, *c.* 6,500 students.

University of Indonesia: Salemba Raya 4, Jakarta, Java; 2,020 teachers, 7,310 students.

Universitas Lambung Mangkurat: Jalan Lambung Mankurat 31, Benjarmasin, Kalimantan.

Universitas Negeri Mataram: Taman Majura, Tjakranegara, Lombok, N.T.B.; *c.* 70 teachers, *c.* 790 students.

Universitas Mulawarman: Jalan Mulawarman 7, Samarinda, East Kalimantan; 54 teachers.

Universitas Nusa Cendana: Kupang, Timor.

Universitas Negeri Pajajaran: Jalan Dipati Ukur 37, Bandung, Java; *c.* 1,920 teachers, *c.* 10,360 students.

Universitas Negeri di Palangka Raya: Complex Pelajar, Palangka Raya.

Universitas Pattimura: Jl. Jenderal Acmad Jani Ambon; *c.* 510 teachers, *c.* 980 students.

Universitas Riau: Pakanbaru, Sumatra; *c.* 475 teachers, *c.* 1,100 students.

University Sjiah Kuala: Darusalam Banda, Atjeh, S.U.

Universitas Negeri Sriwijaja: Bumi Sriwijaya, Palembang; *c.* 230 full-time, *c.* 1,150 part-time teachers, *c.* 2,270 students.

Universitas Sam Ratulangi: Kampus Kleak, Manado; *c.* 310 full-time, *c.* 640 part-time teachers, *c.* 2,930 students.

Universitas Sumatera Utara (*University of North Sumatra*): Jalan Singamangaraja, Teladan, Medan.

Universitas Tanjungpura: Jalan Raja 17, Pontianak.

Institut Teknologi 10 Nopember Surabaya (*Surabaya Institute of Technology*): Jl. Cokroaminto 12A, Surabaya; 484 teachers, 3,250 students.

Udayana State University: Jl. Jendral Sudirman, P.O.B. 105, Denpasar, Bali.

PRIVATE

Universitas 17 Agustus 1945: 46 Jl. Teuku Cik Ditiro, Jakarta; 166 teachers, 860 students.

Universitas Bogor: Jalan Bioskop 31, Bogor; *c.* 60 teachers, *c.* 350 students.

Universitas Jajabaja: Jl. Salemba Raya 12, Jakarta.

Universitas Ibnu Chaldun Bogor: Jalan Papandajan 25, Bogor.

Universitas Ibnu Chaldun: Senen Raya 45-47, Jakarta; *c.* 80 teachers, *c.* 1,000 students.

Universitas Islam Indonesia: Jalan Tjik di Tiro (Terban Taman) No. 1, Yogjakarta, Java; *c* 245, teachers *c.* 5,500 students.

Universitas Islam Jakarta: Jalan Prof. Muh. Yamin 57; *c.* 35 teachers, *c.* 310 students.

Universitas Islam Sjarief Hidajatullah Tjeribon: Jalan Kapten Samadikun, Tjeribon.

Universitas Islam Sumatera Utara (*Islamic University of North Sumatra*): Jalan Singamangaraja, Teladan, Medan; *c* 280 teachers, *c.* 1,250 students.

Universitas Katolik Indonesia "Atma Jaya": P.O.B. 2639 Dak, Jl. Jendral Sudirman, Jakarta; *c.* 230 teachers, *c* 1,170 students.

Universitas Katolik Parahyangan: Jalan Merdeka 32, Bandung; 250 teachers, 3,200 students.

Universitas Krisnadwipajana: Jalan Tegal 10, Jakarta; *c.* 130 teachers, *c.* 2,000 students.

Universitas Kristen Indonesia: Jl. Diponegoro 86, Tromolpos 2, Jakarta; *c.* 425 teachers, *c.* 1,620 students.

Universitas Muhammadijah: Jl. Limau 1, Keb. Baru, Jakarta.

Universitas Nasional (*National University*): Jl. Kalilio 17–19, Jakarta.

Universitas H.K.B.P. Nomensen: Jl. Asahan 4A, Pematang Siantar.

Universitas Kristen Satya Wacana: Jalan Diponegoro 54-58, Salatiga, Java; 211 teachers, 2,184 students.

Universitas Sawerigading: Jalan Sembilan 24, Makassar; *c.* 160 teachers, *c.* 1,370 students.

Universitas Tanjungpura Pontianak: 17 Jalan Tanjungpura Pontianak, Kalimantan Barat; *c.* 155 teachers, *c.* 935 students.

Universitas Tarumanegara: Jalan Let. Jen. S. Parman, Jakarta; 249 teachers, 1,929 students.

Universitas Tjokroaminto Surakarta: Jalan Asrama 22, Surakarta; *c.* 100 teachers, *c.* 4,000 students.

Universitas Trisakti: Jl. Kiai Tapa-Grogol, Jakarta; *c.* 690 teachers, *c.* 6,200 students.

Universitas Veteran Republic Indonesia: Jl. Supratman 1, Makassar.

BIBLIOGRAPHY

GENERAL

BRO, M. H. Indonesia—Land of Challenge (Harper and Row, London, 1954).

FISCHER, L. The Story of Indonesia (Hamish Hamilton, London, 1959).

GRANT, B. Indonesia (Penguin Books, Harmondsworth, 1967).

McVEY, R. T. (ed.). Indonesia (Human Relations Area Files Inc., New Haven, 1967).

MINTZ, J. Indonesia—A Profile (Princeton University Press, 1961).

SMOLSKI, T. Social Welfare in Indonesia (Jakarta, 1956).

WERTHEIM, W. F. Indonesia in Transition (The Hague, 1956).

HISTORY

AZIZ, M. A. Japan's Colonialism and Indonesia (The Hague, 1955).

BROEK, J. A. O. Economic Development of the Netherlands Indies (New York, 1942).

DAHM, BERNARD. History of Indonesia in the Twentieth Century (London, 1970).

DAY, C. The Policy and Administration of the Dutch in Java (Oxford University Press, London, 1967).

GEERTZ, C. Agricultural Involution: The Process of Ecological Change in Indonesia (University of California, 1971).

HUGHES, J. The End of Sukarno (Angus and Robertson, London, 1968).

KAHIN, G. McT. Nationalism and Revolution in Indonesia (Cornell University Press, Ithaca, 1952).

MOSSMAN, J. Rebels in Paradise: Indonesia's Civil War (Cape, London, 1961).

PALMIER, L. H. Indonesia and the Dutch (Oxford University Press, London, 1962).

SCHILLER, A. A. The Formation of Federal Indonesia (The Hague, 1955).

UMBGROVE, J. H. F. Structural History of the East Indies (Cambridge, 1949).

VAN DER KROEF, J. M. The West New Guinea Dispute (Institute of Pacific Relations, New York, 1958).

VITTACHI, TARZIE. The Fall of Sukarno (André Deutsch, London, 1967).

VLEKKE, B. M. H. Nusantara, A History of Indonesia (W. Van Hoeve Ltd., The Hague and Bandung, 1959).

ECONOMICS AND POLITICS

ALLEN, G. C., and DONNITHORNE, A. C. Western Enterprise in Indonesia and Malaya (London, 1957).

ANDERSON, B. R., and McVEY, R. T. A Preliminary Analysis of the October 1, 1965 Coup in Indonesia (Ithaca, 1971).

BARTLETT, A. G. et al. PERTAMINA: Indonesian National Oil (Amerasia, Jakarta, Singapore and Tulsa, 1972).

BIRO PUSAT STATISTIK. Statistical Pocketbook of Indonesia (Jakarta, annually).

BRACKMAN, ARNOLD. Indonesian Communism (Praeger, New York, 1963).
The Communist Collapse in Indonesia (New York, 1969).

BULLETIN OF INDONESIAN ECONOMIC STUDIES (Australian National University, three annually).

DE NEUMANN, A. M. Industrial Development in Indonesia (1955).

FAR EASTERN ECONOMIC REVIEW (Hong Kong, weekly).

FEITH, H. The Decline of Constitutional Democracy in Indonesia (Cornell University Press, Ithaca, 1962).

HATTA, MOHAMMAD. The Co-operative Movement in Indonesia (Ithaca, 1957).

HICKS, G. L., and McNICOLL, G. The Indonesian Economy, 1950–67—A Bibliography (Yale University Press, 1968).

HIGGINS, B. Indonesia's Economic Stabilization and Development (New York, 1957).

INDONESIAN NEWS (Indonesian Embassy, London, monthly).

JOURNAL OF CONTEMPORARY ASIA (London, quarterly).

LEGG, J. D. Sukarno—A Political Biography (London, 1972).

LEV, DANIEL S. The Transition to Guided Democracy: Indonesian Politics 1957-1959 (Ithaca, 1966).

METCALF, J. E. The Agricultural Economy of Indonesia (U.S. Dept. of Agriculture, Washington, 1953).

MORTIMER, R. (ed.). Showcase State: The Illusion of Indonesia's "Accelerated Modernization" (Angus and Robertson, Sydney, 1973).

OEY HONG LEE (Ed.). Indonesia after the 1971 Elections (Oxford University Press, 1974).

PACIFIC RESEARCH (Pacific Studies Centre, Palo Alto, California, two-monthly).

ROEDER, O. G. The Smiling President: President Suharto of Indonesia (Gunung Agung Ltd., Jakarta, 1969).

SIE KWAT SOEN. Prospects for Agricultural Development in Indonesia (Wageningen, 1968).

Laos

PHYSICAL AND SOCIAL GEOGRAPHY

C. A. Fisher

Laos covers an area of 236,800 square kilometres (91,425 sq. miles) consisting almost entirely of rugged upland, except for the narrow floors of the river valleys. Of these rivers much the most important is the Mekong, which forms the western frontier of the country for much of its length.

In the northern half of Laos the deeply dissected plateau surface exceeds 1,500 metres over wide areas, and although the average level of the Annamite Chain which occupies most of the southern half is somewhat lower, its rugged and more densely forested surface makes it no less inhospitable. While on the plateau and in the Annamite Chain the tropical temperatures are considerably mitigated by altitude, the more habitable lowlands experience tropical conditions throughout the year, and receive a total annual rainfall of about 125 cm., most of which falls between May and September.

The natural resources of Laos are extremely meagre. Production of tin, its only significant mineral, remains small.

Laos had an estimated population of 3,257,000 in 1974, of whom about 60 per cent are Lao, living mainly in the western valleys, a further 35 per cent belong to various widely scattered hill tribes, and the rest are either Vietnamese or Chinese. Vientiane, the administrative capital, is the only large town; its population was 176,637 in 1973.

HISTORY

E. H. S. Simmonds

The use of the term "Laos" to designate, as a political entity, a group of states lying, for the most part, between the Mekong river and the frontiers of China and Viet-Nam dates only from the closing years of the nineteenth century when French colonial administration was fully established. However, the known political history of this area reaches back to the fourteenth century by which time a group of small Lao states had formed themselves as independent units out of the decaying empire of the Khmers (*see* History of Cambodia). The mixed ethno-linguistic character of Laos derived from the process of gradual infiltration of various Lao-Thai groups from the north. They established political control over the resident peoples of Mon-Khmer and Indonesian origin, who together with later arrivals, the Yao and the Meo, constitute today the substantial hill tribe minorities.

Pre-Colonial History

In 1563, Sai Setthathirat, the ruler of the Lao state of Lan Chang (Kingdom of a Million Elephants), moved his capital from Luang Prabang in the north to Vientiane on the middle Mekong. Lao power was then at its height and laid claim to large areas of what is today northern and northeastern Thailand as well as north, east and central Laos proper. However, during the second half of the sixteenth century, this first Laotian state fell apart under Burmese and Annamese pressures. During the seventeenth century a second Lao state with some claim to unity reached the zenith of its power under the great ruler King Soulingavongsa. From this period date the earliest Western accounts of the region.

Dynastic quarrels followed upon the death of Soulingavongsa and, from about 1711, the state disintegrated into its constituent principalities of Luang Prabang, Xieng Khouang, Vientiane and Champassak. From this time political disunity in Laos enabled neighbouring states, particularly Annam and Siam, to exercise increasing influence. The Annamese established control over north-east Laos and, following the sack of Vientiane in 1828, large areas of central Laos were placed under Siamese administration. The princely courts of Luang Prabang in the north and Champassak to the south were provided with advisers by Bangkok.

French intervention began in 1885, at first taking advantage of the claims of the Emperor of Annam. This halted and reversed the trend towards Siamese domination. A series of Franco-Siamese agreements signed between 1893 and 1907 brought a degree of unity to Laos for the third time and established its present-day political boundaries. Laotian areas west of the Mekong, at Champassak and opposite Luang Prabang, had been acquired in 1907 and were temporarily ceded to Thailand from June 1941 to January 1947.

The Colonial Period

French colonial possessions in Indochina formed a Federation with its capital at Hanoi, and Laos was incorporated within this framework. Wide federal powers existed in the fields of foreign affairs, defence, finance, customs and public works. The chief French official in Laos was the *Résident-Supérieur* who governed from Vientiane. French *résidents* controlled the provincial government of central and southern Laos, operating through Lao officials at the lower territorial levels.

A vestige of more traditional government continued to exist in the north where the royal line of Luang Prabang was recognized by the French. The king maintained a court and a ruling council which governed three provincial areas subject to the overall control of the French administration. Budgetary arrangements, the formation in 1923 of a Consultative Assembly, and participation in the common federal services were unifying factors, but French rule did little to develop Laos nor did it weld a nation out of the various local and ethnic particularistic groups.

Vietnamese immigration reached a total of 50,000 during the colonial period and the Vietnamese, who engaged in commerce and were employed as artisans, technicians and minor officials in the federal agencies, constituted an influential minority in the urban areas. French rule in the mountainous border areas had to contend with the small-scale but long drawn out dissidence of the hill peoples, notably that of the Kha and Meo groups.

In the Second World War, the Japanese assumed direct control of Indochina in March 1945 and encouraged ideas of independence which met with some opposition from the traditional Lao leaders. In the south Prince Boun Oum of Champassak organized an embryo resistance movement against the Japanese with the aid of French officers. In Luang Prabang the king was forced to declare the independence of his state from France. The activist crown prince was exiled and his influence passed to the viceroy, Prince Phetsarath, a member of the junior branch of the Luang Prabang royal family. Prince Phetsarath, who was not a francophile, established a position for himself and his relatives in Vientiane.

The Beginnings of Independence

At the end of the Second World War in Asia, the Japanese surrender in Laos was taken by the Chinese down to the 16th parallel and by the British below that line. French forces began to regroup in the south under the protection of the British "umbrella" and with the ready co-operation of Prince Boun Oum. The king of Luang Prabang reaffirmed his loyalty to France in August 1945 and accepted the resumption of the protectorate.

However, in Vientiane, Prince Phetsarath declared the unity and independence of the whole of Laos on September 15th. After prolonged negotiations with Luang Prabang the king accepted the provisional Constitution worked out by the independence movement led by Phetsarath and became the first constitutional monarch of an officially united Laos on April 23rd, 1946. This, however, was only a month before the French reoccupation of the northern capital. The French had captured Vientiane on April 24th and the leaders of the young independence movement were forced to flee to Bangkok.

The Lao Issara (Free Laos) movement in exile was dominated behind the scenes by Prince Phetsarath. His brother Prince Souvanna Phouma, who later became the neutralist prime minister, and a half-brother, Prince Souphanouvong, were prominent members. Many important non-royal officials who had been concerned with administration during the period of French rule played major roles in the organization of the Free Laos movement.

During the period of complete disorganization at the end of the Second World War the Communist-led Viet-Minh had begun to spread its influence in Laos, making use of members of the substantial Vietnamese minority. Prince Souphanouvong, a number of other Laotians and some leaders of the hill tribes co-operated with the Viet-Minh from 1945 onwards. In May 1949 Souphanouvong was relieved of his position as head of the independence forces because of his Viet-Minh connections. He retired to the hills and forests with his supporters. His movement became known as Pathet Lao (State of Laos) and he set up a resistance "government" on Lao soil in April 1953 in the northeastern part of the country which was controlled by the Viet-Minh. In the meantime, the more moderate members of the Free Laos movement, conscious of the possibility of a negotiated settlement with France, dissolved the movement in October 1949 and returned to Vientiane.

Franco-Laotian negotiations had begun in August 1946 and they led to the promulgation of a Constitution on May 11th, 1947. Laos now became a single unit within the Federation of Indochina and was governed by a Council of Ministers responsible to an elected National Assembly, under the constitutional rule of King Sisavangvong of Luang Prabang. The French, however, still reserved considerable powers including the appointment of French administrators in each province.

Further negotiations took place in 1949 in the course of which Laos was recognized as independent and as an Associate State of the French Union. Laos now had a measure of external recognition as an independent state and joined certain of the specialized agencies of the United Nations. Returning members of the Free Laos movement found themselves in a lively and fruitful political atmosphere and began to form political parties, the most significant of which was the Progressive Party led by Katay D. Sasorith and Prince Souvanna Phouma.

A further important step was taken in 1953 when the Laniel Government negotiated a Franco-Laotian Treaty of Friendship by which the Kingdom of Laos was recognized as sovereign and independent. Remaining reserve powers were transferred but Laos still remained a member of the French Union and continued to rely on France for defence aid.

The war between France and the Viet-Minh was now reaching crisis point and Vietnamese units drove deeply into Laos in March and December 1953. Prince Souphanouvong's resistance, which had engaged in minor guerrilla activity since 1949, now assumed a suitable posture to play a political role in the peace talks which were to follow the French defeat at Dien-Bien-Phu in May 1954.

At the Geneva Conference, Souphanouvong's Pathet Lao movement did not succeed in its aim of obtaining international recognition but was allotted two northeastern provinces, i.e. Phong Saly and Houa Phan (Sam Neua), as a regroupment area for its forces and supporters pending a political settlement. Ambiguities in this and associated agreements enabled Pathet Lao to retain a stronghold within Laos and thereby preserve and build up its organization until it was able to operate politically on a nation-wide basis.

The Geneva Agreement of 1954 set up an International Control Commission (ICC) composed of Indian, Canadian and Polish members, to supervise the political settlement. In December 1954 the quadripartite economic arrangements were brought to an end and Laos moved closer to Thailand in commercial affairs. A Lao-Thai commercial agreement was signed in July 1955. Laos was admitted as a member state of the United Nations Organization in December 1955 and could now claim full international recognition as an independent state. Unity was, however, not yet achieved because of the refusal of Pathet Lao to agree to reintegration except on its own terms.

From Rapprochement to Polarization

In the absence of a political settlement the Royal Government of Laos went ahead with elections in December 1955 without the participation of Pathet Lao. The Progressive Party emerged victorious and, following the replacement of Katay D. Sasorith by Prince Souvanna Phouma as Prime Minister in March 1956, negotiations were reopened with Pathet Lao. An agreement was signed in August and ratified in December. Royal Government control was established over the whole kingdom and Pathet Lao participated in the political life of the country through Neo Lao Haksat (Lao Patriotic Front), its newly established political party. In November 1957 Prince Souvanna Phouma formed a Government of National Union which included Prince Souphanouvong and a Pathet Lao colleague as ministers.

This rapprochement was achieved at the cost of accepting most of the Pathet Lao demands. It was welcomed by the Communist states but resulted in serious misgivings among the Western powers and their Asian allies, particularly the United States and Thailand. To complete the 1956–57 agreements it was necessary not only to arrange for the resumption of regular civil administration in the provinces of Phong Saly and Houa Phan and to integrate the Pathet Lao forces with the royal army but also to hold supplementary elections. Twenty-one seats were contested in May 1958, raising the number of members of the National Assembly to fifty-nine. Nine of the seats were won by the Neo Lao Haksat (NLHS) and four by Santhiphap (Peace Party), a newly created political organization headed by Quinim Pholsena, a publicist who represented the left wing of the neutralist movement.

This pro-Communist electoral success caused the well-established Progressive Party and the Independents under Phoui Sananikone to draw together into a single party, Lao Luam Lao (Laotian People's Rally). In June a new organization was formed—The Committee for the Defence of National Interests (CDIN)—which drew its membership mainly from civil servants and military officers. For the first time in Laos political parties which could be classed as left and right wing were emerging.

Moves now commenced to restrict the parliamentary activities of leftist politicians. In January 1959 the new Prime Minister obtained from the National Assembly a grant of special powers for a year in order to counter increased North Vietnamese pressure which was alleged to be taking place. During the year the failure of the government's hard line on army integration policy, which resulted in the mass desertion of a Pathet Lao battalion, threatened to reactivate the civil war. NLHS leaders were arrested and held until they escaped in May 1960.

Phoui Sananikone, who was anxious to reshuffle his government to include more moderate members, was forced out of office by CDIN and army pressure. He handed his resignation to King Savang Vathana, who had succeeded on the death of his father on October 29th. A caretaker government was formed and the army, whose strong man, General Phoumi Nosavan, became Minister of Defence, organized elections which were held on April 24th. The resulting government was dominated by CDIN. Thus, in the course of three years, the Lao political scene had changed radically from one in which Prince Souvanna Phouma, a French-educated nationalist of neutralist leanings, had failed in his experimental attempt to form a government of national union and had been replaced by a series of governments of increasingly rightist-militarist tendencies whose international affiliations were with the United States and her Asian allies.

Coup d'Etat and Aftermath

In August 1960, a coup d'état took place in Vientiane. Its leader was Kong Le, a paratroop captain of isolationist and mildly xenophobic views and little political expertise. The task of forming a government which would support a return to neutralist policies fell once again to Prince Souvanna Phouma. There was natural popular support for this attitude in Laos but General Phoumi Nosavan, who set up an opposition group in Savannakhet, in south Laos, commanded United States and Thai support. Souvanna Phouma attempted to gain some countervailing international influence by accepting Soviet help to break a blockade imposed by Thailand. He failed in his efforts to negotiate with Pathet Lao and with Phoumi Nosavan and left Laos for Cambodia on December 9th. Phoumi's troops occupied Vientiane on December 16th after, by Laotian standards, an unusually fierce battle involving several hundred civilian and military casualties. Pathet Lao forces seized the opportunity to make territorial gains in north-east Laos.

Following the capture of Vientiane a government was set up with Prince Boun Oum of Champassak as Prime Minister and Phoumi Nosavan as Minister of Defence. This government was recognized by Thailand, the United States and other Western powers, while a neutralist government recognized by the Communist powers was established by Souvanna Phouma at Khang Khay in north-east Laos in close proximity to the headquarters of the Pathet Lao forces.

Fighting in Laos during the early months of 1961 went on balance in favour of Pathet Lao and the neutralist forces commanded by Kong Le. The clear resumption of the civil war in Laos occasioned international moves which included an Indo-British effort to reconvene the International Control Commission which had been adjourned in 1958, and a Soviet proposal to reconvene the 1954 Geneva Conference. Prince Norodom Sihanouk of Cambodia suggested wider participation and his formula was close to that which was finally accepted.

Efforts made by Britain and the Soviet Union, as co-chairmen of the 1954 conference, to arrange a cease-fire achieved relative success by May and invitations were issued to a new conference in Geneva.

The Geneva Conference 1961–62

The fourteen nations which met in Geneva on May 16th, 1961, were Laos, Burma, Cambodia, the People's Republic of China, Canada, the Democratic Republic of Viet-Nam, France, India, Poland, the Republic of Viet-Nam, Thailand, the U.S.S.R., the United Kingdom and the United States.

Early procedural difficulties were resolved by permitting the presence with equal status of all three Laotian factions of which the leading personalities were the three princes, Boun Oum (royal government), Souphanouvong (Pathet Lao) and Souvanna Phouma (neutralists). However, there was a wide divergence of view between the non-Communist powers who saw the main problem as one of effective international control of the peace, and the Communists who wanted merely a declaration of support for Laotian neutrality not a guarantee and an agreement that the non-Communist side, which was branded as the aggressor, would not interfere in Laos. In this view a "troika" government of all the factions would be set up which would have ultimate control of all matters including inspection.

By the end of the year progress had been made by the drafting committees but the three princes had shown the utmost reluctance in coming together to form a coalition government. This was not achieved until June 1962. In the meantime the civil war continued despite the official cease-fire and the royal government suffered a number of serious reverses and lost control of much territory. The military crisis caused the United States to take special steps to ensure the security of Thailand by a unilateral guarantee. In May United States forces with small Allied contingents provided military backing in north Thailand.

Final agreement was reached at Geneva on July 21st. The 1962 agreement gave much less freedom of supervision, inspection and control to the ICC than had that of 1954, which itself had not been very effective. The unanimity rule which was to apply to major activities of the ICC, as well as to all decisions of the tripartite government, seriously reduced the chances both of effective government and of supervision.

Breakdown in Laos

The Government of National Union headed by Prince Souvanna Phouma was ineffective from the start. Factional rivalries which carried with them opposing forms of external support were not stilled. Through its representatives in government the reactivated NLHS attempted to build up Communist diplomatic representation in Vientiane. On the other hand, state security, especially in the capital, was controlled by the rightist army and police. The chief NLHS leaders soon retired to their stronghold on the Plain of Jars where Kong Le's neutralist forces were also stationed. The programme of national unification and reconstruction had been checked at the first obstacle and early in 1963 the rival factions retained control of the areas they had held before the agreement and consolidated their positions.

Pathet Lao attempted to gain control of the neutralist forces and this rivalry erupted in a series of political assassinations of which the most significant was that of Quinim Pholsena, the Foreign Minister, on April 1st, 1963. In April and May fighting between Pathet Lao and the neutralists resulted in the evacuation of the Plain of Jars by Kong Le's forces. The inadequacy of the protocol arrangements made at Geneva was shown by the failure of the co-chairmen to take joint action and the readiness of the members of the ICC to take different lines on questions of inspection and control.

Attempts at negotiations between the factions were made but broke down over security arrangements for Pathet Lao, which demanded the re-establishment of the mixed police force before its leaders would come to the capital. Pathet Lao also objected to the full powers taken from the National Assembly by Prince Souvanna Phouma in order to carry on day-to-day business. It regarded the National Assembly derived from the 1960 elections as an illegal body and saw Souvanna Phouma's action as a violation of the tripartite unanimity rule.

On April 19th, 1964, there was an attempted coup d'état organized by the right-wing military and police. International diplomatic action was necessary to restore the position of Prince Souvanna Phouma. In this disturbed situation Pathet Lao launched an offensive which finally drove the neutralist forces from north-east Laos. General Kong Le set up his headquarters at Vang Vieng in the hills north of Vientiane.

Further international attempts were made to stabilize the Laotian situation during 1964. France made urgent efforts to bring the Laotian parties together.

In Laos Prince Souvanna Phouma, assured now even of United States support, consolidated his position. General Phoumi Nosavan made a final attempt to take over power in a series of military uprisings between February and April 1965. He retired to Thailand and was subsequently tried for treason *in absentia*. Souvanna Phouma was now able to make progress with a reorganization of the armed forces. A further casualty was General Kong Le who had been showing considerable independence of the government. He went into exile in October 1966 and the neutralist forces were reintegrated under his successor.

On the political front the government made arrangements for further National Assembly elections which were due in 1965. They took place on July 18th, and members were elected by a restricted list of voters numbering some 22,000. This restriction of the franchise to members of the *élite* groups in the country, both military and civilian, required an amendment to the Constitution. Pathet Lao boycotted the election and, in October, called again for a return to tripartite government. The situation in Laos was now one of *de facto* partition. The Mekong valley was controlled by the government while most hill areas were in the hands of Pathet Lao and their Vietnamese backers

Laos and the War in Viet-Nam

Nationalist politicians like Prince Souvanna Phouma had long tried to keep the Laotian and Vietnamese situations separate in the hope that a unified neutral state could be constructed, free from external interference. This had always existed from the North Vietnamese side in varying degrees appropriate to the immediate political or military situation. It was, however, not admitted by the Communists but evidence was produced as a result of the capture of North Vietnamese prisoners in 1964 and 1965. American air reconnaissance, which had been stepped up from May 1964, provided evidence of North Vietnamese supply columns entering Laos. On its side, the royal government received considerable United States military aid and American advisers were again operating with the Lao army following their withdrawal after the Geneva Agreement of 1962. The United States and her Asian allies were also involved in air intervention and bombing.

After the escalation of the war in Viet-Nam the interests of Laos were finally subordinated to the major strategic issue. The hill trails of the Annamite Chain passing through Lao territory were used as a supply route from North to South Viet-Nam. They became known as the "Ho Chi Minh Trail". Much of the military action from 1964 to 1972 resulted from the efforts of North Vietnamese forces to protect these trails with the help of Pathet Lao. United States counteraction was mostly mounted from the air. Anti-government forces, however, maintained pressure and succeeded in gaining territory on balance, thus creating a refugee problem for the Vientiane administration.

During 1969–70 Royal Government forces were able to outflank the Pathet Lao-North Vietnamese alliance and drive their troops off the Plain of Jars in north-east Laos by September 1969. Resettlement of the area began but Pathet Lao and North Vietnamese forces regained the lost territory early in 1970 and laid siege to two strongholds held by the troops of General Vang Pao to the south of the Plain. Wet season (June–November) occupation of the strategic area of the Plain by the Royal Army and subsequent dry season (December–May) recapture by pro-Communist forces became a pattern. Particularly heavy Communist attacks commenced in December 1971.

In the period 1969–72 military operations were increased in intensity in the neighbourhood of Luang Prabang, the royal capital, and on the Bolovens plateau in Southern Laos where North Vietnamese troops were successfully engaged in protecting the Ho Chi Minh trail.

Following the peace negotiations intended to end the war in Viet-Nam, a cease-fire agreement was signed in Laos by royal government and Pathet Lao representatives on February 21st, 1973. Although the cease-fire held, despite minor violations, and prisoners-of-war were exchanged, negotiations to form a provisional coalition government and the joint committees of a National Political Consultative Committee to oversee the problems of a return to peace and to organize a general election for a new National Assembly did not have a successful outcome for many months.

A number of deep differences between the negotiating parties caused delay and considerable right-wing pressure was brought to bear on Prince Souvanna Phouma to dissuade him from signing with the Pathet Lao. The Pathet Lao, uneasy about the personal safety of its members, required neutralization of the royal and administrative capitals of Luang Prabang and Vientiane. This was to be effected by withdrawing the royal forces and replacing them with mixed forces of police and troops drawn equally from both sides. The royal army objected to withdrawal prior to the signing of a final agreement and the implementation of some of the proposals contained in it. The army and many ministers were highly suspicious of proposals to identify "hot spots" of possible conflict and neutralize them by withdrawal. It was felt that the "hot spots" might become a chain and result in the apparent demarcation of a partition line with Pathet Lao taking by far the larger amount of territory.

Eventually, protocols for an agreement were signed on September 14th, and the portfolios of a provisional coalition government were listed. Prince Souvanna Phouma remained as Prime Minister with Prince Souphanouvong, Chairman of the Central Committee of the Lao Patriotic Front, joining him as Deputy Prime Minister and Minister of Foreign Affairs. Ministerial portfolios and posts of under-secretaries of state were equally divided between the opposing parties with a place for some uncommitted "intellectuals", for example, in the Ministry of Justice.

When meetings of joint committee representatives commenced in October to activate the operations of the National Political Consultative Council differences soon emerged again. However, early in December 1973 the neutralization of the capitals was proceeding, and foreign forces were under an obligation to leave within 60 days of the signing of a final agremeent.

The year 1974 was relatively peaceful, and Laos came to be regarded as a state which was adjusting successfully to the new situation developing after the Viet-Nam cease-fire agreements. Beneath the calm surface, peaceful indeed compared with the conditions existing in Cambodia and Viet-Nam, trends favouring a take-over by pro-Communist forces slowly developed. The royal army lost credibility as a force able to provide support for an anti-leftist *coup* and the influence of the rightist ministers in the coalition government began to wane. The political balance had tipped in favour of Pathet Lao, and urban public opinion, especially among the younger elements, was in favour of change.

The cataclysmic events of April and May 1975 in Viet-Nam, with the Communist forces of the North gaining control over the formerly American-supported South, had immediate repercussions in Laos. A miniature offensive by Pathet Lao-controlled troops drove royal army forces back towards the Mekong in Central Laos. In the event, the move was little more than symbolic but the intended effect was achieved. Organized demonstrations against the United States in Vientiane and in the south involved some violence and were a warning to right-wing leaders. The Prime Minister, Prince Souvanna Phouma, held the coalition government together by an arrangement which replaced the once powerful Defence and Finance Ministers, the Deputy Commander-in-Chief and others by a group of five less prominent non-Pathet Lao personalities. This resulted in Pathet Lao dominance in government even though the letter of the agreement was still followed. Moves to reorganize the military forces, giving greater command strength to Pathet Lao, began in June.

Political pressure towards a complete take-over steadily developed, culminating in November in demonstrations calling for an abolition of the monarchy. King Savang Vatthana signed an instrument of abdication on November 29th and the Prime Minister, Prince Souvanna Phouma, resigned. A National Congress of People's Representatives, convened by the NLHS, proclaimed the Lao People's Democratic Republic on December 1st. The new government structure is headed by a President. Kaysone Phomvihane, a long-standing member of the Pathet Lao movement, who was now designated Secretary-General of the People's Revolutionary Party of Laos, became Prime Minister.

From May 1975 onwards many aristocrats and office-holders in former governments and the armed services, both Laotian and Meo, fled the country. The National Political Consultative Council was abolished and a nation-wide administrative reorganization was put in hand. This included arrangements for re-education.

Co-operation with the United States and Thailand was brought to an end as Laos re-aligned itself with other Communist powers. The shift of interest was particularly marked by a high-level official visit to Peking early in March 1976.

ECONOMIC SURVEY

E. H. S. Simmonds

(Revised by the Editor, 1976)

The basic economic activity of Laos is subsistence agriculture which involves over 90 per cent of the population. Wet rice growing is practised along the middle Mekong and in certain other valley areas in north and north-east Laos such as Luang Prabang. Sophisticated irrigation techniques have been little developed and farmers rely for the most part on simple methods of rainfall and flood control. The harvest can be greatly affected by periodical drought as in 1955 or by severe flooding as in 1966.

Land tenure in the valleys still reflects the traditional pattern where land ownership is nominally vested in the state but farmers possess rights of usufruct and inheritance. The land is worked mainly on a family basis but in the more heavily populated districts near the towns there is some share-cropping, often organized on an intra-family or intra-community basis. The water buffalo and oxen required for use on the land and for rural transport are raised in south Laos.

The Lao farmer relies heavily on fish for protein and the fish and rice diet is supplemented by domestic fowls, eggs and pork and many varieties of vegetables and fruit.

In the hill regions dry rice is grown by means of the slash and burn technique which involves the periodic clearing and re-clearing of forest land to maintain fertility. This has caused serious de-forestation in north and north-east Laos, and on the Bolovens plateau in the south. Landholding among the Kha and Meo hill peoples is vested in the community which moves its village site at intervals as fresh jungle land is cleared. The Meo, who prefer to live above 3,000 feet, produce maize as a food in addition to rice.

Marketing

Country markets in Laos are on a very small scale. There is little saleable surplus. In the larger towns, such as Vientiane, food importation is relied on and much produce is brought daily across the Mekong from Thailand by Vietnamese farmers and market-gardeners. General retail stores run by Chinese, Vietnamese and Indians deal in imported merchandise and local handicrafts.

Imports and Exports

Laos needs to import 70,000 tons of rice annually and other essential imports are textiles, pharmaceuticals, petroleum products, and transportation and electrical equipment.

The principal export in terms of value is tin produced from two mines at Phon Tiou in central Laos. A production level of over 1,000 tons per annum (50 per cent metal content) is maintained. Preliminary surveys in north and north-east Laos show that copper, lead, iron, coal and other minerals are present in exploitable quantities.

Timber and other forest products, such as benzoin, have been exported since ancient times. The north-western province of Sayaboury produces teak and other woods. Cardamoms and other spices and food and medicinal oil plants are produced on the Bolovens plateau together with coffee, which is recovering its position as an important export after some years of eclipse owing to disease. Opium is grown in upper Laos, mainly by the Meo people, but the considerable revenue involved cannot be brought effectively into national budgetary calculations, and the trade has been considerably disrupted by the war.

Laos has always had an unfavourable balance of trade; in 1973 the deficit was estimated at 31,000 million old kips. Before the change of regime in 1975, support for essential commodity imports was provided by the United States, and since 1975 Laos had been given aid by its communist allies in the form of the direct provision of essential commodity supplies.

Aid and Development

French aid to Laos continued after independence and France provided major assistance in communications projects, and especially in the expanding education programme.

United States assistance began before independence under the Mutual Security Act of 1951 by arrangement with France. Following the Geneva Agreement of 1954, American aid grew very rapidly. In the economic field this amounted to U.S. $55 million for the period June 1955 to June 1966. Apart from support for the importation of food, the United States supported refugee relief, educational, communications and rural development programmes. An undisclosed amount was provided for the armed services and police.

Finance

In January 1955 the kip replaced the Indochina piastre as the national monetary unit for Laos. The currency has never been stable and in recent years its value in relation to the U.S. dollar declined dramatically. In the early 1970s the free market exchange rate was approximately 500 kips to the U.S. dollar but by June 1976 this had sunk to 14,000 per dollar. The ending of U.S. aid to Laos in 1975 was a major factor in the collapse of the kip with the selling of Lao currency at high black-market exchange rates by refugees also contributing to its decline. In June 1976 the Lao Government introduced a new currency in an attempt to dispel the monetary confusion prevailing since the fall of the Royal Lao administration in 1975. Previously there were two currencies in circulation, the old and the Lao Patriotic Front (LPF) kip. The old kip was about one-eighth of the value of the LPF kip. The new kip is worth 20 old kips and the official exchange rate (based on the official selling rate for the old kip) is 60 to the U.S. dollar. However, this rate is seen as unrealistically low and unofficial exchange rates set the new kip at about one-tenth of that value.

It is hoped that the reform of the currency, together with a tighter control over foreign exchange transactions, will help to control the rate of inflation which in 1972 and 1973 was running at between 25 and 30 per cent. In 1976 the Government had to double the price of rice to 40,000 old kips per sack. But the continuing need to import a whole range of basic materials and manufactures, including fuel, foodstuffs and machinery, and the high level of government spending on development projects, will make this objective extremely difficult to achieve.

Laos participated in the development plan for the Mekong basin from its inception in 1957 under ECAFE. A Japanese-built dam on the Nam Ngum river, north of Vientiane, was opened in December 1971 as the largest of a number of projects planned for Laos. The dam provides irrigation facilities and hydro-electric power. The government of the People's Republic intends to continue the development of hydro-electric resources.

Industry

Without foreign aid a small agricultural country like Laos with a population of about 3,000,000 would be unable to develop the complex infrastructure of a modern state. Even with aid, industry is in the earliest stages of development. Saw-mills are well established. A bottling plant is in operation and tobacco products, matches and rubber shoes are manufactured. France provided finance for a cement factory.

Since the establishment of the People's Republic in December 1975, steps have been taken to set up a state-controlled economy. The new Government has announced its intention to develop agriculture and forestry as the basis for future industrial development.

Communications

Laos suffers from a great lack of effective communications. An internal network of roads was under construction when the Second World War called a halt to development. After independence, the main trade outlet switched from the Saigon to the Bangkok route. A rail link was established from the Laotian border to the Thai capital and this has since been supplemented by a modern road.

Nevertheless, Laos is not a natural unit as far as communications are concerned. The northern and northeastern regions look towards China and north Viet-Nam, and the Chinese and north Vietnamese have been building and repairing road links with Laos. The middle Mekong valley towns look south and west towards Cambodia, south Viet-Nam and Thailand. Luang Prabang, isolated far up the Mekong, has been connected with Vientiane by a mountain road, expensive to build and difficult to maintain on an all-weather basis.

The nature of the Mekong river and its tributaries with their rapids and waterfalls has prevented the establishment of a commercially effective water transport system. It is, in fact, the physical features of Laos that stand in the way of its rapid development as an economic unit. Air transport has naturally been greatly expanded during the last two decades but, in itself, even in times of peace, is not an efficient substitute for effective surface communications.

STATISTICAL SURVEY

AREA AND POPULATION

Area: 236,800 sq. km. (91,400 sq. miles). **Population:** 3,257,000 (estimate for July 1974).

PROVINCES

Luang Prabang	Sayaboury	Attopeu	Borikhane	Champhone*
Xieng Khouang	Saravane	Houaphan (Sam Neua)	Sithandone	Vang Vieng*
Savannakhet	Phongsaly	Khammouane	Sédone	Hongsa*
Houa Khong (Nam Tha)	Vientiane	Champassak	Wapikhamthong	Paklay*

* New provinces established 1973–74.

PRINCIPAL TOWNS
(census 1973)

Vientiane (capital)	176,637	Luang Prabang	44,244
Savannakhet	50,690	Sayaboury	13,775
Pakse	44,860	Khammouane	12,676

Births and Deaths: Average annual birth rate 47 per 1,000; death rate 23 per 1,000 (estimates by National Statistical Office).

Employment (1970): Total economically active population 1,556,000, including 1,218,000 in agriculture (ILO and FAO estimates).

AGRICULTURE

LAND USE, 1971
('000 hectares)

Arable and Under Permanent Crops	950
Permanent Meadows and Pastures	800
Forest Land	15,000
Other Areas	6,930
TOTAL	23,680

Source: FAO, *Production Yearbook 1974.*

PRINCIPAL CROPS
(FAO estimates)

	Area ('000 hectares)			Production ('000 metric tons)		
	1972	1973	1974	1972	1973	1974
Rice (paddy)	665*	665*	665*	817*	883*	900
Maize	35*	36*	36	27*	29	30
Potatoes	3	3	3	15	15	15
Sweet potatoes and yams	3	3	3	15	16	16
Cassava (manioc)	2	1	2	15	13	14
Pulses	9	9	9	12	13	13
Soybeans	4	4	4	4	4	4
Groundnuts	2	2	2	1	1	1
Cottonseed	5	6	6	4.4*	6*	6.4
Cotton (lint)				2.2*	3*	3.2
Sugar cane	2	2	2	8	8	8
Coffee	6	6	6	2.3*	1.8*	1.8
Tobacco	3.7*	3.7	4.1	3.7*	4*	4.3

* Official figures.

Source: FAO, *Production Yearbook 1974*.

LIVESTOCK
('000—FAO estimates)

	1969–70	1970–71	1971–72	1972–73	1973–74
Horses	27	28	29	30	33
Cattle	420	435	435	450	464
Buffaloes	935	940	950	960	1,040
Pigs	1,100	1,150	1,200	1,250	1,292
Goats	34	35	36	37	38
Chickens	11,500	12,000	12,500	13,000	13,999
Ducks	198	190	190	190	194

Domestic elephants: 892 recorded in 1971.

Source: FAO, *Production Yearbook 1974*.

LIVESTOCK PRODUCTS
('000 metric tons, FAO estimates)

	1972	1973	1974
Beef and veal	4	4	4
Buffalo meat	10	11	12
Pig meat	29	30	31
Poultry meat	10	11	12
Edible offals	3.7	3.8	4.0
Cows' milk	5	5	5
Hen eggs	16.0	17.2	18.4
Buffalo hides	2.7	3.0	3.2

Source: FAO, *Production Yearbook 1974*.

FORESTRY

ROUNDWOOD REMOVALS

('000 cubic metres, all non-coniferous)

	1965	1966	1967	1968	1969	1970	1971	1972
Sawlogs, veneer logs and logs for sleepers	68	71	107	69	115	71	72	96
Other industrial wood	62	65	70	70	70	75*	75*	80*
Fuel wood	2,370	2,420	2,480	2,540	2,620	2,690*	2,760*	2,830*
TOTAL	2,503	2,556	2,657	2,679	2,805	2,836	2,907	3,006

* FAO estimate.

Source: FAO, *Yearbook of Forest Products.*

SAWNWOOD PRODUCTION

('000 cubic metres, all non-coniferous)

	1965	1966	1967	1968	1969	1970	1971	1972
TOTAL (incl. boxboards)	30	33	45	4	50	35*	45*	50*

* FAO estimate.

Source: FAO, *Yearbook of Forest Products.*

Fishing: Total catch 20,000 metric tons per year (FAO estimate).

MINING

		1971	1972	1973	1974	1975
Tin concentrates (metal content)	metric tons	672	788	748	612	522

Source: International Tin Council, London.

INDUSTRY

SELECTED PRODUCTS

		1969	1970	1971	1972	1973
Distilled alcoholic beverages	'000 hectolitres	18	18	9	15	24
Cigarettes	million	381	361	381	375	628
Washing powder	metric tons	n.a.	7,000	2,880	2,880	n.a.
Rubber footwear	'000 pairs	864	1,152	1,889	161	180
Clay building bricks	million	27	27	—	137	n.a.
Electric energy	million kWh.	21	12	16	228	245*

* Estimate.

Source: United Nations, *Statistical Yearbook* and *The Growth of World Industry*.

FINANCE

100 at (cents) = 10 bi = 1 new kip.
Coins: 10, 20 and 50 at.*
Notes: 10, 20, 50, 100, 200, 500 new kips.
Exchange rates (June 1976): £1 sterling = 106.4 new kips; U.S. $1 = 60 new kips.
1,000 new kips = £9.39 = $16.67.

Note: The kip was introduced in January 1955, replacing (at par) the Indo-Chinese piastre. From May 1953 the piastre's value was 10 old French francs. The initial exchange rate was thus U.S. $1 = 35 kips (1 kip = 2.857 U.S. cents). In October 1958 the currency was devalued by 56 per cent, the new exchange rate being $1 = 80 kips (1 kip = 1.25 U.S. cents). This rate remained in force until the end of 1963. From January 1964 to November 1971 the official exchange rate was $1 = 240 kips (1 kip = 0.417 U.S. cent), although a free market rate also operated officially at around 500 kips to the dollar. In November 1971 this official free rate was fixed at $1 = 600 kips (1 kip = 0.167 U.S. cent) and this became the rate used to convert the value of foreign trade transactions. The official basic rate of $1 = 240 kips was abolished in April 1972, when the basic and free rates were unified at $1 = 600 kips. A financial (selling) rate of $1 = 840 kips was introduced in May 1972. The currency was devalued in March 1975, when the rates were fixed at $1 = 750 kips (buying) or 1,200 kips (selling). In June 1976 the new kip, worth 20 old kips, was introduced. The official exchange rate was fixed at $1 = 60 new kips. In terms of sterling the exchange rate was £1 = 576 old kips (official) from November 1967 to August 1971; and £1 = 1,563.43 old kips (free market) from December 1971 to June 1972.

* These are the denominations of the old kip, replaced in June 1976. Some of them remain in circulation, with their value adjusted to the new currency. Some of the old notes also remain in circulation.

BUDGET

Twelve months ending June 30th
(million old kips)

Revenue	1970–71	1971–72*	1972–73*	1973–74*
Direct Taxes	804	790	895	865.0
Import and Customs Duties	3,862	5,425	3,700	3,381.0
Registration Tax	180	211	250	280.0
Other Indirect Taxes	1,345	1,875	2,105	2,205.0
Revenue from Services	533	764	857	2,131.2
Other receipts	67	35	201	4,923.3
Total	6,791	9,100	8,008	13,785.5

Expenditure	1970–71	1971–72*	1972–73*	1973–74*
Education and Culture	1,764.3	1,949.5	2,323.2	2,564.0
Social Security and Health	607.0	635.3	711.4	892.9
Public Works	391.8	400.5	454.4	858.8
Defence	9,411.7	9,337.8	11,321.9	14,142.5
State Administration	2,727.3	2,798.1	3,365.6	3,069.5
National Economy	254.5	286.3	305.0	329.4
Debt Services	176.0	325.0	405.0	550.0
Transfers	142.5	156.3	372.9	486.5
Development Expenditure	400.0	400.0	300.0	353.0
Other Expenditure	2,397.8	2,911.2	3,248.1	5,538.9
Total	18,272.9	19,200.0	22,807.5	28,785.5

* Voted estimates.

FOREIGN EXCHANGE OPERATIONS FUND

(million U.S. $)

Contributor	1967	1968	1969	1970	1971	1972	1973
United States	13.8	16.1	16.6	16.1	20.1	16.1	16.1
France	1.7	1.7	1.7	1.7	1.7	1.7	2.3
Japan	1.7	1.7	1.7	2.0	2.3	2.6	3.0
United Kingdom	1.7	1.7	1.7	1.7	1.7	1.8	1.8
Australia	0.6	0.8	0.7	0.7	0.7	0.7	0.9
Total	19.5	22.0	22.4	22.2	26.5	22.9	24.1

Note: The Foreign Exchange Operations Fund was set up in 1964 to attempt to control inflation.

MONEY SUPPLY

(million old kips at December 31st)

	1967	1968	1969	1970	1971	1972	1973
Bank Deposits	1,000	1,068	1,327	1,141	1,231	1,731	3,213
Money in Circulation	10,260	11,294	12,497	14,215	17,723	21,743	23,449

COST OF LIVING

CONSUMER PRICE INDEX, VIENTIANE

(base: 1970=100)

	1966	1967	1968	1969	1971	1972	1973	1974
Food	94.1	99.8	105.5	107.5	100.6	135.8	190.7	289.9
Clothing	86.7	90.0	93.7	97.2	101.4	121.9	146.5	228.4
Rent, fuel and light	85.9	87.9	89.2	94.2	102.5	108.6	128.6	185.4
All Items	85.1	92.0	96.5	99.6	101.3	126.8	165.7	248.1

August 1975: Food 537.9; All items 432.4.

Source: International Labour Office, mainly *Year Book of Labour Statistics*.

EXTERNAL TRADE*

(million old kips)

	1966	1967	1968	1969	1970	1971	1972	1973
Imports	10,017.2	11,796.4	12,878.6	19,854.5	27,329.1	19,739.7	26,205.4	34,298.3
Exports	357.7	1,064.4	1,448.1	1,032.9	1,726.7	1,485.4	1,752.8	3,044.7

* Trade, excluding gold, valued at the rate of 240 kips per U.S. $ until November 1971, when the official free rate was fixed at 600 kips per $.

COMMODITIES

(million old kips)

IMPORTS (Excluding gold)	1970	1971	1972
Animals and Meat	1,196	697	1,569
Vegetables	2,449	2,405	4,749
Fats and Oils	47	67	189
Industrial Food Products	2,864	1,867	2,326
Mineral Products	7,754	5,178	6,857
Chemical Products	1,968	973	1,240
Leather Products	14	13	10
Wood and Wood Products	195	77	67
Paper and Paper Products	549	396	698
Textiles	1,507	1,264	816
Clothing	52	49	32
Ceramic Products	182	180	326
Precious Metals	13	18	261
Metal Products	2,201	1,238	1,696
Machinery	2,597	2,275	2,078
Transport Vehicles	2,322	1,997	2,022
Scientific Instruments	681	489	488
Others	738	557	781
TOTAL	27,329	19,740	26,205

EXPORTS	1970	1971	1972*	1973*
Tin	616.4	762.5	916.9	898.3
Timber	402.5	604.4	572.7	1,939.5
Green Coffee	88.7	13.1	—	15.0
Cardamom	2.0	3.9	3.1	2.4
Leather and Hides	16.1	14.3	16.0	10.1
Others	601.0	87.2	31.4	179.3
TOTAL	1,726.7	1,485.4	1,540.1	3,044.6

* Provisional.

PRINCIPAL TRADING PARTNERS

(million old kips)

IMPORTS	1970	1971	1972
France	2,194.9	1,377.4	1,125.8
Germany, Federal Republic	177.6	341.6	327.9
Hong Kong	398.4	363.6	513.6
Indonesia	4,173.0	2,113.3	2,097.1
Japan	3,925.8	3,843.5	2,469.9
Singapore	1,529.0	1,823.2	1,025.7
China (Taiwan)	266.1	269.0	396.0
Thailand	5,622.8	5,086.0	12,353.7
United Kingdom	675.0	366.2	366.2
U.S.A.	6,647.9	3,143.0	4,298.4
Others	1,718.6	1,012.9	1,231.1
TOTAL	27,329.1	19,739.7	26,205.4

PRINCIPAL TRADING PARTNERS—*continued*]

Exports	1970	1971	1972	1973*
Singapore and Malaysia	689.2	773.7	1,027.2	910.5
Thailand	472.6	634.6	457.0	1,987.3
Hong Kong	44.0	25.5	19.7	73.8
South Viet-Nam	18.6	0.2	—	0.4
TOTAL (incl. others)	1,726.7	1,485.4	1,540.1	3,044.6

* Provisional.

TRANSPORT

VEHICLES IN USE*

	1970	1971	1972	1973
Cars	10,969	12,054	12,765	13,611
Trucks	1,694	2,060	2,230	2,369
Motor cycles	10,365	11,068	12,105	13,162
TOTAL	23,028	25,182	27,100	29,142

* Excluding official vehicles.

CIVIL AVIATION

DOMESTIC SERVICES

	Arrivals			Departures		
	1971	1972	1973	1971	1972	1973
Flights	4,829	6,429	8,303	4,859	6,426	8,303
Passengers	66,774	86,808	186,217	76,597	88,613	167,554
Freight carried (metric tons)	1,719	2,152	3,035	2,610	2,283	2,991

INTERNATIONAL SERVICES

	Arrivals			Departures		
	1971	1972	1973	1971	1972	1973
Flights	782	877	1,285	792	885	1,285
Passengers	16,837	17,503	25,095	16,805	17,807	26,097
Freight carried (metric tons)	465	425	588	130	210	292

Tourism (1973): 12,378 visitors.

EDUCATION

(1973)

	Schools	Teachers and Administrators	Pupils
State Primary	2,018	6,374	240,354
State Secondary	22	399	8,722
Private Primary and Secondary	145	1,224	40,586
State Technical	3	152	1,118
Teacher Training	9	227	4,031
Higher Education	3	106	625
Fine Arts	2	74	283

Source (unless otherwise indicated): Service National de la Statistique, Vientiane.

THE CONSTITUTION

Following the change of regime in December 1975 and the abolition of the monarchy, it was announced that a new constitution would be prepared by the Supreme People's Council.

GOVERNMENT

HEAD OF STATE

President: SOUPHANOUVONG.

SUPREME PEOPLE'S COUNCIL

(*May* 1976)

President: SOUPHANOUVONG.

Vice-Presidents: SISOUNTHONE LOVANSAY, FAYDANG LOBLIAYAO, SITHON KOMMADAN, KHAMSOUK KEOLA.

Secretary-General: KHAMSOUK KEOLA.

Vice Secretary-Generals: XAY PHETRASY, SOUVANNARATH.

Prime Minister: KAYSONE PHOMVIHANE.

Vice-Prime Minister and Minister of Finance: NOUHAK PHOUMSAVANH.

Vice-Prime Minister and Minister of Education, Sport and Religion: PHOUMI VONGVICHIT.

Vice-Prime Minister and Minister of Foreign Affairs: Gen. PHOUNE SIPRASEUTH.

Vice-Prime Minister and Minister of Defence and Supreme Commander of the Lao Liberation Army: KHAMTAY SIPHANDONE.

Ministers to the Prime Minister's Office: SALY VONGKHAMSAO, CHANMY DOUANGPHOUKEO, MAYCHANTANE SENGMANY, SISAVAT KEOBOUNPHANH.

Minister of Interior, Veterans and Social Welfare: SOMSUNE KHAMPHITHOUNE.

Minister of Information, Propaganda, Culture and Tourism: SISANA SISANE.

Minister of Justice: KOU SOUVANNAMETHI.

Minister of Communications, Public Works and Transport: SANAN SOUTHICHAK.

Minister of Health: SOUK VONGSAK.

Minister of Agricultural Production, Forestry and Irrigation: KHAMSOUK SAYGNASENG.

Minister of Industry and Commerce: MAYSOUK SAYSOMPHENG.

Minister of Posts and Telecommunications: KHAMPHENG BOUPHA.

Supreme Counsellor of the President: Ex-King SAVANG VATTHANA.

Counsellor of the Government: SOUVANNA PHOUMA.

There are a further 21 members in the Supreme People's Council: 19 Vice-Ministers, the Chief of the Committee of the Minorities, and the Governor of the National Bank.

PARLIAMENT

The National Assembly was dissolved in April 1975. Elections for local assemblies were held in October and November 1975. A National Congress of People's Representatives, comprising 264 delegates elected by local authorities, was convened in December 1975. The Congress appointed the Supreme People's Council to draft a new constitution.

POLITICAL PARTY

Lao People's Revolutionary Party (LPRP): Vientiane; amalgamation of Lao Patriotic Front and Lao People's Party; Chair. SOUPHANOUVONG; Gen. Sec. of Central Committee KAYSONE PHOMVIHANE; Soc. of Central Committee NOUHAK PHOUMSAVANH; publ. *Siang Pasason*.

DIPLOMATIC REPRESENTATION

EMBASSIES AND LEGATION ACCREDITED TO LAOS

(In Vientiane unless otherwise indicated)

(E) Embassy; (L) Legation.

Algeria: Hanoi, Viet-Nam (E).

Australia: Quartier Phone Xay (E); *Ambassador:* JOHN A. FORSYTHE.

Austria: Bangkok, Thailand (E).

Belgium: Bangkok, Thailand (E).

Bulgaria: Hanoi, Viet-Nam (E).

Cambodia: (E); *Ambassador:* MÉAK TOUCH

Canada: Bangkok, Thailand (E).

China, People's Republic: (E); *Ambassador:* KUO YING.

Cuba: (E); *Ambassador:* R. VALDES.

Czechoslovakia: (E); *Chargé d'Affaires:* F. KAN.

Denmark: Bangkok, Thailand (L).

France: (E); *Ambassador:* GEORGES CARDI.

German Democratic Republic: (E); *Ambassador:* DIETRICH JARCK.

Germany, Federal Republic: (E); *Chargé d'Affaires:* Dr. CLAUS VOLLERS.

Hungary: (E); *Ambassador:* BÉLA BENYEI.

India: (E); *Ambassador:* B. DEVA RAO.

Iran: Bangkok, Thailand (E).

Italy: Bangkok, Thailand (E).

Japan: (E); *Ambassador:* KIYOSHI SUGANUMA.

Korea, Democratic People's Republic: (E); *Ambassador:* RIAN TAICHOUN.

Malaysia: (E); *Chargé d'Affaires:* RAZALI ISMAIL.

Mongolia: Hanoi, Viet-Nam (E).

Nepal: Rangoon, Burma (E).

Netherlands: Bangkok, Thailand (E).

New Zealand: Bangkok, Thailand (E).

Pakistan: Bangkok, Thailand (E).

Philippines: 4 Thadeva Rd. (E); *Ambassador:* JOSÉ M. EVANGELISTA.

Poland: (E); *Ambassador:* F. MUCZEK.

Romania: Hanoi, Viet-Nam (E).

Sri Lanka: Jakarta, Indonesia (E).

Sweden: Bangkok, Thailand (E).

Switzerland: Bangkok, Thailand (E).

Thailand: (E); *Ambassador:* SAWET KOMALABHUTI.

Turkey: Bangkok, Thailand (L).

U.S.S.R.: (E); *Ambassador:* VALENTIN VDOVINE.

United Kingdom: (E); *Ambassador:* DONALD P. CAPE.

U.S.A.: (E); *Chargé d'Affaires:* T. J. CORCORAN.

Viet-Nam: (E); *Ambassador:* LE VAN HIEN.

Yugoslavia: Rangoon, Burma (E).

Laos also has diplomatic relations with Burma, Finland, Indonesia and Israel.

JUDICIAL SYSTEM

Below is the judicial system in operation before the change of regime.

Supreme Court: Vientiane; exercises supervisory jurisdiction over all lower courts.

Court of Appeal: Vientiane; hears civil and criminal appeals from the Criminal Courts and other Courts of First Instance.

Criminal Courts: Vientiane, Pakse and Luang Prabang; appeals can be made from the decisions of these courts to the Court of Appeal and Supreme Court.

There is also a Provincial Tribunal in each of the provincial capitals (14 in all). There are 37 District Justices of the Peace.

RELIGION

The official religion of Laos is Buddhism (Hinayana).

BUDDHISM

His Eminence The Sangharaja, Wat Mai Suwannabhumarama, Luang Prabang.

CHRISTIANITY

Roman Catholic: Vicars Apostolic: Mgr. Thomas Nantha, B.P. 113, Mission Catholique, Vientiane (concurrently Admin. Apostolic of Luang Prabang), Mgr. Thomas Kamphan, Mission Catholique, Pakse, Mgr. Jean-Baptiste Outhay, Khammouane.

PRESS

New Vientiane: P.O.B. 989, Vientiane; f. 1975; semi-official.

Voice of the People: Vientiane; f. 1975; official organ.

PRESS AGENCIES

Lao Presse: B.P. 122, Vientiane; f. 1953; organ of the Ministry of Information.

Foreign Bureaux

Hsinhua (*People's Republic of China*): P.O.B. 898, Vientiane.

United Press International—UPI: Constellation Hotel, Vientiane.

Agence France-Presse and Novosti also have offices in Laos.

PUBLISHERS

Lao Printing office: Samsenthai Rd., Vientiane.

Pakpassak Kanphin: 9–11 Quai Fa-Nguun, Vientiane.

RADIO

Radiodiffusion Nationale Lao: B.P. 310, Vientiane; f. 1951; government-owned; programmes in Lao, French, English, Thai, Kmer and Vietnamese (news only) G.M.T. 23.00–02.30 (03.00 Sat./Sun.), 05.00–14.30 (15.00 Sat./Sun.); two regional stations Luang Prabang and Pakse; Dir.-Gen. (vacant); number of radio sets (1974) 102,000.

FINANCE

(cap.=capital; p.u.=paid up; dep.=deposit; m.=million)

BANKING

Central Bank

Banque Nationale du Laos: Rue Yonnet, Vientiane; f. 1955; central bank; cap. p.u. 290m. kips; dep. 44,842m. kips (Dec. 1974); Governor Thongchanh Upravanh.

TRADE AND INDUSTRY

New regulations for the organization of trade and industry were being prepared in mid-1976.

DEVELOPMENT ORGANIZATION

National Office for Agriculture and Livestock: Vientiane; public enterprise; imports and markets agricultural commodities; produces and distributes feed and animals.

MAJOR INDUSTRIAL COMPANIES

(capital in old kips)

Souk Kanlagna Sawmill: Rue Thong Khankham, Vientiane; f. 1964; export of sawn wood and timber; cap. p.u. 10m. kips.

Khambay Philaphandeth Sawmill: Luang-Prabang to Vientiane Highway; f. 1956; export of sawn wood and timber; cap. p.u. 9.5m. kips.

Lim Soung Houat Sawmill: 195-197 rue Sethathirath, B.P. 548, Vientiane; f. 1963; export of sawn wood and timber; cap. p.u. 50m. kips.

Khambay Philaphandeth Tyre Factory: Luang-Prabang to Vientiane Highway; f. 1969; production of tyres and retreads; cap. p.u. 35m. kips.

Yem Norasing Soap Factory: 188-190 rue Khoun Boulom, Vientiane; f. 1968; production of soaps and detergents; cap. p.u. 300m. kips.

Nang Noune Panyasiri Tobacco Factory: 63 rue Pangkham, Vientiane; f. 1960; manufacture of cigarettes; cap. p.u. 20m. kips.

Nang Sounat Tobacco Factory: 63 rue Pangkham, B.P. 181, Vientiane; f. 1954; manufacture of cigarettes; cap. p.u. 25m. kips.

Nang Kham Thieng Factory: Thadeua to Vientiane Highway; f. 1967; manufacture of seasonings and spices; cap. p.u. 60m. kips.

Thao Xa Khowongsa Factory: 150 rue Nong Bone, Vientiane; f. 1963; tanning and leather production; cap. p.u. 3m. kips.

TRANSPORT

There are no railways in Laos.

ROADS

There are about 6,500 km. of roads. Private operators run local bus services and long-distance services linking Vientiane and Luang Prabang with Saigon (south Viet-Nam), north Viet-Nam and Phnom-Penh (Cambodia). There are also usable roads linking Vientiane with Savannakhet, Phongsaly to the Chinese border, Vientiane with Luang Prabang and Khammouane with Ha Tink (north Viet-Nam). A rail and road project, linking Vientiane with Bangkok and sponsored by the Mekong Development Committee, is under survey.

INLAND WATERWAYS

The River Mekong is Laos' greatest traffic artery. Ferry services are run by government and private operators. The river is interrupted by rapids and is navigable between the following points only (traffic fluctuating seasonally):

Vientiane—Savannakhet (458 km.), ships of 200 gross tons, drawing 1.75 metres at 7 knots.

Savannakhet—Pakse (257 km.), ships of 200 gross tons, drawing 1.75 metres at 12 knots.

Pakse—Khone—Saigon, ships of 500 gross tons. drawing 2.5 metres at 7 knots.

CIVIL AVIATION

Lao Aviation: 2 Rue Pang Kham, B.P. 422, Vientiane.

Aviation Service of the Lao Patriotic Front: f. 1973.

Foreign Airlines

The following foreign airlines also serve Vientiane: Thai Airways and Aeroflot.

TOURISM

Lao National Tourism Department: P.O.B. 122, Samsenthai Rd., Vientiane; administered by an Executive Committee.

DEFENCE

Pathet-Lao Forces: Total strength about 40,000, equipped with Soviet and Chinese made light tanks, armoured cars and howitzers.

Commander-in-Chief: Souphanouvong.

EDUCATION

In 1945 only 1 per cent of the population of Laos were receiving primary education which was in Lao, and only 200 were receiving secondary education which was in French. Government expenditure on education and culture in 1973–74 was 2,564.0 million old kips.

Schooling in Laos is compulsory for six years and there is no age limit. The age of entry into primary school is six and lasts for six years, the duration of the secondary school course is from seven to eight years. Lao has gradually taken over as the medium of instruction in schools and a new type of school based on a comprehensive school system has been introduced with teaching completely in Lao.

About 240,000 children were enrolled in state primary schools in 1973 and 8,700 in state secondary schools. In 1970 there were 5,982 primary school teachers and 318 secondary school teachers, making a 1 : 29 primary school ratio and 1 : 22 secondary school ratio.

The Government has implemented a rapid programme of teacher training such that by 1974 there were 9 colleges with 4,031 students.

There are art school facilities and also teacher training courses which last from five to six years.

UNIVERSITY

Université Sisavangvong: Vientiane; *c.* 2,000 students.

BIBLIOGRAPHY

Berval, René de (Editor). The Kingdom of Laos (France-Asie Presse, Saigon, 1959).

Condominas, G. Essai sur la société lao de la région de Vientiane (Commissariat des affaires rurales, Vientiane).

Ministry of Planning and Co-operation.

Agence de développement de la plaine de Vientiane: Etablissement Public à caractère industriel et commercial (Vientiane, 1970).

Plan Cadre 1969–1974: programme annuel de réalisation 1971–72 (Vientiane, 1971).

Plan de mise en valeur de 6,000 hectares dans la plaine de Vientiane: Plan de développement agricole et rural, Vol. I (Pakpassack Press, Vientiane, 1970).

Plan de mise en valeur de 6,000 hectares dans la plaine de Vientiane: Étude préliminaire de l'établissement d'industries agricoles, Vol. II (Pakpassack Press, Vientiane, 1970).

Dommen, A. J. Conflict in Laos: The Politics of Neutralization (Pall Mall Press, London, 1964).

Lancaster, D. The Emancipation of French Indo-China (Oxford University Press, London, 1961).

Le Bar, F. M., and Suddard, A. Laos, its People, its Society, its Culture (HRAF Press, New Haven, 1960).

Toye, H. Laos—Buffer State or Background (Oxford University Press, London).

USAID. Facts on foreign aid to Laos (Usaid, Vientiane 1971).

See also Cambodia and Viet-Nam.

Malaysia

PHYSICAL AND SOCIAL GEOGRAPHY

C. A. Fisher

Malaysia covers a total of 329,744 square kilometres (127,315 square miles), comprising Peninsular Malaysia with an area of 131,587 square kilometres (50,806 square miles) and Sarawak and Sabah in northern Borneo with areas of, respectively, 124,446 square kilometres (48,049 square miles) and 73,711 square kilometres (28,460 square miles).

While both Peninsular and East Malaysia lie in almost identical latitudes between 1° and 7° N. of the Equator, and have characteristic equatorial climates with uniformly high temperatures and rain at all seasons, there is nevertheless a fundamental difference in their geographical position. For Peninsular Malaysia forms the southern tip of the Asian mainland, and on its western side, facing the sheltered and calm waters of the Straits of Malacca, flanks one of the oldest and most frequented maritime highways of the world, whereas East Malaysia lies off the track of the main shipping routes, along the northern fringe of the remote and consequently retarded island of Borneo.

PHYSICAL FEATURES

Structurally, both form part of the old stable massif of Sunda-land, though whereas the dominant folding in the Malay peninsula is of Mesozoic age that along the northern edge of Borneo dates from Tertiary times. In Peninsular Malaysia the mountain ranges, whose summit levels reach 4,000–7,000 ft. (1,200–2,100 metres), run roughly N.-S. and their granitic cores have been widely exposed by erosion. The most continuous of these is the Main Range which over most of the peninsula marks the divide between the relatively narrow western coastal plain draining to the Straits of Malacca, and the much larger area of mountainous interior and coastal lowland which drains to the South China Sea.

Because of the much greater accessibility of the western lowlands to the main sea-routes, and also of the existence of extensive areas of alluvial tin in the gravels deposited at the break of slope in the western foothills of the Main Range, the strip of country lying between the latter and the western coast of Malaya has been much more intensively developed than the remaining four-fifths of the country. For although tin has long taken second place to rubber, the planting of the latter became concentrated in the vicinity of the roads, railways and other facilities originally developed in connection with the former. In contrast to the placid waters of the west coast, the east coast is open to the full force of the N.E. monsoon during the period from October to March, and the difficulties which this situation has presented to small craft have reinforced the remoteness of the eastern side of the peninsula from the main stream of commercial activity.

In many respects East Malaysia displays similar basic geographical characteristics to eastern Malaya, but in a more extreme form. Thus, its lowlands are mostly wider, its rivers longer and even more liable to severe flooding, its coastline is exposed to the N.E. monsoon and avoided by shipping, and its equatorial forest cover appears even denser and more continuous than that of the peninsula. Moreover, while in general its mountains are of comparable height to those in Malaya, it contains one striking exception in Mt. Kinabalu, a single isolated horst which towers above the Crocker Range of Sabah to an altitude of 13,455 ft. (4,101 metres).

NATURAL RESOURCES

Notwithstanding minor deposits of coal, as well as some gold and other metals, in both Sarawak and Sabah, East Malaysia has nothing comparable in scale with the tin or even the more scattered but considerable high-grade iron resources of Peninsular Malaysia. However, Sarawak and Sabah export petroleum, and copper mining has begun in northern Sabah. Moreover, while there are some useful areas of volcanically enriched soil in eastern Sabah, their remoteness has hitherto militated against the development of any large-scale commercial agriculture there, and although both Sarawak and Sabah produce some rubber this is of trivial importance compared with that of Peninsular Malaysia, and in Sabah is far exceeded in value by the output of commercial timber.

While it must be stressed that Peninsular Malaysia's much greater economic importance, which now rests primarily upon its production of rubber and other tree crops such as palm oil and copra, is the result of accessibility and commercial enterprise rather than of any inherent superiority of soil, this great contrast between Peninsular Malaysia (and in particular the areas west of the Main Range) and East Malaysia (where development is also mostly restricted to a relatively narrow coastal zone) is fundamental to an understanding of the great demographic contrast between the two parts of the country.

POPULATION AND CULTURE

The total population of Malaysia was estimated at 11,759,949 in December 1974, of whom 9,865,635 were in Peninsular Malaysia, giving it an average density of 194.2 per square mile, 804,149 were in Sabah (28.3 per square mile) and 1,090,165 in Sarawak (22.7 per square mile).

However, the difference in density is not the only difference in the populations of the two wings of Malaysia. In Peninsular Malaysia the indigenous population, apart from some 50,000 or so primitive animist peoples, consists of Muslim Malays, though these form only 53 per cent of the total population, which also includes 35 per cent Chinese and a further 10 per cent Indians (an ethnic term which applies to people from India, Pakistan or Bangladesh). In East Malaysia, on the other hand, Malays and other Muslim peoples are confined mainly to the coastal zone while various groups of less advanced peoples occupy the interior. Nevertheless, there is also a large Chinese element in East Malaysia, amounting to 30 per cent of the 1974 estimate in Sarawak and 21 per cent in Sabah, so that in Malaysia as a whole Malays constituted 47 per cent, Chinese 34 per cent, Indians 9 per cent, Borneo indigenes 8.5 per cent and others 1.5 per cent of the population in 1974.

Finally, the contrast between the two parts of the country shows up most sharply of all in respect of urbanization, for while Peninsular Malaysia has at least ten towns of over 50,000 people (including Kuala Lumpur, the national capital, which now exceeds 500,000) East Malaysia has only one, namely Kuching, the capital of Sarawak (with 63,535 in 1970), and the largest town in Sabah is not the capital, Kota Kinabalu (formerly Jesselton, whose population was 40,939 in 1970), but Sandakan (42,249).

HISTORY

J. M. Gullick

The state of Malaysia was established as recently as 1963 but its long history is a significant factor in its present situation. In prehistoric times it was populated by successive waves of migrants from the north. On the arrival of the Malays about five thousand years ago the earlier settlers retreated to the remoter highland areas where they are now represented by small groups of aborigines who still live mainly as hunters and collectors. The first Malays developed a simple agriculture on the lowland and riverine areas. Because of its position across the sea route from India to the Far East the Malay Peninsula was always exposed to contact with foreign traders but their influence was felt on the coast and at the northern isthmus of Kra (part of modern Thailand) and it did not penetrate to the uninhabited interior. The northern part of Borneo was more isolated but subject to the same factors to a lesser extent. In the first millennium of the Christian era contact with India introduced to the Malay culture a number of elements of Indian civilization including the Hindu religion. At this time there was a series of kingdoms in South-East Asia whose economy was based on trade rather than agriculture. In the area of the Straits of Malacca the centre of power shifted in the fifteenth century from the east coast of Sumatra to Malacca where a Malay Sultanate was established about A.D. 1400. Malacca was the last and one of the greatest indigenous kingdoms of South-East Asia and its traditions shaped the Malay States of later centuries.

THE MALAY POLITICAL SYSTEM

Malacca began as an offshoot of another centre of power. According to the "Malay Annals", a classic of Malay literature, a Malay prince from Tumasik (the modern Singapore) established himself at Malacca, then an obscure and unimportant area, at the beginning of the fifteenth century. The new port flourished mightily; its earliest rulers were converted to Islam through contacts with traders from India and the Persian Gulf; they also sent trade missions to the imperial court of China to secure recognition.

The Sultans of Malacca were drawn from a patrilineal royal dynasty and combined in their office attributes of indigenous South-East Asian, Hindu and Islamic royal prerogatives and symbolism. In the government of the state the Sultan was assisted by high officers, to whom were given titles such as Bendahara (Chief Minister), Temenggong (Minister of War and Police) and Shahbandar (Minister of Ports and Trade). These officers were drawn from families of aristocratic but not royal pedigree though on occasion the Sultans took wives from these families. Inevitably there was intrigue and competition for power but the ruling aristocracy as a whole was a caste set above and apart from their subjects. Unlike its successor states Malacca was essentially a centre of power based on regional and foreign trade. To the port of Malacca came traders from other parts of South-East Asia such as Acheh in northern Sumatra and the Celebes, and also merchants from India, the Middle East and China. Their common purpose was to sell the cargoes which they had brought and to purchase from others cargoes for the return voyage. The half-yearly change of prevailing winds under the monsoon climate made this inflow and outflow possible and predictable. The polyglot population of the thriving port was administered through headmen appointed from the main groups. Malacca had influence over many lesser ports on both sides of the Straits but did not possess a territorial empire. The rural population was sparse and agriculture of secondary importance. In its last decades Malacca was weakened by conflict within the ruling class and by dispute with the foreign traders who filled the town. The disaffection of the latter contributed to the fall of Malacca to the Portuguese.

PORTUGUESE, DUTCH AND BRITISH INTERVENTION

Now that the colonial period in South-East Asia fades into historical perspective it can be seen as "the Vasco da Gama Epoch of Asian History" (the sub-title of K. M. Pannikar's *Asia and Western Dominance*). It was an episode prolonged and important but less decisive than perhaps it once seemed in shaping modern South-East Asia. The main effects of European control were, first, to break the sequence of indigenous kingdoms and to disrupt the trade system upon which they had been based; secondly, to delimit colonial spheres of influence and thereby to fix the subsequent boundaries of the national states which are heirs to colonial rule; and lastly to promote economic development and establish the infrastructure of government and other services which that development required; mass immigration from India and China was an incidental consequence of economic development. However, the culture, institutions, values and traditions of the region persisted even in a context of alien cultural and political domination.

First of the European powers to attempt to dominate the region were the Portuguese who came to Malacca as traders in 1509 and as aggressors in 1511.

The seventeenth century saw the arrival of the Dutch as the leading European trading power in South-East Asia. In 1641 Malacca fell to the Dutch and their Johore Malay allies. Although Malacca was always an important link in Dutch communications and trade the main centre of their power was further east in Java. The Dutch pursued the same objectives as the Portuguese before them but by more methodical and systematic means. By diplomacy and the show of force they endeavoured to control the trade of the region. Like the Portuguese they encountered much resistance and evasion. In particular during the early years of the eighteenth century the Dutch came into conflict with the Bugis, a people from the Celebes who for centuries had sailed their ships on trading voyages through the narrow seas of modern Indonesia and Malaysia.

The Bugis were to play a prominent part in the Malay resistance to the Dutch but they were latecomers. On the fall of Malacca to the Portuguese in 1511 the Malacca dynasty removed itself to the southern tip of the Malay peninsula and founded the kingdom of Johore. But the rulers of Johore, harassed during the sixteenth century both by the Portuguese and by the Achehnese of north Sumatra, could never regain the wealth and power of their Malacca predecessors. They were, however, the recognized successors of Malacca. In northern Malaya a branch of the same dynasty had established itself in Perak, destined later to be the major tin-producing area of the peninsula; other Malay states emerged in the north and east; in northern Borneo the long domination of the Malay rulers of Brunei had begun. But these were scattered centres of power lacking a common leadership and sense of purpose. The Bugis leaders took control of the weak and divided Johore, reducing its Malay rulers to puppets and installing themselves as "under kings". Further north in the mid-eighteenth century Bugis established settlements on the west central coast of Malaya and eventually became Sultans of a new State of Selangor. Their attempts to establish a similar hegemony of the small states between Selangor and Malacca were resisted, however, under the leadership of Malay Rajas invited over from the Menangkabau region of Sumatra; thus began the Negri Sembilan confederacy. There had been an offshoot of the Johore dynasty on the Pahang River since the sixteenth century and further still up the east coast the Malay States of Trengganu and Kelantan were within the sphere of influence of Siam. The modern pattern of the peninsular Malay States was emerging but the intervention of European powers prevented any coalescence of Malay States into a confederacy or centre of power without providing an effective European integration of the area.

In the latter part of the eighteenth century Dutch power waned; the British, victorious in India, turned eastwards to South-East Asia and in particular to trade with China. During the period of the Napoleonic War Malacca and then Java passed temporarily from Dutch to British control and Stamford Raffles, with his vision of an imperial mission, made his appearance. In the settlement which followed the war, maritime South-East Asia was in effect divided by the Anglo-Dutch treaty of 1824 into two spheres of influence. Britain took or retained the island of Penang (first acquired from Kedah in 1786), Malacca and also Singapore (acquired from Johore in 1819). These three positions along the west coast of Malaya formed the Straits Settlements; the hinterland of the Malay Peninsula as far north as the undetermined southern boundary of Siamese influence was also within the British sphere. There was also some ambiguity over the line of division in Borneo but in the event James Brooke in Sarawak and the Borneo Company in modern Sabah acquired substantial parts of the territories of the Sultanate of Brunei as the century went on.

Information is fragmentary on the condition of the Malay States as they entered the period of British influence and eventual direct control. Until 1874 it was the object of British policy to avoid involvement in the Malay States; there was no systematic reporting on their condition. Some common features can, however, be discerned. None of the States was a major centre of trade or production; without the essential sinews of public revenue the rulers tended to impotence. The Malay population of the entire peninsula was probably well below half a million and of that total a considerable part was in the Siamese sphere of influence to the north and east. The population was dispersed in small villages along the coasts and up the rivers. The villagers lived by rice cultivation, fishing and the collection of jungle produce such as rattans, gutta percha, sago and fruit. Effective power was in the hands of district chiefs drawn from the ruling aristocracy. The chief might bear some title of office in the Malacca tradition such as Temenggong or Shahbandar but the duties of the office no longer existed. His position was that of a mediaeval baron ruling his fief rather than that of an officer of a royal government. When the office of Sultan fell vacant the ensuing struggle for power might lead to civil war and similar competition arose over the remunerative position of district chief. Along the west coast of the Malay peninsula mining of alluvial tin deposits was becoming the most important source of wealth. From about 1830 mining passed from Malay to Chinese control since the immigrant Chinese were better organized for sustained and large-scale operations. The expansion of Chinese tin mining drew in considerable numbers of labourers imported from China under arrangements made by Chinese merchants in the ports of the Straits Settlements. First Lukut (now in Negri Sembilan) then central Selangor and the Larut tinfields of Perak attracted Chinese in their thousands for lucrative but laborious and crude mining operations. Thus the multi-racial society of western Malaya had its real beginning though, until well into the present century, most of the Chinese were temporary immigrants who eventually returned to China. The expansion of tin mining in the nineteenth century had two significant effects on the Malay States. First, competition for the right to work the most productive tinfields led to fighting between rival groups of Chinese, organized under "secret society" leadership, and also between Malay rulers and chiefs whose tax revenues increasingly came from this source. Secondly, commercial interests in the Straits Settlements, including some European as well as Chinese entrepreneurs, became involved in mining investments in the western Malay States and were accordingly at risk on the outcome of local struggles for power. These conflicts threatened the whole political and economic stability of the western Malay States in the 1860s and early 1870s. The official British policy of non-intervention came increasingly under pressure by interested parties. Elsewhere in eastern Malaya and northern Borneo the absence of these economic stresses permitted a more stable situation to continue.

Apart from the objective of non-involvement in the Malay States British policy also required that no foreign power should intervene in a territory which stood at the "back door" of the Straits ports. In the second quarter of the nineteenth century the main concern of the British authorities in the Straits Settlements was to hold in check Siamese aspirations to extend or consolidate their suzerainty in north-western Malaya. In mid-century there was growing concern among the merchants in the Straits ports about the continuing viability of their position. In its earliest period Singapore had attracted trade from far afield. The establishment of Hong Kong in 1842 and the appearance of the French and Spanish in Indo-China and the Philippines shut out Singapore in the north of the region. Nearer home the Dutch were consolidating their hold on what was to become the Netherlands East Indies and in so doing introducing mercantilist policies to the detriment of Singapore trade. There were fears also that Germany, a formidable competitor and a growing imperial power, might intervene in the British sphere. These factors, added to the increasing impracticability of maintaining peace in the Malay States by remote control, led to demands for a "forward policy" which would bring the economically most important parts of the peninsula under direct British control. In northern Borneo there was at the same time a completely separate but bitter rivalry between Sarawak and the Borneo Company over claims to what remained of the territories of the Sultan of Brunei.

British policy changed abruptly at the end of 1873. Within a few months the troubled and economically important States of west-central Malaya had come under a British protectorate. It was the first step in a sequence of events which was to bring the entire peninsula under direct British rule.

BRITISH RULE IN THE MALAY STATES

The basis of British administration in the Malay States was to be found in the key passage of the Treaty of Pangkor, 1874, whereby under the Residential System, British rule was exercised through British Officers, whose advice must be asked and acted upon by the Malay States in all matters other than those touching Malay religion and custom. In the circumstances of the Malay States in 1874, this was unworkable and the British attempted then to exert a stronger rule in the Malay States. Resentment against British rule led to disturbances in Perak, Selangor and Negri Sembilan and to a Malay revolt in 1875. Nevertheless, the "Residential system" became the basis for British administration until the Second World War. The Residential system was extended from Perak to Selangor, Negri Sembilan and Pahang and together they formed the Federated Malay States (F.M.S.) in 1896.

There remained two zones of Malaya outside the sphere of British rule. The four States of Kedah, Perlis, Kelantan and Trengganu in the north were within the Siamese sphere of influence. Though the British were anxious to extend northwards to carry their boundary up to the narrow Kra Isthmus, Anglo-French rivalry in and around Siam prevented the achievement of this policy. However, by 1909, the European differences were resolved and the four northern States were transferred by Siam to the British sphere. The States accepted British advisers but did not enter the centralized administration of the F.M.S., i.e. they became known as the Unfederated Malay States (U.M.S.). Johore remained independent and avoided becoming a formal protectorate until 1914 when some defects in local administration resulted in the acceptance of a permanent British Adviser in Johore. With this, the unification of the Malay Peninsula under British rule was complete.

Under the British, the Malay political system was preserved though there were minor modifications. The basic framework of political power was maintained though the Sultans and the chiefs felt the loss of national dignity and the forced obedience to law. But the Malay ruling class was reconciled to the Residential system by the scrupulous insistence of the British advisers in distinguishing between the constitutional basis of power and executive control. The Residential system meant government in the name of the Sultan of the State. In addition to the consultative machinery of the State Councils, the early British residents conferred with the Malay rulers, and treated them with due deference as royalty. The unemployed or frustrated aristocrats were converted into civil servants. Malay chiefs were appointed to the honorific sinecure of "Malay Magistrates" in the districts. The young generation of Malay aristocrats was given English education, the main purpose of which was to train them for appointment to the administrative branch of the civil service. The local headman (*Penghulu*) became the main instrument of rural government and was essentially a government servant with a host of administrative chores. Also, the British devised inexpensive means of governing the Malay peasant class. Local police forces were raised to keep order and the police rank and file were recruited almost entirely from the Malay peasantry.

British rule in the Straits Settlement and the Malay States encouraged the immigration of non-Malay communities, particularly the Chinese, into Malaya. By 1921, the Chinese in Malaya numbered 1.2 million, and they formed more than 50 per cent of the total population in Selangor and Perak. At the apex of the Chinese community were the relatively small number of wealthy Chinese merchants in the major ports who financed tin-mining in the Malay States and who imported their countrymen from China to work in the mines. The institutional framework which embraced the community was the "secret society", at one time the dominant form of association among the Malayan Chinese. The secret society provided them with welfare services, economic management, local government and leadership but it also enabled the merchants to dominate, intimidate and exploit the immigrants.

The British administrators had been coping ineffectively with the problems presented by the secret societies primarily because they did not understand the language and customs of the Chinese. An attempt to solve the problem was the establishment of the Chinese Protectorate in 1877 staffed by officers who could speak Chinese. A further move was made in 1889 by the enactment of a Societies Ordinance, which outlawed the secret societies. But though their political power was broken, remnants of the secret societies persisted as undercover criminal organizations. Later, Chinese nationalism in the form of the Kuomintang replaced the secret society as the *imperium in imperio* of the Malayan Chinese community.

NATIONALISM AND PLURALISM

The creation of the State Council was the first move in the evolution of the Malay States towards constitutional monarchy and representative government. It provided contact between the Chinese and the Anglo-Malay régime and was a step towards the acceptance of the non-Malays as Malayans. The proceedings were conducted in Malay in which all members were proficient and in the early years after 1877, the Council was of the utmost value as a forum of Sino-British-Malay discussion. However, the transfer of power from the States to the new federal executive of the F.M.S. in 1895 deprived the State Councils of their usefulness and it left them merely to approve proposals handed down to them from a federal secretariat. Subsequently, the establishment of a Federal Council for the F.M.S. in 1909 was an attempt to restore the balance. When the Council was enlarged in the 1920s to take in Malay unofficial members, it became a political body in which the force of public opinion could be mobilized on local issues to influence the federal bureaucracy. From 1925, various measures of decentralization were proposed, designed to restore to the State governments of the F.M.S. some of the powers and functions which they had lost. Nominated Malay unofficial members of aristocratic status were included in the Federal Council. In the early 1930s a considerable measure of administrative decentralization was achieved from the federal to the State governments of the F.M.S. However, the concept of a larger federation proved unattainable and this was the position until 1941.

The Straits Settlements were governed under a Crown Colony system. There were no Malay rulers and therefore no Anglo-Malay dyarchy. Between the World Wars the educated members of the Chinese and Eurasian communities were admitted to the administrative service but on terms inferior to those of British members. Demands for an elected unofficial majority in the local legislatures of the Straits Settlements were dismissed on the ground that the majority of the population were transient aliens who showed no interest in their government. The Unfederated Malay States remained essentially Malay States in the political sense, subject to British influence rather than control.

The existence of the various communities with conflicting interests and different viewpoints prevented the emergence of a united nationalist movement in the period up to 1942. To the Malays the colonial régime was a bulwark against the economic strength and sheer numbers of the immigrant communities. The Chinese and Indians were preoccupied with their own material interests and in the political developments of their ancestral homelands. Moreover, the Malay aristocracy, which still commanded the loyalty of the mass of the peasantry, was distrustful of the minority of the Malay religious and social reformers. The Chinese middle class gave its support to the Kuomintang (KMT), an externally orientated nationalist movement, but the KMT was circumscribed both by British restrictions on its activities and the communist penetration of the working class.

Under the British there was an intensive Malay preoccupation with Islamic affairs; a new establishment of religious officials appeared both in the capitals and villages. Steamer services made possible the pilgrimage to Mecca to a greater number of the peasantry. Some remained in Mecca or Cairo to prolong their religious education. A consequence was that they brought back the ideas prevalent in the Middle East of reinvigoration of the Islamic peoples through religious reforms. The Malay upper class and the new religious "establishment" opposed such ideas as dangerous. In the period between the two World Wars incipient Malay nationalism took on a secular form and lost its pan-Islamic flavour. This was attributed to the presence of some Indonesian nationalists in the late 1920s and the emergence of a politically conscious group among the Malays. At this time, the Sultan Idris Training College was the main forum of Malay intellectual discussion. It produced an articulate generation of village schoolmasters together with a minority of left-wing political activists. Together with the English-educated Malay civil servants, the Malay society was acquiring a new middle stratum which included the village headmen, the Islamic clergy, landowners, the schoolmasters and the retired civil servants.

The first Malay communal body of a semi-political character was the Singapore Malay Union formed in 1926; in the Straits Settlements the Malays were a small minority without the protection of being subjects of a Malay ruler but they were better educated and more sophisticated than their rural brethren. In the Malay Peninsula between 1937–39 local bodies sprang up under the leadership of Malay public figures and senior civil servants. The first pan-Malayan conference of local Malay associations was held in 1939. They were the origin of the Malay national party after the war. At the same time, the pan-Malaysian left-wing groups formed the Union of Young Malays (*Kesatuan Melayu Muda*—KMM). The anti-British tone of the KMM resulted in their leaders' arrest under defence regulations in 1940.

In the 1920s the Kuomintang government of China extended its influence among the overseas Chinese in order to gain financial support from the latter. In their drive for members and contributions among the Malayan Chinese, the local KMT leaders enlisted the support of the old secret societies and until 1927 they admitted communists to the party. The effect of these KMT activities was to spread among the immigrant Chinese a sense of national solidarity in opposition to European rule. After the split in 1927 within the KMT, the communists broke away to form in April 1930 the Malayan Communist Party. The third group among the Malayan Chinese community was the small but influential group of Straits Chinese. Through the Straits Chinese British Association they sought recognition of their position as a Malayan-domiciled community. They had Western education and experience in the consultative procedures of government. Events external to Malaya in the period 1937–41 had a significant effect on the outlook of the various elements of the Malayan Chinese community. The renewed Japanese attack on China in 1937 evoked strong patriotic feelings which the MCP was able to exploit, and this brought about the rapprochement between the MCP, KMT supporters and the government.

Up to 1942, the forces of tradition in Malaya were rather stronger than in many other Asian countries then under colonial rule. The British régime managed a satisfactory accommodation both with the aristocratic leaders of the Malay community and the influential Chinese merchant class. There was no educated middle class in revolt against these forces. With the important exception of the MCP, no radical or left-wing group had achieved significant influence with the mass of the people. The status quo, however, was upset by the Japanese defeat of the British, which altered the balance between conservatism and change.

THE INDEPENDENCE OF MALAYA

This flow of change led Malaya to eventual independence. The Japanese victory in 1942 and the ensuing occupation (1942–45) was both a traumatic and a catalytic experience. The British had failed to defend the country from foreign attack; their credentials as the protecting power were destroyed. Each of the major communities looked forward to some new régime in which there would no longer be a British umpire between them. Yet, relations between the communities deteriorated owing to Japanese discrimination. The Japanese encouraged Malay and Indian nationalism so long as they could harness it to their own war effort; they encountered resistance from the Chinese led by the communist Malayan People's Anti-Japanese Army (MPAJA). In these years when British policy-makers were cut off from Malaya the British Government became committed to two new objectives for Malaya. First, it was necessary to complete the territorial unification of the whole Malay peninsula (excluding Singapore which was regarded as a distinct and special problem); the second objective was to put all the communities on an equal basis, thus abandoning the distinction between the indigenous Malay population and the other communities with their recent history of immigration and their existing links with the countries of their origin. As soon as the Japanese surrender of September 1945 reopened communications the new plan was promulgated in the form of a "Malayan Union", a unitary State in which the Malay States and their sovereign Malay Rulers would lose all title to constitutional identity; all persons who had made Malaya their home (by various tests of local birth, residence or parentage) were to be citizens of the new state regardless of their origin. The high-handed manner in which these reforms were introduced added to the deep Malay resentment and dislike of the whole concept of the Malayan Union. Opposition galvanized the nascent Malay political associations into the immediate formation of the United Malay National Organization (UMNO) which since 1946 has been the dominant Malay communal party and since 1956 the main government party in office. In face of this opposition the British Government withdrew its Malayan Union proposals and negotiated a Federation of Malaya with the Malay Rulers and political leaders. The Federation (established on February 1st, 1948) was still a union of the whole peninsula (including the former Straits Settlements of Penang and Malacca but not Singapore) under a strong central government. But it also recognized the continued sovereignty of the Malay Rulers in their States and preserved what came to be called the "special position" of their Malay subjects as the indigenous people of the country with appropriate rights.

The Chinese and other non-Malay communities had had no part in these Anglo-Malay negotiations. Their opposition to the Federation of Malaya was predictable but ineffectual. In part this was because the opposition group comprised every element of opinion from conservative to communist but it lacked political organization. There was no real identity of objectives;

mere opposition was not enough to unite such disparate ideologies. The Chinese community was uncertain which course would best suit its interests. The Chinese were less interested in political matters than the Malays; indeed many did not yet fully identify themselves with Malaya rather than China as their homeland. If they continued to follow a constitutional path of co-operation or moderate opposition they were unlikely to secure the equality with the Malays which the shortlived Malayan Union had offered them. Many were therefore tempted to follow the more extreme leadership of the Malayan Communist Party (MCP) which at this time was a legal and important political organization. The MPAJA as the military wing of the MCP had led Chinese opposition to the Japanese and in 1945 it was still an effective cadre with arms prudently dumped in jungle hideouts. The communist victory in China in 1949 further increased the prestige of the movement as the expression of Chinese nationalist feeling—for the same reason communism made little appeal to the Malays. To follow communist leadership was for the Malayan Chinese to commit themselves to extreme policies and to isolate themselves from co-operation with the Malays. The communist leadership itself was sharply divided on the choice of strategy to adopt, i.e. whether to take full advantage of its high standing with non-communist bodies and manipulate a "united front" for communist purposes or whether, following the example of Mao Tse-tung, to launch a direct military attack as a bid for power, beginning from the periphery and moving in to the centre of power at the end.

In 1948 the choice was made of the second alternative and so began the long struggle known in Malaya as "the Emergency". In this campaign small bodies of armed communists operating from jungle hideouts made raids and laid ambushes designed to destroy government control of the remoter parts of the country which were to become "liberated areas" and bases for further extension of communist control. The raiders were much assisted by the supplies and information provided, from fear or loyalty, by Chinese "squatters" settled along the fringe of the jungle zone. After several years of intense effort by numerically superior security forces, the resettlement of squatters in "New Villages" where they could be protected and controlled, and the development of a much improved intelligence system, the government was able to destroy much of the communist forces and to drive the remainder into refuge on the inaccessible border zone between Thailand and northern Malaya. As the communist movement cut itself off by open resistance from the mainstream of legal political activity the main body of the Malayan Chinese grouped itself with some hesitation behind the Malayan Chinese Association (MCA), whose leaders were drawn mainly from the world of Chinese business, traditionally the spokesmen of the community. In 1956 the MCP had the opportunity of negotiating a settlement with the new Alliance government but lost it by asking for too much. The Emergency was formally ended in 1960 but the threat of communism is by no means at an end.

In 1952 the leaders of UMNO and MCA entered into an "Alliance" (to which the Malayan Indian Congress—MIC—was later admitted). Thus a limited coalition of moderate leaders of the three major communities prepared the way for self-government. The constitutional development of the years 1948–56 was an intricate sequence of adjustments in which concessions were exchanged between the communal groups. Throughout this period there was a wholly nominated central legislature (the Federal Legislative Council) in which appointed unofficial members (in fact chosen on the advice of political and other representative bodies) outnumbered but rarely outvoted the government official members. The British High Commissioner was advised in his function of head of the government executive by an Executive Council in which from 1950 onwards certain quasi-ministerial responsibilities were discharged by Malay, Chinese and Indian leaders. It was an embryo cabinet based on a dyarchy in which power was shared between local leaders and the British authorities. In the States there were somewhat similar arrangements under which the Malay Ruler acted as a constitutional monarch and executive power was exercised by a Malay Chief Minister (with slight modifications in the former Settlements of Penang and Malacca). The qualifications for citizenship admitted virtually all Malays and a majority of the adult non-Malay population (on criteria of local birth, parentage, residence and proficiency in the Malay language). The first elections held in 1955 to choose members of the federal and state councils, yielded an overwhelming victory to the Alliance which won 51 out of 52 seats in the federal council and a majority in nine out of eleven state councils. In the ensuing twenty years it has at all times had a similar preponderance. A new constitution whose complexity reflected the issues of inter-communal relationships was introduced. In 1957 the government, which had had powers of internal self-government since 1955, assumed the powers of a fully independent state. The first Prime Minister was Tunku Abdul Rahman, President of UMNO and architect of the inter-communal Alliance coalition. His deputy and eventual successor (in 1970) was Tun Abdul Razak. For many years until his retirement in 1974 the senior Chinese Minister (and Minister of Finance) was Tan Siew Sin, President of the MCA.

Apart from its unsuccessful attempt to come to terms with the MCP the new Alliance government tackled a number of other difficult issues. The Malayan education system was reorganized with a view to the greater integration of the different community schools and the more extended use of the Malay language. Much effort and money was put into a "rural development" programme, and also the opening up of new land for settlement; both were designed to improve the economic position of the Malay community whose sense of their own weakness as compared with the Chinese is one of the basic causes of inter-communal tension. British civil servants who at independence held two-thirds of the senior posts were phased out and replaced by local men.

FORMATION OF MALAYSIA

In the late 1950s the future of Singapore was a matter of increasing concern to the Malayan Government. In the reconstruction after the war Singapore had been excluded from the newly united Malaya because it was felt that Singapore with its preponderance of Chinese population and its concentration of economic power would upset the delicate communal balance in Malaya. Accordingly, Singapore progressed as a separate state by stages to a system of elected legislature and internal self-government (in 1956). But Singapore showed itself politically unstable; its economic survival as a separate state was doubted at this time (wrongly as later events have shown). The Malayan Government came to the view that its own problems of Sino-Malay relations would be eased rather than aggravated if Singapore joined the Federation on terms which gave it reduced representation in the federal parliament but extended local powers of government (as compared with the Malay States). Participation on these terms was welcomed by the People's Action Party (PAP) Government of Singapore headed by Lee Kuan Yew. The British Government, which shared power in Singapore in uneasy partnership with the PAP, also welcomed the scheme and proposed that its remaining territories in northern Borneo, i.e. Sabah and Sarawak (Crown colonies since 1945), and the protected state of Brunei should also join the enlarged federation. To the Malayan Government it seemed—over-optimistically as it turned out—that the Borneo territories with their agricultural populations, some of whom were Malay or at least Malay-speaking Muslims, would fit easily into the enlarged state and counterbalance Singapore. There was some doubt as to whether the peoples of the Borneo territories, politically and educationally far behind Malaya, were ready or willing to join their stronger neighbours. However, the attitudes of the Borneo peoples to the Malaysia scheme were tested first by an Anglo-Malayan body (the Cobbold Commission) and later by a United Nations mission. Both reported in favour of the proposal provided that safeguards were supplied. There was considerable opposition from Indonesia and the Philippines (*see* below "International Relations") but Malaysia was formed in September 1963 to include the eleven States of Malaya, Singapore, Sarawak and Sabah. Brunei at a late stage decided to stay out.

Indonesia then attempted by military means ("Confrontation") to bring down the new and enlarged state but failed. Following the fall from power of President Sukarno a reconciliation was effected in 1966. Singapore proved a disturbing influence on the internal politics of Malaysia as its slogan of "Malaysian Malaysia" afforded a rallying point for those who opposed the Malay predominance in the political system. In August 1965 Singapore was compelled to withdraw from Malaysia as its government saw no other way of avoiding severe communal friction. Relations between the central government of Malaysia and the State governments of Sabah and Sarawak also proved difficult but here the disparity of power led to the supersession of local opponents by more accommodating State governments.

1965-75

The ending of Confrontation, the withdrawal of Singapore and the settlement of disputes in northern Borneo seemed to afford to Malaysia a period of calm and progress. The country had continued to make satisfactory economic progress; its internal government machinery was working reasonably well; the Alliance government had been re-elected in 1964 with a larger majority than it had obtained in the previous elections of 1959. At most times there is little sign in Malaysian public life of inter-communal friction; it is indeed arguable that at most times it is not a major problem; the communities accommodate themselves to each other on the basis that a compromise is inevitable. But this acquiescence is dependent on stability. If it appears that the balance may be upset anxiety wells to the surface. The general election campaign of 1969 was one such occasion. The essence of the compromise is that over a period of time the Malays are to have a greater share in the economy of the country and the Chinese are to move nearer to equality of political rights, i.e. the "special rights" of the Malays are to be diminished. In the election campaign of May 1969 it appeared that the MCA was losing ground among its Chinese electorate to parties disposed to demand a more rapid end to Malay predominance. Malay anxiety at this trend was increased by provocative behaviour. In the end there was serious rioting in which it is believed that several hundred people lost their lives.

In this crisis the constitution was suspended for over a year while the government framed measures to remedy the situation and to prevent recurrence of the disorder. It was at this point that Tunku Abdul Rahman, whose anguish at the disaster had impeded his ability to deal with it effectively, gave way to Tun Abdul Razak as Prime Minister. The Sedition Act was amended to prohibit any public advocacy of changes which would diminish the sovereignty of the Malay Rulers, which since the withdrawal of the Malayan Union in 1947 has been the sheet anchor of the Malay position, or reduce the special rights of the Malays and (in Borneo) other indigenous groups and the citizenship rights of any ethnic group. As an essay in more positive nation building a written National Ideology (*Rukunegara*) was submitted to Parliament for approval. These principles included belief in God, loyalty to King and country, respect for the Constitution, the rule of Law and good behaviour and morality. The next five-year economic development plan (1971–75) included a twenty-year objective, to be attained by 1990, of raising the ownership by indigenous communities (*bumiputra*) to at least 30 per cent of national wealth. The attainment of that object obviously requires that indigenous participation in new or expanded enterprises should exceed 30 per cent. In the political sphere the old Alliance coalition was widened to absorb most of the former opposition parties into a National Front. The purpose here is presumably to harness the energies of the opposition to constructive aims and to bring disputes within the framework of a political coalition rather than let them find expression in open conflict. The only major party now in opposition is the Democratic Action Party (DAP). On this basis the general election of August 1974 gave the National Front a majority in Parliament of 135 to 19 and a majority in every one of the State assemblies (though this result was achieved by questionable tactics in Sabah and Sarawak).

The year 1975 was a disquieting one. The energy of a hard-working Prime Minister, Tun Abdul Razak, was sapped by ill-health. He died in January 1976 and was succeeded by Datuk Hussein bin Onn. The proscribed communist movement showed greater strength by some bold acts of terrorism including the selective assassination of police officers specializing in counter-subversion. The worldwide economic recession halted the steady growth of the Malaysian economy for the first time in some years. The efforts of some of the younger technocrats to strengthen domestic control of foreign enterprises, notably in the petroleum industry, led to some loss of confidence. For the first time since 1969 Malaysia seemed to lose its momentum and sense of direction.

In his first six months as Prime Minister, Datuk Hussein faced a series of controversial issues but, despite some unpopular decisions, he proved to be a resilient politician. When the General Assembly of UMNO, the leading party in the ruling coalition, met in July 1976 Hussein had a firm grip on the reins of government. He launched a strong attack on corruption and mismanagement and appealed for unity among the several factions within the coalition.

INTERNATIONAL RELATIONS

Malaysia has been a significant factor in South-East Asia, being the focal point in the international politics of the Straits of Malacca area during the past two decades. Between 1957 and 1970, Malaysia followed the course of alliance or alignment with the Western Powers, a policy dictated by its colonial past, and economic and security considerations. As a primary producer and a developing country, Malaysia was oriented very much to Britain and the rest of the Commonwealth for trade and assistance. And between 1948 and 1960 and again between 1963 and 1966, when Malaysia was faced with the threats of local communism and Indonesian aggression, it had to rely on the British, Australian and New Zealand military power to successfully deter them.

Malaysia's general orientation in foreign policy until 1970 was one of alliance with the Western Powers and opposition to the Communist bloc. Hence Malaysia supported the United States' involvement in Viet-Nam and became a member of the anti-communist group, the Asian and Pacific Council. It had no diplomatic relations with any communist countries, including the Soviet Union and the People's Republic of China. Within South-East Asia, Malaysia attempted to initiate regional co-operation and was able to establish the Association of South-East Asia or ASA with Thailand and the Philippines in 1961. Two years later, Malaysia together with the Philippines and Indonesia formed Maphilindo. But these groupings were aborted primarily due to the conflicts in the area, and manifestations of these were seen in the hostile policies of the Philippines and Indonesia toward Malaysia; the Philippines pursued a claim over the Malaysian territory of Sabah, and Indonesia wanted the break-up of the federation. Fundamentally there was little in common between these states, while there were contradictory views relating to regional leadership and alliance with external powers.

A shift in Malaysia's foreign policy occurred in 1970. International developments, such as the western military withdrawal and the *détente* within the South-East Asian region, resulted in a re-examination of the efficacy of the policy of alignment. The British decision to withdraw east of Suez and the American decision to reduce its land forces in Viet-Nam reflected the trend towards a new international order in East Asia. The subsequent re-emergence of China and Japan as the additional power-centres in the region was another decisive factor. Within the region, Malaysia negotiated the end of the Indonesian Confrontation, effected the resumption of diplomatic relations with the Philippines and accepted the independence of Singapore. However, the Malaysia-Philippines dispute over Sabah territory remained unresolved and Malaysia-Singapore relations continued to go through difficult adjustments.

Malaysia's foreign policy posture is tending toward non-alignment. The Commonwealth military presence or the so-called Five-Power Defence Arrangement agreed upon by Malaysia, Singapore, the United Kingdom, Australia and New Zealand, is no longer regarded as a viable force to ensure the security of the country from external aggression. The Five-Power Defence Arrangement provides for a token presence of the Commonwealth forces and for immediate consultation in the event of external aggression. Malaysia seeks to develop its non-alignment in the international community and its role in co-operation among the South-East Asian states. It has also established diplomatic relations with the Soviet Union and other East European countries. Malaysia together with Indonesia, the Philippines, Singapore and Thailand established the Association of South-East Asian Nations or ASEAN in 1967 and it is active in such functional groupings as the Ministerial Conference on the Economic Development of South-East Asia and the South-East Asia Ministers of Education Organisation.

In 1974 Malaysia at length established diplomatic relations with communist China; this was the culmination of years of cautious movement towards a normalization of relations with a great power which has a special concern with and influence over one of the two major Malaysian communities. The Malaysian Prime Minister had previously visited Peking and discussed the position of the 200,000 persons of Chinese descent who are not nationals of either country but are resident in Malaysia. The broader objectives of Malaysian foreign policy,i.e. an effective regional association of the South-East Asian countries and the acceptance by the great powers of the "neutrality" of South-East Asia are not yet fully attained. The fall of South Viet-Nam and Cambodia to internal communist attack poses a new uncertainty for Malaysia among other neighbours of those troubled countries.

ECONOMIC SURVEY

Malcolm Caldwell

The primary sector is divided into three groups: (*a*) basically subsistence agriculture, including rice cultivation, hunting and fishing; (*b*) agriculture basically for export, the products requiring a substantial degree of processing—notable in this category are rubber and palm oil; (*c*) mining (notably tin). The last is dealt with in another section. It was estimated in 1970 that in Peninsular Malaysia 49 per cent of the economically active population were in the primary sector, 9 per cent in manufacturing and 42 per cent in the tertiary and other sectors, including an officially estimated 8 per cent unemployed.

from the remarkable expansion of rubber cultivation in the twentieth century. In 1951 rubber alone earned nearly two-thirds (65 per cent) of all Malaya's export receipts, while rubber and tin together earned nearly three-quarters (74.5 per cent). This degree of dependence has diminished since. In 1974 total exports of Malaysia amounted to $M 10,194.7 million, of which rubber earned 30 per cent and palm oil, tin (tin alone 15 per cent compared to 20 per cent in 1967) and petroleum another 36 per cent. Malaysia depends on these commodities for 80 per cent of all export earnings, as in 1961, but the composition has changed.

	PLANTATIONS	MINING	MANUFACTURING	TRANSPORT	GOVERNMENT AND PUBLIC SERVICE
Peninsular Malaysia (1969)	263,600	49,500	120,304*	23,000†	266,700‡
Sarawak (1968)	3,604§	1,201	n.a.	1,829	12,340
	PLANTATIONS		INDUSTRY		GOVERNMENT
Sabah (June 1970)	11,305		15,454		12,235

* Survey of 76 industries accounting for 89 per cent Value Added and 82 per cent of total paid employment.
† Road (July 1969) and Rail (1968) only. ‡ July 1968. § Agriculture and logging only.

Other estimates are given in the tables above and on p. 524.

Another way of looking at this matter is to divide the population into urban (those living in towns with greater than 1,000 population) and rural. On this basis, in 1962 Peninsular Malaysia was 57.3 per cent rural, while Sabah and Sarawak were both over 85 per cent rural. However, some allowance has to be made for those in the rural areas who work for the big "industrial" estates, and for those employed in administration, before one can arrive at a reasonable estimate of the core peasant rural sector. For Peninsular Malaysia this cannot be very much less than half the population. In Sabah and Sarawak, where the core rural sector consists of hunters as well as peasants, it would be about four-fifths.

AGRICULTURE

Export Sector

Malaysia is a case *par excellence* of specialization in a handful of export products. This stems from the economic history of the country, and in particular

Rubber. Malaysia is the world's leading producer of natural rubber, accounting for 35 per cent of the world's total output. In Peninsular Malaysia, 4,186,000 acres were planted with rubber in 1973. This may be compared with the 1,462,000 acres under rice and the 1,036,000 acres under oil palms. This huge rubber acreage is concentrated in a west coast "rubber belt" stretching from southern Kedah to Singapore, the bulk of it in the states of Perak, Selangor, Negri Sembilan and Johore. In 1962 three-fifths of the estate rubber acreage was in European hands; of the two-fifths in Asian hands, 70 per cent was Chinese-owned. The share in Chinese ownership and control has grown steadily in the post-war period. By 1974, 65 per cent of rubber acreage was in smallholder hands, although accounting for only half of the 1.57 million tons of rubber produced.

With so much at stake in rubber, price fluctuations can play havoc with the Malaysian economy. Net export earnings account for about 30 per cent of G.N.P., with rubber accounting for about a third of that. Rubber prices are subject to big swings: in the first quarter of 1974, for instance, prices reached 230 cents per kilo, only to plunge to under 100 cents per kilo at the year's end. The difficulties making themselves felt in the synthetic rubber industry because of the oil crisis (synthetic rubber being an off-shoot of the petro-chemical industry) nevertheless make long-term prospects rosier than at any time since the Second World War.

Synthetic rubber has made efficient rubber cultivation essential in order to minimize costs and keep the natural product competitive. As the United States of America (which at one time consumed three-quarters of the world's natural rubber production), Britain, Federal Republic of Germany, Japan, Canada and other major consumers increasingly turn to synthetics, the Soviet Union, Eastern Europe and China emerge as major customers for Malaysia's rubber.

The rubber industry is the chief employer of labour in Malaysia. In Peninsular Malaysia it accounts for about 30 per cent of the economically active population. If their dependants are taken into account, plus all those employed in rubber trading, transport and other related activities, over 1.5 million people are estimated to depend upon the industry in Peninsular Malaysia and in neighbouring Singapore (home of the Rubber Market, the world's leading emporium in the commodity). The rubber industry is also the largest single source of government revenue and of export revenue, and is the largest single item in Gross Domestic Product by industrial origin.

Nevertheless, diversification is a pressing need in the Malaysian economy. The rubber industry cannot absorb more than an insignificant proportion of those annually coming onto the labour market, and Malaysia's growth rate of population is one of the highest in the world. Moreover, in the long run synthetics must inevitably bring into question the further viability of the industry. Although there is a considerable variety of other plantation and/or export crops grown in Malaysia—including pineapples (generally canned locally before export), tea, and pepper—only one, the palm, is of a magnitude and special importance necessitating brief separate consideration. It will be noted that the palm is, like rubber, a perennial: Malaysia's primary sector is characterized by its dependence upon perennials.

Palm. The oil palm has grown rapidly in significance in recent years, the area planted to it increasing from 304,000 acres in 1966 to 1,036,000 acres in 1973, and the export of palm oil from $M 61 million (2 per cent of Malaysia's total) in 1961 to $M 1,020 million (11 per cent of the total) in 1974. The target is 2 million acres by 1980, with production of 1.6 million tons, half the world total. The oil palm is generally regarded in Malaysia as the most hopeful alternative to the rubber tree, and there has been a certain amount of oil palm planting by rubber growers as an insurance against low prices. Nevertheless, the oil palm requires the outlay of a great deal of capital in expensive installations if the fruit is to be adequately processed, and it is therefore almost entirely an estate crop. However, co-operatives could prove to be the answer to this and in the face of a world shortage—certain to continue for the foreseeable future—of high protein foodstuffs for livestock, the oil palm bids fair to shoulder a significant weight of Malaysia's development for the rest of this century.

Peasant Sector

In turning to the subsistence sector, the principal concern is rice, although in coastal areas fishing forms an important occupation, and in the interiors of Sabah and Sarawak hunting still provides a livelihood for a number of the indigenous peoples. Although some dry rice is still grown, the overwhelming bulk of the rice in Malaysia is cultivated in irrigated paddy fields. In Peninsular Malaysia it may be said as a very rough approximation that about 80 per cent of the Malays are rural dwellers.

In some respects, the rice sector shows healthy trends. Though yields are low by Asian standards, they crept up (for the main season crop) from 3,160 lb. per acre in 1960 to 3,480 in 1973. Largely because of the introduction of double-cropping, Malaysian rice self-sufficiency, 65 per cent in 1965, is now 85 per cent with 90 per cent as an immediate target. This is obviously of great significance in a country with rapidly rising population.

As to landlessness, it is estimated that somewhere between a half and two-thirds of the paddy farmers in Peninsular Malaysia do not own their own paddy land but work as tenants for landlords. Rents charged vary, but despite control legislation are still believed to take from a third to two-thirds of the crop. Indebtedness, which is prevalent throughout the peasant sector, typically arises from the *padi kuncha* system, by which money is borrowed on the condition that the disposable part of the harvest will be sold to the lender at a stipulated price which is well below the prevailing market price. Once indebtedness has been incurred, it is virtually impossible for the peasant farmer to escape from it. Fragmentation occurs in Peninsular Malaysia because of Muslim laws of inheritance, by which the land of the deceased is meticulously divided out among his heirs according to certain fixed principles. This is workable with stable populations, such as characterized earlier times, but not with fast-growing populations. In crowded areas of Peninsular Malaysia fragmentation has resulted in tiny holdings, instances occurring of beneficiaries insisting on legacies of a few square feet. Naturally, fragmentation accelerates both indebtedness and landlessness.

In recent years double-cropping has spread among rice growers in Peninsular Malaysia and although its further adoption has been discouraged by the big rent increases imposed by the landlords of tenants taking up double-cropping, 60 per cent of the area is now double-cropped compared with 10 per cent a decade ago. It is feared that peasant acceptance of the new strains of "miracle" rice, yielding crops up to three or four times those of traditional strains, may be similarly inhibited. In addition, poor peasants are tempted to sell subsidized fertilizers, a necessary input, for immediate cash.

Rural reform, extension of the cultivated area, and higher yields are all, therefore, indicated for the Malaysian peasant sector. In addition, expanding employment opportunities outside agriculture are also urgently required. Indications are not hopeful. Urban unemployment continues to increase. Federal Land Development Authority schemes have been shown to be inadequate in scale and inappropriate in nature. Most significantly there have been in recent years cases of unilateral land seizures by Malay peasants, resulting in clashes with the authorities. The land hunger of "New Village" Chinese has also not been adequately assuaged.

Timber has become one of Malaysia's biggest and most rapidly growing economic sectors. Prices have soared under surging international demand and consumption. However, 1974 proved to be a bad year, demand contracting in response to the international recession. In any case, grave warnings have already been issued by experts that excessive deforestation is resulting in soil degradation and threatening to silt up West Malaysian ports and even close the Straits of Malacca in time.

MINERAL AND POWER RESOURCES

Tin

Until very recently, tin predominated among Malaysia's minerals to an extent comparable with rubber's predominance among agricultural products. However, other minerals have come in the last few years to occupy a significant position. Malaysia is the world's largest producer of tin, just as she is of rubber. In recent years, Malaysian output has accounted for nearly a third of the world's total. Extraction is confined to Peninsular Malaysia, where production of tin-in-concentrates rose from an annual average of 51,800 tons in the five-year period 1956–60 to 75,069 tons in 1968, and then decreased to 67,048 in 1974. The best seams are fast working out.

Production in Malaysia is concentrated in the states of Perak and Selangor (with more than 90 per cent of total output) but there is a scattering of mines elsewhere. More than 86 per cent of production is by dredging and gravel-pumping, capital-intensive methods which help account for the continuing European domination of the industry. The European share in Malaysian tin production actually rose from 57 per cent in 1957 (the year Malaya became independent) to 65 per cent in 1961, with British interests predominant. But more recently, with exhaustion of workable deposits in sight, foreign capital has moved out into other spheres, such as manufacturing industry, and the local stake has increased sharply. American releases of tin from strategic stockpiles were resumed in 1973 after a five-year gap, giving rise to fears of a fall in tin prices. However, on the London Metal Exchange the price of tin per metric ton rose from less than £1,500 in June 1972 to more than £4,200 in September 1974. It quickly fell to below £3,000 and was under £3,500 throughout 1975. Another upward surge in 1976 took the price from about £3,100 in January to a record £4,890 in July. The U.S.A. takes over half of Malaysia's tin production.

Gold, Ilmenite, Bauxite, Iron, Oil

Like most developing countries, Malaysia is still very under-prospected, and therefore it is possible to make only an arbitrary judgement on her mineral resources. However, in addition to tin and iron (to consideration of which I return below), the country already produces and exports significant quantities of gold, ilmenite and bauxite. In 1963 raw gold production reached a peak of 9,116 troy ounces, but by 1975 had declined to 2,484 troy ounces. Production of ilmenite, from which the metal titanium is derived, was 151,105 tons in 1974. Production of bauxite, from which aluminium is refined, increased from 962,497 tons in 1971 to 1,124,722 tons in 1973, but fell to 932,549 tons in 1974 and 692,453 tons in 1975. As far as Malaysia's future is concerned, one of the great advantages of bauxite is that there is a growing tendency for extraction of the 60 per cent or so alumina in the ore to be conducted near the bauxite mines, thus saving the buyers freight on the raw material, while projects are under consideration for having actual refining of the finished metal also adjacent to the mines—if hydro-electric power is locally available.

With recession in the iron industry, Malaysia's mineral potential has had to be reassessed. Fortunately, as early expectations for iron have been disappointed, other developments have helped to compensate. A fourth important bauxite mine, Ramunia Bauxite's second, was activated in March 1971. Prospects for bauxite production exceeding 1.5 million tons per annum in the near future seem excellent. In addition, ESCAP aid is being sought to determine the significance of minerals of economic interest in the beach sand along the east coast of Peninsular Malaysia, in line with developments elsewhere in the region. East Malaysia has similarly been up-graded in terms of mineral potential. The *Geological Survey Malaysia* claims that prospects for Sarawak "have given reasonable grounds for optimism", production at the moment encompasses oil, gold, antimony, building materials (gravel, etc.), and lime. In Sabah, while stone, coral, sand and clay remained the principal products being actively developed, feverish prospecting for copper and oil continued during 1970 and 1971. The five oil companies which hold prospecting licences and leases over areas totalling more than 28,000 sq. miles, again increased their geological and geophysical activities in 1971. Copper is being sought in Mamut and Gunong Nugnkok, Sabah.

Power

As far as power is concerned, Malaysia has both thermal and hydroelectric power stations. Hydroelectric potential is high, and a major project is taking shape in the Cameron Highlands. But the focus here must be on Malaysia's emerging oil industry: production reached 110,000 barrels per day in 1975, enabling a significant net export above domestic needs. It is calculated by PETRONAS, the state oil corporation launched in 1974, that petroleum export revenues should, by 1980, exceed those of the old staples, rubber and tin, combined.

INDUSTRY

As is the case with most ex-colonial countries, Malaysia embarked upon independence with but a rudimentary manufacturing industrial sector at her disposal. There was, however, an industrial sector closely associated with the plantation and mining industries—processing their products for export chiefly—and therefore a supply of skilled labour and experienced entrepreneurs. Since independence the government has chosen to attempt economic development and further industrialization by means of encouraging private enterprise, in particular by encouraging foreign private investment. Since Malaysia has, compared with most of her South-East Asian neighbours, a good record for both political and monetary stability, and a relatively well-developed infrastructure (roads. railways, ports, banking, insurance, etc.), industry has been attracted by the government's inducements, which take the form of tax reliefs, guarantees of fair compensation in case of nationalization, double taxation agreements, and unimpeded repatriation of capital profits and dividends. An Investment Incentives Act in 1968 extended industrial estates then established.

The indigenous industrial sector has two prominent characteristics—it tends to be small-scale. and it is dominated by the Chinese.

Malaysian industry embraces a wide variety of fields. Important categories, outside the sphere of processing and working up rubber, include food, beverages and tobacco; cement and bricks; footwear; saw-milling; rattan, attap and basketware; general engineering, machinery, equipment, electrical machinery and repairs; and a range of other consumer goods. Manufacturing, building and construction together employed about 16 per cent of the economically active population of Malaya in 1970, and although the percentage may be increasing slowly, the rate of growth in Malaysia has failed to keep pace with either urbanization or with the rapidly growing labour force. The foreign firms tend to be capital-intensive, and thus of no relevance to the unemployment problem. Development of a local market is hindered by the poverty of the rural and urban masses. A further question mark hangs over the wisdom of fostering, under the 1971–75 Plan, an artificially large *Bumiputra* (ownership by indigenous communities) component in government-aided or -encouraged industry. There are already indications of resultant inefficiency and corruption.

TRANSPORT

In 1974 there were 2,150 kilometres of railway track in Peninsular Malaysia and in Sabah there were 155 kilometres.

In 1972 there were 17,867 kilometres of road in Peninsular Malaysia and in 1975 1,230,222 vehicles in use. In 1975 there were 59,375 licensed vehicles in Sabah and 72,092 in Sarawak.

Malaysia's ports have undergone considerable extension and improvement in recent years. The principal ports are Penang, Port Klang, Dungun, Telok Anson, Malacca and Port Dickson in Peninsular Malaysia, Sibu and Kuching in Sarawak and Labuan in Sabah.

The state airline, Malaysian Airline System, operates flights to London, the Middle East and within Asia. There are five international airports within Malaysia: three in Peninsular Malaysia and one each in Sabah and Sarawak.

FOREIGN TRADE

As has been noted, Malaysia is peculiarly dependent upon her exports, and therefore upon her trade in general. Exports, which went up by 50 per cent in 1973, rose by only 30 per cent in 1974 to reach $M 10,194.7 million and declined in 1975 to $M 9,218.6 million; the situation with respect to imports was reversed, with a 30 per cent growth in 1973, but 50 per cent in 1974, attaining $M 9,891.2 million. Imports also fell in 1975 to $M 8,503.6 million.

The chief markets for Malaysia's exports in 1975 were, in order of importance, Singapore, the U.S.A., Japan, the Netherlands and the United Kingdom. The main suppliers of imports in 1975 were Japan, the U.S.A., the United Kingdom, Singapore and Australia.

Malaysia has, historically, had a consistently positive balance of trade in visibles, but incurs net international indebtedness on invisibles. For the first time in many years, Malaysia faces balance of payments deficits.

FINANCE

The currency is the Malaysian dollar or ringgit. From December 1971 to the end of 1974 the ringgit appreciated by 16.5 per cent against the yen; 18 per cent against the U.S. dollar; and 31.5 per cent against the £ sterling. Currency has been issued by the central bank (Bank Negara Malaysia) since 1967. A large number of commercial banks operate in the country. Some, mostly Chinese, are indigenous, but branches of foreign banks undertake the major part of the banking business of Malaysia. The oldest overseas banks are also the biggest—the Chartered Bank, the Hongkong and Shanghai Bank, and the Mercantile Bank.

Public finance was until recently conducted with an orthodoxy which ensured the stability of the currency, in marked contrast to the experience of some of Malaysia's Asian neighbours. However, inflation hit 10 per cent in 1973 and 18 per cent in 1974, propelled by rising import prices (imports account for about 50 per cent of Malaysia's G.N.P.), pay increases (politically motivated) to civil servants, teachers and the armed forces; and subsidies (on food and in support of rubber prices, for example). The Federal budget for 1974 provided for $M 3,500 million in recurrent revenues, $M 1,100 million in net domestic borrowing and $M 200 million in net foreign borrowing; recurrent expenditures took $M 3,500 million of this provision while development outlays were fixed at $M 1,400 million.

Foreign Aid

Foreign aid has not, so far, been of any significance to Malaysia. Aid received per capita has been negligible (M$ 3 to M$ 4). However, it may become of greater importance in a future strewn with economic problems.

ECONOMIC DEVELOPMENT

Malaysia's economic fortunes and achievements in the post-war world have been, in many respects, the envy of other developing countries. The Government has been able to undertake considerable expenditures in such vital areas as health and education, and yet at the same time to avoid, until lately, the kind of inflationary erosion of the currency so common in developing countries. The major industry—rubber—has successfully adapted itself to changing international circumstances by prompt and thorough adoption of the fruits of research in the shape of the new high-yield trees. Some diversification has been achieved in the plantation sector, and the industrial base has been expanded.

Yet, with all this, there must be reservations, and disturbing questions occur concerning the country's long-term prospects. A strong reservation must, for example, be made concerning the distribution of the benefits of such economic development as has taken place. According to the Government's own figures, in 1957 the top 20 per cent of the population accounted for nearly half of the total income and the bottom 60 per cent for 30 per cent, while by 1970 the top 20 per cent had 56 per cent and the bottom 60 per cent a mere 25 per cent. Over the same period, the income of the poorest 40 per cent actually fell from $M 75 per household to $M 66.

A further reservation concerns the long-run viability of the mode of development chosen—namely via private, including foreign, enterprise. Peninsular Malaysia, while Malaya, did have five-year plans, but their principal objective was the improvement of the infrastructure, not direct planning and control of industry. The first Malaysia Plan ran from 1966 to 1970, and a second was launched in 1971. The third Plan (1975–1980), announced in July 1976, allowed for an expenditure of M$ 18,100 million, a 90 per cent increase over the previous Plan. The Government is to provide M$ 7,400 million and by private investment the rest, half of which is expected to come from overseas. The Plans have been little more than predictions or forecasts based on an optimistic reading of past trends in the economy. Implementation is left to private enterprise, and the outcome is really a question of the buoyancy or otherwise of world prices for the handful of important export commodities. It has been pointed out by economists that the Malaysian Government might readily raise the capital at its disposal for development were it to staunch some of the huge annual flow out of the country of profits, dividends and other remittances of foreign businesses operating in Malaysia. This flow obviously constitutes a serious drain on the potential investible funds of the country. Moreover, private foreign investors' decisions are quite outside the control of the government, and may as readily be detrimental to Malaysia as beneficial in the future.

Malaysia continues to sustain a favourable "climate" for investment, having to all appearances recovered some of the communal harmony and co-operation shattered by the racial disturbances of 1969. But one consequence with incalculable implications for the future is the greatly stepped-up recruitment from all communities to the guerrilla movement—at one point the Malaysian Communist Party had difficulty providing adequate training for the numbers joining its ranks. So widespread has guerrilla activity become in Peninsular Malaysia that the Government has been compelled to re-adopt a variety of measures reminiscent of those employed during the 1948–60 "Emergency" (for example, regroupment of population). But disruption of economic activity is not now, as it was on the former occasion, a principal aim of guerrilla activity, which is primarily devoted to political work among the peasants (health and educational provision, help in the fields). A feature of the present security situation which must greatly disturb the Government is recruitment from among the land-hungry and deeply indebted Malay peasantry (groups of whom have in recent years on their own initiative unilaterally seized and distributed land); the "Emergency" was always officially treated as a Chinese subversive insurrection, with the other communities hostile to them. In Sarawak, guerrilla activity at one time reached such proportions that a virtual state of martial law prevails, but there has recently been some downturn in clashes.

However, from the Malaysian Government's point of view there are positive features in the present situation. Given the adjustment of American policies in South-East Asia dictated by the U.S. retreat from Indochina, the importance of a strong pro-western government preserving power in Kuala Lumpur assumes greater importance. It seems clear that ASEAN—the Association of South-East Asian Nations (Thailand, Indonesia, the Philippines, Malaysia and Singapore)—will henceforth constitute the front line of the American sphere of political and economic interest in South-East Asia. Sizeable though the remaining British economic interests are in Malaysia, there has been in recent years a steady growth of U.S. (and Japanese) investment. Militarily, British power locally is now negligible, but Washington has shown growing concern for the defence and security of Malaysia. Since 1966 there has been a steady upward movement in the amount of American military aid going to Malaysia, while greatly increased numbers of Malaysians have received American military training, and U.S. military equipment has begun to feature prominently in the Malaysian armed forces. American counter-insurgency experts have also been involved in stimulating research projects relevant to social control.

The United States has shown particular interest in the prospects for bringing in Malaysian off-shore oil, and mineral exploration in general. But, however impressive figures for U.S. (and other foreign) investment may seem on paper and in monetary terms, it is not appropriate to the underlying needs of the Malaysian economy. Unemployment continues to rise steadily, while working-class incomes, rural and urban alike, stagnate—despite the average achieved growth rate in G.N.P. per annum since the mid-sixties of over 6 per cent. Vast and worsening inequalities in wealth point to the heart of the matter. The rich elite display a very high propensity to import, and the substantial foreign economic interests, while siphoning off much in the way of profits, dividends, etc., contribute little to the Malaysian economy. The second Five-Year Plan aims at the creation of a Malay bourgeoisie, in order to mollify communal feelings, but much more relevant would be a programme of labour-intensive "non-profitable" (i.e. in the book-keeping sense) rural improvement schemes and small industries, on the one hand, and very much accelerated and magnified government welfare expenditures on the other. Such radical steps will not, of course, be taken within the framework of the present social structure. Indeed, political signs of apprehension on the part of the ruling groups indicate that the failure of their economic policies to satisfy the aspirations of the urban and rural masses is as evident to them as to their critics.

STATISTICAL SURVEY

Statistics refer to Peninsular Malaysia only unless otherwise stated.

AREA AND POPULATION

	Area (sq. miles)	Population (Census, August 24th–25th, 1970)*			Estimated Population (Dec. 31st, 1974)	1974 Density (per sq. mile)
		Males	Females	Total		
Peninsular Malaysia	50,806	4,434,645	4,374,912	8,809,557	9,865,635	194.2
Sabah	28,460	339,714	313,890	653,604	804,149‡	28.3
Sarawak	48,049	491,731	484,538	976,269	1,090,165	22.7
Total	127,315†	5,266,090	5,173,340	10,439,430	11,759,949‡	92.4

* Excluding transients afloat. † 329,744 square kilometres. ‡ Provisional.

PRINCIPAL RACES

(Estimated as at December 31st, 1974)

	Peninsular Malaysia	Sabah	Sarawak
Chinese	3,481,447	161,861	335,767
Malays	5,274,077	38,967	209,318
Indians and Pakistanis	1,034,577	—	—
Land Dyak	—	—	96,271
Malanau	—	—	58,734
Kadazan	—	211,210	—
Bajau	—	91,270	—
Murut	—	35,096	—
Ibans	—	—	322,488
Other Indigenous	—	150,523	56,223
Other	75,594	115,222	11,364

STATES

	Area sq. miles	Population* 1970 Census	Capital	Population* 1970 Census
Johore	7,330	1,277,180	Johore Bahru	136,396
Kedah	3,639	954,947	Alor Star	66,294
Kelantan	5,765	684,738	Kota Bahru	55,123
Malacca	637	404,125	Malacca Municipality	87,231
Negri Sembilan	2,565	481,563	Seremban	81,465
Pahang	13,886	504,945	Kuantan	43,409
Penang and Province Wellesley	399	776,124	George Town	270,378
Perak	8,110	1,569,139	Ipoh	247,970
Perlis	307	121,062	Kangar	8,761
Sabah	28,460	653,604	Kota Kinabalu	41,061
Sarawak	48,049	976,269	Kuching	63,591
Selangor	3,166	1,630,366	Kuala Lumpur†	451,986
Trengganu	5,002	405,368	Kuala Trengganu	53,344

* 1970 Population and Housing Census of Malaysia (Age Distribution).

† Kuala Lumpur, the capital of Malaysia, was designated a separate federal territory on February 1st, 1974. A new capital for Selangor is to be established at Shah Alam in 1977.

ECONOMICALLY ACTIVE POPULATION
(1970 census)

	Peninsular Malaysia*		
	Males	Females	Total
Agriculture, forestry, hunting and fishing	772,886	451,689	1,224,575
Mining and quarrying	48,203	7,073	55,276
Manufacturing	178,881	73,058	251,939
Construction	55,624	4,238	59,862
Electricity, gas, water and sanitary services	18,732	1,024	19,756
Commerce	224,993	49,611	274,604
Transport, storage and communications	93,852	4,117	97,969
Services	332,158	140,468	472,626
Activities not adequately described	152,417	127,331	279,748
Total	1,877,746	858,609	2,736,355

* Excluding persons seeking work for the first time, numbering 134,594 (80,542 males, 54,052 females).

	Sabah			Sarawak		
	Males	Females	Total	Males	Females	Total
Agriculture, forestry, hunting and fishing	81,997	43,780	125,777	127,187	101,764	228,951
Mining and quarrying	856	33	889	1,029	79	1,108
Manufacturing	5,971	1,108	7,079	13,535	3,468	17,003
Construction	5,803	427	6,230	5,165	176	5,341
Electricity, gas, water and sanitary services	1,279	116	1,395	1,343	67	1,410
Commerce	9,171	2,599	11,770	14,163	3,153	17,316
Transport, storage and communications	6,527	396	6,923	5,769	321	6,090
Services	24,560	7,766	32,326	29,580	8,789	38,369
Activities not adequetely described	8,415	11,910	20,325	11,595	18,826	30,421
Total	144,579	68,135	212,714	209,366	136,643	346,009

AGRICULTURE

LAND USE

('000 acres)

	Rubber	Forest*	Rice	Oil Palm (estates only)
1970	4,260	30,930	1,318	675
1971	4,245	30,400	1,365	769
1972	4,206	30,098	1,414	887†
1973	4,186	27,057	1,462	1,036
1974	n.a.	n.a.	1,476	n.a.

* Square miles.

† Excludes acreage under State Government schemes.

1975: Rubber approximately 2 million hectares.

PRODUCTION

	Rubber (tons)	Rice (tons)	Palm Oil (tons)	Palm Kernel (tons)	Copra (tons)	Coconut Oil (tons)	Coconut Cake (tons)	Tea (lb.)
1972	1,238,275	1,001,930	646,625	134,804	22,878	91,482	74,303	7,417,000
1973	1,442,018	1,105,690	727,618	152,397	20,836	77,058	64,817	7,632,000
1974	1,461,660*	1,163,860	927,445*	191,635*	21,734*	65,134	44,433	6,935,000*
1975	1,392,972	n.a.	1,117,227	228,874	23,406	73,615	48,876	6,594,000

* Provisional.

Sabah‡ (1975—tons): Rubber 31,525, Copra 30,003, Sawlogs 4,978,530†, Sawn timber 3,335.

Sarawak‡ (1975)—tons): Rubber 28,579, Sago flour 22,506, Pepper 29,873, Sawlogs 696,989†, Sawn timber 170,648.

† Tons of 50 cu. ft. ‡ Export figures only.

LIVESTOCK

('000)

	1972*	1973†	1974†
Cattle	328	328	362
Buffalo	220	194	204
Goats	340	290	310
Sheep	41	41	43
Pigs	760	729	790

* FAO estimates.

† *Source:* Veterinary Division, Ministry of Agriculture and Fisheries, Malaysia.

FORESTRY

TIMBER PRODUCTION

		1971	1972	1973	1974	1975
Round timber	'000 solid cu. ft.	252,974	308,331	327,000	347,424	280,332
Poles	,, ,, ,, ,,	3,247	3,439	3,215	4,064	2,632
Charcoal	,, ,, ,, ,,	21,114	18,921	16,679	20,620	16,216
Firewood	,, ,, ,, ,,	4,811	3,855	3,212	4,020	2,518
Sawn timber	'000 tons of 50 cu. ft.	1,740.5	2,210.8	2,492.5	2,486.5	2,440.3

Sarawak (tons of 50 cu. ft.): (1971) 2,169,281 of logs; (1972) 1,759,738 of logs; (1973) 1,803,325 of logs; (1974) 1,568,032 of logs.

FISHING

	Number of Vessels		Landings of Fish (tons)
	Powered	Non-powered	
1970	15,029	5,277	294,296
1971	16,320	4,821	317,973
1972	16,954	4,665	306,209
1973	17,612	4,580	365,375
1974	14,371	3,753	430,495

MINING

PRODUCTION

	Tin-in-Concentrates Tons	Iron Ore Tons	Gold (Raw) Troy Ozs	Ilmenite* Concentrate Tons	Bauxite Tons
1969	72,167	5,151,022	3,152	130,533	786,042
1970	72,630	4,420,143	3,912	219,095	1,056,068
1971	74,253	934,982†	4,491	153,489	1,121,318
1972	75,619	512,571	3,780	151,883	962,497
1973	71,121	509,013	2,730	182,485	1,059,503
1974	67,048	472,998	3,495	15,105‡	1,124,722
1975	63,346	342,702	2,484	110,475‡	692,453

* Exports.

† Two large mines closed down towards the end of 1970.

‡ Provisional.

Sarawak (1975): Crude oil 4,141,689 long tons, Gold 1,192 troy oz.

INDUSTRY

		1972	1973	1974
Rubber:				
Crepe Rubber	tons	113,179	86,070	70,426
Ribbed Smoked Sheets	,,	123,968	151,440	137,909
Foam Rubber (excl. mattresses)	'000 lb.	3,679	4,268	4,578
Foam Rubber Mattresses	,, ,,	6,135	8,444	7,180
Rubber Compound	,, ,,	12,482	15,971	16,751
Tubing and Hoses	,, ,,	40	36	42
Tubing and Hoses, part rubber	,, ,,	1,432	1,446	1,443
Inner Tubes	'000 pieces	4,581	5,411	5,217
Footwear	doz. pairs	1,973,525	1,677,317	1,872,808
Cement	tons	1,142,021	1,257,947	1,342,442
Cigars, Cigarettes, Cheroots and other Manufactured Tobacco	'000 lb.	21,330	24,417	26,495
Aerated Waters and Cordials	'000 gallons	20.579	21,742	23,459

FINANCE

(Malaysia)

100 cents (sen) = 1 ringgit or Malaysian dollar (M$).
Coins: 1, 5, 10, 20 and 50 cents; 1 dollar.
Notes: 1, 5, 10, 50, 100 and 1,000 dollars.
Exchange rates (June 1976): £1 sterling = M$4.53; U.S. $1 = M$2.55.
M$100 = £22.08 = U.S. $39.18.

Note: The Malaysian dollar was introduced in June 1967, replacing (at par) the Malayan dollar. From September 1949 the Malayan dollar was valued at 2s. 4d. sterling (£1 = M$8.5714) or 32.667 U.S. cents (U.S. $1 = M$3.0612). This valuation in terms of U.S. currency remained in effect until August 1971. Between December 1971 and February 1973 the Malaysian dollar was valued at 35.467 U.S. cents (U.S. $1 = M$2.8195). From February to June 1973 the Malaysian dollar's value was 39.407 U.S. cents (U.S. $1 = M$2.5376). In terms of sterling, the exchange rate was £1 = M$7.347 from November 1967 to June 1972. The Malaysian dollar was interchangeable with the Singapore and Brunei dollars until May 1973. Since June 1973 the Malaysian dollar has been allowed to "float". Under legislation passed in July 1975, the Malaysian dollar was officially renamed the ringgit. From September 1975 the ringgit's link with the U.S. dollar was ended and its value determined by changes in a weighted "basket" of currencies of the country's main trading partners. The average market exchange rate (ringgits per U.S. dollar) was: 2.443 in 1973; 2.407 in 1974; 2.402 in 1975.

ORDINARY BUDGET

(million M$)

Revenue	1973	1974	1975 (est.)
Duties, Taxes and Licences	3,045	3,975	4,421
Government Services	115	151	159
Commercial Undertakings*	77	81	88
Rent and Interest	78	127	91
Miscellaneous Receipts	87	51	91
Federal Territory of Kuala Lumpur	—	15	20
Total (incl. others)	3,402	4,400	4,870

* Radio, Television, Civil Aviation and Posts, excluding Telecommunications Department.

Expenditure	1973	1974	1975 (est.)
Defence	654	628	800
Internal security*	297	317	357
Health	254	291	334
Social welfare	10	12	15
Education	804	874	1,098
Posts	41	45	49
Ministry of Transport and Works	50	62	67
Administration	1,118	1,305	1,745
Allocation to States	168	125	130
Total	3,396	3,659	4,595

* Includes expenditure of the following Departments: Ministry of Home Affairs, Royal Malaysia Police, Immigration, Judicial, Prison, Civil Defence and Fire Service.

DEVELOPMENT BUDGET

(million M$)

Expenditure	Peninsular Malaysia	Sabah	Sarawak	Total
1972	1,118	69	55	1,242
1973	1,001	56	71	1,128
1974	1,800	108	142	2,050
1975 (estimates)	2,095	146	165	2,406

SECOND MALAYSIA PLAN 1971–75

PUBLIC SECTOR	million M$
Agriculture and Rural Development	2,073·7
Other Economic Services	3,355·9
Social Services	1,105·1
Defence and Security	1,050·9
General Administration	262·5
TOTAL	7,848·1
PRIVATE SECTOR	6,175·0
GRAND TOTAL	14,023·1

Third Plan (1976–1980): Total expenditure M$18,100 million.

RESERVES AND CURRENCY IN CIRCULATION

(At 30th June—million M$)

	1972	1973	1974	1975
Official Reserves including Gold	2,805	3,224	3,781	3,480
Commercial Banks (Net)	27	−70	−154	−163
Currency in Circulation (Gross)	1,194·5	1,523·1	1,970·3	2,183·6

EXTERNAL TRADE

(Malaysia—million M$)

	1969	1970	1971	1972	1973	1974	1975*
Imports	3,581·9	4,288·4	4,416·2	4,543·2	5,933·9	9,891·2	8,503·6
Exports	5,051·6	5,136·1	5,016·8	4,854·0	7,372·1	10,194·7	9,218·6

* Provisional.

COMMODITIES

(million M$—1975)

IMPORTS	PENINSULAR MALAYSIA	SABAH	SARAWAK	TOTAL MALAYSIA
Food and live animals	1,192·1	123·3	87·6	1,403·0
Beverages and tobacco	60·4	21·5	4·1	86·0
Crude materials, inedible, excluding fuels	520·0	12·5	20·9	554·4
Mineral fuels, lubricants and related materials	827·1	55·1	139·6	1,021·8
Animal and vegetable oils and fats	22·9	2·4	0·8	26·1
Chemicals	660·3	25·5	26·4	712·2
Basic manufactures	1,150·8	158·0	86·2	1,395·0
Machinery and transport equipment	2,444·2	216·2	114·6	2,775·0
Miscellaneous manufactured articles	403·4	36·9	16·7	457·0
Miscellaneous transactions and commodities	56·5	3·8	13·8	73·1
TOTAL	7,338·7	655·2	509·7	8,503·6

COMMODITIES—*continued*]

EXPORTS	PENINSULAR MALAYSIA	SABAH	SARAWAK	TOTAL MALAYSIA
Food and Live Animals	429.6	52.7	110.8	593.1
Beverages and Tobacco	11.2	16.3	0.1	27.6
Crude Materials, inedible, excluding fuels	2,437.0	622.9	160.1	3,220.0
Mineral Fuels, Lubricants and related materials	35.8	79.1	852.2	967.1
Animal and Vegetable Oils and Fats	1,367.3	131.3	7.1	1,505.8
Chemicals and Products	77.3	2.2	0.4	79.9
Basic Manufactures	1,561.6	28.4	34.1	1,624.1
Machinery and Transport Equipment	548.6	21.7	4.7	574.9
Miscellaneous Manufactured Articles	521.7	6.7	0.8	529.2
Miscellaneous Transactions n.e.s.	79.5	7.1	10.3	96.9
TOTAL	7,069.6	968.4	1,180.6	9,218.6

PRINCIPAL COUNTRIES

(million M$—1975)

IMPORTS	PENINSULAR MALAYSIA	SABAH	SARAWAK	TOTAL MALAYSIA
Australia	634.3	18.6	13.7	666.6
China, People's Republic	267.0	48.0	41.2	356.2
Germany, Federal Republic	400.5	17.7	12.3	430.5
Indonesia	172.3	2.6	16.1	191.0
Japan	1,431.0	193.4	83.6	1,708.0
Singapore	530.9	115.8	77.1	723.8
Thailand	303.0	15.3	17.8	336.1
United Kingdom	742.7	59.3	50.0	852.0
U.S.A.	801.4	68.3	38.7	908.4
TOTAL (incl. others)	7,338.7	655.2	509.7	8,503.6

EXPORTS	PENINSULAR MALAYSIA	SABAH	SARAWAK	TOTAL MALAYSIA
Australia	172.0	3.5	3.9	179.4
Canada	94.6	0.1	1.2	95.9
France	160.3	1.7	0.6	142.6
Germany, Federal Republic	353.4	10.7	32.0	396.1
Italy	148.8	0.8	13.8	163.4
Japan	454.9	505.4	365.9	1,326.2
Netherlands	738.9	22.4	8.7	770.0
Singapore	1,425.9	77.5	370.5	1,873.9
U.S.S.R.	243.3	—	—	243.3
United Kingdom	473.4	64.9	15.8	554.1
U.S.A.	1,425.8	41.3	21.0	1,488.1
TOTAL (incl. others)	7,069.6	968.4	1,180.6	9,218.6

TRANSPORT

RAILWAYS

	Total Railway Revenue	Total Railway Expenditure	Paying Coach Mileage	Paying Goods Mileage	Freight Tons	Net Ton Mileage Freight	Passengers	Passenger Miles	Track Mileage
	'ooo Malaysian dollars		'ooo miles		'ooo tons	'ooo ton-miles	'ooo	'ooo miles	miles
1971	68,730	82,179	2,731	3,652	3,633	735,012	5,272	401,851	1,343
1972	76,284	84,276	2,734	3,400	3,328	673,719	5,645	451,479	1,444
1973	78,995	82,255	2,490	3,291	3,401	718,852	5,644	495,611	1,337
1974	87,889	99,256	2,403	2,957	3,413	665,183	5,964	593,290	n.a.
1975	85,854	96,258	2,628	2,292	2,740	467,915	6,105	627,437	n.a.

Sabah

	Passenger-Miles	Freight Ton-Miles
	'ooo	'ooo
1972	17,185	2,566
1973	16,185	1,214
1974	19,137	2,903
1975	20,025	4,225

ROADS

Registration of Vehicles

	Private Motor Cycles	Private Motor Cars	Buses	Lorries and Vans	Taxis
1971	389,133	253,491	6,447	60,543	7,179
1972	435,334	279,300	6,839	64,979	7,256
1973	507,096	316,894	7,274	72,164	7,394
1974	611,822	357,910	7,739	81,584	7,988
1975	722,309	318,014	8,688	92,207	9,004

Sabah: Licensed motor vehicles: 59,375 (1975).

Sarawak: Licensed vehicles: 72,092 (1975).

SHIPPING

Foreign Trade
(vessels over 75 n.r.t.)

	Entered		Cleared	
	No. of vessels	'ooo net registered tons	No. of vessels	'ooo net registered tons
1972	5,242	20,791	5,236	20,765
1973	4,845	20,380	4,819	20,252
1974	4,864	21,411	4,872	21,702
1975	5,198	23,971	5,185	23,913

Sabah (1974): Passengers entered and departed 29,057; Freight loaded and unloaded 5,352,057 tons.

Sarawak (1975)*: Tonnage entered 4,263,000; tonnage cleared 4,331,000.

* Figures refer to vessels over 75 n.r.t. only.

Coastal Trade
(vessels over 75 tons n.r.t.)

	Entered		Cleared	
	No. of vessels	'000 net registered tons	No. of vessels	'000 net registered tons
1971	3,169	1,004,889	3,159	1,008,634
1972	3,263	1,050,230	3,244	1,043,067
1973	3,023	1,163,999	2,785	1,011,607
1974	3,512	1,228,948	3,214	1,061,786
1975	3,843	1,625,389	3,843	1,621,394

CIVIL AVIATION

	Aircraft Landings*		Passengers Landed*		Total Freight Handled ('000 kilos)		Total Mail Handled ('000 kilos)	
	Internal Flights*	International Flights†	Internal Flights*	International Flights†	Landed	Despatched	Landed	Despatched
1969	10,625	8,386	138,787	179,298	1,722	1,372	547	514
1970	11,880	9,407	160,846	243,337	2,028	1,445	514	539
1971	12,770	10,876	196,096	306,489	2,266	1,662	491	751
1972	12,354	14,865	239,837	352,659	2,990	1,832	516	865
1973	12,583	15,690	380,757	515,717	4,889	3,938	692	1,172
1974	13,668	17,797	452,586	556,658	7,517	6,481	912	1,744

* For the years 1969–72 Internal Flights include Singapore but for 1973 and 1974 Singapore flights are excluded. International flights 1969–72 exclude Singapore but Singapore flights are included for 1973 and 1974.

Sabah (1974): Total passengers embarked 532,611; total passengers disembarked 536,518.

Sarawak (1975): Total passengers embarked 347,328; passengers disembarked 336,060.

COMMUNICATIONS MEDIA

	1973	1974	1975
Television sets licensed	313,244	371,692	424,523
Radio receivers in use	347,860	326,797	299,744

TOURISM

	1973	1974	1975
Tourist arrivals	3,058,621	2,655,488	2,602,624

EDUCATION
(1974)

	Establishments	Teachers	Students
Schools:			
Malay Medium	2,709	30,500	1,197,860
English Medium	979	25,167	490,322
Chinese Medium	1,055	14,426	492,440
Tamil Medium	622	3,442	79,814
Vocational and Professional	96	3,921	54,161
Total	5,461	77,456	2,314,597

Sabah (1975)*: *Primary:* schools 780, pupils 125,592; *Secondary:* schools 91, pupils 45,873; *Technical and Vocational:* schools 2.

Sarawak (1974): Total schools 1,321; primary pupils 165,484; secondary students 50,202.

* Government secondary schools with both English and Malay streams are now considered as single schools and not counted twice as in the past.

Source: Department of Statistics, Kuala Lumpur, Kuching and Kota Kinabalu.

THE CONSTITUTION

Supreme Head of State

(YANG DI-PERTUAN AGONG)

The Yang di-Pertuan Agong (King or Supreme Sovereign) is the Supreme Head of Malaysia.

Every act of government flows from his authority although he acts on the advice of Parliament and the Cabinet. The appointment of a Prime Minister lies within his discretion, and he has the right to refuse to dissolve Parliament even against the advice of the Prime Minister. He appoints the Judges of the Federal Court and the High Courts on the advice of the Prime Minister. He is the Supreme Commander of the Armed Forces. The Yang di-Pertuan Agong is elected by the Conference of Rulers, and to qualify for election he must be one of the nine Rulers. He holds office for five years or until his earlier resignation or death. Election is by secret ballot on each Ruler in turn, starting with the Ruler next in precedence after the late or former Yang di-Pertuan Agong. The first Ruler to obtain not less than five votes is declared elected. A Deputy Supreme Head of State (the Timbalan Yang di-Pertuan Agong) is elected by a similar process. On election the Yang di-Pertuan Agong relinquishes, for his tenure of office, all his functions as Ruler of his own State and may appoint a Regent. The Timbalan Yang di-Pertuan Agong exercises no powers in the ordinary course, but is immediately available to fill the post of Yang di-Pertuan Agong and carry out his functions in the latter's absence or disability. In the event of the Yang di-Pertuan Agong's death or resignation he takes over the exercise of sovereignty until the Conference of Rulers has elected a successor.

Conference of Rulers

The Conference of Rulers consists of the Rulers and Governors. Its prime duty is the election by the Rulers only of the Yang di-Pertuan Agong and his deputy. The Conference must be consulted in the appointment of Judges, the Attorney-General, the Elections Commission and the Public Services Commission. The Conference must likewise be consulted and concur in the alteration of State boundaries, the extension to the Federation as a whole of Muslim religious acts and observances, and in any bill to amend the Constitution. Consultation is mandatory in matters affecting public policy or the special position of the Malays and natives of the Borneo States. The Conference also considers matters affecting the rights, prerogatives and privileges of the Rulers themselves.

Federal Parliament

Parliament has two Houses—the Dewan Negara (Senate) and the Dewan Ra'ayat (House of Representatives). The Senate has a membership of 58, made up of 26 elected and 32 appointed members. Each State Legislature, acting as an electoral college, elects two Senators; these may be members of the State Legislative Assembly or otherwise. The Yang di-Pertuan Agong appoints the other 32 members of the Senate. Members of the Senate must be at least 30 years old. The Senate elects a President and a Deputy President from among its members. It may initiate legislation, but all money bills must be introduced in the first instance in the House of Representatives. All bills must be passed by both Houses of Parliament before being presented to the Yang di-Pertuan Agong for the Royal Assent in order to become law. A bill originating in the Senate cannot receive Royal Assent until it has been agreed to by the House of Representatives, but the Senate has only delaying powers over a bill originating from and approved by the House of Representatives. Senators serve for a period of six years, but the Senate is not subject to dissolution. Parliament can by statute increase the number of Senators elected from each State to three. The House of Representatives consists of 154 elected members. Of these, 114 are from Peninsular Malaysia, 24 from Sarawak and 16 from Sabah. Members are returned from single-member constituencies on the basis of universal adult franchise. The life of the House of Representatives is limited to five years, after which time a fresh general election must be held. The Yang di-Pertuan Agong may dissolve Parliament before then if the Prime Minister so advises.

The Cabinet

The Yang di-Pertuan Agong appoints a Cabinet to advise him in the exercise of his functions, consisting of the Prime Minister and an unspecified number of Ministers who must all be members of Parliament. The Prime Minister must be a citizen born in Malaysia and a member of the House of Representatives who, in the opinion of theYang di-Pertuan Agong, commands the confidence of that House. Ministers are appointed on the advice of the Prime Minister. A number of Assistant Ministers (who are not members of the Cabinet) are also appointed from among Members of Parliament. The Cabinet meets regularly under the chairmanship of the Prime Minister to formulate policy.

Public Services

The Public Services, civilian and military, are non-political and owe their loyalty not to the party in power but to the Yang di-Pertuan Agong and the Rulers. They serve whichever government may be in power, irrespective of the latter's political affiliation. To ensure the impartiality of the service, and to protect it from political interference, a number of Services Commissions are established under the Constitution to select and appoint officers, to place them on the pensionable establishment, to decide as to promotion, and to maintain discipline.

The States

With the exception of Malacca, Penang, Sabah and Sarawak, each of the States has a Ruler. The Ruler of Perlis has the title of Raja and that of Negri Sembilan, Yang di-Pertuan Besar. The rest of Their Highnesses are Sultans. The heads of the States of Malacca, Penang and Sarawak are Governors. The Head of State of Sabah is designated Yang di-Pertuan Negara. Each of the 13 States has its own written Constitution, and a single Legislative Assembly. Every State Legislature has powers to legislate on matters not reserved for the Federal Parliament. Each State Legislative Assembly has the right to order its own procedure, and the members enjoy parliamentary privilege. All members of the Legislative Assemblies are directly elected from single-member constituencies. The Ruler or Governor acts on the advice of the State Government, which advice is tendered by the State Executive Council or Cabinet in precisely the same manner as the Federal Cabinet tenders advice to His Majesty the Yang di-Pertuan Agong.

The Legislative authority of the State is vested in the Ruler or Governor in the State Legislative Assembly. The executive authority of the State is vested in the Ruler or Governor but executive functions may be conferred on other persons by law. Every State has an Executive Council or Cabinet to advise the Ruler or Governor, headed by a Chief Minister (in Malacca, Penang, Sabah and Sarawak) or Mentri Besar (in other States), and collectively responsible to the State legislature. Each State in Malaya is divided into administrative districts under a District Officer. Sabah is divided into four residencies: West Coast, Interior, Sandakan and Tawau with headquarters at Kota Kinabalu (formerly Jesselton), Keningua, Sandakan and Tawau respectively. The island of Labuan is administered by a District Officer responsible direct to the State Secretary in Kota Kinabalu. Sarawak is divided into five Divisions, each in charge of a Resident—the First Division, with headquarters at Kuching; the Second Division, with headquarters at Simanggang; the Third Division, with headquarters at Sibu; the Fourth Division, with headquarters at Miri; the Fifth Division, with headquarters at Limbang.

Amendment

From February 1st, 1974, the city of Kuala Lumpur, formerly the seat of the Federal Government and capital of Selangor State, is designated the Federal Territory of Kuala Lumpur. It is administered directly by the Federal Government and returns five members to the Dewan Ra'ayat.

THE GOVERNMENT

THE SUPREME HEAD OF STATE

(His Majesty the Yang di-Pertuan Agong)

His Majesty Sultan YAHAYA PETRA Ibni AL-MARHUM Sultan IBRAHIM (Sultan of Kelantan).

DEPUTY SUPREME HEAD OF STATE

(Timbalan Yang di-Pertuan Agong)

His Royal Highness Sultan Haji AHMAD SHAH Ibni AL-MARHUM Sultan ABU BAKAR (Sultan of Pahang).

THE CABINET

(*June* 1976)

Prime Minister and Minister of Defence: Datuk HUSSEIN bin ONN.

Deputy Prime Minister and Minister of Education: Dr. MAHATHIR bin MOHAMED.

Minister of Communications: Tan Sri V. MANICKAVASAGAM.

Minister of Trade and Industry: Datuk Haji HAMZAH bin Datuk ABU SAMAH.

Minister of Labour and Manpower: Datuk LEE SAN CHOON.

Minister of Lands, Mines and Regional Development: Datuk Haji MOHAMED ASRI.

Minister of Works and Utilities: Datuk Haji ABDUL GHANI GILONG.

Minister of Public Enterprises: Datuk Haji MOHAMED bin YAACOB.

Minister of Health: Tan Sri LEE SIOK YEW.

Minister of Local Government and Federal Territory: Tuan Haji HASSAN ADLI bin Haji ARSHAD.

Minister of Law and Attorney-General: Tan Sri Datuk Haji ABDUL KADIR bin YUSOF.

Minister of Home Affairs: Tan Sri MUHAMMAD GHAZALI bin SHAFIE.

Minister of Science, Technology and Environment: Tan Sri ONG KEE HUI.

Minister of Primary Industries: Datuk MUSA HITAM.

Minister of Welfare Services: Puan Hajjah AISHAH GHANI.

Minister of Housing and Village Development: Encik MICHAEL CHEN WING SUM.

Minister of Culture, Youth and Sports: Datuk ABDUL SAMAD bin IDRIS.

Minister of Finance: Tunku Tan Sri RAZALEIGH HAMZAH.

Minister of Foreign Affairs: Tunku AHMAD RITHAUDDEEN Alhaj bin Tunku ISMAIL.

Minister of Information: Datuk TAIB bun MAHMUD.

Minister of Agriculture: Datuk ALI bin Haji AHMAD.

Minister without Portfolio (under Prime Minister's Department): Tan Sri CHONG HON NYAN.

PARLIAMENT

DEWAN NEGARA

(Senate)

58 members, 26 elected, 32 appointed. Each State Assembly elects two members. The Monarch appoints the other 32 members.

DEWAN RAKYAT

(House of Representatives)

154 elected members, 114 from Peninsular Malaysia, 16 from Sabah and 24 from Sarawak.

(*December* 1974)

PARTY	SEATS
National Front Coalition*	144
Democratic Action Party	9
Social Justice Party (PEKEMAS)	1

*See under Political Parties.

THE STATES

JOHORE

(Capital: Johore Bahru)

The Sultan of Johore: His Royal Highness Sultan ISMAIL Ibni AL-MARHUM Sultan IBRAHIM, D.K. (Selangor), D.M.N., S.M.N., S.P.M.J., S.P.M.K., D.K. (Brunei), K.B.E., C.M.G., D.K. (Pahang), D.K., S.S.I.J., D.K. (Perak).

Chief Minister (The Mentri Besar): Tan Sri Haji OTHMAN bin Haji SA'AD.

STATE ASSEMBLY
(Elected August 1974)

PARTY	SEATS
National Front	31
Democratic Action Party	1
TOTAL	32

KEDAH

(Capital: Alor Star)

The Sultan of Kedah: His Royal Highness Tunku ABDUL HALIM MU'AZZAM SHAH Ibni AL-MARHUM Sultan BADLISHAH, D.K., D.K.H., D.K.M., D.M.N., D.U.K., D.K. (Kelantan), D.K. (Pahang), S.P.M.K.

Chief Minister (The Mentri Besar): Datuk Seri SYED AHMAD bin SYED MAHMUD SHAHABUDDIN, S.P.M.K., J.M.N., J.P.

STATE ASSEMBLY
(Elected August 1974)

PARTY	SEATS
National Front	24
Democratic Action Party	1
Independent	1
TOTAL	26

KELANTAN

(Capital: Kota Bahru)

The Regent of Kelantan: Tengku ISMAIL PETRA Ibni Tuanku Sultan YAHAYA PETRA.

Chief Minister: Datuk Haji MOHD. bin NASIR, D.P.M.K., J.P.

STATE ASSEMBLY
(Elected August 1974)

PARTY	SEATS
National Front	36
TOTAL	36

MALACCA

(Capital: Malacca)

The Governor of Malacca: His Excellency Tun SYED ZAHIRUDDIN bin SYED HASSAN, S.M.N., P.S.M., D.P.M.P., J.M.N.

Chief Minister: Tuan Haji ABDUL GHANI bin ALI.

STATE ASSEMBLY
(Elected August 1974)

PARTY	SEATS
National Front	16
Democratic Action Party	4
TOTAL	20

NEGRI SEMBILAN

(Capital: Seremban)

The Yang di-Pertuan Besar: His Royal Highness Tuanku JA'AFAR Ibni AL-MARHUM Tuanku ABDUL RAHMAN, D.M.N., D.K. (Brunei), D.K. (Kelantan).

Chief Minister (The Mentri Besar): Datuk MANSOR bin OSMAN, Datuk SETIA LELA DI-RAJA, K.M.N., P.J.K.

STATE ASSEMBLY
(Elected August 1974)

PARTY	SEATS
National Front	21
Democratic Action Party	3
TOTAL	24

PAHANG

(Capital: Kuantan)

The Sultan of Pahang: His Royal Highness Sultan AHMAD SHAH Ibni AL-MARHUM Sultan ABU BAKAR.

Chief Minister (The Mentri Besar): Datuk MOHD. bin JUSOH, D.I.M.P., J.S.M.

STATE ASSEMBLY
(Elected August 1974)

PARTY	SEATS
National Front	32
TOTAL	32

PENANG

(Capital: George Town)

The Governor of Penang: His Excellency Tan Sri Haji SARDON bin Hj. JUBIR, S.M.N., P.M.N.

Chief Minister: Dr. LIM CHONG EU.

STATE ASSEMBLY
(Elected August 1974)

PARTY	SEATS
National Front	23
Democratic Action Party	2
PEKEMAS	1
Independent	1
TOTAL	27

PERAK
(Capital Ipoh)

The Sultan of Perak: His Royal Highness Sultan IDRIS AL-MUTAWAKIL ALLAHI SHAH Ibni AL-MARHUM Sultan ISKANDAR SHAH KADDASALLAH, D.K., D.M.N., S.P.M.P., D.K. (Johore), P.K.J., C.M.G., D.K. (Pahang), S.P.C.M.

Chief Minister (The Mentri Besar): Tan Sri Haji MOHD. GHAZALI bin Haji JAWI, P.M.N., D.P.C.M., P.N.B.S.

STATE ASSEMBLY
(Elected August 1974)

PARTY	SEATS
National Front	31
Democratic Action Party	11
TOTAL	42

PERLIS
(Capital: Kangar)

The Raja of Perlis: His Royal Highness Tuanku SYED PUTRA Ibni AL-MARHUM SYED HASSAN JAMALULLIAL, D.K., D.M.N., S.M.N., S.P.M.P., D.K.(M.), D.K. (Selangor), S.P.D.K. (Sabah).

Chief Minister (The Mentri Besar): Datuk JA'AFAR bin HASSAN.

STATE ASSEMBLY
(Elected August 1974)

PARTY	SEATS
National Front	12

SABAH
(Capital: Kota Kinabalu)

Yang di-Pertuan Negara of Sabah: His Excellency Datuk MOHD. INDAN bin KARI.

Chief Minister: Datuk HARRIS SALLEH.

STATE ASSEMBLY
(Elected April 1976)

PARTY	SEATS
Berjaya (elected)	28
Berjaya (nominated)	6
Sabah Alliance	20
TOTAL	54

SARAWAK
(Capital: Kuching)

Governor: His Excellency Tun Datuk Patinggi Tuanku Haji BUJANG bin Tuanku Haji OTHMEN, S.M.N., P.S.M., O.B.E., D.P.

Chief Minister: Datuk Haji ABDUL RAHMAN bin YAKUB, S.P.D.K., P.N.B.S., B.M. (Indonesia), O.S.E.(G.C.), O.S.M.

STATE ASSEMBLY
(Elected August 1974)

PARTY	SEATS
National Front	30
Sarawak National Party*	18
TOTAL	48

* In June 1976 the Sarawak National Party joined the National Front Coalition.

SELANGOR
(Capital: Kuala Lumpur*)

The Sultan of Selangor: His Royal Highness Sultan SALAHUDDIN ABDUL AZIZ SHAH Ibni AL-MARHUM Sultan HISAMUDDIN ALAM SHAH Haji, D.K., D.M.N., S.P.M.S.

Chief Minister (The Mentri Besar): Datuk HORMAT RAFEI.

STATE ASSEMBLY
(Elected August 1974)

PARTY	SEATS
National Front	30
Democratic Action Party	1
Independent	2
TOTAL	33

* Following the amendment to the Constitution (*q.v.*) in which Kuala Lumpur is redesignated as the Federal Territory of Kuala Lumpur, a new Selangor State capital is to be established at Shah Alam in 1977.

TRENGGANU
(Capital: Kuala Trengganu)

The Sultan of Trengganu: His Royal Highness Tuanku ISMAIL NASIRUDDIN SHAH Ibni AL-MARHUM Sultan ZAINAL ABIDIN, D.K., D.K.(M)., D.M.N., S.P.M.T., D.K. (Kelantan), D.K. (Selangor).

Chief Minister (The Mentri Besar): Datuk WAN MOKHTAR bin AHMAD, K.M.N., J.P., P.J.K.

STATE ASSEMBLY
(Elected August 1974)

PARTY	SEATS
National Front	27
Independent	1
TOTAL	28

POLITICAL PARTIES

The National Front: a multiracial coalition of eleven parties; 144 seats in the House of Representatives. The component parties of the National Front are:

United Malay National Organization (UMNO): UMNO Bldg., 39 Jalan Tunku Abdul Rahman, Kuala Lumpur; f. 1946; Pres. (acting) Datuk HUSSEIN bin ONN.

Berjaya (*Sabah People's Union*): Kota Kinabalu Sabah; f. 1975; Pres. (acting) Datuk HARRIS SALLEH.

Malaysian Chinese Association: P.O.B. 626,67 Jalan Ampang, Kuala Lumpur; Pres. Datuk LEE SAN CHOON.

Malaysian Indian Congress (MIC): Bangunan MIC, Jalan Tun Ismail, Kuala Lumpur; f. 1946; Pres. Tan Sri V. MANIKAVASAGAM.

Pan-Malayan Islamic Party: 214-1A, Jalan Pahang, Kuala Lumpur; f. 1951; Pres. Dato Haji MOHAMED bin Haji MUDA.

Parti Gerakan Rakyat Malaysia (GERAKAN): c/o Chief Minister's Office, Bungunan Tunku Syed Putra, Penang; f. 1968; Pres. Dr. LIM CHON EU.

People's Progressive Party of Malaysia (PPP): 23 Hale St., Ipoh, Perak; f. 1955; Pres. KHONG KOK YAT.

Parti Pesaka Bumiputra Bersatu (PPBP): Jalan Satok, Kuching, Sarawak; Pres. Datuk Haji TAIB MAHMUD.

Sarawak United People's Party (SUPP): 7 Central Rd., P.O.B. 454, Kuching, Sarawak; f. 1959; Pres. Tan Sri ONG KEE HUI.

Sarawak National Party (SNAP): 115 Green Rd., Kuching, Sarawak; f. 161; Pres. STEPHEN KALONG NINGKAN.

United Sabah National Organization (USNO): Kota Kinabalu, Sabah; Pres. Tun Datu Haji MUSTAPHA bin Datu HARUN.

Democratic Action Party: 77 Road 20/9, Petaling Jaya, Selangor; f. 1966; Opposition; advocates multiracial Malaysia based on democratic socialism; Chair. Dr. CHEN MAN HIN; Sec.-Gen. LIM KIT SIANG.

Parti Keadilan Masharakat (PEKEMAS): Room 208, Bangunan Tong Khin, Jalan Pasar Baru, Kuala Lumpur; f. 1971; Chair. Dr. TAN CHEE KHOON.

Parti Sosialis Rakyet Malaysia (PSRM): 946 Jalan Bangsar, Kuala Lumpur; Chair. Encik KASSIM AHMAD.

Kesatuan Insaf Tanah Ayer (KITA): National Consciousness Party; 41 Jalan Pasar, Taiping, Perak; Chair. Encik NG HOE HUN.

Independent People's Progressive Party (IPPP): 63 Jalan Baru, Port Dickson, Negri Sembilan; f. 1974; Pres. YAU SZE.

Parti Bisamah: B 286, Yun Phin Bldg., Padungan Rd., Kuching, Sarawak.

DIPLOMATIC REPRESENTATION

HIGH COMMISSIONS AND EMBASSIES ACCREDITED TO MALAYSIA

(In Kuala Lumpur unless otherwise stated)
(HC) High Commission; (E) Embassy.

Algeria: New Delhi, India (E).

Argentina: Bangkok, Thailand (E).

Australia: 44 Jalan Ampang (HC); *High Commissioner:* GRAHAM B. FEAKES.

Austria: 7th Floor, Oriental Plaza Bldg., Jalan Parry, P.O.B. 154 (E); *Ambassador:* Dr. KLAUS RUDOLF ZIEGLER.

Bangladesh: 204-1 Jalan Ampang (HC); *High Commissioner:* Maj.-Gen. K. M. SHAFIULLAH.

Belgium: 2 Jalan Ampang (E); *Ambassador:* P. Y. DE VLEESCHAUWER.

Brazil: Bangkok, Thailand (E).

Bulgaria: Chartered Bank Bldg., Jalan Ampang (E); *Ambassador:* TODOR STOYANOV.

Burma: 7 Jalan Taman U Thant (E); *Ambassador:* U THET TIN.

Canada: AIA Bldg., Jalan Ampang (HC); *High Commissioner:* JOHN A. DOUGAN.

China, People's Republic: 229 Jalan Ampang (E); *Ambassador:* WANG YU-PING.

Cuba: Tokyo, Japan (E).

Czechoslovakia: 6 Liorong Ru, Jalan Ampang (E); *Ambassador:* Dr. MILAN MACHA.

Denmark: 86 Jalan Ampang (E); *Ambassador:* KARL RAAVAD.

Egypt: 118 Jalan Berhala, Brickfields (E); *Ambassador:* ADEL SAMI GUENENA.

Finland: Jakarta, Indonesia.

France: 210 Jalan Bukit Bintang (E); *Ambassador:* FRANCOIS SIMON DE QUIRIELLE.

German Democratic Republic: 2A Pesiaran Gurney (E); *Ambassador:* GUNTER GAHLICH.

Germany, Federal Republic: Bangunan UMBC, 17th Floor, Jalan Suleiman, P.O.B. 23 (E); *Ambassador:* (vacant).

Ghana: Canberra, Australia (HC).

Greece: New Delhi, India (E).

Hungary: Jakarta, Indonesia (E).

India: 19 Malacca St. (HC); *High Commissioner:* S. L. MALIK.

Indonesia: 91 Jalan Campbell (E); *Ambassador:* Drs. MOHAMAD HASAN.

Iran: Bangkok, Thailand (E).

Iraq: 17 Jalan Yap Kuan Seng (E); *Ambassador:* (vacant).

Ireland: New Delhi, India.

Italy: Jalan Ampang (E); *Ambassador:* (vacant).

Japan: AIA Bldg., Jalan Ampang (E); *Ambassador:* EIKICHI HARA.

Jordan: Islamabad, Pakistan (E).

Korea, Democratic People's Republic: 203 Jalan Ampang (E); *Ambassador:* JONG SONG MUN.

Korea, Republic: 422 Circular Rd. (E); *Ambassador:* SANG JIN CHYUN.

Kuwait: Tokyo, Japan (E).

Laos: Bangkok, Thailand (E).

Lebanon: Islamabad, Pakistan (E).

Libya: 6/8 Jalan Langgak Duta (E); *Ambassador:* MOHAMED RAMADAN MAHMOUD.

Mexico: Jakarta, Indonesia (E).

Mongolia: Tokyo, Japan (E).

Morocco: Islamabad, Pakistan (E).

Nepal: Rangoon, Burma (E).

Netherlands: 86 Jalan Ampang (E); *Ambassador:* J. H. DELGORGE.

New Zealand: 6th Floor, Bangunan Sharikat Polis, Jalan Suleiman (HC); *High Commissioner:* J. H. WEIR.

Norway: Jakarta, Indonesia (E).

Pakistan: 132 Ampang Rd. (E); *Ambassador:* HAFIZ MOHD. HABIBULLAH.

Philippines: 1 Changkat Kia Peng (E); *Ambassador:* YUSUF R. ABUBAKAR.

Poland: 4 Jalan Madge (E); *Ambassador:* JERZY MARKIEWICZ.

Qatar: Islamabad, Pakistan.

Romania: Jakarta, Indonesia (E).

Saudi Arabia: 5th Floor, Bangunan Sharikat Polis, Jalan Suleiman (E); *Ambassador:* (vacant).

Singapore: Straits Trading Bldg., Leboh Pasar Besar (HC); *Ambassador:* WEE KIM WEE.

Spain: Bangkok, Thailand (E).

Sri Lanka: 29 Jalan Yap Kuan Seng (HC); *High Commissioner:* K. L. V. ALAGIYAWANNA.

Sudan: New Delhi, India (E).

Sweden: AIA Bldg., Jalan Ampang (E); *Ambassador:* KJELL ARNE FALTHEIM.

Switzerland: 16 Pesiaran Madge (E); *Ambassador:* PETER S. ERNI.

Syria: Jakarta, Indonesia.

Thailand: 206 Ampang Road (E); *Ambassador:* Prince YUDHISTHIRA SVASTI.

Turkey: Regent Hotel (E); (temporary address); *Ambassador:* TURGUT ILKAN.

U.S.S.R.: 263 Jalan Ampang (E); *Ambassador:* V. N. BENDRYSHEV.

United Kingdom: Wisman Damansara, Jalan Samantan (HC); *High Commissioner:* Sir ERIC NORRIS.

U.S.A.: AIA Bldg., Jalan Ampang (E); *Ambassador:* FRANCIS T. UNDERHILL, Jr.

Yugoslavia: 353 Jalan Ampang (E); *Ambassador:* VLATKO COSIC.

Malaysia also has diplomatic relations with Cambodia, Oman and Viet-Nam.

JUDICIAL SYSTEM

The two High Courts, in Malaya and Borneo, have original, appellate and revisional jurisdiction as the federal law provides. Above these two High Courts is a Federal Court which has, to the exclusion of any other court, jurisdiction in any dispute between States or between the Federation and any State; and has special jurisdiction as to the interpretation of the Constitution. There is also unlimited right of appeal from the High Courts to the Federal Court and limited right of appeal from the Federal Court to the Yang di-Pertuan Agong who refers such appeals to Her Britannic Majesty's Privy Council. The High Courts each consist of the Chief Justice and a number of Puisne Judges. The Federal Court consists of the Lord President together with the two Chief Justices of the High Courts and four Federal Judges. The Lord President and Judges of the Federal Court, and the Chief Justices and Judges of the High Courts, are appointed by the Yang di-Pertuan Agong on the advice of the Prime Minister, after consulting the Conference of Rulers.

The Sessions Courts, which are situated in the principal urban and rural centres, are presided over by a President, who is a member of the Federation Legal Service and is a qualified barrister. Their criminal jurisdiction covers the less serious indictable offences, excluding those which carry penalties of death or life imprisonment. Civil cases are usually heard without a jury. Civil jurisdiction of a President Sessions Court is up to $5,000 and Special President's Sessions Courts can hear cases of up to $10,000. The Presidents are appointed by the Yang di-Pertuan Agong.

The Magistrates' Courts are also found in the main urban and rural centres and have both civil and criminal jurisdiction, although of a more restricted nature than that of the Sessions Courts. The Magistrates consist of officers from either the Federation Legal Service or are seconded from the administration to the Judicial Department for varying periods up to three years. They are appointed by the Rulers of the States in which they officiate on the recommendation of the Chief Justice.

Lord President of the Federal Court of Malaysia: Hon. Mr. Justice Tun MOHAMED SUFFIAN bin HASHIM, S.S.M., D.I.M.P., J.M.N. (Brunei), P.J.K., M.A., LL.B., Bar.-at-Law.

Chief Justice of the High Court in Peninsular Malaysia: Tan Sri GILL, S.S., P.S.M.

Chief Justice of the High Court in Sabah and Sarawak: Hon. B. T. H. LEE, (Kota Kinabalu).

RELIGION

Islam is the religion of Malaysia, but every person has the right to practise his own religion. All Malays are Muslims. A small minority of Chinese are Christians but most Chinese follow Buddhism, Confucianism and Taoism Of the Indian community, about 70 per cent are Hindu, 20 per cent Muslim, 5 per cent Christian and 2 per cent Sikh In Sabah and Sarawak there are many animists.

ISLAM

President of the Majlis Islam: Al-Ustaz MOHAMMED MORTAZA bin Haji DAUD.

CHRISTIANITY

ANGLICAN

Bishop of Peninsular Malaysia: The Rt. Rev. J. G. SAVARIMUTHU, B.D., 14 Pesiaran Stonor, Kuala Lumpur 04-08.

Bishop of Sabah: Rt. Rev. LUKE CHHOA HENG SZE, Bishop's House, P.O.B. 811, Kota Kinabalu, Sabah.

Bishop of Kuching: Rt. Rev. BASIL TEMENGONG, Bishop's House, P.O.B. 347, Kuching, Sarawak.

ROMAN CATHOLIC

Archbishop of Singapore: The Rt. Rev. M. OLÇOMENDY, 31 Victoria St., Singapore 7.

Archbishop of Kuala Lumpur: Rt. Rev. DOMINIC VENDARGON, 528 Jalan Bukit Nanas, Kuala Lumpur.

METHODIST

Bishop for Malaysia and Singapore: Rev. T. R. DORAISAMY; P.O.B. 483, Singapore 6; the Church has 40,000 members.

THE PRESS

PENINSULAR MALAYSIA

DAILIES

ENGLISH LANGUAGE

Malay Mail: 31 Jalan Riong, P.O.B. 250, Kuala Lumpur; f. 1896; afternoon; Editor P. J. JOSHUA; circ. 49,000.

Straits Echo: 216 Penang Rd., Penang; f. 1903; morning; Editor WILSON DE SOUZA; circ. 7,000.

New Straits Times: 31 Jalan Riong, P.O.B. 250, Kuala Lumpur 22-03; Editor-in-Chief LEE SIEW YEE; circ. 155,000 in all states of Malaysia.

CHINESE LANGUAGE

Chung Kuo Pao (*China Press*): 139 Jalan Abdul Sarnad, Kuala Lumpur; f. 1946; morning; Publisher NG HON YUEN; Editor S. H. WONG; circ. 36,000.

Kin Kwok Daily News: 21 Panglima St., Ipoh; f. 1940; morning; Editor YAP KOON SEE; circ. 49,000.

Kwong Wah Yit Poh: 2 & 4 Chulia St. Ghaut, Penang; f. 1910; morning; Editor HO KOON GUAN; circ. 34,000.

Malayan Thung Pau: 40 Jalan Lima off Jalan Chan Sow Lin, Kuala Lumpur; Editor CHONG CHEE MENG; circ. 75,400.

Nanyang Siang Pau: 80 Jalan Riong, Kuala Lumpur; f. 1923; morning; Editor CHU CHEE CHUAN; circ. 156,000 (daily), 86,000 (Sunday).

Shin Min Daily News: 82-B Jalan Rodger, Kuala Lumpur; f. 1957; morning; Editor PAUL CHIN; circ. 86,000.

Sin Chew Jit Poh (Malaysia): 54 Jalan Masjid India, P.O.B. 634, Kuala Lumpur; Editor-in-Chief NG CHONG LEE (acting); circ. 135,000.

Sing Pin Jih Pao: 8 Leith St., Penang; f. 1939; morning; Gen. Man. FOO YEE FONG; circ. 28,000.

TAMIL LANGUAGE

Tamil Malar: 10 Jalan Bersekutu, Petaling Jaya; f. 1963; Editor N. T. S. ARUMUGAM PILAI; circ. 13,150.

Tamil Nesan: 37 Jalan Ampang, Kuala Lumpur; f. 1924; morning; Independent Malaysia; Chair. N. M. NAGAPPAN; Editor MURUGU SUBRAMANIAN; circ. 23,000 (daily), 41,000 (Sunday).

MALAY LANGUAGE

Berita Harian: 31 Jalan Riong, P.O.B. 250, Kuala Lumpur; morning; Editor Hj. WAHAB ZAIN; circ. 53,000.

Mingguan Malaysia: 31 Jalan Rd., Kuala Lumpur; Sunday; Editor SALLEH Haji YUSOF; circ. 165,000.

Utusan Malaysia: 46M Jalan Chan Sow Lin, Kuala Lumpur; f. 1965; Editor A. R. KAMALUDDIN; circ. 87,000

Utusan Melayu: 46M Jalan Chan Sow Lin, Kuala Lumpur; morning; Editor ALI SALIM; circ. 50,000.

PUNJABI LANGUAGE

Malaya Samachar: 256 Jalan Brickfields, Kuala Lumpur; f. 1965; evening; Editor TIRLOCHAN SINGH; circ. 2,500.

Navjiwan Punjabi News: 52 Jalan 8/18, Petaling Jaya; Assoc. Editor TARA SINGH.

SUNDAY PAPERS

ENGLISH LANGUAGE

New Sunday Times: 31 Jalan Riong, P.O.B. 250, Kuala Lumpur 22-03; f. 1931; Editor P. C. SHIVADAS; circ. 198,000 copies in all states of Malaysia.

Sunday Gazette: 216 Penang Rd., Penang; f. 1930; morning; Editor CHEAH CHEONG LIN; circ. 8,500.

Sunday Mail: 31 Jalan Riong, P.O.B. 250, Kuala Lumpur; Editor P. J. JOSHUA; circ. 58,000.

MALAY LANGUAGE

Berita Minggu: 31 Jalan Riong, P.O.B. 250, Kuala Lumpur 22-03; Editor Encik A. SAMAD SAID; circ. 71,000 in all states of Malaysia.

Utusan Zaman: 46M Jalan Chan Sow Lin, Kuala Lumpur; Editor AMIR HAMZA; circ. 55,000.

PERIODICALS

English Language

Malayan Forester, The: Malayan Forest Department, Kuala Lumpur; f. 1931; Business Editor Ismail bin Haji Ali.

Malayan Nature Journal, The: P.O.B. 750, Kuala Lumpur; f. 1940 by the Malayan Nature Society; Pres. Dr. F. S. P. Ng; Hon. Editor Dr. C. H. Cheah; Hon. Sec. P. J. Verghese; circ. 800.

Malaysia Warta Kerajaan Seri Paduka Baginda (H.M. Government Gazette): Kuala Lumpur; fortnightly.

Malaysian Agricultural Journal: Ministry of Agriculture and Rural Development, Jalan Swettenham, Kuala Lumpur; f. 1901; twice yearly.

Malaysian Digest: Ministry of Foreign Affairs, Jalan Wisma Putra, Kuala Lumpur; English; twice monthly; airmail edition.

Planter, The: No. 1, Pesiaran Lidcol, off Jalan Yap Kwan Seng, P.O.B. 262, Kuala Lumpur; f. 1919; Incorporated Society of Planters' monthly; Editor M. Rajadurai; circ. 1,800.

Chinese Language

Sin Lu Pao (*New Path News*): P.O.B. 513, Kuala Lumpur; produced by the Psychological Warfare Section; monthly; circ. 50,000 (Chinese), 3,200 (English).

Malay Language

Balai Muhibbah: National Goodwill Council, Kuala Lumpur; Editor Abu Bakar bin Kamat.

Dewan Masyarakat: c/o Dewan Bahasa dan Pustaka, Kuala Lumpur; Editor Encik M. Noor Azam.

Dewan Pelajar: c/o Dewan Bahasa dan Pustaka, Kuala Lumpur; monthly; Editor Saleh Daud.

Filem dan Fesyen: 46M Jalan Chan Sow Lin, Kuala Lumpur; fortnightly; Editor Aimi Jarr.

Guru: Malay School, Jelutong, Penang; f. 1924 by Federation of Malay Teachers' Union of the Federation of Malaya (*Kesatuan Persakutuan Guru Melayu Persakutuan Tanah Melagu*); educational magazine; monthly; Pres. and Editor Mohamed Noor bin Ahmed; circ. 10,000.

Mastika: 46M Jalan Chan Sow Lin, Kuala Lumpur; Malayan illustrated magazine; monthly; Editor Zaharah Nawawi; circ. 12,000.

Pengasoh: Majlis Ugama Islam, Kota Bahru, Kelantan; f. 1925; monthly; Editor Hasan Haji Muhammad; circ. 12,000.

Sinar Zaman: Jalan Tun Perak, Kuala Lumpur; Produced by the Federal Information Services; Editor Abdul Aziz Malim.

Suara Umno: Johore Bahru; Editor Syed Ja'affer bin Hassan Albar; circ. 1,500.

Utusan Film and Sports: 46M Jalan Chan Sow Lin, Kuala Lumpur; weekly.

Utusan Pelajar: 46M Jalan Chan Sow Lin, Kuala Lumpur; fortnightly; Editor Mohd. Salleh Hamzah.

Utusan Radio dan TV: 46M Jalan Chan Sow Lin, Kuala Lumpur; weekly; Editor Mohd. Salleh Yusof.

Wanita: 46M Jalan Chan Sow Lin, Kuala Lumpur; monthly; Editor Nik Rahimah.

Tamil Language

Janobaharl: Brockman Rd., Kuala Lumpur; f. 1946; monthly; produced by Information Services; Editor C. V. Kuppusamy; circ. 25,000.

Solai: Messrs. Solai & Co., Kuala Lumpur; monthly; Editor K. L. Ramanathan; circ. 2,000.

SABAH

DAILIES

Api Siang Pau (*Kota Kinabalu Commercial Press*): P.O.B. 170, 24 Australian Place, Kota Kinabalu; f. 1954; Chinese; Editor Datuk Lo Kwock Chuen; circ. 12,000.

Borneo Times: Tamah Merah, P.O.B. 455, Sandakan; f. 1956; Chinese; Editor Chan Kian Tian; circ. 11,500.

Daily Express: P.O.B. 139, Kota Kinabalu; f. 1963; English and Malay; Editor P. C. Abdu; circ. 25,795.

Hua Chiau Jit Pao (*Overseas Chinese Daily News*): P.O.B. 139, Kota Kinabalu; Chinese; f. 1936; Editor Yeh Pao Tzu, A.M.N.; circ. 27,925.

Kinabalu Daily News: P.O.B. 700, Sandakan; f. 1968; Chinese; circ. 2,000.

Kinabalu Sabah Times: P.O.B. 525, 67 Gaya St., Kota Kinabalu; f. 1947; English; Editor Ignatius P. Daim; circ. 2,096.

Kinabalu Sabah Times: P.O.B. 525, 67 Gaya St., Kota Kinabalu; f. 1963; Chinese; Editor Halim Loy Chee Fatt; circ. 12,000.

Malaysia Daily News: 7 Island Rd., Sandakan; f. 1968; Editor Wong Ching Chiong.

Merdeka Daily News: P.O.B. 332, Sandakan; f. 1968; Chinese; Editor Yam Yue Tung.

Overseas Chinese Daily News: P.O.B. 139, 9 Gaya St., Kota Kinabalu; f. 1936; Chinese; Editor Hii Yuk Sen; circ. 22,670.

Sandakan Jih Pao: P.O.B. 337, Sandakan; f. 1960; Chinese; Editor Chia Siew Yin; circ. 24,000.

SARAWAK

DAILIES

Chinese Daily News: Abell Rd., Kuching; f. 1945; Chinese; Editor Hia Swee Wan; circ. 2,400.

International Times: Abell Rd., Kuching; f. 1965; Chinese; Editor Wee Tin Fatt; circ. 5,000.

Malaysia Daily News: 7 Island Rd., Sibu; f. 1968; Chinese; Editor Wong Seng Kwong.

Miri Daily News: 9-10 Permaisuri Industrial Shophouses, P.O.B. 377, Miri; f. 1957; Chinese; Editor Chai Sze-Voon; circ. 16,000.

Sarawak Siang Pau: P.O.B. 370, Sibu; f. 1966; Chinese; daily; Editor Chee Guan Hock; circ. 5,000.

Sarawak Tribune and Sunday Tribune: 19 Jalan Tun Haji Openg, Kuching; f. 1945; English; Editor Dennis Law; circ. 4,350.

See Hua Daily News: 11 Island Rd., Sibu; f. 1952; Chinese; daily; Editor Lim Yew Seng; circ. 17,000.

Utusan Sarawak: Abell Rd., Kuching; f. 1949; Malay; Editor Mohammed Gol Safar; circ. 5,000.

The Vanguard: 9 Temple St., Kuching; f. 1963; English and Chinese; Editor Desmond Leong Kok Shin; circ. 19,500.

PERIODICALS

Nendak: Borneo Literature Bureau, P.O.B. 1390, Kuching; f. 1967; Iban; monthly; Editor Singki Lintan; circ. 1,385.

Pedoman Ra'ayat: Malaysian Information Service, Kuching; f. 1956; Malay; monthly; Editor M. Deli Abd. Rahman; circ. 6,000.

Pelita Pelajar: Borneo Literature Bureau, P.O.B. 1390, Kuching; f. 1960; English; monthly; Editor CECELIA GOH; circ. 6,000.

Pelita Pelajar: Borneo Literature Bureau, P.O.B. 1390, Kuching; f. 1961; Chinese; monthly; Editor HWANG JUN HIEN; circ. 11,000.

Pemberita: Malaysian Information Office, Kuching; f. 1956; Iban and Chinese; monthly; Editor FREDERICK AUGUST anak ENCHANA; circ. 6,000.

Perintis: Borneo Literature Bureau, P.O.B. 1390, Kuching; f. 1970; Bahasa Malaysia; monthly; Editor PUAN MALIAH ALI MORNI; circ. 5,000.

Sarawak Karang Seminggu: State Information Office, Kuching; weekly; Editor F. A. ENCHANA.

Sarawak Gazette: Govt. Printing Office, Kuching; f. 1870; English; monthly; Editors SAFRI AWANG ZAIDELL, LOH CHEE YIN; circ. 500.

Sarawak Museum Journal: Sarawak Museum, Kuching; f. 1911; English; annually; Editor LUCAS CHIN; circ. 2,000.

Sarawak by the Week: Malaysian Information Services, Mosque Rd., Kuching; f. 1961; weekly; Malay and Iban; circ. 2,700.

NEWS AGENCIES

Bernama (*Malaysian National News Agency*): Bernama, Wisma Belia, Jalan Syed Putra, P.O.B. 24, Kuala Lumpur; f. 1967; general news service, economic service and feature service; teleprinter network between Head Office and regional bureaux and newspaper offices throughout the country; daily output in Bahasa Malaysia and English; Gen. Man. DOL RAMLI.

FOREIGN BUREAUX

Agence France-Presse: 26 Hotel Equatorial, Kuala Lumpur; Correspondent N. G. NAIR.

Associated Press: China Insurance Bldg., 174 Jalan Tuanku Abdul Rahman, Kuala Lumpur; Correspondent H. SUBRAMANIAM.

Cathay Information Service: 239 Jalan Pekeliling, Kuala Lumpur; Dir. SENYUNG CHOW.

Central News Agency: G-4 Sam Mansion, Jalan Tuba, Kuala Lumpur; Representative JACK C. WANG.

Reuters: P.O.B. 841, 133A Jalan Masjid India, Kuala Lumpur; P.O.B. 141, 25 Light St., Penang.

TASS: 297-C Jalan Ampang, Kuala Lumpur; Representative BYTCHKOV STANISLAW.

Thai News Agency: 124-F Burmah Rd., Penang; Kuala Lumpur Representative SOOK BURANAKUL.

United Press International: 95 Jalan Travers, Kuala Lumpur; Representative R. BINGH.

PUBLISHERS

Penang

Kwong Wah Yit Poh Press Bhd.: 2 & 4 Chulia St. Ghaut, P.O.B. 31; f. 1910; Man. OON CHOO KHYE.

National Press, The: 46–48 Prangin Lane; Man. Dir. TAN CHENG TIT; Gen. Man. TAN CHONG HENG.

Phoenix Press Limited: 6–8 Church St.; Man. Dir. TAN CHIN BOON; Dir. OOI SIEW KEE; Man. TAN CHIEW SENG.

Perak

Al-Zainiyah: 66A Assam Kumbang, Taiping; religious books and periodicals.

Caxton Press, The (Ipoh): 130 Belfield St., P.O.B. 140, Ipoh; Man. CYRIL R. LABROOY.

Charles Grenier Sdn. Bhd.: Head Office: 37/39 Station Rd., P.O.B. 130, Ipoh; br. at 8 Medan Pasar, P.O.B. 183, Kuala Lumpur; Man. Dir. H. D. G. JANSZ.

Peter Chong Printers Sdn. Bhd.: 120 Belfield St., Ipoh; f. 1921; publishers, offset/letterpress; printers and stationers; Man. Dir. J. KONG.

Kuala Lumpur

Commercial Press Sdn. Bhd.: 99 Jalan Bandar, Kuala Lumpur; Man. Dir. YUEN SZE KIN.

Federal Publications Sdn. Bhd.: 170 Jalan Sungai Besi, Kuala Lumpur and Times House, River Valley Rd., Singapore 9; educational books; Gen. Man. H. S. KOH.

Longman Malaysia Sdn. Bhd.: 2nd Floor, Wisma Damansara, Jalan Semantan, Damansara Heights, Kuala Lumpur; textbooks, educational materials.

Malaysia Publishing House Ltd.: 279 Jalan Tuanku Abdul Rahman, Kuala Lumpur; br. of *M.P.H. Ltd.* of Singapore.

Marican and Sons (Malaysia) Sdn. Bhd.: 321 Jalan Tuanku Abdul Rahman, Kuala Lumpur; publishers and booksellers.

M. S. Geetha Publishers: 131 Jalan Tuanku Abdul Rahman, Kuala Lumpur 01-08; history, education, reference and textbooks; Man. Dir. SETHU.

Oxford University Press: Bangunan Loke Yew, Jalan Belanda, Kuala Lumpur; history, reference, geography and education; Regional Man. J. A. NICHOLSON.

Peter Chong and Co.: 31 Ampang St., Kuala Lumpur; educational books; Propr. PETER CHONG.

University of Malaya Press Ltd.: University Library, University of Malaya, Kuala Lumpur 22-11; economics, literature, history, philosophy, medicine, politics, social science.

Negri Sembilan

Bharathi Press: 23-24 Jalan Tuan Sheikh, Seremban, P.O.B. 74; f. 1939; Proprs. RAMA SINNIAH, C. RAMASAMY; Man. M. R. N. MUTHURENGAM.

Malay Press, The: 198 Tong Yen Rd., Kuala Pilah; Malay story books.

Peter Chong and Co.: 68 Birch Rd., Seremban; Propr. PETER CHONG.

Association of Southeast Asian Publishers (ASEAP): Kuala Lumpur; f. 1972; comprises 16 publishers from Indonesia, Cambodia, Singapore, Thailand, Philippines and Malaysia; Pres. Encik GHAZALI YUNUS; Sec.-Gen. Encik R. NARAYANA MENON.

Sarawak

Borneo Literature Bureau: P.O.B. 1390, Kuching, Sarawak, and P.O.B. 16, Tanjong Arn, Sabah; sponsored by the State Governments of Sabah and Sarawak; educational, general and children's books in English, Iban, Malay, Chinese and other languages spoken in Sabah and Sarawak; also monthly magazines *Pelita Pelajar* (English and Chinese), *Perintis* (Bahasa Malaysia) and *Nendak* (Iban); Dir. EDWARD ENGGU.

RADIO AND TELEVISION

RADIO

Peninsular Malaysia

Department of Broadcasting: P.O.B. 1075, Angkasapuri, Kuala Lumpur; stations of "Radio Malaysia" are operating at Kuala Lumpur, Penang, Malacca, Ipoh, Kota Bahru, Johore Bahru, Kuantan and Kuala Trengganu; broadcasts 419 hours 20 minutes weekly in Malay, English, Tamil and Chinese (four dialects); Dir.-Gen. Abdullah Mohamed.

Rediffusion (Malaya) Ltd.: subsidiary of Rediffusion Ltd., London; P.O.B. 570, Kuala Lumpur; f. 1949; 2 programmes; Gen. Man. M. J. Bleeck; 18,584 subscribers in Kuala Lumpur; 8,881 subscribers in Penang; 5,996 subscribers in Ipoh.

Sabah

Dept. of Broadcasting (Sabah): P.O.B. 1016, Kota Kinabalu; inaugurated in 1955 and broadcasts programmes 126 hours a week in Malay, English, Chinese (3 dialects), Kadazan, Murut, Indonesian and Bajau; Dir. of Broadcasting, Sabah, Suhaimi Haji Amin.

Note: A television service began in December 1971 for 5 hours daily.

Sarawak

Radio Malaysia (Sarawak): Broadcasting House, Kuching; f. 1954, incorporated as a department of Radio Malaysia 1963; broadcasts 323 hours (1974) in Malay, English, Chinese, Iban, Bidayuh, Melanau and Kayan/Kenyah; Schools Broadcasting Service started 1959; branch stations at Limbang and Sibu; Dir. of Broadcasting, Sarawak, Mohamed Salleh bin Askor, p.b.s.

In September 1974 there were about 326,800 radio receivers in use.

TELEVISION

Radio Television Malaysia: Dept. of Broadcasting, Angkasapuri, Kuala Lumpur; f. 1963; Dir.-Gen. Abdullah Mohamed.

In 1974 there were 371,692 licensed television receivers. Colour television is expected to be introduced by the end of 1976.

FINANCE

(cap = capital; p.u. = paid up; dep. = deposits; m. = million; brs. = branches; M$ = Malaysian dollars.)

BANKING

Central Bank

Bank Negara Malaysia: Jalan Kuching, P.O.B. 922, Kuala Lumpur; brs. at Kuala Lumpur, Pulau Pinang, Kota Kinabalu, Johore Bahru, Kuching; f. 1959; bank of issue; cap. p.u. M$40m., dep. M$1,572m. (Dec. 31st, 1975); Gov. and Chair. Tan Sri Ismail bin Mohamed Ali, p.m.n.; Deputy Gov. Datuk Arshad bin Ayub.

PENINSULAR MALAYSIA

Commercial Banks

Ban Hin Lee Bank Bhd.: 43 Beach St., Penang; f. 1935; cap. p.u. M$6m., dep. M$27.3m. (Dec. 31st, 1975); Chair. Datuk Yeap Hock Hoe; Gen. Man. Goh Eng Toon.

Bank Bumiputra Malaysia Bhd.: P.O.B. 407, 21 Jalan Melaka, Kuala Lumpur; f. 1966; Commercial Bank established by the Government to facilitate capital formation, and provide banking and financial services to all sectors of the economy; 41 brs. including East Malaysia; wide network of corresponding banks throughout the world; cap. M$200m.; cap. p.u. M$40m., dep. M$1,042.7m. (Dec. 31st, 1975); Chair. Senator Kamarul Ariffin Mohd. Yassin.

Bank Buruh Malaysia Bhd.: 2, 4, 6, 8 Jalan Gereja, Kuala Lumpur; f. 1975; cap. p.u. M$10m.; dep. M$5.1m. (Dec. 1975); Chair. P. P. Narayanan; Exec. Dir. S. J. H. Zaidi.

Development and Commercial Bank: 18 Jalan Silang, Kuala Lumpur; f. 1966; 5 brs.; cap. p.u. M$15.0m.; dep. M$69.2m. (Dec. 31st, 1975); Chair. Sir Henry H. S. Lee, Dir. and Gen. O. P. Chan.

Kwong Yik Bank Bhd.: 75 Jalan Bandar, P.O.B. 135, Kuala Lumpur; f. 1913; 6 brs.; cap. p.u. M$8.0m.; dep. M$123.8m. (June 1975); Chair. Inche Azman bin Hashim; Man. Dir. Lim Khin Seong.

Malayan Banking Bhd.: 92 Jalan Bandar, P.O.B. 2010, Kuala Lumpur; f. 1960; cap. p.u. M$45m., dep. M$1,249.9m. (Dec. 1975); 126 brs.; Chair. Tan Sri Taib bin Haji Andak, p.m.n., d.p.m.j.; Exec. Dirs. Azman Hashim, Hooi Kam Sooi.

Oriental Bank Bhd.: P.O.B. 243, 16 Jalan Silang, Kuala Lumpur; f. 1937; 4 brs.; cap. p.u. M$2m., dep. M$29.9m. (Dec. 75); Chair. Tan Sri Haji Hussain bin Haji Mohd. Sidek; Snr. Man. James L. P. Leow.

Pacific Bank Berhad: 145 Jalan Bandar, P.O.B. 43, Kuala Lumpur; f. 1963; 2 brs.; cap. p.u. M$3m., dep. M$34.8m. (Dec. 75); Chair. Raja Tunuda bin Raja Mohamed; Man. Quek Hang Chew.

Public Bank Bhd.: 3rd Floor, Bangunan Yee Seng, 15 Jalan Raja Chulan, Kuala Lumpur; f. 1966; 8 brs.; cap. p.u. M$16m., dep. M$126.7m. (Dec. 75); Chair. Nik Ahmed Kamil; Man. Dir. Teh Hong Piow.

Southern Banking Bhd.: 21 Beach St., Penang; f. 1965; 6 brs.; cap. p.u. M$10m., dep. M$71.5m. (Dec. 75); Chair. Saw Choo Theng; Gen. Man. Saw Bin Sit.

United Asian Bank Bhd.: 4 Jalan Tun Perak, Kuala Lumpur; f. 1973; 19 brs.; cap. p.u. M$10m., dep. M$316.8m. (Dec. 75); Chair. Y. A. M. Tengku Ibrahim Ibni Sultan Abu Bakar; Exec. Dir. K. V. Murthy Yerkadithaya.

United Malayan Banking Corporation Bhd.: Bangunan UMBC, Jalan Suleiman, Kuala Lumpur; f. 1960; 38 brs.; cap. p.u. M$30m., dep. M$910.4m. (June 1975); Chair. Saw Choo Theng; Man. Dir. Kang Kock Seng.

Foreign Banks

Algemene Bank Nederland N.V.: Wisma Sachdev, Jalan Raja Laut, Kuala Lumpur; 1 br.; f. 1888; dep. M$18.3m. (Dec. 1975); Man. W. J. J. Cozijnsen.

Bangkok Bank Ltd.: 105 Jalan Bandar, Kuala Lumpur; f. 1959; dep. M$52.7m. (Dec. 1975); Man. Athit Wasantachat.

Bank of America N.T. and S.A.: P.O.B. 950, 2 Jalan Raja Chulan, Kuala Lumpur; f. 1959; dep. M$49.4m. (Dec. 1975); Man. Richard K. Moss.

Bank of Canton Ltd.: 18 Pudu St., Kuala Lumpur; f. 1957; dep. M$27.6m. (Dec. 1975); Man. Tan Hock Seng, k.m.n.

Bank of Nova Scotia: 41 Jalan Melayu, Bangunan Safety Insurance, P.O.B. 1056, Kuala Lumpur; f. 1973; dep. M$8.1m. (Oct. 31st, 1975); Man. M. C. Johnston.

Bank of Tokyo Ltd:. 22 Medan Pasar, P.O.B. 959, Kuala Lumpur; f. 1959; dep. M$47.6m. (Sept. 30th, 1975); Gen. Man. K. Kagomiya.

Banque de l'Indochine: 44 Jalan Pudu, Kuala Lumpur; 1 br.; f. 1958; dep. 61.6m. (Dec. 1975); Man. R. Mariette.

Chartered Bank: 2 Jalan Ampang, P.O.B. 1001, Kuala Lumpur, 34 brs.; dep. M$1,265.1m. (Dec. 1975); Chief Man. C. Little.

Chase Manhattan Bank, N.A.: 9 Jalan Gereja, P.O.B. 1090, Kuala Lumpur; dep. M$34.8m. (Dec. 1975); 2nd Vice-Pres. Lawrence W. Burr.

Chung Khiaw Bank Ltd.: 10-11 Medan Pasar, Lee Wah Bank Bldg. (2nd Floor), Kuala Lumpur 01-20; 15 brs.; f. 1950; dep. M$353.6m. (Dec. 31st, 1975); Snr. Man. Yoong Yan Pin.

Europaeisch Asiatische Bank AG (*European Asian Bank*): Bangunan Yee Seng, 15 Jalan Raja Chulan, Kuala Lumpur; f. 1968; dep. M$13.6m. (Dec. 31st, 1975); Man. A. G. Coates.

Citibank N.A.: AIA Bldg., 11 Jalan Ampang, P.O.B. 112, Kuala Lumpur; f. 1812; 2 brs.; dep. M$179.3m. (Dec. 1975); Vice-Pres. R. Buenaventura; Operations Man. Ho Chin Piao.

Hong Kong and Shanghai Banking Corporation, The: 1 Benteng, Kuala Lumpur, 35 brs.; dep. M$844.1m. (Dec. 31st, 1975); Man. (Malaysia) D. A. McKnight.

Lee Wah Bank Ltd.: 10-14 Medan Pasar, Kuala Lumpur; f. 1956; 8 brs.; dep. M$149.4m. (Dec. 1975); Man. Tan Siak Tee.

Lloyds Bank International (LBI): Wisma MPI, Jalan Raja Chulan, Kuala Lumpur; Rep. N. Astbury.

Oversea-Chinese Banking Corpn. Ltd.: 30 Jalan Tun Perak, P.O.B. 197 Kuala Lumpur; f. 1932; 23 brs.; dep. M$666.0m. (Dec. 1975); Dir. and Gen. Man. Lin Jo Yan.

Overseas Union Bank Ltd.: Lee Yan Lian Bldg., Jalan Tun Perak, P.O.B. 621, Kuala Lumpur; f. 1958; 10 brs.; dep. M$211.8m. (Dec. 31st, 1975); Man. Ho Mang Chew.

Merchant Banks

Amanah Chase Merchant Bankers Bhd.: P.O.B. 2492, Kuala Lumpur; f. 1975; cap. p.u. M$5.0m.; Chair. Tan Sri Mohd. Shariff bin Abdul Samad; Gen. Man. O. N. Greeves.

Asian & Euro-American Merchant Bankers (M) Bhd.: P.O.B. 1057, Kuala Lumpur; f. 1973; cap. p.u. M$10m. Chair. Tan Sri Taib bin Haji Andak; Man. Dir. Encik Malek Ali Merican.

Asian International Merchant Bankers Bhd.: P.O.B. 988, Kuala Lumpur; f. 1973; cap. p.u. M$5.0m. (Dec. 1974); Chair. Tan Sri Omar Yoke Lin Ong; Gen.-Man. Wong Heng Wool.

Asiavest Merchant Bankers (M) Bhd.: 8th Floor, Oriental Plaza, Jalan Parry, Kuala Lumpur; f. 1975; cap. p.u. M$2.0m.; Chair. Dato Syed Kechik; Deputy Man. Dir. Michael P. Goco.

Bumiputra Merchant Bankers Bhd.: P.O.B. 890, Kuala Lumpur; f. 1972; cap. p.u. M$5.0m.; Chair. Lorrain Esme Osman; Gen. Man. Jan-Otto Van Boetzelaer.

Chartered Merchant Bankers (M) Bhd.: P.O.B. 1001, Kuala Lumpur; f. 1970; cap. p.u. M$3.75m. (Dec. 1974); Chair. Tunku Tan Sri Mohamed bin Tunku Besar Burhanuddin; Man. Christopher M. Meynell.

D. & C. Nomura Merchant Bankers Bhd.: 10th Floor, Oriental Plaza, Jalan Parry, Kuala Lumpur; f. 1974; cap. p.u. M$3.0m. (Dec. 1974); Chair. Tun Sir Henry Hau Shik Lee; Gen. Man. Kunihiko Katayama.

Malaysian International Merchant Bankers Bhd.: P.O.B. 2250, 5th Floor, Bangunan Yee Seng, Jalan Weld, Kuala Lumpur; f. 1970; cap. p.u. M$6.0m. (Oct. 1975); Chair. Geh Ik Cheong; Snr. Man. Dr. Chong Sin Jee.

Pertanian Baring Sanwa Multinational Bhd.: P.O.B. 2362, Kuala Lumpur; f. 1974; cap. p.u. M$3.0m. (Dec. 1974); Chair. Dr. Agoes Salim; Gen. Man. Maurice de Bunsen.

Rakyat First Merchant Bankers Bhd.: P.O.B. 2346, Kuala Lumpur; f. 1974; cap. p.u. M$2.5m. (July 1974); Gen. Man. T. P. Guerin, Jr.

UDA Merchant Bankers Bhd.: P.O.B., 2406 Kuala Lumpur; f. 1975; cap. p.u. M$2.0m.; Chair. Y. B. Datuk Ya'cob bin Hitam; Man. Dir. Abdul Samad bin Ya Hya.

BANKERS' ASSOCIATION

Association of Banks in Malaysia: c/o Malayan Banking Bhd., 92 Jalan Bandar, Kuala Lumpur; Chair. Hooi Kam Sooi; Sec. Chang Yee Hoong.

Association of Merchant Bankers in Malaysia: c/o Malaysian International Merchant Bankers Bhd., 5th Floor, Bangunan Yee Seng, Jalan Raja Chulan, Kuala Lumpur; Chair. Geh. Ik Chong; Sec. Malek Ali Merican.

INSURANCE

Malaysian National Insurance Sdn. Bhd.: 9th Floor, Wisma Yakin, Jalan Melayu, P.O.B. 799, Kuala Lumpur; state-run company handling non-life and general insurance; auth. cap. M$10m.; Chair. A. Rahman Hamidon; Exec. Dir. Abdul Samad Hj Alias.

STOCK EXCHANGE

Stock Exchange of Malaysia and Singapore: 7th Floor, Bangkok Bank Bldg., Jalan Bandar, Kuala Lumpur.

SABAH

Commercial Banks

Bank Negara Malaysia: Kota Kinabalu.

Hock Hua Bank (Sabah) Bhd.: Head Office: Sibu; 59-69 3rd Ave., Sandakan; f. 1961; 2 other brs. in Sabah; cap. p.u. M$47.4m. (Dec. 31st, 1975); Chair. Datuk Ling Beng Siew; Man. Dir. Kwang-Chue Ming.

Malayan Banking Bhd.: Sabah: 55 Jalan Dua, P.O.B. 374, Sandakan.

FOREIGN BANKS

Chartered Bank: Sabah: P.O.B. 99, Kota Kinabalu; Man. J. T. ROGERS; 7 brs.

Chung Khiaw Bank Ltd.: P.O.B. 539, Kota Kinabalu; P.O.B. 902, Sandakan; P.O.B. 111, Tuaran; Man. for Sabah CHOW SHEE SENG, P.G.D.K., O.ST.J.

Hongkong and Shanghai Banking Corpn., The: Man. I. N. MACLEOD; 66 brs.

United Overseas Bank Ltd.: 22 Jalan Tugu, Kampong Ayer, Kota Kinabalu, Sabah; f. 1966; dep. M$9.6m.; Man. YONG KON FAH.

SARAWAK

COMMERCIAL BANKS

Bank Negara Malaysia: Kuching.

Bian Chiang Bank Bhd.: Head Office: 32/33 Jalan Khoo Hun Yeang, P.O.B. 133, Kuching; f. 1956; cap. p.u. M$4.5m.; dep. 13.7m. (Dec. 1975); Chair. Datuk WEE HOOD TECK; Man. TAI FOH LEAN.

Hock Hua Bank Bhd.: Head Office: Central Rd., Sibu; f. 1952; cap. p.u. M$5.0m.; dep. M$116.5m. (Dec. 31st, 1975); brs. throughout Sarawak and Sabah, and in Kuala Lumpur; Chair. Datuk LING BENG SIEW, P.N.B.S.; Man. Dir. Datuk TING LIK HUNG, O.B.E., P.N.B.S.

Kong Ming Bank Bhd.: Head Office: 82 Market Road, P.O.B. 656, Sibu; f. 1964; 3 brs.; cap. p.u. M$2.0m.; dep. M$25.3m. (Dec. 1975); Chair. Datuk LING BENG SUNG; Man. Dir. LING BENG HUI.

Kwong Lee Bank Bhd.: Head Office: 30 Main Bazaar, P.O.B. 33, Kuching; f. 1934; 4 brs.; cap. p.u. M$6.2m.; dep. M$60.9m. (Dec. 1975); Chair. CHAN KUM CHEE; Man. Dir. LAM TIN YUE.

Malayan Bank Bhd.: 24 China St., Miri; 5 brs. throughout Sarawak.

Wah Tat Bank Bhd.: 15 Bank Rd., Sibu; f. 1955; cap. p.u. M$2.0m.; dep. M$21.0m. (Dec. 1975); Chair. CHEW CHOO SING; Man. Dir. CHEW PENG CHENG.

FOREIGN BANKS

Chartered Bank: Sarawak: Jalan Tun Haji Openg, Kuching; brs. at Sibu, Miri, Sarikei, Bintulu and Simanggang.

Hongkong and Shanghai Banking Corporation: brs. in Kuching and Sibu.

Overseas-Chinese Banking Corporation Ltd.: P.O.B. 60, Kuching.

Overseas Union Bank Ltd.: P.O.B. 653, 1 Main Bazaar, Kuching; Man. TAN YORK WEE.

TRADE AND INDUSTRY

CHAMBERS OF COMMERCE

The National Chamber of Commerce of Malaysia: 5th Floor, Wisma Yakin, 5 Jalan Masjid India, Kuala Lumpur; f. 1962; 4 mems., namely Associated Malay, Chinese, Indian Chambers of Commerce of Malaysia; Chair. Y. M. Tengku RAZALEIGH HAMZAH, S.P.M.K.; Sec. JUNUS SUDIN, J.S.M.

PENINSULAR MALAYSIA

Associated Chinese Chambers of Commerce of Malaysia Chinese Assembly Hall, Ground Floor, 1 Jalan Birch, Kuala Lumpur 08-02.

Associated Indian Chambers of Commerce of Malaya: 18 Jalan Tun Perak, P.O.B. 675, Kuala Lumpur; Pres. Sen. Tan Sri S. O. K. UBAIDULLA; Sec. G. S. GILL.

Associated Malay Chambers of Commerce: 5th Floor, Wisma Yakin Bldg., Jalan Masjid India, Kuala Lumpur.

Malacca Chamber of Commerce: 89 Wolferstan Rd., Malacca; f. 1948; Pres. GOH KENG HOW; Sec. C. F. GOMES & Co.; publ. *Bulletin* (quarterly).

Malaysian International Chamber of Commerce and Industry (MICCI): Chartered Bank Chambers, P.O.B. 192, Jalan Ampang, Kuala Lumpur; f. 1908; 245 mem. companies; Pres. C. LITTLE; Exec. Dir. D. C. L. WILSON; publ. *Annual Year Book*.

Penang Branch: Chartered Bank Chambers, P.O.B. 331, Penang, Peninsular Malaysia; f. 1838 as Penang Chamber of Commerce; Chair. J. McKEOWN; Secs. EVATT & Co.

Perak Branch: Chartered Bank Chambers, P.O.B. 136, Ipoh; f. 1911 as Perak Chamber of Commerce; Chair. R. JEFFRESS; Secs. EVATT & Co.

Penang Chinese Chamber of Commerce: 2 Penang St., Penang; f. 1903; Pres. KOH PEN TING, A.M.N.; Sec. CHOY MENG FOOK, P.B., A.M.N.; 900 mems. (1975).

Perak Chinese Chamber of Commerce: 35–37 Hale St., Ipoh; f. 1908; Pres. YEOH KIM TIAN, J.P.; Vice-Pres. LEE LOY SENG, J.P., NG SONG CHOON, J.P.; Hon. Gen. Sec. LAU CHIN SOON; 1,500 mems.

Selangor Chinese Chamber of Commerce: Chinese Assembly Hall, 1st Floor, Birch Rd., Kuala Lumpur; Pres. Tan Sri LEE YAN LIAN, P.M.N., J.M.N.; Exec. Sec. LAI KIM WAT.

Selangor Indian Chamber of Commerce: 63 Jalan Tuanku Abdul Rahman, Kuala Lumpur; Pres. AVTAR SINGH; Hon. Sec. AV. M. JAFFARDEEN.

Chinese, Indian and Malay Chambers of Commerce are also represented in most of the important towns of Peninsular Malaysia.

DEVELOPMENT ORGANIZATIONS

Commonwealth Development Corporation: Head Office: London; Malaysia Office: P.O.B. 494, Kuala Lumpur; Man. R. E. BEACHAM.

Federal Land Development Authority: Jalan Maktab, Kuala Lumpur; f. 1957; to raise the productivity of low income groups and so their earned income and to open up new land for development; Chair. Dato HARUN ARIFIN; Gen. Man. Y. M. R. M. ALIAS; publ. *Annual Report*.

Majlis Amanah Ra'ayat (*Council of Trust for Indigenous People*): 232 Jalan Tuanku Abdul Rahman, Kuala Lumpur; f. 1965 to carry on the manufacture, assembly, processing and marketing of products; to undertake research in industry and joint ventures; Dir.-Gen. Encik SULAIMAN bin OSMAN; Sec. Encik ABU BAKAR bin Haji MOHAMED.

PUBLIC CORPORATIONS

Federal Industrial Development Authority: 5th and 6th Floor, Wisma Damansara, P.O.B. 618, Kuala Lumpur; Dir. Encik MOHD. ZAIN bin Haji ABDUL MAJID.

National Land Finance Co-operative Society Ltd.: 3rd Floor, Oriental Plaza, Jalan Parry, Kuala Lumpur; f. 1960 to mobilize capital from rubber industry workers and others to purchase rubber estates; 60,300 mems.; owns 18 rubber, tea, oil-palm, cocoa and coconut plantations; cap. p.u. M$15.02m.; Pres. Y. A. B. Tun V. T. SAMBANTHAN; Chair. Enche S. S. GOVINDASAMY; Vice-Chair. Dr. C. APPA RAO; Sec. Encik K. R. SOMASUNDARAM.

Malaysian Industrial Development Finance Bhd.: 117 Jalan Ampang, P.O.B. 2110, Kuala Lumpur; f. 1960 by the Government, Banks, Insurance Companies; shareholders include International Finance Corporation, Commonwealth Development Finance Co.; provides capital for industry; marketing services and builds factories; Chair. Tan Sri ISMAIL MOHAMED ALI; Gen. Man. H. F. G. LEEMBRUGGEN.

Perbadanan Nasional Bhd. (PERNAS): 9th Floor, Bank Bumiputra Bldg., 21 Jalan Melaka, P.O.B. 493, Kuala Lumpur; f. 1969; a government sponsored company established to promote trade, property development, construction, mineral exploration, inland container transportation, mining, insurance, industrial development; auth. cap. M$500m.; cap. p.u. M$116.25m.; has eight wholly owned subsidiary companies; Chair. TENGKU Dato SHARIMAN; Man. Dir. A. RAHMAN HAMIDON.

Petronas (National Oil Company): P.O.B. 2444, Jabatan Perdana Menteri, Jalan Datuk Onn, Kuala Lumpur; f. 1974; Chair. TENGKU RAZALEIGH HAMZAH.

INDUSTRIAL AND TRADE ASSOCIATIONS

Federal Agricultural Marketing Authority: Bangunan Wisma Yan, 17-19 Jalan Selangor, Petaling Jaya; f. 1965 to supervise, co-ordinate, improve existing markets and methods of marketing of agricultural produce and seek and promote new markets and outlets for agricultural produce; Chair. Y. B. Datuk Haji ABDULLAH bin MAHMOOD, S.J.M.K., D.P.M.K., J.M.N.

Federation of Malaysian Manufacturers: 4th Floor, Oriental Plaza, Jalan Parry, Kuala Lumpur; Pres. Tengku Tan Sri MOHAMED.

Federation of Rubber Trade Associations of Malaysia: 138 Jalan Bandar, Kuala Lumpur.

Malayan Agricultural Producers' Association: Bangunan Getah Asli, Jalan Ampang, P.O.B. 1063, Kuala Lumpur; f. 1966; 412 mem. estates and 38 factories; Pres. Senator Tan Sri GAN TECK YEOW, P.S.M., J.M.N., M.P.; Dir. CHUNG SHIN CHE, K.M.N.

The Malayan Pineapple Industry Board: P.O.B. 35, Batu 5, Jalan Scudai, Johore Bahru; Suite 2303, 23rd Floor, Ocean Bldg., Collyer Quay, Singapore 1; 17/20 St. Margaret's Mansions, 53 Victoria St., London, SW1H 0EU.

Malaysian Rubber Research and Development Board: 150 Jalan Ampang, Kuala Lumpur 04-06; U.K. Office: 19 Buckingham St., London, WC2N 6EJ; undertakes research into natural rubber production and application; cost benefit analysis; classification, packaging, shipping and handling; responsible for government planning; offices in U.S.A., Australia, Federal Republic of Germany, Austria, Spain, Italy, India, Japan and New Zealand; Controller of Research Dr. B. C. SEKHAR; publs. *Journal of RRIM* (irregular), *Rubber Developments* (quarterly), *Rubber Technology* (quarterly), *Planters Bulletin* (two a month).

The Malayan Rubber Goods Manufacturers' Association: c/o Messrs. Low and Co., 63 Klyne St., Kuala Lumpur.

Malaysia Timber Industry Board: 5th Floor, Wisma Bunga Raya, Jalan Ampang, P.O.B. 887, Kuala Lumpur; to promote, regulate and control the export of timber and timber products from peninsular Malaysia; f. 1968; Chair. Tuan Haji ABDUL MAJID bin Haji MOHAMED SHAHID; Dir.-Gen. ABDUL RAZAK bin ABDUL MAJID; Marketing Dir. AHMAD NAZIREE bin MOHAMED YUSOFF; publs. *Timber Trade Review, Maskayu, Commercial Timbers.*

Rubber Trade Association of Ipoh: 2 Jalan Ali Pitchay, Ipoh.

Rubber Trade Association of Malacca: 128A Wolferston Rd., Malacca.

Rubber Trade Association of Penang: 16 Anson Rd., Penang; f. 1919; 170 mems.; Pres. SAW CHOO THENG; Sec. KOH PEN TING; Treas. TAN HOAY EAM.

Rubber Trade Association of Selangor and Pahang: 138 Jalan Bandar, Kuala Lumpur.

States of Malaya Chamber of Mines: 12 Jalan Tuanku Abdul Rahman, 1st Floor, Wisma Doshi, P.O.B. 2560, Kuala Lumpur; f. 1914; Pres. E. L. DEMPSTER; Vice-Pres. D. H. DAVIDSON; Sec.-Gen. DAVID WONG; no. of mems.: 49 companies, 171 individuals, 3 associations.

Timber Trade Federation of the Federation of Malaya: 2 Lorong Haji Taib Satu, Kuala Lumpur 02-07.

TRADE UNIONS

Malaysian Trades Union Congress: 19 Jalan Barat (First Floor), Petaling Jaya; P.O.B. 457, Kuala Lumpur; f. 1949; 103 affiliated unions, 500,000 mems.; Pres. Dr. P. P. NARAYANAN; Sec.-Gen. S. J. H. ZAIDI; publ. *Suara Buroh* (monthly).

Affiliated Unions with membership over 10,000:

National Mining Workers' Union of Malaya: Bangunan Kesatuan, Kebangsaan Pelombong-Pelombong Malaysia, 84-1B Jalan Sungei Besi, Kuala Lumpur; f. 1955; about 14,000 mems.; Pres. MUNIR bin BUYONG; Gen. Sec. ABDUL HALIM bin MAHMOOD.

National Union of Plantation Workers in Malaya: 2 Jalan Templer, P.O.B. 73, Petaling Jaya, Selangor; f. 1954; about 165,000 mems.; Gen. Sec. P. P. NARAYANAN.

Railwaymen's Union of Malaya: 258A Brickfields Rd., Kuala Lumpur; f. 1960; about 9,000 mems.; Pres. MOHAMED bin ABAS; Gen. Sec. V. BARADAN.

INDEPENDENT FEDERATIONS

Malayan Federation of Clerical and Administrative Staff Unions: Chan Wing Bldg., Mountbatten Rd., Kuala Lumpur; f. 1949; 4 affiliates.

Amalgamated Union of Employees in Government Clerical and Allied Services: 1362 Kandang Kerbau Rd., Brickfields, Kuala Lumpur; about 6,000 mems.; Pres. ABDUL HAMID bin MAT DOM; Gen. Sec. A. H. PONNIAH.

All Malayan Federation of Government Medical Employees Trade Unions: District Hospital, Ipoh; f. 1947; 9 affiliates.

Federation of Government Medical Services Unions: General Hospital, Panang Rd., Kuala Lumpur; 9 affiliates.

Federation of Indian School Teachers' Unions: 5 affiliates.

SABAH

CHAMBERS OF COMMERCE

Chinese Chamber of Commerce: P.O.B. 100, Beaufort; P.O.B. 63, Kota Kinabalu; P.O.B. 14, Keningau; P.O.B. 31, Labuan; P.O.B. 32, Lahad Datu; P.O.B. 28, Papar; P.O.B. 161, Sandakan; P.O.B. 12, Semporna; P.O.B. 164, Tawau; P.O.B. 6, Tenom; P.O.B. 37, Tuaran.

North Borneo United Chinese Chamber of Commerce: P.O.B. 156, Sandakan.

Sabah Chamber of Commerce: P.O.B. 1204, Sandakan; Pres. T. H. Wong.

Sabah United Chinese Chamber of Commerce: P.O.B. 89, Kota Kinabalu.

TRADE UNIONS AND ASSOCIATIONS

Chinese School Teachers' Association: P.O.B. 10, Tenom; f. 1956; 74 mems.; Sec. Vun Chau Choi.

Employees' Trade Union: P.O.B. 295, Sandakan; f. 1955; 40 mems.; Sec. Louis L. Quyn.

Kota Kinabalu Teachers' Association: P.O.B. 282, Kota Kinabalu; f. 1962; 258 mems.; Sec. K. J. Joseph.

Sabah Civil Service Union: P.O.B. 175, Kota Kinabalu; f 1952; 1,356 mems.; Pres. J. K. K. Voon; Sec. Stephen Wong; publ. *Union News Letter*.

Sabah Commercial Employees' Union: P.O.B. 357, Kota Kinabalu; f. 1957; 1,500 mems.; Gen. Sec. Albert Thien Thau Siong.

Sandakan Tong Kang Association: 120 Mile ½, Leila Rd., Sandakan; f. 1952; 86 mems.; Sec. Lai Ken Min.

The Incorporated Society of Planters, (North-East) Sabah Branch: P.O.B. 203, Sandakan; f. 1962; 44 mems.; Chair. A. J. Wong.

CO-OPERATIVES

Co-operatives include general purpose village stores for consumer needs and sale of produce; milling of rice and coffee; paddy storage; rubber curing and sale; buffalo rearing and grazing; sale of meat, vegetables and fish; transport; tractor ploughing; labour contracting; timber extraction; thrift and loan schemes; land purchase and land development.

SARAWAK

CHAMBERS OF COMMERCE

Chinese Chamber of Commerce: 68 Queen's Sq., Marudi, Baram, Fourth Division; 21 Court Rd., Binatang, Third Division; Daro, Third Division; 31 Limbang Bazaar, Limbang, Fifth Division; Matu, Third Division; 28 High St., Miri, Fourth Division; Sarikei, Third Division; Theatre Rd., Mukah, Third Division; 12 Old Rd., Sibu, Third Division; 32 River Rd., Sibuti; Song, Third Division; Marudi Bazaar, Baram, Fourth Division.

Kuching Chinese General Chamber of Commerce: Biang Ching Bank Ltd., Jalan Tuanku Abdul Rahman, Kuching.

South Indian Chamber of Commerce of Sarawak: 37-c India St., Kuching, First Division.

Sarawak Chamber of Commerce: c/o Turquand, Youngs and Co., Lanka Bldg., Khoo Hun Yeang St., Kuching; f. 1950; Chair. Sidi Munan; Vice-Chair. G. N. Shewring.

DEVELOPMENT ORGANIZATIONS

Borneo Development Corporation Sdn. Bhd.: shareholders: Governments of Sarawak and Sabah; Electra House, P.O.B. 342, Power St., Kuching; Sabah Office: P.O.B 721, 1st Floor, Jalan Haji Jacob, Kota Kinabalu.

Sarawak Economic Development Corporation: Electra House, P.O.B. 400, Kuching; f. 1972; statutory organization responsible for economic development in Sarawak; provides agricultural, commercial and industrial credit as well as participating in trading and industrial activities either on its own or jointly with foreign and local entrepreneurs; Chair. Encik Mohd. Amin Haji Satem; Deputy Chair. Encik Sufian Saufi.

Borneo Housing Mortgage Finance Bhd.: Registered and br. office: Electra House, Power St., Kuching; Head Office: 9 Jalan Pantai, Kota Kinabalu, Sabah; jointly owned by State Governments of Sabah and Sarawak; provides long-term loans for housing; auth. cap. M$50m.; loans and dep. M$66m.; Mortgage Securities M$113.5m. (Sept. 1975); Gen. Man. Yap Hyun Phen, B.A. (Hons.); Sec./Accountant Stephen Chan Kin Wing, B.COM., A.C.I.S., A.C.A. (N.Z.).

TRADE UNIONS

Many of the unions are small, catering for wharf labourers working in up-river areas. The largest is:

Sarawak Government Officers' Union: Batu Lintang Rd., P.O.B. 626, Kuching; f. 1946; largest civil service union in Sarawak; Pres. Encik Sarjit Singh Khaira, Vice-Pres. Encik Joseph Yong Kim Kwee; Gen. Sec Encik Sim Teck Chai; publ. *Voice*, circ. 3,000.

MAJOR INDUSTRIAL COMPANIES

The following is a selected list of some of the major industrial organizations in Malaysia:

Alcan Malaysia Berhad: Jalan 13/6, P.O.B. 47, Petaling Jaya, Selangor; manufacturers of aluminium sheet and extruded products; Chair. Mohamed Besar Burhanuddin; Man. Dir. W. G. Fergusson.

Associated Pan Malaysia Cement Sdn. Bhd.: P.O.B. 613, 468 Jalan Ipoh, Kuala Lumpur; cement manufacturers.

Bata (Malaysia) Bhd.: P.O.B 38, 3¼ Mile Kapar Rd., Klang; manufacturers, retailers, wholesalers and exporters of leather, canvas and plastic shoes.

Carrier International Sdn. Berhad: 5 Jalan Kemajuan, Petaling Jaya, Selangor; manufacturers of room air-conditioners, packaged equipment, split systems and air handling units.

Chemical Company of Malaysia Ltd.: 11th Floor, Wisma Damansara, Jalan Semantan, P.O.B. 284, Kuala Lumpur; manufactures concentrated fertilizers and a number of chemicals including chlorine, caustic soda and hydrochloric acid.

Cold Storage (Malaysia) Sdn. Bhd.: P.O.B. 401, 157 Jalan Sungei Besi, Kuala Lumpur; f. 1903; aerated drinks, cordials, sterilized flavoured milks, still drinks, sterilized milk, butter, ghee, margarine, bread, bread products, ice, ice cream, bacon, ham, sausages.

Cycle and Carriage Bintang Sdn. Bhd.: Lot 9, Road 219, Federal Highway, Petaling Jaya, Kuala Lumpur; producers of Mercedes Benz commercial and passenger vehicles.

Dunlop Malaysian Industries Bhd.: P.O.B. 66, 4 Jalan Tandang, Petaling Jaya, Selangor; f. 1961; cap. p.u. M$30.0m.; manufacturers of a complete range of Dunlop tyres and tubes, Dunlopillo and chemical products, sports goods; Man. Dir. Tunku AHMAD YAHAYA; Finance Dir. P. J. REARDON; Marketing Dir. S. R. FOSTER; Works Dir. B. A. MACMILLIAN; 1,700 employees.

Esso Malaysia Bhd.: Chartered Bank Bldg., 2 Jalan Ampang, P.O.B. 601, Kuala Lumpur; refiners and marketers of all classes of petroleum products.

Far East Oxygen & Acetylene Co.: 10 Klang Rd., Kuala Lumpur; manufacture gases for industrial and medical purposes, welding and cutting equipment, sports equipment and fire extinguishers.

Fraser & Neave (Malaya) Sdn. Bhd.: P.O.B. 55, Jalan Foss, Kuala Lumpur; manufacturers of soft drinks and mineral waters.

Glaxo Malaysia Sdn. Bhd.: P.O.B. 11, Petaling Jaya, Selangor; manufacturers of pharmaceuticals, specialized foods and antibiotic preparations.

Goodyear Malaysia Bhd.: P.O.B. 49, Sungei Renggam, Shah Alam, Selangor; manufacturers of tyres, tubes and industrial rubber products.

Guinness Malaysia Bhd.: P.O.B. 144, Petaling Jaya; cap. p.u. M$24m.; manufacturers of Guinness Stout and Gold Harp Lager; Man. Dir. E. S. PALMER.

Hargill Engineering Sdn. Bhd.: Syah Alam Industrial Estate, P.O.B. 50, Sungei Renggam, Selangor; f. 1968; subsidiary of Syarikat Harper Gilfillan Bhd.; manufactures products for mining, transport, the oil industry; Man. Dir. J. B. WOODHOUSE; Sales Dir. CHAN HENG; 350 employees.

Hume Industries (Malaysia) Bhd.: P.O.B. 21, Petaling Jaya, Selangor; manufacturers of asbestos cement products, steel and concrete pipes, prestressed concrete beams and piles.

ICI Paints (Malaysia) Sdn. Bhd.: Jalan 205, Petaling Jaya; manufacturers of a variety of paints.

Lam Soon Oil & Soap Mfg. Sdn. Bhd.: P.O.B. 8, Jalan 205, Petaling Jaya, Selangor; manufacturers of soap, detergents, cooking oil and margarine, copra cakes, crude glycerine, coconut oil, etc.

Lever Brothers (Malaysia) Sdn. Bhd.: Wisma Damansara, P.S. 1015, Kuala Lumpur; manufacturers of soaps, detergents, edible products and toilet preparations.

Malayan Breweries (Malaya) Sdn. Bhd.: Jalan Foss, P.O.B. 55, Kuala Lumpur; manufacturers of beer and stout.

Malayan Cables Bhd.: 10 Jalan Tandang, Petaling Jaya; f. 1957; cap. p.u. M$8.6m.; manufactures a wide range of cables; Dir./Gen. Man. G. H. DUNN; Man. LEE SING KUAN; 350 employees (Feb. 1976).

Malayan Oxygen Sdn. Bhd.: 13 Jalan 222, Petaling Jaya, Selangor; manufacture oxygen, acetylene, nitrogen for industrial and medical purposes.

Malayan Tobacco Co. Bhd.: 178-3 Jalan Sungai Besi, Kuala Lumpur; cigarette manufacturers.

The Metal Box Company of Malaysia Ltd.: P.O.B. 6, Federal Highway, Petaling Jaya, Selangor; manufacturers of plain, lacquered and decorated cans and tin boxes, screw caps, aluminium tubes, polythene, etc.

Pan-Malaysia Cement Works Bhd.: 468-11, D. & E. Jalan Ipoh, P.O.B. 405, Kuala Lumpur; investment holding company.

Paper Products (Malaya) Ltd.: 135, 3½ Ms. Jalan Tampoi, Johore Bahru; manufacturers of paper bags, tissue paper, etc.

PAR Paints Malaysia Sdn. Bhd.: 4, Road 250, P.O.B. 1, Petaling Jaya; paint manufacturers.

Pillar Naco (M) Sdn. Bhd.: 5 Jalan Bersaty, Petaling Jaya; manufacturers of metal window frames, sliding doors, sunscreens etc.

Rothmans of Pall Mall (Malaysia) Bhd.: Virginia Park, Jalan University, Petaling Jaya, Selangor; cigarette manufacturers.

Shell Refining Company (Fed. of Malaysia) Bhd.: Port Dickson, Negri Sembilan; refiners of all classes of petroleum products.

Sissons Paints (East) Sdn. Bhd.: P.O.B. 14, 2 Jalan Kemajuan, Petaling Jaya; manufacture a variety of paints.

Tamco Electrical Engineering Co. (M) Sdn. Bhd.: P.O.B. 156, Petaling Jaya, Selangor; f. 1965; cap. p.u. M$2.4m.; Chair. and Chief Exec. M. M. CHANTLER; 300 employees.

Tasek Cement Bhd.: Tasek Industrial Estate, P.O.B. 254, Ipoh; cement manufacturers.

Terco (Malaya) Sdn. Bhd.: 4 Jalan 217, P.O.B. 36, Petaling Jaya; manufacturers of retreaded tyres.

Tropical Veneer Co. Bhd.: UMBC Bldg., 1st Floor, Jalan Sulaiman, Kuala Lumpur; f. 1969; cap. p.u. M$5.5m.; manufacturers and exporters of various species of wood; Chair. Tan Sri GAN TECK YEOW; Man. Dir. ONG CHIN KUN, S.M.T.; 591 employees (Sept. 1973).

United Engineers (M) Sdn. Bhd.: P.O.B. 115, Sungei Besi Rd., Kuala Lumpur; iron, steel and non-ferrous founders; mechanical, electrical, civil, structural and telecommunication engineers for contract and project schemes.

Wilkinson Process Rubber Co. Ltd.: Batu Caves, Sengalor; rubber processors.

Linatex Far East Division: Suppliers of linatex lined equipment, abrasion and corrosion resistant lining.

TRANSPORT

RAILWAYS

PENINSULAR MALAYSIA

Malayan Railway Administration: P.O.B. No. 1, Kuala Lumpur; Gen. Man. Dato ISHAK bin TADIN, D.P.C.M.

The main line, 787 km. long, follows the west coast and extends from Singapore in the south to Butterworth (opposite Penang Island) to the north.

From Bukit Mertajam, close to Butterworth, the line branches off to the Thai border at Padang Besar where connection is made with the State Railway of Thailand.

The East Coast Line, 526 km. long, runs from Gemas to Tumpat (near Kota Bahru). A 21-km. branch line from Pasir Mas, which is 27 km. south of Tumpat, connects with the State Railway of Thailand at the border station of Sungei Golok.

Branch lines serve railway-operated ports at Port Dickson and Teluk Anson as well as Port Klang and Jurong (Singapore).

Diesel rail car services are operated between Butterworth and Kuala Lumpur. In addition to the normal express services between Kuala Lumpur and Singapore, there is a rapid diesel rail car service. Total distance (1974): 1,659 km.

SABAH

Sabah State Railways: Kota Kinabalu; the length of the railway is 155 km. (1974). The line is of metre gauge and runs from Kota Kinabalu to Melalap serving part of the west coast and the interior; diesel and steam trains are used; Gen. Man. WONG LEN HIN, D.I.P.C.E., GRAD.I.E.

ROADS

In 1972 there were 17,867 kilometres of roads in Peninsular Malaysia.

Automobile Association of Malaysia: P.O.B. 34, Petaling Jaya, Selangor; f. 1932; mems. 12,500 (1974); Chair. Y. A. M. TUNKU SHAHABUDDIN, D.K.; Vice-Chair. P. T. OON; Sec.-Gen. Mrs. K. S. LIM; publs. *A.A.M. News* (monthly), *Handbook* (every 18 months).

SABAH

The Public Works Department has constructed and maintained a network of trunk, district and local roads comprising 299 miles of bitumen, 922 miles of metal (gravel) and 371 miles of earth surface making a total of 1,592 miles up to 1968.

SARAWAK

The State government maintains about 140 miles of hard-surfaced roads, 370 miles of gravelled and 50 miles of earth roads. In addition local authorities maintained some 340 miles of roads.

SHIPPING

PENINSULAR MALAYSIA

The principal ports, which have undergone considerable extension, are Penang, Port Klang, Dungun, Telow Anson, Malacca and Port Dickson. A major port expansion programme, costing M$120 was launched under the second Five-Year Plan (1971–75). It included the reconstruction of the two main ports of Sabah–Kota Kinabalu and of Kuching and Sibu ports in Sarawak.

Malaysian International Shipping Corporation Berhad (*National Shipping Line of Malaysia*): 14th and 15th Floors, Fitzpatrick's Bldg., Jalan Raja Chulan, P.O.B. 371, Kuala Lumpur; f. 1968; fleet of 16 vessels; 3 palm oil carriers on order; regular sailings between Far East and Europe; Chair. KUOK HOCK NIEN; Gen. Man. LESLIE EU; Sec. MAH HON CHOON.

Sharikat Perkapalan Kris Sdn. Bhd. (*The Kris Shipping Company of Malaysia*): Straits Trading Bldg., Kuala Lumpur; fleet of 10 tankers and cargo vessels; services from Malaysia to Thailand; Dirs. R. E. L. WINGATE, M.B.E., GAN TECK YEOW, H. W. LADE, G. H. POSTLETHWAITE; Sec. ABDUL RAHIM ISMAIL.

SABAH

The chief ports are Labuan, Sandakan, Kota Kinabalu, Kudat, Tawau, Sempoma and Lahad Datu. The operation of all ports, except Labuan, is carried out by the Sabah Ports Authority. The Authority also controls the minor port of Kunak which has facilities for loading palm oil in bulk to ocean carriers and a small landing jetty for general cargo from local craft. A three year M$78 million port development programme began in July 1972 covering the ports of Kota Kinabalu and Sandakan.

There are many shipping lines using the ports and the main lines listed below run regular services to and from the State. Local services are maintained by a fleet of coastal steamers and numerous small craft to all ports in Sabah, Brunei and Sarawak.

Director of Marine: Capt. H. M. STANFIELD, Labuan.

Australian West Pacific Lines: From Japanese and Australian ports.

Ben Line: Monthly services to United Kingdom and Europe.

Blue Funnel Line: Monthly services to United Kingdom and Europe.

Iino Line: Monthly services between Japan and West Australia.

Indo-China Steam Navigation Co.: Frequent sailings from East Coast ports to Japan and from Hong Kong.

Kinabalangan/Man Tung Shipping Co.: From Japan, Taiwan and Hong Kong to Sabah ports.

Netherlands Royal Dutch Mail: From United Kingdom and other European ports.

Nissho Line: Service between Sabah, Brunei and Japan.

Norwegian Asia Line: A fortnightly service to Sabah ports from Hong Kong, Japan and Shanghai; also a three-weekly service from Bangkok.

Pacific International Line: From Singapore and West Malaysian ports.

Royal Inter-Ocean Line: From Australian, Indonesian and Thai ports.

Royal Rotterdam Lloyd: From United Kingdom and other European ports.

Shell Tankers Ltd.: West Malaysia, Singapore, Sarawak and Sabah ports with bulk petroleum.

Straits Steamship Co.: Weekly cargo, passenger and mail service from Singapore; agents Harrisons and Crosfield (Sabah) Ltd., Prince Philip Drive, P.O.B. 22, Kota Kinabalu.

SARAWAK

Under the Second Five-Year Plan, work has started on a new port at Pending Point, near Kuching. Port facilities at Sibu will be extended by 1,000 feet.

Ben Line: Sarawak Agents: C.T.C. Shipping Agencies Sdn. Bhd., Sibu and Sarikei; direct sailings U.K./Tanjong Mani, Sarawak.

Blue Funnel and Glen Line: Sarawak Agent: The Borneo Co. (Malaysia), Sendirian Berhad, Kuching and Sibu; direct sailings from Rejang, Sarawak to U.K.

"K" Line: Sarawak Agent: Guthrie Boustead Shipping Agencies Ltd.; regular cargo service: Western Australia/Tanjong Mani, Sarawak.

Norwegian Asia Line: Agents Harper Gilfillan (Borneo) Sdn. Bhd.; direct service Japan–Hong Kong–Sabah–Sarawak, carrying cargo.

Sarawak Steamship Co. Bhd.: 14 Carpenter St., P.O.B. 131, Kuching, Sarawak; operates weekly services to and from Singapore and Port Klang; local shipping company, shipping agents and travel agents.

Polish Ocean Lines: Sarawak Agent: Borneo United Sawmills Sdn. Bhd.; Sibu and Kuching; Australian services: Sydney, Melbourne, Adelaide and Brisbane.

CIVIL AVIATION

Malaysia has five international airports at Kuala Lumpur, Kota Kinabalu, Penang, Johore Bahru and Kuching. In addition there are airports catering for domestic services at Alor Star, Ipoh, Kota Bahru, Kota Trengganu, Kuantan, Malacca and Johore Bahru, in Peninsular Malaysia, Sibu and Miri in Sarawak and Sandakan, Tawau and Labuan in Sabah. There are also numerous smaller airstrips all over Malaysia.

Under the Third Malaysia Plan funds will be allocated for the further development of the following airports to cater for heavier air traffic and larger aircraft: Penang, Kota Kinabalu, Kuching, Kota Bahru, Johore Bahru, Miri and Sandakan.

Malaysian Airline System (MAS) Bhd.: UMBC Bldg., 4 Jalan Sulaiman, Kuala Lumpur; commenced operations in October 1972 as the Malaysian successor to the Malaysia Singapore Airlines (MSA); Chair. Raja Tan Sri MOHAR bin Raja BADIOZAMAN; Gen. Man. SAW HUAT LYE; operates a fleet of 3 Boeing 707, 9 Boeing 737, 10 F.27 and 4 BN-2 to more than 50 international and domestic destinations. Its network consists of flights from Kuala Lumpur to London, Madras, Sydney, Jakarta, Tokyo, Taipei, Hong Kong, Bangkok, Haadyai, Manila, Singapore, Medan, Melbourne and Kuwait.

FOREIGN AIRLINES

The following foreign airlines serve Malaysia: Aeroflot, Air Ceylon, Air India, British Airways, Cathay Pacific Airways, China Airlines, ČSA, Garuda Indonesia Airways, JAL, KLM, PIA, Qantas, Sabena, Singapore Airlines, SAS, Thai International.

TOURISM

PENINSULAR MALAYSIA

Tourist Development Corporation of Malaysia: Ministry of Trade and Industry, P.O.B. 328, Kuala Lumpur; f. 1972; responsible for the co-ordination of activities relating to tourism; formulating recommendations thereon and for promoting tourism overseas; overseas information centres in London, San Francisco, Sydney, Tokyo, Bangkok and Singapore; Chair. Tan Sri PHILIP KUOK.

SABAH

Sabah Tourist Association: P.O.B. 946, Kota Kinabalu; f. 1962; 70 mems.; semi-governmental promotion organization; Chair. SYED KECHIK; Exec. Sec. GAN PO TIAU; publs. *Sabah Tourist Guide* and others.

SARAWAK

Sarawak Tourist Association: Jalan Tun Haji Openg, P.O.B. 887, Kuching.

CULTURAL ORGANIZATIONS

Arts Council of Malaysia: P.O.B. 630, Kuala Lumpur; promotes the accessibility, improvement and utilization of the arts in Malaysia; Pres. Tan Sri M. GHAZALI bin SHAFIE; Chair. KINGTON LOO.

Liberal Arts Society of Malaysia: 10th Floor, Kwong Yik Bank Bldg., Jalan Bandar, Kuala Lumpur; non-profit cultural society for music, drama, etc.; Pres. VINCENT YONG; Sec. ABRAHAM SAMUEL.

ATOMIC ENERGY

In early 1973, the Minister for Technology, Research and Local Government, Datuk ONG KEE HUI announced a M$2 million scheme to finance a nuclear reactor project. The reactor will be used solely for medical, industrial and agricultural research. Several overseas countries have promised assistance.

DEFENCE

Armed Forces (1975): Total strength 61,100; army 51,000, navy 4,800, air force 5,300; military service is voluntary. Paramilitary forces comprise Police Field Force of 15,000; local Defence Corps; Border Scouts about 60,000.

Equipment: The army and navy have mainly British equipment while the air force has Australian fighter-Bombers and French helicopters. Under an agreement concluded in 1974 the U.S.A. will supply 6 C-130H transport aircraft to Malaysia for delivery in 1976.

Defence Budget: The budget for 1975 was M$1,018.4 million (U.S. $445 million).

CHIEFS OF STAFF

Chief of the Armed Forces Staff: Gen. Datuk IBRAHIM bin ISMAIL, D.P.M.J., P.D.K., J.M.N., P.I.S.

Army: Gen. Ungku NAZARUDDIN bin Ungku MOHAMED, J.M.N., P.J.K.

Navy: Commodore Datuk K. THANABALASINGAM, D.P.M.J., G.M.N., S.M.J.

Air Force: Air Commodore Datuk SULAIMAN bin SUJAK, D.P.M.S., J.M.N.

EDUCATION

The first schools were established during the colonial period in Malaysia by public-spirited individuals, charitable organizations and religious missions; these have left their mark on the present pattern of education. Under the 1961 Education Act a National Education Advisory Board is responsible for advising the Minister on all matters pertaining to education.

The education scheme provides nine years of free and compulsory education between the ages of 6 and 15. In 1970 the total enrolment in Malaysian schools was 1,800,000. The Government recognizes two types of schooling: assisted schools, and private schools, which receive no financial aid from the Government and are allowed to operate provided they observe the statutory requirements applicable to assisted schools.

The Government spends over 20 per cent of the total annual budget on education. No school fees are charged in assisted primary schools or in any of the Malay-medium secondary schools, but in other assisted secondary schools fees of $5 a month are charged per pupil, though up to 10 per cent may receive free places. Scholarships are awarded at all levels and there are many scholarship holders studying at universities and other institutes of higher education at home and abroad.

Primary Education

Primary education is provided in Malay, English, Chinese and Tamil; this is intended to preserve the four main cultures of Malaysia and at the same time to establish a national system of education in which the national language gradually becomes the main medium of instruction. As stated in the 1961 Education Act, the Government aimed to make Malay the sole official language ten years after independence. At present half the total of the primary school enrolment is in national schools where Malay is used and the other half in national-type primary schools where English, Tamil or Chinese are used. In 1970 *Bahasa Malaysia*, the national language, was introduced in all national schools. By 1971 all Standard One pupils in national-type English primary schools were using the national language in all subject classes. By 1980 it is expected that the national language will be in use in all secondary schools. Common content syllabuses are used in all schools.

A place in primary school is now assured to every child from the age of 6 onwards, and parents are free to choose the language medium. The total primary school enrolment in 1970 was 1,421,469 and an additional 5,890 classrooms were built for them. In 1970 there were 4,365 primary schools. The primary school course lasts for six years.

Secondary Education

With the abolition of the Malaysian secondary school entrance examination in 1964 children automatically proceed from primary to secondary school to begin a three-year course of comprehensive education culminating in the Lower Certificate of Education examination. This three-year comprehensive course was introduced in the lower classes of secondary schools at the time of the extension of the school-leaving age from 12 to 15, and enables pupils to select the type of further education to which they are most suited, either academic, technical or vocational. Selected pupils in the fifth year of the secondary course are chosen to sit for the sixth-form entrance examination and the successful candidates are then admitted to a two-year course leading to the Higher Certificate of Education, which is a qualifying examination for university entrance. There has been a considerable increase since 1960 in the number of schools. In that year there were only 209; since then the number has increased to 735 by 1970. There has also been a correspondingly large increase in the number of trained teachers over the last decade, *i.e.* from 4,390 to 18,368 in 1970.

Secondary Vocational Schools provide a three-year course and are open to children who have completed the three-year secondary course. Pupils are selected on the results of the Lower Certificate of Education and are taught electrical, mechanical and building trades.

Secondary Technical Schools: Pupils are selected on the basis of the Lower Certificate of Education. The school provides an initial technical education which will enable them to take up a technical career.

Higher Education

The University of Malaya was opened in 1959 and officially established under the University of Malaya Act, 1961. At present there are nine faculties: Arts, Science, Economics and Administration, Engineering, Agriculture, Dentistry, Medicine, Law and Education, with the largest proportion of students taking Arts subjects. The University has undergone a period of extensive development since its opening in all faculties and the number of students is now 8,517 (1974). There are four other universities including the Malay Medium National University of Malaysia.

Teacher Training: There are five residential secondary Teacher Training Colleges in West Malaysia, three in Sarawak and two in Sabah. The basic course lasts two years and the colleges together produce 1,000 trained teachers annually. Owing to the shortage of trained teachers 22 regional training centres were set up where teachers taught part-time and studied. In 1965 there were two non-residential day training colleges, three residential colleges and 11 non-residential day training centres for the training of primary school teachers. The training lasts from two to three years depending on the type of academic qualification.

The number of graduate teachers required in West Malaysia is 2,686 but only 996 were available in 1974; the Government has set a target to train 350 graduate teachers a year to overcome this shortage.

Further Education

The Government provides further education for adults in the form of evening classes.

SABAH AND SARAWAK

Both states now come under the Federal Ministry of Education and are subject to central government financial controls, but still retain a certain degree of control over policy and administration.

Sabah

The policy at present is to provide a place at school for every child of primary school age. In 1975 there were 780 primary schools with an enrolment of 125,592 pupils. There were 88 secondary schools with an enrolment of 43,257 pupils.

Sarawak

Primary schools are run by local authorities, missionary bodies and a large group by Chinese Committees. Apart from the latter that employ Mandarin, all primary schools use English as the language medium. The primary school course, which is not compulsory, lasts six years starting at the age of 6. In 1974 there were 1,321 schools with 165,484 pupils at primary level and 50,202 pupils at secondary level. The intake of pupils at secondary level is somewhat limited at the moment, mainly for financial reasons and because of a shortage of qualified staff. About 30 per cent of primary school pupils selected on the basis of an entrance examination are admitted to Government and aided schools, with English as the teaching medium. The course lasts three years after which an examination selects pupils for higher secondary schools.

UNIVERSITIES

Universiti Kebangsaan Malaysia (*National University of Malaysia*): P.O.B. 1124, Jalan Pantai Baru, Kuala Lumpur; f. 1970; *c.* 100 teachers, *c.* 1,500 students.

University of Malaya: Pantai Valley, Kuala Lumpur; f. 1962; *c.* 760 teachers, *c.* 8,500 students.

Universiti Sains Malaysia (*University of Science*): Minden, Penang; f. 1969; 320 teachers, *c.* 2,500 students.

Universiti Pertanian Malaysia (*University of Agriculture*): Serdang, Selangor; f. 1973; *c.* 170 teachers, *c.* 2,100 students.

National Institute of Technology: Gurney Rd., Kuala Lumpur; f. 1954, university status 1972; 2,000 students.

BIBLIOGRAPHY

GENERAL

ALLEN, R. Malaysia, Prospect and Retrospect (Oxford University Press, London, 1968).

BEGBIE, P. J. The Malayan Peninsula (Oxford University Press, London, 1967).

HARRISON, T. The Malays of South-West Sarawak before Malaysia: a socio-ecological survey (Macmillan, London, 1970).

HO, R. Environment, Man and Development in Malaya (Kuala Lumpur, 1962).

JONES, L. W. The Population of Borneo: a study of the peoples of Sarawak, Sabah and Brunei (Athlone Press, London, 1966).

MCKIE, R. Malaysia in Focus (Angus and Robertson, Sydney, 1963).

PURCELL, V. Malaysia (Thames and Hudson, London, 1965).

ROBEQUAIN, C. Malaya, Indonesia, Borneo and the Philippines (Longmans, London, 1954).

RYAN, N. J. The Cultural Heritage of Malaya (Longman Malaysia, Kuala Lumpur, 1971).

TREGONNING, K. G. North Borneo (H.M.S.O., London, 1960).

WANG, G. Malaysia—A Survey (Pall Mall Press, New York and London, 1964).

HISTORY

BASTIN, J., and WINKS, R. W. (Editors). Malaysia—Selected Historical Readings (Oxford University Press, London, 1967).

BLYTHE, W. The Impact of Chinese Secret Societies in Malaya: a historical study (Oxford University Press, London, 1969).

CLUTTERBUCK, R. The Long, Long War—The Emergency in Malaysia 1948–60 (Cassell, London, 1966).

COUPLAND, R. Raffles of Singapore (Oxford University Press, London, 1946).

COWAN, C. D. Nineteenth Century Malaya (Oxford University Press, London, 1961).

GULLICK, J. M. Malaysia and its Neighbours (Routledge & Kegan Paul, London, 1967).
Malaya (Benn, London, 1963).
Malaysia (Benn, London, 1969).

HAHN, EMILY. James Brooke of Sarawak (Arthur Barker, London, 1953).

KENNEDY, J. A. History of Malaya 1400–1959 (Macmillan, London, 1962).

MILLER, H. The Story of Malaysia (Faber & Faber, London, 1967).

MILLS, L. A. British Malaya 1824–1967 (Oxford University Press, London, 1968).

PARKINSON, C. N. A Short History of Malaya (Singapore, 1954).
British Intervention in Malaya (University of Malaya Press, Kuala Lumpur, 1960).

PRINGLE, R. Rajah and Rebels: the Iban of Sarawak under Brooke rule 1841–1941 (Macmillan, London, 1971).

PURCELL, V. The Chinese in Malaya (Oxford University Press, Oxford, 1948).

ROBINSON, J. B. Transformation in Malaya (Secker and Warburg, London, 1956).

RUNCIMAN, Sir STEVEN. The White Rajahs (Cambridge University Press, 1960).

ROFF, W. The Origins of Malay Nationalism (Yale University Press, 1967).

SIMANDJUNTAK, B. Malayan Federalism 1945–63 (Oxford University Press, Kuala Lumpur, 1969).

WINSTEDT, Sir RICHARD O. Malaya and its History (Hutchinson, London, 1949).

WURTZBURG, C. E. Raffles of the Eastern Isles (Hodder and Stoughton, London, 1954).

YIP, Y. H. The Development of the Tin Industry of Malaya (University of Malaya Press, Kuala Lumpur, 1969).

ECONOMICS AND POLITICS

ALLEN, G. C., and DONNITHORNE, A. G. Western Enterprise in Indonesia and Malaya (Allen and Unwin, London, 1957).

ARIFF, M. O. The Philippines Claim to Sabah (Oxford University Press, Singapore, 1970).

CHOU, K. R. Studies on Savings and Investment in Malaya (Academic Publications, Hong Kong, 1966).

GOH, C. T. The May thirteenth incident and democracy in Malaysia (Oxford University Press, Kuala Lumpur, 1971).

GOULD, J. W. The United States and Malaysia (Harvard University Press, Cambridge, 1969).

KANAPATHY, V. The Malaysian Economy: Problems and Prospects (Asia Pacific Press, Singapore, 1970).

LEE, H. L. Household Saving in West Malaysia and the Problem of Financing Economic Development (Faculty of Economics and Administration, University of Malaya, Kuala Lumpur, 1971).

LIM, C. Y. Economic Development of Modern Malaya (Oxford University Press, Kuala Lumpur, 1967).

LOH, F. S. P. The Malay State 1877–1895; Political Change and Social Policy (Oxford University Press, Singapore, 1969).

MALAYSIA: ECONOMIC PLANNING UNIT. Second Malaysia Plan 1971–1975 (Government Printer, Kuala Lumpur, 1971).

MILNE, R. S. Government and Politics in Malaysia (Houghton Mifflin, Boston, 1967).

OOI, JIN-BEE. Land, People and Economy in Malaya (Longmans, London, 1963).

PURCELL, V. The Chinese in Malaya (Oxford University Press, Kuala Lumpur, 1967).

SCOTT, J. C. Political Ideology in Malaysia: Reality and the Beliefs of an Elite (University of Malaya Press, Kuala Lumpur, 1968).

The Philippines

PHYSICAL AND SOCIAL GEOGRAPHY

C. A. Fisher

The combined surface area of the 7,100 islands which make up the Philippines amounts to 300,000 square kilometres (115,831 square miles). With the intervening seas, most of which rank as Philippines territorial waters, the country extends over a considerably larger area, from above 18° N. to below 6° N. latitude, lying between the South China Sea and the Pacific Ocean.

Of its multitudinous islands some 880 are inhabited and 462 have an area of one square mile (2.6 square kilometres) or more, though the two largest, namely Luzon in the north (104,688 square kilometres (40,420 square miles) and Mindanao in the south 94,630 square kilometres (36,537 square miles), account for 66.4 per cent of its territory, and this figure is raised to 92.3 per cent if the next nine largest (Samar, Negros, Palawan, Panay, Mindoro, Leyte, Cebu, Boho and Masbate) are also included.

PHYSICAL FEATURES

Structurally, the Philippines forms part of the vast series of island arcs which fringe the East Asian mainland and also include Japan, the Ryukyus and Taiwan to the north, and extend into Sulawesi, Irian and other Indonesian islands to the south. Two main and roughly parallel lines of Tertiary folding run roughly N.–S. through Luzon, swing approximately N.W.–S.E. through the smaller islands surrounding the Sabayan, Visayan and Mindoro seas, and resume a N.–S. trend in Mindanao. In addition to these two, a less pronounced N.E.–S.W. pair extend from the central Philippines through Panay and the smaller islands of the Sulu archipelago, ultimately linking up with the similar Tertiary structures of the north-eastern tip of Sabah in East Malaysia.

These major lines of folding largely determine the broad pattern of relief throughout the country. Over most of the islands Tertiary sediments and Tertiary-Quaternary eruptives predominate, and over a dozen major volcanoes are still in the active stage. Nearly all the larger islands have interior mountain ranges, attaining heights typically of 1,200–2,400 metres (4,000–8,000 ft.), but apart from narrow strips of coastal plain few have any extensive lowlands. This is the greatest natural liability from which the country suffers, and it is largely because the central plain of Luzon represents such a significant exception that this island has assumed the dominant role in the life of the country as a whole.

CLIMATE

Because of its mountainous character and its alignment athwart the S.W. monsoon and the N.E. trade winds, the Philippines shows considerable regional variation in both the total amount and the seasonal incidence of rainfall. Thus, in general, the western side of the country gets most of its rain during the period of the S.W. monsoon (late June–late September) whereas on most of the eastern side the wettest period of the year is from November to March when the influence of the N.E. trades is at its greatest, though here, in contrast to the west, there is no true dry season. These differences can be seen by comparing Manila (on the west side of Luzon) which, out of an annual total of 210 cm. (82 in.), receives 110 cm. (47 in.) in July–September and only 15 cm. (6 in.) in December–April, with Surigao (in the north-east of Mindanao) which receives an annual total of 178 cm. (140 in.), 225 cm. (88 in.) of it between November and March inclusive, but with no monthly total falling below the August figure of 12 cm. (4.8 in.) In some sheltered valleys, however, totals may be as low as 102 cm. (40 in.) which, in association with mean annual sea-level temperatures rarely much below 26.7°C. (80°F.) anywhere in the country, makes farming distinctly precarious. On the other hand, a different kind of climatic hazard affects many of the more exposed parts of the country as a result of their exposure to typhoons, which are commonest in the later months of the year, and tend to be most severe in eastern Luzon and Samar.

NATURAL RESOURCES

As has already been implied, the central lowlands of Luzon provide by far the best major food-producing region within the country, and although many of the smaller lowlands are also intensively cultivated, their soils are in most cases of only average fertility and the only substantial areas of lowland offering scope for any important extension of cultivation are in the remote and nearly equatorial island of Mindanao, which has been aptly described as the frontier of the Philippines.

While, as elsewhere in South-East Asia, rice forms the most important single item in the country's agricultural system, its predominance is less marked than in other parts of the region and indeed in several of the islands, partly because of their relatively low rainfall, and partly because of the close cultural link with Latin America, maize is the leading food crop. So far as export crops are concerned the emphasis has hitherto been mainly on sugar, coconuts and, to a lesser extent, abaca (Manila hemp) and tobacco.

Apart from its agricultural potential the country's main natural resources lie in its extensive reserves of timber, particularly good quality hardwoods, and a fairly wide range of metallic minerals, including copper, gold, chromite, iron, and nickel. While none of these has ever yielded any great output, the potentialities, at least of the lateritic iron ores, appear to be considerable.

POPULATION AND CULTURE

With an estimated population of 42,800,000 in 1976, the Philippines had an average density of over 140 to the square kilometre (370 to the square mile), which was nearly double the South-East Asian average and exceeded only by those of North Viet-Nam and Singapore. The shortage of lowland means that much the greater part of the population is concentrated in a relatively small area and, particularly in the lowlands of central Luzon, the resultant pressure is now a serious problem and likely to become increasingly severe owing to the exceptionally high rate of population growth.

Despite the existence of several regional languages spoken by the lowland Filipinos, the latter, who form the great majority of the population, share a basically common culture which is much influenced by Catholicism. In recent decades considerable progress has been made in developing Tagalog, the language of central Luzon, as a national language (Pilipino) though, particularly among the largely mestizo *élite* elements, English is widely used.

Other than the Christian Filipinos, the only large indigenous group comprises the Muslim Moros inhabiting the southern and southwestern peripheries of the country, who form about 5 per cent of the total population. But there are also several much smaller communities of animist hill peoples, mainly in the remoter parts of Luzon and Mindanao, who together form perhaps 6 per cent of the total. By comparison with other parts of South-East Asia, the Chinese population in the Philippines is very small, numbering some 400,000, or about 1.25 per cent.

Largely because of its long history of colonial rule the Philippines now has a widespread scatter of small administrative and market towns. The country's largest town is Manila. At the 1975 census Manila's population was 1,454,352, while the nearby Quezon City, then the country's capital, had 960,341 inhabitants. A local government reform later that year created a new administrative area, Metropolitan Manila, with a population of about 4.5 million (including Quezon). This was designated the national capital in June 1976. Only three other towns, Davao (482,233), Cebu (408,173) and Caloocan (393,251), had populations over 300,000 at the 1975 census.

HISTORY

Renato Constantino

The Filipino people have had the misfortune of being "liberated" four times during their entire history.

First came the Spaniards who "liberated" them from the "enslavement of the devil", next came the Americans who "liberated" them from Spanish oppression, then the Japanese who "liberated" them from American imperialism, then the Americans again who "liberated" them from the Japanese. After every "liberation" the Filipinos found their country occupied by foreign "benefactors".

Philippine history, therefore, is fundamentally the reaction of the Filipinos to colonial policies and their resistance to colonial oppression.

PRE-COLONIAL SOCIETIES

The autonomous communities that the Spanish *conquistadores* encountered in the sixteenth century were communities in transition from a primitive communal state to some form of Asiatic feudalism. The social unit was the *barangay*. While there were some large *barangays* most were small, scattered communities of 100 to 500 persons. They were kinship groups, with only informal contacts with other villages.

Primitive economic units with a system of subsistence agriculture, the *barangays* had no class structure although there were social stratifications. Such stratifications were more marked in the more advanced Muslim communities of the south. *Barangay* chiefs, freemen and "debt peons" were the main strata, but this stratification was not rigid, for chiefs could be deposed, freemen could be reduced to dependence and "debt peons" became freemen after paying their debts.

Pre-Spanish settlements had houses of renewable materials, usually aligned along a riverbank or on a shore. Travel was principally by water; there were no roads nor wheeled vehicles. Agriculture was the principal occupation. There was no separate artisan class. Syllabic writing was confined to the more advanced coastal communities and was used for sending messages rather than for recording purposes. There were no houses of stone and no public buildings. Trade between communities and with Muslim and Chinese traders was on the whole accidental and irregular. The fairly low level of political and social organization made it easy for the Spaniards to conquer the native population and impose their own culture and values.

SPANISH COLONIALISM

Spanish intrusion into the islands, which would later be named Filipinas in honour of Felipe II, began in 1521, when Ferdinand Magellan attempted unsuccessfully to implant Spanish sovereignty. This Spanish adventure was in implementation of the mercantilist policies of Spain which like its rival, Portugal, had embarked on a search for colonies to extract gold and to control the spice trade.

It was not until 1565 that another expedition, headed by Miguel López de Legazpi, arrived from Mexico and finally established a foothold in Manila on the island of Luzon. Spanish control was rapidly extended over the entire country, with the exception of Muslim territory in Mindanao and Sulu and certain mountain communities of Northern Luzon which successfully resisted domination to the end of Spanish rule.

Two characteristics of the colonial power had profound effects on the colony: first, the fact that Spain at the time was in the mercantilist stage of capitalist development and, second, the theocratic character of the Spanish state.

Disappointed in their mercantilist objective of finding rich deposits of gold and silver and a fortune in spices, the Spaniards adopted other means of extracting wealth from their colony. They imposed tributes, conscripted labour, levied on communities assessments of rice and other produce for the needs of the government and the army. Thousands of young men were impressed into the Spanish navy and army. Other thousands were forcibly taken far away from their homes to fell logs for the building of ships or to work in the shipyards.

Until the middle of the eighteenth century, Spanish colonialism was mainly extractive. The economic development of the country was given little importance. Agriculture was neglected. Instead, the main economic activity of the Spanish community was the profitable galleon trade. But, since Manila was merely a transhipment port through which Chinese goods were shipped to Mexico and Mexican silver flowed to the Chinese coast, the galleon trade had practically no effect on the native economy. No Philippine products were developed for export.

Church and State

Although the economy was largely stagnant, profound changes were being effected in the lives of the people, mainly by the Church. The theocratic nature of the Spanish state gave the religious a pre-eminent position in colonial administration. In fact, to bring the light of Christianity to the heathen was solemnly declared to be the primary motivation for Spanish colonization.

Because of the union of church and state and the small number of Spanish colonial officials, the friars from the start took on administrative duties that eventually made them an important part of the exploitative colonial establishment. The friars almost single-handedly effected the resettlement of the scattered *barangays* into more compact and therefore more easily controlled communities, with the church as the physical and psychological centre. Since in most of the smaller towns the friar was the only Spaniard, he assumed so many administrative functions that he had a say in almost every aspect of community life.

To their spiritual and administrative control over the people the friars soon added a third factor: economic power. The religious orders acquired vast landed estates and also profitably engaged in the galleon trade and in internal commerce. As a result of this economic ascendancy, the Church was transformed from a colonial accessory to the principal apparatus of colonial appropriation and exploitation.

A by-product of friar control was cultural poverty. Until the mid-nineteenth century, education was mainly religious instruction under the supervision of the parish priests. Art was purely religious imagery and public entertainment centered on the feast days of patron saints. Spanish was not taught.

Pattern of Resistance

Despite the control over the native mind through religion, the material fact of colonial exploitation urged the people to rise in many unsuccessful revolts. Although these were localized actions at different times and in different areas, two evolving historical threads may be perceived: first, the development and transformation of revolts with religious content and, second, the rise and ebb of élite participation in the people's uprisings.

The religious thread started as nativism, an assertion of the power of the old pagan gods against the Catholic god. Because of the prominence of the Church in the colonial enterprise, the people's protest against their material deprivation and physical oppression was expressed in a rejection of the Catholic religion and a return to their old gods. But, as Catholicism made further inroads, later revolts, while still exhibiting nativistic characteristics and rejecting the friars, adopted more and more of the beliefs and rituals of Catholicism.

The other historical thread began to unfold with the emergence of the local élite. Spanish colonialism gradually transformed the *barangay* chieftains into adjuncts of colonial rule. Administrative responsibilities gave the chiefs colonial privileges as well as opportunities to participate in the exploitation of the people. The chiefs and ex-chiefs and their families constituted the *principalia* (principals) of a community, a prospering upper stratum with colonial sanction.

Thus, the middle of the seventeenth century saw the emergence of a new pattern of native resistance in which *principales* took advantage of mass unrest to advance their own interests. Some exploited the grievances of their followers to extract concessions for themselves from the Spaniards. Others led uprisings to expel the Spaniards from their region so that they could rule in their stead.

Except for the Bohol* revolt, which was sustained for 85 years due to a fortuitous combination of circumstances, the numerous uprisings lasted only briefly. They were conceived and conducted as local revolts triggered by local grievances and they had neither the ideology, the resources nor the organization to wage a prolonged resistance. But, over the years, two aspects

* Island province in East Visayas.

of Spanish colonialism stimulated a trend toward unification of the country; the administrative structure and the uniform oppression which developed a growing awareness of common grievances. However, these were not enough to spark a national revolution for there could be no nation and no national consciousness to wage such a struggle until certain economic developments had occurred to produce a national economy, better communications facilities, and a group of articulators who could project the common grievances and crystallize the aspirations of the people.

The necessary economic developments that ultimately produced the Filipino nation occurred in the period from 1750 to 1850.

Economic Transformation, 1750–1850

Spanish colonialism underwent vital changes after the Seven Years' War with Great Britain. The British occupied Manila from 1761 to 1764. Spain's Latin American colonies revolted and Spain itself was gripped by liberal revolutions. British interests penetrated the Spanish colony. European and American firms also started coming in during the latter part of the eighteenth century. The Philippines was gradually opened to world trade. Spain, responding to the imperatives of an expanding world capitalism, liberalized its former restrictive economic policies. The demand for agricultural products for export, particularly sugar, indigo, tobacco, hemp, rice and coffee quickly fostered the regionalization of production.

The British linked the country to world capitalism but it was the Chinese who acted as the economic solvents in the hitherto stagnant interior, for it was they who gathered the agricultural crops for the foreign traders and sold to the people the goods these same traders brought into the country. When a majority of the Chinese was expelled or killed during the last two of the periodic purges by the Spaniards, the Chinese *mestizos* (sons of Chinese fathers and native mothers but brought up as natives and Catholics) replaced them. The Chinese *mestizos* later relinquished their trading activities to the Chinese when these were again allowed to return and operate in the provinces but by this time the Chinese *mestizos* were already rich enough to shift to agriculture. They merged with, or took over from, the old native *principalia* as community leaders and landowners.

The educational reforms of 1863 opened the doors of higher institutions of learning to the natives. Children of prosperous Chinese *mestizo* and native families studied in Manila; the wealthier families sent their sons to Spain. From these youths emerged the *ilustrados* (the enlightened ones) who were to become the disseminators of Spanish culture and liberal thought and eventually the articulators of the intellectual ferment in the colony.

Reform Movement

Ferment sprang from diverse sectors of the population and was spurred by economic development and the dissemination of liberal ideas. The *creoles* or Españoles-Filipinos (Spaniards born in the Philippines) resented the preferential treatment given to the *peninsulares* (Spaniards born in Spain) in government employment and in the army. They gravitated toward the *ilustrados* who, having prospered, were chafing under the restrictions which the Government continued to impose on them and which inhibited further economic ascendancy. The *ilustrados* also demanded social equality, civil rights and a voice in government.

Economic progress and the liberalized policies on education had increased the number of native priests. Discriminated against by the Spanish friars who monopolized the more lucrative parishes, the native clergy made common cause with the *creole* clergymen in demanding Filipinization of the clergy. This demand became one of the rallying cries of the steadily growing sentiment of nationality, with *creoles* accepting the educated natives as Filipinos.

The growth of the concept of nationhood was coterminous with the development of the concept of Filipino. From a term with narrow racial and élitist connotation (only for Spaniards born in the Philippines), the term Filipino began to include Chinese *mestizos* and urbanized natives whose economic ascendancy in the eighteenth and nineteenth centuries gave them the opportunity to acquire education and Hispanic culture. This made them socially acceptable to the *creoles*, especially since progress had given both groups a common economic base to protect. Later, the *ilustrados*, offsprings of this rising local élite, wrested the term Filipino from the *creoles* and infused it with national meaning to include the entire people. From then on, the term Filipino would refer to the inhabitants of the Philippine archipelago regardless of racial strain or economic status.

The National Revolution of 1896

Progress inevitably produced economic dislocations. Many small landholders lost their lands, the people suffered from rising prices, aggravated by unemployment in those areas where native production could not compete with imported goods. Economic development produced better communications and a national market, both of which made for greater cohesiveness and facilitated the dissemination of protest, thus increasing its scope and intensity. The particular grievances of Philippine-born Spaniards, of the native clergy, of the Chinese *mestizos* and of the indigenous élite swelled the stream of general discontent which finally found more or less systematic articulation in the writings of the *ilustrados*.

The *ilustrados* were reformists. They agitated for better treatment of the colony and its eventual assimilation as a province of Spain. The foremost leader of what is now called the Propaganda Movement was José Rizal. But, although the people revered Rizal and the other reformists, the revolutionary spirit that had been nurtured in centuries of struggle made them decide in favour of revolution rather than reform and separation rather than assimilation.

The people's revolution was launched by the *Katipunan** under the leadership of Andres Bonifacio in August 1896 and quickly spread to the rest of the country. Military successes in Cavite catapulted to prominence then Captain Emilio Aguinaldo and aroused the ambitions of the Cavite† élite who wrested the leadership of the Revolution from Bonifacio. The *Katipunan* organization was discarded and Aguinaldo, now a general, was elected President of the revolutionary government. Aguinaldo and his group eventually compromised the national struggle by consenting to stop hostilities in return for a monetary settlement and exile to Hong Kong.

A few months later, the Spanish-American war broke out and Gen. Emilio Aguinaldo returned to the Philippines. The people had continued their revolution against Spain even after Aguinaldo had abandoned the struggle. With American backing, Aguinaldo reassumed leadership of the movement and proclaimed Philippine independence on June 12th, 1898, placing the country's independence under American protection.

THE FIRST PHILIPPINE REPUBLIC,

The Filipino people pressed their fight against the Spaniards until they were in control of the whole country except Cavite and Manila, which passed to American hands. The Americans made arrogant demands on their supposed allies and colluded with the Spaniards to stage a sham battle so that Manila could be surrendered to the Americans alone. Despite many ominous signs, Aguinaldo continued to declare his faith in the United States.

Aguinaldo was inaugurated President of the Philippine Republic at Malolos in January 1898. But the Malolos Government was a completely *ilustrado* government. Wealthy Manilans, who had shunned Bonifacio's *Katipunan*, had joined the Revolution when it looked as if it just might succeed. Aguinaldo appointed the élite to his cabinet and they dominated the Congress.

AMERICAN OCCUPATION

In the Treaty of Paris of December 1898 Spain ceded the Philippines to the United States for $20 million. The American expansionists now had a free hand to subdue their new colony. Aguinaldo's forces were no match for the American army; after a series of retreats Aguinaldo was captured in March 1901. But the hostilities did not end.

New leaders emerged and the resistance continued into the second decade of the century, although brutally suppressed by the Americans. All political activity was banned.

Despite fierce resistance, American colonial administrators established a civil government. In this the Americans were able to use quite a number of *ilustrados* who declared their acceptance of American rule. These *ilustrados* had occupied prominent positions under the Spanish regime. That Aguinaldo had appointed many of them to his cabinet made them all the more valuable to the Americans as exhibits of Filipino acceptance of the American regime. These men were rewarded with high office in the new dispensation while news of resistance was suppressed.

Colonial Policy

The principal agent of Americanization was the public school system, and the master stroke of educational policy was the adoption of English as the medium of instruction. A people who had long been denied educational facilities under Spain welcomed this development. However, the use of English made possible the introduction of the American public school curriculum, with its American culture and values which had the effect of gradually dissipating the intense feelings of nationalism that had animated the people during the Revolution and the resistance to American occupation. A quasi-American society was eventually established which bore the imprint of the institutions, values and outlook of the colonizing power. The American colonial technique finally earned for the United States the loyalty of millions of Filipinos.

American economic policies in the Philippines represented a compromise between two clashing economic forces in the United States: those interested in trade and economic holdings overseas and those interested in protecting local agricultural production and labour from foreign competition. The first enthusiastically supported colonization; the second opposed it and subsequently agitated for independence for the colony. The agricultural sector, however, concerned itself with colonial policy only when its interests were involved; otherwise, official policy was dictated by the requirements of American commercial and industrial interests.

Exploitation of the colony involved development of the import-export trade and investment principally in the extractive industries. The various economic legislations culminating in the establishment of free trade were all designed to produce an economic climate attractive to American traders and investors and to transform the colony into a source of cheap raw materials and a market for American manufactured goods. Thus, from an 11 per cent share in the value of the import and export trade of the Philippines in 1900, the U.S. share rose steadily to 72 per cent in 1935. And whereas in 1899 the Philippines bought only 9 per cent of its imports from the United States, by 1933 the figure had risen to 83 per cent.

American land policy favoured the traditional landed élite. Agricultural lands were undertaxed and agricultural products exempted from tax assessments in order to encourage export-crop production. Demand for their products under free trade conditions stimulated landowners to enlarge their holdings. The *hacienda* system was therefore strengthened and the tenancy problem worsened.

* "Association of the Sons of the People".

† Province in Southern Luzon.

Colonial Politics

The Filipinization policy which was conceived as a pacification measure but was presented as a policy in pursuance of the American desire to train the Filipinos in the art of self-government gave political power to the landed élite. With the help of property restrictions on suffrage which the Americans imposed, this landed elite acquired political control in the municipal elections of 1905 and emerged in full force in the Philippine Assembly of 1907. Although suffrage was subsequently extended, the élite never lost political power, exercising it either directly or through middle-class professionals whom they sponsored or co-opted. Subsequent gains in Filipinization, a Senate, to take the place of the American-dominated Philippine Commission, and Filipino cabinet members and bureau heads, did not diminish élite control.

The Nacionalista Party, under the leadership of Sergio Osmeña (later supplanted by Manuel L. Quezon), retained a virtual monopoly of political power from the start. All other political groups died away or were absorbed by this party. Fierce political battles occurred only when personal ambition caused a temporary split in Nacionalista ranks.

These basic factors determined the peculiar characteristics of Philippine colonial politics: on the one hand, a colonial master that gave its wards a semblance of democratic power but kept for itself the substance of that power, and on the other, a people still resolute in their desire for independence. In the middle were the Filipino leaders who owed their positions to an electorate faithful to the old goal of independence, and their powers and prerogatives to the colonizer. The political battle-cry was still for "immediate, complete and absolute independence" and many independence missions were sent to the United States but mainly for political effect inasmuch as the idea of immediate and absolute independence had long been tacitly discarded.

Filipino leaders and the class they represented wanted independence eventually but having accepted the concept of tutelage and allowed the development of an economy dependent upon free entry of its raw materials into the U.S. market, they became increasingly reluctant to trade their prosperous dependence for the uncertainties of freedom and preferred to postpone it whenever it appeared to be within reach.

The Philippine Commonwealth (1935–46)

It was therefore more as a result of the agitation of American farm and labour groups that the United States moved to give the Philippines its independence. By 1932 American farm and dairy interests, hard hit by the deep economic crisis, renewed their clamour for immediate Philippine independence so that free trade could be abandoned and tariffs imposed for their protection. The American Federation of Labor, which wanted to exclude cheap Filipino labour, applied pressure. The result was the passage in 1934 of a law which established a Commonwealth and provided for the recognition of Philippine independence after a ten-year transition period. The Philippine Commonwealth was inaugurated on November 15th, 1935, with Manuel L. Quezon as president and Sergio Osmeña as vice-president.

Social Unrest

The masses, although temporarily quiescent after their resistance to American occupation had been crushed, remained faithful to the revolutionary dream of freedom. Poverty, usury, oppressive treatment by landlords, the dispossession of poor farmers, fraudulent titling and other legal trickeries produced a new upsurge of peasant unrest in the 1920s. Ideologically confused and poorly organized, the revolutionary peasant movements of this period were easily suppressed by the Philippine Constabulary which the Americans had organized to police the country.

Unrest was not confined to the rural areas. Urban workers joined labour unions, some of which became increasingly radical. The economic crisis of the late 1920s and early 1930s intensified unionization as well as peasant organization. Large peasant unions based in Central Luzon joined unions of urban workers to form a militant Confederation. Although peasants and workers directed their strikes and other mass actions primarily against their own exploiters, their radical leadership began to project the inter-relationship between their economic demands and the national goal of independence. A number of these radical leaders, headed by Crisanto Evangelista, established the Communist Party of the Philippines in 1930.

Another group called *Sakdal* (Accusation), despite a leadership that was eventually exposed as opportunistic and fascist-inclined, contributed to the politicization of the people. The insights into the colonial establishment that it propagated, its projection of the inter-relationship between colonialism and mass poverty, its denunciation of the élite leaders, and its exposure of the economic strings that the Americans attached to independence all raised the level of consciousness of the people. Because of faulty leadership, however, *Sakdal* staged a violent uprising in 1935 which was quickly suppressed, thus ending a movement whose surprising electoral victories had sparked hopes that a real opposition party might emerge.

President Quezon tried to counter unrest with his Social Justice Program. While some constructive legislation was passed, the programme was essentially intended to placate the masses while reassuring the landowners. In 1938 the Communist Party and the Socialist Party merged. In 1940 this group joined other progressive and Left elements to form the Popular Front which won some modest victories in the provincial and municipal elections of that year.

But as the Second World War was extended to Asia, Left groups joined other organizations in a united front against fascism. Growing class animosities were temporarily set aside, although by no means obliterated, as the Pacific War broke out.

JAPANESE INTERLUDE

The outbreak of the Pacific war altered the course of domestic developments. Contrary to the hopes of most Filipinos, who were sure that the Americans would trounce the Japanese in a matter of weeks, the American forces were driven out of the country after a few months of resistance. The Japanese instituted a new apparatus of control over the Philippines.

The Filipinos eventually resigned themselves to a period of enemy occupation, confident that it was to be temporary. They regarded America's war as their own. While the Filipino people resented the new colonialism, it served only to deepen their loyalty to the United States, on whom, after the initial shock of seeing it defeated by Japan, they pinned their hopes for their liberation.

Spanish religious prejudices and Americanization had developed in the Filipinos an attitude of superiority toward the Japanese (and Asians in general) because the latter were orientals and non-Christian. Filipino prejudices were subsequently confirmed and exacerbated by the cruelties inflicted on the Filipinos by Japanese soldiers.

The Japanese military administration immediately put into operation plans to integrate the Philippines into Japan's "Greater East Asia Co-prosperity Sphere." A segment of the old colonial leadership, left behind by Quezon, was harnessed for this task. Other segments continued their resistance as guerrilla groups or as supporters of resistance groups waiting for the return of U.S. forces. The Commonwealth officials, led by Quezon and his vice-president, Sergio Osmeña, lived in exile in Washington.

Military Rule

The Japanese imposed a very severe form of military rule. Arms were confiscated; civil liberties were curtailed; censorship was established. Only media licensed by the military were allowed to operate. Neighbourhood associations were established for closer control of the population and to facilitate the rationing of basic commodities. Production was geared to the needs of the military. With the Philippines isolated from the rest of the world, with production facilities and agriculture at less than peak performance and with the Japanese occupation forces having first preference and even exporting Philippine produce to Japan, there were severe shortages of vital items for the civilian population.

An aggravating factor was the Japanese attempt to reorient the economy of the country to contribute to Japan's war effort and to be finally integrated into the autarchic scheme of the Japanese empire. Sugar production was limited; instead of being used for export, excess sugar was utilized for the manufacture of alcohol and butanol to fuel Japanese vehicles. A programme was initiated to convert part of the sugar lands into areas for growing cotton for Japan's textile mills. Experimental farms were established for the growing of cotton and the cultivation of Japanese rice. New lands were opened to expand grain production. The military took over the management of public utilities and other firms vital to the war effort, and labour conscription was initiated.

Filipino Collaboration

In early 1942 the Japanese organized an executive commission to carry on the government functions. This commission was drawn from the ranks of former politicians and high-ranking bureaucrats led by Jorge Vargas, Quezon's executive secretary. The native constabulary was re-organized and its ranks bolstered by former prisoners of war. A civico-political organization called *Kalibapi** was organized. This was headed by Benigno Aquino, Sr., a senator of the old regime. The organization was vocally anti-American and aided the Japanese in mobilizing public support for Japanese policies.

On October 14th, 1943, one year and a half after the occupation had begun, the Japanese granted the Philippines independence. The puppet republic joined the East Asia Co-prosperity Sphere. The new Philippine Republic was headed by Jose P. Laurel who had been instructed by Quezon to remain and deal with the occupying forces to protect the people. While on the whole he acquiesced to Japanese demands, he was at the same time trying to protect the people from Japanese abuses. For one thing, he was able to prevent the conscription of Filipinos to fight with the Japanese. Documents would later reveal that Laurel had liaison with some of the guerrilla groups.

Resistance

Soon after the fall of Bataan, various guerrilla groups were formed, most of them under the leadership of former USAFFE† officers, American and Filipino. The resistance of these groups was confined to sporadic skirmishes with Japanese patrols. They held their forces in reserve until instructed by the American command to attack the Japanese in preparation for the American landings.

Only one guerrilla group, the *Hukbalahap*, had a different orientation. Operating in Central and Southern Luzon, its forces fought the enemy throughout the occupation. Coming from the ranks of militant peasants who had been on the verge of revolt just before the Pacific war, and led by Communists and Socialists, the "Huks" were both anti-Japanese and anti-landlord. They did not, however, have clear-cut goals of opposing the return of the Americans. Their struggle was premised on the return of the Commonwealth government.

With the successive defeats of the Japanese in the mid-Pacific, the economic situation in the Philippines quickly deteriorated. Increasingly severe shortages and high inflation made life progressively more miserable. Thousands suffered from malnutrition and in the cities many starved. Economic conditions, the brutality of the army of occupation as well as the popular bias in favour of the Americans and against the Japanese made it impossible for the puppet Republic to gain any acceptance among the people.

During the occupation there was an attempt to expunge from the textbooks American-oriented values. The banning of American jazz and movies

---

* Kapisanan sa Paglilingkod sa Bagong Pilipinas (Association in the Service of the New Philippines).

† United States Armed Forces in the Far East.

‡ Hukbo ng Bayan Laban sa Hapon (People's Anti-Japanese Army).

allowed a modest flowering of Filipino entertainment fare. The use of the national language was encouraged and its importance vis-à-vis English was stressed. Filipinos were constantly exhorted to remember that they were Asians. But none of this made a strong impression on most Filipinos because of their hatred for the Japanese and because their minds were focused on the return of the Americans. American forces entered Manila in February 1945. The war ended officially when Japan surrendered in September 1945.

Return of the Commonwealth, 1945

The return of the Americans was received with nationwide rejoicing. The government-in-exile, headed by Sergio Osmeña who had succeeded Manuel Quezon after the latter's death in 1944, returned to resume the Commonwealth rule. Osmeña faced insurmountable problems: the country was devastated and its production facilities were at a standstill. There was also the question of those who had collaborated with the Japanese.

The Osmeña administration was in a dilemma. On the one hand, there was the problem of rehabilitation and reconstruction which required unity and concentrated effort, and on the other the problem of collaboration which was dividing the nation and distracting its attention from pressing economic and financial problems.

Meanwhile, in Washington, rehabilitation funds were being provided for in a Philippine Rehabilitation Bill. A companion bill defined the trade relations between the Philippines and the United States. This bill provided for free trade for a period of eight years and a graduated tariff schedule for the next 20 years. It also granted Americans parity rights with Filipinos in the exploitation, disposition and utilization of natural resources and the operation of public utilities. This was to be the framework of Philippine-American relations after the grant of independence. The Rehabilitation Act contained a condition that no payment in excess of $500 would be given as war damage unless an agreement was reached by the presidents of the United States and of the Philippines regarding trade relations. But acceptance of this condition would require amendment of the constitution to give Americans rights that the constitution had reserved only for Filipino citizens. Osmeña was forced into an alliance with the Left, led by the Democratic Alliance (DA). The DA was a non-traditional group, a united front of liberals, leftists and anti-collaborationist elements. Besides being strongly anti-collaborationist, the DA stood for a more independent posture vis-à-vis the United States. Osmeña lost the elections of April 1945 and Manuel Roxas, who had been supported by the returning Americans, became the last president of the Commonwealth and on July 4th, 1946, the first president of the Philippine Republic.

In one sense, Roxas' victory represented a break in the monopoly of power of the Nacionalista party which had held sway since the early period of colonial politics. Sections of this party had broken away in the past only to wither away or be re-absorbed once more. Roxas' Liberal Party was also a splitting wing of the Nacionalista Party, but from then on it achieved co-equal status to establish an orthodox two-party system in the Philippines. In a more fundamental sense, however, the two parties merely represented two sections of the same ruling group. Proof of this were the frequent shifts by political figures from one to the other party. Ramon Magsaysay and Ferdinand E. Marcos were both Liberals who won the presidency as candidates of the Nacionalista Party.

THE PHILIPPINE REPUBLIC, 1946–76

Roxas clearly delineated the direction of the new republic. A proud product of the American public school system, with a long career in colonial politics, and the head of a country economically prostrate and still euphoric over its American "liberation", Roxas firmly placed his country "in the glistening wake of America."

Roxas went all out for American parity rights. To secure the amendment of the Constitution, he had to have a 75 per cent vote of Congress. This was attained by unseating the Democratic Alliance Congressmen for alleged election frauds and terrorism. Parity became a reality with the approval of the amendment in a plebiscite held in 1947. A military bases agreement was also concluded, giving the Americans a 99-year lease on areas of Philippine territory. The collaboration issue was buried when Roxas issued an amnesty for all collaborators in 1948. In March 1948 Roxas outlawed the Hukbalahap.

Dissidence and Economic Difficulties

Dissidence in Central Luzon spread as the "Huks," now seeing no possibility of working within the existing framework, stepped up their organizational activities and began combatting government forces in a long-range programme to seize power.

Roxas died in April 1948. Vice-President Elpidio Quirino succeeded Roxas and immediately tried, unsuccessfully, to solve the dissidence problem. He was no more successful with the vast economic problems he had inherited and which were to continue to plague each succeeding president. The war damage payments and other payments from the United States were quickly dissipated in an orgy of spending on nonessentials. The old colonial set-up was restored under parity. Faced with an exchange crisis, the country had to adopt import and exchange controls, limiting importation and the expenditure of foreign exchange. This institution, however, was wracked by corruption although it was able to produce a group of entrepreneurs who would in the future demand more nationalistic policies.

Quirino ran for re-election in 1949 against Jose Laurel, the war-time collaboration leader. Quirino won but wholesale frauds and terrorism further disillusioned the people and brought new strength to the dissident movement now led by the PKP*. In 1950 Quirino was able to arrest almost the entire leadership of the communist party. This feat was credited to his defence secretary, Ramon Magsaysay. The problem

* Partido Komunista ng Pilipinas.

in Central Luzon was defused and many dissidents were either resettled or kept under interdiction.

Magsaysay's star was rising. He was considered by his American backers to be ready to challenge Quirino. When Quirino insisted on running for re-election in 1953, Magsaysay left the Liberal Party to become the standard bearer of the Nacionalistas, whose leaders accepted him due to American pressure. With the backing of the Americans, Ramon Magsaysay became the next president.

Magsaysay did not conceal the fact that he was an American puppet. It was during his term that the South East Asia Treaty Organization (SEATO) was established and Magsaysay was among the first presidents to recognize the regime of Ngo Dinh Diem, his counterpart in South Viet-Nam.

The Nationalist Crusade

The puppetry of Magsaysay encountered in Senator Claro M. Recto the nationalist oppositionist. It was during Magsaysay's term that the parity provisions were extended to the realm of business under the Laurel-Langley Agreement. One of Magsaysay's vote-catching gimmicks, "an artesian well in every barrio," dramatized the American aim of keeping the Philippine economy principally agricultural. This was opposed by proponents of nationalist industrialization led by Recto.

Recto started a nationalist campaign and exposed Magsaysay's pro-American policies. This campaign reached its climax in the presidential elections of 1957, in which Recto was a contender. Magsaysay, however, died in a plane crash a few months before the elections. He was succeeded by his vice-president, Carlos P. Garcia, who won the election in a four-cornered presidential battle. Garcia's administration was characterized by the adoption of nationalistic policies, the principal expression of which was the "Filipino First" policy. This policy was the result of the pressures of the Recto campaign and also of the emergence of a new group of indigenous entrepreneurs who had benefited from controls.

The Trade-Loan Devaluation Cycle, 1961–72

Graft and corruption and the various scandals that rocked the Garcia administration led to its defeat in 1961. The new president, the Liberal Party's Diosdado Macapagal, scrapped controls in return for stabilization loans urged on him by the U.S. Treasury Department and the International Monetary Fund (IMF). Among the conditions of the loan was the devaluation of the peso. Decontrol and devaluation initiated a period of unbalanced neo-colonial trading where deficits in the balance of payments were always remedied by new loans to aid the peso.

Devaluation crippled infant Filipino industries and scuttled plans for nationalist industrialization. Many floundering local industries were bought by American corporations.

Senate President Ferdinand E. Marcos, who left the Liberal Party ranks to become the Nacionalista Party standard bearer, defeated President Macapagal in the elections of November 1965. Marcos' administration has been credited with massive infrastructure programmes. But the trade-loan devaluation cycle, started during the Macapagal administration, continued to take its toll well into the Marcos administration, and its effects have been responsible for many contemporary developments. In February 1970 the peso was allowed to float. Marcos' term saw an increase in American investments covering vital and strategic areas. Many of these investments started as joint venture projects in anticipation of the end of parity in 1974. The deterioration of the economy also featured recurrent shortages in the production of rice. Worldwide inflation adversely affected the country, whose economic and financial policies were geared mainly to strictures by the U.S. and the IMF.

Marcos broke tradition by winning a second term as President in 1969. His second term was marked by frequent demonstrations by students and other protest groups. Demonstrations and protests covered issues from American bases to rural feudalism on the part of the left while right-wing and moderate reformist groups attacked corruption, smuggling and established oligarchies. While disagreeing on many issues, these groups found a common denominator in their opposition to the Marcos administration. Conditions deteriorated to the extent that law enforcement agencies were virtually helpless in curbing crimes. Private armies proliferated and there was rampant smuggling. Increasing violence led to Marcos' suspending *habeas corpus* provisions. There was a nationwide protest against this but the Supreme Court sustained him.

Conditions deteriorated further. There were bombings and reports of attempted assassinations. The Philippine communist party (Maoist) had established a New People's Army (NPA) and the clashes between Christians and Muslims in the south had increased in frequency and magnitude.

During all this period the Constitutional Convention was meeting to draft a new constitution for the country. It became the arena for the conflicts that were agitating the country: the conflict between the nationalists and the anti-nationalists, between those who wanted an end to the Marcos regime after 1973 and those who wanted him or his wife to continue in office, between those who wanted reforms and those who opposed them.

Martial Law

In September 1972, Marcos declared martial law. Leading members of the opposition, from right to left, and journalists critical of the administration were arrested and detained.

Martial law was the first departure in a history of parliamentary government that lasted nearly seven decades. Congress was not convened but work on the new constitution was allowed to continue until its completion. This constitution was submitted to the people in a referendum in 1973. Opponents of the Marcos government questioned the legality of the referendum which they claimed was not free. This question was submitted to the Supreme Court. The court handed down a decision which, although vague, for all purposes sustained the government's contention that the new constitution was operative and the president was within his rights to exercise supreme powers until such time as the interim assembly was convened.

During this period there were constant agitations for the lifting of martial law and the release of detained prisoners. Former president Diosdado Macapagal launched a move to call the interim assembly. But these expressions of opposition have been muted because the media, despite some liberalization compared with the early days of martial law, still operates under martial law constraints.

New thrusts have been made in foreign relations. The People's Republic of China was recognized, along with East European nations, and trade and cultural relations have been opened with the Soviet Union, with full diplomatic relations in the offing. Negotiations were going on between the Philippines and the United States in 1976 on the question of U.S. bases and a trade agreement to replace the Bell Trade Act which expired in 1974.

The government launched a sustained drive to attract foreign investments with generous tax exemption incentives and the promise of cheap labour. Multinationals have responded favourably and have set up subsidiaries in the country. The tourist industry is being promoted as a dollar earner. Local banking institutions have merged and/or entered into joint venture with foreign banking giants. The administration still faces armed opposition from various sectors which range from NPA elements to the Muslim autonomy movement. Sections of the Catholic church have been active in opposing martial law and the restriction of workers' rights.

The country recently played an active rôle in the formal establishment of the Association of South East Asian Nations (ASEAN) which held a summit in March 1976. This organization has been hailed by China, the Soviet Union and the United States but is viewed with suspicion by Viet-Nam.

A dramatic oil find has resulted in feverish activities in the stock exchange. The commercial exploitation of this resource will certainly effect changes in the Philippine foreign posture and will greatly modify internal conditions as well as policy. The direction of change will be conditioned by the manner in which the administration handles its relations with the powers represented by the service contractors and the global companies that control the energy industry of the country.

ECONOMIC SURVEY

T. M. Burley

The Philippines has a land area of 30 million hectares, of which about 12.5 million hectares are reserved as permanent forests. Community, industrial and other non-agricultural sites cover about 5.5 million hectares.

The economy is based largely on agriculture, which provided 27 per cent of the Net Domestic Product in 1973 and employs more than half the labour force. The major food-producing area is the central lowland of Luzon in the north. Rice forms the most important single item in the agricultural system, but its predominance is less marked than in other South-East Asian countries, and in some of the islands corn is a leading food-crop. Coconut and coconut products, sugar, bananas and pineapples are other significant crops. The country is widely forested and timber provides an important export commodity. Mineral deposits include copper, iron ore, manganese, molybdenum, zinc and lead. Gold and silver are also to be found. In the manufacturing sector food and beverage products, chemicals, textiles, tobacco and footwear are the main products. There has been a determined effort to increase the amount of domestic processing of raw materials, particularly timber, copper and copra.

The imposition of martial law in September 1972 has led to more efficiency in economic management and to considerable stability, both economic and social. At the same time, the world rise in commodity prices, particularly of timber, gave the country an unprecedented balance of payments surplus for 1973. Measures designed to create a more favourable climate for business and industry and to attract foreign investment are a feature of the martial law regime. These included the creation of a National Economic Development Authority (NEDA), to determine priorities and incentives for economic growth, and an overhaul of the tariff, customs and taxation codes.

The activities of NEDA, and the Board of Investments (BOI), have necessarily involved greater government interference in the private sector, and this has caused some concern among foreign investors and in domestic business circles. However, the net effect of government intervention has been to rationalize and co-ordinate a generally inefficient commercial and industrial structure, and hence to promote confidence and investment. Revision of the Internal Revenue Code was undertaken to cover a broad range of changes in taxes on income, and on domestic transactions, consumption and transfers. Measures were also taken to attract foreign capital.

According to advanced estimates by NEDA, gross national product (based on 1967 prices) rose again by 5.9 per cent in 1975 to 43,389 million pesos from

40,985 million pesos in 1974. At current prices, the G.N.P. growth rate was 11 per cent, from 110,849 million pesos to 115,530 million pesos.

The 5.9 per cent real G.N.P. growth for 1975 is attributed to the gains in the agriculture, construction and mining and quarrying sectors. In agriculture, good weather and the food production programme combined to outpace the normal growth rate. The value of agricultural production (including fishing and forestry) amounted to 9,915 million pesos, up 3 per cent from 9,626 million pesos in 1974. The overall growth rate for agriculture conceals a 12 per cent increase in production of paddy rice (palay) and a 14 per cent rise for maize (corn) which was offset by declines in livestock and forestry output. Construction in 1975 recorded a real growth of 31.2 per cent, mainly because of massive government spending in infrastructure, which rose by 37.6 per cent to 1,368 million pesos. Manufacturing appeared to be the most sluggish sector in the economy during the year, growing by only 3 per cent to 6,958 million pesos, a performance which was blamed on the decline in the textile and chemical industries. Mining showed a 9.8 per cent growth to 796 million pesos in 1975, mainly because of rising nickel production. However, the output of major minerals such as copper declined by 5.2 per cent. The output value of transport, communications, storage and utilities reached 1,464 million pesos, an increase of 5.8 per cent. The increase was attributed to progress in rural electrification and increases in warehousing capacity to accommodate bumper crops. Commerce, including banking, had a 5.9 per cent growth, to 5,504 million pesos.

Response to incentives caused registered foreign investments in approved projects to amount to 1,558 million pesos in 1974, a 274 per cent rise over 1973 (there is an acknowledged discrepancy between registered capital and the amounts which actually entered the country but the trend has certainly been upwards).

According to the Central Bank, approved foreign investment between 1970 and 1975 totalled $493 million. The U.S.A. was the biggest investor, contributing 44 per cent or $217.2 million, while Japan came second with $117.8 million, 24 per cent of the total investments. Canada was third with $36.3 million or 7 per cent of total capital inflows. Japan, however, exceeded the U.S.A. in investments made in 1975, with a one year capital inflow of $63 million against the $47 million for the U.S.A. Foreign investors concentrated their investments in manufacturing, injecting $223.9 million into the sector (45 per cent of total investments) in 1970–75.

AGRICULTURE

In 1970 there were 8,946,000 hectares under cultivation. In 1974 palay (rough rice) was grown over 3,539,000 hectares, followed by maize (corn), covering 3,062,000 hectares. A third of the rice area is irrigated. Over 2.13 million hectares were planted to coconut in 1972 and a further 447,000 hectares grew sugar cane. Of the other crops, bananas have followed pineapples in displacing abaca (Manila hemp) as a foreign exchange earner (though not in area cropped). Commercial banana production began only in 1969 but in 1975 exports were worth $73 million; canned pineapple exports totalled $35 million.

Land reform is a pressing need. Historically, about two-thirds of the rural work force of 8.3 million was landless and the proportion reached 90 per cent in some areas. Moreover, the small size of farms limited the income potential of both owner and tenant and hindered scope for improved techniques.

The prime emphasis in Philippine agriculture remains the achievement of self-sufficiency in foodgrain production, particularly rice. Government subsidies on fertilizers and generous credit schemes for the purchase of new seed, pesticides and fertilizers are aimed at improving yields: estimates for rice production in 1975 indicate an output increase of about 8 per cent over the previous year but this is entirely due to increased hectarage, with productivity remaining low at 800 kilogrammes per hectare. Other government measures include a major effort to improve the country's rural infrastructure, particularly irrigation and roads.

Rice. The rice crop for 1971/72 suffered from a wide infestation of the extremely pernicious tungro disease. Then flooding in 1972 led to an acute shortage of rice in 1973. Irrigation water is available to only a third of the rice area; this inadequacy, coupled with the scarcity of capital among farmers and low yields, means that the Philippines is still some way from self-sufficiency. With the introduction of higher-yield strains of rice, now cultivated over a fifth of the rice area, self-sufficiency was achieved in 1968, but imports had to be resumed in 1972. Production has increased from 4,415,000 metric tons in 1972/73 to 5,594,000 tons in 1973/74 and 5,660,000 metric tons in 1974/75.

Sugar. In 1973 there were over 20,000 planters, 37 sugar mills (centrals) and over 500,000 hectares planted to sugar cane. Production of raw sugar was a record 2.69 million metric tons in 1973/74 but fell back to 2.63 million tons in 1974/75. After several years of poor output, owing largely to adverse weather, sugar is again the country's major single dollar earner. Exports were worth $581 million in 1975 ($737 million in 1974), from a 1974/75 harvest of 24.6 million tons of cane. Exports, formerly sent almost exclusively to the U.S.A., now enter a diversity of markets.

Coconuts. The Philippines accounts for almost three-quarters of world exports of coconut products. A rapid rise in production, resulting from new planting, increased foreign exchange earnings in 1971 and 1972. Lower output in 1973 and 1974 was more than offset by much higher prices: earnings from copra, coconut oil and dessicated coconut totalled $580 million in 1974 (but only $432 million in 1975). The U.S. duty-free coconut oil quota of 40,000 tons, under the Laurel-Langley Agreement, expired in July 1974 and Europe is now a market equally as important to the Philippines as the U.S.A.

Other rural occupations. Meat output, estimated at 341,251 tons in 1973, continues to lag behind domestic demand and per caput meat supply has declined in recent years. Fishing production, 1.37 million tons in 1975, lags behind domestic demand and about a third of local requirements are met by imports, despite the potential of Philippine waters.

Philippine forests carry an estimated stand of 465 million board feet of valuable hardwoods; at present, only 8.6 million hectares are commercial and less than 200 of the 1,000 commercially useful species of trees are currently being marketed. Moreover, the country's forest resources are being rapidly depleted (an estimated 40 per cent since 1945), mainly owing to shifting cultivation, illegal cutting and inadequate re-afforestation. It is estimated that illegal cutting runs to 20 million board metres annually. Output is exported mainly to Japan and the U.S.A. (earning some $194 million in 1975), and also forms the basis of local plywood and furniture industries. Government policies provided for the gradual phasing out of log exports by 1976 but the total ban was deferred in early 1976 because of the adverse effect on the balance of payments.

Land reform. In September 1972, a Presidential Decree proclaimed the whole country a land reform area. The full implementation of the Agrarian Reform Programme is regarded as an indispensable requirement for the development of not only the agricultural sector but also the overall growth of the national economy. The emancipation of the tenant-farmers of rice and/or maize is to be effected by transferring to them ownership of the land. Under the new provision, the tenant-farmer shall be deemed owner of a portion constituting a family-size farm of five hectares if not irrigated and three hectares if irrigated. Existing holdings of smaller areas are not affected. Landowners will be paid for land given to their tenants based on a pre-determined value and time period. Meanwhile, the Government will provide all possible technical and financial assistance to the tenant-farmers for all phases of farming operations.

The programme was expected to affect an estimated 915,000 farmers and 1.4 million hectares. A succession of new rulings on this highly sensitive issue have made the guidelines on land reform too complex to be administered easily and it appears that only about half of the original 915,000 farmers affected will secure their own land and also that the stated area of a family-style farm represents the maximum not the norm. The latest statistics suggest that the Programme will affect 394,000 tenant farmers and 760,000 hectares. As of October 1975, some 205,000 tenants tilling 362,000 hectares had received Certificates of Land Transfer: these entitle the tenant to receive land, but not until he completes payment, usually over a 15-year period.

MINING

The Philippines has extensive deposits of gold, silver, copper, nickel, iron, lead, manganese and chrome. Mineral production earned some $500 million in 1974 and the Government has given high priority to the development of minerals. As a result, mining has been the fastest-growing productive sector i recent years. In 1971 there were 27 companies en gaged in metal mining, and 67 in non-metal mining Of these, 11 were engaged in copper mining, five i manganese and mercury, five in gold mining, four i iron ore and two in chromite. At the end of 1971 or reserves were estimated at 1,859 million tons of cop per, 2.8 million tons of manganese, 18 million tons o chromite, 3,526 million tons of nickel, 91 million ton of molybdenum and 106 million tons of iron ore. Les than 10 per cent of the total land area has been sur veyed geographically, and some of the richest deposit are untouched. Although there is petroleum seepage oil has not yet been confirmed in commercial quan tities, despite extensive exploration and an upsurg in drilling both on and offshore. Recoverable coa reserves are small and of poor quality.

In 1974 copper constituted about 78 per cent of th total mineral production of the country (exports wer worth $212 million in 1975). Gold production decline by 9 per cent in 1974 but, owing to favourable marke prices, the value went up by 55 per cent and in 197 production increased three-fold. A new giant nicke plant started operation at Surigao in 1974 and is ex pected to earn about $140 million per year in exports With reserves of nickel ore estimated at 3,000 millio tons (1973), it is likely that in a few years nickel wil become as important to the Philippines as copper.

MANUFACTURING

There has been a noticeable change in the composi tion of industrial activities since the mid-1960s Initially, the food component accounted for about a third of total value-added for manufacturing. Late a movement towards intermediate processing activi ties became apparent. This was most pronounced i the manufacture of textiles, concrete products, glass ware, electrical machinery and related products There were marked increases also in the output o cement, chemicals, machine and base metals manu facturers.

While the processing of primary products is th mainstay of secondary industry, there has been a marked growth in the number of assembly plant basically dependent on imported components, al though a number of components are now being pro duced locally under protective tariffs. The structur of industry is still heavily weighted toward the pro duction of consumer goods, and lacks capital good capacity. Investment priorities have shifted emphasi slightly toward investment goods, such as ships diesel engines and machine tools, although th present regime is giving emphasis to more labour intensive and less capital-intensive sectors. The mos significant manufacturing sectors at present include wood processing (423 logging firms, 29 plywoo plants, 22 veneer plants and 13 board plants at end o 1974); petroleum refining (four refineries in 1974 wit a capacity of 274,000 barrels per day); tobacco pro cessing (90 factories, of which 59 produce cigars); tex tiles (77 mills, of which 15 are fully-integrated); pul and paper manufacture (18 mills in 1971, with anothe nine then planned). An export processing zone started at Mariveles in 1970.

INFRASTRUCTURE

Infrastructure development between 1970 and 1972 was held below the level of previous years due to financial constraints and a series of typhoons. From 1973 onwards the boom in government revenue has made possible a notable increase in development spending on infrastructure.

Transport. Despite marked achievements in road construction the road network is still inadequate: in 1975 the total road length was 104,195 kilometres. In 1974 there were 670,292 vehicles in use, of which 397,603 were passenger cars.

Total loans planned by the IBRD for the current highways programme amount to some $65 million. The IBRD will lend a total of $70 million to fund the third highways programme which is expected to be under way late in 1976.

Harbours and ports developments stress the improvement of selected national ports by providing adequate berthing and storage facilities and dredging work. This will enable a more efficient handling of increases in the volume of maritime traffic and changes in vessel characteristics whilst meeting the requirements of an accelerated programme of regional development. Airports are adequate in number, but they are technically deficient. The airports programme centres on improving existing airports.

Communications

Despite the joint efforts of the Government and several private communications firms, demands for telecommunication services in the country are not being fully met. Expansion plans in both sectors may well fill the growing needs for the service. Between 1970 and 1972, about 19 per cent of the Nationwide Telecommunication Expansion and Improvement Project was realized. The present telecommunications programme aims for a co-ordinated telecommunications network and seeks to extend telegraph services to municipalities without communication facilities.

Power

Complete rural electrification is a long-range target of the economic development programme. Between 1970 and 1972 a total of 50 megawatts were generated and 381 kilometres of transmission lines constructed. Immediate efforts are being made to establish an electric co-operative system for every province. Thus the electrification programme is designed to bring about the establishment of a power network throughout the whole country. Apart from some small amounts of coal in Cebu and a few hydro-electric schemes, all power generation has to rely on imported oil.

POPULATION AND EMPLOYMENT

Transcending the needs for infrastructural improvements is a need for a solution to the population and employment problems. Success in slowing population growth and creating wider employment opportunities accessible to a greater number of people is vital to the nation's economic programme. Thus, in the present development efforts one of the key guidelines for accelerating economic growth is the emphasis on programme and policies which will direct investment to labour-intensive industries rather than to highly capital-intensive undertakings in order to absorb as much as possible of the unproductive labour force.

Population

The Philippine population growth rate officially has fallen from 3 per cent per annum in 1970 to 2.85 per cent in 1975 but, even on these disputed figures, remains one of the highest in the world.

A very high fertility among Filipino child-bearing women, a tradition of large families and a culture of children-loving people has contributed immensely to the fast growth of population. A rapid and well-supported health development programme by both the Government and private sector has also influenced the population boom to a great extent.

Employment

Of the country's 1975 population aged 10 years and over (estimated at 29 million), about 14.3 million people or 49 per cent were part of the labour force. The distribution of this labour force by age is especially significant, with those aged 25–44 years comprising 42.7 per cent and those aged 10–24 years 33.1 per cent (the 45–64 years age group comprised only 21.1 per cent) leaving 3.1 per cent for those aged 65 and over. The above statistics emphasize the youthful nature of the labour force: on the other hand, the employment trend shows that more and more persons from the younger group have already returned to school or may have ceased to look for work for lack of job opportunities.

Of the 13,769,000 persons employed (though only 77 per cent worked full time) in 1975, 7,497,000 or 54.7 per cent were in agriculture, forestry and fishing. Employment from May to August is largely seasonal and the work force most heavily affected during this period are the farmers, farm labourers or related agricultural workers. The increasing excess labour pool of urban workers can readily be seen by noting the decline in blue collar workers' real wages which, according to a recent World Bank Report, fell by 20 per cent in 1974. For the first half of 1975, according to Central Bank figures, real wages of skilled workers in Manila declined another 8.5 per cent, while unskilled workers lost another 4.8 per cent of their real wages. Job creation is simply not keeping up with demand for jobs, so excess labour supply is reducing the wage level. (Some 500,000 job seekers enter the labour pool annually.)

FINANCE

Government expenditure has risen sharply in recent years, but attempts to raise taxation were consistently thwarted by congressional opposition. This meant that the Government had to turn to foreign borrowing in an attempt to minimize the need for deficit financing at home. The martial law regime is not similarly constrained, and its revenue position has greatly improved as the result of higher prices for most exports since 1973. Much of this revenue has been spent on agricultural developments with rice farmers as the major beneficiaries of rural credit schemes, fertilizer subsidies and irrigation projects.

Government receipts increased from 1,908.9 million pesos in 1963/64 to an estimated 14,768.5 million pesos in 1974/75. Taxation accounts for the greater bulk of government revenues: from 71.3 per cent in 1963/64 it advanced to over 77 per cent in 1974/75. Expenditure increased from 1,852 million pesos in 1963 to an estimated 17,718 million pesos in 1974/75.

A budgetary cash deficit of 1,625 million pesos for the first five months of fiscal year 1975/76 forced a second reduction in the budget for the year: an austerity budget of 18,800 million pesos replaced the original amount of 24,200 million pesos, thus cutting the expected deficit from 5,000 million pesos to 2,100 million pesos.

As of December 1975 the external debt stood at $3,995.9 million, 37.4 per cent higher than the $2,908.9 million of a year earlier.

Prices

After being relatively stable for the first half of 1972 prices rose following the damage to production and distribution facilities caused by the July-August flooding. Upon proclamation of martial law a more rigid enforcement of price ceilings and intensified efforts at stabilizing the supply situation brought down the prices of consumer goods for some months. However, the rice shortage caused prices to rise again sharply during 1973.

For the year 1972 the consumer price index increased by 8.2 per cent over the average for the previous year. This was lower than the increases for the previous two years, which were recorded at 14.8 per cent and 21.8 per cent respectively.

During 1974 the rate of inflation increased considerably, but food prices rose by only 8 per cent in 1975 compared with 42 per cent in 1974. For all items the corresponding figures were 12 per cent and 51 per cent. The Central Bank said the price increase slowdown in 1975 reflected the Government's success in containing the crippling effects of worldwide inflationary and recessionary pressures. It said the price stabilization policy and several subsidies extended to food related industries appeared to have helped dampen consumer prices movements.

INTERNATIONAL TRADE

In 1972 the Philippines had a trade deficit of $124.1 million, compared with a deficit of $49.6 million in 1971. With the boom in world commodity prices, however, the situation changed radically and in 1973 exports soared to $1,886.3 million, giving a trade surplus of $289.7 million. Exports continued to rise but the growing volume and cost of imports brought about a trade deficit of $418.3 million in 1974 and $1,164.7 million in 1975.

The Philippines' balance of payments showed a current deficit of about $923 million in 1975 compared with the $521 million surplus in 1973.

It was Central Bank borrowing, including the use of the IMF compensatory financing facility, and short-term credits which insured that reserves declined in 1975 by considerably less than $500 million: in fact by only $144 million to $1,360 million. The country's external debt consequently rose to $3,996 million at the end of 1975 compared with $2,909 million a year earlier.

Exports

Between 1972 and 1974 exports increased from $1,106 million to $2,725 million. This dramatic increase is accounted for by rising world commodity prices rather than by expansion of the volume of trade and exports fell to $2,294.5 million in 1975. Earnings from logs and lumber increased from $174.4 million in 1972 to $339 million in 1973 but fell to $246.4 million in 1974 and $194.1 million in 1975. Coconut oil exports rose from $84.7 million in 1972 to $380.7 million in 1974 but fell to $230.3 million in 1975. Rising demand increased the value of copper exports from $190.9 million in 1972 to $393.1 million in 1974, falling to $212 million in 1975. The most dramatic increase, however, was in export earnings from sugar, which rose from $208.6 million in 1972 to $737.4 million in 1974, establishing it as the Philippines' most valuable export, which it remained in 1975, although earnings fell to $580.7 million. In 1975, Japan superseded the U.S.A. as the Philippines' principal market and remained its major source of imports. Together, the U.S.A. and Japan accounted for two-thirds of export earnings in 1975 and provided about half of all imports.

Imports

Imports doubled in value between 1973 and 1974, amounting to $3,143.3 million in the latter year, and increased to $3,459.2 million in 1974. Mineral fuels, non-electric machinery, transport equipment and base metals were the major imports in 1975. A trade surplus of nearly $300 million in 1973 was converted into a deficit of $1,164.7 million in 1975. This will almost certainly be financed from the large amount of credits arranged with international banks in 1974, yet to be significantly drawn upon.

Tourism

Invisible earnings from this source have flourished in recent years but 1975 saw the Philippines' tourist boom slacken slightly: the number of tourists increased from 243,000 in 1973 to 410,000 in 1974 and 502,000 in 1975.

PLANNING

The 1974–78 Five-Year Development Plan is the successor of the 1972–76 plan, revised to take into account more recent developments in the national economy, particularly the major social and economic reforms which have drastically altered the framework in which economic development proceeds. In addition to the general development goal of improving the standards of living of the greater mass of the population, the new Plan sets forth the following objectives: (1) promotion of employment; (2) maximum economic growth feasible; (3) more equitable income distribution; (4) regional development and industrialization; (5) promotion of social development; and (6) maintenance of acceptable levels of price and balance of payments stability.

The gross national product (at constant 1967 prices) is planned to increase at an average annual rate of 7 per cent, accelerating from 6.5 per cent in 1974/75 to 7.5 per cent in 1977/78. From a value of 39,700 million pesos in 1974/75, G.N.P. will total 48,861 million pesos by 1977/78. Assuming a constant population growth of 3.01 per cent, per capita G.N.P. will expand from 927 to 1,077 million pesos by 1977/78. To attain these aggregate targets, investments will have to increase by an average rate of 9.8 per cent per year to reach the level of 10,417 million pesos in 1977/78 from the 1974/75 level of 8,213 million pesos. The share of gross domestic capital formation to G.N.P. will increase from 19.4 per cent in 1974/75 to 21.3 per cent in 1977/78. On the expenditure side, the aggregate demand by households will register an initial value of 28,071 million pesos and will grow at an average rate of 5.1 per cent thus reaching a level of 32,558 million pesos in 1977/78. Its share to G.N.P. will decrease from 70.7 per cent in 1974/75 to 66.6 per cent in 1977/78. Government consumption expenditures, on the other hand, will increase from 3,202 million pesos in 1974/75 to 3,746 million pesos in 1977/78, representing a 5.3 per cent average annual growth rate.

The net domestic product (N.D.P.) is planned eventually to grow by 6.6 per cent at the end of the Plan period. By the end of the Plan period, agricultural production will have increased by 5 per cent, reaching a production level of 11,182 million pesos. The sector's contribution to the N.D.P. will gradually drop from 30.2 per cent in 1974/75 to 29 per cent in 1977/78.

Growth rates for the mining sector will be at a sustained 18 per cent per year as production rises from 897 million pesos in 1974/75 to 1,475 million pesos in 1977/78. The participation rate in the N.D.P. will reach a peak of 3.8 per cent in 1977/78 from the 2.8 per cent level at the start of the Plan period.

In the manufacturing sector, the Plan lays out growth rate targets of 9 per cent for 1974/75 and an annual average of 10 per cent for 1975–78. The sector's output level is projected to expand from 6,730 million pesos in 1974/75 to 8,957 million pesos in 1977/78. Thus, manufacturing will account for an increasing share in total N.D.P., moving from 21.1 per cent in 1974/75 to a high of 23.2 per cent in 1977/78. During the Plan period construction will expand at 10 per cent per year to reach a level of 1,654 million pesos in 1977/78 from an initial value of 1,243 million pesos in 1974/75. The share of the sector in the N.D.P. will increase from 3.9 per cent to 4.3 per cent during the period.

Value added in the combined transportation-communications-utilities sector is set to increase at an average annual rate of 4.9 per cent per year, reaching a peak level of 5.1 per cent in 1977/78. It is expected that the 1977/78 output will be 1,396 million pesos, compared with the 1974/75 value of 1,204 million pesos. The sector's share in the N.D.P. will drop from 3.8 per cent to 3.6 per cent. The level of commercial activities is estimated to rise from 4,907 million pesos in 1974/75 to 5,649 million pesos in 1977/78. The annual growth rate will increase from 4.5 per cent in 1974/75 to 4.8 per cent in 1977/78; the sector's percentage share in N.D.P. will recede from 15.4 per cent to 14.6 per cent. Finally, the services sector will grow from 7,283 million pesos in 1974/75 to 8,351 million pesos in 1977/78 for an average annual increase of 4.5 per cent. The sector will contribute a diminishing share to N.D.P. of 22.8 per cent in 1974/75 to 21.6 per cent in 1977/78.

Exports are projected to grow at the rate of 10 per cent per annum during the Plan period. From a level of $1,216.1 million (measured in 1967 prices) in 1973, they will reach $1,780.6 million in 1977. While the prices of some agriculture-based exports are not expected to improve substantially, an increased volume shipment of these commodities is expected to offset the downward pull of any price deterioration. The main thrust, however, is expected to come from exports of minerals and manufactured goods in view of expanded production, greater inflow of investments into these areas, and the priority status being accorded them. Imports are projected to expand at the rate of 9 per cent in the initial year of the Plan. In the succeeding year, this rate will accelerate to 9.5 per cent, and, thereafter, at 10 per cent. Hence, from a level of $1,340.3 million (at 1967 prices) in 1973, imports are anticipated to rise to $1,953.4 million in 1977. These rates are based on the assumption that import prices will undergo moderate increases owing to inflationary trends in most of the trading partners of the country.

One of the general objectives of the Development Plan is to stabilize prices within reasonable limits. According to the Plan, some price increases cannot be totally discounted so the principal responsibility, therefore, is to keep such price increases to the minimum, preferably below 8 per cent per year.

Three basic agricultural development programmes have been envisioned to raise agricultural productivity, attain self-sufficiency in food production, and raise the level of rural income; namely, agrarian reform, food production, and co-operatives development. For the industrial sector, a programme aimed at promoting employment opportunities, diversifying and expanding manufactured exports, and increasing efforts at regional development has been laid out. Notably, the development of export-oriented industries and of medium and small-scale industries is given top priority. To sustain the overall development effort, the infrastructure programme provides for the setting up of an efficient system of roads, ports, railways and airports, as well as of power-generating, telecommunication and water resource facilities.

While providing the proper setting for development in the economy, efforts will simultaneously be directed towards improving the well-being of individuals through education, employment, housing, social welfare, community development and health services.

Moreover, in view of the growth imbalance among regions, more emphasis will be given to regional development and industrialization. Thus, in addition to the correction of policies which artificially favour a few select areas, the integrated approach to regional development will be utilized. This approach calls for the integration of physical development with the economic, social administrative and financial aspects of development into a common plan for a given area.

New fiscal dating

The official fiscal year has been re-set to begin on January 1st instead of July 1st, starting in 1977. The 1975/76 fiscal period will consequently be extended to the end of this year, with current spending in the extra six months to be up to 50 per cent of the programmed or actual levels in the twelve-month period. The Government's aim is to make development planning easier.

STATISTICAL SURVEY

AREA AND POPULATION

AREA OF ISLANDS

(sq. km.)

Luzon	Mindanao	Samar	Negros	Palawan	Panay	Mindoro	Leyte	Cebu	Bohol	Masbate	Others
104,688	94,630	13,080	12,705	11,785	11,515	9,735	7,214	4,422	3,865	3,269	23,092

Total area: 300,000 sq. km.

Source: National Census and Statistics Office.

POPULATION

Census Enumerations							1975 Density (per sq. km.)
February 15th, 1960	May 6th, 1970			May 1st, 1975			
	Male	Female	Total	Male	Female	Total	
27,087,685	18,250,351	18,434,135	36,684,486	21,018,265	20,812,780	41,831,045	139.4

1976: Population estimate 42,800,000

Source: National Census and Statistics Office.

PRINCIPAL TOWNS

(population at May 1975*)

Manila (capital)†	1,454,352	Angeles	149,968
Quezon City	960,341	Olongapo	143,279
Davao	482,233	Butuan	131,336
Cebu	408,173	Basilan	126,410
Caloocan	393,251	Batangas	125,044
Zamboanga	261,978	Cadiz	124,563
Iloilo	227,374	Iligan	118,038
Bacolod	222,735	San Pablo	116,383
Pasay	186,782	Cabanatuan	113,814
Cagayan de Oro	164,920		

* Preliminary census results.

† Metropolitan Manila (including the former capital Quezon City) was designated the national capital in June 1976. In 1975 the population of Metropolitan Manila was estimated at 4.5 million.

Source: National Census and Statistics Office.

LABOUR FORCE EMPLOYED*
(persons aged 10 years and over)

	1973	1974	1975
Agriculture, forestry and fishing	7,016,000	8,245,000	7,497,000
Mining and quarrying	62,000	44,000	44,000
Manufacturing	1,418,000	1,508,000	1,440,000
Construction	522,000	403,000	418,000
Electricity, gas and water supply	37,000	44,000	42,000
Commerce	1,660,000	1,613,000	1,574,000
Transport, storage and communications	505,000	518,000	527,000
Services	2,013,000	2,085,000	2,190,000
Other activities	29,000	19,000	38,000
TOTAL	13,262,000	14,479,000	13,768,000

* Figures based on labour force sample surveys at May of each year, except for 1975 when figures are for February.

AGRICULTURE

PRINCIPAL CROPS
(July/June—'000 metric tons)

	1969–70	1970–71	1971–72	1972–73	1973–74	1974–75
Rice (rough)	5,233	5,343	5,100	4,415	5,594	5,660
Maize	2,008	2,005	2,013	1,831	2,289	2,568
Coffee	49	50	52	51	53	57
Tobacco*	61	56	56	65	63	62
Cocao	4	4	4	4	4	4
Sugar Cane	18,835	19,957	17,719	21,819	26,085	24,600
Copra	1,656	1,574	1,703	1,698	1,703	1,719
Abaca (Manila hemp)	122	105	110	119	126	134

* Virginia and native.

Source: Bureau of Agricultural Economics; Sugar Quota Administration.

LIVESTOCK
('000)

	1970	1971	1972	1973	1974
Cattle	1,679	1,795	1,933	2,099	2,194
Horses	295	n.a.	n.a.	n.a.	n.a.
Pigs	6,456	7,050	7,742	8,627	8,987
Goats	772	924	1,083	1,248	1,453
Buffaloes	4,432	4,556	4,711	4,937	5,215

Source: Bureau of Agricultural Economics.

FORESTRY

(year ending June 30th)

	1970/71	1971/72	1972/73	1973/74	1974/75
Logs (million board ft.)	4,528	3,568	4,429	4,321	2,273
Lumber (million board ft.)	365	598	449	472	n.a.

Source: Bureau of Forest Development.

FISHING

('000 metric tons)

	1971	1972	1973	1974	1975
Commercial Fishing	382	425	465	471	499
Fish Ponds	98	99	100	113	122
Municipal Fisheries and Sustenance Fishing	543	599	640	684	752
TOTAL	1,023	1,122	1,205	1,268	1,373

Source: Bureau of Fisheries and Aquatic Resources.

MINING

		1971	1972	1973	1974	1975
Manganese	'000 metric tons	5	2	4	1	n.a.
Iron	,, ,, ,,	2,250	2,205	2,255	1,608	1,351
Copper	,, ,, ,,	198	214	221	225	226
Chrome	,, ,, ,,	430	350	580	530	520
Coal	,, ,, ,,	40	40	39	51	105
Salt	,, ,, ,,	235	220	220	196	71
Mercury	'000 flasks of 76 lb.	5	3	2	1	8
Silver	'000 fine ounces	1,939.8	1,847.6	1,891.6	1,706.3	50,373*
Gold	,, ,, ,,	637	606.7	572.3	536.4	15,608*

* Kilogrammes.

Source: Bureau of Mines.

INDUSTRY

		1970	1971	1972	1973	1974
Sugar	'000 metric tons	1,927	2,060	1,817	2,246	2,446
Cement	,, ,, ,,	2,447	3,117	2,903	4,059	3,485
Tobacco*	metric tons	681	713	919	906	1,031
Cigarettes	million	39,671	41,988	45,777	51,194	41,454
Cotton yarn	metric tons	41,916	40,422	26,630	32,225	29,401
Cotton fabrics	million metres	194	183	187	221	183

* Smoking and chewing tobacco.

Source: National Census and Statistics Office.

FINANCE

100 centavos = 1 Philippine peso.

Coins: 1, 5, 10, 25 and 50 centavos; 1 and 5 pesos.

Notes: 1, 2, 5, 10, 20, 50 and 100 pesos.

Exchange rates (June 1976): £1 sterling=13.22 pesos; U.S. $1=7.43 pesos.

100 Philippine pesos=£7.56=$13.45

Note: Prior to January 1962 the official exchange rate was U.S. $1=2.00 pesos but other rates were effective for certain transactions. The multiple exchange rate system was ended in January 1962, when a free market was introduced. In May 1962 the free rate stabilized at $1=3.90 pesos (1 peso=25.64 U.S. cents) and this became the par value in November 1965. In February 1970 a free market was re-introduced and the peso "floated" downward. The average market rate (pesos per U.S. dollar) was: 6.01 in 1970; 6.37 in 1971; 6.67 in 1972; 6.75 in 1973; 6.80 in 1974; 7.27 in 1975. In terms of sterling, the exchange rate between November 1967 and February 1970 was £1=9.36 pesos.

BUDGET

(million pesos—year ending June 30th)

Revenue	1972/73	1973/74*	1974/75*
Tax on income	1,749.6	2,456.7	2,928.0
Import duties	1,438.1	2,349.0	3,228.7
Excises	627.7	943.6	1,454.5
Other taxes	2,808.8	3,642.9	3,790.4
less: Tax receipts apportioned to local governments	−384.9	n.a.	n.a.
Other receipts	901.5	1,670.0	3,366.9
Total (incl. others)	7,140.8	11,062.2	14,768.5

Expenditure	1972/73	1973/74*	1974/75*
Education	1,508.2	1,969.7	2,530.3
Other social services	475.1	664.6	858.2
Agricultural and natural resources	1,292.4	2,894.5	4,043.4
Transport and communications	1,188.0	2,085.5	3,173.4
Other economic services	9,411.0	2,571.6	2,179.3
National defence	846.7	1,232.1	1,583.3
Total (incl. others)	7,941.2	13,933.2	17,718.0

* Estimate.

1976: estimated expenditure 18,700 million pesos.

Source: Budget Commission.

NATIONAL ACCOUNTS

(million pesos—at current prices)

	1973	1974	1975
GROSS DOMESTIC PRODUCT (AT MARKET PRICES)	71,239	99,899	113,521
NET DOMESTIC PRODUCT (AT FACTOR COST)	56,763	79,189	89,376
of which:			
Agriculture	20,004	28,351	31,482
Mining and quarrying	1,692	2,128	1,743
Manufacturing	12,177	19,564	21,984
Construction	1,462	1,948	2,728
Transportation, communications and storage utilities	1,955	2,574	2,988
Commerce	8,268	11,125	12,752
Services	11,205	13,449	15,699
Income from abroad (net)	−344	582	−107
Depreciation allowance	7,583	10,560	12,945
GROSS NATIONAL INCOME	64,002	90,281	102,214
Less: Depreciation allowances	7,583	10,560	12,945
NET NATIONAL INCOME	56,419	79,721	89,269
Indirect taxes less subsidies	6,893	10,200	11,200
NET NATIONAL PRODUCT	63,312	89,921	100,469
Depreciation allowance	7,583	10,560	12,945
GROSS NATIONAL PRODUCT (AT MARKET PRICES)	70,895	100,481	113,414
Balance of exports and imports of goods, services and borrowings (income from abroad)	−1,456	3,082	9,415
Statistical discrepancy	−429	−413	−512
AVAILABLE RESOURCES	69,868	103,976	123,341
of which:			
Private consumption expenditure	49,062	70,639	77,216
Government consumption expenditure	6,255	8,243	10,407
Gross domestic capital formation	14,551	25,094	35,718

Source: National Economic and Development Authority.

GOLD RESERVES AND CURRENCY IN CIRCULATION

(At December 31st)

	1971	1972	1973	1974	1975
Gold Reserves (million U.S.$)	67.1	70.8	44.6	44.6	44.6
Foreign Exchange Holdings of the Central Bank (million U.S.$)	308.3	478.0	992.4	1,457.9	1,316.0
Currency in circulation (million pesos)	2,650.0	3,434.6	3,452.4	4,311.1	4,115.2
Money Supply (million pesos)	5,567.4	6,796.6	8,152.5	10,220.1	9,348.1

Source: Central Bank of the Philippines.

BALANCE OF PAYMENTS

(million U.S.$)

	1970	1971	1972	1973	1974	1975
Merchandise	−7	−38	−125	275	−449	−1,196
Other goods and services	−142	−87	−55	104	−34	−45
Transfer payments	119	134	188	246	276	318
CURRENT BALANCE	−30	9	8	521	−207	−923
Long-term capital movements	105	31	118	135	173	482
Short-term capital movements	167	134	−19	−4	411	303
Changes in reserves	−95	−31	−38	−594	−290	76
CAPITAL BALANCE	177	134	99	−455	294	861
Errors and omissions	−147	−143	−107	−66	−87	62

Source: Central Bank of the Philippines.

INTERNATIONAL INVESTMENTS
(1973—million U.S. $)

	Direct* Private Long-Term	Indirect				
		Public		Private		
		Long-Term	Short-Term	Long-Term	Short-Term	
Net Foreign Investments in the Philippines:						
United States and Canada	60.46	41.73	−76.80	7.10	−45.55	−13.06
OECD Member Countries	−0.73	18.46	−40.31	−1.02	91.58	67.98
All Other Countries	−0.27	10.80	—	−1.62	17.48	26.39
International Institutions	2.40	−14.92	—	2.40	—	−10.12
Unallocated	−5.09	—	—	−0.64	11.14	5.41
Total Foreign Liabilities	−56.77	56.07	−117.11	6.22	74.65	76.60

1975: private foreign investments totalled U.S. $90.17 million.

* Represents direct investments reported through the banking system. This does not include investments made in the form of machinery and equipment.

Source: Central Bank of Philippines.

EXTERNAL TRADE
(million U.S. dollars)

	1970	1971	1972	1973	1974	1975
Imports (f.o.b.)	1,090.1	1,186.0	1,229.6	1,596.6	3,143.3	3,459.2
Exports (f.o.b.)	1,061.7	1,136.4	1,105.5	1,886.3	2,725.0	2,294.5

Source: National Economic and Development Authority.

COMMODITIES
('000 U.S. dollars)

Imports	1971	1972	1973	1974	1975
Textile Yarns and Fabrics	23,372	25,259	47,051	68,902	66,010
Mineral Fuels and Lubricants	141,233	148,825	187,604	653,378	769,886
Non-electric Machinery	255,118	239,930	296,044	424,015	654,871
Base Metals	90,726	112,450	150,447	295,669	212,786
Transport Equipment	122,173	123,691	102,313	265,330	301,591
Dairy Products	38,497	45,564	45,197	74,465	61,789
Cereals	65,098	84,253	111,778	154,946	175,410
Textile Fibres	48,836	45,754	60,344	88,685	77,625
Electric Machinery	66,286	54,008	70,761	105,335	156,944
Explosives and miscellaneous chemicals	56,366	54,345	80,097	113,777	109,282

Exports	1971	1972	1973	1974	1975
Copra	114,040	110,480	165,766	139,784	172,318
Sugar	212,348	208,639	274,718	737,365	580,736
Abaca (Manila Hemp)	12,989	13,099	19,631	37,533	14,544
Logs and Lumber	225,907	174,444	338,965	246,389	194,110
Dessicated Coconut	20,741	17,551	32,456	60,300	30,429
Coconut Oil	103,451	84,269	151,083	380,021	230,299
Iron Ore	1,462	1,272	1,268	24	367
Plywood	25,115	33,747	58,057	26,089	20,602
Copper Concentrates	185,135	190,867	275,246	393,184	212,081
Canned Pineapple	19,683	19,552	19,696	30,625	34,705

Source: Central Bank of the Philippines.

TRADING PARTNERS

('000 U.S. dollars)

	Imports (f.o.b.)			Exports (f.o.b.)		
	1973	1974	1975	1973	1974	1975
Australia	66,422	134,170	125,835	17,015	30,109	31,628
Belgium and Luxembourg	7,796	17,978	20,625	3,960	6,521	4,617
Canada	19,835	41,401	64,807	11,950	12,634	18,565
China (Taiwan)	25,116	78,899	79,622	44,388	28,147	28,703
France	19,297	40,992	61,739	21,030	17,550	23,499
Germany, Federal Republic	76,499	122,581	132,083	63,516	68,491	66,418
Hong Kong	16,847	27,402	32,861	37,678	31,724	27,525
India	2,827	5,813	10,107	507	917	4,836
Indonesia	1,653	4,503	63,100	14,321	9,501	19,631
Italy	8,671	19,864	29,542	7,582	7,569	9,814
Japan	518,519	864,596	966,291	674,523	949,207	864,996
Malaysia and Singapore	22,761	55,136	21,275	20,424	23,045	31,693
Netherlands	15,863	38,673	45,115	90,551	159,951	176,113
Spain	2,301	14,215	7,970	7,867	5,834	7,229
Switzerland	11,253	18,409	27,402	49,892	3,427	4,896
United Kingdom	70,651	132,626	125,412	35,087	56,384	82,328
United States	449,492	732,982	753,622	675,955	1,156,730	654,791

Source: National Census and Statistics Office.

TRANSPORT

RAILWAYS

		1970	1971	1972	1973	1974
Passengers	(thousands)	5,628	4,794	3,955	6,162	8,067
Passenger-kilometres	(million)	752	795	831	805	999
Freight	('000 metric tons)	926	454	287	340	436
Ton-kilometres	(million)	64	102	60	91	100

Source: National Census and Statistics Office.

VEHICLES IN USE

	1971	1972	1973	1974	1975
Passenger Cars	285,063	312,137	322,233	397,603	403,481
Commercial Vehicles	183,097	204,391	239,114	272,689	281,731

Source: Land Transportation Commission.

CIVIL AVIATION

(Philippine Air Lines only—'000)

	1970	1971	1972	1973	1974
Kilometres flown	33,380	28,386	28,114	27,395	33,670
Passenger kilometres	1,261,418	1,264,662	1,357,522	1,587,954	2,389,944
Cargo ton-kilometres	21,027	28,650	33,860	43,089	59,208
Mail ton-kilometres	3,151	3,713	3,635	3,100	3,231

Source: Civil Aeronautics Board.

SHIPPING

('000 metric tons)

	1970	1971	1972	1973	1974
Vessels entered	8,550	8,267	9,317	10,081	8,707
Vessels cleared	7,778	7,617	8,814	9,941	8,893
Goods loaded	15,792	16,148	15,064	16,760	14,532
Goods unloaded	12,539	13,462	13,359	13,923	12,964

Source: Philippine Coast Guard.

TOURISM

	1971	1972	1973	1974	1975
Number of Visitors ('000)	144	166	243	410	502
Average stay (days)	7.3	7.3	7.8	7.8	7.8
Estimated spending ('000 U.S. dollars)	32,133	38,271	67,803	124,242	155,217

Source: Department of Tourism.

COMMUNICATIONS MEDIA

	1974
Radio Stations	15,231
Television Stations	17
Telephones	343,903
Daily Newspapers	24
Total Circulation	1,196,239

Sources: Bureau of Posts and Bureau of Telecommunications.

EDUCATION

(1973)

	SCHOOLS	TEACHERS	PUPILS
Elementary	43,639	255,561	7,784,150
Secondary	3,666	56,019	1,910,625
Collegiate	558	25,976*	810,530

* Excludes teachers in independent state colleges and universities.

Source: Department of Education.

THE CONSTITUTION

(Proclaimed January 17th, 1973)

The following is a summary of the main features of the Constitution.

BASIC PRINCIPLES

Sovereignty resides in the people; defence of the State is a prime duty and all citizens are liable for military or civil service; war is renounced as an instrument of national policy; the State undertakes to strengthen the family as a basic social institution, promote the well-being of youth, maintain adequate social services, promote social justice, assure the rights of workers and guarantee the autonomy of local government.

Other provisions guarantee the right to life, liberty and property, freedom of abode and travel, freedom of worship, freedom of speech, of the press and of petition to the Government, the right of *habeas corpus* except in cases of invasion, insurrection or rebellion, and various rights, before the courts.

SUFFRAGE

All citizens of the Philippines over the age of 18 years, not disqualified by law, resident in the Philippines for at least one year and in their voting district for at least six months, are eligible to vote.

THE PRESIDENT

The President is elected from among the members of the National Assembly for a six-year term, by a majority vote; he ceases to be a member of the Assembly or of any political party; he must be at least 50 years of age; he may not receive any emolument other than that entitled to as the President; he can dissolve the National Assembly, call general elections and, when appropriate, accept the resignation of the Cabinet.

THE NATIONAL ASSEMBLY

Legislative power is vested in the National Assembly; members are elected for six years and must be natural-born citizens, over 25 years of age, literate and registered voters in their district.

Regular elections are to be held on the second Monday of May; the Assembly convenes on the fourth Monday of July for its regular session; it elects a Speaker from among its members; the election of the President and Prime Minister precedes all other business following the election of the Speaker.

Various provisions define the procedures of the Assembly and the rights of its members, among them that the Assembly may withdraw its confidence in the Prime Minister by a majority vote; that no bill shall become law until it has passed three readings on separate days; that every bill passed by the Assembly shall be presented to the Prime Minister for approval, upon the withholding of which, the Assembly may reconsider a bill and, by a majority vote of two-thirds, enable it to become law.

THE PRIME MINISTER AND CABINET

Executive power is exercised by the Prime Ministe with the assistance of the Cabinet; the Prime Minister i elected from the members of the National Assembly by majority vote; he appoints the members of the Cabinet.

The Prime Minister is Commander-in-Chief of the arme forces; he may suspend the writ of *habeas corpus* an proclaim martial law; all powers vested in the Presiden under the 1935 Constitution are vested in the Prim Minister unless the National Assembly provides otherwise

THE JUDICIARY

The Supreme Court is composed of a Chief Justice an 14 Associate Justices, and may sit *en banc* or in two divisions

LOCAL GOVERNMENT

The National Assembly shall enact a local governmen code which shall establish a more responsive and account able local government structure.

CONSTITUTIONAL COMMISSIONS

These are the Civil Service Commission, the Commissio on Elections and the Commission on Audit. The Com mission on Elections enforces and administers all law relating to the conduct of elections and registers an accredits political parties.

THE NATIONAL ECONOMY

The National Assembly shall establish a Nationa Economic Development Authority which shall recommen co-ordinated social and economic plans to the Nationa Assembly and all appropriate governmental bodies Various provisions relating to the public interest i economic matters are set forth.

AMENDMENTS

Amendments and revisions to the Constitution may b proposed by the National Assembly upon a vote of three quarters of its members, or by a constitutional conventior Any amendment or revision is valid when ratified by majority of votes cast in a plebiscite.

TRANSITIONAL PROVISIONS

There shall be an *interim* National Assembly, convene by the incumbent President, who shall continue to exercis his powers under the 1935 Constitution until he calls o the *interim* National Assembly to elect the *interim* Presiden and the *interim* Prime Minister, who shall then exercis their respective powers under the new Constitution. A proclamations, orders, decreees and acts of the incumben President shall remain valid and binding even after th lifting of martial law or the ratification of this Constitutior The present Judiciary shall continue to exercise its power and functions. This Constitution shall take effect immed ately after its ratification by a majority of the votes cas in a plebiscite called for the purpose.

Note: When President Marcos proclaimed the ratification of the new Constitution on January 17th, 1973, following plebiscite, he also proclaimed the suspension of the *interim* National Assembly envisaged by the Constitution and the con tinuation of martial law, in force since September 23rd, 1972. In a referendum held on July 27th–28th, 1973, a majorit voted that President Marcos should continue in office beyond 1973 and complete the reforms he had initiated under marti law. A further referendum in February 1975 gave the President an overwhelming mandate for the continuation of Martial law

THE GOVERNMENT

HEAD OF THE STATE

President: FERDINAND EDRALIN MARCOS (inaugurated December 1965, re-elected November 1969, term of office extended by referendum July 1973).

THE CABINET

(*June* 1976)

Prime Minister: FERDINAND EDRALIN MARCOS.

Secretary of Foreign Affairs: Brig.-Gen. CARLOS P. ROMULO.

Secretary of Finance: CÉSAR E. A. VIRATA.

Secretary of Justice: VICENTE ABAD SANTOS.

Secretary of Agriculture: ARTURO TANCO, Jr.

Secretary of Public Works and Communications: ALFREDO JUINIO.

Secretary of Education and Culture: JUAN L. MANUEL.

Secretary of Labour: BLAS F. OPLE.

Secretary of Agrarian Reform: CONRADO F. ESTRELLA.

Secretary of National Defence: JUAN PONCE ENRILE.

Secretary of Health: CLEMENTE S. GATMAITAN.

Secretary of Trade: TROADIO P. QUIAZON, Jr.

Secretary of Social Welfare: ESTEFANIA ALDABA-LIM.

Secretary of Public Information: FRANCISCO S. TATAD.

Director-General, National Economic Development Authority: GERARDO SICAT.

Secretary for Public Highways: BALTAZAR AQUINO.

Secretary of Tourism: JOSÉ D. ASPIRAS.

Secretary of Industry and Chairman of the Board of Investments: VICENTE PATERNO.

Secretary of Natural Resources: JOSÉ J. LEIDO, Jr.

Secretary of Local Government and Community Development: JOSE A. ROÑO.

Undersecretaries of Youth and Sports Development: GILBERTO DUAVITT, ELPIDIO DOROTEO.

Chairman, National Science Development Board: MELECIO MAGNO.

Chairman of Energy Development Board: GERONIMO VELASCO.

Budget Commissioner: JOSE LAYA.

Presidential Assistant on National Minorities: MANUEL ELIZADE, Jr.

Presidential Assistant: JUAN C. TUVERA.

Presidential Executive Assistant and Civil Service Commissioner: JACOBO C. CLAVE.

NATIONAL ASSEMBLY

Following the suspension of Congress in September 1972 and the proclamation of martial law, a new Constitution (*q.v.*) was proclaimed in January 1973, which provided for an elected National Assembly. This was also suspended, however, in January 1973. A Legislative Advisory Council was to be set up in September 1976 as a substitute for the Interim National Assembly envisaged by the constitution. Its function is to be advisory.

POLITICAL ORGANIZATIONS

Before the imposition of martial law and the suspension of Congress the following political parties were in operation:

Nacionalista Party: Manila; f. 1907; The party represents the right wing of the former *Partido Nacionalista*, which split in two in 1946; Pres. Senator GIL J. PUYAT.

Liberal Party: The party represents the centre-liberal opinion of the old *Partido Nacionalista*, which split in 1946; Leader Senator BENIGNO AQUINO.

Christian Social Movement: Manila; f. 1968; campaigning for liberal social reforms; Pres. RAUL MANGLAPUS.

National Citizens' Party: Manila; Pres. LORENZO TANADA.

Moro National Liberation Front (M.N.L.F.): leads rebellion aimed at securing autonomy for Muslim communities in Southern Philippines; Chair. NUR MISUARI.

DIPLOMATIC REPRESENTATION

EMBASSIES ACCREDITED TO THE PHILIPPINES

(In Metropolitan Manila unless otherwise indicated)

Argentina: Oledan Bldg., Ayala Ave., Makati, Rizal; *Ambassador:* FERNANDO J. TAUREL.

Australia: 5th Floor, China Bank Bldg., Paseo de Roxas, Makati, Rizal; *Ambassador:* D. G. NUTTER.

Austria: Jakarta, Indonesia.

Bangladesh: 8th Floor, Madrigal Bldg., Ayala Ave., Makati, Rizal.

Belgium: 9th Floor, Security Bank Bldg., Ayala Ave., Makati, Rizal; *Ambassador:* LOUIS VANDENBRANDE.

Bolivia: 1007 Makati Ave., Rizal.

Brazil: 6th Floor, Esquerra Bldg., 140 Amorsolo St., Makati, Rizal; *Ambassador:* CARLOS ALFREDO BERNARDES.

Bulgaria: Tokyo, Japan.

Burma: Ground Floor, ADC Bldg., 6805 Ayala Ave., Makati, Rizal; *Ambassador:* U KYAW ZAW.

Canada: 4th Floor, Pal Bldg., 6780 Ayala Ave., Makati, Rizal; *Ambassador:* JOHN ARNOLD IRWIN.

Chile: Tokyo, Japan.

China, People's Republic: Roxas Blvd., Manila; *Ambassador:* KE HUA.

Czechoslovakia: Tokyo, Japan.

Denmark: Jakarta, Indonesia.

Dominican Republic: 454 Shaw Blvd., Mandaluyong, Rizal; *Ambassador:* (vacant).

Egypt: 13th Floor, PAL Bldg., Ayala Ave., Makati, Rizal; *Ambassador:* ABDEL MONEM ZAKI EL SHINNAWI.

Finland: Tokyo, Japan.

France: 5th Floor, Filipinas Life Bldg., 6786 Ayala Ave., Makati, Rizal; *Ambassador:* CHARLES DE LESTRANGE.

Germany, Federal Republic: L & S. Building, 1414 Roxas Blvd., Manila; *Ambassador:* WOLFGANG EGER.

Greece: Tokyo, Japan.

Guatemala: Tokyo, Japan.

Hungary: Tokyo, Japan.

India: Campos Rueda Bldg., 101 Tindalo Bldg., Makati, Rizal; *Ambassador:* P. S. NASKAR.

Indonesia: 5th Floor, Kalayaan Bldg., Salcedo St., Makati, Rizal; *Ambassador:* S. B. ARIOTEDJO.

Iran: Tokyo, Japan.

Israel: Metropolitan Building, 6813 Ayala Ave., Makati, Rizal; *Ambassador:* DANIEL LAOR.

Italy: 7th Floor, Vincente Madrigal Bldg., 6793 Ayala Ave., Makati, Rizal; *Ambassador:* ALBERO SOLERA.

Japan: Sikatuna Bldg., 6762 Ayala Ave., Makati, Rizal; *Ambassador:* MASEO SAWAKI.

Korea, Republic: Rufino Building, 6784 Ayala Ave Makati, Rizal; *Ambassador:* KANG YOUNG KYOO.

Laos: Bangkok, Thailand.

Malaysia: 7th Floor, Architectural Center Bldg., Ayal Ave., Makati, Rizal; *Ambassador:* HAMID BI PAWANCHEE.

Mexico: L. & S. Bldg., 1414 Roxas Blvd., Manila; *Ambassador:* ROBERTO MOLINA-PASQUEL.

Nepal: Tokyo, Japan.

Netherlands: Metropolitan Bldg., 6813 Ayala Ave Makati, Rizal; *Ambassador:* FRANS VON OVEN.

New Zealand: Philippines Bank of Commerce Bldg., 675 Ayala Ave., Makati, Rizal; *Ambassador:* MCLEO PALM CHAPMAN.

Norway: L. & S. Bldg., 1414 Roxas Blvd., Manila; *Ambassador:* FINN S. KOREN.

Pakistan: 3rd Floor, CMI Bldg., 6799 Ayala Ave., Makat Rizal; *Ambassador:* MAQBOOL AHMAD BHATTY.

Poland: Tokyo, Japan.

Portugal: 814 Pasay Rd., San Lorenzo Village, Makat Rizal; *Ambassador:* F. J. DE SOUZA TEIXEIRA D SAMPAYO.

Romania: 1268 Acacia Rd., Dasmairñas Village, Makat Rizal; *Ambassador:* NICOLAE FINANTU.

Saudi Arabia: 8th Floor, Insular Life Bldg., 6781 Ayal Ave., Makati, Rizal; *Ambassador:* AQUIL MOHAMME AQUIL.

Singapore: Room 502, J. M. Tuason Bldg., Ayala Ave Makati, Rizal; *Ambassador:* CHEAM KIM SEANG.

Spain: Mayflower Apartments, 2515 Leon Guinto corne Estrada, Malate, Manila; *Ambassador:* D. CLEOF LIQUINIANO ELGORIAGA.

Sri Lanka: 640 Vito Cruz, Malate, Manila; *Chargé d'Affaire a.i.:* J. OLIVER PERERA.

Sweden: 10th Floor, PAL Bldg., Ayala Ave., Makat Rizal; *Ambassador:* CAI MELIN.

Switzerland: 5th Floor, V. Esquerra Bldg., 5207 Amorsol St., Makati, Rizal; *Chargé d'Affaires a.i.:* ROLF GERBE

Thailand: Oledan Bldg., 131–133 Ayala Ave., Makat Rizal; *Ambassador:* KLOS VISESSURAKARN.

Turkey: Tokyo, Japan.

United Kingdom: L. & S. Bldg., 1414 Roxas Blvd., P.O.I 295, Manila; *Ambassador:* J.A. TURPIN.

U.S.A.: 1201 Roxas Blvd., Manila; *Ambassador:* WILLIA SULLIVAN.

Vatican City: 2140 Taft Ave., Manila (Apostolic Nunciature); *Apostolic Nuncio:* Mgr. BRUNO TORPIGLIANI.

The Philippines also has diplomatic relations with Afghanistan, Algeria, Colombia, Costa Rica, Cuba, Ecuador, El Salvado Honduras, Ireland, Lebanon, Monaco, Nicaragua, Peru, the U.S.S.R., Viet-Nam and Yugoslavia.

JUDICIAL SYSTEM

Supreme Court: Composed of a Chief Justice and 14 Associate Justices. For the purpose of declaring a law or treaty unconstitutional and of imposing the death penalty, at least 10 Justices must concur. For other purposes, the concurrence of 8 Justices is enough.

Chief Justice: FRED RUIZ-CASTRO.

Court of Appeals. Consists of a Presiding Justice and thirty-five Associate Justices.

Presiding Justice: MAGNO GATMAITAN (acting).

In addition to the Supreme Court and the Court of Appeals, several lower courts exist, such as Courts of the First Instance, presided over by district judges, Circuit Criminal Courts, Juvenile and Domestic Relations Courts, City courts and Municipal courts.

Note: All members of the Philippine Bench are appointed by the President.

RELIGION

Iglesia Filipina Independiente (*Philippine Independent Church*): 1327 Alfredo St., Sta. Cruz, Manila; f. 1902; 2.9 million mems. (8 per cent of the population); The Most Rev. ISABELO DE LOS REYES, Jr., S.T.D., D.D., Head Bishop; Rt. Rev. MACARIO V. GA, Bishop Gen. Sec.; Rt. Rev. FEDERICO R. RICO, Bishop Gen. Treas.; publ. *Christian Register*.

ROMAN CATHOLIC CHURCH

Roman Catholicism is the predominant religion of the Philippines, its adherents numbering approximately 80 per cent of the population.

Metropolitan See of Manila: Most Rev. JAIME L. SIN, D.D.

Metropolitan See of Cebu: H.E. Cardinal JULIO R. ROSALES.

Metropolitan See of Nueva Segovia: Most Rev. JUAN C. SISON, D.D.

Metropolitan See of Caceres: Most Rev. TEOPISTO V. ALBERTO, D.D.

Metropolitan See of Lingayen-Dagupan: Most Rev. FREDERICO G. LIMON, D.D.

Metropolitan See of Jaro: Most Rev. ARTEMIO G. CASAS, D.D.

Metropolitan See of Cagayan de Oro: Most Rev. PATRICK H. CRONIN, D.D.

Metropolitan See of Zamboanga: Most Rev. FRANCISCO R. CRUCES, D.D.

Metropolitan See of Lipz: Most Rev. RICARDO VIDAL, D.D.

PROTESTANT CHURCHES

Union Church of Manila: P.O.B. 184 Makati, Rizal.

United Church of Christ in the Philippines: P.O.B. 718, Manila; Gen. Sec. Bishop ESTANISLAO Q. ABAINZA; 175,000 mems.; publs. *United Church Letter*, *Church and Community*.

There are about 3,000,000 Protestants.

MUSLIMS

Chief Imam: Hadji MADKI ALONTO, Governor of Lansao del Sur.

There are about 1,500,000 Muslims.

OTHERS

There are about 43,000 Buddhists and 400,000 Animists and persons of no religion.

THE PRESS

The Philippines had a large and diverse press, with about 15 metropolitan dailies and 175 weeklies, before the imposition of martial law by President Marcos in September 1972, when all newspapers and radio stations were shut down. The President claimed that he had "silenced the media because some were undermining Philippine society and giving aid and comfort to the Communists". A number of reporters, editors and publishers were arrested, and before publication could be resumed the Government's Mass Media Council had to screen staff and give its authorization. The strict controls on content and comment were gradually relaxed, and the Mass Media Council was replaced in May 1973 by a Media Advisory Council, composed of representatives of the various media. In November 1974 controls were further relaxed with the abolition of the Media Advisory Council and its replacement by the all-civilian Philippine Council for Print Media (P.C.P.M.). Newspapers are expected to publish only what the President described as news of "positive national value" and to eschew sensationalism.

DAILIES

Balita: 2249 Pasong Tamo, Makati, Rizal; Tagalog; published by Liwayway Publishing Inc.; Editor DOMINGO QUIMLAT; circ. 90,000.

Bulletin Today: Muralla St., Intramuros, Manila; English; Publisher HANS MENZI; Editor BEN F. RODRIGUEZ; circ. 156,000.

Business Day: West Ave., Quezon City; English; Publisher RAUL LOCSIN; Managing Editor EXEQUIEL MOLINA.

Daily Express: 371 Bonifacio Drive, Port Area, Manila; f. 1971; English and Pilipino editions; Publisher JUAN A. PEREZ, Jr.; Editor ENRIQUE P. ROMUALDEZ; circ. 225,000.

Evening Express: 371 Bonifacio Drive, Port Area, Manila; English; Managing Editor A. P. SANTA ANA.

Evening Post: 13th St., Port Area, Manila; Published by Orient Media Inc.; Editor KERIMA POLOTAN-TUVERA.

Orient Daily News: 489 San Fernando St., Binondo, Manila; f. 1974; English and Chinese; published by The Orient Media Inc.; Editor KERIMA POLOTAN-TUVERA.

The Times Journal: Meralco Ave., Corner Tektite Rd., Pasig, Rizal; English; published by Philippine Journalists Inc.; Editor MANUEL SALAK; circ. 90,000.

United Daily News: 818 Benavides St., Manila; f. 1973; Chinese and English; published by United Daily News Corporation; Editors SY YINCHOW and BEN PEÑARANDA; circ. 20,000.

PERIODICALS

Bannawag: 2249 Pasong Tamo, Makati, Rizal; weekly; Ilocano; published by Liwayway Publishing Inc.; Editor DAVID D. CAMPANANO; circ. 50,000.

Bisaya: 2249 Pasong Tamo, Makati, Rizal; weekly; Cebuano; published by Liwayway Publishing Inc.; Editor NAZARIO BAS; circ. 67,000.

Express Week: 371 Bonitacio Drive, Port Area, Manila; weekly; English; Publisher JUAN A PEREZ; Editor RODOLFO G. TUPAS.

Focus Philippines: Corner Railroad and 13th Sts., Port Area, Manila; Editor KERIMA POLOTAN-TUVERA.

Government Report: P.O.B. 4201, Intramuros, Manila; published by The National Media Production Center, Man. Editor MAX T. RAMOS.

Hiligaynon: 2249 Pasong Tamo, Makati, Rizal; f. 1934; weekly; Ilongo; published by Liwayway Publishing Inc.; Editor FRANCIS J. JAMOLANGUE.

Liwayway: 2249 Pasong Tamo, Makati, Rizal; weekly; Pilipino; published by Liwayway Publishing Inc.; circ. 165,000.

Philippines Today: P.O.B. 4201, Intramuros, Manila; published by The National Media Production Center.

NEWS AGENCIES

Philippines News Agency: 2nd Floor, National Press Club Bldg., Magallenes Drive, Intramuros, Manila; f. 1973; Man. JOSE L. PAVIA; Man. Editor RENATO B. TIANGCO.

FOREIGN BUREAUX

Agence France-Presse: 4th Floor, Globe Mackay—ITT Building, United Nations Ave., Binondo, Manila; Chief of Bureau TEODORO BENIGNO.

AP: L. and S. Building, 1515 Roxas Blvd., P.O.B. 2274, Manila; Chief of Bureau ARNOLD ZEITLIN.

Central News Agency (*Taiwan*): P.O.B. 3585, Room 706, Bank of Philippine Island Building, Binondo, Manila; Bureau Chief JOHN LAI.

Hsinhua (*People's Republic of China*): Roxas Blvd., Manila; correspondent LI YI-CHIEN.

Reuters: 301-B Trade and Commerce Bldg., Juan Luna, Manila; Chief Rep. COLIN BICKLER.

Tass (*U.S.S.R.*): 572 Cypress St., Dasmarinas Village, Makati, Rizal; Correspondent FELIX KONOPIKHIN.

United Press International: 4th Floor, Globe Mackay (ITT) Bldg., 669 United Nations Ave., Ermita, Manila; Bureau Chief VINCENTE MALIWANAG.

PRESS ASSOCIATIONS

National Press Club of the Philippines: Magallanes Drive, Manila; Pres. PAT GONZALES; Sec.-Gen. STEPHEN F. SERGIO.

Manila Overseas Press Club: B. F. Hones Condominiun, Aduana St., Intramuros, Manila; Pres. TEODORO F. VALENCIA.

Publisher's Association of the Philippines, Inc.: c/o Bulletin Today, Romualdez St., Paco, Manila; Pres. HANS MENZI.

PUBLISHERS

Abiva Publishing House: 942 Misericordia, Santa Cruz, Manila; f. 1949; Chair. Mrs. A. Q. ABIVA; Pres. L. Q ABIVA.

Associated Publishers Inc.: 63 Quezon Blvd. Extension, Quezon City, P.O.B. 449, Manila; f. 1952; law, medical and educational books; Pres. J. V. ROXAS.

Atlas Publications: 54A Roces Ave., Quezon City.

Bookman Printing House: 49 Quezon Blvd. Extension, Quezon City.

A. G. Briones & Co.: Room 301 Marvel Bldg., No. 1, 258 Juan Luna Street, Manila; publishes *AB Commercial Directory of the Philippines*.

Bustamente Press Inc.: 155 Panay Ave., Quezon City; f. 1949; textbooks on English, sciences and mathematics; Pres. PABLO N. BUSTAMENTE, Jr.

Capitol Publishing House Inc.: 54 Don Alejandro A. Roces Ave., Quezon City.

Filipino Publishing House Inc.: Scout Reyes St., Quezon City.

R. M. Garcia Publishing House: 903 Quezon Blvd. Ext., Quezon City; f. 1951; distributor and publisher of textbooks and Filipiniana books; Pres. and Gen. Man. ROLANDO M. GARCIA.

L. J. Gonzalez Publishers: P.O.B. 3501, 2 Broadway, Quezon City; f. 1956; magazines and brochures; Man. LUZ J. GONZALEZ.

Industry & Trade Publishers: 5 Martelino St., Quezon City.

Lawyers' Co-operative Publishing Company (Phil.) Inc.: 63 Quezon Blvd. Extension, Quezon City, P.O.B. 449, Manila; Head Office: The Lawyers' Co-operative Publishing Co., Rochester, New York 14603, U.S.A.; estab. in Manila 1913; law, medical and educational books; Pres. JAIME V. ROXAS.

Macaraig Publishing Co. Inc.: 1144 Vermont St., Paco, Manila; f. 1926; textbooks; Pres. SERAFIN E. MACARAIG.

Martinez, Roberto & Sons: 3 España, Quezon City.

Mutual Books Inc.: 465 Shaw Boulevard, Mandalvyong, Rizal 3119; college textbooks on accounting, management and economics; Chair. BENITO PAÑGILINAN.

National Book Store, Inc.: P.O.B. 1934, Rizal Ave., Manila; Pres. ALFREDO C. RAMOS; Gen. Man. SOCORRO C. RAMOS.

Philippine Arts and Architecture: 1346 U.N. Ave., Ermita, Manila.

Philippine International Publishing Co.: 1789 A. Mabini St., Ermita, Manila.

Regal Publishing Co.: 1729 J. P. Laurel Sr., San Miguel, Manila; Man. ALBERTO D. BENIPAYO.

Tamaraw Publishing Co.: 167 Mother Ignacia Ave., Quezon City.

The Macmillan Co.: 1336 Paz St., Paco, Manila.

University Publishing Co.: Central Office, 1128 Washington, Sampaloc, Manila; f. 1936; Dirs. Dr. JOSÉ M ARUEGO and Mrs. CONSTANCIA E. ARUEGO.

RADIO AND TELEVISION

Broadcast Media Council: Manila; replaced the Media Advisory Council and the Bureau of Standards for Mass Media; overseas the broadcast industry in the areas of sales, advertising, programming, research, engineering and manpower development; provides self-regulation for radio and television; issues permits to operate stations for specified periods; provides standards for the industry and rationalizes the Philippine broadcast band; Chair. TEODORO F. VALENCIA.

Kapisanan Ng Mga Brodkaster Sa Pilipinas: Manila; association of broadcasters; acts in liaison with other related agencies on advertising matters and membership considerations; Chair. ANTONIO C. BARREIRO; Pres. TEODORO F. VALENCIA.

Telecommunication Control Bureau: Department of Public Works, Transportation and Communications, Manila; regulates the installation, establishment and operation of all radio stations; and the possession, sale or purchase of radio transmitters and receivers; Dir. CEFERINO S. CARREON (acting).

RADIO

There are 230 radio stations, 40 of which are in the Greater Manila area and the remainder in the provincial areas. The following are the principal operating networks:

Banahaw Broadcasting Corporation: Broadcast Plaza, Bohol Ave., Quezon City; 14 stations; Pres. ALEX LUKBAN; Gen. Man. SALVADOR TAN.

DPI Radio-TV Network: GSIS Building, Arroceros St., Manila; 10 stations; Dir. FLORENTINO DAUZ.

Far East Broadcasting Company: P.O.B. 2041, Manila; f. 1948; 7 stations; operates a home service 24 hours a day, a cultural music station, an overseas service throughout Asia in 73 languages; Pres. ROBERT HANN BROWNE; Dir. FRED M. MAGBANUA, Jr.; publ. *The Signal* (bi-monthly).

Manila Broadcasting Co.: Elizalde Bldg., Ayala Ave., Makati, Rizal; 5 stations; Gen. Man. Atty. EDUARDO L. MONTILLA.

Nation Broadcasting Corporation: 4th Floor, Sikatuna Bldg., Ayala Ave., Makati, Rizal; 19 stations; Pres. and Gen. Man. ABELARDO YABUT, Sr.; Vice-Pres. for Operations CEFERINO BASILIO.

Northern Broadcasting Co.: Suites 408–409 Chateau Makati Bldg., F. Zobel St., Makati, Rizal; 11 stations; Pres. MARCELINO FLORETE; Vice-Pres. for Operations VIC DE VERA; Gen. Man. ANTONIO C. BARREIRO.

Radio Mindanao Network: Suites 411–413 Chateau Makati Bldg., F. Zobel St., Makati, Rizal; 11 stations; Pres. and Gen. Man. HENRY R. CANOY; Vice-Pres. WILFREDO CAMOMOT.

Radio Philippines Network: Broadcast Plaza, Bohol Ave., Quezon City; 16 stations; Pres. EXEQUIEL GARCIA; Gen. Man. SALVADOR TAN.

Radio-Republic Broadcasting System: E. de los Santos Ave., Diliman, Quezon City; Chair. GILBERTO M. DUAVIT; Pres. MENARDO R. JIMENEZ.

TELEVISION

There are five major television networks operating in the country with 17 relay stations. The following are the principal operating television networks:

Banahaw Broadcasting Corporation: Broadcast Plaza, Bohol Ave., Quezon City; 4 stations; Pres. ALEX LUKBAN; Gen. Man. SALVADOR TAN.

GMA Radio Television Arts: E. de los Santos Ave., Diliman, Quezon City; 2 stations; Pres. MEWARDO JIMENEZ; Gen. Man. FEDERICO GARCIA.

GTV—4: Broadcast Plaza, Bohol Ave., Quezon City; 1 station; Government service; Dir. GREG CENDANA.

Intercontinental Broadcasting Corporation: P. Guevarra St., San Juan, Rizal; 8 stations; Gen. Man. JOSE TALARON.

Radio Philippines Network: Broadcast Plaza, Bohol Ave., Quezon City; 6 stations; Pres. EXEQUIEL GARCIA; Gen. Man. SALVADOR TAN.

Republic Broadcasting System: E. de Los Santos Ave., Diliman, Quezon City; Station DZBB-TV; Chair. GILBERTO M. DUAVIT; Pres. MENARDO R. JIMENEZ.

FINANCE

(cap.=capital, p.u.=paid up, dep.=deposits, m.=million, amounts in pesos)

BANKING

The Central Bank of the Philippines supervises the entire financial system.

The financial structure consists of: (1) the banking system: commercial banks, thrift banks (savings and mortgage banks, stock savings and loan associations and private development banks), regional unit banks (rural banks), and specialized and unique government banks such as the Development Bank of the Philippines, and the Land Bank of the Philippines; (2) non-bank financial intermediaries: investment houses and companies, securities dealers, financing companies, fund managers, pawnshops and lending investors.

CENTRAL BANK

Central Bank of the Philippines: A. Mabini corner Vito Cruz, Malate, Manila; f. 1949; cap. 10m.; dep. 7,330m. (March 1976); Gov. and Chair. (Monetary Board) GREGORIO S. LICAROS.

GOVERNMENT BANK

Philippine National Bank (PHILNABANK): P.O.B. 1844, PNB Bldg., Escolta, Manila; government controlled; f. 1916; cap. 701.7m. (Dec. 1974); dep. 6,779m. (March 1976); Chair. J. PONCE ENRILE; Pres. P. O. DOMINGO; Exec. Vice-Pres. M. Y. CONSING; 177 brs. and agencies; 122 mobile banks; 9 overseas offices.

Principal Commercial Banks

Bank of the Philippine islands: P.O.B. 1827 MCC, Makati, Rizal; f. 1851; cap. p.u. 184.6m.; dep. 1,132m. (Sept. 1975); Pres. Alberto de Villa-Abrille; 49 brs.

China Banking Corporation: Corner Dasmariñas and Juan Luna, P.O.B. 611, Manila; f. 1920; cap. 75.3m.; dep. 601.6m. (March 1976); Chair. and Gen. Man. Albino Z. Sy Cip; Pres. George Dee Sekiat; 4 brs.

Commercial Bank and Trust Co. of the Philippines: CBTC Bldg., Ayala Ave., Makati, Rizal; f. 1954; total resources 1,091.5m. (Sept. 1975); Chair. Manuel J. Marquez; Pres. Vicente A. Pacis, Jr.

Far East Bank and Trust Co.: Far East Bank Bldg., Muralla, Intramuros, Manila (P.O.B. 1411); f. 1960; cap. 52m. (Sept. 1973); dep. 872.4m. (March 1976); Chair. José B. Fernandez, Jr.; Pres. A. M. Barcelon; 26 brs.

Filipinas Manufacturers Bank: Ayala Ave., Makati, Rizal; dep. 207.5m. (March 1976); Chair. Romeo R. Eschauz; Pres. Conrado T. Calang.

General Bank and Trust Co.: 560 Quintin Paredes St., Binondo. Manila; f. 1963; Pres. and Chair. Dr. Clarencio S. Yujuico; dep. 276.8m. (March 1976); 22 brs.

Metropolitan Bank and Trust Co.: Ayala Ave., Makati, Rizal; f. 1962; dep. 963.9m. (March 1976); Chair. George S. K. Ty; Pres. Andres V. Castillo; 59 brs.

Pacific Banking Corporation: 460 Quintin Paredes St., Manila; f. 1955; cap. 105.3m. (Oct 1975); dep. 611.2m. (March 1976); Chair. Antonio Roxas Chua; Pres. and Gen. Man. Chester G. Babst; 19 brs.

Philippine Commercial and Industrial Bank: Antonio Building, T. M. Kalaw St., Ermita, Manila; f. 1960; cap. 126.8m.; dep. 581.4m. (Dec. 1975); Chair. Emilio Abello; Pres. Placido L. Mapa, Jr.; 39 brs.

Philippine Trust Co.: Plaza Lacson, Manila; f. 1916; cap. 98.7m. (Dec. 1974); dep. 123.8m. (March 1976); Pres. L. de la Llana; Vice-Pres. Juan S. Pelea; 3 brs.

Philippine Veterans Bank: Bonifacio Drive, Port Area, Manila; f. 1964; loans granted to both veterans and non-veterans; dep. 753.8m. (1975); Chair. Alejo Santos; Pres. Esteban B. Cabanos; 24 brs.

Rizal Commercial Banking Corpn.: 333 Buendia Ave. Extension, Makati, Rizal; f. 1963; cap. 63m.; dep. 533m. (Dec. 1975); Chair. A. T. Yuchengco; Vice-Chair. Alberto M. Meer.

Foreign Banks

Bank of America: 8751 Paseo de Roxas, Makati, Rizal D-708, Manila; Vice-Pres. and Man. David A. Artko.

Chartered Bank: London; 7901 Makati Ave., Makati, Rizal; Man. R. Pudner.

Citibank: 120 Juan Luna St., Binondo, Manila; Vice-Pres. Daniel Jacobson.

Hongkong and Shanghai Banking Corporation: PAL Bldg., Ayala Ave., Makati, Rizal; Res. Man. D. G. Harrison.

Rural Banks

Small private banks established with the encouragement and assistance (both financial and technical) of the Government in order to promote and expand the rural economy in an orderly manner. Conceived mainly to stimulate the productive capacities of small farmers, small merchants and small industrialists in rural areas, and to combat usury, their principal objectives are to place within easy reach and access of the people credit facilities on reasonable terms and, in co-operation with other agencies of the Government, to provide advice on business and farm management and the proper use of credit for production and marketing purposes. The nation's rural banking system consisted of over 781 units in 1975.

Special Banks

Development Bank of the Philippines: DBP Bldg., Corner Makati and Buendia Aves., Makati, Rizal; f. 1947; wholly owned by the Government; provides long-term loans for agricultural and industrial development; Chair. Leonides S. Virata; 56 brs.

In addition there are 24 private development banks.

Land Bank of the Philippines: 6th Floor, B.F. Condominium, Aduana St., Manila; f. 1966; provides financial support in all phases of the Government's agrarian reform programme; Chair. Cesar E. A. Virata; Pres. Basilio Estanislao; 3 brs.

Bankers' Association of the Philippines: 12th Floor, Philbanking Corpn. Bldg., Port Area, Manila; Pres. J. B. Fernandez, Jr.

DEVELOPMENT ORGANIZATIONS

National Economic Development Authority (NEDA): Neda Bldg., Padre Faura, Manila; f. 1973; central planning and policy formulation body for the Philippines, to ensure the better utilization of public resources and to increase economic efficiency; Minister of Econ. Planning Gerardo Sicat.

Agricultural Credit Administration (ACA): 2544 Taft Ave., Manila; wholly government-owned corporation; provides credit extension to farmers.

National Development Company (NDC): Pureza St., Sta. Mesa, Manila; f. 1919; wholly government-owned corporation engaged in the organization, financing and management of subsidiaries and corporations including commercial, industrial, mining, agricultural and other enterprises which may be necessary or contributory to the economic development of the country; Chair. Constante L. Fariñas; Gen. Man. Carlos P. Morales.

Philippine Rural Reconstruction Movement (PRRM): Manila; a non-profit-making, private, civic agency; f. 1952; operates social laboratories in selected Philippine villages in which new and creative approaches to rural development are tested and validated; Human Resource Development centre offers graduate studies in community development and non-formal training for rural leaders; Chair., Board of Trustees Manuel P. Manahan.

Private Development Corporation of the Philippines (PDCP): PDCP Bldg., Ayala Ave., Makati, Rizal; f. 1963 with World Bank assistance; assists private enterprise development in the Philippines, especially of capital markets and managerial skills, total loans 1963–Dec. 1974: foreign currency loans U.S. $121m., peso currency loans 147m. pesos; Chair. and Pres. Roberto T. Villanueva.

STOCK EXCHANGES

Makati Stock Exchange: Ayala Ave., Makati, Rizal; Pres. Jose Campos.

Manila Stock Exchange: Manila Stock Exchange Bldg; Muelle de la Industria and Prensa Sts., Binondo, Manila; f. 1927; 43 mems.; Pres. Enrique Santamaría; Exec. Vice-Pres. Anthony Dee K. Chiong, Jr.; Sec. Simplicio J. Roxas; publs. *MSE Weekly Letter, MSE Pamphlet, MSE Monthly Review, Profile of Philippine Securities.*

Metropolitan Stock Exchange: E. Rodriguez Blvd., Quezon City; Pres. TEOFILO REYES.

INSURANCE

Asian Surety and Insurance Co. Inc.: W. L. Yao Bldg., Manila; Pres. W. LI YAO; fire, casualty, car, marine, personal accident.

Associated Insurance & Surety Co., Inc.: David-M. de Banco. Nacional, Manila; Pres. E. A. SUAREZ.

Capital Insurance and Surety Co. Inc.: P.O.B. 1613, Escolta, Manila; f. 1949; Pres. J. G. GARRDIO; Chair. J. MUÑOZ; fire, casualty, marine, life.

Central Surety & Insurance Co.: 10th Floor, Philippine Banking Building, Port Area, Manila; auth. cap. 5m. pesos; Pres. CONSTANCIO T. CASTAÑEDA; bonds, fire, marine, casualty, motor car, workmen's compensation.

Commercial Insurance and Surety Co., Inc.: 469 Solana St., Intramuros, Manila; non-life insurance.

Commonwealth Insurance Co.: Warner Barnes Bldg., 2900 Faraday Cnr. South Expressway, Makati, Rizal; f. 1935; cap. 4m. pesos; Pres. A. ROXAS; Vice-Pres. E. P. ESTEBAN, J. P. DE GUZMAN.

Domestic Insurance Company of the Philippines: Domestic Insurance Bldg., Port Area, Manila; f. 1946; Pres. A. L. ACHAVAL; Man. J. I. PUEO; fire, marine, motor car, fidelity and surety and allied lines.

Empire Insurance Co.: Prudential Bank Bldg., Ayala Ave., Makati, Rizal; f. 1949; Chair. SERGIO CORPUS; fire, bonds, marine, accident, extraneous perils.

Equitable Insurance Corporation: Equitable Bank Bldg., Juan Luna St., P.O.B. 1103, Manila; Pres. Dr. ROQUE D. YAP; fire, marine, accident, workmen's compensation, car.

Far Eastern Surety and Insurance Co. Inc.: Martinez Bldg., P.O. Box 345, Manila; f. 1934; Pres. ANTONIO TAN KIANG.

FGU Insurance Corporation: Insular Life Bldg., 6781 Ayala Ave., Makati, Rizal, P.O.B. 70, Makati; f. 1963; Chair. E. ZOBEL.

Fidelity and Surety Co. of the Philippines, Inc.: Plaza Lacson, Manila; f. 1912; Pres. PATERNO M. SISANTE.

First Continental Assurance Co. Inc.: Concepcion Bldg., corner Victoria and Muralla Streets, Intramuros, Manila; f. 1960; Pres. G. B. LICAROS, Jr.; fire, marine, motor car, accident, workmen's compensation, bonds.

First National Surety & Assurance Co. Inc.: Insurance Center Bldg., 633 Gen. Luna St., Intramuros, Manila; f. 1950; Pres. and Gen. Man. D. L. MERCADO; all kinds of non-life insurance, bonds and investments.

The Insular Life Assurance Co. Ltd.: Insular Life Bldg., 6781 Ayala Ave., Makati, Rizal, P.O.B. 128, Manila; incorporated 1910; Pres. RAMON A. DIAZ.

Luzon Surety Co. Inc.: 180 David St., Manila; f. 1929; Pres. E. RODRIGUEZ, Sr.

Malayan Insurance Co. Inc.: P.O.B. 3389, 484 Rosario St., Manila; f. 1949; industrial and commercial; Pres. ALFONSO YUCHENGCO; cap. 2,500,000 pesos.

Manila Insurance Company, Inc.: 119 Dasmariñas Street, Binondo, Manila; f. 1917; Pres. JOSÉ P. FERNÁNDEZ; Vice-Pres. CARLOS P. FERNANDEZ.

Manila Surety & Fidelity Co., Inc.: 66 P. Florentino, Quezon City; f. 1945; Pres. Dr. PRECIOSO S. PEÑA; Vice-Pres. Dr. ELISA V. PEÑA.

Manila Underwriters Insurance Co. Inc.: 221 Natividad Bldg., Escolta, Manila; f. 1949; Pres. T. R. FLORO.

Metropolitan Insurance Company: Elizalde Bldg., 141 Ayala Ave., Makati, Rizal; f. 1933; Pres. MANUEL ELIZALDE; Vice-Pres. and Man. G. A. REEDYK; non-life.

National Life Insurance Company of the Philippines: 306 Regina Bldg., Escolta, Manila; Chair. J. V. MACUJA; Pres. B. de LEON.

Paramount Surety and Insurance Co. Inc.: Paramount Bldg., 434 Rosario St., Manila; Pres. TION SIM; fire, marine, casualty, car.

People's Surety & Insurance Co., Inc.: Trade Center Bldg., Cnr. P. Faura and A. Mabini Sts., Manila; f. 1950; Chair. Dr. A. LIBORO; non-life, surety, fidelity.

Philippine American Accident Insurance Co. Inc.: Philamlife Bldg., U.N. Ave., Manila; f. 1961; Chair. W. SWARTZENDRUBER; Pres. M. CAMPOS; Exec. Vice-Pres. W. E. WINEBRENNER; all classes of general insurance.

Philippine American General Insurance Group: Philamlife Bldg., U.N. Ave., Manila; f. 1950; Chair. E. CARROLL; Pres. M. CAMPOS; Exec. Vice-Pres. W. E. WINEBRENNER; all classes of general insurance.

Philippine American Life Insurance Co.: Philamlife Bldg., United Nations Ave., Ermita, Manila; f. 1947; Chair. W. SWARTZENDRUBER; Pres. C. C. ZALAMEA; Exec. Vice-Pres. R. DE LOS REYES.

The Philippine Guaranty Co. Inc.: Insular Life Bldg., 6781 Ayala Ave., Makati, Rizal, P.O.B. 70, Commercial Centre, Makati; f. 1917; Chair. E. ZOBEL.

Philippine Prudential Life Insurance Co. Inc.: Insurance Center Bldg., 633 Gen. Luna St., Intramuros, Manila; f. 1963; Pres. and Gen. Man. D. L. MERCADO; life, health and accident.

Philippine Reinsurance Corporation: 516–517 Bank of Philippine Islands Bldg., Plaza Cervantes, Manila; f. 1958; Chair. SERGIO CORPUS; reinsurance in all branches.

Philippine Surety & Insurance Co. Inc.: 224 Natividad Bldg., Escolta, Manila; Pres. C. MARTIN.

Philippine Underwriters Corpn.: General managers for: Sterling Life Assurance Corpn., Filriters Guaranty Assurance Corpn., F.G.R. Bldg., Buendia Ave., Makati, Rizal; Chair. LUZ B. MAGSAYSAY; Pres. ATTY H. V. RODIS; general insurance.

Pioneer Insurance and Surety Corpn.: Pioneer House, 320 Nueva Corner, Escolta, Manila; f. 1954; cap. p.u. 10m.; Chair. JOHNNY CHENG; Pres. ROBERT COYIUTO.

Provident Insurance Company of the Philippines: 416 Natividad Bldg., Escolta, Manila; Gen. Man. JOSE DE LEON.

Reinsurance Company of the Orient, Inc.: 2nd Floor, Rico House, 126 Arnorsolo St., Makati, Rizal; f. 1956; Pres. JOSE P. ALVENDIA; all classes.

Rico General Insurance Corporation: 2nd Floor, RICO House, 126 Amorsolo St., Legaspi Village, Makati, Rizal; f. 1964; Chair. and Pres. Justice CARMELINO G. ALVENIDA; Gen. Man. ROMEO A. MALLARI.

Rico Life Insurance Co., Inc.: RICO Bldg., 533 United Nations Ave., Ermita, Manila; Chair. CARMELINO G. ALVENDIA; Pres. Hon. JAIME HERNANDEZ; Officer-in-charge MIGUEL P. CRUZ.

Rizal Surety and Insurance Co.: Roman R. Santos Building, Plaza Goiti, Manila; f. 1939; Chair. A. A. SANTOS.

South Sea Surety and Insurance Co. Inc.: 55 M. de Binondo, Manila; f. 1947; Pres. V. L. CO CHIEN.

Standard Insurance Co. Inc.: 5th Floor, Cardinal Bldg., cnr. F. Agoncillo and Herran Sts., Manila; f. 1958; Pres. Mrs. LOURDES T. ECHAUZ.

State Bonding & Insurance Co. Inc.: Jacinto Bldg., 375 Escolta, Manila; cap. p.u. 2.2m.; Chair. N. JACINTO.

Tabacalera Insurance Co., Inc.: Bank of P.I. Bldg., Ayala Ave., Makati, Rizal 3116; f. 1937; Pres. ALEJANDRO ROS DE LACOUR; Chair. MANUEL P. MANAHAN.

Traders' Insurance & Surety Co.: 277 Juan Luna St., Manila; Pres. J. V. Limpe; Gen. Man. J. T. Limpe.

Union Surety & Insurance Co., Inc.: Metropolitan Theatre Bldg., Plaza Lawton, Manila; Pres. R. F. Navarro.

United Insurance Co., Inc.: Padillade los Reyes Bldg., Manila; Pres. I. K. Yang.

Universal Reinsurance Corporation: Insular Life Bldg., 6781 Ayala Ave., Makati, Rizal, P.O.B. 70, Commercial Center, Makati; f. 1971; Chair. Enrique J. Zobel; Pres. Mauro Blardony, Jr.

Visayan Surety and Insurance Corpn.: Vista Bldg., Quiapo, Manila; Pres. F. Go Chan.

Workmen's Insurance Co., Inc.: 6th Floor, G. E. Antonino Bldg., T.M. Kalaw, Ermita, Manila; f. 1961; Chair. Dr. Pacifico E. Marcos; Pres. and Gen. Man. Firmo O. Liwanag; fire, motor vehicle, marine cargo and hull, transportation, accidents, casualty bonds.

World-Wide Insurance & Surety Co. Inc.: 4th Floor, Cardinal Bldg., Corner Herran and F. Agoncillo Streets, Ermita, Manila; f. 1950; affiliated with Standard-Cardinal Life Insurance Companies; Pres. Romeo R. Echauz; fire, marine, motor car, accident, workmen's compensation, loans, mortgages, bonds, aviation.

The majority of the larger British, American and Canadian insurance companies are represented in Manila.

TRADE AND INDUSTRY

TRADING CORPORATIONS

Philippine International Trading Corporation (PITC): 3rd Floor, ITC Bldg., Buendia Cor. Reposo St., Makati, Rizal; f. 1976; government-owned stock corporation to conduct bulk trade in raw materials: Pres. Felimon C. Rodriguez.

Philippine Exporters Trading Corporation (PETLOR): Equitable Bank Bldg., Manila; Private corporation designed to promote exports; Ad interim Pres. Henry Brimo; Vice-Pres. Francisco Wenceslao.

CHAMBERS OF COMMERCE AND INDUSTRY

Chamber of Agriculture and Natural Resources of the Philippines: Med-Dis Bldg., corner Solaña and Real Sts., Intramuros, Manila.

Chamber of Commerce of the Philippines: Magallanes Drive, Intramuros, Manila 2801; f. 1903; 1,420 mems.; Pres. Fred J. Elizalde; Sec.-Treas. R. J. de la Cuesta; publ. *Commerce*.

Federation of Filipino-Chinese Chambers of Commerce Inc.: P.O.B. 23, 6th Floor, Federation Centre, Muelle de Binondo, Manila; Pres. Ralph Nubla.

International Chamber of Commerce of Iloilo: P.O.B. 54, Iloilo City 5901; f. 1924; 63 mems.; Pres. Francisco M. de la Cruz; publ. *Journal*.

Manila Chamber of Commerce Inc.: P.O.B. 763, Room 410, Shurdut Bldg., Intramuros, Manila; f. 1898; 59 mems.; Pres. B. H. Martin; Vice-Pres. M. V. Bane, R. Pudner.

Mandaluyong Chamber of Commerce and Industry: Mandaluyong, Rizal.

Philippines Chamber of Industries: L & S Bldg. No. 2, 1515 Roxas Boulevard, Manila; f. 1950; 675 mems.; Pres. Raul A. Boncan; publ. *Industrial Philippines*.

Philippine Chinese Chamber of Commerce: 1122 Soler, Manila.

There are other Philippine Chambers of Commerce in all the more important towns and seaports.

American Chamber of Commerce of the Philippines Inc.: 6th Floor, SBTC Building, Ayala Ave., Makati, Rizal, P.O.B. 1836, Manila.

Cámara Oficial Española de Comercio (*Spanish Chamber of Commerce*): 510 Romero Salas, Ermita, Manila; f. 1899; Pres. Alejandro Ros; Vice-Pres. Luis Antúnez; publ. *Spanish Economic News* (weekly).

French Chamber of Commerce: P.O.B. 3095, Manila.

EMPLOYERS' ASSOCIATIONS

Base Metals Association of the Philippines: Manila Banking Corpn. Bldg., Ayala Ave., Makati, Rizal; 12 mems.; Chair. Jesús S. Cabarrus; Pres. Sebastian Ugarte; Sec. H. T. Cawile.

Filipino Shipowners' Association: R.212 Magsaysay Bldg., T. M. Kalaw St., Ermita, Manila; f. 1950; 17 mems.; Chair. and Pres. Miguel A. Magsaysay; Exec. Sec. Ramon G. Santillan.

Philippine Cigar and Cigarette Manufacturers Association: 4 L. Avelino St., Parañague, Rizal.

Philippine Coconut Producers Federation, Inc: Suite D. Loreaco Bldg., Vitocruz corner Taft Ave., Manila.

Philippine Copra Exporters Association Inc.: Gabaldon Bldg., 943 Jil Escoda St., Ermita, Manila.

Philippine Sugar Association: Suite 1111, Sikatuna Building, Ayala Ave., Makati, Rizal; f. 1922; Pres. Manuel Elizalde; Exec. Officer and Sec.-Treas Edgardo F. Q. Yap; 17 mems.

Pulp and Paper Manufacturers' Association Inc.: Room 302, Magsaysay Bldg., Teodoro M. Kalan St., Ermita, Manila; f. 1959; Pres. Francisco P. Monge.

Sugar Producers' Co-operative Marketing Association, Inc.: 7th Floor, Kalayaan Bldg., Corner Salcedo and Dela Rosa Sts., Makati, Rizal, P.O.B. 3839, Manila; Pres. A. U. Benedicto; Sec. D. M. Locsin.

Textile Mills Association of the Philippines, Inc. (TMAP): Unit 102, Alexander House, 132 Amorsolo St., Legaspi Village, Makati, Rizal; f. 1956; 52 mems., Pres. Raymundo Lorenzana.

TRADE UNIONS

Federations

Trade Union Congress of the Philippines: Suite 613, Shurdut Bldg., Intramuros, Manila; affiliates include PTGWO, CUGCO, PCWF, etc.; 1 million mems.

Confederation of Citizens Labor Unions (CCLU): R.303 Free Press Building, 708 Rizal Ave., Manila; f. 1951; 21 affiliated unions; Pres. Leon O. Ty.

Confederation of Unions in Government Corporations (CUGC): 10 Roosevelt Ave., Diliman, Quezon City; f. 1956; about 12 affiliates; Pres. Emmanuel Clave.

Federation of Free Workers (FFW): Suite E, Ysmael Apts., 1845 Taft Ave., P.O.B. 163, Manila; f. 1950; affiliated to the Brotherhood of Asian Trade Unions and the

WCL; about 370 affiliated unions and 200,000 mems.; Pres. JUAN C. TAN; Exec. Vice-Pres. RAMON JABAR.

National Association of Trade Unions (NATU): Suite 401, San Luis Terraces, Ermita, Manila; f. 1954; about 27,000 mems.; Pres. IGNACIO P. LACSINA.

National Labour Union Inc.: 3199 Sta. Mesa Blvd., Manila; f. 1929; Pres. EULOGIO R. LERUM; Sec. ANTONIO V. POLICARPIO; 100,000 mems.; publ. *National Labor Unionist* (quarterly).

Philippines Association of Free Labor Unions (PAFLU): 1233 Tecson-Tindalo, Tondo, Manila; f. 1951; 380 affiliated unions, about 75,000 mems.; Pres. CIPRIANO CID; Exec. Sec. ISRAEL DE C. BOCOBO.

Philippines Trade Union Council (PTUC): f. 1954; 49 affiliated unions, about 238,000 mems.; affiliated to ICFTU; Pres. CIPRIANO CID; Gen. Sec. JOSÉ J. HERNANDEZ.

Philippine Transport and General Workers' Organization (PTGWO): Port Area, Manila; 180 affiliates; 45,000 mems.; Pres. ROBERTO S. OCA, Sr.; Sec. JOHNNY S. OCA.

Textile and Allied Workers' Federation: 3,400 mems.; Pres. V. L. ARNIEGO.

MAJOR INDUSTRIAL COMPANIES

CEMENT

Bacnotan Consolidated Industries Inc.: 3rd. floor, Bank of P. I. Bldg., Ayala Ave., Makati, Rizal; f. 1957; manufacture of cement and G. I. sheets; cap. 118 million pesos; 550 employees; Chair. E. O. ESCALER; Pres. F. C. RODRIGUEZ.

Northern Cement Corporation: Sikatuna Bldg., Ayala Ave., Makati, Rizal.

Union Industries Inc.: Ermita Center Bldg., Ermita, Manila.

COCONUT PRODUCTS

Franklin Baker Company of the Philippines: Luzon Stevedoring Bldg., Port Area, Manila. Processors and exporters of desiccated coconut.

Lu Do and Lu Ym Corporation: P.O.B. 18, Tupas St., Cebu City; f. 1896; manufacturer of crude coconut oil, refined edible oil, and laundry soap; cap. 45 million pesos; 700 employees; Pres. C. LU DO.

Philippine Refining Co., Inc.: 1351 United Nations Ave., Manila; f. 1927; detergents, toilet preparations, and food manufacturers; processors of coconut oil; Pres. H. ZAYCO.

MINING

Acoje Mining Co., Inc.: 2283 Pasong Tamo Ext., Makati, Rizal.

Atlas Consolidated Mining and Development Corpn.: A. Soriano Bldg., Paseo de Roxas, Makati, Rizal; f. 1935; mining of mostly copper ore; also magnetite and pyrite ore and precious metals; cap. 896 million pesos; 8,000 employees; Chair./Pres. J. M. SORIANO; Sec. A. R. INFANTE.

Benguet Consolidated Inc.: P.O.B. 7343, Airmails Exchange Office, Manila International Airport, 3120; f. 1903; cap. 50m. pesos; Pres. JAIME V. ONGPIN.

Consolidated Mines Inc.: Consolidated Mines Incorporated Bldg., Makati, Rizal.

Marcopper Mining Corporation: V. Madrigal Bldg., Makati, Rizal.

POWER

Manila Electric Company (Meralco): Lopez Bldg., Meralco Center, Pasig, Rizal. Supplies electric power to Manila and six provinces in Luzon.

National Power Corporation: 161 Bonifacio Drive, Port Area, Manila; f. 1936. A state-owned corporation supplying electric and hydro-electric power to the whole country; Gen. Man. CESAR DEL ROSARIO.

OIL

Philippine National Oil Co.: Chair. GERONIMO VELASCO.

SUGAR

Binalbagan Sugar Co., Inc.: SGV Bldg., Ayala Ave., Makati, Rizal.

Central Azucarera de la Carlota: 141 Ayala Ave., Makati, Rizal.

Hawaiian-Philippine Company: 222 Buendia Ave., Makati, Rizal; f. 1918; raw sugar production and molasses; cap. 50m. pesos; 1,030 employees; Pres. E. G. VORSTER; Man. G. D. GORDON.

Victorias Milling Co., Inc.: 4th Floor, Bank of P.I. Bldg., Ayala Ave., Makati, Rizal; P.B. 762 or C.C.P.O.B. 1211, Makati, Rizal.

Southern Negros Development Corpn.: Femii Bldg., Intramuras, Manila.

TEXTILES

General Textiles Inc.: E. Rodriguez Ave., Ext. Libis, Murphy, Quezon City.

Riverside Mills Corporation: Bo. Rosario, Pasig, Rizal.

Universal Textile Mills Inc.: Barranca, Marikina, Rizal.

TOBACCO

Columbia Tobacco Co., Inc.: 305 J. Rizal, Maudaluyong, Rizal.

La Perla Industries, Inc.: Chengt-saijun Bldg., Quirino Ave., Parañaque, Rizal.

La Suerte Cigar and Cigarette Factory: South Super Highway, Parañaque, Rizal.

WOOD AND WOOD PRODUCTS

Aguinaldo Development Corporation: Adecor Bldg., U.N. Ave., corner Romualdez St., Manila.

Insular Lumber Company (PHILS.), Inc.: P.O.B. 3377, Manila; 15th floor, China Bank Bldg., Paseo de Roxas, Makati, Rizal; Hinoba-an, Negros Occidental (Mills); f. 1904 (U.S.A.), 1966 inc. in Philippines; wood processing, biggest hardwood mill in the world, major exporter of mahogany, sawn lumber and lumber products; cap. 75 million pesos; 1,600 employees; Chair. CARLOS PALANCA, Jr.; Pres. A. M. VELAYO; Vice-Pres. and Gen. Man. M. V. VIÑALON.

L. S. Sarmiento & Co., Inc. and Sarmiento Industries, Inc.: Sarmiento Bldg., 2 Pasong Tamo Extension, Makati, Rizal R.P.; manufacturers and exporters of plywood and panels, lumber and woodwork products.

Sta. Clara Lumber Co., Inc.: 1360 L. Guinto St., Manila.

Zamboanga Wood Products, Inc.: Sarmiento Bldg., P. Tamo Ext., Makati, Rizal.

MISCELLANEOUS

Aboitiz & Co., Inc.: P.O.B. 65, 183 J. Luna St., Cebu City 6401; f. 1920; exporter of copra and hemp, importer to general merchandise, industrial and agricultrual machinery; cap. 100 million pesos; Pres. EDUARDO J. ABOITIZ; Gen. Man. LUIS ABOITIZ, Jr.

Paper Industries Corporation of the Philippines: JMT Bldg., Ayala Ave., Makati, Rizal.

Commonwealth Foods, Inc.: Far East Bank Bldg., Makati, Rizal; cocoa and coffee.

Republic Flour Mills, Inc.: Pioneer St., Pasig, Rizal; f. 1959; food processing, flour mills and poultry farms; 1,000 employees; Pres. and Chief Exec. Officer J. CONCEPCION Jr.; Chair. B. J. SERVER.

Planters Products Cooperative Marketing and Supply, Inc.: Planters Products Bldg., Esteban St., Legaspi Village; fertilizers.

Atlantic Gulf and Pacific Co. of Manila, Inc.: 8th Floor, Oledan Bldg., 131–133 Ayala Ave., Makati, Rizal; iron and steel.

Industrial Textile Mfg. Co. of the Philippines: P.O.B. 942, Manila; manufacturer of polyprophlene woven bags and cloth.

TRANSPORT

RAILWAYS

Philippine National Railways: 943 Claro M. Recto Ave., Manila; f. 1892; government owned; 1,067 km. of tracks (1971); the northern line runs from Manila to San Fernando, La Unión, and the southern line from Manila to Legaspi, Albay; Chair. Col. SALVADOR T. VILLA; Vice-Chair./Man. Dir. Col. NICANOR T. JIMENEZ.

Phividec Railways: P.O.B. 300, Iloilo City, Panay; f. 1906; operated by the Philippine Veterans Investment Development Corpn.; 116 km.; Gen. Man. R. D. DOCTURA.

ROADS

Department of Public Highways: Manila; in June 1975 the Philippines had a total of 104,195 km. of roads. Commissioner BALTAZAR AQUINO.

Philippine Motor Association: P.O.B. 999, Manila; Pres. MANUEL LIM; Vice-Pres. JUAN E. TUASON.

SHIPPING

NATIONAL LINES

Botelho Bulk Transport Corpn.: 8th Floor, Antonino Building, T. M. Kalaw St., Ermita, Manila; f. 1966; 5 vessels; Pres. A. A. R. BOTELHO.

De La Rama Steamship Co., Inc.: P.O.B. 1800, Rizal D-708; Chair. and Pres. ESTEBAN R. OSMENA; services to U.S.A., Hong Kong and Japan.

Eastern Shipping Lines, Inc.: UPL Bldg., Intramuros, Manila; 6 vessels; Pres. Cong. JAMES L. CHIONGBIAN; services to Japan and Philippines.

Lusteveco (Luzon Stevedoring Co.): Tacoma and Second Sts., Port Area, P.O.B. 582, Manila; f. 1909; world-wide tanker and towage operations; fleet of 36 tankers, 182 tugs and 674 barges; Chair. VINCENTE G. PUYAT; Pres. DONALD I. MARSHALL.

Magsaysay Lines, Inc.: Magsaysay Building, 520 T. M. Kalaw St., Ermita, Manila (P.O.B. 21); 4 vessels; Chair. ROBERT C. F. HO; Pres. MIGUEL A. MAGSAYSAY; Shipping agents and brokers.

Maritime Company of the Philippines: 105 Dasmarinas St., (P.O.B. 805), Manila; 9 cargo vessels; Chair. J. P. FERNANDEZ; Man. WILLIAM R. PALOU.

Philippine Ace Lines, Inc.: 230 Shurdut Bldg., Intramuros, Manila; 5 vessels; Gen. Man. LOPE O. ANGANGCO; cargo and liner services to Japan, Europe, South America and U.S.A.

Philippine President Lines Inc.: PPL Bldg., 1000–1046 United Nations Ave., Manila; 12 cargo vessels; Chair. A. MONTELIBANO; Pres. E. T. YAP; services: Chartering, U.S.A., Japan, Europe.

Sweet Lines, Inc.: Pier 6 North Harbour, Manila; 13 passenger-cargo vessels; Pres. L. POH; Gen. Man. P. C. LIM.

Transocean Transport Corpn.: Magsaysay Bldg., 520 T. M. Kalaw St., Ermita, Manila (P.O.B. 3050); 5 cargo vessels; Pres. MIGUEL A. MAGSAYSAY.

United Philippine Lines, Inc.: UPL Bldg., Santa Clara St., Intramuros, Manila; Chair. and Pres. Col. GENEROSO F. TANSECO; Sen. Vice-Pres. and Treas. RENATO M. TANESCO; services to Japan, Hong Kong, and U.S.A.

William Lines, Inc.: Pier 14 North Harbour, Manila; passenger and cargo inter-island service; 11 pass./cargo vessels; Pres. W. L. CHIONGBIAN; Gen. Man. A. S. CHIONGBIAN.

CIVIL AVIATION

In addition to the international airport at Manila, there are eight trunk airports, 23 secondary airports and 90 air-strips in the domestic system. There are plans to start building two new airports at Negros Oriental and at Bokol in 1976, and to improve other airports in the central Visayas region.

Philippine Air Lines Inc. (PAL): PAL Bldg., Ayala Ave., Makati, Rizal, P.O.B. 954 Manila; f. 1946; Chair. and Pres. BENIGNO P. TODA, Jr.; internal services; and to San Francisco, Honolulu, Sydney, Melbourne, Singapore, Hong Kong, Taipei, Tokyo, Bangkok, Karachi, Rome, Amsterdam, Frankfurt; fleet of 9 DC-3, 1 DC-8-63, 2 DC-8-50, 2 DC-8-30, 2 DC-10-30, 9 One-Eleven 500, 11 HS 748, 10 YS-11A.

Manila is also served by the following airlines: Air France, Alitalia, Cathay Pacific Airlines Ltd. (CPA), China Air Lines, Egypt Air, JAL, KLM, Lufthansa German Air Lines, Northwest Orient Airlines (NWA), Pan American, PIA, Qantas, SAS, Singapore Airlines, Swissair and Thai International.

TOURISM

TOURISM

Department of Tourism: Agrifina Circle, Rizal Park, Manila (P.O.B. 3451 Manila).

PRINCIPAL THEATRE COMPANIES

Bayanihan Philippine Dance Company: Philippine Women's University, Taft Ave., Manila; f. 1957; regular programmes; efforts towards a folk dance revival and the emergence of a native dance tradition; occasional subsidies from the Board of Travel and Tourist Industry, government grants for foreign tours; Pres. Dr. HELENA Z. BENITEZ; Exec. Dir. Dr. LETICIA P. DE GUZMAN.

Filippinescas Dance Company: 41 Timog (South) Ave., Quezon City; f. 1957; private company; folkloric ballets in native dance styles; 24 male and female dancers, five instrumentalists; Founder-Dir. Madame LEONOR OROSA GOQUINGCO.

PNC Baranggay Folk Dance Troupe: Philippine Normal College, Taft Ave., Manila; f. 1946; study and propagation of Philippine folk dances, songs and games; national and international performances; Founder-Dir. Mrs. PAZ-CIELO A. BELMONTE.

PRINCIPAL ORCHESTRAS

The Manila Symphony Orchestra: P.O.B. 664, Manila; f. 1926; regular symphonic, opera and ballet programmes; encourages young artists; Music Dir. and Conductor OSCAR C. YATCO.

National Philharmonic Orchestra: Suite B, 2nd Floor, Metropolitan Theatre Bldg., Plaza Lawton, Manila; f. 1960; seasonal symphony concerts; sponsors international operas and ballets; privately financed; Pres., Musical Dir. and Conductor REDENTOR ROMERO.

Celebrity Concerts: Suite B, 2nd Floor, Metropolitan Theatre Bldg., Plaza Lawton, Manila; f. 1964; sponsors appearances of top international concert artists and group attractions not accommodated within the regular season of the National Philharmonic Society of the Philippines; Pres. REDENTOR ROMERO.

ATOMIC ENERGY

National Science Development Board: Bicutan, Taguig, Rizal; the policy-making body for science and technology; the Philippine Atomic Energy Commission and the National Institute of Science and Technology and 5 others are its implementing agencies, while 7 others are attached to it; Chair. FLORENCIO A. MEDINA; Vice-Chair. PEDRO G. AFABLE.

Philippine Atomic Energy Commission: Don Mariano Marcos Ave., Diliman, Quezon City, D-505; f. 1958; the official body dealing with nuclear energy activities in the Philippines, under the supervision of the National Science Development Board. It has a 1,000-kW. swimming pool research reactor for research, training and production of radioisotopes. Its research centre conducts studies in agriculture, biology, medicine, chemistry, physics and nuclear engineering. Technical assistance is received mainly from International Atomic Energy Agency, United States Agency for International Development, Colombo Plan and through bilateral agreements with other nations. Commissioner Dr. LIBRADO D. IBE.

DEFENCE

Armed Forces: Total strength (1975) 67,000 army: 39,000, navy 14,000, air force 14,000; military service is selective; the constabulary numbers 34,900 and reserves total 218,000.

Equipment: The army, navy and air force have American equipment and there are American military bases in the country.

Defence Expenditure: Defence budget (1975/76): 2,900 million pesos (U.S. $407 million).

CHIEFS OF STAFF

Chief of Staff of the Armed Forces: Gen. ROMEO C. ESPINO.

Army: Brig.-Gen. FORTUNATO ABAT.

Navy: Commodore ERNESTO OGBINAR.

Air Force: Brig.-Gen. SAMUEL SARMIENTO.

Constabulary: Maj.-Gen. FIDEL B. RAMOS.

EDUCATION

The 1973 Constitution provides for free compulsory public education at elementary level and in some areas education is free up to secondary level. The organization of education is the responsibility of the Secretary of Education and Culture. The Department under him is responsible for the development and implementation of programmes based on policies formulated by the National Board of Education. The Board of Higher Education assists the NBE with its post-secondary education programmes.

There are both government and non-government schools. The non-government or private schools are either sectarian or non-sectarian. In 1975 the existing administrative Bureaux were abolished and replaced by the Bureau of Elementary Education, the Bureau of Secondary Education and the Bureau of Higher Education.

Basically, education in the Philippines is divided into four stages: pre-school (from the age of 3), elementary school (for 6 or 7 years), secondary or high school (for 4 or 5 years) and higher education (normally 4 years). The public schools offer a general secondary curriculum and there are private schools which offer more specialized training courses. Under a new plan, there is a common general curriculum for all students in the first and second years and more varied curricula in the third and fourth years leading to either college or technical vocational courses. In 1974 the first National College Entrance Examination (NCEE) was taken by 318,521 students.

The education budget for 1973–74 was 1,883.9 million pesos. Total enrolment in 1973–74 was 10,844,719 as against 4,283,197 in 1963–64, an increase of 65 per cent. In 1973–74, 8,405,195 students were enrolled in public schools, 127,774 in vocational schools, 2,210,612 in private schools and 101,138 in State colleges and universities. Some 5,207 adults attended functional literacy courses in the year 1973–74 and 279,144 adults enrolled for adult education classes.

From 1945 to 1971 the number of public school teachers at elementary, secondary and college levels increased from 46,864 to 258,148. The number of private school teachers increased from 1,006 to 63,907. In 1971–72 there was a total of 43,589 public schools and 3,001 private schools.

At the primary level instruction is in English or Pilipino. At the secondary and college levels English is the usual medium, although Pilipino is sometimes used.

UNIVERSITIES

Adamson University: San Marcelino, Manila; *c.* 330 teachers, *c.* 10,150 students.

Angeles University: Angeles City; *c.* 180 teachers, *c.* 4,650 students.

Aquinas University: Legazpi City; 155 teachers, 4,000 students.

Araneta University: Caloocan City, Rizal; 350 teachers, *c.* 12,000 students.

Arellano University: Legarda, Manila; 215 teachers, 7,410 students.

Ateneo de Manila University: Padre Faura, Manila; 580 teachers, 7,900 students.

University of Baguio: Baguio City; 230 teachers, 8,200 students.

Bicol University: Legazpi City; *c.* 400 teachers, *c.* 12,500 students.

Central Luzon State University: Muñoz, Nueva Ecija; *c.* 170 teachers, 3,000 students

Central Mindanao University: Musuan, Bukidnon; *c.* 170 teachers, *c.* 2,800 students.

Central Philippine University: Iloilo City; *c.* 270 teachers, *c.* 6,850 students.

Centro Escolar University: Mendiola, Manila; *c.* 460 teachers, *c.* 10,890 students.

De La Salle College: Taft Avenue, Manila; *c.* 230 teachers, *c.* 3,450 students.

Divine Word University: Tacloban City; *c.* 250 teachers, *c.* 7,550 students.

University of the East: Claro M. Recto, Manila; 1,550 teachers, 64,500 students.

University of the Eastern Philippines: University Town, Northern Samar.

Far Eastern University: P.O.B. 609, Manila 2806; 1,300 teachers, 66,900 students.

Feati University: Santa Cruz, Manila; 850 teachers, 30,000 students.

Foundation University: Dumaguete City: 150 teachers, 3,240 students.

Luzonian University Foundation: Lucena City; 130 teachers, 3,110 students.

University of Manila: Sampaloc, Manila; *c.* 360 teachers, 10,000 students.

Manila Central University: Zurbaran, Manila; 200 teachers, *c.* 6,200 students.

Mindanao State University: Marawi City; *c.* 320 teachers, *c.* 5,800 students.

University of Mindanao: Davao City; *c.* 200 teachers, 18,300 students.

National University: M. Jhocson, Manila.

University of Negros Occidental-Recoletos: Bacolod City; *c.* 220 teachers, *c.* 6,900 students.

University of Northern Philippines: Vigan, Ilocos Sur; *c.* 150 teachers, *c.* 2,300 students.

Notre Dame University of Cotabato: Cotabato City; *c.* 120 teachers, *c.* 3,450 students.

University of Nueve Caceres: Naga City; 260 teachers, *c.* 7,300 students.

University of Pangasinan: Dagupan City; *c.* 330 teachers, *c.* 11,000 students.

Philippine Women's University: Taft Ave., Manila; 555 teachers, *c.* 8,250 students.

University of the Philippines: Diliman, Quezon City; *c.* 2,450 teachers, *c.* 18,000 students.

Manuel L. Quezon University: R. Hidalgo, Manila; *c.* 490 teachers, *c.* 8,430 students.

Saint Louis University: Baguio City; 285 teachers, 10,850 students.

University of San Agustin: Iloilo City; 315 teachers, 9,400 students.

University of San Carlos: Cebu City; *c.* 340 teachers, *c.* 9,500-students.

University of Santo Tomás: España, Manila; *c.* 1,440 teachers, *c.* 33,600 students.

Silliman University: Dumaguete City; 290 teachers, 5,700 students.

University of Southern Philippines: Cebu City; 175 teachers, *c.* 5,900 students.

South Western University: Cebu City; *c.* 350 teachers, *c.* 12,000 students.

University of the Visayas: Cebu City; *c.* 500 teachers, *c.* 20,000 students.

Xavier University: Cagayan de Oro City; *c.* 210 teachers, *c.* 4,260 students.

BIBLIOGRAPHY

GENERAL

CORPUZ, O. The Philippines (Prentice Hall, N. J., 1965).

SAITO, SHIRO. The Philippines: a Review of Bibliographies (University of Hawaii, Honolulu, 1966).

HISTORY

AGONCILLO, TEODORO A. Malolos, the Crisis of the Republic (*University Philosophical Review*, Quezon City, 1960). The Fateful Years (R. P. Garcia, Quezon City, 1965).

ALFONSO, OSCAR M. Theodore Roosevelt and the Philippines; 1897–1908; (University of the Philippines Press, 1970).

BLOUNT, J. H. The American Occupation of the Philippines, 1898–1912 (Malaya Books, Quezon City, 1968).

COCKROFT, J. The Philippines (Angus and Robertson, London, 1968).

COSTA, HORACIO DE LA. The Jesuits in the Philippines, 1581–1768 (Harvard University Press. Mass., 1961)

FELIX, ALFONSO ed. The Chinese in the Philippines (2 vols.), (Solidaridad Publishing House, Manila, 1966).

QUAISON, SERAFIN D. English "Country Trade" with the Philippines, 1644–1765 (University of the Philippines Press, 1966).

ECONOMICS

CASTILLO, A. Philippine Economics (University Book Supply, Manila, (rev. ed.) 1968).

DALISAY, A. M. Development of Agricultural Policy in Philippine Agriculture (Phoenix Publishing House, Manila, 1959).

FABELLA, A. An Introduction to Economic Policy (Philippine Executive Academy, Manila, 1968).

POLITICS AND GOVERNMENT

ALZONA, E. The Filipino Civic Code (Philippines Historical Assoc., Manila, 1958).

BRIONES, N. L. The Constitution of the Republic of the Philippines (Mozar Press, Rizal, 1968).

CORPUZ, O. D. The Bureaucracy in the Philippines (University of the Philippines, Institute of Public Administration, 1957).

CORTES, IRENE R. The Philippine Presidency (University of the Philippines, Law Centre, 1966).

GREGORIO ARANETA MEMORIAL FOUNDATION. Lectures on Constitutional Reforms (Manila, 1970).

LANDE, CARL H. Leaders, Factions and Parties: The Structure of Philippine Politics (Yale University Press, Southeast Asia Studies, Monograph Series No. 6).

MEYER, MILTON W. A Diplomatic History of the Philippine Republic (Universtiy of Hawaii Press, Honolulu, 1965).

Singapore

PHYSICAL AND SOCIAL GEOGRAPHY

C. A. Fisher

(Revised by the Editor, 1976)

The Republic of Singapore is an insular territory of 597 square kilometres (230 square miles) lying to the south of the Malay peninsula to which it is joined by a causeway carrying a road, a railway and a water pipeline across the intervening Straits of Johore.

Singapore Island, which is situated less than 1½° north of the equator, occupies a focal position at the turning point on the shortest sea-route from the Indian Ocean to the South China Sea.

PHYSICAL FEATURES

The mainly granitic core of the island, which rises in a few places to summits of over 100 metres, is surrounded by lower land, much of it marshy, though large areas are now intensively cultivated. Singapore City has grown up on the firmer ground adjacent to the Mt. Faber ridge, whose foreshore provides deep water anchorage in the lee of two small offshore islands, Pulau Blakang Mati and Pulau Brani. In recent years suburban growth has been rapid towards the north and along the eastern foreshore, and since 1961 a large expanse of mangrove swamp to the west of the dock area has been reclaimed to provide the Jurong industrial estate.

POPULATION

The estimated population in mid-1975 was 2,249,900, giving a population density of 3,770 per square kilometre, one of the highest in the world. Of the total, 1,712,800 (76 per cent) were Chinese, 338,800 (15 per cent) Malay and 43,100 (7 per cent) Indian. Forty per cent of the population are under 19 years old. A population of 4,000,000 is projected by the end of the century.

HISTORY

George Thomson

South-East Asia, with its tropical abundance and the accessibility of its islands and peninsulas by sea, has been a major trading area for more than 2,000 years, whether in the gold of the Ancient Greek title of the "Golden Peninsula", or in the rubber, oil or tin of today. Singapore, at the geographical centre of the pattern of sea-ways which still carry the bulk of South-East Asian trade and the trade from Europe and the Indian Ocean to the Pacific Ocean, has added historic achievement to geographical position to become the largest port of South-East Asia, the second largest in Asia, and the fourth largest in the world.

ORIGINS AND EARLY DEVELOPMENT

The original seaport (or Temasek) of Singa-pura (Lion-city in Sanskrit) was founded in 1297 as one of the three kingdoms of the trading empire of Srivijaya, based on Palembang, in South Sumatra. It was destroyed in 1376 by the Majapahit empire based on Java. Singapore Island was never, however, quite deserted and the ruins of the first Singapore remained to be visible to Sir Stamford Raffles of the East India Company when he founded modern Singapore in 1819 as an "emporium" (or in modern phraseology, a departmental store) for the trade of the "Southern Seas", based on three freedoms—from tariffs, from racial discrimination and from piracy, in contrast to the closed mercantilist system of the Dutch who dominated the Malay archipelago from their bases in Java and Malacca. Leased in 1819 from the Sultan of Rhio-Johore, Singapore was taken over in full sovereignty in 1824, and British possession was recognized by the Dutch in return for British withdrawal from Sumatra.

That Raffles' Singapore met a commercial need for the area was shown by the increase in its trade from 1.8 million dollars* in 1821 to 12.1 million dollars in 1825, and by the increase of its population from the 150 on Raffles' arrival to 10,000 by 1823, as the traders of the area, mainly Chinese, moved to Singapore. In 1832, Singapore became the centre of government for the Straits Settlements, which it formed with Penang and Malacca in 1826, because of "its increasing importance, its proximity to Java as well as to those countries to the Eastward from whence the great resort to the island principally arises". The Straits Settlements came under the Presidency of Bengal till 1851 and were transferred to the direct control of the Governor-General.

The next phase of its growth began in the 1850s when the unrest caused by the T'ai P'ing rebellion in China acted as a stimulus for the emigration of Chinese labour at a time when the expansion of tin

* Mexican silver dollars: the common currency in the area for most of the nineteenth century.

mining in Malaya created a demand for labour. In 1867, following the transfer of the powers of the East India Company to the British Government after the Indian Mutiny of 1857, the Colony of the Straits Settlements came directly under the control of the Colonial Office in London. The opening of the Suez Canal in 1869 and the growing use of steamships opened up and consolidated Singapore's position on the Great Marine Trunk Route from London to China, which was increasingly open to Western trade with the establishment of Hong Kong, and with the rapidly modernizing Japan of the Meiji Restoration; while the opening of the international cable telegraph geared Asian production to the world market. And finally, when with the increased pressure from merchant interests in Singapore, and with the growing pressures of competitive imperialisms in South-East Asia, the policy of intervention in the Malay States was inaugurated in 1874, Singapore became the centre of the British operation of that policy which created the stable conditions out of which, on the failure of coffee plantations, the rubber industry was to grow, once Mr. H. M. Ridley, Director of Singapore's Botanic Gardens, had found the method of tapping rubber without savaging the trees. Singapore added a new international role to her already focal position in South-East Asia, as it developed economically under the imperial impetus from Britain, Holland and France. When the protectorates were established over the Federated and Unfederated Malay States, the title of High Commissioner for the Malay States was added to that of the Governor of the Straits Settlements who was based in Singapore (*see* Malaysia: History).

Evolution of an Indigenous Society

Singapore expanded with immigrant alien labour, predominantly from the Treaty Ports of South China, coming to the temporary, rootless social climate of a frontier town. Population grew rapidly—by 43 per cent from 97,111 in 1871 to 139,208 in 1881. As 93.5 per cent of the predominantly Chinese population were males, Singapore grew not through indigenous labour, politically and culturally acclimatized, but through a steady stream of immigrant labour which, by inertia, kept active the political and cultural inheritance of their countries of origin. As the number of women immigrants grew, and as more girls were born in Singapore, this disproportion slowly declined; and the settled Straits-born families grew in number, wealth, importance, and self-consciousness. As rubber and tin expanded after 1900 to meet the new technologies of peace, and of the First World War, there was a further stimulus to immigration which increased the population at the rate of 35 per cent in each of the first two decades of the century. This era of *laissez-faire* ended with the economic crisis of 1929 which seriously damaged the economy and reversed the tide of migration. When the demand for labour again grew, legislation in 1932 limited by quota the immigration of men but not of women; and this gave a stimulus to the immigration of women—190,000 between 1934 and 1939.

An immigration which had always been treated as temporary was on the way to becoming permanent. The new immigrants married in Singapore, and their children were born in Singapore, and automatically became by law citizens of the territory. The instincts of home and the outlook on the future symbolized by the children, turned Malaya-wards, and family ties with Malaya were to challenge family ties with China and India. The Japanese occupation which froze migration, and which made Malaya the country in which, and for which, the people suffered, confirmed this inward-looking trend. The Singapore "Fortress" Base, the building of which in the 1930s gave a new role to Singapore and a new dimension to its economy, fell to the Japanese on February 12th, 1942, and remained under ruthless Japanese occupation until September 1945 when the forces of South-East Asia Command under Lord Louis Mountbatten recovered Singapore after the defeat of the Japanese in Burma by his forces, and the overall surrender of the Japanese Government after the bombing of Hiroshima.

THE POST-WAR PERIOD

Until March 31st, 1946, Singapore was administered by the British Military Administration which, anticipating the future separation of Singapore from Peninsular Malaya, formed Singapore into a separate administrative unit. But it was a different Singapore to which the British régime was restored. The return of British administration never erased the effect on British prestige of the defeat in the Battle of Malaya; with British protection withdrawn, the people had matured as they faced their own individual problems and made their own decisions during the Japanese occupation. The freedom restored after the Japanese occupation was social and economic as well as political, and would not confine itself with a restoration of the *status quo ante*. Sacrifices had established new bases for rights. The part played by the guerrillas, who had mainly been Chinese and Communist raised the issue of the place of the Chinese in the new Malaya, and raised the question of the economic pattern of the new Malaya: these issues were more urgent amid the Chinese preponderance and comparative wealth of Singapore. Finally, the rehabilitation of Singapore was a joint endeavour in which all races played their part. While, therefore, the aim of British policy was a gradual and educative transfer of power, distrusting political activism as inevitably being to the Communist advantage, it thought mainly in terms of the Straits-born group, who alone had citizenship rights at the time. It under-estimated the more intense and increasingly Malaya-directed activity of those more recently, and directly, influenced by events—natural and ideological—in China. The dynamic and direction of this group in which communal frustrations expressed in Communist formulations of ideas and patterns of organization prevailed, were given less by the non-citizen parents, and more by their children in the Chinese-language schools who were full citizens by birth and whose political actions did not wait the adult achievement of the political power of the vote they would inherit at the age of 21. Economically, with large rehabilitation grants and a major British military presence, Singapore quickly regained its entrepôt position and contribution to the economic reactivation of South-East Asia as part of the world economy; and from its profits, the foundation of its welfare services in health, education and housing were firmly laid.

Civil government was restored on April 1st, 1946. The Straits Settlements ceased to exist constitutionally. Penang and Malacca were merged with the nine Malay States into the Malay Union (later, in 1948, the Federation of Malaya) and Labuan was incorporated, after a further period of military administration, in North Borneo in July 1946.

The story of Singapore from 1946 has been of transforming a colonial into a national political system, in face of a determined communist assault and with, till 1957, a predominantly alien-born, non-citizen population; of transforming a dependent, and predominantly commercial economy into a national and increasingly industrial economy; of transforming a clash of cultures into a composition of cultures, a problem focussed on the decisions on the pattern of education; and latterly, with the British decision to withdraw its base by 1971, the establishment of a national defence service of regional relevance in place of a British defence service of imperial relevance.

Constitutional Developments, 1948–65

The first constitutional plan of 1948 was the establishment of conventionally colonial Legislative and Executive Councils with official and nominated majorities led by the Governor, and a minority elected by voluntarily registered British citizens (including all born in Singapore). This, through the Progressive Party, reflected the views mainly of the middle class Straits-born of all communities. It established, in public understanding, the pattern of elections and Parliamentary procedure, and in face of Communist agitation aimed at the non-citizen adult and non-voting citizen minors, gave a focus for political participation in the legislature; and after a constitutional amendment in 1951, for participation in policy formation and administrative control in the Executive Council. Under the new constitution of 1955, a Legislative Assembly was established with 25 out of 32 members elected, a Governor-nominated Speaker, and a Council of Ministers with a minority of officials and responsible to the Legislative Council. Registration as electors was automatic, based on Identity Card counter-foil data, rather than on voluntary action as previously. The register increased fourfold to 300,000, putting the English-educated in a minority. The new unpredictable electorate of 1955, with Emergency controls relaxed, brought to power a Labour Front Government with Mr. David Marshall as Chief Minister, unexpectedly and on a minority basis because of split voting between the Progressive Party and a Democratic party communally organized by the Chinese Chamber of Commerce. The People's Action Party contested the election and won 3 of the 4 seats it fought. 1955–56 were years of sustained Communist political challenge to constitutional processes through their control of the Trade Union Movement and the Chinese Middle Schools. But a resort to force in 1956 brought their defeat by the temporary imposition of military law and by the detention till 1959 of pro-Communist leaders by Emergency Regulation. The independence issue was forced back to the constitutional field. A new constitution was negotiated which in 1959 established full internal self-government by a Cabinet fully responsible to a Parliament of 51 members all elected from one-member constituencies by citizens whose numbers were now virtually coincident with the adult population as a result of a generous Singapore Citizenship Bill of 1957 which added 350,000 to the electorate. Foreign Affairs and Foreign Defence remained the responsibility of the United Kingdom, while responsibility for Internal Security lay with an Internal Security Council, on which the United Kingdom and Singapore each had three members, and the Malayan Government one member who virtually held the casting vote.

The People's Action Party was elected in 1959 with 53 per cent of the votes and 43 seats out of 51, and took office under the Prime Ministership of Mr. Lee Kuan Yew who had been a member of the 1955 Legislative Council, and who continues to be Prime Minister. The Party survived two splits, one based on a personal bid for power, the other on a pro-Communist challenge over the issue of the formation of Malaysia, which led to the formation of the Barisan Sosialis (Socialist Front) which has followed Communist policies. Surviving the second in 1961 by a Parliamentary majority of 1, the Party, after an intensive political campaign, and a referendum in which 71 per cent of votes, under the system of compulsory voting based on Australian experience, favoured joining Malaysia on the terms freely negotiated by the four constituent units and the United Kingdom led Singapore into Malaysia politically on September 16th, 1963 and ended its colonial status. Under the agreement, Singapore retained full responsibility in matters of labour and education, and special provisions were made for the adjustment of Singapore revenue between Federal and Singapore expenditure. Negotiations continued for a Malaysian Common Market for selected commodities, but this never became effective. In September 1963 the P.A.P. was returned to power in a general election, winning 37 seats including 3 with a Malay majority. This success, and their fighting the 1964 Malaysian election in mainland constituencies on a policy of a "Malaysian Malaysia", was met by growing Malay communal reaction which led to the separation of Singapore on August 9th, 1965, entirely on the initiative of the Kuala Lumpur Government which gave only 3 days notice of its decision. On August 9th Singapore proclaimed itself "forever a sovereign democratic and independent nation, founded upon the principles of liberty and justice and ever seeking the welfare and happiness of her people in a more just and equal society".

The Republic of Singapore

Whatever doubts of Singapore's capacity for survival there were at the time of separation, were dispelled in practice. International recognition was achieved by membership of the UN in September

1965, of the Commonwealth in October and of the Afro-Asian group. By a constitutional amendment on December 22nd, 1965, Singapore became a Republic with a President as Head of State.

Separation led to no political turmoil, and in the election of April 1968 the P.A.P. won all 58 of the Parliamentary seats.

In 1971 in anticipation of a General Election and in adjustment to an electorate which had grown in number to 908,382 and to the changed residential pattern created by massive housing developments, 65 constituencies were created and boundaries re-drawn. In the general election of September 2nd, 1972, there was a 91.9 per cent poll and the P.A.P. won all the seats and 69.1 per cent of the votes cast.

A bill was passed on November 3rd, 1972, to give effect to the need defined in the President's speech at the opening of Parliament in October 1972 to ensure that "no surrender of sovereignty or any part thereof by way of incorporation into, or federation with, any other country" would be possible "unless endorsed in a referendum by two-thirds of the electorate". The legislation followed allegations during the 1972 election campaign that foreign interests were financing and manipulating political parties. Legislation was passed to provide that all political parties must have their income and expenditure periodically inspected by Supreme Court Judges to discover whether they have received foreign money. Legislation now ensures national ownership of the Press and its ownership by public companies.

The visit of the Prime Minister, Mr. Lee Kuan Yew, to Kuala Lumpur in March 1972, his first since Singapore's separation from Malaysia in 1965, was followed by the reciprocal visit of Tun Abdul Razak, his first as Malaysian Prime Minister, to Singapore in November 1973. Political rapprochement did not prevent separation of the national economies. In October 1972 the joint airline, Malaysia-Singapore Airlines, divided into two separate lines, Singapore International Airlines and Malaysian Air Services. In June 1973 the two currencies were floated and mutual interchangeability at par ceased. In June 1973 Malaysia established its own stock exchange and in August its own rubber exchange, both of them separate from the Singapore exchanges. Singapore regretted, but accepted, the split. In June, also, the separation of the two banking associations was announced. Consultation has now become informal and regular, and there has been concurrence on issues such as incidents involving subversives, the wish of the Malaysian Government to stabilize the prices of its natural resources, the drug problem and the problem of tankers in the Straits of Malacca and of Singapore.

Following an official visit by Dr. Goh Keng Swee, then Minister of Defence, to Indonesia in October 1972, Mr. Lee paid an official visit in March 1973, his first to Indonesia since the "confrontation" of the period 1963–66, and met President Suharto for the first time. Singapore is the fifth largest investor in Indonesia. A joint venture between Singapore and Indonesia is developing Bataam Island in the Rhio Archipelago. In June 1973 Singapore, Indonesia and Malaysia agreed to limit the draft of vessels sailing in the Straits of Malacca.

During 1973 the new Labour Party Prime Ministers of New Zealand and Australia, Norman Kirk and Gough Whitlam, visited Singapore. New Zealand was welcomed as "part of our wider region". In 1974, the Shah of Iran, Prime Minister Tanaka of Japan, and the Philippines Foreign Minister Carlos Romulo visited Singapore. Mr. Lee Kuan Yew visited Bangkok and Manila to complete his visit to ASEAN partners. Following the fall of President Thieu, Lee Kuan Yew visited the U.S.A. on his return from the meeting of Commonwealth Heads of Government in Jamaica.

Singapore's relations with her neighbours have become increasingly close politically and economically within the context of a strengthening ASEAN which collectively negotiated access to the Common Market for its products and with Japan on the use of natural rubber. ASEAN was also the medium for joint consultation on the recognition of the People's Republic of China and on relations with South Viet-Nam after the defeat of President Thieu.

Singapore's initiatives in its economic and exploratory diplomacy, and the senior visitors to Singapore from Australia, New Zealand, the U.S.A. and South Korea in the first quarter of 1976, reflected the political changes in the area. During April Sinnathamby Rajaratnam, the Foreign Minister, visited Moscow, and the Prime Minister announced a forthcoming good-will mission to China which, however, it was emphasized, reflected no change in the decision that Singapore's diplomatic recognition of the People's Republic of China would follow recognition by Indonesia.

Following a general election in 1970, the new Conservative Government in the U.K. announced its intention "to contribute to Five-Power (i.e. Malaysia, Singapore, Australia, New Zealand and the U.K.) Commonwealth defence arrangements relating to Singapore and Malaysia". The British Far East Command ceased on October 31st, 1971, thus ending Singapore's era as a British naval base. Defence was co-ordinated under a consultative pact on external defence signed on April 16th, 1971, between Singapore and Malaysia, and Australia, New Zealand and the U.K. forming a combined ANZUK force. Following the decision of the Australian Government and the Labour Government in the U.K. in 1974, to withdraw their troops from Singapore, ANZUK was dissolved. The last British troops left in March 1976 and New Zealand troops are to leave by the end of 1977.

Singapore's armed forces, based on National Service, have smoothly and with increasing effectiveness grown to seven active infantry battalions organized in two brigades with tank, artillery and other ancillary units. The Maritime Command controls a unit of fast, missile-armed patrol craft. To the continuing joint Air Command Singapore contributes Hunter and helicopter squadrons as well as the Bloodhound surface-to-air missile and radar system taken over from the British Royal Air Force. National

Service has now been extended to the Police Force in the face of growing urban crime problems.

In education, primary education has been expanded from 6 to 7 years. New sites are being built for the University of Singapore and the Singapore Polytechnic. In 1976 there were three Junior Colleges and one more under construction. The Housing Development Board built 28,000 houses in 1975, a rate of over three per hour; they now house 45 per cent of the population. Hospital facilities are expanding and improving. To meet the growing traffic congestion, admission of private cars to the city centre was restricted in 1975. The Singapore bus service was being drastically reorganized, and the second phase of the mass rapid transport subway scheme was pushed forward.

In 1975 Singapore celebrated ten years of independence. With the constitutional limitation of the life of any one Parliament to five years, a general election must be held before September 1976. In 1975 the electoral register included 951,805 names. In June 1975 the only Cabinet re-shuffle was made. In September a senior Minister of State was found guilty on five charges of corruption. During 1975 there was minor political agitation among university students over squatter problems in Johore, and retrenchment of workers in electronic factories in Singapore. Most of the leaders who were Malaysians were expelled from Singapore. Parliament subsequently passed legislation to reorganize the Students' Union, and requiring that the Political Society of the Union should be registered under the Societies' Act, like any political party. Following increased Communist activity in Malaysia, five members of the Malayan Communist Party and the National Liberation Front, a Communist affiliate, were arrested in August 1975. A further 14 were detained in October, following evidence of MCP recruiting in Singapore, with the possibility of repetition in Singapore of incidents occurring in Malaysia.

ECONOMIC SURVEY

David H. B. Lim

The growth of the Singapore economy further decelerated in 1975 because of persisting recessionary conditions. Real growth in gross domestic product varied from 10 to 12 per cent annually between 1969 and 1973 but in 1974 and 1975 real growth rates were 7 per cent and 4.2 per cent respectively. Per capita G.N.P. in 1975 was S$5,968, compared with S$2,825 in 1970. The main impetus of growth between 1965 and 1975 came from the manufacturing sector. Structurally, the economy was transformed from one of entrepôt trading in the 1950s and early 1960s to entrepôt-manufacturing. The structural changes in the economy have resulted in a contribution of more than 20 per cent by the manufacturing sector to total G.D.P. at factor cost since 1971, compared with only 13 per cent in 1960, while the relative importance of the entrepôt sector has remained stagnant at 10 per cent of G.D.P., having declined from around 20 per cent in 1960. Growth has also been remarkable in the tourist and banking industries. The annual growth rate in the number of tourist arrivals averaged 17.5 per cent between 1970 and 1975, and in 1974 and 1975 Singapore attracted more than a million visitors annually. The Government's policy of developing Singapore into an international financial centre was a big boost to the growth of the banking sector. Both the tourist and banking sectors have enjoyed high annual growth rates of around 20 to 25 per cent since 1970.

PROBLEMS OF DEVELOPMENT

The major concern of public policy during the decade of the 1960s was to accelerate economic growth and the rate of job creation so as to reduce the problem of mounting unemployment and the stagnating entrepôt trade sector which has been the backbone of the economy.

The post-war baby boom of the early 1950s and the inflow of migrants resulted in a population growth rate of 4.4 per cent between 1947 and 1957. The population increased by 507,000 during this 10-year period. In 1957, unemployment stood at around 5 per cent of the labour force and increased steadily to 9.2 per cent in 1966.

Aggravating the situation was the slow rate of income and employment generation by the entrepôt trade sector. With the demise of the European Colonial empires in Indonesia, Malaya and Indochina which were once Singapore's protected hinterland, the newly emerging nations, dictated both by economic and political considerations, have attempted to develop trade services and facilities traditionally provided by the Republic. As a result of such a development, the entrepôt functions have diminished in importance to her neighbours.

At the same time, the industrial relations system was undergoing a turbulent period. Anti-colonial feelings were rife in the 1950s and even after gaining independence in 1957, the activities of politically active trade unions and leftist elements did much damage to the industrial relations system. The early 1960s were characterized by industrial unrest and work-stoppages resulting in massive man-days lost.

Political instability was further evidenced by the stormy relationships of Singapore with neighbouring countries. In 1963, Indonesia launched a policy of confrontation against the formation of Malaysia of which Singapore later became a member. Indonesian confrontation meant the loss of an important trading partner for Singapore. However, two years after forming Malaysia, Singapore was separated from Malaysia due to irreconcilable differences in the political, economic, and social policies of the two countries.

By the end of decade of the 1960s a new problem had arisen. The British Government announced the withdrawal of its forces from Singapore by 1971, a move which resurrected fears of massive unemployment since British military services constituted the Republic's largest single employer. Moreover, it meant the loss of an important source of foreign exchange. U.K. military expenditure had been estimated at more than $400 million a year.

DEVELOPMENT STRATEGY

The People's Action Party (PAP), in power since 1959, has recognized the necessity to adapt to changing circumstances. Since the initiation of the Singapore Development Plan in 1961, the emphasis in development policy has been upon industrialization. However, the basic resources at Singapore's disposal for stimulating economic growth are largely intangibles. The island Republic has very little natural resources and has to obtain almost all its basic requirements, including food, water, and raw materials, from external sources. Further, the population is too small and income levels (estimated at U.S. $1,313 per capita in 1972) are too low to create a significant domestic market. Besides its favourable geographical position and natural harbours, the Republic has the other advantage of having an urbanized, highly literate, and increasingly well-educated population, which appears to be singularly adaptable and responsive to change.

The development strategy leaned heavily on its industrialization programme with simultaneous development of labour and capital resources. The development objectives were to build up a manufacturing sector geared to the export market, to provide suitable social and economic infrastructure, to attract foreign and local capital to industry, to develop technical, managerial and marketing expertise and to train and discipline the labour force.

Two important pieces of legislation were enacted in 1968, the Employment Act 1968 and the Industrial Relations (Amendment) Act 1968. Together these two Acts established the ascendancy of the employer and management over the worker. The scope of collective bargaining was restricted and certain issues like recruitment, dismissal, and retrenchment became non-negotiable and non-arbitrable. Militant unionism and industrial unrest were almost completely eliminated.

Between 1961 and 1971, the value of industrial output increased ninefold. Employment in manufacturing industries increased by more than five times over the same period. A World Bank team reported that "in 1968 Singapore entered a new phase of accelerated growth with boom conditions in private investment and a decline in unemployment, buoyancy of government revenues, the emergence of an overall surplus of savings over investments and a significant build-up of external reserves".

The favourable economic conditions of 1970 to 1972 enabled Singapore to achieve almost full employment and eventually led to a shortage of labour. As a temporary relief measure, work permits were liberally issued to foreigners from nearby countries to meet the excess demand for labour. Most of these migrant workers were unskilled and semi-skilled.

With booming conditions prevailing in the major industrial countries, inflation too became a world-wide phenomenon. The fourfold increase in the price of petroleum further aggravated inflation. The vulnerability of the Singapore economy to external conditions was once more manifested by sharp increases in consumer prices, which rose by nearly 35 per cent in 1973 compared with less than 6 per cent in 1972. Following in the wake of inflation was the threat of an economic recession which began to take its toll on the textiles and electronics industries. Strict credit policies, higher wages, higher costs of raw materials, and excess production in the past adversely affected these industries. With recessionary conditions in Singapore's foreign markets, the demand for these commodities fell steadily. During 1975, 18,000 workers were made redundant.

However, the recession did not affect all sectors similarly. The ship-building industry experienced a mild boom in 1974 because of increased activity in oil explorations around the region. The building of tankers and oil rigs generated income and employment in this sector. In 1975 international competition and cancellation of orders adversely affected the industry. Singapore was fortunate enough to have developed into a distribution and assembling base for South-East Asia as well as a supply and fabrication base for oil and mineral resources development projects in the region. It became the world's third largest oil refining centre, petroleum and coal products accounting for over 40 per cent of total industrial output in 1974.

The discovery of oil in Malaysia contributed to the growth potential of the region as a whole, Indonesia being an oil-producing country already. The policy of the Government to develop the Republic into a financial centre to serve the financial needs of development and growth in this region led to the establishment of more foreign banks and branches in Singapore. Recently, counter-recessionary measures in the form of credit relaxation and the stimulation of the construction industry through public and private expenditure were initiated by the Government. The trading sector has also embarked on an intensive export promotion drive to capture markets in the Middle East, Africa, Europe and the United States while further efforts were taken by the Government to establish more foreign trade missions.

GROWTH AND EMPLOYMENT

Post-war economic development during the decade of the 1950s was characterized by slow growth with intermittent bouts of booms and slumps. The Korean

War Boom of the early 1950s was immediately followed by a mild recession which lasted till 1955 when the foreign trade sector once again was boosted by improved rubber prices. The average growth rate of Gross Domestic Product between 1956 and 1960 has been estimated at 5.4 per cent per annum. The period of political transition in the first half of the decade of the 1960s also marked a period of co-ordinated and planned growth for the Singapore economy stimulated by increased public and private expenditure. Rapid growth was sustained at the rate of 12 per cent per annum between 1968 and 1974 until world-wide recession occurred.

The establishment of such labour intensive industries as textiles and electronics assembly contributed immensely to the rate of labour absorption in the industrial sector. Between 1970 and 1974, employment grew at 5.4 per cent per annum while the labour force increased annually by 4.8 per cent only. The unemployment rate was officially estimated at 4 per cent of the labour force in 1974, increasing to 4.5 per cent in 1975.

INFLATION

The growth of the Singapore economy throughout the 1960s and even until 1972 was achieved with remarkable price stability. Official statistics show that the average annual increase in consumer prices was less than 2 per cent between 1963 and 1972. However, in the 12 months ending December 1973 consumer prices rose by 34.6 per cent, compared with an increase of less than 6 per cent in 1972. Food prices alone rose by 51.6 per cent in 1973. By March 1974 inflation had been brought under control and since February 1975 prices have actually fallen, the result of monetary control, a fall in commodity prices and slackening demand. The consumer price index showed a rise of 11.7 per cent in 1974 and a fall of 0.9 per cent in 1975. The G.D.P. deflator, which provides an indirect and rough indication of average increases in production costs, rose by only 5 per cent in 1975 compared with 11 per cent in 1974.

Inflation has been due to both imported and domestically generated factors. The Republic, being devoid of raw materials and natural resources, has a high propensity to import, which has been further augmented by the needs of rapid growth and economic development since 1968. It has been estimated that 60 per cent of total consumer expenditure is spent on imported goods and that import prices increased by more than 45 per cent in 1974 alone. The vulnerability of the economy to external events can be further seen from the large trade/G.N.P. ratio of 0.65 compared with ratios of 0.06 in the case of the U.S.A. and 0.11 for Japan. Imported inflationary factors have also taken the form of large capital inflow which increased money supply by some 35 per cent in 1972. Furthermore, the oil crisis has added some 10 per cent to production costs.

FOREIGN TRADE

Commodity Trade

Singapore owes its early development and economic prosperity to its function as the trading centre for South-East Asia. Its fine natural harbour and strategic geographical position on the crossroads of international sea-routes have enabled the Republic to develop a port which is now Asia's second largest and the world's fourth. Besides, in the historical development of the colonial empires in the region, Singapore served as an entrepôt port. In consequence Singapore developed into a trading city of a special sort; her economic hinterland comprising, or rather having comprised, agrarian extraction economies. As a trading intermediary Singapore handles well above one-quarter of the region's total foreign trade.

The general expansion in the value of Singapore's imports and exports, which followed the termination of Indonesian confrontation and trade boycott, has continued. Total external trade grew from S$7,755 million in 1960 to S$34,563.8 million in 1974, averaging an 11.5 per cent increase each year, but declined by 7.3 per cent in 1975, when imports totalled S$19,270 million and exports S$12,758 million. The average annual growth rates of imports and exports between 1960 and 1975 were 11 per cent and 9 per cent respectively. Domestic exports, however, grew at about 35 per cent each year between 1970 and 1975 compared with 14.5 per cent for re-exports over the same period. In absolute value terms, domestic exports accounted in 1963 for only S$1,111 million or 32 per cent of total exports but increased to S$7,540 million or 60 per cent of total exports in 1975. This phenomenon has been due to the relative decline in the entrepôt trading functions of the Republic.

Direction and Composition of Trade

Between 1963 and 1974 Singapore's four main trading partners were Japan, the U.S.A., Malaysia and the United Kingdom. Imports from Iran, Kuwait and Saudi Arabia increased by 40 per cent between 1970 and 1975, due mainly to the fivefold increase in the price of oil.

Among the more advanced countries, trade with the U.S.A. and Germany increased most markedly at 48.6 per cent and 48.2 per cent respectively between 1972 and 1973 while the contributions of China and Saudi Arabia showed important increases of 53.7 per cent and 55.0 per cent respectively. Except for trade with Hong Kong, which rose by 36.4 per cent, trade with less developed countries showed less marked expansion. Trade with the rest of South-East Asia accounts for less than 20 per cent of trade.

The major import items in 1975 were machinery and equipment (S$5,046 million), mineral fuels (S$4,734 million), manufactured goods (S$3,510 million) and food and live animals (S$1,654 million). The major exports were machinery and transport equipment, rubber, electrical machinery and petroleum products.

Balance of Payments

Singapore's balance of payments clearly reflects its entrepôt base; commodity trade shows a continuous deficit with sizeable earnings in invisible exports. The deficit on commodity trade continued to worsen in

1975, amounting to S$5,898 million. The widening trade gap was clearly the consequence of rapid industrialization which generated an urgent and greater need for capital goods and raw materials imports in a period of rising prices. The importance of Singapore as a services centre is further borne out by the net surplus on the services and invisibles account which recorded a surplus of S$4,221 million in 1975, mainly from transport services. On the receipts side, preliminary data showed that "invisible" earnings were augmented by a large capital inflow mainly for the private sector. And with the loss of British military expenditure, Singapore has to depend increasingly on capital inflow from abroad to finance rising import requirements. Faced with the growing pressure on the balance of payments, the Singapore Government has actively encouraged the development of the Asian Dollar Market. Private long-term capital stood at S$1,541 million in 1975. The overall payments surplus was S$972 million in 1975 compared with S$718 million in the previous year, due primarily to the widening trade gap and the rising import costs.

Tourist Trade

The tourist industry showed important increases from 1960 in terms of contribution to the G.D.P., rising from 1.5 per cent to 5.8 per cent in 1973. The annual average rate of growth (1960–73) was about 25 per cent.

During 1975, the Republic had a total of 1.2 million visitors, an increase of 7.5 per cent over 1974. The largest proportion of visitors was from Indonesia (18 per cent) while Australian visitors ranked second (17 per cent), Japanese third (10 per cent) and Malaysians were fourth (9 per cent). The other important country was the U.S.A. A notable feature has been the large increase in regional travel, in particular, the marked increase in visitors from Australia, Malaysia, Indonesia and Japan, which together accounted for 54 per cent of total visitors in 1975.

Tourist expenditure rose from S$424 million in 1972 to S$794 million in 1975. Employment in the restaurant and hotel sector increased from 43,000 persons in 1970 to 52,000 in 1975.

Further efforts by the Government to promote intra-regional travel have taken the form of co-operation through the Association of South-East Asian Nations (ASEAN) which has established a permanent committee to ease travel restrictions and increase travel within ASEAN. Singapore has also achieved considerable success as a convention centre of the East. There were 69 tourist-class hotels in 1975, with 9,900 rooms.

AGRICULTURE

The economic structure of Singapore is characterized by an absence of a rural agricultural base. Less than a sixth of the land area is cultivated, more than half under rubber and coconuts, for which prices improved markedly in 1972 and 1973. The relative share of the sector in G.D.P. declined steadily from 6.1 per cent in 1960 to 1.6 per cent in 1975.

MANUFACTURING

Manufacturing activity, stimulated by government industrial promotion efforts, expanded rapidly between 1968 and 1974 at 16 per cent annually. However, in 1974 it grew by only 3.9 per cent and in 1975 declined by 1.6 per cent. Increasing at an average annual rate of 25 per cent, from S$1,140.9 million in 1970 to S$3,416 million in 1975, the growth in manufacturing value added, albeit from a small base, has not been unimpressive. The problem of labour absorption in the mid-1960s has been contained to a large extent through the establishment of labour-intensive industries. The current strategy for the future development of the manufacturing sector is to shift the emphasis to establishing high-technology industries with a more skill-intensive labour mix. Industries which have shown rapid growth in these years include petroleum products, shipbuilding and repairing, basic metals and metal products. The contribution of the relatively higher value-added industries to total manufacturing employment and value-added was evident in 1975, reflecting the changing structure of the manufacturing sector. By 1975 the relatively higher value-added industries, which require higher skills and technology, were providing employment for 55 per cent of the industrial work force and contributing 72 per cent to total value-added in manufacturing.

Employment

The growth in manufacturing employment has been less significant than the growth in manufacturing value added. Increasing at an average annual rate of 9.5 per cent, manufacturing employment rose from 126,361 in 1970 to 203,043 in 1974, but fell to 196,729 in 1975, a decline of 6 per cent.

While growing unemployment in the mid-1960s dictated the use of labour-intensive methods of production, modern industries with their emphasis on mass-production and standardization are inevitably capital-intensive. It appears that the bias has been on relatively capital-intensive industries. Capital expenditure in manufacturing increased at an annual rate of 33 per cent, totalling S$620 million in 1974. The bulk of the increase in employment was in newly established firms; the main stimulus was export expansion. Industries in these categories include textiles, wearing apparel and made-up textile goods, electronic equipment assembling and electronic components manufacturing; others were shipbuilding, paper and paper products (which are more labour-intensive industries). Employment in manufacturing is expected to grow in the long run, especially after the end of the current recessionary conditions.

Export Sales

The growth in direct exports of manufactured goods increased more than sixfold between 1970 and 1974. Total direct exports from manufacturing amounted to S$7,812 million in 1975. While industrial exports appear to have grown at a satisfactory pace, averaging 40 per cent per annum between 1970 and 1974, there has been an actual fall in the proportion of output absorbed by foreign markets before 1971; in 1960 the share of exports in total sales was 36 per cent, in 1967 under 31 per cent and only 28 per cent in 1968. This suggests that early manufacturing growth in Singapore has depended upon the expansion of domestic markets mainly as a result of import-substitution. In 1970 export sales surged upward to account for 40 per cent of total sales, suggesting that import-substitution had reached saturation point. By 1974, export sales accounted for more than 60 per cent of production. For a number of industries, Malaysian markets were important for the growth of export sales. During 1960–68, West Malaysia took more than a third of industrial exports. The distribution of sales of manufactured goods since 1969 shows a markedly different pattern of market shares—one in which foreign markets, particularly the developed nations of the United States, Western Europe and Japan, play a much more important role. The expansion in export sales provided an important stimulus for industrial expansion.

Industries heavily dependent upon export sales for growth included textiles, shirts and wearing apparel, electrical machinery and components and plywood and veneer in which two-thirds of sales were to foreign markets; others were petroleum products (60.6 per cent) and non-ferrous metal basic industries (mainly tin-smelting, 42.7 per cent), other chemical products (48.8 per cent), natural gums (46.6 per cent), non-electrical machinery (48.1 per cent) and transport equipment (44.5 per cent). Two industries—tobacco products and iron and steel basic industries—produced predominantly for the domestic market; the value of export sales of these industries amounted to only 4.9 per cent and 1.4 per cent of total sales respectively. It is significant to note that, on the whole, domestic-oriented industries have shown slower growth rates than those geared to export markets.

Although the initial stimulus to industrial expansion appears to have come from within, given the limitations of the domestic market, it is doubtful whether any massive development of industry can get under way or even present growth rates be sustained unless adequate external markets are found rapidly. It is of paramount importance that costs of production are kept low so that prices of manufactured goods can be competitively maintained overseas.

The current emphasis is on the development of high-technology, export-oriented manufacturing industries and on the active promotion of exports overseas. The lesson that has been learned from the current recession is that labour intensive industries are still important in terms of employment creation and that industrial training by up-grading the skills of the work force would ensure a more optimal utilization of its only natural resource.

Foreign Investment

Recognizing the limited growth potential in production for the domestic market and the difficulties of breaking into the international market, the Government has placed emphasis on the promotion of export-oriented industries, in particular firms from advanced countries which have the requisite know-how and, more important, established marketing channels. Several incentives are offered, including prepared industrial sites (in some cases also ready-made factory buildings), loans and even government equity participation and various tax exemptions.

New foreign investments have undoubtedly been a predominant factor in the recent growth of new industries in Singapore. Panic capital inflow from Hong Kong largely accounted for the spurt of industries established in the early 1970s. However, the main impetus for sustained growth in industry is expected to come from the U.S.A. Among the more notable investments are Jurong Shipyard and National Iron and Steel Mill (both with Japanese participation) and a number of petroleum refineries—*Mobil*, *Esso Standard* and *Caltex*—all representing U.S. capital. Several other firms in electronics, petrochemicals, paper and pulp, fertilizers, watch-making, construction of fishing vessels and other specialized ships and marine structures, prefabricated houses, internal combustion engines, farm implements and machine tools are being established by foreign investors. Besides providing employment, these large firms with international connections exert an enormous impact on the level of technological advancement in Singapore manufacturing.

Total investment commitments in manufacturing amounted to S$828.6 million in 1974 but fell to S$400 million in 1975. More than 76 per cent of these commitments were in the petroleum products and machinery industries. Foreign investments comprised 67 per cent of these commitments in 1975.

To strengthen further the industrialization effort, three institutions were set up in the 1960s. *The Development Bank of Singapore*, with paid-up capital of S$100 million, was set up with the aid of the Investment Bank of the Federal German Government. In addition to financing purely manufacturing undertakings, the Bank's financial scope extends to include service industries contributing to Singapore's development as a regional services and international financial centre. The second institution, a government-sponsored international trading company (*INTRACO*), was established in 1968 to co-ordinate and expedite the search for markets for locally manufactured products. The third institution, the *Jurong Town Corporation*, took over the ownership and management of the vastly extended industrial estates in Singapore.

Oil Refining

Although petroleum refining contributed more than 35 per cent of total manufacturing output in 1975, its contribution to total value added is only 17 per cent. Singapore is the third largest oil-refining centre in the world, with a capacity of one million barrels per day. Oil companies are actively exploring the possibility of diversifying into petrochemicals. Plans to establish a S$2,000 million petrochemical complex are being finalized. The Republic has also become a leading base for offshore oil exploration.

Ship Building and Ship Repairing

Oil exploration activities have boosted this industry tremendously. The transport equipment industry is the third largest in manufacturing in terms of total output. Singapore shipyards are now constructing larger tonnage vessels such as 90,000-ton tankers. Repair and salvage activities continue to make important contributions. Drydocking facilities were also expanded. The out-fitting and servicing of highly sophisticated exploration equipment and rigs have attracted three American companies to set up shipyards in joint ventures with local groups. Singapore is the fourth largest Asian shipbuilder (after Japan, Taiwan and India) and ranks twenty-first in the world. Ship and rig building increased by 16 per cent in 1975. The shipyards employ some 20,000 persons which is twice the number in 1968.

CONSTRUCTION

An important sector which has expanded rapidly in recent years is that of building and construction, some two-thirds of which have been under the aegis of government bodies. Private construction expenditure, augmented by the public contribution, rose from S$116 million in 1961 to S$1,939 million in 1974. Construction activity, particularly in the building of factories, offices and hotels, declined in 1974 and 1975 because of rising construction costs, the shortage of labour and the overall bleak economic prospects. The construction of residential buildings dipped drastically during the last few years because of the credit squeeze and the prohibition of foreigners to own certain types of houses in Singapore. This last move was to curb speculative activity in the property market. Although less markedly, there was also some increase in the Government's housing development programme under the stimulus provided by the Government's new house-ownership schemes for the lower income groups and also in utilities construction and public works which are continuously being expanded and improved. It has been estimated that more than half Singapore's population now lives in public low-cost housing which is equipped with modern amenities. The Housing and Development Board, under its Third Five-Year Building Programme (1970–75), built 91,949 flats and shops. However, in March 1975, 100,000 were still on the accommodation waiting list. New emphasis is being placed on non-residential building construction, mainly factories and commercial offices, which has not kept pace with the rate of establishment of business concerns. The Government's urban renewal scheme, spear-headed by the newly created Urban Redevelopment Authority, has been aimed at clearing slums and derelict buildings and rebuilding parts of the city to ensure optimum land use. These activities have provided continued impetus in the construction sector.

MONEY, BANKING AND FINANCE

The Singapore Dollar

An important monetary development in mid-1967 was the termination of the Currency Agreement which had provided a common currency for the States of Malaya, Singapore and the Borneo territories. At the outset, the Singapore Government sought the co-operation of the Malaysian Government in setting up a joint currency system. However, after prolonged negotiations, the two countries decided to issue separate currencies. Singapore's currency is backed 100 per cent in gold and convertible foreign assets, which rules out the possibility of fiduciary issue. At the end of 1975, total issue of Singapore currency was estimated at S$1,639 million, an increase of 25 per cent over 1974. Against this currency stands total official foreign assets amounting to S$7,500 million. While the rapid rate of accumulation of foreign assets was due in part to sound investments by the Board and rapid economic expansion, it includes also some elements of "hot money" from politically less settled neighbouring countries.

During 1973 the Currency Interchangeability Agreement, which had provided for the free flow and exchange of the Singapore and Malaysian dollars at par, was terminated by the Malaysian Government. Brunei, the third party to the Agreement, subsequently broke off its currency link with Malaysia, maintaining the original agreement with Singapore. Since the currency split the Singapore and Malaysian dollars have fluctuated, within a narrow margin, around the parity level.

Money and Banking

The contribution of banking and insurance services to the G.D.P. rose by 13.2 per cent between 1970 and 1975. Commercial banks have become an increasingly important source of funds for the finance of business activity in Singapore. Total deposits increased by 19 per cent annually between 1970 and 1975, rising to S$7,606 million in 1975, while total bank loans and advances rose from S$731 million in 1962, at an initial stage of the Republic's first attempts at planned development, to S$7,679 million in 1975. The finance of international trade—import, export and wholesale trade—continued to be an important area of banking interest, although the proportion of bank loans going to the sector has fallen from 51 per cent in 1968 to 32 per cent in 1975. Commercial banks have played an important role in the industrialization programme, providing increasing funds for the finance of industrial ventures; loans to the manufacturing sector have risen from S$822 million in 1971 to S$1,953 million in 1975, which is a 21 per cent increase. The willingness of commercial banks to accommodate the demand for loans for industrial expansion indicated a radical departure in commercial banking practices, which by long established custom have been geared to trade financing.

A notable feature of the money supply in recent years has been the tremendous increase in bank money creation, i.e. demand deposits in commercial banks against which cheques can be drawn. At November 30th, 1975, the money supply totalled S$3,383 million, of which S$1,811 million (53.5 per cent) was in the form of demand deposits. To some extent, this indicates the growing sophistication of business transactions in the Republic and the rapid development of the monetized section of the economy.

Against the background of international currency instability and the relative strength of the Singapore dollar, inflows of speculative funds raised the domestic money supply to S$2,413 million by the end of 1972, an increase of 35 per cent over the previous year. In an attempt to curb the inflationary tendency generated, the Monetary Authority of Singapore raised the minimum reserve requirements of banks from 3.5 per cent to 9 per cent.

The Singapore dollar was "floated" in June 1973. In 1975 it weakened against the U.S. dollar compared with 1974, but gained against the Japanese yen, pound sterling, Hong Kong dollar and Malaysian ringgit.

In the early part of 1974, monetary measures taken to check inflation included the raising of interest rate and the introduction of selective credit control. Further steps were taken in 1975 and inflation was virtually halted.

The development of Singapore into an international financial centre proceeded rapidly in 1975. The number of banks operating in Singapore, including offshore banks, rose to 70, an increase of 8. Of the total number of banks, 57 are foreign and only 13 local. There are 21 merchant banks, three of which are foreign.

The Asian Dollar Market

As part of the policy to develop Singapore into an international financial centre, the Asian Dollar Market was established in 1968 to tap the existing pool of "hard currencies" circulating in Asia. Singapore has numerous advantages in this respect: it is the traditional entrepôt port for the region; it has a favourable geographical location which enables it to trade simultaneously in European money markets for several hours daily; it has excellent communication with all major cities of the world; it has a well developed banking system and political and economic stability; and, most important of all, is located within a region with a high growth potential.

The Stock Exchange

Malaysia and Singapore established their own stock exchanges in 1973 thus ending the common Exchange A few months later the joint rubber exchange was also terminated. These developments were to enable the two countries to pursue their independent policies. The Singapore Government enacted the Securities Industry Bill to give it wider powers to investigate manipulation and other abuses in the stock market. A Securities Industry Council was appointed to implement the Act and to develop the capital market. Share prices declined in 1974, revived slightly in early 1975 and declined again.

Public Finance and Development

Government expenditure and revenue statistics indicate clearly the rising prosperity of the period. Total public revenue rose yearly, largely from taxes on incomes and, with the greater range of duties to protect local infant industries, from taxes on production and consumption. These are supplemented substantially by the net earnings of public corporations and other commercial undertakings of government.

Government revenue rose from S$1,219 million in 1970 to S$3,055 million in 1975. Revenue from taxes on income, constituting about 37 per cent of total revenue, rose by an average of 20.9 per cent during this period. The other main source of revenue has been taxes on production and expenditure which represent almost 32 per cent of total government revenue.

The most outstanding feature of public finances in recent years has been the extent of expansion of the Government's influence on the course of domestic business activity and the increasing use of fiscal measures to achieve monetary control. Public capital expenditure rose markedly with the initiation of the First Development Plan in 1961. Capital formation by the public sector rose from S$67 million in 1960 to S$367 million in 1970 and is estimated to have reached S$1,296 million in 1975 (or 27 per cent of gross domestic capital formation). As a result of the rapid rise of public capital, the pattern and rate of investment in the overall economy are substantially influenced by the government contribution. Government stimulus in these years was applied chiefly through public works and building construction, although its participation in other sectors of activity, particularly in industry, also increased significantly.

An interesting development has been the decline in the public share of total capital formation in Singapore, which had fluctuated around a half until the mid-1960s but gradually declined to two-fifths in 1968 and about a quarter since 1971. This indicates that private investment has not only matched the growth in public investment but has, in recent years, continued to expand even more rapidly.

Because of the conservative system of monetary management in the years of colonial rule, a current surplus was always budgeted and realized. Such surpluses have not only financed development expenditures, at least up to 1961, but were sufficiently large to allow a sizeable reserve to be accumulated through the years.

Development outlays have increased rapidly particularly in the last few years, in part as a result of the counter-recessionary moves and the need for further development of the infrastructure. In the past, government expenditures were financed almost entirely from current budget surpluses and in part by running down accumulated reserves, but greater reliance is now being placed on domestic loans and external credit to finance the extended development programmes. Domestic borrowing, chiefly through sale of government long-term bonds, has been augmented by foreign loans and grants from the United Kingdom Government.

Of the Government's intention to increase the public debt substantially over the next few years, it may be said that its sizeable accumulated reserves provide a firm financial base for the Government to run budget deficits financed by spending accumulated overseas assets or proceeds of foreign loans raised on the collateral of these assets.

STATISTICAL SURVEY

AREA

(square km.)

Total	Singapore Island	Offshore Islands
597	558	39

LAND USE

(1975—square km.)

Built-up*	Agricultural	Cultivable Waste	Forest	Marsh and Tidal Waste	Others†
228.4	77.5	95.8	32.4	32.4	130.3

* Includes new industrial sites.

† Includes inland water, open spaces, public gardens, cemeteries, non-built up areas in military establishments and quarries.

POPULATION

ETHNIC GROUPS

('000—mid-1975 estimate)

Chinese	1,712.8
Malays	338.8
Indians	155.2
Others	43.1
Total	2,249.9

BIRTHS AND DEATHS

	Live Births	Deaths
1970	45,934	10,717
1971	47,088	11,329
1972	49,678	11,522
1973	48,269	11,920
1974	43,268	11,674
1975	39,948	11,447

Capital: Singapore City (population 1,327,500 at June 30th, 1974).

EMPLOYMENT

	1973 (September)	1974 (June)	1975 (June)
Agriculture, Forestry, Hunting and Fishing	2,419	21,709	17,372
Mining and Quarrying	1,756	1,748	3,139
Manufacturing	221,117	234,231	218,096
Construction	37,113	42,495	39,181
Electricity, Gas, Water and Sanitary Services	16,058	10,344	8,929
Commerce	128,586	172,650	191,686
Transport, Storage and Communications	56,217	97,519	97,899
Services	146,279	241,710	254,679
Activities not Adequately Defined	n.a.	1,943	2,544
Total All Industries	609,545	824,349	833,525

Note: Data for 1973 were obtained from mandatory labour returns submitted by employers under the Employment Act 1968. The data cover working proprietors, unpaid family workers, employees and other paid workers employed in establishments. Domestic servants and certain categories of own account workers like farmers, fishermen, hawkers, etc., were excluded. Data for 1974 and 1975 were obtained from the 1974 Labour Force Survey which was based on a sample of 8,218 and 7,707 households respectively and covered all categories of workers.

AGRICULTURE

	Area (hectares)			Production			
	1972	1973	1974		1973	1974	1975
Rubber	3,294	3,160	2,391	metric tons	1,205	975	66
Coconuts	2,600	2,400	1,860	million	9	7	7
Fruits	2,588	2,657	2,638	metric tons	18,400	14,645	14,629
Mixed Vegetables	1,367	1,025	} 851	,, ,,	49,550	} 35,825	38,285
Root Crops	1,013	790		,, ,,	6,400		
Tobacco	243	310	279	,, ,,	417	376	311

LIVESTOCK
('000 head)

	1971/72	1972/73	1973/74
Cattle	8*	8*	8*
Buffaloes	3	3	3
Pigs	1,140	1,279	1,186
Goats	2	2	2
Chickens	12,500*	12,786*	13,072*
Ducks	1,657*	1,636*	1,744*

* FAO estimate.

Source: FAO, *Production Yearbook 1974*.

LIVESTOCK PRODUCTS
('000 metric tons)

	1972	1973	1974*
Mutton and lamb	4	2	2
Pig meat	39	37	37
Poultry meat	20*	20*	21
Edible offals	3.5*	2.8*	2.9
Cows' milk	1*	1*	1
Hen eggs	18.9	20.3	20.9
Other poultry eggs	6.0*	5.9*	6.3

* FAO estimates.

Source: FAO, *Production Yearbook 1974*.

FISHERIES

FISH LANDED AND AUCTIONED
(metric tons)

1969	1970	1971	1972	1973	1974	1975
43,704	60,671	62,324	61,855	65,593	64,200	65,803

INDUSTRY

		1973	1974	1975
Rubber Smoked Sheets	metric tons	12,988	10,810	12,905
Remilled Crepe Rubber	,, ,,	107,637	102,168	992,089
Paints	kilolitres	12,843.7	12,468.6	12,692.2
Broken Granite	'000 cu. metres	1,777.9	1,795.3	2,302.1
Bricks	'000 pieces	146,751	141,295	126,111
Cigarettes	'000 kg.	3,483.8	3,431.2	3,241.5
Cheroots	,, ,,	63.2	60.4	47.2
Soft Drinks	'000 litres	101,756.7	106,062.4	113,806.0
Coconut Oil	metric tons	14,490	7,589	15,041
Vegetable Cooking Oil	,, ,,	45,769	37,438	53,099
Animal Fodder	,, ,,	371,863	284,331	234,195
Electricity	million kWh.	3,719.3	3,864.3	4,175.7
Gas	million cu. ft.	344.8	391.1	432.4

FINANCE

100 cents = 1 Singapore dollar (S$).
Coins: 1, 5, 10, 20 and 50 cents; 1 dollar.
Notes: 1, 5, 10, 25, 50, 100, 500, 1,000 and 10,000 dollars.
Exchange rates (June 1976): S$1 = 1 Brunei dollar; £1 sterling = S$4.39; U.S. $1 = S$2.47.
S$100 = £22.78 = U.S. $40.41.

Note: The Singapore dollar (S$) was introduced in June 1967, replacing (at par) the Malayan dollar (M$). From September 1949 the Malayan dollar was valued at 2s. 4d. sterling (£1 = M$8.5714) or 32.667 U.S. cents (U.S. $1 = M$3.0612). This valuation in terms of U.S. currency remained in effect until August 1971. Between December 1971 and February 1973 the Singapore dollar was valued at 35.467 U.S. cents (U.S. $1 = S$2.8195). From February to June 1973 the Singapore dollar's value was 39.407 U.S. cents (U.S. $1 = S$2.5376). In terms of sterling, the exchange rate was £1 = S$7.347 from November 1967 to June 1972. The formal link with the Malaysian dollar, begun in June 1967, ended in May 1973 but the Brunei dollar remains tied to the Singapore dollar. Since June 1973 the Singapore dollar has been allowed to "float". The average exchange rate (Singapore dollars per U.S. dollar) was: 2.809 in 1972; 2.444 in 1973; 2.437 in 1974; 2.371 in 1975.

ORDINARY BUDGET

(S$ million—estimates for year ending March 31st, 1977)

Revenue		Expenditure	
Direct Taxes	1,573.3	General Services	150.1
Indirect Taxes and Taxes on Outlay	724.1	Defence and Justice	859.1
Reimbursements and Sales on Goods and Services	407.9	Social and Community Services	802.7
Income from Investments and Property	226.3	Economic Services	172.8
Others	176.0	Public Debt	456.9
		Unallocable	37.2
		Add: Transfer to Development Fund	625.0
		Surplus	3.8
Total	3,107.6	Total	3,107.6

DEVELOPMENT BUDGET

(S$ million—estimates)

Expenditure	1975/76	1976/77
Transport and Communications	74.2	27.6
Defence	51.9	37.1
Education	92.1	55.9
Health	34.0	30.5
Finance	145.1	131.3
Information and Social Affairs	9.8	13.3
Reclamation and Urban Redevelopment	28.7	36.4
Public Works	58.7	85.8
Loans to:		
Industrial and Commercial Enterprises	281.7	292.9
Jurong Town Corporation	270.3	338.4
Public Utilities Board	54.0	58.0
Housing and Development Board	718.0	792.0
Sentosa Development Corporation	10.0	30.0
Urban Renewal Authority	118.0	100.0
Other Heads	241.7	581.1
Total	2,188.2	2,610.3

OFFICIAL FOREIGN ASSETS

(S$ million, valuation at cost, December 31st)

	1973	1974	1975
Total External Reserves of Monetary Authority (including gold tranche)*	3,137.5	4,083.7	5,681.7
Total External Reserves of Singapore Government and Statutory Authorities	2,662.7	2,419.2	1,804.3

* Figures include foreign assets of the Board of Commissioners of Currency, Singapore, and foreign assets of the Monetary Authority of Singapore.

BALANCE OF PAYMENTS

(S$ million—estimates)

	1973	1974	1975*
Current Account:			
Merchandise:			
Import f.o.b.	11,689.7	18,964.7	17,790.5
Exports f.o.b.	8,418.4	13,423.8	11,892.9
Trade Balance	−3,271.3	−5,540.9	−5,897.6
Service Payments (net)	1,799.0	2,905.8	4,220.6
Total Goods and Services (net receipts)	−1,472.3	−2,635.1	−1,677.0
Transfers (net receipts)	— 10.1	−95.1	−99.4
Balance on Current Account	−1,482.4	−2,730.2	−1,776.4
Capital Movements			
Non-monetary Sector (net)	874.6	1,578.4	1,544.7
Private	848.0	1,577.3	1,540.8
Official	26.6	1.1	3.9
Monetary Sector—Commercial banks (net)	592.5	−420.7	−157.8
Net Errors and Omissions	1,020.5	2,290.9	1,361.4
Total Capital Movements	2,487.6	3,448.6	2,748.3
Net Surplus or Deficit	1,005.2	718.4	971.9

* Preliminary.

EXTERNAL TRADE

(S$ million)

	1971	1972	1973	1974	1975
Imports	8,664.0	9,538.0	12,522.0	20,404.9	19,270.4
Exports	5,371.3	6,149.4	8,906.8	14,154.6	12,757.9

PRINCIPAL COMMODITIES

(including trade with West Malaysia)

(S$ million)

	Imports			Exports		
	1973	1974	1975	1973	1974	1975
Food and Live Animals	1,262.9	1,551.2	1,654.4	617.2	814.0	915.7
Beverages and Tobacco	112.8	117.9	130.3	37.4	38.6	40.9
Crude Materials, inedible, excluding Fuels	1,460.7	1,648.7	1,229.2	2,152.4	2,506.2	1,694.3
Mineral Fuels and Lubricants	1,618.2	4,897.9	4,734.1	1,367.8	3,693.0	3,451.2
Animal and Vegetable Oils and Fats	186.4	391.3	242.0	171.6	358.1	245.5
Chemicals	723.6	1,220.6	1,119.6	393.6	917.1	475.7
Manufactured Goods classified chiefly by Materials	2,526.6	3,591.8	3,510.3	920.1	1,069.9	1,086.5
Machinery and Transport Equipment	3,498.4	5,405.8	5,046.3	1,967.8	2,918.6	2,894.6
Miscellaneous Manufactured Articles	957.5	1,345.9	1,331.3	695.8	807.5	880.4
Commodities and Transactions n.e.s.	165.8	233.8	272.9	583.1	1,031.6	1,073.1

PRINCIPAL TRADING PARTNERS*
(S$ million)

	Imports			Exports		
	1973	1974	1975	1973	1974	1975
Australia	442.1	571.0	661.5	329.2	687.7	637.2
China, People's Republic	573.2	643.9	682.0	128.4	125.8	98.5
Sabah and Sarawak	409.2	625.7	483.0	392.2	586.3	501.1
Germany, Federal Republic	497.0	712.3	636.2	303.4	428.2	481.5
Hong Kong	354.0	470.9	427.8	486.3	901.4	937.0
Japan	2,295.5	3,653.9	3,254.3	713.3	1,610.5	1,112.9
Thailand	312.3	542.6	406.3	201.0	343.2	445.4
United Kingdom	692.7	996.3	956.0	552.5	574.5	539.8
U.S.A.	1,885.6	2,858.1	3,024.0	1,515.3	2,100.7	1,775.4
Peninsular Malaysia	1,630.7	2,060.4	1,755.6	1,220.5	1,761.1	1,687.1

* No figures are available for trade with Indonesia.

TRANSPORT

RAILWAYS

The Malayan Railway system also serves Singapore.

ROADS—VEHICLES REGISTERED

	1973	1974*	1975
Private Cars	187,972	142,674	142,045
Motor Cycles and Scooters	122,714	84,849	83,145
Motor Buses	4,775	4,779	4,935
Goods Vehicles (incl. private)	45,537	36,424	41,363
Others	6,739	8,140	8,890
Total Vehicles on Register	367,737	276,866	280,378

* With effect from January 1974, figures are not comparable with earlier years due to computerization of the records on motor vehicles.

SHIPPING
(Vessels of over 75 net registered tons)

	Ships Entered	Ships Cleared	Cargo Discharged ('000 metric tons)	Cargo Loaded ('000 metric tons)
1972	18,624	18,628	35,651.8	21,412.4
1973	18,948	18,884	38,566.9	22,702.0
1974	19,641	19,617	37,713.6	22,738.9
1975	20,216	20,201	33,032.0	19,067.2

CIVIL AIR TRAFFIC

	Passengers			Mail ('000 Kilograms)		Freight ('000 Kilograms)	
	Arrived	Departed	In Transit	Landed	Despatched	Landed	Despatched
1971	825,712	835,796	344,775	1,282	1,514	10,305	15,401
1972	1,029,214	1,039,252	466,875	1,311	1,589	13,098	17,431
1973	1,350,745	1,373,933	583,850	1,457	1,777	18,853	22,717
1974	1,483,232	1,513,732	631,028	1,557	2,181	23,843	34,285
1975	1,647,081	1,676,963	712,105	1,655	2,818	26,276	39,811

TOURISM

TOURIST EXPENDITURE
(S$ million)

1972	1973	1974	1975
424	573	735	794*

* Preliminary.

In December 1975, there were 69 gazetted tourist hotels, having some 9,900 rooms in operation. Another 3,118 rooms are presently under construction, and are expected to be completed by December 1979. In 1975 1,324,312 tourists visited Singapore.

COMMUNICATIONS MEDIA

Radio Licences issued: (1974) 67,808; (1975) 64,211.

Radio and Television Licences issued: (1975) 280,479.

Rediffusion Subscribers (at Dec. 31st, 1975): 85,567.

DAILY NEWSPAPERS (1975)

		combined circ.
Chinese	4	227,307
English	2	187,278
Malay	1	26,453
Tamil	2	7,139
Malayalam	1	630
Total	10	448,807

EDUCATION

(End—June 1975)

	Institutions*	Students	Teachers†
Primary	391	328,401	11,190
Secondary:			
Academic	114	153,029	6,154
Technical	9	19,802	911
Commercial	1	3,393	55
Technical and Vocational Institutes‡	12	9,830	740
Universities and Colleges	5	18,501	1,646
Total	532	532,956	20,696

* A full school conducting both primary and secondary classes is treated as one primary and one secondary school.

† Including relief teachers but excluding teachers on national service, study leave, scholarship, secondment, etc.

‡ Including Hotel and Catering Training School and School of Printing.

Source: Department of Statistics, Singapore.

THE CONSTITUTION

HEAD OF STATE

The Head of State is the President, elected by Parliament for a four-year term. He normally acts on the advice of the Cabinet.

THE CABINET

The Cabinet, headed by the Prime Minister, is appointed by the President and is responsible to Parliament.

THE LEGISLATURE

The Legislature consists of a Parliament of sixty-five members, presided over by a Speaker who may be elected from the members of Parliament themselves or appointed by Parliament although he may not be a member of Parliament. Members of Parliament are elected by universal suffrage.

A Constitutional Amendment Act was passed in December 1969 setting up a 21-Member Presidential Council chaired by the Chief Justice. This exists to examine legislation to see whether it contains elements which differentiate between racial or religious communities or contains provisions inconsistent with the fundamental liberties of Singapore citizens and report and advise the Government thereon.

CITIZENSHIP

Under the constitution Singapore citizenship may be acquired either by birth, descent or registration. Persons born when Singapore was a constituent State of Malaysia could also acquire Singapore citizenship by enrolment or naturalization under the constitution of Malaysia.

THE GOVERNMENT

HEAD OF THE STATE

President: Dr. BENJAMIN HENRY SHEARES.

THE CABINET

(*July* 1976)

Prime Minister: LEE KUAN YEW.

Deputy Prime Minister and Minister of Defence: Dr. GOH KENG SWEE.

Minister for Science and Technology: Dr. LEE CHIAW MENG.

Minister for Finance: HON SUI SEN.

Minister for Foreign Affairs: SINNATHAMBY RAJARATNAM.

Minister for Labour: ONG PANG BOON.

Minister for Home Affairs and Education: CHUA SIAN CHIN.

Minister for Communications and National Development: LIM KIM SAN.

Minister for Law and the Environment: E. W. BARKER.

Minister for Culture: JEK YEUN THONG.

Minister for Social Affairs: Enche OTHMAN bin WOK.

Minister for Health: Dr. TOH CHIN CHYE.

Minister without Portfolio: YONG NYUH LIN.

PARLIAMENT

The Speaker: Dr. YEOH GHIM SENG, B.B.M., J.P.

A General Election was held in September 1972. The People's Action Party (P.A.P.) was returned in 57 out of the 65 constituencies and in the remaining 8 constituencies, P.A.P. candidates were returned unopposed. The opposition parties received a total of 220,347 votes or 29 per cent of the votes cast.

POLITICAL PARTIES

The following participated in the 1972 general election:

People's Action Party: 143–145 Orchard Rd.; f. 1954; first formed the government of the State of Singapore in 1959; re-elected to power 1963, 1968 and 1972 as government of independent Republic of Singapore; Chair. Dr. TOH CHIN CHYE; Sec.-Gen. LEE KUAN YEW.

Socialist Front (*Barisan Sosialis Malaya*): 436-C Victoria St., Singapore 7; f. 1961; left-wing; formerly members of People's Action Party; seeks to abolish national service, provide free medical services for the poor, reduce taxes and relax the citizenship laws; Chair. Dr. LEE SIEW CHOH; publs. *Barisan* (Chinese), *Plebeian* (English).

Singapore Malays' National Organization (S.M.N.O.): 218E Changi Rd.; reorganized 1967; formerly the United Malays' National Organization in Singapore; seeks to improve conditions for the Malays, to promote Islam and Malay culture, to encourage democracy and racial harmony, to work against colonialism; Chair. Encik AHMAD bin HAJI TAFF.

United National Front: f. 1970; aims to abolish the Internal Security Act, release political detainees and promote a common market between Malaysia and Singapore.

Workers' Party: f. 1971; seeks a new democratic constitution, closer relations with Malaysia and the establishment of immediate diplomatic relations with the People's Republic of China; Leader J. B. JEYARETNAM.

People's Front: f. 1971; favours an independent democratic socialist republic; Chair. LUI BOON POH.

Towards the end of 1974 seven of the opposition parties: the United National Front, the United Front, the Singapore Justice Party, Angkatan Islam, Pekemas, Persatuan Malayu Singapura and the Singapore Chinese Party moved to merge into a United People's Front.

DIPLOMATIC REPRESENTATION

EMBASSIES AND HIGH COMMISSIONS ACCREDITED TO SINGAPORE

(In Singapore City unless otherwise indicated)

(E) Embassy; (HC) High Commission

Argentina: Room L-1, 11th Floor, International Building, 360 Orchard Rd., Singapore 9 (E); *Ambassador:* VALENTIN LUCO.

Australia: 201 Clemenceau Ave. (HC); *High Commissioner:* ROBERT BIRCH.

Austria: Bangkok, Thailand (E).

Bangladesh: 43 Kings Rd., Singapore 10 (HC); *High Commissioner:* KHAWAJA MOHAMMED KAISER.

Belgium: Tower 2202, DBS Bldg., Shenton Way, Singapore 1; *Ambassador:* JAN HELLEMANS.

Brazil: Bangkok, Thailand.

Bulgaria: Room 808/9 Thong Teck Bldg., 15 Scotts Rd., Singapore 9 (E); *Ambassador:* STOYAN VALDIMIROV ZAIMOV.

Burma: 15 St. Martin's Drive (E); *Chargé d'Affaires a.i.:* MYO AUNG.

Canada: 7/8 Floors, Faber House, 230-236 Orchard Rd. (HC); *High Commissioner:* R. K. THOMSON.

Czechoslovakia: Rangoon, Burma (E).

Denmark: Rooms 10, 13/14 Supreme House, 10th Floor, Penang Rd. (E); *Ambassador:* K. RASMUSSEN.

Egypt: 20C and 22C Paterson Rd., Singapore 9 (E); *Ambassador:* Dr. ALI SAMIR SAFOUAT.

El Salvador: Tokyo, Japan (E).

Finland: 15th Floor, Goldhill Plaza (E); *Ambassador:* ORO RITTA (resident in New Delhi, India).

France: 5 Gallop Rd. (E); *Ambassador:* JACQUES GASSEAU.

German Democratic Republic: Colombo, Sri Lanka (E).

Germany, Federal Republic: 12th Floor, Far East Shopping Centre, 545 Orchard Rd. (E); *Ambassador:* HANS DIETRICH.

Greece: Rooms 707/709, 7th Floor, Robina House, Shenton Way, Singapore 1 (E); *Ambassador:* BASIL VITSAXIS.

Hungary: New Delhi, India (E).

India: India House, 31 Grange Rd. (HC); *High Commissioner:* VENCATA SIDDHARTHACHARRY.

Indonesia: "Wisma Indonesia", 1st Floor, 435 Orchard Rd. (E); *Ambassador:* CHAERUDIN TASNING.

Iran: Bangkok, Thailand (E).

Ireland: New Delhi, India (E).

Israel: 7th Floor, Faber House, 236G Orchard Rd. (E); *Ambassador:* ITZHAK LAVAN.

Italy: Rooms 810–812, 8th Floor, Supreme House, Penang Rd. (E); *Ambassador:* FRANCO LUCIOLI OTTIERI DELLA CIAIA.

Japan: 16 Nassim Rd. (E); *Ambassador:* SHINSUKE HORI.

Malaysia: 301 Jervois Rd., Singapore 10 (HC); *High Commissioner:* MOHD YUSSOF BIN ZAINAL.

Nepal: Rangoon, Burma (E).

Netherlands: 10th Floor, International Bldg., 360 Orchard Rd. (E); *Ambassador:* PIET WILLEM HENRI SCHAEPMAN.

New Zealand: 13 Nassim Rd. (HC); *High Commissioner:* ROGER E. B. PEREN.

Norway: 16th Floor, Hong Leong Bldg., 16 Raffles Quay, Singapore 9 (E); *Ambassador:* WILHELM KROGH-FLADMARK.

Pakistan: 510–511 Shaw House, Orchard Rd. (E); *Ambassador:* (vacant).

Philippines: Rooms 505–506, 5th Floor, Thong Teck Bldg., 15 Scotts Rd. (E); *Ambassador:* DELFIN REUTO GARCIA.

Poland: 1st Floor, Bank of China Bldg. (E); *Ambassador:* WIKTOR KINECKI.

Romania: Room E8, 3rd Floor, Maritime Bldg., Singapore 1 (E); *Ambassador:* (vacant).

Spain: Bangkok, Thailand (E).

Sri Lanka: c/o U.S. De Silva & Sons, 92 and 102 Clifford Centre, 24 Raffles Place (HC); *High Commissioner:* (vacant).

Sweden: Rooms 1404–5, 14th Floor, Goldhill Plaza, 187 Thomson Rd. (E); *Ambassador:* ERIC OTTO GUNNARSSON VIRGIN.

Switzerland: Room 705, Shaw House, Orchard Rd. (E); *Chargé d'Affaires a.i.:* MAX LEU.

Thailand: 370 Orchard Rd. (E); *Ambassador:* CHAMNONG PHAHUIRAT.

Trinidad and Tobago: New Delhi, India (HC).

Turkey: Bangkok, Thailand (E).

U.S.S.R.: 51 Nassim Rd. (E); *Ambassador:* YURI IVANOVICH RAZDUKHOV.

United Kingdom: Tanglin Circus (HC); *High Commissioner:* J. P. TRIPP, C.M.G.

U.S.A.: 30 Hill St. (E); *Ambassador:* JOHN H. HOLDRIDGE.

Yugoslavia: 52 Stevens Rd., Singapore 9; *Chargé d'Affaires en pied:* MILUTIN FILIPOVIC.

Singapore also has diplomatic relations with Cambodia and Viet-Nam.

JUDICIAL SYSTEM

A Supreme Court consisting of the High Court, the Court of Appeal and the Court of Criminal appeal was established by the Supreme Court of Judicature Act. The High Court exercises original criminal and civil jurisdiction in appeals from the Subordinate Courts. An appeal from the High Court lies to the Court of Criminal Appeal or the Court of Appeal which exercises appellate jurisdiction. In certain cases, a further appeal lies from the decision of the Court of Criminal Appeal or Court of Appeal, as the case may be, to the Judicial Committee of the Privy Council.

The Subordinate Courts consist of Magistrates' and District Courts which have limited civil and criminal jurisdiction. There is also an Industrial Arbitration Court to regulate labour relations.

The Criminal Procedure Code (Amendment) Act, 1969, enacts that in all cases where the accused is charged with an offence in respect of which punishment by death is authorized by law, the accused shall be tried by a court consisting of two Judges of the High Court, one of whom shall be the presiding Judge. The decision of the Court as to the guilt of the accused in respect of such a charge shall be arrived at unanimously.

The Government Proceedings Act, Chapter 21, enables an individual to sue the Government in tort and contract. Provision is also made for the right of the Government to sue if it had a claim against any person which would, if such claim has arisen between subject and subject, afford ground for civil proceedings.

The administration of justice in Singapore extends also to persons of limited means. There is an Act to make legal aid and advice in Singapore more readily available to persons of limited means, to enable the cost of legal aid or advice to persons to be defrayed wholly or partly out of monies provided by Parliament. Provisions are also made, yet to be implemented, for persons of limited means to apply for legal aid in defence of criminal cases and criminal appeals in which they are the accused. However, a person who is charged with a capital offence and who is unrepresented will have counsel assigned to him out of public funds. This scheme is administered by the Registrar of the Supreme Court.

In its administration of justice, Singapore adheres to "The Rule of Law" as defined in the United Nations Declaration of Human Rights.

Chief Justice: Mr. Justice WEE CHONG JIN.

Puisne Judges: Mr. Justice F. A. CHUA, Mr. Justice A. V. WINSLOW, Mr. Justice CHOOR SINGH, Mr. Justice T. KULASEKARAM, Mr. Justice TAN AH TAN, Mr. Justice DENIS DE COTTA.

RELIGION

The majority of Chinese are Buddhists, Confucians or Taoists. The Malays and Pakistanis are almost all Muslims, while the Europeans and Eurasians are overwhelmingly Christian. Most of the Indian community are Hindu.

BUDDHISM

The Singapore Buddhist Sangha Organization: Headquarters; Pho Kark See, Bright Hill Rd., off Thomson Rd., Singapore 20.

The Buddhist Union: 28 and 39-0 Jalan Senyum, Singapore 14.

The Singapore Buddhist Federation: 50 Lorong 34, Singapore.

World Buddhist Society: 40 Pender Rd., Singapore.

CHRISTIANITY

Anglican Church:

Diocese of Singapore: Bishop of Singapore and Dean of St. Andrew's Cathedral: The Rt. Rev. BAN IT CHIU, LL.B., Bishopsbourne, 4 Bishopsgate, Singapore 10.

Roman Catholic Church—Archdiocese of Singapore: His Grace the Archbishop Mgr. MICHEL OLÇOMENDY, Archbishop's House, 31 Victoria St., Singapore. Archbishop's Secretary: Rev. S. FERNANDEZ.

Methodist Church: Bishop for Malaysia and Singapore: Dr. YAP KIM HAO, P.O.B. 483, Singapore; Comptroller YONG NGIM DJIN.

Brethren Assemblies: Bethesda Gospel Hall, 77 Bras Basah Rd., Singapore 7; f. 1864; Hon. Sec. LIM TIAN LEONG; Bethesda (Katong) Church, 17 Pennefather Rd., Singapore 15; Chair. of Elders and Deacons, Dr. B. CHEW.

Presbyterian Church: Minister Rev. E. M. WHITE, B.A., "B" Orchard Rd., Singapore; f. 1856; 327 mems.; publs. *St. Andrew's Outlook* (twice yearly), Newsletter (monthly).

THE PRESS

In 1974 the Government passed a bill providing for compulsory government vetting of newspaper management. It obliged all newspaper companies to go public.

DAILIES

ENGLISH LANGUAGE

New Nation: Times House, Kim Seng Rd., Singapore 9; f. 1971; Proprs. New Nation Publishing Pte. Ltd.; Independent; Editor PETER LIM HENG LOONG; circ. 36,000.

Straits Times: Times House, Kim Seng Rd.; f. 1845; Man. Editor KHOO TENG SOON; circ. 140,000 (Singapore only).

CHINESE LANGUAGE

Min Pao Daily: 62 Bendermeer Rd., Singapore 12; Man. Dir. LO SUN KI; circ. 52,000.

Nanyang Siang Pau: 307 Alexandra Rd.; f. 1923; morning; Chair. and Chief Editor TAN CHIN HA; circ. 69,700.

Shin Min Daily News: 577 Macpherson Rd., Singapore 13; f. 1967; Chief Editor CHUNG WEN LING; circ. 69,000.

Sin Chew Jit Poh: 128 Robinson Rd.; f. 1929; morning; Exec. Dir. AW IT HAW; Man. WONG YUT WAH; Editor WONG SZU; circ. 140,000 (1973).

MALAY LANGUAGE

Berita Harian: Times House, Kim Seng Rd.; f. 1957; morning; Editor HUSSEIN JAHIDIN (arrested 1976); circ. 17,000.

MALAYALAM LANGUAGE

Malaysia Malayali: 12 Kinta Rd.; Man. Editor V. P. ABDULLAH; circ. 2,000.

TAMIL LANGUAGE

Tamil Malar: 430 Race Course Rd.; Editor T. SELVAGANAPATHY; circ. 9,044.

Tamil Murasu: 139–141 Lavender St.; f. 1936; Editor V. I. VANAM; circ. 8,500.

SUNDAY PAPERS

ENGLISH LANGUAGE

Sunday Nation: Times House, Kim Seng Rd., Singapore 9; Editor CHEONG YIP SENG; circ. 49,000 (Singapore only).

Sunday Times: Times House, Kim Seng Rd., Singapore 9; f. 1931; Editor T. S. KHOO; circ. 155,000 (Singapore only).

MALAY LANGUAGE

Berita Minggu: Times House, Kim Seng Rd.; f. 1957; Editor HUSSEIN JAHIDIN (arrested 1976); circ. 13,000.

PERIODICALS

About 300 periodicals are published in the various languages. The principal ones only are given here.

ENGLISH LANGUAGE

The Asia Magazine: International Bldg., Orchard Rd., 9; f. 1961; distributed by leading English language newspapers in Asia; Editor GEORGE V LIU.

Asia Research Bulletin: Research Private Ltd., 124 Stamford House, Stamford Rd., Singapore 6; political and economic; monthly.

Eastern Trade: P.O.B. 21, Thomson Rd., Singapore 20; f. 1961; business newspaper; fortnightly; Editor Mrs. M. V. GILL.

Her World: Times Publishing Bhd., Magazines and Periodicals Division, 422 Thomson Rd., Singapore 11; f. 1960; woman's monthly; Editor WENDY F. TAYE.

Republic of Singapore Government Gazette: Singapore National Printers (Pte.) Ltd., P.O.B. 485; weekly (Friday).

Singapore Medical Journal: André Publications, Tanglin, P.O.B. 7, Singapore 10; quarterly.

Singapore Trade and Industry: Times Publishing Bhd., Magazines and Periodicals Division, 422 Thomson Rd.; Editor A. A. MORAIS.

Straits Times Annual: Times Publishing Sdn. Bhd., 422 Thomson Rd., Singapore 11; annual.

CHINESE LANGUAGE

Island Literature: Island Society, 23 Cashin St., Singapore 7; quarterly.

MALAY LANGUAGE

Medan Sastera: 745–747 North Bridge Rd., Singapore 7; f. 1964; quarterly; Editor HARUN AMINURRASHID; circ 4,000.

PUNJABI LANGUAGE

Navjiivan National Punjabi News: 5 Albert House, Albert St., P.O.B. 2146; f. 1951; twice weekly, Wednesday and Saturday; Voice of the Sikhs in South-East Asia; Editor DEWAN SINGH RANDHAWA.

NEWS AGENCIES

FOREIGN BUREAUX

Agence France-Presse: 6th Floor, Nehsons Bldg., 24 Peck Seah St., Singapore 2; Correspondent M. K. MENON.

Allgemeiner Deutscher Nachrichtendienst—ADN (*German Democratic Republic*): 10A St. Martin's Drive, Singapore 10; Correspondent HEINER KLINGE.

Antara News Agency: 106A Grange Rd.; Correspondent M. ANWAR RAWY.

Associated Press—AP: G.P.O. Box 44, Room 1001, Robina House, Shenton Way, Singapore 2; Chief KENNETH L. WHITING.

Central News Agency of China: 69 Clover Way, Singapore 20; Correspondent CHI HUA-HUANG.

Czechoslovak News Agency ČETEKA: 1st Floor, M.S.A. Bldg., 77 Robinson Rd.; Correspondent Dr. MIROSLAV OPLT.

Deutsche Presse-Agentur—DPA (*Federal Republic of Germany*): 16 Mount Sinai Rd., Singapore 10; Correspondent ECKHARD BUDEWIG.

Jiji Press: 14K Asia Insurance Bldg.; Correspondent SHINJI NAYA.

Kyodo News Service: (Singapore Bureau), 1103, Marina House, Shenton Way/Palmer Rd., Singapore 2; Correspondent YOICHI YOKOBORI.

Novosti Press Agency (*U.S.S.R.*): 116 University Rd., Singapore 11; Correspondent YURI B. SAVENKOV.

Reuters: P.O.B. 463, 12th Floor, Marina House, Shenton Way; S.E. Asian Man. GORDON HAWSON.

TASS (*U.S.S.R.*): 37, A6 Nassim Rd., Singapore 10; Man. V. I. VOLKOV.

United News of India—UNI: P.O.B. 768; Correspondent E. M. RASHEED.

United Press International—UPI: Suite 69B, Raffles Hotel, Beach Rd., Singapore 7; Man. JOSEPH GALLOWAY.

PUBLISHERS

ENGLISH LANGUAGE

André Publications: Tanglin, P.O.B. 7, Singapore 10; publishes various guides to Asian cities.

Asia Pacific Press Pte. Ltd.: Liat Towers, 514 Orchard Rd., Singapore 9; f. 1969; fiction, religion, university textbooks; Chair. JOHN EDE.

Chopmen Enterprises: 47 The Arcade, Singapore 1; f. 1966; social science, history, textbooks, reference, fiction; Man. Dir. N. T. S. CHOPRA.

Eastern Universities Press Sdn. Bhd.: 112-F, Boon Keng Road, (P.O.B. 1742); 1; f. 1958; biography, history, textbooks; Man. RAYMOND YUEN.

Federal Publications Sdn. Bhd.: Times House, River Valley Rd., Singapore 9; educational books; Gen. Man. KOH HOCK SENG.

Jay-Birch & Co. Ltd.: 22B Penang Lane, P.O.B. 66; publishers to H.M. Forces.

University Education Press: Newton, P.O.B. 96, Singapore 11; books on E. and S.E. Asia, humanities and social sciences; Man. YEO TEO KONG.

MALAY LANGUAGE

Al-Ahmadiah Press: 101 Jalan Sultan; religious books and periodicals; Propr. A. ARIFF.

H.M. Ali Press: P.O.B. 1484, Singapore; books and magazines.

Malaysia Press Snd. Bhd.: 745–747 North Bridge Rd., Singapore 7; f. 1962; general; Dir. and Man. ABU TALIB ALLY.

Pustaka Melayu: 745–747 North Bridge Rd., Singapore 7; f. 1956; Malay educational books; Chief Editor HARUN AMINURRASHID.

Solo Enterprises: 12A Galaxy Cinema Arcade, Singapore 15; general.

CHINESE LANGUAGE

Commercial Press Ltd., The: incorporated in China; Singapore branch: 309 North Bridge Rd.; f. 1897; publishers, stationers and booksellers; school textbooks and magazines; Attorney and Man. DAVID C. N. HSU, F.B.A.A.

Educational Publications Bureau: 175A/177A Outram Park, Singapore 3.

Hong Seng Press: 520 North Bridge Rd.; Man. P. Y. LOOI.

Nanyang Book Co. Ltd.: 20 North Bridge Rd.; f. 1935; school textbooks; publications on South-East Asia; Journal of South Seas Society; Dir. TAN YEOK SEONG.

Wanli Cultural Enterprises: G40 Golden Mile Tower, Singapore 7.

World Book Co. Ltd.: 205–207 South Bridge Rd., Singapore 1.

INDIAN LANGUAGE

India Publishing House: 458 Race Course Rd., Singapore 8.

TAMIL LANGUAGE

Vani Nilayarn: 162 Cross St., Singapore 1.

Visvabharathi Publications: 1 Rappa Terrace, Singapore 8.

RADIO AND TELEVISION

RADIO

Radio Singapore: Ministry of Culture, P.O.B. 1902; f. 1959; broadcasts in English, Chinese (Mandarin and six dialects), Malay and Tamil, over four networks; each language channel broadcasts over one hundred hours weekly; Dir. Mrs. WONG-LEE SIOK TIN.

Rediffusion (Singapore) Private Ltd.: P.O.B. 608; f. 1949; commercial wired broadcasting service, originating two programmes in numerous Chinese dialects and English; over 85,000 subscribers; Man. Dir. J. SNOWDEN.

In 1976 there were 354,000 radio sets and 290,000 television sets.

Far East Broadcasting (F.E.B.A. Ltd.): 130-S Sophia Rd., Singapore 9; f. 1960; Chair. YEO KOK CHENG; Exec. Dir. LAUW KIM GUAN.

TELEVISION

Television Singapore: Ministry of Culture, P.O.B. 1902, Singapore; one station with two separate channels started operations in 1963; total weekly average of 109 hours; education service of 53 hours weekly; services in Malay, Chinese, Tamil and English; Dir. Mrs. WONG-LEE SIOK TIN.

FINANCE

(cap.=capital; p.u.=paid up; dep.=deposits; m.=million; S$=Singapore dollars; brs.=branches.)

BANKING

The Singapore monetary system is co-ordinated by the Monetary Authority of Singapore (MAS) and the Ministry of Finance. The Monetary Authority of Singapore performs all the functions of a central bank, except the issuing of currency, a function which is carried out by the Board of Commissioners of Currency. Legislation due to be passed in 1976 will give the Monetary Authority of Singapore the status of a Central Bank. In 1976 there were 70 banks and 38 representative offices in Singapore. Thirteen banks were fully licenced and 14 foreign banks had restricted offshore banking licences. There are also 21 merchant banks.

Board of Commissioners of Currency: Empress Place, Singapore 6; Chair. The Minister for Finance, HON SUI SEN.

Monetary Authority of Singapore: SIA Building, 77 Robinson Rd., Singapore 1; Chair. HON SUI SEN.

MAJOR COMMERCIAL BANKS

Asia Commercial Banking Corpn.: 106 Robinson Rd.; cap. p.u. S$40m. (1976); dep. S$146m. (1975); Chair. Datuk TAN KIM CHUA; Man. Dir. CHUA PHO TIONG.

Bank of Singapore: 34 Market St.; cap. p.u. S$5m.; dep. S$25m. (1975); Chair. RUNME SHAW; Exec. Dir. TAN TOCK SAN.

Chung Khiaw Bank Ltd.: 59 Robinson Rd.: f. 1950; became a subsidiary of the *United Overseas Bank* (q.v.) in 1971; cap. p.u. S$20m.; dep. S$763m. (Dec. 1973); Vice-Chair./Man. Dir. WEE CHO YAW; Dir. and Gen. Man. ALLAN NG POH MENG; 33 brs.

Four Seas Communications Bank Ltd: 57 Chulia St., 1; incorporated in Singapore 1906; auth. cap. S$50m.; cap. p.u. S$20m.; dep. S$144.6m. (Dec. 1974); Chair./Man. Dir. TAN SIAK KEW, P.J.G.

Industrial and Commercial Bank Ltd., The: ICB Bldg., 2 Shenton Way; f. 1954; cap. p.u. S$9m.; dep. S$147.7m. (Dec. 1974); Chair. TAN PEE CEE; Deputy Chair. and Exec. Dir. Dr. TAN POH LIN.

Lee Wah Bank Ltd.: 63 Robinson Rd., Singapore 1; f. 1920; cap. p.u. S$7.7m.; dep. S$192.5m. (Dec. 1973); Man. Dir. RICHARD K. M. EU; Gen. Man. W. F. CHEN.

Tat Lee Bank: Tat Lee Building, 63 Market St.; cap. p.u. S$36m.; dep. S$50m. (1975); Chair. GOH TJOEI KOK; Pres. GOH SEONG PEK.

Oversea-Chinese Banking Corporation Ltd.: Head Office Bldg., Upper Pickering St.; f. 1932; auth. cap. S$300m.; cap. p.u. S$113.7m. (Dec. 1974); Chair. TAN SRI TAN TUAN; Dir. and Gen. Man. LIN JO YAN; 6 overseas brs.; 39 brs. in Singapore and Malaysia.

Overseas Union Bank Ltd.: Meyer Chambers, Raffles Place; f. 1947; auth. cap. S$ 200m.; cap. p.u. S$55m.; dep. S$1,015.9m. (June 1975); Chair. and Man. Dir. LIEN YING CHOW; 43 brs.

United Overseas Bank Ltd.: 1 Bonham St., Raffles Place, Singapore 1; f. 1935; cap. p.u. S$86.7m.; dep. S$1,774m. (Dec. 1973); Chair. and Man. Dir. WEE CHO YAW; Dir. and Gen. Man. ALLAN NG POH MENG; 23 brs. in Singapore and 4 overseas.

DEVELOPMENT BANK

Development Bank of Singapore Ltd., The: DBS Bldg., Shenton Way, Singapore 1; f. September 1968; functions: providing finance to manufacturing, processing, service and other industries in the form of term loans, equity participation and guarantees; hire-purchase financing and leasing; providing a wide range of merchant banking facilities including underwriting share, debenture and bond issues, syndicating loans, providing advice on corporate structure and financial planning; providing a complete commercial banking service to both corporate and individual clients; cap. S$100m.; dep. S$630m. (Dec. 1974); Pres. HOWE YOON CHONG; Exec. Vice-Pres. DHANA BALAN.

FOREIGN BANKS

Algemene Bank Nederland N.V. (*General Bank of the Netherlands*): 2 Cecil St.; Gen. Man. C. H. J. VAN VUURDEN; Man. P. N. M. GEMKE.

Bangkok Bank Ltd.: 55 New Bridge Rd.; Vice-Pres./Branch Man. ADISORN TANTIMEDH.

Bank of America N.T. & S.A.: 31 Raffles Place; Vice-Pres. and Man. ROBERT CHEN.

Bank of Canton Ltd.: Denmark House, Raffles Quay, Singapore 1; Man. C. P. HUO.

Bank of China: Bank of China Building, Battery Rd.; Man. CHANG CHI HSIN.

Bank of India: 132-136 Robinson Rd.; Man. V. M. NADKARNI.

Bank of Nova Scotia: 1st Floor, Finlayson House; Man. T. L. GIBBS.

Bank of Tokyo Ltd.: Hong Leong Building, 16 Raffles Quay; Man. K. HAYASHI.

Bank Negara Indonesia: 3 Malacca St.; Gen. Man. ROCHMAT TANUSEPUTRA.

Banque de l'Indochine et de Suez: Shenton House, 3 Shenton Way, P.O.B. 246, Singapore 1; f. 1905; Man. A. UTARD.

Barclay's Bank International Ltd.: 1601/3 Shing Kwan House; Man. DONALD PAYNE.

Chartered Bank, The: 28-30 Battery Rd.; Man. GORDEN GEORGE JANES.

Chase Manhattan Bank, N.A.: 4 Shenton Way; 541 Orchard Rd.; 505 Yung An Rd., Jurong; Vice-Pres. and Gen. Man. JOHN D. TAYLOR.

European Asian Bank: Overseas Union Shopping Centre, 50 Collyer Quay, P.O.B. 3941; Man. DONALD E. WHITE.

Hongkong and Shanghai Banking Corporation: Ocean Building, 10 Collyer Quay, Singapore 1; Man. for Singapore A. R. PETRIE.

Lloyds Bank International Ltd.: 14th Floor, Shing Kwan House, 4 Shenton Way; Man. I. A. D. ORR.

Malayan Banking Bhd.: Malayan Bank Chambers, Fullerton Square, 1; Man. J. Y. LIM.

Mitsubishi Bank Ltd.: Podium G 2, DBS Bldg.; Man. OSAMU YAMADA.

Nordic Bank: P.O.B. 1769, Singapore 2; Man. HAAKON MELANDER.

United Malayan Banking Corporation Bhd.: 66–68 South Bridge Rd.; Man. KERMIN TSANG.

STOCK EXCHANGE

Stock Exchange of Singapore: 601 Clifford Centre, Raffles Place, Singapore 1; f. 1930; 74 mems.; Chair. NG SOO PENG; Dep. Chair. ONG TJIN AN; Gen. Man. LIM CHOO PENG; publ. *Singapore Stock Exchange Journal*.

INSURANCE

Export Credit Insurance Corporation: f. 1976; state and privately owned; to insure against non-payment to exporters; cap. p.u. 30m.

Life Business Only:

Asia Life Assurance Society Ltd.: Asia Insurance Bldg., Finlayson Green, P.O.B. 76, Singapore 1; f. 1948; Man. Dir. NG AIK HUAN.

First Life Insurance Co. (Pte) Ltd., The: First Life Bldg., 96–98 Robinson Rd., Singapore 1.

Public Life Assurance Co. Ltd.: 59 Robinson Rd., Singapore 1; f. 1954; Man. FUNG LOK NAM.

General Business Only:

Asia Insurance Co. Ltd.: Asia Insurance Bldg., Finlayson Green, P.O.B. 76, Singapore 1; f. 1923; Man. Dir. NG AIK HUAN.

Industrial and Commercial Insurance Co. Ltd., The: Industrial and Commercial Bank Bldg., 2 Shenton Way, Singapore 1; f. 1958; Man. Dir. Y. K. HWANG.

Insurance Corporation of Singapore Ltd.: Podium 416, DBS Bldg., 6 Shenton Way, Singapore 1; f. 1969; Gen. Man. CHEW LOY KIAT.

Malayan Motor and General Underwriters (Pte.) Ltd.: 3rd Floor, M & G Centre, 154–170 Clemenceau Ave., Singapore 9; f. 1954; Gen. Man. D. A. KEIGHLEY.

Nanyang Insurance Co. Ltd.: 25–26 Circular Rd., Singapore 1; f. 1956; Man. LIM SI HUI.

Overseas Union Insurance Ltd.: 43–47 New Bridge Rd., Singapore 1; f. 1956; Dir. and Gen. Man. MAURICE C. LEE.

People's Insurance Co. of Malaya Ltd.: 66–68 Cecil St., Singapore 1; f. 1957; Man. CHEW CHENG HOI.

Public Insurance Co. Ltd.: 59 Robinson Rd., Singapore 1; f. 1950; Man. FUNG LOK NAM.

Life and General Business:

Great Eastern Life Assurance Co. Ltd.: Great Eastern Life Bldg., 12–16 Cecil St., Singapore 1; f. 1908; Dir. and Gen. Man. N. N. HANDA.

Singapore International Insurance Brokers (Pte.) Ltd.: 10th Floor, Singapore Airlines Bldg., 77 Robinson Rd., Singapore 1; f. 1969; Dir. and Gen. Man. TAN CHENG KAI; Man. Marine Dept. V. RAJARAM.

Overseas Assurance Corporation Ltd.: 5 Malacca St., Singapore 1; f. 1920; Gen. Man. TAN HOAY GIE.

General, Marine and Aviation Business:

Pacific and Orient Underwriters (Pte.) Ltd.: P and O Bldg., Corner Market and Cecil Sts., Singapore 1; f. 1965; Dir. RUDOLPH MENDEZ.

In addition, many foreign insurance companies have offices in Singapore.

TRADE AND INDUSTRY

CHAMBERS OF COMMERCE

Singapore Chinese Chamber of Commerce: 47 Hill St., Singapore 6; Sec. C. M. WONG; publ. *Economic Monthly*.

Singapore Indian Chamber of Commerce: 55-A Robinson Rd., P.O.B. 1038, Singapore 1; f. 1937; 439 mems.; Pres. D. D. SACHDEV; Sec. S. N. DORAI.

Singapore International Chamber of Commerce: Denmark House, Raffles Quay; f. 1837; Chair. J. D. H. NEILL, M.B.E.; Exec. Dir./Sec. T. EAMES HUGHES, C.B.E.; publs. *Economic Bulletin* (monthly), *Showcase* (annual) *Investor's Guide*, Annual and other Reports.

Singapore Malay Chamber of Commerce: No. 101 Jalan Sultan, Singapore 7; Chair. Inche M. GHAZALI CAFFOOR; Hon. Sec. SYED AHMAD SEMAIT.

DEVELOPMENT ORGANIZATIONS

Economic Development Board: Second Floor, Fullerton Bldg., P.O.B. 2692; f. 1961; statutory organization planning and implementing Government's industrialization programme; Chair. NGIAM TONG DOW; Deputy Chair. P. Y. HWANG, I. F. TANG.

Housing and Development Board: National Development Bldg., Maxwell Rd., P.O.B. 702, Singapore 2; f. 1960; public housing authority of Singapore; Chair. MICHAEL FAM; publ. *Annual Report*.

INDUSTRIAL AND TRADE ASSOCIATIONS

Malayan Pineapple Industry Board: Suite 2303, Ocean Building, Collyer Quay, Singapore 1 and 5th Mile, Jalan Scudai, Johore Barhu; f. 1957; controls pineapple cultivation, canning and marketing; Chair. BADRUDDIN bin ABDUL SAMAD.

Rubber Association of Singapore: Rooms 604 and 606, 6th Floor, Chinese Chamber of Commerce Bldg., 47 Hill St., 6; incorporated Oct. 1967; to support, develop and maintain the rubber industry in general, and to conduct a market in Singapore for the sale and purchase of rubber under the arrangements and regulations formulated by the Corporation; Chair. TAN ENG JOO; Exec. Sec. GNOH CHONG HOCK.

Singapore Association of Shipbuilders and Repairers: c/o Keppel Shipyard Ltd., P.O.B. 2169, Singapore; Pres. CHUA CHOR TECK.

Singapore Manufacturers' Association: Colombo Court Bldg., Rooms 213–216, 2nd Floor, North Bridge Rd., Singapore 6; f. 1932; Chair. ONG LENG CHUAN; Deputy Chair. LIM HONG KEAT, TAN I. TONG; publ. *S.M.A. Directory* (annual).

EMPLOYERS' ORGANIZATIONS

The principal ones are:

The Singapore Employers' Federation: 23A Amber Mansions, Orchard Rd.; f. 1948; Pres. E. G. WALLER; Exec. Dir. E. R. BAUM.

Singapore Maritime Employers' Federation: P.O.B. 247; f. 1955; Chair. Capt. M. S. WRIGHT.

TRADE UNIONS

Singapore National Trades Union Congress (SNTUC): Trade Union House, Shenton Way, Singapore; Pres. PHEY YEW KOK; Sec.-Gen. C. V. DEVAN NAIR.

In July 1975 there were 143 registered employees' and employers' unions of which 91 were employees' trade unions (total membership 207,711), two-thirds of which are affiliated to the SNTUC.

CO-OPERATIVES

Singapore has 106 co-operative societies, made up of 42 Thrift and Loan Societies, 8 Employees' Credit Societies, 22 Thrift and Investment Societies, 13 Consumers' Societies, 6 Marketing Societies, 4 Rural Credit Societies, 2 Housing Societies, 2 Co-operative Banks, 1 Co-operative Union and 6 Miscellaneous Societies. These societies have a combined membership of 40,480 with S$19,420,903 as their working capital and S$910,156 as Reserve Fund.

MAJOR INDUSTRIAL COMPANIES

The following are among the major industrial establishments in Singapore in terms either of employment or capital investment.

BUILDING AND BUILDING MATERIALS

Hume Industries (Far East) Ltd.: 13.7 km., Bukit Timah Rd., Singapore 21; auth. cap. S$100m.; manufacturers of asbestos cement and reinforced concrete products, and steel, cast iron and PVC products; Man. Dir. MICHAEL Y. O. FAM; 2,193 employees.

Pilkington (S.E.A.) Pte. Ltd.: 180C Clemenceau Ave., Singapore 9; f. 1971.

Activities include moulding of fibreglass reinforced plastic items such as boats and custom mouldings for architects; responsible for marketing of Pilkington Group products throughout the region.

Man. Dir. J. G. HAMPSON.

Singapore PE Pte. Ltd.: 205 Kallang Bahru, Singapore 12; f. 1961; cap. S$1m.; manufacturers and converters of Polyethylene bags; Man. Dirs. C. P. CHIA, H. JIAN; 150 employees.

ELECTRICAL AND ELECTRONICS

ACMA Electrical Industries Ltd.: Jurong Port Rd., Jurong Town, Singapore 22; f. 1965; cap. S$6.4m.; manufacturers of electrical household appliances; Man. Dir. MARTIN C. W. YUEN.

Digitron Equipments (Pte.) Ltd.: 28C Tanglin Halt Close, Singapore 3; f. 1971; manufacturers of electronic calculators and related electronic consumer products; Dir. CHRIS CHEN; 100 employees.

General Electric (U.S.A.) Appliance Components Pte. Ltd.: 159C Boon Keng Rd., Kallang Industrial Estate, Singapore 12; f. 1970; cap. S$3.9m.; manufactures television components; Man. Dir. C. T. KIMBALL, Jr.; 500 employees.

Pan-Electric Industries Ltd.: 280 Kampong Arang Rd., Singapore 15; f. 1963; cap. S$16m.

Manufacturers of refrigerators, airconditioners, steel windows and metal products; marine salvage, shipbuilding, importers and exporters of aircraft, electrical power station equipment; general and electrical engineering.

Man. Dir. E. KAMIENBURG; 1,000 employees.

Philips Singapore Pte. Ltd.: Lorong 1, Toa Payoh, P.O.B. 340, Singapore 12; f. 1951; cap. S$20m.

Manufacturers of television sets, radios, tape-recorders, household appliances, telecommunication equipment, machinery and tools.

Man. Dir. B. M. LAP; 3,400 employees.

Sanyo Industries (S) Pte. Ltd.: 4 Wan Lee Rd., Jurong Industrial Estate, Singapore 22; f. 1966; cap. p.u. S$800,000.

Manufacturers of electrical household appliances.

Man. Dir. NG GHIT CHEONG; 200 employees.

Setron Ltd.: 10 Dundee Rd., Singapore 3; f. 1963; cap. p.u. S$10.2m.; manufacturers of television receivers, tuner amplifiers, radiograms, tape-recorders and related electronic equipment; Gen. Man. S. K. HUANG; 800 employees.

Singapore Semiconductor Pte. Ltd.: 1022A–1032A Lower Delta Rd., Kampong Tiong Bahru Flatted Factory, Singapore 3; f. 1969; cap. S$500,000.

Manufacturers of semi-conductors, transformers, radios and electronic components.

Man. Dir. WONG CHUN WIN; 500 employees.

FOOD AND BEVERAGES

Sugar Industry of Singapore Ltd.: 34 Jurong Port Rd., Jurong Town, Singapore 22; cap. S$25m.; 290 employees.

METALS AND ENGINEERING

Far East Shipbuilding Industries Ltd.: 39/41 South Bridge Rd., Singapore 1; cap. S$369,000; 303 employees.

Jurong Shipyard Ltd.: Pulau Samulun, Jurong Town, Singapore 22; cap. S$21,184,000; 1,500 employees; shipbuilders and repairers.

The Metal Box Company of Malaysia Ltd.: Registered office: MacDonald House, Orchard Rd., Singapore 9; f. 1949; cap. p.u. S$13,500,000.

Manufacturers and lithographers of cans and tin boxes including aerosol containers, screw caps and closures, decorated advertising show tablets, security printing, etc.

Man. Dir. P. B. BLACKWELL; 1,630 employees.

National Iron and Steel Mills Ltd.: Room 501, 5th Floor, Tat Lee Bldg., 63 Market St., Singapore 1; auth. cap. S$50m.

PETROLEUM

Amoco Far East Oil Co.: 9th Floor, Yen San Bldg., Orchard Rd., Singapore 9; petroleum refining and marketing.

B.P. Refining Co. (S) Ltd.: 1 Pasir Panjang Rd., Singapore; cap. S$22,432,000; 161 employees.

Burmah Oil Orient (Pte.) Ltd.: 11th Floor, Supreme House, Penang Rd., P.O.B. 122, Tanglin Post Office; oil extractors.

Castrol (F.E.) Pte. Ltd.: P.O.B. 35, Bukit Panjang Post Office, Singapore 23; manufacturers of lubricating oils, greases, speciality products and brake fluids.

Esso Singapore Pte. Ltd.: Pulau Ayer Chawan, Singapore 22; petroleum refining.

Gulf Oil Company South Asia: Ming Court Hotel, P.O.B. 641, Singapore 10; petroleum drillers.

Mobil Refining Co. (M) Ltd.: P.O.B. 3025, Singapore; cap. S$192.6m.; 400 employees.

Shell Eastern Chemicals (Pte.) Ltd., Shell Eastern Lubricants (Pte.) Ltd., Shell Eastern Petroleum (Pte.) Ltd., Shell Singapore (Pte.) Ltd.: UOB Bldg., No. 1 Bonham St., Singapore 1; 2,300 employees.

Singapore Petroleum Co. Pte. Ltd.: 4th Floor, Orchard Bldg., 1 Grange Rd., Singapore 9; petroleum marketing, manufacturing and distribution.

Pharmaceuticals

Beecham Pharmaceuticals Pte. Ltd.: Quality Rd., Jurong, Singapore 22; manufacture and sale of pharmaceuticals.

Bristol-Myers (S) Pte. Ltd.: Lau's Arcadia, 217 East Coast Rd., Singapore 15; importers, distributors and manufacturers of pharmaceuticals, toiletries and consumer household goods.

Ciba-Geigy S.E. Asia (Pte.) Ltd.: 1 Third Lokyang Rd., Singapore 22; importers, manufacturers, distributors of Ciba-Geigy products in Singapore and S.E. Asia.

Jack Chia-MPH Limited: 71–77 Stamford Rd., Singapore 6; f. 1927.

Manufacturers and distributors of pharmaceuticals, perfumes, toiletries, confectionery, optical lenses, spectacle frames; also operate timber industries and hotels; subsidiary companies include publishers, retailers, distributors of books and magazines, educational toys, stationery and novelties.

Chair. Jack Chia.

Wellcome (S) Pte. Ltd.: 33 Quality Rd., Jurong Town, P.O.B. 2, Singapore 22; medical and veterinary products, consumer products manufacturers, hygiene service.

Rubber and Leather Products

Bridgestone Singapore Co. (Pte.) Ltd.: 2 Jurong Port Rd., Jurong Town, Singapore 22; cap. S$10m.; 580 employees.

Textiles and Garments

Great Malaysia Textiles Mfg. Co. Pte. Ltd.: 1 Tanglin Halt Close, Singapore 3; cap. p.u. S$1.7m.; *c.* 1,200 employees.

Malaysia Garment Manufacturers Ltd.: 407 Chinese Chamber of Commerce Bldg., 47 Hill St., Singapore 6; cap. S$422,000; 354 employees.

Wing Tai Garment Manufacturers (S) Ltd.: 107 Tampenis Rd., Singapore 19; cap. S$4.2m.; 1,800 employees.

Unitex Singapore Pte. Ltd.: 26 Jalan Tukang, Singapore 22; cap. S$4m.; 300 employees.

Wood and Paper Products

Pan-Malaysia Industries Ltd.: Jalan Papan, Jurong, Singapore 22, P.O.B. 2923; cap. S$4m.; 750 employees.

Singapore Eidai Corpn. Ltd.: 8 Jalan Papan, Jurong, Singapore 22; cap. S$4.2m.; 576 employees.

Starlight Timber Products Pte. Ltd.: Jalan Papan, Jurong, Singapore 22; annual sales S$16m.; 1,100 employees.

Veneer Products Ltd.: Jurong Town, P.O.B. 4, Singapore 22; cap. S$11,427,900; 450 employees.

TRANSPORT

Singapore owes much of its wealth to its situation as a natural centre for sea and air routes.

RAILWAYS

There are 26km. of metre-gauge railway, linked with the Malaysian railways system. The main line crosses the Johore causeway and terminates near Keppel Harbour. Branch lines link it with the industrial estate at Jurong.

ROADS

In 1974 Singapore had a total of 2,155 kilometres of roads of which 1,655 kilometres were asphalt-paved. The road system includes dual carriage-ways, flyovers and expressways.

All roads are maintained by the Public Works Department, 10th Floor, National Development Bldg., Maxwell Rd., Singapore 2.

SHIPPING

Port of Singapore Authority: P.O.B. 300; Chair./Gen. Man. Howe Yoon Chong; Dir. Operations Billie Cheng; Dir. Eng. Services A. Vijiaratnam.

Container port facilities comprise three main berths of 914 metres (13.4 metres LWOST) and a feeder service berth of 213 metres (10.8 metres LWOST) completed in 1970. In addition, there are conventional wharves which include Keppel wharves (4.8 km.), Telok Ayer Basin, Jurong Port, Pasir Panjang wharves and Sembawang Port.

Major Shipping Lines

Neptune Orient Lines Ltd.: Neptune Bldg., 13 Trafalgar St., Singapore 2; f. 1968; liner services on the Far East Freight Conference and Straits/Australia routes; tankers and dry cargo vessels on charter; 17 ships with 3 under construction; total tonnage (including 3 ships under construction) 635,592 d.w.t.; Chair. M. Wong Pak-shong; Man. Dir. Goh Chok Tong.

Austasia Line Pte. Ltd.: 6th Floor, Realty Centre, 15 Enggor St., (P.O.B. 1946); f. 1953; 2 vessels; passenger/cargo services to Australasia and the Far East; Man. N. W. Hornby.

Chip Hwa Shipping & Trading Co. Pte. Ltd.: 45 Telok Ayer St.; tramp service; Man. Dir. Kiat bin Lau.

Everett Steamship Corporation: 11 Collyer Quay, Singapore 1; f. 1951; cargo services to Hong Kong, Indonesia, Burma, India and the Persian Gulf.

Guan Guan Shipping (Pte.) Ltd.: 23 Telok Ayer St., Singapore 1; f. 1955; shipowners and agents; passenger/cargo services to East Malaysia, Indonesia, and the Middle East.

Heap Eng Moh Steamship Company Pte. Ltd.: 1 Finlayson Green, Singapore 1; f. 1931; 3 vessels; passenger/cargo services to Kuching and Sibu.

Hua Siang Steamship Co. Ltd.: 16 Winchester House (1st Floor), Collyer Quay; services to Sarawak—Malaysia; 3 cargo vessels.

Kie Hock Shipping (1971) Pte. Ltd.: 48 Cecil St., Singapore 1; cargo services to South-East Asia, Middle East and Africa; 9 cargo vessels; operates liners, tramps and freighters; Man. Dir. Tay Hock Gwan.

Maersk Line (Singapore) Pte. Ltd.: 19th Floor, UIC Bldg., 5 Shenton Way, Singapore 1; f. 1974; cargo services on Far East/U.S.A. route; operates container and cargo vessels; Man. Dir. Jorgen Lund.

Pacific International Lines Pte.: 45 Market St., Singapore 1; f. 1967; passenger/cargo services to Indonesia, Thailand, Burma, India, Persian Gulf, Middle East, East Africa, China, Japan and Australia; Chair. R. E. L. WINGATE.

Sea-Land Services, Inc.: 156 Cecil St., Far Eastern Bank Building, Singapore 1; f. 1933; liner services to central America and U.S.A.; container service.

Straits Steamship Co. Ltd.: Ocean Building, Singapore 1, f. 1973; services to Thailand, Brunei, East and West Malaysia; 7 vessels; Chair. R. E. L. WINGATE; Sec. T. S. ONG, B.COMM. (MELB.), A.A.S.A.

CIVIL AVIATION

Singapore Airlines Ltd. (SIA): Airline House, Singapore Airport, Singapore; f. 1972; services to London, Seoul, Tokyo, Osaka, Sydney, Brunei, Manila, Madras, Medan, Bangkok, Kuala Lumpur, Hong Kong, Taipei, Perth and Melbourne; fleet of ten Boeing 707, five 737, four 747; Chair. Y. J. M. PILLAY; Man. Dir. LIM CHIN BENG.

Singapore is also served by the following foreign airlines: Aeroflot, Air Ceylon, Air India, Alitalia, Air New Zealand, British Airways, Cathay Pacific Airways, China Air Lines, Czechoslovakian Airlines, Garuda Indonesian Airways, JAL, KLM, Lufthansa, Malaysia Airlines System, Olympic Airways, Philippines Airlines, PIA, Qantas, Sabena, SAS, Swissair, Thai International, Trans Mediterranean Airways, UTA.

TOURISM

Singapore Tourist Promotion Board: Tudor Court, Tanglin Rd., Singapore 10; f. 1964; Chair. RUNME SHAW; Dir. LAM PENG LOON; publs. *Singapore Travel News* (monthly in English and Japanese), *Singapore Weekly Guide* (English).

CULTURAL ORGANIZATIONS

The Singapore Arts Council: c/o National Theatre, Clemenceau Ave., Singapore 9; aims to promote cultural activities and the integration of the Malay, Chinese, Tamil and English cultures; to maintain and improve standards in all forms of art and to serve as co-ordinating body for all cultural societies and associations in the Republic; Pres. LEE KHOON CHOY; Hon. Sec. M. LOGANATHAN.

National Theatre Trust: Clemenceau Ave., Singapore 9; f. 1960; responsible for the management of the National Theatre and the encouragement and development of culture in the Republic; Chair. KWA SOON CHUAN. The Trust established a **National Theatre Company** in 1968.

People's Association: Kallang, Singapore 14; a statutory corporation set up in 1960 for the organization of leisure, the promotion of youth activities and group participation in social, cultural, educational, vocational and athletic activities; operates a network of 172 community centres, 5 holiday camps and a 30-unit holiday complex.

POWER

PUBLIC UTILITIES BOARD

City Hall, St. Andrew's Rd., Singapore 6.

A statutory corporation formed in May 1963 to provide the public with the essential utilities of electricity, water and gas.

The Board's Gross Fixed Assets at the end of 1975 stood at S$1,534.3 million.

The recurrent expenditure for 1975 was $369.9 million, while income and net revenue surplus were $455.7 million and $91 million respectively.

Chairman: LIM KIM SAN.

Acting General Manager: WEE KIAN KOK.

Employees: c. 9,700.

Publs. include *Annual Report, Newsletter*, pamphlets and brochures.

ELECTRICITY

The Electricity Department supplies electricity to homes, schools, industries and roads, both in the city and in rural areas. The annual per capita consumption of electricity in Singapore was 1,633 kWh. in 1975, one of the highest in South-East Asia.

WATER

Singapore's water sources are rivers and impounding reservoirs. The bulk of the water in the reservoirs is collected from protected catchments. The "raw" water is chemically treated, filtered and sterilized with chlorine at the Board's treatment works.

GAS

Gas supplies are piped under regulated pressure into gas mains to serve various parts of the Republic. Areas outside the town gas distribution network are served with liquefied petroleum gas stored in tanks.

DEFENCE

Armed Forces (1975): Total strength 30,000; army 25,000, navy 2,000, air force 3,000; military service lasts 24–36 months. Army reserves number 25,000 and para-military forces comprise 7,500 police, marine and Ghurkha guard batallions; Home Guard 30,000.

Equipment: The army has French tanks and British guns. The navy has patrol boats and landing craft. The air force has mainly British aircraft, but France, Italy and New Zealand have also provided equipment.

Defence Expenditure: The defence budget for 1975–76 was S$613 million.

EDUCATION

Education in Singapore is not compulsory, but all children are entitled to at least six years' free primary education. A recently completed school building programme now ensures a place for every child, though most schools still work a shift system, one functioning in the morning and another in the afternoon.

In June 1975 there were 391 primary schools and 121 secondary (including technical and commercial) schools. Total enrolment was 532,956 in June 1975, approximately a quarter of the population. Of this total, 328,401 were enrolled in primary schools, 176,224 in secondary schools and 16,849 in higher education.

Parents may choose between the four official languages—English, Chinese, Malay and Tamil—as the medium for instruction, but the syllabus and curriculum are uniform. English and Chinese schools are in the majority. Much emphasis is placed on bi-lingualism, and all primary and secondary school children study a second language from their first year.

After six years of primary schooling, successful candidates proceed to secondary schools which offer four-year courses with a technical, academic or commercial bias, leading to the Singapore-Cambridge General Certificate of Education "O" Level Examination. Those who complete this course successfully may follow a 2-year pre-university course leading to the General Certificate of Education "A" Level Examination.

Teacher Training

The total number of teachers in June 1975 was 20,696. The Institute of Education conducts both full and part-time teacher training courses. During the 1975/76 academic year there were 685 students under-going pre-service training.

Higher Education

As of June 1975 there were 12 technical and vocational institutes, including a hotel and catering training school and a school of printing. There are also two technical colleges, one teacher training institute and two universities.

Adult Education

This is an important part of the education programme and covers all aspects—academic, vocational and commercial. More than 30,000 students attended these courses each month in 1975 in 35 centres run by the Adult Education Board.

UNIVERSITIES

University of Singapore: Singapore 10; *c.* 450 teachers, *c.* 5,800 students.

Nanyang University: Singapore 22; 170 teachers, 2,350 students.

BIBLIOGRAPHY

BRACKMAN, ARNOLD. Southeast Asia's Second Front (Pall Mall, London, 1966).

BUCHANAN, IAIN. Singapore in Southeast Asia; An Economic and Political Appraisal (G. Bell, London, 1972).

EMERSON, R. Malaysia, A Study in Direct and Indirect Rule (1937, reprinted, Oxford University Press, Kuala Lumpur, 1966).

GOH, KENG SWEE. The Economics of Modernization and other essays (Asia Pacific Press, Singapore, 1972).

LEE KUAN YEW. The Battle for Merger (Ministry of Culture, Singapore, 1961).

MILLS, L. A. British Malaya 1824–1867 (1925, reprinted, Oxford University Press, Kuala Lumpur, 1968).

NATIONAL LIBRARY, SINGAPORE. Singapore National Bibliography (Government Printing Office, Singapore, 1969). (annual).

OOI JIN BEE and CHIANG HAI DING. Modern Singapore (University of Singapore Press, 1969).

OSBORNE, MILTON. Singapore and Malaysia (Data Paper No. 53, Cornell University, New York, U.S.A., 1964).

PANG, CHENG LIAN. Singapore's People's Action Party (Oxford University Press, Singapore, 1971).

SAW SWEE HOCK. Asian Metropolis: Singapore in transition (University of Pennsylvania and Oxford University Press, 1970).

Singapore Trade and Industry Yearbook (Straits Times Press, Singapore).

THIO, EUNICE (Editor). Singapore 1819–1969 (Journal of South-East Asian History, University of Singapore, March 1969).

TSUJI, M. Singapore, the Japanese Version (Ure Smith, Sydney, Australia, 1960).

WILSON, DICK. East meets West: Singapore (Times Printers, Singapore, 1971).

WONG LIN KEN. The Trade of Singapore, 1819–1869 (Journal of the Malayan Branch, Royal Asiatic Society, 1961).

WURTZBURG, C. E. Raffles of the Eastern Isles (Hodder and Stoughton, London, 1954).

YOU, POH SENG, and LIM CHONG YAH. The Singapore Economy (Eastern Universities Press, 1971).

(*See also* Malaysia.)

Thailand

PHYSICAL AND SOCIAL GEOGRAPHY

C. A. Fisher

Thailand, which was formerly known as Siam, occupies the centre of the South-East Asian mainland, between Burma to the west, Laos and Cambodia to the east, and Peninsular Malaysia to the south. Its total area is 514,000 square kilometres (198,457 square miles).

Of this territory much the greater part lies to the north of the Bight of Bangkok, and hence well removed from the main shipping routes across the South China Sea between Singapore and Hong Kong, though peninsular Thailand, extending south to the Malayan border approximately at latitude 6° N. has a coastline some 600 miles long facing the Gulf of Siam, and a somewhat shorter one facing the Andaman Sea. Between these two the peninsula narrows at the isthmus of Kra to a straight-line distance of only 35 miles between salt water on both sides, and at various times during the last hundred years the possibility has been considered of cutting a canal here to link the Indian Ocean with the South China Sea, thus by-passing Singapore. Although during the late 1960s it seemed that the idea of building such a canal had been finally abandoned as economically unjustifiable, it took on a new lease of life in the early 1970s owing to the rapid increase in shipping congestion in the Straits of Malacca.

PHYSICAL AND CLIMATIC ENVIRONMENT

Apart from peninsular Thailand, which except in the far south consists of mainly narrow coastal lowlands backed by low and well-wooded mountain ranges, the country comprises four main upland tracts —in the west, north, north-east and south-east— surrounding a large central plain drained by the principal river, the Menam Chao Phraya. Because of its central position within mainland South-East Asia, Thailand, while experiencing tropical temperatures throughout its entire area, receives relatively less rainfall than either Burma to the west or most parts of the Indochinese lands to the east. In general, rainfall is highest in the south and south-east, and in the uplands of the west and to some extent in the higher hills in the north, but most of the rest of the country in effect constitutes a rain-shadow area where the total annual fall is below 150 cm. (60 inches).

The western hills are formed by a series of N.–S. ridges, thickly covered by tropical monsoon forest with much bamboo, and drained by the Gwei Noi and Gwei Yai rivers. Although summit levels here are only of the order of 600–900 metres (2,000–3,000 feet), the ridge and furrow pattern makes this generally inhospitable country. In the northern uplands, which represent the southernmost portion of the great Yunnan-Shan-Laos plateau, altitudes are higher than in the west, reaching an upper limit of about 1,500 metres (5,000 feet), and the upland surface is fairly well forested, though the natural cover has clearly deteriorated in many areas as a result of shifting cultivation. But in the four parallel valleys of the Ping, Wang, Yom and Nan rivers, which flow through these uplands and subsequently converge farther south to form the Chao Phraya, there are relatively broad lowlands with a more open vegetation now largely cleared for rice cultivation.

The northeastern plateau, also known as the Korat plateau, is mostly of much lower altitude than the two uplands just described. For while on its western and southern edges it presents a continuous rim usually exceeding 300 metres (1,000 feet) and in places much higher than that, elsewhere it consists of a relatively low and undulating surface, draining eastwards via the Nam Si and the Nam Mun to the Mekong, which flows along its entire northern and eastern edge.

In contrast to most of the other uplands, including the small southeastern area of steep and rugged hills which lie along the northern shore of the Gulf of Siam, and are very heavily forested, the Korat plateau is an area of barely adequate rain, which during the dry season presents a barren and desiccated appearance. Since the main rivers flowing across it rise within this same area of low rainfall, Korat is less favourably placed in respect of irrigation water than the central plain, which, though likewise receiving an annual rainfall of less than 150 cm. (60 inches), is well watered by the Chao Phraya system.

Because of its focal position, its fertile alluvial soils, and the well developed system of natural waterways, the central plain forms by far the most important single region within the country. And within this region, the delta, which begins about 190 kilometres (120 miles) from the coast, enjoys all these advantages to a more pronounced extent, and it is here that both the former capital, Ayudhya, and the present capital, Bangkok, are situated, and that the highest densities of rural population also occur.

NATURAL RESOURCES

As the above remarks imply, Thailand's main natural resources lie in its agricultural potential, and in particular in the capacity of the central plain (and to a lesser extent the Korat plateau) to produce a substantial surplus of rice. In addition, maize and kenaf have also become increasingly important in these areas in recent years, while the more humid and more nearly equatorial coastal plains of southern peninsular Thailand have similarly expanded their production of rubber. It is likewise in the far south, in the areas nearest to Malaya, that Thailand's main mineral wealth, namely tin, is found. Although various other minerals, including wolfram, lead, iron and lignite also occur within the country, none of these is produced on a large scale, and the only other important natural commodity to note is teak, which comes mainly from the northern hills.

POPULATION AND ETHNIC GROUPS

The estimated population at mid-1975 was 42,277,000, an average density of 82 per square kilometre. Although average densities fall to between a quarter and a half of this in the west and north, the total area of really sparsely populated upland is small, and in general the population is much less unevenly distributed than in most other countries in South-East Asia. Similarly, the proportion formed by indigenous minority peoples is low, and apart from some 700,000 Muslim Malays in the far south, a much smaller number of Cambodians near the eastern borders, and a total of 300,000 scattered hill peoples—Meo, Lahu, Yao, Lisu, Lawa, Lolo and Karen—mainly in the far north and west, virtually the entire indigenous population belongs to the Thai ethnic group (which also includes the Shan and Lao) and subscribes to Theravada Buddhism. However, it should be added that the inhabitants of the north-east tend to be closer in speech and custom to the Lao populations on the other side of the Mekong than to those of central Thailand and this sense of difference is aggravated by the lower standards of living in the former area.

By far the largest minority in Thailand consists of the ethnic Chinese who are estimated to number 3.73 million or over 12 per cent of the total population. But in contrast to most other parts of South-East Asia, a very high proportion of this Chinese community has come to identify itself with Thailand, although officially only some 300,000 are now ranked as Thai nationals.

As an overwhelmingly agricultural country Thailand so far shows only a relatively limited degree of urbanization, and apart from the single great complex of Bangkok-Thonburi, which has passed the two million mark, only one other town, namely Chiengmai in the north (65,736) had more than 50,000 in 1960.

HISTORY

David K. Wyatt

When groups of the Thai people began to move into the area of present-day Thailand towards the tenth century, most of the region was under the rule of the Khmer Empire of Angkor. After a number of attempts, one such group at Sukhothai on the northern edge of the great central plain succeeded in asserting its independence early in the thirteenth century, and by the end of that century had extended its rule far down the Malay Peninsula, westwards into lower Burma, and into northern Laos. The region's political centre of gravity, however, shifted towards the south, and in 1350 a rival Thai kingdom was established at Ayudhya which soon gained a dominant position by conquering Angkor in 1369 and 1389 and reducing Sukhothai to vassalage by the end of that century. During the reign of the great King Borommatrailokanat (1448–88), the kingdom's constitution was formalized. The absolute monarchy, imbued with the authority and sanctity of the god-king of classical Indian tradition, lay under the rule of the moral principles of Theravada Buddhism; while the civil and military bureaucracy was firmly established and placed under the central control of the capital. On these institutional foundations the kingdom grew and prospered.

One theme prominent in the history of the Kingdom of Ayudhya is the manner in which it was compelled to come to terms with the world which lay around and outside it. Early conflict with Cambodia over territory to the east and north-east, and with the northern Thai kingdom of Chiengmai over the mountainous lands to the north gradually was extended further afield, until the Thai came into conflict with Burma, and suffered the first sack of Ayudhya in 1569, after which Chiengmai remained under Burmese control for a further two centuries. The growth and development of international trade brought to Ayudhya the Portuguese early in the sixteenth century and Western commercial rivalries in the seventeenth, which grew into an abortive Franco-Siamese alliance during the reign of King Narai the Great (1657–88), when the French, having won to their side the Greek adventurer who was Narai's prime minister, attempted to dominate the kingdom but were expelled after a revolution in 1688. Out of regional conflict and the development of international trade came a strengthening of Ayudhya's control over its export-producing provinces in the south, west, and south-east, and a growing dependence on foreign trade which survived the withdrawal of European traders after 1688. Conflict with the Burmese, however, resumed in the middle of the eighteenth century, and brought about the utter destruction of the Kingdom of Ayudhya in 1767.

Reconstruction

The kingdom was re-constituted militarily by King Taksin, the half-Chinese usurper who reigned at Thonburi from 1767 until his overthrow in 1782; and it was reconstructed politically and economically by the first of the Bangkok kings, Rama I (1782–1809). Increasingly, the kingdom's attention was engaged by a situation of regional conflict which for the first time caught the Thai kingdom between two major powers, Burma and a resurgent Viet-Nam. At issue were Thai hegemony in Laos and Cambodia to the east, and in

Chiengmai in the north. In addition, Thai interests in the northern Malay states, especially Kedah, threatened further to bring the Thai into conflict with the British East India Company. The Thai responded to these difficulties with great sensitivity to changes in international politics, strong military measures in the east and south in the reign of King Rama III (1824–51), and timely concessions to the British in a treaty of 1826 which opened Bangkok to a limited Western trade. In the later years of the reign of Rama III there grew up at court an influential group of men whose interests were closely involved with foreign trade and who were remarkably well-informed of events outside their own country, receptive to Western innovations and learning, and intelligent and practical realists in their attitudes to foreign relations. One of the leaders of this group was the Buddhist monk and royal prince Mongkut, who became King Rama IV in 1851. His party was able to force the country's acceptance of Western demands that Thailand should open her ports to free commercial intercourse with the West; and the modern history of Thailand begins with the Anglo-Siamese Treaty of 1855 which was at once the springboard of rapid economic development, founded on the rice trade, and the signal for a dramatic intensification of colonial threats to Thai independence.

MODERN HISTORY

The policies of King Rama IV and his son King Rama V (Chulalongkorn, 1868–1910) to counter these colonial threats were threefold. First, they attempted by diplomacy carefully to play against each other the Western powers, particularly Britain and France. Secondly, they worked to integrate more securely into the kingdom outlying provinces and dependent states, as in the north, the north-east, Laos, and northern Malaya, lest the local rulers of these areas either defect or by their actions provide the Western powers with excuses for intervention. Thirdly, they worked to modernize the financial, judicial, and administrative institutions of the kingdom both so as to strengthen its ability to resist the West and to meet the standards of justice and efficiency expected of it by the West. Mainly for political reasons, progress in meeting these objectives was painfully slow, and it was not until the late 1880s that fundamental reorganization of the machinery of state could be undertaken. By the death of King Rama V in 1910, these policies had been proven successful by the kingdom's survival; yet survival had been purchased at a high price. National integration had been undertaken too late to prevent the loss of Thai suzerainty over Cambodia (1863–67) and the provinces of Laos to France after the Franco-Siamese conflict of 1893, when Anglo-French rivalry failed to work in Thailand's favour. Likewise, release from some of the most onerous provisions of the treaties with the Western powers, particularly extra-territoriality, could be gained only by further territorial cessions in Laos and Cambodia to France (1904–07) and in Malaya to Great Britain (1909). The loss could have been much worse; and the fact that it was not is due largely to the great reforms of 1889–1910, which gave the kingdom a unified and centralized provincial administration, a modern revenue and financial system, improved communications, and a modern system of education.

King Rama V handed on to his son Vajiravudh, who ascended the throne as King Rama VI in 1910, the basic structure of a modern state. That structure, however, had been created rapidly, and the society's accommodation to it was still imperfect. Economic development had been uneven: large areas of the country, such as the impoverished north-east, were largely untouched by it; and large-scale Chinese immigration had created by 1910 a distinct Chinese community numbering about 800,000 which held a dominant position in the economy. In addition, the growth of modern education and the creation of a national bureaucracy brought into being a new class of men who increasingly demanded a degree of political power which the absolute monarchy did not give them. King Rama VI fostered the development of a modern nationalist feeling and enlarged the role of the new bureaucratic *élite* in the government. His younger brother Prajadhipok, King Rama VII (1925–35), who succeeded to the throne unexpectedly, lacked his predecessors' political skills and tended to be dominated by his uncles, the brothers of Rama V. He wished to grant his kingdom a constitution, but was dissuaded from doing so. By 1930, financial retrenchment still further weakened his support in the bureaucracy, and hastened the formation of a coalition of conservative civil servants, and young military officers, civil servants, and professionals trained abroad, which on June 24th, 1932, staged a *coup d'état* which ended the absolute monarchy and inaugurated a constitutional regime which the king first accepted and then rejected by abdicating in 1935.

Army Rule: 1933–45

The "Promoters" of the coup of 1932, who called themselves the People's Party, included in their number widely diverse elements. Young civilian radicals, led by a university law lecturer, Pridi Phanomyong, attempted to commit their party to radical economic reform, and they were forced out of the government in April 1933. When conservative and royalist forces appeared to be using this move to strengthen their own power, the military wing of the party led by Phraya Phahon Phonphayuhasena and Luang Phibunsongkhram, staged another coup in June 1933, which firmly established the predominance of the army; and their position was further strengthened when they overcame a royalist counter-coup led by Prince Boworadet in October. The Constitution of 1932 provided for a National Assembly of which half the members were appointed by the People's Party and half were elected in a general election in November 1933. As Prime Minister, Phraya Phahon steered the government along a course which was moderate and progressive, particularly in the fields of education and social welfare. At the same time, the importance of the military to the People's Party required that the Assembly grant substantial funds to the army, although these budgets could be justified first in terms of internal and then of external threats to the government's existence. At the end of 1938, amidst growing fears of Japanese expansionism, a rising nationalist feeling directed against the Chinese community, and the growing prestige of authoritarian governments elsewhere in the world, Phraya Phahon lost a vote of confidence in the National Assembly and was succeeded as Prime Minister by Luang Phibunsongkhram, his Minister of Defence since 1934.

The extreme nationalism of Phibun's first government, from 1938 to 1944, was characterized by aggressively anti-Chinese and anti-Western measures, and by the assertion of irredentist claims on the territories lost to France between 1867 and 1907. Taking advantage of France's prostration in 1940, these claims were pressed on the government of French Indochina, and a short war broke out which was settled to Thailand's advantage by Japanese mediation early in 1941, when the Thai were awarded Lao territories on the west bank of the Mekong River and a portion of western Cambodia. The further extension of Thai claims eastwards was forestalled by Japan's virtual occupation of French Indochina in July. When Japanese troops without warning landed at Thai ports on the Gulf of Siam on December 8th, 1941, Prime Minister Phibun was forced fully to commit his government to the Japanese war effort in order to retain for his country a maximum degree of independence. Small forces of Japanese troops were stationed in Thailand throughout the war, but as allied forces rather than as occupying troops. After the Thai declared war on Britain and the United States in January 1942, the Japanese attempted further to gain Thai support by handing over to them the four Malay states ceded to Britain in 1909 and two of the Shan States of Burma, in November 1943. By this time, however, the prospects of a Japanese victory were increasingly dim. Pridi Phanomyong, who at this time was acting as Regent for the boy-king Ananda (Rama VIII, 1935–46), who was at school in Switzerland, was actively working with the anti-Japanese *Free Thai* underground, which was in direct contact with the Allied powers. In August 1944, the resignation of Phibun's government was forced by an adverse vote in the National Assembly. The military clique within the old People's Party was discredited by the reverses of its wartime ally, and a government led by a civilian politician, Khuang Aphaiwong, was installed under the aegis of Pridi.

The Post-War Period

At the close of the war it was vitally necessary for Thailand to avoid being treated as a defeated belligerent. It was to this end that the authoritarian military regime was swept away and a semblance of parliamentary democracy restored. Seni Pramoj, who as Thai Ambassador in Washington during the war had refused to present to the American government Thailand's declaration of war and who had co-operated in establishing Allied links with the Thai underground, replaced Khuang as Prime Minister in September 1945. He skilfully utilized American support and goodwill to moderate the extreme demands of the British and French governments for compensation, and the immediate crisis in Thailand's foreign relations passed with the signing of peace treaties with Britain and France in 1946 which restored the pre-war status; but internal politics quickly heated up. A new Constitution promulgated in May 1946, introduced a bicameral legislature, the lower house of which was fully elected while the upper house was elected by the lower. In the developments which led up to this further change in the internal balance of power, Pridi was forced to come out from behind the scenes and accept office as Prime Minister in March 1946. Pridi was in an exposed position. Some of the concessions which he had to make to regain for Thailand a respectable place in the world community were unpalatable at home; Thailand's international trade had not recovered from the war; and inflation and rampant rice smuggling brought increased official corruption and a weakening of national morale. The death of the boy-king Ananda on June 9th, 1946, an event never fully explained, rebounded against Pridi, who soon had to resign; and he was replaced by a conservative independent, Luang Thamrong Nawasawat, who lacked a secure political following and was unable to act firmly. As successive parliamentary governments showed a continuing inability to deal with mounting problems of corruption and inflation, a return to authoritarian military rule might have been expected; yet the memory of the recent past and the delicacy of Thailand's international relations made the army extremely reluctant to resume an active political role. Finally, in November 1947, an army conspiracy seized power, abrogated the Constitution, and experimented briefly with a new government of Khuang Aphaiwong, who had led the parliamentary opposition to Pridi. In April 1948, however, Khuang was forced from office and Field Marshal Phibunsongkhram again became Prime Minister.

The years 1948–51 were a period of extreme political uncertainty, due partly to considerations of foreign affairs and partly to the fragmentation of the Thai political *élite*. The civilian, liberal politicians were split: Pridi's radicals had been routed after the death of the King, while the Democrat Party resented the light-handed manner in which Khuang, their leader, had been treated. The armed forces were divided both on service lines and within the army itself, younger elements within the latter still distrustful of Phibun's leadership. The government was in need of external support, yet fearful of American disapproval of an avowedly military regime. As the war in Indochina became more intense and Thailand appeared to be the only haven of relative stability in South-East Asia, American economic and military aid was forthcoming. Phibun could afford to ignore the parliament, which through these years was dominated by Khuang's disheartened Democrat Party; but his authority was not sufficiently strong to avert a major split within his own forces. After four abortive coups between 1948 and 1951, Phibun's military rivals were reduced to two men: General Phao Siyanon, Director-General of the para-military Police Department, and General Sarit Thanarat, Commander of the Army in Bangkok. Phibun was caught between these two of his aides, and power began to slip from his hands.

Both external threats to the country's security and internal political instability worked to strengthen the army. Viet-Minh gains in Viet-Nam, Cambodia, and Laos early in 1954 and the prospects of continued subversion on Thailand's frontiers after the execution of the Geneva agreements made the Thai fearful for their safety. They were enthusiastically receptive to the conclusion of the SEATO pact in 1954, and thereafter benefited substantially from increased American military and economic aid. But while Phibun's foreign policy successes grew, his political position at home was still further eroded as the wilful and arbitrary acts of General Phao discredited his regime, and public criticism of the government mounted. On his return from a visit to Europe and America in 1955, Phibun made a dramatic attempt to rally the nation in his favour by legalizing political parties, holding press conferences, and lifting restraints on free speech, in preparation for general elections scheduled for early 1957. The campaign of the massive government party, pledged to Phibun's support, was managed by General Phao, while the chief opposition came from Khuang's Democrat Party and smaller leftist parties based in the North-East. In February 1957, the government barely won a majority of the seats contested, despite flagrant electoral corruption and mismanagement. General Sarit, who had managed to avoid identification with Phibun and Phao, became the rallying point for national discontent, and on September 16th, 1957, staged a bloodless military *coup d'état* which ended the long political career of Phibun.

After new elections in December, an experimental parliamentary government under Sarit's deputy, General Thanom Kittikachorn, was inaugurated while Sarit went abroad for urgent medical attention. The political pressures on the government, however, were great: its supporters and members represented interests too diverse for accommodation and the government was unable to act decisively on the many economic and foreign policy problems facing it. On October 21st, 1958, Sarit returned suddenly from abroad and restored military rule. Field Marshal Sarit's five-year rule was not, however, a return to the politics of the Phibun era. He commanded broad support which was not confined to the armed forces, brought into his government many professional civil servants, and enhanced his authority by encouraging King Bhumibol Adulyadej to play a greater role in the public life of the nation. At the same time, he exercised his authority by acting decisively on the serious problems facing the country.

The achievements of the military governments of Field Marshal Sarit and of Field Marshal Thanom Kittikachorn, who took power on Sarit's death in 1963, were in many ways impressive. Ambitiously planned economic development raised the G.N.P. at a real annual rate of almost 8 per cent in the 1960s, and major programmes for the improvement of communications and social services, particularly education, were successful. Foreign investment and aid contributed substantially to this development, but the key to its success was a leadership hitherto lacking. New stimulus was lent to government efforts by events in neighbouring Indo-China. The dominant fear of the Thai Government in the early and mid-1950s centred on what was felt to be the subversive potential of Thailand's Chinese minority. Some substance was lent to this fear by the creation of a Thai Communist opposition in China with which the exiled Pridi became associated in 1954, and by the creation of a Thai Patriotic Front in China in 1965, as well as by vociferous Chinese support for North Viet-Nam and for insurgent movements in Laos and Cambodia.

Thailand has particularly strong and historic interests in Laos and Cambodia. Her frontiers with both are to some extent artificial, and across them movement by hostile or subversive forces could be easy. The Thai consistently viewed Laotian and Cambodian neutrality as weakness and a threat to Thailand's security. During the Laotian crisis of 1960–62, when Thai-supported rightist forces were losing control, the Thai demanded strong action from the United States, and acquiesced in the Geneva neutralist solution of 1962 only after American troops were sent to North-East Thailand and the American Government secretly pledged further support for the defence of Thailand. As the Viet-Nam war intensified and spread into Laos and then Cambodia by the early 1970s, Bangkok felt that Thailand's fate rested on the outcome. Thanom firmly committed his nation to the American cause by sending Thai military units to fight in Laos and South Viet-Nam, by allowing U.S. aircraft to bomb North Viet-Nam and Laos from bases in Thailand, and by providing support for government forces in Cambodia and Laos.

Period since Indochinese War

The withdrawal after 1973 of U.S. forces from the war in Indochina, followed by the collapse of the Thieu and Lon Nol governments in 1975, brought the Thai to a fundamental re-examination of their foreign policy. Carefully correct relations were established with the new Laos coalition and the new Khmer Rouge Government, the Thai officially requested that all American military personnel leave Thailand by mid-1976, and diplomatic relations were resumed with China in July 1975.

Through this critical period in the early 1970s successive Thai governments were plagued by a rising tide of internal pressures. Insurgency within Thailand, which began in the North-East region in the early 1960s, by the 1970s was endemic in several provinces, from hill-tribe areas in the North to the Malay provinces of the South.

What proved to be even stronger pressure came from Thailand's burgeoning educated urban classes, who forced Thanom's government to experiment briefly with a restoration of parliamentary rule in 1969–71, which failed because of the military's alarm over student agitation, growing insurgency, economic decline, and the course of events in Indochina. Thanom's government, under a new interim constitution restoring military dominance, came under heavy attack by mass demonstrations involving mainly students in 1973. These culminated in massive demonstrations and pitched battles between students and police in mid-October 1973. The country's military, unwilling to move against strong popular opinion, refused to step in to save the government, and Thanom and his deputies were forced to flee the country and were replaced by an interim civilian government led by a university rector, Dr. Sanya Dharmasakti.

The events of 1973 and 1974 suggested that fundamental changes were taking place in the political life of the kingdom. Popular demonstrations occurred in nearly every province on a scale and with an intensity never before seen in Thailand. Marching students were joined by urban labourers and even by disgruntled farmers. Much political energy was channelled into the formation of numerous political parties that contested the elections to the House of Representatives in January 1975. No single party gained a working majority, and several attempts were made to form governments. Seni Pramoj's Democratic Party, in a coalition with two leftist parties, formed a Government in February 1975 but it lasted only two weeks. Seni was succeeded by his brother Kukrit and a 17-party coalition led by the Social Action Party. Kukrit initially won the approval of demonstrating students for his actions to eliminate the American military presence and for negotiating the resumption of diplomatic relations with the People's Republic of China. His government fell in January 1976 over his insistence on a complete American withdrawal, which many Thai regarded as seriously weakening Thailand's defences at a time of great international uncertainty.

New parliamentary elections held in April 1976 returned Seni Pramoj to power, and materially strengthened and stabilized the political scene. Seni's Democratic Party won 114 of the 279 seats; and his coalition, with four other parties of the right and centre, gave him a total of 207 seats. His electoral victory, and the initial policies of his government, indicated a reaffirmation of civilian authority over the military, a lessened willingness to bow to leftist and student pressure, and more cautious and conservative economic and diplomatic policies, including continued close relations with the U.S.A.

ECONOMIC SURVEY

Paul Sithi-Amnuai

In 1975 Thailand's gross national product (G.N.P.) was U.S. $15,000 million and per capita income was about $349, next only to Brunei, Singapore and Malaysia in South-East Asia. Despite rapid industrial development since 1960, about 75 per cent of the population is still engaged in agriculture. With farming being the most self-sufficient of occupations, this has meant that during the mid-1970s, with double-digit inflation in Thailand and worldwide, most people have not suffered any decline in their living standards in real terms. Relative self-sufficiency and the fact that most Thais are not totally dependent on a money economy have meant that in reality the people enjoy a much higher standard of living than that suggested by the per capita income.

Agriculture continues to play a predominant role in the economy, and Thailand has continued to maintain its role as the granary of South-East Asia. It alternates between being the largest and second largest rice exporter of the world (over 1 million tons in 1975) and, including maize (2 million tons in 1975), Thailand is one of the world's largest grain exporters. Rubber (335,000 tons) and tin metal (16,000 tons) were also among Thailand's major exports in 1975, as were kenaf and tapioca products (151,000 tons and 2.2 million tons, respectively). Since 1974 Thai sugar exports have come to play a very significant role in the country's foreign trade. In 1975, for instance, foreign exchange earnings from sugar (593,400 tons valued at U.S. $284 million) made the commodity second only to rice. One of the keys to Thailand's great success as a major world exporter of farm products has been agricultural diversification. Of late the light manufacturing industries have been of some consequence (cement, gunny bags and other textiles). In addition to fertile soil, the country has rich mineral resources, though at present, only tin, lignite, wolfram, lead, antimony, manganese, gypsum, iron ore and fluorite are mined in significant quantities. There are, however, great hopes that oil will be important. Since 1969, several international oil companies were given exploration licences to make test drills in the Gulf of Thailand. Since the fivefold increase in the world price of crude, exploration activities in the Gulf, which is situated in the "oil belt" of this part of the world, have been stepped up. As the preliminary findings have been highly encouraging, there are strong hopes that Thailand will become self-sufficient in this mineral by 1980.

The Role of the Private Sector

Since 1957, the Government has divested itself of most of its industrial enterprises and only maintained monopolies for certain sectors of the economy which it deemed, for development and administrative reasons, essential to the country to keep within the domain of the government. Hence, with a few exceptions, it can be said that free enterprise is the predominant business trend of the country. The result is that about 86 per cent of the G.N.P. is contributed by the private sector. This, coupled with a healthy investment climate (this deteriorated considerably during 1975 because of political instability within and also because of the fall of Indochina), which it has fostered over the years, has attracted vast amounts of foreign investment capital into the country. The economic growth rate since 1965 has been well over 7 per cent per annum in real terms. During 1974, Thailand experienced an economic growth rate of about 4 per cent in real terms. When many economies were declining or stagnating, growth in 1975 was 6.4 per cent.

AGRICULTURE

Agriculture is still by far the most important sector of the economy. Its importance, however, has been on a relative decline as "progress" in the form of industrial development is being achieved. In 1959, agriculture contributed 37.6 per cent of the G.N.P., compared with about 28 per cent in 1975. Agriculture in Thailand is still labour-intensive; of the 45 per cent of the population who constitute the total working population (19.3 million), about 80 per cent, or 15.4 million, are engaged in agriculture.

In the past, weather conditions used to affect the agricultural output of the country. But since the construction of various irrigation projects, as well as the introduction of multiple-cropping projects, the agricultural output has been more consistent.

The total farm land under cultivation is about 30 million acres. The major crops grown and agricultural products of economic importance are described briefly below.

Rice

Rice has been the mainstay of the Thai economy for several decades. However, with agricultural diversification, it has become less important, although it is still the country's largest export earner. The total value of rice exports in 1975 was U.S. $288 million, 12.2 per cent of total export earnings ($2,370 million). Rice exports during the year totalled about 930,000 tons, less than in 1974, and only about half the volume exported during the record year of 1972. Yet total export value in 1975 was more than that of 1972, thanks to the increase in world export prices of the grain.

The planting season for rice is during the "wet" season in Thailand, from June to August, and harvest is from December to February. Over fifty varieties of paddy are grown. The bulk of the rice is grown on "wet" fields, although upland "dry" rice and glutinous rice are also grown, especially in the north-east. In 1974, the total cultivated area of rice paddy was about 47.5 million rais (one rai=0.4 of an acre). Output per rai has been on a constant increase over the years: in 1965 the output was 256 kg. per rai, while in 1975 it was about 302 kg. per rai.

Despite agricultural diversification, rice farming is still the predominant occupation of the rural population, and has an important effect on the urban population since the whole price index of the country is geared to rice prices. When the price of the basic food, i.e. rice, rises, all other prices follow. This is just what has happened since the latter half of 1972, with the annual cost of living index going up at double-digit rates. From time to time, the Government has had to intervene to stabilize rice prices, usually by means of an embargo on rice exports (releasing an increased supply for domestic consumption), as was the case for some months of 1967. Since Thailand is the largest rice exporter of the South-East Asian region, throughout which rice is the staple food, an embargo on Thai rice exports has a detrimental effect on the economies of most countries of the region. Thai rice and its yearly harvest is therefore of the utmost importance, not only to Thailand's overall economy, but to that of the whole region.

Maize

Maize first began to outpace rubber as Thailand's second most important export crop in 1971. While it maintained its position in the following year, it lost out to rubber in 1973 though it soon regained its standing in 1974 during which year about 2.2 million tons were exported, fetching a record U.S. $280 million. In 1975 maize exports of 2 million tons, earning U.S. $281 million, were exceeded in value by sugar exports. Most of the maize still goes to Japan, though since 1969 Taiwan, Singapore and Malaysia have become important markets. The growth of maize cultivation may be attributed to several factors, the most important being the Government's desire to promote a suitable crop in the Central Plain and north-eastern areas of the country; combined with the promotion was a highway building programme (which made the crop accessible to markets); and lastly, a price response by commodity exporters who, realizing the favourable world prices for maize, entered into "forward shipment" contracts for maize exports, and this, in turn, created the demand for the farmer to produce more maize at favourable prices.

Rubber

Grown mainly on smallholdings in southern Thailand, rubber has been superseded by maize and sugar to become the fourth most important crop of the country in 1975, when production was about 346,000 metric tons. While world rubber prices were generally high during 1975, they were nowhere near the 1974 level. In 1975 exports totalled about 335,000 tons, with a value of U.S. $171 million. Production and exports were low from 1970 to 1975. Despite the impressive increase in export value made from 1973 to 1975 as a result of the general increase in commodity prices, the long-term future for natural rubber remains uncertain because of competition from the synthetic product.

Kenaf

In 1975 the production of kenaf, a jute substitute, was about 270,000 tons, the lowest for many years and less than half the 1974 production. Exports earnings of U.S. $32 million were 20 per cent below the 1974 income. Kenaf is one of the more important agricultural export crops of the country. The growing of fibre in large amounts was also responsible for the establishment of several gunny-bag factories, which together produced 95 million units in 1975.

Tapioca

Tapioca (cassava) has been important as an alternative crop for the Central Plain area for some years. Production of tapioca roots increased steadily from 1.7 million tons in 1961 to about 4.8 million tons in 1975. Tapioca is exported in "product" form, namely as chips, flour or meal. In 1975 about 2.25 million tons of various tapioca products were shipped abroad at a value of $183 million.

Sugar

Sugar has become a major crop since the mid-1960s, and especially since 1973. While the production of sugar cane was a mere 3.8 million tons in 1966, production increased more than four-fold in ten years to about 16.5 million tons in 1975. During the year a record 1.25 million tons of raw cane sugar was produced, of which about 593,400 tons was exported, bringing in about U.S. $284 million in foreign exchange, second only to rice.

Miscellaneous Agricultural Products

Apart from rice, rubber, maize, kenaf, tapioca and sugar, Thailand has other important agricultural products, many of which are exported. These products, in 1975, included groundnuts (220,000 tons), mung beans (320,000 tons), soya beans (180,000 tons), sesame (32,000 tons), coconuts (780,000 tons), castor seed (32,000 tons), cotton (40,000 tons), tobacco (120,000 tons) and sorghum (220,000 tons).

Forestry products, which for many years were Thailand's main foreign exchange earners, have now lost their importance in the overall economic structure of the country. Lack of effective conservation (the laws are there, but the policing has been ineffective) made an item like teak, for example, a scarce commodity. In 1971, teak production was close to 300,000 cubic metres, but it has since declined rather rapidly to slightly below 160.000 cubic metres in 1975. Meanwhile, other hard woods have been logged with success. Yangwood had, in 1975, a production figure of about 937,000 cubic metres, and other hard woods totalled 1.7 million cubic metres.

Fishing is also important. The sea fishing catch in 1974 totalled 1.6 million tons while the fresh water catch was about 150,000 tons. Marine prawns, shrimps and crabs contributed another 200,000 tons to bring the overall sea and fresh water catch close to 2 million tons. Thai shrimp and prawns are now widely exported, with Japan as the main market.

MINING AND INDUSTRY

The most important mineral is tin. Production of primary tin metal fell from 22,927 tons in 1973 to 19,827 tons in 1974 and 16,630 tons in 1975. Tin exports fell by 20 per cent to 16,000 tons in 1975, earning U.S. $108 million compared with $150 million in 1974, making it the sixth largest foreign exchange earner, whereas formerly it ranked fourth. Other important minerals mined, with the exception of lignite (500,000 tons), are all exported. Production of tungsten was 4,500 metric tons, of lead ore 3,600 tons, antimony ore 7,200 tons, manganese 25,200 tons, iron 33,000 tons, gypsum 306,000 tons, fluorite 286,000 tons and marl 466,000 tons. Other mineral deposits which are in the process of being mined are zinc and copper.

Manufacturing

Manufacturing, including the construction industry, has become increasingly important to Thailand. In 1959, manufacturing, mining and construction contributed 16.4 per cent of the G.D.P. By 1975, this figure had risen to 24 per cent, despite the fact that the construction sector has been suffering from a slump since 1970.

In manufacturing, Thailand is now self-sufficient in cement (4.2 million tons in 1975), refined sugar (1,250,000 tons) and refined petroleum products (8,500 million litres). Since the beginning of the decade, Thailand has become a net exporter of cement and sugar, with the latter, in particular, fetching exceptionally high prices in 1975. The textile industry has become very important in recent years, with production in 1975 totalling over 540 million square yards of cotton and 300 million square yards of synthetic material. Thailand is now self-sufficient in textiles and has, in fact, become an important exporter though it has had to face some difficult export problems since 1972 because of higher tariff barriers imposed by other countries. Other items produced, but not yet at the level of self-sufficiency, include paper (28,000 tons) and tobacco (22,600 tons). However, many manufacturing industries—with the encouragement of the Government which grants tax exemption to industries obtaining "promoted industry" status—have established plants for manufacturing products using domestic raw materials. The most recent of these include several large textile factories and some food and fruit canneries. There are 12 car assembly plants, and consumer and industrial items now manufactured in Thailand include paint and construction materials, plywood, motor cycles, automobile tyres and batteries, furniture and carpets, and pharmaceutical products.

FOREIGN TRADE

As an "export" economy, trade is important to Thailand, total trade being equivalent to slightly over 50 per cent of the 1975 G.D.P. The main items exported are all, with the exception of tin, agricultural products. All of the commodities mentioned in the section on agriculture are items of Thai export. Apart from these commodities, certain Thai exports of special interest include Thai gems, handicrafts, cotton textiles and silk. Thai silk, though world-famous, in fact ranks very low in the list of Thailand's major exports; this may indicate, perhaps, the overall importance of the raw materials which the country exports, as raw materials normally are of concern only to the traders and not to the general public. Some of these "minor" items of export include (for 1975) kapok fibre (22,000 tons), castor seeds (25,000 tons), cattle (25,000 head), mung beans (90,000 tons), groundnuts (5,400 tons), shrimp (10,000 tons), cement (705,000 tons), hides and skins (2,200 tons), tobacco (18,000 tons), seed lac and stick lac (9,000 tons), eggs (520 tons) and sorghum (160,000 tons).

Imports in 1975 were worth U.S. $3,210 million while total export value amounted to $2,370 million. Unlike most developing countries, Thailand has few import restrictions. Tariffs, however, are high for "luxury" items, such as cameras, air-conditioners and automobiles. A record deficit of $691 million in 1974 was followed by the second largest ever deficit of $640 million in 1975. The 1975 deficit would have been very much larger had it not been that Thailand's export commodities continued to fetch record prices. This helped compensate for the fivefold increase in the cost of imported crude oil. Nevertheless, the level of international reserves fell by $190 million. During 1975 crude oil imports went up to U.S. $535 million, a big jump from the U.S. $179 million of 1973.

FINANCE AND DEVELOPMENT

The relationship between finance and development is closer in Thailand than in many other developing countries. The financial policy of the Government for the past decade may be described as conservative, cautious and non-inflationary. Despite this, Thailand began to feel the impact of world inflation as of the middle of 1972 which was both a year of poor harvests and one during which the baht was devalued in line with the U.S. dollar. Prior to that, domestic prices were exceptionally stable. For instance, the consumer price index between 1965 and 1971 rose from 100.4 points to 115.4 points (October 1964–September 1965=100), averaging an increment of slightly over 2.1 points per annum during that period. In 1972 alone, however, the CPI went up by 9.2 points, accelerating by 11.6 points in 1973 and by about 23 points in 1974. In 1975 inflation was reduced to 5.2 per cent. So, compared with most other countries, the unusual increase in cost of living may be said to be relatively mild. The non-inflationary policy of the financial sector has, in general, made possible actual increments in the standard of living by means of various infra-structural projects directed by the Ministry of Development. Thailand began planning in 1961.

To finance the First Six-Year Plan (1961–66), the Government, employing a cautious financial policy, borrowed locally and from abroad. It did so by selling government bonds and treasury bills to the public. In reality, however, the actual investors in these government bonds were the commercial banks (from deposits of the public), the savings banks, and the central bank, the Bank of Thailand, which made loans to the Government. These local sources of funds, nevertheless, were insufficient to balance the Budget (which had allocated two-thirds to development and the rest to administrative services); consequently, foreign loans became important to Thailand. By the end of 1975, total foreign outstanding debts were equivalent to U.S. $615 million. This amount, however, was not a heavy burden on the external debt service. The main sources of foreign loans have been the World Bank, the United States and West Germany, and as of late, Japan. This combination of local and foreign borrowing was the main thrust of finance in Thailand's development. The First Six-Year Plan was successful. The overall growth rate for the six-year planned period averaged about 8 per cent per year in real terms. The Second Five-Year Plan, 1967–71, involved a government expenditure of about U.S. $2,500 million on implementational projects, top priorities being given to irrigation and power, but transport and education are also important investment items of the Plan.

Thailand initiated her Third Plan in October 1971. The Plan, generally described as more realistic than its predecessors, calls for a total expenditure of U.S. $5,014 million. It places particular emphasis on manpower development, agriculture, national security, industry, export promotion, and the reduction of income disparities.

Having achieved both financial stability and successful planning, Thailand was able to accumulate very attractive reserves of foreign exchange. At the end of 1975, they stood at U.S. $1,369 million or equivalent to about five months' imports. In 1969, Thailand suffered its first balance of payments deficit in many years, at a figure of nearly U.S. $46 million. It was for this reason that increased tariffs were imposed to make imports "more expensive", hoping that this would be a way of helping to bring the balance of payments back into surplus. In 1970 the payments deficit shot up to $132.6 million, though it subsided to a deficit of $16.8 million in 1971, thanks in part to the mid-1970 tax increase on the import of various "luxury" items and also to Thailand's improved export performance. In 1972, however, the payments balance reverted to a surplus of about U.S. $200 million and remained in surplus until 1975, when a deficit of U.S. $75 million was recorded.

Thailand might be said to have joined the group of truly developing countries which have reached the stage of economic "take-off" into becoming fully sustained semi-industrial nations.

STATISTICAL SURVEY

AREA AND POPULATION

Area	Census Population: April 25th, 1960	Census Population: April 1st, 1970	Estimated Population (mid-year): 1972	1973	1974	1975	Density (per sq. km.) 1975
514,000 sq. km.*	26,257,916	34,397,374†	38,580,000	39,787,000	41,023,000	42,277,000	82

* 198,547 square miles. † Excluding adjustment for underenumeration.

Principal towns (1970 census): Bangkok (capital) 1,867,297; Thonburi 627,989; Chiengmai 65,736 (1960).

Births and deaths: Average annual birth rate 43.7 per 1,000; death rate 12.5 per 1,000 (UN estimates for 1965–70).

ECONOMICALLY ACTIVE POPULATION
(labour force sample survey, persons aged 11 and over, July–September 1973)

	Males	Females	Totals
Agriculture, forestry, hunting and fishing	6,569,380	5,701,100	12,270,480
Mining and quarrying	96,970	13,910	110,880
Manufacturing	735,070	466,060	1,201,130
Construction	231,210	26,750	257,960
Electricity, gas, water and sanitary services	44,910	3,530	48,440
Commerce	648,950	743,340	1,392,290
Transport, storage and communications	370,510	13,390	383,900
Services	743,090	632,510	1,375,600
Activities not adequately described	200	1,780	1,980
Total in Employment	9,440,290	7,602,370	17,042,660
Persons seeking work for the first time	27,840	15,200	43,040
Unemployed	28,150	2,700	30,850
Total Labour Force	9,496,280	7,620,270	17,116,550

Source: International Labour Office, *Year Book of Labour Statistics*.

AGRICULTURE

LAND USE, 1971
('000 hectares)

Arable land	12,431
Land under permanent crops	1,496
Permanent meadows and pastures	308
Forest and woodland	28,960
Other land	7,982
Total Land	51,177
Inland water	223
Total	51,400

Source: FAO, *Production Yearbook 1974*.

PRINCIPAL CROPS

	Area Harvested ('000 hectares)			Production ('000 metric tons)		
	1972	1973	1974	1973	1974	1975*
Rice (paddy)	6,780	7,760	7,734	14,898	13,175	n.a.
Maize	997	1,000*	1,120†	2,343	2,400*	n.a.
Sorghum	40	55	60*	130*	280	220
Sweet potatoes	34†	35	36†	319	320†	n.a.
Cassava (manioc)	225†	320†	420†	6,307	3,800*	4,800
Dry beans	215†	200†	230†	210*	250*	n.a.
Soybeans	80	93	102	100	115	180
Groundnuts (in shell)	146*	145*	145*	210	230	220
Cottonseed	81*	61*	60†	40*	33.2	40
Cotton (lint)				20*	16.3*	
Coconuts	n.a.	n.a.	n.a.	730	750†	780
Water melons	35†	35†	36†	420†	450†	n.a.
Sugar cane	140	180†	250†	9,513	13,100	16,500
Bananas	180†	185†	185†	1,250†	1,300†	n.a.
Kenaf (mesta)	370†	540	380†	645	400*	270
Natural rubber	n.a.	n.a.	n.a.	382	379	346

* Unofficial figures. † FAO estimates.

Source: FAO, *Production Yearbook 1974*.

LIVESTOCK

('000 head—FAO estimates)

	1972	1973	1974
Horses	168	166	164
Cattle	4,377*	4,751*	4,800
Buffaloes	5,829*	5,634*	5,700
Pigs	3,884*	4,573*	4,700
Sheep	45	47	48
Goats	32	31	30
Chickens	52,882*	53,000	55,000
Ducks	7,281	7,300	7,400

* Official figures.

LIVESTOCK PRODUCTS

('000 metric tons—FAO estimates)

	1972	1973	1974
Beef and veal	90	92	92
Buffalo meat	51	51	51
Pigmeat	150	170	175
Poultry meat	82	85	88
Edible offals	29.1	31.3	31.8
Cows' milk	4	4	4
Buffalo milk	6	6	6
Hen eggs	120.5	122.0	125.0
Other poultry eggs	57.8	59.3	61.6
Cattle hides	18.0	18.4	18.4
Buffalo hides	12.0	12.0	12.0

Source: FAO, *Production Yearbook 1974*.

FORESTRY

ROUNDWOOD REMOVALS

('000 cubic metres, all non-coniferous)

	1967	1968	1969	1970	1971	1972*	1973*	1974*
Sawlogs, veneer logs and logs for sleepers	2,966	3,279	3,010	2,655	2,725	3,721	3,517	3,517
Other industrial wood	1,480	1,530	1,590	1,640*	1,700*	1,750	1,811	1,871
Fuel wood	13,600	13,900	14,200	14,450*	14,750*	15,050	15,915	16,440
Total	18,046	18,709	18,800	18,745	19,175	20,521	21,243	21,828

* FAO estimate.

Source: FAO, *Yearbook of Forest Products*.

SAWNWOOD PRODUCTION

('000 cubic metres, all non-coniferous)

	1965	1966	1967	1968	1969	1970	1971*	1972*
Sawnwood (incl. boxboards)	1,293	1,206	1,373	1,435	1,306	1,162	1,190	1,923
Railway sleepers	26	39	22	21	36	42	45	29
TOTAL	1,319	1,245	1,395	1,456	1,342	1,204	1,235	1,952

* FAO estimate.

Source: FAO, *Yearbook of Forest Products.*

FISHING

('000 metric tons)

	FRESH-WATER	SEA	TOTAL
1969	90.4	1,179.6	1,270.0
1970	112.7	1,335.7	1,448.4
1971	116.8	1,470.3	1,587.1
1972	131.4	1,548.2	1,679.6
1973	140.9	1,538.0	1,678.9
1974	158.9	1,351.6	1,510.0
1975*	165.0	1,215.0	1,380.0

* Provisional.

Source: Department of Fisheries: Fisheries Record of Thailand.

MINING

		1969	1970	1971	1972	1973
Brown coal and lignite	'000 metric tons	348	400	445	345	361
Crude petroleum	,, ,, ,,	2	10	13	16	6
Iron ore*	,, ,, ,,	277	13	24	16	21
Salt (unrefined)	,, ,, ,,	200	200	160	160	n.a.
Antimony ore*	metric tons	908	2,511	2,380	4,867	3,535
Lead concentrates*	,, ,,	1,692	1,214	1,386	1,612	3,486
Manganese ore*	,, ,,	9,821	8,344	5,111	6,610	11,985
Tin concentrates*	,, ,,	21,092	21,779	21,689	22,072	20,921
Tungsten concentrates*	,, ,,	806	895	2,286	3,329	2,733

* Figures refer to the metal content of ores and concentrates.

Source: UN, *The Growth of World Industry 1973.*

Tin concentrates (metric tons): 20,339 in 1974; 16,406 in 1975.

INDUSTRY

SELECTED PRODUCTS

		1970	1971	1972	1973
Sugar	'000 metric tons	495	640	702	839
Beer	'000 hectolitres	363	321	339	432
Cigarettes	million	15,287	16,078	16,773	19,422
Cotton yarn[1]	metric tons	56,060	10,800	n.a.	n.a.
Woven cotton fabrics[2]	million sq. metres	306	376	402	474
Non-cellulosic continuous filaments[3]	metric tons	1,200	4,800	9,800	16,300
Non-cellulosic discontinous fibres[3]	,, ,,	3,400	5,000	8,200	11,800
Woven fabrics of man-made fibres	million sq. metres	37.5	121.6	174.3	240
Nitrogenous fertilizers	'000 metric tons	11.5	10.3	7.7	8
Liquefied petroleum gas[4]	,, ,, ,,	61	94	163	218
Naphtha[4]	,, ,, ,,	75	25	237	282
Motor spirit (petrol)[4]	,, ,, ,,	511	1,473	960	1,060
Kerosene[4]	,, ,, ,,	138	147	232	195
Jet fuel[4]	,, ,, ,,	269	417	636	552
Distillate fuel oils[4]	,, ,, ,,	995	1,655	1,864	1,902
Residual fuel oils[4]	,, ,, ,,	2,010	2,139	2,730	3,511
Petroleum bitumen (asphalt)[4]	,, ,, ,,	8	118	141	128
Cement	,, ,, ,,	2,626.9	2,770.6	3,377.7	3,706
Crude steel	,, ,, ,,	40	n.a.	n.a.	n.a.
Tin (unwrought): primary	metric tons	22,040	21,742	22,281	22,927
Electric energy	million kWh.	4,545	5,225	6,209	n.a.

1974: Sugar 967,000 metric tons; Beer 4,475,000 litres; Cement 3,923,000 metric tons; Tin 19,827 metric tons.

1975: Sugar 1,250,000 metric tons; Cement 4,200,000 metric tons; Tin 16,630 metric tons.

[1] Excluding yarn made from waste.
[2] After undergoing finishing processes.
[3] *Source:* Textile Economics Bureau,Inc. (New York).
[4] *Source:* Bureau of Mines, U.S. Department of the Interior.

Source: UN, *The Growth of World Industry 1973*.

FINANCE

100 satangs (stangs) = 1 baht.
Coins: ½, 1, 5, 10, 20, 25 and 50 satangs; 1 baht.
Notes: 50 satangs; 1, 5, 10, 20, 100 and 500 baht.
Exchange rates (June 1976): £1 sterling = 36.19 baht; U.S. $1 = 20.40 baht.
1,000 baht = £27.63 = $49.02.

Note: From October 1963 to July 1973 the official exchange rate was U.S. $1 = 20.80 baht (1 baht = 4.8077 U.S. cents). Since July 1973 the baht has had a par value of 5 U.S. cents ($1 = 20.00 baht) while the market rate was fixed at $1 = 20.375 baht (1 baht = 4.9080 U.S. cents) until October 1975 and at $1 = 20.40 baht since November 1975. In terms of sterling, the exchange rate was £1 = 49.92 baht from November 1967 to August 1971; and £1 = 54.20 baht from December 1971 to June 1972.

BUDGET

(million baht, October 1st to September 30th)

Revenue	1972/73	1973/74*	1974/75*
Taxes on income and wealth	3,636†	3,325	4,900
Import duties	6,364	6,600	9,580
Export duties	545	400	1,420
Rice export premium	277	290	1,020
Fiscal monopolies	993	912	1,236
Other indirect taxes	10,459	11,807	16,197
Fees, sales and other charges	1,108	1,032	1,522
Profits and dividends	892	905	968
Other receipts	1,070	1,249	1,038
Total	25,344	26,520	37,881

Expenditure	1972/73	1973/74*	1974/75*
Education	5,918.0	6,953.3	10,287.5
Health	935.9	1,084.0	1,507.6
Other social services	1,589.5	1,611.3	2,312.4
Agriculture	2,482.3	2,938.8	4,152.7
Other economic services	4,222.1	4,304.2	5,990.6
National defence	5,949.6	6,812.8	8,289.2
Total (incl. others)	30,519.4	34,482.0	45,672.2

* Estimate. † Including motor vehicle taxes.

Source: United Nations, *Statistical Yearbook*, quoting the Department of Economic Research, Bank of Thailand.

1975/76: Proposed expenditure totalled 62,000 million baht.

DEVELOPMENT PLANS

(million baht)

REVENUE	SECOND PLAN (1967–71)	THIRD PLAN (1972–76)
Domestic sources	41,440	83,354
Foreign assistance	14,435	16,930
TOTAL	55,875	100,284
EXPENDITURE		
Agriculture and co-operatives	11,300	n.a.
Industry and mining	885	
Power	3,540	
Communications, transport	17,080	
Community development and public utilities	10,250	
Public health	2,570	
Education	6,520	
Commerce	180	
Reserve	3,550	
TOTAL	55,875	100,284

GROSS DOMESTIC PRODUCT

(million baht at current prices)

	1972	1973	1974
Agriculture, hunting, forestry and fishing	49,297	72,976	86,225
Mining and quarrying	2,886	2,880	4,788
Manufacturing	28,007	36,614	47,137
Electricity, gas and water	2,231	2,672	2,842
Construction	7,158	8,358	10,882
Trade, restaurants and hotels	34,162	46,327	60,460
Transport, storage and communications	10,358	12,498	15,534
Finance, insurance, real estate and business services; Community, social and personal services; Government services	28,174	31,835	42,209
	162,273	214,160	270,077
Statistical discrepancy	−202	1,034	−60
G.D.P. IN PURCHASERS' VALUES	162,071	215,194	270,017

BALANCE OF PAYMENTS

(U.S. $ million)

	1971	1972	1973	1974
Merchandise exports f.o.b.	802	1,046	1,531	2,430
Merchandise imports f.o.b.	−1.152	−1,325	−1,856	−2,798
TRADE BALANCE	−350	−279	325	−368
Exports of services	475	544	623	791
Imports of services	−344	−376	−495	−706
BALANCE ON GOODS AND SERVICES	−219	−111	−197	−283
Unrequited transfers (net)	44	39	68	219
BALANCE ON CURRENT ACCOUNT	−175	−72	−129	−64
Direct investment (net)	38	68	80	188
Other long-term capital (net)	36	93	−10	191
Short-term capital (net)	21	34	218	82
BALANCE ON CAPITAL ACCOUNT	95	195	288	461
Net errors and omissions	62	74	74	79
TOTAL (net monetary movements)	−17	197	234	476
Allocation of IMF Special Drawing Rights	14	15	—	—
CHANGES IN RESERVES	−3	212	234	476

Source: IMF, *International Financial Statistics.*

EXTERNAL TRADE

(million baht)

	1969	1970	1971	1972	1973	1974	1975*
Imports c.i.f.	26,891	27,009	26,794	30,875	42,184	64,032	58,433
Exports f.o.b.	14,705	14,772	17,281	22,491	32,226	50,363	48,404

*Provisional

PRINCIPAL COMMODITIES

(million baht)

IMPORTS	1970	1971	1972	1973
Food	1,091	1,032	1,210	1,371
Beverages and Tobacco	303	521	609	415
Crude Materials	1,400	1,757	2,077	3,547
Oils, Mineral Fuels and Lubricants	2,329	2,721	3,116	4,318
Animal and Vegetable Oils and Fats	35	39	46	85
Chemicals	3,505	3,723	4,757	6,848
Manufactured Goods	6,458	5,869	6,517	8,814
Machinery	9,536	8,949	9,716	13,708
TOTAL (incl. others)	27,009	26,794	30,875	42,184

[*continued on next page*

PRINCIPAL COMMODITIES—*continued*]

EXPORTS	1972	1973	1974	1975
Rice	4,437	3,594	9,792	5,848
Rubber	1,862	4,573	5,036	3,437
Tin metal	1,664	2,069	3,071	2,166
Kenaf and jute	1,087	1,054	838	705
Maize	1,939	2,969	6,047	5,611
Teak and other woods	330	747	645	598
Tapioca products	1,560	2,468	3,878	4,469
Sugar	n.a.	1,161	3,757	5,680*

* Unofficial estimates.

Source: Department of Customs.

PRINCIPAL COUNTRIES
(million baht)

IMPORTS	1971	1972	1973	1974
Australia	865	981	1,392	1,904
France	n.a.	499	819	1,511
Germany, Federal Republic	2,075	2,279	3,210	4,675
Italy	428	475	601	1,104
Japan	10,093	11,101	15,078	20,102
Kuwait	447	773	1,278	3,468
Malaysia	185	169	223	181
Saudi Arabia	751	967	981	3,062
Taiwan	748	1,058	1,384	1,541
United Kingdom	2,054	1,620	2,715	2,970
U.S.A.	3,807	4,838	5,915	8,642

EXPORTS	1971	1972	1973	1974
Germany, Federal Republic	641	556	771	1,115
Hong Kong	1,152	1,674	2,362	3,576
Indonesia	248	727	1,496	1,867
Japan	4,277	4,660	8,409	12,853
Malaysia	680	1,047	1,802	2,433
Netherlands	1,385	1,794	2,927	4,328
Philippines	435	580	n.a.	n.a.
Singapore	1,223	1,955	2,661	4,142
Taiwan	517	830	1,289	n.a.
United Kingdom	420	368	622	664
U.S.A.	2,264	2,834	3,252	3,985

TRANSPORT

RAILWAYS
('000)

	1968	1969	1970	1971	1972	1973
Passenger-kilometres	3,913,708	3,964,876	4,152,398	4,295,396	4,449,468	4,771,192
Freight (ton-kilometres)	2,117,609	1,935,162	2,289,672	2,318,897	2,201,493	2,057,132
Freight tons carried	5,136	4,784	5,155	5,144	5,345	4,906

Source: The State Railway of Thailand.

ROADS

('000)

	1968	1969	1970	1971*
Cars	125.6	167.7	212.9	199.4
Lorries and Buses	102.4	119.8	146.2	154.6

* October to September.

SHIPPING

(Port of Bangkok)

	Vessels Entered (number)	Net Registered Tonnage (in ballast)	Vessels Cleared (number)	Net Registered Tonnage (in ballast)	Cargo Tons Unloaded	Cargo Tons Loaded
1970	1,616	1,554,973	1,744	3,677,742	8,681,952	4,963,682
1971	1,566	2,122,036	1,917	3,609,033	9,525,599	6,370,711
1972	1,754	2,866,780	2,350	4,219,983	12,669,746	7,795,597
1973	1,729	2,591,876	2,062	4,683,138	12,586,647	6,976,725

CIVIL AVIATION

(Thai Airways)

	Kilometres Flown	Total Load Ton/ Kilometres	Passengers Carried		Freight Carried	
			Number	Passenger kilometres	Tons	Ton/ kilometres
1970	16,269,838	8,395,616	766,561	717,557,636	6,778.0	7,465,527
1971	17,651,323	14,507,596	700,783	916,738,167	7,777.1	13,273,994
1972	18,907,324	19,696,111	766,938	1,146,647,084	9,165.5	17,217,538

COMMUNICATIONS MEDIA

Telephones (1973)	254,896
Radio sets (1974)	5,100,000
Television sets (1974)	714,000
Daily papers (1974)	27*

* Thai 16, English 3, Chinese 8.

EDUCATION

(1972)

	Schools	Teachers	Students
Kindergarten	74	1,543	42,977
Elementary (Ministry of Education)	563	8,915	222,063
Elementary (Provincial Authority)	26,616	144,624	4,841,484
Municipal	527	9,348	304,851
Secondary (Public)	576	15,842	377,744
General Education (Private)	2,557	49,674	1,179,095
Special Private	1,547	4,382	152,836
Vocational	211	6,593	104,603
Teacher Training	37	4,241	121,160

Source: National Statistical Office, Bangkok (unless otherwise stated).

THE CONSTITUTION

(Promulgated October 7th, 1974)

SUMMARY

Thailand is a kingdom, one and indivisible. The sovereign power belongs to the Thai people, and the country adopts a democratic form of government.

GOVERNMENT

MONARCHY

The person of the King is sacred and inviolable. The King is the head of State and commander-in-chief of the armed forces. He is a Buddhist and upholder of religion. The King exercises executive power through the Council of Ministers, legislative power through the National Assembly and judicial power through the Courts of Justice. He appoints a Privy Council composed of a president and not more than 14 others. In times of national emergency the King may issue decrees with the force of law, or may initiate martial law, for a period of 30 days without the consent of the National Assembly. The King exercises the above powers only in conformity with the provisions of the constitution.

COUNCIL OF MINISTERS

The Council of Ministers is composed of a Prime Minister and not more than 30 Ministers of State, appointed by the King. The Prime Minister must be a member of the House of Representatives, and not less than half of the total number of Ministers must be members of the National Assembly. The Council of Ministers may be removed by a vote of "no confidence" by the National Assembly.

NATIONAL ASSEMBLY

The National Assembly is the legislative body and consists of the Senate and the House of Representatives. It is presided over by a President, who is the President of the House of Representatives and a Vice-President, who is President of the Senate. A bill may be enacted as law only by and with the consent of the National Assembly. To become law a bill must be passed by both houses and receive the signature of the King. The National Assembly holds one or two sessions, lasting 90 days, every year. Extraordinary sessions may be convened by the King or by no less than a third of the total number of members. In certain cases the National Assembly is to hold joint sittings.

Senate

The Senate is composed of 100 members appointed by the King, and confirmed by the President of the Privy Council, for a period of six years. Members of the Senate must be at least 35 years of age. The President and Vice-President of the Senate are appointed by the King in accordance with the members' resolution.

House of Representatives

The House of Representatives is composed of not less than 240 and not more than 300 members elected directly by the people for a term of 4 years. Members must be at least 25 years of age and must belong to a political party. Government employees and members of the armed forces must resign before seeking election. The King may dissolve the House, in which case new elections must be held within 90 days. The President and Vice-President of the House of Representatives are appointed by the King in accordance with the members' resolution.

JUDICIARY

The judicial power is in the hands of the courts, which can be established only by law. Judges are appointed and removed by the King with the consent of a Judicial Committee, composed of the president of the Supreme Court, 3 ex officio and 8 members qualified in law.

CONSTITUTIONAL TRIBUNAL

The Constitutional Tribunal is composed of nine judges, three of whom are appointed by the National Assembly, three by the Council of Ministers and three by the Judicial Committee. Members of the Constitutional Tribunal must be appointed within 60 days of the date of the election of the House of Representatives and vacate office after the next general election. The Constitutional Tribunal has the power to decide the constitutionality of bills before the National Assembly, and the power of judicial review.

RIGHTS, LIBERTIES AND DUTIES OF THE THAI PEOPLE

All persons are equal under the constitution and before the law. Freedom of speech, of the press, of association and of religion are guaranteed under the constitution. Every person has the right to a fundamental education, which the state has the duty to provide. All persons enjoy freedom of choice of occupation and place of dwelling. The right of peaceful assembly, the right of a person in property and the freedom to form political parties are guaranteed under the constitution. Every person has the duty to protect the nation, religion, the King, and the democratic form of government of the constitution, and no person may exercise his rights and liberties adversely to these.

CONSTITUTIONAL AMENDMENTS

Amendments to the constitution may be passed by no less than half the total number of members of the National Assembly with the assent of the King. If the King witholds his assent the matter is to be decided by national referendum.

THE GOVERNMENT

HEAD OF THE STATE

King Bhumibol Adulyadej (King Rama IX), born December 5th, 1927; succeeded to the throne on the death of his brother King Ananda Mahidol, on June 9th, 1946. The Heir-Apparent is Prince Vajiralongkorn, born July 28th, 1952.

PRIVY COUNCIL

Sanya Dharmasakti (President).

Srisena Sombatsiri.

Gen. Luang Suranarong.

Prakob Hutasingh.

Police Maj.-Gen. Arthasidhi Sidhisunthorn.

M. C. Vongsanuwat Devakul.

Gen. Samkan Phaetyakul.

Chaovana Na Silawan.

Chinta Bunya-akom.

M. C. Chakrabandhu Pensiri Chakrabandhu.

Kitti Sihanond.

Charunphan Isarangkun Na Ayuthaya.

M. L. Chirayu Navawongs.

THE CABINET

After the general elections held in April 1976, a coalition government was formed comprising the following parties: Democratic (D), Thai Nation (T), Social Justice (SJ) and Social Nationalist (SN).

(*June* 1976)

Prime Minister and Minister of the Interior: M. R. SENI PRAMOJ (D).

Deputy Prime Minister and Minister of Finance: SAWET PIAMPONEGARN (D).

Deputy Prime Minister and Minister of Agriculture and Co-operatives: Maj.-Gen. PRAMARN ADIREKSARN (T).

Deputy Prime Minister and Minister of Public Health: Air Chief Marshal DAWEE CHULASAPYA (SJ).

Ministers to the Prime Minister's Office: SURIN MASDIT (D), CHUAN LEEK PAI (D).

Minister of Justice: PRASIT KANCHANAWAT (SN).

Minister of Foreign Affairs: PICHAI RATTAKUL (D).

Minister of Education: Maj.-Gen. SIRI SIRIYOTHIN (T).

Minister of Defence: Gen. TAVICH SENIWONG NA AYUDHAYA (D).

Minister of Industry: Maj.-Gen. CHARTICHAI CHOONHAVAN (T).

Minister of Communications: TAVICH KLINPRATOOM (SJ).

Minister of Commerce: DAMRONG LATHAPIPAT (D).

Minister of the State Universities Bureau: NIBHOND SASITHORN (SJ).

Deputy Minister of Finance: Wing Commdr. THINAKORN BHANDHUGRAVI (T).

Deputy Ministers of Agriculture and Co-operatives: KRAISORN TANTIPONG (D), ANNWAT WATANAPONGSIRI (T).

Deputy Ministers of Communications: BOONKERD HIRANKAM (D), PRACHOOM RUTTANAPIAN (SJ).

Deputy Ministers of Interior: KHUNTHONG BHUPIEWDUEN (D), SAMAK SUNDARAVEJ (D), SOMBOON SIRITHORN (D), CHUSSUNGA RIDHIPRASAT (T).

Deputy Ministers of Education: SIDDIK SARIF (D), DABCHAI AKARAJ (T).

Deputy Minister of Public Health: PREECHA MUSIKUL (D).

Deputy Minister of Commerce: KLAI LA-ONMANI (D).

Deputy Minister of Foreign Affairs: LEK NANA (D).

Deputy Ministers of Industry: PAEN SIRIVEJJAPAN (D), BUNHARN SILPA-ACLIA (T).

NATIONAL ASSEMBLY

SENATE

In January 1975 a senate of 100 members was appointed by the King on the advice of the out-going Prime Minister Dr. Sanya Dharmasakti.

HOUSE OF REPRESENTATIVES

Speaker: UTHAI PIMCHAICHON.

A general election was held on April 4th, 1976, with 2,355 candidates from 39 political parties for 279 seats in the House of Representatives. Out of about 20,800,000 eligible voters, about 40 per cent attended the polls.

Election, April 1976

PARTY	SEATS
Prachipat (Democratic)	114
Chart Thai (Thai Nation)	56
Kit Sangkom (Social Action)	45
Dharma Sangkom (Social Justice)	28
Sangkom Chart Niyom (Social Nationalist)	9
Kaset Sangkom (Social Agrarian)	8
Palang Mai (New Force)	3
Palang Prachachon (Populist)	3
Sangkom Niyom (Socialist)	2
Patthana Changwad (People's Development)	2
Others (9 parties)	9
TOTAL	279

POLITICAL PARTIES

In October 1974 political parties were legalized after a three-year ban.

Democratic Party: f. 1946; the oldest political party; monarchist and conservative; Pres. SENI PRAMOJ.

New Force Party: left of centre; advocates a wide range of reforms along social democratic lines; led by KRASAE CHANAWONG.

Social Action Party: conservative; led by KUKRIT PRAMOJ.

Social Agrarian Party: right wing; led by SAWET KHAMPRAKORB.

Social Justice Party: right wing with military elements; led by Air Chief Marshal DAWEE CHULASAPYA.

Social Nationalist Party: right wing with elements of the former United Thai People's Party; led by PRASIT KANCHANAWAT.

Socialist Party of Thailand: left wing; led by Col. SOMKID SRISANGKHOM.

Thai Nation: right-wing with elements of former United Thai People's Party; Leader Maj.-Gen. PRAMARN ADIREKSAN; Deputy Leader Maj.-Gen. SIRI SIRIYOTHIN; Sec.-Gen. Maj.-Gen. CHARTICHAI CHOONHAVAN.

United Socialist Front: amalgamation of six left-wing groups; pledged to abolish the anti-communist laws, create a fairer distribution of wealth, undertake land reform and place major industries under state control; led by KLAEW NORPATI.

DIPLOMATIC REPRESENTATION

EMBASSIES ACCREDITED TO THAILAND

(In Bangkok unless otherwise stated)

Afghanistan: Islamabad, Pakistan.

Argentina: 5th Floor, Thaniya Bldg., 62 Silom Rd.; *Ambassador:* FRANCISCO CARLOS DE POSDA (also accred. to Malaysia).

Australia: 7th Floor, Anglo-Thai Bldg., 64 Silom Rd.; *Ambassador:* M. L. JOHNSTON.

Austria: Maneeya Bldg. (3rd Floor), 518 Ploenchit Rd., P.O.B. 27; *Ambassador:* WALTER DE COMTES (also accred. to Burma, Laos and Singapore).

Bangladesh: Rangoon, Burma.

Belgium: 44 Soi Phya Phipat; *Ambassador:* LUC LEERMAKERS (also accred. to Burma and Laos).

Brazil: 5th Floor, Maneeya Bldg., 518 Ploenchit Rd.; *Ambassador:* JORGE DE OLIVEIRA MAIA (also accred. to Malaysia and Singapore).

Burma: 132 Sathorn Nua Rd.; *Ambassador:* U THEIN MAUNG (also accred. to Laos).

Canada: Thai Farmers Bank Bldg., 142 Silom Rd., P.O.B. 2090; *Ambassador:* (vacant).

Chile: Tokyo, Japan.

China, People's Republic: *Ambassador:* CHAI TSE-MIN.

Cuba: Manila, Philippines.

Denmark: 10 Soi Attakarn Prasit, Sathorn Tai Rd.; *Ambassador:* FRANTZ BONAVENTURA HOWITZ (also accred. to Burma and Laos.)

Dominican Republic: Taipeh, Taiwan.

Egypt: 49 Soi Ruam Rudee, Ploenchit Rd.; *Ambassador:* MOUSTAFA FAHMY EL-ESSAWY.

Finland: New Delhi, India.

France: Custom House Lane, New Rd.; *Ambassador:* GÉRARD ANDRÉ.

Germany, Federal Republic: 9 Sathorn Tai Rd.; *Ambassador:* Dr. EDGAR VON SCHMIDT-PAULI.

Greece: New Delhi, India.

Hungary: Tokyo, Japan.

India: 139 Pan Rd.; *Ambassador:* GUNWANTSINGH J. MALIK.

Indonesia: 600–602 Phetchburi Rd.; *Ambassador:* Maj.-Gen. SOETARTO SIGIT.

Iran: Shell Bldg., 140 Wireless Rd., 9th Floor; *Ambassador:* Dr. MOHSEN S. ESFANDIARY (also accred. to Laos Malaysia and Singapore).

Iraq: Islamabad, Pakistan.

Israel: 31 Soi Lang Suan, Ploenchit Rd.; *Ambassador:* REHAVAM AMIR (also accred. to Laos).

Italy: 92 Sathorn Nua Rd., *Ambassador:* MARIO PRUNAS (also accred. to Laos).

Japan: 1674 New Phetchburi Rd.; *Ambassador:* M. FUJISAKI.

Jordan: New Delhi, India.

Korea, Republic: 956 Rama IV Rd., Olympia Thai Bldg., 1st Floor; *Ambassador:* PARK KUN.

Laos: 193 Sathorn Tai Rd.; *Ambassador:* PHAGNA ANURACK RAJA SENA (also accred. to Burma, Malaysia, Pakistan and the Philippines).

Lebanon: New Delhi, India.

Malaysia: 35 Sathorn Tai Rd.; *Ambassador:* ABDUL RAHMAN BIN ABDUL JALAL.

Nepal: 819 Soi Puengsuk, Sukhumvit Soi 71; *Ambassador:* BHARAT RAJ BHANDARY.

Netherlands: 106 Wireless Rd.; *Ambassador:* FRANS VAN DONGEN (also accred. to Bangladesh and Laos).

New Zealand: Anglo-Thai Bldg., 64 Silom Rd.; *Ambassador:* Hon. E. J. HALSTEAD, T.D. (also accred. to Laos).

Nigeria: New Delhi, India.

Norway: 16 Surasak Rd.; *Ambassador:* FINN SYNNOEVSOEN KOREN (also accred. to Burma).

Pakistan: 31 Soi Nana Nua, Sukhumvit Rd.; *Ambassador:* ABDUL GHAYUR. (also accred. to Laos).

Peru: New Delhi, India.

Philippines: 760 Sukhumvit Rd.; *Ambassador:* Gen. MANUEL T. YAN.

Poland: 16 Soi Chaiyos (11) Sukhumvit Rd.; *Counsellor Chargé d'Affaires a.i.:* B. ZAKRZEWSKI.

Portugal: 26 Bush Lane; *Chargé d'Affaires:* Dr. MANUEL SÁ NOGUEIRA.

Romania: Dacca, Bangladesh.

Saudi Arabia: 2nd Floor, 385 Silom Rd.; *Ambassador:* (vacant).

Singapore: 129 Sathorn Tai Rd.; *Ambassador:* CHI OWYANG.

Spain: 104 Wireless Rd.; *Ambassador:* MARIANO SANZ BRIZ (also accred. to Malaysia and Singapore).

Sri Lanka: 22/1 Soi Sukothai 3, Rajvithee Rd.; *Chargé d'Affaires:* CHANDRA MONARAWALA.

Sweden: 197/1 Silom Rd.; *Ambassador:* ERIC VIRGIN (also accred. to Burma and Laos).

Switzerland: 35 North Wireless Rd.; *Ambassador:* RUDOLF HARTMANN (also accred. to Burma and Laos).

Turkey: 352 Phaholyothin Rd.; *Ambassador:* TÜRGUT ILKAN (also accred. to Laos and Singapore).

U.S.S.R.: 108 Sathorn Nua Rd.; *Ambassador:* BORIS I. ILYECHEV.

United Kingdom: Ploenchit Rd.; *Ambassador:* DAVID L. COLE, C.M.G., M.C.

U.S.A.: 95 Wireless Rd.; *Ambassador:* CHARLES WHITEHOUSE.

Vatican: 217/1 Sathorn Tai Rd.; *Apostolic Pro-Nuncio:* The Most Rev. GIOVANNI MORETTI.

Yugoslavia: 15 Soi 61, Sukhumvit Rd.; *Ambassador:* AZEM ZULFICARI.

Thailand also has diplomatic relations with Algeria, Bulgaria, Cambodia, Czechoslovakia, Gabon, the German Democratic Republic, Iceland, the Democratic People's Republic of Korea, Mongolia, Nicaragua, Papua New Guinea, Qatar, Uruguay. and Viet-Nam.

JUDICIAL SYSTEM

COURTS OF FIRST INSTANCE

Magistrates' Courts (*Sarn Kwaeng*): Function is to dispose of small cases with minimum formality and expense. Judges sit singly.

Juvenile Courts (*Sarn Kadee Dek Lae Yaochon*): original jurisdiction over juvenile delinquency and matters affecting children and young persons. One judge and one woman associate judge form a quorum. There are four courts in Bangkok, Songkla, Nakhon Ratchasima and Chiang Mai.

Civil Court (*Sarn Paeng*): Court of general original jurisdiction in civil and bankruptcy cases in Bangkok and Thonburi. Two judges form a quorum.

Criminal Court (*Sarn Aya*): Court of general original jurisdiction in criminal cases in Bangkok and Thonburi. Two judges form a quorum.

Provincial Courts (*Sarn Changvad*): Exercise unlimited original jurisdiction in all civil and criminal matters, including bankruptcy, within its own district which is generally the province itself. Two judges form a quorum. At each of the five Provincial Courts in the South of Thailand where the majority of the population are Muslims (i.e. Pattani, Yala, Betong, Satun and Narathiwat), there are two Dath Yutithum or Kadis (Muslim judges). A Kadi sits with two trial judges in order to administer Islamic laws and usages in civil cases involving family and inheritance where all parties concerned are Muslims. Questions on Islamic laws and usages which are interpreted by a Kadi are final.

COURT OF APPEALS

Sarn Uthorn: Appellate jurisdiction in all civil, bankruptcy and criminal matters; appeals from all of the Courts of First Instance throughout the country come to this Court. Two judges for a quorum.

SUPREME COURT

Sarn Dika: The final court of appeal in all civil, bankruptcy and criminal cases. The quorum in the Supreme Court consists of three judges. The Court sits in plenary session occasionally to determine cases of exceptional importance and cases where there are reasons for reconsideration or overruling of its own precedents. The quorum for the full Court is half the total number of judges in the Supreme Court.

RELIGION

Buddhism is the prevailing religion. Besides Buddhists, there are some Muslim Malays. Most of the immigrant Chinese are Confucians.

Christians are found mainly in Bangkok and Northern Thailand and number about 150,000, of whom 116,000 are Roman Catholics.

BUDDHIST

Supreme Patriarch of Thailand: Somdij Phra ARIYAVONGFAKHATAYAN.

The Buddhist Association of Thailand: 41 Phra Aditya St., Bangkok; under royal patronage; f. 1934; 3,879 mems.; Pres. Dr. SANYA THAMMASAK.

ROMAN CATHOLIC

Bangkok: Archbishop: Most Rev. MICHAEL MICHAI KITBUNCHU, Assumption Cathedral, Bangrak, Bangkok 5.

Tharé and Nonseng: Archbishop's House, Tharé, Sakonnakhon; Archbishop: Most Rev. MICHEL KIEN SAMOPHITHAK.

Catholic Association of Thailand: 12 Convent Rd., Bangkok.

PROTESTANT

The Church of Christ in Thailand: 14 Pramuan Rd., Bangkok; f. 1934; communicant mems. 27,000; Moderator Rev. TONGKHAM PANTUPONG; Gen. Sec. Dr. KOSON SRISANG; affiliated mission mems.: United Presbyterian (U.S.A.), Disciples of Christ Mission American Baptist, German Lutheran (Marburger), Presbyterian Church of Korea, Church of South India, United Church of Christ in Japan; Member of the World Presbyterian Alliance, East Asia Christian Conference and WCC.

THE PRESS

(In Bangkok unless otherwise stated)

DAILIES

THAI LANGUAGE

Ban Muang: 1 Soi Superhighways Rd.; f. 1972; Editor VIJARN PUKPIBOON; circ. 100,000.

Bangkok News (formerly *Kiattisakdi*): 108 Suapa Rd.; Editor CHARN SINSOOK; circ. 45,000.

Chao Thai: Thai Samaki Co. Ltd., 555 Chakrapatpong Rd., Siyaek Maensrie; f. 1947; Editor CHALERM WUTHIKOSIT; circ. 10,000.

Daily News: 423 Siphya Rd.; f. 1964; Editor-in-Chief SANIT EKACHAI; circ. 230,000.

Dao Siam: Mansion 4, Rajdamnern Ave.; f. 1974; Editor LEK LAKSANAPHOL; circ. 50,000.

Khao Panich (Daily Trade News): Khao Phanit Printing House, Memorial Bridge; Editor CHARAT CHATURAT; f. 1950; circ. 6,000.

Prachathipatai: Mahachon Publications Ltd., 33/28 Soi Phetchburi, Phetchburi Rd.; f. 1933; Editor SANIT THANARAK; circ. 84,000.

Primthai/Thai Post: 1 Dindaeng Rd.; f. 1946; Editor CHAIYONG CHAVALIT; circ. 20,000.

Siam: 15/3 Bangkok-Saraburi Rd., Bangkhen; f. 1972; Editor SURAT ONSATHANUKRAW; circ. 50,000.

Siam Rath: Mansion 6, Rajdamnern Ave.; f. 1950; Editor NOPPORN BUNYARIT; circ. 100,000.

Thai Daily: 311 Phra Sumen Rd.; f. 1968; Editor CHAMONG KAEWSOWATHANA; circ. 38,000.

Thai Rath: 480 Phaholyothin Rd.; f. 1958; Editor KAMPOL VACHARAPOL; circ. 500,000.

ENGLISH LANGUAGE

Bangkok Post: Post Publishing Co. Ltd., 968 Rama IV Rd., Bangkok; Editor MICHAEL J. GORMAN; circ. over 17,000.

Bangkok World: Allied Newspapers Ltd., 968 Rama IV Rd., Bangkok; f. 1957; Editor GRAEME STANTON; circ. 13,000.

The Nation: 5/5–6 Dejo Rd.; f. 1971; Editor SUTHICHAI YOON; circ. 12,000.

CHINESE LANGUAGE

Chia Pao Daily News: 1017 Siphya Crossroads, New Rd.; f. 1968; Editor ENG ENGPICHO; circ. 67,000.

Sakon: 21/1 Phrayi Si Crossroad; f. 1955; Editor YAO TIWA; circ. 9,000.

Sing Sian Wan Pao Daily News: 267 New Rd.; f. 1950; Editor CHANG YI KWANG; circ. 40,500.

Siri Nakorn: 108 Suapa Rd.; f. 1959; Editor PRASIT SIRIWARIWET; circ. 10,000.

Tong Fua Yit Pao: 877–9 New Rd.; f. 1960; Editor SAKHORN KAYAWATT; circ. 20,000.

WEEKLIES

THAI LANGUAGE

Arthit (The Sun): 58 Soi 36, Sukumvit Rd.

Bangkok: 31–7 Lan Luang Rd.; Editor VICHIT ROJANAPRABHA.

Bangkok Time: 37 Bamrung Muang Rd.; Editor CHAROON KUVANONDH.

Dara Thai: 9 Soi Bampen, Tung Mahamek; Editor SURAT PUKAVES.

Darunee (Lady): 7/2 Soi Watanawonge, Rajprarope Rd.; f. 1953; magazine for ladies; Principal Officer CHIT KANPAI; Editor WEERAWAN SUWANVIPATH; circ. 100,000.

Khun Ying: 215 Soi Saynamthip, Sukumvit Rd.; women's magazine.

Mae Sri Ruen: 13/22 Prachatipok Rd.; Editor Mrs. NANTRA RATANAKOM.

Nakorn Thai: 13–22 Soi Wat Hivanruchee, Prachatipok Rd.

Phadung Silp: 163 Soi Thesa, Rajborpit Rd.; Editor AKSORN CHUAPANYA.

Sakul Thai: 58 Soi 36, Sukumvit Rd.; Editor PRAYOON SONGSERM-SWASDI.

Satri Sarn: 83–86 Arkarntrithosthep 2, Prachathipatai Rd.; f. 1948; women's magazine; Editor Miss NILAWAN PINTHONG.

See Ros: 612 Luke Luang Rd.; Editor MANI CHINDANONDH.

Siam Rath Weekly Review: Mansion 6, Rajdamnern Ave.; Editor SAMRUEY SINGHADET.

ENGLISH LANGUAGE

Financial Post: Mansion 4, Rajdamnern Ave., Bangkok.

FORTNIGHTLIES

Chaiya-Pruek: 599 Maitrichit Rd.; f. 1953; Editor ANUJ APAPIROM.

Mae Barnkarn Ruan: 612 Luke Luang Rd.; Editor Mrs. THONG MUAN CHINDANONDH.

Nakorn Thai: 13/3 Prachatipok Rd.; Editor SAKDI RATANAKOM.

Pharp Khao Taksin: 226 Samsen Rd.; Editor LUAN VIRAPHAT.

Saen Sook: 553/9 Sriayuthya Rd.; Editor SUCHATI AMONKUL.

Sena Sarn: Army Auditorium, Ministry of Defence; Editor Lt.-Col. FUEN DISYAVONG.

MONTHLIES

Chao Krung: Mansion 6, Rajdamnern Ave.; Editor NOPPHORN BUNYARIT.

Chaiyapruek: Maitri Chit Rd.; Editor PLUANG NA-NAKORN.

The Dharmacakshu (*Dharma-vision*): Foundation of Mahāmakut Rājavidyālaya, Phra Sumeru Rd., Bangkok 2; f. 1894; Buddhism and related subjects; Editor Group Capt. MEGH AMPHAICHARIT; circ. 5,000.

The Investor: Siam Publications Ltd., 101 Naret Rd., P.O.B. 12-89, Bangkok; f. Dec. 1968; English language; business, industry, finance and economics; Editor TOS PATUMSEN; circ. 6,000.

Kasikorn: Dept. of Agriculture, Bangkhen, Bangkok 9; Editor SAWART RATANAWORABHAN.

The Lady: 77 Rama V Rd.; Editor Princess NGARMCHITR PREM PURACHATRA.

Satawa Liang: 689 Wang Burapa Rd.; Editor THAMRONGSAK SRICHAND.

Thai T.V. Mirror: Thai T.V. Co. Ltd., 73–75 Sow Ching Cha Square; f. 1954; Editor ARCHIN PUNJAPHAN; circ. 20,000.

Thailand Illustrated: Government Public Relations Dept., Rajdamnern Ave., Bangkok 2; Thai and English; Editor Mrs. PAWA WATANASUPT; circ. 2,000.

Villa Wina Magazine: 3rd Floor, Chalerm Ketr Theatre Bldg.; Editor BHONGSAKDI PIAMLAP.

Vithayu Sueksa: Ministry of Education, Rajdamnern Ave.; Editor PLUANG NA-NAKORN.

PRESS AGENCIES

FOREIGN BUREAUX

Agence France-Presse: P.O.B. 1567, Bangkok; Correspondent JACQUES J. ABELOUS.

AP: 103 Pat Pong Rd., Bangkok; Correspondent PETER O'LOUGHLIN.

Central News Agency Inc.: 17 Soi St., Louis 2, Sathorn South Rd., Bangkok; Chief of Bureau CONRAD LU.

Reuters: P.O.B. 877, 53 Nava Bldg., 4–6 General Post Office Lane, Bangkok.

Antara, the Jiji Press and UPI also have bureaux in Bangkok.

PRESS ASSOCIATION

Press Association of Thailand: 299 Nakorn Rassima North Rd., Bangkok; f. 1941; Pres. WASANT CHOOSAKUL

There are other regional Press organizations and two journalists' organizations.

PUBLISHERS

Aksorn Charoen Tasna Ltd.: Bamrung Muang Rd. 195, Bangkok.

Chalermnit Press: 108 Sukumvit Soi 53, Bangkok; f. 1957; dictionaries, history, literature, guides to Thai language, books on Thailand; Mans. Brig.-Gen. M. L. M. JUMSAK and Mrs. JUMSAI.

Pra Cha Chang & Co. Ltd.: Talad Noi 861–3, New Rd., Bangkok.

Prae Pittaya Ltd.: P.O.B. 914, 718 Wang Burapa Rd., Bangkok.

Pramuansarn Publishing House: 703/15-16 Petchburi Rd., Bangkok; f. 1955; general books, fiction and non-fiction, paperbacks, guidebooks, children's books; Man. LIME TAECHATADA.

Ruamsarn: Wang Burapha, Bangkok.

Siam Directory: P.O.B. 1515, Bangkok; history, politics, economics, business directories.

Sie Kan Ka Co. Ltd.: Prayurawong Mansion 198, Mansion 1, Thonburi.

Social Science Association Press: Chula Soi 2, Phya Thai Rd., Bangkok; f. 1961; scholarly books, quarterly magazine; Man. and Editor SULAK SIVARAKSA.

Suekanka Ltd.: Practatipok Road 198, Thonburi.

Suksapan Panit (*Business Organization of Teachers' Institute*): Mansion 9, Rajdamnern Ave., Bangkok; f. 1950; textbooks, children's books, pocketbooks; Man. KAMTHON SATHIRAKUL.

Suriwongs Book Centre: P.O.B. 44, Chiengmai; head office: 116-128 Loy Kraw Rd.; br. office: 134 Suriyong Cinema Arcade; f. 1954; textbooks and general books in Thai; wholesalers and retailers of Thai and foreign books; Man. Proprietor CHAI JITTIDECHARAKS.

Thai Commercial Printing Press: Bangkok; law, administration, politics economics, industry.

Thai Inc.: Mansion 96, Rajdamnern Ave. 2, Bangkok.

Thai Vatnapanis: Maitrijit Rd. 599, Bangkok; children's books, picture books.

RADIO AND TELEVISION

RADIO

Thai National Broadcasting Station: Public Relations Dept., Rajdamnern Ave., Bangkok; f. 1938; under full Government control; Deputy Dir.-Gen. Dr. W. SIWASARIYANOND; services in Thai, English, French, Vietnamese, Chinese, Malay, Laotian and Cambodian.

Ministry of Education Broadcasting Service: Division of Educational Information, Ministry of Education, Bangkok; f. 1954; Dir. of Division MOM LUANG CHINTANA NAVAWONGS; evening programmes for general public; daytime programmes for schools including music, social studies and English.

Pituksuntiradse Radio Stations: Two at Paruksakavun Palace and Bangkhen, Bangkok, two at Nakorn Rachasima and one at Chiengmai; Dir.-Gen. SUCHART P. SAKORN; programmes in Thai.

Radio Station HS1JS: Bang-Sue, Bangkok; controlled by Government, permits advertising; Dir.-Gen. K. KENGRADOMYING.

Voice of Free Asia: Ayutthaya Province; established 1968; 1,000 kW. broadcasting station; operated to broadcast programmes for the Royal Thai and U.S. Governments in Thai, English and several other languages used in the area.

In 1975 there were an estimated 5.4 million radio sets.

TELEVISION

Television of Thailand: Government Public Relations Department, Bangkok; Government controlled; three stations; programmes 12.00 p.m.–16.00 p.m.

Thai Television Co. Ltd.: Mansion B., Rajdamnern Ave., Bangkok; transmissions from 1955, commercial programmes 4.45–12.00 p.m. daily, 10.00 a.m.–12.00 p.m. weekends; Dir.-Gen. Gen. K. PUNNAGUNTA.

Royal Thai Army HSA-TV: Phaholyothin St., Sanam Pao, Bangkok; transmissions over a 75 mile radius since Jan. 1958; daily 17.00–23.00 hours; Sundays 09.00–12.00 and 17.00–23.00 hours; Dir.-Gen. Maj.-Gen. PRASIT CHUNBUN.

In 1975 there were about 761,000 TV receivers in use.

FINANCE

(cap.=capital; p.u.=paid up; dep.=deposits; m.=million; res.=reserves; amounts in baht).

BANKING

CENTRAL BANK

Bank of Thailand: 273 Bang Khunprom, P.O.B. 154, Bangkok; f. 1942; government-owned; cap. 20m.; dep. (Government and banks) baht 8,668m. (April 1976); Gov. SNOH UNAKUL.

COMMERCIAL BANKS

Asia Trust Bank Ltd.: 80-82 Anuwongse Rd., P.O.B. 195, Bangkok; f. 1965; cap. p.u. 95m.; dep. 2,083m. (Dec. 1975); Chair. Princess CHUMBHOT of Nagor Svarga; Pres. WALLOB TARNVANICHKUL; 10 brs.

Bangkok Bank Ltd.: 3-9 Plabplachai Rd., Bangkok; f. 1944; cap. p.u. 1,050m.; dep. 33,731m. (Dec. 1975); Chair. and Pres. CHIN SOPHON PANICH; 146 brs.

Bangkok Bank of Commerce Ltd.: 171 Surawong Rd., Bangkok; f. 1944; cap. p.u. 75m.; dep. 4,016m. (Dec. 1975); Chair. M. R. BOONRUB PHINIJCHONKADI; 97 brs.

Bangkok Metropolitian Bank Ltd.: Suan Mali, Bangkok; f. 1950; cap. 10m.; dep. 4,165m. (Dec. 1975); Chair. and Man. Dir. UDANE TEJAPAIBUL; 38 brs.

Bank of Asia for Industry and Commerce Ltd.: 601 Charoen Krung Rd., Bangkok, P.O.B. 112; f. 1939; cap. p.u.

150.om.; dep. 2,082m. (Dec. 1975); Chair. CHAROON EUARCHUKIATI; Man. SATHIEN TEJAPAIBUL; 10 brs.

Bank of Ayudhya Ltd.: P.O.B. 491, 550 Ploenchit Rd., Bankgok; f. 1945; cap. p.u. 300m.; dep. 5,658m. (Dec. 1975); Chair. Pol. Gen. PRASERT RUJIRAVONGS; Man. Dir. CHUAN RATANARAKS, 72 brs.

Government Savings Bank of Thailand: 470 Phaholyothin Rd., Bangkok 4; f. 1913; cap. 1,241m.; dep. 12,022m. (Dec. 1975); 346 brs.; Chair. IAD NAKORNTHAP; Dir.-Gen. DUSDEE SVASDI-XUTO; publs. *Savings Bank Journal* (bi-monthly), *Annual Report*.

Krung Thai Bank Ltd. (*State Commercial Bank of Thailand*). 260 Yawaraj Rd., Bangkok 1; f. 1966; cap. p.u 600m.; dep. 15,076m. (Dec. 1975); Chair. IAD NAKORNTHAP; Gen. Man. TAMJAI KHAMPHATO; 125 brs.

Laem Thong Bank Ltd.: P.O.B. 131, 289 Suriwong Rd., Bangkok; f. 1948; cap. 12m.; dep. 802m. (Dec. 1975); Man. Dir. SOMBOON NANDHABIWAT; Chair. Police Lt-Gen. TORSAKDI YOMNAK; 3 brs.

Siam City Bank Ltd.: 13 Anuwongse Rd., Bangkok; f. 1941; cap. p.u. 200m.; dep. 4,435m. (Dec. 1975); Chair. CHALERM CHIO-SAKUL; Man. Dir. VISIDTHA SRISOMBOON; 85 brs.

Siam Commercial Bank Ltd., The: 1060 New Petchburi Rd., Bangkok 4, P.O.B. 15; f. 1906; cap. p.u. 100m.; dep. 5,036m. (Dec. 1975); Chair. NAI POONPERM KRAIRIKSH; Gen. Man. PRACHITR YOSSUNDARA; 41 brs.

Thai Danu Bank Ltd.: 393 Silom Rd., Bangkok; f. 1949; cap. p.u. 25m.; dep. 1,116m. (Dec. 1975); Chair. POTE SARASIN; Pres. CHALERM PRACHUABMOH; 10 brs.

Thai Farmers' Bank Ltd.: 142 Silom Rd., Bangkok; f. 1945; cap. p.u. 238m.; dep. 8,892m. (Dec. 1975); Pres. BANCHA LAMSAM; Chair PHRA NITIKARN-PRASOM; 119 brs.

Thai Military Bank Ltd.: Mansion 2, Rajdamnern Ave., Bangkok; f. 1957; cap. p.u. 10m.; dep. 2,060m. (Dec. 1975); Pres. SUKUM NAVAPAN.

Union Bank of Bangkok Ltd.: G.P.O. Box 2114, 624 Yawaraj Rd., Bangkok; f. 1949; cap. p.u. 50m.; dep. 1,767m. (Dec. 1975); Chair. Gen. KRICHA PUNNAKANTA; Man. Dir. BANJURD CHOLVIJARN; 34 brs.

Wang Lee Chan Bank Ltd.: 1016 Rama IV Rd., Bangkok 5; f. 1933; cap. p.u. 12m.; dep. 277m. (Dec. 1975); Chair. TAN SIEW TING; 2 brs.

FOREIGN BANKS

Bank of America N.T. and S.A.: San Francisco; 297 Surawong Rd., P.O.B. 158, Bangkok 5; dep. 746m. (Dec. 1975); Man. R. E. PHILLIPS.

Bank of Canton Ltd.: 197/1 Silom Rd., Bangkok 5; f. 1921; dep. 149m. (Dec. 1975); Man. C. Y. SUN.

Bank of Tokyo Ltd.: 62 Thaniya Bldg., Silom Rd., Bangkok; f. 1962; dep. 710m. (Dec. 1975); Man. M. UNABARA.

Banque de l'Indochine S.A.: Paris; 142 Wireless Rd., P.O.B. 303, Bangkok; f. 1897; dep. 292m. (Dec. 1975); Man. B. AGIER.

Chartered Bank: Rama IV Rd., Saladaeng Circle, Bangkok; f. 1894; dep. 808m. (Dec. 1975); Man. J. R. MEDLEY.

Chase Manhattan Bank, N.A.: New York; 965 Rama 1 Rd., P.O.B. 525, Bangkok; f. 1964; dep 646m. (Dec 1975); Man. HENDRIK STEEN BERGEN.

Four Seas Communications Bank Ltd.: 1378-1380 Songwad Rd., Bangkok; f. 1909; dep. 87m. (Dec. 1975); Man. TAN PUAY LIANG.

Hongkong and Shanghai Banking Corporation, The: Hong Kong; P.O.B. 57, 2 Bush Lane, Siphya, Bangkok; f. 1888; dep. 432m. (Dec. 1975); Man. P. M. RYAN.

Indian Overseas Bank: Madras; 221 Rajawongse Rd., Bangkok; f. 1947; dep. 158m. (Dec. 1975); Man. T. M. U. MENON.

International Commercial Bank of China: Tapei; 95 Suapa Rd. Bangkok; f. 1947; dep. 116m. (Dec. 1975); Man. JAMES C. C. CHENG.

Mercantile Bank Ltd.: Hongkong; P.O.B. 64, Silom Rd., Bangkok; f. 1923; dep. 203m. (Dec. 1975); Man. J. A. ANDERSON.

Mitsui Bank, The: Tokyo; 138 Boonmits Bldg., Silom Rd., Bangkok; f. 1952; dep. 656m. (Dec. 1975); Man. W. MAEDA.

United Malayan Banking Corpn. Ltd.: Kuala Lumpur; 147–151 Suapa Rd., Bangkok; f. 1964; dep. 324m. (Dec. 1975); Man. LIMCHENG LAI.

DEVELOPMENT FINANCE ORGANIZATIONS

Bank for Agriculture and Agricultural Co-operatives (BAAC): 469 Nakornsawan Rd., Bangkok; f. 1956 to provide credit for agriculture; cap. 1,284m.; dep. 2,845m. (Dec. 1975); Chair. PUEY UNGPHAKORN; Man. CHAMLONG TOKTONG.

Government Housing Bank: 77 Rajdamnern Ave., Bangkok; f. 1953 to provide housing finance; cap. 168m.; dep. 219m. (Dec. 1975); Chair. PRASIT NARONGDEJ; Man. MANASAKDI INTARAKOMALYASUT.

Industrial Finance Corporation of Thailand (I.F.C.T.): 101 Naret Rd., Bangkok; f. 1959 to assist in the establishment, expansion or modernization of industrial enterprises in the private sector; to bring about mobilization and pooling of funds and assist in capital market development; makes medium-and long-term loans, underwriting shares and securities and guaranteeing loans; cap. p.u. baht 150m. (Dec. 1975); loans granted 2,985m. on 335 projects (Dec. 1975); Chair. SOMMAI HOONTRAKOOL; Gen. Man. WAREE BHONGSVEJ.

Board of Investment: 88 Mansion 2, Rajdamnern Ave., Bangkok; Sec.-Gen. SOMPORN PUNYAGUPTA.

Small Industries Finance Office (SIFO): 16 Mansion 6, Rajdamnern Ave., Bangkok; f. 1964 to provide finance for small scale industries; cap. 54m. (Dec. 1975); Chair. PRAPAS CHAKKAPHAK; Man. ANEK BOONYAPAKDI.

Thai Development Bank Ltd.: 20 Yukhon 2 Rd., Suanmali, Bangkok; Cable address: Patanabank; cap. p.u. 220m.; dep. 3,275m. (Dec. 1975); 49 brs. throughout Thailand; Chair. SUNTHORN SATHIRATNAI; Man. Dir. CORO TEJAPAIBUL.

STOCK EXCHANGE

Securities Exchange of Thailand (SET): 965 Rama I Rd., Bangkok; f. 1975; 30 mems.; 21 listed firms; 5 authorized firms; Chair. VAREE BHONGSVEJ; Man. Dir. SUKREE KAOCHAROEN.

INSURANCE

Bangkok Insurance Co. Ltd.: The Bangkok Insurance Bldg., 302 Silom Rd., Bangkok; f. 1947; non-life insurance; Chair. CHIN SOPHONPANICH; Man. Dir. CHOOMPORN RUNGSOPINKUL.

Bangkok Union Insurance Co. Ltd.: 27–29 Yukon 1 Rd., Bangkok; f. 1967; Chair. PHORN LIEWPHAIRATANA; Man. Dir. Y. K. TU; Gen. Man. BOONYONG TAYJASANANT.

Borisat Arkanay Prakan Pai Jamkat (*South-East Insurance Co. Ltd.*): South East Insurance Bldg., 315 Silom Rd., Bangkok; f. 1946; Chair. and Exec. Dir. R. S. JOTIKASTHIRA; life, marine, accident, fire, cte.

China Insurance Co. (Siam) Ltd.: 95 Suapa Rd., Bangkok; f. 1948; fire and marine underwriters; cap. (1971) baht 18.5m.; Man. K. Y. Chan.

International Assurance Co. Ltd., The: 291–293 Rajawongse Rd., Bangkok; f. 1952; Chair. Gen. P. Boribhandh Yuddhakich; Man. Dir. V. S. Saman; cap. p.u. 2.5m.; fire, marine, general.

International Life Assurance (Thailand) Ltd., The: 52/4-5-6 Surawong Rd., Bangkok; f. 1951; Chair. (vacant); Gen. Man. Suriyon Raiwa; cap. baht 15m.; life.

Luang Lee Insurance Co. Ltd.: 4219–4225 Chiengmai Rd., Klongsarn, P.O.B. 97, Bangkok-Thonburi Metropolitan City; f. 1933; non-life insurance; cap. baht 5m.; res. baht 8.9m.; Chair. Tan Siew Ting Wanglee; Man. Dir. Suchin Wanglee.

Ocean Insurance Company Ltd.: 1666 Krung Kasem Rd., Bangkok; Man. Dir. Tana Bulsuk; accident, fire, life, marine, motor car.

Shiang Ann Insurance Co. Ltd.: 40–42 Chalermkhet Soi 3, Plabplachai Rd., Bangkok 1; f. 1929; non-life insurance; cap. baht 9m.; res. baht 2m.; Chair. Coro Teja-phaibul; Dir. K. P. Yu.

Sinswad Assurance Co. Ltd.: 167/3–4 Wireless Rd., Bangkok; f. 1946; Chair. B. Sukanich; Man. Dir. C. Prypiroonrojn; cap. p.u. 10m.; fire, casualty, marine.

Syn Mun Kong Insurance Co. Ltd.: 385 Silom Rd., Yong Vanich Bldg. 3rd Floor, Bangkok 5; f. 1951; fire, automobile and personal accident underwriters; Man. Dir. Tanavit Dusdeesurapot.

Thai Commercial Insurance Co. Ltd.: 133/19 (6th Floor) Rajdamri Rd., Bangkok; f. 1940; fire, marine and casualty insurance; cap. baht 5.0m.; res. baht 1.4m.; unearned premium res. baht 1.9m.; Mans. Suchin Wanglee, Surajit Wanglee.

Thai Insurance Co. Ltd.: 933 Maha Chai Rd., Bangkok; est. 1939; Man. Dir. Chalor Thongsuphan.

Thai Life Insurance Co. Ltd.: Mansion 8, Rajdamnern Ave., Bangkok; f. 1942; Man. Dir. Smit Yamasmit.

Thai Prasit Insurance Co. Ltd.: 295 Sriphya Rd., Bangkok; f. 1947; fire, marine, automobile and life insurance; Chair. Tan Eng Ghee; Man. Dir. Saeng Limpan-onda.

Wilson Insurance Co. Ltd.: 5th Floor, Bangkok Bank Rajawongse Branch Bldg., 245-249 Rajawongse Rd., Bangkok; f. 1951; fire, marine insurance; Chair. Chin Sophonpanich; Man. Dir. Choomporn Runsopinkul.

TRADE AND INDUSTRY

CHAMBERS OF COMMERCE

Thai Chamber of Commerce: 150 Rajbopit Rd., Bangkok; f. 1946; 520 mems.; Pres. Nai Charoon Sibunruang; Vice-Pres. Nai Ob Vasuratna, Nai Preecha Tan-prasert, Dr. Somphob Sussangkarn; publs. *Thai Chamber of Commerce Journal* (monthly), *Thai Chamber of Commerce Directory*.

Chiengrai Chamber of Commerce: Chiengrai, North Thailand.

Cholburi Chamber of Commerce: Cholburi, South-East Thailand.

GOVERNMENT ORGANIZATIONS

Forest Industry Organization: 76 Rajdamnern Nok Ave., Bangkok 1; f. 1947; has wide responsibilities concerning all aspects of Thailand's forestry and wood industries; Man. Dir. Krit Samapuddhi.

Rubber Estate Organization: Visuthikasat Rd., Bangkok.

Thai Sugar Organization: Luang Rd., Bangkok.

INDUSTRIAL AND TRADE ASSOCIATIONS

The Association of Thai Industries: "Suriyothai" Bldg., 5th Floor, 260 Phaholyothin Rd., Bangkok 4; f. 1967; 300 mems.; Pres. Maj.-Gen. Pramarn Adireksarn; Vice-Pres. Bunjerd Cholvicharn, Thavorn Porn-prapha, Pong Sarasin.

Jute Association of Thailand: 335 New Rd., Bangkok.

Mineral Industry Association of Thailand: 26 Bangkok Rd., Puket.

Pharmaceutical Association of Thailand: 150 Rajbopit Rd., Bangkok.

Rice Mill Association of Thailand: 233 South Sathorn Rd., Bangkok.

Rice Traders Association of Thailand: 120 N. Sathorn Rd., Bangkok 5.

Rubber Trade Association of Thailand: 150 Rajbopit Rd., Bangkok.

Sawmill Association of Siam: 258/1 Visuthykasat Rd., Bangkok.

The Tapioca Association of Thailand: 291-293 Rajawongse Rd., Bangkok.

Thai Maize and Produce Exporters Association: 52/16-18 Surawongse Rd., Bangkok.

Thai Silk Association: c/o Industrial Promotion Dept., Ministry of Industry, Rama VI Rd., Bangkok.

Thailand Lac Association: 66 Chaleamkatt 1, Bangkok.

Timber Exporters Association: 119/1 Nr. Huachang Bridge, P.O.B. 240, Phaya Thai Rd., Bangkok.

The Union Textile Merchants Association of Thailand: 121/1 Rajawongse Rd., Bangkok.

TRADE UNIONS

Federation of Labour Unions of Thailand (FLUT): Bangkok; Pres. Paisarn Thawatchainand; Vice-Pres. Arom Pongse-Pangan.

TRANSPORT

RAILWAYS

State Railway of Thailand: Yodse, Bangkok; f. 1891; 27,473 permanent employees, 5,481 temporary (Sept. 1975); 3,765 km. of open lines, 3,885 km. of running track and 583 km. of siding track; gauge 1 metre; Chair. PRAPASNA AUYCHAI; Gen. Man. Lt.-Gen. THUEN SARIKHAGANONDHA; Sec. MANI HINSHIRANAN; publ. *Railway Monthly Magazine* (Thai).

ROADS

Total length of primary and secondary roads at the end of 1972 was 17,686 km., of which 72 per cent were paved. Under Thailand's Second Highway Project it is planned to build approximately 90 kilometres of a new two-lane highway to the east of the Nan River and possibly to improve 475 kilometres of feeder roads in the area.

SHIPPING

Port Authority of Thailand: Bangkok; 16 vessels; Chair. Admiral PRAJUM I. MOKAVES, R.T.N.; Dir. Admiral ABHAI SITAKALIN, R.T.N.

Bangkok United Mechanical Co. Ltd.: 144 Sukumvit Rd., Bangkok; coastal services; Pres. P. PRASARTTONG-ORSOTH; Man. C. W. CHAIKOMIN; 1 tanker.

Keat Navigation Co. Ltd.: 19 Thalang Rd., Phuket; Gen. Man. C. UPATISING; 1 cargo vessel.

Oceanic Transport Co. Ltd.: 197/1 Silom Rd., Bangkok; tanker services; Chair. C. J. HUANG; Man. Dir. C. D. SHIAH; 4 tanker vessels.

Oil Fuel Organization of Thailand: Bangkok; river transport; 1 tanker vessel.

Thai Maritime Navigation Co. Ltd.: 59 Yanawa, Bangkok; services from Bangkok to Far Eastern ports; 3 vessels; Chair. Air Chief Marshal DAWEE CHULASAPYA; Gen. Man. G. SAMANANDA.

Thai Mercantile Marine Ltd.: Bangkok Bank Bldg., 4th Floor, P.O.B. 905, 300 Silom Rd., Bangkok; f. 1967; four dry cargo vessels on liner service between Japan and Thailand; Chair. H. E. THANAT KHOMAN; Vice-Chair. CHIN SOPHONPANICH.

Thai Navigation Co. Ltd.: 721 Hongkong Bank Lane, Siphya, Bangkok; f. 1940; services (passenger and freight) between Thailand, Singapore, Malacca and Penang; Man. a.i. Commodore SAWAENG KARNJANA-KANOK.

Thai Petroleum Transports Co. Ltd.: Air France Bldg., 3 Patpong Rd., Bangkok; coastal tanker services; Chair. C. CHOWKWANYUN; Man. Capt. A. MACKAY; 5 vessels.

CIVIL AVIATION

Note: Work has started on a new international airport at Nong Ngu Hao. Costing 2,000–3,000 million baht, it will be completed by 1977. The existing Don Muang airport will be used for military purposes and domestic services from 1977.

Thai Airways International Ltd.: 1043 Phaholyothin Rd., Bangkok 4; f. 1959; international services from Bangkok to Athens, Calcutta, Copenhagen, Dacca, Delhi, Denpasar, Frankfurt, Hong Kong, Jakarta, Kathmandu, Kuala Lumpur, London, Manila, Osaka, Paris, Penang, Rangoon, Saigon, Singapore, Sydney, Tapei and Tokyo; Chair. Air Chief Marshal KAMOL THEJATUNGA; Man. Dir. Air Marshal CHOO SUTHICHOTI; 3 DC-8-63, 6 DC-8-33, 2 DC-10-30.

Thai Airways Co. Ltd.: 6 Larn Luang Rd., Bangkok; f. 1951; operates domestic services and also flies to Panang and Vientiane; Chair. and acting Man. Dir. Lt.-Cdr. PRASONG SUCHIVA; fleet of 9 HS-748, 2 DC-3.

Air-Siam (*Air-Siam Air Co. Ltd.*): P.O.B. 4-155, 1643-5 New Petchburi Rd., Bangkok; f. 1965; 1 B747, 1 DC-10-30, 1 707-120; principal routes: Bangkok–Hong Kong–Fukuoka–Tokyo–Honolulu–Los Angeles; scheduled passenger/freight operator; member of IATA; Chair. H.H. Princess SUDASIRISOBHA; Pres. and Man. Dir. V. VANNAKUL.

Bangkok is also served by the following airlines: Aeroflot, Air Cambodge, Air Ceylon, Air France, Air India, Air Viet-Nam, Alitalia, British Airways, Burma Airway Corpn., Cathay Pacific Airways, China Airlines, EgyptAir, Garuda Indonesian Airways, Japan Air Lines Co., KLM, Korean Airlines, Lufthansa, Pan American, Philippine Air Lines, Quantas, Royal Nepal Airlines, SAS, Singapore Airlines, Swissair, Trans World Airlines, UTA.

TOURISM

The Tourist Organization of Thailand (TOT): Head Office, Mansion 2, Ratchadamnoen Ave., Bangkok 2; f. 1960; Dir.-Gen. Lt.-Gen. CHALERMCHAI CHARUVASTR; Deputy Dir.-Gen. Col. SIRISAK SUNTAROVAT, Col. SOMCHAI HIRANYAKIT; publs. *Thailand Travel Talk* (monthly, English), *Holiday Time in Thailand* (quarterly, English), *TOT's Magazine* (monthly, Thai); overseas offices in New York, Los Angeles, Frankfurt, Sydney and Tokyo.

North Thailand Tourist Promotion Asscn.: Chieng Mai; Pres. Prof. MOMLUANG TUI XUMSAI.

POWER

National Energy Administration: Pibultham Villa, Kasatsuk Bridge, Bangkok 5; Sec.-Gen. NITIPAT JALICHAN.

Electricity Generating Authority of Thailand (EGAT): Man. Dir. KASAME CHATIKAVANIJ.

ATOMIC ENERGY

Office of Atomic Energy for Peace: Srirubsook Rd., Bangkhen, Bangkok 9; Chair. the Prime Minister; Sec.-Gen. Dr. SVASTI SRISUKH.

The National Energy Administration maintains a research reactor and a nuclear institute.

Note: Thailand's first nuclear electricity plant is to be established at Ao Pai in Si Racha district by 1981.

DEFENCE

Armed Forces (1975): Total strength 204,000: army 135,000, navy 27,000, air force 42,000; military service lasts for two years and is compulsory.

Equipment: The armed forces are mainly American-equipped, recent additions to the air force have been T-6 Air Tourer trainers from New Zealand, F-53 fighters and A37B "Skyraider" from the U.S.A.

Defence Expenditure: The amount allocated to defence in the 1976–77 budget was 12,335 million baht ($605 million).

EDUCATION

Compulsory education was first introduced in 1921 in Thailand; however, it was not until 1960 that a national scheme of education was announced by royal proclamation; this was put into force on 1 April 1961. According to the 1960 census the literacy rate of the population over the age of 10 was 70.8 per cent, a 17 per cent increase over the 1947 rate of 53.7 per cent. The 1960 scheme aimed at improving the general standard of education among the people by extending free compulsory education from four to seven years.

There are four types of schools in Thailand: (1) Government schools established and maintained by government funds. (2) Local schools which are created by virtue of the Elementary Education Act and are usually financed by the Government; however, if they are founded by the people of the district, funds collected from the public may be used in supporting such schools. (3) Municipal schools, a type of primary school financed and supervised by the municipality. (4) Private schools set up and owned by private individuals under the provisions of the 1954 Private Schools Act. The National Scheme of Education provides for education on four levels: (1) Pre-School Education (nursery and kindergarten), which is not compulsory and aims at preparing children for elementary education; (2) Elementary Education; (3) Secondary Education; (4) Higher Education. The distribution of schools by types, and numbers of pupils and teachers, can be seen in the Statistical Survey (*above*).

Elementary Education

Starts at the age of 7 and is divided into junior school which consists of four grades and the senior school consisting of three grades, previously known as Junior Secondary Education. From 1955 on the Ministry of Education made an annual provision in the budget so that every district would have at least one primary extension school. These efforts have now spread to the villages, resulting in the opening of about a hundred schools of this type every year.

Secondary Education

Aims at providing knowledge and skills to enable pupils to carry out an occupation or to prepare them for further education. Secondary education is divided into the lower and upper schools, each having no more than three grades. There are three streams: the first, general, stream is designed to give instruction in theoretical subjects and is not concerned directly with occupational skills. The second, vocational, stream is designed to prepare students with knowledge and skills for directly taking up specific occupations. There is also a teacher-training stream at secondary level. In the field of secondary school improvements, an experimental comprehensive school project has been initiated; there were twenty comprehensive schools in 1971. Secondary school enrollment has increased to nearly 17 per cent of the secondary age group in 1971.

Higher Education

At present there are thirteen universities in Thailand, offering both undergraduate and graduate courses in all fields. There remains a shortage of university places, although university enrolment increased to approximately 50,000 in 1973. The enrolment of women, although small, increased faster than that of men. Since 1966 higher education has been expanded and extended to different parts of the country; the above figures include the Prince of Songkla University in the south, founded in 1964, the Open University of Ramkhamhaeng, founded in 1971 and expected to enrol 50,000 students, and the Pra Chom Klao Institute of Technology, now to be the centre of higher technical education in Thailand. In addition, four new Colleges of Education were inaugurated between 1967–69. Other higher education establishments include the various Military and Police Academies providing a standard of training equivalent to that of civil establishments, and teacher-training establishments. In 1974 it was announced that a number of educational institutions which previously offered only post-secondary diploma programmes were to be allowed to award degrees. This would double the number of universities and degree-awarding colleges in Thailand.

Rural Education

Expansion of rural education has been an important project to stem the increasing flow of students to the cities, especially Bangkok. For this purpose the Ministry of Education set up the Regional Education Development Project, including higher education in its terms of reference. The Education Broadcasting Service has been functioning since 1954 to give schoolchildren and teachers as well as the public general education and educational news. In 1958 school broadcasting was begun covering such subjects as civics, music and English. At present over 1,300 schools have made use of this service, which it is hoped to extend, especially to schools in remoter areas.

Much has been done for the improvement in both quality and quantity of vocational training throughout the country. Short-term vocational courses are given in more rural areas, and new multi-vocational mobile schools have been tried out giving such courses as dressmaking, hairdressing, cooking, etc. Another innovation is the Special Agricultural School for the self-help settlements, designed to give such settlers a basic knowledge of agriculture.

UNIVERSITIES

Asian Institute of Technology: P.O.B. 2754, Bangkok; f. 1959; 70 teachers, 400 students.

Chiangmai University: Chiangmai; f. 1963; 700 teachers, 7,100 students.

Chulalongkorn University: Phya Thai Rd., Bangkok; 1,630 teachers, 15,230 students.

Kasetsart University: Bangkhen, Bangkok; 840 teachers, 6,900 students.

Khonkaen University: Khonkaen; f. 1966; 425 teachers, 2,200 students.

King Mongkut's Institute of Technology: Rasburana, Bangkok 6; *c.* 100 teachers, *c.* 1,060 students.

Mahidol University: Siriraj Hospital, Thonburi, Bangkok; *c.* 900 teachers, *c.* 4,320 students.

Prince of Songkla University: Songkla; f. 1964; 280 teachers, 1,060 students.

Ramkhamhaeng University: Hua Mark, Bangkok 10; f. 1971.

Silpakorn University: Na Pra Dhat Rd.; f. 1943; 2,700 students.

Sri Nakharinwirot University: Bangkok; f. 1954; 305 teachers, *c.* 5,000 students.

Thammasat University: Bangkok; 685 teachers, 10,760 students.

BIBLIOGRAPHY

General

AUDRIC, J. Siam: Land of Temples (Robert Hale, London, 1962).

BARNETT, D. The Mask of Siam (Robert Hale, London, 1959).

BARTLETT, N. Land of the Lotus Eaters (The Adventures Club, London, 1959).

BLANCHARD, W. Thailand: Its People, Its Society, Its Culture (Human Relations Area Files, New Haven, 1958).

BLOFELD, P. J. People of the Sun (Hutchinson, London, 1960).

BUSCH, N. F. Thailand: An Introduction to Modern Siam (Van Nostrand, New York, 1959).

COUGHLIN, R. J. Double Identity: The Chinese in Modern Thailand (Hong Kong University Press, Hong Kong, 1960).

CRIPPS, F. The Far Province (Hutchinson, London, 1965).

DE YOUNG, J. E. Village Life in Modern Thailand (University of California Press, Berkeley, 1955).

EXELL, F. K. The Land and People of Thailand (A. & C. Black, London, 1960).

Government of Thailand, Thailand Official Year Book 1968 (Government House Printing Office, Bangkok, 1968).

GRAHAM, W. A. Siam (Alexander Morning, London, 1924).

KRULL, G. Bangkok: Siam's City of Angels (Robert Hale, London, 1964).

NACH, J. Thailand in Pictures (Oak Tree Press, London, 1963).

PENDLETON, R. L., and KINGSBURY, R. C. Thailand: Aspects of Landscape and Life (Duell, Sloan & Pearce, New York, 1962).

SEIDENFADEN, E. The Thai Peoples (The Siam Society, Bangkok, 1963).

SRISVASDI, B. C. The Hill Tribes of Siam (Khun Aroon, Bangkok, 1963).

THOMPSON, V. Thailand: The New Siam (New York, 1941).

WATSON, J. W. Thailand: Rice Bowl of Asia (Garrad Publishing Co., Illinois, 1966).

History

CADY, J. F. Thailand, Burma, Laos and Cambodia (Prentice-Hall Inc., Englewood Cliffs, New Jersey, U.S.A., 1966).

CHAKRABONGSE, Prince CHULA. Lords of Life: the Paternal Monarchy of Bangkok, 1782–1932 (Taplinger, New York and Alvin Redman, London, 1960).

CROSBY, Sir JOSIAH. Siam: The Crossroads (Hollis & Carter, London, 1945).

FISTIE, P. L'Evolution de la Thailande Contemporaine (Paris, 1967).

NUECHTERLEIN, D. E. Thailand and the Struggle for South-East Asia (Cornell University Press, Ithaca, New York, 1965).

WOOD, W. A. R. A History of Siam (Chalermnit, Bangkok, 1959).

Economics and Politics

INGRAM, J. C. Economic Change in Thailand since 1850 (Stanford University Press, Stanford, Calif., 1955).

INSOR, D. Thailand: A Political, Social and Economic Analysis (Allen & Unwin, London, 1963).

MOUSNY, A. The Economy of Thailand: An Appraisal of a Liberal Exchange Policy (Social Science Asscn. Press of Thailand, Bangkok, 1964).

MUSCAT, R. J. Development Strategy in Thailand: A Study of Economic Growth (Pall Mall Press, London, 1966).

NAIRN, R. C. International Aid to Thailand: The New Colonialism (Yale University Press, New York, 1967).

REEVE, W. D. Public Administration in Siam (Royal Institute of International Affairs, London, 1951).

RIGGS, F. W. Thailand: The Modernization of a Bureaucratic Polity (East-West Center Press, Honolulu, 1966).

SIFFIN, W. J. The Thai Bureaucracy: Institutional Change and Development (East-West Center Press, Honolulu, 1966).

SILCOCK, T. H. (ed.). Thailand: Social and Economic Studies in Development (Australian National University Press, Canberra, 1967).

WILSON, D. A. Politics in Thailand (Cornell University Press, New York, 1962).

Viet-Nam

PHYSICAL AND SOCIAL GEOGRAPHY

C. A. Fisher

(Revised by the Editor, 1976)

Viet-Nam covers a total area of 332,559 square kilometres (128,402 square miles) and lies along the western shore of the South China Sea, bordered by the People's Republic of China to the north, by Laos to the west and Cambodia to the south-west.

PHYSICAL FEATURES

The fundamental geographical outlines of the country have been likened to two bags of rice hanging from a pole, with the deltas and immediate hinterlands of the Mekong and Songkoi (Red River) linked by the mountain backbone and adjacent coastal lowlands of Annam.

Of the two rivers which are thus of major significance in the geography of Viet-Nam, the Songkoi, rising like the Mekong in southwestern China, is much the shorter, and its delta, together with that of a series of lesser rivers, forms a total area of some 14,500 square kilometres, which is less than half that of the great Mekong delta in the south. Besides the delta, north Viet-Nam also includes a much more extensive area of rugged upland, mainly in the north and west, which represents a southward continuation of the Yunnan and adjacent plateaux of southwestern China, and forms an inhospitable and sparsely populated divide, some 900 to 1,500 metres high, between north Viet-Nam and northern Laos.

Both the Songkoi and its main right-bank tributary, the Songbo (Black River), flow in parallel N.W./S.E. gorges through this upland before their confluence some 100 kilometres above the apex of the delta, while a third main river, the Songma, also follows a parallel course still farther to the south, beyond which rises the similarly N.W./S.E. trending Annamite Chain or Cordillera. This, in relief if not in structure, constitutes a further prolongation of the massive upland system already described, and extends without a break to within about 150 kilometres of the Mekong delta.

With an average breadth of 150 kilometres, and an extremely rugged and heavily forested surface, at many points exceeding 1,500 metres in altitude, the Annamite Chain, which lies mainly in southern Viet-Nam, provides an effective divide between the Annam coast and the middle Mekong valley of southern Laos and eastern Cambodia. Moreover, from the Porte d'Annam (lat. 18° N.) southwards, the Chain not only reaches to within a few miles of the coast, but also sends off a series of spurs which terminate in rocky headlands overlooking the sea. Thus, along the 1,000-kilometre stretch of coast between latitudes 18° and 11° N., the continuity of the coastal plain is repeatedly interrupted and it dwindles to an average width of less than 16 km. and often to less than half that figure. But thereafter it broadens out to merge with the vast deltaic plain of the Mekong and its associated natural waterways, the whole forming an almost dead flat surface covering some 37,800 square kilometres.

CLIMATE

In forming the western hinterland of the South China Sea virtually from the tropic of Cancer to within 9° N. of the equator, Viet-Nam might be assumed to be wholly within the zone of the tropical monsoon climate. But while the greater part of the country does merit such a designation, and Hué, practically at the mid-point of the coastal zone, has a mean monthly temperature range from 20°C. in January to 30°C. in August, and a total rainfall of 260 cm., of which 165 cm. falls during September–November inclusive, the Songkoi delta in the north is not strictly tropical in the climatological sense. For owing to its exposure to cold northern air during the season of the N.E. monsoon, it experiences a recognizable cool season from December to March, and in both January and February the mean monthly temperatures in Hanoi are only 17°C. This fact is of great practical importance since the cooler weather gives greater effectiveness to the 13–15 cm. of rain which fall during these months, and so makes it possible to raise a "winter" as well as a summer crop of rice in this part of the country.

NATURAL RESOURCES

In terms of agricultural potential, the two deltas are of overwhelming importance.

The uplands offer far less opportunity for supporting population and have been almost completely avoided, not only because of the extremely restricted prospects they afford for wet rice cultivation but also because of their intensely malarial character. These facts are in part inter-related, for the anopheles mosquito, which carries malaria, does not flourish in the muddy water of paddy fields. In respect of mineral wealth, on the other hand, the uplands, particularly in the north, contains a wide variety of lesser metalic ores, and also some useful apatite (a source of phosphates), though economically the most important mineral is in the anthracite field of Quang-Yen, which occurs in an area of Mesozoic folding immediately to the north-east of the Songkoi delta.

Oil has been discovered onshore in the north and offshore in the south.

POPULATION AND ETHNIC GROUPS

Of the two parts of Viet-Nam, the north contains the larger population, with 23,780,375 and an average density of 150 per square kilometre (April 1974 census), compared with the south's 19,954,000 and a density of 115 in 1973. These average densities are, however, very misleading, first because the great majority of the population (and practically all of the Vietnamese proper) in both halves of the country live within the lowlands, and secondly because the lowlands comprise rather more than one-third of the total area of south Viet-Nam, but barely one-sixth of that of north Viet-Nam. Thus, whereas most of the vast Mekong delta supports rural densities varying from 40 to 200 to the square kilometre, the comparable figures for the Songkoi delta are between four and five times as great.

On the other hand it is the south which shows the higher degree of urbanization. The north has only three of the twelve towns which in 1963 had populations exceeding 50,000. In the south the huge Saigon-

fucianism and Mahayana Buddhism also took deep

habitants while the two largest cities of the north, namely the capital, Hanoi, and its port, Haiphong, have 1,200,000 and 500,000 respectively, as estimated in June 1969.

Vietnamese, who are ethnically close kinsfolk of the southern Chinese, form the overwhelming majority of the population. In the north they account for 90 per cent, the remainder including approximately a million Thais and some 400,000 Meo, Tho and Nung tribesmen, nearly all of whom live in the hills of the west and north. In the south the Vietnamese proportion drops to 80 per cent, and in addition there are approximately a million hill peoples, most of whom are collectively referred to as Moi, and about half a million Cambodians mainly near the southwestern border. There are over 800,000 Chinese in the south, primarily concentrated in Cholon, whereas the north, which never afforded comparable opportunities for immigrant middlemen, has a Chinese population of only 100,000.

HISTORY

Ralph Smith

EARLY HISTORY

The Vietnamese trace their history back to the Hung Vuong kings who are said to have ruled in what is now northern Viet-Nam during the third or second millennium B.C. For a long time it was thought that such a dynasty was purely legendary, but recent archaeological work suggests that Viet-Nam had at least some kind of distinctive bronze age civilization, perhaps by 1000 B.C. The earliest written evidence records that a country called Au-Lac in that area was conquered by the first Chinese emperor and founder of the Ch'in dynasty, Shih Huang-ti, about 214 B.C. But its relationship to China at that period was probably rather distant, and its material culture—characterized by the famous "Dong-Son" bronze drums—shows closer affinities with that of Yunnan. After a period of dependence on the south Chinese kingdom of Nan-Yueh (or Nam-Viet) from 207 to 112 B.C., the present northern Viet-Nam became incorporated into the Chinese Han empire and remained effectively a province of China for about a thousand years.

An anti-Chinese revolt led by the Trung Sisters in A.D. 41 was followed by a tightening of control by the Han. Likewise the revolt of Ly Bon in 542 was followed by the T'ang period (618–907), when the province of An-nam ("pacified South") was absorbed even more firmly into the Chinese cultural sphere. During these centuries of Han and T'ang rule, there occurred a gradual fusion of Vietnamese and Chinese ideas and institutions. The Chinese language was introduced, although it did not entirely supplant Vietnamese. The Chinese religions of Taoism, Confucianism and Mahayana Buddhism also took deep root.

When the T'ang empire broke up early in the tenth century South China came under the rule of the independent dynasty of Nan-Han, which in 923 extended its control to Viet-Nam. But that control was not easy to maintain; the Nan-Han army was defeated in 931 and 938, and it is from the latter year, when Ngo Quyen became king, that the Vietnamese usually date their independence from Chinese rule. In 981 the new Sung dynasty of China tried to take advantage of internal Vietnamese conflicts to reimpose Chinese rule, but it too was defeated. During the next four centuries Viet-Nam (or Dai-Viet) gradually developed into a strong and fairly centralized state, with a capital in Hanoi and institutions modelled on those of China. It was not yet wholly "Confucianized" however; Mahayana Buddhism played an important part in the life of court and people, and twentieth-century Vietnamese Buddhists look back to the eleventh and twelfth centuries as the golden age of their religion. Thus, under the dynasties of the Ly (1009–1225) and Tran (1225–1400), Dai-Viet was strong enough to resist further Chinese attempts at reconquest: by the Sung in 1075–77, and by the Yuan (the Mongols) in the years 1282–88. In the late fourteenth and early fifteenth centuries the kingdom went through a period of difficulties, and when a new Chinese attack came in 1407 it succumbed. But not for long; after twenty years the Chinese were once more driven out by Le Loi, founder of the Le dynasty (1428–1789).

Meanwhile, in what is now Central Viet-Nam there flourished the kingdom of Champa, with a culture strongly influenced by Hinduism; as was that of the Khmer (Cambodian) kingdom, to which the whole of the Mekong delta then belonged (though the Cambodians later adopted Theravada Buddhism). The remains of Cham temples dating from the ninth to the thirteenth centuries, very Indian in appearance, still survive along the central Vietnamese coast. The Chams were frequently at war with the Vietnamese, from the tenth century onwards, but on the whole were the losers in most campaigns. Dai-Viet annexed areas of Cham territory in 1070, 1306 and 1470; by the latter year Champa was reduced to a small principality, which was finally extinguished altogether in 1695. But as the Vietnamese kingdom expanded, it found increasing difficulty in maintaining its own unity.

CONFLICTS, DIVISION AND UNIFICATION

The fifteenth century, and especially the reign of Le Thanh Tong (1459–97), was the "golden age" of Confucian culture in Viet-Nam and a period of general stability. But in the early sixteenth century the kingdom began to break up under the stress of conflict between rival clans, one of which established the Mac dynasty (1527–92) but failed to keep control of the whole country. Later the Le were restored to the throne, but not to power. After the intermittent civil war of the sixteenth century, the seventeenth saw a more lasting division of Viet-Nam between two powerful clans: the Trinh in the north and the Nguyen in the south (i.e. central Viet-Nam). The latter resisted a series of Trinh attempts to conquer them (1627–77) and maintained their independence down to 1775. It was the Nguyen who led the way in a further southward expansion. A series of wars with Cambodia beginning about 1658 enabled them to annex much of the lower Mekong delta by 1760, thus establishing their control over the greater part of what is now south Viet-Nam.

In the 1770s, however, the Nguyen were overthrown by a combination of the Tay-Son rebellion, which broke out at Qui-Nhon in 1773, and a new invasion by the Trinh. The whole country was now thrown into a state of civil war, for although the Tay-Son proved capable of establishing a new dynasty and of repelling a Chinese invasion in 1789, they could not bring new stability. The last Nguyen survivor returned to recapture Saigon in 1789, and from there went on to conquer the centre and north by 1802. He proclaimed himself emperor at Hué, with the title Gia-Long, and for the first time in its history the present area of Viet-Nam was brought under the control of a single ruler. It was under Gia-Long (1802–20) and Minh-Mang (1820–41) that Hué acquired the status and the architectural adornments of an imperial capital.

Under Gia-Long the new unity was precarious, and the governors of Tonkin and Cochinchina were allowed considerable independence. Minh-Mang, more orthodox a Confucian than his father, was also more ambitious. When Le Van Duyet, governor of Saigon, died in 1832, the emperor sought to impose a more uniform administrative structure. The immediate consequence was a serious revolt in Cochinchina, lasting from 1833 to 1835; but once it was suppressed Minh-Mang was able to have his way, and for a few years even extended his control to embrace much of Cambodia. At the time of his death, Viet-Nam had the widest extent in the whole of its history. His successor, Thieu-Tri (1841–47), soon lost Cambodia, though he maintained the power of Hué over Viet-Nam itself. But the trend towards centralization and administrative development suffered a set-back with the succession conflict that followed his death, which led to the elevation to the throne of a much younger ruler, Tu-Duc (1847–83). It was in his reign that the Vietnamese came face-to-face with the challenge of imperialist France.

Gia-Long, who had used French advisers in his campaigns before 1802, was willing to tolerate Christianity. Minh-Mang was not, and by 1833 he had instituted a persecution as severe as any the missionaries had faced since they first came to Viet-Nam in the seventeenth century. It was because of this that when Minh-Mang chose to send an embassy to France in 1840, it was refused an audience by the king. The persecution continued under Thieu-Tri and Tu-Duc, and in the meantime French embassies to Hué were brushed aside. Finally, in 1858, a Franco-Spanish fleet attacked Tourane (Danang). The following year the same force directed its attentions to Saigon, and by the end of 1860 the French were virtually in possession of three provinces of Cochinchina. After some hesitation they decided to hold on to them, and their annexation was formally recognized by Tu-Duc in 1862. But relations with the Europeans continued to be bad, and in 1867 the French annexed another three provinces. In 1873 a French force attacked Hanoi and captured the citadel, but then withdrew on orders from home. A new Franco-Vietnamese treaty was signed in 1874, recognizing French possession of all Cochinchina but otherwise giving the French little of substance. It was not until 1882–83 that the French finally occupied Tonkin (Tongking) again, and imposed a treaty of "protection" on the Vietnamese empire. Two years later, after a border war with China, the French secured Chinese recognition of their Protectorate. For although Viet-Nam had been independent of China for the past nine hundred years, it had recognized Chinese overlordship by sending regular tribute for most of that time.

FRENCH RULE AND VIETNAMESE OPPOSITION

Thus by 1885 the whole of Viet-Nam was under French colonial rule: Cochinchina, in the south, as a directly administered colony; Tongking and Annam (the north and centre) as protectorates. In 1887 they were united with Cambodia to form the Indochinese Union, to which Laos was added in 1893. The government-general of the Union was at first somewhat nebulous, but in the years 1897-1901 it was transformed by Paul Doumer into an effective central authority with financial control over the whole of Indochina. The French administration promoted economic development in certain spheres, such as the mining of coal and minerals in Tongking, the cultivation of rubber and other plantation crops in the hill areas, the export of rice from Cochinchina, and the construction of several railways. They also created several new towns, notably Saigon and Hanoi, which for a time were alternate capitals of the Union and which attracted the growth of a small urban, French-educated elite amongst the Vietnamese population. In the countryside, on the other hand, the peasantry did not benefit much from French rule. Their taxes were increased several times from about 1897, without very much attention being paid to helping them to raise productivity. During the 1930s, with the economic slump followed by a new inflation, the economic condition of the peasantry declined seriously and many of the poor and landless villagers became permanently indebted to their richer neighbours. The political developments of the 1930s and 1940s must be seen against this background of social conflict. At the same time the development of French education tended to undermine traditional values and to make economic inequalities more transparent.

Opposition to French rule was essentially "traditional" before about 1900: a long sequence of local risings led by scholars or military men who had had some status in the old society, but who had no effective means of defeating the new régime. The period produced several celebrated heroes: notably Truong Cong Dinh, Phan Dinh Phung and Hoang Hoa Tham. During the first decade of the twentieth century a new opposition movement began, characterized by political associations strongly influenced by the model of Japanese modernization and by Chinese revolutionary aspirations. But an anti-taxation revolt and a nationalist education movement in 1907–08 were both suppressed by the French. The two most prominent leaders of this period spent long years in exile. Phan Chau Trinh, at first imprisoned after the events of 1908, was obliged to live in France and returned only when he was dying in 1926. Phan Boi Chau, who wrote many revolutionary and nationalist pamphlets, lived for a time in China and also visited Japan; he was arrested in Shanghai in 1925 and spent the rest of his life under confinement at Hué.

The growth of constitutionalist opposition to Western colonial rule throughout Asia, from about 1916, was reflected in Viet-Nam by the Constitutionalist Party founded in Cochinchina in 1917. The party participated in elections for the Colonial Council, but was not allowed to operate outside Cochinchina: the French did not permit an all-Indochina constitutional opposition movement comparable to the Congress Party in India. Consequently from about 1925 Vietnamese nationalism began to produce revolutionary organizations, some of which became Communist. In 1930 it also found expression in a number of open revolts. A rising known as the Yen-Bay mutiny, started by the Nationalist Party in Tongking in February 1930, was quickly suppressed; so too was a strike movement in certain areas at the beginning of May. But a peasant movement which developed in summer 1930 in parts of Cochinchina and in Nghe-An, Ha-Tinh and other parts of Annam, reached more serious proportions. It was organized largely by the Indochinese Communist Party, which had grown out of a number of organizations developing from 1925 onwards and was formally founded in 1930. The movement lasted into 1931 and is generally known as the "Nghe-Tinh Soviets". It was the first occasion when the French used air power to maintain control, and it was suppressed with some ferocity. As a result many Communist leaders, including several members of the North Vietnamese politburo after 1954, spent the years 1930–36 in prison.

Political life in the early 1930s was somewhat subdued, but no serious efforts were made towards constitutional advancement until 1936, when the Popular Front government in France allowed an amnesty of political prisoners and a measure of press freedom and open political activity. Among those who took advantage of it to organize meetings and to write articles were Pham Van Dong, Vo Nguyen Giap and Dang Xuan Khu (now known as Truong Chinh). Also during this period a Trotskyist movement grew up, with a strong following in Cochinchina, under the leadership of Ta Thu Thau and Nguyen An Ninh. They joined with the pro-Comintern (Stalinist) Communists in attempting to hold an all-Indochina Congress in 1937, but it was quickly suppressed. With the outbreak of war in Europe in 1939, the various left-wing groups were again banned. The Trotskyist and some Stalinist leaders were imprisoned, and Pham Van Dong and Vo Nguyen Giap escaped eventually to southern China. But in the north, at least, the Communists managed to maintain a secret network of cells throughout the war period under the leadership of Truong Chinh.

A different type of political movement which developed in the south during the 1920s and 1930s was associated with a number of religious sects whose beliefs were partly apocalyptic and partly spiritualistic. The Caodaists, formally established in 1926, founded a "holy see" at Tay-Ninh, although they subsequently split up into a number of smaller sects. The Hoa-Hao Buddhists, who traced their origins back to the Buu-Son Ky-Huong secret society movement of 1913–16, were reorganized by a new leader in 1939. These groups tended to look towards Japan for political inspiration and support. Also during the 1930s there was a more orthodox revival of Mahayana Buddhism in all regions of Viet-Nam, although it did not play an active role in politics until the 1960s. In addition, Catholicism made considerable progress under the French, so that by 1954 there were probably over two million Vietnamese Catholics.

REVOLUTION, WAR AND PARTITION

It is to the period 1941–46 that we must look for the events which have shaped the recent history of Viet-Nam. In 1940 the Japanese obliged the French to allow them to use military facilities in northern Indochina, and in July 1941 they advanced in strength into southern Indochina. Administrative control, however, was left in French hands, with

Admiral Decoux acting as governor and accepting the authority of Vichy France. Among the Vietnamese, pro-Japanese groups gained ground, notably the Cochinchinese sects and the new Dai-Viet (Great Viet-Nam) Party. The Japanese finally overthrew the French administration and disarmed its forces in March 1945, in order to avoid them playing any role that would assist the allies in the closing stages of the war. At Japanese behest, the Emperor Bao-Dai revoked the treaties of 1884–85 which had made Annam and Tongking into protectorates, and proclaimed his independence. It was not until August, however, that he was permitted to revoke the treaties concerning Cochinchina, signed in 1862 and 1874. In April 1945, Bao-Dai appointed a new government headed by the pro-Japanese Tran Trong Kim, which made some effort to institute reforms. But in war conditions, with most communications destroyed by American bombing, it was unable to control the country effectively and could do hardly anything about the famine which had afflicted northern Viet-Nam since late in 1944.

Meanwhile in South China a number of Vietnamese political groups were active, of which the Communists were by far the most effective and the only ones in touch with a solid movement within the country. Their leader in China was Ho Chi Minh, who as Nguyen Ai Quoc had played a significant part in founding the Indochinese Communist Party in 1930 and who now returned from Moscow as its Comintern-appointed leader. In June 1941 a meeting between the Chinese-based leaders and the leaders of the party still active in Tongking, at a place near the border of Viet-Nam and Kwangsi, marked the foundation of the Viet-Nam Doc Lap Dong Minh Hoi (Revolutionary League for the Independence of Viet-Nam), usually known as the Viet-Minh. During the next few years the Communists sought to establish two base areas in northern Tongking and survived a series of French punitive campaigns against them.

In spring 1945, after a period of imprisonment at the hands of the Chinese Nationalists, Ho Chi Minh made contact with the American OSS and obtained their material assistance (although very little in the way of weapons) in expanding his base areas inside Tongking. When the Japanese overthrew the French regime, the Viet-Minh were ready to take advantage of an increasingly chaotic situation, and in August they emerged as the most effective political force within the country.

When the Japanese surrendered, the Viet-Minh decided to act quickly and by August 20th were in control of Hanoi. The next few days saw their flag raised in many provinces throughout the country, and on August 24th Bao-Dai (at Hué) abdicated in their favour. The defeated Japanese acquiesced in this change, and on September 2nd, 1945, Ho Chi Minh, as president of the new provisional government, read the Declaration of Independence which marked the foundation of the Democratic Republic of Viet-Nam. In the next month, the Viet-Minh leaders carried out the first stages of what amounted to a political and social revolution. Inevitably, however, they were stronger in the North, where they had been active throughout the war. In the South they had only a loosely arranged front organization, in which their allies and rivals included the formerly pro-Japanese sects and various other small groups. Their Provisional Committee took over in Saigon but was not very firmly established in power.

The Allies had agreed at the Potsdam Conference that the Japanese surrender would be received by the Chinese in the northern half of Indochina and by the British in the south. This led to the temporary occupation of Viet-Nam by British and by Chinese nationalist forces, respectively south and north of the sixteenth parallel: the first contingents of both arrived about September 20th. In the south, Franco-British co-operation made it relatively easy for the French to recover control in Saigon and to land reinforcements there in October. By the end of the year the British zone was virtually in their hands, apart from a number of rural areas where guerrillas held out; the British themselves left early in 1946. In the north, the French had to negotiate first with the Chinese, who agreed to withdraw in March 1946, and then with the Viet-Minh government in Hanoi. The latter had survived, still under the presidency of Ho Chi Minh, despite the presence of Chinese troops and of various Vietnamese nationalist parties which had Chinese support. Elections for a National Assembly were held in the north, and some parts of the south, in January 1946. The Viet-Minh dominated the polls, although they reserved a number of seats for Nationalist members, and they had the upper hand in the coalition government formed in February 1946. The withdrawal of the Chinese troops in the next few months left the Nationalists with very little power. In the meantime, the regime attempted a number of reforms: it took firm measures to prevent a recurrence of the famine of 1944–45, and it conducted an extensive literacy campaign. The significance of the revolutionary changes in that period has probably been underestimated by Western commentators.

Negotiations between the French and the Viet-Minh permitted the return of a French army to Tongking in the spring of 1946, and culminated in a conference at Fontainebleau in July. But this failed to produce agreement, and a semi-formal *modus vivendi* broke down by the end of the year. The Haiphong incident of November 20th–27th, 1946, was followed by an attempted Viet-Minh rising in Hanoi on December 19th. By then the French had sufficient troops in the north to defeat the rising, and the Viet-Minh withdrew to the countryside to plan a more protracted guerrilla war based on the tactics which Mao Tse-tung had begun to use so effectively in China. Their leaders narrowly escaped capture in 1947, but then began to build up their strength and by 1950 were in a position seriously to challenge the French. On their side, the French decided against the creation of a separate state of Cochinchina in 1946, and began a series of negotiations with Vietnamese anti-Communists (including Bao-Dai) which led to the establishment of the Associated State of Viet-Nam in 1949. If the French could recover firm control over the country, it was to be united under the new régime with France retaining control of defence and other key decisions. The new state had a succession of prime ministers between then and 1954, and was internationally recognized by the Western powers early in 1950. At about the same time, China and the Soviet Union recognized the Democratic Republic of Viet-Nam.

The war situation was transformed in 1950–51. Communist victories in China gave Viet-Nam a common frontier with a Communist state, and the United States responded by offering aid to the French side. The Communist Party re-emerged in 1951 with the holding of a new congress (in the *maquis*) by the newly formed Viet-Nam Workers' (Lao-Dong) Party, and the conflict took on a "cold war" dimension. Despite defeats at Vinh-Yen and Dong-Trieu in early 1951, the Viet-Minh armies gained in strength and by the end of 1953 the French Government was increasingly unable to cope with the situation. The military climax came with the siege of Dien-Bien-Phu, a fortress-encampment near the Laos border, which fell to the Viet-Minh in May 1954.

In the meantime the great powers had agreed on an international conference in Geneva, which began its deliberations on Indochina just as Dien-Bien-Phu fell. On July 21st, 1954, a ceasefire agreement was signed by representatives of the French and Viet-Minh high commands, and an international declaration by 14 governments set forth conditions for an eventual political settlement, including a provision for national elections in July 1956. Both the agreement and the (unsigned) declaration made clear that the partition was purely military and that politically Viet-Nam remained one country. But in effect two zones were created, to be administered by the two existing Vietnamese governments: that of the Democratic Republic in Hanoi, that of the State of Viet-Nam in Saigon, with the seventeenth parallel as the boundary between them. A period of three hundred days was allowed for regroupment, during which between 30,000 and 100,000 people moved north whilst perhaps 800,000 people (mainly Catholics) moved to the South.

SOUTH VIET-NAM

The State of Viet-Nam, originally within the French Union, made an independence agreement with France in June 1954. After the ceasefire agreements at Geneva in July, French forces withdrew, leaving the State's jurisdiction limited to the zone south of 17° N. Complete sovereignty was transferred by France in December 1954.

For a little over twenty years after the Geneva agreements, the area south of the seventeenth parallel remained a separate state with an anti-communist administration supported by the United States. A French community continued to look after its own interests there, notably the large rubber estates north of Saigon. But economically, culturally, and above all militarily, South Viet-Nam moved out of the French world into the American sphere of influence, developing much closer relations with other pro-American states: the Philippines, Thailand, South Korea. It very soon became dependent for its survival on American aid.

From 1954 to 1963, the politics of South Viet-Nam were dominated by Ngo Dinh Diem and his brother Nhu. Coming from a family of Catholic mandarins (a combination characteristic of the colonial period), Diem had been a minister at Hué briefly in 1933 but had since become strongly anti-French, as well as being deeply anti-communist. From the American point of view this made him an apparently ideal choice for leadership of a nationalist state in Viet-Nam, and he became Prime Minister at their behest in June 1954. For the next year and more his position was very insecure; but after careful political manoeuvring and several street battles, he defeated the leaders of the sects and of the Binh-Xuyen secret society that had controlled the Saigon underworld. In October 1955 he was strong enough to hold a referendum, whose result enabled him to depose Bao-Dai and to proclaim himself President of the Republic of Viet-Nam. He went on to repudiate the Geneva declaration and to reject any idea of holding the elections which it had envisaged for July 1956. During the next few years, he set about destroying the Viet-Minh (or, as he labelled it, Viet-Cong) network in the South. By 1959, the Communists and their sympathizers who had remained in the South in 1954 were under severe pressure from the Diem regime; numbers of them were imprisoned, along with many more "suspects". It was probably during 1959 that the Communists, with the approval of Hanoi, decided to fight back by means of a low-level guerrilla war which would at least prevent their total annihilation. By 1960 it became clear that there would be a serious armed confrontation between the two sides, and in December of that year the Communists created the National Front for the Liberation of South Viet-Nam, to unite opposition to Diem.

American determination to prevent any communist advance in South-East Asia led President Kennedy to take a firm line during 1961–62. The Staley Mission to Viet-Nam produced a plan which was implemented during those years, and by the end of 1962 there were about 8,000 American troops serving as advisers to the South Vietnamese army. During 1963 this conflict became even more intense. But by that time American confidence in Ngo Dinh Diem himself was beginning to decline. In May 1963 a Buddhist demonstration in Hué precipitated a conflict between the Catholic President and the Buddhist sects. The Americans withdrew support from Diem, and in November 1963 he was overthrown by a military coup with their tacit approval. But a change of government in Saigon was no solution to the principal problem for the United States: how to protect the Saigon Government against a growing rural guerrilla movement. During the autumn of 1963 the communists adopted a more offensive strategy and by the end of the year the situation for Saigon was precarious. Nor was it easy to create a stable regime with Diem gone. A second military coup in January 1964 brought to power

General Nguyen Khanh. But he retained his dominant position for barely a year, during which he was almost overthrown by the other generals in August 1964 when he tried to make himself president. In February 1965 he was forced out by a group of younger officers led by the air force commander, Nguyen Cao Ky. The last of a series of short-lived military regimes was the National Leadership Committee, established in June 1965, with Lt.-Gen. Nguyen Van Thieu as Chairman and Air Vice-Marshal Ky as Prime Minister.

By that time the Americans had made up their minds to reinforce the Saigon government by sending their own combat troops to fight in Viet-Nam. An incident involving American ships in the Gulf of Tongking in August 1964 enabled President Johnson to obtain virtually a free hand from Congress, and he used the power granted to him at that time to deal with the Vietnamese situation without any formal declaration of war. The number of American forces in Viet-Nam increased from 23,000 at the beginning of 1965 to over half a million by March 1968; in addition, contingents were sent from South Korea, Australia, the Philippines and Thailand. The conflict, as a result, escalated into a war of major proportions, with the Communists obliged to draw increasing support from North Viet-Nam, and beyond that from China and the Soviet Union. In addition to sending troops to the South, the Americans also bombed the North from the air, beginning in March 1965.

Escalation of the war continued during 1966 and 1967, but those years also saw the gradual return of a measure of stability to the political scene in Saigon, where Nguyen Cao Ky defeated a Buddhist revolt during the spring of 1966. Out of the crisis, there emerged the promise of a new constitution for South Viet-Nam, and it came into effect in 1967. As a result General Nguyen Van Thieu was elected President in September 1967, with Marshal Ky as his Vice-President; elections were also held for the upper and lower houses of a legislature based on the American model. Thieu remained the President from October 1967 until April 1975, being re-elected unopposed (after splitting with Marshal Ky) in October 1971.

The war reached a crisis point in January-February 1968, when the Communists launched an offensive to coincide with the lunar New Year (known as *Tet*). It was on a larger scale than any previous operation, and included attacks on Saigon, Hué and several other towns. There was also heavy fighting just south of the seventeenth parallel. The *Tet* offensive, although only a partial success, forced the United States to reconsider its policy. It is now clear that Secretary of Defence Clark Clifford played a key role in the American decision not to send any more troops to Viet-Nam, despite the request of General William Westmoreland, commander of the U.S. Military Assistance Command, for an additional 200,000 men. At the end of March 1968 President Johnson announced a partial cessation of bombing raids over North Viet-Nam, thus opening the way to talks between American and North Vietnamese representatives which began in Paris in May 1968. The following October, Washington and Hanoi agreed to an enlargement of the talks and the United States thereupon ended completely its bombing raids against the North. Heavy bombing continued, however, to be an essential part of American strategy in the South, and the talks led to no decrease in the fighting.

The transfer of power in the U.S.A. from President Johnson to President Nixon and his foreign policy adviser, Dr. Henry Kissinger, marked a turning-point not only for Viet-Nam, in the long run, but for the whole pattern of negotiations on world-wide issues between the United States and the Soviet Union. Almost immediately, on January 25th, 1969, the informal talks in Paris were transformed into a formal conference between representatives of the United States, North Viet-Nam, South Viet-Nam and the National Liberation Front. In June 1969 the NLF was supplemented by the creation of a new Provisional Revolutionary Government of South Viet-Nam. During 1969–70 the war dragged on. The most important change was that the United States began to withdraw its own troops and to pursue a policy of "Vietnamization". At the same time, fears that the North Vietnamese might take advantage of the withdrawal led to a sequence of American moves which tended in fact to intensify the war. The most spectacular was the invasion of Cambodia in April 1970, following an American-instigated plot to overthrow the Government of Prince Sihanouk in Phnom-Penh. Equally important was the "Lam-Son" operation of February 1971 in Laos, which damaged North Vietnamese supply lines even though it ended in South Vietnamese retreat. By this time the communist war effort in the South was very largely dependent on the presence of North Vietnamese regular troops.

In March 1972, with American forces reduced to about 95,000, the North Vietnamese launched a new offensive which led to some of the most intense fighting of the war. Quang-Tri, the northernmost provincial capital in the South, was totally destroyed: after falling to the Communists in May it was recaptured by the South Vietnamese army in September. There was also fierce fighting at An-Loc, north of Saigon, where the offensive was defeated only with the aid of massive American airpower. American troops were not in the forefront of the ground fighting, but the United States reacted to the offensive by renewing its bombing of the North and by mining Haiphong and other harbours. By September it was clear that the situation had reached stalemate, whilst in the United States itself there was mounting pressure to bring the war to a speedy end. Secret meetings in Paris between Dr. Kissinger and Mr. Le Duc Tho of the Vietnamese Politburo had taken place several times since 1969. They now began to bear fruit, following Dr. Kissinger's visit to Moscow in September 1972. By November an agreement seemed to have been reached; but in December 1972, for reasons which have still to be made clear, American planes conducted the heaviest bombing raids of the war against North Viet-Nam. Only after that was the ceasefire agreement finally signed in Paris in January 1973.

The Paris Agreement provided for the complete withdrawal of all American troops from Viet-Nam, together with the return of American prisoners of war, by the end of March 1973. That part of the agreement was largely fulfilled, although the Communists later accused the United States of keeping some military personnel in Viet-Nam disguised as civilians. But the remaining terms of the agreement, including provisions for political freedom in the South and the creation of a national council of reconciliation and concord, were virtually ignored during the next two years. Further talks between Kissinger and Tho produced a supplementary agreement in June 1973, but the effect was only temporary. For the United States the war was over. Since 1961 they had suffered 45,941 combat deaths and over 10,000 deaths from other causes in Viet-Nam, as well as 150,000 casualties serious enough to require hospital treatment. In the same period, probably well over a million Vietnamese on both sides had been killed in the war.

For the Vietnamese, in any case, the war was not yet over. Despite protests by President Thieu, the Paris Agreement provided for a ceasefire in place, with limitations on the introduction of more arms but without any requirement that North Vietnamese forces be withdrawn from the South. Nor was there any provision for American action to enforce the agreement, and in July 1973 the United States Congress made any further American military action in Indochina illegal. The International Commission set up to supervise the ceasefire was not able to prevent frequent outbreaks of fighting between the two sides, whilst the North Vietnamese were now free to make preparations, in their own liberated areas, for an eventual final offensive. Towards the end of 1974, more serious fighting began and in January 1975 the entire province of Phuoc-Long was taken by the Communists. In March their capture of the highland centre of Ban Me Thuet threw the forces of President Thieu completely off balance and led him to order the virtual evacuation of all the Central Highlands. Within weeks the retreat became a rout, so that by the end of March the Communists controlled Hué and Da-Nang and were advancing southwards along the coast. In April they threatened Saigon, overcoming the only significant resistance at Xuan-Loc. Thieu resigned to be succeeded for a few days by his Vice-President and then by Gen. Duong Van Minh. By April 30th, 1975, the Americans had evacuated the last members of their embassy and other personnel and the Communists had entered Saigon. Although not yet formally reunified, Viet-Nam was now controlled entirely by the Communists and its ideological partition was at an end.

NORTH VIET-NAM

During the same twenty-year period following the Geneva Agreements, Viet-Nam north of the seventeenth parallel underwent a political and social revolution under a Communist-led regime. The first steps towards this were already being taken in the liberated areas from 1953, the date of an Agrarian Reform Law designed to revolutionize the pattern of land distribution and of agricultural production. This land reform programme was interrupted during the period immediately after the Geneva Agreement, but was resumed and completed throughout the North in 1955–56. There has been much controversy about the reform, and the Government subsequently admitted a number of excesses in its application, but its object was to eliminate as a class the landlords and rich peasants who—often through money-lending as much as through actual ownership of land—had dominated the economic life of the villages. Land was confiscated and redistributed, and in many cases the former owners were publicly disgraced. The most significant aspect of the reform was that it made possible a social revolution in the countryside. It was followed in 1959–60 by a movement for co-operativization.

In 1955 Ho Chi Minh visited the U.S.S.R. and China and signed aid agreements with both countries, in preparation for a national economic plan for 1956–57. There followed a Three-Year Plan in 1958–60, and a Five-Year Plan beginning in 1961, both of which made some progress towards developing agricultural and industrial production using a limited amount of material and technical aid from the major Communist countries. But these programmes were always accompanied by a sense of frustration that the southern half of the country, with its agricultural surplus, was separated from the North both politically and economically by the Geneva partition and by the impossibility of implementing those parts of the agreement relating to reunification.

The detailed political history of North Viet-Nam since 1954 has yet to be written, and there is still much that is unknown to outsiders. But it is clear that, within the revolutionary framework of the Lao-Dong party and its objectives, there have been several occasions of conflict within the leadership. Probably the first major crisis occurred in 1957, after it became clear that the South was not going to collapse and that the elections envisaged by the Geneva Agreements for 1956 would never be held. There was a conflict of priorities between the desire to press on with socialist revolution in the North, and the policy of "completing the revolution" in the South and bringing about national reunification. It was probably not finally settled until 1960, when the Hanoi leaders decided on a combination of support for the National Liberation Front in the South, and the simultaneous implementation of the Five-Year Plan in the North.

During 1960, indeed, the political life of the Democratic Republic of Viet-Nam took on a more settled pattern. At the beginning of that year a new Constitution came into effect, and in May elections were held for a new National Assembly to take the place of the one elected in 1946. Its first session in July endorsed a new distribution of power and responsibilities amongst the top leaders, whilst the Third National Congress of the Lao-Dong Party in September 1960 established the broad framework of policy within which the country was to develop, despite the ravages of war, over the next fifteen years. A remarkable feature of the party's history throughout the 20 years since 1954 has been the absence of any major purge within its top leadership, and the fact that, apart from the death of Ho Chi Minh in 1969, it was led throughout that period by essentially the same group which founded the Viet-Minh in 1941. This survival of a group of men who have fought for the revolution from the beginning probably explains the smoothness of the succession to Ho Chi Minh when he died in 1969.

The policy adopted in 1960 assumed a substantial measure of economic and military aid from the Soviet Union, which was apparently negotiated by Ho Chi Minh on a visit to Moscow that year. It meant, however, that the Vietnamese, seeking to continue good relations with both the U.S.S.R. and China, were very vulnerable in the face of a growing split between the two major Communist powers. Ho Chi Minh made every effort to avoid a split, but by 1963 it was impossible to prevent it. The Vietnamese were obliged to take sides when the Nuclear Test Ban treaty was signed in August 1963, and by deciding not to sign they were, in effect, choosing China. Relations with the U.S.S.R. consequently became distant until after the fall of Khrushchev in October 1964, and North Viet-Nam went through a "pro-Chinese" phase. The escalation of the war in the South in 1965, however, made it imperative to secure more Soviet aid, and Hanoi sought to steer a difficult middle path of friendship for both Moscow and Peking for the next ten years.

The North was involved in the war as the "rear area" of the NLF, following a decision in 1960 that the South Vietnamese should, in principle, achieve their own revolution, with as much support from the North as they needed. By 1973 there were 150,000 regular North Vietnamese troops in the South, but their status there continued to be denied. The war seriously disrupted life in the North during the years of American bombing, from March 1965 until November 1968, and again in 1972, from May to October and in December. The latter raids were more devastating than the earlier series, but those of December 1972 also involved serious U.S. aircraft losses. During 1965–66, to defend the economy against this aerial bombardment, the Hanoi Government devised a system of decentralized activity which may well have long-term significance for economic development. But by 1969 it became concerned about the possibility that in a more liberal system, capitalist agriculture might again take root. During 1969–70 Truong Chinh led a movement to create higher-level co-operatives and to limit the encroachments of individualism on the collective system. The war in the South again intensified during 1971–72 and, even after the Paris agreement of January 1973, there continued to be a strong emphasis on combining defence and production. A major offensive in early 1975 extended North Vietnamese control over the entire country by May.

Reconstruction and reunification

During 1975–76, in both North and South, the accent was on reconstruction. It was recognized that the South had still to complete the "national democratic" phase of its revolution, whereas the North had long since entered the stage of socialist revolution. There would consequently be continuing differences between their economies and social relationships for some time to come. But the pressures towards administrative unification and the creation of a single framework of economic planning were very strong. Measures were taken to establish control over economic and social life in the South. In May and June 1975, steps were taken to register former members of the "puppet" army and administration, and to re-educate them for life in the new society. The majority appear to have been quickly rehabilitated, but more senior officers and officials were treated less leniently. In some cases political reform study was combined with labour in the fields or elsewhere. Those who refused to register or to co-operate with the new government were regarded as counter-revolutionaries. A few cases of open opposition were reported, but for the most part the new regime established its control without difficulty. Gaining control of the economy presented more serious problems. In August 1975 the private banks were closed, and in September there was a full-scale attack on the "comprador bourgeoisie" who had dominated the Saigon economy under Thieu, and who were now accused of distorting the economy by hoarding commodities. This was followed by a change of currency in September, in order to limit the economic power of those who had savings in old piastres. But by the middle of 1976 there was no attempt to eliminate the "national bourgeoisie" as a class, or to collectvize agriculture.

In May 1975 revolutionary committees were created at all levels in the South, with a Military Management Committee to run the conurbation of Saigon-Giadinh (now renamed "Ho Chi Minh City"). But effective power lay in the southern branch of the Lao-Dong Party, headed by a southern-born member of its Politburo, Pham Hung. The much-publicized "third force" in South Vietnamese politics was not allowed a significant political role and was virtually dissolved and even the Provisional Revolutionary Government did not appear to be a major centre of decision-making once victory was achieved. In November 1975 a reunification conference was held in Saigon, attended by delegations representing the North (led by Truong Chinh) and the South (led by Pham Hung,) at which it was agreed that reunification should take place during 1976. Accordingly, nation-wide elections for a new National Assembly were held in April 1976. The new Assembly met in late June and in early July appointed a single national government, dominated by leaders of the former Democratic Republic, but including members of the former Provisional Revolutionary Government (PRG) in the South. The Assembly adopted the name of Socialist Republic of Viet-Nam for the reunified country, with Hanoi as the capital, and the flag and anthem of North Viet-Nam. A commission was set up to draft a new constitution for the whole country.

ECONOMIC SURVEY

North Viet-Nam, 1954-1975

Alec Gordon

Following the division of Viet-Nam in 1954, the Democratic Republic of Viet-Nam in the north occupied the poorer and over-populated half of a poor and populous country. Not only was the North a food deficit area during the period of French colonial rule, but for climatic reasons it lacked the export earning capacity of the plantations in the South. So whilst the North in peacetime has since established self-sufficiency in food production and has been able to make good use of comparatively rich and varied mineral resources (coal, iron, tin, limestone and phosphate) the possible benefits of a division of labour to assist the early stages of development have had to be foregone by both halves of the country.

In 1960 industry in the North accounted for about 42 per cent of the value of output of industry and agriculture combined. By 1964, this proportion had risen to just over 50 per cent. After two periods of heavy aerial bombardment it seems probable that industry again accounted for just over 50 per cent in 1974.

About 90 per cent of the population of 23.8 million (1974) lived in the countryside. Some 80 per cent of the work force gained a livelihood in agriculture, compared with 8 per cent in industry. Much of the gains from the economic progress of the late 1950s and early 1960s was nullified by an exceptionally high population growth rate of 3.5 per cent per annum. However, by about 1970 it was evident that population growth had been reduced to just 2.9 per cent per annum. Although the urban population is small the rural population is itself heavily concentrated in the Red River Delta and coastal plains. Before the war in South Viet-Nam spread to the North with U.S. bombing in 1965, attempts to resettle the population in hill areas met with varying degrees of success, but during the war a fair amount of permanent resettlement appears to have taken place. Currently, official policy stresses the extension and diversification of agriculture into hill areas rather than population movement as such.

Like most communist countries, North Viet-Nam has had its economic policy debates polarizing frequently on heavy industry versus agriculture. For the most part, however, the policy of "walking on two legs" has predominated. Economic policy has followed the dictum "take industry as the leading force and agriculture as the basis for industrial development". Apart from the period 1960–63, those favouring due weight to light industry and agriculture generally won the day.

AGRICULTURE

Rice

Rice is the main crop although its relative importance has been declining. Previously, over 80 per cent of crop areas used to be under rice. Now the figure is just over 70 per cent. Despite its recognition of the economic and dietetic desirability of crop diversification, the state has always been cautious about doing this at the expense of rice production. Although in normal years the North is no longer a food deficit area, the narrow margin of surplus has restrained the scope to experiment. It was only following the widespread introduction of high yielding and fast growing "miracle rice" strains, that a radical restructuring of the crop pattern became possible, and that in combination with higher rice production.

The cultivable land area is approximately 2 million hectares (i.e. less than 1,000 square metres per head of population) but with extensive double (and sometimes even triple) cropping the area actually cultivated is about 3.5 million hectares. The main rice crop (tenth lunar month) is harvested in October-November over an area of some 1,500,000 hectares which are watered in the rainy season. The secondary rice harvest is in May-June over some 900,000 hectares which rely on irrigation as the crop grows in the dry season. Formerly, the fifth lunar month crop was transplanted in November but has recently been, by and large, replaced by a spring rice crop transplanted in February and still harvested by June. Another crop, harvested in July, covers about 100,000 hectares.

Rice production recovered very rapidly after the end of the war against France and quickly surpassed pre-war levels of gross output and production per head. From 3.5 million tons in 1955, paddy output rose to 5.2 million tons in 1959 as compared with 2.4 million tons in 1939, the pre-war record. The euphoria induced by these early successes together with the use of grossly inflated initial estimates for production in 1959 resulted in wildly optimistic targets being adopted for the first Five-Year Plan approved at the third Party Congress in 1960. In fact, far from showing a further increase, rice production lagged and it was not until 1972 that the 1959 peak was surpassed. There was a serious agricultural crisis in 1963 when output dropped to 4.3 million tons. Meanwhile population growth had continued unchecked (indeed, almost unnoticed as far as the Five-Year Plan was concerned) and paddy production per head fell to 241 kilogrammes. A marked change in economic policy followed and, as United States air attacks began in 1965, rice production was showing an upward trend once again.

For reasons of national security the Vietnamese have published no figures of actual output since 1964, but the indications are that during the first period of U.S. bombing (1965–68) production held up well, although after 1966 it was probably down for three years. Serious flooding in 1969 and 1971 retarded production but 1970 and 1972 had excellent harvests producing an estimated 5.0 and 4.4 million tons of paddy respectively. A notable feature of production since 1971 has been the significant contribution made by high yielding varieties of rice.

Dry food crops

Output of other grain and tuber crops grown in the dry season (maize, sweet potatoes, manioc and beans) rose more rapidly than did rice in the period 1955–68. The area under these crops grew from 400,000 hectares to 700,000 hectares in 1964 and the comparative security offered by growing non-irrigated crops during the aerial bombardment of 1965–69 boosted the acreage further. In terms of paddy, production was 0.7 million tons in 1960, 1.2 in 1962, 1.3 in 1963 and 1.6 million tons in 1965. After 1968, production appears to have fallen away, although there was a big recovery in 1972 when it may have reached 1.8 million tons. These dry crops represent a crucial addition to rice production. By the mid-1960s rice production per head was no better than it had been in the mid-1950s, but production of all dry crops per head had increased significantly. The year 1959 was a peak for rice production and for all food crops together. The peak in paddy was not exceeded until 1972, whereas the total grain and tubers figure was surpassed in 1964. A great part of the dry crops have been grown as a second crop. A significant new departure in 1972 was the use of 100,000 hectares freed by fast maturing rice strains for the growing of dry crops as a *third* annual crop (i.e. as well as the secondary rice crop, not instead of it).

Other agricultural activities

Other crops—particularly fruit and vegetables, but also sugar cane, cotton, jute, coffee and tea—are growing in importance. In 1957 they accounted for 4.5 per cent of the cultivated area but by 1967 this had risen to 10.5 per cent.

Pig rearing, chicken keeping and fish ponds provide virtually the only sources of meat. Pig farming is the only significant agricultural activity in private hands, the pigs being reared on family plots and not on collectively farmed land. They also form a vital contribution to supplies of organic fertilizer.

Another important fertilizer (perhaps one third of total consumption), without mention of which no account of North Vietnamese agriculture would be complete, is the plant *Azolla pinata*. Grown on flooded paddy fields this nitrogen producing plant has been cultivated on a nationwide basis only since 1963.

Land Reform and Collectivization

In the war against France, land reform went little further than rent reduction and the distribution of land belonging to French supporters. In 1955–56 an effective land reform campaign transferred some 800,000 hectares to poor and middle peasants. There were few large holdings in the North and after the reform the average landholding was only 1,300 square metres per head. Economically, the move represented a large redistribution of income. It also destroyed the economic basis of the established rural elite. The campaign extended beyond the redistribution of land to the setting up of peasant tribunals to punish landlords for their past behaviour. The death penalty was used frequently in extreme cases. However, in many important respects the campaign was badly handled by Party cadres. Middle or even poor peasants were classified as landlords and often no account was taken, say, of a landlord's war record in a competitive hunt to discover more and more landlords to punish. A rectification campaign began in 1956, but as the restitution of lost rights involved a further redistribution of landholdings and cattle its short term effect was to add to the chaos. The misdirection of the land reform caused a grave internal political crisis. Nevertheless, it was successful in its main political aim: the destruction of the existing rural élites.

In marked contrast, progress towards collectivization went on very quietly. A decision was taken in 1958 not to await the setting up of heavy industry before rural co-operatives should be organized. A drive to organize the peasants into co-operatives began (under the lead of Truong Chinh) and by 1960 about 85 per cent of peasant families were members of rural co-operatives. However, the great majority were still in "low level" co-operatives (where the co-ops paid rent for the use of their members' land, animals or tools). The pace then slackened and much emphasis was laid on private plots of land. Individual families legally retained 5 per cent of the area of the co-operative for whatever use they chose. However, the food crisis of 1963 provoked a renewed interest in full collectivization. By 1965, 85 per cent of peasant families belonged to "high level" co-operatives (collective farms). This was accompanied by an inflow of manpower and managerial skills into the rural co-operatives together with a marked renewal of collective labour on irrigation projects and the rationalization of the untouched individual plots of paddy into large, conveniently shaped fields. Towards the end of the first period of United States bombing (1965–68) the withdrawal of technically skilled personnel and politically experienced cadres from the countryside to participate in the war effort seriously weakened the organizing capacity of the co-operatives' management. By 1968, in at least one province, about 20 per cent of co-operative land (virtually all the crop area other than for rice) was being privately worked. The halt to the bombing stimulated a further debate on when and how to tackle this problem. The outcome was another victory for the advocates of collective working. The New Statute on Agricultural Co-operatives, which became law in 1969, rendered it illegal for a co-operative to contract out land and work projects to individual families. In addition, it transferred the legal rights of ownership of family plots to the co-operative (although the family still has a right to use this land). To date this collectivist policy prevails and is currently finding expression in the specific nature of North Viet-Nam's "green revolution".

"Green Revolution"

Almost 700,000 hectares of paddy were planted to high yielding varieties of rice (HYV) in 1972. At about a quarter of the rice area, this is one of the highest proportions in Asia. In 1970 there were 130,000 hectares, in 1965 20,000 hectares. Only the secondary rice crop is affected. By a stroke of good luck the first really sizable plantings of HYVs took place in 1971 when the main rice harvest was drastically reduced by severe flooding. This converted what would have been a disastrous crop year into merely a poor one. The HYVs are also fast growing and require the mobilization of labour for transplanting in February instead of in the traditional December period. Organized labour works to provide the necessary additional irrigation, to give intensive care to the new crop, and given Viet-Nam's low output of synthetic fertilizer, is involved in collecting greater amounts of human and animal manure and growing more green fertilizer. At least as important as the high yielding properties of the new rice is its ability to grow quickly. In the "space" created by planting late the intention is to introduce a third annual harvest of various crops. The ability to organize large numbers of peasants on a nation-wide basis in order to transplant rice at a completely new time and to assist and organize them to plant new crops is of crucial importance to the whole undertaking.

MINING AND INDUSTRY

Besides coal, North Viet-Nam has workable deposits of iron, tin, zinc and chromite and probably also of antimony, wolfram, bauxite and manganese; it produces large quantities of phosphate and the extensive areas of limestone are utilized to produce cement, as well as lime for agriculture. The country's reserves of coal were reported in early 1959 as amounting to "several hundreds of millions of tons", of zinc to "several million" and of apatite to around 100 million tons. No on-shore sources of petroleum have been traced. A pre-war report gives 25 million tons of manganese, though this mineral appears never to have been worked to any extent except during the period of Japanese ascendancy. Near Thai-Nguyen the Trai-Cau iron mine, a new undertaking, is said to have reserves of 20 million tons of ore containing 60 per cent iron.

Of these coal is by far the most important. The largest, or anyway the most rewarding deposit, that of the Quang-Yen basin, forms a shallow arc running some 150 kilometres from Sept Pagodes in the west to Tien-Yen in the east, and extending to Ke-Bao island. Secondary deposits, of bituminous and semi-bituminous coal, occur in central Tonkin at Tuyen-Quang and the Phan-Me basin, 15 kilometres north-west of Thai-Nguyen, and along the southern edge of the Tonkin delta between Ninh-Binh and Van-Yen. Quang-Yen coal is an anthracite of high calorific power. Zinc occurs in the massif north of the delta, between the Clear River and the Hanoi-Na-Cham railway. Tin is found in the Pia-Ouac range some 60 kilometres west of Cao-Bang (where it is associated with wolfram). Iron is also found on Ke-Bao island, and antimony in the regions of Mon-Cay, Hongay and Thanh-Hoa. Off-shore prospecting for oil began in 1973.

Pre-1939 Industrialization

Before the Second World War most of the products of this promising mineral infrastructure for an industrial state were exported. It supported, however, two major industries, the cement works at Haiphong and the textile industry run by the *Société Cotonnière de l'Indochine* at Haiphong and Nam-Dinh. The growth of the former was encouraged by the proximity of supplies of limestone and clay, and of course of the coal field, and availability of ocean and river transport. Immediately before the war the works had an annual capacity of 300,000 tons, producing in 1937 235,000 tons of which 53 per cent was exported. The textile industry at that time possessed 30,000 spindles at Haiphong and at Nam-Dinh 54,000 spindles, 1,300 looms and bleaching and dyeing facilities; the Nam-Dinh mill, with some 10,000 hands working irregularly, was the largest single employer of labour in Indochina. In 1937 the *Cotonnière* produced something over 8,000 tons of cotton yarn, most of which went into the cottage weaving industry, 702,000 blankets and 2,212 tons (say 16.5 million metres) of miscellaneous cotton fabrics. Distilleries, with adjoining rice mills, at Hanoi, Nam-Dinh and Hai-Duong and breweries at Hanoi and Haiphong were the only other industrial enterprises of importance.

Industry under the Democratic Republic

"In 1939, the most prosperous year under French domination", wrote the review *Viet-Nam Advances* in January 1959, "modern industry provided only a tenth of the total volume of industrial and agricultural production" (i.e. in the 1959 area of North Viet-Nam). "The three industries which constitute the framework of a heavy industry, namely an iron, a mechanical engineering and a chemical industry, were non-existent. . . . This factor even today compels us to import nearly everything we need in the way of cast iron, steel, various kinds of metals, mechanical tools and accessories, chemical products, etc. . . . On the return of peace, industry in North Viet-Nam was in such a poor state that the share of heavy industry was down to 1.5 per cent of the whole of industrial and agricultural production".

Two official indexes of industrial output give a reasonable picture of overall development up to 1965. A volume of gross production index based on 1939 records 337 for 1965 and a constant prices value of production index (1957=100) records 180 for 1960 and 340 for 1965. These tend to confirm that pre-war production levels were regained about 1957. Thereafter production expanded rapidly despite serious shortcomings in the Three-Year (1958–60) and Five-Year (1961–65) Plans. On the eve of the war against the United States in 1965, state-owned factories accounted for 65 per cent of industrial output, handicraft co-operatives for about 25 per cent and individual handicraft workers about 5 per cent.

Up to 1965 the proportion produced by the handicrafts sector was declining noticeably, but there is reason to believe that it has since increased as a result of wartime damage to, and the dispersal of, large factories, and of the policy of encouraging regional self-sufficiency. At any rate, it was officially claimed that there were 500,000 handicraft workers in the spring of 1973, which is equivalent to the total industrial work force recorded in the 1960 census. Before the start of the bombing the largest industries in terms of output were textiles and food (each about 20 per cent of the total), wood and paper production (15 per cent) and engineering (13 per cent). None of the other branches had reached 10 per cent but there is little doubt that chemicals and iron and steel would have done so but for the effects of aerial bombardment.

The First Five-Year Plan (1961–65) envisaged laying the basis for a socialist and industrial Viet-Nam, to modernize agriculture, to increase manufacturing output and to serve defence needs. But in the euphoric atmosphere of the early days not only were most of the targets adopted over-optimistic but the plan strategy itself appears to have been misconceived. The fact that 45 per cent of Central Government expenditure on investment went to industry by itself does not prove that other sectors were starved. Nor was a pronounced emphasis on heavy industry necessarily ill-judged. But an examination of the "product mix" shows a predominance of capital intensive, late maturing investment. In particular the Thai Nguyen steel works, which took up about one fifth of total government investment in the five years, appears as a costly mistake in timing. Combined with an unrealistic assessment of potential agricultural output, the policy led to the economic crisis of 1963. The big policy changes of 1963 resulted in more realistic targets as well as the altering of the industrial product mix and laying more stress on agriculture.

The main branches of industry in 1974 may be summarized as follows:

Food processing was composed of at least three large modern sugar refineries, fish and fruit canning plants and numerous rice mills all of which were state-owned. A handicrafts sector of small units making bread, confectionery, cooked food, sauces, etc. probably accounted for well in excess of the 20 per cent of this sector which it produced in 1965.

Textiles: Weaving production in 1965 was about 100 million metres of cotton goods coming from two large factories in Nam Dinh and Hanoi, a smaller one in Haiphong and a sizable artisan sector which in 1965 accounted for about a quarter of the total. The handicrafts share has certainly increased since, but following the re-assembly of the dispersed machinery from the mills in Nam Dinh and Hanoi the share of handicrafts will undoubtedly decline once again. A modern knitwear factory exists in Hanoi.

Wood and paper: The two main centres of factory production were Hanoi and Viet Tri. This was the only industry in which the share produced by the handicrafts sector was on a rising trend prior to 1965. Then it accounted for about 20 per cent.

Engineering: There were two large machinery plants in Hanoi and sizeable repair shops in other parts of the country. Small workshops have proliferated since 1965. The industry has built railway locomotives and small ocean-going ships.

Iron and Steel: The Thai Nguyen complex was planned as a small integrated strip mill with an ingot capacity of 300,000 tons. The power plant, coking batteries and the first blast furnace started up late in 1963, and the first steel ingots were cast early in 1965. The rolling mill was, however, incomplete and until the bombing commenced ingot production was shipped to China for rolling. In addition there were electric arc furnaces using scrap in Hanoi and Haiphong and there seemed to be a variety of rural workshops producing pig-iron or melting down scrap.

Energy: Coal output reached 4 million tons in 1965, of which 2 million tons were exported, mainly to Japan.

Electrical capacity from 14 thermal power stations and 4 hydro-electric stations totalled about 200,000 kW. in 1965. Large numbers of small or even mobile plants have since been put into use.

Chemicals: Fertilizers were probably the largest component and about 300,000 tons were produced in 1963. Two modern plants began production in that year, one a superphosphate plant at Lan Thao, the other producing nitrogen at Hac Bac. War-time bombing probably reduced production below that level and the main sources of fertilizers are manures, green fertilizers and imports.

Cement: One of the largest factories of any kind in Viet-Nam was the cement works at Haiphong which produced about 600,000 tons in 1964.

FOREIGN ECONOMIC RELATIONS

Complete figures in terms of value do not appear to have been published for North Viet-Nam's foreign trade. United States official estimates for 1963 value North Viet-Nam's combined imports and exports at around $300 million. Vietnamese sources indicate that export earnings covered about 70–80 per cent of imports. However, the situation created by the war has dated the relevance of these figures.

Some 80–85 per cent of North Viet-Nam's trade was with other communist countries, the other main trade flows being with Japan, Hong Kong and to a lesser extent France. There is now clear evidence that there is a desire to broaden economic relations with other countries. Trade and technical agreements have been worked out with Japan which could be of great importance. An accredited trade mission has been working in Singapore since 1972. And, in an important new departure, the Italian state oil concern, ENI, has been commissioned to carry out exploration for off-shore petroleum over large areas of the Gulf of Tonkin. Coal and cement will probably remain the principal industrial exports and there has recently been considerable emphasis placed on growing tropical products for export and on selling handicraft products abroad.

Economic aid has been considerable and, with the

recent exception of agreements with Sweden and Australia, has been exclusively from communist countries. In the period 1955–65 it amounted to an estimated $1,250 million. Since then military and economic aid have increased. During the war years imports financed by aid alleviated shortages such as the rice shortages in the winter of 1968–69. They have also played an essential role in maintaining the structure of the North's economy by enabling a sufficiently large flow of manufactured goods to be supplied to the agricultural sector.

BOMBING AND RECONSTRUCTION

During the two periods of intensive bombing of North Viet-Nam, 1965–68 and 1972, industrial installations suffered extensive damage in terms of destruction of plant and impairment of output. It is estimated that 70 per cent of North Viet-Nam's industrial capacity was destroyed. Although the dispersal of industry during the war to some extent averted more major destruction, it is clear that the bombing had a severe effect on the development of the North Vietnamese economy.

Reconstruction has been rapid. By the end of 1974 the pre-bombing level of gross national product had been restored. Coal output was still down on 1965 but electricity production was 66 per cent higher. Seaport capacity was intended to be 20 per cent higher in 1975 than in 1964. Plans were that railway carrying capacity in 1975 would equal the 1971 volume. The largest single industrial complex, the Thai Nguyen iron and steel works, produced its first post-bombing steel in 1974. A large new pulp and paper project was initiated and will form the main project of economic aid from Sweden.

The year 1974 produced impressive economic results. Agricultural output rose by 20 per cent and industrial production by 15 per cent. The latter was not unexpected but the rise in agricultural output was particularly welcome in view of the destruction caused by the late floods in 1973. Whilst not being as bad as 1968 or 1971 the main rice harvest in that year was well down and, but for the stability of the secondary harvest of "miracle rice" strains, domestic food supplies would have been disastrously low. However, in 1974 rice production rose by 21 per cent, reaching an estimated 5.5 million tons of paddy. For the main tenth lunar month crop this, by and large, represented recovery but for the 22 per cent increase in output from the fifth month crop it was almost entirely a spectacular net increase in production which bodes well for the future. The outcome of the 1975 "miracle rice" crop in June looked good as the area transplanted rose by 40,000 hectares over 1974 (about 5 per cent). Chemical fertilizer output for the first quarter of 1975 was over 90,000 tons, nearly double the pre-bombing peak.

South Viet-Nam up to 1975

P. H. M. Jones

(Revised by Alec Gordon and the Editor)

AGRICULTURE

Rice Production

Throughout Viet-Nam paddy rice is by far the main crop, in Cochinchina everywhere occupying over 90 per cent and in some districts 100 per cent of the cultivated land. Before the Second World War rice covered 2.2 million hectares in Cochinchina, an increase of a million hectares since the beginning of the century. The record since 1945 was 2.1 million hectares in 1957, during the only peaceful period Viet-Nam had known since 1939. The Saigon Government's Fourth Five-Year Plan (1971–75) envisaged the production of rice increasing from 6.7 million tons in 1971 to 7.2 million tons at the end of the plan period. The area under rice rose from 2,430,000 hectares in the 1969/70 season to 2,720,000 for the 1970/71 season.

The main producing provinces are in West Cochinchina and the region south of the Bassac, the most southerly of the great arms of the Lower Mekong. In the 1880s the French administration built a grid of canals across the country, which served the purposes of drainage and desalinization and of transport of the paddy by junk to Saigon.

During the 1958/59 crop season the province of Ba-Xuyen at the mouth of the Bassac was the largest producer, with production given as 375,000 metric tons from 195,000 hectares. Then came Phong-Dinh (360,000 tons) and An-Giang (350,000 tons), both on the south bank of the Bassac, then Kien-Giang (335,000 tons) and Vinh-Binh (328,000 tons). For 1966/67 the figures for these provinces are given as 413,000, 194,000, 160,000, 221,000 and 275,000 tons respectively, out of a total for Cochinchina of 3.5 million tons, compared with 3.4 million in the earlier year. For all South Viet-Nam paddy production in 1971/72, the best for eight years, totalled 5.6 million metric tons. Average yield per hectare was 2.2 metric tons. However, about 40 per cent of the crop consists of "Java" or floating rice, a variety in parts of Cochinchina near the Cambodian border which are subject to very deep flooding. This can be used only for cattle feed.

Rice Trade

Before 1940 Cochinchina was the world's third largest rice exporter after Burma and Thailand. In the years 1933–37 the exports averaged nearly 1.6 million tons annually. Exports have never since reached this level, but substantial though fluctuating quantities were shipped in some post-war periods. On the other hand, exports fell to 84,000 tons in 1962, the shipment having been prohibited for most of the year in consequence of an over-estimate of the damage done by serious floods in some of the main producing provinces in late 1961. In 1964 exports fell back to 48,000 tons owing to the authorities' desire to maintain sufficient stocks at Saigon to guarantee local supplies, the need being estimated at some 45,000 tons a month, 15,000 for the city itself and 30,000 for the rice-deficit areas of East Cochinchina and Central Viet-Nam. Late in the year Central Viet-Nam was devastated by the worst floods (it was said) for 350 years; then, in 1965, the activities of the insurgent National Liberation Front (NLF) in the Delta region began seriously to impede deliveries.

South Viet-Nam therefore became a rice-importing country. Imports in 1965, mostly under the U.S. Public Law 480 aid programme, totalled 225,000 tons, rising to 653,000 tons in 1968, falling to 325,000 tons in 1969 and rising again to 568,000 tons in 1970. After then the official production statistics (*see* the *Statistical Survey*) left a serious unexplained discrepancy between the amount that could have been consumed locally and taken by the NLF for its own purposes (probably including some export through Cambodia) and the production estimated.

Rubber

Rubber planting in Cochinchina dates from the end of the last century, and by 1937 rubber plantations covered 98,000 ha. in Cochinchina, out of a total for French Indochina of 126,700 ha. The plantations are wholly in the region called East Cochinchina, to the north and east of Saigon, and have the advantage, among others, that they provide an economic use for the poor *terres grises*—the old alluvial soils—of the region. But much rubber is also grown on the rich volcanic *terres rouges* which extend into the adjacent parts of Cambodia.

Most of the production came from the estates of the great French companies, of which four accounted in 1960, after some years of normal working, for about 21,000 metric tons out of a total production for the year of 76,600 tons. The largest producer in that year was the *Société des Plantations des Terres Rouges* (SPTR—7,113 tons from 17,722 hectares of plantations), followed by the *Sté. Indochinoise de Plantations d'Hévéas* (5,775 tons), the *Cie. des Caoutchoucs d'Extrême-Orient* (CEXO—4,675 tons) and the *Sté. Michelin* (3,573 tons). The large estates chiefly produced rubber for Ribbed Smoked Sheets No. 1 and obtained yields of up to 1,500 kilogrammes per hectare. In all, French-owned companies contributed about 87 per cent of the total production.

During 1957–61 replanting, urgently needed after the disruption caused by the previous hostilities, proceeded satisfactorily—1,500 ha. in 1957, 2,000 in 1958, 4,000 in both 1959 and 1960 and 3,000 in 1961. But from 1962 insecurity reduced replanting almost to nothing. Production reached a peak of 79,100 metric tons in 1960, fell to 27,650 metric tons in 1969 but increased to 28,458 in 1970 and to over 30,000 metric tons in 1971. At the beginning of 1971, of a total planted area of 68,000 ha., 57,800 were considered workable and only 30,900 were actually tapped. Production from the plantations of over 500 ha. stood at 68,200 tons in 1960, and at 70,800 tons in 1961, but had fallen to 26,200 tons in January-September 1967. Owing to the post-war insecurity, just under 70 per cent of the trees on the plantations of over 500 ha. were planted before 1946, and 32 per cent were old trees planted before 1930.

From 1962 production was seriously impeded by NLF activity. Though the guerrillas did not normally stop working they prevented replanting (if necessary, by destroying the tractors and bulldozers) and hindered the transport of rubber by road to Saigon. Moreover, from December 1964 fighting took place near Baria in the rubber-growing region south-east of Saigon, and in early 1965 five estates almost completely stopped working as a result of heavy fighting about 80 miles due north of Saigon. At some places the trees were damaged by shell-fire and defoliation, and at others the processing and other technical plant were wrecked. The biggest plantations of all, those of the SPTR and CEXO, slightly to the west, were more or less unaffected at this time but were unable to get their production out or supplies in along the road from Loc-Ninh to Saigon. Between 1971 and 1973 production fell from 37,500 tons to 20,600 tons.

Coffee, Tea and Other Crops

About four-fifths of South Viet-Nam's arable land is under rice. Sweet potatoes (a dry season crop), manioc and maize are grown merely as a substitute for rice on inferior or unirrigable land, or as a cash crop after a poor rice harvest; there is also some production of industrial crops. Before the war coffee was quite extensively grown by the Vietnamese settlers in the Central Highlands; but after the war the crop suffered severely from neglect of the trees, lack of fertilizer and so forth. Despite the disruption brought about by the war, production of coffee was maintained after 1964 and increased from 3,345 metric tons in 1967 to 3,925 metric tons in 1970, which sufficed for local consumption. In 1973 production was about 5,120 tons.

Tea had been grown in Viet-Nam by small cultivators before the French came. Then, in the 1920s, a number of French companies established about 2,500 hectares of tea plantations in the Central Highlands. Methods of cultivation and preparation were improved, with the result that tea production increased from 4,195 metric tons in 1967 to 6,250 metric tons by 1973. Another commercial possibility is bananas. East Cochinchina and the Central Lowlands have also produced some groundnuts and soya beans.

Of the main industrial crops, sugar is cultivated chiefly in the central lowlands between Danang and Cape Varella, and in the river valleys of the Saigon region. Production fell sharply in the war years following 1950, as several irrigation schemes and refineries (notably a refinery at Tuy-Hoa in the Central Lowlands) were destroyed and the farmers converted their cane fields to food crops. The consequent need to import raw and refined sugar cost considerable foreign exchange, and by 1959 the Diem regime had under way an important programme for expanding sugar cane production, including experiments with varieties of Florida-grown cane supplied by the U.S. Department of Agriculture, and the creation of new refineries. Production of sugar cane declined after 1967, but since 1970 there has been some slight improvement; 1973 production reached 529,900 tons.

Coconut trees cover a substantial area on the central coast and in the southern neighbourhood of Saigon. Production of coconut oil in the 1960s averaged about 14,000 tons annually but this was sufficient only for local consumption. Copra is also produced. Another fibre crop, kenaf, was planted for the first time in 1959 in resettlement centres east of Saigon in the provinces of Phuoc-Thanh and Phuoc-Tuy. It was then hailed as the great hope of Vietnamese agriculture, and some 7,000 hectares were planted to kenaf in 1961 with no regard to the possible market, so that area and production have since fallen sharply.

Before 1945 silk-worm raising was fairly extensively practised in the Centre, which had some 5,000 ha. of mulberry trees, and in Cochinchina (1,500 ha.). Subsequently the area fell to 1,500 ha. for the whole of South Viet-Nam. The high price of raw silk in the early 1960s induced the authors of the Second Five-Year Plan to set a target of 14,500 ha. of mulberry trees and a production of 200 tons of raw silk in 1966, but little progress has been achieved.

South Viet-Nam appeared to have excellent prospects for large-scale livestock raising. The semi-amphibious buffalo and the pig are both kept all over the Delta region, and cattle in the Central Lowlands; the latter also thrive in the more temperate Central Highlands. Pigs and buffaloes on the hoof and pork were exported to Hong Kong in 1960–65.

INDUSTRY

Before the war industry in South Viet-Nam was confined to the processing of agricultural produce—rice milling and distilling of rice alcohol in Cholon, sugar refineries at Hiep-Hoa on the Eastern Vaico, Tay-Ninh and Tuy-Hoa. After 1954 industrial development was hindered, as in other Asian countries, by lack of technicians, lack of capital—local capital could make large and rapid profits in the import trade—lack of power supplies and the smallness of the local market. However, the Diem regime set on foot a reasonable programme of industrial development, mostly aimed at import substitution, which after some years showed appreciable results. Thus, thanks partly to strict controls, imports of seven categories of industrial crops and of light industrial goods—rubber products, sugar, textiles, paper, glass, cement and pharmaceuticals—fell from U.S. $126.9 million in 1956 to $73.5 million in 1959.

Textiles

As usual in developing countries, the first efforts were made in the field of textiles. Until 1960 the only substantial production of cotton yarn came from 7,600 spindles at Nam-Dinh in Tonkin, which supplied yarn to a small but rapidly expanding weaving industry comprising 11,730 looms in that year, of which about 7,000 were manually operated, scattered throughout the country. The first large new mill to go up after 1954 started working with 20,000 spindles and 400 automatic looms in 1960. Dyeing and finishing plant were installed in 1962. The company was launched by private Vietnamese and Chinese capital, with U.S. $2,360,000 in foreign exchange from American aid funds for the purchase of equipment. A team of technicians from Taiwan directed the mill's installation and initial running.

A second large textile mill started working near Saigon in 1961, with 17,200 spindles, 300 looms and a dyeing and finishing section; 45 per cent of the capital was American, representing the first important American industrial investment in Viet-Nam. By 1971 there were 4,700 automatic looms and 220,000 spindles in South Viet-Nam.

In order to protect the cottage industry, expansion by the big mills was restricted and no more big mills were to have been authorized for several years, but expansion of some mills in Saigon did take place. Production of cotton fabrics fell from 120.7 million metres in 1965 to 43.2 million metres in 1972, but increased to 75.8 million metres in 1973. Imports of all sorts of fabrics totalled $48 million in 1967, some $25 million in 1968, $20 million in 1969 and fell to $6 million in 1970. Local production of cotton yarn met nearly 70 per cent of the total demand in 1967. From 1968 to 1970 output more than doubled from 4,996 to 11,742 tons.

There is no rayon or nylon spinning industry. Rayon weaving in the early 1970s was mostly a cottage industry, the small firms being grouped into co-operatives possessing 7,200 power looms and 800 hand looms. There were also several medium-sized mills in and around Saigon with some 900 automatic looms. Nylon weaving was carried on by eight firms possessing 1,072 looms and equipped for dyeing and finishing. Two mills, using fibre from Thailand, produced kenaf yarn and bags—for which there was little demand after rice exports ceased—and a cottage industry of some 300 handlooms produced silk cloth from imported yarn. Production of rayon and synthetic fabrics totalled 60.3 million metres in 1970.

Other Industries

A cement plant build by a group of French firms at Ha-Tien on the Gulf of Siam, with a capacity of 300,000 tons of clinker annually, started working in early 1964. Cement production in 1973 was 265,255 tons.

South Viet-Nam's first paper mill (a joint Vietnamese-American project) started working at Bien-Hoa in early 1961, and a second in mid-1963. A joint Vietnamese-French glassware factory producing bottles, tumblers, etc. began working at Khanh-Hoi at the end of 1960.

In 1971 total steel production of South Viet-Nam's three plants at Cholon, Thu Duc and Bien Hoa was

75,000 tons (utilizing military scrap) of billet steel, bars, tubes and wire.

Oil

Following the carrying out of seismic surveys in 1970, the government announced in June 1971 the granting of petroleum exploration and exploitation concessions covering 160,000 square miles of South Viet-Nam's southern coastline off-shore. One definite oilfield was struck in 1974.

Power

The deficiency in the supply of electric power to the Saigon region was to have been solved by the Danhim hydroelectric complex, near Dalat, which was financed out of Japanese war reparations. Construction of the dam started in April 1961 and was completed in 1963, together with an 80,000 kW. power station and a 253-km. transmission line to Saigon. The latter was, however, sabotaged two years later, obliging Saigon to endure regular power cuts, but the situation was partially restored in May 1966 when an American-financed 33,000 kW. thermal plant started working at Thu-Duc.

COMMUNICATIONS

Some 85 per cent of South Viet-Nam's foreign trade passed through Saigon before 1975, and most of the rest through Da-Nang. Saigon is 45 miles from the sea; the wharves stretch 2.5 miles and 26 ships can moor at the buoys or in docking berths simultaneously; the warehouses cover about 100,000 square yards. In addition, the petroleum port at Nhabé, 10 miles downstream, has storage tanks with a capacity of some 200,000 cubic metres.

A high proportion of the imports for U.S. personnel came in by the port established in the 1960s at Cam-Ranh Bay, 200 miles north-east of Saigon, which has been called the finest natural port in Asia. This now comprises two piers, a petroleum jetty and storage area, an airfield and many other facilities for military use. Conveniently located between important sea lanes and the coastal road and railway, Cam-Ranh may have an important commercial future.

After 1962 almost all long-distance passenger traffic was carried by Air Viet-Nam. In 1970 Air Viet-Nam carried 1.26 million passengers. The airline then owned 23 planes including three B727—used on foreign flights—with 20 more on charter from Taiwan companies.

FOREIGN TRADE

Until 1958 France was the largest source of South Viet-Nam's imports, supplying a quarter of the total in that year. Thereafter, restrictions on purchases from France, dictated by distaste for French neutralism, reduced imports from France to a small fraction of the total, while imports from other countries increased. This process was hastened by the enforcement from early 1961 of a prohibition on the use of American aid credits to make purchases from nineteen "advanced" countries. The main beneficiaries of this policy, apart from the United States, were Taiwan and, a little later, South Korea. Thus, by 1963 the U.S. supplied 37 per cent and Taiwan 13 per cent of total imports valued at U.S. $286 million; of these some 60 per cent were financed by American economic aid, 30 per cent from Vietnamese government resources and the rest by credits from Japan, France and elsewhere.

After the cessation of rice shipments, rubber became the largest export commodity but by 1973 was superseded in value by shellfish, mainly shrimps. Other export items are tea, duck feathers and miscellaneous agricultural produce. In 1973 the main markets for South Viet-Nam's exports were Hong Kong, Japan and France, while the main suppliers of imports were the United States (which provided over half), Japan, Singapore and France.

The trade deficit was chronic and huge. In 1973 exports were estimated at 29,700 million piastres and imports at 310,000 million piastres.

FOREIGN AID

From July 1954 to mid-1968 U.S. economic aid to South Viet-Nam totalled about U.S. $4,000 million. Except for a period in 1963 when Washington was bringing pressure on the Ngo Dinh Diem Government, it was practically unlimited except by the country's absorptive capacity. For the fiscal year ending June 30th, 1971, funds allotted came to $604 million, compared with $601 million recorded in the previous fiscal year, owing to a 25 per cent decrease in the cost of the war. In addition to $220 million under the Commercial Import Programme (*see* below), Food for Peace was allocated $162.9 million and Project Aid $221.2 million.

U.S. aid took three forms, non-project and project assistance and development loans. Non-project assistance helped to finance Vietnamese imports either under the Commercial Import Programme ($398 million in 1965/66 and $220 million in 1970/71) or under Public Law 480, Title I. The former paid for all or most of Viet-Nam's imports of fertilizers and other chemicals, machinery, electric equipment, tyres, iron and steel, lorries and tractors, etc.; imports of petroleum products, cement, pharmaceuticals, pulp and paper, non-ferrous metals, sugar and rice of non-U.S. origin were Vietnamese-financed from the beginning of 1967. PL 480, Title I. provided the country with U.S. agricultural surpluses—milk, wheat, flour, rice, tobacco, cotton, etc. Funds allotted under this head totalled $128 million in 1966/67 and $156.7 million in 1968/69, the rise being due to an increase in shipments of rice.

Development loans were made in 1959–61 for such purposes as the supply of equipment and rolling stock for the railways, the construction of the Thu-Duc power station and of a water supply system for Saigon-Cholon completed in 1967.

A certain amount of aid also came from West Germany (chiefly medical and aid to refugees), Australia (including the cost of a modern dairy farm and a variety of supplies under the Colombo Plan and SEATO aid programmes), Japan (medical supplies) and Britain (a loan of £500,000 to purchase British industrial products, made in 1963).

It has been stated that over two-thirds of the American aid simply offset damage caused by the war. The amount spent on direct relief—to refugees, treatment of casualties, etc.—was once running at $80–90 million a year. A very high proportion of the non-project aid was devoted to "economic stabilization", i.e. counteracting the inflation caused by the U.S. troop build-up; these massive imports of food and consumer goods positively discouraged local production. A high proportion also of every sort of aid was simply dissipated by waste, war destruction, misguided employment or diversion of funds.

AFTER THE CEASEFIRE IN 1973

Like the political situation and largely dependent upon it, the economic situation in the Republic of Viet-Nam in 1973 and 1974 was unstable and largely unquantifiable. It was basically an unbalanced and shattered economy, rendered so by the devastation of a long war, by the inflationary effects of the U.S. military presence and the accompanying counter-inflationary policy of cheap aid-financed imports which in turn were followed by the recessionary effects of the withdrawal of American troops and the run down in aid. Massive depopulation of the countryside occurred, as over half the population moved to a non-rural environment: to towns, refugee camps, regroupment centres and around military bases. Refugees moved to escape the effects of ground fighting and as a result of the Saigon Government's attempts to "regroup" the population in order to deny the rival Provisional Revolutionary Government (PRG) access to the rural population and to remove the population from the influence of the PRG.

The economic crisis of the Thieu regime continued during the final year of its existence. Ten devaluations occurred during 1974 and manufacturing industry was estimated to be working at below 50 per cent capacity. The mainstay of the rickety structure, United States aid, although still very large, declined yet again: an estimated U.S. $2,400 million for 1974, compared with $3,100 million and $3,800 million in 1973 and 1972 respectively. Moreover, the continued refusal of the U.S. Senate to accept President Ford's proposals reduced the 1975 appropriations to some $1,300 million. In presenting his 1974–75 budget, the then Minister of Finance specifically abandoned any idea of economic development: "Our objective is how to survive."

Viet-Nam after April 1975

After the communist victory in the south in 1975 great changes, affecting both the economic and the social structures of the country, took place. The impact on the south was most dramatic but in the north, too, the reunification of Viet-Nam set the economy on a new path of development. Although not officially reunified until July 1976, the north and the south had been co-ordinating their economic policies since the end of the war. However, the very different nature of the problems facing the two regions meant that separate policies for the north and south were necessary. While in the north progress towards a more socialist economy continued in 1976, and collectivization in agriculture was extended (in 1975 it was stated that 90 per cent of cultivable land in the north was farmed by co-operatives), in the south the economy remained mixed, with state-run projects working alongside private enterprise. There had been no concerted policy of collectivization of agriculture or of expropriation of landowners by mid-1976. It seemed that the restoration of production levels had been given higher priority than the establishment of socialism.

The Hanoi Government's long-term plans saw the economic roles of the north and south as complementary, with the south providing the bulk of the country's food and agricultural raw materials, with some light industry, and the north being the industrial centre of the country. Realization of these plans will depend on the continuing recovery of the basic sectors of the Vietnamese economy and sufficient stability to allow the plans to develop.

Agriculture

The process of gradual recovery from the effects of the war continued throughout 1975 and 1976 in both north and south Viet-Nam. One of the main priorities was the restoration of agriculture to pre-1965 levels of production. Of the 1 million hectares of arable land abandoned during the war, 500,000 hectares were still to be reclaimed in 1976. However, rice production increased in 1975: 4.7 million tons of rice was produced in the north, compared with 4.3 million tons in 1965. The per capita production, however, fell from 233 kilogrammes to 192 kilogrammes, due to the rapidly growing population. The 1976 production target for the north was set at 5.5 million tons, anticipating improvements in mechanization and the extension of the areas under high-yielding strains. There are plans to expand the irrigation network by 475,000 hectares to a total of 900,000 hectares. It is hoped to make the country self-sufficient in rice within a few years. However, shortages of tools, building materials and draught animals are hampering progress. Livestock levels are expected to increase by 3 per cent in 1976.

In the north fruit-growing for the food-processing industry was still below 1965 levels in 1976, but failure to increase production was in part due to the lack of canning facilities.

Other products, including rubber, timber, coffee, sugar, tobacco and cassava, were included in the programme for expansion of agriculture, particularly in the southern half of the country, which it was hoped would provide raw materials for industrial projects in the north and absorb the surplus labour in the south, where there were an estimated 3.5 million unemployed in early 1976.

Industry

Industrial production in Viet-Nam was making a steady recovery in 1976. In the north only in the following industries had production failed to regain pre-1965 levels: timber, cement, writing paper and sugar. The Thai-Nguyen steel works, badly damaged by American bombing, was producing at its 1965 level of 176,000 tons per year. This constituted only a fraction of north Viet-Nam's estimated steel requirement of one million tons per year. Expansion is taking place in the form of the Gia Sang rolling mill, built with East German aid, which went into production in 1975. Another mill is planned with Chinese assistance. Other projects contributing to the restoration of industrial production are planned, with aid mainly from communist countries but also from Japan, France and Scandinavia. Seventeen engineering works are under construction in the north and two machine tool plants are planned for the south. To encourage the food-processing industry, canning, tea processing and cold storage facilities are planned. The Chinese-aided fertilizer factory at Ha Bac started production in 1975 with a capacity of 240,000 tons. It is hoped to relieve the shortage of building materials by the construction of cement plants with an estimated capacity of 1 million tons, as envisaged in the Five-Year Plan (1976–80) announced in 1976. Textiles are also seen as an area for industrial expansion, with the Government considering buying a polyester manufacturing plant from Japan. In the south it is estimated that two-thirds of the industrial units were operational by the beginning of 1976, but production was hampered by the lack of raw materials. In general, emphasis is being placed on the production of machinery and other heavy industrial products. It is accepted that the output of consumer goods will lag behind for some years to come.

Power

One area where north Viet-Nam has made great advances since the ceasfire of January 1973 is in the output of electricity. In 1975 total output was 950–1,000 million kilowatt hours, compared with 505 million kilowatt hours in 1964. From 1974 to 1975 the increase was 29 per cent. Some 75 per cent of electricity was produced from fossil fuels but the proportion of hydro-electric power is likely to increase with the construction of two hydro-electric stations (with aid from the U.S.S.R.) at Hoa Binh and Song Na. The lack of transmission cables has hampered the distribution of power to rural areas and prevented the full use of its potential.

North Viet-Nam's coal exceeded its 1965 level of 4 million tons in 1975 when an estimated 5 million tons were produced. However, the coal was of poor quality and the slow progress of repairs to railways and harbour installations has prevented a corresponding recovery in coal exports. In 1976 it was planned to increase coal output by 13 per cent.

Foreign Aid

Foreign aid is clearly essential if Viet-Nam's economy is to expand at the rate envisaged by the Second Five-Year Plan (1976–80) announced in early 1976. For many years north Viet-Nam received aid in the form of capital and technology from other communist countries, above all the U.S.S.R., but the Government of the reunited Viet-Nam, established in July 1976, seemed prepared to accept aid and loans from non-communist countries as well, providing that the terms did not conflict with its general policy. Japan is the primary non-communist investor in Viet-Nam and seems likely to play a prominent role in the future development of Viet-Nam's offshore petroleum deposits. Many western countries (including the U.S.A.), as well as the U.S.S.R. and China, have expressed interest in exploring off the south Vietnamese coast and it seems inevitable that Viet-Nam will come to an arrangement with one or more of them. The exploitation of petroleum and natural gas will certainly give a tremendous boost to the economy of Viet-Nam, making the establishment of a petrochemicals industry possible and also improving its balance of payments, bringing in much-needed foreign exchange.

Foreign Trade

It is difficult to gauge how Viet-Nam performed in overseas trade immediately after the end of the war in 1975 because comprehensive figures were not available in 1976. Major changes disrupted the pattern of trade, with an embargo placed on trade with Viet-Nam by the U.S.A., which had formerly been the chief economic support of the south. However, the indications were that Viet-Nam remained heavily dependent on imported manufactured items and certain raw materials. Its major trading partners are the Soviet Union and, among non-communist countries, Japan. It is estimated that south Viet-Nam needs to import 400,000 tons of rice per year, and its only known export of significance in 1975 was shrimps, of which it exported 1,200 tons in the first half of the year.

Finance

Before the end of the war in 1975 the currency of the north was the dông, while the south used the Viet-Nam piastre. The original piastre was introduced in 1955 with an exchange rate of U.S.$1 = 35 piastres. By the time of Saigon's surrender in April 1975 a succession of devaluations had brought the rate to $1 = 755 piastres. In September the PRG introduced a new piastre, worth 500 old piastres, so the exchange rate became $1 = 1.55 new piastres. In November the National Bank announced a rate of 1 piastre = 1.25 dông, an effective devaluation of about 25 per cent. After reunification in July 1976 the economies of the two zones were not fully integrated and it is expected that the two currencies will continue to circulate in their respective areas.

STATISTICAL SURVEY

Note: Some of the data relating to South Viet-Nam may refer only to areas controlled by the former Republic of Viet-Nam. No figures are available for areas under the control of the former Provisional Revolutionary Government.

AREA AND POPULATION

Area: 332,559 sq. km. (128,402 square miles): North Viet-Nam 158,750 sq. km. (61,294 square miles); South Viet-Nam 173,809 sq. km. (67,108 square miles).

Population: North Viet-Nam 23,780,375 (census of April 1st, 1974); South Viet-Nam 19,954,000 (estimate for July 1st, 1973); 22,000,000 (unofficial estimate, 1976).

PRINCIPAL TOWNS

(1973 estimates)

Town	Population	Town	Population
Hanoi (capital)	736,211*	Haiphong	182,490‡
Saigon ("Ho Chi Minh City")	1,825,297†	Can-Tho	182,424
Da-Nang	492,194	Mytho	119,892
Nha-Trang	216,227	Cam-Ranh	118,111
Qui-Nhon	213,757	Vungtau	108,436
Hué	209,043	Dalat	105,072

* 1976 estimate.

† Including Cholon. It is estimated that since April 1975 the population of Saigon has been reduced by 500,000.

‡ 1960 census.

BIRTHS AND DEATHS

North Viet-Nam: Average annual birth rate 41.5 per 1,000; death rate 18.0 per 1,000 (UN estimates for 1965–70).

South Viet-Nam (1969): Annual birth rate 42.7 per 1,000; death rate 8.1 per 1,000 (*Source:* U.S. Department of Commerce. *International Statistical Program Monthly Activities*, December 1971).

EMPLOYMENT

North Viet-Nam (mid-1970); In a total population of 20,757,000, the economically active numbered 10,921,000, including 8,475,000 in agriculture (ILO and FAO estimates).

South Viet-Nam (mid-1970): Total economically active population 9,441,000, including 7,015,000 in agriculture (ILO and FAO estimates).

AGRICULTURE

LAND USE

('000 hectares)

North Viet-Nam

(1966)

Arable and Under Permanent Crops	2,018
Forest Land	7,900
Other Land and Inland Water	5,957
Total Area	15,875

South Viet-Nam

(1973)

Arable Land	3,146
Under Permanent Crops	150
Permanent Meadows and Pastures	2,870*
Forest Land	5,620
Other Land and Inland Water	5,595
Total Area	17,381

* 1962

Source: FAO, *Production Yearbook 1974.*

PRINCIPAL CROPS

North Viet-Nam

(FAO estimates)

	Area Harvested ('000 hectares)				Production ('000 metric tons)			
	1971	1972	1973	1974	1971	1972	1973	1974
Maize	210	200	200	200	230	220	250	250
Rice (Paddy)	2,182*	2,200*	2,200*	2,700	3,900	4,400*	4,100*	4,200
Sugar Cane	19	20	22	22	600	630	660	660
Sweet Potatoes	190	195	196	197	850	860	900	910
Cassava (Manioc)	100	110	110	160	700	780	780	780
Dry Beans	60	60	60	60	15	15	15	15
Other Pulses	74	76	78	80	37	38	39	40
Soybeans	38	38	40	42	19	19	21	23
Groundnuts (in shell)	43	48	50	51	40	46	48	48
Cottonseed	} 20	22	25	25	{ 4.0	4.4	5.0	5
Cotton (Lint)					2.0	2.2	2.5	2.7
Sesame Seed	7	7	7	7	2.9	3.0	3.0	3
Castor Beans	4	4	4	4	2	2	2	2
Onions (dry)	20	20	22	22	51	52	53	54
Water melons	2	2	2	2	22	23	24	25
Coffee	11	10	10	10	2.0	2.0	2.2	2.3
Tea	13	13	10	10	2.8	3.0	3.0	3
Tobacco	4.3	4.3	4.3	4.3	4	4	4	4
Jute	6	6	6	6	6	6	6	6
Kenaf	12	12	12	12	18	16	16	16
Natural Rubber	n.a.	n.a.	n.a.	n.a.	3.2	2.7	2.7	2.7

* Unofficial estimate quoted by FAO.

Source: FAO, *Production Yearbook, 1974.*

South Viet-Nam

	Area Harvested ('000 hectares)				Production ('000 metric tons)			
	1971	1972	1973	1974*	1971	1972	1973	1974*
Maize	31	36	40	75	33.8	41.7	50.5	150
Rice (paddy)	2,625	2,700	2,830	2,900	6,324.2	6,324.2	7,025.1	7,200
Sorghum	14	31	12	12	21	40	13	12
Sweet potatoes	33	38	40	42	230.3	240.5	279	290
Cassava (manioc)	36	32	48	49	270.0	247.3	279.7	300
Dry beans	17*	18*	19*	20	12*	13*	14*	15
Other pulses	45*	45*	46*	47	26*	26*	28*	28
Soybeans	8	8	11	12	8.4	7.1	10.6	12
Groundnuts (in shell)	34	35	39	40	37.0	38.9	44.8	45
Coconuts	} n.a.	n.a.	n.a.	n.a. {	110	102	110*	115
Copra					22.5*	20.5*	23.0*	23
Cabbages	1*	1*	1*	2	32*	33*	35*	36
Onions (dry)	17*	17*	17*	17	58*	60*	60*	60
Water melons	4	3	4*	4	40.0	37.5	40*	44
Sugar cane	13	12	17	17	340.5	331.0	529.9	500
Coffee	9.6	8.5	8.9	9.0	4.4	3.9	5.1	5
Tea	8.5	8.0	7.4	7.5	5.8	5.1	6.3	6
Tobacco	8.7	9.4	11.6	12	8.6	8.4	10.3	12
Natural rubber	n.a.	n.a.	n.a.	n.a.	37.5	20.3	20.6	25

* FAO estimates.

Source: mainly FAO, *Production Yearbook 1974.*

LIVESTOCK

North Viet-Nam

('000—FAO estimates)

	1970–71	1971–72	1972–73	1973–74
Cattle	880	880	890	899
Pigs	6,800	7,100	7,500	7,985
Buffaloes	1,700	1,700	1,730	1,764
Horses	59	60	61	63
Chickens	27,000	28,000	29,000	30,000

Source: FAO, *Production Yearbook 1974.*

South Viet-Nam

	1969/70	1970/71	1971/72	1972/73	1973/74
Cattle	940,000	908,300	897,800	852,500	926,090
Pigs	3,772,000	3,847,500	4,071,500	4,275,000	4,605,440
Buffaloes	627,000	565,250	559,800	500,800	491,280
Sheep	10,000	12,000	12,840	18,530	10,400
Goats	29,000	43,000	43,500	38,200	38,300
Horses	9,000	8,000	8,340	8,070	7,780
Chickens	19,261,000	20,000,000*	19,000,000	23,250,000	25,982,300
Ducks	14,475,000	14,500,000*	16,500,000	18,170,000	20,156,300

* FAO estimate.

LIVESTOCK PRODUCTS

(metric tons)

South Viet-Nam

	1968	1969	1970
Beef, Veal and Buffalo Meat*	19,000	23,000	16,000
Pork, including Bacon and Ham*	56,000	94,000	81,000
Hen Eggs	27,500†	26,000†	25,000†
Cattle and Buffalo Hides	1,975	2,415	2,415

* Commercial production only. † FAO estimate.

FORESTRY

(FAO estimates, '000 cubic metres)

ROUNDWOOD REMOVALS

North Viet-Nam

	1971	1972
Sawlogs, veneer logs and logs for sleepers	500	500
Other industrial wood	650	660
Fuelwood	8,650	8,800
TOTAL	9,800	9,960

SAWNWOOD PRODUCTION

North Viet-Nam

	1971	1972	1973
Coniferous	25	25	25
Non-coniferous	225	225	225
TOTAL	250	250	250

Source: FAO, *Yearbook of Forest Products 1973.*

South Viet-Nam
(cubic metres)

	1968	1969	1970	1971*
Coniferous (soft wood)	15,000	35,000	44,000	44,000
Broadleaved (hard wood)	176,000	273,000	226,000	226,000
TOTAL	191,000	308,000	270,000	270,000

* FAO estimates.

FISHING

(metric tons)
South Viet-Nam

1969	1970	1971	1972	1973
463,800	577,400	587,490	677,718	713,596

North Viet-Nam: Total catch 288,700 metric tons in 1962. For 1963–73 the annual catch has been estimated by the FAO at 300,000 metric tons (inland waters 85,000; Pacific Ocean 215,000).

MINING

North Viet-Nam

		1969	1970	1971	1972	1973
Hard coal*	'000 short tons	3,300	3,300	3,300	2,200	3,300
Salt (unrefined)*	'000 metric tons	150	150	150	150	150
Phosphate rock†	,, ,, ,,	201	455	550	280	500

* *Source:* Bureau of Mines, U.S. Department of the Interior (Washington, D.C.).

† *Source:* International Superphosphate and Compound Manufacturers' Association (London).

Note: No recent data are available for the production of chromium ore (19,400 metric tons in 1960), tin or zinc.

South Viet-Nam: Salt production (metric tons) 1970: 167,610, 1971: 134,182, 1972: 149,218.

INDUSTRY

North Viet-Nam
(estimated production)

		1970	1971	1972	1973
Phosphate fertilizers*	'000 metric tons	65	96	42	50
Cement	,, ,, ,,	500	500	250	500
Electric energy	million kWh.	850	900	650	650

* In terms of phosphoric acid.

Note: No recent figures are available for other industrial production.

Source: UN, *The Growth of World Industry*, 1973 edition.

South Viet-Nam

		1970	1971	1972	1973
Electricity	'000 kWh.	1,214,512	1,340,829	1,482,126	1,627,485
Cotton Yarn	tons	11,742	13,368	9,398	10,422
Jute (Kenaf) Yarn	,,	1,522	1,399	1,061	562
Woven Cotton Fabrics	'000 metres	72,000	76,660	43,244	75,840
Rayon and Synthetic Fabrics	,,	60,317	42,654	36,446	32,588
Refined Sugar	tons	124,443	235,967	225,379	108,824
Brown Sugar	,,	2,974	3,287	2,821	—
Beer	hl.	1,486,666	1,468,910	1,431,790	1,361,630
Carbonated Drinks	,,	1,383,030	1,185,330	1,156,170	979,398
Tobacco Products	tons	9,670	12,163	11,759	9,499
Paper and Paper Preparations	,,	42,823	48,537	46,375	44,308
Glass	,,	18,783	20,779	24,458	18,363
Cement	,,	285,751	263,316	243,172	265,255

FINANCE

North Viet-Nam

100 xu=10 hào=1 dông.

Coins: 1, 2 and 5 xu.

Notes: 2 xu; 1, 2, and 5 hào; 1, 2, 5 and 10 dông.

Exchange rates (June 1976): £1 sterling=4.35 dông (basic rate) or 6.17 dông (non-commercial rate); U.S. $1=2.47 dông (basic rate) or 3.48 dông (non-commercial rate).

100 dông=£23.01=$40.48 (basic rates).

Note: The new dông, equal to 1,000 old dông, was introduced in February 1959. From January 1961 to August 1971 the basic exchange rate was U.S. $1=2.94 dông (1 dông=34.01 U.S. cents). From December 1971 to February 1973 the rate was $1=2.71 dông. In terms of sterling, the basic rate between November 1967 and June 1972 was £1=7.056 dông. In 1961 a commercial exchange rate was established for foreign trade transactions. This was £1=10.08 dông ($1=3.60 dông) until November 1967, after which it was £1=9.00 dông, equal to $1=3.75 dông from November 1967 to August 1971 and $1=3.45 dông from December 1971 to June 1972. This commercial rate has been abolished. The non-commercial exchange rate for tourists from non-Communist countries was $1=4.20 dông until August 1971; $1=3.87 dông from December 1971 to February 1973; and $1=3.48 dông since February 1973.

South Viet-Nam

100 centimes = 1 new Viet-Nam piastre.

Exchange rates (June 1976): £1 sterling=3.48 new piastres; U.S. $1=1.98 new piastres.

100 new Viet-Nam piastres=£28.76=$50.60.

Note: The new piastre, worth 500 old piastres, was introduced in September 1975. The old Viet-Nam piastre had been introduced in January 1955, replacing (at par) the Indo-Chinese piastre. From May 1953 the piastre's value was 10 old French francs, the basic exchange rate being U.S. $1=35 piastres (1 piastre=2.857 U.S. cents). This valuation in terms of U.S. currency remained officially in effect until June 1966, although multiple exchange rates were in use and the effective rate from January 1962 was $1=60 piastres (1 piastre=1.667 U.S. cents). In June 1966 the basic rate became $1=80 piastres (1 piastre=1.25 U.S. cents) but a premium of 38 piastres per dollar made the official market rate $1=118 piastres (1 piastre=0.847 U.S. cent). This remained in force until July 1972, although a rate of $1=275 piastres (1 piastre=0.364 U.S. cent) was introduced for certain transactions on a "parallel" market in October 1970 and extended to all foreign trade in November 1971, when the "parallel" rate was fixed at $1=400 to 410 piastres. In July 1972 the official and "parallel" rates were unified at $1=425 piastres. Subsequently, however, the piastre was frequently devalued and the exchange rates (at December 31st) were: $1=465 piastres (1972); $1=550 piastres (1973); and $1=685 piastres (1974). For converting the value of foreign trade transactions, the average rates were: $1=131.1 piastres in 1971; $1=357.1 piastres in 1972; $1=498.[illegible] piastres in 1973; and $1=630.0 piastres in 1974. In January 1975 the currency was again devalued, the new rate being $1=700 piastres, representing a depreciation of 95 per cent in 13 years. By April 1975 the rate was $1=755 piastres, which remained in effect after the PRG took power. The initial exchange rate for the new currency was thus $1=1.51 piastre (1 new piastre=66.225 U.S. cents). In November 1975 the new piastre was linked to the currency of the Democratic Republic of Viet-Nam, the exchange rate being 1 piastre=1.25 dông. In terms of sterling, the exchange rate was £1=283.2 old piastres (official rate) from November 1967 to October 1970; £1=660 piastres ("parallel" rate) from October 1970 to August 1971; and £1=1,068.34 piastres ("parallel" rate) from December 1971 to June 1972.

BUDGET

North Viet-Nam: The budget for 1975 has been unofficially announced at 6,500 million dông.

EXTERNAL TRADE

North Viet-Nam

SELECTED COMMODITIES*

(U.S. $'000)

IMPORTS	1971	1972	1973
Wheat flour and meal	31,000	20,000	26,000
Sugar (raw)	7,200	8,000	12,000
Natural rubber	450	430	700
Raw cotton	2,800	2,900	3,300
Milk, evaporated and condensed	350	370	450
Coconut oil	600	620	900

EXPORTS	1971	1972	1973
Rice	3,000	3,150	4,300
Bananas (fresh)	400	310	310
Coffee	830	840	1,000
Tea	1,700	1,900	2,000
Groundnuts (shelled)	400	200	280
Groundnut oil	540	580	850
Jute	290	300	300
Sugar (raw)	1,500	1,800	2,000

* FAO estimates.

Source: United Nations, *Statistical Yearbook for Asia and the Pacific 1974.*

SELECTED COUNTRIES

IMPORTS		1973	1974	1975
U.S.S.R.	million roubles	142.9	192.3	158.7
German Democratic Republic	million D.D.R. valuta-marks	30.8	139.6	n.a.
Hungary	million forints	279.2	271.5	n.a.
Hong Kong*	U.S. $'000	n.a.	5,579	3,535
Singapore*	,,	n.a.	4,478	1,111
United Kingdom†	,,	n.a.	603	1,710
Japan	,,	n.a.	20,000§	11,000†

EXPORTS		1973	1974	1975
U.S.S.R.	million roubles	36.9	n.a.	n.a.
German Democratic Republic	million D.D.R. valuta-marks	117.0	33.8	n.a.
Hungary	million forints	n.a.	19.4	n.a.
Hong Kong*	U.S. '000	n.a.	3,049‡	8,246‡
Singapore*	,,	n.a.	1,139	437
United Kingdom†	,,	n.a.	345	50
Japan	,,	n.a.	30,200§	26,700†

* January–August.
† January–November.
‡ Includes re-exports.
§ January–December.

South Viet-Nam

(million old piastres)

	1966	1967	1968	1969	1970	1971	1972	1973
Imports c.i.f.	28,363	43,037	37,271	53,422	44,032	70,104	233,225	310,002
Exports f.o.b.	1,491	1,313	936	954	916	994	5,467	29,607

PRINCIPAL COMMODITIES

Imports	1972 metric tons	1972 '000 old piastres	1973 metric tons	1973 '000 old piastres
Dairy Products	25,442	5,651,120	11,486	6,510,912
Wheat Flour	48,084	1,780,661	35,069	1,679,381
Sugar	165,907	14,215,834	362,000	30,324,095
Rice	271,000	16,707,000	303,000	43,250,000
Tobacco and Cigarettes	16,524	9,721,666	8,804	6,252,749
Cement	651,597	5,912,844	538,692	6,771,828
Petroleum Products	1,844,040	20,720,031	2,110,042	35,003,526
Chemicals	50,446	7,880,513	98,523	11,321,982
Pharmaceuticals	3,234	9,700,109	3,058	12,635,984
Fertilizers	234,173	7,266,809	326,353	18,119,703
Rubber and Rubber Goods	5,581	3,103,849	3,841	2,909,200
Paper and Cardboard	29,007	2,280,688	25,687	4,157,294
Textile Fabrics	7,352	14,610,406	2,734	7,290,013
Yarn	13,895	8,495,548	14,674	14,308,238
Metallurgic Products	212,098	16,042,322	95,254	12,859,489
Machinery and Appliances	20,514	20,873,680	15,067	23,375,955
Electrical Equipment	13,177	14,057,134	6,051	8,200,044
Motor Cars and Parts	15,259	4,590,401	4,652	3,057,683

Exports	1972 metric tons	1972 '000 old piastres	1973 metric tons	1973 '000 old piastres
Shrimps, Crustaceans	1,872	1,599,883	4,236	6,539,536
Feathers for Beds	424	113,031	967	671,263
Bones	517	10,720	2,026	79,565
Tea	601	123,283	694	283,545
Rubber	22,932	1,565,248	19,619	6,358,356
Ceramics	173	18,098	1,244	365,788

Note: Exports of rice are now insignificant.

PRINCIPAL COUNTRIES

(million old piastres)

Imports	1972	1973
U.S.A.	96,000	128,677
China (Taiwan)	17,083	14,318
Japan	45,541	39,483
Korea, Republic	4,660	7,654
France	16,117	22,676
Germany, Federal Republic	4,528	5,107
India	525	643
Italy	4,169	4,532
United Kingdom	1,880	2,043
Portugal	198	253
Thailand	5,650	8,418
Singapore	18,914	32,380
Total (incl. others)	215,265	310,001

Exports	1972	1973
France	1,065	4,202
Germany, Federal Republic	144	612
United Kingdom	155	138
Japan	1,650	6,917
Singapore	316	3,409
Hong Kong	1,340	7,626
Italy	30	418
U.S.A.	229	1,212
Netherlands	25	117
Spain	47	293
China (Taiwan)	51	1,540
Thailand	9	376
Total (incl. others)	5,061	29,697

1974: U.S.A.: Imports U.S. $675 million; Exports U.S. $8 million.

TRANSPORT

North Viet-Nam

INTERNATIONAL SEA-BORNE SHIPPING

(estimated freight traffic in metric tons)

	1969	1970	1971	1972
Goods Loaded . . .	360,000	350,000	500,000	300,000
Goods Unloaded . .	915,000	1,200,000	1,170,000	900,000

Source: United Nations, *Statistical Yearbook 1974.*

Inland Waterways (1960): 27 million freight ton-km.

South Viet-Nam

RAILWAYS

	1971	1972	1973
Passengers ('000 passenger-km.) .	85,657	65,672	170,043
Freight ('000 ton-km.) . .	38,208	6,617	1,214

ROADS

	1971	1972	1973
Passenger cars	74,000	74,600	66,120
Commercial vehicles	90,400	91,250	97,661

SHIPPING

('000 metric tons)

	1970	1971	1972	1973
Goods Loaded . .	904	961	784	1,027
Goods Unloaded .	6,824	6,554	5,614	4,877

CIVIL AVIATION

	1971	1972	1973
International			
Flights	18,039	15,219	8,253
Passengers . . .	746,617	528,489	236,459
Freight (metric tons) .	72,717	105,753	33,747
Mail (,, ,,) .	4,334	7,702	2,713
Domestic			
Flights	85,169	89,572	64,420
Passengers . . .	1,723,823	1,411,073	1,007,677
Freight (metric tons) .	9,116	7,622	5,277
Mail (,, ,,) .	825	1,335	1,561

EDUCATION

North Viet-Nam

(1966–67)

	General	Secondary Vocational	Higher
Schools	10,993	185	28
Teachers	86,495	4,194	5,004
Pupils and Undergraduates*	4,517,600	101,880	48,402
of which: in evening and correspondence courses	1,154,500	9,300	10,743

*1972: Number of students at all grades was 7 million.

South Viet-Nam

(1972/73)

	Schools	Teachers	Pupils
Primary	8,275	65,984	3,290,387
Secondary	1,138	27,547	903,383
Higher	10	1,341	88,617

Sources (unless otherwise indicated): *Nhan Dan* of May 3rd and 4th, 1963; text of the Five-Year Plan as presented to the National Assembly (end April 1963); trade statistics of partner countries; General Statistical Office of the Democratic Republic of Viet-Nam; South Viet-Nam statistics from Institut National de la Statistique, Saigon.

THE CONSTITUTION

Note: The constitution summarized here is that of the Democratic Republic of Viet-Nam. The constitution of the Socialist Republic of Viet-Nam had yet to be drafted in July 1976. However, it is likely to be based on the following provisions, which will remain in force in the interim.

The original constitution of the Democratic Republic was replaced by a revised constitution, adopted in 1960.

Main provisions:

Unity of Viet-Nam: The territory of Viet-Nam is an indivisible whole.

Economic Principles: The economy is directed by a plan, and the state relies on the organs of state, the trade unions and the co-operative sector to assist in fulfilling the plan.

President: elected for four years by the National Assembly. He represents the country in external affairs, and is the supreme commander of the armed forces.

Council of Ministers: consists of the Prime Minister (President), the Vice-Premiers, the Heads of State Commissions and the Director-General of the National Bank. The Council is responsible to the National Assembly.

Special Political Conference: *ad hoc* executive body convened to make important political decisions. The President of the state takes the chair.

National Assembly: elected for the same period as the President. The Assembly is to meet twice a year, or for extraordinary sessions. It elects a President of the Assembly, the President and Vice-President of the state, the Prime Minister and other officials. It discusses economic plans, and among other functions, examines and approves the budget.

Standing Committee of the National Assembly: permanent executive body of the Assembly, and elected by it. It consists of a Chairman, Vice-Chairman, Secretary-General, and members. It is responsible to the National Assembly, and decides questions of election and franchise, and most appointments. It also supervises local government.

Local Government: the country is divided into provinces, and subdivided into districts, cities and towns. There are People's Courts and all these levels, elected locally.

Judicial System: consists of the Supreme People's Court, local People's Courts, and military courts. There are also People's Organs of Control, under the Supreme People's Organ of Control, to secure observance of the laws.

THE GOVERNMENT

President: TON DUC THANG.

Vice-Presidents: NGUYEN LUONG BANG, NGUYEN HUU THO.

COUNCIL OF MINISTERS

(*July* 1976)

Prime Minister: PHAM VAN DONG.

Vice-Premiers: PHAM HUNG, HUYNH TAN PHAT, Gen. VO NGUYEN GIAP, NGUYEN DUY TRINH, LE THANH NGHI, VO CHI CONG, DO MUOI.

Minister of the Interior: TRAN QUOC HOAN.

Minister of Foreign Affairs: NGUYEN DUY TRINH.

Minister of National Defence: Gen. VO NGUYEN GIAP.

Chairman of the State Commission for Planning: LE THANH NGHI.

Vice-Chairman: NGUYEN HUU MAI.

Minister of Agriculture: VO THUC DONG.

Minister for Scientific Work and Agricultural Techniques: NGHIEM XUAN YEM.

Minister of Forestry: HOANG VAN KIEU.

Minister of Water Conservancy: NGUYEN THANH BINH.

Minister of Machinery and Metallurgy: NGUYEN CON.

Minister of Electricity and Coal: NGUYEN CHAN.

Minister of Construction: DO MUOI.

Minister of Communications and Transport: PHAN TRONG TUE.

Minister of Light Industry: VU TUAN.

Minister of Grain and Food Products: NGO MINH LOAN.

Minister of Marine Products: VO CHI CONG.

Minister of Internal Trade: HOANG QUOC THINH.

Minister of Foreign Trade: DANG VIET CHAU.

Minister of Finance: DOA THIEN THI.

Director of the State Bank: HOANG ANH.

Chairman of the State Commission for Prices: TO DUY.

Minister of Labour: NGUYEN THO CHAN.

Minister of Supply: TRAN SAM.

Chairman of the State Commission for Nationalities: LE QUANG BA.

Chairman of the State Commission for Science and Technology: TRAN DAI NGHIA.

Minister of Culture: NGUYEN VAN HIEU.

Minister of Higher and Vocational Education: NGUYEN DINH TU.

Minister of Education: NGUYEN THI BINH.

Minister of Public Health: VU VAN CAN.

Minister for Disabled Soldiers and Social Affairs: DUONG QUOC CHINH.

Minister for Da River Projects: HA KE TAN.

Minister for Oil and Natural Gas: DINH DUC THIEN.

Chairman of the Inspectorate: TRAN NAM TRUNG.

Ministers in charge of Cultural and Educational Work at the Prime Minister's Office: TRAN QUANG HUY.

Minister of the Prime Minister's Office: DANG THI.

Minister, Director of the Secretariat of the Prime Minister's Office: PHAN MY.

NATIONAL DEFENCE COUNCIL

(*July* 1976)

Chairman: TON DUC THANG.

Vice-Chairman: PHAM VAN DONG.

Members: LE DUAN TRUONG CHINH, PHAM, HUNG, Gen. VO NGUYEN GIAP, NGUYEN DUY TRINH, LE THANH NGHI, TRAN QUOC HOAN, VAN TIEN DUNG.

NATIONAL ASSEMBLY

The Sixth National Assembly, the first since 1946 to be based on nationwide elections, was elected on April 25th, 1976. It consisted of 492 deputies, representing 79 electoral units and zones. Its first meeting took place in June and July 1976.

Standing Committee

Chairman: TRUONG CHINH.

Six Vice-Chairmen, 13 permanent members, 2 alternate members.

POLITICAL PARTIES

Dang Lao Dong Viet-Nam (*Viet-Nam Workers' Party*): Hanoi; controlling party in Viet-Nam Fatherland Front; successor to the Communist Party of Indochina; f. 1930; First Sec. LE DUAN; Southern branch leader PHAM HUNG; 620,000 mems.; publs. *Nhan Dan, Hoc Tap*.

Socialist Party: Hanoi; f. 1946; consists mainly of intelligentsia; Gen. Sec. NGUYEN XIEN; publ. *To Quoc*.

Democratic Party: Hanoi; f. 1944; party of the middle classes, and intelligentsia; Sec.-Gen. NGHIEM XUAN YEM.

POLITICAL ORGANIZATIONS

Ho Chi Minh Working Youth Union: 60 Ba Trieu, Hanoi; f. 1931; 2,600,000 mems.; Sec. VU QUANG.

Vietnamese Women's Union: Hanoi; Pres. NGUYEN THI DINH

It was reported in 1976 that the following three organizations were planning to merge:

Viet-Nam Fatherland Front: Hanoi; f. 1955; replaced the Lien-Viet (Popular National Front), the successor to Viet-Nam Doc-Lap Dong Minh Hoi (Revolutionary League for the Independence of Viet-Nam) or Viet-Minh; Chief Spokesman XUAN THUY.

National Front for the Liberation of South Viet-Nam: f. 1960; Pres. NGUYEN HUU THO.

Viet-Nam Alliance of National, Democratic and Peace Forces: f. 1968; Pres. TRINH DINH THAO.

DIPLOMATIC REPRESENTATION

By July 1976 the following countries had formally recognized the United Socialist Republic of Viet-Nam: Belgium, Cambodia, the People's Republic of China, Denmark, France, the Federal Republic of Germany, India, Indonesia, Ireland, Italy, Japan, Laos, Luxembourg, Malaysia, the Netherlands, the Philippines, Singapore, the United Kingdom and the U.S.S.R. It is expected that most of the other countries listed below, which had diplomatic relations with the Democratic Republic of Viet-Nam, will also recognize the new state.

EMBASSIES ACCREDITED TO VIET-NAM
(In Hanoi unless otherwise stated)

Albania: *Ambassador:* ASTRIT MERO.

Algeria: *Ambassador:* (vacant) (also accred. to Bangladesh).

Australia: *Ambassador:* D. G. WILSON.

Belgium: *Ambassador:* GEORGE J. VILAIN XIV.

Bulgaria: *Ambassador:* NIKOLAI TCHERNEV.

Burma: *Ambassador:* HLA SWE.

Cambodia: *Ambassador:* SIEN AN.

China, People's Republic: *Ambassador:* FU HAO.

Cuba: *Ambassador:* RAÚL FORNELL DELGADO.

Czechoslovakia: *Ambassador:* VLADIMIR KUBAT.

Egypt: *Ambassador:* ABDEL KADER KHALIL.

Finland: *Ambassador:* UNTO K. TANSKENEN.

France: *Ambassador:* CHARLES MALO.

German Democratic Republic: *Ambassador:* DIETER DOERING.

Germany, Federal Republic: *Chargé d'Affaires:* DR. PETER TRUHART.

Hungary: *Ambassador:* LAJOS KARSAI.

India: *Ambassador:* (vacant).

Indonesia: *Ambassador:* USEP RANAWIJAYA.

Iraq: *Ambassador:* ALA SHAFIK AL-RAWI.

Italy: *Ambassador:* GIULIANO BERTOLUCCI.

Japan: Room 138, Hotel Thong Nhat, 15 Ngo Quyen; *Ambassador:* TAKAAKI HASEGAWA.

Korea, Democratic People's Republic: *Ambassador:* KIM SANG CHUN.

Laos: *Ambassador:* KHAMPHAY BOUPHA.

Mongolia: *Ambassador:* TSERENDORJ DENDEVYNE.

Netherlands: *Charge d'Affaires:* BASTIAAN R. KORNER.

Pakistan: *Ambassador:* ASHFAQUE AHMED KHAN.

Poland: *Ambassador:* JOSEF PUTA.

Romania: *Ambassador:* TUDOR ZAMFIRA.

Sweden: *Ambassador:* BO KJELLEN.

Switzerland: *Ambassador:* HANS MUELLER.

United Kingdom: 16 Pho Ly Thuong Kiet; *Ambassador:* R. M. TESH, C.M.G.

Yugoslavia: *Ambassador:* EKREM DURIC.

Viet-Nam also has diplomatic relations with Afghanistan, Argentina, Austria, Bangladesh, Burundi, Cameroon, Canada, Denmark, Equatorial Guinea, Finland, the Gambia, Greece, Guinea, Iceland, Iran, Libya, Luxembourg, Madagascar, Malaysia, Mali, Malta, Mauritania, Mexico, Norway, the Philippines, Portugal, Senegal, Singapore, Somalia, Sri Lanka, Sudan, Syria, Tanzania, Thailand, Tunisia, Uganda, Upper Volta, the Yemen Arab Republic, the People's Democratic Republic of Yemen and Zambia. Viet-Nam also recognizes the Palestine Liberation Organization.

JUDICIAL SYSTEM

The Judicial System, based on French lines, has been thoroughly revised since 1954. The Supreme Court in Hanoi is the chief court and exercises civil and criminal jurisdiction over all lower courts. There are People's Courts in District towns, and a number of military courts. The observance of the laws is the concern of the People's Organs of Control, under a Supreme People's Organ of Control.

President of the Supreme Court: PHAM VAN BACH.
Chief Procurator: TRAN HUU DUC.

RELIGION

Traditional Vietnamese religion included elements of all three Chinese religions: Mahayana Buddhism, Taoism and Confucianism. Its most widespread feature was the cult of ancestors, practised in individual households and clan temples. In addition, there were (and remain) a wide variety of Buddhist sects, and the sects belonging to the "new" religions of Caodaism and Hoa Hao; and a Catholic Church.

BUDDHISM

North: A Buddhist organization has existed since 1954, grouping Buddhists loyal to the Democratic Republic.

South: The Unified Buddhist Church, formed in 1964, incorporated several disparate groups, including the "militant" An-Quang group (mainly natives of central Viet-Nam), the group of Thich Tam Chau (mainly northern emigrés in Saigon) and the southern Buddhists of the Xa-Loi temple. The situation since April 1975 is unclear, but one Buddhist group was represented in the National Liberation Front by Thich Thien Hao, head of the Luc-Hoa Buddhist Association.

CAODAISM

Formally inaugurated in 1926, this is a syncretic religion based on spiritualist seances with a predominantly ethical content, but sometimes with political overtones. A number of different sects exist, of which the most politically involved (1940–75) was that of Tay-Ninh. Another sect, the Tien-Thien, has been represented in the National Liberation Front since its inception. Together the sects are said to number two million adepts. They live mostly in the south.

HOA HAO

A new manifestation of an older religion called Buu Son Ky Huong, the Hoa Hao sect was founded by Huynh Phu So in 1939, and at one time claimed 1.5 million adherents in southern Viet-Nam. Its fate since April 1975 is uncertain, in view of its anti-communist stand since 1946.

CATHOLICISM

The Vietnamese Church has existed since the 17th century, and since the 1930s has been led mainly by Vietnamese priests. Many Catholics moved from North to South Viet-Nam in 1954–55 to avoid living under Communist rule, but some remained in the north. There are possibly as many as two million Catholics throughout the country.

ARCHBISHOPS

Hanoi: Cardinal JOSEPH MARIE TRIN NHU KHUE.
Hué: Most Rev. PHILIPPE NGUYEN KIM DIEN.
Saigon: Most Rev. PAUL NGUYEN VAN BINH.

THE PRESS

DAILIES

HANOI

Nhan Dan (*The People*): 71 Hang Trong St.; f. 1946; official organ of the Lao-Dong Party; Editor HOANG TUNG; circ. 100,000.

Quan Doi Nhan Dan (*People's Army*): 7 Blvd. Phan Ding Phung; f. 1950; published by the Army.

Thoi Moi: circ. 25,000.

Thu Do Hanoi: f. 1957; Editor DINH NHO KHOI; circ. 30,000.

There are some 45 regional dailies.

SAIGON

Giai Phong (*Liberation*): 174-6 Vo Thi San St.; f. 1964; organ of the National Front for the Liberation of South Viet-Nam.

Saigon Giai Phong (*Saigon Liberation*): 432 Xo-Viet Nghe-Tinh St.; f. 1975.

Tin Sang (*Morning News*): f. 1963, re-established 1975; independent; Editor NGO CONG DUC.

PERIODICALS

Bulletin of the Medical Association of the Viet-Nam D.R.: Hanoi; illustrated annual in French and English.

Chinh Nghia (*Justice*): Hanoi; Catholic; Weekly.

Cong Giao va Dan Toc (*Catholics and the Nation*): Saigon; f. 1975; Catholic; Weekly; Editor NGUYEN DINH-THI.

Cuu Quoc (*National Salvation*): Hanoi; weekly; f. 1942; organ of the Fatherland Front; Chief Editor NGUYEN TIEU.

Hoc Tap (*Studies*): 28 rue Tran binh Trong, Hanoi; monthly; f. 1954; organ of the Lao Dong Party; circ. 50,000.

Lao Dong (*Labour*): Hanoi; twice weekly; organ of Federation of Trade Unions; circ. 45,000.

Nghien Cuu Kinh Te (*Economic Research*): Hanoi; every two months.

Nghian Cuu Lich Su (*Historical Research*): 38 Hang Chuoi St., Hanoi; organ of Institute of History; Dir. NGHUYEN KHANH TOAN.

Nhan Dan Nong Thong (*Peasantry*): Hanoi; twice weekly; agricultural supplement; circ. 21,000.

Phu Nu Viet-Nam (*Vietnamese Women*): 47 Hang Chuoc, Hanoi; Women's magazine.

Tap Chi Van Hoc (*Review of Literature*): 20 Ly Thai St., Hanoi; f. 1960; organ of Institute of Literature; every two months; Dir. DANG THAI MAI.

Tien Phong (*Vanguard*): 15 rue Ho Xuan Huong, Hanoi; f. 1957; three times weekly; organ of the Youth Movement; circ. 16,000.

To Quoc (*Fatherland*): 53 Nguyen Du St., Hanoi; f. 1946; organ of Viet-Nam Socialist Party.

Van Nghe (*Arts and letters*): 17 Tran Quoc Tuan St., Hanoi; f. 1949; Published by Association for Letters and Fine Art.

Viet-Nam: 79 Ly Thuong Kiet St., Hanoi; f. 1954; illustrated monthly; published by Committee for Cultural Relations with Foreign Countries; Vietnamese, Russian, Chinese, French, Spanish and English; circ. 86,000; Dir. LE BA THUYEN.

Viet-Nam Courier: 46 Tran Hung Dao, Hanoi; monthly; Committee for Cultural Relations with Foreign Countries; English and French editions.

Vietnamese Studies: 46 Tran Hung Dao, Hanoi; quarterly; publ. by Committee for Cultural Relations with Foreign Countries; English and French editions.

NEWS AGENCIES

Viet-Nam News Agency: Hanoi.

FOREIGN BUREAUX

Agence France Presse: 18 Phung Khac Khoan, Hanoi.

Czechoslovak News Agency (Ceteka): 65 Hoang Dieu St. Hanoi.

Novosti Press Agency: APN Representation, 15 Thuyen Quang St., Hanoi.

Polish Press Agency (PAP): B17 Khu Kim Lien, Hanoi.

Prensa Latina: 66 Ngo Thi Nham, Hanoi.

Tass: 23 Cao Ba Quat, Hanoi.

PRESS ASSOCIATION

Viet-Nam Journalists' Association: Hanoi; 2,000 mems.; Sec.-Gen. LU QUY KY.

PUBLISHERS

Su That (*Truth*) **Publishing House:** Hanoi; controlled by the Government; Marxist classics, political and philosophical works.

Foreign Languages Publishing House: Hanoi; controlled by the Government; Chief Editor NGUYEN KHAC VIEN.

Giao Duc (*Educational*) **Publishing House:** Hanoi; Ministry of Education.

Khoa Hoc (*Social Sciences*) **Publishing House:** Hanoi.

Lao Dong (*Labour*) **Publishing House:** Hanoi.

Literary Publishing House: Hanoi; State-controlled.

Pho Thong (*Popularization*) **Publishing House:** Hanoi.

Popular Army Publishing House: Hanoi.

Scientific Publishing House: Hanoi.

Y Hoc (*Medical*) **Publishing House:** Hanoi.

RADIO AND TELEVISION

Voice of Viet-Nam: 58 Quan-Su St., Hanoi; controlled by the Council of Ministers; Home Service in Vietnamese; Foreign Service in English, Japanese, Korean, French, Cambodian, Laotian, Thai, Cantonese and Standard Chinese, and Indonesian; Dir.-Gen. T. LAM.

Radio Saigon Giai-Phong (*Saigon Liberation Radio*): started broadcasts in May 1975.

In 1971 there were 510,000 radio receivers in North Viet-Nam, and in 1972 there were 5 million in South Viet-Nam.

TELEVISION

Television was introduced into South Viet-Nam early in 1966 when the Saigon government station THVN was established with American assistance. In 1972 there were about 1.2 million receivers, many installed in public meeting places.

FINANCE

BANKING

North Viet-Nam

State Bank of Viet-Nam (Viet-bank): 7 Le-Lai St., Hanoi; f. 1951; central bank of issue; 350 branches; Min. Gen. Dir. TA HOANG CO, Vice-Mins. Dep. Gen. Dir. LE DUC, VU DUY HIEU, TRAN DUONG.

Bank of Foreign Trade of Viet-Nam (Vietcombank): 47–49, Ly-Thai-To St., Hanoi; f. 1963; the only bank authorized to deal in the country with foreign currencies and international payments; Chair. TRAN DUONG; Vice-Chair. DAO VIET DOAN, MAI HUU ICH.

South Viet-Nam

All banking activities in Saigon were suspended in May 1975. It was announced in June 1975 that the Viet-Nam National Bank would resume operations under a new governor, responsible to the Provisional Revolutionary Government (PRG), to handle foreign exchange activities. The Viet-Nam Thuong Tin Bank was also reconstituted in June 1975. In November 1975, 27 private banks were permitted to resume limited operations, but not the three main U.S. banks formerly operating in Saigon.

National Bank of Viet-Nam: Saigon; f. 1955; re-organized 1975; functions include: the supply of capital for restoration and development, the settlement of debts, deposits and savings, foreign banking activities; Gov. TRAN DUONG.

Viet-Nam Thuong Tin (*Commercial Credit Bank of Viet-Nam*): Saigon; f. 1955; re-organized 1975; entrusted with certain foreign transactions.

INSURANCE

Viet-Nam Insurance Co. (Baoviet): 7 Ly Thuong Kiet, Hanoi; state company; marine insurance.

TRADE AND INDUSTRY

North Viet-Nam

Chamber of Commerce of Viet-Nam (Vietcochamber): 33 Ba Trieu St., Hanoi; attached organizations are:

Vinacontrol (*Goods Control Office*): 54 Tran Nhan Tong St., Hanoi.

Maritime Arbitration Committee: 33 Ba Trieu St., Hanoi; settles and exercises jurisdiction over disputes arising from sea transportation.

Foreign Trade Arbitration Committee: 33 Ba Trieu St., Hanoi; settles disputes arising from foreign trade transactions between Vietnamese and foreign economic organizations.

All foreign trade activities are directed and controlled by the State through the intermediary of the Ministry of Foreign Trade. To this effect, several National Import-Export Corporations have been set up (*see below*).

FOREIGN TRADE CORPORATIONS

Agrexport (*Viet-Nam National Agricultural Produce and Foodstuffs Export-Import Corporation*): 6 Trang Tien, Hanoi; imports and exports agricultural produce and foodstuffs.

Artexport (*Viet-Nam National Handicrafts and Arts Articles Export-Import Corporation*): 31–33 Ngo Quyen St., Hanoi; deals in craft products and art materials.

Machinoimport (*Viet-Nam National Machinery Export-Import Corporation*): 8 Trang Thi St., Hanoi; imports and exports machinery and tools.

Meranimex (*Viet-Nam National Marine and Animal Products Import and Export Corporation*): 17 Cu Chinh Lan St., Haiphong; exports live animals, salted and frozen meat, eggs, animal feeds, furs and skins, shellfish and seaweed.

Minexport (*Viet-Nam National Minerals Export-Import Corporation*): 35 Hai Ba Trung, Hanoi; exports minerals and metals, quarry products, building materials, chemical products, pharmaceutical products; imports coal, metals, pharmaceutical and chemical products, industrial and building materials, fuels and oils, asphalt, fertilizers, gypsum and cement bags.

Naforimex (*Viet-Nam National Forest and Native Produce Export-Import Corporation*): 19 Ba Trieu St., Hanoi; imports coconut products, rubber and wood and exports oils, forest products and miscellaneous products.

Technoimport (*Viet-Nam National Complete Equipment Import and Technical Exchange Corporation*): 16–18 Trang Thi St., Hanoi; imports industrial plant.

Tocontap (*Viet-Nam National Sundries Export-Import Corporation*): 36 Ba Trieu St., Hanoi; imports and exports consumer goods.

Transaf (*Viet-Nam National Foreign Trade Corporation*): Mo-Guyen St., Hanoi; import and export transactions with foreign co-operative societies and firms in consumer goods; foodstuffs and handicrafts; re-exports; compensation trade; agents for all commercial transactions.

Xunhasaba (*Viet-Nam State Corporation for Export and Import of Books, Periodicals and other Cultural Commodities*): 32 Hai Ba Trung, Hanoi.

Fafim (*Viet-Nam State Film Distribution Enterprise*): 49 Nguyen Trai, Hanoi; export and import of films; organization of film shows and participation of Vietnamese films in international film exhibitions.

All commercial and non-commercial payments to foreign countries are effected through the Bank of Foreign Trade of Viet-Nam.

TRADE UNIONS

Viet-Nam General Federation of Trade Unions: f. 1976 from merger of the Southern Viet-Nam Trade Union Federation and the following.

Tong Cong Doan Viet-Nam (T.C.D.) (*Viet-Nam Federation of Trade Unions*): 82 Tran Hung Dao, Hanoi; f. 1946; 1,200,000 mems.; Pres. Hoang Quoc Viet; Gen. Sec. Nguyen Duc Thuan; publs. *Viet-Nam Trade Unions* (in English, French and Spanish), *Lao Dong*, *Cong Doan*.

TRANSPORT AND TOURISM

North Viet-Nam

RAILWAYS

Viet-Minh National Railways: Hanoi; Government-owned; official information is not available, but lines reported to be in operation are: Hanoi–Haiphong (104 km.), Hanoi–Mukh Nam Quong (162 km.), Hanoi–Thanh Hoa (167 km.), Hanoi–Laokay (296 km.), Dong Anh-Thai Nguyen (51 km.).

ROADS

National Automobile Transport Undertaking: Hanoi; f. 1951; operates long distance and municipal bus services.

There are about 13,400 kilometres of motorable roads.

SHIPPING

Vietfracht (*Viet-Nam Foreign Trade Transportation Corporation*): 74 Nguyen Du St., Hanoi; in charge of all activities concerning sea transportation; charters vessels and books shipping space for principals at home and abroad; canvasses cargo for shipowners; provides regular services to and from South-East Asian ports, mainly Haiphong–Hong Kong–Singapore, Cambodian ports–Heungnam–Chungjin and main Japanese ports; provides services to and from the Black Sea and western and northern Europe; arranges shipments on through bill of lading from Haiphong to any port in the world.

Viet-Nam Ocean Shipping Agency (VOSA): 11 Tran Phu St., Haiphong; in charge of performing all such facilities as may be required for the coming and going of merchant shipping, of loading and unloading operations, lighterage, forwarding and reception of goods, tallying, weighing and measuring, warehousing, reconditioning and repacking of damaged goods; arranging the booking of cargo, the chartering, purchase and sale of vessels and the settlement of marine casualties and insurance.

South Viet-Nam

The following information applies to the situation before April 1975.

RAILWAYS

Viet-Nam Railways: 2 Dien Hong Square, Saigon.

State-owned length of track 1,278 km.; dislocation caused by the war had reduced exploitable length of track to about 684 km. in 1973.

ROADS

There are 6,523 km. of national highways, 3,663 km. of secondary or regional roads, 10,731 km. of other roads; total 20,917.

SHIPPING

There are more than 4,500 km. of navigable waterways of which 2,200 km. are canals.

Nam-Hai: 20 Nguyen-Cong-Tru, Saigon.

Nam-Tien: 114 Vo-Di-Nguy, Saigon.

Viet-Nam Thuy-Bo-Van-Tai Cong-Ty: 10 Ton-Dam, Saigon.

The following foreign lines call at Saigon.

American President Lines: San Francisco, Calif., Getz Bros & Co. (Vietnam), 26–28 Ham Nghi, Saigon.

Compagnie des Messageries Maritimes: 46–48 Tu-Do, B.P. 11, Saigon.

Compagnie Maritime des Chargeurs Réunis: 27–28 Ben Bach Dang, B.P. 137, Saigon.

East Asiatic Company Ltd.: Copenhagen, Saigon.

CIVIL AVIATION

Viet-Nam's principal airport is Gia Lam, near Hanoi. It caters for domestic and foreign traffic and is at present, being extended to take 707s.

Civil Aviation of Viet-Nam (CAVN): Hanoi; f. 1954; Government-owned; controls all services; operates services between Hanoi and Saigon and other internal routes; acquired the equipment and aircraft of Saigon's *Air Viet-Nam* in 1975.

Hang Kong Dan Dung (*People's Airlines*).

The following foreign airlines also serve Viet-Nam: Aeroflot, Civil Aviation administration of China (CAAC) and Interflug. The Vietnamese Government has agreed, in principal, to permit Air France to operate in Viet-Nam.

TOURISM

Vietnamtourism (*Viet-Nam Travel Service*): 54 Nguyen Du St., Hanoi.

DEFENCE

North Viet-Nam

Armed Forces and Equipment (1974): Total 583,000 of which army 570,000; navy 3,000; air force 10,000 (plus para-military forces of 445,000). Equipment is largely of Soviet and Chinese origin and includes about 1,000 tanks and 200 combat aircraft.

Military Service: Two years minimum.

Defence Expenditure: Estimated defence spending (1970): 2,150 million dông (U.S. $584 million).

Chief of Staff, Army: Gen. Van Tien Dung.

Commander-in-Chief of the Armed Forces: General Vo Nguyen Giap.

EDUCATION

The details of the educational system operating in Viet-Nam in 1976 are not available. All education is state-run. Educational institutions in the South, closed in May 1975, were due to re-open later in that year with political courses being held for teachers and students. In North Viet-Nam it is estimated that 10,000 teachers graduate annually.

UNIVERSITIES

University of Cantho: Dailo Hoabinh, Cantho; 105 teachers, about 4,500 students.

University of Hanoi: Hanoi; about 150 teachers; about 1,500 students.

University of Hué: 3 rue le Loi, Hué; 288 teachers, 6,251 students.

University of Saigon: 3 Cong-Tryong Chien-Si, Saigon; f. 1955, reorganized 1975-76; 670 teachers, 63,800 students.

BIBLIOGRAPHY

BATOR, V. Vietnam: a Diplomatic Tragedy (Faber & Faber, London, 1967).

BUTTINGER, J. Vietnam, a Political History (Deutsch, London, 1969).

Vietnam: a Dragon Embattled (Pall Mall Press, London, 1967).

CAMERON, A. W. Viet-Nam Crisis, a Documentary History (1940–56) (Cornell University Press, Ithaca, 1971).

CHALIAND, G. The Peasants of North Vietnam (Penguin Books, Harmondsworth, 1969).

CHEN, K. Vietnam and China 1938–54 (Princeton University Press, Princeton, 1969).

CHESNEAUX, J. Contribution à l'Histoire de la Nation Vietnamienne (Editions Sociales, Paris, 1955).

CHESNEAUX, J., BOUDAREL, G., HEMERY, D. *et al.* Tradition et Revolution au Vietnam (Editions Anthropos, Paris, 1971).

DEVILLERS, P. Histoire du Viet-Nam de 1940 à 1952 (Le Seuil, Paris, 1952).

DEVILLERS, P. and LACOUTURE, J. End of a War, Indochina 1954 (Pall Mall Press, London, 1969).

FALL, B. The Two Viet-Nams, a Political and Military Analysis (2nd edn., Pall Mall Press, London, 1967).

Street Without Joy: Insurgency in Indochina 1946–63 (Pall Mall Press, London, 1963).

Hell in a very Small Place: the Siege of Dien Bien Phu (Pall Mall Press, London, 1967).

FITZGERALD, F. Fire in the Lake: the Vietnamese and the Americans in Vietnam (Little, Brown, Boston, 1972).

HALBERSTAM, D. The Best and the Brightest (Barrie and Jenkins, London, 1973).

HAMMER, E. J. The Struggle for Indochina (Stanford University Press, Stanford, 2nd edn. 1966).

HO CHI MINH. On Revolution: Selected Writings 1920–66. Editor B. B. Fall (Pall Mall Press, London, 1967).

HONEY, P. J. Communism in North Vietnam (MIT Press, Cambridge, 1963).

ISOART, P. Le Phénomène National Vietnamien (Paris, 1961).

LACOUTURE, J. Ho Chi Minh (Penguin Books, London, 1968).

LANCASTER, D. The Emancipation of French Indochina (Oxford University Press, London, 1961).

LE THANH KHOI. Le Viet-Nam, Histoire et Civilisation (Editions de Minuit, Paris, 1955).

MCALEAVY, H. Black Flags in Vietnam (Allen and Unwin, London, 1968).

MCALISTER, J. T. Viet-Nam, the Origins of Revolution (Allen Lane, London, 1970).

MARR, D. G. Vietnamese Anticolonialism, 1885–1925 (University of California, Berkeley, 1971).

MUS, P. Les Vietnamiens et leur Révolution (le Seuil, Paris, 1972).

NGO VINH LONG. Before the Revolution: the Vietnamese Peasants under the French (MIT Press, Cambridge, 1973).

OSBORNE, M. E. The French Presence in Cochinchina and Cambodia: Rule and Response (1859–1905) (Cornell University Press, Ithaca, 1969).

The Pentagon Papers: the Defense Department History of U.S. Decision-making on Vietnam ("Senator Gravel Edition", 4 vols., Beacon Press, Boston, 1971).

PIKE, D. Viet Cong, the Organization and Techniques of the National Liberation Front of South Vietnam (MIT Press, Cambridge, 1966).

RACE, J. War comes to Long An: Revolutionary Conflict in a Vietnamese Province (University of California, Berkeley, 1972).

SANSOM, R. L. The Economics of Insurgency in the Mekong Delta of Vietnam (MIT Press, Cambridge, 1970).

SCIGLIANO, R. South Vietnam, Nation under Stress (Houghton Mifflin, Boston, 1963).

SMITH, R. Viet-Nam and the West (Heinemann Educational, London, 1968).

TABOULET, G. La Geste Française en Indochine, 2 vols. (Paris, 1955–56).

TRUONG BUU LAM. Patterns of Vietnamese Response to Foreign Intervention 1858–1900 (Yale University Press, New Haven, 1967).

TRUONG CHINH. Primer for Revolt (ed. B. B. Fall, Praeger, New York, 1963).

VAN DYKE, J. M. North Vietnam's Strategy for Survival (Palo Alto, 1972).

VO NGUYEN GIAP. People's War, People's Army (Praeger, New York, 1962).

VO NHAN TRI. Croissance Economique de la République Démocratique du Viet-Nam (Hanoi, 1967).

WOODSIDE, A. B. Vietnam and the Chinese Model: a Comparative Study of Vietnamese and Chinese Government in the first half of the Nineteenth Century (Harvard University Press, 1971).

See also Cambodia and Laos.

East Asia

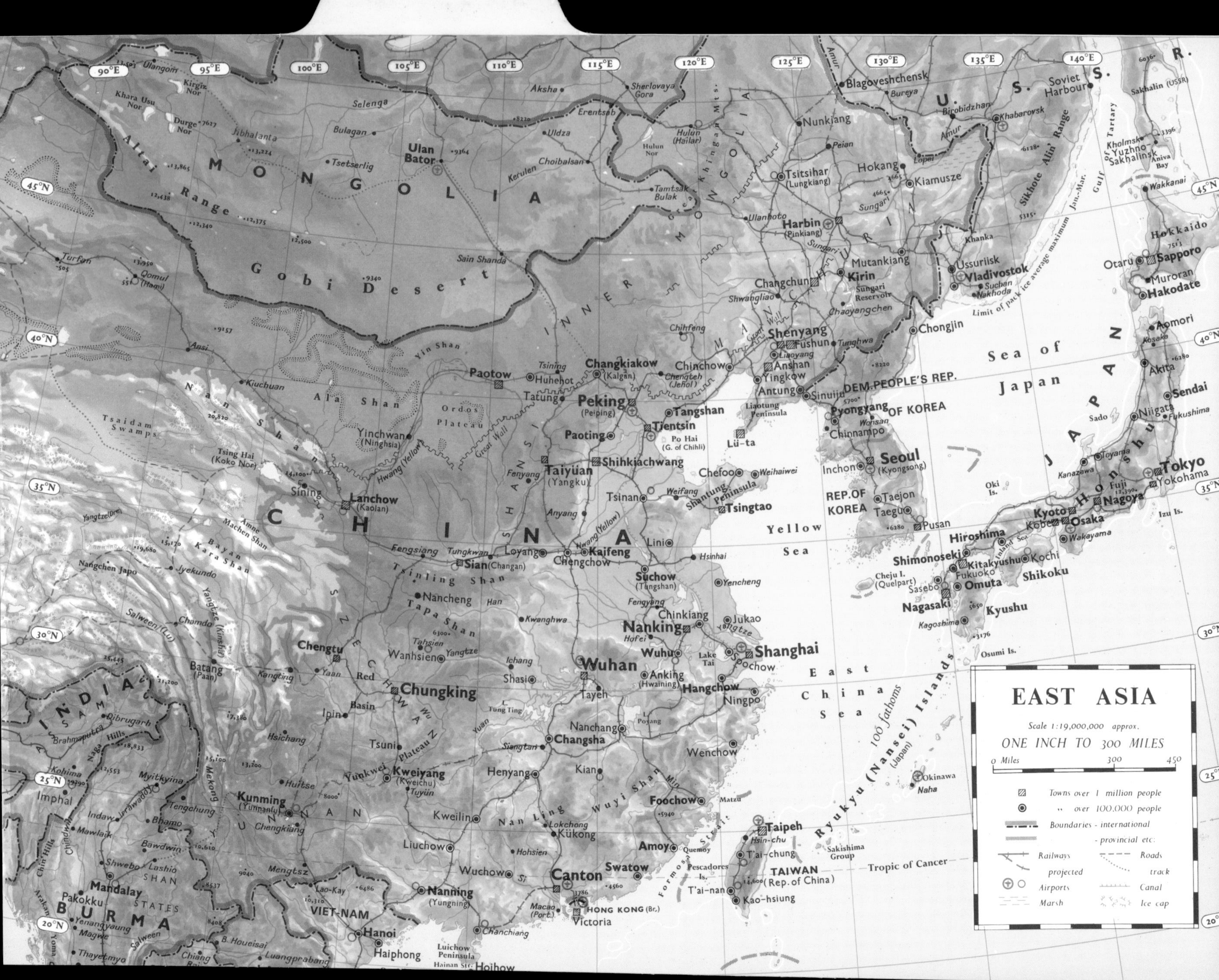
EAST ASIA
Scale 1:19,000,000 approx.
ONE INCH TO 300 MILES
0 Miles 300 450
Towns over 1 million people
" over 100,000 people
Boundaries - international
- provincial etc.
Railways
projected
Roads
track
Airports
Canal
Marsh
Ice cap
MONGOLIA
Gobi Desert
Altai Range
INNER MONGOLIA
MANCHURIA
CHINA
JAPAN
U. S. S. R.
DEM. PEOPLE'S REP. OF KOREA
REP. OF KOREA
TAIWAN (Rep. of China)
VIET-NAM
BURMA
INDIA
Sea of Japan
Yellow Sea
East China Sea
Tropic of Cancer
Ryukyu (Nansei) Islands (Japan)
100 fathoms
Limit of pack ice average maximum Jan.-Mar.
Ulan Bator
Peking (Peiping)
Tientsin
Shenyang
Harbin (Pinkiang)
Seoul (Kyongsong)
Pyongyang
Shanghai
Nanking
Wuhan
Chungking
Chengtu
Canton
HONG KONG (Br.)
Victoria
Taipeh
Tokyo
Osaka
Nagoya
Kyoto
Vladivostok
Hanoi
Mandalay
Kunming (Yunnanfu)
Lanchow (Kaolan)
Sian (Changan)
Taiyuan (Yangku)
90°E
95°E
100°E
105°E
110°E
115°E
120°E
125°E
130°E
135°E
140°E
45°N
40°N
35°N
30°N
25°N
20°N

East Asia

Keith Buchanan

PERSPECTIVE

East Asia, consisting of China, Korea and Japan, contains a population of some 1,000 million; this is twice the population of Europe and three times that of North America. The overall density of population is not high (*ca.* 70 per sq. km.) but the nutritional density, the density per unit-area of cropland, is the highest of any major area of the globe; it locally exceeds figures of 2,800 per sq. km. and for the region as a whole is approximately 420 per sq. km. It will be obvious from these figures that the population is extremely unevenly distributed and one of the most striking features of East Asia is the juxtaposition of uplands that are virtually empty and lowlands that are closely packed with people. This patchiness of population is a reflection of agricultural techniques: all the East Asian civilizations are based on intensive, garden-style, cultivation, mostly on irrigated land and with rice as the dominant crop; population is thus closely tied to the availability of level and irrigable land—the so-called "moist aquatic fringes"—and tends to avoid the uplands. And the absence of techniques of upland livestock rearing such as are typical of Western Europe is another factor explaining the sparse settlement of the upland areas.

Modern economic development is transforming these formerly dominantly agrarian societies and is introducing new contrasts within an area which once showed a high degree of economic homogeneity. These contrasts arise partly from the contrasts in the length of time since the process of modernization was initiated, partly from the contrasts in the framework within which development is taking place. Japan began her emergence as a modern industrial nation a century ago but in China and Korea effective modernization of the whole economy did not begin until after the Second World War. And whereas in Japan economic development has taken place within a largely capitalistic framework, economic development in China has, since 1949, taken place within a planned communist framework. The contrasting priorities and goals of the two systems result in markedly differing patterns of agricultural and industrial activity and in markedly different cultural landscapes; this is dramatically illustrated in Korea where the partition of the country in 1945 was followed by the development of the North along communist lines and of the South along the lines of a free-enterprise system strongly influenced by United States aid and by Japanese investment.

THE PHYSICAL SETTING

East Asia shows an almost unique diversity of environmental conditions. It extends from 55°N. to 17°N., the distance from Moscow to the south of Arabia; it extends from 500 feet below sea level in the depression of Turfan to over 29,000 feet in Mount Everest; it includes continental and insular environments; its climates range from the perpetual frost climates of parts of Tibet to the rain forest climate of Hainan and the extreme south. The concept of duality permeates Chinese thought; it can be extended to the physical and the human geography of East Asia, providing us with a means of organizing and describing the diversity of the region.

The key areas of these East Asian countries are the lowland areas where some four-fifths of the population is concentrated. These include the lowlands of eastern China—those of Manchuria, the Great Plain, the Yangtze valley and the valley of the Pearl River; the narrow coastal lowlands of Korea; and the alluvial lowlands which hug the mountain spine of the Japanese islands. They are of very uneven value. Coldness of climate and shortness of growing season restrict the variety of crops and the possibility of multiple cropping in Manchuria and the northern lowlands of Japan; by contrast, the warmth and humidity of sub-tropical and tropical South China and of southern Japan makes possible multiple cropping of rice, vegetables and a variety of fruits. Soils, too, are variable in quality. The "pioneer fringe" areas of Manchuria include relatively fertile black earths and also less productive podsol soils; in Japan there is a marked contrast between the more productive younger alluvium and the less versatile older alluvial soils of the river terraces; in China the loess-derived alluvium of the Great Plain is a highly productive soil but this and many of the other soils have been built up to their present high level of fertility by man. The productivity of many of these lowlands is dependent on man in another way, for intensive agriculture is dependent on flood control and irrigation and the mastery of East Asia's rivers has been of decisive importance to agricultural development; this applies to the smaller rivers of Japan no less than to the giant rivers of China.

The upland areas are thinly-peopled. In the warmer and humid areas of East China and of Japan they originally carried a forest cover varying from the coniferous forest of the cooler north to the luxuriant broad-leaf forest of the tropical south. For countless centuries, however, this has been ravaged by man; clearing for a transient "robber" agriculture destroyed much of the forest country of central and south China from the seventeenth century onwards while millennia of felling and cutting for fuel, constructional timber and fodder left a scrubby and degraded second-growth vegetation. Only recently has afforestation begun to change the picture, though the uplands, even where climate is favourable, still remain largely marginal to East Asian agriculture. Their soils are thin and fragile and this applies to both the prozols and brown earths of the north and the red and yellow soils of the sub-tropical and tropical south. In the interior of East Asia two types of upland environment are found—the high deserts of the Tibetan plateau characterized by bitter cold throughout the year and the true sand and gravel deserts of the interior basins of China's north-west with their cold winters and hot summers. Settled agriculture in the former area is confined to the limited areas where summer temperatures rise sufficiently high for crop growth, i.e. to the climatically more favoured Tsangpo valley; in the latter to the girdle of oases on the fringes of the desert basins, oases nourished by "exotic" streams rising in the snows and glaciers of mountain ranges such as the Tien Shan or the Altai. Over wide areas, however, the dominant economy is that of pastoral nomadism carried on today within the framework of the pastoral commune. And, in the last fifteen years, new resources have been developed in these formerly marginal areas: oil in the basins of China's north-west, a wide range of metallic minerals, energy sources in the shape of coal and water-power on the outer margins of the uplands. These resources are providing the basis for new patterns of industry and settlement; what were formerly semi-colonial areas are being integrated fully into the national economy.

Physical conditions certainly pose problems throughout the whole of this East Asian area. The area of arable land (or potential arable land) is limited; the vagaries of climate and of river regimes are unpredictable; mineral resources are limited, as in the case of Japan, or only partly known as in the case of China. Yet these problems are not insuperable and in overcoming them the massive human resources of the area are a major factor. As the past development of Japan and the present development of China demonstrate, the huge populations of East Asia, traditionally regarded by the West as a major obstacle to progress, can, given adequate political and social organization, be converted into a factor for progress. What we may term an antagonistic dualism—human needs as opposed to environmental resistances—is resolved by the labour-intensive economies which are one of the distinctive features of East Asia.

The techniques of labour-investment directed towards the remodelling of the physical environment go back far in the history of these "hydraulic civilizations" but have received a new impetus from the ambitious Chinese schemes of terracing and flood control. In Japan, and even more extensively in China, the creation by long centuries of human labour of "micro-plains", of irrigable terraces, has been of critical importance in extending the area of level land suitable for wet rice cultivation. Such terrace systems not only transform undulating or hilly terrain into the ideally flat relief suitable for irrigation, they also control run-off and soil erosion and make possible the accumulation of fine soil transported from higher levels. And the complex systems of irrigation and drainage developed in many of the lowland areas mean that ground-water levels—and thus the conditions of soil formation—are in large measure man-controlled.

The significance of Japanese development and of the Chinese experiment to other "under-developed" countries lies, in part at least, in this use of massed human labour to overcome the apparent limitations posed by the physical environment.

POPULATION

East Asia is usually regarded as an area of Mongoloid peoples, typified by straight black hair, yellowish to brown skin colour and the characteristic "Mongolian eye". Certainly the majority of the population would conform to this stereotype but it should be recalled that the dominance of this group is relatively recent in human terms, that much of East Asia was once the domain of non-Mongoloid peoples and that, if the Ainu of Japan are now an insignificant minority group, the minority peoples of China even today still occupy almost two-thirds of the area of the country. The human geography, no less than the physical geography of the area, thus shows a pronounced duality.

This is less so in the islands; here the aboriginal peoples of Taiwan have been pushed into the forested uplands which form the spine of the island, while in Japan the Ainu, belonging to an early offshoot of the Caucasoid group, have been either absorbed or pushed into the northern island of Hokkaido. On the mainland, however, the deserts and grasslands of sub-humid China, the high plateau of Tibet and much of China's tropical and sub-tropical south are still held by minority peoples. The pattern of distribution and the relationships which evolved between the Han majority and the various minority groups were shaped by the character of Chinese expansion. Until a relatively late date in Chinese history (less than two millennia ago) China south of the Yangtze was a Thai land, held by tribal peoples speaking languages belonging to the Thai group. These folk were gradually displaced southwards as a result of Chinese expansion; some were absorbed, many took refuge in the uplands which were of little interest to the Chinese farmer. Today sizeable blocs of such people remain in South China, the biggest being the Chuang of the Kwangsi Chuang Autonomous Region. Southwestwards, in the hill and basin country of Yunnan, there is a complex intermingling of Han Chinese (occupying the level basins and valleys) with Thai and Mon-Khmer peoples; these tribal groups all form parts of larger groupings overlapping into South-East Asia. By contrast, the minority peoples occupying western China, the Tibetans of the high plateau and the Uighurs, Mongols and related groups of the grasslands and deserts to the north, form compact blocs and still occupy their historic homelands. They were brought under Chinese political and military control as part of China's policy of protecting the settled lands to the east, and Chinese settlement in these areas has been on only a limited scale.

In language, in religion and in their traditional economic life these peoples show major contrasts with the Han Chinese. Their integration has always presented problems and it was not until the introduction of a new "nationalities policy" by the present Chinese government that these problems were effectively tackled. And since, in south-west China, many of these minority groups spread across the frontiers far into South-East Asia the effects of China's nationalities policy will be felt increasingly by the ethnically complex states which share with her a common frontier.

Population: Distribution Patterns

Some two-thirds of the population of East Asia are concentrated into six major areas; these are areas of high agricultural productivity and industrial development and represent the "key economic areas" of the continent's eastern fringe. They are: the lowlands of southern Japan, the coastal lowlands of Korea, the North China Plain (which alone contains over 180 million people), the plains of the Middle and Lower Yangtze, the Red Basin of Szechwan and the lowlands of tropical South China. This pattern has shown a remarkable stability in recent times; the regions of population concentration are, above all, regions of highly intensive land use, and the general result of developments in the countryside—such as the improvement of the irrigation system or the increasing use of fertilizers or machinery—has been to increase the population-supporting capacity of already closely-settled areas. Only in the most recent period have techniques of upland utilization, such as afforestation or the small and highly-localized beginning of an upland livestock industry, begun to indicate what may be a slow revolution in the attitudes to the "unused uplands" of East Asia.

In humid and sub-humid East Asia, that is in Japan, Korea and what is termed "Agricultural China", the population is a long-settled village-dwelling population; in the densely settled areas there is a close-textured pattern of villages, market towns and regional centres. In China, for example, G. W. Skinner sees as the basic unit in the social and economic structure of the countryside the "standard marketing area"; this is the area within walking distance of the market town, an area some 50 sq. km. in size and containing a score of villages; the villages and market towns are in turn tied into a network of "higher-level" market towns, often of considerable antiquity, and, as the Chinese have discovered since 1958, any reorganization of rural life (such as the commune system involved) must if it is to succeed be based on this traditional framework. Only exceptionally is the population dispersed into isolated farmsteads and hamlets; the two most important examples of such settlement are the long-settled province of Szechwan and the area of pioneer settlement in the northern Japanese island of Hokkaido.

There are striking contrasts in the proportion of urban-dwellers in the population as between the countries of East Asia; these contrasts are in large measure a reflection of the contrasts in the economic history of the various countries. In Japan, seven-tenths of the population is classed as "urban" though the inclusion of sizeable rural tracts within the urban areas suggests that this figure is exaggerated. In China slightly under one-fifth of the population was classed as urban in the 1953 census and of these one-quarter was concentrated in the nine major cities which had populations of one million or more; however, as in Japan, even the major cities contained a sizeable non-urban population (in the case of Peking and Nanking approximately one-quarter). In Korea, one-fifth of the population was urban in both North and South in 1950, with a significantly higher proportion in cities of over 100,000 in South Korea; by 1970 about one-third of the population of South Korea was in cities of over 100,000. To the contrasts in proportion of urban dwellers to total population we have to add the contrasts in rhythm of urbanization. Japan has shown, and is likely to continue to show, a progressive increase, and this applies to South Korea.* China, by contrast, appears to be attempting to stabilize the size of her urban population and, after a rapid expansion up to 1960, shows a levelling-off, if not an actual decrease in the size of her urban population. This is part of a deliberate policy of labour-intensive development in the countryside and has been accompanied by an increasing diversion of industrial development away from the "million cities" towards the smaller local and regional centres. Chinese planning, which seeks to attenuate the differences between city and countryside, between town-dweller and peasant, is thus leaving a decisive mark on the distribution of population.

Population: Growth and Changing Composition

The population of East Asia, some 1,000 million in 1975, will, according to the United Nations "medium variant", reach a total of close on 1,370 million by the end of the century; the "high variant" estimate (which assumes that birth rates will fall less sharply) is 1,435 million.

According to the UN estimates ("medium variant"), the population of China (including Taiwan) will grow from 772 million in 1970 to 1,148 million in 2000—an increase of 376 million (or nearly 50 per cent), compared with an increase for Japan, over the same period, of 28.6 million. China's estimated growth rate in 1970–75 was 1.66 per cent per annum, as compared with a growth rate of some 1.2 per cent annually for Japan. Official Chinese policy towards population restriction has veered uncertainly over the last two decades but, even given a strong state-backed policy aimed at smaller families, the growth rate, in absolute figures, is likely to continue at a high level for some years to come since the proportion of young people (and thus of potential parents) in the population is very high; the 1953 census thus showed that over two-fifths of the population was under 18 years of age. Even higher rates of growth seem likely in Korea and Mongolia. The UN estimates suggest that North Korea's population will nearly double between 1970 and 2000, while Mongolia's will rise by more than 110 per cent.

The major economic problems of the area are rooted in this population explosion, the major problems being the biological one of expanding food production to keep pace with population and the economic one of providing employment for a rapidly expanding labour force; the extent of this challenge can be better appreciated if it is recalled that in the past much of East Asia has been plagued by unemployment and under-employment. And to get the

* In addition, Japan's urban population shows an extreme, and growing, concentration—with 57 per cent of the total population living in and around the three cities of Tokyo, Osaka and Nagoya.

Population Estimates 1980, 1990, 2000
(million)

	1980		1990		2000	
	Medium	High	Medium	High	Medium	High
China*	907.6	918.7	1,031.1	1,067.4	1,148.0	1,208.5
Japan	117.5	117.8	126.2	127.1	132.9	134.2
Remainder†	61.9	62.5	75.4	77.8	88.2	93.0
TOTAL	1,087.0	1,099.0	1,232.7	1,272.2	1,369.1	1,435.7

* Including Taiwan. † Hong Kong, Korea, Macau and Mongolia.

situation into perspective it must be stressed that the rate of population growth is considerably in excess of the rate of growth typical of Europe during its period of "economic take-off" in the eighteenth and nineteenth centuries (estimated at 0.6 per cent annually); for this reason, and also because of the much higher initial densities of population in East Asia, European development models have only limited relevance in the developing countries of East Asia. In Japan, whose population structure is more "mature" than that of the other East Asian neighbours, the problem is that of absorbing an increase of some 70 per cent in the male labour force over the period 1950–80; the burden of dependency in the shape of a very large (and economically unproductive) child population will be replaced by a somewhat smaller burden of dependency represented by the increasing number of old people. By contrast, in China and Korea the evidence is that growth rates will continue high (even if family size declines) in the coming decades and that these countries will be characterized by a young age distribution and high juvenile dependency rate. And for the immediate future these countries face the problem of absorbing into their economy increasingly large contingents entering the working age groups; by 1960 the annual increase of these in China was estimated at 7 million, as compared with 4 million during the First Five-Year Plan and 5 million during the Second Five-Year Plan. Of these, only 1 million can be absorbed in the cities; the necessity of absorbing the large residue in the rural areas will dictate a labour-intensive pattern of development for the countryside. Such a policy appears increasingly relevant to the other developing countries of Asia and seems to be the only answer to the threat of massive unemployment and under-employment which many ILO experts foresee in Asia.

Population: Contrasting Economic Patterns

Modern economic development has been uneven in its impact on East Asia, and the contrast in the period over which such development has taken place is reflected in the economic structure of the populations in the countries of the area and in the contribution to the Gross Domestic Product made by each economic sector. Japan, whose economic transformation began during the last third of the nineteenth century, shows the most diversified structure. China and Korea, by contrast, retained a semi-colonial status until almost the middle of the present century; South Korea has subsequently developed within a Western free-enterprise form of economy, China and North Korea on communist lines, with centrally-planned economies. The broad contrasts in the employment pattern of the four major countries are summarized below:

East Asia: Employment by Major Sectors (per cent)

	PRIMARY	SECONDARY	TERTIARY
China	(70)*	—	—
Japan	16	34	50
North Korea	(45)*	—	—
South Korea	50	17	33

* Agriculture only. *Note:* Figures for late 1960s.

The gaps in the statistics available for the East Asian Communist countries, together with the rather different basis of classification, make strict comparison impossible but the general picture is clear. The economic structure of Japan's population is similar to that of the developed economies of the West; agriculture employs less than one-twelfth of the population, the manufacturing and construction industries employ over one-third and the service or tertiary sector over one-half. Seven-tenths of China's population, by contrast, are still peasants (though the spread of small-scale industry in the countryside blurs the distinction between agriculture and industry); modern industry has made major strides as an employer of labour but, according to Western estimates, employed a total of only 8 million even after the Great Leap Forward—and despite marked industrial expansion during 1969–71, it is unlikely that modern industry employed more than 9 million in 1971; for comparison, in Japan total manufacturing employment, in 1971, was about 14 million—over half either "peasant-workers" or employees of small labour-intensive units (in Japan, 0.5 per cent of manufacturing firms employ 30 per cent of the industrial labour force and produce some 53 per cent of the industrial output). In terms of occupational structure Korea, with approximately one-half of the occupied population in agriculture, is transitional between China and Japan; there are major contrasts in the organization of this sector as between North and South Korea, between the collectivized agriculture of the North and the disintegrating individual-peasant economy of the South.

The contribution of the various sectors to the Gross Domestic Product is summarized below:

East Asia: Sectoral Contribution to G.D.P., 1970

	PRIMARY	SECONDARY	TERTIARY
China . .	(40)*	(34)	(26)
Japan . .	12	35	53
North Korea .	23*	67	10
South Korea .	40	23	37

* Including mining.

The table emphasizes the contrasts between the economic development of the two Koreas: rapid industrialization in the North has meant that today industry accounts for two-thirds of the G.D.P. as compared with one-fifth in the South; expressed in another way, in 1946 agriculture accounted for 72 per cent of the combined output value of industry and agriculture in the North, agriculture for 28 per cent, proportions which by 1960 had been reversed (industry 71 per cent, agriculture 29 per cent). In Japan the sector contribution closely parallels the employment distribution, suggesting the high productivity of the agricultural sector. The Chinese data shows that the seven-tenths of China's population employed in agriculture produced less than 40 per cent of G.D.P. The figures (based on American and Chinese estimates) are, however, of doubtful reliability since some experts claim that as early as 1959 the contribution of industry to the national product had begun to equal that of agriculture and the continuing differential growth rates of agriculture and industry will certainly have increased the relative share of industry. Even so, no significant decline in the relative size of the peasant sector is likely in the foreseeable future since it is in intensification of agriculture that Chinese planners appear to see the solution to the problem of absorbing the massive population increase of coming decades.

RESOURCES AND ECONOMIC DEVELOPMENT

Japan

Even though the East Asian region has only limited areas of readily cultivable land these resources are not yet fully taken up except in Japan; in China, by contrast, the reserves of unused arable land total between 100 million and 250 million acres. Again excepting Japan, which is built of young fold mountains, relatively deficient in minerals, the area possesses a mineral endowment sufficiently large and diversified to provide a firm basis for modern industrialization; this endowment includes iron and ferro-alloys, a wide range of non-ferrous metals, and abundant energy resources in the form of coal, oil and hydroelectricity. Most important of all, the area has immense resources of labour and it is through the mobilization of this latter resource that economic development has been initiated in East Asia. Japan in the nineteenth century, China and North Korea almost a century later—the patterns of initial development are strikingly similar; only South Korea seems to have failed to achieve any effective mobilization of her unemployed and under-employed labour resources.

Japanese economic development today is typically regarded as following Western "free enterprise" lines. The meteoric rise of the country as a major industrial, trading and military power was, however, due largely to strong central planning and thorough exploitation of the resources of the human sector. This central control made possible the holding-down of living levels and the financing of industrial development by funds accumulated in the agricultural sector of the economy. And, while the technological basis for industrial development was largely borrowed from the West, the social basis of Japanese life remained semi-feudal and rooted in tradition; the individual counted for little by comparison with the family or the nation, and his immediate well-being was of little consequence by comparison with the ultimate good of the larger community. The whole nation, indeed, worked in an atmosphere of ruthless austerity and with unfaltering loyalty to those who spoke for the Emperor. Such conditions made possible a high rate of accumulation and economic growth while the highly integrated character of industry, dominated by a handful of great family trusts (the *Zaibatsu*), gave Japan a tremendous advantage when competing for world markets. It was these conditions of population mobilization and high degree of central economic control that made possible the emergence of Japan as the most developed nation of East Asia.

There is, however, some truth in the assertion that Japan has been trying to play the role of nineteenth century Britain in the twentieth century world—and trying to do so with resources no larger than those of Italy. For, as became apparent in the 1930s and as is evident still today, given the pressure of population and the narrow resource base, the maintenance of Japan's status is dependent to a large degree upon a highly developed system of trading relations which will ensure the essential raw materials for Japanese industry and provide a dependable outlet for Japanese manufactures. It was these considerations which lay behind the Japanese attempt to create the Co-prosperity Sphere before the Second World War; it is these considerations which underlie the present Japanese trade drive in South-East Asia and the Western Pacific.

By the late sixties Japan had the third largest G.N.P. in the world and was the world's second largest steel producer. In 1968 the country showed an "astounding 14.8 per cent increase" in her growth rate. The phenomenal progress of Japan in the last decade or so has been very heavily dependent on her relationship with the U.S.A. In 1969 Yoshizane Iwasa of the Fuji Bank commented that Japan's present economic prosperity has been made possible "because the United States carried the cost of Japanese defence"; this, however, is only part of the explanation. No less important has been the expenditure of the

U.S. military in Japan and the markets for Japanese goods created by America's involvement in Korea and Indochina. The scale of the former, between 1945 and 1962, was sufficiently great to pay for almost one-fifth of Japanese imports; by 1966–67 the value of direct and indirect war-related contracts had reached 1.7 billion dollars, providing a major boost to the economy. Indeed, if the opportunities offered by the Korean War initiated the Japanese "miracle", the even more massive demands created by the Viet-Nam War have played a major role in boosting Japan's economic progress.* And, since the U.S.A. is the largest market for Japanese goods, the upswing in the American domestic economy as the result of the Viet-Nam War in turn stimulated the Japanese economy. The potential economic dangers of such a heavy dependence on American military activity need no stressing.

For many Japanese the obvious economic alignment might seem to be with the developing giant of mainland Asia—with China. In the words of Tokuma Utsunomiya, Deputy Chairman of the Japan Association for the Promotion of International Trade, "There are many items Japan wants from China, and others that China wants from Japan. If it were not for political pressure, there would be great potential for the development of trade". To avoid such an alignment the United States "is encouraging Japan to re-establish its relationship with the Southeast Asian region of its former East Asian Co-prosperity Sphere, while directing the rest of its overseas activities towards the West". Today South-East Asia supplies two-fifths of Japan's iron imports, nearly all its crude rubber needs and over half of its timber imports; in return, South-East Asia takes two-fifths of Japan's chemical exports and over a quarter of the country's iron and steel and machinery exports. And the proportion of Japanese foreign investment in South-East Asia jumped from 12.8 per cent in 1968 to almost a third in 1970. At the same time the ties with the West were strengthened and this was exemplified by the country's increasing dependence on imports of ores, coal and other raw materials from the U.S.A. and joint U.S.-Japanese ventures in the Pacific world and by Japan's participation in the Pacific Basin Economic Co-operation Community.

The Pacific Basin Council was established in 1967 and brings together senior business executives from the U.S.A., Canada, Australia, New Zealand and Japan. The formation of the Council reflects the displacement of the European powers by the U.S.A. as the dominant force in the Asian-Pacific world;† for the old concept of an "East of Suez", under British (or French/Dutch) hegemony, it substitutes the concept of a "Pacific Basin" linked to North America. Economically and politically a new "Pacific" hierarchy is emerging, with the U.S.A. and then Japan at the apex; these draw resources from the next tier—Canada, Australia, New Zealand—and sell goods in these markets. All five advanced countries are, moreover, attempting to integrate the less developed nations of the Asian/Pacific world into a pattern of trading relations based upon an international specialization of labour within the region.

For the less developed nations of the Asian/Pacific region this means continuing underdevelopment and dependence. And for Japan, as the Japanese themselves saw, it meant that the country was cast in the role of "a senior American client-state active in pursuit of global capitalist objectives and receptive to an American sphere of influence within its own borders."‡

THE LIMITS OF INDEPENDENCE

The subordinate role in which Japan was cast was underlined by the "shock diplomacy" of the Nixon period during which the U.S.A. by-passed Tokyo in elaborating new policies in Moscow and Peking. And the unfolding of America's multipolar diplomacy, which involved playing off the two major Communist powers against one another and against Japan, underlined yet further the U.S. vision of the Japanese role.

The reaction, which can scarcely cause surprise, was a heightening of Japanese nationalist feeling and a trend towards a much more independent economic and military stance. Says one Japanese commentator: "The report of a hearing on future U.S. foreign policy held by the U.S. Congressional Committee on International Affairs (January 28th, 1976) hinted at the possibility of conflicts of interests arising between the U.S. and Japan and predicted that Japan may turn in a nationalistic and neutralist direction. From the Japanese side, too, there are not a few signs corroborating this prediction".§ It is perhaps ironical that this trend towards an assertion of independence is less marked among the opposition groups (traditionally critical of the U.S.-Japanese alliance) than among more conservative groups. In this context the Lockheed bribes scandal has strengthened the hand of ultranationalist right-wing groups who assert that corruption is an inevitable consequence of dependency on the United States.

Yet, as the Japanese have learned over recent years, the possibilities open to them of initiating independent policies are narrowly circumscribed because of their dependence on overseas resources. Their heavy, and increased, dependence on imports makes them highly vulnerable to external pressures—and this is nowhere more clearly demonstrated than in the field of mineral fuels. Before 1950 the country derived 60 per cent of its energy from coal; by 1974, 75 per cent was being derived from oil. And not only was the demand for oil rapidly expanding (estimated consumption in 1975

---

* The rate of growth of G.N.P. was 2.7 per cent in 1965–66, reached a peak of nearly 15 per cent in 1968, and fell to a still high 9.7 per cent in real terms in 1971.

† James Ridgeway comments on the Pacific Rim strategy thus: "The politics are not particularly subtle. . . In one sense it represents an American intrusion into the old Japanese Southeast Asia Co-Prosperity Sphere". *The Last Play: The Struggle to Monopolize the World's Energy Resources* (Mentor, N.Y., 1974), p. 106.

‡ Leon Howell and Michael Morrow: *Asia, Oil Politics and the Energy Crisis* (IDOC/North America, 1974), p. 137.

§ Yamakawa Akio, "Flying Blind in the East China Sea" in *AMPO*, vol. 8, no. 1, March 1976, p. 65.

was 7 million b/d; the estimate for 1985 is 12 million b/d) but some 99 per cent came from imports. Moreover, almost four-fifths of the oil was coming from Middle East sources, involving "a rotation of more than 250 tankers, tailing each other less than 50 miles apart". And quite apart from the dangers of depending on sources in politically unstable areas and on a life-line 8,000 miles long, the large tankers are now experiencing difficulties in making the passage through the Malacca Straits.*

The economic dependence and political vulnerability of the country led Japan to move increasingly into a "resources diplomacy" which made the Japanese Government "a major player in the oil game."

The earliest move was towards securing control of Middle East sources and in 1958 Japan's Arabian oil source was formally established in the Neutral Zone between Kuwait and Saudi Arabia; by 1972 the Khafji field in the area was producing 400,000 b/d. Meanwhile, in 1966 the Petroleum Committee of the Energy Council moved to bring as much oil as possible under Japanese control, setting, in February 1967, the goal that by 1985 Japanese companies should account for 30 per cent of the country's total crude oil demand. Within the next seven years Japanese companies moved into operations in 14 countries but the target of 30 per cent of crude oil from Japanese-controlled sources seemed as remote as ever; by 1972 the proportion was still only 8.5 per cent and several major ventures had proved costly failures; by 1973 Japan's dependence on the major oil companies was, in Jon Halliday's words: "even higher . . . than it was four years earlier when it launched an extensive search for independent supplies."†

The vulnerability of Japan was illustrated by the OPEC settlements of 1971; the price increases had, in the words of Masaji Yamamoto, First Secretary of Japan's Embassy in Singapore, "come as a big shock. We Japanese are very disturbed that we have no say in determining such astronomical costs". The price per barrel for Arabian light "marker" crude was $1.39 in April/June 1971; it rose to $3.65 at the end of 1973 and to $8.00 plus freight in early 1974. (Indonesia's "sweet crude" reached $10.80). That there was a political dimension to the whole issue of petroleum supplies seemed evident to many Japanese; higher oil prices were readily accepted by the U.S.A. because, they held, they were regarded as a quick and easy way of slowing down a dangerously competitive economy.

The insecurity generated was increased by the unilateral decision of Exxon, Mobil, Shell and BP to cut back supplies of crude oil to Japanese refineries by 10–20 per cent in early 1973 and by the refusal of Caltex to renew its crude supply contract with Mitsubishi Oil. And Japanese attempts to turn westwards and obtain large supplies of gas and crude oil from Siberian fields or from China were to fall victim to the U.S.A.'s "detente diplomacy". As the *Economist* reported: "A year ago it seemed that the massive oil and gas wealth of Siberia would fall neatly into the hands of Japan. . . . This week's announcement that the United States is negotiating to drill and buy up to $40 billion of Russian fuel has convinced the resentful Japanese that they have lost out on the bulk of Siberian oil, together with its tied trading market. . . . The Japanese are even more annoyed about American participation in the crude petroleum fields at Tyumen."‡ In the same way, moves towards Sino-Japanese co-operation in the exploitation of both on-shore and off-shore deposits in China seem to be in the process of being undercut by the U.S.A. The economic and trade delegation which left for China in mid-December 1975 carried proposals which would boost imports of Chinese crude from the current level of 8 million tons yearly to 30 million tons by 1980. But in mid-February 1976 it was reported that China was cutting back on oil supplies to Japan and had decided to "export oil to Japan through the American major oil companies. This is one of the points in the new U.S.-China alliance that was established last fall during the visit to Peking of President Ford, as one of the means of keeping Japan under the joint control of the U.S. and China."§ In the light of these events it is clear that, in the field of conventional energy development, Japan's freedom of action is narrowly circumscribed and her biggest achievements have been in South-East Asia; a 1973 agreement with Pertamina will contribute to making Japan the world's largest LNG market.

One of the results of the pressure described above has been a strident campaign for the development of nuclear power||; as the 1974 Energy Council programme stressed: "we must make every effort to secure stable supplies of energy and reduce our dependency on foreign energy resources, namely petroleum." Earlier the General Council on Energy had recommended that nuclear power should be top priority in Japan's energy programme and the revised master plan suggested that nuclear generating capacity should be increased to 60 million kW by 1987. This would mean that the contribution of petroleum to energy production would drop from 77 to 63 per cent and that nuclear power would account for 30 per cent of the electricity generated. As far as uranium

* The problem of the Straits is discussed by Howell & Morrow, *op.sup.cit*, pp. 147 sqq.

† Jon Halliday, *A Political History of Japanese Capitalism* (N.Y., 1975).

‡ *Economist* November 11th, 1972.

§ *New Asia News* (Tokyo) December 19th, 1975; *id* February 27th, 1976. Apart from political motives, we may also see in U.S. oil and gas policy the emerging possibility of U.S. partial dependence on East Asian petroleum resources. Escalating prices and developing technology (notably liquefaction processing and cryogenic shipping) have effectively narrowed the geographic distance between the energy-hungry American West Coast and the oil and gas fields of East Asia. The contract between Pertamina of Indonesia and a subsidiary of the Pacific Lighting Corp. of Los Angeles for the supply of natural gas (Sept. 1973) is perhaps a harbinger of things to come. .

|| See "Japan's People Resist the Nuclear Con Game" and "The Politics of Japan's Uranium Purchase" in *AMPO* vol. 8, no. 1, 1976, pp. 26–37.

supplies are concerned, by the end of 1973 Japan had concluded contracts assuring 80 per cent of her needs over the decade 1975–85 (on the assumption of the 1987 target of 60 million kW).

The plans are ambitious—but whether they are feasible in a country already facing a major pollution crisis is doubtful. They mean the construction of 40 more nuclear reactors to add to the 8 in operation and the 15 under construction or testing, and this prospect of the coastline of Japan dotted with nuclear reactors has triggered off a strong reaction among the various people's resistance movements. This opposition from local people's movements is admitted by the Energy Council to be "the single, most serious bottleneck for our programme".

JAPAN AND THE COSTS OF ECONOMIC GROWTH

And yet, as has been suggested earlier in the Introduction, the very success of the "Japanese economic miracle" has jeopardized the human and ecological future of the whole country and, ultimately, poses the question of whether Japan can sustain for any length of time a policy of economic and political expansion. That the ecological viability of all the industrial societies of the North, capitalist or Soviet, is dubious cannot be denied but, because of the very pace and dimensions of Japanese development, it is in Japan that breakdown seems most imminent. Consider some of the warning signs: that half of Tokyo's residents fear they will personally fall victim to pollution-related disease and 65 per cent believe they will have to wear gas masks in 10 or 15 years' time; that in one industrial suburb of Tokyo 10,000 cases of chronic respiratory disease due to air pollution are reported; that the "officially recognized" total of those affected by Minamata Disease, a form of mercury poisoning resulting from contamination of the marine biomass by industrial waste, totals several hundred, and that the actual total of victims may exceed 10,000 (the disease can be fatal, and in March 1973 a group of 30 families who had suffered were awarded £1.3 million compensation in a case brought against the Chisso fertilizer company); that because of pollution half of the country's commercial fishing grounds are now unfit for fishing. . . . These are but a few of the costs of economic growth.

Between 1962 and 1971 the annual percentage increase in G.N.P., in real terms, was 10.2 per cent. Industry expanded; so did various forms of consumption. The Japanese car-fleet increased eighteen-fold in the 1960s and is expected to increase further, seven and a half-fold, by the end of the century. Demand for steel is estimated at 150 million tons in 1975 and over 200 million tons in 1985, for aluminium at these dates 2.3 million tons and 6.0 million tons, for electricity 530,000 million kWh and more than a million million kWh.

This spiralling rate of expansion, in a resource-poor country such as Japan, can only be maintained by an increasing flow of raw materials. Some of the basic elements in the situation were set out in the Japanese *White Paper on Resources* (1971): from 1966 to 1970 the average annual rates of increase in the demand for raw materials were the highest in the world; against an annual rate of increase in G.N.P. of 12.2 per cent, rates of increase in the demand for oil and iron ore were, respectively, 18.8 per cent and 19.1 per cent. Since 1967 the country has, in fact, been the world's largest importer of raw materials and by 1980 will absorb 30 per cent of the world's exports of raw materials. The weighted average of foreign dependency for 10 critical raw materials meanwhile rose from 71 per cent in 1960 to 90 per cent in 1970; at present the economy is estimated to be living with some 20 days' supply of raw materials for industry available in the country. These considerations help explain what some Japanese experts have termed "the vicious circle of expansionism"—for to maintain a high rate of growth in G.N.P. (and in profits) raw materials must be imported; to import raw materials, foreign exchange has to be earned; to earn foreign exchange, exports have to be expanded faster than imports. . . .

And economic expansion on the Japanese scale makes demands on local resources, too. Freshwater supplies needed in 1975 will be triple the amount needed in 1965 and by 1985 they will be quadruple. The demand for industrial land will double by 1975 and triple by 1985. The external economies found in the great urban agglomerations have tended, predictably, to pull industry towards existing centres in spite of the shortage of land and soaring rents, and it is this concentration that *Shinzenso*, the comprehensive development plans of recent years, have set out to correct. These call for a measure of dispersion into some 11 prospective development areas away from present centres; this dispersion will, it is estimated, mean that one-sixth of the existing limited area of agricultural land will be converted to industrial use by 1985.

Increasingly, however, the costs of this growth are beginning to concern people, and there is an increasing preoccupation with what the *Environmental White Paper* refers to as "the enormous losses to the nation as a whole", losses attributable to what the Japanese term *kogai*. This word is conventionally translated as "environmental pollution" but is also "used to refer to all sorts of things that aren't strictly pollution: factory noise, vibration, obstruction of sunlight, traffic congestion, water shortage and so on. . . ."

Such pollution is often regarded as an unfortunate, difficult-to-avoid side-effect of economic growth, but some conservationists in Japan argue persuasively that neglect of the pollution problem has been as important as wage levels and protectionism in making possible rapid economic expansion. As examples, the pulp and steel industries are quoted. In both cases, the industry is permitted to operate in Japan without the provision for the treatment of toxic wastes which is mandatory in most other developed countries. The cost of anti-pollution installations in the pulp industry is estimated at 10 to 20 per cent of the investment in the plant; the complex anti-pollution devices necessary before the use of the oxygen furnace is permitted in the U.S. or European steel industries are even more costly, representing 20 to 30 per cent of the cost of the total installation. The economic advantage accruing to Japanese industry from this official laxity over pollution control is obvious. And, viewed thus, the facts that Japan has the world's fastest growing economy and the world's most polluted environment are simply two sides of the same process.

DEVELOPMENT VERSUS PEOPLE

The situation in Japan is aggravated by the extreme concentration of population and industry. Half of Japan's 110 million inhabitants are concentrated on 1.7 per cent of the country's area, consisting of lowland areas and especially the coast plains. Agricultural considerations were largely responsible for this pattern but it has been reinforced by the country's industrial development. Following the Second World War Japan became in effect one gigantic "transformation factory", processing imported raw materials. Under these conditions a coastal location became a major advantage and this is well illustrated by the steel industry—almost four-fifths of the steel works are on the coast, as compared with a figure of 22 per cent for the EEC countries and 8 per cent for the U.S.A.

The concentration of industry is not simply in the coastal regions, it is above all a concentration on the shores of the Inland Sea.* The Sea, which is margined by the islands of Honshu, Shikoku and Kyushu, has an area of 18,000 square kilometres and accounts for 70 per cent of the catch from Japan's coastal fisheries. It thus plays an important role in Japan's protein economy yet this role is increasingly compromised by industrialization; indeed, in the opinion of many Japanese experts, the continued discharge of industrial wastes into its waters threatens to convert it into a dead sea. The size of the problem is evident from some statistics of industrial concentration on the coasts of the Inland Sea: in its coastal zone is produced 53 per cent of Japan's steel, 40 per cent of the petroleum refined in Japan, and a high proportion of the nation's petrochemical output, including 35 per cent of the ethylene. It is a zone showing a high concentration of non-ferrous metal refining—63 per cent of the copper refined in the country, 76 per cent of the lead and 13 per cent of the zinc; a zone which produces 44 per cent of the nation's power and a high proportion of the wood pulp and aluminium.

Industrial output has certainly increased; so, too, has pollution. The volume of some of the major atmospheric pollutants increased seven-fold between 1955 and 1972; pollution by liquid wastes discharged directly into the sea has greatly increased. Meanwhile, an indication of the growing deterioration of environmental conditions in the Inland Sea is given by the increasing occurrence of deformed fish (due to heavy-metal accumulation) and of so-called "red tides". These latter are associated with abnormal plankton formation and may on occasion be fatal to aquiculture.† In 1955 there were 7 such tides, in 1965 44, in 1971 136 and in 1974 298.

And to the gradual build-up of pollution due to industrialization must be added the destruction due to accidents, such as the bursting of a reservoir belonging to Mitsubishi Oil in March 1975. This involved a spillage of 40,000 kilolitres of petrol which devastated the surrounding countryside; as a consequence, some $45 million was paid as compensation to fishermen on the Inland Sea whose livelihood had been affected by the spillage.

Says Tsuneo Amano: "The writer Shiba Ryotaro said, on the subject of property speculation, that Japan had been incapable of assimilating capitalism. This remark applies to the totality of business enterprises. Neither the central government nor the local bodies have called a halt to the blind development of industry which is simply another form of colonialism". And at a symposium on environmental problems held at Kyoto in November 1975 Professor Tsuru proposed a three-year ban on all industrial development round the Inland Sea; during this period, he suggested, an interdisciplinary and international commission of enquiry should carry out a thorough assessment of environmental conditions.

That the words of the Environmental White Paper—that "degradation of the environment represents a real threat to each citizen"—are true is thus clearly demonstrated in the cultural and economic "heartland" of Japan—the area around the Inland Sea. And, given that an "increasingly defiant reaction emerging among local communities against construction of new heavy and chemical industrial plants is worsening the situation"‡, it is increasingly doubtful whether the promise of industrial decentralization made by Kakuei Tanaka, the former Prime Minister, offers any real solution to the problem of mounting social and environmental destruction. Indeed, such a programme may aggravate yet further the problem for, as Professor Kazajui Nagasu has pointed out, what it involves is packing an area aggregating 10,000 square kilometres, or one-thousandth of the land area of the United States, with heavy facilities producing a G.N.P. approaching that of the U.S.A.§

Under these circumstances, it becomes clear that, if economic development is to continue, two alternatives are open to Japan. The first is to change to a development model, that is, like the Chinese model, ecologically far less destructive—and such a trend would be particularly welcome to those Japanese who believe that the country should strive for greater self-sufficiency in food supplies. The second—and to date most likely course—is to attempt to stabilize the present situation (unsatisfactory though it is) by "exporting pollution"—in other words, by dispersing

* See Tsuneo Amano, "Pour sauvegarder la mer Intérieur les collectivités concluent des accords anti-pollution avec les entreprises" in *Le Monde Diplomatique*, June 1976, p. 17. I have drawn heavily on this valuable report.

† The "red tide" of August 1972 caused losses of almost $13 million (Tsuneo Amano, *op.cit.*)

‡ Shinichi Kondo, speaking at "Conference on Business opportunities in the Pacific Basin" (Oct. 1973) and cited by Leon Howell and Michael Morrow, *op.sup.cit.*

§ Cited by Leon Howell and Michael Morrow, *op.sup.cit.* p. 108.

the dirtier types of industry to other countries in East or South-East Asia. This, indeed, appears to be the course Japanese industry is adopting. Said Yatsugi Kazuo, speaking of Japanese-South Korea collaboration: "As in the industries in which Japan expects great development in the future—steel, aluminium, oil, petrochemicals, shipbuilding, electronics, plastics, etc., limitations are gradually being experienced in Japan because of coastal land use and anti-pollution measures . . . I wonder whether the Korean side would be able or would like to share the task."*

By 1974 the dispersal of the more pollution-prone industries, and especially industries of the petrochemical group, was well under way. Chisso, the firm at the centre of the Minamata storm, had established a multi-million dollar petrochemical plant at Ulsan, and Mitsui was moving into ethylene production at Yeosu (also in South Korea). In Thailand, Asahi had established a caustic soda and chlorine plant near Bangkok and was claimed responsible for caustic soda, mercury and chlorine contamination of the Chao Phraya River;† Mitsubishi and Mitsui were associated with other firms in the establishment of a giant petrochemical complex at Si Racha in Chonburi Province. In Malaysia, Japan Agricultural Chemical Malaysia was established on Penang Island; among its products was BHC insecticide, outlawed in Japan. And in Singapore and Indonesia a range of Japanese petrochemical firms are either established or contemplating production of PVS, styrene and ethylene.

The pressures faced by Japanese industry are well illustrated by the ethylene industry. Present capacity is 6 million tons annually, but the Industrial Structure Council estimates the 1980 demand at 8 million tons and the 1985 demand at 12 million tons; in addition, demand in 10 other Asian countries will reach 2 million tons in 1980. The Council believes that land could be found in Japan for an additional 6.5 million tons capacity but that environmental factors preclude this construction. After 1976, therefore, most Japanese ethylene plants will be built in developing countries.

Recent development has been possible only because Japan has been able to integrate into her economic living space important sources of raw materials, such as oil and timber, and of man-power (in various South-East Asian countries). Continuing expansion is implicit in the country's overseas investment programmes, arranged largely at the initiative of the Japanese Government. These are clearly integrated into a pattern of global expansion of Japanese business and are linked with large-scale resource extraction projects or storage projects.

The pattern was set out recently by the Industrial Structure Council, an advisory body of the Ministry of International Trade and Industry, in its "Long-term Vision of the Japanese Industrial Structure" and envisages an increase in Japanese overseas investments from $12,600 million in 1974 to $40,900 million in 1980 and $80,700 million in 1985. But whether the societies involved will continue to remain passive in the face of the accelerating degradation of their environment which will result from this exploitation and from the pollution-generating industries that Japan is exporting is doubtful—something underlined by recent student riots in Thailand and by the radical press in Malaysia.‡

"ENOUGH OF THIS LIFE AT BREAKING-POINT . . ."

Uchiyama Takuro has commented: "Japan's high economic growth rate, which had so fascinated the rest of the world, was premised on the availability of cheap imported energy. Moreover, long-term economic planning was based on ever-increasing dependence on foreign oil; under the cabinet of Kakuei Tanaka Japanese policy was to increase oil imports from the 1972 level of 257 million kilolitres to 700–800 million kl by 1985"§. By 1974 the steep rise in world oil prices (which added some $7,000 million to Japan's import bill) demonstrated the danger of this dependence on imported energy. Four-fifths of the oil, we have seen, came from the Middle East, by a long and vulnerable route; two-thirds of it was supplied by the giant U.S. and Anglo-Dutch companies; and attempts by Japan to achieve greater autonomy with regard to energy supplies were fruitless. The "oil crisis", combined with an inflation rate of some 20 per cent, cut the growth rate of the economy to between 2 and 3 per cent per annum—and in what Herman Kahn saw as the emerging "superstate of the year 2000" discussion of long term perspectives became academic. In Christian Sautter's words: "the horizon of the ruling circles is now some two years."

Because of the very pace of development in the 1960s and early '70s "the latent crisis of Western capitalism (inflation, brutal urbanization, pollution) attains in Japan unheard of proportions. During 1973 wholesale prices increased 34 per cent, cost of living by 20 per cent and of housing by 38 per cent. . . . Each day the press reports new pollution-generated diseases. . . . The Japanese have had enough of this life at breaking-point".|| Given these stresses, given the rigidity of the Japanese political system, there has been little possibility of resolving the situation through normal parliamentary channels so that Japanese society, according to Philippe Pons, is increasingly like a boiler without safety valves. Under such circumstances the desperation of the ordinary Japanese finds an outlet in spontaneous "peoples'

* On the dispersal of *Kogai* to South Korea, see Thomas B. Lifson and Tsukamoto Kiyoshi, "Oka mo Umi mo Shindeyuku: Kankoku ni Shinshutsushita Nichi-bei no Kogai" in *Asahi Journal*, June 9th, 1972.

† for details, and reactions of the Thai Government, see Inoue Sumio, "Exporting Pollution: Asahi Glass in Thailand" in *AMPO* No. 18, Autumn 1973.

‡ Says the Kuala Lumpur newspaper *Sin Chew Jit Poh* (August 14th, 1972), speaking of the dispersion into South-East Asia of Japanese polluting industries: "Such pollution must be stopped by all means possible."

§ By 1970 Japanese "energy consumption on a per square kilometre basis rose to eight times that of the U.S. and double that of the United Kingdom". Yamakawa Akio in *AMPO* Vol. 6, No. 1, Winter 1974.

|| Philippe Pons in *Le Monde Diplomatique*, July 1974.

movements" directed against pollution, land speculation, rising prices, movements asserting the right to such essentials as clean air, clean water and sunshine. These movements have become an important force in the country's economy. Their impact on plans for continuing economic expansion has been strong; as one illustration, in 1972 less than one-third of the planned total work on constructing new electric power stations was completed as a result of the opposition of citizens groups.

Such developments as increasing urbanization, the energy problem and the increase in pollution have had their repercussions on the political scene, for the impotence of the establishment parties has given a marked advantage to the Communist Party. The decline in the agricultural population to less than ten millions has weakened the support for the LDP which in any case was losing touch with the electors.* The socialists have suffered from internal divisions and from the inadequacy of their "solutions" to the energy problem. Their strength derived from their stance in foreign affairs but today the problem of relations with the U.S. is overshadowed by the problems of prices, housing, pollution and the general lack of social security. And it is by grass-roots action on these issues that the Communist Party has consolidated its position. Its policy statement emphasizes that it seeks "above all to be realistic and to engage in action directly related to the aspirations of the people"—and this means in one area a struggle against pollution, in another the building of a school, elsewhere pressure for an increase in the number of doctors. . . . The result was seen in the 1972 elections when it received 10.5 per cent of the votes and increased its number of seats in the Lower House from 14 to 39; at the local government level, too, it is increasingly powerful. Today it is described by some observers as the only real spokesman against conservative forces in Japan. There is a certain irony in the fact that Japan's high rate of growth—or the deficiencies and side-effects of this—should have proved a powerful force in the emergence of what is potentially one of the strongest Communist parties in Asia. . . .

Given the growing pressures to shift the emphasis in Japan from development of the economy to the development of the people, given the various external limitations to orthodox development whose impact is beginning to be felt, the next decade may bring major changes in the character of the Japanese economy. This, indeed, is recognized by Japanese businessmen; in the words of a resolution passed at the meeting of Keidanren (Federation of Economic Organizations) held in Tokyo on May 25th, 1976, the nation's economy "now stands at the greatest turning point since the opening of the door in the Meiji era almost a century ago." Faced with the possible emergence of a radical coalition, of a government (to quote the *Japan Times*) "not very friendly to private business", it was suggested that big business should begin consolidating its own power base, separate from this potentially hostile government. Such a policy threatens growing social conflict and a continuation of the style of development which is making for ecological disaster. Yet it is evident to many that, if the Japanese people are to have a future, today's destructive, profit-oriented and "outer-directed" economy must give way to an inner-directed, welfare-oriented and ecologically-viable economy. And, as it does, we may expect to see a growing convergence, because of ecological imperatives, between the two great societies of East Asia, those of Japan and China.

BEYOND TECHNOLOGICAL MONISM

The development of Japan, as the development of the Centre as a whole, has been based increasingly upon capital-intensive and large-scale industrial technologies. These technologies are, above all, high-impact technologies; they are extremely expensive in terms of energy demands; characterized by a high degree of waste, by large-scale ecological destruction and by profound sociological disruption. In spite of the fact that they appear increasingly as an aberration—and one condemned by growing energy costs to an ephemeral existence—they are still regarded by those in power in the Centre as essential for real "development". Moreover, this viewpoint has successfully been "sold" to a majority of the power élites in the Periphery.

Only quite recently, as Robert Jungk has pointed out, has it become possible "to talk not of technology as an absolute, almost preordained, phenomenon with which one must come to terms as if it were a force of nature, but of a multiplicity of possible technologies in which first one group, then another, assumed the dominant role." He continues: "This attitude is slowly beginning to gain ground.† The idea that there may be alternative technologies in itself implies the idea of technological pluralism in place of the until now almost universally accepted technological monism. In each case each social system and each political ideology, indeed each culture, would be free to develop on its own particular line".‡ Yet it is well to recall today, when Japan's success in adopting the technology of the West is driving Western automobile manufacturers to the wall, that perceptive Asian writers have long spoken of, and insisted on the need for, a diversity of technologies, each with its specific cultural, social and psychological roots. In the words of the great Japanese novelist Junichero Tanizaki, over 40 years ago: "I always think how different everything would be if we in the Orient had developed our own science. Suppose for instance we had developed our own physics and chemistry: would not the techniques and industries based on them have taken a different form, would not our myriads of everyday gadgets, our medicines, the products of our industrial art—would

* According to a high official of the LDP in November 1973: "We feel ourselves cut off from our electors. Most of us do not always know what they wish for." Quoted by Philippe Pons.

† For a recent statement see the editorial in *Ceres* (FAO), vol. 9, No. 2, March-April 1976.

‡ From *Impact* (Unesco), quoted in *Technology for Development* (V.C.O.A.D.), 1975, p. 32.

they not have suited our national temper better than they do?"*

That in the past the nations of the Periphery have tended to an uncritical adoption of the technologies of the Centre may be attributed in part at least to the tendency of such nations to define their problems and outline the solutions to these problems in terms of what was most familiar or available to them—which was usually some form of Western technology. Today, Jungk can pose the question "Might there not be an unmistakably Japanese technology, just as there are typically Japanese buildings and clothes?" Today, many nations of the Periphery are beginning to experiment with a range of "alternative" or "appropriate" technologies; these programmes may involve the revival of an old technology, the adaptation of a current one, the invention of a new one or the improvement of a traditional and indigenous technology. And common to all these programmes is the attempt to create a technology compatible with the needs of the small community, a technology which serves rather than dominates those who use it, a technology which, because of the simplicity and ease of maintenance of its essential components, makes possible a large measure of local self-reliance.

China, more perhaps than any other nation, demonstrates the potential of intermediate or alternative technologies in breaking the shackles of poverty and dependence which still hold fast many nations of the Periphery. And, as the Chinese case shows, the role of alternative technologies is not simply an economic one; perhaps even more important than the contribution such technologies may make to production is the role they play in the intellectual emancipation of peasant and worker—for they demonstrate that no ethnic group, no class, has a monopoly of the skills required to initiate self-sustaining growth. Given the appropriate political conditions, the most impoverished of groups can begin the long uphill road from dehumanizing poverty to full human dignity—and for this they need neither massed capital nor imported expertise but rather the full mobilization of the underutilized potential of their own brain and muscle. At the same time we must stress the fundamental importance of political conditions for the Chinese strategy has been favoured by a wide range of social controls which are tied into the structure of political power and the social objectives of the planners. Not least, as David Dickson points out, has been the non-competitive nature of Chinese society which makes possible the sharing and rapid diffusion of new developments in technology and the protection of the markets of small-scale industries.

The contrast between the development processes of the "emerging Japanese super-state" and the nations of the Asian Periphery is a fundamental one and is most clearly evident in the East Asian region. Here the contrast between technological monism and technological pluralism is sharply posed. And whether the criterion be based on energy availability, ecological viability or the possibility of achieving full humanity, the disadvantages of technological monism, of an economy modelled on the developed nations of the White North, become increasingly evident. And for those nations of the Periphery who seek a way out of their underdevelopment the price of failing to strike out along their own, authentic, road of development has been spelled out by François Partant. Says Partant: "In taking as their model the countries who exploit them, the nations of the Third World integrate themselves into the system of exploitation: *they underdevelop themselves for the profit of their model*".†

THE CHINESE EXPERIMENT

The Chinese people in 1949 were faced, as are the peoples of so many emergent countries, with the need to carry through simultaneously an agricultural revolution and an industrial revolution, and to create, virtually from zero, the whole technical and social infrastructure on which a modern nation depends. They had to accomplish these things in the face of a rate of population growth (*ca.* 2 per cent per annum) greatly in excess of that in the West during its period of rapid growth (*ca.* 0.6 per cent), a population growth which was to influence strongly the character of Chinese development policies. Three options were open to them; they could follow the western model of free-enterprise development; they could adopt the Soviet model: or they could pioneer a "Third Way", drawing on the experience of other countries but modifying these models in the light of conditions specific to East Asia. The adoption of the Western model was precluded by the absence of most of the pre-conditions for its successful functioning (such as the availability of capital and of trained personnel) and by the pressure of time—the need to carry through in a matter of years a social and economic transformation which had been spread out over generations in Europe. The Soviet model which had made possible the rapid transformation of the backward peasant society of Russia seemed more attractive, and it was the Stalinist strategy of development which was followed in the Chinese First Five-Year Plan. Agricultural collectivization provided an institutional framework within which resources from the agricultural sector could be channelled towards the building up of the industrial sector; within the industrial sector there was an emphasis on large-scale capital-intensive technology and on the production of capital equipment rather than consumer goods; a high rate of capital accumulation was achieved by drastically holding down consumption levels. The success of the policy in the industrial field is indicated by the rate of growth achieved; according to United States sources, output doubled between 1949 and 1952 (annual growth rate 27 per cent) and doubled again during the First Five-Year Plan (annual growth rate 14 per cent). Increasingly, however, the specific character of the Chinese situation and the contrasts with Russia forty years earlier had to be conceded greater

* Cited in *Manas* (Los Angeles), vol. XXIX, No. 12, March 24th, 1976, p. 3.

† François Partant: *La guérilla économique: les conditions du développement* (Paris, 1976), p. 57 (emphasis in original).

weight, and by 1958 Chinese planners were moving towards a more distinctively Chinese model of development.

"The Great Leap Forward" in 1958 indicated the lines of the new strategy. The most important break with the Soviet model of development was the mass mobilization of the peasantry with the aim of substituting abundant labour for scarce capital; indeed, to turn labour into capital in the shape of public works programmes (such as the expansion of irrigation), agricultural intensification and the widespread development of rural industries. Economic development became "dualistic" with, on the one hand, a modern, large-scale, capital-intensive sector and, on the other, a more or less traditional labour-intensive sector represented by agriculture and commune industry; this is the pattern the Chinese term "walking on two legs". 1958 undoubtedly saw economic excesses, and three years of flood and drought in the early 'sixties cut back severely the rate of economic growth. By 1962, however, the economy had been re-consolidated and the present-day policy of "agriculture as the base and industry as the leading factor" emerged.

KING SOLOMON'S RING

Speaking of China's progress, Curtis Ullerich comments: "China seems to have found the key to accelerated development and to the problem of surmounting material backwardness within humanly acceptable time spans—something which amounts to King Solomon's ring in our time". This is a large claim, especially for a regime described in the authoritative *Financial Times* (July 4th, 1967) as "tottering inexorably towards final collapse"*, and, indeed, until now the recent flow of visiting American experts would have been greeted with scepticism. But that Ullerich's claim is not unrealistic is suggested by J. K. Galbraith's conclusion after his recent visit to China: "There can be no serious doubt that China is devising a highly effective economic system. . . . The Chinese economy isn't the American or European future. But it is the Chinese future. And let there be no doubt: for the Chinese, it works". Let us examine briefly the scale of the Chinese achievement, the achievements on the production front and in the field of social policies. And, in doing this, let us bear in mind the relevance to the poorer countries of Asia and the Third World of China's success in achieving full employment and equitable income distribution at a relatively low level of per capita income.

Perhaps the most striking conclusion reached by Ullerich is that China's per capita G.N.P. has increased fivefold in 20 years, reaching about $250 at the beginning of the 1970s. The total G.N.P. (at 1952 price levels) he estimates at 180,000 million dollars. This is made up as follows:

* Although it is fair to add that four years later the same journal described the same regime as "highly efficient", and the country's economy as "humming away as busily as that of any other Asian developing country".

	($ million)
Agriculture	30,000
Industry	90,000
Services	30,000
Corrective for Undervaluation and Deflation	30,000
G.N.P. AT 1952 PRICES	180,000

The inclusion of a 20 per cent (i.e. $30,000 million) "corrective" to the combined value of the primary, secondary and tertiary sectors is important. It is designed to correct the deflation which makes the Chinese price system unique (deflation between 1952 and 1958 was 1.5 per cent per annum; since 1965 about 1 per cent a year). It is also designed to offset "the systematic underpricing and financial undervaluation of the Chinese physical effort if we schematically translate Chinese figures [of new construction] into monetary terms". It is worth stressing that, as Ullerich points out, this systematic undervaluation of the present-day economic performance implies the promise of much more vigorous expansion once the created assets (whether reclaimed land, new forests or new irrigation systems) "become fully generative in terms of secondary benefits". We may, then, expect even higher growth rates than the annual growth rate of over 10 per cent which seems to have been achieved over the past two decades. We should also stress again that Chinese development efforts have been more oriented towards the elimination of poverty and social inequalities than towards mere production. The expansion of the latter has been impressive—but much less impressive than the highly developed grass-roots system of social services—and this is impossible to quantify.

"AGRICULTURE AS THE BASE . . ."

Asian realities, like the realities of the Third World as a whole, are peasant realities. Yet the highest priority in the majority of development plans tends to be the development of modern capital-intensive industry. The critical employment needs of growing populations are ignored; the stagnation, if not retrogression, of the countryside continues; the gap between industry and agriculture, town and country, technocrat and peasant, widens progressively. The Chinese, as the North Vietnamese and the North Koreans, followed a different path. They accepted the reality of the "enormous mass of concentrated peasant". They realized that poverty could not be eliminated nor a modern economy created by grafting a capital-intensive industrial sector on an unchanged rural base. City and countryside, industry and agriculture, had to be developed in a harmonious relationship. The key to successful development was in the countryside, for only if the productivity of the rural sector were boosted would it be possible to maintain a strong flow of funds towards the industrial sector. And the key to rural development lay in the political motivation of 500 million peasants; "only when the peasants are politically and socially motivated, enthused and directly involved, can agricultural output be set on an expanding course."

This is a policy which has paid off handsomely in recent years. The *Sunday Times* (June 28th, 1970) says of the Green Revolution in the Third World that "while the technical possibility of abolishing hunger now exists, the organizational ability to take full advantage of it and control its social implications is usually missing". This is not the case in China or the other East Asian socialist countries. China was not only experimenting with high yielding varieties (H.Y.V.) a decade before India, but possessed the "organizational ability" to ensure that gains in output went to benefit, not a small and wealthy land-owning group, but the peasant population as a whole. And the diffusion of technology into the countryside, the widespread policy of rural industrialization and the heavy emphasis on self-reliance, have meant that the policy of agricultural development has become largely self-sustaining; some 5,000 small fertilizer factories in the local sector complement the output of giant combines such as those at Taiyuan or Nanking; most of the communes are now producing their own H.Y.V. seed strains. Careful meshing of urban and rural industry, the conversion of under-utilized labour into capital through a policy of mobilizing under-utilized manpower to create a rural infrastructure, the progressive extension of an education system tailored to the needs of a world both peasant and socialist, and decentralization of decision-making, have made possible remarkable achievements in the rural sector. The results? In the words of David Rockefeller, after his mid-1973 visit: "The most impressive thing is the development they made with respect to agriculture in terms of feeding a very large population."* In statistical terms? According to Premier Chou En-lai a cereal production of over 240 million tons†—but this appears to refer only "to the common food grains in the narrower sense", and estimates by Ullerich and others of the overall "grain-equivalent" output (i.e. including colza, soya beans, groundnuts and tubers) produce an "annual gross product figure" of 330–350 million tons. In addition, the rural collectives are held responsible for keeping in stock 18 months' emergency supplies while the central government has built up some 40 million tons of grain as buffer stocks. Says John Gurley: "The Chinese—all of them—now have what is in effect an insurance policy against pestilence, famine, and other disasters". And this is one of the dominating realities not simply of Asia but of the contemporary world.

INDUSTRY: WALKING ON TWO LEGS

The separation of "agriculture" and "industry" in any discussion of China is unreal and is for convenience of treatment only. Today in China there is no clear-cut distinction between these two main sectors—thus field studies in 1966 showed that on some communes 33 to 45 per cent of the total income was being derived from industry. In 1958 it was estimated that this commune-run industry accounted for 10 per cent of China's industrial output. In the succeeding years this sector has greatly expanded, and become much more sophisticated in its output (which ranges from fertilizers and agricultural machinery to transistors and electronic equipment) so that, by 1970, the local sector was accounting for from one half to two-thirds of the production of artificial fertilizers and agricultural implements and 70 per cent of all the processed agricultural produce. The scale of development of these medium and small industries has been illustrated by Roland Berger's comments on Hupeh province. Says Berger: "The province in 1970 opened 2,000 small factories to manufacture, among other things, agricultural implements, tractors, diesel engines and small hydro-electric equipment. Twenty-two local chemical fertilizer factories were commissioned, and during the year construction started on a further 33. In 1956 the province had only three such plants."‡

Chinese industry walks on two legs—and one of these is represented by the small-scale, labour-intensive sector administered by the commune (or the *hsien* or brigade); the other is the centrally administered and capital-intensive state sector. The economic achievements since 1949 have been due not only to the integration of agriculture and industry; they have been due no less to the integration of modern and traditional industry, and of centrally controlled and locally controlled industry. Geographically this style of development has resulted in a landscape very different from that of the non-socialist countries of Asia; industry and modern technology are diffused deep into the countryside, and the concentration of development in a handful of cities, set like islands of the 20th century in a medieval countryside, has been avoided in China.

Because of what has been termed Peking's "studied indifference" to outside evaluations of their achievements, it is not easy to estimate the size of the centrally administered State sector. Oil output, according to a Chinese delegation to OPEC, reached 40 million tons in 1971.§ Steel production in 1970 was *c.* 18 million tons; if steel produced in the local sector is included, a total output of some 30 million tons is probable. Fertilizer production is some 14 million tons (probably excluding commune production). Cotton cloth output in 1970 was 8,500 million metres, making China the world's biggest producer. Isolated statistics, perhaps, but sufficient for us to measure the industrial progress achieved over the last two decades, sufficient to bear out Curtis Ullerich's assessment: "One conclusion is absolutely inescapable: China's rapid and comprehensive advance in the fields of nuclear energy, space technology and aviation is such that it cannot have been performed by a skeletal, ramshackle, industrial apparatus of uncertain but low output capacity. To move ahead in so many

* Quoted in *Ta Kung Pao*, July 5th, 1973.

† This, as *Le Monde* pointed out, is almost three times that of India, although China's population is less than a third larger than that of India.

‡ Roland Berger, "Chinese Cities, Chinese Hamlets: Beckoning a New Generation", in *The Nation* (New York), October 18th, 1971.

§ *Le Monde*, August 11th, 1972.

vital fields at so rapid a pace and with such a massive show of strength calls for a large, efficient and well run-in industrial complex".

The creation of such a complex is the decisive event of our time; the means used to create it of decisive importance to the emerging nations of Asia and of the whole Third World. For what we are concerned with is an economy developing as fast as that of Japan, and without the human and ecological disruption that is the Achilles' heel of Japanese-style development. And it is an economy which, starting from the same level as that of India or other Asian nations, has confronted the challenge of employment and population growth before which the countries of non-socialist Asia are impotent.

"HIS FULL HUMAN POTENTIAL"

Almost 20 years ago René Dumont, the French agronomist, recognized that the major cause of backwardness and poverty in Asia was the failure to utilize, in any meaningful fashion, its greatest resource—the muscles and the minds of its people. Partly, this was because of the prevalence of oppressive social and economic structures; partly because preventable disease caused the wastage of billions of man-days of potential labour; partly because ignorance and illiteracy left the Asian peasant helpless in the face of a hostile physical or social environment. So real social and economic progress demanded not only the breaking of oppressive social structures but also the liberation of the peasant from the diseases which sapped his efficiency and shortened his life, demanded that he have access to an education which would draw out his full human potential.

Land reform and the abolition of capitalism provided the first of these preconditions; the development of the social services, especially the health services and education, provided for the second and third. Within the first decade of the People's Republic many of the diseases which had plagued peasant and townsman were virtually eliminated; these include malaria, most intestinal worm diseases and venereal disease. One of the results of the Cultural Revolution was to shift the emphasis of development to the rural areas and this was especially so in the medical field. By the early 1970s, figures of one medium-level health worker (a so-called "barefoot doctor") for every 600 peasants were claimed; the ratio observed by the writer in 1972 ranged from 1:600 to 1:140 on a range of communes; the number of fully trained doctors varied from 1:5,000 peasants to 1:1,000. Each production brigade has its clinic and most communes have hospitals which can undertake all save the most specialized surgery. Such a medical infrastructure is without parallel in the under-developed world; indeed, the medical provision in some areas is not paralleled in many "developed" societies. Part at least of the secret of China's economic progress is to be found in the elimination of many diseases and, more important, in the creation of an efficient medical infrastructure which has its role not simply in the preventing or curing of disease, but in the promotion of health and well-being.

A UNESCO expert*, writing some seven years ago, described the failure of the conventional education systems in the Third World; it is, he says, "necessary to seek out and find educational structures better adapted to the needs and the resources of the countries of the Third World". China for some years now has been experimenting with such alternative educational structures, and her achievements have an Asia-wide relevance.

Ivan Illich notes how the belief that education is something done at school and something that is very difficult and complex discourages the poor from taking over their own learning. Today the Chinese are demonstrating the fallacy of this belief, and showing how a whole people can take the educational process into its own hands and make of it an integral part of life itself, a means by which the vision of a Good Society is realized. All of China, says John Gurley, is "one great school". There are schools run by factories and schools run by communes, there are day schools for children and evening schools for peasants, there are peasants and workers teaching in schools and universities and teachers and students who spend sizable amounts of time working in the fields and the factories. Everywhere, experimentation and flux, so that generalization is hazardous. But certain broad themes do emerge. There is the close integration of theory and practice, of learning and applying that learning in the factory or the field; there is the high component of productive work which means most schools can be virtually self-supporting financially; there is a rejection of school as a ladder for individual betterment and an emphasis on "serving the people"; above all, there is a strong emphasis on local initiative which echoes the line of a Chinese Communist Party policy document of 1966: "The only method is for the masses to liberate themselves, and any method of doing things on their behalf must not be used."

The pattern is a fluid pattern for, as the Chinese see it, rules or programmes are not made for all time, but the trend is clear and it is a trend which, by liberating the latent potential of young and old, is fashioning that "spiritual atom bomb" of human energy and human creativity of which Mao has spoken. Indeed, in this respect, the Chinese reshaping of their educational system is of greater world significance than China's emergence as a nuclear power or the dramatic transformation of her physical environment; without it, the economic progress we have described would have been impossible.

INTERLUDE: CHINA'S RESOURCES

(Now you see them, now you don't . . .)

As James Cameron observed ironically over 20 years ago: "There were, of course, few mysteries in China for those who had never been there"†—and this applies particularly to the assessment of the resources, both physical and human, on which China's development is based.

---

* Rémi Van Waeyenberghe in *Les Carnets de l'Enfance/Assignment Children* (Unicef, Paris), January 1968.

† James Cameron, *Mandarin Red* (London, 1955), p. 21.

A decade ago the present writer commented: "The riches of the Chinese earth are very great"*. Five years later this assertion was described as "at best misleading, and at worst a dangerous assumption"† China's supposedly great natural wealth, the critic claimed, "may well prove to be one of the myths of the twentieth century"†. By 1976 the Canadian economist Barry Richman could write: "China is abundantly endowed with huge surpluses of a number of minerals". Oil reserves, Richman suggests, could conceivably be double those of Saudi Arabia, while China is one of the best endowed countries in terms of coal, ranks fourth or fifth in the world "just on her *known* natural gas reserves", has nuclear energy and "an abundance of hydro-electric possibilities"‡. Richman foresees a possible Chinese export of over 100 million tons of oil by the mid-1980s and the trading of American "know-how, equipment, and training in return for oil, cash and *finished goods* from China" (emphasis added). Oil exports may be bringing in China about $1,000 million yearly by about 1983; this is the current plan—and it will clearly give the country very considerable scope for manoeuvre in her trading relations with the outside world. In orthodox terms, such export earnings would make possible extensive purchases of foreign equipment and technology; such a policy would, however, depend to a considerable extent on the weight which future Chinese policy gives to environmental considerations (Japan is a warning of the ecological dangers of heavy technological inputs) and to orthodox concepts of efficiency as against revolutionary concepts of equity in shaping the nation's economy.

SOME ENVIRONMENTAL CONSIDERATIONS

Ecological problems, stemming from pollution, may, we have seen, place limits on Japan's industrial expansion. China, by contrast, appears to be escaping the problems of environmental deterioration found in most of the developed capitalist and socialist nations. Partly this is because the country's vast area makes it in any case easier to absorb the side-effects of industrialization than is the case in, say, Japan. Partly it is because the degree of industrialization is less. But more important than either of these facts is the Chinese attitude to waste, an attitude rooted deep in Chinese history and in the character of contemporary China's socio-economic system.

In contrast to the "waste-making" societies of the White North, the Chinese have long been accustomed to a life lived on the very narrowest of resource margins. Neale Hunter has commented perceptively that the Chinese, living close to the earth, know "that the source of their life is in *things*, that they are linked inseparably to their material environment. They believe in matter in a way that few Westerners (perhaps only the minority of peasants that remain) can fully understand. Their philosophy and religion—in ancient times as well as under communism—spring from and never wander far from the material ground of their existence". He adds: "Waste is about the worst word in the Chinese language these days, as it was in China's (and Europe's) past."§

The Chinese preoccupation with frugality (an "obsolete virtue" in the West, as Hunter observes) goes back far into their history and was sharpened by their experience during the Civil War and the struggle against Japan; non-waste was then a precondition for national survival. And in the succeeding years non-waste has been elevated from a simple necessity to a revolutionary virtue. Campaign after campaign stresses the need "to convert all waste to treasure" and emphasizes the need for "comprehensive use", while school children are taught to "struggle against the four wastes—waste material, waste gas, waste water and waste heat". As a Writing Group of the Tientsin Municipal Revolutionary Committee puts it: "There is nothing in the world which is absolute waste. 'Waste' under one condition may be valuable under different ones. 'Waste material' left from one product can become good material for another product. After being transformed and utilized, 'waste material' can become a product or useful material".‖ Today, the Chinese are experimenting with programmes of "multi-purpose use" which involve complexes of factories, each running off the "waste" material of others. They have long reclaimed and recycled materials such as cans, paper and glass, and the human excreta and vegetable waste of cities and towns are composted down, or "re-cycled", so that even today some 80 per cent of the fertilizer used on the land is organic. Garbage disposal has become a major problem in the cities of the West; by contrast, because of the effectiveness of re-cycling by factories and neighbourhood groups, the city of Shanghai (with a metropolitan population of 12 million) has been able to eliminate the old-style garbage collection.

In part at least the environmental movement in the West is motivated by aesthetic considerations; waste and pollution are destructive of the beauty which we feel should be part of life, and, as "environmentalists", we attempt to halt the advancing tide of ugliness. The concern of the Chinese is with a rather different aspect; because life is still austere, because there is still not abundance, they are concerned not with aesthetics but with efficiency of use—and this means eliminating waste.¶

* Keith Buchanan, *The Chinese People and the Chinese Earth* (London, 1966), p. 30.

† Michael Freeberne in *The Changing Map of Asia*, ed. W. G. East, O. H. K. Spate & C. A. Fisher (rev. edn., London, 1971), p. 354.

‡ Barry Richman, "Oil for the Lamps of America", in *The Center Report*, April 1976, p. 15.

§ Neale Hunter, "The good earth and the good society", in *China and Ourselves*, ed. Bruce Douglass and Ross Terrill (Boston, 1969), p. 179.

‖ Cited by Orville Schell, "China's way with waste", in *Ecologist*, Vol. 3, No. 2, February 1973.

¶ Increasing shortage of some basic resources, coupled with a growing awareness that our "Babylonian" consumption levels are quite simply unethical in a world of hunger, will lead to an increasing emphasis on non-waste in our Western ecological/environmental programmes.

The generalization—and application—of this non-waste ethic have clearly been favoured by the socio-economic realities of contemporary China, a country rich in manpower and "relatively poor in automated industrial power". Under these conditions it is economically worthwhile to deploy labour-intensive techniques in a programme of converting waste into usable products. In the developed societies, by contrast, resources have been relatively cheap in relation to labour and, from a cost-effectiveness point of view, re-using or re-cycling has been rarely profitable. Given these latter considerations, it is evident that the application to Japan, or other developed societies, of China's experience in coping with pollution is limited—at least until, as is inevitable, growing resource shortages combine with continuing unemployment to bring about structural changes.

The outstanding example of the ecological efficiency of the Chinese economy, however, has always been the agricultural system. Thus, using as criterion calorie-output against calorie-input, Chinese wet-rice cultivation is the most productive of any farm system, and "one calorie of energy put into the system—largely in the form of food for the farmer—yields about 40 calories in rice".* By contrast, western mechanized agriculture demands a much larger input of calories (in the shape of oil to power tractors and other machinery or to make fertilizers and pesticides) than it yields; it has become, in short, "a gigantic energy sink"†.

Any interruption of the supply of oil, whether through war or the gradual exhaustion of reserves, would have a disastrous impact on Western (and Soviet) food production; China's agriculture would be scarcely affected. And, at a time when the continuing availability of supplies of imported phosphates poses a question-mark over the future of many highly-specialized agricultures, China's high degree of self-sufficiency with regard to plant nutrients is a major source of strength. As we have seen, four-fifths of the fertilizer used is organic and derived from various types of "waste", and in this respect China could provide a model for other developing countries.‡ In the future we are going to have to concern ourselves increasingly with ecological considerations of this kind.

EFFICIENCY OR EQUITY? HUMAN DIMENSIONS OF DEVELOPMENT

These material achievements are considerable and mean a cumulative narrowing of the margin which separates the East Asian socialist states from Japan. Nevertheless, our Western preoccupation with economic criteria may well lead us to overlook the major contrast which is emerging, not only between China and North Korea on the one hand and Japan on the other but also between the East Asian socialist states and the states of the European socialist bloc. The Chinese, and the North Koreans, are striving not only to develop their productive forces but also to create a "new socialist man". The commune, the co-operative, the factory, is more than an economic unit, it is also the basic social and political unit in a new socialist society. Economic growth and the raising of the level of people's welfare is important but welfare is seen less in accumulation of consumer goods than in the development of people whose full creative powers are realized. And progress of any sort is worthless, the Chinese hold, unless all rise together; indeed, they say, rapid economic development is unlikely unless everyone *does* rise together. The classical Western pattern of "building on the best", whether in industry, agriculture or education, is rejected, as is the concept of development as a "trickle-down" process. Rather is the objective of Chinese planning one of involving everyone in the development process, thus "demystifying" the whole problem of economic development and ultimately creating the conditions for much more rapid growth. There can be "big leaps", hold the Chinese, only by putting man at the centre and by thus providing scope for his immense creative potential.

This emphasis on "man" and on the "new socialist man" has been affirmed increasingly strongly since the Cultural Revolution. As John G. Gurley puts it: "Experts are pushed aside in favour of decision-making by 'the masses'; new industries are established in rural areas; the educational system favours the disadvantaged; expertise (and hence work proficiency in a narrow sense) is discouraged; new products are domestically produced instead of being imported 'more efficiently'; the growth of cities as centres of industrial and cultural life is discouraged; steel, for a time, is made by 'everyone' instead of by only the much more efficient steel industry." Such a policy may, as Gurley notes, be dismissed simply as one which sacrifices efficiency to equity but this, he emphasises, misses what is the most important—and revolutionary—aspect of the "Chinese model". This is the conviction "that the resources devoted to bringing everyone into the socialist development process—the effort spent on building on 'the worst'—will eventually pay off not only in economic ways by enormously raising labour productivity, but, more important, by creating a society of truly free men, who respond intelligently to the world around them, and who are happy."

More recently, Barry Richman has drawn attention to the significance, the human significance, of the Chinese success in achieving a society in which people no longer have to worry about "their basic material needs". This achievement of a basic level of security, together with the narrowness of the gap between the high-paid and the low-paid, means, as Richman puts it, "that most of the population can start satisfying their human needs in non-materialistic ways. If people

* See *Ecologist*, Vol. 3, No. 8, August 1973, pp. 289–290.

† See for example, the data given by George Borgstrom in "Food, Feed and Energy", in *Ambio* (Stockholm), Vol. 2, No. 6, 1973.

‡ A study quoted in *Ceres* (March-April 1976) shows that in the Third World countries, the tonnage of soil nutrients available (as animal manure, human excreta, composts, etc.) was "ten times what they used in chemical form. . . and twenty times what they produced".

are turned on by things other than money you need less money to motivate them. Thus, income distribution ties in very closely with the goal of building a cohesive society, a relatively altruistic society, a society without great emphasis on self-interest or material gain."*

In evaluating the Chinese experiment we would do well if we devoted more attention to its human implications. Its downgrading of the specialist and its emphasis on a more versatile "universal man" means that it will be able, with little loss of efficiency, to mobilise its labour force for a variety of tasks and this gives the flexibility needed in most underdeveloped economies. Its emphasis on plain and simple living and mutual aid means that the wasteful dissipation of resources by an elite group which is a barrier to progress over much of Asia is avoided; saving and investment and the growth of the capital stock is promoted. And in its preoccupation with the development of the full human being, its confrontation of the problem of "how men, in an industrial society, should relate to machines and to each other in seeking happiness and real meaning in their lives" it is concerning itself with the basic problem which confronts all industrialized or industrializing societies, whether they be capitalist or socialist. Most analyses of Chinese society ignore these issues—but it is precisely in its attempt to confront and solve such issues that the Chinese experiment becomes of global relevance.

* Barry Richman, *Center Report*, April 1976. It is worth noting that in his earlier work (*Harvard Business Review*, 1967, and *Industrial Society in Communist China*, 1969, pp. 914–916) Richman was extremely sceptical regarding the Chinese policy of using non-material stimuli.

POSTSCRIPT: "SEEK TRUTH, EVEN THOUGH IT BE IN CHINA . . ."

"During a recent conference on extraterrestrial life, American scientists speculated seriously on the possibility of learning from such life how better to cope with our earthly problems. Yet, with few exceptions, these scientists have not concerned themselves with that vast laboratory for social innovation where one-quarter of the human race is addressing itself directly and purposefully to problems that concern the other three-quarters as well. There has been interest in acupuncture and barefoot doctors and native strains of "miracle rice", but how many have seriously investigated China's substantive social experiments—to substitute social service for personal gain as the mainspring of society, to eliminate the "private ownership of knowledge," to introduce self-management in factories and communes, to reduce the age-old tension between rural areas and urban centers, and also between mental work and physical? What proportion of popular and professional writings in the United States are devoted to analyzing this unprecedented social creativity, and what proportion to speculation about Chou's political fortunes or Mao's health and the power struggles over the succession?"

Professor L. S. Stavrianos in *The Nation* (New York), Feb. 8th, 1975.

BIBLIOGRAPHY

ADAMS, RUTH.(ed.) Contemporary China (Vintage, New York, 1966).

ATOMIC SCIENTISTS, BULLETIN OF THE. China after the Cultural Revolution (New York, 1969).

BALDWIN, FRANK (Editor). Without Parallel: The American-Korean Relationship Since 1945 (New York, 1974).

BARTZ, PATRICIA M. South Korea (Oxford, 1972).

BERGER, ROLAND. "Planification 'à la chinoise'" in *Le Monde Diplomatique*, March 1973.

BERGER, ROLAND. "La Politique financière de la Chine" in *Le Monde Diplomatique*, August 1973.

BETTELHEIM, CHARLES, CHARRIÈRE, JACQUES, and MARCHISIO, HÉLÈNE. La construction du socialisme en Chine (Paris, 1965).

BRACHI, PHILIP. "Japan's G.N.P.: Growing . . . Growing . . . Gone" in *Ecologist* (London), September 1972.

BRULÉ, JEAN-PIERRE. China Comes of Age (Penguin, 1971).

BUCHANAN, KEITH. The Transformation of the Chinese Earth (London, 1969).

CHEN, NAI-RUENN. Chinese Economic Statistics: A Handbook for Mainland China (Edinburgh, 1967).

DELEYNE, JAN. L'économie chinoise (Paris, 1971).

DONNITHORNE, AUDREY. China's Economic System (London and New York, 1967).

DUMONT, RENÉ. La Chine surpeuplée: Tiers-monde affamé (Paris, 1965).

ETIENNE, GILBERT. La voie chinoise (Paris, 1962).

FACTS ABOUT KOREA (Foreign Languages Publishing House, Pyongyang, 1962).

FRIEDMAN, EDWARD and SELDEN, MARK (eds.). America's Asia (New York, 1971).

GALBRAITH, J. K. "Galbraith in China" in *Observer Review* July 1st, 1973.

GOUROU, PIERRE (transl. S. H. Beaver). Man and Land in the Far East (London, 1975).

GROSSMAN, BERNHARD. Die Wirtschaftliche Entwicklung der Volksrepublik China (Stuttgart, 1960).

GUILLAIN, ROBERT. Dans trente ans la Chine (Paris, 1965).

GURLEY, J. G. "Capitalist and Maoist Economic Development" in *Bulletin of Concerned Asian Scholars*, April-July 1970 (San Francisco).

HALLIDAY, JON. A Political History of Japanese Capitalism (New York, 1975).

HALLIDAY, JON and MCCORMACK, GAVAN. Japanese Imperialism Today (Penguin, 1973).

HAN SUYIN. China in the Year 2001 (London and New York, 1967).

HEDBERG, HAKAN. Japan's Revenge (London, 1972).

HENLE, H. V. Report on China's Agriculture (FAO, 1974).

HENSMAN, C. R. China: Yellow Peril? Red Hope? (SCM Press, London, 1968).

HINTON, W. Fanshen: A Documentary of Revolution in a Chinese Village (New York, 1966).

Hong Kong Research Project. Hong Kong: A Case to Answer (Nottingham, 1974).

HORN, JOSHUA S. Away with all Pests: An English Surgeon in People's China 1954–69 (New York and London, 1971).

HUDDLE, NORIE and REICH, MICHAEL. "The Octopus that eats its own legs" (Pollution in Japan) in *Ecologist*, August 1973.

JAPAN ECONOMIC RESEARCH CENTRE. The Structure and Development in Asian Economics (Tokyo, 1968).

Japanese Economy in the World—1980 (Tokyo, 1972).

JOINT ECONOMIC COMMITTEE, CONGRESS OF THE UNITED STATES. An Economic Profile of Mainland China (Washington, 1967).

KAROL, K. S. China: The Other Communism (London, 1967; New York, 1968).

KOLB, A. East Asia: The Geography of a Cultural Region (London, 1971).

LIPPIT, VICTOR. "Economic Development and Welfare in China" in *Bulletin of Concerned Asian Scholars*, Summer 1972.

MCCUNE, S. Korea's Heritage (Tokyo, 1966).

MARCH, ANDREW L. The Idea of China (New York, 1974).

MYRDAL, JAN. Report from a Chinese Village (Penguin Books, 1967).

MYRDAL, JAN and KESSLE, GUN. China: The Revolution Continued (London, 1971).

NIPPON: A CHARTED SURVEY OF JAPAN (Japan, 1966).

NOBUO, MATSUOKA. "Pollution Imperialism" in *AMPO* (Tokyo), March 1973.

NORMAN, E. H. Origins of the Modern Japanese State: Selected Writings (edited by JOHN W. DOWER) (New York, 1975).

ORLEANS, LEO A. Professional Manpower and Education in Communist China (Washington, 1961).

PELISSIER, ROGER. Le troisième géant: La Chine (Paris, 1965).

PONS, PHILIPPE *et al.* "Japon: Les 'retombées' politiques d'un certain type de croissance" in *Le Monde Diplomatique*, July 1974.

PONS, PHILIPPE. "Japon: une majorité en crise" in *Le Monde Diplomatique*, April 1975.

RISKIN, CARL. "China's Economic Growth: Leap or Creep?" in *Bulletin of Concerned Asian Scholars*, January 1970.

RISKIN, CARL. "Maoism and Motivation: Work Incentives in China" in *Bulletin of Concerned Asian Scholars*, July 1973.

SCHRAM, STUART (editor). Chairman Mao Talks to the People: Talks and Letters, 1956–71 (New York, 1974).

SCHURMANN, FRANZ. Ideology and Organization in Communist China (Berkeley and Los Angeles, 1966).

SCHURMANN, FRANZ and SCHELL, ORVILLE. Communist China (China Readings 3, Penguin Books, 1968).

SCIENCE FOR THE PEOPLE. China: Science Walks on Two Legs (New York, 1974).

SELDEN, MARK. The Yenan Way in Revolutionary China (Cambridge, Massachusetts, 1971).

SIDEL, RUTH. Women and Child Care in China (New York, 1972).

SIDEL, VICTOR, and SIDEL, RUTH. Serve the People: Observations on Medicine in the People's Republic of China (Boston, 1974).

SNOW, EDGAR. The Other Side of the River (New York and London, 1963).

TUAN, YI-FU. China (The world's landscapes 1, Longmans 1970).

UCHIYAMA, TAKURO. "The Current Status of Nuclear Power Development in Japan" in *AMPO*, Vol. 7, No. 1, Winter 1975.

UI, JUN (ed.). Polluted Japan (Tokyo, 1972).

ULLERICH, CURTIS. "Size and Composition of the Chinese G.N.P." in *Journal of Contemporary Asia* (London) Vol. 2, No. 2 (1972).

ULLERICH, CURTIS. "China's G.N.P. Revisited: Critical Comments on a Previous Estimate" in *Journal of Contemporary Asia* Vol. 3, No. 1 (1973).

WERTHEIM, W. F. Dawning of an Asian Dream (Amsterdam, 1973).

WERTHEIM, W. F., and SCHENK-SANDBERGEN, L. CH. Polarity and Equality in China (Amsterdam, 1973).

WU, YUAN-LI. The Spatial Economy of Communist China (New York and London, 1967).

The Economy of Communist China (New York and London, 1965).

YAMAKAWA, AKIO. "Petroleum and Political Vision: Coming to the Crunch" in *AMPO*, Vol 6, No. 1, Winter 1974.

China

PHYSICAL AND SOCIAL GEOGRAPHY

Michael Freeberne

The third largest country in the world (after the U.S.S.R. and Canada), China's territory covers 9.6 million square kilometres (over three and a half million square miles) and measures about two thousand five hundred miles north to south and three thousand miles from east to west. China and the United States are approximately the same size, but because of China's relief and the comparatively backward state of transport, distance creates major economic and political problems. For example, not only is it difficult to build a dense communications network but also the current policies of industrial re-location are seriously hindered, due to such factors as the long haul for minerals or the distance from the market. Similarly, the vastness of China has made it very hard to provide strong central government from Peking. This is illustrated by the widespread tendency toward localism which became apparent after the onset of the Cultural Revolution in mid-1966. Offsetting these disadvantages is the inestimable psychological pressure which China's bulk exerts over its Asian neighbours.

China's land frontiers extend for a total of 20,000 kilometres (official), in an arc of actual and potential conflict. The eleven countries which share frontiers with China are North Korea, the Soviet Union, Mongolia, Afghanistan, Pakistan, India, Nepal, Bhutan, Burma, Laos and Viet-Nam. Although frontier agreements have been concluded with countries such as Mongolia, Pakistan and Burma since 1949, these have not prevented frontier tensions. The dispute over the boundary between China and India resulted in the border war of 1962. Meanwhile, the most recent Chinese maps show large stretches of the north-eastern boundary with the Soviet Union and the Sino-Soviet boundary in the Pamir area as "un-delimited", whilst border incidents have increased dramatically both in the north-east and north-west since 1960, as in the clashes along Heilungkiang's borders in 1969.

The eastern seaboard is 14,000 kilometres in length. Territorial waters are dotted with over 5,000 islands, ranging from provincial sized Hainan and Taiwan down to minute atolls. Rich in fish, the Territorial waters make an important contribution to the output of aquatic products (marine and fresh water combined), estimated at between five and seven million tons a year. China lacks an important sea-faring tradition, however, partly because the relatively smooth coastline is largely without good natural harbours.

Administratively, China is divided into twenty-two provinces (including Taiwan); five autonomous regions (Inner Mongolia A.R., Ninghsia Hui A.R., Sinkiang Uighur A.R., Kwangsi Chuang A.R., and Tibetan A.R.), and three cities (Peking, Tientsin and Shanghai), all of which are directly under the central government. In addition there are over two thousand counties and cities, which are subdivided into 74,000 people's communes. As the communes have undergone striking changes since their introduction in 1958, much of the effective economic and political organization in China is at production brigade and production team level, which probably frequently coincides with the natural village. Other organizational structures such as macro-economic and military regions may embrace several provinces, whilst tiny urban street organizations complete the administration network.

PHYSICAL FEATURES

Physical size on its own cannot automatically raise China to the rank of a first-class world power. The West regarded China as a land of fabulous wealth at the height of the Ch'ing empire, but in fact the geographical environment presents considerable obstacles to modern development, which if not insurmountable put a brake on progress. For example, a Chinese source published in 1964 reveals that approximately 10 per cent of China's surface is in agricultural use, 10 per cent is forest, 28 per cent is pasture, whilst a further 12 per cent is classified as reclaimable wasteland; this leaves roughly 40 per cent unclassified wasteland.

Relief, configuration and climate are critical in suggesting possible settlement areas and zones suitable for economic development. For the most part high in the west and relatively low in the east, comparison has been made with a three section staircase. The Chinghai-Tibet Plateau at over 4,000 metres is the highest flight; next is an arc of plateaux and basins between 1,000 and 2,000 metres extending eastwards from the Tarim Basin, across Inner Mongolia and the loess lands, then turning south to include the immensely fertile Szechwan Basin, and the Yunnan-Kweichow Plateau; much of the land which constitutes the lowest flight lies below 500 metres and includes the most densely settled areas, such as the middle and lower Yangtze Basin, the North China Plain and the northeastern plain. About a third of China's total area is highland; 26 per cent is plateau land; 10 per cent is hill country; 20 per cent is occupied by basins; but only 12 per cent of the surface is composed of plains.

Watering these plains are rivers which in some moods bring rich harvests, whilst in other years they may cause flooding, or dry up altogether with resulting drought famines, which were frequent before 1949. In the north, the Yellow River is 4,845 kilometres in length and has a drainage basin of 745,000 square kilometres. In central China the Yangtze is 5,800 kilometres long with a massive drainage basin of 1,800,000 square kilometres, covering one-fifth of the country. The shorter Sikiang is the most important river in south China. The long history of flood control and water conservation continues into the contemporary period, as in the case of the taming of the Hwai River, which is a project which has been encouraged by Mao Tse-tung. Flood control, irrigation, navigation and power generation are all stressed in this and similar multi-purpose projects. The Chinese claim that China is high in world ranking in hydro-electric power potential and that the Hengtuan Mountains in the south-west have an "unlimited" potential; what they fail to point out is that this area is difficult of access and economically backward. Indeed China has been characterized as a land which suffers from having either too much water or not enough water, both in terms of regional and seasonal distribution. Since 1969 there has been a national campaign to build small and medium-sized hydro-electric power stations which was said to have doubled the total capacity of rural hydro-electricity stations constructed over the previous twenty years during the winter and spring of 1969–70 alone.

CLIMATE

Climatically, China is dominated by a monsoonal regime. Cold air masses build up over the Asian land mass in winter, and the prevailing winds are offshore and dry. In summer there is a reversal of this pattern, and the rainy season is concentrated in the summer months over the most densely settled parts of the country, in the east and the south. Running from south to north there are six broad temperature zones; tropical and sub-tropical, warm–temperate and temperate, cold–temperate and the Chinghai-Tibet plateau area, which has its own characteristic regime. January is generally the coldest month and July the hottest. There is a great range in winter temperatures—as much as 60°F. between the average for Canton in the south and Harbin in the north. South of the Nanling Mountains January temperatures average around 46°F., but they drop to between 17.5° and minus 4°F. over much of the north-east, Inner Mongolia and the north-west. In summer the temperature difference between Canton and Harbin is only 10°F. and summer temperatures over much of the country average above 68°F.

The summer monsoon brings abundant rain to coastal China, especially in the south and east, but amounts decrease drastically to the north and west. A humid zone covers much of southeastern China and the average annual rainfall is above 30 inches. In the semi-humid zone, extending across the north-east, the North China Plain and the southeastern region of the Chinghai-Tibet Plateau, the average falls to less than 20 inches. The remainder of the Chinghai-Tibet, the Loess, and the Inner Mongolian Plateaux receive only about 12 inches, whilst western Inner Mongolia and Sinkiang receive less than 10 inches and include extensive deserts.

Eighty per cent of the precipitation falls between May and October, with July and August the wettest months. Not infrequently the rain turns the rivers into raging torrents and disastrous floods occur, or alternatively not enough rain falls. In the late 1870s, for instance, four northern provinces were devastated by a drought famine which cost between nine and thirteen million lives. To flood and drought can be added other calamities: typhoons, earthquakes, frosts, hailstorms, plant and animal pests and diseases. The present government attributes the grave economic difficulties of the early 1960s to three main factors, namely the withdrawal of Soviet aid, internal mistakes, and bad weather. The Chinese refer to the years 1959, 1960 and 1961 as the "three bitter years" and they claim that in 1960 and again in 1961 half the agricultural land was affected by natural disasters.

VEGETATION AND NATURAL RESOURCES

During many hundreds of years a great deal of China's natural vegetation has been stripped. The basic contrast is between the forests and woodlands of the eastern half of the country and the grassland-desert complex of the western half. Tree types vary from the tropical rain forests in the south, through evergreen broad-leaved forests, mixed mesophytic forests, temperate deciduous broad-leaved forests, and mixed northern hardwood and boreal coniferous forests in the north. Sixty per cent of China's forest reserves are found in the area of the eastern Mongolian Plateau, the Lesser and Greater Khingan Mountains, and the Changpaishan massif. Other natural forests are located in Yunnan, Kiangsi, Fukien, Kweichow, Szechwan, on Hainan Island, in the Tsinling Mountains and along the eastern edge of the Chinghai-Tibet Plateau. Most of China's forests are largely inaccessible, however, and there is a serious shortage of workable timber.

Due to the widespread destruction of natural vegetation, soil erosion is a major problem. Sheet and gulley erosion are common; water and wind erosion do great damage in the north, whilst water erosion is the chief enemy in the south; also, farming malpractices, such as deep ploughing, have aggravated the situation both historically and since 1949. A recent Chinese source states that about 40 per cent of the total cultivated area comprises "poor" soils: red loams, saline-alkaline soil and some of the rice paddy soils. Thus the legendary fertility of China's soils cannot be taken for granted.

Information concerning mineral wealth is incomplete, but the best available estimates suggest that China is extremely rich in coal and iron ore. Record steel production figures of 23 million tons were claimed for 1972. Between 1966 and 1973 many thousands of small coal mines and pits have been opened, especially in areas south of the Yangtze river. Following a major oil strike at Taching and explorations elsewhere, China has increased its annual production of crude oil from about 3 million tons in 1960 to an estimated 60 million tons in 1974. China has abundant reserves of manganese, tungsten and molybdenum, but is relatively poor in copper, lead and zinc, and nickel supplies are meagre. There are rich resources of salt, moderate reserves of sulphur, whilst phosphates require development; supplies of tin, fluorite, graphite, magnesite, talc, asbestos and barytes are also comparatively good.

HUMAN GEOGRAPHY

According to a statement made by China's Vice-Minister of Health in August 1974 (and repeated by Chou En-lai in January 1975), approximately 800 million people, or more than a fifth of the world's population, live in China. This is a formidable figure in view of the pressures which Chinese numbers have exerted on the Chinese realm in the past, and in view of the continuing problems in the physical environment already outlined. There is, for instance, a striking imbalance in the distribution of population, which is heavily concentrated in the plain and riverine lands of the southeastern half of the country, whilst most of the northwestern half is, by comparison, virtually uninhabited. This results in very high densities of population in the richest areas for settlement, such as the Yangtze delta or the Red Basin of Szechwan. Indeed, 90 per cent of the population inhabit little more than 15 per cent of the country's surface area.

Some 94 per cent of the population are Han Chinese. The remaining 6 per cent belong to one of the national minority groups. Altogether there are over fifty million non-Chinese living within China, chiefly in the peripheral areas beyond the Great Wall, in the north, the north-west and the south-west. There are over fifty different minorities scattered throughout 60 per cent of the country. Ten minorities number more than one million each (the Chuangs, Uighurs, Huis, Yis, Tibetans, Miaos, Manchus, Mongolians, Puyis, and Koreans). There are over seven million Chuangs in Kwangsi, whilst the smallest of all the minorities, the Hochih, from the banks of the Ussuri River, number only about six hundred.

Although so-called autonomous regions (and also districts and counties) have been established, the larger minority groups have presented the central government with serious administrative difficulties. Racial, religious and linguistic problems, as in Muslim Sinkiang and Buddhist Tibet, have resulted in several anti-Chinese uprisings since 1949; these have been forcibly suppressed.

Linguistic differences between the seven main Chinese dialects, as well as between Chinese and minority languages, have proved an intractable issue, despite the adoption of Mandarin as the national language, despite attempts at the simplification of the written language by reducing the number of strokes in individual characters and by romanization, and despite literacy drives. In 1957, Mao Tse-tung forecast that illiteracy would be wiped out by 1963; by 1975 the Chinese had not achieved this goal.

Well over one hundred million people in China live in cities or towns, but this is still predominantly a rural country with possibly 85 per cent of the population living in the countryside. The inequalities in living standards which exist between the "parasitic" cities and the rural areas confront the Chinese with some of their most urgent ideological and practical problems. One answer is to advertise life in the countryside by applauding the progress of model villages like Tachai, a tiny community in the northern province of Shansi.

About eighteen million Chinese live beyond the frontiers of China. These Overseas Chinese are found mostly in South-East Asia. Because of its proximity to the People's Republic and because this part of Asia is rich in items such as rice, oil, timber and rubber, which China lacks in sufficient quantities, some authorities see in the presence of these communities a threat to the security of the area.

The population of China is expanding at a rate of approximately 1.6 per cent a year, and the 1,000 million mark is expected to be topped by about 1987. Three birth control campaigns, in the mid-1950s, in the early 1960s and since 1969, have failed to make any noticeable inroads in the increase in Chinese numbers. Internal migration offers no solution to the population problem.

Despite a record grain harvest of 246 million tons in 1971 and a crop of 240 million tons in 1972, and because the agricultural sector has to provide not only food for a rapidly growing population but also investment for individual growth, population pressure must remain central to all domestic and external issues within the forseeable future.

TAIWAN

The province of Taiwan is one of a mountainous arc of islands offshore from the Asian land mass. Separated from the mainland by the Taiwan Strait (about 90 miles wide at the narrowest point), Taiwan is 13,885 square miles in area, measures 244 miles from north to south and 89 miles from east to west, and straddles the Tropic of Capricorn.

Due to the mountainous character of the relief only about one quarter of the island is cultivated, while forests cover about 55 per cent of the total land area.

The climate is sub-tropical in the north and tropical in the south, being strongly modified by oceanic and relief factors. Apart from the mountainous core winter temperatures average 60°F and summer temperatures about 80°F. Monsoon rains visit the north-east in winter (October to March) but come to the south in summer, and are abundant, the mean annual average rainfall being 101 inches. Typhoons are often serious, particularly between July and September.

The population numbered 16,149,702 in December 1975, giving Taiwan a population density of nearly 450 per square kilometre, one of the highest in the world.

In 1964 the rate of natural increase fell below 3 per cent for the first time; it was 3.7 per cent in 1952 and 1.8 per cent in 1974. The crude birth rate in 1975 was 23 per 1,000 (compared with 46.6 per 1,000 in 1952), and the crude death rate in 1975 was 4.7 per 1,000 (compared with 9.9 per 1,000 in 1952). The death rate is one of the lowest in Asia, and the infant mortality rate (deaths under 1 year of age per 1,000 corresponding to live births) of 20.5 per thousand in 1970 is the lowest in Asia apart from Japan. At the end of 1971,

38.7 per cent of Taiwan's population was under 15 years of age; 56.2 per cent were aged between 15 and 59; and 5.1 per cent of the population was 60 and over. This is a youthful population with over 50 per cent under 20 years of age (1971), and therefore a high potential for growth.

Figures for the population distribution by employment (15 years of age and over) for 1971 showed that agriculture accounted for 42.3 per cent, personal services for 27.9 per cent and manufacturing for 13.9 per cent. However, urban population is increasing with the expansion of industry.

HISTORY

C. P. FitzGerald

China has a long history, but it does not reach quite so far back as is often claimed. The earliest written Chinese records date from the period round 1500 B.C., and recorded history is uncertain and partly legendary until after 1000 B.C. These dates are late for Egypt, Iraq, or Asia Minor. On the other hand, the civilization first appearing in the second millennium B.C. is the direct ancestor of the culture of modern China, the written language is an early form of the present script, and the connection between spoken Chinese of today and that of a remote age can be traced. There is good archaeological evidence that the present-day Chinese, especially in north China, are the descendants of the people of Shang, the first certainly known kingdom of that region. It would not, of course, be historical to speak of "China" and the "Chinese" in this early period. Next to nothing is known of the culture of what is now more than half China, the south, until centuries later. The north China kingdom of Shang was probably confined to the valley of the Yellow River.

In the next age, the first millennium B.C., a new kingdom was established over a much wider area of north China, but was divided into feudal fiefs some of which were very large. This kingdom, or dynasty, the Chou, endured nominally from *c.* 1100 to 221 B.C., but in the later centuries the kings had lost all power and retained only the old capital city. The country was divided among warring feudal lords, the most powerful of which finally set up as independent kings and virtually abolished the nominal overlordship of the King of Chou. Other, originally ethnically different, peoples in the Yangtze valley, acquired Chinese civilization in this age and also established strong states in the south and centre of China. In the same age as the early Chinese philosophers taught and wrote, of which the first was Confucius (died 479 B.C.), the Chinese Feudal System broke down, and a period of intense strife known as the "Age of the Warring States" (481–221 B.C.) ravaged the country both north and south. This was in reality a contest to unite the whole of the Chinese civilized world under one rule, and was ultimately won by a powerful ruthless monarch, king of the western state of Ch'in.

IMPERIAL CHINA

Ch'in had been a state dedicated to war and conquest: its official ideology despised the arts, literature and philosophy, but exalted law, by which was meant a harsh criminal code to which all, rich and poor, noble and serf, were alike subject. When the king of Ch'in had conquered all his rivals (221 B.C.) he proclaimed himself First Emperor, choosing a new and lofty title which we have translated as "emperor" although the Chinese words *Huang Ti* do not have the military connotations of the Latin *imperator*. Once in power the Ch'in applied their own harsh system of government to the whole country, and thereby provoked a violent and fatal reaction. On the death of the First Emperor after a reign of eleven years his incompetent successor was soon engulfed in a national revolt, from which emerged, after several years of civil war, the Han dynasty, which restored the central unified empire but ruled it with more moderate policies and thus established the new form of the state. Before the Ch'in-Han empire there had been no political unity in China; the rule of even the earliest Chou kings had been limited, and the later fiction of an original unified empire, from which the feudal system was a degeneration, is an imaginative reconstruction of largely unknown periods in the light of the reality of the first century B.C.

One of the acts of Ch'in which was most condemned at the time and has subsequently been bitterly denounced by Chinese historians was the "burning of the books"—a decree by which all the works of the philosophers and much other literature were collected and destroyed, in order to crush the intellectual opposition to Ch'in rule. In the Han period scholars laboured, with some success, to restore the lost works, but our knowledge of earlier China has undoubtedly suffered greatly from this proscription. The ancient Chinese did not inscribe on clay tablets, nor carve long inscriptions on stone: they wrote on slips of bamboo, a perishable material which rarely survives long periods of interment. The Han empire, which expanded the frontiers to limits close to those of the present People's Republic, and also extended its conquests far into central Asia, has left very full historical records, which became the model for all later dynastic histories.

Ruling all China for over four hundred years (206 B.C.–A.D. 221) it was contemporary with the great age of the Roman Republic and the first centuries of the Roman Empire. The imperial state as constructed by the Han remained the model for the subsequent regimes, right down to modern times, although innovations and advances in the art of government were made at later times. The Emperor was the supreme and absolute monarch, in theory, and when a vigorous personality occupied the throne, in practice also. He was advised, and often controlled, by a council of ministers chosen from the heads of the civil service, who were thus not politicians but bureaucrats. In Han times the civil service was recruited by recommendation, not yet by public examinations. High officials recommended their followers or clients, but these had to be men of education, usually of some means, and also capable. An incompetent or corrupt official would bring his patron into trouble and disgrace. The hereditary aristocracy of pre-imperial days had been abolished. Only the imperial family and a small number of their eminent supporters held such titles, and after the middle of the Han period these ranks no longer gave any effective jurisdiction over territory, which was divided into units governed by imperial officials. As both the imperial family of the Han dynasty and their early chief supporters were all men of poor origin and low social class, the advent to power of this group made a social revolution almost inevitable. Feudal land tenure vanished, to be replaced by the free ownership of land, and as a consequence the rise of the landlord class and a mixed farming class of free peasants and tenants.

Division and Reunification under the T'ang and Sung

On this basis the Han dynasty retained power for a long period, which was one of rapid and varied development both in the economy and in the art and literature of China. In the early third century A.D. the Han empire collapsed due to a variety of internal tensions and the increasing weakness of the ruling family. Civil wars at first divided the empire into three kingdoms (221–265), then, after a very brief reunion, the empire was invaded in the north by Tartar tribes, who seized the northern provinces. Chinese dynasties ruling from Nanking, held the south, and developed it. This period of division between north and south lasted for more than 250 years (316–589). It was a period of political weakness, but not a "Dark Age". Literature flourished, and in these centuries Buddhism was introduced from India and established a major place in the Chinese civilization, from whence it spread to Japan. In both north and south military power tended to overshadow the civil service, but that institution did not wholly disappear.

Reunion of the empire was accomplished by the short-lived Sui dynasty (589–618) and then consolidated by the great T'ang dynasty (618–907). This period of three hundred years marks what many would call the apogee of the old Chinese civilization (contemporary with the European Dark Ages). The T'ang empire was as extensive as the Han, and at one time also included all Korea. It was governed on the same principles but with significant improvements on Han practice. Public examinations for the choice of civil service candidates came steadily into prominence, displacing the recommendation system. This was partly the T'ang emperors' response to the dangerous power of the highly placed military aristocracy who had dominated the court in the period of the division between north and south. It had the consequence of bringing to power a much larger class of literates who had neither territorial nor military power bases. The T'ang bureaucracy could thus draw on a wide field of talent, and the extent to which it mastered the practice of government is evidenced by the elaborate and detailed census taking in 754, which enumerated the population of China as 52,880,488, a figure which archaeological discovery has proved to be founded on exact and detailed returns of families, in which men, women and children were counted. The second half of the T'ang dynasty was disturbed by a major rebellion, which weakened central government control in the provinces. Art and literature, especially poetry, early forms of the drama and the novel, all flourished during this great age, in which China was also in closer contact with western Asia and Byzantium, as with India and Japan, than ever before.

When the T'ang fell in 907 a short interval of fifty years of confused struggle and separation divided it from the rise of the next great unifying dynasty, the Sung (960–1280). This period is again divided at 1127 when the Sung lost north China to the invading Kin Tartars. The Sung regime differed in some respects from its predecessor. The civil service now reigned supreme, recruited by public examination. Sung rule was rather gentle; disgraced statesmen were sent to govern small provincial towns, not imprisoned or executed, and even rival kings at the foundation of the dynasty were spared if they surrendered. Art excelled, and the Sung is also the age of the reshaping and modernization of Confucianism (finally perfected by the philosopher Chu Hsi), which was the main intellectual interest of the age. The Sung were in fact too civilized for their age; beyond their northern frontier powerful and violent nomadic peoples were emerging and were to break into the empire first in 1127 when they conquered north China, and later, from 1212 to 1280, when the Mongol ruler Genghiz Khan and his successors maintained continuous attacks upon China, both north and south, till they had conquered the whole country and extinguished the Sung dynasty. During that dynasty the economy had made great advances; porcelain was perfected and became the common table ware of China, and was also exported far and wide to Asia and eastern Africa. Silk weaving increased and became an organized industry established in factories (although only using handicraft methods of production). It has been suggested that the Sung economy was approaching the point of "take off" to an industrial revolution. Shipping and overseas commerce were for the first time more important sources of revenue, in the southern Sung, than the land tax.

Mongol and Ming Rule

All this was checked, indeed largely destroyed, by the Mongol conquest which was particularly destructive in north China. Large areas were reduced to uninhabited wilderness, and made into imperial Mongol hunting grounds. A very great number of people perished, either by slaughter or starvation. Europe was soon to learn of the glory of Kubilai Khan, the first Mongol to rule all China. but Marco Polo was in large part describing the surviving prosperity of parts of the Sung empire which had escaped the worst devastation. The Mongols ruled China with foreigners, such as Polo, who took service under the Khans. They came from all over Asia as well as some from Europe, and they did not speak or read Chinese. Consequently, Mongol rule was alien and hated. Chinese in their service were often employed in non-Chinese parts of their empire. The successors of Kubilai were weak and incompetent; in 1368, after less than a century of full control, they were driven out by a large-scale Chinese rebellion, which was finally led and organized by the founder of the following Ming dynasty. The main contribution of the Mongol period to Chinese culture was the rise of the drama, possibly under some foreign inspiration, but essentially the work of Chinese scholars. The widespread Mongol empire of the early Khans, which included Persia, Asia Minor and much of Russia, made communication better for a time that ever before. It was in this age that, thanks to Marco Polo and other travellers, the Europeans for the first time obtained some accurate information about China. Chinese scholars, in the Sung period, using Arab informants, had also gained more knowledge of western Asia and Europe.

The Ming dynasty not only restored Chinese rule, but expanded the limits of the empire. South Manchuria was settled and incorporated, as was Yunnan, at the opposite extremity of the empire. But the land route to the west decayed in importance after the Mongol period, and the sea route round India to the Red Sea and Persian Gulf became more important. Early in the fifteenth century, from 1405 to 1433, the Ming court sent out several large-scale maritime expeditions carrying up to 70,000 men in specially built large ships. These expeditions roamed over the seas south of China, established Ming suzerainty over the kingdoms of Malaya and parts of what is now Indonesia, visited Ceylon, India, Burma, the Philippines, the Persian Gulf, Arabia, the Red Sea, and the east coast of Africa down to Zanzibar, from which region they brought back a live giraffe as a gift to the Emperor. Ming sea power, had it been maintained in the southern seas, would have barred the Portuguese when they arrived seventy years later. But there was a change of policy in Peking: the maritime effort was discontinued and never resumed. Unwittingly, the Ming court thus exposed China to many calamities.

From the middle of the fifteenth century China was also to an increasing extent menaced by the growth of a new power in what is called Manchuria, or the Three Eastern Provinces. The Manchu tribes, kindred of the Kin Tartars who had ruled north China in the late Sung period, were at first tributary to the Ming. From China, through this contact, they acquired a knowledge of governing techniques, literacy, and organization. Late in the sixteenth century they coalesced into a new kingdom which threw off allegiance to the Ming, and before long began to encroach on the Ming territory of south Manchuria, or modern Liaoning province. By the middle of the seventeenth century they had seized this region and were raiding the Great Wall frontier of China proper. In 1644 an internal rebellion overthrew the Ming government in Peking, and the general commanding the frontier army, Wu San-kuei, decided to admit the Manchus rather than acknowledge the rebel chief as a new emperor. Aided by his powerful Chinese army (which could probably have denied them entry to China indefinitely), the Manchus occupied north China, while Wu destroyed the rebels. Later he broke with the Manchus and tried to establish his own dynasty in south China. His death during this campaign enabled the Manchus to conquer south China also. But Manchu rule was not firmly established in the south of China until 1682, nearly forty years after their unopposed entry into Peking. This difference between the history of north and south had great importance for later times. The north had accepted the Manchus, and remained loyal to them; the south had resisted them, and remained hostile and unreconciled. In the first century of Manchu rule the difference was unimportant, although even then moulding Manchu policy. In later times, when the dynasty was losing power, the hostile traditions of the south became the main source of trouble and rebellion from which the failing regime was never delivered.

Manchu (Ch'ing) Dynasty

The Ch'ing, or Manchu dynasty (1644–1912) was the last age of imperial China. In many ways, although a dynasty of alien origin, the Ch'ing were more conservative and traditional than any of their Chinese predecessors. Being of foreign origin, and a small minority in a vast sea of Chinese subjects, they sought to conciliate the Chinese intellectual class, the scholar-officials, by adopting all their opinions and endorsing their outlook. They became more Confucian than the Chinese Confucianists. Had the Ch'ing had no more to contribute than an extreme conservative standpoint and a reverence for Chinese culture which distrusted all change and advance, it is probable that they would not have lasted very long. They had the fortune to produce, within a generation of their accession to the throne, three successive very capable rulers, the Emperors K'ang Hsi (1662–1723), Yung Cheng (1723–1736), and Ch'ien Lung (1736–1796). The first and last of these also reigned for sixty years each. Long reigns are conducive to stability in an authoritarian government. The gains acquired through a period of such stability lasting nearly 150 years were great. Peace was maintained throughout China; only frontier wars, to pacify the nomads of Mongolia, kept the army in good training. The population rose very rapidly; for a time prosperity grew proportionately. New grains and plants, such as maize, the potato and sweet potato introduced through the Philippines from the Americas, added to the productivity of the soil.

But these successes were themselves productive of trouble and danger. The pacification of the Mongolian tribes ended the nomad menace for ever, for at the same time the advance of Russia in Siberia cut off and destroyed the reservoir of nomad power. Consequently, the Manchu army, originally a highly trained and very efficient force, had now no wars to fight, and degenerated. No one at court considered the activity of European shipping on the coasts to be a latent menace; no one heeded the fate of India. The long internal peace is believed to have doubled the population from 100 million to over 200 million. Land became hard to find and prices rose; tenants were rack-rented and free peasants bought or squeezed out. Industry was not developed to meet the rising population and provide new employment. Industry and mining were held to be occupations which, needing some foreign technology, could only prove subversive and anti-Confucian in their operation. The ruling scholar-officials were not trained to engage in this sort of enterprise and the court endorsed their attitude.

Foreign Relations under the Manchus

The court distrusted foreign contacts. These were made in the south, at the great port of Canton above all. But the south had been the most tenacious opponent of the Manchu conquest. Southerners were apt to form secret anti-Manchu societies, to plot rebellion, and to look abroad for aid and comfort. A Chinese navy would have had to be manned largely with southerners and based in the south, so a strong navy could be a danger; better not to have one at all. This left the defence of the country to an antiquated army. The history of Manchu dealings with the foreign traders who were now resorting to China in ever increasing numbers reveals the weakness of Manchu policy. They needed the trade, which was at first very profitable to China. They distrusted the foreign traders, confined them to one port (Canton), forced them to deal only with a selected group of Chinese merchants, hedged them about with innumerable vexatious restrictions, as if they were dangerous pirates. Chinese were forbidden on pain of death to travel overseas.

All these restrictions were imposed without relaxation throughout the eighteenth century, and the otherwise able and enlightened Emperor Ch'ien Lung upheld them. He would not accept any permanent foreign diplomatic representation in Peking; it had never been customary. Foreigners came to pay tribute, were given magnificent gifts, and sent back home. The same treatment was given to the British, Dutch and other embassies who tried to open up relations. The Manchus did not wish to learn about a new world which would upset their basic assumptions and challenge their traditional claims. Tension built up at Canton, and the discovery that opium, produced in India, could have a ready and spreading sale in China, turned the favourable trade balance from China to Britain. Opium was an illegal import; British traders, and their officials, connived at an extensive smuggling trade; Chinese officials were easily corrupted to turn a blind eye and win a share in the profits. Early in the nineteenth century the opium trade was an open scandal and doing great harm to China's economy and to social life. The court was finally induced by earnest and patriotic officials to decree the total suppression of the trade. The resulting action, and high-handed methods employed, touched off the powder keg and brought about the Opium War (1842).

China was defeated; her navy was wholly inadequate to face the British fleets; her old-style army could not overcome the more modern arms of small British landing forces. She was compelled to sue for peace, and this was consummated by the Treaty of Nanking, the first of the "Unequal Treaties" as they came to be called, which established the system of Treaty Ports, concession areas and the right of extraterritorial jurisdiction. This system was to endure for just one century until, in 1942, it was swept away by the Japanese invasion of China. Treaty Ports were cities, not always on the coast, which were designated as places where foreign traders could reside and trade. At such cities they were granted concessions (usually outside the walls) which were under their own government, and beyond Chinese control. Foreigners of the Treaty Powers (who came to include all the subjects of the European powers and the citizens of the U.S.A.) were not subject to Chinese law, but were under the jurisdiction of their own consuls. This was the system of extraterritoriality. Chinese right to impose tariffs on foreign imports was limited to 5 per cent. Foreign Treaty Powers could set up their own postal services in China. It must be recognized that not all of these provisions, harsh though they seem today, were then seen as unreasonable. Much of the system was directly copied from the Capitulations which had long been in force in the Turkish Empire, and which had in fact sprung from Turkish governmental practice. The Turks put all foreigners, subject or alien, under their own laws administered by their own judges. This system had a religious origin. Christians under Christian law, Muslims under Koranic law, Jews under their own. So it was not a great infliction to set up such a system in China.

Concessions were thought necessary because the Chinese populace, especially at Canton, were extremely hostile to foreigners living among them in the city. It was agreed that the system would save trouble and avoid incidents. Chinese law was unreformed and by European standards harsh and cruel. The limitation of tariffs was the most openly "imperialist" condition, but in return the foreign traders paid their dues to representatives of the Peking government, not to local officials. Peking actually gained revenue. It was the condition, not at first implemented, that the foreign powers had the right to station envoys in Peking itself, which the Manchu court most resented and for long evaded. These facts serve to show how far apart were the ideas of Chinese and Europeans at that time. The condition resented by the Manchus was accepted without question by the republicans of the next century; the terms which the Manchus rather willingly conceded were seen as severe encroachments on Chinese sovereign rights.

Reform Movement

It was not, at first, the terms of the Treaty of Nanking which did harm to the Chinese Government of the Ch'ing dynasty; it was the loss of prestige following defeat in war, and defeat in the south, where the population was hostile. Within a few years the great unrest of the south, aggravated by economic pressures, burst out in the T'ai P'ing rebellion (1851–1864). This rebellion swept the south and centre of China, and narrowly failed to capture Peking and dethrone the dynasty. Its leader was a man with some imperfect knowledge of the Christian Protestant religion, who claimed to be a prophet inspired directly by God. Established in Nanking, he ruled the T'ai P'ing Heavenly Kingdom and for a time tried to enforce many advanced reforms, especially in the condition of women and land tenure. But the pressure of the imperial armies was too constant to make these efforts fruitful. At the end Nanking was recaptured; the Heavenly King dying of disease, for which he refused all attention, shortly before the city fell. The salient fact about this campaign was that the Manchu army of the dynasty had been proved useless and the imperial cause was won by Chinese armies commanded by Chinese loyalists. They could not thereafter be disbanded and their commanders became the highest officials of the dynasty, and dominated political life for the next fifty years. The Manchu government now survived on Chinese arms and loyalty; so long as it could command both, it could endure; when these were lost the dynasty had no further resource.

Preserved against all likelihood in the 'sixties, the Manchus were compelled to permit some few modernizing reforms, mainly concerned with the armed forces. These were to be equipped with modern weapons, and arsenals were built. A modern navy was constructed, and its future officers sent to England to serve with the British Fleet and learn their art. This was, in fact, the flaw in the new movement. "Chinese learning as a base, foreign skills for use" was the new slogan. But foreign skills require foreign learning; the young men had to study English, or French; they did not confine their reading to technology, they read about democracy and other strange notions. They became at first reformers; when reform was denied, they became revolutionaries. The patrons of the young students now beginning to be sent abroad were the great officials who had commanded and raised armies to fight the T'ai P'ings, and now exercised unquestioned power. Change and reform were thus built into the power structure, but this could still be obstructed by the supreme authority of the Emperor. For nearly half a century since the death of the Emperor Hsien Feng in 1862 until her own death in 1908 this power was exercised by the Regent, the Empress Dowager Tz'u Hsi, first in the name of her infant son and when he died in youth in that of her infant nephew Emperor Kuang Hsu. She was an able but basically ignorant woman who hated foreign innovations. She did her best to obstruct reform, and she was very successful.

If the great reforming officials of the early 'seventies had had the leadership of the sovereign to back them, as their contemporaries in Japan had, it is at least possible that they might have achieved in China some reformed system not unlike the Meiji system in Japan. China is a larger country and the task harder; but there were plenty of able men willing to undertake it. Instead they had to hold on to power by conciliating the prejudices of an obscurantist court arbitrarily ruled by a strong-minded but conservative woman. When the Emperor Kuang Hsu came of age he tried, in a brief three months in 1898, to implement a programme of sweeping reforms, inspired by young and progressive officials who had gained his confidence. He was never fully free to act, and when it seemed that he might become so, the Empress Dowager emerged from a very partial retirement to carry out a *coup d'état*, imprison the Emperor for the rest of his life, and execute all reformers she could catch. Thus tragically ended the last real hope of reform under the monarchy.

Meanwhile, since the 1870s, China had been steadily suffering the encroachment of the European Powers. Russia had taken the opportunity of the T'ai P'ing war to obtain what is now the Maritime Province of Siberia and land north of the Amur river. These territories had been Manchu, but never Chinese. France had in the 'eighties seized Indochina and forced Peking to renounce its suzerainty. Britain and France together had been at war with China (1858) and had actually occupied Peking, exacting a further "Unequal Treaty". Towards the end of the century Japan entered the lists, and in the war of 1894–95 drove the Chinese out of Korea, and destroyed the new fleet. China had to yield suzerainty over Korea, and also the ports of Talienwan (Dairen) and Lushun (Port Arthur) to Japan. Russia, aided by France and Germany, then put pressure on Japan to give up these two ports to Russia. A government which is laggard in reform at home, and unable to defend itself abroad, is not likely to retain loyalty and support. When the younger generation, towards the turn of the century, realized that reform would be frustrated, and that the country was running the real risk of partition by foreign powers—already "spheres of influence" were openly marked out—there was a sharp turn to revolutionary ideas and action. This movement will for ever be associated with the name of Dr. Sun Yat-sen.

REPUBLICAN CHINA

Sun Yat-sen was a Cantonese, who had been educated from childhood in Hawaii and then took a medical degree at the medical school of Hong Kong, which later became Hong Kong University. His formation was thus largely foreign and Western. Finding that radical reform was unacceptable to the official world of China, he turned revolutionary and republican, and for more than ten years maintained an unceasing effort to stir up rebellion in China. He was for long unsuccessful; but his influence grew steadily among the young Chinese studying abroad, particularly in Japan, where the majority of them went. He built up a party and a secret organization, obtained funds from the overseas Chinese of South-East Asia, always anti-Manchu,. and finally his followers were able to infiltrate the army—the new model army whose officers had also studied abroad. Army officers, who must necessarily learn modern techniques, have in many countries of Asia proved to be the most effective revolutionaries. They at least can command armed support.

Thus, when in 1911 the revolution broke out it was from the first dominated by the army men, a servitude from which it was not to escape for many years. The court had lost further prestige in 1900 by backing the peasant anti-foreign movement known as the Boxer Rebellion, which for a time threatened to massacre the diplomatic corps in Peking, and was finally crushed by an international expedition, which took Peking and drove the court to retreat to the west of China. The southern provinces under their great viceroys refused to follow court policy over the Boxers, and virtually concluded a separate peace with the Foreign Powers. This was a sign of coming disruption which proved a portent. After signing a further humiliating peace the court returned to Peking, and in its last years attempted to put through reforms which might have saved it fifty years earlier. It was too late. When the Empress Dowager died in 1908 no strong character remained to carry on the Regency in the name of the next infant Emperor, Hsuan T'ung or P'u Yi. Within three years the revolution had broken out and the dynasty was doomed.

In its last extremity it called upon the former commander-in-chief Yüan Shih-k'ai, who was out of favour with the new Regent, to save it. The northern troops would only obey their old commander; the southern army had gone over to the revolution. Yüan took command, but he did not intend to save the dynasty; he hoped to set up his own. First he showed by a brief campaign that he was a serious contender, then began to negotiate with the republicans. A deal was soon arranged. Yüan would bring about the peaceful abdication of the dynasty, which would in return be granted very favourable terms, and the republic would elect Yüan to be president. It would seem strange now that the republicans should have trusted Yüan Shih-k'ai, who had already betrayed the Emperor Kuang Hsu to the Empress Dowager in 1898 and was now betraying the Manchu dynasty to the republic. It was at least probable that he would betray the republic in due turn. This did indeed happen. Once the dynasty had accepted the favourable terms for abdication (leaving it the tenancy of the imperial palace and a shadow court with large revenues) Yüan refused to move the capital to Nanking, as had been stipulated. When the first Parliament was called (under conditions of flagrant corruption) Yüan had some of the more able members assassinated, and soon, having obtained a loan from the Foreign Powers without the assent of Parliament, dissolved that body and ruled by decree. Futile and ineffective resistance in the south was speedily crushed. Yüan now moved to obtain support for a new dynasty with himself as Emperor (1914).

The outbreak of the First World War was a factor which worked against this programme. It divided the Foreign Powers, and left Japan a comparatively free hand in Asia. Japan did not approve of Yüan, an old opponent in Korea. By making the famous "Twenty-One Demands", which if accepted would have reduced China to a Japanese protectorate, Japan weakened his prestige, for he dared not refuse all these demands. Japan bribed and armed his secret opponents, his own generals, who were jealous of his pretensions to the throne. On December 25th, 1915, a revolt broke out, and within a few months it was evident that the generals had turned against him, and the projected monarchy was impossible. He renounced his plans, tried to cling to the Presidency, and died in June 1916. His death was soon followed by the contests among his former generals who controlled the provinces. The "warlord era" from 1917 to 1927 was marked by a series of short civil wars fought entirely between rival militarists to gain control of revenues, and above all of the impotent government in Peking, which could dispense the customs revenue collected under foreign supervision to service the foreign loans, but which still left a valuable revenue for whichever general could dominate Peking. The international position of China fell to its lowest point, and within the country there was an increasing breakdown of law and order, banditry, and rural distress. The seeds of revolution in a real sense were rapidly maturing.

Nationalism and Communism

If to foreign observers China had never seemed so chaotic and purposeless, there were, in fact, beneath the surface, forces stirring which were very little understood abroad. In May 1919 the students of Peking, had rioted against the Peking Government's acceptance of the secret deal by which Japan was to acquire the former German leased port of Tsingtao in Shantung. It was generally known that the corrupt politicians and their militarist master had received large sums from Japan for this virtually treasonable decision. The students burnt the house of one of the ministers concerned and, obtaining widespread support from the ordinary citizens and even from the peasants of nearby villages, they forced the government to withdraw from their policy and to authorize the Chinese delegation at the Peace Conference at Versailles to refuse to sign the Treaty. The "May Fourth Movement", as it has become known, spread widely in all parts of China; it was the first sign of a new phase of the revolution, a revolt against Western dictation of China's affairs and fate, the first overt reaction of the generation who had grown up since the empire fell. Today the Communist government commemorates it as the opening of a new era.

In May 1925, six years later, another violent outbreak followed upon the shooting by International Settlement police of student demonstrators in Shanghai. This time the wave of anger, directed against Britain and Japan, was nation-wide. There was a total boycott of British and Japanese trade and enterprise. Hong Kong's labour was withdrawn and its life all but paralysed. Further riots and shootings occurred at Canton, and missionaries were compelled to leave the interior of China. Boycott pickets were established in the Treaty Ports and became an extra-legal militia. The Peking Government and the militarists were helpless and despised spectators of a movement far beyond their understanding or control. The army was a particular target for public criticism; instead of fighting the foreigners to regain China's lost sovereign rights all it did was plunder the people and engage in sordid civil wars. The prestige, such as it was, and the authority of the militarists were greatly damaged by this incident, which was skilfully used both by the Nationalist Party and the newly born Communist

Party to spread their influence and increase their numbers.

Dr. Sun Yat-sen, having failed to obtain any help from the Western Powers to reinstate his government —which he and his followers regarded as the only legal one—had turned to the Soviet Union, who gave him the necessary support in arms, advisers and possibly money. He regained control of Canton in 1923 and swiftly set about the organization of an efficient government and a new model army. In 1921 the Chinese Communist Party had been formally set up at a meeting attended by eleven members, one of whom was Mao Tse-tung. At almost the same time a Chinese Communist Party had been formed in France by students living in Paris. One of the founders was Chou En-lai. The two parties, the Communists still very small, the Nationalists already gaining wide support, co-operated on the basis that Communists might join the Nationalists (Kuomintang) as individuals, but there was no affiliation of the two parties. Aided by the repercussions of May 1925, revolutionary agitation increased rapidly. A change of warlord leadership in Peking induced Sun Yat-sen to hope that the new leader, the Protestant Christian General Feng Yu-hsiang, would co-operate with him and restore legal constitutional government under the Nationalist Party. Dr. Sun went to Peking in the spring of 1925, but found Feng either unwilling to act decisively, or perhaps without the strength to do so. Dr. Sun fell ill and died in Peking. Feng was before long driven from Peking by the reactionary Chang Tso-lin, who had Japanese support, being the warlord of Manchuria.

All hope of peaceful reunion being thus ended, the Nationalist government in Canton prepared for war, which was launched in 1926 against the southern warlords. Success was rapid, and early in 1927 the whole of the middle Yangtze region had fallen into Nationalist hands, and their armies, commanded by Chiang Kai-shek, were approaching Shanghai. Alarmed, the Treaty Powers landed troops to defend the International Settlement. The Shanghai workers and boycott pickets, organized by the Communists, rose and seized the Chinese-governed part of Shanghai, expelling the warlord army. When Chiang's forces arrived they found Chinese Shanghai already in the hands of the revolutionaries, and a critical situation pregnant with acute danger of war with the Foreign Powers. Chiang had close connections with Chinese big business and finance in Shanghai. These people, good Nationalists, and no friends of the plundering warlords, were equally very frightened of social revolution and the Communist-controlled workers. Chiang, knowing he had their support, carried out a sudden coup and massacre of the Communists (from which Chou En-lai narrowly escaped) and broke with the Communist Party. A confused situation followed for several months. Chiang set up his right-wing Nationalist government at Nanking; the former Canton government was now established at Wuhan, further up the Yangtze, and did not at first break with the Communist Party. In much of south China, particularly Hunan province, social revolution, inspired by rural agitators led by Mao Tse-tung, was sweeping the country.

Before long the two Nationalist governments coalesced at Nanking, and Chiang could turn his attention to combating the Communists, who had now taken to the hills, but were still trying, on Russian advice and direction, to take large cities, where proletarian support should be found. This was a Russian error; at that time there was virtually no proletariat in the modern sense outside Shanghai; the workers of the other large cities were handicraftsmen or penniless, half-starved coolie labourers. Neither of these classes was revolutionary. The last of the northern warlords had now been driven from Peking, and the Foreign Powers reluctantly recognized Chiang's Nationalist government in Nanking as the legal government of China. Japan had covertly opposed Chiang at every step, and finally, when their man in Peking, Chang Tso-lin, failed to hold the north, had him blown up in his train as he retreated to Manchuria. Japanese hostility to the Nationalist regime was barely concealed.

From 1929 to 1935 Chiang launched successive extermination campaigns against the Communists, who had now, under the leadership of Mao Tse-tung and Chu Teh, established a Soviet area in the hill country on the Hunan-Kiangsi border. The central committee of the Communist Party remained clandestinely in Shanghai, under strong Russian direction, and was by no means always at one with the rural leadership in Kiangsi. Quarrels, doctrinal disputes, and changes of leadership were frequent, but fortunately for the fighting forces in Kiangsi communications were difficult and these problems were largely ignored by the men on the spot. Chiang's campaigns failed until he devised, on the advice of his German staff officers, the plan of blockading the Kiangsi Soviet and thus forcing the Communists to break out or be starved into surrender. Meanwhile, Chiang was constantly yielding to Japanese pressure in the north. Manchuria had been lost in 1931, and the puppet state of Manchukuo set up. Soon, north China was infiltrated and half detached from Nanking's authority. In 1932 the Japanese used part of the International Settlement at Shanghai to launch an attack on Chinese Shanghai, but met with unexpectedly strong resistance, in the course of which much of the city was destroyed.

The Communists set out on the Long March in 1935 with about 100,000 men and many of their dependants. A year later they reached Yenan, in north Shensi, after marching and counter-marching for more than 6,000 miles, with 30,000 fighting men. But they had not been defeated; and during that epic march Mao Tse-tung had emerged as the unquestioned leader of the Party, a position he has ever since retained. The Party, also, was fully emancipated from long-distance control by Moscow, which had proved uniformly disastrous for several years. This fact should be remembered as background to the later Sino-Soviet dispute. Chiang's armies had attempted to pursue or to intercept the Communist march; they failed to do so effectively, but following on behind they were able to reduce to dependency on Nanking many of the weak remote warlords of the western and south-western provinces who had hitherto remained virtually independent. It seems at least possible that Chiang thought this result more valuable than the destruction of the Communist forces. The Communists found more trouble from the inhospitable remote lands they crossed than from the feeble efforts of the local warlords, who were only too glad to let them through, so long as they then invaded the territory of the next neighbour. Thus they reached Yenan, in the far north-west, difficult to attack, almost impossible to blockade, and close to the areas soon to be threatened by the impending Japanese invasion.

Japanese Invasion

Everyone in China knew that the Japanese were bent on an all-out effort to conquer China; Japan feared that if she waited China would grow strong and she also feared the rise of Communist influence. But the Nanking government was still bent on destroying the Communists before resisting the Japanese. It was not until December 1936, his own army, facing the Communists at Sian in Shensi, mutinied and held him prisoner until he agreed to cease the civil war, that Chiang was forced to agree to the slogans "Chinese do not fight Chinese" and "unite to resist Japanese aggression". The Japanese did not wait; in July 1937 they struck near Peking, and the fighting soon escalated into a large-scale, but still undeclared, war.

In the early stages Nationalist resistance, as at Shanghai and the battle of Taierhchuang in Shantung, had been at times effective; but the weight of Japanese armament was far superior. They had almost unchallenged air power and complete control of the sea. The Nationalist forces were forced back from the coast to the mountainous interior of western China, losing nearly two-thirds of the provinces. The difficulties of forcing the Yangtze gorges halted the Japanese at that point, and the added difficulty of holding vast conquered territories prevented any further advance. In those conquered territories, particularly north China, the Communists were organizing the guerrilla resistance which was soon to shake Japanese authority. The hope of a quick Chinese surrender had faded; Japan was now involved in the Second World War in the Pacific, and here, too, early victory was turning into stalemate and presaged defeat. The Chinese Communists steadily expanded their guerrilla war until large areas were liberated and in these they set up their own administration. Japanese retaliation was brutal and ruthless, forcing the Chinese peasantry to rely on guerrilla groups for their protection. It roused the national consciousness of an indifferent apolitical peasantry, and was the main factor in building the power of the Communist Party to a national level.

COMMUNIST CHINA

The war was ended neither by the still passive resistance of the Nationalists in western China, nor by the activity of the guerrillas, but by the Japanese surrender in the Pacific War. It left China deeply divided. The Nationalists took over from the Japanese in the south and eastern provinces. The Communists controlled the rural north, and cut the communications when the Nationalists flew in men to take over the Japanese-held cities. Civil war loomed close. The U.S.A. sent General Marshal to mediate and build, if possible, a coalition government. He failed; neither side trusted the other, and the demands made by the Nationalist side would have been a death warrant for the Communists. Early in 1946 the dreaded civil war began, but was neither as long nor as destructive as most Chinese feared it would be. From the first it became evident that the Communists were going to win. Their troops fought well under firm discipline; the Nationalist forces had no will to war, and plundered wherever they went. Gross inflation was wrecking the economy, corruption was notorious and fantastic in the Nationalist Government and army, business was almost paralysed, there was nothing that the Nationalists could offer to enlist the support of any social class, not even the capitalists of Shanghai, where government-protected racketeers preyed on business.

Therefore, despite massive American arms supply, full control of the air, and vastly superior numbers, the Nationalist armies were wholly destroyed and defeated in less than three years. Vast numbers surrendered; relatively few were killed in battle. By the end of 1948 the Communists already held all north China and Manchuria; they were on the banks of the Yangtze opposite Nanking. The Nationalist side was no longer united. A large group favoured peace and negotiation. They compelled Chiang to renounce his Presidency, but were not able to shake his under-cover control over many units of the army. The Nanking government tried to secure peace, and nearly did so, but this effort was sabotaged by the agents of Chiang at the last moment, and the acting President Li Tsung-jen was forced into exile. The war resumed, the Communists crossed the Yangtze, took Nanking, then Shanghai, and swept on into the south and west. By the middle of 1949, when the People's Republic was proclaimed on October 1st in Peking, the Communists were the masters of China, and Chiang and his remnant forces were retreating to Taiwan (Formosa), where under American protection they have since then remained (*see* section on Taiwan on p. 714).

Yet the failure to end the war by negotiation did China, and the Communists, one serious piece of harm. It destroyed the continuity of the legitimate internationally recognized government. If the Nanking regime had made peace—any sort of peace—it would have remained the legal government, even if it was now run by the Communists. By failing to win this diplomatic victory the Communists found their new regime subject to recognition, or non-recognition, at the will of foreign states, and their claim to China's seat at the UN disputed by the Nationalist *protégés* of the U.S.A. This situation has continued to be one of the main causes of friction between China and the Western Powers, who in their attitudes to the new China have also been deeply divided. To many of the

Western and in particular the European Powers the fate of China was settled; the Nationalists on Taiwan were no longer significant. To the U.S.A., on the other hand, they were the "real China" and the Communists considered to be Soviet puppets. Thus, the Communist regime started its career with the open ill will of the U.S.A., the doubtful and wary acceptance of Britain and other smaller Western Powers, and the half-hearted and cautious approval of the U.S.S.R. Only two years earlier Stalin had assured the U.S.A. that he recognized only Chiang as the legitimate ruler of China.

Economic and Social Reform

The early policy of the new regime in Peking was necessarily one of national salvage. The economy was at a standstill, communications almost wholly interrupted, inflation rampant, public utilities run down by years of neglect. Even foreign trade was deflected into the supply of quick-selling consumer goods, largely useless to the economy, while valuable exports could not be moved and needed imports could not be paid for. To the general surprise of both Chinese and foreign observers, the new regime, headed by men who had had no urban life nor experience for more than 25 years, tackled these tasks with great skill and expedition. Within weeks the railways were running, and supplying coal to Shanghai in place of the normal seaborne supplies which the Nationalist navy blocked. Inflation was brought under steady control and ended, with a new currency, in the next year. Since then the Chinese currency, subjected to violent fluctuations for longer than living memory, has remained stable. Foreign trade began to revive, cautiously, and limited to imports which the country really required, and to exports which would earn foreign exchange. The restoration of the cities, some of which were still in partial ruins from wartime bombing, and all neglected, insanitary and decaying, was made a high priority. In one year the transformation was profound.

All these things should have been done by any competent government of any political complexion; they were not specifically Communist. But it was, in fact, the Communist government which first undertook them. This gained them widespread popular support, and served to offset other policies less immediately appealing to many people. Land reform was the first major socialist, or Communist, policy implemented. It was at first a simple redistribution of land in equal lots to all cultivators, including the families of former landlords, if still willing to remain and work. With it went the trial and frequent condemnation of those landlords who were accused of maltreating their tenants, oppressing the peasants and dominating the villages with their armed retainers. Not all those found guilty were put to death; probably a larger number were sentenced to terms of imprisonment. It is at least probable that the institution of such courts, rough and ready as their justice often was, prevented a much more widespread and savage vengeance from the peasants, which could have attained the proportions of wholesale massacre.

The Communist Party did not intend to leave the matter at the level of peasant proprietorship of tiny plots. From the first, co-operative work teams were organized to co-ordinate crop sowing and harvesting. Later these were developed into the two stages of co-operative farming, and still later the co-operative farms were grouped together into communes. By these stages private ownership of agricultural land was abolished and replaced by the communal system under which each former owner has a share of the commune's revenue allotted by "work points", based on hours worked. State-owned collective farms are confined to newly opened lands or reclaimed land not previously privately owned. Whatever other defects and difficulties the new land system has encountered, due to bad weather or administrative over-centralization, it can be said with certainty to have achieved two major gains. No peasant family now starves to death in bad times; irrigation and water conservancy with flood control was made possible on a large and beneficial scale by the abolition of smallholdings. These factors enabled the commune system to withstand the great drought years 1960–62 without wholesale famine and thousands of deaths, although not without stern rationing and some malnutrition. In earlier less severe droughts the victims were often numbered by the million.

The Korean War and Relations with the U.S.S.R.

The Korean War has given rise to a large literature, and its origin and the responsibility for its outbreak are still in dispute. Chinese intervention, after the United Nations forces began to move northwards into North Korea, was forewarned, but the warnings were not heeded. To the Chinese this movement was a direct threat to their vital industrial area of south Manchuria (Liaoning province) adjoining Korea. It was also widely feared in China to be the preliminary move to an invasion of China itself. How far the Chinese intervention was intended to reassert Chinese authority, rather than Soviet influence, in Manchuria and in Korea, remains conjectural. Later developments seem to indicate that this consideration was important. It was certainly a consequence of the war, for after the cease-fire the Soviet Union soon renounced the special position which the Chinese had conceded to her in the port of Talienwan (Dairen) and over the railways across Manchuria. In China the effect of the war was to strengthen the prestige of the government which had, for the first time for more than a century, if ever, shown itself able to meet and match a large-scale Western army.

In 1957 the government permitted, in the "Hundred Flowers" movement, open criticism of its methods, if not of its basic policies. The results were probably disconcerting to the authorities. Many criticisms were published in the newspapers which tended to complain of bureaucratic domination by Party cadres, and neglect of expert advice. Others were so openly critical of more fundamental aspects of the regime that the movement was brought to an abrupt stop, and notorious critics were either dismissed from their posts or rusticated. Yet much of what was said made its mark, and led to some change of style in the

Party. The Hundred Flowers, it is now known, was almost contemporary with the first phase of the Sino-Soviet dispute, which grew in violence and bitterness over the years until the two countries have become completely estranged. In origin a quarrel over ideological standpoints, such as the possibility or impossibility of a "parliamentary road to socialism" and the degree of support which should be given to revolutionary peoples' wars, the dispute became in time more concerned with national interests, especially after the U.S.S.R. in 1960 withdrew its technical aid and experts from China. This was a hard blow to the Chinese industrialization, still in mid-course. It has been overcome by the steady development of Chinese technology, as is clearly proved by the Chinese nuclear fission programme and its rapid progress. After a period of border clashes along the Manchurian and Central Asian frontiers in 1969, which seemed to portend a major conflict, negotiations for a settlement of Sino-Soviet differences concerning the border regions opened in Peking in October 1969. However, subsequent relations between the two countries have shown no signs of improvement, and they have continued to confront each other with a barrage of invective and propaganda. The fear of a possible Soviet attack, either using conventional or nuclear weapons, has a strong influence on China's military and diplomatic planning.

All Chinese governments since the fall of the Manchu Dynasty have continued to assert sovereignty over Tibet, although the western two-thirds of the country had been in practice independent since 1912. In 1951 the Communist régime reoccupied the country and placed it under an autonomous region status. In 1961 a rebellion originating in the eastern part of Tibet spread to the reoccupied western part and was followed by the flight of the Dalai Lama, temporal ruler of Tibet, to India. Chinese occupation was consolidated and social changes and reforms imposed. In 1962 the establishment of Chinese forces on the Indian border with Tibet led to disputes upon the position of the undefined and unmarked boundary. China proposed negotiations, but the Indian side rejected them, asserting that the frontier had been established by Britain before Indian independence. The tension escalated into a border war when Indian forces attempted to expel Chinese troops from some disputed positions. The clash resulted in a Chinese victory, which could have led to an invasion of Indian Assam. China unilaterally called off the operations and withdrew to the positions already established before the clash. Soviet verbal support for the Indian claim considerably embittered relations between China and Russia. The frontier dispute remains unsettled, the Chinese holding what they claim is the correct frontier line.

The Cultural Revolution

The programme called the Great Leap Forward, contemporary with the establishment of the commune system in 1958–59, was intended to push Chinese industrialization forward by a great effort to the level of Great Britain. It did not achieve this result, partly because of the great drought of 1960–62, partly because of the Soviet withdrawal of technical assistance. It is suggested that disagreements in the higher leadership following this set-back lie at the bottom of the open political struggle associated with the Cultural Revolution. These problems must be seen in proportion; it is certain that Chinese industrial progress has not attained the level of the Western advanced nations; it is equally evident that enormous transformations of the virtually pre-industrial economy of China have been achieved, and that the essential change to a modern economy has been made.

In 1966, Mao Tse-tung, emerging from a partial seclusion, which has been variously interpreted, launched the "Great Proletarian Cultural Revolution" and raised, to carry it out, the Red Guards, composed for the most part of middle-school children from fourteen to eighteen years old. Contrary to a widespread belief, university students did not form a large proportion of the Red Guards. The movement, at first directed against "old ways of thinking, acting, and working", and leading to attacks on "bourgeois" people of professional and academic standing, was soon directed to an attack upon the leadership of the Communist Party itself, and in particular upon Liu Shao-ch'i the Head of the State and long-time organizer of the Party machine. Mao's aim was to create a new form of Communist society, free from the rigidity and hierarchy of the Communist Party of earlier times. He claimed that unless this were done the whole of Chinese society would slide back, as he saw the Soviet Union sliding, to a bourgeois way of life, with privilege hardening into new class divisions and revolutionary enthusiasm disappearing.

It is admitted that this movement encountered a considerable opposition, but it could not easily be identified. It would not appear that any group openly repudiated the "Thoughts of Mao Tse-tung". Rather many, claiming to be his true followers, still continued practices which others condemned as "revisionist". There was faction brawling, and at times more serious clashes. The army was called upon to maintain order and guard essential installations. The picture remains obscure, due largely to lack of objective news. Certain large and important fields of national life were hardly affected at all. Agriculture, the nuclear fission programme, the revenue collection, and also foreign trade remained outside the battle. Political life was galvanized into violent struggle centred round the "Top Party persons taking the capitalist road", by which were meant Liu Shao-ch'i, Head of the State, and Teng Hsiao-p'ing, Secretary-General of the Communist Party. Liu and Teng, with some others, were dismissed from all posts including that of Head of State, at the Ninth Party Congress of the Chinese Communist Party in April 1969.

The Ninth Congress of the Chinese Communist Party, the first to meet for some years, was convened in Peking in April 1969. It ratified changes in the Constitution including the new power structure of three-part committees which now govern provinces and cities. They are composed of Army, Revolutionary Cadres and Workers. The Army component seems in most cases to hold the predominant positions.

CHINA

Although the Ninth Congress seems to have formally ended the active phase of the Cultural Revolution, and was accompanied by measures disbanding the large Red Guard groups, conflicting factions still existed in the Chinese leadership. One indication was the dramatic fall and death of Marshal Lin Piao, Minister of Defence and proclaimed heir to Mao Tse-tung. In July 1972 the Chinese Government disclosed that Lin Piao had conspired to assassinate Mao Tse-tung and seize power, that his plot was detected, and that he and some companions had died in an aircraft crash in September 1971 while fleeing from China. His companions have not been officially identified nor has the fate of the other senior military persons who have disappeared from public view been officially linked either with the plot or the aircraft accident.

These events have been variously interpreted, but in the years that have followed the Chinese government has waged a propaganda campaign seeking to prove that Lin Piao was an arch-reactionary, comparable to Confucius in antiquity. The situation since his fall was clarified and settled by the decisions of the Fourth National People's Congress, the supreme organ of the Chinese state, in January 1975. The Congress promulgated a new Constitution, superseding that of 1954. One major change is that the Chairman of the Central Committee of the Communist Party becomes commander-in-chief of the armed forces. Mao Tse-tung holds this post. The post of Head of State, whether President or Chairman of the Government, is abolished, which leaves the Chairman of the Central Committee of the Communist Party as the supreme power. No system of succession to this post is laid down; it could be presumed that a new Chairman would be elected by the other members of the Committee.

China and the World

China sees itself as the leader of the Third World against the domination of the two super-powers. The early stages of the Cultural Revolution were marked by extreme xenophobia, but these outbursts are now officially regarded as excesses. A policy of detente has since been pursued, based on the principle of non-interference in the affairs of other nations. Since 1971 successful negotiations for normal diplomatic relations were concluded with several foreign powers, following upon the adoption of the formula devised in the negotiations with Canada by which the Canadian Government "takes note that the Government of the People's Republic of China claims Taiwan to be an integral province of the People's Republic of China". Italy, Chile, Austria and Belgium, as also several west Asian and African states concluded negotiations leading to recognition using this formula or related variants. United States President, Richard Nixon, visited Peking in February 1972. In the summer of 1972 the Prime Minister of Japan, Kakuei Tanaka, paid a state visit to Peking and, in a spectacular reversal of previous Japanese policy, arranged for diplomatic recognition of the People's Republic of China, broke off diplomatic relations with the Nationalist regime on Taiwan, and opened negotiations for a treaty of friendship with China designed to end the long antagonism between the two nations. The question of Chinese representation at the United Nations was resolved in October 1971 with the adoption in the UN General Assembly of an Albanian resolution proposing the People's Republic as one of the five permanent members of the Security Council and the representatives of its Government as the only legitimate representatives of China to the United Nations, and also proposing the expulsion of the representatives of Taiwan from the United Nations.

The Viet-Nam cease-fire agreement in January 1973 opened the way for a further improvement in relations with the U.S.A. A visit by U.S. Secretary of State Dr. Kissinger in February led to the establishment of liaison offices in the respective capitals, and a further visit in November confirmed the progress made. Trade with capitalist countries has also developed dramatically. Relations with the U.S.S.R., on the other hand, showed a marked deterioration, and the Chinese government has organized a potential resistance to aggression both in the form of a militia and of nuclear missiles directed against Russia.

Chou En-lai died in January 1976 and it was assumed that Teng Hsiao-p'ing would succeed him. However, after an apparent split in the Party leadership, Hua Kuo-feng, the Minister of Public Security, was appointed acting Premier in February. A campaign denouncing Teng and others as "capitalist roaders" then developed. Demonstrations in memory of Chou En-lai took place in early April, and were regarded as a display of popular support for Teng. This culminated in serious rioting in Peking, followed by widespread disturbances throughout the country. On April 7th the Politburo published its confirmation of Hua Kuo-feng's appointment as Premier, and Teng Hsaio-p'ing was dismissed from his posts as First Vice-Premier, Vice-Chairman of the Party's Central Committee, member of the Politburo Standing Committee, and Chief of General Staff. Mass demonstrations in favour of the Politburo's decisions were then organized.

Chairman Mao-Tse-tung died in September 1976, leaving no apparent successor.

TAIWAN

The location of the island has determined its history. Situated between the Malayan Archipelago, China and Japan, the island has had a chequered past. The original inhabitants were tribes of Malayan origin. China's relations with the island date from 607 A.D., but the first small Chinese settlements were not established there until the fourteenth century. During the seventeenth century, Portuguese, Spanish, and Dutch traders visited the island from time to time. In 1624 the Dutch settled the southern part. Two years later came the Spanish, who occupied the northern part. In 1642 the Dutch drove out the Spanish and in 1661 the Dutch were driven out by the Chinese Ming loyalist Cheng Cheng-kung (Coxinga) who ruled, with his sons, for 22 years. In 1663 the Manchu Emperor

K'ang-hsi invaded and conquered the island which became a part of his empire until ceded to the Japanese at the end of the Sino-Japanese war of 1895. During the period of independence and Manchu rule, massive immigration from the mainland established the ethnic Chinese character of the island.

As a result of Japan's defeat in the Second World War, Taiwan was returned to China in 1945. The island became one of the thirty-five provinces of the Republic of China. Practically all the exportable surpluses went to China, and Chinese government control replaced that of the Japanese. In 1947 misgovernment by the mainland officials led to a large-scale, but peaceful, political uprising which was repressed with great brutality by the Nationalist government.

Early in 1949 the Nationalist government authorities, driven from the mainland by the Communists, moved to Taiwan's capital, Taipei, along with approximately 2 million soldiers, officials and their dependants. Thus the island's population increased from 6.8 million to 7.5 million in 1950, excluding military personnel numbering 600,000.

Taiwan under the Chinese Nationalist Government

Communist control of the mainland meant the loss of the island's chief market. Taiwan was thus forced to seek a world market, and the economy of the island changed from that of a colony to that of an independent state. The Nationalist government in Taiwan has tried to achieve three major engineering feats: the cross-island highway, the Shihmen Reservoir project, and the port of Kaohsiung on the west coast. These three efforts parallel the three great Japanese achievements: the hydro-electric power plant at Sun-Moon Lake, the irrigation system at Chianan, and the mountain railway. The Nationalist government in Taiwan has achieved a remarkable record and regeneration in the period since 1949 with massive American aid. The years 1951 and 1952 were years of government re-organization. Then followed a four-year period (1953–56) of adjustment and planning. In 1957 and 1958 the cumulative effect of domestic reform and United States aid brought a great improvement in economic and other fields. The prominent developments include the following: the land reform programme, which was internationally acclaimed as a model; the rapid development of industry, with new types of export products, such as bicycles, plate glass, electric fans, plastics, aviation gasoline, and even jeeps and cars, which previously had been unknown in Taiwan; the establishment of a system of nine-year free public education. No longer receiving American economic aid, the economy of the island is prosperous.

In October 1971, the People's Republic of China was admitted to the United Nations in place of Taiwan. Consequently a number of countries broke off diplomatic relations with Taiwan and recognized the People's Republic of China. On establishing diplomatic relations with Peking in March 1972, the British Government issued a communiqué acknowledging " . . . the position of the Chinese Government that Taiwan is a province of China . . . ".

When Japan sought *rapprochement* with Peking in September 1972 Taiwan angrily broke off diplomatic relations with Japan.

In February 1973 the U.S. Government announced that they would continue to maintain diplomatic relations with Taiwan, but at the same time would set up an "American mission" in Peking and allow a "Chinese liaison office" to open in Washington.

President Chiang Kai-Shek died in April 1975. He was succeeded as President by the former vice-president, Dr. Yen Chia-kan, and by his son, General Chiang Ching-kuo, the Prime Minister, as Chairman of Kuomintang, the ruling Nationalist Party of China. Although no immediate dramatic changes are to be expected, President Chiang's death cannot fail to have profound implications for the future status of Taiwan, which the People's Republic of China continues to claim to be that of a province of China.

ECONOMIC SURVEY OF THE PEOPLE'S REPUBLIC OF CHINA

W. Klatt

China ranks first among the nations of the world in numbers and third after the Soviet Union and Canada in area. When looking at China and its problems, one is thus considering a continent rather than a country. No two geographers agree on the division of the country into clearly distinguished economic regions.

Climate and Soil

China proper, i.e. the territory within the Great Wall, is traditionally divided into North China, Central China and South China. In geographical terms these regions may be described as the three main river basins of the nearly 3,000 miles (5,000 km.) long Hwang Ho or Yellow River in the North, the 3,500 miles (5,800 km.) long Yangtze River in the Centre, and the Sikiang (West River), a short river, which flows into the Canton delta in South China. The flow of these rivers is determined by the topography of the country, whose highest elevations are to be found in the west and whose lowlands lie along the Pacific coast.

Man still lives very close to nature in China. The climate is thus an all-important factor in his life. It is marked by great regional contrasts. Through a large part of the year the climate is determined by the extreme ranges of temperature of the Eurasian land mass that lies to the west of China. In winter, cold dry winds, commonly known as winter monsoons, blow from the area of the "Siberian High" towards the Pacific Ocean, carrying with them large amounts of dust that originates in the loess region of northern China. In summer, the continental land mass gets considerably hotter than the ocean and becomes a low-pressure region. Moist air moves from the high-pressure area in the Pacific Ocean and provides ample precipitation during the growing season on the mainland of China, whose climate thus alternates between dry cold continental winters and wet maritime summers. The winter monsoon blows from the north-west in North China, from the north in Central China and from the north-east in South China, whilst the summer monsoon blows, from April to September, from the south and south-east.

Temperatures vary widely from region to region. In northern Manchuria temperature ranges of more than 80°F. (45°C.) are recorded between summer and winter. South China knows no such extremes. Precipitation is marked by similarly great regional variations, ranging from 4 in. (100 mm.) in the Mongolian desert to 80 in. (2,050 mm.) in the south. In South China intense disturbances are quite frequent in late summer, when tropical typhoons strike the coast with winds of exceptionally high velocity and torrential rains that often cause severe damage to shipping and farming. On other occasions large parts of the country are hit by devastating droughts.

The soils of China are as varied as her topography and her climate. From the point of view of the farming industry, the alluvial deposits in the great river basins of the Hwang Ho, the Hwai Ho, the Yangtze and Pearl River have created the most valuable soils. Whilst in North China the soils are most suitable for wheat and cotton growing, under the humid conditions of South China they are leached and short of lime and thus most suitable for paddy (rice) cultivation. On the brown and black soils of the north, wheat and millet (kaoliang) are grown, while on the red and yellow soils of the south tea bushes and tung trees flourish. Over four-fifths of China's cultivated land is estimated to lack nitrogen, over two-fifths to be short of phosphates and one-fifth to be in need of potash. These deficiencies are being reduced by steadily increasing allocations of commercial fertilizers.

Mineral Resources

From the time when Marco Polo reported the Chinese way of burning black stones and forging metals to the recent reports of the New China News Agency, the accounts of China's natural resources have varied from glowing optimism to cautious underestimates. A geological survey undertaken in the 1920s came to the conclusion that China possessed adequate resources for an industrial development in support of agriculture, but not for industrialization on the scale of modern, highly industrialized countries. Cressey saw little likelihood that China would ever rival the industrial areas of the eastern States of North America or of Western Europe.

At that time China's entrepreneurs looked outwards. China's main industrial centres were developed by foreigners who judged her chances of industrialization with the interests of the West European or Japanese markets in mind. This point of view has now been displaced by that of a government set on economic self-reliance instead of international division of labour. Consequently, prospecting has been carried out in areas previously omitted from geological surveys. The results are said to be such that China can claim to have sufficient natural resources to become a major industrial power. The official statements are not always precise, however, as to the degree of certainty about mineral deposits. The distinction between proven, probable and inferred reserves is not always made.

The Chinese authorities claim that the energy reserves amount to 100,000 million tons of coal and 1,200 million tons of mineral oil. In addition there is also said to be a water-power potential of 536 million kilowatts. According to Dr. Wu, "there is no doubt that as a whole reserves in the energy resources sector are adequate to support a highly industrialized economy". Over four-fifths of the total energy produced comes from coal, of which one-fifth is anthracite and four-fifths bituminous coal Almost 80 per cent of the coal deposits known at present are located in north and north-west China. The coal mines exploited in Manchuria and east China at present are not particularly rich in either quantity or quality, but they were chosen because of their vicinity to the areas of principal demand.

Recently, China's oil explorations gained prominence. Originally, geological surveys were carried out with Russian assistance, but since the mid-'60s China has been independent in this respect. The first major oil strike was made at Taching (Heilungkiang). This was followed by discoveries at Shengli (Shantung), Takang (Hopei) and elsewhere (Tsaidam, Karamai, Szechwan).

In the past China has been considered distinctly deficient in reserves of iron ore and thus incapable of creating a major iron and steel industry. However, on the basis of post-war surveys the Chinese authorities claimed in 1957 deposits of more than 12,000 million tons. Almost three-quarters of the deposits known in the past were in Manchuria, but new deposits are said to have been discovered in north-west China, Hainan and Kwangtung. In 1960, according to Dr. Wu, annual estimated production capacities of pig iron, ingot steel and finished steel were 40, 38 and almost 17 million tons respectively. The original centres of the iron and steel industry at Anshan (Manchuria) and Shanghai have been supplemented by new state enterprises at Paotow and Wuhan.

China's main mineral resources are in non-ferrous metals such as tin, molybdenum, tungsten and antimony, which are found mostly in north-west China. These minerals were exploited for a time by the Sino-Soviet joint stock companies, and Chinese tin was sold at one time by the Soviet Union on the London tin market. During that period China's economic geography shifted from the eastern sea shore to the western border. Since the disruption of Sino-Soviet relations a new shift has taken place. The Chinese leaders are now set, more than ever before, on the internal development of the country's natural wealth and of domestic industries which are based on these resources.

Human Resources

One of China's greatest assets is her population. It is at the same time one of her major liabilities. Its size, growth, composition by age and occupation are not known for certain. Between 1949 and 1953 official Chinese reports put the population of the mainland of China at less than 500 million. In April 1953 a decree was issued ordering a nation-wide census of the population. When the census results were released in November 1954, the count showed a population on the mainland of China of 583 million, or almost 100 million more than the figure given by Chou En-lai four years earlier.

Several distinguished Western demographers have analysed the limited data published and have tried to come to a decision as to the degree of accuracy with which the 1953 census can be credited. John Aird of the U.S. Bureau of the Census allows for a possible undercount of 5 to 15 per cent, implying a population in 1953 of at least 613 and at most 685 million. Irene Taeuber found so many flaws in the census technique that she concluded that China remained "the country without statistics". Leo Orleans predicted that "China's population will continue to be an enigma and a subject for academic guessing games for many decades to come". The doubts of the critics as to the validity of the 1953 census results do not imply a charge of falsification, but one of faults committed during the state's first nation-wide census.

The census was carried out at a time when some 100 million villagers (out of a total of 500 million) were said to be benefiting from the redistribution of land set in motion by the agrarian reform law of June 1950. Certain evasions may have occurred in urban areas during the year when the census was taken, but it seems equally probable that rural families eligible under the regulations of the land distribution legislation overstated the number of family members in the village register. It is worth remembering that the village councils which first had a hand in the distribution of land were later consulted in the course of the population census. The exaggeration of the rural population that could have resulted from such practices might thus have exceeded the undercount due to any evasion of registration elsewhere.

The uncertainty as to the increase of China's population since 1953 is just as great as that regarding the census itself. Since 1960 the Chinese authorities seem to have lost count of the number of people to be fed, clothed and housed, to be employed and taxed. For several years, the registration figure for 1957 of 650 million was used without any allowance being made for the increase in birth over death. During the Great Leap Forward and the movement of population which accompanied it, the register was apparently so dislocated that in 1964 re-registration became necessary in certain localities.

Official projections of China's population have been published by the Bureau of Statistics up to the end of 1956. Since then there has been a complete absence of statistical data on the population. Crude birth and death rates are available up to the end of 1957 for China as a whole and for the two main cities, Shanghai and Peking. The sharp decline of the death rate in 1954 coincided with the introduction of rationing. Thus the possibility of deliberate failure to report cases of death for the sake of continued supplies of rationed food and clothing cannot be ruled out. A certain decline in the rate of growth of the population during the years of poor harvests and the separation of families in the communes, followed by a certain increase after 1961 would seem plausible. Mention should be made here of population figures made known by provincial authorities during the Cultural Revolution. At the time of publication in 1967-68 these figures suggested a population of 712 million for China as a whole (including Tibet). They may be taken to represent the best estimates available to the provincial authorities at the end of 1967. If this is the case, China's population at the end of 1970 may be estimated at 750 million. In an atlas, published by the

State Cartographical Institute in Peking in the summer of 1972, China's population was given as 698 million in 1970 (including 15 million in Taiwan), but a little later in the year China's Vice-Premier Li Hsien-nien mentioned to Japanese visitors 750 million as the more likely figure. In August 1974, China's Vice-Minister of Health gave the country's population as "almost 800 million". This statement was repeated by Prime Minister Chou En-lai at the Fourth National People's Congress in January 1975. If this is in fact the correct estimate, at the end of 1975 China's population might have reached slightly more than 800 million.

Labour Force

China is able to mobilize a labour force of at least 350 million able-bodied men and women. This is the largest number of working people in any one country in the world. Its non-agricultural section is still rather small, however, probably less than one-third of the total labour force. Its apparently rapid increase during the first Five-Year Plan and the Great Leap Forward that followed it was in part due to a more complete statistical coverage. At present some 100 million Chinese are employed outside agriculture.

Approximately one-seventh of the total number are "non-productive" workers, i.e. men and women engaged in the all-important service sector of the economy. Employment in the private sector of industry and commerce which in 1949 affected over 20 million has in the meanwhile all but disappeared. Employment in the traditional sectors of the economy, such as handicraft and commerce, has also declined greatly. The "modern" sectors of the economy increased their employment from 8 million registered in 1949 to 44 million in 1958, half of whom were employed in industry proper. By 1970 the number of workers engaged in industry probably exceeded 50 million. The number of women working outside agriculture is still rather small. Even the mobilization of women during the Great Leap Forward brought few female workers into industry, whilst the proportion of women engaged in land reclamation work was as high as 50 per cent. The mass mobilization of labour directed many young people into non-agricultural employment. In some sectors of industry, up to four-fifths of the labour force was under 25 years old. The majority of the 5 million intellectuals reported to be in existence in 1958 were located in the urban areas. The countryside remains starved of brains. A transfer of urban dwellers to the countryside was set in train at the end of the Cultural Revolution. This movement was probably motivated by political considerations rather than labour requirements.

The Agricultural Sector

Agriculture has always been China's main industry. This is still the case today, and it will continue to be so for a long time to come. The success or failure of the farming industry thus has a direct bearing on the country's overall development, its progress in industrialization and the volume and composition of its foreign trade. The agricultural sector probably accounts at present for almost one-third of the nation's total output, and grains alone provide as much as one-sixth, the other sixth consisting of technical crops and animal products. Agriculture still provides work for almost three out of every four, or more than 100 million families. Thus farming continues to be China's largest industry and one of the largest contributors to China's export trade.

The composition of the population adds further proof of the importance of the farming community to the welfare of the nation. At least four-fifths of the population still live in villages, of which there are well over half a million. At the time of the 1953 census over 100 million farm households or about 500 million people were directly connected with the farming industry. As in the meantime the population of China has grown by almost 300 million people and industrial employment has increased little, China is more of an agrarian community today than she was at the time of the Revolution. The development of the farming industry is thus of crucial importance to the future of China.

China's farm land is chiefly used for growing arable crops which occupy nine-tenths of the cropped area. Most of the crops are grown for direct human consumption, fodder and technical crops occupying only a small portion of the total farm area. Although China has more land under rough grass than under arable crops, grazing is no common feature of Chinese agriculture. Little livestock is kept, i.e. approximately one "livestock unit"* per family. At the time of the Japanese invasion of China, the average size of the family farm was 1.70 hectares (4.25 acres), and it declined thereafter owing to increasing pressure on the land. According to a survey of the National Agricultural Research Bureau, more than one-third of all farms were less than 0.67 hectares (1.67 acres), whilst less than one-tenth of all farms were over 3.33 hectares (8.33 acres) in size. Thus, even large farms were small by any but Asian standards.

Farming in China is labour-intensive, resulting in high yields per unit of land, whereas yields per man are still low. On average, every unit of land is cropped one-and-a-half times a year. South of the Yangtze the country is principally under paddy (rice), whilst north of this river it is under wheat, millet and kaoliang. However, various crop combinations and rotations can be found throughout the country. Manchuria (north-east region) is the main pastoral region of China.

In the years preceding the Communist Revolution, the conditions of land tenure left much to be desired. The social structure of the Chinese village was marked by an extreme degree of polarization. At the time of the Japanese invasion of China, more than half the land under cultivation was owned by less than one-tenth of the farm population, whereas at the other end of the social scale two-thirds had to eke out a bare subsistence on less than one-fifth of the land cultivated. Tenants had to pay 50 per cent and more of their gross harvest as rent, and interest rates on short-term loans

* Draught animal = 1.0; cattle = 0.8; pig = 0.2; and sheep or goat = 0.1 livestock unit.

were 30 per cent and more a year. It was thus not difficult to see the likelihood of revolutionary developments when the Kuomintang failed in its attempts to carry out institutional changes.

Industrial Base

Before the Revolution, China's industry was limited to a narrow range of manufacturing plants, most of which were located in the coastal provinces and in some inland river ports. The three industrially developed regions of the north-east (Manchuria), north and east accounted for most of China's manufacturing plants, non-agricultural workers and industrial equipment. Three-quarters of the factories, the non-agricultural workers and the energy used in China were concentrated in Shanghai and Tientsin, the only other manufacturing centres being Tsingtao, Peking, Nanking, Wuhan, Chungking, Canton and Anshan, the Japanese steel town in Manchuria.

After the Revolution, this one-sided location of industry was to be altered in favour of an even distribution throughout the country and a regional decentralization of administrative controls. Major industrial centres were planned in Paotow, Lanchow and other cities. In fact, the shift has been more modest than was originally intended. The eight largest cities are still the same as at the time of the Revolution. "No radical departure from the pre-Communist spatial pattern can be observed from a study of city growth and distribution" (Y. L. Wu, H. C. Ling, G. H. Wu: *The Spatial Economy of Communist China*). This is also true if the yardstick is not the country's urban population, but its industrial capacity. As in the past, over half of this is still to be found in the provinces of Kiangsu, Hopei and Liaoning; and two-thirds is located in the traditional three regions of the north-east, the north and the east. Some industrial development has occurred elsewhere, but the developed industrial regions have retained their position of supremacy. At present Szechwan is given priority in the development plan, and by 1975 one-half of China's industrial output was expected to be produced in the interior of the country.

During the first few years after the Communist seizure of power the damage caused in the Second World War was repaired. Thereafter, during the first plan period, the industrial raw material basis was laid. In the interval between the Great Leap Forward and the Cultural Revolution a modern machine building industry was created, whilst more recently the emphasis has been shifted to the expansion of the chemical industry. Certain industries have grown faster than others. This is true in particular of the industries producing cement, mineral oils and fertilizers, but also of some sections of the machine tool industry—one of the most dynamic sectors of the Chinese economy—without which no modern industrial growth, no expansion of the defence system and no nuclear development would have been possible. Within the last two decades the machine industry expanded at an annual growth rate of almost 20 per cent to become one of the main industrial sectors of the country. After 1960 six new ministries whose responsibility lay chiefly in supplying the armed forces with their equipment were created.

Owing to explorations at Taching, Shengli and Takang, the production of crude oil increased from about 3 million tons in 1960 to apparently as much as 80 million tons in 1975. As refining capacities and transport facilities fall short of requirements, some of the oil may be merely on tap rather than above ground. Since the mid-'60s China has been able to do without imports of oil and oil products from Russia. At first, processing plants were set up and operated by Russian technicians, but lately British, German and Italian refineries and petro-chemical factories have been installed. Some oil is refined close to the oil-fields, but much of it has to be transported by single-track rail, by tanker lorries and by coastal tankers to refineries at Dairen, Shanghai, Fushun, Lanchow, Peking and Nanking. A pipeline of 1,000 kilometres, linking the Taching oilfield with the port of Ching huang tao, has recently been completed. In the absence of suitable port facilities, the 8 million tons of crude oil exported to Japan in 1975 had to be shipped mainly in small vessels.

China's armaments industry is now able to produce for the country's regular and para-military forces of close on 3 million men—not counting the 5 million enrolled in the civilian militia—all manner of hardware, including: medium bombers, fighters, radar equipment, amphibious tanks, destroyers, minesweepers and diesel-propelled submarines. Substantial progress has been reported in the production of intermediate and medium-range ballistic missiles. China is apparently also engaged in testing a nuclear-powered submarine.

In the nuclear field progress has been spectacular. In October 1964, i.e. in the interim period between the defunct second plan and the anticipated third plan, China became the first backward agrarian country to place itself side by side, in the nuclear field, with some of the most highly developed industrial nations in the world. By mid-1976 17 nuclear tests had taken place. Centralized economies, such as that in operation on the Mainland of China, can advance greatly on a narrow front once the political choice has been made, the necessary administrative decisions have been taken and the appropriate allocation of resources has been authorized. By implication, some other sectors, such as the consumer goods industries, had to be given lower priority.

Transport System

Before the Revolution, China's transport system was marked by extreme backwardness. At a density of little more than 2 miles of railways and of waterways and less than 10 miles of highways per thousand square miles of territory, China was less well provided with transport facilities than any other large country in the world. Like industry, the transport system was concentrated in the coastal areas. Three-quarters of the railway net was in the developed regions of the country, and half the railway lines were in Manchuria.

The bulk of China's freight and passenger traffic is

carried by the railways. At the time of the Revolution they handled four-fifths of all freight and over four-fifths of all passenger traffic, the rest being carried by ships or on the highways. These statistics leave out of account, however, the substantial movement of goods and persons by junks and sampans, vehicles pulled by beast or man, push carts and, last but not least, human carriers. The railway system, badly run down during the years of war and civil war and depleted as a result of Soviet dismantling after the war, was restored to its former operational level by 1957. It now amounts to slightly more than 20,000 miles (32,000 km.), of which two-fifths are in Manchuria where, before the last war, the Russians built the railway in the north and the Japanese the one in the south. According to the United Nations Statistical Yearbook, railway transport amounted in 1959 to 46,000 million passenger/kilometres and 265,000 million freight ton/kilometres. Although these are large figures, transport is one of the bottlenecks that holds up economic development. China is unlikely to have at present more than 5,000 locomotives, 5,000 passenger cars and 100,000 freight cars. The average haul is 300 miles (500 km.).

Since the Revolution, the length of the railway system has been increased by about one half. The main extension took place in north-west China. As a result, the profile of China's transport system and domestic economy has been changed substantially. Among the chief railway lines are the following: Peking-Canton Railway: 1,500 miles (2,400 km.); Tientsin-Shanghai Railway: 1,000 miles (1,600 km.); Eastern Chinese Railway, Manchouli-Vladivostok: 1,500 miles (2,400 km.); South Manchuria Railway: 700 miles (1,100 km.); Peking-Mukden (Shenyang) Railway: 800 miles (1,300 km.); Lanchow-Patao Railway: 600 miles (1,000 km.); Chengtu-Chungking Railway: 300 miles (500 km.); North-South trunk line; and East-West trunk line (partly under construction).

Of China's main rivers, the Yangtze is navigable from the western border of the basin of Szechwan and it passes through some of China's most densely populated areas. It connects such important centres as Chungking, Hankow and Nanking with Shanghai and the Pacific Ocean, and it is thus China's most important internal waterway, carrying a freight load of almost 20 million tons a year. The only other rivers of any importance as carriers of freight are the Sikiang (West River) in South China, which serves mainly the ports of Wuchow and Canton and their hinterland of Kwangtung and Kwangsi, and the Sungari River which serves mainly Harbin and northern Manchuria.

Although the coastline is 7,000 miles long, coastal shipping accounts only for a small portion of China's total transport. The country tended to look inwards until the metropolitan powers of Western Europe opened up some of the coastal areas. Much of the coast is shallow and silted up and thus offers only limited opportunities for port facilities. Along the coast of the Yellow Sea, the best natural harbours are the commercial port of Dairen and the naval base at Port Arthur. Other major ports are those of Tientsin and Tsingtao. On the East China Sea lies Shanghai, still China's largest city, although it has lost much of its former importance since the expropriation of all foreign commercial firms and the subsequent departure of most of them. Also on the coast of the East China Sea lie the ports of Ningpo and Wenchow. Along the coast of the South China Sea are the ports of Amoy and Swatow, which have been affected badly by China's conflict with the regime of Chiang Kai-shek in Taiwan. The British Crown Colony of Hong Kong still provides one of China's chief points of contact with the non-Communist world.

The present length of the national and provincial highways, some of which are still not all-weather roads, is 125,000 miles (200,000 km.). Much of the road transport consists of primitive vehicles pulled by mules and donkeys or by hand. More primitive still, many loads are still transported at the two ends of the carrying pole or on the backs of men.

DEVELOPMENT OF THE ECONOMY

With the seizure of power by the Communists in 1949, China left behind its "bourgeois-democratic stage of development", and it entered the era of "proletarian revolution". The country was in a sorry state, devastated by war and civil war and depleted of its industrial equipment, much of which the Russians had dismantled. The years of reconstruction were governed by the "Common Programme", based on Mao Tse-tung's concept of the "New Democracy", a temporary truce between the Communists and the members of the bourgeoisie, in so far as they were not considered hostile to the Revolution.

A central system of control was created in six administrative zones which supervised the work of the counties (hsien) and village groups (hsiang). At the same time, war-damaged industrial equipment was repaired, wholesale and retail prices were stabilized and a uniform system of taxation was introduced. A new currency, the People's currency (Jen-min-pi), replaced the grossly inflated and discredited currency of the National Government (at the rate of 10,000 old units to one yuan). The official rate of exchange was fixed at U.S. $1 = 2.46 yuan or 1 yuan = $0.41; or £1 (pre-1967 devaluation rate) = 6.89 yuan or 1 yuan = 14p*. State trading companies brought the principal movement of goods under control. An agrarian reform, which was carried out with much severity and violence, strengthened the position of the Communist Party in the countryside. Outside agriculture there was at first less interference with the pattern of ownership than had been expected. At the end of the period of reconstruction over one-third of the output of modern industry, two-thirds of the internal trade and almost the entire output of agriculture were still handled by private individuals.

China's entry in 1950 into the Korean war caused severe stresses and strains. Over two-fifths of the state budget was diverted to defence. Yet, at the end of 1952 the economy was said to have recovered to its

* The official exchange rate in June 1976 was U.S. $1=1.97 yuan. Subject to fluctuations, the £ sterling equalled 3.48 yuan.

pre-war level of production. Although actual achievements were more modest than official claims, China was ready to move to her next phase of economic development. Her industrial base was, of course, considerably narrower than that of Russia in 1927. Yet, the "General Line of the State" anticipated the completion, in the course of three five-year plans, of "socialist transformation" of agriculture, handicraft, industry and commerce, and the full industrialization of the country. This concept was approved in 1954 by the National People's Congress and endorsed by the Constitution of the People's Republic of China. Its implementation required a plan.

Planning Mechanism

At the end of 1952, the State Planning Commission was set up. Kao Kang, the powerful chairman of the northeastern administrative region (Manchuria), was its first president. In the summer of 1956 its responsibilities were restricted to long-term planning and the co-ordination of plans, whilst the newly-created State Economic Commission was charged with determining annual plan targets and controlling their fulfilment.

A large number of government agencies are concerned with the implementation of the plan. Central ministries, state commissions and bureaux operate under the Council of State. They are partly in charge of the supply and allocation of factors of production, such as labour, transport and communications, raw materials or manufactured goods. A number of supervisory agencies control the financial and trading activities of the state and the individual. Most important among them is the People's Bank of China with its main office in Peking, its many branches throughout the country, and its numerous ramifications abroad. The Bank controls every aspect of the country's economic and monetary affairs. The financing of foreign trade is handled by the Bank of China, which has overseas branches in London, Hong Kong and Singapore.

It is one of the prime preoccupations of the planners to determine the respective shares of state investment and private consumption. Hence the prominence that is given to the relationship between accumulation and consumption, between the output of producer goods as against that of consumer goods, and between heavy and light industries, of which farming is the largest component part in China. The discussions in the press concerning the problem of balanced growth or the proportional development of the national economy are a reflection of the problems which the central planners have to face. Although temporarily displaced by agriculture, heavy industry invariably has the highest priority, since it provides the foundation of an industrial nation and its national defence. Consumer welfare takes a lower place by comparison, and it is regarded as a by-product of industrialization rather than an integral part of the national plan. The rate of growth of the industries producing capital goods traditionally exceeds those manufacturing consumer goods. Agriculture is expected to produce a surplus with which to finance industrialization. To this end, low prices are paid for farm products which are subject to obligatory deliveries. Industrial wages are fixed at a lower growth rate than labour productivity.

Statistical Services

Statistical services form an integral part of the governmental machine of any industrial state. Before 1949, only a rudimentary collection of statistics gathered by the Bank of China, the National Resources Commission and the Agricultural Research Bureau existed. A Department of Statistics was set up in 1949 under the State Planning Bureau and branch offices were created in the administrative regions. In 1953 it was replaced by the State Statistical Bureau.

The Great Leap Forward threw into confusion what little there was of a functioning statistical administration. Statistical, like other public services, deteriorated when a programme of administrative decentralization coincided with emulation campaigns among urban and rural workers. In some instances, different sets of statistics were obtained from progress reports, surveys and normal returns. By the end of 1958 the falsification of statistical data had reached unheard of dimensions. The output of steel, grain and cotton had allegedly more than doubled within one year. A few months later the government admitted gross exaggerations and scaled down drastically the earlier claims. Even the revised data were unlikely to be correct. In the case of grain two re-counts were said to have taken place after sizeable portions of the crop had in fact been consumed. The true output data are unlikely ever to become known.

Practically no absolute data have been published since 1959 on the fulfilment of output targets and the like. The sparing references made by Chinese leaders to rates of growth have provided little more than orders of magnitude in the case of a few industrial sectors. Nothing firm is known about the output of the farming industry, the extent of foreign trade, the level of urban employment, the trend of wages and prices or many other aspects of the life of the country. No budgets are published any longer. Recently information in quantitative terms has become available for some selected industries, for certain urban and industrial areas and for a few factories, communes and work brigades. An analysis of the mass media reveals that items selected are frequently chosen for publicity reasons rather than for their intrinsic value or representative character. Reports on the use of manpower, on the development of agriculture and the growth of small-scale industries are given prominence, whereas large-scale industrial operations, for both civilian and military purposes, as well as aggregate national data are withheld from the public at home and abroad. Since the end of 1971, a few production figures have been released, but these can hardly be taken as evidence that the statistical services are in full working order except possibly in the narrow area of a few selected industrial sectors. None of the statistical information on man-power, wages, prices, public finance, investment, transport and trade, which is published annually by countries far less developed than China, is available. The New Year's Day editorials (January 1st, 1976) of the three official newspapers (*People's Daily*, *Red Flag* and *Liberation Army Daily*) —traditionally vehicles of information on the year's progress—reported plan fulfilment but gave no quantitative information. However, at the Fourth National People's Congress, held in January 1975, Prime Minister Chou En-lai listed a few industrial production indices (based on unpublished 1964 data) and grain and cotton output indices (based on somewhat questionable data for 1949) (*see Statistical Survey*). It is thus possible to estimate, very roughly, the orders of magnitude of China's economic progress.

The First Development Plan

Work on China's first five-year plan began in 1951, but the plan document was only ready for adoption by the State Council two and a half years after the plan had officially begun in January 1953. Revisions of the plan targets were made at the end of 1954, two years after the formal inauguration of the plan. Whilst it was in operation, the share of capital construction was raised from 30 to 45 per cent of the state budget and from less than one-sixth to well over one-fifth of the national income. Nearly three-fifths of the total investment was allocated to industry, and almost nine-tenths of this sum was earmarked for use in heavy industry. Agriculture was allocated less than one-tenth of total investment, a disproportionately small amount, considering that this sector of the economy had to provide a livelihood for three-quarters of the working population. The investment priorities were reflected in the production targets. The annual growth rate anticipated in agriculture was approximately 4 per cent; in the case of heavy industry it was set at four and a half times the rate expected in farming.

For the most part capital investment depended on internal resources, such as taxes, profits of state enterprises and other forms of domestic savings. However, Soviet aid, though small by all accounts, played a not insignificant part in China's first effort to industrialize. The U.S.S.R.'s contribution consisted in the main of plant equipment, provided on medium-term credit. During the first plan some 150 industrial plants were erected as a result of Soviet assistance. Among them were the heavy industries set up at Anshan, China's original industrial centre, and at the new locations at Wuhan and Paotow. China's industrial base was thus shifted inland from the coastal areas where it had been situated as long as foreign interests determined its location.

The relatively smooth development of the economy was rudely interrupted in the summer of 1955 when, without any warning, the collectivization of farming began. The agrarian reform law of June 1950 had given considerable satisfaction, since almost 50 million hectares (125 million acres) taken from some four million landowners had been distributed among almost fifty million smallholders, poor peasants and landless farm labourers. Half the number of farming households had thus benefited. In the outcome large landowners and poor peasants very nearly disappeared, whilst middle peasants dominated the village scene. Collectivization seemed remote. Yet five years later it was in full swing. The Draft Constitution endorsed by the National People's Congress in 1954 provided for the promotion of producers' co-operatives as the principal means for the transformation of individual farming to collective ownership. Full collectivization was set in train following Mao's report in July 1955 "On the Co-operatization of Agriculture". By the end of the first five-year plan, collectivization had been completed, for all practical purposes, except in some remote hill areas. Collectivization caused considerable disruption in the process of planned economic development. This was all the more the case, since it was accompanied by a transfer of industry and commerce from private hands to the state. By the middle of 1956 all private firms had come under joint state-private operation.

The Second Plan

The second plan was even more ambitious than its forerunner. The gross production of industry, handicraft and agriculture was supposed to increase by 75 per cent, or half as much again as during the first plan. Priority was given, even more than previously, to the output of capital goods whose share in total industrial production was to grow from less than two-fifths in 1957 to one-half in 1962; the share of consumer goods was expected to decline correspondingly. The investment required to meet this programme was to be twice the amount planned during the previous five years.

The second plan was all the more ambitious as the economy had shown signs of strain during the last years of the previous plan. Retrenchment was needed, since the Soviet Union, engaged in pacifying its rebellious and resentful East European neighbours with the aid of long-term credits worth U.S. $1,000 million, was unable to offer China any assistance to speak of. If the pace of China's economic growth was to be maintained, let alone increased, the method of "primitive accumulation" had to be intensified. There was thus no room for any relaxation.

The respite granted during the period of the Hundred Flowers (1956–57) was short-lived. It was overtaken by the Great Leap Forward of 1958. This political campaign, which had no precedent in Communist history, was an attempt to draw on surplus labour, the one and only resource readily available in China. The country's population was organized in rural and urban communes. By the autumn of 1958, some 600,000 small-scale furnaces were said to have been set up, employing over a million people with no previous experience in industrial processes. The steel target of the year was almost doubled. So were other economic goals. At the end of the year, gross industrial output had supposedly increased by 65 per cent within the preceding twelve months.

The targets set for agriculture were equally fantastic. Some 100 million cultivators were said to have been organized for the purpose of building irrigation canals, which were to raise the acreage under wet crops by 30 per cent within one year. At the same time home-produced fertilizers were to be manufactured and deep ploughing, close planting and other new farm techniques were to be introduced on a massive scale. The direction and control of labour in a campaign of such vast dimensions required forms of organization for which there was no precedent. In the autumn of 1958 "People's Communes" were created in the countryside. By the end of 1958 over 700,000 agricultural producer co-operatives, set up only the year before, were reported to have merged into some 26,000 communes with an average of almost 5,000 rural families and 10,000 acres of land.

In 1959 a period of economic and organizational retrenchment began. The second plan was abandoned in 1959, and a year later planning became impracticable altogether. Exaggerated production claims were corrected. Whereas during the Great Leap Forward priority was given to heavy industry, two years later agriculture had precedence over every other sector of the economy. Agriculture was declared to be "the foundation" and industry "the leading factor". Producer goods were supposed to rank behind consumer goods and both in turn behind agriculture, but this order of priorities has to be taken with a pinch of salt. The consumer goods industries were probably not meant to meet primarily the task of "serving the people" but rather the call of the Exchequer to earn some of the foreign exchange needed to meet the cost of the import bill.

By 1960 the communes had ceased to function in all but name. Authority reverted to the production brigades which, not unlike the former agricultural producer co-operatives, supervised the operations of villages in place of the large areas controlled by the communes. Work in the fields was organized by production teams which rarely embraced more than forty households. In some regions farm work even reverted to individual families. Private plots and rural markets, which had been prohibited at the height of the Great Leap Forward, were again allowed to serve as inducements to the rural population to raise "sideline" food production.

It took three years before the set-backs caused during the years of the Great Leap Forward were overcome in agriculture. In the meantime serious shortages occurred in food-deficit areas, particularly at the end of the season when stocks were depleted, if not disposed of altogether. Annual imports of 5–6 million tons of wheat and wheat flour became a regular feature of China's foreign trade pattern. The record was little better in industry. As no production data and no plan or budget were published after 1960, it is difficult to estimate with any degree of certainty the results of industrialization beyond the year 1959. By 1962 some of the basic raw materials and semi-manufactured goods had probably reached or surpassed the levels envisaged by the second plan. Against this, industrial consumer goods—like farm products—lagged behind badly. All in all, during the years covered by the second plan the national product increased less than during the first plan.

The year 1963 marked the end of the period of economic retrenchment, forced upon China by the "three bitter years" (1959–61) of agricultural calamities, the withdrawal of Soviet aid and expertise, and the mismanagement brought about by the Great Leap Forward. In 1964 the economic readjustment, set in train when new economic priorities were set up, was basically completed. In his report to the National People's Congress held at the end of 1964, Chou En-lai, the Prime Minister, was able to speak of a turn for the better. However, while the years of consolidation had borne fruit, the improvement was not maintained. This was all the more significant, since 1966 had been earmarked as the first year of the third five-year plan.

The Delayed Third Plan

The third plan should have started in 1963, but at that time China's economy was too dislocated to permit of any planned operation. This is now publicly admitted. In its editorial of 1 January 1966, the *People's Daily*, the Party's official organ, claimed that the second plan was "basically fulfilled" in 1960, but that during the five following years the national economy was first "readjusted" and later organized for a "new upsurge" so as to create the basis for the third plan. Shortcomings and mistakes were conceded.

In fact, at the start of the new plan, in 1966, the economy was little better off than in 1958; in some respects the situation was even worse. On the whole, China started her third plan in important sectors of the economy at levels of production that were below those reached during the first two years of the second plan. Grain output was hardly greater than in 1957. As the population had increased since then by some 100 million people, in spite of substantial grain imports the diet provided in 1965–66 a mere 2,000 calories, or one-tenth less than a decade earlier. The output of cement, mineral oils and industrial fertilizers surpassed the level of 1958, but in the consumer sector supplies were hardly back to where they had been in 1957.

There had been progress on a narrow front, however. The development following the nuclear explosion of October 1964 is a pointer to some of the priority targets. In June 1967, China exploded her first hydrogen bomb. In the meantime, seventeen nuclear devices have been exploded and sufficient material is available for the production of large numbers of nuclear weapons. The nuclear tests have revealed a considerable degree of sophistication in China's scientific and technological advance in a narrow area to which probably 1 per cent of the country's annual national product is being devoted. The psychological impact of this development on non-industrial nations in Asia has been considerable.

As idle capacities could be utilized, some growth was possible during the third plan, but the lack of industrial equipment and spare parts made itself felt. An increase of gross industrial production by 30 per cent in the course of the five years up to the end of 1970 was the most that could be expected. During the same period of time, the output of the farm industry, which lacks important farm requisites, is unlikely to have increased by more than 15 per cent. This left little for improvement in food supplies and for investment in industry. The control by the State over farm deliveries and urban consumption levels was tight, to meet the needs of industry and the armed forces. Light industry, once placed second behind agriculture and ahead of heavy industry, did not rank quite so high on the list of priorities during the third plan. When it was first raised in status, the Chinese planners appeared to be thinking as much of the export markets as of indigenous consumers in town and country.

In 1957, China was expected to surpass Britain by 1972 in the output of steel, coal, machine tools, cement and chemical fertilizers. Nine years later, the official Party organ expected China to need 20 to 30 years in order to catch up with Western industrial nations. At the end of 1970 China's steel output of approximately 20 kilos per capita equalled one-thirtieth of Britain's production and one-fortieth of that of the United States. By the end of the third plan, China may well have succeeded in ranking among the industrial nations of the world, but she was still far from being an industrialized country. A minimum supply of energy equal to 1.5 tons of coal per capita is necessary to create the preconditions of an industrialized community. In China, energy available per head of population equals approximately 500 kilos of coal.

Capital was the principal bottleneck of the last plan, and inflation could only be averted by strict rationing of consumer goods and tight allocation of industrial materials. Lack of capital restrained the rate of economic growth. "Socialism in one country", as Stalin understood it, or political and economic consensus between China and one of the two great super powers seemed to be the two alternatives on which China's leaders had to reach a decision. The indecision as to which of these alternatives to choose seems to have been one of the sources of conflict that caused the political struggles of the "Great Proletarian Cultural Revolution". Originally it was intended not to interfere with work in the fields and factories, but early in 1967 agricultural and industrial output began to be affected by this nation-wide political upheaval.

Industry was particularly affected by the political dispute between opposing factions. A large number of factories were at a standstill for at least some of the time during the confusing months when the Cultural Revolution was at its height. Leading personalities in industry and administration became casualties of the dispute. Even the nuclear establishment was not spared the effects of the upheaval. General education, vocational training and academic work were also set back.

In the industrial sphere order was restored only in the second half of 1968 when the decline of production was halted. The Ninth Party Congress held in April 1969 brought the Cultural Revolution formally to a close. By the end of the year, industrial production had recovered from the setbacks suffered in the preceding two years. In the course of the decade following the Great Leap Forward, during which production was supposed to double and treble, China's industrial output had probably increased by some 70 per cent or by an average of 5.5 per cent per year. This industrial growth, though far from negligible, was modest when compared with what had been intended in China and with what had been achieved in some other communist and non-communist countries aiming at high rates of economic development. The Cultural Revolution, like the Great Leap Forward, had been responsible for the reduced rate of industrial progress.

The Fourth Plan

The last year of the third plan was one of continued economic recovery and of industrial growth, due largely to improved factory discipline, and labour productivity, resulting in increased output and economic efficiency. At the end of 1970, the third plan was officially declared to have been fulfilled (though no plan targets had ever become known), and the foundation was said to have been laid for the fourth plan, due to start in 1971 (*People's Daily*, January 1st, 1971). No statistical details to support these claims were released. However, Chou En-lai gave the late American journalist Edgar Snow data not previously published, which can be compared with estimates published in Western and Soviet journals. Later some output figures from Chinese sources were reproduced in the United Nations World Economic Survey. On the whole, the Chinese figures, the first in ten years, would seem to be on the high side. Bearing in mind the long period of statistical black-out, the differences may seem to fall within a reasonable margin of error, except in the case of grains and fertilizers, where alien ingredients may have been included in the official production data. In industries where small-scale production is prominent, statistical exaggerations cannot be ruled out either.

No plan targets for 1971–75 were made known but, while the first plan was devoted to the development of the basic industries and the next decade to the machine industry, the chemical and electronics industries are now known to have been added to the list of sectors earmarked for expansion.

The first year of the fourth plan got off to a good start. Industrial capacities were apparently utilized to the full. The administration also seemed to have recovered from the setbacks of the Cultural Revolution. Chou En-lai, the Prime Minister, and Huang Yung-sheng, the Chief of Staff of the People's Liberation Army, being respectively the chief civilian and military executives, seemed to work in harness under the overall direction of Mao Tse-tung and Lin Piao.

The Tenth Party Congress, held in August 1973, was to dispose of the Lin Piao affair. Following his death in the air crash at Undur Khan, his position changed from that of Mao's most intimate comrade-in-arms and successor at the Ninth Party Congress in August 1970 to that of a "plotter, ambitionist, political swindler, renegade and traitor". Little was said at the Tenth Congress about the economic situation. The political report was presented by Chou En-lai and that on the Party constitution by Wang Hung-wen, who had risen rapidly from the rank of branch secretary at a textile mill in Shanghai to the position of Vice-Chairman of the Party and the third most senior man after Mao and Chou. In the newly elected Central Committee the balance of political forces was changed in favour of the Party. This trend was confirmed at the end of the year with the reshuffle of leading military personnel.

The attacks in 1973-74 against Confucius and Confucianism suggested that important issues of policy remained unresolved. At the start of 1974 the internal and external situation could hardly be regarded as stable. Clearly important matters of state had yet to be resolved, although some of them were clarified with China's admission to the United Nations and the visits of President Nixon, Prime Minister Tanaka and Sir Alec Douglas-Home to Peking. The balance of power in the Far East, static for two decades, had shifted in China's favour, but her economy remained that of a "relatively backward" country.

The Fourth National People's Congress, long overdue, was eventually held in secret in January 1975. It led to a political balance between the Party, the Government and the Armed Forces. By the end of 1975 the Plan was said to have been fulfilled, but the growth rate had apparently slowed down. In the preceding decade, total gross agricultural and industrial output had increased at annual rates of 4 and 11 per cent respectively, implying a growth rate of 7.5–8 per cent for total material production (excluding "non-productive" services, which do not figure in Chinese aggregate accounts).

The Fifth Plan

The prospects for a successful start of the Plan (1976–80) seemed promising. However, the arrangements made by Chou En-lai during his terminal illness proved less lasting than was assumed at the time of his death in January 1976. The appointment of Teng Hsiao-p'ing as Chou's successor was fiercely challenged by the "radical" wing of the Party and its most prominent representative, Chiang Ching. As the Chairman's wife, she appeared to use her influence to discredit the acting Premier as an unrepentent "capitalist roader", revisionist and enemy of Mao's concept of "permanent revolution". Apart from personal rivalries, issues of political doctrine and economic strategy were at stake. In industry, the controversy between material incentives and ideological commitment remained a burning issue. In agriculture, the pace at which the mechanization of the communes was to be carried out and side-line production and private trading were to be permitted continued to be matters of public debate. In foreign affairs, antagonism and accommodation in relation to the U.S.A. and the U.S.S.R. were never much below the surface of public controversy. Self-reliance was revived as an important issue of economic policy, though the purchase of foreign plant and technical expertise was not hindered.

Hua Kuo-feng, the man chosen to replace the discredited Teng Hsiao-p'ing, is likely to wield considerable influence in a period of uncertainty. As the experienced Minister of Public Security, Hua must have a unique knowledge of Party and Government personnel. Yet Hua may prove to be no more than an interim office-holder until the issue of the succession is finally settled between the "pragmatists" and the "radicals" within the Chinese leadership. The present political uncertainty is not yet affecting the domestic economy, but a certain retrenchment in overseas commitments has been noted by foreign observers. This may be due to a financial adjustment to foreign exchange currently available rather than a change of foreign economic policy. In any event, only a small portion of the nation's overall performance is likely to be affected, though the purchase of foreign technology is likely to suffer at least a temporary setback. Domestically, the spontaneous demonstration of sympathy for the late Chou En-lai in April 1976 suggests divisions within the rank and file of the Party, the bureaucracy and the factory workers. These public displays of sentiments represent a departure from an apparent political unity which in the past was taken for granted.

Economic priorities seem to have remained largely unchanged during the current five-year period. However, one of the assets on which China will be able to draw increasingly is mineral oil, which will supply a growing portion of the domestic fuel requirements and provide foreign exchange needed for the purchase of industrial equipment and technical know-how. The degree to which self-sufficiency is being achieved in foodstuffs remains uncertain. Official claims of grain output seem to be expressed in terms of "bunker yields" which include alien ingredients. China looks like remaining dependent on grains from abroad, though these may not provide more than, say, 3 per cent of the national food intake. The food bill accounts for about 60 per cent of the urban family's income, and the rural diet absorbs an even larger proportion of the villagers' still meagre household budget. Malnutrition is almost unknown in present-day China, but the financial resources needed to increase the volume and improve the composition of the national diet remain tight. When family planning becomes universally accepted, the per capita supply of foodstuffs is bound to take a turn for the better. In the meantime, the average diet remains short of animal proteins, vitamins and minerals. Other basic necessities are in sufficient supply, but the mass market of items other than necessities is yet to be opened. The activities of foreign firms are likely to remain restricted to capital goods and their use in a rapidly expanding domestic economy.

FOREIGN ECONOMIC RELATIONS

China aims at being self-sufficient in all essentials. This aim has not been realized, however, since substantial imports of grain and equipment have become a regular feature of China's external economic relations. Even so, foreign trade represents only a marginal aspect of the nation's economic life. China's planners do not regard the international division of labour as a factor of importance in their consideration of the country's requirements.

No foreign trade data have been available from official Chinese sources since 1959. China's foreign

trade can, of course, be gleaned from that of her trading partners, but if taken from other countries' import statistics, China's exports are exaggerated by the amounts of freight and insurance that are included in the c.i.f. values recorded by the importers of Chinese merchandise.

If allowance is made for these inaccuracies, China's foreign trade turnover appears to have been equivalent to almost U.S. $14,000 million in 1974 and over U.S. $14,000 million in 1975. This seems a not insignificant achievement when it is borne in mind that China's domestic economy recovered only in 1965 from the set-backs of the early 1960s.

In assessing the increase in foreign trade, the worldwide rise in prices and the devaluation of some of the world's main currencies have to be taken into account. Thus the volume of foreign trade, expressed in pre-crisis prices, increased considerably less than its value, measured in current dollars. Moreover, in an attempt to beat the inflationary trends, China imported and exported more goods than she would have done in normal world market conditions. In real terms, China's foreign trade probably increased between 1971 and 1975 by 15 per cent a year or two to three times as fast as the domestic economy. There are, however, certain signs of foreign trade and overseas commitments slowing down.

As no official estimates exist of China's gross national product, it is difficult to relate the volume of foreign trade to the nation's overall efforts. However, China's foreign trade probably accounts for less than 5 per cent of the gross national product. The degree of economic self-sufficiency is thus high. China accounts for one-fifth of the world's production, but she contributes only 1 per cent to world trade.

State Trading Organizations

Considering the relatively marginal nature of China's trade, the size and competence of her trading organizations may seem surprising. Foreign trading and banking interests were among the first enterprises to be nationalized after the Revolution. Foreign trade became a monopoly of the State, which by 1953 conducted almost all economic operations abroad. However, the fact that all foreign trade is controlled centrally does not exclude a certain flexibility in the face of changing conditions.

The Ministry of Foreign Trade is responsible, directly and through its trading corporations, for negotiating and implementing trade agreements with both Communist and non-Communist countries. In any dealings with the Soviet bloc the rouble is used as the unit of accounting. The £ sterling used to serve for transactions with non-Communist countries but, after the devaluation of sterling in 1967, the Swiss and French francs entered the market for the settlement of commercial accounts. Since the spring fair held in Canton in April–May 1970 the Chinese negotiators have tried to base their trade transactions increasingly on their national currency. Where China is not recognized, trade agencies, missions and offices of the Committee for the Promotion of International Trade (which, though government-controlled, presents itself as an independent commercial body) serve in place of diplomatic representatives, such as trade counsellors and attachés.

The spring and autumn fairs in Canton provide an additional forum for trade contacts which frequently lead to negotiations and agreements. The two strongest Chinese trade agencies covering Asia and Western Europe respectively are located in the China Resources Company in Hong Kong and the Chinese foreign trade mission in Berne, Switzerland (until 1956 in East Berlin). As more and more countries establish direct diplomatic relations with China, the trade sections of her diplomatic missions abroad have gained in importance. The financial aspects of foreign trade are handled by the People's Bank where Communist trading is concerned, and by its subsidiary, the Bank of China, with its overseas branches in London, Hong Kong and Singapore, in the case of East-West trade transactions. Besides financing trade transactions, they handle the sale of Chinese silver, the purchase of foreign exchange, the transfer of overseas Chinese remittances and any other financial business deemed by the political and commercial authorities in Peking to fall within their purview.

Direction of Foreign Trade

The direction of China's foreign trade has undergone dramatic changes in a relatively short period of time. Prior to the Japanese invasion of the Mainland, most of China's trade was tied to the great trading powers in Europe. Only 3 per cent of China's foreign trade was with the Soviet Union. By 1952, almost one-half of China's foreign trade was with the Soviet Union, one-fifth with other countries of the Communist bloc, and only one-third with non-Communist countries.

By 1965, however, the position had been entirely reversed, with the Communist bloc accounting for hardly one-third and the non-Communist countries for 70 per cent of China's total foreign trade. Sino-Soviet trade turnover declined from its peak of U.S. $2,000 million in 1959 to less than $50 million in 1970. By 1975, it had increased five-fold. Developing countries, including Hong Kong, account for one-third of China's trade with non-communist countries and for 25 per cent of that trade if Hong Kong is excluded. In 1975, China's ten chief trading partners, in order of the value of their trade, were: Japan, Hong Kong, the Federal Republic of Germany, France, the United States, Australia, Canada, the United Kingdom, the Soviet Union and Singapore. Hong Kong is the main importer of Chinese goods and China's main source of foreign exchange earnings. China's trade with Communist countries accounts at present for a little more than one-sixth of her total trade turnover. By comparison the shares of Hong Kong, Japan and Western Europe are 10, 26 and 19 per cent respectively.

The commodity composition of China's trade has also undergone significant changes in recent years. As exports are despatched not for their own sake, but so as to pay for essential imports, the composition of the foreign trade tends to vary in accordance with domestic requirements rather than with surplus conditions.

During the period of the first plan approximately half the country's plant equipment and machinery and more than a quarter of other metal goods were of foreign origin. As the factories started operating and raw materials and finished products had to be moved, the dependence on foreign supplies of rubber and mineral oil products made itself felt to an increasing extent. As the farm industry failed to live up to the planners' expectations, the imports of grain and flour tended to determine the whole pattern of foreign trade.

After the withdrawal in 1960 of Soviet technicians and Soviet economic assistance, China, once again, began to take an interest in the possibility of buying plant equipment and technical know-how from Japan and Western Europe. The import of complete Soviet plants dropped within the short span of a few years from U.S. $400 million worth in 1959 to nil in the 1960s. The traumatic effect of this experience cannot easily be exaggerated. Recent Chinese orders for plant and equipment from Western industrialized countries have reached sizeable proportions, and the effect of the re-direction of trade is reflected in the substantial increase of East-West trade. However, in view of the vacillations of the last decade, China's foreign trade cannot be considered as having settled down to a lasting pattern.

In 1974, foodstuffs and raw materials accounted for about one-quarter and one-third respectively of China's exports, the remainder consisting of manufactured goods. On the import side, manufactures accounted for over half of the total whilst foodstuffs and raw materials made up the remainder.

One of the unanswered questions is China's need for foreign grains. In 1974 over U.S. $1,000 million were spent, on approximately 7 million tons of wheat and other grain. At the same time, about 2 million tons of rice were exported.

A new feature of China's foreign trade is the export of crude oil and oil products. After a slow start, in 1974 this new export commodity is likely to have brought China some U.S. $450 million for 4 million tons shipped to Japan and 0.5 million tons sent to Hong Kong, Thailand and the Philippines. In 1975, oil exports doubled in value. If this trend continued, in time mineral oil could be expected to help China to return to a balanced foreign trade pattern and to deferred payments of short duration.

China's foreign trade policies and practices are modelled on those of other Communist countries. Theoretically, exports are to balance imports, but this principle is rarely adhered to. In practice, China has had both surpluses and deficits of sizeable proportions with individual countries and in her overall trading accounts. In her trade with the U.S.S.R. China accumulated between 1950 and 1955 a deficit on trading account of close on U.S. $1,000 million. This debt was repaid through export surpluses. Annual swings usually carry an interest rate of at least 2 per cent where they exceed certain ceilings agreed on between the two parties to a trade agreement. As to prices, the world market usually provides fairly firm guidance. However, in the case of commodities prevented by strategic embargo from reaching China through the normal channels, the Chinese State trading organizations tended to offer prices higher than those operating in the world markets. Conversely, China has been willing at times to accept lower than international prices in her export trade. Any losses as the result of these price concessions are covered by the State budget (of which no details have been published since 1961).

China's trade policy has been highly successful during the last ten years. Early in 1965 she could claim, with justification, to have repaid all her debts to the Soviet Union. The same does not apply, however, to the rest of the world. At present China's overall short-term foreign debt probably stands at about U.S. $500 million. Her gold and hard currency reserves are probably twice as large. China's current debts to Japan, Western Europe and North America are considerable and she will thus have to operate for some time to come on a budget that will dictate strict housekeeping of the limited foreign exchange reserves.

In recent years China has become increasingly active as a donor of economic and technical aid to developing countries. In 1970, when aid became a major instrument of China's foreign policy, 18 aid agreements and protocols were signed. As the list of recipients shows, the selection of targets is largely decided on political grounds. In 1970 China surpassed the Soviet Union in its offers of aid: the equivalent of U.S. $700 million was offered by China as against less than U.S. $300 million by the Soviet Union. In 1971 almost U.S. $470 million worth of aid was granted. In 1970 Tanzania and Zambia were each offered U.S. $200 million for the construction of the Tanzam railway (completed in 1975) linking the copper belt with Dar es Salaam. Pakistan was offered a credit of the same order, some of it being earmarked for a bridge across the Brahmaputra in East Bengal. China officially recognized Bangladesh in August 1975, so this aid will now become available in Dacca. Within the Soviet orbit, China offered Romania a credit of the order of U.S. $200–300 million, thus countering Soviet attempts at interfering in Romania's internal affairs.

ECONOMIC BALANCE SHEET

In view of the uncertainty which has prevailed in many of the urban and industrial areas of China for several years, it is exceedingly difficult (in May 1976) to arrive at any national aggregates that have any meaning. It is even more difficult to look into the future. Nothing is known from official sources about the current value of China's total national product and the size of its chief components. From Western calculations of gross and net national product and of net domestic product, based on official Chinese data, it would appear that China's gross domestic product and expenditure increased (in 1957 prices) from approximately 75,000 million yuan in 1952 to 100,000 million yuan in 1957. This corresponds to an annual growth rate of approximately 6.5 per cent. After 1957, another year of good performance was followed by several years of severe retrenchment, caused by over-investment, errors in the allocation of scarce resources and lack of economic balance.

Economic recovery took place from 1963 onwards. Official claims for agricultural and industrial output seem to imply an increase by the end of 1966 of approximately one-third over and above the level which the gross domestic product had reached in 1957. This would be equal to an annual growth rate of approximately 3 per cent during the decade following the end of the first five-year plan. In the course of the third plan period industrial production, after an initial increase by 10 per cent, dropped in 1967 by about 15 per cent below the level reached in the previous year. At the end of 1969 the level attained in 1966 was exceeded only slightly and in 1970 a further gain of, say, 15 per cent was made. Agricultural production was affected somewhat less by the Cultural Revolution, but this was not true of the supply and distribution of both farm products and farm requisites; nor did it apply to public utilities which were seriously disrupted during the Cultural Revolution. In spite of a shift of emphasis in favour of agriculture, the shares of the chief non-agricultural components in the gross domestic product have probably changed relatively little. The farming industry is likely to absorb two-thirds of the labour force, but to produce somewhat less than one-third of the total product of the nation. A similar amount is generated by the combined efforts of industry, mining, construction and handicraft which employ approximately one-sixth of the labour force. The remainder of the total product and the labour force is accounted for by public utilities, internal and external trade and other services. The use of the gross domestic product may well have undergone some changes. Personal consumption was curtailed during the years of the Great Leap Forward and the recovery that followed it, whilst the gross domestic expenditure devoted to government consumption and government-controlled communal services increased proportionally. During the Cultural Revolution personal consumption was depressed once again, though not as much as during the Great Leap Forward.

As the normalization of economic life which began late in 1968 continued, an increase of industrial production by over 50 per cent during the period of the third plan is likely to have been achieved. This implies an average annual industrial growth rate of 8.9 per cent. Transport, commerce and public services are unlikely to have matched this rate of progress. The record of the economy as a whole continued to depend to a considerable extent on the performance of the farming industry, where nature rather than man still determines the outcome. An increase of 20 per cent over the five-year period or an average of 3.7 per cent a year is likely to have been achieved. In the aggregate this would mean an increase of gross domestic product by almost 40 per cent, or by an average of 6.6 per cent a year: no less than the growth rate attained during the first plan, and more than during the interim period between the first and the third plan. These estimates are more conservative than those given in the latest edition of the Congressional Report on the economy of China, whose contributors seem to have overestimated China's population and economic performance, extrapolating the favourable trends of a few years without allowing sufficiently for the effects of reverses, however temporary.

When the main evidence from western sources is summarized, China's total national product appears to have increased by 4.5 to 5 per cent a year in the two decades since the introduction of the first plan, but the annual growth rate was reduced to about 4 per cent for the years following the end of this plan. During the latter period the national product per capita appears to have increased at an annual rate of about 2.5 per cent. As a substantial part of this growth was skimmed off for public investment and defence, the consumption per capita cannot have increased to the same extent. In conclusion, in spite of the setbacks caused by the Great Leap Forward and the Cultural Revolution, China's economy has expanded at a reasonably high growth rate, although not as fast as was anticipated when the first plan was conceived. Without the upheavals of the 1950s and 1960s, more could have been achieved, particularly if recourse had been had consistently to aid from Russia and the United States, both of whom withheld this help for reasons of their own at crucial periods in China's economic development. On balance, the account given by the *People's Daily* in Peking on January 1st, 1972, remains realistic and relevant: China is a developing country whose economy continues to be relatively backward when compared with the truly industrialized nations of the world.

As to the future, at the Fourth National People's Congress, held in 1975, the late Chou En-lai looked forward to 1980, the end of the next (fifth) five-year plan, when the first era of planning would have created an "independent and relatively comprehensive industrial and economic system", and beyond that to the year 2000, when China's economy would be sufficiently modernized "to put the country in the front rank of the world's nations". These expectations may well materialize, provided that such upheavals as the Cultural Revolution can be avoided, a balance between "traditional" and "radical" forces can be restored and the succession from the present to the future leadership can take place without another political convulsion and the economic setback which it inevitably causes. In mid-1976 a smooth transition following Mao's death seemed doubtful.

ECONOMIC SURVEY OF TAIWAN

Ramon H. Myers

In spite of a severe loss in international status and prestige in recent years, Taiwan's economy exported goods worth more than U.S. $5,200 million in 1975.

Economic growth has been made possible by three developments. First, Taiwan experienced fifty years of enlightened colonial administration under Japan which gave the Chinese Nationalist government in 1945 an economy with a well developed agricultural sector and a network of roads, railways, markets, and public health facilities. Secondly, U.S. aid during the 1950s greatly assisted the Government to control inflation, endure a long-term trade imbalance while new industries were being built, and increase agricultural and industrial production. Finally, after promoting the growth of import-substitution industries during the 1950s, the Government reversed its policies in the early 1960s and initiated steps to develop a modern industrial sector oriented towards world trade.

Post-War Economic Development

Under Japan's colonial rule, Taiwan's economic structure gradually began to shift from a dependency on agriculture to manufacturing. This trend accelerated after the war so that by 1974 only 14 per cent of the goods and services produced originated from agriculture compared to 35 per cent in 1952, whereas manufacturing produced 39 per cent compared to 18 per cent in 1952. The share of the service sector remained unchanged (47 per cent), but it employed 35 per cent of the labour force in 1974 compared to 30 per cent in 1952. This transformation in economic structure is unusual because it was associated with a rapid population growth of 3.5 per cent in the 1950s and a very rapid annual growth of per capita income of 3 and 7 per cent respectively during the 1950s and 1960s.

Although the economy suffered serious dislocation and inflation after the war, by 1952 the Nationalist government had brought inflation under control and revived economic activity to its pre-war level. The government had used grain from U.S. Public Law 480 to stabilize food prices, introduced a land reform to reduce tenant rents and redistribute land to small holders, and spent heavily to expand the infrastructure of public transport, flood control, and agricultural research. The first four-year economic development plan, launched in 1952, favoured building import-substitution industries such as iron and steel, chemicals, machines, tools, and fertilizers. But after 1958 economic policy shifted toward liberalizing trade regulations and encouraging the rapid development of export industries.

Between 1960 and 1973 Taiwan experienced an unprecedented economic boom in which the value of exports rose twenty-fold and real G.N.P. in 1966 prices more than trebled for the same period. Meanwhile, per capita income at 1973 prices was about U.S. $470 in 1973, compared with only U.S. $190 in 1960. A recent study found that the sources for this remarkable growth are technical progress, which explains half of the output growth between 1963–72, and capital accumulation, which accounts for another 36 per cent. The remaining 14 per cent of output growth came from the expansion of the labour supply.

It is significant that prior to 1967 foreign sources played a large role in financing net capital formation expansion, but after 1967 domestic savings financed the entire growth of net capital formation. The structure of capital also changed in the late 1960s shifting from mainly construction items toward a larger share comprised of transport equipment, machinery, and equipment. The expansion of foreign trade is the major reason for Taiwan's rapid capital growth. Eighty per cent of the growth in exports can be attributed to the competitiveness of Taiwan's exports in price and quality in world markets for food, crude materials, machinery, transport equipment, and other manufactured goods. The sources for this competitiveness are to be found in low cost, high skilled labour, efficient management, the strong profit incentive of businessmen, and social and political stability within the country.

This rapid economic boom naturally created new problems. After 1965 farm labour became scarce, and the sudden rise in rural wages began to influence adversely farm costs and product prices. In the early 1970s overcrowding of public transportation and shipping congestion in major ports revealed for the first time that demand had outstripped the capacity of Taiwan's infrastructure to provide the same services as in the recent past. In 1973 the energy crisis and rising import prices threatened to reduce Taiwan's competitiveness in world markets. Domestic prices began to rise rapidly from September 1973 to early 1974. The Central Bank tightened its control over the money supply by raising the rediscount rate and bank deposit interest rates. This action reduced the demand for money and encouraged savings to rise. By late 1974 prices began to level off. Then in 1975 the Government selectively reduced taxes to prevent many key industries from sliding into recession. The problem confronting Taiwan in the 1970s is the same facing other modern states: how to deal effectively with both stagnation and inflation while still maintaining reasonably full employment with rising real per capita income.

RESOURCES

About 68 per cent of the island, estimated at 6,158,975 acres, is still forested with broad-leaved evergreens, coniferous trees, shrub, and bamboo. Only 24 per cent of the land surface is under cultivation. Rapid population growth has increased the cultivated area from 1,665,000 acres in 1910 to 2,124,000 acres in 1940 and a near maximum limit of 2,197,220 acres in 1965. Cultivated soil in Taiwan is mainly of the alluvial type. The fertility of this alluvial soil is rather high, and its physical properties are well-suited for crop-growing.

Mineral resources are poor and it is unlikely that important mineral reserves still remain to be discovered. The chief minerals produced are coal, gold, and sulphur; other resources of importance include copper, petroleum, and salt. Bituminous coal is found in shales and sandstone in the north. At the present rate of coal exploitation, about 4 million tons annually, current coal reserves can be expected to last somewhat less than 50 years.

Manpower

Roughly 45 per cent of Taiwan's population is under 15 years of age, and the economically active portion constitutes only 52 per cent compared to an average of 60 per cent in more advanced countries. According to the 1964 manpower survey, the fully employed labour force totalled 3.6 million out of a population of 12.2 million. Agriculture, forestry, and fisheries absorbed 54 per cent of this labour force, 12 per cent were employed in industry which consisted of mining and manufacturing, and the remaining 34 per cent were in commerce, transport, services and government. Unemployment disappeared in the 1960s but revived again in early 1975 when the growth rate began to slow down. As nearly two-fifths of the population is less than twelve years of age, the government's chief problem has been to finance the growth of education facilities rapidly enough to train this large, youthful population. After 1964 government expenditures for education rose sharply, from 12.4 per cent to 15.5 per cent of government consumption expenditures of gross domestic product.

AGRICULTURE

Until 1965 agriculture produced the largest share of national income, but thereafter its share steadily declined as industrial production expanded rapidly and the growth rate of agricultural production slowed. Land used for food-grain production had been diverted to producing more vegetables, mushrooms and fruit. More farm capital and labour were also shifted to increase the supply of poultry and pigs. But, due to a decline in the agricultural labour force since the mid-1960s, the multiple cropping index also declined slightly. While some farm mechanization had increased, the trend of more costly farm specialization can only mean that food-grain production might not meet future demand, necessitating some importing of food or food price rises. Over 85 per cent of the farms still are less than 3 hectares, and 45 per cent of this number are smaller than 1 hectare. In 1973 the average farm family contained 6.6 persons farming 1.02 hectares, compared with 6.77 persons farming 1.05 hectares in 1965.

Crops

The main crops ranked by acres of cultivation are rice, sugar, sweet potatoes and groundnuts. Rice has accounted for more than half of total farm production and nearly half of the cultivated farm land. However, the acreage used for these main crops has been declining since 1969 as farmers have switched land use to corn and soy beans which are used as feed for hogs and poultry. Farming areas around metropolitan areas are being converted into vegetable and fruit lands. Hog production stood at over a half million in 1973 compared to 224,000 in 1964. The production of hen eggs also doubled for the same period.

Improvements in Yield

Until 1910 the growth of farm production has been accounted for by the expansion of farming inputs such as land, labour and farm capital produced by farmers themselves. Between 1910 and 1970 farm production expanded three times more rapidly than the historical growth trend and new farm capital and technology began to account for roughly half of this output expansion. During this period Taiwan achieved modern agricultural development for the first time. In 1955 the limits of arable, cultivated land were reached, and output can be increased only by raising yields. In 1910 Japan's average rice yield exceeded Taiwan's rice yield by 100 per cent but in 1951/53 by only 50 per cent. In 1963/64 Taiwan's rice yield was the second highest in Asia and double the average yield in South-East Asian countries. The rice growing area increased only 25 per cent between 1938 and 1965 but production rose nearly 70 per cent. Sugar cane yield is still 75 per cent of the 1938 all-time record, but sugar cane is grown on only three-fifths of the 1938 cane-growing area.

The rise in productivity must be attributed to the activities of an efficient farm extension service which provides research and technical assistance to farmers. In 1898 the first agricultural research station was established in Taipei. By 1908 similar stations were located in the five main districts and conducted research to improve seed varieties, control plant disease, correct poor soil conditions and care for livestock. Serving each district station were agricultural associations comprised of local officials, landlords and wealthy farmers. These associations received new seeds and instructions to use them from district associations; they, in turn, introduced the seeds to villages. New seed varieties was the principal factor responsible for the rise in rice and sugar cane yield before 1938. This same research and farm extension system operates today, and its achievements over the past half-century have made the Taiwanese farmers the best informed and most sophisticated, with the exception of the Japanese farmers, in Asia.

In addition to new seeds, there was notable progress achieved in expanding irrigation facilities and using chemical fertilizers, pesticides, and new farm machinery. Irrigated land increased greatly in the 1930s because of the completion of several large reservoirs and numerous networks of canals and ponds started in the 1920s. By 1955 three-fifths of the farm land was irrigated. Before 1940 farmers used night soil and soya bean cake but few chemical fertilizers on their fields. By 1965 farmers had already shifted from using nitrogenous compounds to phosphate and sulphate fertilizer compounds. Taiwan's fertilizer industry now supplies farmers with all the nitrogenous fertilizer required. Pesticides are widely used, and rice dehuskers, rotary tiller ploughs, power-driven sprayers and dusters, pumps, and spacing gauges can be found on many farms. However, less than one quarter of the farming population possess these implements, and the potential is great for elevating yield still further when the majority of farmers own and use these implements.

Land Tenure

One of the most striking post-war changes in the countryside was the creation of a freehold farming class and the elimination of powerful absentee landlords. This was accomplished by a land reform programme carried out between 1949 and 1953. By paying landlords a fair price for their land and encouraging them to invest in urban enterprises, the government induced this class to shift its wealth and energies from farming to finance and industry. By establishing a land bank and providing easy credit terms to tenant farmers, the government made it possible for seven out of every ten households to own their farms compared to three out of ten households before the war. Although the farming population rose from 4,699,000 to 5,999,000 between 1956 and 1968, the share of tenant families declined from 17 to 12 per cent and part-owners from 23 to 20 per cent.

Structural Change and Policy

Between 1953 and 1972 the agricultural share of Gross National Product decreased from 38.0 to 15.7 per cent. For the same period exports of primary and processed agricultural products as a share of total export trade dropped from 92.7 to 17.1 per cent. Such a rapid economic transformation was also accompanied by a great exodus of rural labour to urban occupations. Real wages began to rise rapidly in the late 1960s, and farmers for the first time in history were being confronted by a severe labour scarcity which threatened to persist for a long time to come. Further, the pattern of farm production began to change during the 1960s. The value of rice production, formerly a main staple crop, gradually fell from 44.3 to 31.7 per cent between 1961 and 1970, whereas the value of livestock production over the same period increased from 20.9 to 29.6 per cent.

As a result of these structural changes, the Chinese Government adopted a new agricultural development policy in 1969 aimed at reducing such farm costs as fertilizer, irrigation, interest charges and taxes. Then in September, 1972, Premier Chiang Ching-kuo announced that the Government would spend NT $2,000 million to support the 1969 farm programme. This programme contains measures which seek to improve agricultural marketing and research, accelerate farm mechanization, strengthen the rural infra-structure, and encourage new industries to evolve in rural areas.

INDUSTRY

The shortage of fuel and minerals has not prevented the development of new industries. Between 1946 and 1952 the nucleus of industry constructed by the Japanese during the war slowly recovered. Government import controls and foreign exchange licensing gave importers of intermediate products a premium to be earned. Exports declined, and as imports rose, the productive capacity of the pre-war industries rapidly expanded. Two new industries, textiles and chemicals, also grew rapidly as a result of this programme of protecting infant industries.

By 1954, however, industrial production began to falter. As manufacturers found their inventories rising, idle capacity in plants increased; textile and chemical factories were especially hard hit. In 1958 the Government reversed its former policy and liberalized trade. Import controls on numerous products were removed, and many industries were encouraged to produce for world markets as the Government reduced the costs of products they imported from abroad. The growth rate of manufacturing began to accelerate once again, and between 1961 and 1973 overall manufacturing output expanded at a growth rate of 17 per cent per annum. Between 1974 and 1975 manufacturing output expansion slowed down considerably because of government steps to curb inflation in late 1973 and early 1974. In 1975 the government began giving tax rebates to certain firms and industries to encourage businessmen to eliminate inefficiencies and reduce their unit costs in order to remain competitive in world markets.

The relative value of manufactured products in 1960 was processed food (27 per cent of total), textiles (22), chemical products (21), tobacco and wine (13), timber (5), machinery and ship repairing (3), iron, steel, aluminium and other metals (3), cement and ceramics (2) and other (4). Most of the basic industries are located in Kaohsiung city. Light industries are situated around Taipei which uses the facilities of Keelung harbour to import raw materials such as cotton for nearby textile mills. Industries depending on local agricultural products such as sugar cane, are concentrated in the south. Food processing industries, such as rice hulling, grain milling, manufacturing of edible oil, bean curd, and of condiments, are located in larger cities of the rural areas.

Textiles, plastics, plywood, machine-making and electrical appliance industries have made considerable profits for investors and have successfully tapped overseas markets. These industries fitted well into the Taiwan environment of cheap labour and easy access to raw materials and flourished because production costs were kept low. Other industries such as automobiles, steel and aluminium have not fared as well because of high production costs and poor quality of product.

In 1965 the government designated Kaohsiung as the site for an industrial zone to stimulate investors and businessmen to develop new export industries on the model of Hong Kong's free entrepot economy. A site of 165 acres was set aside for establishing factories which would produce optical equipment, plastics, electrical appliances, chemicals, garments, furniture and packaging materials for export. In late 1973 two additional zones in Nante and Taichung were in operation, with a fourth being planned. There were 290 factories located in these zones, of which 222 were in operation. Their combined investment exceeded U.S. $148 million; they employed 78,000 workers and exported goods valued at U.S. $405 million, about 9 per cent of total exports.

In the late 1960s and early 1970s foreign capital began pouring into Taiwan. Japanese and American businessmen were establishing plants to assemble fabricated products for export to Japan and the American market. But, in April 1974 air services between Taipei and Tokyo by Chinese and Japanese airlines ended as a consequence of Japan's closer diplomatic ties with the People's Republic of China. Taiwan importers have begun to look to sources other than Japan to buy plant equipment and intermediate products. Meanwhile, government action has tried to strengthen existing limited stock companies, increase credit to industry, adjust corporate taxes, and liberalize controls in order to encourage greater efficiency. In 1969–70 a government commission studied possible reforms of the taxation system.

FOREIGN AID

It is admitted that without U.S. economic and military assistance Taiwan's economic recovery would have been protracted and the economy may well have floundered in inflation and stagnated. The Nationalist Government has used economic aid for both agriculture and industry, and there have not been any reported instances of corruption or misuse of aid. Between 1951 and 1965 Taiwan received U.S. $1,465.4 million worth of economic aid. The importance of this aid for economic development can be seen in the financing of capital formation between 1952 and 1960: U.S. aid financed 26 per cent of the total value of capital formed during this period. It was also responsible for closing the annual trade deficit of approximately U.S $100 million. U.S. aid was also used for building the fertilizer industry, financing the Shihmen dam, launching many agricultural programmes, establishing schools and distributing teaching guides. In 1965 the aid programme was terminated, and by 1970 all grants previously earmarked would have run out.

OVERSEAS TRADE

Taiwan depends greatly on trade to obtain raw materials and capital for industrial expansion and consumer goods which she is still unable to produce. Before the war sugar and rice accounted for three-fifths of the island's exports. Food and fibres made up two-fifths of the imports and the remainder consisted of textiles and assorted goods. Industrial development in the post-war period greatly increased the demand for raw materials, semi-finished goods and machinery. Food and fibres now account for less than one-quarter of total imports. Exports have also undergone changes. During the 1950s industrial products in exports averaged less than 21 per cent, but by 1965 they made up over half of the export trade. The share of agricultural raw materials and processed goods has declined but still accounts for about two-fifths of exports. The degree of foreign trade dependency has increased rapidly during the 1960s; by 1970, the ratio of exports and imports to gross national product had risen to 65 per cent as compared to 40 per cent in 1962.

In 1964 an export surplus of U.S. $16 million was achieved for the first time, but this was followed by six years of moderate trade deficit. Then, between 1971 and 1973, large export surpluses accumulated, to be followed by a huge deficit of U.S. $1,327 million in 1974 because of the sudden rise in petroleum prices. This deficit fell to U.S. $620 million in 1975, when the Government initiated various policies to stem domestic inflation.

On the export side the U.S.A. takes the largest share (41 per cent) of Taiwan's exports followed by Japan (12 per cent) and Hong Kong (7 per cent). On the import side Japan supplies 38 per cent of Taiwan's imports followed by U.S.A. and West Germany. Taiwan has recently exported greater quantities of cement, fertilizers and textiles to South-East Asia.

In 1955 the foreign exchange certificate system went into operation and was controlled by the Bank of Taiwan. The system is still in effect today. Foreign exchange proceeds from exports must be sold to the Bank of Taiwan which issues a certificate of foreign exchange settlement of the same value to the seller according to the official exchange rate. Importers must make application with the Bank of Taiwan and submit a certificate of foreign exchange settlement.

Due to rapidly rising prices of imports around the end of 1972, the Government reduced the tariffs on 10 categories of imports which included such commodities as barley, corn, soybeans, molasses, wheat bran, and steel scrap. In March, 1973, the Government removed 2,360 additional items of import from the control list, which means that except for military items, heroin, and precious metals such as gold, trade restrictions on general commodities have been completely removed. In February of the same year the Government set a new rate for the NT dollar at 38 per U.S. dollar instead of the former par value of 40 NT dollars per U.S. dollar.

FINANCE

The Bank of Taiwan serves as the country's central bank and issues notes, controls foreign exchange and makes loans to other banks. In July, 1961, the Central Bank of China resumed its operations in Taipei after 11 years of suspension. It also makes loans to other banks, handles U.S. aid funds and assists the government in its transactions. There are five national banks, three provincial banks and three large commercial banks.

The Bank of Taiwan and the national banks have maintained tight control over the money supply whenever prices began to rise unexpectedly. During the 1960s these institutions allowed the money supply to rise steadily in order to satisfy transactions and speculative demands. But in 1974 restrictions were vigorously applied, with the money supply rising by only 7 per cent, compared with 47 per cent the previous year. Then in 1975 the money supply rose by 26 per cent.

Taiwan operates with a national, provincial and district budget, but the national budget is most important because of the large amount of revenue collected and spent. Government receipts of income tax, estate tax, commodity taxes and monopoly profits account for roughly 64 per cent of total revenue. The remainder comes from profits of public enterprises, sale of foreign exchange certificates, indemnities and fees. Expenditures on national defence and administration as a share of the budget have remained fairly constant over the years at about 80 per cent. Expenditures for education, science, economic development, debt and social welfare comprise the remainder. In 1966 there was a cutback in spending for economic development and an increased amount allocated for defence, administration and education. Previously, budget expenditures had averaged around 14 per cent of national income, but this ratio has now risen to roughly one-fifth.

TRANSPORT

The *Taiwan Railway Administration* is a government enterprise operating 3,749 km. of railway track; there are also 2,838 km. of privately managed railway lines operated by the *Taiwan Sugar Corporation* and the forestry administration. The main line, located in the west, links the port of Keelung in the north with Kaohsiung in the south. Most of the major cities and their industries are served by this line. On the eastern side a 175-km. line connects Hualien with Taitung. Railway passenger traffic increased from 105 million persons in 1956 to 129 million in 1971, and freight hauled for the same period rose from 10.6 to 24.8 million metric tons.

Highways in 1972 totalled 16,404 km. Roads are more developed on the western side of the island, and a four-carriage expressway is planned in the near future to connect Taipei with Kaohsiung. Roads are two-lane and asphalted. In 1960 a cross island highway was completed linking Taichung in the west with Hualien in the east, a distance of more than 117 miles.

The *Taiwan Highway Bureau* is a government enterprise with a fleet of 1,365 buses which operates 73 bus stations with modern facilities. The bus service throughout the island is excellent.

Taiwan's three major harbours of Keelung, Kaohsiung and Hualien handle marine traffic and service ocean vessels of all sizes. The tonnage handled by these harbours between 1960 and 1970 more than trebled.

There are two domestic airlines that provide all major cities of over 100,000 people with air service. Taipei International Airport is a major stop-off for all flights from Japan to South-East Asia and beyond. Seven foreign airline companies use this terminal, and air traffic has increased greatly in the past ten years.

Crowded roads and railways and congested harbours, however, have plagued Taiwan since the late 1960s. The Government has taken steps to correct these bottlenecks. Since November 1973 Keelung harbour has operated at night. Existing harbour facilities are being expanded for Keelung, Hualien and Kaohsiung cities. A new international port near Taichung is under construction. Electrification of Taiwan's west coast railroads, began in 1975, will increase its carrying capacity by one-third and reduce travel time.

POWER

Since 1952 the supply of electricity has increased more than six times because of the construction of dams, hydroelectric stations and thermal power plants. In 1946 the *Taiwan Power Company* was organized to supply electricity and administer electrical rates. This government enterprise manages 32 plants of which 24 are hydroelectric and 8 are thermal with a capacity of 923,420 kilowatts. The power industry is an integrated system with a primary trunk line of 154,000 volts running the length of the island, and a transmission line of 66,000 volts connects this system with the eastern side of the island. There are 12 primary sub-stations sending power to every town and village, even in the remotest rural areas. Power consumption increased from 798 million to 4,300 million kWh between 1952 and 1965. The *Taiwan Power Company* launched four major projects in the early 1960s to increase the supply of electrical energy: the Shihmen dam, Nanpu thermal power unit, and the Shenao thermal unit were completed by 1963.

Because 80 per cent of Taiwan's electrical power is produced by thermal stations, using mainly petroleum, the 1973–74 increase in energy prices created a new source for domestic inflation. The Government introduced a new energy conservation programme in November 1973 with government agencies taking the lead by reducing their power and oil consumption by one-quarter. Rising energy costs are likely to reduce the growth of industrial production, adversely influence exports, and worsen the balance of payments unless cheap, alternative energy is found in the near future. Taiwan is now trying to diversify its sources of energy by investing in nuclear power plants. The first reactor is expected to be operational in October 1976. By the mid-1980s, it is expected that nuclear plants will supply Taiwan with 50 per cent of its electric power.

PEOPLE'S REPUBLIC OF CHINA

STATISTICAL SURVEY

AREA AND POPULATION

AREA ('000 sq. km.) 1967	TOTAL POPULATION (million)			
	1953 (Census)	1968 (Est.)	1974 (Est.)	1975 (Est.)
9,561.0	582.6	712.0*	almost 800.0†	839.0‡

* As announced during the "Great Proletarian Cultural Revolution" (1967–68).

† As stated by Vice-Minister of Public Health, Huang Shu-tse, at the World Population Conference in Bucharest, August 21st, 1974, and by Chou En-lai during the National People's Congress in January 1975.

‡ United Nations estimate, including Taiwan.

PROVINCES AND AUTONOMOUS REGIONS

	LOCATION	AREA ('000 sq. km.)	POPULATION (million) 1953 (Census)	POPULATION (million) 1968 (Est.)*	CAPITAL OF PROVINCE OR REGION	POPULATION OF CAPITAL 1958 (Est.)
PROVINCES:						
Szechwan	SW.	569.0	65.69	70.00	Chengtu	1.13
Shantung	E.	153.3	48.88	57.00	Tsinan	0.88
Honan	C.	167.0	44.22	50.00	Chengchow	0.78
Kiangsu	E.	102.6	41.25	47.00	Nanking	1.45
Hopei	N.	202.7	38.68	47.00†	Tientsin	3.28
Kwangtung	S.	231.4	34.77	40.00	Canton	2.20
Hunan	C.	210.5	33.23	38.00	Changsha	0.71
Anhwei	E.	139.9	30.34	35.00	Hofei	0.36
Hupeh	C.	187.5	27.79	32.00	Wuhan	2.23
Chekiang	E.	101.8	22.87	31.00	Hangchow	0.79
Liaoning	NE.	151.0	23.70	28.00	Shenyang	2.42
Yunnan	SW.	436.2	17.47	23.00	Kunming	0.90
Kiangsi	C.	164.8	16.77	22.00	Nanchang	0.52
Shensi	NW.	195.8	15.88	21.00	Sian	1.37
Heilungkiang	NE.	463.6	11.90	21.00	Harbin	1.59
Shansi	N.	157.1	14.31	18.00	Taiyuan	1.05
Kweichow	SW.	174.0	15.04	17.00	Kweiyang	0.53
Fukien	S.	123.1	13.14	17.00	Foochow	0.62
Kirin	NE.	187.0	11.29	17.00	Changchun	0.99
Kansu	NW.	366.5	11.23	13.00	Lanchow	0.73
Tsinghai	NW.	721.0	1.68	2.00	Hsining	0.15
AUTONOMOUS REGIONS:						
Kwangsi	S.	220.4	19.56	24.00	Nanning	0.26
Inner Mongolia	N.	1,177.5	6.10	13.00	Huhehot	0.32
Sinkiang	NW.	1,646.9	4.87	8.00	Urumchi	0.32
Ninghsia	NW.	66.4	1.70	2.00	Yinchuen	0.09
Tibet	W.	1,221.6	1.27	1.30	Lhasa	0.05
SPECIAL MUNICIPALITIES:						
Peking	NE.	7.1	2.77	7.00	—	4.15
Shanghai	E.	5.8	6.20	10.70	—	6.98
TOTAL		9,561.0	582.60	712.00		36.85

* As announced during the "Great Proletarian Cultural Revolution" (1967–68). † Including Tientsin (4.00).

POPULATION BY RACIAL GROUPS

1953 (Census)—million

Han (Chinese)	547.28
Chuang	6.61
Uighur (Turki)	3.64
Hui	3.56
Yi	3.25
Tibetan	2.77
Miao	2.51
Manchu	2.42
Mongolian	1.46
Puyi	1.25
Korean	1.12
Other	6.72
	582.60

TOWNS OVER 1 MILLION INHABITANTS

1958 (Est.)—million

Shanghai	10.82*
Peking	7.57*
Tientsin	3.28†
Shenyang (Mukden)	2.42
Wuhan	2.23
Canton	2.20
Chungking	2.16
Harbin	1.59
Lü-ta	1.59
Nanking	1.45
Sian	1.37
Tsingtao	1.14
Chengtu	1.13
Taiyuan	1.05
Fushun	1.02

* Official 1970 estimates. † 1968: 4.00.

ECONOMIC INDICATORS

(Estimates)

	1952	1957	1965	1970	1975
	Million				
Population:					
Joint Economic Committee*	570	642	750	836	938
Far East and Australasia	550	600	685	750	825
	1957=100				
Agricultural and Industrial Production:					
Joint Economic Committee (net)*	72	100	119	149	n.a.
Far East and Australasia	75	100	120	150	225
	U.S. $'000 Million				
National Income:					
Joint Economic Committee*	59	82	97	122	n.a.
Far East and Australasia	40	55	70	90	125†
	U.S. $ Per Capita				
National Income:					
Joint Economic Committee*	104	128	129	146	n.a.
Far East and Australasia	75	90	105	120	150†

* U.S. Congress, Joint Economic Committee, *People's Republic of China: An Economic Assessment*, Washington, 1972; *China: A Reassessment of the Economy*, Washington, 1975.

† Pre-1973 U.S. $.

RATES OF ECONOMIC GROWTH
(Estimates)

	PER CENT PER YEAR				
	1952–57	1957–65	1965–70	1957–70	1971–75
POPULATION:					
Joint Economic Committee*	2.5	2.0	2.2	2.0	2.3
Far East and Australasia	1.7	1.8	1.8	1.8	1.9
NATIONAL INCOME:					
Joint Economic Committee*	6.8	2.1	4.7	3.2	n.a.
Far East and Australasia	6.4	3.2	4.5	3.7	6.7
NATIONAL INCOME (PER CAPITA):					
Joint Economic Committee*	4.3	0.1	2.5	1.1	n.a.
Far East and Australasia	4.7	1.4	2.8	2.0	4.6

* U.S. Congress, Joint Economic Committee, *People's Republic of China: An Economic Assessment*, Washington, 1972; *China: A Reassessment of the Economy*, Washington, 1975.

DOMESTIC PRODUCT AND EXPENDITURE
('000 million yüan of 1952—estimates)

	1952	1957	1965	1970	1975
Gross Domestic Product:					
Agriculture	33.5	40.0	40.0	46.0	55.0
Industry, Mining, Construction, Handicrafts	19.0	30.0	45.0	60.0	92.0
Trade, Public Utilities	22.5	30.0	45.0	54.0	73.0
TOTAL	75.0	100.0	130.0	160.0	220.0
Gross Domestic Expenditure:					
Personal Consumption	52.5	65.0	78.0	95.0	130.0
Government Consumption, Communal Services (Communes)	7.5	10.0	19.5	25.0	35.0
Domestic Gross Investment	15.0	25.0	32.5	40.0	55.0
TOTAL	75.0	100.0	130.0	160.0	220.0

AGRICULTURE

AREA HARVESTED
(million hectares)

	1952	1957	1965 (Est.)	1970 (Est.)	1975 (Est.)
Total Grains	112.3	120.9	120.0	126.0	130.0
Rice	28.4	32.2	30.0	32.0	35.0
Wheat	24.8	27.5	26.0	27.5	25.0
Other Grains and Pulses	50.4	50.6	52.0	54.0	55.0
Potatoes	8.7	10.5	12.0	12.5	15.0
Soya Beans	11.5	12.6	9.0	10.0	10.0
Cotton	5.5	5.8	5.0	6.0	6.5

PRODUCTION
(million metric tons)

	1952	1957	1965 (Est.)	1970 (Est.)	1975 (Est.)
Total Grains*	154.5	185.0	185.0	205.0†	230.0
Rice	68.5	86.8	85.0	97.0	110.0
Wheat	18.1	23.7	25.0	31.0	35.0
Other Grains	51.5	52.6	55.0	52.0	60.0
Potatoes*	16.4	21.9	20.0	25.0	25.0
Soya Beans	9.5	10.0	8.0	9.0	10.0
Cotton	1.3	1.6	1.6	2.0	2.5

* Grain equivalent (barn yield).

† Chinese claim: 240; Soviet estimate: 205–210; for 1971: Chinese claim: 246; for 1972: 4 per cent less; for 1973: at or slightly above 1971 level; for 1974: 275 (overstated); for 1975: 280 (overstated).

YIELD
(tons per hectare)

	1952	1957	1965 (Est.)	1970 (Est.)	1975 (Est.)
Total Grains*	1.38	1.53	1.54	1.63	1.77
Rice	2.41	2.70	2.83	3.03	3.14
Wheat	0.73	0.86	0.96	1.13	1.40
Other Grains and Pulses	1.02	1.04	1.06	0.96	1.10
Potatoes*	1.86	2.08	1.66	2.00	1.67
Soya Beans	0.83	0.80	0.90	0.90	1.00
Cotton	0.24	0.28	0.30	0.35	0.38

* Grain equivalent (barn yield).

LIVESTOCK
(million)

	1952	1957	1965 (Est.)	1970 (Est.)	1975 (Est.)
Horses, Donkeys, Mules	19.6	19.8	20.0	20.0	20.0
Cattle and Buffaloes	56.6	65.8	65.0	70.0	80.0
Pigs	89.8	145.9	180.0	200.0	250.0
Sheep and Goats	61.8	98.6	100.0	120.0	150.0

FERTILIZER PRODUCTION AND CONSUMPTION
(million tons of nutrients)

	1970/71	1971/72	1972/73	1973/74	1974/75
Production:					
Nitrogen (N)	1.43	1.85	2.24	2.79	3.09
Phosphates (P_2O_5)	0.78	0.92	1.03	1.24	1.30
Potassium (K_2O)	0.24	0.28	0.30	0.30	0.30
Consumption:					
Nitrogen	3.11	3.14	3.46	4.01	3.92
Phosphates	0.78	0.92	1.04	1.26	1.32
Potassium (K_2O)	0.32	0.34	0.37	0.53	0.56

MINING AND INDUSTRY

		1952	1957	1965 (Est.)	1970* (Est.)	1975 (Est.)
Coal	million tons	66.5	130.7	230.0	255.0	420.0
Iron Ore	,, ,,	4.3	19.4	33.0	45.0	105.0
Pig Iron	,, ,,	1.9	5.7	15.0	20.0	35.0
Crude Steel	,, ,,	1.3	5.3	11.0	15.0	25.0
Crude Petroleum	,, ,,	0.4	1.5	9.0	15.0	80.0
Cement	,, ,,	2.9	6.9	10.5	15.0	35.0
Electricity	'ooo million kWh.	7.3	19.3	45.0	65.0	115.0
Machine Tools	'ooo units	13.7	28.5	57.5	80.0	120.0
Salt	million tons	4.9	8.3	12.5	15.0	18.0
Sugar	,, ,,	0.5	0.9	1.3	1.7	2.3
Vegetable Oils	,, ,,	1.0	1.5	1.8	2.4	2.7
Cotton Yarn	,, ,,	0.7	0.8	0.9	1.4	2.0
Cotton Cloth	'ooo million metres	4.2	5.0	5.2	7.5	8.0
Paper	million tons	0.6	1.2	1.8	2.5	3.0

* Chinese claims: Coal 300–350, Steel 21.0, Petroleum 25.6, Fertilizers 17.0, Cotton Cloth 9.0; Soviet estimates: Steel 15–16, Petroleum 18–19, Fertilizers 10.0, Cotton Cloth 8.0–8.5.

CHOU EN-LAI'S STATISTICS

		Absolute Data*			Indices			Average Annual Growth (%)
		1949	1964	1974	1949	1964	1974	
Population	million	500.0	—	800.0	100	—	160	1.9
Grain production	million tons	108.0	—	259.0	100	—	240	3.5
Cotton production	,, ,,	0.4	—	2.5	100	—	470	7.0
Agricultural output		—	—	—	—	100	151	4.2
Industrial output		—	—	—	—	100	290	11.2
Production:								
Cotton yarn	million tons	—	1.0	1.7	—	100	185	6.4
Coal	,, ,,	—	200.0	382.0	—	100	191	6.6
Steel	,, ,,	—	10.0	22.2	—	100	220	8.2
Electricity	'ooo million kWh.	—	36.0	108.6	—	100	300	11.6
Fertilizers	million tons	—	3.5	15.0	—	100	430	13.0
Artificial fibres	,, ,,	—	n.a.	n.a.	—	100	430	13.0
Tractors	'ooo	—	12.6	78.0	—	100	620	20.0
Petroleum	million tons	—	6.9	51.7	—	100	750	22.5

* Absolute figures derived from indices.

Sources: Joint Economic Committee, *China: An Economic Assessment*, Washington, 1972; *Peking Review*, January 24th 1975.

FINANCE

Renminbi (RMB or "People's Currency"):
100 fen (cents) = 10 chiao (jiao) = 1 Jen Min Piao (People's Bank Dollar), usually called a yüan.
Coins: 1, 2 and 5 fen.
Notes: 10, 20 and 50 fen; 1, 2, 5 and 10 yüan.
Exchange rates (June 1976): £1 sterling = 3.48 yüan; U.S. $1 = 1.97 yüan.
100 yüan = £28.74 = $50.86.

Note: The new yüan, equal to 10,000 old yüan, was introduced in March 1955. The initial exchange rate was U.S. $1 = 2.46 new yüan (1 yüan = 40.65 U.S. cents) and this remained in effect until August 1971. Between December 1971 and February 1973 the official rate was $1 = 2.27 yüan, though an effective rate of $1 = 2.20 yüan was in force from January 1973. Since February 1973 the exchange rate has been adjusted frequently. The rate (at December 31st) was: $1 = 2.04 yüan in 1973; $1 = 1.90 yüan in 1974; $1 = 1.97 yüan in 1975. In terms of sterling, the exchange rate between November 1967 and June 1972 was £1 = 5.904 yüan.

BUDGET

(1960—million yüan)

Revenue		Expenditure	
Taxes on Agriculture	3,300	Economic Development	42,910
Taxes on Industry and Commerce	19,450	Social Services, Culture and Education	8,620
Other Taxes	1,610	Defence	5,800
Receipts from State Enterprises	45,300	Administration	3,170
Other	360	Repayment of Loans	1,200
		Aid to Foreign Countries	500
		Credit Funds allotted to Banks	5,800
		General Reserve	1,700
		Other	320
Total	70,020	Total	70,020

FIRST FIVE-YEAR PLAN 1953–57

The First Five-Year Plan aimed at raising basic industrial and agricultural production. The Government claim that most targets were fulfilled.

SECOND FIVE-YEAR PLAN 1958–62

This plan was prematurely terminated and for a number of years, there were only annual, if any, plans in existence.

THIRD FIVE-YEAR PLAN 1966–70

The Third Plan, delayed by economic and political difficulties, was put into operation in January 1966. No details have been issued.

FOURTH FIVE-YEAR PLAN 1971–75

It was announced that a Fourth Five-Year Plan started in January 1971. No details have yet been issued but a few output data were released at the end of 1971.

FIFTH FIVE-YEAR PLAN 1976–80

No details were available in mid-1976. Agriculture continues to rank high in economic priorities. The exploitation of China's petroleum resources is rapidly changing the country's fuel and power basis and its industrial economy.

A Twenty-Five Year Plan is proposed for 1976–2000.

EXTERNAL TRADE

TRADING AREAS
('000 million U.S. $)

IMPORTS	1957	1965	1970 (Est.)	1974 (Prel.)	1975 (Prel.)
Communist Bloc	0.9	0.5	0.4	0.9	1.0
Developing Countries	0.2	0.4	0.3	1.2	1.1
Developed Countries*	0.2	0.9	1.5	5.3	5.4
TOTAL	1.3	1.8	2.2	7.4	7.5

EXPORTS	1957	1965	1970 (Est.)	1974 (Prel.)	1975 (Prel.)
Communist Bloc	1.1	0.7	0.5	1.4	1.5
Developing Countries	0.2	0.5	0.5	1.6	2.0
Developed Countries*	0.3	0.9	1.1	3.3	3.4
TOTAL	1.6	2.1	2.1	6.3	6.9

* Including Hong Kong.

COMMODITIES
(per cent)

IMPORTS	1957	1965	1970 (Est.)	1973 (Prel.)	1974 (Prel.)
Food, Drink, Tobacco	5	25	16	20	20
Raw Materials and Chemicals	35	30	32	29	27
Manufactured and Semi-Manufactured Goods	60	45	52	51	53
TOTAL	100	100	100	100	100

EXPORTS	1957	1965	1970 (Est.)	1973 (Prel.)	1974 (Prel.)
Food, Drink, Tobacco	30	30	31	33	27
Raw Materials and Chemicals	45	35	26	24	33
Manufactured and Semi-Manufactured Goods	25	35	43	43	40
TOTAL	100	100	100	100	100

PRINCIPAL COUNTRIES

(million U.S. $—based on partner-country statistics)

IMPORTS	1970	1972	1973*	1974*	1975*
Australia	146.5	71.0	147.0	354.7	341.0
Canada	135.3	261.7	284.9	446.1	370.5
Cuba	n.a.	55.0	75.0	80.0	n.a.
Egypt	18.5	45.0	15.0	n.a.	n.a.
France	81.2	58.1	89.6	160.4	374.0
German Democratic Republic	42.3	46.0	49.5	69.4	73.0
Germany, Federal Republic	167.2	165.2	310.1	420.7	522.9
Hong Kong	10.6	18.2	52.8	58.4	35.0
Italy	57.0	77.1	76.3	105.0	144.7
Japan	571.7	609.5	1,041.4	1,988.0	2,258.6
Malaysia and Singapore	50.3	47.5	134.5	147.1	88.0
Pakistan	36.0	17.5	15.0	11.3	n.a.
Poland	26.0	31.0	33.1	44.8	n.a.
Sri Lanka	43.9	27.0	34.8	39.8	59.6
U.S.S.R.	24.9	121.0	134.7	140.0	130.0
United Kingdom	107.0	78.1	206.0	167.7	178.4
United States	—	60.2	656.5	821.4	303.8

EXPORTS	1970	1972	1973*	1974*	1975*
Australia	41.5	51.0	76.5	121.6	98.0
Egypt	15.0	25.0	25.0	n.a.	n.a.
France	69.8	104.9	147.1	183.7	173.5
German Democratic Republic	35.7	46.0	58.9	76.7	97.0
Germany, Federal Republic	84.4	106.2	150.0	192.8	224.4
Hong Kong	467.1	685.5	1,101.1	1,186.6	1,361.2
Italy	63.1	84.7	139.8	116.9	125.9
Japan	253.8	491.6	974.1	1,305.0	1,531.1
Malaysia and Singapore	204.9	210.5	325.0	483.6	433.3
Pakistan	30.0	24.0	45.0	54.2	n.a.
Poland	24.0	58.0	33.8	48.5	n.a.
Sri Lanka	44.8	15.0	26.3	47.8	83.5
U.S.S.R.	21.7	134.0	135.1	140.0	150.0
United Kingdom	80.9	89.0	118.3	156.5	131.9
United States	—	32.2	66.0	114.7	158.3

* Preliminary.

IMPORTS OF GRAIN AND FERTILIZER

(million tons)

	1972/73	1973/77	1974/45	1975/76*
Wheat	5.4	5.7	5.8	2.1
Maize	1.0	2.11	0.4	0.0
Total Grains	6.4	7.8	6.2	2.1
Fertilizers	4.2	4.2	4.1	n.a.

* Preliminary.

CHINA'S ECONOMIC POSITION

(International Comparison)

	Gross National Product ($)	Steel Production (kilos)	Energy Consumption (kilos coal equivalent)
	Per Capita		
	1971	1972	1972
China	160*	33*	567*
India	110	16	186
Japan	2,130	644	3,251
U.S.S.R.	1,400	490	4,767
United Kingdom	2,430	406	5,398
U.S.A.	5,160	663	11,611

* Probably overestimated.

Sources: World Bank Atlas, Washington, 1973; *UN Statistical Yearbook*, New York, 1973.

TRANSPORT

Railways (1959): Freight carried 542 million tons.

Roads (1959): Freight carried by lorry 344 million tons.

Merchant Shipping Fleet (1973): 1.5 million gross registered tons.

Inland and Coastal Shipping (1959): Freight carried 121 million tons.

Civil Aviation: Freight (1959) 1,630,000 ton-kilometres.

COMMUNICATIONS MEDIA

Radio Receivers (1970)	12 million
Television Receivers (1970)	300,000
Newspapers (daily circ.)	12 million
Cinema Attendance (per year)	4,000 million

EDUCATION

(1959)

	Pupils
Primary Schools	90,000,000
Middle Schools	10,900,000
Higher Education Establishments	810,000

University Graduates (1962): 220,000.

Estimates by W. Klatt.

THE CONSTITUTION

The 1954 Constitution of the People's Republic of China was revised by the Tenth National Congress of the Communist Party of China, and a new constitution was adopted by the Fourth National People's Congress on January 17th, 1975. The 106 articles of the 1954 Constitution were reduced to 30, and a number of significant changes in the theory and structure of government were made. The provisions of the 1975 Constitution are as follows:

Preamble

(*Summary*)

Socialist society extends over a fairly long historical period. Throughout this period classes, class contradictions and class struggle exist, as well as the struggle between the socialist and capitalist roads, the danger of a restoration of capitalism and the threat of subversion and aggression by imperialism and social-imperialism. China will never be a super-power. We must strengthen our unity with the socialist countries and with all oppressed peoples and nations, and work for peaceful co-existence with countries having different social systems.

Chapter 1. General Principles

Article 1—The People's Republic of China is a socialist state of the dictatorship of the proletariat led by the working class and based on the alliance of workers and peasants.

Article 2: Communist Party—The Communist Party of China is the core of leadership of the whole Chinese people. The working class exercises leadership over the state through its vanguard, the Communist Party of China.

Marxism-Leninism-Mao Tse-tung thought is the theoretical basis guiding the thinking of our nation.

Article 3: People's Congresses—All power in the People's Republic of China belongs to the people. The organs through which the people exercise power are the people's congresses at all levels, with deputies of workers, peasants and soldiers as their main body.

The people's congresses at all levels and all other organs of state practise democratic centralism.

Deputies to the people's congresses at all levels are elected through democratic consultation. The electoral units and electors have the power to supervise the deputies they elect and to replace them at any time according to provisions of law.

Article 4—The People's Republic of China is a unitary multi-national state. The areas where regional national autonomy is exercised are all inalienable parts of the People's Republic of China.

All the nationalities are equal. Great power chauvinism and local national chauvinism must be opposed.

All the nationalities have the freedom to use their own spoken and written languages.

Article 5—In the People's Republic of China, there are mainly two kinds of ownership of the means of production at the present stage: socialist ownership by the whole people and socialist collective ownership by working people.

The state may allow non-agricultural individual labourers to engage in individual labour involving no exploitation of others, within the limits permitted by law and under unified arrangement by neighbourhood organizations in cities and towns or by production teams in rural people's communes. At the same time, these individual labourers should be guided on to the road of socialist collectivization step by step.

Article 6: The Economy—The state sector of the economy is the leading force in the national economy.

All mineral resources and waters as well as the forests, undeveloped land and other resources owned by the state are the property of the whole people.

The state may requisition by purchase, take over for use, or nationalize urban and rural land as well as other means of production under conditions prescribed by law.

Article 7—The rural people's commune is an organization which integrates government administration and economic management.

The economic system of collective ownership in the rural people's communes at the present stage generally takes the form of three-level ownership with the production team at the basic level, that is, ownership by the commune, the production brigade and the production team, with the last as the basic accounting unit.

Provided that the development and absolute predominance of the collective economy of the people's commune are ensured, people's commune members may farm small plots for their personal needs, engage in limited household sideline production, and in pastoral areas keep a small number of livestock for their personal needs.

Article 8—Socialist public property shall be inviolable. The state shall ensure the consolidation and development of the socialist economy and prohibit any person from undermining the socialist economy and the public interest in any way whatsoever.

Article 9—The state applies the socialist principle: "He who does not work, neither shall he eat" and "From each according to his ability, to each according to his work".

The state protects the citizens' right of ownership to their incomes from work, their savings, their houses, and other means of livelihood.

Article 10—The state applies the principle of taking hold of revolution, promoting production and other work and preparedness against war; promotes the planned and proportionate development of the socialist economy, taking agriculture as the foundation and industry as the leading factor and bringing the initiative of both the central and the local authorities into full play; and improve the people's material and cultural life step by step on the basis of the constant growth of social production and consolidates the independence and security of the country.

Article 11—State organizations and state personnel must earnestly study Marxism-Leninism-Mao Tse-tung thought, firmly put proletarian politics in command, combat bureaucracy, maintain close ties with the masses and whole-heartedly serve the people. Cadres at all levels must participate in collective productive labour.

Every organ of state must apply the principle of efficient and simple administration. Its leading body must be a three-in-one combination of the old, the middle-aged and the young.

Article 12—The proletariat must exercise all-round dictatorship over the bourgeoisie in public life, including all spheres of culture. Culture and education, literature and art, physical education, health work and scientific research work must all serve proletarian politics, serve the workers, peasants and soldiers, and be combined with productive labour.

Article 13—Speaking out freely, airing views fully, holding debates and writing big-character posters are new forms of carrying on socialist revolution created by the masses of the people. The state shall ensure to the masses the right to use these forms to create a political situation in which there are both centralism and democracy, both discipline and freedom, both unity of will and personal ease of mind and liveliness, and so help consolidate the leadership of the Communist Party of China over the state and consolidate the dictatorship of the proletariat.

Article 14—The state safeguards the socialist system, suppresses all treasonable and counter-revolutionary activities and punishes all traitors and counter-revolutionaries.

The state deprives the landlords, rich peasants, reactionary capitalists and other bad elements of political rights for specified periods of time according to law, and at the same time provides them with the opportunity to earn a living so that they may be reformed through labour and become law-abiding citizens supporting themselves by their own labour.

Article 15: Armed Forces—The Chinese People's Liberation Army and the people's militia are the workers' and peasants' own armed forces led by the Communist Party of China; they are the armed forces of the people of all nationalities.

The chairman of the Central Committee of the Communist Party of China commands the country's armed forces.

The Chinese People's Liberation Army is at all times a fighting force, and simultaneously a working force and a production force.

The task of the armed forces of the People's Republic of China is to safeguard the achievements of the socialist revolution and socialist construction, to defend the sovereignty, territorial integrity and security of the state, and to guard against subversion and aggression by imperialism, social-imperialism and their lackeys.

Chapter 2. The Structure of the State

Section I. THE NATIONAL PEOPLE'S CONGRESS

Article 16—The National People's Congress is the highest organ of state power under the leadership of the Communist Party of China.

The National People's Congress is composed of deputies elected by the provinces, autonomous regions, municipalities directly under the central government, and the People's Liberation Army. When necessary, a certain number of patriotic personages may be specially invited to take part as deputies.

The National People's Congress is elected for a term of five years. Its term of office may be extended under special circumstances.

The National People's Congress holds one session each year. When necessary, the session may be advanced or postponed.

Article 17: Functions—The functions and powers of the National People's Congress are: to amend the constitution, make laws, appoint and remove the premier of the State Council and the members of the State Council on the proposal of the Central Committee of the Communist Party of China, approve the national economic plan, the state budget and the final state accounts, and exercise such other functions and powers as the National People's Congress deems necessary.

Article 18: Standing Committee—The Standing Committee of the National People's Congress is the permanent organ of the National People's Congress. Its functions and powers are: to convene the sessions of the National People's Congress, interpret laws, enact decrees, dispatch and recall plenipotentiary representatives abroad, receive foreign diplomatic envoys, ratify and denounce treaties concluded with foreign states, and exercise such other functions and powers as are vested in it by the National People's Congress.

The Standing Committee of the National People's Congress is composed of the chairman, the vice-chairman and other members, all of whom are elected and subject to recall by the National People's Congress.

Section II. THE STATE COUNCIL

Article 19—The State Council is the central people's government. The State Council is responsible and accountable to the National People's Congress and its Standing Committee.

The State Council is composed of the premier, the vice-premiers, the ministers, and the ministers heading commissions.

Article 20: Functions—The functions and powers of the State Council are: to formulate administrative measures and issue decisions and orders in accordance with the Constitution, laws and decrees; exercise unified leadership over the work of ministries and commissions and local organs of state at various levels throughout the country; draft and implement the national economic plan and the state budget; direct state administrative affairs; and exercise such other functions and powers as are vested in it by the National People's Congress or its Standing Committee.

Section III. THE LOCAL PEOPLE'S CONGRESSES AND THE LOCAL REVOLUTIONARY COMMITTEES AT VARIOUS LEVELS

Article 21: Local People's Congresses—The local people's congresses at various levels are the local organs of state power.

The people's congresses of provinces and municipalities directly under the central government are elected for a term of five years. The people's congresses of prefectures, cities and counties are elected for a term of three years. The people's congresses of rural people's communes and towns are elected for a term of two years.

Article 22: Local Revolutionary Committees—The local revolutionary committees at various levels are the permanent organs of the local people's congresses and at the same time the local people's governments at various levels.

Local revolutionary committees are composed of a chairman, vice-chairmen and other members, who are elected and subject to recall by the people's congress at the corresponding level. Their election or recall shall be submitted for examination and approval to the organ of state at the next higher level.

Local revolutionary committees are responsible and accountable to the people's congress at the corresponding level and to the organ of state at the next higher level.

Article 23: Functions—The local people's congresses at various levels and the local revolutionary committees elected by them ensure the execution of laws and decrees in their respective areas; lead the socialist revolution and socialist construction in their respective areas; examine and approve local economic plans,. budgets and final accounts; maintain revolutionary order; and safeguard the rights of citizens.

SECTION IV. THE ORGANS OF SELF-GOVERNMENT OF NATIONAL AUTONOMOUS AREAS

Article 24—The autonomous regions, autonomous prefectures and autonomous counties are all national autonomous areas; their organs of self-government are people's congresses and revolutionary committees.

The organs of self-government of national autonomous areas, apart from exercising the functions and powers of local organs of state as specified in Chapter 2, Section III of the Constitution, may exercise autonomy within the limits of their authority as prescribed by law.

The higher organs of state fully safeguard the exercise of autonomy by the organs of self-government of national autonomous areas and actively support the minority nationalities in carrying out the socialist revolution and socialist construction.

SECTION V. THE JUDICIAL ORGANS AND THE PROCURATORIAL ORGANS

Article 25—The Supreme People's Court, local people's courts at various levels and special people's courts exercise judicial authority. The people's courts are responsible and accountable to the people's congresses and their permanent organs at the corresponding levels. The presidents of the people's courts are appointed and subject to removal by the permanent organs of the people's congresses at the corresponding levels.

The functions and powers of procuratorial organs are exercised by the organs of public security at various levels.

The mass line must be applied in procuratorial work and in trying cases. In major counter-revolutionary criminal cases the masses should be mobilized for discussion and criticism.

Chapter 3. The Fundamental Rights and Duties of Citizens

Article 26—The fundamental rights and duties of citizens are to support the leadership of the Communist Party of China, support the socialist system and abide by the Constitution and the laws of the People's Republic of China.

It is the exalted duty of every citizen to defend the motherland and resist aggression. It is the honourable obligation of citizens to perform military service according to law.

Article 27—All citizens who have reached the age of eighteen have the right to vote and stand for election, with the exception of persons deprived of these rights by law.

Citizens have the right to work and the right to education. Working people have the right to rest and the right to material assistance in old age and in case of illness or disability.

Citizens have the right to lodge to organs of state at any level written or oral complaints of transgression of law or neglect of duty on the part of any person working in an organ of state. No one shall attempt to hinder or obstruct the making of such complaints or retaliate.

Women enjoy equal rights with men in all respects.

The state protects marriage, the family, and the mother and child.

The state protects the just rights and interests of Overseas Chinese.

Article 28—Citizens enjoy freedom of speech, correspondence, the press, assembly, association, procession, demonstration and the freedom to strike, and enjoy freedom to believe in religion and freedom not to believe in religion and to propagate atheism.

The citizens' freedom of person and their homes shall be inviolable. No citizen may be arrested except by decision of a people's court or with the sanction of a public security organ.

Article 29—The People's Republic of China grants the right of residence to any foreign national persecuted for supporting a just cause, for taking part in revolutionary movements or for engaging in scientific activities.

Chapter 4. The National Flag, the National Emblem and the Capital

Article 30—The national flag has five stars on a field of red.

The national emblem: Tien An Men in the centre, illuminated by five stars and encircled by ears of grain and a cogwheel.

The capital is Peking.

THE GOVERNMENT

HEAD OF STATE

The functions of Head of State are exercised by the Standing Committee of the National People's Congress.

STATE COUNCIL

(Appointed by the Fourth National People's Congress, January 17th, 1975)

(*July* 1976)

Premier: HUA KUO-FENG.

Vice-Premiers:

LI HSIEN-NIEN
CHI TENG-KUEI
CHEN YUNG-KUEI
WANG CHEN
KU MU
CHANG CHUN-CHIAO
Gen. CHEN HSI-LIEN
WU KUEI-HSIEN
YU CHIU-LI
SUN CHIEN

Minister of Foreign Affairs: CHIAO KUAN-HUA.

Minister of National Defence: Marshal YEH CHIEN-YING.

Minister in charge of the State Planning Commission: YU CHIU-LI.

Minister in charge of the State Capital Construction Commission: KU MU.

Minister of Public Security: HUA KUO-FENG.

Minister of Foreign Trade: LI CH'IANG.

Minister of Economic Relations with Foreign Countries: Fang Yi.

Minister of Agriculture and Forestry: Sha Feng.

Minister of the Metallurgical Industry: Chen Shao-kun.

First Minister of Mechanical Industry: Li Shui-ching.

Second Minister of Mechanical Industry: Liu Hsi-yao.

Third Minister of Mechanical Industry: Li Chi-tai.

Fourth Minister of Mechanical Industry: Wang Cheng.

Fifth Minister of Mechanical Industry: Li Cheng-fang.

Sixth Minister of Mechanical Industry: Pien Chiang.

Seventh Minister of Mechanical Industry: Wang Yang.

Minister of the Coal Industry: (vacant).

Minister of the Petroleum and Chemical Industry: Kang Shih-en.

Minister of Water Conservancy and Electric Power: Chien Cheng-ying.

Minister of Light Industry: Chien Chih-kuang.

Minister of Railways: Wan Li.

Minister of Posts and Telecommunications: Chung Fu-hsiang.

Minister of Finance: Chang Ching-fu.

Minister of Commerce: Fan Tzu-yu.

Minister of Culture: Yu Hui-yung.

Minister of Education: (vacant).

Minister of Public Health: Liu Hsiang-ping.

Minister in charge of the Physical Culture and Sports Commission: Chuang Tse-tung.

Minister of Communications: Yeh Fei.

SPECIAL AGENCIES OF THE STATE COUNCIL

The People's Bank of China: President Chen Hsi-yu.

Central Meteorological Bureau: Director Meng Ping.

State Oceanography Bureau: Director Chou Shao-t'ang.

Civil Aviation Administration of China (CAAC): Director Kuang Jen-nung.

New China News Agency: Director Chu Mu-chih.

Central Broadcasting Administration: Director-General Mei Yi.

China Travel and Tourism Bureau: Deputy Director Li Ch'uan-chung.

Cultural Group: Head Wu Teh.

Foreign Affairs Bureau: Acting Director Li Po-shih.

Government Officers' Administration Bureau: Director Kao Teng-pang.

Publishing Department: Directors Liu Mei, Wang Chi-sheng.

Scientific and Education Group: Head Liu Hsi-yao.

Supervisory and Guidance Group for Libraries, Museums and Work on Cultural Relics: Acting Director Wang Yeh-chiu.

Staff Office: Acting Director Ting Chiang.

Telecommunications Administration: Director Chung Fu-hsiang.

FOREIGN ECONOMIC RELATIONS ADMINISTRATION SUBORDINATED TO THE STATE COUNCIL

Staff Office for Finance and Trade
China Committee for the Promotion of International Trade
China Council for the Promotion of International Trade
Ministry of Foreign Trade
National Corporations (Export and Import)
Diplomatic Missions
Trade Missions
People's Bank of China
Bank of China
Foreign Economic Relations Commission
Foreign Aid and Technical Assistance Missions

NATIONAL PEOPLE'S CONGRESS

The National People's Congress is the highest organ of state power under the leadership of the Communist Party of China. Its structure and functions are described in Articles 16–18 of the constitution (*see* page 744). The First Session of the Fourth National People's Congress (the Third National People's Congress was held in 1964) was held in Peking from January 13th to 17th, 1975. 2,885 deputies had been elected from all parts of the country and 2,864 deputies attended the Congress.

FOURTH CONGRESS

Permanent Chairmen of Presidium:

Soong Ching-ling
Liu Po-chien
Wu Teh
Wei Kuo-ching
Saifudin,
Kuo Mo-jo
Hsu Hsiang-chien
Marshal Nieh Jung-chen
Chen Yun.
Tan Chen-lin
Li Ching-chuan
Chang Ting-cheng
Tsai Chang
Ulanfu
Ngapo Ngawang-jigme
Chou Chien-jen
Hsu Teh-heng
Hu Chueh-wen
Li Su-wen
Yao Lien-wei

STANDING COMMITTEE

Chairman: (vacant).

Vice-Chairmen:

Yao Wen-yuan
Soong Ching-ling
Liu Po-cheng
Wu Teh
Wei Kuo-ching
Saifudin
Kuo Mo-jo
Hsu Hsiang-chien
Marshal Nieh Jung-chen
Chen Yun
Tan Chen-lin
Li Ching-chuan
Chang Ting-cheng
Tsai Chang
Ulanfu
Ngapo Ngawang-jigme
Chou Chien-jen
Hsu Teh-heng
Hu Chueh-wen
Li Su-wen
Yao Lien-wei

Secretary-General: Chi Peng-fei.

There were 144 members of the Standing Committee in 1975.

PROVINCIAL GOVERNMENTS

REVOLUTIONARY COMMITTEES

Revolutionary Committees were established to administer each of the 29 provinces, special municipalities and autonomous regions in 1967 and 1968 during the "Great Proletarian Cultural Revolution" and received official recognition in the January 1975 constitution.

Province	Chairman of Committee
Szechwan	LIU HSING-YUAN.
Shantung	YANG TEH-CHIH
Honan	LIU CHIEN-HSUN
Kiangsu	HSU SHIH-YU
Hopei	LIU TZU-HOU
Kwangtung	WEI KUO-CHING
Hunan	HUA KUO-FENG
Anhwei	SUNG PEI-CHANG
Hupeh	CHAO HSIN-CHU
Chekiang	NAN PING
Liaoning	TSENG SHAO-SHAN
Yunnan	CHIA CHI-YUN
Kiangsi	CHENG SHIH-CHING
Shensi	LI JUI-SHAN
Kweichow	LI TSAI-HAN
Shansi	WANG CHIEN
Heilungkiang	WANG CHIA-TAO

Province	Chairman of Committee
Fukien	HAN HSIEN-CH'U
Kansu	HSIEN HENG-HAN
Kirin	WANG HUAI-HSIANG
Tsinghai	LIU HSIEN-CHUAN
Special Municipalities	
Peking	WU TEH
Shanghai	CHANG CH'UN-CH'IAO
Tientsin	HSIEH HSUEH-KUNG
Autonomous Regions	
Mongolia (Inner)	YU TAI-CHUNG
Sinkiang	SAIFUDIN
Ninghsia Hui	K'ANG CHIEN-MIN
Tibet	JEN JUNG
Kwangsi	(vacant)

COMMUNIST PARTY

The Chinese Communist Party is defined in the 1975 constitution as "the core of leadership of the whole Chinese people". There are about 28 million members (1974). Although the National People's Congress is the highest organ of state power, it exercises it under the leadership of the Communist Party. The First Plenary Session of the Tenth Central Committee was held in August 1973, and the Second Plenary Session was held from January 8th to 10th, 1975.

TENTH CENTRAL COMMITTEE

Chairman: (vacant).

First Vice-Chairman: HUA KUO-FENG

Vice-Chairmen:
WANG HUNG-WEN
Marshal YEH CHIEN-YING

There are 309 Members and Alternate Members of the Tenth Central Committee.

POLITBURO

Members of the Standing Committee:

WANG HUNG-WEN
Marshal YEH CHIEN-YING
HUA KUO-FENG
CHANG CH'UN-CH'IAO

Other Full Members:

LIU PO-CHENG
CHIANG CHING
HSU SHIH-YU
CHI TENG-KUEI
WU TEH
Gen. LI TEH-SHENG
WANG TUNG-HSING
CHEN YUNG-KUEI
Gen. CHEN HSI-LIEN
LI HSIEN-NIEN
YAO WEN-YUAN
WEI KUO-CHING

Alternate Members: WU KUEI-HSIEN, SU CHEN-HUA, NI CHI-FU, SAIFUDIN.

OTHER POLITICAL BODIES

Kuomintang Revolutionary Committee: Chair. HO HSIANG-NING.

China Democratic League.

China Democratic National Constructional Association.

China Association for Promoting Democracy: Chair. MA HSU-LUN

China Peasants and Workers' Democratic Party: Chair. CHI FANG.

China Chih Kung Tang: Chair. CH'EN CH'I-YU.

Chiu San Society: Chair. HSU TE-HENG.

Taiwan Democratic Self-Government League: Vice-Chair. LI CH'UN-CH'ING.

PROVINCIAL PARTY COMMITTEES

Since November 1970, 29 provincial party committees have been established; the previous party structure was destroyed during the "Great Proletarian Cultural Revolution". The following have been formed:

Province	*First Secretary*
Hunan	Hua Kuo-feng
Kiangsu	Hsu Shih-yu
Kwangtung	Wei Kuo-ching
Liaoning	Tseng Shao-shan
Anhwei	Sung Pei-chang
Chekiang	T'an Ch'i-lung
Kansu	Hsien Heng-han
Honan	Liu Chien-hsun
Shensi	Li Jui-shan
Tsinghai	Liu Hsien-chuan
Kirin	Wang Huai-hsiang
Hupeh	Chao Hsin-chu
Fukien	Liao Chih-kao
Shantung	Yang Teh-chih
Shansi	Wang Chien
Kweichow	Lu Jui-lin
Hopei	Liu Tzu-hou
Yunnan	Chia Chi-yun
Szechwan	Chao Tzu-yang
Heilungkiang (Manchuria)	Wang Chia-tao
Kiangsi	Cheng Shih-ching
Special Municipalities	
Shanghai	Chang Ch'un-ch'iao
Peking	Wu Teh
Tientsin	Hsieh Hsueh-kung
Autonomous Regions	
Sinkiang	Saifudin
Mongolia (Inner)	Yu Tai-chung
Tibet	Jen Jung
Ninghsia Hui	K'ang Chien-min
Kwangsi	(vacant)

THE PEOPLE'S LIBERATION ARMY

Apart from its strategic role as a defensive force, the People's Liberation Army is closely tied to the political leadership of the country and is recognized in the constitution as having an important part to play in civil life. It is divided into eleven major Military Regions, and further divided into a number of Military Districts.

Commander-in-Chief: (vacant).

Chief of General Staff: (vacant).

Chief of the General Political Department (Chief Political Commissar): Chang Ch'un-ch'iao.

Political Commissar: Hsiang Chung-hua.

Commander, PLA Navy: Hsiao Ching-Kuang.

Commander, PLA Air Force: Ma Ning.

Head, Armament Department, General Logistics Department: Yuan Hua-ping.

Military Region	*Commander*
Canton	Hsu Shih-yu
Chengtu	Chin Chi-wei
Foochow	(vacant)
Kunming	Wang Pi-cheng
Lanchow	Han Hsien-chu
Nanking	Ting Sheng
Peking	Chen Hsi-lien
Shenyang	Li Te-sheng
Sinkiang	Tsao Ssu-ming
Tsinan	Tseng Ssu-yu
Wuhan	Yang Te-chih

DIPLOMATIC REPRESENTATION

EMBASSIES ACCREDITED TO THE PEOPLE'S REPUBLIC OF CHINA
(Peking)

Afghanistan: *Ambassador:* Mohamed Assaf Sohail.

Albania: *Ambassador:* Behar Shtylla.

Algeria: *Ambassador:* Mohamed Cherif Sahli (also accred. to Mongolia).

Argentina: *Ambassador:* Dr. Eduardo Bradley.

Australia: 47 San Li Tun; *Ambassador:* Dr. Stephen Fitzgerald.

Austria: *Ambassador:* Franz H. Leitner.

Belgium: *Ambassador:* Jacques Groothaert.

Benin: *Chargé d'Affaires:* (also accred. to the Democratic People's Republic of Korea).

Brazil: *Chargé d'Affaires a.i.*

Bulgaria: *Chargé d'Affaires a.i.*

Burma: *Chargé d'Affaires a.i.* (also accred. to Mongolia).

Cameroon: *Ambassador:* Clement Langue Toobgny.

Canada: *Ambassador:* John Small.

Chad: *Chargé d'Affaires a.i.*

Congo People's Republic: *Ambassador:* Claude-Earnest Ndalla.

Cuba: *Chargé d'Affaires a.i.*

Cyprus: *Chargé d'Affaires a.i.*

Czechoslovakia: *Ambassador:* Stanislav Kohousek.

Denmark: *Chargé d'Affaires a.i.*

Egypt: *Ambassador:* Salah el Den A. el Abd.

Equatorial Guinea: *Chargé d'Affaires a.i.*

Ethiopia: *Chargé d'Affaires a.i.*

Finland: *Ambassador:* Veli Helenius.

France: *Ambassador:* Claude Arnaud.

Gabon: *Ambassador:* Christophe Boupana.

Gambia: *Chargé d'Affaires a.i.*

German Democratic Republic: *Ambassador:* HELMUT LIEBERMANN.

Germany, Federal Republic: *Ambassador:* ROLF PAULS.

Greece: *Chargé d'Affaires a.i.*

Guinea: *Ambassador:* KAMANA ANSOU (also accred. to Pakistan).

Guyana: *Ambassador:* (to be appointed).

Hungary: 14 San Li Tun, Peking 2; *Ambassador:* JÓZSEF HALASZ.

Iceland: *Chargé d'Affaires a.i.*

India: *Chargé d'Affaires a.i.:* KOCHERIL RAMAN NARAYANAN.

Iran: *Ambassador:* ABBAS ARAM.

Iraq: *Chargé d'Affaires a.i.:* OTHMAN HUSSEIN AL-ANI.

Italy: *Ambassador:* FOLCO TRABALZA.

Jamaica: *Chargé d'Affaires a.i.*

Japan: *Ambassador:* HEISHIRO OGAWA.

Korea, Democratic People's Republic: *Ambassador:* HYUN JUN KENK.

Kuwait: *Chargé d'Affaires a.i.*

Laos: *Ambassador:* (to be appointed).

Lebanon: *Ambassador:* ELIE J. BONSTANY.

Madagascar: *Chargé d'Affaires a.i.*

Malaysia: *Chargé d'Affaires a.i.*

Maldives: *Chargé d'Affaires a.i.*

Mali: *Ambassador:* ASSANE GUINDO.

Malta: *Chargé d'Affaires a.i.*

Mauritania: *Ambassador:* MOHAMED A. O. KHARACHY (also accred. to Pakistan).

Mauritius: *Chargé d'Affaires a.i.*

Mexico: *Ambassador:* EUGENIO A. ROCH.

Mongolia: *Ambassador:* DONDOGIYN TSEVEGMID (also accred. to Pakistan).

Morocco: *Ambassador:* ABDELLATIF LAKHMIRI.

Nepal: 27 Kan Mein Hutung; *Ambassador:* CHELTRA BIKRAM RAMA.

Netherlands: 2 San Li Tun; *Ambassador:* J. J. DERKSEN.

New Zealand: *Chargé d'Affaires a.i.*

Nigeria: *Ambassador:* J. TANKO YUSUF.

Norway: *Ambassador:* OLE AALGAARD.

Pakistan: 16 San Li Tun; *Ambassador:* Khwaja MOHAMMAD KAISER.

Peru: *Chargé d'Affaires a.i.*

Philippines: *Chargé d'Affaires:* RAFAEL GONZALEZ.

Poland: *Ambassador:* WITOLD RODZINSKY.

Qatar: *Chargé d'Affaires a.i.*

Romania: *Ambassador:* AUREL DUMA.

Senegal: *Ambassador:* ALY DIOURI.

Sierra Leone: *Chargé d'Affaires a.i.*

Spain: *Ambassador:* ANGEL SANZ BRIZ.

Sri Lanka: *Ambassador:* D. B. R. GUNAWARDENA (also accred. to Mongolia).

Sudan *Ambassador:* FAKREDDINE MOHAMED.

Sweden: *Ambassador:* KAJE BJORK.

Switzerland: *Ambassador:* OSCAR ROSETTI.

Syria: *Ambassador:* YOUSSEF CHAKRA.

Tanzania: *Ambassador:* JOB LUSINDE (also accred. to the Democratic People's Republic of Korea).

Thailand: *Ambassador:* KASEMSAMORSORN KASEMSRI (also accred. to the Democratic People's Republic of Korea).

Togo: *Chargé d'Affaires a.i.*

Turkey: *Chargé d'Affaires a.i.*

Uganda: *Chargé d'Affaires a.i.*

U.S.S.R.: *Ambassador:* VASILY TOLSTIKOV.

United Kingdom: *Ambassador:* EDWARD YOUDE.

* **U.S.A.:** Liaison Office; *Head:* THOMAS GATES.

Venezuela: *Chargé d'Affaires a.i.*

Viet-Nam: *Ambassador:* NGUYEN TRONG VINH (also accred. to Pakistan).

Yemen Arab Republic: *Ambassador:* ABDOL WAHED AL-KHERBASH.

Yemen, People's Democratic Republic: *Chargé d'Affaires a.i.:* ABDULLA ABODAH HAMAM.

Yugoslavia: *Ambassador:* A. ORESCHANIN.

Zaire: *Ambassador:* ANREA SYLVESTER MASIYE.

Zambia: *Ambassador:* PHILEMON NGOMA.

China also has diplomatic relations with Bangladesh, Botswana, Cambodia, Cape Verde, Fiji, Mozambique, Niger, Surinam and Trinidad and Tobago. Consular relations have been established with San Marino and Luxembourg.

* Liaison office opened in 1973, preparatory to establishment of full diplomatic relations, when the problem of U.S. recognition of Taiwan is resolved.

JUDICIAL SYSTEM

The general principles of the Chinese judicial system are laid down in Article 25 of the January 1975 constitution.

PEOPLE'S COURTS

Supreme People's Court: Peking; f. 1949; the highest judicial organ of the State. Directs and supervises work of lower courts.

President of the Supreme People's Court: CHIANG HUA; term of office four years.

Vice-Presidents: HO LAN-CHIEH, HSING YI-MIN, TSENG HAN-CHOU, WANG-TEH-MAO, CHANG CHIH-JANG, CH'EN CHI-HAN, WANG WEI-KANG, WU TE-FENG, T'AN KUAN-SAN.

Special People's Courts.

Local People's Courts.

PEOPLE'S PROCURATORATES

Supreme People's Procuratorate: Peking; acts for the National People's Congress in examining government departments, civil servants and citizens, to ensure observance of the law; prosecutes in criminal cases.

Chief Procurator: CHANG TING-CHENG elected by N.P.C. for four years.

Deputy Chief Procurators: HUANG HUO-HSING, CHANG SU.

Local People's Procuratorates: undertake the same duties at the local level. Ensure that the judicial activities of the people's courts, the execution of sentences in criminal cases, and the activities of departments in charge of reform through labour, conform to the law; institutes, or intervenes in, important civil cases which affect the interest of the State and the people.

RELIGION

The practice of religious belief is not encouraged. Below are listed the dominant religions which prevailed before 1949.

ANCESTOR WORSHIP

Ancestor worship is believed to have originated with the deification and worship of all important natural phenomena. The divine and human were not clearly defined; all the dead became gods and were worshipped by their descendants. The practice has no code or dogma and the ritual is limited to sacrifices made during festivals and on birth and death anniversaries.

CONFUCIANISM

Confucianism is a philosophy and a system of ethics, without ritual or priesthood. The respects accorded Confucius are not paid to a prophet or god, but to a great sage whose teachings promote peace and good order in society and whose philosophy encourages moral living. The teachings of Confucius were officially criticized at the Fourth National People's Congress in January 1975.

TAOISM

China Taoist Association: Peking; Chair. CH'EN YINGNING.

Taoism originated as a philosophy expounded by Lao Tse, born 604 B.C. The establishment of a religion was contrary to his doctrines, but seven centuries after his death his teachings were embodied into a ritual.

BUDDHISM

Chinese Buddhist Association: f. 1953; Pres. SHIROB-JALTSO; Sec.-Gen. CHAO P'U-CH'U.

Buddhism was introduced in China from India in A.D. 61, and now bears little resemblance to the religion in its original form, a number of native Chinese legends, traditions, rites and deities having been added. The "secularization" of Buddhist monasteries has resulted in the evacuation of many, particularly in Tibet.

ISLAM

China Islamic Association: Peking; f. 1953; Chair, BURHAN SHAHIDI.

According to Muslim history, Islam was introduced into China in A.D. 651. Its number of adherents in China is estimated at about 10 million, chiefly among the Uighur and Hui people.

CHRISTIANITY

During the 19th century and the first half of the 20th large numbers of foreign Christian missionaries worked in China. The Chinese People's Republic has steadily discouraged all foreign influences in Chinese religious affairs.

Roman Catholic Church: Catholic Mission, Si-She-Ku, Peiping, Hopeh.

THE PRESS

Only the major newspapers and periodicals are listed below and only a very restricted number are allowed abroad.

PRINCIPAL DAILIES

Hunan Daily: Changsa, Hunan.

Kwangming Daily (*Kwangming Ribao*): Peking; f. 1949.

Liberation Army Daily (*Jiefangjun Bao*): Peking; f. 1949; official organ of the P.L.A.

Liberation Daily (*Jiefang Ribao*): Shanghai; f. 1949.

Peking Daily (*Beijing Ribao*): Peking.

People's Daily (*Renmin Ribao*): Wang Fu Ching St., Peking; f. 1948; organ of the Communist Party of China; 200 staff including 70 foreign affairs specialists; Editor YAO WEN-YUAN; circ. 3,400,000.

Reference News (*Tsan Kao Hsiao Hsi*); Peking; reprints from foreign newspapers; circ. 8,000,000.

Szechwan Daily: Chengtu, Szechwan.

Takong Daily (*Wen Hui Pao*): Shanghai.

Tibet Daily: Lhasa, Tibet.

PERIODICALS

China Pictorial: Peking, monthly; published in 16 languages, including English.

China Reconstructs: China Welfare Institute, Peking; monthly, economic, social and cultural affairs; illustrated; English, Spanish, French, Russian and Arabic.

Chinese Literature: Yu Cheou Hong, Peking 37; literary; includes reproductions of art works; monthly in English and French.

Peking Review: Peking 37; weekly; English, French, Spanish, Japanese and German.

Red Flag (*Hung Chi*): monthly; official organ of the Chinese Communist Party; Editor (vacant).

NEWS AGENCY

Hsinhua (New China) News Agency: 26 Kuo Huei Chieh, Peking; f. 1937; offices in all large Chinese towns and some foreign capitals; Dir. CHU MU-CHIH.

China News Service: Peking; f. 1952; supplies news for overseas Chinese newspapers and magazines and those printed in Hong Kong and Macao; service in Chinese.

FOREIGN BUREAUX

Agenzia Nazionale Stampa Associata (ANSA): Ban Gong Lou 2-81 San Li Tun, Peking; Italian news agency; Agent ADA PRINCIGALLI.

Bulgarian Telegraph Agency (BTA): Bulgarian Embassy, Peking; Bureau Chief YORDAN BOZHILOV

Reuters: 2–21 Ban Gong Lou, San Li Tun, Peking.

The following are also represented: Agence France-Presse, Czechoslovak News Agency (Četeka) and Tass.

PUBLISHERS

Publishing is carried on by central and local government departments, universities, scientific and learned societies, trade unions and cultural bodies, as well as by state and private publishing houses. All publishing is controlled by the Propaganda Department of the Party Central Committee.

Publishing Department: Peking; special agency of the State Council; undertakes the major part of book publishing in China.

China Youth Publishing House: Peking; f. 1953; books and periodicals.

Chung Hua Book Co.: Peking; state publishers; specializes in Chinese classics.

Commercial Press: Peking; state publishers; specializes in translation of foreign books on philosophy and social sciences.

Foreign Languages Press: Peking 37; state publishing house; publishes books and periodicals in foreign languages reflecting political, economic and cultural progress in People's Republic of China.

Guozi Shudian (*China Publications Centre*): P.O.B. 399, Peking; publishes periodicals, textbooks, etc. in English; import and export house.

Hsinhua (New China) Book Agency: Peking; since 1951 this agency has functioned as a national enterprise, publishing and distributing books for the State under the auspices of the Ministry of Culture and co-ordinating the activities of all other publishing houses.

National Minorities Publishing House: publishes books in Tibetan, Kazakh, S.E. language group, etc.

People's Educational Publishing House: Shanghai,

People's Literature Publishing House: Peking; Shanghai.

People's Physical Culture Publishing House: Peking, sports books and pictorial magazines.

Popular Press: caters for peasants.

San Lien Publishers: Peking; a state publishing house; general and political.

Workers' Press: Peking; publishing house of All China Federation of Trade Unions.

Writers' Publishing House: Peking; a state enterprise publishing reprints of Chinese literature.

Youth Publishing House: Peking.

RADIO AND TELEVISION

RADIO

Central Broadcasting Administration: Outside Fu Hsing Men, Peking; Dir.-Gen. MEI YI; controls the Central People's Broadcasting Station.

Central People's Broadcasting Station: Hsi Chang An Chieh 3, Peking; has five relay stations broadcasting 1,450 hours per week; also controls 117 local stations; domestic service in Chinese, Cantonese, Tibetan, Tai, Amoy, Hakka, Foochow dialect, Kazakh, Uighur, Mongolian and Korean; foreign service in English, Esperanto, French, German, Indonesian, Italian, Japanese, Portuguese and Spanish.

In 1972 there were about 10 million radio licences.

TELEVISION

Central People's Television Broadcasting Section: Peking Bureau of Broadcasting Affairs of the State Council; f. 1958.

There are thirteen television stations at Peking (2), Harbin, Shanghai, Canton, Tientsin, Changchung, Mukden (Shenyang), Sian, Taiyuan, Hofei, Nanking and Wuhan; also twelve experimental stations.

In 1972 there were an estimated 200,000 television receivers.

FINANCE

BANKING

People's Bank of China: 22 Hsi Chiao Min Hsiang, Peking; f. 1948; the state bank of the People's Republic of China; more than 34,000 brs.; Pres. CHEN HSI-YU; Vice-Pres. CHIAO PEI-HSIN.

Bank of China: 108 Hsi Chiao Min Hsiang, Peking; f. 1912; handles foreign exchange and international settlements; Gen. Man. KUNG YIN-PING.

Agricultural Bank of China: Peking; f. 1963; functions directly under the State Council and handles State agricultural investments; Pres. HU CHING-YUN.

People's Construction Bank of China: Ministry of Finance, Peking; f. 1954 to make payments for capital construction according to plan and budget approval by the State; issues short-term loans to State contractors.

Bank of Communications: Hsi Chiao Min Hsiang, Peking; f. 1908; operates for the Ministry of Finance; handles State investments in the joint state-private enterprises. Chair. JUNG TZU-HO; Gen. Man. CHANG PIN-CHIH.

Chekiang First Bank of Commerce Ltd.: 222 Kiangse Rd., Shanghai; f. 1948; 3 brs.

China and South Sea Bank Ltd.: 110 Hankow Rd., Shanghai; f. 1920; Chair. OEI KIEN-SOC.

Kincheng Banking Corporation: Shanghai; f. 1917; Gen. Man. TSE YAO-HWA.

National Commercial Bank Ltd.: Shanghai; f. 1907.

Shanghai Commercial and Savings Bank Ltd.: 50 Ningpo Rd., Shanghai; f. 1915.

FOREIGN BANKS

Chartered Bank: 10 Clements Lane, London, EC4N 7AA; f. 1853; P.O.B. 2135, 185 Yuan Ming Yuan Lu, Shanghai.

Hongkong and Shanghai Banking Corporation: 1 Queen's Rd. Central, Hong Kong; f. 1865; 185 Yuan Ming Yuan Rd., P.O.B. 151, Shanghai.

Oversea-Chinese Banking Corporation Ltd.: Upper Pickering St., Singapore 1; f. 1932; brs. in Amoy and Shanghai; Chair. Tan Sri TAN CHIN TUAN.

INSURANCE

China Insurance Company Ltd.: 34 Fa Ti Lu, Peking; f. 1931; freight and transport insurance and reinsurance.

People's Insurance Company of China, The: 34 Fa Ti Lu, Peking; f. 1949; hull, marine cargo, aviation, motor, fire and reinsurance, etc.

Tai Ping Insurance Co. Ltd.: 34 Fa Ti Lu, Peking; general insurance.

TRADE AND INDUSTRY

EXTERNAL TRADE

The structure of the administration of Foreign Economic Relations is given under "Government", *above*.

Ministry of Economic Relations with Foreign Countries: Peking; f. 1972; Minister FANG YI; Vice-Ministers HAN TSUNG-CHENG, CH'EN MU HUA, CHUNG YU-YI, HSIEH HUAI-TEH.

China Council for the Promotion of International Trade: Hsi Tan Bldg., Hsi Chang An Chieh, Peking; f. 1952; encourages foreign trade; arranges Chinese exhibitions at home and abroad; Chair. WANG YAO-TING; Vice-Chair. LI CHUAN.

EXPORT AND IMPORT CORPORATIONS

Subordinate to the Ministry of Foreign Trade.

China National Foreign Trade Transportation Corporation: Erh Li Kou, Hsi Chiao, Peking; arranges customs clearance, deliveries, forwarding and insurance.

China National Native Produce Animal By-products Import and Export Corporation: 82 Tung An Men St., Peking.

China National Cereals, Oils and Foodstuffs Import and Export Corporation: 82 Tung An Men St., Peking.

China National Chartering Corporation: Erh Li Kou, Hsi Chiao, Peking; chartering of ships.

China National Chemicals Import and Export Corporation: Erh Li Kou, Hsi Chiao, Peking; deals in rubber, petroleum, chemicals and drugs.

China National Complete Plant Export Corporation: Soochow Hutung, Peking.

China National Instruments Import and Export Corporation: Peking; Deputy Dir. CHENG CHI-HSIEN.

China National Light Industrial Products Import and Export Corporation: 82 Tung An Men St., Peking.

China National Machinery Import and Export Corporation: Erh Li Kou, Hsi Chiao, Peking.

China National Metals and Minerals Import and Export Corporation: Import Bldg., Erh Li Kou, Hsi Chiao; Peking; f. 1961; incorporating the former China National Metals Import Corporation and China National Minerals Corporation; Dir. HSIEH SHOU-TIEN.

China National Native Produce and Animal By-Products Import and Export Corporation: 82 Tung An Men St., Peking.

China National Technical Import Corporation: Erh Li Kou, Hsi Chiao, Peking; exports and imports; whole-plant projects and equipment.

China National Textile Import and Export Corporation: 82 Tung An Men St., Peking; Man. Dir. CHEN CHENG-CHUNG.

Guozi Shudian: P.O.B. 399, Peking; exporters of books and periodicals.

Sinofracht Ship Chartering and Broking Corporation: Erh Li Kou, Hsi Chiao, Peking.

Waiwen Shudian: P.O.B. 88, Peking; f. 1964; importers of books and periodicals.

INTERNAL TRADE

Central Administration of Industry and Commerce: Peking; under the direct supervision of the State Council; Dir. HSU TI-HSIN.

All-China Federation of Industry and Commerce: Peking; f. 1953; helps industry and traders to execute government policy; Sec.-Gen. HSIANG SHU-HSIANG; Members: Provincial Associations of Industry and Commerce; All-China Federation of Co-operatives; Central Organizations of the Joint State-Private Enterprises.

TRADE UNIONS

All-China Federation of Trade Unions: 1 Fu Chien St., Peking; f. 1948; affiliated to W.F.T.U.; organized on an industrial basis; 22 affiliated national industrial unions; membership is voluntary but some social benefits are open only to trade unionists; trade unions administer state social insurance; mems. about 16 million; Chair. LIU NING-YI.

TRADE FAIR

Chinese Export Commodities Fair: Canton; twice-yearly 15th April–15th May, 15th October–15th November.

TRANSPORT AND TOURISM

RAILWAYS

Ministry of Communications: Peking; controls all railways through regional divisions. The railway network has been extended to all provinces and regions except Tibet, where construction is in progress, and totalled over 36,000 km. in 1965, in addition to special railways serving factories and mines. Some of the major routes are Peking–Canton, Tientsin–Shanghai, Manchouli–Vladivostok, Chiaotso-Chihcheng. and Lanchow–Patao.

Note: An underground system for Peking is under construction which will run for 24 km. One route and 16 stations have been completed.

ROADS

There are about 500,000 km. of paved and unsurfaced roads. Four major highways have recently been completed linking Lhasa with Szechwan, Sinkiang, Kokonor and Katmandu. Further construction of mountain roads is under way.

INLAND WATERWAYS

General Inland Navigation Bureau: Controls river and canal traffic. There are 160,000 km. of inland waterways in China, 48,000 of which are open to steam navigation. The main rivers are the Yellow, Yangtze and Pearl.

The Yangtze is navigable by vessels of 10,000 tons as far as Wuhan, over 1,000 km. from the coast. Smaller vessels can continue to Chungking. Over one-third of internal freight traffic is carried by water.

SHIPPING

Ministry of Communications: Peking.

The greater part of China's shipping is handled in nine major ports: Dairen (Talien), Chinhuangtao, Hsinkang Tsingtao, Lienyunkang, Shanghai, Whampoa, Canton and Chanchiang (Liuchow). Two-thirds of the handling facilities are mechanical, and harbour improvement schemes are constantly in progress.

China Ocean Shipping Company: Chang An Rd., Peking; br. offices: Shanghai, Canton, Tientsin; the only Chinese line which operates its own shipping outside territorial waters; also operate chartered foreign ships.

FOREIGN LINES SERVING CHINA

Blue Funnel Line: Liverpool; services to Shanghai.,

Glen Line: London; services to Chinese ports.

CIVIL AVIATION

Civil Aviation Administration of China (CAAC): 15 Chang An St. East, Peking; f. 1950; controlled by General Bureau of Civil Aviation; Dir.-Gen. MA JEN-HUI; fleet of 5 Viscounts, 19 Ilyushin-18, 58 Ilyushin-14, 5 Ilyushin Il-62, 6 Boeing 707-320C, 4 707-320B, 2 Antonov An-24, one An-12, 26 Li-2, 300 An-2, 13 Super Frelon, 3 Trident 1E, 12 Trident 2E; 21 Trident 2E, 2 Trident 3B on order; 3 Concordes on option

China operates air routes totalling 43,200 km. 25,600 km. of which are internal. External flights are operated as follows: Peking–Tokyo, Peking–Karachi–Ankara–Athens–Rome, Peking–Teheran–Bucharest–Tirana, Peking–Shenyang–Pyongyang, Canton–Hanoi, Kunming–Rangoon, Peking–Moscow.

FOREIGN AIRLINES

Aeroflot: Moscow; 15 Chang An St. East, Peking; twice weekly service Moscow–Irkutsk–Peking.

Air France: Paris; Hotel Hsin Chiao, Room 355, Peking; twice-weekly service Paris–Athens–Karachi–Peking.

Civil Aviation Administration of the Democratic People's Republic of Korea: Pyongyang; c/o CAAC, Peking; weekly service Shenyang-Peking-Pyongyang.

Ethiopian Airlines: Addis Ababa; c/o CAAC, Peking; weekly service via Bombay to Peking.

Pakistan International Airlines Corporation: Karachi; c/o CAAC, Peking; London–Karachi–Islamabad–Peking–Shanghai, twice weekly.

Iran Air: c/o CAAC, 117 Wusze St., P.O.B. 644, Peking; twice-weekly service, Tokyo–Peking and Teheran.

Japan Airlines: Tokyo; Rm. 6087, Peking Hotel, Peking; flights Tokyo–Peking, Shanghai–Osaka–Tokyo.

Swissair: Rm. 6089, Peking Hotel, Peking; weekly service London-Geneva-Athens-Bombay-Peking.

There are plans for the following airlines to operate flights into China: Alitalia, British Airways, Canadian Pacific Airlines and Lufthansa.

TOURISM

China International Travel Service (Lüxingshe): Hsitan Building, Peking; makes travel arrangements for foreign parties; brs. in Canton, Shanghai and Hong Kong.

Chinese People's Association for Friendship with Foreign Countries: Peking; Pres. WANG PING-NAN; Vice-Pres. YANG CHI, TING HSUEH-SUNG, LI EN-CHIU, LIN LIN; Sec.-Gen. TING HSEUH-SUNG.

ATOMIC ENERGY

China was believed to have a total of about 40 nuclear reactors in operation at the end of 1966.

Atomic Energy Institute: Academia Sinica, Peking; contains an enriched uranium heavy water reactor and a cyclotron.

Atomic Research Centre: Tarim Basin, Sinkiang; f. 1953; Dir. WANG KAN-CHANG.

Military Scientific Council: Peking; Dir. Dr. CHIEN HSUEH-SAN.

Nuclear Institute of the Academia Sinica: Academia Sinica, 3 Wen Tsin Chen, Peking; Dir. CHEN SAN-CHIANG.

Tsinghua University: Peking; f. 1911; has built its own nuclear reactor; Prof. of Physics CHAO CHUNG-YAO.

DEFENCE

Armed Forces and Equipment (1975): Total 3,250,000; army 2,800,000, navy 230,000 (including naval air force and 28,000 marines), air force 220,000. The army is equipped with some early Soviet-made tanks and artillery but mostly with its own manufactured weapons. The navy has some 50 submarines and a variety of other vessels mainly deployed in three fleets, the North Sea (150 vessels), the East Sea, i.e. around the Chinese coast (500 vessels), and the South Sea mainly around North Viet-Nam and the Gulf of Tonkin (200 vessels). The air force has 3,800 combat planes including some Soviet aircraft. China also has 20–30 IRBM and about 50 MRBM. In addition to these forces there are about 300,000 security and border troops.

Defence Expenditure: Since 1960 China has issued no budget figures. Speculative estimates put defence spending at between U.S. $4,000 million and U.S. $12,000 million.

Military Service: Army 2–4 years; air force 3–5 years; navy 4–6 years.

CHIEFS OF STAFF

Chief of Staff (People's Liberation Army): (vacant).

Air Force Commander: MA NING.

Navy Commander: HSIAO CHING-KUANG.

Director-General, Political Department of the People's Liberation Army: CHANG CH'UN-CH'IAO.

EDUCATION

The aim of education in People's China is the transformation of society by the development of new patterns of thought and the discarding of traditions which hamper the growth of the communist state, together with the aim of training people in those disciplines which are dictated by the needs of the State. Experiment and changes of plan have characterized the period since 1949. Education policy has veered between the conflicting aims of the pursuit of scientific knowledge seen as an end in itself, and the abandonment of book learning in favour of practical experience. Ideology and indoctrination play a prominent part in educational curricula. Recently the Great Proletarian Cultural Revolution has sparked off a further reorganization and reorientation of the system, with still greater emphasis on student and worker participation, communist ideology and physical labour.

Historical Background

Education was fostered, in traditional Chinese society, both as a noble profession and as the principal means of professional advancement. Confucian thought emphasized the moral content of education, while scholarship was the principal qualification for entry to the administrative class. But because of the excessive respect accorded to scholars the administrative system came gradually to be over-conservative, and began to lose touch with reality. From the Ming period (1368–1644) onwards, state control over the educational system was tightened, and the examination system became stylized; the result was the degeneration of the civil service into a bureaucracy uninformed by intelligence or breadth of vision.

Educational reform in China came after her defeat in the war with Japan (1895), when examinations for the civil service were abolished, and western science was introduced, along with more modern methods of teaching and teacher training Mission schools were established by British, American and other groups, and study abroad began to be encouraged, first in Japan, later in Western Europe, U.S.A. and the Soviet Union. After the establishment of the Republic in 1927 the school system came to be modelled on that of the U.S.A., and heavier emphasis was put on technological subjects, while study of the Chinese classics was largely abandoned. Between 1932 and 1944 the proportion of children receiving primary education rose from 20 to 75 per cent. Government measures attempted to standardize the school system, to simplify the written language, and to reorganize the universities and independent colleges, raising their standards of entrance and unifying courses of study. Many new universities were established in the years immediately following the Sino-Japanese war (1937–45).

Educational System of the People's Republic

Education in China today is based on the two principles of fulfilling the need for trained manpower and developing the student into the communist ideal of the all-round man: worker, intellectual and soldier. The two principles have not always been given equal weight; indeed, the conflict between the two ideals is the key to understanding many of the ideological disputes of the past two decades. During the "Hundred Flowers" campaign of 1956–57 education in an atmosphere of free discussion was actively encouraged; more recently, however, politics has come to take precedence over content, and knowledge has suffered at the expense of proletarian socialism. Alongside book learning, physical work is promoted; this is to break down the traditional contempt for manual labour among the educated classes. This trend has the added advantage of releasing school buildings for double-shift teaching, and encouraging modern attitudes in agriculture and industry.

Administrative Reorganization, 1949–54

One of the most immediate consequences of the Communist victory in 1949 was the reorganization of education, particularly at higher levels, to eliminate content deemed superfluous, replacing it with constructive courses oriented to the new concept of society. An early task was the careful examination of textbooks and their replacement, particularly in social sciences, by translations from Soviet texts considered more suitable. Following on from this, a major campaign was undertaken to reorient the thinking of teachers, from 1951 to 1952, urging them to change their attitude towards study for its own sake, and conscientiously to attempt to serve the masses. At this time the majority of private schools were closed down or taken over by the State. Higher education, following the Soviet model, became specialized along those channels which served the needs of Chinese society, and very few of the universities retained the broad spectrum of courses in all subjects typical of western institutions.

Between 1952 and 1954 primary education was shortened and simplified to a single five-year curriculum, but the experiment was soon abandoned as inadequate, and a return made to the former two-tier, six-year programmes. In the Constitution of 1954, responsibility for education was divided between two Ministries, one for Education covering primary and middle schools and adult classes, and the other for Higher Education including within its mandate upper secondary, higher and technical education.

In an informal sense, Communist Party control of the school system has in the past been assured by the Party branches and cadres which act as the local authority for interpreting official policy. It is not clear whether the establishment of the Red Guards from among secondary school students has affected this system of control; it seems likely that many schools are now run by committees of workers and students.

Outside the State educational system, factories, communes and similar organizations are encouraged to develop their own teaching institutions, the "people's schools". Most are work-schools in which labour pays for tuition.

Somewhat surprisingly, only higher education in China is free. Both State and people's schools charge some form of fees.

Pre-School Education

Kindergartens are regarded as important in introducing the child to ideas which will shape his thought in later life, and they have economic significance in releasing women for productive work. In general it is believed that the number of schools exceeds the available capacity of trained teachers, though rapid training courses were in hand in 1967 to relieve the burden on unskilled staff.

Primary Education

Primary education grew fourfold in the first decade of the People's Republic. No figures have been published since 1958, though in 1965 it was claimed that between 35 and 50 per cent of rural youths had completed a primary course. The curriculum for the five-year course includes Chinese language, arithmetic, geography, history and music. Songs and slogans, parades and demonstrations provide the main ideological content of the curriculum; classes in language and history are illustrated by examples chosen for their political significance. Pupils spend several weeks of the year working on communes.

The increase in educational establishments since 1949 has been caused mainly by the expansion of people's schools, staffed and attended part-time by young people. Standards in these schools do not always meet official requirements, and legislation in March 1966 was aimed at improving this situation.

In State primary schools classes number between 40 and 60 pupils. Teachers are assisted by class leaders and row leaders chosen from among the students.

Secondary Education

The middle school course of general education lasts four to five years and it is divided into two separate phases. Entry and departure are controlled by examination. The curriculum includes more science, mathematics, foreign languages and political study and discussion than before. As with primary education, much of the expansion of secondary facilities in the 1960s was in the field of people's schools giving technical instruction through work-study. Within the State system there is also a division between general and vocational schools, the latter being almost all part-time work-study institutions. A few full-time vocational schools give a two- to three-year course, but most work-study schools give part-time courses lasting up to four years. The curriculum includes politics, Chinese language and mathematics. In addition to specialized practical instruction pupils spend several weeks of the year working in factories.

Although no complete statistics have been published since 1958 (when there were 8.5 million students in general middle schools and 3.5 million in vocational middle schools), it is known that a considerable expansion has taken place in vocational education. According to U.S. sources there were about 10,000 agricultural middle schools and 1,000 industrial schools in 1964, and the trend towards practical instruction has certainly been consolidated by the Cultural Revolution of 1966–68. Since the late 1950s large numbers of middle school graduates (over 40 million by 1965) have been sent to work on farms in order to deploy their knowledge to good advantage.

At 16, all pupils are expected to work in factories, on communes or in the army.

Higher Education

In the field of higher education the conflict between education for specialist skills and correct political indoctrination reaches its apogee. Many changes of emphasis and orientation have taken place in educational policy in recent years, making a coherent picture difficult to achieve. Most of the higher institutes, out of an estimated total of 800, are specialist colleges; some provincial upper secondary schools have been given the name university. Only about twenty western-style universities can be identified, giving wide-ranging courses in the arts and sciences. Outstanding among these are the Universities of Peking and Nanking, founded in 1898 and 1923 respectively. Both are strongly developed in the sciences.

Entrance to university education was formerly by examination, with family and political background playing a necessary but subordinate role in selection. But since 1966 students of proletarian origin showing close familiarity with the writings of Mao Tse-tung have been given preference, while in the prevailing atmosphere of anti-intellectualism formal qualifications have counted for little. Recruitment to the universities is only after two years, i.e. 16–18, and is based on educational standards, political level and work achievements. Courses are expected to be cut to two or three years. Entrance examinations have been abandoned in favour of admitting students selected from the workers, peasants and soldiers themselves. University teachers are also to be involved in direct urban or rural labour to ensure that they may adapt their academic knowledge to Chinese economic requirements.

Courses in higher institutions are determined largely by national requirements for various specialized skills. In 1958 over 40 per cent of graduates qualified in education, 24 per cent in engineering and technology, 7.5 per cent in medicine, 6.4 per cent in pure sciences, 5.7 per cent in letters, 4.9 per cent in agriculture and 3.3 per cent in finance and economics. All students must in addition to their normal courses study politics, economics, Marxist philosophy, Communist Party history and one foreign language, normally Russian or English. No degrees are awarded on graduation.

Since 1966 the introduction of part-time work-study at university level has begun to be applied, in a strong attempt to combat *élitism* among intellectuals. Courses have been shortened to accommodate this change of emphasis. Those schools and colleges which had gained prestige for the quality of their courses, such as Peking Medical College, or Shanghai's Tong-ji University, have suffered most drastically by the new policy; far from being praised as centres of professional excellence, they are now discredited as "over-specialized". In a speech in August 1968 Mao Tse-tung called on workers and peasants to take over and run schools and universities under the guidance and direction of the Army. It may be that this was a veiled call for a return to discipline and order after two years of upheaval and change.

Teacher Training

The special position of the teacher in Chinese society has been eroded and attacked by the Communist regime. Teachers are expected to ensure political conformity in their classes as well as educational progress. In 1961 official figures indicated a total of three million teachers for a total of 100 million pupils in full-time schools. Many of the teachers are recent graduates of secondary and even of primary schools. Teacher training is mostly undertaken in specialist secondary schools, in which political training is stressed—the political content of teacher-training curricula may be as much as one-third. Special schools and short courses are among many methods employed to increase the available resources of teaching manpower and to raise standards among existing teachers.

Special Schools

Much of China's educational effort is devoted to part-time and spare-time systems, both for professional training and ideological dissemination. This has been one of the remarkable features of Communist policy and is justifiably recognized as a major achievement in the mobilization of manpower and resources. Almost all the special schools are people's schools set up by factories, government agencies, street committees, communes and similar organs. Many of the government schools also provide extension classes, and a few special institutes provide correspondence courses. Content and standards are closely adapted to local conditions. In addition, television has been adopted in urban areas to provide a "TV University" offering specialized lectures to classes assembled at convenient reception points. Students who register for the classes must check in regularly to the reception point and are expected to continue their studies by spare-time reading. Secondary diplomas may be gained by attending a four-year TV course.

General Outlook

The overall level of literacy in China is difficult to assess; probably it is over 60 per cent; it was claimed in 1960 that by 1957 67 per cent of the counties and municipalities had eliminated illiteracy. But in a largely rural population the provision of any kind of schooling to outlying districts is still a difficulty, and the relapse from partial literacy to inability to read for lack of practice is clearly a continuing problem.

At the other end of the scale, no picture of Chinese education would be complete without some consideration of the higher apparatus of scientific research and policy. Planning of research lies with the State Scientific and Technological Commission, which is directly responsible to the State Council. The execution of almost all significant research is carried out under the auspices of the Chinese Academy of Sciences, founded in 1949 and still headed by the veteran leader Kuo Mo-jo in late 1968. The Academy has the status of a Ministry within the government hierarchy. Since 1956 when the Scientific Commission produced its research development programme, all research has been guided along highly specialized lines designed to give China the edge over her international rivals in fields chosen for their appropriateness to her needs. It is in this light that such achievements as the synthetization of insulin in 1966 and the successful detonation of a nuclear ballistic missile at the end of the same year must be viewed. Such triumphs are designed to bring China prestige and at the same time to solve some of the economic and strategic problems she has had to face since the breakdown of good relations with the U.S.S.R. early in the 1960s.

Current Directives

In October 1967 the Communist Party Central Committee ordered that all schools and universities which had been closed down in June 1966 to allow students to take part in the Cultural Revolution should reopen immediately. A similar order issued in February had produced only limited results; a third of the schools in Peking were still closed in September, and *Wenhui Bao* admitted that in Shanghai "the regular functioning of education had not yet begun", as some teachers were afraid to return to the schools, and the pupils refused to accept others. The shortage of teachers was aggravated by the purge that had taken place in the earlier stages of the Cultural Revolution; *Peking Daily* reported in March 1968 that 20 per cent of the staffs of Peking schools and universities had been dismissed.

Reports of the promised changes in the educational system in the Chinese press in November 1967 stated that the length of courses would be shortened to four years' primary, five years' secondary and two to four years' university or technical education. All senior pupils and students would be required to spend at least half their time on farm or factory work, in addition to studying Mao's thought and receiving military training. In the selection of students, if facilities were limited, priority would be given to the children of workers, peasants and soldiers. Knowledge of Mao's thought would govern advances to higher education and ensure earlier graduation, and foreign language study would include Mao's works in translation. Examinations would be abolished in schools; in universities they would be tests of reasoning rather than memory, the use of reference material being permitted.

More recently an official directive, published by *People's Daily* in July 1968, proposed that all college graduates should take part in manual work in farms or factories for four to five years in order to earn "qualification certificates" before commencing technical work. Those who showed correct ideological and political attitudes would then be selected for higher technical training. It is made clear by the Chinese sources that all these proposals are designed to prevent the emergence of an intellectual *élite*, divorced from the thoughts and attitudes of "proletarian politics, the worker and peasant masses, and production". What is not clear is how far these proposed policies have been put into practical effect. But for the time being, in theory at least, China's educational policy is committed to the revolutionary road of "Socialist consciousness and culture".

UNIVERSITIES

Amoy University: Amoy, Fukien.

Central Institute for Nationalities: Peking.

China Scientific and Technical University: Hofei.

Chungshan Medical College: Canton.

Chungshan University: Canton.

East China Water Conservancy College: Nan-ching.

Futan University: Shanghai, Kiangsu.

Hunan University: Changsha, Hunan Province.

Kirin University: Changchun, Kirin.

Liaoning College of Finance and Economics: Shenyang, Liaoning Province.

Nankai University: Tientsin, Hopei.

Nanking University: Nanking, Kiangsu.

Nanking Engineering College: Nanking.

Nanking Medical College: Nanking.

Peking University: Peking, Hopei.

Peking Aeronautical College: Peking.

Peking Medical College: Peking.

People's Liberation Army Military and Political College: Peking.

Shensi University: Sian, Shensi.

Sun Yat-Sen University: Canton.

Tientsin University: Tientsin.

Tsinghua University: Peking; 2,600 teachers.

Tungchi University: Shanghai; c. 2,000 students.

Wuhan University: Wuchang, Hupei.

CHINA (TAIWAN)

STATISTICAL SURVEY

AREA AND POPULATION

Area (sq. km.)	Population (Dec. 1975)*		Births and Deaths (1975)			
	Total	Taipei	Births	Birth Rate (per '000)	Deaths	Death Rate (per '000)
35,981.44	16,149,702	2,043,318	367,647	23.0	75,061	4.7

* Excluding armed forces and foreigners.

Other Towns (population at December 31st, 1975): Kaohsiung 998,919; Taichung 546,838; Tainan 523,568; Keelung 341,383.

AGRICULTURE

PRINCIPAL CROPS
('000 metric tons)

	1972	1973	1974	1975
Rice	2,440.3	2,254.7	2,452.4	2,494.1
Sweet potatoes	2,927.7	3,203.8	2,788.1	2,403.4
Asparagus	106.6	112.5	111.1	80.1
Soybeans	60.2	60.6	66.9	61.9
Maize	70.5	84.2	107.1	137.9
Tea	26.2	28.6	24.2	26.1
Tobacco	16.4	17.9	17.7	18.1
Groundnuts	94.0	97.9	93.9	91.5
Cassava (manioc)	324.7	328.1	376.3	278.7
Sugar cane	7,091.9	7,474.5	8,896.5	7,630.4
Bananas	366.4	422.5	333.6	196.6
Pineapples	334.4	328.0	307.9	319.0
Citrus fruit	290.6	331.7	360.9	347.8
Vegetables	1,703.6	1,881.1	1,938.9	2,226.1
Mushrooms	85.5	64.3	61.4	48.8

Livestock (1975): Cattle 249,329, Pigs 3,314,823, Goats 191,434.

LIVESTOCK PRODUCTS

		1972	1973	1974	1975
Beef	metric tons	4,425	5,592	4,754	4,295
Pigmeat	,, ,,	428,068	522,661	462,484	395,334
Goatmeat	,, ,,	1,196	1,334	1,188	1,340
Chicken	'000 head	44,683	48,955	50,015	56,044
Duck	,, ,,	17,003	13,819	17,518	18,599
Goose	,, ,,	2,797	2,736	2,720	2,697
Turkey	,, ,,	1,152	1,209	1,245	1,314
Milk	metric tons	22,932	37,640	41,879	46,189
Duck eggs	'000	494,833	515,494	437,014	478,756
Hen eggs	,,	715,307	762,875	797,162	980,332

FORESTRY
(1975)

Total Area (hectares)	Timber Production (cubic metres)
2,224,472*	854,731

*Pending a resurvey of reserves.

FISHERIES
(1975—metric tons)

Deep Sea	326,707
Inshore	295,920
Coastal	29,746
Ponds	127,577
Total	779,950

INDEX OF AGRICULTURAL PRODUCTION
(1971=100)

Inclusive of 139 products and includes forestry, livestock and fishing production.

1970: 98.7; 1971: 100; 1972: 102.6; 1973: 108.0; 1974: 108.5; 1975: 106.3.

MINING*

	1973	1974	1975
Coal	3,327,107	2,934,427	3,140,578
Gold (hectograms)	6,904	7,108	6,877
Silver (hectograms)	28,982	10,212	1,926
Electrolytic copper	6,649	9,859	8,539
Pyrite	11,216	10,452	14,175
Crude petroleum (kilolitres)	167,734	209,975	214,788
Natural gas (cubic metres)	1,454,303	1,586,701	1,574,543
Salt	385,681	368,228	268,149
Gypsum	3,534	2,443	3,054
Sulphur	5,595	3,310	5,476
Marble (cubic metres)	283,191	312,593	531,746
Talc	23,124	13,517	12,050
Asbestos	5,308	3,596	1,737
Dolomite	126,432	135,426	135,952

* Amounts in metric tons unless otherwise specified.

INDUSTRY

SELECTED PRODUCTS

		1973	1974	1975
Wheat flour	'000 metric tons	452.0	595.6	425.9
Refined sugar	,, ,, ,,	791.9	813.9	705.5
Alcoholic beverages (excl. beer)	'000 hectolitres	1,246.2	1,459.0	1,586.7
Cigarettes	million	19,292	19,000	20,816
Cotton yarn	'000 metric tons	96.3	111.2	130.9
Paper	,, ,, ,,	465.1	463.2	421.7
Sulphuric acid	,, ,, ,,	609.1	547.1	395.5
Synthetic fibres	,, ,, ,,	178.3	190.7	282.7
Motor spirit (petrol)	,, ,, ,,	1,017.7	1,065.0	1,122.1
Diesel oil	,, ,, ,,	1,777.6	1,648.2	1,714.9
Cement	,, ,, ,,	6,096.2	6,171.4	6,795.6
Pig iron	,, ,, ,,	150.0	111.1	66.8
Steel ingots	,, ,, ,,	507.5	569.6	520.0
Transistor radios	'000 sets	14,530.1	12,945.7	6,654.6
Television receivers	,, ,,	4,542.0	4,036.2	2,935.0
Ships	'000 gross tons	341.2	355.7	294.6
Electric energy	million kWh.	19,805	20,536	22,894
Liquefied petroleum gas	'000 metric tons	452.0	249.7	249.9

INDEX OF INDUSTRIAL PRODUCTION
(1971=100)

Inclusive of mining, manufacturing, construction, public utilities.

1970: 80.6; 1971: 100; 1972: 121.0; 1973: 144.2; 1974: 142.1; 1975: 150.4.

FINANCE

100 cents=1 New Taiwan dollar (NT $).

Coins: 10, 20 and 50 cents; 1 and 5 dollars.

Notes: 1, 5, 10, 50 and 100 dollars.

Exchange rates (June 1976): £1 sterling=NT $67.41; U.S. $1=NT $38.00.

NT $100=£1.483=U.S. $2.632.

Note: Multiple exchange rate systems were in operation from 1951 to August 1959. From March 1956 the certificate rate (used for foreign trade transactions) was U.S. $1=NT$24.78 (NT$1=4.04 U.S. cents). In 1958 the rate became U.S. $1=NT$36.38 (NT$1=2.75 U.S. cents). In August 1959 the currency was devalued and the exchange rate fluctuated close to U.S. $1=NT$40.00 (NT$1=2.50 U.S. cents), which became the par value in September 1970. Foreign trade was valued at this rate from January 1961 and it became the official basic rate in June 1961, though from October 1963 a selling rate of U.S. $1=NT$40.10 came into force. These rates remained in effect until February 1973. Since February 1973 the exchange rate (par value) has been U.S. $1=NT$38.00 (NT$1=2.63 U.S. cents). In terms of sterling, the exchange rate was £1=NT$96.00 from November 1967 to August 1971; and £1=NT$104.23 from December 1971 to June 1972.

BUDGET
(1974–75—NT$ million)

Revenue	
Taxes	84,389
Monopoly Profits	13,052
Non-Tax Revenue from Other Sources	29,642
Total	127,083

Expenditure	
General Government and Defence	49,601
Reconstruction and Communications	14,746
Social Development	12,657
Education	20,716
Debt Service	3,269
Enterprise Fund	15,907
Others	2,644
Total	119,540

Sixth Four-Year Economic Development Plan (1973–76): G.N.P. to increase to U.S. $11,600 million by the end of 1976; per capita income to increase by about 80 per cent to U.S. $550 and a projected annual economic growth rate of 9.5 per cent. Major projects under the plan are in the fields of power generation, which is to increase by 12.1 per cent per year, and traffic volume of transportation and communications (9.5 per cent per annum increase). Total investment will amount to U.S. $12,057 million (at 1972 constant prices).

NATIONAL ACCOUNTS
(NT$ million at current prices)

	1973	1974	1975*
Gross Domestic Product (at market price)	388,699	524,655	547,994
Net Domestic Product (at factor cost)	303,689	410,599	428,219
of which:			
Agriculture and Fisheries	45,726	64,303	69,647
Mining	3,118	4,596	4,783
Manufacturing	98,281	122,873	115,666
Electricity	5,140	9,058	10,978
Construction	15,158	21,286	24,107
Transport and communications	18,498	24,630	24,722
Commerce	64,500	93,673	95,861
Net National Product (National Income)	303,536	410,422	427,473
Gross National Product	388,583	524,478	547,247
Balance of exports and imports of goods and services	21,764	−42,581	−18,667
Available External Resources (end of year)	71,353	70,432	69,522

* Preliminary estimates.

EXTERNAL TRADE

(NT $ million)

	1971	1972	1973	1974	1975
Imports . . .	73,941.9	100,791.4	145,078.6	265,395.3	224,758.1
Exports . . .	79,906.4	116,648.5	167,383.4	209,675.5	201,078.6

PRINCIPAL COMMODITIES

(NT $ million)

Imports	1973	1974	1975
Wheat (unmilled)	2,481.1	6,325.9	4,063.5
Maize (unmilled)	4,865.4	6,459.1	8,100.0
Soybeans	6,201.4	5,879.1	8,412.6
Logs	13,788.6	8,571.6	5,586.3
Wool	1,019.5	508.6	720.7
Crude petroleum	3,784.3	27,257.3	23,732.4
Raw cotton	5,067.5	7,143.8	7,238.6
Synthetic fibres	2,023.7	2,440.0	1,092.7
Synthetic fabrics	720.2	1,147.5	855.6
Distillate fuels	1,270.1	4,393.3	5,300.8
Polymers and copolymers	2,482.2	3,324.5	2,062.6
Iron and steel sheets	2,235.4	5,103.3	2,838.0
Stainless and heat-resistant steel	976.3	1,461.9	923.2
Iron and steel scrap	2,247.6	4,371.5	2,034.1
Spinning, weaving, knitting, etc. machines	5,734.4	15,813.5	4,840.9
Electrical switchgear	2,455.6	2,883.5	2,225.3
Television receivers	3,120.1	3,145.2	1,653.9
Radio receivers	2,019.0	1,969.3	1,313.7
Ships for breaking	2,354.0	6,330.6	4,646.2
Total (incl. others)	145,078.6	265,395.3	224,758.1

Exports	1973	1974	1975
Fresh, chilled or frozen fish	2,284.6	2,141.8	5,374.0
Fresh bananas	1,112.6	744.7	778.7
Canned mushrooms	1,833.1	1,634.5	1,796.4
Canned asparagus	2,008.2	3,226.9	2,960.4
Raw sugar	3,126.5	10,834.8	8,649.5
Cotton fabrics	8,065.1	5,873.2	5,190.9
Synthetic yarn and thread	3,762.9	5,784.2	6,498.8
Synthetic fabrics	1,565.6	901.1	903.9
Plywood	8,620.6	6,568.6	5,006.6
Clothing	18,058.6	22,185.0	21,958.0
Plastic footwear	6,108.1	6,891.4	7,887.7
Leather footwear	1,788.8	2,548.8	2,964.7
Iron and steel bars and rods	362.6	235.0	820.9
Calculating machines	744.1	702.4	1,416.0
Television receivers	12,349.1	14,717.4	9,354.4
Radio receivers	6,495.8	8,366.2	6,155.0
Plastic articles	9,990.5	5,398.4	5,175.3
Dolls and toys	2,419.2	3,221.1	2,484.2
Total (incl. others)	167,383.4	209,675.5	201,078.6

PRINCIPAL TRADING PARTNERS

(NT $ million)

	Imports			Exports		
	1973	1974	1975	1973	1974	1975
Australia	3,884.9	6,285.4	6,101.6	4,099.1	7,243.9	4,762.7
Canada	1,070.1	2,467.0	1,823.5	6,512.3	7,785.8	6,888.1
Germany, Federal Republic	7,767.1	18,101.5	14,095.3	8,199.0	11,608.3	11,989.0
Hong Kong	3,809.2	4,458.9	2,711.9	11,270.7	12,822.9	13,703.8
Indonesia	3,873.3	6,784.4	6,378.0	4,504.7	4,830.2	6,746.2
Iraq	30.9	26.6	n.a.	0.4	8.9	n.a.
Italy	1,062.1	2,555.5	1,630.9	1,987.5	2,453.5	1,865.9
Japan	54,646.1	84,389.4	68,304.3	31,640.5	31,987.8	26,269.4
Korea, Republic	1,607.1	2,573.7	2,245.0	2,036.7	6,042.3	4,536.6
Malaysia and Singapore	3,391.0	5,138.1	3,521.4	6,114.1	7,333.3	6,973.9
Philippines	2,112.2	1,762.1	1,253.1	1,101.7	1,752.9	3,109.8
Saudi Arabia	1,597.9	12,749.9	8,687.7	949.1	2,289.9	4,447.3
Thailand	2,177.9	6,735.2	2,649.1	2,426.7	2,612.5	2,566.7
United Kingdom	2,800.0	6,009.4	4,823.5	4,277.5	5,687.4	5,216.6
U.S.A.	36,410.8	64,004.3	62,280.3	63,864.0	77,188.4	69,053.8
Vietnam, South	228.3	195.4	n.a.	1,116.3	1,300.8	n.a.
Total (incl. others)	145,078.6	265,395.3	224,758.1	167,383.4	209,675.0	201,078.6

TRANSPORT

Railways (1975): Passengers 146,808, Passenger/km. 8,287,176; Freight 35,219,000 metric tons, Ton/km. 2,702,212.

Roads (1975): Passengers 1,930,567, Passenger/km. 19,007,062; Freight 88,872,000 metric tons, Ton/km. 3,838,154.

Shipping (1975): Imports 23,328,883 metric tons, Exports 4,300,575 metric tons.

Civil Aviation (1975): Passengers entered and departed 5,677,531.

Tourism (1975): Total visitors 853,140.

COMMUNICATIONS MEDIA

December 1975: Radio Receivers 1,486,376; Television Receivers 912,942; Telephones 774,233 subscribers.

EDUCATION

(1974–75)

	Schools	Full-time Teachers	Pupils
Pre-school	660	3,084	110,403
Primary	2,354	62,109	2,406,531
Secondary (incl. Vocational)	968	56,753	1,433,755
Higher	100	13,320	282,168
Special	6	400	2,844
Supplementary	312	3,426	159,456
Total (incl. others)	4,400	139,092	4,395,157

Sources: Directorate-General of Budgets, Accounts and Statistics; Inspectorate-General of Customs, Taipei.

THE CONSTITUTION

The form of government incorporated in the Constitution follows the five-power system envisaged by Dr. Sun Yat-sen, which has the major features of both cabinet and presidential government. The following are the chief organs of government:

National Assembly: Composed of elected delegates; meets to elect or recall the President and Vice-President, to amend the Constitution, or to vote on proposed Constitutional amendments submitted by the Legislative Yuan.

President: Elected by the National Assembly for a term of 6 years, and may be re-elected for a second term (the two-term restriction is at present suspended). Represents country at all state functions, including foreign relations; commands land, sea, and air forces, promulgates laws, issues mandates, concludes treaties, declares war, makes peace, declares martial law, grants amnesties, appoints and removes civil and military officers, and confers honours and decorations. He also convenes the National Assembly, and subject to certain limitations, may issue emergency orders to deal with national calamities and ensure national security.

Executive Yuan: Is the highest administrative organ of the nation and is responsible to the Legislative Yuan; has five categories of subordinate organization:

Executive Yuan Council
Ministries and Commissions
Secretariat
Government Information Office and Personnel Administration Bureau
Directorate-General of Budgets, Accounts and Statistics.

Legislative Yuan: Is the highest legislative organ of the state, composed of elected members; holds two sessions per year; is empowered to hear administrative reports of the Executive Yuan, and to change Government policy.

Judicial Yuan: Is the highest judicial organ of state and has charge of civil, criminal, and administrative cases, and of cases concerning disciplinary measures against public functionaries (*see* Legal System).

Examination Yuan: Supervises examinations for entry into public offices, and deals with personal questions of the civil service.

Control Yuan: Is a body elected by local councils to impeach or investigate the work of the Executive Yuan and the Ministries and Executives; meets once a month, and has a subordinate body, the Ministry of Audit.

THE GOVERNMENT

THE HEAD OF STATE

President: Dr. Yen Chia-kan.

Secretary-General: Cheng Yin-fun.

THE EXECUTIVE YUAN

(*July* 1976)

Prime Minister: Gen. Chiang Ching-kuo.

Deputy Prime Minister: Hsu Ching-chung.

Secretary-General: Philip C. C. Chang.

Minister of the Interior: Chang Feng-hsu.

Minister of Foreign Affairs: Shen Chang-huan.

Minister of National Defence: Kao Kuei-yuan.

Minister of Finance: Walter Fei Hua.

Minister of Education: Tsiang Yien-si.

Minister of Justice: Wang Tao-yuan.

Minister of Economic Affairs: Sun Yun-suan.

Minister of Communications: Lin Chin-sheng.

Ministers Without Portfolio: George K. C. Yeh, Yu Kuo-hwa, Li Lien-chun, Chow Shu-kai, Lee Teng-hui, Li Kwoh-ting, Henry Yu-shu Kao, Hsu Chin-teh, Chiu Chuang-huan.

Chairman of the Overseas Chinese Affairs Commission: Mo Sung-nien.

Chairman of the Mongolian and Tibetan Affairs Commission: Tsui Chui-yien.

Director-General of the Government Information Office Ding Mou-shih.

Other Yuan

President of Legislative Yuan: Nieh Wen-ya.

President of Judicial Yuan: Tien Chun-chin.

President of Examination Yuan: Yang Liang-kung.

President of Control Yuan: Yu Chun-hsien.

OTHER MINISTERS

Minister of Personnel: Shih Chueh.

Minister of Examinations: Choong Kow-kwong.

Minister of Audit: Chang Tao-ming.

PARLIAMENT

NATIONAL ASSEMBLY

Following the general election held on December 23rd 1972, the National Assembly in 1976 had 1,282 life members and 53 new members elected for 6 years. Delegates meet to elect or recall the President and Vice-President, to amend the Constitution or to vote on Constitutional amendments submitted by the Legislative Yuan.

LEGISLATIVE YUAN

The Legislative Yuan is the highest legislative organ of state. In the elections held throughout China in 1948 members elected to the Legislative Yuan totalled 760. Following general elections held on December 23rd, 1972, membership in 1976 comprised 389 life members and 36 elected for 3 years.

CONTROL YUAN

The Control Yuan exercises powers of impeachment and censure, and powers of consent in the appointment of the President, Vice-President and the grand justices of the Judicial Yuan, and the president, vice-president and the Members of the Examination Yuan (*see* the Constitution).

POLITICAL PARTIES

Kuomintang (KMT) (*Nationalist Party of China*): 11 Chung Shan S. Rd., Taipei; f. 1894; aims to overthrow Communist rule in China and promote constitutional government; mems. 1,000,000; Chair. Gen. CHIANG CHING-KUO; Sec.-Gen. CHANG PAO-SHU; Deputy Sec.-Gen. CHIN HSIAO-YI, HSUEH JEN-YANG, LIN CHIN-SHENG.

Young China Party: Taipei; f. 1923; aims: to recover and maintain territorial sovereignty; to safeguard the Constitution, and democracy; to better international understanding between free China and the free world.

China Democratic Socialist Party: Taipei; f. 1932; aims: to promote democracy; to protect fundamental freedoms; to promote public welfare and social security.

DIPLOMATIC REPRESENTATION

EMBASSIES ACCREDITED TO THE REPUBLIC OF CHINA

(In Taipei unless otherwise stated)

Bolivia: Tokyo, Japan.

Central African Republic: 22, Lane 242, Chien Kuo N. Road; *Ambassador:* SIMON PIERRE KIBANDA.

Colombia: 14, Lane 161, Nan Ya Li Tien Mu; *Chargé d'Affaires a.i.:* HERNANDO RICARDO.

Costa Rica: 11A Lane 23, Rd. 3, Tien Mou; *Ambassador:* EDGAR SÁNCHEZ.

Dominican Republic: 54 Nanking E. Rd.; *Ambassador:* ADOLFO R. CAMARENA (also accred. to Thailand).

El Salvador: Tokyo, Japan.

Guatemala: 6, Lane 44, Chien Kuo N. Rd.; *Ambassador:* Col. AGUSTÍN DONIS KESTLER.

Honduras: Tokyo, Japan.

Ivory Coast: Tokyo, Japan.

Jordan: 11E Ai Chun Mansion, 120-23 Chung Hsiao E.; *Ambassador:* ANWAR NASHASHIBI.

Korea, Republic: 72 Jen Ai Rd., Sec. 3; *Ambassador:* KIM KAE-WON.

Liberia: Tokyo, Japan.

Nicaragua: 3rd Floor, 270 Chung Shan Rd., Section 6; *Ambassador:* R. GARCÍA LECLAIR.

Panama: 3rd Fl., 307 Shih Pai Rd., Sec. 2; *Ambassador:* RICARDO E. CHIARI.

Paraguay: Tokyo, Japan.

Saudi Arabia: 7 Alley 8, Lane 27, Jen Ai Rd., Sec. 4; *Chargé d'Affaires a.i.:* FAWZI A. SHOBOKSHI.

South Africa: *Ambassador:* WILLIAM PRETORIUS.

U.S.A.: 2 Chung Hsiao West Rd., Sec. 2; *Ambassador:* LEONARD UNGER.

Uruguay: 3 Alley 6, Lane 142, Jen Ai Rd., Sec. 3; *Chargé d'Affaires:* EDISON BOUCHATON.

Vatican: 6 Lane 63, Chin Shan St.; *Papal Nuncio:* Right Rev. Monsignor EDWARD CASSIDY.

Taiwan also has diplomatic relations with Barbados, Haiti, Lesotho, Libya, Malawi, Nauru, Swaziland, Tonga and Western Samoa.

JUDICIAL SYSTEM

Judicial Yuan: Pres. TIEN CHUN-CHIN; Vice-Pres. TAI YEN-HUI; Sec.-Gen. CHENG TEH-SHOW; is the nation's highest Judicial organ, and the interpreter of the Constitution and national laws and ordinances. Its judicial powers are exercised by:

Supreme Court: Chief Justice TSIEN KUO-CHENG; court of appeal for civil and criminal cases.

Administrative Court: Chief Justice DAVID DING-YU CHOW; aims at the redress of administrative wrongs.

Committee on the Discipline of Public Functionaries: Chair. KU RU-SHING; metes out disciplinary measures to persons impeached by the Control Yuan.

The interpretive powers of the Judicial Yuan are exercised by the Council of Grand Justices nominated and appointed for nine years by the President of the Republic of China with the consent of the Control Yuan. The President of the Judicial Yuan also presides over the Council of Grand Justices.

The Ministry of Justice of the Executive Yuan has jurisdiction over district and high courts.

RELIGION

BUDDHISM

Buddhists belong to the Mahayana and Theravada schools. Leaders Venerable PAI SHENG, Venerable NAN TING, Venerable YIN SHUNG. The Buddhist Association of Taiwan has 1,900 group members and more than 5,750,000 devotees.

TAOISM

Leader CHANG EN-PU. There are about 3,300,000 devotees.

ISLAM

Leader Haji KHALID T. C. SHIH. About 41,000 adherents.

CHRISTIANITY

Roman Catholic: Archbishop of Taipei STANISLAUS LOKUANG, D.S.T., D.PH., D.C.L., Archbishop's House, P.O.B. 7-91, Taipei; 53,954 adherents.

Episcopal: There are about 2,000 adherents; Bishop of Taiwan (Episcopal Church of America) Rt. Rev. JAMES T. M. PONG, 1-105-7 Hangchow S. Rd., Taipei.

Tai-can Ki-tok Tiu-Lo Kau-Hoe (Presbyterian Church in Taiwan): 89-5 Chang-Chun Rd., Taipei; f. 1865; Gen. Sec. Rev. C. M. KAO; 70,000 adult mems., constituency 170,000.

THE PRESS

DAILIES

TAIPEI

Central Daily News: 83 Chung Hsiao West Rd., Section 1; f. 1949; morning; official Kuomintang paper; Publisher TSU SUNG-CHIU; Editor HSUEH SHIN-YUNG; circ. 300,000.

China Daily News (*Northern Edition*): 131 Sungkiang Rd.; morning; Chinese; f. 1948; Publisher HSIAO TSE-CHENG; Pres. TSU SUNG-CHIU; Editor-in-Chief FUNG AI-KUN; circ. 40,000.

China News: 177 Hsinyi Rd., Section 2; f. 1949; afternoon; English; Publisher S. LO; Editor-in-Chief W. T. TING; circ. 18,000.

China Post: 8 Fushun St.; f. 1952; morning; English; Publisher NANCY YU HUANG; Editor TSENG FU-SENG; circ. 22,500.

China Times: 132 Da Li St.; f. 1950; morning; Chinese; general and financial; Chair. and Publisher CHI-CHUNG YU; Editor TSANG YUAN-HOU; circ. 450,000.

Chung Cheng Pao: 111 Lin Sen South Rd., Taipei; f. 1948; morning; armed forces; Publisher CHANG CHI-HEH; Editor HOU CHIEN-WEN; circ. 5,000.

Economic Daily News: 555 Chung Hsiao E. Rd., Section 4; f. 1967; morning; Publisher WANG TIH-WU; Editor WU PU-CHUAN.

Hua Pao: 100 Wuchang St., Section 2; f. 1968; afternoon; tabloid; Shanghai dialect; Publisher CHU TING-YUN; Editor HUANG CHUAN-TAO.

Independent Evening Post: 15 Chinan Rd., Section 2; f. 1947; afternoon; Chinese; Publisher WU SAN-LIEN; Editor-in-Chief CHANG SHU-BEN; circ. 50,000.

Mandarin Daily News: 10 Fuchow St.; f. 1948; morning; Dir. HUNG YEN-CHIU; Editor YANG RUU DET; circ. 70,000.

Min Tsu Evening News: 235 Kunming St.; f. 1950; afternoon; Chinese; Publisher WANG CHENG-YUNG; Editor CHAO YU-MING; circ. 120,000.

Shin Sheng Pao: 110 Yenping S. Rd.; f. 1945; morning; Chinese; Publisher LEE PAI-HUNG; Editor STONE Y-SHIH; circ. 300,000.

Ta Chung Daily News (*Everybody's Daily*): 21–2 Cheng-teh Rd.; f. 1968; Chinese; Publisher CHIEN WEN-FA; Editor CHIN HSI-JEN; circ. 10,000.

Ta Hua (Great China) Evening News: 53 Kwan Chien Rd.; f. 1950; afternoon; Publisher KENG HSIU-YEH; Editor PAN PIN; circ. 50,000 (weekday), 60,000 (Sunday).

United Daily News: 555 Chung Hsiao East Rd., Section 4; f. 1953; morning; Publisher WANG TIH-WU; Editor WANG CHI-PU; circ. 400,000.

Young Warrior Daily: 3 Hsin Yi Rd., Section 1; f. 1952; morning; Chinese; armed forces; Publisher HSIAO TAO-YING; Editor CHANG CHU-AN; circ. 60,000.

PROVINCIAL DAILIES

Cheng Kung Evening News: Kaohsiung; 24 Chiao Nan Rd., Chiao Nan Village, Chiao Tou Hsiang; f. 1956; afternoon; Publisher CHIEN CHANG; Editor CHEN CHANG-CHANG.

Chien Kuo Daily News: Makung; 36 Min Sheng Rd.; f. 1949; morning; Publisher YANG TYNG-YUN; Editor CHANG YEN-HSU; circ. 15,000.

China Daily News (*South Edition*): Tainan; 2 Cheng Kung Rd.; f. 1946; morning; Publisher HSIAO TZE-CHENG; Editor LIN WEN-HSING; circ. 115,000.

Chung Kuo Daily News: Taichung; 1, Lane 45, Shuang Shi Rd., Section 2; f. 1956; morning; Publisher CHEN SHEN-CHI; Editor KU HUNG-TSUAN; circ. 30,000.

Chung Kuo Evening News: Kaohsiung; 243 Hsin Lo St.; f. 1955; afternoon; Publisher YANG NIEN-CHU; Editor TSENG SU-TSU; circ. 20,000.

Hsin Wen Pao: Kaohsiung; f. 1949; morning; Publ. HOU PING-YUAN; Editor HSU CHANG; circ. 100,000.

Keng Sheng Pao: Hualien; 36 Wuchuan Rd.; f. 1947; morning; Publ. HSIEH YING-YI; Editor CHEN HSING; circ. 5,000.

Matsu Daily News: Matsu; f. 1951; morning; Publisher SUN FENG-CHEN; Editor LIN DZ-SHIU.

Min Sheng Daily News: Taichung; 51 Minchu Rd.; f. 1946; morning; Publisher HSU TSANG-CHU; Editor HUANG JO-YUN; circ. 7,000.

Min Tsung Daily News: Keelung; 189 Hsin Erth Rd.; f. 1950; morning; Publisher LI JUI-PIAO; Editor YAO TA-CHANG; circ. 3,000.

Quemoy Daily News: f. 1965; morning; Publisher YAO HEIANG-CHIU; Editor WU WEI-HO.

Shang Kung Daily News: Chiayi; 216 Kuo Hua St.; f. 1953; morning; Publ. Lin Fu-ti; Editor Liu Kuei-nan; circ. 16,000.

Ta Han Daily News: Taitung; f. 1972; Publ. Lin Tsao-keng; Editor Li Su.

Taiwan Daily News: Taichung; 16 Nai Hsin Rd., Tali Hsiang; morning; f. 1964; Publisher Fu Chao-chu; Editor Yao Ta-chung; circ. 100,000.

Taiwan Times: Kaohsiung; 61 Lane 40 Jen Ai Rd., Fengshan; Publisher Wu Chi-fu.

SELECTED PERIODICALS

Chen Kuang: 6 Lane 6, Lien Yun St., Taipei; f. 1952; monthly arts magazine; Chinese; Publisher Wu Ka-shui; Chief Editor Wu Kai-shuh.

Continent Magazine: 5-2 Roosevelt Rd., Section 2, Taipei; f. 1950; archaeology, history and literature; fortnightly; Publ. Hsu Kou-pao; circ. 3,000.

Taiwan Pictorial: 20 Chungking S. Rd., Section 2, Taipei; f. 1951; general illustrated; monthly; Chinese; Publr. Chow Tien-kou; Editor-in-Chief Chang Ming; circ. 70,000.

Taiwan Trade Monthly: P.O.B. 1642, Taipei; f. 1964; Publisher J. F. Chang; circ. 8,000.

NEWS AGENCIES

Central News Agency: 209 Sungkiang Rd., Taipei 104; f. 1924; 9 br. offices and 20 overseas offices; 462 mems.; issues daily, morning, evening and financial editions, mimeographed bulletin in English: *Express News:* Chair. Ma Hsin-yeh; Editor Chuan-hou Hu.

Chiao Kwang News Photo Service: 28 Tsian Rd., Section 2, Taipei.

China Youth News Agency: 131 Tun Hua N. Rd., Taipei; Dir. Lu Ling-kwei.

Foreign Bureaux

UPI: CNA Bldg., 209 Sungkiang Rd., Taipei; Bureau; Chief Shullen Shaw.

AP and Jiji Press are also represented.

PRESS ASSOCIATION

Taipei Journalists Association: 131 Sung Chiang Rd., Taipei; 1,675 mems. representing editorial and business executives of newspapers and broadcasting stations; publ. *Chinese Journalism Yearbook*.

PUBLISHERS

Cheng Chung Book Company: 20 Hengyang Rd., Taipei; humanities, social sciences, natural sciences, medicine, technology, fine arts.

Chung Hwa Book Co.: 94 Chungking S. Rd., Section 1, Taipei; f. 1911; publisher, printers and booksellers for humanities, social sciences, natural sciences, medicine, fine arts, school books; Gen. Man. D. S. Hsiung.

Commercial Press: 37 Chungking S. Rd., Section 1, Taipei.

Eastern Publishing Co. Ltd.: 121 Chungking S. Rd., Section 1, P.O.B. 75, Taipei; geography, maps, agriculture, gardening, fiction, technology.

Far East Book Co.: 66–1, 10th Floor, Chungking S. Rd., Section 1, Taipei; art, education, history, physics, mathematics, literature, school books, Chinese/English, English/Chinese dictionaries.

Fu-Hsing Book Co.: 44 Huai Ning St., Taipei; art, archaeology, geography, education, history, cookery, technology, economics, school books.

Great China Book Corporation: 66 Chungking S. Rd., Section 1, Taipei; f. 1952; education, history, agriculture, politics, fiction, technology, economics, textbooks and reference books; Chief Dir. Hsieh Chung-liu; Man. Hseih Yu.

Hua Kuo Publishing Co.: 6 Lane 180, Section 1, Ho-ping East Rd., Taipei; f. 1950; Publr. T. F. Wang.

San Min Book Co.: 77, 1st Sec., Chung Ching So. Rd., Taipei; f. 1953; literature, history, philosophy, social and humanitarian sciences; Man. Ko Chun-chin.

Tah Chung Book Co.: 37–1, Chung Shan N. Rd., 2nd Section, Taipei; hygiene, music, physics, technology, economics.

World Bock Co.: 99 Chungking S. Rd., Section 1, Taipei.

RADIO AND TELEVISION

RADIO

Broadcasting stations are mostly privately owned, but the Ministry of Communications determines power and frequencies and supervises the operation of all stations, whether private or governmental. In August 1975 there were 1,484,095 radio receivers. Principal networks:

Broadcasting Corporation of China: 53 Jen Ai Rd., Section 3, Taipei 106; f. 1928; 5 Services: Domestic (3 networks), Mainland and Overseas (all AM); FM, Stereo and TV production; 23 stations, 78 transmitters, 85 frequencies; 18 languages and dialects; total power output 2,607 kW.; Pres. Lee Shih-feng; Chair. Mah Soo-lay.

Cheng Sheng Broadcasting Corporation: 7–8th Floors, Chungking S. Rd., Section 1, Taipei; f. 1950; 18 stations in 7 locations; Pres. Lee Lien; Gen. Man. Tu Hsin-shih.

Fu Hsing Broadcasting Corporation: P.O.B. 799, Taipei; 35 stations in 12 locations; Dir. T. Pin-Sun.

TELEVISION

In August 1975 there were 911,849 television sets.

Taiwan Television Enterprise Ltd.: 10 Pa Te Rd., Sec. 3, Taipei; f. 1962; Chair. Lim Peck-siu; Pres. Carl Liu; publ. *TTV* (weekly).

China Television Company Ltd.: 53 Ren-Ai Rd., Section 3, Taipei; f. 1969; Chair. Ku Feng-hsiang; Pres. Penney Tung; publ. *CTV* (weekly).

Chinese Television Service Ltd.: 100 Kung Fu S. Rd., Taipei; f. 1971; Chair. Ran In-ting; Pres. Liu Hsien-yun; publ. *CTS* (weekly).

FINANCE

(cap.=capital; p.u.=paid up; dep.=deposits; m=million)

BANKING

Central Bank

Central Bank of China: 21 Paoching Rd., Taipei; f. 1928; issuing bank; Gov. Kuo-hwa Yu; Deputy Gov. Liang Kuo-shu.

National Banks

Bank of Communications: 91 Heng Yang Rd., Taipei; cap. NT $900m.; dep. NT $8,153m. (Dec. 1974); Chair. C. K. Ma; Gen. Man. T. C. Pan.

Bank of Taiwan: 120 Chungking S. Rd., Section 1, Taipei 100; f. 1946; cap. NT $1,000m.; dep. NT $42,305m. (Dec. 1974); Chair. M. S. Chen; Pres. Ronald H. C. Ho; publ. *Bank of Taiwan Quarterly* (Chinese).

Co-operative Bank of Taiwan: 75-A Kuan Chien Rd., Taipei; f. 1946; primary function: to act as central bank for co-operatives, and as major agricultural credit institution; 55 brs., 9 sub-brs., 11 agents and 288 correspondents; cap. NT $400m.; dep. NT $27,673m. (Dec. 1974); Chair. Chiao-jung Mung; Pres. Po-chin Yen.

Farmers Bank of China: 53 Huai Ning St., Taipei; f. 1933; cap. NT $900m.; dep. NT $4,103m. (Dec. 1974); Chair. Tang Tsung; Pres. F. M. Hsu.

International Commercial Bank of China: 152 Chungshan Rd. N., Section 1, Taipei 104; f. 1912; cap. NT $780m.; dep. NT $1,841m. (Dec. 1974); Chair. P. S. Lim; Pres. Tsung To Way; publs. *Economic Review* (bi-monthly), *Monthly Economic Survey*.

Land Bank of Taiwan: 46 Kuan Chien Rd., Taipei; f. 1946; cap. NT $450m.; dep. NT $18,222 (Dec. 1974); Chair. Sing-min Yeh; Gen. Man. C. T. Chang; publ. *Quarterly Journal*.

Commercial Banks

Central Trust of China: 49 Wu Chang St., Section 1, Taipei; f. 1935; cap. NT $900m.; dep. NT $987m. (Dec. 1974); Chair. An-Chi Lu; Pres. Dr. I-shuan Sun.

Chang Hwa Commercial Bank Ltd.: 38 Section 2, Tsuyu Rd., Taichung; f. 1905; cap. NT $500m.; dep. NT $23,277m. (Dec. 1974); Chair. Chin-chuan Wu; Pres. San-mu Huang; 95 branches.

First Commercial Bank: 30 Chungking S. Rd., Section 1, Taipei; f. 1899; cap. NT $544m.; dep. NT $33,507m. (June 1975); Chair. C. C. Chen; Pres. Chung-ching Cheng; 97 branch offices.

Hua Nan Commercial Bank Ltd.: 33 Kaifeng St., Section 1, Taipei; f. 1919; cap. NT $420m.; dep. NT $20,534m. (Dec. 1974); Chair. Y. L. Lin; Pres. T. P. Kao.

Overseas Chinese Commercial Banking Corporation: 102 Heng Yang Rd., Taipei; f. 1961; general and foreign exchange banking business; cap. p.u. NT $999m.; Chair. Lamko Chua; Gen. Man. C. Y. Wu.

Foreign Banks

American Express International Banking Corpn.: Taipei.

Bangkok Bank Ltd.: 24 Chungshan N. Rd., 2nd Section, P.O.B. 22419, Taipei; Asst. Vice-Pres./Man. A. Wasantachat.

Bank of America NT and SA: 43 Kuan Chien Rd., Taipei; Man. William L. Dafoe.

Chase Manhattan Bank: 72 Nanking E. Rd., Section 2, Taipei.

Chemical Bank: 261 Nanking E. Rd., Section 3, Taipei.

Continental Bank: 62 Nanking E. Rd., Section 2, Taipei.

Dai-Ichi Kangyo Bank: Head Office; Tokyo.

First National City Bank: Head Office: New York, N.Y., U.S.A.; 53 Nanking East Rd., Section 2, Taipei; Resident Vice-Pres. R. Lee Sherrill.

Irving Trust Company: 10 Chungking S. Rd., Section 1, Taipei.

Metropolitan Bank and Trust Co.: 52 Nanking E. Rd., Section 1, Taipei.

Toronto Dominion Bank: 20 Pa Teh Rd., Section 3, Taipei.

United California Bank: 97 Nanking E. Rd., Section 2, Taipei.

DEVELOPMENT CORPORATION

China Development Corporation: 131 Nanking East Rd., Section 5, Taipei 105; f. 1959 as privately owned development finance company to assist in creation, modernization, and expansion of private industrial enterprises in Taiwan, to encourage participation of private capital in such enterprises, and to help to promote and develop a capital market; cap. NT $400m.; Chair. P. S. Lim; Pres. Yen Shen.

Since the establishment of the C.D.C., industry has become increasingly important in the Taiwan economy, manufactured goods have emerged as significant exchange earners, and the private sector has played an increasing role in industrial development.

STOCK EXCHANGE

Taiwan Stock Exchange Corporation: 9th Floor, City Bldg., 85 Yen-ping South Rd., Taipei; f. 1962; 35 mems.; Pres. T. Y. Tsai; Chair. K. P. Chao.

INSURANCE

Cathay Insurance Co. Ltd.: 90 Nanyang St., Taipei; Chair. Tin-li Lin.

China Insurance Co. Ltd.: 58 Wu-Chang St., Section 1, Taipei; Chair. H. P. Chen; Gen. Man. T. L. Cho.

Central Trust of China, Insurance Dept.: 49 Wuchang St., Taipei; fire, marine, casualty, export, life insurance.

China Mariners' Assurance Corporation Ltd.: 4 Kuan Chien Rd., Taipei.

Tai Ping Insurance Co. Ltd.: 42 Hsu Chang St., Taipei; f. 1929; Chair. Tung Han-cha.

Taiwan Life Insurance Co. Ltd.: 45 Kuan Chien Rd., Taipei; Chair. M. H. Chou; Gen. Man. P. S. Wan.

TRADE AND INDUSTRY

CHAMBERS OF COMMERCE

American Chamber of Commerce in the Republic of China: Room N-1012, Chia Hsin Bldg. II 96, Chung Shan N. Rd., Section 2, Taipei; Exec. Dir. Herbert Gale Peabody.

General Chamber of Commerce of the Republic of China: 162-28 Hsin Yi Rd., Section 3, Taipei.

TRADE AND INDUSTRIAL ORGANIZATIONS

China Productivity Centre: 62 Sining South Rd., Taipei; f. 1955; Gen. Man. S. C. Kao.

Chinese National Association of Industry and Commerce: 4th Floor, Roosevelt Rd., Section 1, Taipei; Chair. Chen-fu Koo; Sec.-Gen. Richard C. Y. Wang.

Chinese National Federation of Industries: 162 Shin Yee Rd., Section 3, Rose Bldg., 3rd Floor, Taipei; Chair. Y. S. Pan.

Industrial Development and Investment Centre: 5th Floor, 53 Hwaining St., Taipei; f. 1959 to assist investment and planning; Dir. Lawrence Lu.

Taiwan Handicraft Promotion Centre: Hsu Chow Rd., Taipei; f. 1956; Chair. K. C. Wang; Gen. Man. Phillip P. C. Liu.

Trading Department of Central Trust of China: 49 Wuchang St., Section 1, Taipei; assists the Government in promoting foreign trade and handling exports and domestic sales for public and private enterprises.

TRADE UNIONS

Chinese Federation of Labour: 7–2 Jen Ai Rd., Section 3, Taipei; f. 1948; mems.: 1,123 industrial unions representing 710,000 workers; Chair. Chou Hsueh-hsiang; Gen. Sec. Shui Hsiang-yun.

National Federations

Chinese Federation of Postal Workers: 4th Floor, 99 Kweilin Rd., Taipei; f. 1930; 10,931 mems.; Pres. Shui Hsiang-yun.

Chinese National Federation of Railway Workers: 7 Alley 10, Lane 4, Ching Chow St., Taipei; 25,202 mems.; Chair. Chang Jui-ming.

National Chinese Seamen's Union: 25 Nanking East Rd., Section 3, Taipei; f. 1913; over 49,560 mems.; Pres. Hong Dah-ih; publ. *Chinese Seamen's Monthly* (in Chinese).

Taiwan Federation of Salt Miners: 40-2 Wancheng Rd., Chingmei, Taipei; about 6,000 mems.

Taiwan Federation of Textile and Dyeing Workers' Union (TFTDWU): 2 Lane 64, Chung Hsia E. Rd., Section 2, Taipei; f. 1957; 37,000 mems.; Chair. H. P. Sung.

Regional Federation

Taiwan Federation of Labour: 21 Chengte Rd., Taipei; 440,300 mems. and 35 affiliates; Chair. B. C. Wu; Sec.-Gen. S. W. Kuo.

CO-OPERATIVES

By the end of 1974 there were 3,234 co-operatives with a total membership of 1,512,657 people and total capital of NT$264,373,980. Of the specialized co-operatives, the most important were consumers (2,618 co-ops., 1,137,682 mems., cap. NT $26,905,806), credit (77 co-ops., 417,558 mems., cap. NT $575,801,574), and co-operative farms (176 co-ops., 18,588 mems., cap. NT $16,377,867).

The centre of co-operative financing is the Co-operative Bank of Taiwan, owned jointly by the Taiwan Provincial Government and 632 co-operative units (*see* Finance section). The Co-operative Institute (f. 1928) and the Co-operative League (f. 1940), which has 416 institutional and 14,448 individual members, exist to further the co-operative movement's national and international interests; and departments of co-operative business have been set up at the Taiwan Provincial Chung Hsing University and other colleges.

RURAL RECONSTRUCTION

Joint Commission on Rural Reconstruction (JCRR): 37 Nanhai Rd., Taipei; f. 1948; provides technical and financial assistance to Government in rural reconstruction programmes aiming to improve rural living standards, to increase agricultural production, to develop self-help among the rural population, to strengthen services of agricultural agencies and organizations, and to mobilize volunteers for rural programmes; Chair. Dr. Robert C. T. Lee; Commrs. Dr. W. C. Clark, Dr. Y. S. Tsiang; Sec.-Gen. You-tsao; library of 11,941 vols.; publs. general reports (yearly), technical papers (irregular), news releases (irregular).

MAJOR INDUSTRIAL COMPANIES

STATE ENTERPRISES

The following are the major state enterprises operating in Taiwan under the Ministry of Economic Affairs:

China Fisheries Corporation: 25 Tung Shan St., Taipei; f. 1955; Pres. P. K. Liu; Gen. Man. Y. C. Lee; employees: 700.

Chinese Petroleum Corporation: 83 Chung Hwa Rd., P.O.B. 135, Taipei; f. 1946; natural gas, aviation fuel, motor and diesel oil, kerosene, lubricants, etc.; refinery at Kaohsiung; Chair. K. S. Liu; Pres. S. N. Hu; employees: 14,764.

Taiwan Aluminium Corporation: 15 Chengkung 2nd Rd., P.O.B. 19, Kaohsiung; f. 1946; aluminium sheets, foils, door and window frames, castings and finished products, etc.; Chair. C. H. Sun; Pres. C. Y. Chang; employees: 3,353.

Taiwan Fertilizer Co.: 101 South Yenping Rd., Taipei; manufacturers of fertilizers, urea, ammonium sulphate, calcium super-phosphate; Pres. T. J. Chen.

Taiwan Machinery Manufacturing Corporation: 25 Kung Yuen 2nd Rd., P.O.B. 30, Kaohsiung; f. 1946; machine manufacturing, shipbuilding and repairing, prefabricated steel frameworks, steel iron casting, various steel products; Pres. S. C. Wang; Gen. Man. E. T. Wang; employees: 2,636.

Taiwan Power Co.: 39 Hoping E. Rd., Section 1, P.O.B. 171, Taipei; electricity generating company; Chair. Chia-yu Yang; Pres. Lan-kao Chen.

Taiwan Shipbuilding Corporation: P.O.B. 150, Keelung; f. 1919; shipbuilding and repairing up to 130,000 d.w.t.; machinery manufacture; Chair. C. F. Tann; Pres. H. P. Yen; employees: 4,200.

Taiwan Sugar Corporation: 25 Paoching Rd., Taipei; f. 1946; sugar, yeast powder, molasses, alcohol, bagasse board, vegetable oil, hogs and cattle; Chair. Y. T. Chang; Pres. Y. P. Yu; employees: 14,971.

PRIVATE COMPANIES

The following is a selected list of some of Taiwan's major industrial enterprises in the private sector:

Canned Food

Hwa Chen Canned Food: 4 Nanking E. Rd., Section 1, P.O.B. 1583, Taipei; f. 1957; variety of canned foods, particularly fruits; factory at Tainan; Pres. C. T. Chen; Gen. Man. K. P. Fuang; employees: 1,204.

Wei Chuan Foods Corporation: 19 Nanking W. Rd., Taipei; f. 1953; milk products and condensed milk, canned foods and soya sauce; Pres. L. H. Huang; Gen. Man. C. L. Lee; employees: 1,815.

Cement

Taiwan Cement Corporation: 113 Chung Shan N. Rd., Section 2, Taipei; f. 1946; cement manufacturers and exporters; plant at Suao; Pres. Lim Peck Siu; Gen. Man. Koo Chen-fu; employees: 2,840.

Chemicals

Formosa Chemicals and Fibre Corporation: 456 Chung Shan Rd., Changhwa; f. 1965; manufacturers of chemicals, pulp, rayon staple, yarns, cloth and nylon filament; Pres. Yung-ching Wang; employees: 5,400.

Kaohsiung Ammonium-Sulphate Corporation Ltd.: 100-2 Chung Shan 3rd Rd., P.O.B. 52, Kaohsiung; f. 1951; manufacturers of ammonium sulphate and nitrate, anhydrous ammonia, nitric and sulphuric acid, etc.; employees: 1,100.

Engineering and Motorworks

Tatung Co.: 22 Chung Shan N. Rd., Section 3, Taipei; f. 1918; electric fans, air conditioners, refrigerators, transformers, motors, televisions, electric razors, etc.; Chair. T. S. Lin; Pres. W. S. Lin; employees: 15,000.

Yue Loong Motor Co. Ltd.: 16 Sin Yan St., Taipei; f. 1953; cars, diesel engines, motor scooters and spare parts; Pres. T. L. Yen; employees: 1,650.

Iron and Steel

Tang Eng Iron Works Co. Ltd.: 2 Chen Kong 1st Rd., P.O.B. 47, Kaohsiung; f. 1940; steel bars, iron and steel casting, concrete products, red bricks, car body fabrication; Pres. S. C Wu; Gen. Man. Y. Y. Bao; employees: 2,845.

Taiwan Iron Manufacturing Corporation: 30 Wenhua Lane, Zenten Li, Hsitsu Chen, Taipei Hsien; f. 1952; steel bars and pig iron; Pres. Cheng Fon-yuan; Gen. Man. Kuo Chin-ta; employees: 1,010.

Mining

Taiwan Metal Mining Corporation: Chin-Qua-Shih, Keelung; f. 1955; gold, silver, copper, pyrite, coal, copper and brass strips; Chair. Yao Chen; Pres. Y. L. Wang; employees: 2,150.

Tai Yang Mining Co.: 88 Chung Hwa Rd., Taipei; f. 1948; gold, silver, copper, coal; Pres. C. H. Yen; employees: 4,473.

Plywood and Timber

Lin Shan Hao Plywood Corporation: 150 Hoping W. Rd., Section 2, Taipei; f. 1938; factories at Kaohsiung and Chiayi; Pres. and Gen. Man. T. S. Lin; employees: 2,300.

Fu Shing Manufacturing & Lumber Co.: 9th Floor, 53 Nanking East Rd., Section 2, Taipei; f. 1949; Chair. P. L. Cheng; Gen. Man. T. S. Chow; employees: 1,500.

Textiles and Synthetic Fibres

China Wool Textiles Inc.: 115 Po Ai Rd., P.O.B. 950, Taipei; f. 1953; yarns, worsted fabrics, knitted garments; Pres. T. T. Hsiao; Gen. Man. N. T. Cheng; employees: 1,407.

East Asia Textile Ltd.: 5 Nanking E. Rd., Section 1, Taipei; f. 1957; cotton yarns, spun rayon yarns, blended yarns, corduroy and velveteen; Pres. Liang-fa Huang; Gen. Man. Tou Kou; employees: 1,600.

Far Eastern Textile Ltd.: 128 Yen Ping S. Rd., Taipei; f. 1951; cotton/polyester yarn, piece goods, shirts, underwear, pyjamas, polyester pants/suits; Chair. Y. Z. Hsu; Pres. W. Y. Hsu; employees: 9,500.

Lio Ho Cotton Weaving Mill Co. Ltd.: 73 Chang An W. Rd., Taipei; f. 1948; cotton yarn and cloth and ready-made garments; Pres. K. C. Tsung; employees: 2,010.

New Taiwan Spinning Co. Ltd.: 72 Hwaining St., Taipei; f. 1954; synthetic and blended yarns, poplin, gingham, flannel, shirting and fishing net; Pres. C. T. Lee; Gen. Man. K. Lin; employees: 1,513.

Tai Yuen Textile Co. Ltd.: 8th Floor, 150 Nanking East Rd., Section 2, Taipei; f. 1951; yarn, cloth, garments and sewing thread; Pres. Vivian Wu; Gen. Man. T. L. Yen; employees: 5,600.

Tainan Spinning Co. Ltd.: 511 Yu-Nung Rd., Tainan; f. 1955; cotton, blended and synthetic yarns, etc.; Pres. San Len Wu; Gen. Man. Siu Chi Wu; employees: 1,605.

Miscellaneous

Chinaimex Industry Development Inc.: P.O.B. 39–542, Taipei; f. 1976; exporters of machinery, industrial products, foodstuffs, frozen foods, etc.; Pres. T. L. Chen; Gen. Man. Willi Chen.

Nan Ya Plastics Fabrication Co. Ltd.: 201 Tung Hwa N. Rd., Taipei; f. 1958; P.V.C. compound, imitation glass, floor tiles, folding doors, window blinds etc.; 4 divisions; Chair. Y. C. Wang; employees: 7,000.

Taiwan Salt Works: 13 Chung-Yi Rd., Tainan; Pres. C. Wu; employees: 1,320.

TRANSPORT

RAILWAYS

Taiwan Railway Administration: 2 Yen Ping N. Rd., Section 1, Taipei; a public utility under the provincial government of Taiwan, it operates both the west line and east line systems with a route length of 2,176.2 km.; the west line is the main trunk line from Keelung in the north to Kaohsiung in the south, with several branches; the east line runs down the east coast linking Hualien with Taitung; the electrification of the main trunk line and the construction of the north link between Suao and Hualien are scheduled for completion in 1978; Man. Dir. T. N. Chen.

There are also 2,838.4 km. of private narrow-gauge railroads operated by the Taiwan Sugar Corporation, the Taiwan Forestry Administration and the Taiwan Metal Mining Corporation. These railroads are mostly used for freight but they also provide public passenger and freight services which connect with those of T.R.A.

ROADS

Taiwan Highway Bureau: 70 Chung Hsiao West Rd., Section 1, Taipei; Dir.-Gen. JEFFERSON F. CHANG.

There were 16,404 km. of highways in 1972, most of them asphalt-paved, representing about 50 km. of road per 100 sq. km. of land. There is a national omnibus service operated by the Bureau.

SHIPPING

Kaohsiung is Taiwan's chief port, handling over two-thirds of the country's external commerce. Keelung, near Taipei, is the country's second port.

China Merchants' Steam Navigation Co.: Enterprise Bldg., 9th Floor, 46 Kuan Chien Rd., Taipei; 6 tankers, 15 cargo vessels; tanker services worldwide; Chair. C. C. TSAO.

China Union Lines Ltd.: 3rd Floor, 46 Kwan Chien Rd., Taipei; f. 1948; 10 cargo vessels, 5 bulk carriers, 1 banana carrier; liner and tramp services; Chair. K. P. YANG; Pres. C. CHAO.

Evergreen Marine Corp.: 63 Sungkieng Rd., Taipei; f. 1968; 5 bulk carriers, 2 containers, 12 cargo vessels; services from Far East to India, Pakistan, Persian Gulf, Red Sea, Central South America and the Caribbean; Chair. Y. F. CHANG; Gen. Man. F. H. YEH.

Far Eastern Navigation Corp. Ltd.: 7th Floor, 10 Chungking S. Rd., Section 1, P.O.B. 1120, Taipei; 2 cargo vessels, 1 bulk carrier; Chair. W. H. E. HSU.

First Steamship Co. Ltd.: 42 Hsu Chang St., 7th Floor, Taipei; 7 cargo vessels; worldwide service; Chair. H. C. TUNG; Gen. Man. S. C. CHU.

Great Pacific Navigation Co. Ltd.: 79 Chung Shan Rd. North, Section 2, Taipei; 8 fruit carriers, 3 dry cargo vessels; fruit and general cargo services to Japan; Pres. CHA-MOU CHEN.

Taiwan Navigation Co. Ltd.: 6 Chungking S. Rd., Section 1, Taipei; f. 1947; 5 cargo, 4 bulk carriers, 1 reefer; 1 passenger vessel; Chair. H. L. HUANG; Pres. T. W. CHEN.

Yangming Marine Transport Corp.: Enterprise Bldg., 46 Kuan Chien Rd., Taipei; 11 cargo vessels, 4 bulk carriers.

CIVIL AVIATION

China Air Lines Ltd. (CAL): 26 Nanking Rd. East, Section 3, Taipei; f. 1959; has operated since 1965 as the national airline of the Republic of China; scheduled passenger and cargo services are operated from Taipei to Hong Kong, San Francisco, Bangkok, Manila, Singapore, Kuala Lumpur, Honolulu, Los Angeles and Jakarta; domestic services throughout Taiwan; fleet comprises 6 Boeing 707, 3 727, 1 747, 3 Caravelles, 1 YS-11A, 1 C-47, 1 C-123; Chair. Gen. H. S. HSU; Vice-Chair. Gen. BEN Y. C. CHOW; Pres. Gen. CLIFF YEN-CHUN LOUIE.

Far Eastern Air Transport Corporation: 15 Nanking E. Rd., Section 3, Taipei; f. 1957; domestic services; fleet: 2 Caravelle, 6 Viscount, 2 Herald, 4 DC-3, 3 Beech 18, 5 Bell 212, 1 Bell 206, 4 Jet-Ranger; Chair. K. T. SIAO; Pres. T. C. HWOO.

There is an international airport at Taipei which is served by the following foreign airlines: Cathay Pacific, Korean Air Lines, North-west Orient, Singapore Airlines, Thai International.

TOURISM

Tourism Bureau, Ministry of Communications: 9th Floor, 280 Chung Hsiao E. Rd., Section 4, Taipei; f. 1960; Chair. Maj.-Gen. K. H. CHU.

Taiwan Visitors Information Service: 2 Lane 18, St. 110, Tienmu 1st Rd., Taipei; f. 1966; Dir. Y. C. HSU.

China Tourism Development Corporation: Taipei; f. 1969; state-owned; cap. NT $100 million.

In 1975, there were 853,000 foreign visitors to Taiwan.

CULTURAL ORGANIZATIONS

PRINCIPAL OPERAS

Foe Hsing Chinese Opera: 177 Neihu Rd., Section 2, Neihu; f. 1957; Dir. MA CHING-JUI.

Ta Peng Chinese Opera: No. 1 Special, Sungkiang Rd., Taipei; f. 1965; Dir. CHANG CHING-CHIU.

PRINCIPAL ORCHESTRA

Taiwan Symphony Orchestra: 293 Chin Wu Rd., Taichung; f. 1945; Government body under Taiwan Provincial Dept. of Education; Music Dir. Prof. DENG HAN-CHING.

ATOMIC ENERGY

Atomic Energy Council: 6th Floor, BCC Bldg., 53 Jen A. Rd., Section 3, Taipei; Chair. CHIEN SHIH-LIANG; Seci V. CHEN-HWA CHENG; publs. *Nuclear Science Journal* (quarterly), *Chinese AEC Bulletin* (every 2 months).

Biological and Medical Isotope Laboratory: Department of Biochemistry, National Defence Medical Centre, P.O.B. 7432; f. 1957; fall-out and irradiation studies.

Industrial Technology Research Institute, Union Industrial Research Laboratory: 1021 Kuan-Fu Rd., Hsin-Chu, Taiwan 300; food preservation studies etc.

Institute of Nuclear Energy Research (INER), AEC: P.O.B. 3, Lung Tang, Tao-Yuan; f. 1968; national research centre.

National Taiwan University: Taipei; equipped with Cockroft-Walton accelerator and an isotope laboratory.

National Tsing-Hua University, College of Nuclear Science: 855 Kuan-Fu Rd., Hsin-Chu, Taiwan 300; f. 1956; various studies.

Nuclear Medical Centre, Veterans General Hospital: Shih-Pai, Taipei; diagnosis and treatment using various radio-isotopes.

DEFENCE

Armed Forces (1975): Total strength 494,000; army 340,000, navy 37,000, and a marine corps of 35,000, air force 82,000. Military service is for 2 years.

Equipment: The army is equipped with U.S. manufactured weapons including medium and heavy tanks, armoured personnel carriers, heavy guns and surface-to-air missiles. The navy largely comprises destroyers, escort vessels, minesweepers and landing craft. The air force has 206 combat planes including tactical aircraft, interceptors, transports, trainers and some helicopters.

Defence Expenditure: Defence spending for 1975–76 is estimated at NT $38,000 million.

Chief of the General Staff: Gen. LAI MING-TANG.

EDUCATION

The educational policy of the Chinese Republic, as set out in the Constitution, places the stress on national morality, the Chinese cultural tradition, scientific knowledge and the ability to work and to contribute to the community. Hence the Government efforts in education have been mainly directed towards (*a*) promoting advanced study in higher institutions of learning, (*b*) stepping up the in-service training of teaching staff to enable them to keep abreast of the times, (*c*) to co-ordinate education to the economic and social needs of the country.

Elementary Education

Pre-school kindergarten education is optional, though in 1974–75, 110,403 children attended kindergartens and kindergartens attached to primary schools. In 1968 an educational development programme was begun; this extended compulsory and free education for children of school-age to 9 years. Children above school-age and adults who have had no education whatsoever receive supplementary education in the form of supplementary courses of four to six months and six months to one year's duration, which are held in the central elementary schools. Primary education has expanded in recent years; in 1974–75 there were 2,354 schools with 62,109 teachers and 2,406,531 pupils.

Secondary Education

Secondary, including vocational, education has shown substantial growth in past years with 968 schools and 1,433,755 pupils enrolled in the 1974–75 academic year with 56,753 teachers.

Secondary education involves two types of school: senior high and vocational. Senior high schools admit junior high school graduates and prepare them for higher education. They offer a three-year programme. Vocational schools also offer a three-year programme and provide training in agriculture, fisheries, commerce and industry. With the extension of compulsory education to secondary school, the secondary school entrance examinations have been abolished.

Higher Education

In 1974–75 there were 101 universities, junior colleges and independent colleges. Most of them offer postgraduate facilities. Students are selected by entrance examination under the joint sponsorship of private and public universities. The great majority of courses are of four years duration; junior colleges run five-year courses and admit junior high school leavers. The 1974–75 enrolment was 282,168 students with 13,320 teachers. In order to utilize the existing educational facilities to the full, colleges and universities have to set up night departments and conduct summer courses.

Under a 1963 plan the university curriculum has been revised in order to adapt Taiwan's higher education to modern academic research at the higher level. As part of the government policy to promote advanced education and academic standards, it has been encouraging existing universities to set up graduate schools with special budgets made available for the purpose. In 1975 there were 156 graduate schools, of which 56 were in science and engineering, 51 in the humanities and social sciences, 20 in agriculture, 10 in medicine, and the remainder in the fields of education, law and fine arts.

The government also encourages the establishment of overseas Chinese institutes of higher learning for the study of Chinese learning as a means of promoting international understanding. Recently rules have been considerably relaxed to allow more students to go abroad for further education, though a larger number are sent to Europe and Latin America than to the U.S.A.

Government lectureships and research professorships have been established to encourage Chinese scholars abroad to return to Taiwan. In 1974 a total of 486 graduates returned to teach or undertake research.

Teacher Training

The government attaches great importance to the improvement of teacher training in schools and universities and in-service courses have been running since 1959. In 1975 there were seven teachers' junior colleges. They provide a five-year course which is open to junior high school leavers. High school teachers are trained at the National Taiwan Normal University and a teachers' college.

Adult Education

The main aim has been to raise the literacy rate and standard of general knowledge. In 1975 there were 312 supplementary schools with an enrolment of 159,456. Chinese language, general knowledge, arithmetic, music and vocational skills are taught.

Radio and television also play an important part in the expansion of education. The Chinese Television Service and the Educational Broadcasting Station are both run by the Ministry of Education to broadcast cultural and educational programmes, the former for 2¼ hours daily and the latter 10 hours daily.

UNIVERSITIES

(June 1975)

Fu-jen Catholic University: Hsinchuang, Taipei; 9,320 students.

National Central University: Chung-li; 986 students.

National Chengchi University: Mucha 116, Taipei; 706 teachers, 5,936 students.

National Cheng Kung University: Ta-Hsueh Rd., Tainan; 820 teachers, 7,502 students.

National Chiao Tung University: Hsing Chu; 1,514 students.

National Chung Hsing University: 250 Kuokuang Rd., Taichung; 1,222 teachers, 9,667 students.

National Taiwan Normal University: 162 East Ho Ping Rd., Section 1, Taipei; 1,295 teachers, 8,550 students.

National Taiwan University: 1 Roosevelt Rd., Taipei; 1,838 teachers, 12,852 students.

National Tsing Hua University: Kuang Fu Rd., Hsinchu; 217 teachers, 807 students.

Soochow University: Wai Shuang Hsi, Shihlin, Taipei; 808 teachers, 7,558 students.

Tunghai (Christian) University: Taichung; 353 teachers, 3,133 students.

BIBLIOGRAPHY

GENERAL

BARNETT, A. D. China on the Eve of the Communist Takeover (Thames & Hudson, London, 1963).
China after Mao (Princeton University Press, 1967).
Cadres, Bureaucracy and Political Power in Communist China (Columbia University Press, New York, 1968).

BERTON, P., and WU, E. Contemporary China. A Research Guide (The Hoover Institution on War, Revolution and Peace, Stanford, Calif., 1967).

BLOODWORTH, D. Chinese Looking Glass (Secker and Warburg, London, 1967).

CHEN, JEROME. Mao Papers, Anthology and Bibliography (Oxford University Press, 1970).

CHEN, T. H. E. (Ed.). The Chinese Communist Regime, Documents and Commentary (Praeger, New York, 1967).

DAWSON, R. The Chinese Chameleon (Oxford University Press, London, 1967).
(Ed.), The Legacy of China.

DEUTSCHER, ISSAC. Russia, China and the West (Oxford University Press, 1969).

FAIRBANK, J. K. China: The People's Middle Kingdom and the U.S.A. (Harvard University Press, 1967).

FRANKE, W. China and the West (Blackwell, Oxford, 1968).

GEOFFROY-DECHAUME, F. China Looks at the World (Faber, London, 1967).

GRAY, J., and CAVENDISH, P. Chinese Communism in Crisis (Pall Mall Press, London, 1968).

HSUEH, CHUN-TU. Revolutionary Leaders of Modern China (Oxford University Press, 1970).

KAROL, K. S. China: The Other Communism (Heinemann, London, 1967).

KIRBY, E. S. (Ed.). Contemporary China (Hong Kong University Press, Hong Kong, 1956).

KLATT, W. The Chinese Model. A Political, Economic and Social Survey (Hong Kong University Press, Hong Kong, 1965).

KONINGSBERGER, H. Love and Hate in China (Cape, London, 1967).

KUO, PING-CHIA. China—New Age and New Outlook (Penguin, London, 1956).

MAO TSE TUNG. Selected Works (London, 1964).

MEHNERT, K. Peking and Moscow (Weidenfeld and Nicolson, London, 1964).

MENDE, T. China and her Shadow (Thames & Hudson, London, 1960).

NORTH, R. C. Chinese Communism (Weidenfeld and Nicolson, London, 1967).

PLESSIER, R. The Awakening of China (Secker and Warburg, London, 1967).

PURCELL, V. China (Benn, London, 1962).

SALISBURY, H. E. Orbit of China (Secker and Warburg, London, 1967).

SCHRAM, S. R. Political Thoughts of Mao Tse-tung (New York and London, 1963).
Mao Tse-tung (Penguin, London, 1966).

SEBES, J. Russia, Mongolia, China (London, 1919, revised edition 1964).

SNOW, E. Red Star Over China (Gollancz, London, 1937).

HISTORY

BIANCO, LUCIEN. Origins of the Chinese Revolution, 1915–1949 (Stanford University Press, U.S.A., 1972).

BRANDT, C., SCHWARTZ, B. I., and FAIRBANK, J. Documentary History of Chinese Communism (Harvard University Press, Cambridge, Mass., and London, 1962).

CHASSIN, L. M. The Communist Conquest of China (Weidenfeld and Nicolson, London, 1966).

CHEN, J. Mao and the Chinese Revolution (Oxford University Press, London, 1965).

CHEN, J. (Ed.). Mao Papers: anthology and bibliography (Oxford University Press, London, 1971).

FAN, K. H. The Chinese Cultural Revolution (Monthly Review Press, London, 1967).

FEUERWERKER, A., MURPHEY, R., and WRIGHT, M. C. (Eds.). Approaches to Modern Chinese History (California University Press and Cambridge University Press, 1967).

FITZGERALD, C. P. Revolution in China (Cresset Press, London, 1952).
China: A Short Cultural History (Cresset Press, London, revised edition, 1964).
Birth of Communist China (Penguin Books, London, 1964).

FITZGERALD, S. China and the Overseas Chinese: a study of Peking's changing policy 1949–70 (Oxford University Press, London, 1971).

GRIFFITHS, W. E. The Sino-Soviet Rift (Cambridge, Mass., and London, 1964).

HINTON, W. Hundred Day War (Monthly Review Press, New York and London, 1972).

HOLT, E. The Opium Wars in China (Putnam, London, 1964).

HUDSON, G. F., LOWENTHAL, R., and MACFARQUAR, R. The Sino-Soviet Dispute (New York, 1961).

LATOURETTE, K. S. A History of Modern China (Penguin Books, London, 1954).
The Chinese: Their History and Culture (Macmillan, New York, 1964).

LOEWE, M. Everyday Life in Early Imperial China (Batsford, London, 1968).
Records of Han Administration, Vols. I & II (Cambridge University Press, London).

MCALEAVY, H. A Modern History of China (Weidenfeld and Nicolson, London, 1967).

MENDE, T. The Chinese Revolution (Thames & Hudson, London, 1961).

MOSELEY, G. China: Empire to People's Republic (Batsford, London, 1968).

SCHWARTZ, B. I. Chinese Communism and the Rise of Mao (Harvard University Press, Cambridge, Mass., 1951).

TUNG, CHI MING. An Outline History of China (Peking, 1959).

TWITCHETT, D. C. Financial Administration under the T'ang Dynasty (Cambridge University Press, London).

WALEY, A. The Opium War through Chinese Eyes (Allen & Unwin, London, 1958).

WALKER, R. L. China under Communism—the First Five Years (New Haven, 1955).

WILSON, DICK. The Long March 1935 (Hamish Hamilton, London, 1971).

ZAGORIA, D. S. The Sino-Soviet Conflict 1956–61 (Princeton University Press, 1962).

GEOGRAPHY

BUCHANAN, K. The Chinese People and the Chinese Earth (Bell, London, 1966).

The Transformation of the Chinese Earth (Bell, London, 1970).

CRESSEY, C. China's Geographic Foundations: A Survey of the Land and its People (McGraw Hill, New York, 1934).

CRESSEY, G. B. Land of the 500 Million—A Geography of China (New York, 1955).

TREGEAR, T. R. A Geography of China (University of London Press, 1965).

ECONOMICS

BARNETT, A. D. Communist Economic Strategy: The Rise of Mainland China (National Planning Association, New York, 1959).

BUCK, J. L. Land Utilization in China (Chicago University Press, Chicago, 1937).

BUCK, J. L., DAWSON, O. L., and WU, Y. L. Food and Agriculture in Communist China (The Hoover Institution, Praeger, New York, 1966).

CHANDRASEKAR, S. China's Population (Hong Kong University Press, Hong Kong, 1959).

CHAO, K. Agricultural Production in Communist China 1949–1965 (University of Wisconsin Press, Madison, Milwaukee, 1970).

CHAO, K. C. Agrarian Policy of the Chinese Communist Party (Asia Publishing House, London, 1960).

CHEN, N. R. Chinese Economic Statistics (Edinburgh University Press, Edinburgh, 1967).

CHEN, N. R., and GALENSON, W. The Chinese Economy under Communism (University Press, Edinburgh, 1969).

CHENG, C. Y. The Machine-Building Industry in Communist China (Edinburgh University Press, 1972).

DAWSON, O. L. Communist Agriculture: Its Development and Future Potential (Praeger, New York, 1970).

DONNITHORNE, A. China's Economic System (Allen & Unwin, London, 1967).

ECKLUND, G. Financing the Chinese Government Budget (Edinburgh University Press, Edinburgh, 1967).

ECKSTEIN, A. The National Income of Communist China (The Free Press, Glencoe, Ill., 1961).

Communist China's Economic Growth and Foreign Trade (McGraw-Hill, New York, 1966).

ECKSTEIN, A., GALENSON, W., and LIU, T. C. Economic Trends in Communist China (University Press, Edinburgh, 1968).

EMERSON, J. P. Non-Agricultural Development in Mainland China (Bureau of Census, U.S. Dept. of Commerce, Washington, D.C., 1965).

Sex, Age and Level of Skill of the Non-Agricultural Labor Force of Mainland China (Bureau of Census, U.S. Dept. of Commerce, Washington, D.C., 1965).

HOLLISTER, W. W. China's Gross National Product and Social Accounts 1950–1957 (The Free Press, Glencoe, Ill., 1958).

HOU, C. M. Foreign Investment and Economic Development in China 1840–1937 (Harvard University Press, 1966).

HSIA, R. Economic Planning in Communist China (Institute of Pacific Relations, New York, 1955).

HUGHES, T. J., and LUARD, D. E. T. The Economic Development of Communist China 1949–1960 (Oxford University Press, London, 1961).

KIRBY, E. S. Introduction to the Economic History of China (Allen & Unwin, London, 1954).

KIRBY, E. S., *et al.* Contemporary China. Vols I–VI (Hong Kong University Press, Hong Kong, 1956ff).

LI, C. M. The Economic Development of Communist China (California University Press, Berkeley, 1959).

The Statistical System of Communist China (California University Press, Berkeley, 1962).

LIU, T. C., and YEH, K. C. The Economy of the Chinese Mainland: National Income and Economic Development 1933–1959 (Princeton University Press, Princeton, 1965).

MAH, F. H. The Foreign Trade of Mainland China (Edinburgh University Press, 1972).

ORLEANS, L. A. Professional Manpower and Education in Communist China (National Science Foundation, Washington, D.C., 1960).

Every Fifth Child: The Population of China (Eyre Methuen, London, 1972).

PERKINS, D. H. Agricultural Development in China 1368–1968 (University Press, Edinburgh, 1969).

REMER, C. F., *et al.* International Economics of Communist China (Michigan University Press, Ann Arbor, 1959).

TREGEAR, T. R. Economic Geography of China (Butterworths, London, 1970).

U.S. CONGRESS: Joint Economic Committee, People's Republic of China: An Economic Assessment (U.S. Government Printing Office, Washington, 1972).

WU, Y. L. An Economic Survey of Communist China (Bookmen Associates, New York, 1956).

Economic Development and the Use of Energy Resources in Communist China (Praeger, New York, 1963).

The Steel Industry of Communist China (Praeger, New York, 1965).

The Economy of Communist China (Pall Mall Press, London, 1965).

WU, Y. L., LING, H. C., and WU, G. H. The Spatial Economy of Communist China: A Study in Industrial Location and Transportation (Praeger, New York, 1967).

YIN, H. L., and YIN, Y. C. Economic Statistics of Mainland China (Harvard University Press, Cambridge, Mass., 1960).

STATISTICAL INFORMATION

A Great Decade: Statistical Information on Communist China's Economic Growth in the First Ten Years (Peking, 1959).

Ten Great Years: Statistics of the Economic and Cultural Achievements of the People's Republic of China (Peking, 1960).

TAIWAN

GENERAL

BANK OF AMERICA. Focus on Taiwan (San Francisco, 1968).

GODDARD, W. G. Formosa: A Study in Chinese History (Macmillan, London, 1966).

HSU, LONG-HSUEN, and CHANG, MING-KAI. History of the Sino-Japanese War (Chung Wu Publishing Co., 1971).

ECONOMY

CHANG, HAN-YU, and MYERS, R. H. Japanese Colonial Development Policy in Taiwan 1895–1906: A Case of Bureaucratic Entrepreneurship (*The Journal of Asian Studies*, Vol. XXII, No. 4, 1963).

CHANG, KOWEI. Economic Development in Taiwan (Cheng Chung Co., Taipei, 1968).

CHINA YEAR BOOK. Annual.

GURTOV, M. Recent Developments on Formosa (*The China Quarterly*, No. XXXI, 1967).

HO, C. S., and others. Economic Minerals of Taiwan, Geological Survey of Taiwan, 1963.

HO, YHI-MIN. Agricultural Development of Taiwan: 1903–1960 (Vanderbilt University Press, Tennessee, 1966).

JACOBY, N. H. An Evaluation of U.S. Economic Aid to Free China 1951–1965 (Praeger, New York, 1967).

KAO, CHARLES HSI-CHUNG. An Analysis of Agricultural Output Increase on Taiwan 1953–1964 (*The Journal of Asian Studies*, Vol. XXVI, No. 4, 1967).

MINISTRY OF INTERIOR AND COUNCIL FOR INTERNATIONAL ECONOMIC CO-OPERATION AND DEVELOPMENT. Labor Laws and Regulations of the Republic of China (Taipei, 1965).

MYERS, R. H. Economic Growth and Population Change in Taiwan (*The Malayan Economic Review*, Vol. VIII, No. 2, 1963).

SHEN, TSUNG-HAN. Agricultural Development on Taiwan since World War II (Mei Ya Publication Inc., Taipei, 1971).

TAIWAN AGRICULTURAL YEARBOOK. Department of Agriculture and Forestry, Provincial Government of Taiwan (Annual).

TAIWAN. STATISTICAL DATA BOOK. Directorate-General of Budgets, Accounts and Statistics (Annual).

TANG, H. S., and HSIEH, S. C. Land Reform and Agricultural Development in Taiwan (*The Malayan Economic Review*, Vol. VI, No. 1, 1961).

Hong Kong

PHYSICAL AND SOCIAL GEOGRAPHY

Michael Freeberne

(Revised by the Editor, 1976)

Hong Kong's teeming population is crowded into a total area of only 403.8 square miles. The Crown Colony is situated off the south-east coast of China, to the east of the mouth of the Pearl river, between latitudes 22° 9′ and 22° 37′ N. and longitudes 113° 52′ and 114° 30′ E. Hong Kong includes the island of Hong Kong, ceded to Britain by China in 1842, the Kowloon peninsula, ceded in 1860, and the New Territories, which are part of the mainland leased to Britain in 1898 for a period of ninety-nine years, together with Deep Bay and Mirs Bay and various outlying islands. The fine anchorages between the capital of Victoria on the northern shore of Hong Kong island and Kowloon, provided an ideal situation for the growth of one of the world's leading entrepôt ports.

Physical Features

Hong Kong Island is roughly eleven miles long and between two and five miles wide. An irregular range of hills rises abruptly from the sea; several peaks are over 1,000 ft. in height, and Victoria Peak reaches 1,809 ft. Granites, basalt and other volcanic rocks account for the main geological formations. These rocks are most common, too, on Lantau and Lamma islands and in the Kowloon peninsula and New Territories, which are mostly hilly, rising to 3,144 ft. in Tai Mo Shan, and have rugged deeply indented coastlines. The Colony is poor in minerals and largely stripped of natural vegetation. Flat land and agricultural land is everywhere scarce. Reclamation of land from the sea for building purposes is very important, and the new land is used for housing and factories, as well as projects like the extension of the runway of Kai Tak international airport.

Climate

The climate of Hong Kong is tropical monsoon. Winter lasts from October to April, when the winds are from the north or north-east, whilst during the summer months from May to September south or southwesterly winds predominate. Average daily temperatures are highest in July with 28°C. and lowest in February with 15°C. The wet summer is very humid. Annual rainfall averages 2,169 mm., over two-thirds of which falls between June and September. Devastating typhoons occasionally strike in summer, taking an especially heavy toll amongst the squatter colonies which crowd some of the hill-sides.

Notwithstanding the high rainfall it has proved difficult to supply sufficient domestic and industrial water, and recently water has been piped from neighbouring Kwangtung Province in China. The Plover Cove reservoir, inaugurated in 1969, and holding 37,000 million gallons, trebled Hong Kong's reservoir capacity. A further hazard which frequently threatens the sub-standard housing of the large refugee population is the danger of fire and disease, despite the brave housing and health schemes of the government.

POPULATION

The population of Hong Kong at the beginning of 1976 was estimated at 4,400,000, an average density of 4,187 per square kilometre. However, average density in the New Territories in 1971 was only 468 per square kilometre, whereas for Hong Kong Island and Kowloon it was 17,098, and in the Mong Kok district 154,677. These higher figures represent some of the highest population densities in the world.

Hong Kong has experienced an extraordinary growth in population. About 58 per cent of the population in 1976 was born in Hong Kong. Between 1841, when only about 2,500 people lived on the island, and 1941, the colony received wave after wave of migrants; then the population was estimated at about 1.5 million. There was a drastic reduction during the Japanese occupation in the early 1940s, but by 1949 the population had grown to 1,857,000. After the establishment of the People's Republic of China in 1949 large numbers of refugees arrived in Hong Kong, where the rate of natural increase was already high. About 1.22 million people had been resettled in multi-storey estates by the end of 1972. More than 98 per cent of the population are Chinese, on the basis of language and place of origin. The Cantonese are the largest community.

Land Use

Seventy-six per cent of Hong Kong's land area is marginal land; 11.5 per cent comprises built-up areas; and 12.5 per cent is in agricultural use. Only the alluvial soils around Yuen Long in the Deep Bay area have any depth. Hong Kong belongs to the frost-free double-cropping rice zone of East Asia. Increasingly, however, more profitable forms of land utilization are replacing rice: market gardens, including vegetables, fruit and cut flowers for the dense urban populations; poultry farms and fish ponds.

HISTORY

N. J. Miners

The area of the present colony was acquired in three stages. The First Opium War of 1840–42 began after the Chinese Commissioner in Canton had seized and destroyed large stocks of opium held by the British traders there, who then left the city. The British Government demanded compensation and a commercial treaty, and an expedition was despatched to enforce these demands. During the hostilities a naval force occupied the island of Hong Kong, which was ceded to Britain "in perpetuity" by the Treaty of Nanking of 1842. As soon as this was ratified the colony was formally proclaimed in June 1843.

Continuing disputes between Britain and China over trade and shipping led to renewed warfare in 1856. This was ended by the Convention of Peking of 1860, by which the peninsula of Kowloon on the mainland opposite the island was annexed.

In 1895 China was defeated by Japan, and the Western powers seized the opportunity to exact further concessions. Britain obtained a 99-year lease of the mainland north of Kowloon together with the adjoining islands, on the ground that this was needed for the colony's defence. These New Territories increased the area of the colony from 43 to 400 square miles. The terms of the 1898 Convention of Peking allowed the existing Chinese magistrates to remain in the Old Walled City of Kowloon, but in 1899 they were unilaterally expelled by the British on the pretext that they had encouraged resistance to the British occupation. The Chinese Government protested at the time and reasserted a claim to jurisdiction over this small area in 1933, 1948 and 1962, though this interpretation of the 1898 Convention has been rejected by the Hong Kong courts.

Since 1949 spokesmen for the People's Republic of China have asserted that all the unequal treaties forced upon China in the days of its weakness are no longer recognized as binding; but the treaties of 1842, 1860 and 1898 have not yet been formally abrogated. After admission to the United Nations in 1971, Peking's permanent representative informed the Special Committee on Colonialism that "Hong Kong and Macao are part of Chinese territory occupied by the British and Portuguese authorities. The settlement of the questions of Hong Kong and Macao is entirely within China's sovereign right and does not at all fall under the ordinary category of colonial territories. . . . The Chinese Government has consistently held that they should be settled in an appropriate way when conditions are ripe".

In deference to China's wishes, Hong Kong and Macao were deleted from the list of colonial territories. However, the United Kingdom still considers the treaties to be valid. All leases of Crown land in the New Territories terminate on June 27th, 1997, three days before the expiry of the British lease.

Early Development to 1945

The main reason for the British occupation of Hong Kong in 1841 was its magnificent harbour. Attracted by its free port status, the entrepôt trade between the West and China grew steadily for the next 100 years. The great trading companies set up their headquarters under the British flag; banks, insurance companies and other commercial enterprises were established to serve the China traders as well as shipbuilding, ship-repairing and other industries dependent on the port. At the same time the population grew from about 5,000 in 1841 to more than 500,000 in 1916 and over a million by 1939, of which fewer than 20,000 were non-Chinese. Chinese were allowed free access and the flow of migrants increased whenever China was disturbed by wars or rebellions, reversing itself when peaceful conditions had been restored on the mainland. Apart from the settled farming population of the New Territories, relatively few Chinese regarded Hong Kong as their permanent home until after the Second World War. Most came to trade or seek employment and then returned to their home-towns. Europeans were similarly transient, whether they were government officials or in private employment. Few, apart from some Portuguese from Macao and Eurasians, considered Hong Kong their permanent home.

The colony's administration followed the usual Crown Colony pattern, with power concentrated in the hands of a Governor advised by nominated Executive and Legislative Councils on which government officials had an overall majority over the unofficial members. The first unoficial members were appointed to the Legislative Council in 1850, and the first Chinese in 1880; the first unofficials in the Executive Council were appointed in 1896, and the first Chinese in 1926. In 1894 and 1916 the British merchants pressed for an unofficial majority in the Legislative Council and the election of some or all of the unofficials on a franchise confined to British subjects, citing the constitutional progress made in other colonies; but on both occasions the British Government was unwilling to allow the Chinese majority to be politically subjected to a small European minority. A Sanitary Board was set up in 1883 and this was made partly elective in 1887. In 1936 it was renamed the Urban Council, though its powers were not significantly increased.

Little of note happened in Hong Kong throughout this period, apart from commercial expansion, land reclamation, the building of reservoirs and minor squabbles between British officialdom and the trading community. There were a number of large-scale strikes in the early 1920s, notably that of 1925/26 which closed the port for several months, but, other than these incidents, anti-foreigner agitation in China had little effect on Hong Kong's prosperity.

The outbreak of war in Europe in the late 1930s led

to an increase in defence expenditure, which forced the institution of income and profits tax for the first time; this wartime expedient was made permanent in 1947. Japanese forces occupied most of the Chinese province of Kwangtung, north of the colony, in 1938, and in December 1941 invaded Hong Kong, which was forced to surrender. The Japanese occupation lasted three years eight months until August 1945, when the Japanese authorities handed power back to the surviving colonial officials who had been interned with the rest of the British community throughout the occupation. A British naval force arrived in late August to set up an interim military administration, thus forestalling pressures from the United States Government for Hong Kong to be handed back to China.

The Post-War Period

After the loss of Hong Kong in 1941 a planning unit was set up in London to prepare for the post-war rehabilitation of the colony. Its members staffed the interim military administration, which restored public services on a minimum basis. During the war the colony's population had dropped to about 600,000 as a result of privation and mass deportations by the Japanese. The population quickly regained pre-war levels and then rose to about 2,000,000 in 1950 as a result of a massive influx of refugees from the civil war in China. The pressures caused by this inflow forced the colony to abandon its policy of free access and the frontier was closed in 1950. Since then, movement over the border has largely been controlled by the Chinese authorities who have usually limited immigration into Hong Kong to a quota of roughly 50 per day, with the exception of 1962 when the frontier was unexpectedly opened and 120,000 refugees were allowed to leave. Individual escapers also attempt to enter clandestinely. Until 1974 those who succeeded in eluding the frontier guards were allowed to remain, but since then any illegal immigrants apprehended near the frontier have been handed back to the Chinese authorities.

The United Kingdom recognized the new Communist Government of China in 1950, having heavily reinforced the garrison in Hong Kong in 1949 to deter any possible Chinese attack. The only serious violation of the frontier occurred in 1967. Since the early 1970s the garrison has been run down at successive British defence reviews. From 1976 it will consist of four infantry battalions (three of them Gurkha) and supporting services, together with the locally-raised Hong Kong Regiment. British troops are mainly occupied with patrolling the border and also provide a back-up for the police in internal security operations.

The Hong Kong Government at first hoped that the refugees would return to China when stability was restored there, but this did not happen. The problem of feeding them and providing employment was made worse by the outbreak of the Korean war in 1950 which led to the imposition of an embargo on the export of strategic goods to China and gravely damaged Hong Kong's entrepôt trade. However, the refugees provided a pool of docile, hard-working labour. Local businessmen and industrialists who had fled from Shanghai took advantage of this and, by making use of the colony's existing financial infrastructure and worldwide trading connections, they re-oriented the economy to manufacturing for export. The value of domestic exports fluctuated during the 1950s but there were continued rapid increases in the 1960s.

Government revenue has risen in line with the growth of the economy, from HK $195 million in 1948/49 to an estimate of over HK $6,000 million in 1975/76. Over this period tax increases have been minimal. The greatest increase in revenue, from HK $2,000 million to HK $6,000 million, occurred between 1970 and 1975. Between 1961 and 1971 there was only one year of deficit (in 1965/66) in spite of the fact that all capital expenditure was financed out of current revenue. From 1971 there was a rapid expansion in the social services: for example, education expenditure more than doubled from HK $498 million in 1970/71 to HK $1,145 million in 1974/75, and expenditure on social welfare went up seven times from HK $36 million to HK $262 million in the same period. The oil crisis and world depression, which began in 1974, put a check on this expansion in 1974/75 and resulted in the first budget deficit for nine years. This led the Financial Secretary to budget for small deficits in both 1975/76 and 1976/77 rather than cut back drastically on planned expenditure.

Apart from education, most social service expenditure has been on housing. The refugees put an immense strain on all public services and the newcomers were left to build themselves shanty towns which spread over the hillsides. A devastating fire at one of these shanty towns in 1953 spurred the Government into a resettlement programme; huge estates were built with rooms allocated on the scale of 25 square feet (2.3 square metres) for each adult. The early designs provided few amenities, as the main consideration was speed of erection. The housing programme has continued steadily since then with an added boost in 1972 when a ten-year programme to house a further 1,500,000 people, mainly in new towns in the New Territories, was announced. At the same time various government housing agencies were amalgamated in a new Housing Authority to take over the planning, construction and management of all public housing in Hong Kong. The latest estates are being built to improved standards, with separate washrooms and kitchens for each family and a space allocation of 50 square feet per adult. At the end of 1975 over 1,800,000 people, 43 per cent of the population, were living in government estates.

Since 1945 the people of Hong Kong have shown a marked apathy towards any form of political activity or agitation for democratic self-government. This political calm has been disturbed only three times: in 1956 by faction fights between communist and nationalist supporters; in 1966 there were three nights of rioting sparked off by a fare increase on the cross-harbour ferry; and for several months in 1967 there were disturbances and bomb attacks, led by communist sympathizers inspired by the example of the Cultural Revolution in China. Since then, relations with China have greatly improved and China seems content to allow capitalism to flourish in Hong Kong so long as it enjoys a favourable balance of trade and payments with the colony. Estimates of China's foreign exchange earnings vary up to U.S. $1,500 million per year or more, enough to finance about 40 per cent of China's trade with non-communist countries. In 1973 the Chinese Government proposed to the United Kingdom that an official representative should be appointed in Hong Kong, but talks on this were suspended after disagreement over the precise status and title of the official.

Administrative and Political Developments

Civil government was restored after the Japanese occupation in May 1946. The returning governor promised a greater measure of self-government and, after inviting suggestions from the public, proposed that an elected municipal council with wide powers over local affairs in the urban area should be set up. The detailed bills to implement this proposal were not published until June 1949, but then the unofficial members of the Legislative Council objected that reforms of their council to provide for elected members and an official majority should have priority, and voted unanimously against the plan. Consultations were recommenced and continued for the next three years; but, in the absence of widespread agitation for changes and amid the continuing uncertainty over the colony's future caused by the communist victory in China in 1949, reform was abandoned in 1952 and has not been revived since.

Instead, the number of unofficial members on the Legislative Council has been successively increased, to 8 in 1951, 13 in 1964 and 15 in 1973. In 1976 eleven of these unofficials were Chinese. All are nominated by the Secretary of State for Foreign and Commonwealth Affairs in Britain, on the advice of the Governor. The number of official members has also been increased to keep their numbers equal to the unofficials. In the last resort, since the Governor is a member of the Council, the officials could outvote the unofficials, but in practice the official majority has not been used to overrule the unanimous view of the unofficials since 1953. The unofficials also form a Finance Committee which meets in private to scrutinize in detail all government expenditure proposals. Since 1945, if the unofficials have rejected any item, the administration has always taken this as final.

The number of unofficial members on the Executive Council was increased to eight in 1966, thus outnumbering the six official members. In 1976 half the Council were Chinese (six unofficials and one official). The Governor is empowered to reject the advice given to him by the majority of the Council, but in fact is most unlikely to do so.

The British Government and parliament retain the power to legislate for the colony, to veto ordinances passed by the Legislative Council, and to issue mandatory instructions to the Governor. The veto has not been invoked since 1913 and the power to legislate is confined almost entirely to matters which concern the United Kingdom's international or Commonwealth obligations. Hong Kong is normally allowed to run its internal affairs without reference to Britain. It has drawn up its own budget since 1958. When sterling was devalued in November 1967 a new rate for the Hong Kong dollar was fixed locally in the light of the colony's special position. In July 1972 the rate of exchange was pegged to the U.S. dollar and in November 1974 the Hong Kong dollar was allowed to "float". Hong Kong is free to diversify its reserves, and the proportion held in sterling dropped from 99 per cent in 1970 to less than 40 per cent in 1976.

The Urban Council was reorganized in 1973 with 12 appointed and 12 elected members, and responsibility for public health and sanitation, recreation, amenities and cultural services in the urban area. The franchise is restricted: about 500,000 are entitled to vote, but in recent years fewer than 40,000 have bothered to register and fewer than 12,000 have voted in the biennial elections. The Reform Club and the Civic Association run candidates but voting is largely on the basis of personalities. The limited functions performed by the Council do not arouse widespread interest.

Since 1968 the urban area has been divided into ten city districts, each run by an administrative officer with a small staff, who is responsible for explaining government policy and receiving local complaints. Grievances can also be aired at the ward offices of the Urban Council, and at the Office of the Unofficial Members of the Executive and Legislative Councils (UMELCO). The interests of the indigenous inhabitants of the New Territories are served by an elected advisory body, the *Heung Yee Kuk*. Though it has no executive powers it is heard with the greatest respect by the administration and has been successful in obtaining very generous compensation terms when the Government resumes land for development.

In 1973 revelations of widespread corruption in the police force led to the establishment of the Independent Commission Against Corruption (I.C.A.C.). Its energetic investigations have led to the conviction and imprisonment of a number of police officers and businessmen.

ECONOMIC SURVEY

M. P. Gopalan

The Year of the Dragon, 1976, marked the end of two years of virtual stagnation for Hong Kong's economy. The Government and the private sector had been pumping millions of dollars into construction, property development and vital infrastructure. A 9 per cent increase in real growth for the year was predicted. Such forecasts were based not only on internal elements in the economy, but also on such external factors as the expected upturn in Hong Kong's major export outlets in the industrialized West.

The total value of visible imports and exports (domestic exports plus re-exports) is almost twice the size of the gross domestic product. (In 1974 visible imports and exports together were valued at HK $65,393 million, compared with the G.D.P. of HK $33,842 million.) Income (in the sense of value added) derived from visible exports is equivalent to almost half the G.D.P. (and it can thus be demonstrated statistically that the rate of growth of demand in Hong Kong's principal export markets has a significant bearing on the rate of growth of the colony's economy. (Over the period 1969–74, domestic exports to North America and Western Europe, at current prices, grew at a rate of 15 per cent per annum, while the G.D.P., again at current prices, grew at 17 per cent per annum.) Finally, half the consumption and investment expenditure, which is itself generated by the income derived from the exports, is represented by its visible import content. In 1974 consumption (HK $28,465 million) and investment (HK $7,302 million) added up to HK $35,767 million, of which 50 per cent was the import content. If the invisible imports and exports (the transactions connected with tourism and mercantile and financial services) and the capital transactions are added to the visible imports and exports, it is estimated that the total money flows in and out of Hong Kong probably account for as much as six times the G.D.P.

The buoyant outlook for 1976 was all the more significant because the previous year had been a period of dual distresses, of inflation and recession, for most of the world. The oil crisis compounded the problems. But the colony's economy once again proved its resilience and adaptability to a changing economic environment.

The 1976/77 budget is based on the premise that "the economy is in good shape in terms of external cost competitiveness and the stock of money." The colony's exports, imports and re-exports during January–March 1976 went up by 51 per cent, 39 per cent and 36 per cent respectively compared with the corresponding period of 1975. The financial scene was brighter at the beginning of 1976. The money supply, M1 (i.e., cash with the non-bank public plus demand deposits) and M2 (i.e. M1 plus time and savings deposits), respectively stood at HK $14,779 million and HK $41,837 million at the end of January 1976, up 29 per cent and 20 per cent over the corresponding month of 1975.

The rate of inflation for 1976/77 was forecast at 6 per cent, up from the 1.2 per cent of 1975/76. Total exports and imports by volume are expected to increase by 8 per cent and 12 per cent, respectively, leaving a visible trade deficit of HK $4,600 million.

The official preliminary estimate of Hong Kong's nominal G.D.P. for 1975 was placed at HK $35,407 million, an increase of 2.8 per cent over 1974. Compared with increases of 12.5 per cent in 1974 and 26.8 per cent in 1973, this is the lowest growth rate since the mid-1960s. In real terms G.D.P. rose 0.8 per cent during 1975 to HK $19,428 million (at 1966 prices). Per capita G.D.P. at current prices remained unchanged at HK $8,109 (U.S. $1,642) in 1975. From 1971 to 1975, per capita income increased at an average rate of 11.7 per cent per annum at current prices, or 3.1 per cent in real terms.

AGRICULTURE AND FISHING

Hong Kong aims to become as self-sufficient as possible in the production of fresh foods such as vegetables, fish, pigs and poultry. A large proportion of the people's requirements is already being met, even though only 12 per cent of the total land area is used for farming, and less than 2 per cent of the working population is involved in fishing. China remains Hong Kong's major source of imports of agricultural and food products.

The 1971 census showed that farmers comprised only 2.09 per cent of the total economically active population of Hong Kong, and fishermen made up another 1.88 per cent. Hong Kong's fishing fleet catches about 92 per cent of all fresh marine fish eaten in the territory, and local pond fish farmers produce some 12 per cent of the freshwater fish consumed. Agricultural production is limited by the availability of suitable land rather than by numbers of people in the industry. Farmers in the New Territories produce about 43 per cent of the vegetables consumed, some 52 per cent of the total live chicken requirements, and about 12 per cent of all pigs slaughtered.

Common crops are vegetables, flowers, rice, fruit and other field crops. The value of crop production increased from HK $89 million in 1963 to HK $283 million in 1975, a rise of 218 per cent. Vegetable production accounts for more than 87 per cent of the total value, having increased from HK $58 million in 1963 to HK $245 million in 1975.

Rice is the staple food of the southern Chinese. Two crops of rice per year can be grown on land where water is adequate. The normal yield from an acre of two-crop rice land is about two tons, or up to five tons with high fertilizer use and high-yielding strains. The area of rice land dropped from 23,353 acres in 1954 to 2,750 acres in 1975. Rice production continues to give way to intensive vegetable production, which gives a far higher return where there is adequate water and good road access.

The main vegetable crops are white cabbage, flowering cabbage, lettuce, Chinese kale, radish, watercress, leaf mustard, spring onion and chive. They grow all the year round, with the peak production period in the cooler months. The area of land under vegetables and flowers increased from 2,250 acres in 1954 to 12,290 acres in 1975.

As there is insufficient land for extensive grazing, pigs and poultry are the principal animals reared for food. Although locally produced pigs represented only 12 per cent of total pigs killed in 1975, their value was HK $74 million.

With an annual production value of HK $160 million, the poultry industry, including ducks, pigeons and quail, is continuing to develop on a more sophisticated basis. Farmers are adopting advanced methods of management and successfully adapting them to local conditions, taking the process through from locally bred chicks to table birds with both local breeds and imported hybrids.

The total quantity of fish and fishery products increased from 121,500 metric tons (valued at HK $316 million) in 1970 to 150,400 metric tons (valued at HK $523 million) in 1975. This is an increase of 24 per cent by quantity and 65 per cent by value. Marine fish landings in 1975 amounted to 95,000 metric tons at a wholesale value of HK $316 million. This represented 92 per cent of the local consumer demand.

The fishing fleet consists of 5,600 vessels, of which 92 per cent are mechanized. An estimated 47,000 fishermen work the fleet, with a large proportion of vessels being owner-operated.

INDUSTRY

Light industry (of which textiles, electronics and plastics are the most important) continues to dominate Hong Kong's manufacturing sector. Establishments producing textiles and clothing, electronics, plastic products and toys account for about 70 per cent of the total industrial work force and more than 70 per cent of the total domestic exports. These industries are likely to maintain their lead for a few more years. The Government is, however, encouraging industries with a high technological content and those which can supply raw materials for local industry.

In the earlier months of 1975, as a result of the world-wide recession, textiles (except clothing), electronics and plastics were particularly hard hit by the fall in consumer demand in some of their most important export markets, and this led to a reduction in employment. But by mid-year demand was recovering and by the third quarter most factories were able to re-engage labour and resume full-time working. Factories producing clothing and watches and clocks managed to withstand the effects of the recession particularly well and certain sectors of these industries produced substantially more than in the previous year.

Of 120 representative factories producing a range of products, the majority employed more labour in 1975 than in 1974. Ninety-two of them had increased the value of their production in the first three months of 1976. The majority reported that orders on hand and the average value of orders were both higher than a year before. Over 50 per cent of those factories were expecting demand to increase in both the first and second halves of 1976 and just under 50 per cent predicted a further increase in 1977.

About 8.7 per cent of Hong Kong's workers in manufacturing industries (totalling 678,857 in December 1975) are employed in factories owned or partly owned by overseas interests, and several new subsidiaries of overseas companies were in the course of being established at the end of 1975. In order to broaden Hong Kong's industrial base, the Government increased its efforts to promote industrial investment and sent missions to Australia, the United Kingdom and the U.S.A. during 1975. In a further move to encourage the development of a wider range of industries, the Government decided to construct Hong Kong's first industrial estate for land-intensive industries in the New Territories.

Textiles

Despite the drop in overseas orders in the early part of 1975, the textiles industry remained the mainstay of Hong Kong's economy, employing approximately 50 per cent of the manufacturing workforce and accounting for about 54 per cent of domestic exports. The world economic recession affected the spinning, weaving and finishing sectors of the industry, with most factories operating below capacity for several months. Employment was relatively low, although by the end of the year there was a substantial improvement compared with the first quarter. The new multi-fibre restraint agreement concluded with the European Economic Community in July under the GATT Multi-Fibre Textiles Arrangement caused some disruption to production.

The spinning sector, operating about 895,300 spindles, contains some of the most modern factories in the world. Although many mills operated below capacity for much of the year, the production of cotton yarn in 1975 was 357 million lb., compared with 328 million lb. the previous year; man-made fibre yarn and cotton and man-made fibre blended yarn dropped by 18 per cent to 60 million lb.; and woollen and worsted yarn was 13 million lb., compared with 14 million lb. in 1974. Most of the yarn produced was used by local weavers.

In 1975 the 26,575 looms in the weaving sector produced 847 million square yards of fabrics of various fibres and blends, compared with 805 million square yards in 1974. As in previous years the bulk of the production, 87 per cent, was of cotton. The knitting sector exported 15 million lb. of fabrics, of which 62 per cent was of man-made fibres and 38 per cent of cotton. A large part of the production of knitted fabrics of all fibres was used by local clothing manufacturers.

The finishing sector provides sophisticated supporting facilities to the spinning, weaving and knitting sectors. It handles a large amount of textile fabrics for bleaching, dyeing, printing and finishing. Output in early 1975 was considerably affected by the difficulties experienced during the year in the spinning and weaving sectors of the textiles industry.

Clothing continued to be the largest sector of the industry, employing about 34 per cent of Hong Kong's manufacturing workforce and accounting for 45 per cent of all domestic exports. During the year the clothing industry manufactured an increasing variety of high-quality items and kept up to date with the latest trends in fashion. The textiles industry was the sector least affected by the world economic recession. Hong Kong's domestic exports of clothing in 1975 were valued at HK $10,202 million, 17 per cent more than in 1974.

Other Light Industries

Although the electronics industry maintained its position in 1975 as the second largest export earner, it was one of the industries most affected by the international recession. Many electronics factories operated below capacity for much of the year and some were forced to suspend operation. But there was an improvement during the second half of the year due to increased overseas demand for certain electronic products, particularly pocket calculators. The industry comprises 460 factories employing 51,570 workers, and its products include computer memory systems, transistors, integrated circuits and semiconductors, tape recorders, transistor radios, desk and pocket calculators, television aerials and television sets. Hong Kong's domestic exports of electronic products in 1975 were valued at HK $2,683 million, 11 per cent less than in 1974.

The plastic industry had another difficult year. Although there was an adequate supply of plastic raw materials available at stable prices, there was a decrease in consumer demand in overseas markets for most plastic products. The industry comprises 3,437 firms with a workforce of 63,706. It produces a wide range of items, the most important being: toys and dolls; plastic household articles; artificial flowers, foliage and fruit; and footwear. In 1975, domestic exports of plastic products were valued at HK $1,979 million, 16 per cent less than in 1974.

Other significant light industries produce watches, clocks and accessories; travel goods; metal products; and electrical machinery, apparatus and appliances. Most of the factories in the watches, clocks and accessories industry maintained or increased their production and an increasing number of watch factories now manufacture electronic digital quartz watches.

Hong Kong's heavy industry includes shipbuilding and repair, aircraft maintenance and repair, steel rolling and manufacture of machinery and machine tools. Proposals for construction of an oil refinery and petrochemical complex were put into abeyance in view of the present over-capacity in the industry and the uncertain world economic situation.

The construction industry reported completion of 569 buildings at a cost of HK $1,890 million in 1975, compared with 645 buildings at HK $1,869 million in the previous year. In 1973, 713 buildings were constructed at a cost of HK $1,383 million.

Work began on the underground mass transit railway which will cost HK $5,000 million. Following the Japanese consortium's decisions to cease negotiations for a formal contract for building the railway's initial system, the Government decided to modify the plans. The new rail system comprises 9.7 miles of route, linking the Central District of Hong Kong Island to Kwun Tong in Kowloon. The system is scheduled to commence partial operation in 1979 and to be fully operational by 1980.

Overseas Investments

At the end of 1975, there were at least 271 factories in Hong Kong either fully or partly owned by overseas interests—an increase of 9.7 per cent over 1974. These establishments employed a total labour force of 59,607 or 8.7 per cent of total employment in the colony's manufacturing industry. The total direct investment involved was about HK $1,730 million. The main sources of overseas investment continued to be the United States, Japan, Britain, Thailand, Singapore and Australia. The principal industries involved were textiles and electronics although new investment was generally in other fields, such as light to medium engineering and chemicals.

LABOUR AND WAGES

In December 1975 a total of 678,857 workers were employed in 31,034 establishments in the manufacturing sector. The largest number of the labour force—351,880—were engaged in weaving, spinning, knitting, and manufacture of garments and made-up textile goods. The plastics and electronics industries were the next two largest employers.

The 1971 population census revealed a total working population of 1,582,849 in Hong Kong—1,049,989 male and 532,860 female. The main distribution of the work force was: manufacturing 677,498; services 312,173; commerce 208,604; construction and engineering 168,773; transport and communications 114,722; agriculture, forestry and fishing 62,975; public utilities 8,870; mining and quarrying 4,518; and other industries 24,716.

Most semi-skilled and unskilled workers in the manufacturing industries are piece-rated, although daily rates of pay are common. Men and women receive the same rates for piece-work, but women are generally paid less when working on a time-basis.

Daily wages for the manufacturing industries at the end of 1975 ranged from $18.50 to $65.30 for skilled workers; $14 to $40 for semi-skilled workers and $13 to $28.50 for unskilled workers. Many employers provide their workers with free accommodation, subsidized meals, or food-allowances, good attendance bonuses, paid rest-days, and a Lunar New Year bonus of one month's pay.

The Factories and Industrial Undertakings Ordinance and its regulations control the hours and conditions of work in industry. Since December 1971, the maximum hours of work for women and young people, aged 16 and 17, employed in industry have been eight hours a day and 48 hours a week. In addition to establishing maximum daily working hours, the regulations limit overtime and provide for weekly rest-days, and rest-breaks for women and young people. Maximum overtime was reduced to 250 hours per year from January 1975 and to 200 hours from January 1976.

Young people aged 14 and 15 may work eight hours a day in industry with a break of one hour after five hours' continuous work and no overtime is allowed. Children under the age of 14 are prohibited from working in industry, and no woman or young person is allowed to work at night or underground. A number of large factories, however, were authorized in 1970 to employ women at night. There are no restrictions on hours of work for men.

Labour Relations

At the end of 1975 there were 356 unions, 111 independent and the others belonging to two major organizations.

With the exception of a small neutral and independent segment, most employees' unions are either affiliated to or associated with one of two local federations which are registered as societies and bear allegiance to opposing political groups. The Hong Kong Federation of Trade Unions is a left-wing organization. Most of the members of its 67 affiliated unions are concentrated in shipyards, textile mills and public utilities. A further 29 unions, nominally independent, are friendly towards the federation and participate in its activities. The Hong Kong and Kowloon Trades Union Council has right-wing sympathies. Most of the members of its 84 affiliated unions and of the nine nominally independent unions which generally support the Trades Union Council are employed in the catering and building trades. The Trades Union Council is affiliated to the International Confederation of Free Trade Unions. Although the majority of workers are organized, employees and employers generally maintain industrial peace. The Labour Relations Ordinance, which aims at improving labour-management relations, gives the Government the right to intervene in trade disputes so that efforts can be made to defuse potentially damaging situations arising out of such disputes.

In September 1975, 9.1 per cent of Hong Kong's estimated labour force of 1,947,000 was unemployed. The labour force includes 64.2 per cent of the total population aged between 14 and 64. However, there was a significant improvement in the unemployment situation during the last quarter of 1975.

EXTERNAL TRADE

Hong Kong's total trade reached $63,304 million in 1975 compared with $64,156 million in the previous year. Imports were valued at $33,472 million compared with $34,120 million; domestic exports $22,859 million compared with $22,911 million; and re exports $6,973 million compared with $7,124 million.

Hong Kong is almost entirely dependent on imported resources to meet the needs of its people and the extensive requirements of its diverse industries. Although domestic supplies of agricultural produce and fish are substantial, imports of foodstuffs amounted to $6,283 million, or 19 per cent of imports in 1975, constituted the major part of the food consumption. The principal items were rice and other cereals, live animals, fruit and vegetables, fish and fish preparations, meat and meat preparations and dairy products and eggs. Imports of raw materials and semi-manufactures valued at $13,581 million, or 41 per cent of total imports, included textile fibres, yarn and fabrics, base metals, plastic moulding materials and paper and paperboard. Imported capital goods totalling $4,340 million, or 13 per cent of total imports, were mainly machinery and transport equipment, while retained imports of consumer goods were composed largely of precious stones, consumer durables and textile made-ups. Fuel imports, valued at $2,033 million, represented 6 per cent of imports.

Japan continued to be the principal supplier of imports in 1975, providing 21 per cent of the total. China came second, supplying 20 per cent of total imports and 52 per cent of all imported foodstuffs. The United States supplied a further 12 per cent. Other important sources of imports were Taiwan, Singapore, the United Kingdom, the Federal Republic of Germany, Switzerland and the Republic of Korea.

Domestic exports consisted almost entirely of manufactured goods, emphasizing the importance of the manufacturing sector in Hong Kong. Textile and clothing exports accounted for 54 per cent of the total, while sales of miscellaneous manufactured articles, mainly toys and dolls, artificial flowers, jewellery and goldsmiths' and silversmiths' wares, umbrellas and metal watch bands, made up an additional 15 per cent. Exports of electrical machinery, apparatus and appliances, mainly transistorized radios, electronic components and parts for computers, transistors, diodes, and semi-conductor integrated circuits, accounted for a further 12 per cent. Other light manufactured products such as fabricated metal goods, travel goods, watches and clocks, electronic calculators and footwear were also important exports.

The direction and level of Hong Kong's export trade is influenced principally by economic conditions and commercial policies in its main overseas markets. Despite some diversification of products and markets, exports are still concentrated in few products and outlets. During 1975, 62 per cent of domestic exports by value went to the United States and the European Economic Community. The United States alone absorbed 32 per cent. The Federal Republic of Germany took 13 per cent (11 per cent in 1974); and the United Kingdom 12 per cent (the same as in 1974). Other important markets were Australia, Japan, Canada, Singapore, the Netherlands and Sweden. Exports to some members of the Organization of

Petroleum Exporting Countries (OPEC) like Nigeria and Saudi Arabia, with newly acquired purchasing power, showed remarkable increases.

Hong Kong's traditional entrepôt trade was about 23 per cent by value of total exports in 1975. Japan was still the largest re-export market, followed by Singapore, Taiwan, Indonesia and the United States. The principal commodities re-exported were machinery and transport equipment, textiles and clothing, diamonds, watches and clocks, crude vegetable materials, medicinal and pharmaceutical products and dyeing, tanning and colouring materials. The principal sources of re-exports were China, Japan and the United States.

Hong Kong practises the rules of the General Agreement on Tariffs and Trade (GATT) and the only trade restrictions are those required by international obligations. Most prominent among these are restraints on textile exports to most major trading partners. A bilateral agreement was concluded in 1975 with the European Economic Community, whereby exports of certain textiles from Hong Kong to the EEC were placed under restraint. The agreement came into effect in July 1975 and will expire at the end of 1977. Bilateral agreements were also concluded with Australia, Austria, Canada and Sweden.

A generalized scheme of preferences, to come into effect on January 1st, 1976, was authorized in the U.S.A. in 1975. Hong Kong was a beneficiary.

FINANCE

Hong Kong enjoys a high degree of financial autonomy despite its political status of merely a crown colony. This has enabled it to develop an independent financial system in which taxation is minimal and budgets are scrupulously balanced every year. The Hong Kong dollar is one of the stablest currencies in the region.

The colony is financially self-supporting, apart from the cost of its external defence, to which it makes a substantial contribution. Under an agreement covering the five years from April 1971 to March 1976, Hong Kong is making a contribution in kind and in cash amounting to £40 million. About £28 million of this contribution will be spent in the colony on capital works and on the maintenance of buildings which will revert to Hong Kong if no longer required by the armed forces. A new defence cost accord was to take effect on April 1st, 1976.

Compared with budgeted revenue and expenditure of HK $6,184 million and HK $6,615 million for 1975/76, the Government's revised estimates of revenue and expenditure for 1975/76 stood at HK $6,015 million and HK $6,222 million, respectively. Thus the officially estimated deficit was lowered from HK $431 million to HK $207 million. To finance the deficit, the Government has already raised a total of HK $264.1 million via five-year Hong Kong dollar bonds (HK $247.4 million), a Eurodollar loan for new coinage (HK $15.3 million) and grants from abroad for Vietnamese refugees (HK $1.4 million).

The deficit for 1975/76 may ultimately amount to less than HK $50 million. For the first nine months of 1975/76, revenue and expenditure were HK $4,167 million and HK $4,204 million, leaving a deficit of only HK $37 million. Reduced public spending was largely attributable to a shortfall of $393 million in capital public works programme expenditures. Substantial declines in contract prices for materials and wages, an unusually rainy summer and delays in the delivery of equipment from overseas all contributed to the shortfall.

The budget for 1976/77 provides for revenue and expenditure of HK $6,857 million and HK $7,212 million, leaving a deficit of HK $355 million. This takes into account additional revenue of HK $136 million to be generated by an increase in the corporate profits tax, estate duty, general rates and stamp duty; the imposition of a Business Registration Fee for "shelf" companies; and an increase in excise duty on petrol and automotive diesel fuel.

Education claims a 19 per cent share of proposed expenditure for 1976/77. Other social services (medical, housing, social welfare and labour) account for 18 per cent of planned expenditure. Transport, roads and civil engineering will consume 14 per cent.

For the three fiscal years 1977/78 to 1979/80, revenues of nearly HK $7,640 million, HK $8,930 million and HK $9,130 million are forecast, while expenditures are expected to total HK $7,950 million, HK $8,560 million and HK $9,140 million, respectively. This will result in overall deficits of HK $310 million, HK $170 million and HK $10 million for the forecast period.

Hong Kong's accumulated fiscal reserves stood at HK $2,484 million at the end of 1975, up 16.3 per cent from 1974. These "free reserves" were expected to reach HK $2,626 million by April 1976.

Bank deposits increased during 1975 to $36,343 million at December 31st, which represents a net increase of 17 per cent over the previous year. Loans and advances increased by 19 per cent to reach $35,075 million at December 31st. Monthly bank clearings averaged $32,793 million.

At the end of 1975 there were 74 licensed banks in Hong Kong with a total of 703 banking offices, an increase of 72 offices during the year. In addition, there were 80 representative offices of foreign banks. Banks in Hong Kong have branches and correspondents throughout the world and offer a comprehensive service of the highest order.

Share prices of companies listed on the colony's four stock exchanges moved up slightly during 1975. However, the total turnover of HK $10,335 million represented a decrease of 8.1 per cent as compared with the previous year.

On August 13th, 1975, the Legislative Council passed a resolution approving in principle the establishment of a Commodity Exchange in Hong Kong. The draft Commodity Exchange Bill was to be enacted some time in 1976.

TOURISM

The tourist industry is one of Hong Kong's largest sources of foreign revenue and in 1975 its gross earnings were estimated at HK $2,976 million. This was 5.8 per cent more than in the previous year. There were some 1.3 million visitors, an increase of 0.4 per cent over 1974.

Japan continued to provide the largest number of tourists, but their proportion dropped to 29 per cent. There was a steady increase in visitors from South-East Asia, which accounted for nearly 25 per cent of all tourists. Economic uncertainty in the U.S.A. reduced the proportion of American visitors to 14 per cent, but the ever-increasing numbers of Australians and New Zealanders amounted to nearly 11 per cent of the total. Europe remained stable in providing 12 per cent of the tourists, but the figures for individual European countries showed some marked fluctuations.

THE YEARS AHEAD

The colony's Financial Secretary projected an annual average growth of between 6 and 7 per cent for the second half of the 1970s; in the first five years an average growth of 7.4 per cent a year was achieved. His assumption is that "the recovery in world trade will not continue for very long, mainly because it has started with all major countries experiencing inflation rates considerably higher than were considered acceptable ten years ago. The recovery will tend to lift these rates and it would be unusual if this did not call forth some response. I do not see 1977, therefore, as a year of accelerating growth for Hong Kong. While 1976 will see a growth rate modestly above trend, I consider that 1977 will probably start slightly better than trend, but will close with the growth rate starting to slow down. In other words, 1977 will probably be one of those rare years of average growth."

Earlier, in another exercise in economic forecasting, the Financial Secretary stated that Hong Kong would experience an annual growth rate of 6.7 per cent during the ten years ending 1985. His reasons for such an assumption were: firstly, "the average rate for the past ten years is influenced by the exceptional experience of 1974/75 when our economy has paused. Over the eight years ending 1973 the rate was 7.7 per cent. Secondly, the historical experience of most other economies is that, for one reason or another, a fast-growing, working population is associated with a fast rate of growth of productivity. Thirdly, the conditions which result in a high capital/labour ratio (and a high ratio of gross domestic capital formation to the G.D.P.) will still apply. To offset the disadvantages of having to procure all raw materials from abroad and ship their finished products to distant markets, manufacturers must be continually concerned with cost efficiency. They have no alternative and, although wage costs are to some degree flexible downwards in periods of low growth, competitiveness depends increasingly on investment in up-to-date plant and equipment."

STATISTICAL SURVEY

AREA AND POPULATION

Area (sq. miles)				Population (Mid-1975)	
Total	Hong Kong Island	Kowloon and Stonecutters Island	New Territories (leased)	Total	Chinese (approx.)
403.8*	29.2	4.1	370.5	4,366,600	98 per cent.

* 1,046 square kilometres.

DISTRIBUTION OF POPULATION
(Provisional census figures—March 9th, 1971)

Hong Kong Island	Kowloon	New Kowloon	Marine	New Territories
996,183	716,272	1,478,581	79,894	665,700

REGISTERED BIRTHS AND DEATHS
(1975)

Births		Deaths	
Number	Rate per '000	Number	Rate per '000
78,200	18.3	21,191	4.9

ECONOMICALLY ACTIVE POPULATION
(Census of March 9th, 1971)

	Employed			Unemployed*		
	Males	Females	Total	Males	Females	Total
Agriculture, hunting, forestry and fishing	40,855	22,120	62,975	1,327	428	1,755
Mining and quarrying	3,404	1,114	4,518	89	38	127
Manufacturing	439,189	316,345	755,534	6,245	2,732	8,977
Electricity, gas and water	8,143	727	8,870	41	20	61
Construction	76,904	6,254	83,158	2,131	139	2,270
Trade, restaurants and hotels	194,049	59,876	253,925	3,034	769	3,803
Transport, storage and communications	105,993	8,729	114,722	4,540	110	4,650
Finance, insurance, real estate and business services	30,603	10,469	41,072	242	39	281
Community, social and personal services	138,114	95,245	233,359	1,517	2,626	4,143
Activities not adequately described	12,735	11,981	24,716	15,723	6,271	21,994
Total	1,049,989	442,860	1,582,849	34,889	13,172	48,061

* Excluding persons seeking work for the first time, numbering 23,997 (12,022 males, 11,975 females).

In December 1975, 678,857 workers were employed in the manufacturing sector.

AGRICULTURE

LAND USAGE
(1975)

	Area (sq. miles)	Percentage of Whole	Remarks
Built-up (urban areas) . . .	49.0	12.1	Includes roads and railways.
Woodlands	49.3	12.2	Natural and established woodlands.
Grass and Scrub Lands . .	237.3	58.6	Natural grass and scrub, including Plover Cove reservoir.
Badlands	16.8	4.1	Stripped of cover; granite country; capable of regeneration.
Swamp and Mangrove Lands .	4.8	1.2	Capable of reclamation.
Fish Ponds	5.6	1.4	Fresh and brackish water fish farming.
Arable	42.0	10.4	Includes orchards and market gardens.

AGRICULTURAL PRODUCTION*
(HK $'000)

	1973/74	1974/75
Crops:		
Flowers†	24,501	26,001
Fruit	10,719	10,288
Vegetables	224,608	191,595
Rice (Paddy)	12,399	5,284
Rice straw	2,812	2,030
Field crops	6,718	6,236
Livestock:		
Pigs	67,902	85,171
Cattle	3,788	3,055
Milk (Fresh)	22,975	23,014
Chickens	113,396	102,991
Hen eggs	23,141	20,348
Ducks	25,092	21,773
Pigeons	6,633	6,760

* Financial year ending March 31st.

† Including pot plants and blossom trees.

FISHERIES
(HK $'000 1974)

Marine Fish (total landings)	368,079
Pond Fish	28,959
Oysters (edible)	1,090

LIVESTOCK
(Estimate 1974/75)

Cattle	12,566
Water Buffaloes	590
Pigs	386,300
Chickens	3,670,690
Ducks	247,480
Geese	5,010
Quail	340,200
Pigeons (pairs)	119,380

MINING
(metric tons)

	1974	1975
Iron Ore*	159,737	167,200
Kaolin	3,320	1,490
Quartz	351	761
Feldspar	5,566	2,059

* 50–56 per cent iron concentrate.

INDUSTRY
(December 1975)

	Establishments	Employed
Food Manufacture	813	12,551
Textile Manufacture	2,433	103,684
Footwear and Clothing	3,792	197,890
Printing and Publishing	1,229	18,171
Rubber Products	282	5,884
Fabricated Metal Products	3,557	49,643
Manufacture of Machinery	841	9,771
Electrical Apparatus	564	60,553
Transport Equipment	94	10,450
Transport, Storage and Communications	70	23,002
Total (all industries)	20,671	625,634

FINANCE

100 cents = 1 Hong Kong dollar (HK $).

Coins: 5, 10 and 50 cents; 1 dollar.

Notes: 5, 10, 50, 100 and 500 dollars.

Exchange rates (June 1976): £1 sterling = HK $8.78; U.S. $1 = HK $4.94.

HK $100 = £11.39 = U.S. $20.23.

Note: From September 1949 to November 1967 the Hong Kong dollar was officially valued at 1s. 3d. sterling (£1 = HK $16.00) or 17.5 U.S. cents (U.S. $1 = HK $5.714). On November 18th, 1967, the Hong Kong dollar was devalued, in line with sterling, to 15 U.S. cents (U.S. $1 = HK $6.667) but, four days later, it was revalued at 1s. 4½d. or 6.875p (£1 = HK $14.545), worth 16.5 U.S. cents (U.S. $1 = HK $6.061) until August 1971. The relationship to sterling remained unchanged and a rate of U.S. $1 = HK $5.582 (HK $1 = 17.91 U.S. cents) came into operation in December 1971. After sterling was allowed to "float" in June 1972, the Hong Kong dollar was devalued in July 1972, when the central exchange rate became U.S. $1 = HK $5.65 (HK $1 = 17.70 U.S. cents). This was retained until February 1973, after which the central rate was U.S. $1 = HK $5.085 (HK $1 = 19.666 U.S. cents) until November 1974, since when the Hong Kong dollar has been "floating". For 1975 the average value of the Hong Kong dollar was 20.18 U.S. cents.

BUDGET*

(HK $ million—Estimates)

Revenue	1974/75	1975/76
Duties	479.3	555.1
Rates	424.0	536.9
Internal revenue	2,626.8	2,768.8
Licences	165.1	193.1
Fees and receipts	247.9	353.0
Water	181.4	208.4
Revenue from properties and investments	496.8	436.2
Land sales	289.1	356.6
Postal services	185.9	218.5
Airport and air services	181.2	235.9
Reimbursements	534.6	161.4
Total (incl. others)	5,983.3	6,184.0

Expenditure	1974/75	1975/76
Education	193.7	194.2
Housing	229.8	122.2
Medical and health	359.7	379.7
Miscellaneous services	318.3	371.0
Police	375.7	422.6
Public Works Department	283.0	285.2
Public works recurrent	289.8	323.7
Public works non-recurrent	1,597.1	1,600.9
Social Welfare Department	203.9	264.9
Subvention: education	701.2	797.0
Subvention: medical	169.7	188.4
University and polytechnic	253.5	290.8
Total (incl. others)	6,453.2	6,615.4

* Financial year ending March 31st.

CURRENCY IN CIRCULATION

(HK $ million)

1971	2,932.1
1972	3,378.2
1973	3,712.4
1974	3,866.8
1975	4,427.0

EXTERNAL TRADE

(HK $ million)

	1972	1973	1974	1975
Imports	21,764	29,005	34,120	33,472
Exports	15,245	19,474	22,911	22,859
Re-exports	4,154	6,525	7,124	6,973

PRINCIPAL COMMODITIES
(HK $ million)

IMPORTS	1973	1974	1975
Food	4,914	6,111	6,113
Live Animals	832	1,118	1,149
Meat	521	618	675
Dairy Products and Eggs	347	443	487
Fish	632	628	662
Cereals	1,101	1,326	1,087
Fruit and Vegetables	961	1,198	1,267
Beverages and Tobacco	579	540	583
Crude Materials	2,101	2,360	2,500
Textile Fibres and Waste	1,223	1,290	1,523
Other Animal and Vegetable Crude Materials	533	602	616
Mineral Fuels, etc.	791	2,133	2,126
Petroleum and Petroleum Products	757	2,066	2,048
Chemicals	2,204	2,892	2,496
Chemical Elements and Compounds	347	537	464
Medicinal and Pharmaceutical Products	377	437	412
Plastic Materials	751	983	702
Manufactured Goods	9,779	10,174	9,828
Textile Yarn, Fabrics, Made-up Articles, etc.	4,856	4,576	4,792
Non-Metallic Mineral Manufactures	2,298	2,248	2,186
Iron and Steel	682	974	713
Paper, Paperboard, etc.	720	898	710
Machinery and Transport Equipment	4,925	5,624	5,643
Non-Electric Machinery	1,455	1,738	2,015
Electric Machinery	2,737	3,316	2,885
Transport Equipment	734	570	743
Other Manufactures	3,523	4,004	3,892
Clothing	617	532	518
Scientific Instruments, Photographic and Optical Goods, Watches and Clocks, etc.	1,443	1,946	1,828

EXPORTS	1973	1974	1975
Food	301	299	351
Fish	150	140	183
Cereals	29	28	29
Fruits and Vegetables	31	33	39
Sugar, Sugar Preparations and Honey	10	10	10
Miscellaneous Food Preparations	72	80	84
Beverages and Tobacco	32	47	52
Tobacco and Tobacco Manufactures	26	41	48
Crude Materials	267	397	215
Textile Fibres and Waste	18	27	22
Metalliferous Ores and Metal Scrap	146	241	117
Chemicals	171	201	192
Dyeing, Tanning and Colouring Materials	30	34	44
Medicinal and Pharmaceutical Products	48	52	47
Manufactured Goods	3,213	3,781	3,079
Textile Yarn, Fabrics, Made-up Articles, etc.	2,352	2,737	2,145
Non-Metallic Mineral Manufactures	170	161	174
Iron and Steel	51	88	17
Manufactures of Metals (others)	521	641	605
Machinery and Transport Equipment	2,898	3,674	3,332
Electric Machinery, Apparatus, etc.	2,622	3,296	2,787
Other Manufactures	12,540	14452	15,565
Clothing	7,454	8,752	10,202
Footwear	266	311	256
Sanitary, Heating, Lighting Fixtures and Fittings	257	302	251

PRINCIPAL COMMODITIES—*continued*]

RE-EXPORTS	1973	1974	1975
Food	493	513	559
Fruits and Vegetables	146	160	188
Coffee, Tea, Spices, etc.	104	104	77
Sugar, Sugar Preparations and Honey	6	12	58
Cereals	109	69	23
Crude Materials	527	628	538
Oil Seeds, Oil Nuts and Kernels	13	13	17
Other Animal and Vegetable Crude Materials	358	421	360
Chemicals	746	927	902
Dyeing, Tanning and Colouring Materials	189	204	252
Medicinal and Pharmaceutical Products	235	280	258
Manufactured Goods	2,752	2,514	2,259
Textile Yarn, Fabrics, Made-up Articles, etc.	1,081	930	790
Non-Metallic Mineral Manufactures	1,382	1,163	1,132
Machinery and Transport Equipment	776	950	1,035
Machinery other than Electric	312	358	480
Electric Machinery, Apparatus, etc.	382	485	451
Other Manufactures	1,084	1,370	1,485
Clothing	187	213	216
Scientific Instruments, Photographic and Optical Goods, Watches and Clocks, etc.	517	723	841
Other Manufactured Articles	326	369	341

PRINCIPAL TRADING PARTNERS

(HK $ million)

IMPORTS	1973	1974	1975
Australia	697	760	742
Belgium and Luxembourg	340	342	407
China, People's Republic	5,634	5,991	6,805
France	432	427	460
Germany, Federal Republic	1,114	1,193	1,034
Japan	5,853	7,142	6,991
Pakistan	626	434	652
Singapore	958	1,889	1,921
Switzerland	910	1,121	943
Taiwan	1,686	1,765	1,943
Thailand	548	809	725
United Kingdom	1,716	1,942	1,715
U.S.A.	3,702	4,621	3,961

EXPORTS	1973	1974	1975
Australia	771	1,298	1,034
Canada	512	619	775
Germany, Federal Republic	1,902	2,444	2,860
Indonesia	187	230	143
Japan	1,065	1,061	956
Netherlands	411	504	496
New Zealand	192	299	179
Singapore	536	626	624
Sweden	324	389	471
Taiwan	390	362	236
Thailand	129	176	119
United Kingdom	2,814	2,768	2,778
U.S.A.	6,825	7,422	7,334

RE-EXPORTS	1973	1974	1975
Belgium and Luxembourg	94	113	100
Indonesia	528	615	589
Japan	1,429	1,023	964
Korea, Republic	278	278	286
Macao	214	231	211
Nigeria	29	74	117
Philippines	124	193	231
Singapore	737	862	928
Switzerland	158	201	231
Taiwan	673	692	600
United Kingdom	90	162	112
U.S.A.	461	514	555
Viet-Nam, South	65	58	22

TRANSPORT

(1975)

RAIL TRAFFIC

(Kowloon-Canton railway, British section)

Passengers	13,451,826
Freight (metric tons)	1,482,297

ROAD TRAFFIC

(Motor Vehicle Registrations)

Private Cars	114,260
Goods Vehicles	31,660
Motor Cycles (including scooters)	22,290
Taxis	4,754
Crown Vehicles (excl. H.M. Forces)	3,907
Buses	3,710
Public Light Buses	4,307
Private Light Buses	1,447
Public Cars	1,283
TOTAL (incl. others)	188,018

CIVIL AIR TRAFFIC

	1973/74	1974/75	1975/76
Passengers:			
Arrivals	1,787,791	1,792,340	1,962,610
Departures	1,875,152	1,871,122	2,055,841
Freight (in metric tons):			
Arrivals	39,603	34,317	42,994
Departures	61,117	69,804	108,721

MARINE TRAFFIC

		Ocean-going	River Steamers	Junks
Vessels entered	number	7,406	1,813	9,553
Tonnage entered	'000 n.r.t.	32,776	1,997	1,602
Passengers landed	number	6,285	2,035,545	n.a.
Passengers embarked	"	5,096	2,031,268	n.a.
Cargo tons landed	d.w.t.	11,672,508	1,285	998,665
Cargo tons loaded	"	4,839,634	2,558	154,636

TOURISM

	1973	1974	1975
Visitors	1,291,950	1,295,462	1,300,836
Hotel rooms	11,316	13,190	13,448

COMMUNICATIONS MEDIA

(1975)

Telephones	837,023
Television Sets	805,000*
Periodicals	226
Daily Newspapers	107

* Estimate.

EDUCATION

(1975)

Schools	Pupils
Kindergarten	146,965
Primary	660,922
Secondary	415,691
Post-Secondary	11,584
Adult Education	65,081
Special Education	5,675

Source: Hong Kong Government, *Official Statistics*.

THE CONSTITUTION

The Government of Hong Kong, which consists of the Governor, the Executive Council and the Legislative Council, is constituted under the authority of Letters Patent and Royal Instructions.

The Executive Council is consulted by the Governor on all important administrative questions. In addition to five *ex officio* members, there are eight unofficial members (of whom six are Chinese), and one nominated official member, who is Chinese.

The Legislative Council, which advises on and approves the enactment of the Colony's laws and approves all expenditure from public funds, consists of four of the *ex officio* members who sit on the Executive Council, ten other official members and fifteen unofficial members (these include eleven Chinese). A finance committee comprising all the unofficial members meets in private to scrutinize all government expenditure proposals; two subcommittees deal with public works capital expenditure, and with government staff increases.

THE GOVERNMENT

Governor: Sir CRAWFORD MURRAY MACLEHOSE, G.B.E., K.C.M.G., K.C.V.O.

EXECUTIVE COUNCIL

(*June* 1976)

President: The GOVERNOR.

Ex Officio Members:

The Commander British Forces Lt.-Gen. Sir JOHN ARCHER, K.C.B., O.B.E.
The Colonial Secretary Sir DENYS ROBERTS, K.B.E., Q.C., J.P.
The Financial Secretary C. P. HADDON-CAVE, C.M.G., J.P.
The Attorney-General J. W. D. HOBLEY, C.M.G., Q.C., J.P.
The Secretary for Home Affairs D. C. BRAY, C.V.O., J.P.

Nominated Official Member: Dr. G. H. CHOA, C.B.E., J.P.

Unofficial Members:

Sir YUET-KEUNG KAN, C.B.E., J.P.
Sir SIDNEY GORDON, C.B.E., J.P.
WOO PAK-CHUEN, C.B.E., J.P.
SZETO-WAI, C.B.E., J.P.
Dr. CHUNG SZE-YUEN, O.B.E., J.P.
ANN TZE-KAI, C.B.E., J.P.
G. M. SAYER, J.P.
OSWALD CHEUNG, O.B.E., Q.C., J.P.

LEGISLATIVE COUNCIL

President: The Governor.

Ex Officio Members: The Colonial Secretary, The Attorney-General, The Secretary for Home Affairs, The Financial Secretary.

Nominated Official Members:

J. J. ROBSON, C.B.E., J.P.
Dr. G. H. CHOA, C.B.E., J.P.
D. AKERS-JONES, J.P., M.A.
I. M. LIGHTBODY, C.M.G., J.P.
D. H. JORDAN, C.M.G., M.B.E., J.P.
LI FOOK-KOW, C.M.G., J.P.
L. M. DAVIES, C.M.G., O.B.E., J.P.
K. TOPLEY, C.M.G., J.P.
I. R. PRICE, T.D., J.P.
D. W. MCDONALD, J.P.

Unofficial Members:

WILSON T. S. WANG, O.B.E., J.P.
ROGERIO LOBO, O.B.E., J.P.
Mrs. C. J. SYMONS, O.B.E., J.P.
P. G. WILLIAMS, O.B.E., J.P.
JAMES WU MAN-HON, O.B.E., J.P.
HILTON CHEONG-LEEN, O.B.E., J.P.
LEE QUO-WEI, O.B.E., J.P.
LI FOOK-WO, O.B.E., C.M.G., J.P.
J. H. BREMRIDGE, O.B.E., J.P.
Dr. HARRY S. Y. FANG, O.B.E., J.P.
Mrs. KWAN KO SIU-WAH, M.B.E., J.P.
LO TAK-SHING, J.P.
FRANCIS Y. H. TIEN, O.B.E., J.P.
OSWALD CHEUNG, O.B.E., Q.C., J.P.
Dr. S. Y. CHUNG, C.B.E., J.P.

POLITICAL ORGANIZATIONS

The **Reform Club** and **Civic Association,** which worked in alliance between 1961 and 1964, stand for moderate constitutional changes in Hong Kong's Government.

The **Communists** and **Kuomintang** (Nationalist Party of China, based in Taiwan) also maintain organizations.

JUDICIAL SYSTEM

The Supreme Court consists of a Court of Appeal and of a High Court.

The High Court of Justice has unlimited jurisdiction in civil and criminal cases, the District Court having limited jurisdiction. Appeals from these courts lie to the Court of Appeal, presided over by the Chief Justice and consisting of two Justices of Appeal. Appeals from Magistrates' Courts are heard by a High Court judge.

Supreme Court:

Chief Justice: Sir GEOFFREY G. BRIGGS, Q.C.

Justices of Appeal: Hons. A. A. HUGGINS, W. F. PICKERING.

High Court Judges:

Hons. A. M. MCMULLIN
P. F. X. LEONARD
SIMON F. S. LI
J. P. TRAINOR
D. CONS
M. J. MORLEY JOHN
E. G. BABER
T. L. YANG

District Courts: There are 13 District Judges with Courts in Victoria, Kowloon and the New Territories.

Magistrates' Courts: There are 43 Magistrates' Courts.

RELIGION

The Chinese population is predominantly Buddhist, although Confucianism and Taoism are also practised. The three religions are frequently found in the same temple. There are more than 440,000 Chinese Christians and a number of Muslims and Jews.

ANGLICAN

Bishop of Hong Kong: Rt. Rev. J. GILBERT H. BAKER, Bishop's House, 1 Lower Albert Rd.

ROMAN CATHOLIC

Bishop of Hong Kong: JOHN BAPTIST CHENG-CHUUNG WU, Catholic Mission, 16 Caine Rd., Hong Kong.

THE PRESS

DAILY NEWSPAPERS

English Language

Hongkong Standard: News Building, 635 King's Rd.; f. 1949; Editor-in-Chief P. V. NATHAN; circ. (weekday and Sunday) 32,000.

South China Morning Post: Tong Chong St., P.O.B. 47; Editor ROBIN HUTCHEON; circ. 55,000.

The Star: 19–21 Pennington St., Causeway Bay; f. 1965; evening; Editor G. JENKINS; circ. 40,000.

English and Chinese

Daily Commodity Quotations: Marina House, Queen's Rd., Central; f. 1948; morning; commercial news; Editor EDWARD IP.

Chinese Language

Ching Pao: 141 Queen's Rd. East, 3rd Floor; f. 1956; Editor CHAN HA TZE; circ. 90,000.

Chiu Yin Pao: 458 Lockhard Rd., 11th Floor; f. 1950; morning; Editor KWONG LAI; circ. 25,000.

Chun Pao (*Truth Daily*): 29–33 Gage St.; evening; Editor MAK YIH-TONG.

Chung Ying Daily News: 29-33 Gage St., 2nd floor; f. 1946; morning; Editor CHAN KU-LEONG

Fai Po (*Express*): News Bldg., 633 King's Rd., 5th Floor, North Point; f. 1963; morning; Editor KWONG YAN-CHUN.

Hong Kong Evening Post: 5–13A New St.; f. 1969; Editor LEE KAM-SIK.

Hong Kong Sheung Po (*Hong Kong Commercial Daily*): 28–30 Wing Lok St.; f. 1952; morning; Editor-in-Chief H. CHEUNG; circ. 110,000.

Hong Kong Shih Pao (*Hong Kong Times*): 64–66 Gloucester Rd.; f. 1949; morning; right-wing; expresses the views of the Chinese Nationalist Government in Taiwan; Editor T. Y. TONG.

Hsin Sheng Wan Pao (*New Life Evening Post*): 171–173 Hennessy Rd.; f. 1945; independent; Editor and Gen. Man. K. C. CHAN; circ. 30,000.

Hsin Wan Pao (*New Evening Post*): 342 Hennessy Rd.; f. 1951; left-wing; Editor LO FU.

Hung Look Yat Po: 37 Gough St.; f. 1939; morning; Prop. YAM TAT NIN; circ. 40,000.

Kung Sheung Man Po (*Industrial and Commercial Evening News*): 18 Fenwick St.; f. 1930; evening; Editor TAM TAT FU; circ. 48,000.

Kung Sheung Yat Po (*Industrial and Commercial Daily News*): 18 Fenwick St.; f. 1925; morning; independent; Editor NELSON LIU; circ. 70,200.

Ming Pao: 651 King's Rd., 9th Floor; f. 1959; morning and evening; Editor LOUIS CHA; circ. 200,000.

Sing Pao: 101 King's Rd.; morning; circ. 300,000; Editor YU KEE PING.

Sing Tao Jih Pao: 635 King's Rd., North Point; f. 1938; morning; Editor CHOW TING; circ. 50,000.

Sing Tao Wan Po: 635 King's Rd.; f. 1938; evening; Editor TENG BIK CHUEN.

The Star: 19–21 Pennington St., Causeway Bay; f. 1965; evening; Editor G. JENKINS; circ. 100,000.

Ta Kung Pao: 342 Hennessy Rd.; f. 1951; morning; left-wing; Editor LI HSIA WEN; circ. 30,000.

Tin Tin Yat Pao: 14 Westlands Rd., Quarry Bay; f. 1960; Editor C. K. TONG; circ. 75,000.

Wah Kiu Man Po: 110 Hollywood Rd.; f. 1945; evening; independent; Editor SHUM CHO-SANG; circ. 49,561.

Wah Kiu Yat Po (*Overseas Chinese Daily News Ltd.*): 110 Hollywood Rd.; f. 1925; morning; independent; Chief Editor HO KIN CHEUNG; circ. 74,390.

Wen Wei Po: 197–199 Wanchai Rd.; morning; left-wing; Editor-in-Chief LI TSE-CHUNG.

SUNDAY NEWSPAPERS

English Language

South China Morning Post: P.O.B. 47; Editor ROBIN HUTCHEON; circ. 34,000.

Sunday Examiner: Catholic Centre, 15–18 Connaught Rd. Central; f. 1946; religious (R. Catholic); Editor Fr. A. BIRMINGHAM.

Chinese Language

Asia Weekly: 407 Asian House, 1 Hennessy Rd.; f. 1964; Editor WARREN LEE.

PERIODICALS

English Language

Apparel: Connaught Centre, 3/F., Connaught Rd., Hong Kong; f. March 1969; published by the Hong Kong Trade Development Council; concerned with new developments in local manufacturing of garments; bi-annual; circ. 17,000; Editor ANDREW SIMPSON.

Asia Magazine: New Industrial Bldg., Tong Chong St., Quarry Bay; f. 1961; general interest; Sunday supplement distributed to English language newspapers; Editor ARNOLD ABRAMS.

Asia Pictorial: 82 Yee Wo St., 2nd Floor; f. 1954; independent monthly; general; Editor CHANG KUO-SIN; circ. 20,000.

Asian Building and Construction: c/o Far East Trade Press Ltd., 4th Floor, Toppan Building, 22 West Land Rd., Quarry Bay; f. 1938; monthly; Editor GEORGE MITCHELL.

Asian Business and Industry: c/o Far East Trade Press Ltd., 1908 Prince's Bldg., Des Voeux Rd., Central; monthly; Publisher MICHAEL BRIERLEY; Editor PHILIP DION.

Asian Journal of Modern Medicine: 1908 Prince's Bldg., Des Voeux Rd. Central; f. 1964; monthly; Editor Dr. W. J. ORAM, F.R.C.S.; Man. Editor R. P. NAYAR; circ. 20,093.

Asian Product News: c/o Far East Trade Press Ltd., 1908 Prince's Bldg., Des Voeux Rd., Central; monthly; Editor Y. L. V. SHARMA.

Eastern Horizon: 3rd Floor, 472 Hennessy Rd.; f. 1960; independent bi-monthly; devoted to art and culture; Editor LEE TSUNG-YING; circ. 20,000.

Far Eastern Economic Review: 406-410 Marina House, P.O.B. 160; f. 1946; weekly; Editor DEREK DAVIES; circ. 26,500.

Gregg's Medical Directory: c/o Far East Trade Press Ltd., 1908 Prince's Bldg., Des Voeux Rd. Central; annual.

Hong Kong Builder Directory: c/o 704 Lee Hing Bldg., Des Voeux Rd. Central; f. 1935; annual.

Hong Kong Enterprise: Connaught Centre, 3/F., Connaught Rd., Hong Kong; f. Oct. 1967; published by the Hong Kong Trade Development Council; concerned with new developments in local manufacturing; monthly; Editor ANDREW SIMPSON; circ. 55,000.

Hong Kong Government Gazette: Beaconsfield House, Queen's Rd. Central; weekly.

Modern Asia: P.O.B. 770; f. 1967; business, government and industry; 10 issues yearly; circ. 24,000.

The Reader's Digest (Asian Edn.): Reader's Digest Asia Ltd., 22 Westlands Rd., Quarry Bay; f. 1963; general topics; monthly; sold throughout Asia; Editor ELIZABETH G. COOPER; circ. 310,000.

Textile Asia: c/o Business Press Ltd., Tak Yan Commercial Bldg., 30-32 D'Aguilar St.; f. 1970; monthly; Editor-in-Chief KAYSER SUNG; circ. 15,000.

Travelling Magazine: Room 903, Yat Fat Building, 44 Des Voeux Rd. Central; f. 1965; monthly; Publisher SHAU-FU POK; circ. 50,500.

World Today: P.O.B. 5217, Kowloon; monthly; circ. 55,000.

Chinese Language

Hong Fook (*Pictorial Happiness*): monthly.

Hsin Kar Ting (*New Home*): monthly.

Kar Ting Sang Wood (*Home Life Journal*): 326 Jaffe Rd. f. 1950; every ten days; Editor TONG BIG CHUEN; circ. 30,000.

Kung Kao Pao: Catholic Press Bureau, Grand Buildings; weekly; f. 1928; religious (R. Catholic).

The Reader's Digest (Chinese Edn.): Reader's Digest Association Far East Ltd., 22 Westlands Rd., Quarry Bay; f. 1965; general topics; monthly; sold throughout Asia; Chief Editor Miss LIN TAI-YI; circ. 250,000.

Sin Chung Hwa Pictorial: monthly.

Sing Tao Weekly: 179 Wanchai Rd.

Sinwen Tienti (*Newsdom Weekly*): Room 903, Yat Fat Building, 44 Des Voeux Rd. Central; f. 1945; weekly; Publisher SHAU-FU POK; circ. 60,550.

Tien Wen Tai: (*Observatory Review*) 60 Leighten Rd., 6th Floor; f. 1936; alternate days; Editor Gen. CHEN HSIAO-WEI; circ. 20,000.

Travelling Magazine: Room 903, Yat Fat Building, 44 Des Voeux Rd. Central; f. 1966; monthly; Publisher SHAU-FU POK; circ. 50,500.

Tse Yau Chun Hsin (*Freedom Front*): weekly.

Tsing Nin Wen Yu (*Literary Youth*): monthly.

Tung Sai (*East and West*): fortnightly.

PRESS AGENCIES

Pan-Asia News Agency: Printing House, 6 Duddel St. (P.O.B. 836); f. 1949; Editor-in-Chief BRUCE LEE.

New Zealand Press Association: 708 Gloucester Building; Correspondent DEREK ROUND.

FOREIGN BUREAUX

Reuters: P.O.B. 430, 707/9 Gloucester Bldg., 7th Floor, Des Voeux Rd., Central.

The following agencies also have offices in Hong Kong: AFP, Antara, AP, Central News Agency of China, DPA, Jiji Press, Kyodo News Service, and UPI.

PUBLISHERS

Asia Press Ltd.: 88 Yee Wo St., Causeway Bay; f. 1952; books and magazines; Pres. CHANG KUO-SIN; Gen. Manager CHEN LIU-TO.

Business Press Ltd.: 501 Yip Fung Bldg., 2-12 D'Aguilar St.; f. 1970; textiles periodicals and economics papers; Man. Dir. KAYSER SUNG.

Chung Chi Publications: Chung Chi College, The Chinese University of Hong Kong, Shatin, New Territories; f. 1961; history, philosophy, Asian studies, history of science, *Chung Chi Journal*, etc.

Far East American Publishing Co.: 25A Robinson Rd.; geography, travel, politics, fiction.

Far East Trade Press Ltd.: 1908 Prince's Bldg., Des Voeux Rd. Central; trade magazines and directories; Publisher and Man. Dir. MICHAEL BRIERLEY.

Hong Kong University Press: 94 Bonham Rd., University of Hong Kong; f. 1955; scholarly and general; Dir. G. W. BONSALL, M.A., M.L.S.

Longman Group (Far East) Ltd.: Taikoo Sugar Refinery Compound, Quarry Bay; arts, geography, history, education, literature, school books.

PUBLISHERS' ASSOCIATION

Hong Kong Printers' Association: 48–50 Johnston Rd. 1/F, Wanchai; f. 1939; 287 mems.; Pres. LEE YAT NGOK; Chair. HO WAI CHUEN.

RADIO AND TELEVISION

RADIO

Radio Television Hong Kong: Broadcasting House, Broadcast Drive, Kowloon Central Post Office, Box 200; f. 1928; public service broadcasting department of the Government; services in English and Chinese; television division (RHKTV), producing public affairs programmes in English and Chinese, to be carried by local commercial stations; Dir. B. HAWTHORNE.

Hong Kong Commercial Broadcasting Co. Ltd.: P.O.B. 3000, Hong Kong; f. 1959; broadcasts in English and Chinese; Man. Dir. G. HO.

British Forces Broadcasting Service: BFPO 1, Hong Kong; f. 1971; Controller J. M. CAMPBELL, A.M.B.I.M.; Programme Organizer Capt. (QGO) KISHOR KUMAR GURUNG.

In 1972 there were an estimated 725,000 radio receivers in use.

TELEVISION

Rediffusion Television Ltd.: Television House, 81 Broadcast Drive, Kowloon; f. 1973; a member of the Rediffusion group of companies; operates two commercial wireless television services (English and Chinese) on CCIR 625 line PAL System 1; 110,000 subscribers; Man. Dir. STEVE HUANG; Acting Controller of Programmes ROBERT LEUNG.

Hong Kong Television Broadcasts Ltd.: P.O.B. K100, 77 Broadcast Drive, Kowloon; f. 1967; 2 colour networks; Man. Dir. A. K. W. EU.

Commercial Television Ltd.: P.O.B. 4707, Broadcast Drive, Kowloon; Deputy Chair. GEORGE HO.

In January 1976 there were 857,000 television receivers in use.

FINANCE

Of the Colony's 74 licensed banks in 1975, 13 were Communist banks, including the Bank of China. Fifty-one of the banks were authorized to deal on the official foreign exchange market. The remainder were non-authorized and deal on the free market.

BANKING

Banking Commission: 1604 Hang Chong Bldg., 5 Queen's Rd. Central; f. 1964; Commissioner A. D. OCKENDEN; Chief Banking Inspector C. D. W. MARTIN; Senior Banking Officer C. S. LEUNG; publs. monthly banking statistics and other information connected with the banking system.

ISSUING BANKS

Chartered Bank: 4–4A Des Voeux Rd., Central; 69 brs.

Mercantile Bank Ltd.: 1 Queen's Rd., Central Hong Kong; cap. p.u. £2.94m.; dep. £137m.; Chair. G. M. SAYER.

Hongkong and Shanghai Banking Corporation: 1 Queen's Rd. Central, P.O.B. 64; f. 1865; cap. issued and p.u. HK $867m. (1975); dep. HK $22,511m. (1975); Chair. G. M. SAYER.

HONG KONG BANKS

Bank of Canton Ltd.: 6 Des Voeux Rd. Central; incorp. in Hong Kong in 1912; cap. p.u. HK $12.4m.; total resources (1974) HK $1,107m.; Chief Man. E. H. BURRELL; Chair. HUO PAO-TSAI.

Bank of East Asia Ltd.: 10 Des Voeux Rd. Central; incorp. in Hong Kong in 1918; cap. p.u. HK $47.2m. dep. (1974) HK $1,393m.; Chair. Hon. Sir Y. K. KAN C.B.E., LL.D.(Hon.), J.P.

Chekiang First Bank Ltd.: Prince's Bldg., 3 Statue Square; f. 1950; cap. p.u. HK $10m.; dep. (1974) HK $355m.; Chair. and Man. TE-CHUAN LI.

China and South Sea Bank Ltd.: 77–83 Queen's Rd. Central; Man. HUANG CHEN-YING.

Chiyu Banking Corporation Ltd.: 80 Des Voeux Rd. Central; f. 1947.

Dao Heng Bank Ltd.: 17–19 Bonham Strand East, Hong Kong; f. 1921; Chair. and Man. Dir. TANG PANG YUEN; cap. HK $20m.; resources HK $1,069.6m. (1974).

Hang Seng Bank Ltd.: 77 Des Voeux Rd., Central; cap. p.u. HK $132m.; dep. HK $5,446m. (1975); Chair. S. H. HO, M.B.E.

Hong Kong Chinese Bank Ltd., The: The Hong Kong Chinese Bank Bldg., 61-65 Des Voeux Rd., Central; f. 1955; cap. HK $45m.; dep. HK $189m. (1975); 6 brs.; Chair. and Gen. Man. The Hon. Sir SIK-NIN CHAU, Kt., C.B.E., J.P., LL.D.; Dir. and Deputy Gen. Man. KAI-YIN CHAU, J.P.

Hong Kong Industrial and Commercial Bank: 10 Queen's Rd. Central; f. 1964

Hong Kong Metropolitan Bank Ltd.: 40-42 Des Voeux Rd. Central, P.O.B. 14612.

Hong Kong and Swatow Commercial Bank Ltd.: 48A Bonham Strand, West.

Kwong On Bank Ltd.: 137–141 Queen's Rd. Central, Hong Kong; f. 1938, inc. 1954; cap. HK $20m.; dep. HK $618m. (1974); Chair. and Gen. Man. LEUNG KWAI-YEE; 8 brs.

Nanyang Commercial Bank Ltd.: 1A Des Voeux Rd. Central; f. 1949; cap. p.u. HK $50m.; res. HK $26m.; resources HK $1,041m. (Dec. 1974); Chair. and Gen. Man. CHUANG SHIH PING; 9 brs.

Overseas Trust Bank Ltd.: 5E Ice House St.; cap. p.u. HK $100m.; dep. HK $822m.; Man. Dir. TSAO YAO.

Shanghai Commercial Bank Ltd.: 12 Queen's Rd. Central; f. 1951; incorp. in Hong Kong; cap. HK $25m. (1974); dep. HK $1,176m. (1974); Chair. K. P. CHEN; Gen. Man. K. K. CHEN.

Wing On Bank Ltd.: 22 Des Voeux Rd. Central; incorp. in Hong Kong in 1931; cap. p.u. HK $25m.; dep. HK $489.9m. (1975); Chair. LAMBERT KWOK; Chief Man. LAMSON KWOK; 11 brs.

FOREIGN BANKS

Algemene Bank Nederland N.V.: Holland House, 9 Queen's Rd. Central; Man. R. VELTEMA.

American Express International Banking Corpn.: Union House, 9–25 Chater Rd.; Resident Vice-Pres. T. M. DE'ATH; Man. J. H. GIDWANI.

Bangkok Bank Ltd.: 26–30 Des Voeux Rd. West; Vice Pres. and Man. SANYA PALANANTANA.

Bank of America N.T. and S.A.: San Francisco; St. George's Building, 2 Ice House St., Hong Kong.

Bank of China: Peking; 2A Des Voeux Rd. Central; Man. LI CHUO-CHIH.

Bank of Communications: Peking; 3A Des Voeux Rd. Central.

Bank of India: Bombay; Dina House, 3-5 Duddell St., P.O.B. 13763; Man. J. N. KARANI.

Bank Negara Indonesia 1946: Jakarta; 25 Des Voeux Rd. Central.

Bank of Tokyo Ltd.: Sutherland House, 3 Chater Rd., Hong Kong; 691–697 Nathan Rd., Kowloon.

Banque Belge Pour l'Etranger S.A.: 11 Queen's Rd. Central; 9 brs.

Banque de l'Indochine et de Suez: Paris 8e; Hang Seng Bank Bldg., 19th floor 77 Des Voeux Rd. Central.

Banque Nationale de Paris: Central Bldg., 21–27 Queen's Rd. Central; f. 1966.

Barclays Bank International Ltd.: Connaught Centre, Connaught Rd. Central (P.O.B. 295); Chief Man. J. THRESH.

Chase Manhattan Bank, N.A.: 15 Queen's Rd. Central, P.O.B. 104; 720 Nathan Rd., Kowloon; Gen. Man. ERIC W. P. HASSELMAN.

China State Bank Ltd.: 11B Queen's Rd. Central.

Chung Khiaw Bank Ltd.: 15–18 Connaught Rd. Central.

Thomas Cook and Son (Continental and Overseas) Ltd.: 1236 Union House, Hong Kong and 223 Tung Ying Bldg., 100 Nathan Rd., Kowloon.

Equitable Banking Corporation: Manila; Hong Kong Br.: 4 Duddell St.

European Asian Bank: P.O.B. 3193, Hong Kong.

First National City Bank: New York City; Hong Kong P.O.B. 14; Vice-Pres. R. A. FREYTAG.

Four Seas Communications Bank Ltd.: Singapore; 36 Bonham Strand West.

Indian Overseas Bank: Madras; 7–9 Duddell St.; Man. J. P. MOSES.

Korea Exchange Bank: 1st Floor, Loke Yew Bldg., 50–52 Queen's Rd. Central; 2 brs.

Malayan Banking Berhad: Hong Kong Office: 1st Floor, Pacific House, 20 Queen's Rd., Central; Kowloon br.: 227 Nathan Rd.

National Bank of Pakistan: Karachi; Hong Kong br.: 129 Central Bldg., Queen's Rd., Central; Kowloon br.: 7 Chatham Rd.

National Commercial Bank Ltd.: Shanghai; Hong Kong Br.: 1–3 Wyndham St.

Oversea-Chinese Banking Corpn. Ltd.: Head Office: Singapore; Hong Kong Office: Edinburgh House, 13B Queen's Rd. Central; Kowloon Office: Alhambra Bldg., 383 Nathan Rd.

Overseas Union Bank: Singapore; 14–16 Pedder St.

Sanwa Bank Ltd.: Head Office: Fushimimachi 4-chome, Osaka; Hong Kong br.: 30–32 Connaught Rd. Central.

Sin Hua Trust, Savings and Commercial Bank, Ltd.: Peking; Marina House, 17 Queen's Rd. Central; f. 1914; Man. SU TSAN SING.

Sumitomo Bank Ltd.: Osaka; 5 Queen's Rd. Central.

United Commercial Bank: Hong Kong; Prince's Bldg., 5 Statue Square.

United Overseas Bank Ltd.: Incorp. in Singapore; Hong Kong br.: Mongkok Commercial Centre, 16 Argyle St., Kowloon; Man. H. T. Peng.

Bank Association

The Exchange Banks' Association, Hong Kong: c/o The Hong Kong and Shanghai Banking Corporation, 1 Queen's Rd. Central; f. 1897; an association of major banks with the purpose of representation with official bodies and the co-ordination of the banking services offered by its members; Chair. J. L. Boyer.

STOCK EXCHANGES

Far East Exchange Ltd.: Room 201, China Building, Queen's Rd. Central, Hong Kong; f. 1969; 346 mems.; Chair. Ronald Fook-Shiu Li.

Hong Kong Stock Exchange Ltd.: 21st Floor, Hutchison House; Chair. F. R. Zimmern; Sec. R. A. Witts; Publs. *Daily Quotations, Weekly Report, Monthly Gazette, Year Book.*

Kam Ngan Exchange: 7th floor, Connaught Centre, Connaught Rd. Central; f. 1970; 346 mems.; Chair. Woo Hon Fai; publs. *Daily Quotation, Monthly Bulletin.*

Kowloon Stock Exchange: f. Jan. 1972; 175 mems.; Chair. Peter P. F. Chan.

TRADE AND INDUSTRY

CHAMBERS OF COMMERCE

Hong Kong General Chamber of Commerce: Union House, 9th Floor, P.O.B. 852; f. 1861; 2,000 mems.; Chair, H. P. Foxon.

Chinese General Chamber of Commerce: 24 Connaught Rd. Central; f. 1900; 6,000 mems.; Chair. Tong Ping Tat.

Hong Kong Junior Chamber: 24 Ice House St., 4th Floor; f. 1950; 400 mems.; Pres. Peter C. Tsang; Sec.-Gen. Eric Low; publ. *Harbour Lights.*

Kowloon Chamber of Commerce: Liberty Ave., Kowloon; Pres. Chea Pak-cheong.

Indian Chamber of Commerce: Dina House, 5A Duddell St., P.O.B. 2742; f. 1952; 326 mems.; Chair. R. K. Sood; Sec. S. Arunadri Ram.

EXTERNAL TRADE ORGANIZATIONS

Hong Kong Trade Development Council: Connaught Centre, Connaught Rd., Hong Kong; f. 1966; a statutory body to promote, assist and develop Hong Kong's overseas trade, with particular reference to exports; and to make such recommendations to the Government as it sees fit in relation to any measures which it considers would achieve an increase in Hong Kong's trade; overseas offices in Australia, Austria, Canada, Fed. Repub. of Germany, Italy, Japan, Netherlands, Sweden, Switzerland, U.K., U.S.A.; Chair. T. K. Ann; Exec. Dir. L. Dunning; publs. *Hong Kong Enterprise* (monthly), *Apparel* (bi-annual), *Toys* (annual).

Hong Kong Exporters' Association: P.O.B. K1864; Office: 626 Star House, Kowloon; f. 1955; 134 mems. consisting of the leading merchants and manufacturing exporters of Hong Kong; Chair. I. Macaulay; Vice-Chair. N. J. Sousa, O. J. Nicholl; Sec. Mary Dalby.

INDUSTRIAL ORGANIZATIONS

Hong Kong Productivity Council, The: Rooms 512–516, Gloucester Bldg., Des Voeux Rd. C.; f. 1967 to promote increased productivity of industry and to encourage more efficient utilization of resources; established by statute and supported by Hong Kong Government, of which the executive body is the *Hong Kong Productivity Centre*; mems.: not more than 21, appointed by the Governor, of which 4 represent management, 4 represent labour, 2 represent academic or professional interests and no more than 14 are public officers; Chair. of Council Dr. the Hon. Sir S. Y. Chung, C.B.E., J.P., Chair. of Exec. Cttee. Dr. Hon. S. Y. Chung, O.B.E., J.P.; Exec. Dir. W. H. Newton; publs. *Hong Kong Productivity News* (monthly, bilingual), *Industry data Sheets* (yearly bilingual), *Hong Kong Industrial Directory* (yearly bilingual).

Federation of Hong Kong Industries, The: Eldex Industrial Bldg., 12th. Floor, Unit A, 21 Ma Tau Wei Rd., Hung Hom, Kowloon; f. 1960; about 1,000 individual mems., divided into 21 groups according to type of industry; Chair. Hon. James H. Wu, O.B.E., J.P.; Deputy Chair. M. C. Tang.

Chinese Manufacturers' Association of Hong Kong, The: 64–65 Connaught Rd. C.; f. 1934; seeks to promote and protect industrial and trading interests; over 2,000 mems.; Pres. C. P. Hung; Sec.-Gen. J. P. Lee; publs. *Monthly Bulletin, Annual Report, Directory of Members.*

Federation of Hong Kong Cotton Weavers: Room 1041 Union House Central, Hong Kong; f. 1957; 39 mems.

Hong Kong Cotton Spinners' Association: 1038 Union House; f. 1955; 31 mems.

Hong Kong Jade and Stone Manufacturers' Association: Hang Lung House, 16th Floor, 184–192 Queen's Rd. Central; f. 1965; Pres. R. Y. C. Lee.

Employers' Federation of Hong Kong: 909 Union House, Chater Rd., P.O.B. 2067; f. 1947; 136 mems.; Chair. J. G. Oliver; Vice-Chair. J. H. W. Salmon; Sec. and Treas. J. A. Cheetham.

TRADE UNIONS

In 1975 there were 356 trade unions in Hong Kong, 111 independent and the others affiliated to the following organizations:

Hong Kong and Kowloon Trades Union Council (TUC): Labour Bldg., 11 Chang Sha St., Kowloon; f. 1949; 84 affiliated unions, mostly covering the catering and building trades; supports the Republic of China; affiliated to ICFTU; Gen. Sec. Wong Yiu Kam.

Hong Kong Federation of Trade Unions (FTU): 142 Lockhart Rd., 3rd Floor; f. 1948; 67 affiliated unions, mostly concentrated in the shipyards, seafaring, textile mills and public utilities, and 29 nominally independent unions which subscribe to the policy and participate in the activities of the FTU; left-wing supporting the Chinese People's Government.

CO-OPERATIVES

Registrar of Co-operatives: The Director of Agriculture and Fisheries, 393 Canton Rd., Kowloon; as at March 31st, 1974 there were 423 Co-operatives with a membership of 22,580 and paid-up capital of HK $1,782,576.

Co-operative Societies

(socs. = societies; mems. = membership; cap. = paid-up share capital in HK $; feds. = federations)

Agricultural Credit: socs. 9, mems. 255, cap. $39,280.
Apartment Owners': socs. 2, mems. 159, cap. $10,950.

Better Living: socs. 23, mems. 1,789, cap. $31,930.
Consumers': socs. 11, mems. 2,529, cap. $19,575.
Farmers' Irrigation: socs. 1, mems. 68, cap. $340.
Federation of Fishermen's Societies: feds. 4, member-socs. 56, cap. $5,425.
Federation of Pig Raising Societies: fed. 1, member-socs. 30, cap. $1,050.
Federation of Vegetable Marketing Societies: fed. 1, member-socs. 28, cap. $5,500.
Fishermen's Credit: socs. 60, mems. 1,333, cap. $31,310.
Fishermen's Credit and Housing: socs. 2, mems. 101, cap. $665.
Housing: socs. 236, mems. 5,042, cap. $1,391,600.
Pig Raising: socs. 30, mems. 1,507, cap. $134,300.
Salaried Workers' Thrift and Loan: socs. 6, mems. 736, cap. $10,266.
Vegetable Marketing: socs. 31, mems. 8,705, cap. $107,997.

MARKETING ORGANIZATIONS

Fish Marketing Organization: f. 1945; statutory organization to control wholesale fish marketing; in 1975 landings marketed through wholesale fish markets totalled 88,990 metric tons valued at HK $232m.

Vegetable Marketing Organization: f. 1946; Government agency to collect vegetables and handle wholesale marketing; loan fund to farmers; during 1975 64,865 metric tons of vegetables, valued at HK $89m. were sold through the organization.

DEVELOPMENT CORPORATIONS

Hong Kong Housing Authority: 1, Ma Tau Kok Rd., Kowloon; Chair. Hon. I. M. LIGHTBODY, C.M.G., M.A.; Vice-Chair. and Dir. of Housing DONALD P. H. LIAO, O.B.E., B.ARCH., Dip. L.D.

Hong Kong Housing Society: P.O.B. 845; f. 1948 as an offshoot of the Hong Kong Council of Social Service; incorporated by ordinance in 1951; voluntary organization managing 22,594 flats and shops accommodating 141,454; Chair. Hon. Sir DOUGLAS CLAGUE, C.B.E.

Kadoorie Agricultural Aid Association: f. 1951; assists farmers in capital construction by technical direction and by donations of livestock, trees, plants, seeds, fertilizers, cement, road and building materials, farming equipment, etc.; grounds for livestock breeding, orchards, vegetable and flower gardens open to public.

Kadoorie Agricultural Aid Loan Fund: f. 1954; in conjunction with the Hong Kong Government, provides interest-free loans to assist farmers in the development of projects. At March 31st, 1973, the balance of normal loans was HK $4,722,300.

J. E. Joseph Trust Fund: c/o Director of Agriculture and Fisheries, Canton Rd. Govt. Offices: 12th-14th Floor, 393 Canton Rd., Kowloon, Hong Kong; f. 1954; grants credit facilities to farmers; up to March 31st, 1975 the accumulated total of loans amounted to HK$31,258,320.

MAJOR INDUSTRIAL COMPANIES

The following are some of Hong Kong's leading industrial organizations, arranged in alphabetical order:

Chiap Hua Flashlights Ltd.: 23 Bailey St., Hunghom, Kowloon.

China Light & Power Co. Ltd.: 147 Argyle St., Kowloon; electricity suppliers; generating station at Kowloon; Chair. L. KADOORIE.

Gilman & Co. Ltd.: G.P.O.B. 56, Hong Kong; subsid. of Inchcape & Co. Ltd., London; importers, exporters, engineers, shipping, insurance and travel agents; Man. Dir. H. P. FOXON; 1,100 employees.

Hong Kong Electric Co. Ltd.: Electric House, 44 Kennedy Rd., P.O.B. 915, Hong Kong; power stations at North Point and Ap Lei Chau; Chair. Hon. P. G. WILLIAMS, O.B.E., J.P.

Hong Kong Spinners Ltd.: 1501 Prince's Bldg., Chater Rd., Hong Kong; cotton yarn; Man. Dir. T. Y. WONG, Man. Z. D. WOO.

Hutchison International Ltd.: Hutchison House, Murray Rd., Hong Kong; commercial, industrial, aviation, shipbuilding, investment holding and dealing company; Chair. Hon. Sir DOUGLAS CLAGUE, C.B.E.; Deputy Chair. and Chief Exec. W. R. A. WYLLIE.

Kader Industrial Co. Ltd.: 24 Tanner Rd., North Point, Hong Kong; plastic goods including dolls, toys, household articles, table-wares and unbreakable chairs; Man. Dir. H. C. TING.

Shun Fung Ironworks Ltd.: Manning House, Hong Hong; steel ingot, steel bars, casting, etc.; factory at Kowloon; Dirs. L. Y. LEUNG, Y. C. FU, D. Q. CHEUNG.

Senca Industries Ltd.: 34 Tai Yau St., San Po Kong, Kowloon; manufacturers of consumer goods including aluminium, brass, steel and plastic flashlights, battery lanterns, transistorized flashing lights, etc., electronic products and also precision machinery for industrial use; Man. Dir. Dr. The Hon. S. Y. CHUNG.

Swire Group: John Swire and Sons (HK) Ltd.: Union House, 9 Connaught Rd Central, Hong Kong; shipping managers and agents, airline operators, marine and aviation engineering, trading, insurance, property development, operators of offshore drilling rigs, and manufacturers of soft drinks and paints, packagers and distributors of sugar; Chair. and Man. Dir. Hon. J. H. BREMRIDGE.

W. Haking Industries (Mechanics & Optics) Ltd.: 981 King's Rd., North Point, Hong Kong; binoculars, field and opera glasses, telescopes, microscopes, cameras and other optical equipment.

Wheelock Marden & Co. Ltd.: 5th Floor, Lane Crawford House, Hong Kong; shippers, importers and agents; Chair. J. L. MARDEN; Deputy Chair. P. J. GRIFFITHS; Man. Dirs. W. J. LEES, H. W. LEUNG.

Winner-Soco Group: c/o Soco Textiles (HK) Ltd., Yu To Sang Bldg., Queen's Rd., Central, Hong Kong; cotton spinners; importers of raw cotton and exporters of cotton yarn and finished cotton piecegoods; Man. Dirs. W. H. CHOU, T. K. ANN, H. C. TANG.

Yangtzekiang Garment Manufacturing Co. Ltd.: 22 Tai Yau St., San Po Kong, Kowloon; clothing manufacturers; Man. Dir. S. K. CHAN.

TRANSPORT

Transport Commissioner: I. F. C. MACPHERSON.

RAILWAYS

Kowloon-Canton Railway: the line is 22 miles long and runs from the terminus at Kowloon to the Chinese frontier at Lowu. Through passenger services to China have been in abeyance since 1949; all passengers are obliged to change trains at the frontier. Mail and goods wagons, however, travel through without transshipment. Work began in 1974 on the introduction of a double track for the first seven miles of route from Hung Hom to Sha Tin; it is expected to be completed in 1977. The construction of an oil terminal at Fo Tan commenced in 1976. A marshalling yard at Lowu is being built to improve the situation for passengers visiting China. An investment programme of about HK $1,100m. has been formulated for implementation over the next ten years; Gen. Man. R. E. GREGORY, C.ENG., M.I.MECH.E., F.P.W.I.

An underground railway system is due to come into operation in 1980.

ROADS

There are 653.5 miles of officially maintained roads, 210.22 on Hong Kong Island, 194.56 in Kowloon and New Kowloon and 248.72 in the New Territories. Almost all of them are concrete or asphalt surfaced.

FERRIES

Four steamers and 11 hydrofoils operate between Hong Kong and Macao.

Star Ferry Company Ltd.: Kowloon; operates passenger ferries between the Kowloon Peninsula and the main business district of Hong Kong; Gen. Man. H. M. G. FORSGATE; Sec. D. T. NOLAN.

Hong Kong and Yaumati Ferry Co. Ltd.: Hong Kong; 14 passenger and two car ferry services within harbour limits and 13 services to outlying districts (including recreational and excursion services). Operates a fleet of 86 vessels.

SHIPPING

Regular services are maintained by 20 shipping lines to Europe and 20 lines to North America. Other lines serve Australia, New Zealand, South Africa, South America and the Asian ports.

SHIPPING LINES

Agana Line Ltd.: c/o Jardine, Matheson & Co. Ltd., P.O.B. 70.

Alfred Shipping & Trading Co. Ltd.: Li Po Chun Chambers, 13th Floor, Des Voeux Rd. Central; agents for American Export Isbrandtsen Lines; Pres. ALFRED HSIEH.

American President Lines Ltd.: 2018 Connaught Centre, Connaught Rd. Central.

Australia-West Pacific Line: c/o Everett Steamship Corpn. S/A, 20th floor, Connaught Centre, Connaught Rd., Central; Man. M. J. MITCHELL.

Australian National Line: c/o Jardine, Matheson and Co. Ltd., P.O.B. 70.

Ben Line Steamers Ltd.: Chartered Bank Bldg.

British India Steam Navigation Co. Ltd. (Calcutta/Japan Service): c/o Jardine, Matheson & Co. Ltd., P.O.B. 70.

Canadian Pacific Steamships Ltd.: 1702 Union House, P.O.B. 17; Man. C. H. CHAN.

China Navigation Co. Ltd.: Union House, 9 Connaught Rd. Central; f. 1873; Man. Dir. A. D. MOORE.

Chinese Maritime Trust (1941) Ltd.: Hutchison House; Man. D. T. YUI.

Clan Line: c/o Jardine Matheson & Co. Ltd., P.O.B. 70.

Columbia International: c/o Jardine, Matheson & Co. Ltd., P.O.B. 70.

Compagnie Maritime des Chargeurs Réunis (H.K. Branch): 916 Union House, P.O.B. 13364.

Dominion Navigation (Bahamas) Ltd.: c/o Jardine, Matheson & Co. Ltd., P.O.B. 70.

Eastern Africa National Shipping Line Ltd.: c/o Jardine, Matheson & Co. Ltd., P.O.B. 70.

East Asiatic Co. Ltd.: 19th floor, Connaught Centre, Connaught Rd., Central.

Everett Steamship Corporation, S/A: Connaught Centre, 20th floor, Connaught Rd., Central; Gen. Man. T. C. LAMB; Asst. Gen. Man. J. C. SWIFT.

Gibb Livingston & Co. Ltd.: P.O.B. 55.

Glen Line Ltd.: Agents: Swire Shipping Agencies Ltd., Union House, P.O.B. 1.

Gold Star Line Ltd.: Head Office: Kobe, Japan; Hong Kong Office: 8th floor, South China Bldg., 1-3 Wyndham St.

Hapag-Lloyd A.G.: c/o Jebsen & Co. Ltd., Prince's Bldg., Ice House St.

Hesco (Hong Kong) Ltd.: Jardine House; f. 1970; Chair. G. B. GODFREY; Man. Dir. H. CHEN.

Indo-China Steam Navigation Co. Ltd., The: c/o Jardine, Matheson & Co. Ltd., P.O.B. 70.

Kuwait Shipping Co. (S.A.K.): c/o Jardine, Matheson & Co. Ltd., P.O.B. 70.

W. R. Loxley & Co. Ltd.: P.O.B. 84.

Lykes Bros. Steamship Co. Inc.: c/o Jardine, Matheson & Co. Ltd., P.O.B. 70.

Cie. des Messageries Maritimes: Union House, 11 Connaught Rd.; P.O.B. 53.

Moller Group: 12th Floor, Union House.

Nedlloyd and Hoegh Lines: c/o Getz Bros., Edinburgh House, Queen's Rd. Central.

Neptune Orient Lines Ltd.: c/o Jardine, Matheson & Co. Ltd., P.O.B. 70.

Norwegian Asia Line: c/o Thoresen & Co., Union House, P.O.B. 6; Man. Dir. T. VINDE.

Pacilloyd Shipping Co. Ltd.: Jardine House; f. 1970; Chair. G. B. GODFREY; Man. Dir. H. CHEN.

Phoenix Container Liners Ltd.: Gen. Man. Gilman and Co. Ltd., P.O.B. 56.

P & O S.N. Co.: c/o Mackinnon Mackenzie & Co. of Hong Kong Ltd., P. & O. Building.

R.I.L. (Hong Kong) Ltd.: 219–232 Prince's Bldg., Ice House St., P.O.B. 45; agents for various Dutch shipping lines and all airline bookings.

Royal Mail Line: c/o Jardine, Matheson & Co. Ltd., P.O.B. 70.

C. F. Sharp & Co., S/A: 30-36 Caxton House, 1 Duddell St.

South African Marine Corp. Ltd. (Safmarine): c/o Jardine, Matheson & Co. Ltd., P.O.B. 70.

States Steamship Co.: Agents: Jardine, Matheson & Co. Ltd., P.O.B. 70.

Sun Hing Shipping Co. Ltd.: 8th & 9th floors, South China Bldg., 1–3 Wyndham St.; Man. Partner SIMON LEE.

Swedish American Line: Agents: Gilman & Co. Ltd., P.O.B. 56; cruise vessels.

Union-Castle Mail Steamship Co. Ltd.: c/o Jardine, Matheson & Co. Ltd., P.O.B. 70.

United States Lines Inc.: 616 Union House.

Wallem & Co. Ltd.: P.O.B. 40, 34/36th Floors, Gammon House, Harcourt Rd., Central; Man. Dir. A. J. HARDY.

World-Wide (Shipping) Ltd.: 21st Floor, Prince's Bldg., Hong Kong; Chair. Y. K. PAO.

CIVIL AVIATION

Director of Civil Aviation: R. E. DOWNING, J.P.

Cathay Pacific Airways Ltd.: Union House, 9 Connaught Rd.; f. 1946; Parent Company John Swire & Sons Ltd., London; amalgamated with Hong Kong Airways 1959; services to 15 major cities in the Far East (services to Saigon were suspended May 1975) and to Perth, Sydney (Australia) using a fleet of 2 Lockheed

Tristar L-1011S and 4 Boeing 707-320Bs, 8 Boeing 707-320Cs; unduplicated route miles 19,499; Chair. J. H. BREMRIDGE; Man. Dir. D. R. Y. BLUCK.

In addition, thirty foreign airlines serve Hong Kong.

The airport runway has been expanded to accommodate supersonic aircraft.

TOURISM

Hong Kong Tourist Association: 35th floor, Connaught Centre, Connaught Rd. Central, Hong Kong; f. 1957; co-ordinates and promotes the tourist industry; has Government support and financial assistance; 11 mems. of the Board representing Government and the tourist industry; Chair. J. H. BREMBRIDGE, J.P.; Exec. Dir. J. PAIN; Sec. ALEC H. B. CHEUNG, A.C.I.S., A.M.B.I.M., publ. *Hong Kong Travel Bulletin.*

In 1975, there were some 1.3 million visitors to Hong Kong.

LEADING ORCHESTERA AND OPERA COMPANIES

The Hong Kong Philharmonic Society Ltd.: City Hall; Chair. ALEX WU; Music Dir. LIM KEK-TJIANG; Gen. Man. SO HAU-LEUNG.

The Hong Kong Society for the Promotion of Chinese Opera: c/o Hong Kong Arts Centre, 3 Yung Ping Rd., 4/F, Causeway Bay; Chair. Mrs. HELGA BERGER-WERLE.

Tai Ping Theatre: 421 Queen's Rd. West, Hong Kong; Tai Ping Amusement Co.; Cantonese Opera; Gen. Man. I. H. YUEN.

Chun Chau Chap Chinese Operatic Research Society: 14 Hart Ave., Kowloon; Mandarin Opera; Man. K. Z. LEE.

EDUCATION

The main concern of the Hong Kong education authorities has been to extend and subsidize primary education, which is non-compulsory at present, and also to increase the number of secondary school places. In 1946, in order to cope with the post-war population pressure, it was necessary to adopt the shift system of morning and afternoon sessions which has had to be continued down to the present day for the majority of primary schools. Schools in Hong Kong fall into three main categories: those wholly maintained by the government; those run by private non-profit making bodies with government financial aid; and those run independently by private organizations. There are also specialized schools for handicapped children run by government and voluntary organizations. In 1975 they provided education for 5,675 children.

Pre-primary and Primary Schools

Kindergarten and pre-primary schools are run by private bodies without government assistance for children between the ages of three and six. In 1975 there were over 800 such schools with an enrolment of 146,965. The age of entry into primary school is six and the schools provide a six-year course of basic primary education. During 1971 fees were abolished in all Chinese language government primary schools, and a form of compulsory primary education was introduced. Since 1965 with the doubling of free places in primary schools and also the introduction of a system of subsidizing places in private schools, every child of primary school age is ensured of a place. The government maintains five primary schools for English-speaking children, as Chinese tends to be the medium of instruction at primary school level. At post-primary level a dual system of educational instruction has been developed using English as the second language in English schools. At the completion of the primary course a secondary school entrance examination selects suitable pupils for government-aided secondary schools. It is proposed to increase the vocational training possibilities for children who fail to gain admission to secondary schools.

Secondary Schools

In 1975 there were 415,691 pupils in secondary schools. There were five types of secondary schools in Hong Kong: Anglo-Chinese grammar schools, pre-vocational schools, secondary modern schools, the Chinese middle schools and the secondary technical schools. The Certificate of Education may be taken after a five-year course; a further course of one or two years leads to Matriculation. The secondary modern schools provide shorter courses with higher vocational content. The Government aims to provide three years of aided secondary education for children in the 12-14 age group by 1979, and aided places for 40 per cent of pupils between 15 and 16 years.

Higher Education

Higher education is provided at the University of Hong Kong and the Chinese University which together had 8,073 students in 1975. The Polytechnic is wholly government-maintained and is the principal centre for technical education. In 1975, 20,932 students enrolled for full and part-time courses, from higher apprenticeship to higher diploma level. Technological training is also provided by the Morrison Hill Technical Institute, which had 14,000 students in 1974–75, and four other Technical Institutes are in advanced stages of development.

Teachers' Training

There are three government-run colleges of education which provide training for teachers of primary schools and the lower classes in secondary schools. The total number of students in 1975 was 3,299 and the government provides interest-free loans and grants for poor students. All three colleges offer full-time courses of 2 years duration, with a third-year course for specialist non-graduate teachers. Both universities also provide a post-graduate course in education of one year's duration.

UNIVERSITIES

University of Hong Kong: Hong Kong; 400 teachers, 3,714 students.

Chinese University: Shatin, New Territories; 339 teachers, 3,347 students.

BIBLIOGRAPHY

GENERAL

COLLIS, M. Foreign Mud (Faber, London, 1946).
The Great Within (Faber, London, 1946).

DAVIS, S. G. Hong Kong in its Geographical Setting (Collins, London, 1949).

ENDACOTT, G. B. Government and People in Hong Kong, 1841–1962: A Constitutional History (Hong Kong University Press, 1964).

GLEASON, G. Hong Kong (Robert Hale, London, 1964).

HONG KONG GOVERNMENT, Annual Reports (H.M.S.O., London, and Government Publications Centre, Hong Kong).

HOPKINS, KEITH (Ed.). Hong Kong: The Industrial Colony (Oxford University Press, Hong Kong, 1971).

HUGHES, R. Hong Kong: Borrowed Place, Borrowed Time (Andre Deutsch, London, 1976).

INGRAMS, H. Hong Kong (H.M.S.O., London, 1952).

JARVIE, IAN C. (Ed.). Hong Kong: A Society in Transition (Routledge and Kegan Paul, 1969).

MINERS, N. J. The Government and Politics of Hong Kong (Oxford University Press, 1975).

SIMPSON, C. Asia's Bright Balconies (Angus and Robertson, Sydney, 1962).

HISTORY

CARRINGTON, C. E. The British Overseas (Cambridge, 1950).

ENDACOTT, G. B. A History of Hong Kong (Oxford University Press, London, 1958).

GREENBERG, M. British Trade and the Opening of China 1800–1842 (Cambridge University Press, London, 1951).

LUARD, E. Britain and China (Chatto and Windus, London, 1962).

LUFF, J. The Hidden Years: Hong Kong 1941–1945 (South China Morning Post, Hong Kong, 1967).

MILLS, A. British Rule in Eastern Asia (Oxford University Press, London, 1942).

SAYER, G. R. Hong Kong: Birth, Adolescence and Coming of Age (Oxford University Press, London, 1937).

ECONOMY

ALLEN, G. C., and DONNITHORNE, A. G. Western Enterprise in Far Eastern Economic Development (Allen & Unwin, London, 1955).

CHOU, K. R. The Hong Kong Economy: A Miracle of Growth (Academic Publications, Hong Kong, 1966).

SZCZEPANIK, E. F. The Economic Growth of Hong Kong, (Oxford University Press, London, and Hong Kong, University Press, 1958).

Japan

PHYSICAL AND SOCIAL GEOGRAPHY

John Sargent

(Revised by the Editor, 1976)

The Japanese islands lie off the Asian continent in an arc stretching from latitude 45° N. to latitude 35° N., covering a land area of 377,483 square kilometres. The Tsushima Strait, which separates Japan from Korea, is nearly 120 miles wide, while 500 miles of open sea lie between Japan and the nearest point on the coast of the Chinese mainland.

Four large and closely grouped islands—Hokkaido, Honshu, Shikoku, and Kyushu—constitute 98 per cent of the territory of Japan, the remainder being made up by a large number of smaller islands.

PHYSICAL FEATURES

The Japanese archipelago belongs to a belt of recent mountain building which extends around the rim of the Pacific Ocean, and which is characterized by frequent volcanic activity and crustal movement. Around the fringes of the western Pacific, this belt takes the form of a complex series of island arcs, stretching southwards from the Aleutians and including Japan. In the Japanese islands, the Kurile, Kamchatka, Bonin, Ryukyu, and Korean arcs converge. Where two or more of these major arcs meet, as in Hokkaido and in central Honshu, conspicuous knots of highland occur. In the latter area, the Japan Alps, which rise to over 10,000 feet, form the highest terrain in the country, although the highest single peak, Mount Fuji (12,388 ft.), is an extinct volcano unrelated to the fold mountains of the Alps.

Three major zones of active volcanoes and hot springs occur: in Hokkaido, in northern and central Honshu, and in southern Kyushu. Further evidence of crustal instability is provided by the occurrence, each year, of over a thousand earth tremors. Earthquakes strong enough to cause damage to buildings are, however, less frequent, and occur, on average, once every five years.

While the major arcs determine the basic alignment of the main mountain ranges, complex folding and faulting has resulted in an intricate mosaic of landform types, in which rugged, forested mountains alternate with small pockets of intensively cultivated lowland.

In the mountains, short, fast flowing torrents, fed by meltwater in the spring and by heavy rains in the summer, have carved a landscape which is everywhere characterized by steep and sharply angled slopes. Narrow, severely eroded ridges predominate and rounded surfaces are rare. Although the mountain torrents provide many opportunities for the generation of hydroelectric power, marked seasonal changes in precipitation cause wide fluctuations in the rate of flow, and consequently hinder the efficient operation of hydroelectric plant throughout the year.

The extreme scarcity of level land is one of the salient features of the geography of Japan. In a country where the population was the sixth largest in the world in 1976, only 16 per cent of the total land area is cultivable. Thus, the small areas of lowland, which contain not only most of the cultivated land but also all the major concentrations of population and industry, are of vital importance.

Most Japanese lowlands consist of small coastal plains which have been formed through the regular deposition of river-borne alluvium. On encountering the low-lying land of the coastal plain, the typical torrent becomes a sluggish river which meanders across the gently sloping surface of the plain, to terminate in a shallow estuary. The river bed is usually raised above the surface of the surrounding plain, and the braided channel is contained by levees, both man-made and natural. Most alluvial plains are bounded inland by rugged upland, and many are flanked by discontinuous benches of old and poorly consolidated alluvial material. None of the alluvial plains of Japan is extensive: the Kanto, which is the largest, has an area of only 5,000 sq. miles. Many plains are merely small pockets of nearly level land, closely hemmed in by the sea and the steeply sloping mountains.

The coastline of Japan is long and intricate. On the Pacific coast, where major faults cut across the prevailing grain of the land, large bays, flanked by relatively extensive alluvial plains, are conspicuous features. Three of these bay-head plains—the Kanto, the Nobi, and the Kansai—contain over a third of the population of the country, and over half of its industrial output. Farther west along the Pacific coast, two narrow channels lead into the sheltered waters of the Inland Sea, which occupies a zone of subsidence between Shikoku and western Honshu. By contrast with the Pacific coasts, the Japan Sea coastline is fairly smooth. The overall insularity of Japan may be indicated by reference to the fact that very few parts of the country are more than sixty miles from the sea.

CLIMATE

While relief conditions in Japan often impose severe limits upon economic activity, climatic conditions are, on the whole, more favourable. The summers of Japan are of sufficient warmth and humidity to allow the widespread cultivation of paddy rice; yet cold, dry winters clearly differentiate Japan from those countries of sub-tropical and tropical Asia, where constant heat prohibits prolonged human effort.

JAPAN

The climate of Japan, like the climates of the rest of Monsoon Asia, is characterized by a marked seasonal alternation in the direction of the prevailing winds. In winter, in association with the establishment of a centre of high atmospheric pressure over Siberia, cold dry air masses flow outwards from the continent. During their passage over the Japan Sea, these air masses are warmed in their lower layers, and pick up moisture, which, when the air masses rise on contact with the Japanese coast, is precipitated in the form of snow. Thus, winter weather along the Japan Sea coastlands is dull, cloudy, and characterized by heavy falls of snow. By contrast, the Pacific side of the country experiences cold dry weather, with low amounts of cloud. Near the Pacific coast, winter temperatures are ameliorated by the influence of the warm Kuro Shio sea current.

Besides this contrast between the two sides of the country, a latitudinal variation in temperature, similar to that of the Atlantic seaboard of the United States, is also apparent. Thus, north of latitude 38° N., average January temperatures fall below 32°F., and reach 20°F. in Hokkaido. In this northern zone, winter weather conditions prohibit the double cropping which is elsewhere characteristic of Japanese agriculture. South of latitude 38° N., January temperatures gradually rise, reaching 40°F. at Tokyo, and 44°F. at Kagoshima in southern Kyushu.

After mid-March, the winter pattern of atmospheric circulation begins to change, with high pressure developing over the Aleutians, and low pressure over Siberia. In association with these unstable conditions, the first of the two annual rainfall maxima occurs, with the onset of the Bai-u rains in June. By July, however, the high pressure centre to the east of Japan has fully developed, and, with low pressure prevailing over the continent, a southeasterly flow of warm moist air covers the entire country. On the Pacific coast, August temperatures rise to over 80°F., and the weather becomes unpleasantly hot and humid. To the north, however, August temperatures are lower, reaching only 66°F. in Hokkaido.

In late August and early September, the Pacific high pressure centre begins to weaken, and the second rainfall maximum occurs, with the arrival of typhoons, or tropical cyclones, which travel northwards to Japan from the equatorial regions of the Pacific Ocean. These severe storms, which frequently coincide with the rice harvest, cause widespread damage.

By October, high pressure has again developed over Siberia, and the northwesterly winter monsoon is consequently re-established.

Annual precipitation in Japan varies from 33 in. in eastern Hokkaido to over 120 in. in the mountains of central Honshu, and in those parts of the Pacific coast which are fully exposed to the force of the late summer typhoons.

RESOURCES

Although nearly 70 per cent of the total area of Japan is forested, not all of the forest cover is commercially valuable, and large areas of woodland must be preserved to prevent soil erosion. Because many houses are still built of wood, the domestic demand for timber is high, and the home output is supplemented by imports.

In terms of value, and, since 1972, also of volume, the Japanese fish catch is the world's largest. In Japan, fish still supplies a large proportion of the protein content of the average diet, and demand is therefore high. Rich fishing grounds occur in both the Japan Sea and the Pacific to the east of Japan.

Japan is poorly endowed with mineral resources, and industry is heavily dependent upon imported raw materials and fuels. Japan's coal is of poor to medium quality, and seams are thin and badly faulted. The two main coalfields are located towards the extremities of the country, in Hokkaido and in northern Kyushu. In 1975, coal output amounted to 19.0 million tons. Japanese coal deposits are particularly weak in coking coal, much of which is imported, mainly from the United States and Australia.

The small Japanese oilfields, which are located in north-east Honshu, supply only 2 per cent of the domestic demand. The remaining 98 per cent, which now constitutes Japan's biggest import category in terms of value, is shipped from the Middle East.

In 1969, Japanese domestic iron ore production, including ironsand, was 1.9 million tons in contrast to imports of 83.2 million tons. Japan is thus heavily dependent on foreign ores, imported mainly from Australia, Brazil and India.

A wide variety of other minerals is mined, but none exists in large quantities. Japan is self-sufficient only in sulphur.

POPULATION

The population of Japan in 1975 was 111,934,000, according to preliminary census results, giving it an average density of nearly 300 per square kilometre. However, only 16 per cent of the land area is cultivable lowland and the population density in these areas is among the highest in the world.

Three conspicuous urban-industrial concentrations, centred upon Tokyo, Osaka and Nagoya, contain more than a third of the population of Japan. With ten cities containing populations of one million and over in 1975, and a further 78 with populations of between 200,000 and 1 million, Japan is by far the most urbanized country in Asia. Tokyo, the capital of Japan and one of the four largest cities in the world, had a population of 8,642,000. Osaka, with 2,778,975, was the second largest city, followed by Yokohama, with 2,621,648, and Nagoya, with 2,079,694. Kyoto, Kobe, Sapporo, Kita Kyushu, Kawasaki and Fukuoka also have populations of over one million.

In 1867, on the eve of modernization, the population of Japan was already approximately 30 million, a level at which it had stood for the preceding 150 years. With industrialization, population increased rapidly and by 1930 had reached 65 million. After the Second World War, the population policy initiated by the Japanese government succeeded in drastically lowering the rate of population increase, and since 1954, the growth rate has closely corresponded to the rates prevailing in Western Europe.

Apart from the very small number of Ainu, a people who exhibit certain Caucasian characteristics, the Japanese population has been, since early times, ethnically and linguistically uniform. The racial origins of the Japanese are still obscure, but both Mongolian and southern Pacific strains are observable in the present-day population.

HISTORY

Richard Storry

ANTIQUITY AND THE MIDDLE AGES

It is generally agreed that the ancestors of the Japanese must have been immigrants from the mainland of Asia. It is also claimed that there was probably some migration to Japan from the islands of South-East Asia. But the whole subject is still one of pure conjecture. What does seem undeniable is that the forbears of the dwindling little Ainu communities of Hokkaido once occupied the whole country and were in fact the original inhabitants. Be that as it may, an elaborate mythology surrounds the origins of Japan and the Japanese. This declares, for example, that the country itself was created by the gods, and that the first emperor was a direct descendant, in the fifth generation, of the sun goddess. In modern times it was only after the national collapse in 1945 that such legends could be subjected to critical comment in print or public speech. For the belief in the special creation of Japan, and in the unique ancestry of the imperial family, was taught in classrooms all over the land. To question such propositions was to be guilty of something close to blasphemy.

Yamato Period

At all events, what seems to have happened is that the invading immigrants from Asia, who no doubt crossed over from Korea, gradually forced their way eastward from Kyushu along the shores of the Inland Sea; until, around the beginning of the Christian era, they found themselves in the fertile Kansai plain (the modern Kyoto-Osaka region). Here, in the Yamato district, they established an ordered society under chieftains who became priest-kings, dedicated to the cult of the Sun.

This early Japanese society was profoundly influenced by the civilizations of Korea and China. The Chinese ideographic script is only one important and very striking example of many cultural importations from or through Korea. Of even greater significance was the introduction of Buddhism in the sixth century A.D. It was at this stage that the existing body of religious practices, associated with sun worship and animism, became known as Shinto, or "The Way of the Gods". Neither the theology of Buddhism nor the ethics of Confucianism (another import from the continent) made Shinto superfluous. Old beliefs existed side by side with the new. And in course of time, as one would expect, Chinese ideas of religion, of morality, of artistic excellence, of good government, of sound agriculture, were adapted to Japanese conditions and thus suffered a degree of change in the process.

Nara and Heian Periods

At the beginning of the eighth century Nara became the capital, being built on the contemporary Chinese model. This was the heyday of the early Buddhist sects in Japan; and the splendid temples surviving at Nara have a particular interest today, since they are the best remaining examples anywhere of Chinese architecture of the T'ang period. Nara was meant to be a permanent capital. But this was in fact Heian-kyo, later to be known as Kyoto, founded in 794 and constructed, like Nara, on the model of the Chinese capital. It was to be the home of the Japanese imperial family until 1868.

The establishment of this city marks the opening of the Heian age (794–1185), a period remarkable for the artistic sophistication of the court and metropolitan aristocracy. No better picture of a society has been drawn than the elegant portrait of Heian life and manners depicted by the eleventh-century court lady, Murasaki Shikibu, in *Genji Monogatari*, "The Tale of Genji". Its fascination is perennial. This masterpiece, it should be noted, is the reflection of an exquisite culture already characteristically Japanese, even though the debt to China and Chinese modes may be immense.

By the middle of the twelfth century effective power in Kyoto was in the hands of a warrior household, the Taira. Their great rivals were another family, the Minamoto. The strife between the two gave rise to many later epics; and the story of Taira-Minamoto rivalry has never ceased to appeal to the imagination of the Japanese. At first the Taira carried all before them; and Kiyomori, the head of the family, ruled Japan in the emperor's name for a generation. But after his death in 1181 the tables were turned; and in a final battle, in 1185, the Minamoto annihilated their enemies. Thereafter the leader of the Minamoto, Yoritomo, set up a new system of government, known as the *Bakufu* (literally, "camp office"), at Kamakura in the east of the country, far from the imperial capital. The emperor gave Yoritomo the title, *Sei-i Tai Shogun*, or "Barbarian-subduing generalissimo"—usually abbreviated, in Western publications on Japan, as "shogun".

Kamakura Period

The original purpose of Yoritomo's *Bakufu* was the control and administration of the Japanese warrior class, which was now a distinctive entity, and one that was rapidly becoming all-powerful in society. Here was a striking contrast with the situation in China, where the fighting man as such tended to be despised, or at least was held in relatively low esteem by comparison with those who had risen by competitive examination to the peaks of the government service. The Japanese fighting man was already a member of an *élite* class by the twelfth century. The true rulers of the country from that time forward, to a period well within living memory, would tend nearly always to belong to the warrior class. Not for a moment did this class seek to overthrow the imperial dynasty. The idea was indeed unthinkable, since the emperor's line was descended from the sun goddess. So ceremonious respect was always paid to the Kyoto court; but it was exceptional, and usually a sign of uncharacteristic weakness, for any warrior administration to allow the reality of power to slip back into the hands of the imperial household. Every shogun governed in the emperor's name and received his appointment from the emperor.

The Kamakura *Bakufu* lasted until well into the fourteenth century. Yoritomo was a man of exceptional energy, organizing ability, and ruthlessness, who did not hesitate to pursue a vendetta against his own younger half-brother Yoshitsune, who as a military commander had been chiefly responsible for the ultimate defeat of the Taira. Yoritomo died in 1199. His successors in the office of shogun were leaders of inferior calibre, and the *Bakufu* was run by the house of Hojo, related to the Minamoto by marriage. It was the Hojo who rallied the country in resistance to the Mongol invasions of 1274 and 1281. Japanese martial courage was a vital element in the discomfiture of the invaders; but the decisive factor, both in 1274 and 1281, seems to have been the storms which wrecked the Mongol ships lying off the coast. With some justice the Japanese described the great typhoon of 1281 as a *Kami-kaze*, or "Divine Wind".

Some fifty years later both the Hojo family and the Kamakura *Bakufu* were overthrown in the course of a civil war. The climax occurred in 1331 when, with their enemies overrunning Kamakura, the Hojo and their supporters—more than 800 in all—committed *seppuku*, the formal term for the act of hara-kiri, the warrior's suicide by self-disembowelling.

Muromachi Period

Over the succeeding 250 years and more there was great disorder, including much bitter fighting in and near Kyoto. A new *Bakufu* was established, this time in the Muromachi district of the capital, with members of the Ashikaga house (of the Minamoto line) holding office as shogun. From the fall of Kamakura to the latter half of the sixteenth century political events, so often shaped by domestic warfare, are extremely complicated. They require, however, no elaboration here. It should be noted only that Ashikaga power was on the whole limited, and that this was a period in which, thanks to the troubled times, established families were ruined and new men, leading new warrior households, rose to eminence, often from nothing. Yet these two and a half centuries of feudal disorder should not be thought of as Japan's equivalent of the English anarchy in the period of Stephen and Matilda. It was by no means an unrelieved Dark Age. It was marked not only by civil war but also by economic growth and artistic achievement. For the breakdown of central government gave at least some provincial lords the freedom and incentive to embark on foreign trade on their own account, especially with China. One consequence of this commerce was a substantial importation in the fifteenth century of copper cash from China; which promoted the growth of money instead of rice as a medium for exchange. At the same time painting, classical drama, architecture, landscape gardening, ceramics, the tea ceremony, flower arrangement—a great deal of what is recognized today as Japan's magnificent cultural heritage—blossomed in these stormy years. Here Zen Buddhism, in all its manifestations, played a central part. Japan presented a paradoxical scene of savagery and civilization, of barbarism and beauty, intertwined.

TOKUGAWA RULE

Effective central government and internal peace were not finally secured until the early years of the seventeenth century, after Ieyasu founded the Tokugawa *Bakufu* in Yedo (the modern Tokyo), giving the whole country a domestic order that would endure until the coming of American and European men-of-war in the 1850s. Tokugawa Ieyasu built on the work already performed by two notable captains, Oda Nobunaga (1534–82) and Toyotomi Hideyoshi (1536–98). The former contrived, before his death, to unify about half the provinces of Japan. Hideyoshi, the son of a foot-soldier, was one of Nobunaga's commanders. Within ten years of Nobunaga's death he made himself master of the whole country, with the help of a wise and cautious ally in the shape of Tokugawa Ieyasu. Once Japan was under his control (in the emperor's name, of course) Hideyoshi dispatched a host of warriors against Korea, his ambition being to threaten China itself. This venture was a failure. Korea was devastated but could not be permanently conquered and held.

"The Closed Country"

After Hideyoshi's death Ieyasu lost little time in making his own position supreme. He defeated his most formidable rivals in battle in 1600, and three years later he was appointed shogun by the emperor. The history of Japan in Ashikaga days taught him, no doubt, the lesson that the shogun's government was best conducted, like Yoritomo's regime, well away from Kyoto. At any rate he made Yedo castle the headquarters of his administration.

Ieyasu and his immediate descendants adopted a number of important measures to buttress the dominant position of the Tokugawa house (a branch of the seemingly indestructible Minamoto line). Their basic concern was to make sure that no provincial lord or coalition of lords should ever be able to challenge the *Bakufu*. Careful watch at all times was kept on those lords considered to be unreliable. But a more effective way of controlling all feudatories was the rule, strictly enforced, that they spend part of every year in the shogun's capital at Yedo. It was also decreed that when a lord returned to his own province he must leave his wife and family behind him, in Yedo.

Moreover, the Tokugawa *Bakufu* adopted a policy of severe national isolation. From 1628 only the Chinese and Dutch were allowed in, as traders; and their commerce was confined to the port of Nagasaki, where the handful of Dutch merchants was restricted to the tiny island of Deshima. No other foreigners were granted access. No Japanese was permitted to go abroad. Vessels above a certain tonnage could not be built. The modest foreign trade at Nagasaki was a Tokugawa monopoly, controlled by officials appointed by Yedo.

This situation, of what was called *sakoku* or "the closed country", was in sharp contrast with the state of affairs in the previous century. For when, from 1543 onwards, Portuguese traders and missionaries had begun to appear in Japanese waters they had been received with goodwill. More than this, the Christian missionaries had made considerable headway in south-west Japan, especially in Kyushu. They were nearly all of them Jesuits, picked men, who impressed the Japanese by their high standards of personal conduct, by their sincerity, and by their intellectual capacity. Over the years they made thousands of converts. But both Hideyoshi and Ieyasu came to be suspicious of the new faith, which seemed scarcely compatible with many of Japan's own religious practices. Furthermore, it was perceived that in the Philippines Spanish missionary endeavour had gone hand-in-hand with Spanish invasion and conquest. Erratic and capricious at first, persecution of Christianity came to be conducted with brutal efficiency as the seventeenth century advanced. Christians refusing to recant faced painful torments and death.

National isolation was not broken until 1853 and 1854, when Commodore Perry's squadron of American warships paid visits to Yedo (now Tokyo) Bay. On his second visit Perry secured *Bakufu* consent to the opening of two ports and the acceptance at a future date of a resident American consul. The door having been forced ajar it was soon widened. Other powers lost no time in following the example of the United States; and a decade after Perry's expedition a community of foreign diplomats and traders had settled on Japanese soil.

While none of Japan's leaders really welcomed this intrusion by the West, some were implacable in their hostility, insisting that the "barbarians" be expelled. Others perceived the weakness of their country and argued that it must come to terms with the situation, learning the techniques of modern Western civilization. Only then would Japan attain the necessary power to hold her own. At the cost of much humiliation—a great deal of pride had to be swallowed—the second, more realistic, course was adopted as the national policy.

THE RISE OF IMPERIAL JAPAN

Modernization followed the domestic transformation known as the Meiji Restoration. The Tokugawa shogunate had lost face from the moment the first concessions were made to Perry and other intruders. Eventually, in 1868, the much weakened *Bakufu* was overthrown by provincial lords from the south-west, acting in concert and impelled by a coalition of their own most vigorous, far-sighted, warrior retainers. The emperor, still in his teens, was persuaded to leave Kyoto for Yedo, which was renamed Tokyo and became the new capital. Nominally, full governing powers were "restored" to the ancient monarchy; but the young emperor, Meiji, reigned rather than governed. Real power was exercised by an oligarchy composed almost entirely of the provincial warriors (all of them young or still in the prime of life) who had engineered the downfall of the shogunate. These men, the Meiji modernizers, dominated Japanese politics, actively or from their retirement, for the best part of fifty years. They pushed their country out of feudalism into the late nineteenth century world of battleships, telegraphs, steam technology, and Great Power politics. The pace of modernization, the abolition of so many cherished customs and privileges (such as the warrior's right to wear two swords) inevitably gave acute offence to many conservatives. There was more than one unsuccessful armed rising against the government in the decade following the Restoration of 1868.

On the other hand, the Meiji leaders were equally unsympathetic with those who called for guarantees of human rights and individual liberty, together with popular participation in central and local government. It was a question of priorities. Even when such demands were not considered to be actually subversive they were held to be premature. "A rich country and strong military forces"—this was the slogan of the modernizers in the early years. Factories and blast furnaces must come before freedom and the ballot box.

The heritage of Confucian ethics, with their strong emphasis on loyalty to seniors and superiors, fortified the traditions of Shinto, with its veneration of the imperial house, in sustaining a spirit of harmony and hard work, deeply influencing the great majority of the people. Educational indoctrination played a great part here. The Meiji government founded an impressive structure of schools, colleges, and universities. Primary education was compulsory and free. All came under the aegis of the state, in one way or another. State schoolmasters were civil servants, and therefore loyal vassals of the emperor. In 1890 the emperor issued his famous *Rescript on Education*, an exhortation commending the nation's fundamental ethical code to all young people. The Rescript, stressing the patriotic virtues of obedience and self-sacrifice, was read aloud in all schools on days of national festival and commemoration.

A Constitution promulgated in 1889, setting up a bicameral parliament, represented a concession by the oligarchy to the growing demand for some kind of national legislative assembly. But the powers of the Diet (as the new parliament was known) were modest.

Nevertheless, the party leaders in the Diet soon became a serious irritant to the government.

Wars with China and Russia

Domestic political squabbles, however, were put aside in the face of a crisis with China over Korea, in 1894, which led to a war in which Japan won spectacular victories on land and sea. By the Treaty of Shimonoseki (1895) China surrendered to Japan the island of Formosa and the Liaotung peninsula in South Manchuria, including Port Arthur. Within a few days Japan was forced by Russia, Germany and France to waive her claim to the Manchurian prize. A few years later Russia established herself in control of Port Arthur and its hinterland. Revenge came in 1904, when Japan took the gamble of waging war on Russia. But the Anglo-Japanese Alliance (concluded in 1902) meant that Russia's ally, France, could not intervene unless she was prepared to fight England also. The Russo-Japanese War of 1904–05 was a much more costly affair for Japan in men and material resources than the Sino-Japanese War ten years earlier. But Japan's victories, including the destruction of the Tzar's Baltic Fleet off Tsushima in May, 1905, were dramatic. Asia in particular was deeply moved by what happened. The hegemony of the white race seemed to be shaken by Russia's defeat in the East.

THE TAISHO ERA

The death of Emperor Meiji in 1912 was decidedly a landmark, the end of a not inglorious chapter. For the Meiji era is Japan's Victorian age, when despite set-backs and disappointments everything seemed to move forward. The new emperor proved to be mentally unstable, and in 1921 his eldest son, Crown Prince Hirohito, became Regent, succeeding to the throne at the end of 1926.

The period 1912–26 is known as the Taisho era, after the title chosen for the reign of Meiji's successor. It is noteworthy for three important developments and one shocking disaster. In the first place, thanks to the World War of 1914–18, the nation's economic power began to swell in dynamic fashion, as the Japanese shipyards, factories, and foundries were overwhelmed with orders from the Allied countries. There were demands, too, from markets in Asia and Africa which could no longer be supplied by British and German exporters. Secondly, as Britain's ally, Japan invaded and occupied Germany's leased territory in Shantung, China. This brought Japan firmly into China's affairs. The temptation to dictate to China could not be resisted, with the result that Chinese dislike and distrust of Japan increased dramatically, souring the relations between the two countries for years to come. Thirdly, Lenin's triumph in Russia gave some impetus to movements of protest created by the contrast in the standards of living between those who had done well out of the war and the poorer sections of the urban working class. Left-wing groups began to obtain a measure of representation in the Diet. But those who called themselves Communists faced continual harassment by the police and were not allowed to form a legal party. Marxism, however, became fashionable in the academic world. In parts of Tokyo, at any rate, the old-fashioned virtues of patriotism and loyalty seemed faintly outmoded; democracy appeared to be coming into vogue.

And then there occurred the disaster. In September 1923 more than half the city of Tokyo and the whole of Yokohama were destroyed in a series of earth tremors and subsequent fires. In recorded history there has been no comparable natural disaster so calamitous in loss of life and destruction of property.

THE PRE-WAR SHOWA PERIOD

After Emperor Taisho's death (1926) his successor chose as the title for the new reign two Chinese characters, Sho Wa, which can be translated as "Bright Harmony". But the years that followed belied the promise implicit in these words. As the decade of the 1920s ended the clouds gathered in the sky. A prime minister (Hamaguchi) was shot and wounded by a nationalist fanatic in 1930, and died some months later from his injuries. In 1932 another prime minister (Inukai) was assassinated; and in 1936 two former premiers (Saito Makoto and Takahashi Korekiyo) were shot down in their homes by parties of mutinous troops. These and other instances of domestic bloodshed and violence were among the more lurid symptoms of a wave of irrational nationalist hysteria prompted partly by events on the continent of Asia and in part by the economic consequences for Japan of the world depression, which hit the country hard at the beginning of the 1930s. Unrest and dissatisfaction exploded in anger against Diet politicians, wealthy capitalists, and liberal-minded men at the palace and in other influential positions. Public opinion came to regard such figures as weak-kneed, corrupt, and incompetent. The man in uniform, on the other hand, was back in favour, and in power. For in the early autumn of 1931 Japanese forces in South Manchuria carried out a coup against the Chinese in Mukden, and this soon developed into the forcible seizure of all Manchuria.

The army and navy had long enjoyed a key position at the apex of government. For the minister of war and the navy minister were invariably active officers of their respective services. If the army disliked the policy of a cabinet it could usually make its opposition felt by requiring the minister of war to resign. Again, no general on the active list would defy his own service by taking office in a cabinet of which the army disapproved. The same considerations applied to the navy and navy minister. But the army was the more powerful service. During the 1930s indeed it was the single most powerful force shaping the destinies of the country; although the Constitution was never overtly modified, much less overruled.

Expansion in Asia

Condemned by the League of Nations for aggression in Manchuria, Japan left that body in 1933. Manchuria became a puppet state (Manchukuo), an appanage of the empire, only in name more independent than Formosa, or Korea, which had been annexed in 1910. Domination of Manchuria led to involvement in North China; and out of this came undeclared war in the summer of 1937. By the end of that year Japan and China were locked in a combat that would not end until 1945. Chiang Kai-shek resisted with determination, retreating from Nanking to Wuhan, and then, further up the Yangtze, to Chungking in the far west. As the war continued, Japan's relations with other powers underwent a change. She drew closer to Nazi Germany and Fascist Italy, eventually joining them in a full alliance in September 1940. Increasingly, both Great Britain and the United States, powers which supported the Chinese government in Chungking, were seen as potential enemies. The Soviet Union, with whom Japan always expected to be at war sooner or later, dealt some hard blows when Soviet forces clashed with the Japanese on the Manchuria-Outer Mongolia frontier region in 1939.

In July 1941 Vichy France agreed to the Japanese occupation of bases in the Saigon area—bases in northern French Indochina had been occupied by Japan in the previous year. The move southward seemed a clear threat to both Malaya and the Dutch East Indies. It indicated, too, that for the time being at least Japan was not going to join her ally Germany in the assault on the Soviet Union. There was a quick response by the British Commonwealth, the United States, and the Netherlands, in the form of a virtual embargo on all trade with Japan. This was serious; for it meant that oil imports into that country must cease. Japanese-American talks in Washington led nowhere. It was decided in Tokyo to break the embargo by force, rather than accept American pressure for a withdrawal of troops from Indochina and from most, if not all, of the Chinese mainland.

The Sino-Japanese War of 1894–95 and the Russo-Japanese War of 1904–05 had started with surprise attacks by the Japanese navy. In December 1941, Japan followed the same strategy, attacking not only Pearl Harbor in Hawaii but also Hong Kong, Malaya, and the city of Singapore.

THE PACIFIC WAR

For the first six months it was victory all the way. Hong Kong, Malaya, Singapore, Java and the Indies, the Philippines, Burma and the Andamans, New Britain and the Solomons—all these fell to Japanese arms.

But there had been a grave miscalculation of the spirit and resources of the nation's principal enemies. Allied submarines, American island-hopping strategy, and superior fire-power turned the tables on Japan. From early summer in 1944 it was defeat all the way—in the Pacific, on the eastern frontier of India, in Burma, in the Philippines, in Okinawa. By midsummer 1945 the position was desperate. American air raids had inflicted fearful punishment. The merchant fleet, like the battle fleet, had practically ceased to exist. Germany was out of the war. The Soviet Union was an unknown but menacing factor, returning no answer to pleas that Moscow should act as a mediator. The civilian population, exhausted and undernourished, drilled with bamboo spears against the day of invasion, hoping to match the heroism of the *kamikaze* suicide pilots.

The Potsdam Proclamation at the end of July 1945 seemed to leave the government unmoved, although in reality the premier, the aged Admiral Suzuki, was seeking ways and means of ending the war short of abject capitulation. On August 6th the first atomic bomb laid waste Hiroshima. On August 9th the second descended on the suburbs of Nagasaki. Between those dates the Soviet army invaded Manchukuo at several points in great strength.

In this supreme crisis the nation's leaders were divided between those who favoured surrender (with the proviso that the monarchy be maintained) and those who were ready to fight on in spite of everything. It was the emperor, invited to give an unprecedented decision of his own, who tipped the balance by declaring that the Potsdam terms must be accepted.

THE OCCUPATION

U.S. General Douglas MacArthur represented all the Allies in Japan, but the Occupation was nevertheless an almost exclusively American undertaking and to a very great extent MacArthur went his own way, took his own decisions, with or without the agreement of Washington. He rejected the view that the Japanese would be better off without the age-old institution of the monarchy. He felt that the emperor was a stabilizing factor in a society shaken to its roots by the capitulation. This view was correct. But popular regard for the emperor no longer rested on the belief that he partook of divinity because of his descent from the sun goddess. The capitulation—something hardly imagined, even as a nightmare, by most of the people up to August 1945—had shattered the old concept of the state, so intimately bound up with Shinto mythology. When the emperor formally renounced his "divinity" at the beginning of 1946 it created little interest among most Japanese.

In ruling Japan MacArthur acted through the Japanese Government, a procedure that worked smoothly in nearly every instance. Between conquerors and conquered there was indeed a harmony that nobody could have foreseen during the years of warfare. The Japanese, however, can be intensely pragmatic. The events of 1945 seemed to demonstrate that their own way of conducting affairs was inefficient and harmful to themselves. So when the Americans arrived, and once it was clear that their general behaviour was by no means vengeful and oppressive, the Japanese were ready to be their pupils in all manner of activities. During what can be described as the honeymoon period of the Occupation—let us say the first two years—the Americans, exemplifying Democracy triumphant, could do little wrong in the eyes of at least the younger generation in Japan.

Political, Economic and Social Reforms

The watchwords of the Occupation, in the early days especially, were disarmament and democratization. A new Constitution, promulgated in 1946, reflected both these aims. One clause (Article 9) stated that the Japanese people renounced war; and it went on to say that "land, sea, and air forces, as well as other war potential, will never be maintained". A further clause (Article 66) laid down that the prime minister and his cabinet colleagues must be civilians. The other Articles of the Constitution reflected the authentic spirit of North American democracy, with full emphasis on the rights of the individual. Sovereignty of the people was declared. The emperor was made "the symbol of the State and of the unity of the people", and it was affirmed that he derived his position "from the will of the people".

Although undeniably the concoction of American brains, the post-war Constitution captured the imagination of the Japanese. To this day its defenders are sufficiently numerous to make it unlikely that the Constitution will be so radically amended as to change its basic character. Amendment requires the assent of two-thirds of the members of both houses of the Diet, confirmed by a referendum of the people as a whole. So far, conservative governments, wishing to undertake some revision, have been unable to secure the necessary two-thirds majority in the houses of the Diet.

Another measure of profound social and political importance, instigated by MacArthur's headquarters, was the Land Reform. Scores of thousands of tenant farmers were able to obtain ownership of the land they cultivated. Up to the war a depressed class, the farmers of Japan, thanks to the Land Reform, became firm, if not always satisfied, upholders of the political *status quo*. Left-wing parties found the farming vote difficult to entice. The average farmer, freed from the burden of rent and assured of sales for his crop at guaranteed prices, was not impressed by advocates of collectivization and other projects of agrarian socialism.

A drastic purge, often unfair to those affected, barred from public office of any kind all those held to have participated in planning and supporting aggressive war. Whole categories came under the ban. After some years, however, a great many of these "purgees" —the majority in fact—were "rehabilitated".

The educational system was reformed from top to bottom. In terms alike of organization and syllabus it was reworked to a pattern resembling that of the United States. The famous Rescript, needless to say, was discarded; and there was a thorough revision of school-books concerned with history, political science, and ethics.

These manifold changes, not far short of revolutionary in character, were liberating in their effects; but they also caused a good deal of confusion. All established authority, including, of course, male authority in the household, was called in question. "Since the war only two things have become stronger —women and nylon stockings." So runs a favourite Japanese saying. If the post-war freedom of women (who now had the vote and married property rights) may be regarded as an unmixed blessing, it is undeniable that the weakening of traditional, basically Confucian, ethics led to a painful increase in the crime rate—juvenile crime especially.

Political freedom gave the parties of the Left an opportunity to exploit the changes that had occurred, and to make them even more far-reaching. But except for the period between May 1947 and March 1948, when a coalition cabinet under the socialist Katayama was in office, electoral success always attended the conservative parties. Until the end of 1954 the political scene was dominated by Yoshida Shigeru; and even after his retirement the old man was influential, as adviser to successive cabinets, up to his death in 1967.

Consolidation of Relations with the West

As the international situation hardened into the Cold War the attitude of MacArthur's headquarters underwent a subtle but definite change. The emphasis shifted from reform to rehabilitation; and whereas at first the Japanese Left were looked upon as a progressive, liberating force this point of view was no longer fashionable among MacArthur's entourage after about 1947. In particular, as the armies of Mao began to gain ground in China, and as it became clear that American influence on the Chinese mainland might soon be eliminated, the importance of Japan as part of the free world was perceived with growing clarity. After the Korean War broke out in the summer of 1950 it seemed all the more desirable, and in fact urgent, to nourish the revival of Japan. In other words Japan was now regarded not as a recent enemy but rather as a new friend and junior ally. In these circumstances the disarmament clause of the Constitution appeared as an embarrassment. In practice, however, it was to be blandly ignored. The first steps in rearmament were taken in 1950, after war had started in Korea, when MacArthur authorized the Yoshida cabinet to recruit gendarmerie (the National Police Reserve) of 75,000 men.

The Occupation lasted up to the end of April 1952. This was much longer than had been planned. For soon after his basic reforms had been introduced, MacArthur had decided that the situation called for a treaty of peace. When he was dismissed by President Truman in 1951 the Japanese feared that progress towards a peace treaty would be checked. However, in September 1951 the treaty was concluded between Japan and 48 nations (but not the Soviet Union) at San Francisco. It was a magnanimous settlement, free from punitive clauses, although Japan's territorial losses were confirmed. On the same day a bilateral security pact was signed by Japan and the United States. In this Japan asked the U.S. to retain their forces in and around the Japanese islands as a defence against outside attack. When all the signatories of the San Francisco Treaty had ratified the document, it came into force; and in the spring of 1952 Japan became once again formally an independent state.

DEMOCRATIC JAPAN—"ECONOMICS BEFORE POLITICS"

The story since 1952 has been one of astonishing material success, bringing solid practical benefits to the Japanese people in terms of the comfort and enjoyment of their daily lives. The speed and extent of this economic leap forward was something that few had predicted, even after it was clear that the Korean

War was going to put industry on its feet again. The problems facing the country in the early 1950s seemed too great to encourage much optimism about the future. The population, after all, was approaching the figure of 100 million. The China market was lost; and so was the market in Korea. The Soviet Union had put a stop to nearly all Japanese fishing in the seas between Hokkaido and Kamchatka—where the richest harvest of salmon and crab was garnered before the war, for both home consumption and the export trade. Above all, the nation was very poorly endowed with natural resources. It seemed logical to expect that recovery, although real, would be fairly modest.

But a number of factors worked in Japan's favour. During the post-war years, for example, the importance of primary products, of raw materials, declined—thanks to the development of synthetic products. And new discoveries, in various parts of the world, of oil and iron ore helped to create a buyer's market. Thus, the loss of access to the high-grade coal and ore of Manchuria and North China was less vexatious than had been feared.

Nevertheless, these and other factors would have been of minor significance had they not been intelligently utilized. The real secret of the country's success lay elsewhere. It may be summed up in the words of Yoshida Shigeru, written shortly before his death:

> It was the diligence, initiative, and creative ability of the Japanese people that enabled them to exploit the advantages offered. The precept "God helps those who help themselves" was certainly valid for post-war Japan. The economic rehabilitation and advance of Japan was due less to political factors than to hard toil and good fortune.
>
> *Japan's Decisive Century: 1867–1967* (Praeger, New York, 1967).

Fundamentally, it was "hard toil" by a literate, and indeed technologically well-educated, population which made Japan a world leader in shipbuilding, the world's third greatest producer of steel (with a production exceeding that of the United Kingdom, France and Western Germany combined), and a striking example of *speed* in economic growth which other industrial societies have so far failed to emulate.

Since independence it has been government policy (in Tokyo's own words) "to give priority to economics over politics". For instance, in foreign affairs the close association with America has been sustained; and a revised security pact was concluded and ratified in 1960 against shrill and determined popular criticism expressed in repeated street demonstrations on a massive scale. Moreover, the government has frequently announced its support of American policy in Viet-Nam. Yet there has been a refusal, quite firm and consistent, to adopt more positive measures. Japan has rejected the idea that she should join any regional defence organization. Although a conscientious member of the United Nations, she has declined to participate in any active peace-keeping role by contributing a detachment—or even observers—to a UN military force. No doubt to the disappointment of Washington, the Japanese never considered for a moment that they might follow South Korea's example and send a contingent to Viet-Nam. The fact is that such a display of national power would be political suicide. The conservative cabinets—of the *Jiyu-Minshuto* (Liberal-Democratic) party—have maintained their political ascendancy through the 1950s and 1960s on the strength of their remarkable success in running the economy. The recollection of what total war meant to them has not faded from the consciousness of the Japanese, although a new generation has grown to manhood since 1945. Although Japan is now a well-armed state, at least in conventional non-nuclear weapons, the distaste for militarism is still deep enough, and the pacifism symbolized by Article 9 still strong enough, to turn the voters against a government which became involved in any commitment beyond the country's own shores.

If Japan has a definable, short-term, foreign policy goal it is to regain possession of the southern Kuriles. The Soviet Union so far has shown little sign of giving way over the Kuriles, which have been theirs since the Surrender. The Ryukyu Islands, including Okinawa, were returned to Japanese sovereignty by the U.S.A. in May 1972.

A single event can be taken as a symbol of the final triumphant recovery of national morale. This was the Tokyo Olympiad of 1964, when in bright autumn sunshine the emperor opened the Games in the presence of athletes from 94 countries. Yet only a day or two later, for those who looked to the future, an ominous incident occurred. The Chinese tested their first atomic bomb.

This action by Peking, and the later tests, inevitably had an effect on the Japanese attitude towards the People's Republic of China. Under strong pressure from the Americans the Yoshida cabinet in 1951 had agreed to recognize Chiang Kai-shek's administration in Taiwan as the legitimate government of China; and the policy of not recognizing Peking continued. But it had always been realized that some kind of satisfactory relationship must be established, sooner or later, with Communist China. For Japan to be at loggerheads with her huge neighbour was dangerous in the past and could be much more perilous in the future. So despite the value they attached to their vital economic ties with the United States, the Japanese always hoped that somehow they could strengthen their very tenuous commercial links with Peking. Japanese of all political opinions tended to feel a sense of shame for Japan's past misdeeds in China; and the industrialization of China by the Communists was viewed with sympathetic interest, because China seemed to be doing at last what Japan had done sixty or seventy years earlier.

But to a people who had suffered, uniquely, the horrors of atomic attack China's nuclear tests came as a severe shock, recalling—though on a less intense scale—the revulsion that swept the country in 1954, when Japanese fishermen were drenched by the fall-out from America's hydrogen bomb test at Bikini. An important consequence in Japan of the Chinese tests has been the eradication of the sense of guilt for earlier aggression against China.

In 1970 the first world exhibition held in Asia opened at Osaka and, from March to September, attracted vast crowds of visitors. Expo 70, a notable success, seemed to epitomize Japan's remarkable "economic miracle". Yet in the same year pollution of the environment, by industry and its products (especially the motor-car), became the main topic of public interest. At the very moment of high economic achievement the people of Japan showed signs of dissatisfaction with the frustrations and dangers that technology had produced. Industrial smog in the great cities, at its worst in the summer of 1970, was seen as a real menace to the health of the ordinary citizen; and there was an unprecedented outcry in the press and mass media. The future of the Liberal-Democratic party, which was returned to power in the elections of 1969 and 1972, may well rest upon the government's success or failure in dealing with the problem of urban pollution.

The Sato government's victory at the polls in 1969 was due in great part, no doubt, to satisfaction at the agreement reached with America on Okinawa. But the conservatives' success also reflected the growing public revulsion against the extreme left-wing student violence that disturbed universities and colleges in all parts of Japan during 1968 and 1969. This turmoil, which on occasions spilled over into the streets far beyond the precincts of the universities, was often savage, involving arson and much destruction of property. Certain incidents, particularly a two-day battle in 1969 between mobile police squads and students at Tokyo University, attracted world-wide publicity. Although 1970 appeared to be a relatively quiet year, on the campus front, the traditional relationship between teachers and students, deriving ultimately from Confucian ethics, had incurred such damage that many older people feared that the national educational structure was fatally undermined.

In the summer of 1972 Premier Sato resigned, having held the office of Prime Minister for a longer period than any of his predecessors. To succeed him the ruling Liberal-Democratic Party voted into office Kakuei Tanaka, Minister of Trade and Industry, a largely self-made man, noted for his dynamic political style. This was soon confirmed when he announced his intention of visiting Peking in order to establish an entirely new relationship with mainland China.

Premier Tanaka's visit to Peking in September 1972 was an event of great historic importance; for it involved not only the recognition of the People's Government of China as the only legitimate government of China, but also the termination of Japan's diplomatic links with the Chinese Nationalist Government in Taiwan. Moreover, both sides at Peking declared their intention to negotiate a Sino-Japanese Treaty of Friendship.

Japan's new China policy was hailed with enthusiasm by nearly all political groups in Japan. Great interest was also aroused by a plan, *The Remodelling of the Japanese Archipelago*, which had been worked out by Mr. Tanaka before he became Prime Minister. This was a best-seller when published as a book and it was widely believed that the proposals contained in the plan would form the basis of the Government's domestic policies. One of the major proposals was the movement of industry to less developed parts of the country, to remedy over-concentration on the Pacific coast.

The success of his visit to China and the interest in his domestic plans were among the factors believed to have influenced Mr. Tanaka to decide on an early dissolution of the House of Representatives. The House was dissolved in November 1972 and elections held in the following month. The Liberal-Democratic Party was returned to power, though with a reduced majority. Important gains were made by left-wing parties, including Communist victories in all six districts of Osaka. The Prime Minister formed a new Cabinet, in which only six portfolios were unchanged.

Early in 1973 Mr. Tanaka attempted to introduce a reform of the electoral system but an Opposition boycott forced him to abandon the proposal. By the autumn the Government's popularity had greatly diminished. Mr. Tanaka had been unable to check Japan's rampant inflation (consumer prices rose 12 per cent in the year to August 1973) and he was blamed for the rush of speculative activities which followed publication of his plans for relocating industry. Following the death of the Finance Minister, Kiichi Aichi, in November, Mr. Tanaka carried out another extensive Cabinet reshuffle, dismissing 11 Ministers. Announcing the new appointments, the Prime Minister said that they were made to tide Japan over "the most difficult time in our postwar economic history".

This was a reference to a series of events late in 1973, when Japan's rapid economic growth, sustained over more than 20 years, became seriously threatened. Following the Middle East war in October, the governments of Arab oil-producing countries agreed to reduce the output of crude petroleum as a means of putting pressure on countries supporting Israel. The oil cutback exposed Japan's vulnerability to outside pressures, due to the country's dependence on imported raw materials. In November Japanese industry was asked to reduce oil consumption by 10 per cent. Later the Japanese Government made an announcement concerning its Middle East policy which was widely interpreted as taking a pro-Arab stance, resulting from Japan's need to ensure continuing oil supplies from Arab states. In December the Deputy Prime Minister made a three-week tour of eight Middle East countries, with the hope of developing closer ties. Nevertheless, more stringent legislation was introduced to control energy consumption by industry and the public.

These setbacks also affected the strength of Japan's currency. Following the 10 per cent devaluation of the U.S. dollar in February 1973, the Japanese yen (valued at 308 per dollar since December 1971) was allowed to "float" and immediately showed an appreciation of about 14 per cent against U.S. currency. A rate of around 265 yen per dollar was maintained until November 1973, when the oil crisis threatened the Japanese economy. The yen was effectively devalued three times in November and again in January 1974, when the exchange rate was allowed to settle at 300 yen per dollar. The yen subsequently strengthened a little and by March the dollar was valued at less than 280 yen.

Meanwhile, Japan continued to pursue its aim of gaining greater recognition as a world power. In September 1972 it was reported that the Japanese Government was to make a bid for a permanent seat on the United Nations Security Council.

During September and October 1973 the Prime Minister and other Japanese officials made a four-nation tour, visiting France, Britain, Western Germany and the Soviet Union. The Soviet visit produced a joint communiqué which included agreement to resume in 1974 the deadlocked negotiations for the conclusion of a peace treaty. The main stumbling block to the signing of this treaty has been the Soviet occupation of the northern Kurile Islands. Relations with Moscow thus remain lukewarm, despite provisional agreements on joint efforts to develop Soviet oil and gas fields. Japan's relations with China were further strengthened in December 1973, when a three-year trade agreement was initialled, though plans for Sino-Japanese air services remained deadlocked over the issue of Taiwan. Another tour by the Prime Minister, this time to South-East Asia, took place in January 1974. This was marked by hostile demonstrations, notably in Thailand and Indonesia, directed against Japan's economic penetration of the region.

What some commentators interpreted as a turning-point in Japan's post-war politics took place in July 1974, when the House of Councillors' election occurred. This Upper House election is held every three years, for half the seats in the House. The July election reduced the overall majority of the Liberal-Democratic Party in the House from 26 to 7. This blow to the government party's position harmed Premier Tanaka's standing in the country, and this was undermined further when the Prime Minister came under strong criticism as a result of allegations, originally made in a prominent monthly journal, that he had used irregular means to amass his personal fortune. A political storm blew up, and late in November Mr. Tanaka announced his intention to resign. His successor, appointed early in December 1974, was Takeo Miki, who had been Deputy Prime Minister but had left the Government soon after the House of Councillors' election.

Mr. Miki seems to have been a popular choice, judged by the evidence of national opinion polls. He had the reputation of being rather to the left of his party, and he was not associated in the public eye with "money power". The standing of the Liberal-Democratic Party was severely damaged in February 1976 by allegations of leading politicians' and businessmen's involvement in a financial scandal concerning massive bribes accepted from the Lockheed Aircraft Corporation, a leading U.S. aerospace company. In July 1976 the former Liberal-Democratic Prime Minister, Kakuei Tanaka, was arrested on charges concerning the "Lockheed scandal".

Although suffering from recession, the economy showed signs of revival in 1975. The trade balance that year was healthy, and the rate of inflation showed a marked decrease. Wage increases, very high early in 1974, were held at a lower level in 1975; and there was a prospect of Japan's entering once more upon a period of growth, although the rate of growth would be at a much lower figure than in the boom years of the 1960s.

In 1975 and the first half of 1976 Japan maintained a position of virtual balance, if not immobility, *vis-à-vis* her powerful neighbours, China and the Soviet Union. No progress was made towards an agreement with the latter on the northern islands' question (Southern Kuriles, Shikotan and Habomai), and the desired treaty of peace and friendship with Peking had yet to be negotiated. However, a Tokyo-Peking air agreement symbolized a further move by Japan in the direction of closer relations with the People's Republic of China.

ECONOMIC SURVEY

Hisao Kanamori

Japan has a total area of 377,483 square kilometres and a population of 112 million (1975); the population density is about 300 persons per square kilometre. Much of the land is mountainous; 66 per cent of the total area is forest, 14 per cent cultivated land, 3 per cent wilderness, and 16 per cent other. The percentage of cultivated land to the total area is low compared with that in European nations (30–40 per cent). There is a large variety of mineral resources, but the quantity is meagre except for limestone and sulphur. Hence, Japan has to depend heavily on imported minerals; the percentage of imports to total domestic consumption in 1975 was 100 per cent for oil, bauxite and iron ore, 97 per cent for copper ore, and 83 per cent for coking coal. Having thus a large population but little cultivated land and meagre mineral resources, Japan cannot increase her national income unless she promotes manufacturing industries, increases the export of industrial products and thereby finances the imports of the necessary foodstuffs and raw materials.

GROSS NATIONAL PRODUCT

Japan's gross national product was U.S. $480,000 million in 1975; this amount is the second largest in the world, after the United States (the nations in the Soviet bloc are excluded). However, the gross national product per capita was either thirteenth or fourteenth among the countries of the world.

The contributions of principal industries to the net national product are agriculture, forestry and fisheries 6 per cent, manufacturing industry 28 per cent, and services 50 per cent. The weight of agriculture, forestry and fisheries, though high compared with that in the United States, the United Kingdom and West Germany, has decreased markedly in recent years, to less than half of that for 1960, as shown in the accompanying table, whereas the percentage for services has increased.

NET NATIONAL PRODUCT
(percentage distribution)

	1960	1974
Agriculture, Forestry and Fisheries	15	6
Mining	2	1
Manufacturing	29	28
Construction	6	9
Electricity, Gas, Water Supply, Transportation and Communications	9	7
Wholesale and Retail Trade	16	20
Banking, Insurance and Real Estate	9	11
Services	11	14
Public Administration	4	5

The composition of the gross national expenditure is shown below. A notable feature is the high percentage of investment (32 per cent for 1975) and the low percentage of consumption expenditure (57 per cent). The percentage of investment is higher than that in any other industrial nation of the world. Among the various sectors of investment, the percentage of private equipment investment is particularly high, amounting to 14 per cent of the gross national expenditure in 1975.

GROSS NATIONAL EXPENDITURE
(percentage distribution)

	1960	1975
Private Consumption	56	57
Government Consumption	9	11
Gross Domestic Capital Formation	35	32
of which:		
Fixed Capital Formation	31	31
Increase in Stocks	4	1

In the distribution of the national income, employees' income in 1974 was 63 per cent (*cp.* 50 per cent in 1960), the unincorporated enterprises income 19 per cent (*cp.* 26 per cent in 1960), and the private corporations income 17 per cent (*cp.* 15 per cent in 1960). The percentage of the employees' income is low and that of the unincorporated enterprises income high compared with those in the United States and the European nations. The reason is that in Japan the proportion of employees in the total working population is still low, there being numerous small enterprises and farms under private management. Compared to a decade ago, however, the percentage of the employees' income has increased considerably.

The most remarkable feature of the post-war Japanese economy has been the high rate of economic growth.

The percentage increases of G.N.P. in real terms over the previous year were as follows:

	per cent		per cent
1966	9.8	1971	7.3
1967	12.9	1972	9.1
1968	13.4	1973	9.9
1969	10.8	1974	−1.2
1970	10.9	1975	2.1

The rate of increase of the gross national product in real terms was highest in 1968, 13.4 per cent. The average annual growth rate from 1960 to 1970 was 10.7 per cent. The principal causes of such high growth are the brisk equipment investment, the abundant labour, the active adoption of foreign techniques, the high rate of savings and the success in expanding exports.

In 1974, however, real G.N.P. fell for the first time. This aroused speculation as to whether the era of Japan's high economic growth had come to an end. It appears, however, that the decline of G.N.P. in 1974 was a temporary phenomenon attributable to the vast increase in crude oil prices in the autumn of 1973. It is believed, therefore, that after a period of adjustment to higher oil prices the Japanese economy will resume growth, if not at a rate as high as in the past, at least at a rate higher than the growth rate of European economies.

AGRICULTURE, FORESTRY AND FISHERY

Until the end of the Second World War, approximately half of Japan's cultivated land was owned by landlords to whom the tenants paid rent in kind. By the post-war land reform, absentee landlords were forbidden to own land, and the holding of a resident landlord was limited to 1 hectare. As a result, 95 per cent of the total cultivated area came into the possession of owner-farmers.

Japan's labour force in agriculture totalled 6.2 million in 1975. There were 4.95 million farmhouses, and the cultivated area per farmhouse was only 1.1 hectares. Labour-intensive farming characterizes Japanese agriculture; the productivity per unit area is very high, about three times that in Italy and West Germany, according to a survey by the OECD. Nevertheless, only 12 per cent of the farmhouses are exclusively engaged in farming; the rest combine farming with employment in other industries.

Production and Distribution

The most important agricultural product is rice, amounting to 36 per cent of agricultural output in 1975. A large variety of other products—wheat, sweet potatoes, potatoes, soya beans, radishes, cabbages, mandarin oranges, apples, persimmons, pears, etc.—are grown. The domestic self-supply rate (the percentage of domestic products in the total supply of edible agricultural products) is about 72 per cent. Under the Staple-Food Management Law of Japan, the price of rice is set by the Government. Every year, the Government sets the price of rice, and how much it should be becomes an important political issue. At present, rice is overproduced, and the Government is endeavouring to decrease production.

About 70 per cent of Japan's total area is covered by forest. Although there is a large variety of trees—cedar, Japanese cypress, pine, Japanese oak, beech, etc.—56 per cent of domestic timber requirements had to be imported in 1975. As an import item, timber ranked second only to petroleum in value.

In fishing, Japan's catch in 1974 was 10,773,000 metric tons, higher than for any other country and over 15 per cent of the world total. However, because of labour shortage and the limited area for deep-sea fishing, the catch is increasing only slowly.

INDUSTRY

Japan's mineral resources are rich in variety but meagre in quantity. While the domestic output of limestone, sulphur, etc. suffices for domestic demand, total needs for bauxite, crude oil and iron ore, 97 per cent for copper ore, and 83 per cent for coking coal, have to be met by imports.

Manufacturing

Manufacturing is Japan's major industry. There were 13.3 million employed in manufacturing in 1975. Industrial production is concentrated into four regions, Tokyo-Yokohama, Osaka-Kobe, Nagoya and northern Kyushu, which together produce 50 per cent of Japan's total output. The concentration in the Tokyo-Yokohama region, in particular, is mounting.

A comparison of the output of major products (1974) with those abroad shows that Japan is top in the production of ships, second in automobiles (passenger cars only), synthetic fibres, paper, cement and synthetic resins, third in steel and fourth in cotton yarn; altogether, Japan ranks about third in industrial production, after the United States and the Soviet Union.

The percentage distribution of various industries in the total shipments (1974) is shown below. Compared with 1950, the weight of the machine-building industry has increased markedly and that of the textile industry has fallen off; thus, Japanese industry is undergoing a drastic compositional change.

COMPOSITION OF INDUSTRY
(percentage distribution of shipments)

	1950	1974
Metals	16	20
Machinery	14	33
Chemicals	14	15
Foodstuffs	13	10
Textiles	24	5
Ceramics	3	3
Others	15	14

Machinery and Consumer Goods. Machinery production has become the most important industry because, as the result of rapid economic growth, there has been an increasing demand for machine tools, industrial machines, heavy electric equipment, etc. Also, as the standard of living has risen, the demand for durable consumer goods such as automobiles, TV sets, cameras, transistor radios, tape recorders, etc., has increased. The automobile industry, in particular, has shown a spectacular development in recent years. Japan's production of passenger cars ranks second in the world, and the production of buses and trucks was in first place in 1974. Passenger cars are not yet widespread in Japan—one car to 6.6 persons (1975)—but the domestic demand for them is mounting rapidly; in 1975, the production of passenger cars was 6.6 times the production in 1965. The export of passenger cars to the United States, Australia, Thailand, etc., is also increasing rapidly.

The development of the light machinery industry, such as cameras, transistor radios, TV sets, tape recorders, etc., is also remarkable and such products now constitute important export items.

Shipbuilding. Japan's pre-war tradition has been used to advantage in the shipbuilding industry. Labour is cheap and, moreover, extensive technical innovations have been made in the post-war years. Hence, Japan's shipbuilding industry has an outstanding competitive strength in the international market. It produces about 50 per cent of the total output of the world. Over 80 per cent of Japan's output is exported.

Iron and Steel. The leading metal industry is the iron and steel industry. Formerly it was not considered a profitable industry for Japan, since she has such meagre domestic supplies of iron ore and coking coal, and insufficient capital. However, after 1950, large-scale, modern iron foundries were constructed, and as a result the Japanese iron and steel industry gained competitive strength; in the mid-1970s it was Japan's greatest export industry. Its equipment is among the most advanced in the world. More than a third of the output is exported, and 52 per cent of the export is for the American market. As for the raw materials, iron ore is imported from Australia, Brazil and India, and coal from the United States, Canada and Australia.

Chemicals. The chemical industry has developed with chemical fertilizers such as ammonium sulphate as the principal products, but recently petroleum chemical products have been increasing rapidly. Unlike the United States, Japan has no supply of waste gas from large-scale oil refineries or natural gas, so volatile oil is decomposed instead. Despite this handicap in raw materials, the petroleum chemical industry is developing dramatically.

Textiles. The textile industry was the earliest to develop in Japan. Up to the 1920s, raw silk was Japan's most important export item. Even in the mid-1970s, Japan's production of raw silk amounts to 40 per cent of world output, but its export has decreased drastically; since 1966, Japan has been importing raw silk.

The cotton industry, too, was a major industry in pre-war Japan, but as a result of the development of synthetic fibres and the growth of the cotton industry in the People's Republic of China, India and Hong Kong, Japan's production and export have become stagnant. On the other hand, the synthetic fibre industry, established upon the tradition of the pre-war cotton and rayon industries, is manifesting a great competitive strength. The principal products are nylon and polyester; the technique is mostly adopted from foreign companies such as *Dupont* and *I.C.I.*, but vinylon is produced by domestic techniques. Japan's output of synthetic fibre amounts to about 15 per cent of the world total, and ranks second in the world after the United States.

Ceramics. In the ceramic industry, the production of chinaware is well developed; the principal products are tableware, tiles and porcelain insulators; 30 per cent of the output is exported, the chief market being the United States.

BALANCE OF PAYMENTS

Japan's international balance of payments is shown in the *Statistical Survey*; a characteristic feature of Japan's balance of payments is that foreign currency earned by trade is applied to the payments of freightage, patent fees, etc., and to overseas investment. However, in 1974 the trade balance registered a deficit because of the high price of oil.

In 1969, 1970, 1971 and 1972, Japan's overall balance of payments registered a large surplus. Japan's exports, when averaged over the past decade, have been increasing at a very high rate, about 19 per cent per year. Imports have been increasing at the high rate of 13 per cent, but since the rate of increase of exports exceeds that of imports, Japan's balance of payments surplus is increasing. The exchange rate, set at 360 yen to the dollar in 1949, was maintained until August 1971. In December the yen was revalued (*see Statistical Survey*) following a very large surplus on the balance of payments in 1971. While the balance of payments registered a deficit in 1973, 1974 and 1975, it is expected to reach a surplus in 1976.

Foreign Trade

Japan's exports in 1975 totalled U.S. $55,753 million. The principal export items are listed in the *Statistical Survey*; the products of the metal and machinery industries such as iron and steel, ships, automobiles, radios, television sets, etc., rank high. Before the Second World War, the principal export items were raw silk, green tea, cotton fabrics, ceramics, toys, etc., and even after the War, cotton fabrics were the largest export item until 1955. However, the development of heavy industries in Japan has brought about a rapid change in the composition of exports.

The principal imports are listed in the *Statistical Survey*. The most valuable item is crude oil, followed by wood. Other major imports are the raw materials for the iron and steel and textile industries. The import of raw materials amounts to 17 per cent of total imports, that of fuel 44 per cent, that of foodstuffs about 15 per cent, and that of manufactured goods only about 20 per cent.

In both exports and imports the trade with the United States is the largest, amounting to 20 per cent of the total trade (*see* the *Statistical Survey*). Exports to Asian countries such as South Korea and the Philippines are also considerable.

In imports, the U.S.A. is followed by Saudi Arabia, Iran, Australia, Indonesia and Canada. From Australia, Japan imports wool, coal, iron ore, etc.; trade relations between the two nations have rapidly become close in recent years. From Saudi Arabia and Iran, Japan imports petroleum, and from Canada, non-ferrous metal ore, wheat, wood, etc. Imports from the Soviet Union are also important because of large imports of wood, coal and cotton.

In Japan, about 97 per cent of imports have been liberalized. Liberalization of capital was carried out fairly extensively in August 1971 and May 1973. Only five types of industry have not been liberalized.

Invisible Trade

The deficit in the invisible trade balance is due to the large deficits in freightage, patent fees and the expenses of overseas branch offices. The tourist balance, too, registers a deficit; in 1975 Japan's revenue from tourism and other travel was only U.S. $252 million while the expenditure on travel amounted to $1,367 million. In 1975, 851,675 foreign visitors entered Japan of which over a third were Americans. Receipts from the United States Forces amounted to about $733 million in 1975.

The long-term capital balance, too, shows an excess of payments over receipts. The reasons are: (1) direct investment in Japan is restricted in order to protect domestic industries; (2) the United States is restricting the outflow of long-term capital; (3) Japan's exports to developing nations are made on a deferred payment basis. Most of Japan's direct investments abroad aim at obtaining raw materials such as crude oil from the Arab countries, iron ore and coal from Australia and wood from Alaska. The amount of direct investment was U.S. $1,761 million in 1975.

LABOUR AND LIVING STANDARDS

Post-war Japan was faced with the problem of surplus labour, but as a result of high economic growth the demand for labour increased, and in the 1960s labour shortage became a serious problem. Because of the labour shortage, the average wage began to increase at the high rate of about 10 per cent per year. As a result, labour began to move from the farming villages—where the unemployed had collected—to the cities. Service charges too, which had been extremely low in Japan, began to rise rapidly. A number of minor enterprises which had managed to do business on cheap labour went out of business. Even in the prosperity of the 1960s, bankruptcies of minor enterprises continued to increase. Thus, the change from excess to shortage of labour has transformed many aspects of the Japanese economy. The labour shortage is expected to become even more acute in the future because the birth rate in Japan has dropped since the 1950s, the 1975 rate of 17.1 per thousand being little higher than in the United States and Europe.

The trade unions in Japan are mostly organized enterprise by enterprise, and these form federations by industries. The federations, in turn, are organized into larger groups; typical ones are *Sohyo* which had a membership of 4.6 million in 1975, and *Domei* (2.3 million). Trade unionists amount to 33 per cent of total employed workers.

Standard of Living

The standard of living in Japan is improving. In 1975 the average monthly income (before tax) of a city worker's household (3.82 persons per household) was U.S. $787; the average monthly wage of a labourer was U.S. $573. However, the rate of savings (the percentage of savings in the disposable income) in workers' households is very high, 23 per cent.

As for the quality of national living, the average daily calorie intake of a Japanese in 1974 was quite low compared with that in the United Kingdom (3,130 calories in 1973) or in the United States (3,316 calories in 1973). On the other hand, the average consumption of textiles in 1973 was 19.8 kilogrammes, higher than in Western Europe. Durable consumer goods are remarkably widespread; 90 per cent of households in Japan possess colour television sets, 98 per cent washing machines, and 97 per cent refrigerators (1975). The percentage for automobiles is still low, 41 per cent, but it has been increasing rapidly in recent years.

The least developed aspect is housing. Because of the concentration of population into urban areas, the price of land has risen markedly, and this impedes the construction of houses. The number of inhabitants per room is 0.9, very high in comparison with 0.6 in the United Kingdom and the United States.

Another serious problem is the rise in consumer prices; during the period 1965–72 they rose by 5.5 per cent per year on average. The reason is that the prices of agricultural products and service charges rose, although the prices of industrial products were stable. The increase in the rate of consumer prices accelerated in 1973, 1974 and 1975, at 12, 25 and 12 per cent, respectively.

FINANCIAL, MONETARY AND ECONOMIC POLICIES

In Japan, economic activities are conducted on principles of free economy. Adjustments of business trends and economic growth rates are made mainly through financial and monetary policies.

Government expenditure occupies about 21 per cent of the gross national expenditure; the percentage is not high, for military expenses and social security expenses borne by the government are small. Taxes (direct and indirect) are also low, amounting to only 20 per cent of the national income. Direct taxes such as personal income and corporation tax account for 66 per cent of the total and indirect tax 34 per cent. Government finance was more or less balanced up to 1961, but since then government expenditure has increased and exceeded revenue. Accordingly, public bonds have been issued; the weight of public bonds in the general account is 26 per cent in the fiscal year 1975. A conspicuous feature of the present Japanese economy is that, while private enterprises have extremely modern equipment, public utilities such as roads, hospitals and schools are undeveloped. Moreover, pollution such as the contamination of rivers and the air, smog, noise, etc., is becoming a serious problem. In future, more funds need to be applied to public works and to measures against pollution. How to finance these social improvements is the major difficulty.

The Implementation of Government Policy

Basic monetary policies such as a change in the official discount rate and the reserve rate are decided by the central bank, the Bank of Japan. It also issues bank notes, makes loans to other banks, discounts bills, purchases and sells bonds. Other banks wholly financed by the Government are the Development Bank of Japan, the Export-Import Bank, the Smaller Enterprise Loan Corporation, the People's Finance Corporation, the Agriculture, Forestry and Fishery Loan Corporation, etc. Private banks comprise 76 commercial banks and numerous small banking facilities for minor enterprises and agricultural and forestry industries.

One of the characteristics of Japan's monetary affairs is that commercial banks receive large loans from the Bank of Japan, while industrial and commercial enterprises, in turn, borrow heavily from commercial banks. In the enterprises' capital, 14 per cent was owned capital and 86 per cent borrowed capital in 1974, the major part of the latter being borrowed from banks. The reasons are: (1) The enterprises expanded so rapidly that they could not procure enough funds through internal capital accumulation alone; (2) sufficient capital could not be raised through shares because the capital market was undeveloped; (3) Japan's tax system is such that it is more profitable for the enterprises to borrow the funds from banks than to try to raise them by issuing stocks. This heavy dependence on borrowed capital is one of the reasons why the enterprises are liable to instability in periods of business fluctuations. On the other hand, it increases the efficacy of monetary policies, which are chiefly effected through a change in the rate of interest by the Bank of Japan. Further, to tighten the money market, the Bank of Japan may directly set a limit to the loans to be made by commercial banks.

The Government, in 1976 introduced a five-year project (1976–80) called "economic plan for the second half of the 1970s". At the beginning of each year, the Government publishes the economic outlook for the year. This forms the basis of the Government's economic policies, but, for private economic activities, it merely serves as a guide; the Government does not directly control private economic activities on the basis of this programme. The five-year plan sets the average annual growth rate for the period at 6.25 per cent.

STATISTICAL SURVEY

AREA AND POPULATION

Area		Population ('000) at October 1st.†		
		Total	Male	Female
377,483·74 square kilometres	1971*	105,014	51,529	53,485
	1972	107,332	52,639	54,693
	1973	108,710	53,331	55,379
	1974	110,049	54,010	56,039
	1975‡	111,934	55,089	56,845

*Excluding Okinawa Prefecture, formerly the U.S.-occupied Ryukyu Islands (area 2,196 sq. km.), which reverted to Japan on May 15th, 1972.

† Excluding foreign military and civilian personnel and their dependents.

‡ Preliminary result of 1975 census.

Source: Bureau of Statistics, Office of the Prime Minister.

PRINCIPAL CITIES*

(October 1st, 1975 census—preliminary)

Tokyo (capital)†	8,642,800
Osaka	2,778,975
Yokohama	2,621,648
Nagoya	2,079,694
Kyoto	1,461,050
Kobe	1,360,530
Sapporo	1,240,617
Kitakyushu	1,058,067
Kawasaki	1,015,022
Fukuoka (Hukuoka)	1,002,214
Hiroshima	852,607
Sakai	750,671
Chiba	659,344
Sendai	615,473
Amagasaki	545,762
Higashiosaka	524,731
Okayama	513,452
Kumamoto	488,053
Hamamatsu	468,886
Kagoshima	456,818
Nagasaki	450,195
Shizuoka	446,952
Himeji	436,099
Niigata	423,204
Funabashi	423,106
Gifu	408,699
Nishinomiya	400,590
Tonaka	398,363
Kanazawa	395,262
Kurashiki	392,770
Wakayama	389,677
Yokosuka	389,559
Sagamihara	377,341
Matsuyama	367,313
Kawaguchi	345,547
Matsudo	344,552
Utsunomaya	344,417
Urawa	331,145
Takatsuki	330,571
Iwaka	330,210
Fukuyama	329,779
Omiya	327,696
Hachioji	322,558
Asahikawa	320,526
Oita	320,236
Ichikawa	319,272
Hakodate	307,447
Nagano	306,643
Suita	300,949
Takamatsu	298,997
Hirakata	297,618
Naha	295,091
Toyama	290,145
Toyohashi	284,597
Kochi	280,960
Shimonoseki	266,596
Fujisawa	265,938
Keriyama	264,610
Aomori	264,187
Yao	261,642
Akita	261,242
Nara	257,482
Machida	255,303
Neyagawa	254,316
Sasebo	250,723
Maebashi	250,241
Toyota	248,774
Yokkaichi	247,000
Fukushima	246,531

* Except for Tokyo, the data for each city refer to an urban county (*shi*), an administrative division which may include some scattered or rural population as well as an urban centre.

† The figure refers to the 23 wards (*ku*) of the old city. The population of Tokyo-to (Tokyo Prefecture) was 11,669,167.

BIRTHS, MARRIAGES AND EDATHS

	Births	Birth Rate (per '000)	Marriages	Marriage Rate (per '000)	Deaths	Death Rate (per '000)
1971*	2,000,973	19.2	1,091,229	10.5	684,521	6.6
1972*	2,038,682	19.3	1,099,984	10.4	683,751	6.5
1973	2,091,983	19.4	1,071,923	9.9	709,416	6.6
1974	2,029,989	18.6	1,000,455	9.1	710,510	6.5
1975	1,901,450	17.1	941,628	8.5	702,281	6.3

* Excluding Okinawa Prefecture.

Source: Ministry of Health and Welfare.

EMPLOYMENT
(annual average in '000)

	Population 15 Years Old and Over	Labour Force: Total	Labour Force: Employed	Labour Force: Unemployed	Not in Labour Force
1971*	79,700	51,780	51,140	640	27,790
1972*	80,510	51,820	51,090	730	28,510
1973	82,080	52,990	52,330	670	28,870
1974	83,000	52,740	52,010	720	30,000
1975	83,910	52,770	51,780	990	30,850

* Excluding Okinawa Prefecture.

	1972*	1973	1974	1975
All Industries ('000)	51,090	52,330	52,010	51,780
Agriculture and Forestry	7,050	6,560	6,280	6,150
Fishery and Aquatic Culture	490	470	450	430
Mining	160	130	140	160
Construction	4,310	4,640	4,590	4,730
Manufacturing	13,780	14,360	14,170	13,340
Wholesaling, Retailing, Finance, Insurance and Real Estate	11,970	12,360	12,520	12,860
Transport, Communications and Public Utility	3,540	3,690	3,610	3,590
Services	7,970	8,220	8,250	8,490
Government Service	1,750	1,790	1,900	1,940

* Excluding Okinawa Prefecture.

Source: Bureau of Statistics.

AGRICULTURE

PRINCIPAL CROPS
('000 metric tons)

	1972	1973	1974	1975
Rice (rough)*	11,889	12,144	12,292	13,165
Barley	324	216	233	211
Wheat†	284	202	232	241
Potatoes, Sweet and Irish	5,520	4,963	4,377	4,679
Silk Cocoons	105	108	102	91
Soybeans	127	118	133†	126
Tobacco	145	157	151	166

* Twelve months ending October of year stated.

† Twelve months beginning April 1st of year stated.

LIVESTOCK
('000)

	Cattle	Sheep	Goats	Horses	Pigs
1973	3,598	17	137	79	7,490
1974	3,650	16	124	66	8,018
1975	3,644	12	111	43	7,684
1976	3,723	10	57	36	7,459

LIVESTOCK PRODUCTS
(metric tons, excluding Okinawa)

	1971	1972	1973	1974	1975
Beef and veal*	296,173	317,445	245,769	320,672	352,880
Pig meat*	843,244	885,306	970,520	1,077,307	1,039,170
Poultry meat†	570,784	686,827	775,414	833,307	851,615
Cows' milk	4,820,000	4,939,000	4,908,000	4,868,000	4,963,000
Butter‡	47,699	43,792	42,189	38,816	41,888
Cheese‡	42,906	44,578	43,661	51,673	53,746
Hen eggs†	1,801,319	1,794,076	1,800,186	1,798,553	1,787,899
Raw silk	19,684	19,137	19,317	18,936	20.169
Pig skins	92,068	91,300	98,100	n.a.	n.a.

*Figures refer to the inspected production of meat from indigenous animals, i.e. from animals slaughtered under government supervision.

†Including Okinawa from 1974.

‡Industrial production only (i.e. butter and cheese manufactured at milk plants), excluding farm production.

Source: Ministry of Agriculture and Forestry.

FORESTRY

INDUSTRIAL ROUNDWOOD
('000 cubic metres)

	Sawn Timber	Pulp	Pit Props	Plywood	Others	Total
1970	27,362	6,566	727	778	9,918	45,351
1971	26,325	6,019	573	855	11,481	45,253
1972	26,433	4,427	476	890	10,888	43,114
1973	26,102	3,712	369	810	10,591	41,584
1974	22,382	3,781	363	796	11,546	38,874

Source: Ministry of Agriculture and Forestry.

FISHING

('000 metric tons, live weight, including Okinawa)

	1971	1972	1973	1974
Salmon	141.9	121.7	139.0	135.5
Flounders, halibuts, soles, etc.	345.7	356.7	388.6	356.3
Alaska pollack	2,655.6	3,035.3	3,020.9	2,855.6
Pacific sand launce	271.9	194.9	194.0	299.4
Atka mackerel	147.1	180.6	115.0	142.9
Pacific saury (Skipper)	190.3	196.6	406.3	135.5
Japanese jack mackerel	270.9	152.2	128.4	166.1
Pacific herring	150.8	59.5	79.8	72.8
Japanese pilchard (sardine)	57.4	57.9	296.9	351.7
Japanese anchovy	350.7	369.7	335.3	287.5
Skipjack tuna (Oceanic skipjack)	193.2	246.7	321.4	346.4
Chub mackerel	1,252.7	1,188.3	1,134.0	1,330.5
Other fish	2,060.7	2,104.0	2,218.7	2,193.0
TOTAL FISH	8,088.9	8,264.1	8,778.3	8,673.1
Crustaceans	140.4	144.9	147.4	177.2
Pacific cupped oyster	193.8	217.4	229.9	211.5
Japanese (Manila) clam	126.4	115.6	114.5	137.7
Japanese flying squid	364.3	465.3	334.1	327.7
Other molluscs	418.0	470.3	450.9	513.8
Other sea creatures*	38.4	35.9	38.3	34.5
TOTAL AQUATIC ANIMALS*	9,370.2	9,713.5	10,093.4	10,075.6
Seaweeds	541.4	515.6	606.5	656.1
Other aquatic plants	47.6	45.7	47.7	41.7
TOTAL CATCH*	9,959.2	10,274.8	10,747.6	10,773.4
of which:				
Atlantic Ocean	298.1	280.5	312.5	295.9
Indian Ocean	69.8	56.4	44.2	47.2
Pacific Ocean	9,440.2	9,772.0	10,212.4	10,250.8
Inland waters	151.1	165.9	178.5	179.4

* Excluding whales, dolphins, etc.

Sources: FAO, *Yearbook of Fishery Statistics*; Ministry of Agriculture and Forestry.

MINING

		1971	1972	1973	1974	1975
Coal	'000 metric tons	33,432	28,098	22,414	20,333	18,999
Lignite	,, ,, ,,	134	102	85	75	61
Zinc	,, ,, ,,	294	281	264	241	254
Iron	,, ,, ,,	830	799	729	542	602
Iron Pyrites	,, ,, ,,	3,792	2,590	2,068	1,959	1,698
Manganese	,, ,, ,,	284	260	189	167	158
Quartzite	,, ,, ,,	7,513	7,668	9,067	9,395	8,767
Limestone	,, ,, ,,	124,701	134,197	164,374*	160,789*	143,857*
Titanium	metric tons	2,376	2,115	n.a.	n.a.	n.a.
Chromite	,, ,,	31,642	24,819	23,174	25,858	23,149
Copper	,, ,,	121,029	112,114	91,258	82,135	84,905
Lead	,, ,,	70,586	63,449	52,889	44,248	50,566
Gold Ore	kg.	7,939	7,559	6,008	4,346	4,463
Crude Oil	million litres	879	833	817	785	705
Natural Gas	cu. metres	2,433,457	2,475,055	2,595,037	2,572,125	2,435,998

* Including Okinawa Prefecture.

Source: Ministry of International Trade and Industry.

INDUSTRY

SELECTED PRODUCTS

		1972*	1973	1974	1975
Wheat flour[1]	'000 metric tons	3,583.0	3,752.6	3,706.7	3,903.1
Sugar	,, ,, ,,	2,608	2,771	2,479	n.a.
Distilled alcoholic beverages[1]	'000 hectolitres	4,124	4,324	4,442	n.a.
Beer[1]	,, ,,	35,113.7	38,434.8	36,434.8	n.a.
Cigarettes[1]	million	256,008	269,929	292,370	287,000
Cotton yarn (pure)	metric tons	527,155	524,780	480,433	431,739
Cotton yarn (mixed)	,, ,,	27,985	30,118	30,987	28,744
Woven cotton fabrics (pure and mixed)	million sq. metres	2,264.1	2,380.4	2,163.5	2,124.4
Flax, ramie and hemp yarn	metric tons	3,728	3,676	2,524	
Jute yarn	,, ,,	65,181	58,899	50,773	30,935
Linen fabrics	'000 sq. metres	22,767	23,976	18,778	
Jute fabrics	,, ,,	74,807	60,402	38,095	35,132
Woven silk fabrics (pure and mixed)	,, ,,	189,743	188,453	166,550	168,472
Wool yarn (pure)	metric tons	164,580	161,691	109,334	142,244
Wool yarn (mixed)	,, ,,	31,829	36,699	26,514	
Woven woollen fabrics (pure and mixed)[2]	'000 sq. metres	478,619	469,770	356,618	356,695
Rayon continuous filaments	metric tons	82,670	91,158	84,497	79,318
Acetate continuous filaments	,, ,,	36,311	37,122	31,128	23,930
Rayon discontinuous fibres	,, ,,	367,900	383,423	328,715	255,602
Acetate discontinuous fibres[3]	,, ,,	24,956	27,327	29,069	32,039
Woven rayon fabrics (pure and mixed)[2]	million sq. metres	1,146.7	1,175.6	885.4	755.6
Woven acetate fabrics (pure and mixed)[2]	,, ,, ,,	124.8	123.6	102.9	83.0
Non-cellulosic continuous filaments	metric tons	502,820	592,127	522,560	490,634
Non-cellulosic discontinuous fibres	,, ,,	613,845	716,321	651,769	570,569
Woven fabrics of non-cellulosic fibres[2,4]	million sq. metres	2,717.9	2,922.1	2,621.5	2,411.1
Leather footwear[5]	'000 pairs	46,453	49,517	49,302	49,095
Mechanical wood pulp	'000 metric tons	1,302.8	1,403.4	1,446.0	1,337.2
Chemical wood pulp[6]	,, ,, ,,	8,155.3	8,719.5	8,593.7	7,292.5
Newsprint	,, ,, ,,	2,059.6	2,105.7	2,232.8	2,160.3
Other printing and writing paper	,, ,, ,,	2,448.3	2,819.8	2,937.4	2,771.5
Other paper	,, ,, ,,	2,963.5	3,296.7	3,273.5	2,779.0
Paperboard	,, ,, ,,	6,176.3	7,753.2	7,202.6	5,889.7
Synthetic rubber	metric tons	819,365	967,467	857,945	788,687
Motor vehicle tyres	'000	78,080	87,746	81,954	83,300
Rubber shoes	'000 pairs	88,729	95,717	77,857	66,834
Ethylene (Ethene)	'000 metric tons	3,851.2	4,170.7	4,175.8	3,399.0
Propylene (Propene)	,, ,, ,,	2,653.2	2,824.8	2,729.5	2,314.0
Benzene (Benzol)	,, ,, ,,	1,852.1	1,995.3	1,997.4	1,608.2
Toluene (Toluol)	,, ,, ,,	832.9	918.5	899.9	657.0
Xylenes (Xylol)	,, ,, ,,	929.3	1,058.1	1,142.2	894.8
Methyl alcohol (Methanol)	,, ,, ,,	1,084.6	1,221.2	1,058.5	719.0
Ethyl alcohol (Grain alcohol)	'000 hectolitres	2,288	2,403	2,366	n.a.
Sulphuric acid (100%)	'000 metric tons	6,713.6	7,115.6	7,126.5	6,000.2
Caustic soda (Sodium hydroxide)	,, ,, ,,	2,987.9	3,231.4	3,161.6	2,948.4
Soda ash (Sodium carbonate)	,, ,, ,,	1,307.6	1,363.3	1,327.0	1,123.1
Ammonium sulphate	,, ,, ,,	2,110.5	2,108.7	2,077.8	2,125.5
Nitrogenous fertilizers (a)[7]	,, ,, ,,	2,173	2,275	2,294	n.a.
Phosphate fertilizers (b)[7]	,, ,, ,,	772	724	845	n.a.
Plastics and synthetic resins	,, ,, ,,	8,194	9,384	9,553	n.a.
Liquefied petroleum gas	,, ,, ,,	8,121	8,829	8,646	7,925
Naphtha	million litres	26,919	31,255	30,424	26,348
Motor spirit (Gasoline)[8]	,, ,,	24,712	27,432	27,224	28,904
Kerosene	,, ,,	16,979	22,985	22,120	20,624
Jet fuel	,, ,,	3,391	4,141	3,220	3,331
Gas oil	,, ,,	14,489	18,028	17,031	16,102
Heavy fuel oil	,, ,,	118,702	139,416	136,764	128,742
Lubricating oil	,, ,,	2,455	2,757	2,458	2,037
Petroleum bitumen (Asphalt)	'000 metric tons	4,578	5,226	4,699	n.a.
Coke-oven coke	,, ,, ,,	36,247	44,301	45,632	51,942†
Gas coke	,, ,, ,,	4,421	4,715	4,787	
Cement	,, ,, ,,	66,292	78,118	73,108	65,517
Pig-iron	,, ,, ,,	74,054.7	90,007.5	90,437	86,877
Ferro-alloys[9]	,, ,, ,,	1,743.2	2,035.0	2,266.9	2,139.4

[*continued on next page*

SELECTED PRODUCTS—*continued*]

		1972*	1973	1974	1975
Crude steel	,, ,, ,,	96,900.2	119,321.6	117,131	102,314
Aluminium (unwrought): primary	,, ,, ,,	1,014.9	1,102.7	1,124.0	1,016.2
secondary[10]	,, ,, ,,	411.6	536.5	518.4	n.a.
Electrolytic copper: primary	metric tons	737,737	870,263	917,795	818,861 (primary and secondary)
secondary	,,	72,218	80,519	78,254	
Refined lead (unwrought): primary	,,	217,016	219,102	218,288	194,217 (primary and secondary)
secondary[11]	,,	6,210	8,934	9,672	
Zinc (unwrought): primary[12]	,,	795,164	833,554	836,492	701,794 (primary and secondary)
secondary[12]	,,	13,834	10,440	14,318	
Calculating machines	'000	4,546.3	10,326.0	15,875.9	n.a.
Radio receivers	,,	26,833	24,484	18,027	14,188
Television receivers	,,	14,303	14,414	13,406	26,640
Steel ships and boats	'000 gross reg. tons	12,834	14,189	17,540	n.a.
Passenger motor cars	'000	4,022.3	4,470.6	3,931.8	4,567.9
Lorries and trucks[13]	,,	2,241.5	2,573.9	2,575.2	2,337.2
Motorcycles, scooters and mopeds	,,	3,565.2	3,763.1	4,510	3,801
Cameras: photographic	,,	5,318	5,685	6,644	7,281
cinematographic	,,	1,596.0	1,613.6	1,577.0	1,306.0
Watches and clocks	,,	58,187	68,674	68,815	56,810
Construction: new dwellings started[14]	,,	1,807.6	1,905.1	1,316.1	1,356.3
Electric energy[1]	million kWh	414,291	468,511	460,705	n.a.
Manufactured gas: from gasworks	million cu. metres	2,651	3,127	3,800	n.a.
from cokeries	,, ,, ,,	1,089	1,138	1,147	n.a.

* Excluding Okinawa prefecture.

† Coke of all grades (52,553,000 metric tons in 1974).

[1] Twelve months beginning April 1st of the year stated.

[2] Including finished fabrics.

[3] Including cigarette filtration tow.

[4] Including blankets made of synthetic fibres.

[5] Sales.

[6] Including pulp prepared by semi-chemical processes.

[7] Figures are in terms of (a) nitrogen, 100%, and (b) phosphoric acid, 100%.

[8] Including aviation gasoline.

[9] Including silico-chromium.

[10] Including alloys.

[11] Excluding recovered lead bullion.

[12] The 1975 figure comprises electrolytic, distilled and rectified zinc (849,897 metric tons in 1974).

[13] Including three-wheeled vehicles.

[14] Including buildings and dwelling units created by conversion.

FINANCE

1,000 rin = 100 sen = 1 yen.
Coins: 1, 5, 10, 50 and 100 yen.
Notes: 500, 1,000, 5,000 and 10,000 yen.
Exchange rates (June 1976): £1 sterling = 531.5 yen; U.S. $1 = 299.3 yen.
1,000 yen = £1.881 = $3.341.

Note: From April 1949 to August 1971 the official exchange rate was U.S. $1 = 360 yen. Between December 1971 and February 1973 the rate was 308 yen per $. Since February 1973 the yen has been allowed to "float", though the exchange rate was maintained at around 265 yen to the $ until November 1973. For converting the value of foreign trade transactions, the average rates were: $1 = 350.7 yen in 1971; $1 = 272.2 yen in 1973; $1 = 291.5 yen in 1974; $1 = 296.8 yen in 1975. In terms of sterling, the exchange rate was £1 = 864 yen from November 1967 to August 1971; and £1 = 802.56 yen from December 1971 to June 1972.

GENERAL BUDGET

Twelve months ending March 31st.
(million yen)

Revenue	1973–74	1974–75	1975–76
Taxes and Stamps	13,365,522	15,035,865	13,461,000
Public Bonds	1,766,200	2,159,983	5,480,000
Monopoly Profits	356,638	342,508	337,060
Others	1,273,618	2,840,767	1,559,098
Total	16,761,978	20,379,123	20,837,158

Expenditure	1973–74	1974–75	1975–76
Social Security	2,220,418	3,125,723	4,032,248
Education and Science	1,643,293	2,308,494	2,698,335
Defence	953,201	1,225,251	1,367,424
Public Works	2,560,397	3,071,815	3,313,668
Local Finance	3,205,148	4,156,577	3,330,160
Pensions	471,252	590,106	755,852
Miscellaneous	3,724,594	4,611,827	5,339,471
Total	14,778,303	19,099,793	20,837,158

INTERNATIONAL RESERVES

(U.S. $ million at December 31st)

	1969	1970	1971	1972	1973	1974	1975
Gold	413	532	738	801	891	905	865
IMF Special Drawing Rights	—	146	307	461	513	529	520
Reserve position in IMF	627	973	532	620	639	739	804
Foreign exchange	2,614	3,188	13,783	16,483	10,203	11,347	10,627
Total	3,654	4,840	15,360	18,365	12,246	13,519	12,815

May 31st, 1976: Total reserves $15,210 million.

Source: Ministry of Finance.

MONEY SUPPLY*

('000 million yen at December 31st)

	1969	1970	1971	1972	1973	1974	1975
Currency outside banks	4,319.1	5,097.8	5,957.7	7,706.1	9,113.3	10,730.9	11,578.6
Demand deposits	13,963.4	16,261.7	21,735.4	26,820.0	31,198.2	34,220.3	38,370.1
TOTAL MONEY	18,282.5	21,359.5	27,693.1	34,526.1	40,311.5	44,951.2	49,948.7

April 30th, 1976 ('000 million yen): currency outside banks 10,626.2; demand deposits 39,669.2; total money 50,295.4.

* Excluding Okinawa prefecture prior to 1972.

COST OF LIVING

Consumer Price Index*

(Average of monthly figures. Base: 1970=100)

	1966	1967	1968	1969	1971	1972	1973	1974	1975
Food (incl. beverages)	77.6	81.3	86.5	91.7	106.0	110.1	124.4	158.9	179.5
Housing	83.1	87.1	90.3	94.0	104.8	109.1	120.0	151.6	162.7
Rent	76.1	81.8	85.7	92.1	108.4	117.1	127.0	136.7	149.7
Fuel and light	97.4	96.9	97.8	98.2	103.7	105.3	111.0	142.1	161.3
Clothing	81.7	84.0	87.7	92.0	109.0	115.0	139.7	172.3	182.7
Others	81.3	84.4	89.0	93.9	105.9	111.7	120.1	143.3	164.1
ALL ITEMS	80.6	83.8	88.2	92.9	106.1	110.9	123.9	154.2	172.4

May 1976: Food 195.0; all items 187.6.

* Excluding Okinawa prefecture.

NATIONAL ACCOUNTS

('000 million yen at current prices)

	1971	1972	1973	1974	1975
Government final consumption expenditure	6,864.9	8,155.8	10,054.5	13,186.8	16,221.3
Private final consumption expenditure	41,217.4	47,177.7	56,670.4	69,859.3	82,326.5
Increase in stocks	1,873.0	1,847.6	3,600.2	5,200.6	1,751.2
Gross fixed capital formation	27,209.3	31,289.6	40,685.7	45,473.1	44,711.0
TOTAL DOMESTIC EXPENDITURE	77,164.6	88,470.7	111,010.8	133,719.8	145,010.0
Exports of goods and services	9,475.1	9,795.9	11,305.5	18,290.7	n.a.
Less Imports of goods and services	7,270.9	7,672.2	11,285.0	19,285.3	n.a.
GROSS DOMESTIC PRODUCT	79,368.8	90,594.5	111,031.3	132,725.2	n.a.
Factor income received from abroad	421.0	580.7	820.6	1,162.5	n.a.
Less Factor income paid abroad	536.1	563.5	790.8	1,414.8	n.a.
GROSS NATIONAL PRODUCT	79,253.6	90,611.7	111,061.0	132,472.8	144,915.0
Less Consumption of fixed capital	10,627.0	12,376.4	14,800.5	17,234.4	n.a.
	68,626.6	78,235.3	96,260.5	115,238.4	n.a.
Statistical discrepancy	745.2	1,414.1	639.1	−1,376.3	n.a.
NATIONAL INCOME IN MARKET PRICES	69,371.8	79,649.4	96,899.0	113,862.1	n.a.

GROSS DOMESTIC PRODUCT BY ECONOMIC ACTIVITY*

('000 million yen at current prices)

	1971	1972	1973	1974
Agriculture and livestock	3,170.9	3,515.8	4,131.2	4,976.4
Forestry and logging	579.7	612.9	820.0	883.1
Fishing	815.2	883.7	1,053.9	1,218.0
Mining and quarrying	561.2	547.9	698.5	814.6
Manufacturing	26,493.4	29,825.5	38,871.6	45,549.3
Electricity, gas and water supply	1,452.3	1,558.0	1,609.2	2,009.9
Construction	5,389.4	6,793.4	8,307.8	9,195.1
Wholesale and retail trade	13,061.8	14,984.2	20,842.3	23,368.7
Transport, storage and communications	5,641.7	6,965.9	8,377.8	8,851.9
Banking and insurance	4,222.8	5,069.7	6,452.3	9,249.4
Real estate	4,841.1	6,302.8	8,061.1	8,298.8
Public administration and defence	2,561.1	3,107.5	3,754.1	5,067.8
Other producers and services†	11,286.9	12,912.3	16,049.4	18,721.2
SUB-TOTAL	80,077.5	93,079.6	119,029.2	138,204.2
Less Imputed bank service charge	2,519.5	2,597.2	2,727.5	1,548.6
SUB-TOTAL	77,558.0	90,482.1	116,271.7	136,655.6
Inventory valuation adjustment	397.8	−692.1	−7,055.0	−7,250.4
G.D.P. IN PURCHASERS' VALUES	77,955.8	89,790.0	109,216.7	129,405.2

* Estimates made on a basis which has not yet been reconciled with the Japanese system of national accounts. The figures are therefore not strictly comparable with those shown in the previous table.

† Including hotels, restaurants and community, social and personal services.

BALANCE OF PAYMENTS—ALL FOREIGN COUNTRIES

(U.S. $ million)

	1974			1975		
	CREDIT	DEBIT	BALANCE	CREDIT	DEBIT	BALANCE
Goods and Services:						
Merchandise f.o.b.	54,480	53,044	1,436	54,734	49,706	5,028
Freight	2,871	3,031	−160	3,128	2,725	403
Insurance on merchandise	130	239	−109	135	252	−117
Non-merchandise insurance	472	491	−19	649	687	−38
Other transportation	2,677	5,056	−2,379	3,166	5,550	−2,384
Tourists	139	787	−648	163	834	−671
Other travel	96	571	−475	89	533	−444
Investment income	3,562	4,013	−451	3,616	3,889	−273
Military transactions	704	} 78	654	733	} 76	734
Other government services	28			77		
Other private services	1,352	3,607	−2,255	1,742	4,306	−2,564
TOTAL	66,511	70,917	−4,406	68,232	68,558	−326
Unrequited Transfers:						
Private transfer payments	162	246	−84	178	272	−94
Reparations	—	37	−37	—	42	−42
Other government transfers	27	193	−166	19	239	−220
TOTAL	189	476	−287	197	553	−356
TOTAL CURRENT ACCOUNT	66,700	71,393	−4,693	68,429	69,111	−682

[*continued on next page*

BALANCE OF PAYMENTS—ALL FOREIGN COUNTRIES—*continued*]

(U.S.$ million)

	1974			1975		
	CREDIT	DEBIT	BALANCE	CREDIT	DEBIT	BALANCE
Capital Flows:						
Long-term Capital:						
Direct investments	202	2,012	−1,810	226	1,763	−1,537
Trade credits (net)	—	672	−672	−26	29	−55
Loans (net)	−232	1,136	−1,368	166	1,295	−1,129
Securities (net)	−865	141	−1,006	1,518	24	1,494
External bonds	177	97	80	1,321	86	1,235
Others (net)	901	—	901	280		280
BALANCE			−3,881			−288
Short-term Capital:						
Trade credits (net)	1,256	—	1,256	—	1,022	−1,022
Others (net)	522	—	522		116	116
BALANCE ON CAPITAL ACCOUNT			−2,103			−185
NET ERRORS AND OMISSIONS		43	−43		584	−584
OVERALL BALANCE (NET MONETARY MOVEMENTS)			−6,839			−2,676
of which:						
Gold and foreign exchange reserves			1,272			−703
Others			−8,111			−1,973
of which: commercial banks			−8,200			−1,880

Source: Bank of Japan.

BALANCE OF PAYMENTS—REGIONAL SUMMARY 1974

(U.S.$ million)

	WORLD	U.S.A.	OECD COUNTRIES IN EUROPE*	COMMUNIST COUNTRIES	OTHER TERRITORIES	INTERNATIONAL INSTITUTIONS
Goods and Services:						
Merchandise f.o.b.	1,436‡	1,893	3,630	1,179	−5,331	—
Transportation	−2,539	−1,348	−909	20	−302	—
Insurance	−128	−10	−28	−3	−87	—
Travel	−1,123	−201	−445	−29	−448	—
Investment income	−351	−615	−449	34	540	89
Government services	654	685	−20	1	−16	4
Other private services	−2,255	−1,019	−601	−11	−624	
TOTAL	−4,406‡	−615	−1,178	1,191	−6,268	93
Unrequited Transfers:						
Private	−84	−12	−16	0	−56	0
Government	−203	−66	−1	0	−84	−52
TOTAL	−287	−78	−17	0	−140	−52
TOTAL CURRENT ACCOUNT	−4,693‡	−693	1,111	1,191	−6,408	41
Long-term Capital:						
Direct investments	1,810	392	304	1	955	—
Trade credits	678	136	−87	277	352	
Loans	1,368	−38	17	38	1,177	52
Securities	1,006	458	434	0	155	−41
External bonds	−80	4	−84	—	—	
Others	−901	−34	13	−2	−1,050	172
TOTAL	−3,881	−918	−877	−314	−1,589	−183
BASIC BALANCE†	−8,574‡	−1,611	234	877	−7,997	−142

* Including Turkey.
† Excluding short-term capital movements (net credit $1,778 million) and errors and omissions (net debit $43 million).
‡ Including unallocated (net credit $65 million).

Source: Bank of Japan.

JAPANESE DEVELOPMENT ASSISTANCE

(U.S. $'000)

	1971	1972	1973	1974
Official:				
Bilateral Grants:				
Donations	125,400	170,600	220,100	198,600
Reparations	97,700	135,000	162,900	135,100
Technical Assistance	27,700	35,600	57,200	63,500
Direct Loans	306,700	307,200	545,100	681,800
TOTAL	432,000	477,800	765,200	880,400
Capital Subscriptions or Grants to International Agencies	78,700	133,300	245,800	245,800
TOTAL	510,700	611,100	1,011,000	1,126,200
Other Government Capital:				
Export Credits	271,700	266,300	254,000	8,300
Direct Investment Capital	136,300	264,700	569,800	798,500
Loans to International Agencies	243,100	325,400	355,100	−17,900
TOTAL	651,100	856,400	1,178,900	788,900
TOTAL OFFICIAL	1,161,800	1,467,500	2,189,900	1,915,100
Private:				
Export Credits	494,000	190,600	440,100	148,700
Direct Investments	356,200	844,300	3,072,100	874,700
Loans to International Agencies	125,400	217,400	135,300	15,100
Donations to non-profit Organizations	3,100	5,600	6,800	8,700
TOTAL	978,700	1,257,900	3,654,300	1,047,200
GRAND TOTAL	2,140,500	2,725,400	5,844,200	2,962,300

EXTERNAL TRADE*

(U.S. $ million)

	1968	1969	1970	1971	1972	1973	1974	1975
Imports c.i.f.	12,987	15,024	18,881	19,712	23,471	38,314	62,110	57,863
Exports f.o.b.	12,972	15,990	19,318	24,019	28,591	36,930	55,536	55,753

* Excluding the payment of reparations and all trade in gold, silver and goods valued at less than $100. Also excluded are fish and other marine products landed directly from the high seas. Beginning May 15th, 1972, figures include the trade of Okinawa prefecture, formerly the U.S.-occupied Ryukyu Islands.

Source: Ministry of Finance.

PRINCIPAL COMMODITIES
(U.S. $ million)

Imports c.i.f.	1972	1973	1974	1975
Food and live animals	3,433.7	5,765.7	7,759.4	8,366.1
Meat and meat preparations	356.0	834.1	482.7	658.7
Fresh, chilled or frozen meat	335.8	800.5*	450.9*	n.a.
Fish and fish preparations	567.3	993.0	1,021.1	1,195.1
Fresh and simply preserved fish	543.4	934.9*	956.8*	n.a.
Cereals and cereal preparations	1,106.7	2,034.4	3,474.8	3,271.2
Wheat and meslin (unmilled)	361.2	659.9	1,210.8	1,117.0
Maize (unmilled)	378.8	740.4*	1,194.8*	n.a.
Sugar, sugar preparations and honey	517.4	544.8	1,295.9	1,814.9
Sugar and honey	513.7	540.3*	1,290.4*	n.a.
Raw sugar	445.1	433.8	1,156.4	1,686.3
Beverages and tobacco	173.3	243.4	363.0	448.8
Crude materials (inedible) except fuels	7,114.3	12,082.3	14,136.0	11,482.2
Oil-seeds, oil nuts and oil kernels	668.3	1,072.1	1,308.3	1,357.7
Soya beans (excl. flour)	474.2	771.5	882.3	940.3
Wood, lumber and cork	1,740.3	3,428.4	3,706.7	2,639.0
Rough or roughly squared wood	1,536.6	3,003.1	3,205.3	2,271.7
Coniferous sawlogs and veneer logs	851.0	1,523.0*	1,490.7*	n.a.
Non-coniferous sawlogs and veneer logs	661.8	1,433.7*	1,643.7*	n.a.
Textile fibres and waste	1,347.7	2,187.3	1,861.3	1,524.5
Wool and other animal hair	487.5	1,108.3*	549.6*	n.a.
Sheep's and lambs' wool (greasy)	403.4	873.4	457.0	412.7
Cotton	619.6	707.9	1,046.9	846.8
Raw cotton (excl. linters)	609.4	693.8	1,023.3	827.8
Metalliferous ores and metal scrap	2,487.6	4,033.4	5,328.4	4,416.6
Iron ore and concentrates	1,275.0	1,652.2	2,076.4	2,197.7
Non-ferrous ores and concentrates	1,011.3	1,879.1*	2,641.0*	n.a.
Copper ores and concentrates (excl. matte)	514.2	1,167.5	1,628.6	808.5
Mineral fuels, lubricants, etc.	5,715.1	8,326.5	24,895.2	25,640.9
Coal, coke and briquettes	1,079.5	1,356.4	2,877.2	3,474.3
Coal (excl. briquettes)	1,078.1	1,353.6	2,864.0	3,454.4
Petroleum and petroleum products	4,466.4	6,726.0	21,161.5	20,995.2
Crude and partly refined petroleum	3,927.5	6,000.0	18,898.5	19,643.8
Crude petroleum	3,635.3	5,627.5*	17,757.4*	n.a.
Petroleum products	538.9	726.0	2,263.1	1,351.3
Residual fuel oils	344.9	450.4	1,306.7	671.1
Gas (natural and manufactured)	169.2	244.2	856.5	1,171.5
Animal and vegetable oils and fats	77.2	176.4	243.0	177.6
Chemicals	1,148.0	1,865.2	2,668.1	2,057.3
Chemical elements and compounds	356.7	645.7	1,023.3	742.0
Basic manufactures	2,134.5	4,526.8	5,150.2	3,643.1
Textile yarn, fabrics, etc.	389.5	1,137.5	1,001.8	772.1
Non-ferrous metals	922.0	1,669.3	2,036.4	1,284.5
Machinery and transport equipment	2,376.2	3,142.2	4,290.8	3,830.8
Non-electric machinery	1,311.9	1,815.7	2,322.3	2,058.2
Electrical machinery, apparatus, etc.	478.9	803.9	1,091.2	1,004.5
Transport equipment	585.4	522.7	877.3	768.1
Miscellaneous manufactured articles	1,129.6	2,021.2	2,431.6	1,989.5
Clothing (excl. footwear)	157.9	577.3	827.2	538.3
Other commodities and transactions	168.7	163.7	173.3	226.8
Re-imports	147.4	137.6	143.2	195.0
Total	23,470.7	38,313.6	62,110.5	57,863.1

* Provisional.

Source: The Summary Report, Trade of Japan.

[*continued on next page*

Principal Commodities—*continued*]

(U.S. $ million)

Exports f.o.b.	1972	1973	1974	1975
Food and live animals	646.9	823.2	820.9	721.3
Beverages and tobacco	18.8	18.2	25.3	38.7
Crude materials (inedible) except fuels	477.0	680.1	1,100.5	825.6
Mineral fuels, lubricants, etc.	73.9	92.4	248.2	220.5
Animal and vegetable oils and fats	26.8	36.2	87.3	48.8
Chemicals	1,784.3	2,147.0	4,059.0	3,888.8
Chemical elements and compounds	854.5	849.2	1,852.0	1,679.3
Organic chemicals	654.5	623.6	1,442.4	1,231.3
Plastic materials, etc.	535.9	649.1	1,151.9	996.0
Products of polymerization, etc.	431.0	494.8*	886.5*	n.a.
Basic manufactures	8,264.3	10,663.0	18,732.5	17,533.5
Textile yarn, fabrics, etc.	2,186.6	2,450.2	3,079.8	2,920.6
Textile yarn and thread	511.5	579.2	810.6	580.6
Woven textile fabrics (excl. narrow or special fabrics)	1,417.0	1,574.5	1,946.5	1,995.9
Fabrics of synthetic (excl. regenerated) fibres	814.5	1,000.3	1,264.5	1,300.0
Iron and steel	3,610.3	5,304.0	10,757.7	10,176.5
Ingots and other primary forms	194.1	811.4*	1,808.8*	n.a.
Bars, rods, angles, shapes, etc.	464.4	693.6	2,164.9	1,577.5
Universals, plates and sheets	1,941.1	2,526.1	4,162.8	3,241.6
Universals and heavy plates and sheets	410.5	508.9*	1,147.5*	n.a.
Thin plates and sheets (uncoated)	914.2	1,274.7	1,836.0	1,194.0
Tubes, pipes and fittings	694.3	886.7	1,849.8	3,322.5
Welded (excl. cast iron) tubes and pipes	316.5	422.3*	985.6*	n.a.
Non-ferrous metals	272.8	307.3	1,143.5	539.9
Other metal manufactures	997.8	1,210.1	1,789.3	1,801.1
Machinery and transport equipment	13,653.7	18,193.9	25,260.9	27,390.2
Non-electric machinery	3,083.9	4,335.5	5,947.8	6,729.0
Office machines	490.0	803.9	727.3	776.5
Textile and leather machinery	425.7	651.0*	903.1*	n.a.
Electrical machinery, apparatus, etc.	3,725.7	4,716.0	5,844.1	6,132.9
Electric power machinery and switchgear	469.8	612.1*	838.9*	n.a.
Telecommunications apparatus	2,183.9	2,663.1	3,097.0	3,315.7
Television receivers	565.0	608.2	719.0	782.8
Radio receivers	1,033.1	1,242.6	1,358.9	1,324.0
Transport equipment	6,844.1	9,142.4	13,469.0	14,528.3
Road motor vehicles and parts	4,109.9	4,889.8	7,327.5	8,105.3
Passenger cars (excl. buses)	2,235.8	2,648.1	3,509.5	4,022.9
Lorries and trucks	654.6	837.3*	1,505.5*	n.a.
Motorcycles and parts	907.0	945.2	1,513.1	1,276.9
Motorcycles	829.7	855.2	1,394.4	1,156.8
Ships and boats	2,399.1	3,818.9	5,599.7	5,998.2
Ships and boats (excl. warships)	2,314.3	3,702.3*	5,386.2*	n.a.
Miscellaneous manufactured articles	3,387.8	3,886.8	4,391.1	4,351.8
Scientific instruments, watches, etc.	1,085.4	1,382.5	1,884.8	2,009.1
Scientific instruments and photographic equipment	771.7	969.6	1,319.6	1,367.6
Musical instruments, sound recorders, etc.	883.5	1,100.3*	1,125.5*	n.a.
Sound recorders, phonographs and parts	713.0	890.0	877.0	787.7
Sound recorders and phonographs	676.2	814.0*	796.2*	n.a.
Other commodities and transactions	257.6	389.2	810.1	733.6
Re-exports	252.6	381.9	809.2	725.4
Total	28,591.1	36,930.0	55,535.8	55,752.8

* Provisional.

Source: The Summary Report, Trade of Japan.

PRINCIPAL TRADING PARTNERS*

(U.S. $ million)

IMPORTS C.I.F.	1972	1973	1974	1975
Australia	2,205.2	3,495.0	4,025.0	4,156.1
Brazil	249.4	452.9	657.2	883.2
Brunei	101.7	282.7	884.8	1,021.2
Canada	1,148.9	2,014.8	2,675.7	2,498.8
China, People's Republic	491.1	974.0	1,304.8	1,531.1
China (Taiwan)	421.9	890.7	955.2	811.6
Cuba	145.4	182.7	443.7	343.2
France	300.7	537.6	592.4	500.8
Germany, Federal Republic	681.1	1,116.2	1,454.4	1,139.0
India	407.6	574.9	658.2	657.9
Indonesia	1,197.5	2,213.7	4,571.5	3,430.3
Iran	1,489.7	1,921.6	4,766.2	4,977.8
Italy	156.7	294.6	462.2	365.2
Korea, Republic	426.0	1,207.3	1,568.0	1,308.0
Kuwait	548.3	585.3	2,131.9	2,011.7
Malaysia	395.5	776.3	979.0	691.4
New Zealand	248.5	417.4	402.2	367.3
Nigeria	80.0	189.0	448.9	278.3
Philippines	470.4	820.2	1,104.8	1,121.0
Saudi Arabia	901.2	1,386.4	5,238.3	6,135.1
Singapore	120.9	223.0	619.0	399.0
South Africa	398.9	521.9	763.4	868.2
Switzerland	229.6	378.9	453.3	417.2
Thailand	252.1	393.6	685.8	723.7
U.S.S.R.	593.9	1,077.7	1,418.1	1,169.6
United Arab Emirates	225.9	552.5	2,116.0	1,774.0
United Kingdom	500.8	760.8	877.7	810.5
U.S.A.	5,851.6	9,269.6	12,682.2	11,608.1
TOTAL (incl. others)	23,470.7	38,313.6	62,110.5	57,863.1

EXPORTS F.O.B.	1972	1973	1974	1975
Australia	728.4	1,192.9	1,998.1	1,738.9
Belgium and Luxembourg	343.6	380.6	485.5	560.2
Brazil	395.3	611.5	1,389.1	927.1
Canada	1,104.0	998.9	1,587.3	1,150.8
China, People's Republic	608.9	1,039.5	1,984.5	2,258.6
China (Taiwan)	1,090.6	1,641.8	2,009.0	1,821.7
France	283.4	360.6	736.2	699.2
Germany, Federal Republic	930.3	1,270.8	1,497.9	1,660.7
Greece	393.4	471.8	496.9	336.7
Hong Kong	909.7	1,117.9	1,359.9	1,378.2
India	239.8	338.7	594.7	471.4
Indonesia	615.5	902.4	1,450.3	1,849.8
Iran	321.7	484.2	1,013.6	1,854.3
Iraq	31.0	49.1	473.5	818.8
Korea, Republic	979.8	1,789.1	2,656.1	2,247.7
Liberia	1,022.0	1,594.6	2,344.7	2,585.3
Malaysia	263.9	447.9	708.0	566.1
Netherlands	424.3	524.1	1,054.5	726.3
New Zealand	165.3	266.6	484.5	393.1
Norway	215.0	454.2	470.9	522.8
Panama	412.6	606.9	1,018.2	1,114.0
Philippines	457.4	620.3	911.2	1,026.2
Saudi Arabia	237.8	388.8	677.0	1,350.8
Singapore	701.5	929.9	1,387.9	1,523.7
South Africa	364.1	595.6	959.5	871.9
Thailand	522.2	720.0	951.2	958.7
U.S.S.R.	504.2	484.2	1,095.6	1,626.2
United Kingdom	979.4	1,357.2	1,529.7	1,473.2
U.S.A.	8,847.7	9,448.7	12,799.4	11,148.6
TOTAL (incl. others)	28,591.1	36,930.0	55,535.8	55,752.8

* Imports by country of production; exports by country of last consignment.

TOURISM

	Foreign Visitors	Money Received (U.S. $ million)	Japanese Travellers Abroad	Tourist Payments Abroad (U.S. $ million)
1972	723,744	201	1,392,045	774
1973	784,691	209	2,288,966	1,252
1974	764,246	235	2,335,530	1,358
1975	851,675	252	2,466,326	1,367

TRANSPORT

NATIONAL RAILWAYS

	Passengers (million persons)	Freight (million ton-km.)
1970	6,534	62,435
1971	6,659	61,250
1972	6,724	58,561
1973	6,871	57,405
1974	7,113	51,583

PRIVATE RAILWAYS

	Passengers (million persons)	Freight (million ton-km.)
1970	9,850	988
1971	9,837	997
1972	10,061	963
1973	10,185	932
1974	9,166	869

ROADS
(licensed vehicles—'000)

	Cars	Buses	Lorries	Special Purpose Vehicles	Total
1971–72	10,915.3	196.9	8,943.0	404.2	20,459.3
1972–73	12,964.3	205.9	9,484.4	460.5	23,115.1
1973–74	14,551.9	213.8	9,919.3	514.9	25,199.9
1974–75	16,044.3	218.7	10,281.0	557.4	27,101.5

SHIPPING
(International Sea-borne Traffic)

	Entered	
	Number	'000 net tons
1968	28,234	159,957
1969	30,475	180,646
1970	33,401	208,061
1971	35,557	224,032
1972	36,243	248,362
1973	39,389	283,991
1974	39,915	298,118

MERCHANT FLEET
(registered at June 30th)

	Vessels	Displacement ('000 g.t.)
1972	9,433	34,929
1973	9,469	36,785
1974	9,974	38,708
1975	9,932	64,479

CIVIL AVIATION

	Passengers Carried ('000)	Passenger/Km. (million)	Freight Ton/Km. ('000)*
(Domestic Lines Only)			
1971–72	16,418	10,349	68,559
1972–73	18,830	12,663	101,748
1973–74	22,663	15,426	130,359
1974–75	25,342	17,589	127,764
(International Services)			
1971–72	2,082	8,129	488,864
1972–73	2,303	10,613	556,724
1973–74	2,499	11,997	664,882
1974–75	2,297	12,035	662,357

* Freight includes mails.

COMMUNICATIONS MEDIA

('000)

	1972†	1973	1974	1975
Radio Receivers	70,794	n.a.	n.a.	n.a.
Television Subscribers	24,433	24,925	25,573	25,832
Daily Newspaper Circulation*	38,162	39,847	40,006	40,513

* At October 10th, morning or evening edition only.

†Excluding Okinawa Prefecture.

Source: Japan Statistical Yearbook.

EDUCATION

(1975)

	INSTITUTIONS	TEACHERS	STUDENTS
Primary Schools	24,652	415,039	10,364,855
Secondary Schools	10,751	234,832	4,762,444
High Schools	4,946	222,733	4,332,719
Technical Colleges	65	5,758	47,955
Junior Colleges	513	36,071	353,784
Graduate Schools and Universities	420	147,294	1,734,082

Sources: Research and Statistics Division, Minister's Secretariat, Ministry of Education.

THE CONSTITUTION

(Summary of the Constitution promulgated November 3rd, 1946, in force May 3rd, 1947)

The Emperor: Articles 1–8. The Emperor derives his position from the will of the people. In the performance of any State act as defined in the constitution, he must seek the advice and approval of the Cabinet though he may delegate the exercise of his functions, which include: (i) the appointment of the Prime Minister and the Chief Justice; (ii) promulgation of laws, cabinet orders, treaties and constitutional amendments; (iii) the convocation of the Diet, dissolution of the House of Representatives and proclamation of elections to the Diet; (iv) the appointment and dismissal of Ministers of State and as well as the granting of amnesties, reprieves and pardons and the ratification of treaties, conventions or protocols; (v) the awarding of honours and performance of ceremonial functions.

Renunciation of War: Article 9. Japan renounces for ever the use of war as a means of settling international disputes.

Articles 10–40 refer to the legal and human rights of individuals guaranteed by the constitution.

The Diet: Articles 41–64. The Diet is convened once a year, is the highest organ of State power and has exclusive legislative authority. It comprises of the House of Representatives (491 seats) and the House of Councillors (252 seats). The members of the former are elected for four years whilst those of the latter are elected for six years, one half of whom retire after three years. If the House of Representatives is dissolved, a general election must take place within 40 days and the Diet must be convoked within 30 days of the date of the election. Extraordinary sessions of the Diet may be convened by the Cabinet when one quarter or more of the members of either House request it. Emergency sessions of the House of Councillors may also be held. A quorum of at least one third of the Diet members is needed to carry on Parliamentary business. Any decision arising therefrom must be passed by a majority vote of those present. A bill becomes law having passed both Houses except as provided by the constitution. If the House of Councillors either vetoes or fails to take action within 60 days upon a bill already passed by the House of Representatives, the bill becomes law when passed a second time by the House of Representatives, by at least a two-thirds majority of those members present.

The Budget must first be submitted to the House of Representatives. If, when it is approved by the House of Representatives, the House of Councillors votes against it or fails to take action on it within 30 days, or failing agreement being reached by a joint committee of both Houses, a decision of the House of Representatives shall be the decision of the Diet. The above procedure also applies in respect of the conclusion of treaties.

The Prime Minister and other government Ministers are responsible to the Diet and may be impeached as provided by law.

The Executive: Articles 65–75. Executive power is vested in the cabinet consisting of a Prime Minister and such other Ministers as may be appointed. The Cabinet is collectively responsible to the Diet. Members of the Cabinet are designated from among members of the Diet by a resolution thereof.

If the House of Representatives and the House of Councillors disagree, and if no agreement can be reached even through a joint committee of both Houses, provided for by law, or the House of Councillors fails to make designation within 10 days, exclusive of the period of recess, after the House of Representatives has made designation, the decision of the House of Representatives shall be the decision of the Diet.

The Prime Minister appoints and may remove other Ministers, a majority of whom must be from the Diet. If the House of Representatives passes a no-confidence motion or rejects a confidence motion, the whole Cabinet resigns unless the House of Representatives is dissolved within 10 days. When there is a vacancy in the post of Prime Minister, or upon the first convocation of the Diet after a general election of members of the House of Representatives, the whole Cabinet resigns.

The Prime Minister submits bills, reports on national affairs and foreign relations to the Diet. He exercises control and supervision over various administrative branches of the Government. The Cabinet's primary functions (in addition to administrative ones) are to: (a) administer the law faithfully; (b) conduct State affairs; (c) conclude treaties subject to prior (or subsequent) Diet approval; (d) administer the civil service in accordance with law; (e) prepare and present the budget to the Diet; (f) enact Cabinet orders in order to make effective legal and constitutional provisions; (g) decide on amnesties, reprieves or pardons. All laws and Cabinet orders are signed by the competent Minister of State and countersigned by the Prime Minister. The Ministers of State, during their tenure of office, are not subject to legal action without the consent of the Prime Minister. However, the right to take that action is not impaired.

Articles 76–95. Relate to the Judiciary, Finance and Local Government.

Amendments: Article 96. Amendments to the Constitution are initiated by the Diet, through a concurring vote of two-thirds or more of all the members of each House and are submitted to the people for ratification, which requires the affirmative vote of a majority of all votes cast at a special referendum or at such election as the Diet may specify.

Amendments when so ratified must immediately be promulgated by the Emperor in the name of the people, as an integral part of the Constitution.

Articles 97–99 outline the Supreme Law, while Articles 100–103 consist of Supplementary Provisions.

THE GOVERNMENT

HEAD OF THE STATE

His Imperial Majesty HIROHITO, Emperor of Japan; succeeded to the throne December 25th, 1926.

THE CABINET

(*July* 1976)

Prime Minister: TAKEO MIKI.

Deputy Prime Minister, Minister of State and Director-General of the Economic Planning Agency: TAKEO FUKUDA.

Minister of Justice: OSAMU INABA.

Minister of Foreign Affairs: KIICHI MIYAZAWA.

Minister of Finance: MASAYOSHI OHIRA.

Minister of Education: MICHIO NAGAI.

Minister of Health and Welfare: MASAMI TANAKA.

Minister of Agriculture and Forestry: SHINTARO ABE.

Minister of International Trade and Industry: TOSHIO KOMOTO.

Minister of Transport: MUTSUO KIMURA.

Minister of Posts and Telecommunications: ISAMU MURAKAMI.

Minister of Labour: TAKASHI HASEGAWA.

Minister of Construction: NOBORU TAKESHITA.

Minister of Home Affairs, Chairman of National Public Safety Commission, Director-General of Hokkaido Development Agency: HAJIME FUKUDA.

Minister of State and Chief Cabinet Secretary: ICHITARO IDE.

Minister of State, Director-General of the Prime Minister's Office, Director-General of Okinawa Development Agency: MITSUNORI UEKI.

Minister of State and Director-General of the Administrative Management Agency: YUZO MATSUZAWA.

Minister of State and Director-General of the Defence Agency: MICHITA SAKATA.

Minister of State and Director-General of the Science and Technology Agency: YOSHITAKE SASAKI.

Minister of State and Director-General of the Environment Agency: TATSUO OZAWA.

Minister of State and Director-General of the National Land Agency: SHIN KANAMARU.

Governor of Okinawa Prefecture: CHOBYO YARA.

PARLIAMENT

THE DIET

The Diet consists of two Chambers—the House of Councillors (Upper House)—which replaces the old House of Peers—and the House of Representatives. The 491 members of the House of Representatives are elected for a period of four years (subject to dissolution). For the House of Councillors, which has 252 members, the term of office is six years, half the members being elected every three years.

HOUSE OF COUNCILLORS

Speaker: YUZO SHIGEMUNI.

(*February* 1976)

PARTY	SEATS
Liberal Democrat	129
Socialist	62
Komeito	24
Communist	20
Democratic Socialist	10
Independent and others	7

HOUSE OF REPRESENTATIVES

Speaker: MITSUJIRO ISHII.

(*February* 1976)

PARTY	SEATS
Liberal Democrat	274
Socialist	114
Communist	39
Komeito	30
Democratic Socialist	20
Independent	1
Vacancies	13

POLITICAL PARTIES

The Political Funds Regulation Law is the basis of political organization in Japan. It provides that any organization which wishes to support a candidate for an elective public office must be registered as a political party. There are over 10,000 registered parties in the country, mostly of local or regional significance. National politics are still largely factional in character, but since the introduction of the western pattern of parliamentary democracy in the 1946 Constitution, a restricted number of major parties has formed, grouping the principal pressure groups and personal followings. The conservative Liberal-Democratic Party has the support of big business and the rural population, and holds a majority of seats in the Diet; it is also by far the richest of the political parties. Support for the two socialist parties comes from the intelligentsia, the trades unions, and younger urban voters, and the proportion of votes for these parties combined has increased slowly at each election since 1952. The split between the two parties reflects a longstanding division between supporters of a mass popular party (now represented by the D.S.P.) and those seeking a class party on Marxist lines. The Communist Party of Japan has split since 1964, the official party being independent and supporting neither the U.S.S.R. nor China. In the 1969 elections the militant religious organization Sokagakkai increased its representation in the Diet through its political wing Komeito, although this was reduced in the 1972 elections, which produced gains for the Socialists and Communists. There are also a number of small extreme right-wing political organizations.

Liberal-Democratic Party (Jiyu-Minshuto): 7, 2-chome, Hirakawacho, Chiyoda-ku, Tokyo; f. 1955; programme includes the establishment of a welfare state, the build-up of industrial development, the levelling up of educational and cultural systems and the revision of the Constitution where necessary; follows a foreign policy of alignment with U.S.A.; 226,800 mems. (1975); Pres. TAKEO MIKI; Sec.-Gen. YASUHIRO NAKASONE; publ. *Jiyu Shimpo* (weekly).

Socialist Party of Japan (Nihon Shakaito): 1-8-1, Nagata-cho, Chiyoda-ku, Tokyo; f. 1945; aims at the establishment of collective non-aggression and mutual security system, including Japan, the U.S.A., the U.S.S.R. and China; 40,000 mems. (1975); Chair. TOMOMI NARITA; Sec.-Gen. MASASHI ISHIBASHI; publ. *Shakai Shimpo* (twice a week).

Komeito (*Clean Government Party*): 17 Minamimotomachi, Shinjuku-ku, Tokyo; f. 1964; based on middle-of-the-road principle and humanitarian socialism, promotes policies in best regard of "dignity of human life"; 120,000 mems. (1975); Founder DAISAKU IKEDA; Chair. YOSHIKATSU TAKEIRI; Sec.-Gen. JUNYA YANO; publs. *Komei Shimbun* (daily), *The Komei* (monthly), *Komei Graphic* (bi-monthly).

Democratic Socialist Party (Minshu-Shakaito): Shiba Sakuragawa-cho, Minato-ku, Tokyo; f. 1961 by Right-Wing Socialists of the Social Democratic Party of Japan; aims at the pursuit of an independent foreign policy; 35,000 mems. (1975); Leader KAZUYUKI KASUGA; Sec.-Gen. SABURO TSUKAMOTO; publs. *Shukan Minsha* (daily), *Gekkan Kakushin* (monthly).

Communist Party of Japan: Sendagaya 4-26-7, Shibuya-ku, Tokyo; f. 1922; independent; over 300,000 mems. (1975); Chair. (Central Committee) SANZO NOSAKA; Chair. (Presidium) KENJI MIYAMOTO; Chief Sec. TETSUZO FUWA; publs. *Akahata* (daily and weekly), *Zen-ei* (monthly), information Bulletin for abroad (irregular).

DIPLOMATIC REPRESENTATION

EMBASSIES ACCREDITED TO JAPAN

(In Tokyo unless otherwise stated)

(E) Embassy.

Afghanistan: Rm. 503, Olympia Annexe Apartments, 31-21, Jingumae 6-chome, Shibuya-ku (E); *Ambassador:* ALI AHMAD POPAL (also accred. to the Republic of Korea).

Algeria: Shibusawa Bldg., 3-5-4 Shiba-koen, Minato-ku (E); *Ambassador:* BRAHIM GHAFA.

Argentina: Chiyoda House, 17-8 Nagata-cho 2-chome, Chiyoda-ku (E); *Chargé d'Affaires:* JUAN JANIER RINALDINI.

Australia: 1-14, Mita 2-chome, Minato-ku (E); *Ambassador:* K. C. O. SHANN.

Austria: No. 17, Kowa Building, 2-7 Nishi-Azabu 1-chome, Minato-ku (E); *Ambassador:* Dr. FRANZ WEIDINGER (also accred. to the Republic of Korea).

Bangladesh: 15-19, Minami Aoyama 1-chome, Minato-ku (E); *Ambassador:* ABDUL MUNTAQUIM CHAUDHURY (also accred. to the Republic of Korea).

Belgium: 5, Niban-cho, Chiyoda-ku (E); *Ambassador:* RAOUL DOOREMAN.

Bolivia: House No. 2, 13-9, Ooi 7-chome, Shinagawa-ku (E); *Ambassador:* Dr. WALTER MONTENEGRO (also accred. to Taiwan and the Republic of Korea).

Brazil: 3rd and 4th Floor, Aoyama Daiichi Mansion, 4-14, Akasaka 8-chome, Minato-ku (E); *Ambassador:* HELIO DE BURGOS CABAL.

Bulgaria: 36-3, Yoyogi 5-chome, Shibuya-ku (E); *Ambassador:* RUMEN SERBEZOV (also accred. to the Philippines).

Burma: 8-26, Kita-Shinagawa 4-chome, Shinagawa-ku (E); *Ambassador:* U THAUNG LWIN.

Canada: 3-38, Akasaka 8-chome, Minato-ku (E); *Ambassador:* BRUCE I. RANKIN.

Central African Republic: 8-11-43, Akasaka, Minato-ku (E); *Ambassador:* ANTOINE M'BARY-DABA (also accred. to the Republic of Korea).

Chile: 14-2, Shoto 1-chome, Shibuya-ku (E); *Ambassador:* CARLOS BESA LYON (also accred. to the Philippines).

China, People's Republic: 4-5-30 Minami Azabu, Minato-ku (E); *Ambassador:* CHEN CHU.

Colombia: 9-10 Minami-Aoyama 5-chome, Minato-ku (E); *Ambassador:* JOSÉ MARÍA VILLARREAL (also accred. to the Republic of Korea).

Costa Rica: Mamiana Mansions, 44 Mamiana-cho, Azabu, Minato-ku (E); *Ambassador:* GERMÁN GAGO PÉREZ (also accred. to the Republic of Korea).

Cuba: 6-2, Hiro 2-chome, Shibuya-ku (E); *Ambassador:* MARIO GARCÍA INCHAUSTEGUI (also accred. to Malaysia and Thailand).

Czechoslovakia: 4-6-1 Shiba Koen, Minato-ku; *Ambassador:* Dr. RUDOLF KOZUZNIK (also accred. to the Philippines).

Denmark: Denmark House, 17-35, Minami-Aoyama, 4-chome, Minato-ku (E); *Ambassador:* TYGE DAHLGAARD (also accred. to the Republic of Korea).

Dominican Republic: 2-28, Shiroganeidai 3-chome, Minato-ku (E); *Ambassador:* Dr. ALVARO LOGRONO BATLLE (also accred. to the Republic of Korea).

Ecuador: Azabu Sky Mansion, Room 101, 19-13 Minami Aabu 3-chome, Minato-ku (E); *Chargé d'Affaires a.i.:* ADOLFO H. ALVAREZ (also accred. to the Republic of Korea).

Egypt: 5-4, Aobsdai 1-chome, Meguro-ku (E); *Ambassador:* Dr. MOHSEN ABDEL-KHALEK.

El Salvador: Yurakucho Bldg., Room 1019, 5, Yurakucho; 1-chome, Chiyoda-ku (E); *Ambassador:* WALTER BENEKE MEDINA (also accred. to Taiwan, the Republic of Korea and Singapore).

Ethiopia: 2-13, Akasaka 8-chome, Minato-ku (E); *Ambassador:* ATO MILLION NEQNIQ (also accred. to the Republic of Korea).

Finland: 2-7, Roppongi 3-chome, Minato-ku (E); *Ambassador:* OSMO LAVES (also accred. to the Republic of Korea and the Philippines).

France: 11-44, Minami-Azabu 4-chome, Minato-ku (E); *Ambassador:* JEAN-PIERRE BRUNET.

Gabon: 16-2, Hiroo 2-chome, Shibuya-ku (E); *Ambassador:* SIDOINE MOUGNON.

German Democratic Republic: Akasaka Mansion 7-5-16 Akasaka, Minato-ku; *Ambassador:* HORST BRIE.

Germany, Federal Republic: 5-10, Minami-Azabu 4-chome, Minato-ku (E); *Ambassador:* Dr. WILHELM G. GREWE (also accred. to Mongolia).

Ghana: 15-12, Higashi Gotonda, 5-chome, Shinagawa-ku (E); *Ambassador:* C. O. C. AMATE.

Greece: 4th Floor, Green Fantasia Bldg., 11-11, Jungumae 1-chome, Shibuya-ku (E); *Ambassador:* JEAN C. CAMBIOTIS (also accred. to the Republic of Korea and the Philippines).

Guatemala: 17-1, Shoto 1-chome, Shibuya-ku (E); *Ambassador:* CARLOS ENRIQUE MOLINA MUÑOZ (also accred. to the Republic of Korea and the Philippines).

Guinea: Hirakawa Bldg., 1-11-28 Nagata-cho, Chiyoda-ku (E); *Ambassador:* MAMADY LAMINE CONDÉ.

Honduras: 2-25, Minami-Azuba 4-chome, Minato-ku (E); *Ambassador:* CÉSAR MOSSI SORTO (also accred. to Taiwan and the Republic of Korea).

Hungary: 1-29, Nakameguro 1-chome, Meguro-ku (E); *Ambassador:* ERNŐ HORVÁTH (also accred. to the Philippines and Thailand).

Iceland: Bonn/Bad Godesberg, Federal Republic of Germany.

India: 2-11, Kudan-Minami 2-chome, Chiyoda-ku (E); *Ambassador:* ERIC GONSALVES.

Indonesia: 2-9, Higashi Gotanda 5-chome, Shinagawa-ku (E); *Ambassador:* Lt.-Gen. ANTONIUS JOSEF WITONO SARSANTO.

Iran: 10-32, Minami-Azabu 3-chome, Minato-ku (E); *Ambassador:* ABDUL HOSSEIN HAMZAVI (also accred. to the Republic of Korea and the Philippines).

Iraq: Rms. 185, Greenleaves Hill, 17-12 Sarugaku-cho, Shibuya-ku (E); *Ambassador:* KAHTAN LUTFI ALI.

Ireland: No. 25, Kona Bldg., 7 Sanban-cho, 8-chome, Chiyoda-ku (E); *Ambassador:* DAVID NELIGAN.

Israel: 3, Niban-cho, Chiyoda-ku (E); *Ambassador:* SHAUL RAMATI.

Italy: 5-4, Mita, 2-chome, Minato-ku (E); *Ambassador:* CARLO PERRONE CAPANO.

Ivory Coast: 2nd Floor, Aoyama Tower Bldg., 2-24-15 Minami Aoyama, Minato-ku (E); *Ambassador:* PIERRE N. COFFI (also accred. to Taiwan and the Republic of Korea).

Jordan: 4A, B, Chiyoda House, 17-8 Nagatacho 2-chome, Chiyoda-ku (E); *Ambassador:* AMER ABDEL KADER SHAMMOUT (also accred. to the Republic of Korea).

Korea, Republic: 2-5 Minami Azabu 1-chome, Minato-ku (E); *Ambassador:* YOUNG SUN KIM.

Kuwait: 13-12, Mita 4-chome, Minato-ku (E); *Ambassador:* TALAT YACOUB AL-GHOUSSEIN (also accred. to Malaysia).

Laos: 3-21, Nishi-Azabu 3-chome, Minato-ku (E); *Ambassador:* LANE PATHAMMAVONG.

Lebanon: Azabu Tokyo Apts. No. 95, 47, Azabu, Mamiana-cho, Minato-ku (E); *Ambassador:* Dr. ALIF GEBARA.

Liberia: 1, Kioiocho, Chiyoda-ku (E); *Ambassador:* ERNEST EASTMAN (also accred. to Taiwan and the Republic of Korea).

Libya: 5-36-21 Shimouma, Setagaya-ku (E); *Chargé d'Affaires:* SAID A. ALHAZHAZI.

Madagascar: 3-25 Moto Azabu 2-chome, Minato-ku (E); *Ambassador:* APOLINAIRE ANDRIATSIAFAJATO.

Malaysia: 20-16, Nanpeidaimachi, Shibaya-ku (E); *Ambassador:* LIM TAIK CHOON.

Mali: Moscow, U.S.S.R.

Mexico: 15-1, Nagata-cho 2-chome, Chiyoda-ku (E); *Ambassador:* MANUEL ALVAREZ LUNA (also accred. to the Republic of Korea).

Mongolia: Pine Crest Mansion, 21-4 Shoto, Kamiyama-cho, Shibuya-ku (E); *Ambassador:* SONOMDORJIIN DAMBADARJAA (also accred. to Malaysia).

Morocco: 5th and 6th Floors, Silver Kingdom Mansion, 16-3 Sendagaya 3-chome, Shibuya-ku (E); *Ambassador:* ABDELSAM TADLAOUI (also accred. to the Republic of Korea).

Nepal: 17-1, Higashi Gotonda 5-chome, Shinagawa-ku (E); *Ambassador:* YADAV PRASAD PANT (also accred. to the Republic of Korea and the Philippines).

Netherlands: 1, Sakae-cho, Shiba, Minato-ku (E); *Ambassador:* Dr. CARL DIETRICH BARKMAN.

New Zealand: 20-40, Kamiyama-cho, Shibuya-ku (E); *Ambassador:* T. C. LARKIN.

Nicaragua: 2-3, Roppongi 4-chome, Minato-ku (E); *Chargé d'Affaires:* Lic. FRANCISCO J. DIESCOTO BROCKMANN (also accred. to the Republic of Korea).

Nigeria: 2-19-7 Uehara, Shibuya-ku (E); *Ambassador:* PETER LOUIS UDOH.

Norway: 12-2, Minami-Azabu 5-chome, Minato-ku (E); *Chargé d'Affaires:* DAG BRYN (also accred. to the Republic of Korea).

Pakistan: National Azabu Apt. 5-2, Minami-Azabu, 4-chome, Minato-ku; *Chargé d'Affaires:* SHUJAAT HASAN KHAN.

Panama: 8-6 Minami-Azabu, 3-chome, Minato-ku (E); *Ambassador:* JOSÉ NAPOLEON FRANCO CASANOVA (also accred. to the Republic of Korea).

Papua New Guinea: Room 313, 3rd Floor, Mita Kokusai Bldg., 1-4-28 Mita, Minato-ku, Tokyo 108; *Chargé d'Affaires:* V. S. MARAGAU.

Paraguay: 2-6-29 Hiroo, Shibuya-ku (E); *Ambassador:* DESIDEIRO MELANIO ENCISO (also accred. to Taiwan, the Republic of Korea and Pakistan).

Peru: Higashi 4-4-27 Shibuya-ku; *Ambassador:* JORGE VELANDO UGARTECHE (also accred. to Taiwan and the Republic of Korea).

Philippines: 6-15, Roppongi 5-chome, Minato-ku (E): *Ambassador:* ROBERTO S. BENEDICTO.

Poland: 13-5, Mita 2-chome, Meguro-ku (E); *Ambassador*; STEFAN PERKOWICZ (also accred. to the Philippines).

Portugal: Olympia Annex Appt. 306, 31-21, Jungamae 6-chome, Shibuya-ku (E); *Chargé d'Affairés:* ANTÓNIO DE OLIVEIRA CASCAIS.

Qatar: Hiroo Towers, 1-12 Minami Azabu 4-chome, Minato-ku (E); *Ambassador:* HAMAD MANSOUR AL HAJIRI.

Romania: 3-1, Aobadai 2-chome, Minato-ku (E); *Ambassador:* NICOLAE FINANTU.

Saudi Arabia: 4-18, Moto-Azabu 3-chome, Minato-ku (E); *Chargé d'Affaires:* ABDUL RAHMAN AL-BAIZ (also accred. to the Republic of Korea).

Singapore: Room 1518, Kasumigaseki Bldg., 2-5 Kasumigaseki 3-chome, Chiyoda-ku (E); *Ambassador:* WEE MON CHENG.

Spain: 3-29, Roppongi 1-chome, Minato-ku (E); *Ambassador:* Don JOSÉ ARRAGONES.

Sri Lanka: 14-1, Akasaka 1-chome, Minato-ku (E); *Ambassador:* BERNARD P. TILAKARATNA.

Sudan: Yada Mansion, 6-20 Minami Aoyama 6-chome, Minato-ku (E); *Ambassador:* EL-BAGHIR ABDEL-MUTAAL.

Sweden: 10-3, Roppongi 1-chome, Minato-ku (E); *Ambassador:* BENGT ODEVALL.

Switzerland: 9-12, Mimami-Azabu 5-chome, Minato-ku (E); *Ambassador:* PIERRE CUENOUD.

Tanzania: 21-9, Kamiyoga 4-chome, Setagaya-ku (E); *Ambassador:* GEORGE NHIGULLA.

Thailand: 14-6, Kami-Osaki 3-chome, Shinagawa-ku (E); *Ambassador:* Dr. SOMPONG SUCHARITKUL.

Trinidad and Tobago: New Delhi, India.

Turkey: 5th Floor, Yashica Bldg., 27-8 Jingumae, 6-chome, Shibuya-ku (E); *Ambassador:* CELAL EYICEOGLU (also accred. to the Philippines).

Uganda: 2-2 Shoto 2-chome, Shibuya-ku; *Chargé d'Affaires a.i.:* SAMUSONI TWINE BIGOMBE.

U.S.S.R.: 2-1-1 Azabudai, Minato-ku (E); *Ambassador:* DMITRI STEPANOVICH POLYANSKY.

United Arab Emirates: Kotsu Anzen Kyoiku Centre Bldg., 24-20 Minami Azabu 3-chome, Minato-ku (E); *Ambassador:* AHMED SALIM AL-MOKARRAB.

United Kingdom: 1, Ichiban-cho, Chiyoda-ku (E); *Ambassador:* Sir MICHAEL WILFORD, K.C.M.G.

U.S.A.: Chancery, 10-5, Akasaka 1-chome, Minato-ku (E); *Ambassador:* JAMES D. HODGSON.

Uruguay: 5-26, Akasaka 9-chome, Minato-ku (E); *Ambassador:* ALBERTO RODRÍGUEZ.

Vatican City: 9-2, Sanbancho, Chiyoda-ku (Pro-Nunciature); *Apostolic Pro-Nuncio:* Archbishop IPPOLITO ROTOLI.

Venezuela: 11-23, Minami Azabu 3-chome, Minato-ku (E); *Chargé d'Affaires:* ROBERTO H. PALACIOA GONZALES (also accred. to the Republic of Korea).

Viet-Nam: 50–11 Moto Yoyogi-Cho, Shibuya-ku; *Ambassador:* NGUYEN GIAP.

Yemen, People's Democratic Republic: 12-12 Akasaka 8-chome, Minato-ku (E); *Chargé d'Affaires a.i.:* SALEH AHMED SALEH.

Yugoslavia: 7-24, Kitashinagaway 4-chome, Shinagawa-ku (E); *Ambassador:* MIROSLAV KREACIC.

Zaire: 5th Floor, Odakyn Minami Aoyami Bldg., 8-1 Minami Aoyama 7-chome, Minato-ku (E); *Ambassador:* Brig.-Gen. LEONARD MULAMBA NYNYI WA KADIMA (also accred. to the Republic of Korea).

Zambia: 3-19-8 Pakanawa, Minato-ku (E); *Ambassador:* LOMBE PHYLLIS CHIBESAKUNDA.

Japan also has diplomatic relations with Bahrain, Barbados, Benin, Botswana, Burundi, Cameroon, Chad, the Congo People's Republic, Cyprus, Fiji, the Gambia, Guyana, Haiti, Jamaica, Kenya, Lesotho, Luxembourg, Malawi, Maldives, Malta, Mauritania, Mauritius, Nauru, Niger, Oman, Rwanda, San Marino, Senegal, Sierra Leone, Somalia, South Africa, Swaziland, Syria, Togo, Tonga, Tunisia, the Upper Volta and the Yemen Arab Republic.

JUDICIAL SYSTEM

The basic principles of the legal system are set forth in the Constitution, which lays down that the whole judicial power is vested in a Supreme Court and in such inferior courts as are established by law, and enunciates the principle that no organ or agency of the Executive shall be given final judicial power. Judges are to be independent in the exercise of their conscience, and may not be removed except by public impeachment, unless judicially declared mentally or physically incompetent to perform official duties. The judges of the Supreme Court are appointed by the Cabinet, the sole exception being the Chief Justice, who is appointed by the Emperor after designation by the Cabinet.

The Court Organization Law, which came into force on May 3rd, 1947, decreed the constitution of the Supreme Court and the establishment of four types of inferior court—High, District, Family (established January 1st, 1949), and Summary Courts. The constitution and functions of the courts are as follows:

THE SUPREME COURT

This court is the highest legal authority in the land, and consists of a Chief Justice and fourteen associate judges. It has jurisdiction over the following matters:

(1) **Jokoku** (appeals).

(2) **Kokoku** (complaints), prescribed specially in codes of procedure.

It conducts its hearings and renders decisions through a Grand Bench or three Petty Benches. Both are collegiate bodies, the former consisting of all justices of the Court, and the latter of five judges. A Supreme Court Rule prescribes which cases are to be handled by the respective Benches. It is, however, laid down by law that the Petty Bench cannot make decisions as to the constitutionality of a statute, ordinance, regulation, or disposition, or as to cases in which an opinion concerning the interpretation and application of the Constitution or of any laws or ordinances is at variance with a previous decision of the Supreme Court.

Chief Justice: TOMOKAZU MURAKAMI.

Secretary-General: KAZUO YASUMURA.

INFERIOR COURTS

High Court

A High Court conducts its hearings and renders decisions through a collegiate body, consisting of three judges, though for cases of insurrection the number of judges must be five. The Court has jurisdiction over the following matters:

(1) **Koso** appeals from judgments in the first instance rendered by District Courts, from judgments rendered by Family Courts, and from judgments concerning criminal cases rendered by Summary Courts.

(2) **Kokoku** complaints against rulings and orders rendered by District Courts and Family Courts, and against rulings and orders concerning criminal cases rendered by Summary Courts, except those coming within the jurisdiction of the Supreme Court.

(3) **Jokoku** appeals from judgments in the second instance rendered by District Courts and from judgments rendered by Summary Courts, except those concerning criminal cases.

(4) Actions in the first instance relating to cases of insurrection.

District Court

A District Court conducts hearings and renders decisions through a single judge or, for certain types of cases, through a collegiate body of three judges. It has jurisdiction over the following matters:

(1) Actions in the first instance, except offences relating to insurrection, claims where the subject matter of the action does not exceed 300,000 yen, and offences liable to a fine or lesser penalty.

(2) **Koso** appeals from judgments rendered by Summary Courts, except those concerning criminal cases.

(3) Complaints against rulings and orders rendered by Summary Courts, except those coming within the jurisdiction of the Supreme Court and High Courts.

Family Court

A Family Court handles cases through a single judge in case of rendering judgments or decisions. However, in accordance with the provisions of other statutes it conducts its hearings and renders decisions through a collegiate body of three judges. A conciliation is effected through a collegiate body consisting of a judge and two or more members of the conciliation committee selected from among citizens.

It has jurisdiction over the following matters:

(1) Judgment and conciliation with regard to cases relating to family as provided by the Law for Adjudgment of Domestic Relations.

(2) Judgment with regard to the matters of protection of juveniles as provided by the Juvenile Law.

(3) Actions in the first instance relating to adult criminal cases of violation of the Labour Standard Law, the Law for Prohibiting Liquors to Minors, or other laws especially enacted for protection of juveniles.

Summary Court

A Summary Court handles cases through a single judge, and has jurisdiction in the first instance over the following matters:

(1) Claims where the value of the subject matter does not exceed 300,000 yen (excluding claims for cancellation or change of administrative dispositions).

(2) Actions which relate to offences liable to fine or lesser penalty, offences liable to a fine as an optional penalty, and certain specified offences such as habitual gambling and larceny.

A Summary Court cannot impose imprisonment or a graver penalty. When it deems proper the imposition of a sentence of imprisonment or a graver penalty, it must transfer such cases to a District Court, but it can impose imprisonment with hard labour not exceeding three years for certain specified offences.

A Procurator's Office, with its necessary number of procurators, is established for each of these courts. The procurators conduct searches, institute prosecutions and supervise the execution of judgments in criminal cases, and act as representatives of the public interests in civil cases of public concern.

RELIGION

The traditional religions in Japan are Shintoism and Buddhism. Neither is exclusive, and many Japanese subscribe at least nominally to both. Since the war a number of new religions based on an amalgamation of Shinto, Buddhist, Taoist, Confucian and Christian beliefs have grown up.

SHINTOISM

Shintoism is an indigenous cult of nature and ancestor worship. It is divided into two cults: national Shintoism, which is represented by the shrines; and sectarian Shintoism, which developed towards the end of the Tokugawa Shogunate. In 1868, Shinto was designated a national religion, and all Shinto shrines acquired the privileged status of a national institution. After the adoption of the present constitution in 1947, however, complete freedom of religion was introduced, and state support of Shinto was banned. There are an estimated 80,000 shrines, 200,000 priests and approximately 80,000,000 adherents.

BUDDHISM

World Buddhist Fellowship: Rev. RIRI NAKAYAMA, Hozenji Buddhist Temple, 1115, 3-chome, Akabane-cho, Kita-ku, Tokyo.

CHRISTIANITY

In 1969 the number of Christians was estimated at 875,000, with 5,000 churches and 20,000 clergy. Twenty-two universities are maintained by Christian communities.

In 1940 the Religious Organization Law was passed, according to which a religious body must possess at least 50 churches and 5,000 adherents in order to be recognized. Many of the numerous Christian sects united in order to obtain recognition. The Law was repealed at the end of the war and certain groups returned to their original status. The following are the largest groups:

Roman Catholic Church: Archdiocese of Tokyo: Sekiguchi, 3-chome, 16-15, Bunkyo-ku, Tokyo 112; suffragan sees at Sapporo, Sendai, Yokohama, Urawa, Niigata; Archbishop of Tokyo Mgr. PETER SEIICHI SHIRAYANAGI; Archdiocese of Nagasaki: 1 Otsu Minami-Yamate-cho, Nagasaki; suffragan sees at Kagoshima, Fukuoka, Oita and Naha (Okinawa); Archbishop of Nagasaki Mgr. JOSEPH A. SATOWAKI; Archdiocese of Osaka: 1-55, Nishinomiya-shi, Hyogo-ken; suffragen sees at Kyoto, Hiroshima, Takamatsu; Nagoya; Archbishop of Osaka Mgr. PAUL Y. TAGUCHI, 357,478 adherents.

United Church of Christ in Japan: Japan Christian Center, Room 31, 3-18 Nishi Waseda 2-chome, Shinjuku-ku, Tokyo 160; f. 1941; union of 34 Presbyterian, Methodist, Congregational, Reformed and other denominations; Moderator Rev. ISUKE TODA; Vice-Moderator Rev. ICHIRO ONO; Sec. Rev. CHIKARA DEGUCHI.

Japanese Orthodox Church: Holy Resurrection Cathedral (Nicolai-Do), 1-3, 4-chome, Surugadai, Kanda, Chiyoda-ku, Tokyo 101; Primate H.E. Most Rev. THEODOSIUS, Archbishop of Tokyo and Metropolitan of All Japan; 24,680 adherents.

Nippon Sei Ko Kai (*Anglican-Episcopal Church*): 4-21, Higashi 1-chome, Shibuya-ku, Tokyo; in Communion with the Church of England; est. as Province of the Anglican Communion 1887; 52,147 mems.; Primate Most Rev. JOHN NAOHIKO OKUBO (Bishop of Kita-Kanto); 10 other diocesan bishops.

OTHER RELIGIONS

There are an estimated 5,000,000 adherents of other religions, with 1,200 shrines and temples and 15,000 priests.

THE "NEW RELIGIONS"

Many new cults have grown up in Japan since the end of World War II. Collectively these are known as the New Religions (*Shinko Shukyo*). The most important are as follows:

Soka Gakkai: **32 Shinano-machi, Shinjuku-ku, Tokyo; f. 1930; the lay society of Orthodox Nichiren Buddhism; membership 7½ million households; Buddhist group aiming at individual happiness and world peace;** Pres. DAISAKU IKEDA; publs. include: *Selected Works of Daisaku Ikeda, The Human Revolution, Vols. 1-7, Science and Religion, Essays on Life, Reflections on Civilization, Encyclopedia of Buddhist Philosophy, Vols. 1–8, Choose Life—Dialogues between Arnold Toynbee and Daisaku Ikeda, Dialogue with the Juvenile, Seikyo Shimbun* (daily), *Dai-byaku Renge* (monthly), *Seikyo Graphic* (weekly), *Seikyo Times* (English language monthly), *East and West—Dialogue with Richard E. Coudenhove-Kalevgi.*

Rissho Kosei-kai: 11-1, Wada 2-chome, Suginami-ku; Tokyo 166; f. 1938; Buddhist laymen; Pres. Rev. NIKKYO NIWANO; 4 million mems. in Japan and U.S.A.

THE PRESS

The average circulation of Japanese dailies is 57,820,000 copies, the highest in the world after the U.S.S.R. and the U.S.A., and the circulation per head of population is highest at 528 copies per thousand inhabitants. The three newspapers with the largest circulations are the *Asahi Shimbun* (combined circ. 5.5 million), *Mainichi Shimbun* (4.6 million) and *Yomiuri Shimbun* (5.9 million). There are three other influential papers, *Nikon Keizai Shimbun, Chunichi Shimbun* and *Sankei Shimbun*, with a combined circulation of over 1.5 million. These papers together account for 41.4 per cent of the total circulation of Japanese newspapers. A notable feature of the Japanese press is the number of weekly news journals.

Technically the Japanese press is highly advanced, and all three of the major newspapers are issued in simultaneous editions in the main centres.

PRINCIPAL DAILIES

Tokyo

Asahi Evening News: 8-5 1-chome, Tsukiji, Chuo-ku; f. 1954; evening; English language; Editor Y. Kitamura; circ. 37,000.

Asahi Shimbun: 6-1, 2-chome, Yuraku-cho, Chiyoda-ku, 100; f. 1888; Editor T. Hitotsuyangi; circ. morning 3,281,725, evening 2,314,291.

Business Japan: Sankei Bldg., 7-2, 1-chome, Otemachi, Chiyoda-ku; f. 1955; Pres. Y. Kobayashi; Man. Editor Ken Yanagisawa; circ. 63,000.

Daily Sports: 1-39, 2-chome, Ikenohata, Taito-ku; f. 1955; morning; Man. Editor S. Ueda; circ. 367,424.

Daily Yomiuri, The: 1-2-3, Ginza, Chuo-ku; f. 1955; English; Editor Hideo Ueno; circ. morning 37,000.

Dempa Shimbun: 11-15, Higashi Gotanda, 1-chome, Shinagawa-ku; f. 1950; morning; Editor H. Sasaki; circ. 200,000.

Denki Kikai Kogyo Shinbun: 11-15, 1-chome, Higashi Gotanda, Shinagawa-ku; f. 1958; morning; Editor T. Ajiki; circ. 45,000.

Hochi Shimbun: 29, 2-chome, Hirakawa-cho, Chiyoda-ku; f. 1871; morning; Chair. I. Furuto; Editor T. Noguchi; circ. 1,094,204.

Japan Times, The: 5-4, 4-chome, Shibaura, Minato-ku; f. 1897; morning; English; Pres. Y. Higashiuchi; Editor M. Ogawa; circ. 49,200.

Komei Shimbun: 17 Minami-motomachi, Shinjuku-ku, organ of the Komeito political party; circ. 800,000. Sunday edition 1,400,000.

Mainichi Daily News, The: 1-1-1 Hitotsubashi, Chiyoda-ku; f. 1922; English language; morning; Gen. Man. and Editor Hitoshi Ohnishi; circ. 60,000 (*see* also under Osaka).

Mainichi Shimbun: 1-1, 1-chome, Hitotsubashi, Chiyoda-ku; f. 1872; Editor M. Gomi; circ. (all editions) morning 4,492,700, evening 2,570,700.

Naigai Sports: Nikkei Insatsu Bldg., 14, 2-chome, Kayabacho, Nihonbashi, Chuo-ku; f. 1962; evening; Man. Editor S. Yui; circ. 329,408.

Naigai Times: 5, 3-chome, Ginza, Chuo-ku; f. 1949; evening; Pres. Tsai Chang Keng; Man. Editor S. Tamaki.

Nihon Keizai Shimbun: 9-5, 1-chome, Otemachi, Chiyoda-ku, Tokyo; f. 1876; morning, evening and weekly (English editions: The Japan Economic Journal), economic news; Pres. J. Enjoji; Chief Editor Y. Takeyama; circ. morning 1,046,300, evening 1,056,500.

Nihon Kogyo Shimbun: 7-2, 1-chome, Otemachi, Chiyoda-ku: f. 1933; morning business and financial; Pres. Y. Kobayashi; Man. Editor T. Masaki; circ. 425,000.

Nihon Nogyo Shimbun: 2-3 Akihabara, Taito-ku, Tokyo 110; f. 1928; agricultural; Man. Editor O. Gunji; circ. morning 320,000.

Nikkan Kogyo Shimbun (*Industrial Daily News*): 8-10, 1-chome, Kudan-kita, Chiyoda-ku; f. 1945; morning; Ed. Dir. A. Kato; circ. 600,000.

Nikkan Sports: 5-10, 3-chome. Tsukiji, Chuo-ku; f. 1946; Chair. G. Kawada; Editor F. Okazaki; morning; circ. 617,061.

Sankei Shimbun, The: 7-2, 1-chome, Otemachi, Chiyoda-ku; f. 1933; Editorial Dir. T. Nagata; circ. morning 2,027,000, evening 1,254,005.

Sankei Sports: 7-2, 1-chome, Otemachi, Chiyoda-ku; f. 1963; Man. Editor T. Kitagawa; circ. morning 317,407.

Shipping and Trade News: Tokyo News Service Ltd., 10 Ginza Nishi, 8-chome, Chuo-ku, Tokyo 104; f. 1949; English language; Man. Editor M. Chihaya; circ. 17,250.

Sports Nippon: 1-1, 1-chome, Hitotsubashi, Chiyoda-ku; f. 1950; Dir. Y. Miyamoto; Man. Editor Y. Araj; morning; circ. 594,310.

Tokyo Shimbun: 3-13, 2-chome, Konan, Minato-ku; f. 1942; Pres. M. Kato; Man. Editor F. Yamanaka; circ. morning 930,000, evening 640,000.

Tokyo Sports: 5-10, 3-chome, Tsukiji, Chuo-ku; f. 1959; Pres. M. Nagata; Man. Editor H. Hirota; circ. evening 566,780.

Tokyo Times: 1, 1-chome, Higashi-Shimbashi, Minato-ku; f. 1946; Pres. and Man. Editor Y. Tukoma; circ. morning 250,000.

Yomiuri Shimbun: 7-1, 1-chome, Otemachi; f. 1874; Propr. T. Shoriki; Pres. M. Mutai; Man. Editor J. Hasegawa; morning and evening; circ. (all editions) morning 5,884,962, evening 3,536,638, (Tokyo) morning 3,634,348, evening 2,328,713.

Osaka District

Asahi Shimbun: 3, 3-chome, Nakano-shima, Kita-ku; f. 1879; Man. Editor Ichiro Yasutake; circ. morning 2,019,556, evening 1,264,453.

Daily Sports: 18 1-chome, Kitadori, Edobori, Nishi-ku, Osaka; f. 1948; morning; Editor Y. Morisawa; circ. 527,648.

Hochi Shimbun: 46 Nozaki-machi, Kita-ku; f. 1964; morning; Chief Editor H. Unno; circ. 213,115.

Kansai Shimbun: 31 Hashizume-cho, Uchihon-cho, Higashi-ku; f. 1950; evening; Editor K. Kimura; circ. 110,500.

Mainichi Daily News, The: 36, 2-chome, Dojima-kami, Kita-ku, Osaka; f. 1922; Editor T. Nakao; circ. 21,560 (*see* also under Tokyo).

Mainichi Shimbun: 36, 2-chome, Dojima-kami, Kita-ku; f. 1882; Editor D. Yamanouchi; circ. morning 1,544,427, evening 917,321.

Nihon Keizai Shimbun: 1, 1-chome, Komabashi, Higashi-ku; f. 1950; Editor K. Suzuki; circ. morning 416,003, evening 294,439.

Nikkan Sports: 92-1, 5-chome, Hattori-kotu-bukicho, Toyonaka City; f. 1950; Editor K. Matsui; circ. 391,143.

Osaka Nichi-nichi Shimbun: 69, 1-chome, Edobori-kitadori, Nishi-ku; f. 1946; evening; Pres. H. NOBEKIN; Man. Editor M. ABE; circ. 64,012.

Osaka Shimbun: 27, Umeda-cho, Kita-ku; f. 1922; evening; Pres. TERUMI NAGATA; Editor S. HIRAYOSHI; circ. 156,086.

Sankei Shimbun: 27, Umeda-cho, Kita-ku; f. 1933; Man. Editor A. AOKI; circ. morning 1,007,700, evening 555,908.

Sankei Sports: 27 Umeda-machi, Kita-ku; f. 1955; Editor K. NAGAO; circ. morning 323,521.

Shin Kansai: 2-3 3-chome, Minami, Oyodo-cho, Ovodo-ku; f. 1946; Rep. Dir. H. MORIGUCHI; Man. Editor S. NAGAI; evening; circ. 147,000.

Shin Osaka: 36 Kawaguchi-cho, Nishi-ku; f. 1946; Man. Editor K. FURUKAWA; circ. evening 29,808.

Sports Nippon: 2-3 Minami, 3-chome, Oyodo-cho, Oyodo-ku; f. 1949; Man. Editor A. HONDA; circ. morning 485,926.

Yomiuri Shimbun: 77 Nozaki-cho, Kita-ku; f. 1952; Pres. T. KURIYAMA; Man. Editor G. SAKATA; circ. morning 1,879,900, evening 1,216,100.

KANTO DISTRICT (Outside Tokyo)

Chiba Nippo (*Chiba Daily News*): 14-10, 4-chome, Chu-ku, Chiba City; f. 1957; Pres. I. KUBO; Editor K. TSURUOKA; circ. 92,984.

Ibaragi: 2-15 Kitami-machi, Mito City, Ibaraki; f. 1891; Man. Editor T. MIKURA; circ. 88,700.

Jyomo Shimbun: 90 Furuichi-machi, Maebashi City, Tochigi; f. 1886; morning; Editor M. SAKURAI; circ. 126,090.

Kanagawa Shimbun: 23 2-chome Otomachi, Naka-ku, Yokohama City; f. 1942; morning; Editor F. SHIMOYAMA; circ. 177,866.

Shimotsuke Shimbun: 4-11 Hon-cho, Utsunomiya City, Tochigi; f. 1884; morning; Man. Editor T. FUKUSHIMA; circ. 123,543.

Tochigi Shimbun: 2502, 1-chome Shimotomatshuri, Utsunomiya City; f. 1949; Editor E. TAKAHASHI; circ. 81,525.

TOHOKU DISTRICT (Northeast Honshu)

Akita Sakigake Shimpo: 2-6, 1-chome, Omachi, Akita-shi, Akita, f. 1874; Chair. S. HITOMI; Man. Editor I. ANDO; circ. morning 173,559, evening 173,559.

Daily Tohoku: 3 Bancho, Hachinohe, Iwate; f. 1945; morning; Editor S. SATO; circ. 65,580.

Fukushima Minpo: 21, Sakae-cho, Fukushima; f. 1892; morning and evening; circ. morning 177,064, evening 13,662; Editor Y. SATO.

Fukushima Minyu: 9-9, Naka-Machi, Fukushima City; Man. Editor H. SAITO; circ. morning 126,995, evening 10,593.

Iwate Nippo: 3-7, Uchimaru, Morioka, Iwate; f. 1938; Editor D. TADA; circ. morning 157,515, evening 157,515.

Kahoku Shimpo: 2-28, 1-chome, Hsutsubashi, Sendai City, Miyagi; f. 1897; Man. Editor Y. NIKAIDO; circ. morning 367,127, evening 157,714.

Too Nippo: 2-11, 2-chome, Shin-machi, Aomori; f. 1888; morning and evening; circ. 151,804 and 150,680; Man. Editor T. KUSUMI.

Yamagata Shimbun: 5-12, 2-chome Hatago-cho, Yamagata City; f. 1876; Pres. Y. HATTORI; Chief Editor K. OKAZAKI; morning and evening; circ. 145,200.

CHUBU DISTRICT (Central Honshu)

Asahi Shimbun: 3-3, 1-chome, Sakae, Naka-ku, Nagoya; f. 1935; Man. Editor H. ISHIHARA; circ. morning 440,037, evening 304,115.

Chubu Keizai Shimbun: 24-1 Hijie-cho, Nakamura-ku, Nagoya; f. 1946; Man. Editor K. NAITO; circ. 165,222.

Chunichi Shimbun: 6-1, 1-chome Sannomaru Naka-ku, Nagoya; f. 1942; Editor N. WAKAMATSU; circ. morning 1,710,200, evening 842,500.

Chunichi Sports: 6-1, 1-chome, Sannomaru, Naka-ku, Nagoya City; f. 1954; morning; Chief Editor M. FUKAMI; circ. 430,000.

Gifu Nichi-nichi Shimbun: 9 Imakomachi, Gifu City; f. 1879; morning and evening; Pres. M. SUGIYAMA; Man. Editor Y. TAMADA; circ. morning 134,282, evening 75,436.

Mainichi Shimbun: 1, 4-chome, Horinouchi-machi, Nakamura-ku, Nagoya; f. 1935; Man. Editor H. YAMANOUCHI; circ. morning 295,501, evening 170,702.

Nagoya Times: 3-10, 1-chome, Maruno-uchi, Naka-ku, Nagoya City; f. 1946; evening; Man. Editor I. KIMI; circ. 117,200.

Shinano Mainichi Shimbun: 657 Minamiagata-cho, Nagano; f. 1873; Man. Editor K. KOMIYAMA; circ. morning 164,728, evening 32,726.

Shizuoka Shimbun: 1-1, 3-chome, Toro, Shizuoka City; f. 1941; Man. Editor S. FUJITA; circ. morning 462,018, evening 462,179.

Yamanashi Nichi-Nichi Shimbun: 6, 2-chome, Kitaguchi, Kofu City; f. 1872; morning; Man. Editor Y. TAKAMURO; circ. 123,293.

HOKURIKU DISTRICT (North Coastal Honshu)

Fukui Shimbun: 1-14, 1-chome, Haruyama, Fukui City; f. 1889; Man. Editor T. FUKUDA; circ. morning 126,653, evening 15,243.

Hokkoku Shimbun: 5-1, 2-chome, Korinbo, Kanazawa, Ishikawa; f. 1893; Man. Editor S. NUKUI; circ. morning 194,984, evening 89,469.

Hokuriku Chunichi Shimbun: 7-15, 2-chome, Korinbo, Kanazawa; Editor H. IWAYA; circ. morning 85,219, evening 16,688.

Kita Nihon Shimbun: 2-14 Yasuzumi-cho, Toyama-shi, Toyama; f. 1940; Man. Editor H. MATSUDA; circ. morning 153,000, evening 42,000.

Niigata Nippo: 189-3 Ichiban-cho, Higashinaka-dori, Niigata City; f. 1942; Editor K. NAKAJIMA; circ. morning 332,281, evening 101,870.

Yomiuri Shimbun: 4-5 Shimonoseki-machi, Takaoka City; f. 1961; Man. Editor N. SHIROISHI; circ. morning 109,728, evening 14,382.

KINKI DISTRICT (West Central Honshu)

Hyogo Shimbun: 3-25 Minato-machi, Hyogo-ku, Kobe; f. 1946; evening; circ. 94,257; Editor J. IWASA.

Ise Shimbun: 34-9, Hon-cho, Tsu City, Mie; f. 1878; morning; Man. Editor F. NAITO; circ. 91,410.

Kobe Shimbun: 4, 7-chome, Kumoidori, Fukiai-ku, Kobe City; f. 1898 Man. Editor S. NAKAO; circ. morning 428,335, evening 231,900.

Kyoto Shimbun: 239 Shoshoi-machi Ebisugawa-kitairu, Karasuma-dori, Nakakyo-ku, Kyoto; f. 1942; Chief Editor K. NODA; circ. morning 378,212, evening 302,429.

Wakayama Shimpo: 5, 4-chome, Komatsubara-dori, Wakayama; f. 1940; morning; Editor H. AKAI; circ. 65,000.

CHUGOKU DISTRICT
(Western Honshu)

Bocho Shimbun: 3 Kifune-cho, Shimonseki; f. 1941; morning; Pres. S. KAWAMURA; Man. Editor K. TAGUCHI; circ. 48,600.

Chugoku Shimbun: 7-1 Dobashi-cho, Hiroshima City, Hiroshima; f. 1892; Pres. A YAMAMOTO; Man. Editor K. HIRAOKA; circ. morning 434,878, evening 110,690.

Sanyo Shimbun: 1-23, 2-chome, Yanagi-cho, Okayama; f. 1879; Man. Editor A. KAGA; circ. morning 310,931, evening 79,587.

Shimane Shimbun: 14-3 Sodeshi-machi, Matsue, Shimane; f. 1942; morning; Chief Editor T. NAKAMOTO; circ. 65,500.

Yamaguchi Shimbun: 16. Higashiyamamoto-cho, Shimonoseki; f. 1946; Pres. K. OGAWA; Editors Y. KODAMA, Y. HAGIWARA; circ. 34,700.

SHIKOKU ISLAND

Ehime Shimbun: 12-1, 1-chome, Otemachi, Matsuyama, Ehime; f. 1876; Chair. Y. HIRATA; Man. Editor I. MATSUSHITA; circ. morning 179,859, evening 40,256.

Kochi Shimbun: 2-15, 3-chome, Honcho, Kochi City; f. 1904; Man. Editor H. KOMATSU; circ. morning 151,329, evening 91,959.

Shikoku Shimbun: 15-1, Nakono-machi, Takamatsu; f. 1889; Man. Editor Y. SAKANE; circ. morning 130,103, evening 20,907.

Tokushima Shimbun: 32-1 Saiwai-cho, Tokushima; f. 1941; Man. Editor K. SUGIMOTO; circ. morning 165,127, evening 40,203.

HOKKAIDO ISLAND

Asahi Shimbun: 1-1, 1-chome, Nishi, Kita Nijo, Sapporo City; f. 1959; Man. Editor M. OKEMOTO; circ. morning 161,119, evening 110,321.

Hokkai Times: 6, 10-chome, Minami-Ichijo, Nishi, Chuo-ku, Sapporo City; f. 1946; morning and evening; Man. Editor M. TAKAYASU; circ. morning 97,093, evening 47,442.

Hokkaido Shimbun: 6, 3-chome, Odori-Nishi, Sapporo; f. 1942; Editor T. YAMAKAWA; circ. morning and evening 800,000.

Mainichi Shimbun: 1, 6-chome, Kita-Nijo, Sapporo; f. 1959; Editor Z. WATANAKE; circ. morning 151,600, evening 82,900.

Nikkan Sports: 10, Minami-Ichijo, Nishi, Chuo-ku, Sapporo; f. 1962; morning; Pres. U. CHIZAKI; Man. Editor T. AKASAKA; circ. 92,000.

Yomiuri Shimbun: 11 Nishi, 1-chome, Minami-Sanjo, Sapporo; f. 1959; Editor H. TANAKA; circ. morning 189,948, evening 95,574.

KYUSHU ISLAND

Asahi Shimbun: 12-1, 1-chome, Sunatsu, Kokura-ku, Kita-Kyushu City; f. 1935; Man. Editor Y. WAKABAYASHI; circ. morning 738,486, evening 249,134.

Fukunichi: 2-1, 1-chome, Imaizumi-machi, Fukuoka; f. 1946; evening; Editor M. KIMURA; circ. 127,781.

Kagoshima Shimpo: 7-28 Jonan-cho, Kagoshima; f. 1959; morning; Editor N. KUWAHARA; circ. 47,000

Kumamoto Nichi-nichi Shimbun: 2-33 Kamidori-cho, Kumamoto-shi, Kumamoto; f. 1942; Editor H. AMANO; circ. morning 183,277, evening 48,893.

Mainichi Shimbun: 13-1, Konya-machi, Kokura Kita-ku, Kitakyushu; f. 1935; Man. Editor AKIRA HINO; circ. morning 615,000, evening 245,300.

Minami Nihon Shimbun: 1-2 Yasui-cho, Kagoshima-shi, Kagoshima; f. 1881; Man. Editor J. YAMASHITA; circ. morning 217,060, evening 35,698.

Miyazaki Nichinichi Shimbun: 1-33, 1-chome Takachihodori, Miyazaki; f. 1940; Man. Editor S. HIRASHIMA; circ. 123,923.

Nagasaki Jiji Shimbun: 6-24 Dajima-machi, Nagasaki; f. 1904; Man. Editor S. IWAMURA; circ. morning 65,153.

Nagasaki Shimbun: 6-24 Dejima, Nagasaki; f. 1889; Man. Editor Y. IKEMOTO; circ. morning 140,345; evening 140,559.

Nishi Nippon Shimbun: 4-20, 1-chome, Tenjin, Fukuoka; f. 1887; Man. Editor T. HANADA; circ. morning 614,219, evening 257,101.

Oita Godo Shimbun: 7-15, 3-chome, Funai-cho, Oita f. 1886; Man. Editor S. MASAMITU; circ. morning 142,633, evening 142,633.

Saga Shimbun: 3-8, 1-chome, Matsubara, Saga City; f. 1884; morning; Man. Editor S. NISHIMURA; circ. 92,242.

Shin Kyushu: 1-3 Kiyotaki-cho, Moji, Fukuoka; f. 1946; morning Man. Editor S. KITAJIMA; circ. 73,164.

Sports Nippon: 4-1, 1-chome, Kiyotaki-cho, Moji-ku, Kita-Kyushu; Man. Editor S. KITAJIMA; morning; circ. 151,063.

Yomiuri Shimbun: 1-11 Meiwa-machi, Kokura-ku, Kita-Kyushu; Man. Editor T. AOKI; circ. morning 648,700, evening 180,300.

OKINAWA PREFECTURE

Okinawa Times: P.O.B. 293, Naha, Okinawa; f. 1948; Japanese: morning and evening; Pres. KAZAFUMI UECHI; Man. Editor SEIKO HIGA; circ. 132,500.

Ryukyu Shimpo: P.O.B. 15, Naha, Okinawa; f. 1893; Japanese; morning and evening; Pres. SHUI IKEMIYAGI; Editor S. HOKAMA; circ. 90,548.

Morning Star: P.O.B. 282, Naha, Okinawa; English; Editor GENE SALZGAVER; circ. 15,000.

WEEKLIES

Asahi Graphic: Asahi Shimbun Publishing Co., Yurakucho, Chiyoda-ku, Tokyo; f. 1923; pictorial review; Editor MICHITO ITO; circ. 200,000.

Asahi Journal: Asahi Shimbun Publishing Co., Yurakucho, Chiyoda-ku, Tokyo; review.

Economist: 1-1-1 Hitotsubashi; Chiyoda-ku, Tokyo; f. 1923; published by the Mainichi Newspapers; Editorial Chief NOZOMU SEKINE; circ. 117,000.

The Gijitsu Journal: 8-10 Kudan kita, 1-chome, Chiyodaku, Tokyo; f. 1959; industrial technology.

Japan Company Handbook: 1-4 Hongoku-cho Nigonbashi, Chuo-ku, Tokyo; in English, published by *The Oriental Economist*.

Nipon Shogyo: 1-13-8 Bakuro-cho. Chuo-ku, Tokyo; f. 1895; Exec. Dir. SHIGETOSHI MATSUNAGA; circ. 35,000.

Oriental Economist: 1-4, Hongoku-cho, Nihonbashi, Chuo-ku. Tokyo; f. 1934; economics, politics; English edition; Pres. KIYOSHI UKAJI.

Shukan Asahi: Asahi Shimbun Publishing Co., 2–3 Yurakucho, Chiyoda-ku, Tokyo; circ. 1,300,000.

Shukan Bunshun: 3 Kioi-cho, Chiyoda-ku, Tokyo; f. 1959; general; circ. 550,000.

Shukan Sankei: 1–3 Otemachi, Chiyoda-ku, Tokyo; general.

Shukan Shincho: 71 Yarai-cho, Shinjuku-ku, Tokyo; general; circ. 910,000.

Shukan Yomiuri: 3-3 Ginza Nishi, Chuo-ku, Tokyo; Editor S. HARA; general.

Student Times: Japan Times Inc., 4-5-4 Shibaura, Minato-ku, Tokyo; English language.

Sunday Mainichi: 11-1 Yuraku-cho, Chiyoda-ku, Tokyo; circ. 1,200,000.

Tenji Mainichi: 2-36 Dojima, Kita-ku, Osaka; f. 1922; in Japanese braille; Editor MICHITOSHI ZENIMOTO; circ. 11,000.

Toyo Keizai Shimpo: 1-4 Hongkoku-cho, Nihonbashi, Chuo-ku, Tokyo; f. 1895; weekly; economics; Pres. K. UKAJI; circ. 100,000.

PERIODICALS

Airview: 601 Kojun Building, 6 Ginza, Tokyo; f. 1946; monthly; Editor E. SEKIGAWA.

Alpinist: 3-13, 2-chome, Konan, Minato-ku, Tokyo; f. 1942; circ. 100,000; Editor S. TAZAWA; monthly.

Asahi Camera: Yurakucho, Chiyoda-ku, Tokyo 100; f. 1926; photography; monthly; Editor AKIRA OKAMI; circ. 200,000.

Bijutsu Techô: Bijutsu Shuppan-sha, 15 Ichigaya Honmura-cho, Shinjuku-ku, Tokyo; f. 1948; monthly; fine arts.

Bungaku: Iwanami Shoten, 5-5, 2-chome, Hitotsubashi, Chiyoda-ku, Tokyo; f. 1933; Editor YOSHIYA TAMURA.

Bungei-Shunju: 3 Kioi-cho, Chiyoda-ku, Tokyo; f. 1923; popular monthly; general.

Chuo Koron: 2-1 Kyobashi, Chuo-ku, Tokyo; f. 1886; monthly; political, economic, scientific and literary; Chief Editor KINJIRO SASAHARA.

Design: Bijutsu Shuppanh-sha, 15 Ichigaya-honmura-cho, Shinjuku-ku, Tokyo; f. 1955; monthly; covers all aspects of design.

Fujin Koron: Chuo Koron-sha, 1, 2-chome, Kyobashi, Chuo-ku, Tokyo; women's literary monthly.

Geijitsu Shincho: 71 Yarai-cho, Shinjuku-ku, Tokyo; f. 1950; monthly; fine arts, music, architecture, drama and design; Editor-in-Chief SHOZO YAMAZAKI.

Gekkan Rodo Mondai: Nippon Hyoron Sha 14 Sugumachi, Shinjuku-ku, Tokyo; labour problem monthly.

Gengo-Seikatsu: Chikuma-shobo, Chiyoda-ku, Tokyo; f. 1951; language and life monthly; Editor NAOO HARADA; circ. 10,000.

Horitsu Jiho: 14 Sugamachi, Shinjuku-ku, Tokyo; law journal.

Ie-no-Hikari (*Light of Home*): 11 Funagawara-cho, Ichigaya, Shinjuku-ku, Tokyo; f. 1925; monthly; rural and general interest; Pres. RYOHEI ADACHI; Editor NAOMICHI MURATANI; circ. 1,300,000.

Industries of Japan: Mainichi Newspapers, Tokyo; f. 1952; Editor YOSHIMASA SUMINO.

Japan Almanac: Mainichi Newspapers, Tokyo; f. 1972; English yearbook on Japan; Editor YOSHIMASA SUMINO.

The Japan Architect: 31-2, Yushima 2-chome, Bunkyo-ku, Tokyo 113; f. 1956; monthly; international edition of *Shinkenchiku*; Editor SHOZO BABA; Publisher YOSHIO YOSHIDA; circ. 17,000.

Japan Economic Yearbook: Nihonbashi, Tokyo; in English; published by *The Oriental Economist*.

Japan Electric Engineering: 11-15 Higashi Gotanda, 1-chome, Shinagawa-ku; monthly; circ. 60,000.

Japan Electric Industry: 11-15 Higashi Gotanda, 1-chome, Shinagawa-ku; monthly; circ. 65,000.

Japan Quarterly: Asahi Shimbun-sha, Yuraku-cho, Chiyoda-ku, Tokyo; in English; Exec. Editor YUICHIRO KOMIWAMI.

Jitsugyo No Nihon: Ginza Nishi, Chuo-ku, Tokyo; semi-monthly; economic and business.

Junkan Yomiuri: 3-1 Ginza Nishi, Chuo-ku, Tokyo; f. 1942; three times monthly.

Kagaku: Iwanami Shoten, publishers 2-5-5 Hitotsubashi Chiyoda-ku, Tokyo; f. 1931; Editor YOKO NATORI.

Kagaku Asahi: 2-6-1 Yuraku-cho, Chiyoda-ku, Tokyo; f. 1941; scientific; Editor SHINYA ITO; monthly.

Kagakushi-Kenkyu: Department of Humanities, Tokyo Institute of Technology, 2-12-1, O-okayama, Meguro-ku, Tokyo; quarterly Journal of the History of Science Society of Japan.

Keizai Hyoron: 14 Sugamachi, Shinjuku, Tokyo; economic review.

Keizaizin (*Home Economics*): Kansai Economics Federation, Shin-Dai-Bldg., Dojima-Hamadori, Kita-ku, Osakao economics; monthly; Editor Y. MIYANO.

Kikanhanga: Bijutsa Shuppan-sha, 15 Ichigaya-honmura-cho, Shinjuku-ku, Tokyo; f. 1968; quarterly; covers all aspects of printing.

Kokka: Asahi Shimbun Publishing Co., 3, 2-chome, Yuraku-cho, Chiyoda-ku, Tokyo; Far Eastern art, monthly.

Mizue: Bijutsu Shuppan-sha, 15 Ichigaya-honmura-cho, Shinjuku-ku, Tokyo; f. 1905; monthly; fine arts.

Museum: Bijutsu Shuppan-sha, 15 Ichigaya-Honmura-cho, Shinjuku-ku, Tokyo; f. 1951; monthly bulletin of Tokyo National Museum.

Nogyo Asahi: 2-3 Yuraku-cho, Chiyoda-ku, Tokyo; monthly; scientific.

Ongaku no Tomo: Kagurazaka 6-30, Shinjuku-ku, Tokyo; music; monthly.

The Pacific Community: Jiji Press Ltd., Central P.O.B. 1007, Tokyo; f. April 1969; political, economic, diplomatic, cultural, military, etc.; quarterly (Jan., April, July, Oct.) in English; Editor KIKUO SATO; Man. Editor NORIO IGUCHI; circ. 6,000.

Seibutsu-Kagaku (*Biological Sciences*): edited and publ. by the Japanese Inst. of Biological Sciences, c/o Dept. of Biology, Ochanomizu University, P.O. Koishi-kawa, Tokyo 112; f. 1949; quarterly.

Sekai: Iwanami Shoten 3, 2-chome, Kanda, Hitotsubashi, Tokyo; f. 1946; reviews; monthly; Editor RYOSUKE YASUE.

Shincho: 71 Yarai-cho, Shinjuku-ku, Tokyo; literary; monthly; Editor JUICHI SAITO; circ. 30,000.

Shinkenchiku: 31-2, Yushima 2-chome, Bunkyo-ku, Tokyo 113; f. 1924; monthly architectural journal; Editor SHOZO BABA; Publisher YASUGORO YOSHIOKA; circ. 48,000.

Shiso (*Ideology*): Iwanami Shoten 3, 2-chome, Kanda, Hitotsubashi, Tokyo; f. 1921; Editor TORU MIDORIKAWA; monthly.

Shizen (*Nature*): Chuo Koron Sha, 1, 2-chome, Kyobashi, Chuo-ku, Tokyo; scientific monthly.

Shosetsu Shincho: Shincho-sha, 71 Yarai-cho, Shinjuku-ku, Tokyo; f. 1945; monthly; literature; Chief Editor TOSHIO SATO.

Shufu to Seikatsu: 1-2 Nishi Kanda, Chiyoda-ku, Tokyo; monthly: women's magazine.

So-en: Bunka Publishing Bureau, 1-22, 3-chome, Yoyogi, Shibuya-ku, Tokyo; fashion monthly; Chief Editor ISAO IMAIDA; circ. 400,000.

Statistical Monthly (*Toyo Keizai Tokei Geppo*): published by *The Oriental Economist*, 1-4 Hongoku-cho, Nihonbashi, Chuo-ku, Tokyo; f. 1895.

Sûgaku (*Mathematics*): Mathematical Society of Japan, c/o Faculty of Science, University of Tokyo; f. 1947; quarterly.

Tenbo: Chikuma-Shobo, Chiyoda-ku, Tokyo; f. 1964; general; monthly; Editor NADO HARADA; circ. 30,000.

Yama-To-Keikoku (*Mountain and Valley*): 1-1-33 Shiba-Daimon, Minato-ku, Tokyo; monthly; mountain climbing.

Yomiuri Nenkan (*Yomiuri Yearbook*): published by Yomiuri Shimbun, Ootemachi, Chiyoda-ku, Tokyo 100; f. 1946, general year book and almanac; Editor K. YAMADA.

Zosen: Tokyo News Service Ltd., 10 Ginza Nishi, 8-chome, Chuo-ku, Tokyo; monthly, in English; shipbuilding.

NEWS AGENCIES

Jiji Tsushin-Sha (*Jiji Press*): 1-3 Hibiya Park, Chiyoda-ku, Tokyo; f. 1945; general news service by facsimile; Man. Dir. TATURO SATO; publ. *Yearbook*.

Kyodo Tushin (*Kyodo News Service*): 2 Aoi-cho Akasaka, Minato-ku, Tokyo; f. 1945; supplies press, radio and television with foreign and domestic news; Pres. SHINTARO FUKUSHIMA; Chief Editor M. NAGAYO.

Radiopress Inc.: 7 Ichigaya, Shinjuku-ku, Tokyo; f. 1945; Pres. K. NAKADA; Man. Editor T. NAKADATE.

Soviet News: Tokyo; monitors Radio Moscow broadcasts.

Sun Telephoto: Palaceside Bldg., 1-1, 1-chome, Hitotsubashi, Chiyoda-ku, Tokyo; f. 1952; Pres. K. MATSUOKA; Man. Editor Y. YAMAMOTO.

FOREIGN BUREAUX

Tokyo

ABC: Asahi Bldg., 6-7, Ginza, 6-chome, Chuo-ku; Bureau Chief IRWIN M. CHAPMAN.

ADN News Agency (*German Democratic Republic*): 9-9, 4-chome, Jingu-mae, Shibuya-ku; Correspondent OTTO MANN.

Agence France-Presse: Asahi Shimbun Shinkan, 3-2 chome Yurakucho, Chiyoda-ku; Bureau Chief PIERRE BRISARD.

ANSA: Kyodo Tsushin Kaikan, 2 Aoi-cho, Akasaka, Minato-ku; Correspondent MARIA ROMILDA GIORGIS.

Antara: Kyodo News Service Bldg., No. 2, Aoicho Akasaka, Minato-ku; Bureau Chief ALADDIN.

AP: Asahi Shimbun Bldg., 2-3, Yuraku-cho, Chiyoda-ku, Bureau Chief H. HARTZENBUSCH.

Bulgarian News Agency: 1-10, 5-chome, Minami Aoyama, Minato-ku 107; Correspondent DANIELA KANEVA.

Central News Agency of China: 5-6 Iidabashi, 1-chome, Chiyoda-ku; Bureau Chief LEE CHIA.

Czechoslovak News Agency: 5-13, Jingumae 4-Chome, Shibuya-ku; Bureau Chief IVO STOLC.

Deutsche Presse-Agentur (dpa): Shisei Kaikan, Room 202, Hibiya 2, Chiyoda-ku; Bureau Chief GERHARD MENNING.

Hapdong News Agency: Kyodo Press Bldg., 2 Aoi-cho, Minato-ku; Bureau Chief SANG KWON LEE.

Hungarian News Agency: 5-13, 4-chome, Jingumae, Shibuya-ku 150; Correspondent BÉLA ELIAS.

Keystone: 12-3, Koji-machi, Chiyoda-ku; Bureau Chief H. J. ABRAHAMS.

Interpress (*Poland*): Daikan-yama Plaza Annex, 24-7, Sarugaku-cho, Shibuya-ku; Correspondent YOLANTA LICZBINSKA.

New China News Agency: 35-23, 3-chome, Ebisu, Shibuya-ku 150; Correspondent KAO TI.

Novosti: 3-9-13, Higashi-gotanda, Shinagawa-ku; Bureau Chief A. M. LAZAREV.

Prensa Latina: 1-26, 3-chome, Moto Azabu, Minato-ku 106; Correspondent VICTORIO M. COPA.

Reuters: Kyodo Tsushin Kaikan, 2 Akasaka, Aoi-chi, Minato-ku; Chief Representative MICHAEL NEALE.

Sisa News Agency: 1-14-12 Shinkawa, Chuo-ku; Bureau Chief WHA BONG SHINN.

Tass: 1-5, Hon-machi, Shibuya-ku; Bureau Chief VICTOR ZATSEPIN.

UPI: Palaceside Bldg., 1-1 Hitotsubashi 1-chome, Chiyoda-ku; Man., North Asia, ARNOLD B. C. DIBBLE.

PRESS ASSOCIATIONS

Nihon Shinbun Kyokai (*Japan Newspaper Pnblishers and Editors Association*): Shiseikaikan Building, Hibiya Park, Chiyoda-ku, Tokyo 100; f. 1946; mems. include 172 companies, including 112 daily newspapers, 8 news agencies 51 radio and TV companies, and 1 non-daily newspaper; Pres. TOMOO HIROOKA; Sec.-Gen. MASAAKI KASAGI; publs. *The Japanese Press* (annual), *Shimbun Kenkyu* (monthly), *Shimbun Kyokai Ho* (weekly), *Nihon Shimbun Nenkan* (annual), *Shimbun Insatsu Gijutsu* (quarterly), *Shimbun Keiei* (quarterly).

Foreign Correspondents' Club of Japan: 1-2, Marunouchi 2-chome, Chiyoda-ku, Tokyo, Japan 100.

Japan Magazine Publishers' Association: 7, 1-chome, Kanda Surugadai, Chiyoda-ku, Tokyo.

PUBLISHERS

KYOTO

Jimbun Shoin: Takakura-Nishi-Hairu, Bukkoji-dori, Shimokyoku; f. 1922; literary, philosophy, history, fine art; Pres. MUTSUHISA WATANABE.

TOKYO

Baifukan Co. Ltd.: 4-3-12 Kudan Minami, 4-chome, Chiyoda-ku; f. 1924; mathematics, natural and social science, technology; Pres. K. YAMAMOTO.

Bijutsu Shuppan-Sha: 15 Ichigaya Honmura-cho, Shinjuku-ku; f. 1906; art and architecture; Pres. ATSUSHI OSHITA.

Chijin Shokan 2-112 Totsuka-machi, Shinjuku-ku; Science and technical, agriculture, geography; Pres. ISAMU KAMIJO.

Chuokoron-sha Inc.: 2-1, Kyobashi, Chuo-ku; f. 1886; philosophy, history, sociology, literature; Pres. HOJI SHIMANAKA.

Froebel-Kan Co. Ltd.: 3-1 Kanda Ogawa-machi, Chiyoda-ku; f. 1907; juvenile, educational, music; Pres.KENSUKE SUGANO;

Fukuinkan Shoten: 1-1-9, Misaki-cho, Chiyoda-ku, Tokyo; f. 1950; juvenile, education, religion; Pres. TADASHI MATSUI.

Gakken Co. Ltd.: 4-40-5, Kamiikedai, Ohta-ku; f. 1946; juvenile, education, reference; Man. Dir. HIROSHI FURUOKA.

Hakusui-Sha: 3-24 Kanda-Ogawa-machi, Chiyoda-ku; f. 1915, general literature, science and languages; Pres. TEISHI KUSANO.

Heibon Sha: 4-1 Yonbancho, Chiyoda-ku; f. 1914; encyclopaedias, art, history books, Japanese and Chinese literature, etc.; Pres. KUNIHIKO SHIMONAKA.

Hokuseido Press, The: 3-12, Kanda-Nishiki-cho, Chiyoda-ku; f. 1914; Pres. JUMPEI NAKATSUCHI; regional non-fiction.

Ie-No-Hikari Association: 11 Funagawara-cho, Ichigaya, Shinjuku-ku; f. 1925; agriculture, education; Pres. RYOHEI ADACHI; Man. Dir. YOSHIRO TAKAHASHI.

Iwanami Shoten: 2-5-5, Hitotsubashi, Chiyoda-ku; f. 1913; natural and social sciences, literature, history, geography; Pres. YUJIRO IWANAMI.

Kanehara & Co. Ltd.: 31-14, 2-chome Yushima Bunkyo-ku, Tokyo 113-11; f. 1875; medical, agricultural, engineering and scientific; Pres. HIDEO KANEHARA.

Kodansha Ltd.: 2-12-21, Otowa 2-chome, Bunkyo-ku, Tokyo 112; f. 1909; art, education, children's picture books, fiction, cookery, encyclopaedias, dictionaries, paperbacks in Japanese; weekly, monthly and quarterly magazines; Pres. SHOICHI NOMA.

Kyoritsu Shuppan Co. Ltd.: 6-19 Kobinata, 4-chome, Bunkyo-ku, Tokyo 112; f. 1926; scientific and technical; Pres. MASAO NANJO.

Maruzen Company Ltd.: 3-10, Nohonbashi, 2-chome, Chuo-ku; f. 1869; general; Pres. SHINGO IIZUMI; Man. Dirs. KIYOSHI SAKURAI; MASAO NAKATA.

Misuzu Shobo Publishing Co.: 3-17-15, Hongo, Bunkyo-ku: f. 1947; fine art, science, medicine, politics; Pres. TAMIO KITANO; Man. Dir. TOSHITO OBI.

Nikkan Kogyo Shimbun: 1-8-10 Kudan Kita, 1-chome, Chiyoda-ku, Tokyo 102; f. 1911, revived 1945; technical, business and management, dictionaries; Pres. IKUTARO YOSHIKAWA.

Nippon Hyoron Sha: 14 Suga-machi, Shinjuku-ku; law, economics, sociology, business; Pres. MIOKICHI SUZUKI.

Obunsha Co. Ltd.: 55 Yokodera-cho Shinjuku-ku; f. 1931; textbooks, reference books, general science and fiction; magazines; audio-visual aids; Pres. YOSHIO AKAO.

OHM-Sha Ltd., The: 3-1 chome, Kanda-Nishiki-cho, Chiyoda-ku; f. 1914; engineering, technical and scientific; Pres. S. MITSUI; Man. Dir. K. TOBE.

Ongaku No Tomo Sha Corpn.: 6-30, Kagurazaka, Shinjuku-ku; f. 1941; music books, magazines and scores; Chair. KEIZO HORIUCHI; Pres. SUNAO ASAKA.

Risosha: 46 Akagashita-machi, Shinjuku-ku; f. 1927; philosophy, religion, social science; Pres. S. OHE.

Sanseido (*Sanseido Publishing Co.*): 1-1, Kanda-Jinbo-cho, Chiyoda-ku; dictionaries, education, languages, science, sociology; Pres. MASAKAZE OGURA.

Seibundo-Shinkosha Publishing Co. Ltd.: 1-chome Nishikicho, Kanda Chiyoda-ku, Tokyo; f. 1912; technical and scientific, agriculture, history, geography; Pres. and Man. Dir. SHIGEO OGAWA.

Shinkenchiku-Sha Ltd.: 31-2, Yushima,, 2-chome, Bunkyo-ku; f. 1925; architectural; Editor and Publisher Y. YOSHIOKA; Man. Dir. Y. YOSHIDA.

Shogakukan Publishing Co. Ltd.: 2-3, Hitotsubashi, Chiyoda-ku; f. 1922; juvenile, education, geography; Pres. T. OHGA.

Shokokusha Publishing Co. Inc.: 25 Saka-machi, Shinjuku-ku; f. 1932; architectural, technical and fine art; Chair. G. SHIMOIDE; Pres. G. SHIMOIDE; Man. Dir. K. KOMPARU.

Shufunotomo Co. Ltd.: 6, 1-chome, Surugadai, Kanda, Chiyoda-ku, Tokyo; f. 1916; domestic science, juvenile, fine art, gardening, handicraft, cookery; monthly women's magazine; Pres. KAZUO ISHIKAWA.

Shunju-Sha Co. Ltd.: 2-18-6 Sotokanda, Chiyoda-ku; f. 1918; philosophy, religion, literary, economics, music, etc.; Man. R. KANDA.

Taishukan Shoten: 3-24, Kanda-Nishiki-cho, Choyoda-ku; f. 1918; reference, language, sport, Buddhism, audio-visual aids, dictionaries; Chair. KATASHI INOUE; Pres. TOSHIO SUZUKI.

Tokyo News Tsushiu-Sha: 8-10 Ginza-Nishi, Chuo-ku; f. 1947; sociology, economics, general non-fiction; Pres. I. OKUYAMA.

University of Tokyo Press: 7-3-1 Hongo, Bunkyo-ku; f. 1951; humanities, history, sociology, economics, politics, science; Man. K. ISHII.

Yama To Keikoku Sha Co. Ltd.: 1-1-33, Shiba-Daimon, Minato-ku;, f. 1930 mountaineering, skiing and travel books; Pres. K. KAWASAKI.

Yamakawa Shuppan Sha: 1-13-13, Uchi-kanda, Chiyoda-ku; history, education, dictionaries, textbooks; Pres. SHIGEJI NOZAWA.

Yuhikaku Co.: 17, 2-chome, Kanda Jimbo-cho, Chiyoda-ku; f. 1877; social sciences; Dir. T. EGUSA; Man. S. EGUSA.

Zeimukeiri Kyokai: 3-53-9, Totsuka-machi, Shinjuku-ku; law, economics, business, sociology, education; Pres. HANGO OTSUBO.

Zenkoku Kyodo Shuppan: 1-10-32, Wakaba, Shinjuku-ku; agriculture, sociology, economics; Pres. KINNOSUKE ONAKA.

Japan Book Publishers Association: 6 Fukuro-machi, Shinjuku-ku; Tokyo.

Publishers Association for Cultural Exchange: 2-1, Saruga-ku-cho, 1-chome, Chiyoda-ku, Tokyo.

RADIO AND TELEVISION

There were an estimated 70,794,000 radio receiving sets in 1972 and 25,563,999 televisions in 1974.

Nippon Hoso Kyokai, N.H.K. (*Japan Broadcasting Corporation*): Broadcasting Centre, 2-2-1 Jinnan, Shikuya-ku, Tokyo; f. 1925; Chair. Board of Govs. S. KUDO; Pres. KICHIRO ONO.

N.H.K. is a non-commercial public corporation whose Governors are appointed by the government. Five (2 TV and 3 radio) networks and 5,039 stations cover the country, the TV ones equipped for colour broadcasting, equally divided between general and educational networks; central stations at Tokyo, Osaka, Nagoya, Hiroshima, Kumamoto, Sendai, Sapporo and Matsuyama. The Overseas Service broadcasts in 21 languages.

National Association of Commercial Broadcasters in Japan: Bungei Shunju Bldg., 3, Kioicho, Chiyoda-ku, Tokyo 102; Pres. YOSOJI KOBAYASHI; Exec. Dir. KAZUO SUGIYAMA; Sec.-Gen. NAGATO IZUMI; association of 107 companies (90 TV companies, 17 radio companies. Among 90 TV companies, 36 operate radio and TV) with 180 radio stations and 1,832 TV stations. They include:

Asahi Broadcasting Corp.: 2-2 Oyodo-Minami, Oyodo-ku, Osaka; Chair. T. HIRAI.

Far East Network (AFRTS): H.Q.S. A.P.O. San Francisco Ca. 96268; serves U.S. forces in Japan; 5 stations (Tokyo, Okinawa, Misawa, Iwakuni, Sasebo) operate 24 hours; 5 TV stations (Misawa, Iwakuni, Sasebo, Cp. Zama and Okinawa); 1 FM station (Okinawa); Commander Lieut.-Col. FRANK J. MORRIS, U.S.A.F.

Nippon Cultural Broadcasting, Inc.: 1-5, Wakabo-cho, Shinju-ku, Tokyo; Pres. S. TOMODA.

Nippon System, Inc.: 7, 1-chome, Yuraku-cho, Chiyoda-ku, Tokyo; Chair. K. UEMURA; Pres. N. SHIKANAI.

Nihon Short-Wave Broadcasting Co.: 9-15 Akasaka 1-chome, Minato-ku, Tokyo; Pres. M. NAKAJIMA.

Okinawa Hozo Kyokai (*Okinawa Public Broadcasting System*): Service Centre 342, Sobe, Naha, Okinawa; Pres. C. KABIRA; Vice-Pres. H. TANIGUCHI.

Okinawa Television Broadcasting Co. Ltd.: 2-32-1 Kume, Naha, Okinawa; f. 1958; Pres. Y. YAMASHIRO; Man. Dir. Y. TOMITA.

Ryukyu Broadcasting Corporation Ltd.: 2-3-1, Kumoji, Naha, Okinawa; Pres. T. TOMA.

Tokyo Broadcasting System, Inc.: 5-3-6, Akasaka, Minato-ku, Tokyo; f. 1951; Chair. JUNZO IMAMICHI; Pres. HIROSHI SUWA.

There are also 77 commercial stations operated by Radio Tokyo, Asahi Broadcasting Co., Nippon TV Network Co., Nippon Educational TV Co. and others, including:

NET Television Network Co. Ltd.: 4-10, 6-chome Roppongi, Minato-ku, Tokyo; f. 1957; Chair. YOSHIO AKAO; Pres. MAKOTO TAKANO.

YTV—Yomiuri Telecasting Corporation: 2-74 Iwaicho, Kita-ku, Osaka; f. 1957; 18 hrs. broadcasting a day, of which 62 hrs. per week in colour; Pres. Y. MUTAI; Exec. Dir. T. OKANO; Programme Man. U. TANAKA.

Regular colour television transmissions started in 1960.

TELEVISION NEWS AGENCIES

NET-Ashi Productions Ltd.: 6-4-10 Roppong, Minato-ku Tokyo; f. 1958; Pres. T. FUJII.

Kyodo Television News: 7 Kawata-cho, Ichigaya, Shinjuku-ku, Tokyo; f. 1958; Chair. R. NOZAWA; Pres. N. AIZAWA.

FINANCE

BANKING

(cap.=capital; p.u.=paid up; dep.=deposits; m.=million; amounts in yen)

Japan's central bank and note-issuing body is the Bank of Japan, founded in 1882. More than half the credit business of the country is handled by approximately one hundred commercial banks and three long-term credit institutions, collectively designated "All Banks". The most important of these are the thirteen city banks, many of which have a distinguished history, reaching back to the days of the *zaibatsu*, the private entrepreneurial organizations on which Japan's capital wealth was built up before the Second World War. Although the *zaibatsu* were abolished as integral industrial and commercial enterprises during the Allied Occupation, the several businesses and industries which bear the former *zaibatsu* names, such as Mitsubishi, Mitsui and Sumitomo, continue to flourish and to give each other mutual assistance through their respective banks and trust corporations. Among the commercial banks, one, the Bank of Tokyo, specializes in foreign exchange business, while the Industrial Bank of Japan provides a large proportion of the finance for capital investment by industry. The Japan Long-Term Credit Bank also specializes in industrial finance; the work of these two privately-owned banks is supplemented by the government Japan Development Bank.

The Government has established a number of other specialized organs to supply essential services not performed by the private banks. Thus the Japan Export-Import Bank advances credits for exports of heavy industrial products and imports of raw materials in bulk. A Housing Loan Corporation assists firms building housing for their employees, while the Agriculture, Forestry and Fisheries Finance Corporation gives loans to the named industries for equipment purchases. Similar services are provided for small businesses by the Small Business Finance Corporation.

An important part is played in the financial activity of the country by co-operatives, and by the many small enterprise institutions. Each prefecture has its own federation of co-operatives, with the Central Co-operative Bank of Agriculture and Forestry as the common central financial institution. This Central Co-operative Bank also serves as an agent for the government's Agriculture, Forestry and Fisheries Finance Corporation.

The commonest form of savings is through the government-operated Postal Savings System, which collects petty savings from the public by means of the post office network. The funds thus made available are used as loan funds by the government financial institutions, through the government's Trust Fund Bureau.

Clearing houses operate in each major city of Japan, and total 80 institutions. The largest are those of Tokyo and Osaka.

Central Bank

Nippon Ginko (*Bank of Japan*): 2-2-1 Hongoku-cho, Nihonbashi, Chuo-ku, Tokyo; f. 1882; cap. 100m., dep. 4,154,660m. (March 1975); Gov. Teiichiro Moringa Vice-Gov. Michikazu Kono.

Principal Commercial Banks

Bank of Fukuoka Ltd.: 12-18 Kamikawabata-machi, Hakata-ku, Fukuoka; f. 1945; cap. 5,000m., dep. 915,202m. (March 1975); Chair. Gojiro Arikawa; Toshiaki Yamashita.

Bank of Okinawa: 1-42 Miebashi, Naha, Okinawa; cap. 1,650,000m., dep. 158,396,116m. (March 1975); Pres. Hiroshi Senaga.

Bank of the Ryukyus Ltd.: 1-13 Kumoji 1-chome, Naha, Okinawa; f. 1948; cap. 2,001m., dep. 197,680m. (Sept. 1974); Pres. Shuei Sakahama.

Bank of Tokyo Ltd.: 1-6-3, chome, Nihombashi Hongoku-cho, Chuo-ku, Tokyo; f. 1946; specializes in foreign exchange business; cap. p.u. 60,000m., dep. 4,568,154m. (Sept. 1975); Chair. Sumio Hara; Pres. Soichi Yokoyama.

Dai-Ichi Kangyo Bank Ltd.: 6-2 1-chome, Marunouchi, Chiyoda-ku, Tokyo; f. 1971; cap. p.u. 71,000m., dep. 6,772,218m. (March 1975); Chair. Kaoru Inouye; Pres. T. Yokota.

Daiwa Bank Ltd.: 21 Bongomachi, 2-chome, Higashi-ku, Osaka; f. 1918; cap. p.u. 48,000m., dep. 2,463,808m. (March 1975); Chair. Mitsuru Kume; Pres. Susumu Furukawa.

Fuji Bank Ltd.: 1-chome, Otemachi, Chiyoda-ku, Tokyo; f. 1880; cap. p.u. 66,000m., dep. 6,939,928m. (March 1976); Chair. of Board and Pres. Takuji Matsuzawa.

Hokkaido Takushoku Bank Ltd.: 7 Nishi, 3-chome, Odori, Chuo-ku, Sapporo-city; f. 1900; cap. 20,000m. dep. 1,734,864m. (March 1975); Chair. Tetsuo Nakahara; Pres. Takei Tojo.

Hokuriku Bank Ltd.: 2-26, Tsutsumichodon 1-chome, Toyama; f. 1943; cap. 15,000m., dep. 1,122,949m. (March 1975); Pres. Seisuke Mase.

Industrial Bank of Japan Ltd.: 3-3 Marunouchi 1-chome, Chiyoda-ku, Tokyo 100; f. 1902; cap. 64,000m.; dep. 1,411,451m. (March 1975); Chair. Isao Masamune; Pres. Kisaburo Ikeura.

Kyowa Bank Ltd.: 5-1, Marunouchi, 1-chome, Chiyoda-ku, Tokyo; f. 1945; cap. 32,000m. dep. 2,885,535m. (March 1975); Pres. Yoshiaki Irobe; Chair. Shuichi Shinohara.

Mitsubishi Bank Ltd.: 7-1 Marunouchi, 2-chome, Chiyoda-ku, Tokyo; f. 1919; cap. 66,000m., dep. 6,565,919m. (March 1976); Chair. Wataru Tajitsu; Pres. Toshio Nakamura.

Mitsui Bank Ltd.: 1-2 Yuraku-cho 1-chome, Chiyoda-ku, Tokyo; f. 1876; cap. p.u. 40,000m., dep. 3,899,344m. (March 1975); Chair. Goro Koyama; Pres. Joji Itakura.

Nippon Kogyo Ginko (*The Industrial Bank of Japan Ltd.*): 3-3 Marunouchi 1-chome, Chiyoda-ku, Tokyo 100; f. 1902; medium- and long-term financing of industrial enterprises in Japan; cap. p.u. 64,000m., dep. 1,411,451m.; loans and discounts 4,408,593m. (March 1975); Chair Isao Masamune; Pres. Kisaburo Ikeura.

Saitama Bank Ltd.: 9-15, Takasago 2-chome, Urawa, Saitama Prefecture; f. 1943; cap. 22,680m., dep. 2,148,455m. (March 1975); Chair. Tadateru Matsudaira; Pres. Kyosuke Nagashima.

Sanwa Bank Ltd.: 10 Fushimimachi, 4-chome, Higashi-ku, Osaka 541; f. 1933; cap. 66,000m., dep. 6,288,538m. (March 1976); Chair. T. Watanabe; Pres. T. Murano.

Sumitomo Bank Ltd.: 22, 5-chome, Kitahama, Higashi-ku, Osaka; f. 1895; cap. 66,000m., dep. 5,765,390m. (March 1975) Chair. Shoze Hotta; Pres. Kyonosuke Ibe.

Taiyo Kobe Bank Ltd., The: 56 Naniwa-cho, Ikutaku, Kobe; f. 1973; cap. p.u. 49,000m., dep. 4,653,270m. (March 1976); Chair. Kazuyuki Kohno; Pres. Shinichi Ishino.

Tokai Bank Ltd.: 21-24, Nishiki, 3-chome, Naka-ku, Nagoya; f. 1941; cap. p.u. 54,500m., dep. 4,788,641m. (March 1976); Chair. and Pres. Shigemitsu Miyake.

Government Credit Institutions

Agriculture, Forestry and Fisheries Finance Corporation: 9-3, Otemachi 1-chome, Chiyoda-ku, Tokyo; f. 1953; finances plant and equipment investment; cap. 171,379m.; Pres. Seizo Takeda; Vice-Pres. Hajime Iwao.

Central Bank for Agriculture, Forestry and Fisheries Co-operatives: 182-1 Matsuo, Naha, Okinawa; cap. 11.4m., dep. 20.8m. (June 1969); Pres. Genpei Oshiro.

Central Bank for Commercial and Industrial Co-operatives (*Shoko Chukin Bank*): Yaesu 6-5, Chuo-ku, Tokyo; f. 1936 to provide normal banking services to facilitate finance for smaller enterprise co-operatives and other organizations formed mainly by small- and medium-scale enterprises; 20,871 affiliated orgs.; cap. p.u. 50,200m., dep. 577,527m. (June 1973); Pres. Hajime Takagi; Vice-Pres. Makoto Watanabe; publ. *Shoko Kinyu* (Commerce-Industry Financing, monthly).

Central Co-operative Bank for Agriculture and Forestry (*Norinchukin Bank*): 1-8-3 Ohtemachi, Chiyoda-ku, Tokyo; f. 1923; apex organ of financial system of agricultural, forestry and fisheries co-operatives; receives deposits from individual co-operatives, federations and agricultural enterprises; extends loans to these and to local government authorities and public corporations; adjusts excess and shortage of funds within co-operative system; issues debentures, invests funds and engages in other regular banking business; 13,183 mems.; cap. p.u. 20,000m., dep. and debentures 3,292,246m.; Pres. Shinkichi Katayanagi; Vice-Pres. Kanichi Ohshima; publs. *The Central Co-operative Bank Review* (quarterly), *Statistics of Agricultural Finance in Japan* (irregular).

Export-Import Bank of Japan, The: 1-9-1 Otemachi, Chiyoda-ku, Tokyo; f. 1950 to supplement or encourage the financing of exports, imports and overseas investment by ordinary financial institutions; cap. p.u. 639,300m., dep. 2,249,024m. (Sept. 1973); Pres. Satoshi Sumita.

Housing Loan Corporation: 10-4, 1-chome, Koraku, Bunkyo-ku, Tokyo; f. 1950 to provide long-term capital for the construction of housing at low interest rates; cap. 97,200m.; funds disbursed 1,783,116m. (end March 1970); Pres. Kiyoshi Asamura; Vice-Pres. Toshihide Takahashi; publs. *Housing Loan Report* (monthly), *Housing Loan Annual Report*, *Business Statistics* (annual), *Guidance of Loans for Housing* (annual), *Table of the Housing Loan Corporation's Business* (annual).

Japan Development Bank, The: 9-1, 1-chome, Otemachi, Chiyoda-ku, Tokyo; f. 1951; provides long-term loans; subscribes for corporate bonds; guarantees corporate obligations; invests in specific projects; borrows funds from Govt. and abroad; issues external loan bonds; cap. 760m.; loans outstanding (March 1975) $9,774,248; Gov. EIICHI YOSHIOKA; Vice-Gov. TAKATOMO WATANABE.

Long-Term Credit Bank of Japan Ltd., The: 2-4, Otemachi 1-chome, Chiyoda-ku, Tokyo; f. 1952; cap. p.u. 34,000m., dep. and debentures 2,829,875m. (Sept. 1972); Pres. BINSUKE SUGIURA; Chair. KAZUO MIYAZAKI.

Medical Care Facilities Finance Corporation: 2 Nibancho, Chiyoda-ku, Tokyo; f. 1960; cap. and dep. 11,500m.; Pres. MASAYOSHI YAMAMOTO.

Okinawa Development Finance Corporation: Kokuba Bldg., 21-1, 3-chome, Kumoji, Naha; f. 1972; cap. 24,544m. (May 1972); Pres. HIROSHI SATAKE.

The Overseas Economic Co-operation Fund: 1-1 Uchisaiwaicho, 2-chome, Chiyoda-ku, Tokyo; f. 1961; cap. U.S. $192.62m. (Sept. 1970); Pres. Dr. SABURO OKITA.

People's Finance Corporation: 1-9-3 Ohtemachi, Chiyoda-ku, Tokyo; f. 1949 to supply business funds particularly to very small enterprises among those sections of the population who are unable to obtain loans from banks and other private financial institutions; cap. p.u. 20,000m.; 4,208 mems.; Pres. YASUSHI SAWADA; Vice-Pres. NOBUKUNI YOSHIDA; publ. *Chosageppo* (monthly research report in Japanese).

Small Business Finance Corporation: 9-3, 1-chome, Ohtemachi, Chiyoda-ku, Tokyo; f. 1953 to lend equipment funds and long-term operating funds (directly or indirectly through agencies) which are necessary for the promotion of small businesses (capital not more than 100m., or not more than 300 employees) but which are not easily secured from other financial institutions; cap. p.u. 25,210m. (March 1973) wholly subscribed by Government; Gov. EIICHI YOSHIOKA; Vice-Gov. SHINICHI ARAI; publs. *Financial Statistics Quarterly*, *Monthly Bulletin of Small Business Finance Corporation.*

PRINCIPAL TRUST BANKS

Mitsubishi Trust and Banking Corporation: 4-5, 1-chome, Marunouchi, Chiyoda-ku, Tokyo; f. 1927; cap. 27,500m., dep. 3,444,433m.; Pres. YOSHIHIRO AKAMA.

Mitsui Trust and Banking Co. Ltd.: 1-1, Nihonbashi-Muromachi, 2-chome, Chuo-ku, Tokyo 103; f. 1924; cap. 90,080m., dep. 3,927,881m. (March 1976); Pres. SENKICHI SHONO.

Sumitomo Trust and Banking Co. Ltd.: 15, 5-chome, Kirahama, Higashi-ku, Osaka; f. 1925; cap. 25,000m., dep. 3,016,723m. (1974); Pres. SEN-ICHI OKUDAIRA.

Yasuda Trust and Banking Co. Ltd., The: 2-25, 1-chome, Yaesu, Chuo-ku, Tokyo; f. 1925; cap. 22,000m., dep. 2,300,818m. (March 1975); Pres. SHOJI KAMAI.

FOREIGN BANKS

Algemene Bank Nederland N.V.: Amsterdam (head office); Fuji Bldg., 3-2-3 Marunouchi, Chiyoda-ku, Tokyo 100, C.P.O. Box 374; brs. in Kobe, Osaka.

American Express International Banking Corpn.: New York, 6th Floor, Chamber of Commerce Bldg., 2-2, Marunouchi, 3-chome, Chiyoda-ku, Tokyo 100.

Bangkok Bank Ltd.: Bangkok; Mitsui Bldg. 6th Annex, 8-11, Nihonbashi Muromachi, 2-chome, Chuo-ku, Tokyo; Man. PHAIBUL INGHKAVAT.

Bank of America—National Trust and Savings Association: San Francisco; Shin Marunouchi Bldg., 4, 1-chome Marunouchi, Tokyo; brs. in Yokohama, Osaka and Kobe.

Bank of China: 4-2, 1-chome, Marunouchi, Chiyoda-ku, Tokyo.

Bank of India Ltd.: Bombay; Mitsubishi Denki Bldg., 2-3, Marunouchi 2-chome, Chiyoda-ku, Tokyo; br. also in Osaka.

Bank Indonesia: Head Office: Jakarta; 8-1, Yuraku-cho, 1-chome, Chiyoda-ku, Tokyo.

Bank of Korea: Seoul; Room 611 Hibiya Park Building, 1 Yuraku-cho 1-chome, Chiyoda-ku, Tokyo.

Bank Negara Indonesia: Head Office: 1 Jalan Lada, Jakarta; Kosusai Bldg., Room 1, Marunouchi, Chiyoda-Ku, Tokyo; brs. Hong Kong, Singapore and offices in London and New York.

Banque de l'Indochine: Paris; Tokyo, Central, P.O. Box 314.

Barclays Bank International Ltd.: Mitsubishi Building, 5-2 Marunouchi; 2-chome, Chiyoda-ku, Tokyo; (C.P.O.B. 466); Man. C. STEVENS.

Central Trust of China: Taipei, 5th Floor, Togin Bldg., 4-2 Marunouchi, 1-chome, Chiyoda-ku, Tokyo 100; f. 1935; Vice-Pres. and Man. YUAN-LING PEI.

Chartered Bank: London; 2-3, 3-chome, Marunouchi, Tokyo; brs. in Kobe, Osaka, Yokohama.

Chase Manhattan Bank, N.A.: New York; AIU Bldg., 1-3 Marunouchi 1-chome, Chiyoda-ku, Tokyo 100; Itoh Bldg., 47, 4-chome, Higashi-ku, Osaka 541; Vice-Pres. and Gen. Man. FRANK E. SALERNO.

Continental Illinois National Bank and Trust Company of Chicago: Tokyo Branch: Mitsui Seimei Bldg., 2-3 Ohtemachi, 1-chome Chiyoda-ku; Vice-Pres. J. H. BRINCKMANN; Man. J. H. LERCH; Osaka branch; 35-11 Hiranomachi, 3-chome Higashi-ku; Man. T. DE HAAN.

First National Bank of Chicago: Chicago; Tokyo Branch, 409 Fuji Bldg., 2-3, 3-chome, Marunouchi, Chiyoda-ku, Tokyo; Vice-Pres. and Gen. Man. KEVIN G. WOELFLEIN.

First National City Bank: New York; 2-1 Ohtemachi 2-chome, Chiyoda-ku, Tokyo 100; brs. in Osaka, Yokohama, Nagoya, Camp Zama.

Hong Kong and Shanghai Banking Corporation: Hong Kong; 1-2, Marunouchi 2-chome, Chiyoda-ku, Tokyo.

The Korea Development Bank: 6-1 Marunouchi 1-chome, Chiyoda-ku, Tokyo (Head Office Seoul).

Korea Exchange Bank: Seoul; New Kokusai Bldg., 4, 3-chome, Marunouchi, Chiyoda-ku, Tokyo; Second Shinsaibashi Bldg., 23-1, 4-chome, Sueyoshibashidori, Minami-ky, Osaka; f. 1950 (present name adopted 1968); Dir. BONG-EUN KIM; Man. YOON SUP HONG.

Lloyds Bank International Ltd.: 5-2, 2-chome, Marunouchi, Chiyoda-ku (C.P.O.B. 464); Man. A. B. BUCHANAN.

Manufacturers Hanover Trust Co.: New York; 21st Floor, Asahi Tokai Bldg., 6-1, Ohtemachi 2-chome, Chiyoda-ku, Tokyo; Vice-Pres. and Man. JACQUES R. STUNZI.

Mercantile Bank Ltd.: Hong Kong; P.O.B. Central 86, 450-91 Nagoya; f. 1892; cap. p.u. Stg. £2,940,000; Nagoya Man. S. BOAG.

Morgan Guaranty Trust Co.: New York; New Yurakocho Bldg., 11, 1-chome, Yuraku-cho, Chiyoda-ku, Tokyo 100; Vice-Pres. and Gen. Mans. G. DENHAM, E. CHALONER.

BANKERS' ASSOCIATION

Federation of Bankers' Associations of Japan: 1-3-1, Marunouchi, Chiyoda-ku, Tokyo; f. 1945; 73 member associations; Chair. JOJI ITAKURA; Vice-Chair. SHIGEO MATSUMOTO; publs. *Zenkoku Ginko Tempo*

Ichiran (list of bank offices in Japan), annual; *Zenkoku Ginko Yakuin Meibo* (list of members of Boards of Directors of all banks in Japan), annual; *Tegata Kokan Tokei-Nempo* (annual statistics of Clearing House); *Kinyu* (Finance); *Banking System in Japan* (occasional in English).

Regional Banks Association of Japan: 3-1-2 Uchikanda, Chiyoda-ku, Tokyo 101.

Tokyo Bankers' Association Inc.: 1-3-1 Marunouchi, Chiyoda-ku, Tokyo; f. 1945; 78 member banks; Chair. Joji Itakura.

STOCK EXCHANGES

Tokyo Stock Exchange: 6, 1-chome, Nihonbashi-Kabuaocho, Chuo-ku, Tokyo; f. 1949; 83 mems.; Pres. Hiroshi Tanimura; publs. *Securities* (monthly), *TSE Monthly Statistics Report, Annual Statistics Report.*

Hiroshima Stock Exchange: 14-18, Kanayama-cho, Hiroshima; f. 1949; 15 mems.; Principal Officer Shigeru Akagi.

Fukuoka Stock Exchange: 55, Tenjin-cho, Fukuoka.

Nagoya Stock Exchange: 3-17, Sakae-Sanchome, Naka-ku, Nagoya; f. 1949; Pres. Takumi Yoshihashi; Man. Dir. Isamu Inagaki.

Osaka Securities Exchange: 2-chome, Kitahama, Higashi-ku, Osaka 541; f. 1949; 53 regular mems. and 5 Nakadachi mems.; Pres. Minoru Tomita; Chair. Sunao Takeuchi; publs. *Investment* (bi-monthly), *Monthly Statistical Report, Annual Statistical Report, O.S.E. Official Quotation Daily.*

INSURANCE

The principal companies are as follows:

Life

Asahi Mutual Life Insurance Co.: 7-3, 1-chome, Nishi-Shinjuku, Shinjuku-ku, Tokyo; f. 1888; Pres. Ryuhei Takashima.

Chiyoda Mutual Life Insurance Co.: 19-18, Kamimeguro 2-chome, Meguro-ku, Tokyo; f. 1904; Pres. Shojiro Kayano.

Daido Mutual Life Insurance Co.: 1-23-101 Esaka Suitashi, Osaka 564; f. 1902; Pres. T. Masumura; Senior Man. Dir. E. Fukumoto.

Daihyaku Mutual Life Insurance Co., The: 4-go, 1-ban, 3-chome, Shibuya, Shibuya-ku, Tokyo; f. 1914; Pres. D. Kawasaki.

Dai-ichi Mutual Life Insurance Co., The: 13-1, Yurakucho 1-chome, Chiyoda-ku, Tokyo; f. 1902; Chair. Tsunehisa Yada; Pres. Ryoichi Tsukamoto.

Fukoku Mutual Life Insurance Co.: 6, 3-chome, Kudan, Chiyoda-ku, Tokyo; f. 1923.

Kyoei Life Insurance Co. Ltd.: 4-2 Hongokucho, Nihonbashi, Chuoku, Tokyo; f. 1947; Pres. Masayuki Kitoku; cap. 70m.

Meiji Mutual Life Insurance Co.: 2-chome, Marunouchi, Chiyoda-ku, Tokyo; f. 1881; Chair. Yoshitomi Seki.

Mitsui Mutual Life Insurance Co.: 1-2-3 Ohtemachi, Chiyoda-ku, Tokyo; f. 1927; Pres. Takahiro Tajima.

Nippon Dantai Life Insurance Co. Ltd.: 1-2-19, Higashi, Shibuya-ku, Tokyo; f. 1934; Pres. Takeo Hirakura.

Nippon Life Insurance Co.: 7, 4-chome, Imabashi, Higashi-ku, Osaka; f. 1889.

Nissan Mutual Life Insurance Co.: Aobadai 3-6-30, Meguro-ku, Tokyo; f. 1909; Pres. Masao Fujimoto.

Okinawa Mutual Life Insurance Co.: 1-46 Kumoji; Pres. Seikun Maeda.

Ryukyu Mutual Life Insurance Co.: 1-42 Miebashi, Naha; Pres. Noburu Kazaku.

Sumitomo Mutual Life Insurance Co.: 16, 2-chome, Nakanoshima, Kita-ku, Osaka; f. 1926; Chair. Taizo Ashida; Pres. Masaaki Arai; Senior Man. Dirs. T. Yuasa, S. Oshima.

Taisho Mutual Life Insurance Co.: 7, 1-chome, Yurakucho, Chiyoda-ku, Tokyo; f. 1913; Pres. Shigeji Yamanoda.

Taiyo Mutual Life Insurance Co.: 8, 2-chome, Edobashi, Nihonbashi, Chuo-ku, Tokyo.

Toho Mutual Life Insurance Co.: 3-1, 3-chome, Ginza, Chuo-ku, Tokyo; f. 1898; Chair. Seizo Ohta; Pres. Benjiro Ohta.

Tokyo Mutual Life Insurance Co.: No. 5-2, 1-chome, Uchisaiwaicho, Chiyoda-ku, Tokyo; f. 1895; Pres. Kiichi Kimura.

Yamato Mutual Life Insurance Co.: 1, 1-chome, Uchisaiwaicho, Chiyoda-ku, Tokyo; f. 1911; Pres. Kohei Maeyama.

Yasuda Mutual Life Insurance Co., The: P.O.B. 28, Shinjuku, Tokyo 160-91; f. 1880; Chair. Hajime Yasuda; Pres. M. Mizuno.

Non-Life

Asahi Fire and Marine Insurance Co. Ltd.: 6-2 Kajicho 2-chome, Chiyoda-ku, Tokyo; f. 1951; Pres. Tomio Vematsu.

Chiyoda Fire and Marine Insurance Co. Ltd.: 3-1, 1-chome, Kyobashi, 1-chome, Chuo-ku, Tokyo; f. 1898; Chair. Shotaro Kamiya; Pres. Tsunejiro Tejima.

Daido Fire and Marine Insurance Co. Ltd.: 14-8, 1-chome, Kumoji, Naha-shi, Okinawa; Pres. Yusho Vezu.

Daiichi Mutual Fire and Marine Insurance Co.: 5-1, Nibancho, Chiyoda-ku, Tokyo; f. 1949; Pres. N. Nishihara; Chair. Y. Naruse.

Dai-Tokyo Fire and Marine Insurance Co. Ltd., The: 1-6, Nihonbashi, 3-chome, Chuo-ku, Tokyo; f. 1918; incorporating Tokyo Movable Property Fire and Toshin Fire; Pres. Kin-ichi Akita; Vice-Pres. Sei-ichi Sorimachi.

Dowa Fire and Marine Insurance Co. Ltd.: 61 Shinmei-cho, Kita-ku, Osaka; f. 1944; Chair. Takashi Otsuki; Pres. Tsuyoshi Hosoi.

Fuji Fire and Marine Insurance Co. Ltd.: 3, 2-chome, Sueyoshibashi-dori, Minamiku, Osaka; f. 1918; Pres. Isamu Watanabe.

Japan Earthquake Reinsurance Co. Ltd.: 6-5, 3-chome, Kanda Surugadai, Chiyoda-ku, Tokyo; Pres. H. Segami.

Koa Fire and Marine Insurance Co. Ltd.: 5, 1-chome, Nihonbashi Muromachi, Chuo-ku, Tokyo; f. 1944; Pres. S. Maetani; Chair. Katsumi Yamagata.

Kyoei Mutual Fire and Marine Insurance Co.: 18-8, 1-chome, Shimbashi, Minato-ku, Tokyo; f. 1942; Pres. Shugo Tanaka.

Kyowa Fire and Marine Insurance: 1-46 Banchi, Kumoji-cho, Naha-City; f. 1963; Pres. Yosho Uezu.

Nichido Fire and Marine Insurance Co. Ltd.: 3-16, 5-chome, Ginza Chuo-ku, Tokyo; f. 1914; incorporating Toho Fire; Pres. T. Kubo.

Nippon Fire and Marine Insurance Co.: 2-10, Nihonbashi, 2-chome, Chuo-ku, Tokyo 103; f. 1892; Pres. Yasutaro Ukon.

Nissan Fire and Marine Insurance Co. Ltd.: 9-5, 2-chome, Kita-Aoyama, Minato-ku, Tokyo; f. 1911; Chair. YOSHITSUGU OISHI.

Nisshin Fire and Marine Insurance Co. Ltd.: 5-1, 1-chome, Otemachi, Chiyoda-ku, Tokyo; f. 1908; Pres. SEIJI KAJINISHI; Senior Man. Dirs. TEIJIRO INOUE, MASAO NAKAMURA.

Sumitomo Marine and Fire Insurance Co. Ltd.: 3-5, Yaesu 1-chome, Chuo-ku, Tokyo; f. 1944; Pres. Y. MOROKUZU.

Taisei Fire and Marine Insurance Co. Ltd., The: 11 Kanda Nishiki-cho, 2-chome, Chiyoda-ku, Tokyo; f. 1950; Pres. TOKIO NODA.

Taisho Marine and Fire Insurance Co. Ltd.: 5, 1-chome, Kyobashi, Chuo-ku Tokyo; f. 1918; member of Mitsui group of companies; Pres. AKIO HIRATA; Exec. Dir. N. MISAWA.

Taiyo Fire and Marine Insurance Co.: 5, Tori 3-chome, Nihonbashi, Chuo-ku, Tokyo; f. 1951; Pres. M. KABURAGI; Man. Dir. K. KANEKO.

Toa Fire and Marine Insurance Co.: 6-5, 3-chome, Kanda Surugadai, Chiyoda-ku, Tokyo; f. 1940; Pres. Y. YASUDA.

Tokio Marine and Fire Insurance Co. Ltd. (*Tokio Kaijo*): 2-1, 3-chome, Marunouchi, Chiyoda-ku, Tokyo; f. 1879; Chair. GENZAETION YAMAMOTO; Pres. MINORU KIKUCHI.

Toyo Fire and Marine Insurance Co.: 2-1, 1-chome, Yurakucho, Chiyoda-ku, Tokyo; f. 1950; Pres. T. KAKEHASHI; Chair. YASUSABURO HARA.

Yasuda Fire and Marine Insurance Co. Ltd.: 5-4, Otemachi Itchome, Chiyoda-ku, Tokyo; f. 1887; Pres. T. MIYOSHI.

In addition to the commercial companies, the Post Office runs life insurance and annuity schemes.

INSURANCE ASSOCIATIONS

Life Insurance Association of Japan (*Seimei Hoken Kyokai*): New Kokusai Bldg., 4-1, 3-chome, Marunouchi, Chiyoda-ku, Tokyo; f. 1908; 20 mem. cos.; Chair. K. KAZUNO; Exec. Dir. H. FURUKAWA; Man. Dir. T. NAKAZAWA.

Marine and Fire Insurance Association of Japan: Non-Life Insurance Building, 9, 2-chome, Kanda Awaji-cho, Chiyoda-ku, Tokyo; f. 1907; 22 mems.; Pres. MINORU KIKUCHI; Vice-Pres. TSUNEJIRO TEJIMA; Exec. Dir. FUMIO IMAI; Man. Dirs. SHIRO YOSHIMI, SADABUMI NISHIZAWA.

Fire and Marine Insurance Rating Association of Japan: Sonpo Kaikan, 9, 2-chome, Kanda Awajicho, Chiyoda-ku, Tokyo; f. 1948; Pres. YASUTARO UKON; Exec. Dir. TSUTOMU SAITO.

TRADE AND INDUSTRY

CHAMBERS OF COMMERCE AND INDUSTRY

Japan Chamber of Commerce and Industry, The (*Nippon Shoko Kaigi-sho*): 2-2, 3-chome, Marunouchi, Chiyoda-ku, Tokyo; f. 1922; mems. 473 local Chambers of Commerce and Industry; the central organization of all chambers of commerce and industry in Japan; Pres. SHIGEO NAGANO, K.B.E.; publs. *Standard Trade Index of Japan* (annual), *Japan Commerce and Industry* (bi-annual).

Kobe Chamber of Commerce and Industry, The: Kobe CIT Center Bldg., 2-1, Hamabe-dori 5-chome, Fukiai-ku, Kobe 651; f. 1878; mems. 4,799; Pres. MASASHI ISANO; Man. Dir. SHIRO HATA; publs. *Kobe Directory* (annual), *Current Economic Survey of Kobe* (annual), *The Trade Bulletin* (weekly).

Kyoto Chamber of Commerce and Industry: Karasuma-dori Ebisugawa agaru, Nakakyo-ku, Kyoto 604; f. 1882; mems. 7,149; Pres. HIROUMA MORISHITA; Man. Dir. KUNIO SHIMAZU; publs. *Kyoto Business Directory*, *Members Report* (monthly in Japanese), *Kyoto Directory of manufacturers, exporters, and importers* (annual), *The Trade Opportunities* (twice monthly), *IGS* (International Goodwill Shop), *Member List* (annual).

Nagoya Chamber of Commerce and Industry: 10-19, Sakae 2-chome, Naka-ku, Nagoya; f. 1881; mems. 5,631; Pres. MOTOO TSUCHIKAWA; Man. Dir. RYOJIRO KURITA.

Osaka Chamber of Commerce and Industry: 58-7, Uchi-hommachi Hashizume-chome, Higashi-ku, Osaka; f. 1878; mems. 19,324; Pres. ISAMU SAHEKI; Sen. Man. Dir. TAKEHISA IZUCHI; publs. *Chamber* (Japanese, monthly), *Osaka* (English, quarterly), *List of Members* (Japanese), *Daisho Shimbun* (Japanese newspaper), *Osaka Business Directory* (English), *List of Overseas Chambers of Commerce and Industry*, *Economic Organizations* (English). *Guide to Osaka Merchandise* (English), *Yearbook of Osaka Economy* (Japanese) and *White Paper on Wages in Osaka* (Japanese).

Ryukyu Chamber of Commerce and Industry: 1-49 Kumecho, Naha, Okinawa; Pres. KOTARO KOKUBA.

Tokyo Chamber of Commerce and Industry, The: 2-2, Marunouchi 3-chome, Chiyoda-ku, Tokyo; f. 1878; mems. 13,700; Pres. SHIGEO NAGANO; Man. Dir. EIJI KAGEYAMA.

Yokohama Chamber of Commerce and Industry, The: 11, Nihon-Odori, Nakaku, Yokohama; f. 1880; mems. 5,200; Pres. TAKASHI IHARA; Dir. and Gen. Sec. MASAO KAWAMURA; publs. *Yokohama Economic Statistics* (Japanese and English, annual), *Monthly Report* (Japanese) and *Chamber's News* (Japanese, monthly).

FOREIGN TRADE ORGANIZATIONS

Association for the Promotion of International Trade, Japan: Nippon Bldg., 5th Floor, No. 2-6-2, Ohtemachi, Chiyoda-ku, Tokyo; for the promotion of private trade with the People's Republic of China, the Democratic Republic of Korea, Albania and Viet-Nam; handles 90 per cent of Sino-Japanese trade; Pres. A. FUJIYAMA; Chair. TEIJI HAGIHARA.

China-Japan Memorandum Trade Office: Ishiba, Kotohira-cho, Minato-ku, Tokyo; responsible for official trade with People's Republic of China; Chair. KAHEITA OKAZAKI.

Council of All-Japan Exporters' Association: Kikai Shinko Kaikan Bldg., 5-8 Shibakoen 3-chome, Minato-ku, Tokyo.

Japan External Trade Organization—JETRO: 2 Akasaka Aoi-Cho, Minato-ku, Tokyo; est. 1958; information for foreign firms, investigation of foreign markets, exhibition of Japanese commodities abroad, etc.; Pres.

KICHIHEI HARA; Vice-Pres. KIMITAKA MURAKAMI; publs. *Trade and Industry of Japan* (monthly), *Japan Trade Bulletin* (every ten days), etc.

Japan Foreign Trade Council, Inc. (*Nippon Boeki-Kai*): 6th Floor, World Trade Center Bldg., 4-1, 2-chome, Hamamatsu-cho, Minato-ku, Tokyo 105; f. 1947; 410 mems.; Pres. TATSUZO MIZUKAMI; Man. Dir. NAOJI HARADA; Exec. Dir. ZENJI KYOMOTO; publ. *Bulletin* (in Japanese).

Society for Trade with the U.S.S.R.: Tokyo; f. 1967; Pres. SHIGEO HORIE.

PRINCIPAL GENERAL TRADING COMPANIES

C. Itoh & Co. Lyd.: 4 Nihonbashi Hon-cho, 2-chome, Chuo-ku, Tokyo; f. 1858; cap. 34,913m. yen; exporters and importers of agricultural products, machinery, iron and steel, textiles, chemical products, foodstuffs, etc.; Pres. SEIKI TOZAKI.

Mitsubishi Corporation: 2-6-3 Marunouchi, Chiyoda-ku, Tokyo; f. 1950; cap. 33,480m. yen; exporters and importers of agricultural products, machinery, iron and steel, chemical products, textiles, foodstuffs, etc.; Chair. CHUJIRO FUJINO; Pres. BUN-ICHIRO TANABE.

Marubeni Corporation: 4-2 Ohtemachi, 1-chome, Chiyoda-ku, Tokyo; f. 1858; cap. 30,250m. yen; exporters and importers of iron and steel, machinery, textiles, etc.; Pres. TAIICHIRO MATSUO.

Mitsui & Co. Ltd.: 1-2-9 Nishi Shinbashi, Minato-ku, Tokyo; f. 1947; cap. 22,881m. yen; exporters and importers of iron and steel, machinery, textiles, chemicals, foodstuffs, etc.; Pres. YOSHIZO IKEDA.

Nissho-Iwai Co. Ltd.: 2-4-5 Akasaka, Minato-ku, Tokyo; f. 1928; cap. 15,400m. yen; exporters and importers of iron and steel products, machinery, textiles, chemicals, foodstuffs, etc.; Pres. YOSHIO TSUJI.

Sumitomo Shoji Kaisha Ltd.: 2-2 Hitotsubashi, 1-chome, Chiyoda-ku, Tokyo; f. 1919; cap. 15,686m. yen; exporters and importers of iron and steel, machinery chemical products, foodstuffs, etc.

TRADE ASSOCIATIONS

Fertilizer Traders' Association: Daiichi Saegusa Bldg., 10-5, Ginza 5-chome, Chuo-ku, Tokyo.

Foreign Film Importers-Distributors' Association of Japan: Shochi-ku Kaikan, 13-5 Tsukiji, 1-chome, Chuo-ku, Tokyo.

Japan Agricultural Products Exporters' Association: 12-3, 2-chome, Shimbashi, Minato-ku, Tokyo.

Japan Automobile Importers' Association: c/o Friend Bldgs., 2-4-11 Nagata-cho, Chiyoda-ku, Tokyo.

Japan General Merchandise Exporters' Association: 4-1, Hamamatsu-cho, 2-chome, Minato-ku, Tokyo; f. 1953; 850 mems.; Pres. KYUZABURO JUBA.

Japan Lumber Importers' Association: Yushi Kogyo Bldg., No. 13-11, Nihonbashi 3-chome, Chuo-ku, Tokyo.

Japan Sugar Import and Export Council: Ginza Gas-Hall, 9-15, 7-chome, Ginza, Chuo-ku, Tokyo.

Japan Tea Exporters' Association: 81-1 Kitaban-cho, Shinzuoka, Shinzuoka Prefecture.

Japan Timber Exporters' Association: Mitsui Bldg. 9-1, 1-chome, Ironai, Otaru, Hokkaido, Japan 047.

TRADE FAIR

Tokyo International Trade Fair Commission: 16, 4-chome, Harumi, Chuo-ku, Tokyo (C.P.O. Box 1201, Tokyo).

PRINCIPAL INDUSTRIAL ORGANIZATIONS

GENERAL

Industry Club of Japan: 4-6, Marunouchi, 1-chome, Chiyoda-ku, Tokyo; f. 1917 to develop closer relations between industrialists at home and abroad and promote expansion of Japanese business activities; *ca.* 1,600 mems.; Pres. KOGORO UEMARA; Exec. Dir. GINICHI YAMANE.

Japan Commercial Arbitration Association: Tokyo Chamber of Commerce and Industry Bldg., 2-2, 3-chome, Marunouchi, Chiyoda-ku, Tokyo; f. 1950; 1,025 mems.; provides facilities for adjustment, conciliation and arbitration in international trade disputes; Pres. SHIGEO NAGANO; Man. Dir. TADATOSHI FUKUSHIMA; publ. monthly and quarterly journals.

Japan Committee for Economic Development (*Keizai Doyukai*): Kogyo Club Bldg., 1-4-6, Marunouchi, Chiyoda-ku, Tokyo; an influential group of business interests concerned with national and international economic and social policies.

Japan Federation of Economic Organizations—KEIDANREN (*Keizaidantai Rengo-kai*): 9-4, Otemachi, 1-chome, Chiyoda-ku, Tokyo, 100; f. 1946; private non-profit association to study domestic and international economic problems; mems. 107 professional organizations, 769 firms (Sept. 1973); Pres. TOSHIO DOKO; Dir.-Gen. TEIZO HORIKOSHI.

Japan Federation of Smaller Enterprises: 2-4 Kayabacho, Nihonbashi, Chuo-ku, Tokyo.

Japan Productivity Centre (*Nihon Seisansei Honbu*): 3-1-1 Shibuya, Shibuya-ku, Tokyo: f. 1955; 9,000 mems.; concerned with management problems; Chair. KOHEI GOSHI; Exec. Dir. TAKEO TAMARUSHIMA; publ. *Japan Productivity News* (weekly).

Nihon Keieisha Dantai Renmei—NIKKEIREN (*Japan Federation of Employers' Associations*): 4-6, Marunouchi 1-chome, Chiyoda-ku, Tokyo; f. 1948; covers 95 member organizations, Man. Dirs. MASARU HAYAKAWA, YOSHINOBU MATSUZAKI; Sec.-Gen. ICHIRO MIYAMOTO; publs. *Nikkeiren News* (quarterly, English), *Nikkeiren Times* (weekly, Japanese).

FISHING AND PEARL CULTIVATION

Japan Coastal Trawler Fisheries Association: Showa Kaikan, 1, Sannen-cho, Chiyoda-ku, Tokyo; f. 1948; Pres. KASUKE HOSONO.

Japan Fisheries Association (*Dai-nippon Suisan Kai*): Sankaido Bldg., 9-13, Akasaka 1, Minato-ku, Tokyo.

Japan Pearl Export and Processing Co-operative Association: 7, 3-chome, Kyobashi, Chuo-ko, Tokyo, f. 1951, 130 mems.

Japan Pearl Exporters' Association: 122 Higashi-machi Ikuta-ku, Kobe; Tokyo branch: 7, 3-chome Kyobashi, Chuo-ku, Pres. ATSUSHI KANAI.

Japan Pearl Promoting Society: 7, 3-chome, Kyobashi Chuo-ku, Tokyo; f. 1956.

National Federation of Fishery Co-operative Associations, The: Sankaido Bldg., 1-9-13 Akasaka, Minato-ku, Tokyo.

Ryukyu Fisheries Co-operatives Federation: 2-211 Maejima-cho, Naha, Okinawa; 41 member co-operatives (July 1969); Pres. YUKEN TOME.

TEXTILES

Central Raw Silk Association of Japan, The: 7, 1-chome, Yuraku-cho, Chiyoda-ku, Tokyo.

Japan Chemical Fibres Association: Mitsui Bekkan, 3, Nihonbashi Muromachi, 3-chome, Chuo-ku, Tokyo.

Japan Cotton and Staple Fibre Weavers' Association: 8-7, Nishi-Azabu 1-chome, Minato-ku, Tokyo.

Japan Export Clothing Manufacturers' Association: 4, Utsubo 2-chome, Nishi-ku, Osaka; f. 1956; 698 mems.; promotion and internal policy body for the manufacture of cotton clothing for export; Pres. K. KONDO; publ. *JECMA News* (Japanese), *Directory* (English).

Japan Knitted Goods Manufacturers' Association: 6, Nihonbashi Yoshi-cho, 1-chome, Chuoku, Tokyo, Japan 103.

Japan Silk Association, Inc.: Sanshi Kaikan, 7, 1-chome Yurakucho, Chiyoda-ku, Tokyo; f. 1959; mems. 10 asscns.; Pres. MINORU KOBAYASHI.

Japan Silk and Rayon Weavers' Association: 15-12, Kudankita 1-chome, Chiyoda-ku, Tokyo.

Japan Silk Spinners' Association: Mengyo Kaikan Building, 8, 3-chome, Bingo Machi, Higashi-ku, Osaka; f. 1948; 97 member firms; Chair. RYOJUN MATSUMOTO; publ. *Monthly Report*.

Japan Staple Yarn Merchants' Federation: 2, 1-chome, Nihonbashi Kobune-cho, Chuo-ku, Tokyo.

Japan Textile Council: Sen-i-Kaikan Bldg., 9, 3-chome, Nihonbashi Honcho, Chuo-ku, Tokyo; f. 1948; mems. 24 asscns.; publs. *Textile Yearbook*, *Textile Statistics* (monthly), *Textile Japan* (annual in English).

The Japan Textile Machinery Manufacturers' Association: Room No. 310, Kikai Shinko Bldg., 3-5-8 Shiba Koen, Minato-ku, Tokyo; f. 1951; Pres. NOBUYOSHI NOZAKI.

Japan Wool Industry Conference: Sen-i-Kaikan, 9, 3-chome, Nihonbashi Hon-cho, Chuo-ku, Tokyo.

Japan Wool Spinners' Association: Sen-i-Kaikan 9, 3-chome, Nihonbashi Hon-cho, Chuo-ku, Tokyo; f. 1958; Chair. S. ABE; Man. Dir. H. SAKAI; publ. *Statistical Data on the Wool Industry in Japan* (monthly).

Japan Worsted and Woollen Weavers' Association: Sen-i-Kaikan 9, 3-chome, Nihonbashi Hon-cho, Chuo-ku, Tokyo; f. 1948; Chair. S. OGAWA; Man. Dir. K. OHTANI.

PAPER AND PRINTING

Japan Paper Association: Kami-Parupu Kaikan Bldg., Ginza 3-chome, 9-11 Chuo-ku, Tokyo; f. 1946; 112 mems.; Pres. S. KANEKO; Dir.-in-Chief M. MATSUNAGA.

Japan Paper Exporters' Association: 9-11, Ginza, 3-chome, Chuo-ku, Tokyo.

Japan Paper-Products Exporters' Association: 18-2, 1-chome, Higashi-Komagata, Sumida-ku, Tokyo; f. 1959; Exec. Dir. KIYOSHI SATOH.

Japan Paper-Products Manufacturers' Association: 18-2. 1-chome, Higashi-Komagata, Tokyo; f. 1949; Exec, Dir. KIYOSHI SATOH.

Japan Printers' Association: 1-16-8, Shintomi, Chuo-ku, Tokyo; Pres. KAICHI SAWAMURA; Exec. Dir. FUMIO SANGU.

Machine-Made Japanese Paper Industry Association: 9-11, Ginza, 3-chome, Chuo-ku, Tokyo.

CHEMICALS

Federation of Pharmaceutical Manufacturers' Associations of Japan: 9, 2-chome, Nihonbashi Hon-chu, Chuo-ku, Tokyo.

Japan Perfumery and Flavouring Association: Nitta Bldg., 8, 8-chome, Ginza, Chuo-ku, Tokyo.

Japan Chemical Industry Association: Tokyo Club Bldg., 2-6, 3-chome, Kasumigaseki, Chiyoda-ku, Tokyo; f. 1948; 207 mems.; Pres. HIDEO SHINOJIMA.

Japan Cosmetic Makers' and Wholesalers' Association: 1-13-8, Nihonbashi Bakuro-cho, Chuo-ku, Tokyo; f. 1895; 365 mems.; publ. *The Nihon Syogyo* (weekly).

Japan Gas Association: 38 Shiba Kotohira-cho, Minato-ku, Tokyo; f. 1912; Pres. HIROSHI ANZAI; Man. Dir. Y. SHIBASAKI; publ. *Monthly Journal*.

Japan Inorganic Chemical Industry Association: Sanko Bldg., 1-13-1 Ginza Chuoku, Tokyo; f. 1948; Pres. KAN-ICHI TANAHASHI.

Japan Pharmaceutical, Medical and Dental Supply Exporters' Association: 3-6, Nihonbashi-Honcho 4-chome, Chuo-ku, Tokyo 103; f. 1953; 181 member firms; Pres. CHOBEI TAKEDA; Man. Dir. MITSUO SASAKI.

Japan Urea and Ammonium Sulphate Industry Association: Hokkai Bldg., 1-3-13 Nihombashi, Chuo-ku, Tokyo.

The Photo-Sensitized Materials Manufacturers' Association: 2, Kanda Nishiki-cho, 2-chome, Chiyoda-ku, Tokyo.

Society of Synthetic Organic Chemistry, Japan: Echiso Bldg., 39-7, 2-chome, Hongo, Bunkyo-ku, Tokyo; f. 1942; 4,814 mems.; Pres. Y. IWAKURA; Man. S. NAKAMURA; publ. *Monthly Journal*.

MINING AND PETROLEUM

Asbestos Cement Products Association: Takahashi Bldg., 10-8, 7-chome, Ginza, Chuo-ku, Tokyo; f. 1937; Chair. KOSHIRO SHIMIZU.

Cement Association of Japan, The: Hattori Bldg., 1, 1-chome, Kyobashi, Chuo-ku, Tokyo; f. 1948; 20 member companies; Chair. B. OHTSUKI; Exec. Man. Dir. H. KUROSAWA; publ. *Cement and Concrete* (monthly, Japanese), *Cement Statistics in Japan* (annual, English), *Semento Gijutsu Nenpo* (annual in Japanese), *Review of General Meeting—Technical Session* (annual, English).

Japan Coal Association: Nikkatsu Kokusai Kaikan, 1, 1-chome, Yuraku-cho, Chiyoda-ku, Tokyo.

Japan Mining Industry Association: Shin-hibiya Bldg., 3-6, 1-chome, Uchisaiwai-cho .Chiyoda-ku, Tokyo 100; f. 1948; 91 member companies; Pres. S. OMOTO; Vice-Pres. G. MORI; Dir.-Gen. S. ICHIJO.

Petroleum Association of Japan: Keidanren Kaikan, 5, 1-5-7 Ohtemachi, Chiyoda-ku, Tokyo; f. 1955; 22 mems.; Pres. SHINGO FUJIOKA; Man. Dir. KINZABURO IKEDA.

METALS

Japan Brass Makers' Association: 1-12-22, 1-chome, Tsukiji, Chuo-ku, Tokyo; f. 1948; 81 mems.; Pres. K. UEMATSU; Man. Dir. T. WADA.

Japan Iron and Steel Federation: Keidanren Kaikan, 1-9-4 Ohtemachi, Chiyoda-ku, Tokyo; f. 1948; Chair. Y. INAYAMA; Pres. SHIGEO NAGANO.

Japan Light Metal Association: Nihonbashi Asahiseimei Bldg., 1-3, Nihonbashi 2-chome, Chuo-ku, Tokyo 103, f. 1947; 180 mems.; publs. *Aluminium* (monthly), *JLMA News* (every ten days). *Magnesium* (monthly).

Japan Stainless Steel Association: Tekko Kaikan Bldg., 16, Nihonbashi Kayaba-cho, 3-chome, Chuo-ku, Tokyo; Pres. JUNGABORO NAKAJIMA; Exec. Dir. HIROSHI SATO.

The Kozai Club: 3-16 Kayabacho, Chuo-ku, Tokyo; f. 1947; mems. 33 manufacturers, 94 dealers; Pres. YOSHIHIRO INAYAMA.

Steel Castings and Forgings Association of Japan (JSCFA): Tekko Bldg., 8-2, 1-chome, Marunouchi, Chiyoda-ku, Tokyo 100; f. 1972; mems. 98 companies, 110 plants; Exec. Dir. KYOZO IWAMURA.

MACHINERY AND PRECISION EQUIPMENT

Electronic Industries Association of Japan: Tosho Bldg., 2-2, 3-chome, Marunouchi, Chiyoda-ku, Tokyo; f. 1948; mems. 520 firms; Pres. KOJI KOBAYASHI; publs. *Denshi* (Electronics) (monthly), *Index of Japanese Electronic Manufacturers and Products* (annual, English), *Electronic Industry in Japan* (annual, English).

Japan Camera Industry Association: Mori Building Ninth, 3, 1-chome, Shiba-Atago-cho, Minato-ku, Tokyo; f. 1954; Pres. KAZUO TASHIMA.

Japan Electric Association: 1-7-1 Yurakucho, Chiyoda-ku, Tokyo 100; f. 1921; Pres. MICHIO YOKOYAMA; publs. *Daily Electricity, Journal of the Japan Electric Association, Production and Electricity, Monthly Report on Electric Power Statistics.*

Japan Electrical Manufacturers' Association: 4-15, 2-chome, Nagata-cho, Chiyoda-ku, Tokyo; f. 1948; mems. 152 firms; Pres. S. MAEDA; Exec. Dir. K. IWASAKI; publ. descriptive information on Japanese Electrical Machinery (in English).

Japan Farm Machinery Manufacturers' Association: Kikai Shinko Kaikan Bldg., 5-8, Shiba Koen, 3-chome, Minato-ku, Tokyo.

The Japan Machinery Federation: Kikai Shinko Bldg., 5-8-3 Shiba Koen, Minato-ku, Tokyo.

Japan Machine Tool Builders' Association: Kikai Shinko Bldg., 5-1-21 Shibakoen, Minato-ku, Tokyo; f. 1951; 105 mems.; Exec. Dir. K. SUGIYAMA.

Japan Measuring Instruments Industrial Federation: Japan Metrology Bldg., 1-25 Nando-cho, Shinjuku-ku, Tokyo.

Japan Microscope Manufacturers' Association: c/o Olympus Optical Co. Ltd., 43-2, Hatagaya, 2-chome, Shibuya-ku, Tokyo; f. 1946; mems. 26 firms; Chair. K. KANBE.

Japan Motion Picture Equipment Industrial Association: Kikai-shinko Bldg., 3-5-8, Shibakoen, Minato-ku, Tokyo.

Japan Optical and Precision Instrument Manufacturers' Association: Kikai-Shinko Kaikan, 5-8 Shiba Park 3, Minato-ku, Tokyo 105; f. 1946; 200 mems.; Gen. Man. Y. TSUDA; publ. *Guidebook*.

Japan Photographic Equipment Industrial Association: Shin-Kaede Bldg., 3-3, 2-chome, Uchikanda, Chiyoda-ku, Tokyo.

Japan Power Association: Daido Building, 7-13, 1-chome, Nishi-Shimbashi, Minato-ku, Tokyo; f. 1950; 82 mems., Pres. GORO INOUYE; Sec. SACHIO TANAKA; publ. *Power* (quarterly).

Japan Society of Industrial Machinery Manufacturers: Kikai-Shinko Kaikan, 3-5-8, Shibakoen, Minato-ku, Tokyo; f. 1948; 307 mems.; Chair. KENKICHI TOSHIMA.

TRANSPORT MACHINERY

Japan Association of Rolling Stock Manufacturers: Tekko Bldg., 1-1 Marunouchi, Chiyoda-ku, Tokyo.

Japan Auto Parts Industries Association: 1-16-15 Takanawa, Minato-ku, Tokyo; f. 1948; mems. 350 firms; Pres. K. FUJIOKA; Man. Dir. T. KUROME; publs. *Auto Parts* (monthly, Japanese), *Japia Statistical Issue and Buyer's Guide* (annually, Japanese).

Japan Automobile Manufacturers Association, Inc.: Ohtemachi Bldg., 6-1 Otemachi 1-chome, Chiyoda-ku, Tokyo; f. 1967 in succession to the Automotive Industrial Asscn.; mems. 14 firms; Pres. E. TOYODA; Man. Dir. T. NAKAMURA.

Japan Bicycle Industry Association: 9-15 Akasaka 1-chome, Minato-ku, Tokyo.

Japanese Shipowners' Association: Osaka Bldg., 2-2 Uchisaiwaicho, 1-chome, Chiyoda-ku, Tokyo.

Shipbuilders' Association of Japan: 35 Shiba-Kotohiracho, Minatoku, Tokyo; f. 1947; 50 mems.; Pres. RENZO TAGUCHI; Man. Dir. HAJIME YAMADA.

The Ship Machinery Manufacturers' Association of Japan: Sempaku-Shinko Bldg., 35, Shiba Kotohira-cho, Minato-ku, Tokyo; f. 1956; 270 mems.; Pres. MAKOTO ISOGAI.

The Society of Japanese Aerospace Companies Inc. (*SJAC*): Chiyoda Bldg., 1-2, Marunouchi 2-chome, Chiyoda-ku, Tokyo; f. 1952; reorganized 1974 as Corporation aggregate; 127 mems., 18 assoc, mems.; Pres. KIYOSHI YOTSUMOTO; Exec. Dir. KOZO HIRATA; publs. *Monthly Report* (in Japanese), *Directory of the Aerospace Industry in Japan* (English, annual), *The Aircraft Industry Year Book* (Japanese, annual).

MISCELLANEOUS

Association of Tokyo Exporting Toy Manufacturers: 4-16-3, Higashi-Komagata Sumida-ku, Tokyo; f. 1948; 150 mems.; Pres. S. SATO.

Canners' Association of Japan: Marunouchi Bldg., 18, 2-chome, Marumouchi, Tokyo.

Communication Industries Association of Japan: Sankei Bldg., 1-7-2 Otemachi, Chiyoda-ku, Tokyo; f. 1948; Pres. KOJI KOBAYASHI; Exec. Dir. SHUZO OHIZUMI; 201 mems.; publs. *Tsushin-Kogyo* (monthly in Japanese), *Communications and Electronics Japan* (biennial, English).

Japan Construction Materials Association: Kenchiku Kaikan Bldg., 19-2, 3-chome, Ginza, Chuo-ku, Tokyo; f. 1947; Pres. KENTARO ITO; publ. *Construction Material Industry* (monthly).

Japan Plywood Manufacturers' Association: Meisan Bldg., 17-18, 1-chome, Nishishimbashi, Minato-ku, Tokyo; f. 1948; 251 mems.; Pres. HIROTADA DANTANI.

Japan Pottery Manufacturers' Federation: 32 Nunoike-cho, Higashi-ku, Nagoya; f. 1931; 50 mem. asscns.; Pres JUKURO MIZUNO; Man. Dir. K. MITSUI

Japan Raw Fur Association: 2, 4-chome, Tsukiji, Chuo-ku, Tokyo.

Japan Rubber Manufacturers Association, The: Tobu Bldg., 1-5-26, Moto Akasaka, Minato-ku, Tokyo; f. 1950; 200 mems.; Pres. YOSHIO SHIMASAKI.

Japan Sewing Machine Exporters' Association: 13 Sakamachi, Shinjukuku, Tokyo.

Japan Spirits and Liquors Makers Association: Koura Bldg., 7th Floor, 2 Nihombashi Kayabacho, 1-chome, Chuo-ku, Tokyo 103.

Japan Sugar Refiners' Association: 5-7 Sanbancho, Chiyoda-ku, Tokyo; f. 1949; 20 mems.; Man. Dir. ICHIRO FURUNISHI; Man. KIYOHISA NAGAMIYA; publs. *Sato Tokei Nenkan* (Sugar Statistics Year Book), *Kikan Togyoshiho* (Quarterly Sugar Journal).

Japan Watch and Clock Association: Nomura Bldg., 2, 2-chome, Otemachi, Chiyoda-ku, Tokyo.

Motion Picture Producers' Association of Japan: Sankei Kaikan Bldg., 7-2, 1-chome, Otemachi, Chiyoda-ku, Tokyo; Pres. SHIRO KIDO.

Ryukyu Industrial Federation: 468 Asato, Naha, Okinawa; Pres. M. NAKADA.

Ryukyu Agricultural Co-operatives Federation: 284 Kohagura, Naha, Okinawa; 80 member Co-operatives (July 1969); Pres. YUKEN TOME.

Ryukyu Contractors Association: 1-35 Miebashi, Naha, Okinawa; 223 member contractors (Aug. 1969); Pres. KOTARO KOKUBA.

TRADE UNIONS

A feature of Japan's trade union movement is that the unions are in general based on single enterprises, embracing workers of different occupations in that enterprise, rather than organizing the workers of the same trade in different enterprises on an industry-wide basis.

PRINCIPAL FEDERATIONS

Nihon Rodo Kumiai Sohyogikai—SOHYO (*General Council of Trade Unions of Japan*): 8-2 Shiba-park, Minato-ku, Tokyo; 4.6 million mems. (1975); Pres. TOSHIKATSU HORII; Sec.-Gen. A. IWAI.

Major Affiliated Unions

National Council of Local and Municipal Government Workers' Unions (*Jijiro*): approx. 704,000 mems.; Pres. M. KURIYAMA.

Japan Teachers' Union (*Nikkyoso*): 550,000 mems.; Pres. S. MIYANOHARA.

National Railway Workers' Union (*Kokuro*): approx. 218,000 mems.; Pres. YOSHIO KAMBE.

Japan Postal Workers' Union (*Zentei*): approx. 238,000 mems.; Pres. F. TAKARAGI.

General Federation of Private Railway Workers, Unions (*Shitetsuzoren*): approx. 240,000 mems., Pres. T. HORII.

National Metal and Machine Trade Union (*Zenkoku Kinzoku*): approx. 202,000 mems.; Pres. S. TSUBAKI.

Japan Telecommunication Workers' Union (*Zendentsu*): approx. 184,000 mems.; Pres. T. KASAHARA.

National Federation of Iron and Steel Workers' Unions (*Tekko Roren*): approx. 200,000 mems.; Pres. K. MITO.

Japanese Federation of Synthetic Chemistry Workers' Unions (*Goka Roren*): approx. 122,000 mems.; Pres. K. OTA.

Japan Broadcast Corporation Workers' Union (*Nipporo*): approx. 111,000 mems.; Chair. TETSU UEDA.

Japan Coal Miners' Union (*Tanro*): approx. 68,000 mems.; Pres. T. YAMAMOTO.

All-Japan Free Workers' Union (*Zennichi Jiro*): approx. 221,000 mems.; Pres. FUMIO WADA.

National Forest Labour Union (*Zenriya*): approx. 74,000 mems.; Pres. TAKESHI TAMURA.

Japan Federation of Municipal Transportation Workers' Unions (*Toshikotsu*): approx. 70,000 mems.; Pres. ATSUSHI MIYAHARA.

All-Japan Agriculture and Forestry Ministry's Workers' Union (*Zen Norin*): approx. 57,000 mems.; Pres. T. WATARAI.

Zen Nihon Rodo Sodomei Kaigi—DOMEI (*Japanese Confederation of Labour*): 20-12 Shiba, 2-chome, Minato-ku, Tokyo; f. 1964; 2.1 million mems.; affiliated to ICFTU; Pres. MINORU TAKITA; Vice-Pres. SEIJI AMAIKE; Sec.-Gen. TAKUMI SHIGEEDA.

Affiliated Unions

Japan Federation of Textile Workers' Unions (*Zensendomei*): Pres. MINORU TAKITA; Gen. Sec. TADANOBU USAMI; 516,578 mems.

National Federation of Metal Industry Trade Unions (*Zenkindomei*): Pres. SHIGEO IBORI; Gen. Sec. SEIJI AMAIKE; 220,000 mems.

All Japan Seamen's Union (*Kaiin*): Pres. YUTAKA NABASAMA; 142,900 mems.

Federation of Japan Automobile Workers' Unions (*Jidosharoren*): Pres. ICHIRO SHIOJI; Gen. Sec. SHOZO AKAGI; 129,540 mems.

Federation of Electric Workers' Unions of Japan (*Denroren*): Pres. CHOZUI KAMEYAMA; Gen. Sec. SOOICHI SUZUKI; 127,798 mems.

Japanese Federation of General Trade Unions (*Ippan Domei*): Pres. MISAO MASUHARA; Gen. Sec. TSUTAR SATOH; 105,772 mems.

Japanese Federation of Chemical and General Workers' Unions (*Zenkadomei*): Pres. SHIGEO MURAO; Gen. Sec. KEITARO NAKAJIMA; 72,790 mems.

Japan Federation of Transport Workers' Unions (*Kotsuroren*): Pres. ISAMU YAMAMOTO; Gen. Sec. KENJI NAGASAWA; 67,877 mems.

General Federation of Shipbuilding Workers' Unions (*Zosensoren*): Pres. MASASHICHI MOTOI; Gen. Sec. HARUZO NISHIMOTO; 56,512 mems.

Mitsubishi Heavy Industry Workers' Union Council (*Domei-Mitsubishi*): Pres. AKIRA KINOSHITA; Gen. Sec. KOSHIRO MIKI; 40,800 mems.

National Union of Coal Mine Workers (*Zentanko*): Pres. TAKUMI SHIGEEDA; Gen. Sec. EIJI HAYADATE; 35,137 mems.

National Federation of Food Industry Workers' Unions (*Zenshokuhindomei*): Pres. GENJIRO TSURUTA; Gen. Sec. EIJI OHSEKO; 27,820 mems.

Federation of Japanese Metal Resource Workers' Unions (*Shigenroren*): Pres. TOHRU ENDO; Gen. Sec. KAZUHIRO IIOKA; 12,530 mems.

National Council of Paper and Pulp Workers' Unions "NPU" (*Domeizenkamipa*): Pres. ICHIRO MICHIKAWA; Gen. Sec. HIDEKA HOSOKAWA; 7,937 mems.

National Cinema and Theatre Workers' Union (*Zen-Eien*): Pres. ISAO MASUDA; Gen. Sec. HIROSHI HARIU; 3,220 mems.

Preparatory Council of National Federation of Dockers' Unions (*Kowandomei Jumbikai*): Chair. SADAO HISATSUNE; 800 mems.

Japan Emigration Service Workers' Union (*Kaigai-Ijuroso*): Pres. TADAO IMAMURA; Gen. Sec. MASAJI SAITO; 300 mems.

Japanese Federation of National Railway Workers' Unions (*Shinkokuro*): Pres. EIETSU SUGAWARA; Gen. Sec. KOOICHI TANIMURA; 74,360 mems.

All Japan Special Post Office Labour Union (*Zenyusei*): Pres. TSUTOMU NAKAMURA; Gen. Sec. HIDEMASA FUKUI; 28,840 mems.

National Tax Office Employees' Union (*Kokuzeiroso*): Pres. YASUJI NAKAZAWA; Gen. Sec. MUTSUO SHIMIZU; 10,200 mems.

National Forest Workers' Union of Japan (*Nichirinro*): Pres. KAZUO KUMAI; Gen. Sec. YASUO YAMADA; 10,062 mems.

New Nippon Telephone and Telegram Workers' Union (*Dendenshinro*): Pres. JOTARO TANI; Gen. Sec. TADAO IKEDA; 250 mems.

Domei's Local Federations (*Chihodomei*): 200,000 mems.

Fraternal Organizations

National Council of Government and Public Corporation Workers' Unions (*Zenkanko*): Chair. EIETSU SUGAWARA; 150,000 mems.

National Council of Democratic Unionists (*Zenkokuminren*): Chair. SHIMPACHI KUDO; 300,000 mems.

Churitsu Rode Kumiai Renraku Kaigi—CHURITSU ROREN (*Liaison Council of Neutral Trade Unions*): 4-9, 1-chome, Shiba, Minato-ku, Tokyo; f. 1964; over 1,400,000 mems.; Gen. Sec. SHIGERU OKAMURA.

Major Affiliated Unions

National Federation of Cement Workers' Unions (*Zenkoku Semento*): 29-2, 5-chome, Shinbashi, Minato-ku, Tokyo; approx. 22,000 mems.; Pres. YORIO ABE; Sec.-Gen. MANJI YAMAMOTO.

National Federation of Electric Machine, Tool and Appliance Workers' Unions (*Denki Roren*): 13-10, 3-chome, Minami-Ohoi, Shingawa-ku, Tokyo; f. 1964; approx. 440,000 mems.; Pres. SHINRYO KIYOTA; Sec.-Gen. TARIKICHI SEKI.

Japanese Federation of Food and Allied Workers' Unions (*Shokuhin Roren*): 4-9, 1-chome, Shiba, Minatoku, Tokyo; approx. 92,000 mems.; Pres. SHIGERU OKAMURA.

National Federation of Life Insurance Employees' Unions (*Zenseiho*): 6 Kabuto-cho, 3-chome, Nihonbashi, Chuo-ku; approx. 82,000 mems.; Pres. JUNNOSUKE TANABE.

All-Japan Shipbuilding and Engineering Union (*Zenzosen*): 60-5, Sendagaya-3, Shibuya, Tokyo; f. 1964; 52,000 mems.; Pres. ISAO HASEGAWA; Sec.-Gen. NABEZO OHODE; publ. *Zenzosenkikai* (3 times monthly).

Zenkoku Sangyobetsu Rodo Kumiai Rengokai—SHIN SAMBETSU (*National Federation of Industrial Trade Unions*): Tokyo; approx. 70,000 mems.

MAJOR NON-AFFILIATED UNIONS

Tokyo

All-Japan Federation of Automobile Workers' Unions (*Zenkoku Jidosha*): f. 1962; approx. 120,000 mems.; Pres. KAZUO ITO; Sec.-Gen. TATSUYA KUBO.

Federation of City Bank Employees' Unions (*Shiginren*): c/o Yaesu, Chuo-ku; approx. 130,000 mems.; Pres. T. FURUKAWA.

Federation of Textile Clothing Workers' Unions of Japan (*Sen-i Roren SOHYO*): Katkura Bldg., 3-2 Kyobashi, Chuo-ku; approx. 25,000 mems.; Pres. KENZO OGUCHI.

National Federation of Mutual Bank Employees' Unions (*Zenso Ginren*): 40 Higashi Matsushita-cho; approx. 28,000 mems.; Pres. K. ISHIKAWA; Sec.-Gen. S. SAKAI.

Japan Council of Construction Industry Employees' Unions (*Nikkenkyo*): 5, 3-chome, Kanda-Kaji-cho, Chiyoda-ku; f. 1954; approx. 30,000 mems.; Pres. T. KUROMUSHA; Gen. Sec. N. RIOJA.

Labour Council of Governmental Special Corporations (*Seryokyo*): c/o Nichijuo 14, 1-chome, Kudan, Chiyoda-ku; approx. 19,000 mems.; Pres. K. TAKIZAWA.

All-Japan Damage Insurance Employees' Unions (*Zensonpo*): c/o Morizui Bldg., 3, 2-chome, Kyobashi, Chuo-ku; approx. 38,000 mems.; Pres. T. UEDA.

All-Japan Day Workers' Union (*Zennichijiro*): 3-22-10, Zoshigava Toshimaku, Tokyo; f. 1947; approx. 153,000 mems.; Pres. FUMIO WADA; publs. *Jikatabi* (weekly), *Gakusku* (monthly).

National Council of Medical Treatment Workers' Unions: approx. 49,000 mems.

Federation of Tokyo Metropolitan Government Workers' Unions (*To Roren*): c/o Tokyo-to Office, Marunouchi, Chiyoda-ku; approx. 120,000 mems.; Pres. U. OKAMOTO; Sec.-Gen. T. NAKAGAWA.

Japan Federation of Teachers (*Zenkyoren*): approx. 47,000 mems.; Pres. MASAO SUZUKI; Sec.-Gen. T. KIRUCHI.

Japan High School Teachers' Union (*Nikkokyo*): c/o Kyoiku Kakika, Hitotsubashi, Kanda, Chiyoda-ku; f. 1950; approx. 48,000 mems.; Pres. K. OGASAWARA.

Japan National Railways Locomotive Workers' Union: 3-2-13 Nishi-Gotanda, Shinagawa-ku, Tokyo; f. 1951; approx. 59,000 mems.; publ. weekly newsletter.

NATIONAL COUNCILS

Co-ordinating bodies for unions whose members are in the same industry or have the same employer.

Zenkoku Shogyo Rodo Kumiai Kyogi-kai—Zen Shokyo (*National Council of Commerce Workers' Unions*): 1-2 Nishi-Ginza, Chuo-ku, Tokyo; approx. 153,652 mems.; Gen.-Sec. TATSUO MATSUDA.

Zenkoku Kinyu Kikan Rode Kumiai Kyogi-kai—Zen Kinyu (*National Council of Finance Industry Workers' Unions*): 1-2 Nishi-Ginza, Chuo-ku, Tokyo; approx. 120,000 mems.; Sec.-Gen. MASAYA OKABE.

Zen Nippon Shokuhin Rodo Kumiai Rengo-kai—Shokuhin Roren (*Japanese Federation of Food and Allied Workers' Unions*): 1-4-9 Shiba, Minato-ku, Tokyo; f. 1954; approx. 94,000 mems.; Chair. SHIGERU OKAMURA.

Nihon Kankocho Rodo Kumiai Kyogi-kai—Kankoro (*Liaison Organization of Public Workers' Unions*): Sohyo Kaikan, Shiba Koen, Minato-ku, Tokyo; approx. 2,500,000 mems. from SOHYO affiliates; Sec.-Gen. REIICHIRO TOYOTA.

Zen Nippon Kotsu Unyu Rodo Kumiai Kyogi-kai—Zenkoun (*All-Japan Council of Traffic and Transport Workers Unions*): c/o Kokutetsu Rodo Kaikan, 2-1 Marunouchi, Chiyoda-ku, Tokyo; f. 1947; about 800,000 mems.; Pres. TOSHIKATSU HORII; Gen. Sec. ICHIZO SAKAI.

National Council of Government Enterprise Workers' Unions: Tokyo; approx. 1,000,000 mems.

National Liaison Council of Shipping and Harbour Workers' Unions: Tokyo; approx. 200,000 mems.

Kokusai Jiyuroren Kameikumiai Linkai (*Co-ordinating Committee of the I.C.F.T.U. Affiliated Unions in Japan*): c/o Kawatc Bldg., 5-8, 1-chome, Nishi-Shimbashi, Minato-ku, Tokyo; about 2,400,000 mems.; Gen. Sec. EIICHI OCHIAI.

CO-OPERATIVE ORGANIZATION

National Federation of Purchasing Associations—ZEN-KOREN: 5-12 Omotemachi, Chiyoda-ku, Tokyo; principal agricultural co-operative federation; collective purchase and sale of agricultural materials and produce.

MAJOR INDUSTRIAL COMPANIES

The following are the leading 75 industrial companies in Japan ranked by sales, according to *The Fortune 300 Directory* (1972). The information is compiled from the companies themselves and from the *Diamond Japan Business Directory*.

Nippon Steel Corporation: 6-3 Otemachi 2-chome, Chiyoda-ku Tokyo 100; f. 1970; sales 229,360m. yen.

Chair. SHIGEO NAGANO; Pres. TOMISABURO HIRAI; employees: 80,000.

Hitachi Ltd.: New Marunouchi Building 5-1, 1-chome, Chiyoda-ku, Tokyo; f. 1910; cap. 127,932m. yen.

Manufacture and sale of electric utility apparatus and electrical equipment, consumer products, communications and electronics equipment, measuring instruments, industrial machinery, rolling stock, wire, cable and other products.

Chair. KENICHIRO KOMAI; Pres. HIROKICHI YOSHIYAMA; employees: 163,063.

Toyota Motor Co. Ltd.: 1, Toyota-cho, Toyota, Aichi; f. 1937; cap. 51,200m. yen.

Manufacture of passenger cars, trucks and parts.

Pres. EIJI TOYODA; employees: 44,000.

Mitsubishi Heavy Industries Ltd.: 5-1, Marunouchi, 2-chome, Chiyoda-ku, Tokyo; f. 1950; cap. 100,472m. yen.

Shipbuilding, ship repairing, prime movers, chemical machinery, industrial machinery, heavy machinery, rolling stock, precision machinery, steel structures, construction machinery, refrigerating and air-conditioning machinery, agricultural machinery and engines, aircraft, special purpose vehicles, space systems.

Principal subsidiary companies in Japan and Brazil and other countries; Chair. F. KONO; Pres. SHIGEICHI KOGA; employees: 76,000.

Nissan Motor Co. Ltd.: 17-1, 6-chome, Ginza, Chuo-ku, Tokyo; f. 1933; cap. 54,020m. yen.

Manufacture and sale of automobiles, rockets, textile machinery, other machines and appliances and parts.

Chair. KATSUJI KAWAMATA; Pres. TADAHIRO IWAKOSHI; employees: 52,407.

Matsushita Electric Industrial Co. Ltd.: 1006 Kadoma, Kadoma, Osaka 571; f. 1918; cap. 50,325m. yen.

Manufacture and sales of electrical and electronic home appliances, including radio, television receivers and parts, communication equipment, medical equipment, batteries, electric light bulbs, and electric motors.

Ten major subsidiary companies in Japan; manufacturing and sales companies in 26 countries.

Chair. ARATORO TAKAHASHI; Pres. MASAHARU MATSUSHITA; employees: 47,000.

Tokyo Shibaura Electric Co. Ltd. (Toshiba): 72, Horikawa-cho, Saiwai-ku Kawasaki City, Kanagawa Pref.; f. 1904; cap. 293,393m. yen.

Manufacture, sale and export of electric appliances, apparatus and instruments; heavy electric machinery.

Overseas offices in 24 countries; Pres. KEIZO TAMAKI; employees: 73,000.

Nippon Kokan K.K. (*Japan Steel & Tube Corporation*): 1-1-2, Marunouchi, Chiyoda-ku, Tokyo 100; f. 1912; cap. 102,058m. yen (Mar. 1975).

Manufacture and sale of pig iron, steel ingots, tubes, plates, sheets, bars and shapes, special steels and ferro-alloys, coal derived chemicals, chemical fertilizers, refractories and slag wool, fabricated steel constructions, ships, shipping machinery and boilers, rolling stock, industrial machinery.

Pres. HISAO MAKITA; employees: 40,806.

Sumitomo Metal Industries Ltd.: 5-15, Kitahama, Higashiku, Osaka; f. 1897; cap. 82,976m. yen.

Manufacture and sale of pig iron, steel ingots, steel bars, shapes, wire rods, tubes, pipes, castings, forgings, rolling stock parts.

Fifty subsidiary companies in Japan; 7 offices abroad; Pres. NOBORU INUI; employees: 30,887 (1974).

Kobe Ltd.: 3-18,, 1-chome, Wakinohama-cho, Fukiai-ku, Kobe; f. 1905; cap. 101,285m. yen. (May 1975).

Manufacture and sale of iron, steel and non-ferrous metals and their alloys, cast iron, cast and forged steel, cast and forged non-ferrous metals and their by-products; electrodes, industrial and chemical machinery and appliances.

Chair. YOSHIMI INOUE; Pres. HIROAKI SUZUKI; employees: 36,000.

Mitsubishi Electric Corporation: Mitsubishi Building, Marunouchi, Tokyo; f. 1921; cap. 58,882m. yen.

Manufacturing and sales of electrical machinery and equipment (for power plant, mining, ships, locomotives and other rolling stock, aircraft), domestic electric appliances, radio communication equipment, radio and television sets, meters and relaying equipment, fluorescent lamps, lighting fixtures, refrigerators, lifts, electric tools, sewing machines.

Chair. KEN OKUBO; Pres. SADAKAZU SHINDO; employees: 57,000.

Taiyo Gyogyo (Taiyo Fishery) Co. Ltd.: 1-5-1 Marunouchi, Chiyoda-ku, Tokyo; f. 1880; cap. 15,000m. yen.

Whaling, fishing, processing and sale of agricultural, marine and meat products; canned and frozen salmon, crab, etc.; food processing, marine transport, export and import; refrigeration, ice production and cold storage; manufacture and sale of pharmaceuticals, organic fertilizers and sugar; culture and sale of pearls; breeding and sale of mink.

Sixty-nine subsidiary companies in Japan in fishery, oil, shipping, heavy industry, transport, food processing and the Taiyo Baseball Team; overseas subsidiaries.

Pres. KENKICHI NAKABE; employees: 12,000.

Ishikawajima-Harima Heavy Industries Co. Ltd.: 4 Ote-machi, 2, Chiyoda-ku, Tokyo; f. 1889; cap. 38,855m. yen.

Shipbuilding and ship repair service; manufacture, sale of and repair service for ship turbines and boilers, aircraft gas turbines, atomic power equipment, hauling equipment, iron and steel manufacturing plant, mining and civil engineering machinery, hydro- and thermal electric generating equipment, pneumatic and hydraulic machinery, chemical plant, steel structures.

Chair. TOSHIWO DOKO; Pres. RENZO TAGUCHI; employees: 38,000.

Kawasaki Steel Corporation: 1-28, Kitahonmachi-dori 1-chome, Fukiai-ku, Kobe 651.; f. 1950; cap. 120,856m. yen.

Manufacture and sale of plates, sheets, structural steels, tubular products, castings and forgings, welding electrodes, prefabricated products and iron powder.

Pres. ICHIRO FUJIMOTO; employees: 37,909.

Idemitsu Kosan Co. Ltd.: 1-1, 3-chome, Marunouchi, Chiyoda-ku, Tokyo; f. 1911; cap. 1,000m. yen.

Manufacture and sale of petroleum products and petrochemicals and related enterprises.

Chair. KEISUKE IDEMITSU; Pres. MASAMI ISHIDA; employees: 8,100.

Mitsubishi Chemical Industries Ltd.: 5-2 Marunouchi 2, Chiyoda-ku, Tokyo; f. 1934; cap. 38,750m. yen.

Manufacture and sale of coke and coal-tar derivatives, dyestuffs and intermediates, caustic soda, organic solvents and chemicals, reagents, ammonia derivatives, inorganic chemicals, pesticides and herbicides, fertilizers and food additives.

Pres. HIDEO SHINOJIMA; Exec. Vice-Pres. IKUO IWASAKI, RYUTARO HASEGAWA; employees: 10,000.

Honda Motor Co. Ltd.: 27-8, 6-chome, Jingumae, Shinjuku-ku, Tokyo; f. 1948; cap. 24,350m. yen.

Manufacture of automobiles, motorcycles, power tillers, general purpose engines, and portable generators.

Nine wholly-owned foreign subsidiaries in nine different countries; Pres. KIYOSHI KAWASHIMA; Vice-Pres. KIHACHIRO KAWASHIMA; employees: 24,918.

Toray Industries Inc.: 2-chome, Nihonbashi-Muromachi, Chuo-ku, Tokyo 103; f. 1926.

Manufacturers of nylon, Toray Tetoron (polyester fibre), Toraylon (acrylic fibre), Torayca (carbon fibre), plastics and chemicals.

Chair. KIZO YASUI; Pres. TSUGUHIDE FUJIYOSHI; employees: 19,000.

Nippon Electric Co. Ltd.: 33-1, Shiba Gochome, Minato-ku, Tokyo 108; f. 1899; cap. 40,000m. yen.

Manufacture and sale of telephone, video communications systems, carrier transmission, radio communication and broadcasting, satellite, data processing equipment, electron tubes and semi-conductors, electronic equipment, domestic electric appliances.

Pres. KOJI KOBAYASHI; employees: 55,000.

Kawasaki Heavy Industries Ltd.: Nissei-Kawasaki Bldg., 61-1 Nakamachidori 2-chome, Ikuta-ku, Kobe; f. 1896; assets 525,212m. yen.

Manufacture and sale of shipbuilding, rolling stock, aircraft, machinery, steel structure, engines and motorcycles.

Chair. MASASHI ISANO; Pres. KIYOSHI YOTSUMOTO; employees: 35,187.

Asahi Chemical Industry Co. Ltd.: Hibiya-Mitsui Bldg., 12 1-chome, Yurakucho, Chiyoda-ku, Tokyo; f. 1931; cap. 218,044m. yen.

Manufacture and sale of synthetic fibres, chemical fibres, acrylonitrilemonomer, plastics, synthetic rubber, explosives, construction materials, foods and fine chemicals.

Pres. KAGAYAKI MIYAZAKI; employees: 19,514.

Kanebo Ltd.: 3-80 Tomobuchi-cho, Miyakojima-ku, Osaka; f. 1889; cap. 17,036m. yen.

Manufacture, bleaching, dyeing, processing and sale of cotton yarns, cloth and thread, worsted and woollen yarns, woollen fabrics, nylon and polyester yarns and fabrics, carpets, spun silk yarns, silk thread spun from waste, silkworm eggs, silk fabrics, rayon staple, spun rayon yarns and fabrics, synthetic resins; cosmetics, pharmaceuticals, foodstuffs and household goods.

Pres. JUNJI ITOH; employees: 18,350.

Toyo Kogyo Co. Ltd.: P.O.B. 18 Hiroshima 730-91; f. 1920; cap. 25,704m. yen.

Manufacturing and sale of "Mazda" passenger cars and three and four wheel commercial vehicles; "Toyo" rock drills, machine tools, gauge block and coated sand. Manufacturing agreement with Perkins Engines (diesel) of U.K.

Twenty-eight subsidiary companies at home; subsidiaries in Australia, Belgium, the U.S.A. and Canada; Pres. KOHEI MATSUDA; employees: 32,000.

Nippon Mining Co. Ltd.: 3 Akasaka Aoi-cho, Minato-ku, Tokyo; f. 1905; cap. 24,600m. yen.

Mining, refining and sale of non-ferrous alloys; drilling, refining and sale of petroleum; metal processing and general chemical production.

Chair. TAKAHARU KAWAI; Pres. SHONOSUKE NIWANO; employees: 7,096.

Unitika Ltd.: 4-68, Kitakyutaro-machi, Higashi-ku, Osaka 541; f. 1889; assets 22,883,125m. yen.

Manufacture and sale of synthetic and natural fibres and fabrics; production of plastic resin and film; plant and machinery engineering.

Pres. SHINROKURA KODERA; employees: 17,000.

Sumitomo Chemical Co. Ltd.: 15, 5-chome, Kitahama Higashi-ku, Osaka; f. 1913; cap. 63,958m. yen.

Manufacture and sale of chemical fertilizers, dyestuffs, pharmaceuticals, agricultural chemicals, intermediates, coal tar, organic and inorganic industrial chemicals, synthetic resins, processed resins, aluminium and other electro-chemical products; planning and installation advice for equipment of industrial chemical plants.

Eight subsidiary companies; Pres. NORISHIGE HASEGAWA; employees: 16,265.

Toyobo Co. Ltd.: 8 Dojima Hamadori, 2-chome, Kita-ku, Osaka 530; f. 1882; cap. 29,203m. yen.

Manufacture and dyeing, bleaching, printing, finishing and sale of cotton yarns and fabrics, woollen and worsted yarns and fabrics, polyester yarns and fabrics and various artificial fibres; manufacture and sale of films, resins and biochemicals.

Chair. KUNIO KAWASAKI; Pres. ICHIJI OHTANI; employees: 22,606.

Sanyo Electric Co. Ltd.: 18 Keihan Hon-dori, 2, Moriguchi City, Osaka-ken; f. 1947; cap. 61,215m. yen.

Manufacture and sale of electrical and electronic machinery and appliances—refrigerators, washing machines, electric fans, television and radio sets, bicycle dynamos, bicycle accessories, dry batteries, flashlights, etc.

Pres. KAORU IUE; employees: 16,644.

Komatsu Ltd.: 3-6, 2-chome, Akasaka, Minato-ku, Tokyo; f. 1921; cap. 25,739m. yen.

Manufacture of bulldozers, motor graders, shovel loaders, dump trucks, forklift trucks, snow vehicles, presses, dozer shovels and tunnel boring machines.

Pres. RYOICHI KAWAI; employees: 24,491.

Hitachi Shipbuilding & Engineering Co. Ltd. (Hitachi Zosen): 1-1-1 Hitotsubashi, Chiyoda-ku, Tokyo; f. 1881; cap. 30,409m. yen.

Shipbuilding, ship repairing, remodelling and scrapping; manufacture of diesel engines and turbines, marine auxiliary machinery and fittings. Manufacture of industrial machinery and plant for chemicals, paper, petroleum, sugar, cement and iron, steel bridges and steel structures, environmental equipment, offshore equipment.

Thirty subsidiary companies at home; Pres. TAKAO NAGATA; employees: 25,000.

Maruzen Oil Co. Ltd.: 3 Nagahoribashisuji 1, Minami-ku, Osaka; f. 1933; cap. 16,425m. yen.

Import, refining and sale of petroleum; production and sale of petro-chemicals.

Pres. KAZUO MIYAMORI; employees: 6,343.

Kubota Ltd.: 22 Funade-cho, 2 Naniwa-ku, Osaka; f. 1890; cap. 48,366m. yen.

Manufacture and sale of cast iron pipes, steel ingot moulds, general castings, internal combustion engines, machine tools, measuring instruments, tractor, tiller, planting machine and general farming equipment, home and utilities, asbestos sheet, manufacturing, sale and installation of plant, flood gates and other steel structures, building materials.

Pres. KEITARO HIRO; employees: 18,600.

Teijin Ltd.: 1-1, 2-chome, Uchisaiwai-cho, Chiyoda-ku, Tokyo, and 11, Minami Hommachi, 1-chome, Higashi-ku, Osaka; f. 1918; cap. 31,493m. yen.

Manufactures of fibres, yarns and fabrics from polyester fibres (Teijin Tetoron), nylon, polyvinyl chloride fibre (Teijin Teviron), acetate, acrylic fibre (Teijin Beslon), polycarbonate resin (Panlite), acetate resin (Tenex), petro-chemicals, pharmaceuticals.

Fifty-three subsidiary companies; Pres. SHINZO OHYA; Vice-Pres. TOMOO TOKUSUE, SEIICHIRO WATANABE; employees: 12,399.

Kirin Brewery Co. Ltd.: Kashiwabara Building, 4, 1-chome, Kyobashi, Chuo-ku, Tokyo; f. 1907; cap. 24,763m. yen.

Production and sale of beer and soft drinks.

Pres. ASAJIRO TAKAHASHI; employees: 7,704.

Isuzu Motors Ltd.: 22-10 Minami-oi 6-chome, Shinagawa-ku, Tokyo; f. 1937; cap. 38,000m. yen.

Manufacture and sale of trucks, buses, special purpose vehicles, passenger cars and internal combustion engines.

Pres. TOSHIO OKAMOTO; employees: 14,127.

ToaNenryo Kogyo Kabushiki Kaisha: 1-1 Hitotsubashi 1-chome, Chiyoda-ku, Tokyo; f. 1939; cap. 14,714,662,950 yen.

Petroleum refining.

Principal subsidiary companies: Nichimo Sekiyu, Tonen Sekiyu, Kagaku Co. Ltd.; Chair. N. NAKAHARA; Pres. M. NAMBU; employees: 2,134 (as of June 30th, 1970).

Showa Denko K.K.: 13-9, Shiba Daimoncho 1-chome, Minato-ku, Tokyo 105; f. 1939; assets 312,670m. yen.

Manufacture and sale of aluminium, petrochemical products, fertilizers and thermochemical products.

Pres. HARUO SUZUKI; employees: 9,356.

Mitsubishi Rayon Co. Ltd.: 8, 2-chome, Kyobashi, Chuo-ku, Tokyo; f. 1933; cap. 16,353m. yen.

Manufacture of rayon staple fibre, spun rayon yarn and fabrics, acrylic fibre, yarn and fabrics, methancrylate resin, anti-static solutions.

Principal subsidiary companies: Mitsubishi Acetate, Mitsubishi Vonel, Nitto Chemical, Union Carbide; Pres. KISABURO SHIMIZU; Vice-Pres. SHUZO KANAZAWA; employees: 6,868.

Furukawa Electric Co. Ltd.: 6-1 Marunouchi 2-chome, Chiyoda-ku, Tokyo; f. 1884; cap. 12,533m. yen.

Manufacture and sale of electric wires and cables, non-ferrous metal products.

Chair. KIYOSHI UYEMATSU; Pres. JIRO SUZUKI; employees: 9,500.

Ube Industries Ltd.: 7-2 Kasumigaseki 3-chome, Chiyoda-ku, Tokyo 100; f. 1942; cap. 113,035m. yen.

Mining, production, processing and sale of coal, iron ore, limestone, silica, clay, chemical fertilizers, tar products, sulphuric acid, nitric acid, oxalic acid, ammonium nitrate, ammonia, pharmaceuticals, cement, caprolactam, high pressure polythylene, industrial machinery and equipment, cast steel products, cast iron products, iron and steel bars.

Pres. KANICHI NAKAYASU; Vice-Pres. TOYOZO FUJIMOTO; employees: 13,972.

Sony Corporation: 7-35, Kitashinagawa 6-chome, Shinagawa-ku, Tokyo 141; f. 1946; assets 179,086m. yen.

Manufacture and sale of television sets, radios, tape recorders, etc.

Chair. MASARU IBUKA; Pres. AKIO MORITA; employees: 16,615.

Takeda Chemical Industries Ltd.: 27 Doshomachi, 2 Higashi-ku, Osaka; f. 1925; cap. issued 24,300m. yen.

Manufacture and distribution of pharmaceuticals, industrial chemicals, cosmetics, food additives; enriched foods and drinks, agricultural chemicals, fertilizers.

Chair. KANZABURO MORIMOTO; Pres. SHINBEI KONISHI; employees 13,000.

Sumitomo Electric Industries Ltd.: 15, 5-chome, Kitahama, Higashi-ku, Osaka; f. 1911; cap. 18,069m. yen.

Manufacture of electric wires and cables, high carbon steel wires; sintered alloy products; rubber and plastic products; disc brakes; radio-frequency products.

Chair. ISAMU SAKAMOTO; Pres. MASAO KAMEI; employees: 11,484 (as of Sept. 1974).

Fujitsu Ltd.: Furukawa Sogo Bldg., 6-1, Marunouchi 2-chome, Chiyoda-ku, Tokyo 100; f. 1935; assets 337,505m. yen.

Manufacture and sale of electronic computers and data, processing equipment, telephone equipment, etc.

Pres. HIROSHI SEIMIYA; employees: 32,063.

Mitsubishi Oil Co. Ltd.: 1 Kotohira-cho, Shiba, Minato-ku, Tokyo; f. 1931; cap. 15,000m. yen.

Refining, import and marketing of petroleum products and petrochemicals.

Pres. TAKEO WATANABE; employees: 2,986.

Snow Brand Milk Products Co. Ltd.: 13 Honshio-cho-Shinjuku-ku, Tokyo; f. 1950; cap. 7,500m. yen (March 1974).

Manufacture of liquid milk, condensed and powdered milk, butter, cheese, ice-cream, infant foods, instant foods, margarine, fruit juices, frozen foods, imported wine distribution.

Chair. YOSHIICHI KODAMA; Pres. YOICHI YAMAMOTO; employees: 10,830.

Bridgestone Tire Co. Ltd.: 1 Kyobashi 1-chome, Chuo-ku, Tokyo; f. 1931; cap. 14,546m. yen.

Manufacture of all kinds of rubber tyres and tubes, transmission and conveyor belts and hoses, foam rubber, polyurethane foam, golf balls.

Chair. KANICHIRO ISHIBASHI; Pres. SHIGEMICHI SHIBAMOTO; employees: 18,400.

Mitsui Shipbuilding & Engineering Co. Ltd.: 6-4, Tsukiji 5-chome, Chuo-ku, Tokyo 104; f. 1937; cap. 30,335m. yen.

Shipbuilding and industrial machinery.

Pres. ISAMU YAMASHITA; employees: 16,565.

Fuji Electric Co. Ltd.: 1-2-1, Yurakucho, Chiyoda-ku, Tokyo; f. 1923; cap. 21,145m. yen.

Manufacture and sale of electrical equipment.

Chair. CHOHEI AIDA; Pres. FUKUSHIGE SHISHIDO; employees: 20,853.

Suzuki Motor Co. Ltd.: P.O.B. 116, Hamamatsu 430; f. 1920; cap. 12,000m. yen.

Manufacture and sale of cars and motor cycles, outboard motors, mini-houses and bicycles.

Pres. JITSUJIRO SUZUKI; Senior Man. Dir. OSAMU SUZUKI; employees: 10,000.

Mitsui Mining and Smelting Co. Ltd.: 1-1, 2-chome, Nihonbashi-Muromachi, Chuo-ku, Tokyo; f. 1950; assets 401,897m. yen.

Copper and zinc and related products.

Pres. SHIMPEI OMOTO; employees: 7,846.

Asahi Glass Co. Ltd.: 1-2, Marunouchi 2-chome, Chiyoda-ku, Tokyo; f. 1907; cap. 33,505m . yen.

Manufacture and sale of flat glass, TV bulbs, alkali and other chemicals, and refractories.

Associated and subsidiary companies in Thailand and India; Pres. HIDEAKI YAMASHITA; employees: 11,490.

Nisshin Steel Co. Ltd.: 4-1, 3-chome, Marunouchi, Chiyoda-ku, Tokyo; f. 1928; cap. 32,400m. yen.

Manufacture of ordinary steel, stainless steel, special steel and various secondary products.

Pres. NOBUO KANEKO; employees: 10,000.

Ajinomoto Co. Inc.: 6 Kyobashi 1-chome, Chuo-ku, Tokyo 104; f. 1909; cap. 8,304m. yen.

Manufacture and sale of seasonings, oil products, food-stuffs, etc.

Numerous subsidiaries and overseas offices; Pres. KYOJI SUZUKI; employees: 6,062.

Mitsui Toatsu Chemicals Inc.: Kasumigaseki Bldg., Kasumigaseki, Chiyoda-ku, Tokyo; f. 1933; cap. 21,952m. yen.

Industrial chemicals, fertilizers and resins, etc.

Pres. TOSHIO SUEYOSHI; employees: 9,903.

Sharp Corporation: 22-22 Nagaikecho, Abeno-ku, Osaka 545; f. 1912; cap. 11,552m. yen.

Manufacture and sale of TV sets, acoustic equipment, domestic electrical appliances, industrial machines and medical equipment.

Pres. AKIRA SAEKI; employees: 20,000.

Mitsubishi Metal Corporation: 5, Otemachi 1-chome, Chiyoda-ku, Tokyo 100; f. 1950; cap. 22,500m. yen.

Copper, zinc and metal-processed products.

Pres. YOSHIHIRO INAI; employees: 10,338.

Meiji Milk Products Co. Ltd.: 6, Kyobashi 2-chome, Chuo-ku, Tokyo 104; f. 1917; cap. 7,957m. yen.

Dairy products.

Pres. MASANORI ONO; Exec. Vice-Pres. KEIJO FUJIMI; employees: 6,282.

Honshu Paper Co. Ltd.: 12-8, 5-chome Ginza, Chuo-ku, Tokyo; f. 1949; cap. 4,256m. yen.

Paper, board, and lumber products.

Associated company in Canada; Pres. TOSHIRO KAWAGUCHI; employees: 5,500.

Morinaga Milk Industry Co. Ltd.: 33-1, 5-chome Shiba, Minato-ku, Tokyo; f. 1917; cap. 6,000m. yen.

Manufacture of condensed milk, powdered milk, butter, cheese, ice-cream, liquid milk.

Offices in cities all over Japan; Chair. ISAMU OHNO; Pres. HEIHACHI INO; employees: 5,141 (1975).

Fuji Photo Film Co. Ltd.: 26-30, Nishiazabu 2-chome, Minato-ku, Tokyo 106; f. 1934; cap. 11,599m. yen.

Films and photographic materials.

Chair. SETSUTARO KOBAYASHI; Pres. KUSUO HIRATA; employees: 10,139.

Hino Motors Ltd.: 1-1, Hinodai 3-chome, Hino-shi, Tokyo 191; f. 1942; cap. 12,480m. yen.

Diesel trucks and buses, cars.

Pres. MASANOBU MATSUKATA; employees: 6,800.

Kuraray Co. Ltd.: 8 Umeda, Kita-ku, Osaka 530; f. 1926; cap. 10,000m. yen.

Chemical fibres, chemicals.

Pres. TSUGIO OKABAYASHI; employees: 11,000.

Jujo Paper Co. Ltd.: Shin Yurakucho Bldg., 12-1, Yurakucho 1-chome, Chiyoda-ku, Tokyo 100; f. 1949; cap. 9,200m. yen.

Printing paper, newsprint, non-carbon paper, etc.

Chair. SAICHIRO KANEKO; Pres. KENICHI SHIBUYA; employees: 6,800.

Nisshin Flour Milling Co. Ltd.: 19-12 Koami-cho, Nihonbashi, Chuo-ku, Tokyo; f. 1900; cap. 6,600m. yen.

Production and sale of wheat flour, formula feeds and prepared mixes.

Chair. YOSHIO ISHII; Pres. HIDESABURO SHODA; employees: 3,121.

Fuji Heavy Industries Ltd.: Subaru Bldg., Shinjuku, Tokyo; f. 1953; cap. 10,000m. yen.

Cars, bus bodies, aeroplanes, etc.

Pres. EICHI OHARA; employees: 13,482.

Sumitomo Shipbuilding and Machinery Co. Ltd.: 2-1, Ohtemachi 2-chome, Chiyoda-ku, Tokyo; f. 1934; cap. 17,453m. yen.

Industrial machinery and shipbuilding.

Pres. TSUNESABURO NISHIMURA; employees: 11,980

Nippon Suisan Kaisha Ltd.: 6-2, Otemachi 2-chome, Chiyoda-ku, Tokyo; f. 1943; cap. 10,000m. yen.

Marine, fisheries and fish products.

Chair. MASATAK SUZUKI; Pres. JUUROO OSOEKAWA; employees: 11,000.

Nippondenso Co. Ltd.: 1-1 Showa-cho, Kariya-shi, Aichi-ken; f. 1949; cap. 7,668m. yen.

Car electrical equipment, air conditioners, radiators, fuel injection pumps, instruments, sparking plugs, etc.

Pres. TAKEAKI SHIRAI; employees: 19,760.

Shiseido Co. Ltd.: 5-5, Ginza 7-chome, Chuo-ku, Tokyo, cap. 5,400m. yen.

Cosmetics and soap.

Pres. NOBUKAZU FUKUHARA; employees: 13,000.

Dainippon Ink and Chemicals Inc.: 3, Nihombashi Tori 3-chome, Chuo-ku, Tokyo; f. 1937; cap. 10,000m. yen.

Printing inks, chemicals, building materials, etc.

Pres. KATSUMI KAWAMURA; employees: 5,731.

Toppan Printing Co. Ltd.: 5, Taito 1-chome, Taito-ku, Tokyo 110; f. 1908; cap. 14,300m. yen.

General printing.

Pres. KAICHI SAWAMURA; employees: 9,685.

Daishowa Paper Manufacturing Co. Ltd.: 133 Imai, Fuji-shi, Shizuoka-ken 417; f. 1921; cap. 8,500m. yen.

Paper and board.

Pres. RYOEI SAITO; employees: 5,423.

Sumitomo Metal Mining Co. Ltd.: 11-3, 5-chome, Shimbashi, Minato-ku, Tokyo; f. 1950; cap. 12,963m. yen.

Copper, nickel, ferro-nickel, etc.

Pres. AKIRA FUJISAKI; employees: 4,027.

Oji Paper Co. Ltd.: 7-5, Ginza 4-chome, Chuo-ku, Tokyo 104; f. 1949; cap. 11,063m. yen (Sept. 1974).

Newsprint, packing paper and printing paper.

Chair. KEIJI NAKAJIMA; Pres. FUMIO TANAKA; employees: 4,836.

TRANSPORT

RAILWAYS

Japanese National Railways (J.N.R.): 1-6-5, Marunouchi, Chiyoda-ku, Tokyo; f. 1949 as a public corporation; underwent reorganization, August 1970; 1.067 guage; the 1.435 gauge, very high speed, Shinkansen line (733 km.) linking Tokyo with Yokohama, Nagoya, Kyoto and Shin-Osaka was completed in 1964; this line was extended to Okayama in 1972, and further construction to Hakata in Kyushu is due to be completed shortly. Further extension links are scheduled for construction between Tokyo and Morioka, Niigata and Nanta; 20,924 km. of track, 6,685 km. of 1,067 gauge is electrified; Pres. M. FUJII; Exec. Vice-Pres. K. INOUE; Vice-Pres. Engineering M. TAKIYAMA.

PRINCIPAL PRIVATE COMPANIES: 6,593 km. of track of which 5,607 km. are electrified.

Hanshin Electric Railway Co. Ltd.: 8, Umeda-cho, Kita-ku, Osaka; f. 1899; Pres. CHUJIRO NODA.

Hankyu Corporation: 41, Kakuta-cho, Kitaku, Osaka; f. 1907; links Osaka, Kyoto, Kobe and Takarazuka; Pres. KAORU MORI.

Keihan Electric Railway Co. Ltd.: 47-5, 1-chome, Kyobashi, Higashi-ku, Osaka; Pres. S. MURAOKA.

Keihin Kyuko Electric Express Railway Co. Ltd.: 10-18 Takanawa 4-chome, Minato-ku, Tokyo; Pres. HARUO SATO.

Keio Teito Electric Railway Co. Ltd.: 48, 3-chome, Shinjuku, Shinjuku-ku, Tokyo; Pres. S. INOUE.

Keisei Electric Railway Co. Ltd.: 10-3, 1-chome, Oshiage Sumidaku, Tokyo; f. 1909; Pres. C. KAWASAKI; Man. Dir. IKUJIRO FUKUDA.

Kinki Nippon Railway Co. Ltd.: 1, 6-chome, Uehom-machi, Tennoji-ku, Osaka; f. 1910; Pres. EIZO IMAZOTO.

Kobe Municipal Rapid Transit: Municipal Traffic Bureau, Kobe.

Kyoto Rapid Transit: Hanku Dentetsu Company, Kyoto.

Nagoya Railroad Co. Ltd.: 223, 1-chome, Sashima-cho, Nakamura-ku, Nagoya-shi; Pres. MOTOO TSUCHIKAWA.

Nankai Railroad Co.: 12, Rokuban-cho, Nanbashinchi, Minami-ku, Osaka; Pres. D. KAWAKATSU.

Nippon Express Co. Ltd.: 12-9, 3-chome, Sotokanda, Chiyoda-ku. Tokyo; f. 1937; Pres. T. SAWAMURA; Vice-Pres. S. HIROSE, G. HOSOI; cap. 46m.

Nishi Nippon Railroad Co. Ltd.: 12-1 Tenjin-cho, Fukuoka; serves northern Kyushu; Pres. HIROTSUGU YOSHIMOTO.

Odakyu Electric Railway Co. Ltd.: 28, 2-chome, Yoyogi, Shibuya-ku, Tokyo; Pres. N. ANDO.

Sapporo Rapid Transit: Municipal Transportation Bureau, Sapporo, Hokkaido; 12 km. in length, further 45 km. to be completed in 1986.

Seibu Railway Co. Ltd.: 16-15, 1-chome, Minami-Ikebukuro, Toshima-ku, Tokyo; f. 1912; Pres. SHOJIRO KOJIMA; Vice-Pres. YOSHIAKI TSUTSUMI, SEIJ, TSUTSUMI; Senior Man. Dir. IWAO NISUGI.

Teito Rapid Transit Authority: 19-6, 3-chome, Higashi Ueno, Taito-ku, Tokyo; f. 1941; underground railway service for Tokyo; Pres. M. ARAKI.

Tobu Railway Co. Ltd.: 2, 1-chome, Oshiage, Sumida-ku, Tokyo; Pres. KAICHIRO NEZU.

Tokyu Corporation: 26-20 Sakuragaoka-cho, Shibuya-ku, Tokyo; f. 1922; Pres. NOBORU GOTOH.

Yokohama Rapid Transit: Municipal Transportation Bureau, Yokohama; total planned length of 61 km. of which 12 km. were completed in 1971.

SUBWAYS AND MONORAILS

Subway service is available today in four major cities, Tokyo, Osaka, Kobe and Nagoya, with a combined network of over 200 km. New subway services were inaugurated in Yokohama and Sapporo, the latter in time for the Winter Olympics in 1972. Most new subway lines are directly linked with existing J.N.R. or private railway terminals which connect the cities with suburban areas.

Japan started its first monorail system on a commercial scale in 1964 with straddle-type cars between downtown Tokyo and Tokyo International Airport, a distance of 13 km. In 1969, the total monorail mileage was 24 km. Work started in 1971 on the 34-mile Seikan Tunnel (electric rail only) linking Honshu island with Hokkaido.

Tokyo Underground Railway: Teito Rapid Transit Authority, 19-6 Higashi Ueno, 3-chome, Taito-ku, Tokyo; f. 1941; Pres. M. ARAKI; total length 163.2 km. (March 1975); and Transportation Bureau of Tokyo Metropolitan Government, 2-13 Yurako-cho, Chiyoda-ku, Tokyo; f. 1960; Dir.-Gen. K. SAITO; length 40.5 km.; combined length of underground system 164.4 km.

ROADS

In March 1973 Japan's road network extended to 1,059,200 km. Plans have been made to cover the country with a trunk automobile highway network with a total length of 7,600 km. expected to be completed by 1985.

A 190 km. stretch of trunk highway links Nagoya and Kobe (Meishin Expressway) and a 346 km. joins Nagoya and Tokyo (Tomei Expressway). The Nagano–Gifu section in the mountainous region of Nagano was completed in 1975, when the Enasan tunnel, part of the same route, also came into operation.

There is a national omnibus service, 54 publicly operated services and 294 privately operated services.

SHIPPING

Shipping in Japan is not nationalized but is supervised by the Ministry of Transport. On June 30th, 1974, gross registered tonnage totalled 38,708,000.

PRINCIPAL COMPANIES

Daiichi Chuo Kisen Kaisha: 7-3 Nihonbashi-Dori, Chuo-ku, Tokyo; f. 1960; fleet of 24 vessels; bulk ore and oil carriers; Pres. KOTARO TSUCHIKANE.

Japan Line Ltd.: Kokusai Bldg., 1-1, 3-chome, Marunouchi, Chiyoda-ku, Tokyo; f. 1948; container ship, tanker, liner, tramp and specialized carrier services; Pres. H. MATSUNAGA.

Japan Marine Products Co.: 3, 2-chome, Marunouchi, Chiyoda-ku, Tokyo; cargo and tanker services; fleet of 15 vessels; Pres. H. NAKAI; Vice-Pres. T. ITO, O. KAJIYAMA; Man. Dirs. Y. NAGASAWA, T. TSUAKI, T. MURAKAMI.

Kansai Steamship Co. Ltd.: 1 Soze-cho, Kita-ku, Osaka; f. 1942; fleet of 39 vessels; tramp, cargo/passenger services to Far East, Philippines and Australia; Pres. SHIGERU HASEGAWA.

Kawasaki Kisen Kaisha (*K Line*): 8 Kaigan-dori, Ikuta-ku, Kobe; f. 1919; fleet of 91 vessels; cargo, tanker and bulk ore carrying services worldwide; Chair. Motozo Hattori; Pres. M. Adachi.

Mitsui O.S.K. Lines Ltd.: 3-3, 5-chome, Akasaka, Minato-ku, Tokyo; f. 1964 by merger of Mitsui Steamship Co. and O.S.K.; fleet of 300 vessels; cargo, tanker and ore carrying services world-wide; Pres. Yoshio Shinoda.

Nippon Yusen Kafushiki Kaisha: 3-2, Marunouchi, 2-chome, Chiyoda-ku, Tokyo; merged with Mitsubishi Steamship Co. 1964; fleet of 172 vessels; world-wide cargo, tanker and bulk carrying services, including six main container routes; Chair. Y. Ariyoshi; Pres. S. Kikuch.

Nissho Shipping Co. Ltd.: 2-1, Marunouchi, 2-chome, Chiyoda-ku, Tokyo; fleet of 18 vessels; tanker, lumber and ore carrying services to Arabian Gulf, North America, Philippines, New Caledonia, Chile; Pres. J. Matsushima.

Okinawa Kisen Kaisha: 2-226, Maejima-cho, Naha, Okinawa; Pres. Kokichi Kokuba.

Ryukyu Kaiun Kaisha: 1-5, 1-chome, Nisi Naha, Okinawa; Pres. Mashi Azama.

Ryukyu Unyu Company: 1-1, Nishi-Honmachi, Naha, Okinawa; Pres. Tadoyoshi Miyara.

Western Pacific Corporation Import and Export Shipping Agents: P.O.B. 42, Naha, Okinawa; Pres. M. R. R. Conn.

The Sanko Steamship Co. Ltd.: Shinyurakucho Bldg., 12-1, Yuurakucho, 1-chome, Chiyoda-ku, Tokyo; f. 1934; fleet of 35 owned and 211 chartered vessels; overseas tramping (cargo and oil); Pres. Kotaro Kameyama.

Sankyo Kaiun Co. Ltd.: Miki Bldg., No. 5, 3-chome, Nihonbashi Edobashi, Chuo-ku, Tokyo; fleet of 15 vessels; liner and tramp services to the Far East; Pres. H. Ikemura; Man. Dir. S. Shiraishi.

Shinwa Kaiun Kaisha Ltd.: 1-3, Kyobashi, Chuo-ku, Tokyo; f. 1950; fleet of 39 vessels; ore carrying, cargo and tanker services to Pacific, Far East and U.S.; Pres. Hiroshi Miwa.

Showa Shipping Co. Ltd.: 1, 4-chome, Nihonbashi, Muromachi, Chuo-ku, Tokyo; f. 1964 by merger of Nippon Oil Tanker Co. Ltd. and Nissan Steamship Co. Ltd.; cargo, tanker, tramping and container services worldwide; Chair. Toshiharu Matsue; Pres. Sotaro Yamada; Vice-Pres. Daijiro Eshii.

Taiheiyo Kaiun Kabushiki Kaisha (*The Pacific Transportation Co. Ltd.*): Room 314, Marunouchi Bldg., 4-1, 2-chome, Chiyoda-ku, Tokyo; fleet of 15 vessels, cargo and tanker services; Pres. S. Yamaji.

Yamashita-Shinnihon Steamship Co., Ltd.: 1-1, Hitotsubashi, 1-chome, Chiyoda-ku, Tokyo 100; f. 1917, as Yamashita Steamship Co., Ltd., merger with Shinnihon Steamship Co., Ltd. 1964; fleet of 55 vessels; liner and tramp services to U.S. Far East, etc.; Chair. S. Yamashita; Pres. T. Hori.

CIVIL AVIATION

Japan Air Lines—JAL (*Nihon Koku Kabushiki Kaisha*). 7-3, 2-chome, Marunouchi, Chiyoda-ku, Tokyo 100; f. 1951; operates domestic and international services from Tokyo to Honolulu, Los Angeles, San Francisco, Vancouver, Anchorage, New York, Seoul, Pusan, Khabarovsk, Hong Kong, Manila, Bangkok, Jakarta, Kuala Lumpur, Singapore, Sydney, Guam, New Delhi, Teheran, Beirut, Calcutta, Karachi, Cairo, Rome, Frankfurt, Hamburg, Copenhagen, Amsterdam, Moscow, Paris, Mexico City, Athens, Bombay, Shanghai, Peking and London; Pres. Shizuo Asada; fleet of 2 Boeing 727, 26 Boeing 747, 45 DC-8, 3 Falcon 20, 3 Beech B 18.

Japan Domestic Airlines Co. Ltd.: Tokyo International Airport, Haneda, Tokyo; f. 1964; passenger services throughout Japan; fleet of three Boeing 727, fifteen YS-11; Pres. Tatsuhiko Kawabuchi.

All Nippon Airways: 2-5, Kasumigaseki 3-chome, Chiyoda-ku, Tokyo; domestic passenger and freight services; Pres. Tokuji Wakasa (arrested July 1976); fleet of 23 Boeing 727, 14 Boeing 737, 14 TriStar, and 30 YS-11.

Southwest Airlines Co. Ltd. (*Nansei Koku KK*): 306-1, Aza Kagamizu, Naha, Okinawa; operates inter-island service in Okinawa; Pres. Masao Masumo; fleet of 5 YS-11A, 2 Twin Otter.

Toa Domestic Airline Co.: Tokyo International Airport, 9-1, 1-chome, Haneda-Kuko, O'hta-ku, Tokyo: f. 1971 domestic scheduled services to 35 cities in Japan, including Tokyo and Osaka; Pres. Isamu Tanaka; fleet of 29 YS-11A, 11 DC-9-41, 2 Boeing 727-100, 8 Kawasaki Bell 47G, 2 Hughes 500.

Tokyo is served by the following foreign airlines: Aeroflot, Air France, Air India, Air Siam, Alitalia, British Airways, CAAC, Cathay Pacific Airways Ltd., Air Canada, EgyptAir, Garuda Indonesian Airways, Iran Air, KLM, Korean Airlines, Lufthansa, Northwest Orient Airlines, Philippine Airlines, PIA, Sabena, Singapore Airlines, Pan American, Qantas, SAS, Swissair, Thai Airways International, Varig.

TOURISM

Japan National Tourist Organization: Tokyo Kotsu Kaikan Bldg., 2-13 Yuraku-cho, Tokyo; Pres. Saburo Ohta.

Japan Travel Bureau Inc.: 6-4, Marunouchi 1-chome. Chiyoda-ku, Tokyo; f. 1912; approx. 13,000 mems.; Chair. T. Nishio; Pres. H. Tsuda; Exec. Vice-Pres. M. Kanematsu, M. Hata; publ. *JTB Travel Newsletter* (quarterly).

Department of Tourism: 2-1-3 Kasumigaseki, Chiyoda-ku, Tokyo; f. 1946; inner department of the Ministry of Transport; Dir.-Gen. Akira Takano.

THEATRES

Kabukiza Theatre: Ginza-Higashi, Tokyo; national Kabuki theatre centre.

National Theatre of Japan (*Kokuritsu Gekijo*): 13 Hayabusa-cho, Chiyoda-ku, Tokyo 102; f. 1966; Pres. Seiichiro Takahashi; Chief. Dir. Sakuo Teranaka; Dirs. Kosaburo Shibata, Jiro Osaragi, Yukiso Mirshima.

Nissei Theatre: 1-12 Yuraku-cho, Chiyoda-ku, Tokyo; f. 1963; drama, opera and concerts; mems. 300; Gen. Dir. Keita Asari.

MUSIC FESTIVAL

Osaka International Festival: Osaka; joined European Asscn. of Music Festivals 1966.

POWER

Projected supply of primary energy, in terms of million kilolitres of petroleum:

	1970	1975	1985
Hydroelectricity .	19.9	22.2	26.4
Atomic Energy .	1.5	8.0	60.1
Coal . . .	51.4	55.1	56.5
Petroleum . .	161.7	246.2	446.9

In face of the increasing demand for energy supply, Japan's energy policy is to seek low-cost energy sources and to stabilize the supply. The aim is to make energy supplies autonomous, with the government playing a leading part in promoting technological development and developing overseas resources.

ELECTRICITY

In terms of electric power generation Japan ranks fourth in the world. Similarly, in terms of hydroelectric power generation, she ranks fourth (after U.S.A., Federal Republic of Germany and U.S.S.R.).

Production (1974): 460,705m. kWh.

DISTRIBUTION

There are 47 wholesale organizations. The largest of these is:

The Electrical Power Development Co. Ltd.: 1, 1-chome, Marunouchi, Chiyoda-ku, Tokyo; f. 1952 with government assistance; Pres. OSAMU FUJINAMI.

Regional Corporations

The Hokkaido Electric Power Co. Inc.: 2, 1-chome, Odori-Higashi, Sapporo; Pres. TSUNEJI IWAMOTO.

The Tohoku Electric Power Co. Inc.: 7-1, 3-chome, Ichibaucho, Sendai City, Miyagi Pref.; f. 1951; Pres. and Dir. TSUTOMU WAKABAYASHI.

The Tokyo Electric Power Co. Inc.: 5-1, 1-chome, Uchisaiwai-cho, Chiyoda-ku, Tokyo; Pres. KAZUTAKA KIKAWANDA.

The Chubu Electric Power Co. Inc.: 10, Toshin-cho, Higashi-ku, Nagoya; Pres. OTOSABURO KATO.

The Hokuriku Electric Power Co. Inc.: 3-1, Sakurabashi-dori, Toyama, 930; f. 1951; cap. 43,562m. yen; Pres. KEIGO HARATANI.

The Kansai Electric Power Co. Inc.: 5, Nakanoshima 3-chome, Kita-ku, Osaka; f. 1951; Chair. YOSHISHIGE ASHIHARA; Pres. SEIZO YOSHIMURA.

The Chugoku Electric Power Co. Inc.: 4-33, Komachi, Hiroshima; Pres. MIKIO SAKURAUCHI.

The Shikoku Electric Power Co. Inc.: 2, Marunouchi, Takamatsu; Pres. TSUNENORI YAMAGUCHI.

The Kyushu Electric Power Co. Inc.: 1, 2-chome, Watanabedori, Fukuoka; Pres. KIYOSHI KAWARABAYASHI.

NATURAL GAS

Production (1972): 2,475,055 cu. metres.

MAJOR COMPANIES:

Osaka Gas Co. Ltd.: 5-1, Hiranomachi, Higashiku, Osaka; Chair. TAKEJIRO IGUCHI; Pres. NAGATOMI FUJISAKA.

Saibu Gas Co. Ltd.: 9-1 Kego Okitamachi, Fukuoka City; Pres. MIYAICHI YAMASAKI.

Toho Gas Co. Ltd.: 60, Sakuradacho, Atsutaku, Nagoya; Pres. KIYOSHI AOKI.

Tokyo Gas Co Ltd.: 1-3 Yaesu, Chuo-ku, Tokyo; Pres. HIROTOSHI HONDA.

ATOMIC ENERGY

Japan's atomic energy development programme began towards the end of 1955 with the government's enactment of the Basic Law of Atomic Energy, and setting up the Atomic Energy Commission of Japan. In 1956 the first research centre, Japan Atomic Energy Research Institute, was established in Tokai village, Ibaraki prefecture. In 1962 the Nuclear Ship Development Agency was established, and in 1967 the Power Reactor and Nuclear Fuel Corporation was established to develop advance thermal reactors and fast breeder reactors, as well as nuclear fuels.

Four nuclear power stations were in operation by 1971 and nine more were expected to become operational by 1975 with a combined capacity of 3,600 MWe.

Japan is an active member of the IAEA. She also has Co-operation Agreements on Atomic Energy with the U.S., U.K. and Canada. Through these agreements, various collaborations such as the exchange of technological information, supply of nuclear fuel and instruments, etc., have been carried out. The nine regional electricity companies of Japan have engaged foreign firms to undertake prospecting and mining for uranium in North America on their behalf.

Projected Generating Capacity: 1975: 6,000 MW; 1985: 30,000–40,000 MW.

Japan Atomic Energy Commission (JAEC): 2-2-1 Kasumigaseki, Chiyoda-ku, Tokyo; policy board for research, development and peaceful uses of atomic energy; Commissioners: GORO INOUYE, TOSHINOSUKE MUTO, EIICHI TAKEDA, AKIRA MATSUI, EIZO TAZIMA, TASABURO YAMADA.

Atomic Energy Bureau (AEB): Science and Technology Agency, 2-2-1 Kasumigaseki, Chiyoda-ku, Tokyo; central administrative agency; Dir. TOSHIHAM NARITA.

Japan Atomic Energy Research Institute (JAERI): 1-1-13 Shinbashi, Minato-ku, Tokyo; six reactors for training, isotope production and research; f. 1956; Pres. EIJI MUNEKATA; Vice-Pres. HIROSHI MURATA.

Fund for Peaceful Atomic Development of Japan: 1-1-13, Shinbashi, Minato-ku, Tokyo; education of the Japanese people in understanding atomic energy and its applications; Pres. REINOSUKE SUGA.

Japan Atomic Industrial Forum (JAIF): 1-1-13, Shinbashi, Minato-ku, Tokyo; collates the activities of private industry in connection with peaceful uses of atomic energy; Chair. REINOSUKE SUGA.

PRINCIPAL JAERI ESTABLISHMENTS

Radioisotope Centre: The University of Tokyo, Yayoi 2-11-16, Bunkyo-ku, Tokyo.

Tokai Research Establishment: Tokai-mura, Naka-gun, Ibaraki-ken; Dir. KENZO YAMAMOTO.

Takasaki Radiation Chemistry Research Establishment; 1233 Watanuki-cho, Takasaki-shi, Gumma-ken.

Oharai Establishment: Narita-machi, Oharai-cho, Higahiibaraki-gun, Ibaraki-ken.

CONTRACTORS

The First Atomic Power Industry Group (FAPIG): Nissho-Iwai Bldg., 4-5, Akasaka 2-chome, Minato-ku, Tokyo 107; f. 1957; constructed the Tokai Power Station for JAPCO; member firms mostly belong to the Furukawa, Kawasaki and Suzuki groups; Chair. H. MAEDA.

Mitsubishi Atomic Power Industries, Inc.: Ohtemachi Bldg., 6-1, 1-chome Ohtemachi, Chiyoda-ku, Tokyo 100; set up 1958 to construct nuclear reactors and power plants and to fabricate nuclear fuel; is building the reactor for Japan's first atomic powered ship, Takahama Unit No. 2, Ohi Unit No. 1, No. 2 and Mihami Unit No. 3 nuclear power plants of the Kansai Electric Power Co. Inc., Ikata Unit No. 1 nuclear power plant of Shikoku Electric Power Co. Inc., and Genkai Unit No. 1 nuclear power plant of Kyushu Electric Power Co. Inc.; mems. 24 firms, mostly members of the Mitsubishi group; Pres. EITARO ISHIHARA.

Nippon Atomic Industry Group Co. Ltd. (NAIGCO): 13-12, Mita, 3-chome, Minato-ku, Tokyo 108; f. 1958; set up to construct atomic energy facilities; mems. 36 firms, mostly members of the Toshiba and Mitsui group; Pres. TOSHIO DOKO.

Sumitomo Atomic Energy Industries, Ltd.: Horiuchi Bldg., 6-1, 2-chome, Kandakajmachi, Chiyoda-ku, Tokyo; f. 1958; set up to utilize nuclear materials and build necessary instrumentation; mems. 37 firms, mostly members of Sumitomo group; Pres. KAISUKE OSUMI.

Tokyo Atomic Industrial Consortium (TAIC): Hitachi Bldg., 4-6 Surugadai Kanda, Chiyoda-ku, Tokyo; set up to utilize nuclear materials and build necessary instrumentation; mems. 26 firms, mostly members of Hitachi group; Chair. K. KOMAI.

INDUSTRIAL RESEARCH

Electric Power Development Company (EPDC): 8-2, Marunouchi, 1-chome, Chiyoda-ku, Tokyo; f. 1952; almost entirely government-owned corporation devoted to promoting the development mainly of large-scale hydro-power resources. construction of thermal and nuclear power projects and to wholesaling the generated power to nine privately-owned power companies; also overseas engineering assistance in the development of water resources; Dir. MASATOSHI SAKAI.

The Japan Atomic Power Company (JAPC): 1-6-1, Otemachi, Chiyoda-ku, Tokyo; private consortium building nuclear power plants; Japan's first commercial nuclear unit of 166,000 kW.; advanced Calder Hall type at Tokai Power Station, Ibaraki Prefecture opened 1966; second unit at Tsuruga Power Station of 357,000 kW. BWR opened in 1970 in Tsuruga City; third unit at Tokai No. 2 Power Station of 1,100,000 kW. BWR to be opened 1977; Pres. TOMIICHIRO SHIRASAWA.

Japan Nuclear Ship Development Agency (JNSDA): 35 Shiba-Kotohira, Minato-ku, Tokyo; f. 1963; designing, navigating and constructing an 8,214-ton training and special cargo ships; Pres. SHUICHI SASAKI.

Power Reactor and Nuclear Fuel Development Corporation (PNC): 9-13, 1-chome Akasaka, Minato-ku, Tokyo; f. 1967; public corporation for developing advanced thermal reactor and fast breeder reactor, and for prospecting, mining, manufacture and processing of nuclear fuel; Pres. S. KIYONARI.

Chubu Electric Power Co.: 10-1 Toshin-cho, Higashi-ku, Nagoya; one of the nine electric utilities operating in Japan, plans to add 11,850,000 kW. by 1978, including nuclear power; Pres. OTOSABURO KATO.

Hitachi Company Ltd.: Kawasaki-shi, Kanagawa-ken; swimming-pool reactor.

Kansai Electric Power Co.: 5 Nakanosh-ima 3-chome, Kita-ku, Osaka; Fukui, Mihama Unit 1 (340 mW) went into commercial operation in Nov. 1970, Mihama Unit 2 (500 mW) and Takahama Units 1 and 2 (826 mW) will become operational in 1972, 1974 and 1976 respectively; Pres. S. YOSHIMURA.

Mitsubishi Electric Co. Ltd.: Tokai-mura, Naka-gun, Ibaraki-ken; swimming-pool reactor.

Tokyo Electric Power (TODEN): 1-3, 1-chome, Uchisaiwaicho, Chiyoda-ku, Tokyo; has a nuclear power station at Fukushima which will have 6 generating units in 1976; Chair. K. KIKAWADA; Pres. H. MIZUNO.

Tokyo Shibaura Electric Co. Ltd.: 13-12, 3-chome Mita, Minato-ku, Tokyo 108; 100 kW. swimming-pool reactor; Man. Y. KANAIWA.

ACADEMIC RESEARCH

Kinki University: Fuse-shi Osaka-fu; U.T.R.-type reactor.

Kyote University: Yoshida Honmachi, Sakyo-ku, Kyoto; swimming-pool type reactor at Osaka.

Musashi Institute of Technology: Ozenji, Kawasaki-shi, Kanagawaken; f. 1963; research reactor of Triga II type.

National Institute of Radiological Sciences (NIRS): 9-1, 4-chome, Anagawa, Chiba-shi; f. 1957; research on effects and medical uses of radiation and training of researchers; Dir. KEISUKE MISONO; publs. *Hosha-Sen Kagaku* (Radiology, monthly), *Annual Report NIRS* (English), *Radioactivity Survey data* (English, quarterly).

DEFENCE

Armed Forces and Equipment (1975): Total 236,000: army, 155,000; navy, 39,000; air force, 42,000. The army is equipped with U.S. made weapons including medium tanks, AA guns, 7 surface-to-air missiles (SAM) groups. The navy has 15 submarines, a guided missile destroyer as well as a number of frigates, minesweepers, torpedo boats, landing craft and other vessels. There is also a naval air component comprising 120 aircraft. The air force has 445 combat aircraft plus trainers, helicopters and 4 missile battalions. With the reversion of Okinawa to Japan in May 1972, a total of 2,900 Japanese military personnel were deployed there in December. By the end of June 1973 an air control and warning group was stationed there together with 9 Hercules and Hawk air defence missiles. The systems formerly under U.S. control were transferred to Japanese control when it assumed responsibility for Okinawa's air defence on July 1st, 1973.

Military Service: Voluntary.

Defence Expenditure: Defence Budget 1975–76: 1,327,300 million yen ($4,484 million).

Chairman of the Joint Staff Committee of the National Defence Agency: Gen. H. KINUGASA.

EDUCATION

The standard of literacy among the Japanese has been almost 100 per cent since before the turn of the century.

Before the Government Order of Education in 1872, the form of education for commoners was based on Buddhist temple schools called *terakoya*. Around the middle of the 19th century, there were nearly 16,000 terakoya schools. The noble families had their own form of education by private tutors and governesses. But in 1886 four years primary education was made compulsory and by the turn of the century, higher education beyond the age of 18 was made available. In 1908 the primary school course was made compulsory for six years. By 1920 more than 90 per cent of the school-age children were attending primary schools.

Immediately after World War II, with the introduction of democratic ideas into Japanese education, the educational system and policies underwent extensive reforms including the adoption of the 6-3-3-4 system. The Fundamental Law of Education of 1947 sets forth the central aims of education as follows: the bringing up of self-reliant citizens with respect for human values and equality of educational opportunity based on ability.

The law prohibits discrimination based on race, creed, sex, social status, economic position or family background. Co-education is authorized under the state education system. It also emphasizes political knowledge and religious tolerance, and prohibits any link between political parties or religious groups and state education. The school year lasts from April to March and is divided into three terms.

One of the striking features of education in Japan today is the increased competition to enter good universities. Though the standards vary, the system is on a dual basis with both private and public schools from primary level to university. The general standards of education in Japan are very high, especially in mathematics and foreign languages.

The Ministry of Education administers education at all levels and provides guidance, advice and financial assistance to local authorities. In each of the forty-seven prefectures and over three thousand municipalities, boards of education are responsible, in the former, for upper secondary schools, and special schools; while municipal boards maintain public elementary and lower secondary schools. The annual average percentage of the total expenditure devoted to education in the past ten years was about 21 per cent. Each level of government provides for its own education with funds derived from its own revenue including taxes. The central government may also grant subsidies where appropriate.

The government offers a scholarship system to promising poor students. Approximately 314 students in upper secondary schools, colleges, and universities are currently receiving financial assistance, and are expected to return the money in 20 years after graduation.

Steadily increasing numbers of young people from Asian countries are coming to Japan for technical training at scientific and technological institutes and at factories.

Pre-School Education

There were 11,564 kindergartens and approximately 16,000 day nurseries for children between the age of 3 and 5 in 1972 in which 3,281,544 children were enrolled; about 60 per cent of the former are mainly run privately whilst the latter are operated by local authorities.

Elementary and Lower School Education

All children between 6 and 15 are required to attend six-year elementary schools (Shogakko) and three-year lower secondary schools (Chugakko). All children are provided with text-books free of charge, while children of needy families are assisted in paying for school lunches and educational excursions by the government and the local bodies concerned. There is almost 100 per cent enrolment; 10,364,855 pupils in 24,652 primary and 4,762,444 pupils in 10,751 lower secondary schools in 1975.

Secondary Education

There are three types of course available: full-time, part-time and correspondence. The first lasts three years and the other two both last four years. There is a government plan to make education compulsory up to the age of 18, which may come into effect shortly. There were in 1975, 4,946 upper secondary schools in Japan, with an enrolment of 4,332,719.

Higher Education

There were 420 universities and graduate schools, and 578 junior and technical colleges in 1975. The universities offer courses extending from 3 to 4 years and in most cases postgraduate courses for a master's degree in 2 years and a doctorate in 3 years. Junior colleges offer 2- or 3-year courses, credits for which can count towards a first degree. The technical colleges admit lower secondary school students. The number of students in universities and graduate schools in 1975 was 1,734,082, and in junior and technical colleges, 401,739.

Teacher Training

There are facilities for teacher training in both universities and junior colleges. The total number of students in 1972 was 154,347.

Special Education

In 1972 there were 469 schools for the handicapped, of which there are 108 for the deaf, 75 for the blind, at kindergarten, primary, secondary and high school levels. Primary and secondary education for the blind, the deaf, the mentally retarded and the physically handicapped are also compulsory.

UNIVERSITIES

NATIONAL UNIVERSITIES

Chiba University: 1-33 Yayoicho, Chibashi; 830 teachers, 6,379 students.

Gumma University: 3 Showa-Machi, Maebashi-city; 573 teachers, 4,173 students.

Hirosaki University: 1 Bunkyo-cho, 036 Hirosaki City, 500 teachers, 3,916 students.

Hiroshima University: 1-1-89 Higashi-senda-machi, Hiroshima; 1,328 teachers, 9,194 students.

Hitotsubashi University: Kitatama-gun, Tokyo; 139 teachers, 2,617 students.

Hokkaido University: Nishi 5, Kita 8, Sapporo; 1,814 teachers, 10,410 students.

Ibaraki University: 2127 Watarimachi, Ibaraki Pref., Mito; 481 teachers, 5,346 students.

Kagawa University: 121 Saiwai-Cho Takamatsu-Shi, Kagawa-Ken; 280 teachers, 2,893 students.

JAPAN

Kagoshima University: Uerata-cho, Kagoshima; 759 teachers, 7,286 students.

Kanazawa University: 1-1 Marunouchi, Kanazawa City; 732 teachers, 5,587 students.

Kobe University: Rokko, Nada-ku, Kobe; 1,049 teachers, 9,992 students.

Kokusai University: Yamatoza, Koza, Okinawa; 35 teachers, 1,914 students.

Kumamoto University: Kurokami-machi, Kumamoto; 700 teachers, 5,500 students.

Kyoto University: Yoshida-hommachi, Sakyo-ku, Kyoto; 628 professors, 15,164 students.

Kyushu University: Hakozaki, Fukuoka City, Fukuoka Prefecture; 1,851 teachers, 11,162 students.

Nagasaki University: 1-14 Bunkyo-cho, Nagasaki; 620 teachers, 4,000 students.

Nagoya University: Furo-cho, Chikusa-ku, Nagoya; 1,530 teachers, 8,564 students.

Nara Women's University: Kita-Uoya-Nishi-Machi, Nara City; 306 teachers, 1,215 students.

Niigata University: Asahimachidori 1-Bancho, Niigata; 920 teachers, 6,395 students.

Ochanomizu Women's University: 1-1, 2-chome, Otsuka, Bunkyo-ku, Tokyo; 239 teachers, 1,698 students.

Okayama University: Tsushima, Okayama; 958 teachers, 6,574 students.

Okinawa University: Kokuba, Naha, Okinawa; 27 teachers, 2,835 students.

Osaka University: 36 Joancho, Kita-ku, Osaka; 551 professors, 8,448 students.

Osaka University of Foreign Studies: 8-chome Uehonmachi Tennoji-ku, Osaka; 130 teachers, 1,754 full-time students.

Shimane University: 1060 Nishikawatsu-cho Matsue-chi, Shimane-Ken, 267 teachers, 3,097 students.

Shinshu University: Asahi 3-1-1, Matsumoto, Nagano-ken; 932 teachers, 6,050 students.

Shizuoka University: Oaya 836, Shizuoka-Shi 422; 540 teachers, 7,085 students.

Tohuku University: Katahiracho, Sendai; 2,500 teachers, 10,500 students.

University of Tokushima: 6 Shinkura-cho, 2-chome, Tokushima-shi, Tokushima-ken; 699 teachers, 3,520 students.

The University of Tokyo: Hongo, Bunkyo-ku, Tokyo; 3,753 teachers, 18,956 students.

Tokyo Medical and Dental University: 5-45, 1-chome, Yushima, Bunkyo-ku, Tokyo; 590 teachers, 1,250 students.

Tokyo University of Education: 3-29-1 Otsuka, Bunkyo-ku, Tokyo; 500 teachers, 5,000 students.

Tokyo University of Foreign Studies: 51 Nishigawara; 4-chome, Kita-ku, Tokyo; 116 teachers, 2,246 students.

Tottori University: 1, 5-chome, Tachikawa-cho, Tottori City; 606 teachers, 3,040 students.

Toyama University: 3,190 Gofuku Toyama City; 376 teachers, 4,145 students.

University of the Ryukyus: 1, 3-chome, Tonokura-cho, Naha, Okinawa; 504 teachers, 4,582 students.

Wakayama University: 278 Sekido, Wakayamasi; 191 teachers, 2,241 students.

Yamagata University: 1-4-12 Koshirikawa-machi, Yamagata City; 450 teachers, 4,500 students.

Yamaguchi University: Shimmichi, Yamaguchi; 768 teachers, 6,200 students.

Yamanashi University: Kofu City, 4-4-37 Takeda; 327 teachers, 2,855 students.

Yokohama National University: 702 Ohokahachi, Minamiku, Yokohama; 416 teachers, 6,103 students.

PUBLIC, PREFECTURAL AND MUNICIPAL UNIVERSITIES

Fukushima Medical College: Fukushima City; 234 teachers, 575 students.

Kyoto Prefectural University of Medicine: 465, Kajii-cho Kawaramachi, Hirokoji, Kamikyo-ku, Kyoto; 222 teachers, 583 students.

Mie Prefectural University: Torii-cho, Tsu.

Nagoya City University: 1 Kawasumi, Mizuho-cho, Mizuho-ku, Nagoya; 379 teachers, 1,723 students.

Nara Medical University: 840 Shijo-cho, Kashihara-shi, Nara; 250 teachers, 430 students.

Osaka City University: 459 Sugimotocho, Sumiyoshi-ku, Tokyo; 855 teachers, 6,448 students.

University of Osaka Prefecture: 804 Mozu-Umemachi 4-cho, Sakai, Osaka; 635 teachers, 4,567 students.

Osaka Women's University: Tezukayama 3-chome, Sumiyoshi-ku, Osaka; 80 teachers, 565 students.

Sapporo Medical College: S.1, W.17, Sapporo City; 297 teachers, 565 students.

Attached Institute: *Cancer Research Institute*: f. 1952; Dir. H. TSUKUDA.

Shizuoka College of Pharmacy: 2-2-1 Oshika, Shizuoka-shi; 86 teachers, 542 students.

Tokyo Metropolitan University: 1-1-1 Yagumo, Meguro-ku, Tokyo; 588 teachers, 4,465 students.

Wakayama Medical College: 9 Kuban-cho, Wakayama City; 241 teachers, 422 students.

Yokohama Municipal University: 4646 Mutsuura-machi, Kanazawa-ku, Yokohama; 300 teachers, 3,000 students.

PRIVATE UNIVERSITIES

Aoyama-Gakuin University: 4-4-25 Shibuya, Shibuya-ku, Tokyo 150; 340 teachers, 17,130 students.

Azabu Veterinary College: 1-17-71 Fuchinobe, Sagamihara City, Kanagawa; 65 teachers, 1,000 students.

Bukkyo University: 96 Kitahananobo-cho, Murasakino, Kita-ku, Kyoto; 200 teachers, 3,900 students.

Chuo University: 3-9 Kanda-Surugadai, Chiyoda-ku, Tokyo; 1,328 teachers, 35,055 students.

Dai-ichi College of Pharmacy: 93 Tamagawa-cho, Takamiya, Fukuoka City; 85 teachers, 924 students.

Daito Bunka University: 1-9-1 Takashimadaira, Itabashi-ku, Tokyo; 150 teachers.

Doshisha University: Karasuma Imadegawa, Kamikyo-ku, Kyoto; 392 teachers, 20,217 students.

Doshisha Women's College: 602 Genbu-cho Teramachi-Nishiiru, Imadegawa-dori, Kamikyo-ku, Kyoto; 200 teachers, 2,800 students.

Fukuoka University: 11 Nanakuma, Fukuoka; 463 teachers, 21,356 students.

Gakushuin University: 1-1057 Mejiro-cho, Toshima-ku, Tokyo; 195 teachers, 6,228 students.

Hanazono University: 1-Hanazono Kitsujikita-cho, Ukyo-ku, Kyoto.

Hannan University: 4-35 5-chome Amami, Higashi, Matsubara City, Osaka; 54 full time, 70 part-time teachers, 2,398 students.

Hiroshima Jogakuin College: 13-1, Higashi 4-chome, Ushita, Hiroshima City; 50 teachers, 900 students.

Hokkai Gakuen University: 8-60, Asahimachi, Sappro, 062; 157 teachers, 6,300 students.

Hosei University: 17-1 Fujimi 2-chome, Chiyoda-ku, Tokyo; 425 teachers, 29,000 students.

International Christian University: Osawa, Mitaka-shi, Tokyo; 87 teachers, 1,400 students.

Iwate Medical University: 19-1 Uchimaru, Morioka, Iwate; 349 teachers, 1,488 students.

Japan Women's University: Mejirodai, Bunkyo-ku-Tokyo; 178 teachers, 3,519 students.

The Jikei University School of Medicine: 3-25-8 Nishi Shinbashi Minato-ku, Tokyo 105; 851 teachers, 1,206 students.

Kagoshima College of Economics: 8850 Shimofukumotocho, Kagoshima; 63 teachers, 2,300 students.

Kanagawa University: 3-chome Rokkaku-Bashi, Kanagawa-ku, Yokohama; 200 teachers, 10,000 students.

Kansai University: 3-35 Yamate-cho 3-chome, Suita-shi, Osaka; 477 teachers, 24,980 students.

Kanto Gakuin University: Muutsuura 4834 Kanzawa-ku, Yokohama; 409 teachers, 7,572 students.

Keio University: Mita, Minato-ku, Tokyo; 1,056 teachers, 25,827 students.

Kinki University: 321 Kowakae, Higashiosaka, Osaka; 441 teachers, 23,683 students.

Kogakuin University: 24 Tsunohazu 2-chome, Shinjuku-ku, Tokyo 160; 240 teachers, 7,700 students.

Kokugakuin University: 10-28 Higashi 4-chome, Shibuya-ku, Tokyo; 562 teachers, 13,057 students.

Komazawa University: Komazawa 1-chome, Fukazawamachi, Setagaya-ku, Tokyo; 360 teachers, 19,000 students.

Konan University: Okamoto Motoyama-cho, Higashi Nada-ku, Kobe City; 175 teachers, 5,000 students.

Koyasan University: Koyasan, Ito-gun, Wakayama-ken; 31 teachers, 415 students.

Kurume University: 67 Asahi-machi, Kurume-shi, Fukuoka-ken, 392 teachers, 3,961 students.

Kwansei Gakuin University: Uegahara, Nishinomiya-shi, Hyogo-ken; 268 teachers, 14,466 students.

Kyoto Women's University: 17 Kita Hiyoshi-cho, Imakumano, Higashiyama-ku, Kyoto; 115 teachers, 2,187 students.

Kyoto College of Pharmacy: 5-Nakauchi-cho, Misasagi Yamashina Higashiyama-ku Kyoto; 45 teachers, 1,483 students.

Matsuyama University College of Commerce: Bunkyo-cho, Matsyama 790; 150 teachers, 4,136 students.

Meiji University: Kanda-Surugadai 1-1, Chiyoda-ku, Tokyo-To; 1,427 teachers, 33,313 students.

Meiji Gakuin University: 1-2-37 Shirokanedai, Minato-ku, Tokyo; 410 teachers, 12,000 students.

Meijo University: Yagoto-Urayama, Tenpaku Showa-ku, Nagoya; 470 teachers, 18,000 students.

Miyagi Gakuin Women's College: 1-6, Chuo 4-chome, Sendai City; 126 teachers, 1,529 students.

Nanzan University: 18 Yamazato-cho, Showa-ku, Nagoya 466; 170 teachers, 4,655 students.

Nihon University: 6-16 Nishi-Kanda, 2-chome, Chiyoda-ku, Tokyo City; 2,268 teachers, 102,179 students.

Nippon Dental College: 9-20 1-chome, Fujimi, Chiyoda-ku. Tokyo; 347 teachers, 2.151 students.

Notre Dame Women's College: 1-2 Minami Nonogami-cho, Shimogamo, Sakyo-ku, Kyoto; 37 full-time, 56 part-time, teachers, 1,050 students.

Rikkyo University: Nishi-Ikebukuro, Toshima-ku, Tokyo; 725 teachers, 12,822 students.

Rissho University: 160 4-chome, Higashi-Osaki, Shinagawa-ku, Tokyo; 98 teachers, 3,536 students.

Ritsumeikan University: Kyoto-shi, Kamikyo-ku, Hirokoji-dori Termachi; 289 teachers, 21,160 students.

Ryukoku University: Fukakusa-Isukamoto-cho, Fushimi-ku, Kyoto, 582 teachers, 10,774 students.

University of the Sacred Heart: Hiroo 4-chome, 3-1 Shibuya-ku, Tokyo; 164 teachers, 1,725 students.

Saitama University: 255 Shimo Okubo Urawa City; 385 teachers, 4,640 students.

Science University of Tokyo: 1-3 Kagurazaka, Shinjuku-ku, Tokyo; 226 teachers, 8,294 students.

Seijo University: 6-1-20 Seijo, Setagaya-ku, Tokyo; 123 full-time, 137 part-time teachers, 3,494 students.

Seisen Women's College: 3-chome, 16 Ban 21 Go, Higashi-Gotanda, Shinagawa-ku, Tokyo; 107 teachers, 1,277 students.

Senshu University: Chiyoda-ku Kanda Jinbo-cho, Tokyo-to; 153 teachers, 11,624 students.

Showa Women's University: 1-chome, Taishido, Setagaya-ku, Tokyo; 110 teachers, 1,981 students.

Sophia University: Chiyoda-ku, Kioicho 7, Tokyo; 774 professors, 9,665 students.

Takachiho College of Commerce: 2-19-1 Ohmiya Suginami-ku, Tokyo; 53 teachers, 1,710 students.

Takushoku University: 3-4-14 Kobinata Bunkyo-ku, Tokyo; 208 teachers, 7,034 students.

Tamagawa University: 6-1-1 Tamagawa Gukuen Machida-shi, Tokyo; 411 teachers, 5,298 full-time students.

Tenri University: 1050 Somanouchi-cho Tenri City, Nara; 244 teachers, 2,248 students.

Tohoku Gakuen University: 1 Minami-Rokken-Cho, Sendai; 193 teachers, 8,761 students.

Tokai University: 2-28 Tomigaya, Shibuya-ku, Tokyo; 921 teachers, 26,648 students.

Tokyo College of Economics: 7-1 chome, Minamicho, Kokubunji, Tokyo 185; 200 teachers, 8,000 students.

Tokyo College of Pharmacy: 600 Kashiwagi 4-chome, Shinjuku-ku, Tokyo; 168 teachers, 3,076 students.

Tokyo Women's Medical College: 10 Kawada-cho Shinjuku-ku, Tokyo; 441 teachers, 594 students.

Toyo University: 5-28-20 Hakusan, Bunkyo-ku, Tokyo; 393 full-time teachers, 20,889 students.

Tsuda-Juku Women's College: 11491 Tsuda-Machi, Kodaira City, Tokyo; 80 teachers, 2,500 students.

Waseda University: Totsuka-Machi, Shinjuku-ku, Tokyo; 2,100 teachers, 41,523 students.

TECHNOLOGICAL UNIVERSITIES

Akita University: 1-1 Tegata Gakuencho, Akita City; 498 teachers; 3,000 students.

Chubu Institute of Technology: 1200 Matsumoto-cho, Kasugai-shi Aichi Prefecture; 159 teachers, 5,230 students.

Ehime University: Himata-cho, Matsuyama 790; 490 teachers.

Fukui University: Makinoshima-cho, Fukui.

Gifu University: Monzen-cho, Naka-cho, Kakamigahara-shi, Gifu-Ken.

Himeji Institute of Technology: Idei Himeji, Hyogo; 133 full-time, 28 part-time teachers, 1,100 students.

Iwate University: 3-18-8 Ueda, Morioka, Iwate; 291 teachers, 3,366 students.

Kobe University of Mercantile Marine: Fukae, Honjo-cho, Higashimada-ku, Kobe.

Kyoto University of Industrial Arts and Textile Fibres: Matsugasaki-Hashigamicho, Sakyo-ku, Kyoto.

Kyushu Institute of Technology: 752 Nakabaru, Tobata, Kitakyushu; 97 teachers, 1,954 students.

Miyazaki University: 100 Funatsuka-cho, Miyazaki; 328 teachers, 2,311 students.

Muroran Institute of Technology: 17 Mizumoto-cho, Muroran.

Nagoya Institute of Technology: Gokisho-cho, Showa-ku, Nagoya; 580 teachers; 4,000 students.

Sagami Institute of Technology: 1-1 Nishi Kaigan Tsujido, Fujisawa City; 200 teachers, 1,500 students.

Tokyo Electrical Engineering College: Kanda-Nishikicho, Chiyoda-ku, Tokyo; 500 teachers, 7,000 students.

Tokyo University of Agriculture: 1-1-1 Sakuragaoka, Setagaya-ku, Tokyo; 444 teachers, 7,805 students.

Tokyo University of Agriculture and Technology: 1-8 Harumi-cho, 3-chome, Fucho-shi, Tokyo.

Tokyo Institute of Technology: 12-1 Ookayama, 2-chome, Meguro-ku, 734 teachers, 4,315 students.

Tokyo University of Fisheries: Konan 4-5-7, Minato-ku; Tokyo.

Tokyo University of Mercantile Marine: Echujima 2-1-6 Fukagawa Koto-ku, Tokyo; 99 full-time teachers, 843 students.

University of Telecommunications: 14 Kojima-cho, Chofu, Tokyo; 104 full-time teachers, 1,950 students.

BIBLIOGRAPHY

GENERAL

BALLON, ROBERT. Doing Business in Japan (Sophia University with Tuttle, Tokyo, 1967).

BUNCE, W. K. Religions in Japan (Tuttle, Tokyo).

EARLE, ERNEST. The Kabuki Theatre (Secker & Warburg, London, 1956).

GUILLAIN, ROBERT. The Japanese Challenge (Hamish Hamilton, 1970).

ISHIDA, R. Geography of Japan (Kokusai Bunka Shinkokai, Tokyo, 1961).

KAHN, HERMAN. The Emerging Japanese Superstate (André Deutsch, London 1971).

KATSUMATA, S. Gleams from Japan (Kenkyusha, Tokyo, 1952).

KEENE, D. Modern Japanese Literature (Thames & Hudson, London, 1956).

KOBAYASHI, N., and ADAMS, T. F. M. The World of Japanese Business (Ward Lock, London).

MUNSTERBERG, H. The Arts of Japan (Tuttle, Tokyo).

NORMAN, E. H. Japan's Emergence as a Modern State (Institute of Pacific Relations, New York, 1940).

RITCHIE, D. The Land and People of Japan (A. & C. Black, London, 1958).

SANSOM, G. B. Japan, A Short Cultural History (Cresset Press, London, 1946).

SHIGEMITSU, M. Japan and Her Destiny: My Struggle for Peace (trans. by Oswald White; Hutchinson University Press, London).

SMITH, BRADLEY. Japan, History in Art (Weidenfeld & Nicolson, London, 1964).

THOMSEN, H. The New Religions of Japan (Tuttle, Tokyo, 1963).

TSUNODA DE BARY, KEENE. Sources of the Japanese Tradition (Columbia University Press, New York, 1958).

YANAGA, CHITOSHI (Dr.). Big Business in Japanese Politics (Yale U.P. 1971).

YAMAMOTO, Y. Approach to Japanese Culture (Kokusai Bunka Shinkokai, Tokyo).

Kokusai Bunka Shinkokai, Bibliography of Standard Reference Books for Japanese studies with descriptive notes in 6 vols. (Tokyo, 1963).

POLITICS

BORTON, H. Japan between East and West (Harper and Brothers, New York).

MAKI, JOHN M. Government and Politics in Japan (Frederick A. Praeger, New York).

MARUYAMA, MASAO. Thought and Behaviour in Modern Japanese Politics (Oxford University Press, London, 1963).

MCNELLY, THEODORE. Contemporary Government of Japan (Allen & Unwin, London, 1964).

REISCHAUER, E. O. The United States and Japan (Harvard University Press, Cambridge, Mass.).

MINISTRY OF JUSTICE. The Civil Code of Japan.

SCALAPINO, R. A. Parties and Politics in Contemporary Japan.

YANAGA, CHITOSHI. Japanese People and Politics (John Wiley, New York).

YOSHIDA, SHIGERU. Japan's Decisive Century (Praeger, New York, 1967).

ECONOMICS

ALLEN, G. C. Japan's Economic Expansion (Oxford University Press, London, 1965).

BOLTHO, ANDREA. Japan: An Economic Survey 1953–1973 (Oxford University Press, 1976).

COHEN, JEROME B. Japan's Postwar Economy (Indiana University Press, Bloomington).

International Aspect of Japan's Situation (Council of Foreign Relations, London, 1957).

LEVINE, S. B. Industrial Relations in Postwar Japan (University of Illinois Press, Urbana, Illinois).

OKITA, SABURO. The Rehabilitation of Japan's Economy and Asia (Ministry of Foreign Affairs, London, 1956).

The Co-operative Movement in Japan, by the Asia Kyokai (Maruzen, Tokyo).

Japan Economic Year Book (*The Oriental Economist*, Tokyo).

The New Long Range Economic Plan of Japan (1961–70), Compiled by Economic Planning Agency (Government Printing Bureau).

HISTORY

AKITA, GEORGE. Foundations of Constitutional Government in Modern Japan, 1868–1900 (Harvard University Press, Mass., 1967).

BERGAMINI, DAVID. Japan's Imperial Conspiracy (Heinemann, London, 1971).

BORTON HUGH. Japan's Modern Century (New York Ronald Press, 1955).

BOXER, C. R. The Christian Century in Japan (Cambridge University Press, London, 1964).

BUTOW, ROBERT J. Tojo and the Coming of the War (Princeton University Press, New Jersey, 1960).

BUTOW, R. J. Japan's Decision to Surrender (Stanford University Press, California, 1954).

BYAS, HUGH. Government by Assassination (Allen & Unwin, London, 1943).

GREW, JOSEPH C. Ten Years in Japan (Hammond, London, 1944).

IKE, NOBUTAKE. The Beginnings of Political Democracy in Japan (Johns Hopkins Press, Baltimore, Md., 1950).

KAJIMA, MORINOSUKE. The Emergence of Japan as a World Power, 1895–1925 (Prentice-Hall International, 1970).

KAWAI, KAZUO. Japan's American Interlude (Chicago University Press, 1960).

MOSLEY, LEONARD. Hirohito (Weidenfeld & Nicolson, 1966).

MORRIS, IVAN. The World of the Shining Prince (Oxford University Press, London, 1964).

NISH, IAN. The Story of Japan (Faber, London, 1968)

REISCHAUER, E. O. Japan Past and Present (Duckworth, London, 1964).

SANSOM, G. B. A History of Japan (Cresset Press, London, 1958–64).

The Western World and Japan (Cresset Press, London, 1950).

SADLER, A. L. Maker of Modern Japan, the life of Tokygawa Ieyasu (Allen & Unwin, London, 1937).

STORRY, RICHARD. A History of Modern Japan (Penguin, 1968, 5th edn.).

TAKEUCHI, TATSUJI. War and Diplomacy in the Japanese Empire (Allen & Unwin, London, 1936).

YANAGA, C. Japan since Perry (McGraw Hill, New York. 1949).

Korea

PHYSICAL AND SOCIAL GEOGRAPHY

John Sargent

(Revised by the Editor, 1976)

The total area of Korea is 220,284 square kilometres (85,052 square miles), including North and South Korea and the demilitarized zone between them. North Korea has an area of 120,538 square kilometres (46,540 square miles), and South Korea an area of 98,484 square kilometres (38,025 square miles). The demilitarized zone covers 1,262 square kilometres (487 square miles).

The Korean peninsula is bordered to the north by the People's Republic of China, and has a very short frontier with the U.S.S.R. in the north-east.

PHYSICAL FEATURES

Korea is predominantly an area of ancient folding, although in the south-east, where a relatively small zone of recent rocks occurs, a close geological similarity with Japan may be detected. Unlike Japan, the peninsula contains no active volcanoes, and earthquakes are rare.

Although, outside the extreme north, few mountains rise to more than 5,000 ft., rugged upland, typically blanketed in either pine forest or scrub, predominates throughout the peninsula. Cultivated lowland forms only 20 per cent of the combined area of North and South Korea.

Two broad masses of highland determine the basic relief pattern of the peninsula. In the north, the Changpai Shan and Tumen ranges form an extensive area of mountain terrain, aligned from south-west to north-east, and separating the peninsula proper from the uplands of eastern Manchuria. A second major mountain chain runs for almost the entire length of the peninsula, close to, and parallel with, the eastern coast. Thus, in the peninsula proper, the main lowland areas, which are also the areas of maximum population density, are found in the west and south.

The rivers of Korea, which are short and fast-flowing, drain mainly westwards into the Yellow Sea. Of the two countries, North Korea, with its many mountain torrents, is especially well endowed with opportunities for hydroelectric generation. Wide seasonal variations in the rate of flow, however, tend to hamper the efficient operation of hydroelectric plants throughout the year.

In contrast with the east coast of the peninsula, which is smooth and precipitous, the intricate western and southern coasts are well endowed with good natural harbours, an asset which, however, is partly offset by an unusually wide tidal range.

CLIMATE

In its main elements, the climate of Korea is more continental than marine, and is thus characterized by a wide seasonal range in temperature. In winter, with the establishment of a high pressure centre over Siberia and Mongolia, winds are predominantly from the north and north-west. North Korea in winter is extremely cold, with January temperatures falling, in the mountains, to below 8°F. Owing to the ameliorating influence of the surrounding seas, winter temperatures gradually rise towards the south of the peninsula, but only in the extreme southern coastlands do January temperatures rise above freezing point. Winter precipitation is light, and falls mainly in the form of snow, which, in the north, lies for long periods.

In the southern and western lowlands, summers are hot and humid, with July temperatures rising to 80°F. In mid-summer, violent cloudbursts occur, often causing severe soil erosion and landslides. In the extreme north-east, summers are cooler, and July temperatures rarely rise above 64°F.

Annual precipitation, over half of which falls in the summer months, varies from below 25 in. in the north-east to over 60 in. in the south.

NATURAL RESOURCES

Although 70 per cent of the total area of Korea is forested, high quality timber is virtually limited to the mountains of North Korea, where extensive stands of larch, pine, and fir provide a valuable resource. Elsewhere, excessive felling has caused the forest cover to degenerate into poor scrub.

Korea is fairly well provided with mineral resources, but most deposits are concentrated in the north, where large-scale mining operations were begun by the Japanese before the Second World War. In North Korea, the main iron mining areas are found south of Pyongyang, and in the vicinity of Chongjin in the extreme north-east.

Throughout Korea, many other minerals, including copper, lead, zinc, tungsten, gold, silver and asbestos, are mined.

POPULATION

In 1975, the population of North Korea was 15,852,000 at mid-year, according to United Nations estimates, while that of South Korea was 34,708,542 at October 1st, according to preliminary census results, giving a combined total of more than 50 million. The population of Korea has grown rapidly since 1956, when the combined total was 31.3 million.

Population density in 1975 was higher in South Korea (913 per square mile) than in North Korea (341 per square mile), but mean density figures conceal the crowding of population on the limited area of agricultural land, which is a salient characteristic of the geography of South Korea.

In 1970, 40 per cent of the population of South Korea was concentrated in cities with populations of 100,000 and over. Seoul, the capital of South Korea, had a population of 6,889,470 in 1975; Pusan, with 2,454,051, was the second largest city, followed by Taegu with 1,311,078 and Inchon with 799,982. Recent estimates are not available for the cities of North Korea, but the population of the administrative district of Pyongyang, including the capital, was estimated at 1,364,000 in 1966. Both Chongjin, the leading port of the north-east coast, and Hungnam probably have populations which are well in excess of 150,000.

HISTORY

Andrew C. Nahm

FROM EARLY TIMES TO 1945

A Korean legend says that the divine spirit granted the desire of a bear to become human, and the union of the two gave birth to Tan'gun, who founded the first "kingdom" of the Koreans in 2333 B.C., uniting the tribal groups in northern Korea and adjacent Manchuria. Recent archaeological discoveries, however, indicate that various nomadic tribes of the Tungusic people, with their Ural-Altaic tongue, shamanic religion and a paleolithic culture, made a southward move from eastern Siberia into Manchuria and Korea about 30,000 years before Christ. This south-easterly migration was due, perhaps, to population increase, a scarcity of hunting and grazing grounds or to a search for less rigorous climatic zones. Stone Age remains are plentiful throughout Korea, particularly in the north-west region. Korea's inhabitants during this period were a vigorous, hardy people with a strong ethnic and tribal identity.

Bronze tools and weapons were introduced from China, perhaps at the end of the Shang period (about 1122 B.C.) of the Middle Kingdom. With the arrival of bronze culture, the Sinification of the Korean peninsula began. Toward the end of the third century B.C., a warrior named Wiman, who consolidated his power in southern Manchuria, extended his domination into the peninsula, and established a capital in the fertile river basin surrounding present-day Pyongyang in about 190 B.C. Meanwhile, contacts between Korea and China increased, bringing the Korean peninsula more and more to the attention of the latter. Finally, in 108 B.C., Emperor Wu of the Han dynasty of China invaded Korea and established four Chinese commandaries in the territory of the kingdom Wiman to secure China's northern frontiers against various nomadic tribes whom the Chinese called "the northern barbarians". The most important of the Chinese commandaries was Lo-lang (Nangnang in Korean) in the north-western plain of Korea, with its capital near the present city of Pyongyang. From Lo-lang the Chinese culture was transmitted to the people in Korea. Though Chinese domination continued in north-west Korea, other tribes settled in the river valleys of the north-east and on the southern plains of the peninsula.

The Three Kingdom Period

Despite the Chinese presence, some of the tribes, including the Puyo tribesmen of the peninsula and Manchuria, managed to retain an independent existence. In about 37 B.C. these tribes were welded into the Kingdom of Koguryo, a kingdom which steadily incorporated the territories which China had controlled. In A.D. 313 the end of Chinese domination in Korea came with the destruction of Lo-lang by Koguryo, whose territory covered not only the northern half of the peninsula, but also the southern part of Manchuria. This expansionistic kingdom, with its capital at Pyongyang, constituted a threat to other tribal groups in the central and southern parts of Korea.

Perhaps to ward off this northern threat, the tribes in the southern half of Korea forged themselves into three loosely organized federations, Chin-Han, Ma-Han and Pyon-Han. (The present-day name of the Republic of Korea, which is Tae-Han Minguk, or Hanguk, traces its origin to these federations.) In about 18 B.C. the tribal federation in the central part was transformed into the Kingdom of Paekche, following the formation in about 57 B.C. of the Kingdom of Silla, in the south-eastern part of Korea, with its capital at present-day Kyongju. The growing pressure from the north, particularly following the destruction of the Chinese commandary of Lo-lang by Koguryo, forced the Paekche kingdom to move in a south-westerly direction.

Facing the growing power of Koguryo, the kingdoms of Paekche and Silla formed an alliance in the early fifth century A.D., and they managed to check the aggressive move on the part of Koguryo for a while. However, the alliance was soon broken and the power struggle grew intense among the three kingdoms. It was during this period of conflict that Paekche nurtured a Buddhist civilization in Japan. Meanwhile, the warriors of Koguryo managed successfully to defeat the invading forces of the Sui dynasty of China in 612 and in 614. The T'ang dynasty, which succeeded the Sui in 618, suffered similar defeats in 644, 646, 658 and 659. But Koguryo was weakened and Silla, seizing the opportunity, allied itself with the T'ang and destroyed Paekche first in 663, and then Koguryo five years later. Thus, in 668, a unified nation of the Korean people emerged for the first time and was to last until 1945.

The Three Kingdom period may be regarded as the most important epoch in the development of Korea as a distinct nation and people. During this period, not only rapid political transformation occurred, but also an agricultural economy and a new pattern of social life of the people developed. Meanwhile the Bronze Age gave way to the Iron Age. Buddhism, an important unifying force, contributed greatly to the development of art, architecture, literature and technology in Korea. At the same time, the secular culture of China (Confucian, Taoistic and other thoughts and systems) exerted a great influence on the development of ideas and literature as well as the political and social institutions of Korea.

The Unified Silla and Koryo Periods

The Kingdom of Silla lasted 270 years following the unification of Korea, the first 150 years constituting a golden age in Korean history. The fusion of Paekche, Koguryo and Silla culture, and the increasing contact with China, produced rich art and magnificent masterpieces of architecture and sculpture. Buddhism flourished as Confucian learning and institutions grew, and the poetry and songs of the Korean people were born. But, as warring clans created political havoc, political decline set in. Abuses of political power, misuse of funds, exploitation of the peasants and the usurpation of privilege by the members of the aristocracy brought about peasant revolts. Power struggle within the court created a chaotic situation and weakened central authority. In 892 a small state, called Later Paekche, was set up by rebels, while a monk named Kungye established the rival state of Later Koguryo in 901. Wang Kon, one of the officers of Kungye, removed the monk from power, and founded a new dynasty of his own named Koryo, with its capital at Kaesong, in 918. In 935 the last king of Silla submitted to Wang Kon and the short-lived Later Paekche was destroyed by Wang Kon the following year.

The Koryo dynasty, which lasted until 1392, brought about the greater Sinification of political and social institutions of Korea. Koryo, from which the Western name for Korea was derived, brought its administrative system closer to that of China. The dynasty's bureaucracy was strengthened with the creation of a new, closed hereditary aristocracy which monopolized political power, despite the introduction of the Chinese system of civil service examinations. The capital of Kaesong, a replica of Ch'ang-an, the former capital of China, rivalled the model itself in many ways. Chinese laws became appropriated by the Sinicized bureaucracy, manned by a salaried officialdom.

The founder of Koryo and his successors systematically stratified the people into two large units below the officialdom: the tax-paying commoners and the landless peasants and slaving population called the "lowborn". The "lowborn" class included government and private slaves and labourers.

Although the manufacturing of the renowned Koryo celadon ware reached its zenith during this period, commerce failed to develop, as international trade, which flourished during the Silla period, declined almost completely. With the exception of the capital, where commercial shops flourished, commerce was carried out solely by pedlars and at periodic markets where people bartered rather than bought with cash.

Buddhism became the state religion, and the monastic movement and Buddhist culture made great strides. The rise of Buddhist study, nurtured by many members of the aristocracy who themselves became monks, witnessed the construction of magnificent temples , as well as the invention (or improvement) of printing.

With the increase of Chinese cultural influence, not only did the arts develop rapidly, but scholarship in historical studies grew. As a result, such important historical sources as *History of the Three Kingdoms* and *Memorabilia of the Three Kingdoms* were produced by Korean scholars in the twelfth and thirteenth centuries, respectively.

Almost from the beginning, Koryo was beset by external problems. The Mongols, the Khitans and the Jurchens to the north steadily increased their pressure, and Koryo suffered the first disaster when the Khitans descended upon Koryo in the 990s. In order to strengthen its northern defences, the Koryo Government constructed a "great wall" across its northern border, excluding the north-eastern portion of the Korean peninsula. The Jurchens swept down in the early twelfth century and occupied this unprotected area.

Discontent began festering among the military leaders as power struggles within the ruling class began. In 1170 warfare among military leaders broke out, joined by slave rebellions. Finally, in 1199, the military dictatorship of the Ch'oe family was established and lasted until 1256.

During its political and social turmoil Koryo was invaded by the Mongols under Genghis Khan, and in 1231 the Mongols forced the Koreans to capitulate. Not satisfied with Koryo's attitudes toward the Mongols, the aggressors invaded Korea again in 1259, and forced Mongol suzerainty upon Korea. During the Mongol domination, which lasted a century, new cultural horizons were opened up, bringing Korea into contact with knowledge of astronomy, mathematics and other sciences, as well as the arts of those areas of western Asia and Europe under Mongol control. Meanwhile, the Chu-hsi school of Neo-Confucianism was introduced to Korea. The Korean nation paid a high price for the Mongols' two attempted invasions of Japan, which both ended in disaster.

Corruption, revolving around the control by the Buddhist monks and temples of land and revenues, became rampant, and rivalry between the newly arrived *Son* (*Zen*) Buddhism and Mahayana Buddhism grew. Military leaders and aristocrats who had managed to retain influence under the Mongols exploited the peasantry ruthlessly.

The anti-Mogol sentiment grew stronger as the Mongol empire began to crumble. The Mongol dynasty of Yuan in China was overthrown by the founder of the Ming dynasty in 1368, but the Koryo dynasty remained loyal to the Mongols until Yi Song-gye, a general who led the expeditionary force of Koryo against anti-Mongol forces to the north, rebelled against the Government.

Returning to the capital with his rebel troops, General Yi put the Koryo dynasty completely under his control, and instituted ambitious economic and social reforms while pursuing a pro-Ming foreign policy. Opposition to General Yi's land policy grew, and the power struggle within the Government continued. But in 1392 General Yi overthrew the Koryo dynasty and established the Yi dynasty which was to last until 1910. He named his kingdom Choson ("The Land of the Morning Calm"), resurrecting the ancient name of Korea.

The Yi Dynasty

The new dynasty of Yi Song-gye, with its new capital at Seoul, ruled Korea for 518 years. During this period many reforms, initiating the modern transformation of Korea, were instituted. For the first time the entire Korean peninsula came under the rule of a single government in Seoul. The kingdom was divided into eight provinces.

An efficient administrative structure was established during the reign of the first monarch and his immediate successors. The major organs of the Government were a State Council, a Royal Secretariat and the six ministries of personnel, revenue, rituals, defence, justice and public works. Five other important state organs were two offices of Censors, the Office of Special Counsellors, the Office of the Royal Lecturers and the Office of Superintendent of Education.

Recognizing the supremacy of China, Korean monarchs avoided the usage of the imperial title until the end of the Yi dynasty. At the same time, the Yi dynasty strengthened the tributary relations with China.

Neo-Confucianism became the state creed, and government officials were required to observe the rules of Confucian bureaucratism and behaviour. A significant step taken by the Yi dynasty was the subordination of military officers to civilian rule, although the founder of the dynasty himself was a military figure.

The new land policy which the Yi dynasty instituted marked the beginning of a modern landlordism when the land granted to meritorious subjects or officials became taxable. Although some tax-free estates existed, the era of large tax-free estates ended as the size of landlord holdings became modest and the number of landholders increased. However, the bulk of the farming population possessed no land. The Buddhist church, which had been one of the largest landholders during the Koryo period, was deprived of any rights to hold agricultural lands.

The class structure was also transformed. The scholar-gentry class, high-ranking members of the officialdom who were landholders, constituted the aristocracy. Beneath it were petty government functionaries and professional specialists in medicine, science and technology, and foreign languages; the "common people", which included tenant farmers, artisans and merchants; and the "lowborn", which included farm hands, domestic servants and slaves, labourers and people such as actors, shaman priests and priestesses, butchers, grave diggers, tanners, etc. Although merchants and pedlars were included in the "commoner" class, the strong anti-commercialism of Confucianism relegated merchants into the "lowborn" group. Such a class structure remained almost intact until the very end of the Yi period.

The adoption of the Neo-Confucianism of Chu-hsi as the state creed caused strong anti-Buddhist feelings, and Buddhist monks and nuns moved to Korea's remote regions and hinterland. No Buddhist temples were allowed to be built in the capital until the end of the dynasty. Meanwhile, the rise of Confucianism and the strengthening of the civil service examination system nurtured the growth of educational institutions and scholarship. A Confucian university, four official schools in the capital, and official schools in provincial capitals were the centres of learning. Private schools played an important role in the development of scholarship in Korea. It was in these private schools that reformists of the eighteenth and nineteenth centuries rose, advocating political, economic and social reforms. The Inner Royal Library (*Kyujanggak*), established in the eighteenth century, played a significant role in the advancement of the intellectual movement in Korea.

One of the most outstanding intellectual and creative achievements of the early Yi period was the institutionalization in 1446 of Korean script in a scientific phonetic system, commonly called *Han'gul* ("Korean Letters"), by the fourth monarch, King Sejong. King Sejong, a scholar, encouraged other scholars to study science and technology. The manufacture of moveable type and printing tools occurred during this period of intellectual and creative dynamism. Meanwhile, volumes of legal compendiums were compiled, and historical studies resulted in the publication of such valuable sources as *Essential History of Koryo* and *General Outline of History of Korea* during the fifteenth century.

Toward the end of the fifteenth century, the Court was torn by a struggle for power, as well as ideological conflicts involving the royal family, the gentry and Confucian scholars. In addition to the power struggle, factional controversies among scholars over the interpretation of Neo-Confucianism erupted. As a result, there were four great purges of hundreds of *literati* between 1491 and 1545.

Internal turmoil, caused by battling officials and scholars, was detrimental to domestic stability, but the foreign invasion of the sixteenth and seventeenth centuries drastically weakened the dynastic rule and devastated social and economic life. The Japanese invasions of 1592 and 1597, under Toyotomi Hideyoshi, whose ambition was to conquer Korea and humiliate China, inflicted a mortal wound from which the Korean society never recovered. Despite brilliant naval victories against Japan, nearly the entire Korean peninsula was terrorized by Japanese warriors. The Chinese assistance of Korea and the death of Toyotomi Hideyoshi ended the Korean-Japanese wars in 1597. But the aftermath of the seven-year war, with a period of intermittent peace negotiations, was a weakening of the social fabric and a decrease in population as a vast number of artisans and technicians were forcibly taken to Japan by the invaders. China's Ming dynasty, which provided military assistance to Korea, also suffered a fatal economic setback.

In 1627 the Manchus, who had been fostering their power in Manchuria, invaded Korea and forced the Korean Government to accept vassalage. The Manchus further weakened Korea by forcing it to supply food, soldiers and labourers for the Manchus' invasion of China. The Yi dynasty turned against the Manchus, resulting in the second invasion by the Manchus in 1637, which constituted a death-blow to the Yi dynasty. Korea remained a tributary state to the Manchus, who conquered China and established the Ch'ing dynasty in 1644.

It was not until the introduction of Roman Catholicism to Korea by the annual tribute envoys to the Ch'ing court in the second half of the eighteenth century that interest in Western religion and science began to grow in Korea. Subsequently, a Chinese and several French missionaries entered Korea illegally and spread Christianity, giving birth to two significant intellectual movements, the *Sohak* ("Western Learning") and the *Sirhak* ("Practical Learning"). Many discontented Confucian official-scholars and some leading Confucian scholars became attracted to the new religion. Unfortunately, the Korean scholars were more attracted to Christian thought than to Occidental science and technology, and Korea's "Western Learning" failed to promote modern and scientific studies, manufacturing technology or social transformation. Moreover, with no trading ports open to the merchants of the West, Korea was not exposed to the civilization of the West. The apathy of the masses, as well as the opposition of Orthodox Confucianism to Christianity as a subversive force, did not allow the "Western Learning" in Korea to become a catalytic force for the transformation of society. The number of converts to the new religion, however, grew steadily.

A more important intellectual movement than the "Western Learning" was that of the school of "Practical Learning", which emerged during the middle of the eighteenth century. The decline of factionalism under the enlightened reigns of Yongjo (1724–76) and Chongjo (1776–1800) enabled scholars with a nationalistic and progressive outlook to come forward, advocating political and educational reform, social justice, and economic reconstruction. Such scholars as Chong Yak-yong (pen-name Tasan), a leading figure in the "Western Learning" movement, attacked corrupt and inefficient government and bureaucrats, while criticizing the "empty learning" of Neo-Confucianists. They expressed a strong nationalistic sentiment as they emphasized the study of Korea's traditional culture and the strengthening of its own identity and independence. Their philosophy of government insisted that its primary function was the promotion of the people's welfare and the maintenance of peaceful order. The *Sirhak* painters initiated a new movement when they produced a genre art that depicted Korean life of the times.

The conservative Confucian scholars who controlled the Government refused to adopt proposals made by the *Sirhak* scholars, and the Yi dynasty was unable to lessen the Government's weaknesses or social decay. The economic situation worsened, with population increase and a rising tax burden.

The worsening economic and social conditions, coupled with the misuse of political power by corrupt Confucian officials, gave impetus to peasant rebellions that arose throughout the country in the late eighteenth and early nineteenth centuries. Those peasant rebellions, in the north-west particularly, created serious problems for the Government. A far more serious problem which the Government faced was that of the *Tonghak* ("Eastern Learning"), which emerged around 1860. Ch'oe Che-u, its founder and his followers criticized political corruption, economic mismanagement and social injustice, and, while preaching salvation through faith in the "Eastern Learning", opposed "Western Learning". In 1863 the Government arrested Ch'oe (who was later executed) and many of his followers. The "Eastern Learning" sect, however, grew steadily among the poverty-stricken peasant population in the southern provinces, and was destined to create more serious problems for the Government in later years.

Korea encountered increasing foreign problems as Western mercantilism spread rapidly in Asia in the nineteenth century. Its official isolationistic policy was proclaimed in 1871.

Japan, where a revolution had overthrown the Tokugawa Shogunate in 1867, made several requests to the Korean Government for the renewal of diplomatic and commercial relations, suspended almost completely since the Japanese wars of 1592 and 1597. The Korean refusal brought about a Japanese military threat which the Korean Government was unable to repel and it concluded a diplomatic treaty along commercial agreements in 1876.

Traditional Korea was dominated by the ideas of Confucianism, spread throughout all social classes and creating a uniformity of custom and thought. Society was highly stratified, and the highest social status was that of the *literati* which provided bureaucrats for the Government; commerce was disdained, the artisan looked down upon, and technology minimized. Korea's foreign relations during the traditional period were chiefly with China and Japan.

The Demise of the Korean Nation

Korea, under unimaginative and inefficient government controlled by pro-Chinese conservatives, with its weak social and economic foundation, an ill-prepared military and ever-increasing discontent among the masses, was destined to encounter growing danger to national survival as well as domestic crisis. During the 1870s the young Queen Min and her allies successfully ousted the reform-minded and nationalistic Regent (*Taewon'gun*), and established absolute domination over the boy king, Kojong, and his Government in Seoul. Meanwhile, conflict between China and Japan grew over Korea's sovereignty: Japan recognized Korea's sovereignty in the 1876 treaty, but China did not. The growing economic strength of the Japanese in Korea only aggravated the Sino-Japanese relations. A new group of progressive scholars emerged under the leadership of Kim, Ok-kyun and Pak Yong-hyo, preaching the promotion of national independence and the modernization of Korea.

The Chinese intervened in Korea in 1882 to crush the military insurrection in which the deposed Regent attempted to regain power. The pro-Chinese group of Queen Min was restored to power. The Chinese military intervention, however, stimulated the rise of nationalistic sentiment in Korea, particularly among the progressive scholars, who sought assistance not only from Japan, but also from the United States, which concluded a treaty with Korea in 1882, marking the opening of Korea to the West.

The harder the progressives (who were known as the *Kaehwadang*, or the "Party of Modernization") attempted to bring about urgently needed reforms, the stronger the opposition grew. They managed to gain the support of the Japanese minister to Korea, and, in an attempt to establish a new government under King Kojong and to institute reform similar to those in Japan, they staged a palace coup in December 1884. Their slogans included political reform, economic development, strong military and cultural progress, and social justice. A second Chinese military intervention quickly crushed the new Government, and for the second time restored Queen Min. The majority of the progressives were killed but a handful fled to Japan and the United States.

The Japanese leaders regarded the re-assertion of Chinese direct suzerainty over Korea as intolerable, for they were fearful that it would lead to the domination of Korea by a Western power such as Russia. The majority opinion of the Japanese Government leaders was that Korea's safe existence was the guarantee for Japan's security. Japanese antagonism toward China grew, and led to the Sino-Japanese War of 1894–95, from which Japan emerged a victor and an undisputed power in East Asia.

Although the treaty ending the war stated that Korea was an independent nation, Korea did not secure complete independence, as the military occupation by the Japanese during the war led to increased Japanese domination of Korea. King Kojong's so-called *Kabo* Reform of 1894–95 was more or less a reluctant gesture to accommodate heavy pressure which the Japanese brought upon him. He was even forced to form a pro-Japanese administration "for the sake of national progress and independence".

The Triple Intervention of Russia, Germany and France in 1895 forced Japan to cancel the agreement in which China agreed to lease the Liaotung territory to Japan for 25 years. The weakened Japanese stand against the European powers prompted the rise of a pro-Russian group supported by Queen Min. The Japanese minister to Korea was determined to maintain the position which Japan had gained. He had Queen Min assassinated and forced the Korean Government to restore a pro-Japanese cabinet. The killing of the queen by Japanese soldiers and a few Korean collaborators only strengthened anti-Japanese sentiment on the part of the Korean Government. King Kojong was spirited out of his palace to the nearby Russian Legation in 1896, and a Korean-Russian alliance was formed against Japan.

At this point a new group of young reform advocates emerged, preaching the spirit of independence to save the nation, not by relying on external powers, but by promoting national unity, economic and military strength and a high cultural level among the people. It was a movement for national salvation through self-strengthening and the enlightenment of the people. Its leader, Dr. So Chae-p'il (Philip Jaisohn), who had fled to the United States in 1884, returned to Korea and formed the Independence Club in co-operation with young progressives such as Yi Sung-man (Syngman Rhee), Yi Sang-jae, and Yun Ch'i-ho.

These reformists of the Independence Club were critical of the Government's domestic and foreign policy, and demanded a wide range of reforms. Meanwhile, other groups also arose and advocated national reconstruction.

An awakening of intellectuals, accompanying the ever-increasing number of newspapers, journals, and reform societies, marked the opening of a new chapter in Korean history. The voices of reform advocates grew louder as the cultural influence of the West increased and more and more modern schools came into being. But the Government, in the hands of the unenlightened conservatives, was unwilling to accommodate the desires of reform advocates. Under the strong pressure exerted by the Independence Club and other reform groups, the Government modified its relationship with the Russians. The king, after returning from the Russian Legation to his palace in 1897, inaugurated reform measures, including the renaming of the nation as the Empire of Tae-Han and the adoption of the Western calendar and system of weights and measures.

The growth of Russian influence and of the nationalistic spirit in Korea aroused Japanese concern. While Japanese individuals were agitating for the adoption of an aggressive policy toward Korea and Russia by the Japanese, the Government leaders themselves sought a suitable solution to the Korean question. As a result, the Anglo-Japanese Alliance was formed in 1902 and Japanese attitudes toward Russia stiffened. Meanwhile, the Russians pursued an equally determined policy to extend their influence and control in Asia. This rivalry led to the Russo-Japanese War of 1904–05, which was disastrous for Korea even though it had declared its neutrality. Korea, under Japanese military occupation, helplessly concluded a series of agreements with Japan during the war. Although the treaty ending the war guaranteed Korea's independence, Japan's *de facto* control over Korea, and an understanding between the U.S.A.

and Japan (the Taft-Katsura Agreement) in 1905, led to the establishment of a Japanese protectorate over Korea. Three years after the Japanese replaced the Korean emperor in 1907, the Japanese forced the last ruler of Korea to sign the treaty by which Japan annexed the country on August 22nd, 1910.

The Japanese Colonial Period

The Japanese colonial period lasted from 1910 to 1945. Although the Japanese imperial decree issued at the time of Japan's annexation of Korea stated that the Koreans would be treated in the same way as Japanese subjects, the Korean people were subjected to military rule and deprived of rights and privileges constitutionally guaranteed to the Japanese. The Government-General of Korea in Seoul was headed by army generals, except from 1919 to 1931, and oppressive police rule drove the people into virtual slavery. The Koreans lost their freedom and rights, and their lands were also taken away by the Japanese under various pretexts. Every aspect of the life of the Koreans was controlled by the Japanese gendarmeries and nationalized police.

During the period of colonial rule Korean leaders and students at home and abroad launched an independence movement, culminating in the celebrated March First movement of 1919. On March 1st that year the Declaration of Independence of the Korean people was proclaimed. The peaceful independence movement, however, was met with brutal retaliation by the Japanese military and police. Over 7,500 Koreans were killed and over 50,000 imprisoned. The uprising lasted over a month as it spread into the remotest corners of the country, but it did not remove the Japanese imperialistic rule from Korea.

The Japanese aims in Korea were threefold: the use of human and natural resources in Korea to aid the economic development of Japan, the assimilation of the Koreans into Japanese culture, and the construction of a strong basis for continental expansion. With these objectives, the Japanese developed the Korean economy and expanded educational facilities to train "loyal, obedient, and useful subjects" of the Japanese emperor. The Korean economy was dominated by the Japanese, and Korea remained the chief supplier of food and manpower to Japan. The development of higher and secondary education was kept to a minimum, and training programmes were aimed at the production of cheap labourers with limited skills.

The cultural assimilation programme was aimed at the destruction of the Korean cultural heritage. The use of the Korean language was first discouraged, and then forbidden; Christianity was allowed to exist but only under severe restrictions; Shinto shrines and Japanese Buddhist temples were built everywhere. Koreans were forced to abandon Korean names and adopt Japanese names.

The industrialization and modern economic development of Korea came only after the Japanese launched their aggression against China when, in 1931, Manchuria was occupied by the Japanese. The war with China that broke out in 1937 led to the greater exploitation of Korea by the Japanese. The outbreak of World War II only intensified Japanese control and exploitation of Korea.

In Shanghai (and later in Chungking) the Provisional Government of the Republic of Korea in exile, which was established in April 1919 under the presidency of Dr. Syngman Rhee, led the national restoration movement of the rightist nationalists, while the nationalists who turned to Communism maintained their struggle against the Japanese near the north-eastern regions of Korea as well as in the border regions of Manchuria and the Soviet Union. The *Singanhoe* ("New Shoot Society") and other rightist and leftist organizations in Korea made gallant, but futile, efforts aganist Japanese rule.

The Liberation from Japan and the Division of Korea

The Soviet Union entered the Pacific War against Japan in August 1945 and later in the month the Japanese surrendered to the Allies. The Cairo Declaration of December 1943, issued by the British and American leaders and Chiang Kai-shek of China, had stated that "in due course Korea shall become free and independent". The Soviet leader, Marshal Stalin, accepted the Cairo agreement, but proposals made by the Americans in 1945 led to the division of Korea after the Japanese surrender into two military zones, controlled by the United States and the Soviet Union: the area south of the 38th parallel line under American occupation and the northern area under Soviet occupation.

The Japanese governor-general in Korea persuaded Yo Un-hyong, a prominent left-wing nationalist (Socialist), to form a political body to maintain law and order at the end of the Japanese colonial rule in co-operation with the colonial government. The Committee for the Preparation of the National Construction of Korea was thus organized. This Committee, headed by Yo, included right-wing as well as left-wing nationalists, with only ultra-right-wing nationalists abstaining from it. After Japan's surrender, Korean political prisoners were freed and the Committee began to function as a government. Provincial, district and local committees were organized to maintain law and order. On September 6th, two days before the arrival of American occupation forces, the Committee called a "National Assembly" and established the People's Republic of Korea, claiming jurisdiction over the whole country. Meanwhile, Soviet troops which entered Korea in early August quickly moved southward as they crushed Japanese resistance, and within a month the entire northern half of Korea came under Soviet occupation.

The American occupation authority swiftly disarmed the Japanese and accepted the surrender of Korea from the last Japanese governor-general. But, unlike the Soviet general in the north, the American general refused to recognize the authority of the Committee or the legitimacy of either the People's Republic or the Provisional Government of the Republic of Korea in exile in China, waiting to return to Korea. The United States Army Military Government in Korea (USAMGIK) was established and lasted until August 1948.

Exiled political leaders returned to Korea toward the end of 1945, Dr. Rhee from the United States, Kim Ku and Dr. Kim Kyu-sik from China, and Kim Il-sung and other Communists from Manchuria and China. Pak Hon-yong, a Communist who had been released from the Japanese prison, quickly formed the Korean Communist Party in South Korea. Freedom of political activity permitted by the American military government resulted in a proliferation of political parties and social organization of all political orientation, each vying for prominence. The military government attempted vainly to bring about a coalition of moderate nationalists and non-communist leftists. The Americans continued to antagonize the conservative right-wing nationalists.

In December 1945 representatives of the United Kingdom, the United States and the Soviet Union entered into the Moscow Agreement, providing for a five-year trusteeship for Korea under a four-power regime (China was the fourth power), with the view to establish an independent and united nation of Korea. Despite violent anti-trusteeship demonstrations, the Allied occupation authorities resolved to implement the Moscow plan. Then, suddenly, the Communists throughout Korea changed their stand in favour of the Moscow plan, splitting the Korean people into two opposing camps.

The trusteeship issue created a bitter and bloody struggle between nationalists and Communists in South Korea, and caused the downfall of the nationalist group under a long-time freedom fighter, Cho Man-sik, in the north. With the fall of the nationalists, Kim Il-sung, a Communist who returned to Korea with the Soviet army and the assistance of the Soviet occupation authority, gained control. The communization of the northern half began as many nationalists fled to the south.

In South Korea left-wing political and labour organizations created serious political and economic problems, aggravating further the poor economic conditions in the American zone. Communist-directed labour strikes became widespread, and terrorism of both right-wing and left-wing organizations became rampant. The severe winter of 1945 hit the people hard, with commodity shortages and high unemployment.

A Joint U.S.-U.S.S.R. Commission was formed to establish a national government of Korea in consultation with Korean political and social organizations. The first session of the Joint Commission was held in Seoul in March–May 1946. The Soviet delegate insisted that only "democratic" organizations should participate and that only organizations which supported the Moscow Agreement were "democratic". It became clear that the Soviet Union intended to establish a national government of Korea dominated by Communists.

In May 1947 the second session of the Joint Commission in Pyongyang similarly failed to achieve any agreement and in June the Commission's business was suspended indefinitely.

Realizing that the establishment of the Korean unity and its national government was a remote possibility, the American occupation authority began to adopt various plans for South Korea. The Soviet occupation authority likewise proceeded to establish its puppet regime under Kim Il-sung. All anti-Soviet and anti-communist organizations were either broken up or put under communist leadership. A communist monolithic state began to emerge in the north as Kim Il-sung formed his own party in defiance of Pak Hon-yong, a long-standing leader of the communist movement in Korea, whose Korean Communist Party had its headquarters in Seoul.

In South Korea the Americans established the South Korean Interim Legislative Assembly under a moderate nationalist in late 1946, and in May 1947 the South Korean Interim Government was created, with another moderate nationalist as its head. These actions were bitterly criticized by conservative right-wing leaders such as Dr. Syngman Rhee and Kim Ku. The relationship between the Americans and the right-wing nationalists worsened while terrorist activities created an extremely uneasy situation. Several prominent right-wing leaders, as well as Yo Un-hyong, a moderate leftist, were assassinated. Neither the Interim Legislative Assembly nor the Interim Government was effective or had independent power. Meanwhile, the economic hardships of the people grew worse. The two political institutions that the Americans created were regarded by the conservative nationalists as American puppets to prolong the American military occupation of Korea.

In September 1947 the United States Government, realizing the impossibility of settling the Korean issue with the Soviet Union, placed the Korean question before the United Nations and discarded the Moscow plan. The United Nations General Assembly formed the UN Temporary Commission on Korea in November and authorized it to conduct a national election in Korea to create a national government for the whole country.

The UN decision was welcomed by the Americans and by most people in South Korea. The Soviet occupation authority and the Korean Communists in the north, however, rejected the UN plan, and did not allow the UN Temporary Commission to visit North Korea. It soon became apparent that the UN plan would not work in the whole of Korea, and the Commission adopted an alternative plan to hold elections in those areas where it was possible, namely in South Korea only. It was assumed by the Commission that UN-sponsored and supervised elections would be held in the north in the near future, that a national assembly created by the first democratic elections in Korea would represent the entire country, that the Government to be established would be that of all Korea, and that the people in the north would elect their representatives to the national assembly later. With the establishment of the Government of Korea, the Allied occupation was to be terminated.

Whereas the right-wing nationalists welcomed such an alternative plan, the moderate and progressive nationalists, such as Kim Kyu-sik, the head of the Democratic Independence Party, as well as an extreme right-wing nationalist, Kim Ku, vehemently opposed it. Opposition stemmed from the fear that it would turn the temporary division of Korea into a permanent political partition. The group's representatives visited North Korea and talked with Kim Il-sung and other Communists who were equally adamant against the UN plan, but failed to achieve their objective.

Dr. Rhee's National Society for the Acceleration of Korean Independence, which included some 50 right-wing political organizations (of which the strongest was the Korean Democratic Party), was anxious to end foreign occupation of Korea by any means. Knowing that the Soviet authorities in the north had already begun to transfer real power to the Supreme People's Assembly and the Central People's Committee, both established in early 1947, Dr. Rhee's society advocated the immediate independence of South Korea from Allied control. The bitter controversy over the new UN plan divided the people in the south as tension rose.

The UN-sponsored elections held in the south in May 1948 created a new National Assembly, heavily dominated by conservative right-wing members. About 7.5 million people, or 75 per cent of the electorate, voted in the midst of communist-inspired strikes and boycotts. They elected 198 of 210 representatives from the south, while 100 unfilled seats in the 310-member National Assembly were to be occupied by the north Korean representatives later.

In August 1948 the communists in the north held an election (in which, according to a North Korean statement, "77.52 per cent of the 8.7 million eligible voters in South Korea" also participated) and established the new 527-member Supreme People's Assembly (including 360 "South Korean representatives") for Korea. Kim Il-sung was appointed Premier of the Democratic People's Republic of Korea (D.P.R.K.), proclaimed on September 9th, 1948.

The National Assembly in South Korea drew up a democratic constitution for the Republic of Korea. (The North Korean Supreme People's Assembly had already drafted a constitution for the D.P.R.K. in April 1948 and it was ratified by the new Supreme People's Assembly in September 1948.) The South Korean constitution combined features of the American presidential and the British parliamentary systems. Dr. Rhee was elected by the National Assembly to be the first President of the Republic of Korea, whose legitimacy was immediately recognized by the United Nations. On August 15th, 1948, the Republic of Korea was inaugurated, and the American occupation came to an end.

Arriving unprepared and with no specific plans for Korea, the United States occupation authority and its military government achieved very little in terms of promoting any democratic institutions or way of life, establishing a social order or providing economic necessities. South Korea, which had been mainly an agricultural region with only light industries, began to suffer as the shortage of fertilizers, coal and electricity developed, for nearly 90 per cent of these critical goods had been manufactured in the north. The north Korean supply of electricity to the south ended toward the end of 1947.

Korea, which had been the supplier of raw materials and manpower to Japan, had almost no establishments producing drugs, medical supplies and other necessary consumer goods, which had formerly come from Japan. The flooding of South Korea with refugees from the north aggravated the already severe shortage of housing, food, clothing and fuel. As poor diet and lack of clothing and medical supplies increased, the health problem became critical.

When the political, economic and social problems grew, aggravated by left-wing activity, the American military government became more and more oppressive, betraying its pledge to guarantee freedom of political action. The rapidly growing anti-American sentiments among the people, due to increasing hardships in life, induced more and more Americans to develop a strong antagonism toward the people. American political tutelage to prepare the Koreans to enjoy democracy, as well as to establish a unified, independent Korean nation, failed completely. The Koreans learned neither the principles of democracy nor those of social equality from the American soldiers.

The only positive contributions the American occupation made were in the fields of press, culture and education. The granting of freedom of the press brought about the revival of Korean newspapers which had been non-existent under the Japanese since 1937. (There was a Korean language newspaper printed by the Japanese colonial government after 1937.) The encouragement and freedom given to the Koreans to develop their own educational and cultural institutions resulted in the growth of the number of schools at all levels, theatrical groups and societies and traditional art. The increase in the number of higher and secondary educational institutions was phenomenal, and a vast number of young Koreans, to whom education beyond the primary level was denied by Japanese policy, flooded colleges and universities as well as high schools. The rate of illiteracy dropped from about 75 per cent to approximately 35 per cent.

THE KOREAN WAR, 1950-53*

American forces were withdrawn from South Korea in June 1949, leaving only a small advisory group. South Korea's own forces were weaker than those of the north, which had been built up with Soviet help. As a result of failure to agree on measures for reunification, Korea was effectively divided into two political entities, each claiming to have legitimate jurisdiction over the whole country. Tension and rivalry between them culminated in the Korean War, beginning when

* This section on the Korean War was contributed by the Editor.

a North Korean force of over 60,000 troops, supported by Soviet-built tanks, crossed the 38th parallel and invaded the south on June 25th, 1950. Four days later the North Koreans captured Seoul, the South Korean capital. American forces, whose assistance was requested by the Seoul Government, arrived on June 30th.

In response to North Korea's attack, the United Nations mounted a collective defence action in support of South Korea. Armed forces from 16 UN member states, attached to a unified command under the U.S.A., were sent to help repel the invasion. Meanwhile, the North Koreans continued their drive southwards, advancing so strongly that they soon occupied most of South Korea, leaving UN troops confined to the south-east corner of the peninsula. Following sea-borne landings by UN forces at Inchon, near Seoul, in September 1950, the attackers were driven back and UN troops advanced into North Korea, capturing Pyongyang, the capital, in October and reaching the Chinese frontier on the Yalu River in November.

In October 1950 the People's Republic of China sent in troops to assist North Korea. In November a force of 200,000 Chinese crossed the Yalu River into North Korea and forced the evacuation of South Korean and UN troops. The Chinese advanced into South Korea but were driven back by a UN counter-attack in April 1951.

Peace negotiations began in July 1951 but hostilities continued, inconclusively, until an armistice agreement was made on July 27th, 1953. The war caused more than 800,000 casualties in South Korea and enormous damage to property. The 1953 ceasefire line, roughly along the 38th parallel, remains the boundary between North and South Korea, with a narrow demilitarized zone separating the two countries.

SOUTH KOREA

The First Republic, 1948-60

The Republic of Korea was formally inaugurated on August 15th, 1948. Two months later, a communist-inspired military rebellion broke out in south-western Korea. The key leaders of the Communist Party had already fled to the north, but the strength of the South Korean Workers' (Communist) Party, which went underground, was considerable. The Sunch'on-Yosu rebellion, as it is known, was put down, but it demoralized the nation. In October 1949 the South Korean Workers' Party was outlawed, and eight months later, in June 1950, the North Korean invasion came.

The second South Korean presidential election was due in 1952, while the war was in progress. President Rhee had had sharp disagreements with the National Assembly, and it appeared that the latter would not re-elect him. In July 1952, employing strong pressure tactics, including police repression, he forced the National Assembly to adopt a constitutional amendment instituting election of the president by popular rather than National Assembly election. He won an overwhelming majority in the national election held in August.

The National Assembly elections two years later gave Rhee's Liberal Party a substantial majority. Taking advantage of this, another constitutional amendment was passed; the most important changes were the exemption of Rhee from the two-term constitutional limitation in the office of the president, the succession of the vice-president to the presidency should the incumbent die, and the abolition of the post of prime minister.

In the 1956 presidential election, a new opposition Democratic Party, founded in 1955, nominated contenders for the offices of president and vice-president. The sudden death of the presidential candidate of the opposition party assured victory for Dr. Rhee, but the Democratic candidate, Chang Myou, defeated the Liberal Party candidate for the vice-presidency.

As corruption among government officials and members of the Liberal Party and police pressures increased, a widespread desire for change grew, particularly among the urban voters. In the 1958 National Assembly elections, the Democratic Party increased its seats substantially. Aware of the danger of losing its absolute control, the Liberal Party-dominated National Assembly repealed local autonomy laws and filled politically important local posts with Liberal Party appointees. Chiefs of police were also chosen from the supporters of the Liberal Party.

The fourth presidential election was due in March 1960. Three weeks before the election the Democratic Party presidential nominee died, again assuring the re-election of Dr. Rhee. However, the election of the Liberal Party vice-presidential candidate was uncertain and Liberal Party leaders employed the National Police and corrupt means to assure the election of their candidate, Yi Ki-bung. Popular reaction against corrupt and fraudulent practices grew and riots and student demonstrations erupted throughout the country, particularly in the southern area, culminating in the student uprising of April 19th, 1960.

Martial law was declared and troops were mobilized. However, the troops elected to remain neutral, refusing to act against the demonstrators who were demanding the resignation of the president, the nullification of the March election results, fundamental political reform and the removal of corrupt politicians and profiteers from the Government. Demonstrations and riots continued every day from April 19th to 25th.

On April 26th, President Rhee and his cabinet resigned. A caretaker government was set up under Ho Chong, the Minister for Foreign Affairs, and in mid-June the National Assembly adopted a constitutional amendment establishing a strong parliamentary system, reducing the presidency to a figurehead chief of state, and resurrecting the office of prime minister. In August the National Assembly named Yun Po-son president and Chang Myon prime minister responsible to the lower house of the Assembly, and the Second Republic emerged.

With the exception of the Land Reform Law of 1949, and besides mere survival during the communist-inspired army rebellion in 1949 and the Korean War, the corrupt and inefficient government of the First Republic recorded no positive success. It made no efforts to relax the tension between the north and the south, and it failed to settle outstanding issues with Japan. Its economic programmes were at best poorly designed, paid inadequate attention to the welfare of the people, and so received no economic aid from the United States. Its military, which became another political arm (along with the National Police), was ill-prepared and soldiers were poorly trained, supplied and paid. It failed to inspire the people or promote the confidence and unity of the people. It is true that economic recovery began around 1959, but such recovery was offset by the political corruption and economic profiteering of officials and members of the ruling party.

The Second Republic

The Second Republic was handicapped from the start: it had no mandate from the people and both President Yun Po-son and Prime Minister Chang were men of intellectual and scholarly interests with mild dispositions, lacking fortitude and practical tactics. The Chang administration was indecisive in dealing with former leaders of the Rhee regime and seemed too tolerant toward left-wing radicals. It was unable to deal effectively with ideological and social cleavage between political and sectional groups, while gaining no new support or the loyalty of the people.

The sudden gaining of power by the Democratic Party created tension among factions within the Party, resulting in sharp divisional alignments. No suitable solutions to economic and social problems were forthcoming. With the exception of the stillborn Five-Year Plan, the Chang administration failed to tackle the country's serious economic problems. Meanwhile, new demonstrations erupted as the influence of the communists among the students grew. Agitation by students for direct negotiations with North Korean students, aimed at reunification of the country, created anxiety and turmoil. Stronger party discipline was finally achieved in early spring of 1961, and efforts were made to curb both corruption and public demonstrations, but the danger to national security increased as food and job shortages worsened.

Military Rule

On May 16th, 1961, a military revolution, led by a small group of young army officers headed by Maj.-Gen. Park Chung Hee, overthrew the ill-destined and ineffective Chang administration. The United States was indecisive about intervening on behalf of the Chang Government, and leaders of the Korean armed forces gave their support to the revolutionary group.

The revolutionaries set up a military junta, dissolved the National Assembly, forbade all political activity, and declared martial law, banning student demonstrations and censoring the press. They persuaded Lt.-Gen. Chang Do-yong, the Army Chief of Staff who remained neutral, to become the chairman of the Supreme Council for National Reconstruction which they created. President Yun remained in office, but the Government was in the hands of the military. Pledges by the revolutionaries were issued, upholding anti-communism and adherence to the United Nations, and calling for stronger ties with the United States and the free world, the eradication of corruption and graft, the extinction of street violence and social evils, and rejuvenation of national spirit. It also pledged the construction of a self-supporting economy, a solid foundation for a new and truly democratic republic, as well as the early restoration of civilian rule.

The Supreme Council acted as a legislative body, and a National Reconstruction Extraordinary Measures Law was adopted as a substitute for the constitution. In July 1961 a series of disagreements between Gen. Park and Gen. Chang led to the dismissal of the latter. Gen. Park took over the chairmanship of the Supreme Council and, when President Yun resigned in March 1962, Gen. Park was appointed Acting President.

In August 1961 Gen. Park announced that political activity would be permitted in early 1963 to pave the way for the restoration of a civilian government. A constitutional amendment was passed by national referendum in December 1962, restoring a strong presidential system while limiting presidential office to two four-year terms. The executive branch was to be headed by a Prime Minister appointed by the President. A unicameral National Assembly was to be elected every four years.

In January 1963 the revolutionaries formed the Democratic Republican Party and nominated Gen. Park as its presidential candidate. In mid-March a plot to overthrow the military government was allegedly uncovered and the acting President announced that a plebiscite would be held on a four-year extension of military rule. The reaction was strongly negative, and in July civilian government within a year was promised. In August Gen. Park retired from the army and became an active presidential candidate of the Democratic Republican Party. Freedom of political activity was restored for those not charged with past political crimes.

The opposition forces were badly split. Former President Yun eventually emerged as the principal contender against Gen. Park, as the candidate of the Civil Rule Party. The election in October gave Gen. Park victory by a narrow margin, with a minority of the votes cast. National Assembly elections, held in November, gave a major victory to the Democratic Republican Party, although it received only 34 per cent of the vote. Civilian constitutional rule was restored on December 17th, 1963, with the inauguration of President Park and the convening of the Assembly.

The Third Republic, 1963-72

The Government of the Third Republic faced a series of difficulties. In March 1964 large student demonstrations broke out in Seoul, protesting against corruption and economic hardship, although the ostensible cause was the negotiations with Japan on normalizing relations. Tension gradually mounted and in June martial law was declared in the Seoul area. In April 1965 demonstrators protested against a Korean-Japanese normalization treaty and South Korea's dispatch of troops to South Viet-Nam.

In the May 1967 presidential election Park defeated Yun again, by a large margin. The Democratic Republican Party won a substantial majority of seats in the new National Assembly elected in June. When election irregularities involving the ruling party were uncovered, the opposition New Democratic Party demanded the nullification of the election results and called for a new election. Failing in this, its members refused to participate in Assembly action. A compromise was finally reached in early 1968 and the opposition party members returned. In September 1969 the Assembly adopted an amendment of the constitution, allowing for a third term of office to the incumbent president due to the existence of extraordinary national emergency, while the members of the New Democratic Party were boycotting the session for the second time. A referendum approved the amendment in October, paving the way for President Park to run for the seventh presidential election, held in April 1971, in which he defeated Kim Dae-jung, nominee of the New Democratic Party.

The Fourth Republic, 1972-

President Park, facing sudden changes in the international situation due to the Sino-American détente, proclaimed martial law in October 1972, dissolved the National Assembly and suspended the 1962 constitution. A new constitution was proposed by the Extraordinary State Council and approved in a referendum in November. The new constitution gave the president greatly expanded powers, authorizing him to issue emergency decrees and establish the National Conference for Unification (NCU) and a new National Assembly. The NCU, composed of 2,359 members elected in December 1972 was established for a six-year term, to be responsible for Korean reunification and for electing the president. President Park was re-elected for a six-year term by the Conference's first meeting.

An election was held in February 1973 for 146 representatives to serve a six-year term in the National Assembly. The new unicameral body of 219 members, including 73 elected for three years by the NCU on the President's recommendation, was convened in March. Of the 146 directly elected members, 71 represented the Democratic Republican Party (the Government party); 52 represented the New Democratic Party (the opposition party); and two were from the Democratic Unification Party (a splinter opposition group); and 21 were independents. The 73 NCU appointees to the Assembly were members of the newly formed Revitalization Reform Society.

A series of political incidents which attracted international attention erupted during 1973. In July a clergyman and 14 others were arrested in Seoul on a charge of subversion for distributing leaflets at an Easter sunrise service calling for "a revival of democracy" and "an overthrow of dictatorial government". Due to world-wide press attention and public pressure, all of them were released in October. In August the most outspoken opponent of the South Korean Government, Kim Dae-jung, was whisked away from Tokyo to Korea and was put under house arrest. Kim, President Park's opponent in the 1971 presidential election, had left South Korea shortly before the imposition of martial law in October 1972 and campaigned in the United States and Japan against the Government of President Park. This incident estranged the United States, Japan and North Korea. Despite the South Korean Government's denial of complicity in the kidnapping, Japan deferred further economic aid to South Korea until the Kim case was satisfactorily settled. At the same time, the North Korean co-chairman of the South and North Coordinating Committee demanded that his counterpart be replaced, accusing him of engineering the abduction of Kim.

The most serious incident of all was the anti-government rally in October by about 300 students of the Seoul National University. The demonstration, the first for two years, demanded an end to "fascist intelligence rule and government infringement of basic human rights". Other demonstrations followed throughout the country and in December civic and religious leaders began to collect signatures for a petition to amend the constitution, a move which attracted support from intellectuals. In January 1974 President Park issued decrees ending this campaign and reinforcing the emergency measures.

While undergoing extreme economic hardships, due to the oil shortage at home and the worldwide economic recession, South Korea in 1974 was engulfed by increasing political dissent against the rule by four emergency decrees of January and April 1974, banning anti-government activities and agitation for constitutional reform and imposing tight economic control. Not only the opposition New Democratic Party but a large number of students, reporters, writers, religious leaders and university professors joined the movement against the Government and its emergency measures while demanding an immediate revision of the constitution. Many were arrested and tried, and a large number of schools were temporarily closed.

In August President Park's wife was killed in an assassination attempt against the president. In the following two months the four decrees were repealed. Following that, the opposition New Democratic Party, with Kim Yong-sam as its head, pressed more strongly for constitutional reform and demanded the release of political prisoners.

In September President Park carried out a major cabinet reshuffle, appointing new men to key posts such as chief of the presidential bodyguard unit, CIA Director, Ministers of Home Affairs, Justice, Education, Construction, Finance, Transportation, Communications, Public Information and the Board of Unification.

The visit to Korea by U.S. President Ford in late November 1974 boosted the morale of the Korean

Government which had been concerned with the growing negative attitudes of the U.S. Congress towards South Korea. Meanwhile, the Government was faced with a hardening of the Japanese Government's attitude due to South Korea's trial of Kim Dae-jung on charges connected with 1971 election violations, the trials of two Japanese citizens in South Korea on charges of anti-government subversive activity, and violent anti-Japanese demonstrations in Korea after Mrs. Park's assassination by a Korean from Japan. Negotiations between Seoul and Tokyo towards the end of the year relaxed the tension somewhat.

In 1975 there were two diplomatic setbacks. In August 1975 the UN Security Council refused to consider South Korea's application for membership. The U.S.A. also informed the Security Council that it was prepared to dissolve the UN Command in South Korea as of January 1976 if appropriate arrangements could be made to provide for maintenance of the 1953 Korean Armistice Agreement. Later in August the ministerial conference of 78 non-aligned nations voted to admit North Korea, North Viet-Nam, and the Palestine Liberation Organization but denied participation to South Korea.

After the communist military victories in Indochina in 1975, the U.S.A. pledged to uphold the 1954 mutual defence treaty with South Korea, but the U.S. Congress has displayed concern over the apparent violation of human rights in countries supported by U.S. military and economic aid, including South Korea. Thus there has been talk of scaling down U.S. involvement in South Korea. Korean-Japanese relations improved after the change of regime in South Viet-Nam in April 1975.

The most notable internal development in South Korea during 1975 was the institution in May of a Presidential Emergency Measure for Safeguarding National Security and Public Order. This measure was ostensibly the result of President Park's increased concern for national security, stimulated by what was perceived as a mounting threat of aggression from North Korea as a result of the visit of Kim Il-sung to Peking in the spring of 1975, following the communist take-over in South Viet-Nam. The new measure imposed further prohibition on the opposition to the 1972 constitution, banned student demonstrations or public defamation of current Emergency Measures. Virtually all opposition activity was effectively forbidden. Violators were subject to arrest, detention, search or seizure and measures taken against them were not subject to judicial review.

NORTH KOREA

Strong nationalist leadership with potentially large popular support was at hand in North Korea when World War II ended. It consisted chiefly of democratically-inclined, Western missionary-educated individuals, of whom the most outstanding leader was Cho Man-sik. Following the surrender of Japan in August 1945, the Japanese governor in Pyongyang handed over control to Cho and a newly-formed Provincial People's Committee, which had its national headquarters in Seoul. Later in August the first Soviet troops reached Pyongyang. In contrast to the American occupation policy in South Korea, they accepted the legitimacy of the Committee, and later also approved Cho as chairman of the Five Provinces Administrative Bureau, set up to act as the indigenous government organ for North Korea. However, the Soviet authorities insisted that half the members were to be communists.

In September, Kim Il-sung, a young communist, who had led a guerrilla group of Korean communists in south-eastern Manchuria, returned to Korea with Soviet troops. Kim, however, had to cope with the "domestic" communists, who had been released from Japanese prisons or had re-emerged from their underground bases. They challenged Kim Il-sung's group, commonly known as the "Kapsan" or "partisan" faction. In the early power struggle among the communists, Hyon Chun-hyok, the leader of the "domestic" faction was assassinated in September 1945 by Kim Il-sung's men.

Three groups of communists returned to North Korea after the liberation from Japan: one associated with the Soviet Army known as the "Soviet" faction, one from Manchuria known as the "Kapsan" or "partisan" faction, and one from Yenan, in China, under the leadership of Kim Tu-bong. Kim Tu-bong and his Korean Independence League from Yenan were latecomers who encountered a struggle for power against Kim Il-sung's tightly formed "partisan" faction. The "domestic" faction, which lost its leader, began to decline.

Shortly after he was officially introduced to the people by Cho Man-sik as a "national hero", in early October, Kim Il-sung formed the North Korean Central Bureau of the Korean Communist Party in order to build his political position. A confirmed Marxist, known to and apparently trusted by the Soviet occupation authority, Kim was given covert Soviet support.

To counteract the new communist organization, Cho Man-sik organized the Korean Democratic Party which received the backing of the majority of the people, particularly intellectuals and Christians. The uncompromising stand by Cho against the Moscow plan for a five-year trusteeship of the four Allied powers, however, led to his resignation in January 1946 as chairman of the Five Provinces Administrative Bureau. He was promptly placed under house arrest. Many members of the Korean Democratic Party fled to South Korea, leaving North Korea in the hands of the communists.

After the departure of the nationalists, a North Korean Provisional People's Committee was established in February 1946 with Kim Il-sung as chairman and Kim Tu-bong as vice-chairman. The Soviets gave government status to the Committee. The election of Kim Tu-bong as vice-chairman was a recognition of his strength, but Kim Il-sung was unwilling to share his power with Kim Tu-bong.

Realizing this, Kim Tu-bong formed the New People's Party in March to expand his power base, and despite no Soviet assistance, managed to increase his party's membership. Kim Il-sung preferred to control the new party rather than challenge it, while Kim Tu-bong realized that unification of the two powerful political organizations would give him a better chance to gain control over North Korea. As a result, the North Korean Central Bureau of the Korean Communist Party and the New People's Party merged in July 1946 to form the North Korean Workers' Party, with Kim Tu-bong as its chairman and Kim Il-sung as its vice-chairman. Real power, however, was in the hands of the latter since the former had received no support from the Soviet occupation authority. The new party of the two Kims systematically broke up the "domestic" faction of the communists.

In the spring of 1947 the Supreme People's Assembly was established as the highest legislative organ in North Korea, and the Assembly in turn established an executive branch called the Central People's Committee. Kim Tu-bong assumed the chairmanship of the Assembly, and Kim Il-sung was made Premier. The Committee's first major act was to direct land reform. This was completed during March and April. No attempts were made to establish collective farms, except for several experimental co-operative farms. The farm land which was distributed to landless peasants became the private property of the cultivators. It was not until the end of the Korean War in 1953 that the agricultural "co-operativization" programme was inaugurated. Land reform was followed by the nationalization of industry, transport, communications and financial institutions.

In early 1948 Pak Hon-yong and leaders of his South Korean Workers' (Communist) Party, fled from the south when the party was outlawed by the American occupation authority. Pak Hon-yong, who had been enjoying strong support from the "domestic" faction as leader of the Korean Communist movement in the south, felt that he, instead of Kim Il-sung, should lead the movement in Korea. Dislocated from his power basis in South Korea, Pak Hon-yong was unable to achieve his objectives, and he grudgingly accepted a subordinate position to that of Kim Il-sung. It was reported later by the North Koreans that, anxious to regain his leadership, Pak urged Kim Il-sung to launch a war against South Korea in 1950.

The Democratic People's Republic of Korea

After refusing to allow the United Nations Temporary Commission on Korea to visit North Korea and conduct elections, Kim Il-sung established a separate pro-Soviet state there. In August a so-called national election was held in the north for a new Supreme People's Assembly. The newly created Assembly, with Kim Tu-bong as chairman of its Presidium, drafted a constitution, ratified it on September 8th, and proclaimed the Democratic People's Republic of Korea (DPRK) on September 9th. Kim Il-sung was named Premier, while Pak Hon-yong was made Vice-Premier and Minister for Foreign Affairs.

In June 1949 the merger of the North Korean Workers' Party of Kim Il-sung and Kim Tu-bong and the South Korean Workers' Party of Pak Hon-yong brought about a unified communist party called the Korean Workers' Party, with Kim Il-sung as its chairman and Pak Hon-yong as its vice-chairman. The merger, however, eliminated Pak's autonomous status.

The establishment of the DPRK made the temporary military division of Korea a permanent political partition.

As the United Nations and democratic nations recognized the Government of the Republic of Korea in the south, the Soviet Union and its satellites recognized the Government of the DPRK in the north. The Soviet Union announced the withdrawal of Soviet troops from North Korea, completing the process in December 1949. However, a large number of Soviet advisers in various fields remained in North Korea.

During 1950 North Korea substantially increased the size and strength of its armed forces with Soviet supplies. In June 1950 the North Korean invasion of the south initiated the bloody Korean War (*see* above), inflicting great damage on both sides. During and after the unsuccessful attempt to conquer South Korea, Kim Il-sung purged many of his enemies, including Pak Hon-yong. They were made scapegoats for Kim Il-sung's failure to achieve the forcible reunification of Korea. Thus Kim Il-sung's dictatorial rule emerged.

Conflict among the surviving communist leaders, however, did not end and Kim Tu-bong, who survived a series of purges, remained a formidable figure. Kim Il-sung's economic reconstruction programme, which emphasized the development of heavy industry, met strong opposition from Kim Tu-bong and his supporters.

The debate lasted until 1956, when Tu-bong fell from power. Meanwhile, the Yenan faction attacked the personality cult of Kim Il-sung; he counter-attacked, forcing some Yenan communists to flee to China. China and the U.S.S.R. effected a temporary reconciliation, but leaders of the Yenan faction were systematically relegated to less important posts or eased entirely out of power. By 1958 it ceased to pose any further threat.

In October 1972 the Fifth Central Committee of the Korean Workers' Party proposed amendments to the constitution. To effect these changes, general elections were held in December to choose deputies to the Fifth Supreme People's Assembly, and to provincial, city and county people's assemblies. The newly elected representatives, who held the first session of the new Assembly in late December, unanimously adopted the new constitution and elected Kim Il-sung and Kim Il as President and Premier respectively. For the first time, the North Korean Constitution stated that the capital was Pyongyang and not Seoul.

The new constitution created the Central People's Committee, headed by the President, as the highest organ of state, and the State Administrative Council, headed by the Premier, to replace the former cabinet.

In 1973 North Korea became a member of the World Health Organization, a United Nations body, and gained observer status at the United Nations. The observer status nullified both the branding of North Korea as an aggressor in 1950 and the view that the Government of South Korea was the only lawful government in Korea. Both Koreas were invited to the UN General Assembly in November 1973 for a debate on the Korean question. North Korea was also given membership in the United Nations Conference on Trade and Development in May 1973. However, North Korea failed to terminate the United Nations Command in Korea and the United Nations Commission for the Unification and Rehabilitation of Korea (UNCURK), established in 1950 and 1953 respectively.

The Central Committee of the Korean Workers' Party held its eighth plenary session in February 1974 and launched the "Three Great Revolutions": ideological, technical and cultural. It emphasized the promotion of a self-oriented, self-reliant and independent ideology, or *juche* thought. Kim Il-sung's birthday was declared a new national holiday. The Supreme People's Assembly, meeting in March, proposed in a letter to the U.S. Congress the conclusion of a peace treaty between the U.S.A. and North Korea to replace the Korean Armistice Agreement of 1953. It also advocated the removal of all foreign troops from South Korea.

The Korean Workers' Party reorganized the structure of the cabinet and reshuffled its membership twice in 1974. A newly created seventh vice-premiership went to Ho Dam, concurrently Minister for Foreign Affairs. Kim Yong-ju, brother of Kim Il-sung, who had been regarded as heir apparent, was demoted in the party hierarchy, while Kim Il-sung's only surviving son, Kim Chung-il, rose in rank as a possible successor to his father. Significantly a military leader, Gen. O Jin-u, also rose in rank within the party.

The 1974 United Nations Assembly abolished UNCURK but the North Koreans failed to achieve their aims to abolish the United Nations Command and remove U.S. forces from South Korea, or make the stationing of U.S. troops in South Korea illegal.

North Korea emphasized the importance of increasing solidarity with international revolutionary forces, giving priority to strengthening ties with socialist and third world countries; establishing diplomatic relations with more nations, including South Korea's allies; securing membership in international organizations; and winning the support and, if possible, allegiance of overseas Koreans. North Korea succeeded in widening its diplomatic and commercial arena in more countries, including South Korea's former allies such as Sweden and Pakistan.

One of North Korea's major objectives in 1975 was the intensification of diplomatic activity to strengthen ties between non-aligned nations. The most notable diplomatic event was Kim Il-sung's visit to Peking, when North Korea's position on the Korean question was supported by the Chinese, who nevertheless failed to endorse an aggressive plan against South Korea. Subsequent visits by Kim to Mauritania, Bulgaria and Yugoslavia consolidated the DPRK's diplomatic objectives but no invitation from Moscow was received.

Two North Korean victories were claimed in 1975: one when the ministerial conference of the non-aligned nations in Lima, Peru, voted to accept its application for participation; the second when it received enough votes in the First Committee of the UN General Assembly to adopt a pro-North Korean resolution. This resolution was later passed by the full General Assembly.

ECONOMIC SURVEY OF NORTH KOREA

T. M. Burley

The land area of the Democratic People's Republic of Korea, 120,538 square kilometres, represents just over half the total area of Korea: its population (estimated by the National Unification Board at 15.9 million for 1974) is about 31 per cent of the Korean total and is thought to be growing by 2.4 per cent a year. About 75 per cent of the country is mountainous, and in 1974 the cultivable area was only 2,170,000 hectares or 17 per cent of the total. Farmland per household averages 1.6 hectares and a generally harsh climate restricts agriculture to one crop each year. The Korean War of 1950-53 wrecked the country's industry and caused a fall of 12 per cent for the population overall and 17 per cent for the male population. However, North Korea possesses most of the peninsula's minerals and a trained and notably energetic work force.

"The achievements of the North Korean economy in 1973 and the projected goals for 1974 were detailed in the report of Finance Minister Kim Gyong Ryon at the Third Session of the Fifth Supreme People's Assembly, March 22nd, 1974. The report claims that the industrial output of North Korea increased by 19 per cent in 1973—an increase of 1.6 times over 1970, and that during the past three years industrial output has been averaging a 17 per cent annual growth rate. The total amount of state budgetary revenues and expenditures for 1974 are estimated at 9,801,110,000 won respectively. Minister Kim indicated that investments in capital construction from the state budget would increase 1.5 times over 1973 and this increase would guarantee reliable fulfilment of the Plan prior to schedule. The increase, he indicated, would lay the foundation for attaining ten major goals of economic construction in the years of the next plan: 12 million tons of steel; one million tons of non-ferrous metal; 100 million tons of coal; 50,000 million kWh. of electric power; 20 million tons of cement; 5 million tons of machinery and equipment; 5 million tons of marine products; 5 million tons of chemical fertilizer; 100,000 *chongbo* of reclaimed tideland; and 10 million tons of grain. Minister Kim further stated that reduction in the prices of manufactured goods (effective March 1st, 1974) would give each household an average monthly benefit of 22 won and the abolition of all taxes (effective April 1st, 1974) would increase the beneft by 6 won. Based on these figures, the real income of the average household increased from 73 won to 101 won per month. North Korea's claim that it is the first country in the history of mankind to abolish taxation must be tempered by the realization that revenue from taxes constituted only 1.9 per cent of state income in 1973." (Young C. Kim in *Asian Survey*.) *Note:* One *chongbo* equals 2.45 acres.

The Central Statistical Board, reporting on progress of the Six-Year Plan (1971–76), stated that the national income in 1974 was 1.7 times the 1970 figure. The average monetary income of co-operative farmers was 2,360 won per household in 1974, far surpassing the target of 1,800 won envisaged in the Plan. Following price cuts in manufactured goods, prices of consumer goods dropped by an average of 30 per cent in 1974. In the four years from 1971 to 1974, the real income per household of factory and office workers rose 1.5 times and that of peasants 1.6 times. Differences in living conditions between urban and rural dwellers are apparently receiving special attention: the introduction of bus services to villages has been completed and 87 per cent of water supply works in rural districts had been carried out by the end of August 1975.

Growth in industrial output during the 1960s averaged 12.6 per cent a year. Under the Six-Year Plan, industrial production is to grow by about 14 per cent annually between 1971 and 1976. Some 70 per cent of the expected gain in industry should come from improved labour productivity. In 1973 industrial output is reported to have risen by 19 per cent, bringing the average growth for the first three years of the Plan to 17 per cent. The 1974 increase is reported as 17.3 per cent. Priorities for investment in 1975 were in transport and mining. These are vital sectors in the economy: bottlenecks in the former are major causes of North Korea's present trade problems, while productivity in the latter is extremely low compared with most other heavy industries.

AGRICULTURE

Arable land is concentrated in the relatively flat western provinces; on the east coast the mountains come close to the sea. In 1960 paddy covered 510,000 hectares or nearly 27 per cent of the arable area, compared with 21 per cent in 1946, thanks to intensive irrigation efforts. By January 1959 "the individual peasant economy had been eliminated and one million peasants' households organized into 3,800 co-operatives". North Korean agriculture was now to embark on a revolution of Chinese origin, chiefly designed to raise yields and reduce the area sown to food crops, and comprising the multiplication of irrigation schemes, mechanization and electrification, deep ploughing, close planting and heavy use of fertilizer.

Irrigation and mechanization are considered vital for agricultural progress. An important project, the Ujidon irrigation system, was opened in 1961: it comprises the Suhjeung reservoir, said to be the largest in the country and able to irrigate 38,000 hectares of land in South and North Hwanghai provinces. In South Hwanghai the Chungdan project was planned to irrigate 20,000 hectares and to power small hydro-electric stations to generate current for the villages built along the Western plains area up to the Chinese frontier. North Korean agriculture appears to be seriously short of labour, so that mechanization has received high priority. During 1960 the whole countryside was said to have 6,313 tractors (12,500 in terms of 15 h.p. units); by 1974, the respective totals were 20–30,000 and 75,000.

According to FAO estimates, annual output of cereals was about 5.5 million metric tons in both 1970 and 1971. Despite unprecedented bad weather, 1972 output was similar to that of 1971. In 1973 and 1974 agricultural output improved and the 1974 grain harvest may have reached 7 million tons, with average rice yields reaching 6 tons per hectare. Maize production is put at 1.8 million tons from 860,000 hectares. In an effort to boost agricultural output further, land reclamation in central areas is being given priority: some 200,000 hectares are involved. Fishpond farming prospects have a key role to play in meeting the target production level for aquatic items of 5 million tons per year: about 1.7 million tons were produced in 1975. Currently, emphasis is being placed on fruit production involving an area of 300,000 *chongbo*.

MINING

The regime estimates North Korea's coal deposits at 7,900 million metric tons, the principal collieries being in the region immediately north of Pyongyang. In 1970 coal output was estimated at about 27.5 million tons, by including 4.5 million tons of lignite. Coal production remains the focal point of economic development: it received a 60 per cent increase in investment in 1974 and output recorded a 20 per cent increase over 1973 to reach an estimated 50 million tons. The Suchang and Yonghung mines were the principal beneficiaries of the increased investment.

According to the *Mining Annual Review*, North Korea produces about 9 million tons of iron ore (gross weight) annually. The mines, at Musan, Unryul, Toksong, Tokhyon, Chaeyong and Hasong, are to be expanded, and new mines are to be developed. Substantial investments in iron ore mining in 1974 increased the annual capacity of the Musan mine to 5.5 million tons and this will be further increased to over 6.5 million tons. New mines are being opened up at Toksong and Sohaeri; the country's reserves total about 2,000 million tons of low-grade ore.

Annual production of magnesite is put at 1.5 million tons and North Korea claims to lead the world in magnesite deposits. Dressing plants at the Booyoon nickel mine, capable of concentrating 280,000 tons of ore annually, and at the Manduk copper mine, an annual concentrating capacity of 560,000 tons of ore, started working in 1964; ore output is apparently inadequate for the copper plant, so about 50,000 tons of concentrates are imported annually.

Lead, zinc, tungsten, mercury, phosphates, gold, silver and sulphur are also mined. About 100,000 tons of zinc ore and 65,000 tons of lead ore are produced each year. The zinc ore is smelted within the country, the annual output being around 65,000 tons, whereas part of the lead ore is shipped abroad for smelting. Under the Six-Year Plan for 1971–76, an aluminium smelter with an annual capacity of 20,000 tons is being built; three small aluminium plants are already in production at Hungnam, Chinnampo and Tasado. Under a long-term barter agreement North Korea is supplying substantial quantities of barite to the Soviet Union. Cement is of increasing importance; several new plants have been built, including one with the capacity of 5 million tons; 1975 output is estimated at 15 million tons.

MANUFACTURING

Metallurgy

Production of steel was claimed to be 158 kilogrammes per capita in early 1972. In 1975 output reportedly approached 4 million metric tons. The Hwanghai Iron Works, whose facilities include a bloom rolling shop with a capacity of 400,000 tons annually, will be displaced as the country's biggest iron and steel centre when "the world's leading metallurgical centre" is established at the Kim Chaek Iron Works. Here, construction of a blast furnace, a melting shop and an HR mill, as well as sinter and coking plant, was to have been completed in 1975. In a bid to increase North Korea's annual steel output to 12 million tons in the next few years, Kangson steelworks is to be expanded, a melting shop is to be constructed at Chongjin works, and a new works is to be built at Taedonggang.

Machine Building

Machine tool output in 1970 was 10,400 units, increasing by 180 per cent in 1971 and exceeding the target of 30,000 units in 1972. The industry currently manufactures large-size machines, such as 6,000-ton presses, 50,000-kW. generators, 25-ton trucks, tractors, excavators, 300-h.p. bulldozers, electric and diesel locomotives and ships of up to 20,000 tons, as well as aggregate plant for power stations and metallurgical and chemical factories.

Chemicals

This industrial sector, and especially fertilizers, has received much attention. Output of chemical fertilizers per caput was put at 108 kilogrammes in March 1972 (total output in 1970 was 1.5 million tons). Recent developments include a fertilizer factory with a capacity of 1 million tons per year and a 360,000-ton urea plant. The chemical fertilizer industry's annual capacity is now put at 3 million tons. A French-built petrochemical complex north of Pyongyang should be operational in 1976 and will produce ethylene, polyethylene and acrylo-nitrite. The crude petroleum needed by the plant will come from nearby refineries built by the Soviet Union. In 1974 the plant was able to produce a wide range of synthetic resins. By late 1966 the artificial fibre industry was said to supply two-thirds of the country's output of fibres. A vinalon plant near Hungnam, with an annual capacity of 20,000 tons, was completed in 1961; a factory completed in 1962 at Chongjin produces 30,000 tons of staple fibre and rayon annually, while one at Sinuiju, completed in 1966, produces 20,000 tons of staple fibre from reeds and maize stalks. Vinylchloride production rose by 10 per cent in 1973 and current capacity is 80,000 tons, as is the case for vinalon. Plants have recently been constructed for the production of vinylchloride (50,000 tons) and polyethylene (25,000 tons).

Textiles

The industry has been intensively developed, especially on the artificial side; in 1960 it contributed 16.8 per cent of industrial output by value. In 1963 there were "over a dozen modern mills run by the Central Government" and several hundred "local" mills. Under the Seven-Year Plan (1961–67) "textile mills with 50,000–100,000 spindles, woollen fabrics mills with 30,000 spindles, flax fabric with 15,000 spindles and other textile mills" made their appearance and, by the end of 1970, it was claimed that the annual output of textile fabrics had reached about 350 million metres. A figure of 600 million metres is claimed for 1974.

Transport

In 1974 it was claimed that one half of the rail system of 4,380 kilometres had been electrified. Diesel traction has been introduced on the Pyongyang–Kaesong and Pyongyang–Haeju lines and some railway sections on the east coast, and railway lines have been laid in new sections of 420 kilometres, including the Namsinuiju–Tokhyon and Unpa–Cholgwang sections. Light rails have been replaced with heavy rails in sections extending over 1,070 kilometres. Such ports as Nampo, Hungnam and Chongjin have been reconstructed and expanded. Pipelines, cableways and belt conveyors have been introduced, notably the large-scale Musan-Chongjin pipeline for transporting concentrated ores and the long-distance belt conveyor line at the Unryul mine.

Power

Production of electric power in 1975 was estimated at 30,000 million kWh. In 1970 it was put at 16,500 million kWh. The 1970 production came mainly from a network of over 1,000 newly-built medium-sized and small power stations, but the construction of a number of large power plants raised installed electricity capacity to 3.7 million kW in 1973. It is claimed that all villages are now supplied with electricity; the per capita output of electricity was 1,184 kWh. in 1972.

FOREIGN TRADE

North Korea's imports totalled U.S. $372 million and exports $317 million in 1970; for 1973 the comparable figures were $600 million and $500 million. In 1970 three countries, China, the Soviet Union and Japan, accounted for 71.8 per cent of exports and 61.8 per cent of imports. Communist-bloc countries accounted for about 85 per cent of trade in 1974, but trade with the non-communist world is growing rapidly. For example, following the establishment of diplomatic relations with Sweden in 1973, Swedish companies made a number of major sales to North Korea. Total Swedish sales up to mid-1976 probably exceeded 1,000 million Swedish kronor. Japan, however, remains the largest non-communist market; in 1972, trade between the two countries was valued at $131,754,000, or 2.23 times the 1971 level, and in that year North Korea sold goods worth $38,311,000 to Japan (up 273 per cent on 1971). In 1974 Japan exported goods worth $230 million to North Korea but this fell to $180 million in 1975. Japanese goods were dominated by textile products, iron and steel and machinery. North Korea's principal exports were coal and other minerals.

A combination of low prices for North Korea's exports, transport bottlenecks and soaring import prices, including the cost of petroleum bought from the Soviet Union and China, precipitated a balance of payments crisis in 1975. The balance with Western trading partners had been transformed from an $18 million surplus in 1970 to a $430 million deficit in 1974 (including $200 million owed to Japan and $150 million to France). Debts to communist countries have been estimated at $700 million. Efforts to re-schedule debt repayments were abortive until February 1975, when a two-year moratorium was achieved in respect of $22.5 million owed to Sweden.

FINANCE

According to the Finance Minister, government revenue in 1972 totalled 7,430.3 million won. This represented a 16.9 per cent increase over 1971 and exceeded anticipated revenue by 0.8 per cent. Expenditure in 1972 reached 7,388.6 million won, or 17.2 per cent greater than in 1971, but only 0.1 per cent greater than the target figure.

For 1973 both expenditure and revenue were estimated to be 8,543.5 million won. Of the 1973 expenditure, 15 per cent was allocated to national defence, compared with 30 per cent in 1970. Per capita income in 1974 was estimated at U.S. $313, based on a G.N.P. of $4,820 million.

PLANNING

The Seven-Year Plan (1961–67) arrived at an industrial output in 1967 3.2 times greater than that of 1960, representing an average annual increase of 18 per cent, compared with the 36.6 per cent claimed for 1957–60. Soviet aid seems to have been suspended in 1963–64, a serious matter since North Korea probably relies heavily on the U.S.S.R. for equipment and credit for its capital construction; also, in 1966 the Plan was extended for three years to 1970, in view of the need to build up armaments, and new construction projects were "frozen".

In late 1971 the Government announced a Six-Year Plan (1971–76) which envisages a rise in output of textiles of 50–60 per cent, of paper production by 80 per cent, processed meats by 400 per cent, processed vegetables by 1,370 per cent, aluminium products by 180 per cent, glassware by 420 per cent, porcelain by 130 per cent, and clocks and watches by 150 per cent. An overall increase over the six-year period of 160 per cent is expected. Specific targets include 70 million shoes, 126,000 refrigerators, 27,000 machine tools, 2.9 million tons of fertilizers, 8 million tons each of cement and iron ore, 51 million tons of coal and 3.9 million tons of steel.

In 1974 a shift of emphasis in planning policy became apparent. Rather greater emphasis was to be given to consumer goods but this was to be achieved by importing plant, not actual goods. Thus, for example, a watch factory was bought from Switzerland. Some 120 such plants are being set up to produce a range of items including fabrics, knitwear, footwear and processed foods.

ECONOMIC SURVEY OF SOUTH KOREA

T. M. Burley

One of the most densely populated countries of Asia, with a population (1975 census) of 34,708,542, South Korea recorded an average population density of 349 per square kilometre (on an area of 98,484 square kilometres). Annual population growth has been reduced from 2.8 per cent in 1960–65 to 2.1 per cent in 1970 and 1.7 per cent in 1975. Economic growth has been rapid in recent years: labour is abundant and cheap (wage rates are one-quarter those of neighbouring Japan), yet with high educational standards. Of the economically active population of about 13 million in 1975, 12,478,000 were in employment. In 1974 46.2 per cent were employed in the agricultural sector, while manufacturing employed 16.7 per cent. The annual per capita income in 1975 was $531, compared with $483 in 1974, and is more than double the 1971 level ($253).

During the Second Five-Year Plan period (1967–71), the average annual economic growth rate was 11.4 per cent, compared with 8.3 per cent during the First Five-Year Plan period (1962–66). Based on 1970 prices, the economy grew by 7 per cent in real terms in 1972 (compared with 9.2 per cent in 1971), the lowest increase since 1965. All sectors were in decline in 1972. In contrast, 1973 was a boom year, with gross national product (G.N.P.) increasing by 16.5 per cent. Due to the energy crisis, growth slumped to 8.6 per cent in 1974 and a rate of only 7.4 per cent was expected for 1975. Agriculture, forestry and fisheries together accounted for 25.5 per cent of G.N.P. in 1974 but mining and manufacturing (29.3 per cent) now comprise the dominant industrial sector: preliminary figures for 1975 indicate little change, with sectoral shares of 25.7 per cent and 29.1 per cent respectively. In 1975 agriculture and fisheries grew by 6.2 per cent, due mainly to a good grain harvest; the mining and manufacturing sector grew more slowly than in previous years, recording a 11.8 per cent increase.

AGRICULTURE

As of 1974, 46.2 per cent of the work force (5,584,000 people) were employed in agriculture, forestry and fisheries. About a quarter of the land area (2.3 million hectares) is cultivated and a further two-thirds (6.6 million hectares) is classified as forest land. Much forest land has been devastated by indiscriminate tree felling, and the resultant soil erosion has caused considerable damage to croplands and irrigation reservoirs. South Korea's agriculture is mainly concentrated along river basin areas, with rice as the principal crop.

Agriculture, forestry and fisheries recorded an average annual increase of only 1.2 per cent in real value in 1967–71. By 1974 the sector contributed only 25.5 per cent of G.N.P. compared with 28.8 per cent in 1971. The priority given to urban industrial development has forced many farmers off the land (the farm population fell from 16 million in 1967 to 13.4 million in 1974) but population pressures still necessitate fragmentation of land holdings to an average of about 0.9 of a hectare per farm household. Recent good harvests have boosted farm incomes but generally the rural environment is not conducive to increased productivity through mechanization, and farming still relies heavily on manual labour with the help of bullocks (only 15,000 large tractors are in use).

Only two agricultural products, raw silk and leaf tobacco, are important export earners. They bring in about U.S. $1,100 million annually. In contrast, food imports in 1974 cost $818.2 million, including $450.7 million for rice and wheat, which the country has the capacity to produce itself.

The need for a sound agricultural base was recognized by the Third Five-Year Economic Plan (1972–76), which laid stress on improving the living standards of the rural population, raising provincial productivity, and laying the foundation for productive facilities in rural areas. Emphasis is placed on four comprehensive river basin development projects, improvement of irrigation, a primary products development plan, a field re-arrangement plan, mechanization of farms, expansion of product storage and processing centres, electrification of farm houses, and improvement of health services.

The Government has also tried to enlarge the cultivable land area through reclamation schemes: by 1981 the proposed reclamation projects could supplement cultivable land areas by about 265,000 hectares, although only 27,700 hectares of the reclaimed land would be for paddy. Reclamation is expensive but, by the target year of 1981, projections also indicate that 178,000 hectares of existing farmland would be diverted for industrial sites and social infrastructure.

For 1976 the Ministry of Agriculture and Fisheries launched a 250-day rice farming operation across the country, with a view to producing 4,896,000 tons of paddy rice. The Ministry also decided to provide 11,796 million won to assist various projects aimed at increasing the rice output. Of the amount, 491 million won would go for anti-blight operations and 5,000 million won for prizes to farmers with bumper rice harvests. The grain production target for 1976 was set at 8,622,000 tons, an increase of 6 per cent over the 1975 output of 8,134,000 tons. The target consisted of 4,896,000 tons of rice, 2,185,000 tons of barley, 372,000 tons of soybeans, 840,000 tons of potatoes, and 203,000 tons of miscellaneous cereals.

Production of major food items dominates agricultural output but it is still far from fulfilling domestic demands, meeting only 71.2 per cent of food grain requirements in 1974. In the early 1970s food grain demand increased annually by 3.4 per cent but output increased by only 0.8 per cent annually. In 1974 domestic output of rice was 4,445,000 tons (rising to 4,669,000 tons in 1975) and that of barley 1,705,000 tons. Wheat, soybeans and potatoes are also produced in quantity. In 1974 there were 1.8 million cattle and a similar number of pigs.

Rice production per unit of planted area is high compared with most Asian countries, but is still only about 85 per cent of the Japanese performance. Favourable weather conditions, combined with increased use of chemical fertilizers, the use of lime and intensified irrigation works have contributed to such attainments. However, the quantity of chemical fertilizers used is still about half of the level which is considered optimum (250 kilogrammes per hectare) and its composition also has yet to be optimized.

The Government is aware of the importance of producing more food. Top priorities are placed on wider utilization of high-yielding seeds, intensification of irrigation projects and overall land re-arrangement schemes. By 1971, 74 per cent of the total paddy area had been provided with irrigation; by the end of the Third Plan this figure should reach 90 per cent. The Government has also initiated a scheme to increase the production of rice and to narrow income differences between agricultural and non-agricultural sectors of the economy by the continuous increase of government purchasing prices of rice. The other objective is to reduce consumption of rice and/or substitute other grains so as to attain self-sufficiency in grains.

Sericulture

Climatic and farm labour conditions are ideal for low-cost production of high quality cocoons. Rapidly increasing demand for Korean silk further stimulated the industry and, in 1971, 50 million new mulberry trees were planted. In that year output of cocoons was estimated at 24,000 metric tons and the production of raw silk totalled 2,329 tons. Exports of silk were worth a record $73 million in 1973 but declined to $60 million in 1974 and then to only $21 million in 1975 as increasingly severe cutbacks were initiated by Japan, the principal customer.

Fisheries

South Korea possesses abundant fishery resources in near waters, and opportunities for profitable fishing operations in distant waters are available. In recent years South Korea has emerged as one of the world's leading ocean-fishing nations; tuna is the principal ocean fish caught; shellfish are among the most valuable items in the on-shore catch. Fisheries output in 1973 was 1,686,000 metric tons or 30 per cent more than in 1972. The deep-sea fleet caught 361,000 tons in 1973. Exports of fishery products in 1975 were worth U.S. $416 million, compared with $290 million in 1974. The deep-sea fishing fleet has grown from 65 vessels totalling 11,000 gross tons in 1965 to over 550 vessels totalling some 200,000 tons. It operates in all the world's oceans. A new deep-sea fishing base at Ulsan, with its associated fish-processing plants, is designed to handle 150,000 tons annually. Masan port is also being developed into a major fisheries centre, with the ability to handle 2,000 tons of fish at any one time. On-shore fishing is hampered by pollution but progress is being made with fish culture in controlled conditions: eels, mudfish and, most important, shellfish are being produced in this way. On-shore production of 100,000 tons per year was expected to rise to 250,000 tons by 1976, when some 1,000 hectares of culture sites should be in production.

Forest Products

Timber resources have been depleted in the past by indiscriminate felling. Afforestation and related soil erosion schemes have arrested the devastation but the forestry sector currently makes only a small contribution to timber supplies: in 1970 the output of lumber reached 833,000 cubic metres, compared with domestic demand of 4,656,000 cubic metres. By 1975 output had improved to an estimated 1,060,000 cubic metres. The country's modern plywood and veneer plants rely primarily on logs imported from Indonesia and the Philippines. Rapid growth occurred in the 1960s; a peak of 1,916 million cubic metres was attained in 1973; but output fell to 1,573 million cubic metres in 1974 because of recession. In 1975, however, output recovered to an estimated 1,875 million cubic metres. Paper production, from over 60 mills, of which twelve are large-scale plants, remained buoyant in 1974 since it was not an export-orientated industry. Production of newsprint stood at 150,500 tons, up 20.8 per cent on 1973. Estimated production for 1975 was 145,000 tons.

MINING

Mining and quarrying contributed 70,700 million won to G.N.P. in 1974, one per cent of the total. Nevertheless, South Korea has about 50 different kinds of mineral resources, and a new five-year natural resources development plan, announced in 1973, envisages a concentration of exploration activity on six items: iron ore, copper, lead, zinc, gold and silver. So far, of identified "mineral rich" areas, only one-third have been surveyed in detail, and a further 9,600 square kilometres remain to be investigated.

Conspicuous by its absence is petroleum. South Korea has ambitious plans for petroleum exploration in its offshore areas, and Gulf, Caltex and Shell have each contracted to explore and develop areas off the west or south coasts. Offshore boundary disputes with Japan and China prevent further leasing, however, but an agreement with Japan awaits ratification. A national oil company was set up in 1974 to oversee exploration activities.

Coal. Mostly in the form of anthracite, coal is one of the leading mineral resources in South Korea, but cheap oil stagnated demand in the 1960s. The Government released 7,600 million won during 1971 for the development of coal mining and allowed a 15 per cent increase in coal prices. As a result, output started to expand from its former average of about 12.5 million tons per year, but real growth, stimulated by the energy crisis, is only just beginning. Output in 1974 reached 15,263,000 metric tons and is planned to reach 17.5 million tons in 1975. As evidence of the Government's determination to boost coal output, the leading producer (the state-owned Daihan Coal Corporation) is to get U.S. $83 million in 1975–77. The resultant modernization of equipment will double output to 9.5 million tons. Geological surveys show that there are about 1,309 million tons of coal deposits, of which about one-fifth is exploitable.

Iron ore. Reserves are estimated to be about 80.4 million tons. Ninety per cent or more of the iron ore deposits are magnetite. During 1968 output increased by 18.8 per cent compared with the 1966 level and produced 842,000 tons. However, in 1971, output totalled only 442,000 tons; subsequently, it improved to reach 625,000 tons by 1974.

Tungsten. Reserves are widely distributed over the entire country; the most recent survey estimated that underground resources amount to some 300,000 tons, of which two-thirds are exploitable. In 1975, some 20 tungsten mines were in operation, among which the Sangdong mine is the largest in the world. A processing plant completed in 1972 was capable of processing 1,350 tons annually. Output is expanding steadily, reaching 4,200 tons in 1974.

Non-metallic mineral products. South Korea is one of the principal sources of natural graphite, and almost all of the production is for export. In 1968, 73 mines were in operation, and estimated reserves of amorphous graphite were put at 30 million tons and of crystalline graphite at 2.6 million tons. In 1972 South Korea produced 41,000 tons of amorphous graphite (75–87 per cent carbon) and 200 tons of crystalline graphite. Comparable figures for 1974 were 103,000 tons and 1,200 tons. There are about 40 operating fluorite mines: during the Second Plan period about 230,000 tons were produced, of which about 80 per cent was exported. It is estimated that there are 1.8 million tons of fluorite deposits in terms of 70 per cent concentrate. Output in 1974 of fluorite concentrate was 33,000 tons. Limestone is abundant and cement is produced in large quantities: 9.3 million tons in 1974, of which 1.5 million tons were exported. Kaolin production is substantial: in 1974 output totalled 484,000 tons.

MANUFACTURING INDUSTRY

During the immediate post-war years some unsuccessful attempts were made to develop manufacturing industries. Development of key industries, such as chemical fertilizers, oil refining and cement production, were neglected and most requirements were met by foreign aid. When South Korea launched its First Five-Year Economic Development Plan in 1962, high priority was given to development of manufacturing industry and the share of the sector in G.N.P. increased from 13.5 per cent in 1961 to 18.6 per cent in 1966. During the Second Five-Year Plan (1967–71), manufacturing industry grew by 17.8 per cent per year and represented 22.8 per cent of G.N.P. in 1971. In subsequent years its performance was equally impressive. In 1973 manufacturing contributed 1,290,000 million won, a quarter of the G.N.P. The sector grew by 30.9 per cent in that year and, despite the slow down in the economy, still achieved a 16.1 per cent growth rate in 1974, almost double that of the overall G.N.P. Between 1970 and 1974 the manufacturing index recorded a 138 per cent growth; the most buoyant branches of industry during this period were textiles (including leather), fabricated metals (including machinery and electronics), iron and steel, and paper.

Expansion of private investment and rapidly growing exports, as well as increased government investment and consumption demand, stimulated growth. Although the country's rapid industrial growth was basically the result of private entrepreneurship, it was actively promoted and guided by the government's credit policy and fiscal incentives. The government's industrial development efforts concentrated on promoting export industries and some key import substitution sectors such as cement and fertilizers and, more recently, basic metals and petrochemical industries. The Foreign Capital Inducement Law allows investors duty free importation of necessary capital goods and raw materials, a five-year tax holiday, reduced taxes after this period, repatriation of profits and freedom from labour problems. Management control of a joint venture is permitted, even when the shares held by the foreigner would not give a controlling interest—this applies until the investment is paid off, which normally takes no longer than five years, such is the high profit rate experienced. (Often the Government will guarantee a specific rate of profit.)

Import substitution, previously the main goal of South Korea's industrialization, has in recent years been overshadowed by the all-out export drive. The government's trade liberalization policy, and large investments from various sources, are clearly reflected in its growth achievements in recent years. The Second Five-Year Plan emphasized import substitution, and large-scale investments in iron and steel, petrochemicals, fertilizers and cement have either been completed or are planned with the aim of eliminating most of those imports as soon as possible. Key projects in the investment plan for the rest of the present Plan period were the construction of an integrated iron and steel plant at Pohang, and the establishment of a petrochemical complex on the south-east coast. It was intended that the sector should grow at rates similar to those achieved during the past half decade. It should be noted that many of the major industrial projects such as the naphtha cracker and the integrated steel works are close to or below the minimum efficient size, and thus are high cost producers. The Government is aware of this and is prepared to subsidize output where necessary to maintain producers' competitive strength against foreign suppliers.

Textiles

Textiles account for about 20 per cent of the country's manufacturing industries. Cotton, silk and wool textile industries have a long history; products of rayon and other man-made fibres appeared only in the 1960s. As an export-orientated industry, textiles have benefited from government aid and encouragement. In 1974 the cotton spinners possessed 1.5 million spindles and there are plans to increase the number to 2,680,000 by 1979. A key role is to be played by what is claimed to be the world's largest cotton spinning and weaving plant at Chongbu.

The production index for textiles, weaving apparel and leather goods was 238.6 in 1973 (1970=100), compared with 125.3 in 1971. Production of cotton yarn increased from 94,951 metric tons in 1971 to 103,014 tons in 1973. Output of cotton fabrics totalled 264.4 million square metres in 1973, compared with 233.8 million square metres in 1971; the comparable figures for synthetic fabrics were 332.1 million square metres and 151.1 million square metres. Production of synthetic fibre yarn rose from 70,523 tons in 1971 to 120,855 tons in 1973. Silk fabric production went up from 8.1 million square metres to 15.5 million square metres in the period 1971–73.

Such boom conditions did not persist in 1974: over-expansion of the textile industry in South Korea and other countries, especially Taiwan, caused a crisis of over-production: about 50,000 Korean textile workers are reported to have been laid off. Textile exports for 1974 amounted to U.S. $1,476 million, a gain of 33.8 per cent on the previous year, but in 1973 the value of exports had grown by 114.5 per cent. Output of cotton and synthetic fabrics fell in 1974 to 261.4 million square metres and 313.9 million square metres respectively and cotton fabrics fell again in 1975 to 242.8 million square metres. Synthetic fabrics, which had fallen by only 5.5 per cent in 1974, increased by 38.5 per cent in 1975 to 434.8 million square metres. Yarn production in 1975 stood at 133,596 tons (cotton) and 220,508 tons (synthetic) respective gains over 1974 of 3.1 per cent and 45.7 per cent. Silk fabric output in 1975 was 16.7 million square metres, up 20 per cent on 1974.

Petroleum Refining

Petroleum increased its share of South Korea's energy demand from one-tenth to one-third between 1965 and 1975, and the import bill for crude oil rose by over 500 per cent. Demand for petroleum products rose from 38,600 barrels per day (b/d) in 1965 to an estimated 260,000 b/d in 1974, reflecting primarily the expanding needs of industry for fuel oil. Demand is met from imports processed at the three local refineries which, at the end of 1974, had a combined capacity of 425,000 b/d. The Ulsan plant, partly owned by the nationalized Korea Oil Corporation, was opened in 1964, and had a capacity of 210,000 b/d at the end of 1974, while a refinery owned by Lucky Chemicals and Caltex went on stream in 1968 at Yosu: the capacity of this refinery was 160,000 b/d at the end of 1974. A third refinery, at Inchon, went on stream in mid-1972 with a capacity of 55,000 b/d; it is owned by Union Oil and a number of local interests. Construction of a fourth refinery, with a capacity of 60,000 b/d, was expected to start at Kwangyong Bay at the end of 1975.

Chemicals

In the 1950s chemical industries were mostly confined to the output of consumer goods which required relatively simple operations, but in the 1960s the character of the industry changed as plants producing chemical fertilizers and several basic chemicals (soda ash, ammonia and methanol) started operation. The output of chemical products in 1975 had increased by 126 per cent over 1970 as a result of expanded production of polyvinylchloride, carbide, dyestuffs, pharmaceuticals, cosmetics, etc. Output in 1975 included 503,154 tons of sulphuric acid, 924,666 tons of urea and about 800,000 tons of ammonia.

The focal point of activities is the Ulsan petrochemical complex. It is based on a naphtha cracking centre, owned and operated by Korea Oil Co., which produces 100,000 tons of ethylene per year (the annual capacity can be increased to 150,000 tons.) Downstream facilities include a 33,000-ton caprolactam plant, a 24,000-ton aceta-idehyde plant and a 30,000-ton ethanol plant. A second petro-chemical complex is to be established by Dow Chemical while Union Carbide is to build a $14 million plant to produce industrial gases. However, new construction is focused on a major chemical complex, including eight fertilizer plants and a methanol plant, near Yosu on the southern coast. The project will be dominated by a urea plant with an annual capacity of 495,000 tons, an ammonium plant with an annual capacity of 330,000 tons, and a methanol plant with an annual capacity of 330,000 tons.

Metallurgy

Although 1975's growth was held to only 3.8 per cent by the effects of the recession, output of steel ingots exceeded 2 million metric tons in 1975. However, output of steel plates and sheets was only an estimated 860,000 tons compared with 1,294,000 tons for 1974. Local crude steel demand in 1974 was estimated at 3.8 million tons. The Pohang Iron and Steel Co. (POSCO) operates the country's only integrated steel-making plant which was inaugurated in 1973: its production capacity will be doubled to 2.6 million tons in 1977 and to 8 million tons in the 1980s. The complex includes a steel plate factory, a hot melting iron plant, and plants capable of producing steel slabs and hot coils, billets and foundry pig-iron.

There are refineries for the production of copper, tungsten, gold and lead. Plans for six non-ferrous refineries have been announced; they include facilities for zinc at Sakpo and for aluminium at Ulsan. A copper smelter is also planned.

Machine Building

Machine building in the 1960s was limited to light machinery products, light agricultural machinery and equipment, and simple metal-working machinery, such as lathes and cotton gins. During the Second Plan period, the construction of new plants made possible the production of industrial machinery, metal-working machinery, communications equipment, motor vehicles, ships and other transport equipment, and internal combustion engines.

The production of electrical machinery and appliances soared after 1970, largely owing to increased domestic consumption and increased exports. The electronics sector led the way: in 1972–74 production of radio receivers doubled to reach 3,692,000 (and then 4,280,000 in 1975) while TV sets were up 378 per cent at 1,164,000 (1,215,000 in 1975). Production of electric motors in 1974 exceeded half a million for the first time and reached an estimated 550,000 in 1975.

The expansion in electronics in part reflects the impact of government investment (envisaged at 33,100 million won in 1974) to boost the value of output to over U.S. $1,600 million, or 36 per cent greater than in 1973. It was envisaged that 21 new factories would be built and a second electronics industrial complex established, devoted to telecommunications equipment, computers and medical appliances. In 1975, some 400 electronics factories employed over 100,000 staff: their contribution to G.N.P. was about 6 per cent or nearly one-fifth of the manufacturing sector's contribution.

In 1975 the motor vehicle industry saw the inauguration of manufacturing, as opposed to assembly, operations at Ulsan. Here, a completely integrated plant, costing over $40 million, has the capacity to build 1,000 passenger cars per week by the end of 1975. In 1975 national output of motor vehicles totalled 36,848, 21 per cent more than in 1974.

Plans to expand the nation's shipbuilding capacity to almost 6 million d.w.t., making South Korea one of the 10 largest shipbuilding nations in the world, have been frustrated by the world recession. The outstanding achievement in 1975 was the re-opening of Hyundai Shipbuilding Co.'s new shipyard at Ulsan: its capacity of about 1.5 million d.w.t. will be eventually increased to 4 million d.w.t. The expanded yard will provide employment for about 20,000 workers. South Korea's other major shipbuilders, the Korean Shipbuilding and Engineering Co. (KESC), is building a yard at Okpo Bay on Koje Island (by the 1980s the Government plans no fewer than four separate shipbuilding complexes there). The shipyard, capable of building super-tankers with a displacement of 1 million gross tons, will have an annual capacity of five 300,000-ton tankers and six 150,000-ton tankers. Some 4,500 people will be employed, slightly more than the total at KESC's Pusan yard, which has just been expanded with the completion of a 900,000 d.w.t. drydock and a 150,000 d.w.t. building dock.

INFRASTRUCTURE

Transport

During 1974 the railways carried 8,796 million metric ton-kilometres of freight traffic, compared with 7,488 million in 1970. During the same year passenger-kilometres amounted to 10,532 million as against 9,819 million in 1970. In 1974 the country's railway lines totalled 5,644 kilometres. However, the railway's volume share of total freight traffic fell from 30 per cent in 1970 to 25 per cent in 1974. In contrast, the share carried by road increased from 59.5 per cent in 1970 to about 67 per cent in 1974.

There were 1,013 kilometres of expressways in 1973 out of a total paved road network of 44,613 kilometres. A $90 million loan from the World Bank will help South Korea to improve and modernize its road system. The network of all-weather paved highways between major population centres will be expanded by about 800 kilometres, including the construction of 195 kilometres of four national highways. Most of the road sections are near the fast-growing cities of Seoul, Daegu, Masan and Pohang. In addition, nine national highways totalling 600 kilometres will be paved and improved. Feasibility studies will be made for future highway projects covering 1,200 kilometres.

There was only one motor car per 461 inhabitants in 1973 but passenger traffic in the nation's capital, Seoul, is now benefiting from a mass-transit railway system reaching out to the satellite cities of Inchon, Suwon and Songbuk and from electrification of the 348 route-kilometres to Bukpyong. In 1975 Korean Air Lines carried about 2 million passengers and 55,000 tons of cargo on its domestic and international routes.

Ports. In the 10 years from the middle 1960s the capacity of South Korea's ports increased fivefold to 50 million tons per year; in the next 10 years, annual capacity is planned to increase to 230 million tons.

Electricity. At the end of 1971 generating capacity stood at 2.7 million kW.; it rose to 4.5 million kW. in 1974. Output was 14,826 million kWh. in 1973, rising to 19,837 million kW. in 1975. The revised energy development plan for 1974–81 provides for 19 new hydro-electric power stations (total capacity 1,460 MW), 4 nuclear (2,395 MW) and 7 thermal stations (1,860 MW). The first nuclear plant (600 MW) is due to go into operation in 1976; by 1986, over 5 million kW. will be nuclear. Twelve hydro power stations currently under construction have a capacity of 2.2 million kW.; by 1986 a further 12 are to be built.

Industrial estates. In an effort to stimulate exports, the Government has established a number of industrial estates, several of which are especially designed for foreign companies. The latest and largest, at Pukpyong, covers 16.5 square kilometres and will have a modern port able to handle vessels of up to 50,000 gross tons. The next largest (180 hectares) is the Masan Free Export Zone (MAFEZ); as part of a plan to triple activity of 1989, the Government is spending $15 million to develop the site into the prime concentration of economic activity in the southern part of the country. By the second half of 1974

MAFEZ factories were to be exporting goods at a rate of $300 million per annum. The zone is a 100 per cent bonded area and, in addition to normal investment incentives, all duties and taxes are waived.

INTERNATIONAL TRADE

Exports. For 1975 the f.o.b. value of South Korea's exports was U.S. $5,427 million, a 21.7 per cent increase over 1974. This was somewhat below the Government's target of $6,000 million and suggests that much of the increase can be attributed to rising prices. Exporters did not benefit from the 16.7 per cent devaluation of the won in December 1974 as much as was anticipated. The increased won income that exporters received as a result of devaluation was eroded by buyers' demands for substantial discounts. At the same time exporters faced increases in the won cost of imported raw materials and energy inputs.

Imports. A 61.6 per cent increase in f.o.b. value occurred in 1974 but for 1975 the increase was only 10.4 per cent, from $6,852 million to $7,150 million. Until 1975 mounting demand for imports was generated to supply necessary raw materials for the rapidly growing production of export commodities. It was further stimulated by increasing domestic demand, activated by both liberalization of imports and income growth. The industrial growth of recent years has required further imports. For 1975, however, a combination of export stagnation and domestic austerity contained this upward trend.

Trading partners. Trade with Japan fell sharply in 1975: only 22.8 per cent of exports by value went to Japan, compared with 30.9 per cent in 1974 and a peak of 38.5 per cent in 1973. Japan supplied over 40 per cent of imports by value in 1972 and 1973 but by 1975 the proportion had fallen to only 34 per cent. Depressed business conditions in Japan were a prime cause but the situation has been exacerbated by the trade war developing between the two countries: silk was the first to suffer but some two dozen Korean export products are now finding it difficult to enter Japan. In return, Korea is raising tariff barriers against Japanese goods, notably machinery items.

Invisible Exports

Tourism. In 1972 more than 370,000 tourists (mostly Japanese) spent $83 million in Korea, compared with a mere 125,000 spending $32 million in 1969. To meet this boom, 10,000 new hotel rooms now augment the former 6,000 rooms. Korea's accessibility, low prices (especially following the yen revaluation) and aggressive promotion of its scenic and other tourist attractions have stimulated the influx of Japanese visitors. However, the 1974 recession resulted in only 520,000 arrivals, compared with 679,221 in 1973; earnings also fell to $158 million, compared with $253 million in 1973. There was a recovery to 633,000 visitors in 1975 but earnings fell again, to $136 million.

Shipping. To boost foreign exchange earnings further, the Government is determined that the bulk of trade will be carried on South Korean vessels. The national fleet is being expanded to 6 million d.w.t. by 1980, a fourfold increase over 1975. By 1980 it is hoped that Korean vessels will be carrying half the nation's international trade, compared with the present quarter share. To boost foreign exchange earnings from shipping in the short term, discriminatory legislation virtually excludes the use of non-Korean ships for export cargo if a Korean vessel is available. In 1975 the fleet carried 41.5 million tons of cargo, earning $306.4 million.

FINANCE

Fiscal Policy

The Government wants the public sector to play a major role in the mobilization of domestic financial resources because a large part of investment in the near future will be in social overhead capital, requiring public outlays. To fulfil its financial needs, an aggressive fiscal policy has been formulated and the budget expanded to support rapid economic development and at the same time maintain a monetary balance. By 1974, the budget had exceeded 1,000,000 million won and a 21.5 per cent increase was planned for 1975. Defence needs continue to inflate the budget's general government sector: expenditure increased from 184,300 million won in 1973 to 221,645 million won in 1974, for example. Tax revenues increased greatly due to the enforcement of newly revised tax laws: in 1974 internal taxes represented 73 per cent of government revenue and most of the extra funds required for 1975 were to be derived from taxes. Nevertheless, South Korea's ratio of tax burden to G.N.P. is still relatively low (about 15 per cent), compared with that of other developing countries.

Under the 1976 budget, defence expenditure amounted to 704,488 million won, a 52.2 per cent increase over 1975 and 34.6 per cent of government expenditure (compared with 27.4 per cent for 1975). Appropriations for the loans and investments category and economic development increased by 52 per cent to 540,200 million won, while salaries and pensions for government employees were put at 325,300 million won. General internal taxes were to rise by 44 per cent and provide 59.6 per cent revenue in 1976. In addition, a considerable portion of the defence payments were to be covered by the new defence tax, revenue amounting to 214,477 million won or 10.5 per cent of revenues.

In mid-1975 the Government announced a wide range of new taxes intended to raise about $410 million in a year, specifically for defence expenditure. The new levies are intended to remain in force until 1980 and include a 2.5 per cent surcharge on imports (except on those of raw materials brought in for export industries and authorized foreign investors), an increase in indirect taxes by 10 to 30 per cent, higher income and corporation taxes, an increase in property registration and inheritance levies, higher postal charges and a new levy of 0.2 per cent on the value of farm land. The net effect will be to increase the overall tax burden from 15.6 per cent to 17.8 per cent.

Investment

The Government calculated its investment plan for 1975 at 2,384,843 million won, an increase of 11.8 per cent over 1974. However, the share of government investments in G.N.P. represented a drop of 4 per cent from the 30 per cent in 1974. By industry, 260,692 million won was to go to primary industry, 678,417 million won to the mining and manufacturing industry, and 1,473,084 million won to tertiary industry (up 53.2 per cent, 55 per cent and 26.3 per cent respectively, from the 1974 levels). In secondary industry, 651,305 million won was allocated to manufacturing and 27,112 million won to mining (up 55.1 per cent and 53.5 per cent respectively from 1974).

The share of investment in the G.N.P. during the Second Five-Year Plan period was 30.4 per cent and that of overseas savings 14.9 per cent, compared with 16.9 per cent and 10.2 per cent, respectively, recorded in the First Plan period. The ratio of domestic savings was 15.5 per cent of G.N.P.

Foreign investment in 1972 exceeded U.S. $110 million, a record which was soon broken, for in the first six months of 1973 investment totalled $169 million. The sharp increase was largely attributable to an investment rush by the Japanese following the yen revaluation. For 1973 foreign investment approvals totalled $314 million but 1974 produced only $140 million and 1975 $194 million. In line with the Government's policy to place emphasis on the attainment of long-term soft loans with low interest rates, the public loans obtained in 1975 rose by $193.5 million over the $456.5 million of a year before. However, the amount of commercial loans decreased by 53.8 per cent from $1,086.9 million in 1974. The increase in public loans is attributed to the inducement of long-term foreign loans from the World Bank and the Asian Development Bank.

Foreign Indebtedness

South Korea's foreign exchange reserves totalled U.S. $1,542 million at the end of 1975, up by $492 million from the end of 1974. In 1975 Korea repaid long-term foreign obligations (maturities of three years and more) of $692 million. Repayments in 1976 were expected to amount to slightly more than $1,000 million, indicating a debt service ratio of around 14 per cent (at the end of 1975 it was 13.1 per cent).

The long-term external debt was expected to rise to $5,830 million by the end of 1975, up 34 per cent from the end of 1974. The increased borrowing was to help pay for the higher cost of imported petroleum and to help finance ambitious growth plans.

Foreign bankers, who had just completed a syndicated $200 million balance-of-payments loan to South Korea, were unwilling to advance additional funds on a long-term basis. As a result, South Korea had to increase its short-term borrowings and to rely more heavily on public lending facilities, such as the World Bank and the International Monetary Fund. In late 1975 a private research study concluded that Korea's foreign indebtedness had reached unmanageable proportions, which would lead to a debt crisis unless averted by large doses of U.S. aid or a severe austerity programme.

South Korean officials have disclaimed the conclusions as gross exaggeration but there is no denying that the nation will have problems meeting its debt obligations. Debt rescheduling and the discouragement of imports should, however, tide South Korea over until the expected worldwide economic revival improves its export and foreign investment picture.

Long-term capital inflow loans and investments in 1976 are expected to total $1,800 million: $830 million in public loans, $830 million in commercial loans and $140 million in investments. Of this, nearly $1,400 million is in the pipeline (already committed in previous years), leaving a balance of $436 million expected from new agreements. Overseas fund-raising on a commitment basis is expected to reach $2,300 million: $1,400 million in public loans, $748 million in commercial loans and $170 million in investments. This plan continues the trend of an almost 2 : 1 ratio between public and commercial loans.

Money Supply

The volume of money supply at the end of 1971 was 358,000 million won, an increase of 16.4 per cent over 1970. In the subsequent boom the money supply increased to 519,400 million won at the end of 1972 and then to 730,300 million won in 1973, a jump of 104 per cent in two years. Expansion slowed to 29.5 per cent in 1974 and 25.0 per cent in 1975. A greater increase had been expected, mainly from huge loans to be made for heavy industry, construction, export financing, etc. On the other hand, the Government withdrew 116,300 million won in loans it had extended to banks through the Bank of Korea. The reserve base of the Bank of Korea rose with the money supply and, by the end of 1973, was double its level at the end of 1971. Government measures to combat the 1974 recession caused the reserves to stabilize at around 600,000 million won in 1974. The reserves of the commercial banks stood at about half this level. Banknotes and coin issued in 1973 by the Bank of Korea totalled 353,644 million won, a rise of 44.5 per cent over 1972. This fell to below 300,000 million won by May 1974 but subsequently moved upwards again, mirroring the pace of inflation and the inability of the Government's fiscal measures to bring it under control. At the end of 1974 currency in circulation totalled 410,500 million won; deposit money totalled 535,200 million won. Respective totals for 1975 were 507,200 million and 674,600 million won. The money supply in 1975, at 1,181,800 million won, was one-quarter greater than in 1974.

Following consultations with the International Monetary Fund, the domestic credit ceiling for 1973 was set at 1,885,000 million won. This represented a 23.9 per cent increase over 1972, which itself was 30 per cent up on 1971. But this was quickly overtaken by events. Outstanding domestic credits at the end of 1974 totalled 2,983,500 million won, a 52 per cent increase over 1973. Another big jump, to 3,934,400 occurred in 1975.

The money market in Korea is characterized by its dual structure: an organized market and an unorganized one, commonly known as the "curb market". The former covers official financial institutions regulated and controlled by the Government; and it is still limited in its operations. Most short-term financing has been provided by the banks as direct loans. Discounting of bills is comparatively very small in volume while commercial papers were issued only by the commercial banks and bought by the Bank of Korea. There had been, therefore, a lack of an intermediary link between investors having short-term idle funds and enterprises in need of short-term financing. Estimated at a volume of over 350 million won in July 1972 (or more than 90 per cent of the money then in circulation), the curb market, by comparison, has been very active, and it is essentially a short-term money market, since the majority of loans mature in less than three months. Due to their anonymous and discreet nature, the magnitude of curb market operations has never been accurately quantified.

Wages and Prices

Between 1961 and 1971, real wages increased by an annual average of 8.8 per cent but by 1971 the average manufacturing wage was only U.S. $40 per month. At that time the Bank of Korea estimated that an urban family of four needed $90 per month to meet its expenses: by 1974 this had risen to $130 but the average monthly wage had increased to only $55.

It seems probable that the past docility of Korean workers is coming to an end and that the growing gap between the rich and poor, and the example set by unions in foreign firms, will lead to increasing wage demands. In January 1974 the Government waived income taxes for wage-earners receiving less than 50,000 won per month: about 80 per cent of the work force benefited; however, a subsequent pension scheme involved a 3 per cent deduction from all salaries to create a fund of 32,500 million won.

The wide-ranging price stabilization law introduced in April 1973, followed by an investigation into distribution margins on over 100 major products, was overtaken by events. The won devaluation at the end of 1974 heralded a shift in government price control policy to give the market mechanism a much greater role. Soaring world commodity prices and the oil crisis caused the wholesale price index to rise by 44.6 per cent in 1974 and by 20.2 per cent in 1975. Comparable consumer price rises were 26.4 per cent and 25.4 per cent.

PLANNING

The original targets of the Third Five-Year Development Plan (1972–76) were distorted by the oil crisis and world trade recession. However, the broad planning policy and objectives still hold good. For the last year of the Plan the economic strategy calls for moderate growth, strict control on imports and prices, and a strong campaign to promote domestic savings. It is not as optimistic as in previous years: the economy is expected to grow by only 7–8 per cent in real terms and official policy is to hold inflation at 10–12 per cent (though 15–20 per cent is a more realistic target). Industrialization is given the prime emphasis, with the main growth in the tertiary sector being in activities which support industrialization.

The Outlook to 1981

Following the oil crisis and the resulting slow-down in growth, government economic planners have been re-examining their basic assumptions relating to long-term economic development. The resulting changes in outlook and policies are reflected in a set of recently published economic guidelines, which are intended as the basic framework for the fourth economic plan (for 1977–81), due to be announced in August 1976.

Under new guidelines, the target for average annual growth in real G.N.P. will be approximately 9 per cent, instead of the original projection of 7 per cent, but substantially the same as the advance estimate for the 1972–76 plan (8.6 per cent). The intention is create a largely self-supporting growth structure which will involve rapid development in basic and export industries, infrastructure and the achievement of self-sufficiency in grain. In order to provide the necessary resources, efforts will be made to shift a larger proportion of G.N.P. into investment: there will also be a faster increase in the investment rate. Foreign credit and loans are also expected to expand, although net receipts of foreign capital are not likely to reach the level of the preceding plan period, because of an increase in the debt servicing burden. It is recognized that it will be impossible to maintain the growth of exports at the last few years' level but, because of a significant slow-down in the rise of imports, the final year of the plan will see a visible trade surplus of about $100–200 million. The rate of inflation is forecast to fall from the 1975 target of 20 per cent to 15 per cent in 1977 and to 8 per cent in 1978.

Industrial development. Government plans through to 1980 were outlined in May 1973. Based on a target of $1,000 per capita income, the plans included a ten-fold increase in steel refining capacity to 10 million tons, a twenty-fold expansion in shipbuilding capacity to 5 million tons, and a thirteenfold increase in oil refining to 5 million barrels. Cement production in 1980 would be 16 million tons, vehicle output would reach 500,000 units, and the installed capacity of electricity would rise from 3.9 million kW to 10 million kW.

The heavy and chemical industries development programme had the key role to play through the establishment of the following six industry bases in the southern part of the country: steel (a second mill, near Pusan), general chemicals (at Yosu, as already announced), non-ferrous metals (lead, zinc and aluminium refining near Ulsan), general machinery (near Masan), shipbuilding (the Koje Island project), and electronics (near Taegu).

According to the latest plans, the real growth of

the economy will be slowed to 8.5 per cent a year during the last three years of the 1971–76 economic plan. However, for the subsequent five years, the Government is thinking in terms of an average annual increase of 11 per cent, which would bring per capita G.N.P. in current prices to $970 in 1980 as against $251 in 1971. The 1980 export target has been raised from $5,300 million to $10,000 million. This will require a 25 per cent average annual increase and implies a rise of $1,100 million to $4,600 million in the target originally set for the end of the current six-year plan.

Investment in oil facilities is expected to be of major importance in the coming years. South Korea is strategically located with respect to Japan (and to China) and Japanese interests wish to exploit its locational advantage. Already proposed is the world's largest crude oil depot—to be located near Pusan with a six million kilolitres capacity—and a $100 million oil refinery, with a 150,000 barrels per day capacity, at Ulsan. Both projects would operate on a re-export basis with Japan as the principal market.

In line with the Plan's accent on rationalizing the economy, investment was to be concentrated in heavy industry and in agriculture. As regards the latter, electrification of rural areas is to be achieved by 1977, and all highways will be paved by 1980, by which time farmers' incomes should reach 1.3 million won. Eight industrial promotion districts have been designated in an effort to persuade industry to re-establish itself in smaller urban areas in predominantly agricultural regions.

The strategy of industrial development revolves around substantial fiscal support, private initiatives strongly supported by the Government's various measures, expansion of social overhead capital investment so as to smooth out the flow of economic activities, a dynamic balance of payments policy including activated flows of foreign capital into productive investments, rapid export expansion particularly of manufactured goods, and considerably fewer restrictive import schemes to cope with the rapid economic changes in both internal and the external sectors.

Korea possesses a dual economy: the foreign-financed, export-orientated and modern sector, and the larger sector suffering from limited investment, old-fashioned techniques and labour intensive activities. This dual nature results in many imbalances—in particular, the Government has concentrated most infrastructural investment in the urban areas, particularly Seoul. Elsewhere, transport, housing, schools, medical care, etc., leave much to be desired. However, investment funds available to the Government are limited, in no small measure by the low level of domestic savings, and export earnings are needed to pay off the overseas debt burden. (About 50 per cent of each export dollar has to be allocated to repay debts and to finance imports—primarily for the export industries whose value-added function is principally derived from labour inputs.)

DEMOCRATIC PEOPLE'S REPUBLIC OF KOREA

STATISTICAL SURVEY

AREA AND POPULATION

Area*	Population					
	Official Estimates‡		UN Estimates (mid-year)			
	Dec. 31st, 1960	Oct. 1st, 1963	1972	1973	1974	1975
120,538 sq. km.†	10,789,000	11,568,000	14,660,000	15,053,000	15,450,000	15,852,000

* Excluding the demilitarized zone between North and South Korea, with an area of 1,262 square kilometres (487 square miles).

† 46,540 square miles.

‡ *Source:* Institute of Economics of the World Socialist System, Moscow.

ADMINISTRATIVE DISTRICTS
(Population '000—December 1966)

North and South Pyongan	3,474
North and South Hwanghae	2,294
North and South Hamgyong	3,032
Pyongyang City (including metropolitan area)	1,364
Kangwon	1,050
Chagang	739
Yanggand	422
Kaesong	265

PRINCIPAL CITIES
(estimated population 1974)

Pyongyang (capital)	1,500,000
Chongjin	300,000
Kaesong	240,000
Hungnam	200,000

Source: Far Eastern Economic Review, *Asia 1975 Yearbook.*

BIRTHS AND DEATHS

	Births (per '000)	Deaths (per '000)
1960	38.5	10.5
1961	36.7	11.5
1962	41.1	10.8
1963	42.7	12.8

1965–70 (UN estimates): Average annual birth rate 38.8 per 1,000; death rate 11.2 per 1.000.

EMPLOYMENT

	1959 %	1963 %
Factory Workers	37.2	40.2
Office Workers	13.4	15.1
Peasants on Co-operatives	45.7	42.8
Handicraftsmen in Co-operatives	3.3	1.9
Others	0.4	—
	100.0	100.0

Total employment (1964): 2,092,000 (incl. 780,000 women).

Total labour force (mid-1970): In a population of 13,674,000, the economically active numbered 5,898,000, including 3,138,000 in agriculture (FAO and ILO estimates).

AGRICULTURE

LAND USE, 1960
('000 hectares)

Arable and under permanent crops	1,894*
Forest Land	8,970†
Other land and inland water	1,190
Total Area	12,054

* Excluding temporary meadows and pastures.

† Including rough grazing. Data taken from the world forest inventory carried out by the FAO in 1958.

PRINCIPAL CROPS
(FAO estimates)

	Area Harvested ('000 hectares)			Production ('000 metric tons)		
	1972	1973	1974	1972	1973	1974
Wheat	80	80	80	72	73	74
Rice (paddy)	685	695	700	3,000	3,300	3,300
Barley	170	170	180	360	350	360
Maize	860	860	900	1,840	1,840	2,000
Rye	8	8	8	7	7	7
Oats	83	85	85	60	65	65
Millet	470	480	490	380	400	410
Sorghum	65	65	65	55	55	60
Potatoes	165	165	170	1,040	1,050	1,100
Sweet potatoes	39	40	40	290	300	320
Pulses	350	360	360	200	215	215
Soybeans	405	410	428	235	250	260
Cottonseed	} 15	15	15 {	6	6	6
Cotton (lint)				3	3	3
Tobacco	33	33	33	40	40	40
Hemp fibre	8	8	8	2.3	2.3	2.3

Source: FAO, *Production Yearbook 1974*.

LIVESTOCK
(FAO estimates—'000)

	1971/72	1972/73	1973/74
Horses	28	30	32
Asses	13	3	3
Cattle	750	760	767
Pigs	1,400	1,450	1,491
Sheep	195	200	205
Goats	175	178	187

Source: FAO, *Production Yearbook 1974*.

LIVESTOCK PRODUCTS
(FAO estimates, metric tons)

	1972	1973	1974
Beef and Veal	20,000	20,000	20,000
Mutton and Lamb	1,000	1,000	1,000
Goats' Meat	1,000	1,000	1,000
Pigmeat	70,000	73,000	75,000
Poultry Meat	18,000	20,000	22,000
Edible Offals	7,734	7,917	8,066
Cows' Milk	18,000	19,000	19,000
Hen Eggs	60,000	63,000	64,800
Raw Silk	1,350	1,350	1,380
Cattle Hides	3,150	3,192	3,224

Source: FAO, *Production Yearbook 1974*.

FORESTRY

ROUNDWOOD REMOVALS
(FAO estimates, '000 cubic metres)

	1972	1973	1974
Coniferous (soft wood)	3,330	3,330	3,330
Broadleaved (hard wood)	1,670	1,670	1,670
Total	5,000	5,000	5,000

Source: FAO, *Yearbook of Forest Products*.

Sea Fishing: Total catch 800,000 metric tons per year (FAO estimate).

MINING

(estimated production)

		1971	1972	1973	1974
Hard coal	'ooo metric tons	24,300	27,300	30,000	33,000
Lignite and brown coal	,, ,, ,,	6,200	6,700	7,000	7,900
Iron ore‡	,, ,, ,,	8,500	8,600	8,900	9,400
Copper ore*	,, ,, ,,	13	13	13	15
Lead ore*	,, ,, ,,	80	80	90	101
Magnesite	,, ,, ,,	1,700	1,800	1,800	2,000
Tungsten concentrates*	metric tons	2,150	2,150	2,150	2,150
Zinc ore*	'ooo metric tons	140	150	160	162
Salt	,, ,, ,,	550	550	550	550
Phosphate rock	,, ,, ,,	275	300	360	650
Sulphur†	,, ,, ,,	200	200	200	200
Graphite	,, ,, ,,	75	75	75	75
Silver	'ooo troy oz.	700	700	700	700
Gold	,, ,, ,,	160	160	160	160

Note: No recent data are available for the production of molybdenum ore and asbestos.

* Figures relate to the metal content of ores and concentrates.

† Figures refer to the sulphur content of iron and copper pyrites, including pyrite concentrates obtained from copper, lead and zinc ores.

‡ Gross weight. The estimated metal content (in 'ooo metric tons) was: 4,268 in 1971; 4,318 in 1972; 4,420 in 1973.

Source: Bureau of Mines, U.S. Department of the Interior.

INDUSTRY

(estimated production—'ooo metric tons)

	1971	1972	1973	1974
Nitrogenous Fertilizers (*a*)*	220	230	240	250
Phosphate Fertilizers (*b*)*	98	105	81	113
Coke†	2,200	2,200	2,200	2,200
Cement†	4,800	5,300	5,800	6,400
Pig Iron and Ferro-alloys†	2,500	2,600	2,700	3,000
Crude Steel†	2,400	2,500	2,600	2,900
Refined Copper (unwrought)†	13	13	13	15
Lead (primary metal)†	70	75	80	95
Zinc (primary metal)†	100	120	130	132

* Figures for fertilizer production are unofficial estimates quoted by the FAO. Output is measured in terms of (*a*) nitrogen or (*b*) phosphoric acid.

† *Source:* Bureau of Mines, U.S. Department of the Interior.

SIX-YEAR PLAN 1971–76

		Reported 1970 Targets	1976 Targets	Reported Rate of Fulfilment, Aug. 31st 1975 %
Electricity	million kWh.	16,500	28–30,000	102
Coal	million tons	27·5	50–53	101
Iron Ore	,, ,,	7·2	n.a.	n.a.
Pig and Granulated Iron	,, ,,	2·3	3·5–3·8	92
Crude Steel	,, ,,	2·2	3·8–4·0	86
Rolled Steel	,, ,,	1·7	2·8–3·0	}
Chemical Fertilizers	,, ,,	1·5	2·8–3·0	109
Cement	,, ,,	4–4·5	7·5–8·0	91
Magnesium Clinker	,, ,,	n.a.	1·6	n.a.
Grain	,, ,,	5–7	7·0–7·5*	n.a.
Textiles	mill. metres	350–400	500–600	116
Chemical Fibres	000 tons	80–100	50	n.a.
Synthetic Resin	,, ,,	60–70	n.a.	n.a.
Tractors	numbers	n.a.	21,000	101
Machine Tools	,,	n.a.	27,000	111
Refrigerators	,,	n.a.	126,000	n.a.

* Of which 3.5 is rice.

SIX-YEAR PLAN 1975–80

		1980 Targets
Cement*	million metric tons	20
Cereal	,, ,, ,,	10
Coal	,, ,, ,,	100
Electricity	million kWh.	50,000
Fertilizer	million metric tons	5
Land reclamation	'000 hectares	100
Machinery†	million metric tons	5
Marine products†	,, ,, ,,	5
Non-ferrous metals	,, ,, ,,	1
Steel	,, ,, ,,	12

* Of which 5 million metric tons for export.
† 1978 targets.

FINANCE

100 chon (jun) = 1 won.
Coins: 1, 5 and 10 chon.
Notes: 50 chon; 1, 5, 10, 50 and 100 won.
Exchange rates (June 1976): £1 sterling = 1.775 won (basic rate), 3.775 won (tourist rate) or 6.16 won (trade rate); U.S. $ = 1.009 won (basic rate), 2.128 won (tourist rate) or 3.472 won (trade rate).
100 won = £56.34 = $99.11 (basic rates).

Note: The new won, equal to 100 old won, was introduced in February 1959. From 1958 the basic exchange rate was U.S. $1 = 120 old won. The initial basic rate of $1 = 1.20 new won (1 won = 83.33 U.S. cents) remained in force until August 1971. From December 1971 to February 1973 the basic rate was $1 = 1.105 won (1 won = 90.48 U.S. cents). In terms of sterling, the basic rate was £1 = 2.88 won from November 1967 to June 1972. In January 1961 a commercial exchange rate was established for foreign trade transactions. This is fixed at £1 = 6.16 won, equal to $1 = 2.20 won until November 1967. The commercial rate, tied to sterling, was $1 = 2.567 won from November 1967 to August 1971; and $1 = 2.364 won from December 1971 to June 1972. The tourist rate was the same as the commercial rate until February 1973, since when it has been $1 = 2.128 won.

BUDGET
(million won)

	1969	1970	1971	1972	1973*
Revenue	5,995·4	n.a.	6,357·4	7,430·4	8,543·5
Expenditure	5,995·4	n.a.	6,301·7	7,388·6	8,543·5

* Estimate.

EXTERNAL TRADE

APPARENT EXPORTS OF SELECTED MINERAL COMMODITIES*

(metric tons)

	1971	1972
Iron ore and concentrate	449,838	527,081
Pig iron and cast iron	122,245	135,702
Steel, semi-manufactures	108,800	93,600
Lead metal and alloys, all forms	17,551	36,109
Zinc:		
Ore and concentrate	12,135	3,508
Metal and alloys, all forms	46,983	52,221
Cement	358,000	428,000
Clay products, refractory	375,500	341,800
Magnesite	568,023	522,777
Coal and coal briquettes	72,587	61,667

* Compiled from import data of partner countries.

Source: U.S. Department of the Interior, *Bureau of Mines Minerals Yearbook, 1973.*

PRINCIPAL COUNTRIES

(U.S. $ million at June 1975 rates)

	Exports		Imports	
	1974	1975	1974	1975
Australia	—	—	16.3	9.2††
Austria	1.0	0.8†	26.7	9.7†
Belgium/Luxembourg	7.9	—	19.5	—
Canada	0.1	0.4‖	48.2	4.8‖
Denmark	—	—	—	20.9‖
Finland	3.6*	0.4‡	34.4*	0.1‡
France	38.3	n.a.	118.3	n.a.
German Democratic Republic	24.7	48.1§	89.0	65.0‖
Japan	109.0	65.0	252.0	181.0
Netherlands	4.0*	2.5‡	10.7*	1.3‡
Singapore	7.2	11.2	20.6	7.4
Switzerland	—	0.5**	—	10.2**
Sweden	—	0.2§	—	55.0§
United Kingdom	5.2	3.1‖	33.4	1.4‖

* 11 months. † Jan./June. ‡ Jan./Aug. § Jan./Sept.

‖ Jan./Oct. ** Jan./Nov. †† July/June.

Source: Ostasiatischer Verein EV, Hamburg.

TRANSPORT

INTERNATIONAL SEA-BORNE SHIPPING
(estimated traffic, '000 metric tons)

	1970	1971	1972
Goods loaded	1,300	1,010	1,050
Goods unloaded	420	380	300

Source: United Nations, *Statistical Yearbook 1974*.

EDUCATION

(1966–67)

	Schools	Teachers	Pupils
Primary	4,064	22,132	1,113,000†
Middle	3,335	30,031	704,000†
Technical	1,207	12,144	285,000†
Higher Technical	500*	5,862	156,000†
University and Colleges	129*	9,244	200,000*

* 1970. † 1964–65.

1974: (Estimates): schools 10,000; pupils 3,000,000 (primary 1,500,000, secondary 1,200,000, tertiary 300,000).

Sources (unless otherwise stated): Society for Cultural Relations with Foreign Countries, Pyongyang; *Far Eastern Economic Review*, Hong Kong; *Korea Today*, Pyongyang; The American University *Area Handbook for North Korea* 1969.

THE CONSTITUTION

(adopted December 27th, 1972)

The following is a summary of the main provisions of the Constitution.

Articles 1-6: The Democratic People's Republic is an independent socialist State (Art. 1); the revolutionary traditions of the State are stressed (its ideological basis being the *Juche* idea of the Workers' Party of Korea) as is the desire to achieve national reunification by peaceful means on the basis of national independence.

Articles 7-10: National sovereignty rests with the working people who exercise power through the Supreme People's Assembly and People's Assemblies at lower levels, which are elected by universal, secret and direct suffrage.

Articles 11-17: Defence is emphasised as well as the rights of overseas nationals, the principles of friendly relations between nations based on equality, mutual respect and non-interference, proletarian internationalism, support for national liberation struggles and due observance of law.

Articles 18-48: Culture and education provide the working people with knowledge to advance a socialist way of life. Education is free and there are universal and compulsory one-year pre-school and ten-year senior middle school programmes in being.

Articles 49-72: The basic rights and duties of citizens are laid down and guaranteed. These include the right to vote (for those over the age of 17), to work (the working day being eight hours), to free medical care and material assistance for the old, infirm or disabled, to political asylum. National defence is the supreme duty of citizens.

Articles 73-88: The Supreme People's Assembly is the highest organ of State power, exercises exclusive legislative authority and is elected by direct, equal, universal and secret ballot for a term of four years. Its chief functions are: (i) adopts or amends legal or constitutional enactments; (ii) determines State policy; (iii) elects the President, Vice-President, Secretary and members of the Central People's Committee (on the President's recommendation); (iv) elects members of the Standing Committee of the Supreme People's Assembly, the Premier of the Administration Council (on the President's recommendation), the President of the Central Court and other legal officials; (v) approves the State Plan and Budget; (vi) decides on matters of war and peace. It holds regular and extraordinary sessions, the former being twice a year, the latter as necessary at the request of at least one-third of the deputies. Legislative enactments are adopted when approved by more than half of those deputies present. The Standing Committee is the permanent body of the Supreme People's Assembly. It examines and decides on bills; amends legislation in force when the Supreme People's Assembly is not in session; interprets the law; organizes and conducts the election of Deputies and judicial personnel.

Articles 89-99: The President as Head of State is elected for four years by the Supreme People's Assembly. He convenes and presides over Administrative Council meetings, is the Supreme Commander of the Armed Forces and chairman of the National Defence Commission. The President promulgates laws of the Supreme People's Assembly and decisions of the Central People's Committee and of the Standing Committee. He has the right to issue orders, to grant pardons, to ratify or abrogate treaties and to receive foreign envoys. The President is responsible to the Supreme People's Assembly.

Articles 100-106: The Central People's Committee comprises the President, Vice-President, Secretary and Members. The Committee exercises the following chief functions: (a) directs the work of the Administration Council as well as organs at local level; (b) implements the constitution and legislative enactments; (c) establishes and abolishes Ministries, appoints Vice-Premiers and other members of the Administration Council; (d) appoints and recalls ambassadors and defence personnel; (e) confers titles, decorations, diplomatic appointments; (f) grants general amnesties, makes administrative changes; (g) declares a state of war. It is assisted by a number of Commissions dealing with Internal Policy, Foreign Policy, National Defence, Justice and Security and other matters as may be established. The Central People's Committee is responsible to the Supreme People's Assembly's Standing Committee.

Articles 107-114: The Administration Council is the administrative and executive body of the Supreme People's Assembly. It comprises the Premier, Vice-Premiers and such other Ministers as may be appointed. Its major functions are the following: (i) directs the work of Ministries and other organs responsible to it; (ii) works out the State Plan and takes measures to make it effective; (iii) compiles the State Budget and gives effect to it; (iv) organizes and executes the work of all sectors of the economy as well as transport, education and social welfare; (v) concludes treaties; (vi) develops the armed forces and maintains public security; (vii) may annul decisions and directives of State administrative departments which run counter to those of the Administration Council. The Administration Council is responsible to the President, Central People's Committee and the Supreme People's Assembly.

Articles 115-132: The People's Assemblies of the province (or municipality directly under central authority), city (or district) and county are local organs of power. The People's Assemblies or Committees exercise local budgetary functions, elect local administrative and judicial personnel and carry out the decisions at local level of higher executive and administrative organs.

Articles 133-146: Justice is administered by the Central Court—the highest judicial organ of the State, the local Court, the People's Court and the Special Court. Judges and other legal officials are elected by the Supreme People's Assembly. The Central Court protects State property, Constitutional rights, guarantees that all State bodies and citizens observe State laws and executes judgements. Justice is administered by the court comprising one judge and two people's assessors. The Court is independent and judicially impartial. Judicial affairs are conducted by the Central Procurator's Office which exposes and institutes criminal proceedings against accused persons. The Office of the Central Procurator is responsible to the Supreme People's Assembly, the President, and the Central People's Committee.

Articles 147-149: These articles describe the national emblem, the national flag and designate Pyongyang as the capital.

THE GOVERNMENT

(*June* 1976)

President: Marshal KIM IL SUNG.

Vice-Presidents: KIM IL, CHOE YONG KUN, KANG RYANG UK, KIM DONG GYU.

CENTRAL PEOPLE'S COMMITTEE

Members:

KIM IL SUNG
KIM IL
CHOE YONG KUN
KANG RYANG UK
PAK SUNG CHUL
CHOE HYON
O JIN U
KIM DONG GYU
KIM YONG CHU
KIM CHUNG NIN
HYON MU GWANG
YANG HYON SOP
KIM MAN GUM
LI GUN MO
CHOE JAE U
LI JONG OK
RIM CHUN CHU
YON HYONG MUK
O TAE BONG
RYU JANG SIK
HO DAM
KIM BYONG HA

Secretary: RIM CHUN CHU.

ADMINISTRATION COUNCIL

Premier: PAK SUNG CHUL.

Vice-Premiers:

KIM MAN GUM
CHOE JAE U
NAM IL
HO DAM
LI GUN MO
CHONG CHUN GI,
HONG SONG NAM
KIM YONG CHU
KIM CHUNG IL
KONG JIN TAE
SO GWAN HI

Chairman of the State Planning Commission: HONG SONG NAM.

Chairman of the Heavy Industry Commission: LI JONG OK.

Chairman of the Machine-building Industry Commission: KYE HYONG SUN.

Chairman of the Light Industry Commission: (vacant).

Chairman of the Agricultural Commission: SO KWAN HI.

Chairman of the Transport and Communication Commission: KANG SONG SAN.

Chairman of the Commission for the Service of the People: KIM HYONG KU.

Minister of the People's Armed Forces: Gen. O JIN U.

Minister of Foreign Affairs: HO DAM.

Minister of Public Security: LI CHIN SU.

Minister of the Ship Machine-building Industry: HAN SONG YONG.

Minister of the Chemical Industry: KIM HWAN.

Minister of Fisheries: KIM YUN SANG.

Minister of the Building Materials Industry: MUN BYONG IL.

Minister of Higher Education: SON SONG PIL.

Minister of Common Education: RYU KUM SON.

Minister of Culture and Art: LI CHANG SON.

Minister of Finance: KIM GYONG PYON.

Minister of Commerce: LI SANG SON.

Minister of Foreign Trade: KYE UNG TAE.

Minister of External Economic Affairs: CHONG SONG NAM.

Minister of Construction: PAK IM TAE.

Minister of Labour Administration: CHONG DU HWAN.

Minister of Public Health: PAK MYONG PIN.

Secretary of the Administration Council: (vacant).

PARLIAMENT

SUPREME PEOPLE'S ASSEMBLY

(Fifth Session held December 25th–29th, 1972)

Chairman: HWANG JANG YOP.

Vice-Chairmen: HONG GI MUN, HO JONG SUK.

Deputies: The 457 Deputies of the fifth Supreme People's Assembly were elected on December 13th, 1972.

STANDING COMMITTEE

Chairman: HWANG JANG YOP.

Vice-Chairmen: HONG GI MUN, HO JONG SUK.

Secretary: CHON CHANG CHOL.

Members (*June* 1976): SO CHOL, HAN IK SU, CHON CHANG CHOL, PAK SHIN DOK, KIM YONG NAM, CHONG JUN GI, RYOM TAE JUN, KIM SONG AE, KIM I HUN, LI YONG BOK, YUN GI BOK, LI DU CHAN, KANG SONG SAN, O HYON JU, CHON SE BONG, LI MYON SANG.

POLITICAL PARTIES

The Workers' Party of Korea: Pyongyang; f. October 10th, 1945; the ruling party; leads Democratic Front for the Reunification of the Fatherland; membership: 1,600,000; General Secretary of the Central Committee: KIM IL SUNG; publs. *Rodong Sinmun* (newspaper), *Gunroja* (theoretical journal).

Chondoist Chongu Party: Pyongyang; f. 1946; mem. of Democratic Front for the Reunification of the Fatherland; supports policies of Workers' Party.

The Democratic Front for the Reunification of the Fatherland: Pyongyang; f. 1949; a united national front organization embracing patriotic political parties and social organizations for reunification of North and South Korea.

Members of the Central Committee:

KIM RYO JUNG, KANG RYANG UK, HAN DUK SU, SO CHOL, LI GUK RO, KO JUN TAEK.

Korean Democratic Party: Pyongyang; f. 1945; mem. of Democratic Front for the Reunification of the Fatherland; supports policies of the Workers' Party; Chair. KANG YANG UK.

DIPLOMATIC REPRESENTATION

EMBASSIES ACCREDITED TO THE DEMOCRATIC PEOPLE'S REPUBLIC OF KOREA

(Pyongyang unless otherwise stated)

Albania: *Ambassador:* GACHO CHOLLAKU.

Algeria: *Chargé d'Affaires a.i.:* BENNAYADA KATOUROU.

Benin: Peking, People's Republic of China.

Bulgaria: *Ambassador:* K. KELCHEV.

Burma: *Ambassador:* THAKIN CHAN TUN.

Burundi: *Ambassador:* (vacant).

Cambodia: *Ambassador:* SIM SON.

China, People's Republic: *Ambassador:* LI YUN-CHUAN.

Congo People's Republic: *Ambassador:* DIEUDONNÉ ITOUA.

Cuba: *Ambassador:* ANGEL FELAS MORENO.

Czechoslovakia: *Ambassador:* MARTIN MACUCH.

Denmark: *Ambassador:* J. A. W. PALUDAN.

Egypt: *Chargé d'Affaires a.i.:* MOHAMED SADEK RAGAB.

Finland: *Ambassador:* MARTI JOHANNES SALOMIES.

German Democratic Republic: *Ambassador:* FRANZ EVERHARTZ.

Guinea: *Ambassador:* ABOUBACAK CAMARA.

Hungary: *Ambassador:* FERENC SZABÓ.

India: *Ambassador:* R. K. JERATH.

Indonesia: *Chargé d'Affaires a.i.:* LOGAHANG ZOOST WILLEM FRISO.

Iran: *Ambassador:* AHMED ALI BAHRAMI.

Iraq: *Chargé d'Affaires a.i.:* MOHAMMED R. AL ZABERI.

Laos: Peking, People's Republic of China.

Madagascar: *Ambassador:* RAKOTOFIRINGA CRESCENT SOLOHERY.

Mali: *Ambassador:* SINALY THERA.

Malta: *Ambassador:* JOSEPH L. FORACE.

Mauritania: *Ambassador:* AHMED OULD MENNEYA.

Mongolia: *Ambassador:* OCHIRYN TSEND.

Nepal: *Ambassador:* CHETRA BICKRAM RANA.

Norway: Peking, People's Republic of China.

Pakistan: Munsudong; *Ambassador:* ANWAR SAEED.

Portugal: *Ambassador:* MÁRIO VICOSO NEVES.

Romania: *Ambassador:* DUMITRU POPA.

Rwanda: *Ambassador:* NYANDWI THARCISSE.

Senegal: *Ambassador:* ALY DIOUM.

Somalia: *Ambassador:* MOHAMED ISMAIL KAHIN.

Sweden: *Ambassador:* KAJ BJOVK.

Syria: *Ambassador:* YASSIR FARRA.

Tanzania: Peking, People's Republic of China.

Thailand: *Ambassador:* KASEMSAMORSORN KASEMSRI (also accred. to the People's Republic of China).

Togo: *Ambassador:* AKAKPO AHIANYO ANANIKUMA.

U.S.S.R.: *Ambassador:* GLEB ALEXANDROVICH KRIULIN.

Viet-Nam: *Ambassador:* TRUNG NAM.

Yemen Arab Republic: *Ambassador:* ABDOU OTHMAN MOHAMMED.

Yemen, People's Democratic Republic: *Ambassador:* (vacant).

Yugoslavia: *Ambassador:* SVETISLAV VUĆIC.

Zaire: *Ambassador:* KIMASI MATWIKU BASAULA.

Zambia: *Ambassador:* ANDREYA SYLVESTER MASIYE.

The Democratic People's Republic of Korea also has, or has agreed to establish, diplomatic relations at ambassadorial level with Afghanistan, Austria, Botswana, Cameroon, the Comoros, Equatorial Guinea, Ethiopia, Fiji, the Gambia, Ghana, Guinea-Bissau, Jamaica, Jordan, Kenya, Libya, Maldives, Mozambique, Niger, Nigeria, Papua New Guinea, Singapore, Sudan, Switzerland, Uganda, the Upper Volta and Venezuela.

The Democratic People's Republic of Korea also has, or has agreed to establish, diplomatic relations with Argentina, Bangladesh, Cape Verde, Costa Rica, Guyana, Iceland, Liberia, Malaysia, Mauritius, Poland, São Tomé and Príncipe, Sierra Leone, Sri Lanka and Tunisia.

JUDICIAL SYSTEM

The judicial organs include the Central Court, the Court of the Province (or city under central authority) and the People's Court. Each court is composed of judges and people's assessors.

Central Court: Pyongyang; the Central Court is the highest judicial organ and supervises the findings of all courts.

President: Pang Hak Se.

Central Procurator's Office: supervises work of procurator's offices in provinces, cities and counties.

Procurator-General: Chong Dong Chol.

Procurators supervise the ordinances and regulations of all ministries and the decisions and directives of local organs of state power to see that they conform to the Constitution, laws and decrees, as well as to the decisions and orders of the Cabinet. Procurators bring suits against criminals in the name of the state, and participate in civil cases to protect the interests of the state and citizens.

RELIGION

The traditional religions are Buddhism, Confucianism, Shamanism and Chundo Kyo, a religion peculiar to Korea combining elements of Buddhism and Christianity.

BUDDHISM

Korean Buddhist Federation: Pyongyang; Chairman An Sook Yong.

THE PRESS

PRINCIPAL NEWSPAPERS

Jokook Tongil: Pyongyang; organ of the Committee for the Peaceful Unification of Korea.

Joson Inmingun (*Korean People's Army*): Pyongyang; f. 1948.

Kyowon Shinmoon: Ministry of General Education.

Minjoo Chosun: Pyongyang; government organ; 6 issues per week; Editor-in-Chief Chae Jun Byong.

Nongup Keunroja: Pyongyang; Central Committee of the Korean Agricultural Working People's Union.

Pyongyang Shinmoon: Pyongyang; general news.

Rodong Chongyon: Pyongyang; organ of the Central Committee of the Socialist Working Youth League of Korea; 6 issues per week.

Rodong Sinmun (*Labour Daily*): Pyongyang; f. 1945; organ of the Central Committee of the Workers' Party of Korea; daily; Editor-in-Chief Kim Gi Nam; circ. 1,000,000.

Rodongja Shinmoon: Pyongyang; General Federation of Trade Unions of Korea.

Saenal: Pyongyang; League of Socialist Working Youth of Korea.

Sonyon Sinmun: Pyongyang; League of Socialist Working Youth of Korea.

Tongil Sinbo: Pyongyang; non-affiliated.

PERIODICALS

Principal Periodicals

Chijilkwa Jiri: Pyongyang; organ of the Geology and Geography Committee of the Korean Academy of Sciences; every two months.

Chollima: Pyongyang; popular magazine; monthly.

Choson (*Pictorial*): Pyongyang; social, economic, political and cultural; monthly.

Choson Munhak: Pyongyang; organ of the Central Committee of the Korean Writers' Union; monthly.

Choson Yesul: Pyongyang; organ of the Central Committee of the Korean Dramatists' and Dancers' Unions; monthly.

Hwahakkwa Hwahak Kongop: Pyongyang; organ of the Hamhung branch of the Korean Academy of Sciences; every two months.

Kunroja: Pyongyang; organ of the Central Committee of the Workers' Party of Korea; monthly.

Kwahakwon Tongbo: Pyongyang; organ of the Standing Committee of the Korean Academy of Sciences; every two months.

Munhwaohaksup: Pyongyang; published by the Publishing House of the Academy of Social Sciences; quarterly.

Punsok Hwahak: Pyongyang; organ of the Central Analytical Institute of the Korean Academy of Sciences; quarterly.

Suhakkwa Mulli: Pyongyang; organ of the Physics and Mathematics Committee of the Korean Academy of Sciences; quarterly.

FOREIGN LANGUAGE PUBLICATIONS

The Agricultural Working People of Korea: Pyongyang; English, French and Russian; every two months.

The Democratic People's Republic of Korea: Foreign Languages Publishing House, Pyongyang; illustrated news; Chinese, English, French, Japanese, Korean, Russian and Spanish; monthly.

Foreign Trade: Foreign Trade Publishing House, Oesong District, Pyongyang; economic developments and export promotion; English, French, Japanese, Russian and Spanish; monthly.

Korea: Pyongyang; pictorial in Chinese and Russian; monthly.

Korea Today: Foreign Languages Publishing House, Pyongyang; current affairs; Chinese, English, French, Russian and Spanish; monthly.

Korean Stamps: Pyongyang; English, French and Russian; published by the Philatelists' Union of the DPRK; monthly.

The Korean Trade Unions: Pyongyang; English, French and Russian; every two months.

Korean Woman: Pyongyang; English, French and Russian; quarterly.

Korean Youth and Students: Pyongyang; English, French and Russian; every two months.

New Korea: Pyongyang; Russian and Chinese.

The Pyongyang Times: Pyongyang; English; weekly.

NEWS AGENCIES

Korean Central News Agency: Pyongyang; sole distributing agency for news in Korea; Dir. Kim Sung Kul; publs. *Korean Central News Agency* (daily), *Photo Dispatch, Daily Release* (English and Russian), *Korean Year Book.*

Foreign Bureau

Tass is the only foreign agency with a bureau in Pyongyang.

PUBLISHERS

Pyongyang

Academy of Sciences Publishing House: Central District Nammundong; f. 1953; publs. *Kwahakwon Tongbo* (Journal of the Academy of Sciences of the D.P.R. of

Korea) bi-monthly; *Kwahakgwa Kwahakgoneop* (Journal of Chemistry and the Chemical Industry) bi-monthly; also quarterly journals of Geology and Geography; Metals; Biology; Analytic Chemistry; Mathematics and Physics; and Electricity.

Academy of Social Sciences Publishing House.

Agricultural Books Publishing House: Pres. Li Hyun U.

Economic Publishing House.

Educational Books Publishing House.

Foreign Languages Publishing House: Pres. L. Ryang Hun.

Foreign Trade Publishing House: Oesong District.

Higher Educational Books Publishing House: Acting Pres. Shin Jong Sung.

Industry Publishing House.

Korea Publications Export and Import Corpn.: Oesong District; export and import of books, periodicals, postage stamps and records.

Korean Worker's Party Publishing House.

Mass Culture Publishing House.

Medical Science Publishing House.

Photo Service.

Publishing House of the General Federation of Literary and Art Unions.

Transportation Publishing House: f. 1952; Acting Editor Paek Jong Han.

RADIO

Korean Central Broadcasting Committee: Pyongyang; programmes relayed nationally with local programmes supplied by local radio committees. Loudspeakers are installed in factories and in open spaces in all towns. Home broadcasting hours: 0500 to 0200 hrs. Foreign broadcasts are in Russian, Chinese, English, French, Spanish, Arabic and Japanese.

A television network is now in operation in the main cities and is to be extended to cover the whole country.

FINANCE

BANKING

Central Bank

Korean Central Bank: Nammundong, Central district, Pyongyang; f. 1946; sole issuing and control bank.

Foreign Trade Bank of the Democratic People's Republic of Korea: Namoondong, Central District, Pyongyang; f. 1963; state bank; operates payments with foreign banks and control of foreign currencies; Pres. Bang Ki Yong.

Korean Industrial Bank: Pyongyang; f. 1964; operates short-term loan, saving, insurance work, guidance and control of financial management of co-operative farms and individual remittance.

INSURANCE

State Insurance Bureau: Pyongyang; handles all life, fire, accident, marine, hull insurance and reinsurance as the national enterprise.

Korea Foreign Insurance Co. (*Chosunbohom*): Central District, Pyongyang; branches in Chongjin, Hungnam, Nampo, Haiju and Rajin, and agencies in foreign ports; handles all foreign insurance.

TRADE AND INDUSTRY

Korean Committee for the Promotion of International Trade: Pyongyang; Sec.-Gen. Pak Se Chan.

Korean Council of the Central Federation of Consumption Co-operative Trade Union: Pyongyang.

Korean General Merchandise Export and Import Corporation: Pyongyang.

Korean British Trade Council (Pyongyang): 68, Queen St., London EC 4N5AB; f. 1974; Sec.-Gen. R. B. Thomas.

TRADING CORPORATIONS

Pyongyang

Korea Botonggang Trading Corporation: Oesong District; foodstuffs, arts and crafts, ready-made suits and optical equipment.

Korea Daesong Trading Corpn.: Central District; machinery and equipment, chemical products, textile goods, agricultural products, etc.

Korea First Machinery Export and Import Corpn.: Sosong District; machine tools, automobiles and tractors, ships and fittings, compressors, etc.

Korea Hwanggumsan Trading Corporation: Central District; food products, confectionery, leather goods, animal products and other agricultural goods.

Korea Hyopdong Trading Corporation: Oesong District; fabrics, glass products, ceramics, chemical goods, building materials, foodstuffs, machinery, etc.

Korea Jei Equipment Export Corporation: Central District; machine plant.

Korea Jei Equipment Import Corporation: Central District; hydro-power and thermal-power plants, machine building plants, transport and communication equipment.

Korea Jeil Equipment Export Corporation: Central District; economic and technical co-operation.

Korea Jeil Equipment Import Corporation: Central District; ferrous and non-ferrous metallurgical plants, building materials, mining plants.

Korea Jesam Equipment Import Corporation: Central District; chemical, textile, pharmaceutical and light industry plant.

Korea Joyang Trading Corpn.: Central District; metallurgical machinery and equipment, mining tools, diesel engines, machine instruments, etc.

Korea Kumgang Trading Corporation: Central District; raw silk, knitted goods, fabrics, embroideries, spinning and weaving machinery.

Korea Kumsusan Trading Corpn.: Central District; petroleum and its products, cement and building materials, fertilizers, household goods, etc.

Korea Maibong Trading Corporation: Central District; non-ferrous metal ingots and their products, non-metallic minerals, agricultural and marine products.

Korea Marine Products Export and Import Corporation: Central District; canned, frozen, dried, salted and smoked fish, fishing equipment and supplies.

Korea Myohyang Trading Corporation: Oesong District; processed fruits and vegetables, wines and liquors, chemical products, consumer products.

Korea Paekgumsan Trading Corpn.: Central District; solid fuels, metallic and non-metallic minerals, precious stones, etc.

Korea Pyongyang Trading Co. Ltd.: Central District, P.O.B. 550; one-side and barter trade; pig iron, steel, magnesia clinker, textiles etc.

Korea Rungra Export and Import Corporation: Tongdaewon District; one-side, barter and triangular trade; food and animal products, machinery.

Korea Taebo Trading Corporation: Oesong District; ceramics, PVC products, hardware, household goods, ornaments, and consumer products.

Korea Technical Corporation: Central District; scientific and technical co-operation.

Korea Third Machinery Export and Import Corpn.: Sosong District; electrical machinery and appliances, cables, medical instruments etc.

Korea Vegetables Export Corporation: Oesong District; vegetables, fruit and their products.

Korea Zung Oi Trading Co. Ltd.: Central District, P.O.B. 540; one-side and barter trade; metallic and non-metallic minerals, clinker, marine and agricultural products, etc.

TRADE UNIONS

General Federation of Trade Unions of Korea: Pyongyang; f. 1945; total membership (1970) 2,200,000; 10 affiliated unions; Chair. Ryom Tae Jun; publs. *Rodongja Shinmoon, Rodongja, Korean Trade Unions.*

General Federation of Literature and Arts of Korea: Pyongyang; f. 1961; Chair. of Central Committee Li Ki Yong.

Branch unions:

Korean Painters' Union: Pyongyang; Chair. Chong Kwan Chul.

Korean Writers' Union: Pyongyang; Chair. Chun se Bong.

Korean Cameramen's Union: Pyongyang; Chair. Ko Ryong Jin.

Korean Dancers' Union: Pyongyang; Chair. Pak Kyong Ja.

Korean Drama Workers' Union: Pyongyang; Chair. Li Jai Duk.

Korean Film Workers' Union: Pyongyang; Chair. Li Jong Soon.

Korean Musicians' Union: Pyongyang; Chair. Li Myun Sang.

General Federation of Agricultural and Forestry Technique of Korea: Chung Ku-yuck Nammundong, Pyongyang; f. 1946; publ. *Nong-oup Kisyl* (monthly journal of technical information on agriculture).

General Federation of Industrial Technology of Korea: Pyongyang; f. 1946; 65,368 mems.

Korean Agricultural Working People's Union: Pyongyang; f. 1965 to replace former *Korean Peasants' Union*; 2,400,000 mems.; Chair. Central Committee Kim I. Hun.

Korean Architects' Union: Pyongyang; f. 1954; 500 mems.; Chiar. Kim Jung Hi.

Korean Democratic Lawyers' Association: Pyongyang; f. 1954; Pres. Kim Hyung Kun.

Korean Democratic Scientists' Association: Pyongyang; f. 1956.

Korean Journalists' Union: Pyongyang; f. 1946; Chair. Chong Jun Gi.

TRANSPORT

Railway: 10,500 km. of track; steam, diesel and electric trains, through services to Peking and Moscow. Electric traction has been introduced on all trunk lines, including those between Pyongyang and Sinuiju and Pyongyang and Rajin.

Rivers: Yalu and Daidong, Dooman and Ryesung are the most important commercial rivers. Regular passenger and freight services: Manopo-Chosan-Soopoong; Chungsoo-Shinuijoo-Dasado; Nam-po-Jeudo; Pyongyang-Nampo.

Shipping

Korea Foreign Transportation Corpn.: Central District, Pyongyang; arranges transportation of export and import cargoes, (transit goods and charters).

Korean-Polish Maritime Brokers Co. Ltd.: Moranbong District, Pyongyang; maritime trade with a number of foreign ports.

Korea Tongae Shipping Co.: Oesong District, Pyongyang; arranges transportation by Korean vessels.

Civil Aviation

Civil Aviation Administration of the Democratic People's Republic of Korea: Stalin St., Pyongyang; internal and external services; fleet: Il-14, Il 18, An-24.

Services are also provided by *C.A.A.C.* and *Aeroflot.*

TOURISM

Korean International Tourist Bureau: "Ryohaengsa" Pyongyang.

DEFENCE

Armed Forces and Equipment (1975): Total 467,000: army 410,000; navy, 17,000; air force, 40,000. The army is equipped with Soviet material including medium and heavy tanks, AA guns and surface-to-surface and surface-to-air missiles. The navy has a few old Soviet submarines as well as a large number of motor, torpedo and patrol boats, some armed with missiles. The air force has 588 combat aircraft largely Soviet MiGs. In addition to the above forces, there are also 50,000 security and border guards and a People's Militia with an estimated strength of 1.5 million.

Military Service: Army 5 years, navy and air force 3/4 years.

Defence Expenditure: Defence spending for 1974 was estimated at 1,578 million won ($770 million). The defence budget for 1976–77 was substantially increased.

Chief of the Korean People's Army: Gen. O Jin U.

Director of the Political Bureau of the KPA: Col.-Gen. Han Ik Su.

UNIVERSITY

Kim Il Sung University: Pyongyang; f. 1946; 900 teachers, over 16,000 full and part-time students.

REPUBLIC OF KOREA

STATISTICAL SURVEY

AREA AND POPULATION

Area*	Census Population				
	October 1st, 1966	October 1st, 1970	October 1st, 1975 (preliminary)		
			Total	Male	Female
98,758 sq. km.†	29,192,726	31,465,654	34,708,542	17,451,946	17,256,596

* Excluding the demilitarized zone between North and South Korea, with an area of 1,262 sq. km. (487 sq. miles.)

† 38,131 sq. miles. The figure indicates territory under the jurisdiction of the Republic of Korea on December 31st, 1973, surveyed on the basis of land register.

PRINCIPAL TOWNS

(1975 Census, preliminary figures)

Soul (Seoul—capital)	6,889,470	Masan	371,937	Cheongju	192,734
Pusan (Busan)	2,454,051	Chonchu (Jeonju)	311,432	Jinju (Jingu)	154,676
Taegu (Daegu)	1,311,078	Seongnam	272,329	Gunsan	154,485
Inchon (Incheon)	799,982	Ulsan	252,639	Chuncheon	140,521
Kwangchu (Gwangju)	607,058	Suweon	224,177	Jeju	135,189
Taejon (Daejeon)	506,703	Mokpo	192,927	Yeosu	130,641

ECONOMICALLY ACTIVE POPULATION*

(1975 Average)

	Males	Females	Total
Employed Persons:			
Agriculture, forestry and fishing	3,172,000	2,253,000	5,425,000
Mining and quarrying	55,000	5,000	60,000
Manufacturing	1,450,000	775,000	2,225,000
Construction	486,000	25,000	511,000
Services	2,326,000	1,303,000	3,629,000
Total in employment	7,489,000	4,341,000	11,830,000
Unemployed	395,000	115,000	510,000
Total	7,884,000	4,456,000	12,340,000

* Excluding armed forces.

AGRICULTURE

PRINCIPAL CROPS
('000 metric tons)

	1972	1973	1974	1975
Wheat	241.3	162.4	135.9	135.6
Barley	751.1	662.4	665.7	878.1
Naked Barley	1,213.4	1,115.4	1,038.9	1,240.2
Maize	53.7	61.1	58.2	59.8
Foxtail (Italian) Millet	30.9	30.1	29.4	25.2
Rice (paddy)	3,933	4,190	4,417.0	4,627.3
Potatoes	459	470	469.2	674.8
Sweet Potatoes and Yams	1,879	1,669	1,449.6	1,953.2
Onions: Green	71	72	75.5	92.3
Dry	119.6	91.5	128.0	113.2
Tomatoes	56	57	55.3	77.4
Cabbages	869	822	950.6	878.8
Cucumbers and Gherkins	104	98	112.7	121.3
Melons	91	95	111.6	119.6
Water Melons	149	145	175.2	169.1
Apples	261	291	297.3	310.1
Pears	50	52	56.5	59.7
Peaches	80	84	88.6	88.2
Grapes	48	57	59.2	57.7
Soybeans	224	246	318.6	310.6
Tobacco	115.9	111.6	95.1	104.2

Source: Economic Planning Board, Bureau of Statistics, Seoul.

LIVESTOCK
(recorded numbers at December)

	1971	1972	1973	1974	1975
Cattle	1,280,000	1,338,200	1,486,200	1,777,700	n.a.
Pigs	1,332,500	1,247,600	1,594,700	1,818,300	n.a.
Goats	128,000	152,200	194,100	252,900	250,200
Sheep	3,000	3,600	3,800	4,850	5,800
Horses	12,900	10,800	10,300	10,300	9,000
Rabbits	363,600	421,200	587,000	848,400	n.a.
Chickens	25,903,100	24,537,400	23,071,000	18,814,200	n.a.
Ducks	252,000	224,300	483,100	491,400	498,800
Geese	11,000	10,324	9,670	10,714	10,000
Turkeys	1,900	2,000	4,000	11,800	6,800
Beehives	99,900	105,300	125,400	157,800	151,000

LIVESTOCK PRODUCTS
(metric tons)

	1972	1973	1974	1975
Beef and Veal*	40,229	43,919	51,506	70,292
Pork	90,230	90,126	95,353	106,956
Poultry Meat	54,266	51,801	53,269	55,594
Other Meat	1,596	2,962	2,205	3,306
Cows' Milk	79,852	104,082	126,901	162,345
Goats' Milk	1,428	1,287	980	984
Hen Eggs	140,000	125,000	137,750	144,800
Honey	1,305	1,525	1,944	1,842
Raw Silk	3,656	3,721	4,955	5,364
Fresh Cocoons	26,800	30,980	37,178	36,091
Cattle Hides	4,977†	5,544†	6,990	10,290

* Inspected production only, i.e. from animals slaughtered under government supervision.

† FAO estimate.

FISHING

('ooo metric tons)

	1971	1972	1973	1974	1975
Fish	726.8	947.7	1,121.7	1,406.6	1,450.6
Shellfish	147.8	160.6	211.6	163.0	274.7
Sea plants	117.2	128.8	224.2	335.8	246.8
Others	81.9	106.5	129.0	120.8	162.9
TOTAL	1,073.7	1,343.6	1,686.5	2,026.2	2,135.0

MINING

		1972	1973	1974	1975
Anthracite	'ooo metric tons	12,403	13,571	15,290	17,585
Iron ore	,, ,, ,,	414	466	493	524
Copper ore	metric tons	14,041	15,933	21,569	25,681
Lead ore	,, ,,	23,443	23,654	20,094	19,854
Zinc ore	,, ,,	74,636	96,638	84,532	91,333
Molybdenum ore	,, ,,	141	131	162	152
Tungsten ore	short tons	3,573	4,057	4,545	4,772
Gold (refined)	kg.	533	444	728	369
Silver (refined)	,,	51,738	46,353	40,661	46,470

INDUSTRY

SELECTED PRODUCTS

		1972	1973	1974	1975
Wheat flour	'ooo metric tons	1,399.8	1,401.2	1,162.0	1,146.8
Refined sugar	,, ,, ,,	205.2	303.5	283.5	332.0
Margarine	metric tons	14,790	16,565	18,515	25,645
Beer	'ooo hectolitres	976.0	1,282.3	1,608.7	1,772.8
Cigarettes	million	49,665	49,169	49,625	52,498
Cotton yarn (pure and mixed)	metric tons	91,256	103,014	130,226	133,596
Woven cotton fabrics (pure)[1]	'ooo sq. metres	201,189	264,400	261,446	242,776
Woven silk fabrics (pure)	,, ,, ,,	12,032	15,536	13,888	16,669
Yarn of synthetic fibres	metric tons	91,882	120,855	150,805	220,508
Synthetic fabrics	'ooo sq. metres	204,372	332,084	313,935	434,831
Plywood	'ooo cubic metres	1,668.4	1,915.9	1,573.3	1,853.9
Newsprint	metric tons	113,651	124,561	150,517	150,095
Rubber tyres[2]	'ooo	1,087.9	1,575.3	2,048.2	2,658.3
Sulphuric acid	metric tons	414,862	453,961	474,196	503,154
Caustic soda	,, ,,	32,427	39,617	45,154	59,826
Soda ash	,, ,,	72,573	84,402	97,028	127,103
Urea fertilizer	,, ,,	690,826	698,078	811,980	924,666
Liquefied petroleum gas	million litres	142.9	215.6	287.0	375.9
Naphtha	,, ,,	1,212.5	1,703.7	2,117.6	2,388.4
Motor spirit (petrol)	,, ,,	942.8	1,039.2	702.5	663.5
Kerosene	,, ,,	426.5	479.7	396.2	627.4
Aviation oil	,, ,,	669.6	581.8	642.1	675.9
Distillate fuel oil	,, ,,	2,329.4	2,840.8	2,925.5	3,309.5
Bunker C oil	,, ,,	7,091.1	8,324.1	8,674.5	9,409.7
Residual fuel oil	,, ,,	578.2	626.3	510.1	508.0
Cement	'ooo metric tons	6,486.3	8,174.7	8,841.5	10,129.3
Pig iron	,, ,, ,,	6	454.6	986.9	1,186.3
Crude steel	,, ,, ,,	585.1	1,157.1	1,934.7	2,009.8
Radio receivers	'ooo	1,858.1	3,271.9	3,691.8	4,280.2
Television receivers	,,	307.6	816.4	1,164.0	1,215.2
Passenger cars (assembly)	number	8,856	12,695	8,837	17,672
Electric energy	million kWh.	11,839	14,826	16,835	19,837

[1] After undergoing finishing processes. [2] Tyres for passenger cars and commercial vehicles.

FINANCE

100 chun (jeon) = 1 hwan = 1 won.
Coins: 1, 5, 10, 50 and 100 won.
Notes: 1, 5, 10, 50, 100, 500, 1,000, 5,000 and 10,000 won.
Exchange rates (June 1976): £1 sterling = 858.6 won; U.S. $1 = 484.0 won.
10,000 won = £11.65 = $20.66.

Note: The new won was introduced in June 1962, replacing the hwan at the rate of 1 new won = 10 hwan. The hwan had been introduced in February 1953, replacing the old won at the rate of 1 hwan = 100 old won. The official exchange rate was initially U.S. $1 = 100 hwan but subsequently the hwan was frequently devalued. From February 1961 the exchange rate was $1 = 1,300 hwan. The initial rate of $1 = 130 new won (£1 sterling = 364 new won) remained in force until May 1964, after which the won's value was allowed to fluctuate in a free market. The official buying rate was $1 = 255 won (£1 = 714 won) from May 1964 to March 1965. For the next three years the rate was around 270 to 275 won per U.S. dollar, declining to 281 won per dollar (£1 = 674 won) by the end of 1968 and then to more than 300 won per dollar by November 1969. Depreciation of the won continued and in June 1971 the currency was officially devalued, the new buying rate being $1 = 370 won (£1 = 888 won). Further depreciation followed, despite the devaluation of the U.S. dollar in December 1971, and the buying rate was $1 = 400 won by June 1972. Thereafter the won's value held steady at around that rate (but unchanged by a further dollar devaluation in February 1973) until December 1974, when a new rate of $1 = 484 won was introduced. The average market rates of won per U.S. dollar were: 271 in 1966; 270 in 1967; 276.3 in 1968; 288.4 in 1969; 310.4 in 1970; 350.1 in 1971; 394.0 in 1972; 398.5 in 1973; 406.0 in 1974.

BUDGET
(million won, fiscal years)

REVENUE	1973	1974	1975*	1976*
Internal taxes	439,121	717,976	991,658	1,212,635
Customs duties	82,371	126,697	169,941	203,862
Monopoly profits	57,000	69,000	135,500	178,000
Contribution from government enterprises (net)	63,579	109,713	147,813	155,379
Other receipts	121,821	162,252	174,714	205,917
TOTAL	763,892	1,185,638	1,619,626	1,955,793

* Estimates.

EXPENDITURE	1973	1974	1975*	1976*
National defence	183,469	296,846	462,794	704,448
General expenditures	276,271	401,944	589,463	719,026
Fixed capital formation	121,293	172,895	296,053	335,833
Other expenditures	249,805	460,462	667,067	652,927
	830,838	1,332,147	2,015,337	2,412,274
Net lending	23,499	24,507	38,962	34,813
TOTAL	854,337	1,356,654	2,054,339	2,447,087

* Estimates.

THIRD FIVE-YEAR ECONOMIC PLAN 1972–76
(At 1970 constant market prices)

		1970	1972	1976	1976/1970 (%)	Average growth rate (1972–76)
G.N.P.	'000 million won	2,562.0	3,071.8	4,257.1	166.2	8.6
Agriculture, forestry and fishing	,, ,, ,,	727.8	800.9	955.2	131.2	4.5
Mining and manufacturing	,, ,, ,,	555.3	737.5	1,186.6	213.7	13.0
Social and other services	,, ,, ,,	1,278.9	1,533.4	2,115.3	165.4	8.5
Consumption	,, ,, ,,	2,130.5	2,528.2	3,343.6	156.9	7.4
Gross investment	,, ,, ,,	667.6	776.5	1,060.7	158.9	7.6
Exports	U.S. $ million	1,379	2,005	4,058	294.3	—
Imports	,, ,,	2,177	2,755	4,532	208.2	—

GOLD RESERVES AND MONEY SUPPLY

(At year's end)

		1973	1974	1975
Gold reserves	U.S. $'000	4,636	4,653	4,702
Currency in circulation	million won	311,399	410,526	507,186
Monetary deposits	,, ,,	418,898	535,181	674,559
Total money supply	,, ,,	730,297	945,707	1,181,745

BALANCE OF PAYMENTS

(U.S. $ million)

	1974			1975*		
	Credit	Debit	Net	Credit	Debit	Net
Merchandise:						
Exports f.o.b.	4,515.1	—	4,515.1	4,979.1	—	4,979.7
Imports f.o.b.	—	6,451.9	−6,451.9	—	6,577.5	−6,577.5
Trade balance	—	1,936.8	−1,936.8	—	1,597.8	−1,597.8
Non-monetary gold	—	—	—	—	—	—
Freight and insurance	94.8	428.6	−333.8	130.4	440.1	−309.7
Other transport	134.0	140.5	−6.5	154.8	201.9	−47.1
Travel	153.3	27.6	125.7	140.6	30.7	109.9
Investment income	82.9	324.6	241.7	148.3	452.4	−404.1
Military transactions	155.5	—	155.5	146.2	—	146.2
Other government services	5.9	43.9	−38.0	10.7	71.2	−60.5
Other private services	211.4	180.9	30.5	240.9	215.5	25.4
TOTAL GOODS AND SERVICES	5,352.9	7,598.0	−2,245.1	5,851.6	7,989.3	−2,137.7
Unrequited transfers:						
Private	209.3	55.5	153.8	221.3	64.8	156.5
Central government	68.8	0.2	68.6	70.5	3.0	67.5
TOTAL CURRENT ACCOUNT	5,631.0	7,653.7	−2,022.7	6,143.4	8,057.1	−1,913.7
Private long-term capital	740.8	−91.4	832.2	1,113.4	−8.0	1,121.4
Private short-term capital	−46.7	−1.3	−45.4	747.9	68.3	679.6
Local government capital	42.6	—	42.6	1.8	—	1.8
Central government capital	110.9	7.5	103.4	318.5	14.2	304.3
Deposit money banks	791.8	524.4	267.4	250.9	−60.3	311.2
TOTAL CAPITAL ACCOUNT	1,638.4	439.2	1,200.2	2,432.5	14.2	2,418.3
Net errors and omissions	27.9	—	27.9	—	187.9	−187.9
BALANCE (net monetary movements)	—	794.6	−794.6	316.7	—	316.7

* Preliminary estimate.

Source: Bureau of Statistics, Economic Planning Board, *Monthly Statistics of Korea.*

EXTERNAL TRADE

(U.S. $'000)

	1971	1972	1973	1974	1975
Imports	2,394,320	2,522,002	4,240,277	6,851,848	7,274,434
Exports	1,067,607	1,624,088	3,225,025	4,460,371	5,081,016

PRINCIPAL COMMODITIES
(U.S. $'000)

IMPORTS	1972	1973	1974	1975
Wheat and meslin (unmilled)	128,136	256,621	297,562	293,651
Rice	102,965	83,965	153,112	195,118
Raw sugar	36,449	63,015	131,490	185,387
Crude rubber	22,498	46,700	75,475	57,908
Wood	140,826	311,641	343,523	268,773
Pulp	35,016	64,935	111,097	74,831
Raw cotton	85,477	112,426	189,450	248,992
Artificial fibres	47,127	83,457	74,387	38,868
Petroleum and petroleum products	217,746	296,217	1,020,259	1,339,274
Organic chemicals	92,065	137,248	294,756	339,066
Plastic materials	45,247	60,686	92,752	91,578
Textile yarn and thread	43,592	108,069	78,641	50,418
Textile fabrics (woven)	64,940	152,274	141,248	148,211
Iron and steel ingots	101,067	197,039	236,473	128,180
Iron and steel plates and sheets	22,933	43,491	81,505	85,888
Power generating machinery	84,976	35,007	81,830	113,709
Textile machinery	34,192	147,308	186,542	167,145
Electric power machinery	61,694	52,464	93,065	107,629
Telecommunications apparatus	48,739	76,739	102,424	105,372
Thermionic valves, tubes, etc.	67,489	162,005	218,489	187,193
Aircraft	34,089	106,693	72,785	169,706
Ships and boats (excl. warships)	79,721	51,023	392,239	245,629
TOTAL (incl. others)	2,522,022	4,240,277	6,851,848	7,274,434

EXPORTS	1972	1973	1974	1975
Fish (fresh, chilled or frozen)	32,489	56,756	74,183	242,376
Crustacea and molluscs	32,109	45,438	49,696	65,438
Tobacco (unmanufactured)	12,619	22,111	46,711	66,258
Raw silk (not thrown)	53,943	72,844	59,828	20,988
Rubber tyres and tubes	10,324	18,500	59,797	82,158
Plywood	153,623	273,188	163,409	206,407
Textile yarn and thread	43,881	85,813	117,851	204,986
Cotton fabrics (woven)	34,849	56,489	54,861	50,496
Textile fabrics	88,311	261,794	276,067	355,127
Cement	12,718	19,619	48,946	68,922
Iron or steel sheets	68,122	129,526	233,281	74,300
Electrical machinery	125,150	312,512	474,213	441,619
Transport equipment	14,307	24,042	121,142	183,669
Textile clothing (not knitted)	151,479	314,636	414,235	484,030
Outer garments (knitted)	153,941	118,516	108,512	106,857
Footwear	55,405	106,371	179,547	191,213
Wigs and false beards	73,810	81,536	72,007	75,262
TOTAL (incl. others)	1,624,088	3,225,025	4,460,371	5,081,016

PRINCIPAL TRADING PARTNERS
(U.S. $'000)

Imports	1972	1973	1974	1975
Australia	47,346	89,575	129,338	204,756
Canada	35,995	82,545	115,702	150,175
France	47,798	46,903	35,508	137,338
Germany, Federal Republic	66,931	132,030	140,318	192,695
Indonesia	64,040	153,289	165,369	146,809
Japan	1,031,085	1,726,901	2,620,551	2,433,603
Kuwait	93,511	83,407	257,230	553,479
Malaysia	48,950	132,389	160,548	122,796
Saudi Arabia	87,704	154,183	670,488	605,359
Taiwan	47,875	55,394	107,688	161,973
United Kingdom	73,869	68,932	90,418	123,041
U.S.A.	647,225	1,201,884	1,700,816	1,881,144
Total (incl. others)	2,522,022	4,240,277	6,851,848	7,274,434

Exports	1972	1973	1974	1975
Australia	9,191	27,101	71,289	63,005
Belgium	13,359	40,278	27,500	40,265
Canada	58,915	124,881	166,764	197,347
Germany, Federal Republic	51,195	120,338	241,781	312,238
Hong Kong	72,382	117,724	151,153	181,993
Indonesia	21,467	32,380	55,157	51,359
Iran	9,010	16,343	42,107	125,690
Japan	407,876	1,241,539	1,380,196	1,292,904
Netherlands	32,976	57,207	106,657	128,968
Singapore	10,074	30,460	48,527	58,278
Taiwan	16,131	40,942	50,754	62,880
United Kingdom	28,680	74,960	106,685	161,770
U.S.A.	758,975	1,021,182	1,492,168	1,536,287
Total (incl. others)	1,624,088	3,225,025	4,460,371	5,081,016

TOURISM

	Visitors
1971	232,785
1972	370,656
1973	679,221
1974	517,590
1975	632,846

TRANSPORT

RAILWAYS
('000)

	1972	1973	1974	1975
Passengers	137,301	143,009	184,602	254,571
Freight (metric tons)	31,547	37,762	39,708	42,758

ROADS

	1973	1974	1975
Passenger Cars	78,334	76,462	84,212
Trucks	64,584	76,833	82,862
Buses	18,871	20,060	21,818

SHIPPING

('000 metric tons)

	1973	1974	1975
Loaded	17,712	19,085	21,547
Unloaded	41,545	44,656	45,242

CIVIL AVIATION

	Domestic Services			International Services		
	1973	1974	1975	1973	1974	1975
Passengers	1,269,081	990,826	902,105	1,368,792	1,188,548	1,475,711
Freight (kg.)	8,497,170	5,743,283	5,379,676	50,969,200	61,828,845	86,707,016
Mail (kg.)	232,607	95,131	239,829	4,669,215	4,751,369	3,692,742

EDUCATION

(1975)

	Schools	Teachers	Pupils
Kindergarten	611	2,153	32,032
Primary schools	6,367	108,126	5,559,074
Middle schools	1,967	46,917	2,026,823
High schools	1,152	35,755	1,123,017
Junior technical schools	88	2,565	58,500
Junior colleges	10	160	3,787
Junior teachers' colleges	16	791	8,504
Colleges and universities	72	10,080	208,986
Graduate schools	82	162	13,870

General Sources: Bureau of Statistics of the Republic of Korea, except where otherwise indicated.

THE CONSTITUTION

A new constitution was approved by national referendum in November 1972. The main provisions are summarized below.

THE GOVERNMENT

The President: The President is to be elected by the National Conference for Unification for a period of six years and may be elected for an unlimited number of such terms. In times of national emergency and under certain conditions the President shall have power to take necessary emergency measures in all matters of State. He may, in time of war, armed conflict or similar national emergency, declare martial law in accordance with the provisions of law. He is authorized to take directly to the people important issues through national referenda, and may dissolve the National Assembly at will. He is empowered to appoint members at all levels of the judiciary and may discipline them in cases of misconduct.

The State Council: The State Council shall be composed of the President, the Prime Minister and no more than 25 and no less than 15 others appointed by the President, and shall deliberate on policies that fall within the power of the executive.

The National Assembly: The National Assembly is to be unicameral with a membership as determined by law, two-thirds of whom are to be elected by direct popular vote, and the remainder chosen by the National Conference for Unification. Regular sessions are to be held once a year for a maximum period of 90 days and two special sessions of not more than 30 days each may be held at the request of the President or one-third of the total members. In addition the President may, in extraordinary circumstances, convene an emergency session. The term of office of those members elected by popular vote shall be six years, those elected by the National Conference sitting for three years. The legislative power shall be vested in the National Assembly. It has the power to recommend to the President the removal of the Prime Minister or any other Minister. The National Assembly shall have the authority to pass a motion for the impeachment of the President or any other public official.

The National Conference for Unification: This shall be elected by direct popular vote and shall be composed of no fewer than 2,000 and no more than 5,000 delegates, whose term of office shall be six years. The National Conference for Unification is to be the supreme representative body for national consensus on matters concerning national unification. It shall elect the President and one-third of the members of the National Assembly and shall make the final decision on any draft amendments to the constitution passed by the National Assembly.

The Constitution Committee: The Constitution Committee shall be composed of nine members appointed by the President, three of whom shall be appointed from persons elected by the National Assembly and three from persons nominated by the Chief Justice. The term of office shall be six years. It shall pass judgment upon the constitutionality of laws upon the request of the Court, matters of impeachment and the dissolution of political parties. In these judgments the concurrence of six members or more shall be required.

The Judiciary: The courts shall be composed of the Supreme Court, which is the highest court of the State, and other courts at specified levels (for further details *see* Judicial System, page 914). When the constitutionality of a law is a prerequisite to a trial the Court shall request a decision of the Constitution Committee. The Supreme Court shall have the power to pass judgment upon the constitutionality or legality of administrative decrees, and shall have final appellate jurisdiction over military tribunals.

Political Parties: The establishment of political parties shall be free and the plural party system guaranteed. However, a political party whose aims or activities are contrary to the basic democratic order may be dissolved by the Constitution Committee.

Constitutional Amendments: A motion to amend the Constitution shall be proposed by the President or by a majority of the total members of the National Assembly. Proposed amendments by the President are to be decided by national referendum. Those put forward by the National Assembly shall become effective when passed by a two-thirds majority thereof, having also received confirmation by the National Conference for Unification.

FUNDAMENTAL RIGHTS

Under the constitution all citizens are equal before the law. Freedom of speech, press, assembly and association are guaranteed, as are freedom of choice of residence and occupation. No state religion is to be recognized and freedom of conscience and religion is guaranteed. Citizens are protected against retrospective legislation, and may not be punished without due process of law.

Besides legal limitations on certain of these rights as provided for in specific provisions of the constitution, there is a general clause stating that rights and freedoms may be restricted by law when this is deemed necessary for the maintenance of national security, order or public welfare.

THE GOVERNMENT

President: General Park Chung Hee (re-elected December 23rd, 1972.)

THE CABINET

(*June* 1976)

(Democratic Republican Party)

Prime Minister: Choi Kyu Hah.

Deputy Prime Minister and Chairman of the Economic Planning Board: Dr. Nam Duck Woo.

Minister of Foreign Affairs: Park Dong Jin.

Minister of the Interior: Kim Chi Yol.

Minister of Finance: Kim Yong Whan.

Minister of Justice: Whang Son Dok.

Minister of Defence: Su Chong Chul.

Minister of Education: Yoo Ki Choon.

Minister of Agriculture and Fisheries: Choi Kak Kyu.

Minister of Commerce and Industry: Chang Ye Choon.

Minister of Construction: Kim Jae Kyu.

Minister of Health and Social Affairs: Shin Hyon Hwak.

Minister of Transport: Choi Kyong Nok.

Minister of Communications: Park Won Keun.

Minister of Information and Cultural Affairs: Kim Seong Jin.

Minister of Science and Technology: Choi Hyong Sup.

Minister of Government Administration: Shim Heong Sun.

National Unification Board: You Sang Uine.

Ministers without Portfolio: Shin Hyong Shik, Min Pyong Kwon.

NATIONAL ASSEMBLY

Party	Seats: February 1973 Elections	Seats: June 1976
Democratic Republican Party	141	143
New Democratic Party	57	50
Democratic Unification Party	3	3
Independents	14	12
	215	208

Speaker of the National Assembly: Gen. Chung Il Kwon.

NATIONAL CONFERENCE FOR UNIFICATION (NCU)

(*see* also under the Constitution)

(Elected December 22nd, 1972)

Area	Electoral Districts	Delegates
Seoul	67	303
Pusan	24	104
Kyonggi .	207	280
Kangwon	111	145
Chungbuk	107	127
Chungnam	185	231
Chonbuk .	168	200
Chonnam	242	312
Kyongbuk	268	354
Kyongnam	236	278
Cheju	15	25
Total	1,630	2,359

POLITICAL PARTIES

Democratic Republican Party: 30-90 Huam-dong, Yongsan-gu, C.P.O.B. 196, Seoul; f. 1963; Government Party; 1,359,863 mems.; President Gen. PARK CHUNG HEE; Chair. RHEE HYO SANG; Sec.-Gen. KIL JOUN-SIK; publs. *The Democratic Republican Forum, The D.R.P. Bulletin, Policy Quarterly.*

Democratic Unification Party: 115, Samkak-dong, Chung-ku, Seoul.

New Democratic Party: 103 Kwanhun-dong, Chongno-gu, Seoul; main opposition party formed 1967 by the Sinhan and Minjung Parties; Pres. (vacant).

Unified Socialist Party (*Tongsa Dang*): 14-47 Dongja-dong, Chung-ku, Seoul; Leader AHN TACK-SU.

DIPLOMATIC REPRESENTATION

EMBASSIES ACCREDITED TO THE REPUBLIC OF KOREA

(Seoul unless otherwise stated)

Afghanistan: Tokyo, Japan.

Argentina: 135-53, Itaewon-dong, Yongsan-Ku; *Ambassador:* (vacant).

Australia: 5th Floor Kukdong-Shell House, 58-1 Shinmoonro 1-ka, Chongro-ku; *Ambassador:* J. R. HOLDICH.

Austria: Tokyo, Japan.

Bangladesh: Tokyo, Japan.

Belgium: 1-37 Hannam-dong, Yongsan-ku; *Ambassador:* GASTON JENEBELLY.

Bolivia: Tokyo, Japan.

Brazil: 3rd Floor, New Korea Hotel Bldg., 192-11, 1-ka, Ulchiro, Choong-ku; *Ambassador:* JOACHIM DE ALMEIDA SERRA.

Canada: 9th Floor, Hankook Ilbo Bldg., Chongro-kuh; *Ambassador:* JOHN A. STILES.

Central African Republic: Tokyo, Japan.

Chile: 142-5 Itaewon-dong, Yongsan-ku; *Ambassador:* LEOPOLDO FONTAINE NAKIN.

China (Taiwan): 83, 2-ga, Myong-dong, Chung-ku; *Ambassador:* CHU FU-SUNG.

Colombia: Tokyo, Japan.

Costa Rica: Tokyo, Japan.

Denmark: Tokyo, Japan.

Dominican Republic: Tokyo, Japan.

Ecuador: Tokyo, Japan.

El Salvador: Tokyo, Japan.

Ethiopia: Tokyo, Japan.

Finland: Tokyo, Japan.

France: 30 Hap-dong, Sudaimum-ku; *Ambassador:* RÉMY TEISSIER DU CROS.

Gabon: 1802 Garden Tower, 98-78 Wunni-dong, Chongro-ku; *Ambassador:* VALENTIN OBAME.

Germany, Federal Republic: 9th Floor, Dae Han Bldg., 75 Sosumun-dong, Sudaimun-ku; *Ambassador:* DR. KARL LENTERITZ.

Greece: Tokyo, Japan.

Guatemala: Tokyo, Japan.

Honduras: Tokyo, Japan.

India: San 2-1, Bokwang-dong, Yongsan-ku; *Ambassador:* S. M. AGA.

Indonesia: 258-87, Itaewon-dong, Yongsan-ku; *Ambassador:* SARWO EDHIE WIBOWO.

Iran: Tokyo, Japan.

Israel: 308-9 Dongbinggo-dong, Yongsan-ku; *Ambassador:* AMNON BEN YOHANAN.

Italy: 1-169, 2-ga, Shinmun-ro, Chongno-ku; *Ambassador:* GIULIANO BERTUCCIOLI.

Ivory Coast: Tokyo, Japan.

Japan: 18-11 Chunghak-dong, Chongno-gu; *Ambassador:* AKIRA NISHIYAMA.

Jordan: Tokyo, Japan.

Liberia: Tokyo, Japan.

Madagascar: Washington D.C., U.S.A.

Malaysia: 726 Hannam-dong, Yongsan-gu; *Ambassador:* JOHN DENIS DE SILVA.

Mexico: Tokyo, Japan.

Morocco: Tokyo, Japan.

Nepal: Tokyo, Japan.

Netherlands: 1-85 Tongbinggo-dong, Yongsan-gu; *Ambassador:* (vacant).

New Zealand: 26th Floor, Samilro Bldg., 10 Kwanchul-dong, Chrongro-ku; *Ambassador:* THOMAS CEDRIC LARKIN.

Nicaragua: Tokyo, Japan.

Norway: Tokyo, Japan.

Panama: Tokyo, Japan.

Paraguay: Tokyo, Japan.

Peru: Tokyo, Japan.

Philippines: 258-25 Itaewon-dong, Yongsan-ku; *Ambassador:* BENJAMIN T. TIRONA.

Saudi Arabia: Tokyo, Japan.

Spain: Garden Tower Apt., 1201, 98-78 Wooni-dong, Chongro-ku; *Ambassador:* JOSÉ M. AGUADO.

Sweden: 13th Floor, Tae-Yang Bldg. 60, 1-ka, Myung-dong, Chongro-ku; *Ambassador:* GUNNAR HECKSCHER.

Switzerland: 32-10 Songwol-dong, Sodaemun-gu; *Ambassador:* PIERRE CUENOUD.

Thailand: House 127, New Itaewon, Yongsan-ku; *Ambassador:* PAYONG CHUTIKUL.

Turkey: 330-294, Sungbuk-dong, Sungbuk-ky; *Ambassador:* MELIH ERCIN.

United Kingdom: 4 Chung-dong, Sudaimum-ku; *Ambassador:* W. S. BATES, C.M.G.

U.S.A.: 82 Sejong-no, Chongno-gu; *Ambassador:* RICHARD L. SNEIDER.

Uruguay: 47-1, Dongbinggo-dong, Yongsan-ku; *Chargé d'Affaires:* JUAN CARLOS PEDEMONTE.

Vatican: 2 Kungjung-dong, Chongno-ku; *Apostolic Pro-Nuncio:* REV. LUIGI DOSSENA.

Venezuela: Tokyo, Japan.

Zaire: Tokyo, Japan.

The Republic of Korea also maintains diplomatic relations with Benin, Cameroon, the Gambia, Guyana, Iceland, Maldives Malta, Mauritius, Pakistan, Qatar, Rwanda, Senegal, Sierra Leone, Uganda and the Upper Volta.

JUDICIAL SYSTEM

Supreme Court: this is the highest court consisting of no more than 16 Justices including the Chief Justice. The Chief Justice is appointed by the President with the consent of the National Assembly for a term of six years. Other Justices of the Supreme Court are appointed for ten years by the President on the recommendation of the Chief Justice. It is empowered to receive and decide on appeals against decisions of the Appellate courts in civil and criminal cases. It is also authorized to act as the final tribunal to review decisions of courts-martial, and to try election cases.

Appellate Courts: three courts situated in Seoul, Taegu and Gwangju with three chief, 20 senior and 50 other judges. Has appellate jurisdiction in civil and criminal cases and can also pass judgment on administrative litigation against government decisions.

District Courts: established in all major cities with 11 chief, 76 senior and 280 other judges. Exercise jurisdiction over all civil and criminal cases in the first instance.

Family Court: there is one Family Court, in Seoul, with a Chief Judge and Judges and Probation Officers. This deals with domestic relations and juvenile delinquency.

Courts-Martial: these exercise jurisdiction over all offences committed by members of the armed forces and their civilian employees. Also authorized to try civilians accused of military espionage or interference with the execution of military duties.

THE SUPREME COURT

Chief Justice: MIN POK-KI.

Justices: HONG SUN-YOP, LEE YONG SOP, CHU CHAE HWANG, HAHN WHAN JIN, AHN BYONG SU, KANG AHN HEE, YIM HANG JUN, LA KIL JO, KIM YONG CHOL, YI IL KYU, KIM YUN HAENG, YI BYONG HO, KIM YOUNG SAE, MIN MOON KEE, YANG BYUNG HO.

Director of Court Administration: KIM BYUNG-HWA.

RELIGION

The traditional religions are Buddhism, Confucianism, Taoism and Chundo Kyo, a religion peculiar to Korea combining elements of Buddhism and Christianity.

RELIGIONS
(as of October 1975)

	Temples or Churches	Priests	Believers
Buddhism .	5,692	19,982	11,972,930
Confucianism .	256	11,944	4,723,493
Protestantism .	16,089	19,066	4,019,313
Roman Catholicism	2,319	3,952	1,012,209
Chundo Kyo .	140	1,629	815,385
Others . .	1,500	8,387	2,732,823

Source: Ministry of Information and Cultural Affairs.

Buddhism: Korean Buddhism has 18 denominations. The Chogye-jong is the largest Buddhist order in Korea being introduced from China in 372 A.D. The Chogye Order accounts for over half the 11,972,930 Korean Buddhists. It has also more than 1,400 out of 5,692 Buddhist temples. Leader The Venerable LEE SO-ONG.

Roman Catholic: Archbishop of Seoul: H.E. Cardinal STEPHEN SOU-HWAN KIM, Archbishop's House, 2-Ga 1, Myong Dong, Chung-gu, Seoul.

Protestant: Anglican Church in Korea: Bishop of Seoul Rt. Rev. PAUL C. LEE, D.D., C.B.E., 3 Chong Dong, Seoul; Bishop of Taejon Rt. Rev. MARK BAE, P.O.B. 22, Taejon; Bishop of Pusan Rt. Rev. WILLIAM CHOI.

THE PRESS

DAILIES*

Chosun Ilbo: 61, 1-ga, Taepyeong-ro 1, Chung-gu, Seoul; f. 1920; morning, weekly and children's editions; independent; circ. (morning edn.) 405,000; Chair. IL-YOUNG BANG; Pres. WOO-YOUNG BANG; Editor KIM YONG-WON.

Dong-A Ilbo (*The Oriental Daily News*): 139 Sechong-ro, Chongno-gu, Seoul; f. 1920; evening; independent; circ. 800,000; Pres. KIM SANG MAN; Editor HONG SEUNG-MYUN.

Hankook Ilbo: 14 Chunghak-dong, Chongno-gu, Seoul; f. 1954; morning; independent; circ. 350,000; Publr. CHANG KANG-JAE; Editor KIM KYUNG-HWAN.

Ilgan Sports (*The Daily Sports*): 14 Chunghak-dong, Chonngo-ku, Seoul; f. 1969; circ. 280,000; Publr. CHANG KANG-JAE; Editor KAE CHANG-HO.

Joong-ang Ilbo: 58-9 Seosomun-dong, Seodaemun-gu, Seoul; f. 1975; evening; Publr. HONG CHIN-GI; Editor CHO DONG-OH.

The Korea Herald: 31, 1-ga, Taepyong-no, Seoul; f. 1953; English; morning; independent; Pres. WON KYUNG-SOO; Editor-in-Chief KIM YONG-SOO.

The Korea Times: 14 Chunghak-dong, Chongno-gu, Seoul; f. 1950; morning; English; independent; circ. 120,000; Publr. CHANG KANG-JAE; Editor CHUNG TAE-YUN.

Kyunghyang Shinmun: 22 Chong-dong, Seoul; f. 1946; evening; independent; circ. 300,000; Publisher HWAN-UI YI; Editor CHI-KEUN CHOI.

Meil Kyung Je Shinmun (*The Daily Economic News*): 50 So Kong Dong, Chungku, Seoul; Publr. and Pres. CHUNG JIN KEE.

Seoul Economic Daily: 14 Chunghak-dong, Chongno-ku, Seoul; Publr. CHANG KANG-JAE.

Seoul Shinmun: 31, 1-ga, Taepyeong-no, Seoul; f. 1945; evening; independent; circ. 320,000; Pres. KIM SHONG-KYU; Man. Ed. JAE HEE NAM.

Shin-A Ilbo: 39-1 Seosomun-dong, Seodaemun-gu, Seoul; f. 1965; evening; Publr. CHANG KI-BONG; Editor LIM SEUNG JUNE.

Sonyon Dong-A: 139 Sechong-ro, Chongno-ku, Seoul; children's; circ. 118,300.

* TOTAL CIRCULATION (1975): 2,346,300 copies.

WEEKLIES

Korean Business Review: 28th Floor, Samilro Bldg., 10 Kwanchul-dong, Chongro-ku, Seoul; organ of the Federation of Korean Industries.

Weekly Chosun: 61 Taepyong-ro 1, Chung-ku, Seoul; circ. (weekly) 170,000 (*see under* Dailies).

The Weekly Hankook: 14 Chunghak-dong, Chongno-ku, Seoul; f. 1964; Editor CHUNG KYONG-HEE; circ. 400,000.

The Women's Weekly: 14 Chunghak-dong, Chongno-ku, Seoul.

SELECTED MONTHLIES

Donghwa News Graphic: 43-1, 1-ga, Pildong, Chung-gu, Seoul; f. 1958; Publisher BAE SANG-MO.

FKTU News: Federation of Korean Trade Unions, 20, Sogong-dong, Chung-gu, Seoul; labour; f. 1958; Publisher LEE CHAN-KYU.

Hyundae Munhak: 136-46 Yunji-dong, Chongno-gu, Seoul; f. 1955; literature; Chief Editor YUN HYUN CHO; circ. 115,000.

Shin Dong-A (*New Far East*): 139 Sejong-ro, Chongno-gu. Seoul; f. 1931; general; Editor YI JUN-WOO; circ. 56,500.

Wolkan Joong-ang (*Monthly Joong-ang*): 58-9 Seosomun-dong, Seodaemun-gu, Seoul.

The Yosong Dong-A (*Women's Far East*): 139 Sejong-ro, Chong-gu. Seoul; f. 1933: women's magazine; Editor YI MUN-HWAN ;circ. 92,000.

NEWS AGENCIES

Hapdong News Agency: 108-4, Susong-dong, Chongno-ku, Seoul; f. 1945; Editor's Press Services and Overseas Commentary Service; Pres. PARK YONG KON; Editor YOO SEUNG-BUM.

Orient Press: 188, Chungjin-dong, Chongno-ku, P.O.B. 1039, Seoul; Pres. HONG SEUNG-HI; Chair. KIM SUNG-KONG; Sen. Man. Dir. YIM CHOL-KYU.

FOREIGN BUREAUX

Agence France-Press (AFP): 188, Chongjin-dong, Chongno-ku, Seoul; Correspondent YU SU-JONG.

ANSA: c/o Orient Press, 135 Namdaimoonro 2/KA; Correspondent KIM KYU WHAN.

AP: 108-4 Susong-dong, Chongro-ku, Seoul; Correspondent K. C. HWANG.

Central News Agency of China: 108-4, Susong-dong, Chongno-ku, Seoul; Correspondent LI TAI-FANG.

Jiji Press: 58-9 Sosomun-dong, Sodaemun-gu, Seoul; Correspondent MORITA HACHIRO.

Kyodo News Service: Kyodonews Seoul, c/o Hapdong News Agency, 108-4 Susong-dong, Chongno-ku, Seoul; Correspondent EJAWA KOJI.

Reuters: 108-4, Susong-dong, Chongno-ku, Seoul; Correspondent YI SI-HO.

United Press International (UPI): 188, Chongjin-dong, Chongno-ku, Seoul; Correspondent KIM CHUN-HWAN.

PRESS ASSOCIATIONS

The Korean Newspapers Association: Room 205, 206 The Press Centre of Korea, 31, 1-ga, Taepyeong-ro, Jung-gu, Seoul; 36 mems.; Pres. KIM CHONG-KYU.

PUBLISHERS

Chang-jo Sa: 92 Sinmunro 2-ka, Chongno-ku, Seoul; Man. Dir. DEOK KYO CHOE.

Dankook University Press: 578-18 Hannam-dong, Yongsan-ku, Seoul.

Dong-A Publishing Co., Ltd.: West Gate, Seoul; f. 1956; Pres. KIM SANG-MOON; Man. Dir. PARK YOUNG-KI; dictionaries, text books, reference books and general.

Eul-yoo Publishing Co.: 46-1 Susong-dong, Chongno-ku, Seoul 110; Man. Dir. CHIN SOOK CHUONG; educational.

Ge Mong Sa: 12-23 Kwangchul-dong, Seoul; Dir. WON DAE KIM; juvenile literature and educational books.

Hak Won Sa: 106 Yangpyung-dong-5 ka, Yeongdeungpo-ku, Seoul; f. 1945; Pres. ICK-TAL KIM; encyclopaedia and general.

Hollym Corporation: 4-5 Kwan Chul-dong, Chongro-ku, Seoul; f. 1963; Man. Dir. YONG WON KIM; fiction, literature, biography, history.

Hwimoon Publishing Co.: 30 Kyunji-dong, Chongro-ku, Seoul; f. 1961; Man. Dir. DONG WON KIM; fiction, biography, history, philosophy, religion.

Hyeon-Am Sa: 66-13 Won Nam-dong, Chongro-ku, Seoul; f. 1951; Man. Dir. CHO SANG WON; history, philosophy.

Il Cho Kak: 9 Gongpyung-dong, Chongno-ku, Seoul; Man. Dir. MANNYUN HAN; educational.

Ilji Sa: 37 Gyueonji-dong, Jongro-gu, Seoul; f. 1956; SEONG JAE GIM; fiction, literature, reference, text books.

Jung Eum Sa: 3-2 Hoehyeon-dong, 1-ka, Chung-ku, Seoul; Man. Dir. YONG HAE CHOE; fiction, literature, travel.

Korea University Press: 1 Anam-dong, Seongbuk-ku, Seoul.

Kyohak Sa: 92 Sunhwa-dong, Soedaemun-ku, Seoul; Man. Dir. CHEOL U YANG; educational.

Minjungseogwan Publishing Co.: 35 Tongeu-dong, Chongro-ku, Seoul; Chair. BYUNG JUN LEE; Pres. NAM-WONU; textbooks, dictionaries and general.

Panmun Book Co.: 40 Chongno 1-ka, Chongno-ku, Seoul; Man. Dir. IK HYUNG LIU.

Sam Joong Dang Publishing Co.: 41-3 Dongja-dong, Chung-ku, Seoul; Man. Dir. JAE SOO SEO.

Se Kwang Publishing Co.: 147 Chongno 3-ka, Chongro-ku, Seoul; f. 1953; Man. Dir. YOON MIN EUN; music.

Seoul National University Press: 139 Dongsung-dong, Chongno-ku, Seoul.

Tamgu Dang Book Centre: 101-1 Kyung woon-dong, Seoul; Pres. HONG SUK-U; Man. Dir. YOH WOON-HAK; history; fine arts, reference, text books.

PUBLISHERS' ASSOCIATION

Korean Publishers' Association: 105-2 Sagan-dong, Chongno-ku, Seoul; f. 1947; Pres. MAN NYUN HAN; Vice-Pres. YUNG BIN MIN, CHONG SUNG MOON; Sec.-Gen. KYUNG HOON LEE; Publs. *The Korean Books Journal* (monthly), *Korean Publication Yearbook*.

RADIO AND TELEVISION

There are 48 radio and 13 television stations, of which the following are the most important:

RADIO

Korean Broadcasting System (KBS): Yejangdong 8, Chung-ku, Seoul; publicly-owned corporation with 16 local broadcasting and 34 relay stations; overseas service in Korean, English, Arabic, Indonesian, Chinese, Japanese, Vietnamese and Russian; Dir.-Gen. HONG KYONG-MO.

Munhwa Broadcasting Corporation (MBC) Network: 22, Chong-dong, Sodaemun-ku, Seoul; station in Seoul and 19 throughout country; Pres. YI HWAN-UI.

Pusan MBC: 2 3-ka, Chungang-dong, Chung-ku, Pusan; Pres. KIM CHONG-SIN.

Taegu MBC: 2-174, Tongsong-ro, Chung-ku, Taegu; Pres. SOL HAN-JUN.

Radio Station HLKX: C.P.O.B. 5255, Seoul; f. 1956; religious, educational station operated by Evangelical Alliance Mission, P.O.B. 969, Wheaton, Ill. 60187, U.S.A.; programmes in Korean, Chinese, Russian, Mongolian and English; Dir. W. S. WINCHELL.

Christian Broadcasting System (CBS): 136-46 Yonchi-dong, Chongno-ku, Seoul; independent religious semi-commercial station with four network stations in Taegu, Pusan, Kwangju and Iri; programmes in Korean; Pres. CHAE KYUNG OH.

Tong-yang Broadcasting Co. (TBC): 8-9 Seosomun-dong, Seoul; commercial; Man. Dir. Kim Duck-Po; Dir. Park Moo Sung.

Dong-A Broadcasting System (DBS): P.O.B. Kwang Hwa Moon 250, 139 Sejong-no, Chongno-ku, Seoul; f. 1963; commercial; Pres. Sang Man Kim; Dir.-Gen. Dong Soo Lee.

American Forces Korea Network: Head Office: Seoul; Mil. Address: A.P.O. San Francisco, 96301, U.S.A.; f. 1950; 7 originating stations and 8 relay stations; broadcasts 24 hours a day; Commanding Officer Lt.-Col. Malcolm G. McDonald; Production Chief Ed Masters.

There are about 4,000,000 radio receivers (1974).

TELEVISION

Korean Broadcasting System (KBS): Yejangdong 8, Chung-ku, Seoul; government corporation; Dir. Hong Kyong-Mo.

Munhwa Broadcasting Corporation (MBC)-TV Network: 22, Chong-dong, Sodaemun-ku, Seoul; station in Seoul and 8 throughout country; Pres. Yi Hwan-Ui.

Pusan MBC-TV: 53-17, 4-ka, Chungang-dong, Chung-ku, Pusan; Pres. Chong Sun-Min.

Taegu MBC-TV: 2-174, Tongsong-ro, Chung-ku, Taegu; Pres. Sol Han-Jun.

Tong-yang Broadcasting Co. Ltd.: (TV-AM-FM): 58-9 Seosomun-dong, Seoul; commercial; Pres. Kim Tuk-po; Exec. Dir. Park Moo-sung.

American Forces Korea Network: Head Office: Seoul; Mil. Address: A.P.O. San Francisco, 96301, U.S.A.; f. 1957; key station in Seoul; 70 hours weekly (*see above*, Radio).

In 1974 there were 1,500,000 receiving sets.

FINANCE

(cap.=capital; p.u.=paid up; dep.=deposits; res.=reserves; m.=million; amounts in won)

BANKING

Central Bank

Bank of Korea: 110, 3-ka, Namdaemun-ro, Chung-ku, Seoul; f. 1950; res. 11,257m. (Dec. 1974); 13 domestic brs., 7 overseas offices; Gov. Kim Sung-Whan; Deputy Gov. Pac Soo Kon; publ. *Annual Report, Review of Korean Economy, Monthly Economic Review*, etc.

National Banks

Choheung Bank: 14, 1-ka, Namdaemun-ro, Chung-ku, Seoul; f. 1897; cap. p.u. 15,000m., dep. 277,101m. (Sept. 1975); Pres. Koh Tai-jin; Exec. Vice-Pres. Lee Kang-Won.

Commercial Bank of Korea: 111-1, 2-ka, Namdaemun-ro, Chung-ku, Seoul; f. 1899; cap. p.u. 12,000m., dep. 245,150m. (Sept. 1974); Pres. Kim Bong-Eun; Vice-Pres. Lee Dong-Soo.

Korea First Bank: 53-1, 1-ga, Chungmu-ro, Jung-gu, Seoul 100; f. 1929; cap. p.u. 15,000m., dep. 287,608m. (July 1975); Pres. Kim Joon Sung; Exec. Vice-Pres. Lee Nam Jin.

Hanil Bank: 130, 2-ka, Namdaemun-ro, Chung-ku, Seoul; f. 1932; cap. p.u. 10,000m., dep. 253,126m. (Sept. 1974); Pres. Yoon Soungdoo; Vice-Pres. Kim Jung-Ho.

Seoul Bank: 116-1, Sokong-dong, Chung-ku, Seoul; f. 1959; cap. p.u. 11,200m., dep. 148,081m. (Sept. 1974); Pres. Kim Young-Duck; Vice-Pres. Lee Young (to merge with Korea Trust Bank in August 1976).

Citizen's National Bank: 9-1, 2-ka, Nandaemun-ro, Chung-ku, Seoul; f. 1962; cap. p.u. 2,500m., dep. 119,395m.; Pres. Suh Jung-Kook; Vice-Pres. Pai Sook.

Korea Development Bank: 140-1, 2-ka, Namdaemun-ro, Chungro-ku, Seoul; f. 1954; cap. p.u. 17,822m., dep. 110,612m.; Gov. Kim Won-Ki; Deputy Gov. Sim Won-Taik.

Korea Exchange Bank: Samilro bldg., 10 Kwanchul-dong, Chong-ku, Seoul; f. 1967; cap. p.u. 30,000m., dep. 264,297m.; Pres. Kim Bong-Eun; Vice-Pres. Hong Wan-Mo

Korea Housing Bank: 61-1, 1-ka, Taepyung-ro, Chung-ku, Seoul; f. 1967; cap. p. u. 6,140m., dep. 36,870m.; Pres. Lee Sang-Duk; Vice-Pres. Park Si-Heun.

Medium Industry Bank: 36-1, 2-ka, Ulchiro, Chung-ku, Seoul; f. 1961; cap. p.u. 3,059m., dep. 111,655m.; Pres. Pae Soo-Kon; Vice-Pres. Kim Won.

Local Banks

Cheju Bank: 1349 Ido-ri, Cheju; f. 1969; cap. p.u. 600m., dep. 7,346m.; Pres. Kim Bong-Hack; Vice-Pres. Kim In-Mook.

Chungbook Bank: 9-3, 1-ka, Bookman-ro, Chung-ju; f. 1971; cap. p.u. 1,000m., dep. 5,600m.; Pres. Kim Jai-Hun; Vice-Pres. Sung Nak-Kyum.

Chungchung Bank: 92 Chung-dong, Taejun; f. 1968; cap. p.u. 600m., dep. 9,062m.; Pres. Kim Jung-Sung; Vice-Pres. Kim Wan-Sub.

Junbook Bank: 1-108, Kyungwan-dong, Junju; f. 1969; cap. p.u. 700m., dep. 6,669m.; Pres. Chai Ju-Hwan; Vice-Pres. Kim Ji-Wan.

Kangwan Bank: 72-3, Unkyo-dong, Chunchon; f. 1970; cap. p.u. 600m., dep. 5,063m.; Pres. Jang Kwan-Sick; Vice-Pres. Chai Jai-Sun.

Kwangju Bank: 6, 3-ka, Chungjang-ro, Dong-ku Kwangju; f. 1968; cap. p.u. 700m., dep. 10,111m.; Pres. Jin Kang-Hyun; Vice-Pres. Son Sung-Nam.

Kyungki Bank: 9-1, Sa-dong, Chung-ku, Inchon; f. 1969; cap. p.u. 2,000m., dep. 27,523m.; Pres. Yoo Je-Kook; Vice-Pres. Kim Jin-Hwan.

Kyungnam Bank: 172, Chang-dong, Masan; f. 1970; cap. p.u. 1,000m., dep. 12,214m.; Pres. Choi Hi-Yul; Vice-Pres. Yoo Sang-Won.

Pusan Bank: 8, 1-ka, Sinchang-dong, Chung-ku, Pusan; f. 1967; cap. p.u. 8,100m., dep. 70,877m.; Pres. Suh Jai-Sick; Vice-Pres. Park Jang-Kil.

Taegu Bank: 20-3, Namil-dong, Chung-ku, Taegu; f. 1967; cap. p.u. 6,000m., dep. 37,055m.; Pres. Kim Jung-Sung; Vice-Pres. Nam Ok-Hyun.

Association

Bankers' Association of Korea: 4, 1-ka, Myung-dong, Chung-ku, Seoul; mems. 13 financial institutions; Chair. Kim Sung-Whan (Gov. Bank of Korea); Sec.-Gen. Song Se-Keun.

Foreign Banks

Central Trust of China: Head Office: Taiwan; Seoul Office C.P.O. 361, Seoul; Rep. Joel H. H. Wang.

Chartered Bank: Samsung Building, 50 1-ka, Ulchiro, Choong-ku, Seoul; P.O. Box Kwangwhamun 259, Seoul; Man. H. H. LILLER.

Chase Manhattan Bank, N.A.: New York; Seoul Branch: 50, 1-ka, Ulchiro, Choong-ku, C.P.O. Box 2249; Vice-Pres. and Man. VICTOR J. REIZMAN.

Dai-Ichi Kangyo Bank Ltd.: Kal Bldg., No. 502, 118, 2-ka, Namdaemun-ro, Chung-ku, Seoul.

Bank of Tokyo: 6, 1-chome, Nihombashi Hongokucho, Chuo-ku, Tokyo, Japan; Seoul.

First National City Bank: 28, Sokong-dong, Chung-ku, and 8 1-ka, Shinchang-dong, Chung-ku, Pusan, Seoul.

Mitsubishi Bank Ltd.: 188-3, 1-Ka, Ulchiro, Chung-ku, Seoul; f. 1967; Man. TAKEO FUNABASHI.

DEVELOPMENT AGENCY

Korea Development Finance Corporation: 12th Floor, The Cho Heung Bank Bldg., 14, Namdaemun-ro 1-ka, Chung-ku, Seoul; f. 1967; assists in the development of private enterprise by medium- and long-term financing including loans, guarantees and purchase of equities; cap. p.u. 3,000m. won; Chair. HONG CHAI-SUN; Pres. KIM CHIN -HYUNG.

INSURANCE

PRINCIPAL COMPANIES

Ankuk Fire and Marine Insurance Co. Ltd.: 50, 1-ka, Ulchi-ro, Chung-ku, Seoul; P.O.B. 469; f. 1952; Pres. YUNG KI SOHN; Man. Dir. KYUNG SHIK SOHN.

Dae Han Fire and Marine Insurance Co. Ltd.: 75 Susomun-dong, Sudaemun-ku, Seoul; f. 1946; premium income (1971-72) 1,070m. won, res. 1,023m. won; (Dec. 1971) Pres. CHI BOK KIM; Vice-Pres. BONG IK LEE.

Dai Han Life Insurance Co.: P.O.B. 290, Seoul; f. 1946; Gen. Man. CHANG HO IM.

Eastern Marine and Fire Insurance Co., The: 8-1 Namdaemun-ro, 2-ka Chung-ku, Seoul; f. 1955; Pres. CHUN KYU CHOI.

First Fire and Marine Insurance Co. Ltd., The: 18, 1-ga, Namdaemoon-ro, Chung-ku, C.P.O. Box 530, Seoul; f. 1949; Pres. YE CHUL LEE.

Haedong Fire and Marine Insurance Co. Ltd.: 199-50, 2-ka, Ulchi-ro, Choong-ku, Seoul; f. 1953; Pres. DONG MAN KIM; Exec. Man. Dir. HYOIL KIM.

Korean Reinsurance Corporation: C.P.O. Box 1438, Seoul; f. 1963; auth. cap. 3,000m. won; Pres. YANG-HO LEE; Vice-Pres. CHONG-CHIN LEE.

Koryo Fire and Marine Insurance Co. Ltd.: 84-8, 2-ka, Chong-ro, Chongro-ku, Seoul; f. 1948; auth. cap. 500m. won; Pres. WOO-POONG LEE; Man. Dir. YOON-BOK LEE.

Oriental Fire and Marine Insurance Co. Ltd.: 19, 1-ka, Tae Pyong-ro, Chung-ku, P.O.B. 230, Kwanghwamoon, Seoul; f. 1922; cap. p.u. 1,000m. won (1972); Chair. CHOONG HOON CHO; Pres. IN WAN CHUNG.

Pan Korea Insurance Co.: 77 Sokong-dong, Chung-ku, Seoul; f. 1959; premium income U.S. $12,372m., res. U.S. $3,120,000; Pres. TAE HO CHO; Man. Dir. KYO SUN KIM.

Shindong-A Fire and Marine Insurance Co. Ltd.: 43, 2-ka, Taepyung-ro, Chung-ku, Seoul; f. 1946; premium income U.S. $8,000,000, res. U.S. $4,147,000 (1974); Chair. SANG BOK KIM; Pres. SOON JIP AHN.

TRADE AND INDUSTRY

CHAMBERS OF COMMERCE AND INDUSTRY

Korea Chamber of Commerce and Industry: 111 Sokong-dong, Choong-ku, Seoul; f. 1894; total mems. over 200,000; 37 local chambers; promotes modernization of industry and stimulates regional trade and investment; Pres. SUNG KON KIM; publs. *Korean Business Directory, K.C.C.I. News, Chamber Review.*

Gwangju Chamber of Commerce and Industry: 7, 2-ka, Kumnam-dong, Gwangju, Chunnam Province.

Inchon Chamber of Commerce and Industry: 3, 3-ka, Songhak-dong, Inchon, Kyonggi Province.

Jeonju Chamber of Commerce and Industry: 80, 3-ka Chungang-dong, Jeonju, Chunbuk Province.

Masan Chamber of Commerce and Industry: 4, 1-ka, Chungang-dong, Masan, Kyoungnam Province.

Pusan Chamber of Commerce and Industry: 36, 2-ka, Daegyo-dong, Jung-gu, Pusan; f. 1888; 1,830 mems.; Pres. SUK-CHIN KANG; Exec. Vice-Pres. BUM-SOO AHN.

Taegu Chamber of Commerce and Industry: 197 Sinchun-Dong, Taegu; f. 1904; about 30,000 mems.; Pres. IL YONG OH; Exec. Vice-Pres. JONG WANG LEE; publs. *Review of Taegu Economy* (monthly).

Taejon Chamber of Commerce and Industry: 142-2 Eun Haeng Dong, Taejon; f. 1933; 8,000 mems.; Pres. KWANG PYO HONG; Vice-Pres. BONG SEOK YANG, DEOK YUNG SONG; publ. *Taejeon Sang Gong* (monthly).

FOREIGN TRADE ORGANIZATIONS

Korea Export Industrial Corporation: 188-5 Kuro-dong Youngdungpo-ku, Seoul; f. 1964; encourages industrial exports, provides assistance and operating capital, market surveys; Chair. CHOI MYUNG-HUN.

Korean Trade Promotion Corporation (KOTRA): 10-1, 2-ka, Huehyun-dong, Chung-gu, Seoul; f. 1962; Pres. AHN KWANG HO; publs. *Korean Trade, Korean Trade and Investment.*

Korea Cotton Textiles Export Association: 131, Da-dong, Chung-ku, Seoul; f. 1965; overseas br. Brussels; Pres. KIM YONG-JOO.

Korea Electronic Products Exporters Association: 10-1, 2-ka, Hoehyun-dong, Chung-ku, Seoul; f. 1970; mems. 128 companies; Chair. PARK SUNG-CHAN.

Korean Hair Goods Export Association: 12-14, Kwanchul-dong, Chongro-ku, Seoul; f. 1966; Pres. SUH JANG-UIK.

Korean Knitted Goods Exporters Association: 10-1, 2-ka, Hoehyun-dong, Chung-ku, Seoul; f. 1965; overseas brs. New York, Rotterdam; Pres. KIM YONG-SUN.

INDUSTRIAL ORGANIZATIONS

Agriculture and Fishery Development Corporation—AFDC: 13-8 Noryangjin-dong, Kwanak-ku, Seoul, C.P.O. Box 3212; f. 1967 to develop principal producing areas for various agricultural and fisheries produce, to develop and encourage processing, preservation and marketing of such products and to cement links among activities relating to the production, processing, preservation, marketing and consumption of such goods; thereby to elevate income levels of farming and fishing communities; principal exports: canned mushroom, oysters, tomato juice, white peaches, tobacco, silk; cap. U.S. $20m.; Pres. JUNG OH-KIM; Exec. Vice-Pres. CHAI KWAN SHIK.

Federation of Korean Industries: 28th Floor, Samilro Bldg., 10 Kwanchul-dong, Chongro-ku, Seoul; f. 1961; conducts research and survey work on domestic and overseas economic conditions and trends; makes recommendations on important economic matters to the government and other interested parties; exchange of economic and trade missions with other countries with a view to exploring markets and fostering economic co-operation; sponsoring of regular business conferences with friendly countries; mems. 228 companies and 54 business asscns.; Pres. KIM YONG-WAN; Exec. Vice-Pres. IP SAM KIM; Dir.-Gen. TAI YEOP YOON; Sec.-Gen. NEUNG SUN YOON; publs. *Kyong Hyup* (monthly), *Korean Business Review* (every two months), *Federation of Korean Industries* (annual), *Korean Economic Yearbook*, *FKI Bulletin* (weekly), *FKI Membership directory* (annual), *Korean Economic Yearbook* (annual).

Korean Development Association: 340, 2-ka, Taepyeong-ro Jung-gu, Seoul; f. 1965; economic research; mems. 38 companies; Pres. KWON TACK-SANG.

Korea Productivity Centre: 10, 2-ka, Pil-tong, Chung-gu, Seoul; f. 1957; business consultancy services, economic research; mems. 173 companies; Pres. EUN BOK RHEE; Chair. SUK CHUN LIM; publ. *Journal* (monthly).

Korea Traders Association: 10-1, 2-ka, Hoehyon-dong, Chung-gu, Seoul; f. 1946; Pres. CHOONG HOON PARK; Vice-Pres. POM SIK OH; publs. *Korean Trade News* (daily), *Korean Trade Directory* (annual).

Construction Association of Korea: 31-23, 1-ka, Taepyung-ro, Chung-ku, Seoul; f. 1959; national licensed contractors' association; mems. 650 companies; Pres. CHOI CHONG-WHAN.

Daehan Coalmines Association: 1-27, Soopyo-dong, Chung-ku, Seoul; f. 1949; Pres. WOO SUNG-WHAN.

Korea Electronic Industries Association: 163, 2-ka, Ulchiro, Chung-ku, Seoul; f. 1967; Pres. PARK SUNG-CHAN.

Korea Food Industry Association Inc.: 59-23, 3-ka, Chungmuro, Chung-ku, Seoul; f. 1969; mems. 21 companies; Pres. CHUN JOONG-YOON.

Korea Petroleum Association: 59-23, 3-ka, Chungmu-ro' Chung-ku, Seoul; f. 1956; mems. 78 companies; Chair. PARK MAN-HI.

Korea Sericultural Association: 15-1, Kwanchul-dong, Chongro-ku, Seoul; improvement research and promotion of sericulture; Pres. LEE WON-YOUNG.

Korea Shipowners Association: 10-3, Buckchang-dong, Chung-ku, Seoul; f. 1960; mems. 337 companies; Pres. CHU YO-HAN.

Korea Steelmakers Association: 11th Fl., Ankuk Bldg., 175-87 Ankuk-dong, Chongro-ku, Seoul; f. 1963; Pres. CHUN SUN-HAN.

Mining Association of Korea: 35-24, Tongui-dong, Chongru-ku, Seoul; f. 1918; mems. 219 companies; Pres. HWANG KY-RYONG.

Spinners' and Weavers' Association of Korea: 43-8 Kwanchul-dong, Chongro-ku, Seoul; f. 1947; Pres. BAI DUCK-JIN.

CO-OPERATIVES

National Agricultural Co-operative Federation (N.A.C.F.): 75, 1-ka, Chunjung-ro, Sudaemun-ku, Seoul; f. 1961; purchase, supply, marketing, utilization and processing, mutual insurance, banking and credit services, education and guidance, research and surveys, international co-operation. Pres. YOUN HWAN KIM; Vice-Pres. SANG KYUM KO; cap. 2,800 million won (Dec. 1971); publs. *Agricultural Yearbook*, *Agricultural Co-operative Monthly Survey*, *New Farmer* (monthly), *Marketing of Agriculture Products*.

Central Federation of Fisheries Co-operatives: 88, Kyeongun-dong, Chongro-ku, Seoul; f. 1962; Pres. CHANG DUK HEE.

Federation of Korea Knitting Industry Co-operatives: 48, 1-ka, Shinmun-ro, Chongro-ku, Seoul; f. 1960; Pres. KI SANG-DO.

Korea Woollen Spinners and Weavers Co-operative: 11-3, Kwanchul-dong, Chongro-ku, Seoul; f. 1964; Pres. SOHN TAI-GON.

National Federation of Medium Industry Co-operatives: 138-1, Kongpyong-dong, Chongro-ku, Seoul; f. 1962; Chair. KIM BONG-JAI; Vice-Chair. YONGWOON WON; publ. *Medium Industry News*.

EMPLOYERS' ASSOCIATION

The Korean Employers' Association: 10, Kwanchul-dong, Chongro-ku, Seoul; f. 1970; Pres. KIM YONG-JOO.

TRADE UNIONS

Federation of Korean Trade Unions (F.K.T.U.): 20 Sokong-dong, Chung-ku, Seoul; f. 1946; Pres. BAE SANG HO; Gen. Sec. PARK YOUNG SUNG; 17 unions are affiliated with a membership of 630,374 (June 1974); affiliated to ICFTU; publ. *FKTU News* (monthly); major affiliated unions are:

National Auto Workers' Union: 213 Ulchiro 5-ka, Chung-ku, Seoul; Pres. SON CHANG SOO; 99,043 mems.

National Chemical Workers' Union: Seoul; Pres. CHUNG DONG HO; 62,856 mems.

National Dock Workers' Union: 2-5, Dodong 1-ka, Chung-ku, Seoul; Pres. CHUNG HAN JOO; 19,658 mems.

National Mine Workers' Union: 15-8, Pildong 2-ka, Chung-ku, Seoul; Pres. HAN KEE SOO; 37,987 mems.

National Printing Workers' Union: 20 Sokong-dong, Chung-ku, Seoul; Pres. KIM SANG KON; 5,204 mems.

National Railway Workers' Union: 40, 3-ka, Hangkang-ro, Yongsan-ku, Seoul; Pres. CHO MYUNG HYUN; 33,157.

National Seamens' Union: 15 Tongkwang-dong 2-ka, Pusan; Pres. HONG GUN PYO; 56,012 mems.

National Textile Workers' Union: 60 Myong-dong, Chung-ku, Seoul; Pres. BANG SOON CHO; 87,230 mems.

MAJOR INDUSTRIAL COMPANIES

The following are some of Korea's major industrial companies, arranged by sector:

CEMENT

Asia Cement Manufacturing Co. Ltd.: 75 Seosomoon-dong, Chung-ku, Seoul; f. 1957; cap. p.u. 3,102m. won; manufactures and exports Portland cement, clinker, construction materials, plywood, miscellaneous garments etc.; Pres. LEE BYUNG MOON; Man. Dir. LEE BYUNG MOO; employees: 704.

Hanil Cement Manufacturing Co. Ltd.: 64-5, 2-ka, Chungmu-ro, Chung-ku, Seoul, Korea; f. 1961; cap. 1.53m. won; sells and exports Portland cement with an annual capacity of one million tons; Pres. HUH CHAE-KYUNG; Vice-Pres. LEE JOON-GIU; employees: 557.

Hyundai Cement Co. Ltd.: 157 Sejong-ro, Chongro-ku, Seoul; f. 1964; manufacture of Portland cement and various building materials; Pres. CHUNG SUN YUNG.

Korea Cement Manufacturing Co. Ltd.: 112-5 Sogong-dong, Chung-ku, Seoul; f. 1956; cap. p.u. 1,000m. won; manufactures and sells Portland cement (annual capacity of 500,000 tons), ready-mixed concrete and pulp and asbestos boards (annual capacity 6 million sheets); Pres. SANG-SOON LEE; Vice-Pres. SI-DONG YOO; employees: 925.

Ssangyong Cement Industrial Co. Ltd.: 24, 2-ka, Zuh-dong, Chung-ku, Seoul; f. 1962; cement manufacturers; mine excavating, exporting and importing, civil engineering; Pres. CHIN BONG-HYUN.

CHEMICALS AND FERTILIZERS

Chinhae Chemical Co. Ltd.: 61-3, 2-ka, Chungmu-ro, Chung-ku, Seoul; f. 1965; cap. p.u. U.S. $50m.; manufacturers of urea and various NPK complex fertilizers with annual production capacity of about 300,000 tons; Pres. CHOI SE-IN; Exec. Vice-Pres. M. A. LEWANDEWSKI; employees: 700.

Honam Fertilizer Co. Ltd.: 199-63, 2-ka, Ulchi-ro, Chung-ku, Seoul; f. 1955; manufacturers of fertilizers and chemicals; Rep. YUN GUN KIM.

Korea Explosives Co. Ltd.: 12-1, Seosomun-dong, Seodaemun-ku, Seoul; f. 1952; manufacturers of dynamite and other explosives, safety fuses, electric detonators, mineral products and chemicals; Pres. CHONG HEE KIM.

Korea Petrochemical Industrial Co. Ltd.: 95-1, 3-ka, Namdaemoon-ro, Seoul; f. 1970; cap. p.u. U.S. $8,300,000; manufacturers of polypropylene resin with an annual capacity of 45,000 metric tons, and related products; Pres. LEE CHUNG-NIM; Exec. Vice-Pres. K. ISHINABE; employees: 185.

Lucky, Ltd.: 18th and 19th Floor, Dae Woo Bldg., 3-106, 1-ka, Jung-ku, Do-dong, Seoul; f. 1947; manufacturers and exporters of chemical goods, food and food additions, synthetic detergent, fats and oils; Pres. SHIN KOO HUH.

Tong Shin Chemical Products Co. Ltd.: 601 Shiheung-dong, Yongdungpo-ku, Seoul, f. 1935; manufacturers of rubber products, zinc ingots; Rep. SU DUCK HYUN.

ELECTRICAL AND ELECTRONICS

Gold Star Co. Ltd.: Lucky Bldg., 282 Yang-dong, Chung-ku, Seoul (International P.O.B. 2530, Seoul); f. 1958; cap. p.u. U.S. $7m.; manufacturing, import and export of electrical appliances and communication equipment; Chair. KOO CHA-KYUNG; Pres. PARK SUNG-CHAN; employees: 8,000.

Hanyung Industrial Co. Ltd.: 4 Dangsan-dong, 5-ka, Yondungpo-ku, Seoul; f. 1962; cap. p.u. U.S. $8m. (3,200m. won); manufacturers of electrical apparatus, transformers, motors, pumps; Pres. HEUNG MAN CHO; Vice-Pres. GUN CHUL SHIN; employees: 810.

Samsung Electronics Co. Ltd.: 416 Maetan-dong, Suwon, Gyunggi-do, Seoul; f. 1969; cap. p.u. U.S. $5m.; manufacturers wide range of electronic goods, including TV, radio, calculators, tape recorders, refrigerators; Pres. HOON CHULL SHIN; employees: 2,500.

POWER AND TRANSPORT

Hanjin Transportation Co. Ltd.: 118, 2-ka, Namdaemun-ro, Chung-ku, Seoul; f. 1945; transporting and stevedoring; Rep. CHO CHOONG-HOON.

Hyundai International Inc.: 115, Samkag-dong, Chung-ku, Seoul; f. 1962; exporters and importers, world-wide tramp service, manufacture of automobile parts and building materials; Rep. CHUNG IN YUNG.

Hyundai Motor Co.: 55-4 Suhsomun-dong, Suhdaemun-ku, Seoul; f. 1967; assembling and manufacture of Ford cars, trucks and buses; Rep. CHUNG SE YUNG.

Korea Electric Company: 5, 2-ka, Namdaemun-ro, Chung-ku, Seoul; f. 1961; cap. U.S. $205.38m. (63,668m. won); generation, transmission and distribution of electric power, and development of electric power sources; output: 7,740 kWh. sold in 1970; Pres. KIM JAI-HUYN; employees: 12,021.

Shinjin Motor Co. Ltd.: 62-10, 2-ka, Chungmu-ro, Chung-ku, Seoul; f. 1955; manufactures buses, jeeps and parts; Pres. KIM CHANG-WON.

TEXTILES, SILK AND SYNTHETIC FIBRES

Cheil Wool Textile Industrial Co. Ltd.: 50, 1-ka, Eulji-ro, Chung-ku, Seoul; f. 1954; production of worsted and spun synthetic fibres; import and export; Chair. CHO WOO DONG.

Chonbang Co. Ltd.: 42 Changgyo-dong, Chung-ku, Seoul; f. 1952; manufacturers of cotton and blended yarns and fabrics; garments; Pres. KIM CHANG-SUNG.

Daewoo Industrial Co. Ltd.: 3-60, 1-ka, Do-dong, Chung-ku, Seoul; f. 1967; manufacture of clothes, sporting and leather goods; Pres. KIM WOO-CHONG.

Dainong Co. Ltd.: Chinyang Building 125-1, 4-ka, Chungmu-ro, Chung-ku, Seoul f. 1955; manufacturers of cotton and synthetic fibre products; import and export; Pres. PARK YONG-HAK.

Hanil Synthetic Fibre Ind. Co. Ltd.: 58-7 Suhsomun dong, Sudaemun-ku, Seoul; f. 1964; manufacturers and exporters of synthetic fibre; Pres. KIM HAN-SOO.

Ilshin Spinning Co. Ltd.: 75 Suhsomun dong, Sudaemun-ku, Seoul, Korea; f. 1961; cap. 600m. won; cotton spinning and production of yarn and fabrics; one subsidiary company in Korea with dyeing and finishing factories; import and export; Chair. HYUNG N. KIM; Pres. CHANG H. KIM; employees: 2,500.

Keumsung Textile Co. Ltd.: 130, 3-ka, Chongro, Chongro-ku, Seoul; f. 1948; manufacturers of cotton products and man-made fibres; Rep. YONG HARK PARK.

Korea Nylon Company Ltd.: 35-34 Tongeu-dong, Chongro-ku, Seoul; f. 1957; manufacturers of nylon filament yarn; Rep. WON CHUN LEE.

Korea Silk Co. Ltd.: 118, 2-ka, Namdaemun-ro, Chung-ku, Seoul; f. 1946; manufacturers of raw silk, silk and synthetic fabrics, rubber, leather, canvas and vinyl shoes, boots and sandals; Pres. KIM YOUNG-WOO.

Sun Kyong Ltd.: 65-7, Kyunji-dong, Changro-ku, Seoul; f. 1956; weaving, dyeing, texturing and finishing of polyester fabrics; import and export; Pres. CHOI MOO-HYUN.

Tae Kwang Industrial Co. Ltd.: 90 Koosuh-dong, Dongnae-ku, Pusan; f. 1961; cap. p.u. U.S. $4m.; manufacturers, exporters and importers of fabrics, blankets, Acrylic yarns and fibres; Pres. YONG LEE EAM; Man. Dir. YUN PARK KYUNG; employees: 4,000.

MISCELLANEOUS

Boo-Kook Steel and Wire Co. Ltd.: 1179 Hwamyung-dong, Pusanjin-ku, Pusan, P.O.B. 277; f. 1956; cap. p.u. U.S. $3m.; manufacturers and exporters of high carbon steel wire, steel wire rope, aircraft cable etc. with monthly production capacity of 2,000 tons; Pres. KIM HYUN TAI; Man. Dir. KIM YOUNG SOO; employees: 700.

Chunusa Co. Ltd.: 81 Sokong-dong, Chung-ku, Seoul; f. 1947; exporters, importers and marine transportation services; deal in electronic goods and clothing; etc.; CHUN TAIK-BO.

Dae Lim Industrial Co. Ltd.: 14-26, Dongja-dong, Yongsan-ku, Seoul; f. 1939; general contractor for all construction fields, engineering. Pres. JOUNG IK LEE.

Dai Han Coal Corporation: International P.O. Box 1057, Seoul; f. 1950; 13,789 mems.; Gov. KIM HYO-YONG.

Donkguk Steel Mill Co. Ltd.: 135-1, 2-ka, Namdaemun-ro, Chung-ku, Seoul; f. 1954; manufactures iron and steel; Pres. CHANG SANG-TAI.

Hanil Development Co. Ltd.: 118, 2-ka, Namdaemun-ro, Chung-ku, Seoul; f. 1968; construction, electrical work, mining, gas and petroleum transport; Pres. TAE CHANG-HEE.

Hankuk Glass Industry Co. Ltd.: 75 Suhsomun-dong, Sudaemun-ku, Seoul; f. 1957; cap. U.S. $2.4m. (650m. won); manufacturers of flat glass, figured glass and tube glass, Seoul and Pusan; output: U.S. $6.18m. (including exports); one subsidiary company in Korea; Pres. CHOI TAI-SUP; employees: 900.

Hyundai Construction Co. Ltd.: 178 Sejong-ro, Chongro-ku, Seoul; f. 1950; design and construction of industrial plants, power plants, water resources development, highways, bridges, tunnels, railways, subways, building, dredging, harbour development, airports and steel fabrication, shipbuilding and repairing, manufacture and sale of ship products; Pres. CHUNG-IN YUNG.

Inchon Heavy Industry Co. Ltd.: 16, 1-ka, Ulchi-ro, Chung-ku, Seoul; f. 1962; manufacturers of steel goods; Rep. DONG CHOON LEE.

Inchon Iron and Steel Co. Ltd.: 1-1, Songhyun-dong, Dong-ku, Inchon; f. 1964; manufactures iron and steel products; Pres. SONG YO-CHAN.

Keang Nam Enterprises Ltd.: 151, 2-ka, Inhyun-dong, Chung-ku, Seoul; f. 1951; construction, marine and land transport, vehicle maintenance, labour service, manufacture of souvenirs; Pres. CHEUHG WON-SUNG.

Korea Marine Industry Development Corporation: Baeje Bldg., 55-4 Sursomoon-dong, Chung-ku, Seoul; f. 1963; cap. p.u. U.S. $2,653,402; owns and operates 163 fishing boats engaged in deep-sea fishing (tuna) with annual catches of about 68,701 metric tons; Pres. YUN GUN KIM; Man. Dir. SOO JONG KIM; employees: 2,989.

Korea Shipbuilding and Engineering Corporation: 55-4 Susomun-dong, Sudaemun-ku, I.P.O.B. 1520, Seoul; f. 1937; private; Korea's major shipbuilder, yards at Busan and Okpo; vessels up to 1m. D.W.T., steel structures, rolling stock; Pres. RYUN NAMKOONG; Man. Dir. STEPHEN S. K. KIM.

Kumyang Trading Co. Ltd.: Central P.O.B. 160, 93-33 Bookchang-dong, Chung-ku, Seoul; f. 1959; cap. U.S. $1m.; manufacturers of socks, exporters and importers; Pres. KIM CHO SOON; Dir. JIN YOUNG SIK; employees: 489.

Lotte Moolsan Co. Ltd.: 25-5, Chungmu-ro, Chung-ku, Seoul; f. 1968; manufactures aluminium foil, import and export; Pres. SHIN KYUK-HO.

Oriental Brewery Co. Ltd.: 13, 4-ka, Chongro, Chongro-ku, Seoul; f. 1952; cap. p.u. 3,000m. won; manufacturers and exporters of beer; Pres. SOOCHANG CHUNG; employees: 780.

Taihan Electric Wire Co. Ltd.: 84-18, 5-ka, Namdaemun-ro, Chung-ku, Seoul; f. 1937; manufacturers of electric wires and cables; Pres. SULL WON-RYANG.

Whashin Industrial Co. Ltd.: 21-9 Cho-dong, Chung-ku, Seoul; f. 1926; cap. 2,000m. won; exporters, importers, domestic sales of textiles, electrical consumer products, commercial air-conditioning equipment and other merchandise; 8 subsidiary companies; Pres. HEUNG-SIK PARK; Vice-Pres. JOONG-KIL KIM; employees 5,500.

TRANSPORT

RAILWAYS

Korean National Railroad: Head Office: 3, 1-ka, Doding, Chung-gu, Seoul; f. 1963; operates, as a separate entity under the Ministry of Transportation, all railways and railway repair shops in the Republic of Korea: total route mileage of 5,541 km. (1973); Dir-Gen. YONG LEE; Deputy Dir.-Gen. JONG HYOK YOON.

Seoul Rapid Transit: Metropolitan Rapid Transit Construction Bureau, Seoul; work in progress since 1971 on 10 km. rapid transit line; Dir. MYUNG NYUN KIM.

ROADS

In 1973 there were about 43,581 kilometres of roads of which 7,820 were paved. A network of motorways (1,013 km. in 1973) links all the principal towns, the most important being the 428 km. Seoul-Pusan motorway. Further highways in Yeongdong and Donghae are under construction.

Korea Highway Corporation: 3-106, 1-ka, Do-dong, Choong-ku, Seoul; f. 1969; responsible for construction and maintenance of toll roads; Pres. KI SUK PARK; Exec. Vice-Pres. KWANG SUP YIM.

SHIPPING

Office of Marine Affairs: Seoul; f. 1955; supervises all branches of shipping. Chief ports: Pusan, Inchun, Mookmo, Masan, Yusoo, Goonsan. Ships of U.S., British, Japanese, Dutch and Norwegian lines call at the principal ports.

Far Eastern Marine Transport Co. Ltd.: 55-4, Sosomun-dong, Sodaemun-ku, Seoul; f. 1952; 5 cargo vessels; Pres. RYUN NAMKOONG.

Korea Shipping Corporation Ltd.: Daehan Ilbo Building, 340, 2-ka Taepyung-ro, Seoul (P.O.B. International 1164); f. 1950; 21 cargo vessels; world-wide transportation service and shipping agency service in Korea; Pres. CHU YO-HAN; Vice-Pres. SEH HYUCK RYU.

Korea United Lines, Inc.: 50-10, 2-ka, Chungmu-ro, Chung-ku, Seoul; f. 1967; world-wide transportation with bulk carriers; Pres. LEE CHUNG-NIM.

Pan Ocean Bulk Carriers Ltd.: Daehan Bldg., 75 Seosomun-dong, Seoul; f. 1965; 8 tankers; transportation of petroleum products; Pres. K. S. PARK; Man. Dir. Capt. H. H. PARK.

Samyang Navigation Co. Ltd.: 32-2, Mukyo-dong, Chung-ku, Seoul; f. 1966; 3 tankers; Chair. HAN BYUNG-KI.

CIVIL AVIATION

Korean Air Lines: P.O.B. 864 Central, Seoul; KAL Bldg., No. 114, 2-ka Namdaemun-ro, Chung-ku, Seoul; f. 1962 by the Korean Government; transferred 1969 to the *Hanjin Group*; the only scheduled airline in the Republic of Korea, serves 10 major domestic cities and flies to Tokyo, Fukuoka, Osaka, Taipei, Hong Kong, Bangkok, Manila, Singapore, Honolulu, Los Angeles, Paris and Zurich; Pres. CHOONG HOON CHO; fleet: 5 Fokker F-27, 4 B-707/320C, 1 DC-8, 3 B-727, 1 YS-11, 1 B-747F, 2 B-747B, 2 707-720, 3 DC-10, 3 A-300B.

The following foreign airlines also serve Seoul: Cathay Pacific Airways, China Airlines, Japan Air Lines, Northwest Orient Airlines, Singapore Airlines, Flying Tiger.

TOURISM

Korea Tourist Association: room 502, Hanil Bldg., 132-4, 1-ka, Bongrae-dong, Chung-ku, Seoul; f. 1963; federation of travel enterprises including major hotels, restaurants, travel agents and tourist shops; publishes and distributes travel literature; Pres. JWAH KYUM KIM.

Korea Tourist Bureau (KTB): 9th Floor, Hotel Koreana. 61 Taepyongno, 1-ka, C.P.O. Box 3533; f. 1912; Chair, KUKWHAN SUL; Pres. BONKEUN KOO.

ATOMIC ENERGY

Korea's first atomic power plant at Gori is scheduled to go into operation in 1977 with a generating capacity of 595 mW. There are further plans to build an atomic power plant each year after 1979.

Atomic Energy Commission: Ministry of Science and Technology, Seoul 110; nine members; Minister and Vice-Minister of Science and Technology become chairman and vice-chairman respectively; responsible for fundamental plans and policies, furtherance of research and training of personnel; Chair. CHOI HYUNG SUP; Vice-Chair. LEE CHANG SUK.

Atomic Energy Bureau: Ministry of Science and Technology, Seoul 110; f. 1973; administrative agency with three divisions; Planning, Radiation Safety and Nuclear Reactor; Dir. LEE BYOUNG WHIE.

Korea Atomic Energy Research Institute: P.O.B. 7, Cheong Ryang, Seoul; f. 1973, incorporating Atomic Energy Research Institute, Radiological Research Institute, and Radiation Agriculture Research Institute; responsible for management, control, development, production and utilization of nuclear energy, environmental and cancer research; Triga Mark II (100 kW.) and Triga Mark III (2 mW.) reactors; Pres. YOON YOUNG KU; Vice-Pres. CHOO CHAI YANG.

Korea Atomic Industrial Forum: f. 1972; Chair. CHU CHANG KYUN; Dir.-Gen. PARK IK-SOO.

DEFENCE

Armed Forces: Total strength 625,000; army 560,000, navy 20,000 and a marine corps of 20,000, air force 25,000. There are also para-military forces, i.e. a local defence militia, the Homeland Reserve Defence Force totalling about 2 million.

Equipment: The army is equipped with American material including medium and heavy tanks; armoured personnel carriers and armoured cars; up to 203mm. guns and surface-to-surface and surface-to-air missiles. The navy has mostly destroyers, frigates, landing ships, patrol boats and other escort and coastal vessels. The air force has 216 combat aircraft, some equipped with missiles. The last remaining contingent of ROK troops, numbering 37,000, were withdrawn from South Viet-Nam in December 1972. About 43,000 U.S. personnel are based in South Korea and five-year programme costing $4.83 million to modernize army barracks and to renew and renovate air bases there was announced by President Nixon in July 1972.

Military Service: Army/Marines, 2½ years; Navy and Air Force 3 years.

Defence Expenditure: Estimated defence spending for 1975 was 353,100 million won ($719 million).

Joint Chief of Staff: Gen. HAN SHIN.

Chief of Staff ROK Army: Gen. ROH JAE-HYEN.

Chief of Staff Air Force: Gen. OK MAN-HO.

Chief of Naval Operations: Adm. KIM SANG-KILL.

Commanding General of the Marines: Gen. LEE BYONG-MOON.

EDUCATION

During the second half of the nineteenth century western ideas and education were introduced into Korea by foreign missionaries, who established many modern schools. Under the influence of these new ideas as well as the internal development caused by social changes, the government adopted a more modern education system, and after 1895 established various types of modern school. During the Japanese colonial period many more modern schools were established, though educational opportunities for Koreans were strictly limited, particularly at the secondary and higher levels, and only a little over 57 per cent of school-aged Korean children attended elementary school. Japanese was the official language, and the speaking, reading and writing of Korean was discouraged and finally in 1941 forbidden in all schools. Consequently at independence 78 per cent of the population was illiterate.

Thus in 1945, when Korea regained her independence, there were only 19 institutes of higher education, 2,834 elementary and 165 secondary schools. A modern system of education was formulated, providing six years free elementary education, and was embodied in the Constitution of the Republic of Korea in 1948. Although elementary education was stated to be compulsory it was impossible to achieve this fully owing to the overwhelming problems of shortage of funds, teachers and school facilities. During the Korean War, 1950–53, over 50 per cent of the educational facilities were destroyed and once again the educational system had to be rebuilt. The basic needs were to rebuild and repair school facilities, to train teachers, to continue the programme for the eradication of illiteracy, and to introduce a vocational education programme as an aid to the economy. With public participation, and the help of welfare organizations such as UNESCO much has been done.

Elementary Education

Elementary education consists of kindergartens, civic schools, and elementary schools:

Kindergartens are for children between the ages of three and six and cover one to two years. In 1975 there were 611 kindergartens, but all but five were privately owned though subject to some governmental control; 33,707 children were enrolled, which represents only a limited number of the total children eligible.

As a result of the government's five-year plan of educational development launched in 1962 the attendance rate of the total school-aged population was raised to 98.1 per cent. The criteria for the curriculum of all elementary schools, both public and private, are established by the Ministry of Education though local authorities are encouraged to develop curricula that will meet the needs of individual communities. Korean language, arithmetic, social studies, natural science, music, art, moral education and physical education are taught in classes during 22–31 hours a week. In 1975, there were 6,374 elementary schools.

Civic schools are for children who are beyond the compulsory attendance age and for illiterate adults. There are two separate classes, the children's education being a three-year course covering in condensed form the basic requirements of the elementary six-year course, while the adult course covers 200 hours or more. The number of civic schools has decreased with the implementation of the six-year course.

Secondary Education

Secondary education is divided into two three-year units, middle and high school, which are generally administered as separate institutions. They are fee-paying and therefore not compulsory, and are generally segregated. The Ministry of Education is to abolish the compulsory entrance examination to middle schools. Since independence the number of secondary schools has greatly increased: in 1945 there were 413 schools with 178,599 pupils and in 1975 there were 3,124 secondary schools with 3,158,232.

Middle schools: In 1975 there were 1,935 middle schools, with 2,031,025 pupils and 45,667 teachers. The basic curriculum includes moral education, the Korean language, Korean history, mathematics, social studies, art, music, physical education, foreign languages including English, and vocational training.

High Schools: In 1975 there were 1,153 high schools, with 981,209 students (twice as many boys as girls). In the past the curriculum has been largely limited to the courses required for entrance into the various colleges, and the prestige of a particular school was in proportion to the number passing the entrance examination. But now increasing emphasis is laid on a well-rounded curriculum with a wide variety of subjects. Many high schools have evening sessions for students who work an eight-hour day and then start school at five o'clock.

Vocational Education

Much emphasis is placed on vocational education, particularly in the light of the country's economic needs. Elementary vocational education begins in middle school and for children who cannot afford a secondary education there are technical trade and higher technical trade schools at middle and high school level which offer vocational training; they are nearly all private and offer one- to three-year courses. There are also higher civic schools for elementary school leavers. In middle schools, five hours a week are spent in vocational training, from a variety of courses. Increasing attention is being paid to developing vocational high schools. While encouraging the growth of vocational education, the government is also trying to control the number of academic schools so that the eventual ratio of academic to vocational schools will be 4 : 6. Comprehensive schools have been set up as a means of solving this problem and they have become increasingly popular since they provide courses in academic subjects, general machine shops, home economics, agriculture and science.

Higher Education

The first modern institutions of higher education were established at the end of the nineteenth century with the arrival of foreign missionaries. The founding of Soong Sil college in Pyongyang in 1907 and Ewha Women's College in 1910 marked the beginning of modern college education, and were followed by others after the annexation of Korea by Japan in 1910, though higher education for Koreans was discouraged. In 1945 there were only 19 colleges and one university.

There are three types of higher institution: the junior college which provides two-year courses, and colleges and universities which provide four- or six-year courses. A university consists of three or more colleges, one of which must be a college of natural sciences and another a graduate school. In 1976 201,723 students were enrolled in 154 colleges, universities and graduate schools. With the exception of about 20 universities and colleges for women, higher education in Korea is co-educational.

The Ministry of Education sets minimum standards for the curricula, teaching staff, physical facilities and equipment. The colleges are free to formulate their own curricula, which are then subject to ministerial approval. However, all colleges teach some subjects of general culture; they include the Korean language, foreign languages, outline of philosophy, cultural history, outline of natural science and physical training, which have to total one-third of the number of required subjects. Physical education plays a very important role at all levels of Korean education and is one of the main requirements in the national examinations.

Colleges and universities have expanded rapidly during recent years, though often at the expense of planning and quality. Reforms are now being made and government regulations are strictly enforced. The Ministry of Education proposes to improve the facilities at national universities, to extend financial subsidies for private institutions, and to create ties between national universities and industrial corporations for co-ordination in research. Until recently the majority of enrolments have been in the liberal arts faculties, but since the restoration of civilian rule in 1963 greater emphasis has been placed on technical and scientific education; 50–60 per cent of university enrolments are now in natural and applied sciences.

Higher Technical Education: With the task of rebuilding the economy after the period of Japanese rule, there was a great demand for artisans, engineers, businessmen, experts in fishery and agriculture as well as technicians in all fields. At present there are 41 engineering and professional colleges, most of them attached to universities and situated in the capital. There are also thirteen colleges of agriculture and ten colleges of commerce, several of which include departments of public and business administration.

Teacher Training: In 1961 there were three types of teacher training institution, the normal schools for elementary teachers, the two-year teachers' colleges and the four-year colleges of education, for secondary school teachers. In 1962 in order to improve the quality of teachers the normal schools were up-graded to two-year colleges, and the two-year colleges for secondary school teachers were abolished. There are now sixteen two-year colleges and 24 four-year colleges of education, of which 18 are private. Tuition is free and monthly allowances are allocated to students of national teaching colleges on condition that they teach in a national school for a period equal to the duration of their training. In 1975 there were 39,692 students under training.

Social Education

Before 1970 social education was divided into education for illiterates and training courses in trades and vocations. Since 1970 emphasis has been on technical education and mental development. Owing to the success of the Third Economic Development Plan and the growth of national income, the Government is changing its social education policy towards strengthening the moral education of the nation, in particular that of the younger generation.

UNIVERSITIES

Chonnam National University: Kwang Joo, Chollanam Do; 321 teachers, 5,800 students.

Chosun University: Kwang Joo; 247 teachers, 4,140 students.

Chungang University: Huksuk Dong, Seoul; 200 teachers, 6,800 students.

Chungnam National University: Taijon; 270 teachers, 1881 students.

Chunpuk National University: Chun-Joo, Cholla Puk Do; 4,020 students.

Dan Kook University: 8 Hannam-Dong, Yongsam-ku, Seoul.

Dong A University: 13-ka, Dong-Daesin-Dong, Seo-ku, Pusan; 187 professors, 5,452 students.

Dongguk University: 26, 3-ka, Pil Dong, Seoul; 300 teachers, 4,700 students.

Ewha Women's University: Daihyun-Dong, Seoul; 747 teachers, 8,210 students.

Hankuk University of Foreign Studies: 270 Rimoon-Dong, Dongdaemoon-ku, Seoul; 251 teachers, 3,440 students.

Hanyang University: 8-2 Haengdang-Dong, Sung dong-ku, Seoul; 640 teachers, 9,200 students.

Jeon Buk National University: 2-22 Rue 2, Jouk-gm, Jeon Buk.

Kon-Kuk University: Sung-dong ku, Seoul; 112 teachers, 8,000 students.

Korea University: Anam-Dong, Seoul; 425 teachers, 10,250 students.

Kyung Hee University: Hoeki Dong, Seoul; 580 teachers, 10,000 students.

Kyungpuk National University: Taegu; 360 teachers, 6,575 students.

Myong Ji University: Seosomun-dong, Seodaemun-ku, Seoul; 180 teachers, 2,300 students.

Pusan National University: Dong Nae-ku, Pusan; 300 teachers, 3,374 students.

Seoul National University: Sim-Rim Dong, Seoul; 1,200 teachers, 14,000 students.

Sogang University: 1, Siasudong, Mapoku, P.O.B. 1142, Seoul; 155 teachers, 2,290 students.

Sookmyung Women's University: Chungpa-Dong, Seoul; 200 teachers, 3,300 students.

Sung Jun University: 135 Sang Do-Dong Seoul; 98 teachers, 1,876 students.

Sung Kyun Kwan University: Myung Ryun Dong, Seoul; 364 teachers, 4,836 students.

Woo Sok University: 42nd St., Myung-Yung-Dong, Chong-No-Koo, Seoul.

Yeungnam University: 317-1 Tae-Myung-Dong, Nam-ku, Taegu; 206 teachers, 7,680 students.

Yonsei University: Sodaemoon-ku, Seoul; 628 teachers, 10,082 students.

BIBLIOGRAPHY

GENERAL

BRANDT, VINCENT S. R. A Korean Village between Farm and Sea (Harvard University Press, Cambridge, Mass., 1971).

CHAE, KYUNG OH. Handbook of Korea (Pageant Press, New York, 1958).

THE CHINA QUARTERLY. North Korea (April-June 1963, London).

ECKHARDT, A. A History of Korean Art (Goldston, London, 1929).

Koreanische Musik (Deutsche Gesellschaft für Natur- und Völkerkunde Ostasiens, Tokyo, 1930).

HAKWONSA. Korea, its land, people and culture of all ages (Seoul, 1960).

HENDERSON, G. Korea: The Politics of the Vortex (Harvard University Press, Cambridge, Mass., 1960).

LEE, CHONG-SIK. The Politics of Korean Nationalism (California University Press, Berkeley, 1963).

LEE, P. Korean Literature: Topics and Themes (Arizona University Press, Tucson, 1965).

MCCUNE, E. The Arts of Korea: An Illustrated History (Charles E. Tuttle, Tokyo and Rutland, 1962).

MCCUNE, G. Korea Today (Harvard University Press, Cambridge, Mass., 1950).

NAHM, ANDREW C. (ed.) Korea and the New Order in East Asia (The Center for Korean Studies, Western Michigan University, Kalamazoo, 1974).

(ed.) Studies in the Developmental Aspects of Korea (The Center for Korean Studies, Western Michigan University, Kalamazoo 1969).

OLIVER, R. T. Syngman Rhee (Robert Hale, London, 1955).

OSGOOD, C. The Koreans and their Culture (Ronald Press, New York, 1951).

PYUN, YUNG TAI. Korea: My Country (Korean Pacific Press, 1953).

SCALAPINO, R. A. North Korea Today (Praeger, New York and London, 1963).

THOMPSON, R. Cry Korea (Macdonald, London, 1952).

HISTORY

BERGER, C. The Korea Knot: A Military-Political History (Pennsylvania University Press, Philadelphia, 1957).

CALDWELL, J. C. The Korea Story (Chicago, 1952).

CHO, SOO SUNG. Korea in World Politics 1940-1950 (Cambridge University Press, London, 1967).

CLARK, C. A. Religions of Old Korea (H. Revell, New York, 1932).

CONROY, F. H. The Japanese Seizure of Korea, 1868–1910 (Pennsylvania University Press, Philadelphia, 1960).

HAN SUNGJOO. A History of Korea (Eulyoo Pub. Co., Seoul, 1972).

HARRINGTON, FRED H. God, Mammon and the Japanese (The University of Wisconsin Press, Madison, Wisconsin, 1944).

HULBERT, H. B. History of Korea (Routledge, London, 1962).

KEUN, HAN WOO. A History of Korea (Eulyoo Publishing Company, Seoul, 1972).

KIM, C. I. EUGENE, and KIM, HAN-KYO. Korea and the Politics of Imperialism, 1876–1910 (University of California Press, 1970).

KIM SE JIN. The Politics of Military Revolution in Korea (University of North Carolina Press, 1971).

MCKENZIE, F. A. Korea's Fight for Freedom (Fleming H. Revell, New York, 1920).

MEAD, E. G. American Military Government in Korea (New York, King's Crown Press, 1951).

NAHM, ANDREW C. (ed.) Korea Under Japanese Colonial Rule (The Center for Korean Studies, Western Michigan University, 1973).

NELSON, M. F. Korea and the Old Orders in Western Asia (Louisiana State University Press, Baton Rouge, 1945).

OH, JOHN K. C. Korea: Democracy on Trial (Cornell University Press, Ithaca, N.Y., 1968).

RIDGWAY, M. B. The War in Korea (Barrie & Rockliff, London, 1968).

RUTT, RICHARD. James Scarth Gale and his History of the Korean People (Royal Asiatic Society, Korea Branch, Seoul, 1972).

SCALAPINO, ROBERT A. and LEE, CHONG-SIK. Communism in Korea (University of California Press, Berkeley, Los Angeles, London, 1972).

SOHN, POW-KEY et al. The History of Korea (Korean National Commission for UNESCO, Seoul, 1970).

SUH, DAE-SOOK. The Korean Communist Movement 1918–1948 (Princeton University Press, New Jersey, 1967).

THOMAS, R. C. W. The War in Korea 1950–53 (Gale & Polden, Aldershot, 1954).

WRIGHT, EDWARD R. (ed.) Korean Politics in Transition (University of Washington Press, Seattle, Wash. 1975).

ECONOMICS AND GEOGRAPHY

GRAJDANZEV, A. J. Modern Korea (New York, 1944).

LEE, HOON K. Land Utilization and Rural Economy in Korea (University of Chicago Press, Chicago, 1936).

MCCUNE, S. Korea's Heritage: A Regional and Social Geography (Charles E. Tuttle, Tokyo and Rutland, 1966).

REEVE, W. D. The Republic of Korea: A Political and Economic Study (Oxford University Press, London, 1963).

RUDOLPH, P. North Korea's Political and Economic Structure (Institute of Pacific Relations, New York, 1959).

Macao

Frank H. H. King

GEOGRAPHY

Macao has an area of 15.5 square kilometres, comprising the peninsula of the Chinese district of Fo Shan and the two small islands of Taipa and Colôane which together lie some 64 kilometres west across the Canton River estuary from Hong Kong. The climate is tropical.

Official statistics gave a population of 260,000 in mid-1975, based on a 1.2 per cent annual growth since the last official census in 1970, but most observers agree that the real figure should exceed 300,000.

HISTORY

The territory was established as one of several trading posts by the Portuguese as early as 1537; records of continuous settlement begin in 1557. Driven by trade and missionary zeal, the Portuguese developed Macao as a base for their operations both in China and Japan, and penetration during Japan's "Christian century" involved close relations with Macao. However, sovereignty remained vested in China, the Chinese residents remained subject to a Chinese official, and Macao's Portuguese administration, virtually autonomous for the first two hundred years, concerned itself with the governance of the Portuguese and, until the establishment of Hong Kong, with the growing presence of other European trading nations. The Portuguese paid an annual rent to China.

Macao was an uncertain base for an expanded China trade. The Catholic administration was unfriendly to Protestants, the Chinese authority was too close and restrictive, and the opium question and growing restlessness of the "private" merchants undermined a system which had developed during the years of controlled and relatively limited "company" trade.

The ceding of Hong Kong to Britain in 1842 revealed China's weakness and in 1845 Portugal declared Macao a free port. In the consequent disputes the Macao Governor, Ferreira do Amaral, was assassinated, Portugal drove out the Chinese officials, and the settlement became Portuguese territory. This unilateral declaration was recognized by China in 1887 in return for provisions intended to facilitate the enforcement of its customs laws, particularly in regard to opium, by the Imperial Maritime Customs.

However, Macao's establishment as a colony did not restore prosperity. With the silting of its harbour, the diversion of its trade to Hong Kong, and the opening of the treaty ports as bases of trade and missionary work, Macao was left to handle the local distributive trade, while developing a reputation as a base for smuggling, gambling and other unsavoury activities. With the closing of the Hong Kong–China border in 1938, Macao's trade boomed, but the prosperity was short-lived as the colony soon became isolated as the only European settlement on the China coast not occupied by the Japanese during the Second World War.

In 1951 Macao was declared an overseas province of Portugal and elected a representative to the Portuguese legislature. Macao's economic prosperity depended largely on the gold trade, illegal in Hong Kong, on gambling and tourism, and on an entrepôt business with China.

Recent political developments

Macao's tranquility was disrupted by communist riots in 1966–67 inspired by the Cultural Revolution in mainland China. These were contained only after the Macao Government signed an agreement with Macao's Chinese Chamber of Commerce outlawing the activities of Chinese loyal to the Taiwan regime, which Portugal continued to recognize, paying compensation to the families of Chinese killed in the rioting, and refusing entry to refugees from China.

But the nature of the settlement made it clear that China wished the Portuguese administration to continue, and on admission to the United Nations the Peking Government affirmed that it regarded the future of both Hong Kong and Macao as an internal matter.

After the military coup in Portugal in April 1974 Macao's was the only governor of an overseas territory retained in office. China refused to discuss the future of Macao with Portugal and the revolutionary leaders became convinced that there was no demand for an independence which China would not, in any case, have tolerated. Nevertheless the revolution caused considerable political activity in Macao. The Centro Democratica de Macau (CDM) was established to press for radical political reform and the purging of those connected with the former regime. The conservative Association for the Defence of the Interests of Macao (ADIM) was established and in April 1975 defeated the CDM's candidate for Macao's representative to the Lisbon assembly. The Macao electorate reaffirmed its conservative bias when, under the constitutional arrangements, over 65 per cent voted for right-wing parties in the Lisbon constituency.

Colonel Garcia Leandro, who succeeded Nobre de Carvalho at the end of his much-extended term as governor in late 1974, dealt at first with the CDM, but his assertion that Macao needed capitalism and was not ready for socialism, his failure to force through the election of the CDM candidate, and his quick grasp of the essential realities of Macao's relations with China, alienated him from the local supporters of the Portuguese revolutionary left.

In February 1976, according to constitutional changes granting Macao greater autonomy, Macao became a special territory of Portugal with a Governor of ministerial rank, appointed by the President of Portugal, to whom he is responsible. In Macao the Governor is the executive authority; the new Legislative Assembly has 17 members of whom 6 are elected on a proportional basis, 6 elected indirectly from designated organizations, and 5 appointed by the Governor. A two-thirds majority is needed to veto executive decrees. International relations remain the responsibility of the President of Portugal, but even this can be delegated, and it is expected that Macao will negotiate its own economic agreements, subject in some instances to the virtually assured approval of the Portuguese president. The partly elected Municipal Council remains to handle the routine problems of the city of Macao; an appointed council administers the islands. Macao, however, lost its representative in the Portuguese legislature; the two governments are separate although Portuguese in Macao may vote in Portuguese elections.

Portuguese military forces left Macao at the end of 1975 and local police units and the fire brigade were unified as the Security Forces of Macao. In 1976, the CDM was weakened with the expulsion from Macao of many of its supporters, while the ADIM, still important, remained closely associated with business interests, and a new panel of "independents", young officials and professionals, were offering a serious threat to the established "civic associations" in the forthcoming elections. As a result of an independent but parallel change the Catholic Church, which played an important role in the spread of Christianity under the Portuguese flag, became directly subject to the Holy See and not to the Portuguese Church through Goa.

However, unlike Hong Kong, the Chinese community has throughout remained separate. Thus of the officially estimated 260,000 residents in mid-1975 only some 3,500 electors, almost all "Portuguese", have registered.

Electoral politics are virtually the monopoly of the "Portuguese", defined as those culturally identified with Portugal and, almost without exception, Catholic. The Chinese will certainly be fully represented in the appointed and "indirectly-elected" categories in the new Legislative Assembly. Thus the anomalous position of a Chinese population on China's very borders voting for a non-Communist party may be avoided.

The administration of Macao remains Portuguese. The Lisbon Government will continue to subsidize the territory. The Education Director plans the development of Portuguese language instruction. While government dependence on Church co-operation in social welfare and medical matters will continue, government departments talk of expanding their role beyond the "Portuguese" into the Chinese community linking with and co-operating with long-standing Chinese institutions to the extent this is administratively feasible and acceptable to the Chinese community.

In July 1976, the conservative ADIM won a decisive victory in the first elections to the New Legislative Assembly, gaining four of the six elective seats.

International relations. The People's Republic of China regards Macao as Chinese territory under a Portuguese administration. In Western legal terms Macao is a territory and Portugal is sovereign. In both cases it is certain that Macao has no international personality itself and that its relations are subject to the *de jure* approval of the President of Portugal and the *de facto* tolerance of China. As a self-governing territory far from Portugal, Macao may seek to play some role in the region, at least to the extent of attending non-political conferences. Macao has already sent out trade missions and negotiated trade agreements.

Macao was closely watched by China during the period of leftist strength in Portugal in 1975, for the activities of the Moscow-oriented Communist Party were naturally suspect. At the same time the Soviet Union tried to embarrass China with the existence of a "colony" on its borders.

Of more immediate importance, perhaps, are Macao's relations with Hong Kong. A new tax imposed by Hong Kong in 1975 on travellers to and from Macao brought forth protests; the tax was lowered but not cancelled. With thousands of Hong Kong residents visiting Macao annually, the territory's police administration is concerned with the possibility of the spread of activities of the Hong Kong based Triad Societies, secret groups involved in organized crime, particularly drug-peddling.

ECONOMIC SURVEY

In 1976 Macao was recovering from the world trade recession and the uncertainty about its own future after the military coup in Portugal in April 1974, which had caused unemployment, a fall in real wages and a decline in tourist spending in 1975.

Tourism

Despite efforts to diversify the economy, Macao remained heavily dependent on tourism and the related gambling industry, with clientele coming mainly from Hong Kong at weekends. After Hong Kong, most tourists come from Japan, the U.S.A. and Australia. Figures for the first half of 1976 indicate that the number of tourists for the whole year could be a record. In 1976 a new six-year contract was made with the Sociedade de Turismo e Diversoes de Macau (STDM), a syndicate controlling gambling in Macao and its biggest source of income, employing 10,000 people in a wide range of activities including all the big hotels. Under the new contract, which came into effect in June 1976, the syndicate's annual rent to the Government was increased from 9 million Hong Kong dollars to HK $30 million and it was also obliged to invest HK $30 million annually in the economy.

The STDM's contribution to the budget may be as high as 30 per cent, while its overall contribution to the economy equals that of the ordinary budget as officially recorded. Efforts are being made to broaden the base of the tourist industry, to encourage longer stays and to bring visitors from overseas to visit the territory's historical and religious monuments. Nevertheless, there are plans for resort developments on Colôane, the more modest of which may soon be implemented. Completion of the Macau-Taipa bridge in late 1974 is leading to the integration of Macao's economy and development plans are focusing on the islands.

Finance

One indicator of Macao's economic health confirms an optimistic forecast. The pataca, Macao's currency, used to be quoted at par with the Hong Kong dollar; early in 1975 it declined on the open market and by 1976 was at a 20 per cent discount, reflecting in part lack of confidence in the Portuguese escudo, since Macao's reserves were heavily invested in Portugal as well as in Hong Kong. After the signing of the STDM agreement, in May 1976 the pataca was quoted at an 11 per cent discount, a rate probably satisfactory to the Government. Essential commodities are imported at more favourable rates, while 25 per cent of exchange earnings must be surrendered at par. This is, therefore, a reasonable time for the scheduled consideration of a central bank and for the establishment of a monetary system independent of the escudo and more openly related to the Hong Kong dollar, one of the world's strongest currencies.

The new constitutional arrangements of February 1976 imply that Macao will become economically independent of Portugal, but for the immediate future a budgetary subsidy will be continued. Additional funds for social welfare, especially for refugees, and educational expenditures are also available from United States social welfare and religious agencies, from various other Church sources and elsewhere.

Trade

Macao's once flourishing gold trade disappeared with the 1974 legalization in Hong Kong and the focus changed to manufactures, which as late as 1969 were virtually confined to fireworks and matches. There has recently been a spillover from Hong Kong industrialists who, partly seeking a new quota-base and partly recognizing the real facilities of nearby Macao, have established textiles, plastics and other manufacturing enterprises.

The loss of markets in former Portuguese African possessions had already been offset by the growth of exports to EEC countries and to the United States, and Macao's exports (excluding re-exports) increased by 10 per cent in 1974; in 1975 they rose a further 24 per cent to 684 million patacas. Retained imports declined 13 per cent in 1974 but rose 22 per cent to 791 million patacas in 1975. In 1975, trade, including the important transit trade, totalled 1,670 million patacas. Hong Kong continued as Macao's principal supplier in 1975, especially for textile manufactures, while the People's Republic of China, the source of food and other consumer articles, ranked second. Imports from Portugal declined while those from the United Kingdom and the U.S.A. both doubled. Reflecting improved EEC quotas, exports to Western European countries increased significantly during 1975, although exports to Italy and Portugal not unexpectedly declined. France, the Federal Republic of Germany, the U.S.A. and Hong Kong were Macao's most important markets as exports to former Portuguese territories, especially in Africa, continued to decline. Macao had succeeded in increasing the value of its exports even during 1974, but the recovery in 1975 was marked.

Industry and Power

With the emigration of trained professionals and others in unsettled 1974 and 1975, skilled labour is at a premium and the lack of water on the islands reinforces the view that industrial development must now be selective, with government priority for more sophisticated manufacturing such as electronics. The chronic electricity shortage was temporarily solved with the installation of three 15-kilowatt diesel generators; in January 1977 two 25-megawatt steam-operated generators will come into operation on Colôane in the first stage of a long-term development.

The year 1975 produced mixed results in manufacturing industry, with the main gains found in knitwear and clothing: 1,907 and 13,174 metric tons respectively. At the end of 1974 there were 21,300 employed in 1,127 registered establishments, most of them of the small, traditional type, indicating a source of potential manpower should investment permit the expansion of the modern sector. Macao actively seeks new markets with official trade delegations, but is more selective in attracting direct investment due to the restraints previously discussed.

Development

Ambitious plans are being drawn up for the improvement of housing and for a satellite town on the nearer island of Taipa. Development of water supplies depends on China, where facilities sometimes suffer from the same water shortfall as in the territory itself. A scheme to reclaim 35 hectares of land in Macao's outer harbour has been temporarily suspended, but other capital works are being built, particularly a container pier to facilitate links with Hong Kong's growing containerized trade and another pier to permit direct shipment of fuel for Colôane's new generator station. This latter may be a prelude to a major port development at Ka Ho.

Communications

The bulk of Macao's trade must be routed via Hong Kong with transshipment, although satellite container service has already been inaugurated. Some trade takes place directly with the neighbouring counties of Kwangtung Province in the People's Republic of China, and considerable local exchange, both of products and of people, occurs. However, the bulk of Macao's visitors arrive from Hong Kong on one of the half-hourly hydrofoils, the new jetfoils, or the three ferryboat services.

STATISTICAL SURVEY

AREA AND POPULATION

Area	Population 1970 Census	Mid-1975 Official Estimate
15.5 sq. km.	248,636	260,227

	Births	Marriages	Deaths
1972	2,750	138	1,539
1973	2,686	165	1,410
1974	2,781	168	1,579
1975	2,583	171	1,398

AGRICULTURE

LIVESTOCK

(metric tons—slaughtered)

	1973	1974	1975
Cattle	409	398	556
Buffaloes	407	296	375
Pigs	5,132	4,683	5,108
Total	5,948	5,377	6,039

FISHING*

(metric tons)

	1971	1972	1973
Fish	3,735	3,780	4,044
Crustaceans and molluscs	6,562	6,361	6,609
Total	10,297	10,141	10,653

* landed.

INDUSTRY

(metric tons)

	1972	1973	1974	1975
Wine	2,168	1,994	1,549	1,807
Ice	20,730	23,419	24,629	n.a.
Woven fabrics and textiles	943	1,005	875	754
Knitwear	1,643	1,423	1,629	1,907
Footwear	1,050	1,852	1,448	1,034
Clothing	10,988	9,932	10,690	13,174
Furniture	505	579	953	n.a.
Explosives and pyrotechnic products	3,287	2,211	988	722
Optical articles	405	447	281	110
Electric energy (million kWh.)*	81.9	93.7	109.0	n.a.

* Consumption.

FINANCE

100 avos=1 pataca.
Coins: 5, 10 and 50 avos; 1, 5 and 20 patacas.
Notes: 5, 10, 50, 100 and 500 patacas.
Exchange rates (June 1976): £1 sterling=12.73 patacas; U.S. $1=7.14 patacas.
100 patacas=£7.85=$14.00.

Note: From January 1968 to February 1973 the pataca was valued at 4.80 Portuguese escudos. The exchange rate was U.S. $1=5.990 patacas from January 1968 to August 1971; and $1=5.677 patacas from December 1971 to February 1973. In terms of sterling, the rate was £1=14.375 patacas from January 1968 to August 1971; and £1=14.793 patacas from December 1971 to June 1972. The Hong Kong dollar (June 1976: £1 sterling=H.K. $8.78; U.S. $1=H.K. $4.94) also circulates freely in the province.

BUDGET
('000 patacas)

Revenue	1975
Ordinary	91,157
Direct taxes	11,192
Indirect taxes	4,470
Industries with special tributary conditions	13,657
Taxes—revenue from sundry services	5,275
Private domain, State firms and industries—participation in profits	19,332
Earnings from capital, shares and bonds of banks and companies	—
Reimbursements and restitutions	12,152
Consignments of receipts	25,079
Extraordinary:	32,872
Development Plan	32,872
Total	124,029

Expenditure	1975
Ordinary:	91,157
Provincial debt	5,412
Provincial government and national representation	1,393
Retirements, pensions, etc.	7,300
General administration and inspection	25,944
Treasury services	1,868
Justice services	2,367
Development services	13,647
National defence—armed forces	3,899
Marine services	7,319
General charges	21,929
Previous periods	80
Extraordinary:	32,872
Development Plan	32,872
Total	124,029

CURRENCY IN CIRCULATION
('000 patacas at December 31st)

	1972	1973	1974	1975
Notes	80,860	96,205	98,724	116,632
Coins	9,486	11,884	13,321	19,172
Total	90,346	108,089	112,045	135,804

EXTERNAL TRADE
(million patacas)

	1972	1973	1974	1975
Imports (retained)	592.5	750.3	648.7	791.3
Exports (excluding re-exports)	409.7	497.1	551.2	683.9

PRINCIPAL COMMODITIES

('000 patacas)

IMPORTS	1972	1973	1974	1975*
Pigs	18,229	18,423	19,466	15,858
Eggs	5,744	7,600	13,199	7,718
Fresh fruit	11,364	20,046	22,866	21,498
Rice	12,811	10,828	12,946	17,458
Canned meat	13,110	15,381	12,793	7,877
Tobacco (manufactured)	11,111	12,235	13,626	16,046
Marble	2,717	14,334	5,719	3,480
Cement (incl. clinker)	4,238	8,539	9,237	5,993
Plastic materials	12,024	10,419	5,970	5,585
Carded wool yarn	89,685	145,799	101,623	97,619
Woven cotton fabrics	48,373	63,438	56,370	121,856
Woven fabrics of cellulose fibres	55,865	40,799	53,233	71,734
Clothing	18,079	24,722	18,967	10,375
Passenger cars	6,551	10,749	8,231	6,776
Fuel oil	6,030	5,787	7,190	n.a.
Medicines	5,085	5,443	5,361	n.a.
Wood, wood products and charcoal	9,652	11,590	8,559	n.a.
Paper and cardboard	11,706	10,794	7,445	n.a.
Ceramic products	9,804	16,003	14,108	n.a.
Casting and soft iron; steel	17,638	18,191	13,847	n.a.
Machinery and apparatus	16,642	38,392	32,390	n.a.
TOTAL (incl. others)	592,525	750,298	648,716	791,304

*Provisional.

EXPORTS	1972	1973	1974	1975*
Fresh fish	9,153	8,995	7,193	10,824
Shrimps	6,198	11,560	12,622	15,121
Ice	7,270	1,137	340	n.a.
Pyrotechnic products	13,701	8,762	2,901	2,295
Leather manufactures	4,788	5,677	4,140	3,450
Woven fabrics of cellulose fibres	6,663	6,533	2,402	1,455
Knitwear and other made-up goods, elastic, without rubber	70,484	120,404	108,423	177,564
Clothing	196,611	212,031	286,362	361,430
Handkerchiefs	13,175	19,233	18,665	8,950
Clothes for bed, table and other domestic uses	12,380	12,876	15,059	4,270
Footwear	7,559	10,775	8,737	6,196
Porcelain ware	3,540	5,892	13,286	8,839
Optical articles	13,189	19,140	12,826	4,171
TOTAL (incl. others)	409,734	497,065	551,213	683,924

*Provisional.

PRINCIPAL COUNTRIES

('000 patacas)

IMPORTS	1972	1973	1974	1975
China, People's Republic	153,844	195,965	163,320	151,017
Hong Kong	398,671	501,454	419,902	565,250
Japan	9,418	14,868	14,735	12,788
Portugal	6,152	5,568	16,194	5,448
United Kingdom	5,041	6,601	6,927	13,061
U.S.A.	7,085	12,524	12,604	24,031
TOTAL (incl. others)	592,525	750,298	648,716	791,304

[*continued on next page*

PRINCIPAL COUNTRIES—*continued*]

EXPORTS	1972	1973	1974	1975
Angola	18,477	27,932	14,226	7,914
Belgium-Luxembourg	11,647	23,617	19,854	26,947
East Timor	3,350	5,083	5,887	2,930
France	77,075	79,624	87,461	145,522
Germany, Federal Republic	46,105	61,955	86,834	96,052
Hong Kong	44,679	47,493	55,539	68,929
Italy	18,527	23,303	34,299	26,845
Japan	9,370	20,384	23,753	12,236
Mozambique	15,368	12,722	7,846	9,645
Netherlands	7,058	12,474	25,757	42,155
Portugal	34,148	55,741	51,504	43,412
Sweden	6,758	8,447	7,360	20,703
United Kingdom	1,623	13,316	10,331	40,304
U.S.A.	95,944	77,512	56,815	75,902
TOTAL (incl. others)	409,734	497,065	551,213	683,924

TRANSPORT

ROADS

(Vehicles in use)

	1971	1972	1973	1974
Passenger cars	3,949	4,861	5,664	6,489
Trucks and buses	759	1,010	1,170	1,240
Motor cycles	1,638	2,576	3,638	4,374

SHIPPING

	1972	1973	1974	1975*
Vessels entered:				
Number	19,691	22,673	23,341	23,399
'000 g.r.t.	5,796	6,845	6,970	7,286
Freight (metric tons):				
Unloaded	338,518	374,991	298,746	374,050
Loaded	67,457	57,777	146,588	286,412
Passengers:				
Embarked	1,960,886	2,275,582	2,229,774	2,153,948
Disembarked	1,967,665	2,278,608	2,234,520	2,157,770

* Provisional.

EDUCATION

(1974/75)

	SCHOOLS	TEACHERS	STUDENTS
Kindergarten	38	119	4,118
Primary	51	558	17,907
Secondary:			
High schools	25	466	7,006
Technical schools (commercial and industrial)	5	74	694
Other*	9	66	554

* Including one school of arts and five training schools for public staff.

Note: These figures probably understate totals, due to the failure of all Chinese schools to report.

Sources: Instituto Nacional de Estatística, Banco Nacional Ultramarino, Repartição Provincial dos Serviços de Estatística, Macao.

THE CONSTITUTION

The constitution of Macao is embodied in an organic statute of Portugal promulgated in February 1976.

Macao, comprising the town of Nome de Deus de Macau (God's Name of Macao) and the Taipa and Colôane islands, has administrative, economical, financial and legislative autonomy.

The sovereignty organs of Portugal, except the Law Courts, are represented in the territory by the Governor. In foreign relations and international agreements or conventions, Macao is represented by the President of Portugal who may delegate to the Governor if the matters concern the territory only.

The judicial power is independent and it is regulated by legislation enacted in Portugal.

The Governor

The Governor is nominated after the local population is consulted and dismissed by the President of Portugal to whom he is responsible politically. He has a rank similar to a Minister of Government in Portugal.

The Secretaries-Adjunct

The Secretaries-Adjunct, up to five in number, are nominated and dismissed by the President of Portugal on the Governor's proposal. Each has a rank similar to a Secretary of State of Government in Portugal.

They exercise the executive powers which have been delegated by the Governor.

The Superior Council of Security

The Superior Council of Security works in conjunction with the Governor who presides over it. It comprises the Secretaries-Adjunct, the Commander, Second-Commander and Chief of General Staff of the Security Forces, and three deputies elected by the Legislative Assembly. Its duties are to settle and to co-ordinate directives relating to the security of the territory.

The Legislative Assembly

The Legislative Assembly comprises 17 deputies with a mandate of three years. Five deputies are appointed by the Governor from among residents of recognized reputation, six are elected by direct and universal suffrage and six elected by indirect suffrage.

The President of Portugal can dissolve the Assembly in the public interest on the Governor's recommendation.

The Consultative Council

The Consultative Council is presided over by the Governor and has five elected members (two elected by the members of the administrative bodies and from among them, one by organizations representing moral, cultural and welfare interests, and two by associations with economic interests; three statutory members (the Secretary-Adjunct for the Civil Administration Services, the Attorney of the Republic and the Chief of Finance Services); and two members nominated by the Governor.

Judicial System

Ordinary justice is administered directly from Portugal.

Under the superintendence of the Attorney of Portugal are the Delegate of the Attorney of the Republic, the Delegation of the Attorneyship of the Republic, the Services of Registries and of Notarial Affairs, the Judiciary Police, and the Cabinet of the Government's Juridical Consultation.

Finance

Macao draws up its own budget, which is annual and unitary.

The issuing bank of Macao will be the Government's banker of the territory.

The annual public accounts of the territory must be submitted to the judgment of the Administrative Law Court.

Public Services

The public services of Macao are private organizations and they can constitute autonomous entities, with or without juridical personality.

THE GOVERNMENT

Governor: Col. José Eduardo Martinho Garcia Leandro.

Secretaries:

Public Works and Communications: Vasco Joaquim Rocha Vieira.

Social and Cultural Affairs: Vitor Manual de Oliveira Santos.

Economic Affairs: Dr. Ramiro de Andrade Fonseca de Almeida.

There is a consultative committee of *ex-officio* and nominated members, the latter representing the Chinese community, "moral and cultural" interests and economic interests.

LEGISLATIVE ASSEMBLY

Seventeen members, 5 appointed by the Governor, 6 elected directly and 6 indirectly, serve for three years.

POLITICAL GROUPS

There are no political parties but a number of civic associations exist. The three represented in the Legislative Assembly are: the conservative Association for the Defence of the Interest of Macao (ADIM), the Centro Democratico de Macau (CDM), a reformist group and the moderate Group to Study the Development of Macao (GSDEC).

JUDICIAL SYSTEM

Courts of First Instance. These administer the Legal Code of Metropolitan Portugal. Cases may be finally referred to the Court of Second Instance and the Supreme Court in Lisbon.

RELIGION

Bishop of Macao: Rev. Vicar Capitular Arquimínio Rodrigues da Costa.

ROMAN CATHOLIC

There are 6 parishes and 3 missions for the 30,000 Catholics.

The majority of the Chinese residents probably profess Buddhism, and there are numerous Chinese places of worship.

THE PRESS

Portuguese

Notícias de Macau: Calçada do Tronco Velho 6, Macao; f. 1947; daily; independent; Dir. Dr. António Maria da Conceiçao; (suspended).

Boletim Oficial: Caixa Postal 33, Macao; f. 1838; weekly. government publication; Dir. Alexandre da Silva.

Gazeta Macaense: Avenida do Infante D. Henrique 3, Macao; daily; Dir. Leonel Borralho.

O Clarim: Rua Central 26, Macao; f. 1948; twice weekly; Dir. Father José Barcelos Mendes.

Confluencia: Rua Francisco Xavier Pereira, Edificio Vila Verde, Macao; twice monthly; Dir. José Florencio Pereira Chan.

Democracia em Marcha: Sede do CDM, Avenida da Republica, Macao; irregular; Dir. José da Silva Maneiras.

Chinese

Jornal "Va Kio": 7–9 Rua da Alfândéga, Macao.

Ou Mun: Rua Almirante Sérgio, 30–32, Macao.

Si Man: Avenida Almeida Ribeiro, 107–1°, Macao.

Tai Chung: Rua dos Mercadores, 136–2°, Macao.

Seng Pou: Travessa da Caldeira, 11, Macao.

RADIO

Emissora de Radiodifusão de Macau: Macao; government station; programmes in Portuguese (6 hours daily) and Chinese (4 hours daily); Dir. Carlos Figueiredo.

Emissora Vila Verde: Rua Francisco Xavier Pereira 123, Macao; private commercial station; programmes in Chinese; Dir. Ho Yin.

In 1971 there were 12,000 radio receivers in Macao.

There is no television in Macao.

FINANCE

Issuing Bank

Banco Nacional Ultramarino: f. 1864; est. in Macao 1902; Head Office: Rua do Comércio 84, P.O.B. 2069, Lisbon 2; 2 Avenida Almeida Ribeiro, Macao.

Commercial Banks

Hongkong and Shanghai Banking Corporation: Sucursal de Macao, Apt. 476, Rua da Praia Grande, 2 (Edifício Montepio), Macao.

Overseas Trust Bank Limited: Avenida do Infante D. Henrique, 51–53, Macao.

Banco de Cantão, S.A.R.L.: Rua de Cinco de Outubro, 134, Macao.

Banco Weng Hang, S.A.R.L.: 21 Avenida Almeida Ribeiro, Macao.

Banco Tai Fung, S.A.R.L.: Avenida Almeida Ribeiro, 28, Macao; Pres. Ho Yin.

Banco Seng Heng, S.A.R.L.: Avenida Almeida Ribeiro, 142, Macao.

Banco Hang Sang, S.A.R.L.: Avenida Almeida Ribeiro, 56 r/c, Macao.

Banco do Oriente, S.A.R.L.: Edifício Sintra, Macao.

Banco Comercial de Macau, S.A.R.L.: Rua da Praia Grande, 16, Macao.

Nam Tung Ngan Hong: Avenida Almeida Ribeiro, 1, Macao.

Banco Pacífico: Avenida do Infante D. Henrique, 33–35, Macao.

There are also seven registered dealers in exchange.

INSURANCE

The following Portuguese companies are represented in Macao:

Companhia de Seguros Comércio e Indústria, S.A.R.L.: Agents: H. Nolasco & Cia. Lda., P.O.B. 223, Macao (Head Office: Rua Arco do Bandeira-12, Lisbon).

Companhia de Seguros Tagus, S.A.R.L.: Agents: F. Rodrigues (Suc. Res.) Lda., Rua da Praia Grande 71, P.O.B. 2, Macao (Head Office: Rua do Comércio 40-64, Lisbon).

Companhia de Seguros Ultramarina, S.A.R.L.: Agents: H. Nolasco & Cia. Lda., P.O.B. 223, Macao (Head Office: Rua da Prata 108, Lisbon).

TRADE AND INDUSTRY

CHAMBERS OF COMMERCE

Associação Comercial de Macau: Pres. Ho Yin.

Associação dos Exportadores de Macau: Pres. Union Trading.

Associação Industrial de Macau: Pres. Peter Pan.

Associação das Agencias de Turismo de Macau: Pres. Pedro Hynman Lobo.

TRANSPORT

ROADS

There were 33 km. of roads in 1974.

SHIPPING

There are no shipping agencies for international lines.

Hydrofoils and ferry-services operate a regular service during daylight between Macao and Hong Kong.

TOURISM

Centro de Informação e Turismo: Government Palace, Rua da Praia Grande, Macao; there were 2.2 million visitors to Macao in 1975.

Macao Tourist Information Bureau: 1522 Star House, Kowloon, Hong Kong.

BIBLIOGRAPHY

Braga, J. M. The Western Pioneers and their Discovery of Macao (Imprensa Nacional, Macao, 1949).

Coates, A. Prelude to Hong Kong (Routledge and Kegan Paul, London, 1966).

Jesus, C. A. Montalto de. Historic Macao (Salesian Printing Press, Macao, 1926).

Mongolia

PHYSICAL AND SOCIAL GEOGRAPHY

Charles Bawden

The Mongolian People's Republic occupies an area estimated at about 600,000 square miles in east central Asia. It is bordered by only two other states, the U.S.S.R. along its northern frontier and China along the considerably longer southern frontier.

PHYSICAL ENVIRONMENT

For the purpose of geographical description Mongolia may be divided into five regions. In the west is the Altay area, where peaks covered with eternal snow reach up to over 15,000 ft. To the east of this lies a great depression dotted with lakes, some of salt water and some of fresh. Some of these, such as Uvs nuur (1,300 square miles) and Hövsgöl nuur (1,025 square miles), the latter being quite important for navigation, reach a considerable size. Thirdly, the north-central part of the country is occupied by the Hangay-Hentiy mountain complex, enclosing the relatively fertile and productive agricultural country of the Selenge-Tuul basin. This has always been the focus of what cultural life existed in the steppes of north Mongolia: the imperial capital of Karakorum lay here and the ruins of other early settlements are still to be seen. To the east again lies the high Mongolian plateau reaching to the Chinese frontier, and to the south and east stretches the Gobi or semi-desert.

Water is unevenly distributed. In the mountainous north and west of the country large rivers originate, draining into either the Arctic or the Pacific. A continental watershed divides Mongolia, and the much smaller rivers of the south drain internally into lakes or are lost in the ground.

Climate

The climate shows extremes of temperature between the long cold dry winter and the short hot summer during which most of the year's precipitation falls. In Ulan Bator the maximum summer temperature may lie around 92°F. and the minimum winter temperature around −50°F. Annual precipitation is variable but light. For example, in 1956 Ulan Bator had some 7.5 in., and in 1960 about 12. However, rain is liable to fall in sudden heavy showers or more prolonged outbursts in mid-summer, particularly in July, with severe flooding and damage to towns and bridges. The bitter winter weather is relieved by the almost continuous blue sky and sunshine. Mongolia is liable to severe earthquakes, especially in mountainous regions, but the population is too widely scattered for heavy losses to be caused.

POPULATION

Mongolia is very sparsely inhabited. The population was estimated at 1,468,600 in January 1976, or about two persons per square mile. It is not correct to regard the Mongols as essentially nomadic herdsmen, though stock-movement (*otor*), sometimes covering large distances, is a regular feature of rural life. Of the total population, over 45 per cent live in towns, more than half of these in the capital Ulan Bator (Ulaanbaatar). Moreover, there is a definite shift towards living in permanent settlements in the rural areas, which it is national policy to encourage through capital investment in rural building. There are some 300 such settlements, inhabited by about 22 per cent of the population. The population is, relatively speaking, homogeneous. Some 87 per cent of the people are Mongols, and of these the overwhelming majority belong to the Khalkha (Halh) group. The only important non-Mongol element in the population is that of the Kazakhs, a Turkish-speaking people dwelling in the far west, and representing slightly over five per cent of the whole. The population has grown steadily over recent years: since 1963 it has increased by nearly 31 per cent. As a result there is a preponderance of young people: 65.6 per cent of the population is aged 30 or under. The official language is Mongol, written nowadays in an adaptation of the Cyrillic script. Mongol is quite different from both Russian and Chinese, its geographic neighbours, but does show certain similarities, perhaps fortuitous, to Turkish, Korean and Japanese. Several Mongol dialects beside the dominant Khalkha are spoken in the Republic, and in the Kazakh province of Bayan-ölgiy Kazakh is the first language, most people being bi-lingual in Mongol.

HISTORY

Charles Bawden

Today only a minority of Mongols live in the Mongolian People's Republic, the one independent Mongol state. Apart from the related Buryat and Kalmyk peoples who are to be found within the U.S.S.R. in their own autonomous republics near Lake Baykal and on the lower Volga respectively, many true Mongols dwell outside the M.P.R., most of them in the Inner Mongolia Autonomous Region of the Chinese People's Republic. (Information on the present size of this Region, on administrative boundaries, national composition and living conditions, is extremely scanty.) This division came about in the following way. In the early seventeenth century the Manchus, expanding southwards from Manchuria towards their ultimate conquest of all China, passed through what came to be called Inner Mongolia, which lay across their invasion routes. Many of the Mongol princes allied themselves with the Manchus, sometimes cementing such alliances by marriages, others submitted voluntarily to them, while yet others were conquered. In 1636, after the death of Ligdan Khan, the last Mongol emperor, the subordination of these princes to the new rising dynasty was formalized. The princes of Khalkha or Outer Mongolia maintained a sort of client relationship towards the Manchus for a further half-century, but in their turn lost their independence at the Convention of Dolonnor in 1691. The Manchus had, in 1688, entered Khalkha to expel Galdan, the ruler of the west Mongol Oirats who was both terrorizing the Khalkhas and challenging the Manchus for supremacy in this area. With Galdan defeated, the three great princes of Khalkha, and the Javdzandamba Hutagt, or Living Buddha of Urga, the head of the lamaist church in Mongolia, had to accept Manchu overlordship.

Outer Mongolia was administered by the Manchus as a separate area from Inner Mongolia. A fourth princedom (*aymag*) was created in addition out of the existing three in 1725 and soon afterwards the princedoms were renamed Leagues and removed from the jurisdiction of the hereditary princes to be administered by Mongol League Heads appointed by the Li Fan Yüan or Colonial Office in Peking. Within the League organization Mongolia was divided into about a hundred banners and a number of temple territories, while the Living Buddha owned a huge number of serfs scattered about here and there. This state structure survived the fall of the Manchus in 1911 and lasted until the foundation of the M.P.R. in 1924. In spite of their dependence on Peking, however, the Mongols always considered themselves allies of the Manchus, not subjects on the same level as the Chinese, and made good use of this distinction when the Manchu dynasty lost the throne of China.

Autonomous Mongolia

The beginnings of the existence of contemporary Mongolia can be traced back to 1911. In that year the fall of the Manchus enabled the Mongols to terminate their association with China. With some political and military support from Russia a number of leading nobles proclaimed Mongolia an independent monarchy, and the throne was offered to the Living Buddha. The new government, in an unrealistic excess of euphoria, invited all Mongols everywhere to adhere to the new state, but this involved them in conflict with China, which held on to Inner Mongolia. Nor did they obtain much useful support from Russia which was bound by secret treaties with Japan not to obstruct the latter's interests in Inner Mongolia, and which in any case was reluctant to engage in a doubtful pan-Mongolist adventure. An inconclusive war with China dragged on for a couple of years until in 1915 Russian, Chinese and Mongol representatives, meeting at Kyakhta (Hiagt) on the Russo-Mongol border, agreed to the reduction of Mongolia's state of independence to one of autonomy under Chinese suzerainty. At this time autonomous Mongolia consisted more or less of the present territory of the M.P.R., the only substantial difference being the accession of Dariganga in the south-east at the time of the 1921 revolution. Inner Mongolia, Barga and the Altay district of Sinkiang were to remain under Chinese control, while Tannu Tuva, after a brief period of independence as a "People's Republic" was annexed by the U.S.S.R. during the Second World War.

Autonomous Mongolia was a theocratic monarchy, and during the few years of its existence very little happened to change the conditions inherited from Manchu times. Russian advisers did begin to modernize the Mongol army and to bring some sort of order into the fiscal system. Some primary schools and a secondary school were opened, some children, including the future dictator Choybalsan, were sent to study in Russia, and the first newspaper appeared. But the state structure, the feudal organization of society and the administration of justice remained more or less as they had been, while the church managed to consolidate and enhance its position of privilege. Though legally subject to Chinese suzerainty, Mongolia was, in fact, a Russian protectorate. When Russian power and prestige in Central Asia were sapped by the collapse of the Tsarist empire and the outbreak of revolution, this dependence of Mongolia became very apparent, and China lost no time in reasserting her authority. By mid-1919 the abrogation of autonomy was being discussed by the Mongol Government and the Chinese resident in Urga, the capital, but the process was brutally accelerated by the arrival in Mongolia of General Hsü Shu-tseng who, with a large military force at his disposal, forced the capitulation of the Mongols in early 1920.

The Revolutionary Movement

Towards the end of 1919 two revolutionary clubs had been founded in Urga: the next year these amalgamated to form the Mongol People's Party. There was no long-standing revolutionary tradition in Mongolia, which perhaps explains how it was that the Mongol revolution fell so completely under Soviet control. The members of the clubs included men of varied social origin, lamas such as Bodoo the Premier of 1921 who was liquidated in 1922, government servants, workers, soldiers such as Sühbaatar, and returned students from Russia, such as Choybalsan. They had the sympathy of several prominent nobles through whom they were able to approach the King, while at the same time they acquired some knowledge of Marxism from their acquaintance with left-wing Russian workers in Urga. The first real contacts with Soviet Russia took place in early 1920 when a Comintern agent, Sorokovikov, came to Urga to assess the situation. It is therefore not surprising to find that the aims of the revolutionaries were at this time fairly moderate. First of all they desired national independence from the Chinese, then an elective government, internal administrative reforms, improved social justice, and the consolidation of the Buddhist faith and church. With Sorokovikov's approval they planned to send a delegation to Russia to seek help against the Chinese. They obtained the sanction of the King, and carried with them a letter authenticated with his seal. They were, in fact, authorized only to obtain advice from the Russians, not to negotiate actual intervention.

In their absence from Mongolia the situation was complicated by the incursion into the country of White Russian forces under Baron Ungern Sternberg. At first the Mongol authorities and the people welcomed the White Russians who dislodged the oppressive Chinese, and with the help of Ungern the King was restored to the throne. However, Ungern's brutalities soon turned the Mongols against him. More important, the Soviet agents dealing with the Mongol delegation were able to use Ungern's apparent ascendancy over the Urga regime to extract far-reaching concessions. They made the offer of help conditional upon the establishment in Urga later of a new government friendly to them. In March 1921 the first congress of the Mongol People's Party was held at Kyakhta on Soviet territory, and a provisional revolutionary government was also set up there in opposition to the legal authorities in Urga who had sponsored the delegates who now abandoned them. This provisional government gathered a small band of partisans who, with much more significant Soviet forces, entered Mongolia, defeated Ungern, and then marched on Urga. Here, in July 1921, a new government was proclaimed, under the restored King. The monarchy existed now, however, in name only. Mongolia came more and more under Soviet direction. A secret police force was set up and in 1922 the first of a long series of political purges took place. When, in 1924, the King died, a People's Republic was proclaimed with a constitution modelled on that of the Soviet Union.

The Mongolian People's Republic

Mongolia was now in name a People's Republic, the second socialist state in the world, but her primitive stage of development posed daunting problems. An unproductive church which commanded deep loyalty from the people weighed heavily on the economy and was a powerful ideological opponent of communism. Local separatism, especially in the far west, took years to overcome, and in some outlying parts local government could not be established till 1928 or 1929. Moreover, it was easy for disillusioned herdsmen to trek with their herds over the frontiers into China, and there were considerable losses of population by emigration. The country suffered from almost total illiteracy, and of those who could read and write many were in fact lamas whose skill was in Tibetan and not Mongol. The country's economy depended exclusively on extensive animal herding. Trade and crafts were in the hands of foreigners, almost all of them Chinese. There was no banking system, no national currency, no industry and no medical service in the modern sense. Finally, most of those men who were politically experienced and capable of running the local administration were lamas or nobles, two classes whom the revolutionary regime aimed at annihilating in time.

Thus the stage of economic, social and intellectual development which Mongolia had reached was far below the U.S.S.R.'s, and her capacity for independent action was practically nil against her one international partner, the immeasurably more powerful U.S.S.R. She was willy-nilly caught up with Soviet interests and developments and her history over the next two decades shows the same progression of events as characterized Stalin's U.S.S.R. At first, until 1928, there ensued a few years of semi-capitalist development, during which the privileges of the nobility and clergy were not gravely tampered with. In international contacts, too, the Mongols reached out to France and Germany. However, parallel with the rise of Stalin and the swing to the left in the U.S.S.R. there developed in Mongolia what came to be known as the "leftist deviation". All foreign contacts except with the U.S.S.R. were cut off. The U.S.S.R. monopolized Mongolia's trade in which she had hitherto had only a modest share. Between 1929 and 1932 an unprepared programme of collectivization ruined the country's economy, stocks of cattle dropping by at least one-third. A vicious anti-religious campaign did much to turn people against the Party, and in 1932 uprisings broke out which, particularly in west Mongolia, reached the proportions of civil war, and necessitated the intervention of the Soviet army. Thousands of Mongols deserted the country with their herds. This disastrous course was reversed only on the direct instructions of the Soviet Communist Party in June 1932. Leaders who until then had been enthusiastic leftists, such as Genden who became Premier and was later "unmasked" as a "Japanese spy" and liquidated by Choybalsan, now swung to a more moderate line, and under what was termed the "New Turn Policy" private ownership of cattle and private trade were again encouraged, and the Church was treated more gently. However, from 1936 onwards Mongolia fell under the dictatorship of Marshal

Choybalsan (died 1952), whose methods were indistinguishable from those of Stalin. The lamaist church was utterly destroyed with much loss of life and property, and most of the old guard of revolutionaries, politicians, high military officers and intellectuals were liquidated on charges, usually of treasonable plotting with the Japanese, which have since been acknowledged to have been quite false. This massive elimination of all opposition made it possible for Choybalsan to declare in 1940 that Mongolia could begin the transition from "democratic revolution" to "socialism". Party and government were now staffed by a new body of very young men, *protégés* of Choybalsan, some of whom, such as the present leader, Tsedenbal, have continued uninterruptedly in office until today.

The progress made by 1940 had been mostly negative, consisting in the elimination of old social groupings and the redistribution of wealth confiscated from the former nobles, liquidated in and after 1929, and the Church. A certain amount of reconstruction had been achieved, in the fields of education, medical services, communications and industry, but it was not until well after the Second World War that any drastic programme of modernization was to be attempted in Mongolia. One reason for this tardiness was the threat posed by the Japanese in Manchuria, which meant that most of the Soviet expenditure in Mongolia was devoted to a military build-up. It is significant that the only railway to be built in pre-war years served the base of Choybalsan in east Mongolia. Only after the war was Mongolia's main economic region, the centre, around Ulan Bator, to be connected with the Trans-Siberian line.

Post-War Political Developments

Mongolia escaped the worst of the Second World War, though suffering some effects. The Japanese in Manchuria had for some years been probing the defences of Mongolia, and in the summer of 1939 they provoked a series of battles on the Khalkha River (Halhyn Gol) in which they were heavily defeated by Soviet and Mongol troops. From then on a truce reigned until August 1945 when Mongolia followed the U.S.S.R. in declaring war on Japan. Mongol forces advanced as far as the Pacific coast of China, but were soon afterwards withdrawn, and the only advantage Mongolia drew from her belated participation in the war was the labour of a number of Japanese prisoners. On the debit side, imports from the U.S.S.R. almost dried up during the war years, and Mongolia herself made a heavy contribution to the Soviet war-effort, though she herself was never at war with Germany. As a result there was practically no economic progress. The one important event in Mongolia's history at this time was the recognition of her independence by China in January 1946 after a plebiscite the previous October had called for confirmation of the *status quo*. However, Mongolia's international position of isolation in unique dependence on the U.S.S.R. did not change until the communization of eastern Europe and the success of the Communists in China provided her with a new and ready-made field of diplomatic activity. Between October 1948 and March 1950 she exchanged diplomatic recognition with all the then existing communist states except Yugoslavia (1956), and thereafter with a number of non-aligned countries such as India, Burma and Indonesia. The United Kingdom was the first Western European state to recognize Mongolia. Mongolia was admitted to the United Nations in 1961.

Mongolia still looks mainly to the U.S.S.R. for guidance and help in her affairs in spite of her wider international contacts. In 1946 she abandoned her traditional alphabet in favour of a form of the Cyrillic script. Russian is the most widely known foreign language. Most of those students who study abroad do so in the U.S.S.R., while many textbooks are translated from Russian. But most important, Mongolia's party and state structure, public institutions, educational system, journalism and publications are clearly based on the Soviet model, while economic planning proceeds in close consultation with Soviet experts. Mongolia's alignment with the U.S.S.R. in the Sino-Soviet dispute was predictable, as was also her support of Soviet action in the 1968 Czechoslovak crisis. The official press continues to adopt a sharp anti-Maoist line. China is accused, among other things, of carrying out a colonialist policy in its minority areas, including Inner Mongolia, and, in Tsedenbal's words, of openly preparing for war with the U.S.S.R. and Mongolia.

The partial thaw which was initiated in the U.S.S.R. by Nikita Khrushchev was imitated in Mongolia, where the cult of personality was denounced in 1956 and again in 1962, and several of the leaders put to death in the 1930s were rehabilitated. Contacts with non-communist foreigners were permitted, a small tourist industry was built up, controls on publications somewhat relaxed. An individual feature of this period has been the reassertion of feelings of Mongolian nationalism, which for twenty years had been repressed. Since 1936 the existence of pre-revolutionary culture in Mongolia had been systematically denied. Nothing was taught of old Mongol literature in schools, no old books were reprinted, and party agents went round the countryside collecting and destroying old manuscripts as being contrary to contemporary ideology. After 1956 this policy was modified. School curricula, while still insisting that children be given a communist education which was to convince them of the inevitable victory of communism, were liberalized so far as to include extracts from ancient literature once more. The Committee of Sciences (from 1961, Academy) was able to begin quite an ambitious programme of research and publication in the fields of literature, history and linguistics, and to organize in 1959 the First International Congress of Mongolists. This was the first, and so far only occasion on which scholars from the Western world, the Soviet bloc and China have conferred together in Mongolia. This renascence of national sentiment has been rebuffed from time to time when it clashed with Soviet requirements of greater international communist conformity. The most blatant example of such interference came in 1962 when the Mongols celebrated the 800th anniversary of the birth of Genghiz Khan. The event was translated into the international sphere since the Chinese, for reasons of their own, also celebrated this event in Inner Mongolia. The enthusiasm provoked in Mongolia was seen by Moscow, and in more orthodox quarters in Mongolia itself, as manifesting excessive feelings of nationalism at the expense of "proletarian internationalism", and the celebrations were abruptly called off. Early in 1963 an ideological conference was held in Ulan Bator with the participation of a strong Soviet delegation, in order to reassert the correct political line. A further feature of political life in Mongolia during the 1960s was its brittle quality. On four occasions high party and government officials, hitherto respected comrades, were "unmasked" and dismissed on multiple charges of inefficiency, arrogance, dishonesty, corruption and so on.

In June 1974, Premier Yumjaagiyn Tsedenbal became Head of State, succeeding Jamsrangiyn Sambuu who died in May 1972. The new Premier, Jambyn Batmönh, was a comparative newcomer to political life.

With the increasing complexity of modern life, Mongolia faces the twin problem of making its legislation known to the public and ensuring observance of the law, and of exercising effective control over the work of individuals and enterprises. The importance of educating the public in their legal responsibilities, particularly those under the recent Labour Law, and of preventing crime and maintaining law and order, was stressed in one of the main speeches, that by Vice-Premier Tsevegmid, at the June 1974 meeting of the Great Hural. On the other front, a nation-wide system of control is being built up, with elective "groups" or "posts" in each enterprise. By February 1975, 2,171 groups and 1,618 posts, comprising over 30,000 individuals, were said to be at work. Among their tasks are those of promoting the fulfilment of the state plan, uncovering and correcting lapses of all sorts, reinforcing labour discipline, and safeguarding public property.

Asian Buddhist leaders have set up an "Asian Buddhists' Committee for the Furtherance of Co-operation" under the chairmanship of S. Gombojav, abbot of the Gandan lamasery in Ulan Bator. However, manifestations of interest in religion and religious practices are still sharply condemned as and when they become apparent among the population.

ECONOMIC SURVEY

Charles Bawden

From 1948 the Mongol economy has been developed under a series of Five-Year Plans with large-scale assistance from other communist countries, principally the countries now forming COMECON. The two salient features of post-war development have been the completion of the transition to the socialist system of production, and a rate of economic expansion very much faster than was achieved in the first thirty years of the Republic.

Agriculture: Collective and State Farms

After the catastrophe of the period of leftist deviation, animal herding, the mainstay of Mongolia's economy, had reverted to private enterprise, and apart from taking compulsory deliveries of produce during the war years the government had kept its hands off the herds. Small-scale mutual help in carrying out certain tasks was practised, and some herdsmen joined together in small producers' associations, but under the New Turn Policy the formation of co-operatives was discouraged. By 1952 the existing co-operatives contained only 280,000 animals out of a national stock of nearly 23 million. However, collectivization of herding had by 1947 again become a matter of policy and in that year the Central Committee of the Party was given the task of examining the situation. Although collectivization is said to have been carried out voluntarily by the herdsmen, the initiative came from the Party, and propaganda and economic compulsion were widely used to persuade people to join. Thus, state loans were granted to newly-formed co-operatives, discriminatory rates of taxation were imposed on individuals who owned large herds and similarly differential norms of compulsory deliveries of produce were set. The collectivization programme reached its peak in 1958 and by April 1959 all but a tiny minority of herdsmen had been collectivized. Great attention was paid to the Soviet *kolkhoz* system in organizing the Mongol co-operatives. These are quite different in character from the earlier producers' associations. They are of considerable size, and are units of local administration as well as economic units. Labour is regulated by means of work books issued to each member, who receives pay according to his work. All families are allowed to retain a certain number of private animals. Produce is purchased by the state which also grants loans to the co-operatives. Internally, each co-operative is organized into a number of permanent brigades, each with its own territory and headquarters and its own special tasks. The brigade in its turn contains a number of bases, each base consisting usually of two households living in felt tents and looking after a number of animals.

An innovation in the Mongolian rural economy has been the development of large-scale agriculture. This did not affect any previous pattern of economic activity, and from the start was organized as a direct state venture. Ten state farms existed in 1940 and 46 state farms and "fodder farms" in 1973. In and after 1959 the area ploughed up increased sharply as large tracts of virgin land were opened, but the sown area was smaller in 1970 than in 1965. Increasing attention is to be paid to mechanization and the introduction of scientific methods. The division of activity between the 268 herding co-operatives and the state farms is not a strict one. Co-operatives also engage in field work, especially fodder growing, and in craft work, while state farms are also expected to supply good breeding animals. The principal crops produced by the state farms are cereals, potatoes and vegetables.

Though still of major importance, Mongolia's rural economy, and in particular its main sector, animal-herding, continues to lag, as was stressed by Premier Tsedenbal in a speech in February 1971. However, the catastrophic losses of animals suffered in 1967 and 1968 through *dzud* (spring starvation when the winter-weakened beasts fail to break through the hard snow-cover to reach the available grazing) are said to have been made good by mid-1973. The perennial problem of poor quality of production in both the rural economy and industry, which is regularly aired in the press, was the subject of a national discussion held in June 1973. Certain sectors showed improvement, but attention was drawn to continuing grave defects and their bad effect not only upon domestic consumers but also with regard to Mongolia's export plans. The quality of sheep skins produced in certain provinces was much below the standard of 10 years ago, for example, while field crops showed a sharp decline in quality as compared with 1969. To some extent this decline could be attributed to climatic vagaries, but D. Gombojav, a Vice-Chairman of the Council of Ministers, blamed other factors as well. He said that the main causes for the poor quality of rural production were failure to observe national standards and technical directives, poor technical and labour discipline, and failure to establish proper standards of control. Another factor was complacency at the beginning of a planned period of work, succeeded by rush and emergency action towards the end. However, in reviewing the rural economy in June 1974, Tsedenbal noted some improvements. Twelve per cent more young animals had been produced than in 1973, while both barrenness in females and unproductive losses had been drastically reduced. In January 1975, the net increase in livestock for the year was estimated at 771,500 (1971: 117,700). Poor weather conditions resulted in a grain yield of only 354,700 tons, 10 per cent less than planned, and in a poor potato crop. In 1975, by contrast, 536,000 tons of grain were harvested, well above the planned figure.

A new theme, and one repeatedly developed in the press in the last year or two, is that of the importance of nature conservancy. This problem is assuming critical importance even in Mongolia's under-developed territory. Two aspects especially are stressed—forest protection and control of hunting. Proper methods of forestry are regularly urged and much reafforestation has been achieved, but good intentions are too often frustrated by local indifference and laziness. Woods are cleared in wholesale fashion and not replanted, young wood is cut for fuel, cut wood is left to rot unused, and negligence leads to bad forest and pasture fires. New laws concerning water and forests were promulgated in July 1974.

Industry

Large-scale industry has developed only since the revolution. Before the revolution most manufactured requisites had been imported or were made locally, chiefly by Chinese craftsmen. In the 1920s technicians from Western Europe were engaged to help develop Mongolia's infant industry. In particular they built a power station and a brickworks. But after the swing to the left in 1929 only Soviet aid and expertise were welcome, and in pre-war years industrial growth was slow. Only one enterprise of any size was commissioned, the Industrial Combine in Ulan Bator, which commenced production in 1934 of leather goods and felts. Industry has developed in two channels. Co-operative industry has a much smaller output than state industry. It produces many items needed for domestic use, as well as providing repair services. Since the war, the state-operated industry has expanded rapidly, given Mongolian conditions, and many new enterprises have been commissioned.

Mongolia has received enormous aid from her political allies, without which her industrial advance, modest though it is in world terms, could not have been envisaged. For a while, in the 1950s, it seemed as if China was hoping to challenge the U.S.S.R.'s leading position in Mongolia, using the weapon of economic aid. A first gift of 160 million roubles in 1955 was followed by the dispatch of Chinese labourers to help Mongolia's inadequate and under-trained labour force. Exact numbers are not available, but in the peak years of 1959 and 1960 several thousands of Chinese were working on diverse projects, building apartment blocks, laying roads and irrigation systems, and so on. Many had their families with them. As the Sino-Soviet rift widened, the Chinese labourers began to leave Mongolia, till by mid-1964 most had gone home. To some extent the loss of these workers has been made good by the supply of Soviet construction troops, working principally in Ulan Bator, the Darhan area and Choybalsan, where a third industrial area is planned. However, the break with China had other adverse effects. Chinese consumer goods, in particular silk and cloth, which were plentiful in 1959, were, by 1968, no longer available. The drastic drop in railway through-goods traffic between the U.S.S.R. and China also meant a considerable loss of state revenue.

For purposes of immediate and long-range economic planning, the MPR is considered as comprising three economic regions—Central, Western and Eastern, of which the first is the most significant. There are also a number of sub-regions.

The principal centres of industry in Mongolia are both in the central economic region, at Ulan Bator and Darhan, half-way between the capital and the Soviet frontier. Both centres are situated in the area of densest population and have direct road and rail communication with the U.S.S.R. Both have their own coal supplies also, Ulan Bator at Nalayh, and Darhan at an open cast mine at Sharyn Gol, to which it is linked by a new rail spur. Light producing and service industries are to be found elsewhere in the country: coal is mined in each of the provinces, for example, and an important vehicle repair station has been opened in Hovd. However, the two centres mentioned account for most of Mongolia's production in terms of electric power, capital materials such as cement, bricks and wall panels, and consumer goods—food, drink, leather goods, china, sweets, soap and so on.

Perhaps the most important event in the development of Mongolia's economy during 1973 was the signing in February of a treaty on joint Soviet-Mongol exploitation of copper and molybdenum deposits at Erdenet Ovoo in Bulgan province. A joint Mongol-Soviet enterprise, "Mongolsovsvetmet", is being set up for this purpose. The deposits are located near Hangal sum, about two hours' journey by road to the west of Darhan, and thus accessible to transport routes. A concentration plant, and a town to house 10,000 workers is under construction. The Salhit-Erdenet ovoo railway line, linking the new complex with the main rail system, went into operation on October 4th, 1975. This promises to be the largest scale exploitation of ores in the Republic.

Mongolia has no single major industry. She continues to rely heavily on imports from abroad to satisfy both capital construction and consumer demand. Nevertheless, home production increases annually, in a race, as it were, with the rapidly rising population. But to judge from a reading of the press, underuse of machinery, waste of energy and raw materials, poor deployment of labour, and inefficient application of technology and scientific knowledge, as well as what is termed slack labour discipline, appear to be a chronic drag on the progress of the economy. Criticisms similar to those voiced by Tsedenbal in 1966 at the 15th Party Congress continue to be uttered, as for example, by Ts. Gürbadam, Chairman of the Permanent Planning and Budget Commission of the Great Hural, in late 1975, in summing up the year's achievements and introducing the national plan for 1976.

Starting in 1968 a number of enterprises have been going over to what is termed the "new planned management economic system". Press articles on this topic stress that the Mongol system is much indebted to Soviet and Hungarian experience in this field. The "new system" aims at increased output, higher productivity and profitability, etc., to be promoted by the "scientific organization of labour", and by material rewards and incentives which take account not only of quantitative plan fulfilment as previously, but also of considerations of quality, economy in use of raw materials, discovery and use of "concealed resources", reduction in unnecessary movement and in wasted hours, and so on. The new system is being applied not only to industrial enterprises but to others as well.

A drive for increased initiative was begun in 1971 jointly by the State Committee for Labour and Wages and the State Commission for New Initiatives. Prizes have been awarded to individuals who submitted new ideas for innovations in work processes, but difficulty has been experienced in translating some of the accepted ideas into action. As part of this system, and in an effort to improve accounting procedures, information-flow, internal work-evaluation and price-fixing, etc., Mongolia is experimenting with "industrial co-operatives" (*uildverleliyn negdel*) which appear to be groupings of enterprises within an industry. Soviet experience is being drawn upon.

Foreign Trade

Trade is almost entirely with the countries of the "socialist bloc" but concrete figures are not available. Progress is being made towards economic integration within Comecon. Mongolia exports mainly primary products and imports industrial goods and equipment. Nearly 60 per cent of her exports consist of raw materials, including hides, furs and wool. Raw foodstuffs and food products, including livestock, meat and meat products, account for another 30 per cent. Industrial consumer goods, including leather goods, make up only 6 per cent. The main imports are consumer goods (33 per cent), machinery and equipment (26.5 per cent), fuels, minerals and metals (14 per cent), and food products (13.6 per cent). Apart from this, the Mongol armed forces are equipped from Soviet bloc countries.

Power and Transport

Fuel of many types is used in Mongolia. At one end of the scale is the new thermal power station at Darhan, built with Soviet help and designed to serve the north-central region through a power line stretching from Sühbaatar to Ulan Bator. *Aymag* (provincial) centres may have thermal power stations or diesel generators, and in smaller rural centres small diesel generators are the rule. Domestic heating in apartment blocks in Ulan Bator is by central town-heating from the power station. Elsewhere wood, roots, bushes and dried animal dung are used for domestic firing. Transport shows a similar range of sophistication. Ulan Bator is linked with the U.S.S.R. (Moscow direct and via Irkutsk) and distant provincial centres by turbo-prop aircraft. The direct Trans-Siberian rail route from Moscow to Peking now traverses Mongolia, and there is another link between the Trans-Siberian and the town of Choybalsan. Otherwise long-distance transport is mainly by lorry or Soviet-built *gazik* (jeep-type vehicle), but horse, ox and camel carts are still widely used, even in Ulan Bator, and camels are employed as beasts of burden. Periodically a call is made for greater use of local animal transport. Water transport is not of great significance.

Plan Fulfilment

The fifth Five-Year Plan for 1971-75 was published in the form of proposals in April 1971 and confirmed by the 16th Party Congress which was held in June. During 1975, the final year of the fifth plan, considerable attention was being paid to the problem of increasing production while effecting economies. This was to be achieved partly through the promotion and development of the familiar device of "socialist competition" and also through the further device of "augmented plans" (*ugtvar tolovlogoo*). The latter appear to be a formalization of the tasks assumed by an enterprise in addition to its normal obligations.

Many *aimaks* published their additional targets early in 1975. Extra production was to be achieved within the limits of material and labour resources authorized for the original level. In connection with the recently promulgated Labour Law, but also with the aim of engaging workers more fully in the implementation of the state plan, regulations for trades union committees, made in 1960, were replaced by a new set in July 1974. Among the duties allotted to these bodies was the direction of the "local courts", primary-level local elective courts which deal with minor offences, and which are also intended to persuade, in a friendly manner, individuals with backward or anti-communist views, to change their attitudes. There are now over 1,000 of these courts, first introduced under a decision of the Great Hural of 1960.

The basic directive for the Sixth Five-Year National Economic and Cultural Plan for 1976–80 was published by the Central Committee of the Mongol People's Revolutionary Party in April 1976, preparatory to discussion later in the year at the 17th plenary meeting of the Party. The basic aims of the new plan were to increase the social product, to raise profitability, to improve quality in all branches of economy and culture, and on this basis to improve the material conditions and raise the cultural level of the population. There was thus no fundamental change in the national policy of the Fifth Five-Year Plan, and the main interest of the plan resided in its more detailed provisions. In the rural economy great emphasis was laid on the development of agriculture, with a sharp increase in the production of grain, potatoes and vegetables forecast. To achieve this, it was intended to bring 230,000 hectares of virgin land under cultivation, and to establish eleven new state farms, together with other new agricultural enterprises. The area of irrigated farmland was to be increased by at least two and a half times by 1980. A range of measures was also proposed to increase the numbers of livestock and to raise productivity. In industry, the main aims were to increase reserves of power, to improve product quality and to raise productivity with the intention of providing a better domestic supply of goods and increasing exports. In this respect, a new opencast coal mine at Baga nuur in the Central Economic Region, deserves mention. According to the Plan, the output was estimated at some two million tons by 1979, and the new mine would be linked by rail to the main system via Maan't; geological prospecting and exploitation of mineral resources would be developed, the Erdenet ovoo enterprise would come into operation, and zinc deposits at Salhit in the Central Region would be exploited. Industrial production as a whole would rise by up to 65 per cent, with labour productivity rising by up to 38 per cent. There would be an increase of 25 per cent in the number of hospital beds, no doubt in part a reflection of Mongolia's rapidly growing population. Emphasis was laid upon measures to be taken for the closer integration of Mongolia's economy within COMECON. In particular, the question of the exploitation of Mongolia's mineral wealth, within the linked plan for socialist economic integration, was to be elaborated in association with interested member countries of COMECON. Further co-operation with socialist countries in the fields of education, health, culture, art and sport, was planned.

The five years, 1976–80, were expected to be a decisive stage in Mongolia's transition from an agrarian-industrial state to an industrial-agrarian state.

STATISTICAL SURVEY

Revised by **A. J. K. Sanders**

AREA AND POPULATION

Area (sq. km.)	Population	
	Total (1976)	Ulan Bator (1974)
1,565,000	1,468,600	310,000

Average expectation of life (1975): 65 years (death rate between 9 and 10 per 1,000).

ADMINISTRATIVE REGIONS

Province (Aymag)	Area ('000 sq. km.)	Provincial Districts (sum)*	Population ('000)†	Provincial Centre
Arhangay	55	17	72.3	Tsetserleg
Bayanhongor	116	19	52.4	Bayanhongor
Bayan-ölgiy	46	12	58.1	Ölgiy
Bulgan	49	14	37.4	Bulgan
Dornod (Eastern)	122	13	42.9	Choybalsan
Dornogov' (East Gobi)	111	14	30.9	Saynshand
Dundgov' (Central Gobi)	78	15	30.7	Mandalgov'
Dzavhan	82	22	70.8	Uliastay
Gov'-altay	142	17	47.4	Altay
Hentiy	82	20	40.1	Öndörhaan
Hovd	76	15	54.0	Hovd
Hövsgöl	101	23	74.8	Mörön
Ömnögov' (South Gobi)	165	15	26.4	Dalandzadgad
Övörhangay	63	18	66.8	Arvayheer
Selenge	43	12	42.7	Sühbaatar
Sühbaatar	82	13	35.3	Baruun urt
Töv (Central)	81	24	63.6	Dzuun mod
Uvs	69	19	60.3	Ulaangom

* January 1st, 1970. † 1969 census.

EMPLOYMENT

(% of total employees in material production—1975)

Industry and construction	22.4
Agriculture	45.1
Transport and communications	5.6
Trade	6.4
Other	20.5

AGRICULTURE

SOWN AREAS

('000 hectares)

	1972	1973	1974	1975
All crops	475.3	488.6	495.0	501.3

PRINCIPAL CROPS

('000 metric tons)

	1972	1973	1974	1975
Cereals	232.0	516.4	354.7	525.0
Fodder crops . . .	n.a.	620.0	n.a.	536.3
Hay	600.0	808.9	838.6	874.6

LIVESTOCK

('000)

	1960	1965	1970
Sheep	12,101.9	13,838.0	13,311.7
Goats	5,631.3	4,786.3	4,204.0
Horses	2,502.7	2,432.6	2,317.9
Cattle	1,905.5	2,093.0	2,107.8
Camels	859.1	684.7	633.5
TOTAL . .	23,000.5	23,834.6	22,574.9
Pigs	10.9*	19.6	10.7
Poultry	104.4*	179.0	132.6

* 1961.

Total livestock: 22,692,600 in 1971; 23,109,100 in 1972; 23,541,100 in 1973; 24,313,200 in 1974; 24,450,500 (est.) in 1975.

STATE PROCUREMENTS OF AGRICULTURAL PRODUCTS

		1960	1965	1970
Cattle	'000 tons live weight	48.3	41.7	42.3
Sheep	,, ,, ,, ,,	69.0	79.0	77.4
Goats	,, ,, ,, ,,	18.3	22.4	16.3
Horses	'000 head	38.8	86.7	88.8
Milk	million litres	94.6	89.7	63.2
Wool	'000 tons	14.8	18.6	18.5
Camel hair	,, ,,	3.8	3.4	3.2
Cattle hides	'000	196.1	248.6	291.0
Sheep skins	,,	1,277.3	1,839.4	2,232.5
Marmot pelts	,,	1,034.2	1,208.8	1,201.0
Squirrel skins	,,	140.3	112.8	35.6
Fox skins	,,	34.3	49.5	41.4

INDUSTRY

INDUSTRIAL PRODUCTION

		1960	1965	1970
Electricity	million kWh.	106.4	242.0	493.0
Coal	'ooo tons	618.8	989.5	1,997.4
Fluorspar	„ „	40.3	49.6	76.9
Bricks	million	77.5	43.6	61.7
Lime	'ooo tons	17.3	15.3	28.4
Sawn Timber	'ooo cu. metres	151.7	187.0	382.6
Felt	'ooo metres	295.2	445.8	550.1
Leather Footwear	'ooo pairs	904.3	1,403.0	1,618.8
Matches	million boxes	32.7	4.5	35.0
Woollen Fabric	'ooo metres	229.1	514.1	623.7
Flour	'ooo tons	26.3	77.1	83.3
Meat	„ „	13.1	19.6	34.9
Fish	tons	815.0	357.3	337.5
Butter	'ooo tons	4.8	4.1	2.9
Vodka	'ooo litres	909.3	978.6	2,691.4
Beer	„ „	1,129.4	1,712.0	1,801.1

EMPLOYEES IN INDUSTRY
('ooo)

	1960	1965	1970
Power	0.6	1.5	2.6
Coal	2.3	2.6	2.6
Petroleum	0.4	0.4	0.4
Non-ferrous Metallurgy and Ore Mining	0.4	0.6	0.5
Engineering and Metal-working	0.8	1.5	2.3
Chemicals	0.7	0.8	0.9
Building Materials	3.7	3.5	5.9
Timber and Wood-working	3.9	6.2	6.2
Glass and Porcelain	0.2	0.2	0.4
Textiles	1.1	2.2	2.2
Tanning, Furs and Shoes	3.5	4.6	5.0
Printing and Publishing	1.2	1.7	1.8
Food Industry	5.0	9.2	8.8
TOTAL	35.3	39.9	45.8

ELECTRICITY CONSUMPTION
('ooo kWh.—1968)

Gross Generation	381,701.6
Industry	157,523.6
Agriculture	17,232.3
Forestry	37.8
Construction	8,027.6
Transport	13,914.1
Communications	8,622.0
Trade, Procurement and Supply	10,136.5
Housing and Utilities	86,265.0
Science, Education, Culture	13,909.1
Health, Welfare, Sport	6,395.5
Other	7,120.5
Own Use	28,063.5
Loss in Circuit	24,454.1

BUILDING MACHINERY

	1960	1965	1970
Excavators	71	103	181
Scrapers	20	35	25
Bulldozers	68	118	165
Cranes	17	233	391

HOUSING CONSTRUCTION

	1960	1965	1970
Completed ('ooo sq. m.)	91.0	80.2	85.8

FIFTH FIVE-YEAR PLAN (1971–75)

Agriculture

	Growth 1971–75 (%)
Livestock (to 25 million)	11
on State Farms	20
Agricultural Co-operatives	12
Gross Animal Husbandry Production	14–16
Milk Yields	15
State Procurement:	
Meat	15
Wool	13
Milk	25
Fodder Production	60
Area under Fodder Crops	80
Gross Crop Production	60
Grain	26.7
Potatoes	70
Vegetables	120
Crop Procurement	50.60
Crop Yields:	
Grain	23
Potatoes	41
Vegetables	46

	Planned Increase 1971–75 (units)
Livestock-breeding Farms	21
Cattle Sheds	20,000
Wells	6,000
Farm Machinery Service Stations	50
Tractors	4,300
Grain Combines	1,000
Lorries	1,400
Tractor and Lorry Trailers	2,000
Special Motor Vehicles	400

Annual Production Targets for 1975

Coal ('000 tons)	2,500–2,600
Leather Footwear ('000 pairs)	2,200–2,500
Woollen Cloth ('000 sq. metres)	1,300
Carpets (sq. metres)	300,000
Felt for Yurts (metres)	550,000
Felt Boots (pairs)	415,000

Note: Power station capacity to be put into operation 1971–75 is to total 65,000 kW.

Industry

	Growth 1971–75 (%)
Volume of Production (9.3% a year)	56
Fuel and Power Industry Output	40
Coal Production	50–55
Electricity Generation	48
Mining Industry Production	150
Building Materials Industry Production	60
Walling Materials	70
Cement	110
Concrete and Ferroconcrete Articles	40
Timber and Wood-working Industry Production	39
Factory-made Standard Housing	70
Light Industry Production	52
Leather, Footwear and Fur Production	42
Printing Industry	22.4
Metal-working Industry	40
Chemicals and Pharmaceuticals	100
Food Industry Output	66
Meat and Meat Products	74
Dairy Produce	100
Bakery Products	40
Confectionery	70
Flour	40
Output of Industrial Co-operatives	30
Sewn Goods	70
Yurt Frames	200
Crockery	270

Industrial Productivity

	Growth 1971–75 (%)
Power Industry	32.4
Coal Industry	31.0
Mining	13.0
Building and Assembly Organizations	41.1
Building Materials Industry	40.0
Timber and Wood-working Industry	35.5
Light Industry	24.9
Food Industry	50.0
Industrial Co-operatives	41.1

FIFTH FIVE YEAR PLAN (1971-75)—*Continued*]

GROSS CAPITAL INVESTMENT

	1971–75 (%)
Agriculture	35.0
Industry	23.0
Education, Health, Science, Culture, Housing	22.0
Transport and Communications	10.0
Capital Construction	4.6
Trade and Catering	2.3

Note: During the 1971–75 period 390,000 sq. metres of housing was to be built with central capital investment.

WAGES, TRADE, SERVICES

	GROWTH 1971–75 (%)
Average Wage	7.5
Retail Trade Turnover	24.0
Public Catering	20.0
Book Trade	25.0
Service Industry	30.0
Hospital Beds	17.6
Physicians	30.0

FINANCE

100 möngö = 1 tögrög (tughrik).

Coins: 1, 2, 5, 10, 15, 20 and 50 möngö; 1 tögrög.

Notes: 1, 3, 5, 10, 25, 50 and 100 tögrög.

Exchange rates (June 1976): £1 sterling = 5.91 tögrög; U.S. $1 = 3.36 tögrög.

100 tögrög = £16.92 = $29.76.

Note: Prior to August 1971 the basic exchange rate was U.S. $1 = 4.00 tögrög (1 tögrög = 25 U.S. cents). Between December 1971 and February 1973 the rate was $1 = 3.684 tögrög (1 tögrög = 27.14 U.S. cents). In terms of sterling, the basic exchange rate from November 1967 to June 1972 was £1 = 9.60 tögrög.

BUDGET 1976
(million tögrög)

REVENUE	
Turnover Tax, Price Differences	1,979.6
Deductions from Profits, Fixed Payments	749.9
Revenue from Forestry and Hunting	84.5
Income Tax from Rural Co-operatives	13.0
Social Insurance	125.0
Other Taxes	35.5
TOTAL	2,987.5

EXPENDITURE	
National Economy	1,134.1
Social and Cultural Services	1,281.6
Administration	131.8
Defence	407.0
Unspecified	18.0
TOTAL	2,972.5

EXTERNAL TRADE

COMMODITIES (%—1970)

	Export	Import
Machinery and Equipment	0.3	26.5
Fuels, Minerals, Metals	5.2	14.2
Chemicals, Fertilizers, Rubber	—	5.4
Building Materials	0.9	1.8
Raw Materials of Plant and Animal Origin, excl. Foodstuffs	58.2	2.1
Raw Materials for Production of Foodstuffs	19.7	0.3
Foodstuffs	9.7	13.5
Industrial Consumer Goods	6.0	32.9
Total	100.0	100.0

COUNTRIES (%)

	1960	1965	1970
Exports	100.0	100.0	100.0
to Socialist Countries	99.7	99.2	99.1
including:			
CMEA	94.0	92.7	94.4
Others	5.7	6.5	4.7
to Capitalist Countries	0.3	0.8	0.9
Imports	100.0	100.0	100.0
from Socialist Countries	99.8	99.2	99.1
including:			
CMEA	75.9	94.4	97.3
Others	23.9	4.8	1.8
from Capitalist Countries	0.2	0.8	0.9

Mongolia's Trade Within CMEA

Approximately 95 per cent of Mongolia's trade is with CMEA countries.

	Exports			Imports		
	1967	1968	1969	1967	1968	1969
U.S.S.R. (million roubles)	n.a.	47.8	47.5	n.a.	174.5	176.6
Bulgaria (million leva)	2.6	1.9	n.a.	2.9	2.5	n.a.
Czechoslovakia (million Czech crowns)	49.0	46.0	n.a.	66.0	57.0	n.a.
German Democratic Republic (million marks)	n.a.	12.2	16.7	n.a.	26.4	22.1
Hungary (million foreign exchange forints)	n.a.	24.5	23.7	n.a.	71.0	49.5
Poland (million złotys)	n.a.	17.1	17.0	n.a.	14.5	14.1
Romania (million lei)	n.a.	9.1	10.9	n.a.	11.3	12.6

Note: **Trade between Mongolia and China in 1970 and 1971 has been estimated at U.S. $1,000,000 each way in both years.**

Mongolian-Soviet trade turnover (about 85 per cent of all Mongolia's trade), 1971: 240 million roubles; 1972: 290 million; 1973: 338.5 million; 1974: 404.3 million; 1975 (estimate): 509.4 million. In 1974 Mongolian exports to the U.S.S.R. were worth 119.1 million roubles and imports from the U.S.S.R. 285.2 million roubles.

TRANSPORT

FREIGHT TURNOVER (million ton/km.)

	1960	1965	1970	Growth 1971–75* (%)
Rail	3,036.3	900.3	1,527.6	25.0
Road	201.4	417.8	610.5	20.0
Water	2.6	3.1	3.7	n.a.
Air	0.8	1.2	1.5	n.a.
Total	3,241.1	1,322.4	2,143.3	24.4

FREIGHT CARRIAGE

(million tons)

	1960	1965	1970
Rail	3.9	2.4	4.7
Road	3.4	8.9	9.7
Water	0.02	0.02	0.03
TOTAL	7.3	11.3	14.4

PASSENGER TURNOVER

(million passenger/km.)

	1960	1965	1970	GROWTH 1971–75* (%)
Rail	0.4	0.4	0.7	13.0
Road	17.6	28.5	51.4	28.0†
Air	0.05	0.1	0.2	10.0
TOTAL	18.0	29.0	52.3	21.8

Note: Air route length in 1969: 31,000 km.

* Five-Year Plan. † Urban transport.

COMMUNICATIONS MEDIA

	1960	1965	1970
Post Offices	230	376	401
Telephone Exchanges	36	67	93
Telephones ('000)	5.6	11.8	19.5
Radio Relay Stations	44	134	141
Radio Sets ('000)	19	82.7	99.8
Television Sets ('000)	—	—	20
Telephone and Telegraph Lines ('000 km.)	13.8	14.1	16.8

	GROWTH 1971–75* (%)
Length of Telephone and Telegraph Lines	51.1
Capacity of Telephone Exchanges	21.7
Number of Television Sets	100.0

* Five-Year Plan.

EDUCATION

	Institutions			Teachers ('000)		
	1965	1970	1975	1960	1965	1970
General Schools	557	593	561	5.7	6.9	8.7
Secondary Specialized	18	19	22	0.6	0.6	0.7
Higher	7	5	6	0.6	0.6	0.7

STUDENTS
('000)

	1972/73	1973/74	1974/75
General	261.1	274.5	302.9
Secondary specialized	11.1	11.3	12.9
Technical	n.a.	11.6	13.3
Higher	8.9	10.1	12.8
Total	281.1	307.5	341.9

THE CONSTITUTION

The Mongolian People's Republic is a sovereign democratic state of working people. All land, natural resources, factories, transport and banking organizations are state property. In addition to state ownership the people have co-operative ownership of public enterprises, especially in livestock herding. A limited degree of private ownership is also permitted.

The supreme state power is the People's Great Hural (Assembly), which is elected every four years by universal, direct and secret suffrage of all citizens over the age of 18; the last elections took place in June 1973. It has the power of amending the Constitution (by a two-thirds majority), adopting laws, formulating the basic principles of policy and approving the budget and economic plans. Its Presidium consists of a Chairman (who is Head of State), First Vice-Chairman, a Vice-Chairman, a Secretary and seven members. The functions of the Presidium are to interpret legislation and issue decrees, ratify treaties and appoint or dismiss (with the approval of the People's Great Hural) the members of the Council of Ministers.

The Council of Ministers is the highest executive power and consists of the Chairman, First Vice-Chairmen, Vice-Chairmen, Ministers and Chairmen of State Commissions.

Local government is exercised by Hurals and their executive committees at Aymag (Province) and Somon (County) levels.

THE GOVERNMENT

HEAD OF STATE

Chairman of the Presidium of the People's Great Hural: YUMJAAGIYN TSEDENBAL.

First Vice-Chairman of the Presidium of the People's Great Hural: SONOMYN LUVSAN.

THE COUNCIL OF MINISTERS

(*June* 1976)

Chairman: JAMBYN BATMÖNH.

First Deputy Chairmen: DAMDINJAVYN MAYDAR (Chairman, State Committee for Science and Technology), TÜMENBAYARYN RAGCHAA.

Vice-Chairmen:

CHOYNORYN SÜREN.

MYATAVYN PELJEE.

Chairman, Commission for CMEA Affairs DAMDINY GOMBOJAV.

Chairman, Commission for Construction and Architecture SONOMYN LUVSANGOMBO.

Chairman, Committee for Higher and Special Secondary Education DONDOGIYN TSEVEGMID.

Chairman, State Planning Commission DUMAAGIYN SODNOM.

Minister of Agriculture: MANGALJAVYN DASH.

Minister of Fuel and Power Industry: PUNSALMAAGIYN OCHIRBAT.

Minister of Geology and Mining Industry: CHOYJINGIYN HURTS.

Minister of Light and Food Industries: PAAVANGIYN DAMDIN.

Minister of Construction and Building Materials Industry: ORONY TLEYHAN.

Minister of Forestry and Woodworking Industry: DAMDINGIYN TSEDEN.

Minister of Transport: BATMÖNHIYN ENEBISH.

Minister of Water Economy: BAVUUDORJIYN BARS.

Minister of Communications: DAHYN GOTOV.

Minister of Trade and Procurement: DUNJMAAGIYN DORJGOTOV.

Minister of Foreign Trade: YONDONGIYN OCHIR.

Minister of Finance: TSENDIYN MOLOM.

Minister of Foreign Affairs: LODONGIYN RINCHIN.

Minister of Defence: Army Gen. BATYN DORJ.

Minister of Public Security: Lt.-Gen. BUGYN DEJID.

Minister of Education: DENDZENGIYN ISHTSEREN.

Minister of Health: DAR'SÜRENGIYN NYAM-OSOR.

Minister of Communal Economy and Services: ORSOOGIYN NYAMAA.

Minister of Justice: DONOYN PÜREV.

Chairman, People's Control Committee: LEGDENGIYN DAMDINJAV.

Head, Central Statistical Directorate: DAMIRANJAVYN DZAGASBALDAN.

Chairman, Board of State Bank: DARIYN DANDZAN.

Chairman, State Committee for Labour and Wages: MYATAVYN LHAMSÜREN.

Chairman, State Committee for Information, Radio and Television: SEREETERIYN PÜREVJAV.

President, Academy of Sciences: BADZARYN SHIRENDEV

Chairman State Committee for Foreign Economic Relations (Minister): DANGAASÜRENGIYN SALDAN.

Head, Civil Defence Directorate: Maj.-Gen. CHOYJIVIYN TÜMENDEMBEREL.

Director of Administration, Council of Ministers: BALDANGIYN BADARCH.

First Deputy Chairman, State Planning Commission (Minister): BYAMBYN RINCHINPELJEE.

Chairman, State Committee for Prices and Standards: DASHIYN BYAMBASÜREN

Minister of Culture: SANDAGIYN SOSORBARAM.

PARLIAMENT

PEOPLE'S GREAT HURAL

Presidium

Chairman: YUMJAAGIYN TSEDENBAL.

First Vice-Chairman: SONOMYN LUVSAN.

Vice-Chairman: TSAGAANLAMYN DÜGERSÜREN.

Secretary: TSEDENDAMBYN GOTOV.

Members: NAMSRAYN LUVSANRAVDAN, SANJIYN BATAA, DONDOVIYN YONDONDÜYCHIR, GOMBOJAVYN OCHIRBAT, CHOYJILYN PUREVJAV, SONOMYN UDVAL, LODONGIYN TÜDEV.

Chairman of the People's Great Hural: N. LUVSANCHÜLTEM.

Chairman of the Executive Committee of the Parliamentary Group: D. TSEVEGMID.

POLITICAL PARTY

Mongolian People's Revolutionary Party: Ulan Bator; f. 1921; total membership 66,933 (June 1976).

The Central Committee elected at the XVIIth Congress in June 1976 had 91 members and 61 candidate members.

First Secretary of the Central Committee: YUMJAAGIYN TSEDENBAL.

Members of the Political Bureau and Secretaries of the Central Committee: NYAMYN JAGVARAL, DEMCHIGIYN MOLOMJAMTS, SAMPILYN JALAN-AAJAV, DAMDINY GOMBOJAV.

Members of the Political Bureau: TÜMENBAYARYN RAGCHAA, DAMDINJAVYN MAYDAR, NAMSRAYN LUVSANRAVDAN (also Chairman of the Party Central Committee), JAMBYN BATMÖNH.

Candidate Members of the Political Bureau: TÜMENBAYARYN RAGCHAA, BAT-OCHIRYN ALTANGEREL.

Secretary of the Central Committee: SANDAGIYN SOSORBARAM.

Director of the Institute of Party History: BADAMTARYN BALDOO.

Director of the Higher Party School: BAYTATSYN HURMYETBYEK.

DIPLOMATIC REPRESENTATION

EMBASSIES ACCREDITED TO MONGOLIA

(Res.) Resident in Ulan Bator.

Afghanistan: Moscow, U.S.S.R.
Algeria: Peking, People's Republic of China.
Argentina: Moscow, U.S.S.R.
Australia: Moscow, U.S.S.R.
Austria: Moscow, U.S.S.R.
Bangladesh: Moscow, U.S.S.R.
Belgium: Moscow, U.S.S.R.
Bulgaria: *Ambassador:* KOSTADIN GEORGIEV GYAUROV.
Burma: Peking, People's Republic of China.
Canada: Moscow, U.S.S.R.
China, People's Republic: *Ambassador:* CHANG WEI-LIEH (Res.).
Congo People's Republic: *Ambassador:* PIERRE NGUONIMBA NKZARI.
Cuba: *Ambassador:* RICARDO A. DANSA SIGAS.
Czechoslovakia: *Ambassador:* VLADIMIR BARTOS (Res.).
Denmark: Moscow, U.S.S.R.
Egypt: Moscow, U.S.S.R.
Finland: Moscow, U.S.S.R.
France: *Ambassador:* GEORGES DE BOUTEILLER.
German Democratic Republic: *Ambassador:* B. HANDWERKER (Res.).
Germany, Federal Republic: Tokyo, Japan.
Greece: Moscow, U.S.S.R.
Guinea: Moscow, U.S.S.R.
Hungary: *Ambassador:* ISTVÁN KADAS (Res.).
India: Moscow, U.S.S.R.
Indonesia: Moscow, U.S.S.R.
Iran: Moscow, U.S.S.R.
Italy: Moscow, U.S.S.R.
Japan: Moscow, U.S.S.R.
Korea, Democratic People's Republic: *Ambassador:* KIM YONG-HA (Res.).
Laos: Moscow, U.S.S.R.
Malaysia: Moscow, U.S.S.R.
Mali: Moscow, U.S.S.R.
Mauritania: *Ambassador:* ABDALLAHI OULD SIDYA.
Nepal: Moscow, U.S.S.R.
Netherlands: Moscow, U.S.S.R.
New Zealand: Moscow, U.S.S.R.
Norway: Moscow, U.S.S.R.
Pakistan: Moscow, U.S.S.R.
Poland: *Ambassador:* ROMAN GAJZLER (Res.).
Portugal: Moscow, U.S.S.R.
Romania: *Ambassador:* TRAIAN GIRBA (Res.).
Sri Lanka: Peking, People's Republic of China.
Sweden: Moscow, U.S.S.R.
Switzerland: Moscow, U.S.S.R.
Thailand: *Ambassador:* ARUN PHANUPHONG.
Turkey: Moscow, U.S.S.R.
U.S.S.R.: *Ambassador:* A. I. SMIRNOV (Res.).
United Kingdom: *Ambassador:* MYLES WALTER PONSONBY (Res.).
Viet-Nam: *Ambassador:* NGUYEN XUAN HOA (Res.).
Yugoslavia: *Ambassador:* DRAGO NOVAK (Res.).

Diplomatic relations have also been established with Bahrain, Cape Verde, the Central African Republic, Cyprus, Ethiopia, Ghana, Guinea-Bissau, Iceland, Iraq, Kuwait, Liberia, Libya, Mexico, Morocco, Mozambique, Nigeria, Papua New Guinea, the Philippines, São Tomé and Príncipe, Senegal, Singapore, Somalia, Sudan, Syria, Tanzania, the People's Democratic Republic of Yemen and Zaire.

JUDICIAL SYSTEM

Justice is administered by the Supreme Court, the City Court of Ulan Bator, 18 aymag (provincial) courts and local somon (county) courts. The Chairman and members of the Supreme Court are elected by the People's Great Hural for a term of four years; other judges are elected by local Hurals for terms of three years. The Procurator of the Republic is also appointed by the People's Great Hural for a term of four years. A Ministry was set up in 1972.

Minister of Justice: DONOYN PÜREV.

Chairman of the Supreme Court: RAVDANGIYN GÜNSEN.

Procurator of the Republic: JARANTAYN AVHIA.

RELIGION

Religious freedom is guaranteed by the Constitution. Traces survive of Buddhism of the Tibetan variety.

Bandido Hamba Lama: Ulan Bator; Head of the Gandandegchilen Monastery (the only active temple of Mongolia): SAMAAGIYN GOMBOJAV.

THE PRESS

The following are the most important newspapers and periodicals:

NEWSPAPERS

Ünen (*Truth*): Nayramdlyn Gudamj 24, Ulan Bator; f. 1920; organ of the Central Committee of the Mongolian People's Revolutionary Party and M.P.R. Council of Ministers; daily except Mondays; Editor-in-Chief TSENDIYN NAMSRAY; circ. (1970) 11,000.

Ediyn Dzasag (*Economics*): Ulan Bator; f. 1974; organ of the Central Committee of the Mongolian People's Revolutionary Party; 24 issues a year; Editor D. SÜRENJAV.

Hödölmör (*Labour*): Ulan Bator; f. 1947; organ of the Central Council of Trade Unions; 144 issues a year.

Pionyeriyn Ünen (*Pioneers' Truth*): Ulan Bator; f. 1943; organ of the Central Council of the D. Sühbaatar Pioneers' Organization of the Central Committee of the Revolutionary Youth League; 48 issues a year; Responsible Editor Ts. DASHDONDOV; circ. 132,000.

Sotsialist Hödöö Aj Ahuy (*Socialist Agriculture*): Nayramdlyn Gudamj 24, Ulan Bator; f. 1961; weekly; circ. 14,000.

Ulaan Od (*Red Star*): Ulan Bator; f. 1930; paper of the Ministries of Defence and Public Security; 104 issues a year; Responsible Editor Col. J. YADMAA.

Utga Dzohiol Urlag (*Literature and Art*): Ulan Bator; f. 1954; organ of the Writers' Union and Ministry of Culture; weekly; Editor S. ERDENE.

Dzaluuchuudyn Ünen (*Young People's Truth*): Ulan Bator; f. 1924; organ of the Central Committee of the Revolutionary Youth League; 144 issues a year; Editor S. BATAA.

Shine Hödöö (*New Countryside*): Ulan Bator; f. 1970; weekly.

There are also 18 provincial newspapers, published biweekly by provincial Party and executive committees, including one in Kazakh (**Jana Ömir** (*New Life*) in Bayanölgiy Aymag). Ulan Bator, Nalayh, Erdenet and Darhan cities and the Ulan Bator Railway also have their own newspapers. **Ulaanbaataryn Medee** (*Ulan Bator News*) was founded in 1954 and has 208 issues a year. Its editor is G. DUGAR.

PERIODICALS

Ajilchin (*Worker*): Ulan Bator.

Akadyemiyn Medee (*Academy News*): Lenin St., Ulan Bator; f. 1933; journal of the Mongolian Academy of Sciences.

Ardyn Tör (*People's Government*): Ulan Bator; f. 1949; organ of the Presidium of the People's Great Hural; 6 issues a year; Editor Ts. GOTOV.

Barilgachin (*Builder*): Ulan Bator; published by Council of Ministers' Construction and Architecture Commission; 4 issues a year; Editor J. DZUHAA.

BNMAU—yn Huul', Dzarlig Togtoolyn Emhetgel (*Collection of MPR Laws, Decrees and Regulations*: Ulan Bator; f. 1926; irregular.

Dürsleh Urlag (*Fine Arts*): Ulan Bator; 4 issues a year.

Dzalgamjlagch (*Successor*): Ulan Bator; 6 issues a year.

Dzaluu Üye (*Young Generation*): Ulan Bator; 6 issues a year; Editor H. BATAA.

Dzuragt Huudsan Sonin (*Illustrated News*): Ulan Bator.

Ediyn Dzasgiyn Asuudal (*Economic Questions*): Ulan Bator; 6 issues a year; Editor-in-Chief Ts. GÜRBADAM.

Erüül Mend (*Health*): Ulan Bator; 4 issues a year.

Holboochin (*Communications Worker*): Ulan Bator; organ of the Ministry of Communications.

Hödöö Aj Ahuy (*Agriculture*): Ulan Bator; 4 issues a year.

Hödöö Aj Ahuyn Dzuragt Hundas (*Agriculture Illustrated*): Ulan Bator; 16 issues a year.

Hudaldaaniy Medeelel (*Trade Information*): Ulan Bator; published by Ministry of Trade and Procurement; 4 issues a year; Editor-in-Chief S. JIGJIDSÜREN.

Hüüdhdiyn Hümüüjil (*Children's Education*): Ulan Bator; published by Ministry of Education; 6 issues a year; Editor N. TSEVGEE; circ. 23,400.

Kino Medee (*Cinema News*): Ulan Bator; organ of Mongol Kino.

MAHN—yn Töv Horoony Medee (*MPRP Central Committee News*): Ulan Bator; published by MPRP Central Cttee.

Mongol Uls (*Mongolia*): Ulan Bator; f. 1956; 12 issues a year; published by State Cttee. for Information, Radio and T.V.; Editor-in-Chief CH. CHIMID.

Mongolyn Anagaah Uhaan (*Mongolian Medicine*): Ulan Bator.

Mongolyn Emegteychüüd (*Mongolian Women*): Ulan Bator; f. 1925; 4 issues a year; Editor-in-Chief T. DOLJIN.

Mongolyn Hudaldaa (*Mongolian Trade*): Ulan Bator; 4 issues a year.

Mongolyn Üyldverchniy Evlel (*Mongolian Trade Union*): Ulan Bator; published by Central Council of Mongolian Trade Union Federation; 4 issues a year; Editor B. MYAGMARJAV.

Namyn Am'dral (*Party Life*): Ulan Bator; f. 1923; organ of the Central Committee of the Mongolian People's Revolutionary Party; 12 issues a year; Editor-in-Chief GOMBO-OCHIRYN CHIMID.

Nayramdal (*Friendship*): Ulan Bator; organ of the Mongolian-Soviet Friendship Society.

Oyuun Tülhüür (*Key to Knowledge*): Ulan Bator; 4 issues a year.

Shinjleh Uhaan Am'dral (*Science and Life*): Mongolian Academy of Sciences, Ulan Bator; f. 1935; magazine published by the Society for the Dissemination of Scientific Knowledge; 6 issues a year; Editor-in-Chief D. ÖLDZIY.

Sotsialist Huul' Yos (*Socialist Law*): Ulan Bator; journal of the Procurator's Office, Supreme Court and Ministry of Justice; 4 issues a year.

Sportyn Medee (*Sports News*): Ulan Bator; published by Central Council of Mongolian Physical Culture and Sport Society; 54 issues a year; Editor G. TSERENDASH.

Soyol (*Culture*): Ulan Bator; f. 1945; published by Ministry of Culture; 4 issues a year; Editor P. DAVAASAMBUU.

Surgan Hümüüjüülegch (*Educator*): Ulan Bator; published by Ministry of Education; 6 issues a year; Editor N. TSEVGEE.

Teevriyn Medeelel (*Transport Information*): Ulan Bator; published by Ministry of Transport; quarterly.

Tonshuul (*Woodpecker*): Nayramdlyn Gudamj 24, Ulan Bator; f. 1935; humorous magazine published by the editorial office of *Ünen*; 24 issues a year; Editor G. DELEG; circ. 35,000.

Tsog (*Spark*): Ulan Bator; f. 1944; political and literary magazine of the Union of Writers; 6 issues a year; Responsible Editor D. TARVA.

Tyehnik, Tyehnologiyn Medee (*News of Techniques and Technology*): Ulan Bator; published by Council of Ministers' State Cttee. for Prices and Standards; 4 issues a year; Editor D. TSERENDORJ.

Uhuulagch (*Agitator*): Ulan Bator; f. 1931; published by MPRP Central Cttee.; 18 issues a year; Editor P. PERENLEY; circ. 30,800.

FOREIGN LANGUAGE PUBLICATIONS

Foreign Trade of Mongolia: Nayramdlyn Gudamj 24, Ulan Bator; annual, published by the Ministry of Foreign Trade; English and Russian; Editor-in-Chief D. NATSAGSAMBUU.

Novosti Mongolii (*News of Mongolia*): Sühbaataryn Talbay 15, Ulan Bator; f. 1942; newspaper published by Montsame in Russian; 104 issues a year; Editor-in-Chief D. ARIUNBOLD.

Mongolia: Moscow; English edition of *Mongol Uls*; 6 issues a year.

Mongoliya (*Mongolia*): Ulan Bator; Russian edition of *Mongol Uls*; 12 issues a year; Editor-in-Chief CH. CHIMID.

Menggu Xiaozibao (*News of Mongolia*): Ulan Bator; newspaper published by Montsame in Chinese; 52 issues a year.

News from Mongolia: Ulan Bator; information bulletin published by Montsame's Foreign Service, Sühbaataryn Talbay 9; 52 issues a year.

Les Nouvelles de Mongolie: Ulan Bator; French edition of *News from Mongolia*.

PRESS AGENCY

Montsame (Mongol Tsahilgaan Medeeniy Agentlag): Mongolian Telegraph Agency, Sühbaataryn Talbay 9, Ulan Bator; f. 1957; government owned; publs. (*see* above). Tass and Novosti maintain representatives in Ulan Bator.

PUBLISHING

State Publishing Committee: Ulan Bator; f. 1921; in overall charge of all publishing; Editor-in-Chief T. SODNOMDARJAA.

There are also publishing houses in each province, and other publishing organs in Ulan Bator. The Mongolian People's Republic publishes about 500 books a year in a total print of 7 million.

RADIO AND TELEVISION

RADIO

Ulan Bator Radio: State Committee for Information, Radio and Television, P.O.B. 365, Ulan Bator; programmes in Mongolian (two), Russian, Chinese, English, French and Kazakh; Chair. of the State Committee SEREETERIYN PÜREVJAV; Head of Foreign Service L. GÜNSEN.

Loudspeakers 85,400 (1974), sets 114,400 (1974).

TELEVISION

A television centre has been built by the U.S.S.R. at Ulan Bator, and a television service was opened in November 1967. Daily transmissions (for Ulan Bator and Darhan areas only), comprising locally-originated material and/or relays of Moscow programmes via the Molniya satellite and the Orbita ground station. A 1,900 km. radio relay line to be built from Ulan Bator to Altay and Ölgiy will provide STD telephone links and television services for Western Mongolia. Dir. of Television MAGSARYN CHOYJIL.

Television sets 27,100 (1974).

FINANCE

State Bank of the Mongolian People's Republic: Oktyabriyn Gudamj 6, Ulan Bator; f. 1924; 65 brs.; Chair. of Board DARIYN DANDZAN.

Insurance is covered by a non-contributory scheme administered by the State Directorate for Insurance of the Ministry of Finance; Head J. PÜREVDORJ.

TRADE AND INDUSTRY

All trade and industry is concentrated in the hands of the state, either through direct state ownership or through co-operatives.

Ministry of Trade and Procurement: Ulan Bator; Minister DUNJMAAGIYN DORJGOTOV.

Central Council of Mongolian Trade Unions: Ulan Bator; branches throughout the country; Chair. GOMBOJAVYN OCHIRBAT; Head of Foreign Department G. JIGJIDSÜREN; 272,000 mems. (1975); affiliated to WFTU.

CO-OPERATIVES

Federation of Agricultural Production Associations (Co-operatives): Ulan Bator; body administering the 257 agricultural co-operatives throughout the country; Chair. of Council MANGALJAVYN DASH (Minister of Agriculture); Secretary D. RINCHINSANGI.

Industrial co-operatives have now been absorbed into the state industrial structure. Industrial production associations are gradually being established under various ministries; they are not co-operatives but groupings of allied enterprises (flourmilling, leather processing, etc.)

FOREIGN TRADE

The Mongolian People's Republic has trading relations with over 20 countries. The Ministry of Foreign Trade is responsible for the foreign trade monopoly and controls the operations of several importing and exporting companies

Minister of Foreign Trade: YONDONGIYN OCHIR.

There are four specialized import and export organizations dealing in trade with foreign countries.

Mongoleksport: Export of Mongolian goods.

Mongolraznoimport: Import of consumer goods.

Mongoltekhnoimport: Import of machinery and equipment, other than motor vehicles, fuels and lubricants.

Avtonefteimport: Import of motor vehicles, fuels and lubricants.

Mongolbook: Export of Mongolian publications.

Chamber of Commerce of the Mongolian People's Republic: Nayramdlyn Gudamj 24, Ulan Bator; f. 1960; is responsible for establishing economic and trading relations, contacts between trade and industrial organizations both at home and abroad and assists foreign countries; organizes commodity inspection, press information and international exhibitions and fairs at home and abroad; Pres. D. Hishgee; Gen. Sec. H. Yondon.

TRANSPORT

RAILWAYS

Ulan Bator Railway: Ulan Bator; Dir. V. Sukachev; Deputy Dir. N. Tserennorov.

External Lines: from the Soviet frontier at Naushki Sühbaatar (connecting with the Trans-Siberian Railway) to Ulan Bator on to the Chinese frontier at Dzamyn-üüd/Erhlien and connecting with Peking (total length 1,115 km.).

Branch: from Darhan to Sharyn Gol coalfield (length 68 km.); branch from Salhit near Darhan westwards to Erdenet (Erdenetiyn-ovoo open-cast copper mine) in Bulgan Province (length about 170 km.).

Eastern Railway: Choybalsan; from the Soviet frontier at Borzya/Ereentsav to Choybalsan (length 237 km.).

There are three international train services a week, Moscow–Ulan Bator and Moscow–Ulan Bator–Peking, and return. There is a twice-weekly service between Ulan Bator and Choybalsan and return, via the Trans-Siberian railway. There is a Mongolian service from Ulan Bator to Moscow and return once a week.

Mongolia's railways account for nearly 70 per cent of total freight turnover.

ROADS

Main roads link Ulan Bator with the Chinese frontier at Dzamyn üüd/Erhlien and with the Soviet frontier at Altanbulag/Kyakhta. A road from Chita in the U.S.S.R. crosses the frontier in the east at Mangut/Onon (Öldziy) and branches for Choybalsan and Öndörhaan. In the west and north-west, roads from Biysk and Irkutsk in the U.S.S.R. go to Tsagaannuur, Bayan-ölgiy Aymag, and Hanh, on Lake Hövsgöl, respectively. The total length of these and other main roads is about 8,600 km. The length of asphalted roads is now approaching 1,600 km., almost entirely in towns. The first section of a hard-surfaced road between Ulan Bator and Bayanhongor was completed in 1975. The road from Darhan to Erdenet is also be be surfaced. Inter-provincial and intra-provincial traffic goes across country in most cases.

There are bus services in Ulan Bator and other large towns, and lorry services throughout the country on the basis of 25 motor transport depots, mostly situated in provincial centres.

INLAND WATERWAYS

Water transport plies Lake Hövsgöl and the River Selenge (474 km. navigable) in the northern part of the country. Tugs and barges on Lake Hövsgöl transport goods brought in by road to Hanh from the U.S.S.R. to Hatgal on the southern shore.

CIVIL AVIATION

Mongolian Civil Air Transport (MIAT): Ulan Bator; f. 1956; internal services to most provincial centres and many county centres; thrice-weekly service from Ulan Bator (Buyant-Uhaa) to Irkutsk; equipment includes An-24, Il-14, An-2, Mi-4, Ka-26; Head of Chief Directorate for Civil Aviation Maj.-Gen. S. Sanjmyatav.

Aeroflot: Moscow and Ulan Bator; thrice-weekly service from Ulan Bator to Moscow and return by Tu-154A.

TOURISM

Juulchin: Ulan Bator; f. 1960; the official foreign tourist service bureau, managed by the Ministry for Foreign Trade; Dir. T. Tseren-ochir.

There were 2,300 foreign tourists in the period Jan.-Oct. 1975.

DEFENCE

Armed Forces and Equipment (1973): Total strength 29,000; army 28,000, air force 1,000. There are also about 18,000 frontier guards and security police. Military service is for 2 years. The armed forces have Soviet equipment comprising in the case of the army medium tanks, armoured personnel carriers, heavy artillery including howitzers and AA guns. The air force has no combat aircraft but uses transports, trainers and helicopters in support of the army. It also has some surface-to-air missiles.

Defence Expenditure: Estimated defence spending for 1976 is 407 million tögrög ($127 million).

Chief of Staff of the Mongolian People's Army: Maj.-Gen. Choyndongiyn Pürevdorj.

EDUCATION

The organization and administration of education in the Mongolian People's Republic is the responsibility of the Ministry of Education and the State Committee for Higher and Special Secondary Education.

Kindergartens

Some 18 per cent of children aged 3 to 7 attend kindergartens, of which there were planned to be 549 in 1975.

General Education Schools

General education schools offering primary (4 years), incomplete secondary (7 years) or complete secondary education (10 years) were planned to accommodate 302,900 pupils in 1975. In 1974, it was planned to ensure incomplete secondary education for all children of school age, and provide such schools in 80 per cent of Mongolia's counties (somons). In the 1973–74 school year, the 550 general education schools had a total teaching staff of 10,800.

Boarding Schools

In 1974, 18 boarding schools for nearly 11,000 rural children were to be built, raising the number of children of nomadic herdsmen going to school to 47,700, 45.6 per cent of the total. In 1975, another 30 boarding schools were to be built, for 50,700 herdsmen's children. A 10 per cent increase in funds for feeding boarding school children was approved in 1975.

Special Secondary Schools

Special secondary schools and vocational technical schools, which had over 20,000 pupils in 1974, train personnel for the service industries, and vehicle drivers and machine operators for industry and agriculture.

Higher Education

In 1973, 10,100 students were studying at the Mongolian State University and at technical colleges. Higher education also is provided at special colleges for Party cadres and army officers, and at the Mongolian Teacher Training College. The Mongolian State University has nine faculties: physics and mathematics, natural sciences, engineering and economics, building engineering, social sciences, philology, economics, geology and geography, and energy and mechanics. The technical colleges train doctors, veterinary surgeons, and agricultural specialists. In 1974, of 24,600 graduates of general education schools, 1,900 were accepted by higher education establishments and 3,000 by technical colleges. In 1975, it was planned to accept a total of 6,000 from among 28,500 graduates.

Education Abroad

Each year, some 1,000 Mongolian students study abroad, mostly at Soviet universities, colleges and technical colleges.

UNIVERSITY

Mongolian State University: Ulan Bator; Rector Prof. NAMSRAYN SODNOM; over 350 teachers, 3,000 students.

BIBLIOGRAPHY

GENERAL

MURZAYEV, E. M. Die Mongolische Volksrepublik (Gotha, 1954). *Physical Geography* (translation from a Russian original, Mongol'skaya Narodnaya Respublika).

SANDERS, A. J. K. The People's Republic of Mongolia: A General Reference Guide (Oxford University Press, London, 1968).

THIEL, ERICH. Die Mongolei (Munich, 1958). *Comprehensive handbook.*

JAGVARAL, N. (Editor). The Mongolian People's Republic (Ulan-Bator, 1956). *Official publication* (available in English, French and Russian).

HISTORY

BAWDEN, C. R. The Modern History of Mongolia (Weidenfeld and Nicolson, London, and Praeger, New York, 1968).

DE RACHEWILTZ, I. Papal Envoys to the Great Khans (Faber and Faber, London, 1971).

FRANCIS, JOHN DE (Trans.). Ma Ho-t'ien: Chinese Agent in Mongolia (Baltimore, 1949).

FRITERS, G. Outer Mongolia in its International Position (Allen and Unwin, 1951).

SAUNDERS, J. J. The History of the Mongol Conquests (Routledge and Kegan Paul, London, 1971).

HEISSIG, W. A. Lost Civilisation (Thames and Hudson, London, 1964).

KOROSTOWETZ, I. J. Von Cinggis Khan zur Sowjetrepublik (Berlin and Leipzig, 1926).

LATTIMORE, OWEN. Nationalism and Revolution in Mongolia (E. J. Brill, Leiden, 1955). *English translation of the official life of the revolutionary leader, Sühbaatar with introduction.*

Nomads and Commissars (Oxford University Press, London, 1962).

Studies in Frontier History, Collected Papers 1929–58 (Oxford University Press, London, 1962).

MAYSKIY, I. M. Mongoliya nakanune revolyutsii (Moscow, 1960).

MURPHY, G. G. S. Soviet Mongolia (University of California, 1966).

RUPEN, R. A. Mongols of the Twentieth Century, Vol. 1 (History), Vol. 2 (Bibliography) (Indiana University and Mouton and Co., The Hague).

The Mongolian People's Republic (Hoover Institution Studies, Stanford, 1966).

TANG, PETER. Russian and Soviet Policy in Manchuria and Outer Mongolia, 1911–31 (Durham, North Carolina, 1959).

TRAVEL, ETC.

BISCH, J. Mongolia, Unknown Land (Allen and Unwin, London, 1963).

HASLUND, H. Tents in Mongolia (London, 1935).
Mongolian Journey (Routledge and Kegan Paul, 1949).

JISL, L. Mongolian Journey (Batchworth Press, London, 1960).

LATTIMORE, OWEN. Mongol Journeys (Cape, 1941).

MONTAGU, I. Land of Blue Sky (Dennis Dobson, London, 1956).

The U.S.S.R. in Asia.

The U.S.S.R. in Asia

SOVIET CENTRAL ASIA

G. E. Wheeler

PHYSICAL AND SOCIAL GEOGRAPHY

Soviet Central Asia is the term now usually applied to the territory occupied by the Kazakh, Uzbek, Tadzhik, Kirghiz and Turkmen S.S.Rs. (Soviet Socialist Republics). Soviet writers, however, include only the last four in this term, the Kazakh S.S.R. being regarded as a separate region. The whole area is bounded on the north by Western Siberia, on the south by Iran and Afghanistan, on the east by the Sinkiang-Uygur Autonomous Region of China, and on the west by the Caspian Sea.

Physically Soviet Central Asia can be divided into four regions: the *steppe*, consisting of the northern part of the Kazakh S.S.R.; the *semi-desert* consisting roughly of the rest of the Kazakh S.S.R.; the *desert region* lying to the south of the semi-desert and reaching the Iranian frontier in the west and the Chinese frontier in the east; and the *mountain region* of which the main features are the Pamirs and the Tien-shan. Vegetation is sparse, being confined to a belt of wooded steppe in the north-east, the grasslands of the Kazakh S.S.R., hardy perennials such as saxaul in the deserts, and a variety of trees and plants along the river valleys and in the piedmont zones. In proportion to the vast areas of desert and mountains, the area of cultivated and populated land is very small.

CLIMATE

The climate is "continental", with hot summers and cold winters. In the north of the Kazakh S.S.R. January temperatures may fall as low as minus 60°F., while in the extreme south the climate is sub-tropical with average shade temperatures reaching 104°F. Precipitation is low throughout the whole region: in the semi-desert most of the rain falls in summer, while in the south most rain falls in March. Heavy falls of snow are uncommon except in the mountainous districts.

POPULATION

At the census held in January 1970, the total population of the region was 32,801,000 and by January 1976 it had risen to an estimated 37,900,000. Of the increase of nearly 10 million between the 1959 and 1970 censuses, 8.5 million was accounted for by natural increase and 1.2 million by immigration. In 1970, Asians constituted 64 per cent of the population, compared with about 60 per cent in 1959. Before the coming of the Russians, the most meaningful distinction for the indigenous population was not as between nationalities or even ethnic groups, but as between nomad and settled peoples. The nomads were in fact exclusively of Turkic origin speaking closely related Turkic languages—Kazakhs, Kirghiz and to a lesser extent Turkmens. The settled peoples contained both Turkic (Uzbek and Turkmen) and Iranian (Tadzhik) elements. Until the first half of the nineteenth century there was a marked difference in the way of life followed by the nomad and settled elements, urban culture being entirely confined to the settled people occupying the oases and valleys. During the last 50 years, however, the nomads have been to a large extent stabilized and cultural differences have tended to become much less. Anthropologically the peoples of Central Asia may be grouped as follows. The Uzbeks (9.2 million) and the Tadzhiks (2.1 million) belong to the Caucasoid race; they are brachycephalic, of medium height and have dark hair and eyes. Some Mongoloid features can be found among them. The Kazakhs (5.3 million) and the Kirghiz (1.5 million) belong to the South Siberian type formed as a result of the mingling of the Central Asian Mongoloids with the ancient Caucasoid population of the Kazakh Steppe. The Karakalpaks (236,000) occupy a position midway between the Uzbeks and Kazakhs, somewhat closer to the latter. The Turkmens (1.5 million) are in a somewhat different class. They have predominantly Caucasoid physical features, but they are dolichocephalic and considerably taller than the Uzbeks and Tadzhiks.

There are a number of other smaller Asian communities including Uygurs, Dungans (Chinese Muslims),—whose numbers increased from 95,000 to 173,000 and from 22,000 to 39,000 respectively between 1959 and 1970, partly as a result of an influx from Sinkiang—Koreans, Arabs and Baluchis. The large but scattered Tatar community of 1,038,000 includes the Crimean Tatars expelled from the Crimea in 1944. The Jewish community numbers about 154,000. In 1970 the non-Asian population totalled roughly 11.3 million, of whom the Russians, numbering 8.5 million, were the most numerous and indeed the most numerous of all the nationalities living in the region after the Uzbeks (9.1 million in the five republics). Most of the remaining non-Asians are Ukrainians and Belorussians, but there is known to be a total of approximately one million Germans, mainly in the Kazakh, Kirghiz and Tadzhik S.S.R.s, and 61,000 Poles in the Kazakh S.S.R.

In spite of the very large number of non-Muslims (Russians and Ukrainians) living side by side with the local population there has been remarkably little inter-marriage and in general the two communities keep apart from each other during their leisure hours.

HISTORY

Little is known of the history of Soviet Central Asia before the 8th century, when the Arabs extended their conquest of Iran to Transoxania, the land between the Amu-Dar'ya and Syr-Dar'ya rivers. During the 9th century most of Transoxania became part of the Persian Samanid empire. After the downfall of the Samanids in 999, the desert and oasis regions were mainly ruled by various Turkic Muslim dynasties, the most important being the Seljuks and the Khorezm Shahs. From 1137 to 1212 Transoxania and the region to the west of the Syr-Dar'ya were dominated by a Tungusic people, the Kara-Kitays. During the whole of this period the Kazakh Steppe remained in possession of Turkic nomads who were never conquered by the Arabs. The Mongol invasion, which began in 1220, included the whole of the desert and semi-desert regions and part of the Kazakh Steppe. By the middle of the 14th century all the Mongol rulers had become Turkicized and embraced Islam. Thenceforward, the whole region remained under the rule of various Turkic Muslim dynasties until the coming of the Russians. The principal of these dynasties was that of Timur (Tamerlane) which dominated the whole of the southern part of the region until, at the beginning of the 16th century, it was overthrown by the Uzbek dynasty of Shaibani. This came to an end in 1655 when it broke up into various khanates of which the principal were Kokand, Bukhara and Khiva.

The Russians began to encroach on the Kazakh Steppe in the first half of the 18th century. It took them over 100 years to pacify the Kazakhs, and during this time they established themselves on the Chinese frontier in Semirech'ye (now the western part of the Kirghiz S.S.R.). In the second half of the 19th century they continued their advance southwards capturing the city of Tashkent in 1865. During the next 20 years Russian rule was extended to the frontiers of Afghanistan and Iran; the whole of the khanate of Kokand was annexed and the khanates of Bukhara and Khiva reduced to a state of vassalage. Samarkand, Timur's ancient capital, was annexed to Russia in 1868. The warlike Turkmens were finally subdued after the battle of Geok Tepe in 1881. Although essentially military in character, Tsarist rule was not oppressive and it brought peace and security to the whole region. Roads and railways were built and economic conditions greatly improved. Little was done in the way of education: compulsory primary education was not introduced, nor were any universities established. Religion and existing local traditions and customs were not interfered with, the official view being that, faced with the superior Russian civilization, Islamic culture would eventually die of inanition. The main defects of the Tsarist administration were first that it made no provision for the eventual grant of self-government to the local population and consequently made no attempt to train an indigenous civil service or armed forces. Secondly, it allowed, and indeed encouraged, large-scale settlement of Russian and Ukrainian peasants without any proper organization or regard for the local population.

During the chaos which followed the collapse of the Imperial administration in 1917, attempts were made by the local population to set up national governments. These were unsuccessful owing to their lack of administrative experience and armed forces and to the presence of over two million Russian and Ukrainian settlers. By 1924, the new Soviet regime had re-established military control over the whole region and in the same year embarked on a fundamental re-organization of the administrative system. This involved the final liquidation of the semi-independence of the former khanates of Bukhara and Khiva and the eventual creation of the existing five Soviet Socialist Republics.

ADMINISTRATION

According to the Constitution of 1936, the five Republics are regarded as fully sovereign states forming part of the U.S.S.R. but with the theoretical right of secession. Each Republic is named after the majority indigenous nationality. In 1970 this varied from 66 per cent of Turkmens in the Turkmen S.S.R. to 32 per cent of Kazakhs in the Kazakh S.S.R. The system of Republican administration is uniform throughout the U.S.S.R., each Republic having a president, a Council of Ministers and an elected Supreme Soviet or Parliament. Each Republic has representatives in both Chambers of the U.S.S.R. Supreme Soviet in Moscow. Paramount control of all political, economic and cultural activities, and of defence and foreign policy is exercised by the Communist Party. All the Republics have their own Communist Parties, but these are integral parts of the "indivisible" Communist Party of the Soviet Union. Either the First or the Second Secretary of each Republican Party is always a non-native, usually a Russian. The Republics are subdivided into oblasts and rayons; the Autonomous Soviet Socialist Republic of Kara-Kalpakiya is included in the Uzbek S.S.R. and the Autonomous Oblast of Gorno-Badakhshan (the Pamirs) in the Tadzhik S.S.R. There are no national military formations: conscription into the Soviet Armed Forces is universal, and conscripts are liable for service anywhere in the Soviet Union or abroad.

COMMUNICATIONS

The Imperial Russian Government had established a good road and railway system and adequate port facilities in the Caspian and Aral Seas. They had founded a number of large and flourishing towns in the Kazakh Steppe where none had been before, and they had developed and modernized those in the southern part of the region. All these achievements were inherited and further developed by the Soviet regime, which in addition successfully expanded the modern irrigation system, a field in which the Tsarist government had made little progress. Major works of railway construction undertaken by the Soviet regime include the Turksib Railway connecting the Central Asian and Trans-Siberian systems, the Mointy-Chu stretch west of Lake Balkhash, the Amu-Dar'ya Valley line from Chardzhou to Kungrad, recently extended to Makat on the Gur'yev-Kandagach line, and the so-called Friendship Railway from Aktogay on the Turksib to the Chinese frontier, where it was designed to connect with a Chinese railway. By 1970, however, the Chinese section was still unfinished. A large number of entirely new towns has been built, including the capitals of the Tadzhik and Kirghiz S.S.Rs., Dushanbe (formerly Stalinabad) and Frunze. The irrigation works undertaken in Central Asia by the Soviet Union are among its greatest material achievements. One of the many major projects to be completed all over the region is the Kara-Kum Canal stretching from the Amu-Dar'ya river to Ashkhabad, a distance of over 500 miles. A further extension to Krasnovodsk is planned and work has begun on it. In 1972 survey work was begun on the diversion of the waters of the Ob and Irtysh rivers into a 2,500 km. navigable canal, which will also irrigate six million hectares of arid land in the Uzbek, Kazakh and Turkmen republics. The first section, to Karaganda, was brought into service in 1975.

SOCIAL CONDITIONS

The process of modernization and westernization which has affected most of Muslim Asia during the past 50 years has been greatly speeded up in Soviet Central Asia by the energetic and often arbitrary steps taken by the Soviet Government. Most of these steps have had a beneficial effect on material living conditions, particularly in the urban areas. In respect of standard of living, public health, employment, travel facilities and equality of opportunity the Muslim peoples of Central Asia are probably still better off than those of the adjoining non-Soviet Muslim countries. With the great improvement which has taken place in living conditions in the latter during the past ten years the gap has tended to diminish. Owing to travel restrictions on foreigners, impartial observation of conditions in the rural areas is impossible, and Soviet reporting provides evidence that these are still very primitive in certain districts.

The old tribal and clan social structure of the local inhabitants is tending to disappear, although it is often observed that members of a single enterprise such as a collective farm belong to one tribe or clan. The political organization of the people into national republics, although originally artificial and evidently intended by the authorities to remain so, is now showing signs of crystallization.

RELATIONS WITH NEIGHBOURING COUNTRIES

During the Tsarist regime there was considerable freedom of movement across the frontiers between Russian Central Asia and the adjoining countries of Iran, Afghanistan and China, in all of which countries live large numbers of people of the same nationalities. For example, in Afghanistan there are over two million Tadzhiks and over one million Uzbeks; in the Sinkiang-Uygur Autonomous Region of China there are half a million Kazakhs and smaller communities of Tadzhiks, Kirghiz and Uzbeks; in Iran there are over 200,000 Turkmens. In the early years of the Soviet regime some attempt was made to attract these elements into the newly formed Soviet Republics. These attempts were unsuccessful and were abandoned. At present, the frontiers are closely guarded by a special force maintained for the purpose. Since the Sino-Soviet dispute assumed serious proportions in 1960, numerous frontier violations and incidents have been reported by both Soviet and Chinese governments. According to Soviet reports, in 1962 some 60,000 Kazakhs and Uygurs, mainly old people and children, migrated into Soviet territory from the Ili district of the Sinkiang-Uygur A.R. During 1970 negotiations took place in Peking with the object of resolving differences. But no result has been reported as far as is known. There has still been no progress in the frontier negotiations in Peking.

CULTURE AND EDUCATION

After the Arab Muslim conquests of the 8th century Islamic culture spread rapidly throughout the settled districts of the region and more gradually and less effectively among the nomad elements. The main effects of Islam were on law, social customs and language. Such education as there was before the Russian invasion was exclusively in the hands of the Muslim clergy and was mainly conducted in Arabic. Before the Mongol conquests of the 13th century, the written official language had been Arabic and to a minor extent Persian, but during the 13th and 14th centuries a written Turkic language called Chaghatay was developed. This used the Perso-Arabic script and a large Persian and Arabic loan vocabulary. Chaghatay served as a kind of written *lingua franca*, but the spoken languages remained fairly distinct and had considerable oral literatures.

The Tsarist government interfered little in religious and cultural matters. The Soviet regime, on the other hand, pursued from the beginning an active policy of cultural regimentation. Apart from the development of a complete primary, secondary and higher educational system from which religious instruction was completely excluded, it instituted and maintained a propaganda campaign against the belief and practice of Islam and against all customs and traditions directly or indirectly associated with it. Efforts have been made to develop the arts (literature, music, painting and sculpture) on socialist-realist lines. In 1930, the Perso-Arabic script in which all local languages were formerly written was abolished in favour of a Latin script, and this, in 1940, was changed to a series of cyrillic scripts. The aim has been to modernize and enrich the languages so as to suit them for modern cultural and scientific requirements. At the same time, the declared object is to make Russian "the second mother-tongue" of the local peoples. This object may be defeated by the rapid development of the local languages, which should eventually replace Russian as the medium of higher education and of communication. The effect of the language reforms on literature has been very great. Poetry, once the main literary medium, has largely lost its place to prose-writing on Soviet Russian lines. The press has been greatly developed and every republic has a large number of newspapers and periodicals in Russian and the vernacular languages. All are extensively used as vehicles for official propaganda. By Asian standards the quality of printing and production is high.

The development of education is one of the main Soviet achievements in Central Asia. In 1917 the proportion of literates did not exceed five per cent. It is now claimed that over 90 per cent of the population are literate, having completed four years at school. While this may be an exaggeration, there can be no doubt that the standard of literacy and of higher and technical education in Soviet Central Asia is far higher than that of any other Muslim country in the world, and indeed, higher than any Asian or African country with the exception of Japan and Israel. With the introduction of compulsory primary education in 1930, the old Muslim schools (*mektebs*) and higher educational establishments (*medresehs*) had disappeared. Later, a single *medreseh* was opened in Bukhara for the purpose of training clerical functionaries, and this is the only establishment of its kind in the Soviet Union. The capital of each of the Republics has its own university, the Uzbek S.S.R. having an additional one in Samarkand. A new university was opened in Karaganda in 1972. In the late 1950s the Muslim nationalities were still markedly under-represented in higher education in the Soviet Union, but the gap narrowed appreciably in the 1960s, and by 1970 the total number of Kazakh and Kirghiz students was proportionate to their numbers in the population. The Uzbeks, Tadzhiks and Turkmens, however, were still under-represented. The main reason for this state of affairs seems to lie in the relatively small number of women among Uzbek, Tadzhik and Turkmen students (33, 24 and 23 per cent respectively of the total). Among the Kazakhs, women accounted for 45 per cent of the student body in 1970, and among the Kirghiz 43 per cent (the all-Union figure was 49 per cent).

In spite of strenuous Soviet efforts to eliminate Islamic culture, there are many indications that Islam remains the predominant cultural influence in the whole area.

ECONOMIC SURVEY

Before the Revolution the economy was almost exclusively agricultural, industry being confined to a small amount of cotton ginning and to the mining of copper and coal. Since the Revolution there has been a great expansion of industry, particularly since the Second World War, when a large number of factories with their trained personnel were transferred to Central Asia from the West. Cotton still dominates the agricultural economy, supplying all the U.S.S.R.'s domestic wants and a substantial surplus for export. In spite of frequent failures in organization, the New Lands campaign in the Kazakh S.S.R. inaugurated in 1953 is proving a useful additional source of wheat for the whole Union. Animal husbandry is of considerable and increasing importance. The deposits of copper, lead, zinc, and chrome in the Kazakh S.S.R., and of such rare metals as mercury and antimony in the Kirghiz S.S.R., are the largest in the Soviet Union and make it almost self-sufficient in these respects. The Kazakh S.S.R. also possesses one-sixth of Soviet coal stocks as well as considerable iron ore mines. The whole area now has almost one-third of the Union's reserves of natural gas, one-fifth of the hydro-energy resources and considerable reserves of oil (mainly in the Turkmen and Kazakh S.S.R.s). The output of the growing chemical and fertilizer industry is still relatively small, but it has great future potentialities. The most important achievement in engineering has been the establishment of the Uzbek textile machinery industry, which is now producing 68 per cent of all the spinning and 100 per cent of the roving machinery made in the Soviet Union. Apart from heavy industry, such light industries as textile manufacture and the canning of food products have been greatly expanded.

The economic organization of Central Asia has varied from the complete centralization advocated by Stalin to alternate processes of decentralization and recentralization favoured by Khrushchev. The last step of the latter before his downfall in 1964 was the creation of various Central Asian economic agencies which superseded the Republican Councils of National Economy (*Sovnarkhoz*) instituted by him in 1957. These new agencies were clearly unpopular in the republics and were abolished by his successor as an ostensible concession to republican opinion. The Republican Councils of National Economy were temporarily restored, but in October 1965 the whole of this system was abolished and the former centralized administration of industry and planning was restored but with a greater degree of flexibility than before.

There are recent indications that a serious unemployment problem is resulting from the very high rate of natural increase in the native population and the mechanization of agriculture, particularly in cotton-growing.

THE KAZAKH SOVIET SOCIALIST REPUBLIC

INTRODUCTION

The Kazakh Republic was formed as an Autonomous Republic within the Russian Federation on August 26th 1920, and reconstituted as a Union Republic on December 5th, 1936. It has an area of 2,717,300 sq. km. and a population of 14,170,000 (January 1st, 1975). Of these 32.6 per cent are Kazakhs, 43.2 per cent Russians, 7.2 per cent Ukrainians and 2.2 per cent Tatars (1970 census). The population density is 5.1 persons per square kilometre. Alma Ata, the capital, has a population of 837,000. In size the Kazakh Republic (Kazakhstan) is second only to the Russian Federation. It extends from the Volga to the Altai Mountains and from the Siberian plains to the Central Asian deserts. Kazakhstan has a frontier with the People's Republic of China to the south-east.

The number of towns and industrial communities in Kazakhstan has increased greatly in recent years. The Kazakh settlement of Baikonur, in the heart of the Steppes, is world famous as the launching place of the Soviet spaceships.

STATISTICS

POPULATION

BIRTHS AND DEATHS

	Birth Rate (per '000)	Death Rate (per '000)
1960	36.7	6.5
1970	23.3	6 0
1971	23.8	6 0
1972	23.5	6.3
1973	23.2	6.5

AGRICULTURE

Agriculture in Kazakhstan is varied and intensive. It is one of the greatest regions of the U.S.S.R. for the production of grain and other agricultural crops.

Besides sheep and horses, cows, camels, goats, pigs and poultry are raised. Kazakhstan produces 22.3 per cent of Soviet wool, 18.2 per cent of grain, 6.8 per cent of meat and 4.8 per cent of milk.

In 1974 there were 1,472,000 persons engaged in agriculture on 437 collective farms and 1,783 state farms.

CROP PRODUCTION
('000 tons)

	1960	1970	1971	1972	1973
Grain	15,511	22,200	21,085	27,696	27,687
Maize	116	151	162	204	199
Rice	23.1	274.0	308	371	428
Cotton	86	105	296	292	313
Sugar Beet	1,148	2,239	2,129	2,464	2,346
Sunflower	38	78	90	91	91
Potatoes	1,265	1,892	1,710	1,988	1,913
Vegetables	390	776	792	822	906
Fruit	70	206	169	246	155
Grapes	16	60	112	134	98

LIVESTOCK
('000)

	1960	1971	1972	1973	1974
Cattle	5,501	7,500	7,469	7,629	7,890
of which:					
Cows	2,055	2,657	2,730	2,766	2,723
Pigs	1,759	2,700	2,709	2,726	3,791
Sheep	27,618	31,233	32,596	33,510	34,609
Poultry	19,700	29,700	31,800	33,200	35,100

ANIMAL PRODUCTS
('000 tons)

	1960	1970	1971	1972	1973
Meat	545	874	927	907.8	958.4
Milk	2,457	3,881.8	3,900	3,928	4,173.8
Eggs (million)	851	1,681.2	2,013	2,200	2,387.0
Wool	65.3	92.8	94.1	92.1	99.6

INDUSTRY AND MINING

The Kazakh economy combines heavy industry with food and light industries. The extractive industry, as well as the chemical and construction industries, is also well developed. Kazakhstan occupies third place in the U.S.S.R. in the volume of industrial production, and a total of 1.1 million people are actively engaged in industry.

PRODUCTION

		1970	1971	1972	1973
Pig Iron	'000 tons	1,766	2,528	3,366	3,500
Steel	,, ,,	2,225	3,252	4,024	4,800
Oil	,, ,,	13,200	16,023	18,000	20,300
Coal	,, ,,	61,500	67,300	74,500	79,800
Metal-Cutting Lathes	number	2,302	2,436	2,500	2,600
Natural Gas	million cu. metres	2,093	2,747	3,500	4,800
Electric Power	million kWh.	34,600	37,800	41,300	44,000
Mineral Fertilizers	'000 tons	1,957	2,822	3,300	4,200
Cement	,, ,,	5,653	5,991	6,100	6,300
Cotton Fabrics	million sq. metres	64.1	65.8	79.8	82.1

EDUCATION

The literacy of the population of Kazakhstan between the ages of 9 and 49 is 99.7 per cent. According to the census of 1973, 52.2 per cent of people over the age of 9 have received higher or secondary education.

(1973–74)

	INSTITUTIONS	STUDENTS
Secondary Schools	10,057	3,365,000
Secondary Specialized Schools	205	223,500
Higher Schools (incl. Universities)	46	205,800

GOVERNMENT

SUPREME SOVIET

Chairman: S. E. Esenov.

Presidium President: Sabir Niyazbekov.

COUNCIL OF MINISTERS

Chairman: Baiken A. Ashimov.

POLITICAL ORGANIZATIONS

Kazakh Communist Party: Alma Ata; 609,033 mems.; First Secretary of the Central Committee DINMOHAMMED A. KUNAYEV.

Komsomol Leninist Young Communist League of Kazakhstan: Alma Ata; 1,453,479 mems.; First Sec. Z. KAMALITDENOV.

JUDICIAL SYSTEM

Supreme Court

ALMA ATA

Chairman of the Supreme Court: K. E. MYNBAEV.

Procurator: U. S. SEITOV.

THE PRESS

There are 385 newspapers published in the Kazakh S.S.R., including 146 published in Kazakh. The daily circulation is 4,735,000 copies (1,616,000 in Kazakh). One hundred and sixty-eight periodicals are published, including 29 in Kazakh, with a total circulation of 44,600,000 copies (22,800,000 in Kazakh).

PRINCIPAL NEWSPAPERS

Kazakhstanskaya Pravda (*Pravda of Kazakhstan*): Alma Ata; f. 1920; organ of the Kazakhstan Communist Party, Supreme Soviet and Council of Ministers; six times weekly; in Russian; Editor F. P. MIKHAYLOV.

Leninchil Zhas (*Leninist Youth*): Alma Ata; f. 1921; organ of the Central Committee of the Leninist Young Communist League of Kazakhstan; five times weekly; in Kazakh; Editor S. BERDIKULOV.

Leninskaya Smena (*Leninist Rising Generation*): Alma Ata; f. 1922; organ of the Central Committee of the Leninist Young Communist League of Kazakhstan; five times weekly; Editor F. EGNATOV.

Sotsialistik Kazakhstan (*Socialist Kazakhstan*): Alma Ata; f. 1919; organ of the Kazakh Communist Party, Supreme Soviet and Council of Ministers; six times weekly; in Kazakh; Editor U. BAGAEV.

SELECTED PERIODICALS

(Published monthly unless otherwise indicated)

Ara (*Bumble-bee*): Alma Ata; f. 1956; published by the Publishing House of the Central Committee of the Kazakh Communist Party; in Kazakh and Russian; satirical.

Baldyrgan (*Sprout*): Alma Ata; f. 1958; journal of the Central Committee of the Leninist Young Communist League of Kazakhstan, illustrated; for pre-school and first grades of school; in Russian.

Bilim zhane enbek (*Knowledge*): f. 1960; journal of the Central Committee of the Leninist Young Communist League of Kazakhstan; popular science and technology; in Kazakh.

Kazakhstan Aielderi (*Woman of Kazakhstan*): Alma Ata; f. 1925; journal of the Central Committee of the Kazakh Communist Party; popular women's magazine; in Kazakh.

Kazakhstan Kommunist (*Communist of Kazakhstan*): Alma Ata; f. 1921; published by the Publishing House of the Central Committee of Kazakhstan Communist Party; in Kazakh.

Kazakhstan Mektebi (*Kazakh School*): Alma Ata; f. 1925; journal of the Ministry of Education of the Kazakh S.S.R.; organization of public education; in Kazakh.

Kazakstannyn Auyl Shrushylygy (*Agriculture of Kazakhstan*): Alma Ata; f. 1936; journal of the Central Committee of the Communist Party of Kazakhstan; organization of work on collective farms; in Kazakh.

Kooperator Kazakstana (*Kazakhstan Co-operator*): Alma Ata; f. 1958; published by the Central Committee of the Communist Party of Kazakhstan; journal of the Union of Consumers' Societies of the Kazakh S.S.R.; trade organizations; in Russian.

Madamet hana Turmys (*Culture and Life*): Alma Ata; f. 1958; published by the Kazakhstan Publishing House; journal of the Kazakh S.S.R. Ministry of Culture; popular illustrated; in Kazakh.

Narodnoe khozyaistvo Kazakhstana (*National Economy of Kazakhstan*): Alma Ata; f. 1926; journal of the State Planning Committee of the Council of Ministers of the Kazakh S.S.R.; theory and practice of planning and managing of the national economy of the Republic; in Russian.

Partiinaya Zhizn Kazakhstana (*Party Life of Kazakhstan*): Alma Ata; f. 1931; published by the Publishing House of the Central Committee of the Kazakhstan Communist Party; political; in Russian.

Prostor (*Wide Horizons*): Alma Ata; f. 1935; journal of the Kazakh S.S.R. Union of Writers; fiction; in Russian.

Russkiy Yazyk v Kazakhskoy Shkole (*Russian Language in the Kazakh School*): Alma Ata; f. 1962; journal of the Ministry of Education of the Kazakh S.S.R.; linguistic problems; in Russian.

Vestnik Selskokhozyaistvennoy Nauki (*Herald of Agricultural Science*): Alma Ata; f. 1958; published by the "Kaynar" (Spring) Publishing House; journal of the Ministry of Agriculture of the Kazakh S.S.R.; problems of agriculture in different zones of Kazakhstan; in Russian.

Zhuldyz (*Star*): Alma Ata; f. 1928; published by the Publishing House of the Central Committee of the Kazakh Communist Party; journal of the Kazakh S.S.R. Union of Writers; fiction; in Kazakh.

Zhurnal Mod (*Fashion Magazine*): Alma Ata; f. 1958; published by the "Dom Modely Odezhdy" (Fashion House) Publishing House; twice a year; everyday fashions; in Russian.

NEWS AGENCY

KAZTAG (*Kazakh Telegraph Agency*): Alma Ata.

PUBLISHERS

1,658 books were published in 1973, 606 in Kazakh.

Kainar (Spring) Publishing House: Alma Ata, Kashgharskaya ul. 64; books and booklets about agriculture; Dir. A. K. BEKTEMISOV.

Kazakhstan Publishing House: Alma Ata 9, Ul. Sovetskaya 50; political and popular editions; Dir. M. K. MAMASHANOV.

Zhazushy (Writer) Publishing House: Alma Ata, Kommunisticheskii prospekt 105; fiction; Dir. A. G. DJUMABAEV.

CULTURE

PRINCIPAL THEATRES

State Academic Drama Theatre: Alma Ata; Dir. and Producer A. MAMBETOV.

Kazakh Academic Opera and Ballet Theatre: Alma Ata, Kalinina 112; Dir. K. N. SHALABAEV.

Russian Dramatic Theatre: Alma Ata; Dir. G. I. VAISMAN.

THE KIRGHIZ SOVIET SOCIALIST REPUBLIC

INTRODUCTION

Kirghizia was made an Autonomous Republic on February 1st, 1926, and attained the status of a Union Republic on December 5th, 1936. It has an area of 198,500 sq. km. and a population of 3,294,000 (January 1st, 1975). Of these 43.8 per cent are Kirghiz, 29.2 per cent Russians, 10.6 per cent Uzbeks, 4.1 per cent Ukrainians and 2.4 per cent Tatars (1970 census). Frunze, the capital, has a population of 486,000 (1975). The Kirghiz Republic is situated at the junction of two gigantic mountain systems, the Tien-shan and the Pamirs, and is noted for its severe natural beauty and amazing range of climate. In the south-east there is a frontier with the People's Republic of China.

STATISTICS

POPULATION

BIRTHS AND DEATHS

	Birth Rate (per '000)	Death Rate (per '000)
1960	36.8	6.1
1970	30.5	7.4
1971	31.6	7.0
1972	30.5	7.4
1973	30.6	7.6

AGRICULTURE

The Kirghiz were formerly wandering herdsmen. They have now settled on the land, taken up agriculture and built up their own industry. Kirghizia produces wheat, cotton, tobacco, southern hemp, kenaf, essential oil plants and poppy. Grape- and fruit-growing and silkworm breeding also have an important place in the economy.

Livestock raising is the main branch of agriculture. The wealth of the Republic is made up of its herds of cattle, flocks of fine-fleece sheep and droves of horses.

In 1974 there were 329,000 people engaged in agriculture on 225 collective farms and 121 state farms.

CROP PRODUCTION

('000 tons)

	1960	1970	1971	1972	1973
Grain	429	1,001	1,018	1,171	1,255
Rice	3 1	3.2	1	1.8	2
Leguminous Plants	0 4	3.0	2	1.6	2
Cotton	126	187.2	197	189	217.8
Sugar Beet	1,194	1,683.9	1,562	1,828	1,851
Potatoes	113	106	280	322	289.7
Vegetables	84	191	218	246	242
Fruit	34	85	67	149	124
Grapes	9	21	25	41	38.6

LIVESTOCK
('000)

	1960	1971	1972	1973	1974
Cattle	739	914.6	924.6	935.8	945.3
of which:					
Cows	293	378.6	382	383	387.3
Pigs	199	243.9	291	283	288.5
Sheep	5,996	9,450.7	9,521	9,691	9,818
Poultry	7,200	7,300	6,900	7,200	7,600

ANIMAL PRODUCTS
('000 tons)

	1960	1970	1971	1972	1973
Meat	100	226.8	137	136.9	142.3
Milk	401	545.6	562	575.4	600.3
Eggs (million)	163	268.0	297	305.5	316.3
Wool	14.6	26.9	28.3	28.5	30.6

INDUSTRY AND MINING

The construction of roads and the introduction of air transport have assisted the growth of industry. There are deposits of lead ore and oil and Kirghizia is one of the country's main suppliers of mercury and antimony. There are machine-building, instrument-making, oil, gas, and food industries.

PRODUCTION

		1969	1971	1972	1973
Steel	'000 tons	1.9	6.3	6.1	6.9
Oil	,, ,,	285.9	292	277	243
Coal	,, ,,	3,564	3,741	3,827	3,910
Metal-Cutting Lathes	number	2,273	2,035	2,292	2,479
Natural Gas	million cu. metres	340.7	383	395	396
Electric Power	million kWh.	3,519	3,877	4,060	4,270
Cars	number	12,000	15,100	15,710	16,100
Cement	'000 tons	n.a.	1,011	1,029.1	1,048

EDUCATION

The literacy of the population of Kirghizia between the ages of 9 and 49 is 99.7 per cent. According to the census of 1973, 50.9 per cent of people over the age of 9 have received higher or secondary education.

(1973–74)

	INSTITUTIONS	STUDENTS
Secondary Schools	1,803	842,000
Secondary Specialized Schools	36	42,100
Higher Schools (incl. Universities)	9	48,700

GOVERNMENT

SUPREME SOVIET

Chairman: B. Djamgertchinov.

Presidium President: Turabay K. Kulatov.

COUNCIL OF MINISTERS

Chairman: Akhmatbek S. Suyumbaev.

POLITICAL ORGANIZATIONS

Kirghiz Communist Party: Frunze; 104,155 mems.; First Secretary of the Central Committee T. Usubaliev.

Komsomol Leninist Young Communist League of Kirghizia: Frunze; 306,577 mems.; First Sec. A. A. Rismendiev.

JUDICIAL SYSTEM

Supreme Court

Frunze

Chairman of the Supreme Court: A. Supataev.

Procurator: A. M. Satarov.

THE PRESS

There are 92 newspapers published in the Kirghiz S.S.R., including 53 published in Kirghizian. The daily circulation is 1,032,000 copies (597,000 in Kirghizian). Fifty periodicals are published, including 19 in Kirghizian, with a total circulation of 27,200,000 copies (8,300,000 in Kirghizian).

PRINCIPAL NEWSPAPERS

Komsomolets Kirghizii (*Member of the Leninist Young Communist League of Kirghizia*): Frunze; f. 1938; organ of the Central Committee of the Leninist Young Communist League of Kirghizia; three times weekly; Editor I. Novitsky.

Leninchil Zhash (*Leninist Youth*): Frunze; f. 1926; organ of the Central Committee of the Leninist Young Communist League of Kirghizia; three times weekly; in Kirghizian; Editor K. Osmonaliev.

Sovettik Kyrghyzstan (*Soviet Kirghizia*): Frunze; f. 1924; organ of the Central Committee of the Kirghiz Communist Party, Supreme Soviet and Council of Ministers; six times weekly; in Kirghizian; Editor G. G. Tursunov.

Sovietskaya Kirghizia (*Soviet Kirghizia*): Frunze; f. 1925; organ of the Kirghiz Communist Party, Supreme Soviet and Council of Ministers; six times weekly in Russian and Kirghizian; Editor P. S. Denisyuk.

SELECTED PERIODICALS

(Published monthly unless otherwise indicated.)

Ala-Too (*Ala-Too Mountains*): Frunze; f. 1931; published by the "Ala-Too" Publishing House; journal of the Kirghiz S.S.R. Union of Writers and Ministry of Culture; novels, short stories, plays, poems of Kirghizian authors and translations into Kirghizian; in Kirghizian.

Chalkan (*Stinging-nettle*): Frunze; f. 1955; published by the "Ala-Too" Publishing House; in Kirghizian; satirical.

Kommunist (*Communist*): Frunze; f. 1926; published by the "Ala-Too" Publishing House; in Kirghizian; political.

Kyrgyzstan Ayaldary (*Women of Kirghizia*): Frunze; f. 1951; journal of the Central Committee of the Kirghiz Communist Party; popular; in Kirghizian.

Kyrgystandyn Ayyl Charbasy (*Agriculture of Kirghizia*): Frunze; f. 1955; published by the "Ala-Too" Publishing House; journal of the Ministry of Agriculture of the Kirghiz S.S.R.; progressive system of farming; in Kirghizian.

Literaturnyi Kirghizstan (*Literature of Kirghizia*): Frunze; f. 1955; published by the "Ala-Too" Publishing House; journal of the Central Committee of the Leninist Young Communist League and Union of Writers of Kirghiz S.S.R.; fiction; bi-monthly; in Russian.

Sovetskoe Zdravookhranenie Kirgizii (*Soviet Public Health System of Kirghizia*): Frunze; f. 1938; published by the "Ala-Too" Publishing House; journal of the Ministry of Public Health of the Kirghiz S.S.R.; medical experimental work; bi-monthly; in Russian.

NEWS AGENCY

KIRTAG (*Kirghiz Telegraph Agency*): Frunze.

PUBLISHER

Kirghizstan Publishing House: Frunze, Ul. Bokombaeva 99; political and fiction; Dir. A. S. Stamov.

CULTURE

PRINCIPAL THEATRES

State Drama Theatre: Frunze; Dir. T. Tokoldashev.

Russian Drama Theatre: Frunze; Dir. N. K. Angarov.

Academic Opera and Ballet Theatre: Frunze, Dubovy Park; Dir. S. U. Usupov.

THE TADZHIK SOVIET SOCIALIST REPUBLIC

INTRODUCTION

The Tadzhik Republic was formed as an Autonomous Republic on October 14th, 1924, and attained the status of a Union Republic on October 16th, 1929. It has an area of 143,100 sq. km. and a population of 3,385,000 (January 1st, 1975). Of these, 56.2 per cent are Tadzhiks, 23 per cent Uzbeks, 11.9 per cent Russians and 2.4 per cent Tatars (1970 census). Dushanbe, the capital, has a population of 436,000 (1975). The Tadzhik Republic (Tadzhikistan) includes the Gorno-Badakshan Autonomous Region (Khorog). It is a mountainous region including the greater part of the Pamirs where the tallest peaks in the Soviet Union are located. Afghanistan lies to the south.

STATISTICS

POPULATION

BIRTHS AND DEATHS

	Birth Rate (per '000)	Death Rate (per '000)
1960	33.5	5.1
1970	34.7	6.4
1971	36.8	5.7
1972	35.3	6.3
1973	35.6	7.2

AGRICULTURE

Large irrigation projects have been carried out, making it possible to cultivate cotton, vegetables, hemp, kenaf, groundnuts, sugar-beet and essential oil crops in addition to rice, wheat and maize, the main grain crops. Sheep-breeding is the most developed branch of animal husbandry.

In 1974 there were about 340,000 people working on 251 collective farms and 123 state farms.

CROP PRODUCTION
('000 tons)

	1960	1970	1971	1972	1973
Grain	166	219.9	144	223	230
Rice	10.2	27.2	29	31	32
Cotton	399	726.5	788	742.3	805
Potatoes	31	67	76	94.8	94.9
Vegetables	49	197.1	272	231.6	235.7
Fruit	84	146	176	215	185
Grapes	44	95	114	64.6	109

LIVESTOCK
('000)

	1960	1971	1972	1973	1974
Cattle	683	1,009.3	1,035	1,062	1,076
of which: Cows	264	400.0	397	405	412
Pigs	80	76.3	93	95	98
Sheep	2,183	2,182.0	2,712	2,645	2,777

ANIMAL PRODUCTS
('000 tons)

	1960	1970	1971	1972	1973
Meat	47	59·9	68	70·7	73·9
Milk	203	285·3	305	314·6	351
Eggs (million)	91	125·6	157	166·4	187
Wool	4·6	5·1	4.8	5	5·3

INDUSTRY AND MINING

Coal, oil, gas, ozocerite, lead, zinc, tungsten, bismuth, gold, silver, mountain crystals and building materials have been found in this area. Tadzhikistan has cotton gins, food factories, mining, metal-working, engineering, electrical engineering and chemical industries. The capital has factories manufacturing tractor and automobile spare parts, cotton gins, silk reeling and woollen mills.

PRODUCTION

		1970	1971	1972	1973
Oil	'000 tons	181	192	198	226
Coal	,, ,,	886.9	889	900	900
Natural Gas	million cu. metres	387.6	n.a.	498	520
Electric Power	million kWh.	3,145	3,367	3,548	3,779
Mineral Fertilizers	'000 tons	252	261	324	373
Cement	,, ,,	872	941	967	975
Cotton Fabrics	million sq. metres	n.a.	76.2	77·7	85·3
Silk Fabrics	,, ,, ,,	n.a.	41	42·6	46·5

EDUCATION

The literacy of the population of Tadzhikistan between the ages of 9 and 49 is 99.6 per cent. According to the census of 1973, 49 per cent of people over the age of 9 have received higher or secondary education.

(1973–74)

	Institutions	Students
Secondary Schools	3,200	885,000
Secondary Specialized Schools	39	37,400
Higher Schools (incl. Universities)	9	47,600

GOVERNMENT

SUPREME SOVIET

Chairman: M. Mirshakarov.

Presidium President: M. Kholov.

COUNCIL OF MINISTERS

Chairman: R. Nabiev.

POLITICAL ORGANIZATIONS

Tadzhik Communist Party: Dushanbe; 87,492 mems.; First Secretary of the Central Committee D. R. Rasulov.

Komsomol Leninist Young Communist League of Tadzhikistan: Dushanbe; 263,004 mems.; First Sec. U. G. Usmanov.

JUDICIAL SYSTEM

Supreme Court

Dushanbe

Chairman of the Supreme Court: S. Kurbanov.

Procurator: V. A. Bulgarin.

THE PRESS

There are 60 newspapers published in the Tadzhik S.S.R., including 50 published in Tadzhik. The daily circulation is 958,000 copies (663,000 in Tadzhik). Forty-eight periodicals are published including 16 in Tadzhik, with a total circulation of 26,180,000 copies (about 6 million in Tadzhik).

PRINCIPAL NEWSPAPERS

Kommunist Tadzhikistana (*Tadzhik Communist*): Dushanbe; f. 1929; organ of the Tadzhik Communist Party, Supreme Soviet and Council of Ministers; six times weekly; in Russian; Editor A. R. Rumyantsev.

Komsomolets Tadzhikistana (*Member of the Leninist Young Communist League of Tadzhikistan*): Dushanbe; f. 1938; organ of the Central Committee of the Leninist Young Communist League of Tadzhikistan; three times weekly; in Russian; Editor N. Tabarov.

Komsomoli Tochikistoni (*Member of the Leninist Young Communist League of Tadzhikistan*): Dushanbe; f. 1930; organ of the Central Committee of the Leninist Young Communist League of Tadzhikistan; three times weekly; in Tadzhik; Editor M. Abdurakhmanov.

Tochikistoni Sovieti (*Soviet Tadzhikistan*): Dushanbe; f. 1925; organ of the Tadzhik Communist Party; the Supreme Soviet and the Council of Ministers; six times weekly in Tadzhik; Editor Sh. Saidov.

SELECTED PERIODICALS

(Published monthly unless otherwise indicated.)

Khochgii Kishlŏki Tochikiston (*Agriculture of Tadzhikistan*): Dushanbe; f. 1947; journal of the Ministry of Agriculture of the Tadzhik S.S.R.; problems of agriculture; in Tadzhik.

Khorpushtak (*Hedgehog*): Dushanbe; f. 1953; journal of the Central Committee of the Tadzhik Communist Party; in Tadzhik; fortnightly; satirical.

Kommunisti Tochikiston (*Communist of Tadzhikistan*): Dushanbe; f. 1936; published by the Publishing House of the Central Committee of the Tadzhik Communist Party; in Tadzhik; political.

Maktabi Soveti (*Soviet School*): Dushanbe; f. 1930; journal of the Ministry of Public Education of the Tadzhik S.S.R.; theory of pedagogical science; in Tadzhik.

Mashal (*Torch*): Dushanbe; f. 1952; journal of the Central Committee of the Leninist Young Communist League and Republican Council of the Pioneer Organization named after V. I. Lenin of the Tadzhik S.S.R.; fiction for 10–15 years; in Tadzhik.

Sadon Shark (*The Voice of the East*): Dushanbe; f. 1924; journal of the Tadzhik S.S.R. Union of Writers; fiction; in Tadzhik.

Zanoni Tochikiston (*Women of Tadzhikistan*): Dushanbe; f. 1951; journal of the Central Committee of the Tadzhik Communist Party; popular; in Tadzhik.

Zdravookhranenie Tadzhikistana (*Tadzhikistan Public Health System*): Dushanbe; f. 1954; journal of the Ministry of Public Health of the Tadzhik S.S.R.; problems of improvement of medical help; bi-monthly; in Russian.

NEWS AGENCY

TADZHIKTAG (*Tadzhik Telegraph Agency*): Dushanbe.

RADIO

Radio Dushanbe: Broadcasts in Tadzhik and Persian.

PUBLISHER

In 1973, 645 books were published, 325 in Tadzhik.

Irfon (Knowledge) Publishing House: Dushanbe, Ul. Shevchenko 21; political and fiction; Dir. A. E. Kahhori.

CULTURE

PRINCIPAL THEATRES

Academic Drama Theatre: Dushanbe; Dir. L. N. Kuznetzov.

Russian Drama Theatre: Dushanbe; Dir. A. A. Eroshenko.

State Academic Opera and Music Theatre: Dushanbe, pl. Moskvy; Dir. A. S. Samadov.

THE TURKMEN SOVIET SOCIALIST REPUBLIC

INTRODUCTION

The Turkmen Republic was formed on October 27th, 1924. Turkmenia, the southernmost republic in the Soviet Union, is situated in the south-west of Central Asia. It is bounded on the north by Kazakh S.S.R., on the north-east by the Uzbek S.S.R., on the south by Iran, and the south-east by Afghanistan. To the west lies the Caspian Sea. The Republic has an area of 488,100 sq. km. and a population of 2,495,000 (as of January 1st, 1975). Of these, 65.6 per cent are Turkmen, 14.5 per cent Russian, 8.3 per cent Uzbeks and 3.2 per cent Kazakhs (1970 census).

The Kara-Kum, one of the largest Central Asian deserts, occupies more than four-fifths of the territory and irrigation is therefore of prime importance to this desolate land. The capital, Ashkhabad, has a population of 289,000 (1975). The mostly densely populated districts are the valleys of the rivers Amu-Darya and Murgab and the foothills of Kopet-Dag, and the oases of Khorezm, Tedzen, Atrek and Ashkhabad, where there are up to 300 inhabitants per sq. km. It is extremely sparse in the vast desert lands. However, the discovery of rich mineral deposits has caused many settlements to develop even in the most arid districts.

STATISTICS

POPULATION

BIRTHS AND DEATHS

	Birth Rate (per '000)	Death Rate (per '000)
1960	42.4	6.5
1970	35.2	6.6
1971	34.7	6.7
1972	33.9	7.2
1973	34.3	7.2

AGRICULTURE

Agricultural areas occupy almost half of the territory. The fourth section of the Great Kara-Kum Canal was due to be completed in 1975. The first stage is 850 km. long and stretches from the Amu-Darya river to Geok-Tepe. It supplies water for Ashkhabad and has already provided irrigation for more than 160,000 hectares of desert land; it is also used for shipping. Thanks to its special climatic conditions, Turkmenia is able to grow large quantities of long-staple cotton. Sowing and cultivating operations are fully mechanized. Sheep-breeding is also important.

In 1974 there were 294,000 people engaged in agriculture on 330 collective farms and 55 state farms.

CROP PRODUCTION
('000 tons)

	1960	1970	1971	1972	1973
Grain	19	82	100	114.4	126.9
Rice	0.1	15.3	17	18.2	20
Cotton	363	868	920	931.5	1,007.5
Potatoes	5	13	12	11.2	12
Vegetables	68	150	168	166.8	190
Fruit	28	57	61	50	35
Grapes	24	36	38	25	55

LIVESTOCK
('000)

	1960	1971	1972	1973	1974
Cattle	365	400	455	459	489
of which: Cows	143	200	191	193	202
Pigs	47	69	89.1	99.1	109
Sheep	4,647	4,291	4,438	3,933	4,365

ANIMAL PRODUCTS
('000 tons)

	1960	1970	1971	1972	1973
Meat	51	47.6	52	54.7	60.6
Milk	126	187	195	197.4	217.9
Eggs (million)	56	122.2	145	135.0	148.7
Wool	15.9	14	13.7	12.1	14.4

INDUSTRY AND MINING

Oil is the basic source of wealth of Turkmenia. It also has gas, chemical and other industries based on locally available raw materials. Mirabilite is being extracted in the Kara-Bogaz-Gol Bay on the Caspian and deposits of sulphur are worked in the heart of the Kara-Kum Desert. The Turkmen Republic is the country's biggest supplier of ozocerite. The textile, silk-spinning and food industries are rapidly expanding. Machine-building is the newest branch of heavy industry. Output includes electrical engineering equipment, bulldozers and ventilators.

PRODUCTION

		1970	1971	1972	1973
Oil	'000 tons	14,487	15,535	15,941	16,171
Natural Gas	million cu. metres	13,107	16,899	21,313	28,645
Electric Power	million kWh.	1,657	1,877	1,830	2,347
Cement	'000 tons	n.a.	454	463	534
Cotton Fabrics	'000 sq. metres	n.a.	17,910	17,910	19,665

EDUCATION

The literacy of the population of Turkmenia between the ages of 9 and 49 is 99.5 per cent. According to the 1973 census, 49.6 people over the age of 9 have received higher or secondary education.

(1972–73)

	Institutions	Students
Secondary Schools	1,800	634,000
Secondary Specialized Schools	30	28,300
Higher Schools (incl. Universities)	6	29,600

GOVERNMENT

SUPREME SOVIET

Chairman: (vacant).
Presidium President: ANNA M. KLYCHEV.

COUNCIL OF MINISTERS

Chairman: BALLY IAZKULIEV.

POLITICAL ORGANIZATIONS

Turkmen Communist Party: Ashkhabad; 70,690 mems.; First Secretary of the Central Committee M. N. GAPUROV.

Komsomol Leninist Young Communist League of Turkmenia: Ashkhabad; 249,231 mems.; First Sec. T. B. DURDYEV.

JUDICIAL SYSTEM

Supreme Court

ASHKHABAD

Chairman of the Supreme Court: B. MOKHAMEDKULIEV.
Procurator: A. U. VASILYEV.

THE PRESS

There are 27 newspapers published in the Turkmen S.S.R., including 16 published in Turkmenian. The daily circulation is 726,000 copies (553,000 in Turkmenian). Thirty-four periodicals are published, including 14 in Turkmenian, with a total circulation of 9,400,000 copies (9,200,000 in Turkmenian).

PRINCIPAL NEWSPAPERS

Komsomolets Turkmenistana (*Member of the Leninist Young Communist League of Turkmenia*): Ashkhabad; f. 1938; organ of the Central Committee of the Leninist Young Communist League; three times weekly; in Russian; Editor A. DANILEVICH.

Soviet Turkmenistani (*Soviet Turkmenia*): Ashkhabad; f. 1920; organ of the Turkmen Communist Party, Supreme Soviet and Council of Ministers; six times weekly in Turkmenian; Editor M. BADAEV.

Turkmenskaya Iskra: Ashkhabad; f. 1924; Russian organ of the Turkmen Communist Party, Supreme Soviet and Council of Ministers; six times weekly; Editor M. D. MEDVEDEV.

Yash Kommunist (*Young Communist*): Ashkhabad; f. 1925; organ of the Central Committee of the Leninist Young Communist League of Turkmenia; three times weekly; in Turkmenian; Editor KH. DIVANGULIEV.

SELECTED PERIODICALS

(Published monthly unless otherwise indicated.)

Ashkhabad (*City of Ashkhabad*): Ashkhabad; journal of the Turkmen S.S.R. Union of Writers; popular; bi-monthly; in Russian.

Pioner (*Pioneer*): Ashkhabad; f. 1926; journal of the Central Committee of the Leninist Young Communist League and the Republican Council of the V. I. Lenin Pioneer Organization of the Turkmenian S.S.R.; fiction for 10–15 years; in Turkmenian.

Soviet Turkmenistanynyn Ayallary (*Women of Soviet Turkmenia*): Ashkhabad; f. 1952; journal of the Central Committee of the Turkmenian Communist Party; popular; in Turkmenian.

Tokmak (*Beetle*): Ashkhabad; f. 1925; journal of the Central Committee of the Turkmenian Communist Party; satirical; in Turkmenian.

Turkmenistan Kommunisti (*Communist of Turkmenia*): Ashkhabad; f. 1925; United Publishing House of Newspapers and Journals; political; in Turkmenian.

Turkmenistanyn oba Khozhlygy (*Agriculture of Turkmenia*): Ashkhabad; f. 1957; edition of the Ministry of Agriculture of the Turkmen S.S.R.; intensification of work in agriculture; in Turkmenian.

Sovet edebiyaty (*Soviet Literature*): Ashkhabad; f. 1928; published by the Turkmenskoe Obyedinennoe (Turkmenian United) Publishing House; journal of the Turkmenian S.S.R. Union of Writers; fiction; in Turkmenian.

NEWS AGENCY

TURKMENTAG (*Turkmen Telegraph Agency*): Ashkhabad.

PUBLISHER

In 1973, 545 books were published, 284 in Turkmenian.

Turkmenistan Publishing House: Ashkhabad, Ul. Gogolya 17-a; political and fiction; Dir. B. KH. KHALMURADOV.

CULTURE

PRINCIPAL THEATRES

Academic Drama Theatre: Ashkhabad; Dir. and Producer A. KUNMAMEDOV.

Russian Dramatic Theatre: Ashkhabad; Dir. I. K. INTSEN.

Opera and Ballet Theatre: Ashkhabad, Engelsa 93; Dir. M. A. ALLANUROV.

THE UZBEK SOVIET SOCIALIST REPUBLIC

INTRODUCTION

The Uzebek Republic was formed on October 27th, 1924. It has an area of 447,400 sq. km. and a population of 13,695,000 (January 1st, 1975). Of these, 65.5 per cent are Uzbeks, 12.5 per cent Russians, 4.9 per cent Tartars, 4.0 per cent Kazakhs, 3.8 per cent Tadzhiks and 2.0 per cent Kara-Kalpaks (census 1970). Tashkent, the capital, has a population of 1,595,000 (1975). The Autonomous Soviet Socialist Republic of Kara-Kalpakiya (capital Nukus) is part of the Uzbek Republic. Uzbekistan is situated in the south-eastern part of the Soviet Union, in the heart of Central Asia, and has a short frontier with Afghanistan in the south. Turkmenia lies to the south-west, Kazakhstan to the north, Kirghizia to the east and Tadzhikistan to the south.

STATISTICS

POPULATION

BIRTHS AND DEATHS

	Birth Rate (per '000)	Death Rate (per '000)
1960	39.9	6.0
1970	33.5	5.5
1971	34.5	5.4
1972	33.2	6.1
1973	33.7	6.4

AGRICULTURE

Cotton holds the leading place in agriculture with two-thirds of all land under cotton. Sugar beet and groundnuts are grown under irrigation while the main grain crops are rice, wheat and maize.

In 1974 there were 1,540,000 persons engaged in agriculture on 1,009 collective farms and 445 state farms.

CROP PRODUCTION
('000 tons)

	1960	1970	1971	1972	1973
Wheat	330	409	185	294	344
Maize (Grain only)	76	70	79	143	150
Rice	58.8	187.1	204	238.9	279
Leguminous Plants	1	1	1	1	1
Cotton	2,949	4,666	4,511	4,710	4,908
Potatoes	165	184	158	185.3	197
Vegetables	383	787	834	975	1,020
Fruit	296	410	240	426	663
Grapes	195	310	259	296	300

LIVESTOCK
('000)

	1960	1971	1972	1973	1974
Cattle	2,274	2,907	2,995	2,996	3,060
of which: Cows	931	1,183	1,191	1,192	1,209
Pigs	401	296	362	363	375
Sheep	8,677	7,541	7,755	7,756	8,281

ANIMAL PRODUCTS
('000 tons)

	1960	1970	1971	1972	1973
Meat	182	208	223	222	237
Milk	872	1,333	1,453	1,480	1,695
Eggs (million)	468	860	990	1,031	1,121
Wool	24.3	22.0	21.9	20.8	23

INDUSTRY AND MINING

Uzbekistan is rich in minerals such as copper, gold and bauxites, as well as oil and gas. The Republic's streams and rivers are a potential source of hydro-electric power and contain many commercially valuable fish. Uzbekistan is the U.S.S.R.'s main supplier of cotton.

PRODUCTION

		1970	1971	1972	1973
Steel	'000 tons	389	399	399	403
Coal	,, ,,	3,747	3,811	3,907	4,275
Oil	,, ,,	1,805	1,753	1,921	1,318
Natural Gas	million cu. metres	32,100	33,653	33,700	37,100
Electric Power	million kWh.	18,300	21,300	23,000	26,200
Tractors	number	n.a.	n.a.	17,600	19,100
Cotton Fabrics	million sq. metres	n.a.	n.a.	170.2	173.8
Silk Fabrics	,, ,, ,,	n.a.	n.a.	66	72

EDUCATION

The literacy of the population of Uzbekistan between the ages of 9 and 49 is 99.7 per cent. According to the 1973 census, 53.8 per cent of people over the age of 9 have received higher or secondary education.

(1973–74)

	Institutions	Students
Secondary Schools	9,600	3,646,000
Secondary Specialized Schools	177	172,200
Higher Schools (incl. Universities)	40	233,400

GOVERNMENT

SUPREME SOVIET

Chairman: B. Kh. Sirajdinov.

Presidium President: Nazar M. Matchanov.

COUNCIL OF MINISTERS

Chairman: N. D. Khudaiberdyev.

POLITICAL ORGANIZATIONS

Uzbek Communist Party: Tashkent; 431,536 mems.; First Secretary of the Central Committee Sharaf R. Rashidov.

Komsomol Leninist Young Communist League of Uzbekistan: Tashkent; 1,312,783 mems.; First Sec. E. Gafurjanov.

JUDICIAL SYSTEM

Supreme Court

Tashkent

Chairman of the Supreme Court: S. Kh. Pulatkhodjayev.

Procurator: M. Burikhodjaev.

THE PRESS

There are 230 newspapers published in the Uzbek S.S.R., including 144 published in Uzbek. The daily circulation is 3,952,000 copies (3,014,000 in Uzbek). One hundred and twenty-four periodicals are published, including 31 in Uzbek, with a total circulation of 120,808,000 (about 85.6 million in Uzbek).

PRINCIPAL NEWSPAPERS

Esh Leninchil (*Young Leninist*): Tashkent; f. 1925; organ of the Central Committee of the Leninist Young Communist League of Uzbekistan; five times weekly; in Uzbek; Editor R. Shogulomov.

Komsomolets Uzbekistana (*Member of the Leninist Young Communist League of Uzbekistan*): Tashkent; f. 1926; organ of the Central Committee of the Leninist Young Communist League of Uzbekistan; five times weekly; in Russian; Editor V. Tyurikov.

Pravda Vostoka (*Eastern Truth*): Tashkent; f. 1917; organ of the Uzbek Communist Party, Supreme Soviet and Council of Ministers; six times weekly; in Russian; *Editor:* N. Timofeyev.

Soviet Uzbekistoni (*Soviet Uzbekistan*): Tashkent; f. 1918; organ of the Uzbek Communist Party, Supreme Soviet and Council of Ministers; six times weekly; in Uzbek; Editor M. Koriev.

SELECTED PERIODICALS

(Published monthly unless otherwise indicated)

Fan va Turmush (*Science and Life*): Tashkent; f. 1939; published by the "Fan" (Science) Publishing House; journal of the Uzbek S.S.R. Academy of Sciences; popular scientific; in Uzbek.

Gulistan (*Flourishing Area*): Tashkent; f. 1967; journal of the Central Committee of the Communist Party of the Uzbek S.S.R.; fiction; in Uzbek.

Gulkhan (*Bonfire*): Tashkent; f. 1952; journal of the Central Committee of the Leninist Young Communist League, Ministry of Education and Republican Council of the V. I. Lenin Pioneer Organization of the Uzbek S.S.R.; illustrated fiction; for 10–14 years; in Uzbek.

Guncha (*Small Bud*): Tashkent; f. 1958; journal of the Central Committee of the Leninist Young Communist League and the Republican Council of the Pioneer Organization of the Uzbek S.S.R.; illustrated; for 5–10 years; in Uzbek.

Mushtum (*Fist*): Tashkent; f. 1923; published by the "Soviet Uzbekistoni" newspaper; satirical; in Uzbek; fortnightly.

Obshchestvennie nauki v Uzbekistane (*Social Sciences in Uzbekistan*): Tashkent; f. 1957; published by the "Fan" (Science) Publishing House of the Uzbek S.S.R. Academy of Sciences; history, oriental studies, archaeology, economics, ethnology, etc.; in Russian.

Partiya Turmushi (*Party Life*): Tashkent; f. 1958; published by the Publishing House of the Central Committee of the Uzbek Communist Party; political; in Uzbek and Russian.

Saodat (*Happiness*): Tashkent; f. 1950; journal of the Central Committee of the Uzbek Communist Party; popular for women; in Uzbek.

Shark Yulduzi (*Star of the East*): Tashkent; f. 1933; journal of the Uzbek Union of Writers; fiction; in Uzbek.

Sovet Maktabi (*Soviet School*): Tashkent; f. 1925; published by the "Uchitelj" (Teacher) Publishing House; journal of the Ministry of Education of the Uzbek S.S.R.; improvements to the educational system; in Uzbek.

Uzbekiston (*Uzbekistan*): Tashkent; published by the Publishing House of the Central Committee of the Uzbek Communist Party; journal of the Central Committee of the Uzbek Communist Party; popular; illustrated; in Uzbek.

Uzbekiston Kishlok Khuzhaligi (*Agriculture of Uzbekistan*): Tashkent; f. 1925; journal of the Ministry of Agriculture of the Uzbek S.S.R.; cotton-growing, cattle-breeding, forestry; in Uzbek.

Uzbekiston Kommunisti (*Communist of Uzbekistan*): Tashkent; f. 1925; published by the United Publishing House of the Central Committee of the Uzbek Communist Party; political; in Uzbek and Russian.

Uzbek tili va adabieti (*Uzbek Language and Literature*): Tashkent; f. 1958; published by the "Fan" (Science) Publishing House; journal of the Uzbek S.S.R. Academy of Sciences; articles on history and modern development of the Uzbek language, folk-lore, etc.; in Uzbek; twice monthly.

Zvezda Vostoka (*Star of the East*): Tashkent; f. 1933; published by the Publishing House of the Central Committee of the Uzbek Communist Party; fiction; Russian translations from Arabic, Hindi, Turkish, Japanese, etc.

NEWS AGENCY

UZTAG (*Uzbek Telegraph Agency*): Tashkent.

PUBLISHERS

In 1973, 1,889 books were published, 936 in Uzbek.

Esh Gvardiya (Young Guard) Publishing House: Tashkent, Ul. Navoi 30; books and journals for the young; Dir. A. V. Vakhabov.

Fan (Science) Publishing House: Tashkent, Ul. Gogolya 70; books and journals in all fields of science; Dir. U. U. Yusupov.

Meditsina (Medicine) Publishing House: Tashkent, Ul. Navoi 30; all branches of medical sciences; Dir. U. G. Saipov.

Uzbekistan Publishing House: Tashkent, Ul. Navoi 30; various; Dir. D. U. Yunuzov.

Tashkent Publishing House: Tashkent, Ul. Navoi 30; fiction; Dir. F. U. Yunusov.

RADIO

Radio Tashkent: Broadcasts in Uzbek, English, Urdu, Persian and Arabic.

CULTURE

PRINCIPAL THEATRES

Academic Drama Theatre: Tashkent; Dir. E. Musabekov.

State Academic Opera and Ballet Theatre: Tashkent, ul. Pravdy Vostoka 31; Dir. M. R. Rachmanov.

Russian Dramatic Theatre: Tashkent, Dir. S. R. Leikina.

PRINCIPAL ORCHESTRA

State Symphony Orchestra: Tashkent; Conductor Z. V. Shakhnazakov.

THE SOVIET FAR EAST AND SIBERIA

E. Stuart Kirby

The term Siberia is applied to the whole northern part of the U.S.S.R. in Asia, excluding Soviet Central Asia. It extends 8,000 kilometres from the Ural mountains to the Pacific and over 3,000 kilometres from its southern borders to the Arctic. It has an area of 12.5 million square kilometres, 56 per cent of the area of the Soviet Union.

CLIMATE

Climate is extreme: winters are arctically cold and the brief summer is tropically hot. Some areas are subject to earthquakes.

NATURAL RESOURCES

Siberia is the world's greatest untapped area of natural resources, notably coal, petroleum and natural gas.

POPULATION

The population of Siberia in 1970 was 25,400,000, an average density of two people per square kilometre, which was only a sixth of the average for the U.S.S.R. as a whole. In fact, large areas of the region are uninhabited and over 75 per cent of the population are classified as urban dwellers. The leading cities are very large and modern. Among the fastest growing are Novosibirsk (1.2 million people in 1970, three times the 1939 figure), Omsk (825,000, also three times pre-war), Krasnoyarsk (650,000, over three times pre-war) and Irkutsk (450,000, about 80 per cent greater than in 1939). Others of these proportions include Khabarovsk, Vladivostok, Komsomolsk and Blagoveshchensk. Yakutsk, far to the north, has over 100,000 inhabitants (double the pre-war total) and the remote mining centre of Noril'sk about 140,000. The population is concentrated mainly in the south, which has a less severe climate and is much more developed. Only a small minority live in remote settlements in the Arctic and sub-Arctic zones.

The indigenous, aboriginal or "native" peoples of Siberia are a small minority within the rural portion. Siberia is a distinctly Russian land (including considerable numbers of Ukrainians and Byelorussians from western Russia-in-Europe, Balts and other Soviet "westerners", besides the dominant Great Russians or Muscovites). The other races have a significance equivalent to that of the Indians and Eskimos in North America. Their societies are mostly on a tribal basis, extremely variegated and dispersed. Throughout history, moreover, the Russians have freely intermarried with them: pure strains are quite rare.

The largest indigenous groups, the Yakuts and the Buryats (a branch of the Mongols), constitute Autonomous Soviet Republics of their own with populations, respectively, of about 800,000 and 700,000, as do the Tuvinians (250,000) but even in those areas, with massive influxes of Russians in the Soviet period, Russians have come to form a marked majority. Their predominance, even numerically (not to speak of their political and cultural effect), is still more marked in the outlands. There seem to be about two million Russians in the northern areas of Siberia, where the minor nationalities can now be numbered only as a few tens of thousands, all to some extent assimilated (in various senses of the term) to Soviet Russianism. The complexity of the question may be illustrated as follows: 27 groups of "native peoples" of Siberia are enumerated in the Soviet censuses; in 1970 they totalled just over a million, of whom 30 per cent were Buryats, another 30 per cent Yakuts and 20 per cent Tuvinians. The remaining 20 per cent were thus of twenty-four nationalities, ranging in size from 65,000 Khakasy (in the Krasnoyarsk area) down to 400 Aleuts (out in the north Pacific).

HISTORY

In 1584 the Cossack Yermak defeated the Tartars under Khan Kuchum, whose capital (in Western Siberia) was called Sibir'. This name is the derivation of Siberia. Some etymologists construe it to mean "the Sleeping Land". Yermak, and many small bands of Russian adventurers in the three centuries after him, moved swiftly eastward across the whole continent. Generally they met with little resistance from the resident tribes who were mostly primitive and small (only the Yakuts and Buryat Mongols remained numerous and distinctive enough to be effective still today). Gradually the Cossacks made settlements; on the general pattern of colonial expansion, in time merchants, prospectors, farmers, exiles and prisoners, also bandits and pirates, flowed in considerable but not large numbers over the conquered territories.

The Russian eastward movement soon came into collision with the great Empire of China. A chain of Russian forts or stockades (*ostrog*), serving at the same time as trading posts, centres of administration and the collection of tribute-taxes, reached to the coast of Okhotsk by 1639. This line of communications touched the Upper Amur, but at its eastern end swung considerably towards the north of the present Chinese frontier. More than two hundred years earlier, the Ming dynasty of China had pre-empted southerly parts of what is now the Soviet Far East; by 1411 they had claimed sovereignty and suzerainty as far north as the mouth of the Amur river.

This point is material to the present dispute between the People's Republic of China and the U.S.S.R., as the Peking government demands discussion of such claims. Moscow's first point of reply is that China's presence in or possession of that area has, from the beginning right up to now, been at best nominal. There has never been any significant settlement of Chinese in the disputed territories (the Soviet case continues), there was only remote control from Peking, sporadic visitations of magistrates or tax-gatherers occurred occasionally, as did punitive expeditions against a few and barbarous native tribes whereas the Russians made a systematic initial development of settlements on a more "progressive" basis, a true assimilation of the area (*osvoyenie*).

By the end of the sixteenth century the Ming power had declined until it was contained within China's Great Wall; the Russians established settlements on the Amur, though their main drive was still deflected north-eastwards towards Kamchatka rather than south-eastwards towards what is now Vladivostok.

In 1644 the Manchu dynasty overthrew the Mings and proceeded to subjugate Tibet, Sinkiang (Chinese Turkestan) and Mongolia as well as China proper. Advancing to the river Amur, in 1683–85, they attacked and destroyed a number of Russian settlements along its northern bank. Negotiations at Nerchinsk—a place significantly to the west in Russia, to which the Manchus deployed 15,000 soldiers—resulted in a treaty loosely defining the border between the two countries as a line from the river Argun' northeastwards to the Okhotsk Sea, including all the present-day Maritime and Amur provinces and the southern half of Khabarovsk, also leaving Sakhalin within the Chinese domain. The Manchus had desired all the territory up to Lake Baikal and the river Lena while the Russians had wished the river Amur to be the boundary. Subsequently, the Russians were able to increase their strength and became interested also in the caravan trade and missionary links with China. Through the Treaty of Kiakhta in 1727 they obtained the cession by China of nearly 40,000 square miles of territory, bringing the frontier approximately to the present line between the U.S.S.R. and the Mongolian People's Republic.

In the nineteenth century it was the turn of the Manchu dynasty to go into decline and of Russia to undergo a degree of modernization. Bold Russian leaders repossessed the Amur lands (about 185,000 square miles); the Treaty of Peking in 1860 ceded also to the Tsar some 135,000 square miles east of the river Ussuri, which became Russia's Maritime province, besides marking the Sino-Russian border in Sinkiang. On the consolidation of the Soviet power in Siberia in 1919, the new Communist government in Moscow repudiated "unequal treaties" and Tsarist seizures of alien territory; but subsequently Soviet spokesmen have asserted that Lenin himself stipulated reservations about the meaning of these terms and as to which territories were actually in question.

In any case no retrocessions have been made to China; at the present time the Soviet Government considers all its boundary problems to be "settled", not open to any fundamental renegotiation. Meanwhile massive Chinese immigration into Manchuria (China's "Three North-eastern Provinces") had begun well before the time of the Russian Revolution; by then, however, Russian, Japanese and other interests were established in such strength and rivalry that Manchuria in the early twentieth century was dubbed "the cockpit of Asia". The Russo-Japanese war of 1905 resulted in something like a partition of Manchuria between the two countries; the Japanese went on to establish their puppet Empire of Manchoukuo as a main base in their wars in China, East Asia and the Pacific in the 1930s and the first half of the 1940s.

In the last days of World War II, after the atomic bombs had already fallen on Japan, Soviet forces rapidly occupied Manchuria, Japanese Sakhalin, North Korea and the Kurile Islands. Their campaign in Manchuria was particularly well organized in terms of the latest weaponry and logistics—a feature contributing to present-day Russian confidence that they can deal effectively with anything the Chinese could do against them though, in 1945, they were facing an already attenuated and demoralized Japanese garrison. Mao Tse-tung's forces took Manchuria in the wake of the Soviet Army. In the following ten years there was a "honeymoon" of Sino-Soviet political and economic collaboration followed, at the end of the 1950s, by a dramatic "divorce".

The estrangement became open in 1962–63 at the time of the Cuban crisis when Peking denounced Khrushchev for conceding to the U.S.A. and Moscow retorted scathingly about China's irresponsible "adventurism" with regard to distant areas contrasting with its hypocrisy in not doing anything itself about the "liberation" of Taiwan, Hong Kong and Macao. The Communist Party of China brought the "unequal treaties" into this dispute, with special reference to nine such compacts under which China had made cessions to various Powers, including Tsarist Russia, desiring the Soviets to join in pressing for a general settlement regarding all these and also to admit to the world that the present Sino-Soviet frontiers were created by unequal treaties and should be renegotiated. Some observers take the view that this verbal admission, without any actual territorial changes, would have been enough to satisfy Chinese pride or Maoist principle; others, notably the Moscow authorities, are, however, positive that China is swept by a fury not merely of irridentism but of aggressive expansionism.

Immediately in 1963 the Soviet Government refused to admit the Chinese demand for frontier reconsideration, asserting that it had no territorial disputes with any country—the inference being (as it still continues to be) that it regards its frontiers with China as fixed. Negotiations begun in 1964 in Peking, with a less acute focus than the foregoing, made no progress. Though there have sporadically been local and partial transactions regarding practical matters of river-navigation and the like, these have been interspersed with armed clashes.

RELATIONS WITH FOREIGN COUNTRIES

In the mid-1970s trade with China continued at a low ebb. China and the U.S.S.R. were vying for commercial and other influence on Japan. Communist successes in the area formerly called Indochina, followed by apparent U.S. withdrawal to a new perimeter on the eastern rim of the region, may result in the whole of East and South-East Asia becoming a general arena of Sino-Soviet competition or conflict in various forms. At the western end of East Asia, the U.S.S.R. developed close and friendly relations with India. In May 1976 India resumed diplomatic relations with China.

In the Soviet polity, the U.S.S.R.'s gigantic base in Siberia will increasingly provide an advantageous position and a great deal of material strength. Accordingly the U.S.S.R. is committedly keen on the economic and industrial development of Siberia, on grandly planned lines. In recent years it has let it be understood that it would broadly welcome the partnership and collaboration, for development in Siberia, of Japan and the Western industrial countries.

ECONOMIC SURVEY

Development

The dimensions of distance are enormous and all-important. Since both the markets and the sources of supply, as well as the source of administrative decisions (right down to matters of minor detail), are so far away, Siberian development is very expensive. The expense is increased by the need to pay well and to provide good living conditions, as incentives to induce workers to migrate to the outlands. At all seasons the upkeep of installations (roads, railways, water pipes, telecommunications, airfields, bridges, dwellings, vehicles and everything else that is exposed to the climate) makes this a high-cost economy.

Rewards have to be correspondingly high. Thus the first common illusion to be dispelled is perhaps that Siberia is a poor or depressed area. It is for the most part, although having pockets of comparative poverty like any other region of the world, not only rich in available and potential resources but comparatively rich in current per capita income, which ranges from about double to about treble the levels in European Russia in money terms. Offset by high prices, and often by inadequate availabilities, average income is still high (by Soviet standards) on any net calculation. Equally high, by the Soviet scale at least, are other indicators, such as the provision of living space per family or per person, and a variety of "fringe benefits". Siberia is generally the most affluent region of the Soviet Union and an integral and important part of the nation, as is demonstrated by the heavy and increasing investment there.

These totals represent a slightly rising share in the total investment in the U.S.S.R. as a whole: 14 per cent in 1941–50 (the same proportion as in 1918–40), 15 per cent in 1941–50 and over 16 per cent in 1961–70. From 1971 the proportion was to be raised, according to some indications, such as the statement that Siberia would receive a quarter of all the capital investment in the U.S.S.R. during the next several years.

Industry

In the 1960s overall industrial output in the U.S.S.R. increased by just over 50 per cent. West Siberia performed similarly, being just below this national average for the first half of the decade but just above it for the second. East Siberia was, however, 10 per cent above the average for the whole country, achieving growth of nearly 61 per cent in 1961–65 and nearly 60 per cent in 1966–70. In contrast, the Soviet Far East, although exceeding the national average for the decade by 4 per cent, slipped a little in the second half, growing by 59 per cent in 1961–65 but only 49 per cent in 1966–70.

The ninth Five-Year Plan (1971–75) showed a falling-off in industrial expansion in Siberia, or rather a concentration on the completion and improvement of existing projects, without initiating any large new ones. The basics in the Soviet scale of priorities are broadly the following: Siberia produces about 18 per cent of the U.S.S.R.'s electric power, 10 per cent of its petroleum, 5 per cent of its natural gas, over 30 per

Capital Investment in Siberia
(Under successive Five-Year Plans; in millions of roubles)

	1951–55	1956–60	1961–65	1966–70
West Siberia	4,700	9,400	13,900	20,300
East Siberia	3,500	7,500	12,000	15,800
Soviet Far East	4,000	6,200	9,500	14,600
TOTAL	12,200	23,100	35,400	50,700

cent of its coal, 8 per cent of its iron and steel, 5 per cent of fertilizers, over 30 per cent of commercial timber and 25 per cent of sawnwood, and 12 per cent of cement. In gold and diamonds, Siberia accounts for practically the whole Soviet output, and in non-ferrous metals a large proportion, although figures are kept secret.

Agricultural results appear, however, to be as poor as elsewhere in the Soviet Union, though Siberia has significant agro-industries, producing 10 per cent of the nation's factory output of meat and 12 per cent of its butter. It also supplies over 30 per cent of the U.S.S.R.'s fish and 40 per cent of canned fish. In the domain of consumer goods, Siberia is even weaker than other parts of the Soviet Union. Light industry has never had any strong part in Soviet planning for Siberia; consumer goods have to be brought there from Russia-in-Europe, and to a lesser extent from Soviet Central Asia, at very high transport cost and in rather poor and irregular selections. Thus Siberia produces only about one per cent of the U.S.S.R.'s woollen fabrics, 4 per cent of silk fabrics, 5 per cent of footwear and minor amounts of all other consumption goods.

Siberia's engineering industries are still mainly in its western part but there are some old-established centres all through Siberia to the Far East. They are everywhere advancing, although Siberia must still draw mainly on European Russia for machinery. The chemical industries present broadly the same picture, with great additional prospects for petrochemical industries in connection with oilfield developments. At all points in the spectrum of activity, transport and labour are the most basic problem of Siberia, at the ground level of operational necessities.

Mining and Power

The key point, in the Soviet view, is the provision of plentiful electricity; it is proposed to apply this also to agriculture, by using it to warm the soil as well as to drive all the machinery. Abundant electricity could certainly bring about a prodigious transformation of the conditions of life and work in Siberia. The necessary power is fortunately available, in considerable quantities at present, possibly in great abundance in the future. Siberia is extremely rich in coal, hydroelectric potential and even in firewood, not to mention the existence of less traditional sources of power, like geothermal (volcanic) sites and tidal energy, which are under continued study and development. That nothing is unconsidered or impossible is instanced by the construction of an isolated atomic-power plant at Bilibino, an extremely remote mining area at the western end of the Chukot district at the farthest north-eastern end of the country.

The Kuznetsk basin in West Siberia, with a scheduled output of 135 million tons of bituminous coal in 1975, one-third greater than in 1965, represents some 16 per cent of all Soviet coal production and is second only to the great Don basin in the Ukraine; but it has about four times the reserves of the latter, and produces at less than half the cost.

East Siberia has vast tracts of inferior but useful lignite, mainly for local use, in the Kansk-Achinsk fields (which feed other industrial districts), those of Cheremkhovo (which supply the Angarsk area) and another far to the north at Noril'sk, which furnishes hard coal and coking coal for the industrial complex there. The significance of all but the last of these is, however, changing, as oil displaces coal in the neighbouring industries, and nearly all the Trans-Siberian Railway has been electrified. The Soviet Far East has prodigious reserves of coal but these are remote and mining would be relatively expensive. Existing workings are, in large part, open-cast surface exploitations such as the Raichikhinsk brown coals in the Amur province, which account for nearly 40 per cent of the output in the Soviet Far East. A similar proportion, some of it in harder coal, has come from the Maritime province. Some of the older fields there, around Suchan in the Vladivostok area, are exhausted but new supplies are coming in from the Ussuri area. The biggest reserves of coal (about one-third of all the U.S.S.R.'s, said to be the largest potential coalfield in the world, containing over 2,500 million tons) and the freshest hopes are in the vast northern hinterland of the Yakut Autonomous Republic, particularly those around Chul'man, which include coking coal, hitherto obtained in comparatively minor quantities from Sakhalin.

Petroleum has become of major significance. West Siberia has proven reserves of 1,000 million tons; its output reached 85.5 million tons in 1973. Soviet enthusiasts expect this to become one of the world's leading oilfields. The deposits, or the sedimentary areas which may bear oil, extend all the way from just north of Tyumen' and Tomsk northward to the Arctic Ocean. A strip of similar sedimentary deposit extends from a point about 200 kilometres north of Markovo, a similar distance west of the northern tip of Lake Baikal, for about 500 kilometres north of Markovo, which is already a centre of some oilfield activity. There is another, even more inaccessible deposit about 300 kilometres from north to south and 150 kilometres wide, straddling the Arctic Circle about 300 kilometres north of the last-mentioned sedimentary area. Beyond the Arctic Circle, farther east in an even more remote and inhospitable region, there is a third and much larger area not yet exploited, reaching some 500 kilometres inland from the 1,000 kilometres of Arctic coast between the Yana and Kolyma rivers. Yet another potential "sweep" of the same kind covers both the east and west coasts of Kamchatka and reaches northwards to the area of Anadyr.

Of all these, only the area north of Tyumen' has yet been substantially developed. In fairly imminent prospect of development is a similar area, some 900 kilometres across from east to west and 500 kilometres from north to south, around Ust' Vilyui, north of Yakutsk, already worked for the production especially of natural gas. All these sedimentary areas are, of course, possible major sources of either natural gas or petroleum. Developed for many years for the latter, and recently for the former, is a much smaller area in the northern end of the island of Sakhalin. There are some offshore prospects around that island.

To utilize and consolidate what has been developed, a considerable network of oil and gas pipelines already exists in West Siberia, linking it also with European Russia to the west and Irkutsk to the east, while more are under construction and planned. One from West Siberia all the way to Khabarovsk and Vladivostok was proposed a few years ago but postponed, and another is proposed from the Ust' Vilyui field to the same destinations. Usefully functioning is the double oil pipeline from northern Sakhalin to Komsomolsk on the upper Amur, and a gas pipeline is being added.

Current outputs

The table below gives recent scales of output in the main categories of industrial energy.

Large and increasing quantities of iron ore and non-ferrous metals are produced. A notable potential source of copper, for example, is in the Udokan range some 600–700 kilometres north-west of Chita, said to be larger than the fields of southern Africa. This is a remote permafrost area but an annual output of nearly half a million tons of copper ore is already claimed. There are nickel, tin, tungsten, bauxite (an annual output of a million tons of aluminium is claimed), cobalt, lead and zinc, gold (the volume of output is secret but the U.S.S.R. sold 32 tons on the world market in 1970 and larger amounts in following years; Siberia is the main source), diamonds (also a matter of high secrecy, but output is claimed to have exceeded that of South Africa), vanadium, beryllium and a number of other minerals essential to current advanced technologies.

Labour

Because of the limited population, labour shortage is one of the key problems of Siberian development. Efforts to utilize female labour are one persistent feature. A high proportion of the population consists of young people. Workers on contracts of up to five years create a high rate of labour turnover. (In recent years the former restrictions on personal mobility within the U.S.S.R. have been removed for Soviet citizens).

Hence there have been many allusions to the "drain of people" out of Siberia. In overall terms, this is belied by population figures. The flow of migration varies with the subsidies and higher wage-rates offered. In 1960 the Soviet Government abolished the "wage differentials" for the "northern regions", reducing rates there to the levels in the European Soviet Union. In each of the following years, one-quarter or one-third of the labourers emigrated from certain parts of Siberia until the differentials were restored in 1967, when a distinct net inflow resumed at once, though there are occasional effluxes from particular areas, especially of such groups as construction workers, roadbuilders and stevedores.

However, on the whole, there is net immigration. Much of the movement is internal within Siberia. The instability of the working population, as well as its absolutely small numbers relative to the current and potential tasks in the region, can be quite crippling: in the Tyumen' oilfields (at the westernmost point of West Siberia, a crucial development area) about half the workforce "departed" during the 1960s. They were largely replaced by current recruitment but this was costly. Production was "destabilized" and the new recruits from other parts of the country appeared less trained and less acclimatized.

	Oil (million metric tons)	Natural Gas ('000 million cubic metres)	Electric Power ('000 million KWh.)
West Siberia	1 (1965) 31 (1971) 85 (1973) 120 (1975 *target*)	2.5 (1965) 10 (1970)	23 (1960) 44 (1970)
East Siberia	n.a.	n.a.	16 (1960) 74 (1970)
Soviet Far East	3 (1973)	1 (1971)	5 (1960) 14 (1970)

* Sakhalin only.

BIBLIOGRAPHY

HISTORY

ARMSTRONG, T. E. Russian Settlement in the North (Cambridge University Press, 1975).

CAROE, O. Soviet Empire (Macmillan, London, 1953).

CONOLLY, V. Siberia Today and Tomorrow (Collins, London, 1975).

CURZON, N. The Russians in Central Asia (Longmans, London, 1889).

DALLIN, D. J. The Rise of Russia in Asia (Hollis & Carter, London, 1950).

Soviet Russia and the Far East (Hollis & Carter, London, 1948).

HAMBLY, G. (Ed.). Central Asia (in the Universal History Series) (Weidenfeld & Nicolson, London, 1970).

HOLDSWORTH, M. Turkestan in the Nineteenth Century (Central Asian Research Centre, London, 1959).

KERNER, R. J. The Urge to the Sea. The Course of Russian History: The Role of Rivers, Portages, Ostrogs, Monasteries and Furs (California University Press, Berkeley and Los Angeles, 1946).

LANTZEFF, G. V. Siberia in the Seventeenth Century (California University Press, Berkeley, 1943).

PARK, A. Bolshevism in Turkestan 1917–1927 (Columbia University Press, New York, 1957).

PARKER, W. H. An Historical Geography of Russia (University of London Press, 1968).

PIERCE, R. Russian Central Asia 1867–1917 (California University Press, Berkeley, 1960).

PIPES, R. The Formation of the Soviet Union (Harvard University Press, Cambridge, Mass., 1954).

RAEFF, M. Siberia and the Reforms of 1822 (Washington University Press, Seattle, 1956).

SEMYONOV, Y. The Conquest of Siberia (Routledge, London, 1944).

TREADGOLD, D. W. The Great Siberian Migration: Government and Peasant in Resettlement from Emancipation to the First World War (Princeton University Press, 1957).

WHEELER, G. E. The Modern History of Soviet Central Asia (Weidenfeld and Nicolson, London, 1964).

ECONOMY

COLE, J. P., and GERMAN, F. C. A Geography of the U.S.S.R. The Background to a planned Economy (Butterworth, London, 1961).

CONOLLY, V. Beyond the Urals (Oxford University Press, London, 1967).

KIRBY, E. S. The Soviet Far East (Macmillan, London, 1971).

KRYPTON, C. The Northern Sea Route and the Economy of the Soviet Union (Methuen, London, 1956).

NATO, Division of Economic Affairs, Report of Round Table on the Exploitation of Siberia's Natural Resources (Brussels, 1974).

NOVE, A., and NEWTH, J. A. The Soviet Middle East (Allen & Unwin, London, 1967).

THIEL, E. The Soviet Far East. A Survey of its Physical and Economic Geography (Methuen, London, 1957).

GENERAL

BECKER, S. Russia's Central Asian Protectorates: Bukhara and Khiva 1865–1925 (Harvard University Press, Cambridge, Mass., 1967).

BENNIGSEN, A., and QUELQUEJAY, C. Evolution of the Muslim Nationalities of the U.S.S.R. and their Linguistic Problems (Central Asian Research Centre, London, 1961).

KIRBY, E. S. Russian Studies of China: Progress and Problems of Soviet Sinology (Macmillan, London, 1975).

KOLARZ, W. The Peoples of the Soviet Far East (George Philip, London, 1954).

Religion in the Soviet Union (St. Martin's Press, New York, 1962).

RAKOWSKA-HARMSTONE, T. Russia and Nationalism in Central Asia: the case of Tadzhikistan (John Hopkins Press, 1970).

SALISBURY, H. E. The Coming War between Russia and China (Pan Books, London, 1969).

SMIRNOV, N. A. Islam and Russia (Central Asian Research Centre, London, 1956).

STEPHAN, J. J. Sakhalin: A History (Oxford University Press, 1971).

WHEELER, G. E. Racial Problems in Soviet Muslim Asia (Oxford University Press, 2nd edition, 1962).

ZENKOVSKY, S. A. Pan-Turkism and Islam in Russia (Harvard University Press, Cambridge, Mass., 1960).

CENTRAL ASIAN REVIEW. Central Asian Research Centre, London, quarterly.

Australasia and the Pacific Islands

AUSTRALASIA
Scale 1: 17,000,000 approx
ONE INCH TO 430 MILES
0 Miles 645
Towns over 1 million people
,, over 100,000 people
Boundaries - international
- provincial etc.,
Railways
Roads
track
Sand desert
Marsh
Airports
Salt pan
Feet
16,000
10,000
6,000
3,000
1,500
1,000
600
300
Sea Level
Land Depression
Equator
Tropic of Capricorn
A U S T R A L I A
I N D O N E S I A
P A C I F I C O C E A N
Coral Sea
Tasman Sea
Arafura Sea
Timor Sea
Banda Sea
Flores Sea
Molucca Sea
Great Australian Bight
Great Barrier Reef
Solomon Islands (Br.)
New Hebrides (Br.-Fr. Condominium)
Loyalty Is. (Fr.)
New Caledonia (Fr.)
Fiji Is.
NEW ZEALAND
NORTH ISLAND
SOUTH ISLAND
TASMANIA
WEST IRIAN
PAPUA
NEW GUINEA
NORTH EAST NEW GUINEA
WESTERN AUSTRALIA
NORTHERN TERRITORY
SOUTH AUSTRALIA
QUEENSLAND
NEW SOUTH WALES
VICTORIA
Celebes (Sulawesi)
Bismarck Archipelago
Great Dividing Range
Great Sandy Desert
Gibson Desert
Great Victoria Desert
Simpson Desert
Nullarbor Plain
Lake Eyre
Darwin
Perth
Adelaide
Melbourne
Sydney
Canberra
Brisbane
Newcastle
Hobart
Auckland
Wellington
Christchurch
Port Moresby
Nouméa
Suva
Alice Springs
Townsville
Broken Hill
100 fathoms

Australasia

A. E. McQueen

The concept of "Australasia"—the nations of New Zealand and Australia—is more firmly established in history than it is spoken of today. Both countries are nations of relatively recent settlement, both are populated with people of predominantly British stock, both have the semi-dependent economies which accompany a common economic base, the supplying of pastoral products to northern hemisphere markets. It is this very complementary nature of their economies which at times strains the concept of Australasia as a unit; the many points which are in common can lead as much to competition—especially in trade—as they can lead to closer union.

EARLY SETTLEMENT

Australia was unknown to the rest of the world until 1606, when a Dutch explorer arrived in the Gulf of Carpentaria; after that year other Dutch sailors looked at various parts of the coast, but were not sufficiently impressed to encourage settlement. General exploration in the Pacific during the eighteenth century created interest in adventurers from other lands, especially Britain, and in 1770, after a six-month visit to New Zealand, James Cook landed at Botany Bay, later part of New South Wales. By the precision of his charting and exploration he dispelled a number of vague assumptions held in Britain about land masses in the South Pacific; it was then up to the British Government to decide whether such distant lands were of any value.

The answer was supplied in terms of a social problem which faced the British Government—where to send convicts now that the American colonists would no longer accept them. In 1787 transportation to Australia was approved; and on January 26th, 1788, Governor Phillip, with a party of 1,030 of whom 736 were convicts, landed in New South Wales. It was not an auspicious beginning for the new colony, and the problems of crop-growing with local climate and soils did not ease the strains of existence in a society where a majority were involuntary settlers. There were few experienced farmers among the newcomers; social and economic conditions were such that there was little incentive for a successful British farmer to migrate. The system of land grants was such that by the turn of the century most land was held by a few officers who, using capital acquired by devious means, had bought out nearly all the smallholders; much of the land was held merely as a capital resource rather than to be used for productive purposes. Only in relatively few cases did agricultural development take place, one notable example being on the estate of John Macarthur, an officer who arrived in Sydney in 1790. He was later to import Merino sheep, and along with others of his time, provide the foundations of the Australian fine-wool flocks.

The first settlement of New Zealand was accomplished in rather more dignified circumstances. After a brief visit by the Dutchman Abel Tasman in 1642, Cook was the next to appear on the scene to carry out a thorough exploration of much of the coastline in 1769. Eight years later his journal was published and New Zealand became much more widely known. Explorers from other nations—particularly France—visited various parts of the country in following decades; but by 1800 commercial activities had also begun in the form of whaling, sealing, flax-cutting and the cutting of timber for ships' repairs. The missionaries quickly followed, their aim being to work amongst the native Maori people whose initial association with Europeans had not always been happy. The differences between the Maori and the Australian aboriginal, and the stories of European association with each group, provide a point of some contrast between the two countries.

THE INDIGENOUS PEOPLES

It has been suggested, from a study of Polynesian place names, that the first Maoris came to New Zealand from the Society Islands in the fourteenth century. They brought with them some plants, animals, a language, and a quite complex culture. By applying what they already knew of plant-growing and food-gathering they gradually developed an economy closely in balance with the environmental conditions of their new home. Most of the tribal groups developed bases in areas where food could easily be grown or gathered, factors which led to the much higher proportion of Maori population in the more temperate North Island than the South Island. Not all tribes lived by the same means; some were primarily agriculturalists, others gathered their food from bush or sea. There was exchange of products between various tribes; there was, within most tribes, a wide range of skills such as weaving, building construction, and use of the wedge, lever and skid. But no money was used; gift and counter-gift operated by tribal chiefs (a much more complex system than barter) was the nearest substitute. And at the basis of all this was land over which the tribe rather than the individual had complete rule and to which was attached extremely deep spiritual associations. It was a complex society and economy; one in which the intrusion of the market economy and different values of the nineteenth century European visitors to New Zealand was to have a sharp and at times deleterious effect.

The Australian aborigines were, in some senses, a much more simple community. They are thought to be of South Asian origin, essentially refugee groups driven out from south India and Malaya at a time when much of the Indonesian land bridge still existed and the ocean crossing to Australia was much shorter than it is today. The earliest groups were pushed southward to Tasmania; later tribes settled mainly along the eastern coast.

The aborigines were semi-nomadic, obtaining their food by hunting and gathering. Unlike the Maori, they had no permanent settlements; their only animal was the dog. Their possessions were limited to those needed for survival—weapons, a drinking vessel, perhaps a very little clothing; their time was almost entirely taken up with gathering the means to survive. But they did have a complex mythology and extensive rituals based on ancestor worship which to a great extent governed their behaviour, both as individuals and as a group. It was a social system evolved over a very long period but which did not rest upon the same degree of economic development and tribal interchange as was the case with the Maori.

Relations with the Europeans

The British government had good intentions toward the aborigines, but rarely were these intentions translated into action. As European settlement advanced, so were the aborigines pushed back into the interior; and there was little compunction about killing any natives who dared to trespass on what was originally their hunting ground. The loss of land, introduction of new diseases, and occasional slaughter reduced the aboriginal population sharply; the Tasmanian tribe, of some 2,000, is now extinct. Aborigines are still, today, concentrated in the interior, some working (at lower rates of pay than their European counterparts) on outback stations. Others live in, or near, country towns, and a few have moved to the cities; their numbers (some 50,000 full-blood, about the same of half-castes) have not been large enough in a community of some 13.4 million to stir the national conscience until very recent years. To most Australians the aboriginal remains as something of a curiosity, something rarely seen, a distant fellow-Australian who by the misfortunes of history is part of an under-privileged group in the modern market economy.

The Maori has not been as easily disposed of in New Zealand society. The first association of any note with Europeans took the form of trading with whalers and sealers in the late eighteenth and early nineteenth centuries; this developed particularly in the Bay of Islands, where whalers of many nations called for stores and rest. Introduced diseases took their toll; and in the economic sphere there were marked changes which cut across the established social structure of the Maori community. The use of the steel fish hook, for example, seriously affected the status and skills of craftsmen who had formerly worked in bone, shell, and wood. Although this breaking-down process took some time, the effect of association with the European was to eliminate or modify many quite basic aspects of Maori life.

Estimates of Maori population before and after the European arrived vary widely, but there is sufficient evidence to indicate that disease, the use of muskets and a general disruption of Maori life caused a sharp drop in numbers. It is thought that there were between 120,000 and 160,000 in 1840; Cook's estimate, or rather informed guess, was 400,000. In the mid-nineteenth century the generally depressed state of mind of Maori leaders and their people caused some observers to consider that the people were doomed to extinction as an ethnic group; but from the 1890s onwards the figures rose steadily until after 1945 the Maori had one of the highest rates of natural increase in the world.

The year 1840, in both Maori history and the history of New Zealand, is an important date. In that year the Treaty of Waitangi was signed; under it the sovereignty of New Zealand was granted by a large number of chiefs to the Queen of England, so passing the economic foundation of Maori life—land—to the control of an authority not only outside Maori control, but outside the country itself. Disputes over land were to be the cause of bloodshed between Maori and settler—or the colonial army—for much of the next three decades. Yet it was during this period that there could also be observed the change in New Zealand's function from that of a handy place to service traders to a country suitable for settlers. Under various settlement schemes—the most notable being the Wakefield schemes under which shiploads of settlers were brought to a number of infant ports to set up farm-based settlements—the European population grew quickly during the 1840s. The original intention of the *New Zealand Company's* plans—to transplant to the new colony a British farming structure—was not successful, partly because, like Australia, few well-established British farmers saw any need to travel 12,000 miles to start a livelihood over again in very primitive conditions. Most of the settlers were poor, and unskilled, with only a smattering of tradesmen among them; the result was a direction of effort not into British-type farming, but into a wide range of activities embracing commerce and pastoral farming rather than agriculture. It was in this respect that the Maoris were most valuable to the new settlers, because they had quickly adopted new techniques of production such as wheat- and potato-growing, the use of horses, metal tools and agricultural equipment, all within the context of a market economy. The Maori in some parts of the country therefore became important and very efficient as a food-supplier; indeed it is often held that without the help and co-operation of the Maori the early settlements of New Zealand could not have survived.

The contrasts are drawn. New Zealand, settled five decades later than Australia, under private rather than state-promoted auspices; the settlers came to a country where a highly adaptable native community held skills of great value to the newcomers. The relationship was not always easy; occasional strains are still apparent a century or more later, and the Europeans' treatment of the Maori and his land was, in the early years, rarely very chivalrous. But a community of New Zealanders has slowly emerged, one the minority of predominantly rural origin, the other with urban roots. The Maori is—and has been for decades—moving to the towns, to produce an inter-racial relationship which is more one of integration than assimilation. This is the second major phase of Maori-European relationships; it has speeded up since 1945, and has produced tensions which will take generations to overcome in some urban areas. The solutions lie in education, full employment (for there is a high component of unskilled labour in the Maori labour force) and inter-marriage, already widely practised. As in any matter of social change, the ultimate answer—a largely integrated community—is generations away. But at least the broad aims are in sight, and are publicly discussed—and to an observer of the Australian scene, these objectives would seem to be the less prominent points in national policy toward the aborigines.

In Australia, the number of natives was smaller; their presence was of little or no value to the first settlers because, unlike the Maori, they could not offer the food supplies so badly needed in the early days. The foundation was thus laid for an attitude of oversight, though more recent decades have seen some action on the part of various governments to remedy the neglect of previous generations. The result, in Australasian terms, is an aspect of social geography containing distinct contrasts, rooted in the very earliest years of settlement. Australia in the future will probably remain an almost entirely "white" population; the additions and variations to their community will be from Europe. Europeans will also add to the New Zealand community, but there will be a distinctive characteristic in the presence, largely integrated into the market economy, of the Maori and, as a result of very recent migration from the Pacific Islands, a considerable group of Islanders. It has been predicted that, within a few decades, there will be few New Zealanders without a Maori relative; can the same, even on a more limited scale, be said for the Australian and the aboriginal?

ECONOMIC GEOGRAPHY: NATIONS OR COLONIES?

The first decades of the nineteenth century in Australia were taken up with exploring and occasionally settling coastal areas, and discovering what lay in the interior. These journeys of discovery involved quite incredible hardship, and cost many lives; the results were often negative in the sense that those who returned were able to report only upon the barren and useless qualities of the land they had seen. It was not until about 1860 that the capabilities of the Australian continent could be fairly assessed from a basis of knowledge rather than theory.

In the meantime, however, the more easily accessible land in the east and south was being settled, and the wool trade, for long a staple of the Australian economy, was well under way in the first quarter of the century. In 1821, 175,000 pounds of wool, of a quality equal to the best available in Europe, were sent to Britain. Large-scale land companies received charters under which settlers were to be brought out and the holdings developed in return for the huge land grants. In 1830 the granting of land for nothing was stopped; but with enormous areas still unoccupied, men acquired flocks of sheep and moved out in search of land—the men who were to become known as "squatters". These at first illegal settlers were formally recognized as landholders in 1836; by 1840 "there were 763 . . . legal squatting stations in New South Wales, carrying some 350,000 cattle and 1,200,000 sheep, looked after by a population of 6,664, nearly half of whom were convict servants" (A. G. L. Shaw). Life was hard, and not always successful; but it is to the squatters that Australia must look for its prosperity up to the 1850s. Their production helped to establish not only a skilled farming population and a steady wool trade with Britain, but all the commercial and merchant activities in the cities which go with such a trade. And, if the trading links were those of a colony, the society which the squatters brought into being was peculiarly Australian; there was little tradition of the landed gentry on the English pattern, but rather a fiercely independent, and sometimes wealthy, farming group which began to move into the political scene. There was no inherent respect for the established order; it was a group which argued a case on its particular merits, with but passing reference to the precedents of the society in whose image some had fondly hoped it would grow.

Squatters, or their local equivalent, were not unknown in New Zealand, although the different environment dictated that the holdings were much smaller. But land was the big attraction from the 1840s on, especially in the eastern South Island and the few other parts of the country where grass was the natural vegetation. New Zealand's native bush was regarded largely as an obstacle to development, except where it provided the raw materials for building and local shipbuilding. But the attraction of land, on both sides of the Tasman, did not mean that the population was essentially a rural one. Mid-century New Zealand had a population of some 22,000; the census of 1858 showed barely a third of the labour force as "agriculturalists and pastoralists", with most of the remainder being in work which was essentially urban. Wool, grain, and "vegetables, etc." were the leading exports in 1855, and although exports were to decline briefly later in the decade, the foundations for the market and export economy were firmly laid. Australia, too, was an urbanized community at mid-century, with economic activity more centralized than in New Zealand's case; each colony (equivalent to the present States) had grown from a single centre, significantly the major and at times only port for exports and imports. In both countries the growth of railways was to underwrite the role of major ports as the import-export centres for each State or region; the history of the growth of the various railway systems is one of linking hinterlands to ports, rather than region to region. This tendency was even more marked in Australia where, for a variety of political and historical reasons, no two contiguous States have the same railway gauge. The costs of double handling between railway systems were sufficient to tie effectively all parts of a particular state to its capital even where the distance to another capital was shorter, a situation which was not rationalized to any extent until more flexible road transport began to operate over longer distances.

In brief, the foundations had been laid in the best nineteenth century tradition in both Australia and New Zealand for the supply of some foodstuffs and wool, the raw materials of pastoralism, to Britain. It was a pattern which was to develop, with true Victorian fluctuations in the terms of trade, until well into the twentieth century—indeed, both nations are still fundamentally dependent upon the exports of primary produce, the major current difference from earlier days being the lesser importance of Britain as a market, and the greater variety of items being produced from the land.

Developments in Rural Economy in the late Nineteenth Century

After the introduction of the fine-woolled sheep, refrigeration was the greatest boon to the nineteenth century Australasian export trade, enabling meat, and later dairy produce, to be transported safely through the tropics to northern markets. But more than this, refrigeration applied to the trade from both countries helped to bring about certain basic changes in land use and in the very structure of rural society, particularly in New Zealand.

Until the 1890s the smallholder was not a notable part of the Australasian rural scene; the economies of grazing for wool just did not encourage it—quite apart from the institutional heritage in both countries which had actively discouraged it in all but a few areas. The introduction of refrigeration, however, encouraged more intensive types of farming such as dairying and fattening stock for killing, and other technological improvements, such as improved methods of milk processing in the dairy industry, encouraged higher output and better payment to the farmers. These changes were more notable in New Zealand where the environment and rate of grass growth was kinder to this type of farming; and it was in New Zealand that social change came to the aid of technology in 1894 with the establishment of the Advances to Settlers Office, under which money could be loaned to small farmers at low interest rates. In 1892 the Department of Agriculture was established, its main purpose being to assist farmers with advice on farming techniques; it also provided inspection and grading services.

All this encouraged the expansion of the smallholder, particularly in the dairying areas of the North Island. Much of the land was new, and had to be broken in from bush or scrub; in other cases larger landholders subdivided their holdings. Dairy factories, and their associated settlement of factory workers, were established in many parts of Taranaki and the Waikato, and to a lesser extent elsewhere; the main breed of sheep changed from the wool-bearing Merino to a variety of cross-breds and other breeds which produced both meat and wool. The typical New Zealand farm emerged as one of a few hundred acres, with the farmer and his family doing almost all the work around the property. The period around the turn of the century laid the foundations for the second and major era of farming and indeed economic development in New Zealand. The booms and busts associated with the gold rushes of the 1860s, the violent fluctuations which affected the economy because of the almost total lack of financial controls associated with nineteenth century economic administration—all these more extreme features began to be modified in a rural and urban scene in which there was more stability than ever before as a result of state intervention in farm development and the associated political and social changes.

In Australia in the 1890s the changes on the rural scene were somewhat different. There had been some encouragement for the smallholder in terms of refrigeration and other developments; but refrigeration brought as much assistance to the larger landholder running beef in northern areas as it did to anyone else. There was not the same institutional assistance to the small man; intensive farming in Australia was beginning to appear as the means of producing more specialist crops, such as in the case of vineyards, horticulture, and sugar, rather than the more traditional farm products. Sugar had been commercially planted in Queensland as far back as the 1860s; but as a labour-intensive activity, sugar-farming called for an application of manpower far beyond local resources, so the problem had been solved by importing Kanakas from the South Sea Islands. It was a refined form of slavery; the survivors were eventually repatriated, and the Queensland sugar industry became a case study of "white settlement in the tropics". Traditionally, labour-intensive tropical crops grown on a large scale since then, such as cotton on the controversial Ord scheme, have been worked by mechanical means as far as possible; the least that can be said for the "White Australia" policy is that it was, at least after the Kanakas episode, consistent, until liberalizing moves of the early 1970s.

The Early Years of Nationhood

It was at the turn of the century—on 1st January 1901—that Australia became a nation, not just a group of colonies. Federation brought upon the Commonwealth government the problems of association with six States, widely separated and each with a considerable history of its own, as well as a vast expanse of relatively barren land in the Northern Territory. The problems of a two-tier governmental system have not been eased in the last seventy years; although perhaps the issues have been clarified by continuing debate and argument. The inter-State divisions in terms of attitudes as much as in terms of any trading patterns, were not to be seriously diminished until the irritations of the railway gauge problem could be overcome, first with motor transport, and later with the opening of the standard-gauge link between New South Wales and Victoria in 1962 and its extension through to Perth in 1969.

In both political and economic terms Australia and New Zealand experienced a period of consolidation around the turn of the century. Terms of trade improved, at least in the short term; and in the years prior to the First World War attention moved to some extent from the rural to the urban scene. Certain industries had by this time lost their essentially small-town characteristics, and disputes between labour and management were evidence of pressure groups developing as a result of a large labour force and a more clearly defined occupational structure; and the growth of mining, both for coal and for other minerals, established a milieu in which union activities flourished. But the First World War diverted the nation's energies; New Zealand suffered, in proportion, more casualties than did Belgium, the country on which many of the battles were fought; nearly half of an eligible male population of 250,000 volunteered or were called up for service. The picture was similar in Australia; 417,000 men enlisted, 60,000 died as a result of war service; the total casualty rate was the highest of any British force. It is difficult to measure the losses, in terms of potential leadership and in the more general activities in the labour force, which the two nations suffered by this exercise in devotion to Britain; in both countries it is said with some merit that the lack of inspiration in political leadership and developmental thinking in the inter-war years was in large part due to this demographic wastage.

In an economic sense, nationhood came closer in the post-war years; prices for primary produce in New Zealand were underwritten to a limited extent, and the attitude developed amongst some sections of the farming community that the variations in the auction system which generally prevailed for the disposal of their produce might not always be in their best interests—especially as the distance from the major markets meant that there was little control over the final price. But again international events intervened, this time in the shape of the Great Depression; New Zealand, along with Australia, suffered high rates of unemployment, and jolts to the orthodoxy of economic thinking. If the Depression had any positive effects, however, it was to encourage New Zealand's leaders to take some steps toward a greater control of internal economic activities, especially through the establishment of a central bank in 1933. Welfare measures were improved later in the decade; industrialization became a matter of government policy, propounded with a rather greater attention to polemic than economic folklore. All told, the various policies were a series of rapid steps toward nationhood, steps to which leaders had been pushed by external forces as much as by any pressures from within.

To some extent, New Zealand's growing-up process was lagging behind Australia's; it had achieved comparable status of late adolescent nationhood immediately after the First World War. Australia had been quicker to look to industry as an economic expression of this status; protective tariffs had been imposed with increasing severity during the 1920s. Investment in land, however, was not ignored, because this was still the economic underpinning; assistance to returned soldiers and other agricultural development schemes in the 1920s cost a lot more money than they were likely to return, especially where settlers were put into holdings which were far too small to be economic. The Australian economy boomed at a stage when, as a country, there were the signs of increasing maturity; a high rate of urbanization if in rather raw towns by European standards, and industrial growth, all supported by good returns from the sale of farm produce. The Depression showed up the structural weaknesses behind the apparently healthy facade; the supreme dependence on selling a few products in a few markets, the prime feature of economic existence in Australasia, once again took its toll.

THE POST-WAR YEARS

The geography of Australasia since 1945 has been a geography of prosperity. The war-year period (1939–45) saw a steady demand for the sale of all the goods the countries could produce for sale overseas, it absorbed the backlog of unemployment which was the heritage of the Depression in both countries, and it called into being new industries, new skills, and new jobs. Both countries once again contributed men to a war which was, in the main, fought far from their shores—although Japanese raiders touched both countries, Australia with more than just passing reference. But in economic terms the Second World War gave a boost to both nations, affecting them in a manner according to the particular stage of growth each had achieved.

Australia in 1939 had an industrial structure which could fairly be described as fragmented. There was an efficient iron and steel industry, there were particular strengths in metal-working, chemical and other basic industries; yet local manufacturers and consumers were still heavily dependent upon imported raw materials and production equipment as well as ideas in design. It was a nation in search of a future, still strongly wedded to the pastoral heritage but perceiving, however dimly, that this could not provide the economic answer in the long-term future. The war pushed Australia into industry, and in the years afterwards the push became a "pull" from within. The circumstances of the time dictated that there was a level of internal demand, a size of consumer and industrial market, a propensity to invest (particularly from overseas), and a confidence in the future—all of which combined to move industry to a position in which it became firmly established as part of the national economy. Industry was no longer a local activity looking to regional or State markets; it became a major factor in breaking down introverted State attitudes, as industry in Australia to be successful on a large scale must transgress State boundaries. It began to look for new export markets and found a major outlet in a long-established trading partner across the Tasman.

The Second World War also gave a boost to New Zealand industry; new products and new factories survived the artificial conditions of wartime shortages to fit, at times uneasily, into a manufacturing industry structure which was puny alongside the rural and farm-processing industries. Good prices for farm produce, especially at the time of the 1951 wool boom, led New Zealanders to think seriously about a secondary sector alongside the primary and propulsive sector. The backlog of public works investment, created by depression and war, maintained a demand for labour, materials and services which strained the country's employment resources to the full; until 1967 unemployment was confined to a tiny group of hard-core "unemployables". During the 1950s occasional warning signs appeared; import licensing was imposed and withdrawn as overseas reserves rose and fell; but by a combination of good luck and astute management economic survival continued to be accepted as a matter of course rather than as a result of an active development policy.

Then, in 1957, a rather worse than usual crisis occurred; largely coincidentally a new government was elected, a government with rather clearer ideas than the former administration about where the country's future lay. The result, briefly, was an exercise in crash industrialization, a conscious effort to add new pillars to the economic structure. The joint objectives of this move were stated to be the saving of overseas funds, the maintenance of full employment, and the addition of some diversity to an economic scene of at times depressing dependence on the sale of a few products; and even taking into account the expensive failures which it included, it was an unorthodox but on balance positive step forward out of economic adolescence. What is more, the activities of these years and the rather half-hearted follow-up moves by the previous government which was returned to power in 1960, aroused debate on the whole issue of industrialization. Manufacturers became established as a pressure group; industrial services were set up; and by the mid 1960s New Zealanders were beginning to question the long-held view that nothing but farm produce could be properly made within their shores. A new iron and steel plant began production in 1969; a pulp and paper industry established in the mid-1950s finds ready export markets; and manufacturers in other fields, assisted by various tax and other incentives, find that they can sell a variety of goods successfully in a number of overseas markets.

New Zealand-Australia Co-operation

In some respects New Zealand's industrial development matched Australia's of the mid-1950s—but now that it is catching up, a basic and early-mentioned point emerges once again; the nations are moving to a position of competition with each other as they try to sell "non-traditional" products in new markets, and especially as Australia looks to her smaller neighbour as an outlet for manufactured goods. The common ties in defence and foreign policy, strengthened after 1945, perhaps needed some economic underpinning; and, not without opposition from Australian dairy and fat-stock farmers and New Zealand manufacturers, the New Zealand-Australia Free Trade Agreement was signed in 1965. The Agreement—NAFTA as it has come to be known—in its early stages did little more than formalize existing trade patterns (heavily in Australia's favour) and lay down a negotiating framework for lowering or eliminating duties without excessive harm to affected activities on the other side of the Tasman. The devaluation of November 1967 brought New Zealand currency to parity with Australian, and helped to bring the balance rather less against New Zealand; but NAFTA continues to be eyed warily as the leaders of the two countries firmly declare that there is no possibility of economic or political union. Australasia, as a concept, works in terms of geography, history, and some defence policies; but in economics, as in the attitudes of the Tasman neighbours to each other, Australasia is a framework which calls for caution and negotiation rather than open-hearted association.

Australia

PHYSICAL AND SOCIAL GEOGRAPHY

A. E. McQueen

Australia covers 7,682,300 square kilometres (2,966,150 square miles). Nearly 39 per cent of its land mass lies within the tropics; Cape York, the northernmost point, is only 10° S. of the equator. At the other extreme, the southern limit of the mainland lies at 39° S. or, if Tasmania is included, at 44° S., a distance on the mainland alone of 1,959 miles from north to south. From east to west Australia is 2,489 miles broad.

CLIMATE AND VEGETATION

The wide latitudinal range as well as the size and compact shape of Australia produce a climate with widely varying effects in different parts of the country. The climatic differences can be assigned generally to latitude, and therefore to its liability to influence rainfall either from tropical rain-bearing air masses or from the westerly wind belt which affects the southern areas of Australia. It is important to note, too, that the average elevation of the land surface is only about 900 ft.; nearly three-quarters of Australia is a great central plain, almost all of it between 600 and 1,500 ft. above sea level, with few high mountains. The Dividing Range, running parallel to most of the east coast, is the most notable—the highest peak, Kosciusko, reaches 7,313 ft. This general lack of mountains, coupled with the moderating effects of the surrounding oceans, means that there are fewer abrupt regional climatic changes than would be found on land masses in comparable latitudes in other parts of the world.

The northern part of the continent except the Queensland coast comes under the influence of summer tropical monsoons. This produces a wet summer as the moist air flows in from the north-west; but winter is dry, with the prevailing wind coming from the south-east across the dry interior. Both the north-east and north-west coasts are liable to experience tropical cyclones between December and April, and these storms, with accompanying heavy rain, will occasionally continue some distance inland.

On the other hand, the southern half of Australia lies in the mid-latitude westerly wind belt for the winter half of the year; consequently winter is the wet season. Winter rainfall in the south-east and south-west corners of Australia and Tasmania are particularly high—at least by Australian levels—with maximum falls occurring on the windward sides of the mountains in each area. Rainfall decreases rapidly inland with distance from the coast, with the result that parts of central Australia record some very low annual average rainfall figures; the area of lowest average annual rainfall is the 180,000 sq. miles around Lake Eyre in South Australia which receives an average of some 4-6 in. a year. At the other extreme lies Tully (17° 55′ S.), on the east coast of Queensland, with an annual average of 177 in. Overall, few parts of Australia enjoy abundant rainfall; and even where occasional heavy falls are recorded the unreliability of its seasonal distribution may well count against its value in terms of pasture growth. Only south-west Western Australia, western Tasmania and Victoria south of the divide can be counted as areas of reliable precipitation; elsewhere reliability decreases away from the coast, with wide variations being recorded at stations such as Whim Creek (20° 52′ S., 117° 51′ E.) where 29.41 in. have been recorded in a single day, but only 0.17 in. were recorded in all of 1924.

Very high temperatures are experienced during the summer months over the central parts of the country and for some distance to the south, as well as during the pre-monsoon months in the north. Australia's insular nature and other features tend to hold temperatures at a rather lower general level than other southern hemisphere land areas in the same latitudes but temperatures are high enough to produce an evaporation rate, especially in inland areas, which in turn is high enough to exert a marked influence on soil and vegetation patterns. In much of the interior xerophytic plant species adapted to very dry and variable conditions, such as spinifex, salt bush, blue bush and dwarf eucalyptus, are capable of supporting a limited cattle population. Between these arid areas and the zones of higher rainfall lie the semi-arid plains on which the main vegetation is mulga (*Acacia*) and mallee scrub (*Eucalyptus spp*) in which several stems rise from a common woody base. It is this type of land that carries most of the sheep in New South Wales and Western Australia; it is also here, as well as in the still drier interior, that the major effects of drought are felt—and drought occurs with sufficient regularity to have a limiting effect upon the long-term stock population. In the last hundred years Australia has suffered from at least seven major droughts affecting most of the country, as well as several others causing severe losses in particular areas. The economic effects of these climatic vagaries are felt throughout the economy.

In the colder southeastern areas the length of the growing season is mainly dependent upon temperatures, but elsewhere the availability of soil moisture is the major variable. The growing season lasts for 9 months or more along the east coast and in south-western Australia; elsewhere, and especially in the interior, there are wide variations according to both the intensity and seasonal distribution of rainfall. Underground water supplies are fairly widespread in the semi-arid parts of Australia, including the resources of the Great Artesian Basin, fed from inland slopes of the mountain to make one of the largest such catchments in the world. In some areas, notably the Barkly Tableland, stock-raising is largely dependent upon bore water.

SOILS AND LAND USE

Soils do little to ease the problems of the Australian pastoralist. They are very diverse in both type and origin, and are of low natural fertility over large areas due to the great geological age of Australia and the subsequent poor qualities of the parent materials. Climate has a marked effect on soil type with seasonal dessication and surface erosion coinciding with the extreme dry and wet seasons which affect much of the continent. Salinity and alkalinity are also problems, especially in arid southern Australia; investigations into these factors, as well as into more complex aspects of maintaining and building up soil fertility, form a continuing part of the Commonwealth Scientific and Industrial Research Organization's soil research programme, a programme conducted as part of the broad government assistance schemes to improve the overall productivity of Australia's farmlands.

These various physical influences combine to give a generalized pattern of land use which falls into three broad zones. The first comprises some 70 per cent of the land area, and covers all central Australia, reaching the coast along the shores of the Bight and in north-west Australia. About one-third of the area is desert, useless for farming; the rest is of only marginal value for pastoral activities, and then only in the areas close to the rather more favourable conditions of the second zone. This second zone covers only some 17 per cent of Australia, and contains a wide variety of climate and soil types; it is included within a broad belt up to 200 miles wide extending from the Eyre peninsula paralleling the east coast, and across the northern part of Australia to the Kimberleys. In this zone most farming is practised in the temperate part of the area, including more than 90 per cent of all wheat sown; the zone also supports some 40 per cent of the nation's sheep, 30 per cent of the beef cattle and 20 per cent of the dairy cattle.

The third general zone comprises a belt of land along the east coast from Cairns southward and then westward to south-east South Australia, all of Tasmania, south-west Western Australia and a small part of the Northern Territory around Darwin. Much of this zone (which covers some 15 per cent of the continent) is of broken relief; in the remaining areas the pattern of land use is quite complex. In the northern parts beef grazing dominates, but in the remainder most forms of cropping and livestock production are found. Nearly all Australia's forests are within this zone, as are almost all of the dairying, sugar, fat-lamb, horticulture and high-producing beef cattle areas. The potential for pasture improvement, especially in the southern areas, is considerable.

Just as land-based wealth is concentrated in a relatively small part of the continent, so are the human resources.

POPULATION

Australia's population in mid-1975 was only 13,502,300: a density of just over 4.5 persons per square mile, one of the lowest national figures in the world. The reasons for the sparse average population density can be found, first, in the physical geography of the continent, and, second, in its history of settlement—itself a function in time of the physical geography.

As with land use, so with population, Australia can be divided into three broad zones corresponding in many respects to those outlined in the last section; one-third almost unpopulated, another third sparsely populated, and the final third containing the great majority of the people. This distribution pattern means that any discussion of "averages" in terms of population densities is of only limited value; this is specially so when the proportion of each State's population living in the respective State capitals is revealed (see *Statistical Survey*). The concentration of population within each state is matched by a concentration, on a national scale, in the south-east of Australia. New South Wales and Victoria contain 63 per cent of the nation's population; if Tasmania is added, the proportion rises to 66 per cent. Over the country as a whole settlement is closely related to the areas of moderate rainfall and less extreme temperatures, a pattern initiated by the early growth of towns and cities based on a predominantly pastoral farming community dependent upon farm exports for a livelihood. The result has been the rapid growth of settlement around major ports on which State railway systems were centred, and a subsequent development of manufacturing industry at these port centres where imported raw materials were available, where a skilled labour force could be found, and where distribution facilities to all parts of the respective States were readily available. Only in Queensland and Tasmania did this basic pattern vary to any extent; in Queensland because of the widespread distribution of intensive farming (especially sugar) along a coast well serviced with ports, and in Tasmania because the more dispersed distribution of agricultural and other resources called into being a number of moderate-sized towns and commercial centres.

The occupational distribution of the labour force (see *Statistical Survey*) is, not unnaturally, that of a highly urbanized community.

The majority of the population is from European stock; about 50,000 full-blood and 50,000 half-caste aborigines are concentrated mainly in the interior.

HISTORY

E. J. Tapp

COLONIZATION

The continent of Australia was first discovered by the Dutch in the early half of the seventeenth century, but was left in the undisturbed possession of its few widely scattered palaeolithic aborigines until 1770 when the English navigator, Captain James Cook, charted some of its shores and took possession of its eastern half. The annexation was timely, for a few years later the British Government was confronted by a penal problem consequent upon the forced cessation of transportation to the North American colonies which in 1776 had broken away. To relieve the subsequent congestion of convicts in gaols and hulks the government adopted the suggestion that felons be sent to the newly acquired territory of New South Wales. Accordingly, in 1787, Captain Arthur Phillip sailed in command of the "First Fleet" to establish a penal settlement at Port Jackson (Sydney).

For several years this lonely "gaol" struggled desperately against a harsh, niggardly environment, the constant threat of starvation and internal factions. To ease the pressure on the scanty resources of Port Jackson a branch settlement was established on Norfolk Island, and in 1803 to forestall French designs a further extension of the penal settlement was made on Van Diemen's Land (Tasmania). Fortunately, Australia was spared from being no more than a penal settlement by the introduction of fine-wool sheep in 1796 and by the penetration in 1813 of the forbidding Blue Mountains to the inviting and endless plains beyond. Such developments led to a broadening of English policy to admit of land settlement by emancipists, discharged prison guards and a trickle of free migrants. Even under the sterner conditions of Van Diemen's Land settlement developed and extended to spill over in the 1830s into Port Phillip district of the mainland.

Meanwhile, in 1829 in far Western Australia an entirely free English colony was attempted by private entrepreneurs on the Swan River. Lack of good leadership and planning led to failure and to intervention by the British Government to rescue the misguided settlers from their wretched predicament. For years what remained of the colony languished in the doldrums for want of labour.

From the lessons learnt from the failure of the Swan River settlement South Australia was founded in 1837 on the principles of systematic colonization put forward by Edward Gibbon Wakefield. Here too insufficient preparation caused several years of financial stringency and ultimately necessitated official intervention: but under the vigorous governorship of Captain George Grey and with the opening up of fertile country for wheat growing, South Australia, aided by a locally invented harvester, entered upon an era of steady prosperity.

Political and Economic Developments 1840–1901

So too did New South Wales which by this time was developing rapidly and supporting scattered settlements of pastoralists. Shortly after the establishment of a penal colony in Moreton Bay (Brisbane) squatters opened up the rich and extensive Darling Downs. By 1840 the free settlers of the colony forced the British Government to end the convict transportation system to New South Wales. Ten years later when the Australian colonies were given power to make their own constitutions, they lost little time in doing so. During the 1850s the five colonies of New South Wales, Tasmania (after 1853), South Australia, Victoria and Queensland, the latter two having been separated from New South Wales in 1850 and 1859 respectively, all gained a wide measure of representative and responsible government, including vote by ballot and manhood suffrage. The demand for self-government was largely stimulated by the discovery of gold and by the great flood of immigrants which came to swell the population. Many of them, inflamed by reform and revolutionary movements in Europe, not only quickened and diversified the purely pastoral economy but introduced radically new social and economic forces which were to have lasting effect. As the gold miners' resistance at Eureka (Victoria) in 1854 against overbearing authority tragically showed, their demands for greater democratic freedom could not be brooked. In education the new spirit worked to break down a dual system of national and denominational schools, and by the 1870s the principle of free, secular and compulsory education through government schools had been adopted. Church schools were allowed to keep open but without government subsidies. From the sharpening and clash of conflicting interests there emerged a colonial democracy, militant in tone, placing a premium upon egalitarianism, fiercely independent and brusquely indifferent to the pretensions, but not to the acquisition, of wealth.

After the first flush of the gold-rush period the increased demand for land led in the 1860s to a series of Selection Acts in New South Wales and Victoria which unlocked vast areas for settlement. Unfortunately, the intractable nature of much of the country, drought and the malpractices of squatters partly defeated the purpose of these Acts and intensified sectional bitterness. The eastern colonies were rescued from years of frustration and social conflict by railway construction, by improved yields from the use of superphosphates, by the invention of refrigeration in the 1880s and at the end of the century by the discovery of drought-resistant varieties of wheat. The prosperity of the Australian colonies in the 1870s and 1880s was general, for by this time Western Australia had, partly through a belated recourse to transportation to solve its labour shortage, achieved some measure of economic stability and independence. Prosperity, however, intensified the forces making for colonial separatism. Different railway gauges and conflicting fiscal policies, especially between free trade New South Wales and protectionist Victoria, were symptomatic of an intense and narrow parochialism that gave little thought to the morrow. Yet, cutting across colonial borders and differences were social divisions which in the hands of trade unions hardened into a lasting pattern of employer-employee antagonism and led to much industrial strife in eastern Australia. A series of bitterly fought strikes, the failure of banks and a prolonged drought, which halved the flocks of sheep, brought to an end an era of carefree expansion and prodigal expenditure of men and money. Only Western Australia, through a timely discovery of rich gold deposits at Kalgoorlie and Coolgardie, escaped the depression of the 1880s.

Notwithstanding their primary absorption in internal and domestic matters the eastern colonies towards the end of the century began to show concern for their external relationships. Since their inception all the Australian colonies had subscribed to two basic assumptions, *viz.* that the continent must be preserved for British settlement only and that the purity of the white race must be safeguarded. For long Queensland and New South Wales had been apprehensive of the activities of the French in the south-west Pacific; but they were roused to a sense of danger and dismay when, following the occupation by Germany of the northern half of New Guinea, Queensland's annexation of the southern half was disavowed by the Colonial Office. Of a more general social and economic nature was the Chinese problem which had begun in the 1840s with the importation of cheap coolie labour to replace the convict assignees. With the gold rushes tens of thousands of Asiatics, mainly Chinese, poured into the country to create explosive racial situations on the gold fields. The fiercely competitive practices of the Chinese intensified racial antipathy, and the Colonial Governments' attempts to restrict their entry provoked the intervention of the British Government. Perturbed at such exclusionist policies against a nascent power she wished to placate, Great Britain forced the repeal of the restrictions. But popular feeling in Australia against Asiatic immigration continued to grow and to give rise to alarmist talk of a "Yellow Peril". To labour unions in particular the Chinese were a threat to wages and conditions of employment, so that by the end of the century a white Australia had emerged with sufficient support to insist upon restriction of Chinese immigration.

The Commonwealth of Australia

The common dangers from without served to strengthen arguments for closer political integration among the colonies. Federation had often been discussed and an abortive attempt at colonial union had been made with the Federal Council of Australasia in 1884. But subsequent events were to give federation a sense of urgency. Alarmed at the defenceless position of Australia and acutely aware during times of depression of the folly of tariff barriers against each other's goods, colonial statesmen rose above their parochial loyalties and gave expression to mounting public opinion in a series of federation conventions. Common characteristics and interests triumphed over their differences; and in 1901 five Australian colonies federated to form the Commonwealth of Australia, leaving Western Australia to join a few years later. Adopting a system of parliamentary executive, the constitution provided for specific powers for the Federal Government and left the residual powers with the States. It gave what the colonies wanted, union but not unity.

The first Commonwealth Parliament lost no time in dealing with matters of common concern. One of its first actions was to give legislative sanction to the White Australia policy in the Immigration Restrictions Bill of 1901. This caused the repatriation of Pacific islanders (Kanakas) employed in the Queensland sugar cane fields. Federation brought for the first time a uniform fiscal policy of protection for the whole of Australia. In 1906 a Commonwealth Court of Conciliation and Arbitration was established to deal with labour disputes extending beyond the borders of any State. An early decision of that Court laid down the basic wage as "the normal needs of the average employee regarded as a human being living in a civilized community". With the Labour Party in power after 1909, the Commonwealth Bank was established and a Federal land tax was imposed. At the same time Australia's growing sense of nationhood was reflected in its insistence upon a separate Australian navy and in the introduction of compulsory military training.

In spite of such defence measures and the Prime Minister's pledge that Australia would support Great Britain "to the last man and the last shilling", the country was ill-prepared in 1914 for the full consequences of its almost automatic committal to the war effort. Twice did its mercurial wartime leader, Mr. W. M. (Billy) Hughes, try to carry referenda to conscript manpower for war service; but in two bitterly fought campaigns, in which a powerful Irish element with strong *Sinn Fein* sympathies took a leading part, conscription was rejected; and the Labour Party, seriously divided on the issue, fell from office. For all that, the part Australia played in the war was vigorous and substantial, both in men and material. In the ill-fated Gallipoli campaign her troops, in conjunction with the New Zealanders (together known as the Anzacs) won by their valour laurels for their country. Not only did the war toughen the national fibre but it strengthened the forces making for national unity and gave Australia an enhanced status among the nations of the world. Recognition of this status was made when along with the other Dominions she secured the right of separate representation at the Versailles peace conference and of independent membership of the League of Nations. As a member she was entrusted with the mandate over the ex-German territory in New Guinea and with a share in the mandate over the phosphate island of Nauru.

THE INTER-WAR YEARS

Throughout Australia the war had so disturbed and changed the structure of the economy as to create lasting problems. In the struggle fought on the home front for concerted action, liberalism had been the chief casualty. Never strongly entrenched among vigorously intolerant communities, it fell victim to the clash between capital and labour, which even before the war had ended had resulted in open conflict. The exigencies of war had strengthened and developed heavy and secondary industries in the eastern States. From the consequent development of large industrial monopolies on the one hand and the trade unions on the other came class bitterness and hostility, leading to an era of lock-outs and strikes which continued well after the war. But the fillip given to the Australian economy was such as to cause the Federal Government to set up a tariff board to protect secondary industries and to secure a well balanced commercial and industrial development of the country. Yet too often tariff protection gave shelter to obsolete or obsolescent plants.

In general the 1920s were years of prosperity and economic expansion. High prices for her primary products of wool and meat enabled Australia to spend freely on public works. During this period over 300,000 immigrants were absorbed into the labour force. At the same time, the opening up of some of the back-country and the attempted development of the Northern Territory by the Federal Government led to a revised appraisal of Australia's resources. The popular conception of Australia Unlimited was replaced by more cautious estimates of her economic and demographic potentialities. This too was a period in which the States, freed from the unifying bonds of war, tended to assume a more parochial outlook. In Western Australia this even went to the length of a short-lived movement for secession. In Queensland, and New South Wales in particular, a newly formed Country Party gave support to fissiparous political trends manifest in New State movements.

By 1928 a hardening of trade and financial conditions had strengthened the position of the Federal Government. After eight years of endless wrangling and before that twenty years of uncertainty the States entered into a financial agreement with the Commonwealth by which the Federal Government took over all State debts. But so dependent was Australia's economy upon that of Great Britain in particular that she could not escape the world depression which developed in the early 1930s. A slump in export prices and a sudden cessation of overseas borrowing gave rise to widespread unemployment and distress. Unfortunately for Australia the crisis had developed at a time when she was facing serious problems arising out of a shortage of overseas funds. To meet the emergency the Commonwealth and State Governments imposed drastic deflationary policies involving 20 per cent reduction in wages and a 25 per cent depreciation of the Australian pound. Feverish attempts were made to balance budgets in all States except New South Wales where the problems were tackled by the Labor Government by such unorthodox methods as repudiation of interest on overseas loans that they led to a constitutional crisis and the dismissal in 1932 of the State Premier. To honour the State's obligations the Commonwealth paid the interest in default and furnished the amount from the State Treasury. With nearly 30 per cent of union labour unemployed, Australia sought desperately to find markets and economic security. The Ottawa Trade Agreement of 1932 gave her preferential treatment for dried fruits, dairy produce and sugar in return for reduced duties on English goods. But at best the Agreement afforded only a breathing space in which to find new markets outside the British Commonwealth and Empire. Such efforts led to a trade diversion policy in which reciprocal trade treaties were made with Japan, China, the United States and Egypt in addition to some European countries.

Meanwhile, with her customary predilection for practice rather than theory, Australia struggled out of the depression, so far as the home front was concerned, by trial and error. No longer was she able to shelter inefficient secondary industries; they either had to improve their methods or close down. On the other hand, the restrictions on imports stimulated the growth of some industries. To offset the prevailing low returns the Federal Government gave bounties to wheat farmers, but failed to secure increased powers for marketing and aviation. Yet trade gradually expanded and when in 1937 an end was put to a tariff war with Japan temporary advantages were gained for Australian wool and textiles. Greater internal investment replacing public borrowing abroad contributed to expansion and stability in secondary production.

Foreign Affairs

The depression and her efforts at recovery quickened Australia to a keener awareness of her position in world affairs. Not unnaturally in the absence of international tension isolationist tendencies had re-emerged, but never to the point of making Australia complacently indifferent to her foreign commitments and defence. Not only did she honour the Washington disarmament agreement of 1922 by reducing her naval armaments, but she administered New Guinea in the spirit of the mandate and continued to support the League of Nations. This did not prevent her, especially under a non-Labor Federal Government, from still placing her faith in Great Britain and from contributing towards the British naval base under construction at Singapore. With traditional loyalties to Great Britain unimpaired, Australian statesmen saw little need at the 1926 Imperial Conference to try and define the Dominion Status enjoyed by members of the British Commonwealth. Hence, Australia was in no hurry to adopt the Statute of Westminster of 1931 which granted complete autonomy to the various self-governing Dominions.

Yet world events in the late 1930s were for Australia charged with a new sense of urgency. She could not but be apprehensive at the rapid industrial rise of Japan and of her military conquests in Manchuria. Although reluctant to support the imposition of sanctions upon Italy for unprovoked aggression in Abyssinia, she became increasingly concerned with defence problems, especially in view of the deterioration of the international situation and the impotence of the League of Nations to deal with it. Even the Labor Party, which when in power had suspended compulsory military training, urged stronger air defence. The government under Mr. J. A. Lyons placed its trust in full co-operation with Great Britain and in a balanced development of all armed services. Though remote from the scene of European events Australia watched the gathering storm with fatalistic calm and generally supported every move made by the British Government to prevent it breaking. When it did in 1939, Australia never hesitated to throw in her lot with that of the Mother Country and to place her navy at the disposal of the British Admiralty.

THE SECOND WORLD WAR

Australia entered the Second World War with more maturity and greater realism than she had the First. Although she still harboured old illusions as to her defence and did not yet fully appreciate the nature of the new forces to her north, she was aware that she could no longer escape the consequences of her geographical position in the Pacific. Without delay she began to mobilize all her resources. The United Australia Party, which was in power, invited the Labor Party to form a coalition for the duration of the war, but with its traditional opposition to conscription the Labor Party rejected the offer on the grounds that the interests of democracy could best be safeguarded even in war by a vigilant opposition. With the assistance of State governments the Commonwealth enforced vigorous measures for the prosecution of the war effort. Controls were imposed on exchange, imports, prices and investments, while her wheat and wool were bought up by Great Britain. In 1941 the State governments agreed to surrender their taxing powers for the duration of the war and to accept in return single uniform taxation by the Commonwealth Government.

But the United Australia Party sat uneasily in government. Apart from appointing Australian ministers to Washington and Tokyo, its record was undistinguished, and after losing strength at the 1940 Federal elections it surrendered its precarious tenure of office to the Labor Party under Mr. John Curtin in the following year. With the sudden entry in 1942 of the Japanese on the side of the Axis Powers the Australian Government was charged with unprecedented responsibility. For the first time in her history Australia was faced with the threat of imminent invasion. The fall of Singapore shattered the somewhat pathetic faith she had placed in that bastion of defence and in the British navy. The immediate public reaction was a stiffening of support for the Federal Government's demand for a more direct voice in the determination of Allied war policy. This not being forthcoming, the Prime Minister insisted upon the return from the Middle East of Australian forces to defend Australia. At the same time he turned to the United States for aid. Response was immediate; and General Douglas MacArthur was ordered to escape from the beleaguered Philippines and to make of Australia a base from which to conduct combined service operations to drive back the Japanese. To implement this plan hundreds of thousands of American troops poured into eastern Australia together with much lend-lease assistance. The Commonwealth accelerated her war effort by enforcing manpower direction and tightening control over wages and profits. This policy of austerity was wholeheartedly endorsed in 1943 at the Federal elections.

With Allied victory nearer in Europe and the Japanese invasion turned back in the south-west Pacific, the Federal Government in 1943 began to plan for post-war reconstruction. Although its successful war policy carried it some distance towards planning for peace, the Federal Government met with opposition from the States which, while weakened by the centralizing wartime trends, still clung to their not inconsiderable powers. In this they were supported by the general public which refused the Commonwealth the special powers that it sought to give effect to its post-war planning. For all that, the State governments supported the Federal Government's attempt to avoid another post-war depression by a policy of full employment, and co-operated in settling ex-servicemen on the land, in housing, in the continuation of price control and in reconstruction training.

THE POST-WAR PERIOD

All this post-war development had the full support of the Labor Party which was in power in most of the States as well as in the Commonwealth. But in regarding the post-war era as the critical period in which they should consolidate their gains, trade unions were often at odds with Federal and State governments. Communist-inspired strikes seriously embarrassed an unsympathetic Federal Labor Government which was at the same time being pressed on all sides for the relaxation of wartime controls. The first concessions were made in 1946 when building controls were handed back to the States. But to prevent inflation resulting from the removal of restrictions and to preserve a favourable trade balance drastic cuts were made in dollar imports. In 1947, the new Labor Prime Minister, Joseph Chifley, sought to control the machinery of credit by nationalizing through the forced purchase of their shares the trading banks of Australia. In this he was thwarted by the opposition of the private banks which successfully appealed against the Banking Act to the Privy Council of the Sovereign, which was the final Court of Appeal in all civil cases. Further setbacks to increased Federal control were met when the Australian people rejected a request by referendum for special powers to control rents and prices. Bowing to the public will, the Federal Government in 1948 abandoned all economic controls, but instead sought to set up a social welfare state. Social security measures, such as increased child endowments (first introduced during the war), old age, widow and invalid pensions and hospital benefits, commended themselves to an ageing population appreciative of the blessings of social security but at the same time reluctant to forego the attractions of free enterprise.

Notwithstanding such concessions, return to peace and an era of rising prices hastened the fall of the Federal Labor Government. Not even his own personal popularity and successful handling of a paralyzing coal strike were sufficient to save Mr. Chifley and his party at the 1950 elections. Addressing itself mainly to the business sections of the community and playing on public fears of socialization and regimentation, the newly formed Liberal Party was returned to office to form a coalition government with the Country Party. Wartime rationing was abolished and, with the help of a U.S. $100 million loan from the International Bank for Reconstruction and Development, irrigation, land clearance and increased power schemes were undertaken. But the Senate or upper house, which has never operated as it was intended as a safeguard for the member States but has tended to follow the party lines of the lower house, remained predominantly Labour and therefore opposed to the legislation of the new government. At a double dissolution of the Federal Parliament Mr. R. G. Menzies, the new Prime Minister, secured at the following elections clear majorities in both houses and an endorsement of his policies. Yet in spite of the mandate it had given the government, the public in its dislike of the politics of proscription rejected Mr. Menzies' proposals to deal more effectively with Communism. But the Korean war provided support for firmer anti-Communist policies, including secret ballot in trade union elections. Meanwhile, spiralling inflation consequent upon a spectacular rise in wool income intensified industrial unrest which did not abate until lower wool prices stabilized the economy.

Among the chief sufferers from inflation were the State governments which had to bargain fiercely for the annual Commonwealth "hand-outs". Yet when in 1953 they were offered the return of their taxing powers they preferred to leave the unpopular task of raising money to Canberra. More and more was being expected of the Federal Government, and in 1953 it introduced a health scheme to include anti-T.B. treatment, hospital, medical and pharmaceutical benefits. But in 1970 the Government introduced a national health scheme to reduce the cost of medical and hospital services to the public. Increased public and State demands forced the Federal Government to press its constitutional powers to their limit. In the bold and imaginative Snowy Mountains water conservation and hydroelectric scheme, begun in the 1950s, involving the three States of New South Wales, Victoria and South Australia, it undertook the administration and paid the cost of about £500 million.

Although by the mid-1950s Labor had gained popular support in all State governments, except in South Australia where the electoral system is weighted in favour of rural constituencies, the Liberal-Country Coalition rode comfortably into Federal office again in 1955 on a buoyant economy. Again, in 1958, Mr. Menzies was returned not only with slightly increased gains but with a badly needed Senate majority which he had lost. This enabled him to reform the banking system and make the Reserve Bank of Australia the central bank for the Commonwealth.

Meanwhile, torn by internal dissension, its public image marred in 1954 by a spy case and split by an anti-Communist, Catholic-led group which formed itself into the Democratic Labor Party, the Australian Labor Party retired into the political wilderness to lick its wounds. Economic prosperity, full employment and rising wages had blunted the force of much of Labor's original appeal. Even the resignation of its controversial leader, Dr. H. V. Evatt, and his succession by Mr. A. Calwell, a Roman Catholic, made little difference to the fortunes of the party. The political tide had also turned against Labor by the early 1960s in all States including even New South Wales, a hitherto Labor stronghold, but in 1970 the party was returned to power in South Australia.

It was undoubtedly the serious division in the Labor Party and fear of its extremists, especially in Victoria, which allowed Mr. Menzies in 1966 to retire gracefully after sixteen consecutive years of office as Prime Minister. His successor, Mr. H. Holt, although his Liberal Party was returned to office, was unable to secure referendum support to break the constitutional numerical nexus between the Senate and the House of Representatives. After Holt's tragic drowning at the end of 1967, the Federal Government was led by John Gorton, a former prominent Liberal senator, while the leadership of the Labor Opposition was in the strengthening hands of Mr. Gough Whitlam. A move to increase the membership of the House of Representatives was defeated in a national referendum. Growing disillusionment with existing political parties led in 1969 to the formation of a short-lived and ineffectual Australia Party. At that year's Federal elections the Liberal-Country Party under John Gorton lost heavily and was returned to office with a bare working majority. Bitter internal party strife led to the replacement of Mr. Gorton by William McMahon in March 1971. Yet it was high time for wider change, for neither the Government nor its leader was popular. Their uncertain and timid handling of inflation, together with growing industrial unrest arising out of penal clauses of the Arbitration Act, proved their downfall. At the Federal elections in December 1972 the Labor Party under Gough Whitlam decisively gained the Treasury benches after 23 years of Liberal-Country Party control.

With the moral support of Labor Governments in the States of South Australia, Western Australia and Tasmania, and more importantly the trade union movement under its new (1969) and dynamic president, R. J. Hawke, the Labor Government began life in a general euphoria of great expectations. But Labor's attempts to promote socialistic legislation were frustrated by a hostile Senate, so that after the rejection of a Supply Bill the Prime Minister in 1973 ordered a dissolution of both the House of Representatives and the Senate. The results were disappointing for the Government. Not only was its majority in the House of Representatives reduced, but a stalemate resulted in the Senate and four referenda seeking constitutional reform were rejected by the electorate. In addition the Democratic Labor Party accelerated its long slide to virtual eclipse. Nor could the Liberal Party take much comfort from the result; discredited and weakened by internal dissension, it replaced its leader, Billy Snedden, by Malcolm Fraser in March 1975.

However, the Federal Labor Government's attempt

to do too much too quickly led to political disaster. In July 1975 the Deputy Prime Minister, Dr. James Cairns, was removed from office for an irregular move to raise loans of up to $A4,000 million, mainly from Arab sources, to develop the country's mineral resources. Following this, the Government was trenchantly attacked for its lavish spending and borrowing policies. To add to the Government's embarrassment, both the Queensland and New South Wales Governments failed to observe the normal convention of filling vacant Senate seats with nominees of a like political persuasion to those being replaced, thus giving the Federal Opposition a slight but critical Senate majority. With supply repeatedly blocked by a hostile Senate, which constitutionally has the power to pass or reject money bills, Parliament was deadlocked in an intolerable crisis. In a surprise intervention on November 11th the Governor-General, Sir John Kerr, dismissed Prime Minister Whitlam and dissolved both Houses of Parliament. This unprecedented, much debated and much criticized use of his powers incurred for the Governor-General and his office much public odium which is likely to have lasting effects.

In the meantime, the bitterly fought general election in December resulted in a landslide victory for the Liberal-Country Party and a humiliating defeat for Whitlam and the Labor Party. With an overwhelming majority of 55 (91 seats compared with Labor's 36) in the House of Representatives and a majority of 6 in the Senate, the new Prime Minister, Malcolm Fraser, had a clear mandate to embark on a policy of retrenchment and economy to reduce the rate of inflation and Australia's overseas indebtedness. This rejection of Labor has predictably been reflected in Victoria, where the sitting Liberal Government was returned in March 1976. However, in May 1976, Labor regained power in New South Wales with a slim majority after 13 years out of office. In general, the States have successfully resisted attempts to erode their powers and, with the election of a Federal Government more favourably disposed towards decentralization than the Labor Government, the importance of State Governments may increase.

Australia and the World

More particularly has Australia become alive not only to the strategic importance but to her obligations to Papua and New Guinea over which it exercised control and a United Nations Trusteeship mandate respectively. In the face of earlier Indonesian expansionist designs in West Irian (then Dutch West New Guinea) and of United Nations' criticism as to her treatment of the dependent peoples in the Trust Territory of New Guinea, Australia initiated a policy for both territories of gradual preparation for eventual independence. In 1963 a House of Assembly was set up, providing for an elective native majority.

With the gradual transfer of power from Canberra, Papua New Guinea (as it became known) secured self-government in December 1973 and became independent in September 1975, with the blessing and guaranteed specific support of Australia.

The assumption of such responsibilities towards her dependent peoples has partly quickened the greater maturity Australia has shown since the Second World War in international affairs. Under the vigorous and independent direction of Dr. H. V. Evatt, the Federal Labor Government, while maintaining co-operation with the United Kingdom and with the British Commonwealth of Nations, laid greater store by the United Nations. If somewhat stridently assertive, Australia has in her keen awareness of her vulnerability insisted upon a greater measure of control over policy in the Pacific. As a preliminary measure in 1944 she entered into a regional agreement with New Zealand. At the same time the Federal Government emphasized the need to raise living standards in the under-privileged countries of South-East Asia with whose radical nationalist movements it has shown open sympathy.

But with the fall of the Labor Party from Federal power in 1949 the shift of political emphasis under Robert Menzies returned to the British Commonwealth. With a pragmatic rather than a doctrinaire approach to world affairs and with less confidence in untried Asian nationalism, Liberal-Country Party Governments failed to accord diplomatic recognition to the Government of Communist China and sought mainly to contain Communism in South-East Asia. Hence, Australia was a prime mover in the Colombo Plan of 1950 designed to give economic and technical aid to non-Communist Asian peoples. In addition, moreover, to large sums spent on the rehabilitation of South Viet-Nam and technical assistance in South Korea, she made (1970) a loan of about £25 million to Indonesia for economic development. In 1974 she gave $2.5 million worth of rice to Indonesia to alleviate severe shortage there and seeks generally to be complementary rather than competitive with her nearest neighbour.

Her own security is based upon a collective defence treaty that along with New Zealand she made in 1951 with the United States. This ANZUS Pact was supplemented in 1954 by the South East Asia Treaty Organization (SEATO) of 1954. In 1960, with the assistance of Britain and France, the Woomera rocket range was established in South Australia, but disappointing results have led to a decline in its launching activities.

In the growing recognition that it would have to rely heavily on the American alliance for its defence, Australia agreed in 1963 to the establishment of a U.S. radio communication station at North Cape in Western Australia, in 1967 to the construction of a secret defence research station at Pine Gap in the centre of the continent and in 1975 to an American navigational station in Australia. Heavy reliance on the United States for its defence left Australia with little option but to send about 8,000 troops to aid the Americans in South Viet-Nam in the late 1960s. But in face of widespread opposition to conscription and to involvement in the war in South-East Asia, Australia, in line with American policy, withdrew all its troops and defence aid from South Viet-Nam at the end of 1972.

To help safeguard its northern approaches, especially in view of Britain's prospective withdrawal of armed forces east of Suez, Australia has by agreement with their owner assumed sovereignty over the strategically placed Cocos Islands and begun the establishment of a naval base in Cockburn Sound, Western Australia. It has also given support to the American defence base at Diego Garcia in the British Indian Ocean Territory. In addition, Australia has purchased from the U.S.A. 25 F.111 swing-wing military aircraft, and commenced the construction of two submarines.

With the advent of the Labor Government at the end of 1972, Australia entered upon a new and more independent foreign policy. As the richest and most powerful country in the South-West Pacific, her Prime Minister was able to declare that Australia had no need to be subservient to any country, not even the United States. On the other hand, she lost no time in establishing full diplomatic relations with the People's Republic of China and later with the German Democratic Republic. Along with New Zealand, with whom she has strengthened ties, Australia protested against French nuclear testing in the South Pacific and successfully brought a case against France before the International Court of Justice.

In international affairs Australia is aspiring to the status of a middle power with its security lying in the equilibrium among the U.S.A., the U.S.S.R. and China. But it is in the defence arrangements of South-East Asia that it hopes to play a leading role. To that end, and with lessening emphasis on military pacts, it has supported a scheme of the Association of South-East Asian Nations (ASEAN) for the neutralization of the region. In early 1976 it recognized the new communist government in Laos and in March 1976 concluded a new co-operation and friendship treaty with Japan. In opposition to apartheid policies it has cancelled wheat exports to Rhodesia and has banned participation in racially-selected sports teams from South Africa.

Although relations with the United Kingdom remain essentially unimpaired, Australia has treated its post of High Commissioner in London as of less importance than hitherto. A recently established honours system for Australia was retained by the incoming Liberal-Country Party Government, which also restored the bestowal of British Crown honours abolished by the Labor Government.

Social Development

Among the most difficult and pressing of Australia's social problems is that of the aborigines. In recent years, the public conscience has been quickened by the realization of the white man's inhumanity to Australia's earliest inhabitants. After nearly two centuries of indifference and neglect, the Liberal-Country Party Government gave the 140,000 of aboriginal descent, who live primarily in the Northern Territory, Queensland and Western Australia, the franchise and social benefits hitherto denied them. In 1971, the Federal Senate admitted its first aboriginal senator. But aborigines are beginning seriously to question the wisdom of Federal paternalism and assimilation into the white community. Instead, they are pressing strongly for rights to native lands. In consequence, the Federal Labor Government has placed a better deal for the aborigines high on its list of domestic priorities, for as the Prime Minister has fairly observed, "Australia's treatment of her aboriginal people will be the thing upon which the rest of the world will judge Australia and the Australians". Accordingly, a Cabinet Minister with exclusive responsibility for aboriginal affairs has embarked upon a vigorous new policy designed to end discriminating State practices and to afford better educational opportunities for aboriginal children, including teaching in their own language. In May 1976 the first aboriginal state governor was appointed, to assume office in South Australia in December.

In the wider educational and cultural life of the community there has been, partly through the infusion of new "blood" and Australia's greater involvement in world affairs generally, a more marked sophistication and maturity. Since World War II, the number of universities has grown, through generous Federal Government subsidies to the States, to 16, which include a post-graduate Institute of Advanced Studies in Canberra. Again, largely through Federal assistance, Colleges of Advanced Education have been established in all States. By 1973 the Federal Government had become the dominant economic influence in education, a field which once belonged exclusively to the States, and in 1974 it made grants to private schools subject to the right of inspection.

In keeping with its egalitarian philosophy, the Labor Government established a universal contributory system of social security, but a voluntary health insurance scheme (Medibank), which it also inaugurated, was modified by the Liberal-Country Party Government in 1976 to make it less acceptable to those with annual incomes of more than $A11,000, about one-third of all taxpayers.

To provide for natural disasters, such as bushfires and floods (which are almost endemic to Australia) and cyclones (the worst of which in the nation's history hit Darwin in December 1974, making 20,000 people homeless), the Federal Government is to introduce a comprehensive insurance scheme.

Stringent Federal economic measures taken in May 1976 will cut planned Government expenditure by $2,500 million, but they are unlikely to impair the ample social welfare provisions for all citizens.

ECONOMIC SURVEY

C. G. F. Simpkin

Australia ranks high internationally in terms of income per head, which averaged U.S. $5,884 in 1974. This was slightly below the level for the U.S.A. but higher than the levels of the Federal Republic of Germany, Canada, Belgium and Denmark.

Something like 8 per cent of national income came from farming, 4 per cent from mining, 7 per cent from construction, 28 per cent from manufacturing (including power) and 23 per cent from transport and trade. Australia thus merits the description given by Professor H. D. Arndt as a small, rich industrial country (small because its population in 1975 was only 13.5 million). But growth of real income has been rather slow, averaging about 4 per cent a year since 1959, not much more than twice the corresponding rate of population increase.

Industrial development has been especially marked since the early 1960s. Between 1962/63 and 1972/73 farming grew in real terms by only 1.8 per cent a year but manufacturing showed an average annual increase of 5.1 per cent, about the same rate as for construction and also for trade and transport. Mining grew by 14.1 per cent a year, following important discoveries of iron ore, petroleum and other minerals.

These developments were strongly reflected in Australia's external trade. In 1962/63 farm products accounted for 80 per cent of total export earnings, manufactures for 13 per cent and minerals for 7 per cent. By 1974/75 farming's share had dropped to 48 per cent, and the shares of manufactures and minerals had each risen to 26 per cent. Over this period, moreover, exports of goods and services increased from 14.6 per cent of gross national product (G.N.P.) to 16.9 per cent; imports, reflecting capital inflows, rose from 13.9 to 16.9 per cent of G.N.P.

PRIMARY INDUSTRIES

Farming

Much of Australia is barren desert so that little more than two-fifths of its area is used for farming. Only 1 per cent of the area of nearly 3 million square miles is under crops and only a twelfth of that crop land is irrigated. Droughts and other harsh climatic changes cause large seasonal variations in many farming outputs, and they are also subject to considerable fluctuations of value through variations in world prices for wool, wheat, sugar and other products. It is better, therefore, to make comparisons on a quinquennial rather than an annual basis. Between 1968/69 and 1972/73, pastoral activities contributed about $A1,700 million to the average annual gross value of farming outputs, crops $A1,600 million and dairying $A600 million; all other types of farming contributed a mere $A200 million.

Much the most important pastoral activity is sheep farming, spread over all states and accounting for three-fifths of the gross value of pastoral outputs. Between 1968/69 and 1972/73 wool was four times the gross value of lamb and mutton, but beef was three times their value. Meat as a whole, therefore, has been as important as wool in the gross value of pastoral production.

The figure of $A600 million for the average annual gross value of dairy production includes pig farming, although this has become almost a separate industry. Its contribution was about a sixth of the total. Milk products contributed two-thirds, the largest items being liquid milk, for domestic consumption, and butter. Butter output has fluctuated around a fairly static average since the mid-1950s while cheese production has had a markedly rising trend. Pig production has also grown fairly rapidly as pig numbers trebled between 1951 and 1973. Cattle numbers doubled over the same period. Poultry farming has also become a separate industry. In 1972/73 the gross value of its outputs was $A204 million, or 4 per cent of that for farming as a whole. This, too, is a rapidly growing industry.

Wheat is the most important crop, grown on a large scale in all states. It is especially vulnerable to climatic changes but, since 1955, the output has more than doubled with growing world demands for grain exports. In 1972/73, a bad year, it contributed only $A348 million (or 7 per cent) to gross farming output but in 1974/75, a good year, its contribution was $A1,187 million (or 21 per cent). Barley, the next most important cereal crop, contributed $A91 million in 1972/73 and $A264 million in 1974/75. Other cereals include sorghum, oats, rice, maize, rye and various millets, but their combined contribution in 1974/75 was only $A181 million. The most important industrial crop is sugar cane, grown in suitable coastal regions of Queensland and northern New South Wales. Its output has trebled since the mid-1950s but it is subject to wide fluctuations of price which raised the gross value of its output from $A230 million in 1972/73 to $A479 million in 1974/75, not far short of half the corresponding value of wheat production. Other industrial crops, of which the most important are tobacco and cotton, contributed only $A106 million to the gross value of farming production in 1972/73. About a third of the gross value of crops comes from vegetables and fruits. Fruits are the most important category, with a gross value of $A224 million in 1972/73, not including grapes, whose value was $A65 million. Vegetables, mainly potatoes, tomatoes and onions, contributed $A183 million.

Forestry

Australia is not well endowed with forests as little more than 5 per cent of its area is potentially or actually productive forest. Nearly all of this is natural forest, four-fifths of it dominated by eucalypts. There is a surplus of hardwoods for domestic requirements but a considerable deficiency of conifers, made up by imports. The gross value of forest products in 1972/73 was $A145 million, most of which consisted of logs from eucalypts or related species. There are coniferous plantations of mainly exotic species, but they cover only 484,000 hectares of a total forest area of 42,503,000 hectares.

Fishing

Fishing had a gross value of output of $A102 million in 1972. This is insufficient for local requirements so that Australia has to import about two-fifths of domestic consumption. Lobsters and prawns comprise more than half the gross value of fishery products, while oysters (which are commercially cultured in New South Wales and Queensland) and mussels provide somewhat less than a fifth. Imports supply half of local needs for fresh, frozen and canned fish.

Mining

Australia is at least self-sufficient in most important minerals and has far more than domestic requirements of aluminium, black (hard) coal, copper, iron ore, lead, manganese, natural gas, silver, tin, titanium, tungsten, zinc and zircon. Its main deficiencies, although reserves are uncertain, are in crude petroleum, asbestos, cobalt, graphite, fluorite, magnesite, mercury, molybdenum, nitrates, platinum, potassium salts and sulphur.

The gross value of mineral products in 1972/73, before the later boom and slump, was nearly $A2,000 million, excluding bauxite and nickel, for which adequate estimates are not available. Metallic minerals contributed almost half this recorded value, coal and petroleum a third, and other non-metallic minerals about an eighth. The most important recorded contributions were made by iron ore ($A395 million), black coal ($A391 million), petroleum ($A312 million), copper ($A156 million), lead ($A81 million), zinc ($A62 million), rutile ($A37 million) and tin ($A33 million). Gold contributed $A26 million, and gems, mainly opals and sapphires, $A41 million.

Australia has long been an important producer of lead, zinc and copper, and also had enough iron ore for most domestic requirements. Between 1962 and 1972 there was modest growth of lead and zinc outputs, mostly from the Broken Hill mines of New South Wales and the Mount Isa mine in Queensland. This mine also produced most of the copper output, which trebled over the decade.

Such growth was overshadowed by discoveries of huge reserves of iron ore in Western Australia. These were responsible for increasing output of iron ore from less than 5 million metric tons (gross weight) in 1962 to 75 million tons in 1972/73 and to 99 million tons in 1974/75. Australian iron ore has an average iron content of 65 per cent. Great, highly mechanized mines have had to be developed in remote, inhospitable places, with associated construction of habitable towns, ports and railways. Much foreign capital has flowed in to finance all this, and long-term marketing contracts have had to be negotiated with Japanese and other importers of iron ore to justify such investment.

Almost equally exciting was the discovery of a major oilfield in Bass Strait. This increased Australia's output of crude petroleum from only 2.5 million cubic metres in 1968/69 to 20.7 million in 1972/73 and 23.1 million in 1974/75, by which time the country had become 70 per cent self-sufficient in petroleum. By then, too, nearly 5 million cubic metres of natural gas per year were also being produced, not only from Bass Strait but also from new fields in South Australia and Western Australia, the big potential of which in the latter state has yet to be tapped. The other important mineral for power is coal, and Australia's output of black coal (including waste) rose from 25 million tons in 1962 to 60 million tons in 1972/73 and to 70 million tons in 1974/75. This expansion resulted from development of both new and old fields in Queensland and New South Wales. Most of the brown coal is in Victoria, and in 1972/73 production was 24 million tons. Huge deposits of uranium, another important source of power, have also been found in the Northern Territory, but their exploitation has just begun.

Big discoveries of nickel have been made in Western Australia, and also of bauxite in that state, the Northern Territory and Queensland. Output of nickel concentrates increased from 36,104 tons (metal content) in 1972/73 to 49,106 tons in 1974/75. Both a smelter and a refinery have recently been built in Western Australia to process the ore. Output of bauxite increased from 14.7 million tons in 1972/73 to 18.5 million tons in 1973/74 and to 20.5 million tons in 1974/75.

Tin output has also increased through new discoveries and better exploitation of old ones. It rose from 2,758 metric tons (metal content) in 1962 to 11,754 tons in 1972/73. The main deposits are in Queensland, New South Wales and Western Australia. Queensland and New South Wales also produce most of the rutile output, which increased from 119,000 tons in 1962 to 319,000 tons in 1972/73. Other notable mineral discoveries in recent years include manganese, phosphates, tungsten and a variety of other mineral sands besides rutile.

MANUFACTURING

In 1972/73 manufacturing contributed 24 per cent of Australia's gross national product, and absorbed about 30 per cent of the civilian labour force. Of the manufacturing sectors, food, beverages and tobacco was easily the most important, yielding 23.4 per cent of manufacturing's contribution to G.N.P. Textiles yielded only 3 per cent, and clothing and footwear only 4.6 per cent. Wood and its products, including paper and printing, yielded 12.6 per cent and chemicals, petroleum and coal products 11.3 per cent. Comparable figures for other sectors were: non-metallic mineral products 4.7 per cent, basic metal products 8.5 per cent, fabricated metal products 7.2 per cent, transport equipment 9.5 per cent, other machinery and equipment 11.4 per cent, and miscellaneous manufacturing 4.8 per cent. Chemicals, metals, machinery and equipment thus formed nearly half of the gross product of manufacturing, which strengthens the claim that Australia has become an industrialized country.

Within the food, beverages and tobacco sector, processing of meat, milk, cereals and vegetables account for nearly half the gross added value. Processing of sugar, together with confectionery, may account for something less than an eighth but separate figures for sugar are not published.

Clothing is much the biggest category in the textiles and clothing group, contributing three-fifths of its added value; women's garments are twice as important as men's. The value of knitwear is about a third that of clothing and the value of footwear about three-tenths. Fabric production is half the value of clothing, and fairly evenly divided between cottons, woollens, synthetic fabrics and other products such as carpets, felt products, canvas, rope and cordage. The spinning part of this sector is about as important as the fabric part, but here synthetic fibres are nearly four times as important as wool, and cotton spinning is quite a minor activity. Notable features of the clothing and footwear industries are a high proportion of female labour employed (76 per cent) and a relatively low capital-labour ratio (18 per cent of the average for manufacturing). Textile industries have a much smaller proportion of female labour (44 per cent) and a markedly higher relative capital-labour ratio (67 per cent). The food, beverage and tobacco group was even less dependent on female labour (26 per cent) and had a relatively high capital-output ratio (128 per cent). Concentration ratios (i.e. percentages of turnover accounted for by the four largest enterprise groups) were also low: 11 per cent for clothing and footwear, 37 per cent for textiles, but only 12 per cent for food, beverages and tobacco.

Wood products had both a relatively low capital-labour ratio (44 per cent) and a low concentration ratio (7 per cent). These ratios were also low (60 per cent and 23 per cent) for printing and publishing. But they were high (187 per cent and 91 per cent) for paper and paper products, and very high (345 per cent and 90 per cent) for pulp, paper and paperboard. Added value contributions were about equal for wood products and printing, and twice that of paper products.

Within the chemical sector the largest category was pharmaceuticals, with an added value of $A141 million in 1972/73. Fertilizers had an added value of $A88 million and other agricultural chemicals one of $A19 million. Soap and detergents had about the same values, $A77 million and $A74 million, followed by cosmetics with $A62 million. Concentration and capital-labour ratios are high for basic chemicals generally, and well above Australian averages in the case of soaps and detergents, as in that of ammunition and explosives.

The petroleum refining sector had an added value of $A111 million. It is highly capital-intensive, and has a considerable degree of concentration associated with the operation of multinational enterprises. Local refineries supply over 90 per cent of Australian consumption of motor spirit, aviation turbine fuel, power kerosene, industrial diesel fuel, automatic distillate and liquefied natural gas. The only petroleum product for which they fail to supply two-thirds of the local market is aviation gasolene. Since 1969 Australia's imports of crude petroleum have halved in volume and domestic crude accounts for 70 per cent of the total input. Since then, however, combined exports of crude and refined products have quadrupled to reach a value of $A162 million in 1974/75.

Australia is naturally more self-sufficient in non-metallic mineral products. Over three-quarters of the added value for this sector comes from the production of bricks, cement, concrete and glass, and half of it from cement and concrete together. Capital intensity is relatively high for cement, and well above the average level for concrete and bricks.

Basic metal products are dominated by iron and steel, which account for more than two-thirds of the sector's total added value. By far the largest producer of iron and steel is the Broken Hill Proprietary, although this huge company also has important interests in petroleum and a range of other basic metals. Here activities comprise smelting, refining and further processing of copper, aluminium, lead, zinc and silver, all highly concentrated and capital-intensive. This whole sector supplies more than 93 per cent of the local market for its products, and exports about a fifth of its outputs.

Fabricated metal products had an added value of $A866 million in 1972/73, compared with $A1,005 million for basic metal products themselves. By far the biggest contribution came from structural steel, followed by architectural metal products, and then by boiler and plate work.

Four-fifths of the added value for the transport equipment sector comes from the motor industry. Helped by various sorts of protection it supplied about three-quarters of the local market for motor vehicles and parts in 1971/72, although it later suffered stronger competition from Japanese and European manufacturers. It is not regarded as an efficient industry, partly because of the undue proliferation of models for a relatively small market, and only a small part of its output is exported. Nor is it a very capital-intensive industry in Australia, although necessarily a fairly concentrated one. Remaining types of transport equipment are ships and boats, locomotives and rolling stock.

Other machinery and equipment covers a wide range of activities, among which the leading categories are, in order of importance, industrial machinery, television and radio receivers, refrigerators and other household appliances, and electrical machinery. Domestic outputs supply about 70 per cent of the local market for such products, and only 8 per cent of these outputs are exported. Miscellaneous manufactures are mainly rubber tyres, plastic floor coverings, plastic sheeting and leather. Imports account for less than a fifth of local supplies of such manufactures, and exports are less than 5 per cent of local outputs. In this sector only the manufacture of rubber tyres can be regarded as both capital-intensive and highly concentrated.

On the whole, Australian manufactures are highly protected. In 1970 the weighted average rate of duty on imports of finished manufactures was 28 per cent, compared with 7.7 per cent for the U.S.A., 9.1 per cent for EEC countries and 12.9 per cent for Japan. The average rate of effective protection was 35 per cent in that year, and the most highly protected sectors were clothing (83 per cent), metal products (73 per cent), transport equipment (57 per cent) and other machinery (44 per cent). Manufacturing, nevertheless, is not generally a very profitable activity. The mean ratio of operating profit to funds employed was only 12.6 per cent in 1973/74, a better than average year. On this criterion, the most profitable sectors (with a ratio of 20 to 31 per cent) were soap, tobacco, cosmetics, timber, milling, footwear and sugar, while the least profitable sectors (with a ratio below 8 per cent) were meat products, glass and rubber. A major reason for the moderate profitability of manufacturing industries is their high labour costs. High wages are not, in general, matched by high productivity, and many working days are lost by strikes. In 1972, days lost through industrial disputes averaged 10.2 per 100 employees in engineering, metals, vehicles, etc. and 5.4 in other types of manufacturing, compared with a general average of 4.5 for all industries. This, moreover, was a good year; the general average was 6.9 in 1971 and 13 in 1974.

EXTERNAL TRANSACTIONS

Australia is markedly dependent on the rest of the world. Since 1960 the ratio of exports of goods and services to gross domestic product has varied from 14 to 18 per cent, while the ratio of imports to G.D.P. has ranged from 13 to 18 per cent.

Food, beverages and tobacco (mainly wheat, meat and sugar) have provided a fairly steady proportion of merchandise exports, usually at somewhat over a third. Wool's proportion fell dramatically from 36 per cent in 1962/63 to 9 per cent in 1974/75, but that for iron ore and other basic metal ores has risen even more dramatically, from less than 3 per cent in 1962/63 to 13 per cent in 1974/75. Coal also rose from 1 to 8 per cent of exports over this period. Manufactures have risen from 14 to 27 per cent of merchandise exports. The largest category has been basic manufactures, in which metal products bulk large with a rise from 9 to 13 per cent. Chemicals rose from 1 to 6 per cent, and machinery and transport equipment from 2 to 7 per cent.

Australia's most important customers are Japan, the U.S.A. and the United Kingdom, but there have been marked changes in their relative shares of exports. Between 1962/63 and 1974/75, Japan's share rose from 16 to 28 per cent, that of the U.S.A. fell moderately from 12 to 10 per cent, and that of the United Kingdom fell sharply from 19 to 6 per cent. New Zealand is now a more important export market for Australia than the United Kingdom and the most important single market for Australia's manufactured exports. Exports to Europe were 38 per cent of the total in 1962/63, falling to 21 per cent in 1974/75. After the United Kingdom, the main European market is the Federal Republic of Germany, which took 4 per cent in 1974/75 while France took 2 per cent, and Italy slightly less. Perhaps the most striking feature about Australia's direction of trade is its large and growing involvement with the Pacific basin; this area took three-fifths of exports in 1962/63 and three-quarters in 1974/75. Excluding Japan, the U.S.A. and New Zealand, the rise was from 26 to 31 per cent. Exports to China have fluctuated greatly with its needs for imported wheat, of which Australia is a major supplier when necessary.

On the import side, the largest category has been machinery and transport equipment, although this includes such major consumer goods as television sets, radios and other electronic goods as well as passenger cars. Cars and trucks rose from 3.6 per cent of merchandise imports in 1966/67 to 7.2 per cent in 1974/75, and so were largely responsible for the slight rise in the share of this whole category from 33 per cent in 1962/63 to 38 per cent in 1974/75. Chemicals, over the same period, rose from 7 to 10 per cent of imports. Mineral fuels, despite the exploitation of a major local oilfield, fell only slightly in value terms, from 10 to 9 per cent; but the volume of crude petroleum and petroleum products imported fell by nearly a third so that rising oil prices were a major factor. Owing to high protective duties, imports of clothing were relatively small at 2 to 3 per cent of the total. But they increased so damagingly to the local industry after the 25 per cent tariff cut in 1973 that quotas were imposed, to the particular detriment of developing countries in East Asia. There has been a relative fall in imports of paper products from 9 to 3 per cent. Imports of iron and steel manufactures have been fairly steady at the low rate of 2 to 3 per cent, and imports of food, beverages and tobacco plus inedible crude materials (except fuels) have also been steady at about a tenth of the total.

The Pacific basin is the major area for Australia's external trade. Its contribution rose from 42 per cent of imports in 1962/63 to 54 per cent in 1974/75. This rise is almost wholly due to an increase in trade with Japan, whose share increased from 6 to 18 per cent. That of the U.S.A. was steady at 21 per cent, and New Zealand had little more than 2 per cent. The United Kingdom's share fell markedly from 31 to 15 per cent, as it was partly replaced in the Australian market by other EEC countries, whose share rose from 11 to 14 per cent. The most important supplier among these countries is the Federal Republic of Germany, which had a share of 7 per cent in 1974/75.

For some years Australia has had a substantial deficit on current external account, averaging $A405 million per year in 1960–64, $A882 million per year in 1965–69, and falling back to $A467 million per year in 1970–74, when it was about 8 per cent of export receipts, compared with 18 per cent in 1960–64 and 28 per cent in 1970–74. These fluctuations were accompanied by heavy capital inflows during the later 1960s, when Australia had great new opportunities for mining investment, followed by an attractive real estate boom and a stable currency which together attracted some of the "hot" international money of the early 1970s.

From 1965 to 1969 there was an apparent net inflow of $A4,700 million of private capital, three-fifths of it for direct investment. Net external borrowing by federal and state governments was only $A83 million, and net monetary movements were about twice that amount. Over the next five years, private capital inflows were steady, and two-thirds of them went to direct investment. Government net borrowing rose to a mere $A237 million, but monetary movements accounted for $A2,300 million of capital receipts in the balance of payments.

INFLATION, EMPLOYMENT AND GOVERNMENT POLICY

Australia was strongly affected by the world explosion of prices during 1973 and 1974. Its annual increase of consumer prices rose from a low average of 3 per cent over 1965–69 to 9 per cent in 1973, then to 15 per cent in 1974 and a further 15 per cent in 1975. External influences played their part as import prices rose by 40 per cent in 1974 and by 31 per cent in 1975. Export prices, after rising by 30 per cent in 1973, rose by 17 per cent in both 1974 and 1975. Wages (as measured by average male weekly earnings) rose at somewhat lesser rates; by 12 per cent in 1973, 22 per cent in 1974 and 17 per cent in 1975.

None of this would have been possible without large increases of the domestic money supply. Defined in the widest sense, this increased by 13 per cent in 1972, 23 per cent in 1973, 13 per cent in 1974 and 17 per cent in 1975. But, in considering the major components of these big increases of the money supply, it is best to use figures for fiscal years ending June 30th. Between 1969/70 and 1971/72 money increased by 25 per cent or $A3,534 million. Inflows of foreign exchange (associated with external finance for mining, real estate and other development, plus speculative inflows associated with uncertainty about world exchange rates) came to $A2,366 million; but there were offsetting reductions of about $A1,600 million in "other" Reserve Bank liabilities. Credit expansion by trading and savings banks accounted for $A2,290 million of monetary expansion, and Government debt operations for only $A409 million.

There was a much more rapid expansion of money over the next three fiscal years, altogether by 81 per cent or $A11,351 million. Bank loans increased by $A7,853 million, and Government debt operations contributed another $A2,883 million to this huge monetary expansion.

The major jump in lending by trading and savings banks occurred during 1972/73, when boom conditions were strong. Thereafter more stringent monetary policy, together with a deterioration of economic activity, kept their growth to about the same rate as domestic inflation.

But there was a sudden and large deterioration in public finance. The federal deficit, which had been only $A292 million in 1973/74, rose to $A2,561 million in 1974/75 and was predicted to reach $A2,798 million in 1975/76. By February 1976, however, it had reached $A4,522 million for the first eight months of the fiscal year and, although there would be a seasonal rise in company tax collection, might have become more than $A4,000 million for the whole year, or a fifth of federal outlays. The major cause was a sudden growth of government spending, especially on social services and welfare, by the Labor Government which held power from December 1972 to November 1975. Its Liberal-Country Party successor has seemed determined to reduce both federal spending and taxation, but no substantial results are likely to be achieved until the 1976/77 fiscal year.

Contrary to its expectation, the Labor Government had to cope both with serious inflation and rising unemployment. During the first year it was in power, unemployment was 2.2 per cent of the civilian labour force, then thought to be an uncomfortably high rate. From mid-1974, however, the rate increased to reach 4.6 per cent in February 1975 and was still 4.5 per cent in March 1976. Nor was there official optimism about its falling at all quickly. Unemployment reflected a deterioration in economic activity. Real G.D.P. rose by 5.6 per cent in 1973/74, a fairly normal rate for Australia, but fell slightly in the following year and had not recovered up to the December quarter of 1975. Most of the deterioration, moreover, was in non-farm G.D.P. because export prices for cereals, sugar, dairy produce and fruits remained at high levels, as have their export volumes. Slump conditions have been severe in the farming sector only for wool and meat producers, and they, too, have increased volumes of output.

Manufacturing production reached a peak in the latter half of 1973 and, after keeping to a satisfactory level until mid-1974, fell by 7 per cent from then until November 1975. Falls were particularly heavy for building and construction materials (20 per cent) and for chemicals (14 per cent), and above average for both industrial and electrical machinery. These falls reflected a sharp drop in real private capital formation. New housing investment dropped by a third, although it began to recover slowly from the June quarter of 1975. Other building and construction, however, had a more or less continuous fall of about a sixth up to mid-1975, and investment in capital equipment one of the same order. It has been widely recognized that the most worrying recent feature of the economy from the standpoint of short-term recovery is this depression of private investment. It is also worrying from the standpoint of long-term growth, more particularly because it has been associated with a sharp decline in mineral exploration and development. Steps have been taken to raise investment allowances for tax exemption, and to remove some official discouragements to mining activity.

Consumer expenditures, in real terms, also slackened

from mid-1973 to late 1974, and made only a sporadic recovery in 1975. Partly for this reason, there was a heavy accumulation of stocks, which gave place to some dispersal early in 1975. The automobile industry was especially hard hit as registrations of new motor vehicles dropped by a fifth between February and November 1975, although they began a modest recovery after that, and additional protection against imported cars also helped the industry. Such help was also extended to the clothing industries, which began to recover after June 1975.

Early in 1976 there was no hopeful sign of consumption boom, and still less of an investment boom. Unemployment remained high, and inflation was still far from being under control. The only hopeful signs for reducing inflation were a steadying of import prices and a slackening of wage increases to an equivalent annual rate of 11 per cent in the December quarter of 1975. But the equivalent rise in the consumer price index was 14 per cent and the slackening of wage inflation had owed something to a widely accepted principle of wage indexation, imposed by the Arbitration Commission. Such acceptance was weakened in 1976 through modifications sought by the new Government, and indexation has come under open challenge by some unions and some employers' groups.

There was agitation, too, about the Australian exchange rate. Since late 1974 this has been determined on a daily basis by the Reserve Bank, in accordance with changes in a weighted average for currencies of trading partners. Between February 1975 and April 1976 the Australian dollar accordingly depreciated by 10 per cent against the U.S. dollar and by 6 per cent against the Japanese yen, although it appreciated by 19 per cent against sterling. But mineral exports were severely hit by low world prices and by steeply rising local costs. Farmers also had an interest in further devaluation, and some manufacturers wished to have the extra protection that devaluation would incur. More impartial commentators agreed with the official line taken by the Treasurer in January: that there was no justification for devaluation in regard to the balance of payments, or foreign reserves, and that it would make still more difficult the task of reducing inflation to a comfortable rate.

STATISTICAL SURVEY

NOTE.—The Australian statistical year usually ends in June.

AREA

(sq. km.)

Total	New South Wales	Victoria	Queensland	South Australia	Western Australia	Tasmania	Northern Territory	Australian Capital Territory
7,682,300*	801,600	227,600	1,727,200	984,000	2,525,500	67,800	1,346,200	2,400

* 2,966,150 square miles.

POPULATION

(June 30th, 1975)

Total	New South Wales	Victoria	Queensland	South Australia	Western Australia	Tasmania	Northern Territory	Australian Capital Territory
13,502,317	4,789,563	3,673,368	1,997,170	1,234,078	1,122,559	406,123	87,584	191,872

At the census of June 1971, there were 106,208 persons who considered themselves to be of Aboriginal origin.

PRINCIPAL CITIES*

POPULATION (June 30th, 1975)

Canberra (national capital)†	210,600
Sydney (capital N.S.W.)	2,922,760
Melbourne (capital Victoria)	2,661,400
Brisbane (capital Queensland)	958,800
Adelaide (capital S. Australia)	899,300
Perth (capital W. Australia)	787,300
Newcastle	363,010
Wollongong	211,240
Hobart (capital Tasmania)	164,010
Geelong	129,651

* Statistical divisions or districts.

† Includes the municipality of Queanbeyan in New South Wales.

BIRTHS, MARRIAGES AND DEATHS

(1975)

	Births	Marriages	Deaths
New South Wales	80,783	36,970	40,512
Victoria	61,897	27,710	29,461
Queensland	36,425	15,282	16,444
S. Australia	19,944	9,844	9,947
W. Australia	20,349	9,068	8,014
Tasmania	6,981	3,206	3,340
N. Territory	2,128	376	569
Aust. Capital Ter.	4,375	1,461	732
Total	232,882	103,917	109,019

MIGRATION

	Arrivals			Departures			Net Increase
	Males	Females	Total	Males	Females	Total	
1970	613,899	412,776	1,026,675	548,353	355,448	903,801	122,874
1971	625,066	453,732	1,078,798	581,510	412,683	994,193	84,605
1972	608,730	501,940	1,110,670	597,765	485,059	1,082,824	27,846
1973	696,212	594,148	1,290,360	676,190	573,752	1,249,942	40,418
1974	809,372	687,157	1,496,529	762,529	647,115	1,409,408	87,121

EMPLOYMENT*
('000 persons at June)

	1973	1974	1975
Forestry, fishing and hunting	15.0	14.9	15.9
Mining	75.1	76.8	80.8
Manufacturing	1,287.4	1,331.4	1,204.8
Electricity, gas and water	99.2	99.5	101.1
Construction	399.4	404.7	411.5
Transport, storage and communications	341.7	356.5	358.0
Wholesale and retail trade	925.4	969.2	955.7
Finance, insurance, real estate and business services	365.1	387.9	379.5
Public administration and defence	205.9	219.0	243.5
Community services	638.3	681.0	727.4
Entertainment, recreation, restaurants, hotels and personal services	250.4	265.7	274.5
Total	4,602.9	4,806.5	4,752.7
Private	3,438.8	3,602.7	3,457.1
Government	1,164.1	1,203.8	1,295.5

* Wage and salary earners in civilian employment. Excludes defences force and employers in agriculture and private domestic service.

AGRICULTURE

AREA OF CROPS
('000 hectares)

	1971–72	1972–73	1973–74	1974–75
Cereals for grain:				
Wheat	7,138	7,604	8,948	8,308
Oats	1,241	995	1,182	897
Barley	2,535	2,140	1,894	1,826
Maize	78	59	46	51
Sugar cane	234	242	226	297
Potatoes	40	37	34	38
Vineyards	67	69	70	71
Fruit	123	116	109	103

PRODUCTION

		1971–72	1972–73	1973–74	1974–75
Wheat for grain	'000 metric tons	8,510	6,434	11,902	11,357
Oats for grain	,, ,, ,,	1,275	736	1,107	874
Barley for grain	,, ,, ,,	3,066	1,727	2,398	2,513
Maize for grain	,, ,, ,,	214	139	106	133
Sugar cane	,, ,, ,,	19,391	18,928	19,278	20,418
Wine	'000 litres	291,090	279,944	294,666	n.a.

FRUIT

(metric tons)

	1972/73	1973/74	1974/75
Apples	431,252	334,701	367,974
Apricots	43,560	37,230	27,337
Bananas	123,752	124,679	118,188
Oranges	351,674	309,851	340,810
Peaches	116,074	81,112	90,507
Pears	190,105	162,093	157,973
Plums and Prunes	27,373	23,057	23,172

LIVESTOCK

('000)

	1972–73	1973–74	1974–75	1975–76*
Cattle	29,101	30,839	32,793	33,655
Sheep	140,029	145,173	151,652	148,770
Pigs	3,259	2,505	2,197	2,183

Horses: 456,000 in 1970.

* Preliminary.

DAIRY PRODUCE

		1971–72	1972–73	1973–74	1974–75
Whole Milk	million litres	7,079	6,952	6,756	6,489
Factory Butter	million kg.	195	185	175	161
Factory Cheese	,, ,,	81	93	96	99
Processed Milk Products (whole milk equivalent)	million litres	586	542	535	575

OTHER LIVESTOCK PRODUCTS

('000 metric tons)

	1972–73	1973–74	1974–75
Beef and Veal	1,438	1,310	1,534
Mutton	435	221	250
Lamb	278	235	269
Pig Meat	236	211	175
Poultry Meat	160	191	189
Hen Eggs	201	204	n.a.
Wool: greasy	735	701	793
clean	415	400	449

1975/76: Wool (greasy) 721,000 metric tons.

MINING*

(July 1st to June 30th)

		1972/73	1973/74	1974/75
Coal (black)	'000 metric tons	59,755	59,344	70,142
Coal, brown (lignite)[1]	" " "	20,922	23,258	24,441
Coal, brown (briquettes)	" " "	1,228	1,164	1,092
Bauxite	" " "	14,702	18,545	20,522
Zircon[2]	metric tons	247,545	290,519	317,219
Iron	'000 metric tons	47,204	57,801	60,360
Lead	" " "	385	370	417
Zinc	" " "	507	441	508
Copper	" " "	199	247	236
Titanium[3]	" " "	712	679	840
Tin	metric tons	11,754	10,599	10,165
Tungsten[4]	" "	1,876.0	1,427.8	1,575.6
Crude petroleum	'000 cubic metres	20,669	23,096	23,096
Natural gas	million cubic metres	3,713	4,360	4,633
Gold	kilogrammes	20,002	16,271	15,061
Silver	"	670,492	674,359	709,092
Nickel	metric tons	36,104	42,247	49,106

* Figures for metallic minerals represent metal contents based on chemical assay, except figures for bauxite, which are in terms of gross quantities produced.

[1] Excludes coal used in making briquettes.

[2] In terms of zircon (ZrO_2) contained in zircon concentrates.

[3] In terms of TiO_2 contained in rutile, ilmenite and leucoxene.

[4] In terms of WO_3 contained in scheelite and wolfram concentrates.

INDUSTRY

(1973/74)

	Establishments at end of Year	Persons Employed*	Turnover ($m.)
Food, Beverages and Tobacco	4,249	204,172	6,820.3
Textiles	897	54,619	1,161.5
Clothing and Footwear	3,180	109,968	1,441.8
Wood, Wood Products and Furniture	6,038	85,677	1,601.3
Paper and Paper Products, Printing	3,683	108,034	2,143.4
Chemical, Petroleum and Coal Products	1,169	67,107	2,396.4
Non-Metallic Mineral Products	1,911	55,456	1,358.0
Basic Metal Products	642	98,149	3,866.2
Fabricated Metal Products	5,434	119,040	2,269.5
Transport Equipment	1,608	158,880	3,055.9
Other Machinery and Equipment	5,001	198,971	3,606.4
Miscellaneous Manufacturing	3,332	78,371	1,526.3

* Includes working proprietors.

Note: Direct comparisons with figures for previous years are not possible because of changes in the census units, the scope of the census and the items of data.

INDUSTRIAL PRODUCTION

(July 1st to June 30th)

		1972/73	1973/74	1974/75
Steel (Ingots)	'000 metric tons	7,209	7,504	8,017
Electric Motors (<1 h.p.)	'000	3,439	4,371	4,219
Clay Bricks	million	1,881	2,051	1,698
Sulphuric Acid	'000 metric tons	2,266	2,434	1,770
Nitric Acid	metric tons	149,092	185,646	173,970
Radios	'000	880	939	285
TV Sets	,,	397	447	465
Motor Vehicles	,,	455	471	456
Cotton Yarn	'000 metric tons	26	29	24
Cotton Cloth	'000 sq. metres	46,391	50,361	41,364
Tinplate	'000 metric tons	243	355	317
Electricity	million kWh.	64,802	69,743	73,933
Cement	'000 metric tons	5,097	5,412	5,086

FINANCE

100 cents = 1 Australian dollar ($A).
Coins: 1, 2, 5, 10, 20 and 50 cents.
Notes: 1, 2, 5, 10, 20 and 50 dollars.

Exchange rates (June 1976): £1 sterling = $A1.443; U.S. $1 = 81.4 Australian cents.
$A100 = £69.28 = U.S. $122.90.

Note: The Australian dollar was introduced in February 1966, replacing the Australian pound (exchange rate: £A1 = U.S. $2.24 from September 1949) at the rate of $A2 = £A1. From February 1966 to August 1971 the exchange rate remained at $A1 = U.S. $1.12 (U.S. $1 = 89.29 Australian cents). Between December 1971 and December 1972 the par value of the Australian dollar was U.S. $1.216 (U.S. $1 = 82.24 Australian cents), though the effective mid-point exchange rate was $A1 = U.S. $1.191. Revaluations were made in December 1972 ($A1 = U.S. $1.275), in February 1973 ($A1 = U.S. $1.4167) and in September 1973 ($A1 = U.S. $1.4875). This last valuation remained in effect until September 1974, since when the Australian dollar has been allowed to "float". Its value immediately fell to U.S. $1.31, representing an effective devaluation by 11.9 per cent. For converting the value of foreign trade transactions, the average value of the Australian dollar was: U.S. $1.134 in 1971; U.S. $1.192 in 1972; U.S. $1.423 in 1973; U.S. $1.441 in 1974; U.S. $1.310 in 1975. In terms of sterling the exchange rate was £1 = $A2.143 ($A1 = 9s. 4d. or 46.67p) from November 1967 to December 1971; and £1 = $2.188 from December 1971 to June 1972.

FEDERAL GOVERNMENT BUDGET*

($A million, year ended June 30th)

Revenue	1974/75	1975/76†
Receipts:		
Taxation	14,084	17,608
Interest, rent and dividends	1,174	1,482
Other	6	27
Financing transactions	2,567	2,798
Total	17,831	21,915

Expenditure	1974/75	1975/76†
Net expenditure on goods and services		
Current expenditure:		
Defence	1,444	1,643
Other	2,032	2,587
Capital expenditure	410	567
Transfer payments and net advances:		
To State and local government authorities	6,409	8,470
Cash benefits to persons	4,321	5,700
Interest paid	887	1,011
Other	2,329	1,938
Total	17,831	21,915

* Figures represent the combined transactions of the Consolidated Revenue Fund and the Loan and Trust Funds.
† Estimates.

STATE GOVERNMENT FINANCES*

($A million, year ended June 30th)

	Receipts†		Expenditure	
	1974/75	1975/76‡	1974/75	1975/76‡
New South Wales	2,452	3,063	2,493	3,064
Victoria	1,752	2,106	1,767	2,126
Queensland	1,113	1,394	1,121	1,400
South Australia	789	1,051	781	1,051
Western Australia	734	981	743	981
Tasmania	269	321	282	326
Totals	7,109	8,916	7,187	8,948

* For all States except Victoria the figures cover the Consolidated Revenue Funds. The figures for New South Wales also include the transactions of the Public Transport Commission and the Maritime Services Board. The figures for Victoria cover its Consolidated Revenue Fund, excluding the Works and Services section. In all cases the transactions of the Loan and Trust Funds are excluded.

† Figures include payments to the States by the Federal Government of grants for specific and general purposes.

‡ Estimates.

NATIONAL ACCOUNTS

($A million)

	1972/73	1973/74	1974/75
Gross Domestic Product	41,830	50,669	59,003
Indirect taxes *less* subsidies	4,229	5,350	6,671
Gross Domestic Product at Factor Cost	37,601	43,319	52,332
of which:			
Agriculture forestry and fishing	2,992	4,325	n.a.
Mining	1,427	1,667	n.a.
Manufacturing	8,875	10,480	n.a.
Electricity, gas and water	1,298	1,462	n.a.
Construction	3,042	3,465	n.a.
Transport, storage and communication	2,915	3,450	n.a.
Wholesale and retail trade	5,661	6,787	n.a.
Public administration and defence	1,724	2,115	n.a.
Community services, entertainment, etc., and personal services	4,590	5,663	n.a.
Other	6,145	7,236	n.a.
Less Imputed bank service charge	1,068	1,331	1,625
Depreciation allowances	3,292	3,588	3,991
Domestic Factor Incomes	34,309	41,731	48,341
Indirect taxes *less* subsidies	4,229	5,350	6,671
Net income paid overseas	408	311	457
National Income (at Market Prices)	38,130	46,770	54,555
Expenditure on Gross Domestic Product	41,830	50,669	59,003
of which:			
Private final consumption expenditure	24,836	29,072	34,541
Government final consumption expenditure	5,441	6,756	9,092
Gross fixed capital expenditure	10,055	11,920	14,152
Increase in stocks	−340	1,602	836
Statistical discrepancy	216	1,195	547
Export of goods and services	6,949	7,774	9,782
Less Import of goods and services	5,327	7,650	9,947

OFFICIAL RESERVE ASSETS

(June 30th—$A million)

	1973	1974	1975
Gold	220	210	238
SDR's	200	150	89
IMF Gold	143	149	156
Foreign Exchange	3,684	3,051	3,010
TOTAL	4,248	3,560	3,493

CURRENCY IN CIRCULATION

(June 30th—$A million)

	1973	1974	1975
Coins	205.3	225.4	250.4
Notes	1,757.8	2,146.1	2,557.1
TOTAL	1,963.1	2,371.5	2,807.5

BALANCE OF PAYMENTS

($A million)

	1973/74			1974/75		
	Credit	Debit	Balance	Credit	Debit	Balance
Goods and Services:						
Merchandise	6,688	5,753	935	8,434	7,662	772
Non-monetary gold	30		30	56	—	56
Transportation	680	1,165	−485	937	1,513	−576
Travel	162	341	−179	213	405	−192
Investment income	509	1,150	−641	392	1,037	−645
Government n.e.s.	89	116	−27	100	150	−50
Other services	130	271	−141	152	302	−150
Total	8,288	8,796	−508	10,284	11,069	−785
Transfer Payments:						
Private	223	253	−30	324	242	82
Central Government		290	−290	—	350	−350
Total	223	543	−320	324	592	−268
CURRENT BALANCE		—	−827			−1,054
Capital and Monetary Gold:						
Non-Monetary:						
Government transactions (net)	—	4	4	—	24	−24
Private investment	472	188	284	845	109	736
Marketing authorities investment	—	95	−95	—	59	−59
Total	472	287	185	845	192	653
Monetary:						
Changes in official reserve assets	384	—	384	460	—	460
Allocation of Special Drawing Rights		—			—	—
Other offical monetary institutions transactions	50	—	50	4	—	4
Other	154	—	154	47	—	47
Total	588	—	588	511		511
Balancing item	53	—	53	—	110	−110
CAPITAL BALANCE			826	—		1,054

Note: Any discrepancies between totals and sums of components in the above table are due to rounding.

CURRENT BALANCES—REGIONAL

($A million)

	1971/72	1972/73	1973/74
United Kingdom:			
Exports f.o.b.	439	565	436
Imports f.o.b.	762	682	756
Invisibles (net)	−434	−429	−571
Balance on Current Account	−751	−616	−892
Other EEC:			
Exports f.o.b.	473	661	649
Imports f.o.b.	508	533	786
Invisibles (net)	−106	−137	−178
Balance on Current Account	−141	−9	−315
Other Sterling Area:			
Exports f.o.b.	902	1,020	1,306
Imports f.o.b.	456	497	873
Invisibles (net)	−162	−131	−113
Balance on Current Account	286	391	320
U.S.A.:			
Exports f.o.b.	612	715	723
Imports f.o.b.	889	805	1,334
Invisibles (net)	−365	−455	−553
Balance on Current Account	−641	−545	−1,163
Japan:			
Exports f.o.b.	1,358	1,925	2,145
Imports f.o.b.	606	688	1,036
Invisibles (net)	7	−3	−13
Balance on Current Account	759	1,234	1,096
Other Non-sterling:			
Exports f.o.b.	946	1,130	1,435
Imports f.o.b.	572	603	968
Invisibles (net)	−186	−231	−346
Balance on Current Account	197	296	120
Unallocated:			
Exports f.o.b.	—	—	—
Imports f.o.b.	—	—	—
Invisibles (net)	−6	−6	−2
Balance on Current Account	−6	−6	−2
TOTAL:			
Exports f.o.b.	4,741	6,015	6,694
Imports f.o.b.	3,792	3,808	5,753
Invisibles (net)	−1,251	−1,462	−1,778
Balance on Current Account	−302	745	−836

Note: Any discrepancies between totals and sums of components in the above table are due to rounding.

OVERSEAS INVESTMENT

($A million)

INFLOW

	U.K.	U.S.A.	Canada	Other Countries	IBRD	Total
1969–70	257	307	27	273	−20	844
1970–71	505	467	46	500	−16	1,503
1971–72	339	559	38	512	−16	1,433
1972–73	64	28	7	334	−10	423
1973–74	69	100	18	188	−7	367

OUTFLOW

	U.K.	New Zealand	U.S.A. and Canada	Papua New Guinea	Other Countries	Total
1969–70	32	8	2	83	8	133
1970–71	− 2	20	1	54	15	89
1971–72	−13	20	11	87	30	141
1972–73	− 5	24	38	50	32	110
1973–74	34	20	27	48	79	224
1974–75	33	47	12	−12	53	133

FOREIGN AID EXTENDED BY AUSTRALIA*
($A million)

	Year Ended June			
	1971	1972	1973	1974
Government Transfer Payments:				
Papua New Guinea	123	132	158	197
Other Foreign Aid and Contributions	62	73	94	93
Total	185	206	252	290

* Official only; excludes transfers by private persons and organizations to overseas recipients.

EXTERNAL TRADE
($A million, twelve months ending June 30th)

	1969–70	1970–71	1971–72	1972–73	1973–74	1974–75
Imports	3,881	4,150	4,008	4,121	6,085	8,083
Exports	4,137	4,376	4,893	6,214	6,914	8,673

COMMODITIES
($A'000)

Imports	1972/73	1973/74	1974/75
Producers' Materials for use in:			
Building and Construction	167,084	253,509	239,039
Rural Industries	47,880	70,668	114,981
Motor Vehicle Assembly	228,760	289,096	413,498
Other Manufacturing	1,269,279	2,027,585	2,511,907
Capital Equipment:			
Producers' Equipment	855,892	1,096,963	1,678,030
Road Vehicles and Chassis	193,853	329,951	526,472
Railway Equipment, Ships, Aircraft	69,382	113,336	144,400
Finished Consumer Goods:			
Food, Beverages and Tobacco	171,073	232,684	280,547
Clothing and Accessories	88,180	172,002	232,989
Other	736,561	1,045,623	1,384,173
Fuels and Lubricants†	68,933	123,712	234,314
Auxiliary Aids to Production	93,505	119,938	156,248
Munitions, etc.	81,530	152,024	47,309
	4,071,911	6,027,091	7,963,908
Non-Merchandise Trade	48,816	57,913	119,191
Total	4,120,727	6,085,004	8,083,099

† Excludes crude petroleum, which is included in "Other Producers' Materials".

Exports	1972/73	1973/74	1974/75
Food and Live Animals	1,934,412	2,179,310	2,970,257
Butter	61,986	41,880	33,833
Cheese and Curd	21,688	28,936	34,639
Bacon and Hams	406	574	695
Meat of Bovine Animals	652,874	636,152	322,883
Meat of Sheep, Lambs and Goats	119,723	80,783	65,674
Pork	17,117	8,053	1,614
Dried Fruits	28,516	19,989	21,412
Preserved Fruit and Preparations	55,265	51,720	40,885
Wheat	273,096	517,114	1,034,396
Flour	13,108	21,821	50,611
Barley	38,512	68,463	186,682
Sugar	249,770	223,257	644,574
Beverages and Tobacco	15,167	17,053	19,138
Crude Materials, inedible, except Fuels	2,116,445	2,220,973	2,146,744
Wool (greasy)	1,064,209	1,062,237	663,870
Wool (scoured, etc.)	66,258	94,327	89,622
Sheep and Lamb skins (excl. pieces)	109,397	91,545	61,664
Mineral Fuels, Lubricants and Related Materials	340,989	456,888	834,477
Animal and Vegetable Oils and Fats	30,598	44,885	55,811
Chemicals	271,441	348,365	478,812
Manufactured Goods, classified chiefly by material	645,545	852,117	1,151,009
Machinery and Transport Equipment	498,302	446,864	564,975
Miscellaneous Manufactured Articles	98,298	101,896	124,651
Commodities and Transactions not classified according to kind	262,508	246,042	326,889
Total	6,213,704	6,914,395	8,672,762

PRINCIPAL TRADING PARTNERS

($A '000)

	Exports		Imports	
	1973/74	1974/75	1973/74	1974/75
Belgium-Luxembourg	59,379	73,543	57,437	73,026
Canada	173,465	288,906	191,819	217,100
China, People's Republic	162,550	253,967	71,857	81,150
Egypt	76,401	134,573	454	345
Finland	8,484	2,426	26,772	39,821
France	199,060	175,069	80,156	139,838
Germany, Federal Republic	181,287	308,503	450,836	580,039
Hong Kong	114,074	105,179	159,603	172,240
India	99,300	83,160	52,876	57,840
Indonesia	106,467	175,251	16,550	18,693
Italy	132,816	150,042	140,540	208,818
Japan	2,158,141	2,396,265	1,084,968	1,420,862
Kuwait	18,496	30,819	98,937	118,618
Malaysia	117,637	194,370	69,565	58,800
Netherlands	89,430	145,898	83,842	123,399
New Zealand	449,085	529,270	168,077	183,910
Pakistan	7,969	86,490	12,282	5,386
Papua New Guinea	133,042	193,806	39,614	34,179
Philippines	79,228	99,721	16,234	24,147
Poland	50,010	51,426	8,915	9,074
Saudi Arabia	24,315	27,863	53,169	171,136
Singapore	147,677	206,480	82,082	126,905
South Africa	90,280	97,861	36,629	43,930
Sri Lanka	15,390	45,148	9,448	12,834
Sweden	20,873	34,581	109,475	183,229
Switzerland	15,609	9,391	90,844	104,790
Taiwan	76,505	80,950	114,048	113,103
Thailand	50,627	49,444	9,922	16,150
U.S.S.R.	154,215	243,086	5,895	6,376
United Kingdom	457,499	474,838	848,662	1,214,426
United States of America	749,797	831,496	1,348,012	1,668,181
Viet-Nam, South	8,097	9,634	562	575
Other Countries	687,190	1,083,306	544,922	854,179
Total	6,914,395	8,672,762	6,085,004	8,083,099

TRANSPORT

		1970/71	1971/72	1972/73	1973/74
Railways:					
Route kilometres		40,269	40,323	40,474	40,406
Passengers	'000	452,530	403,816	377,233	373,618
Goods and livestock	'000 metric tons	87,307	88,671	92,481	96,966
Roads:					
Motor vehicles registered	'000	5,039	5,325	5,634	5,986
Overseas shipping:					
Tonnage entered	'000 tons	58,820	53,144	62,628	n.a.
Tonnage cleared	,, ,,	51,399	53,492	62,031	n.a.
Air transport, internal services:					
Kilometres flown	'000	114,605	115,931	121,606	135,209
Passengers carried		6,340,036	6,629,316	7,502,892	8,857,654
Freight	metric tons	91,401	89,883	94,426	112,654
Mail	,, ,,	9,916	10,137	10,114	9,916
Air transport, overseas services:					
Kilometres flown	'000	70,346	66,270	64,823	69,062
Passengers carried		839,629	885,548	1,054,929	1,295,457
Freight	metric tons	21,455	20,961	23,239	27,328
Mail	,, ,,	2,819	2,841	2,791	2,912

TOURISM

	1971	1972	1973	1974
Number of Visitors (Arrivals)*	432,393	426,403	472,124	532,683

* i.e. intending to stay less than one year.

COMMUNICATIONS MEDIA

(At June 30th—'000)

	1972	1973	1974	1975
Telephones:				
Services in Operation	2,978	3,147	3,361	3,529
Instruments in service	4,400	4,659	5,000	5,267
Radio Licences*†	2,758	2,814	2,851	—
Television Licences*†	2,939	3,013	3,022	—
Combined Licences†	2,420	2,493	2,546	

* Includes combined radio and television licences.

† Figures no longer collected. Radio and television licenses were abolished in September 1974.

EDUCATION

(1975)

	Institutions	Teaching Staff†	Students
Government Schools	7,266	123,441	2,297,979
Non-Government Schools	2,140	28,990	621,301
Universities	18	11,153	148,338
Colleges of Advanced Education*	78	8,767	122,557
Private Teachers' Colleges	16	n.a.	3,843

* Includes all former government teachers' colleges.

† Full-time staff plus full-time equivalents of part-time staff.

Source: Australian Bureau of Statistics, Belconnen, A.C.T. 2616.

THE CONSTITUTION

PARLIAMENT

The legislative power of the Commonwealth is vested in a Federal Parliament, consisting of the Queen, represented by the Governor-General, a Senate, and a House of Representatives. The Governor-General may appoint such times for holding the sessions of the Parliament as he thinks fit, and may also from time to time, by Proclamation or otherwise, prorogue the Parliament, and may in like manner dissolve the House of Representatives. This power is limited by strict, although unwritten, constitutional understanding, and it is rare for such decisions to be made at the sole discretion of the Governor-General. After any general election Parliament must be summoned to meet not later than thirty days after the day appointed for the return of the writs.

THE SENATE

The Senate is composed of ten Senators from each State, two Senators representing the Northern Territory and two representing the Australian Capital Territory. The Senators are directly chosen for a period of six years by the people of the state, voting as one electorate, and are elected by proportional representation. They retire by rotation, half from each State on June 30th of each third year. The Senate may proceed to the dispatch of business notwithstanding the failure of any State to provide for its representation in the Senate.

If a Senator vacates his seat before the expiration of his term of service, the Houses of Parliament of the State for which he was chosen shall, in joint session, choose a person to hold the place until the expiration of the term or until the election of a successor. If the State Parliament is not in session, the Governor of the State, acting on the advice of the Executive Council, may appoint a Senator to hold office until Parliament reassembles, or until a new Senator is elected.

THE HOUSE OF REPRESENTATIVES

In accordance with the Constitution, the total number of members of the House of Representatives must be as nearly as practicable double that of the Senate. The number in each State is in proportion to population, but under the Constitution must be at least five. At present the House of Representatives is composed of 127 members, which includes two members for the Australian Capital Territory and one member for the Northern Territory. Until recently these members, though able to join in all debates, were entitled to vote only on matters affecting their Territories; full voting rights were extended to the members for the Australian Capital Territory in 1967 and to the member for the Northern Territory in 1968.

Members are elected by universal adult suffrage and voting is compulsory. Qualifications for Commonwealth franchise are possessed by any British subject, not under 18 years of age, subject to certain disqualifications (e.g. if of unsound mind), who has lived in Australia for six months continuously.

Members are chosen by the electors of their respective electorates by the preferential voting system.

The duration of the Parliament is limited to three years.

Qualification for membership of the House of Representatives is possessed by any British subject 18 years of age or over who has resided in the Commonwealth for at least three years and who is, or is qualified to become, an elector of the Commonwealth.

THE EXECUTIVE GOVERNMENT

The executive power of the Federal Government is vested in the Queen, and is exercised by the Governor-General, assisted by an Executive Council of Ministers of State, known as the Federal Executive Council. These Ministers are, or must become within three months, members of the Australian Parliament.

THE JUDICIAL POWER

The judicial power of the Commonwealth is vested in the High Court of Australia, in such other Federal Courts as the Australian Parliament creates, and in such other courts as it invests with Federal jurisdiction.

The High Court consists of a Chief Justice and not less than two other Justices, appointed by the Governor-General in Council. (There are at present a Chief Justice and six other Justices.) It has both an original and an appellate jurisdiction.

The High Court's original jurisdiction extends to all matters arising under any treaty, affecting representatives of other countries, in which the Commonwealth of Australia or its representative is a party, between States or between residents of different States or between a State and a resident of another State, and in which a writ of *mandamus*, or prohibition, or an injunction is sought against an officer of the Commonwealth of Australia. It also extends to matters arising under the Constitution or involving its interpretation, and to any other matters empowered by the Australian Parliament.

The appellate jurisdiction extends to appeals from all judgments, decrees, orders and sentences of its own Justices exercising original jurisdiction, of any other Federal Court or court exercising Federal jurisdiction and of the Supreme Court of any State or any other State court from which an appeal lies to the Queen in Council. In 1968 appeals from the High Court to the Queen in Council were abolished in all matters involving the Constitution and laws made by the Australian Parliament, as well as from all Federal Courts other than the High Court.

An amendment of the Conciliation and Arbitration Act assented to on June 30th, 1956, altered the structure of the arbitration machinery by separating the judicial and arbitral functions. The Australian Industrial Court was set up to deal with judicial matters under the Act and the Australian Conciliation and Arbitration Commission to handle the function of conciliation and arbitration.

The Australian Industrial Court is composed of a Chief Judge and eleven other Judges. The Australian Conciliation and Arbitration Commission comprises a President, Deputy Presidents, Commissioners, and a number of Conciliators. Jurisdiction in bankruptcy and insolvency is administered by the Federal Court of Bankruptcy or State Courts of Insolvency, or State Courts exercising Federal jurisdiction. There is a Supreme Court in the Australian Capital Territory and in the Northern Territory. State courts, including courts of summary jurisdiction, are invested with Federal judicial power, principally to deal with offences created by Federal statutes.

THE STATES

The Commonwealth Constitution safeguards the Constitution of each State by providing that it shall continue as at the establishment of the Commonwealth, except as altered in accordance with its own provisions. When a State law is inconsistent with a law of the Commonwealth, the latter prevails, and the former is invalid to the extent of the inconsistency. However, the legislation of the Australian Parliament is limited in the main to those matters which are listed in section 51 of the Constitution, while the States possess, as well as concurrent powers in those matters, residual legislative powers enabling them to legislate in any way for "the peace, order and good Government" of their respective territories.

The States may not, without the consent of the Commonwealth, raise or maintain naval or military forces, or impose taxes on any property belonging to the Commonwealth, nor may the Commonwealth tax State property. The States may not coin money.

The Commonwealth may not enact any law for establishing any religion or for prohibiting the exercise of any religion, and no religious test may be imposed as a qualification for any office under the Commonwealth.

The Commonwealth is charged with protecting every State against invasion, and, on the application of a State Executive Government, against domestic violence.

Provision is made under the Constitution for the admission of new States and for the establishment of new States within the Commonwealth.

ALTERATION OF THE CONSTITUTION

Proposed laws for the amendment of the Constitution must be passed by an absolute majority in both Houses of Parliament, and not less than two or more than six months after its passage through both Houses the proposed law must be submitted in each State to the qualified electors.

In the event of one House twice refusing to pass a proposed amendment which has already received an absolute majority in the other House, the Governor-General may, notwithstanding such refusal, submit the proposed amendment to the electors. If, in a majority of the States a majority of the electors voting approve the proposed law and if a majority of all the electors voting also approve, it shall be presented to the Governor-General for Royal Assent.

No alteration diminishing the proportionate representation of any State in either House of the Parliament, or the minimum number of representatives of a State in the House of Representatives, or increasing, diminishing or altering the limits of the State, or in any way affecting the provisions of the Constitution in relation thereto, shall become law unless the majority of the electors voting in that State approve the proposed law.

A Constitutional Convention was convened in September 1973 to review the Commonwealth Constitution. Following this, standing committees were set up to inquire into certain areas of the Australian Constitution.

NEW SOUTH WALES

The executive power is vested in the Governor, appointed by the Crown, who is assisted by a Cabinet.

The legislative power is vested in a Parliament of two Houses, the Legislative Council and the Legislative Assembly. The former consists of sixty members, elected at a joint sitting of both Houses of Parliament, for a term of twelve years, fifteen members retiring every three years. The Legislative Assembly consists of ninety-nine members, and sits for three years.

VICTORIA

The legislative authority is vested in a bicameral Parliament: the Upper House, or Legislative Council, of thirty-six members, elected for six years, and the Lower House, or Legislative Assembly, of seventy-three members, elected for three years. One-half of the members of the Council retire every three years.

In the exercise of the executive the Governor is assisted by a Cabinet of responsible Ministers. Not more than five members of the Council and not more than thirteen members of the Assembly may occupy salaried office at any one time.

Provision has been made for the imminent re-division of the State into eighty-one electoral districts, each returning one Member, and into twenty-two electoral provinces, each returning two Members.

QUEENSLAND

Legislative power rests with a unicameral Parliament composed of eighty-two members elected from eighty-two districts for a term of three years.

SOUTH AUSTRALIA

The Constitution vests the legislative power in a Parliament elected by the people and consisting of a Legislative Council and a House of Assembly. The Council is composed of twenty-two members, half of whom retire every three years. Their places are filled by new members elected under a system of proportional representation, with the whole State as a single electorate. The executive has no authority to dissolve this body.

The forty-seven members of the House of Assembly are elected for three years from forty-seven electoral districts.

The executive power is vested in a Governor, appointed by the Crown, and an Executive Council consisting of twelve responsible Ministers.

WESTERN AUSTRALIA

The administration is vested in the Governor, a Legislative Council and a Legislative Assembly.

According to the present Constitution, the Legislative Council consists of thirty members, each of the fifteen provinces returning two members. Election is for a term of six years, and one-half of the members retire every three years.

The Legislative Assembly consists of fifty-one members, elected for three years, each representing one electorate. Proposals to enlarge both the Legislative Assembly and the Legislative Council are to be considered in 1976.

The entire management and control of the unalienated lands of the Crown in Western Australia is vested in the State Legislature.

TASMANIA

The executive authority is vested in a Governor, appointed by the Crown and acting upon the advice of a Legislative Council and House of Assembly. The Council consists of nineteen members who sit for six years, retiring in rotation. There is no power to dissolve the Council. The House of Assembly has 35 members elected for five years (soon to be reduced to four).

NORTHERN TERRITORY

By a Federal Act of 1974 a Legislative Assembly (sitting at Darwin) was set up, consisting of 19 elected members. The Northern Territory is administered on behalf of the Commonwealth Government by the Administrator and the Department of Northern Australia in Darwin. In addition, the Legislative Assembly is given the power to make Ordinances for the peace, order and good government of the Northern Territory.

AUSTRALIAN CAPITAL TERRITORY

The Australian Capital Territory, within which the Seat of Government is situated, is administered by the Federal Government. Under legislation passed by the Parliament the Governor-General is given power to make Ordinances for the peace, order and good government of the Territory. There is established in the Territory an elected Legislative Assembly, consisting of 18 elected members, which may advise the Government on matters affecting the Territory.

THE GOVERNMENT

(*August* 1976)

Head of State: H.M. Queen ELIZABETH II.

Governor-General: H.E. the Rt. Hon. Sir JOHN KERR, K.C.M.G., K.ST.J.

FEDERAL EXECUTIVE COUNCIL

INNER CABINET

Prime Minister: Rt. Hon. J. MALCOLM FRASER.

Deputy Prime Minister and Minister for National Resources and Overseas Trade: Hon. J. DOUGLAS ANTHONY.

Treasurer: Hon. PHILLIP REGINALD LYNCH.

Minister for Primary Industry and Leader of the House: Hon. IAN MCCAHON SINCLAIR.

Vice-President of the Executive and Leader of the Government in the Senate, Minister for Administrative Services: Senator the Hon. REGINALD GREIVE WITHERS.

Minister for Industry and Commerce: Senator the Hon. ROBERT COTTON.

Minister for Employment and Industrial Relations and Minister Assisting the Prime Minister in Public Service Matters: Hon. ANTHONY AUSTIN STREET.

Minister for Transport: Hon. PETER NIXON.

Minister for Education and Minister Assisting the Prime Minister in Federal Affairs: Senator the Hon. JOHN CARRICK.

Minister for Foreign Affairs: Hon. ANDREW PEACOCK.

Minister for Defence: Hon. DENIS JAMES KILLEN.

Minister for Social Security: Senator the Hon. MARGARET GUILFOYLE.

OTHER MINISTERS

Minister for Environment, Housing and Community Development: Hon. KEVIN EUGENE NEWMAN.

Attorney-General: Hon. ROBERT ELLICOTT, Q.C.

Minister for Business and Consumer Affairs: Hon. JOHN HOWARD.

Minister for Postal and Telecommunications and Minister Assisting the Treasurer: Hon. ERIC LAIDLAW ROBINSON.

Minister for Health: Hon. RALPH HUNT.

Minister for Immigration and Ethnic Affairs: Hon. MICHAEL MACKELLAR.

Minister for the Northern Territory and Minister Assisting the Minister for National Resources: Hon. ALBERT EVAN ADERMANN.

Minister for Aboriginal Affairs: Hon. ROBERT IAN VINER.

Minister for the Capital Territory: Hon. ANTHONY STALEY.

Minister for Construction and Minister Assisting the Minister for Defence: Hon. JOHN ELDEN MCLEAY.

Minister for Repatriation: Senator the Hon. PETER DREW DURACK.

Minister for Science: Senator the Hon. JAMES WEBSTER.

ADMINISTRATORS OF TERRITORIES

Northern Territory: ERIC F. DWYER (acting).

Norfolk Island: CHARLES I. BUFFETT, M.B.E. (acting).

Cocos (Keeling) Islands: R. J. LINFORD.

Christmas Island: W. WORTH.

FEDERAL PARLIAMENT

Elections for both Houses were held on December 13th, 1975.

SENATE

(*July* 1976)

President: Sen. the Hon. CONDOR LAUCKE.

Chairman of the Committees: Sen. the Hon. THOMAS DRAKE-BROCKMAN.

Leader of the Government: Sen. the Hon. REGINALD G. WITHERS.

Leader of the Opposition: Sen. the Hon. KENNETH WRIEDT.

	SEATS
Liberal-National (Country) Party coalition	35
Labor Party	27
Independents	2
TOTAL	64

HOUSE OF REPRESENTATIVES

(*July* 1976)

Speaker: Hon. WILLIAM SNEDDEN.

Chairman of the Committee: PHILLIP E. LUCKOCK

Leader of the House: Hon. IAN SINCLAIR.

Leader of the Government: Rt. Hon. J. MALCOLM FRASER.

Leader of the Opposition: Hon. E. GOUGH WHITLAM.

	SEATS
Liberal Party	68
National (Country) Party	23
Labor Party	36
TOTAL	127

STATE GOVERNMENTS

NEW SOUTH WALES

Governor: H.E. Sir RODEN CUTLER, V.C., K.C.M.G., K.C.V.O., C.B.E., K.ST.J.

LABOR MINISTRY

(*May* 1976)

Premier: Hon. NEVILLE K. WRAN, Q.C., M.L.A.

Deputy Premier and Minister for Public Works, Ports and Housing: Hon. LAURIE J. FERGUSON, M.L.A.

Treasurer: Hon. JOHN B. RENSHAW, M.L.A.

Minister for Transport and Highways: Hon. PETER F. COX, M.L.A.

Attorney-General: Hon. FRANCIS J. WALKER, LL.M., M.L.A.

Minister for Mines and Energy: Hon. PATRICK D. HILLS, M.L.A.

Minister for Industrial Relations and Vice-President of the Executive Council: Hon. DAVID P. LANDA, LL.B., M.L.C.

Minister for Decentralization, Development and Primary Industries: Hon. DONALD DAY, M.L.A.

Minister for Education: Hon. ERIC L. BEDFORD, B.A., M.L.A.

Minister for Local Government and Planning: Hon. HENRY F. JENSEN, M.L.A.

Minister for Lands and Environment: Hon. WILLIAM F. F. CRABTREE, M.L.A.

Minister for Health: Hon. KEVIN J. STEWART, M.L.A.

Minister for Consumer Affairs and Co-operative Societies: Hon. SYDNEY D. EINFELD, M.L.A.

Minister of Justice and Minister for Services: Hon. RONALD J. MULOCK, LL.B., M.L.A.

Minister for Sport, Recreation and Tourism: Hon. KENNETH G. BOOTH, M.L.A.

Minister for Conservation and Water Resources: Hon. ALAN R. L. GORDON, M.L.A.

Minister for Youth and Community Services: Hon. REX F. JACKSON, M.L.A.

Minister assisting the Premier: Hon. WILLIAM H. HAIGH, M.L.A.

LEGISLATURE

Legislative Council: Pres. Hon. Sir HARRY VINCENT BUDD; Chair. of Committees Hon. THOMAS S. MCKAY, B.A., LL.B.

Legislative Assembly: Speaker Hon. LAWRENCE BORTHWICK KELLY; Chair. of Committees THOMAS JAMES CAHILL.

VICTORIA

Governor: H.E. Hon. Sir HENRY WINNEKE, K.C.M.G., O.B.E.

LIBERAL MINISTRY

(*March* 1976)

Premier, Treasurer and Minister of the Arts: Hon. RUPERT J. HAMER, E.D.

Deputy Premier and Minister of Education: Hon. L. H. S. THOMPSON, C.M.G.

Chief Secretary: Hon. VANCE O. DICKIE, M.L.C.

Minister of Transport: Hon. JOSEPH A. RAFFERTY.

Minister of Agriculture: Hon. I. W. SMITH.

Minister of Public Works: Hon. ROBERTS C. DUNSTAN, D.S.O.

Minister of Social Welfare and for Youth, Sport and Recreation: Hon. BRIAN J. DIXON.

Minister of Water Supply and Minister of Forests: Hon. FREDERICK J. GRANTER, M.L.C.

Minister for Conservation, Minister of Lands and Minister of Soldier Settlement: Hon. WILLIAM A. BORTHWICK.

Minister of Fuel and Power and Minister of Mines: Hon. J. C. M. BALFOUR.

Minister for Local Government and Minister for Federal Affairs: Hon. ALAN J. HUNT, M.L.C.

Minister for State Development and Decentralization and Minister of Tourism: Hon. DIGBY G. CROZIER, M.L.C.

Minister of Housing and Minister for Planning: Hon. GEOFFREY P. HAYES.

Minister of Health: Hon. WILLIAM V. HOUGHTON, M.L.C.

Minister of Labor and Industry and Minister of Consumer Affairs: Hon. ROBERT R. C. MACLELLAN.

Minister for Special Education: Hon. ALAN H. SCANLAN.

Minister of Immigration and Assistant Minister of Health: Hon. WALTER JONA.

Attorney-General: Hon. HADDON STOREY, Q.C., M.L.C.

LEGISLATURE

Legislative Council: Pres. Hon. WILLIAM G. FRY, M.L.C.; Chair. of Committees Hon. WILLIAM M. CAMPBELL, M.L.C.; Clerk of the Council ALFRED R. B. MCDONNELL, J.P.

Legislative Assembly: Speaker Hon. Sir KENNETH WHEELER, K.B.; Chairman of Committees IAN FRANCIS MCCLAREN, O.B.E., Clerk of the Assembly J. H. CAMPBELL.

QUEENSLAND

Governor: H.E. Air Marshal Sir COLIN T. HANNAH, K.C.M.G., K.B.E., C.B., K.ST.J.

LIBERAL (L)-NATIONAL (COUNTRY) PARTY (CP) COALITION MINISTRY

(*July* 1976)

Premier: Hon. JOHANNES BJELKE-PETERSEN, M.L.A. (CP)

Treasurer and Deputy Premier: Hon. Sir GORDON W. W. CHALK, K.B.E., LL.D., M.L.A. (L).

Minister for Education and Cultural Activities: Hon. V. J. BIRD (CP).

Minister for Industrial Development, Labor Relations and Consumer Affairs: Hon. F. A. CAMPBELL, M.L.A. (L).

Minister for Mines and Energy: Hon. R. E. CAMM, M.L.A. (CP).

Minister for Health: Hon. Dr. L. R. EDWARDS (L).

Minister for Justice and Attorney-General: Hon. W. E. KNOX, M.L.A. (L).

Minister for Transport: Hon. K. W. HOOPER, M.L.A. (L).

Minister for Local Government and Main Roads: Hon. R. J. HINZE (CP).

Minister for Lands, Forestry, National Parks and Wildlife Services: Hon. K. B. TOMKINS (CP).

Minister for Tourism and Marine Services: Hon. T. G. NEWBERY (CP).

Minister for Works and Housing: Hon. N. E. LEE (L).

Minister for Primary Industries: Hon. V. B. SULLIVAN, M.L.A. (CP).

Minister for Community and Welfare Services and Minister for Sport: Hon. J. D. HERBERT (L).

Minister for Police: Hon. A. M. HODGES (CP).

Minister for Water Resources: Hon. NEVILLE T. E. HEWITT, M.M., A.F.M., M.L.A. (CP).

Minister for Aboriginal and Islanders' Advancement and Fisheries: Hon. C. A. WHARTON (CP).

Minister for Survey, Valuation, Urban and Regional Affairs: Hon. WILLIAM D. LICKISS (L).

LEGISLATURE

Legislative Assembly: Speaker Hon. J. HOUGHTON; Chair. of Committees Hon. W. D. HEWITT; Clerk C. GEORGE.

SOUTH AUSTRALIA

Governor: H.E. Sir MARK OLIPHANT, K.B.E., F.R.S., K.ST.J.

Governor-designate: Sir DOUGLAS NICHOLLS, O.B.E. (from December 1st, 1976).

LABOR MINISTRY

(*July* 1976)

Premier and Treasurer: Hon. DONALD A. DUNSTAN, Q.C.

Deputy Premier, Minister of Works and Minister of Marine: Hon. JAMES DESMOND CORCORAN.

Minister of Mines and Energy and Minister for Planning: Hon. HUGH R. HUDSON.

Minister of Health and Chief Secretary: Hon. D. H. L. BANFIELD, M.L.C.

Minister of Transport and Minister of Local Government: Hon. G. T. VIRGO.

Minister of Lands, Minister of Irrigation, Minister of Repatriation and Minister of Tourism, Recreation and Sport: Hon. T. M. CASEY, M.L.C.

Minister of Education: Hon. D. J. HOPGOOD, PH.D.

Minister of Agriculture, Minister of Forests and Minister of Fisheries: Hon. B. A. CHATTERTON, M.L.C.

Minister of Labor and Industry: Hon. JOHN D. WRIGHT.

Minister of Community Welfare: Hon. R. G. PAYNE.

Attorney-General and Minister of Prices and Consumer Affairs: Hon. P. DUNCAN, LL.B.

Minister for the Environment: Hon. D. W. SIMMONS, D.F.C., A.U.A.

LEGISLATURE

Legislative Council: Pres. and Chair. of Committees Hon. FRANK J. POTTER, B.A., LL.B.; Clerk of the Parliaments and of the Legislative Council IVOR J. BALL, A.A.S.A., A.C.I.S.

House of Assembly: Speaker Hon. E. CONNELLY; Chair. of Committees GILBERT R. A. LANGLEY; Clerk AUBREY F. R. DODD.

WESTERN AUSTRALIA

Governor: Air Chief Marshal Sir WALLACE KYLE, G.C.B., C.B.E., D.S.O., D.F.C.

LIBERAL (L)-NATIONAL (COUNTRY) PARTY (CP)
COALITION MINISTRY
(*July* 1976)

Premier, Treasurer and Minister Co-ordinating Economic and Regional Development: Hon. Sir CHARLES COURT, O.B.E., M.L.A. (L).

Deputy Premier, Minister for Works, Water Supply and the North West: Hon. D. H. O'NEIL, M.L.A. (L).

Minister for Justice, Chief Secretary and Leader of the Government in the Legislative Council: Hon. N. MCNEILL, B.SC., M.L.C. (L).

Minister for Agriculture: Hon. R. C. OLD (CP).

Minister for Transport, Traffic and Police: Hon. R. J. O'CONNOR, M.L.A. (L).

Minister for Education, Cultural Affairs and Recreation: Hon. G. C. MACKINNON, M.L.C. (L).

Minister for Labor and Industry, Consumer Affairs and Immigration: Hon. W. L. GRAYDEN, M.L.A. (L).

Minister for Industrial Development, Mines, Fuel and Energy: Hon. A. MENSAROS, M.L.A. (L).

Minister for Local Government, Urban Development and Town Planning: Hon. E. C. RUSHTON, M.L.A. (L).

Minister for Lands, Forests and Tourism: Hon. K. A. RIDGE, M.L.A. (L).

Minister for Health and Community Welfare: Hon. N. E. BAXTER, M.L.C. (CP).

Minister for Housing, Conservation and the Environment, Fisheries and Wildlife: Hon. P. V. JONES, M.L.A. (CP).

Attorney-General and Minister for Federal Affairs: Hon. IAN G. MEDCALF, E.D., LL.B., M.L.C. (L).

LEGISLATURE

Legislative Council: Pres. Hon. ARTHUR FREDERICK GRIFFITH; Chair. of Committees and Deputy Pres. Hon. JACK HEITMAN.

Legislative Assembly: Speaker Hon. ROSS HUTCHINSON, D.F.C.; Chair. of Committees and Deputy Speaker IAN DAVID THOMPSON.

TASMANIA

Governor: H.E. the Hon. Sir STANLEY BURBURY, K.B.E., K.ST.J.

LABOR MINISTRY
(*July* 1976)

Premier and Treasurer: Hon. WILLIAM ARTHUR NEILSON, M.H.A.

Deputy Premier, Chief Secretary and Minister for Planning and Reorganization: Hon. DOUGLAS ACKLEY LOWE, M.H.A.

Attorney-General and Minister for Police and Emergency Services: Hon. BRIAN KIRKWALL MILLER, M.L.C.

Minister for Lands and Works and Minister for Tourism and Immigration: Hon. MICHAEL T. C. BARNARD, M.H.A.

Minister for Education, Recreation and the Arts and Minister for National Parks and Wildlife: Hon. NEIL LEONARD CHARLES BATT, M.H.A.

Minister for Agriculture and Fisheries: Hon. ERIC W. BARNARD, M.H.A.

Minister for Transport and Minister for Racing and Gaming: Hon. GEOFFREY DONALD CHISHOLM, M.H.A.

Minister for Health: Hon. HEDLEY DAVID FARQUHAR, M.H.A.

Minister for Industrial Development and Minister for Forests and Mining: Hon. STEWART CHARLES HILTON FROST, M.H.A.

Minister for Housing and Social Welfare: Hon. DARRELL JOHN BALDOCK, M.H.A.

LEGISLATURE

Legislative Council: Pres. Hon. C. B. M. FENTON; Chair. of Committees J. H. DIXON; Clerk of the Council G. B. EDWARDS.

House of Assembly: Speaker Hon. HARRY HOLGATE. Chair. of Committees KENNETH E. AUSTIN; Clerk of the House B. G. MURPHY.

NORTHERN TERRITORY

(*see* Constitution)

Minister for the Northern Territory: Hon. ALBERT ADERMANN.

Acting Administrator: ERIC F. DWYER.

POLITICAL PARTIES

Australian Labor Party: Ainslie Bldg., 39 Ainslie Ave., Canberra, A.C.T. 2601; f. 1891, for the democratic socialization of industry, production, distribution and exchange; Leader of the Federal Parliamentary Labor Party the Hon. E. GOUGH WHITLAM, Q.C., M.H.R.; National Pres. ROBERT J. L. HAWKE; Gen. Sec. DAVID COMBE.

Liberal Party of Australia: Federal Secretariat, National Headquarters Bldg., cnr. Blackall and Macquarie Sts., Barton, Canberra 2600; f. 1944; the Party supports freedom of enterprise, social justice and initiative. It has always maintained uncompromising opposition to doctrinaire socialism and communism. Party Leader the Rt. Hon. MALCOLM FRASER, Federal Pres. R. J. SOUTHEY, C.M.G.

National (Country) Party of Australia: John McEwen House, National Circuit, Barton, A.C.T. 2600, f. 1916; name changed from Country to National Party 1975; principal objectives are the betterment of conditions in rural and agricultural communities through improved marketing facilities, more effective Parliamentary representation of country people, the encouragement of desirable immigrants, and the promotion of the study of all matters relating to agricultural and primary production.

Federal Parliamentary Leader Rt. Hon. JOHN DOUGLAS ANTHONY; Gen. Sec. JAMES W. CUMING; publ. *The Countryman*.

Australian Democratic Labor Party: 561-7 George St., Sydney; formed 1956 following a split in the Australian Labor Party; Pres. L. BROSNAN; Gen. Sec. JOHN KANE.

Australia Party: 1 Arundel St., Glebe, N.S.W. 2037; f. July 1969 "to satisfy an urgent need for an alternative in the political management of Australia"; successor to the *Australian Reform Movement*; advocates friendly relations with all countries, parliamentary and educational reform, environmental policies for an equilibrium economy; supports policies designed to promote social justice and eliminate discrimination within the confines imposed by private enterprise; mems. over 3,000 (1974); National Convenor JOHN SIDDONS.

Communist Party of Australia: 4 Dixon St., Sydney, N.S.W., Australia 2000; f. 1920; independent of both Soviet and Chinese influence; Pres. L. CARMICHAEL; Sec. L. AARONS; publ. *Tribune* (weekly).

Communist Party of Australia (Marxist-Leninist): 168 Day St., Sydney, N.S.W. 2000; f. 1967 after split in Communist Party of Australia; supports Chinese principles; Chair. E. F. HILL.

Farm and Town Party: Horsham, Vic.; f. March 1972; advocates economic justice for rural people; Chair. A. C. EVERETT.

Socialist Party of Australia: 111 Sussex St., Sydney, N.S.W.; f. 1971; aims: to bring about a socialist society in Australia through public ownership of the means of production and working-class political power. Aims to build a united front of workers allied to other progressive forces. Fosters international co-operation; Pres. P. CLANCY; Gen. Sec. P. SYMON.

DIPLOMATIC REPRESENTATION

EMBASSIES AND HIGH COMMISSIONS ACCREDITED TO AUSTRALIA

(Canberra unless otherwise stated.)

(HC) High Commission.

Afghanistan: Tokyo, Japan.

Argentina: 58 Mugga Way, Red Hill, A.C.T. 2603; *Ambassador:* RAÚL DESMARAS-LUZURIAGA.

***Austria:** 107 Endeavour St., Red Hill, A.C.T. 2603; *Ambassador:* Dr. FRIEDRICH HOESS.

***Bangladesh:** 43 Hampton Circuit, Yarralumla, A.C.T. 2600 (HC); *High Commissioner:* Air Vice-Marshal A. KARIM KHANDKER.

Belgium: 19 Arkana St., Yarralumla, A.C.T. 2600; *Ambassador:* ELI LUYCKX.

***Brazil:** 127 Mugga Way, Red Hill, A.C.T. 2603; *Ambassador:* MIGUEL ALVARO OZORIO DE ALMEIDA.

Bulgaria: Jakarta, Indonesia.

***Burma:** 85 Mugga Way, Red Hill, A.C.T. 2603; *Ambassador:* Dr. NYI NYI.

Canada: Commonwealth Ave., A.C.T. 2600 (HC); *High Commissioner:* JAMES J. MCCARDLE (also accred. to Fiji).

Chile: 93 Endeavour St., Red Hill, A.C.T. 2603; *Ambassador:* RENATO GARCIA.

China, People's Republic: 247 Federal Highway, Watson, A.C.T. 2602; *Ambassador:* WANG KUO-CHUAN.

Czechoslovakia: Jakarta, Indonesia.

***Denmark:** 24 Beagle St., Red Hill, A.C.T. 2603; *Ambassador:* MOGENS WARBERG.

Egypt: 125 Monaro Crescent, Red Hill, A.C.T. 2603; *Ambassador:* AHMED W. MARZOUK.

Fiji: 9 Beagle St., Red Hill, A.C.T. 2603 (HC); *High Commissioner-Designate:* EPELI KACIMAIWAI.

***Finland:** 83 Endeavour St., Red Hill, A.C.T. 2603; *Ambassador:* Dr. AKE BACKSTROM.

France: 6 Darwin Ave., Yarralumla, A.C.T. 2600; *Ambassador:* ALBERT TRECA

***German Democratic Republic:** 12 Beagle St., Red Hill, A.C.T. 2603; *Ambassador:* HANS RICHTER.

Germany, Federal Republic: 119 Empire Circuit, Yarralumla, A.C.T. 2600; *Ambassador:* Dr. H. BLOMEYER-BARTENSTEIN.

Ghana: 44 Endeavour St., Red Hill, A.C.T. 2603 (HC); *High Commissioner:* V. E. WOOD (also accred. to Malaysia).

***Greece:** 22 Arthur Circle, Forrest, A.C.T. 2603; *Ambassador:* NICHOLAS DIAMANTOPOULOS

Guatemala: Tokyo, Japan.

Hungary: 108 Buxton St., Deakin, A.C.T.; *Ambassador:* Dr. Z. KAZMER.

India: 92 Mugga Way, Red Hill, A.C.T. 2603 (HC); *High Commissioner:* Dr. S. SINHA.

Indonesia: 8 Darwin Ave., Yarralumla, A.C.T. 2600; *Ambassador:* HER TASNING.

***Iran:** 14 Torres St., Red Hill, A.C.T. 2603; *Ambassador:* ALI-REZA HERAVI.

Iraq: Tokyo, Japan.

***Ireland:** 2nd Floor, Bank House, Civic Square, A.C.T. 2608; *Ambassador:* FLORENCE O'RIORDAN.

Israel: 6 Turrana St., Yarralumla, A.C.T. 2600; *Ambassador:* MICHAEL ELIZUR.

Italy: 12 Grey St., Deakin, A.C.T. 2600; *Ambassador:* Dr. PAOLO CANALI.

Japan: 112 Empire Circuit, Yarralumla, A.C.T. 2600; *Ambassador-Designate:* YOSHIO OKAWARA.

Jordan: Tokyo, Japan.

Korea, Democratic People's Republic: 3 Mugga Way, Forrest, A.C.T. 2603; *Chargé d'Affaires a.i.:* JIN SONG DOK (relations suspended November 1975).

Korea, Republic: 55 Mugga Way, Red Hill, A.C.T. 2603; *Ambassador:* SUK CHAN LO.

Kuwait: Tokyo, Japan.

***Laos:** 113 Kitchener St., Garran, A.C.T. 2605; *Chargé d'Affaires a.i.:* TIAO SOUPHAN-THAHEUANGSI.

Lebanon: 1 Arkana St., Yarralumla, A.C.T. 2600; *Ambassador:* ANTOINE YAZBECK.

Malaysia: 71 State Circle, Yarralumla, A.C.T. 2600 (HC); *High Commissioner:* Dr. AWANG BIN HASSAN.

Malta: 261 La Perouse St., Red Hill, A.C.T. 2603 (HC); *High Commissioner:* J. L. FORACE.

***Mexico:** 1 Beagle St., Red Hill, A.C.T. 2603; *Ambassador:* JOSÉ GAMAS-TORRUCO.

Mongolia: Tokyo, Japan.

Nepal: Tokyo, Japan.

Netherlands: 120 Empire Circuit, Yarralumla, A.C.T. 2600; *Ambassador:* R. C. PEKELHARING.

New Zealand: Commonwealth Ave., A.C.T. 2600 (HC); *High Commissioner:* ERIC CHAPMAN.

Nigeria: Canberra Rex Hotel, Northbourne Ave., A.C.T. 2601 (HC); *High Commissioner-Designate:* E. O. FOWORA.

***Norway:** 3 Zeehan St., Red Hill, A.C.T. 2603; *Ambassador:* CARL O. JORGENSEN.

***Pakistan:** 59 Franklin St., Forrest, A.C.T. 2603; *Ambassador:* RIAZ PIRACHA.

Papua New Guinea: 97 Endeavour St., Red Hill, A.C.T. 2603 (HC); *High Commissioner:* O. OALA-RARUA.

***Peru:** 104 La Perouse St., Griffith, A.C.T. 2603; *Ambassador:* Dr. ENRIQUE FERNADEZ DE PAREDES.

***Philippines:** 1 Moonah Place, Yarralumla, A.C.T. 2600; *Ambassador:* GREGORIO G. ABAD.

Poland: 10 Vancouver St., Red Hill, A.C.T. 2603; *Ambassador:* E. WISNIEWSKI.

***Portugal:** 13 Charlotte Street, Red Hill, A.C.T. 2603; *Ambassador:* Dr. ANTÓNIO CABRITA MATIAS.

Romania: Tokyo, Japan.

Senegal: New Delhi, India.

Singapore: 81 Mugga Way, Red Hill, A.C.T. 2603 (HC); *High Commissioner:* PUNCH COOMARASWAMY.

South Africa: Corner of State Circle and Rhodes Place, Yarralumla, A.C.T. 2600; *Ambassador:* J. B. MILLS.

***Spain:** 8 Timbarra Crescent, O'Malley, A.C.T. 2606; *Ambassador:* ALBERTO PASCUAL VILLAR.

***Sri Lanka:** 35 Empire Circuit, Forrest, A.C.T. 2603 (HC); *High Commissioner:* T. S. FERNANDO.

Sweden: Turrana St., Yarralumla, A.C.T. 2600; *Ambassador:* PER LIND.

Switzerland: 7 Melbourne Ave., Forrest, A.C.T. 2603; *Ambassador-Designate:* MARCEL GROSSENBACHER.

Thailand: 15 Mugga Way, Red Hill, A.C.T. 2603; *Ambassador:* VIVADH NA POMBEJRA.

Turkey: 60 Mugga Way, Red Hill, A.C.T. 2603; *Ambassador:* HIKMET BENSAN.

U.S.S.R.: 78 Canberra Ave., Griffith, A.C.T. 2603; *Ambassador:* ALEKSANDR BASOV.

United Kingdom: Commonwealth Ave. (HC); *High Commissioner:* Sir DONALD TEBBIT, K.C.M.G.

U.S.A.: Chancery, Yarralumla, A.C.T. 2600; *Ambassador:* JAMES W. HARGROVE.

Uruguay: 22 Bougainville St., Manuka, A.C.T. 2603; *Chargé d'Affaires a.i.:* AUGUSTO WILD.

Vatican: St. Anne's Convent, Key St., Campbell, A.C.T. 2601; *Apostolic Pro-Nuncio:* Mgr. Dr. GINO PARO.

Viet-Nam: 92 Endeavour St., Red Hill, A.C.T. 2603; *Chargé d'Affaires a.i.:* PHAN KHE DINH.

Yugoslavia: 11 Nuyts St., Red Hill, A.C.T. 2603; *Ambassador:* UROS VIDOVIC.

* Also accredited to New Zealand.

Australia also has diplomatic relations with Algeria, Barbados, Bolivia, Botswana, Colombia, Costa Rica, Cyprus, the Dominican Republic, Ecuador, Ethiopia, Guyana, Haiti, Iceland, Kenya, Liberia, Luxembourg, Madagascar, Mauritius, Monaco, Nauru, Panama, Paraguay, Saudi Arabia, Sudan, Swaziland, Tanzania, Tonga, Trinidad and Tobago, Uganda, Venezuela, Western Samoa and Zambia.

JUDICIAL SYSTEM

The judicial power of the Commonwealth is vested in a Federal Supreme Court, the High Court of Australia, consisting of a Chief Justice and six Justices and such other courts as the Commonwealth Parliament may create. Parliament can also vest certain Federal jurisdiction in State courts. The High Court has original jurisdiction in all matters arising under treaties or affecting representatives of other countries, and in certain matters in which the Commonwealth or the States are concerned. It also hears and determines appeals from judgments of its own Justices exercising original jurisdiction, and from judgments of any other Federal Court or of the Supreme Court of any State. In 1968 appeals from the High Court when acting in a Federal capacity to the Judicial Committee of the Privy Council were ended but appeals direct from Australian States in non-Federal matters have continued. Each State has a Supreme Court as well as a combination of lesser courts.

FEDERAL COURTS

HIGH COURT OF AUSTRALIA

Chief Justice: Rt. Hon. Sir GARFIELD EDWARD JOHN BARWICK, G.C.M.G.

Justices:

Rt. Hon. Sir EDWARD ALOYSIUS MCTIERNAN, K.B.E.
Rt. Hon. Sir HARRY TALBOT GIBBS, K.B.E.
Hon. Sir. NINIAN MARTIN STEPHEN, K.B.E.
Hon. Sir ANTHONY FRANK MASON, K.B.E.
Hon. KENNETH SYDNEY JACOBS
Hon. LIONEL KEITH MURPHY

AUSTRALIAN CONCILIATION AND ARBITRATION COMMISSION

President: Hon. Sir JOHN COCHRANE MOORE.

AUSTRALIAN INDUSTRIAL COURT

Chief Judge: Hon. Sir JOHN ARMSTRONG SPICER, Kt.

FEDERAL BANKRUPTCY ADMINISTRATION

Judges:

Hon. BERNARD B. RILEY (New South Wales).
Hon. CHARLES A. SWEENEY, C.B.E. (Victoria).

NEW SOUTH WALES

SUPREME COURT

King and Elizabeth Streets, Sydney.

Chief Justice: Hon. L. W. STREET.

President of the Court of Appeal: Hon. A. R. MOFFITT.

Chief Judge in Equity: Hon. N. H. BOWEN.

Chief Judge at Common Law: Hon. R. L. TAYLOR.

Chief Judge of Family Law Division: Hon. D. M. SELBY, E.D.

Masters: E. N. DAWES, G. S. SHARPE.

Prothonotary: J. E. NOONAN.

VICTORIA

SUPREME COURT

Chief Justice: Hon. Sir. JOHN MCINTOSH YOUNG, K.C.M.G.

Masters: C. P. Jacobs, m.b.e., S. H. Collie, E. N. Bergere, G. S. Brett.

Prothonotary: P. S. Malbon.

QUEENSLAND

Supreme Court

Southern District (Brisbane)

Chief Justice: Hon. Sir Mostyn Hanger, k.b.e.

Senior Puisne Judge: Hon. C. G. Wanstall.

Registrar and Prothonotary: J. T. Munro.

Central District (Rockhampton)

Puisne Judge: Hon. J. L. Kelly.

Registrar: G. D. Roberts.

Northern District (Townsville)

Puisne Judge: Hon. J. P. G. Kneipp.

Registrar: R. J. Keane.

SOUTH AUSTRALIA

Supreme Court

Chief Justice: Hon. J. J. Bray, ll.d.

Master: J. Boehm.

WESTERN AUSTRALIA

Supreme Court

Chief Justice: Hon. Sir Lawrence W. Jackson, k.c.m.g

Master and Registrar: G. T. Staples, ll.b.

TASMANIA

Supreme Court

Chief Justice: Hon. G. S. M. Green.

Master and Registrar: C. G. Brettingham-Moore, m.c., ll.b.

AUSTRALIAN CAPITAL TERRITORY

Supreme Court

Senior Judge: Hon. R. W. Fox.

Registrar: Z. Hartstein.

NORTHERN TERRITORY

Supreme Court

Senior Judge: W. E. S. Forster.

Master: J. P. Morrison.

RELIGION

CHURCH OF ENGLAND IN AUSTRALIA

There are over 4.1 million members of the Church of England in Australia. The national office of the Church of England in Australia is: General Synod Office, P.O.B. Q190, Queen Victoria Bldgs., York St., Sydney 2000.

Primate of Australia, Archbishop of Melbourne and Metropolitan of Victoria: Most Rev. Frank Woods, k.b.e., m.a., d.d., m.a., th.d.

Archbishop of Sydney and Metropolitan of New South Wales: Most Rev. Marcus L. Loane, m.a., d.d.

Archbishop of Brisbane and Metropolitan of Queensland: Most Rev. Felix R. Arnott, m.a., th.d.

Archbishop of Perth and Metropolitan of Western Australia: Most Rev. Geoffrey T. Sambell, b.a., th.soc.

Archbishop of Adelaide and Metropolitan of South Australia: Most Rev. Keith Rayner, b.a., ph.d., a.c.t., th.l.

ROMAN CATHOLIC CHURCH

There are over 3.4 million Roman Catholics in the 31 dioceses of Australia.

The Apostolic Pro-Nuncio: H.E. The Most Rev. Dr. Gino Paro, d.d., j.c.d., tit. Archbishop of Torcello, St. Anne's Convent, Key St., Campbell, A.C.T. 2601.

Archbishops

Adelaide	Most Rev. James W. Gleeson, d.d.
Brisbane	Most Rev. Francis R. Rush, d.d.
Canberra and Goulburn	Most Rev. Thomas Vincent Cahill, d.d., ph.d.
Hobart	Most Rev. Guilford Young, d.d.
Melbourne	Most Rev. Thomas F. Little, s.t.d.
Perth	Most Rev. Launcelot John Goody d.d. ph.d.
Sydney	His Eminence Cardinal James Darcy Freeman.

OTHER CHURCHES

Baptist Union of Australia: P.O.B. 132, Balwyn, Vic. 3103; Pres.-Gen. Rev. Dr. G. N. Vose, ph.d., th.m., b.a., b.ed.; Sec. Rev. R. K. Smith; 49,780 mems.; 700 churches; publs. *Australian Baptist* (fortnightly) and State papers (monthly).

Congregational Union of Australia: 15 Russell St., Eastwood, N.S.W. 2122; f. 1892; 15,400 mems.; Pres. Rev. Principal K. B. Leaver; Sec. Rev. H. T. Wells; publ. *The Australian Congregationalist* (monthly).

Lutheran Laymen's League of Australia: Lutheran Church House, 54 O'Connell St., North Adelaide, 5006; f. 1966, by amalgamation; 155,000 mems., 371 clergy; Pres. Rev. L. B. Grope, d.d.; Sec. Rev. H. F. W. Proeve, b.a.; runs various seminaries and missions; publs. *The Lutheran* (official organ; fortnightly), *Encounter* (for youth), *Lutheran Women, Lutheran Men, Children's Friend, Prism* (all monthly), *Lutheran Theological Journal* (quarterly), *Lutheran Year Book*.

Greek Orthodox Church: Greek Orthodox Archdiocese, 242 Cleveland St., Redfern, Sydney, N.S.W. 2016; leader in Australia, Archbishop Stylianos; 380,000 mems.; Archdiocesan offices in Melbourne and Adelaide; Greek Orthodox Communities throughout Australia.

Methodist Church of Australasia: The General Conference, 130 Little Collins St., Melbourne, Vic. 3000; 1 million adherents; Pres-Gen. Rev. W. D. O'Reilly, m.a., m.ed., dip.soc.st.; Sec. Gen. Rev. M. G. Wilmshurst.

Presbyterian Church of Australia: 156 Collins St., Melbourne, Vic. 3000; over 1 million mems.; Clerk of Gen. Assembly Rev. L. Farquhar Gunn.

Salvation Army in Australia: 69 Bourke St., Melbourne 3000; Territorial Commander Commissioner Henry J. Warren; Chief Sec. Col. Bramwell Lucas.

JUDAISM

Great Synagogue: Elizabeth St., Sydney; f. 1831; Senior Minister Rabbi Raymond Apple; Sec. Isaac N. Goodman, j.p., 166 Castlereagh St., Sydney, N.S.W.

THE PRESS

Australia's legislation relating to the Press varies in different States.

Under the law concerning contempt of court, since the court takes jurisdiction from the time the accused is arrested, to publish names or photographs before proceedings begin may draw heavy penalties. Though accurate reporting of a case while it is being tried is privileged, and has been known to extend to a degree of scandal, a judge is empowered to ban all reports until the conclusion of the case. Though this legislation is intended to protect the interest of the accused, it frequently hinders the journalist.

Each state has its legislation against obscene publications, which is particularly severe in the State of Queensland, whose broadly defined Objectionable Literature Act of 1954 covers a wide range of offences.

The libel law ranges from seditious libel for matter liable to cause a breach of the peace, or for excessive abuse of government officials, to defamatory libel. The most frequently cited defences are "fair comment and criticism" and "true and public benefit". Certain government agencies have privilege.

All newspapers in the state capitals are owned by limited companies. The trend towards concentration of ownership has led to the development of three principal groups of newspapers. Economic conditions have necessitated the extension of the activities of newspaper companies into related spheres, magazine and book publishing, radio and television, etc. The main groups are as follows:

The Herald and Weekly Times Group: 44 Flinders St., Melbourne; Chair. Sir PHILIP JONES: controls *The Herald* and *Sun News-Pictorial* (Melbourne), *The Bendigo Advertiser, The Geelong Advertiser, West Australian Daily News* (Perth), and also has holdings in several magazines and radio and television companies.

The John Fairfax Group: 235 Jones St., Broadway, P.O.B. 506, Sydney, N.S.W. 2001; Chair. Sir WARWICK FAIRFAX; with its subsidiary Associated Newspapers Ltd., controls *The Sydney Morning Herald, The Sun, National Times, Australian Financial Review* and the *Sun-Herald* (Sydney), *The Canberra Times* and *Illawarra Mercury* (Wollongong); also has radio and television interests.

News Ltd.: 2 Holt St., Surry Hills, Sydney 2010; Chair. Sir NORMAN YOUNG; Man. Dir. RUPERT MURDOCH; controls *Adelaide News* (Adelaide), *The Australian, Daily Mirror* and *Sunday Mirror* (Sydney), *The News* (Darwin), *Sunday Sun* (Brisbane), *The Sydney Daily Telegraph* and *Sunday Times* (Perth) and *Truth* (Melbourne); also has a 50 per cent share with Herald and Weekly Times Group in the *Sunday Mail* (Adelaide); also publish suburban and country newspapers.

Also of some importance are the following:

Consolidated Press Group: 168 Castlereagh St., Sydney; controls *The Maitland Mercury*, and magazines including *The Australian Woman's Weekly* and *The Bulletin.*

David Syme & Co. Ltd., Melbourne: of which John Fairfax Ltd. owns 53 per cent; publishes *The Age* and other newspapers in Victoria.

The total circulation of Australia's daily newspapers was very high in 1972 at about 5,282,000 copies per issue, or 408 for every 1,000 inhabitants. Weekly papers are even more popular as they more successfully penetrate to the remoter parts of the country, whereas metropolitan dailies meet competition from small local papers. The circulation of newspapers has traditionally been almost entirely confined to the state in which each is produced. The only exceptions, which may fairly claim a national circulation, are the dailies *The Australian* and *Australian Financial Review*, and the weeklies, *The Bulletin*, the *National Times* and the *Nation Review.*

The main newspaper centres are Sydney, where the morning *Daily Telegraph* competes with the *Morning Herald*, and the evening *Daily Mirror* competes with *The Sun*, and Melbourne, where *The Age* competes with *The Sun News-Pictorial*, both morning papers. Perth, Adelaide and Brisbane each have only one major morning and one major evening paper.

Among the daily papers most respected for their serious news treatment should be mentioned the *Sydney Morning Herald, The Age* (Melbourne), *The Australian, The Canberra Times* and the *Australian Financial Review.* The most popular dailies include Melbourne's *Sun News-Pictorial* (646,404) and *Herald* (480,800), Sydney's *Daily Telegraph* (331,930), *Sun* (364,288) and *Daily Mirror* (369,153), *Sydney Morning Herald* (272,404) and Brisbane's *Courier Mail* (265,343), and Adelaide's *Advertiser* (230,062).

NEWSPAPERS

Australian Capital Territory

The Canberra Times: 18 Mort St., Braddon, Canberra; f. 1926; morning; Editor I. R. MATHEWS; circ. 38,652.

New South Wales

DAILIES

The Australian: Nationwide News Ltd., 2 Holt St., Surry Hills, P.O.B. 4245, Sydney 2010; f. 1964; national daily; edited in Sydney, published simultaneously in Sydney, Melbourne, Adelaide and Brisbane; Proprietor RUPERT MURDOCH; Editor L. HOLLINGS; circ. 152,765.

Australian Financial Review: 235 Jones St., Broadway, P.O.B. 506, Sydney; f. 1951; Mon. to Fri.; Editor P. ROBINSON; Man. Editor V. J. CARROLL; circ. 43,000.

Daily Commercial News: P.O.B. 1552, Sydney, N.S.W. 2001; f. 1912; News Editor D. DUGAN.

Daily Mirror: 2 Holt St., Surry Hills, Sydney 2010 f. 1941; evening; Man. Dir. K. R. MURDOCH; Editor H. LENZENER; circ. 369,153.

Daily Telegraph: 2 Holt St., Surry Hills, Sydney; f. 1879; independent; morning; Editor S. GALVIN; circ. 331,930.

Newcastle Morning Herald: 28–30 Bolton St., Newcastle, N.S.W. 2300; f. 1858; morning; Editor J. C. HOOKER; circ. 64,229.

The Newcastle Sun: 28-30 Bolton St., Newcastle, N.S.W. 2300; f. 1918; evening; Gen. Man. B. NOACK; Editor K. BROCK; circ. 31,224.

The Sun: 235 Jones St., Broadway, P.O.B. 506, Sydney 2001; f. 1910; evening; Editor I. L. ARNOLD; circ. 364,288.

The Sydney Morning Herald: 235 Jones St., Broadway, P.O.B. 506, Sydney 2001; f. 1831; morning; Editor G. E. W. HARRIOTT; circ. 272,404.

SUNDAY AND WEEKLY NEWSPAPERS

Nation Review: 777B George St., Sydney 2000; f. 1958; independent, progressive weekly; circ. 45,488.

National Times: 235 Jones St., Broadway, Sydney 2001; f. 1971; Sunday; Editor MAX SUICH; circ. 101,034.

Sun-Herald: 235 Jones St., Broadway, P.O.B. 506, Sydney 2001; f. 1953; Sunday; Editor F. R. PETERSON; circ. 683,865.

Sunday Mirror: 2 Holt St., Surry Hills, Sydney 2010; f. 1961; Editor P. WOMBELL; circ. 493,941.

Sunday Telegraph: 2 Holt St., Surry Hills, Sydney 2010; f. 1938; Editor O. THOMSON; circ. 638,482.

VICTORIA

DAILIES

The Age: 250 Spencer St., Melbourne (cnr. Lonsdale St.); f. 1854; Independent liberal; morning; Man. Dir. C. R. MACDONALD; Editor LESLIE CARLYON; circ. 216,507.

The Herald: 44 Flinders St., Melbourne; f. 1840; evening; Editor J. A. FITZGERALD; circ. 480,800.

Sun News-Pictorial: 44 Flinders St., Melbourne; f. 1922; morning; Editor J. A. T. MORGAN; circ. 646,404.

WEEKLY NEWSPAPERS

Melbourne Sunday Press: 250 Spencer St., Melbourne; f. 1973; Editor DALLAS SWINSTEAD; circ. 97,692.

Sporting Globe: 44 Flinders St., Melbourne, Vic. 3000; f. 1922; Weds. and Sats.; Editor A. DUNN.

Sunday Observer: 1 Newton St., Richmond 3121; f. 1971; Editor J. SORELL; circ. 163,000.

Truth: 402 La Trobe St., Melbourne 3001; f. 1902; Sunday; Editor R. GORDON.

QUEENSLAND

DAILIES

Courier-Mail: Campbell St., Bowen Hills, Brisbane; f. 1933; morning; Editor J. R. ATHERTON; circ. 265,343.

Telegraph: Campbell Street, Bowen Hills, Brisbane; f. 1872; evening; Editor L. K. S. HOGG; circ. 172,867.

SUNDAY NEWSPAPERS

Sunday Mail: Campbell St., Bowen Hills, Brisbane; f. 1933; Editor H. G. TURNER; circ. 375,000.

Sunday Sun: Mirror Newspapers Ltd., cnr. Brunswick and McLachlan Sts., Fortitude Valley, Brisbane; f. 1971; Editor R. RICHARDS; circ. 288,515.

SOUTH AUSTRALIA

DAILIES

Advertiser: 121 King William St., Adelaide 5000; f. 1858; morning; Editor-in-Chief D. F. COLQUHOUN; circ. 230,062.

News: 116 North Terrace, Box 1771 G.P.O., Adelaide 5001; f. 1923; evening; Mon. to Sat.; Man. Dir. and Editor RONALD R. BOLAND; circ. 164,588.

SUNDAY AND WEEKLY NEWSPAPERS

Sunday Mail: 116–120 North Terrace, Adelaide 5000; f. 1912; Editor GEOFF JONES; circ. 258,589.

WESTERN AUSTRALIA

DAILIES

Daily News: 125 St. George's Terrace, Perth; f. 1882; evening, Mon.-Fri.; circ. 123,319; Editor D. O'SULLIVAN.

West Australian: Newspaper House, St. George's Terrace, Box D 162 PO, Perth; f. 1833; morning; Editor M. C. UREN; circ. 237,239.

SUNDAY AND WEEKLY NEWSPAPERS

The Countryman: Newspaper House, St. George's Terrace, Perth; f. 1885; Thurs.; a farmers' magazine, with pages for women; circ. 18,040; Editor G. A. BOYLEN.

Sunday Independent: cnr. Briggs and Swansea Sts., East Victoria Park, Box 40 PO, Bentley, Perth 6102; f. 1969; Sunday; Man. Editor MICHAEL WORNER; circ. 80,000.

Sunday Times: 34-36 Stirling St., Perth; f. 1897; Man. Dir M. W. JAMES; Editor F. DUNN; circ. 233,333.

Weekend News: 125 St. George's Terrace, Perth; f. 1960; weekly (Saturday); Editor J. R. DAVIES; circ. 100,260.

TASMANIA

DAILIES

Advocate: P.O.B. 63, Burnie, Tas.; f. 1890; morning; circulates in N.W. and W. Tasmania; circ. 21,973; Editor D. J. CHERRY.

Examiner: 71–75 Paterson St., Launceston; f. 1842; morning; Independent; Gen. Man. B. J. MCKENDRICK; Editor F. G. N. EWENCE; circ. 35,458.

Mercury: 91–93 Macquarie St.. Hobart; f. 1854; morning Editor D. N. HAWKER; circ. 55,675.

WEEKLY NEWSPAPERS

Advocate Weekender: P.O.B. 63, Burnie, Tas.; f. 1968; Saturday afternoon; circulates in N.W. and W. Tasmania; Editor D. J. CHERRY; circ. 16,700.

Saturday Evening Mercury: 91-93 Macquarie St., Hobart; f. 1954; Editor P. J. HOBBS; Gen. Man. B. J. MCKENDRICK; circ. 37,569.

Sunday Examiner-Express: 71–75 Paterson St., Launceston; f. 1924; Editor F. G. N. EWENCE; circ. 36,859.

Tasmanian Farmer: P.O.B. 63, Burnie, Tas.; f. 1946; Thurs.; Editor D. J. CHERRY; circ. 3,500.

NORTHERN TERRITORY

DAILY

Northern Territory News: 46 Mitchell St., P.O.B. 675, Darwin 5794; f. 1952; Mon. to Fri.; Man. Dir. B. R. YOUNG; Editor J. F. BOWDITCH; circ. 12,298.

SELECTED PERIODICALS

WEEKLIES AND FORTNIGHTLIES

The Advocate: 143 a'Beckett St., Melbourne; f. 1868; Thurs.; Catholic; Editor Miss E. RENNICK; circ. 23,000.

Australasian Post: 61 Flinders Lane, Melbourne, 3000; f. 1946; illustrated; factual, general interest, particularly Australiana; mainly for male readers; Mon.; circulates throughout Commonwealth; Editor J. HUGHES; circ. 275,000.

The Australian Miner: P.O.B. 349, Manuka, A.C.T. 2603; f. 1969; mining and related subjects; weekly; Editor I. HUNTLEY; circ. 18,500.

Australian Women's Weekly: 168 Castlereagh St., Sydney; f. 1933; Wed.; Editor ITA BUTTROSE; circ. over 830,000.

The Bulletin: 54 Park St., Sydney; f. 1880; Wed.; Editor TREVOR KENNEDY.

Current Affairs Bulletin: University of Sydney; Sydney 2006; f. 1952; monthly; Editor Dr. D. CROWLEY.

Incentive: P.O B. 349, Manuka, A.C.T. 2603; f. June 1965; weekly; Australian and overseas economics, politics, business, money market, statistics; Editor MAXWELL NEWTON.

Listener-In T.V.: 44 Flinders St., Melbourne; f. 1925; Thurs.; circ. 110,700; Editor D. W. MCLAUGHLIN.

The Medical Journal of Australia: 71-79 Arundel St., Glebe, N.S.W. 2037; f. 1914; weekly; Editor Dr. R. R. WINTON; circ. 18,000.

New Idea: 32 Walsh St., Melbourne; weekly; women's magazine; Editor R. PERRY.

News Weekly: G.P.O. Box 66A, Melbourne 3001; f. 1943; Wed.; political and trade union affairs in Australia; int. affairs, particularly Indian Ocean and South East Asian area; National Civic Council organ; Man. Dir. G. A. MERCER; Editor E. S. MADDEN; circ. 16,500.

Pix/People: P.O.B. 164, Beaconsfield, N.S.W. 2015; f. 1938; weekly; circ. 180,000; Editor K. FINLAY.

Queensland Country Life: 432 Queen St., Brisbane; f. 1935; Thurs.; circ. 30,787; Editor MALCOLM MCCOSKER.

Stock and Land: Stock and Land Publishing Co. Pty. Ltd., Box 82, North Melbourne 3051; f. 1914; weekly; livestock, land and wool market journal; official newspaper of Associated Stock and Station Agents of Melbourne, Man. Editor C. T. DEB. GRIFFITH; circ. 24,000.

TV Times: 630 George St., Sydney, N.S.W. 2000; publ. by Australian Broadcasting Commission; f. 1958; Editor C. DAY.

TV Week: 32 Walsh St., Melbourne; f. 1957; Mon.; national; Editor FRANK CROOK.

Weekly Times: 44 Flinders St., Melbourne 3000; f. 1869; farming, gardening, country life and sport; Weds.; Editor J. BALFOUR BROWN; circ. 106,000.

Woman's Day: P.O.B. 161, Beaconsfield, N.S.W. 2014; Sat.; circulates throughout Australia and New Zealand; Editor MARY FALLOON; circ. *c.* 557,000.

The Worker: 236-238 Elizabeth St., Brisbane; f. 1890; alternate Mons.; official organ of the Australian Workers' Union in Queensland; Editor J. P. DUNN; circ. 44,562.

MONTHLIES AND OTHERS

Archaeology and Physical Anthropology in Oceania: University of Sydney, N.S.W.; f. 1966; three issues a year; Editor A. P. ELKIN.

Architecture in Australia: 33A McLaren St., North Sydney; f. 1917; official journal of the Royal Australian Institute of Architects; 6 issues a year (Feb., April, June, Aug., Oct., Dec.); Editor ANNE LEONHARD; circ. 7,200.

Australian Cricket: Modern Magazines Pty. Ltd., Ryrie House, 15 Boundary St., Rushcutters Bay, N.S.W. 2011; f. 1968; monthly, October–March inclusive.

Australian Current Taxation: Service and Cases: Butterworths Pty. Ltd., 586 Pacific Highway, Chatswood, 2067; f. 1936; monthly; Editors F. C. BOCK, E. F. MANNIX, D. W. HARRIS.

Australian Home Beautiful: 44–74 Flinders St., Melbourne; f. 1925; monthly; Editor A. J. HITCHIN.

Australian House and Garden: 142 Clarence St., Sydney; monthly; building, furnishing, decorating, handicrafts, gardening, etc.; Editor MARIA QUINN.

Australian Journal of Biological Sciences: C.S.I.R.O., 372 Albert St., East Melbourne, Vic. 3002; f. 1953; alternate months; Editor B. J. WALBY.

Australian Journal of Botany: C.S.I.R.O., 372 Albert St., East Melbourne, Vic. 3002; f. 1953; alternate months; Editor-in-Chief B. J. WALBY.

Australian Journal of Chemistry: C.S.I.R.O., 372 Albert St. East Melbourne, Vic. 3002; f. 1953; monthly; Editor B. J. WALBY.

Australian Journal of Pharmacy: 18–22 St. Francis St., Melbourne; f. 1886; monthly; official journal of the associated pharmaceutical organizations of Australia; Editor S. L. DICKSON; Man. I. G. LLOYD; circ. 10,000.

Australian Journal of Physics: C.S.I.R.O., 372 Albert St., East Melbourne, Vic. 3002; f. 1953; alternate months; Editor B. J. WALBY.

Australian Journal of Politics and History: University of Queensland, St. Lucia, Qld. 4067; f. 1955; 3 times a year; Editor G. GREENWOOD.

Australian Journal of Soil Research: C.S.I.R.O., 372 Albert St., East Melbourne, Vic. 3002; f. 1963; three times yearly, at irregular intervals; Editor B. J. WALBY.

Australian Journal of Zoology: C.S.I.R.O., 372 Albert St., East Melbourne, Vic. 3002; f. 1953; four times a year; Editor-in-Chief B. J. WALBY.

Australian Law Journal: 301 Kent St., Sydney; f. 1927; monthly; Editor J. G. STARKE, Q.C.; Asst. Editor Dr. D. HODGSON.

Australian Left Review: Box A247, Sydney South P.O. 2000; f. 1966; bi-monthly.

Australian Quarterly: Australian Institute of Political Science, Science House, 157 Gloucester St., Sydney, N.S.W. 2000; f. 1929; quarterly; Editor HUGH PRITCHARD.

Australian University: Melbourne University Press, Carlton, Vic. 3053; f. 1962; 3 times a year; Editor Dr. S. W. COHEN.

Australian Wildlife Research: C.S.I.R.O., 372 Albert St., East Melbourne, Vic. 3002; f. 1974; twice yearly; Editor-in-Chief B. J. WALBY.

The Australian Worker: 321 Pitt St., Sydney, N.S.W.; f. 1891; monthly; published by D. F. AUSTIN; circ. 105,000.

Commerce, Industrial and Mining Review: Invicta Publications, Box 142, Bentley, W.A. 6102; quarterly; Man. M. J. MURPHY.

Economic Record: Economics Dept., University of Melbourne, Parkville, Melbourne, Vic. 3052; f. 1925; four times a year; journal of Economic Society of Australia and New Zealand; Joint Editors Prof. S. J. TURNOVSKY, Prof. L. R. WEBB.

Electronics Australia: P.O.B. 163, Beaconsfield, N.S.W. 2014; f. 1939; technical, radio, television, hi-fi and electronics; monthly; Editor-in-Chief W. N. WILLIAMS; Editor J. ROWE.

Historical Studies: Department of History, University of Melbourne, Parkville, Victoria 3052; f. 1940; twice yearly, April and October; Editor N. D. MCLACHLAN.

Journal of Pacific History: Australian National University, P.O.B. 4, Canberra, A.C.T. 2600; f. 1966; bi-annual; Editors W. N. GUNSON, D. A. SCARR.

Manufacturers' Monthly: 74 Clarence St., Sydney 2000; f. 1961; circ. 11,440.

Meanjin Quarterly: University of Melbourne, Parkville, Melbourne, Victoria 3052; f. 1940; quarterly; literature, art, discussion; Editor J. H. DAVIDSON.

The Methodist: 139 Castlereagh St., Sydney, N.S.W.; published by the Methodist Church in N.S.W.; monthly on Sat.; Editor Mrs. KATH WHITBY; circ. 25,500.

Modern Motor: 15 Boundary St., Rushcutters Bay, N.S.W.; f. 1954; monthly; Editor JOHN CRAWFORD; circ. 79,000.

New Horizons in Education: c/o Dept. of Education, University of Sydney, Sydney, N.S.W. 2006; f. 1938; published twice a year by the World Education Fellowship; Editors K. D. WATSON, G. WILLIAMS.

Oceania: The University of Sydney, Sydney, N.S.W. 2006; f. 1930; social anthropology; quarterly; Editor A. P. ELKIN.

Open Road: 151 Clarence St., Sydney; f. 1927; official journal of National Roads and Motorists' Assn. (N.R.M.A.); every second month; Editor B. GIULIANO; circ. 994,280.

Overland: G.P.O. Box 98a, Melbourne, Victoria 3001; f. 1954; literary; Editor S. MURRAY-SMITH.

Pacific Islands Monthly: 29 Alberta St., Sydney, N.S.W. 2000; f. 1930; specialist journal dealing with current affairs in the South Seas; Editor and Publisher STUART INDER; Man. J. G. BERRY.

Progress: 31 Hardware St., Melbourne, Vic. 3000; economics; monthly; Editors A. R. HUTCHINSON, G. A. FORSTER.

Queensland Countrywoman: 89–95 Gregory Terrace, Brisbane; f. 1929; monthly journal of the Queensland Country Women's Association; Editor Mrs. G. J. PENNYCUICK.

Queensland Geographical Journal: 177–179 Ann St., Brisbane, Queensland; annual of The Royal Geographical Society of Australia, Queensland, Inc.; Sec. J. H. GRIFFITHS, J.P., F.R.G.S.A.

Search-Science Technology and Society: Science House, 157 Gloucester St., Sydney 2000; f. 1970; journal of Australian and N.Z. Association for the Advancement of Science; monthly; Hon. Editor J. B. DAVENPORT; Sec. Exec. Editor E.F.F. WHEELER; circ. 4,300.

South Pacific Bulletin (*Bulletin du Pacifique du Sud*): South Pacific Commission Publications Bureau, 720 George St., Sydney, N.S.W. 2000; f. 1951; quarterly in English and French; official journal of the South Pacific Commission; Editor C. E. BIRCHMEIER.

Walkabout: Sungravure Pty. Ltd., Box 164, Beaconsfield, N.S.W. 2014; f. 1934; monthly; magazine of Australian way of life; published on behalf of Australian National Travel Association; Editor-in-Chief K. FINLAY; circ. 38,000.

World Review: University of Queensland Press, P.O.B. 42, Brisbane University, St. Lucia, Qld. 4067; f. 1962; three times a year; published under the auspices of the Australian Institute of International Affairs, Queensland; Editor DENIS WRIGHT.

Your Garden: 61 Flinders Lane, Melbourne, 3000; monthly; Editor N. MOODY; circ. 87,554.

PRESS AGENCIES

Australian Associated Press: 291 George St., Sydney; f. 1935; owned by principal daily newspapers of Australia; Chair. E. J. L. TURNBULL; Joint Man. Dirs. A. H. MCLACHLAN and E. J. L. TURNBULL; Gen. Man. D. P. HOOPER.

Australian United Press Ltd.: 44 Flinders St., Melbourne 3000; f. 1928; Chair. A. F. JENKINS.

FOREIGN BUREAUX

The following foreign bureaux are represented in Sydney: ANSA, Associated Press, DPA, Jiji Press, New Zealand Press Association, Reuters, Tass and UPI. Antara Indonesian News Agency is represented in Canberra; Kyodo News Service is represented in Melbourne.

PRESS ASSOCIATIONS

Australian Journalists Association: 36 Chalmers St., Sydney, N.S.W. 2000; f. 1910; 8,000 mems.; Gen. Sec. S. P. CROSLAND; publ. *The Journalist*; circ. 7,500.

Australian Newspapers Council: 44 Pitt St., Sydney; f. 1958; membership 13, confined to metropolitan daily or Sunday papers; Pres. B. A. WILLIAMS; Sec. B. G. OSBORNE.

Australian Provincial Press Association: 33 Rathdowne St., Carlton 3053, Vic.; f. 1906; Pres. B. A. KAESEHAGEN; Sec. K. B. LAURIE.

New South Wales Country Press Association: Newspaper House, 44 Pitt Street, Sydney; f. 1900; 117 mems.; Sec. COLIN C. JENKINS.

Provincial Press Association of South Australia Incorporated: 130 Franklin St., Adelaide; f. 1912; represents South Australian country newspapers; Pres. D. TAYLOR; Sec. M.R. TOWNSEND.

Queensland Country Press Association: 307 Queen St., Brisbane; Pres. M. EASTWOOD; Sec. A. D. MORRIS.

Regional Dailies of Australia Ltd.: 247 Collins St., Melbourne 3000; f. 1936; Chair. C. M. MANNING; Chief Exec. Officer R. W. SINCLAIR.

Tasmanian Press Association Pty. Ltd.: 71–75 Paterson St., Launceston; Sec. B. J. MCKENDRICK.

Victorian Country Press Association Ltd.: 33 Rathdowne St., Carlton 3053, Vic.; f. 1910; Pres. F. V. GANNON; Exec. Dir. K. B. LAURIE; 115 mems.

Western Australian Provincial Press Association: 97 Colin St., West Perth 6005; Sec. J. F. OCKERBY.

PUBLISHERS

The following is a list of the principal book publishers.

Addison-Wesley Publishing Co.: 31 Albany St., Crows Nest, N.S.W. 2065; educational, scientific, technical, juvenile; Gen. Man. W. DOUGLAS.

Angus and Robertson Publishers: 102 Glover St., Cremorne Junction, N.S.W. 2090; f. 1884; fiction, general and children's; Dir. RICHARD WALSH.

Edward Arnold (Australia) Pty. Ltd.: 373 Bay St., Port Melbourne, Victoria 3207; all categories; Dirs. W. B. M. HUNTER, B. BENNETT, B. FORDHAM.

Australasian Medical Publishing Co. Ltd.: 71–79 Arundel St., Glebe, N.S.W. 2037; f. 1913; scientific, medical and educational; Man. JAMES G. ASTLES.

Australasian Publishing Co. Pty.: Corner of Bridge Rd. and Jersey St., Hornsby, N.S.W. 2077; f. 1937; Man. A. S. M. HARRAP; fiction, educational; children's books, general.

Australia and New Zealand Book Co. Pty. Ltd.: 23 Cross St., Brookvale, N.S.W. 2100; general non-fiction, technical, scientific; Exec. Chair. GEOFFREY M. KING.

Australian Government Publishing Service: 109 Canberra Ave., Griffith, A.C.T. 2603; Publishing Dir. B. P. SHURMAN.

Australian National University Press: P.O.B. 4, Canberra, A.C.T. 2600; f. 1966; scholarly; publishes 30–40 new books annually; Acting Dir. Miss P. CROFT.

S. John Bacon Pty. Ltd.: 12–13 Windsor Ave., Mount Waverley, Melbourne, Vic. 3149; f. 1938; theology and Christian education, educational; Man. Dir. J. F. BACON; Man. R. M. LOGAN.

B. T. Batsford (Australia) Pty. Ltd.: 23 Cross St., Brookvale, N.S.W. 2100; general, leisure, travel, art and crafts, textbooks; Dir. JOHN R. FERGUSON.

Butterworths Pty. Ltd.: 586 Pacific Highway, Chatswood, N.S.W. 2067; f. 1912; law, medical, scientific and accountancy publications; Chair. K. E. WELDON; Man. Dir. P. CHEESEMAN.

Cambridge University Press (Australia) Pty. Ltd.: 296 Beaconsfield Parade, Middle Park, Vic. 3206; scholarly and educational; Chair. G. O'D. CROWTHER; Man. Dir. BRIAN W. HARRIS.

Cassell Australia Ltd.: 31 Bridge Rd., Stanmore, N.S.W. 2048; f. 1963; educational and general; Gen. Man. W. J. MACKARELL.

Cheshire Publishing Pty. Ltd.: 346 St. Kilda Rd., Melbourne 3004; also in Sydney, Brisbane and Adelaide; educational at all levels; information and reference; Man. Dir. B. J. RIVERS; Man. Editor F. CHURCH.

Collins, Wm., Publishers Pty. Ltd.: 36 Clarence St., Sydney, N.S.W. 2000; offices in Melbourne, Brisbane and Hackney, South Australia; regd. in Australia 1946; fiction, non-fiction, religious, Bibles, children's, reference, paperbacks; Man. Dir. K. W. WILDER.

Currawong Publishing Co. Pty. Ltd.: P.O.B. 222, Sydney 2001; f. 1940; general, mainly non-fiction; Dirs. K. P. MOSS, P. A. CULLEN.

Encyclopaedia Britannica (Australia) Inc.: 300 Castlereagh St., Sydney, N.S.W. 2000; reference, education, art, science and commerce; Man. Dir. J. D. BATES.

Georgian House Pty. Ltd.: 296 Beaconsfield Parade, Middle Park, Melbourne; f. 1943; general, including educational; Man. Dir. B. W. HARRIS.

Golden Press Pty. Ltd.: 2–12 Tennyson Rd., Gladesville, Sydney, N.S.W. 2111; children's, general non-fiction, education; Gen. Man. H. RICHARDSON.

Granada Publishing Australia Pty. Ltd.: 117 York St., Sydney, N.S.W. 2000; general; Man. Dir. M. L. JOHNSON.

Hamlyn Books Pty. Ltd.: South Creek Rd., Dee Why West, N.S.W. 2099; reference, non-fiction, practical, children's; Man. Dir. PETER MCGILL.

Harcourt Brace Jovanovich Group (Australia) Pty. Ltd.: 40 Whiting St., Artarmon, N.S.W. 2064; educational, technical, scientific, medical; Man. Dir. ANTHONY CRAVEN.

The Hawthorn Press Pty. Ltd.: 601 Little Bourke St., Melbourne 3000; f. 1945; poetry, biography, history, reference, religion, secondary textbooks; Man. JOHN GARTNER.

Wm. Heinemann Australia Pty. Ltd.: 60 Inkerman St., St. Kilda, Vic. 3182; f. 1948; Australian history, biography and travel, fiction and general; Man. Dir. JOHN BURCHALL.

Heinemann Educational Australia Pty. Ltd.: 24 River St., South Yarra, Vic. 3141; Chair. ALAN HILL, C.B.E.; Man. Dir. NICHOLAS HUDSON.

Hicks Smith and Sons Pty. Ltd.: 301 Kent St., Sydney, N.S.W. 2000; educational and general; Dir. G. W. WALLIS-SMITH.

Hodder and Stoughton (Australia) Pty. Ltd.: Corner of Bridge Rd., and Jersey St., Hornsby, N.S.W. 2077; offices in Melbourne, Brisbane and Doubleview, Western Australia; fiction, general, educational, technical, children's; Man. Dir. E. COFFEY.

Horwitz Group Books Pty. Ltd.: 506 Miller St., Cammeray, N.S.W. 2062; fiction, reference, educational, Australiana, general; imprints: *Horwitz Publications*, *Martin Educational*; Man. Dir. L. J. MOORE; Deputy Man. Dir. and Financial Dir. M. C. PHILLIPS.

Hutchinson Group (Australia) Pty. Ltd.: 30–32 Cremorne St., Richmond, Victoria 3121; Man. Dir. PETER M. TAYLOR.

Jacaranda Press Pty. Ltd.: 65 Park Rd., Milton, Queensland 4064; general, educational, technical and cartographic; Man. Dir. JOHN COLLINS.

Lansdowne Press Pty. Ltd.: 37 Little Bourke St., Melbourne 3000; f. 1960; general books; Man. Dir. PETER MCGILL; Man. JOHN CURTAIN.

The Law Book Company Ltd.: 301 Kent St., Sydney; f. 1869; legal and commercial textbooks, legal reports and journals; Chair. and Man. Dir. D. W. POTTER.

Longman Australia Pty. Ltd.: 427 Riversdale Rd., Hawthorn East, Victoria 3123; f. 1947; mainly educational; Man. Dir. W. P. KERR.

Lothian Publishing Co. Pty. Ltd.: 4-12 Tattersalls Lane, Melbourne, 3000; f. 1905; Dirs. LOUIS A. LOTHIAN, K. A. LOTHIAN, L. N. JUPP; general, practical, educational.

McGraw-Hill Book Co. Australia Pty. Ltd.: 4 Barcoo St., Roseville E., Sydney, N.S.W. 2064; general; Dir. D. J. HINTON.

Macmillan Company of Australia Pty. Ltd.: 107 Moray St., South Melbourne; f. 1967; general and educational; Man. Dir. BRIAN STONIER.

Melbourne University Press: 932 Swanston St., Carlton, Vic. 3053; f. 1923; academic, educational, Australiana, general (all fields except fiction and children's); Chair. Prof. A. G. AUSTIN; Dir. P. A. RYAN.

Thomas Nelson (Australia) Ltd.: 19-39 Jeffcott St., West Melbourne, Vic. 3003; all categories; Man. Dir. A. KNIGHT.

New South Wales University Press Ltd.: P.O.B. 1, Kensington, N.S.W. 2033; general, especially educational; Gen. Man. DOUGLAS HOWIE.

Outback Press Pty. Ltd.: 40 Gore St., Fitzroy, Vic. 3065; fiction, non-fiction, children's; Dir. ALFRED MILGROM.

Oxford University Press: 7 Bowen Crescent, Melbourne 3004; f. 1908; general, including fiction; Dir. D. C. CUNNINGHAM.

Penguin Books Australia Ltd.: 487/493 Maroondah Highway, Ringwood, Vic. 3134; general paperbacks; Man. Dir. J. W. MICHIE; Chief Editor J. HOOKER.

Pergamon Press (Australia) Pty. Ltd.: 19a Boundary St., Rushcutters Bay, N.S.W. 2011; educational, general, scientific; Chair. I. R. MAXWELL, M.C.; Deputy Chair. R. MCLEOD; Dir. Dr. ANDREW FABINYI, O.B.E.

Pitman Publishing Pty. Ltd.: 158 Bouverie St., Carlton, Vic. 3053; f. 1968; secretarial and management sciences, art, photographic, educational, technical, general; Chair. Sir GEORGE PATON; Man. Dir. PHILIP J. HARRIS.

Prentice-Hall of Australia Pty. Ltd.: P.O.B. 151, Brookvale, N.S.W. 2100; textbooks, popular trade books, reference; Man. Dir. P. F. GLEESON.

Reed (A. H., and A. W.) Pty. Ltd.: 53 Myoora Rd., Terrey Hills, Sydney, N.S.W. 2084; Head Office, Wellington, N.Z.; f. 1907; books on Australia and New Zealand, educational, general; Chair. J. H. RICHARDS; Man. Dir. (Australia) J. M. REED.

Rigby Ltd.: 30 North Terrace, Kent Town, S.A. 5067; f. 1859; general and educational; Chair. Sir DONALD BRADMAN; Man. Dir. J. L. TAINTON.

Rydge Publications Pty. Ltd.: 74 Clarence St., Sydney 2000; f. 1928; Man. Dir. NORMAN B. RYDGE Jr.; Chief Exec. T. J. STOREY.

Science Research Associates Pty. Ltd.: 82-84 Waterloo Rd., North Ryde, N.S.W. 2113; educational; Chair. and Man. Dir. C. R. CARNACHAN.

Sydney University Press: Press Building, University of Sydney, Sydney, N.S.W. 2006; f.1 964; scholarly, academic and educational books and journals; Dir. MALCOLM TITT.

Thames and Hudson (Australia) Pty. Ltd.: 86 Stanley St. West Melbourne, Vic. 3003; art and general; Gen. Man. H. LONGMUIR.

Transworld Publishers (Aust.) Pty. Ltd.: 380 Lonsdale St., Melbourne, Vic. 3000; general, fiction, juvenile, education.

University of Queensland Press: P.O.B. 42, St. Lucia 4067, Queensland; f. 1948; scholarly and general cultural interest; microfilm, audio-visual programmes; Man. FRANK W. THOMPSON; Senior Editor ANN LAHEY.

University of Western Australia Press: Nedlands, W.A. 6009; f. 1954; educational, secondary and university, technical and scientific, scholarly, humanities; Man. V. S. GREAVES.

Ure Smith Pty. Ltd.: 176 South Creek Rd., Dee Why West, Sydney, N.S.W. 2099; f. 1930; general; a division of Books for Pleasure Pty. Ltd.; Gen. Man. M. C. N. HENRY.

Wiley, John, and Sons Australasia Pty. Ltd.: 1-7 Waterloo Rd. North Ryde, N.S.W. 2113; technical, scientific, educational; Man. Dir. P. SEARLE.

Wren Publishing Pty. Ltd.: 2 Palmer St., South Melbourne, Vic. 3205; general and educational; Man. Dir. DENNIS WREN.

PUBLISHERS' ASSOCIATION

Australian Book Publishers Association: 163 Clarence St., Sydney, N.S.W. 2000; f. 1949; about 100 mems.; Pres. JOHN MICHIE; Dir. G. A. FERGUSON, C.B.E.

RADIO AND TELEVISION

Australian Broadcasting Control Board: 570 Bourke St., Melbourne; f. 1949; Chair. M. F. E. WRIGHT; Vice-Chair. J. E. NEARY, O.B.E.; W. L. C. DAVIES (member), E. N. WILLIAMS, M.B.E., M. J. SOUTER (part-time members); B. J. CONNOLLY (Sec.).

The Australian Broadcasting Control Board is responsible for planning the provision, and ensuring acceptable technical standards, of both commercial and national broadcasting and television stations and for the programme standards of the commercial broadcasting and television stations.

Australian Broadcasting Commission: 145–153 Elizabeth St., P.O.B. 487, Sydney, N.S.W. 2001; Chair. Sir HENRY BLANDE; Vice-Chair. Dr. E. HACKETT; Gen. Man. T. S. DUCKMANTON, C.B.E.

The programmes for the national broadcasting and national television services are provided by the state-owned and non-commercial Australian Broadcasting Commission. All studio technical services are manned by the A.B.C.; transmitting stations in both broadcasting and television are manned by the Postmaster-General's Department staff. Radio: 86 medium-wave stations, fons FM, six domestic and one overseas (Radio Australia) short-wave stations. Television: one national network of six metropolitan channels with 77 regional transmitters and 54 translators.

The A.B.C. maintains membership of the Asian Broadcasting Union, the Commonwealth Broadcasting Association and the British Commonwealth Newsfilm Agency (Visnews). The A.B.C. is also an Associate Member of the European Broadcasting Union.

RADIO

Federation of Australian Commercial Broadcasters: P.O.B. 294, Milsons Point, Sydney, N.S.W. 2061; Federal Dir. D. L. FOSTER; Federal Sec. J. H. FINLAYSON.

The commercial services are provided by stations operated by companies and individuals under licences granted and renewed by the Minister for the Media. They rely for their income on the broadcasting of advertisements and the publicity. On June 30th, 1974, there were 118 commercial broadcasting stations in operation.

MAJOR COMMERCIAL BROADCASTING STATION LICENSEES

Adelaide Central Methodist Mission, Inc.: 43 Franklin St., Adelaide, S.A.; operates stations in Adelaide, Port Augusta, Whyalla and Berri.

Advertiser Broadcasting Network: 121 King William St., Adelaide; operates station 5A.D. in Adelaide and regional stations 5P.I. and 5S.E. in other parts of the State.

Amalgamated Wireless (Australasia) Ltd.: 47 York St., Sydney; operates stations at Sydney, Grafton, Goulburn, Albury, Bendigo, Townsville, Cairns and Launceston; Chair. Sir LIONEL HOOKE; Man. Dir. J. A. L. HOOKE.

Associated Broadcasting Services Ltd.: 290 La Trobe St., Melbourne 3000; f. 1957; operates stations at Shepparton, Warragul and Warrnambool; Chair. SIDNEY J. A. KEMP; Gen. Man. R. W. ELLENBY.

Commonwealth Broadcasting Corporation Pty. Ltd.: 365 Kent Street, Sydney; operating station 2UW, Sydney, key station of Commonwealth Broadcasting Network; stations at Brisbane, Toowoomba, Rockhampton and Maryborough.

Consolidated Broadcasting System (W.A.) Pty. Ltd.: 283 Rokeby Rd., Subiaco, W.A.; operates stations 6GE Geraldton, 6KG Kalgoorlie, 6AM Northam and 6PM Perth; Man. DES MCDONALD.

Findlays Broadcasting Services Pty. Ltd.: 28A Erina St., P.O.B. 665G, Launceston, Tasmania; operates Tasmanian Broadcasting Network radio stations 7BU-7AD-7SD, N. Tasmania, Australia.

The Herald and Weekly Times Ltd.: 44–74 Flinders St., Melbourne 3000; operates television station HSV7 and radio station 3DB.

Radio Broadcasting Network of Queensland: 27 Wharf St., Brisbane, Qld.; operates stations at Longreach, Mount Isa, Darling Downs, Charleville and Greater Brisbane area.

Victorian Broadcasting Network Ltd.: "The Age" Chambers, 239 Collins St., Melbourne, Vic.; operates stations at Hamilton, Maryborough, Sale and Swan Hill.

2 TM Management Pty. Ltd.: Radio Centre, Calala, Tamworth, N.S.W.; controls stations 2 TM Tamworth, and 2 MO Gunnedah and operates 2AD Armidale and 2RE Taree through the New England network.

TELEVISION

Federation of Australian Commercial Television Stations: 167 Kent St., Sydney, N.S.W. 2000.

The commercial television service is provided by stations operated by companies under licences granted and renewed by the Postmaster-General. There were on June 30th, 1975, 48 commercial television stations in operation. Colour services came into operation in most areas in March 1975.

Principal Commercial Television Station Licensees

Amalgamated Television Services Pty. Ltd.: T.V. Centre, Epping, N.S.W.; operates one station at Sydney, ATN7; f. 1956; Gen. Man. E. F. Thomas.

Austarama Television Pty. Ltd.: cnr. Springvale and Hawthorn Rds., Nunawading, Vic. 3131; operates station ATV-O at Melbourne.

Ballarat and Western Victoria Television Ltd.: Box 464, Ballarat; f. 1962; operates BTV Channel 6, and translators Channel 9 (Warrnambool), Channel 11 (Portland) and Channel 7 (Nhill); Chair. A. C. Pittard; Gen. Man. J. L. Stapp.

Brisbane TV Ltd.: Box 604J, G.P.O., Brisbane; started full-scale telecasting 1959, from station BTQ; Man. Murray Norris.

Broken Hill Television Ltd.: P.O.B. 472, Broken Hill, N.S.W. 2880; Chair. P. Martin; Man. Dir. J. M. Sturrock; Station Man. K. R. Boucher.

Canberra Television Ltd.: P.O.B. 21, Watson, A.C.T. 2602; f. 1962; Gen. Man. G. K. Barlin.

Country Television Services Ltd.: Radio and T.V. Centre, Bathurst Rd., Orange, N.S.W.; f. 1962; operates country stations CBN-8, CWN-6, 2GZ Orange and 2NZ Inverell; Gen. Man. E. Yelf.

Darling Downs TV Ltd.: Mt. Lofty, Toowoomba, Qld.; f. 1962; operates country stations DDQ-10, SDQ-4 and Channel 5, Toowoomba; Gen. Man. L. R. Burrows.

Far Northern Television Ltd.: 101 Aumuller St., Cairns, Qld.; f. 1966 to operate station FNQ; Chair. C. K. Carmody.

General Television Corporation Pty. Ltd.: 22–46 Bendigo St., P.O.B. 100, Richmond, Vic. 3121; f. 1957; operates station GVT-9 at Melbourne; Gen. Man. D. J. Evans.

Goulburn-Murray Television Ltd.: 290 La Trobe Street, Melbourne; f. 1961; operates country station GMV-6, Shepparton; Chair. Sidney J. A. Kemp; Gen. Man. Peter L. Twomey.

Herald-Sun TV Pty. Ltd.: 44–47 Flinders St., Melbourne 3000; f. 1956; operates station HSV-7 in Melbourne; parent company, The Herald and Weekly Times Ltd.; Chair. R. H. Sampson; Gen. Man. R. P. Casey.

Mackay Television Ltd.: Box 496 P.O. Mackay, Qld.; f. 1965; operation of station MVQ6 commenced August 1968; Gen. Man. R. J. H. Scott.

Murrumbidgee Television Ltd.: Remembrance Driveway, Griffith, N.S.W. 2680; f. 1965 to operate station MTN; Gen. Man. W. R. Gamble.

Newcastle Broadcasting and Television Corporation Ltd.: Mosbri Crescent, Newcastle, N.S.W.; f. 1962; operates country station NBN-3; Chair. Lawford Richardson; Gen. Man. K. W. Stone.

Northern Rivers Television Ltd.: Pacific Highway, Coff's Harbour, N.S.W.; operates stations NRN-11 and RTN-8.

Northern Television (TNT9) Pty. Ltd.: Watchorn St., Launceston, Tas.; f. 1962; operates Tasmanian country station TNT-9.

Queensland Television Ltd.: Box 72, G.P.O., Brisbane, Qld.; f. 1958; started operating station QTQ-9 in Brisbane 1959; Gen. Man. J. W. McKay.

Riverina and North East Victoria TV Ltd.: Television Centre, Lake Albert Rd., Wagga Wagga, N.S.W. 2650; f. 1964; operates country stations RVN-2 and AMV-4.

Rockhampton Television Ltd.: Dean Street, Rockhampton, Qld.; f. 1963; operates country station RTQ-7; Gen. Man. B. Saunders.

South Australian Telecasters Ltd.: Adelaide; f. 1965; operates a commercial TV station in Adelaide.

South East Telecasters Ltd.: P.O.B. 821, Mount Gambier; f. 1962; operates country station SES-8; Chair. G. T. Barnfield; Gen. Man. A. B. Noblet.

South Western Telecasters Ltd.: P.O.B. 112, Bunbury, W.A. 6230; f. 1967 to operate country stations BTW-3 and GSW-9; Man. B. F. Hopwood.

Southern Television Corporation Ltd.: 202 Tynte St., North Adelaide; f. 1958; station NWS-9 at Adelaide; Gen. Man. Rex Heading.

Spencer Gulf Telecasters Ltd.: P.O.B. 305, Port Pirie, S.A 5540; f. 1968; stations GTS-4, 5 and 8; Man. E. L. Downing.

Sunraysia Television Ltd.: P.O.B. 1157, Mildura, Vic.; f. 1965 to operate country station STV-8; Chair. C. D Lanyon; Gen. Man. B. McLean.

Swan Television Ltd.: Hayes Ave., Tuart Hill, W.A. 6060; f. 1965; operates station STW-9 in Perth; Man. Dir. L. J. Kiernan.

Tasmanian Television Limited: 52 New Town Rd., Hobart; f. 1959; started operating TVT-6 at Hobart, May 1960; Man. Dir. E. G. McRae; Gen. Man. D. L. Carter.

Telecasters North Queensland Ltd.: S.G.I.O. Bldg., Lower Denham St., P.O.B. 1016, Townsville, Qld. 4810; f. 1962; operates country station TNQ-7.

Television Corporation Limited: 168–174 Castlereagh Street, Sydney, N.S.W.; f. 1956; operates station TCN-9 at Sydney; majority shareholding in GTV channel 9 at Melbourne; Gen. Man. (TCN) G. C. Chapman; Man. Dir. L. A. Mauger; Chair. R. C. Packer.

Television New England Ltd.: P.O.B. 317, Tamworth, N.S.W.; f. 1965; operates stations NEN-9 and ECN-8; Chair. H. Joseph; Gen. Man. M. M. Moroney.

Television Wollongong Transmissions Ltd.: Fort Drummond, Mount St. Thomas, Wollongong, N.S.W.; f. 1962; operates station WIN-4, Channels 3 (Wollongong) 6 (Bega), 11 (Moruya), Gen. Man. W. Lean.

TV Broadcasters Ltd.: 125 Strangways Terrace, North Adelaide, S.A. 5006; f. 1958; station ADS-7 at Adelaide; Gen. Man. J. M. Fowler; Film Programme Man. I. Woodward; Executive Producer S. Pippos; News Edi or C. Wood; Chief Engineer N. Sawyer.

TVW Limited: P.O.B. 77, Tuart Hill, W.A. 6060; commercial stations TVW-7 at Perth and SAS-10 at Adelaide, started operations 1959; Man. Dir. J. W. Cruthers.

United Telecasters Sydney Ltd.: P.O.B. 10, Lane Cove, Sydney 2066; operates station TEN, Sydney; Gen. Man. I. G. Holmes.

Universal Telecasters Qld. Ltd.: Box 751, G.P.O., Brisbane 4001; f. 1965; operating TVQ, Channel O; Gen. Man. R. G. Archer.

Victorian Broadcasting Network Ltd.: P.O.B. 240, Lily St., Bendigo, Vic.; f. 1961; operates country stations BCV-8, Bendigo, BCV-11 Swan Hill, and GLV-10, Gippsland, on relay; relays programme to STV-8, Mildura; Exec. Dir. F. A. McManus.

V.B.N. Ltd.: Prince's Highway, Traralgon, Vic.; f. 1962; operates country station GLV-10.

Wide Bay-Burnett TV Ltd.: Granville, Maryborough, Qld.; f. 1965; operates station WBQ-8, Channel 1, Sunshine Coast; Gen. Man. Muir Daniel.

FINANCE

BANKING

cap. = capital; p.u. = paid up; dep. = deposits; m. = million) ($A = $ Australian)

Central Bank

Reserve Bank of Australia: 65 Martin Place, Sydney, N.S.W. 2000; f. 1911; sole bank of issue for Australia and Territories; has separate dept. for commodity marketing finance; cap. $A49.4m.; res. funds $A18.8m.; dep. and other accounts $A2,904.5m. (June 1975); Gov. H. M. Knight; Deputy Gov. D. N. Sanders.

Commonwealth Banks

Commonwealth Banking Corporation: G.P.O. Box 2719, Pitt St., and Martin Place, Sydney, N.S.W. 2000; f. 1960; Government-run controlling body for three member banks: Commonwealth Trading Bank, Commonwealth Savings Bank and Commonwealth Development Bank (*below*); Chair. Prof. L. F. Crisp; Man. Dir. R. S. Elliott.

Commonwealth Trading Bank of Australia: Pitt St. and Martin Place, Sydney 2000; est. 1953 to take over business of General Banking Division of Commonwealth Bank of Australia; cap. $A14.8m.; dep. $A3,128m. (June 1975); Gen. Man. J. F. Lavan.

Commonwealth Savings Bank of Australia: Pitt St. and Martin Place, Sydney, N.S.W. 2000; est. 1912; dep. $A4,848m. (June 1975); Gen. Man. I. R. Norman, M.B.E.

Commonwealth Development Bank of Australia: Prudential Bldg., 39 Martin Place, Sydney, N.S.W. 2000: f. 1960; loans and equipment finance outstanding $A339.9m. (June 1975); Gen. Man. Alwyn Richards.

Development Bank

Australian Resources Development Bank Ltd.: 379 Collins St., Melbourne, Victoria 3000; f. 1967 by major Australian trading banks with support of Reserve Bank of Australia to marshal funds from local and overseas sources for the financing of Australian participation in projects of national importance; cap. p.u. $A3m.; dep. $A295m. (Sept. 1974); Chair. T. B. C. Bell; Gen. Man. R. G. McCrossin.

Trading Banks

The Bank of Adelaide: 81 King William St., Adelaide, S. Australia; f. 1865; cap. p.u. $A31.505m.; dep. $A232.443m. (1975); Principal Offices in Adelaide, Sydney, Melbourne, Brisbane, Perth, Canberra and Hobart; Chair. Hon. Sir Arthur Rymill, M.L.C.; Joint Gen. Mans. L. R. Clifford, K. B. Wright.

Bank of New South Wales: 60 Martin Place, Sydney, N.S.W.; f. 1817; cap. p.u. $A107.47m.; dep. $A4,344.7m. (1974); Pres. Sir John Cadwallader; Chief Gen. Man. Sir Robert Norman.

Bank of Queensland Ltd.: 115 Queen St., Brisbane; f. 1874; cap. p.u. $A2.75m.; dep. $A33m. (1974); Chair. E. W. Savage; Gen. Man. A. N. Murrell.

Commercial Bank of Australia Ltd.: 335–339 Collins St., Melbourne, Vic.; f. 1866; cap. p.u. $A31.66m.; dep. $A2,249m. (June 1975); 800 brs. in Australia and New Zealand; Chair. Sir Thomas Webb; Man. Dir. D. W. Stride.

Commercial Banking Co. of Sydney Ltd.: 343 George St., Sydney, N.S.W.; f. 1834; cap. p.u. $A40.115m.; dep. $A2,350.728m. (1975); 540 brs.; Chair. Sir Gregory B. Kater; Man. Dir. G. F. Bowen.

National Bank of Australasia Ltd.: 271–285 Collins St., P.O.B. 84A, Melbourne, Vic. 3001; f. 1858; group cap. p.u. $A68.9m.; dep. $A3,430m. (Sept. 1974); Chair. Sir James Forrest; Group Gen. Man. T. C. B. Bell.

Rural and Industries Bank of Western Australia: 54–58 Barrack St., P.O.B. E 237, Perth, W.A. 6001; f. 1945; cap. $A22.2m.; dep. $A361.1m. (March 1975); Chair. C. E. Collins.

Rural Bank of New South Wales: 52–56 Martin Place, Sydney, N.S.W. 2000; 216 offices in N.S.W.; correspondent banks in eighteen countries; cap. $A19.74m.; res. $A67.0m.; dep. $A918.6m.; Pres. A. Oliver, C.M.G.; Sec. Brian Herbert.

State Bank of South Australia: 51 Pirie St., Adelaide, S. Australia; f. 1896; cap. $A197,236,155; dep. $A 78,824,038 net (June 1975); Chair. G. F. Seaman, C.M.G., B.EC., A.U.A., F.A.S.A.; Gen. Man. J. C. Taylor.

Savings Banks

Bank of New South Wales Savings Bank Ltd.: 60 Martin Place, Sydney; f. 1955; cap. p.u. $A14m.; dep. $A1,146m. (1971); Chair. Sir John Cadwallader; Chief Man. W. Twycross.

The Savings Bank of South Australia: King William St., Adelaide, S.A.; f. 1848; assets $A753.7m. (1975); 142 brs.; Chair. G. H. P. Jeffery; Gen. Man. A. G. Shepherd.

Savings Bank of Tasmania: Collins St., Hobart, Tasmania; f. 1845; Pres. H. A. Cuthbertson; Gen. Man. R. H. Taylor.

State Savings Bank of Victoria: 233 Collins St., Melbourne, Vic. 3000; f. 1842; dep. $A2,257.6m.; total resources $A2,510.5 (June 1975); 522 brs.; Chair. Prof. Donald Cochrane, C.B.E., PH.D., B.COM.; Gen. Man. D. Ross.

Foreign Banks

Australia and New Zealand Banking Group Ltd.: New Zealand Head Office: 196 Featherston St., Wellington; 300 brs. throughout Australia, New Zealand and the Pacific; Man. Dir. C. H. Rennie; Chief Gen. Man. M. Brunckhorst.

Bank of New Zealand: branches at Sydney and Melbourne; Dir. S. E. Wilson.

Banque Nationale de Paris: 12 Castlereagh St., Sydney; f. in Australia 1881; cap. 500m. FF.; dep. 93,000m. FF.; branches in Sydney, Melbourne, Perth, Brisbane; Gen. Man. L. Jalabert.

Barclays Australia Ltd.: 21st Floor, 1 Castlereagh St., G.P.O. Box 3357, Sydney, N.S.W. 2001; f. 1972; cap. £6m.; Chair. Sir David Griffin Gen. Man. Noel George Ellis; br. in Melbourne.

STOCK EXCHANGES

Australian Associated Stock Exchanges: 60 Martin Place, Sydney, N.S.W. 2000; f. 1937; mems. Stock Exchanges in the six capital cities; Exec. Dir. Ronald L. Coppel.

The Brisbane Stock Exchange: M.M.I. Bldg., 344 Queen St., Brisbane; f. 1885; 45 mems.; Chair. W. A. Park; Man. G. P. Chapman; Sec. D. G. Slater.

Hobart Stock Exchange: 86 Collins St., Hobart; f. 1891.

Stock Exchange of Adelaide Ltd.: 55 Exchange Place, Adelaide, S.A.; f. 1887; 60 mems.; Chair. T. N. Phillips; Gen. Man. S. E. Banks.

Stock Exchange of Melbourne Ltd.: 351 Collins St., Melbourne; f. 1859 (inc. 1970); 169 mems.; Chair. J. C. Johnston, c.b.e.; Gen. Man. R. B. Lee.

Stock Exchange of Perth Ltd.: Exchange House, 68 St. George's Terrace, Perth; f. 1889; 32 mems.; Chair. T. W. Hogan; Gen. Man. P. J. Unsworth.

Sydney Stock Exchange: 20 O'Connell St., Sydney; f. 1871; 144 mems.; Chair. J. H. Valder; Gen. Man. P. W. Marshman; publ. *Australian Stock Exchange Journal* (monthly).

PRINCIPAL INSURANCE COMPANIES

Aetna Life of Australia and New Zealand Ltd.: Head Office: 2 Help St., Chatswood, N.S.W. 2067; Man. Dir. J. H. Maxwell.

A.F.G. Insurances Ltd.: 277–287 William St., Melbourne 3000; f. 1922; fire, accident, marine; Chair. T. L. Webb; Gen. Man. Gordon Dobbs.

A.G.C. (Insurances) Ltd.: A.G.C. House, Philip and Hunter Sts., Sydney, N.S.W.; f. 1938; Chair. N. H. Routley, c.b.e.; Gen. Man. E. H. Wood.

Ajax Insurance Co. Ltd.: 105 Queen St., Melbourne, Vic.; f. 1934; Dir. E. F. Bunny (Chair.); Gen. Man. H. L. Williams.

AMEV Life Assurance Co. Ltd.: 15 O'Connell St., Sydney; f. 1958; Chair. A. J. de Montfort; Gen. Man. R. G. Glading.

A.M.P. Fire & General Insurance Co. Ltd.: A.M.P. Bldg., Sydney Cove, N.S.W. 2000; f. 1958; Chair. Sir Theo Kelly, o.b.e.; Man. Dir. J. K. Staveley.

The Australian Alliance Assurance Co.: 440 Collins St., Melbourne, Vic.; f. 1862; Man. Dir. R. A. Sinclair.

Australian Equitable Insurance Co. Ltd.: 4th Floor, 140 Arthur St., North Sydney, N.S.W. 2060; f. 1952; fire, marine, accident; Chair. Robert D. Somerville, ll.b.; Gen. Man. J. D. C. Wood.

Australian Mutual Fire Insurance Society Ltd.: 109 Pitt St., Sydney; Temple Court, 428 Collins St., Melbourne; Chair. A. L. Brend.

The Australian National Assurance Co. Ltd.: 408/410 Collins Street, Melbourne 3000; f. 1922; Managing Dir. D. G. Pettigrew.

Australian Natives' Association Insurance Co. Ltd.: 28–32 Elizabeth Street, Melbourne; f. 1948; fire, general; Chair. R. J. Joseph, o.b.e.; Man. Dir. L. D. Brooks.

Australian Reinsurance Co. Ltd.: 325 Collins St., Melbourne, Vic. 3000; f. 1962; reinsurance; Chair. R. S. Turner, c.b.e.; Gen. Man. J. H. Winter.

The Chamber of Manufactures Insurance Ltd.: 368-374 St. Kilda Rd., Melbourne 3004; f. 1914; Chair. E. R. Beattie; Gen. Man. G. P. Sutherland.

City Mutual General Insurance Ltd.: 66 Hunter St., Sydney; f. 1889; Chair. M. J. O'Neill; Gen. Man. R. J. Lawson.

City Mutual Life Assurance Society Ltd.: 60–66 Hunter St., Sydney, N.S.W.; f. 1878; Chair. Sir John O'Neill, c.b.e.; Gen. Man. P. C. Wickens, m.a., ll.m., f.i.a.

The Colonial Mutual Fire Insurance Co. Ltd.: 440 Collins St., Melbourne, Vic.; f. 1878; Chair. J. M. Baillieu; Dir. R. A. Sinclair.

The Colonial Mutual Life Assurance Society Ltd.: 330 Collins St., Melbourne, Vic. 3000; f. 1873; Chair. W. D. Brookes, c.b.e., d.s.o., a.e.a.; Gen. Man. J. L. Greig, f.a.s.a., f.i.c.s.

Commercial Union Assurance Co. of Australia Ltd.: Temple Court, 428 Collins Street, Melbourne; f. 1960; fire, accident, marine, life; Chair. Sir Edward Cohen; Gen. Man. A. L. Brend.

Co-operative Insurance Co. of Australia Ltd.: Fourth Floor, 500 Collins St., Melbourne, Vic. 3000; f. 1918; Gen. Man. G. F. Scarth.

Copenhagen Reinsurance Company (Aust.) Ltd.: 1 Castlereagh St., Sydney; f. 1961; reinsurance; Chair. F. M. D. Jackett; Man. D. F. Burke.

Equitable Life and General Insurance Co. Ltd.: Head Office: 80 Alfred St., Milsons Point; f. 1921; cap. p.u. $A590,000; Gen. Man. G. E. N. Rogers.

FAI Insurance Ltd.: FAI Insurance Bldg., 185 Macquarie St., Sydney 2000, f. 1960; Chair. L. J. Adler; Sec. R. L. Herman.

Farmers and Settlers' Co-operative Insurance Co. of Australia Ltd.: Pearl Assurance House, 1–7 Castlereagh St., Sydney, N.S.W.; f. 1914; Gen. Man. W. A. Wilson.

Government Insurance Office of N.S.W.: 60–70 Elizabeth St., Sydney, N.S.W.; Gen. Man. R. M. Porter, a.c.i.s., a.a.s.a., a.a.i.i.

Gre Insurance Ltd.: 604 St. Kilda Rd., Melbourne; fire, marine, accident; Gen. Man. K. Gilbert.

Manchester Unity Fire Insurance Co. of Victoria Ltd.: Cnr. Swanston and Collins Sts., Melbourne; fire, accident; Chair. R. E. Daymon; Sec. and Man. M. W. Campbell.

Manufacturers' Mutual Insurance Ltd.: 60–62 York St., Sydney, N.S.W. 2000; f. 1914; workers' compensation, fire, general accident, motor and marine; Chair. J. M. Burnett, c.b.e.; Gen. Man. F. T. Grose.

Mercantile & General Life Reassurance Co. of Australia Ltd.: Swire House, 8 Spring St., Sydney; f. 1957; life reassurance; Chair. G. B. Kater; Gen. Man. S. R. B. France.

Mercantile Mutual Insurance Co. Ltd.: 117 Pitt St., Sydney, N.S.W.; f. 1878; Chair. M. C. Davis; Man. Dir. W. M. Cowper.

Mercantile Mutual Life Insurance Co. Ltd.: 50 Hunter St., Sydney, N.S.W.; f. 1895; Chair. M. C. DAVIS; Gen. Man. A. E. M. GEDDES, B.A., B.COM., F.I.A., A.A.S.A.

M.L.C. Fire & General Insurance Co. Ltd.: Victoria Cross, North Sydney, N.S.W. 2060; f. 1958; Chair. G. W. E. BARRACLOUGH; Gen. Man. C. W. LEPAGE.

Mutual Life and Citizens' Assurance Co. Ltd.: P.O.B. 200, North Sydney 2060; f. 1886; Chair. B. J. D. PAGE, B.A., LL.B.; Gen. Man. M. H. ALLEN, B.A., LL.B.

National & General Insurance Co. Ltd.: 100 New South Head Rd., Edgecliff, N.S.W.; f. 1954; fire, marine, general; Chair. P. H. FINLEY, O.B.E., D.F.C.; Gen. Man. R. W. MANN.

National Co-operative Insurance Society Ltd.: 799–801 Hunter Street, Newcastle West, N.S.W.; f. 1947; fire, householders, motor car, accident; Chair. A. F. J. SMITH; Gen. Manager L. C. BOYD.

National Mutual Casualty Insurances Ltd.: 447 Collins St., Melbourne; f. 1961; accident, sickness; Chair. G. M. NIALL; Man. P. R. SHIPMAN.

National Mutual Fire Insurance Co. Ltd.: 447 Collins Street, Melbourne; f. 1957; fire, accident, marine; Chair. G. M. NIALL; Gen. Man. H. G. WALKER, B.C.E., F.I.A.; Man. K. N. FISK, A.A.I.I.

National Mutual Life Association of Australasia Ltd.: 447 Collins St., Melbourne, Vic.; f. 1869; Chair. G. M. NIALL; Gen. Man. R. L. BIENVENU, D.F.C., F.I.A.

New Zealand Victoria Life Ltd.: 79 Pitt St., Sydney, N.S.W.; Chair. A. G. WILSON, O.B.E.; Gen. Man. J. R. MARKLEY.

Northumberland Insurance Co. Ltd.: 52–58 Clarence St., Sydney, N.S.W.; f. 1955; fire, marine, accident; Chair. R. E. M. HUTCHESON; Gen. Man. T. G. WHITBREAD.

Phoenix Assurance Co. of Australia Ltd.: 414 Collins St., Melbourne; 32–34 Bridge St., Sydney; f. 1931; Chair. G. A. SAMUEL; Gen. Man. H. A. PARKER.

Phoenix Life Assurance Co. of Australia Ltd.: 32–34 Bridge St. Sydney; incorporated in New South Wales, 1968; Chair. L. E. TUTT, Jnr.; Gen. Man. H. A. PARKER.

QBE Insurance Group Limited: 82 Pitt St., Sydney; f. 1970; cap. p.u. $A11.8m.; Chair. J. F. R. LAWES; Gen. Man. R. R. M. MORGAN.

Regent Insurance Ltd.: 277–287 William St., Melbourne 3000; f. 1959; fire, general; Chair. H. F. STOKES; Chief Man. KEITH MCMORRON.

Reinsurance Co. of Australasia Ltd.: 1 York St., Sydney; f. 1961; reinsurance, fire, accident, marine; Chair. Sir JOHN MARKS, C.B.E.; Gen. Man. W. C. STEVENS.

Royal-Globe Life Assurance Co. Ltd.: 440 Collins Street, Melbourne; f. 1960; life; Chair. and Man. Dir. R. A. SINCLAIR.

South British United Life Assurance Co. Ltd.: Cnr. Hunter and O'Connell Sts., Sydney; f. 1921; Man. Dir. W. J. DOWD.

Southern Pacific Insurance Co. Ltd.: 80 Alfred St., Milsons Point, N.S.W. 2061; f. 1935; fire, accident, marine; Chair. C. H. V. CARPENTER; Chief Gen. Man. B. A. SELF.

Sun Alliance Insurance Ltd.: 22 Bridge St., Sydney 2000; office in Jakarta; fire, accident and marine insurance; Man. Dir. D. G. PETTIGREW.

Switzerland Life Assurance Society Ltd.: 457 Little Collins St., Melbourne, Vic. 3000; f. 1960; life. accident; Chair. and Man. Dir. W. W. PISTERMAN; Gen. Man. J. N. BAYLIS; Actuary and Gen. Sec. D. L. LOADER.

T & G Fire and General Insurance Co. Ltd.: Collins and Russell Sts., Melbourne; f. 1958; Chair. H. D. STEWART; Gen. Man. M. A. KEMP.

T and G Mutual Life Society Ltd.: Collins and Russell Sts., Melbourne, Vic.; f. 1876; Gen. Man. K. T. BLAMEY, O.B.E., E.D.

Underwriting & Insurance Ltd.: 578 St. Kilda Rd,. Melbourne 3004; f. 1930; life, fire, accident; Chair. H. V. NAPIER; Gen. Man. D. J. SLEE.

United Insurance Co. Ltd.: George and Hunter Streets, Sydney, N.S.W.; f. 1862; Chair. Sir JOHN DUNLOP; Gen. Man. J. O. LEWIS.

Unity Life Assurance Ltd.: 20 Bridge St., Sydney; f. 1959; Chair. BLAKE PELLY, O.B.E.; Gen. Man. A. BARNETT.

VACC Insurance Co. Ltd.: 464 St. Kilda Rd., Melbourne, Vic. 3004; f. 1930; Chair. J. C. E. VAN HERWERDEN; Gen. Man. A. C. STUBBS.

Vanguard Insurance Co. Ltd.: 127 Kent St., Sydney, N.S.W.; f. 1951; fire, marine, accident; Chair. Sir. P. SPENDER; Man. Dir. G. COMEL.

The Victory Reinsurance Co. of Australia Ltd.: 491-493 Bourke St., Melbourne; f. 1956; reinsurance, fire, accident, marine, life; Chair. Sir RUPERT CLARKE, Bt.; Sec. D. R. BIRD.

Western Australian Insurance Co. (Canberra) Ltd.: Head Office: 60–62 York St., Sydney, N.S.W.; workers' compensation, fire, general accident, motor and marine; Chair. J. M. BURNETT, C.B.E.; Man. Dir. F. T. GROSE.

ASSOCIATIONS

Australian Insurance Association: 11th Floor, 82 Pitt St., Sydney, N.S.W. 2000; f. 1968; Pres. PARIS CHAMBERS; Sec. I. J. FREW, B.E.C., A.A.S.A.

Australian Insurance Institute: 257 Collins St., Melbourne; f. 1919; Pres. I. M. GAMBLE, F.A.I.I., A.I.F.A., F.A.I.M.; Sec. K. M. LEE, B.COM., B.ED., M.A.C.E.; 36,974 mems.

Council of Fire and Accident Underwriters of Australia, Council of Marine Underwriters of the Commonwealth of Australia: 335–337 Flinders Lane, Melbourne, Vic. 3000; also 210 George St., Sydney, N.S.W. 2000.

The Institute of Actuaries of Australia and New Zealand Swire House, 8 Spring St., Sydney; f. 1897; Pres. J. G. RUTHERFORD F.I.A.; Sec. R. V. CAREY, M.A.; 575 mems.

The Life Offices' Association of Australia: 303 Collins St., Melbourne, Vic. 3000; Exec. Dir. N. E. RENTON.

TRADE AND INDUSTRY

CHAMBERS OF COMMERCE

International Chamber of Commerce: Suite 22, 26 O'Connell St., Sydney, N.S.W. 2001.

Australian Chamber of Commerce: Brisbane Ave., Barton A.C.T. 2600; f. 1901; Dir. R. PELHAM THORMAN, B.A. (Cantab.); membership includes Chambers of Commerce in Sydney, Melbourne, Canberra, Brisbane, Adelaide, Perth, Hobart, Newcastle, Darwin, Gove, Tamworth, Cairns, Ingham, and State Federations of Chambers of Commerce in N.S.W., Victoria, Queensland, South Australia, Western Australia and Tasmania.

Adelaide Chamber of Commerce: 54 Currie St., Adelaide, S.A.

Brisbane Chamber of Commerce Inc.: Qantas House, 288 Queen St., Brisbane, Qld.; f. 1868; Dir. C. ROBERTSON, F.C.I.S., F.A.S.A.; publ. *The Voice of Business.*

Chamber of Commerce and Industry, South Australia, Inc.: 12–18 Pirie St., Adelaide, S.A. 5000; 3,996 mems.; Gen. Man. C. W. BRANSON, B.EC., DIP.COMM., A.A.S.A., F.A.I.M., J.P.; publ. *Journal of Industry* (monthly).

Hobart Chamber of Commerce: 130 Collins St., Hobart, Tasmania; f. 1851; Dir. B. A. JENNINGS; publ. *Hobart Commerce.*

Launceston Chamber of Commerce: 57 George St., Launceston, Tasmania; f. 1849; Pres. J. T. SCOTT.

Melbourne Chamber of Commerce: 60 Market St., Melbourne, Vic. 3000; f. 1851; Exec. Dir. A. L. LOVELL.

Perth Chamber of Commerce (Inc.): 14 Parliament Place, West Perth, West Australia; f. 1890; 950 mems.; Dir. P. C. FIRKINS.

Sydney Chamber of Commerce Inc.: 161 Clarence St., Sydney, N.S.W.; f. 1826; Dir. D. COX.

AGRICULTURAL AND INDUSTRIAL ORGANIZATIONS

The Australian Agricultural Council: Dept. of Agriculture, Canberra, A.C.T.; f. 1934 to provide means for consultation between individual States and Commonwealth on agricultural production and marketing (excluding forestry and fisheries), to promote the welfare and standards of Australian agricultural industries and to foster the adoption of national policies in regard to these industries; 10 mems. comprising the 6 State Ministers for Agriculture and the Commonwealth Ministers for Agriculture and Northern Territory; Sec. G. C. POWER.

Standing Committee on Agriculture: f. 1927; associated as an advisory body with the Australian Agricultural Council additional functions are the co-ordination of agricultural research and of quarantine measures relating to pests and diseases of plants and animals; 13 mems. comprising the 6 State Directors of Agriculture and heads of Commonwealth Departments with a direct or indirect interest in agriculture; Chair. Dr. J. M. HARVEY (Dir.- Gen. Dept. of Primary Industries, Qld.); Sec. G. C. POWER.

There is also a Standing Committee on Soil Conservation associated with the Council.

Australian Dairy Corporation: Dairy Industry House, 576 St. Kilda Rd., Melbourne, Vic. 3004; promotes export of dairy produce; Chair. A. A. S. WEBSTER.

Australian Export Development Council: c/o Dept. of Trade and Industry, Canberra, A.C.T. 2600; advises the government on all aspects of export promotion and development; Chair. D. H. FREEMAN.

Australian Industry Development Corporation: 218 Northbourne Ave., Canberra, A.C.T. 2601; f. 1970; a Commonwealth Statutory Authority providing a wide range of financial facilities including loan and equity financing to promote the development of Australian manufacturing and mining industries, and supporting local participation in the ownership and control of industries and resources; brs. in Sydney and Melbourne; cap. p.u. $A50m.; Chair. Sir ALAN WESTERMAN, C.B.E.

Australian Meat Board: P.O.B. 4129, Sydney, N.S.W.; Chair. Col. M. MCARTHUR.

Australian Wheat Board: Ceres House, 528 Lonsdale St., Melbourne, Vic.; f. 1939; only internal wheat marketing authority; export wheat and flour; 14 mems.; Chair. J. P. CASS, O.B.E.; Gen. Man. L. H. DORMON, O.B.E.; publs. *Wheat Australia* (every 2 months), *Annual Report.*

Australian Wool Corporation: Wool House, 578 Bourke St., Melbourne, Vic. 3000; f. 1973; responsible for wool marketing, research and testing; board of 10 mems. (chairman, 4 wool growers, 4 from commerce, 1 Govt. mem.); Chair. A. C. B. MAIDEN, C.B.E.

Australian Wool Industry Conference: 447 Collins St., Melbourne, Vic. 3000; composed of 25 mems. each from the Australian Woolgrowers' and Graziers' Council and the Australian Wool and Meat Producers' Federation; participates in selection/nomination of Australian Wool Corporation members and advises Minister for Agriculture on financial and other aspects of wool research and marketing; Independent Chair. D. D. VON BIBRA, O.B.E.

Department of National Development: Tasman House 26–30 Farrell St., Canberra City, A.C.T. 2601; functions include the assessment and development of natural resources, mining and non-ferrous metallurgical industries; undertaking geological and geophysical surveys and investigations as well as geographical and resources mapping; Man. Dir. A. E. CREBBIN; Sec. L. F. BOTT, D.S.C.

Australian Minerals Council: Tasman House, 26–30 Farrell St., Canberra, A.C.T. 2601; functions include the progressive development of mining and minerals; Chair. Minister for National Development.

EMPLOYERS' ORGANIZATIONS

The Australian Council of Employers' Federations: 505 Little Collins St., Melbourne; f. 1903; comprises the employers' federation of States and Territories; Pres. D. A. NOAKES; Exec. Dir. G. POLITES.

Associated Newsagents' Co-op. Ltd.: 169 Bonds Rd., Punchbowl, N.S.W. 2196; Gen. Man. J. C. LAFOREST.

Australian Jewellers' Association: 21 Burwood Rd., Hawthorn, Vic.; f. 1906; 750 mems.; Sec. E. A. LEWIS.

Dairy Farmers Co-operative Ltd.: 700 Harris St., Ultimo, N.S.W. 2007; Sec. J. B. SHARPE.

Film Production Association of Australia: 3rd Floor, 129 York St., Sydney, N.S.W.; f. 1972; 50 mems.; Pres. R. PASCOE; Exec. Dir. G. E. FARRAR.

Graziers' Association of New South Wales: G.P.O. Box 1068, 56 Young St., Sydney 2000; f. 1890; publs. *Muster* (monthly), *The Pastoral Employment Guide.*

Master Builders' Association of New South Wales, The: P.O.B. 234, Newtown, N.S.W. 2042; f. 1873; 1,800 mems.; Exec. Dir. R. L. ROCHER; publ. *Builder N.S.W.* (monthly).

Meat and Allied Trades Federation of Australia: National Secretariat; Paul Bldgs., 33–35 Pitt St., Sydney 2000; f. 1928; Pres. T. J. JACKMAN, M.B.E.; Chief Exec. Officer E. W. HORTON.

Metal Trades Industry Association of Australia: 105 Walker St., North Sydney; National Pres. A. N. EDWARDS; Nat. Dir. and Chief Exec. R. G. FRY.

Metropolitan and Suburban Dairymen's Association: Old Windsor Rd., Parklea, N.S.W.; f. 1903; Pres. D. H. CROSBY; Acting Sec. I. S. JENKINS.

New South Wales Flour Millers' Council: Kindersley House, Box 2125 G.P.O., 20 O'Connell St., Sydney; Sec. H. K. BRAY.

Timber Trade Industrial Association: 155 Castlereagh St., Sydney 2000; f. 1940; 530 mems.; Sec./Man. H. J. MCCARTHY.

United Farmers' and Woolgrowers' Association of New South Wales: 32 York St., Sydney; f. 1962; 375 rural brs.; 24,000 mems.; direct representation on marketing boards, commodity cttees, education councils, etc.; provides co-operative buying facilities, special insurance rates, etc.; annual conference in July elects General Council of 40; Gen. Pres. R. H. BLACK; Gen. Sec. B. F. REGAN; publ. *United Farmer* (monthly); has own radio programme weekly.

MANUFACTURERS' ORGANIZATIONS

Australian British Trade Association: P.O.B. 141, Manuka, A.C.T. 2603; Dir. D.C. DOUGLAS, O.B.E., B.COM., A.A.S.A.

Associated Chambers of Manufactures of Australia: Industry House, Canberra; f. 1904; Dir.-Gen. W. J. HENDERSON; 21,000 mems.

Australian Industries Development Association: P.O.B. 1576, Canberra, A.C.T. 2601; Dir. W. CALLAGHAN.

Australian Manufacturers' Export Council: Industry House Canberra; f. 1955; Exec. Officer G. M. CARR.

Chamber of Commerce and Industry, South Australia Inc.: 12 Pirie St., Adelaide, S. Australia 5000; f. 1869; Gen. Man. C. W. BRANSON, B.EC., DIP.COMM., A.A.S.A. (Senior), F.A.I.M., J.P.; 4,000 mems.; publ. *Journal of Industry*.

Chamber of Manufactures of New South Wales: 60 York St., Sydney, N.S.W.; f. 1885; Dir. NOEL J. MASON.

Confederation of Western Australian Industry, Inc.: P.O.B. H515, Perth, W.A.; Dir. F. J. MALONE; Deputy Dir. J. R. COOKE.

Queensland Chamber of Manufactures: Manufacturers House, 375 Wickham Terrace, Brisbane, Qld. 4000; f. 1911; 1,500 mems.; Gen. Man. R. D. BLUCHER.

Tasmanian Chamber of Industries: Industry House, Cnr. Charles and Cameron Streets, Launceston, Tasmania; f. 1898; Exec. Dir. L. M. TROUNCE.

Tasmanian Chamber of Manufactures: Manufacturers' Bldg., Cnr. Charles and Cameron Streets, Launceston, Tasmania; f. 1898; (acting) Gen. Man. E. C. ILES.

The Victorian Chamber of Manufactures: Industry House, 370 St. Kilda Rd., Melbourne, Vic. 3004; f. 1877; 6,500 mems.; Dir. B. H. B. POWELL.

PRINCIPAL TRADE UNIONS

Australian Council of Trade Unions (A.C.T.U.): 254 La Trobe St., Melbourne, Vic.; f. 1927; Pres. R. J. HAWKE; Sec. H. J. SOUTER; the organization includes a branch in each State generally known as a Trades and Labour Council; over 150 Trade Unions are affiliated to the A.C.T.U. and its branches.

Administrative and Clerical Officiers' Association: 75 King St., Sydney, N.S.W. 2000; Gen. Sec. M. J. CAMPBELL.

Amalgamated Engineering Union: 126 Chalmers St., Surry Hills, N.S.W. 2010.

Amalgamated Postal Workers' Union of Australia: 4 Goulburn St., Sydney, N.S.W. 2000.

Australian Builders' Labourers' Federation: 4 Goulburn St., Sydney, N.S.W. 2000.

Australian Insurance Staffs Federation: 59 Hardware St. Melbourne, Vic. 3000.

Australian Railways Union: 377 Sussex St., Sydney, N.S.W. 2000.

Australian Teachers' Federation: 300 Sussex St., Sydney, N.S.W. 2000.

Australian Textile Workers' Union: 54 Victoria St., Carlton, Vic. 3050; Gen. Pres. L. A. NORTH, M.L.C.; Gen. Sec. W. A. C. HUGHES.

Australian Transport Officers' Association and Federation: 327 Sussex St., Sydney, N.S.W. 2000.

Australian Workers' Union: MacDonell House, 321 Pitt St., Sydney, N.S.W.; f. 1886; Pres. E. WILLIAMS; Gen. Sec. F. V. MITCHELL; mems. 165,000; the A.W.U. affiliated with the A.C.T.U. in 1967.

Building Workers' Industrial Union of Australia: 535 George St., Sydney, N.S.W. 2000; f. 1945; Pres. F. MCCAULEY; Gen. Sec. P. M. CLANCY; mems. 50,000.

Commonwealth Public Services Association: 26 King St., Sydney, N.S.W. 2000.

Electrical Trades Union of Australia: Federal Council, 262 Castlereagh St., Sydney, N.S.W. 2000; f. 1919; Pres. U. E. INNES; Gen. Sec. C. O. DOLAN; mems. 64,000.

Federated Clerks' Union of Australia: 17 Anthony St., Melbourne, Vic. 3000.

Federated Ironworkers of Australia: 188 George St., Sydney, N.S.W. 2000.

Federated Municipal Employees' Union: 54 Victoria St., Melbourne, Vic. 3000.

Federated Tobacco and Cigarette Workers' Union: 18 Balfour Rd., Kensington, N.S.W. 2033.

Hospital Employees' Federation: 240 Macquarie Rd., Greystanes, N.S.W. 2145.

Meat Industry Employees' Association: 377 Sussex St., Sydney, N.S.W. 2000.

Miscellaneous Workers' Union: Federal Council: 377 Sussex St., Sydney, N.S.W. 2000.

Postal Telecommunications Technicians' Association: 300 Sussex St., Sydney, N.S.W. 2000.

Printing and Kindred Industries Union: 377 Sussex St., Sydney, N.S.W. 2000.

Public Service Professional Officers' Association: 377 Sussex St., Sydney, N.S.W. 2000.

Seamen's Union of Australia: 289 Sussex St., Sydney, N.S.W. 2000.

Sheet Metal Workers' Union: 300 Sussex St., Sydney, N.S.W. 2000.

Transport Workers' Union of Australia: 4 Goulburn St., Sydney, N.S.W. 2000.

Vehicle Builders Employees' Federation of Australia: 377 Sussex St., Sydney, N.S.W. 2000.

Waterside Workers' Federation of Australia: 377 Sussex St., Sydney, N.S.W. 2000.

MAJOR INDUSTRIAL COMPANIES

The following are some of the major industrial and trading companies, arranged by sector.

MINING AND METALS

Alcoa of Australia Ltd.: 535 Bourke St., Melbourne, Victoria; cap. $A75m.

Bauxite miner and producer of alumina. Refineries at Pinjarra and Kwinana in Western Australia. Producers of aluminium ingot and fabricators of aluminium extrusions, tube, rod, bar, sheet, plate and foil. Smelting and semi-fabricating plant at Point Henry, Victoria.

Chair. Sir JAMES FORREST; Man. Dir. W. PORTER, Jnr.; employees: 4,000.

BH South Ltd.: 459 Collins St., Melbourne, Vic. 3000; f. 1918; cap. $A15.4m.

Copper and zinc mining at Cobar, N.S.W., by Cobar Mines Pty. Ltd. and copper mining at Kanmantoo, S.A., by Kanmantoo Mines Ltd. Copper smelting and refining at Port Kembla, N.S.W., by the Electrolytic Refining & Smelting Co. of Australia Ltd. Phosphate mining started 1975 in N.W. Qld. by Queensland Phosphate Ltd. Mineral exploration.

Five main subsidiary companies; Chair. and Exec. Dir. J. M. TYLER; Exec. Dir. (Phosphates) L. D. THOMSON; employees (incl. subsidiaries): 1,161.

British Phosphate Commissioners: 515 Collins St., Melbourne; mine phosphate on behalf of the New Zealand, U.K., and Australian governments, from Ocean Island, Central Pacific; are also managing agents for Christmas Island Phosphate Commission for mining at Christmas Island and for distribution from there and from Ocean Island, Nauru, etc., to Australia and New Zealand; Commissioners: Sir ALLEN BROWN, C.B.E. (Australia); W. D. M. BREMNER (New Zealand); Sir ALEXANDER WADDELL, K.C.M.G., D.S.C. (U.K.); Gen. Man. A. E. GAZE.

The Broken Hill Proprietary Co. Ltd.: 140 William St., Melbourne, Vic. 3000; f. 1885; cap. $A600m.

Mining, iron and steelmaking, oil and natural gas, exploration and development, shipbuilding. Operates in every state of Australia, the Northern Territory, Papua New Guinea, Taiwan and Malaysia. Exploration activities in Indonesia, New Britain, Bougainville and New Zealand. Three fully integrated iron and steel works at Newcastle and Port Kembla in N.S.W. and Whyalla in South Australia; iron making and steel rolling at Kwinana, Western Australia. Total raw steel production: 8.0m. tons; oil 64.8m. barrels; iron ore 21.7m. tons; Eleven collieries at Newcastle and Port Kembla and two in Central Queensland, at Leichardt and Cook; output: 7.2m. tons (year ending May 31st, 1975).

Twenty-four subsidiary companies; twelve major associated companies; overseas offices in Auckland, Lae, London, Manila, New York, Singapore and Tokyo; Chair. and Dir. of Admin. Sir IAN MCLENNAN; Man. Dir. J. C. MCNEILL; employees; 63,000.

Comalco Ltd.: 95 Collins St., Melbourne, Vic. 3000; cap. $A74.75m.; inc. 1960; public co. 1970.

Provides management services to an intregated group of mining and metal companies.

Chair. D. J. HIBBERD; Man. Dir. A. V. LORCH; Chief Gen. Man. A. L. ELLIS; employees 6,500.

Consolidated Gold Fields Australia Ltd.: Gold Fields House, Sydney Cove, N.S.W. 2000; cap. $A27.1m.

Numerous mining interests throughout Australia and New Zealand.

Chair. Sir BRIAN MASSEY-GREENE; Man. Dir. B. C. RYAN.

Conzinc Riotinto of Australia Limited: 95 Collins Street, Melbourne 3001; f. 1973; cap. issued $A144.3m.

CRA is a mining, development and investment company and, through its subsidiary and associate companies, has wide and various interests in most metals and minerals of economic importance, principally copper, iron ore, lead-zinc, aluminium, uranium, nickel, coal, petroleum and natural gas. The CRA group operates mining and processing ventures which extend into fabrication, distribution and marketing. Active exploration and research programmes are maintained. CRA's principal interests are in: Bougainville Copper Ltd., 53 per cent owned (copper); Australian Mining and Smelting Ltd., 73.5 per cent owned (lead/zinc); Hamersley Holdings Ltd., 54 per cent owned (iron ore); Comalco Ltd., 45 per cent owned (bauxite); IOL Petroleum Ltd., 53.4 per cent owned; and Mary Kathleen Uranium Ltd., 51 per cent owned.

Chair. and Chief Exec. R. H. CARNEGIE; Deputy Chair. F. F. ESPIE, O.B.E.

EZ Industries Ltd.: 390 Lonsdale Street, Melbourne, f. 1956; cap. $A36m.

Operates as a holding company for the wholly-owned operating subsidiaries, Electrolytic Zinc Company of Australasia Ltd., The Emu Bay Railway Company Ltd., A–Z Metals Australia Ltd. and EZ America Ltd. Electrolytic Zinc has lead/zinc mines and a concentrating mill on the West Coast, and zinc and fertilizer works at Risdon, near Hobart, Tasmania. Emu Bay's main operation is the transport of concentrates produced at the West Coast mines of the Electrolytic Zinc Company and the Mount Lyell Mining and Railway Co. Ltd. to Burnie for shipment. A–Z Metals Australia Ltd., and EZ America Ltd. act as marketing organizations for zinc metal and cadmium in Europe and the U.S.A. respectively.

Four subsidiaries: Chair. Sir EDWARD COHEN; employees of subsidiaries: approx. 3,100.

John Lysaght (Australia) Ltd.: 50 Young Street, Sydney; P.O.B. 196, G.P.O., Sydney 2001; f. 1921; cap. $A50m.

Manufacture of coated and uncoated steel sheets and coils; roofing, walling and floor decking, electrical laminations; major plants at Westernport and Port Kembla; other factories and centres in each of the capital cities of Australia and in Townsville, Darwin, Rockhampton, Albury and Devonport.

Ten subsidiary companies inc. abroad; Chair. E. B. GOSSE; Man. Dir. H. J. PEARCE; employees: 6,800.

Metal Manufactures Ltd.: 168 Kent Street, Sydney, N.S.W.; f. 1916; cap. $A37.9m.

Manufacturers of copper and other non-ferrous wire, strand and tubes, covered wire and strip cables, and steel cored aluminium conductors. Main works at Port Kembla, N.S.W.; works in Maribyrnong, Victoria, Elizabeth, S.A., Strathpine, Queensland, Melville, W.A.

Eight wholly-owned subsidiary companies and five partly-owned subsidiaries, all at home; Man. Dir. L. R. POTTER; Exec. Dir. (Operations) Dr. D. R. STEWART; employees: 6,500.

M.I.M. Holdings Ltd.: 160 Ann St., Brisbane, Queensland; f. 1970; cap. $A142.9.

Mining and milling of silver-lead, zinc and copper and smelting of copper and silver-lead at Mount Isa,

Queensland, refining of copper at Townsville, Queensland, and of crude lead at Northfleet, Kent, U.K.; total ores treated 1974–75: 7.5m. tons; production 1974–75: crudelead 132,000 tons; blister copper 160,000 tons; zinc concentrate 221,000 tons; mining of coal at Scottville, Queensland (1974–75) 449,000 tons.

Chair. Sir James Foots; employees: 7,400.

North Broken Hill Ltd.: 459 Collins Street, Melbourne 3000, Victoria; f. 1912; cap. $A100m.

Mines and treats lead, silver and zinc ore at Broken Hill, New South Wales, for the production of lead and zinc concentrates. Engaged in exploration activities in most states of Australia.

Chair. M. L. Baillieu; Exec. Dir. R. L. Baillieu; employees: 1,154.

Tubemakers of Australia Ltd.: 1 York Street, Sydney, N.S.W.; f. 1964; cap. $A40m.

Manufacturing and trading company with four product divisions, several partly-owned companies and one fully-owned subsidiary company.

Man. Dir. J. G. Gosse; employees: 7,500.

Western Mining Corporation Ltd.: 459 Collins St., Melbourne, Vic. 3001; f. 1933; cap. $A90.8m.

Mining of nickel, iron ore, gold, talc, uranium, aluminium, coal and mineral sands.

Chair. and Man. Dir. A. H. Parbo; employees: 4,800.

MOTOR VEHICLES

Chrysler Australia Ltd.: 1284 South Rd., Clovelly Park, South Australia; issued cap. $A21.3m.

Manufacturers of cars and trucks, service parts, accessories, air conditioning equipment, industrial engines. Branches in Milperra (N.S.W.), Prahran (Victoria), Kewdale (Western Australia).

Chair. R. A. Perkins; Man. Dir. I. E. Webber; employees: 7,400.

Ford Motor Company of Australia Ltd.: 1735 Sydney Rd., Campbellfield, Victoria; f. 1925; cap. $A56m.

Manufactures for sale in domestic and export markets passenger and commercial motor vehicles, tractors, construction equipment, implements and parts and accessories. Plant locations: Homebush (N.S.W.), Campbellfield, Geelong, Ballarat (Victoria), Eagle Farm (Queensland), North Freemantle (Western Australia).

Chair. and Man. Dir. B. S. Inglis; employees: *c.* 13,000.

Ford Sales Company of Australia Ltd.: 1735 Sydney Rd., Campbellfield, Victoria; f. 1963; cap. $A6m.

Sells through dealer agents throughout Australia motor vehicles manufactured and assembled by Ford Motor. Offices in Melbourne, North Sydney, Brisbane, Adelaide, and North Fremantle.

Chair. and Man. Dir. B. S. Inglis; employees: *c.* 300.

General Motors-Holden's Ltd.: 241 Salmon Street, Port Melbourne, Vic. 3207; f. 1926; cap. $A140m.

GMH is a wholly-owned subsidiary of General Motors Corporation. Manufactures Holden, Torana, Gemini and Statesman passenger vehicles and Holden commercial vehicles, and Holden engines for marine and industrial use. Produces (through Isuzu Motors Ltd.) Bedford commercial vehicles. Manufacture and distribution of spare parts and accessories. Manufacture and distribution of Terex earth-moving equipment. Plant locations: Fishermen's Bend, Disco, Dandenong and Lang Lang (all in Victoria), Pagewood (N.S.W.), Acacia Ridge (Qld.), Woodville, Elizabeth and Birkenhead (S.A.).

One subsidiary company; Man. Dir. C. S. Chapman; employees: 23,431 (1975).

International Harvester Company of Australia Pty. Ltd.: 171-205 City Road, South Melbourne; f. 1912; cap. $A20m.

Manufacturers and marketers of tractors, farm equipment, trucks etc.; works at Geelong, Dandenong and Port Melbourne.

One subsidiary company at home; Chair. and Man. Dir. John B. Camp; employees: 4,000.

Leyland Motor Corporation of Australia Ltd.: 893–931 South Dowling St., Waterloo, N.S.W. 2017.

Manufacturers, assemblers and distributors of cars, light and heavy commercial motor vehicles and marine engines; importers and distributors of selected high class motor cars made by the parent company, the British Leyland Motor Corporation Ltd. of England. Branches: Pressed Metal Corp., Enfield, N.S.W.; Reevesby, N.S.W.; Airport West, Victoria; Footscray, Melbourne; British Leyland Co. Pty. Ltd., Western Australia.

Chair. J. R. Barber; Deputy Chair. J. O. Martin; Man. Dir. P. J. North.

Repco Ltd.: 630 St. Kilda St., Melbourne 3004, Vic.

Manufacturer of automotive components and service equipment, accessories, hand and machine tools, industrial products and services. Largest suppliers of original equipment to vehicle manufacturers in Australia; has overseas manufacturing and/or merchandising operations in: England, New Zealand, Canada, India, South Africa, Singapore, Hong Kong and U.S.A.

There are also associated companies in Australia, South Africa, Singapore, Hong Kong and India; Man. Dir. Peter I. Rosenblum; employees: 12,000.

PETROLEUM

Ampol Petroleum Ltd.: 84 Pacific Highway, North Sydney 2060; f. 1936; cap. $A60.8m.

Produces approx. 5,500 barrels of crude oil per day from Barrow Island, West Australia and imports approx. 45m. barrels of crude per year; refines this crude, together with 14m. barrels of indigenous crude, in Ampol Brisbane Refinery; transports crude and refined products in two company-owned tankers, markets more than 500m. gallons a year through 2,200 service stations and to industry.

Six subsidiary companies; all at home; Chair. and Chief Exec. W. M. Leonard; Man. Dir. A. E. Harris; Chief Gen. Man. R. C. H. Mason; employees: 2,600.

The British Petroleum Company of Australia Ltd.: BP House, 1 Albert Rd., Melbourne 3004, Victoria; f. 1962; cap. $A60m.

The Holding Company for the BP Group Companies in Australia; wholly-owned by The British Petroleum Company Ltd., England. Activities in Australia: refining, marketing, exploration, transportation of petroleum products and fertilizer production. Refineries operate at Kwinana in Western Australia (110,000 bbls./day) and at Crib Point on Westernport Bay, Vic. (60,000 bbls./day).

Eleven subsidiary companies; Chair. J. Darling; Man. Dir. M. R. Rendle; employees: 4,200.

Esso Australia Ltd.: Esso House, 127 Kent St., Sydney, N.S.W.; cap. $A30m.

All spheres of the petroleum business. Branches in N.S.W., Victoria, Queensland, South Australia, Western Australia. The parent company is the Exxon Corporation through Esso Eastern Inc..

Five subsidiary companies; six associated companies; Chair. and Man. Dir. R. J. Kruizenga; employees: 1,800.

Mobil Oil Australia Ltd.: 2 City Road, Melbourne, Victoria 3205; f. 1895; cap. $A50m.

Marketers in Australia and the Pacific Islands of a full range of petroleum products. Principal offices in Melbourne, Sydney, Brisbane, Adelaide, Perth, Hobart, Fiji, New Caledonia and Tahiti. Total revenues for 1974: $A382m.

Subsidiary companies: 5 at home, 1 in Papua New Guinea; Chair. and Man. Dir. J. B. LESLIE.

Petroleum Refineries (Australia) Pty. Ltd.: 2 City Road, Melbourne, Victoria 3205; cap. $A10m.

Petroleum refiners. The company operates a refinery at Altonia, near Melbourne, producing 100,000 barrels daily and a refinery at Port Stanvac, near Adelaide, producing up to 72,000 barrels daily.

Chair. J. B. LESLIE; Man. Dir. W. R. YEO; employees: 552.

Shell Australia Limited: Shell Corner, 155 William St., Melbourne C.1, P.O.B. 872K; cap. $A70m.

Manufactures and markets petroleum and petroleum products and chemicals.

Fourteen subsidiary companies, Chair. L. T. FROGGATT.

H. C. Sleigh Ltd.: 160 Queen Street, Melbourne, Victoria; cap. $A43.8m.

Petroleum marketers, oil exploration, shipping, exporting and aviation. Branches in New South Wales, South Australia, Queensland, Western Australia, Tasmania and United Kingdom.

Twenty-two subsidiary companies; Chair. and Man. Dir. P. H. SLEIGH; Deputy Man. Dir. Dr. M. H. SEARBY; employees: 2,418.

RUBBER

Dunlop Australia Ltd.: 108 Flinders St., Melbourne 3000, Vic.; cap. $A88.7m.

Manufacturer and distributor. Six operative groups: Dunlop Automotive and Industrial, P.O.B. 21, Port Melbourne: tyres, automotive rubber products, batteries, belting, hoses, irrigation and water purification units; Dunlop Textiles/Clothing, P.O.B. 18, East Brunswick, Vic. 3057: knitted and woven fabrics, clothing, domestic textiles and furnishings, blankets, fabric printing and dyeing; Dunlop Footwear, P.O.B. 199, N. Melbourne, Vic. 3051: footwear; Dunlopillo, P.O.B. 277, Clayton, Vic. 3168: mattresses, innerspring bases, latex and polyurethane foam, steel framed furniture; Dunlop-Slazenger, G.P.O. Box, 4001, Sydney, N.S.W. 2001: sporting goods, under-water equipment and marine sportswear; Ansell, P.O.B. 18, Richmond, Vic. 3121: latex dipped and cured rubber goods.

Chair. Sir ROBERT BLACKWOOD; Man. Dir. L. M. JARMAN; employees: 21,000.

The Goodyear Tyre and Rubber Co. (Australia) Ltd.: 4 Yurong Street, Sydney, N.S.W.; cap. $A16.6m.

Manufacturers of tyres and tubes, industrial rubber products, general rubber products, fan belts, shoe soling; adhesives, Goodyear aviation products, film packaging; distributors of Goodyear chemical products. Branches in New South Wales, South Australia, Queensland, Western Australia, Victoria and Tasmania.

Chair. J. P. MILES; employees: 3,500.

Olympic Consolidated Industries Ltd.: 393 Swanston Street, Melbourne, Victoria 3000; cap. $A40m.

Manufacture of tyres and tubes for cars and trucks, electric wires and cables for transmission and telecommunication, conveyor and transmission belting, industrial nylon and plastics and polyurethane foam products, thermal insulation contracting; operates over 170 tyre service stations and retreading factories throughout Australia; main factories at Melbourne, Brisbane, Tottenham, Lilydale and Footscray.

Four subsidiary companies, all at home; Chair. and Chief Exec. IAN F. BEAUREPAIRE; Deputy Man. Dir. E. R. BOMPHREY; employees: 6,300.

PAPER AND PULP

Australian Paper Manufacturers Ltd.: South Gate, South Melbourne, Vic. 3205; f. 1868; cap. $A112m.

Australia's top producer of woodpulp, paper and paperboard; Mills at Botany (N.S.W.), Fairfield, Maryvale and Broadford (Victoria), Petrie (Queensland), Spearwood (W. Australia), and Port Huon (Tasmania). More than 64,600 hectares of established softwood and hardwood (eucalypt) plantations in Victoria, Queensland and N.S.W. plus extensive holdings of natural forest.

Subsidiary companies: 9 at home, 1 in New Zealand; Chair. P. J. V. RAMSDEN; Man. Dir. J. G. WILSON; Deputy Man. Dir. S. D. M. WALLIS.

Associated Pulp and Paper Mills Ltd.: 459 Collins Street, Melbourne, Victoria; G.P.O. Box 509H, Melbourne, Victoria 3001; f. 1936; cap. $A40.42m.

Manufacture of various papers and boards as well as paper merchandising and converting, forestry, farming and mining and production of filler and superfine coating clays. Paper mills at Burnie and Wesley Vale, Tasmania, Shoalhaven, New South Wales, and Ballarat, Victoria. Sawmills in north-west Tasmania and woodchip mill at Long Reach, Tasmania. Production (1973-74): pulp, 88,245 metric tons; paper, 210,462 metric tons; sawn timber, 39,290 cubic metres; particleboard, 2,540,000 square metres; total sales (1973-74): $A 139.2 million.

Twenty-two subsidiary companies in Australia; employees: 5,550; Chairman W. D. BROOKES, C.B.E., D.S.O., Man. Dir. W. H. THORNTON.

FOOD AND DRINK, ETC.

Allied Manufacturing and Trading Industries Limited (Amatil): Box 145, G.P.O., Sydney, N.S.W. 2001; f. 1927; cap. $A66.9m.

Tobacco, cigarette and cigar production, printing and packaging, food and beverage production, light engineering and extensive pastoral interests.

Eighty-eight subsidiary companies, 80 at home, 8 abroad; Chair. T. J. N. FOLEY, C.B.E.; Deputy Chair. H. WIDDUP; employees: over 13,000.

Cadbury Schweppes Australia Ltd.: 636 St. Kilda Rd., Melbourne, Vic. 3004; f. 1971; cap. $A17.31m.

Manufacture and distribution of chocolate and sugar confectionery, jams, soft drinks, fruit juices and milk bar syrups.

Chief Exec. M. B. GIFFORD; Joint Man. Dirs. R. A. DELOHERY, J. R. URQUHART; employees: 4,860.

Carlton and United Breweries Ltd.: 16 Bouverie St., Carlton, Victoria; cap. $A67m.

Thirty subsidiary companies; Chair. Sir EDWARD COHEN; Gen. Man. L. J. MANGAN; employees: 3,500.

Henry Jones (IXL) Ltd.: 20 Garden St., South Yarra, Vic. 3141; f. 1909; shareholders funds $A40m.

Jam manufacturers, fruit and meat canners, vegetable, juice, tomato and frozen food processors. Interests in shipping, timber, hop growing, television and radio

Major interests are in Australia, South Africa, Great Britain and Hong Kong. Group turnover $A65m. annually.

Subsidiary companies: 33 at home, 7 in South Africa, 2 in Great Britain; Chair. T. MARCUS CLARK; Man. Dir. J. D. ELLIOTT.

Petersville Australia Ltd.: Wellington Rd., Mulgrave, Vic. 3170; f. 1929.

Processor of vegetables, ice cream, dairy products, meat and pastries. Manufacturer of sheet metal and refrigeration products. Importers of gourmet foods.

Chair. Sir CHARLES MCGRATH, O.B.E.; Man. Dir. J. S. SHAW; employees 5,500 (approx.).

Tooth & Co. Ltd.: Kent Brewery, Broadway, N.S.W.; cap. $A70.3m.

Brewers, wine and spirit merchants.

Chair. G. J. CULLEN, M.B.E.; Vice-Chair. D. M. CARMENT; Man. Dir. H. T. ALCE.

Unilever Australia Export Pty. Ltd.: 1-33 Macquarie St., Sydney, N.S.W. 2000; Box No. 1590 G.P.O., Sydney, N.S.W. 2001.

Marketing ice cream, food, edible oils, toiletries, soap and detergents.

Fourteen subsidiary companies; employees: 5,440.

MISCELLANEOUS

Australian Consolidated Industries Ltd.: 550 Bourke St., Melbourne, Vic.; f. 1872; auth. cap. $A100m.

Manufacturers and distributors of glass containers, sheet, decorative rolled and wire reinforced glass, lighting ware, pressed and blown glassware and pyrex ovenware, fibreglass insulants and textiles, polythene piping, corrugated fibre containers—Australia, New Zealand, South-East Asia, Papua New Guinea and Fiji.

One hundred and twenty-two subsidiary companies, 50 in Australia, 72 abroad (N.Z., Fiji, Papua New Guinea, Indonesia, Singapore, Malaysia and Hong Kong); Chair. Sir JAMES FORREST; Gen. Man. R. W. BRACK; employees: 21,800.

Blue Metal Industries Ltd.: 6 O'Connell St., Sydney, N.S.W. 2000; f. 1952; cap. $A28.59m.

Quarrying, aggregates, road bases and sand; manufactures many building and road materials; timber, road transport, general engineering, mining. Concrete and mining activities in Indonesia and Malaysia.

Man. Dir. R. A. ROBSON.

Brambles Industries Ltd.: Gold Fields House, 1 Alfred St., Sydney Cove, N.S.W. 2000; f. 1875; cap. $A24.8m.

Materials movement and distributions, including industrial plant hire, equipment pools, scheduled freight forwarding by road, rail, sea and air, heavy haulage, logistical support programmes for major projects, marine towage and transportation, pollution control services, etc.

Chief Exec. Officer WARWICK J. HOLCROFT; employees: 5,000.

CSR Ltd.: 1 O'Connell St., Sydney, N.S.W. 2000; f. 1855; issued, cap. $A121m.

Sugar milling, refining and marketing, manufacture of building and construction materials, mining and mineral exploration, industrial chemicals and gases, distillery products, sheep, cattle, shipping, macadamia nuts, research and development.

Thirty-one subsidiary companies; Chair. Sir JOHN DUNLOP; Gen. Man. R. G. JACKSON; employees: 12,000.

Commonwealth Industrial Gases Ltd., C.I.G.: 46 Kippax St., Surry Hills, N.S.W.

Manufacturers and suppliers of industrial and medical gases, electric and gas welding equipment and consumables, safety equipment, medical equipment, ground engaging tools, food freezing equipment, paint sprays and safety equipment. Industrial and medical gas plants throughout Australia; equipment and welding consumables factories in Melbourne. Overseas subsidiaries in Papua New Guinea, Fiji, Indonesia and Thailand, each with its own gas manufacturing facilities.

Man. Dir. J. A. DAVIDSON; employees: 3,952.

Containers Ltd.: 265–275 Franklin St., Melbourne, Vic. 3001; f. 1950.

Manufacture of metal food and beverage cans, aerosols, plastic containers and other packaging material.

Man. Dir. R. J LANGMAN; Gen. Man. L. N. PRICE; employees: 4,800.

F. & T. Industries Ltd.: 228 Victoria Parade, East Melbourne, Vic. 3002.

Manufacturers of all kinds of specialized building materials and bricks, clay pipes, corrosion control systems, felts, non-wovens, vinyl floor coverings, PVC furnishing fabrics, electrical accessories, plastic houseware, containers and toys, rubber carpet underlays. Custom plaster moulders.

Ten subsidiary companies in Australia; two abroad; Chair. Sir JOHN MARKS; Man. Dir. R. N. MILLAR; employees: 7,000.

Herald and Weekly Times Ltd.: 44-74 Flinders St., Melbourne, Victoria; f. 1902; cap. $A28.2m.

Newspaper proprietors, publishers, printers, radio and television broadcasters.

Thirteen subsidiary companies; Chair. Sir PHILIP JONES; employees: 3,500.

ICI Australasia Ltd.: ICI House, 1 Nicholson St., Melbourne, Vic.; 62 per cent owned by Imperial Chemical Industries, United Kingdom.

Fifty-nine subsidiary companies; Chair. and Man. Dir. D. R. ZEIDLER, C.B.E., Man. Dir. A. W. HAMER; Sec. R. L. WILSON.

Kodak (Australasia) Pty. Ltd.: 173 Elizabeth St., Coburg, Vic. 3058.

Manufacturers of sensitized photographic materials, photographic chemicals and equipment; distributors and retailers. Branches in Victoria, New South Wales, Queensland, South Australia, Western Australia and Tasmania.

One subsidiary company in New Zealand; Chair. and Chief Exec. Officer K. E. ALLEN; employees: 3,500,

McPherson's Ltd.: 500 Collins St., Melbourne, Victoria.

Distributors of industrial products and machine tools. Also manufacturers of pumps for industrial and agricultural purposes, mechanical fasteners, and cold formed parts, cutting tools, fence and gate fittings, friction materials. Branches in Melbourne, Sydney, Brisbane, Adelaide and Perth.

Chair. W. D. MCPHERSON; Man. Dir. M. B. ADDISON employees: 5,000.

RETAIL AND WHOLESALE TRADE

G. J. Coles & Co. Ltd.: 236 Bourke St., Melbourne, Victoria; cap. $A60.6m.

Variety chain stores, supermarkets and food stores, Branches in all states.

Three grocery subsidiary companies; Chair. and Man. Dir. N. C. COLES; employees: 38,000.

Dalgety Australia Ltd.: 38 Bridge St., Sydney, N.S.W. 2000; cap. $A30m.

Wool selling brokers, stud stock specialists, livestock exporters, finance, produce salesmen, suppliers of graziers' and farmers' merchandise and agricultural seeds requirements, wholesale merchandisers, shipping and travel agents, stevedores, insurance agents, pastoralists, exporters. Branches throughout Australia.

Twenty-two subsidiary trading companies in Australia; Chair. and Man. Dir. W. J. VINES, C.M.G.; Sec. J. S. BURGESS.

Elder Smith Goldsbrough Mort Ltd.: Elder House, 27–39 Currie St., Adelaide, South Australia; cap. $A34.86m.

Importers and exporters, wool brokers, general merchants, land and livestock insurance, shipping and travel agents, ship chartering brokers, fruit exporters, station owners, trustees and executors, merchant bankers, rural and real estate financiers, steel and metal distributors, char manufacturers, coastal marine service, stevedoring and general transport operators. Branches in Sydney, Melbourne, Brisbane, Perth, at over 350 main country towns throughout Australia and in London, Tokyo, Osaka and Hong Kong.

Five main subsidiary companies; Chair. Sir NORMAN YOUNG; Deputy Chair. J. I. N. WINTER; Man. Dir. and Chief Exec. H. C. SCHMIDT; employees: 4,990.

David Jones Ltd.: 86-108 Castlereagh St., Sydney, N.S.W.; f. 1838; cap. $A40m.

Retail departmental storekeepers with six stores located in Sydney and suburbs, twenty-two stores in other major Australian cities and towns. Twelve stores trading under name of Buffums in California, U.S.A. and one manufacturing interest, Selby Shoes (Aust.) Ltd. (footwear), whose output is distributed through group's retail stores.

Chair. CHARLES B. LLOYD JONES; employees: 12,500.

The Myer Emporium Ltd.: 314-336 Bourke St., Melbourne, Vic. 3000; f. 1925; cap. $A93.45m.

Holding company of the largest group of department and discount stores in the Southern Hemisphere. Current sales over $A759m. p.a.

Major department stores in all States. Overseas buying offices maintained in Paris, Frankfurt, Milan, Osaka, Tokyo, Hong Kong and London.

Chair. K. B. MYER; Man. Dir. K. C. STEELE; employees: 32,172.

Waltons Ltd.: George, Park and Pitt Sts., Sydney, N.S.W.; f. 1926; cap. $A23.2m.

Department store chain retailers.

Chair. JOHN S. WALTON; employees: 9,000.

Woolworths Ltd.: 534 George St., Sydney, N.S.W.; cap. $A53.3m.

Chain store proprietors.

Chair. Sir THEO KELLY, O.B.E.; Joint Gen. Mans. W. B. DEAN, H. P. SIMONS; employees: 34,000.

TRANSPORT

Australian Transport Advisory Council: Civic Permanent Building, Allara St., Canberra, A.C.T. 2600; f. 1946; Chairman: the Minister for Transport; Members: Minister for Northern Australia, Minister for the Capital Territory, State Ministers of Transport and Roads; Observers: the New Zealand Minister for Transport; formed to discuss transport matters, promote co-ordination of development and maintain research.

RAILWAYS

Before July 1975 there were seven government-owned railway systems in Australia. The six States each had their own railways and the Commonwealth Railways operated four railways on behalf of the Australian Government. On July 1st the Australian National Railways Commission was formed to incorporate the Commonwealth Railways and any railway systems acquired from the States. The Tasmanian Government Railways and the non-urban section of the South Australian Government Railways are being transferred to the new Commission.

Australian National Railways Commission: 325 Collins St., Melbourne, Vic. 3000; Chair. K. A. SMITH, O.B.E.; Sec. H. N. TURNER; a statutory Authority operating 3,595 km. of railways of both 1,435 and 1,067 mm. gauge in addition to those being transferred to the Commission by the State governments (*see* above). An 831 km. line between Tarcoola, Southern Australia, and Alice Springs is scheduled for completion in 1980.

Public Transport Commission of New South Wales: 11–31 York St., Sydney 2000; administers government transport services in N.S.W.; 9,753 km. train network, with 11 km. under construction; Chief Commissioner (vacant); Acting Sec. A. R. COLEMAN.

Queensland Railways: 305 Edward St., Brisbane; operates 9,621 km. of 1,067 mm. track.

South Australian Railways: G.P.O. Box 2351, Adelaide, S.A. 5001; Railway Bldg., North Terrace, Adelaide; f. 1856; operates 3,884 km. of track; Railways Commissioner M. L. STOCKLEY.

Tasmanian Railways: Box 624F, G.P.O., Hobart, Collins St., Hobart; operates 831 km. of 1,067 mm. gauge track; Gen. Man. G. J. DINEEN; Sec. R. G. BARBER.

Victorian Railways: 67 Spencer St., Melbourne 3000; f. 1856; operates 5,508.66 miles of track; Chair. A. G. GIBBS; Gen. Man. I. G. HODGES.

Western Australian Government Railways: Perth, W.A.; operates passenger and freight transport services mainly in the south of Western Australia; 6,075 route km. of track, 6,652 bus route km. and 3,426 truck route km. of road services; Commissioner R. J. PASCOE; Sec. A. E. WILLIAMS.

ROADS

At the end of 1971 there were 902,218 km. of roads, including 104,610 km. of main roads.

SHIPPING

Commonwealth of Australia: Australian National Line: (Australian Shipping Commission); 65–79 Riverside Ave., South Melbourne, Vic. 3025; (P.O.B. 2238T); Chair. N. G. JENNER; Gen. Man. R. D. ROBIN; services: Australian coastal trade and passenger and car services between mainland and Tasmania; overseas container services to Europe, United Kingdom, United States, Hong Kong, Philippines, Korea and Japan; 33 vessels.

Adelaide Steamship Co. Ltd.: 123 Greenhill Rd., Unley S.A. 5061; f. 1875; Gen. Man. K. W. Russell; Sec. H. R. Goode.

Ampol Petroleum Ltd.: 84 Pacific Highway, North Sydney, N.S.W.; Chair. W. M. Leonard; bulk carriage of oil from Indonesia to Brisbane; 4 vessels.

Associated Steamships Pty. Ltd.: 94 William St., Melbourne; f. 1964; wholly-owned subsidiary of Bulkships Ltd.; owns 1 container ship, 1 bulk carrier and 1 general cargo vessel; operates 2 container ships and 4 bulk ships on demise charter; manages 5 oil tankers and 1 bulk carrier; Chair. Sir Ian Potter; Man. Dir. A. Carmichael; Gen. Man. P. W. Naughton.

Associated Steamships Pty. Ltd., is also a 50 per cent partner with Overseas Containers Australia Pty. Ltd. in Australia's first container transport undertaking, *Seatainer Terminals Ltd.*

Bulkships Ltd.: 94 William St., Melbourne; f. 1958; associate company of McIlwraith McEacharn Ltd., The Adelaide Steamship Co. Ltd., Thomas Nationwide Transport Ltd.; owns 3 bulk carriers and 1 bulk carrier/roll-on, roll-off vessel; managed by wholly-owned subsidiary company Associated Steamships Pty. Ltd.; Chair. Sir Ian Potter; Man. Dir. A. Carmichael; Gen. Man. P. W. Naughton.

John Burke Pty. Ltd.: MacQuarrie St., Teneriffe, P.O.B. 509, Fortitude Valley; Chair. D. B. Hill; 5 vessels; coastal services.

Burns, Philp and Co. Ltd.: 7 Bridge St. (P.O.B. 543), Sydney, N.S.W.; Chair. and Man. Dir. J. D. O. Burns; Gen. Man. M. O'Connor.

Garnew Shipping Pty. Ltd.: 22 Mount St., Perth, W.A.; Man. Dir. R. D. G. Agnew.

Howard Smith Industries Pty. Ltd.: 269 George St., Sydney; Chair. Wm. Howard-Smith; Gen. Man. N. T. Griffin; 17 vessels, including 12 tugs.

McIlwraith McEacharn Ltd.: Scottish House, 90 William St., Melbourne, Vic.; Chair. Sir Ian Potter; Gen. Man. A. D. Campbell; tug and shipowners, liner and tramp-ship agents; agency for coal exports and coke-selling.

Mason Shipping Co. Pty. Ltd.: Smiths Creek, Cairns; 4 vessels; coastal services.

Western Australian Coastal Shipping Commission (State Shipping Service): 6–10 Short St., Fremantle, P.O.B. 394; Chair. F. N. Jones; Gen. Man. G. A. Petersen.

CIVIL AVIATION

Ansett Airlines of Australia Ltd.: 489 Swanston St., Melbourne, Vic.; f. 1936; commercial airline operators; passenger and cargo air services throughout Australia and to Papua New Guinea; fleet includes 4 Boeing 727–100, 8 727-200, 2 727-100 C, 12 DC-9-30, 11 Fokker F.27, 4 Electra, 11 Sikorsky S-61N and 1 JetRanger; Chair. and Man. Dir. Sir Reginald M. Ansett, K.B.E.; Gen. Man. F. Pascoe, C.B.E.

Ansett Airlines of N.S.W. Ltd. (*Division of Ansett Transport Industries (Operations) Pty. Ltd.*): Kingsford Smith Airport, Mascot, Sydney, N.S.W. 2020; f. 1934; operates extensive services from Sydney to N.S.W.; fleet includes 2 Fokker F.27-500 and 4 F.27-200; Gen. Man. P. Stedman.

Ansett Airlines of South Australia: Adelaide Airport, S. Australia; services in South Australia between Adelaide and Kangaroo Island, Port Lincoln, Whyalla, Ceduna, Mount Gambier and Broken Hill; fleet of 3 Fokker F.27; Gen. Man. L. Connelly.

Connair Pty. Ltd.: 51 Todd St., (P.O.B. 1), Alice Springs, N.T. 5750; f. 1938; operations commenced 1939; RPT operator with services throughout Northern Territory and to Queensland, Western Australia and South Australia; charter and maintenance services also available; fleet of 4 DC3, 6 Heron (Lycoming); Chair. E. J. Connellan; Gen. Man. P. W. Levin.

East-West Airlines Ltd.: P.O.B. 249, Tamworth, N.S.W. 2340; f. 1947; routes total 9,725 km.; services to N.S.W., Queensland, Victoria and the Northern Territory; aerial surveys and exploration activities; Chair. D. M. Shand; Gen. Man. J. G. Riley; operates 7 Fokker Friendships.

MacRobertson Miller Airline Services: International House, 26 St. George's Terrace, Perth, W.A. 6000; began operations 1955; a division of Ansett Transport Industries (Operations) Pty. Ltd.; Gen. Man. Capt. C. N. Kleinig; F.28 jet services Perth-Darwin, via North West ports; mainline domestic services using F-28 and Twin Otter throughout Western Australia and to Darwin, Gove and Groote Eylandt in the Northern Territory; fleet: 2 Twin Otter, 5 Fokker F.28.

Qantas Airways Ltd.: Qantas House, 70 Hunter St., Sydney, N.S.W. 2000 (P.O.B. 489); f. 1920; Chair. Sir Lenox Hewitt, O.B.E.; Gen. Man. K. Hamilton; services: Sydney–London via Middle East and Europe, Sydney–U.S.A. and Canada, Sydney–Japan, Sydney–Hong Kong via Manila, Sydney–Port Moresby (Papua New Guinea) via Brisbane, Sydney–Johannesburg via Mauritius, various routes across the Tasman Sea to New Zealand, Sydney–Noumea and Norfolk Island; fleet: 11 Boeing 747-238B, 13 Boeing 707-338C, 2 Douglas DC-4, 1 HS-125.

Trans-Australia Airlines (TAA): 50 Franklin St. (P.O.B. 2806AA), Melbourne 3000; f. 1946; operated by Australian National Airlines Commission (Chair. K. H. Vial); routes totalling approx. 69,488 km. to 52 ports in every Australian State; Gen. Man. L. L.McKenzie C.B.E., D.F.C.; fleet includes 11 Boeing 727, 12 Douglas DC-9, 14 Fokker F.27 and 7 DHC Twin Otter.

The following foreign airlines serve Australia: Aer Lingus, Air Canada, Air France, Air India, Air New Zealand, Alitalia, British Airways, Canadian Pacific, Cathay Pacific, JAL, KLM, Lufthansa, MEA, Malaysian Airlines System (MAS), Northeast Orient Airlines, Olympic Airways, Pan American, South African Airways, SAS, Swissair, TWA and UTA.

TOURISM

Australian Tourist Commission: 414 St. Kilda Rd., Melbourne, Vic. 3004; f. 1967; Government organization for encouraging overseas and domestic tourists; Chair. ALAN GREENWAY; Gen. Man. K. A. McDONALD; offices in Sydney, London, Auckland, Los Angeles, New York, Tokyo, Frankfurt-am-Main.

CULTURAL ORGANIZATION

Australia Council: P.O.B. 302, North Sydney, N.S.W. 2060; f. 1975 to replace the Australian Council for the Arts.

PRINCIPAL THEATRES

The Australian Ballet: 11 Mount Alexander Rd., Flemington, Victoria 3031; f. 1962 by the Australian Ballet Foundation; 50 full-time dancers; Artistic Dir. ANNE WOOLLIAMS; Administrator PETER F. BAHEN.

Australian Elizabethan Theatre Trust: 153 Dowling St., Potts Point, N.S.W.; f. 1954; controls and administers Elizabethan Sydney Orchestra and Elizabethan Melbourne Orchestra, The Marionette Theatre of Australia and the Theatrical Services Division; also major national entrepreneur touring overseas and handling Australian companies and artists on a national basis; financed by subsidies from Commonwealth and State Governments and city councils of approximately $A3,000,000 per annum, and private donations and subscriptions; Pres. Sir JAMES DARLING, C.M.G., O.B.E.; Chair. Sir IAN POTTER; Gen. Man. JEFFRY JOYTON-SMITH.

The Australian Opera: 569 George St., Sydney; f. 1955; full-time professional opera company, tours throughout Australia; 175 singers and staff mems.; annual seasons in each state capital, country tours; Chair. CHARLES J.BERG, O.B.E.; Gen. Man. JOHN WINTHER.

Sydney Opera House Trust: Box 4274 G.P.O., Sydney, N.S.W. 2001; f. 1961 to manage Sydney Opera House as a performing arts complex and convention centre; Gen. Man. FRANK BARNES.

PRINCIPAL ORCHESTRAS

Australian Broadcasting Commission: 145–49 Elizabeth St., Sydney, N.S.W.; f. 1932; organizes more than 750 concerts and recitals each year throughout Australia; has established a major symphony orchestra in each of the six State capitals, as well as a national training orchestra based in Sydney.

Melbourne Symphony Orchestra: Melbourne, Vic.; f. 1947; 87 mems.; Man. G. S. WRAITH; Chief Conductor HIROYUKI IWAKI.

Queensland Symphony Orchestra: f. 1947; 65 mems.; Man. ROBERT SHEPHERD; Chief Conductor PATRICK THOMAS.

Adelaide Symphony Orchestra: f. 1946; 64 mems.; Man. L. G. CASEY; Chief Conductor ELYAKUM SHAPIRRA.

West Australian Symphony Orchestra: f. 1947; 57 mems.; Man. CARL EDWARDS; Chief Conductor DAVID MEASHAM.

Tasmanian Symphony Orchestra: f. 1948; 42 mems.; Man. Mrs. JUNE FISHER; Chief Conductor VANCO CAVDARSKI.

Sydney Symphony Orchestra: Sydney, N.S.W.; f. 1946; 96 mems.; Man. COLIN DUNTON; Chief Conductor WILLEM VAN OTTERLOO.

All orchestras listed are maintained and administered by the A.B.C. with, in addition, small subsidies from State and municipal authorities.

FESTIVALS

Adelaide Festival of Arts: Adelaide Festival Centre, King William Rd., Adelaide, S.A. 5000; f. 1960; biennial; international; performing, visual and creative arts; Artistic Dir. ANTHONY STEEL.

Festival of Perth: Perth, W.A.; f. 1953; annual; concerts, plays, opera, dancing, art exhibitions, jazz, poetry and prose, by Australian and international artists; Chair. Prof. A. J. F. BOYLE; Exec. Officer J. BIRMAN.

ATOMIC ENERGY

Australian Atomic Energy Commission: 45 Beach St., Coogee, N.S.W. 2034; Chair. R. W. BOSWELL, O.B.E., M.SC.; Deputy Chair. Sir LENOX HEWITT, O.B.E., B.COM., F.A.S.A., F.C.I.S., L.C.A.; Mem. Prof. H. MESSEL, B.A., B.SC., PH.D.; Sec. A. D. THOMAS M.SC.; publs. Annual Report, *Atomic Energy in Australia* (quarterly journal).

The Commission is concerned with scientific research, development of practical uses of atomic energy, the training of scientists and engineers, the discovery and production of uranium, the production of radioisotopes and radiopharmaceuticals.

HIFAR: 10 mW. research reactor; critical 1958; for testing materials and radio isotope production.

MOATA: 100 kW. research reactor; critical 1962; provides neutron radiography, uranium analysis and general activation services and beams and irradiation space for physical chemistry and materials research.

Australian Institute of Nuclear Science and Engineering: Lucas Heights, New South Wales; the Institute supports university research and training projects in all branches of nuclear science and engineering. Its membership comprises seventeen Universities and A.A.E.C.; Pres. (1975-76) Prof. P. A. PARSONS; Exec. Officer E. A. PALMER.

Australian School of Nuclear Technology: Private Mail Bag, PO, Sutherland, N.S.W. 2232; provides courses for Australian and overseas students in nuclear technology, radioisotope techniques and applications, health physics, siting and hazards evaluation of nuclear power plants, etc.; Chair. J. L. SYMONDS.

The following universities have facilities for nuclear research and training: Universities of Adelaide, New South Wales, Newcastle, Queensland, Sydney and Tasmania, The Australian National University, Flinders, University of South Australia and La Trobe University.

DEFENCE

Armed Forces (1975): Total strength 69,100; army 31,300, navy 16,200, air force 21,600; military service is voluntary.

Equipment: The army has British medium tanks and scout cars and American helicopters. Other material includes heavy artillery and light aircraft. The navy comprises mainly destroyers, minesweepers and patrol boats as well as an aircraft carrier. The air force has 151 combat aircraft mostly of British, French and American manufacture.

Defence Expenditure: Defence expenditure for 1974/75 was $A1,568.4 million (U.S. $2,331 million). The defence budget for 1976/77 is $A1,900 million.

Chair. Chiefs of Staff Committee: Admiral Sir VICTOR SMITH, K.B.E., C.B., D.S.C.

Chief of the Naval Staff: Vice-Admiral H. D. STEVENSON, C.B.E.

Chief of the Air Staff: Air Vice-Marshal J. A. ROWLAND, D.F.C., A.F.C., B.E.

Chief of the General Staff: Lt.-Gen. FRANK G. HASSETT, C.B., C.B.E., D.S.O., M.V.O.

EDUCATION

Compulsory education was first established in Victoria by the 1872 Education Act, which was followed by similar acts in Queensland in 1875, in New South Wales and South Australia in 1880 and in Tasmania and Western Australia in 1893. After the federation of the 6 states was established in 1901 each state retained responsibility for education. The responsibility for framing educational policy and putting it into effect rests with the Minister of Education, and an Education Department headed by a director general deals with all aspects of education within each state. Although the state systems are not identical they have many similar features. The education of people in isolated areas is an important problem, although only a small proportion of Australia's school-age children live in remote districts. The Australian government gives high priority to equality of educational opportunity. School attendance in Australia is compulsory and free between the ages of 6-15 (16 in Tasmania) for all children except those exempted on account of distance, for whom a special form of education is provided. The academic year, which is divided into 3 terms, begins at the end of January or the beginning of February in schools and at the end of February or March in universities and ends in December for the long vacation. The Federal Government has now assumed full responsibility for education in the Australian Capital Territory and the Northern Territory. It also makes very substantial contributions to the States for recurrent and capital expenditure in both governmental and non-governmental schools. Since 1974 the Federal Government, by agreement with the States, has become responsible for the full financing of higher education throughout Australia. In the academic year 1974-75 the Federal Government provided $A1,545 million for education and the State Governments $A1,732 million.

Government Schools

In 1975 there were 7,266 government primary and secondary schools with an enrolment of 2,297,979 children and 123,441 teachers, of whom about half are women.

Pre-school. Only a small proportion of Australian children attend pre-school centres or kindergartens. Such centres are sometimes run by church bodies and private groups, more frequently by Government-subsidized Kindergarten Unions. These rely heavily on voluntary helpers and local financial support and also conduct training centres for training pre-school teachers.

Although compulsory education does not start until the age of six most children start school at five, attending infants' school or classes attached to the primary school. Primary schools are generally mixed and cater for children up to the age of twelve to thirteen with 4½–5 hours of daily instruction. Syllabuses are prescribed by the Educational departments, although teachers are to a certain extent free to modify courses to suit local circumstances. Progression from primary to secondary school is automatic on completion of the primary school course.

Secondary education is largely co-educational, although in the larger cities segregated schools are not uncommon. Children are grouped in classes according to the subjects that they intend to pursue. In the past, metropolitan high schools provided courses on traditional academic lines with the aim of preparing pupils for qualifying examinations to higher education. Curricula vary in each state but usually include English Language and Literature, or two foreign languages, mathematics, chemistry and physics and other natural and social sciences. However, while a purely academic course is still available it is becoming increasingly common for high schools to be of the comprehensive type. In more sparsely populated areas secondary classes are sometimes attached to a primary school, but the tendency is more and more to bring children in by bus from outlying areas to high schools in the nearest town.

Junior technical, agricultural area and rural schools offer up to four years of the secondary course and a curriculum combining general education with subjects related to their special emphasis.

Public examinations are being phased out in Australian schools. Intermediate examinations have been abolished and already in one state, Queensland, the formal public examination marking the completion of secondary education has been abolished. A variety of forms of assessment, including periodic tests and examinations in class are used to help teachers assess students' abilities and performance. Alternative methods are being developed for the selection of students for tertiary study, which use objective tests in conjunction with teacher assessment in the final year of a student's secondary schooling.

The Education Acts of all states provide for the formation of groups of parents and citizens attached to particular schools to promote the interests of the school by co-operation with the teachers. In several states the general maintenance of school buildings, equipment, and grounds is a statutory responsibility of the parent groups and costs are covered by Government grants. In 1974 the Federal

Government replaced its former scheme of secondary scholarships awarded on merit with a secondary allowance scheme under which grants, subject to a means test, are given to the States to encourage all children to complete the final two years of secondary schooling.

Private Schools or Independent Schools

In 1975 there were 621,301 pupils attending 2,140 private schools with 28,990 teachers. Approximately one child in four attends private schools which are fee-paying. The majority of non-government schools are conducted by various religious denominations, and many of the larger ones make provision for boarders; courses in private schools are similar to those in state schools. More than 80 per cent of the total number of private schools are Roman Catholic schools, which form a highly developed system, usually run on a diocesan basis under the general direction of the Bishop. In 1973 there were 1,754 Roman Catholic schools with 491,775 pupils, of which more than a quarter were at secondary level.

Special Education for Children in Isolated Areas

Education in isolated areas has been provided for in a variety of ways. In areas where there are sufficient children of school age, a school may be formed with all primary grades in one room, under the control of one teacher. Children who complete their primary education in such a school and cannot afford a secondary school education may take secondary correspondence lessons under the teacher's supervision. At one time over a third of Government schools were of this type, but now all state education departments are closing schools with small enrolments. Instead, pupils are transported each day by bus to a consolidated school in the nearest large centre of population. These schools provide primary instruction and from two to four years of post-primary instruction. The curriculum usually has a bias towards practical activities of the locality. All states have systems of subsidies, whereby transport is made available free or at a concession rate for children who have to travel daily to school. For children whose homes are too far from a secondary school to allow daily travel some states run hostels or give financial assistance to privately owned hostels, while others pay boarding allowances to the holders of scholarships. In 1973 the Federal Government introduced the Isolated Children Allowance Scheme, under which allowances are payable to the parents of all children of school age who live more than ten miles from the nearest school of appropriate standard and more than three miles from the nearest transport to that school.

Correspondence Schools have been established in each capital city to meet the needs of children whose daily attendance at school is prevented by distance or illness. These schools originally began with primary grades only but were soon expanded to secondary level and it is now possible to do a complete matriculation course. Correspondence schools are free and postage on books is paid both ways except in some states where tuition at secondary level is charged. As many as 20,000 children including Australian children overseas receive instruction each year through correspondence courses.

Schools of the Air, first established in 1950, are an attempt to give the outback children of school age some of the benefits of school life and at the same time to supplement correspondence education. Using the two-way wireless equipment first developed by the Royal Flying Doctor Service, children hundreds of miles apart take part in the same lesson, and teacher and pupil can talk directly with each other.

Higher Education

Since January 1st, 1974, all Australian students gaining entry to an approved tertiary institution receive maintenance grants, subject to a means test, under the Tertiary Education Allowances Scheme. At the same date all tuition fees for approved tertiary courses were abolished. Various other forms of Financial assistance to students are available from the Australian Government and the State Government.

Universities: Australian universities are autonomous institutions, though members of their respective state governments are among the members of their governing bodies. There are 18 universities and 78 colleges of advanced education. In 1975 the enrolment was 148,338 in the former and 122,557 in the latter. Most of the courses are full-time day courses lasting from three to six years, though some may be taken by part-time evening study. Some of the universities have limited systems of external tuition, whereby students in country areas may do certain courses by correspondence; in Queensland a highly developed system of correspondence tuition has been formed and external students in the larger Queensland country towns receive tutorial assistance at university centres. Postgraduate research facilities are available at all Australian universities and assistance is available either in the form of research grants from the universities themselves, or from the scheme of Commonwealth postgraduate awards.

Colleges of Advanced Education: This term covers a wide variety of institutions, other than universities, which provide Higher Education, including Technical Colleges, Institutes of Technology, Teachers' Colleges and Agricultural Colleges.

Technical education is available in Technical Colleges and Institutes of Technology. Technical Colleges provide craftsman and artisan training in the apprenticeship trades. The Institutes of Technology provide degree or diploma courses giving advanced training in the technical professions.

There is an increasing provision of sandwich courses, though the practice varies from state to state, and in some colleges and institutes courses may be completed wholly by evening study. In addition most colleges provide short diploma and refresher courses as well as courses of general interest. Many, too, provide correspondence courses at both trade and professional level.

Agricultural Colleges: There are eight state agricultural colleges; they are residential and administration in four of the states is by the Department of Agriculture. The minimum entrance requirement is the passing of matriculation subjects, and the course is of two to three years' duration, covering both theoretical and practical aspects of agricultural work, and leading to a diploma in agriculture.

Teachers' Colleges: There are 41 colleges in all. Primary, infants and in some cases, junior secondary teacher trainees complete a three-year course. Secondary state teachers are generally required to do a three-year degree, followed by a one-year diploma in education course. At several universities students can undertake a four-year Bachelor of Education course, which includes professional training. Teacher trainees for state service are recruited mainly at leaving Certificate or Matriculation level; they receive a living allowance during training, and the cost of their training is borne by the state department of education. In return they are required to enter into a bond to serve that Department for a specified period, varying according to the length of training received. The Federal Government also provides scholarships not subject to a bond for teacher trainees entering the Commonwealth Teaching Service. The number of students undertaking teacher training in 1973 was 55,262, and of these 27,625 were enrolled at single-purpose teachers' colleges. There are also private teacher training colleges including Roman Catholic ones and twelve kindergarten training colleges.

Adult Education is used mainly to refer to non-vocational education in which adults participate voluntarily. There are also continuation classes for teaching English to newly arrived migrants, and the State Education Departments and the Australian Broadcasting Corporation colloborate to provide a combined radio and correspondence course in English. At the end of 1973 33,718 adult immigrants were enrolled in continuation classes and over 7,000 were participating in the various radio and correspondence courses.

UNIVERSITIES

University of Adelaide: Adelaide, S.A. 5001; f. 1874; 686 teachers, 9,595 students.

The Australian National University: Canberra, A.C.T. 2600; f. 1946; 780 teachers, 5,272 students.

Flinders University of South Australia: Bedford Park, S.A. 5042; f. 1966; 314 teachers, 3,868 students.

Griffith University: Nathan, Qld. 4111; f. 1971; 91 teachers, 835 students.

James Cook University of North Queensland: Townsville, Qld.; f. 1970; 202 teachers, 1,854 students.

La Trobe University: Bundoora, Vic. 3083; f. 1964; 471 teachers, 8,569 students.

Macquarie University: North Ryde, N.S.W. 2113; f. 1964 570 teachers, 9,800 students.

University of Melbourne: Parkville, Melbourne; 1,000 teachers, 15,500 students.

Monash University: Clayton, Victoria; f. 1961; 956 teachers, 13,249 students.

Murdoch University: Murdoch, Western Australia; f. 1973; 110 teachers, 1,515 students.

University of New England: Armidale, N.S.W. 2351; f. 1954; 480 teachers, 7,883 students.

The University of New South Wales: Kensington, N.S.W. 2033; f. 1948; 1,090 teachers, 18,254 students.

University of Newcastle: Newcastle, N.S.W. 2308; f. 1965; 326 teachers, 4,501 students.

University of Queensland: Brisbane, Qld. 4967; f. 1969; 1,248 teachers, 18,215 students.

University of Sydney: Sydney, N.S.W. 2006; f. 1850; *c.* 1,200 teachers, 17,358 students.

University of Tasmania: Hobart; 280 teachers, 3,399 students.

University of Western Australia: Nedlands, W.A. 6009; f. 1911; 636 teachers, 9,804 students.

University of Wollongong: Wollongong, N.S.W.; f. 1975; 136 teachers, 2,159 students.

BIBLIOGRAPHY

GENERAL

AUSTRALIA: YEARBOOK OF THE COMMONWEALTH OF AUSTRALIA (Commonwealth Bureau of Census and Statistics, annually).

AUSTRALIAN ENCYCLOPEDIA.* 10 vols. (Grolier Society, Sydney, 1965).

BEAN, C. E. W. On the Wool Track (Angus and Robertson, Sydney, 1963).

CROWLEY, F. K. Modern Australia in Documents: 1901-1970 (Melbourne, Wren, 1974).

DAVIES, A. F. (Ed.). Australian Society; a sociological introduction (2nd edn., Melbourne, Cheshire, 1970).

HORNE, D. The Next Australia (Angus and Robertson, Sydney, 1970).

LEEPER, G. W. (Ed.). The Australian Environment (C.S.I.R.O., in association with Melbourne University Press, 4th edn., 1970).

PALFREEMAN, A. C. The Administration of the White Australia Policy (Melbourne University Press and Cambridge University Press, London, 1967).

ROBINSON, K. W. Australia, New Zealand and the South-West Pacific (University of London Press, 1960).

SPATE, O. H. K. Australia (Nations of the Modern World Series, Benn, London, 1968).

VENTURINI, V. G. (Ed.). Australia: a survey. With a foreword by Sir Keith Hancock (Wiesbaden, Otto Harrassowltz, 1970).

WARD, R. B. The Australian Legend (Melbourne, O.U.P., 2nd edn., 1966).

* New edition in preparation.

HISTORY

CLARK, C. M. H. A Short History of Australia (Heinemann, London, rev. edn., 1969).

GREENWOOD, G. (Ed.). Australia: a Social and Political History (Angus and Robertson, Sydney, 3rd edn., 1968).

HANCOCK, Sir KEITH. Australia (Jacaranda Press, Brisbane, 1961).

O'BRIEN, E. The Foundation of Australia (1786–1800): a study of eighteenth-century English criminal practice and penal colonization (Angus and Robertson, Sydney, 1950).

SHAW, A. G. L. The Story of Australia (Faber, London, 3rd edn., 1967).

SHAW, A. G. L., and NICOLSON, H. D. Australia in the Twentieth Century (Angus and Robertson, Sydney, 1967).

POLITICS

CRISP, L. F. Australian National Government (rev. edn., Melbourne, Longman, 1970).

LONDON, H. I. Non-White Immigration and the "White Australia" Policy (Sydney, Sydney University Press, 1970).

MILLAR, T. B. Australia's Foreign Policy (Sydney, Angus and Robertson, 1968).

MILLER, J. D. B. Australian Government and Politics; an introductory survey (4th edn., London, Duckworth, 1971).

MOORE, J. H. (Ed.). The American Alliance: Australia, New Zealand and the United States: 1940–1970 (Melbourne, Cassell, 1970).

TEICHMANN, M. (Ed.). New Directions in Australian Foreign Policy; ally, satellite or neutral? (Melbourne, Penguin Books, 1969).

WHITINGTON, D., and CHALMERS, R. Inside Canberra: a guide to Australian federal politics (Adelaide, Rigby, 1971).

ECONOMY

ANDREWS, J. A. Australia's Resources and their Utilisation (University Press, Sydney, rev. edn., 1970).

COGHILL, I. G. Australia's Mineral Wealth (Melbourne, Sorrett Publishing, 1971).

CORDEN, W. M. Australian Economic Policy Discussion: a survey (Melbourne, Melbourne University Press, 1968).

DOWNING, R. I. National Income and Social Accounts; an Australian Study (Melbourne University Press, 12th edn., reprinted with supplement, 1971).

FITZPATRICK, B. C. British Imperialism and Australia 1783–1833: an economic history of Australasia (Sydney, Sydney University Press, 1971).

FITZPATRICK, B. C. The British Empire in Australia: an economic history, 1834–1939 (Melbourne, Macmillan, 1969).

ISAAC, J. E. (Ed.) and FORD, G. (Ed.). Australian Labour Relations: readings (2nd edn., Melbourne, Sun Books, 1971).

KARMEL, P. H. The Structure of the Australian Economy (Cheshire, Melbourne, rev. edn., 1966).

NANKERVIS, F. T. Descriptive Economics; Australian Economic Institutions and Problems (Longmans, Melbourne, 7th edn., 1966).

PALMER, G. R. A Guide to Australian Economic Statistics (Macmillan, Melbourne, 2nd edn., 1966).

New Zealand

PHYSICAL AND SOCIAL GEOGRAPHY

A. E. McQueen

(Revised by the Editor, 1976)

New Zealand lies 1,600 kilometres (1,000 miles) south-east of Australia. It consists of two main islands, North Island with an area of 114,500 square kilometres (44,200 square miles) and South Island with an area of 150,700 square kilometres (58,170 square miles), plus Stewart Island to the south, with an area of 1,750 square kilometres (625 square miles), and some smaller islands. North and South Islands are separated by the Cook Straits, which are about 30 kilometres (20 miles) wide at the narrowest point. The total area of New Zealand is 268,676 square kilometres (103,736 square miles).

CLIMATE

There are three major factors affecting the climate of New Zealand, particularly so far as pasture growth is concerned.

The first is the country's situation in the westerly wind belt which encircles the globe. The main islands lie between 34° S. and 47° S., and are therefore within the zone of the eastward moving depressions and anti-cyclones within this belt. The second factor is the country's location in the midst of a vast ocean mass, which means that extremes of temperature are modified by air masses passing across a large expanse of ocean. It also means that abundant moisture is available by evaporation from the ocean, and rainfall is considerable and fairly evenly distributed throughout the year. The mean annual rainfall varies from 13 ins. east of the Southern Alps to over 300 ins. west of the Alps, but the average for the whole country lies between 25 and 60 ins.

The third factor is more of local significance: the presence of a chain of mountains extending from south-west to north-east through most of the country. The mountains provide a barrier to the westward moving air masses, and produce a quite sharp climatic contrast between east and west. The rain shadow effect of the mountains produces in certain inland areas of the South Island an almost continental climate, although no part of New Zealand is more than 80 miles from the sea.

Because of this generally "maritime" influence the temperature range is fairly small; the annual range of mean monthly temperatures in western districts of both islands is about 15°F., elsewhere from 17° to 20° except in inland areas of the South Island where it may be as high as 25°. The mean temperatures for the year vary from 59° in the far north to 54° about Cook Strait and 49° in the south. With increasing altitude, mean annual temperatures fall about 3° per 1,000 ft.

Snow is rare below 2,000 ft. in the North Island, and falls for only a few days a year at lower altitudes in the South Island. Rainfall and temperature combine to give a climate in which it is possible to graze livestock for all the year at lower altitudes in all parts of the country, and at higher altitudes, even in the South Island, for a considerable part of each year. Pasture growth varies according to temperature and season, but varies from almost continual growth in North Auckland to between 8 and 10 months in the South Island.

PHYSICAL FEATURES

Altitude and surface configuration are important features affecting the amount of land which is readily available for farming. Less than one-quarter of the land surface lies below the 650 ft. contour; in the North Island the higher mountains (those above 4,000 ft.) occupy about 10 per cent of the surface, but in the South Island the proportion is much greater. The Southern Alps, a massive chain including 16 peaks over 10,000 ft., run for almost the entire length of the island. The economic effect of the Southern Alps as a communications barrier has been considerably more than in the case of the North Island mountains; their rain-shadow effect is also significant for land use, as the lower rainfall, while giving a reduced growth rate, also produces the dry summers of the east coast plains which are major grain-growing areas. In addition, the wide expanses of elevated open country of lower rainfall have led to the development of large-scale pastoral holdings, and it is the South Island high country which produces almost all New Zealand's fine wools, particularly from the Merino sheep.

Other physical features with economic significance include rivers, lakes and earthquakes. Most New Zealand rivers are of little use for navigation but they are of vital importance for hydroelectric power production, with their high rate of flow and reliable volume of ice-free water. Many of the larger lakes of both islands, most of which are situated at quite high altitudes, are also important in power production, acting as reservoirs for the rivers upon which the major stations are situated. Earthquakes are a particular risk along a zone west of the Southern Alps, through Wellington and thence north-east to Napier and Wairoa. Their economic significance lies in the extra strengthening which must be incorporated into buildings, particularly larger commercial structures, and the risk to main communication lines. The degree of earthquake activity in New Zealand is often regarded as roughly similar to that in California, and very much less intense than in Japan or Chile.

NATURAL RESOURCES

In general geological terms, New Zealand is part of the unstable circum-Pacific Mobile Belt, a region where, in parts, volcanoes are active and where the earth's crust has been moving at a geologically rapid rate. Such earth movements, coupled with rapid erosion, have formed the sedimentary rocks which make up about three-quarters of the country. New Zealand also includes in its very complex geology schist, gneiss, and other metamorphic rocks, most of which are hundreds of millions of years old, as well as a number of igneous rocks. In such a geologically mobile country the constant exposure of new rock has led to young and generally fertile soils.

Within this broad pattern a variety of minerals has been found, many of them, however, in only very small deposits. Non-metallic minerals, such as coal, clay, limestone and dolomite are today both economically and industrially more important than metallic ores; but new demands from industry, and a realization that apparently small showings of more valuable minerals may well indicate much larger deposits, have led to a surge of prospecting since the early 1960s. One of the most successful results so far has been the proving of iron sand deposits on the west coast of the North Island. This development, along with the discovery of a satisfactory method of processing the sands, has paved the way to the founding of an iron and steel industry which began production in 1969. But knowledge of New Zealand's economic geology is still far from complete; in many respects the concentration upon farming had led the nation to believe that there were no economically attractive mineral resources, and the exploration and prospecting at present being carried out by both local and overseas firms is only now shattering the illusion that the nation's only worthwhile natural resource is its climate and soil. A particularly notable discovery in 1970 was a large natural gas field, off the South Taranaki coast. Further drilling is now taking place in the same area and work has now begun on pipelines to bring the gas to major centres.

When the first European settlers came to New Zealand they found two-thirds of the land's surface covered by forest. Today only about one-fifth of that forest remains, most of it kept as reserve or as national parks. The rest has been felled, much of it with little regard for land conservation principles. Out of today's total forested area of some 15.4 million acres, 14.0 million acres are still in indigenous forest, much of it unmillable protection forest; it is towards the 1.4 million acres of man-made exotic forest that New Zealand now looks as the major source of building timber and raw material for rapidly developing pulp and paper and other forest product industries. These activities are based at present largely on the extensive exotic forests of the Bay of Plenty—Taupo region, near the centre of the North Island.

POPULATION

At the last census in March 1971 New Zealand's population was 2,862,631, a 6.9 per cent increase over the previous census in 1966 (June 1975 estimate 3,086,900). Nearly 80 per cent of the population live in cities, boroughs or townships with populations greater than 1,000. In terms of international comparisons the population is small, density (29 per sq. mile in 1975) is low, the growth rate is average, and the degree of urbanization is high.

The majority of the population is of European origin; in June 1975 there were an estimated 252,700 indigenous Maoris.

Between 1926 and 1945 an average annual increase in population of 1.1 per cent was recorded, one of the lowest rates in the country's history. Since 1945, however, the rate of population growth has been maintained at a high level—a trend supported by both a high level of natural increase and immigration. A high post-war birth rate, which reached a peak of 26.99 per thousand in 1961, contrasts with a death rate of between 8 and 9 per thousand, one of the lowest in the world. This high rate of increase has been complemented by a steady influx of immigrants, some of them assisted to New Zealand by the Government. The total number of immigrants increased annually until 1952–53, since when there have been large variations in the immigration rate, the net increase in 1960, for example, being only 3,200 while in 1962 it was nearly 19,000. A major factor influencing the level of immigration is the level of economic activity; when prosperity declines, the number of government-assisted and privately sponsored immigrants falls sharply.

The processes of economic development have dictated a steadily increasing concentration of population, farm products processing, and industrial output in the major cities, especially within the North Island. Larger towns contain more of the population than other urban areas. In 1901 10 per cent of the population lived in towns of over 25,000; in 1921, 24 per cent; in 1971, 67 per cent of the population lived in urban areas with populations over 25,000. Conversely, the relative importance of towns with less than 5,000 people has declined steadily since 1901, and the number of people living in rural areas has steadily diminished as a proportion of the total population.

HISTORY

E. J. Tapp

COLONIZATION

In 1642 the islands of New Zealand were discovered and named by the Dutch navigator, Abel Tasman. He found and left them in possession of the Maoris, a neolithic Polynesian people who came, it is thought, from tropical Oceania several centuries before. After Tasman's visit they remained for a century and a quarter undisturbed and secure in their tribal lives until 1769 when they were rediscovered by Captain James Cook. He reported so favourably upon their lands that when a penal colony was established in New South Wales free settlers lost little time in making trading contact with them in search of timber and flax. They were soon followed by sealers and whalers who found the adjacent waters rich hunting grounds. From the consequent fugitive contacts that were made white settlement developed in the far northern district of the Bay of Islands. There the licentious and unscrupulous conduct of traders and whalers gave New Zealand a sinister reputation while traffic in firearms wrought terrible havoc among the natives in their hitherto comparatively harmless tribal warfare.

Concern for the welfare of the natives led in 1814 to the establishment of an Anglican mission in the Bay of Islands by the senior chaplain at Port Jackson (Australia), the Reverend Samuel Marsden. So precarious was its position that for years it exercised little influence. Finally, after repeated appeals from missionaries and traders the British Government in 1833 appointed a Resident for New Zealand. But so inadequate were his authority and power that "the man of war without guns", as the Maoris contemptuously called him, was quite unable to maintain law and order. In the meantime, trade and settlement increased, and in England sufficient interest was aroused to cause Edward Gibbon Wakefield, the systematic colonizer, to establish the *New Zealand Company* for planned settlement in the islands. Its dispatch of settlers, fear of the French and repeated representation from missionaries and merchants, finally forced the British Government to abandon its policy of minimum intervention and to empower Captain James Hobson to take possession of New Zealand as Lieutenant-Governor under the Government of New South Wales. Accordingly, in 1840 Hobson landed in the Bay of Islands and concluded the Treaty of Waitangi with Maori chiefs. By this treaty the natives were confirmed in their right to their lands, of which in return for the Queen's protection they gave her the exclusive right of purchase. By such prompt action Hobson checked unbridled land speculation and restricted a French colonizing venture to settlement at Akaroa, in the South Island, under the British flag. After a brief foster-father connection with New South Wales, New Zealand in 1842 became a separate colony with Hobson its first Governor.

Meanwhile, undue haste by *New Zealand Company* settlers to lay claim to a valley in the north of the South Island led to a disastrous clash with its native inhabitants. At the same time Maoris in the far north, fearing for their lands and their way of life, openly rebelled against the *pakeha* (European). Until Captain George Grey arrived as Governor attempts at suppression were abortive. But by vigorous attack and with a promise to uphold the Treaty of Waitangi, he not only ended the war but won the esteem of the Maoris.

Elsewhere, largely through the activities of the *New Zealand Company*, colonization went on apace. Several hundred West of England farmers landed in Taranaki to found the settlement of New Plymouth. In the South Island, where there were but few Maoris, a Scottish Free Church colony was established in 1848, and two years later a Church of England settlement was made on the Canterbury Plains. Assuming that such colonists would expect this, the British Government in 1846 passed an Act conferring representative institutions on New Zealand. But, thinking the Act premature, the autocratic Governor Grey delayed until 1852 the introduction of self-government, which provided for a General Assembly for the whole of New Zealand and for six Provincial Councils. Four years later the colony secured responsible government, but for twenty years it was in most matters controlled by the Provincial Councils.

THE YEARS 1850-1918

During the first two decades of the period the North Island was troubled by war with the Maoris. In 1860 European ignorance of the nature of the tribal ownership of land provoked bitter fighting in Taranaki which spread like fire in the fern over much of the island. Under astute leadership the Maoris drew together to present a united front to *pakeha* encroachment. In spite of its pacific overtures the Government was for suppressing the Maoris, and even the return of Grey for a second term of office failed to restore peace. At every turn the natives harassed soldier and settler alike until by about 1870, their resources at an end, organized resistance gradually ceased. Although quelled and his spirit temporarily broken, the Maori had earned for his skill and bravery the lasting respect of the *pakeha*.

In the South Island, meanwhile, the English and Scottish settlements, untroubled by war, made rapid progress. The discovery of gold in 1861 in Otago and on the West Coast in 1865 greatly quickened the pace of development. More important in the long run was the impact made by tens of thousands of gold diggers from Australia and North America. Politically their influence was of particular significance, for, free of regional attachments, they encouraged a national rather than a narrow provincial outlook. This tendency was assisted by better communications, inter-island steamship service and the telegraph. By 1870 the prosperity of the South and the pacification of the North Island made a bold policy of economic expansion uniquely opportune. With supreme confidence and foresight Julius Vogel, the Colonial Treasurer (who was to become Premier in 1872-75) borrowed from London nearly £20 million during the next ten years for an extensive scheme of public works. An unwitting pioneer of the social welfare state, Vogel established the Government Life Insurance and the Public Trust organization. In the 1860s and 1870s, independently of the Government, the Bank of New Zealand and several large mercantile companies had already been established.

In the wake of capital came about 100,000 migrants to build roads and railways and to open up the country, especially the Canterbury plains for wheat. Pioneering in the backblocks entailed much privation and hardship, but determined settlers were soon pasturing sheep and laying the foundations of much of New Zealand's future prosperity. In all this development Vogel and the entrepreneurs were favoured by high prices for their exports. Moreover, so disruptive of parochial loyalties were the economic advances and the centripetal forces set up so weakened the Provincial Councils that in 1876 Vogel abolished them. In the following year came free, compulsory and secular education for the whole country.

By 1878 the Vogel boom was over, the spending spree ended. Instead, the high cost of public works and falling export prices combined to bring New Zealand to the brink of disaster. Only a policy of stringent economy tided the colony through the long depression of the 1880s. Of a population that had grown to half a million, thousands left to enjoy the prosperous conditions in Australia. Recovery came slowly, but with more settled conditions in the North Island primary production increased steadily. To this revival nothing gave such a fillip as did the commercial application in 1882 of refrigeration, an invention which not only helped to rescue the colony from its financial predicament but which shaped the whole pattern of New Zealand's future development.

In politics hard times had fostered radicalism and ousted the Conservatives from office in favour of the Liberals with their concern for the artisan and small farmer. This tendency was strengthened by the failure of the great Australasian maritime strike of 1890 and the subsequent recourse of labour to the ballot box for reform. With its support the Liberal Government not only stepped in to save the Bank of New Zealand from collapse but embarked upon an era of unprecedented social activity. Strongly influenced by the Fabian socialism of William Pember Reeves, the Premier, R. J. ("Dick") Seddon, a rugged pragmatist, introduced such far-reaching reforms as to make the New Zealand worker the best protected in the world. Within a few years Seddon carried through legislation which provided for better factory conditions, accident compensation, shorter working hours and payment for overtime, compulsory conciliation and arbitration in industrial disputes, and finally, in 1898, old age pensions. In addition land hunger was appeased by legislation which made possible subdivision of large holdings and which imposed a graduated tax on unimproved land values. Such empirical humanitarianism earned for New Zealand a reputation as an advanced social laboratory. By the end of the century she had in fact so outdistanced the Australian colonies in social legislation as to make her little disposed to accept the invitation to join the Commonwealth of Australia. With urban development fostering secondary industries to supplement the main agricultural and pastoral activities of the people, including the Maoris, whose self-confidence was rapidly being restored, few saw any merit in union with Australia.

Foreign Affairs

So absorbed had she become with her own domestic problems that New Zealand had taken little interest in external affairs. For a few brief years she had, under the audacious imperialism of Vogel, espoused a policy of "Oceania for the Anglo-Saxons", but with little encouragement from Britain, enthusiasm for it died. From her very beginnings she had with unquestioning loyalty placed implicit trust in the Mother Country for her protection. After 1887 she contributed regularly towards the British navy and sent a volunteer contingent to the South African War. At the outbreak of the First World War she gave Britain immediate and generous support. Her armed forces played an active part in the various theatres of war, especially at Gallipoli. At home the war itself made little difference to the life of the average New Zealander; business was as usual. The Labour Party opposed the introduction of conscription for military service. High prices for primary exports and the stimulus that the war gave to their production greatly strengthened the economy.

Generally the war quickened New Zealand's maturity in more ways than one. Her separate representation at the Peace Conference and independent membership of the League of Nations enhanced her international prestige. From the spoils of war she gained the mandate over ex-German Samoa and shared with Australia and the United Kingdom the mandate for the phosphate island of Nauru. For all that, she took little interest in imperial or foreign affairs and preferred to remain as close as possible to Britain.

THE INTER-WAR PERIOD

After the war, under conditions of general prosperity and full employment, New Zealand resumed a selective assisted migration policy which increased the population by nearly 70,000 by 1928 when the intake temporarily ceased. As trade conditions hardened the Government intervened more and more to control the nation's economy. It offered expert advice and financial assistance to step up production. The many dairy farmers who had banded together to establish co-operative butter and cheese factories were content to let the Government organize the marketing of their produce overseas. Increasingly too did the public turn to the Government for aid when in 1928 the first signs of depression appeared. To meet the growing unemployment and unfavourable balance of trade the leader of the United Party, Sir Joseph Ward, proposed to borrow £70 million with which to prime the economy. But, although elected to office, the party was unable to cope with a deteriorating situation. Far from raising tens of millions, the Government was put to the less spectacular tasks of setting up relief works and of rationalizing the rail and road transport system to effect economies. A coalition Government of United and Reform Parties proceeded on orthodox lines to reduce expenditure on defence and to halt railway construction. Faced with a mounting army of unemployed, the Government imposed emergency taxes of a direct and indirect nature and also reduced salaries and wages of public servants. It also declared a moratorium on war debts and converted many of its bonds at lower rates of interest. Along with the other Dominions New Zealand committed herself to the Ottawa Agreement of 1932 in her search for economic recovery, and for the benefit of the primary producer depreciated the New Zealand pound by 25 per cent.

But in spite of all these palliatives the depression grew worse instead of better. Trade had so contracted that in one year (1931) income from exports fell by 40 per cent. Confidence in the Government was badly shaken, for by 1935 the number of unemployed had risen to 70,000. Disorder and rioting broke out in the major cities, and labour unrest was rife throughout the country. Strikes even occurred among the unemployed. The working classes and small farmers complained that the Government failed to consider welfare as against wealth. In 1935 small farmers combined with the working classes to return the Labour Party to power with a substantial majority.

It was a radical political change which only desperate conditions could have provoked. Nevertheless, with the increase in urban development, the Labour Party had steadily gained in strength until it had become the official parliamentary opposition. Extremist elements, which had made an unsuccessful bid for party leadership, had mellowed with the years to play a prominent part in the Labour Government. Imbued with much of the idealism of the old Liberal Party, the Government was now eager to take over where Seddon had left off. Under its leader, Michael Savage, prices of essential commodities were fixed. The dairy farmer was given a guaranteed price for his butter and cheese which were marketed by the Government both at home and abroad. The scourge of unemployment was tackled by the introduction of large-scale public works such as road and railway construction. The State offered the right to work at a fixed basic wage and made trade union membership compulsory. Salary and wage cuts were restored and a forty-hour week was introduced to increase the demand for labour. To cope with the acute housing shortage the Government set up a special department to undertake a most ambitious and exemplary building programme. These various and extensive undertakings were financed by means of increased taxation and public loans. In 1936 the Government bought out the private shareholders of the Reserve Bank, which had been set up two years previously, and thus secured control over currency and exchange rates.

Out of the privately controlled *National Mortgage Corporation* it built up the *State Advances Corporation*, but otherwise it interfered little with secondary industry. Partly because of the vigorous and successful Government attacks on the evils of the depression, and partly because of the general improvement in trading conditions in all countries, at the end of three years Colin Clark, the eminent economist, could point to New Zealand farmers as the "best off" in the world; and he further declared that "no other country has made such a bold departure from the old fashioned fatalistic outlook towards depression or taken such positive steps to promote and maintain employment and income".

It was no undeserved tribute; and, when in 1937 the Labour Government went to the country seeking a mandate for advanced social legislation, a grateful public granted it willingly. The Government then began to build upon the social legislation of the 1890s to complete the welfare state. In 1938 a Social Security Act was passed which gave the Government sweeping powers of paternalism. It provided for free general practitioner services, medicine, hospital treatment and maternity benefits, and for family allowances and increased old age pensions. To finance such comprehensive insurance a special tax was levied on all incomes and supplemented by grants from ordinary revenue. Fortunately, these were years of prosperity with high prices for exports. But although her economic recovery was real enough, New Zealand was so prodigal of her funds that by 1939 they had become so depleted by heavy withdrawals to meet overseas commitments and by the flight of private capital that to stave off a crisis the Government restricted imports and controlled the export of capital.

THE PERIOD SINCE 1939

Such attempts to insulate New Zealand against forces inimical to the welfare state were aided by the advent of the Second World War, which intensified the demand and raised prices for exportable products. The war itself was accepted with fatalistic fortitude by a people who had become progressively disillusioned by the failure of the League of Nations to keep the peace. With a sober appraisal of New Zealand's position in the Pacific her Government had invited Australia and Britain to a defence conference before hostilities began. The Mother Country's declaration of war in 1939 was felt to be as binding on New Zealand as it had been in 1914. A special war cabinet was formed on the basis of a coalition of all parties. The Premier, Peter Fraser, concentrated the economic policy around the objective of stabilization, and in this he was largely successful. Conscription was introduced for overseas service, essential commodities were rationed and the country's resources were mobilized for the war effort. But the rationalizing of manpower in 1942 provoked a crisis in the coal mining industry and caused the Government to take over the mines. Incensed at what it regarded as the Government's capitulation to the coal miners, the National Party withdrew from the war cabinet. With the entry into the war of Japan the country quickly responded to meet the dire threat of imminent invasion, but even after the attack on Pearl Harbor she did not recall her troops from the Middle East. The forty-hour week was suspended and in 1943 thousands of men were released from the armed forces to increase food and factory production and thereby assist the United States in its overall Pacific campaign.

Political Developments since 1945

After the war the Government immediately tackled problems of rehabilitation and reconstruction. Although rationing of butter and meat continued for many years, most controls were soon removed. In 1945 the Labour Government, in spite of much opposition, nationalized the Bank of New Zealand, the Dominion's largest trading bank. But at the 1946 elections it lacked the vote of the small farmers and only the support of the four Maori electorates, which Labour had sedulously cultivated, enabled it to live another day and make minor additions to its social security programme. In the face of widespread industrial troubles which it was powerless to subdue, and embarrassed by a Communist splinter group, Labour at the 1949 elections lost office to the National Party under Mr. S. G. Holland.

Astute enough to realize that no government dare tamper with the social security legislation, the Prime Minister contented himself with removing artificial brakes on prices and imports. With the full approval of the Labour opposition the Government abolished the Legislative Council, which as a council of review had gradually declined in importance. It returned the coal mines to private ownership and withdrew subsidies on certain commodities. But attempts to peg prices failed to prevent inflation. In the consequent social unrest extremists refused to abide by the principle of compulsory arbitration, and the Government brought in troops to break a prolonged waterfront strike. Public feeling ran high over the Prime Minister's handling of the crisis, but at a surprise election in 1951 he secured an unequivocal endorsement of his policy.

So little now separated the two major parties that public interest in politics declined. At the 1954 general elections the Labour Party, bankrupt of ideas, was unable to wrest the reins of office from the National Party with its more liberal policy towards private enterprise. Growing dissatisfaction with both parties was evident in the surprising support (11 per cent of the votes cast) given to the newly formed Social Credit Party. In 1955 import controls were relaxed only to be replaced a year later by credit restrictions to limit spending. At the general elections in 1957 the Labour Party, by outbidding its opponents on income tax rebates and larger security payments, gained a narrow victory under its veteran leader, Walter Nash.

Almost immediately the Labour Government was embarrassed by pressing economic problems. Falling prices for meat and dairy produce led to an adverse balance of trade and an alarming depletion of the country's overseas reserves. To avert a crisis and to stave off unemployment the Government re-imposed import licensing and exchange control and raised over £30 million in London and Australia and another £20 million internally. Although these measures arrested the decline, the Government's "black budget" of 1958, a further attempt to restore economic balance, sealed the fate of Labour and at the elections in 1960 the National Party under Mr. K. J. Holyoake regained the Treasury benches. Among the more important changes that followed was the appointment in 1962 of a Parliamentary Commissioner (Ombudsman) to enquire into public complaints arising from administrative decisions of the Government. Relatively stable economic conditions enabled the National Party to be returned to power in 1966. At the next General Election in 1969 Keith Holyoake, although managing to retain office, lost ground to Labour. Neither the paternalism and sober conservatism of John Marshall, who succeeded Sir Keith Holyoake when he stepped down from office in February 1972 after twelve years as Prime Minister, nor the advent of a new Values Party prevented a major swing in November 1972, when Labour swept into office under Norman Kirk. His vigorous and forthright leadership, especially in the field of foreign policy, was, however, cut short in August 1974 by his untimely death. His successor, Wallace Rowling, who found himself opposed by a new leader of the National Party, Robert Muldoon, in place of the deposed Mr. (now Sir) John Marshall, continued his predecessor's policy but less forcefully.

Playing on fears of national disaster consequent on Labour's heavy overseas borrowing policy with its inflationary effects, the opposition leader, Robert Muldoon, campaigned on the promise of a more attractive and egalitarian superannuation policy than that offered by the Government. The much rejuvenated National Party roundly defeated the less well organized and positive Labour Government at the general elections of November 1975. In an almost unprecedented, surprising and disastrous swing against it, Labour lost 23 seats, including those of 5 Cabinet members.

Recent Foreign and Domestic Affairs

In world affairs New Zealand has become very conscious of her position as a Pacific Power. Her first major step in independent policy was made in 1944 with the Canberra Pact, a mutual security agreement with Australia. In 1947 she adopted at long last the Statute of Westminster, which granted her complete autonomy and freedom of action in international affairs. As a strong supporter of the UN, in 1950 she sent troops to its force in Korea. Although not without misgivings at the exclusion of Great Britain, in 1952 she joined Australia and the United States in the ANZUS defence treaty, and two years later became a member of the South East Asia Treaty Organization (SEATO). To give effect to her treaty commitments New Zealand sent a military unit to Malaya in 1955 and combined with Australia in an ANZAC unit in Viet-Nam. Along with Australia she has undertaken to maintain forces in Singapore and Malaysia to combine with what British forces remain in the area for the safeguarding of the political *status quo.* In the Pacific she has assisted Western Samoa (over which she exercised a UN Trusteeship Agreement until 1962) towards its independence, and has shown increasing interest in the islands to her north, some of which are legally part of New Zealand. Especially has she been involved in the establishment of the new University of the South Pacific in Fiji and in the measures effected for the independence in 1970 of that island group. In 1965 New Zealand was elected to the UN Security Council and in 1967 she applied sanctions against Rhodesia, but was reluctant to press its anti-apartheid policy to effective lengths.

The Labour Government which took office in December 1972 followed a more independent foreign policy than its predecessor. While maintaining the ANZUS treaty as the main plank of defence, it began to phase out its military commitments under SEATO and was intent instead on non-military objectives in South-East Asia. It established diplomatic relations with the People's Republic of China and the Democratic Republic of Viet-Nam. New Zealand protested strongly against French nuclear testing in the South Pacific in 1973 and 1974. With Australia it injected more financial aid into the South Pacific Commission.

To some extent these policies were halted, if not reversed, by the National Government which came to power in December 1975. The Prime Minister, Robert Muldoon, reaffirmed New Zealand's dependence on the U.S.A. and expressed fears of Soviet naval expansion in the area.

New Zealand has grown more responsive to the needs and aspirations of native peoples in the South Pacific. Since the mid-1950s some 30,000 Polynesians from the Cook, Tonga and Tokelau islands have migrated to New Zealand, mainly to the city of Auckland, where they have found a ready labour market. Unfortunately, lack of education and preparation for a new environment have created social problems which have led to restrictive Government measures, especially against the many illegal Polynesian immigrants. Meanwhile, the quarter of a million Maoris in New Zealand's population of 3 million have shown signs of Maori nationalism. For all that, the assimilation of the Maori proceeds peacefully through education and intermarriage.

In 1975 the Labour Government mounted an Education Development Conference, in which 50,000 people took part, to ascertain needs for change in the school system. Partly as a result, the integration of private schools into the State school system is beginning. Growing interest in Maori culture and language has led to their being more actively taught and promoted in schools and universities. To the six universities has recently been added a medical school at the University of Auckland, to supplement the medical school of the University of Otago in Dunedin. In 1976 education was being affected by government budgetary cuts. Finally, New Zealanders generally view with misgivings prospective visits from nuclear-powered ships and the building of nuclear energy plants in the country. The days of unbridled prosperity and complacency are over, giving way to a more sober and realistic appreciation of the domestic situation and of New Zealand's place in world affairs.

ECONOMIC SURVEY

J. W. Rowe

The New Zealand economy is characterized by a high degree of dependence upon agriculture, especially livestock farming, and the export of agricultural products, notably temperate foodstuffs. Although this degree of specialization exposes the country to major fluctuations in external earnings and in recent decades has not been conducive to rapid economic growth, it is fundamental to the comparatively high standard of living still enjoyed by the average New Zealander. Concentration on extensive pastoral farming, in which New Zealand has a comparative advantage owing to its benign climate and low population density, and the development of it to a high state of efficiency have yielded productivity levels not so far matched except in hydro-electric generation and forestry.

Apart from climate and water power, New Zealand is not well endowed with readily exploitable natural resources. Coal is abundant but not of high quality and there are vast deposits of iron sands but these are proving difficult to process. Natural gas has been discovered in large quantities but far from population centres and with the main field in deep water, so exploitation and transport will be expensive. Petroleum has not been found in commercially interesting amounts. New Zealand's natural resources do not have to serve a large population but the elongated shape of the country, its division into two main islands and the ruggedness of most of its terrain, along with the low density of settlement, make for high internal transport costs. The smallness of the domestic market is a major obstacle to higher productivity in secondary industry, yet the population increase necessary to achieve significant economies of scale in manufacturing would almost eliminate agricultural exports which provide the great bulk of the foreign exchange upon which industry relies for raw materials and capital equipment. The relatively great distances separating New Zealand from all other countries of any size (except Australia, which is at much the same stage of development) makes it difficult to expand the local market for manufactures by exporting on a large scale.

Strenuous efforts have indeed been made since the mid-1940s to promote manufacturing and thereby diversify the economy in order to insulate it to some degree from fluctuations in traditional export markets, but these efforts have not greatly lessened New Zealand's dependence upon wool, meat and dairy products. Since the emphasis until recently has been on import substitution rather than exports, the protection accorded to manufacturing may partly explain the country's indifferent growth record. On the other hand, it would have been very difficult to maintain virtually full employment throughout this period without a greatly expanded manufacturing sector.

Despite its key position in the economy, agriculture accounted for only 10 per cent of net output in the mid-1970s. This proportion had fallen by a third since the mid-1960s. Other sectoral contributions did not change greatly in the same decade. In the earlier post-war years the share of manufacturing rose a little but that of the services sector as a whole much more rapidly, both at the expense of agriculture.

STRUCTURE OF THE NEW ZEALAND ECONOMY IN 1976

(% contribution to gross domestic product)

Agriculture	10
Other primary industries	2
Manufacturing	27
Public utilities	4
Construction	6
Transport, etc.	8
Distribution	19
Business services	12
Social services	12

In the decade from the mid-1960s labour productivity in the economy as a whole rose by an average of about 1.5 per cent a year, with agriculture and the services group showing virtually no growth whereas manufacturing achieved an average annual increase of 3 per cent. The greatest achievement was in the public utilities sector. Manufacturing in the earlier post-war years also registered relatively high productivity growth (from a low base in most cases) and agriculture had a good record until the early 1970s.

PRIMARY INDUSTRY

Agriculture

Farming and associated processing industries play a far greater part in the New Zealand economy than in most developed countries because of their export orientation. In 1975 there were 9.7 million cattle, including 2.1 million dairy cows, and 55.3 million sheep. Grasslands have been developed to the point where good dairy farms carry more than one cow per acre throughout the year, without winter stabling and with minimal supplementation of grass in the diet. This high carrying capacity is sustained only by intensive use of artificial fertilizers, mainly phosphates.

Sheep farming is fairly evenly distributed but dairying is concentrated in the North Island, particularly in its upper half which has two-thirds of New Zealand's cows.

In the mid-1970s sheep accounted for about a third of gross agricultural output, cattle for a sixth, dairy products a quarter and all other farm products another quarter. The post-war period has seen a relative decline in the importance of wool, owing to falling prices, and a switch from dairying to beef production, associated with the development of markets for beef in North America and Japan. Domestic consumption accounts for about 40 per cent of New Zealand's output of beef and mutton, 20 per cent of butter and cheese, and 10 per cent of lamb and wool.

Cropping, fruit growing, horticulture and miscellaneous farming activities are of increasing importance. New Zealand is virtually self-sufficient in wheat, while barley, maize, peas and potatoes are other significant crops, but only for the local market. Seeds are grown in quantity mainly for export, and apple and pear production is also export-orientated. There is, too, a growing export of frozen or tinned vegetables, mainly to Australia. Tobacco cultivation has long been fostered as a means of import substitution so that New Zealand now produces half its needs. Hop production is also substantial.

There has been virtually no increase in the area of land used for farming since the early twentieth century. Numbers employed in farming have hardly increased for 70 years, although total population has more than trebled. The volume of agricultural exports, nevertheless, has outpaced population because of increasing investment in land improvement, farm machinery and better livestock. More recently, however, there has been a marked slackening in agricultural production and exports, the level of the former, in volume terms, being little higher in the mid-1970s than a decade previously. This may be explained partly by the disproportionate increase in the costs of processing farm products compared with the trend in their gross return.

Forestry

Forestry has reached maturity since the mid-1950s, as the first man-made forests have come to maturity and the area of replacement forest has greatly expanded. In the nineteenth century timber was an important export but, until the 1950s, almost all the trees logged were indigenous and seldom replaced, mainly because they were slow-growing species. The first large-scale plantings of exotic trees were in the 1920s and it soon became clear that the species best suited to New Zealand was *Pinus radiata*, a conifer which is rapidly becoming the dominant tree in New Zealand, except in protected residual indigenous forests. Annual planting is being steadily increased so that forestry and associated processing industries will progressively increase in importance.

Fishing

Fishing is not a major industry and seems unlikely ever to become so, despite considerable efforts to foster its development. Marine fish and rock lobsters are the main products but oyster farming is being promoted.

Mining

The future of mining and its associated processing industries is less assured. Coal mining will probably be rejuvenated following the enormous increase in petroleum prices in 1973–74; coal reserves are estimated at 1,000 million tons. Natural gas will become economically significant once Maui off-shore gas is "landed". However, both these operations are likely to prove very costly, and the greatly preferable alternative of finding oil in quantity seems increasingly unlikely. When Maui gas is on-stream, in a few years' time, it will be used partly for electricity generation and to a lesser extent for reticulation as a premium fuel. The scale and pattern of easily accessible industrial demand is such that there will be sufficient left for a petrochemical industry based on natural gas.

SECONDARY INDUSTRY

Manufacturing contributed over a quarter of gross domestic product in 1975 and employed about the same proportion of the labour force. In recent years output has been growing at an average annual rate of 5 to 6 per cent. Processing primary products accounts for a fifth of manufacturing, the remainder covering a wide range of activities, characterized by orientation towards the domestic market, reliance on imports and small-scale operations. This situation owes much to various import controls which have been in force since 1938. Although invoked for balance of payments reasons, they have been retained to protect local industry. This protectionist policy has been successful to the extent that domestic production accounts for a high proportion of finished manufactures available in New Zealand but it has made manufacturing very dependent on imports of raw materials, semi-finished goods and fuel, as well as plant and equipment.

Strong and somewhat indiscriminate encouragement of import substitution in a small domestic market has militated against industrial efficiency. Only half of manufacturing output comes from factories employing more than 100 workers and those employing more than 500 workers account for only a fifth. Furthermore, many of the latter are in the primary products processing sector. Prices for domestic manufactures often exceed corresponding import prices by a half, and domestic costs of production are sometimes twice those in advanced industrial countries.

However, exports of manufactures have recently increased markedly, even excluding forest products, the stimulus afforded by export incentives and the 1967 devaluation having proved lasting.

Two of New Zealand's largest industrial enterprises are N.Z. Forest Products Ltd. and Tasman Pulp and Paper Company. Both produce large quantities of sawn timber and chemical pulp; the former also produces kraft and other coarse papers and the latter newsprint and mechanical (groundwood) pulp. They are largely responsible for exports of timber (mainly to Japan) and pulp and paper (mainly to Australia). More recently a large refiner ground wood mill has been established by a Japanese-New Zealand consortium, again almost entirely for export.

Another large enterprise of recent origin is New Zealand Steel Ltd., which is exploiting iron sand deposits with the benefit of a secure domestic market. It plans to produce the bulk of New Zealand's steel requirements by the mid-1980s in association with Pacific Steel Ltd. A World Bank Report criticized the plans as contemplating an excessive range of products, at least some of which could be produced for a small domestic market only at unduly high cost.

No such criticism can be made of the Australian-Japanese consortium which operates a large aluminium smelter based on cheap power (from a state-owned hydro-electric station) and Queensland alumina. The great bulk of the resulting metal is exported to assured markets in Australia and Japan. Aluminium fabrication and semifabrication have also expanded substantially in recent years.

TERTIARY INDUSTRY

Power

Abundant rainfall and a mountainous terrain associated with large lakes give New Zealand a big hydro-electric potential. Electricity output is about 20,000 million kWh. per year, with hydro-electricity contributing 15,000 million kWh. The main thermal stations are fired by coal and oil/gas. There is also a large geothermal station with a capacity comparable with that of both the main thermal stations. The two main islands are linked by two-way direct current cables so virtually the whole country is served by the grid.

Oil consumption and electricity generation both increased greatly between the mid-1960s and mid-1970s, the latter doubling and the former more than doubling. Following the 1973 increase in oil prices, it was decided to fire future thermal power stations with natural gas or coal.

Construction

The construction industry in New Zealand has three distinct parts: dwelling construction, predominantly of timber in single units; commercial and industrial construction, notably of middle-rise office buildings; and heavy earth-moving work associated with bridge, dam and road construction. Since the mid-1960s the industry as a whole, and especially its residential component, has been subject to marked cyclical fluctuations about a slowly falling trend.

Transport

Sea transport has given increasing trouble, with the exception of goods carried on inter-island ferries. Urban passenger transport and all passenger transport by rail are facing increasing problems of patronage, service and cost, with losses as the normal consequence. Higher fuel and labour costs are forcing a rationalization of the country's over-generous internal airline network. There are also three international airports but one handles traffic to Australia only. The motor car is ubiquitous in New Zealand and it has taken great increases in petrol prices to cause even a minor reduction in petrol consumption.

INTERNATIONAL TRADE AND PAYMENTS

In 1950 the United Kingdom took nearly two-thirds of New Zealand's exports; in 1974/75 it accounted for 22 per cent but remained the largest single market. Similarly for imports, the importance of the United Kingdom has greatly diminished, to 19 per cent compared with 60 per cent in 1950. The next largest export markets in 1974/75 were Australia, Japan and the U.S.A., each taking nearly an eighth of exports. Australia was the main source of imports in 1974/75, supplying 20 per cent of the total, followed by the United Kingdom, Japan with 14 per cent and the U.S.A. with 13 per cent. The relative importance of Australia, Japan and the U.S.A. has increased since 1950 but that of Japan, with which there was virtually no trade in 1950, has grown most spectacularly.

Primary producers have a major say in the marketing of their products. The Dairy Board regulates the internal marketing of butter and cheese and both acquires and markets all exports of dairy products, being particularly concerned in the last few years to market these more widely. The Meat Producers' Board controls grading of export meat, negotiates shipping freights, allocates cargo space and organizes shipments. It has also taken the initiative in promoting sales in non-traditional markets. Through its efforts and otherwise, a greater range of meat products is now more widely marketed, very recent developments being the opening up of markets for mutton in the Middle East. The Wool Marketing Corporation fixes minimum prices for various types of wool and participates in auctions to ensure that these prices are maintained. It may also trade on its own account. An Apple and Pear Marketing Board buys all such fruit grown in New Zealand and markets the crops both internally and externally. There are similar authorities for honey, eggs, potatoes, citrus fruit and milk for local consumption.

Tourism has earned increasing amounts of foreign exchange in recent years. Australia supplies over half the tourists and the U.S.A. is the next most important country of origin.

In the late 1960s there were misgivings about export prospects, especially for products sold mainly in the United Kingdom, because of the likelihood that Britain would sooner or later join the agriculturally protectionist European Economic Community. These misgivings returned in 1974 but in between there was a remarkable surge of export income, attributable to a temporary shortage of most farm products. Prices for all major exports rose in 1971-74 but more recently most of New Zealand's major exports slumped in price and so far only wool has recovered strongly.

In recent years there have been disturbing signs of stagnation, if not decline, in the volume of traditional exports. Exports of forest products and miscellaneous manufactures have been rising in volume and value but not sufficiently to increase exports overall. For both traditional and non-traditional exports there is increasing concern about the implications of domestic inflation.

Throughout most of the 1960s New Zealand had a steadily increasing deficit on current account but the situation improved dramatically after the 1967 devaluation. Two years of current account surpluses were followed by deficits for a further two years. The short-lived export boom referred to above yielded another surplus. However, the rise in export income and concurrent upsurge in government expenditure generated such an internal boom that the current account showed a small deficit in 1973/74 and an enormous one in 1974/75.

The latest deterioration in the external trading position has thus been due partly to lower export prices and sagging export volumes but mainly to soaring import costs. Because New Zealand relies heavily on petroleum products it was affected more severely than most other countries by the 1973/74 oil price increases but the payments imbalance which developed in 1974 owed most to sharply rising internal expenditure in 1973 and 1974. This spilled over into imports and other overseas expenditure because there was virtually no restriction on the latter and the import controls in force at the time covered a relatively small proportion of imports, i.e. those competitive with local industry. Most raw materials, semi-processed goods and capital equipment were exempt so there was scope for a surge in imports—partly for inventory. Even for items under control, extra licences had been issued quite freely, partly in recognition of rapid increases in supply prices.

With the assistance of heavy overseas borrowing, private as well as public, New Zealand has been able to cover its external deficit without having to deflate the economy too severely. The New Zealand dollar was devalued by 15 per cent in August 1975 as much to reduce the size of the subsidies to farmers which would otherwise have been necessary as to correct the short-term balance of payments position.

From 1949 to 1961 the New Zealand pound was at par with sterling, with a value of U.S. $2.80. In October 1961 the parity was adjusted to U.S. $2.78 and this rate was not disturbed by conversion in July 1967 to a decimal currency based on the New Zealand dollar, equivalent to half a pound or U.S. $1.39. However, when the United Kingdom devalued in November 1967 New Zealand devalued to a greater extent to establish parity with the Australian dollar (U.S. $1.12 until August 1971 and U.S. $1.216 from December 1971). This parity was, however, lost when Australia unilaterally revalued its currency in December 1972. The New Zealand dollar's fixed relationship with the United States dollar was ended in July 1973, when a trade-weighted daily "float" was introduced, involving the currencies of New Zealand's main trading partners. Subsequently the New Zealand dollar was revalued in September 1973 but devalued in September 1974 and August 1975.

OVERALL ECONOMIC PERFORMANCE

The overall performance of the New Zealand economy in recent years has been unimpressive, with a record of slow growth in real terms, rapid inflation and recurring balance of payments difficulties. Real gross domestic product per head rose by less than 2 per cent a year on average from the mid-1950s to the mid-1970s and even this rate shows signs of slowing down. Allowance for deterioration in the terms of trade during those 20 years further reduces the rate of growth in effective terms.

Because New Zealand has a relatively large external trade sector and most of its exports are subject to major price fluctuations, the terms of trade has always been a key variable. Furthermore, prices of imports and exports tend to be determined externally, with New Zealand having little influence on them. In 1974/75 the terms of trade deteriorated very sharply to a level lower than any since the 1930s. This arose partly from a marked fall in export prices (except for dairy products) and partly from a massive rise in import prices, which in turn stemmed directly and indirectly from earlier and concurrent rises in oil prices. In 1975/76 the terms of trade recovered somewhat.

Export and import prices have a major effect on internal prices because most export commodities are also consumed internally and the export market determines prices. In addition, the attempt by organized labour to increase its share of national income in the early 1970s markedly accelerated the rate of inflation. From the mid-1950s consumer prices rose by an average of 5 per cent per annum. However, in the 1970s inflation rates roughly doubled. For the 12 months to June 1976 the consumer price index is likely to show an increase of about 20 per cent but this reflects in part fiscal measures which should have been taken earlier and may signal the beginning of a gradual slow-down of inflation.

New Zealand's greatest economic problem is the long standing tendency for expenditure abroad to exceed income from abroad. In 1974/75 the excess reached crisis proportions, with a balance of payments deficit on current account equivalent to 15 per cent of G.N.P. This was an extraordinary swing after several years of surpluses or moderate deficits, and was the outcome of a spectacular increase in internal spending and stock accumulation during that year. In 1975/76 the deficit was reduced to 10 per cent of G.N.P. and in 1976/77 it is hoped that it will come down to 5 per cent. In earlier years import licensing would have been extended in such circumstances but this time an attempt is being made to restore external stability by reducing demand without generating too much unemployment.

As in previous post-war efforts to achieve balance in external transactions, full employment is being accorded high priority. The Government operates special work schemes for some of those who would otherwise be unemployed. In mid-1976 the total number unemployed was over one per cent of the work force, higher than at most other times since the 1930s but low by world standards. Unless New Zealand adopts more labour-intensive patterns of production, or import dependence is reduced or the terms of trade soon improve, the level of unemployment is likely to rise.

In recent years the proportion of total private income going to salary and wage-earners has risen sharply, mainly at the expense of farmers but to some extent at the expense of capital returns. Salary and wage-earners are, of course, increasing as a proportion of total population but there has also been a shift from capital to labour.

It is tempting to link this with the decline in total private saving which paralleled the worsening balance of payments situation in the mid-1970s. However, a decline in public sector self-financing of capital expenditure was also a factor. The years 1974/75 and 1975/76 also saw a relative increase in the public sector's claim on the private sector on account of current expenditure. Within the public sector itself central government was increasingly obliged to transfer resources to territorial and other local authorities because the latter lack the automatically increasing flow of funds which a progressive (personal) income tax structure so conveniently provides. At the same time there is a tendency for local or regional authorities to assume responsibility for a greater proportion of total public sector expenditure.

ECONOMIC POLICY

Up to 1968 problems of internal inflation and external imbalance were mainly attributable to excess demand associated with weak fiscal and monetary policies. Following the 1967 devaluation and the earlier introduction of major tax concessions to companies which succeeded in promoting non-traditional exports, the external position improved dramatically. Fiscal policy was also more effective in 1969 and 1970 but in the latter year it proved impossible to hold down public sector spending because of sharp rises in import prices after the 20 per cent devaluation of 1967 and disturbingly large rises in wages.

The arbitration system had long succeeded in moderating wage increases sufficiently to prevent serious cost inflation. But when consumer prices rose sharply after the devaluation and the Arbitration Court made a nil general wage order in June 1968, unions virtually abandoned the system to seek wage increases by direct negotiation, supported by strike action. Average hourly earnings (exclusive of overtime) rose by 8 per cent in the year ended March 1970 and by 21 per cent in the following year. As a result of these increases and a sharp rise in import prices, consumer prices rose by 11 per cent in 1970/71.

Dramatic recognition of the new problem of cost inflation came in late 1970 with a six months' freeze of prices and a Stabilization of Remuneration Authority to control wages and salaries. During the latter part of 1971 and early 1972 the Authority had some success in moderating wage rises and, for this and other reasons, the annual increase in consumer prices fell to 5 per cent in 1972. However, 1972 was an election year, and the Budget both reduced tax rates on personal incomes and greatly increased social security benefits as well as other types of public spending, greatly increasing the deficit before borrowing.

The election of November 1972 was won by the Labour Party, which abolished the Stabilization of Remuneration Act as inconsistent with socialist principles. It maintained price controls, however, and the New Zealand dollar was revalued twice in the hope of moderating the inflationary impact of import price rises. Some attempt was also made in the 1973 budget to check inflation by other means but public sector spending again increased. Price control was extended and a limit was placed on the amount of extra wage costs that an employer could recover in higher prices. Further moves were made to curb inflation and growing industrial unrest, including a short-term price freeze, a general wage order and a subsequent wage freeze for nearly a year. However, by this time wages had again increased substantially in the nine months between the two periods of compulsory restraint.

Steps had previously been taken for a "voluntary" farm income stabilization scheme, the proceeds of which were to be "frozen" by the Reserve Bank, but this and other devices to prevent sudden rises in export receipts from irreversibly boosting incomes in general were quite inadequate for the last export boom. By the time it had passed subsidies were needed for many farmers. By early 1975 restraints on wages, combined with mild demand deflation (stemming mainly from the fall in farm income and a cutback in industrial investment), were beginning to take effect, but this was an election year, traditionally marked by fiscal ease. Government expenditure was boosted to such an extent in relation to income that the resulting shortfall more than offset the deflationary pressures associated with falling export incomes and mounting balance of payments deficits. Wage restraints were maintained but made politically acceptable partly by further deferring the inevitable increases in the prices of several key goods and services provided by government, either subject to "stabilization" arrangements or outright subsidies.

Steps towards a more effective fiscal policy were taken in 1968, only to be retraced in the excitement of the external and internal boom of the early 1970s which roughly coincided with the brief return to power of the Labour Government. Monetary policy remained static until early 1976, when interest rates were allowed to rise significantly on government stock and most other controlled securities, and a good deal of freedom was restored to the financial system and the trading banks in particular. In mid-1976 the indications were that the reforms were having the desired effects, uncontrolled interest rates having first gone up but later receded a little. The yield on government stock was still too low to attract willing lenders but this would not be the case if the rate of inflation could be reduced. A major aim of the exercise is to slow down the growth of financial institutions on the fringe of the controlled institutions, and thereby increase the ambit of effective government control. It is, however, likely that the New Zealand monetary and financial system will remain more subject to detailed regulation than in most Western countries.

Economics and politics are inseparable, such are the effects of inflation and wide swings in the terms of trade. In particular, organized labour appears to be endeavouring consciously to obtain and retain a greater share of national resources. This effort coincides with slow productivity growth and deteriorating external trading conditions. It is also unfortunate, but perhaps equally inevitable, that a much wider range of social demands are being made of central and local government, many of which are inimical to economic growth. Thus, although the economy's capacity to sustain rising material living standards is increasingly in doubt, claimants are becoming more demanding.

STATISTICAL SURVEY

AREA AND POPULATION

Area	Census	Estimated Population (at June 30th)			
	March 1971	1972	1973	1974	1975
268,676 sq. km.*	2,862,631	2,904,871	2,962,911	3,026,000	3,086,900

* 103,736 square miles.

On June 30th, 1975, total population included an estimated 252,700 Maoris.

CHIEF CENTRES OF POPULATION

(Estimate at April 1st, 1975)

Wellington (capital)	354,660	Christchurch	326,410
Auckland	796,660	Hamilton	152,740
Dunedin	120,890		

BIRTHS, MARRIAGES AND DEATHS

	Live Births*		Marriages		Deaths*	
	Number	Rate (per '000)	Number	Rate (per '000)	Number	Rate (per '000)
1965	60,178	22.9	21,702	8.3	22,976	8.7
1966	60,188	22.5	22,949	8.6	23,778	8.9
1967	61,169	22.4	23,515	8.6	23,007	8.4
1968	62,284	22.6	24,057	8.7	24,464	8.9
1969	62,564	22.5	24,971	9.0	24,161	8.7
1970	62,207	22.1	25,953	9.2	24,840	8.8
1971	64,704	22.7	27,199	9.5	24,309	8.5
1972	63,215	21.8	26,868	9.2	24,801	8.5
1973	60,727	20.5	26,274	8.9	25,314	8.5
1974	59,336	19.6	25,412	8.4	25,261	8.4
1975	56,638	18.4	25,434	8.4	25,113	8.1

* Data for births and deaths are tabulated by year of registration rather than by year of occurrence.

Expectation of life: Males 68.19 years; females 74.30 years (1965–67).

IMMIGRATION AND EMIGRATION*

(April 1st to March 31st)

	1967/68	1968/69	1969/70	1970/71	1971/72	1972/73	1973/74	1974/75
Long-term immigrants	30,660	23,225	26,825	39,377	45,099	54,651	69,815	65,900
Long-term emigrants	28,472	29,802	29,822	31,958	37,546	35,483	42,338	43,461

* Figures refer to non-residents intending to remain in New Zealand, or New Zealand residents intending to remain abroad, for more than one year.

EMPLOYMENT

(April 1975)

('000)

	Males	Females	Total
Agriculture, Hunting, Forestry and Fishing	125.7	15.8	141.5
Mining and Quarrying	4.3	0.2	4.5
Manufacturing Industry	218.0	76.9	294.9
Electricity, Gas and Water	13.6	1.5	15.1
Construction	91.4	3.3	94.7
Wholesale and Retail Trade	111.3	82.8	194.1
Transport, Storage and Communications	89.8	20.8	110.6
Finance, Insurance, Real Estate, etc.	42.9	33.6	76.5
Community, Social and Personal Services	134.0	127.7	261.7
Total in Industry	831.0	362.6	1,193.6
Armed Forces in New Zealand	10.3	0.7	11.0
Registered Unemployed	1.9	1.2	3.1
Total Labour Force	843.2	364.5	1,207.7

AGRICULTURE

PRINCIPAL CROPS

(April 1st to March 31st)

	Area ('000 hectares)			Production ('000 metric tons)		
	1971/72	1972/73	1973/74	1971/72	1972/73	1973/74
Wheat	107	108	73	389	398	248
Oats	16	15	18	50	47	59
Barley	96	74	81	336	257	250
Maize	15	13	18*	116	102	132
Peas	23	21	25*	58	59	64*
Potatoes	8	9	9*	242	238	238*

* Provisional.

LIVESTOCK

('000 at January 31st)

	1973	1974	1975	1976†
Dairy cows in milk	2,190	2,140	2,080	2,188
Total cattle	9,088	9,415	9,653	9,433
Breeding ewes	41,017	40,366	41,108*	n.a.
Total sheep	56,684	55,883	55,320*	n.a.
Total pigs	507	507	500	n.a.

* As at June 30th. † Provisional.

LIVESTOCK PRODUCTS

('000 metric tons, April 1st to March 31st)

	1971/72	1972/73	1973/74	1974/75
Beef	389.6	423.8	377.9	n.a.
Veal	20.3	21.7	26.8	n.a.
Mutton	195.8	215.1	192.9	n.a.
Lamb	378.9	341.0	304.6	n.a.
Pig meat	40.6	35.3	34.4	n.a.
Offal	57.1	60.2	53.4	n.a.
Liquid milk (million litres)	6,048	5,823†	5,674†	5,909†
Butter (creamery)	245.8	239.0†	215.9†	240.1†
Cheese	104.3	101.1†	89.0†	88.6†
Preserved milk*	257.85	246.58	263.38	301.79†
Casein	40.27	46.19	36.46	34.49†
Wool: greasy	322	309	285	294
clean	229.9	220.5	203.5	213

* Skim-milk powder, condensed and powdered whole-milk, butter-milk powder.
† Provisional.

FORESTRY

SAWNWOOD PRODUCTION

('000 cubic metres, April 1st to March 31st)

Species	1969/70	1970/71	1971/72	1972/73	1973/74	1974/75
Rimu and miro	325.4	325.4	303.1	281.0	288.2	271.5
Matai	36.1	26.9	17.7	18.3	17.1	17.1
Douglas fir	129.8	124.1	144.2	157.3	177.2	147.3
Kahikatea	34.9	30.0	30.8	28.4	26.4	28.9
Exotic pines	1,189.7	1,265.0	1,167.6	1,234.4	1,470.3	n.a.
Total (incl. others)	1,805.4	1,850.9	1,747.5	1,785.5	2,054.7	2,085.6

FISHERIES

		Quantity			Value ($NZ '000)		
		1972	1973	1974	1972	1973	1974
Marine fish	'000 metric tons	40.1	44.8	48.6	6,819	8,546	10,269
Oysters	,, ,, ,,	8.3	10.6	10.1	1,628	2,101	2,450
Rock lobster	,, ,, ,,	4.6	4.8	3.6	8,145	9,487	7,053
Other	,, ,, ,,	5.2	6.5	6.8	717	1,408	2,065
Total	,, ,, ,,	58.2	66.7	69.1	17,309	21,542	21,837

MINING

		1972	1973	1974
Hard coal	'000 metric tons	534	422	} 2,564
Lignite	,, ,, ,,	1,647	2,046	
Gold	kilogrammes	420.2	343.5	146.5
Silver	,,	973.2	1,529.7	56.4
Petroleum (crude)	'000 cu. metres	178	205	220
Natural gas	million cu. metres	353.3	419.78	484.11
Iron sands	'000 metric tons	1,380	2,181	2,352
Silica sand	,, ,, ,,	110	124	148
Limestone	,, ,, ,,	3,131	3,717	3,672
Salt	,, ,, ,,	59	103	55

INDUSTRY

Selected Commodities

		1973	1974	1975
Canned meat	metric tons	3,647	4,367	4,223
Flour	,, ,,	207,784	212,553	219,251
Refined sugar	,, ,,	155,332	168,398	148,066
Biscuits	long tons	27,321	26,050	28,437
Jam*	,, ,,	5,166	4,674	7,697
Canned fruit*	,, ,,	23,122	19,632	17,902
Canned vegetables*	,, ,,	17,318	19,841	21,243
Soap flakes and powder	,, ,,	9,889	11,890	9,290
Beer and stout	'000 gallons	83,612	86,020	92,611
Wool yarn	'000 lb.	41,810	42,769	39,979
Woollen and worsted piece goods	'000 sq. yds.	4,412	5,770	3,781
Refrigerators	number	229,638	246,248	262,389
Washing machines	,,	73,476	83,364	91,690
Lawn mowers	,,	94,688	101,233	98,769
Radios	,,	124,524	169,426	163,628
Tobacco	metric tons	949	867	811
Cigarettes	million	6,004	5,889	6,488
Chemical fertilizers	metric tons	2,607	2,268	1,801
Cement	,, ,,	1,058	1,110	1,074
Passenger cars	number	72,346	67,667	67,457
Trucks, vans, buses	,,	13,951	12,557	12,897

* Year ended June.

FINANCE

100 cents = 1 New Zealand dollar ($NZ).

Coins: 1, 2, 5, 10, 20 and 50 cents.

Notes: 1, 2, 5, 10, 20 and 100 dollars.

Exchange rates (June 1976): £1 sterling = $NZ1.799; U.S. $1 = $NZ1.014.

$NZ100 = £55.59 = U.S. $98.60.

Note: The New Zealand dollar was introduced in July 1967, replacing the New Zealand pound at the rate of £NZ1 = $NZ2. From October 1961 the New Zealand pound had a value of U.S. $2.78, so the initial value of the New Zealand dollar was U.S. $1.39 (U.S. $1 = 71.9 NZ cents). This remained in force until November 1967, after which the exchange rate was $NZ1 = U.S. $1.12 (U.S. $1.12 = 89.3 NZ cents) until August 1971. From December 1971 to February 1973 the par value of the New Zealand dollar was U.S. $1.216 (U.S. $1 = 82.2 NZ cents), though the effective mid-point rate was $NZ1 = U.S. $1.195. From February to July 1973 the exchange rate was $NZ1 = U.S. $1.351 (U.S. $1 = 74.0 NZ cents). In terms of sterling, the exchange rate was £1 = $NZ2.143 ($NZ1 = 9s. 4d. or 46.67p.) from November 1967 to December 1971; and £1 = $NZ2.180 from December 1971 to June 1972. The fixed relationship with the U.S. dollar was ended in July 1973, since when the basis for the New Zealand dollar's valuation has been a weighted "basket" of currencies of the country's main trading partners. In September 1973 the New Zealand dollar was revalued by 10 per cent against this "basket" (becoming equivalent to U.S. $1.478) but in September 1974 it was effectively devalued by about 6.2 per cent, and in August 1975 by 15 per cent. For converting the value of foreign trade transactions, the average value of the New Zealand dollar was: U.S. $1.136 in 1971; U.S. $1.195 in 1972; U.S. $1.363 in 1973; U.S. $1.401 in 1974; U.S. $1.215 in 1975.

BUDGET

($NZ million, April 1st to March 31st)

INCOME	1974/75	EXPENDITURE	1974/75
Income Tax	2,136	Administration	400
Estate and Gift Duty	41	Defence	163
Land Tax	3	Foreign Affairs	51
		Development of Industry	297
Total Direct Taxation	2,181	Education	527
		Social Services	789
Customs Duty	229	Health	492
Beer Duty	46	Transport and Communications	211
Sales Tax	235	Debt Services and Miscellaneous Investment Transactions	284
Payroll Tax	1		
Racing Duty	22		
Other Stamp Duties	26	Total Net Expenditure	3,214
Other	21		
Total Indirect Taxation	580		
Total Taxation Receipts, Consolidated Revenue Account	2,761		
Highways Tax	105		
Total Taxation	2,865		
Interest, Profit and Miscellaneous Receipts	155		
Borrowing	194		
TOTAL	3,214	TOTAL	3,214

WORKS EXPENDITURE

($NZ million)

	1973–74	1974–75	1975–76 (est.)
Electricity	99.0	146.4	160.0
Forest Development	5.7	6.4	7.5
Land Utilization	3.7	6.5	7.8
Housing	18.2	67.7	122.0
Public Buildings	12.5	16.9	28.8
Railways	15.1	16.4	22.0
Transport	6.8	4.2	7.7
Roads	101.5	116.6	124.9
Education	77.3	88.3	110.9
Post Office	36.9	47.4	56.5
Health and Hospital Building	2.3	2.2	4.3
Defence	7.5	7.9	5.1
TOTAL (incl. others)	420.4	557.3	708.1

NATIONAL INCOME AND EXPENDITURE

($NZ million)

	1972–73	1973–74	1974–75*
NATIONAL INCOME AT FACTOR COST	6,489	7,468	8,162
Indirect taxation	603	687	717
Subsidies	−101	−134	−132
NATIONAL INCOME AT MARKET PRICES	6,991	8,020	8,747
Depreciation	534	607	674
GROSS NATIONAL PRODUCT	7,525	8,628	9,421
EXPENDITURE ON G.N.P.:			
Personal expenditure on consumer goods and services	4,617	5,067	5,734
Public authority current expenditure	1,117	1,329	1,596
Gross domestic capital formation in N.Z.	1,639	2,067	2,510
Change in stocks	13	282	960
Exports of goods and services	1,952	2,238	2,120
Imports of goods and services	−1,693	−2,223	−3,364
EXPENDITURE ON GROSS DOMESTIC PRODUCT	7,386	8,745	10,800
Net factor payments to rest of world	−120	−132	−135
EXPENDITURE ON GROSS NATIONAL PRODUCT	7,525	8,628	9,421

* Provisional.

Currency in Circulation: $NZ352.2 million (December 31st, 1975).

OVERSEAS RESERVES

($NZ million at March 31st)

	ASSETS OF N.Z. BANKING SYSTEM	OVERSEAS SECURITIES		GOLD	IMF		TOTAL RESERVES
		Treasury-held	Other Government-held		RESERVE POSITION	SPECIAL DRAWING RIGHTS	
1972	331.4	186.3	18.9	0.7	47.5	45.1	629.9
1973	561.9	235.0	22.3	0.7	52.1	45.1	917.2
1974	477.1	182.1	21.7	0.7	45.1	51.9	778.5
1975	281.8	230.9	23.9	0.7	n.a.	4.8	542.1
1976*	370.0	274.0	26.3	0.7	n.a.	9.7	680.7

* Provisional.

BALANCE OF PAYMENTS

($NZ million, April 1st to March 31st)

Summary of Current Account	1973/74			1974/75*		
	Credit	Debit	Balance	Credit	Debit	Balance
Merchandise transactions f.o.b.	1,862.0	1,582.8	279.2	1,618.1	2,576.6	−958.5
Non-monetary gold	—	—	—	—	—	—
Transport	194.2	294.4	−100.2	266.3	396.3	−130.0
Travel	78.5	143.4	−64.9	107.0	180.3	−73.3
Insurance	7.3	20.8	−13.5	23.8	25.2	−1.4
International investment income	82.9	214.8	−131.9	72.3	207.3	−135.0
Government transactions	31.1	52.0	−20.9	36.4	69.3	−32.9
Miscellaneous receipts and payments	57.7	127.5	−69.8	61.3	114.1	−52.8
Transfers	122.9	96.1	26.8	123.1	128.8	−5.7
Balance on Current Account	2,436.6	2,531.8	−95.2	2,308.3	3,697.9	−1,389.6

* Provisional.

Summary of Capital Account	1973/74 Increase in		1974/75* Increase in	
	Assets	Liabilities	Assets	Liabilities
Long-term Capital (Private):				
Overseas direct investment in New Zealand	—	152.7	—	163.5
New Zealand direct investment overseas	15.5		14.5	—
Other long-term capital movements	—	37.9	—	208.1
Long-term Capital (Government):				
Government investments	13.8	—	104.1	
Public debt		−58.1		300.9
Local Authority debt	—	−0.5	—	−0.7
Asian Development Bank:				
Holdings of N.Z. securities	—	1.1		1.3
Encashment of securities	0.4	—	0.2	—
N.Z. subscription	1.9		2.1	—
Other	—	35.7	0.1	39.5
Monetary Institutions:				
Reserve Bank of New Zealand	5.4		−45.1	106.0
Reserve Bank of New Zealand and Other Banks:				
Assets of N.Z. banking system	46.8	—	−218.7	—
Special Drawing Rights of IMF addition to official reserves	—	—	−47.2	—
Official Export Credits	0.3	—	3.4	—
Short-term Capital (Government):				
Government cash balances	—	—		—
Other	−38.4	—	−89.6	—
Other Short-term Capital Movements including Errors and Omissions	42.8	—	—	193.5
Balance on Capital Account	−95.2		−1,389.6	

* Provisional.

REGIONAL BALANCES ON CURRENT ACCOUNT*

(1974/75—$NZ million)

	United Kingdom	Australia	United States and Canada	EEC Countries	Other Countries	International Organizations	Total All Countries
Merchandise transactions (f.o.b.)	−195.5	−357.5	−227.7	−40.9	−136.9	—	−958.5
Transport	−61.2	3.1	−18.8	−26.9	−26.2	—	−130.0
Travel	−32.5	−5.6	−4.8	−3.5	−26.9	—	−73.3
Insurance	−8.8	−0.6	6.1	0.5	1.4	—	−1.4
International investment income	−40.0	−39.2	−40.0	−4.5	−6.3	−5.0	−135.0
Government transactions	−0.8	−3.2	1.4	−2.9	−26.8	−0.6	−32.9
Miscellaneous	−21.8	1.8	−15.8	−4.5	−12.5	—	−52.8
Transfers	35.5	−0.3	3.8	2.6	−37.7	−9.6	−5.7
Balance on Current Account	−325.1	−401.5	−295.7	−80.1	−272.0	−15.2	−1,389.6

* Provisional.

EXTERNAL TRADE

($NZ '000)

Twelve months ending June 30th.

	1969/70	1970/71	1971/72	1972/73	1973/74*	1974/75*
Imports c.d.v.†	944,324	1,070,567	1,152,736	1,282,185	1,842,263	2,470,434
Exports f.o.b.	1,086,661	1,131,719	1,374,956	1,791,979	1,787,563	1,612,607

* Provisional. † Current domestic value.

PRINCIPAL COMMODITIES

($NZ'000)

Imports (current domestic value)	1972/73	1973/74*	1974/75*
Food and live animals	67,120	85,838	124,595
Beverages and tobacco	15,424	19,762	21,600
Crude materials (inedible) except fuels	53,723	77,027	94,660
Mineral fuels, lubricants, etc.	76,876	169,997	316,958
Animal and vegetable oils and fats	2,789	7,869	11,022
Chemicals	167,907	246,859	288,268
Basic manufactures	316,042	492,157	618,280
Machinery and transport equipment	466,621	597,549	800,950
Miscellaneous manufactured articles	100,614	132,351	172,441
Other commodities and transactions	15,069	12,855	21,659
Total	1,282,185	1,842,263	2,470,433

* Provisional.

Exports (f.o.b., excluding re-exports)	1972/73	1973/74*	1974/75*
Meat and meat preparations	540,912	534,849	439,729
Butter	137,087	107,152	122,345
Cheese	79,194	61,805	48,423
Fruit and vegetables	30,771	35,866	40,194
Hides, skins and pelts	95,933	67,207	62,691
Wool	424,641	363,410	262,470
Sausage casings	14,209	16,607	18,297
Tallow	9,729	13,851	15,611
Casein	22,028	28,556	14,652
Pulp, paper and paper board	36,420	51,801	80,275
Total (incl. others)	1,758,688	1,744,741	1,548,715

Re-exports ($NZ'000): 1972/73 33,281; 1973/74* 42,822; 1974/75* 63,892.

* Provisional.

PRINCIPAL TRADING PARTNERS
($NZ '000)

Imports	1972/73	1973/74†	1974/75†
Australia	323,468	449,313	502,639
Bahrain	6,017	11,122	10,354
Belgium/Luxembourg	7,080	13,505	17,416
Canada	34,643	44,665	48,898
France	12,824	18,115	24,340
Germany, Federal Republic	50,969	86,767	110,553
Hong Kong	20,011	40,780	33,664
India	10,936	14,821	19,783
Iran	9,776	18,594	95,146
Italy	16,211	29,541	39,018
Japan	166,736	248,047	335,625
Malaysia	8,080	11,750	9,098
Netherlands	16,074	28,418	36,926
Sweden	12,283	15,581	21,726
Switzerland	12,780	17,857	25,699
United Kingdom	303,582	350,921	465,078
U.S.A.	145,857	224,984	329,939
Total (incl. others)	1,282,185	1,842,263	2,470,434

Exports*	1972/73	1973/74†	1974/75†
Australia	131,163	171,789	187,523
Belgium/Luxembourg	42,679	35,789	16,341
Canada	42,414	52,436	45,081
China, People's Republic	5,953	16,952	10,183
Fiji	17,789	20,253	23,393
France	61,717	37,802	43,398
Germany, Federal Republic	51,230	41,046	41,900
Hong Kong	15,564	17,247	17,219
Italy	31,620	26,835	20,969
Japan	231,489	248,789	186,756
Malaysia	16,910	18,412	20,973
Netherlands	39,781	46,848	36,090
Peru	16,795	21,302	27,964
Philippines	19,049	25,907	29,199
Poland	16,795	13,715	10,597
U.S.S.R.	30,192	38,146	45,410
United Kingdom	480,173	365,790	344,079
U.S.A.	275,498	295,343	183,847
Total (incl. others)	1,771,761	1,757,405	1,569,429

* Excluding ships' stores, specie and gold. † Provisional.

TOURISM

(1974/75)

From	Visitors ('000)
Australia	208.0
U.S.A.	48.1
United Kingdom	23.6
Canada	12.1
Japan	8.2
Western Europe	9.7
Other Countries	48.2
Total	358.0

In the year ending March 31st, 1975, 215,090 tourists visited New Zealand.

TRANSPORT

RAILWAYS

Year Ending March 31st	Passenger Journeys ('000)		Goods Carried ('000 metric tons)				Net Metric Ton-Km. (million)
	Railway	Motor*	Timber	Livestock	Agricultural Lime	Total (incl. others)	
1973	18,565	20,866	2,103	103	201	12,127	3,064.9
1974	18,944	20,947	2,256	77	203	13,167	3,627.5
1975	18,894	20,768	2,222	67	142	12,883	3,608.2

* Railway Department's motor services only.

ROADS: MOTOR VEHICLES LICENSED

(as at March 31st)

	1973	1974	1975
Private cars	1,032,228	1,091,160	1,142,326
Lorries	194,654	200,127	206,776
Buses and service cars	3,100	3,054	3,130
Trailers	256,281	279,650	304,883
Motor cycles and power cycles	72,648	87,410	93,977
Other vehicles	94,047	104,207	106,285
Total	1,652,958	1,765,608	1,857,377

SHIPPING

	Entered				Cleared			
	Overseas		Coastal		Overseas		Coastal	
	Vessels	Net Tonnage ('000)	Vessels	Net Tonnage ('000)	Vessels	Net Tonnage ('000)	Vessels	Net Tonnage ('000)
1973	4,030	21,034	8,736	10,992	4,036	21,058	8,724	11,040
1974	3,831	20,536	8,390	11,281	3,817	20,397	8,371	11,379
1975*	3,692	20,098	8,257	11,081	3,688	19,976	8,290	11,207

*Provisional.

CIVIL AVIATION
(Scheduled Services)

	1972	1973	1974	1975
Domestic				
Passengers carried ('000)	1,652	2,005	2,255	2,312
Passenger kilometres ('000)	726,276	891,877	1,004,232	1,033,678
Freight carried (tonnes)	67,300	63,600	64,000	61,200
Freight tonne-kilometres ('000)	19,509	21,931	23,731	24,539
Mail tonne-kilometres ('000)	1,128	1,218	1,447	1,617
International				
Passengers carried ('000)	731	915	1,117	1,179
Freight carried (tonnes)	15,833	21,091	27,668	30,877
Mail carried (tonnes)	1,648	1,867	2,084	2,270

COMMUNICATIONS MEDIA

	March 1975
TV Sets Licensed	790,599
Daily Newspapers	41
Telephones per 100 people	49

EDUCATION

(1974)

	Institutions	Pupils	Teachers
Pre-School	1,041	51,814	1,819
Primary (State and Private)	2,747	441,462	20,086
Intermediate	131	82,211	n.a.
Secondary (State and Private)	345	208,596	10,980
Teacher Training	13	8,004	535
University	7	39,949	2,679

Source: Department of Statistics, Wellington 1.

THE CONSTITUTION

Head of State

Executive power is vested in the Queen and is exercisable by her personal representative, the Governor-General.

In the execution of the powers and authorities vested in him the Governor-General must be guided by the advice of the Executive Council; but if in any case he sees sufficient cause to dissent from the opinion of the Council, he may act in the exercise of his powers and authorities in opposition to the opinion of the Council, reporting the matter to the monarch without delay, with the reasons for his so acting.

Executive Council

The Executive Council consists of the Governor-General and all the Ministers. Two members, exclusive of the Governor-General or the presiding member, constitute a quorum. The Governor-General appoints the Prime Minister and, on the latter's recommendation, the other Ministers.

House of Representatives

Parliament comprises the Crown and the House of Representatives.

The number of members constituting the House of Representatives is eighty-seven—eighty-three drawn from general seats and four from Maori seats. They are designated "Members of Parliament".

Parliaments sit for three-year terms.

Everyone over 18 may vote in the election of members for the House of Representatives. Since August 1975 any person, regardless of nationality, ordinarily resident in New Zealand for 12 months or more and resident in an electoral district for one month or more is qualified to be registered as a voter. Compulsory registration of all electors except Maoris was introduced at the end of 1924; it was introduced for Maoris in 1956.

There are 83 European electoral districts and four Maori electoral districts. As from August 1975 any person of the Maori race, which includes any descendant of such a person, who elects to be considered as a Maori for the purposes of the Electoral Act may enrol on the Maori roll for that particular Maori electoral district in which that person resides.

By the Electoral Amendment Act, 1937, which made provision for a secret ballot in Maori elections, Maori electors were granted the same privileges, in the exercise of their vote, as general electors.

In local government, with some minor exceptions, there is a wider electoral franchise, non-residential rate payers also being eligible to vote.

THE GOVERNMENT

Head of State: H.M. Queen Elizabeth II.

Governor-General and Commander-in-Chief: Sir Edward Denis Blundell, G.C.M.G., G.C.V.O., K.B.E.

THE MINISTRY

(*July* 1976)

Prime Minister and Minister of Finance: Rt. Hon. Robert D. Muldoon.

Deputy Prime Minister, Minister of Foreign Affairs, Minister of Overseas Trade and Minister of National Development: Hon. Brian E. Talboys.

Minister of Labour and Minister of State Services: Hon. John B. Gordon.

Minister of Agriculture and Fisheries and Minister of Maori Affairs: Hon. Duncan MacIntyre, D.S.O., O.B.E., E.D.

Minister of Trade and Industry: Hon. Lance Adams-Schneider.

Minister of Justice: Hon. David Thomson, M.C., E.D.

Minister of Housing, Minister of Regional Development and Deputy Minister of Finance: Hon. George Gair.

Minister of Education and Minister of Science and Technology: Hon. Leslie Gandar.

Minister of Health and Minister of Immigration: Air Commodore the Hon. T. Frank Gill, C.B.E., D.S.O.

Minister of State: Rt. Hon. Sir Keith Holyoake, G.C.M.G., C.H.

Minister of Transport, Minister of Civil Aviation and Meteorological Services and Minister of Railways: Hon. Colin McLachlan.

Minister of Works and Development: Hon. William Young.

Minister of Energy Resources, Minister of Electricity and Minister of Mines: Hon. Eric Holland.

Minister of Defence and Minister of Police: Hon. Allan McCready.

Minister of Social Welfare: Hon. Herbert J. Walker.

Minister of Internal Affairs, Minister of Local Government, Minister of Recreation and Sport, Minister of Civil Defence and Minister for the Arts: Hon. D. Alan Highet.

Attorney-General, Minister of Customs, Minister of Statistics and Associate Minister of Finance: Hon. Peter Wilkinson.

Minister of Lands, Minister of Forests and Minister for the Environment: Hon. Venn Young.

Minister of Tourism: Hon. Henry Lapwood.

Postmaster-General and Minister of Broadcasting: Hon. Hugh Templeton.

PARLIAMENT

THE HOUSE OF REPRESENTATIVES

Speaker: Hon. Sir Roy Jack.

Chairman of Committees: J. R. Harrison.

Leader of the Opposition: Rt. Hon. Wallace E. Rowling.

Clerk of the House: C. P. Littlejohn.

GENERAL ELECTION, November 29th, 1975

Party	Votes	Votes (per cent)	Seats
National Party	760,462	47·20	55
Labour Party	636,322	39·50	32
Social Credit League	119,123	7·39	—
Values Party	83,211	5·17	—
Others	3,755	0·23	—
Informal	8,231	0·51	—

POLITICAL PARTIES

Labour Party: P.O.B. 6146, Te Aro, Wellington; f. 1916; The policy of the Party is the maximum utilization of the Dominion's resources for organizing an internal economy to distribute goods and services so as to guarantee to every person able and willing to work an adequate standard of living.

New Zealand Pres.: C. M. Bennett.
Gen. Sec.: J. F. Wybrow.
Parliamentary Leader: Wallace E. Rowling.

New Democratic Party: Nelson; f. May 1972; aims to dismantle the centralized government and restore maximum freedom for each individual to control his environment.

Leader: J. B. O'Brien.

New Zealand National Party: Corner Customhouse Quay and Hunter St., Wellington 1; f. 1936; The National Party represents the Conservative and Liberal elements in New Zealand politics. In office 1949–57, 1960–72 and 1975–, the Party stands for maintenance of democratic government, and the encouragement of private enterprise and competitive business, coupled with maximum personal freedom.

Parliamentary Leader: Hon. ROBERT D. MULDOON, M.P.

Gen. Dir. and Sec.: P. B. LEAY.

Communist Party of New Zealand: 37 St. Kevin's Arcade, Auckland; pro-Chinese; 300 mems.; Gen. Sec. VICTOR WILCOX; publ. *People's Voice* (weekly).

Social Credit League: 170 Cuba St., Wellington 1; f. 1954; aims to cut taxes and increase social security benefits through the "use and ownership of the people's own credit" under a national credit authority; 10,000 mems.; publ. *New Guardian* (monthly).

Leader: B. C. BEETHAM.

Socialist Unity Party: Box 1987, Auckland; f. 1966; Marxist socialist; Pres. G. H. ANDERSEN; Sec. GEORGE JACKSON; publ. *New Zealand Tribune* and *Socialist Politics*.

Values Party: National Secretariat, 139 Elliott St., Papakura; f. May 1972; humanist party; Leader REG CLOUGH; Deputy Leader CATHY WILSON.

DIPLOMATIC REPRESENTATION

EMBASSIES, HIGH COMMISSIONS AND LEGATION ACCREDITED TO NEW ZEALAND

(In Wellington, unless otherwise indicated)

(E) Embassy; (HC) High Commission; (L) Legation.

Argentina: Government Life Insurance Building, Customhouse Quay, P.O.B. 1621 (E); *Chargé d'Affaires a.i.:* NICOLAS E. LEDESMA.

Australia: I.C.I. House, Molesworth St., I, P.O.B. 12145 (HC); *High Commissioner:* COLIN T. MOODIE.

Austria: Canberra, Australia (E).

Bangladesh: Canberra, Australia (HC).

Belgium: Dominion Farmers' Institute Bldg., Featherston St., I, P.O.B. 3841 (E); *Ambassador:* HERMAN J. MATSAERT.

Brazil: Canberra, Australia (E).

Burma: Canberra, Australia (E).

Canada: I.C.I. House, Molesworth St., I, P.O.B. 12049 (HC); *High Commissioner:* CLIVE E. GLOVER.

Chile: 2nd Floor, Europa House, Featherston St., I, P.O.B. 3861 (E); *Ambassador:* ERNESTO JOBET OJEDA.

China, People's Republic: 2–6 Glenmore St. (E); *Ambassador:* PEI TSIEN-CHANG.

Czechoslovakia: 12 Anne St., Wadestown, I, P.O.B. 2843 (L); *Chargé d'Affaires a.i.:* (vacant).

Denmark: Canberra, Australia (E).

Egypt: 13th Floor, Dalmuir House, The Terrace, I, P.O.B. 9257 (E); *Ambassador:* A. W. MARZOUK.

Finland: Canberra, Australia (E).

France: 3rd Floor, Northern Building Society Bldg., 105 Customhouse Quay, I, P.O.B. 1695 (E); *Ambassador:* ALBERT DE SCHOENEN.

German Democratic Republic: Canberra, Australia (E).

Germany, Federal Republic: 3 Claremont Grove, I, P.O.B. 1687 (E); *Ambassador:* Dr. OTTO SOLTMANN.

Greece: Canberra, Australia (E).

Hungary: Jakarta, Indonesia (E).

India: Lamphouse Chambers, 49 Willis St., I, (HC); *High Commissioner:* L. N. RAY.

Indonesia: 11 Fitzherbert Terrace (E); *Ambassador:* SOETIKNO LOEKITODISASTRO.

Iran: Canberra, Australia (E).

Ireland: Canberra, Australia (E).

Israel: P.O.B. 2171 (E); *Ambassador:* HAIM RAPHAEL.

Italy: 24 Grant Rd., Thorndon, I, P.O.B. 463 (E); *Ambassador:* BENEDETTO FENZI.

Japan: 18A Oriental Terrace (E); *Ambassador:* HIDEHO TANAKA.

Korea, Republic: 7th Floor, Molesworth House, 101 Molesworth St., P.O.B. 12115 (E); *Ambassador:* CHOON HEE KANG.

Laos: Canberra, Australia (E).

Malaysia: Chase-NBA House, 163–165 The Terrace (HC); *High Commissioner:* K. THARMARATNAM.

Mexico: Canberra, Australia (E).

Mongolia: Tokyo, Japan (E).

Nepal: Tokyo, Japan (E).

Netherlands: Fifth Floor, Shell House, The Terrace, I, P.O.B. 840 (E); *Ambassador:* J. A. KERNKAMP.

Norway: Canberra, Australia (E).

Pakistan: Canberra, Australia (E).

Papua New Guinea: Construction House, 82 Kent Terrace, I, P.O.B. 9746, Courtenay Place (HC); *High Commissioner a.i.:* WILSON S. EPHRAIM.

Peru: Canberra, Australia (E).

Philippines: Canberra, Australia (E).

Poland: 17 Upland Rd., Kelburn, 5 (E); *Ambassador:* EUGENIUSZ WISNIEWSKI (resident in Canberra).

Portugal: Canberra, Australia (E).

Romania: Tokyo, Japan (E).

Singapore: 1st Floor, Molesworth House, 101 Molesworth St., I, P.O.B. 12242 (HC); *High Commissioner:* CHAN KENG HOWE.

Spain: Canberra, Australia (E).

Sri Lanka: Canberra, Australia (HC).

Sweden: 17th Floor, Aurora House, 48–64 The Terrace, P.O.B. 1800 (E); *Ambassador:* STEN G. AMINOFF.

Switzerland: Panama House, 22–24 Panama St., P.O.B. 386 (E); *Chargé d'Affaires:* FRITZ ADAMS.

Thailand: 2 Burnell Avenue, I, P.O.B. 2530 (E); *Ambassador:* SRISWARD PUNKRASIN.

U.S.S.R.: 57 Messines Rd., Karori, 5 (E); *Ambassador:* O. P. SELYANINOV.

United Kingdom: Reserve Bank Bldg., 2 The Terrace, I, P.O.B. 1812 (HC); *High Commissioner:* HAROLD SMEDLEY, C.M.G., M.B.E.

U.S.A.: I.B.M. Centre, 151–165 The Terrace, I, P.O.B. 1190 (E); *Ambassador:* ARMISTEAD I. SELDEN, Jnr.

Vatican City: Apostolic Nunciature, 112 Queen's Drive, Lyall Bay, 3, P.O.B. 14044; *Apostolic Pro-Nuncio:* The Most Rev. ANGELO ACERBI.

Yugoslavia: 24 Hatton St., Karori, 5 (E); *Ambassador:* Dr. B. KARAPANDZA.

New Zealand also has diplomatic relations at consular level with Costa Rica, Ecuador, El Salvador, Iceland, Nauru, South Africa, Tonga, Turkey, Venezuela, Viet-Nam and Western Samoa.

JUDICIAL SYSTEM

The Judicial System of New Zealand comprises a Court of Appeal, a Supreme Court, an Industrial Court and a Compensation Court. There are also Magistrates' Courts, having both civil and criminal jurisdiction.

Chief Justice: Rt. Hon. Sir RICHARD WILD, K.C.M.G.

THE COURT OF APPEAL

President: Rt. Hon. Sir CLIFFORD PARRIS RICHMOND

Registrar: D. V. JENKIN

Judges:
Rt. Hon. Sir RICHARD WILD, K.C.M.G. (ex-officio)
Rt. Hon. Sir CLIFFORD RICHMOND
Rt. Hon. Sir OWEN WOODHOUSE
Hon. ROBIN BRUNSKILL COOKE

THE SUPREME COURT

Judges:
Rt. Hon. Sir RICHARD WILD, K.C.M.G.
Hon. ALAN CLIFFORD PERRY
Hon. JOHN NIGEL WILSON
Hon. LESTER FRANCIS MOLLER
Hon. GRAHAM DAVIES SPEIGHT
Hon. CLINTON MARCUS ROPER
Hon. JOHN CHARLES WHITE
Hon. DAVID STUART BEATTIE
Hon. JAMES PETER QUILLIAM
Hon. DUNCAN WALLACE MCMULLIN
Hon. PETER THOMAS MAHON
Hon. JOHN BARRY O'REGAN
Hon. MUIR FITZHERBERT CHILWELL
Hon. MAURICE EUGENE CASEY
Hon. EDWARD JONATHAN SOMERS
Hon. JOSEPH AUGUSTINE ONGLEY

COMPENSATION COURT

Judge: Hon. A. P. BLAIR

INDUSTRIAL COURT

Judge: Hon. R. D. JAMIESON
Employers' Representative: W. N. HEWITT
Employees' Representative: W. C. MCDONNELL
Registrar: B. P. GRAY

RELIGION

CHURCH OF ENGLAND
(Province of New Zealand)

Archbishop: Most Rev. A. H. JOHNSTON, LL.D., L.TH.; Bishop's House, 322 Cobham Drive, Hamilton.

Provincial Secretary: J. C. COTTRELL, J.P., P.O.B. 800, Christchurch.

ROMAN CATHOLIC CHURCH
Archbishop

Wellington . The Most Rev. REGINALD J. DELARGEY, P.O.B. 198, Wellington 1.

OTHER DENOMINATIONS

Baptist Union of New Zealand: 185–187 Willis St., Wellington 1 (P.O.B. 27-390); f. 1882; Pres. of Union R. H. FRENCH; Gen. Sec. Rev. HUGH NEES; 17,901 mems.

Churches of Christ in New Zealand (Associated): 156 High St., Lower Hutt; 12,500 mems.; Gen. Sec. H. C. BISCHOFF; publs. *N.Z. Christian.*

Congregational Churches (*The Congregational Union of New Zealand*): f. 1883; Chair. Rev. J. B. CHAMBERS, M.A.; Treas. A. I. LAM, B.COMM.; Sec. Mrs. J. B. CHAMBERS (28 Wright St., Wellington 2); 478 mems.

Methodist Church of New Zealand: Connexional Headquarters: Box 931, Christchurch; 27,563 communicant mems; General Sec. Rev. W. R. LAWS, M.A., B.D.; Gen. Sec. Overseas Division Rev. W. G. TUCKER (Auckland).

Presbyterian Church of New Zealand: Dalmuir House, 114 The Terrace, Wellington 1; Moderator Rt. Rev. Dr. IAN BREWARD; Assembly Exec. Sec. Rev. W. A. BEST; Moderator of Maori Synod T. TAKAO; 82,548 communicant mems.; 580,400 under pastoral care; publ. *The Outlook* (monthly).

Salvation Army: Territorial Headquarters: 204–206 Cuba St., Wellington (P.O.B. 6015); approx. 19,000 mems.; Territorial Commander: Lieut.-Commissioner Dr. HARRY WILLIAMS, O.B.E.; Chief Sec. Colonel ERNEST R. ELLIOT.

Maori Denominations: there are several Maori Churches in New Zealand with a total membership of over 30,000—Ratana Church of New Zealand, Ringatu Church: Church of Te Kooti Rikirangi, Absolute Maori Established Church, United Maori Mission.

THE PRESS

NEWSPAPERS AND PERIODICALS

DAILIES

Auckland Star: Shortland St., P.O.B. 1409, Auckland 1; f. 1870; evening; Editor ROSS SAYERS; circ. 136,000.

Christchurch Star: P.O.B. 1467, Christchurch; f. 1868; Independent; evening; Editor M. B. FORBES; circ. 70,000.

The Daily News: P.O.B. 444, New Plymouth; f. 1857; morning; Editor R. J. AVERY; circ. 21,000.

The Daily Post: P.O.B. 1442, Rotorua; f. 1886; evening; Editor I. F. THOMPSON; circ. 15,700.

Daily Telegraph: P.O.B. 173, Napier; f. 1871; evening; Editor D. G. CONLY; circ. 18,030.

The Dominion: Dominion Building, Mercer St., Box 1297, Wellington; f. 1907, morning; Editor J. A. KELLEHER; circ. 78,550.

Evening Post: Willis St., P.O.B. 3740, Wellington; f. 1865; Independent; Editor J. M. ROBSON; circ. 101,600.

Evening Standard: P.O.B. 3, Palmerston North; f. 1880; evening; Editor R. D. WATSON; circ. 26,000.

Evening Star: P.O.B. 517, Dunedin; f. 1863; Editor P. J. STEWART; circ. 30,000.

The Hawke's Bay Herald Tribune: Karamu Rd., Box 180, Hastings; f. 1937; independent conservative; evening; Editor E. G. WEBBER; circ. 19,495.

Nelson Evening Mail: P.O.B. 244, Nelson; f. 1866; evening; Editor G. D. SPENCER; circ. 17,409.

New Zealand Herald: P.O.B. 32, Auckland; f. 1863; morning; Editor J. F. W. HARDINGHAM; circ. 235,000.

Northern Advocate: Water St., P.O.B. 210, Whangarei; f. 1875; evening; Man. Dir. B. W. CRAWFORD; circ. 17,097.

Otago Daily Times: Lower High St., P.O.B. 181, Dunedin; f. 1861; morning; Editor E. ALLAN AUBIN; circ. 43,000.

The Press: Cathedral Square, Box 1005, Christchurch; f. 1861; morning; Editor N. L. MACBETH; circ. 74,000.

Southland Times: P.O.B. 805, 67 Esk St., Invercargill; f. 1862; morning and afternoon; Editor P. M. MULLER; circ. 33,381.

Timaru Herald: Sophia St., P.O.B. 46, Timaru; f. 1864; morning; Editor G. J. GAFFANEY; circ. 16,442.

Waikato Times: Victoria St., P.O.B. 444, Hamilton; f. 1872; Independent; evening; Editor and Man. Dir. P. V. HARKNESS; circ. 37,171.

WEEKLY AND OTHER NEWSPAPERS

Best Bets: P.O.B. 1327, Auckland; sporting; circ. 54,000.

Christchurch Star Sports Edition: Box 2651, Christchurch; Saturday evening; circ. 37,000.

Economic News: Universe Press Agency, 201 Lambton Quay, Hamilton Chambers, P.O.B. 1026, Wellington; f. 1954; Editor Miss S. H. ELLIOTT.

8 O'Clock: P.O.B. 3697, Auckland; sports results and features, weekend news, etc.; Saturday evening; Editor NEIL ANDERSON; circ. 115,000.

Mercantile Gazette of New Zealand: 8 Sheffield Cres., P.O.B. 27, Christchurch; f. 1876; economics, finance, management, stock market, politics; Editor J. D. WATSON; circ. 24,000.

New Zealand Gazette: Dept. of Internal Affairs, Wellington; f. 1840; Thursday; Clerk T. COUSINS.

New Zealand Listener: P.O.B. 3140, Bowen State Building, Wellington; f. 1939; Monday; radio and television programmes; feature articles; Editor IAN CROSS; circ. over 223,000.

New Zealand Tablet: 24 Filleul St., Dunedin; f. 1873; Wednesday; Roman Catholic; Editor J. P. KENNEDY, O.B.E.; circ. 12,435.

New Zealand Truth: 23–27 Garrett St., P.O.B. 1122, Wellington; f. 1904; Tuesday; international and local news and comment; sports; finance; women's interests; Independent; Editor R. S. GAULT; circ. 242,700.

New Zealand Woman's Weekly: P.O.B. 1409, Auckland; f. 1934; Monday; family magazine, general interests; Editor JEAN WISHART; circ. over 230,000.

North Shore Times Advertiser: P.O.B. 33-235, Takapuna, Auckland 9; twice weekly; Editor Mrs. P. M. GUNDRY; circ. 42,000.

Sportsweek: P.O.B. 1034, Wellington; circ. 25,000.

Star 7 O'Clock: Box 517, Dunedin; Saturday evening.

The Sunday Times: Dominion Bldg., Mercer St., Wellington; f. 1965; Editor F. A. HADEN; circ. 143,000.

Taieri Herald: P.O.B. 105, Mosgiel; Editor J. F. FOX; circ. 4,700.

Te Aroha News: P.O.B. 131, Te Aroha; f. 1883; bi-weekly; Editor P. J. REILLY.

Waihi Gazette: P.O.B. 130, Waihi; Editor R. L. DARLEY.

Wairarapa News: P.O.B. 18, Carterton; f. 1869; Editor R. M. ROYDHOUSE.

Waitara Times: West Quay, Waitara; f. 1960; Editor B. L. OLDFIELD.

Zealandia: P.O.B. 845, Auckland; f. 1934; Thursday; Roman Catholic; Editor Rev. D. J. HORTON; circ. 19,500.

OTHER PERIODICALS

Better Business: P.O.B. 793, Auckland; f. 1938; monthly.

Board and Council: P.O.B. 807, Auckland; f. 1921; Local Authorities Review; monthly.

Church and People: P.O.B. 10345, The Terrace, Wellington; monthly; Editor S. G. DINNISS; circ. 10,000.

Comment: P.O.B. 1746, Wellington; f. 1959; quarterly; Independent; Editors S. ZAVOS and P. J. DOWNEY.

Journal of the Polynesian Society: P.O.B. 10323, The Terrace, Wellington; f. 1892; the anthropology, ethnology, philology, history and antiquities of the Polynesians and other related peoples; Editor Dr. M. McLEAN; circ. 1,500.

Management: P.O.B. 3159, Auckland; f. 1954; business; 1st of month; Editor SHANE C. NIBLOCK, circ. 7,000.

Monthly Abstract of Statistics: Dept. of Statistics, Private Bag, Wellington; f. 1914; monthly; official; Editor E. A. HARRIS, Govt. Statistician.

Motorman: Fourman Holdings Ltd., P.O.B. 1343, Wellington; f. 1957; motoring monthly; Editor DAVID HALL.

Nation: P.O.B. 957, Wellington; f. 1911; monthly; current topics; Editor M. W. LEAMAN; circ. 30,000.

New Zealand Dairy Exporter: P.O.B. 1001, Wellington; Editor J. D. McGILVARY; circ. 22,000.

New Zealand Economist: P.O.B. 5173, Wellington; business and investment; Editor DENIS WEDERELL.

The New Zealand Farmer: P.O.B. 1409, Auckland 1; f. 1885; twice monthly; Editor RONALD VINE; circ. 26,000.

New Zealand Financial Times: P.O.B. 1367, Wellington; f. 1930; finance, investment, business; Man. Editor E. C. MARRIS.

NZIA Journal: New Zealand Institute of Architects, P.O.B. 438, Wellington; f. 1905; bi-monthly; Man. Ed. C. J. G. McFARLANE.

New Zealand Journal of Agriculture: P.O.B. 32, Auckland; f. 1910; monthly; Editor D. WHITE; circ. 30,000.

New Zealand Journal of Science: Department of Scientific and Industrial Research, P.O.B. 9741, Wellington 1; f. 1958; chemistry, engineering, mathematics, meteorology, physics; quarterly; Editor J. G. GREGORY.

New Zealand Law Journal: Butterworths of New Zealand Ltd., 26–28 Waring Taylor St., Wellington; fortnightly.

New Zealand Manufacturer: Private Bag, Glen Innes, Auckland; monthly; circ. 3,700.

New Zealand Medical Journal: P.O.B. 181, Dunedin; f. 1887; twice monthly; Editor R. G. ROBINSON, G.M., CH.M., F.R.C.S.

New Zealand Methodist: P.O.B. 2986, Auckland; f. 1871; fortnightly; Editor Rev. JOHN BLUCK, M.A., B.D.; circ. 52,000.

New Zealand Motor World: P.O.B. 1, Wellington; f. 1936; bi-monthly; official organ of 14 automobile associations, 9 caravan clubs; Man. Editor R. A. HOCKING; circ. 94,000.

New Zealand Science Review: P.O.B. 1874, Wellington; f. 1942; every 2 months; Editor R. F. BENSEMAN.

New Zealand Sports Digest: P.O.B. 1034, Wellington; f. 1949; monthly; Editor B. F. O'BRIEN; circ. 24,000.

New Zealand Woman: P.O.B. 957, Dunedin; circ. 32,500.

Otago Farmer: P.O.B. 105, Mosgiel; fortnightly; Editor J. F. FOX; circ. 5,300.

Pacific Islands Trade News: 4 Kingdon St., Newmarket 1; circ. 22,000.

Pacific Viewpoint: Victoria University, Private Bag, Wellington; Editors Prof. R. F. WATTERS, Dr. J. M. KIRBY; circ. 1,050.

Public Services Journal: P.O.B. 5108, Wellington; monthly; circ. 49,000.

Reader's Digest: P.O.B. 3372, Auckland; monthly; circ. 165,000.

Straight Furrow: P.O.B. 1654, Wellington; f. 1933; fortnightly; Editor M. A. BERRY; circ. over 39,000.

Students' Digest: P.O.B. 1198, Wellington; monthly; circ. 40,700.

Te Ao Hou (*The New World*): Box 2390, Wellington; f. 1952; Maori and English; quarterly; Editor JOY STEVENSON; circ. 7,200.

Thursday Magazine (inc. N.Z. Family Doctor): P.O.B. 32, Auckland; fortnightly; circ. 62,500.

World Affairs: UN Asscn. of N.Z., Box 1011, Wellington; f. 1945; quarterly; Editor W. E. ROSE.

NEWS AGENCIES

New Zealand Press Association: Newspaper House, 93 Boulcott St., Wellington; f. 1879; non-political; Chair. H. N. BLUNDELL; Man. Editor H. L. VERRY.

South Pacific News Service (SPNS): 161-165 Willis St., Wellington; f. 1948; Man. Dir. E. W. BENTON.

FOREIGN BUREAU

Reuters: New Zealand Press Association, Newspaper House, 1 Boulcott St., Wellington.

PRESS COUNCIL

New Zealand Press Council: P.O.B. 1066, Wellington; f. September 1972; Chair. Sir ALFRED NORTH.

PRESS ASSOCIATIONS

Newspaper Publishers' Association of New Zealand (Inc.): Newspaper House, P.O.B. 1066, 93 Boulcott St., Wellington; f. 1898; 45 mems.; Pres. J. A. BURNET; Exec. Dir. M. J. THOMPSON.

Commonwealth Press Union (New Zealand Section): P.O.B. 180, Hastings; Chair. E. G. WEBBER, M.B.E.; Sec. M. C. MUIR (P.O.B. 573, Gisborne).

PUBLISHERS

Auckland University Press: Private Bag, University of Auckland, Auckland; f. 1966; Man. Editor R. D. McELDOWNEY.

Board and Council Publishing Co. Ltd.: Tingey's Bldg., P.O.B. 807, Auckland; f. 1921; Editor-Man. E. D. BENNETT.

Butterworths of New Zealand Ltd.: 26–28 Waring Taylor St., Wellington.

Cassell & Co. Ltd.: P.O.B. 36013, Northcote Central, Auckland 9; Man. Miss M. GIBSON.

Christchurch Caxton Press: P.O.B. 25088, 119 Victoria St., Christchurch 1; f. 1936; poetry, prose.

Collins (William) (New Zealand) Ltd.: P.O.B. 1, Auckland; Man. Dir. D. BATEMAN.

Commercial Print Ltd.: 127–131 Park Rd., Miramar, Wellington; f. 1911; Chair. I. JACKSON.

Heinemann Educational Books (N.Z.) Ltd.: P.O.B. 36-064, Auckland; f. 1969; educational, technical, academic; Man. Dir. D. HEAP.

Hodder and Stoughton Ltd.: P.O.B. 39038, Auckland West; Man. Dir. R. J. COOMBES.

Hutcheson, Bowman and Stewart Ltd.: P.O.B. 9032, 15–19 Tory St., Wellington.

Hutchinson Publishing Group Ltd.: P.O.B. 2281, Auckland; Gen. Man. N. G. STURT; Man. Dir. C. HANNA.

Independent Newspapers Ltd. (Holding Company): Dominion Building, 27-35 Mercer St.; P.O.B. 2595, Wellington; operating divisions: Wellington Publishing Group (Wellington); Independent Publishers Group (Hamilton); Blundell Group (Wellington); all groups publish daily and/or weekly newspapers and magazines; Chair. H. N. BLUNDELL; Sec. J. W. CROOK.

Longman Paul Limited: C.P.O. Box 4019, Auckland 1; Dirs. W. P. KERR, PHOEBE MEIKLE, L. V. GODFREY, P. M. M. WRIGHT.

New Zealand Council for Educational Research: P.O.B. 3237, Wellington; f. 1934; scholarly books, research monographs, bulletins, educational texts, research summaries, academic journal; Chair. Prof. C. G. N. HILL; Dir. J. E. WATSON.

Oxford University Press: P.O.B. 11-344, Wellington; Man. Dir. R. GOODERIDGE.

Pegasus Press Ltd.: 14 Oxford Terrace, P.O.B. 2244, Christchurch; f. 1948; publishers and printers; fiction, poetry, history, art and education; Man. Dir. ALBION WRIGHT; Editor ROBIN MUIR.

Pelorus Press Ltd.: MK Bldg., 21 Great South Rd., Newmarket, Auckland (P.O.B. 26-065 Epsom); f. 1947; Dirs. G. T. ANSTIS, T. J. ANSTIS, J. R. ENSOR, R. C. HASZARD.

Reed, A. H. and A. W. Ltd.: 182 Wakefield St., Wellington (head office), and at Auckland, Christchurch, Sydney, Melbourne and London; f. 1907; general books, educational books, records relating to Australia, New Zealand and the South Pacific; Chair. M. J. MASON.

Sporting Publications (A. H. Carman): 7 Kowhai St., Linden, Tawa; sports annuals.

Sweet and Maxwell (N.G.) Ltd.: 238 Wakefield St., Wellington; Man. Dir. K. M. McBEN.

University of Otago Press: P.O.B. 56, Dunedin; f. 1958.

Whitcoulls Ltd.: 111 Cashel St., Christchurch; N.Z. general and educational books; brs. throughout New Zealand, Australia, and in London; Gen. Man. P. E. BOURNE.

Wise, H., and Co. (New Zealand) Ltd.: 27 St. Andrew St., Dunedin; f. 1865; publishers of maps and street directories, N.Z. Guide and N.Z. Post Office Directories; Man. J. A. DECOURCY.

RADIO AND TELEVISION

The Broadcasting Council of New Zealand (BCNZ), established in 1975, supervises the independent operating corporations, Radio New Zealand (RNZ), Television Service One (TV1) and Television Service Two (TV2), and provides transmission facilities for them. It also receives licence revenues and allocates them to the corporations. Each corporation keeps its own revenue from commercial advertising. Colour broadcasting began in 1973.

Broadcasting Council of New Zealand (BCNZ): Broadcasting House, Bowen St., Wellington; f. 1975; six members including the chairmen of the three corporations; Chair. Sir ALISTER McINTOSH.

Radio New Zealand: P.O.B. 98, Wellington; f. 1975; controls 26 community radio stations, 3 public radio networks (one of which is a commercial network comprising 22 stations) and a short-wave service directed primarily to the south-west Pacific islands and south-eastern Australia. It also manages the New Zealand Symphony Orchestra and associated concerts on behalf of the BCNZ. The non-commercial National Programme broadcasts 24 hours a day; Chair. P. J. DOWNEY; Dir.-Gen. GEOFFREY WHITEHEAD.

Television Service One: Avalon Television Center, P.O.B. 30355, Lower Hutt, Wellington; f. 1975; colour television network covering almost the whole country; broadcasts for approximately 95 hours per week; commercial for 5 days a week; Chair. R. G. COLLINS; Dir.Gen. ALAN MORRIS.

Television Service Two: Television House, Durham Street West, Auckland; f. 1975; available to 74 per cent of the population; operates for approximately 77 hours per week; commercial for 5 days a week; Chair. K. G. FRASER; Dir. Gen. ALLAN MARTIN.

Commercial radio has been operating in New Zealand since 1970. In 1976 there were seven privately-owned commercial radio stations, depending entirely on commercial revenue but operating under the supervision of the BCNZ.

In October 1971, when the radio licence fee was abolished, there were 712,794 licensed radio sets. In November 1975 there were 816,979 licensed television sets.

FINANCE

(cap.=capital; p.u.=paid up; dep.=deposits; m.=million; $NZ=$ New Zealand)

BANKING

CENTRAL BANK

Reserve Bank of New Zealand: P.O.B. 2498, 2 The Terrace, Wellington; f. 1934; became State-owned institution 1936; Bank of Issue; dep., demand $NZ504.5m., term $NZ124.3m. (1975); Gov. A. R. LOW; Deputy Gov. R. W. R. WHITE.

COMMERCIAL BANKS

Bank of New Zealand: Lambton Quay, Wellington (P.O.B. 2392); f. 1861; cap. subs. and p.u. $NZ26.5m; dep. $NZ1,173.7m. (1975); Chair. L. N. ROSS, C.M.G.; Gen. Man. B. H. SMITH.

Bank of New Zealand Savings Bank Ltd.: Lambton Quay, P.O.B. 2392, Wellington; f. 1964; cap. subs. and p.u. $NZ1m.; dep. $NZ177m. (March 1975); Chair. L. N. ROSS, C.M.G.; Gen. Man. B. H. SMITH.

National Bank of New Zealand Ltd.: 8 Moorgate, London, EC2R 6DB; 170–186 Featherston St., Wellington; cap. p.u. £3.5m. sterling; dep. £331.1m. sterling (Oct. 1974); Chair. Lord LLOYD; Gen. Man. in New Zealand J. MOWBRAY.

National Bank of New Zealand Savings Bank Ltd.: P.O.B. 1791, Wellington; f. 1964; auth. cap. $NZ2m.; dep. $NZ76.0m. (Oct. 1973); Man. A. A. K. GRANT.

FOREIGN BANKS

Australia and New Zealand Banking Group Ltd.: 196 Featherston St., Wellington; incorporates ANZ Savings Bank Ltd.; New Zealand Gen. Man. K. R. PORTER.

Commercial Bank of Australia: 335–339 Collins St., Melbourne, Victoria; 328–330 Lambton Quay, Wellington.

Bank of New South Wales: 318-324 Lambton Quay, Wellington; f. 1817; Chief Man. for New Zealand F. A. SCHULTE.

Bank of Tokyo Ltd.: 109–117 Featherston St., Wellington 1.

SAVINGS BANK

Post Office Savings Bank: 49 Willis St., Wellington 1.

STOCK EXCHANGES

Auckland Stock Exchange: 82–84 Albert St., Auckland; Chair. MARTIN I. HARRIMAN; Sec. D. S. WRIGHT.

Christchurch Stock Exchange Ltd., The: P.O.B. 639, Christchurch; Chair. J. R. WIGNALL; Sec. P. F. MAPLES.

Dunedin Stock Exchange: P.O.B. 483, Dunedin; Chair. H. R. WILSON; Sec. K. R. SELLAR.

Wellington Stock Exchange: P.O.B. 767, Corner Grey and Featherston Sts., 1; Chair. W. R. HOCKING; Sec. T. D. McTAGGART.

INSURANCE

Government Life Insurance Office: P.O.B. 590, Wellington 1; f. 1869; Commissioner L. L. DAVIS; Deputy Commissioner and Actuary H. D. PEACOCK, F.I.A.

State Insurance Office: Lambton Quay, Wellington 1; fire branch f. 1905, accident branch f. 1925; Gen. Man. N. R. AINSWORTH.

A.A. Mutual Insurance Company: P.O.B. 1348, Wellington; f. 1928; Chair. J. C. BATES; Sec. F. C. SULLY.

A.M.P. Fire and General Insurance Company (N.Z.) Ltd.: 86/90 Customhouse Quay, Wellington; f. 1958; Chair. Sir CLIFFORD PLIMMER, K.B.E.; Man. N. B. WILCOX; fire, accident, marine, general.

Colonial Mutual Life Assurance Society Ltd.: Customhouse Quay, P.O.B. 191, Wellington; Man. R. P. MARTELL; life, accident, sickness, staff superannuation.

Commercial Union Assurance: 142 Featherston St., P.O.B. 2797, Wellington; Gen. Man. W. S. MANSFIELD; fire, accident, marine, life.

Export Guarantee Office: EXGO State Insurance Bldg., Lambton Quay, Wellington 1; f. 1964; Gen. Man. N. R. AINSWORTH.

Farmers' Mutual Insurance Association: Harvest Court, George St., Dunedin; f. 1904; Chair. T. G. McNab; Gen. Man. J. D. Wilde; fire and accident.

Metropolitan Life Assurance Company of N.Z. Ltd.: 79 Willis St., Wellington 1; f. 1962; Chair. D. St. Clair Brown; life.

National Insurance Company of New Zealand Ltd., The: Europa House, 109–117 Featherston St., Wellington 1; f. 1873; Chair. J. P. Cook; Gen. Man. J. S. Hodgkinson; Sec. J. Morton, A.C.A. (N.Z.).

National Mutual Group of Companies: National Mutual Centre, 153–161 Featherston St., P.O.B. 1692, Wellington; Man. S. R. Ellis; life, fire, accident, marine, personal accident, sickness.

New Zealand Counties' Co-operative Insurance Company Limited: Local Government Bldg., Lambton Quay, Wellington, C.1; f. 1942; Chair. R. A. Hutchinson; Gen. Man. T. M. McKewen, O.B.E.; fire, accident, fidelity guarantee, motor.

New Zealand Insurance Company Ltd., The: Auckland; f. 1859; Chair. L. N. Ross, C.M.G.; Gen. Man. D. G. Hare.

New Zealand Municipalities Cooperative Insurance Company Limited, The: Local Government Bldg., 114–118 Lambton Quay, Wellington; f. 1960; Chair. E. M. H. Kemp, M.B.E.; Gen. Sec. K. F. J. Bryant, B.COM., A.C.A.; fire, motor vehicle, all risks, accident.

Norwich Union Life Insurance Society Ltd.: 132–138 Featherston St., Wellington 1.

Phoenix Assurance Co. of New Zealand Ltd.: 125–127 Featherston St., P.O.B. 894, Wellington; Gen. Man. A. W. Hall, F.C.I.I.; fire, accident, marine, life.

Primary Industries Insurance Company Ltd., The: 70 Queen St., P.O.B. 1943, Palmerston North; f. 1957; Chief Exec. Officer J. Hackett; fire, accident, motor vehicle, marine, life.

Provident Life Assurance Company Ltd.: 125-127 Featherston St., P.O.B. 894, Wellington, C.1; f. 1904; Chair. R. C. B. Greenslade; Gen. Man. A. W. Hall.

Prudential Assurance Co. Ltd.: 332–340 Lambton Quay, P.O.B. 291, Wellington; Man. (life br.) C. C. Hough; Man. (fire, accident, marine br.) J. T. Paterson; life, fire, accident, marine.

Queensland Insurance Co. Ltd.: Huddart Parker Bldg., Wellington 1.

The Security and General Insurance Company (N.Z.) Limited: 126 The Terrace (P.O.B. 3544), Wellington; f. 1960; Chair. Sir Robert Crichton-Brown; Sec. D. Brady; fire, accident, motor.

S.I.M.U. Mutual Insurance Association: 29–35 Latimer Square, Christchurch; f. 1926; Chair. E. J. Bradshaw.

South British Insurance Company Ltd. (New Zealand): South British Bldg., Shortland St., Auckland; f. 1872; Chair. K. B. Myers; Group Gen. Man. D. L. Bullock.

TRADE AND INDUSTRY

CHAMBERS OF COMMERCE

Associated Chambers of Commerce of New Zealand: Molesworth St., Thorndon 1; Pres. B. N. Vickerman; Dir. G. L. Hawthorne; publ. *New Zealand Commerce* (monthly).

Chambers of Commerce are organized in most major towns, including the following:

Ashburton Chamber of Commerce (Inc.): P.O.B. 271, Ashburton; f. 1924; Pres. W. R. Anstiss; Sec. N. J. Johnson; 86 mems.

Canterbury Chamber of Commerce: Cnr. Oxford Terrace and Worcester St., Christchurch 1; f. 1859; Pres. J. G. Grigor; Sec. P. L. Bush; 1,920 mems.; publ. *Economic Bulletin* (monthly).

Hastings Chamber of Commerce: P.O.B. 144, Hastings; f. 1907; 205 mems.; Pres. F. G. Darroch; Sec. R. C. Cole; publs. *Newsletter* (monthly), *Review* (annual).

Invercargill Chamber of Commerce (Inc.): P.O.B. 311, Invercargill; f. 1863; Pres. T. McKenzie; Sec. A. S. Alsweiler; 200 mems.; publ. *Annual Report and Statement of Accounts.*

Kawerau Chamber of Commerce Inc.: P.O.B. 19, Kawerau, Bay of Plenty; Pres. M. G. Dippie; Sec.-Treas. Mrs. J. Markland; 57 mems.; publ. *Newsletter* (quarterly).

Napier Chamber of Commerce Inc.: P.O.B. 259, Napier; f. 1882; Pres. E. A. Miller; Sec. H. M. Swinburn; 151 mems.; publ. *Newsletter* (monthly).

Otago Chamber of Commerce Inc.: 123 Princes St., P.O.B. 908, Dunedin; f. 1861; Pres. G. W. T. Christie; Sec. Miss E. M. Waigth; 515 mems.; publs. *Newsletter* (monthly), *Annual Report.*

Palmerston North Chamber of Commerce Inc.: Construction House, 275 Broadway Ave., P.O.B. 1791, Palmerston North; f. 1898; Pres. B. K. Plimmer; Sec. W. L. May; 320 mems.; publ. *Newsletter* (bi-monthly).

Rotorua Chamber of Commerce Inc.: P.O.B. 1049, Rotorua; f. 1924; Pres. R. W. C. Wearne; Sec. J. A. W. de Vos; 150 mems.; publ. *Newsletter* (irregular).

Wanganui Chamber of Commerce and Industry Inc.: P.O.B. 88, Wanganui; f. 1885; Pres. B. T. Ireton; Sec. B. Sutcliffe; 129 mems.; publs. *Newsletter, Annual Report and Statement of Accounts.*

Wellington Chamber of Commerce: Commerce House, 126 Wakefield St., Wellington; f. 1856; Pres. D. A. Graham; Dir. G. W. Annand; Sec. R. J. F. Airey; 900 mems.; publs. *Voice of Business* and *Information and Trade Enquiry Bulletin* (every two months), *Register of Members* (yearly), *Annual Report.*

MANUFACTURERS' ORGANIZATIONS

Auckland Manufacturers' Association, The: P.O.B. 28-245, Remuera, Auckland 5; f. 1886; Pres. F. Bruell; Dir. J. Whatnall; 1,150 mems.

Canterbury Manufacturers' Association: P.O.B. 13-152, Armagh, Christchurch; f. 1879; Dir. I. D. Howell; 675 mems.

New Zealand Manufacturers' Federation (Inc.): Industries House, Courtenay Place and Allen St., Wellington 1.

Otago-Southland Manufacturers' Association Inc.: P.O.B. 5118; Moray Place, Dunedin; Pres. H. H. Saunders; Dir. J. G. Crawford; 240 mems.

Wellington Manufacturers' Association: P.O.B. 9234, Wellington; f. 1895; Pres. J. D. Todd; Dir. W. L. Gardner; 700 mems.

DEVELOPMENT ORGANIZATIONS

Development Finance Corporation: P.O.B. 3090, Wellington; f. 1964 to provide medium- and long-term finance for the establishment of new, and the expansion of existing, industries especially in developing regions; and for the promotion of exports; cap. p.u. $NZ10m.

Export-Import Corporation: f. 1974; undertakes export and import of goods and services and trade promotion activities; advisory service; may act as buying and selling agent for government and undertake trade transactions on its behalf.

The New Zealand Bureau of Importers and Exporters (Inc.): Chandris House, 9–11 Lower Albert St., Auckland 1.

PRODUCERS' ORGANIZATIONS

Auckland Vegetable and Produce Growers' Society Ltd.: 17 Overton Rd., Papatoetoe, Auckland; 553 mems.; Pres. I. A. Knight; Sec. A. McDell.

Federated Farmers of New Zealand: 7th Floor, Commercial Union House, Featherston Street, P.O.B. 715, Wellington, C.1; f. 1945; Pres. W. N. Dunlop; Sec. J. G. Pryde; 39,000 mems.; publ. *Straight Furrow* (fortnightly).

Meat Producers' Board: P.O.B. 121, Wellington, C.1; f. 1922; Chair. C. Hilgendorf; Sec. W. L. Keen; 9 mems.; publ. *Meat Producer* (monthly).

National Beekeepers' Association of New Zealand Inc.: Williams Parking Bldg., Boulcott St., Wellington, 1; f. 1913; Pres. I. J. Dickinson; Sec. G. A. Beard; 1,000 mems.; publ. *N.Z. Beekeeper*.

New Zealand Animal By-Products Exporters' Association: 95–99 Molesworth St., Wellington; 23 mems.; Sec. G. A. Turner.

New Zealand Berryfruit Growers' Federation (Inc.): Securities House, P.O.B. 10232, Wellington; Pres. J. G. Weedon, Jr.; Sec. D. W. Goble; 426 mems.

New Zealand Dairy Board: (Statutory Board—13 members); Massey House, Lambton Quay, Wellington 1; f. 1961; Chair. A. L. Friis, c.m.g.; Sec. J. P. McFaull.

New Zealand Fruitgrowers' Federation Ltd.: Huddart Parker Bldg., Wellington, C.1; f. 1915; Gen. Man. C. R. Macleod; publ. *The Orchardist of New Zealand*.

New Zealand Poultry Board: P.O.B. 379, Wellington 1; f. 1933; Chair. L. G. Bedford; Gen. Man. M. R. K. Cowdrey; Sec. B. J. Waymouth; 7 mems. (2 Government and 5 producer); publ. *N.Z. Poultry World* (monthly).

New Zealand Vegetable and Produce Growers' Federation (Inc.): Securities House, The Terrace, Wellington 1; Pres. R. H. Blackmore; Gen. Sec. D. W. Goble; 4,250 mems.

New Zealand Wool Board: 138–141 Featherston St., P.O.B. 3248, Wellington; f. 1944; 9 mems.; Chair. J. Clarke; Gen. Man. A. F. Cassie; Deputy Gen. Man. and Sec. G. H. Drees.

New Zealand Wool Marketing Corpn.: 18 Brandon St., Wellington 1; f. 1972; operates a support scheme for wool growers; Man. Dir. H. L. M. Peirse.

Pork Industry Council: P.O.B. 4048, Wellington; Chair. K. W. W. Sewell; Chief Exec. Officer G. A. Beard; publ. *Pork Industry Gazette*; circ. 3,500.

PRINCIPAL EMPLOYERS' ASSOCIATIONS

New Zealand Employers' Federation (Inc.): 95-99 Molesworth St., Wellington; f. 1902; links district employers' associations and other national industrial organizations; Pres. J. E. S. Hammond; Vice-Pres. D. G. R. Sutcliffe, E. J. Brenan; Exec. Dir. P. J. Luxford.

Auckland Fruit and Vegetable Retail Asscn. Inc.: P.O.B. 2081, Auckland; f. 1936; 325 mems.; Sec. W. Fong.

Auckland Master Bakers and Pastrycooks: Blacketts Bldg., Shortland St., Auckland 1; 117 mems.; Sec. R. S. Harrop.

Auckland Master Builders' Association: 22-24 Hobson St., P.O.B. 2856, Auckland, C.1; f. 1898; 440 mems.; Pres. A. V. Wiles; Man. G. F. Knowles.

Auckland Master Plumbers' Association (Inc.): 26 Albert St., Auckland; 330 mems.

Canterbury Master Builders' and Joiners' Association (Inc.): Shaw Savill Bldg., 220 High St., P.O.B. 359, Christchurch; 1,350 mems.; Sec. N. M. West.

New Zealand Dental Employers: 95–9 Molesworth St., Wellington; 773 mems.; Sec. G. A. Turner.

New Zealand Engineering Employers Federation: 95-9 Molesworth St., Wellington; 316 mems.; Sec. P. J. Luxford.

New Zealand Fibrous Plaster Manufacturers: 95-9 Molesworth St., Wellington; 73 mems.; Sec. G. A. Turner.

New Zealand Fruitgrowers I.U. of Employers: 95-9 Molesworth St., Wellington; 550 mems.; Sec. P. J. Luxford.

New Zealand Master Builders' Federation (Inc.): 80–82 Kent Terrace, Wellington 1.

New Zealand Motor Body Builders Asscn. Inc.: 95-9 Molesworth St., Wellington; 682 mems.; Sec. G. A. Turner.

New Zealand Retailers' Federation (Inc.): P.O.B. 12086, 101–103 Molesworth St., Wellington; 9 mem. asscns.; Exec. Dir. Barry I. Purdy.

New Zealand Sheepowners: Commercial Union House, 140–144 Featherston St., Wellington; 350 mems.; Pres. M. O'B. Loughnan; Sec. R. B. McLuskie.

New Zealand Timber Industry Employers' Union (Inc.): 95–99 Molesworth St., Wellington; 250 mems.; Man. W. F. Coady.

Painting Contractors' Association of Auckland (Inc.): 26 Albert St., P.O.B. 3999, Auckland; 140 mems.; Sec. J. W. Veale, a.c.a.

Wellington and Hutt Valley Master Builders' and Joiners' Association (Inc.): 77 Abel Smith St., P.O.B. 6048, Wellington; 300 mems.; Sec. R. A. Krebs.

TRADE UNIONS

The New Zealand Federation of Labour: F.O.L. Bldg., Lukes Lane, Wellington 1; f. 1937; Pres. Sir Tom Skinner; Sec.-Treas. W. J. Knox; affiliated to ICFTU.

Principal Affiliated Unions

National Union of Railwaymen: P.O.B. 858, Wellington; f. 1886; 16,000 mems.; Pres. R. J. Doherty; Gen. Sec. N. A. Collins; publ. *N.Z. Railway Review* (monthly).

New Zealand Carpenters and Related Trades Industrial Union of Workers: 6 St. Martin's Lane, P.O.B. 3868, Auckland; 4,000 mems.; Pres. J. Gillies; Sec. P. Purdue; publ. *Level*, circ. 4,200.

New Zealand Clerical Employees' Association: Cnr. Marion and Vivian Streets, Wellington; f. 1938; Pres. E. E. Bell; Vice-Pres. T. Brass; Sec. Chief Exec. D. Jacobs; publ. *Paper Clip*; circ. 40,000.

New Zealand Dairy Factories and Related Trades Union: 333 Te Rapa Rd., Hamilton; f. 1937; 5,168 mems.; Sec. S. I. Wheatley.

New Zealand Engineering, Coachbuilding, Aircraft, Motor and Related Trades Industrial Union of Workers: 123 Abel Smith St., Wellington; 40,000 mems.; Nat. Sec. J. A. BOOMER.

New Zealand Food Processing and Chemical Union: 314 Willis St., Wellington 1.

New Zealand Meat Workers and Related Trades Union: Trade Union Centre, 197 Armagh St., Christchurch; 20,000 mems.; Sec. F. E. MCNULTY.

New Zealand Printing and Related Trades Industrial Union of Workers: Labour Party Bldg., 101 Vivian St., Wellington, P.O.B. 6413, Te Aro, Wellington; f. 1862; 11,500 mems.; Pres. W. H. CLEMENT; Sec. G. C. DITCHFIELD; publ. *Imprint*.

New Zealand Public Service Association: Investment House, Whitmore St., Wellington 1.

New Zealand Shop Employees Federation: P.O.B. 1914, Christchurch; 16,000 mems.; Nat. Sec. B. ALDERDIC.

New Zealand Waterside Workers' Federation: 220 Willis St., Wellington 1; Sec. E. G. THOMPSON.

New Zealand Workers' Union: 79 Manchester St., Fielding; 16,000 mems.; Gen. Sec. D. J. DUGGAN; publ. *Bulletin* (quarterly).

North Island Electrical Workers' Union: Wellington; 7,500 mems.; Pres. C. T. LYNCH; Sec. A. J. NEARY.

United Mineworkers of New Zealand: Taylorville, West Coast, S.I.; Pres. A. V. PRENDIVILLE; Sec. J. WHITE.

MAJOR INDUSTRIAL COMPANIES

The following are the major industrial enterprises in New Zealand, ranked by capital:

N.Z. Forest Products Ltd.: Private Bag, Auckland; f. 1935; cap. $NZ64m.

Company has at Penrose two wallboard mills and associated remanufacturing and woodgrain printing departments, a mineral fibre board plant, a multiply paper bag factory and a polyethylene extrusion plant. At Kinleith are timber mills, two kraft pulp mills, a paper mill, veneer mill, shook mill and chemical extraction and a plywood mill. At Whakatane is a timber mill and a paperboard mill and at Mataura a paper mill.

Chair. Sir REGINALD SMYTHE; Man. Dir. A. W. MACKNEY; employees: 8,355.

Tasman Pulp and Paper Co. Ltd.: Kawerau, Bay of Plenty; cap. $NZ23m.

Manufacturers of newsprint, sulphate pulp, sawn timber, turpentine and Tall oil.

Chair. J. C. FLETCHER; Man. Dir. W. W. OLSEN; Sec. I. G. CLINKARD.

Challenge Corporation Ltd.: Challenge House, 105 The Terrace, Wellington, 1; f. 1861; cap. $NZ35m.

Through main subsidiaries: stock and station agents, woolbrokers, woolscourers, livestock and bloodstock salesmen, seed merchants, real estate and insurance agents, suppliers of farm equipment and finance, wine and spirit merchants, agricultural seed merchants, motor vehicle dealers, manufacturers of motor mowers, bicycles, turf care equipment, distributors of industrial and farm machinery, manufacturers of pumps, camping and outdoor living equipment, distributors of liquefied petroleum gas and accessory equipment, home appliance retailers, national wholesalers of pharmaceuticals, veterinary supplies, hardware, residential land developers, financiers for customer credit, plant and equipment leasing and related investments, money market dealers and merchant bankers; through main associated companies: national department store chain owners, development and management of shopping centres and office building, distributors of motor vehicles. Chair. R. R. TROTTER; employees: 5,000.

Fletcher Holdings Ltd.: Great South Rd., Penrose 6, Auckland; cap. $NZ26.7m.

Manufacturers of sawn timber, doors, particle board, plywood and other wood products, wire, metal culverts, long-run roofing, bituminous products, plastic sheeting, linseed oil, lucerne pellets, air-conditioning components. Also involved in medium and heavy construction, housing, heavy engineering, medical and scientific wholesaling, steel sales, machine tools, property development, shopping centre management and hire.

Fifteen New Zealand and nine international subsidiary companies, forty-eight associated companies; Chair. and Man. Dir. J. C. FLETCHER; employees: 6,300.

New Zealand Breweries Ltd.: 15-17 Murphy St., P.O.B. 211, Wellington, N.1; f. 1923; cap. $NZ23m.

Brewers, bottlers and hotelkeepers. Branches in Auckland, Palmerston North, Wellington, Christchurch, Hamilton and Dunedin.

Six associated companies; Chair. Sir CLIFFORD PLIMMER, K.B.E.; Gen. Man. J. MACFARLANE.

U.E.B. Industries Ltd.: 1-11 Short St., P.O.B. 37, Auckland 1; f. 1948; cap. $NZ39.5m.

Manufacturers of tufted and woven carpets and carpet yarn. Also manufacturers of cardboard container and carton packaging lines, polystyrene, wood-wool and cement slabs, etc.

Four subsidiary companies at home, four abroad; Man. Dir. G. S. PHILLIPS; employees: 4,550.

New Zealand Refining Co. Ltd.: P.O.B. 44, Whangarei; f. 1961; cap. $NZ12m.

The company operates Whangarei Refinery at Marsden Point, which refines petrol, diesel oils, fuel oils and bitumen.

Gen. Man. S. BOUMA; employees: 184.

ICI New Zealand Ltd.: ICI House, Molesworth St., Wellington (P.O.B. 1592); f. 1935; auth. cap. $NZ16m.

Importers and manufacturers of agricultural and horticultural chemicals, polyester resins, medical and veterinary pharmaceuticals, alkalis, general chemicals, plastics, explosives, metals, salt, pigments, coated fabrics, dyestuffs, slide fasteners, wallpapers; factories—Lower Hutt, Mount Maungarui, Christchurch, Auckland and Levin.

Seven subsidiary companies, all at home; Chair. and Man. Dir. D. B. GREEN; employees: 638.

Winstone Ltd.: 69–77 Queen St., Auckland; f. 1864; cap. $NZ23m.

Holding company for subsidiaries in the supply and manufacture of materials for the construction industry, quarry owners and processors of metal aggregates and sands; glass merchants; land developers; residential housing developers; forestry owners and timber merchants; road and civil engineering contractors.

Chair. A. H. WINSTONE; Man. Dir. K. O. JARVIS; employees: 3,900.

New Zealand Steel Ltd.: Private Bag, Glenbrook, South Auckland; cap. $NZ30m.

Manufacturers of iron-sand concentrate, sponge iron, steel, galvanized sheet and pipe.

Chair. F. R. A. HELLABY.

New Zealand Refrigerating Co. Ltd.: 159 Hereford St., 1, Christchurch; f. 1881; cap. $NZ8.7m.

Manufacturers of frozen meat, tallow, wool, hides, pelts, casings, preserved meat; exporters of frozen meat.

Chair. C. S. PEATE; Vice-Chair. W. G. V. FERNIE; employees: 475.

General Foods Corporation (NZ) Ltd.: P.O.B. 18221, Glen Innes, Auckland; f. 1938; cap. $NZ10m.

Manufacturers and distributors of ice cream, frozen and other foods and drinks; commercial refrigeration equipment; refrigerated transport operator.

Man. Dir. F. W. ORR; Gen. Man. R. C. FYFE; employees: 2,500.

Note: Merged with Wattie Industries Ltd. (*See below*).

New Zealand Farmers' Fertilizer Co. Ltd.: 31-33 Great South Road, Remuera 5, Auckland; f. 1916; cap. $NZ14.7m.

Manufacturer of fertilizers, sulphuric acid, copper sulphate, sulphate of alumina, chrome sulphate; supplier of pumice and pumice building blocks. Chair. P. C. I. CROOKES; Man. Dir. P. G. RIDDELL; employees: 530.

Cable Price Downer Ltd.: C.P.D. House 108 The Terrace, C.1, Wellington; f. 1854; authorized cap. $NZ20.5m.; issued and p.u. cap. $NZ14.286m.

Holding company for the Cable Price Downer Group of Companies.

Chair. A. L. MCLEAN.

Wattie Industries Ltd.: Corner of King St. and Fitzroy Ave., Hastings; f. 1934; cap. $NZ26.5m.

Food processing and industrial supplies.

Holding company for Wattie Group comprising: J. Wattie Canneries Ltd., General Foods Corpn. (N.Z.) Ltd., Cropper—NRM Ltd. and subsidiaries; Chair. D. F. MCLEOD; Man. Dir. G. J. WATTIE; employees: 6,952.

Alex Harvey Industries Ltd.: 752 Gt. South Rd., 6, Auckland; f. 1886; cap. $NZ50.6m.

Manufacturers of glass bottles and jars, tube vials, bent glass, domestic and commercial glassware and lightingware, metal and tin containers, food beverage aerosol and general line cans, torches, pails and drums, closures, injection and blow moulded bottles, containers and vials, industrial bulk containers, mouldings and extrusions, plastic closures, plastic pipe, tube and pipe fittings, polythene drainage pipe, rigid PVC pipe, rigid plastic sheet, polythene film, bags and shrink film, cellophane and polythene bags, gummed tape, reinforced aluminium foil insulation, laminated plastics, wallboards, corrugated and solid fibres containers, boxes, fibreglass wool, aluminium sliding doors and windows, insect screens for doors and windows, roof tiles, metal bathroom equipment, office equipment, shelving, kitchen hardware and utensils, commercial and stationery printers.

Seventy-four operating units; Chair. H. N. AVERY; Gen. Man. C. M. CAIRNS.

Golden Bay Cement Co. Ltd.: The Third Floor, Conference Chambers, Farish St., C.1, Wellington; f. 1909; cap. $NZ11.1m.

Manufacturers of cement and cement paint.

Chair. IAN T. COOK; employees: 450.

Dominion Breweries Ltd.: "Waitemata House", Cnr. Albert and Wyndham Sts., 1, Auckland; f. 1930; cap. $NZ10m.

Brewers, bottlers, wine and spirit merchants, hotel proprietors.

Chair. L. J. STEVENS; Man. Dir. Sir HENRY KELLIHER.

New Zealand Newspapers Ltd.: 20 Shortland St., 1, Auckland; f. 1870; cap. $NZ4.6m.

Newspaper proprietors. Branches in Auckland and Christchurch.

Chair. T. H. LEYS; Man. Dir. N. P. WEBBER.

Southland Frozen Meat and Produce Export Co. Ltd. (The): 12 Esk St., Invercargill; f. 1882; cap. $NZ4.5m.

Freezing works proprietors. Manufacturers of frozen meat, sliped wool, pickled pelts, hides, tallow, casings, meat meal.

Chair. A. F. GILKISON; employees: 1,600.

Feltex New Zealand Ltd.: 96-98 Anzac Avenue, Auckland.

Manufacturers of carpets, underlays, mattresses, pillows, tyres, tubes, retreads, general rubber goods, plastic foam, floor tiles, footwear and footwear components, wools and yarns, elastic, laces, polyester ropes, webbings, steel furniture, moulded and extruded plastic products, glues and marine coatings and sports equipment.

Chair. I. D. REID; Man. Dir. G. E. PEARCE; Gen. Man. N. H. CHAPMAN; employees: 6,663.

Steel and Tube Company of New Zealand Ltd.: UDC House, The Terrace, C.1, Wellington; cap. $NZ9.4m.

Holding company.

Five subsidiary companies; Chair. F. H. KEMBER.

TRANSPORT

RAILWAYS

New Zealand Government Railways: Wellington, 1; are under the jurisdiction of the Minister of Railways; 4,797 km. open (at March 31st, 1975); Minister of Railways Hon. COLIN MCLACHLAN; Gen. Man. T. M. SMALL; Deputy Gen. Man. J. W. DEMPSEY.

ROADS

National Roads Board: P.O.B. 12-041, Wellington North; est. 1953; Chair. Hon. WILLIAM YOUNG, Minister of Works and Development; Sec. D. J. CHAPMAN.

The Board consists of ten members nominated to represent various interests; it is advised by District Roads Councils. New Zealand is divided into 22 geographical Roads Districts, each of which is administered by a Roads Council. The Board and Councils are responsible for the Administration of State Highways. Maintenance and construction expenditure of these highways is met in full from the National Roads Fund.

Rural roads and Borough streets are the full responsibility of County, Borough and City Councils, which are assisted in meeting expenditure on maintenance and construction by the National Roads Board.

There were 91,158 km. of roads in 1975.

SHIPPING

New Zealand Ports Authority: Wellington; f. 1968; to foster an integrated and efficient ports system for New Zealand and to keep under review a national ports plan for the development of ports and harbours. Chair. Hon. J. K. McAlpine; Mems. A. T. Gandell, Capt. J. B. McGowan, Hon. J. Mathison, F. A. Reeves.

PRINCIPAL COMPANIES

New Zealand Shipping Corporation: UDC House, 104 The Terrace, Wellington 1; f. 1973 by the government to establish and operate shipping services; two container vessels serve the United Kingdom and a roll-on roll-off service is operated by a third ship between Auckland, Lyttelton and Dunedin.

Anchor Shipping and Foundry Co. Ltd.: Wakefield Quay, P.O.B. 1007, Port Nelson; f. 1862; services Wellington–Picton, Nelson–Westport–Greymouth; New Plymouth, Wanganui, Raglan, Portland, Onehunga, Motueka, Tarakohe, Napier, Gisborne; 4 vessels in service; Chair. H. G. West; Gen. Man. A. K. Gellatly.

Holm Shipping Co. Ltd.: Huddart Parker Bldg., Wellington; fleet of 11 cargo vessels; coaster and Pacific Islands services; Chair./Man. Dir. Capt. J. H. Holm, D.F.C.; Gen. Man. Capt. I. A. McKay; brs. in Auckland, Onehunga, Lyttleton and Christchurch.

P. and O. (NZ) Ltd.: Maritime Bldg., Customhouse Quay, Wellington; f. 1873; services New Zealand–United Kingdom via Panama Canal; 28 vessels in service; Man. Dir. G. Hunter.

Shaw Savill and Albion Co. Ltd.: corner Customhouse Quay and Brandon St., Wellington; f. 1858; cargo services New Zealand–United Kingdom via Panama Canal, Mediterranean and Europe, South America and West Indies. Passenger services United Kingdom–New Zealand via Panama, New Zealand–United Kingdom via South Africa, Panama, Caribbean; Gen. Man. for New Zealand M. J. Smith.

Union Steam Ship Company of N.Z. Ltd.: 38 Customhouse Quay, P.O.B. 1799, Wellington; f. 1875; cargo services between New Zealand and the Pacific Islands; also passenger and cargo services on New Zealand coast; cargo services between New Zealand and Australia and on Australian coast; 1 passenger, 16 conventional cargo vessels, 9 roll-on-roll-off cargo vessels; Chair. Sir Peter Abeles.

CIVIL AVIATION

There are international airports at Auckland, Christchurch and Wellington. The latter two are used for flights to Australia and internal flights only.

Air New Zealand Ltd.: Air New Zealand Hse., 1 Queen St., Auckland; f. 1940; services to Australia, Fiji, South Pacific Territories, Hong Kong, Singapore, U.S.A.; Chair. C. J. Keppel; Gen. Man. Chief Exec. M. R. Davies; fleet of 6 DC-8-52, 6 DC-10-30, 1 DC-10-30 on order.

Mount Cook Airlines: 47 Riccarton Rd., Christchurch; f. 1920; domestic services throughout New Zealand; Man. Dir. H. R. Wigley; fleet of 3 HS-748, 1 DC-3, 1 Goose, 6 BN-2A Islanders, 17 Cessna, 4 Widgeon, 2 FU-24.

New Zealand National Airways Corporation: P.O.B. 96, Wellington; f. 1947; operates regular daily services to all parts of New Zealand; Chair. C. W. Mace; Chief Exec. and Gen. Man. D. A. Patterson; fleet of 9 Boeing 737, 5 Vickers Viscounts V807, 15 Friendship F27; publs. *NAC's New Zealand* (circ. 41,000), *Skylines* (circ. 3,500).

Safe Air Ltd.: P.O.B. 244, Blenheim; f. 1951; operates scheduled passenger and cargo services; Chief air freight carrier in N.Z.; Pres. J. Sawers; Chair. L. G. Hucks; Gen. Man. D. P. Lynskey; fleet of 2 Argosy 200, 11 Bristol Freighters 31.

The following foreign Airlines serve New Zealand: American Airlines, British Airways, Lan-Chile, Pan Am, Qantas, U.T.A.

TOURISM

New Zealand Tourist and Publicity Department: P.O.B. 95, Wellington; f. 1901; National Tourist Office; Gen. Man. J. E. Hartstonge; offices in Auckland, Wellington, Christchurch, Dunedin, Invercargill, Rotorua and Queenstown.

New Zealand National Travel Association Inc.: Hume House, 152 The Terrace, Wellington; represents tourist industry interests; Chief Executive A. C. Staniford; publ. *New Zealand Holiday, Faces of Travel* (both quarterly).

CULTURAL ORGANIZATION

Queen Elizabeth II Arts Council: P.O.B. 6032, Te Aro, Wellington; f. 1964 in succession to the Arts Advisory Council; a statutory body which administers state aid to the arts; Chair. Hamish Keith; Dir. Malcolm Rickard.

MUSIC

Music Federation of New Zealand (Inc.): P.O.B. 3391, Wellington; f. 1950; arranges about 275 concerts a year, about one third by overseas groups, for its 19 member societies (which include Fiji), 32 associated regional organizations and in schools; active educational work includes organization of a nationwide school chamber music contest, master classes, etc.; mems. approx. 9,500; Pres. A. Hilton; Administrator Miss E. Airey; publ. *Theme* (annually).

The New Zealand Ballet and Opera Trust: P.O.B. 6682, Wellington; Chair. W. N. Sheat, O.B.E.; Dir. Una Kai; Gen. Man. G. C. Atkinson.

New Zealand Symphony Orchestra: P.O.B. 2092, Wellington; under direction of Radio New Zealand; public and broadcast concerts throughout New Zealand; 90 mems.

ATOMIC ENERGY

New Zealand Atomic Energy Committee: c/o D.S.I.R., Private Bag, Lower Hutt; responsible to the Minister of Science for advising Government on the development of peaceful uses of atomic energy in New Zealand; Chair. C. K. STONE; Exec. Sec. J. T. O'LEARY.

New Zealand Institute of Nuclear Sciences: DSIR, Private Bag, Lower Hutt; administered by the Department of Scientific and Industrial Research; facilities available to other government departments and to the universities; operates a 3 MeV Van de Graaff accelerator; Dir. T. A. RAFTER, M.SC., D.SC.

Department of Health: P.O.B. 5013, Wellington; radiation protection; advised by the Radiological Advisory Council.

National Radiation Laboratory: 108 Victoria St., P.O.B. 25099, Christchurch; branch of the Department of Health; radiation protection, licensing, measurement standards, practical services and research; Dir. H. J. YEABSLEY

University of Auckland: P.O.B. 2175, Auckland; research and training; operates 4MV Tandem Electrostatic accelerator.

University of Canterbury: Private Bag, Christchurch; research and training.

University of Otago: P.O.B. 56, Dunedin; research and training.

Victoria University of Wellington: P.O.B. 196, Wellington; research and training.

DEFENCE

Armed Forces (1975): Total strength 12,685; army 5,525 (excluding 5,618 active Territorials), navy 2,850 air force 4,310. Military service is voluntary though this is supplemented with twelve weeks selective national service in the army.

Equipment: The army has scout cars of British manufacture; medium tanks, armoured personnel carriers, and artillery. The navy has a small number of frigates armed with surface-to-air missiles; other craft include minesweepers and patrol boats. The air force has 36 combat aircraft and some helicopters.

Defence Expenditure: Defence expenditure for 1975–76 was $NZ179.2 million (U.S. $233 million).

Chief of the Defence Staff: Lieut.-Gen. Sir R. J. H. WEBB, K.B., C.B.E.

Chief of Staff (Army): Maj.-Gen. H. R. F. HOLLOWAY, C.B.E.

Chief of Staff (Navy): Rear-Adml. E. C. THORNE, C.B.E.

Chief of Staff (Air Force): Air Vice-Marshal R. B. BOLT, C.B.E., D.F.C., A.F.C.

EDUCATION

The present system of education in New Zealand is based mainly on the 1877 Education Act which provided compulsory, free education on a national and secular basis for both Europeans and Maoris between the ages of five and thirteen; in 1944 the school-leaving age was raised to fifteen. The Department of Education is responsible for the curriculum and for education on a national scale, although there is still a certain amount of local and regional control. A ratio of one teacher to 35 pupils in primary and intermediate schools was scheduled by 1975. The rate of expansion in secondary schools has been increassd by the growing number of pupils staying on at school after the age of 15. A new sixth-form schedule of one teacher to 20 pupils was introduced in 1970.

Elementary Education

Pre-school

Children under the age of five may be enrolled at free kindergartens or play centres controlled by local associations which are voluntary bodies formed for the purpose. In 1974 there were 1,041 kindergartens and play centres and together they catered for 51,184 children.

Primary Education

Primary school is compulsory from the age of six, although children may start at the age of five. All state primary schools are coeducational and provide a six-year course. In 1974 there were 441,462 pupils at state primary and private primary schools. There were 2,747 primary schools including more than 300 private primary schools. The curriculum includes English, mathematics, geography history, arts and crafts, science, physical education, health education and music. After the six-year primary course the pupils complete the final two years of primary school education either at the same school, or at an *intermediate school*. An intermediate school is a centrally situated school usually holding 300 to 600 pupils between eleven and thirteen years of age. Such schools make it possible to classify the pupils into groups of approximately equal ability and to provide a good range of optional courses. In 1974 there were 82,211 pupils at 131 intermediate schools and intermediate departments.

Secondary Education

At the age of thirteen children go to secondary schoo where they are obliged to stay until they are fifteen; all children are entitled to free secondary education until the end of their nineteenth year. At secondary level all district high schools and three-quarters of the state secondary schools are co-educational, while the remaining quarter and nearly all the private secondary schools are segregated. The syllabus at secondary school is made up of common core subjects like English, social studies, general science, elementary mathematics, music, arts, crafts, and physical education, plus a degree of specialization in the remaining subjects which complete the course. Some of these are of a practical nature, akin to technical education. In larger cities there are one or two schools which provide some technical education while the remainder have an academic bias with little or no technical education provided. District high schools are state primary schools with a secondary top and the basic course is academic as in the normal secondary school. In 1974 a total of 208,596 pupils received secondary education but the majority of pupils leave school at the end of their third or fourth year. The School Certificate examination is taken at the end of the third or fourth year of secondary school. Pupils who pass subjects in this examination go on to a year in the sixth form where, after a satisfactory year's work, they can be awarded a Sixth Form Certificate or University Entrance Certificate. High School Certificates are awarded after a five year course to pupils who have successfully completed an advanced course of two years and have been awarded a School Certificate.

Academic bursaries may be granted to pupils of above average ability who are obliged to live away from home in order to obtain tuition in all the subjects of their choice in the S.C.E. There are 400 awards each year tenable for up to three years, as well as special sixth-form bursaries tenable for two years.

Rural Education

In order to give children in country districts the advantage of special equipment and the more specialized teaching of larger schools, the consolidation of the smaller rural schools has been undertaken wherever this is practicable. In certain cases boarding allowances are granted to pupils living in areas where there are no convenient transport services enabling them to attend school.

Correspondence Schools

Since 1922 correspondence classes have been conducted for the education of children in very remote areas and those of missionaries and New Zealand Government servants abroad. The correspondence school also provides a number of other courses for part-time education, particularly for the teaching diploma.

Maori Education

There is a continued increase in Maori enrolment, particularly at secondary school level, and a steady increase in the numbers of Maori children attending pre-school institutions. The period of stay of Maori secondary pupils remains considerably shorter than that for other pupils. In 1973 there were 20,797 Maori pupils at secondary school level. Recognized play centres provided for 2,913 Maori children out of a total enrolment of 20,792 in July 1973, and kindergartens for 2,706 out of a total of 28,580. In addition, some Maori pre-school children were enrolled in primary schools for special pre-school programmes.

In 1973 there were 96,381 Maori children receiving education, of which 479 were enrolled scholarship-holders at public and private secondary schools.

Maori Education Foundation (MEF): The MEF was established in 1961 to promote and encourage the better education of Maoris and for providing financial assistance to further this end with Government grants.

Pacific Islands Education Foundation: In 1972 the Pacific Islands Polynesian Education Foundation was established. This Foundation will have similar purposes to the MEF and will benefit New Zealand born Pacific Island Polynesians or those residing permanently in New Zealand.

Technical Institutes and Community Colleges

Technical Institutes: Both theoretical and practical training for apprentices are available at twelve Technical Institutes throughout the country.

Technical education at higher level for technicians is growing steadily. Courses leading to national certificates have been provided in engineering, draughting, science, building, quantity surveying and others. Bursaries are available for suitably qualified students wishing to take approved full-time courses at technical institutes.

A Technical Correspondence Institute has nearly 300 full-time tutors and provides courses in some 769 subjects. In 1973, 17,679 students were enrolled at the TCI.

Community Colleges: An amendment to the 1877 Education Act in 1974 provided a legal basis for the establishment of community colleges. These will be established in provincial centres where there is some need for technical education. However, these colleges will assume the broader role of further education to meet the education needs of adults in each particular community.

Universities

At present New Zealand has six universities, at Auckland, Hamilton, Palmerston North, Wellington, Christchurch and Dunedin, plus a constituent agricultural college of the University of Canterbury at Lincoln. The state supports the universities and acts through the Universities Grants Commission. This body advises the Government of the needs of university education and research in New Zealand and determines the allocation of grants of money to meet those needs. It is also responsible for the awarding of scholarships which are tenable for three to six years, depending on the minimum full-time study necessary for the completion of the course. Students are selected for university on the basis of the university entrance examination. About 12 per cent of pupils leaving secondary school go to university. The approximate number of first year students in New Zealand universities each year is 9,000 while the approximate number of graduates is 6,000. Degrees in New Zealand universities (other than advanced or full-time professional degrees) usually permit part-time as well as full-time study. Massey University runs a large external degree teaching function. In 1974 there were 39,949 students enrolled at the universities, of whom approximately 3,000 were external students. There was a teaching staff of 2,679 full-time teachers.

Some adult education is provided in universities by University Extension courses. These do not usually lead to qualification. The major provider of continuing education is the secondary school evening class programme.

Teacher Training

In 1974 there were 8,004 students undergoing primary and secondary teacher training in seven teachers' colleges. Since 1971 most students follow a three-year course leading to the Trained Teacher's Certificate. University graduates take an alternative course lasting one year. In order to meet future staffing requirements due to the rapidly increasing school population special one-year training schemes have been established for selected adult trainees followed by one year as probationary assistants before they are granted a teacher's certificate. In 1974 there were 21,905 fully-trained state and private primary school teachers.

UNIVERSITIES

University of Auckland: Princes St., Auckland; 560 teachers, 9,493 students.

University of Canterbury: P.O.B. 1471, Christchurch; 371 teachers, 6,732 students.

Massey University: P.O. Palmerston North; 400 teachers, 6445 students.

University of Otago: Dunedin; 500 teachers, 6,377 students.

Victoria University of Wellington: Private Bag, Wellington; 421 teachers, 6,696 students.

University of Waikato: Hamilton; 168 teachers, 2,928 students.

Lincoln College: Canterbury; constituent college of University of Canterbury; 125 teachers, 2,050 students.

BIBLIOGRAPHY

GENERAL

CUMBERLAND, K. B., and WHITELAW, J. S. New Zealand (Longman, London, 1970).

McLINTOCK, A. H. (ed.). An Encyclopaedia of New Zealand (Government Printer, Wellington, 1966).

GUTHRIE-SMITH, W. H. Tutira; the story of a New Zealand sheep station, 4th edn. (Reed, Wellington, 1969).

LARKIN, T. C. New Zealand's External Relations (Oxford University Press, London, 1962).

NEW ZEALAND, MINISTRY OF FOREIGN AFFAIRS. New Zealand Foreign Policy: statements and documents 1943–1957 (Government Printer, Wellington, 1972).

ROSS, A. (ed.). New Zealand's Record in the Pacific Islands in the Twentieth Century (Longman Paul for the New Zealand Institute of International Affairs, Auckland, 1969).

SCHWIMMER, E. G. (ed.). The Maori People of the Nineteen-Sixties . . . (Paul, Auckland, 1968).

SCOTT, K. J. The New Zealand Constitution (Clarendon Press, Oxford, 1962).

TAYLOR, C. R. H. A Bibliography of Publications on the New Zealand Maori (Oxford University Press, London, 1971).

HISTORY

BEAGLEHOLE, J. C. The Discovery of New Zealand (Oxford University Press, London, 1961).

CONDLIFFE, J. B. New Zealand in the Making (Allen and Unwin, London, 1959).

LISSINGTON, M. P. New Zealand and Japan 1900–1941 (Government Printer, Wellington, 1972).

LLOYD PRICHARD, M. F. An Economic History of New Zealand until 1939 (Collins, Auckland, 1970).

OLIVER, W. H. The Story of New Zealand (Faber, London, 1963).

SIMKIN, C. G. F. The Instability of a Dependent Economy; Economic Fluctuations in New Zealand 1840–1914 (Oxford University Press, London, 1951).

SINCLAIR, K. A History of New Zealand (Oxford University Press, London, 1961).

SUTCH, W. B. The Quest for Security in New Zealand (Oxford University Press, Wellington, 1966).

ROSS, ANGUS. New Zealand's Aspirations in the Pacific in the Nineteenth Century (Clarendon Press, Oxford, 1964).

TAPP, E. J. Early New Zealand: Relations with Australia (Melbourne University Press, 1958).

ECONOMY

BLYTH, C. A. (ed.). The Future of Manufacturing in New Zealand (Oxford University Press, London, 1964).

BRIGHT, T. N. Banking Law and Practice in New Zealand (Sweet and Maxwell, Wellington, 1969).

CORNWALL, J. P. M. Planning and Forecasting in New Zealand (Oxford University Press, London, 1965).

LLOYD PRICHARD, M. F. Economic Practice in New Zealand, 1954–55 to 1967–68 (Collins, Auckland, 1970).

MARRIS, E. C. New Zealand Investment Guide (New Zealand Financial Times, Wellington, rev. edn., 1970).

NEW ZEALAND, DEPARTMENT OF AGRICULTURE. Agriculture in New Zealand (Government Printer, Wellington, 1972).

NEW ZEALAND, TOWN AND COUNTRY PLANNING DIVISION. National Resources Surveys, Parts I–VII (Government Printer, Wellington, 1959–71).

RIMMER, J. O. (ed.). Marketing in New Zealand (Hicks Smith, Wellington, 1972).

Other Territories

CHRISTMAS ISLAND   COCOS (KEELING) ISLANDS

CHRISTMAS ISLAND

Christmas Island covers an area of about 135 square kilometres and lies 360 kilometres south of Java Head in the Indian Ocean. The nearest point on the Australian coast is North West Cape.

Administration was transferred from Singapore to Britain on January 1st, 1958, pending final transfer to Australia. It became an Australian territory on October 1st, 1958. The island has no indigenous population. At June 30th, 1975, the total population was 3,032 (1,735 Chinese, 888 Malays, 316 Europeans and 93 others). Nearly all the residents are employees of the British Phosphate Commissioners and their families. The recovery of phosphates is the sole economic activity, and exports were 1,426,276 tons of phosphates and 2,168 tons of phosphate dust for the year ending June 30th, 1975.

Administrator: W. Worth.

Supreme Court: Judge: The Hon. Mr. Justice E. A. Dunphy.

Christmas Island Broadcasting Station: Lower Drumsite; daily broadcasting service.

There were 2,000 radio sets in 1975.

Christmas Island Phosphate Commission: 515 Collins St., Melbourne, Vic. 3000, Australia. The British Phosphate Commissioners are the managing agents of the Christmas Island Phosphate Commission. Commissioners: Sir Allen Brown, c.b.e. (Australia), W. D. Bremner (New Zealand), W. B. Marston (joint Commissioner). The Commission controls phosphate mining on the Island as well as the export and distribution of phosphate.

Transport: Australian Government charter aircraft operate a three-weekly service from Perth. The British Phosphate Commissioners conduct a cargo-shipping service to Singapore and Australian ports. They also operate flights from Singapore and Malaysia to Christmas Island.

COCOS (KEELING) ISLANDS

The Cocos (Keeling) Islands are 27 in number and lie 2,768 kilometres north west of Perth in the Indian Ocean. The islands, which have an area of 14 square kilometres, form a low-lying coral atoll, densely covered with coconut palms. The population on June 30th, 1975, was 604, comprising 92 persons on West Island and 512 on Home Island, the only inhabited islands in the group.

The islands were declared a British possession in 1857 and came successively under the authority of the Governor of Ceylon (1878) and the Governor of the Straits Settlements (1886); they were annexed to the Straits Settlements and incorporated with the Settlement (later Colony) of Singapore in 1903. Administration of the islands was transferred to the Commonwealth of Australia in November 1955.

On July 23rd, 1975, the Official Representative Ordinance 1955–61 was repealed and replaced by the Administration Ordinance 1975. This provided for the appointment of an Administrator by the Governor–General of Australia.

Administrator: R. J. Linford.

Supreme Court, Cocos (Keeling) Islands: Judge: The Hon. Mr. Justice E. A. Dunphy.

Radio Cocos: daily services from 15.30; to 23.30 Man. R. W. Pilsbury.

There were 650 radio receivers in 1975.

The main economic activity is the production of copra. Total exports in 1974/75 were 300 tonnes.

Australian Government charter aircraft carry passengers, supplies and mail to and from the Cocos every three weeks. Cargo vessels, also chartered by the Government, deliver supplies, usually at six-monthly intervals.

The Pacific Islands

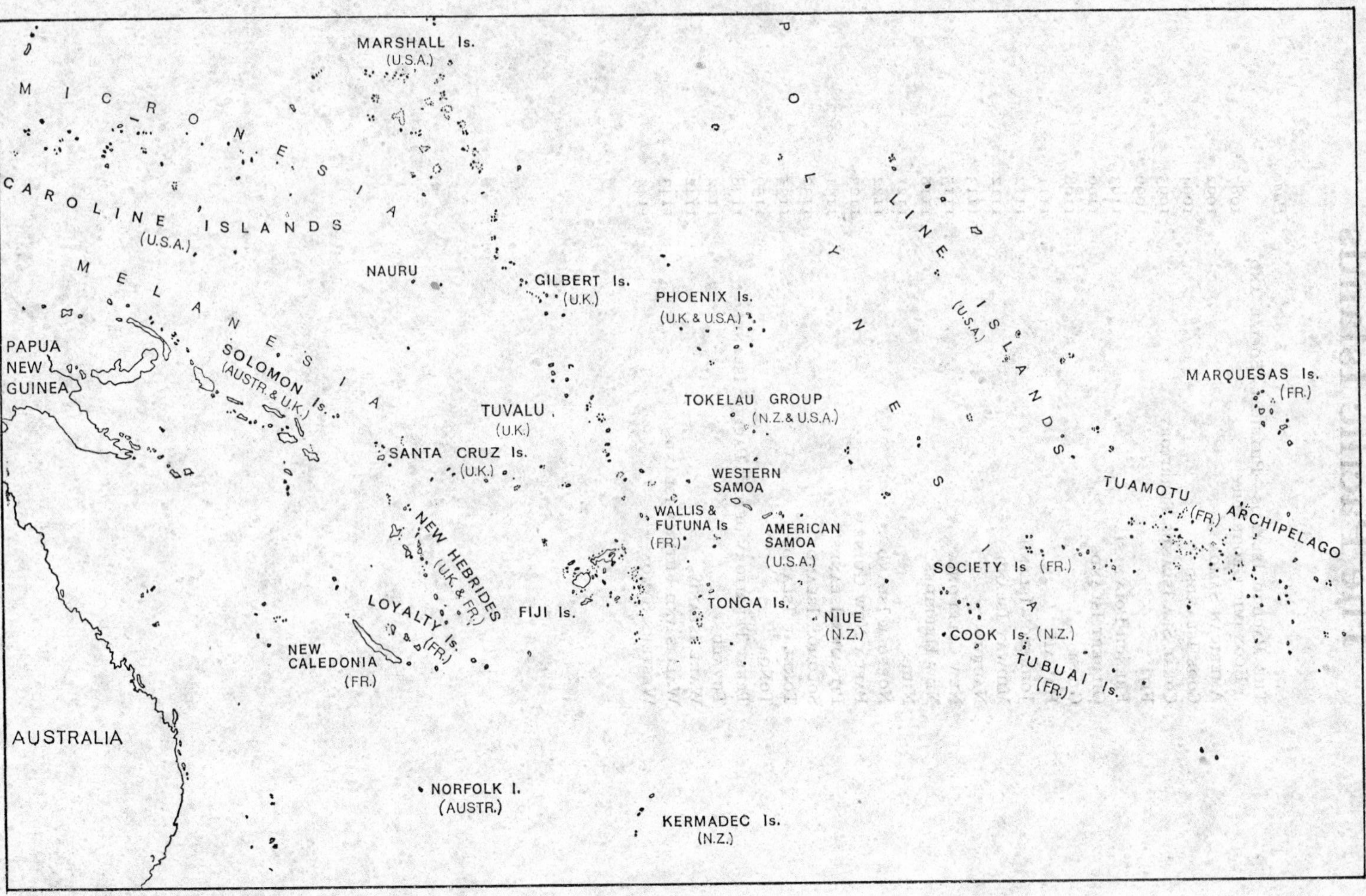

The Pacific Islands.

The Pacific Islands

Bryant J. Allen

The Pacific Ocean occupies a third of the earth's surface. Within it are located many thousands of islands, more than in all the rest of world's seas combined. The numerousness of Pacific islands, and their widespread distribution, gives rise to a great variety of physical, social and economic environments. Their location relative to the continents and larger islands which border the Pacific and which include North and South America, Japan, China, the Philippines, Indonesia, Australia and New Zealand, continues to influence political and economic conditions in them. Their small size and physical isolation has rendered them vulnerable to influences from the rest of the world. Rapid and often traumatic ecological, social, economic and political changes have occurred throughout the Pacific following penetration by European and Asian explorers and colonists, a process which is still under way, as improved communications and the neo-colonialism of mining, investment and tourism bring the Pacific Islands closer to the modern world.

A number of broad classifications of Pacific Islands exist. The islands may be divided into continental islands, high islands, low islands and atolls. The people of the Pacific may be divided into Melanesians, Polynesians and Micronesians. Melanesians occupy the larger islands in the south-west, Irian Jaya and Papua New Guinea, the Solomons, the New Hebrides, Fiji and New Caledonia. Polynesians live on islands which are located over an immense area from Hawaii in the north to Easter Island in the south-east to New Zealand in the south-west. In the central Pacific, Polynesians occupy the major groups of Tonga, Samoa, the Society Islands including Tahiti, and the Cook Islands, as well as numerous small atolls. The Micronesians live in the north, central and west Pacific in the Mariana, Caroline, Marshall and Gilbert groups.

The islands may be also divided into politically dependent and independent states. The dependent states are governed wholly or partially by colonial administrations owing allegiance to the United Kingdom, France, the U.S.A., Australia and New Zealand. Islands which fall into this category are the Solomon Islands, Pitcairn Islands, Gilbert Islands and Tuvalu (formerly Ellice Islands) (the United Kingdom); the New Hebrides (the United Kingdom and France); New Caledonia, Tahiti, Society Islands, the Tuamotu, Austral, Gambier and Marquesas groups, Wallis and Futuna (France); the Tokelau, Cook and Niue Islands (New Zealand); Caroline, Marshall and Mariana Islands, Guam and American Samoa (U.S.A.); and Hawaii, a state of the United States.

Former dependencies which have achieved political independence are Papua New Guinea (from Australia in 1975); Tonga (from the United Kingdom in 1970); Fiji (from the United Kingdom in 1970); Western Samoa (from New Zealand in 1962); and Nauru (from the United Nations and Australia in 1968). Irian Jaya, the western half of the island of New Guinea, is a province of Indonesia and will not be considered in this section; New Zealand and the Philippines are also excluded.

PHYSICAL GEOGRAPHY

No agreement exists on the origin of the Pacific basin. One hypothesis suggests the basin is the result of shrinkage and depression of the earth's crust, while another argues the gradual expansion of the earth, the emergence of new rocks on the ocean floors and the drift of continental land masses on great plates, has created the great oceans of the world, of which the Pacific is the largest.

The physical features of the Pacific basin are better known. The basin is from four to six kilometres deep and roughly circular in shape. The boundary is in most places the continental margin, but elsewhere it is obscured in a jumble of island arcs and fragmented continental blocks. The north half of the basin forms one relatively deep unit between five and six kilometres deep, and the southern half another shallower one. The north is characterized by a number of enormous volcanoes and numerous clusters of smaller ones. The crust here is broken by very long faults. The south is deformed by a series of very long broad arches or rises with associated block and wrench faulting. Island arcs and deep trenches occur along the margins of the basins and parallel to them, archipelagoes of volcanic islands and clusters of submarine volcanoes occur in all parts of the basins but most are in the west and south-west.

These structures give rise to a number of characteristic island types. West of the so-called andesite-line, representing the farthest eastward limit of the continental blocks of Asia and Australia, are islands formed on the broken edges of the continental blocks. These continental islands have foundations of ancient folded and metamorphosed sediments which have been intruded by granites. Vulcanism has overlain these rocks with lavas, tuff and ash, and transgressions by the ocean have lain down softer and younger marine sediments. Erosion has resulted in plains, deltas and swamps along the modern coastline. New Guinea is the best example of these continental islands; it is dominated by a massive central cordillera within which lie dissected and flat floor montane valleys. The highest peak in the island is over 5,000 metres. Active volcanoes exist along the north coast and in the New Guinea islands. North and south of the central mountains are broken hills and vast swamps. The coastal pattern is one of small coastal plains alternating with low river terraces, high marine terraces, coastal hills and steep mountain slopes plunging straight into the sea. The largest rivers of all the Pacific Islands are found here. The Fly is navigable by motorized vessels for about 800 kilometres and the Sepik for 500. Other continental islands are Fiji, the Solomons, the New Hebrides and New Caledonia.

The high islands of the central Pacific are composed almost entirely of volcanic materials, together with reef limestone and recent sediments. The islands are the peaks of the largest volcanoes in the world. The Hawaiian volcano of Mauna Loa, for example, rises nine kilometres from the ocean floor and is over 200 kilometres in diameter. Characteristic landforms of the high islands are striking peak and valley forms, with old volcanic cores often eroded to form fantastic skylines. Waterfalls, cliff faces and narrow beaches, with fringing coral reefs complete the pattern. High islands in the Pacific include Hawaii, Samoa, Tahiti and the Marquesas, Rarotonga in the Cook Islands, and Ponape and the northern Mariana Islands.

Low islands are of two types: some are volcanic islands which have been eroded, while others are raised atolls, which resemble sea-level reefs, but which are now elevated above modern sea-level. Caves and sinkholes occur widely. Small pockets of soil occur within the limestone rocks. Surface water is uncommon. Examples of low volcanic islands include Aitutaki in the Cook Islands and Wallis Island. Raised coral islands include some of the islands of the Tuamotu, Society, Cook, Line, Tokelau, Marshall, Caroline and Gilbert Islands groups. Low islands with raised reefs are also common. One of the best examples is Mangaia in the Southern Cook group, which has a central core of volcanic rock 180 metres high surrounded by an unbroken kilometre wide band of coral limestone raised 70 metres above the present sea-level. A new fringing reef now surrounds the island.

The fourth island form are the atolls, roughly circular reefs of coral limestone, partly covered by sea water on which there are small islands made up of accumulations of limestone debris, and within which there occur a lagoon of calm water. Atoll islets are commonly less than three metres above the high-tide level. It is generally agreed that atolls have developed on the tops of volcanoes which now no longer protrude above sea-level. Atolls vary in size from the Rose Atoll near Samoa which is about 3 kilometres by 3 kilometres to the Kwajalein Atoll in the Marshall Islands which is over 60 kilometres long. Sources of fresh water are rain and a freshwater lens which is frequently found floating on salt groundwater beneath the islets. Hurricanes and typhoons frequently sweep over atolls, partially or completely destroying islets.

Climate

Five atmospheric circulation regions have been identified in the Pacific. A middle latitude area is characterized by the occurrence of extra-tropical cyclones with characteristic distinctive frontal weather systems. The Marianas and the western Hawaiian Islands sometimes receive this type of weather in the northern winter. The trade winds regions where at least 60 per cent of prevailing winds are from the north-west in the northern hemisphere and the south-east in the southern hemisphere, lie in an arc from the west coast of Mexico through Hawaii to the Marshall Islands in the north, and from the west coast of South America across the Marquesas and Tuamotus to the Society Islands. In these areas distinct wet and dry zones appear on larger islands, Hawaii being a good example. The monsoon area occurs to the far west and influences few of the Pacific Islands. The weather of Papua New Guinea is influenced, however, and a wet season and a dry season are distinguishable, although they are by no means as sharp as the term "monsoon" implies. A doldrums area occurs in a poorly defined band south of the equator in an arc extending east from the Solomon Islands to the Phoenix Islands. Finally, a hurricane zone exists in the northern Pacific west from Panama in an arc which includes the Marshall, Caroline and Mariana Islands. A similar zone occurs in the south extending from the Tuamotus west across the Cooks, Samoa, Tonga and Fiji to the north-east Australian coast.

Rainfall in the Pacific is geographically most variable; some islands are semi-arid while others are very wet. In the northern Pacific, for example, Midway receives a mean annual rainfall of 1,194 mm. and Honolulu 550 mm. Further south Yap receives 3,023 mm., Palau 3,900 mm., Ponape 4,700 mm. and Fanning 2,054 mm. In the eastern Pacific near the equator islands are frequently barren. Rainfall decreases from west to east along the equator; Nauru receives 2,050 mm., Ocean Island 1,930 mm. and Christmas Island 950 mm. Further south in an arc extending east from New Guinea to the Society Islands in the Central Pacific average annual rainfall varies from between 3,500 mm. in the west to 2,000 mm. in the east. In Papua New Guinea altitude and local relief influence climate. Areas exposed to the north-west and south-east winds receive over 5,000 mm. of rain, while inland areas cut off from moist air masses may receive less than 1,500 mm. On the south-eastern coast east and west of Port Moresby average annual rainfall is less than 1,000 mm.

Soils, minerals, vegetation

Geology, soil, altitude, landforms, location and climate are all combined in the creation of the widely varying physical environments of Pacific islands. Continental islands exhibit the widest range of environments, from high alpine grasslands, through montane forest, and lowland rainforest to savannah and mangrove swamps. They also contain the richest deposits of minerals: nickel, chrome and manganese are mined in New Caledonia, gold and copper in New Guinea. The high volcanic islands contain no known minerals of commercial value. Terrain is frequently a limit to cultivation, although soils are in general heavily leached and of low fertility, with low mineral and humus content. Raised coral islands lack groundwater and soils are shallow and often scattered in pockets. Phosphate deposits are mined from the coral in limestone on Nauru and Ocean Islands and were formerly mined on Makatea in the Society Islands. The atolls contain only sparse resources. Soil development is often nil, fresh water difficult to obtain and foodplants other than coconuts and pandanus nuts difficult to cultivate. Special techniques are used to cultivate taro, but storms or high sea-levels frequently destroy gardens. The atolls provide the most tenuous existence for man in the Pacific.

The flora and fauna of the Pacific Islands are unbalanced in comparison with the continents in that many major categories of plants have not reached the islands. A few ancestral immigrants have given rise to the entire endemic biota. Lack of ecological competition appears to have resulted in genera developing many more species than plants on continental land masses have been able to produce.

PREHISTORY, CULTURE AND SOCIETY

The continental and oceanic Pacific islands were never linked by land bridges to the Asian continent and the Indonesian islands east of Bali and west of New Guinea form a frontier zone between a realm of placental mammals and marsupial mammals, the Wallace Line. Prehistorians argue therefore that man, a placental mammal, is an intruder in the Pacific. The first men to immigrate across the Wallace Line are believed to have been *Homo sapiens* approaching the modern form. The people of the interior of New Guinea are classified as Australoid populations which are thought to have begun moving into the area from Indonesia about 30,000 years ago. Until 5,000 years or so ago, archaeological evidence points to the Pacific east of the Bismarck Archipelago being devoid of human settlement. Between 4,000 and 2,000 years ago, people who are thought to have lived in north-eastern Indonesia and the Philippines, and who had descended from a Mongoloid stock, spread into the Pacific and along the coasts of the continental islands, intermarrying with the existing Australoid populations of eastern Indonesia and New Guinea. Modern Melanesians, Polynesians and Micronesians are thus to varying degrees the outcome of the mixing of these early Australoid and Mongoloid stocks.

Thus the Melanesians who inhabit the island chains from the Solomons eastwards to Fiji are basically an Australoid group, while the Fijians are a more intermediate group. Polynesians tend towards the Mongoloid end of the continuum and Micronesians more so. The actual pattern, however, is far more complex than this simple description.

Origins of the three groups may also be evidenced in their cultures. The Polynesians are culturally and linguistically the most homogenous. Polynesian societies are basically patrilineal and genealogically ranked, with elaborate hierarchical systems of rank and class, best developed on the Hawaiian, Tongan and Society Islands. Micronesian societies are mainly matrilineal, with the exception of Yap and the Gilberts. Melanesia is culturally the most diverse area of all. Hereditary ranking occurs in Fiji, but in many areas, especially in Papua New Guinea, status is achieved rather than inherited. Most groups are patrilineal, but matrilineal societies occur in the New Guinea Islands, the Solomons and the New Hebrides.

Throughout the Pacific, the pre-contact subsistence economy was based on the vegetative propagation of root and tree crops, together with fishing and some pig husbandry and hunting. The only domesticated animals were dogs, pigs and fowls but all three were not present everywhere in the region. The major root crops, taro and yam, have Asian origins, but one, the sweet potato which was grown in New Guinea, Hawaii, Marquesas, Society and Easter Island groups prior to European contact, has a South American origin. Shifting cultivation was the main agricultural technique in most areas, although the intensity of land use and the periodicity of cycles varied widely in relation to population densities. In New Caledonia and parts of Polynesia, notably Hawaii, Tahiti and the Cook Islands, taro was cultivated in relatively elaborate, terraced, irrigated gardens.

Short distance ocean voyaging was well-established in Polynesia and Micronesia before European contact, with large double-hulled canoes and navigation based on stars, wave patterns, bird flights and inherited geographical knowledge. Large ocean-going and coastal canoes were also used in Papua New Guinea and Fiji.

Over 1,000 different languages are spoken in the Pacific Islands, more than 700 being found in Papua New Guinea and the Solomon Islands. They belong to two groups, the non-Austronesian phyla found in Papua New Guinea (and in scattered pockets in Indonesia), and the Austronesian phyla, which are spoken in coastal Papua New Guinea, most of island Melanesia, all of Polynesia and Micronesia (as well as in parts of Indonesia, the Philippines, South-East Asia and Madagascar).

To summarize, existing evidence suggests Papua New Guinea was settled before 30,000 years ago by ancestral Australoid populations who were followed about 3,000 years ago by Austronesian speakers of Mongoloid stock who probably brought pottery, horticulture and pigs to Papua New Guinea. Intermixing occurred, followed by further movements east to New Caledonia and the New Hebrides. Fiji was then settled by people who carried with them a pottery technology previously established in Papua New Guinea and islands to the east, and further movements into the Pacific Ocean took place. During the last 2,500 years further intermixing has occurred in Melanesia while Polynesian and Micronesian populations have had less interaction.

American Samoa

PHYSICAL AND SOCIAL GEOGRAPHY

American Samoa comprises the seven islands of Tutuila, Tau, Olosega, Ofu, Aunuu, Rose and Swains. They lie in the South Central Pacific along latitude 14° S. at about longitude 170° W., some 2,300 miles south-west of Hawaii. Swains Island lies 210 miles to the north-west of the main group. They are high volcanic islands with rugged interiors and little flat land except along the coasts.

The population at the 1970 census was 28,000, of whom over 25,000 lived on Tutuila.

The islands are peopled by Polynesians and are thought to have been the origin of many of the people who now occupy islands further east. The Samoan language is believed to be the oldest form of Polynesian speech in existence. Samoan society developed an intricate hierachy of graded titles comprising titular chiefs and orator chiefs. One of the striking features of modern Samoa is the manner in which these titles and the culture before European contact remains a dominant influence. Most of the population are Christians.

HISTORY

The Samoan islands were first visited by Europeans in the 1700s, but it was not until 1830 that missionaries from the London Missionary Society settled there. In 1878 the then independent Kingdom of Samoa gave the United States the right to establish a naval base at Pago Pago. Britain and Germany were also interested in the island, but Britain withdrew in 1899 leaving the Western islands for Germany to govern until 1914. The chiefs of the eastern islands ceded their lands to the United States in 1904 and the island officially became an American territory in 1922.

American Samoa is administered by a Governor, appointed by the United States, and a legislature comprising a Senate and a House of Representatives. The Senate is made up of chiefs, or *matai*, from 18 districts and the House of 20 members elected by universal adult suffrage. Prior to 1963 emigration to Hawaii and the United States, California in particular, was common. A tuna canning plant was built at Pago Pago in 1953 and processes fish from Japanese vessels. The US naval base there is another major source of employment. Tourism is also an important industry and Pago Pago is a major mid-Pacific stop-over for large passenger aircraft. The American Samoan economy and urban life is oriented strongly toward the United States.

STATISTICAL SURVEY

Area: 76.1 square miles.

Population (1970 census): Total 28,000; Ofu 411, Olosega 410, Tau 1,317, Tutuila 25,357, Swains 74, Aunuu, Rose (uninhabited); Pago Pago (capital, on Tutuila Island) 2,291. Total population (1973): 29,296.

Agriculture (1974-metric tons, FAO estimates): Coconuts 9,500, Taro 7,000, Bananas 3,000. Papayas, pineapples and breadfruit are also grown.

Livestock (1974-FAO estimates): Chickens 38,000, Pigs 8,000, Goats 8,000.

Industry (1973): Canned Fish $64,000,000. Electricity 55.7 million kWh. worth $1.6 million.

Currency: United States currency: 100 cents=1 U.S. dollar ($). Coins: 1, 5, 10, 25 and 50 cents; 1 dollar. Notes: 1, 2, 5, 10, 20, 50 and 100 dollars. Exchange rates (June 1976): £1 sterling=U.S. $1.77; $100= £56.37.

Budget (1973): Local Revenue $9,836,000; Congressional grants and direct appropriation $30,411,000; Other receipts $3,510,000; Total receipts $33,921,000.

External Trade (1973—U.S. $): *Imports:* $35,952,859; *Exports:* $66,576,005.

Transport (1973): *Roads:* Cars 2,064, Trucks 69, Taxis 89; *Shipping:* Ships entered 1,042; cleared 1,051; *Civil Aviation*: Planes arriving at Pago Pago airport 6,036; Passenger arrivals and departures 165,250.

THE CONSTITUTION

American Samoa is administered by the United States Department of the Interior. According to the 1966 constitution executive power is vested in the Governor, who is appointed by the Secretary of the Interior, but his authority is limited in favour of the legislature. The President of the Senate and the Speaker of the House of Representatives have an equal voice with the Governor in choosing heads of Departments. Local government is carried out by indigenous officials. The Fono (Legislature) consists of two Houses. The Senate is composed of 18 members elected according to Samoan custom from local Chiefs. The House of Representatives consists of 20 members elected by popular vote. The Fono meets twice a year, in February and July, for not more than 30 days and at such special sessions as the Governor may call. Since 1972 several referenda on proposals for the popular election of a Governor and Lieut.-Governor for the territory have rejected the plans.

THE GOVERNMENT

Governor: Earl B. Ruth.

Lieutenant-Governor: Frank Barnett.

There are numerous executive departments.

JUDICIAL SYSTEM

High Court: Consists of four Divisions: Appellate, Trial, Probate and Land and Title. Appellate Division has limited original jurisdiction and hears appeals from the other three. Trial Division hears original cases $300 and over in civil as well as criminal cases. It serves as appellate court for 59 District Courts; Traffic Courts; Small Claims Court. Land and Title Division hears cases involving communal land questions and disposition of Matai titles to family litigants.

Chief Justice: William J. McKnight, III.

Associate Justice: Leslie Jochimsen.

RELIGION

The population is largely Christian. Roman Catholics come under the jurisdiction of the Vicar Apostolic for Samoa and the Tokelau Islands (Catholic Mission, Apia, Western Samoa), Cardinal Pio. Protestant denominations active in the Territory include the Congregational Christian Church, the Methodist Church, the Church of Jesus Christ of the Latter-Day Saints, Assemblies of God, Church of the Nazarene, Seventh Day Adventists and Jehovah's Witnesses.

THE PRESS

Daily Bulletin: Office of Samoan Information, Pago Pago; English; daily; circ. 6,500.

Samoa News: P.O.B. 57, Pago Pago; twice a week; circ. 3,000.

RADIO AND TELEVISION

RADIO

Radio Station WVUV: Pago Pago; former government-administered station leased to Radio Samoa Ltd. in 1975; programmes in English and Samoan; 113 hours a week.

TELEVISION

KVZK: Pago Pago; f. 1964; Government-owned station administered by the Department of Education; programmes in English and Samoan; operates on channels 2, 4, 5, 8, 10 and 12 for seven hours a day, broadcasting instructional programme for school use; channels 4 and 5 for six hours daily for adult education, public information, entertainment; channel 4 for 10 hours, channel 5 for six hours, on Saturday and Sunday; Gen. Man. Richard W. Stevens.

In 1975 there were 27,000 radio sets and 5,000 television sets.

FINANCE

BANKING

Bank of Hawaii: Pago Pago, Tutuila; f. 1969; Pres. Wilson P. Cannon; Man. Dennis K. Pearson.

First National City Bank: P.O.B. 2599, Pago Pago, Tutuila.

Development Bank of American Samoa: Pago Pago, Tutuila; f. 1969; cap. $3m.; a government-owned non-commercial undertaking; Chair. and Pres. William H. Cravens.

TRADE AND INDUSTRY

DEVELOPMENT

Office of Economic Development and Planning *and* The Economic Development Commission: Pago Pago; f. 1969 by legislative action; two offices co-ordinate economic development.

American Samoa Development Corporation: Pago Pago; f. 1962; financed by Samoan private shareholders; a luxury hotel employing 115 people has been built.

Division of Agricultural Development and Extension Services: f. 1973 out of other departments to co-ordinate agricultural development on behalf of the Department of Agriculture.

INSURANCE

G.H.C. Reid and Co. Ltd.

Burns Philp (SS) Company Ltd.

Hartford Insurance Co.

Richard Gebauer.

TRANSPORT

ROADS

There are about 38 miles of paved and 5 miles of secondary roads.

Non-scheduled commercial buses operate a service over 42 miles of main and secondary roads.

SHIPPING

Pacific Far East Lines Inc.: 50 Young St., Sydney, Australia; ships call every three weeks *en route* from the U.S.A. and Canada to New Zealand, Australia and Tasmania, and on return journey also.

There are various other passenger services originating from the U.S. Pacific coast and from Australia (mainly Sydney) and New Zealand, that call at Pago Pago. A number of inter-island boats operate frequently between Western and American Samoa.

CIVIL AVIATION

Continental Airlines: P.O.B. 138, Saipan, Mariana Islands; services to the U.S. Pacific territories and to Japan.

Pan American World Airways: P.O.B. 728, Pago Pago; service to Honolulu, Tahiti and New Zealand.

Polynesian Airlines Ltd.: P.O.B. 280, Pago Pago 96799; twice-daily service to Western Samoa; also three times weekly to Tonga and four times weekly to Fiji.

Air New Zealand: Pago Pago; twice-weekly service to New Zealand.

EDUCATION

Education is compulsory from the age of 6 to 18. The Government maintains 27 consolidated elementary schools, 4 senior high schools and 1 community college. It also operated in 1973 156 village early childhood education centres. Total enrolment in elementary and secondary public schools (1972/73): 8,207 pupils; 390 teachers. The community college had more than 700 students in 1973 and at that time there were altogether nearly 1,000 students in higher education. Total educational enrolment in 1973 was over 12,000.

Cook Islands

PHYSICAL AND SOCIAL GEOGRAPHY

The 14 inhabited and one uninhabited islands of the Cook Islands are located midway between Samoa and Tahiti. The Cooks form two groups; the Northern Cooks which are all atolls, and include Pakapuka, Rakahanaga and Manihiki, and the Southern Cooks, including Aitutaki, Mangaia and Rarotonga, which are all volcanic islands. The total area of all the islands is 240 square kilometres. In 1974 it was estimated that the population was about 20,000, of whom over half live on Rarontonga.

HISTORY

The Cook Islands were proclaimed a British Protectorate in 1888 and a part of New Zealand in 1901. On August 4th, 1965, they became a self-governing territory in free association with New Zealand. The people are British subjects and New Zealand citizens. The Premier elected in 1965, Albert Henry, has retained power, but in the 1975 elections met his stiffest opposition thus far.

ECONOMY

Economic and agricultural development on the Cook Islands has always suffered from isolation and smallness. All forms of exports, but in particular fresh fruit, oranges, bananas, tomatoes and pineapples, have been hindered by lack of shipping and inadequate marketing in New Zealand metropolitan centres.

The islands receive a large proportion of their revenue in the form of aid from New Zealand and remittances sent back to the islands by migrants. A New Zealand owned plant cans pineapple and orange juice near Ararua, reducing dependency on fresh fruit markets.

The outstanding feature of the Cook Islands is the migration of outer islanders into Rarotonga and from there to New Zealand, where, until 1976, Cook Islanders enjoyed free entry as New Zealand citizens. In 1975 more Cook Islanders lived in New Zealand than in the islands. Migrants have tended to work in the timber towns of Kawerau and Tokoroa, in the Auckland metropolitan area, in Wellington and in the meat packing industry in Southland.

STATISTICS

AREA
(acres)

Rarotonga 16,602, Mangaia 12,800, Atiu 6,654, Mitiaro 5,500, Mauke 4,552, Aitutaki 4,461, Penrhyn 2,432, Manuae 1,524, Manihiki 1,344, Pukapuka 1,250, Palmerston 500. Total area 90.3 square miles.

POPULATION

At the intercensal population count taken on December 1st, 1973, the population totalled 20,348: 10,302 males and 10,046 females.

Rarotonga*	11,115	Mitiaro	332
Aitutaki	2,574	Nassau	118
Atiu	1,368	Palmerston	80
Mangaia	1,954	Penrhyn	561
Manihiki	385	Pukapuka	753
Manuae	21	Rakahanga	343
Mauke	743	Suwarrow	1

Takutea is uninhabited.

* Including the capital, Avarua.

AGRICULTURE

PRODUCTION*
(metric tons–1974)

Coconuts	10,500	Mangoes	2,000
Cassava	4,000	Avocados	1,000
Citrus fruits	4,000	Sweet potatoes	1,000
Bananas	2,000	Copra	960

* FAO estimates.

Livestock (1974–FAO estimates): Horses 1,000, Pigs 3,000, Poultry 62,000.

EMPLOYMENT

Most of the working population are engaged in agriculture, services and commerce. There are two clothing factories, a fruit canning factory and two factories manufacturing handicrafts. A tourist industry is developing, with nine hotels and motels completed and further construction under way.

CO-OPERATIVES

There are over 70 active co-operatives, covering such activities as village and school savings, credit, processing and marketing, supply, audit, and development.

FINANCE

New Zealand currency: 100 cents=1 New Zealand dollar ($NZ).

Coins: 1, 2, 5, 10, 20 and 50 cents.
Notes: 1, 2, 5, 10, 20 and 100 dollars.

Exchange rates (June 1976): £1 sterling=$NZ1.799; U.S. $1=$NZ1.014; $NZ100=£55.59=U.S. $98.60.

Note: For previous changes in the exchange rate, *see* the chapter on New Zealand.

BUDGET
($NZ'000)

	Revenue	Expenditure	New Zealand Budgetary Assistance
1972	3,928	5,578	1,650
1973	4,469	6,119	1,650
1974	4,348	7,442	1,838
1975/76*	7,724	12,056	4,333

* Fifteen months to March 1976.

Principal sources of revenue: Import and export duties, sales tax, stamp sales, income and welfare tax.

Primary items of expenditure: Education, public health, public works.

EXTERNAL TRADE
(1971)

Total Imports: $4,947,000, principal items are foodstuffs, piece goods, timber and cement.

Total Exports: $2,070,000, principal items are tomatoes, mother-of-pearl, copra, citrus fruits, fruit juices and canned fruit preparations, clothing, handicrafts.

Trade is chiefly with New Zealand, the EEC, Japan, the U.S.A., Hong Kong and Australia. Imports from New Zealand represented 76.27 per cent of total imports in 1970.

GOVERNMENT

Executive authority is vested in Her Majesty the Queen in right of New Zealand. The Chief Justice of the High

Court in the Cook Islands is temporarily representing the Queen. The New Zealand Government is represented by the New Zealand representative, who resides on Rarotonga.

Executive Government is carried out by a Cabinet consisting of a Premier, six Ministers and two Deputies to the Premier. The Cabinet is collectively responsible to the Legislative Assembly.

THE CABINET

(*July* 1976)

Premier, Minister for Government and Central Administration, External Affairs, Outer Islands Affairs, Police, Immigration, National Development Corporation, National Provident Fund, Civil Aviation, Housing and Civil Defence: Hon. Sir ALBERT HENRY.

Minister for Finance and Postmaster-General: Hon. G. A. HENRY.

Minister for Agriculture, Marine, Natural Resources and Science and Industrial Research: Hon. W. ESTALL.

Minister for Justice, Lands and Survey and Internal Affairs: Hon. T. A. HENRY.

Minister for Supportive Services and Electricity: Hon. I. AKARURU.

Minister for Health and Education: Hon. Dr. J. WILLIAMS.

Minister for Trade, Industries and Commerce, Tourism and Shipping: Hon. G. ELLIS.

LEGISLATIVE ASSEMBLY

The Legislative Assembly consists of 22 members elected by universal suffrage every four years from a common roll for both Maoris and Europeans and is presided over by a Speaker.

Speaker: Mrs. MARGUERITE STORY.

President of the House of Arikis: PARUA ARIKI.

Each of the main islands has an Island Council.

In the December 1974 elections the Cook Islands Party won 14 seats against the Democratic Party's 8 seats.

POLITICAL PARTIES

Cook Islands Party: Rarotonga; the government party; 19 representatives in the Legislative Assembly; Leader Sir ALBERT HENRY.

Democratic Party: P.O.B. 202, Rarotonga; opposition party; Leader Dr. TOM DAVIS.

JUDICIAL SYSTEM

High Court; Land Court; Land Appellate Court.

The High Court exercises civil and criminal jurisdiction throughout the Cook Islands. The Land Court is concerned with litigation over land and titles. The Land Appellate Court hears appeals over decisions of the Land Court.

Chief Justice of the High Court: G. J. DONNE.

Judge of the Land Court: J. J. MACCAULEY.

RELIGION

Main groups are Cook Islands Christian Church (Congregational), Roman Catholic, Latter Day Saints and Seventh Day Adventists.

Roman Catholic:

Bishop of Rarotonga: Most Rev. JOHN H. M. RODGERS.

THE PRESS

Cook Islands News: daily government newspaper.

Photo News: weekly government newspaper published by the Cook Islands Broadcasting and Newspaper Corporation.

The Weekender: P.O.B. 202, Rarotonga; f. 1974; opposition weekly.

RADIO

Cook Islands Broadcasting and Newspaper Corporation: Rarotonga; broadcasts in English and Maori; Gen. Man. MICHAEL DROLLET.

There were 7,000 radio sets in 1975.

TRANSPORT

Ships from New Zealand, the United Kingdom, Japan and the U.S.A. call at Rarotonga. The New Zealand Shipping Corporation operates fortnightly services between the Cook Islands and New Zealand ports. An international airport was opened at Rarotonga in 1973. There is an internal air service (Cook Islands Airways), operating between Rarotonga and Aitutaki. Passenger flights to and from New Zealand are made via Air N.Z. Ltd. thrice weekly—twice direct and once via Fiji. One flight from New Zealand per week continues to Tahiti, returning to Rarotonga the next day.

EDUCATION

In 1975 there were 29 government schools, four of which were high schools. They had 6,075 pupils.

Free secular education is compulsory for all children between the ages of 6 and 15.

Secondary education is provided at Tereora College in Rarotonga and junior high schools on Aitutaki, Mangaia and Atiu. Under the New Zealand Training Scheme, the New Zealand Government offers education and training in New Zealand, Fiji and W. Samoa for secondary and tertiary education, career training and short-term in-service training. At 31st March 1973 there were 75 long-term students under this scheme.

Coral Sea Islands Territory

The Coral Sea Islands Territory was created in May 1969 and is composed of a number of islands situated east of Queensland between the Great Barrier Reef and 157° 10' E. longitude. The islands had been acquired by the Commonwealth by acts of sovereignty over a number of years. All are very small and they include Cato Island, Chilcott Islet in the Coringa Group, and the Willis Group. Three members of the Commonwealth Bureau of Meteorology are stationed on one of the Willis Group, but the remainder of the islands are uninhabited.

The Act constituting the Territory did not establish an administration on the islands but provides means of controlling the activities of those who visit them. The possibility of exploration for oil on the continental shelf and the increasing range and scope of international fishing enterprises made desirable such an administrative framework and system of law. The Governor-General is empowered to make ordinances for the peace, order and good government of the Territory, and the Supreme Court and Court of Petty Sessions of Norfolk Island have jurisdiction in relation to the Territory.

Fiji

PHYSICAL AND SOCIAL GEOGRAPHY

The total area of Fiji, including the Rotuma group, is 18,376 square kilometres. The Fiji group comprises four main islands, Viti Levu, Vanua Levu, Tavenui and Kadavu; in addition there are numerous smaller islands, atolls and reefs, numbering in all about 400, of which fewer than 100 are inhabited.

Fiji is characterized by racial diversity. The indigenous Fijian population fell sharply during the 1850s due to measles and influenza epidemics in which thousands died. Only in the 1950s did it begin to recover and by the 1970s was increasing at over 3 per cent a year. The Indian population has always increased rapidly.

In 1975, the estimated population was 569,468, of whom 250,883 were Fijians and 288,408 were Indians.

HISTORY

The first documented sighting of the islands by a European was that of Abel Tasman in 1643. The first Europeans to settle on the islands were sandalwood traders, missionaries and shipwrecked sailors; under their influence local fighting and jealousies reached unprecedented heights, until by the 1850s, one chief, Thakombau, had gained a tenuous influence over the whole of the western islands. Thakombau ran foul of American interests during the 1850s and turned to the British for assistance, unsuccessfully at first, but in 1874 Britain agreed to a second offer of cession, and Fiji was proclaimed a British possession. Fiji became independent in October 1970.

The racial diversity, compounded by actions of the past colonial administrations, presents Fiji with one of its most difficult problems. The colonial government consistently favoured the Fijian population, protecting them from exploitation and their land from alienation but allowed the importation of foreign labour. Approximately 80 per cent of the islands are owned by Fijian communities, but over 90 per cent of the sugar crop, Fiji's largest export, is produced by Indians usually on land leased from Fijians. Until recently, Indians were poorly represented politically, while Fijians had their own administrative and judicial systems.

In the 1970s signs of racial tension and unrest in the Indian community were apparent, but since independence Indian and Fijian leaders appear to have settled their differences. In the national parliament of 52 seats, 12 Fijians and 12 Indians are elected from communal rolls which are mutually exclusive and 10 Fijians and 10 Indians are elected from national rolls on which all citizens are represented. The Prime Minister in 1976 is a Fijian, Sir Kamisese Mara, who leads a Cabinet of 14 ministers.

ECONOMY

Sugar, Fiji's most important export crop, was first planted in the 1860s. In 1880, the Colonial Sugar Refining Company of Australia (CSR) built their first mill near Suva and by 1900, three more mills were in operation. CSR planted large areas of sugar under a plantation system, initially using indentured labour from the Solomons and the New Hebrides. When this source became restricted, labour was imported from India. (The British government protected the Fijian villagers and they could not be forced to work). The first group of Indians arrived in 1879 and had the choice of repatriation or of remaining in Fiji at the end of their indenture. By 1920 40,000 had decided to stay.

Fiji's economy deteriorated between 1973 and 1975. The balance of payments declined rapidly and the country suffered an inflation rate of about 20 per cent. Between 1974 and 1975 the cost of oil imports increased by 150 per cent and fertilizer for the sugar industry by 65 per cent. Sugar markets remained unstable, while tourism, Fiji's second most important industry, was adversely affected by rising travel costs. Fiji's trade deficit increased by 20 per cent to 72 million Fiji dollars between 1973 and 1974 and special drawing rights had to be negotiated with the World Bank.

Many Fijians of all races are becoming increasingly concerned by the growing influence of foreign countries, in particular Australia and the U.S.A., in Fiji's economy and society. One of the first major decisions of the new government was to nationalize CSR. In March 1973, after protracted negotiations, the government purchased CSR's interests in South Pacific Sugar Mills Ltd. for 10 million Fiji dollars, to gain control over this most important industry. However, heavy foreign investment continues. The tourist industry in particular, it is argued, is causing a breakdown in traditional life and values, and is benefiting ordinary Fijians very little.

STATISTICAL SURVEY

Area: 18,736 square kilometres (including the Rotuma group).

POPULATION

	1966 Census	June 30th, 1975 Estimate
Fijians	202,176	250,883
Indians	240,960	288,408
Part Europeans	9,687	10,125
Rotumans	5,797	6,952
Other Pacific Islanders	6,095	6,905
Chinese	5,149	4,045
Europeans	6,590	2,030
Others	273	120
Total	476,727	569,468

Suva (capital): 1966 census: 54,157, 1971 estimate: 60,000.

EMPLOYMENT

	1972	1973	1974
Agriculture and fishing	2,782	3,443	3,901
Mining	1,745	1,748	1,963
Manufacturing	9,828	10,116	11,840
Electricity, gas and water	1,441	1,727	1,659
Construction	8,239	9,454	8,291
Wholesale and retail trade, restaurants and hotels	9,887	9,668	10,014
Transport, storage and communications	5,225	4,909	6,180
Finance, insurance, real estate and business	2,026	2,601	3,341
Community, social and personal services	17,226	17,810	19,809
TOTAL	58,399	61,476	66,998

AGRICULTURE

(metric tons)

	1972	1973	1974
Sugar cane	2,238,000	2,500,000†	2,300,000†
Coconuts	270,000*	268,000*	273,000†
Cassava†	88,000	89,000	89,000
Copra	28,798	28,250*	30,000†
Rice (paddy)	17,000	16,000	18,000*
Sweet potatoes†	16,000	16,000	16,000
Bananas	5,000*	4,000†	4,000†

* Unofficial figure. † FAO Estimate.

Source: FAO Production Yearbook, 1974.

Livestock (1974—FAO estimates): Horses 33,000, Cattle 165,000, Pigs 30,000, Goats 57,000, Poultry 594,000.

Fishing (metric tons): 1972 4,800, 1973 5,100, 1974 4,261.

INDUSTRY

		1972	1973	1974	1975
Beef	tons	2,835	3,199	3,120	2,438
Sugar	,,	298,000	296,000	269,000	n.a.
Copra	,,	29,000	27,000	27,000	22,000
Coconut oil	,,	18,000	16,000	17,000	15,000
Soap	,,	3,547	3,983	4,791	3,883
Cement	,,	89,000	91,000	84,000	72,000
Paint	'ooo gallons	244	329	306	243
Beer	,, ,,	2,242	2,634	3,303	3,452
Soft drinks	,, ,,	520	538	800	n.a.
Cigarettes	million	360	406	442	472
Timber	'ooo cu. ft.	3,922	4,328	5,279	4,609
Matches	'ooo gross boxes	130	153	147	139
Gold	'ooo fine oz.	76	80	69	69

MINING

(1974)

		PRODUCTION	VALUE IN $F
Gold	fine oz.	68,890	8,621,188
Silver	fine oz.	27,101	103,112
Limestone	tons	123,006	307,515
Crushed metal	cu. yds.	250,904	878,164

FINANCE

100 cents = 1 Fiji dollar ($F).

Coins: 1, 2, 5, 10, 20 and 50 cents.

Notes: 50 cents; 1, 2, 5, 10 and 20 dollars.

Exchange rates (June 1976): £1 sterling = $F1.602; U.S. $1 = 90.03 Fiji cents.

$F100 = £62.41 = U.S. $110.72.

Note: The Fiji dollar was introduced in January 1969, replacing the Fiji pound at the rate of £F1 = $F2. From November 1967 the exchange rate was £1 sterling = £F1.045 (£F1 = U.S. $2.2966) so the new rate was £1 sterling = $F2.09, with the Fiji dollar valued at U.S. $1.1483 (U.S. $1 = 87.08 Fiji cents) until August 1971. The link with sterling was maintained and the exchange rate was $F1 = U.S. $1.2467 (U.S. $1 = 80.21 Fiji cents) from December 1971 to June 1972, when the British currency was allowed to "float". The Fiji dollar also "floated", the exchange rate continuing at £1 = $F2.09 until October 1972. The rate was £1 = $F1.98 from October 1972 to September 1973; and £1 = $F1.89 from September 1973 to February 1974. In February 1974 the link with sterling was broken and a new exchange rate of $F1 = U.S. $1.25 (U.S. $1 = 80 Fiji cents) was established. This remained in effect until April 1975, since when the Fiji dollar has been valued in relation to a weighted "basket" of the currencies of the country's main trading partners.

BUDGET

($F'000 estimate)

Revenue	1975	1976	Expenditure	1975	1976
Customs duties and port dues	44,713	47,481	Public debt charges	16,082	23,351
Income tax and direct revenue	46,625	55,748	Pension and gratuities	2,603	2,735
Interest	1,560	1,510	Works annually recurrent	8,481	10,655
Income from property and entrepreneuring	9,209	15,302	Contributions to capital	—	—
			Departmental expenditure	74,941	90,941
Total	102,107	120,041	Total	102,107	127,682

CURRENCY IN CIRCULATION

($F'000)

1970	1971	1972	1973	1974	1975
11,162	13,075	14,246	15,699	21,572	27,394

CONSUMER PRICE INDEX

(Base: January 1974 = 100)

	1974	1975
Food	111.6	125.4
Housing	107.0	118.4
Household operations	108.0	123.6
Clothing and footwear	106.7	132.4
Transport	109.9	136.3
All items	108.6	122.8

EXTERNAL TRADE

($F)

	1971	1972	1973	1974
Imports	111,563,868	131,347,000	174,645,000	219,331,000
Exports	61,769,000	64,601,000	74,426,000	95,369,000

PRINCIPAL COMMODITIES

Imports	1974–$F
Electrical Machinery and Goods	14,776,659
Machinery, other than electrical	12,609,335
Transport Equipment	7,834,220
Fabrics	14,064,009
Iron and Steel	8,191,796
Food	41,302,257
Fuel	34,490,161
Clothing	5,158,325
Tape Recorders	3,432,166
Watches	4,919,791

Exports	1975*–$F'000
Sugar	97,200
Gold	8,580
Coconut oil	4,560
Molasses	1,330
Coconut meal	370
Green ginger	450
Veneer sheets	650
Biscuits	430
Cement	570
Lumber	250
Silver	50

* Provisional.

Re-exports	1974—$F
Fuel	14,932,481
Fish	2,513,220
Textile Yarns and Fabrics	2,851,167
Clothing	792,903

PRINCIPAL TRADING COUNTRIES

(1974–$F)

Imports	
Australia	66,529,253
Canada	1,147,293
Germany, Federal Republic	2,966,917
Hong Kong	7,274,181
India	3,592,503
Iran	1,132,750
Japan	39,297,962
Netherlands	2,051,388
New Zealand	24,525,735
Singapore	18,588,077
United Kingdom	21,748,312
U.S.A.	9,350,705

Exports	
Australia	12,279,215
Canada	3,000,117
Germany, Federal Republic	444,736
Japan	476,946
New Zealand	8,191,043
Singapore	3,157,580
Tonga	3,620,421
United Kingdom	37,066,000
U.S.A.	32,081,650
Western Samoa	3,728,917

Transport (1974): *Shipping:* Entered 522 ships, 2,624,000 tons. *Civil Aviation:* Landed 197,592 passengers; Departed 204,288; Transit passengers 222,035. **Tourism:** (1974) 181,077 visitors, Receipts $F60.6 million; (1975) 165,000 visitors, Receipts $F71.9 million (estimate).

EDUCATION

(1972)

	Schools	Students
Primary	635	130,440
Secondary	87	21,079
Vocational and Technical	22	1,277
Teacher Training	3	426
Medical	1	215

There are also 69 Fiji Government scholarship holders in higher education abroad (1973).

Source: Bureau of Statistics, Suva.

THE CONSTITUTION

The Constitution is set out in the Fiji (Independence) Order of 1970. It contains provisions relating to the protection of fundamental rights and freedoms, the powers and duties of the Governor-General, the Cabinet, the House of Representatives, the Senate, the Judiciary, the Public Service and finance.

It provides that every person in Fiji regardless of race, place of origin, political opinion, colour, creed or sex is entitled to the fundamental rights of life, liberty, security of the person and protection of the law, freedom of conscience, expression, assembly and association; protection for the privacy of his home and other property and for the deprivation of property without compensation. The enjoyment of these rights, however, is subject to the proviso that they do not prejudice the rights and freedom of others, or the public interest.

GOVERNMENT

Governor-General: The Queen appoints a Governor-General as her representative in Fiji.

The Cabinet: The Cabinet consists of the Prime Minister, the Attorney-General and any other Minister whom the Governor-General might appoint on the advice of the Prime Minister. The Governor-General appoints as Leader of the Opposition in the House of Representatives either the leader of the largest Opposition party or, if there is no such party, the person whose appointment would be most acceptable to the leaders of the Opposition parties in the House.

Parliament: The Fiji Parliament consists of a Senate and a House of Representatives. The Senate has 22 members: 8 nominated by the Council of Chiefs, 7 nominated by the Prime Minister, 6 nominated by the Leader of the Opposition and one nominated by the Council of the Island of Rotuma. Their appointments are for a six-year term. The President and Deputy President of the Senate are elected from members who are neither Ministers nor Assistant Ministers. The House of Representatives has 52 members: 27 elected on the communal roll and 25 on the national roll (a cross-voting system by which all races vote together). The House elects a Speaker and a Deputy Speaker from among its non-ministerial members.

THE GOVERNMENT

Governor-General: Ratu Sir GEORGE CAKOBAU, G.C.M.G., O.B.E., J.P.

THE CABINET

(*July* 1976)

Prime Minister: Rt. Hon. Ratu Sir KAMISESE KAPAIWAI TUIMACILAU MARA, P.C., K.B.E., M.A.

Deputy Prime Minister and Minister for Home Affairs: Ratu Sir PENAIA GANILAU, K.B.E., C.M.G., C.V.O., D.S.O., E.D.

Attorney General: Sir JOHN N. FALVEY, K.B.E., Q.C.

Minister of Finance: CHARLES A. STINSON, O.B.E.

Minister for Fijian Affairs and Rural Development: Ratu WILLIAM B. TOGANIVALU.

Minister of Labour: Ratu DAVID TOGANIVALU.

Minister of Education, Youth and Sports: PENIAME NAQASIMA.

Minister for Commerce, Industry and Co-operatives: EDWARD BEDDOES.

Minister for Urban Development, Housing and Social Welfare: M. RAMZAN, M.B.E.

Minister of Lands, Mines and Mineral Resources: SAKEASI WAQAVAVALIGLAGI.

Minister of Health: JAMES S. SINGH, M.B.E.

Minister of Agriculture, Fisheries and Forests: Ratu JOSUA B. TOGANIVALU.

Minister of Information: JONE NAISARA.

Minister for Communications, Works and Tourism: JONATI MAVOA.

PARLIAMENT

THE SENATE

Twenty-two member appointed Senate.

President: ROBERT MUNRO.

Deputy President: Ratu LIAVI VOLAVOLA.

HOUSE OF REPRESENTATIVES

Speaker: VIJAY R. SINGH.

Deputy Speaker: MOSESE QIONIBARAVI.

Leader of the Opposition: SIDDIQH KOYA.

HOUSE OF REPRESENTATIVES

(General Election, April 1972)

PARTY	SEATS
Alliance	33
National Federation	19
	52

Note: Since 1972 two members have resigned from the Alliance and sit as independents.

PROVINCIAL GOVERNMENT

There are fourteen provinces, each headed by a chairman.

POLITICAL PARTIES

Alliance Party: multi-racial; government party; 31 members of the House of Representatives; Leader Rt. Hon. Ratu Sir KAMISESE K. T. MARA, K.B.E., M.A.; publ. *Nation.*

National Federation Party: G.P.O. Box 228, Suva; f. 1963; fusion of two parties: the Federation, which was mainly Indian but multi-racial, and the National Democratic Party, a purely Fijian party; 19 members in the House of Representatives, comprising official opposition; Leader SIDDIQH M. KOYA; mems.: approx. 40,000.

Nationalist Party: f. 1974; seeks more representation for Fijians in Parliament and for general reforms in their favour; Leader SAKIASI BUTADROKA.

DIPLOMATIC REPRESENTATION

EMBASSIES AND HIGH COMMISSIONS ACCREDITED TO FIJI

(E) Embassy; (HC) High Commission.

Australia: Suva (HC); *High Commissioner:* H. W. BULLOCK.

France: Suva (E); *Chargé d'Affaires a.i.:* JEAN DOUTRELANT.

India: Suva (HC); *High Commissioner:* BHAGWAN SINGH.

New Zealand: Suva (HC); *High Commissioner:* G. K. ANSELL.

United Kingdom: Civic Centre, Stinson Parade, P.O.B. 1355, Suva (HC); *High Commissioner:* JAMES STANLEY ARTHUR.

U.S.A.: Suva (E); *Chargé d'Affaires a.i.:* VANCE HALL.

Fiji also has diplomatic relations with Argentina, the Bahamas, Bangladesh, Belgium, Canada, the People's Republic of China, Denmark, Egypt, the German Democratic Republic, the Federal Republic of Germany, Indonesia, Israel, Japan, the Democratic People's Republic of Korea, the Republic of Korea, Malaysia, Mexico, the Netherlands, Norway, Pakistan, Papua New Guinea, the Philippines, Romania, Senegal, Singapore, Sweden, Turkey and the U.S.S.R.

JUDICIAL SYSTEM

The law in force in Fiji consists of the Constitution of Fiji as set out in the Fiji Independence Order of 1970, the Ordinances in force on 10th October, 1970, the Acts of the Parliament of Fiji enacted after that date, and subject thereto, and to certain qualifications, the Common Law, Rules of Equity and the statutes of general application which were in force in England on January 2nd, 1875.

Justice is administered by the Fiji Court of Appeal, the Supreme Court, the Magistrates' Courts and certain Provincial and Tikina (District) Courts. The Supreme Court of Fiji is the superior court of record presided over by the Chief Justice. The Fiji Court of Appeal hears appeals from the Supreme Court and the High Court of the Western Pacific.

Chief Justice: Hon. Mr. Justice CLIFFORD GRANT.

Puisne Judges: Hon. G. MISHRA, Hon. T. TUIVAGA, Hon. K. A. STUART, Hon. J. T. WILLIAMS.

Ombudsman: Hon. MOTI TIKARAM.

RELIGION

Most Fijians are Christians, mainly Protestant. The Indians are mostly Hindus.

Anglican: Bishop in Polynesia Rt. Rev. JABEZ LESLIE BRYCE; Bishop's House, Box 35, G.P.O., Suva.

Methodist Church: G.P.O. Box 357, Suva; Pres. Rev. S. A. TUILOVONI; Sec. Rev. I. NABULIVOU.

Roman Catholic Archbishop: Most Rev. PETERO MATACA; Archbishop's House, P.O.B. 393, Suva.

THE PRESS

NEWSPAPERS AND PERIODICALS

Fiji Holiday: Fiji Times and Herald Ltd., P.O.B. 1167, Suva; f. 1968; monthly; Editor MARAIA BROWN; circ. 19,000.

Fiji Royal Gazette: Government Printer, P.O.B. 98, Suva; f. 1874; Fridays.

Fiji Samachar: P.O.B. 151, Suva; f. 1923; Hindustani; weekly; Editor S. M. BIDESI, Jr.; Man. N. P. GANDHI; circ. 4,000.

Fiji Sandesh: Patel Arcade, Suva; f. 1965; Hindi; weekly; Editor V. L. MORRIS.

Fiji Sun: Newspapers of Fiji Ltd., Suva; f. 1974; English; daily.

Fiji Times: P.O.B. 1167, Suva; f. 1869; English, daily; Gen. Man. J. MURRANT; circ. 20,000.

Jagriti: Pacific Periodicals Ltd., P.O.B. 9, Nadi; Editor R. K. SHARMA; circ. 5,500.

Jai Fiji: P.O.B. 109, Lautoka; f. 1959; Hindi; Thursdays; Editor K. P. MISHRA; circ. 7,800.

Kisan Mitra: P.O.B. 46, Lautoka; f. 1961; Hindi; weekly.

Nai Lalakai: P.O.B. 1167, Suva; f. 1962; publ. by Fiji Times and Herald Ltd.; Fijian; weekly; Editor LUKE VUIDREKETI.

Na Mata: Fijian Affairs Office, Suva; f. 1876; Fijian; monthly.

Pacific Review: Suva; f. 1949; English and Fijian; weekly; Editor P. GAUNDER.

Shanti Dut: P.O.B. 1167, Suva; f. 1935; publ. by Fiji Times and Herald Ltd.; Hindi; weekly; Editor GURUDAYAL SHARMA.

Sunday Sun: Newspapers of Fiji Ltd., Suva; f. 1974; English; weekly.

Tovata (*Nation*): published by Alliance Publications, P.O.B. 1373, Suva; English and Fijian (Natovata); fortnightly; Editor ESALA RASOVO.

Volagauna: P.O.B. 597, Suva; f. 1952; Fijian; weekly; Editor JIOJI R. QALILAWA.

Western Herald: Fiji Times Group Ltd., Lautoka; f. 1974; weekly.

RADIO

Fiji Broadcasting Commission (Radio Fiji): P.O.B. 334, Broadcasting House, Suva; f. 1954; broadcasts from ten stations; two each at Suva, Lautoka, Rakiraki, Sigatoka and Labasa; in English, Fijian and Hindi; Chair. W. G. J. CRUICKSHANK, O.B.E.; Gen. Man. HUGH LEONARD.

The number of radio sets in 1975 was 300,000.

FINANCE

BANKS

Central Monetary Authority: arbiter on banking affairs in Fiji and will form the basis of a central bank; Gen. Man. IAN CRAIK.

Savings Bank of Fiji: Head Office: P.O.B. 1166, Suva; 60 brs.

FOREIGN BANKS

Australia and New Zealand Banking Group Ltd.: P.O.B. 179, Suva; Man. J. H. GARLAND.

Bank of Baroda Ltd.: India; P.O.B. 57, Suva; Man. A. N. DESAI.

Bank of New South Wales: P.O.B. 283, Suva; Chief Man. L. W. ULLMAN.

Bank of New Zealand: P.O.B. 177, Suva; Man. for Fiji A. L. WILLIAMS.

Barclays Bank International: Dominion House, Thomson St., Suva; Man. J. J. LAING.

First National City Bank: P.O.B. 216, 66 Thomson St., Suva; f. 1970.

INSURANCE

Fiji Insurance Co. Ltd.: Fiji Development Bank Centre, P.O.B. 1080, Victoria Parade, Suva.

GRE Insurance Ltd.: Honson Bldg., 68 Thomson St., Suva.

TRADE AND INDUSTRY

DEVELOPMENT CORPORATIONS

Commonwealth Development Corpn.: Fiji and Western Pacific Islands Office, P.O.B. 161, Suva.

Fijian Development Fund Board: P.O.B. 122, Suva; f. 1951; the Fund was established at the request of the Fijian Provincial Councils; funds derived from payments of £10 a ton from the sales of copra; deposits credited to the producing group or individual at 2½ per cent interest for use in Fijian development schemes; July 1971, deps. $F701,577; Chair. Ratu Sir GEORGE K. CAKOBAU; Sec. P. J. UNDERHILL.

Fiji Development Bank: Suva; f. 1967 as successor to Agricultural and Industrial Loans Board (f. 1952); finances the development of natural resources, transportation and other industries.

Fiji Development Company Ltd.: P.O.B. 161, Suva; f. 1960; subsidiary of the Commonwealth Development Corporation; Man. J. H. SAND.

Land Development Authority: c/o Ministry of Agriculture, Fisheries and Forests, Suva; f. 1961 to co-ordinate development plans.

MARKETING ORGANIZATIONS

Fiji Sugar Corporation Ltd.: P.O.B. 283, Suva; buyer of sugar cane and raw sugar manufacturer.

Fiji Sugar Marketing Co.: Suva; Chief Exec. ERIC JONES.

CO-OPERATIVES

In 1971 there were about 800 registered co-operatives.

EMPLOYERS' ORGANIZATION

Fiji Employers' Consultative Association: P.O.B. 575, Suva; represents 132 of the principal employers in the Dominion; Pres. G. S. BARRACK; Dir. J. GRUNDY.

TRADE UNIONS

Fiji Trades Union Congress: P.O.B. 989, Suva; affiliated to ICFTU; 24 affiliated unions; over 20,000 mems.; Pres. JOVECI GAVOKA; Nat. Sec. JAMES R. RAMAN.

Largest affiliated unions:

Fiji Sugar and General Workers' Uniou: Lautoka; Gen. Sec. RAM DAYAL; 2,509 mems.

Fiji Waterside Workers' and Seamen's Union: f. 1974; Gen. Sec. TANIELA VEITATA.

Public Employees' Union: P.O.B. 781, Suva; over 7,000 mems.; Gen. Sec. JOVECI GAVOKA.

Fiji Council of Trade Unions: split from Fiji Trades Union Congress.

At the end of 1972 37 trade unions were registered.

TRANSPORT

RAILWAYS

Fiji Sugar Corporation Railway: P.O.B. 283, Suva; 644 km. of track, serving cane-growing areas at Ba, Lautoka and Penang on the island of Viti Levu; also Labasa on the island of Vanua Levu.

ROADS

There are 702 miles of main roads, 286 miles of secondary roads, 561 miles of country roads and 19 miles of residential roads, all maintained by the Government.

SHIPPING

There are ports of call at Suva, Lautoka and Levuka, which are served by passenger and cargo lines *en route* to Europe and America from Australia and New Zealand (Shaw Savill Lines and Sofrana Unilines), Japan (Daiwa Line) and the United Kingdom (Burns Philp Co.). In 1975 a new operation, Pacific Line Ltd., started services between Fiji and New Zealand and Western Samoa. A South Pacific regional shipping venture, in which Fiji is to be a partner, may commence operations in 1976.

CIVIL AVIATION

Air Pacific Ltd.: Air Pacific House, Corner of MacArthur and Butt Streets, Suva; f. 1951; domestic services within Fiji Islands, and services to Western Samoa, Tonga, Nauru, the Solomon Islands, the Gilbert Islands and Tuvalu, the New Hebrides, Papua New Guinea, Brisbane and Auckland; fleet of 1 BAC 1-11/475, 1 New Trislander, 3 HS 748s and 4 DH Herons; Chair. C. G. HOWSON; Gen. Man. S. H. QUIGG.

Fiji Air Services: internal airline which carried 27,000 passengers in 1974; owned jointly by Hawker de Havilland and the Fijian government.

There is an international airport at Nadi and a domestic airport at Nausori. International airlines operating through Nadi include Qantas, Air New Zealand, British Airways, Pan American, UTA, Air India, American Airlines, Canadian Pacific Airlines and Japan Airlines. Fiji Air Service Ltd. provides an internal charter service, based at Nausori.

EDUCATION

Education is not yet free but is heavily subsidized by the Government. Free primary education was introduced in Class 1 in 1973 and will be extended to an additional class each year. Some grants are given in case of hardship and all basic textbooks are provided free at primary school level. Secondary education lasts for 4 or 5 years and leads to the Fiji Junior Certificate examination in the second year, the New Zealand or Cambridge School Certificate examination in the third or fourth year and the New Zealand University Entrance examination in the fourth or fifth year. Higher education is provided at the University of the South Pacific.

In 1975 164,000 children, about 30 per cent of the national population, attended school. About 95 per cent of all children aged six to thirteen attend school full-time. There were 125,900 children in the 647 primary schools and 38,100 in the 79 secondary schools. There were six private primary schools and two private secondary schools. In early 1976 the Government was employing 4,000 teachers and there were 80 teachers in private schools.

There are three teacher training colleges and a new one is to be built at Lautoka. In 1972 there were 22 vocational and technical institutions including the Derrick Technical Institute at Suva with 428 students in 1975, the Fiji School of Medicine in Suva with 213 students and the Fiji College of Agriculture at Koronivia with 110 students. The University of the South Pacific was established in 1968 and by 1976 had 1,709 students and 210 staff.

Estimated government expenditure on education in 1975 was $F22 million compared with $F15 million in 1974.

UNIVERSITY

The University of the South Pacific: G.P.O. Box 1168, Suva; 120 teachers, 1,709 students.

French Polynesia

GEOGRAPHY

French Polynesia is an Overseas Territory of France containing six island groups: Society, Tuamotu, Austral, Gambier, Marquesas and Rapa. The Society Islands comprise the Windward group to the south-east, including Tahiti and Moorea, and the Leeward group about 160 kilometres north-west, which includes Huahine, Raiatea, Borabora and Maupiti. The Tuamotu group comprises 78 islands scattered east of the Society group in a line stretching north-west to south-east about 1,500 kilometres. The Gambier Islands, 1,600 kilometres south-east of Tahiti, are made up of the islands of Mangareva and Taravai and two others. The Austral or Tubuai group, 640 kilometres south of Tahiti, include Ruruta, Tubuai and Raevaevae. Rapa is 770 kilometres south-east of Tubuai. The Marquesas Islands are 1,450 kilometres north-east of Tahiti and comprise a northern group, which includes Nuku Hira, and a southern group.

HISTORY

The islands of French Polynesia were first visited by Europeans during the sixteenth century by Spanish and Portuguese explorers. Dutch and British explorers followed during the 1700s. Descriptions of Tahiti and other Society Islands by Wallis, who first visited in 1767, and Captain James Cook and his officers, gave rise in Europe to a vision of a new Arcadia in the South Pacific, the "islands of love", a romantic view which has drawn Europeans to the islands. In fact, European discovery dealt the Tahitian and other island groups' populations a severe blow. Disease caused rapid declines in population and inter-island and inter-group warfare killed many others.

Tahiti was made a French protectorate in 1842 and a colony in 1880. The other groups were all annexed during the last 20 years of the nineteenth century. The islands were governed from France under a decree of 1885 until 1957, when it became an Overseas Territory with a Governor in Papeete, the capital on Tahiti. A council and members of a territorial assembly were elected in five *circonscriptions* to assist the governor. The assembly has no legislative power; it may issue requests to the governor, but these have no legal force unless consented to by the French Government. There have been attempts at a greater degree of autonomy since 1958, but all have been turned down by France. In 1972, 44 communes were established within the Territory, each with its own budget and power to handle its own internal affairs.

Nuclear testing on Mururoa Atoll since 1970 has caused local unrest in Tahiti and protests from other Pacific nations.

ECONOMY

The influx of large numbers of French military personnel and the creation of many more employment and commercial opportunities has severely distorted the economy, to the extent that many islanders believe a French withdrawal from Tahiti would cause an economic disaster. Migration into Tahiti and the military bases from outer islands has created a larger group of people who no longer have the subsistence skills of previous generations. Tourism, which was the island's major industry before the nuclear tests, will not be able to maintain the economy in its present state without massive outside investment.

STATISTICS

Area: 4,200 sq. km. **Population** (Census of February 8th, 1971): 119,168 (Native 86 per cent, Asiatic 10 per cent, European 4 per cent); Papeete (capital) 25,342; estimated total population (1973): 120,000.

Agriculture (1974–metric tons): Copra 18,000, Coconuts 140,000, Roots and tubers 19,000 (Cassava 6,000), Citrus fruits 2,000 (all FAO estimates).

Livestock (1974–FAO estimates): Cattle 13,000, Horses 2,000, Pigs 15,000, Goats 4,000, Sheep 3,000, Poultry 198,000.

Fishing (1974): 2,386 metric tons landed.

Industry: annual output of Mother of Pearl is about 100 metric tons, Beer 64,000 hl.

Currency: 100 centimes = 1 franc de la Communauté française du pacifique (franc CFP or Pacific franc). Coins: 50 centimes; 1, 2, 5, 10, 20 and 50 francs CFP. Notes: 100, 500, 1,000 and 5,000 francs CFP. Exchange rates (June 1976): 1 franc CFP = 5.5 French centimes; £1 sterling = 153.18 francs CFP; U.S. $1 = 86.35 francs CFP; 1,000 francs CFP = £6.53 = $11.58.

Budget (1976–estimate): 14,000 million francs CFP.

Aid from France (FIDES 1966–70): Local section 1,535 million francs CFP, General section 292 million francs CFP. France assured a loan of 2,300 million francs CFP in 1974.

External Trade (1975—million francs CFP): *Imports:* 22,317.0 (Cereals, Petroleum Products, Metal Manufactures), principal suppliers: France 12,148.5, U.S.A. 3,848.1; *Exports:* 1,968.9 (Copra, Vanilla, Mother of Pearl, Coffee, Citrus Fruits), principal client: France 1,663.3.

Tourism (1971): 63,222 visitors, excluding cruise passengers and excursionists (35,250).

Shipping (port of Papeete—1973): ships entered 589, net displacement 1,577,000 registered tons, freight loaded 34,437 metric tons, freight unloaded 441,671 metric tons, passenger arrivals 1,159, passenger departures 1,212.

Civil Aviation (Faa airport, Papeete—1973): aircraft arrivals and departures 38,167, freight handled 4,254 metric tons, passenger arrivals 254,400, passenger departures 234,899, mail loaded and unloaded 358 metric tons.

Education (1973): Pupils: Primary: 34,253; Secondary: 6,585; Technical: 880.

THE GOVERNMENT

(*July* 1976)

Governor: CHARLES SCHMITT.

Secretary-General: JEAN RENÉ GARNIER.

COUNCIL OF GOVERNMENT

President: The Governor.

Councillors (elected by the Territorial Assembly): EMILE LECAILL, CHARLES TAUFA, JACQUES TEUIRA, MARC MAMAATUAIHUTAPU.

TERRITORIAL ASSEMBLY

Elected every five years on the basis of universal suffrage.

President of the Territorial Assembly: GASTON FLOSSE.

ELECTIONS
(*May* 1975)

PARTY	SEATS
U.T.-U.D.R.	10
Independents	7
Te Ea Api	5
Pupu Here Aia	5
Non-Party	3

Representative to the National Assembly: (vacant).

Representative to the Senate: POUVANAA A. OOPA.

POLITICAL PARTIES

Union Tahitienne-Union pour la Nouvelle République (U.T.-U.N.R.): 103 Rue Bréa, Papeete; f. 1958; Pres. GASTON FLOSSE.

Pupu Here Aia: Papeete; f. 1965; 7–8,000 mems.; Pres. JOHN TEARIKI.

Te Ea Api: Papeete; Leader FRANCIS SANFORD.

Pupu Tiama: Papeete; Leader MICHEL LAW.

Ia Mana Te Nuaa: Papeete; f. 1976; socialist.

Judicial System: Tribunal Supérieur d'Appel, Tribunal de Première Instance, Justice de Paix, Tribunal Mixte de Commerce, Tribunal du Travail; Section of the Tribunal de Première Instance at Uturoa; Procureur attached to the Tribunal Supérieur d'Appel and Head of Judicial Service R. GIRARD; Pres. Tribunal Supérieur d'Appel Y. PEGOURIER; Procureur attached to the Tribunal de Première Instance G. AMADEO; Pres. Tribunal de Première Instance J. JUPPE.

Religion: 50 per cent of the population are Protestants, 34 per cent Roman Catholics. Pres. Conseil Supérieur des Eglises Tahitiennes (Protestant) Pastor SAMUEL RAAPOTO. Archbishop of Tahiti (Roman Catholic) Mgr. MICHEL COPPENRATH. There are also small Sanito, Mormon, Adventist and Jehovah's Witness missions.

PRESS AND BROADCASTING

Papeete

Le Canard Tahitien: rue Clapier; satirical weekly; Dir. Mme LIENARDS.

La Dépêche de Tahiti: Société Polynésienne de Presse, B.P. 50; f. 1964; daily; Dir. PHILIPPE MAZELLIER.

Le Journal de Tahiti: rue des Remparts, B.P. 600; f. 1962; daily; Dir. MICHEL LEFEVRE; largest circulation in French Polynesia.

Les Nouvelles: B.P. 629; f. 1956; daily; Propr. R. BRISSAUD.

Reef: B.P. 966; f. 1966; bi-monthly; English; general and tourist information; Editor BOB DIXON; circ. 10,000.

Sports Tahiti: rue des Remparts, B.P. 600; f. 1969; twice weekly; Editor HENRY BOUQUET.

Tahiti Bulletin: Immeuble Laguesse, Place Notre Dame, B.P. 912; f. 1967; daily; English; Editor V. K. BOYACK.

Radio-Télé-Tahiti: B.P. 125, 410 rue Dumont d'Urville, Papeete; f. 1951 as Radio-Tahiti, television service began 1965; run by France Région Trois, Paris; daily programmes in French and Tahitian; in 1975 there were 60,000 radio receivers and 14,000 television sets; Dir. LOUIS-MARIE COHIC.

FINANCE

BANKS

Banque de l'Indochine: 96 blvd. Haussmann, Paris 8, France; 2 place Notre-Dame, Papeete; brs. in Papeete (Quai Galliéni) in Faa, Pirae and Uturoa.

Banque de Tahiti S.A.: B.P. 1602, rue Paul Gauguin, Papeete; f. 1969; affiliated to Bank of Hawaii, Honolulu, and Crédit Lyonnais, Paris; cap. 100m. frs. CFP; dep. 2,608m. frs. CFP (1974); Pres. G. PRADERE-NIQUET; Man. M. BARNIER.

Société de Crédit et de Développement de l'Océanie (SOCREDO): B.P. 130, Papeete; f. 1959; cap. 120m. CFP, dep. 1,784m. CFP; Pres. R. QUESNOT; Dir.-Gen. JEAN VERNAUDON.

TRADE AND INDUSTRY

Papeete

Chambre de Commerce et d'Industrie de la Polynésie Française: B.P. 118; f. 1880; 18 mems.; Pres. CHARLES T. POROÏ; Sec.-Gen. RAMON H. DEXTER; publs. *Les Nouveaux Objectifs*, *Revue Mensuelle* (monthly).

Chambre d'Agriculture et d'Elevage: B.P. 626; f. 1886; 10 mems.; Pres. HUGH LAUHLIN.

Union Territoriale des Syndicats de la Confédération Générale du Travail "Force Ouvrière": Sec.-Gen. W. BREDIN.

Centrale des Travailleurs Chrétiens du Pacifique: B.P. 333; f. 1946; Pres. CHRISTIAN BODIN; Sec.-Gen. JEAN-BAPTISTE VERNIER.

Syndicat Autonome des Fonctionnaires Indépendants: f. 1948; Sec.-Gen. Mlle A. LAGARDE.

Syndicat des Eleveurs de Bovins: B.P. 1325; f. 1951; 80 mems.; Pres. SYLVAIN MILLAUD.

Syndicat des Armateurs: Pres. A. BLOUIN.

Union Patronale: B.P. 317; f. 1948.

TRANSPORT

ROADS

There are 215 km. of bitumen-surfaced and 368 km. of stone-surfaced roads.

SHIPPING

Papeete

Agence Tahiti Poroï: B.P. 83; f. 1958; commission agents, exporters and importers; Dir. ROBERT WAN.

Compagnie des Messageries Maritimes: P.O.B. 96, Papeete-Tahiti; cargo ship services between Europe, the Far East, Madagascar, East Africa, Oceania and Australia; agents for French Line, Farrell Lines, Holland America Line, Lloyd Triestino, Norwegian America Line, Shaw Savill Line, Sitmar Line, Chevron Shipping Corporation, West Cruise Lines, Lauro Lines, Dominion Far East Line, German Atlantic Line.

Pacific Islands Transport Line: Agents: Agence Maritime Internationale Tahiti, B.P. 274, Papeete-Tahiti; services every six weeks to Pago Pago, Apia, Los Angeles, San Francisco, Vancouver.

Other companies operating services to, or calling at, Papeete are: Chandris Lines, Karlander, South Pacific United Lines, China Navigation Co., Nedlloyd, Union Steam Ship Co., Bank Line and Silk and Boyd.

CIVIL AVIATION

Air Polynésie: P.B. 314, Papeete; f. 1953; inter-islands services to Huahine, Raiatea, Bora Bora, Rangiroa, Manihi, Ua-Huka, Moorea, Maupiti, Tubuai, Takapoto, Ruruta, Tetiaroa Moorea, and Hiva-oa; Gen. Man. J. Lesné; fleet of 3 Fairchild F-27A, 3 Twin Otter, 1 BN-2A Islander. *Air Tahiti* operates internal services between Tahiti and Moorea Island and some inter-territorial services.

Six international airlines serve Tahiti: Air New Zealand, Pan American Airways Inc., Qantas Airways, Union des Transports Aériens, Air France, LAN-Chile.

TOURISM

Office de développement du Tourisme de la Polynésie Française: B.P. 65, Papeete.

Syndicat d'Initiative de la Polynésie Française: B.P. 326, Papeete.

Gilbert Islands

GEOGRAPHY

The Gilbert Islands consist of 33 coral atolls and islands totalling 655 square kilometres scattered over 4.14 million square kilometres of ocean. There are 16 Gilbert Islands, 8 Phoenix Islands 8 Line Islands, and Ocean Island (Banaba) lying off the Gilberts. Gilbert Islanders are Micronesians.

HISTORY

The Gilbert and Ellice Islands Colony was established in 1915 following the proclamation of a British protectorate over the Gilbert Islands in 1892. The Colony was governed from the Solomon Islands until January 1972 when a separate government, directly responsible to the United Kingdom, was appointed. On October 1st, 1975, the Ellice Islands were allowed to break away from the Colony to form the Territory of Tuvalu with its capital on Funafuti Atoll.

In 1975 the British Government refused to recognize as legitimate an independence move by the people of Ocean Island (Banaba) who have been in litigation with the British Government since 1971 over revenues derived from exports of phosphate. The discovery of the guano deposits on the 600 hectare Ocean Island was a prime motive in Britain's annexation of the island. Since 1920 the British Phosphate Commissioners, a consortium of the British, Australian and New Zealand governments, have been mining phosphate for use as a fertilizer in Australia and New Zealand. Open-cast mining so adversely affected the island's environment that the Banabans, who were removed from the island during the Second World War, were resettled on Rabi Island, 2,600 kilometres away in the Fiji group, and became citizens of Fiji in 1970. They claim to have been unjustly deprived in the past of their true share of the income from phosphate exports (the phosphate was marketed well below world prices in Australia and New Zealand). By 1973 they had won 50 per cent of the Gilbert and Ellice Islands Colony revenues but they maintained that no serious consideration had been given to the underpayment of past royalties and the British Phosphate Commissioners have not agreed to make good the environmental damage caused by mining. Their case was heard in the High Court between April and December 1975 and a decision is expected in 1976. Banaban leaders are also seeking international backing for the independence of Ocean Island. The British Government has argued that the phosphate revenues should be spread over the whole Gilbert Islands group.

The Gilbert Islands are to obtain internal self-government on November 1st, 1976, with full independence to follow in 1978.

ECONOMY

Some 300,000 metric tons of phosphate are exported annually from Ocean Island by the British Phosphate Commissioners. Copra is the only other export. Most islanders are fully engaged in subsistence activities.

STATISTICAL SURVEY

Area: Land area: 655.27 square kilometres.

Population (1973 census): 51,932; Tarawa (capital) 17,188.

Agriculture (1974–metric tons): Coconuts 25,200, Copra 7,200.

Mining (1972): 511,000 metric tons of phosphate rock mined.

Employment (1972): Phosphate Mining (Ocean Island and the Republic of Nauru) 1,264, Government Service 1,280, Development Authority 1,360.

Finance: Australian currency: 100 cents = 1 Australian dollar ($A). Coins: 1, 2, 5, 10, 20 and 50 cents. Notes: 1, 2, 5, 10, 20 and 50 dollars. Exchange rates (June 1976): £1 sterling = $A1.443; U.S. $1 = 81.4 Australian cents; $A100 = £69.28 = U.S. $122.90. *Note:* For previous changes in the exchange rate, *see* the chapter on Australia.

Budget (1974): Revenue $A19,973,540; Expenditure $A19,973,540; Development Programme (1976) $A4,998,659.

External Trade (1973): Imports $A7,546,230; Exports $A23,735,698 (including 521,530 tons of phosphate, 11,657 tons of copra).

Trade is mainly with Australia, Fiji, the United Kingdom, Japan and New Zealand.

Transport: *Roads:* There are about 400 miles suitable for motor vehicles. *Shipping:* The Government and the Development Authority maintain a fleet of six passenger/freight vessels for administrative business. During 1975 114 overseas vessels called at the Islands.

ADMINISTRATION

The Gilbert Islands administration consists of a House of Assembly of 28 elected members, the Deputy Governor, the Attorney-General and the Financial Secretary. The Council of Ministers consists of the Chief Minister, not fewer than four nor more than six Ministers appointed from among the elected members of the House of Assembly, the Deputy Governor, the Attorney-General and the Financial Secretary.

COUNCIL OF MINISTERS

(*July* 1976)

Governor: H.E. John H. Smith, C.B.E.

Deputy Governor: H. Layng.

Attorney-General: G. L. Pimm.

Financial Secretary: P. W. Reardon, O.B.E.

Elected members

Chief Minister: Naboua Ratieta.

The Minister of State in the Chief Minister's Office: Ibeata Tonganibeia.

Minister of Commerce and Industry: Otiuea Tanentoa.

Minister of Communications, Works and Utilities: Bwebwetake Areieta.

Minister of Education, Training and Culture: Roniti Teiwaki.

Minister of Health and Welfare: Tekarei Russell.

Minister of Local Government and Rural Development: Teweia Uaruta.

Local Government is by Island Councils elected by universal adult suffrage with a staff of permanent Local Government Officers responsible for education, health, sanitation, local police, bye-laws and local taxation etc. The Councils are financially assisted by Central Government in specific fields.

JUDICIAL SYSTEM

High Court, Senior Magistrates Court, Magistrates Courts and Island Courts: all administer English and Colony law with varying extents of jurisdiction.

Lands Courts: have exclusive jurisdiction in matters connected with land, the administration of estates and certain other powers.

Attorney-General: G. L. Pimm.

Senior Magistrate: K. Drennan.

Registrar and Clerk in Senior Magistrates Court: Kakaiwa Kirimaua.

RELIGION

Protestant, Roman Catholic, Seventh-Day Adventist, Baha'i and Church of God communities are represented.

Roman Catholic: Bishop of Tarawa Most Rev. Pierre Guichet.

RADIO

Gilbert Islands Broadcasting Service: Broadcasting Office, Tarawa; f. 1954; two transmitters; government run; over 5,000 receivers in use in 1973; programmes in Gilbertese, Ellice and English; Chief Publicity Officer Kaburoro Tanielu.

FINANCE

BANKING

Bank of New South Wales: Bairiki, Tarawa; f. 1970 (incorporating the *Government Savings Bank*).

TRADE AND INDUSTRY

British Phosphate Commissioners: hold a concession on Ocean Island for phosphate mining.

The Gilberts Copra Co-operative Society Ltd.: Betio, Tarawa; f. 1975; the sole exporter of copra; 7 committee mems.; 18 member Co-operative Societies; Chair. Tioti Taia; Sec. David Brechtefeld.

Development Authority: statutory body responsible for carrying out development projects in the Islands. Also concerned with travel, shipping, water supply, power generation, building construction, the hotel trade, civil engineering and vehicle and plant repairs.

CO-OPERATIVE SOCIETIES

In 1973 there were 51 co-operative societies; 40 consumer-marketing societies, 4 secondary societies and 7 others. Total membership 21,399.

TRADE UNIONS

There are five registered trade unions.

TRANSPORT

ROADS

Wherever practicable, roads are built on all atolls and connecting causeways between islets are also being built as funds and labour permit.

SHIPPING

Vessels owned or chartered by the British Phosphate Commissioners visit Ocean Island about six times a month. Australian cargo vessels call at Tarawa every six weeks and United Kingdom cargo ships every four months. Ships call at Tarawa to collect copra every two or three months and at Christmas, Fanning and Washington Islands twice a year. Vessels of the Columbus Line en route from U.S.A. and Australia call at Tarawa at approximately six weekly intervals. There is an irregular service from Tarawa to Suva, Fiji by Government vessels, and a two-monthly service to Fiji and to the Marshall Islands. Ships owned by the Daiwa Line operate a ten to twelve-weekly service from Japan, and tankers bring fuel from Fiji.

CIVIL AVIATION

Air Pacific maintains a weekly service from Nadi to Funafuti/Tarawa/Nauru and return. It also operates a twice-weekly service between Tarawa and three other islands in the Gilberts. Air Nauru also provides services. A regular charter service between Honolulu, Christmas Island and Tarawa began in early 1976. There are seven airfields in the Islands.

EDUCATION

(1973)

Schools are run by the Government and the Churches; Primary Schools 133; total enrolment 14,194; Secondary Schools 5; total enrolment 833; Teacher Training College 1; Theological Colleges 2; total number of teachers 500 in all establishments. (Information refers to the Gilbert Islands and Tuvalu).

Guam

Guam, the largest of the Mariana Islands, was ceded to the U.S.A. by Spain in 1898. It is situated about 1,500 miles south-east of the Philippines.

Magellan discovered the islands in 1521 and they were colonized by Spain in 1668. When Spain ceded Guam to the U.S.A. it sold the other Mariana Islands to Germany. Japan obtained a League of Nations mandate over the German islands in 1919. In 1941 it seized Guam but the island was retaken by American forces in 1944.

Guam is under the jurisdiction of the U.S. Department of the Interior. In 1970 the Guamanians elected their first Governor and in 1972 a new law gave Guam one delegate to the U.S. House of Representatives. The delegate may vote in Committee but not on the House floor.

The economy is based on the export of copra, fish and handicrafts. Tourism is a growing source of revenue.

STATISTICAL SURVEY

Area: 209 square miles.

Population (1974): 105,641. Servicemen and dependants, about 24,500. Capital: Agaña.

Agriculture: Production (1974): Fruits and vegetables 3.5 million lb.; Eggs 2,436,000 dozen; Pigs 10,463 head; Cattle 2,771 head; Fish 201,000 lb.

Industry: Construction companies, retail stores, watch assembly factories, soft drink bottling plants and tourist facilities are the major employers in private industry. The island's economy, once basically military-oriented, is quickly becoming civilian with the rapid growth in tourism. The Government of Guam is the island's largest single employer.

Tourism: No. of visitors ('000): (1971) 119.1; (1972) 185.4; (1973) 242.7; (1974) 260.6.

FINANCE

United States currency: 100 cents = 1 U.S. dollar ($).

Coins: 1, 5, 10, 25 and 50 cents; 1 dollar.

Notes: 1, 2, 5, 10, 20, 50 and 100 dollars.

Exchange rates (June 1976): £1 sterling = U.S. $1.77; $100 = £56.37.

BUDGET
(1974—U.S. $ million)

Revenue		Expenditure	
Income Taxes	66.03	Current Operating Programmes:	
Gross Receipts Tax	21.09	General Government	14.81
Real Estate Property Tax	3.08	Public Safety	5.44
Other Local Taxes	2.98	Highways	
Licences and Permits	0.80	Personnel Benefits	4.17
Court Fines and Forfeits	0.36	Conservation of Health	3.68
Use of Money and Property	1.08	Social and Community Services*	5.02
Federal Grants-in-Aid	11.51	Public Schools	34.88
Charges for Current Services	5.05	Public Library	0.36
Other Revenues	0.65	Recreation	0.61
		Protection and Development of Resources	3.76
		Utilities, Hospitals and Other Enterprises	18.50
		Repayment of Rehabilitation Loans	—
		Previous Years' Operating Encumbrances	2.12
		Capital Improvement Projects	2.38
		Other Continuing Projects	1.91
		Appropriated Receipts	1.73
		Total Expenditure	99.07
Total Revenue	112.63	Overall Surplus	13.56

* Includes sanitation and waste removal.

External Trade: Imports (1973) $211.1 million; Exports (1973) $10.9 million.

Shipping: Vessels entered (1973) 950; Freight (1973) entered 885,300 tons, cleared 668,200 tons, in transit 138,500 tons.

THE CONSTITUTION

Guam is governed under the Organic Act of Guam of 1950, which gave the island statutory local power of self-government and made its inhabitants citizens of the United States, although they cannot vote in national elections. Their delegate to the House of Representatives is elected every two years. Executive power is vested in a civilian Governor, first elected in 1970. Elections for the governorship occur every four years. The government has 14 executive departments, whose heads are appointed by the Governor with the consent of the Guam Legislature. The Legislature consists of 21 members elected by popular vote every two years. It is empowered to pass laws on local matters, including taxation and fiscal appropriations.

THE GOVERNMENT

Governor: Ricardo Jerome Bordallo.

Lieutenant-Governor: Rudolph Guerrero Sablan.

LEGISLATURE

Speaker: Joseph F. Ada.

Elections: November 1974. The Republican Party won 12 seats, the Democratic Party 9 seats.

JUDICIAL SYSTEM

District Court of Guam: Judge appointed by the President. The court has the jurisdiction of a district court of the United States in all cases arising under the law of the United States and original jurisdiction over such other cases arising in Guam as the Guam Legislature does not transfer to courts of its own creation. Appeals may be made to the Court of Appeals for the Ninth Circuit and to the Supreme Court of the United States.

Presiding Judge: Hon. Cristobal C. Duenas.

Clerk of Court: Edward L. G. Aguon.

There are also the Superior Court, the Police Court, Traffic Court, Juvenile Court and the Small Claims Court.

RELIGION

About 96 per cent of the population is Roman Catholic, although other Christian denominations are represented. Roman Catholic Bishop of the Diocese of Agaña (Bishop's House, Cuesta San Ramon, Agaña) Most Rev. Felixberto C. Flores, d.d., o.f.m.cap.

THE PRESS

Pacific Daily News: P.O.B. DN, Agaña; f. 1950; daily except Sunday; Editor Joseph Murphy; circ. 19,700.

Pacific Dateline: P.O.B. DN, Agaña; f. 1971; daily; evening; Editor Thomas Brislin; circ. 1,400.

Pacific Sunday News: P.O.B. DN, Agaña; f. 1950; Sunday; Editor Joseph Murphy; circ. 19,500.

Pacific Voice: Agaña; Sunday; Ed. John L. Mitchell; circ. 5,500.

RADIO AND TELEVISION

RADIO

Radio Guam (KUAM): P.O.B. 368, Agaña; relays N.B.C., C.B.S. and A.B.C. programmes; Pres. H. Scott Killgore; Exec. Vice-Pres. William B. Nielsen.

There were 100,000 radio receivers in 1975.

TELEVISION

Guam-Agaña (KUAM-TV): P.O.B. 368, Agaña; relays N.B.C., C.B.S. and A.B.C. programmes; operates colour service; Pres. H. Scott Killgore; Exec. Vice-Pres. William B. Nielsen.

KGTF: P.O.B. 3615, Agaña; educational programmes; Dir. Iris Muna.

There were 10,000 television receivers in 1975.

BANKING

American Savings and Loan Association: P.O.B. 811, Agaña; Pres. William Thomasson.

Bank of America National Trust and Savings Association: San Francisco, Calif., U.S.A.; P.O.B. BA, Agaña, Guam 96910; 2 agencies; Man. D. L. Raggio.

Bank of Guam: P.O.B. 3988, Agaña; Pres. Jesus Leon Guerrero.

Bank of Hawaii: Honolulu, Hawaii, U.S.A.; P.O.B. BH, Agaña, Guam 96910; Vice-Pres. and District Administrator W. M. Ord.

Bank of Tokyo of California: P.O.B. 3367, Agaña.

Chase Manhattan Bank of New York: P.O.B. AE, Agaña; Man. F. J. McGinity.

First National City Bank of New York: Agaña; Gen. Man. Stephen H. Stull.

First Hawaiian Bank: Honolulu, Hawaii, U.S.A.; P.O.B. AD, Agaña; Vice-Pres. E. W. Schaartt.

Guam Savings and Loan Association: P.O.B. 2888, Agaña; Pres. Joseph Flores.

TRADE AND INDUSTRY

PRINCIPAL TRADE UNIONS

International Operating Engineers Local No. 3.

Guam Federation of Teachers.

American Communications Association (Teamsters).

Transport Workers Union.

DEVELOPMENT

Guam Economic Development Authority (GEDA): P.O.B. 3280, Agaña, Guam 96910.

TRANSPORT

ROADS

There are 183 miles of paved and 47 miles of improved roads.

SHIPPING

Tucor Services Inc.: P.O.B. 6128, Tamuning, Guam 96911; General Agents for numerous tankers, dry cargo, passenger and fishery companies; Gen. Man. Capt. Alex Roth, Jnr.

Micronesian Interocean Line Inc.: P.O.B. 365, Agaña; Man. Filemon Go.

Pacific Navigation System: P.O.B. 7, Agaña; f. 1946; Pres. Kenneth T. Jones, Jr.

Pacific Far East Line (Guam) Ltd.: P.O.B. EE, Agaña 96910; Vice-Pres. and Gen. Man. ROBERT E. HAHN.

Atkins Kroll (Guam) Ltd.: Agents: PNS, P.O.B. 7, Agaña; Man. DAVID PORTER.

CIVIL AVIATION

Pan American World Airways: Skinner Plaza, P.O.B. BB, Agaña; Dir. KENNETH S. SITTON.

Continental-Air Micronesia: P.O.B. 138, Saipan, Mariana Islands, 96950; Gen. Man. B. DUGGAN.

Japan Air Lines: P.O.B. 7659, Tamuning, 96911; Dir. TARO KANAI.

TOURISM

Guam Visitors Bureau: P.O.B. 3520, Agaña 96910.

There were 260,600 tourists in 1974. Total expenditure was about $90 million.

EDUCATION

There were 35 public and 18 private schools operating on the island in 1974, including seven senior high schools (4 private, 3 public). At September total school enrolment was 33,240. School attendance is compulsory.

UNIVERSITY

University of Guam: P.O.B. EK, Agaña, Guam 96910; 250 teachers, 3,727 students.

Hawaii

PHYSICAL AND SOCIAL GEOGRAPHY

The Hawaiian Islands of the central northern Pacific are comprised of volcanic and coral islands formed by the peaks of huge undersea volcanoes, covering a total land area of 16,641 square kilometres. They form a chain from Hawaii in the south-east (10,414 square kilometres) through Maui (1,886 square kilometres), Molokai (671 square kilometres), Oahu (1,551 square kilometres) to Kauai (1,432 square kilometres) in the north-west. Further west a series of small islands including Midway, the only inhabited island, which lies just east of the International Date Line, complete the chain. Active volcanoes are the outstanding physical feature of the Hawaiian Islands.

The Hawaiian population is multi-racial. The Polynesian population was estimated to be 142,050 in 1823. This had fallen to 56,900 by 1872. In 1974 the total population of the islands was 847,000 of which Hawaiians were only 16 per cent. Organized immigration of non-Polynesian groups into Hawaii began in the 1890s with Portuguese from Madeira and the Azores. They were followed by Americans, Europeans, Puerto Ricans, Indians, Chinese, Japanese, Koreans and Filipinos. European, Japanese, Chinese, Filipino and Hawaiian are major identifiable present day groups.

HISTORY

The Hawaiian Islands were probably the last of the Pacific Islands to be settled by Polynesians. Oral history suggests that until about 1300 AD contacts were maintained between Tahiti and Hawaii. There followed, however, a long period of isolation in which the Hawaiian Polynesian culture developed its own characteristic features.

Captain James Cook is the first documented European to have visited the islands. He landed at Waimea on Kauai Island in 1778, but was killed at Kealakeku on Hawaii during a return visit in 1779. Hawaiian history from contact until June 1900, when it became officially a United States Territory, is one of the virtual destruction of the indigenous Polynesian culture by missionary, commercial and political intervention by outsiders and the sharp reduction of the indigenous population by disease. Russian, Spanish, British, French and American interests all vied for favours with the islands' rulers during the 1800s, while independent traders and entrepreneurs supplied arms to various chiefs in an attempt to gain a foothold for their enterprises. The four chiefdoms in existence in 1782 had been reduced to one under Kamehameha I by 1820. Kamehameha's first wife became a nominal Christian in 1823 and Christianity rapidly became a national religion, which increased the disintegration of the old society. Gradually United States influence became entrenched. Internal insurrections and unrest in the 1890s led to annexation by the United States in 1900.

Hawaii was the 50th state admitted to the United States (in 1959). Hawaiians are United States citizens and may move freely between Hawaii and the mainland.

ECONOMY

The most important early commercial activities in the islands were sandalwood trading and whaling. Sugar, the most important agricultural export, was first cultivated for sale in 1802, but became important during the 1870s. By 1930 over one million metric tons per year were being exported and this rate is maintained in the 1970s. The sugar is grown on intensive plantations, many of which are irrigated. Pineapples were first cultivated commercially in the 1900s. Exports are more than 30 million cases of canned fruit and juice, produced by nine major companies employing about 20,000 people. Other agricultural products include livestock, coffee, rice, cut flowers, bananas, silk, cotton, tobacco, vanilla and groundnuts. Fishing and fish processing is a well developed industry. Secondary industries are largely linked to Hawaii's important agricultural base and include fertilizer and can plants and an oil refinery. A handicraft industry has developed in response to the tourist industry. Tourism is the most important industry on the islands, with over 1 million visitors a year, earning over U.S. $400 million a year, more than all agricultural exports together. Hawaii is also the centre for the unified command of all United States Armed Forces in the Pacific, an activity which contributes significantly to the economy.

STATISTICAL SURVEY

AREA AND POPULATION

Area	Population	
	Census 1970	Estimate 1974
16,705 sq. km.*	768,561	847,000

* 6,450 sq. miles.

MAIN TOWNS

(1970 census)

Honolulu (capital)	324,871	Kaneohe	29,903
Kailua	33,783	Hilo	26,353

FINANCE

100 cents=1 United States dollar ($).
Coins: 1, 5, 10, 25 and 50 cents; 1 dollar.
Notes: 1, 2, 5, 10, 20, 50 and 100 dollars.
Exchange rates (June 1976): £1 sterling=U.S. $1.77; U.S. $100=£56.37.

BUDGET
(1973/74)

Revenue: U.S. $989,507,000; **Expenditure:** U.S. $990,859,000.

COST OF LIVING
Honolulu
(1967=100)

	1973	1974
Food	135.2	158.7
All items . . .	128.3	141.8

CONSTITUTION AND GOVERNMENT

Hawaii has been a State of the U.S.A. since 1959 and the U.S. Constitution and Government institutions apply.

JUDICIAL SYSTEM

Hawaii comes under the jurisdiction of the Ninth Circuit of the U.S. judicial system.

PRESS

In 1975, there were 7 morning, 4 evening and 2 Sunday newspapers.

Honolulu Advertiser: 605 Kapiolani Blvd., Honolulu, Hawaii 96813; f. 1856; morning; Editor GEORGE CHAPLIN; circ. 75,000.

Honolulu Star-Bulletin: 605 Kapiolani Blvd., Honolulu, Hawaii 96813; f. 1912; evening; Editor A. A. SMYSER; circ. 75,000.

Honolulu Star-Bulletin and Advertiser: 605 Kapiolani Blvd., Honolulu, Hawaii 96813; f. 1962; Sundays; circ. 183,040.

FINANCE

BANKING

Bank of Hawaii: 111 South King St., Honolulu 96813; f. 1897; cap. $70.7m.; dep. $946.8m. (Dec. 1974); Chair. and Chief Exec. CLIFTON D. TERRY; Pres. WILSON P. CANNON, Jr.

First Hawaiian Bank: 165 South King St., Honolulu, Hawaii 96813; f. 1929; cap. U.S. $15.2m.; dep. U.S. $839.6m. (June 1974); Pres. JOHN D. BELLINGER.

TRANSPORT

CIVIL AVIATION

Aloha Airlines Inc.: P.O.B. 30028, Honolulu International Airport, Hawaii 96820; f. 1946; inter-Hawaiian island services; Chair. HUNG WO CHING; Pres. KENNETH F. C. CHAR; fleet of 7 Boeing 737s.

Hawaiian Airlines Inc.: P.O.B. 30008, Honolulu International Airport, Honolulu, Hawaii 96820; f. 1929; inter-Hawaiian island services; Pres. Chair. and Chief Exec. JOHN H. MAGOON, Jr.; fleet of 10 Douglas DC-9.

UNIVERSITY

University of Hawaii: Honolulu, Hawaii; 1,612 teachers; 19,320 students.

Johnston Island

Johnston Island lies in the Pacific, south-west of Hawaii. It has an area of less than half a square mile and in 1970 had a population of 1,007. It is administered by the U.S. Air Force.

Midway Islands

The Midway Islands consist of Sand Island and Eastern Island in the North Pacific, 1,150 miles north-west of Hawaii. They have an area of about two square miles and in 1970 had a population of 2,220. They are administered by the U.S. Navy Department.

Nauru

Nauru is a small island in the Central Pacific with an area of 8.2 square miles. Lying about 1,300 miles north-east of Australia, Nauru has a warm and pleasant climate. About half the population are Nauruans, most of them belonging to the Nauruan Protestant Church. The national flag (proportions 2 by 1) is blue, divided by a horizontal gold bar, with a 12-pointed white star at the lower left.

HISTORY

A former German colony, the island was occupied by Australia during the 1914–18 war. The island continued under the administration of Australia under a League of Nations mandate which also named the United Kingdom and New Zealand as co-trustees. Between 1942 and 1945, Nauru was occupied by the Japanese. In 1947, the island was placed under United Nations Trusteeship, with Australia as the administering power on behalf of the Governments of Australia, New Zealand and the United Kingdom. The UN Trusteeship Council proposed in 1964 that the indigenous people of Nauru be resettled on Curtis Island, off the Queensland coast. This offer was made in anticipation of the progressive exhaustion of the island's phosphate deposits. The Nauruans elected to remain on the island, and studies were put in train in 1966 for the shipping of soil to the island to replace the phosphate rock. Nauru received a considerable measure of self-government in January 1966, with the establishment of Legislative and Executive Councils, and proceeded to independence on January 31st, 1968. The Head of State is the President, who governs the Republic, assisted by a Cabinet; legislative power is vested in an elected parliament.

ECONOMY

The island's only industry is phosphate mining, which is manned largely by indentured labour. About four-fifths of the area is phosphate-bearing rock, but deposits are expected to be exhausted by 1992, by which time, it is hoped, Nauru will be able to derive economic security from its shipping and civil aviation services and from its proposed role as a tax haven for international business.

STATISTICAL SURVEY

Area: 8.2 square miles.

Population (June 30th, 1972): Total 6,768 (Nauruan 3,471, Other Pacific Islanders 1,787, Chinese 883, European 627).

Agriculture and Livestock (1974–FAO estimates): Coconuts 1,700 metric tons; Chickens 4,000, Pigs 2,000.

Employment: Total 2,473 (Administration 845, Phosphate Mining 1,408, Other activities 220).

Finance: Australian currency: 100 cents = 1 Australian dollar ($A). Coins: 1, 2, 5, 10, 20 and 50 cents. Notes: 1, 2, 5, 10, 20 and 50 dollars.

Exchange rates (June 1976): £1 sterling = $A1.443; U.S. $1 = 81.4 Australian cents. $A100 = £69.28 = U.S. $122.90. *Note:* For previous changes in the exchange rate, *see* the chapter on Australia.

Budget (1975–76—$A): Estimated revenue: $45,510,600; Estimated expenditure: $26,674,000.

Imports (1970–71) ($A): Total $4,502,123 (from Australia $4,148,435).

Exports (1968–69): Phosphate only, 2,186,000 tons. Exports to Australia 1,424,050 tons, United Kingdom 73,800 tons, New Zealand 526,950 tons, Japan 161,200 tons. Phosphate exports (metric tons): 2,200,000 in 1969/70; 1,913,000 in 1970/71; 1,906,000 in 1971/72.

THE CONSTITUTION

Protects the fundamental rights and freedoms and provides for a Cabinet responsible to a popularly elected Parliament. The President of the Republic is elected by Parliament from among its members. The Cabinet is composed of five members including the President, who presides. There are eighteen members of Parliament, including the Cabinet. Voting is compulsory for those over 20 years of age, except in certain specified instances.

The highest judicial organ is the Supreme Court and there is provision for the setting up of subordinate courts with designated jurisdiction.

There is a Treasury Fund from which monies may be taken by Appropriation Acts.

A Public Service is provided for with the person designated as the Chief Secretary being the Commissioner of the Public Service.

THE GOVERNMENT

(*July* 1976)

President: HAMMER DEROBURT, O.B.E., M.P.

CABINET

Minister of External Affairs, Minister of Internal Affairs, Minister of Island Development and Industry and Minister of Civil Aviation: HAMMER DEROBURT, O.B.E., M.P.

Minister of Health and Education: The Hon. AUSTIN BERNICKE, M.P.

Minister of Works and Community Services and Minister Assistant to the President: The Hon. R. BURARO DETUDAMO, M.P.

Minister of Finance: The Hon. JAMES ATEGAN BOP, M.P.

Minister of Justice: The Hon. JOSEPH DETSIMEA AUDOA, M.P.

PARLIAMENT

Elected December 15th, 1973.
18 members.

Speaker: The Hon. K. AROI, M.P.

DIPLOMATIC REPRESENTATION

EMBASSIES AND HIGH COMMISSIONS ACCREDITED TO NAURU

(E) Embassy; (HC) High Commission.

Australia: Nauru (HC): *High Commissioner:* A. L. FOGG.

Japan: Canberra, Australia (E); *Ambassador:* KENZO YOSHIDA.

New Zealand: Suva, Fiji (HC); *High Commissioner:* G. K. ANSELL.

U.S.A.: Canberra, Australia (E); *Ambassador:* GREEN MARSHALL.

The United Kingdom is represented by the Australian High Commissioner. Nauru also has diplomatic relations at consular level with China (Taiwan).

JUDICIAL SYSTEM

SUPREME COURT

Chief Justice: His Honour Mr. Justice IAN ROY THOMPSON.

DISTRICT COURT

Resident Magistrate: RICHARD LAWRENCE DA SILVA.

RELIGION

About 43 per cent of Nauruans are adherents of the Nauruan Protestant Church. The Sacred Heart of Jesus Mission (Roman Catholic) is also represented.

PRESS AND RADIO

Bulletin: Local news; fortnightly; Editor P. L. JONES; circ. 1,000.

Radio Nauru: f. 1968; government-owned and not used for commercial purposes; broadcasts in English and Nauruan to an estimated (January 1975) audience of 6,500; Man. DAVID AGIR; Broadcasts Officer SAMUEL BILLEAM.

There were 3,600 radio sets in 1975.

FINANCE

BANKING

Bank of New South Wales: 341 George St., Sydney, N.S.W., Australia; br. in Nauru.

INSURANCE

Nauru Insurance Corporation: P.O.B. 82, Nauru; f. 1974; Sole licensed insurer in Nauru; Man. Dir. D. J. HARRISON.

TRADE AND INDUSTRY

Nauru Phosphate Corporation: Nauru, Central Pacific; f. 1969; Chair. R. S. LEYDIN, C.B.E.; Man. Dir. R. S. LEYDIN, C.B.E.; Dirs. P. COOK, T. W. STAR, C. E. RESEIGH; Sec. A. C. WESTBURY; The Corporation operates the phosphate industry of the Republic of Nauru on behalf of the Nauruan people. It is responsible for the mining and marketing of phosphate.

TRADE UNION

The Nauruan Workers' Organization: f. 1974 to represent the interests of a substantial section of Nauru's employees; Chair. BERNARD DOWIYOGO; Sec. DETONGA DEIYE.

TRANSPORT

There are 3½ miles of 3 ft. gauge railway to serve the phosphate workings. A sealed road, 12 miles long, circles the island, and another serves Buada District.

Registered Vehicles (June 30th, 1972): 1,534.

Shipping (1971–72): Ships calling 89; g.r.t. 1,479,600.

Nauru has its own *Nauru Pacific Line* which operates regular six-weekly passenger and cargo services between Melbourne and Sydney and Nauru, Majuro (U.S. Trust Territory of the Pacific Islands), Guam and Tarawa (Gilbert Islands); also services from San Francisco and Honolulu to Majuro and Ponape (U.S. Trust Territory), and from Sydney and Melbourne to New Guinea, Guam and Ponape; owns six ships; three more are on charter.

Air Nauru: f. 1970; operates twice weekly services linking Nauru with Melbourne, Hong Kong, Japan (Kagoshima), Tarawa, Majuro, Nouméa, Okinawa, Guam, Ponape and Honiara. It operates a once weekly service between Nauru and Western Samoa, Fiji, Taipei and the New Hebrides (Vila); Pres. HAMMER DE ROBURT; fleet: 2 Fokker Fellowship F.28, 1 Boeing 737 and 1 Boeing 727.

EDUCATION

(1971)

Primary: 10 schools, 65 teachers, 1,118 pupils.

Secondary: 2 schools, 29 teachers, 364 pupils.

New Caledonia

New Caledonia is a long narrow island 16,750 square kilometres in area, south and slightly west of the New Hebrides. The nearby Loyalty Islands, which are administratively part of New Caledonia, are 2,353 square kilometres in area. Rugged mountains divide the west of the main island from the east and there is little flat land.

The population in 1975 was estimated at 128,000, of which 40 per cent were indigenous Melanesians, 40 per cent European (mainly French) and 20 per cent Asian and Polynesian, the former mainly Vietnamese and Javanese and the latter from Wallis, Futuna and Tahiti.

HISTORY

New Caledonia became a French Territory in 1853 when the island was annexed as a dependency of Tahiti. In 1884 a separate administration was established, and in 1946 it became an Overseas Territory of the French Republic.

Early European settlers on New Caledonia quickly set about alienating Melanesian land, which involved iniquitous legislation and physical violence in putting down rebellions by Melanesians, the last of which took place in 1917. Further seizures of land followed as punishment. Cattle grazing practised by the Europeans disrupted indigenous agriculture and today large areas of formerly irrigated taro terraces lie abandoned.

From 1856 to 1946 two separate administrations existed for Melanesians and expatriates. In 1956 New Caledonia was included in the Loi Cadre legislation; the old Conseil Générale was replaced by an Assemblée Territoriale of 30 members elected by universal adult sufferage. The Governor retains control of all French national departments and the Gendarmerie Nationale but otherwise there is substantial self-government. Moves towards increased autonomy were slowed in 1963, apparently as a result of the Algerian rebellion.

The dominant political party, the Mouvement de l'Union Calédonienne, first formed in 1953, began as a combination of Melanesians and European small business, farming and wage and salary earners. It has been strongly opposed by the Société le Nickel, the major mining consortium, but has won every election since 1953. In July and September 1974 there were demonstrations and unrest against metropolitan France. A general strike was held in October 1974 for greater local control of the mines. The Territorial Assembly includes representatives from seven political parties, three advocating autonomy and four against. Three extremist groups are known to exist, two comprised solely of Melanesians and one including Europeans. A number of bombings have occurred.

ECONOMY

In 1867 and 1870 nickel was discovered and a fusion works was established near Nouméa in 1887. Cobalt and chrome were found in 1875. Since then, New Caledonia has been strongly influenced by the presence of large-scale mining enterprises. Because local labour proved too unreliable, large numbers of New Hebrideans, Japanese, Vietnamese and Javanese were imported to work the mines. By 1921 4,000 Asians were resident.

After 1946, Melanesians began to move into the towns and to the mines, where heavy capitalization increased productivity. Further expansion absorbed more labour from rural areas and the high wages paid to nickel workers threatened all forms of rural production and eliminated chrome and cobalt mining, removing almost all forms of non-urban employment, particularly in the northern part of the island. New Caledonia possesses the world's largest known nickel deposit and has the third largest nickel production, after the U.S.S.R. and Canada. The vulnerability of such a narrowly based economy was demonstrated in 1973 when, after enjoying a boom from 1969, nickel exports and revenues fell, resulting in a sharp depression and public unrest.

STATISTICS

Area: 19,103 sq. km.; **Population** (Jan. 1975 estimates): 128,000. Melanesians 54,500, Europeans (mainly French) 53,750, Wallisians 9,280, Polynesians 6,169, Others 4,250; Nouméa (capital) 60,000 (1973).

Employment (December 1972): Commerce 4,951, Public and Semi-Public Sector 3,940, Metallurgy 3,593, Building 4,863, Mines 3,204, Transport (regularly employed) 1,696, Domestic Servants 1,825, Other Industries 4,016, Professions 1,457, Agriculture, Forestry and Stock-breeding 634; 2,980 employers.

Agriculture (1974—metric tons): Maize 1,000, Potatoes 1,000, Copra 2,000, Coffee 1,500, Sweet Potatoes and Yams 12,000, Taro 3,000, Cassava 4,000, Coconuts 26,900 (all FAO estimates).

Livestock (1974–FAO estimates): Cattle 124,000, Pigs 21,000, Goats 14,000, Horses 8,000, Sheep 6,000, Poultry 177,000.

Mining and Metallurgy (1974—metric tons): Nickel Ore 7,015,000, Chrome Ore (Giobertite) 1,099 (1971), Nickel Matte 18,837, Ferro Nickel 48,533.

Currency: 100 centimes = 1 franc de la Communauté française du pacifique (franc CFP or Pacific franc). Coins: 50 centimes; 1, 2, 5, 10, 20 and 50 francs CFP. Notes: 100, 500, 1,000 and 5,000 francs CFP. Exchange rates (June 1976): 1 franc CFP = 5.5 French centimes; £1 sterling = 153.18 francs CFP; U.S. $1 = 86.35 francs CFP; 1,000 francs CFP = £6.53 = $11.58.

Budget (1975): Revenue 9,990,331,000 francs CFP; Expenditure 9,698,606,000 francs CFP.

Aid from France (francs CFP, 1971): State Budget 3,949,416,216; Local section of FIDES 206,360,108; General section of FIDES 185,617,159.

External Trade (1975—million francs CFP): *Imports:* 27,048.6 (incl. 11,396.2 from France): *Exports:* 22,380.2 (Nickel 4,877.2, Nickel Matte 4,533.4, Ferro-Nickel 11,766.2), incl. 13,464.2 to France.

Roads (1969): Motor Vehicles 27,451, Motor Cycles 10,045, Tractors 454.

Shipping (1974): Vessels entered 596, Freight entered 1,265,366 metric tons, Freight cleared 3,592,511 metric tons, Passenger arrivals 42, Departures 143.

Civil Aviation (1973): Passenger arrivals and departures 129,138, freight handled 4,600 metric tons, postal traffic handled 351 metric tons.

Tourism (1974): 24,008 visitors.

Education (1974): 38,500 in full-time education. Primary Schools: 240; Secondary schools: 8 (1973).

THE GOVERNMENT

(*July* 1976)

Governor: JEAN-GABRIEL ERIAU.

Secretary-General: CLAUDE ERIGNAC.

COUNCIL OF GOVERNMENT

President: JEAN-GABRIEL ERIAU.

Members:

CHARLES ATITI
FRANÇOIS NEOERE
JACQUES LAFLEUR
CLAUDE MEYER
MARC OINEMOIN

Representative to the National Assembly: ROCH PIDJOT.

Representative to the Senate: LIONEL CHERRIER.

Representative to the Social and Economic Council: ROGER LAROQUE.

TERRITORIAL ASSEMBLY

President: YANN CELENE UREGEI.

GENERAL ELECTION
(*August* 1975)

PARTY	SEATS
Union Calédonienne	12
Entente Démocratique et Sociale	7
Mouvement Libéral Calédonien	5
Union Démocratique	4
Mouvement Populaire Calédonien	2
Union Multiraciale de la Nouvelle Calédonie	2
Union Progressiste Multiraciale	2
Front Populaire Calédonien	1
	35

POLITICAL PARTIES

Entente Démocratique et Sociale: Pres. ROGER LAROQUE; Vice-Pres. MICHEL KAUMA, JACQUES LAFLEUR.

Mouvement Libéral Calédonien: Leaders JEAN LEQUES, GEORGES NAGLE.

Mouvement Populaire Calédonien: Leader ALAIN BERNUT.

Union Calédonienne: Leader MAURICE LENORMAND.

Union Démocratique: Leader RENÉ HENIN; Pres. DICK UKEIWE.

Union Multiraciale: Leader YANN CELENE UREGEI.

Union Progressiste Multiraciale: Leader ANDRÉ GOPEA.

Front Populaire Calédonien: Leader PIERRE ISSAMATRO.

JUDICIAL SYSTEM

Cour d'Appel: Nouméa; First Pres. B. RAYMOND; Procureur Général M. REMMY.

Tribunal of First Instance: Nouméa; Pres. V. DELMÉE; Procureur de la République E. VERILHAC.

RELIGION

The population is Christian, Roman Catholics comprising some 63 per cent. There is a substantial Protestant minority.

Roman Catholicism: The Archdiocese of Nouméa comprises New Caledonia and the Loyalty Islands; Archbishop of Nouméa Most Rev. EUGENE X. KLEIN.

PRESS, RADIO AND TELEVISION

L'Avenir Calédonien: 10 rue Gambetta, Nouméa.

Les Calédoniens: Nouméa; f. 1975; radical left weekly; Publr. J.-P. CAILLARD.

Le Drapeau: 21 rue Jules Ferry, Nouméa.

La France Australe: B.P. 25, Nouméa; f. 1889; daily; Dir.-Gen. MICHEL GERARD; circ. 8,500.

Le Journal Calédonien: 32 rue Colnett, B.P. 831, Nouméa.

Le Semeur Calédonien: B.P. 170, Nouméa; f. 1953; Catholic fortnightly; circ. 2,000.

Les Nouvelles Calédoniennes: Librairie JPL, 34 ave. de la République, Nouméa.

Nouméa Soir (Le Bulletin du Commerce): 13 rue de la Somme, Nouméa; f. 1899; Dir. ANDRÉ LEGRAS.

Radio Nouméa: B.P. 327, Nouméa; f. 1942; Government station; daily programmes in French; 60,000 radio sets in 1975; Dir. R. LE LEIZOUR.

Télé Nouméa: B.P. 327, Nouméa; 15,000 television sets in 1975.

BANKS

Banque de l'Indochine et de Suez: f. 1975 by merger; rue de l'Alma et ave. Foch, B.P. 32, Nouméa.

Banque Nationale de Paris: 60 ave. de la Victoire, B.P. K.3, Nouméa.

Banque de Paris et des Pays-Bas: 33 rue de l'Alma, B.P. J3, Nouméa.

Société Générale: 56 ave. de la Victoire, B.P. G2, Nouméa.

TRADE AND INDUSTRY

Chambre de Commerce: B.P. 10, Nouméa; f. 1880; 12 mems.; Pres. JEAN CHEVAL; Vice-Pres. JEAN LANCHON; Sec. Treas. ANDRÉ DE BÉCHADE; publ. *Bulletin* (monthly).

Chambre d'Agriculture: B.P. 111, Nouméa; f. 1909; 18 mems.; Pres. M. ROGER PENE.

TRADE UNIONS

Fédération des Cadres et Collaborateurs de Nouvelle-Calédonie: B.P. 478, Nouméa; Pres. and Sec.-Gen. F. VIANNENC; trade union organization which includes the following:

Syndicat Général des Cadres et Assimiles de Nouvelle-Calédonie: Sec.-Gen. E. OLIVEAU.

Syndicat Général des Cadres du Commerce de Nouvelle-Calédonie: Sec.-Gen. G. JORE.

Fédération Patronale de Nouvelle-Calédonie et Dépendances: 16 rue d'Austerlitz, B.P. 466, Nouméa; f. 1936; groups the leading companies of New Caledonia for the defence of professional interests, co-ordination, documentation and research in socio-economic fields; Pres. RENÉ FAURE; Sec.-Gen. M. DEMENE.

Syndicat des Ouvriers et Employés de Nouvelle-Calédonie: Sec.-Gen. M. DRAYTON.

Union des Syndicats Autonomes: Sec.-Gen. R. JOYEUX.

Syndicat des Fonctionnaires, Agents et Ouvriers des Services Publics: Sec.-Gen. CHRISTY ANDRÉ.

Fédération des Syndicats des Mines Nouvelle-Calédonie: Sec.-Gen. M. BENETEAU.

Syndicat des Travailleurs d'Outre-Mer: Sec.-Gen. M. BASTIEN.

TRANSPORT

Roads: there are a total of 4,600 km. of roads in New Caledonia, of which 300 are bitumen-surfaced, 1,880 stone-surfaced and 2,500 tracks.

Shipping: Services from Sydney to Nouméa are maintained by *Chargeurs Calédoniens* and *Sofrana Unilines* (cargo only), and from Europe to Nouméa by *Hamburg/Sued* and *Messageries Maritimes*; services calling at Nouméa are maintained by *Karlander* (Sydney–New Hebrides), *Polynésia* (Sydney–New Hebrides), *South Pacific United Lines* (Sydney–Tahiti), *Nauru Pacific Line*, *China Navigation Co.* (Hong Kong–South Pacific), *Nedlloyd* (Europe–South Pacific), *Daiwa Line* (Japan–South Pacific), *Union Steam Ship Co.* (New Zealand), *Sofrana-Unilines* (Sydney), *Royal Viking Line* (Sydney), *P & O Lines* (Sydney) and *Bank Line* (Europe–South Pacific).

Civil Aviation: *Air Calédonie:* 6 rue de Verdun, B.P. 212, Nouméa; f. 1955; services throughout New Caledonia and to the Loyalty Islands; fleet of three Twin Otters, three Islanders, one Cherokee 6; Pres. HENRI MARTINET.

Foreign airlines serving New Caledonia are: Air Nauru, Air New Zealand, Air Pacific, Norfolk Island Airlines, Qantas and UTA.

TOURISM

Association calédonienne pour le dévelopment du tourisme—ASCADETO: Nouméa.

Office du Tourisme de la Nouvelle-Calédonie: B.P. 688, Nouméa.

New Hebrides

The New Hebrides is an archipelago of some 70 islands stretching from south of the Solomon Islands to the east of New Caledonia, 800 kilometres in all. The islands range in size from 25 hectares to 3,600 square kilometres. The islands have rugged mountainous interiors with narrow coastal strips where most of the inhabitants dwell. Three islands have active volcanoes on them. Estimates for 1975 place the population at 96,532 of whom over 90 per cent are New Hebrideans. Other races represented include Europeans, Chinese and Polynesian migrants. Approximately 65 per cent of New Hebridean adult males are full-time subsistence gardeners, producing small amounts of copra, coffee and cocoa.

The New Hebrides are governed by an Anglo-French Condominium which was established in 1906. Under this arrangement each power is responsible for its own citizens and other non-New Hebrideans who choose to be *"ressortissant"* of either power. Indigenous New Hebrideans may not claim either British or French citizenship. One result is two official languages, two police forces, three public services, three courts of law, three currencies, three national budgets, two resident commissioners in Vila, the capital, and two district commissioners in each of the four Districts.

Local political initiatives began after the Second World War and originated in New Hebridean concern over the alienation of native land. More than 36 per cent of the New Hebrides is owned by foreigners. Nagriamel, one of the first political groups to emerge, had its source in cult-like activities. In 1971 Nagriamel leaders petitioned the United Nations to prevent more land sales at a time when land was being sold to American interests for development as tropical tourist resorts. In 1972 the New Hebrides National Party was formed with support from Protestant missions and covert support from British interests. In response French interests formed the Union des Communautés Néo-Hébridaises in 1974. Discussions in London in 1974 resulted in the setting up of a Representative Assembly of 42 members, of whom 29 are elected by universal adult sufferage, nine (three British, three French and three New Hebridean) by economic interests, Chambers of Commerce and rural co-operatives, and four by the traditional chiefs. In elections in November 1975 the National Party, which had campaigned on an independence-in-1977, pro-British platform, won 17 of the elective seats, the remaining 12 going to the Union Party which strongly opposed independence. The support for the National Party alarmed many foreign residents, for in the two days following the elections, funds worth about six million Australian dollars were transferred out of the country. After the election Nagriamel leaders on Santo called for separate and immediate independence for that island and again sent representatives to the United Nations where they received strong support from Fiji for the right to New Hebridean self-determination. However, the Anglo-French Government replied that neither would unilaterally abdicate responsibility to the people of the New Hebrides. Meanwhile the economy continues to be increasingly influenced economically by the nearby French territory of New Caledonia.

STATISTICS

Area: 14,763 square kilometres (12 large and 60 small islands between 13°–21° S. and 166°–170° E., forming a double chain of islands about 440 miles long).

Population (1967 Census): 77,982 (73,937 indigenes), Vila (capital) 7,738, Santo 2,564. Est. population at December 31st, 1975: 96,532, Vila 16,604.

Employment: The native population is mainly engaged in peasant agriculture, producing both subsistence and cash crops. Most Europeans are employed in commerce or government service.

Agriculture: 150,000 acres are cultivated; there are 750,000 acres of forests. Production (1974-metric tons): coconuts 177,900, copra 24,500 (FAO estimates); (1975) copra 27,000; meat 634; small quantities of cocoa and coffee.

Livestock (1974-FAO estimates): Cattle 90,000, Pigs 62,000 Goats 7,000, Poultry 123,000.

Fishing: 8,000 metric tons landed in 1974 (FAO estimate); (1975) 5,218 metric tons frozen fish.

Mining: (1975) 46,520 tons of manganese exported.

Finance: Australian and local currency are both legal tender.

100 cents = 1 Australian dollar ($A). Coins: 1, 2, 5, 10, 20 and 50 cents. Notes: 1, 2, 5, 10, 20 and 50 dollars. Exchange rates (June 1976): £1 sterling = $A1.443; U.S. $1 = 81.4 Australian cents; $A100 = £69.28 = U.S. $122.90. *Note:* For previous changes in the exchange rate, *see* the chapter on Australia.

100 centimes = 1 New Hebrides franc (franc néo-hébridais). Exchange rates (June 1976): 1 NH franc = 6.1875 French centimes; £1 sterling = 136.16 NH francs; U.S. $1 = 76.75 NH francs; 1,000 NH francs = £7.34 = U.S. $13.03.

The currencies are locally interchangeable at the rate of $A1 = 95 NH francs.

Condominium Budget (1975): Revenue 737 million FNH; Expenditure 102 million FNH.

British Budget (1974–75): Revenue $A4,450,453; Expenditure $A4,220,528.

French Budget (1975 estimate): 9 million FNH.

External Trade (1975): *Imports:* 2,496 million NH francs (chief items rice, canned foods, beer and wines, building materials, petrol and fuel oils, clothing, textiles, machinery, vehicles and spares). *Exports:* 787.5 million NH francs (chief items frozen fish, copra; others: timber, manganese, cocoa, frozen and canned beef). Principal trading partners are Australia, France, Japan and U.S.A.

Transport (1975): *Roads:* 4,389 vehicles. *Shipping:* 333 ships called at New Hebrides ports. *Aviation:* 1,113 aircraft landed.

Tourism: In 1975 42,969 cruise ships passengers arrived in the New Hebrides and a further 15,838 visitors arrived for longer stays. Visitors are mainly from Australia and and New Caledonia.

THE CONSTITUTION

In 1902, Joint Deputy Commissioners were appointed by Britain and France and in 1906 an Anglo-French Convention established the Condominium as a Joint Administration. Citizens of the two Powers enjoy equal rights of residence, personal protection and trade. Each Power retains sovereignty over its nationals and business corporations. There is no Territorial sovereignty and natives bear no allegiance to either Power.

There are three elements in the structure of administration: the British National Service, the French National

Service and the Condominium (Joint) Departments. An Advisory Council, established in 1957, was presided over by the Resident Commissioners, until, following talks in 1974, Britain and France agreed to the establishment of a Representative Assembly of 42 members which replaced it in 1975.

More than half the islands have local authorities and in 1975 the municipal authorities of Vila and Santo were created.

THE GOVERNMENT

British High Commissioner: EDWARD N. LARMOUR, C.M.G. (resident in London).

French High Commissioner: JEAN-GABRIEL ERIAU (resident in Nouméa, New Caledonia).

The High Commissioners are joint and equal heads of the Administration acting locally through British and French Resident Commissioners. The Joint Administration consists of the British National Service, the French National Service and certain Condominium services, including Treasury, Customs and Inland Revenue, Public Works and Transport, Posts and Telephones, Radio, Lands, Survey, Ports and Harbours, Civil Aviation, Agriculture and Meteorology. A rough balance is kept between nationalities in numbers appointed.

BRITISH NATIONAL ADMINISTRATION

Resident Commissioner: JOHN S. CHAMPION, O.B.E.

FRENCH NATIONAL ADMINISTRATION

Resident Commissioner: ROBERT GAUGER.

REPRESENTATIVE ASSEMBLY

A 42 member Representative Assembly was established in 1974. Twenty-nine members are elected by universal adult suffrage, nine (three British, three French and three New Hebridean) by economic interests (three each from British and French interests in the Chamber of Commerce and three representing the rural co-operative movement) and four by the traditional chiefs. The members are elected for a three-year term.

The Assembly is presided over by the two Resident Commissioners who are not bound to enact resolutions unacceptable to them in their executive capacity unless these resolutions are confirmed by a two-thirds majority of all the Assembly's members.

In the elections held in November 1975 the National Party won 17 of the 29 elected seats, the Union des Communautés Néo-Hébridaises won 10 and the coalition formed by Nagriamel and the Mouvement Autonomiste des Nouvelles-Hébrides won 2 seats.

POLITICAL PARTIES

National Party: f. 1972; aims at independence from Franco-British administration and more power for the indigenes and for the return of their lands; Pres. Rev. WALTER LINI.

Union des Communautés Néo-Hébridaises: f. 1974; for legal reform and increased involvement of the indigenous Melanesian population in the territory's affairs; Pres. JEAN-MARIE LEYE.

Mouvement Autonomiste des Nouvelles-Hébrides: f. 1974; aims to involve Melanesians in creating a political structure similar to those existing in New Caledonia and French Polynesia; Pres. AIMÉE MALERE.

Nagriamel: f. 1963; rural party aiming at return of land to indigenes; Leader JIMMY STEVENS.

JUDICIAL SYSTEM

CONDOMINIUM COURTS

The Joint Court: comprises a neutral President, a British Judge and a French Judge assisted by a neutral Public Prosecutor, a Registrar and a Native Advocate.

President: (vacant).

British Judge: (vacant).

French Judge: L. CAZENDRES.

Courts of First Instance: In each District. Composed of British and French District Agents sitting with one assessor.

NATIONAL COURTS

For all suits between non-natives, except for certain land claims.

NATIVE COURTS

Composed of one of the two Agents of the District sitting with two native assessors. Their jurisdiction covers all offences peculiar to natives under the police and administrative regulations and by the code of native laws.

RELIGION

Most of the inhabitants are Christian. Twelve Protestant groups are represented, including Presbyterian and Church of Melanesia (Anglican). The Roman Catholic Church is also well established.

Church of Melanesia: Bishop: The Rt. Rev. D. A. RAWCLIFFE; Lolowai, Longana.

Roman Catholic: Bishop of Port Vila: (vacant). Apostolic Administrator PIERRE MARTIN; B.P. 59, Port Vila.

THE PRESS

There are no independent daily or weekly newspapers.

New Hebridean Viewpoints: quarterly journal published by New Hebrides National Party, Aoba.

New Hebrides News: British Residency; f. 1955; fortnightly; circ. 2,900.

Nabanga: French Residency; f. 1975; fortnightly tabloid; circ. 2,500.

RADIO

Radio Vila: P.O.B. 110, Port Vila; f. 1966; broadcasts in English, French and Pidgin; Mans. J. HASTIE, C. LASSALAS.

In 1975 there were 15,000 receivers.

FINANCE

New Hebrides is rapidly developing as a tax-haven. There are a growing number of banks, exempted from tax, largely administered by trust companies. Bank Gutzwiller, Kurz, Bungener Overseas (Ltd.), Banque de l'Indochine et de Suez, Barclays DCO, Commercial Banking Company of Sydney, Bank of New South Wales, Commonwealth Savings Bank of Australia (agency), National Bank of Australia, Hong Kong and Shanghai Bank, Australia and New Zealand Bank have branches in the New Hebrides.

TRANSPORT

ROADS

In 1974 there were 340 miles of roads, 200 miles of which consisted of seasonal earth motor tracks.

SHIPPING

The principal ports are Vila and Santo.

Messageries Maritimes: regular service to France, French Oceania, Australia and New Caledonia at three-to four-week intervals.

Burns Philp (New Hebrides) Ltd.: agents for regular services linking the New Hebrides with Australia, the Solomon Islands and New Guinea.

P. & O. Lines: operate cruise services from Sydney.

There are also other passenger and cargo services linking the New Hebrides with the United Kingdom, Australia and New Zealand.

CIVIL AVIATION

The principal airports are Bauer Field (Efate) and Pekoa (Santo).

Union des Transports Aériens: seven services per week to and from New Caledonia, one weekly to Wallis.

Air Pacific: service thrice weekly linking Fiji and Brisbane via the New Hebrides and New Caledonia.

Air Nauru: weekly link with Nauru, connecting with Japan and Hong Kong.

Air Melanesia: P.O.B. 72, Hong Kong and New Zealand House, Vila; f. 1966; operates internal regular and charter service under the auspices of New Hebrides Airways and Société Française Air Hébrides, a subsidiary of Union des Transports Aériens.

EDUCATION

There are no joint services. The National Service Education Department supervises 125 primary schools, three secondary schools and a teacher-training college. There are some 8,000 pupils enrolled in French schools and over 10,000 in British institutions, and an increasing share of the cost of running English speaking mission schools is being borne by the British Administration. The French Administration run two lycées at Vila and Santo and 47 primary schools, two with secondary facilities.

Primary education is not free but only nominal fees are charged and primary education is available for most children.

Niue

Niue is a coral island of 259 square kilometres, located about 480 kilometres east of Tonga and 930 kilometres west of the Southern Cook Islands. It is a self-governing dependency of New Zealand. Niueans have free entry to New Zealand and a sizeable resident Niuean community exists there. Emigration is continuing. Vegetables, fruit, copra and handicrafts are exported to New Zealand. New Zealand aid is being employed to establish a bee industry and to introduce dairy and beef cattle for local consumption. A small forestry project is also being undertaken. The population in 1975 was 4,048.

STATISTICS

Area: 259 sq. km. (100 sq. miles).

Population: 4,048 (estimate, December 1975).

The birth rate in 1975 was 41.3 per 1,000 and the crude death rate 6.0. The infant mortality rate per 1,000 live births was 12.5.

EMPLOYMENT

Under a current programme the Agriculture Department is rehabilitating the coconut industry and developing grass land, cattle and other farming operations. The Niue government is the major employer, however, and most workers are employed by government departments. There is no unemployment problem.

AGRICULTURE

The main crops are coconuts, taro, yams, limes, cassava (manioc), kumara and passion fruit. About 51,000 of the island's 64,000 acres are used for agriculture and over 13,000 acres are merchantable forest. The main livestock are beef cattle, pigs and poultry.

FINANCE

Currency: 100 cents=1 New Zealand dollar ($NZ). For details, *see* the Cook Islands.

BUDGET
($NZ, April 1st to March 31st)

	Revenue	Expenditure	New Zealand Subsidy
1973/74	375,089	2,407,137	1,495,313
1974/75	410,778	3,237,813	2,367,822
1975/76	579,407	3,700,123	2,516,000

Revenue is raised mainly from import and export duties, sale of postage stamps, court fines and income tax.

EXTERNAL TRADE

($NZ '000)

	1973	1974	1975
Imports	721.0	1,151	2,095
Exports	136.5	168	197

Export items include copra, plaited ware, honey, passion fruit and limes.

New Zealand takes most of Niue's export (nearly 73 per cent in 1975) and provides a large part of the island's imports (nearly 79 per cent in 1975). The main imports are foodstuffs, vehicles and spares, building materials, and oil and petrol.

GOVERNMENT

In October 1974 Niue gained self-government in free association with New Zealand. The latter, however, remains responsible for Niue's defence and external affairs and will continue economic and administrative assistance. Executive government in Niue is through the Premier, assisted by three Ministers. Legislation is carried out by the Niue Assembly but New Zealand, if called upon to do so by the Assembly, will also legislate for the island. There is a New Zealand representative in the territory.

New Zealand Representative: W. J. Ashwell.

THE CABINET

(*July* 1976)

Premier and Member for Finance and Government Administration: Hon. Robert R. Rex.

Member for Agriculture, Economic Development and Education: Hon. M. Y. Vivian.

Member for Health, Justice, Radio and Post Office: Hon. Dr. E. Lipitoa.

Member for Works, Police and Tourism: Hon. F. F. Lui.

JUDICIAL SYSTEM

The High Court: exercises civil and criminal jurisdiction in Niue.

The Land Court: is concerned with litigation over land and titles.

Land Appellate Court: hears appeals over decisions of the Land Court.

RADIO

Niue Broadcasting Division: Administrative Department, P.O.B. 67, Alofi; broadcasts in Niue and English.

There were 650 radio sets in 1975.

TRANSPORT

There are 77 miles of all-weather roads and 66 miles of access and plantation roads. At March 31st, 1976, there were 739 registered motor vehicles of which 497 were motor cycles, 205 cars and 37 trucks. The best anchorage is an open roadstead at Alofi, the largest of Niue's 13 villages. A shipping service is maintained with New Zealand via Tonga, Fiji and Samoa on a regular four-weekly basis.

An airstrip of 5,400 ft., capable of taking most types of aircraft except modern jet aircraft, and a twice-weekly air service from New Zealand, via Fiji, Tonga and Western Samoa, is operated by Air N.Z. Ltd. and Polynesian Airlines Ltd.

EDUCATION

There are 8 primary schools and 1 secondary. Education is free and compulsory between the ages of six and fourteen but most children remain at school until sixteen. In December 1975 there were 1,343 children attending school. There were also 45 students undertaking long-term education or training in New Zealand under the auspices of the New Zealand Training Scheme.

Norfolk Island

Norfolk Island is about 8 km. long and 4.8 km. wide and was discovered by Captain Cook in 1774. The island was used as a penal settlement from 1788 to 1813 and again from 1825 to 1855. It was a separate Crown Colony until 1897, when it became a Dependency of New South Wales. In 1913 it was transferred to the Australian Government. Area: 3,440 hectares; Estimated population (June 30th, 1975): 1,870.

THE GOVERNMENT

ADMINISTRATION

Acting Administrator: C. I. BUFFETT, M.B.E.

The Administrator is appointed by the Governor-General of Australia. The Norfolk Island Council acts as an advisory body to the Administrator, who is its Chairman. The eight members are elected by adult franchise. Legislation must be referred to the Council for its advice.

JUDICIAL SYSTEM

Supreme Court of Norfolk Island; appeals lie to the **High Court of Australia.**

Judges: The Hon. Mr. Justice P. JOSKE, C.M.G., The Hon. Mr. Justice E. A. DUNPHY.

PRESS AND RADIO

Norfolk Islander: "Greenways Press", Queen Elizabeth Ave.; f. 1965; weekly; circ. 1,100; Co-Editors Mr. and Mrs. T. LLOYD.

Norfolk Island News: Collins Head Rd.; f. 1975; weekly; Proprietor and Editor E. HOWARD.

Norfolk Island Broadcasting Service: Norfolk Island Administration; Broadcasting Officer Mrs. S. RYVES.

There were 1,150 radio receivers in 1975.

ECONOMIC ACTIVITIES

The climate is suitable for the cultivation of a variety of crops and for grazing; the volcanic soil is chemically rich but presents many difficulties to the farmer, especially the steep terrain and the porosity of the soil. The situation is aggravated by over-cultivation, over-grazing and erosion. About 405 hectares are arable. The main crops are bean seed, Kentia palm, cereals, vegetables and fruit. Some flowers and plants are grown commercially. The Administration is increasing the area devoted to Norfolk Island pine and hardwoods. Seed of the Norfolk Island pine is exported.

Imports (year ending June 30th, 1975): $6,172,174, mainly from Australia.

Exports (1975): $621,017.

Budget (year ending June 30th, 1975): Revenue $1,408,054; Expenditure $1,077,753.

Banking: There are branches of the Commonwealth Trading Bank, the Commonwealth Savings Bank of Australia, the Bank of New South Wales Trading Bank and the Bank of New South Wales Savings Bank.

Trade Association: Norfolk Island Chamber of Commerce.

TRANSPORT

There are about 80.5 km. of roads, including 29 km. of sealed road. Regular air services operate between Sydney and Auckland and Norfolk Island. There are also regular shipping services from Sydney and New Zealand. A small tanker from Nouméa (New Caledonia) delivers petroleum products to the island.

Papua New Guinea

PHYSICAL AND SOCIAL GEOGRAPHY

Papua New Guinea consists of the eastern part of the island of New Guinea and some smaller islands, including the Bismarck Archipelago (mainly New Britain, New Ireland and Manus) and the northern part of the Solomon Islands (mainly Bougainville and Buka). It covers a total area of 461,691 square kilometres. The climate is hot and humid throughout the year, with an average maximum temperature of 33°C. and an average minimum of 22°C.

In 1974 the population was estimated at 2,693,200. The rate of population growth is very high at between 2.7 and 3.5 per cent a year.

HISTORY

New Guinea was divided in 1828. The west was administered until 1949 as part of the Netherlands East Indies and from 1949 until 1962 as the Nederlands Nieuw Guinea. In 1963, after military action by Indonesia, the territory became provisionally Daerah Irian Barat and became part of Indonesia by an "act of free choice" in August 1962. It is known as Irian Jaya, a province of Indonesia.

The southern part of the eastern end of New Guinea became British New Guinea in 1906 after the establishment of a British Protectorate in 1884 and annexation in 1886. Australia administered what became the Territory of Papua until 1949, when it was joined, under one administration, with New Guinea. The northern part of the eastern end of the island became Schutzgebiet Kaiser-Wilhelmsland und Bismarck-archipel in 1884, part of the Schutzgebiet Deutsch Neu-Guinea in 1899, the Mandated Territory of New Guinea in 1919 and the Trust Territory of New Guinea in 1946. Australian troops "invaded" Rabaul in 1914 and relieved the Germans of the territory. Australia administered the area until 1942 when much of it fell under Japanese administration until 1945. In December 1973 the Territory of Papua New Guinea became internally self-governing and on September 16th, 1975, became the independent nation of Papua New Guinea.

Moves towards earlier rather than later self-government and independence for Papua New Guinea were begun by the Pangu political party, the leader of which is the present Prime Minister, Michael Somare. Between December 1973 and September 1975, however, a coalition government headed by Pangu members in the House of Assembly postponed the planned independence date of December 1st, 1974, because of disagreement over the post-independence constitution. The main differences between the constitutional planning committee which drafted the constitution and the Government were over rights of citizenship and the decentralization of power through the creation of provincial governments and assemblies. The constitutional planning committee was chaired by a Catholic priest, Fr. John Momis, from Bougainville, an island where pressure for decentralization existed to the point of Momis's resignation from the committee and the House of Assembly and a unilateral declaration of independence by Bougainville (the site of the huge Panguna copper mine, controlled by a Rio Tinto-Zinc Corporation subsidiary, Conzinc Rio Tinto), on September 1st, 1975. The Government persuaded the House of Assembly to accept the constitution as amended and independence followed on September 16th.

The pre-independence difficulties faced by the central government typify the problems faced by the country as a whole, one year after independence. Although broad cultural similarities occur among groups in the Papuan coastal, New Guinea highlands, New Guinea coastal, New Guinea islands and Bougainville regions, local group sympathies are strong and in rural areas, where approximately two million of the 2.5 million indigenous population are living, understanding of national issues is low or non-existent. The new Government inherited from Australia a highly bureaucratic, centralized administration unsuited to a country in which communications are so difficult and national awareness so low. Strong pressure from the provinces during 1975 and 1976 resulted in the Government replacing the provisions for decentralized provincial governments in the constitution. In May 1976, after small scale disturbances on Bougainville, the leaders of the province, which had been calling itself the Independent Republic of the North Solomons, agreed to negotiate with the central Papua New Guinea government on terms for Bougainville's inclusion as a self-governing province within Papua New Guinea. Provincial government elections were held in July and August 1976. In June 1976 four other provinces were granted the power to form provincial governments, although the proposed relationship between central and provincial governments are not clear.

A National Parliament was elected in February 1972. It has 102 members elected by universal adult suffrage. There are 20 ministers including the Prime Minister, and an inner Cabinet of 10 ministers. The government is a loose coalition of three main political parties, with the opposition made up of one main party, and a number of independents supporting both groups. Papua New Guinea is administered at three levels. Local government councils were introduced in the 1950s. In 1976 over 160 councils were in existence involving almost the total population. The councils are empowered to levy taxes and make rules. However, many councils are too small to operate efficiently and rely heavily on funds and administrative assistance from the central government. Councils are finding increasing difficulty collecting personal taxes.

In 14 of the 20 provinces, Area Authorities have been set up. Their main function is to advise central government on development priorities in their provinces. Members of the Authorities are drawn from local government councils. Pressure for real decentralization of decision-making has come from Area Authorities which have asked that their status be changed to that of Provincial Governments.

A national health plan was drawn up in 1974. Health is worst in rural areas, in the Highlands region and among young children. The plan proposes shifting expenditure away from expensive services in urban areas toward rural health centres and aid posts.

ECONOMY

Road construction is a most important part of development plans. Approximately seven million kina was spent on new roads in 1974–75, with emphasis on trunk and development roads. Feeder roads have been constructed with funds earmarked for rural improvement. Loans from the World Bank and the Asian Development Bank are being used on extending the national highway network, with the ultimate object of a trans-national highway linking Port Moresby with the Highlands and the north coast.

Telecommunications are highly developed. Broadcasting is the principal means of mass communication. The National Broadcasting Commission operates a national service in

English and local services in the two main *lingua franca*, Pidgin and Hiri Motu, as well as local languages.

High rainfall and relief give Papua New Guinea the potential to generate large amounts of hydro-electricity. The Ramu River project stage I has been completed at a cost of K30 million and has a capacity of 45 MW. Eventually this project will generate 255 MW. A feasibility study is being undertaken on the Purari River at Wabo by Japanese and Australian interests for a 1,500 MW powers tation and dam estimated to cost about K700 million.

Another area of likely development is the Ok Tedi and associated copper deposits in the Telefomin area of the West Sepik and Western Provinces. Exploration was begun by the Kennecott Corporation which discovered an ore body of up to 300 million metric tons averaging 0.9 per cent copper at Ok Tedi, and other lower grade deposits nearby. The area is 800 km. from the coast (by river), 2,700 metres above sea level and receives over 10,000 mm. of rain per year, so severe engineering and transport problems must be overcome before any extraction. A government agency is negotiating with Broken Hill Proprietary of Australia, after Kennecott withdrew, complaining that the government was demanding too much in royalties and equity.

Towns in Papua New Guinea grew at an annual rate of 16.4 per cent between 1966 and 1971, mainly as a result of rural-urban migration .Employment in the towns is not available to many who seek it, and urban services cannot cope with the migrants when they arrive. Migrant "shanty" towns are already a feature of all the major urban areas. Services are being extended to these settlements and materials and loans for housing improvement are being made available. Existing forecasts suggest towns will grow by an average of 9.4 per cent between 1971 and 1986, which will alter the present rural-urban population distribution from 11 per cent in urban areas in 1971 to 23 per cent in 1986. One serious problem facing all towns is lack of land, and the unwillingness of village owners to sell land to the government for urban development.

Population growth in the mid-1970s was outstripping growth in employment opportunities. The adult urban population grew by 15.4 per cent per annum between 1966 and 1971 while urban wage employment grew at only 13.4 per cent per annum. Between 1971 and 1975 wage employment opportunities declined further and there is high unemployment. Before 1975 Australia was providing direct assistance towards the costs of administering the country, as well as funding specific development projects. Following independence, this aid was reduced sharply. While copper prices remained high, royalties from the Bougainville mine provided slightly in excess of 60 per cent of the national internal receipts, but with the fall in copper prices in 1975, it became apparent that the country was living beyond its means. Cuts in funds to government departments during 1976 resulted in a marked reduction in government services in all fields, which was in turn felt in all sectors of the economy. Falling prices on international markets for those agriculture commodities which Papua New Guinea exports, copra, coffee, cocoa and rubber, exacerbated the problem.

As yet no clearly stated political ideology has emerged in Papua New Guinea. Foreign investment is sought and encouraged on the one hand, but fears of neo-colonialism and domination of the economy by overseas interests are frequently expressed. Rural development is a government aim, but most government spending per head of population occurs in towns, which are growing rapidly, and it is in urban areas that the best living conditions, services and educational facilities are to be found. A marked rural-urban migration pattern has developed, with the best educated people being drawn from the villages into the towns where they are fast forming an urban élite. Papua New Guinea enjoys one advantage that many developing countries do not: about 90 per cent of the population are employed in the subsistence, non-monetarized sector of the economy to varying degrees, and provide themselves with almost all their daily requirements of food, clothing and shelter. However, even this advantage is being rapidly whittled away by rapid population growth.

STATISTICAL SURVEY

AREA AND POPULATION

Area (sq. km.)			Population (estimate for June 30th, 1974)		
Mainland	Islands	Total	Indigenous	Non-indigenous	Total
394,766	66,925	461,691*	2,654,000	39,200	2,693,200

* 178,260 square miles.

Administrative Capital: Port Moresby, with a population of 76,507 (including 16,944 non-indigenous) at July 7th, 1971.

Births and Deaths: Average annual birth rate 42.4 per 1,000; death rate 19.1 per 1,000 (UN estimates for 1965–70).

INDIGENOUS EMPLOYMENT

(1972)

Primary Production	35,999
Mining and Quarrying	4,101
Manufacturing	10,121
Building and Construction	11,553
Transport, Communications and Storage	7,719
Commerce	9,418
Personal Service (Hotels, Cafés and Amusements)	3,496
Others	37,607
TOTAL	120,014

Total economically active (June–July 1966): 1,255,953 indigenous (648,681 males, 607,272 females).

AGRICULTURE

PRINCIPAL CROPS

('000 metric tons)

	1972	1973	1974
Rice (paddy)	2†	2*	2*
Sorghum	3*	3*	3*
Sweet potatoes	380*	388*	400*
Cassava (Manioc)	77*	80*	82*
Taro (Coco yam)	205*	210*	215*
Yams	155*	160*	165*
Other roots and tubers	260*	270*	280*
Pulses	19*	19*	19*
Groundnuts (in shell)	2*	2*	2*
Coconuts	760*	800*	800*
Copra	136†	140*	140*
Sugar cane	420*	430*	440*
Pineapples	7*	7*	8*
Bananas	840*	860*	880*
Coffee (green)	34.0†	39.0†	40.8†
Cocoa beans	29.3	23.7†	30.5†
Tea	2.8†	3.0†	3.2†
Natural rubber	5.8	5.9†	6.0*

* FAO estimate. † Unofficial figure.

Source: FAO, *Production Yearbook 1974.*

LIVESTOCK

	1972	1973*	1974*
Cattle	78,000	80,000	83,000
Goats	15,000*	15,000	15,000
Horses	1,000*	1,000	1,000
Pigs	1,100,000*	1,120,000	1,150,000
Chickens	990,000*	1,020,000	1,040,000

* FAO estimates.

Source: FAO, *Production Yearbook 1974.*

FORESTRY

ROUNDWOOD REMOVALS

('000 cubic metres)

	1970	1971	1972	1973	1974
Hardwood (non-coniferous)	434	645	767	767*	767*
Softwood (coniferous)	70	74	74	74*	74*
Fuelwood	4,250	4,350	4,450	4,450*	4,450*

* FAO estimates.

Source: FAO, *Yearbook of Forest Products 1963–74.*

SEA FISHING

('000 metric tons)

	1966	1967	1968	1969	1970	1971	1972	1973	1974
Total catch	15.0	15.0	15.4	16.1	18.7	33.3	29.9	48.5	52.7

Source: FAO, *Yearbook of Fishery Statistics 1974.*

MINING

(July 1st to June 30th)

		1970/71	1971/72	1972/73
Gold . . .	fine oz.	22,277	25,353	23,029
Silver . . .	fine oz.	16,897	18,923	17,816
Copper . .	tons	n.a.	140,779	495,088

FINANCE

100 toea=1 kina.
Coins: 1, 2, 5, 10 and 20 toea; 1 kina.
Notes: 2, 5 and 10 kina.
Exchange rates (June 1976): 1 kina=1 Australian dollar; £1 sterling=1.443 kina; U.S. $1=81.4 toea.
100 kina=£69.28=U.S. $122.90.

Note: The kina was introduced in April 1975, replacing (at par) the Australian dollar ($A). Australian currency remained legal tender until December 31st, 1975. The kina continues to be at par with the Australian dollar. Figures in this survey are sometimes expressed in Australian dollars. For previous changes in the exchange rate, *see* the chapter on Australia.

BUDGET

('000 kina, twelve months ending June 30th)

Revenue	1973/74	1974/75
Customs and excise . .	39,990	50,004
Other taxation . . .	61,397	89,502
Australian Government grant	135,269	156,282
Loan fund	41,387	50,330
Other revenue . . .	34,981	45,079
Total . .	313,024	391,196

Expenditure	1973/74	1974/75
Departmental	132,379	n.a.
Capital Works and Services .	50,028	n.a.
Other Expenditure . .	122,244	n.a.
Total . .	304,651	400,289

EXTERNAL TRADE*

(million kina, July 1st to June 30th)

	1966/67	1967/68	1968/69	1969/70	1970/71	1971/72	1972/73	1973/74	1974/75
Imports†	127.4	145.3	150.5	213.1	254.6	256.4	228.8	228.9	417.9
Exports f.o.b. . . .	52.3	69.4	74.4	92.8	101.2	126.4	228.6	482.1	428.5

* Figures include outside packaging and migrants' and travellers' dutiable effects but exclude gold, some parcel post and arms, ammunition and other equipment for military use.

† Imports are valued f.o.b. or at current domestic value in the exporting country, whichever is higher.

PRINCIPAL COMMODITIES
('000 kina)

Imports	1972/73	1973/74
Food and live animals . .	47,734	57,404
Beverages and tobacco .	5,025	4,289
Crude materials, except fuel .	749	769
Mineral fuels, lubricants etc.	11,102	19,642
Animal and vegetable oils and fats . .	357	471
Chemicals . . .	12,435	13,624
Manufactured goods . .	39,214	38,964
Machinery and transport equipment . .	73,533	61,666
Miscellaneous manufactured articles . .	21,791	22,202
Miscellaneous commodities and transactions . .	13,556	6,950

Exports	1973/74	1974/75*
Copra	23,672	29,287
Cocoa beans . . .	23,338	40,377
Coffee	28,847	33,513
Rubber	3,563	2,575
Tea	2,602	3,828
Timber (logs) . . .	11,588	7,480
Plywood . . .	3,571	2,663
Tuna	10,189	n.a.
Crayfish and prawns . .	3,432	n.a.
Copra oil . . .	13,761	14,286
Palm oil . . .	2,685	6,785
Copper ore and concentrates	311,909	236,657

* Preliminary.

PRINCIPAL TRADING PARTNERS
('000 kina)

Imports	1971/72	1972/73
Australia . . .	141,330	123,507
Germany, Fed. Rep. .	4,598	3,459
Japan	38,009	35,647
United Kingdom . .	11,415	9,242
U.S.A.	20,232	20,973

Exports (incl. gold)	1971/72	1972/73
Australia . . .	53,245	46,059
Germany, Fed. Rep. .	17,590	17,590
Japan	21,377	81,440
United Kingdom . .	13,264	11,365
U.S.A.	10,710	11,455

TRANSPORT

LICENSED VEHICLES
(December 1972)

Cars and station wagons .	20,057
Commercial vehicles .	14,673
Motor cycles . . .	3,047
Tractors	1,921

SHIPPING FREIGHT

		1970–71	1971–72	1972–73
Vessels entered	'000 gross reg. tons	3,545	n.a.	3,443
Vessels cleared	,, ,, ,, ,,	3,434	n.a.	3,452
Cargo unloaded	'000 long tons	1,498	1,620	1,526
Cargo loaded .	,, ,, ,,	865	933	1,585

CIVIL AVIATION*
(Twelve months ending June 30th, 1973)

Internal Flights	
Scheduled Services:	
Passengers embarked . .	514,788
Freight carried (short tons) .	8,141
Mail carried (short tons) .	1,085
Charter Services:	
Passengers embarked . .	221,186
Freight carried (short tons) .	20,211
Mail carried (short tons) .	112

Overseas Flights	
Passengers embarked . . .	219,616
Freight carried (short tons) . .	4,440
Mail carried (short tons) . . .	667

* Preliminary.

THE CONSTITUTION

A new constitution came into effect on September 16th, 1975, when Papua New Guinea became independent.

PREAMBLE

The national goals of the Independent State of Papua New Guinea are: integral human development, equality and participation in the development of the country, national sovereignty and self-reliance, conservation of natural resources and the environment and development primarily through the use of Papua New Guinean forms of social, political and economic organization.

BASIC RIGHTS

All people are entitled to the fundamental rights and freedoms of the individual whatever their race, tribe, places of origin, political opinion, colour, creed or sex. The individual's rights include the right to freedom, life and the protection of the law, freedom from inhuman treatment, forced labour, arbitrary search and entry, freedom of conscience, thought, religion, expression, assembly, association and employment, and the right to privacy. Papua New Guinea citizens also have the following special rights: the right to vote and stand for public office, the right to freedom of information and of movement, protection from unjust deprivation of property and equality before the law.

THE NATION

Papua New Guinea is a sovereign, independent state. There is a National Capital District which shall be the seat of government.

The constitution provides for various classes of citizenship. The age of majority is 19 years.

HEAD OF STATE

Her Majesty the Queen of Great Britain and Northern Ireland is Queen and Head of State of Papua New Guinea. The Head of State takes precedence in rank over all other persons in Papua New Guinea and the Governor-General takes precedence in rank immediately after the Head of State. The Head of State appoints and dismisses the Prime Minister on the proposal of Parliament and other ministers on the proposal of the Prime Minister and the Governor-General, Chief Justice and members of the Public Service Commission on the proposal of the National Executive Council. All the privileges, powers, functions, duties and responsibilities of the Head of State may be had, exercised or performed through the Governor-General.

GOVERNOR-GENERAL

The Governor-General must be a citizen who is qualified to be a member of Parliament or who is a mature person of good standing who enjoys the respect of the community. No one is eligible for appointment more than once unless Parliament approves by a two-thirds majority. No one is eligible for a third term. The Governor-General is appointed by the Head of State on the proposal of the National Executive Council in accordance with the decision of Parliament by simple majority vote. He may be dismissed by the Head of State on the proposal of the National Executive Council in accordance with a decision of the Council or of an absolute majority of Parliament. The normal term of office is six years. In the case of temporary or permanent absence, dismissal or suspension he may be replaced temporarily by the Speaker of the House of Assembly until such time as a new Governor-General is appointed.

THE GOVERNMENT

The Government comprises the National Parliament, the National Executive and the National Judicial System.

National Parliament

The National Parliament is the House of Assembly, a single chamber legislature of members elected from single-member open or provincial electorates and not more than three nominated members who are appointed on a two-thirds absolute majority vote of Parliament. The National Parliament has 102 members elected by universal adult suffrage. The normal term of office is five years. There is a Speaker and a Deputy Speaker, who must be members of Parliament and must be elected to these posts by Parliament. They cannot serve as Ministers concurrently.

National Executive

The National Executive comprises the Head of State and the National Executive Council. The Prime Minister, who presides over the National Executive Council, is appointed and dismissed by the Head of State on the proposal of Parliament. The other ministers, of whom there shall be not fewer than six nor more than a quarter of the number of members of the Parliament, are appointed and dismissed by the Head of State on the proposal of the Prime Minister. The National Executive Council consists of all the ministers, including the Prime Minister, and is responsible for the executive government of Papua New Guinea.

National Judicial System

The National Judicial System comprises the Supreme Court, the National Court and any other authorized courts. The judiciary is independent.

The Supreme Court consists of the Chief Justice, the Deputy Chief Justice and the other judges of the National Court. It is the final court of appeal. The Chief Justice is appointed and dismissed by the Head of State on the proposal of the National Executive Council after consultation with the Minister responsible for justice. The Deputy Chief Justice and the other judges are appointed by the Judicial and Legal Services Commission. The National Court consists of the Chief Justice, the Deputy Chief Justice and no less than four nor more than six, other judges.

The Constitution also makes provision for the establishment of the Magisterial Service and the establishment of the posts of Public Prosecutor and the Public Solicitor.

THE STATE SERVICES

The constitution establishes the following State Services which, with the exception of the Defence Force, are subject to ultimate civilian control.

National Public Service

The Public Service is managed by the Public Service Commission which consists of not fewer than four members appointed by the Head of State on the proposal of the National Executive Council. The Commission is responsible to the National Executive Council.

Police Force

The Police Force is subject to the control of the National Executive Council through a Minister and its function is to preserve peace and good order and to maintain and enforce the law. There shall be a Commissioner of Police who shall be responsible for the superintendence, efficient organization and control of the Force.

Papua New Guinea Defence Force

There shall be no office of Commander-in-Chief of the

Defence Force. The Defence Force is subject to the superintendence and control of the National Executive Council through the Minister of Defence. The functions of the Defence Force are to defend Papua New Guinea, to provide assistance to civilian authorities in a civil disaster, in the restoration of public order or during a period of declared national emergency.

The fourth State Service is the PARLIAMENTARY SERVICE.

The Constitution also includes sections on Public Finances, the office of Auditor-General, the Public Accounts Commission and the Ombudsman Commission, and the declaration of a State of National Emergency.

THE GOVERNMENT

Head of State: H.M. Queen ELIZABETH II.

Governor-General: Sir JOHN GUISE, G.C.M.G., K.B.E.

NATIONAL EXECUTIVE COUNCIL

(*July* 1976)

Prime Minister: MICHAEL THOMAS SOMARE.

Minister for Justice and Minister assisting the Prime Minister with Provincial Affairs and Local Government: EBIA OLEWALE.

Minister for Primary Industry: BOYAMO SALI.

Minister for Culture, Recreation and Youth Development: MOSES SASAKILA.

Minister for Foreign Affairs and Overseas Trade and Minister for Defence: Sir MAORI KIKI, K.B.E.

Minister for Education: KOBALE KALE.

Minister for the Environment and Conservation: STEPHEN TAGO.

Minister for Finance: JULIUS CHAN, C.B.E.

Minister for Health: Sir PAUL LAPUN.

Minister for Natural Resources: (vacant).

Minister for Labour, Commerce and Industry: GAVERA REA.

Minister for Transport, Works and Supply: BRUCE JEPHCOTT.

Minister for Police: JOHN POE.

Minister for Posts and Telegraphs: KAIBELT DIRIA.

Minister for Housing and Supply: YANO BELO.

Minister for Public Utilities: DONATUS MOLA.

Minister for Corrective Institutions and Liquor Licensing: PITA LUS.

Minister for Information and Broadcasting: Dr. REUBEN TAUREKA.

Minister for Provincial Affairs: OSCAR TAMMUR.

HOUSE OF ASSEMBLY

Speaker: BARRY HOLLOWAY.

Nominated Members: None appointed (the Papua New Guinea Act provides for the appointment of up to 3).

Elected Members: 102 (2 new seats were established in 1976, but previously 82 represented open electorates and 18 represented regional electorates).

POLITICAL PARTIES

Pangu Pati: f. 1967; urban-based; Senior party in National Coalition; Leader MICHAEL SOMARE.

Country Party: f. 1974 with aid of National Country Party of Australia, and composed of Coalition and Opposition backbenchers; stresses rural development. Leader SINAKE GIREGIRE.

People's Progress Party: f. 1970; member party in National Coalition; Chair. JULIUS CHAN, C.B.E.

National Party: P.O.B. 6545, Boroko; member party in National Coalition; Leader THOMAS KAVALI; Sec. BAVUNKE KAMAN.

United Party: f. 1969; main opposition party in House of Assembly; was opposed to early independence and stands for retaining links with Australia; Leader Sir TEI ABAL.

The Papuan republican movement comprises two major organizations: Papua Besena, led by Josephine Abaijah, and the Eriwo Development Association, led by Simon Kaumi. Associated with the movement are the Papua Black Power Movement and the Socialist Workers' Party.

DIPLOMATIC REPRESENTATION

(E: Embassy; H.C.: High Commission)

Japan: Port Moresby (E.); *Ambassador:* KOICHIRO YAMAGUCHI.

United Kingdom: United Church Building, 3rd Floor, Douglas St., Port Moresby, P.O.B. 739 (H.C.); *High Commissioner:* G. W. BAKER, M.B.E.

U.S.A.: Port Moresby (E.); *Ambassador:* MARY OLMSTED.

Papua New Guinea also has diplomatic relations with Australia, Fiji, India, Indonesia, the Republic of Korea, Malaysia, Mexico, New Zealand, the Philippines, Romania, Singapore, Thailand and the U.S.S.R.

JUDICIAL SYSTEM

Supreme Court of Papua New Guinea: Chief Justice The Hon. Sir THOMAS SYDNEY FROST.

Registrar: RICHARD C. H. TEO.

The National Court is the highest judicial authority in the country. Appeals may be made from decisions of a single judge to the Supreme Court. District Courts deal with summary and non-indictable offences. In addition, Local Courts deal with minor offences, including matters regulated by native custom and are open to all races. They have limited jurisdiction in land matters. Wardens Courts have jurisdiction over civil cases respecting mining or mining lands and offences against mining laws. Cases involving land are heard by the Land Titles Commission from which appeals lie to the National Court. Children's Courts deal with cases involving minors.

RELIGION

The indigenous population is pantheistic. There are many Missionary Societies.

ANGLICAN

Bishop of New Guinea: Rt. Rev. G. DAVID HAND, M.A., Box 806, Port Moresby.

ROMAN CATHOLIC

Archbishop of Madang: Most Rev. ADOLPH NOSER, S.V.D., Archbishop's Residence, P.O., Alexishafen, Madang.

Archbishop of Port Moresby: Most Rev. HERMAN TOPAIVU, Catholic Mission, P.O.B. 82, Port Moresby.

Archbishop of Rabaul: Most Rev. JOHANNES HÖHNE, M.S.C., Archbishop's House, P.O.B. 414, Rabaw.

ECUMENIST

The United Church in Papua New Guinea and the Solomon Islands: P.O.B. 3401, Port Moresby; f. 1968 by union of the Methodist Church in Melanesia, the Papua Ekalesia and United Church, Port Moresby; 90,000 communicant mems.

THE PRESS

Lae Nius: Lae; f. 1974; twice weekly; Man. Editor PAUL COX; circ. 5,000.

Papua New Guinea Post-Courier: P.O.B. 85, Port Moresby; f. 1969; independent; daily; Editor DOUGLAS LOCKWOOD.

Our News: Office of Information, Prime Minister's Department, P.O.B. 2312, Konedobu; f. 1960; fortnightly in English; circ. 17,000.

Wantok: Catholic Mission, Wewak; fortnightly in Pidgin; aimed at rural readership; Editor Father MIHALIC; circ. 9,000.

There are numerous news sheets and magazines published by Local Government Councils, Co-operative Societies, Missions and government departments. They are variously in English, Pidgin, Motu and vernacular languages.

PRESS AGENCY

International News Service Papua New Guinea: P.O.B. 5050, Boroko; f. 1969; Man. Editor JOHN L. RYAN.

RADIO AND TELEVISION

National Broadcasting Commission of Papua New Guinea: P.O.B. 1359, Boroko; f. 1973; broadcasting in English, Pidgin, Hiri Motu and ten major vernaculars; Chair. SAM PINIAU; Dir. of Programmes CAROLUS KETSIMUR.

Television New Guinea: P.O.B. 5050, Boroko; f. 1970; Exec. Dir. JOHN L. RYAN.

The Papua New Guinea Service of Radio Australia is also received.

There were 110,000 radio sets in 1975.

FINANCE

CENTRAL BANK

Bank of Papua New Guinea: P.O.B. 121, Douglas St., Port Moresby; f. 1973; bank of issue; cap. $A5 m.; dep. $A26.9 m. (June 1974); Gov. HENRY TOROBERT; Deputy Gov. P. S. FERGUSON; Sec. E. TOKAIVOVO.

COMMERCIAL BANKS

Australia and New Zealand Banking Group Limited: Port Moresby; Man. T. A. WHITEMAN.

Bank of New South Wales (P.N.G.) Ltd.: Port Moresby; Chief Man. L. J. RITSON.

Bank of South Pacific Ltd.: P.O.B. 173, Douglas St., Port Moresby; f. 1974; subsidiary of the National Bank of Australasia; cap. K2 m.; Chair. Sir JAMES FORREST; Chief Man. F. B. ELLIOTT.

Bank of Australia: Port Moresby and Rabaul.

Papua New Guinea Banking Corporation: P.O.B. 78, Port Moresby; f. 1974; cap. K.10m.; dep. K.85m. (June 1975); Man. Dir. W. H. CLARK; Sec. R. J. WILSON.

DEVELOPMENT BANK

Papua New Guinea Development Bank: P.O.B. 6310, Boroko; f. 1965; cap. $A24m.; f. 1967; Man. Dir. A. R. REDMAN.

SAVINGS AND LOAN SOCIETIES

Registry of Savings and Loan Societies: P.O.B. 121, Port Moresby: 136 Savings and Loan Societies; mems. 68,188; total funds A$4,478,230; loans outstanding A$2,903,369; investments A$729,655; 60 Savings Clubs: mems. 4,612; total funds A$70,195.

INSURANCE

There are branches of several of the principal Australian and United Kingdom insurance companies in Port Moresby, Rabaul, Lae and Kieta.

TRADE AND INDUSTRY

INDUSTRIAL AND DEVELOPMENT ORGANIZATIONS

Department of Business Services: government body providing advisory service to extensive system of industrial co-operatives.

Investment Corporation: f. 1975; government body formed to support local enterprise and to purchase shares in foreign businesses operating in Papua New Guinea.

National Investment and Development Authority (NIDA): f. 1975; statutory body formed to protect indigenous enterprises and employment; to register foreign investment and to regulate it both in quantity and in regard to specific sectors.

TRADE UNIONS

Papua New Guinea Trade Union Congress: Port Moresby; co-ordinates majority of trade unions; Pres. TONY ILA; Sec. TOM COLLINS.

Bank Officials' Association of Papua New Guinea: c/o Dept. of Labour, Port Moresby; Pres. M. S. MORE; Sec. D. J. THACKERAY.

Bougainville Mineworkers' Union: Kieta, Bougainville; Pres. HENRY MOSES.

Goroka Workers' Association: c/o Radio Goroka, Goroka; f. 1964; Pres. M. KAUTIL; Sec. F. KOMBUGUN; 91 mems.

Lae Miscellaneous Workers' Union: P.O.B. 1103, Lae; Pres. SAM MIMILONG; 5,000 mems.

Madang Workers' Association: c/o Dept. of Labour, Madang; f. 1961; Pres. P. NAIME; Sec. A. MALAMBES; 388 mems.

Manus District Workers' Association: c/o Dept. of Labour, Port Moresby.

Milne Bay Workers' Association: c/o Milne Bay Native Societies Asscn. Ltd., Samurai; f. 1965; Pres. P. MATASARORO; Sec. J. FIFITA; 445 mems.

New Ireland District Workers' Association: P.O.B. 25, Kavieng; Pres. A. ABOM; Sec. M. CHILCOTT; 292 mems.

Northern District Workers' Association: c/o Dept. of Labour, Popondetta; f. 1965; Pres. P. AREK; Sec. P. SORODA; 220 mems.

Papua New Guinea Teachers' Association: P.O.B. 6546, Boroko; f. 1971; Pres. Ms. R. KEKEDO; Industrial Officer R. PRICE; publs. *Teacher*; 10 newsletters per year; 10,500 mems.

Police Association of Papua New Guinea: P.O.B. 903, Port Moresby; f. 1964; Pres. Sub-Insp. L. DEBESSA; Gen. Sec. J. SHIELDS; 3,000 mems.; publ. *Kumul*.

Port Moresby Workers' Association: P.O.B. 123, Port Moresby; f. 1961; Pres. OALA OALA RARUA; Sec. A. T. CHAPMAN; 50 mems.

Public Service Association: P.O.B. 2033, Konedobu, Port Moresby; brs. at other PNG centres; f. 1947; 18,560 mems.; Pres. (*a.i.*) J. AOAE; Gen. Sec. J. T. LEMEKI; publ. *PSA Bulletin*.

Rabaul Workers' Association: P.O.B. 688, Rabaul; Pres. JAMES KALULA; Sec. K. J. BOTT; 1,052 mems.

Senior Police Officers' Guild: P.O.B. 2085, Konedobu; f. 1968; Pres. B. A. BEATTIE; Sec. K. R. GASCOIGNE; 50 mems.

Timber Workers' Association of Wau-Bulolo: P.O.B. 105, Bulolo; f. 1964; Pres. ROMPIER SIMAN; Sec. GEORGE NIMAGI; 667 mems.

Western Highlands District Workers' Association: c/o Dept. of Labour, Mount Hagen; Pres. JAMES T. OVIA; Sec. JOSEPH AVAKA; Treas. BEN PUKARE; 260 mems.

Wewak Workers' Association: c/o Dept. of Labour, Wewak; f. 1964; Pres. J. BULA; Sec. Y. WRINDIMA; 393 mems.

TRANSPORT

ROADS

In 1974 there were over 12,000 km. of surfaced roads in Papua New Guinea, of which over 3,600 were classified as highways or trunk roads. There are plans to extend the national highway with the aim of completing a trans-national highway linking Port Moresby with the Highlands and the north coast.

SHIPPING

Papua New Guinea has 13 major ports and a coastal fleet of about 300 vessels.

Regular passenger and cargo services to Australia are maintained by Conpac (Burns Philp and Co. Ltd. and Australia West Pacific Line), China Navigation Co. Ltd., Karlander New Guinea Line Ltd., and Austasia Line, Amplex New Guinea Line, Keith Holland Shipping Co., Farrell Lines, New Guinea Express Lines and New Guinea Australia Lines. Various ships of these companies also call at Asian ports. The Bank Line provides a regular cargo service between the Territory and Europe, while the New Zealand Export Line operates regular services between Papua New Guinea, New Zealand and the Pacific Islands. Farrell Lines also operate services from the United States and Canada.

CIVIL AVIATION

An international airport is being built at Port Moresby with Australian finance and another, at Lae, to handle medium-sized jets, is expected to be operational at the same time: late 1976.

Air Niugini: P.O.B. 84, Port Moresby; f. 1973; the national airline, using aircraft chartered from Ansett Airlines of Australia and Trans-Australia Airlines (TAA) operates, in conjunction with Qantas, services between Papua New Guinea and Australia; also operates services to the Solomon Islands and Indonesia; fleet of 10 Fokker F-27, 12 DC-3, 1 Boeing 720B; Gen. Man. BRYAN GREY.

Panga Airways Ltd.: P.O.B. 1335, Lae; f. 1949; helicopter and aircraft services; bases at Lae, Rabaul, Kavieng and Hoskins; Exec. Dir. K. H. GODDARD; Gen. Man. J. M. CRUIKSHANK.

Talair Pty. Ltd.: P.O.B. 108, Goroka; f. 1952; regular services to about 90 Papua New Guinea and Solomon Islands airports and charter service; fleet of 26 Twin Otter and Cessna Twin; also acquired fleet of 23 aircraft by takeover in 1975; Man. Dir. R. D. BUCHANAN, M.H.A.

Ansett Airlines runs a service from Australia to Papua New Guinea, and Qantas operates 4 flights a week between Sydney and Port Moresby, two calling at Brisbane. Qantas also provides services between Papua New Guinea and Singapore. Air Pacific operates between Fiji and Port Moresby. Internal services are provided by Bougainville Air Services Pty. Ltd. as well as by Air Niugini.

DEFENCE

On March 6th, 1975, the Papua New Guinea Government took over the Papua New Guinea Defence Force from Australia. The force comprises two infantry battalions, a patrol boat squadron and landing craft. Air-support is still provided by Australia but the Defence Force expects to run its own air operations by the end of 1976.

EDUCATION

Education from pre-school to tertiary level is available in Papua New Guinea although facilities are still inadequate and unevenly distributed. There are about 650 primary schools, 70 secondary schools, 35 tertiary institutions, including teacher training colleges and religious institutions, and two universities.

An average of 58 per cent of primary school age children attend school. In some areas, such as East New Britain and Port Moresby, almost all children attend school whereas in others, such as the Highlands provinces, as few as 34 per cent do. Access to higher education ranges from 7 per cent in the Eastern Highlands to almost 50 per cent in East New Britain.

It is hoped to place greater emphasis on teaching vocational and agricultural skills at village schools.

UNIVERSITIES

University of Papua New Guinea: P.O.B. 1144, Boroko, Port Moresby; 238 teachers, 2,343 students.

Papua New Guinea University of Technology: P.O.B. 793, Lae; 100 teachers, 1,100 students.

Pitcairn Islands

The Pitcairn Islands consists of Pitcairn Island and three uninhabited islands, Henderson, Ducie and Oeno. Pitcairn, situated at 25°04'S and 130°06'W and about halfway between Panama and New Zealand, has an area of 4.5 square kilometres and a population of 67 in 1975. The economy is based on subsistence agriculture, fishing, handicrafts and the sale of postage stamps. The Pitcairn Islands are administered by the British High Commission in New Zealand, with the High Commissioner acting as Governor, in consultation with an Island Council of four elected, five nominated and one ex-officio members.

Governor: HAROLD SMEDLEY, C.M.G., M.B.E. (British High Commissioner in New Zealand).

Commissioner: REGINALD HICKS.

ISLAND COUNCIL

Island Magistrate: IVAN CHRISTIAN.

Island Secretary (*ex-officio*): BEN CHRISTIAN.

Members: BRIAN YOUNG, TOM CHRISTIAN, OSCAR CLARK, STEVE CHRISTIAN, THELMA BROWN, FLORENCE YOUNG, Pastor J. NEWMAN, T. WHIU.

Solomon Islands

GEOGRAPHY

The Solomon Islands comprises the major islands of Choiseul, Santa Isabel, New Georgia, Malaita, Guadalcanal and San Cristobal, plus numerous small islands, totalling 29,785 square kilometres in area. Much of the Solomon Islands remains under dense tropical rainforest; extensive tracts of native and introduced grassland cover the northern plains of Guadalcanal. The total population in 1976 was 196,708, which included 1,300 Europeans, 700 Chinese, about 2,000 Micronesians resettled from the Gilbert Islands and about 5,300 Polynesians from the Polynesian "outliers" in the western Pacific near the Solomons. The rate of population growth is very high.

HISTORY

First European contacts with the island economy in the 1500s caused little change. It was not until the nineteenth century that traders, whalers and missionaries began to establish outposts on the main islands. Forcible recruiting of labour, spread from the New Hebrides to the Solomons during the 1860s. The Solomons became a British Protectorate in 1893, and until 1952 were governed from Fiji.

The British Solomon Islands Protectorate became the Solomon Islands on January 2nd, 1976. In 1960 a Legislative Council and Executive Council were set up with an appointed membership. These bodies were revised in 1964 to provide for a council of three ex-officio, eight official, eight elected and two nominated members. Further revisions in 1967 and 1970 increased the number of elected members to 14. After general elections in 1973, a new Governing Council of 24 elected members was constituted and a ministerial system introduced. Solomon Mamaloni, leader of the People's Progress Party (PPP), was elected Chief Minister in August 1974. Following the announcement of self-government in January 1976, arrangements for independence in July or August 1977 were tentatively proposed. Immediately before the announcement the Chief Minister resigned, the Cabinet was radically re-organized and Solomon Mamaloni was re-elected. The new cabinet contained five members of the PPP's former opposition, the United Solomon Islands Party, After a general election in June 1976, which was not fought on party lines, a new Chief Minister, Peter Kenilorea, was chosen by the Assembly.

ECONOMY

In an attempt to diversify the economy away from the single export crop copra, a number of resource surveys were carried out during the 1950s and 1960s.

A heavily mineralized area at Betilonga and in the Sutakiki Valley has been investigated for gold, silver and copper and an asbestos deposit at Kumboro on Choiseul has been surveyed. On Rennell and Wagina Islands bauxite mining seems certain to go ahead. The companies involved are the Mitsui Mining and Smelting Company of Japan and Conzinc Rio Tinto of Australia. On Bellona Island an estimated 10 million metric tons of phosphate rock is under investigation. The other main resource in the Solomons is timber. Rice and cattle farming are being developed on the grasslands, the latter largely in association with investment from Australia.

STATISTICS

Area: Land 29,785 square kilometres.

Population (1976 census): 196,708; Honiara (capital) 14,993.

Employment (1974): Persons in paid employment 13,384.

Agriculture (1975): Copra 26,051 tons; Cocoa 1,175 tons; Rice 1,257 tons; Timber (logs) 7.9 million cu. ft.; Cattle 22,668 head.

Fishing: 11,585 metric tons landed in 1974.

Finance: Australian currency: 100 cents=1 Australian dollar ($A). Coins: 1, 2, 5, 10, 20 and 50 cents. Notes: 1, 2, 5, 10, 20 and 50 dollars. Exchange rates (June 1976): £1 sterling=$A1.443; U.S. $1=81.4 Australian cents; $A100=£69.28=U.S. $122.90. *Note:* for previous changes in the exchange rate, *see* the chapter on Australia. The Solomon Islands will possibly introduce a new currency in 1977.

Budget (1976): Estimated revenue is $A18.42 million recurrent (including British Development Aid of $A5.75 million, aid from other countries of $A2.41 million and Grant-in-Aid to the recurrent expenditure from the United Kingdom of $A1.6 million).

External Trade (1975): *Imports:* $A22,273,000 (mainly machinery and transport, food and manufactured articles); *Exports* $A11,851,000 (mainly fish, timber, copra, marine shells, scrap metal, manufactured tobacco, cocoa). Imports were mainly from Australia, and exports to Japan and Western Europe.

THE CONSTITUTION

The 1974 constitution established the office of Governor of the Protectorate. It introduced a Legislative Assembly, whose 24 elected members choose a Chief Minister who in turn chooses his Ministers from the Legislature to form a Council of Ministers. The members of the Council of Ministers are collectively responsible to the Legislative Assembly for any advice given to the Governor. The Governor is responsible for defence, external affairs, internal security and the public service, and enjoys certain discretionary powers. Internal self-government was instituted on January 2nd, 1976, with independence to follow 12 to 18 months later. Early in 1976 an Order in Council was made to increase the Legislative Assembly from 24 to 38 members and a General Election was held in June 1976 returning this increased number.

Governor: Sir Donald C. C. Luddington, K.B.E., C.M.G., C.V.O.

THE GOVERNMENT

(*July* 1976)

Chief Minister: Peter Kenilorea.

Minister of Home Affairs: Francis Billy Hilly.

Minister of Foreign Trade, Industries and Labour: Pulepada Ghemu.

Minister of Health and Welfare: Daniel Ho'ota.

Minister of Education and Cultural Affairs: Mariano Kelesi.

Minister of Agriculture and Lands: Sethuel James Kelly.

Minister of Finance: Benedict Kinika.

Minister of Works and Public Utilities: John Tepaika.

Minister of Natural Resources: Paul John Tovua.

COUNCIL OF MINISTERS

The Council consists of the Chief Minister, who is the President of the Council, and eight other ministers.

LOCAL GOVERNMENT COUNCILS

The number of Local Councils was reduced from 9 to 8 in 1975 when the Makira and Ulawa Councils were amalgamated. These councils cover almost the whole country and vary widely in size and wealth. All the members of the Local Councils are elected by universal adult suffrage. The majority of the Councils' revenue derives from an annual basic rate. Honiara is the only town with a town council.

POLITICAL PARTIES

In 1976 there were four political parties. They are the People's Progress Party (PPP), the United Solomon Islands Party (USIPA) and two newly formed parties: the Nationalist Party, a political association connected with the Solomon Islands General Workers' Union, and the Melanesian Action Party.

JUDICIAL SYSTEM

The High Court is a Superior Court of Record with jurisdiction and powers as prescribed by the Solomon Islands Constitution or by any law for the time being in force in the Solomon Islands. The Judges of the High Court are the Chief Justice, resident in the Solomon Islands and employed by their government, and Puisne Judges, who are non-resident and visit the territory as and when necessary, as prescribed by the Governor. Appeals from this Court go to the Fiji Court of Appeal and ultimately, in certain cases, to Her Majesty in Council.

In addition there are Magistrates' Courts staffed by lay magistrates exercising limited jurisdiction in both civil and criminal matters. There are also Native Courts staffed by elders of the native communities which have jurisdiction in the areas of established native custom, petty crime and local government by-laws. In 1975 a Customary Lands Appeals Court was established to hear land appeals from local courts.

Chief Justice of the High Court: R. B. Davis, O.B.E.

RELIGION

Most of the people are Christian, and the remainder still follow their traditional animism.

Church of Melanesia (Anglican): Archbishop of Melanesia: The Very Rev. N. K. Palmer.

Roman Catholic: Bishop of Honiara, Most Rev. Daniel Stuyvenberg, S.M., C.B.E.

Methodist: Bishop of Solomon Islands, Rev. John Pratt.

THE PRESS

Solomon News Drum: f. 1975; Government Information Service; weekly.

There is no local independent commercial newspaper, although efforts have been made to establish one. There is a monthly or two-monthly journal of comment, the *Kakamora Reporter*, which is produced by a small committee and has a significant circulation among educated Solomon Islanders. There is one other regular periodical published by the Melanesian Mission (Anglican).

RADIO

In early 1976 the only broadcasting service on the Solomon Islands was owned and operated by the Government. However, it is planned to make this service a Statutory Corporation in late 1976.

Daily transmission (on VQO–1030 KHz, VQO5–5020 KHz and VQO9–9545 KHz) are mainly in Pidgin with a certain amount of simple English. Almost 50 per cent of the programming is produced from locally recorded material. The Solomon Islands Broadcasting Service (SIBS) operates a Schools Broadcasting Service with 14 hours of programmes a week. Other programmes include the national news, prepared by the Government Information Service and world news from the BBC and Radio Australia.

FINANCE

BANKING

Australia and New Zealand Banking Group Ltd.: Honiara.

Commonwealth Banking Corporation of Australia: Honiara.

Hong Kong and Shanghai Banking Corporation: Honiara; P.O. Gizo, Western Solomons.

Solomon Islands Agricultural and Industrial Loans Board: Honiara.

INSURANCE

About ten of the principal British insurance companies maintain agencies in the territory.

TRADE AND INDUSTRY

Solomon Islands Chamber of Commerce: P.O.B. 64, Honiara.

Solomon Islands Copra Board: P.O.B. 454, Honiara; sole exporter of copra; agencies at Yandina and Gizo.

CO-OPERATIVE SOCIETIES

In 1976 there were 233 primary co-operative societies working mostly outside the capital.

TRANSPORT

ROADS

There were 283 miles of main road in 1976. Road construction and maintenance is difficult because of the nature of the country, and what roads there are serve as feeder roads to the main town of an island. Honiara now has a main road running about 40 miles each side of it along the north coast of Guadalcanal, and Malaita has a road 98 miles long running north from Auki and around the northern end of the island to the Lau Lagoon, where canoe transport takes over; and one running south for 17 miles to Bina. On Makira a road has been built linking Kira Kira and Kakoragana, a distance of 34 miles.

SHIPPING

Regular shipping services (mainly for freight) exist between the Solomons and Australia (Sydney and Brisbane), New Zealand, Bougainville (Kieta), Hong Kong, Japan and U.K./Continent ports. Internal shipping is provided by 33 ships of the government marine fleet and about 120 commercial vessels. Gross tonnage is 3,620. The two main ports are at Honiara and Gizo. The ports are controlled by the Solomon Islands Ports Authority.

Solomon Islands Ports Authority: P.O.B. 307, Honiara; Chair. M. Kelesi.

Shipping services to the Solomon Islands are provided by the Bank Line (monthly services to and from Europe), the Daiwa Navigation Co. (to and from Japan each month via Pacific ports), Japan South Pacific (regular five-weekly service to Japan), New Guinea Australia Line (three-weekly services from Australia via Papua New Guinea), and Sofrano (regular six-weekly services to New Zealand, Papua New Guinea and the New Hebrides). Several cruise lines also call at the Solomons. The chief ones are Shaw Savill Line, Sitmar Line and Dominion Far East Line. Oil tankers also call to supply the Solomons.

CIVIL AVIATION

Solomon Islands Airways Ltd. (Solair): P.O.B. 23, Honiara; internal services and charter. Fleet of 1 Beechcraft Baron, 1 Britten-Norman Islander and 1 Beechcraft Queen-Air.

International air services to the Islands are provided by Air Pacific.

TOURISM

Solomon Islands Tourist Authority: P.O.B. 321, Honiara f. 1972; Chair. F. Saemala.

EDUCATION

In 1975 28,219 children attended the 266 aided and 78 private primary schools and 1,535 children attended the six secondary schools. In 1976 an additional 800 students attended the four new secondary schools which provide practical two year courses in technical and commercial subjects, mainly subsistence village agriculture. By 1980 the country is to have 20 new secondary schools.

Tokelau Islands

The Tokelau group consists of three atolls, Atafu, Nukunono and Fakaofo, which lie 300 miles north of Western Samoa.

The islands became a British protectorate in 1877. At the request of the inhabitants Britain annexed the islands in 1916 and included them within the Gilbert and Ellice Islands Colony. In 1925 the United Kingdom Government transferred administrative control to the Governor-General of New Zealand. In 1946, the Group was officially designated the Tokelau Islands and in 1948 sovereignty was transferred to New Zealand. From 1962 until the end of 1971 the High Commissioner for New Zealand in Western Samoa was also the Administrator of the Tokelau Islands. In November 1974 the administration of the Tokelau Islands was transferred to the Ministry of Foreign Affairs in New Zealand.

STATISTICS

AREA (acres)

ATAFU	NUKUNONU	FAKAOFO	TOTAL
500	1,350	650	2,500

POPULATION

Total (September 1975): 1,603 (Atafu 564, Nukunonu 374, Fakaofo 665).

FINANCE

Currency: 100 cents=1 New Zealand dollar ($NZ). For details, *see* the Cook Islands.

BUDGET
(April 1st to March 31st)

1975/76: Revenue $NZ 62,625; Expenditure $NZ 540,022.

Financial aid from New Zealand totalling $NZ1,400,000 for three years 1974/75 to 1976/77 was announced in February 1974.

Revenue is derived mainly from copra export duty, import duty, and sale of postage stamps. Expenditure is devoted mainly to the provision of social services, particularly health, education, and agriculture.

EXTERNAL TRADE

In 1975/76 copra exports totalled $NZ74,171. There were no other exports. The main imports are foodstuffs, building materials and kerosene.

TRANSPORT

The Group is visited five or six times per year by vessels under charter.

GOVERNMENT

The administration of the Tokelau Islands is the responsibility of the Ministry of Foreign Affairs in New Zealand. The Secretary of Foreign Affairs is the Administrator and certain powers are delegated to a Senior Administrative Officer (formerly District Officer) and senior officers of the Ministry of Foreign Affairs. By agreement with the government of Western Samoa, the office of the Tokelau Islands administration is based in Apia.

LOCAL GOVERNMENT

There is a *Faipule* (who is also the magistrate) on each island who is democratically elected by the people triennially. He is responsible to the Administrator and presides over the Council of Elders (*Fono*).

RELIGION

On Atafu and Fakaofo most inhabitants are members of the London Missionary Society; on Nukunonu all are Roman Catholic.

EDUCATION

The Administration and Churches co-operate in this field. There are three schools, one on each atoll. In 1975 there were 34 trained Tokelauan teachers on the islands. The New Zealand government supplies all educational equipment. Schools receive daily radio broadcasts from the Western Samoan Education Department. Scholarships are awarded for secondary and tertiary education in Western Samoa, Fiji and New Zealand.

Tonga

GEOGRAPHY

The Kingdom of Tonga, which is located in the central South Pacific east of Fiji and south of Samoa, comprises about 150 islands, totalling 700 square kilometres in area. The islands lie in two lines, those to the west being volcanic and those to the east being coral islands. They are divided into three groups, Vava'u in the north, Ha'apai and Tongatapu in the south. In 1975 the population of Tonga was estimated to be 100,105, more than half of whom were resident on Tongatapu. The inhabitants of the islands are Polynesians.

HISTORY

From about the 10th century Tongan society developed a lineage of sacred chiefs, who gradually became effective rulers. Since European contact, the chiefs have become known as kings. In 1900 Tonga became a British Protected State; in 1958 and 1967 it gained increased control over internal affairs and in June 1970 became fully independent.

ECONOMY

The economy is based on agriculture. Coconuts and bananas form the bulk of Tonga's exports. Two five-year development plans, for 1965-70 and 1970-75, both aimed at stimulating coconut production and tourism. Every adult male is allotted 3.3 hectares of land in which to garden, plus a building site in his village, although all land remains the property of the Crown. Alienation of land is forbidden.

There is a high rate of migration to New Zealand and Australia. Unemployed Tongans in New Zealand and illegal immigrants in Australia have caused both countries to restrict the entry of Tongans to those with return tickets or guaranteed employment. A marked imbalance in the Tongan population and a lack of skilled labour in the islands have been secondary outcomes of these movements.

STATISTICAL SURVEY

Area: 700 square kilometres. There are about 150 islands.

Population: 1975 estimate 100,105; Nuku'alofa (capital) 25,000 (1973 estimate).

Agriculture (1974, metric tons, FAO estimates): Coconuts 115,000, Sweet Potatoes 77,000, Cassava 26,000, Copra 13,500, Bananas 4,000, Oranges 2,000.

Livestock (1975): Pigs 39,882, Horses 7,727, Cattle 6,396.

Currency: 100 seniti (cents) = 1 pa'anga (Tongan dollar). Coins: 1, 2, 5, 10, 20 and 50 seniti; 1 and 2 pa'anga Notes: 50 seniti; 1, 2, 5 and 10 pa'anga. Exchange rates (June 1976): £1 sterling = $T1.385; U.S.$1 = 78.1 Tongan cents. $T100 = £72.19 = U.S. $128.00.

Budget ($T'000): (1974-75): Revenue 5,530.2; Expenditure 4,772.6; (1975-76 estimate): Revenue 5,256.6; Expenditure 5,896.6.

External Trade (1974-75 estimate): *Imports:* $T12,970,600 (mainly food and textiles); *Exports:* $T4,613,200 (mainly copra and bananas). Trade is chiefly with the Commonwealth.

Transport: *Roads* (1974): Commercial Vehicles 785, Private Vehicles 427, Motor Cycles 248; *Shipping* (1974): Tonnage entered and cleared 611,281 tons; *Civil Aviation* (1974): Aircraft arriving 399.

THE CONSTITUTION

The Constitution of Tonga is based on that granted in 1875 by King George Tupou I. It provides for a government consisting of the Sovereign, a Privy Council and Cabinet, a Legislative Assembly and a Judiciary. Limited law-making power is vested in the Privy Council and any legislation passed by the Executive is subject to review by the Legislature.

The Privy Council is appointed by the Sovereign and consists of the Sovereign and the Cabinet.

The Cabinet consists of a Prime Minister, a Deputy Prime Minister, other Ministers and the Governors of Ha'apai and Vava'u.

The Legislative Assembly consists of the Speaker (President), the Cabinet, the Representatives of the Nobles (7) and the elected Representatives of the People (7). Franchise is open to all male literate Tongans of 21 and over who pay taxes, and all female literate Tongans aged 21 and over. There are elections every three years, and the Assembly must meet at least once every year.

Elections to the Assembly were held in May 1975.

THE GOVERNMENT

The Sovereign: H.M. King Taufa'ahau Tupou IV, G.C.V.O., K.C.M.G., K.B.E.

CABINET

(*July* 1976)

Prime Minister, Minister of Foreign Affairs, Agriculture, Tourism and Telegraphs and Telephones: H.R.H. Prince Fatafehi Tu'ipelehake, C.B.E.

Deputy Prime Minister and Minister of Lands: Hon. Tuita.

Minister of Police: Hon. 'Akau'ola.

Minister of Education and Works: Hon. Dr. S. Langi Kavaliku.

Minister of Industries, Commerce and Labour: Hon. the Baron Vaea.

Minister of Health and Acting Minister of Finance: Hon. Dr. Sione Tapa.

Governor of Ha'apai: Hon. Va'ehala.

Governor of Vava'u: Hon. Ma'afu Tupou.

DIPLOMATIC REPRESENTATION

EMBASSIES AND HIGH COMMISSIONS ACCREDITED TO TONGA

Embassy (E); High Commission (HC).

Australia: Suva, Fiji (HC); *High Commissioner:* H. W. Bullock.

Belgium: Wellington, New Zealand (E); *Ambassador:* H. Matsaert.

Canada: Wellington, New Zealand (HC); *High Commissioner:* Clive E. Glover.

France: Wellington, New Zealand (E); *Ambassador:* Albert de Schonen.

India: Suva, Fiji (HC); *High Commissioner:* Bhagwan Singh.

Japan: Wellington, New Zealand (E); *Ambassador:* Hideho Tanaka.

Korea, Republic: Canberra, Australia (E); *Ambassador:* SUK-CHAN LO.

New Zealand: Apia, Western Samoa (HC); *High Commissioner:* PAUL COTTON.

United Kingdom: Nuku'alofa, Tonga (HC); *High Commissioner:* HUMPHREY ARTHINGTON-DAVY, O.B.E.

U.S.A.: Wellington, New Zealand (E); *Ambassador:* ARMISTEAD I. SELDEN, Jnr.

Tonga also has diplomatic relations with the U.S.S.R.

JUDICIAL SYSTEM

There are Magistrates' Courts, a Land Court, Supreme Court and Court of Appeal.

There are eight Magistrates, and appeals from the Magistrates' Courts are heard by the Supreme Court. In cases which come before the Supreme Court the accused, or either party in a civil suit, may elect for a jury trial. The Chief Justice is resident in Tonga and appeals from the Supreme Court are heard by the Privy Council as a Court of Appeal. The Chief Justice is Judge of the Supreme Court and of the Land Court in which he sits with a Tongan assessor.

Chief Justice and Judge of the Land Court: H. STEAD ROBERTS.

RELIGION

The Tongans are Christian, 77 per cent belonging to sects of the Wesleyan faith. There is also a small number of Roman Catholics. Fourteen denominations are represented in total.

Roman Catholic: Bishop of Tonga Most Rev. PATELISIO PUNOU-KI-HIHIFO FINAU, Bishop's House, P.O.B. 1, Nuku'Alofa.

PRESS AND RADIO

Press: *The Chronicle:* A weekly newspaper, sponsored by the Government; f. 1964; Editor S. H. FONUA; circ. (Tongan) 4,300, (English) 1,200.

There is a regular issue of Church newspapers by the various missions.

Radio: *Tonga Broadcasting Commission:* P.O.B. 36, Nuku'alofa; started operating July 1961, government and commercially sponsored; programmes from two 10 kW. medium wave 1020 kHz transmitters in English and Tongan with some Fijian and Samoan; Man. DAVID PORTER. In 1975 there were 15,000 receivers.

FINANCE

BANKING

Bank of Tonga: P.O.B. 924, Nuku'alofa; owned by Government of Tonga, Bank of Hawaii, Bank of New Zealand and Bank of New South Wales; full commercial banking facilities; dep. over $T5 million; Chair. Mr. TAIT (Bank of N.S.W.).

TRADE AND INDUSTRY

DEVELOPMENT ORGANIZATION

Commodities Board: non-profit making organization formed to incorporate the Copra, Construction and Produce Divisions (formerly Boards); Chair. H.R.H. Prince TU'IPELHAKE; Dir. F. V. SEVELE, PH.D.

Copra Division: P.O.B. 27, Nuku'alofa; f. 1941; non-profit making board controlling the export of coconut and all coconut products; Chair. Minister of Agriculture.

Construction Division: P.O.B. 28, Nuku'alofa; f. 1958 to carry out the construction programme of the Copra Board as well as those of government, local bodies and private concerns; commission agents for imports and exports; Chair. H.R.H. Prince TU'IPELEHAKE, C.B.E.

Produce Division: P.O.B. 84, Nuku'alofa; formerly the Tonga Produce Board; non-profit making organization controlling the export of bananas, pineapples, water melons, taros and other root crops, fresh vegetables, kava and cured vanilla beans on behalf of growers; Gen. Man. A. JOHANSSON.

In 1974 the first co-operative society registered under the Agricultural Organization Act was set up.

TRANSPORT

ROADS

There are about 120 miles of all-weather metalled roads on Tongatapu and 44 miles on Vava'u. Total mileage in Tonga including fair-weather-only dirt roads: 271.

SHIPPING

The chief ports are Nuku'alofa and Neiafu on Vava'u.

Regular services are maintained by:

Union Steam Ship Co. of New Zealand Ltd.: P.O.B. 4, Nuku'alofa; f. 1875; fortnightly passenger and cargo services between Auckland, Fiji, Samoa and Tonga; six-weekly cargo service from Australia to Fiji, Samoa and Tonga.

Bank Line: Burns Philp (South Sea) Co. Ltd., Nuku'alofa; approximately six-weekly cargo services to the United Kingdom.

Pacific Navigation Co.: P.O.B. 81, Nuku'alofa; formerly Tonga Shipping Agency; maintains a service from Sydney (Australia) to Nuku'alofa with the vessel *Tauloto*, a fortnightly service between Auckland (New Zealand) and Nuku'alofa with the vessels *Aoniu* and *Frysna*, a monthly scheduled service between Suva (Fiji) and Nuku'alofa and local inter-island services; Acting Gen. Man. SIONE FALETAU.

Local ships connect all the islands.

CIVIL AVIATION

Tonga is served by Fua'amotu Airport, 13 miles from Nuku'alofa, limited seaplane facilities at Nuku'alofa and airstrips at Vava'u and Ha'apai.

Tonga Internal Air Service: P.O.B. 91, Nuku'alofa; operates services to the Vava'u, 'Eva, Ha'apai and Tongatapu islands.

Air Pacific, based in Fiji, and Polynesian Airlines, based in Western Samoa serve Tonga.

TOURISM

Tonga Tourist and Development Co.: P.O.B. 91, Nuku'alofa, Tonga.

Tonga Visitors' Bureau: P.O.B. 37, Nuku'alofa.

EDUCATION

Free state education is compulsory between the age of 6 and 14 and the Government and other Commonwealth countries offer scholarships for higher education abroad. There are about 180 schools, about two thirds of which are government schools and the rest mission schools, with over 40,000 pupils. There is one teacher training college.

Estimated government expenditure on education in 1974/75 was $T692,242.

Trust Territory of the Pacific Islands

GEOGRAPHY

The U.S. Trust Territory of the Pacific Islands consists of over 2,000 islands covering less than 2,600 square kilometres of land and scattered over 7,500,000 square kilometres of ocean. Most of the islands lie in a band which begins about 800 kilometres east of the Philippines and stretches 4,800 kilometres east across the Pacific towards Hawaii. In the far west are the Palau group, with Yap and Ulithi slightly to the north and east, comprising together the Western Caroline Islands. Further east, Truk and Ponape form the Eastern Carolines. The Marshall islands lie further east again. The Mariana Islands stretch from Guam 800 kilometres almost due north to 20° latitude.

Only about 100 of the islands are large enough to be inhabited. The population of the trust territory is about 115,000. Most live on the largest islands in the districts of Palau, Truk, Yap, Ponape and Saipan.

HISTORY

First European contacts were Iberian. Magellan sailed through the islands in the 1500s and the Spanish maintained a presence in the Mariana Islands from 1700 until the Spanish-American war in 1898. The indigenous population was all but completely destroyed by disease and violent conquest and the modern population is made up from an intermixing of the Spanish and native Chamorro population.

In the Caroline Islands intensive contacts did not begin until the 1800s and in some areas, notably the Palau group, until the early 1900s.

In 1885 Germany took over control of the Marshall Islands and in 1898 bought the rest of the territory, except Guam, from Spain. German administration ended in 1914 when Japan occupied the islands. In 1920 Japan received a mandate from the League of Nations to administer the islands, and remained in control until being forcibly ejected by United States military forces in 1944 and 1945.

Under the Germans, and more so under the Japanese, a policy of colonization and exploitation of natural resources was followed. Fishing and agriculture, in particular copra and sugar production, were encouraged and sugar mills and fish processing plants were established. The Micronesians were involved mainly as labourers in most enterprises, but many moved out of subsistence production completely. With the Japanese military expansion before 1942, the islands became increasingly populated with Japanese and Okinawans.

After the 1942-45 war, almost all of the Japanese were repatriated. Their colonial towns and almost the whole of their pre-war economy disappeared and many islanders were forced to revert to subsistence farming or rely on United States aid. The Mariana islanders were removed to Saipan where, with no access to fishing or agricultural resources, they lived in poverty.

Between 1947 and 1951 the islands were administered by the U.S. Navy. Bikini and Eniwetok in the Marshall Islands were used for nuclear bomb experiments in 1946 and 1948, and are still uninhabited. In 1951 the Trust Territory administration was set up to administer the islands, although the Marianas remained under military rule until 1962. The civil administration operated under an inadequate budget and little development occurred until 1962. Apart from subsistence agriculture and fishing, the only money-earning activities were government employment and the sale of vegetables, copra, trochus shell and scrap metal left over from the war. Immigration and visits by outsiders were severely restricted.

In 1962 the islands' budget was doubled and further increased in following years. Schools, hospitals, housing, roads, airstrips and port facilities were built or upgraded. Public services were expanded and incomes rose, although the greater part was provided by the U.S.A.

Since 1970, tourism has overtaken copra and sugar to become the most important industry in the islands. About half of all tourists come from the U.S.A. and a third from Japan. The Marianas receive 68 per cent of tourists and have the best tourist facilities.

Since 1965, there have been increased demands for local autonomy. In that year the Congress of Micronesia was formed, and in 1967 a commission to examine the future political status of the islands was established. In 1970 it declared Micronesians' rights to sovereignty over their own lands, self-determination, the right to form their own constitution and to revoke any form of free association with the United States. Two problems face the islands in this respect. The first is how to form a unified country out of the widely scattered islands and the nine linguistic and cultural groups which occupy them. Internal distrust and mutual suspicion are high between the islanders. The second problem involves the strategic position of many of the islands and the importance the U.S.A. places on maintaining military bases there.

In 1969 talks began which produced in 1974 a draft agreement on the formation of a Government of Micronesia which will give the Trust Territory greater independence from the U.S.A. However, the latter will retain responsibility for defence and foreign affairs and will continue to provide aid. In 1975 the northern Mariana islanders voted for closer integration with the U.S.A. In March 1976 U.S. President Ford signed the Northern Marianas Commonwealth Covenant. This Covenant will come into force when the Trusteeship Agreement is terminated.

STATISTICAL SURVEY

Area: Total area of the Territory: 3 million square miles; Land area: 717 square miles; the largest islands are Babelthuap (153 square miles) in Palau District and Ponape Island (129 square miles) in Ponape District.

Population (1972): Total 114,645; Mariana Islands 13,381, Marshall Islands 24,248, Palau 13,025, Ponape 23,723, Truk 32,738, Yap 7,536. 1975 estimate: 115,000. Administration centre: Saipan, Mariana Islands.

Agriculture: The chief crops are Coconut, Breadfruit, Bananas, Taro, Yams, Cocoa, Pepper and Citrus. Subsistence crop production predominates and, except for copra from all districts and vegetables from the Mariana Islands, little is marketed. Production (1974-metric tons, FAO estimates): Coconuts 82,600, Copra 9,500, Cassava 5,000, Sweet Potatoes 3,000, Bananas 2,000.

Livestock (1974-FAO estimates): Pigs 17,000, Cattle 16,000, Goats 6,000, Poultry 160,000.

Fishing (1974): 3,360 metric tons landed.

FINANCE

United States currency: 100 cents = 1 U.S. dollar ($).
Coins: 1, 5, 10, 25 and 50 cents; 1 dollar.
Notes: 1, 2, 5, 10, 20, 50 and 100 dollars.
Exchange rates (June 1976): £1 sterling = U.S. $1.77; $100 = £56.37.

BUDGET
(1972–73—U.S. $)

Revenue		Expenditure	
Territorial Taxes, Fees and Licences	4,455,327	General Administration	4,799,648
Miscellaneous Income	310,521	Construction	16,283,318
Reimbursements	936,335	Legal and Public Safety	2,105,059
Grant from U.S. Congress	59,362,000	Health	7,070,941
Carried over	13,903,313	Education	12,020,620
		Other	30,532,862
Total	79,605,496	Total	62,812,448

TRADE

External Trade (1973): *Imports:* $30 million est. (including foodstuffs $8.9 million, beverages $3.04 million, building materials $2.88 million). *Exports:* $1.9 million (including copra $946,765, fish $525,715, handicrafts $191,451, and vegetables $102,071).

TRANSPORT
(1973)

Roads: Trucks 428; pickups 1,962; sedans 5,290; jeeps 611; motorcycles, etc. 623; other motor vehicles 309.

Shipping: Passengers 1,546 (TransPacific Lines Inc.); Freight 140,132 tons; other American vessels also entered and cleared in external trade.

Civil Aviation: Passengers flown 149,120; Passenger miles flown 80,596,000. Freight flown 7,988,897 lb.; freight ton miles flown 3,356,847.

EDUCATION
(1973)

	Schools	Pupils
Elementary	224	30,751
High School	27	7,174
MOC* (Secondary Programme)	1	72

* Micronesian Occupational Centre. Also provides post-secondary and adult education. During 1973 871 Micronesian students were pursuing post-secondary courses outside the Trust Territory.

THE CONSTITUTION

The Trust Territory of the Pacific Islands is a United Nations Trusteeship administered by the United States of America. Executive and administrative authority is exercised by a High Commissioner, appointed by the President of the United States with the consent and approval of the U.S. Senate. The High Commissioner is under the direction of the Secretary of the Interior. The High Commissioner is represented in each district by a District Administrator and has his headquarters at Saipan, Mariana Islands.

Legislative authority is vested in the Congress of Micronesia, a bicameral legislature consisting of the Senate and the House of Representatives. There are twelve Senators, two elected at large from each of the six districts for a term of four years. The House of Representatives has twenty-one members elected for two-year terms from single-member election districts of approximately equal population. The present apportionment of Representatives is: Mariana Islands District, three; Marshall Islands District, four; Palau District, three; Ponape District, four; Truk District, five; and Yap District, two.

The Mariana Islands, Marshall Islands, Palau, Ponape, Truk, and Yap Districts have formally constituted legislatures. Local governmental units are the municipalities and villages. Elected Magistrates and Councils govern the municipalities. Village government is largely traditional.

Talks which began in 1969 produced in 1974 a draft agreement on the formation of a Government of Micronesia, which will give the Trust Territory greater independence from the United States. However, the latter will retain responsibility for defence and foreign affairs and will continue to provide aid. In June 1975 the northern Mariana Islands voted for closer integration with the U.S.A. In March 1976 President Ford signed the Northern Marianas Commonwealth Covenant. This Covenant will come into effect when the Trusteeship Agreement is terminated. The population of the other island groups has not as yet settled its attitude to the proposed future constitution.

THE GOVERNMENT

Acting-High Commissioner: The Hon. PETER T. COLEMAN.

Director of Resources and Development: EUSEBIO RECHUCHER.

Director of Public Works: KOICHI L. WONG.

Director of Education: DAVID RAMARUI.

Director of Finance: (vacant).

Director of Health Services: MASAO KUMANGAI, M.D.

Director of Personnel: PODIS PEDRUS.

Director of Public Affairs: STRIK YOMA.

Director of Transportation and Communications: (vacant).

Attorney-General: DANIEL HIGH.

District Administrators: FRANCISCO C. ADA (Mariana Islands), OSCAR DE BRUM (Marshall Islands), THOMAS REMENGESAU (Palau), LEO A. FALCAM (Ponape; acting), JUAN A. SABLAN (Truk), EDMUND GILMAR (Yap).

Under the proposals for the Trust Territory's future status it is planned that a Government of Micronesia should replace the present administration.

CONGRESS OF MICRONESIA

President of the Senate: Hon. TOSIWO NAKAYAMA.

Speaker of the House of Representatives: Hon. BETHWEL HENRY.

DISTRICT LEGISLATURES

Mariana Islands District Legislature: 16 members serving for three years.

Marshall Islands District Legislature: 24 members serving for two years.

Palau District Legislature (*Olbiil era Kelulau*): 16 chiefs (non-voting members) and 28 elected representatives serving for four years.

Ponape District Legislature: 24 representatives elected for four years (terms staggered).

Truk District Legislature: 27 members, serving for three years.

Yap District Legislature: 20 members, 12 elected from the Yap Islands proper and 8 elected from the Outer Islands of Ulithi and Woleai, for a two-year term.

JUDICIAL SYSTEM

The Trust Territory laws derive from the Trusteeship Agreement, certain applicable laws of the United States and Executive Orders of the President, Secretarial Orders of the Secretary of the Interior, laws and regulations of the Government of the Trust Territory, District Administrator's orders and enactments of the Congress of Micronesia and district legislative bodies approved by the High Commissioner, and municipal ordinances. Recognized customary law has full force where it does not conflict with aforementioned laws.

High Court: Appellate and Trial Divisions; Chief Justice Hon. HAROLD W. BURNETT; Associate Justices Hon. ARVIN H. BROWN, Hon. DON WILLIAMS, Hon. ROBERT A. HEFNER.

District Courts: 3 judges Mariana Islands; 3 Marshall Islands; 3 Palau; 5 Ponape; 4 Truk; 3 Yap.

Community Courts: a number in each District; 103 judges.

RELIGION

The population is predominantly Christian, mainly Roman Catholic.

Catholic Church: The Bishop of the Diocese of Agaña (Guam), Most Rev. Bishop FELIXBERTO C. FLORES, D.D., has ecclesiastical jurisdiction in the territory.

Protestantism: Marshall Islands and Eastern Caroline Islands: U.S. effort under the auspices of the United Church Board for World Ministries (475 Riverside Drive, New York City, N.Y. 10027); Pacific Regional Sec.: Rev. PAUL GREGORY.

Western Carolines: under auspices of the Liebenzell Mission of Germany and the U.S.A.; Rev. PETER ERMEL, Truk, Caroline Islands 96942.

THE PRESS

Highlights: newsletter from Office of the High Commissioner; semi-monthly; circ. 9,700.

Marianas Variety News and Views: f. 1972; P.O.B. 231, Saipan, Mariana Islands 96950; Marianas district weekly; independent; English, Chamarro; circ. 2,000.

Micronesian Independent: Marshall Islands; f. 1970; weekly; Editors JOE MURPHY, MIKE MALONE; circ. 2,500 throughout Micronesia.

Micronesian Reporter: Public Information Office; journal of Micronesia; 4 times a year; circ. 5,300.

Tia Belau: P.O.B. 569, Koror, Palau; f. 1972; bi-weekly; independent; Editor MOSES ULUDONG; circ. 1,000.

RADIO AND TELEVISION

All stations are government owned, broadcasting between 6 a.m. and midnight daily.

RADIO

Station KJQR: Saipan, Mariana Is. 96950; programmes in English and Chamorro; 1 kW; Man. R. SABLAN.

Station WSZA: Colonia, Yap, W. Caroline Is. 96943; programmes in English and Yapese; 1 kW; Man. A. YUG

Station WSZB: Koror, Palau, W. Caroline Is. 96940; member of the Micronesian Broadcasting System; 1 kW; 18 hours a day; Man. H. RODAS.

Station WSZC: Moen, Truk, E. Caroline Is. 96942; programmes in English and Trukese; 5 kW; Man. K. PETER.

Station WSZD: Kolonia, Ponape, E. Caroline Is. 96941; programmes in English, Kusaiean and Ponapean; 10 kW; Man. H. JOHNNY (Acting).

Station WSZE-AM-FM: Saipan, Mariana Is.; commercial station owned by Micronesian Broadcasting Corpn.

Station WSZO: Majuro, Marshall Islands 96960; owned and operated by the Government of the Trust Territory of the Pacific Islands; programmes in English and Marshallese; 1 kW broadcasts on 1440 kc.; on the air 18 hours a day Monday to Friday, 16 hours on Sundays and holidays; Station Man. LAURENCE N. EDWARDS.

TELEVISION

WSZE/WSZF-TV: Saipan, Mariana Is. 96950; two-channel commercial station owned by Micronesian Broadcasting Corpn., broadcasts 6 hours of American shows daily.

In 1975 there were 72,000 radio receivers and 3,000 television sets.

FINANCE

BANKING

Bank of America, National Trust and Savings Association: Saipan Branch, P.O.B. 67, Saipan, Mariana Islands 96950; Man. DALE BRANCHCOMB; brs. also in Truk and Majuro, Marshall Islands.

Bank of Hawaii: brs. in Kwajalein (Marshall Is.), Koror, Ponape, Saipan, Yap, Wake, Midway.

Banking services for the rest of the territory are available in Guam, Hawaii and on the U.S. mainland.

INSURANCE

There are two firms on Saipan which sell insurance:

Micronesian Insurance Underwriters Inc.

Microl Corporation: P.O.B. 267, Saipan, Mariana Islands 96950.

CO-OPERATIVES

Mariana Islands: Mariana Islands District Co-operative Association, Rota Producers, Tinian Producers Association.

Palau: Palau Fishermen's Co-operative, Palau Boatbuilders' Association, Palau Handicraft and Woodworkers' Guild.

Ponape: Ponape Federation of Co-operative Associations (P.O.B. 100, Ponape ECI, 96941), Ponape Handicraft Co-operative, Ponape Fishermen's Co-operative, Uh Soumwet Co-operative Association, Kolonia Consumers and Producers Co-operative Association, Kitti Minimum Co-operative Association, Kapingamarangi Copra Producers' Association, Metalanim Copra Co-operative Association, PICS Co-operative Association, Mokil Island Co-operative Association, Ngatik Island Co-operative Association, Nukuoro Island Co-operative Association, Kusaie Island Co-operative Association, Pingelap Consumers Co-operative Association.

Truk: Truk Co-operative, Faichuk Cacao and Copra Co-operative Association, Pis Fishermen's Co-operative, Fefan Women's Co-operative.

Yap: Yap Co-operative Association (P.O.B. 159, Colonia Yap 96943, Western Caroline Islands), Yap Shipping Co-operative Association.

Co-operative organizations have been set up for the sale of school supplies and sundries, one at the Truk High School and one at the Ponape High School.

TRANSPORT

ROADS

Macadam and concrete roads are found in the more important islands. Other islands have stone and coral surfaced roads and tracks.

SHIPPING

Most shipping in the Territory is government-organized. Six vessels are operated by Micronesia Interocean Lines Inc. and other private carrier services are being set up with government subsidies.

Micronesia Interocean Lines Inc.: P.O.B. 468, Saipan, Mariana Islands 96950; f. 1968.

Marshall Islands Import-Export Co.: Marshall Islands District; service began 1956; carry more than half the inter-district trade; 2 motor vessels; deal with imports from U.S., Japan and Australia.

Ponape Federation of Co-operative Asscns.: P.O.B. 127, Kolonia, Ponape; inter-island tramp.

Saipan Shipping Co.: Mariana Islands District; services Guam, Micronesia and Far East.

Truk Transportation Co.: Box 99, Moen, Truk; f. 1967; inter-island tramp; Pres. MASATAKA MORI.

Yap Shipping Co-operative Asscn.: Palau and Yap; inter-island tramp.

CIVIL AVIATION

Continental-Air Micronesia: P.O.B. 198, Saipan, Mariana Islands 96950; f. 1966; owned by United Micronesia Development Association (60 per cent), Continental Airlines (30 per cent), Aloha Airlines (10 per cent); provides internal and some external services; Chair. CARLTON SKINNER; Pres. DONALD BECK.

Air Nauru also serves the territory and *Air Pacific* provides another internal service.

Tuvalu

The former Gilbert and Ellice Islands Colony, situated in the South-West Pacific around the point where the International Date Line cuts across the Equator, was divided on October 1st, 1975, into the two territories of the Gilbert Islands and Tuvalu (the former Ellice Islands), after a referendum held in August 1974 in the Ellice Islands resulting in a clear majority in favour of separate status as Tuvalu.

Tuvalu comprises nine islands scattered over 1.06 million square kilometres of ocean south of the Gilbert Islands. It was administered by the existing Gilbert and Ellice Islands Council of Ministers until January 1st, 1976, after which it formed its own cabinet and legislative assembly, run along similar lines to that of the Gilbert Islands and based at the capital, Funafuti. The Deputy Governor of the former Gilbert and Ellice Islands is also Her Majesty's Commissioner in Tuvalu. The United Kingdom will finance capital projects and help to meet the recurrent costs of government.

STATISTICS

Land area: 24.6 square kilometres.

Population: (1973 census): 5,887.

Economy: A subsistence level economy based on fish and coconuts.

Finance: Australian currency: 100 cents = 1 Australian dollar ($A). Coins: 1, 2, 5, 10, 20 and 50 cents. Notes: 1, 2, 5, 10, 20 and 50 dollars. Exchange rates (June 1976): £1 sterling = $A1.443; U.S.$1 = 81.4 Australian cents; $A 100 = £69.28 = U.S.$122.90.

Note: For previous changes in the exchange rate, *see* the chapter on Australia.

Budget: (1976): Expenditure $A1,687,150 of which $A839,090 is British grant-in-aid. The remainder, $A850,060, is expected to comprise personal tax revenue of $A50,000, customs duties of $A125,000 and philately and coinage $A360,000.

Development: (1976): $A1,761,970 derived from grant and loan funds. Some of this will be used to build an administrative centre at Funafuti.

The Government is planning to spend $A758,980 on home affairs, including shipping and works, $A354,280 on social services and education and $A42,030 on commerce and natural resources.

THE CONSTITUTION

The Constitution of Tuvalu provides for a Commissioner in Tuvalu responsible for external affairs, defence, internal security, finance and the public service, and for the establishment of a House of Assembly.

The House of Assembly comprises 8 elected members and 2 ex-officio members, the Financial Secretary and Attorney General, presided over initially by the Commissioner until a Speaker is elected. The elected members would elect from their own number a Chief Minister on whose advice two further members would be appointed to serve as ministers in a cabinet which would also include the two ex-officio members and would be chaired by the Commissioner. The existing Ellice representatives in the Gilbert and Ellice Islands Colony Assembly would continue to serve as the first elected members of the Tuvalu Assembly as new elections are not scheduled until October 1977.

GOVERNMENT

(*July* 1976)

Commissioner: Thomas H. Layng.

Ex-officio members: G. L. Pimm, P. W. Reardon, O.B.E.

Elected Members

Chief Minister and Minister of Home Affairs: Hon. Toalipi Lauti.

Minister for Social Services: Hon. Taui Finikaso.

Minister for Commerce and Industries: Hon. Tomu Sione.

RADIO

Radio Tuvalu: Funafuti; began broadcasting in October 1975.

TRANSPORT

Civil Aviation: Air Pacific maintains a weekly service from Fiji to Tuvalu and the Gilbert Islands.

Wake Island

Wake Island and its neighbours, Wilkes and Peale Islands, lie in the Pacific on the direct route from Hawaii to Hong Kong about 2,000 miles west of Hawaii and 1,290 miles east of Guam. The group is 4.5 miles long, 1.5 miles wide and covers less than three square miles. In 1970 the population was 1,647. The U.S.A. took formal possession in 1899 and since 1972 the group has been administered by the U.S. Air Force.

Wallis and Futuna Islands

This self-governing French Overseas Territory comprises two groups: the Wallis Islands, including Uvea and 22 islets on the surrounding reef, and, to the southeast, Futuna (or Hooru), comprising the two small islands of Futuna and Alofi. Wallis is 159 square kilometres in area and has a population of about 7,000; Futuna and Alofi have an area of 115 square kilometres. Wallis and Futuna, located north of Fiji and west of Samoa, are inhabited by Polynesians.

A French Protectorate since 1888, the Islands chose by referendum in December 1959 to become an Overseas Territory. In July 1961 they were granted this status. In 1975 talks started on changing the status of the territory to that of an Overseas Department.

Copra, which formerly provided the main cash income for the islands, has been seriously affected by rhinoceros beetle; most monetary income on the island is derived from government employment and remittances sent home by islanders employed in New Caledonia.

Area (sq. km.): Wallis Island 159, Futuna Island and Alofi Island 115, total of all islands 274.

Population: 9,900: Wallis Island 7,000 (chiet town Mata-Utu), Futuna Island 2,900; Alofi Island uninhabited; about 11,000 Wallisians and Futunians live on New Caledonia and in the New Hebrides.

Agriculture: the principal export crop is copra. Yams, taros, bananas and arrowroot and other food crops are also cultivated.

Livestock (1972): 300 horses, 350 cattle, 3,000 pigs.

Currency: 100 centimes=1 franc de la Communauté française du pacifique (franc CFP or Pacific franc). Exchange rates (June 1976): 1 franc CFP=5.5 French centimes; £1 sterling=153.18 francs CFP; U.S. $1=86.35 francs CFP; 1,000 francs CFP=£6.53=$11.58.

Budget (1975): 97,142,900 francs CFP.

External Trade (1969): *Imports:* 125 million francs CFP; *Exports:* 2 million francs CFP.

Government: *Administrateur Supérieur* Yves Arbellot-Repaire; President of Territorial Assembly Sosefo Makape Papillo; Representative to National Assembly Benjamin Brial; Representative to Senate Sosefo Makape Papillo.

Religion: The entire population is nominally Catholic; Bishop of Wallis and Futuna Mgr. Lolesio Fuahea.

Shipping: Services to Nouméa (New Caledonia), Suva (Fiji), Port Vila and Santo (both in the New Hebrides).

Aviation: *Union des Transports Aériens (UTA):* Wallis Island; twice-monthly service to Nouméa, New Caledonia. *Air Fiji:* Charter services to the Wallis and Futuna Islands from Suva.

Education (1973): 2,700 pupils in 9 State-financed primary and lower secondary schools.

Western Samoa

Western Samoa comprises the two large islands of Savai'i and Upolu and the two small islands of Manono and Apolima. These high volcanic islands, with rugged interiors and little flat land except along the coasts, lie in the South Pacific 1,500 miles north of New Zealand.

The islands are peopled by Polynesians and are thought to have been the origin of many of the people who now occupy islands further east. The Samoan language is believed to be the oldest form of Polynesian speech in existence. Samoan society developed an intricate hierarchy of graded titles comprising titular chiefs and orator chiefs. One of the striking features of modern Samoa is the manner in which these titles and pre-contact culture remain a dominant influence. Most of the population have become Christians.

The Samoan islands were first visited by Europeans in the 1700s but it was not until 1830 that missionaries from the London Missionary Society settled there. The eastern islands (now American Samoa) were ceded to the United States in 1904 but Western Samoa was occupied by New Zealand in 1914 and the League of Nations granted a mandate over the territory to New Zealand in 1920

Despite independence it still has strong links with New Zealand where many Samoans now live and where many others received their secondary and tertiary education.

The population of Western Samoa in 1974 was estimated at 155,000, three quarters of whom live on Upolu. The capital, Apia, on Upolu, had a population of 29,089 in 1971. Western Samoa's main exports are copra, cocoa, dessicated coconut and bananas which are shipped to New Zealand, Australia and Great Britain.

Western Samoa has had a legislative assembly since 1948. Since independence on January 1st, 1962, the islands have been governed under a parliamentary system with a head of state, Prime Minister and Cabinet. The 1973 elections were won by Fiame Mata'afa Faumui Mulinuu who was first elected Prime Minister in 1962 but who lost the position in 1970 to Tupua Tamasese Lealofi. Fiame Mata'afa Mulinuu remained Prime Minister until his death in 1975 when Tupua Tamasese Lealofi was recalled to complete the term of office. In March 1976 Tupuola Taisi Efi was elected Prime Minister.

STATISTICAL SURVEY

AREA AND POPULATION

AREA
(square miles)

Total	Savai'i	Upolu
1,097	662	433

POPULATION
1966

Total	Upolu	Savai'i	Apia (capital)
131,552	95,344	36,208	25,391

Average annual rate of increase (1961–66): 2.8 per cent.
Population (census of November 3rd, 1971): 146,635.
Estimated population (December 1974): 151,251.

EMPLOYMENT

	1966	1971
Agriculture, forestry and fishing	26,160	25,410
subsistence	24,030	22,850
cash	2,130	2,560
Manufacturing and construction	1,360	2,440
Trade and commerce	1,770	2,420
Transport and communications	840	1,250
Government and services	5,160	6,230
TOTAL	35,290	37,740

AGRICULTURE

PRINCIPAL CROPS
(metric tons)

	1972	1973	1974
Taro (coco yam) .	14,000*	15,000*	15,000*
Coconuts . .	170,000	135,000	170,000*
Sugar cane . .	2,000*	2,000*	2,000*
Bananas . .	12,000	11,000*	11,000*
Cocoa beans . .	2,400	2,000	2,000

* FAO estimate.

Copra (metric tons): 20,500 in 1972; 15,500 in 1973; 20,000 (FAO estimate) in 1974.

Source: FAO, *Production Yearbook 1974.*

Livestock (1974 FAO estimates): Pigs 45,000, Cattle 21,000, Horses 3,000, Poultry 93,000.

Fishing (1973 estimate): 9,000 metric tons.

Industry: The chief industries include the production of sawnwood, soap, cabinets, biscuits and clothing.

FINANCE

100 sene (cents) = 1 tala (Western Samoan dollar).
Coins: 1, 2, 5, 10, 20 and 50 sene.
Notes: 1, 2 and 10 tala.
Exchange rates (May 1976): £1 sterling = 1.443 tala; U.S. $1 = 81.3 sene.
100 tala = £69.77 = U.S. $123.07.

Note: The tala was introduced in July 1967, replacing the Western Samoan pound at the rate of £WS1 = 2 tala. This changeover coincided with a similar move in New Zealand. The Western Samoan pound had been introduced in January 1962, replacing (at par) the New Zealand pound. From October 1961 the pound was valued at U.S. $2.78 so the initial value of the tala was $1.39 ($1 = 71.9 sene). The market rate was fixed at 1 tala = U.S. $1.387 (U.S. $1 = 72.11 sene). This valuation remained in effect until August 1971. From December 1971 to February 1973 the central rate was 1 tala = $1.51 ($1 = 66.24 sene) and the market rate originally 1 tala = $1.478 and later 1 tala = $1.485. From February 1973 to October 1975 the central rate was 1 tala = $1.677 ($1 = 59.62 sene) and the market rate 1 tala = $1.649 ($1 = 60.66 sene). Since October 1975 the tala's direct link with the U.S. dollar has been broken and it is pegged to a "basket" of currencies (as used by New Zealand). In terms of sterling, the central exchange rate between November 1967 and June 1972 was £1 = 1.726 tala.

BUDGET
('000 tala)

Revenue	1970	1971	1972
Tax on income and wealth . . .	784	849	1,275
Customs . . .	3,542	4,127	4,731
Other tax revenue .	29	—	—
Other receipts . .	2,242	2,834	2,880
Total . .	6,597	7,810	8,886

Expenditure	1970	1971	1972
Economic services .	812	958	1,217
Social services .	1,762	1,901	2,342
Other current expenditure . . .	2,030	2,660	2,962
Investments . . .	2,221	2,642	3,809
Total . .	6,825	8,161	10,330

Source: UN Economic and Social Commission for Asia and the Pacific, *Statistical Yearbook.*

CURRENCY IN CIRCULATION
('000 tala)

	1971	1972	1973	1974
Coins . .	126.0	144.2	168.8	195.3
Notes . .	634.2	774.5	1,157.8	1,288.0

EXTERNAL TRADE
(million tala)

	1971	1972	1973	1974
Imports	9.61	13.04	14.43	15.87
Exports	4.52	3.39	4.00	7.01

PRINCIPAL COMMODITIES
(tala)

Imports	1972	1973
Meat and meat preparations	822,405	1,004,710
Cereals and cereal preparations	955,536	703,907
Fish and fish preparations	429,826	558,722
Sugar, sugar preparations and honey	457,514	526,255
Petroleum and petroleum products	418,089	568,712
Rubber manufactures	124,007	530,944
Textile yarn, fabric and manufactured articles	694,543	727,027
Non-ferrous metals	666,993	653,548
Machinery	469,828	789,494
Electrical machinery	2,018,983	1,368,784
Transport equipment	813,169	1,094,927
Miscellaneous	796,738	914,697
Total	13,044,274	14,435,069

Exports	1972	1973
Fruit and vegetables	215,991	450,851
Coffee, tea, cocoa	896,376	1,072,989
Oil seeds, nuts and kernels	1,380,135	1,645,282
Wood, lumber, cork	568,251	549,492
Total	3,355,947	3,786,137

PRINCIPAL COUNTRIES
('000 tala)

	1973		1974	
	Exports	Imports	Exports	Imports
Australia	33	3,023	146	3,272
Hong Kong	—	318	—	556
Fiji	218	788	42	738
Federal Republic of Germany	713	441	1,079	2
Japan	73	1,826	70	2,052
Netherlands	548	70	798	101
New Zealand	1,439	4,770	3,269	5,676
United Kingdom	33	839	456	1,618
U.S.A.	273	1,222	625	1,661

TRANSPORT
ROADS

Vehicles Registered	1974
Passenger Cars and Buses	536
Private Cars and Lorries	1,200
Motor-Cycles	115

TOURISM

1973: 9,377 visitors. 1974: 9,073 visitors.

EDUCATION

(1974)

	Government	Mission	Total
Pupils:			
Primary	27,259	4,142	31,401
Intermediate	6,365	917	7,282
Secondary*	2,267	1,616	3,883
Teachers:			
Primary and intermediate	1,050	180	1,130
Secondary†	97	49	146

* Including the Trades Technical Institute.

† Including vocational and teachers' training establishments.

COMMUNICATIONS

In 1973 there were approximately 2,000 telephones in use.

THE CONSTITUTION

HEAD OF STATE

The office of Head of State is held by His Highness Malietoa Tanumafili, who will hold this post for life. After that the Head of State will be elected by the Legislative Assembly for a term of five years.

EXECUTIVE POWER

Executive power lies with the Cabinet, consisting of a Prime Minister, supported by the majority in the Legislative Assembly, and eight Ministers selected by the Prime Minister. Cabinet decisions are subject to review by the Executive Council, which is made up of the Head of State and the Cabinet.

LEGISLATIVE POWER

Since the General Election of February 25th, 1967, the Legislative Assembly has consisted of 47 members, two of whom are Europeans. It has a three-year term and the Speaker is elected from among the members. Samoans and Europeans have separate electoral rolls; the Europeans are elected by universal adult suffrage and the Samoans by the Matai (elected family leaders).

THE GOVERNMENT

HEAD OF STATE

O le Ao o le Malo: H.H. Malietoa Tanumafili II, c.b.e., Fautua of Maliena.

CABINET

(*July* 1976)

Prime Minister, Minister of External Affairs and Local and District Affairs and Attorney General: Tupuola Taisi Efi.

Minister of Economic Affairs, Economic Development, Industries and Trade, Forests and Fisheries: Asi Eikeni.

Minister of Justice, Labor, Police, Youth, Sport and Cultural Affairs: Ulualofaiga Talamaivao Niko.

Minister of Works: Letiu Tamatoa.

Minister of Agriculture: Fuimaono Mimio.

Minister of Finance and Customs: Vaovasamanaia Filipo.

Minister of Communications and Transport and Health: Tofaeno Tile.

Minister of Education: Lilomaiava Niko.

Minister of Lands and Land Survey and Broadcasting: Mano Togamau.

PARLIAMENT

LEGISLATIVE ASSEMBLY

Speaker: Leota Leuluaialii I. Ale.

Deputy Speaker: Hon. Teo Fetu.

Samoan Members: 45 representing 41 territorial constituencies.

Individual Voters: 2.

DIPLOMATIC REPRESENTATION

EMBASSIES AND HIGH COMMISSIONS ACCREDITED TO WESTERN SAMOA

(In Wellington, New Zealand, unless otherwise indicated)
(E) Embassy; (HC) High Commission.

Australia: Suva, Fiji (HC); *High Commissioner:* H. W. Bullock.

Canada: (HC); *High Commissioner:* Clive E. Glover.

France: (E); *Ambassador:* Albert de Schonen.

India: (HC); *High Commissioner:* P. S. Naksar.

New Zealand: Apia (HC); *High Commissioner:* Paul Cotton.

United Kingdom: Nuku'alofa, Tonga (HC); *High Commissioner:* Humphrey Arthington-Davy, o.b.e.

U.S.A.: (E); *Ambassador:* Armistead I. Selden, Jr.

Western Samoa also has diplomatic relations with the People's Republic of China.

JUDICIAL SYSTEM

The Supreme Court consists of a Chief Justice and a Puisne Judge. It has full jurisdiction for both criminal and civil cases. Appeals lie with the Court of Appeal.

Chief Justice: Hon. LILOMAIAVA NIKO.

Registrar: F. J. THOMSEN.

The Court of Appeal consists of a President (the Chief Justice of the Supreme Court), and of such persons possessing qualifications prescribed by statute as may be appointed by the Head of State. Any three judges of the Court of Appeal may exercise all the powers of the Court. A Judge of the Court cannot sit on the hearing of an appeal from any decision made by him.

The Magistrates Court consists of a Magistrate and two senior Samoan Judges, assisted by seven junior Samoan Judges.

Magistrate: W. A. WILSON.

The Land and Titles Court has jurisdiction in respect of disputes over Samoan land and succession to Samoan titles. It consists of the President (who is also Chief Justice of the Supreme Court) assisted by five Samoan associate judges and assessors; P.O.B. 33, Apia.

Registrar: AUELUA F. ENARI.

RELIGION

The population is almost entirely Christian.

PROTESTANT CHURCHES

Congregational Christian Church in Samoa: Tamaligi, Apia; Elder Deacon FUIMAONO ASUEMU.

Methodist Church in Samoa: Rev. LENE MILO.

Church of Jesus Christ of Latter-Day Saints: Pres. RALPH RODGERS, L.D.S. Mission, P.O.B. 197, Apia.

Seventh-Day Adventist Church: Box 600, Apia; f. 1895; mission territory constituted by American Samoa and Western Samoa; adherents (1975 est.) 2,343; Pres. Pastor I. F. PUNI; publ. one bi-monthly magazine.

Congregational Church of Jesus in Samoa: Rev. SOLOMONA SIULAGI, Fataogo, Apia.

Anglican Church: Rev. H. H. BUTLER; P.O.B. 16, Apia.

ROMAN CATHOLIC COMMUNION

Bishop of Samoa and Tokelau: H.E. Cardinal PIO TAOFINU'U, Cardinal's Residence, Box 532, Apia, Western Samoa.

THE PRESS

Samoa Times, The: Apia, Western Samoa; weekly, independent, bi-lingual newspaper; Editor FAALOGO P. FAALOGO; circ. 5,000.

Savali: P.O.B. 193, Apia; f. 1904; fortnightly; government publication; Samoan and English; Man. and Editor KALATI MOSE; circ. 6,500.

South Seas Star: Box 242, Apia; f. 1971; weekly (Wed.); Man. Editor LEOTA PITA; English Editor S. FIGIEL; Samoan Editor POUVI SU'A; circ. 3,000.

RADIO

Western Samoa Broadcasting Service: Broadcasting Dept., P.O.B. 200, Apia; commenced operation and broadcasts 1948; broadcasts in English and Samoan on 1420 kc./s. and 10,000 watts power; Dir. J. W. MOORE. In 1973 there were some 50,000 radio sets in use.

There is a radio communications station at Apia. Radio telephone service connects Western Samoa with American Samoa, Fiji, New Zealand, Australia, Canada, U.S.A., U.K. and other overseas countries.

FINANCE AND TRADE

Bank of Western Samoa: Apia; f. 1959; cap. p.u. 750,000 tala; dep. 5,784,000 tala (Oct. 1975); Chair. L. N. ROSS, C.M.G.; Man. W. W. ANSELL.

Development Bank of Western Samoa: Apia; f. 1974 by Parliamentary legislation to foster economic development of the territory.

CO-OPERATIVES

In 1966 there were 8 registered co-operatives, and 13 credit unions.

TRANSPORT

Public Works Department: Apia; Dir. of Works M. A. E. ADAMS.

ROADS

There are 582 miles of roads in the islands, of which 81 miles are bitumen surfaced. Main roads total 251 miles, secondary roads 90 miles, and plantation roads 220 miles.

SHIPPING

There are regular passenger and cargo services from Australia and New Zealand via Fiji and other Pacific territories. There is a monthly cargo service from Japan and a five/six weekly service from the U.S.A. There is also a direct service to the United Kingdom. Nauru state shipping line makes regular calls at Apia, Western Samoa.

CIVIL AVIATION

Polynesian Airlines Ltd.: P.O.B. 599, Beach Rd., Apia; daily air services to Pago Pago (capital of American Samoa) connect with services to Tahiti, New Zealand and the U.S.A.; three services weekly to Nadi (Fiji), one a week to Niue Island; three services weekly to Nuku' alofa (Tonga); aircraft: 2 HS 748; Chair. E. ANNANDALE; Gen. Man. N. C. WISELEY.

Services between Western Samoa and other Pacific territories are also run by *Air Pacific* and *Air Nauru*.

EDUCATION

The education system is divided into primary, intermediate and secondary and is based on the New Zealand system. In 1971 there were 159 primary, 39 intermediate and 15 secondary schools attended by a total of over 34,000 pupils. In 1974 there were 42,066 children attending school. There are also a trades' training institute, teacher's training college and a college for tropical agriculture. Western Samoa has also joined other Governments in the area in establishing the regional University of the South Pacific.

BIBLIOGRAPHY

ADAMS, A., and JOESTING, E. An Introduction to Hawaii (5 Associates, San Francisco, 1964).

ALPERS, A. Legends of the South Seas (Murray, London, 1970).

An Ethnographical Bibliography of New Guinea (Australian National University Press, Canberra, 1968).

BAIN, K. R. The Friendly Islanders (Hodder & Stoughton, London, 1967).

BARROW, T. Art and Life in Polynesia (Phaidon Press, London, 1972).

BURNS, Sir ALAN. Fiji (H.M.S.O., London, 1963).

CAMMACK, F. M., and SAITO, S. Pacific Island Bibliography (Scarecrow Press, New York, 1962).

CARMICHAEL, P., and KNOX-MAWER, J. A World of Islands (Collins, London, 1968).

COCKCROFT, J. Polynesian Islands of the South Pacific (Angus & Robertson, London, 1968).

COPPELL, Dr. W. G. A Bibliography of the Cook Islands (Australian National University Press, Canberra, 1970).

CUMBERLAND, K. B. Southwest Pacific (Whitcombe & Tombs, Christchurch, 1954).

DAY, A. GROVE. Pacific Islands Literature (University of Hawaii, Honolulu, 1972).

DERRICK, R. A. The Fiji Islands (Government Printer, Suva, 1951).

Economy of Western Samoa 1968 (Government Printer, Apia, Western Samoa).

EASON, W. J. E. A Short History of Rotuma (Government Printer, Suva, 1951).

ELLIS, Sir ALBERT. Ocean Island and Nauru (Angus & Robertson, Sydney, 1935).

FERDINAND-LOP, S. Les Possessions françaises du Pacifique (Paris, 1933).

FIRTH, R. W. We, the Tikopia (Cambridge University Press, 1936).

FISK, E. K. (Editor). New Guinea on the Threshold (Australian National University Press, Canberra, 1966).

GARDNER, R., and HEIDER, K. G. Gardens of War (Andre Deutsch, London, 1969).

GORSKY, B. Island at the End of the World (Rupert Hart-Davies, London, 1966).

GRATTAN, C. H. The Southwest Pacific since 1900 (Univ. of Michigan Press, Ann Arbor, 1963).

GRAY, J. A. C. American Samoa (United States Naval Institute Press, 1960).

GRIMBLE, Sir ARTHUR. A Pattern of Islands (London, 1952).
Return to the Islands (London, 1957).
Migrations, Myth and Magic from the Gilbert Islands, edited by Rosemary Grimble (Routledge and Kegan Paul, London, 1972).

HADFIELD, E. Among the Natives of the Loyalty Group (London, 1920).

HANDY, E. S. C. History and Culture in the Society Islands (Bishop Museum, Honolulu, 1930).

HASTINGS, P. (Editor). Papua New Guinea (Angus and Robertson, London, 1971).

Introducing the British Pacific Islands (H.M.S.O., London, 1951).

Islands of the South Pacific (Lane Books, California, 1966).

IRWIN, G. Samoa (Cassell, London, 1965).

IVENS, W. G. The Island-Builders of the Pacific (London, 1930).

JOESTING, E. Hawaii (W. W. Norton, New York, 1972).

KENNEDY, T. F. A Descriptive Atlas of the Pacific Islands (A. H. & A. W. Reed, Wellington, 1967).

KNIBBS, S. G. C. The Savage Solomons as they Were and Are (London, 1929).

LANGDON, R. Island of Love (Cassell, 1959).

LEA, D. A. M., and IRWIN, P. G. New Guinea, the Territory and Its People (Oxford University Press, Melbourne, 1967).

LETT, L. Papua, its People and its Promise (Melbourne, 1944).

LEWIN, P. E. The Pacific Region; a bibliography of the Pacific & East Indian Islands (Royal Empire Society, London, 1944).

LOHSE, B. Australia and the South Seas (Oliver & Boyd, Edinburgh, 1959).

LUKE, Sir HARRY. From a South Seas Diary (Nicholson and Watson, London, 1945).

MCGRATH, W. A. New Guineana or books of New Guinea (U.F.M. Press, Port Moresby, 1965).

MAIR, L. P. Australia and New Guinea (Christophers, London, 1948).

MAUDE, H. E. Of Islands and Men (Oxford University Press, Melbourne, 1968).

MEAD, M. Coming of Age in Samoa (1928).
Growing up in New Guinea (1930).

MOOREHEAD, A. The Fatal Impact: The Invasion of the South Pacific 1767–1840 (Hamish Hamilton, London, 1966).

O'REILLY, P. G. F. Bibliographie méthodique, analytique et critique de la Nouvelle-Calédonie (Publs. Soc. Océanist, 1955).
Bibliographie méthodique, analytique et critique des Nouvelles-Hébrides (Publs. Soc. Océanist, 1958).

O'REILLY, P. G. F., and REITMAN, F. Bibliographie de Tahiti et de la Polynésie française (Musée de l'Homme, Paris, 1967).

PRICE, Sir GRENFELL. The Challenge of New Guinea (Angus & Robertson, London, 1965).

REED, K. E. The High Valley (George Allen & Unwin, London, 1960).

REED, S. W. The Making of Modern New Guinea (Philadelphia, 1943).

ROBINSON, K. W. Australia, New Zealand and the South west Pacific (University of London Press, 1960).

ROLLIN, L. Les Iles Marquesas (Paris, 1929).

ROTH, G. K. Fijian Way of Life (edited by G. B. Milner, Oxford University Press, Melbourne, Revised, 1973).

SNOW, P. A. Best Stories of the South Seas (Faber and Faber, London, 1967).

Bibliography of Fiji, Tonga and Rotuma (Australian National University, Canberra, and Miami University Press, 1969).

SOUTER, G. New Guinea. The Last Unknown (Angus & Robertson, London, 1964).

STANNER, W. E. H. The South Seas in Transition (Australian Publishing Co., Sydney, 1953).

Statistical Year Book 1969 (Government Printer, Apia, Western Samoa).

THOMPSON, L. Guam and its People (San Francisco, 1941).

TODD, I. Island Realm (Angus & Robertson, Sydney, 1974).

TUDOR, J. (Editor). Pacific Islands Year Book and Who's Who (Pacific Publications, Ltd., Sydney, 1968).

WENKAM, R. Maui: The Last Hawaiian Place (Friends of the Earth, San Francisco, 1970).

WOOD, A. H. History and Geography of Tonga (Nuku' alofa, 1938).

Other Reference Material

WHO'S WHO IN THE FAR EAST AND AUSTRALASIA

A

Abdul Jamil, Tan Sri, P.M.N., P.J.K.; Malaysian civil servant and fmr. diplomatist; b. 14 Jan. 1912; ed. Clifford School and Oxford Univ., England.
Joined Admin. Service 32; State Sec. Perlis 51-52; State Financial Officer, Selangor 54-55, State Sec. 56; Chief Minister of Selangor 57-59; Deputy Sec. to the Treasury 59-61; Sec. to Fed. Treasury 61-64; Chief Sec. to Malaysian Govt., Head of Home and Foreign Service, Sec. to the Cabinet 64-67; High Commr. in U.K. 67-71; Chair. Penang Port Comm.; Vice-Chair. Malaysian Red Cross; Chair. Nat. Family Planning Board; Vice-Pres. Malaysian Lawn Tennis Assen.; Hon. LL.D. (Univ. of Malaysia) 68.
Jamnor, 32 Jalan Kia Peng, Kuala Lumpur, Malaysia.

Abdul Rahman, Tunku ibni Al-Marhum Sultan Abdul Hamid Halim Shah, C.H., B.A.; Malaysian politician; b. 8 Feb. 1903; ed. St. Catharine's Coll., Cambridge, and Inner Temple, London.
Appointed to Executive and Legislative Councils, as unofficial mem. 52; Leader, Fed. Legislative Council; Chief Minister and Minister for Home Affairs 55; first Prime Minister and Minister of External Affairs, Federation of Malaya Aug. 57-Feb. 59, Aug. 59-Sept. 63; Prime Minister and Minister of External Affairs, Malaysia Sept. 63-Sept. 70; Minister of Information and Broadcasting 63-64; Minister of Culture, Youth and Sports 64; Dir. and script writer for film *Raja Bersiong* 68; leader successively of United Malay National Organization and Alliance Party; Sec.-Gen. of Islamic Conf. 69-72; numerous foreign honours.
Kuala Lumpur, Malaya, Malaysia.

Abdulgani, Roeslan; Indonesian diplomatist, civil servant and politician; b. 1914; ed. Teacher Training Coll., Surabaya.
Active in Nat. Youth Movement seeking independence from Dutch; active in anti-Japanese underground during Japanese occupation; Editor *Bakti* (in East Java) 45; Sec.-Gen. Ministry of Information 47-53; Sec.-Gen. Ministry of Foreign Affairs 53-56; Del. to UN 51, 56, 66; Sec.-Gen. Afro-Asian Conf., Bandung 55; headed Del. to Suez Conf. 56; Minister of Foreign Affairs 56-57; mem. Constituent Assembly 57-; Vice-Chair. Nat. Council 57-59; Vice-Chair. Supreme Advisory Council 59-62; Co-ordinating Minister and Minister of Information 63-65; Deputy Prime Minister for Political Institutions 66; Perm. Rep. to UN 67-71; Vice-Pres. UN Gen. Assembly 69; Consultant, Nat. Defence and Security Council; Indonesian medals; several hon. degrees; mem. PNI (Indonesian Nat. Party).
Publs. *In Search of Indonesian Identity, The Bandung Spirit, Indonesian and Asian-African Nationalism, Pantja-Sila: The Prime Mover of the Indonesian Revolution, Hero's Day: In Memory of the Fighting in Surabaya on 10 November 1945, Impact of Utopian-Scientific and Religious Socialism on Indonesian Socialism, 25 Years: Indonesia and the UN, Personal Experiences During the Japanese Occupation.*
c/o Ministry of Foreign Affairs, Jakarta, Indonesia.

Abdullah, Sheikh Mohammad; Indian politician; b. 1905; ed. Kashmir and Aligarh (U.P.).
Founder of Kashmir Muslim Conf., later Kashmir Nat. Conf., for representative govt. in Kashmir 38; Pres. All-India States People's Conf. 46; led popular movement opposing rule of Maharajah of Kashmir 46; detained 46-47; Head, Interim Govt. 47; mem. Indian del. to UN 48; Prime Minister of Jammu and Kashmir 48-53; in detention 53-58, 58-64, 65-68; mem. Indian Constituent Assembly 49; fmr. Leader, Plebiscite Front Party; Chief Minister of Jammu and Kashmir Feb. 75-; Leader, State Congress Party Feb. 75-.
Soura, Srinagar, Kashmir, India.
Telephone: 3809.

Abdullah bin Ali, D.P.M. (Johore), K.M.N.; Malaysian diplomatist; b. 31 Aug. 1922; ed. Raffles Coll., Singapore.
Johore Civil Service; Malaysian Civil Service; Malaysian Foreign Service 57-; service in India, Australia, Indonesia, Ethiopia, Morocco, Singapore, Fed. Repub. of Germany; Chief of Protocol, Ministry of Foreign Affairs 69-71, concurrently Deputy Sec.-Gen. (Admin. and Gen. Affairs) 70-71; High Commr. in Singapore 71-75; Amb. to Fed. Repub. of Germany 75; High Commr. in U.K. Nov. 75-.
Malaysian High Commission, 45 Belgrave Square, London, SW1X 8QT; Home: 3 Hans Street, London, S.W.1, England.
Telephone: 01-245-9221 (Office); 01-235-3355 (Residence).

Abe, Kobo; Japanese novelist and playwright; b. 7 March 1924; ed. Tokyo Univ.
Twenty-fifth Akutagawa Prize 51, Post-War Literature Prize 49, Yomiuri Literary Prize 62, Kishida Prize for Drama 58.
Publs. *Owarishi Michino Shirubenni* (The Road Sign at the End of the Road), *Akai Mayu* (Red Cocoon) 49, *Kabe-S. Karumashi No Hanzai* (The Crimes of S. Karma, Esq.) 51, *Gaki Domei* (Hunger Union) 54, *Seifuku and other plays* (The Uniform) 55, *Doreigari* (Hunt for a Slave) 55, *Kemonotachi wa Kokyo o Mezasu* (Animals are Forwarding to Their Natives) 57, *Dai Yon Kanpyoki* (The Fourth Unglacial Period) 59, *Yurei wa Kokoni Iru* (Here is a Ghost) 59, *Ishi no Me* (Eyes of Stone) 60, *Suna no Onna* (The Woman in the Dunes) 62, *Tanin no Kao* (The Face of Another) 64, *Omaenimo Tsumi Ga Aru* (You are Guilty Too) 65, *Enomoto Buyo* (Buyo Enomoto) 65, *The Ruined Map* 69, *Inter Ice Age 4* 70, *Warau Thuki* (Smiling Moon).
1-22, Wakaba Cho, Chofu City, Tokyo, Japan.

Abe, Shintaro; Japanese journalist and politician.
Member House of Reps. 58-; Private Sec. to Prime Minister Nobusuke Kishi; fmr. Deputy Sec.-Gen. Liberal Democratic Party, fmr. Vice-Pres. LDP Diet Policy Cttee.; Minister of Agriculture and Forestry, Dec. 74-.
Ministry of Agriculture and Forestry, Tokyo, Japan.

Acharya, Bejoy Krishna; Indian civil servant and diplomatist; b. 1 May 1912; ed. Calcutta Univ. and Univ. Coll., London.
Joined I.C.S. 36; Chief Minister, Tripura State 48-49; Deputy Sec. in Ministries of Industry, External Affairs 49-51; Deputy High Commr. for India in East Pakistan 51-54; Minister and Political Rep. to Cambodia 55-56, Foreign Service Inspector, External Affairs 56, Joint Sec. External Affairs 57-59; Ambassador to Czechoslovakia and Romania 59-62, to Morocco and Tunisia 62-64; High Commr. in Canada 64-66, in Pakistan 69-71; Amb. to Brazil, Bolivia and Venezuela 66-68; Vigilance Commr., W. Bengal, Calcutta 71-72; Cen. Vigilance Commr., Govt. of India, New Delhi 72-.
3 Dr. Rajendra Prasad Road, New Delhi, India.

Adams-Schneider, Lance Raymond, M.P.; New Zealand politician; b. 1919; ed. Mt. Albert Grammar School.
Manager, Taumarunui dept. store; served in Second World War, N.Z. Medical Corps; Vice-Chair. Nat. Party in Waitomo electorate; mem. South Auckland Div. Exec.; M.P. for Hamilton 59-; Minister of Broadcasting, Minister Asst. to Minister of Customs until 69; Minister of Customs, Asst. Minister of Industries and Commerce 69-72; Minister of Health and Social Welfare 72; Opposition Spokesman on

37

Health and Social Welfare 72-74, on Trade, Industry and Customs 74-75; Minister of Trade and Industry Dec. 75-. Parliament Buildings, Wellington, New Zealand.

Adarkar, Bhaskar Namdeo, M.B.E., M.A.; Indian economist; b. 18 May 1910; ed. Wilson Coll., Bombay and Gonville and Caius Coll., Cambridge.
Agent, Bank of India Ltd., Bombay 38; Research Officer to the Economic Adviser to the Govt. of India 38-40, Chief Research Officer 40-41; Under-Sec. to the Govt. Commerce Dept. 41-43; Asst. Economic Adviser to the Govt. 43-45, Deputy Economic Adviser 45-49; mem. Indian Tariff Board 49 and 50-52; Sec. Reconstruction Cttees. 41-43, mem. Tariff Comm. 52-57; Exec. Dir. Int. Monetary Fund 57-61; Joint Sec. Ministry of Commerce and Industry 61-63; Additional Sec. Ministry of Economic and Defence Co-ordination Feb.-Aug. 63, Ministry of Finance Sept. 63-65; Deputy Gov. Reserve Bank of India 65-69, Gov. 70-75; Custodian, Central Bank of India 71-72, Chair., Man. Dir. 72-74; Chair. Maharashtra State Road Corpn. 74-.
Publs. include *Indian Tariff Policy, Devaluation of the Rupee, The Gold Problem, History of the Indian Tariff.*
Gulestan, Cuffe Parade, Colaba, Bombay 5, India.
Telephone: 21-18-67.

Adermann, (Albert) Evan; Australian (b. British) politician; b. 10 March 1927, Kingaroy, Queensland.
Public accountant; mem. House of Reps. 72-; opposition spokesman on customs and excise June 74-, assisting spokesman on trade, resources allocation and decentralization June 74-; mem. Joint Cttee. on Public Accounts 73-74; Minister for the Northern Territory Dec. 75-; mem. Gen. Admin. Cttee. Jan. 76-; Nat. Country Party.
Parliament House, Canberra, A.C.T. 2600; Howard Chambers, Queen Street, Nambour, Queensland; Home: 29 Oxleigh Crescent, Nambour, Queensland, Australia.

Adiseshiah, Malcolm Sathianathan, M.A., PH.D.; Indian economist; b. 18 April 1910; ed. Madras, London and Cambridge Univs.
Professor of Econs., Calcutta and Madras Univs. 30-46; Assoc. Gen. Sec. Int. Student Service 46-48; Deputy Dir. Exchange of Persons Service, UNESCO 48-50; Dir. Dept. of Tech. Assistance, UNESCO 50-54; Asst. Dir.-Gen. UNESCO 55-63, Deputy Dir.-Gen. 63-70; Dir. Madras Inst. of Devt. Studies 71-75; Vice-Chancellor, Univ. of Madras 75-.
Publs. *Demand for Money* 38, *Agricultural Economic Development* 41, *Handicraft Industries* 42, *Rural Credit* 43, *Planning Industrial Development* 44, *Restless Nations* 62, *War on Poverty* 63, *Non-political UN* 64, *Welfare and Wisdom* 65, *Economics of Indian Natural Resources* 66, *Education and National Development* 67, *International Role of the University* 68, *Unesco and the Second Development Decade* 69, *Let My Country Awake* 70, *It is Time to Begin* 71, *Techniques of Perspective Planning* 72, *Plan Implementation Problems and Perspective* 73, *Science in the Battle Against Poverty* 74, *Towards a Functional Learning Society* 75.
74 Second Main Road, Gandhinager, Adyar, Madras 20, South India.

Adjie, Lieut.-Gen. Ibrahim; Indonesian army officer and diplomatist; b. 24 Feb. 1923; ed. Acad. for Officers, Indonesian Volunteer Army, Fort Benning, Staff and Command Coll.
Commanding Officer, Indonesian Volunteer Army 42-45, People's Security Forces 45; Battalion Commdr. 46, Chief-of-Staff 2nd Regiment, West Java Territory 47; Deputy Commdr. Sub-Territory VII (Sumatra) 48; Mil. Gov. South Tapanuli 49; Chief of Staff 1st Div., North Sumatra 54; Mil. Attaché, Yugoslavia 56-59; Chief of Staff, Siliwangi Corps 59, Commdg. Gen. 60-66; Chair. Nat. Front, West Java 60-66; Amb. to the U.K. 66-70; retd. from Army Jan. 75; numerous awards including 12 mil. honours.
Publs. *Doctrines of Total People's Defence and Territorial Warfare* 60, *Doctrines of Territorial Management* 60, *National Alertness* 66.
c/o Ministry of Foreign Affairs, Jakarta, Indonesia.

Ahmed, Aziz, O.B.E.; Pakistani civil servant, politician and diplomatist; b. 1906; ed. Cambridge Univ.
Sub-Divisional Officer, Bengal 34-37; Dir. Debt Conciliation Bengal 37-39; District Magistrate, Raj Shahi District 39-41; Registrar Co-op Socs., Bengal 41-43; Dir. Procurement, Dept. of Civil Supplies, Bengal 43-44, Joint Sec. (Planning) 44-46; Deputy Sec. Indian Dept. of Agriculture 46-47; Chief Sec. to Govt. of E. Pakistan 47-52; Sec. to Cabinet, Central Govt., Pakistan 52-56; Sec. to various Ministries, then Sec.-Gen. to Govt. of Pakistan 56-59; Amb. to U.S.A. 59-63; Sec. to Govt. of Pakistan Ministry of Foreign Affairs 63-66; Chair. Press Trust of Pakistan; Minister of State for Foreign Affairs and Defence 73-; cabinet mem. Feb. 76-; Hilal-i-Pakistan, Hilal-i-Azam, Sitara-i-Pakistan.
Ministry of Foreign Affairs, Islamabad; Home: 55 Clifton, Karachi 6, Pakistan.

Ahmed, Fakhruddin Ali, B.A.; Indian barrister and politician; b. 13 May 1905; ed. St. Stephen's Coll., Delhi, St. Catharine's Coll., Cambridge, and Inner Temple, London.
Called to Bar; went to Assam 28; joined Indian Nat. Congress 31; mem. Assam Pradesh Congress Cttee. 36-, All-India Congress Cttee. 36-; Minister of Finance and Revenue, Assam 38-39; detained 40, 42-45; Advocate-Gen. of Assam 46-52; mem. Rajya Sabha 54-57, 66-67, of Assam Assembly 57-66; Minister of Finance, Law, Community Devt. and Panchayyats in Assam Govt. 57-66, of Local Self-Govt. 57-62; Union Minister of Irrigation and Power 66, of Educ. 66-67, of Industrial Devt. and Company Affairs 67-70, of Internal Trade 69-70, of Agric. 70-74; Pres. of India Aug. 74-; mem. Del. to UN 57; leader, Del. to FAO Council 71, 73; Vice-Chair. Assam Sports Council; Pres. All-India Lawn Tennis Asscn., Asia Lawn Tennis Fed.; Hon. LL.D. (Guru Nauak Univ.) 74, (Gauhati Univ.) 75, (Kurukshetra Univ.) 76.
Office of the President, Rashtrapati Bhavan, New Delhi, India.

Ahmed, Khandakar Moshtaque; Bangladesh lawyer and politician; b. 1918; ed. Dacca Univ.
Joined Quit India movement 42; imprisoned 46; collaborated with Sheikh Mujibur Rahman in Bengali language movement, later in Awami League; imprisoned several times by Pakistan authorities; Minister of Foreign Affairs, Law and Parl. Affairs in Govt. of Bangladesh April-Dec. 71 (in exile in India), of Law, Parl. Affairs and Land Revenue 71-72, of Power, Irrigation and Flood Control 72-74, of Trade and Commerce 74-75; Pres. of Bangladesh, also Minister of Defence and Home Affairs Aug.-Nov. 75; living in Bangladesh.

Aida, Chohei; Japanese business executive; b. 22 Feb. 1898; ed. Kobe Univ.
Chairman, Fuji Electric Co., Ltd.
Fuji Electric Co., Ltd., 1-1, Ranabeshinden, Kawasaki City, Kanagawa Prefecture, Japan.

Aikyo, Mitsuo; Japanese mining executive; b. 3 Jan. 1908; ed. Hitotsubashi Univ.
Former Pres. Mitsubishi Metal Mining Co., Chair. 71-.
Mitsubishi Metal Mining Co. Ltd., 5-2, Ohtemachi, 1-chome, Chiyoda-ku, Tokyo, Japan.

Aitmatov, Chingiz; Soviet (Kirghiz) writer; b. 1928; ed. Kirghiz Agricultural Inst.
Writer 52-; First Sec. of Cinema Union of Kirghiz S.S.R. 64-69, Chair. 69-; Candidate mem. Central Cttee. of C.P.

of Kirghiz S.S.R.; Lenin Prize for *Tales of the Hills and the Steppes* 63; State Prize 68.
Publs. include stories: *Face to Face, Short Stories, Melody* 61, *Tales of the Hills and the Steppes* 63; novels: *Djamilya* 59, *My Poplar in a Red Kerchief* 60, *Camel's Eye, The First Teacher, Farewell Guilsari.*
Kirghiz Branch of Union of Writers of U.S.S.R., Ulitsa Pushkina 52, Frunze, Kirghiz S.S.R., U.S.S.R.

Akama, Yoshihiro; Japanese banker; b. 2 Dec. 1916, Tokyo; ed. Tokyo Univ.
Managing Dir. Mitsubishi Trust & Banking Corpn. 65-69, Senior Man. Dir. 69-70, Deputy Pres. 70-71, Pres. 71-.
Mitsubishi Trust & Banking Corporation, 4-5, 1-chome, Marunouchi, Chiyoda-ku, Tokyo; Home: 4-15-22 Komagome Toshimaku, Tokyo, Japan.
Telephone: 03-917-5755.

Akatani, Genichi; Japanese United Nations official; b. 29 Sept. 1918, Taipei; ed. Univ. of Oxford and Sophia Univ., Tokyo.
Joined Japanese Foreign Service 45; Second Sec., Paris 54, First Sec. 55; Head, East-West Trade Div., Econ. Affairs Bureau, Ministry of Foreign Affairs 58; Counsellor, Washington, D.C. 61-66; Counsellor, Public Information Bureau, Ministry of Foreign Affairs 66-72; Asst. Sec.-Gen. for Public Information, UN June 72-; del. to several sessions of UN Gen. Assembly.
United Nations, First Avenue, New York, N.Y. 10017, U.S.A.

Akhund, Iqbal Ahmad, M.A.; Pakistani diplomatist; b. Aug. 1924, Hyderabad; ed. Bombay Univ.
Entered Pakistan Foreign Service 49, served in Canada, Spain, Netherlands, Saudi Arabia, Malaysia and New York (UN); Personal Sec. to Minister of Foreign Affairs 56-58; Dir. and Dir.-Gen. Ministry of Foreign Affairs 64-66, 66-68; Amb. to Egypt 68-71, to Yugoslavia 71-72; Perm. Rep. to UN May 72-; Vice-Pres. Econ. and Social Council 74, Pres. 75.
Permanent Mission of Pakistan to United Nations, Pakistan House, 8 East 65th Street, New York, N.Y. 10021, U.S.A.

Akilandam, Perungalur Vaithialingam (*pseudonym* Akilon); Indian Tamil writer; b. 27 June 1922; ed. Maharaja's Coll., Pudukkottai.
Writer 40-; in Indian Post & Telegraph Dept. 45-58; freelance writer 58-65; Sec. Tamil Writers' Asscn., Tiruchy 53-57; Sec. Gen. Fed. of All-India Tamil Writers 62-65; Dir. Tamil Writers' Co-op. Soc. 63-; mem. Tamil Advisory Board, Sahitya Akademi 64-; Producer, Spoken Word in Tamil, All-India Radio, Madras 65-; Pres. Tamil Writers Asscn. 67; Kalai Magal Prize for *Penn* 46, Tamil Akademi Award for *Nenjin Alaigal* 53, Sahitya Akademi Award for *Vengaiyin Maindan* 63, Tamil Nadu Govt. Award for *Kayalvizhi* 68, for *Erimalai* 73.
Publs. include novels: *Penn* 46, *Snehithi* 50, *Nenjin Alaigal* 53, *Pavai Vilakku* 58, *Vengaiyin Maindan* 61, *Ponmalar* 64, *Kayalvizhi* 64, *Chittirap Paavai* 67; short stories: *Sakthivel* 47, *Nilavinilay* 50, *Vazhi Pirandhadu* 52, *Sahodara Andro?* 63, *Nellore Arisi* 67, *Erimalai* 70.
171 Lloyds Road, Madras 14, India.
Telephone: 81968.

Ali, (Chaudhri) Mohamad, M.SC.; Pakistani politician; b. 15 July 1905; ed. Lahore and Univ. of Punjab.
Lecturer in Chemistry, Islamia Coll., Lahore 27-28; joined Indian Accounts and Audit Service 28; Accountant-Gen., Bahawalpur 32-36; entered Govt. of India service 36; Under-Sec. Finance Dept. 38-39; Deputy Financial Adviser 39-43; Joint Financial Adviser, Ministry of Supply 43-45; Financial Adviser War and Supply 45-47; mem. Steering Cttee. of Partition Council 47; Sec.-Gen. to Govt. of Pakistan 47-51; Minister of Finance 51; Minister of Finance and Econ. Affairs 54-55; Prime Minister and other portfolios 55-56; Leader Nizam-e-Islam Party; retd. from politics 69.
Publ. *The Emergence of Pakistan* 67.
86-D/1, Gulberg III, Lahore, Pakistan.
Telephone: 81434.

Ali, H. A. Mukti; Indonesian specialist in comparative religion; b. 1923, Central Java; ed. Indonesia, Karachi, Pakistan and McGill Univ., Canada.
Vice-Chancellor, AIN "Sunan Kalijaga", Jogjakarta; Minister of Religious Affairs Sept. 71-.
Publs. *Modernization of Islamic Schools, Comparative Religion, Its Method and System.*
Ministry of Religious Affairs, J. L. M. Husni Thamrin 6, Jakarta; Home: Perumahan Dinas Pejabat Tinggi 1, Jakarta, Indonesia.

Ali, S. Osman; Pakistani banker and civil servant; b. 1 July 1912; ed. Univs. of Madras and Oxford.
Indian Civil Service 34-66; Chief Presidency Magistrate, Madras 43-45; Deputy Sec. of Home Dept., Govt. of India 45-46, of Cabinet Secr. 46-47, of Cabinet Secr. of Govt. of Pakistan 47-49, Joint Sec. 49-52; Joint Sec. Ministry of Commerce 52-58, Sec. (also in Ministry of Industries) 59-62; Sec. for Econ. Affairs 62-66; Amb. to Belgium, Luxembourg and EEC, Perm. Rep. to UN Office at Geneva 66-68; Exec. Dir. IBRD, IDA, IFC 68-72; fmr. Man. Dir. Pakistan Industrial Credit and Investment Corpn.; Gov. State Bank of Pakistan Dec. 75-; leader dels. in trade negotiations and to GATT, UNCTAD, ECOSOC; fmr. Chair. Advisory Cttee. for UNCTAD; Sitara-i-Quaid-i-Azam 58, Sitara-i-Pakistan 64.
State Bank of Pakistan, Central Directorate, I, I. Chundrigar Road, Post Box No. 4456, Karachi, Pakistan.

Ali, Sadiq, B.A.; Indian politician; b. 1910; ed. Allahabad Univ.
Permanent Sec., All-India Congress Cttee. 38-48; mem. Lok Sabha 50-58, Rajya Sabha 58-70; Gen. Sec. Indian Congress Party 58-64, 66-69; Pres. Opposition Congress Party 71-73; Chair. Gandhi Smarak Sangrahalaya Samiti 66-; Chief Editor *Political and Economic Review* 67-71.
Publs. *Know Your Country, Congress Ideology and Programme, Culture in India, General Elections 1957, Towards Socialist Thinking in Congress.*
Gandhi National Museum and Library, Rajghat, New Delhi, India.

Allen, Percy B., M.P.; New Zealand politician; b. 1913; ed. Te Aroha and Rotorua.
Deputy Chair. Rotorua Branch of Nat. Party; M.P. Bay of Plenty 57-75; Minister of Works and Minister in Charge of Police 63-69, 72; Minister of Works and Minister of Electricity 69-72.
c/o Parliament Buildings, Wellington, New Zealand.

Amatayakul, Manu, LIC.RER.POL.; Thai diplomatist and Barrister-at-law; b. 1912; ed. Chulalongkorn Univ., Univ. of Berlin and Univ. of Berne.
Lecturer in Public Finance, Econs., Journalism, Chulalongkorn Univ., lecturer in Int. Law, Thammasat Univ. 42-47; Deputy Chief Thai Perm. Del. to UN 47-50; Dir.-Gen. UN Dept., Ministry of Foreign Affairs 53-59; Prof. of Int. Relations, Chulalongkorn Univ. 55-58; Prof. of Int. Law and Law of Treaties, Thammasat Univ. 69-70; mem. Thai Del. to UN Gen. Assembly 47-49, 53, 58, 61; mem. Civil Aviation Board of Thailand 53-59; Amb. to U.S.S.R. 59-63, to Spain 63-65; Dir.-Gen. of Treaty and Legal Dept., Ministry of Foreign Affairs 65-70; Legal Adviser to Prime Minister 69-70; Amb. to Brazil and Peru 70-71, to Italy -75; Special Grand Cordon of Most Noble Order of Crown of Thailand 65, and other decorations.
Publs. *Umwandlung der Währungspolitik Europas von*

1918–1939, *Kreditpolitik Europas*, *United Nations*, and other works.
Home: 69 Prongchai Road, Mahamek, Bangkok, Thailand. Telephone: 862427; 861473.

Amerasinghe, Hamilton Shirley; Ceylonese diplomatist; b. 18 March 1913; ed. Royal Coll., Colombo and Ceylon Univ. Coll.
Ceylon Civil Service 37; Sec. to Minister of Health, Ceylon 41-46; Resident Manager, Gal Oya Development Board 50-52; Counsellor, Washington 53-55; Controller of Establishments, General Treasury, Ceylon 55-57; Alt. Del. Ceylon Del. to UN 57; Controller of Supply, Cadre and Finance, General Treasury, Ceylon 58; Perm. Sec. to Ministry of Nationalised Services and Chair. Port (Cargo) Corpn., Colombo 58; Sec. to Treasury and Perm. Sec. Ministry of Finance 61-63; Dir. Bank of Ceylon 62-63; High Commr. of Ceylon in India 63-67; Perm. Rep. to UN 67-; Pres. UN Conf. on Law of the Sea 73-; Chair. UN Cttee. on Peaceful Uses of the Sea Bed and Ocean Floor beyond Nat. Jurisdiction 69, 70, 71, 72, 73; Chair., UN Ad Hoc Cttee. on the Indian Ocean 73.
Permanent Mission of Sri Lanka to United Nations, 630 Third Avenue, New York, N.Y. 10017; Home: Apartment 5SW, 1155 Park Avenue, New York, N.Y. 10028, U.S.A.

Amir Machmud, Lt.-Gen.; Indonesian army officer and politician; b. 21 Feb. 1923, Cimahi, West Java; ed. Technical School, Army Staff Coll. (SSKAD).
Several army posts 43-65, including Deputy Chief of Staff Dwilora Command I 61, Commdr. Mil. Territory X, Lambung Mangkurat, S. Kalimantan 62-65, Commdr. Mil. Territory V/Djaja 65; promoted to rank of Lt.-Col. 57, Col. 61, Brig.-Gen. 64, Maj.-Gen. 66, Lt.-Gen. 70; Minister of Home Affairs, Pembangunan (Devt.) Cabinet 69; Chair. of govt. body for the implementation of Act of Free Choice in W. Irian (now Irian Jaya) according to New York Agreement on Irian Jaya 69; implemented general elections 71; Minister of Home Affairs 73-.
Department of Home Affairs, Jalan Veteran, Jakarta, Indonesia.

Amritanand, Rt. Rev. Joseph; Indian ecclesiastic; b. 17 Feb. 1917; ed. Forman Christian Coll., Lahore and Bishop's Coll.
Ordained Deacon 41, Priest 43; Bishop of Assam 49-62, of Lucknow 62-70, Bishop of Calcutta 70-, also of Durgapur 72-74.
Bishop's House, 51 Chowringhee Road, Calcutta 700071, India.

An P'ing-sheng; Chinese politician.
Provincial Cadre in Kwangtung 55, Vice-Gov. Kwangtung 56-61; Sec. Kwangsi CCP Cttee. 61-67, 71-75, First Sec. 75-; Vice-Chair. Kwangsi Revolutionary Cttee. 68-.
People's Republic of China.

Anand, Bal Krishan, M.B., B.S., M.D.; Indian physiologist; b. 19 Sept. 1917; ed. Government Coll. and K.E. Medical Coll., Lahore.
Professor of Physiology, Lady Hardinge Medical Coll., New Delhi 49-57; All India Inst. of Medical Sciences, New Delhi 57-; Pres. XXVI Int. Congress of Physiological Sciences, New Delhi 74; Rockefeller Foundation Fellow at Yale Univ. School of Medicine 50-51; Fellow, Indian Acad. of Medical Sciences, Nat. Inst. of Sciences (F.N.I.); Indian Council of Medical Research Senior Research Award 62; Watumull Foundation Award in Medicine 61; Sir Shanti Swaroof Bhatnagar Memorial Award for Scientific Research in Medicine 63; Padma Shri 69; Medical Council of India Silver Jubilee Research Award 69.
All India Institute of Medical Sciences, Ansari Nagar, New Delhi 16, India.

Anand, Mulk Raj, PH.D.; Indian author and critic; b. 12 Dec. 1905; ed. Punjab and London Univs.
Active in Nationalist and Gandhi movements; lecturer, London County Council; B.B.C. broadcaster; film script writer, British Ministry of Information; edited (56) various magazines, Leverhulme Fellow for Research in Hindustani literature; Editor *Marg* magazine, India; mem. India Nat. Acad. of Letters, Indian Nat. Acad. of Arts, Indian Nat. Book Trust; Tagore Prof. of Art and Literature, Panjab Univ., Chandigarh; fmr. Chair. Nat. Acad. of Art, New Delhi; Padma Bhushan 67.
Publs. Novels: *Morning Face*, *Private Life of an Indian Prince*, *Confession of a Lover*, *Untouchable Coolie*, *The Barbers' Trade Union*, *Seven Summers*, etc.; Essays: *Apology for Heroism*, *Lines Written to an Indian Air*, etc.
Jassim House, 25 Cuffe Parade, Colaba, Bombay 5, India.

Anderson, Dame Judith, D.B.E.; Australian actress; b. 10 Feb. 1898, Adelaide; ed. Norwood High School.
Stage debut in *A Royal Divorce*, Theatre Royal, Sydney 15; went to New York 18; stage appearances have included: *The Dove*, *Behold the Bridegroom*, *Strange Interlude*, *Mourning becomes Electra*, *Come of Age*, *The Old Maid*, *Hamlet*, *Macbeth*, *Family Portrait*, *Tower Beyond*, *Three Sisters*, *Medea*; films: *Rebecca*, *Edge of Darkness*, *Laura*, *King's Row*, *Spectre of the Rose*, *The Red House*, *Pursued*, *Tycoon*, *Cat on a Hot Tin Roof*, *Macbeth*, *Don't Bother to Knock*, *The Chinese Prime Minister* (TV) 74.
c/o Actors' Equity of New York, 165 West 4th Street, New York, N.Y.; 808 San Ysidro Lane, Santa Barbara, Calif. 93103, U.S.A.

Anderson, Hon. Sir Kenneth McColl, K.B.E.; Australian politician; b. 11 Oct. 1909.
Army service 41-45; prisoner-of-war for 3½ years; Mayor of Ryde 49-51; elected to Legislative Assembly of New South Wales 50-53; mem. Senate 53-; temporary Chair. of Cttees. of the Senate 56-64; Minister for Customs and Excise 64-68, for Supply 68-70, for Health 71-72.
Australian Parliament Offices, Australian Government Centre, Chifley Square, Sydney, N.S.W. 2000, Australia.

Angami, T. N.; Indian politician; b. 1913.
Served in Indian Army overseas during Second World War; in Indian Civil Service 46-50; Chair. *De facto* Nagaland Legis. Assembly 61-63; Speaker Nagaland Legis. Assembly 64-66; Chief Minister Nagaland 66-67, 67-69; Minister of Public Works and Electricity 69-74.
c/o P.O. Kohima, Nagaland, India.

Ansell, Graham Keith, B.A.; New Zealand diplomatist; b. 2 March 1931, Lower Hutt, New Zealand; ed. Horowhenua Coll., Palmerston North Boys' School and Victoria Univ., Wellington.
Department of Industries and Commerce 48-51, of External Affairs 51-56; Second Sec., High Comm. to Canada 56-59; Asst., then Acting Head, Econ. and Social Affairs Div., Dept. of External Affairs 59-62; Deputy High Commr., Australia 64-68; Head, Econ. Div., Ministry of Foreign Affairs 68-71; Minister, N.Z. Embassy, Japan 71-73; High Commr., Fiji 73-, concurrently to Nauru 74-.
New Zealand High Commission, Suva; Home: 1 Marou Road, Suva, Fiji.

Ansett, Sir Reginald Myles, K.B.E.; Australian company executive; b. 13 Feb. 1909.
Chairman and Man. Dir. Ansett Transport Industries Ltd. and subsidiaries, Ansett Transport Industries (Operations) Pty. Ltd. (Trading as Ansett Airlines of Australia, Ansett Airlines of New South Wales, Ansett Airlines of S. Australia, Ansett Freight Express, Ansett Pioneer, Aviation Engineering Supplies, N.I.C. Instrument Co., Barrier Reef Islands, Macrobertson Miller Airline Services, Mildura Bus Lines, Ansett General Aviation, Ansair, Ansett Motors, Ansett Television Films, Provincial Motors), Ansett Niugini Enterprises Ltd., Ansett Hotels Pty. Ltd., Austarama Television Pty. Ltd., Universal Telecasters Queens-

land Ltd., Wridgways Holdings Ltd., Ansett Hotels (P. & N.G.) Pty. Ltd., Ansett Brewarrawa Holdings Pty. Ltd., Albury Border Transport Pty. Ltd., Transport Industries Insurance Co. Ltd., J. Sist and Co. Pty. Ltd.; Dir. Van Dusen Aircraft Supplies Australia Ltd., Diners Club Ltd.
489 Swanston Street, Melbourne, Victoria, Australia.

Anthony, Rt. Hon. (John) Douglas; Australian farmer and politician; b. 31 Dec. 1929; ed. Murwillumbah High School, The King's School, Paramatta, and Queensland Agricultural Coll.
Member House of Reps. 57-, Exec. Council 63-72, Minister for the Interior 64-67, of Primary Industry 67-71; Leader of Country Party 71-; Minister for Trade, Deputy Prime Minister 71-72; Deputy Prime Minister, Minister for Overseas Trade Nov. 75-, also Minister for Minerals and Energy Nov.-Dec. 75, for Natural Resources Dec. 75-; Privy Councillor 71.
Parliament House, Canberra, A.C.T., Australia.

Anwar Sani, Chaidir; Indonesian diplomatist; b. 19 Feb. 1918, Padang; ed. Univ. of Leiden.
Joined Indonesian Foreign Service 50; First Sec., Paris 50-52; Ministry of Foreign Affairs 52-55; Counsellor, Cairo 55, Peking 55-57; Ministry of Foreign Affairs 57-60; Minister, Counsellor, New Delhi 60-64; Ministry of Foreign Affairs 64-70; Amb. to Belgium and Luxembourg and Head, Indonesian Mission to EEC 70-72; Perm. Rep. to UN March 72-.
Permanent Mission of Indonesia to the United Nations, 733 Third Avenue, 11th Floor, New York, N.Y. 10017, U.S.A.

Aramaki, Torao; Japanese business executive; b. 22 Nov. 1902; ed. Yokohama Nat. Univ.
President, Isuzu Motors Ltd.
Isuzu Motors Ltd., 6-22-10, Minami-Oi, Shinagawaku, Tokyo; Home: 2-3-7, Ikeda, Kawasaki City, Kanagawa Pref., Japan.
Telephone: Kawasaki 32-4610.

Arifov, Ubai Arifovich; Soviet physicist; b. 1909; ed. Samarkand Pedagogical Acad.
Director Physico-Technical Inst., Uzbek Acad. of Sciences 45-56; mem. Acad. of Sciences of Uzbekistan 56-; Dir. Inst. of Nuclear Physics of Uzbek Acad. of Sciences 56-62, Pres. 62-66; Dir. Inst. of Electronics 66-; Editor *Doklady Acad. Nauk Uzbekskej S.S.R.*, later mem. editorial board; Chief Editor *Helio-technology* 65-; Order of Lenin, Biruni Prize, other medals and orders of U.S.S.R.
Publs. More than 150 scientific works and about 150 publs.
Observatorskaya, 85 Institute of Electronics, Tashkent, U.S.S.R.

Armstrong, John Ignatius; Australian politician; b. 6 July 1908, Sydney; ed. Marist Brothers High School, Darlinghurst.
Member, Sydney City Council 34, Chair. 63-65; Senator for N.S.W. 38-62; Govt. Rep., Nat. Film Board 45-49; Minister for Supply and Devt. 46-49, and mem. Commonwealth Rationing Comm.; Minister in Charge Royal Visit 48; Deputy Opposition Leader, Senate 51-56; Lord Mayor of Sydney 65-67; High Commr. to the U.K. 72-75.
47 Beach Road, Collaroy, N.S.W., Australia.

Arnaud, Claude; French diplomatist; b. 9 Nov. 1919, Voiteur (Jura); ed. Univs. of Dijon, Lyon and Paris.
Attaché, Washington 45-46; Office of Resident-Gen. in Morocco 46-51; First-Sec. Bonn 52-55; Econ. Dept., Foreign Office, Paris 55-59; Counsellor, Chargé d'Affaires, Belgrade 59-62; Minister-Counsellor, Perm. Mission to UN 62-65; Amb. to Laos 66-68, to Kenya 68-69; Dir. European Dept., Ministry of Foreign Affairs 69-72, Deputy Dir. for Political Affairs 72-75; Amb. to People's Repub. of China 75-; Chevalier Légion d'Honneur, Croix de Guerre 39-45.
French Embassy, Peking, People's Republic of China; and 3 rue La Perouse, Paris, France.

Arthur, James Stanley, B.SC.; British diplomatist; b. 3 Feb. 1923; ed. Anderson Educ. Inst., Shetland Isles, Trinity Acad., Edinburgh and Liverpool Univ.
Ministry of Educ. (later Dept. of Educ. and Science) 47-66, Private Sec. to Parl. Sec. 49-51, Principal Private Sec. to Minister 60-63; Foreign Office 66-67; Counsellor, High Comm., Kenya 67-70; Deputy High Commr. in Malta, G.C. 70-73; High Commr. in Fiji 74-.
British High Commission, Suva, Fiji; and c/o Foreign and Commonwealth Office (Fiji), King Charles Street, London, S.W.1, England.

Aryal, Krishna Raj, M.ED., M.A.; Nepali politician; b. Dec. 1928, Kathmandu; ed. Durbar High School, Tri-Chandra Coll., Allahabad Univ., India.
Lecturer, Nat. Teachers' Training Centre 54-56; Prof. of Educ., Coll. of Educ. 56-59; Editor *Education Quarterly* 56-59, *Nabin Shikshya* 56-59; Founder, Admin. and Principal Shri Ratna Rajya Laxmi Girls' Coll. 61-71; Asst. Minister for Educ. 71-72, Minister 72-75, concurrently Pro-Chancellor, Tribhuvan Univ. 73-75; Minister of Foreign Affairs April 75-; Gorakha Dakhinbahu, Second Class; Grand Officer of Yugoslav Star, Second Class; Grand Cordon of Yugoslav Star, First Class; Order of the Million Elephants (Laos).
Publs. *Monarchy in the Making of Nepal* (in English), *Education for Development of Nepal* (in English), *Facts of Interest* (series in Nepali).
Ministry of Foreign Affairs, Singha Durbar, Kathmandu; Home: Gaihiri Dhara, Kathmandu, Nepal.

Asada, Shizuo; Japanese aviation official; b. 13 Oct. 1911; ed. Law Dept., Tokyo Imperial Univ.
Dir. Bureau of Shipping, Ministry of Transport 58-61; Admin. Vice-Minister of Transport 61-63; Senior Vice-Pres. Japan Air Lines 63-69, Exec. Vice-Pres. 69-71, Pres. 71-.
Japan Air Lines, 7-3, Marunouchi 2-chome, Chiyoda-ku, Tokyo 100; Home: 30-19, Seijo 6-chome, Setagaya-ku, Tokyo 157, Japan.

Asai, Koji; Japanese banker; b. 3 Aug. 1902, Ishikawa Pref.
Joined The Sumitomo Bank 25, Man. Dir. 52, Senior Man. Dir. 58, Deputy Pres. 63, Pres. 71-73; Dir. Fed. of Bankers' Asscns. of Japan, Osaka Bankers' Asscn.
12-5 Hamacho, Ashiya-City, Hyogo Prefecture, Japan.

Asamov, Salakhitdin; Soviet politician; b. 1930; ed. Moscow Veterinary Acad.
Member C.P.S.U. 56-; zoo-technician, Dir. Nishan State Stud Farm, Karshi District, Surkhandarya Region 51-61; party official and Minister of Agriculture of Uzbek S.S.R. 61-64, also Chair. Samarkand Regional Soviet of Working People's Deputies; First Sec. Kashkadarya Regional Cttee. of C.P. of Uzbekistan 64-71; Chair. Exec. Cttee. Tashkent Regional Soviet of Working People's Deputies 71-; mem. Central Cttee. of C.P. of Uzbekistan; Deputy to U.S.S.R. Supreme Soviet 66-70.
Tashkent Regional Soviet of Working People's Deputies, Tashkent, U.S.S.R.

Asano, Teiji; Japanese business executive; b. 1906; ed. Tohoku Imperial Univ.
Joined shipbuilding dept., Mitsui & Co. 30; entered Tamano Shipyard Ltd. (predecessor of Mitsui Shipbuilding & Engineering Co. Ltd.) 48; Man. Dir. Mitsui Shipbuilding & Engineering Co. 58, Senior Man. Dir. 65, Vice-Pres. 68, Chair. of Board 70-.
Mitsui Shipbuilding & Engineering Co. Ltd., 6-4, Tsukiji 5-chome, Chuo-ku, Tokyo, Japan.
Telephone: 543-3111.

Ashihara, Yoshinobu, B.A., M.ARCH., D.ENG.; Japanese architect; b. 7 July 1918; ed. Univ. of Tokyo and Harvard Univ. Graduate School.
Worked in architectural firms, Tokyo 46-52; in Marcel Breuer's firm, New York 53; visited Europe on Rockefeller Travel Grant 54; Head, Yoshinobu Ashihara, Arch. and Assocs. 55-; Lecturer in Architecture, Hosei Univ., Tokyo 55-59, Prof. of Architecture 59-65; visited Europe and U.S.A. to study exterior space in architecture 60; Prof. of Architecture, Musashino Art Univ., Tokyo 64-70; Prof. Univ. of Tokyo 70-; Visiting Prof., School of Architecture and Building, Univ. of New South Wales, Australia 66, Univ. of Hawaii 69; Award of Architectural Inst. of Japan for Chuo-Koron Building 60; Special Award of Architectural Inst. of Japan for Komazawa Olympic Gymnasium 65; Ministry of Educ. Award for Japan Pavilion *Expo 67*, Montreal; NSID Golden Triangle Award (U.S.A.) 70, Order of Commendatore (Italy) 70.
Works include: Chuo-Koron Building, Sony Building, Komazawa Olympic Gymnasium 65, Japanese Pavilion, Expo 67, Montreal, Fuji Film Building 69.
Publ. *Exterior Design in Architecture* 70.
Y. Ashihara, Architects and Associates, 7th Floor, Sumitomo-seimei Shibuya Building, 31-15 Sakuraga-okacho, Shibuya-ku, Tokyo; Home: 47 Nishihara-3, Shibuya-ku, Tokyo, Japan.

Askarov, Asanbai; Soviet politician; b. 1922; ed. Frunze Teachers' Training Coll. and Higher Party School of C.P.S.U. Central Cttee.
In Educational Service 39-42; Soviet Army 42-46; Party Official 46-51, 54-58; Chair. Djambul Regional Soviet of Working People's Deputies 58-59; First Sec., Djambul Regional Cttee., Communist Party of Kazakhstan 59-65; First Sec. Alma Ata Regional Cttee., C.P. of Kazakhstan; mem. Central Cttee. of C.P.S.U. and of Central Cttee. of Kazakhstan C.P. 65-; Alt. mem. Bureau of Central Cttee., C.P. of Kazakhstan; Deputy to U.S.S.R. Supreme Soviet; mem. Mandate Cttee., Soviet of Nationalities of U.S.S.R. Supreme Soviet; Chair. Youth Affairs Comm. 74-; mem. C.P.S.U. 44-.
Alma Ata Regional Committee, Communist Party of Kazakh S.S.R., Alma Ata, U.S.S.R.

Askin, Hon. Sir Robert William, G.C.M.G.; Australian politician; b. 4 April 1909; ed. Sydney Technical High School, New South Wales.
Former bank official; war service; mem. N.S.W. Legislative Assembly 50-; Deputy Leader N.S.W. Liberal Party 54-59, Leader 59-; Premier and Treas. of N.S.W. 65-74.
86 Bower Street, Manly, Sydney, New South Wales, Australia.

Asri bin Haji Muda, Datuk Haji Mohamed, S.P.M.K.; Malaysian politician; b. 10 Oct. 1923.
Former teacher; Acting Sec.-Gen. Pan-Malayan Islamic Party 49-54, Commr., Kelantan 54-61, Vice-Pres. 61-64, Pres. 64-; mem. Kelantan State Assembly 59-68, Speaker 64-68; mem. Parl. 59-68; mem. Nat. Unity Council 69-; Minister of Land Devt., Mines and Special Functions 72-76, of Land, Mines and Regional Devt. March 76-; Deputy Chair. Nat. Council for Islamic Affairs 73-.
Ministry of Land, Mines and Regional Development, Kuala Lumpur, Malaysia.

Aston, Hon. Sir William John, K.C.M.G.; Australian politician; b. 19 Sept. 1916, Sydney; ed. Randwick Boys' High School.
Mayor of Waverley 52; Mem. of Parl. for Phillip 55-61, 63-72; Deputy Govt. Whip 59-61, 63-64, Chief Govt. Whip 64-67; mem. and Deputy Chair. Joint Select Cttee. on New and Perm. Parl. House 65-72; Chair. House of Reps. Standing Orders Cttee.; Chair. Joint House Cttee.; Chair. Joint Cttee. on Broadcasting of Parl. Proceedings 67-72; Speaker, House of Reps. 67-72; Leader Del. to Interparl. Union Conf., Ottawa 65; Dir., Astyle Pty. Ltd., Kolotex (Holdings) Ltd., Nelson McCarthy (Aust.) Ltd.
46 Carrington Road, Waverley, N.S.W., Australia.
Telephone: 38-6737.

Azad, Bhagwat Jha, M.A., B.L.; Indian politician; b. 28 Nov. 1922; ed. TNB Collegiate School, TNB Coll., Patna Coll., Patna Univ.
Joined "Quit India" movement 42, sentenced to four years' imprisonment; Pres. Bihar State Students Congress 50; Sec. to Students and Econs. Depts. of Bihar State Congress 50-51; mem. All-India Congress Cttee. 52-, Lok Sabha 52-; Minister of State for Educ. 67-69, for Labour and Rehabilitation 69-71; mem. Public Accounts Cttee. for Foreign, Defence and Econ. Affairs.
7 Ashoka Road, New Delhi, India.

Azimov, Pigam Azimovich; Soviet specialist in Turkmenian language and literature; b. 1915; ed. Ashkhabad Pedagogic Inst.
Member C.P.S.U. 39-; at Ashkhabad Pedagogic Inst. 48-50; at Turkmenian State Univ. 50-65; mem. Turkmenian Acad. of Sciences 51-, Pres. 66-; several U.S.S.R. decorations.
Presidium of the Turkmenian Academy of Sciences, 15 Gogol Street, Ashkhabad, U.S.S.R.

Aziz, Shaikh Abdul; Bangladesh politician.
Minister of Agriculture, Local Govt., Rural Devt. and Co-operatives 72; Minister of Information and Broadcasting March-Nov. 73, of Posts, Telegraph and Telephone 73-74.
c/o Ministry of Posts, Telegraph and Telephone, Dacca, Bangladesh.

Aziz, Ungku Abdul; Malaysian economist and university administrator; b. 28 Jan. 1922, London, England; ed. Raffles Coll. and Univ. of Malaya, Singapore, Waseda Univ., Tokyo, Univ. of Pittsburgh, U.S.A.
Johore State Civil Service; Lecturer in Econs., Univ. of Malaya, Singapore until 52; Head, Dept. of Econs., Univ. of Malaya, Kuala Lumpur 52-61, Dean of Faculty 61-65, Vice-Chancellor 68-; Pres. Nat. Co-operative Org. (ANGKASA) March 71, Asscn. of S.E. Asian Insts. of Higher Learning 73-75; Chair. Asscn. of Commonwealth Univs. 74-; mem. of Council, Soc. for Int. Devt. 71-74; Trustee, Asian Inst. of Technology 71-77; corresp. mem. advisory board, *Modern Asian Studies* 73-75; mem. Econ. Asscn. of Malaysia, Scientific Comm. of Int. Council of Research in Co-operative Devt., Int. Asscn. of Agricultural Economists, Joint Advisory Cttee. of FAO, UNESCO and ILO; mem. Nat. Consultative Council and Nat. Unity Advisory Council, Govt. of Malaysia; Ordre des Arts et des Lettres (France) 65; Fellow, World Acad. of Arts and Sciences 65-.
Office of the Vice-Chancellor, University of Malaya, Kuala Lumpur 22-11, Malaysia.
Telephone: Kuala Lumpur 54400.

B

Babayev, Sabir; Soviet composer; b. 1920; ed. Tashkent Conservatoire.
Executive mem. Uzbek Composers' Union; Sec. Soviet Composers' Union.
Principal works: Two Suites for Symphony Orch. 46-48; Two Poems and *Festival Overture* for folk instrument orch. 50-52; Concerto for chang (Uzbek folk instrument) and orch. of folk instruments 52; Cantata, *Cotton Farmers of Uzbekistan* 55, *Segokh* (symphonic poem on folk themes) 56; *Love of Motherland* (musical drama) 57, *During the Festival* (symphonic poem) 58, *Khamza* (opera) 61, *Uzbek Poetic Songs* 66.
Uzbek Composers' Union, Tashkent, U.S.S.R.

Bahadur K. C., Kaisher; Nepalese educationist and diplomatist; b. 28 Jan. 1907; ed. St. Paul's Mission School, St. Xavier's Coll., Calcutta, and Univ. Coll., Calcutta.
Translator and Lecturer, Tri-Chandra Coll. 30-32; research in MS., inscriptions and sculpture, Nepal 32-45; Nepalese Resident in Tibet 46-50; Sec. Ministry of Educ., Health and Local Self Govt. 56-61; Del. to UN 56-57, UNESCO 60; Ambassador to People's Repub. of China, concurrently to Mongolian People's Repub. and Burma 61-65, also to Repub. of Indonesia and Kingdom of Laos 62-65; Chair. Nepal Public Service Comm. 66-70; awarded Italian Order of Merit 53; Order of the Ghurkas (1st Class) of King Mahendra 62.
Publs. *Countries of the World* 35, *Ancient and Modern Nepal* 53, *Materials for the Study of Nepalese History and Culture* 58, *Judicial Customs of Nepal, Part I* 58, *Eroticism in Nepalese Art* 60, *Introduction to Kathmandu and Patan* 61, *Universal Value of Nepalese Aesthetics, Part I and II* 61-62, *Nepal after the Revolution of* 1950 75, trans. of *Kiratarıniye, Nepal and her Neighbours* 74.
636 Kamal Pokhari, Kathmandu, Nepal.
Telephone: 11696.

Bahadur, Raj, B.SC., M.A., LL.B.; Indian lawyer and politician; b. 21 Aug. 1912; ed. Agra Coll. and St. John's Coll., Agra.
Member Cen. Advisory Cttee. Bharatpur State 39-42, Municipal Comm. 41-42; resigned to join "Quit India" Movement; mem. Rep. Assembly 43; Sec. Assembly Praja Parishad Party 43-48; Gen. Sec. Matsya Union Congress Cttee. 48-49; Pres. Bharatpur Bar Asscn. 48-51; mem. Indian Constituent Assembly for Bharatpur 48, Lok Sabha 48-; Sec. Congress Party in Lok Sabha 50-52; Deputy Minister, later Minister of State for Communications 51-56; led Indian del. to 10th Session of Int. Civil Aviation Organization, Caracas; Minister of Communications 56-57, Minister of State for Transport and Communications 57-62, for Transport 62-64; Minister of Transport 64-66, of Information and Broadcasting 66-67; Advocate, Supreme Court of India 67; Amb. to Nepal 68-71; Minister of Parl. Affairs, Shipping and Transport 71-73, of Communications 73-74, also Union Minister of Tourism and Civil Aviation 74-; mem. Rajasthan P.C.C. and All-India Congress Cttee.; Congress Party; awarded Tamrapatra 74.
P.C.C. and All-India Congress Cttee.; Congress Party.
Ministry of Tourism and Civil Aviation, New Delhi; and Basan Gate, Bharatpur, India.

Ballmer, Ray Wayne, M.SC.; American mining executive; b. 1926, New Mexico; ed. N.M. School of Mines, Mass. Inst. of Technology.
Held senior posts with Kennecott Copper Corpn., U.S.A., with responsibilities in Ariz. and Bingham Canyon, Utah operations; now Man. Dir. Bougainville Copper Ltd. and Dir. Bougainville Mining Ltd., responsible for design, construction and commissioning of Bougainville copper operation.
Bougainville Copper Limited, 95 Collins Street, Melbourne, Australia.

Bam, Arvind Shankar, B.SC.; Indian civil servant and United Nations official; b. 12 March 1918; ed. Fergusson Coll., Poona, and King's Coll., London.
Entered Civil Service 41, Asst. Collector, Dharwar 42-44; Special Officer, Civil Supplies, Darjeeling 44-45; District Controller of Civil Supplies, Jalpaiguri 45-46; Asst. Collector, Broach 46-47; Under-Sec., Home Dept., Govt. of Bombay April-Aug. 47, Deputy Sec. 47-49; First Collector and District Magistrate, Kolhapur 49-52; Dep. Sec. Ministry of Rehabilitation, Calcutta 52-57; Controller for Iron and Steel 57-61; Chair. Tea Board, Govt. of India 61-65; Gen. Man. Indian Airlines Corpn. Dec. 65-Nov. 66, Chair. and Gen. Man. Dec. 66-June 67; Resident Rep. of UN Devt. Programme in Yugoslavia 67-74, in Liberia 74-; Leader, Indian Steel Del. to ECAFE 60; Leader, Indian Tea Del. to U.S., Canada, Australia, New Zealand and Singapore 62.
Resident Representative of United Nations Development Programme P.O. Box 274, Monrovia, Liberia.
Telephone: 26019 and 26032 (Office); 26551 (Residence).

Bandaranaike, Felix Dias; Ceylonese politician; b. 1931.
Minister of Finance and Parl. Sec. to Minister of Defence and of External Affairs July 60-62; Minister without Portfolio Nov. 62-May 63, of Agriculture, Food and Co-operatives May 63-65; Minister of Public Admin., Local Govt. and Home Affairs 70-75, of Justice 72-, of Finance Sept. 75-.
Ministry of Finance, Colombo, Sri Lanka.

Bandaranaike, Sirimavo Ratwatte Dias; Ceylonese politician; b. 17 April 1916; ed. St. Bridget's Convent, Colombo.
Widow of the late S. W. R. D. Bandaranaike (Prime Minister of Ceylon 56-59); Pres. of Sir Lanka Freedom Party 60-; Prime Minister, Minister of Defence and External Affairs 60-65; mem. Senate until 65; mem. Parl. and Leader of Opposition 65-70; Prime Minister, Minister of Defence and External Affairs May 70-, also Minister of Planning and Econ. Affairs, and of Plan Implementation July 73-.
Horagolla, Nittambuwa, Sri Lanka.

Bandzar, Jambalyn; Mongolian diplomatist; b. 10 July 1922; ed. Mongolian State Univ., Ulan Bator.
Secondary school teacher 46-48; local govt. posts 48-50; First Sec., Moscow 50-54; Head of Dept., Ministry of Foreign Affairs 54-56; First Sec., Prague 56-58; Head of Dept., Ministry of Foreign Affairs, and Deputy Foreign Minister 58-60; Amb. to Hungary 60-64; Permanent Rep. of Mongolian People's Repub. to UN 66-68; Amb. to France 69-72, to Poland 72-.
Embassy of the Mongolian People's Republic, Warsaw, Poland.

Banerji, Shishir Kumar, B.A.; Indian diplomatist and administrator; b. 21 Oct. 1913; ed. Univ. of Allahabad and New Coll., Oxford.
Indian Civil Service 37-; Deputy Commr. Central Provinces 37-46; Sec. Civil Supplies, Central Provinces Govt. 46-47; First Sec. and later Chargé d'Affaires, Iran 47-49; Deputy Sec. Ministry of External Affairs 49-51; Deputy High Comm., Lahore 51-54; Consul-Gen., San Francisco 54-56; Chair. UN Visiting Mission to British and French Togolands 55; Envoy to Syria 56, Amb. 57-58; High Commr. in Malaya 58-59; Joint Sec., Ministry of External Affairs 60-61, Chief of Protocol 61-64, Chief Inspector of Indian Missions abroad 64; Ambassador to Federal Republic of Germany 64-67, to Japan 67-70; Sec. Ministry of Foreign Affairs 70-72; Lieut-.Gov. of Goa, Daman and Diu 72-.
Cabo Raj Niwas, Goa, India.

Bannikov, Nikolai Vasilyevich; Soviet politician; b. 1914; ed. Kuibyshev Industrial Inst.
Shop Mechanic, then Man., later Chief Mechanic, then Dep. Dir. of factory, and Party Organizer of C.P.S.U. Central Cttee. at a Kuibyshev factory 37-45; Party Official 45-59; Second Sec., Karaganda Regional Cttee. of Communist Party of Kazakhstan 59-62, Second Sec. 63-; also mem. Central Cttee. of C.P. of Kazakhstan, Alt. mem. of C.P.S.U. Central Cttee., and Deputy to U.S.S.R. Supreme Soviet; mem. C.P.S.U. 40-, First Sec. Irkutsk Regional Cttee. 68-.
Irkutsk Regional Committee, Irkutsk, U.S.S.R.

Bansal, Ghamandi Lal, M.A., LL.B.; Indian commercial executive; b. 3 Dec. 1914; ed. A.V. Mission School, Ranikhet, Government Intermediate Coll., Almora, and Lucknow Univ.
Former Dir. State Bank of India; mem. Indian Parl.

52-57; Sec.-Gen. Fed. of Indian Chambers of Commerce and Industry, All-India Organization of Industrial Employers, Indian Nat. Cttee. of Int. Chamber of Commerce 54-75; Chair. Governing Body of Shri Ram Coll. of Commerce.
Publ. *India and Pakistan—An Analysis of Economic, Agricultural and Mineral Resources.*
28 Ferozeshah Road, New Delhi 1, India.

Barker, E. W., M.A., LL.B.; Singapore politician; b. 1920; ed. Raffles Coll., Singapore, St. Catharine's Coll., Cambridge and Inner Temple, London.
Practised law in Singapore 52-64; Assemblyman in constituency of Tanglin 63-; Speaker of Singapore Legislative Assembly 63-64; Minister for Law 64-65; Minister for Law and Nat. Devt. 65-75, for Law and Environment June 75-.
Ministry for Law and Environment, Law Division. St. Andrews Road, Singapore.

Barnard, Lance Herbert; Australian politician; b. 1 May 1919, Launceston, Tasmania; ed. Launceston Technical Coll.
Qualified as teacher and served in Educ. Dept.; mil. service 40-45, Australian Cadet Corps 45-54; M.P. 54-75; State Pres. Tasmanian Branch, Australian Labor Party 66-67, and 70-73; Deputy Leader, Parl. Labor Party 67-74; Deputy Prime Minister 72-74, Minister for Defence 72-75; Amb. to Sweden, Finland and Norway Sept. 75-; mem. Joint Public Accounts Cttee. 56-58, Fed. Parl. Labor Party Exec. 58-67; Del., Parl. Asscn. Group Conf., London 62; mem. Commonwealth Immigration Advisory Council; mem. Joint Parl. Cttee. on Foreign Affairs 67-69, Joint Select Cttee. on the Defence Forces Retirement Benefits Legislation 70-71.
Publ. *Australian Defence—Policy and Programmes.*
Australian Embassy, 12 Sergels Torg, Box 40 046, 103 42, Stockholm, Sweden; Home: 8 Lantana Avenue, Launceston, Tasmania, Australia.

Barr, Morris Alfred, LL.D.; Australian international business exec. and admin.; b. 23 Dec. 1922; ed. Scotch Coll., Melbourne Univ. and Melbourne Conservatorium of Music.
Member editorial staff Melbourne *Argus*; served with Australian Imperial Forces, mem. Far Eastern Liaison Office; Head, Melbourne Conservatorium of Music 48; with English-Speaking Union 51-; Dir. of Programmes 59-64, Dir.-Gen. 64-69; Partner and Dir. Int. Operations, Winner Marketing Communications 69-; Int. Co-ordinator Winston Churchill Memorial Trust 60-65; Chair., Man. Dir. Associated Consultants Construction Ltd. 69-; Trustee, Univ. of Louisville (Humphrey Centenary Scholarship Trust); Chair. Australian Musical Asscn.
106 Gloucester Place. London, W.1; Home: 16 Park Place Villas, London, W.2, England; 6 Walker Street, Balwyn, Melbourne, Australia.
Telephone: 01-935 4253.

Barwick, Rt. Hon. Sir Garfield Edward John, P.C., G.C.M.G., B.A., LL.B.; Australian lawyer and fmr. politician; b. 22 June 1903; ed. Sydney Univ.
Admitted to N.S.W. Bar 27, Victoria Bar 45, Queensland Bar 58; Pres. N.S.W. Bar Asscn. 50-52, 55-56, Law Council of Australia 52-54; mem. Fed. House of Reps. for Parramatta 58-64; Attorney-Gen. 58-64; Acting Minister for External Affairs 59, 60, Minister 61-64; Chief Justice of Australia 64-; Chancellor Macquarie Univ. March 67-; Pres. Australian Inst. of Int. Affairs 72-; Hon. LL.D. (Sydney).
Office of the Chief Justice, High Court of Australia, Sydney; and Mundroola, George Street, Careel Bay, Sydney, Australia.

Ba Saw, U; Burmese diplomatist and fmr. politician; b. 17 Nov. 1914; ed. Govt. High School, Kyaukpyu, and Ananda Coll., Colombo, Sri Lanka.
Joint Editor Burma Propaganda Office, British Ministry of Information (Far Eastern Bureau), New Delhi 43; guerrilla training in India and Ceylon 44; leader resistance campaign in Southern Arakan 44; mem. Patriotic Burmese Forces (PBF); formed Kyaukpyu District Anti-Fascist People's Freedom League and People's Volunteer Organization (Pres. and mem. Exec. both orgs); mem. Constituent Assembly for Kyaukpyu North 48-50; Special District Commr. Kyaukpyu District 50-51; elected to Union Parl. for Kyaukpyu (South) 51-62; Minister for Minorities and Refugee Welfare 52-53, for Relief Resettlement and Social Welfare 53-56, for Religious Affairs and Social Welfare 56-58, for Social Welfare and Religious Affairs, Union Culture, Health, Immigration and Nat. Registration 60-62; Amb. to Thailand and the Philippines 62-64, to U.S.S.R., Romania, Poland, Czechoslovakia and Hungary 64-68, to U.K., Sweden, Norway and Denmark 68-71, to Fed. Repub. of Germany 71-76, concurrently accred. to Finland 72-76, and to EEC 73-76.
Ministry of Foreign Affairs, Rangoon, Burma.

Basnayake, Hema Henry, Q.C.; Ceylonese judge; b. 3 Aug. 1902; ed. St. Aloysius Coll., Galle, and St. Joseph's Coll., Colombo.
Admitted to the Bar 27; Crown Counsel 32; Commr. for preparing new revised edition of Legislative Enactments of Ceylon 37-38; Asst. Legal Draftsman 39; Senior Crown Counsel 44; Acting Solicitor-Gen. 45, Jan 46; Acting Attorney-Gen. 46, 47; mem. Local Govt. Service Comm. 45-47; Solicitor-Gen. 46; Puisne Justice 47-51; Attorney-Gen. 51-55; Acting Chief Justice 55; Chief Justice 56-64; Chair. Board of Trustees, Ceylon Univ. Sangharama and Vihara Trust, Musaeus Girls Coll., Kalutara Bodhi Trust: Pres. Child Protection Soc., Crippled Children's Aid Asscn., Sri Lanka Human Ecology Asscn.; Vice Pres. St. John Ambulance Asscn.; Pres. Ceylon Farmers' Asscn., Maha Bodhi Soc. of Sri Lanka, Int. Comm. of Jurists (Sri Lanka Section); Chair. Water Resources Board of Sri Lanka.
Publ. *Legislative Enactments of Ceylon* 38, 56.
Elibank House, Elibank Road, Colombo 5, Sri Lanka.

Bastyan, Lieut.-Gen. Sir Edric (Montague), K.C.M.G., K.C.V.O., K.B.E., C.B.; British army officer and governor; b. 5 April 1903; ed. Royal Military Coll., Sandhurst.
Army career began as Second Lieut. Sherwood Foresters 23, rising to Chief Admin. Officer, Eighth Army 43; Maj.-Gen. in charge Admin., Allied Land Forces, S.E. Asia 44-45; Imperial Defence Coll. 46; Maj.-Gen. in charge Admin., British Army of the Rhine 46-48; employed on special duties, War Office 49; Chief of Staff, Eastern Command 49-50; Dir. of Staff Duties, W.O. 50-52; Commdr. 53rd (Welsh) Infantry Division (T.A.) and Mid-West District 52-55; Vice-Adjutant-Gen. War Office 55-57; Lieut.-Gen. 57; Commdr., British Forces, Hong Kong 57-60; retd. 60; Gov. of South Australia 61-Oct. 68; Gov. Tasmania 68-73; Hon. Col. Royal South Australia Regiment 61; Hon. Air Commodore, R.A.A.F.; K.St.J. 61; Hon. Col. Royal Tasmanian Regt. 68.
c/o Government House, Hobart, Tasmania, Australia.

Ba Swe, U; Burmese politician; b. 19 April 1915, Tavoy; ed. Rangoon Univ.
Member of exec. cttee. Rangoon Univ. Students' Union (RUSU) 37-38; co-founder, People's Revolutionary Party 39; Sec.-Gen. All Burma Student Union and RUSU 39-40, Pres. RUSU 40-41; detained by British 40-41; Chief of Civil Defence, Rangoon 42-45; leader Anti-Fascist People's Freedom League (AFPFL), detained by Japanese 45; participated in resistance 45; Sec.-Gen. Socialist Party 45, AFPFL 47-51, Vice-Pres. 52; Pres. Burma TUC 48-63; mem. Chamber of Deputies for Taikkyi 52-56, for Lanmadau 56-62; Minister for Defence and Mines 52-56; Chair. Asian Socialist Conf. 52-54, 54-56, 56-58; Prime Minister

56-57; Deputy Prime Minister for Defence and Law and Order 57-58; Pres. Stable AFPFL; detained by Revolutionary Council 63-66; Yugoslav Banner, First Class, Noble order of the White Elephant (Thailand), Star of Revolution, First Degree.
84 Innes Road, Rangoon, Burma.

Bateman, Leslie Clifford, C.M.G., D.SC., PH.D., F.R.S., P.S.M.; British scientist; b. 21 March 1915; ed. Univ. Coll.; London, and Oriel Coll., Oxford.
Chemist, British (later Natural) Rubber Producers' Research Asscn., England 41-53, Dir. of Research 53-62; Controller of Rubber Research and Chair. Malayan Rubber Research and Devt. Board 62-74; Colwyn Medal 62 and Jubilee Foundation Lecturer 71, Inst. of the Rubber Industry; Hon. D.Sc. (Malaya) 68, (Aston) 72; Fellow, Univ. Coll., London 74.
Publs. Editor and contributor to *The Chemistry and Physics of Rubber-like Substances* 63; numerous publs. in Journal of Chem. Soc. etc., and on the technoeconomic position of the natural rubber industry.
3 Palmerston Close, Welwyn Garden City, Herts. AL8 7DL, England.

Batten, Jean Gardner, C.B.E.; New Zealand pioneer airwoman; b. 1909; ed. Cleveland House Coll., Auckland.
Obtained flying licence 30, commercial pilot's licence 32; made solo flights England-India 33, England-Australia (woman's record) 34, Australia-England (first woman to complete return flight) 35, England-Brazil (world record 61¼ hours; fastest crossing of S. Atlantic 13¼ hours; first England-S. America and solo S. Atlantic flight by woman) 35, England-Auckland, New Zealand (first direct flight, 11 days 45 minutes, establishing record England-Australia solo 5 days 21 hours, Australia-New Zealand over Tasman Sea 9 hours 29 minutes) 36, Australia-England (solo record 5 days 18 hours 15 minutes) 37; many trophies and medals; Chevalier Légion d'Honneur; Officer Order of Southern Cross of Brazil; City of Paris Medal 71; Jean Batten Archive established at Royal Air Force Museum, Hendon, London 72.
Publ. *My Life* 38.
c/o Barclays Bank, 25 Charing Cross Road, London, W.C.2, England.

Baxter, Sir John Philip, K.B.E., C.M.G., B.SC., PH.D., M.I.CHEM.E., F.R.A.C.I., M.I.E. (Aust.), F.A.A.; Australian chemical engineer and educationalist; b. 7 May 1905; ed. Hereford, and Birmingham Univ.
Research Dir.-Gen. Chemicals Division I.C.I. and Dir. Thorium Ltd. -49; Prof. of Chemical Engineering N.S.W. Univ. of Technology 49-53, Dir. 53-54, Vice-Chancellor (now Univ. of New South Wales) 55-69; Chair. Atomic Energy Comm. 57-72; Chair. Sydney Opera House Trust 68-.
1 Kelso Street, Enfield, N.S.W., Australia.
Telephone: 7474261.

Beale, The Hon. Sir Howard, K.B.E., Q.C., B.A., LL.B.; Australian lawyer, diplomatist and company director; b. 1898; ed. Univ. of Sydney.
Called to the Bar 25; Queen's Counsel 50; R.A.N. 42-45; Liberal mem. for Parramatta, House of Reps. 46-58; mem. Commonwealth Parl. Public Works Cttee. 47-49; Cabinet Minister in Menzies' Govt. 49-58, Minister for Information and Transport 49-50, for Supply 50-58, and of Defence Production 56-58 and Minister-in-Charge of Atomic Energy Comm. and Aluminium Production Comm. 50-58; Acting Minister for Immigration 51-52, 53, 54, for Nat. Development 52-53, for Air 52, for Defence 57; mem. Australian Defence Council, Cabinet Defence Preparations Cttee., Cabinet Cttee. on Uranium and Atomic Energy 50-58; Amb. to U.S.A. 58-64; Alternate Gov. Int. Monetary Fund 60, 62, 64; Del. to ANZUS Council 58, 59, to Colombo Plan Conf. 58, to UN 59, to SEATO Conf. 59, 60, to World Food Congress 63; Pres. Arts Council of Australia 64-68; Woodward Lecturer, Yale Univ. 60, Regents' Visiting Prof., Univ. of California 66, Marguette Univ. 67, 69; now Dir. and Adviser to various Australian, British and U.S. industrial and financial corporations; Hon. LL.D., Kent Univ., Ohio 59, Marguette Univ. 69; Hon. D. H. Lit., Nebraska 62.
1-4 Marathon Road, Darling Point, 2027, Australia.

Beazley, Kim Edward, M.A.; Australian politician; b. 30 Sept. 1917, Northam, W. Australia; ed. Perth Modern School, Claremont Teachers' Coll., Univ. of W. Australia, Australian Nat. Univ.
Worked as schoolteacher and tutor until 45; mem. Parl. for Fremantle, W. Australia 45-; mem., Vice-Chair. Joint Parl. Cttee. on Foreign Affairs 67-70; Minister of Educ. 72-75; opposition spokesman on educ. and defence Jan.-March 76; resigned; mem Council, Australian Nat. Univ. 51-72, Australian Inst. of Aboriginal Studies 64-72, Advisory Council, Australian Commonwealth Scientific and Industrial Research Org. (CSIRO) until 72; fmr. Vice-Pres. Teachers' Union, Councillor Australian Teachers' Fed.; del. to Commonwealth Parl. Asscn. Conf., Nigeria 62; Labor Party.
Parliament House, Canberra, A.C.T. 2600; Home: 1 Thomson Road, Claremont, W.A. 6010, Australia.

Beeby, Clarence Edward, C.M.G., M.A., PH.D.; New Zealand educationist and administrator; b. 16 June 1902; ed. Christchurch Boys' High School, Canterbury Coll., Univ. of New Zealand, University Coll., London, and Univ. of Manchester.
Lecturer in Philosophy and Education, Canterbury Univ. Coll., Univ. of N.Z. 23-34; Dir. N.Z. Council for Educational Research 34-38; Asst. Dir. of Education, Education Dept., N.Z. 38-40; Dir. of Education 40-60 (on leave of absence 48-49); Asst. Dir.-Gen. of UNESCO 48-49; Ambassador to France 60-63; leader N.Z. Dels. to Gen. Confs. of UNESCO 46, 47, 50, 53, 54, 56, 58, 60, 63; Hon. Counsellor of UNESCO 50; mem. of UNESCO Exec. Board 60-63, Chair. 63; Research Fellow, Harvard Univ. 63-67; Chair. UNESCO Evaluation Panel for World Functional Literacy Projects 67-70; Commonwealth Visiting Prof., Univ. of London 67-68; Consultant to Australian Govt. on educ. in Papua and New Guinea 69; Educ. Consultant to Ford Foundation in Indonesia 70-75; Consultant to UNDP (Malaysia) 76; mem. Council of Consultant Fellows, Int. Inst. for Educ. Planning, Paris 72-; Hon. LL.D., Hon. Litt.D.; Order of St. Gregory (First Class); Mackie Medal (ANZAAS) 71.
Publs. *The Intermediate Schools of New Zealand* 38, *Entrance to University* (with W. Thomas and M. H. Oram) 39, *The Quality of Education in Developing Countries* 66, *The Qualitative Aspects of Educational Planning* (ed.) 69.
New Zealand Council for Educational Research P.O. Box 3237, Wellington; 73 Barnard Street, Wellington, New Zealand.

Benawa, Abdul Raouf; Afghan writer and administrator; b. 1913; ed. Ganj Public School, Kandahar.
Mem. Language Dept. Afghan Acad. 39; mem. Words Dept. Afghan Acad. and Asst. Information Dept. 40; Dir. Publication Dept. Afghan Acad. 41; Gen. Dir. *Pushtu Tolana*; Sec. Afghan Acad. and Dir. *Kabul* magazine; proprietor of weekly magazine *Hewad*; mem. History Dept. 50, Dir. Internal Publ. Dept. 51, Gen. Dir. 52; Press Attaché India 53-56; Pres. Radio Kabul 56-63; Press and Cultural Counsellor, Cairo 63-.
Publs. *Women in Afghanistan, Mir Weiss Neeka, Literary Sciences, Pushtu Songs, De Ghanamo Wazhai, Pushtoonistan, A Survey of Pushtoonistan, Rahman Baba, Pir mohammad-Kakar, Khosh-hal Khan se Wai. Pushtoo Killi,* Vol. 4, *Kazim Khan-e-Shaida*; translations: *Mosa-fir Iqbal, Geetan-Jali Tagoor, Da Darmistatar Pushtoo Seerane,*

Leaders of Pashtoonistan, History of Hootaki, Preshana afkar (poem), *Da zra khwala, Pashto writers today* (2 vols.), *Pashto reader for schools, Pachakhan* (A leader of Pashtoni), *Landei* (public poems); plays: *I-Zoor gonahgar* (Old criminal), *Ishtebah* (confusion), *Kari bar asal, Aashyanae aqab, Zarang, Chaoki der khater, Hakoomat baidar.*
Afghan Embassy, Cairo, Egypt; and Ministry of Information and Culture, Kabul, Afghanistan.

Benedicto, Roberto S., A.A., LL.M.; Philippine lawyer, banker and diplomatist; b. 17 April 1917; ed. Univ. of the Philippines, George Washington Univ., U.S.A.
Major in the Philippines Armed Forces 41-45; Acting Provincial Fiscal, Negros Occidental 45; Prof. Commercial Law, Far Eastern Univ. 48-55; Gov. Devt. Bank of the Philippines 57-59; Exec. Vice-Pres., Treas., Philippines Commercial and Industrial Bank 62-65; Pres., Vice-Chair. Philippine Nat. Bank 66-70; Amb. to Japan 72-; mem. Monetary Board, Cen. Bank of the Philippines; Legion of Merit, Rep. Community Chest of Greater Manila.
Embassy of the Philippines, 6-15, Roppongi 5-chome, Minato-ku, Tokyo, Japan; Home: 1420 San Marcelino, Malate, Manila, Philippines.

Bengzon, Cesar, B.A., LL.B.; Philippine judge; b. 29 May 1896; ed. Ateneo de Manila and Univ. of the Philippines.
Law Clerk, Bureau of Justice 19, Special Attorney, then Asst. Attorney 20, Solicitor-Gen. 31; Dean and Prof. of Law, Univ. of Manila 28-32; Under-Sec. of Justice and Chair. Board of Pardons 33; Assoc. Justice, Court of Appeals 36; Assoc. Justice, Supreme Court 45; Prof. of Law, Univ. of Santo Tomás and Philippine Law School 48-54; Chair. Senate Electoral Tribunal 50-57; Chief Justice Supreme Court 61; Judge, Int. Court of Justice, The Hague 66-76; mem. Philippine Acad. of Sciences and Humanities 64-; Pres. Philippine Section, Int. Comm. of Jurists 64, 66; mem. Nat. Research Council 64-, American Judicature Soc. 65, Philippine Soc. of Int. Law 65-; LL.D. h.c. Univ. of Manila 57, Ateneo de Manila Univ. 64, Univ. of the Philippines 64.
c/o International Court of Justice, The Hague, Netherlands.

Bennett, Lieut.-Col. Sir Charles Moihi To Arawaka, D.S.O., M.A., DIP.ED., DIP.SOC.SC.; New Zealand diplomatist; b. 1913; ed. Univ. of N.Z. and Exeter Coll., Oxford.
Schoolmaster 37; Staff mem. New Zealand Broadcasting Service 38-39; service with New Zealand Army in U.K., Greece, Crete, North Africa, commanding Maori Battalion from Alamein to Tunis, 39-46; Staff mem. War Histories Section, Internal Affairs Dept., mem. Ngarimu Scholarship Fund Board 47-50; Asst. Controller Maori Welfare Division, Maori Affairs Dept. 51-57, Dir. 57-58; mem. State Literary Advisory Cttee., New Zealand Parole Board 51; New Zealand High Commr. to Malaya (the first Maori to lead an overseas Mission) 59-63; Asst. Sec. Dept. of Maori Affairs, Wellington 63-69; Vice-Pres. New Zealand Labour Party 70-72, Pres. 73-75, retd. Dec. 75.
33A High Street, Rotorua, New Zealand.

Betham, Hon. Gustav Frederick Dertag, O.B.E.; Western Samoan politician and businessman; b. 11 April 1915; ed. Newton West School and Seddon Memorial Technical Coll., Auckland, N.Z.
Western Samoan Public Service 32-39; O. F. Nelson & Co. Ltd. (Gen. merchants) 39-47; Man. Samoa Printing & Publishing Co. 47-49; Man. Dir. Greenline Service Ltd. 49-52; merchant 53-; mem. Legislative Council of Western Samoa 48-71; Minister of Finance 61-70, also of Econ. Devt., Inland Revenue and Customs; mem. Exec. Council 61-70; Gov. for W. Samoa, Asian Devt. Bank (ADB) 66-70; Sec.-Gen. South Pacific Comm. 71-75; del. to numerous int. corpns.
Nouméa, New Caledonia, South Pacific.

Bewoor, General Gopal Gurunath; Indian army officer and diplomatist; b. 11 Aug. 1916; ed. Dehra Dun Mil. Coll., Staff Coll., Quetta.
Commissioned 37; Instructor, Staff Coll., Quetta 47; served 2nd Dogra Regiment 47-48; Commdr. infantry brigade 52; Dir. Personnel Services, Army H.Q. 53; Del. to UN Gen. Assembly 56; Commdr. infantry brigade 57; promoted Maj.-Gen., Chief of Staff Western Command 59; G.O.C. infantry div. 61; Dir. Mil. Training, H.Q. 63; promoted Lieut.-Gen., Corps Commdr. Eastern Theatre 64; Deputy Chief of Army Staff 67; G.O.C.-in-C. Southern Command 69-73; Chief of Army Staff Jan. 73-75; Col. 11 Gurkha Rifles 60-75, retd. June 75; Amb. to Denmark 76-; Param Vishisht Seva Medal 69; Padma Bhushan 72.
Embassy of India, Vangehusvej 15, 2100 Copenhagen Ø, Denmark.

Bhabha, Cooverji Hormusji, M.A., B.COM., J.P.; Indian businessman; b. 22 July 1910; ed. St. Xavier's Coll. and Sydenham Coll. of Commerce, Bombay.
Fellow St. Xavier's Coll. 32-34; Fellow and Lecturer in Banking Law and Practice, Sydenham Coll. of Commerce 32-33; J.P. 38-; Commerce mem. Govt. of India Sept. 46, mem. Works, Mines and Power Nov. 46; Minister of Commerce, Govt. of India, Aug. 47-April 48; Leader Indian del. to World Trade Conf. Havana 47 (elected Vice-Pres. of Conf.); Chair. United Carbon India Ltd., Kelvinator of India Ltd.; Dir. Investment Corpn. of India, Tata Power Co. Ltd., Tata Chemicals Ltd., Swadeshi Co. Ltd., Spencer & Co. Ltd.
Commerce (1935) Ltd., Manek Mahal, 90 Veer Nariman Road, Bombay 20; 49 Cuffe Parade, Colaba, Bombay 5, India.

Bhagat, Bali Ram; Indian politician; b. 1922; ed. Patna Coll.
Secretary Bihar Provincial Congress Cttee. 49; mem. Provisional Parl. 50-52, Lok Sabha 52, Speaker Jan. 76-; Parl. Sec. Ministry of Finance 52-55; Deputy Minister for Finance 55-63; Minister of State for Planning 63-67, for Defence March-Nov. 67, for External Affairs 67-69, for Foreign Trade and Supply 69-70; Minister for Steel and Heavy Industry 70-71.
Office of the Speaker, Lok Sabha, New Delhi, India.

Bhagat, Dhanraj; Indian sculptor; b. 20 Dec. 1917; ed. Khalsa High School and Mayo School of Arts, Lahore.
Teacher, Mayo School of Arts 39 and 44; Lecturer in Sculpture, Delhi Polytechnic Art Dept. 46-60, Senior Lecturer 60-62, Asst. Prof. 62-, Prof. 68; numerous comms. throughout India; works in stone, wood, plaster, cement, and metal-sheet; nine one-man sculpture shows in India 50-67; exhibitions abroad in London and Paris 48, East European countries 55 and 58, U.S.A. 54, Fed. Repub. of Germany 58, São Paulo 62, South Africa 65, London and Ghent 66; mem. Delhi Silpi Chakra; mem. Nat. Cttee. of the Int. Asscn. of Plastic Arts, Paris; Nat. Award, Lalit Kala Akademy 61.
College of Art, 22 Tilak Marg, New Delhi; and H 20, New Delhi South Extension Part 1, New Delhi, India.

Bhagavantam, Suri, M.SC.; Indian scientist and university professor; b. 1909; ed. Nizam Coll., Hyderabad and Madras Univ.
Professor of Physics, Andhra Univ. until 48; Scientific Liaison Officer, B.C.S.O. and Scientific Adviser to Indian High Commr. in U.K., London 48-49, Prof. of Physics, Osmania Univ. 49-52, Vice-Chancellor and Dir. Physical Laboratories 52-57; Dir. Indian Inst. of Science, Bangalore 57-62; Scientific Adviser to Minister of Defence 61-69; Chair. Bharat Electronics Ltd., Cttee. on Org. of Scientific Research; Vice-Pres. Int. Union of Pure and Applied Physics; Dir. Hindustan Aeronautics India Ltd.; Hon. D.Sc., F.N.I. and F.A.Sc.
Publs. *Scattering of Light and Raman Effect* 40, *Theory of*

Groups and Its Application to Physical Problems 52, *Crystal Symmetry and Physical Properties* 66.
Indian Institute of Science, Bangalore 560012, India.
Telephone: 81698.

Bhandari, Sunder Singh, M.A., LL.B.; Indian politician; b. 12 April 1921, Udaipur, Rajasthan; ed. Sirohi, Udaipur and Kanpur.
Advocate, Mewar High Court, Udaipur 42-43; Headmaster, Shiksha Bhawan, Udaipur 43-46; Divisional Pracharak, Rashtriya Swayamsewak Sangh, Jodhpur 46-51; Provincial Sec. Bharatiya Jana Sangh (People's Party), Rajasthan 51-57; All India Sec. Bharatiya Jana Sangh 61-65, 66-67, All India Organizing Sec. 65-66; mem. Rajya Sabha 66-72; Leader, Jana Sangh Group in Rajya Sabha 67-68; Gen. Sec. Bharatiya Jana Sangh 67-.
Bharatiya Jana Sangh Office, Vithal Bhai Patel Bhawan, Rafi Marg, New Delhi; Panchayati Nohara, Udaipur, Rajasthan, India.
Telephone: 383349 (New Delhi); 495 (Udaipur).

Bhargava, Vashishtha, M.SC.; Indian judge; b. 5 Feb. 1906; ed. Univ. of Allahabad.
Joint Magistrate 30-35; Civil and Sessions Judge 36-37; District and Sessions Judge 37-47; Additional Commr. for Food and Supplies, Govt. of Uttar Pradesh 47-48; Legal Remembrancer and Judicial Sec. 48-49; Puisne Judge, High Court, Allahabad 49-66, Chief Justice Feb.-July 66; Judge Supreme Court of India 66-71; Chair. Sugar Industry Inquiry Comm. 71-74.
A 16/3 Vasant Vihar, New Delhi 110057, India.

Bhatia, Prem Narain; Indian journalist and diplomatist; b. 1911; ed. Government Coll., Lahore, and Punjab Univ.
Army Service, Second World War; Dir. of Public Information, Bengal Government 45-46; Political Correspondent *The Statesman* (Calcutta and New Delhi) 46-58; Public Relations Adviser, Indian Embassy, Moscow 48; Editor *The Tribune*, Ambala 59; Resident Editor *The Times of India*, Delhi 60-62; Delhi Editor *The Indian Express* 63-65; India Corresp. *The Guardian* (Manchester and London); High Commr. in Kenya 65-68, Singapore 69-72; Editor-in-Chief and Dir. India News and Features Alliance 73-.
Publs. *All My Yesterdays, Indian Ordeal in Africa.*
Jeevan Deep Building, Parliament Street, New Delhi, India.

Bhatt, Ravishanker, B.A., M.A.; Indian merchant banker; b. 13 Dec. 1909; ed. Samaldas Coll., Bhavnagar, Bombay School of Economics and Sociology and London School of Economics.
Secretary, Industrial Investment Trust Ltd., 36-40; Sec. Diwan's Office, Bhavnagar State, subsequently Nayab Diwan (finance and railway) 40-47; Finance Officer, Oriental Govt. Security Life Assurance Co. Ltd. 48-53; Man. Dir. Bombay State Finance Corpn. 53-57; mem. Govt. of India Tariff Comm. 57-60; Exec. Dir. Indian Investment Centre 60-64, Chair. 72-; Chair. Unit Trust of India 64-72; Dir. Steel Authority of India; Chair. SAIL Int. (subsidiary of Steel Authority); Adviser, Merchant Banking Div., State Bank of India; mem. Cen. Advisory Council of Industries, Small Industries Board; Chair. Govt. of India Advisory Cttee. on Control of Capital Issues 73-; Chair. Ahmedabad Electricity Co. Ltd.; Dir. Premier Automobiles Ltd., Atul Products Ltd., Industrial Investment Trust Ltd., Steel Authority of India, State Bank of India; Hon. Fellow, London School of Econs.
Publs. *Capital for Medium and Small-Scale Industries*; various articles on economic and financial subjects.
Ewart House, Homi Mody Street, Bombay-1, India.
Telephone: 253756.

Bhattacharyya, Bhabani, PH.D.; Indian author and journalist; b. 10 Nov. 1906; ed. Patna and London.
Press Attaché at Indian Embassy in Washington 49-50; Asst. Ed. *The Illustrated Weekly of India*, Bombay 50-52; mem. Indian cultural del. to U.S.S.R. 51; mem. Nat. Acad. of Literature; Sec. Tagore Commemorative Volume Soc.; Univ. of N.Z. Prestige Award; Del. Harvard Int. Seminar 59, Harvard-Japanese Seminar, Tokyo 60; Indian Nat. Acad. of Letters Award 67; Asia Foundation Research Award 66-67; Ford Foundation Award 69; Senior Specialist, Inst. of Advanced Projects, East-West Center, Honolulu 69-70; Visiting Prof. Univ. of Hawaii 71-72; Walker-Ames Prof. Univ. of Washington 73; Visiting Prof. Washington State Univ. at Pullman 75.
Publs. *Some Memorable Yesterdays, Indian Cavalcade, The Golden Boat*, and the novels *So Many Hungers, Music for Mohini, He Who Rides A Tiger, A Goddess Named Gold, Shadow from Ladareh* (novels translated into 16 European languages), *Towards Universal Man, Gandhi, the writer.*
3 Otley Court, Glan Tai, Manchester, Mo. 63011, U.S.A.

Bhattacharyya, Birendra Kumar, B.SC., M.A.; Indian journalist and writer; b. 16 March 1924; ed. Jorhat Government High School, Cotton Coll., Gauhati, Calcutta Univ. and Gauhati Univ.
Former Science Teacher, Ukrul High School, Manipur; Editor *Ramdhenu* 51-61, *Sadiniya Navayung* 63-67; Exec. mem. Sanjukta Socialist Party, Assam; Sahitya Akademi Award for Assamese Literature 61.
Publs. novels: *Iyaruingam* (won Akademi Award), *Rajpathe Ringiai* (Call of the Main Street), *Mother, Sataghai* (Killer); collections of short stories: *Kolongajioboi* (Still Flows the Kolong), *Satsari* (Necklace).
Kharghuli Development Area, Gauhati 1, Assam, India.

Bhave, Acharya Vinoba; Indian philosopher and savant; b. 11 Sept. 1895, Gagoda, Maharashtra; ed. in Gagoda, Baroda Coll., Vadodara.
Worked with the late Mohandas Gandhi; founder and leader of Bhoodan movement for voluntary land reform by land gifts and communal ownership; leader of Shanti Sena movement for resolution of conflicts and econ. and social reform; host of nat. seminar to discuss the state of emergency 76.
Publs. *Talks on the Gita* 60, *The Essence of the Quran* 62, *Democratic Values* 63, *Steadfast Wisdom* 66, *The Essence of Christian Teachings* 66.
Sarva Seva Sangh, Rajghat, Varanasi, U.P., India.

Bhaya, Hiten, M.A.; Indian business executive; b. 29 Feb. 1920, Muzaffarpur, Bihar; ed. Patna Univ.
Joined Indian Navy Armament Supply Org. and trained in Royal Naval Establishments in Ceylon and U.K.; Dir., Naval Armaments, Naval H.Q. 55-59; joined Industrial Management Pool 59, Dir. Purchase and Stores, Bhilai Steel Plant 59-61; Sec. Hindustan Steel 61-67, Gen. Man. Alloy Steels Plant, Durgapur 67-70, Dir. Hindustan Steel, in charge of Commercial Operations 70-72, Chair. Hindustan Steel Ltd. 72-; Dir. Bokaro Steel Ltd., Heavy Eng. Corpn. Ltd., Indian Iron and Steel Co. Ltd.; mem. Exec. Cttee., Int. Iron and Steel Inst., Brussels, Council of Indian Statistical Inst., Calcutta, Nat. Council of Applied Econ. Research, New Delhi.
Hindustan Steel Ltd., P.O. Hinoo, Ranchi-2; Home: 16 New Road, Calcutta-27, India.

Bhumibol Adulyadej; King of Thailand; b. 5 Dec. 1927, Cambridge, Mass., U.S.A.; ed. Bangkok and Lausanne, Switzerland.
Youngest son of Their Royal Highnesses Prince and Princess Mahidol of Songkhla; succeeded his brother, the late King Ananda Mahidol, June 46; married Her Majesty the present Queen Sirikit, daughter of H.H. the late Prince Chandapuri Suranath, 28th April 1950; formal Coronation 5th May 50; three daughters, H.R.H. Princess Ubol Ratana, b. 51, H.R.H. Princess Sirindhorn, b. 55, H.R.H. Princess Chulabhorn, b. 57; one son, H.R.H. Crown Prince Vajiralongkorn, b. 52.
Chitralada Villa, Bangkok, Thailand.

Bhutan, King of (*see* Wangchuk, Jigme Singhye).

Bhutto, Mumtaz Ali, M.A.OXON; Pakistani politician; b. 13 March 1933, Pir Buksh Bhutto; ed Christ Church, Oxford.
Called to Bar, Lincoln's Inn; practised law, High Court, Karachi Bench 59-61; mem. Nat. Assembly from Larkana 65-, Movt. against Pres. Ayub Khan 66-69; founder mem. Pakistan People's Party 67; imprisoned by Ayub Khan 68; Gov. of Sind 71-72, Chief Minister 72-73; Minister of Communications, Govt. of Pakistan Oct. 74-.
Village Pir Buksh Bhutto, Taluka Ratodero District, Larkana, Pakistan.

Bhutto, Zulfiqar Ali; Pakistani lawyer and politician; b. 5 Jan. 1928, Larkana; ed. Univ. of Calif. (Berkeley), Christ Church, Oxford and Lincoln's Inn, London.
Lecture in Int. Law, Univ. of Southampton 52-53; Teacher of Constitutional Law, Sind Muslim Law Coll., and also private law practice 53-58; mem. del to U.N. General Assembly 57, leader 59, 60, 63, 65, 66; leader del. to UN Conf. on Law of the Sea 58; Minister of Commerce 58-60, of Minority Affairs, Nat. Reconstruction, of Information, of Fuel, Power and Natural Resources, of Kashmir Affairs 60-62; mem. Nat. Assembly 62-; Minister of Foreign Affairs, of Industries and Natural Resources 63-66; Chief Del. Indo-Pakistan talks on Kashmir 62-63, leader del. to UN Security Council debate on Kashmir 64, on Indo-Pakistan war 65; Sec. Gen. Pakistan Muslim League 64; attended Afro-Asian Foreign Ministers Conf. Algeria 65; Founder Chair. Pakistan People's Party 67; led popular movement against Pres. Ayub Khan 68; political arrest Nov. 68, released Feb. 69; elected leader of Pakistan People's Party 70; Deputy Prime Minister and Minister of Foreign Affairs 71; Pres. 71-73, Minister of Foreign Affairs and Defence 71-, of Atomic Energy 72-; Chief Martial Law Admin. 71-72; Pres. Nat Assembly 72-; Prime Minister 73-; Chair. Islamic Summit Conf., Lahore 74.
Publ. *The Myth of Independence* 69.
Office of the Prime Minister, Islamabad, Pakistan.

Bingham, Colin William Hugh; Australian journalist; b. 10 July 1898; ed. Townsville Grammar School and Queensland Univ.
Foreign Corresp. *Sydney Morning Herald* 43-48, Assoc. Ed. 57-61, Acting Ed. 57-58, Ed. 61-65; mem. Australian Broadcasting Comm.'s Advisory Cttee. (N.S.W.) 68-72, Metropolitan Council Workers' Educational Asscn. (N.S.W.) 70-74; Wilkie-Deamer Memorial Newspaper Address 65; Jubilee Lecture Queensland English Asscn. 73; Ford Memorial Prize for Verse (three times), Queensland Univ.
Publs. Two volumes of verse 25, 29, *Men and Affairs* 67, *The Affairs of Women* 69, *Decline of Innocence and Other Poems* 70.
30 Arnold Street, Killara, Sydney, Australia.
Telephone: 4982970 (Sydney).

Binh, Nguyen Thi (*see* Nguyen Thi Binh).

Birendra Bir Bikram Shah Dev; King of Nepal; b. 28 Dec. 1945, Kathmandu; ed. St. Joseph's Coll., Darjeeling, Eton Coll., England, Univ. of Tokyo and Harvard Univ.
Has travelled extensively throughout Europe, North and South America, U.S.S.R., Iran, Japan, China and several African countries; Grand Master and Col.-in-Chief, Royal Nepalese Army 64; Chief Scout, Nepal Boy and Girl Scouts; Chair. Nepal Asscn. of Fine Arts; came to the throne 31 Jan. 72, crowned Feb. 75.
The Royal Palace, Kathmandu, Nepal.

Bista, Kirti Nidhi, M.A.; Nepalese politician; b. 1927; ed. Tri-Chandra Coll., Kathmandu and Lucknow Univ.
Assistant Minister for Education 61-62, Minister for Educ. 62-64, for Foreign Affairs 64; Vice-Chair. Council of Ministers and Minister for Foreign Affairs and Educ. 64-66; Vice-Chair. Council of Ministers and Minister for Foreign Affairs and Econ. Planning 66-67; Deputy Prime Minister and Minister for Foreign Affairs and Educ. Jan. 67-68; Prime Minister, Minister of Finance, General Administration and Palace Affairs 69-73; Leader Nepalese Dels. to UN Gen. Assemblies 64, 65, 66, and to UNESCO Gen. Confs. 62, 64, 66, 68, and to various other confs.; accompanied H.M. the King on many State visits; mem. Royal Advisory Cttee. 69-70; Order of the Right Hand of Gurkhas (First Class), Order of Merit of Fed. Repub. of Germany, French Legion of Honour.
Kshetra Pati, Kathmandu, Nepal.

Bjelke-Petersen, Johannes; Australian politician; b. 13 Jan. 1911, Dannevirke, New Zealand.
Farmer; mem. Queensland Legislative Assembly 47-; Minister for Works and Housing, Queensland 63-68; Deputy Leader Country Party (later Nat. Party) of Queensland 68, Leader Aug. 68-; Premier of Queensland 68-.
Premier's Department, Brisbane, Queensland, Australia.

Blackwood, Sir Robert (Rutherford), Kt., M.C.E., B.E.E., F.I.E.A.; Australian business executive; b. 3 June 1906, Melbourne; ed. Melbourne Church of England Grammar School, Melbourne Univ.
Testing Officer, Engineering School, Univ. of Melbourne 28-30, Lecturer Agricultural Engineering 31-33, Prof. of Mechanical Engineering 47; Research Engineer Dunlop Australia Ltd. 33-36, Technical Man. 37-46, Gen. Man. 48-66, Chair. Board of Dirs. 72-; Chair. Interim Council, Monash Univ. 59-61, First Chancellor 61-68; Dir. Humes Ltd. 66-; Chair. Board of Dirs., Steel Mains Pty. Ltd. 70-; Pres. Nat. Museum of Victoria Council 70-, Royal Soc. of Victoria 73-75; Trustee, Asian Inst. of Technology, Bangkok 67-; Peter Nicol Russell Memorial Medal 66, Hon. LL.D. (Monash).
Publs. *Monash University: The First Ten Years* 68, *Beautiful Bali* 70, and scientific papers.
8 Huntingfield Road, Middle Brighton, Victoria 3186, Australia.
Telephone: 92-5925.

Blundell, Sir (Edward) Denis, G.C.M.G., G.C.V.O., K.B.E.; New Zealand lawyer and diplomatist; b. 29 May 1907, Wellington; ed. Waitaki High School and Trinity Hall, Cambridge.
Called to the Bar 29; Barrister and Solicitor, Wellington 30-68; Senior Partner, Bell, Gully and Co.; Served with N.Z.E.F. 39-44; High Commr. in U.K. 68-72; Amb. to Ireland 68-72; Gov.-Gen. of New Zealand 72-; Chair. Royal Comms. on Parl. Salaries 61, 64, 67-68; Chair. Air Services Licensing Authority 52-62; Pres. N.Z. Cricket Council 57-60, of "Birthright" 61-68, of N.Z. Law Soc. 62-68; fmr. Dir. N.Z. Shipping Co. Ltd., N.Z. Breweries Ltd. and others; Kt.St.J.
Government House, Private Bag, Wellington, New Zealand.

Boediardjo, Air Marshal; Indonesian air force officer and politician; b. 16 Nov. 1921, Magelang, Central Java; ed. Dutch elementary and secondary schools, aviation school and R.A.F. Staff Coll., Andover, U.K.
Entered Air Force 45, Air Commodore 62, Air Vice-Marshal 64, Air Marshal 70-; Air Attaché, Indonesian Embassy, U.A.R. 56; Accredited Air Attaché to Govt. of Iraq and Jordan 58; Asst. to Chief of Staff, Air Force Dept. 61; Deputy Minister, Commdr.-in-Chief for Logistics Affairs 63; Amb. to Cambodia 65; Minister of Information 68-73; numerous Indonesian military awards and medals of merit from govts. of Yugoslavia, Egypt, Cambodia and the Netherlands.
32 Teuku Umar, Jakarta, Indonesia.

Bolkiah Mu'izuddin Waddaulah, H.H. Sultan Hassanal, D.K., P.S.P.N.B., P.S.N.B., P.S.L.J., S.P.M.B., P.A.N.B.; Sultan of Brunei; b. 15 July 1946; *s.* of former Sultan Sir Muda

Omar Ali Saifuddin, K.C.M.G.; ed. privately, and Victoria Inst., Kuala Lumpur, Malaysia, and Royal Military Acad., Sandhurst.
Appointed Crown Prince and Heir Apparent 61; Ruler of State of Brunei Oct. 67-; Hon. Capt. Coldstream Guards 68; Sovereign and Chief of Royal Orders instituted by Sultans of Brunei.
Istana Darul Hana, Brunei.

Bonynge, Richard; Australian conductor; b. 1930, Sydney.
Trained as a pianist; debut as conductor with Santa Cecilia Orchestra, Rome 62; conducted first opera *Faust*, Vancouver 63; has conducted in most of leading opera houses; Artistic Dir., Principal Conductor Sutherland/Williamson Int. Grand Opera Co., Australia 65; Artistic Dir. Vancouver Opera Asscn. 74-; Musical Dir. Australian Opera 75-.
Has conducted *La Sonnambula, La Traviata, Faust, Eugene Onegin, L'Elisir d'Amore, Orfeo* 67, *Semiramide*, Florence 68, *Guilio Cesare, Lucia*, Hamburg, New York 69-71, *Norma and Orfeo* 70, *The Tales of Hoffmann* 73, Sydney Opera House 74.
Major recordings include *Alcina, La Sonnambula, Norma, Beatrice di Tenda, I Puritani, Faust, Semiramide, Lakmé, La Fille du Régiment, The Messiah, Don Giovanni, Les Huguenots, L'Elisir d'Amore, Lucia, Rigoletto, The Tales of Hoffmann, Thérèse* (Massenet), numerous orchestral works, ballet including *Giselle, Coppelia, Sylvia, Nutcracker*.
c/o Ingpen and Williams, 14 Kensington Court, London, W.8, England.

Border, Lewis Harold, M.V.O.; Australian diplomatist; b. 16 April 1920; ed. The Armidale School, Armidale, and Univ. of Sydney.
Australian Army 41-45; entered Australian Diplomatic Service 45, served Japan, Switzerland, India and Washington, D.C. 47-59; Amb. to Burma 63-65, to Republic of Viet-Nam 66-68; Australian High Commr. in Pakistan and Amb. to Afghanistan 68-70; Deputy Sec. Dept. Foreign Affairs 71-75; Amb. to Fed. Repub. of Germany 75-.
Australian Embassy, Bonn-Bad Godesberg I, Kölnerstrasse 107, Federal Republic of Germany.

Borodin, Andrei Mikhailovich; Soviet veterinary surgeon and politician; b. 1912; ed. Alma Ata Zoo-Veterinary Inst.
Acting Veterinary Surgeon on state farm, and Veterinary Surgeon for an agricultural combine in Kazakhstan 32-39; exec. post, Agricultural Dept., Kustanai Region, Kazakh S.S.R. 39-42; exec. Party and local govt. posts 42-45; Asst. Head of Dept., Central Cttee., C.P. of Kazakhstan, then First Deputy Minister of Agriculture and Procurements, Kazakhstan S.S.R. 45-53; Rep. of U.S.S.R. Ministry of Procurements for Kazakh S.S.R. 53-56; First Sec., Akmolinsk Regional Cttee., C.P. of Kazakhstan 56-57; Minister of Agriculture, then Vice-Chair., State Planning Cttee., Kazakh Council of Ministers 57-58; at H.Q. of Central Cttee., C.P. of Kazakhstan 58-59; First Sec., Kustanai Regional Cttee., C.P. of Kazakhstan; mem. Central Cttees. of C.P.S.U. and of C.P. of Kazakhstan 59-; Deputy to U.S.S.R. Supreme Soviet 62-; mem. C.P.S.U. 41; Hero of Socialist Labour, Order of Lenin, Hammer and Sickle Gold Medal, etc.
Kustanai Regional Committee, Communist Party of Kazakhstan, Kustanai, U.S.S.R.

Borooah, Dev Kanta, LL.B.; Indian politician; b. 22 Feb. 1914, Dibrugarh (Assam); ed. Nowgong Govt. School and Banaras Hindu Univ.
Secretary, Assam P.C.C. 38-45; Editor *Dainik, Assamiya* and *Natun Asamiya* (daily newspapers); mem. Constituent Assembly 49-51, Lok Sabha 52-57; mem. Legislative Assembly of Assam 57-60, Speaker, 60; Chair. Oil Refinery 60; mem. Assam Legislative Assembly 62-66, 67; Minister of Educ. and Co-operation 62; Chair. Oil India 68; Gov. of Bihar 71-73; Union Minister of Petroleum and Chemicals 73-74; Pres. Indian Nat. Congress Party 74-; del. to Commonwealth Conf., UN Gen. Assembly and mem. several Indian dels. visiting overseas countries.
Publ. a volume of poetry in Assamese.
Raj Bhavan, Patna, Bihar, India.

Borrie, Wilfred David, O.B.E., M.A.; British (b. New Zealand) demographer; b. 2 Sept. 1913; ed. Waitaki Boys High School, Oamaru, New Zealand, Univ. of Otago, N.Z. and Cambridge Univ.
Lecturer, Social History and Econs., Sydney Univ. 44-46, Senior Lecturer 46-47; Research Fellow, Research School of Social Sciences, Australian Nat. Univ. 49-52, Reader 52-57, Prof. and Head of Dept. of Demography 57-68, 73-; Dir. of Research School 68-73; Vice-Pres. Int. Union for Scientific Study of Population 61-63; Pres. Social Science Research Council of Australia 62-64, Australian Council of Social Services 63-64; Chair. Population Comm., UN 65-69; mem. Immigration Planning Council of Australia 65-; Fellow, Acad. of the Social Sciences in Australia 71-, Australian Coll. of Educ. 72-.
Publs. *Population Trends and Policies* 47, *Immigration* 48, *Italians and Germans in Australia* 54, *The Cultural Integration of Immigrants* (Part I and General Editor) 59, *Australia's Population Structure and Growth* (with G. Spencer) 65, *The Growth and Control of World Population* 70.
Department of Demography, Australian National University, P.O. Box 4, Canberra, A.C.T., Australia 2600.
Telephone: 49-2306.

Bose, Vivian, B.A., LL.B.; Indian jurist; b. 9 June 1891; ed. Dulwich Coll., England, and Pembroke Coll., Cambridge.
Called to Bar, Middle Temple, London 13; practised at Nagpur Bar, India 13-36; Principal, Univ. Coll. of Law 24-30; Govt. Advocate and Standing Counsel to Govt. of Central Provinces and Berar 30-36; Additional Judicial Commr., Nagpur 31-36; Puisne Judge, Nagpur High Court 36-49, Chief Justice, Nagpur High Court 49-51; Puisne Judge, Supreme Court of India 51-56, retd. 56, ad hoc Judge 58-59; mem. Int. Comm. of Jurists 58-, Pres. 59-66, Hon. Pres. 66-; Chief Commr. for India, Boy Scouts Asscn. 48-49, Nat. Commr. 59-62.
Henessy Road, Nagpur 1, Maharashtra, India.

Boun Oum Na Champassak, Prince; Laotian politician; b. 11 Dec. 1911, Champassak; ed. Lycée Chasseloup Laubat, Saigon.
Member resistance movement against Japanese 41-45; Pres. Del. of 1946 for Franco-Lao Co-operation; renounced right of succession to South Laotian throne in interests of Lao Unity; Prime Minister 49-50; Pres. Nat. Assembly which negotiated independence 49; Pres. Revolutionary Cttee., Anti-Communist League of Savannakhet after *coup d'état* of 1960; Prime Minister, Pres. Nat. Assembly 61-62; del. of H.R.H. for Gen. Inspection of the Kingdom 62; Minister of Religion 66-72.
c/o Ministry of Religion, Vientiane, Laos.

Bowen, Nigel Hubert, B.A., LL.B., Q.C.; Australian lawyer and politician; b. 26 May 1911, Summerland, British Columbia, Canada; ed. King's School, Sydney, and St. Paul's Coll., Univ. of Sydney.
Admitted to N.S.W. Bar 36, Victoria Bar 54; Q.C. 53; Editor *Australian Law Journal* 46-58; Vice-Pres. Law Council of Australia 57-60; Lecturer, Univ. of Sydney 57-58; Pres. N.S.W. Bar Council 59-61; mem. of Parl. 64-73; Attorney-Gen. 66-69; Minister of Educ. and Science 69-71; Attorney-Gen. March-Aug. 71; Minister of Foreign Affairs Aug. 71-72; Judge, N.S.W. Court of Appeal 73-, Chief Judge in Equity June 74-; head of del. to UN Conf. on Human Rights, Vice-Pres. 68; head of del. to UNESCO

Conf. on Cultural Policies 70, to UN Gen. Assembly 71, 72; Liberal.
Judges' Chambers, Supreme Court, Sydney, N.S.W., Australia.

Boyd, Arthur Merric Bloomfield; Australian painter; b. 24 July 1920; ed. State School, Murrumbeena, Victoria.
Taught painting and sculpture by parents and grandfather; painted and exhibited in Australia 37-59, in England 59-; designed for theatre, Melbourne 55-57, ballet, Edinburgh Festival and Sadler's Wells 61, Covent Garden 63; Retrospective Exhibition, Whitechapel Gallery, London 62, Adelaide 64, Edinburgh and London 69; exhibited Australia 71, London 73; Creative Arts Fellowship, Australian Nat. Univ. 71.
c/o Commercial Bank of Australia Ltd., 34 Piccadilly, London, W. 1, England.

Brack, Robert William, B.A., F.A.I.M.; Australian business executive; b. 1921; ed. Telopea Park High School, Canberra and Melbourne Univs.
With Dept. of Trade and Customs 38-41; served 8th Div. A.I.F. 41-45, P.O.W. Singapore and Thailand; Aust. High Commr.'s Office, London 49-51, 56-57; Aust. Embassy, Washington 52-53; Asst. Comptroller Gen. of Customs, Canberra 59-63; Collector of Customs for N.S.W. 63-64; Commercial Man. Aust. Consolidated Industries Ltd. 64-66, Asst. Gen. Man. 66-67, Gen. Man. 67-, Dir. 74-; Dir. Alex Harvey Industries Ltd., Malaysian Containers Berhad, Thai Glass Industries Ltd., Singapore Glass (1974) Ltd.; Chair. Pak Pacific Corpn. Pty. Ltd.; Dir. of many other cos.
Australian Consolidated Industries Ltd., 550 Bourke Street, Melbourne, Victoria 3000; Home: 2 Evans Court, Toorak, Victoria 3142, Australia.

Brand, Sir David, K.C.M.G., M.L.A.; Australian politician; b. 1 Aug. 1912; ed. Govt. School, Mullewa, Western Australia.
Mem. Western Australian Legislative Assembly for Greenough 45-; Hon. Minister for Housing, Forests and Local Govt. 49; Minister for Works, Water Supply and Housing 50; Leader of the Opposition and Parliamentary Leader, Liberal and Country Party 57-59; Premier, Treasurer and Minister for Tourists, Govt. of Western Australia 59-71; Leader of the Opposition 71-72.
Home: 24 Ednah Street, Como; and Parliament House, Perth, Western Australia.

Brand, Lindsay Brownfield, O.B.E., M.A., A.I.A.; Australian financial official; b. 29 Nov. 1916, Melbourne; ed. Univ. of Melbourne.
With Bureau of Census and Statistics, Canberra 39-40, 46-54; Served, Royal Australian Navy 40-46; with Australian Treasury 54-70, 75-; Sec. Australian Loan Council 55-70; mem. Decimal Currency Board 63-68; Exec. Dir. IMF 70-75.
The Treasury, Canberra, A.C.T. 2600, Australia.

Bryant, Gordon Munro, B.A., DIP.ED., E.D., M.P.; Australian politician; b. 3 Aug. 1914, Lismore; ed. Frankston High School, Melbourne Univ.
War service; school teacher until 55; mem. Parl. 55-; Minister of State for Aboriginal Affairs 72-73, of Capital Territory 73-75; mem. Council, Nat. Library of Australia 64-73, 76-; fmr. Senior Vice-Pres. Fed. Council for the Advancement of Aborigines and Torres Strait Islanders; del. to Inter-Parl. Union Conf., Commonwealth Parl. Assen.; Efficiency Decoration; Labor Party.
486 Sydney Road, Coburg, 3058 Victoria; Home: Bannockburn Road, Lower Plenty, 3084 Victoria, Australia.

Bullen, Keith Edward, M.A., B.SC., PH.D., SC.D., F.R.S.; Australian university professor; b. 29 June 1906; ed. Auckland Grammar School and Auckland Univ., New Zealand, and St. John's Coll., Cambridge.
Master, Auckland Grammar School, New Zealand 26-27; Lecturer in Mathematics, Auckland Univ. 27-31, 34-40; Special Lectureship, Hull Univ. 33; Senior Lecturer in Mathematics, Melbourne Univ. 40-45; Prof. of Applied Mathematics, Univ. of Sydney 46-71, Emeritus Prof. 71-; Pres. Int. Assen. of Seismology and Physics of Earth's Interior 54-57; Vice-Pres. Int. Union of Geodesy and Geophysics 63-67, Int. Scientific Cttee. for Antarctic Research 58-62; Chair. Int. Cttee. for Standard Earth Model 71-75; Chair. Australian Nat. Cttee. for Int. Geophysical Year 55-60; Convenor, Australian Nat. Cttee. for Antarctic Research 58-62; Foreign Assoc. U.S. Nat. Acad. of Sciences; Foreign Hon. mem. American Acad. of Arts and Science, Hon. mem. Royal Soc. of New Zealand; Pontifical Academician; Foundation Fellow, Australian Acad. of Science; Hon. Fellow, Royal Soc. of N.S.W.; Gold Medal, Royal Astronomical Soc. 74 and numerous other medals; Hon. D.Sc. (Auckland) 63, (Sydney) 76.
Publs. *Introduction to the Theory of Seismology* 47 (3rd edn. 65), *Introduction to the Theory of Mechanics* 49 (8th edn. 71), *Seismology* 54, *The Earth's Density* 75.
Department of Applied Mathematics, University of Sydney, Sydney 2006; and 132 Fuller's Road, Chatswood, N.S.W., 2067 Australia.
Telephone: Sydney 41-7649 (Home).

Bunting, Sir (Edward) John, Kt., C.B.E., B.A.; Australian civil servant; b. 13 Aug. 1918, Ballarat, Vic.; ed. Trinity Grammar, Trinity Coll., Melbourne Univ.
Assistant Sec., Prime Minister's Dept. 49-53; Official Sec. Australian High Comm., London 53-55; Deputy Sec., Prime Minister's Dept. 55-58, Sec. 59-68; Sec. Dept. of Cabinet Office 68-71, Prime Minister's Dept. 71-; Sec. to Australian Cabinet 59-75; High Commr. in U.K. Feb. 75-.
Australian High Commission, Australia House, Strand, London, W.C.2; Residence: 45 Hyde Park Gate, London, S.W.7, England; Home: 3 Wickham Crescent, Red Hill, A.C.T., 2603, Australia.

Burbury, Sir Stanley Charles, K.B.E., LL.B.; Australian state governor; b. 2 Dec. 1909; ed. Univ. of Tasmania.
Barrister; Solicitor-Gen. Tasmania 52; Chief Justice of Tasmania 56-73; Gov. of Tasmania Dec. 73-; Pres. Nat. Heart Foundation of Australia 67-73; Dir. Winston Churchill Memorial Foundation 67-73; Hon. LL.D. (Tasmania).
Government House, Hobart, Tasmania, Australia.

Burke, Samuel Martin, B.A. (HONS.), M.A., F.R.S.A.; Pakistani diplomatist; b. 3 July 1906; ed. Govt. Coll., Lahore, and School of Oriental Studies, London.
Indian Civil Service 31-47; District Officer and District and Sessions Judge; Pres. Election Tribunal, Punjab 46; Pakistani Foreign Office 48-49; served as Sec. to Pakistani Del. to Inter-Dominion Confs. with India 48 and 49; Counsellor to Pakistani High Comm. in London 49-52; Minister in Washington 52-53; led Special Missions to Dominican Republic and Mexico 52; Chargé d'Affaires, Rio, Brazil 53; mem. UN Cttee. on Contributions 53-55; Deputy High Commr. for Pakistan in United Kingdom 53; Minister to Sweden (concurrently to Norway, Denmark and Finland) 53-56; Ambassador to Thailand and Minister to Cambodia and Laos 56-59; mem. Pakistani Del. to SEATO Council Meetings 57, 58, 59; High Commr. in Canada 59-61; led Special Mission to Argentina 60; Prof. and Consultant in South Asian Studies, Dept. of Int. Relations, Univ. of Minnesota 61-; Sitari-i-Pakistan.
Publs. *Zafrulla Khan: The Man and His Career, Pakistan's Foreign Policy, Mainsprings of Indian and Pakistani Foreign Policies.*
10 Lantern Close, Roehampton, London, S.W.15, England.

Burnet, Sir Frank Macfarlane, O.M., K.B.E., F.R.S., SC.D., F.R.C.P., F.R.A.C.P., F.A.C.P.; Australian scientist; b. 3 Sept. 1899; ed. Melbourne Univ.

Resident Pathologist, Melbourne Hospital 23-25; Beit Fellow for Medical Research at Lister Inst., London 26-27; Asst. Dir. Walter and Eliza Hall Inst. for Medical Research 28-31 and 34-44, Dir. 44-65; Dunham Lecturer, Harvard Medical School 44; Croonian Lecturer, Royal Society 50; Herter Lecturer, Johns Hopkins Univ. 50, Flexner Lecturer at Vanderbilt Univ. 58; Chair. Board of Trustees, Commonwealth Foundation 66-69; Foreign mem. Royal Swedish Acad. of Science 57; Foreign Assoc. Nat. Acad. of Sciences, U.S.A. 54; Copley Medal Royal Society 59, Nobel Prize for Medicine 60; Pres. Australian Acad. of Sciences 65-69; Hon. F.R.C.S.Eng.
Publs. *Biological Aspects of Infectious Disease* 40, *Production of Antibodies* 49, *Viruses and Man* 53, *Principles of Animal Virology* 55, *Enzyme, Antigen and Virus* 56, *Clonal Selection Theory of Immunity* 59, *Integrity of the Body* 62, *Auto-Immune Diseases* (with I. R. Mackay) 63, *Changing Patterns* 68, *Cellular Immunology* 69, *Dominant Mammal* 70, *Immunological Surveillance* 70, *Genes, Dreams and Realities* 71, *Walter and Eliza Hall Institute 1915-65* 71, *Auto-Immunity and Auto-Immune Disease* 72, *Intrinsic Mutagenesis* 74.
48 Monomeath Avenue, Canterbury, Victoria, Australia.
Telephone: 834526.

Bushell, John Christopher Wyndowe, C.M.G.; British diplomatist; b. 27 Sept. 1919.
R.A.F. 39-45; Foreign Office 45; Second Sec., British Embassy, U.S.S.R. 46, Italy 48; Foreign Office 51; NATO Defence Coll. 53; Foreign Office 54; Deputy Sec.-Gen. Baghdad Pact Org. (later CENTO), Baghdad and Ankara 57; Foreign Office 59; Counsellor and Political Adviser to C.-in-C. Middle East Command, Aden 61; Counsellor and Head of Chancery, del. to NATO 64; seconded to Cabinet Office 68; Minister and Deputy Commdt., British Mil. Govt., Berlin 70; Amb. to Repub. of Viet-Nam 74-75; sabbatical year, SOAS, London Univ. 75-76; Amb. to Pakistan 76-.
British Embassy, Diplomatic Enclave, Islamabad, Pakistan.

Butement, William Alan Stewart, C.B.E., D.SC., C.ENG., F.I.E.E., F.INST.P., F.A.I.P., F.I.R.E.E. (Aust.), Australian scientist; b. 18 Aug. 1904; ed. Scots Coll., Sydney, Australia, Univ. Coll. School, Hampstead and London Univ.
Scientific Officer, War Office 28-39; Asst. Dir. Scientific Research, Ministry of Supply 39-47; First Chief Superintendent, Research Establishment and Rocket Range, Woomera, Australia 47-49; Chief Scientist, Australian Dept. of Supply 49-66; Dir. Plessey Pacific 67-.
Publ. *Precision Radar* 45-46.
Plessey Pacific, 9-25 Commonwealth Street, Sydney, N.S.W. 2000; and 5A Barry Street, Kew, Victoria, Australia.
Telephone: 421186 (Office); 868375 (Home).

C

Cadwallader, Sir John, Kt.; Australian business executive; b. 25 Aug. 1902, Melbourne; ed. Sydney Church of England Grammar School.
Managing Dir. Mungo Scott Pty. Ltd. until incorporation of Allied Mills Ltd. 19-49; Chair. and Man. Dir. Allied Mills Ltd. 49-; Dir. Bank of New South Wales 45, Pres. 59-; Chair. Bushells Investments Ltd. 63-; Dir. Queensland Insurance Co. Ltd. 46-74.
27 Marian Street, Killara 2071, N.S.W., Australia.
Telephone: 49-1974.

Cairns, James Ford, PH.D.; Australian politician; b. 4 Oct. 1914, Carlton, Victoria; ed. State Schools, Univ. of Melbourne.
Junior Clerk, Australian Estates Co. Ltd. 32-35; with Victoria Police Detective Force 35-44; Australian Infantry Forces 44-46; Senior Lecturer of Econ. History, Univ. of Melbourne 46-55; mem. House of Reps. for Yarra 55-69, for Lalor 69-; Minister for Overseas Trade 72-74, of Secondary Industry 72-73; Deputy Prime Minister 74-75; Fed. Treas. Dec. 74-June 75; Minister of Environment and Conservation June-July 75; mem. Fed. Parl. Labor Party Exec. 60-62, 64-75; del. to IPU Conf., Paris 71; Labor Party.
Publs. *Australia* 52, *Living with Asia* 65, *The Eagle and the Lotus* 69, *Silence Kills* 70, *Tariffs and Planning* 71, *The Quiet Revolution* 72.
21 Wattle Road, Hawthorn 3122, Australia.

Cakobau, Ratu Sir George Kadavulevu, G.C.M.G., O.B.E.; Fijian politician; b. 1911; ed. Queen Victoria School Fiji, Newington Coll. Australia, Wanganui Tech. Coll. New Zealand.
Military service 39-45; mem. Great Council of Chiefs 38-72, Legislative Council 51-70; Minister of Fijian Affairs and Local Govt. 70-71, without Portfolio 71-72; Gov.-Gen. of Fiji 73-; Kt.St.J.
Government House, Suva, Fiji.

Cameron, Clyde Robert; Australian politician; b. 11 Feb. 1914; ed. Gawler High School, South Australia.
Worked in shearing sheds 28-38; Organizer Adelaide Branch, Australian Workers' Union 38, Sec. 41-49; Fed. Vice-Pres. AWU 42-50; Industrial Officer 44-48; mem. House of Reps. for Hindmarsh 49-; mem. Fed. Parl. Labor Party Exec. 53-; Minister for Labour 72-75, also for Immigration 74-75; mem. S.A. Broadcasting Advisory Cttee. 45-49, 64-75; Pres. S.A. Branch, Australian Labor Party 46-48; Labor Party.
c/o Parliament House, Canberra, A.C.T., Australia.

Cao Van Bo; Vietnamese politician; b. 1908, Vinh Long Province; ed. studied electronics in France.
Technical Director for several industrial firms in France; joined French resistance during World War II; politically active in overthrow of Diem Govt. 63; detained for joining opposition movements 65, 67; joined NLF 68; Minister of Econ. and Finance, Provisional Revolutionary Govt. of S. Viet-Nam May 75-June 76.

Carnegie, Roderick Howard, B.SC., M.A. (OXON.), M.B.A.; Australian mining executive; b. 27 Nov. 1932; ed. Trinity Coll. Melbourne Univ., New Coll. Oxford, Harvard Business School Boston, U.S.A.
Associate McKinsey and Co., Melbourne and New York 59-64, Principal Assoc. 64-68, Dir. 68-70; Dir. Conzinc Riotinto of Australia Ltd. 70, Joint Man. Dir. 71-72, Man. Dir. 72-74, Chief Exec. 72-, Chair. 74-; Dir. Rio Tinto-Zinc Corpn. Ltd., Bougainville Copper Ltd., Hamersley Holdings Ltd., Australian Mining and Smelting Co. Ltd., Comalco Ltd., and several other cos. in the CRA group.
Conzinc Riotinto of Australia Ltd., 95 Collins Street, Melbourne 3000; Home: 15 St. Georges Road, Toorak, Victoria 3142, Australia.

Carrick, Hon. John Leslie; Australian politician; b. 4 Sept. 1918, Sydney; ed. Sydney Technical High School, Univ. of Sydney.
Army service 39-48; prisoner-of-war 42-45; mem. Citizen Mil. Force 48-51; Gen. Sec. N.S.W. Div. of Liberal Party of Australia 48-71; mem. Senate 71-; mem. Senate Standing Cttee. on Educ., Science and the Arts 71-75, on Foreign Affairs and Defence 71-75, Joint Cttee. on Foreign Affairs 71-72, on Foreign Affairs and Defence 73-75; opposition spokesman for federalism and intergovernment relations 75; Minister for Housing and Construction, for Urban and Regional Devt. Nov.-Dec. 75; Minister for Educ. and Minister assisting the Prime Minister in Fed. Affairs Dec. 75-.
Parliament Building, Canberra, A.C.T. 2600, Australia.

Casey, Baron (Life Peer, cr. 60), of Berwick (Victoria) and the City of Westminster; **Richard Gardiner Casey,** K.G., P.C., G.C.M.G., C.H., D.S.O., M.C.; Australian politician and diplomatist; b. 29 Aug. 1890, Brisbane, Queensland; ed. Melbourne and Cambridge Univs.
Political Liaison Officer between British and Australian Govts. in London 24-30; mem. Fed. House of Reps. 31-40, 49-60; Asst. Treas. to Commonwealth Govt. 33-35; Treas. of the Commonwealth 35-39, and Min. of Development 37-39; Privy Councillor 39; Min. for Supply and Development 39-40; resgnd. from Parl. and Cabinet on appointment as first Min. to U.S.A. 40-42; British Min. of State Resident in Middle East 42-44; Gov. of Bengal 44-46; Federal Pres. Liberal Party of Australia 47-49; Minister of Supply 49; Minister in Charge of C.S.I.R.O. 49-60; Minister of Nat. Development 50; Minister for External Affairs 51-60; mem. Exec. C.S.I.R.O. 60-65; Gov.-Gen. Australia 65-69; Kt.St.J.
Publs. *An Australian in India* 46, *Double or Quit* 49, *Friends and Neighbours* 54, *Australian Foreign Policy* 54, *Personal Experience 39-46* 62, *The Future of the Commonwealth* 63, *Australian Father and Son* 66, *Australian Foreign Minister—The Diaries of R. G. Casey 1951-60* 72.
Edrington, Berwick, Victoria 3806, Australia.

Cavanagh, James Luke; Australian politician; b. 21 June 1913, S. Australia; ed. Primary School.
Trades Union Sec. 46-62; Senator 62-; Minister of Works 72-73, of Aboriginal Affairs 73-75, of Police and Customs June-Nov. 75.
1 King William Street, Adelaide, S.A. 5000; Home: 17 Hennessy Terrace, Rosewater, S. Australia 5013, Australia.
Telephone: 47-22-41 (Home).

Chagla, Mahomedali Currim, B.A.; Indian barrister, diplomat and politician; b. 30 Sept. 1900; ed. St. Xavier's High School and Coll., Bombay, and Lincoln Coll., Oxford.
President Oxford Asiatic Soc. 21; Pres. Oxford Indian Majlis 22; called to Bar (Inner Temple) 22; Prof. of Constitutional Law, Govt. Law Coll., Bombay 27-30; Hon. Sec. Bar Council of High Court of Judicature, Bombay 33-41; Puisne Judge Bombay High Court 41-47; Chair. Legal Education Cttee. 48; Vice-Chancellor, Bombay Univ. 47; Chief Justice, High Court, Bombay 47-58; Del. to UN 46; Pres. Bombay Branch Royal Asiatic Soc. 47-58; Gov. of Bombay 56; Judge, Int. Court of Justice 57; mem. Law Commission 55-58; Ambassador to U.S., Mexico and Cuba 58-61; High Commissioner in the United Kingdom, Ambassador to Ireland 62-63; Minister of Educ., Govt. of India 63-66, of External Affairs 66-Aug. 67; Pres. Indian Council for Cultural Relations; Vice-Pres. Sahitya Akademi 67-69; Leader Rajya Sabha; Chair. Life Insurance Corpn. Inquiry Comm. 58; mem. Sikh Grievances Enquiry Comm. 61; Leader Indian del. to UN Security Council 64-65, to UNESCO 64, to Gen. Assembly 65, to Commonwealth Educ. Conf. 64; Hon. Fellow, Lincoln Coll., Oxford 61; Hon. LL.D. (Hartford, Temple, Boston, Leningrad and Punjab Univs., Dartmouth Coll., Hindu Benares Univ.).
Publs. *The Indian Constitution* 29, *Law, Liberty and Life* 50, *The Individual and the State, An Ambassador Speaks* 62, *Education and the Nation, Unity and Language, Roses in December—an Autobiography.*
Pallonji Mansion, New Cuffe Parade, Bombay 5, India.

Chakravarti, Subramaniam, M.A.; Indian state governor; b. 30 Aug. 1910, Madras; ed. Hindu High School and Presidency Coll., Madras, London School of Econs. and Trinity Coll., Cambridge.
Joint Sec. Ministry of Transport 48-49; Chief, Industry Div., UN Econ. Comm. for Asia and Far East 50-51; Devt. Commr. and Sec. Planning and Devt. Dept., Govt. of Andhra Pradesh 55; Admin., Nagarjunsagar Project 55-59; Principal, Nat. Inst. of Study and Research in Community Devt., Mussoorie 59-62; Sec., Ministry of Community Devt. and Co-operation 63-65, Ministry of Food, Agriculture, Community Devt. and Co-operation 66, Ministry of Transport 67-69, Ministry of Educ. and Youth Services 69-70; Gov. Himachal Pradesh 71-; fmr. del. to many int. confs. including ECAFE, UNICEF and UNESCO.
Raj Bhavan, Simla 4; and 19 G Road, Maharani Bagh, New Delhi 14, India.
Telephone: 3440 (Office); 3152 (Home).

Chakravarty, Birendra Narayan, B.SC.; Indian diplomatist; b. 20 Dec. 1904; ed. Presidency Coll., Calcutta Univ., Univ. Coll., London, School of Oriental Studies, London.
Joined Indian Civil Service 29; held various appointments in Bengal districts and Bengal Secretariat; Finance Sec., Bengal Govt. 44; Sec. to Gov., West Bengal 47; Chargé d'Affaires, Embassy of India, Nanking Feb.-June 48; Head of the Indian Liaison Mission, Tokyo, with personal rank of Minister 48-49; Joint Sec., Ministry of External Affairs 49-51; Sec. (Commonwealth Relations) 51-52; Ambassador to Netherlands 52-54; Senior Alt. Chair. Neutral Nations Repatriation Comm., Korea 53; Acting High Commr. to U.K. 54; High Commr. to Ceylon 5-56; Special Sec. Ministry of External Affairs 56-60; High Commr. to Canada 60-62; Perm. Rep. to UN 62-65; Gov. of Haryana 67-.
Publ. *India Speaks to America.*
Office of the Governor of Haryana, Chandigarh; and 19, G. Road, Maharani Bagh, New Delhi 14, India.

Champassak, Sisouk Na; *see* Na Champassak, Sisouk.

Chan, Julius, C.B.E.; Papua New Guinea politician; b. 29 Aug. 1939, Tanga, New Ireland; ed. Maurist Brothers Coll., Ashgrove, Queensland and Univ. of Queensland, Australia.
Co-operative Officer, Papua New Guinea Admin. 60-62; Man. Dir. Coastal Shipping Co. Pty. Ltd.; mem. House of Assembly 68-, Deputy Speaker, Vice-Chair. Public Accounts Cttee. 68-72; Parl. Leader, People's Progress Party 70; Minister of Finance and Parl. Leader of Govt. Business 72-; Gov. for Papua New Guinea and Vice-Chair. Asian Devt. Bank 74-; Fellowship mem. Int. Bankers' Asscn. Inc., U.S.A. 76-.
Ministry of Finance, Central Government Offices, Post Office, Wards Strip, Papua New Guinea.

Chandavimol, Abhai, M.A. (CANTAB.); Thai education expert and politician; b. 16 Feb. 1908; ed. Suan Kularb School, Bangkok, Imperial Service Coll., Windsor, Gonville and Caius Coll., Cambridge Univ. and Inner Temple, London.
Teacher 25-28, 35-36; Sec. Dept. of Physical Educ. 36-43; Chief Private School Div. 43-47; Asst. Dir.-Gen. Dept. of Gen. Educ. 47-51; Dir.-Gen. Dept. of Physical Educ. 51-52, Dept. of Elementary and Adult Educ. 52-61; Under-Sec. of State for Educ. 61-68; Deputy Minister of Educ. 70-71, Minister of Educ. 72-74; Senator 75-; mem. Boy Scouts World Cttee. 65-71; Order Crown of Thailand, Order of the White Elephant; Bronze Wolf, Boy Scouts World Cttee.
Senate (Vudhi Sabha), Bangkok; Home: 85 Rajatapan Lane, Makkasan, Bangkok 4, Thailand.

Chandra, Satish, M.A., B.SC.; Indian business executive and fmr. politician; b. 1917; ed. S.M. Coll., Chandausi, Govt. Agricultural Coll., Kanpur, and Bareilly Coll., Bareilly (Agra Univ.).
Indian Nat. Congress 36-; mem. Indian Constituent Assembly 48-50, Provisional Parl. 50-52, Lok Sabha 52-62; Parl. Sec. to Prime Minister 51-52; Union Dep. Minister for Defence 52-55, for Production 55-57, for Commerce and

Industry 57-62; Chair. Indian Airlines Corpn. and Dir. Air-India 63, 64; Chair. British India Corpn. Ltd., The Elgin Mills Co. Ltd., Cawnpore Textiles Ltd., Cawnpore Sugar Works Ltd., Champarun Sugar Co. Ltd., Saran Engineering Co. Ltd. 62-, also fmr. Chair. and Man. Dir. Fertilizer Corpn. of India; Dir. other cos.
Chitrakut, Parbati Bagla Road, Kanpur, U.P., India.

Chandrasekhar, Sripati, M.A., M.LITT., M.SC., PH.D., Indian economist and demographer; b. 22 Nov. 1918; ed. Univ. of Madras and Columbia, New York and Princeton Univs.
Visiting Lecturer, Univ. of Pa. and Asia Inst., New York 44-46; Prof. of Economics, Annamalai Univ. 47-50 Dir. Demographic Research UNESCO, Paris 47-49; Prof. of Economics and Head of Dept., Baroda Univ. 50-53; Nuffield Fellow, London School of Economics 53-55; Dir. Indian Inst. for Population Studies 56-67; mem. Rajya Sabha 64-70; Minister of State for Health and Family Planning 67-Nov. 67, for Health, Family Planning and Urban Devt. 67-70; Research Prof. of Demography, Univ. of Calif.; Fellow, Battelle Research Centre 71-72; Distinguished Visiting Prof. of Sociology, Calif. State Univ. 72-73; Visiting Prof. of Demography and Public Health, Univ. of Calif., Los Angeles 73-74, Regents Prof., Santa Barbara 75; Vice-Chancellor, Annamalai Univ., Chidambaram 75-; Editor *Population Review*; Hon. D.Litt. (Univs. of Redlands, Kurukshetra), Hon. M.D. (Budapest), Hon. D.Sc. (Univ. of the Pacific); Watumull Award for distinguished work in Indian demography 64; Kaufman Award 69.
Publs. *India's Population* 46, *Census and Statistics in India* 47, *Indian Emigration* 48, *Hungry People and Empty Lands* 52, *Population and Planned Parenthood in India* 55, *Infant Mortality in India* 59, *China's Population* 59, *Communist China Today* 61, *Red China: An Asian View* 62, *A Decade of Mao's China* (Editor) 63, *American Aid and India's Economic Development* 65, *Asia's Population Problems* 67, *Problems of Economic Development* 67, *India's Population: Fact, Problem and Policy* 68, *Infant Mortality, Population Growth and Family Planning* 72, *Abortion in a Crowded World* 74.
Vice-Chancellor's Lodge, Annamalainagar, South India; 8976 Cliffridge Avenue, La Jolla, Calif. 92037, U.S.A.

Chandrasekharan, Komaravolu, M.A., M.SC., PH.D.; Indian mathematician; b. 21 Nov. 1920; ed. Presidency Coll., Madras, and Inst. for Advanced Study, Princeton, U.S.A.
Prof. Eidgenössische Technische Hochschule, Zürich; Sec. Int. Mathematical Union 61-66, Pres. 71-74; Vice-Pres. Int. Council of Scientific Unions 63-66, Sec.-Gen. 66-70; mem. Scientific Advisory Cttee. to Cabinet, Govt. of India 61-66; Visiting Lecturer, American Math. Soc. 63; Fellow, Nat. Inst. of Sciences of India, Indian Acad. of Sciences; Foreign mem. Finnish Acad. of Science and Letters 75; Padma Shri 59; Shanti Swarup Bhatnagar Memorial Award for Scientific Research 63; Ramanujan Medal 66.
Publs. *Fourier Transforms* (with S. Bochner) 49, *Typical Means* (with S. Minakshisundaram) 52, *Lectures on the Riemann Zeta-function* 53, *Analytic Number Theory* 68, *Arithmetical Functions* 70.
Eidgenössische Technische Hochschule, 8006 Zürich, Rämistrasse 101; Home: Hedwigstrasse 29, 8032 Zürich, Switzerland.
Telephone: 53-96-86.

Chandy, Kanianthra Thomas, M.A., LL.M.; Indian business executive; b. 1913; ed. London Univ.
Law practice; Hindustan Lever Ltd., Dir. 56-62; Dir. of Research Hyderabad Admin. Staff Coll. 57; Dir. Indian Inst. of Management, Calcutta 62-66; Chair. Food Corpn. of India 66-68, Hindustan Steel Ltd. 68-72, Kerala State Industrial Devt. Corpn. Ltd. 72-; Pres. Calcutta Management Asscn.; Vice-Pres. Kerala State Planning Board; Chair. Kerala State Textile Corpn. Ltd., Board of Govs. Indian Inst. of Technology (IIT), Exec. Council Nat. Metallurgical Laboratory, Jamshedpur, All-India Board of Management Studies, Nat. Productivity Council, New Delhi, Board of Apprenticeship Training; first Vice-Chair. Asian Productivity Org., Chair. May 76-; Dir. Int. Iron and Steel Inst., Brussels, Belgium; mem. Board of Govs. Indian Insts. of Management, Calcutta and Bangalore, Council of IITs, All India Council of Technical Educ.; fmr. mem. Univ. Grants Comm., Nat. Planning Council.
P.O. Box 105, Trivandrum I, Kerala, India.

Chang Ch'ih-ming; People's Repub. of China.
Political Commissar, 4th Field Army, People's Liberation Army 50; Political Commissar in Gen. Logistics Dept., Cen.-South Mil. District, PLA 54; re-assigned to Cen. Mil. Org. 54; Lieut.-Gen. PLA 55; Pres. Logistics Inst., PLA 60; Deputy Dir., Gen. Logistics Dept., PLA 65, Political Commissar 67-.

Chang Ch'ing-fu; People's Republic of China.
Vice-Minister of Forestry 56-58; Minister of Finance 75-.

Chang Ching-yao; army officer, People's Repub. of China.
Commander Kwangtung Mil. District, People's Liberation Army 73-.

Chang Ch'un-chi'ao; People's Repub. of China; b. *circa* 1911.
Director East China Gen. Branch, New China News Agency 50; Dir. *Liberation Daily*, Shanghai 54; Alt. Sec. CCP Shanghai 64, Sec. 65; Chair. Shanghai Revolutionary Cttee. 67; Deputy Head Cen. Cultural Revolution Group 67; First Political Commissar Nanking Mil. Region, People's Liberation Army 67-; mem. Politburo, 9th Cen. Cttee., CCP 69; First Sec. CCP, Shanghai 71-; mem. Standing Cttee. of Politburo, 10th Cen. Cttee. of CCP 73, 75-; Vice-Premier, State Council Jan. 75-; Dir.-Gen. Political Dept., PLA 75-.

Chang Chung; army officer, People's Repub. of China.
Commander Kansu Mil. District, People's Liberation Army 67-; Vice-Chair. Kansu Revolutionary Cttee. 68; Sec. CCP Kansu 72.

Chang Dai-chien; Chinese painter; b. 1 April 1899; ed. Chui-ch'ing School, Chungking and under Li Ch'ing, Shanghai.
Member Cttee. first Nat. Exhbn. of Fine Arts 29; Prof. Central Univ. Nanking 36; moved to Argentina 52; first one-man exhbn. Peking 34, then Shanghai 36, Chungking 39, 40, Chengtu 43, Shanghai 46, 47, Hong Kong 48, 62, New Delhi and Hyderabad 50, Buenos Aires 52, Tokyo 55, 56, Museum of Modern Art, Paris 56, Salon Nationale, Paris 60, Brussels 60, Athens 60, Madrid 60, Geneva 61, São Paulo 61, Singapore 63, Kuala Lumpur 63, New York 63, Cologne 64, Grosvenor Gallery, London 65; represented at Paris Exhbn. of Chinese Painting 33, London 35, UNESCO Exhbn., Paris 46; Gold Medal, Int. Council of Fine Arts, N.Y. 58.
Major works: *The Lotuses*, Jeu-de-Paume Museum, Paris 33, copied two hundred frescoes, caves of Tun-huang 40, *Giant Lotus* 45, twelve major works, Perm. Exhbn. Contemporary Chinese Art, Cernuschi Museum 59, Lotus Painting, Museum of Modern Art, New York 61.
P.O. Box 249, Mogi das Cruzes, São Paulo, Brazil.

Chang Hai-t'ang; army officer, People's Repub. of China.
Deputy Chief of Staff Liaoning Mil. District, People's Liberation Army 59, Deputy Commdr. 60, Commdr. 72-; Maj.-Gen. PLA 59; Vice-Chair. Liaoning Revolutionary Cttee. 72.

Chang Hsien-yueh; People's Repub. of China.
Lieutenant-General, People's Liberation Army 55; Deputy Dir., Gen. Logistics Dept., PLA 64-.

Chang Lin-pin; People's Repub. of China.
Deputy Dir., Gen. Logistics Dept., People's Liberation Army 50-; Lieut.Gen. PLA 55; Alt. mem. 9th Cen. Cttee. of CCP 69, 10th Cen. Cttee. 73.

Chang P'ing-hua; People's Repub. of China; b. 1903, Hunan.
Political Commissar in 120th Div. 47; Sec. CCP Wuhan 49-52; Third Sec. CCP Hupeh 55-56, Second Sec. 56, Sec. 57-59; Alt. mem. 8th Cen. Cttee. of CCP 56; First Sec. CCP Hunan 59-67; First Political Commissar Hunan Mil. District, People's Liberation Army 60; Sec. Cen.-South Bureau, CCP 66-67; Deputy Dir. Propaganda Dept., CCP 66; criticized and removed from office during Cultural Revolution 67; Vice-Chair. Shansi Revolutionary Cttee. 71; Sec. CCP Shansi 71; Sec. CCP Hunan 73, Second Sec. 74-; mem. 10th Cen. Cttee. of CCP 73.

Chang Shu-chih; army officer, People's Repub. of China.
Commander Honan Mil. District, People's Liberation Army 64-; Deputy Commdr. Wuhan Mil. Region, PLA 70; Sec. CCP Honan 71; mem. 10th Cen. Cttee. of CCP 73.

Chang Ts'ai-ch'ien; army officer, People's Repub. of China.
Guerrilla leader in Hupeh, Honan, Anhwei and Hunan 46; Chief of Staff Hupah Mil. District, People's Liberation Army 50; Lieut.-Gen. PLA 58; Deputy Commdr. Nanking Mil. Region, PLA 58-70; mem. 9th Cen. Cttee. of CCP 69, 10th Cen. Cttee. 73; Deputy Chief of Staff PLA 71-.

Chang Tsung-hsun; Chinese army officer; b. 1898, Shensi; ed. Whampoa Mil. Acad.
Graduated 1925; Div. Commdr. Red Army 29; Chief of Staff, 4th Front Army on "Long March" 34; Brigade Commdr. 37; Alt. mem. 7th Cen. Cttee. 45; Deputy Commdr. First Field Army, PLA 49-54, Deputy Chief of Gen. Staff 54-75; Alt. mem. 8th Cen. Cttee., CCP 56; visited Eastern Europe 59; Dir. Gen. Logistic Dept., PLA 75-.
People's Republic of China.

Chang Wei-hsun; Chinese civil servant and United Nations official.
Formerly in Foreign Relations Dept., Ministry of Health, Peking; Asst. Dir.-Gen. World Health Org. (WHO), in charge of family health and health services divs. 73-.
World Health Organization, Avenue Appia, 1121 Geneva, Switzerland.

Chao Hsin-chu; Chinese party official.
Secretary, CCP Hupeh 57-65; Vice-Gov. Hupeh 58-64; Vice-Minister of Culture 65; criticized and removed from office during Cultural Revolution 66; rehabilitated as a "leading cadre" in Inner Mongolia 72; Vice-Chair. Provincial Revolutionary Cttee. and Sec. CCP, Hupeh 73, Chair. Revolutionary Cttee. and First Sec., Hupeh 75.
People's Republic of China.

Chao Tzu-yang; People's Repub. of China.
Secretary-General S. China Sub-Bureau, CCP 50-54, Third Sec. 54-55; Third Deputy Sec. CCP Kwangtung 55, Sec. 62, First Sec. 65-67; Political Commissar Kwangtung Mil. District, People's Liberation Army 64; Sec. Cen.-South Bureau, CCP 65-67; criticized and removed from office during Cultural Revolution 67; Vice-Chair. Inner Mongolia Revolutionary Cttee. 71; Sec. CCP Inner Mongolia 71, CCP Kwangtung 72; Vice-Chair. Kwangtung Revolutionary Cttee. 72; mem. 10th Cen. Cttee. of CCP 73; First Sec. CCP Kwantung 74; Chair. Kwantung Revolutionary Cttee. 74.

Charusathiara, Field-Marshal Prapas; Thai army officer and politician; b. 25 Nov. 1912; ed. Chulachomklao Royal Military Acad. and National Defence Coll.
Army service 32-, rose to Gen. 60; Minister of Interior 57-71, Deputy Prime Minister 63-71, Army Deputy Commdr. and Deputy Supreme Commdr. 63-64, Supreme Commdr. 64-73; Deputy Supreme Commdr. Armed Forces Sept.-Oct. 73; Vice-Pres. and Rector Chulalongkorn Univ. 61; mem. Nat. Exec. Council 71-72; Dir. of Security Council (Defence and Interior) 71-72; Deputy Prime Minister, Minister of Interior 72-73; Crown of Thailand (Highest Class).
Publs. *The Role of the Ministry of the Interior in the Development of National Security, The Role of the Ministry of Interior in Maintenance of National Peace and Order.*
Taiwan.

Chatterjee, Dwarka Nath, B.A.; Indian diplomatist; b. 2 Nov. 1914; ed. Calcutta Univ., King's Coll., London, London School of Economics and School of Oriental Studies, London.
Army Service 40-47; Indian Foreign Service 47-; First Sec., Paris 48-49, London 49-54; Deputy Sec., Ministry of External Affairs 54-55; Deputy High Commr. in Pakistan 56-58; Consul-Gen., Geneva 58-59; Minister, Washington 59-62; Amb. to Congo (Kinshasa) 62-64; High Commr. in Australia 65-67; Acting High Commr. in U.K. 67-68, Deputy High Commr. 68-69; Amb. to France 69-.
15 rue Alfred Dehodencq, 75016 Paris, France.

Chatterji, Suniti Kumar, M.A., D.LIT. (London); Indian educationist, philologist and writer; b. 26 Nov. 1890; ed. Calcutta, School of Oriental Studies, London, and Univ. of Paris.
Khaira Prof. of Indian Linguistics and Phonetics, Calcutta Univ. 22-52, Emeritus Prof. of Comparative Philology 52-; Visiting Prof., Univ. of Pa., U.S.A. 51-52; Chair., Upper House, West Bengal State Legislature 52-65; Nat. Prof. of India in Humanities 65-; Pres. Sahitya Akademi Aug. 69-; Pres. Bangiya Sahitya Parishad, fmr. Pres. Asiatic Soc., Calcutta, Linguistic Soc. of India; hon. mem. Société Asiatique, Paris, American Oriental Soc., Norwegian Acad. of Sciences, Royal Siam Soc., Utrechts Genootschap van Kunst en Wetenschappen, Ecole Française de l'Extrême Orient, Linguistic Soc. of America; Fellow, Indian Council for Cultural Relations 61-, etc.; awarded Padma-Vibhushan 63; Hon. D.Lit. (Univs. of Rome, Delhi, Calcutta, Osmania, Visva-Bharati, Ravindra-Bharati, Nava-Nalanda Buddhist Univ.).
Publs. *Origin and Development of the Bengali Language* 26, 71, *Dvipamaya Bharat* 40 (2nd edn. 64), *Indo-Aryan and Hindi* 42 (2nd edn. 60), *Kirata-jana-Krti or the Indo-Mongoloids* 51, 74, *Africanism* 60, *Indianism and the Indian Synthesis* 62, *Languages and Literatures of Modern India* 64, *Dravidian* 66, *People, Language and Culture of Orissa* 66, *Balts and Aryans* 68, *India and Ethiopia* 69, *World Literature and Tagore* 71, *Iranianism* 72, *Jayadeva* 74, and other works in English, Bengali and Hindi.
"Sudharma", 16 Hindusthan Park, Calcutta 29, India.
Telephone: 46-1121 (Home); 45-5319 (Office).

Chattopadhyaya, Harindranath; Indian poet, dramatist, musician and actor; b. 1898; ed. U.K., Germany, U.S.A. and U.S.S.R.
Studies drama under Stanislavsky and Meyerholdt; pioneer modern Indian theatre; leader progressive movt. in literature; producer of film, *Azadi* (Freedom); author of script for *Legend of Gautama Buddha* 42 and *Abul Hassan* (musical comedy); mem. of Lok Sabha (Parliament) 52.
Publs. *The Coffin, Feast of Youth, Ancient Wings, Grey Clouds and White Showers, Poems and Plays, Five Plays in Verse, Five Plays in Prose, Dark Well, The Divine Vagabond, Horizon—Ends, Edgeways and the Saint, Lyrics, Blood of Stones, Perfume of Earth, Magic Tree, Crossroads, Life and Myself* (Vol. I: Autobiography), *Hunter of Kalahasti* (play), *Treasury of Poems, Land of the New Man, The Toy-Maker of Kondapalli* (play), *Spring in Winter* (lyrics), etc.
3 Krishna Iyer Street, Nungumbakam, Madras, India.

Chau, Hon. Sir Sik-Nin, Kt., C.B.E., M.B., B.S., D.O.M.S., D.L.O., J.P.; Hong Kong business executive; b. 1903; ed. St. Stephen's Coll., Hong Kong, Univs. of Hong Kong, London and Vienna.
Chairman, Hong Kong Productivity Council; Pres. Fireworks Co. Ltd. (Taiwan), Hong Kong Model Housing Soc., Hong Kong Marine Food Co. Ltd., The Hong Kong Chinese Bank Ltd., State Trading Corpn. (Far East) Ltd., Kowloon Motor Bus Co., Man Lee Cheung Co. Ltd., Pioneer Trade Devt. Co. Ltd., Repulse Bay Enterprises Ltd., Far East Insurance Co. Ltd., Nin Fung Hong, Oriental Express Ltd., Sik Yuen Co. Ltd., Atherton Co. Ltd., Yin Bong Ltd., Marquise Industrial Estate Co. Ltd., Swiss Watch Case Center Ltd., H.K. and Kowloon Land and Loan Co. Ltd., Hong Kong Cttee. for Osaka World *Expo 1970*; Vice-Pres. Hong Kong Anti-Tuberculosis Asscn.; dir. numerous companies; official, educational and philanthropic orgs.; Hon. LL.D. (Hong Kong Univ.).
3547 Hatton Road, Hong Kong.

Chaudry, Fazal Elahi (*see* Elahi Chaudry, Fazal).

Chaudhry, Air Marshal Zafar Ahmad; Pakistani fmr. air force officer; b. Aug. 1926, Sialkot; ed. Punjab Univ., R.A.F. Coll., British Joint Services Staff Coll. and Imperial Defence Coll.
Commissioned, Royal Indian Air Force (fighter pilot) 45; has held various important staff and command appointments in the Pakistan Air Force; Asst. Chief of Air Staff (Operations) until 71; Chief Exec., Pakistan Int. Airlines (PIA) 71-72; Chief of Staff, Pakistan Air Force 72-74, retd.; Sitara-i-Quaid-i-Azam 65.
c/o Air Force Headquarters, Peshawar, Pakistan.

Chaudhuri, Gen. Joyanto Nath, O.B.E.; Indian army officer; b. 10 June 1908; ed. Highgate School and Royal Military Coll., Sandhurst.
Served Indian 7th Cavalry, Middle East and Burma 39-45; Military Gov. Hyderabad 48-49; fmr. G.O.C.-in-C. Indian Southern Command; Commdr. Goa Operation 62; Chief of Indian Army Staff Nov. 62-June 66; High Commr. in Canada 66-69; Visiting Prof. McGill Univ. 69; Int. Inst. for Strategic Studies, London 71; Chair. and Man. Dir. Andrew Yule & Co., Calcutta 73-; awarded Padma-Vibhushan, Hon. D.Sc., Hon. LL.D.
Publs. *Operation Polo, Arms, Aims and Aspects.*
The Cavalry Club, 127 Piccadilly, London, England; c/o Grindlays Bank, 10 Parliament Street, New Delhi, India.

Chaudhuri, Naranarain (Sankho), B.A.; Indian sculptor; b. 25 Feb. 1916; ed. Armanitoba High School, Dacca and Bishwa Bharti Santiniketan, West Bengal.
Freelance artist 47-; Chief, Dept. of Sculpture, Maharaja Sayajirao Univ. of Baroda 51-, Prof. 57-, Dean of the Faculty 66-68; mem. Lalit Kala Akademi 56-; mem. Int. Sculptors Symposium, Yugoslavia 61; Exhibited São Paulo Biennale 61, one-man exhbns. Bombay and Delhi; numerous Indian awards.
Major Works: Sculptures, All-India Radio, Delhi 55, Statue of Mahatma Gandhi, Rio de Janeiro, and works in collections in India, U.K. and U.S.A.

Chaudhuri, Nirad Chandra, B.A.; Indian writer; b. 23 Nov. 1897; ed. Calcutta Univ.
Former Asst. Editor *The Modern Review* (Calcutta); fmr. Sec. to Sarat Bose (Leader of Congress Party, Bengal); fmr. Commentator, All-India Radio; has contributed to *The Times, Encounter, New English Review, The Atlantic Monthly, Pacific Affairs;* also contributed to Indian papers *The Statesman, The Illustrated Weekly, The Hindustan Standard, The Times of India;* Duff Cooper Memorial Prize for *The Continent of Circe* 67.
Publs. *The Autobiography of an Unknown Indian* 51 (published as *Jaico*, India 64), *A Passage to England* 59, *The Continent of Circe* 65, *Woman in Bengali Life* (in Bengali) 68, *Scholar Extraordinary: The Life of Professor the Rt. Hon. Friedrich Max Müller P.C.* 74, *Clive of India* 75.
P. and O. Buildings, Nicholson Road, Delhi-6, India.

Chaudhury, Mahendra Mohan, B.A., B.L.; Indian politician; b. 12 April 1908, Nagaon, Assam; ed. Cotton Coll., Gauhati, and Earle Law Coll., Gauhati.
Admitted to Barpeta Bar 36; joined freedom struggle under Mahatma Gandhi, imprisoned 32, 41 and 42; mem. Assam Legis. Assembly 46; Sec. Assam Congress Parl. Party; Parl. Sec. 47; Advocate of Assam High Court 49; Cabinet Minister, Assam 50-55; Pres. Assam Pradesh Congress Cttee. 55-56; Gen. Sec. All India Congress Cttee. 56-57; mem. Rajya Sabha 56, 72; Speaker Assam Legis. Assembly 58; Chief Minister of Assam 70-72; Gov. of Punjab May 73-.
Publs. *Life of Mahatma Gandhi, Life and Philosophy of Acharya Vinoba Bhave.*
Raj Bhavan, Punjab, Chandigarh, India.
Telephone: 24481, 24400.

Chavan, Yeshwantrao Balwantrao, B.A., LL.B.; Indian politician; b. 12 March 1913; ed. Rajaram Coll., Kolhapur, and Law Coll., Poona.
Practised law at Karad; directed underground movement in Satara District 42-43; arrested 43-44; Pres. District Congress Cttee., Satara; Sec. Maharashtra Provincial Congress Cttee. 48-50; mem. Bombay Legislative Assembly and Parl. Sec. 46; started a Marathi daily, *Prakash*, at Satara; Minister for Civil Supplies 52, later Minister of Local Self-Govt. and Forests; Chief Minister, Bombay State 56-60, Maharashtra State 60-62; mem. Bombay Legislative Assembly 57-60; Treas. Working Cttee. All-Indian Congress 58; Minister of Defence, India 62-66, of Home Affairs 66-70; Minister of Finance 70-74, of External Affairs Oct. 74-; mem. Indian Nat. Congress Party.
Ministry of External Affairs, New Delhi; 1 Racecourse Road, New Delhi, India.

Ch'en Chang-feng; army officer, People's Repub. of China.
Deputy Commdr. Kiangsi Mil. District, People's Liberation Army 67, Commdr. 73-; Sec. CCP Kiangsi 73.

Ch'en Hsi-lien, Gen.; army officer, People's Repub. of China; b. 1913, Hungan, Hupeh; ed. Red Army Acad.
Joined CCP 27; Battalion Commdr. 31-33; on Long March 34-35; Regimental Commdr. 37; Commdr. 3rd Army Corps, 2nd Field Army 49; Mayor of Chungking 49; Commdr. of Artillery Force, People's Liberation Army 51; Gen. 55; Alt. mem. 8th Cen. Cttee. of CCP 56; Commdr. Shenyang Mil. Region, PLA 59-73; Sec. N.E. Bureau, CCP 63-67; Chair. Liaoning Revolutionary Cttee. 68; mem. Politburo, 9th Cen. Cttee. of CCP 69, Politburo, 10th Cen. Cttee. 73; First Sec. CCP Liaoning 71; Commdr. Peking Mil. Region, PLA 74-; Vice-Premier State Council 75-.

Ch'en Ming-yi; army officer, People's Repub. of China.
Deputy Commdr. Tibet Mil. Region, People's Liberation Army 55, Commdr. 71-; Maj.-Gen. PLA 57; Vice-Chair. Tibet Revolutionary Cttee. 68; Sec. CCP Tibet 71.

Ch'en Tsai-tao; army officer, People's Repub. of China; b. 1908, Macheng, Hupeh.
Guerrilla leader 27; Commdr. 4th Army 34, 2nd Column, Cen. Plains Field Army 44; Commdr. Honan Mil. District, People's Liberation Army 49, Wuhan Mil. Region, PLA 54-67; Gen. 55; Leader of Wuhan Incident uprising (an anti-Maoist army revolt during Cultural Revolution, for which he was criticized and removed from office) 20 July 67; Deputy Commdr. Foochow Mil. Region, PLA 73-.

Ch'en Yun; politician, People's Repub. of China; b. 1905, Ching-pu, Kiangsu.
Joined CCP 25; Trades Union activist 25-27; mem. 6th Cen. Cttee. of CCP 31; on Long March 34-35; Deputy Dir. Org. Dept., CCP 37, Dir. 43; Dir. Peasants Dept., CCP 39;

mem. 7th Cen. Cttee. of CCP 45; Vice-Premier 49-75; Minister of Heavy Industry 49-50; Sec., Secr. of Cen. Cttee., CCP 54; Vice-Chair. CCP 56-69; mem. Standing Cttee., Politburo of CCP 56-69; Minister of Commerce 56-58; Chair. State Capital Construction Comm. 58-61; mem. 9th Cen. Cttee. of CCP 69, 10th Cen. Cttee. 73.

Ch'en Yung-kuei; People's Repub. of China; b. Shiyang, Shansi.
National Model Worker; Sec. CCP Tachai Production Brigade, Shansi 63-; Vice-Chair. Shansi Revolutionary Cttee. 67; mem 9th Cen. Cttee. of CCP 69; Sec. CCP Shansi 71; mem. Politburo, Cen. Cttee. of CCP 73; Vice-Premier State Council 75-.

Ch'eng Chun; Chinese air force officer.
Commander, 35th Army, 10th Army Corps, 3rd Field Army, People's Liberation Army 49; Deputy Commdr. Fukien Mil. District 50; Lieut.-Gen. PLA Air Force 55; Deputy Commdr. PLA Air Force 57-.
People's Republic of China.

Chi P'eng-fei; politician, People's Repub. of China; b. 1910, Yung-chi, Shensi; ed. Mil. Medical Coll.
Joined Communist Party 31; on Long March in Medical Dept., Red Army 35; Deputy Political Commissar, Army Corps, 3rd Field Army 50; Amb. to German Democratic Repub. 50-55; Vice-Minister of Foreign Affairs 55-72; Acting Minister of Foreign Affairs 68-72, Minister 72-74; mem. 10th Cen. Cttee., CCP 73.

Chi Teng-k'uei; People's Repub. of China.
First Sec. CCP Loyang District, Honan 59; Alt. Sec. CCP Honan 66; Vice-Chair. Honan Revolutionary Cttee. 68; Alt. mem. Politburo, 9th Cen. Cttee. of CCP 69; mem. Politburo, 10th Cen. Cttee. of CCP 73; First Political Commissar, Peking Region, People's Liberation Army 74-; Vice-Premier State Council 75-.

Chia Chi-yun; Chinese party official.
Deputy Dir. State Statistical Bureau 54-58, Dir. 58-61; Sec. S.W. Bureau of Cen. Cttee. CCP 61-67; Sec. CCP Szechuan 63; First Sec. CCP Kweichow 65; criticized and removed from office during Cultural Revolution 67; Chair. Yunnan Revolutionary Cttee. 75-; First Sec. CCP Yunnan 75-.
People's Republic of China.

Chiang Ch'ing; People's Repub. of China; b. 1914, Chucheng, Shantung; *m.* Mao Tse-tung (*q.v.*) 1939; ed. Shantung Experimental Drama Acad., Tsinan.
Librarian, Tsingtao Univ. 33; film actress 34-38; joined CCP 37; Instructor Lu Hsun Art Acad., Yenan 39; Head of Cen. Film Admin. Bureau, Propaganda Dept., CCP 49; with Ministry of Culture 50-54; Organizer of Reforms in Peking Opera 63; First Deputy Head of Cen. Cultural Revolution Group 66; leading pro-Maoist activist in propaganda work during Cultural Revolution 65-69; mem. Politburo, 9th Cen. Cttee. of CCP 69, Politburo, 10th Cen. Cttee. 73, 75.

Chiang Ching-kuo, Gen.; Chinese politician; b. 18 March 1910; ed. Sun Yat-sen Univ., Moscow, and U.S.S.R. Military and Political Inst.
Eldest son of the late Gen. Chiang Kai-shek; Admin. Commdr. for South Kiangsi 39-45; Foreign Affairs Commdr. of Mil. and Political Admin. for N.E. China 45-47; Deputy Econ. Control Supervisor for Shanghai 48; Chair. Kuomintang Taiwan Province H.Q. 49-50; Dir., Gen. Political Dept., Ministry of Nat. Defence 50-54; mem. Central Revision Cttee. of Kuomintang 50-52; Minister without Portfolio 63; Deputy Minister of Nat. Defence 64-65; Minister of Nat. Defence 65-69; Deputy Sec.-Gen. Nat. Defence Council 54-67; Chair. Nat. Gen. Mobilization Cttee.; mem. Standing Cttee. of Kuomintang; Vice-Premier 69-72, Premier 72-; Sec.-Gen. Kuomintang 75-.
18 Chang An East Road, 1st Section, Taipei, Taiwan.

Chiang Hua; People's Repub. of China; b. Hupeh.
Guerrilla activist with New 4th Army, CCP 40; Mayor of Hangchow 49-51; Deputy Sec. CCP Chekiang 52-55, First Sec. 52-68; Alt. mem. 8th Cen. Cttee. of CCP 56; First Political Commissar Chekiang Mil. District, People's Liberation Army 56-68; Prof. of Political Theories, Chekiang Univ. 58; Sec. E. China Bureau 65; criticized and removed from office during Cultural Revolution 68; Alt. mem. 10th Cen. Cttee. of CCP 73.

Chiang Kai-shek, Madame (Soong Mayling), LL.D., L.H.D.; Chinese sociologist; ed. Wellesley Coll., U.S.A.
Married Chiang Kai-shek 27 (died 75); first Chinese woman appointed mem. of Child Labour Comm.; inaugurated Moral Endeavour Asscn.; established schools in Nanking for orphans of revolutionary soldiers; fmr. mem. Legislative Yuan; served as Sec.-Gen. of Chinese Comm. on Aeronautical Affairs; Dir.-Gen. New Life Movement; founded and directed Nat. Chinese Women's Asscn. for War Relief and Nat. Asscn. for Refugee Children; accompanied husband on mil. campaigns; Founder and Dir. Cheng Hsin Rehabilitation Center for Post-Polio Crippled Children; Chair. Board of Dirs. Fu Jen Catholic Univ.; mem. Board of Govs. Nat. Palace Museum; Hon. Chair. American Bureau for Medical Aid to China and Cttee. for the promotion of the Welfare of the Blind; Patroness Int. Red Cross Cttee.; Hon. Chair. British United Aid to China Fund and United China Relief; First Hon. Mem. Bill of Rights Commemorative Soc.; first Chinese woman to be decorated by Nat. Govt. of China, awards include Gold Medal of Nat. Inst. of Social Sciences; L.H.D. (John B. Stetson Univ., Bryant Coll., Hobart and William Smith Colls.); LL.D. (Rutgers Univ., Goucher Coll., Wellesley Coll., Loyola Univ., Russell Sage Coll., Hahnemann Medical Coll., Univs. of Michigan and Hawaii, and Wesleyan Coll., Macon; Hon. F.R.C.S. (Eng.).
Publs. *China in Peace and War* 39, *China Shall Rise Again* 39, *This Is Our China* 40, *We Chinese Women* 41, *Little Sister Su* 43, *The Sure Victory* 55, *Madame Chiang Kai-shek: Selected Speeches* 58-59, *Selected Speeches* 65-66, *Album of Chinese Orchid Paintings* 71, *Album of Chinese Bamboo Paintings* 72, *Album of Chinese Landscape Paintings* 73.
c/o The President's Residence, Taipei, Taiwan.

Chiang Wei-ch'ing; Chinese party official; b. Kiangsu.
Deputy Political Commissar, People's Liberation Army, Nanking 49; Second Sec. CCP Kiangsu 53-55, First Sec. 56-68; Alt. mem. 8th Cen. Cttee. of CCP 56; First Political Commissar Kiangsu Mil. District, PLA 60-68; Sec. E. China Bureau, CCP 66; criticized and removed from office during Cultural Revolution 68; Alt. mem. 10th Cen. Cttee. of CCP 73; First Sec. CCP Kiangsi 75.
People's Republic of China.

Chiang Yee, B.SC., F.R.A., H.L.D., D.LITT., D.ARTS; Chinese artist, calligrapher and author; b. 19 May 1903, Kiukiang; ed. Nat. South Eastern Univ., Nanking.
Lecturer in chemistry, Nat. Univ., Shanghai; district gov. of Kiukiang and Yushan (Kiangsi province), Tangtou and Wuhu (Anhui province); emigrated to London 33; worked as writer and artist 33-; lecturer in Chinese, School of Oriental Studies, London Univ. 35-38; in charge of Chinese section, Wellcome Inst. of the History of Medicine 38-40; designed decor and costumes for Sadlers' Wells performance of *The Birds* 42; after World War II went to live in America; paintings at this time include *The Tops of New York Skyscrapers Appeared Above the Evening Clouds*; curator of Chinese ethnology, Peabody Museum, Salem, Mass. 56-; Ralph Waldo Emerson Fellow in Poetry, Harvard Univ. 58-59; Prof. of Chinese Studies, Columbia Univ., New York 60-; mem. American Acad. of Arts and Sciences, etc.; works in numerous collections including Fogg Art Museum, Cambridge, Mass., Utah

State Univ. Museum, Logan; recent exhibitions include City Hall, Hong Kong 72, Australian Nat. Univ. 72.
Publs. *A book of poems in Chinese* 35, *The Chinese Eye* 35, *Chinese Calligraphy* 38, *A Chinese Childhood* 40, *Chinese Painting* 53, *One hundred quatrains of Chung-Ya* 55, *Chinese Ch'an Poetry* 66, the *"Silent Traveller"* series: *The Silent Traveller in Lakeland* 37, *in London* 38, *in Wartime* 39, *in Yorkshire Dales* 41, *in Oxford* 44, *in Edinburgh* 46, *in New York* 50, *in Dublin* 55, *in Paris* 56, *in Boston* 59, *in San Francisco* 64, *in Japan* 70, *in Australia* 76; mainly for children: *Birds and Beasts* 39, *Chinpo and The Giant Pandas* 39, *Chinpo at The Zoo* 41, *Lo Cheng, the boy who wouldn't keep still* 41, *The Men of The Burma Road* 42, *A Story of Ming* 43, *Dabbitse* 44, *Yebbin* 47.
520 West 123 Street, New York, N.Y. 10027; c/o W. W. Norton Co., 55 Fifth Avenue, New York, N.Y. 10003, U.S.A.

Chiang Yu-an; army officer, People's Repub. of China.
Commander Ninghsia Mil. District, People's Liberation Army 72-.

Chiao Hung-kuang; army officer, People's Repub. of China.
Commander Kwangsi Mil. District, People's Liberation Army 67-; Political Commissar PLA Air Force, Kwangsi 67; Vice-Chair. Kwangsi Revolutionary Cttee. 68.

Ch'iao Kuan-hua; politician, People's Repub. of China; b. 1908, Yen-cheng, Kiangsu; ed. Tsinghua Univ., Peking and Univ. of Tübingen, Fed. Repub. of Germany.
Director S. China Branch, New China News Agency 46-49; Deputy Dir., Gen. Office, Cen. People's Govt. 49-54; Asst. to Minister of Foreign Affairs 54-64; Vice-Minister of Foreign Affairs 64-74, Minister Nov. 74-; Head of Chinese del. to Sino-Soviet Border talks 69; Leader of del. to UN Gen. Assembly 71; mem. 10th Cen. Cttee. of CCP 73.

Ch'ien Cheng-ying; People's Repub. of China; b. 1922; ed. Tatung Univ., Shanghai.
Vice-Minister of Water Conservancy 52-58, of Water Conservancy and Electrical Power 58; Minister of Water Conservancy and Electrical Power 75-.

Ch'ien Chih-kuang; People's Repub. of China.
Vice-Minister of Textile Industry 49; Minister of Light Industry 75-.

Chikami, Teruomi; Japanese banker; b. 11 Aug. 1902, Tokyo, Japan; ed. Tokyo Univ.
Managing Dir. The Mitsubishi Trust and Banking Corpn. 58, Senior Man. Dir. 62, Deputy Pres. 64, Pres. 65-71, Chair. 71-74; Blue Ribbon Medal 68; Second Order Merit, Order of the Sacred Treasure 74.
The Mitsubishi Trust and Banking Corporation, 4-5, 1-chome, Marunouchi, Chiyoda-ku, Tokyo; Home: No. 503 Town House Akasaka, 8-5-25 Akasaka, Minato-ku, Tokyo, Japan.

Ch'in Chi-wei; army officer, People's Repub. of China. b. Hung-an, Hupeh.
Company Commdr. Red Army 31; Deputy Commdr. Yunnan Mil. District, People's Liberation Army 54; Deputy Commdr. Kunming Mil. Region, PLA 55, Commdr. 58; Lieut.-Gen. PLA 55; Sec. CCP Yunnan 66-68; Commdr. Chengtu Mil. Region, PLA 73-; mem. 10th Cen. Cttee. of CCP 73.

Chipp, Hon. Donald Leslie, B.COM, A.A.S.A.; Australian politician; b. 21 Aug. 1925, Melbourne, Victoria; ed. Northcote High School.
R.A.A.F. 43-45; Registrar, Commonwealth Inst. of Accountants and Australian Soc. of Accountants 50-55; Chief Exec. Officer Olympic Civic Cttee. 55-56; Councillor, City of Kew 55-61; mem. House of Reps. 60-; Minister for Navy and Minister in charge of Tourist Activities 66-68, Minister for Customs and Excise 69-72; Minister assisting Minister for Nat. Devt. 71; Minister for Social Security, Health, Repatriation and Compensation Nov.-Dec. 75; Liberal.
Parliament House, Canberra, A.C.T. 2600; Home: 60 Bluff Road, Black Rock, Victoria 3195, Australia.
Telephone: 62-2521 (Office).

Chit Myaing, U; Burmese retd. army officer and diplomatist; b. Oct. 1922; ed. Univ. of Rangoon.
Joined Burma Independence Army under Gen. Aung San 42; Leader of Burmese Forces, Tharawaddy District during Liberation Movt. 45; Battalion Commdr. 48; Mil. Insp. 50, Brigade Commdr. 50; Insp.-Gen., Ministry of Immigration and Nat. Registration 58-60; Commdr. Army Staff Coll. 61; Minister of Trade and Industry 63-64; retd. from Army 67; Amb. to Yugoslavia 68-71, to U.K. 71-75; Sithu (Order of Burma).
c/o Ministry of Foreign Affairs, Rangoon, Burma.

Cho, Kiyoko Takeda, PH.D.; Japanese historian; b. 20 June 1917, Kobe; ed. Kobe Jogakiun Coll., Olivet Coll., Michigan, Columbia Univ., Union Theological Seminary, New York, and Univ. of Tokyo.
National Sec. for Univ. and Coll. Students, Japan YWCA 47-53; Prof. Int. Christian Univ. 53-65; Research Assoc. in Asian Studies, Princeton and Harvard Univs. 65-67; Dean, Coll. of Liberal Arts, Int. Christian Univ. 67-69, Prof. of History, Dean of Graduate School 70-74; Dir. Inst. of Asian Cultural Studies 71-; mem. Exec. Cttee. World Student Christian Fed.; Pres. World Council of Churches 71-75; Senior Assoc. Fellow, St. Anthony's Coll., Oxford 75-76.
Publs. *Conflict in Concept of Man in Modern Japan* 59, *The Emperor System and Educational Thought* 64, *Indigenization and Apostasy: Traditional Ethos and Christianity* 67, *The Genealogy of Apostates: the Japanese and Christianity* 73, *Comparative Modernization Theories*; has translated works of Reinhold Niebuhr into Japanese.
1-59-6 Nishigahara Kita-Ku, Tokyo 114, Japan.

Choi Kyu Hah; Korean politician; b. 16 July 1919; Wonju City, Kangwon-do; ed. Kyungg High School, Seoul, Tokyo Coll. of Educ., Japan, and Nat. Daedong Inst., Manchuria.
Professor, Coll. of Educ., Seoul Nat. Univ. 45-46; Dir. Econ. Affairs Bureau, Ministry of Foreign Affairs 51-52; Consul-Gen. Korean Mission, Japan 52-57, Minister 59; Vice-Minister of Foreign Affairs 59-60; Amb. to Malaysia 64-67; Minister of Foreign Affairs 67-71; Special Asst. to the Pres. for Foreign Affairs 71-75; Acting Prime Minister Dec. 75-; Chair. Korean del. to UN Gen. Assembly 67, 68, 69; del. to numerous int. confs. 55-; decorations from Ethiopia, Panama, El Salvador, Malaysia, Repub. of Viet-Nam, Tunisia and Belgium; Order of Diplomatic Service Merit; Hon. Litt. Dr. (Hankook Univ. of Foreign Studies, Seoul).
Office of the Prime Minister, Seoul; and 7-17, 1-ga, Myongnyun-dong, Chongnogu, Seoul, Republic of Korea.

Chou Chien-jen; biologist, People's Repub. of China; b. 1887, Shaohsing, Chekiang.
Founder mem. China Asscn. for Promoting Democracy 45; Vice-Gov. of Chekiang 51-54, Gov. 58-68; Vice-Minister of Higher Educ. 54-58; Vice-Chair. Standing Cttee., Nat. People's Congress 65-; Vice-Chair. Chekiang Revolutionary Cttee. 68; mem. 9th Cen. Cttee. of CCP 69, 10th Cen. Cttee. 73.

Chou Jung-hsin; Chinese government official.
Second Sec. N. China Bureau, CCP Cen. Cttee. 50-52; Vice-Minister of Building 52-58; Pres. Chekiang Univ. 58-60; Vice-Minister of Educ. 61-63; Acting Sec.-Gen. State Council 63-65; criticized and removed from office during Cultural Revolution 67; Minister of Educ. 75-.
People's Republic of China.

Chow Shu-kai; Chinese diplomatist; b. 21 Aug. 1913, Hupeh, China; ed. National Central Univ., Nanking and Univ. of London.
Chinese Consul, Manchester, England 44-45; Assoc. Prof. of Int. Relations, Univ. of Nanking 46-47; Deputy Dir. Information Dept., Ministry of Foreign Affairs 47-49; Minister, Chargé d'Affaires, Manila 53-55; Deputy Minister of Foreign Affairs 56-60; Cabinet Minister and Chair. Overseas Chinese Affairs 60-62; Amb. to Spain 63-65, to U.S.A. 65-71; Minister of Foreign Affairs 71-72, without Portfolio 72-.
Executive Yuan, Taipei, Taiwan.

Chowdhury, Abu Sayeed, M.A., B.L.; Bangladesh lawyer, administrator and diplomatist; b. 31 Jan. 1921, Negbari (Tangail); ed. Calcutta Univ. and Lincoln's Inn, London.
Member del. to UN Gen. Assembly 59; Advocate-Gen., E. Pakistan 60; mem. Constitution Comm. 60-61; Judge, Dacca High Court July 61; Chair. Cen. Board for Devt. of Bengal 63-68; Vice-Chancellor, Univ. of Dacca 69-71; Amb.-at-large and Head, Bangladesh Missions in London and New York April 71-Jan. 72; Pres. of Bangladesh 72-73; Special Govt. Rep. in charge of Foreign Relations and int. agencies 74; now in U.K.

Chu Mu-chih; journalist, People's Repub. of China.
Deputy Dir. New China News Agency 54-72, Dir. 72-; Vice-Chair. Nat. Journalists Asscn. 60; mem. 10th Cen. Cttee. of CCP 73.

Chu Yao-hua; army officer, People's Repub. of China.
Major-General Fukien Mil. District, People's Liberation Army 64; Commdr. 68-; Vice-Chair. Fukien Revolutionary Cttee. 68.

Chuang Tse-tung; Chinese government official.
Former world table-tennis champion; Minister of Physical Culture and Sports 75-.
People's Republic of China.

Chung Fu-hsiang; Chinese government official; b. Kwangsi.
Vice-Minister of Posts and Telecommunications 53-57, of Second Ministry of Machine Building 57-58, of First Ministry of Machine Building 58-61, of Posts and Telecommunications 62-67; criticized and removed from office during Cultural Revolution 67; Minister of Posts and Telecommunications 75-.
People's Republic of China.

Chulasapya, Air Chief Marshal Dawee; Thai air force officer and politician; b. 8 Aug. 1914, Thon Buri; ed. Mil. Acad. (now Chulachomklao), Flying Training School and Command and Gen. Staff Coll. Fort Leavenworth, U.S.A.
Fighter pilot, Royal Thai Air Force 36; intelligence work and studies abroad during World War II; Dir. of Intelligence 48-55; Acting Dir. Civil Aviation 48-55; Air Marshal 55; Chief of Air Staff 55-61; Air Chief Marshal 57; Chief of Staff, Supreme Command 61-63; SEATO Mil. Adviser 61-63; rank of Gen. and Admiral 63; Special Officer, First Royal Guard Infantry 63; Deputy Minister of Defence 63-69; Minister of Communications 69-71; Chair. Thai Maritime Navigation Co. 69-74; Dir. of Nat. Devt., Agriculture and Communications in Nat. Exec. Council 71; Minister of Agriculture and Co-operatives 72-73, of Defence 73-74; fmr. Chair. Joint Chiefs of Staff of Nat. Security Command; fmr. Deputy Dir. Communist Suppression Operations Command; concurrently Deputy C.-in-C. Armed Forces and Acting Supreme Commdr. 73; retd. 74; mem. House of Reps. for Mae Hong Son April 76-; leader Social Justice Party 76-; Deputy Prime Minister, Minister of Public Health April 76-; Medal of Courage 72, numerous other awards.
Ministry of Public Health, Bangkok, Thailand.

Chung Il Kwon, Gen.; Korean army officer (retd.), diplomatist and politician; b. 21 Nov. 1917; ed. Military Acad. of Japan, U.S.A. Command and General Staff Coll., Harvard and Oxford Univs.
Former Army Chief of Staff, Chair. Joint Chiefs of Staff; Amb. to Turkey, France, U.S.A., concurrently to Brazil, Colombia, Argentina, Chile, Paraguay and Ecuador; Prime Minister 64-70, concurrently Minister of Foreign Affairs 66-67; Chair. Democratic Republican Party 72-73; Speaker Nat. Assembly 73-.
91-19 Oksu-dong, Sungdong-ku, Seoul, Republic of Korea.

Chung Yul Kim; Korean diplomatist and former air force officer; b. 1917; ed. Japanese Military Acad.
Commandant, Republic of Korea Air Acad. 49, Chief of Staff, Korea Air Force 49-52, 54-56; Chief, Korean Liaison Group to United Nations Command, Tokyo 53; Special Asst. to Minister of Nat. Defence 54, Minister of Nat. Defence 57-60; Amb. to U.S.A. 63-68; mem. of Nat. Assembly 67-71; Chief Commdr. Legion of Merit, Order of Military Merit Taeguk.
c/o Ministry of Foreign Affairs, Seoul, Republic of Korea.

Clark, Colin Grant, M.A.; Australian economist; b. 2 Nov. 1905; ed. Dragon School, Oxford, Winchester Coll., and Brasenose Coll., Oxford.
Assistant Social Surveys of London 28-29, of Merseyside 29-30; Economic Advisory Council 30-31; Lecturer, Cambridge Univ. 31-37; Visiting Lecturer, Univs. of Sydney, Melbourne and Western Australia 37-38; Under-Sec. of State for Labour and Industry, Dir. Bureau of Industry, Financial Adviser to Treasury, Queensland 38-52; Dir. Inst. for Research in Agricultural Economics, Oxford 53-69; Research Fellow, Mannix Coll., Monash Univ. 69-; Fellow Brasenose Coll., Oxford; Fellow Econometric Soc.; Hon. Sc.D. (Milan), D.Litt. (Oxford); Hon. D.Econ. (Tilburg).
Publs. *The National Income, The Conditions of Economic Progress, The Economics of 1960, Welfare and Taxation, British Trade in the Common Market, Economics of Irrigation, National Income of Australia* (with J. G. Crawford) 38, *Australian Hopes and Fears* 58, *Population Growth and Land Use* 67, *The Economics of Irrigation* 67, *Starvation or Plenty* 70, *The Myth of Overpopulation* 72, *The Value of Agricultural Land* 73.
Mannix College, Monash University, Clayton, Victoria, Australia.

Coelho, Vincent Herbert, B.SC.; Indian diplomatist; b. 20 July 1917; ed. Madras Univ.
Indian Audit and Accounts Service 42, later Indian Foreign Service; Asst. Financial Adviser (Supply Dept.) 44-45; Under-Sec. Ministry of Finance 45-46; Under-Sec. Cabinet Secr. 46-47; Private Sec. to Prime Minister 47-48; Foreign Service 48-; First Sec. Berne 48-49; Trade Commr., Alexandria 49-50; Consul-Gen., Goa 51-54; Deputy Sec. Ministry of External Affairs 54-57; Chargé d'Affaires, Ankara 57-59; Joint Sec. Ministry of External Affairs 59-63; Amb. to Brazil 63-65; Indian Political Officer in Sikkim 66-67; Sec. Ministry of External Affairs 68-70; Amb. to Japan 70-72; High Commr. to Sri Lanka 72-76.
c/o Ministry of External Affairs, New Delhi, India.

Cole, Sir David Lee, K.C.M.G., M.C.; British diplomatist; b. 31 Aug. 1920, Newmarket, Suffolk; ed. Cheltenham Coll. and Sidney Sussex Coll., Cambridge.
Royal Inniskilling Fusiliers, Second World War; Dominions Office 47; U.K. Del. to United Nations, New York 48-51; First Sec., British High Comm., New Delhi 53-56; Private Sec. to Sec. of State for Commonwealth Relations 56-60; Head, Personnel Dept., Commonwealth Relations Office 61-63; Dep. High Commr. in Ghana 63-64, Acting High Commr. 63; High Commr. in Malawi 64-67; Minister (Political), High Comm., New Delhi, 67-70; Asst. Under-

Sec. of State, Foreign and Commonwealth Office 70-73; Amb. to Thailand 73-.
British Embassy, Ploenchit Road, Bangkok, Thailand; and c/o Foreign and Commonwealth Office, London, S.W.1, England.

Concepcion, Roberto, A.A., LL.B.; Philippine lawyer; b. 7 June 1903, Manila; ed. San Beda Coll. and Univ. of Santo Tomás.
Private practice 25-29; Asst. Attorney, Office of the Attorney-Gen. 29-38; successively Asst. Solicitor-Gen., Judge of First Instance, Under-Sec. of Justice, Assoc. Justice of Court of Appeals; Assoc. Justice of Supreme Court 54, Chief Justice and Chair. Presidential Electoral Tribunal 66-73; Prof. of Law at several leading univs.; active in many local and int. orgs. engaged in the promotion of the rule of law; rep. of the Philippines at several int. confs.; Knight Grand Cross of Rizal; Hon. D.C.L. (Univs. of Santo Tomás and the Philippines, St. Louis Univ. and San Beda Coll.).
Publs. Various lectures and papers, etc.
Integrated Bar of the Philippines, 915 Quezon Boulevard Ext., Quezon City; Home: 18 Kitanlad, Quezon City, Philippines.
Telephone: 97-23-88 (Office); 62-32-73 (Home).

Condliffe, John Bell, M.A., D.SC., LL.D., LITT.D.; American economist; b. 23 Dec. 1891; ed. Canterbury Coll. of New Zealand, Gonville and Caius Coll., Cambridge.
Professor of Economics Canterbury Coll. 20-26; Research Sec. Inst. of Pacific Relations, Hawaii 27-31; Visiting Prof. of Economics Univ. of Michigan 30-31; mem. Economic Intelligence Service L.N. 31-37; Prof. of Commerce London Univ. 37-39; Prof. of Economics Univ. of California 40-58; Adviser Indian Nat. Council of Applied Econ. Research 59-60; Senior Economist Stanford Research Inst. 61-67; Associate Dir. Div. Economics and History, Carnegie Endowment for Int. Peace 43-47: mem. Royal Econ. Soc., Soc. of Australia and N.Z.; Fellow, A.A.A.S. 53; Howland Memorial Prize Yale Univ. 39, Wendell Wilkie Prize 50, Sir James Wattie Prize 72; Gold Cross, Royal Order of Phoenix (Greece).
Publs. *New Zealand in the Making* 30 (revised 58), *Problems of the Pacific* 27, 29, *China Today—Economic* 32, *World Economic Survey* 31-37, *Reconstruction of World Trade* 40, *Agenda for a Post-War World* 42, *Commerce of Nations* 50, *The Welfare State in New Zealand* 59, *The Development of Australia* 63, *Foresight and Enterprise* 65, *The Economic Outlook for New Zealand* 69, *Te Rangi Hiroa: The Life of Sir Peter Buck* 71, *Defunct Economists* 74.
1641 Canyonwood Court 1, Walnut Creek, Calif. 94595, U.S.A.

Connelly, Michael Aynsley B.COM., F.C.A., C.M.A,; New Zealand politician; b. 21 Feb. 1916; ed. Univ. of Otago.
Served World War II; mem. of Parl. for Riccarton 56-69, for Wigram 69-; served on numerous parl. cttees.; fmr. Christchurch City Councillor; fmr. Pres. Canterbury Savings Bank, now Trustee; Minister of Police 72-73, of Customs 72-74, Assoc. Minister of Finance, Minister in charge of Statistics 74-75; Minister of Works and Devt. 75-Nov. 75; fmr. mem. Lincoln Coll. Council; Pres. Adult Cerebral Palsy Soc.; Chair. Exec. Cttee., Canterbury Provincial Bldgs. Board; Vice-Pres. N.Z. Greyhound Racing Asscn.; Patron, N.Z. Fed. of Roller Skating, Ferrymead Museum of Science and Industry.
Parliament Buildings, Wellington; Home: 40 Nortons Road, Christchurch, New Zealand.

Coombs, Herbert Cole, A.C., F.A.A., M.A., PH.D.; Australian retd. administrator; b. 24 Feb. 1906; ed. Univ. of Western Australia and London School of Economics and Political Science.
Assistant Economist, Commonwealth Bank of Australia 35; Economist to Commonwealth Treasury 39; mem. Commonwealth Bank Board 42; Dir. of Rationing 42; Dir.-Gen. of Post-War Reconstruction 43; Gov. Commonwealth Bank of Australia 49-60; Chair. Commonwealth Bank Board 51-60; Gov. Reserve Bank of Australia 60-68, Chair. Reserve Bank Board 60-68; Chair. Australian Council for Aboriginal Affairs 68-76; Chair. Australian Council for the Arts 68-74; Chair. Royal Comm. on Australian Govt. Admin. 74-76; Chancellor Australian Nat. Univ. 68-76, Visiting Fellow 76-; Fellow, Australian Acad. of the Humanities, Australian Acad. of the Social Sciences; Hon. LL.D. (Melbourne, Sydney, Australian Nat. Univ.), Hon. D.Litt. (Western Australia), Hon. Fellow, London School of Econs.
Publ. *Other People's Money, The Fragile Pattern: Institutions and Man;* co-author *Conservation.*
119 Milson Road, Cremorne, N.S.W. 2090, Australia.

Cooray, H.E. Cardinal Thomas B., PH.D., D.D., B.A. (LOND.); Ceylonese ecclesiastic; b. 28 Dec. 1901; ed. Univ. Coll., Colombo and Anglicum Univ., Rome.
Ordained priest 29; Titular Archbishop of Preslavo and Co-adjutor Archbishop of Colombo 45; Archbishop of Colombo 47-; mem. Pontificial Comm. for Canon Law; created Cardinal 65; Pres. Ceylon Bishops Conf.
Archbishop's House, Colombo 8, Sri Lanka.
Telephone: 95471.

Cope, James Francis; Australian politician; b. 26 Nov. 1907, Sydney.
Active in Australian Labor Party, holding many exec. positions 30-; alderman Redfern Council 48-; Hon. Treas. and del. to Fed. Council of Australian Glassworkers' Union 53-55; mem. House of Reps. for Cook 55, then Watson, then Sydney 69-; Parl. Public Accounts Cttee. 56-72; temp. Chair. of Cttees. 67-72; Speaker, House of Reps. 73-75.
13 William Street, Redfern, N.S.W., Australia.

Corea, Gamani, M.A., D.PHIL.; Ceylonese economist and civil servant; b. 4 Nov. 1925; ed. Royal Coll., Colombo, Corpus Christi Coll., Cambridge, and Nuffield Coll., Oxford.
Director, Planning Secr. and Sec. Nat. Planning Council 56-60; Dir. of Econ. Research and Asst. to Gov. of Central Bank of Ceylon 60-65; Perm. Sec. to Ministry of Planning and Econ. Affairs 65-70; Deputy Gov. Central Bank of Ceylon 70-; Consultant to Sec.-Gen., UN Conf. on Trade and Devt.; fmr. Chief, UN Econ. Mission to British Honduras; fmr. Chair. UNCTAD Expert Group on Int. Monetary Issues; fmr. Pres. Section F, Ceylon Asscn. for Advancement of Science, Consultative Cttee. Asian Agricultural Survey, Asian Devt. Bank; Chair. Expert Group on Int. Monetary Reform and Developing Countries 69; Pres., Ceylon Asscn. for Advancement of Science 71; Chair. Expert Panel on Devt. and Environment 71; Senior Adviser to Sec.-Gen. UN Conf. on Human Environment 71; Chair. UN Cttee. for Devt. Planning 72-74, UN Cocoa Conf. 72, ECAFE Group on Review and Appraisal of 2nd Devt. Decade 71, 72; Amb. to EEC and the Benelux countries 73-74; Sec.-Gen. UN Conf. on Trade and Devt. (UNCTAD) 74-; Chair. Marga Inst.; Research Fellow, Int. Devt. Research Centre, Canada 72; Visiting Fellow, Inst. of Devt. Studies, Univ. of Sussex 72, Nuffield Coll., Oxford Univ. 73.
Horton Lodge, 21 Horton Place, Colombo 7, Sri Lanka.

Corner, Frank Henry, M.A.; New Zealand diplomatist; b. 17 May 1920; ed. Victoria Univ. of Wellington.
First Sec., Washington, D.C. 48-51; Senior Counsellor, London 52-58; Deputy Sec. of External Affairs 58-62;

Perm. Rep. to UN 62-67; Amb. to U.S.A. 67-72; Sec. of Foreign Affairs 73-.
Ministry of Foreign Affairs, Wellington, New Zealand.

Cotton, Hon. Robert Carrington, A.A.S.A.; Australian politician; b. 29 Nov. 1915, Broken Hill, N.S.W.; ed. St. Peter's Coll., Adelaide.
Former Fed. Vice-Pres. Liberal Party of Australia, State Pres. Liberal Party, N.S.W. 57-60, Acting Pres. 65; Senator for N.S.W. 65-; leader del. to IPU confs., Majorca and Geneva 67; Chair. Cotton's Pty. Ltd., Broken Hill; Minister of State for Civil Aviation 69-72, Minister of Manufacturing Industry, Science and Consumer Affairs Nov.-Dec. 75, of Industry and Commerce Dec. 75-; Liberal.
The Senate, Parliament House, Canberra, A.C.T.; Carrington Park, Oberon, N.S.W. 2787, Australia.

Court, Hon. Sir Charles Walter Michael, KT., O.B.E.(MIL.), M.L.A., F.C.A., F.C.I.S.; Australian politician; b. 29 Sept. 1911, Crawley, Sussex, England; ed. Perth, Australia.
Founder Partner, Hendry, Rae & Court, chartered accountants 38, served Australian Imperial Forces 40-46, rank of Lt.-Col.; mem. Legis. Assembly for Nedlands 53-; Deputy Leader of Opposition, W. Australian Parl. 57-59; Minister for Railways, 59-67, for Industrial Devt. and the N.W. 59-71, for Transport 65-66; Deputy Leader of Opposition 71-72, Leader 72-73; Premier, State Treas., Minister Co-ordinating Econ. and Regional Devt., W. Australia April 74-; State Registrar (W. Australia) Inst. of Chartered Accountants in Australia 46-52; Senator Junior Chamber Int. 71; Hon. Col. W. Australia Univ. Regt. 69; Hon. LL.D. W. Australia Univ. 69; Australian Mfrs. Export Council Award 70, Inst. of Production Engs. Award 71; Liberal.
Publs. many papers on industrial, economic and resource development matters.
Premier's Department, 32 St. George's Terrace, Perth, W. Australia 6000; Home: 46 Waratah Avenue, Dalkeith, W. Australia 6009, Australia.
Telephone: Perth 25-3749 (Office); 86-1257 (Home).

Crawford, Sir John Grenfell, Kt., C.B.E., M.EC.; Australian administrator; b. 4 April 1910; ed. Univ. of Sydney.
Lecturer in Rural Economics, Univ. of Sydney 34-42; Economic Adviser, Rural Bank of N.S.W. 35-46; Adviser, Dept. of War Organization of Industry 42-43; Dir. of Research, Commonwealth Ministry of Post-War Reconstruction 43-46; Dir. Commonwealth Bureau of Agricultural Economics 45-50; Commonwealth Wool Adviser 49-55; Sec. Dept. of Commerce and Agriculture, Canberra 50-56, Dept. of Trade 56-60; Dir. School of Pacific Studies, Australian Nat. Univ. 60-67 and Fiscal Adviser to Univ., Vice-Chancellor of ANU 68-73; Chancellor, Univ. of Papua New Guinea 72-75; Consultant to IBRD; Vice-Chair. Commonwealth Econ. Enquiry 63-64; Gov. Canadian Int. Devt. Research Centre 70-; Chair. Tech. Advisory Cttee. advising IBRD, FAO, etc. on Int. Research in Agric. 71-; Chancellor, ANU 76-; Walter and Eliza Hall Fellow 33-35; Commonwealth Fund Fellow, U.S.A. 38-40; Farrer Medallist (and Orator) 57; Fellow, Australian Inst. of Agricultural Science 58; ANZAAS Medal 71; Hon. D.Sc., Hon. D.Ec., Hon. LL.D., etc.
Publs. *National Income of Australia* (with Colin Clark) 38; Editor and author *Australian War-Time Agriculture* 54; *Australian Trade Policy 1942-1949: A Documentary History* 68.
32 Melbourne Avenue, Deakin, A.C.T. 2600, Australia.

Crean, Frank, B.A., B.COM., A.A.S.A.; Australian accountant and politician; b. 28 Feb. 1916, Hamilton, Victoria; ed. state schools, Melbourne Univ.
Income Tax Assessor for ten years; mem. Victoria Legislative Assembly for Albert Park 45-47, for Prahran 49-51; mem. Parl. for Melbourne Ports 51-; mem. Fed. Parl. Labor Party Exec. 56-, Deputy Leader July 75-Jan. 76; mem. Privileges Cttee. 67-; Fed. Treas. 72-74; Minister for Overseas Trade 74-75; Deputy Prime Minister July-Nov. 75.
Publ. *Government and Politics* (with Byrt) 73.
Parliament House, Canberra, A.C.T.; and 106 Harold Street, Middle Park, Vic. 3206, Australia.

Critchley, Thomas Kingston, A.O., C.B.E.; Australian diplomatist; b. 27 Jan. 1916; ed. North Sydney Boys' High School and Sydney Univ.
Assistant Econ. Adviser, Dept. of War Organization of Industry 43-44; Head, Research Section, Far Eastern Bureau, New Delhi, British Ministry of Information 44-46; Head, Economic Relations Section, Dept. of External Affairs, Canberra 46-47; Australian Rep. UN Cttee. of Good Offices on Indonesian Question 48-49; rep. UN Comm. for Indonesia 49-50; Acting Australian Commr. Malaya 51-52; Australian rep. on UNCURK 52-54; Head, Pacific and Americas Branch, Dept. of External Affairs, Canberra 54-55; Commr. Fed. of Malaya 55-57, High Commr. 57-63, High Commr. in Malaysia 63-65; Senior External Affairs Rep., High Comm., U.K. 66-69; Amb. to Thailand and SEATO 69-74; High Commr. of Papua New Guinea 74-75; Australian High Commr. Sept. 75-.
Australian High Commission, Port Moresby, Papua New Guinea.

Crocker, Walter Russell, C.B.E.; Australian politician and fmr. diplomatist; b. 25 March 1902; ed. Balliol Coll., Oxford, Univ. of Adelaide, Australia, and Stanford Univ., California.
With British Colonial Service 30-34, L.N. and I.L.O. 34-40; served army 40-46; with UN 46-49; Prof. of Int. Relations, Australian Nat. Univ. 49-52, Acting Vice-Chancellor 51; High Commr. for Australia in India 52-55; Amb. to Indonesia 55-57; High Commr. in Canada 57-59; High Commr. in India 59-62 and Amb. to Nepal 60-62; Amb. to the Netherlands and Belgium 62-65; Amb. to Ethiopia and High Commr. to Kenya and to Uganda 65-67; Amb. to Italy 67-70; Lieut.-Gov. of S. Australia 73-; Croix de Guerre, Order of the Lion (Belgium), Knight Grand Cross of Italy.
Publs. *The Japanese Population Problem* 31, *Nigeria: Critique of Colonial Administration* 36, *On Governing Colonies* 46, *Self-Government for Colonies* 49, *Can the UN Succeed?* 51, *The Racial Factor in International Relations* 55, *Nehru* 66, *Australian Ambassador* 71.
8 Fowler's Road, Glen Osmond, S.A. 5064, Australia.

Cutler, Sir (Arthur) Roden, V.C., K.C.M.G., K.C.V.O., C.B.E., K.ST.J., B.EC.; Australian public servant and diplomatist; b. 24 May 1916; ed. Sydney High School and Univ. of Sydney.
Justice Dept. N.S.W. (Public Trust Office) 35-42; army war service 40-42; State Sec. Returned Servicemen's League N.S.W. 42-43; mem. Aliens' Classification and Advisory Cttee. to advise Commonwealth Govt. 42-43; Asst. Deputy Dir. of Security Service N.S.W. 43; Commonwealth Asst. Commr. of Repatriation 43-46; High Commr. in New Zealand 46-52, in Ceylon 52-55; Minister to Egypt 55-56; Sec.-Gen. SEATO 57; Chief of Protocol, Dept. of External Affairs, Canberra 57; State Pres. Returned Servicemen's League, A.C.T.; High Commr. in Pakistan 59-61; rep. to independence of Somalia 60; Consul-Gen., New York 61-65; del. to UN Gen. Assembly and rep. Fifth Cttee. 62, 63, 64; Amb. to the Netherlands 65-66; Gov. N.S.W. 66-; Hon. LL.D. (Sydney Univ.), Hon. D.Sc. (Univs. of N.S.W. and of Newcastle); Hon. Col. Royal N.S.W. Regt., Sydney Univ. Regt.; Hon. Air Commdr. No. 22 Sqdn. R.A.A.F.
Government House, Sydney, N.S.W., Australia.

D

Dahanayake, Wijeyananda; Ceylonese politician; ed. Richmond Coll. Galle and St. Thomas' Coll., Mount Lavinia.
Trained teacher; elected to Galle Municipal Council 35, Mayor of Galle 39, 40 and 41; elected to the State Council for Bibile 44; M.P. 48-; Minister of Education 56-59; Prime Minister Sept. 59-March 60; Minister of Home Affairs 65-June 70; mem. Nat. State Assembly 72-; founded Ceylon Democratic Party 59.
c/o House of Representatives, Colombo, Sri Lanka.

Dalai Lama (Tenzin Gyatso); Tibetan ruler and religious leader; b. 6 July 1935, Taktser, Amdo Province.
Born of Tibetan peasant family in Amdo district of Chhija Nangso Province; enthroned at Lhasa 40; rights exercised by regency 34-50; fled to Chumbi in S. Tibet on Chinese invasion 50; negotiated agreement with China 51; Hon. Chair. Chinese Buddhist Assen. 53-59; Del. to N.P.C. 54-59, Vice-Chair. Standing Cttee.; mem. Nat. Cttee. C.P.P.C.C. 51-59; Chair. Preparatory Cttee. for the Autonomous Region of Tibet 55-59; left Tibet for India after abortive resistance to Chinese 59; Dr. of Buddhist Philosophy 59; Supreme Head of all Buddhist sects in Tibet.
Publs. *My Land and People* 62, *Losar Migje* (The Opening of the Wisdom-Eye) 63, *Umai Dhemig* (Key to the Middle Way) 71.
Thekchen Choling, Dharmsala Cantt., Kangra District, Himachal Pradesh, India.

Daly, Frederick Michael; Australian politician; b. 13 June 1912, Currabubula, N.S.W.; ed. Christian Brothers' Coll., Waverley, Sydney.
Member, House of Reps. for Martin 43-49, for Grayndler 49-75; Opposition Party Whip 50-56; Minister of Services and Property, Leader of House 72-75; mem. Joint Cttee. on A.C.T. 67, Deputy Chair. 70; mem. Commonwealth Immigration Advisory Cttee. 70-71; del. to IPU Conf., Brussels 61, to Commonwealth Parl. Assen. Conf., Nassau 68, Malawi 72, London 73, Sri Lanka 74; Labor Party.
Parliament House, Canberra, A.C.T., Australia.

Dăng Quang Minh; Vietnamese politician; b. 2 Nov. 1909, Vinh Long Province, S. Viet-Nam.
Propaganda and resistance work against French rule 27-, Cantho Province and Nam Bo District 45-54, arrested 30, 40, and imprisoned for many years; mem. Nat. Liberation Front (NLF) Central Cttee., S. Viet-Nam 64-; Head of Perm. NLF Mission in Moscow 65-69; Amb. of Provisional Revolutionary Govt. of Repub. of S. Viet-Nam to U.S.S.R. 69-June 73.
Moscow, G/99 Karmanitsky per 6/8, U.S.S.R.

Dange, Shripad Amrit; Indian trade union leader and politician; b. 10 Oct. 1899.
Took a prominent part in organizing Textile Workers' Unions in Bombay; arrested on many occasions for trade union and political activity; sentenced to twelve years' transportation in the Meerut conspiracy trial; released 36; imprisoned 39-43; Pres. Girni Kamgar Union; Pres. All-India T.U.C. 43-45; Del. to W.F.T.U. Paris 45, Moscow 46; Vice-Pres. W.F.T.U. 48, mem. Exec. Bureau; Editor and Founder of *Socialist* 22, first Marxist paper in India; Editor and Founder of *Kranti*, first working class paper in Marathi language; mem. Legislative Assembly, Bombay 46; imprisoned 48-50; Gen. Sec. All-India TUC 56-; mem. Lok Sabha 57-62, 67-72; Chair. Nat. Council, Communist Party of India 62-; Order of Lenin 74.
Publs. *Gandhi versus Lenin* 21, *Hell Found* 27, *Literature and the People* 45, *India from Primitive Communism to Slavery* 49, *One Hundred Years of Our Trade Unions* 52, *Mahatma Gandhi and History* 68, *When Communists Differ* 70, etc.
9 Kohinoor Road, Dadar, Bombay 400014; Ajoy Bhavan, Kotla Marg, New Delhi 110004, India.

Daoud, Lieut.-Gen. Mohammad; Afghan army officer and politician; b. 18 July 1909; ed. Habibia Coll. Kabul, Precadet School Kabul, and in France.
Governor of Kandahar 32; Gov. and C.-in-C. Eastern Provinces 34; C.-in-C. Central Forces and Mil. Schools 37-; suppressed revolt of 45; Prime Minister 53-63, concurrently Minister of Defence and of the Interior; led coup deposing King Mohammed Zahir Shah July 73; Pres. of Afghanistan July 73-, concurrently Prime Minister, Minister of Defence and of Foreign Affairs; renounced royal title July 73.
Office of the President, Kabul, Afghanistan.

Dark, Eleanor; Australian author; b. 26 Aug. 1901; ed. Sydney.
Won Australian Literature Soc. Gold Medal for *Prelude to Christopher* 34, and for *Return to Coolami* 36.
Publs. *Prelude to Christopher* 34, *Return to Coolami* 36, *Sun across the Sky* 37, *Waterway* 38, *The Timeless Land* 41, *The Little Company* 45, *Storm of Time* 48, *No Barrier* 53, *Lantana Lane* 59.
Varuna, Katoomba, New South Wales, Australia.
Telephone: Katoomba 378.

Darmojuwono, Cardinal Justine; Indonesian ecclesiastic; b. 2 Nov. 1914.
Ordained Priest 47; Archbishop of Semarang 63-; created Cardinal by Pope Paul VI 67; mem. Congregation of Sacraments and Divine Worship; mem. Secr. for Non-Christians; Chair. Conf. of Indonesian Bishops; Bishop of Indonesian Armed Forces.
Jalan Pandanaran 13, Semarang, Java, Indonesia.

Das, Sudhi Ranjan, B.A., LL.B.; Indian judge; b. 1 Oct. 1894; ed. Tagere's School, Santiniketan, Bangabasi Coll., Calcutta and Univ. Coll., London.
Called to Bar, Gray's Inn 18, to Calcutta Bar 19; Lecturer Univ. Law Coll. Calcutta; Additional Judge, High Court, Calcutta 42, Puisne Judge 44; Chief Justice East Punjab High Court (Simla) 49-50; Judge Fed. Court of India 50; Judge Supreme Court of India 50-55; Chief Justice of India 56-59; Vice-Chancellor, Visva-Bharati Univ. 59-66; Vice-Pres. Indian Council for Cultural Relations 64-65; Chair. Statesman Ltd. 68-; edited *Mulla's Transfer of Property Act.*
Swapanpuri, Kalimpong, West Bengal; and 18 Penn Court, Calcutta 27, India.
Telephone: Calcutta 45-7565.

Das Gupta, Bimal; Indian artist; b. 27 Dec. 1917; ed. Krishnalth Collegiate School, Berhampore, W. Bengal, and Govt. Coll. of Arts and Crafts, Calcutta.
Originally painted landscapes in water colours; is now avant-garde painter in oils; Senior Lecturer in Painting, Coll. of Art, Delhi 63-; paintings in Nat. Gallery of Modern Art, New Delhi, Nat. Gallery of Poland, Warsaw, Berlin Museum, Pilnitz Gallery, Dresden, Hermitage Gallery, Leningrad; one-man exhbns. in Delhi, Calcutta, Bombay, Madras Amritsar, Mysore, Berlin, Poland, London, New York, Cairo, Moscow, Belgrade and Paris; exhibited at São Paulo Biennale, and int. exhbns. in Japan, New York and U.S.S.R.
E 13 Motibag II E Block, New Delhi, India.

Das Gupta, Prodosh Kusum, B.A.; Indian sculptor and art gallery director; b. 10 Jan. 1912; ed. Univ. of Calcutta, Government Schools of Arts and Crafts, Lucknow and Madras, Royal Acad. of Arts, London and Ecole de Grand Schaumère, Paris.
Founder, Calcutta Group (pioneer org. of modern art in India) 43, Sec. 43-51; Reader and Head, Dept. of Sculpture,

Baroda Univ. 50; Prof. of Sculpture, Govt. Coll. of Arts and Crafts, Calcutta 51-57; Dir. Nat. Gallery of Modern Art, New Delhi 57-70; Pres. Third Congress, Int. Asscn. of Arts, Vienna 60; mem. Indian Artists' Dels. to U.S. and U.S.S.R.; represented India in int. sculpture competition *The Unknown Political Prisoner*, Tate Gallery, London; works in Nat. Gallery of Modern Art, New Delhi, Madras Museum, Acad. of Fine Arts Gallery, Calcutta and in private collections in India and abroad.
Publs. *My Sculpture, Temple Terracottas of Bengal, Fallen Leaves*, and numerous articles on art.
5 Jatin Das Road, Calcutta 29, India.

Daud, Lieut.-Gen. Mohammed (*see* Daoud).

Daultana, Mian Mumtaz Muhammad Khan; Pakistani diplomatist and fmr. politician; b. 23 Feb. 1916; ed. Punjab Univ. and Corpus Christi Coll., Oxford Univ.
President Indian Majlis, Oxford Univ. 36-37; called to the Bar 39; Punjab Legislative Assembly, Muslim League Party Rep. 43, re-elected 51, Rep. from Sialkot Mohammedan Rural Constituency 46; Gen. Sec. Punjab Provincial Muslim League 44-47; mem. All-India Muslim League Cttee. of Action 46; mem. Indian Constituent Assembly 46, and first Pakistan Constituent Assembly 47; Finance Minister, Punjab 47; Pres. Punjab Muslim League 48; Chief Minister of the Punjab 51-53; Minister for Defence, Central Govt. Oct.-Dec. 57; Pres. Council Muslim League 67-72; participated Round Table Conf. as a mem. Democratic Action Cttee. 69; mem. Nat. Assembly 70; Amb. to the U.K. 72-.
Embassy of Pakistan, 35 Lowndes Square, London, SW1X 9JN, England.

Davidson, Alan Eaton, C.M.G.; British diplomatist; b. 30 March 1924; ed. Leeds Grammar School, Queen's Coll. Oxford.
Royal Naval Volunteer Reserve, Lieut. 43-46; Foreign Service 48-; served U.S.A. 50-53, the Netherlands 53-55, Foreign Office 55-59; First Sec. British Property Comm., later Head of Chancery, British Embassy, Egypt 59-61; Head of Chancery and Consul, Tunisia 62-64; Foreign Office 64, Counsellor 65, Head of Cen. Dept. 66-68; Head of Chancery, del. to NATO 68-71; seconded as Visiting Fellow, Centre for Contemporary European Studies, Univ. of Sussex 71-72; Head of Defence Dept., FCO 72-73; Amb. to Laos 73-.
Publs. *Seafish of Tunisia and the Central Mediterranean* 63, *Snakes and Scorpions Found in the Land of Tunisia* 64, *Mediterranean Seafood* 72, *The Role of the Uncommitted European Countries in East-West Relations* 72, *Fish and Fish Dishes of Laos* 75.
British Embassy, Vientiane, Laos; Home: 45 Lamont Road, World's End, London, S.W.10, England.

Davidson, James Alfred, O.B.E.; British diplomatist; b. 22 March 1922; ed. Christ's Hospital, Royal Naval Coll., Dartmouth.
Royal Navy 39-60; commanded H.M.S.S. *Calder* and *Welfare*; Commdr. 55; retd. 60; called to Bar 60; Commonwealth Relations Office (later FCO) 60-, served Trinidad, Cambodia; Chargé d'Affaires, later Deputy High Commr. Bangladesh 72-73; High Commr. in Brunei 75-.
British High Commission, Bandar Seri Begawan, Brunei; Home: Little Frankfield, Seal Chart, Kent, England.

Davis, Owen Lennox, B.A., LL.B.; Australian diplomatist; b. 12 April 1912; ed. King's School, Sydney and Sydney Univ.
Barrister-at-Law 38-40; Australian Forces (Capt.) 40-45; joined Australian Dept. of External Affairs 46; First Sec. Washington 48-51, Karachi 52-53; Acting High Commr., Wellington, N.Z. 54-55; Senior External Affairs Rep., London 57-59; Australian High Commr. to S. Africa 59-61, Amb. 61-62; Amb. to Brazil 62-64; Asst. Sec. Ministry of External Affairs 65-66, First Asst. Sec. 67-69; Amb. to Belgium and EEC 69-72, concurrently to Luxembourg 70-72; Amb. to Mexico 72-74; Amb. and Perm. Rep. to UN, Geneva 74-.
Permanent Mission of Australia to the Office of the United Nations at Geneva, 56 Rue de Moillebeau, Petit Saconnex, 1211 Geneva 19, Switzerland.

Dehlavi, Samiulla Khan, M.A.; Pakistani diplomatist; b. 14 Sept. 1913; ed. Univs. of Bombay and Oxford.
Joined Indian Civil Service 38, served in Province of Bengal, later District Magistrate, Tipperah and Chittagong, E. Pakistan; later in Pakistani Foreign Office; Deputy Sec. Ministry of Foreign Affairs and Commonwealth Relations 50; Chargé d'Affaires *a.i.*, Paris 50-53; Joint Sec. Ministry of Foreign Affairs and Commonwealth Relations 53-57; Amb. to Italy, concurrently to Tunisia 57-61; Foreign Sec. 61-63; Amb. to U.A.R., also to Libya and Yemen 63-65, to Switzerland, concurrently to Albania 65-66; High Commr. in U.K. 66-68; Amb. to France and UNESCO 68-72, to U.S.S.R. and concurrently to Finland and Mongolia 72-75, to Fed. Repub. of Germany June 75-; leader del. to ILO, mem. of Cttee. for Elimination of Racial Discrimination and other confs.; del. to UN Gen. Assembly; Sitara-i-Pakistan; Grand Cross of Merit (Italy); Hilal-i-Quaid-e-Azam.
Pakistan Embassy, Bonn-Bad Godesberg, Rheinallee 24, Federal Republic of Germany.

Delacombe, Sir Rohan, K.C.M.G., K.C.V.O., K.B.E., C.B., D.S.O., K.ST.J.; British administrator and former army officer; b. 25 Oct. 1906, Malta; ed. Harrow, Royal Mil. Acad., Sandhurst, and Staff Coll., Camberley.
Served in Egypt, North China, India, active service 37-39, in Palestine, France, Norway, Normandy, Italy 39-45; Deputy Mil. Sec., War Office 53-55; G.O.C. 52 Lowland Div. 55-58; Major-Gen. 56; G.O.C., Berlin 59-62; retd. 62; Gov. Victoria, Australia 63-May 74; Administrator of Australia on four occasions 71-74; freeman City of Melbourne; Hon. LL.D. (Melbourne, Monash).
Shrewton Manor, Salisbury, Wilts., England.
Telephone: Shrewton 253 (Home).

Desai, Hitendra Kanaiyalal, B.A., LL.D.; Indian politician; b. 9 Aug. 1915 in Surat; ed. Bombay Univ. faculties of Economics and Law.
Took part in anti-British political activities; imprisoned 30, 41, 42-43; set up private legal practice in Surat 39; elected mem. Surat Municipal Council 39-57; mem. Bombay Legislative Ass. 57-60; Minister of Educ., Bombay 57-60; Minister of Revenue, Gujarat State 60, later Home Minister; Leader of the House Gujarat Assembly 60-; Chief Minister of Gujarat 65-72; mem. Congress Party, elected to Supreme Exec. 68; Pres. Gujarat Pradesh Congress Cttee. 75-.
Dugnala, Shahibag, Ahmedabad 4, Gujarat, India.

Desai, Khandubhai Kasanji; Indian politician; b. 23 Oct. 1898; ed. High School, Bulsar and Wilson Coll.
Joined Non-co-operation Movement under Gandhi 20; taught at Gujarat Vidyapith Nat. Inst.; with Labour Union, Ahmedabad 21; elected to Bombay Assembly 37 and to Constituent Assembly 46; served with many Cttees. in the Ministries of Commerce, Industries, Railways and Labour; mem. of Congress Working Cttee.; Dir. Industrial Finance Corpn. and Employers' State Insurance Corpn.; Minister of Labour 54-57; founded Indian Nat. Trade Union Congress 47, Pres. for three years, and fmr. Gen.-Sec.; mem. Fiscal Comm. 48; Chair. Oil India Ltd. 61-68; Gov. of Andhra Pradesh 68-75.
c/o Raj Bhavan, Hyderabad, Andhra Pradesh, India.

Desai, Morarji Ranchhodji; Indian politician; b. 29 Feb. 1896; ed. Bulsar and Wilson Coll., Bombay.
Served in the Provincial Civil Service in the Bombay Presidency 18-30; joined Civil Disobedience Movement led by Mahatma Gandhi 30, and was convicted for it;

mem. of All-India Congress Cttee. since 31; Sec. Gujarat Provincial Congress Cttee. 31-37, 39-46; Min. for Revenue and Forests 37-39; imprisoned for Quit India Movement for about five years; Home and Revenue Minister, Bombay 46-52; Chief Minister of Bombay 52-56; Union Minister for Commerce and Industry 56-58, Finance Minister 58-63; Chair. Admin. Reforms Comm. 66-67; Deputy Prime Minister and Minister of Finance 67-69; mem. Congress Party Parliamentary Board 63; Treas. of Congress 50-58; mem. All-India Congress Cttee. until Nov. 69; Chair. Parliamentary Group, Congress Party (Opposition) Nov. 69-; detained June 75; Hon. Fellow, Coll. of Physicians and Surgeons, Bombay; Hon. LL.D. (Karnatak Univ.).
5 Dupleix Road, New Delhi, India.

Deshmukh, Sir Chintaman Dwarkanath, Kt., C.I.E., B.A.; Indian administrator and banker; b. 14 Jan. 1896. ed. Elphinstone Coll., Bombay, and Jesus Coll., Cambridge.
Served in Central Province and Berar as Asst. Commr.; Under-Sec. to Govt.; Deputy Commr. and Settlement Officer 19-30; Sec. to second Round Table Conf. 31; Revenue and Financial Sec. Govt. of Central Province and Berar 32-39; Joint Sec. Dept. of Education; Health and Lands Officer on Special Duty, Finance Dept.; Custodian Enemy Property April-Oct. 39; Sec. Central Board of Reserve Bank of India 39-41, Deputy Gov. 41-43, Gov. 43-49; del. to World Monetary Conf. 44, Gov. IMF, IBRD 46-49, Chair. 50; Pres. Indian Statistical Inst. 45-64; financial rep. of Govt. of India in Europe and America 49-50; mem. Planning Comm.; Minister of Finance, Govt. of India 50-56; Chair. Univ. Grants Comm. 56-61; Chair. Nat. Book Trust 57-60; Hon. Fellow, Jesus Coll., Cambridge 52; Chair. Admin. Staff Coll. of India, Hyderabad 60-73; Pres. India Int. Centre, New Delhi 59-; Vice-Chancellor, Univ. of Delhi 62-67; mem. Board of Trustees, UN Inst. for Training and Research 65-70, Vice-Chair. 66-70; Chair. Cen. Sanskrit Board 67-68; Pres. Indian Inst. of Econ. Growth 65-74, Council for Social Devt. 66, Population Council of India 70-; Ramon Magsaysay Award 59; Hon. LL.D. (Princeton, New Jersey, Leicester and 13 Indian Univs.).
"Rachana", Bagh Amberpet, University Road, Hyderabad 500768, Andhra Pradesh, India.

Devkota, Rajeshwar; Nepalese writer, journalist and politician; b. 1930; ed. Sanskrit Coll., Varanasi.
Member Nat. Panchayat (legis. chamber of Nepal) 63-, Chair. 64-67; Asst. Minister of Educ. 63-64; Asst. Minister of Agriculture, Forestry and Land Reform 64, Minister 67-68; Leader, Del. to FAO Conf., Rome 67, Del. to Inter-Parl. Union Conf., Monaco 70; Chair. Nat. Panchayat July 71; mem. Standing Cttee. State Council July 71; Trishakti Patta (First Class).
National Panchayat, Kathmandu, Nepal.

Dey, Mukul Chandra, F.R.S.A., A.R.C.A.; Indian artist; b. 23 July 1895; ed. Santiniketan School (Bengal).
Studied art in Calcutta with Dr. Abanindra Nath Tagore, in Japan, with James Blanding Sloan in Chicago, and in London; exhibited Indian Soc. of Oriental Art, Calcutta 13, Tokyo 16, Art Int., Chicago 16; studied Slade School of Art, London 20; scholarship Royal Coll. of Art, London 20-22; Art Teacher King Alfred School, Hampstead 20-21; Lecturer Indian Art, L.C.C. London 25-27; Royal Acad. 22-23; 1st one-man show, London 27; executed murals Wembley Exhbn., London 25; exhibited Philharmonic Hall, Berlin 26, Indian Soc. of Oriental Art, Calcutta 28; Principal Govt. School of Art, Calcutta; Officer-in-Charge Art Section and Keeper Govt. Art Gallery, Indian Museum, Calcutta; Trustee Indian Museum 28-43; Founder Mukul Dey Art Gallery at Kalika 44; Fulbright Visiting Prof. of Art in U.S.A. 53-54; Curator Nat. Gallery of Modern Art, Govt. of India, New Delhi 55-57; exhbn., Commonwealth Inst., London 60; works acquired by British Museum, Metropolitan Art Museum, New York 70, Philadelphia, Prince of Wales Museum, Bombay, Lahore; Award and Cert. of Honour in Painting, Rabindra Bharati Univ., Calcutta 71-72; Deva-De-Dev.
Works include paintings, portraits, drypoint-etchings, engravings, copies of frescoes in Ajanta and Bagh Caves, Pollonaruwa temples, Sri Lanka, Sittanavasal caves, S. India, British Museum, London, etc.
Publs. *12 Portraits* 17, *My Pilgrimages to Ajanta and Bagh* 25 and 51, *My Reminiscences* 38, *15 Drypoints* 39, *20 Portraits* 43, *Portraits of Mahatma Gandhi* 48, *Birbhum Terracottas* 60, *Indian Life and Legends* Vol. I 74.
Kalika Art Gallery, P.O. Santiniketan, West Bengal, India.

Dey, Surendra Kumar, M.SC.; Indian electrical engineer and politician; b. 13 Sept. 1906; ed. Zilla School, Rangpur, Bengal Engineering Coll., Purdue and Michigan Univs., U.S.A.
Rose from position of Sales Engineer to Divisional Man. for India, Burma and Ceylon with Victor X-ray Corpn. (India) Ltd. 32-47; Hon. Technical Adviser, Ministry of Rehabilitation 47-52; built township of Nilokheri, a pilot experiment in agro-industrial development; mem. of Exec. United Council for Relief and Welfare 49-53; Admin., Community Projects Admin., mem. Central Board, Bharat Sewak Samaj 52-56; Minister for Community Devt. 56-58, for Co-operation and Community Devt. 59-65, of Mines and Metals 66-67; worked as Special Adviser to Administrator UNDP on global mission of rural devt. in continents; Pres. All India Panchayat Parishad 68-73; Special Consultant UNROD, Dacca, Bangladesh 72-73; mem. Akhil Bharatya Congress Rachanatmak Karya Samiti, Youth Advisory Cttee. (All-India Congress Cttee.); Hon. LL.D. (Univ. of Michigan); awarded Padma Bhushan 55; Congress Party.
Publs. *The Quest, Fragments Across, Missing Link, Planning for Life, Random Thoughts I, II and III, Community Development, Panchayati Raj, Nilokheri, Community Development: A Chronicle, Power to the People?—A Chronicle of India* 47-67.
"Bul Bul", 5-Lajpatrai Marg, Lajpatnagar-IV, New Delhi 24, India.

Dhavan, Shanti Swarup; Indian judge, diplomatist and administrator; b. 2 July 1905; ed. Government Coll., Lahore, Forman Christian Coll., Lahore, Emmanuel Coll., Cambridge, Middle Temple, London, and Univs. of Bonn and Heidelberg.
Former Pres. Cambridge Union; Advocate, Allahabad High Court; Lecturer in Law, Univ. of Allahabad 40-54; Senior Standing Counsel, Govt. of Uttar Pradesh 56-58; Puisne Judge, Allahabad High Court 58-67; High Commr. of India in U.K. 68-69; Gov. of West Bengal 69-71; mem. Law Comm. of India 72-; Pres. Uttar Pradesh Section, Indo-Soviet Cultural Soc. 65-67; delivered the Lal Bahadur Sastri Memorial Lecture on Nat. Integration, Trivandrum 73.
15 Safdarjang Road, New Delhi; and 28 Tashkent Marg, Allahabad, Uttar Pradesh, India.

Dhillon, Gurdial Singh; Indian politician; b. 6 Aug. 1915, Amritsar; ed. Govt. Coll. Lahore, Univ. Law Coll. Lahore.
Law practice 37-47; army service; active in Congress and Akali Dal movements; imprisoned twice before independence in 1947; journalist and co-founder, Punjab daily *Virman* 47-52; Chief Editor Urdu daily *Sher-e-Bharat* 47-52; Man. Dir. Sikh Newspaper Ltd.; founder mem. Fed. of Working Journalists of India; mem. Punjab Legis. Assembly 52-67, Deputy Speaker 52-54, Speaker 54-62, Sec.-Gen. and Chief Whip Congress Legis. Party 64-67; Punjab State Minister of Transport 65-66; mem. Lok Sabha 67-, Chair. Parl. Cttee. on Public Undertakings 68-69, Speaker 69-75; Minister of Transport and Shipping

Nov. 75-; fmr. mem. A.I.C.C.; Pres. Commonwealth Speakers' Conf. 70, Chair. Standing Cttee. of Commonwealth Speakers 71-73; mem. Exec. Commonwealth Parl. Asscn. 69-, Vice-Pres. 73-74, Pres. 74-Nov. 75; Pres. IPU Conf. 69, mem. Exec. Cttee. IPU 69-72, Pres. Oct. 73-; mem. Syndicate Punjab Univ. 60-, Fellow 68-69, now Dean Faculty of Law; mem. Syndicate and Fellow, Guru Nanak Univ. 70-.
Ministry of Transport, New Delhi, India.

Diah, Burhanudin Mohamad (husband of Herawati Diah, *q.v.*); Indonesian journalist and diplomatist; b. 1917; ed. Taman Siswa High School, Medan, Sumatra and Ksatrian School for Journalism, Bandung, Java.
Asst. Editor daily *Sinar Deli*, Medan 37-38; free-lance journalist 38-39; Chief of Indonesian Information Desk, British Consulate-Gen. 39-41; Editor-in-chief Indonesian monthly *Pertjaturan Dunia dan Film* 39-41; radio commentator and editorial writer daily *Asia Raya* 42-45; Editor-in-chief daily *Merdeka* 45-49, 68-; Chair. elect Indonesian Journalists Asscn.; Pres. Merdeka Press Ltd., Masa Merdeka Printing Presses; active in political movement, especially during Japanese occupation; Chair. New Youth (underground) movement and jailed by Japanese in 42 and again in 45; active in forcing proclamation of Indonesian Independence Aug. 45; mem. Provisional Nat. Cttee., Republic of Indonesia 45-49; mem. Provisional Indonesian Parl. 54-56; mem. Nat. Council 57-59; Amb. to Czechoslovakia (concurrently to Hungary) 59-62, to U.K. 62-64, to Thailand 64-66; Min. of Information 66-68; Vice-Chair. Press Council of Indonesia 70-.
Office: Jalan M. Sangadji, Jakarta; Home: Jalan Diponegoro, Jakarta, Indonesia.

Diah, Herawati, B.A. (wife of Burhanudin Mohamad Diah, *q.v.*); Indonesian journalist; b. 1917; ed. Barnard Coll. (Columbia Univ.).
Announcer and feature writer, Indonesian Radio 42; Sec. to Minister of Foreign Affairs, Republic of Indonesia Sept.-Dec. 45; reporter daily *Merdeka* 46; Editor *Minggu Merdeka* Jan.-July 47 (when it was banned by Dutch authorities); reporter *Merdeka* 47-48; Editor *Madjalah Merdeka* 48-51, of *Minggu Merdeka* May 51, *Keluarga* (Family) 53-59, of *Indonesian Observer* 55-59; Founder, Dir. Foundation for Preservation of Indonesian Art and Culture 67-.
Jalan Diponegoro, Jakarta, Indonesia.

Dias, Anthony Lancelot, B.A., B.SC.(ECON); Indian civil servant; b. 13 March 1910, Poona; ed. Deccan Coll., Poona, London School of Econs. and Magdalene Coll., Cambridge.
Entered Indian Civil Service 33; Sec. Educ. Dept. 52-55, Agricultural Dept. 55-57, Home Dept. 57-60; Chair. Bombay Port Trust 60-64; Sec. Dept. of Food, Ministry of Food and Agriculture 64-70; Lieut.-Gov. of Tripura 70-71; Gov. of West Bengal Aug. 71-; mem. Board of Govs., Int. Devt. Research Centre, Ottawa, Canada; Padma Vibhushan 70.
Raj Bhavan, Calcutta, West Bengal, India.
Telephone: 23-5641.

Dikshit, Uma Shankar; Indian politician and journalist; b. 12 Jan. 1901, Ugo, Uttar Pradesh; ed. Govt. School and Christchurch Coll., Kanpur.
Secretary, Kanpur City Congress Cttee. and mem. Uttar Pradesh Congress Cttee. 20-25; imprisoned for participation in Non-Co-operation Movt. 21-23; Pres. Uttar Bharatiya Sabha and Hindi Bhashi Sammedan 25-30; active in underground movt. 32, imprisoned 30, 32-33; Hon. Sec. Hindustani Prachar Sabha, Bombay 34-41; joined Quit India Movt. 42, detained until 44; Custodian, Evacuee Property, New Delhi 48-52; Hon. Adviser, Nat. Small Industries Corpn. 56; Man. Dir. Associated Journals Ltd., Lucknow 57-; mem. Rajya Sabha 61-76; Minister of Health and Family Planning 71-73, of Home Affairs 73-74, without Portfolio Oct. 74-Feb. 75, of Shipping and Transport Feb.-Nov. 75; Gov. of Karnataka 75-.
Office of the Governor, Bangalore, Karnataka, India.

Diwakar, Ranganath, LL.B., M.A.; Indian author and politician; b. 1894; ed. Bombay Univ.
Teacher and Prof. of English 16-20; founded *Karmaveer* (Kannada weekly paper) 21, editor until 30, now sole trustee of People's Education Trust, Hubli, controlling *Karmaveer* and *Samyukta Karnatak* (Kannada daily paper) and *Kasturi* (monthly Kannada paper); Pres. Karnatak Provincial Congress Cttee. 30-34; mem. Constituent Assembly 46; Min. of Information and Broadcasting 48-52; Gov. of Bihar 52-57; Chair. Gandhi Smarak Nidhi 57-, and Peace Foundation, New Delhi 59-; imprisoned for sedition (during freedom movement) 21-23, 24-26, 30-32, 40, 44; took part in civil disobedience 41; mem. of Rajya Sabha 62-69.
Publs. In English: *Satyagraha—Its History and Technique* 46, *Glimpses of Gandhiji* 49, *Satyagraha in Action* 49, *Upanishads in Story and Dialogue* 50, *Satyagraha—Pathway to Peace* 50, *Mahayogi* (biography of Aurobindo Ghose), *Saga of Satyagraha* 70; and many books in Kannada and Hindi on religion, philosophy, and other subjects.
2 Residency Road, Bangalore 25, Mysore State, India.

Djojohadikoesoemo, Soemitro; Indonesian economist and politician; b. 29 May 1917, Kebumen, Central Java; ed. Netherlands School of Econs., Rotterdam and the Sorbonne, Paris.
Assistant to Prime Minister of Indonesia 46; Pres. Indonesian Banking Corpn. 47; Chargé d'Affaires, Washington, D.C. 49-50; Minister of Econ. Affairs 50-51; Minister of Finance 52-53, 55-56; Prof. and Dean, Faculty of Econs., Univ. of Indonesia, Jakarta 51-57; left the country after the PRRI/Permesta armed rebellion 58-67; Minister of Trade 68-73; Minister of State for Research 73-.
Ministry of State for Research, Jakarta, Indonesia.

Doi, Shozaburo; Japanese banking executive; b. 23 Dec. 1907, Yonago City; ed. Aoyama Gakuin Univ.
Joined the Mitsui Trust & Co. Ltd. 29; Dir. The Mitsui Trust & Banking Co. Ltd. 58, Pres. 68-71, Chair. 71-; Dir. Mitsui Petroleum Devt. Co. Ltd. 69-, Mitsui Ocean Devt. Co. Ltd. 70-, Mitsui Devt. Co. 71-; Auditor The Developer Sanshin Co. Ltd. 71-, Mitsui Alumina Co. Ltd. 72-; Insp. Japan Medical Foods Asscn. 72-.
The Mitsui Trust and Banking Co. Ltd., 1-1, Nihombashi Muromachi 2-chome, Chuo-ku, Tokyo 103; and 3-7 Higashi-Tamagawa 2-chome, Setagaya-ku, Tokyo, Japan.
Telephone: 720-5656.

Doko, Toshio; Japanese business executive; b. 15 Sept. 1896; ed. Tokyo Inst. of Industrial Science, Univ. of Tokyo.
With K.K. Tokyo Ishikawajima Shipyard 20; with Ishikawajima Shibaura Turbine Co. Ltd. 36, Pres. 46; elected Pres. Ishikawajima Heavy Industries Co. Ltd. 50, Chair. of Board 64- (now Ishikawajima-Harima Heavy Industries); Dir. Tokyo Shibaura Electric 57, Pres. 65-; Ishikawajima do Brasil Estaleiros S.A. 59-; Vice-Pres. Fed. of Econ. Orgs., Pres. 74-; Nat. Order of Cambodia, Medal of Honour with Blue and Navy Ribbons, Order of Southern Cross (Brazil), First Class Order of the Sacred Treasure.
Tokyo Shibaura Electric Co. Ltd., 1-6 1-chome, Chiyoda-ku, Tokyo, Japan.

Dorji-Khangsarpa of Chakhung, Kazi Lhendup; Indian (Sikkimese) politician; b. Sept. 1904, Pakyong; ed. Enchey School, Gangtok and Rumtek Monastery.
Head Lama, Rumtek Monastery 22-30; founder of various schools in W. Sikkim in collaboration with his brother the late Kazi Phag Tshering; founded Sikkim Praja Mandal 45, elected Pres. 45; Pres. Sikkim State Congress 53-58;

led del. to India 54; founded Sikkim Nat. Congress 62; Exec. Councillor for Agriculture, Animal Husbandry and Transport Authority 70-72; tour of Europe 72; Pres. Joint Action Council, later Sikkim Congress (merger of Sikkim Janta Congress and Sikkim Nat. Congress) 73-; Chief Minister and Leader of Sikkim Assembly April 74-.
Publs. Various articles on the need for democratization of Sikkim, usually in *Bulletin of the Sikkim Congress*.
Chief Minister's Residence, Government of Sikkim, Gangtok, Sikkim; Chakhung House, Kalimpong, West Bengal, India.

Douglas, Roger Owen, A.C.A., C.M.A.; New Zealand; chartered accountant and politician; b. 5 Dec. 1937; ed. Auckland Grammar School, Univ. of Auckland.
Formerly Co. Sec. Bremworth Carpet Co., Auckland; mem. Manukau City Council 65-68; mem. of Parl. for Manukau 69-; Postmaster-Gen. 72-74; Minister of Broadcasting 72-75, in charge of Govt. Life Insurance Office 72-Nov. 75, of Housing 74-Nov. 75, of Customs March-Nov. 75.
c/o Parliament Buildings, Wellington; Home: 8 Frank Place, Manurewa, Auckland, New Zealand.

Doulatram, Jairamdas, B.A., LL.B.; Indian politician; b. 21 July 1891.
Joined Indian Home Rule Movement 16; took part in Gandhi's Satyagraha Movement 19; mem. All-India Congress Cttee. 27-40; Editor *The Bharatvasi* 19-20; participated in Gandhi's Non-Co-operation Movement 20-21; imprisoned for sedition 21-23; Editor *The Hindustan Times*, Delhi 25-26, Gandhi's *Young India* 30; mem. Bombay Legislative Council 27-29; joined Satyagraha Movement for Indian Freedom 30; imprisoned twice during Civil Disobedience Movement 30 and 32, released 34; Gen. Sec. Indian Nat. Congress 31, Acting Pres. I.N. Congress 34, mem. Congress Working Cttee. 29-40; Chair. Textile Labour Wage Enquiry Cttee. 38; detained in prison during "Quit India" Movement 42-45; mem. All-India Village Industries Board 41-46, Indian Constituent Assembly 46-50; Gov. of Bihar 47; Minister of Food and Agriculture Govt. of India 48-50; Gov. of Assam 50-56; Chief Editor *Collected Works of Mahatma Gandhi* 57-59; mem. Governing Body Gandhi Peace Foundation 58-70; mem. Rajya Sabha 59-.
Rajya Sabha, Parliament House, New Delhi 1; Home: 14 Tughlak Road, New Delhi 11, India.

Downer, Hon. Sir Alexander Russell, K.B.E., M.A., F.R.S.A., Barr.-at-Law; Australian diplomatist; b. 7 April 1910; ed. Geelong Grammar School, Victoria, Brasenose Coll., Oxford, and Inner Temple, London.
Served with Australian Imperial Forces 40-45; prisoner of war of Japanese 42-45; Liberal Mem. Australian House of Representatives 49-64; mem. Parl. Foreign Affairs Cttee. 52-58; mem. of Constitutional Review Cttee. 56-59; Rep. of the Australian Parl. at the Coronation of H.M. Queen Elizabeth II 53; Minister of State for Immigration 58-63; High Commr. for Australia in the United Kingdom 64-72; a gov. English-Speaking Union 73; Freeman of City of London 65; Hon. LL.D. (Birmingham Univ.) 73.
26-27 Queen's Gate Gardens, London, S.W.7, England; Martinsell, Williamstown, S.A., Australia.

Drake-Brockman, Hon. Thomas Charles; Australian politician; b. May 1919, Toodyay, W. Australia; ed. Guildford Grammar School, Perth.
R.A.A.F. 41-45; Pres. Wool Exec., Farmers Union of W. Australia; Vice-Pres. Australian Wool and Meat Producers Fed. 57-58; mem. Senate 58-, Chair. of Cttees. 76-; Minister of State for Air 69-72, for Aboriginal Affairs and Admin. Services Nov.-Dec. 75; Distinguished Flying Cross.
Parliament House, Canberra, A.C.T. 2600, Australia.

Drysdale, Sir (George) Russell, Kt.; British-born Australian artist; b. 7 Feb. 1912; ed. Geelong Grammar School, Victoria, Australia.
Art studies in Melbourne, London and Paris; works in New York Metropolitan Museum of Art, Nat. Gallery, London, Tate Gallery, London, Nat. Galleries of New South Wales, Victoria, South Australia, etc.; mem. Australian Soc. of Artists; mem. Commonwealth Art Advisory Board 62-; Dir. Pioneer Sugar Mills Ltd.
Publ. (with Jock Marshall) *Journey Among Men* 62.
Bouddi Farm, Kilcare Heights, Hardy's Bay, N.S.W., Australia.

Dua, Indar Dev, B.A., LL.B.; Indian judge; b. 4 Oct. 1907, Marden (now in Pakistan); ed. Christian Coll., Lahore, Law Coll., Punjab and Punjab Univ.
Practised at the Bar, Lahore High Court 33-47, Punjab High Court 47-58; Judge, Punjab High Court 58, Delhi High Court 66; Chief Justice, Delhi High Court 67-69; Judge of the Supreme Court 69-73; Lokayukta (Ombudsman), State of Rajasthan 73-.
Lokayukta, 11 Civil Lines, Jaipur, India.

Duan, Le (*see* Le Duan).

Duckmanton, Talbot Sydney, C.B.E.; Australian broadcasting executive; b. 1921; ed. Newington Coll., Stanmore, New South Wales, Sydney Univ. and Australian Administrative Staff Coll.
Australian Army and Air Force Service; Australian Broadcasting Comm. 39-, Man. for Tasmania 53-57, Controller of Admin. 57-59, Asst. Gen. Man. (Admin.) 59-64, Deputy Gen. Man. 64-65, Gen. Man. 65-; Vice-Pres. Asian Broadcasting Union 70-73, Pres. 73-; Trustee, Visnews Ltd. 65-; mem. Council Australian Admin. Staff Coll. 69-, Australian Film Devt. Corpn. 70-75, Australian Council for the Arts 73-75, Australia Council 75-; Pres. Commonwealth Broadcasting Assen. 75-.
Australian Broadcasting Commission, Broadcast House, 145-153 Elizabeth Street, Sydney, 2000 N.S.W., Australia.
Telephone: 310211.

Dügersüren, Mangalyn; Mongolian diplomatist; b. 15 Feb. 1922; ed. Inst. of International Relations, Moscow.
Schoolmaster 41-44; studies in Moscow 44-51; Deputy Head, later Head of Dept., Ministry of Foreign Affairs, Mongolia 51-53; Sec. of Central Cttee. of Mongolian Revolutionary Youth League 53-54; Deputy Minister of Justice 54-56; Deputy Minister of Foreign Affairs 56-68; Amb. to India 58-62; First Deputy Minister of Foreign Affairs 62-63, Minister of Foreign Affairs 63-68; Perm. Rep. to UN 68-72; Perm. Rep. UN Office at Geneva and other int. orgs. Aug. 72-; mem. Central Cttee. of Mongolian People's Revolutionary Party.
Permanent Mission of the Mongolian People's Republic, 5 chemin des Crettets, Conches, 1231 Geneva, Switzerland.

Dunstan, Donald Allan, Q.C., LL.B.; Australian lawyer and politician; b. 21 Sept. 1926, Fiji; ed. St. Peter's Coll. and Univ. of Adelaide, S. Australia.
Practised law for two years in Fiji, returned to S. Australia; mem. S. Australia Parl. for Norwood 53-; mem. S. Australia Labor Party Exec. 55, Junior Vice-Pres. 58, Senior Vice-Pres. 59, Pres. S. Australian Branch of Labor Party 60; del. to Fed. Exec. of Labor Party 60-64; Attorney-Gen., Minister of Aboriginal Affairs and Social Welfare, S. Australia 65; Premier, Treasurer, Minister of Housing 67-68; Leader of Opposition 68-70; Premier, Treasurer 70-; Minister of Devt. and Mines 70-73.
Premier's Department, P.O. Box 2343, Adelaide, South Australia 5001; Home: 15 Clara Street, Norwood, South Australia 5067, Australia.

Duong Van Minh, Lieut.-Gen.; Vietnamese army officer and politician; b. 1916; ed. French Lycée, Army General Staff School, Paris, and U.S. Army Command School.
French Colonial Army 40-52, Prisoner-of-War; Major, Vietnamese Army 52; Campaign against Binh Xuyen bandits 55, Viet Cong guerillas 56-62; Military Adviser to Pres. Diem 62-63; led *coup d'état* against Diem Nov. 63; Chair. Revolutionary Council Oct. 63-Jan. 64; Head of State Jan.-Oct. 64; lived in Bangkok 64-68; made unsuccessful attempt to stand as Presidential candidate June 67; returned to Saigon Oct. 68; Pres. 28-30 April 75.
98 Hong-Thap-Tu, Saigon, Viet-Nam.

Dy, Francisco Justiniano, M.D., M.P.H.; Philippine public health administrator; b. 17 Sept. 1912; ed. Univ. of Philippines and School of Hygiene and Public Health, Johns Hopkins Univ., U.S.A.
Research Asst. and Instructor, Inst. of Hygiene, Univ. of Philippines 38-41; U.S. Army 42-45; Senior Surgeon, U.S. Public Health Service 45-46; Consultant and Chief of Malaria Division, U.S. Public Health Service Rehabilitation Programme in Philippines 46-50; Prof. of Malariology and Chair. Dept. of Parasitology, Inst. of Hygiene, Univ. of Philippines 50-52; Deputy Chief, Malaria Section, World Health Org. (WHO), Geneva 50-51; Regional Malaria Adviser, WHO, for W. Pacific Region 51-57; Dir. of Health Services, WHO Regional Office for W. Pacific 58-66, Regional Dir. of WHO for W. Pacific July 66-; Prof. of Community Medicine, Univ. of Philippines June 69-; mem. Nat. Research Council of Philippines; Distinguished Service Star (Philippines); Legion of Merit, with Oak Leaf Cluster (U.S.A.).
Regional Office for the Western Pacific, World Health Organization, P.O.B. 2932, Manila; Home: 901 E. de los Santos Avenue, Quezon City, Philippines.
Telephone: 59-20-41.

E

Eccles, Sir John Carew, Kt., M.B., B.S., D.PHIL., F.R.A.C.P., F.R.S.N.Z., F.A.A., F.R.S.; Australian research physiologist; b. 27 Jan. 1903; ed. Melbourne Univ., Magdalen Coll., Oxford.
Rhodes Scholar 25; Junior Research Fellow, Exeter Coll., Oxford 27-32, Staines Medical Fellow 32-34; Fellow and Tutor, Magdalen Coll., Oxford, lecturer in physiology 34-37; Dir. Kanematsu Memorial Inst. of Pathology, Sydney, Australia 37-43; Prof. of Physiology, Otago Univ., New Zealand 44-51, Australian Nat. Univ., Canberra 51-66; at AMA/ERF Inst. for Biomedical Research, Chicago 66-68; at State Univ. of New York at Buffalo 68-75; Waynflete lecturer, Oxford 52; Herter lecturer, Johns Hopkins Univ., Baltimore 55; Foreign Hon. mem. American Acad. of Arts and Sciences, Accademia Nazionale dei Lincei, Deutsche Akad. der Naturforscher Leopoldina (Cothenius Medal); mem. Pontifical Acad. of Sciences, American Philosophical Soc.; Ferrier Lecturer, Royal Soc. 60; Pres. Australian Acad. of Science 57-61; Hon. Fellow Exeter Coll. and Magdalen Coll., Oxford, Hon. Fellow New York Acad. of Sciences; Hon. Sc.D. (Cambridge, Tasmania, Univ. British Columbia, Gustavus Adolphus Coll.), Hon. LL.D. (Melbourne); Hon. M.D. (Charles Univ., Yeshiva Univ.); Hon. D.Sc. (Oxford); Royal Medal, Royal Soc. 62, Nobel Prize for Medicine 63.
Publs. *Reflex Activity of the Spinal Cord* (in collaboration) 32, *Neurophysiological Basis of Mind* 53, *Physiology of Nerve Cells* 57, *Physiology of Synapses* 64, *The Cerebellum as a Neuronal Machine* 67, *Inhibitory Pathways of the Central Nervous System* 69, *Facing Reality* 70, *The Understanding of the Brain* 73, *The Self and its Brain* 76.
Ca' a la Gia', CH 6611 Contra (Ticino), Switzerland.
Telephone: 093-672931.

Edwards, Air Commodore Sir Hughie Idwal, K.C.M.G., V.C., C.B., D.S.O., O.B.E., D.F.C.; Australian administrator; b. 1 Aug. 1914, Fremantle, W. Australia; ed. Fremantle Boys' School.
Cadet, R.A.A.F. 35-36; R.A.F. Officer (mentioned in despatches) 36-63; Dir. Aust. Selection (Pty.) Ltd. 64-73; Gov. of W. Australia 74-75.
42 New Beach Road, Darling Point, N.S.W. 2627, Australia.

Egami, Fujio, D.SC.; Japanese biochemist; b. 21 Nov. 1910, Tokyo; ed. Univ. of Tokyo and in Strasbourg and Paris.
Associate Prof. of Biochem., Nagoya Univ. 42-43, Prof. of Biochem. 43-60; Prof. of Biochem., Univ. of Tokyo 58-71, Saitama Univ. 68-71; Dir. Mitsubishi-Kasei Inst. of Life Sciences 71-; mem. Science Council of Japan 49-72, Vice-Pres. 66-69, Pres. 69-72; Chemical Soc. of Japan Prize 54; Officier de l'Instruction Publique (French Govt.) 54; Asahi Culture Prize 67; Japan Acad. Prize 71; Légion d'Honneur 72.
Publs. *Biochemistry of Nucleic Acids, Biochemistry of Heteropolysaccharides, Enzyme Biochemistry, Microbiological Chemistry, Discovery of Ribonuclease* T_1.
Mitsubishi-Kasei Institute of Life Sciences, 11 Minamiooya, Machida-shi, Tokyo, Japan.
Telephone: 0427-26-1211, Ext. 38 (Office); 0423-81-9212 (Home).

Elahi Chaudhry, Fazal, B.SC., M.A.(ECONS.), LL.B.; Pakistani lawyer and politician; b. 1 Jan. 1904, Gujrat District; ed. Muslim Univ., Aligarh.
Joined Gujrat Bar 29; mem. Gujrat District Board 31-53; joined Muslim League 43; mem. Punjab Legislative Assembly 46-56; Parl. Sec. Punjab Govt. 47-48, Minister for Educ. and Health 48-56; mem. W. Pakistan Assembly 56, Speaker 56-58; mem. Nat. Assembly 62-, Senior Deputy Speaker 64-70, Speaker 71-73; joined Pakistan People's Party 71; President of Pakistan Aug. 73-; Hilal-e-Quaid-e-Azam 67.
The Presidency, Rawalpindi, Pakistan.

Ellicott, Robert James, Q.C.; Australian lawyer and politician; b. 15 April 1927, Moree, N.S.W.; ed. Fort Street Boy's School and Univ. of Sydney.
Admitted to Bar in N.S.W. 50, Victoria 60; Q.C. 64; Commonwealth Solicitor-Gen. 69-73; mem. House of Reps. for Wentworth, N.S.W. 74-; opposition spokesman on consumer affairs and commerce 74-75; Attorney-Gen. Dec. 75-; Liberal Party.
Parliament Buildings, Canberra, A.C.T. 2600, Australia.

Enderby, Keppel Earl, Q.C., LL.M.; Australian lawyer and politician; b. 26 June 1926; ed. Dubbo High School, Univs. of Sydney and London.
Practising barrister; Lecturer, Examiner, in Commercial Law, Sydney Technical Coll. 55-62; Senior Lecturer in Law, Australian Nat. Univ. 63-65; mem. House of Reps. for A.C.T. 70-74, for Canberra 74-75; del. to Fed. Exec. of Australian Labor Party 71-, Chair. Econs. Cttee., Health Cttee.; mem. House of Reps. Privileges Cttee. 73-75; Minister for A.C.T. and Northern Territory 72-73, of Secondary Industry and Supply 73-74, for Mfg. Industry 74-75; Attorney-Gen. and Minister for Customs and Excise Feb.-Nov. 75.
Publ. *Courts Martial Appeals in Australia* (Fed. Law Review) 64.
32 Endeavour Street, Red Hill, A.C.T., Australia.

Espie, Frank Fletcher, O.B.E.; Australian mining engineer; b. 1917, Bawdwin, Burma; ed. St. Peter's Coll., Adelaide, Adelaide Univ.
Served 9th Div., AIF, N. Africa and New Guinea rising to rank of Capt. 40-45; Underground Man., then Mine Supt., Zinc Corpn.-New Broken Hill Consolidated Mines 43-57, Asst. Gen. Man. for Production 57-61; Gen. Man. Comalco Products, Yennora, Sydney 61-62, Gen. Man. Industrial

Div., CRA 64-65; successively Exec. Dir., Man. Dir., Chair. of Dirs., Bougainville Copper Ltd. and Bougainville Mining Ltd. 65-; Exec. Dir. Conzinc Riotinto of Australia Ltd. 68-74, Deputy Chair. 75-; Chair. Australian Mining and Smelting Co. Ltd., Mary Kathleen Uranium Ltd.; Dir. Rio Tinto Zinc Corpn. Ltd., London.
Bougainville Copper Ltd., 95 Collins Street, Melbourne, Australia.

Etemadi, Noor Ahmad; Afghan diplomatist; b. 22 Feb. 1921 in Kandahar; ed. Istiqlal Lyceum and Kabul Univ.
Started public service in Ministry of Educ.; Asst. Chief of Protocol, Ministry of Foreign Affairs 46, Dir. of Econ. Relations 53-57, Dir.-Gen. of Political Affairs 57-63, Sec.-Gen. 63, has also served in London and Washington, D.C.; Amb. to Pakistan 65; Minister of Foreign Affairs 65-67, concurrently First Deputy Prime Minister 66-67; Prime Minister and Minister of Foreign Affairs 67-71; Amb. to Italy 72-73, to U.S.S.R. 73-; mem. Loya Jirgah 64, mem. Constitutional Drafting Cttee.
Embassy of Afghanistan, Ul. Vorovskogo 42, Moscow, U.S.S.R.

Everingham, Douglas Nixen, M.B., B.S.; Australian medical practitioner and fmr. politician; b. 25 June 1923; ed. Fort Street School, Univ. of Sydney.
Resident medical officer in gen. and mental hospitals 46-53; gen. practice 53-67; mem. House of Reps. 67-75; Minister of Health Dec. 72-Nov. 75.
Publs. *Chemical Shorthand for Organic Formulae* 43, *Critique of Bliss Symbols* 56, *Braud Inglish Speling* 66.
50 Corberry Street, Rockhampton 4700, Queensland, Australia.

Eyre, Dean Jack; New Zealand politician; b. 8 May 1914; ed. Hamilton High School and Auckland Univ.
Founder, D. J. Eyre & Co. 36 (now Airco (N.Z.) Ltd.); naval service, World War II; M.P. 49-68, Minister of Industries, Commerce and Customs 54, of Social Security, and of Tourist and Health Resorts 56-57, of Housing and State Advances 57, of Defence 57, of Police 60-63, Minister of Defence 60-66, of Tourism and Publicity 60-66; High Commissioner of New Zealand to Canada Aug. 68-73; Lieut. R.N.V.R.; National Party.
c/o Ministry of External Affairs, Wellington, New Zealand.

F

Fabinyi, Andrew, D.PHIL., O.B.E., F.R.S.A.; Australian publisher; b. 27 Dec. 1908; ed. Minta Gymnasium and Pazmany Univ., Budapest, Hungary.
British Publishers' Rep. in Hungary 33-39; Publishing Manager, F. W. Cheshire Pty. Ltd. 39-54; Australian Army Educ. Service 42-46; Publishing Dir. F. W. Cheshire Pty. Ltd. 54; Pres. Australian Book Fair Council 55-60, Victorian Branch of Library Asscn. of Australia 55, 59, 65, 66, Public Libraries Div. of Library Asscn. of Australia 62; Dir. Lansdowne Press Pty. Ltd. 62-69; Pres. Australian Book Publishers' Asscn. 65, 66; mem. Exec. Cttee. for Econ. Development of Australia 65-; mem. of the General Council (Fed.) Library Asscn. of Australia 67; Chair. of Australian Inst. of Int. Affairs, Victoria Branch 68-69, Australian Book Trade Advisory Cttee. 67-68; Pres. Australian Inst. of Int. Affairs, N.S.W. Branch 71-73, Chair. Communications Cttee. 70-; mem. Australian Nat. Comm. for UNESCO 70-; Deputy Chair. Cheshire Group Publishers and Booksellers 67-68, Chair. 68-69; Man. Dir. F. W. Cheshire Publishing Pty. Ltd. 67-69; Dir. Jacaranda Press 66-69; Man. Dir. Pergamon Press (Aust.) Pty. Ltd. 69-75, Dir. 75-; Chair. Australian Book Publishers Asscn. Book Export Devt. Cttee. 71-73; Redmond Barry Award, Australian Library Asscn. 74; Research Fellow, Univ. of N.S.W. 75-.
116 Grosvenor Road, Lindfield, N.S.W. 2070, Australia.

Fairbairn, David Eric, D.F.C.; Australian grazier and politician; b. 3 March 1917, Claygate, Surrey, England; ed. Geelong Grammar School and Jesus Coll., Cambridge.
Farmer and grazier, Woomargama, nr. Albury, N.S.W. until 71; R.A.A.F., Second World War; mem. House of Reps. 49-75; Minister for Air 62-64; Minister for Nat. Devt. 64-69, and Leader in House 66; Chair. Joint Parl. Cttee. on Foreign Affairs 70-71; Minister for Educ. and Science March-Aug. 71, for Defence 71-72; opposition spokesman on nat. devt. 73-74; mem. N.S.W. State Liberal Party Exec. 73-75; Liberal.
2/3 Tasmania Circle, Forrest, A.C.T. 2603, Australia.

Fairfax, Sir Vincent Charles, Kt., C.M.G.; Australian business executive; b. 26 Dec. 1909, Cambooya, Queensland; ed. Geelong Grammar School, Victoria and Brasenose Coll., Oxford.
Military service 40-46; Royal Flying Doctor Service 54-71; Dir. Bank of N.S.W. 53, John Fairfax Ltd. 56; Dir. Australian Mutual Provident Soc. 56, Chair. 66; Chair. Stanbroke Pastoral Co. Pty. Ltd. 64; Chair. Australian Section, Commonwealth Press Union 50-73; Chair. Boys Brigade 50, Pres. 73; Chief Commr. Scout Asscn. N.S.W. 58-68, for Australia 69-73; mem. Council Royal Agricultural Soc., N.S.W. 50-, Treas. 59, Pres. 73; Deputy Pres. Royal Agricultural Soc. of Commonwealth 66; mem. Church of England Property Trust 50-71, Council Art Gallery Soc. of N.S.W. 53-69, Glebe Admin. Board 62-73; Trustee, Walter and Eliza Hall Trust 53.
550 New South Head Road, Double Bay, N.S.W. 2028, Australia.

Fairfax, Sir Warwick (Oswald), Kt., M.A.; Australian newspaper executive; b. 1902; ed. Geelong Grammar School, St. Paul's Coll. Sydney Univ. and Balliol Coll., Oxford.
Joined staff of John Fairfax and Sons Ltd. (*The Sydney Morning Herald, The Sun Herald, The Sun, The Australian Financial Review, The National Times* and other publs.) 25, Dir. 27, Man. Dir. 30, Chair. 56-; Chair. Associated Newspapers Ltd.; Dir. David Syme and Co. Ltd.; Vice-Pres. Australian Elizabethan Theatre Trust; mem. Council Australian Nat. Univ.
Publs. *Men, Parties and Policies* 43, *The Triple Abyss: Towards a Modern Synthesis* 65; Ed. *A Century of Journalism* (*The Sydney Morning Herald*) 31; plays: *A Victorian Marriage, Vintage for Heroes, The Bishop's Wife.*
John Fairfax and Sons Ltd., Box 506, G.P.O. Sydney; Fairwater, 560 New South Head Road, Double Bay, Sydney, N.S.W. 2028; Harrington Park, Narellan, N.S.W. 2567, Australia.

Fan Tzu-yu; politician, People's Repub. of China.
On Long March in Dept. of Supplies, 2nd Front Army 34-35; Champion of Swimming Contest for Generals in People's Liberation Army Units 60; Maj.-Gen., Gen. Logistics Dept., PLA 64; Minister of Commerce 71-.

Fang, Roland Chung, B.A., M.A.; Chinese scholar; b. 1902; ed. Tsing Hua Coll., Peking, Calif. and Stanford Univs.
Professor of English Literature, Central Univ. Nanking 28-30; Prof. of English Literature and Head of English Dept., Wuhan Univ. 31-44; Visiting Prof. Trinity Coll. Cambridge Univ. 44-46; Prof. of English and Head of Dept. of Foreign Languages, Chekiang Univ. 47-51, Chekiang Teachers' Coll. 51-52; Prof. Anhwei Univ. 52-53, East China Teachers' Univ., Shanghai 53-54, Futan Univ., Shanghai 54-56; Head, English Dept., Shanghai Inst. of Foreign Languages 57-.
Publs. *Book of Modern English Prose* (2 vols.) 34, *Studies in English Prose and Poetry* 39, *A Chinese Verse Translation of Shakespeare's Richard III* 59, *Complete Works of*

Chaucer translated into Chinese 62, *Chaucer's Canterbury Tales* (revised edn.) 63.
Shanghai Institute of Foreign Languages, Shanghai, People's Republic of China.

Fang Yi; politician, People's Repub. of China; b. 1909, Fukien.
Editor Commercial Press, Shanghai 30; on Long March 34; Sec.-Gen. N. China People's Govt. 48; Vice-Gov. of Shantung 49, of Fukien 49-52; Deputy Mayor of Shanghai 52-53; Vice-Minister of Finance 53-54; with Embassy of People's Repub. of China, Hanoi 54-61; Alt. mem. 8th Cen. Cttee. of CCP 56; Dir. of Bureau for Econ. Relations with Foreign Countries, State Council 61-64; Chair. Comm. for Econ. Relations with Foreign Countries 64-68; Alt. mem. 9th Cen. Cttee. of CCP 69; Minister of Econ. Relations with Foreign Countries 69-; mem. 10th Cen. Cttee. of CCP 73.

Fateh, A. F. M. Abul, M.A.; Bangladesh diplomatist; b. 28 Feb. 1926; ed. Dacca Univ.
Carnegie Fellow in Int. Peace 62-63; Pakistan Foreign Service 49-71; Third Sec. Pakistan Embassy, France 51-53, High Comm. Calcutta, India 53-56; Second Sec. Embassy, U.S.A. 56-60; Dir. Ministry of Foreign Affairs, Karachi 61-65; First Sec., Czechoslovakia 65-66; Counsellor, New Delhi, India 66-67; Deputy High Commr., Calcutta 68-70; Amb. to Iraq 71; Adviser to Acting Pres. of Bangladesh July 71; Foreign Sec. of Bangladesh Jan. 72; Amb. to France 72-75; High Commr. in U.K. 76-.
Bangladesh High Commission, 28 Queen's Gate, London, SW7 5JA, England.
Telephone: 01-584-0081.

Faulkner, Arthur James; New Zealand politician; b. 20 Nov. 1921; ed. Otahuhu District High School.
Member of Parl. for Roskill 57-; undertook fact-finding missions to S. Viet-Nam, Indonesia, Malaysia, Thailand, Singapore and the Philippines 63, 67; visited U.S.A. 65 study tour of Britain to discuss EEC 69; Minister of Defence and concurrently in charge of War Pensions and Rehabilitation 72-74, of Labour and State Services 74-Nov. 75; Pres. N.Z. Labour Party May 76-.
c/o Parliament Buildings, Wellington; Home: 1 Invermay Avenue, Mt. Roskill, Auckland 4, New Zealand.

Feng Yu-lan; philosopher, People's Repub. of China; b. 1895, Tang-ho, Honan; ed. China Acad., Shanghai, Peking Univ. and Columbia Univ., U.S.A.
Professor of Philosophy Chung-chou Univ., Kaifeng 23, Tsinghua Univ. 25-52; Dean, Coll. of Arts, Tsinghua Univ. 33; Visiting Prof. Univ. of Pennsylvania, U.S.A. 46-47; Dir. Research Dept. of History of Chinese Philosophy, Peking Univ. 54; Prof. Peking Univ. 61-68.
Publs. *The Philosophy of Life* 24, *A Kind of Outlook on Life* 24, *A History of Chinese Philosophers* (3 parts) 30, 33, 36, *The New Neo-Confucianism* 38, *The New World* 39, *The New Teachings of the World* 40, *The New Origin of Men* 42, *The New Origin of Truth* 42, *The New Understanding of Speech* 48, *A Short History of Chinese Philosophy* 48.

Feng Yung-shun; People's Repub. of China.
Major-General People's Liberation Army 57; Deputy Dir., Gen. Ordinance Dept., PLA 57; Deputy Dir., Gen. Logistics Dept., PLA 69-.

Fenner, Frank John, M.B.E., M.D., F.R.C.P., F.A.A., F.R.S.; Australian research biologist; b. 21 Dec. 1914; ed. Thebarton Technical High School, Adelaide High School, Adelaide Univ.
Medical Officer, Hospital Pathologist, Australian Forces 40-43, Malariologist 43-46; Francis Haley Research Fellow, Walter and Eliza Hall Inst. for Medical Research, Melbourne 46-48; Travelling Fellow, Rockefeller Inst. for Medical Research 48-49; Prof. of Microbiology, Australian Nat. Univ. 49-73; Dir. John Curtin School of Medical Research, Australian Nat. Univ. 67-73, Dir. Centre for Resource and Environmental Studies 73-; David Syme Prize, Melbourne Univ. 49; Harvey Lecturer, Harvey Soc. of N.Y. 58; Overseas Fellow, Churchill Coll., Cambridge 61-62; Mueller Medal 64, Britannica Australia Award 67; Matthew Flinders Lecturer 67, Fogarty Scholar, Nat. Insts. of Health (U.S.A.) 71 and 74.
Publs. about 100 scientific papers, mainly on acidfast bacilli and pox viruses, *The Production of Antibodies* (with F. M. Burnet) 49, *Myxomatosis* (with F. N. Ratcliffe) 65, *The Biology of Animal Viruses* (2 vols.) 68, 2nd edn. 74, *Medical Virology* (with D. O. White) 70, 2nd edn. 76.
Centre for Resource and Environmental Studies, Australian National University, Canberra, A.C.T., Australia.
Telephone: 49-4588.

Fernando, Hugh Norman Gregory, O.B.E., B.A., B.C.L.; Ceylonese judge; b. 17 Nov. 1910; ed. St. Joseph's Coll., Colombo, Trinity Coll., Kandy, and Balliol Coll., Oxford.
Barrister of Gray's Inn (London); Legal Draftsman, Ceylon 50-54; Commr. of Assizes and Puisne Justice, Supreme Court 54-66; Chief Justice of Sri Lanka 66-74; Officer Administering the Govt. of Ceylon Oct. 67; Leader, Ceylon Del. to Afro-Asian Legal Consultative Cttee. 62; Chair. Cheshire Homes Foundation, Sri Lanka, Appeal for Children Fund, Sri Lanka; Hon. Master of the Bench (Middle Temple); Master of the Bench (Gray's Inn).
129 Macarthy Road, Colombo 7, Sri Lanka.

Fernando, Thusew Samuel, C.B.E., Q.C., LL.B.; Ceylonese judge; b. 5 Aug. 1906; ed. Royal College, Colombo, Univ. Coll., Colombo, Univ. Coll., London, and Lincoln's Inn, London.
Crown Counsel 36-52; Solicitor-Gen., Ceylon 52-54; Attorney-Gen. 54-56; Justice, Supreme Court of Ceylon 56-68; Pres. Int. Comm. of Jurists, Geneva 66-; mem. Int. Cttee. of Inst. on Man & Science, New York; Pres. Court of Appeal of Sri Lanka 71-73; mem. Constitutional Court 72; High Commr. in Australia and New Zealand 74-.
High Commission of Sri Lanka, 35 Empire Circuit, Forrest, A.C.T. 2603, Australia; Home: 3 Cosmas Avenue, Barnes Place, Colombo 7, Sri Lanka.

Finlay, Allan Martyn, Q.C., PH.D., LL.M.; New Zealand lawyer and politician; b. 1 Jan. 1912; ed. Otago Boys' High School, Otago Univ., London School of Economics and Harvard Law School.
Research Asst., League of Nations 38; Private Sec. to various N.Z. Govt. Ministers 39-43; M.P. 46-49, 63-; Dir. Tasman Empire Airways Ltd. 58-61; Vice-Pres. N.Z. Labour Party 56-59, Pres. 60-63; Attorney-Gen., Minister of Justice, of Civil Aviation and Meteorological Services 72-Dec. 75, concurrently Minister in charge of Publicity 74; mem. N.Z. Law Revision Comm. 68.
Publs. *Third Party Contract* 39, *Social Security in New Zealand* 40.
Parliament Buildings, Wellington; and 9 Central Terrace, Wellington, New Zealand.
Telephone: 767-739.

Fitzgerald, Dr. Stephen; Australian scholar and diplomatist; b. 1938; ed. Australian Nat. Univ., Canberra.
Formerly with Dept. of Foreign Affairs (until 66); Fellow, Dept. of Far Eastern History, Australian Nat. Univ., Deputy Head Contemporary China Centre until 73; Amb. to People's Repub. of China April 73-.
Ministry of Foreign Affairs, Canberra, A.C.T., Australia.

Fleming, Allan Percy, O.B.E.; Australian librarian; b. 5 March 1912; ed. State School, Scotch Coll. and Univ. of Melbourne.
Journalist 32-39; War Service as Lt.-Col. 39-46; Dir. Joint Intelligence Bureau, Dept. of Defence 47-48; Controller Joint Service Orgs. 48-58; Trade Commr., Paris 59-62; First Asst. Sec. Dept. Trade and Industry, Canberra, 62-66;

Special Commercial Adviser London 67; Del. to GATT Conf. 61 and UNCTAD Confs. 63-66; Pres. UNCTAD Board Sept. 65; Commonwealth Parl. Librarian 67-70; Nat. Librarian 70-73.
National Library of Australia, Canberra, A.C.T. 2600; 60 Gellbrand Street, Campbell, Canberra, A.C.T. 2603, Australia.

Fleming, Charles Alexander, O.B.E., F.R.S., F.R.S.N.Z., D.SC.; New Zealand geologist and paleontologist; b. 9 Sept. 1916; ed. Kings Coll., Auckland and Auckland Univ. Coll.
Joined N.Z. Geological Survey as Asst. Geologist 40, becoming Paleontologist and later Chief Paleontologist; published research on geological and biological topics, mainly on history of life in N.Z.; has taken part in expeditions to subantarctic islands; Pres. Royal Soc. N.Z. 62-66; Chief Paleontologist, N.Z. Geological Survey (Dept. of Scientific and Ind. Res.); Pres. Australian and N.Z. Asscn. for Advancement of Science 68-69, Ornithological Soc. of N.Z. 45; Corresp. Fellow, American Ornithologists Union; Commonwealth Fellow, Geological Soc. of London; Foreign mem. American Philosophical Soc.; Hector and Hutton Medals of Royal Soc. of N.Z.; Walter Burfitt Medal of Royal Soc. of N.S.W., ANZAAS Medal 72.
Publs. *Checklist of New Zealand Birds* (editor) 53, Hochstetter's *Geology of New Zealand* (translator and editor) 59, *Stratigraphic Lexicon: New Zealand* (editor) 59, *Marwick's Illustrations of New Zealand Shells* 66, and over 200 research papers on N.Z. geology, paleontology, zoology and biogeography.
Office: New Zealand Geological Survey, P.O.B. 30368, Lower Hutt; Home: "Balivean", 42 Wadestown Road, Wellington, New Zealand.
Telephone: 699-059 (Office); 737-288 (Home).

Foots, Sir James (William), Kt.; Australian industrialist; b. 12 July 1916; ed. Coburg and Univ. High Schools, Melbourne and Melbourne Univ.
Mining engineer 38-45, with North Broken Hill Ltd. 38-43, Allied Works Council 43-44, Lake George Mines Ltd. 44-45, Zinc Corpn. Ltd. 46-54; Asst. Gen. Man. Zinc Corpn. and New Broken Hill Consolidated Ltd. 53-54; Gen. Man. Mount Isa Mines Ltd. 55-56, Dir. 56-, Man. Dir. 66-70, Chair. 70-; Chair. and Chief Exec. M.I.M. Holdings Ltd. 70-; Dir. Bank of New South Wales 71-, Thiess Holdings Ltd. 71-; mem. Senate Queensland Univ. 70-; Pres. Australian Mining Industry Council 74, 75; mem. Australasian Inst. of Mining and Metallurgy, Pres. 74.
M.I.M. Holdings Limited, G.P.O. Box 1433, Brisbane, Queensland 4001, Australia.

Forbes, Alexander James, M.C., D.PHIL.; Australian politician; b. Dec. 1923, Hobart, Tasmania; ed. Knox Grammar School, Sydney, St. Peter's Coll., Adelaide, Royal Mil. Coll., Duntroon, and Univ. of Oxford.
Served with 2nd Australian Mountain Battery, New Guinea and Bougainville 42; mem. British Occupation Forces, Japan 46, on attachment to British Army 46-47; student, Adelaide Univ. 47-50; a resident tutor, St. Mark's Coll., Adelaide 51; travelling scholarships until 54; Lecturer in Political Science, Univ. of Adelaide 54-56; Liberal mem. Parl. for Barker 56-; Minister for the Army and Minister Assisting the Treas., also responsible for Navy 63-64; Minister for Health 66-71, for Immigration 71-72; Opposition Spokesman on Defence 73-Dec. 75; mem. Council, Australian Nat. Univ. 61-63; Pres. S. Australia Branch, Australian Inst. of Int. Affairs 60-62.
Walkerville, Adelaide, S. Australia, Australia.

Ford, John Archibald, C.M.G., M.C., M.A. (OXON.); British diplomatist; b. 19 Feb. 1922, Newcastle-under-Lyme; ed. St. Michael's Coll. Tenbury, Sedbergh School, Oriel Coll. Oxford.
Served in Royal Artillery 42-46; joined Foreign Service 47; Third Sec., British Legation Budapest 49-52, Third Sec. and Resident Clerk, Foreign Office 52-54, Private Sec. to Perm. Under-Sec. of State 54-56; Consul, San Francisco 56-59; seconded to Treasury 59; attended course at Admin. Staff Coll. Henley 59; First Sec. and Head of Chancery, Bahrain 59-61; Asst., Foreign Office Personnel Dept. 61-63; Head of Establishment and Org. Dept., Diplomatic Service 64-66; Counsellor (Commercial), Rome 66-70; Asst. Under-Sec., F.C.O. 70-71; Consul Gen. New York and Dir.-Gen. British Trade Devt. in U.S.A. 70-75; Amb. to Indonesia May 75-.
British Embassy, Jalan M. H. Thamrin 75, Jakarta, Indonesia; Foreign and Commonwealth Office (Jakarta), London, S.W.1, England.

Forrest, Sir James Alexander, Kt.; Australian industrialist; b. 10 March 1905, Kerang, Victoria; ed. Melbourne Univ.
Partner, Hedderwick Fookes & Alston, Solicitors 33-70, Consultant 70-73; served R.A.A.F. and Dept. Aircraft Production 42-45; Chair. Australian Consolidated Industries Ltd. 53-, Nat. Bank of Australasia Ltd. 59-, Chase-N.B.A. Group Ltd. 69-, Alcoa of Australia Ltd. 70-; Dir. Australian Mutual Provident Soc. 61-, Chair. Victorian Branch Board 57-; Dir. Western Mining Corpn. Ltd. 70-; mem. Council Monash Univ. 61-71, Royal Children's Hosp. Research Foundation and Victoria Law Foundation.
19th Floor, AMP Tower, 535 Bourke Street, Melbourne, Victoria 3000; Home: 11 Russell Street, Toorak, Victoria 3142, Australia.

Fou Ts'ong; Chinese pianist; b. 10 March 1934; ed. Shanghai and Warsaw.
First performance, Shanghai 53, concerts in Eastern Europe and U.S.S.R. 53-58; London debut 59, concerts in Europe, North and South America, Australia and Far East.
28 Rosecroft Avenue, London, N.W.3, England.

Frame Clutha, Janet Paterson; New Zealand writer; b. 1924; ed. Oamaru North School, Waitaki Girls' High School, Dunedin Training Coll. and Otago Univ.
Hubert Church Award for New Zealand Prose; New Zealand Scholarship in Letters 64, Burns Fellow Otago Univ. Dunedin.
Publs. *Lagoon* 51, *Owls do Cry* 57, *Faces in the Water* 61, *The Edge of the Alphabet* 62, *Scented Gardens for the Blind* 63, *The Reservoir* (stories), *Snowman, Snowman* (fables), *The Adaptable Man* 65, *A State of Siege* 67, *The Pocket Mirror* (poetry), *The Rainbirds* 68, *Intensive Care* 71, *Daughter Buffalo* (novel) 72.

Fraser, (John) Malcolm, M.A. (OXON.); Australian politician; b. 21 May 1930; ed. Melbourne Grammar School and Oxford Univ.
Member Joint Parl. Cttee. of Foreign Affairs 62-66; Chair. Govt. Members' Defence Cttee.; Sec. Wool Cttee.; mem. Council of Australian Nat. Univ., Canberra 64-66; Minister for the Army 66-68; Minister for Educ. and Science 68-69, 71-72, for Defence 69-71; Leader Liberal Party March 75-; Prime Minister Nov. 75-.
Parliament House, Canberra, A.C.T., Australia.

Fraser, William Alex; New Zealand politician; b. 28 July 1924, Dunedin; ed. King Edward Technical Coll., Dunedin, Seddon Memorial Technical Coll., Auckland.
Joined R.N.Z.A.F. 43; mem. Parl. for St. Kilda 57-; held office in Dunedin South Branch of Labour Party; Dunedin City Councillor 53-56; Pres. Associated Trustee Savings Bank of N.Z. 63-66; Minister of Housing 72-74, of Defence Sept. 74-Nov. 75.
Parliament Buildings, Wellington; Home: 141 Surrey Street, Forbury, Dunedin, New Zealand.

Freeman, H.E. Cardinal James Darcy; Australian ecclesiastic; b. 19 Nov. 1907, Sydney; ed. Christian Brothers' High School, Sydney, St. Columba's Coll., Springwood and St. Patrick's Coll., Manly.

Ordained Priest 30; Private Sec. to H.E. Cardinal Gilroy, Archbishop of Sydney 40-46; Auxiliary Bishop of Sydney 57; Bishop of Armidale 68; Archbishop of Sydney 71-; created Cardinal March 73; Knight of the Holy Sepulchre.
St. Mary's Cathedral, Sydney, N.S.W., Australia.
Telephone: 232-3788.

Freer, Warren Wilfred; New Zealand politician; b. 27 Dec. 1920; ed. Auckland Grammar School.
Journalist 36-43; mem. Parl. for Mount Albert 47-; Minister of Trade and Industry, of Energy Resources 72-Nov. 75.
Parliament Buildings, Wellington, New Zealand.

Fujimoto, Ichiro, B.ENG.; Japanese iron and steel executive; b. 21 Jan. 1909; ed. Tokyo Univ.
Joined Kawasaki Dockyard Co., Ltd. 32, Man. Rolling Dept., Fukiai Works 45; Dir. Kawasaki Steel Corpn. and Asst. Gen. Man. of Fukiai Works 53-55, Gen. Man. of Fukiai Works 55-57; Man. Dir. Kawasaki Steel Corpn. 57-62, Senior Man. Dir. 62-64, Exec. Vice-Pres. 64-66, Pres. July 66-; Hattori Award for contribution to devt. of Japanese iron and steel industry 64.
Kawasaki Steel Corporation, Kitahonchodori, Fukiyaku, Kobe, Japan.

Fujioka, Shingo; Japanese oil executive; b. 27 June 1901; ed. Keio Univ. Tokyo.
Director and Gen. Man. Kawasaki Refinery, Mitsubishi Oil Co. Ltd. 50-55, Man. Dir. Mitsubishi Oil Co. Ltd. 55-61, Pres. 61-; mem. Cttee. World Petroleum Conf. 61-, Petroleum Deliberative Council 63-; Chair. Japan Petroleum Asscn.; Blue Ribbon Award 63.
Mitsubishi Oil Co. Ltd., 1 Shiba-Kotohiracho, Minato-ku, Tokyo 105, Japan.

Fujisaki, Akira, LL.B.; Japanese business executive; b. 1 May 1917, Kagoshima; ed. Tokyo Imperial Univ.
Joined Sumitomo Mining Co. Ltd. (later Sumitomo Metal Mining Co. Ltd.) 41, Controller 64, Dir. 67, Man. Dir. 70, Pres. 73-.
Sumitomo Metal Mining Co. Ltd., 11-3, 5-chome, Shimbashi Minato-ku, Tokyo; Home: 2-7-14, Nishi-Kamakura, Kamakura-shi, Kanagawa Prefecture, Japan.
Telephone: 03-434-2211 (Office); 0467-32-6233 (Home).

Fujisawa, Tokusaburo; Japanese banker; b. 13 Sept. 1907; ed. Tokyo Univ. of Commerce.
Bank of Japan 30-62, Chief of Admin. Dept. 52-54, of Foreign Exchange Dept. 54-56, Bank of Japan Rep., New York 56-58, Chief of Bank Relations and Supervision Dept. 58-59, Dir. Bank of Japan, concurrently Man. Osaka Branch 59-62; Vice-Pres. the Export-Import Bank of Japan 62-70; Pres. Tokyo Small Business Investment Co. 70-.
Office: Tokyo Small Business Investment Co., 2-47 Kabuto-cho, Nihonbashi-ku, Tokyo; Home: 13-10, No. 3 Naka-ochiai, Shinzyuku-ku, Tokyo, Japan.
Telephone: 952-0760.

Fujiyama, Aiichiro; Japanese businessman and politician; b. 1897; ed. Keio Univ.
Pres. Dai Nippon Sugar Manufacturing Co. 34, and Nitto Chemical Industry 37; Pres. Japan Air Lines 51, Adviser 53-; Pres. Japan and Tokyo Chambers of Commerce 51-57; Foreign Minister 57-60; mem. Council, Int. Chamber of Commerce 54-; Dir. Int. Telegraph and Telephone Co. 53-; Pres. Japan Fed. UNESCO Asscns. 51-; Pres. Advertising Fed. 53-; Pres. Society for Economic Co-operation in Asia 54-61; Minister of Foreign Affairs 57-60; mem. House of Reps. 58-; State Minister in charge of Econ. Planning Board 61-62, 65-66; Pres. Asscn. for the Promotion of Int. Trade 73-.
Publs. *Shacho gurashi Sanju-nen* 52, *Okyaku-shobai* 53, *Kuchibeni-kara kikansha-made* 53.
21-1-1, Shirogane-dai, Minato-ku, Tokyo, Japan.

Fukuda, Hajime; Japanese politician; b. 1902; ed. Tokyo Univ.
Reporter, Political Editor, Kyodo News Service; mem. House of Reps. for Fukui Pref. 49-; fmr. Parl. Vice-Minister of Labour; Minister of Int. Trade and Industry 62, for Home Affairs 72-73, for Home Affairs, Chair. Nat. Public Safety Comm., Dir.-Gen. Hokkaido Devt. Agency Dec. 74-; Liberal-Democratic Party.
c/o House of Representatives, Tokyo, Japan.

Fukuda, Takeo; Japanese politician; b. 14 Jan. 1905; ed. Tokyo Imperial Univ.
With Ministry of Finance 29-50, Deputy Vice-Minister 45-46, Dir. of Banking Bureau 46-47, Dir. Budget Bureau 47-50; mem. House of Reps. 52-; Chair. Policy Board, Liberal-Democratic Party, Sec.-Gen. 66-68; fmr. Minister of Agriculture and Forestry; Minister of Finance 65-Dec. 66, 68-71; Minister of Foreign Affairs 71-July 72; Minister of State, Dir.-Gen. Admin. Management Agency Dec. 72-73; Minister of Finance Nov. 73-74, Deputy Prime Minister and Dir. Econ. Planning Agency Dec. 74-.
Office of the Director, Economic Planning Agency, Tokyo; 1-247 Nozawa-machi, Setagaya-ku, Tokyo, Japan.

Fukuhara, Nobusaku, D.SC.; Japanese business executive; b. 12 Nov. 1911, Ginza, Chuo-ku, Tokyo; ed. Yokohama Technical Coll. (now Yokohama Nat. Univ.) and Duke Univ., U.S.A.
Shiseido Co. Ltd. 32-, Dir. 52, Man. Dir. 62, Senior Man. Dir. 73, Pres. 75-; Dir. Fed. of Econ. Orgs. 75-; Exec. Dir. Japan Fed. of Employers' Asscns. 75-; Counsellor, Japan Chemical Industry Asscn. 75-; mem. Presidium, Int. Fed. of Socs. of Cosmetic Chemists 73-.
Shiseido Company Ltd., 7-5-5 Ginza, Chuo-ku, Tokyo; Home: 2-18-5 Minami-senzoku, Ohta-ku, Tokyo, Japan.
Telephone: 572-5111 (Office); 727-3902 (Home).

Funahashi, Masao; Japanese business executive; b. 3 May 1913, Aichi Pref.; ed. Tokyo Univ.
Manager of Purchasing Dept., Furukawa Electric Co. Ltd. 59, of Finance and Accounting Dept. 61, Man. Dir. 68, Exec. Dir. 71, Vice-Pres. 73, Pres. 74-.
6-1, Marunouchi 2-chome, Chiyoda-ku, Tokyo, Japan.
Telephone Tokyo (03) 213-0811 (Office).

G

Gajendragadkar, Pralhad Balacharaya, M.A., LL.D.; Indian jurist; b. 16 March 1901, Satara, Maharashtra; ed. Karnatak Coll. Dharwar, Deccan Coll. Poona, Law Coll. Poona, Bombay Univ.
Appellate Side Bar, Bombay 26-; Editor *Hindu Law Quarterly*; judge Bombay High Court 45-57, Supreme Court of India 57-64, Chief Justice 64-66; Vice-Chancellor Bombay Univ. 66-71; Hon. Chair. Law Comm. 71-; Chair. and Pres. of many bodies; mem. Univ. Grants Comm. and various bodies; numerous lectures; Sir Jehangir Ghandy Medal for Industrial Peace 69; Padma Vibhushan 72; Hon. LL.D. (Karnatak).
Publs. Sanskrit text and English trans. of Nanda Pandit's *Dattaka Mimamsa, Law, Liberty and Social Justice, Kashmir—Retrospect and Prospect, Jawaharlal Nehru—a Glimpse of the Man and His Teachings, The Constitution of India—its Philosophy and Basic Postulates, Secularism and the Constitution of India.*
Law Commission, Shastri Bhavan, Dr. Rajendra Prasad Road, New Delhi 1; Home: 12 Tughlak Road, New Delhi, India.

Gandar, Leslie Walter; New Zealand sheep farmer and politician; b. 26 Jan. 1919, Wellington; ed. Wellington Coll. and Victoria Univ., Wellington.
R.N.Z.A.F. 40-44; sheep farming 45-; mem. Pohangina

County Council 52-69, Chair. 59-69; mem. M'tu Catchment Board 56-68; mem. Massey Univ. Council 63, Chancellor 70-75; Minister of Educ., Science and Technology Dec. 75-. Parliament Buildings, Wellington; Home: Moorlands, No. 6 RD, Feilding, New Zealand.

Gandhi, Indira Priyadarshini; Indian politician; b. 19 Nov. 1917, Allahabad; ed. in India, Switzerland, Visva Bharati Univ., Somerville Coll., Oxford Univ.
Daughter of late Pandit Jawaharlal Nehru; founded Vanar Sena, a children's organization to aid Congress non-cooperation movement 29; joined Congress 38; imprisoned for thirteen months 42; hostess for her father 46-64; worked in riot areas under Mahatma Gandhi 47; Minister for Information and Broadcasting, New Delhi 64-66, Prime Minister 66-, Chair. Planning Comm. 66-, Minister of Atomic Energy 67-, of External Affairs 67-69, of Finance 69-70, of Home Affairs 70-73, of Information and Broadcasting 71-74, of Space 72-, of Electronics 73-, of Planning Jan. 75-, of Defence Nov.-Dec. 75; mem. Rajya Sabha 64-67, mem. Lok Sabha 67-, Leader, Congress Parl. Party 67-; Founder-Pres. Bal Sahayog, New Delhi; Pres. Training Centre for Vagrant Boys, Allahabad; Vice-Pres. Indian Council of Child Welfare; Chair. Standing Cttee. Children's Film Soc.; mem. Standing Cttee. Cen. Social Welfare Board, Children's Book Trust; mem. Working Cttee., All-India Congress Cttee., Pres. Women's Dept., mem. Cen. Electoral Board, Youth Advisory Board; Pres. All-India Congress Party 59-60; mem. UNESCO Exec. Board 60; Deputy Pres. Int. Union of Child Welfare; Howland Memorial Prize, Yale Univ. 60; Hon. D.Litt. (Agra), Hon. D.C.L. (Oxford) 71, Hon. D.Sc. (U.S.S.R. Acad. of Sciences) 76; Bharat Ratna Award 71.
Publ. *Indira: the Speeches and Reminiscences of Indira Gandhi* 75.
Office of the Prime Minister, New Delhi 11, India.

Ganilau, Ratu Sir Penaia Kanatabatu, K.B.E., C.M.G., C.V.O., D.S.O., E.D.; Fijian politician; b. 28 July 1918; ed. Queen Victoria School, Fiji.
Clerk, Fiji Civil Service 37-41; Capt. 4th Battalion, Fiji Mil. Forces 40-46; Asst. Rehabilitation Officer 46; District Officer in Overseas Colonial Service 48-53; Fiji Mil. Forces, Malaya 53-56; C.O. 1st Battalion, Malaya 56, Roko 57; mem. Legis. Council 58-63; Sec. for Fijian Affairs 65-70; Minister for Home Affairs 70-72; Leader of Govt. Business in the Senate 70-72; Minister for Communications, Works and Tourism 72-75; Deputy Prime Minister 73-; Minister of Home Affairs 75-.
Ministry of Home Affairs, Suva, Fiji.

Gapurov, Mukhamednazar; Soviet politician; b. 1922; ed. Chardzhou Pedagogic Inst.
Soviet Army 41-43; Young Communist League and Party work 43-57; mem. C.P.S.U. 44-; First Sec. Chardzhou District C.P. Turkmenian S.S.R. 57-61; Chair. of Council of Ministers and Minister of Foreign Affairs of Turkmenian S.S.R. 63-69; First Sec. Cen. Cttee. of C.P. Turkmenian S.S.R. 69-; mem. Presidium Cen. Cttee. C.P. Turkmenian S.S.R.; Deputy to Supreme Soviet of the U.S.S.R. 62-; mem. Planning and Budgetary Comm., Soviet of the Union, U.S.S.R. Parl. Group; Alternate mem. Cen. Cttee. C.P.S.U. 66-71, mem. 71-.
Central Committee of the Communist Party, Ashkhabad, Turkmenian S.S.R., U.S.S.R.

Garland, Ransley Victor, M.P., B.A., F.C.A., F.C.I.S.; Australian politician; b. 5 May 1934, Perth; ed. Hale School and Univ. of W. Australia.
Councillor, Claremont Town Council 63-70; Deputy Mayor of Claremont 68-69; Senior Vice-Pres. Liberal Party of W. Australia 65-69; mem. House of Reps. April 69-; Chair. Taxation Cttee. 70-71, 73-75; mem. Parl. Cttee. on Pharmaceutical Benefits 70; Minister of State for Supply 71-72; Minister assisting the Treas. 72; Acting Minister for Customs and Excise 72; Chief Opposition Whip 74-75; Minister for Posts and Telecommunications and Minister Assisting the Treas. Dec. 75-Feb. 76; leader del. to IPU Conf. 71; mem. Parl. Cttees. on Prices, Standing Orders and Privileges 73, 74, 75; Parl. Adviser to Mission to UN Gen. Assembly 73.
Parliament House, Canberra, A.C.T. 2600; 191 St. George's Terrace, Perth, W.A. 6000; Richardson Avenue, Claremont, W.A. 6010, Australia.
Telephone: (092) 22-2400; (092) 31-3632.

Gates, Thomas Sovereign, Jr.; American politician; b. 10 April 1906; ed. Univ. of Pennsylvania.
Associated with Drexel and Co. 28-, partner 40-53; Under-Sec. for Navy 54-57; Sec. for Navy 57-59; Sec. of Defence 59-61; Naval Reserve Officer 42-45; Chair. Exec. Cttee. Morgan Guaranty Trust 61-62, 65-68, 69-71, Pres. 62-65, Dir. 71-; Head of U.S. Liaison Office, People's Republic of China 76-; Dir. Bethlehem Steel Corpn. 70-, Campbell Soup Co., Cities Service Co., Gen. Electric Co., Insurance Co. of North America, Scott Paper Co. and Smith Kline & French Laboratories; Trustee, Univ. of Pa. and Acad. of Political Science; Bronze Star, Yale; Hon. LL.D. (Columbia and Yale Univs., and Univ. of Pa.).
United States Liaison Office, Peking, People's Republic of China; Home: Mill Race Farm, Devon, Pa. 19333, U.S.A.

Ghosh, Amalananda, M.A.; Indian archaeologist; b. 3 March 1910; ed. A.B. High School, Banaras, Queen's Coll., Banaras, Univs. of Allahabad and London.
Assistant Supt., Archaeological Survey of India 37-44, Supt. 44-50; Deputy Dir.-Gen. for Exploration, Archaeological Survey of India 50-52; Joint Dir.-Gen. of Archaeology in India, Archaeological Survey of India 52-53, Dir.-Gen. 53-68; UNESCO Consultant on Archaeology to Govts. of Qatar 68, Bahrain 68, Saudi Arabia 69, Yemen Arab Republic 70; Fellow Indian Inst. of Advanced Study 68-71; Visiting Prof. of Indian Culture, Univ. of Indonesia 73-74; Hon. mem. Int. Congress for Prehistoric and Protohistoric Sciences; Corresp. mem. Int. Council on Museums, Int. Cttee. on Monuments, Artistic and Historical Sites and Archaeological Excavation; Vice-Pres. Royal India, Pakistan and Ceylon Soc., London; Hon. Fellow, Soc. of Antiquities of London; Fellow, Deutsches Archäologisches Inst.; Hon. Corresp., Archaeological Survey of India; Padma Sri 62.
Bankuli, Gurgaon Road, New Delhi 110037, India.
Telephone: 39-2318.

Ghosh, Tushar Kanti, B.A.; Indian journalist; b. 21 Sept. 1898; ed. Calcutta Univ.
Editor *Amrita Bazar Patrika*; former Pres. Indian Journalists' Asscn.; Pres. Andhra Journalists' Conf., Guntur 37; All-India Printers' Conf., Poona 39; former Pres. Indian and Eastern Newspaper Society, All-India Newspaper Editors' Conf., United Press of India; Chair. Press Trust of India; founder *Jugantar*, Calcutta, *Northern Indian Patrika, Allahabad* and *Amrita* (Bengali weekly); Chair. Commonwealth Press Union, Indian Section; mem. Exec. Cttee., Int. Press Inst.; Padma Bhushan 64.
Amrita Bazar Patrika City Office, 3 Chittaranjan Avenue, Calcutta 13, India.
Telephone: 23-2838.

Giap, General Vo Nguyen (*see* Vo Nguyen Giap, General).

Gilroy, His Eminence Cardinal Sir Norman Thomas, K.B.E.; Australian ecclesiastic; b. 22 Jan. 1896; ed. St. Columba's Coll., Springwood, and Urban Coll., Rome.
Ordained priest 23; Bishop of Port Augusta 34-37; Coadjutor Archbishop of Sydney 37-40; Archbishop of Sydney, Metropolitan 40-71; retd. Aug. 71; created Cardinal Feb. 46.
St. John Vianney Villa, Market Street, Randwick, N.S.W. 2031, Australia.

Giri, Dr. Tulsi; Nepalese politician; b. Sept. 1926.
Deputy Minister of Foreign Affairs 59; Minister of Village Development 60; Minister without Portfolio 60; Minister of Foreign Affairs, the Interior, Public Works and Communications 61; Vice-Chair. Council of Ministers and Minister of Palace Affairs 62; Chair. Council of Ministers and Minister of Foreign Affairs 62-65; mem. Royal Advisory Cttee. 69-74; Adviser to the King 74-; Prime Minister, Minister of Palace Affairs and Defence Dec. 75-.
Jawakpurdham, District Dhanuka, Nepal.

Giri, Varahagiri Venkata; Indian fmr. head of state, lawyer and diplomatist; b. 10 Aug. 1894, Berhampur; ed. Nat. Univ. of Ireland.
Trade Union leader for many years; fmr. Gen. Sec. and Pres. All-India Railwaymen's Fed.; twice Pres. All-India Trade Union Congress; Indian workers' del. to Int. Labour Conference Geneva 27; workers' rep. Second Round Table Conf., London 31; mem. Central Legislative Assembly 34-37; Minister of Labour Industries, Commerce and Co-operation, Madras 37-39, 46-47; High Commr. for India in Ceylon 47-51; Minister of Labour, Govt. of India 52-54 (resigned Sept. 54); Gov. Uttar Pradesh 57-60, Kerala 60-65, Mysore 65-67; Vice-Pres. of India 67-69, Acting Pres. May-Aug. 69, Pres. 69-74; state visits to numerous countries in Asia, Europe and Africa; Pres. Indian Conf. of Social Work 58-60; Hon. D.Litt. (Banaras Hindu, Lucknow and Andhra Univs.); Hon. LL.D. (Agra, Moscow, Bulgaria and Bratislava Univs.).
Publs. *Industrial Relations, Labour Problems in Indian Industry, Jobs For Our Millions.*
Girija, 1 Third Block, Jayanagar, Bangalore 56011, India.

Glenn, Sir (Joseph Robert) Archibald, Kt., O.B.E., B.C.E., F.I.E. (AUST.), M.I.CHEM.E.; Australian businessman; b. 24 May 1911, Sale, Victoria; ed. Scotch Coll., Melbourne, Melbourne and Harvard Univs.
Chief Engineer ICIANZ (now ICI Australia Ltd.) 47-49, Gen. Man. 49-53, Man. Dir. 53-73, Chair. 63-73; Dir. Imperial Chemical Industries Ltd. 70-75; Chair. Fibremakers Ltd. 63-73, IMI Australia Ltd. 73-, IC Insurance Australia Ltd. 73-; Dir. Alcoa Australia Ltd. 73-, Hill Samuel Australia 73-, Tioxide Australia Ltd. 73-; Dir. Bank of New South Wales 67-; Chair. Council, Scotch Coll.; Chancellor, La Trobe Univ., Melbourne 66-72; Gov. Atlantic Inst. of Int. Affairs.
ICI House, P.O. Box 4311, Melbourne 3001; Home: 3 Heyington Place, Toorak 3142, Victoria, Australia.

Goh Keng Swee, B.A., B.SC.(ECON.), PH.D.; Singapore politician; b. 6 Oct. 1918; ed. Raffles Coll., London Univ.
Vice-Chairman People's Action Party; elected Legislative Assembly from Kreta Ayer Div. and Minister for Finance 59-65; initiated Singapore's industrialization plan, the establishment of Econ. Devt. Board; Minister of Defence 65-67; Minister of Finance 67-70; Minister of Defence 70-, concurrently Deputy Prime Minister 72-; mem. Governing Council, Asian Inst. for Econ. Devt. and Planning, Bangkok 63-66; Hon. Fellow of the London School of Econs.; Ramon Magsaysay Award for Govt. Service 72; Order of Sikatuna, Philippines.
Publ. *Economics of Modernization and Other Essays* 72.
Ministry of Defence, Minden Road, Tanglin, Singapore 10.

Gokhale, Hari Ramachandra; Indian politician; b. 1917; ed. at Baroda and Bombay.
Former political worker and trade unionist; subsequently practised law and was Judge of Bombay High Court 62-66; mem. Lok Sabha 71-; Minister of Law and Justice 71-, of Company Affairs 74-.
Shastri Bhavan, Dr. Rajendra Prasad Road, New Delhi 1; and 12 Janpath, New Delhi 11, India.

Gooneratne, Tilak Eranga, B.A.; Ceylonese civil servant and diplomatist; b. 27 March 1919; ed. St. John's Coll., Panadura, Sri Lanka, Ceylon Univ., and Ceylon Law Coll.
Joined Ceylon Civil Service 43; Asst. Sec. Ministry of External Affairs 47-51; Govt. Agent, Trincomalee 51-54, Matra 54-56; Registrar Gen. Marriages, Births and Deaths 56-58; Dir.-Gen. of Broadcasting and Dir. of Information, Ceylon 58-60; Commr. Co-operative Devt. 60-63; Acting Perm. Sec. Ministry of Commerce and Trade 63; Dir. of Econ. Affairs 63; Deputy Sec. to Treasury 63-65; Pres. Colombo Plan Council for Technical Co-operation in South and South East Asia 64-65; Ceylon Del. to UN Gen. Assembly 64-65; Deputy Sec.-Gen. Commonwealth Secr., London 65-70; High Commr. in U.K. 70-75; Amb. to EEC (also accred. to Belgium) 75-.
Publs. *An Historical Outline of the Development of the Marriage and Divorce Laws of Ceylon, An Historical Outline of the Development of the Marriage and Divorce Laws Applicable to Muslims in Ceylon, Fifty Years of Co-operative Development in Ceylon.*
Embassy of Sri Lanka, 21-22 avenue des Arts, 1040 Brussels, Belgium.

Goonetilleke, Sir Oliver Ernest, G.C.M.G., K.C.V.O., K.B.E., K.ST.J., B.A., LL.D., F.R.S.A., F.R.E.S.; Ceylonese politician; b. 20 Oct. 1892; ed. London Univ.
Assistant Auditor for Railways, Ceylon 21; Asst. Colonial Auditor 24-31; Colonial Auditor 31; Auditor-Gen. July 31; Ceylon Govt. Del. to Int. Railway Congress, Cairo 33; Chair. Retrenchment Comm. Ceylon 38; Civil Defence and Food Commr. 42; mem. Ceylon War Council 42; Financial Sec. Govt. of Ceylon 45-47; Home Minister 47; High Commr. in U.K. 48-51; Minister of Home Affairs 51-52, of Agriculture and Food 52-53, of Civil Defence 53, also Leader of the Senate; Minister of Finance 54; Gov.-Gen. of Ceylon 54-62; Vice-Pres. Royal Inst. of Int. Affairs; Dir. and Chair. of numerous companies; Underwriting mem. Lloyd's, London; sentenced *in absentia* to four years' imprisonment Feb. 76.
14 Albion Gate, Hyde Park Place, London, W.2, England.

Gopal-Ayengar, Anekal Ramaswamiengar, M.SC., M.A., PH.D., F.A.SC., F.N.A.; Indian biologist; b. 1 Jan. 1909; ed. Univs. of Mysore and Toronto.
Lecturer in Botany, Mysore Univ. 33-38; Vincent Massey Fellow, Univ. of Toronto 38-39; Senior Instructor, Univ. of Toronto 41-45, Kettering Research Fellow, Barnard Skin and Cancer Hospital and Research Assoc., Washington Univ., St. Louis, Mo. 45-47; Chief Research Cytologist, Tata Memorial Hospital, Bombay 47-51; Head, A.E.C. Unit on Cell Biology 48-51; Senior Int. Research Fellow, Lady Tata Trust and Research Assoc., Chester Beatty Research Inst., London and Inst. for Cell Research, Karolinska Inst., Stockholm 51-53; Chief Scientific Officer and Head, Biological and Medical Divs., Atomic Energy Establishment, Trombay (AEET) 60-62; Dir. Biology Group (AEET) 62-67; Expert, Radiation Cttee. of World Health Org. (WHO) 58-73; mem. Int. Cttee. on Experimental Studies on Human Cancer, Comm. for Exptl. Oncology; Rep. for South-East Asia on Genetics Section of Int. Union of Biological Sciences (IUBS) and Int. Cell Research Org. 63-66; Chair. Nat. Cttee. for Biophysics 62-; Pres. Indian Soc. of Genetics and Plant Breeding 63-64 and Comm. on Radiation Biophysics of Int. Union for Pure and Applied Physics (IUPAP) 65-69; Associated with Int. Soc. for Cell Biology, New York Acad. of Sciences and American Assen. for Cancer Research; Dir. Bio-Medical Group 68-71; Emer. Dir. and Bio-Medical Adviser A.E.C. 71-; official of numerous scientific orgs.; Pres. Indian Assen. for Radiation Protection (IARP) 69-72; mem. Editorial Board *Radiation Botany* and *Biophysik*; Fellow, Indian Acad. of Sciences; J. H. Bhabha Prize 48; Padma Shri 67; D.Sc. h.c. (Mysore), Sc.D. h.c. (Hannover).
8B Atomic Energy Officers Apartments, Little Gibbs Road, Malabar Hill, Bombay 400006, India.

Gopalan, A. K., M.P.; Indian politician; b. 1 Oct. 1904, Mavilai, Cannanore; ed. Cannanore, Malabar and Kerala. Deputy Leader Communist Group in Parl. 57, Leader 52, 62, 67; Main Opposition Group Leader in Parl. 71; Sec. Nat. Council C.P. of India; Pres. All India Kisan (Peasants) Sabha; mem. Polit Bureau CPI(M), Exec. Cttee. of Trade Union Int. of Agricultural Forestry and Plantation Workers; Editor *New Kerala*; detained then released July 75.
Publs. *Kerala, Past and Present, Autobiography, I Saw a New World.*
4 Ashoka Road, New Delhi, India.
Telephone: 382870.

Gopallawa, William, M.B.E.; Ceylonese politician; b. 17 Sept. 1897, Dullewa, Matale; ed. Dharmarajah Coll., St. Anthony's Coll., Kandy and Law Coll., Colombo.
Enrolled as Proctor of Supreme Court 24; mem. and later Chair. Matale Urban Council 27-39; Municipal Comm. Kandy 39-52, Colombo 52-57; Amb. to People's Repub. of China 58-61, to U.S.A., Cuba and Mexico 61-62; Gov.-Gen. of Ceylon, March 62-72; Pres. Repub. of Sri Lanka 72-; Chancellor, Univ. of Sri Lanka; LL.D. (Univs. of Ceylon and Vidyalankara) 62; D.Litt. (Vidyodaya Univ.) 62.
President's House, Colombo, Sri Lanka.
Telephone: Colombo 27821.

Gordon, Hon. John Bowie (Peter); New Zealand politician; b. 1921, Stratford; ed. St. Andrew's Coll., Christchurch, Lincoln Coll.
R.N.Z.A.F. 41-44, mentioned in despatches; Pres. West Otago Branch Federated Farmers; mem. first Nat. Hydatids Council; Chair. Dir. of Heriot Transport 51-54; Dir. Farmers' Mutual Insurance 51-60, N.Z. Board Shaw Savill 56-60; toured U.K., Scandinavia and U.S. under Nuffield Scholarship 54; visited U.S. under U.S. State Dept. Foreign Leadership Award 64; M.P. for Clutha 60-; Minister of Transport and Railways 66-72, of Marine and Fisheries 72, of Labour and of State Services Dec. 75-; National Party.
Parliament House, Wellington, New Zealand.

Gorton, Rt. Hon. John Grey, P.C., M.P., M.A.; Australian politician; b. 9 Sept. 1911; ed. Geelong Grammar School and Brasenose Coll. Oxford.
Served Royal Australian Air Force during Second World War, severely wounded; Councillor Kerang Shire 47-52, Pres. of Shire 49-50; Senator for State of Victoria 49-68, Govt. Leader in Senate 67-68; Minister for Navy 58-63; Minister Assisting Minister for External Affairs 60-63; Minister-in-Charge of Commonwealth Scientific and Industrial Research Org. (C.S.I.R.O.) 62-68; Minister for Works and Minister-in-Charge of Commonwealth Activities in Educ. and Research 63-66; Minister for Interior 63-64, for Works 66-67; Minister for Educ. and Science 66-68; Prime Minister of Australia 68-71; Minister of Defence and Deputy Leader of Liberal Party March-Aug. 71; mem. House of Reps. 68-; mem. Parl. Liberal Party Executive until 75; Liberal Party Spokesman on Environment, Conservation and Urban and Regional Devt.; Deputy Chair. Parl. Joint Cttee. on Prices 73-74; Independent May 75-.
Parliament House, Canberra, A.C.T. 2600, Australia.

Gosse, Edmund Barr, M.A. (CANTAB.); Australian company director; b. 14 July 1915, Perth; ed. St. Peter's Coll., Adelaide, Trinity Hall, Cambridge.
Chairman, John Lysaght (Aust.) Ltd., 67-; Man. Lysaght's Works, Newcastle 53-63; Dir. Guest, Keen and Nettlefolds (Overseas) Ltd.; mem. Iron & Steel Inst., U.K.; Dir. ICI Australia Ltd.
27 Sutherland Crescent, Darling Point, N.S.W. 2027, Australia.

Grace, Sir John Te Herekiekie, K.B.E., M.V.O., J.P.; New Zealand farmer, company director and diplomatist; b. 28 July 1905; ed. Wanganui Technical Coll. and Te Aute Coll., Hawke's Bay.
Member N.Z. Geographic Board 52-70; mem. N.Z. Historic Places Trust 56-57; Vice-Pres. and Dominion Councillor N.Z. Nat. Party 59-64, 65-66; mem. Lake Rotoaira Trust 56-70; Vice-Pres. Wanganui Public Museum 60-61; mem. N.Z. Maori Purposes Fund Board 61-70, N.Z. Maori Educ. Board of Trustees 61-70, N.Z. Nature Conservation Council 63-70, N.Z. Adult Educ. Council 64-70, Taupo Forest Trust, N.Z. 68-70, Taupo Basins Reserves Cttee. 68-70; High Commr. in Fiji 70-74; mem. Lake Taupo Reserves Board 75-.
Publ. *Towharetoa.*
32 McFarlane Street, Wellington; Te Waka, Parapara Road, R.D. 3, Wanganui, New Zealand.

Gracias, H.E. Cardinal Valerian, D.D., M. AGG., J.P.; Indian ecclesiastic; b. 23 Oct. 1900; ed. St. Patrick's High School, Karachi, St. Joseph's Seminary, Mangalore, Papal Seminary, Kandy, and Gregorian Univ., Rome.
Secretary to the Archbishop 29-36; Chancellor of the Archdiocese 29; Editor *Messenger of the Sacred Heart* 35; Co-editor *The Examiner* 38; Rector of the Pro-Cathedral, Bombay 41; Titular Bishop of Tannis and Auxiliary to the Archbishop of Bombay 46-50; Archbishop of Bombay 50-; created Cardinal by Pope Pius XII 53; mem. Sacred Congregations for the Oriental Church, of Sacraments and De Propaganda Fide; fmr. Pres. Catholic Bishops' Conf. of India; mem. Council for Implementation of the Constitution on the Sacred Liturgy, and Comm. for Revision of Code of Canon Law and Secretariat for Non-Christians; awarded "Padma Vibhushan" by Pres. of India 66.
Publs. *Features of Christian Life, Heaven and Home, The Vatican and International Policy, The Decline of Public Morals: The Chief Duties of Christians as Citizens.*
Archbishop's House, Nathalal Parekh Marg, 400001 Bombay, India.
Telephone: 213131/2/3.

Grassby, Albert Jaime; Australian politician; b. 12 July 1926, Brisbane, Queensland; ed. schools in Australia, Univ. of California.
Specialist Officer, Information Dept., CSIRO 48; Specialist Officer, Agricultural Extension Service, N.S.W. 50; Exec. Officer, Irrigation Research and Extension Org., N.S.W. 53; mem. N.S.W. Parl. for Murrumbidgee 65-69; mem. House of Reps. for Riverina 69-74; Minister of Immigration 72-74; Special Govt. Adviser on Community Relations 74-75; Commr. for Community Relations 75-; Commdr. Order of Solidarity of the Repub. of Italy 70, Knight Grand Cross of Mil. Order of St. Agata of Paterno 74, Citation, Univ. of Santo Thomas (Philippines).
Publs. *Four Faces of Griffith* and several papers on population and immigration, irrigation and agricultural devt. in Australia.
Parliament House, Canberra, A.C.T.; Home: Yambil Street, Griffith, N.S.W., Australia.

Green, Marshall, B.A.; American diplomatist; b. 27 Jan. 1916, Holyoke, Mass.; ed. Groton School, and Yale Univ.
Private Sec. to American Amb. to Japan 39-41; Lieut. U.S. Navy 42-45; U.S. Foreign Service 45-; Third Sec., Wellington, N.Z. 46-47; Japanese Desk Officer, State Dept., Washington 47-50; Second, later First Sec., Stockholm 50-55; Nat. War Coll. 55-56; Policy Planning Adviser, Far East, State Dept. 56-59; Minister-Counsellor, Seoul 60-61; Consul-Gen., Hong Kong 61-63; Deputy Asst. Sec. of State, Far East 63-65; Amb. to Indonesia 65-69; Asst. Sec. of State for E. Asian and Pacific Affairs 69-73; Amb. to

Australia 73-; Meritorious Service Award, Nat. Civil Service League Career Service Award.
American Embassy, Yarralumla, Canberra, A.C.T. 2600, Australia; and c/o Department of State, Washington, D.C. 20520, U.S.A.

Greenwood, Ivor John, Q.C., LL.B.; Australian politician; b. 15 Nov. 1926, Melbourne; ed. Scotch Coll., Melbourne.
Admitted to Victorian Bar 51; Vice-Pres. Victorian State Exec. of Liberal Party 66-68; Senator from Victoria 68-; Minister for Health 71; Attorney Gen. 71-72; Deputy Leader of the Opposition, Senate 72-75; Attorney-Gen. and Minister for Police and Customs Nov.-Dec. 75; Minister for Environment, Housing and Community Devt. Dec. 75-July 76; Deputy Leader of the Govt. in the Senate; Liberal.
The Senate, Canberra, A.C.T.; and 8 Marlborough Avenue, Camberwell, Victoria 3124, Australia.

Gresford, Guy Barton, B.SC., F.R.A.C.I.; Australian science administrator; b. 7 March 1916; ed. Hobart High School, Royal Melbourne Technical Coll., Trinity Coll., Univ. of Melbourne, and School of Administration, Harvard Univ.
Officer in Charge, Australian Scientific Liaison Office, London 42-46; Asst. Sec. (Australian) Commonwealth Scientific and Industrial Research Org. 47-52, Sec. (Physical Sciences) 52-59, Sec. 59-66; Dir. for Science and Technology, UN 66-73; Sec. UN Advisory Cttee. for Application of Science and Technology to Devt. 66-73; Senior Adviser on Science, Technology and the Environment, Australian Dept. of Foreign Affairs 73-; Harkness Fellow Commonwealth Fund of New York 57.
Department of Foreign Affairs, Canberra, A.C.T., Australia.

Grover, Amar Nath, M.A., LL.B.; Indian judge; b. 15 Feb. 1912, Shwebo (British Upper Burma); ed. Univs. of Punjab, Lahore and Cambridge and Middle Temple, London.
Called to Bar 36; Barrister, High Court, Lahore 36-47, later at High Court of E. Punjab, Simla and Chandigarh; Judge, High Court, Punjab 57-68; mem. Punjab Bar Council 54-57; Judge, Supreme Court of India 68-73; now working as a consultant; mem. Exec. Cttee. of Int. Law Assen., Indian Law Inst.; mem. World Peace Through Law Centre.
Publs. several articles on various branches of law.
132 Sundirnagar, New Delhi 110003, India.
Telephone: 70 118.

Guerrero, León María; Philippine diplomatist; b. 24 March 1915; ed. Ateneo de Manila, Philippine Law School, Manila.
Associate Editor, Philippines Free Press 35-40; with Office of Solicitor-Gen. 40; served army 40-45; Chief of Protocol, Dept. of Foreign Affairs 46; Legal and Legislative Counsel, Philippines Senate 48; Under-Sec. of Foreign Affairs 54; Ambassador to Great Britain (concurrently Minister to Norway, Sweden, Finland and Denmark) 54-61, to Spain 61-66, to India (concurrently to Nepal, Afghanistan) 66-72, to Mexico (concurrently to Colombia, Costa Rica, Ecuador, El Salvador, Guatemala, Honduras, Nicaragua, Panama and Venezuela) 73-; Chair. Philippine Trade Mission to Fed. Repub. of Germany 55; Vice-Chair. Int. Sugar Council 59, Chair. 60; Vice-Chair. Philippine Del. to UNCTAD 68; Grand Cross Knights of Rizal (Philippines), Dannebrog (Denmark), Lion of Finland, Order of Isabel la Católica (Spain).
Publs. *Twilight in Tokyo* 46, *Passion and Death of the USAFFE* 47, *Report from Europe* 50, *The Young Rizal* 52, *Our Foreign Relations* 52, *Alternatives for Asians* 57, *An Asian on Asia* 58, *Noli Me Tangere* (translation) 60, *El Filibusterismo* (translation) 61, *El Si y El No* 63, *The First Filipino* 63, *The Philippine Revolution* (trans.) 69, *Prisoners of History* 72.
Philippine Embassy, 125 Sierra Torrecillas, Lomas de Chapultepec, Mexico 10, D.F., Mexico.

Guha, Phulrenu, D.LITT.; Indian social and political worker; b. 13 Aug. 1911; ed. Calcutta and Paris Univs.
Participated in Freedom Movement from early days; social worker for over forty-five years; Sec. United Council for Relief and Welfare; Gen. Sec. and Vice-Pres. All India Women's Conf.; Chair. W. Bengal State Social Welfare Advisory Board; Pres. India Council for Child Welfare; Chair. Cttee. on Status of Women in India; mem. Rajya Sabha 64-70; Union Minister of State for Social Welfare 67-70; mem. Cottage Industries Cen. Social Welfare Board; Pres. Karmakutir, W. Bengal Assen. for Social Health, S. Calcutta District Congress Cttee. (CC); Chair. W. Bengal Council for Child Welfare; mem. All-India CC, W. Bengal Pradesh CC; Adviser Indian Inst. of Social Welfare and Business Management; attended many seminars and confs.
Publs. articles on social problems, lectures on social and political problems.
55/5 Purna Das Road, Calcutta 29, India.

Guise, Sir John, G.C.M.G., K.B.E.; Papua New Guinea politician; b. 29 Aug. 1914, Milne Bay; ed. Anglican School, Dogura, Milne Bay Province.
Sergeant-Major, Royal Papua New Guinea Constabulary 46-57; mem. Legis. Council 61-63, House of Assembly 64-75, Speaker 68-71; Deputy Chief Minister 72-75, Minister of the Interior, later of Agriculture 72-75; Gov.-Gen. of Papua New Guinea Sept. 75-; Hon. LL.D.
Government House, Konedobu, Port Moresby, Papua New Guinea.

Gujral, Inder Kumar, M.A.; Indian politician and diplomatist; b. 4 Dec. 1919, Jhelum (now in Pakistan); ed. Forman Christian Coll. and Hailey Coll. of Commerce in Lahore, Punjab Univ.
Jailed for participation in freedom fight 30-31 (and again during Quit India movement 42); helped nat. effort for rehabilitation of displaced persons; Minister of State for Communications and Parl. Affairs 67-69, for Information, Communications and Broadcasting 69-71, for Works, Housing and Urban Devt. 71-72, for Information and Broadcasting 72-75, for Planning 75-76; Amb. to U.S.S.R. April 76-; mem. Rajya Sabha 70-76; Vice-Pres. New Delhi Municipal Cttee. for five years; helped organize Citizens Cttee. for Civil Defence; mem. All India Cen. Citizens Council, Sec. Resources Sub-Cttee.; mem. All India Congress Cttee.; rep. at IPU Conf. in Canberra; Founder-Pres. Delhi Arts Theatre; Treas. Fed. of Film Socs. of India; Vice-Pres. Lok Kalyan Samiti; Co-Chair. Asian Regional Conf. of Rotary Int. 58.
Indian Embassy, Ul. Obukha 68, Moscow, U.S.S.R.; Home: 9 Motilal Nehru Marg, New Delhi 110011; 67 Model Town, Jullundur City, Punjab, India.

Guna-Kasem, Pracha; Thai diplomatist; b. 29 Dec. 1934, Bangkok; ed. Dhebsirinda School, Bangkok, Marlborough Coll., England, Oxford and Yale Univs.
Ministry of Foreign Affairs 59-; Chief of Section, Political Div. of Dept. of Int. Org. 60-61, Second Sec. SEATO Div. 62-63; alt. mem. for Thailand, SEATO Perm. Working Group 62-63; Embassy in Egypt 64-65; Chief of Foreign News Analyses Div. of Information Dept., concurrently in charge of press affairs 66-69, Chief of Press Div. 70-71, Dir.-Gen. of Information Dept. 73-75; Consul-Gen. in Hong Kong 71-73; Perm. Rep. to UN Sept. 75-; fmrly. Special Lecturer, Thammasat Univ.; mem. del. to UN Gen. Assembly 62, 68, 70, 74, to 2nd Afro-Asian Conf., Algeria 65, to SEATO Council 66.
Permanent Mission of Thailand to the United Nations, 20 East 82nd Street, New York, N.Y. 10028, U.S.A.

Gunaratne, Victor Thomas Herat, L.M.S., D.T.M. & H., D.P.H., M.R.C.P.(E.), F.R.C.P.(E.); Ceylonese international health official; b. 11 March 1912, Mellowagara; ed. Ceylon Medical Coll., London School of Hygiene and Tropical Medicine, and Univ. of Edinburgh Medical School.
Acting Deputy Dir. Public Health Services, Ceylon 59-61; Deputy Dir. Ceylon Medical Services 61-64; Dir. Health Services, Govt. of Ceylon 64-67; Pres. World Health Assembly 67; Dir. WHO Regional Office for S.E. Asia; Fellow, Royal Coll. of Physicians of Edinburgh, Sri Lanka Public Medical Assen.; Hon. Fellow, Indian Acad. of Medical Sciences 75, Ceylon Coll. of Physicians 76.
Publs. Articles in professional journals.
WHO Regional Office for South-East Asia, World Health House, Ring Road, Indraprastha Estate, New Delhi 1, India.
Telephone: 270181.

Gunn, Sir William Archer, K.B.E., C.M.G., J.P.; Australian grazier and company director; b. 1 Feb. 1914; ed. The King's School, Parramatta, New South Wales.
Chairman Int. Wool Secr. 61-73, Australian Wool Board 63-72, Queensland Advisory Board Devt. Finance Corpn. 62-72; Chair. Cattle Investments Ltd., Livestock Management Pty. Ltd., Gunn Devt. Pty. Ltd., Eagle Corpn. Ltd.; Dir. Rothmans of Pall Mall (Australia) Ltd., Grazcos Co-operative Ltd., Clausen Steamship Co. (Australia) Pty. Ltd., Walter Reid & Co. Ltd., Gunn Rural Management Pty. Ltd.; mem. Commonwealth Bank Board 52-59, Reserve Bank Board 59-, Australian Meat Board 53-66, Australian Wool Bureau 51-63 (Chair. 58-63), Australian Wool-growers Council 47-60 (Chair. 55-58), Graziers Fed. Council of Australia 50-60 (Pres. 51-54), AustralianWool-growers and Graziers Council 60-65, Export Devt. Council 62-65, Exec. Council, United Graziers Assen. of Queensland 44-69 (Pres. 51-59), Australian Wool Testing Authority 58-63; Golden Fleece Achievement Award (Nat. Assen. of Wool Manufacturers of America) 62; Award of the Golden Ram (Nat. Wool Growers Assen. of S. Africa) 73.
Office: Wool Exchange, 69 Eagle Street, Brisbane; Home: 98 Windermere Road, Ascot, Queensland 4007, Australia.
Telephone: Brisbane 221-4044 (Office); Brisbane 68-2688 (Home).

H

Haddon-Cave, Charles Philip, M.A., C.M.G.; British colonial administrator; b. 6 July 1925; ed. Univ. of Tasmania, King's Coll., Cambridge Univ.
With Colonial Admin. Service 52-; successively posted in Kenya, Seychelles and Hong Kong; Financial Sec., Hong Kong 71-.
Colonial Secretariat, Central District, Hong Kong; Home: 45 Shouson Hill, Hong Kong.

Hadiwijaya, Toyib; Indonesian agriculturist and politician; b. 12 May 1919, Ciamis, W. Java; ed. Middelbare Landbouwschool Bogor, Faculty of Agriculture, Bogor, Univ. of Indonesia and special studies in U.S.A., Europe and Asia.
Assistant plant pathologist, Inst. for Plant Diseases, Dept. of Agriculture, Bogor 39-48; Student and Instr. of Plant Pathology, Faculty of Agric., Univ. of Indonesia, Bogor 48-55, Asst. Prof. 55-56, Prof. 56-; Dean of Faculty of Agric. 57-62; mem. Regional Rep. Council, W. Java 60-62; Minister of Higher Educ. and Science 62-64; Amb. to Belgium and Luxembourg 65-66; Pres. Bogor Agric. Univ. 66-70; Minister of Plantations 67-68, of Agric. 68-; mem. Board of Trustees Int. Inst. for Rice Research, Los Banos, Philippines 70-74; Chair. and mem. of numerous advisory cttees.; chief del. to several int. confs.
Publs. Many scientific publs. and papers in Indonesian, Dutch, English and French.
Ministry of Agriculture, 11 Taman Cut Meutia, Jakarta, Indonesia.

Hagihara, Yusuke, DR. SC.; Japanese astronomer; b. 28 March 1897; ed. Tokyo, Cambridge and Harvard Univs.
Assistant, Tokyo Univ. 21, Asst. Prof. 23, Prof. of Astronomy 35-57; Rockefeller Fellowship 28-29; Harvard Observatory Research Assoc. 38; Dir. of Tokyo Astronomical Observatory 46-57 (Visiting Prof. Chicago Univ 52), Emeritus 57; Prof. of Astronomy, Tohoku Univ. 57-60; Consultant Smithsonian Astrophysical Observatory 61-; Pres. Utsunomiya Univ. 60-64; mem. Science Council of Japan 49-59, Japan Acad. 43-, F.R.A.S. 28-; Pres. Physico-Mathematical Soc. of Japan 42; Pres. Astronomical Soc. of Japan 49-53; mem. Standing Cttee. of Int. Astronomical Union 28-, Vice-Pres. 61-67; Chair. of Comm. on Celestial Mechanics 61-67; official mem. Int. Scientific Radio Union 50-60; H.I.M. Decoration for Cultural Merit 54, Watson Medal (Nat. Acad. of Sciences of U.S.A.) 60; Lecturer Yale Univ. Summer Inst. on Dynamical Astronomy 60, 61, 62, 64, 65.
Publs. *Foundation of Celestial Mechanics I* 47, *Beyond Nebulae* 49, *General Astronomy* 55, *Astronomy* 56, *Stability in Celestial Mechanics* 57, *The Stability of the Solar System* (in *The Solar System*, Vol. 3, ed. Kuiper) 61, *Theories of Equilibrium Figures of a Rotating Homogeneous Mass* 70, *Celestial Mechanics Vols. I–IV*, 70, 72, 74, 75.
Himonya 6-chome, 3-7 Meguro-ku, Tokyo, Japan.
Telephone: 712-7800.

Haguiwara, Toru; Japanese diplomatist; b. 25 May 1906; ed. Tokyo Imperial Univ.
Entered diplomatic service 28; Chief of several sections of the Ministry of Foreign Affairs 40-46; Dir. Treaties Bureau, Ministry of Foreign Affairs 46-50; Chief of Japanese Govt. Overseas Agency, Paris 50-52; Rep. of Japan to various confs. of UN, UNESCO, WHO, GATT 52-67; Minister to France 52; Envoy and Minister to Switzerland 52, Amb. 55-57; Amb. to Canada 57-61, to France 61-67; Commr.-Gen. of Govt. for *Expo* 70 68-71; Adviser to the Minister for Foreign Affairs 71-; mem. of OECD Trade Group 71-72; Pres. 17th UNESCO Gen. Conf. 72, 3rd Extraordinary Gen. Conf. 73; mem. Int. Civil Service Comm., UN 74-.
Publs. include two books on Diplomatic History of World War II 49, and the Peace Treaty 51.
Office: Room 982, Hotel New Japan, Tokyo; Home: 502, Shinsaka 40 Apartments, Akasaka 8-10-24, Minato-ku, Tokyo, Japan.
Telephone: 580-1387 (Office); 401-0055 (Home).

Haksar, Ajit Narain, B.A., M.B.A.; Indian tobacco executive; b. 11 Jan. 1925; ed. Doon School, Dehra Dun, Allahabad Univ., Harvard Univ., U.S.A.
Training with J. Walter Thompson Co., N.Y. 46-48; joined India Tobacco Co. Ltd. (fmrly. The Imperial Tobacco Co. of India Ltd.) as Asst. Marketing 48; seconded to British-American Tobacco Co. Ltd., London 48-50; Marketing Dir. Board of India Tobacco 66, Deputy Chair. 68, Chair. 69-; Chair. Local Board, Indian Leaf Tobacco Devt. Co. Ltd.; Chair. Board of Govs. Indian Inst. of Technology; Gov. Indian Inst. of Management; non-exec. Chair. Webstar Ltd.; Dir. Reserve Bank of India and Industrial Devt. Bank of India; mem. Court of Govs., Admin. Staff Coll. of India, Hyderabad, Calcutta and Doon School, Dehra Dun; non-official mem. Special Cttee. Civil Supplies, State Advisory Cttee. for Territorial Army (W. Bengal); Past Pres. Bengal Chamber of Commerce and Industry.
Office: 37 Chowringhee, Calcutta 16; Home: 24B Raja Santosh Road, Calcutta 27, India.
Telephone: 24-8141 (Office); 45-7696 (Home).

Halstead, Eric Henry, E.D., M.A., B.COM., F.C.A.(N.Z.), F.C.I.S.; New Zealand politician and company director; b. 26 May 1912; ed. Auckland Univ. Coll. and Teachers' Training Coll.
Major N.Z. Forces Middle East and Italy 39-45; head of Commercial and Accountancy Dept., Seddon Memorial Technical Coll. 45-49; Mem. of Parl. (mem. of National Party) 49-57; Minister of Social Security and Minister-in-Charge of Tourist and Health Resorts 54-56; Minister-Asst. to the Prime Minister 54-57, concurrently Minister of Industries and Commerce and of Customs 56-57; partner Mabee, Halstead and Co.; Pres. Auckland Savings Bank; Dir. Air New Zealand Ltd. 65-70; mem. Council Univ. of Auckland 61-70; Amb. to Thailand and Laos 70-73; rep. to SEATO 70-73, to ECAFE Confs. 71-73; mem. Board Asian Inst. of Technology 70-74, Deputy Chair. 72-74; Business Consultant and Co. Dir. 74-.
Publs. *Modern Bookkeeping, Junior Commercial Practice.*
5 Pere Street, Remuera, Auckland, New Zealand.
Telephone: 545-083.

Hamada, Shoji; Japanese potter; b. 9 Dec. 1894, Tokyo; ed. Tokyo Technical Coll., Kyoto Ceramic Experimental Inst.
Went to St. Ives, Cornwall, England to work with Bernard Leach, constructed first *noborigama* kiln in western world 20; first one-man exhbn. Patterson Gallery, London 23; moved to Japan 24; first one-man exhbn. Japan 25; f. Japanese Folkcraft Museum with Soetsu Yanagi and Kanjiro Kawai 36; cultural mission to Europe with Naoya Shiga and Soetsu Yanagi, attended Dartington Hall Int. Craft Conf., England 52; Dir. Japanese Folkcraft Museum 62-; Japanese del. to Japan-U.S. Cultural and Educ. Conf., Wash. 63; Dir. Japan Folkcraft Soc. 74; mem. Soc. Japanese Painters (kokyga Kai) 25-; mem. Council for Protection of Cultural Properties of Japan 57-; designated Holder of Intangible Cultural Property (Living National Treasure) of Japan 55; Medal of Honour with Purple Ribbon of Japan 64; Hon. D.F.A. Michigan State Univ. 67; Okinawa Times Prize 68; Order of Culture of the Emperor of Japan 68; Hon. Citizen of Mashiko 69; other awards.
Publs. *A Catalogue of the Works of Kenkichi Tomimoto, Kanjiro Kawai and Shoji Hamada* 40, *The Catalogue, Shoji Hamada* (ed. Soetsu Yanagi) 61, *The Works of Shoji Hamada 1921–1969* 69, *77 Tea Bowls of Shoji Hamada* 72.
3387 Mashiko, Mashiko Machi, Haga Gun, Tochigi Ken, Japan.
Telephone: 028572-2036.

Hamengkubuwono IX, H.R.H. Sultan Dorodjatun; Indonesian ruler; b. 12 April 1912; ed. Univ. of Leiden.
Inaugurated Sultan of Jogjakarta 40; Mil. Gov. of Special Territory with rank of Maj.-Gen. of the Army) 45-49; Head of Special Territory 46; Gov., Head of Special Territory 59; mem. Provisional People's Consultative Assembly Aug. 59, Titular Gen. of the Army 60; Minister of State Oct. 46-49; Minister of Defence and Co-ordinator of Domestic Security Aug.-Dec. 59; Defence Minister, Cabinet of the Repub. of the United States of Indonesia Dec. 49, 53; Deputy Prime Minister 50-April 51; Curator Univ. of Gajah Mada Dec. 51; Chair. Supervisory Comm. for the Apparatus of the State Aug. 59; Minister and Head, Body for Controlling State Finance 64; First Minister for Econ. and Financial Affairs in the Presidium and Deputy Prime Minister 66-68; State Minister for Econ. Affairs, Finance and Industry 68-73; Vice-Pres. 73-; Chair. Indonesian Olympic Cttee. 51, Tourist Inst. 56, Asian Games Fed. 58, Indonesian Tourist Council 62-; Chair. Session, Econ. Comm. for Asia and the Far East (ECAFE) 57, Nat. Preparatory Cttee. for New York World Fair 63; Chief Del. of Indonesia, Pacific Area Travel Asscn. (PATA), U.S. 58, UN First World Conf. of Int. Travel and Tourism, Rome 63; Medal of the Guerilla, Medal of Loyalty to the Independence and the Order of the White Elephant (Thailand); Hon. titles of Maha Putra (Spes Patria) and Pramuka Agung (Supreme Boy Scout).
Office of the Vice-President, Jakarta; and Medan Merdeka Selatan 6, Jakarta, Indonesia.

Hamer, Alan William; Australian business executive; b. 27 Nov. 1917, Melbourne; ed. Oxford Univ.
Joined ICI Australia, England 41, returned to Australia 42; associated with setting up of new plants; Works Man. Yarraville plant 50-56; Controller Technical Dept. 56-59, Dir. 59-68; Chair. ICI Group of Cos., India 68-71, concurrently non-exec. Dir. ICI Australia Board; Man. Dir. ICI Australia Ltd. 71-; Chair. Australian Fertilizers Ltd., Consolidated Fertilizers Ltd., Fibremakers Ltd.; Dir. ICI New Zealand; Rhodes Scholarship 37.
ICI Australia Limited, ICI House, 1, Nicholson Street, Melbourne, Australia.

Hamer, Rupert James, LL.M.; Australian solicitor and politician; b. 29 July 1916, Kew, Vic.; ed. Melbourne and Geelong Grammar Schools, Univ. of Melbourne.
Joined Australian Imperial Forces 40; C.O. Vic. Scottish Regt., Citizen Mil. Forces 54-58; mem. Vic. Legislative Council for E. Yarra 58-71; Minister for Immigration, Vic. 62-64, for Local Govt., Vic. 64-71; mem. Vic. Legislative Assembly for Kew 71-; Chief Sec., Deputy Premier, Vic. 71-72, Premier, Treas. and Minister of the Arts Aug. 72-.
Office of the Premier of Victoria, Melbourne, Victoria, Australia.

Hamid, Agha Abdul; Pakistani civil servant; b. 2 Aug. 1912; ed. Govt. Coll., Lahore, and Emmanuel Coll., Cambridge.
Joined Indian Civil Service 35, Asst. Commr. 37; Deputy Dir.-Gen. All-India Radio 42-45; Deputy Registrar, later Registrar of Co-operative Socs. 45-47; Sec. to late Liaquat Ali Khan, Prime Minister of Pakistan 48-51; Prime Minister of Kalat State 51-53, Baluchistan State Union 53-54; Joint Sec. to Central Cabinet 54-55, Joint Sec. in Charge of Ministry of Information and Broadcasting 55-56; Joint Sec. Cabinet 56-58, Cabinet Sec. 58, 66-68; Commr. in Peshawar 59-60; Administrator 60-61; Dir. Civil Service Acad. 61-66; Chair. Central Public Service Comm. 66; Asst. Sec.-Gen. for Public Information, UN 68-72; UN Commr. for Namibia 70-73; Founder, later Sec. and Chair. Karachi Fine Arts Soc.; fmr. Chair. Pakistan Arts Council; Pres. Pakistan Section of Int. Asscn. of Art Critics; Sitara Quaid-i-Azam.
Publs. *Majlis, Scrutiny.*
c/o Ministry of Foreign Affairs, Rawalpindi, Pakistan.

Hammond, Dame Joan Hood, D.B.E., C.M.G.; Australian singer (retd.); b. 24 May 1912, Christchurch, New Zealand; ed. Presbyterian Ladies Coll., Pymble, Sydney and Sydney Conservatorium of Music.
Former mem. Sydney Philharmonic Orchestra and sports writer, *Daily Telegraph*, Sydney; first public (singing) appearance, Sydney 29; London debut in *Messiah* 38; operatic debut, Vienna 39; has appeared as guest artist at Royal Opera House, Covent Garden, Sadlers Wells, Vienna State Opera, Bolshoi Theatre, Moscow, New York City Center, Netherlands Opera, Barcelona Liceo, etc.; world tours have included Europe, U.S.A., Canada, Australasia, India, S. Africa and U.S.S.R.; repertoire includes: *Aïda, Madame Butterfly, Tosca, Othello, Don Carlos, La Traviata, La Bohème, Turandot, Tannhäuser, Lohengrin*, and *Die Zauberflöte*; records for HMV (fmrly. for Colombia); Coronation Medal 53; Sir Charles Santley Award, Worshipful Co. of Musicians 70.
Publ. *A Voice, A Life.*
Private Bag 101, Geelong Mail Centre, Victoria 3221, Australia; also c/o Bank of New South Wales, Sackville Street, London, W.1, England.

Han Hsien-ch'u; army officer, People's Repub. of China; b. 1908, Hunan.
Regimental Commdr. 38; Commdr. 40th Army, 4th Field Army 49; Deputy Commdr. Hunan Mil. District, People's Liberation Army 49-50; Chief of Staff Chinese People's Volunteers in Korea 52; mem. Nat. Defence Council 54; Alt. mem. 8th Cen. Cttee. of CCP 56; Gen. 60; Commdr. Foochow Mil. Region, PLA 60-73; Chair. Fukien Revolutionary Cttee. 68; mem. 9th Cen. Cttee. of CCP 69; First Sec. CCP Fukien 71; mem. 10th Cen. Cttee. of CCP 73; Commdr. Lanchow Mil. Region, PLA 74-.

Hanif Khan, Mohammed; Pakistan politician.
Minister of Information and Broadcasting Feb. 76-.
Ministry of Information and Broadcasting, Rawalpindi, Pakistan.

Hanif Khan, Rana Mohammad; Pakistan politician; b. 1921, Garh Shankar, E. Punjab; ed. Govt. Coll., Ludhiana.
Called to the Bar, Lincoln's Inn, London 55; legal practice, Shahiwal 55-; mem. Pakistan People's Party 70-; mem. Nat. Assembly 70-; Minister of Labour, Works and Local Bodies Dec. 71-74, of Finance, Planning and Devt. Oct. 74-.
National Assembly, Islamabad, Pakistan.

Hannah, Air Marshal Sir Colin Thomas, K.C.M.G., K.B.E., C.B., KT. ST. J.; Australian administrator; b. 22 Dec. 1914, Menzies, W.A.; ed. Perth Boys' School, Hale School, Perth and R.A.A.F. Coll.
R.A.A.F. Staff, London 47-49; Dir.-Gen. of Personnel 51-54; Imperial Defence Coll. 55; Senior Air Staff Officer, R.A.F. Far East 56-59; Dir.-Gen. Plans and Policy 59-61; Deputy Chief of Air Staff 61-64; Air Officer Commdg. Operational Command 65-68, Support Command 68-69; Chief of Air Staff 70-72; Gov. of Queensland March 72-; Dr. h.c. (Griffith Univ.) 75.
Government House, Brisbane, Queensland 4001, Australia.

Hanumanthaiya, Kengal; Indian politician; b. Feb. 1908, Kengeri, Mysore State; ed. Maharaja Coll., Univ. of Mysore and Poona Law Coll., Bombay Univ.
Delegate to Indian Nat. Congress, Madras Session 27; advocate practice 33-36; work in Congress as full-time worker 36-; mem. Mysore Rep. Assembly 40-; Sec. Congress Party, Mysore Rep. Assembly 40-44, Leader 44-49; imprisoned seven times during fight for freedom of India; mem. Mysore Constituent Assembly, Constituent Assembly of India 48, Provisional Parl. of India, Cttee. of Constituent Assembly to draft Model Constitution for Indian States, Cttee. on Abolition of Caste Nomenclatures; mem. Mysore Legislative Assembly 52- and Leader, Congress Party; Chief Minister, Mysore State March 52-Aug. 56; Chair. Mysore Educ. Reforms Cttee.; fmr. Pres. Post and Telegraph Workers' Union, S. India, Pres. Mil. Eng. Staff Workers' Union, S. Region; M.P. 62-; Chair. Punjab Admin. Reforms Comm. 64-65, Admin. Reforms Comm., Govt. of India 67; Deputy Leader of Congress Party 67-68; mem. Working Cttee. of All India Congress Cttee. 69; Minister of Law and Social Welfare, Govt. of India 70-71; mem. Perm. Court of Arbitration, The Hague June 70-; Minister of Railways, Govt. of India 71-73; mem. Indian Coffee Board.
"Kengal Krupa", Bellary Road, Bangalore 6, India.
Telephone: 22324.

Hara, Sumio; Japanese banker; b. 7 March 1911, Yokosuka, Kanagawa; ed. Faculty of Law, Tokyo Imperial Univ.
Joined Ministry of Finance 34; Deputy Dir. Budget Bureau 53-56; Dir.-Gen. of the Tax Bureau 56-60; Commr. Nat. Tax Admin. Agency 60-62; Deputy Pres. The Bank of Tokyo Ltd. 62-65, Pres. 65-73, Chair. 73-; Chair. Bank of Tokyo (Switzerland) Ltd., Zurich 71-; Dir. and Vice-Chair. of Board, Partnership Pacific Ltd., Sydney 69-; Chair. Private Investment Co. for Asia (PICA) S.A., Panama 75-; Commr. External Devt. Co-operation Council (Prime Minister's Office) 69-; Exec. Dir. Fed. of Econ. Orgs. 65-; Trustee, Japan Cttee. for Econ. Devt. 65-; Vice-Pres. Japan Tariff Asscn. 68-; mem. Directing Cttee. Asscn. Int. pour la Promotion et la Protection des Investissements Privés en Territoires Etrangers 70-; Vice-Pres. and Dir. Japan ESCAP Asscn. 73-; Special Adviser to the Pres. Japan Chamber of Commerce and Industry 75; mem. Rockefeller Univ. Council, Trilateral Comm. 73-, Int. Advisory Board, Sperry Rand Corpn. N.Y. 74-, Council of American-Japan Soc. Inc. 74-76, Japan-U.S. Econ. Council.
Bank of Tokyo Ltd., 1-1, Nihombashi Muromachi 2-chome, Chuo-ku, Tokyo; Home: 26-14, Tsutsujigaoka, Midori-ku, Yokohama, Kanagawa, Japan.
Telephone: 03-270-8111 (Office); 045-981-7507 (Home).

Harjono, Maj.-Gen. Piet; Indonesian industrial executive and fmr. army officer; b. 1919.
Posts in financial admin. of armed forces 52-66, Ministry of Finance 66-76; acting Pres.-Dir. Pertamina March 76-.
P.N. Pertamina, 2-4-6 Perwira, Jakarta, Indonesia.

Harry, Ralph Lindsay, C.B.E.; Australian diplomatist; b. 10 March 1917, Geelong, Victoria; ed. Tasmania and Lincoln Coll., Oxford.
Department of External Affairs 41-; Private Sec. to Minister of External Affairs; Asst. Official Sec., Canada 43-45; Second Sec., later First Sec., Washington, D.C., U.S.A. 45-49 (at UN, New York 47-48); Dept. of External Affairs, Canberra 49-53; Consul-Gen. in Switzerland 53-56; rep. in Singapore, Brunei, Sarawak and Borneo 56-57; seconded to Ministry of Defence 58-59; Asst. Sec. Ministry of External Affairs 60-66; Amb. to Belgium and the EEC 66-68, to Repub. of Viet-Nam 68-70, to Fed. Repub. of Germany 71-75, to UN May 75-; fmrly. mem. UN Cttee. drafting Universal Declaration of Human Rights and leader del. to UN Conf. on the Law of the Sea.
Permanent Mission of Australia to the United Nations, Dag Hammarskjöld Plaza, 885 Second Avenue, 16th Floor, New York, N.Y. 10017, U.S.A.

Harun, Tun Datu Haji Mustapha bin Datu, O.B.E., K.V.O.; Sabah (Malaysian) administrator; b. 1918.
Member Legislative Council of North Borneo 54-63; mem. Exec. Council 56-63; Chair. Sabah (North Borneo) Nat. Council; Chair. and Leader United Sabah Nat. Org.; Yang Di-Pertuan Negara (Head of State) of Sabah 63-67, Chief Minister 67-76; served on Malaysia Solidarity Consultative Cttee. and Inter-Govt. Cttee. on Malaysia; Life mem. Commonwealth Parl. Asscn.; mem. Royal Commonwealth Soc., London; mem. Nat. Unity Council.
United Sabah National Organization, Kota Kinabalu, Sabah, Malaysia.

Hasan, Mubashir, PH.D.; Pakistani civil engineer and politician; b. 1922, Panipat, Punjab; ed. Govt. Coll., Lahore, Engineering Coll., Lahore, Columbia Univ. and State Univ. of Iowa, U.S.A.
Member of Staff, Civil Engineering Dept., Engineering Coll., Lahore (subsequently Univ. of Engineering and Technology) 43, later Prof. and Head of Dept. until 62; private practice, Lahore 62-67; joined Pakistan People's Party 67; arrested for political activities 68, 69; mem. Nat. Assembly 70-; Minister of Finance, Econ. Affairs and Devt. 71-74.
National Assembly, Islamabad, Pakistan.

Hasegawa, Norishige; Japanese industrialist; b. 8 Aug. 1907; ed. Tokyo Imperial Univ.
Sumitomo Chemical Co. 31-, Dir. 51-, Man. Dir. 56, Vice-Pres. 63-65, Pres. 65-; Vice-Pres. Fed. of Econ. Orgs. (Keidanren); mem. Econ. Council, Office of the Prime Minister, Industrial Structure Council of Ministry of Int. Trade and Industry, Advisory Cttee. Japanese Nat. Railways; Exec. Councillor Osaka Chamber of Commerce

and Industry; Standing Dir. Kansai Econ. Fed.; mem. Exec. Cttee., Japan-U.S. Econ. Council; Japan Nat. Chair. Japan-New Zealand Businessmen's Conf.; mem. Japan Comm. of Trilateral Comm.; Standing Dir. Japan Fed. of Employers' Asscns.; mem. Visiting Cttee., Center for Int. Studies, M.I.T.; Deputy Chair. Japan C.I.O.S. Asscn.; Pres. Japan Chemical Industry Asscn., Japan Greece Soc., Kansai Philharmonic Soc.; Trustee, Univ. of the Sacred Heart; Chair. Mount Pleasant Chemical Co. Ltd.; Pres. Nippon Asahan Aluminium Co. Ltd.; many other directorships and affiliations; Medal for Distinguished Industrialist of Osaka Prefecture 68, Blue Ribbon Medal 69, Commdr. Order of the Phoenix (Greece) 75.
Sumitomo Chemical Co., 15, 5-chome, Kitahama, Higashi-ku, Osaka, Japan.
Telephone: (06) 203-1231.

Hasegawa, Takashi; Japanese politician; b. 1 April 1912; ed. Waseda Univ.
Editor Kyushu daily paper; Private Sec. to Minister of State; mem. House of Reps. 53-; Deputy Minister of Education 61-62; Vice-Chair. Public Relations Cttee., Liberal Democratic Party 63, Chair. 66; Minister of Labour Dec. 73-; Dir. Japan Athletic Asscn.
8-903, Yonban-cho, 9-chome, Chiyoda-ku, Tokyo, Japan.

Hasluck, Rt. Hon. Sir Paul Meernaa Caedwalla, P.C., G.C.M.G., G.C.V.O., M.A.; Australian historian, diplomatist and politician; b. 1 April 1905; ed. Western Australia Univ.
Member Editorial staff *The West Australian*; Lecturer in History Western Australia Univ.; mem. staff Australian Dept. of External Affairs 41-47; Sec. Canberra Conf. Jan. 44; Adviser on Australian del. to Wellington Conf. Nov. 44; Adviser British Commonwealth Meeting London April 45; Adviser San Francisco Conf. April 45; Australian del. Exec. Cttee. of United Nations Preparatory Comm. London Aug. 45; alt. del. Preparatory Comm. Nov. 45; del. General Assembly Jan. and Sept. 46; Dir. post-hostilities Div., Australian Dept. of External Affairs April 45; Counsellor Australian Mission UN H.Q. Mar. 46; Acting Rep. of Australia on Security Council and Atomic Energy Comm. July 46; Research Reader in History, Univ. of W. Australia 48; mem. Commonwealth Parl. as Liberal M.P. 49-69; Minister for Territories 51-63, of Defence Dec. 63-April 64, of External Affairs 64-69; Gov.-Gen. 69-74; Fellow, Royal Australian Historical Acad., Australian Acad. of the Humanities, Acad. of Social Sciences in Australia; Kt.St.J.
Publs. *Into the Desert* 39, *Black Australians* 42 (2nd edn. 70), *Workshop of Security* 47, *The Government and the People, 1939-1945*, 2 vols. (Australian Official War History) 52, 69, *Native Welfare in Australia* 53, *Collected Verse* 70, *An Open Go* 72, *The Poet in Australia* 75, *A Time for Building* 76.
95 St. George's Terrace, Perth, Western Australia.

Hassan, Tan Sri Syed Zahiruddin bin Syed, G.C.V.O., J.M.N., S.P.M.P., P.J.K.; Malaysian state governor; b. 11 Oct. 1918, Perak; ed. Raffles Coll., Singapore.
Malay Officer 45-47; Deputy Asst. District Officer, Krian 48, Asst. District Officer 51; Asst. District Officer, Tanjong Malim 53, Ipoh 54; Second Asst. State Sec., Perak 55, Registrar of Titles and Asst. State Sec. (Lands) 56; District Officer, Batang Padang, Tapah 57; Deputy Sec. Public Services Comm. 58; Principal Asst. Sec., Federation Establishment Office 60; State Sec. Perak 61; Perm. Sec. Ministry of Agriculture and Co-operatives 63, Ministry of Educ. 66; Dir.-Gen. Public Services Comm. 69; Chair. Railway Services Comm. 72-; High Commr. to United Kingdom 74-75; Governor of Malacca 75-; mem. Special Cttee. on Superannuation, Board of Govs. Malay Coll., Interim Council of Nat. Inst. of Technology, Central Board; Vice-Pres. Subang National Golf Club.
Office of the Governor, Malacca, Malaysia.

Hassett, Gen. Francis George, A.C., C.B.E., C.B., D.S.O. M.V.O.; Australian army officer; b. 11 April 1918, Sydney; ed. Canterbury High School and Royal Mil. Coll. of Australia, Duntroon.
Lieutenant, Darwin Mobile Force 39; Australian Imperial Force Middle East and S. W. Pacific Area 39-45, Adjutant Aust. Infantry Bn., Brigade Maj. 18th Aust. Infantry Brigade, G.S.O.1 3rd Aust. Div.; Commdr. Korea 51-52; Dir. Mil. Artillery, Royal Mil. Coll. Duntroon with rank of Col. 53-58; Mil. Sec. Army H.Q. 58-60; Commdr. (Brig.) Malaya 60-63; Imperial Defence Coll. London 63; Deputy Chief of the Gen. Staff and 5th mem. Mil. Board (Maj. Gen.) 64-66; Head, Aust. Joint Services Staff, London 66-68; G.O.C. Northern Command 68-70; Head, Army Re-org. and Planning Staff 70-71; Vice-Chief of Gen. Staff 71-73, Chief of Gen. Staff 73-75, of Defence Force Staff 76-.
Department of Defence (Army Office), Russell Offices, Canberra, A.C.T., 2600; Home: 42 Mugga Way, Red Hill, A.C.T. 2603, Australia.

Hathi, Jaisukhlal; Indian politician; b. 19 Jan. 1909.
Senior Advocate, Indian Supreme Court; mem. Constituent Assembly 46-47; mem. Provisional Parl.; Chief Sec. Saurashtra 48; mem. Rajya Sabha 52-57, 62-, Lok Sabha 57-62; Deputy Minister of Irrigation and Power 52-62; Minister of State for Labour and Employment April-Nov. 62; Minister of Supply 62-64; Minister of State in Ministry of Home Affairs 64-66, also Minister of Defence Supplies 65-66; Minister of State for Defence 66-67; Minister for Labour and Rehabilitation 67-69; Deputy Leader, Congress Party in Parl. 72-74; Chair. Cttee. on Subordinate Legislation Rajya Sabha; Vice-Pres. Bharatiya Vidya Bhavan, Bar Asscn. of India.
Bharatiya Vidya Bhavan, K. Munshi Marg, Bombay 400007, India.

Hattori, Motozo; Japanese shipping executive; b. 1 Jan. 1905; ed. Kyoto Imperial Univ.
Kawasaki Kisen Kaisha Ltd., Kobe 31-, Rep. New York Branch 40-41, Sub-Man., Santiago, Chile 41-42, Man. 42-43, Sub-Man., later Man. Operating Section, Kobe 43-46; Gen. Man. Operating and Chartering Dept. 46, Dir. 47-49, Exec. Dir. 49-50, Pres. 50-73, Chair. 73-; Pres. Kawasaki Steamship Co., New York 55-, Kawasaki (London) Ltd. 56-70; official of other firms and business orgs.
Kawasaki Kisen Kaisha Ltd., 8 Kaigan Dori, Ikuta-ku, Kobe, Japan.

Hattori, Seitaro; Japanese international bank official; b. 23 June 1920; ed. Tokyo Imperial Univ.
Joined Ministry of Finance 42; Liaison Office, Ministry of Finance 47-53; London Rep., Japan Monopoly Corpn. 53-64, Dir. Faculties Div. 64-65, Sales Div. 65-66; Deputy Dir. Int. Finance Bureau, Ministry of Finance 66-68; Alt. Exec. Dir. Int. Monetary Fund 68-70; Exec. Dir. for Burma, Ceylon, Japan, Laos, Malaysia, Nepal, Singapore and Thailand, Int. Bank for Reconstruction and Devt. (World Bank), IFC and IDA 70-73; Counsellor Nat. Westminster Bank, Tokyo 73-; Alt. Rep., Japanese Del. to UNCTAD II, New Delhi 67.
National Westminster Bank, Mitsubishi Building, Marunouchi 2-chome, Chiyoda-ku, Tokyo 100, Japan.

Hawke, Robert James Lee, B.A., LL.B., B.LITT.; Australian trade union executive; b. 9 Dec. 1929, Bordertown, S. Australia; ed. Univs. of Western Australia and Oxford.
Research Officer and Advocate, Australian Council of Trade Unions 58-70, Pres. Jan. 70-; Senior Vice-Pres. Australian Labor Party 71-73, Pres. July 73-; mem. Board of Reserve Bank of Australia 73-; mem. Nat. Labor Advisory Council, Governing Body Int. Labor Org.
Australian Council of Trade Unions, 5th Floor, 254 La Trobe Street, Melbourne, Victoria 3000, Australia.

Hay, David Osborne, C.B.E., D.S.O., B.A.; Australian public servant; b. 1916; ed. Geelong Grammar School, Brasenose Coll., Oxford and Melbourne Univ.
Joined Australian Dept. of External Affairs 39 and rejoined 46 after army service 39-45; Del. to UN 49 and 50; served Ottawa 50-52; attended Imperial Defence Coll. London 54; Minister to Thailand 55-56, Ambassador 56-57, concurrently Rep. to SEATO; Asst. Sec. Department of External Affairs 57-61; High Commr. to Canada 61-64; Amb. and Perm. Rep. of Australia to the UN 63-65; Ministry of External Affairs 65-66, Administrator, Territory of Papua and New Guinea 67-70; Sec., Dept. of External Territories 70-73; Defence Force Ombudsman 73-.
10 Hotham Crescent, Deakin, A.C.T., Australia.
Telephone: 731705 (Canberra).

Hayaishi, Osamu, M.D., PH.D.; Japanese biochemist; b. 8 Jan. 1920, Stockton, Calif., U.S.A.; ed. Osaka High School, Osaka Univ.
Assistant Prof., Dept. of Microbiology, Washington Univ. School of Medicine, St. Louis 52-54; Chief, Toxicology, Nat. Inst. of Arthritis and Metabolic Diseases, Nat. Insts. of Health, Bethesda 54-58; Prof. Medical Chem. Dept., Kyoto Univ. 58-, Molecular Biology Dept. of Inst. for Chem. Research 59-76; Prof. Physiological Chem. and Nutrition Dept., Tokyo Univ. 70-74; Prof. Inst. of Scientific and Industrial Research, Osaka Univ. 75-; Foreign Hon. mem. of American Acad. of Arts and Sciences 69; Foreign Assoc. U.S. Nat. Acad. of Arts and Sciences 69; mem. Japan Acad. of Sciences 74, New York Acad. of Sciences 75; Hon. mem. American Soc. of Biological Chemists 74; Award of Japan Soc. of Vitaminology 64, Award of Matsunga Science Foundation 64, Asahi Award for Science and Culture 65, Award of Japan Acad. of Sciences 67, of Fujiwara Science Foundation 75; Bronze Medal (City of Paris), Order of Culture 72.
Publs. *Oxygenases* 62, *Molecular Mechanisms of Oxygen Activation* 73, *Molecular Oxygen in Biology* 73, and nearly 300 scientific reviews and articles.
Department of Medical Chemistry, Kyoto University Faculty of Medicine, Sakyo-ku, Kyoto 606; Home: 23 Kita-chanoki-cho, Shimogamo Sakyo-ku, Kyoto, Japan.
Telephone: 075-751-2111 (Office); 075-781-1089 (Home).

Hayakawa, Tokuji; Japanese business executive.
Chairman, Sharp Corporation.
Sharp Corporation, 22-22 Nagaikecho, Abenoku, Osaka, Japan.

Hayden, William George, B.ECONS.; Australian politician; b. 23 Jan. 1933, Brisbane, Queensland; ed. Brisbane State High School, Univ. of Queensland.
Police constable, Queensland 53-61; mem. Parl. for Oxley 61-; mem. Queensland Central Exec., Australian Labor Party 65-; Parl. Spokesman on Health and Welfare 69-72; Minister of Social Security 72-75; Treas. June-Dec. 75; mem. Select Cttee. on Pharmaceutical Benefits 70; Labor Party.
Parliament House, Canberra, A.C.T.; Home: 16 East Street, Ipswich, Queensland 4305, Australia.

Hegde, Sadanand K., M.A., B.L.; Indian judge; b. 11 June 1909, Kawdoor, Mysore.
Advocate 35; Govt. Pleader and Public Prosecutor 47-51; mem. Parl. 52-57; Judge, High Court of Mysore 57; Chief Justice, Delhi High Court 66; Judge Supreme Court of India 67-74.
10 Tughlak Road, New Delhi; also 244 Palace Upper Orchards, Bangalore 6, India.
Telephone: 617715 (New Delhi); 26337 (Bangalore).

Heinze, Sir Bernard Thomas, Kt., M.A., F.R.C.M.; Australian professor of music and conductor; b. 1 July 1894; ed. Univ. of Melbourne, Royal Coll. of Music, London and Schola Cantorum, Paris.
Appointed to academic staff, Univ. of Melbourne 24; Ormond Prof. of Music, Univ. of Melbourne 25-57; Dir.-Gen. of Music for Australian Broadcasting Co. 29-32; Conductor, Royal Melbourne Philharmonic Society 28-, Melbourne Symphony Orchestra 33-46, Victoria Symphony Orchestra 33-56; Dir. State Conservatorium of N.S.W. 57-66; conductor for Australian Broadcasting Comm.; Chair. Commonwealth Assistance to Australian Composers 67-, Music Advisory Cttee., Australian Council for the Arts 69-; Officer, Order of the Crown (Belgium); Order of Polonia Restituta 72; Hon. LL.D. (Univ. of British Columbia), Mus. Doc. (Univ. of W. Australia).
101 Victoria Road, Bellevue Hill, Sydney, N.S.W. 2023, Australia.

Henry, Sir Albert Royle; Cook Islands (New Zealand) politician; b. 11 June 1907; ed. Auaura School, Aitutaki.
Clerk, teacher, labourer, storeman, Labour Party and Industrial Union work in New Zealand; co-founder Cook Islands Soc. (N.Z.) Inc.; Premier, Cook Islands 65-, also Minister for Govt. and Cen. Admin., External Affairs, Outer Island Affairs, Police, Immigration, Nat. Devt. Corpn., Nat. Provident Fund, Civil Aviation, Shipping, Housing and Civil Defence.
Office of the Premier, Rarotonga, Cook Islands.

Hibberd, Donald James, O.B.E.; Australian business executive; b. 1915; ed. Fort St. Boys' High School, Sydney, Univ. of Sydney.
Formerly First Asst. Sec., Treasury Dept., Canberra; Man. Dir. Comalco Ltd. 60-69, Chair. and Chief Exec. 69-; Vice-Chair. Queensland Alumina Ltd. 64-; mem. Board, Reserve Bank of Australia 66-; Chair. Munich Reinsurance Co. of Australia Ltd. 70-; Council mem., Univ. of Melbourne 67-; Pres. Australian Mining Industry Council 72-73.
Comalco Ltd., 95 Collins Street, Melbourne; Home: Apartment 13-2, Domain Park, 193 Domain Road, South Yarra, Australia.

Hidayatullah, Mohammed, O.B.E., M.A.; Indian judge; b. 17 Dec. 1905; ed. Government High School, Raipur, Morris Coll., Nagpur, Trinity Coll., Cambridge, and Lincoln's Inn, London.
Advocate, Nagpur High Court 30-46; Advocate-Gen. C.P. and Berar 43-46; Puisne Judge 46-54; Dean of Faculty of Law, Nagpur Univ. 49-53; Chief Justice, Nagpur High Court 54-56; Chief Justice, Madhya Pradesh High Court 56-58; Judge, Supreme Court of India 58-68; Chief Justice of India 68-70; Acting Pres. of India 69; Hon. Bencher, Lincoln's Inn; Mitchell Fellow, State Univ. of Buffalo; Hon. LL.D. (Univ. of the Philippines) 70, (Ravishankar Univ.) 70, (Rajasthan Univ.) 76; Silver Elephant and War Service Badge 47; Bronze Medal for Gallantry 69; Order of the Yugoslav Flag with Sash 71; Kt. of Mark Twain 75.
Publs. *Democracy in India and the Judicial Process, The South-West Africa Case, Mullah's Mahomedan Law* (editor, 17th edn.), *A Judge's Miscellany*.
112 Walkeshwar Road, Bombay 6 W.B., India.
Telephone: 369798.

Highet, Hon. David Allan; New Zealand businessman and politician; b. 27 May 1913, Dunedin; ed. Otago Boys' High School and Otago Univ.
Practised as chartered accountant, Wellington 42-60; Gen. Man. L. J. Fisher & Co. Ltd., Auckland 60-64; Senior Partner, Cox, Elliffe, Twomey, Highet & Co. (Chartered Accountants), Auckland 64-; Wellington City Councillor 54-59; mem. Parl. for Remuera 66-; Minister of Internal Affairs, of Local Govt., of Civil Defence and Assoc. Minister of Social Welfare 72, of Internal Affairs, of Local Govt., of Recreation and Sport, for the Arts Dec. 75-.
28 Burwood Crescent, Remuera, Auckland, New Zealand.
Telephone: 549-507.

Hilaly, Agha, M.A., S.PK.; Pakistani diplomatist; b. 20 May 1911; ed. Madras and Cambridge Univs.
Entered Civil Service 36; apptd. Under-Sec. to Finance Ministry, Govt. of Bengal; transferred to pre-partition Govt. of India and served as Under-Sec. in Ministries of Agriculture, Food and Commerce 41-47; Deputy Sec. Pakistan Foreign Ministry 47-51, Joint Sec. 51-54; attended several Int. Confs. as Sec.-Gen. of Pakistan dels.; Amb. to Sweden, Norway, Denmark and Finland 56-59, to U.S.S.R. (concurrently Minister to Czechoslovakia) 59-61; High Commr. in India and Amb. to Nepal 61-63; High Commr. in U.K. and Amb. to Republic of Ireland 63-66; Amb. to U.S.A. 66-71 (concurrently to Mexico and Venezuela, High Commr. in Jamaica); mem. Board of Dirs. State Bank of Pakistan 72-; Chair. Board of Govs. Pakistan Inst. of Strategic Studies 73-.
25C Block 6, P.E.H.C. Society, Karachi 29, Pakistan.
Telephone: 411767 (Home).

Hillary, Sir Edmund Percival, K.B.E.; New Zealand mountaineer and explorer; b. 20 July 1919; ed. Auckland Grammar School and Univ. of Auckland.
Went to Himalayas on N.Z. Garwhal expedition 51, when he and another were invited to join the British reconnaisance over Everest under Eric Shipton; took part in British expedition to Cho Oyu 52, and in British Mount Everest Expedition under Sir John Hunt 53, when he and Tenzing reached the summit on May 29th; Leader N.Z. Alpine Club Expedition to Barun Valley 54; N.Z. Antarctic Expedition 56-58, reached South Pole Dec. 57; Leader Himalayan Expeditions 61, 63, 64; Pres. Volunteer Service Abroad in New Zealand 63-64; built a hospital for Sherpa tribesmen, Nepal 66; has built 12 schools for Nepalese hillmen 60-70; Leader climbing expedition on Mount Herschel, Antarctica 67; Dir. Field Educ. Enterprises of Australasia Pty. Ltd.; Polar Medal 58; Gurkha Right Hand (1st Class); Hon. LL.D. Victoria Univ., British Columbia 69, Victoria Univ., Wellington 70.
Publs. *High Adventure* 55, *The Crossing of Antarctica* (with Sir Vivian Fuchs) 58, *No Latitude for Error* 61, *High in the Thin Cold Air* (with Desmond Doig) 63, *Schoolhouse in the Clouds* 65, *Nothing Venture, Nothing Win* (autobiog). 75.
278A Remuera Road, Auckland, New Zealand.

Hirai, Tomisaburo, LL.B.; Japanese business executive; b. 13 Dec. 1906, Tokyo; ed. Tokyo Imperial Univ.
Joined Ministry of Commerce and Industry 31, Perm. Vice-Minister, Int. Trade and Industry 53; Exec. Counsellor, Yawata Iron and Steel Co. Ltd. 56, Dir. Admin. Bureau, Yawata Works 56, Dir. 56, Man. Dir. 58, Senior Man. Dir. and Gen. Supt. Yawata Works 62, Exec. Vice-Pres. 67; after merger with Fuji Iron and Steel Co. Ltd., Exec. Vice-Pres. Nippon Steel Corpn. 70-73, Rep. Dir. and Pres. 73-; Chair. Japan-Brazil Econ. Cttee., Fed. of Econ. Orgs. 74; Pres. Japan Overseas Enterprise Asscn. 74; Blue Ribbon Medal 73.
11-4, 1-chome, Kakinokizaka, Meguro-ku, Tokyo, Japan.

Hiraizumi, Wataru; Japanese politician; b. 26 Nov. 1929; ed. Tokyo Univ., Univs. of Grenoble and Aix-Marseilles, Ecole Nat. de l'Admin., Paris.
Member of Foreign Service 51-64; mem. House of Councillors 65-; fmr. Parl. Vice-Minister of Science and Technology; Vice-Pres. Kajima Corpn. 70-71; State Minister, Dir.-Gen. of Science and Technology 71-; Vice-Pres., Kajima Inst. for Int. Peace; currently Vice-Chair. Special Cttee. for Int. Cultural Exchange and mem. Policy Planning Cttee., Liberal-Democratic Party.
Room 329, House of Councillors, Tokyo; Home: 9-15, Haraī-kata-matchi Shinjuku, Tokyo, Japan.

Hirata, Kusuo; Japanese business executive; b. 7 Sept. 1909, Ooita; ed. Kwansei Gakuin Univ.
With Daicel Ltd. 33-34; joined Fuji Photo Film Co. Ltd. 34, Man. Finance Dept. 50-62, Dir. 54-64, Man. Planning Div. 62-66, Man. Dir. 64-69, Man. Sales Div. 66-71; Senior Man. Dir. 69-71; Pres. Fuji Photo Film Co. Ltd. 71-; Blue Ribbon Medal 74.
Fuji Photo Film Co. Ltd. 26-30, Nishiazabu 2-chome, Minato-ku, Tokyo; Home: 48-12, Utsukushigaoka 2-chome, Midori-ku, Yokohama-shi, Kanagawa, Japan.
Telephone: 03-406-2111 (Office); 045-911-1771 (Home).

Hiratsuka, Masunori, M.A., LITT.D.; Japanese educationist; b. 1907; ed. Tokyo Imperial Univ.
Lecturer, Aoyama Gakuin Theological School 31-36, Ferris Seminary 32-36, St. Paul Univ. 36-39, Hiroshima Higher Normal School 39-40, Prof. 40-44; Prof. Faculty of Letters, Kyushu Imperial Univ. 44-49, Faculty of Educ. 49-63, leave of absence 60, Dean of Faculty of Educ. 54-56, Dir. Research Inst. of Educ. and Culture 56-63; Dir. Dept. of Educ., UNESCO, Paris 60, Prof. 56-63, Emer. 64; Dir.-Gen. Nat. Inst. for Educational Research 63-; mem. Cen. Advisory Council on Educ., Council on Curriculum Revision, Council on Social Educ., Japan Educ. Soc. (Gov. of Board), Japan Educ. Philosophy Soc., Japan Educ. History Soc., Gov. Board of UNESCO Inst. for Educ. in Hamburg, World Council of Comparative Educ.; Chair. Japan Comparative Educ. Soc., Nat. Asscn. of Research Inst. for Educ., Gov. Board of Nat. Educ. Hall; Pres. Japanese Nat. Comm. for UNESCO 72-; Chair. Emer. Baiko Women's Univ.; Commdr. Palmes Académiques (France) 61.
Publs. *The Educational Thought of the Old Testament* 35 and 57, *History of Education in Japan* 38, *History of Modern Education in China* 44, *Future of Japan and Moral Education* 59, *Future of Japanese Education* 64.
Kokuritsu Kyoiku Kenkyusho (NIER), 6-5-22 Shimo-meguro, Meguro-ku, Tokyo, Japan.

Hiro, Keitaro; Japanese business executive; b. 7 Dec. 1908, Hyogo; ed. Ritsumeikan Univ.
Teacher, Okhura Commercial High School 38-43; Chief, Accounting Dept., Kubota Ltd. 46, Man. Financial Dept. 50, Dir. Financing 51, Man. Dir. 53, Senior Man. Dir. 60, Pres. 71-; Dir. Japan Productivity Asscn. 61, Osaka Industrialist Asscn. 61, Kansai Management Asscn. 61; Blue Ribbon Medal
Kubota Ltd., 22 Funadecho, 2-chome, Naniwa-ku, Osaka; Home: 15-32, Takakura-cho, Nishinomiya City, Hyogo, Japan.
Telephone: 06-648-2111 (Office); 0798-22-3191 (Home).

Hirohito, Emperor of Japan; b. 29 April 1901.
Son of Emperor Taishô, married 24 Princess Nagako Kuni; Regent 21-26; succeeded 26; heir H.I.H. Crown Prince Akihito (Tsugunomiya), b. 33, married Michiko Shoda 59; Fellow Royal Soc. (U.K.) 71.
Publs. Nine books on plant and marine biology.
The Imperial Palace, Tokyo, Japan.

Hirota, Hisakazu; Japanese steel executive; b. 7 May 1899; ed. Univ. of Kyoto.
Sumitomo Steel Works 23, Dir. Sumitomo Metal Industries Ltd. 46-, Man. Dir. 47, Senior Man. Dir. 47-49, Pres. 62, Chair. 73-; Adviser to Pres.; Pres. Kansai Productivity Center; "Ranju Hosho" Decoration, Order of the Rising Sun.
No. 27-5, 1-chome, Tsukaguchi-cho, Amagasaki-city, Hyogo-ken, Japan.

Hla Han, Col., M.B., B.S., D.P.H.; Burmese politician; b. 26 Sept. 1918; ed. Rangoon and Liverpool Univs.
Served in Burma National Army and Resistance 42-45; joined Burma Medical Corps 49; Dir. Medical Services, Ministry of Defence 55-; promoted Colonel 58; mem. Revolutionary Council 62-74, Council of State March 74-; Minister for Health and Educ. 62-74; Minister for Foreign Affairs 70-72; Star of Independent Sithu (First Class).
Council of State, Rangoon, Burma.

Hla Maung, U Thado Thiri Thudhamma; Burmese diplomatist; b. 20 Sept. 1911; ed. Rangoon Univ.
Deputy-Sec. Ministry of Foreign Affairs 42-45; founder and a leader of the Anti-Fascist People's Freedom League (A.F.P.F.L.); Parl. Sec. to Minister for Forests and Agriculture, later transferred to Minister for Home and Judicial Affairs 47; mem. Constituent Assembly; then Amb. to Thailand 48-51, concurrently to Indonesia 50-51; Amb. to People's Republic of China 51-58, concurrently Minister to Mongolia 57; Amb. to Israel 58-61, to the U.K. 61-68, concurrently to Norway, Sweden and Denmark 63-68; Amb. to U.S.A. 68-70; Amb. to Ceylon 70-71.
c/o Ministry of Foreign Affairs, Rangoon, Burma.

Ho Kuang-yu; army officer, People's Repub. of China.
Major-General, Deputy Commdr. Kweichow Mil. District, People's Liberation Army 58, Commdr. 66-; Vice-Chair. Kweichow Revolutionary Cttee. 67; Deputy Sec. CCP Kweichow 71.

Ho Yu-fa; army officer, People's Repub. of China.
Deputy Commdr. Kirin Mil. District, People's Liberation Army 67, Commdr. 68-; Vice-Chair. Kirin Revolutionary Cttee. 68; Sec. CCP Kirin 71.

Holyoake, Rt. Hon. Sir Keith (Jacka), G.C.M.G., C.H., P.C., M.P.; New Zealand politician and farmer; b. 11 Feb. 1904; ed. Tauranga, Hastings, Motueka.
Nelson Provincial Pres. Farmers' Union 30-41; Pres. N.Z. Hop Marketing Cttee. 38-41; Dominion Vice-Pres. Farmers' Union 40-50; mem. Dominion Exec. Farmers' Union 40-50; mem. N.Z. Tobacco Growers' Fed. and N.Z. Fruit Exporters' Asscn.; M.P. 32-; Deputy Leader of Opposition 47; Deputy Prime Minister and Minister of Agriculture 49-57; Prime Minister Sept.-Dec. 57; Leader of Opposition 57-60; Prime Minister 60-Feb. 72, Minister of Foreign Affairs 60-Nov. 72, of State Dec. 75-; N.Z. rep. at Farmers' World Conf., London 46; Chair. Gen. Council FAO 55; Nat. Party; Hon. LL.D. (Victoria Univ., N.Z.) 66, Hon. LL.D. (Agric.) (Seoul Nat. Univ.) 68; Hon. Freeman City of London.
52 Aurora Terrace, Wellington N.I., New Zealand.

Hon Sui Sen; Singapore politician; b. 16 April 1916, Penang; ed. St. Xavier's Inst., Penang, and Raffles Coll., Singapore (now Univ. of Singapore).
Joined Straits Settlements Civil Service 39, subsequently transferred to Singapore Admin. Service; Perm. Sec., Office of the Prime Minister and Perm. Sec., Econ. Devt. Div., Ministry of Finance 59-61; Chair. Econ. Devt. Board 61; Chair. and Pres. Devt. Bank of Singapore Ltd. 68; mem. Parl. April 70-; Minister for Finance 70-; Meritorious Service Medal 62, Malaysia Medal 64, Distinguished Service Order 67; Hon. D.Litt. (Univ. of Singapore) 69.
Ministry of Finance, 5th Floor, Fullerton Building, Singapore 1; 35 Malcolm Road, Singapore 11, Singapore.

Honda, Chikao; Japanese newspaper executive; b. 1899; ed. Waseda University.
Joined *Osaka Mainichi* 24, Editor-in-Chief 45-48; Pres. Mainichi Newspapers 48-; fmr. Pres. Japanese Newspaper Publishers' and Editors' Asscn. (Nihon Shimbun Kyokai).
126 Hara-machi, Bunkyo-ku, Tokyo, Japan.

Honda, Soichiro; Japanese business executive; b. 17 Nov. 1906.
Garage apprentice 23, opened own garage 28; Owner and Head, Piston Ring Production Factory 39; started producing motor cycles 48; Pres. Honda Motor Co. until 73, Dir. and Supreme Adviser 73-; Hon. D.Eng. (Michigan Tech. Univ.) 74.
Honda Motor Company, 27-8, 6-chome, Jingumae Shibuya-ku, Tokyo, 150, Japan.

Hongladarom, Sunthorn, M.A.; Thai international official; b. 23 Aug. 1912; ed. Thepsirin School, Bangkok, Weymouth and Brighton Colls., England and Cambridge Univ.
With Ministry of Education 37-40; Chief of Foreign Div., Dept. of Information 40-47; Asst. Sec.-Gen. of Council of Ministers 48-50; Sec.-Gen. of Nat. Econ. Council 50-57; Amb. to Fed. of Malaya 57-59; Minister of Econ. Affairs 59; Minister of Finance 59-65; Deputy Minister of Nat. Devt. 63; Minister of Econ. Affairs 65-68; Amb. to the U.K. 68-69, to the U.S.A. 69-72; Sec.-Gen. S.E. Asia Treaty Org. (SEATO) 72-; Rector of Chiengmai Univ. 66; Fellow of Econ. Devt. Inst., Int. Bank of Reconstruction and Devt.; Knight Grand Commdr. Order of White Elephant and Order of Chula Chom Klao; Hon. LL.D.
SEATO, P.O. Box 517, Bangkok, Thailand.

Hope, Alec Derwent, O.B.E.; Australian poet; b. 21 July 1907; ed. Sydney and Oxford Univs.
Former Lecturer Sydney Teachers' Coll. and Senior Lecturer Melbourne Univ.; Prof. of English Canberra Univ. Coll. 50-60, Australian Nat. Univ. 60-68; Library Fellow, Australian Nat. Univ. 69-72 (retd.); Fellow Australian Acad. of the Humanities; Arts Council Prize 65, Britannica-Australia Award 66, Levinson Prize for Poetry 69, Ingram Merrill Award 69, Robert Frost Award 76; Hon. D.Litt. (Australian Nat. Univ.) 72, (Univ. of New England) 73, (Monash Univ.) 76.
Publs. *The Wandering Islands* 55, *Poems* 60, *The Cave and the Spring* 65, *New Poems* 69, *A Mid-summer Eve's Dream* 70, *Dunciad Minor* 70, *Collected Poems 1930–1970* 72, *Native Companions* 73, *A Late Picking* 75; verse and criticism in numerous magazines, including *Meanjin, Southerly, M.U.M., Hermes, Quadrant, The Hudson Review, The Southern Review* and *Australian Literary Studies.*
66 Arthur Circle, Canberra, A.C.T., Australia.
Telephone: Canberra 73-1342.

Hori, Shigeru; Japanese politician; b. 20 Dec. 1901; ed. Chuo Univ.
Political Reporter in Hochi and Tonichi newspapers 24-28; Sec. to Minister of Agriculture; mem. House of Reps. 44-; successively Parl. Vice-Minister of Commerce and Industry, mem. Exec. Board Japan Progressivist Party, Sec.-Gen. of Democratic Party; Minister of Labour 50; Chief Cabinet Sec. 51; Minister of Agriculture and Forestry 53; Minister of Construction Nov. 67; Chief Cabinet Sec. (Dir.-Gen. of Cabinet Secr.) 68-71; Dir. Admin. Management Agency 73-74; mem. Exec. Board Liberal Democratic Party 53.
39-16, Gohongi, 1-chome, Meguro-ku, Tokyo, Japan.

Hori, Taro; Japanese finance official; b. 25 Dec. 1917, Kyoto; ed. Tokyo Imperial Univ.
Entered Ministry of Finance 43; Dir. Int. Org. Div. 60-61; Dir. Foreign Capital Div. 61-65; rep. of Ministry of Finance and Consul, New York, Financial Counsellor, Japanese Embassy, U.S.A. 65-68; Special Adviser to Minister of Econ. Planning 68-70; Exec. Dir. Honshu-Shikoku Bridge Authority 70-73; Special Adviser to Minister of Finance, Special Asst. to Minister of Foreign Affairs 74-; Exec. Dir. IBRD 73-.
Publ. *GATT Analysis and Prospect.*
International Bank for Reconstruction and Development, Washington, D.C. 20433; Home: 2 Kittery Court, Bethesda, Maryland 20034, U.S.A.
Telephone: 365-0894 (Home).

Horikoshi, Teizo, LL.B.; Japanese business executive; b. 13 Dec. 1898; ed. Tokyo Imperial Univ.
Entered Bank of Japan 24, Dir. 47-; Deputy Dir. Econ. Stabilization Agency 47; Sec.-Gen. Japanese Nat. Cttee. of Int. Chamber of Commerce 50; Exec. Dir. and Sec.-Gen. Fed. of Econ. Orgs. 54-; auditor, Toho Mutual Life Insurance Co. 59-; Pres. Securities and Exchange Council, Ministry of Finance 61-; Pres. Nippon Usiminas Co. Ltd. 65-; Hon. C.B.E. (U.K.) 66.
270 Kyodo-machi, Setagaya-ku, Tokyo, Japan.

Hossain, Kamal, M.A., B.C.L., D.PHIL.; Bangladesh politician; b. 20 April 1937, Calcutta; ed. St. Gregory's High School and Coll., Dacca, Univ. of Notre Dame, Indiana (U.S.A.), and Queen's Coll. and Nuffield Coll., Oxford, England.
Called to the Bar, Lincoln's Inn, London 59; practising lawyer, Dacca High Court 59-75; lecturer in constitutional and int. law, Univ. of Dacca 61-68; Sec. Bangladesh (fmrly. Pakistan) Law Inst. 70-75; mem. Faculty of Law, Univ. of Dacca; Chair. Bangladesh Inst. of Law and Int. Affairs 72-75; Minister of Law and Parl. Affairs 72-73, of Foreign Affairs 73-75, also of Natural Resources, Research and Atomic Energy 74-75.

Hotta, Shozo; Japanese banker; b. 23 Jan. 1899, Nagoya; ed. Dept. of Econs., Kyoto Imperial Univ.
Joined Sumitomo Bank Ltd. 26, Man. Tokyo Branch 45, Chief Man. 47, Man. Dir. and Deputy Pres. 47, Pres. 52-71, Chair. 71-; Dir. Nippon Electric Co. Ltd., Sumitomo Real Estate Co. Ltd., Mitsui-OSK Lines Ltd.; Auditor, Kansai Oil Co. Inc., Asahi Breweries Ltd.; Adviser to Kansai Electric Power Co. Inc., Sumitomo Electric Industries Ltd., Sumitomo Atomic Energy Industries Ltd.; Adviser to Ministry of Foreign Affairs; Vice-Chair. Bankers' Asscn., Osaka; Exec. Dir. Japan Fed. of Econ. Org. (Keidanren); Deputy Pres. Japan Asscn. for *Expo 70*; Pres. Japan-Spanish Soc.; Roving Amb. in Europe 57; leader of govt. mission to EFTA countries 67; visited Latin America 67, Europe 68 on behalf of Minister in charge of *Expo 70*; Blue Ribbon Medal; Commdr. Orden de Isabel la Catolica (Spain).
The Sumitomo Bank Ltd., P.O.B. 45, Osaka Central, 530-91, Japan.

Hou Youn; Cambodian politician; b. 1928.
Former deputy Nat. Assembly in Prince Sihanouk's party, *Sangkum Reastr Nyum* (Popular Socialist Community); left *Sangkum* party, went underground and became active in *Khmers Rouges* 67; Minister of Interior, Co-operatives and Communal Reforms Royal Govt. of Nat. Union of Cambodia (GRUNC) 70-76 (in exile 70-75, in Phnom-Penh 75-76); mem. Politburo Nat. United Front of Cambodia (FUNC) 70-, rep. in N.W. Cambodia 70-75.
Front uni national du Cambodge, Phnom-Penh, Cambodia.

Howson, Peter, F.A.I.M.; Australian politician; b. 22 May 1919; ed. Stowe School and Trinity Coll., Cambridge.
War service 40-46 (mentioned in despatches 42); Staff Man. Foy and Gibson Stores Ltd. 50, Dir. 51-55; Dir. Eagley Mills Ltd. 55, Cleckheaton (Yorkshire) Ltd. 61-64; mem. House of Reps. 55-72; Minister for Air 64-68; Minister assisting the Treas. 66-68; Minister for the Environment, Aborigines and the Arts, Minister-in-Charge for Tourism 71-72; Pres. Royal Victorian Eye and Ear Hospital 56-64; Chair. Exec. Cttee. Commonwealth Parl. Asscn. 68-70, Australian Foundation for the Prevention of Blindness 69-71, Australian Deafness Council 74-; Liberal.
Publ. 23rd Roy Milne Memorial Lecture: *Australia in the World Environment*.
40 Kensington Road, South Yarra, Melbourne, Victoria, Australia.

Hsiang Chung-hua; army officer, People's Repub. of China.
Deputy Political Commissar, People's Liberation Army Armoured Force 53, Political Commissar 58; Lieut.-Gen. 55; Deputy Chief of Staff PLA 71-; Alt. mem. 10th Cen. Cttee. of CCP 73.

Hsiao Ching-kuang; army officer, People's Repub. of China; b. 1904, Changsha, Hunan; ed. Hunan Provincial Normal School, Sun Yat-sen Univ. and Red Army Coll., Moscow, U.S.S.R.
Joined Communist Youth League and CCP 20; Instructor Whampoa Mil. Acad. 24; Political Commissar 5th Army Corps 31; on Long March 34-35; Commdr. Cavalry, Red Army 38; Alt. mem. 7th Cen. Cttee. of CCP 45; Commdr. Hunan Mil. District, People's Liberation Army 49; Commdr. PLA Navy 60-; Vice-Minister of Nat. Defence 54-; mem. 8th Cen. Cttee. of CCP 56, 9th Cen. Cttee. 69, 10th Cen. Cttee. 73.

Hsieh Ch'en-hua; army officer, People's Repub. of China.
Commander Shansi Mil. District, People's Liberation Army 67-; Vice-Chair. Shansi Revolutionary Cttee. 68, Chair. 69; First Sec. CCP Shansi 71; Alt. mem. 10th Cen. Cttee. of CCP 73.

Hsieh Hsueh-kung; People's Repub. of China.
Shansi Provincial People's Govt. 50-52; Vice-Minister of Foreign Trade 52-58; Pres. Peking Foreign Trade Coll. 54-58; Sec. CCP Hopei 58-68; Sec. N. China Bureau 63-68; Chair. Tientsin Revolutionary Cttee. 67; mem. 9th Cen. Cttee. of CCP 69; First Sec. CCP Tientsin 71-; mem. 10th Cen. Cttee. of CCP 73.

Hsien Heng-han; People's Repub. of China.
Regimental Political Commissar 34; Deputy Political Commissar Tsinghai Mil. District, People's Liberation Army 49; Lieut.-Gen. 55; Political Commissar Lanchow Mil. Region, PLA 57-; Chair. Kansu Revolutionary Cttee. 68; mem. 9th Cen. Cttee. of CCP 69; First Sec. CCP Kansu 71-; mem. 10th Cen. Cttee. of CCP 73.

Hsin Chun-chieh; army officer, People's Repub. of China.
Commander Hupeh Mil. District, People's Liberation Army 70-; Vice-Chair. Hupeh Revolutionary Cttee. 71.

Hsiung Shih-i; Chinese author; b. 14 Oct. 1902; ed. Teachers' Coll., Nat. Univ. Peking.
Associate Man. Chen Kwang Theatre, Peking 22; Prof. Agricultural Coll., Nanchang 23; Editor, Commercial Press. Shanghai 26, Special Editor 28; Prof. Chung Shan Univ., Nanchang 27; Man. Dir. Pantheon Theatres Ltd., Shanghai 29; Prof. Min Kuo Univ., Peking 30; Sec. China Soc., London 33, Hon. Sec. 35; Chinese del. to Int. PEN Congress 34, 35, 38, 39, 40, 47, to Int. Theatre Inst. Congress 48; lecturer, Cambridge Univ. 50-53; Dean, Coll. of Arts, Nanyang Univ. 54-55; Man. Dir. Pacific Films Co. Ltd., Hong Kong 55-; Chair. Board of Dirs. Standard Publishers Ltd., Hong Kong 61-; Pres. Tsing Hua Coll., Hong Kong 63-; Hon. Ph.D.
Publs. in English: *Lady Precious Stream* 34, *The Romance of Western Chamber* 35, *The Professor from Peking* 39, *The Bridge of Heaven* 43, *The Life of Chiang Kai-shek* 48, *The Gate of Peace* 49, *The Story of Lady Precious Stream* 50, *Book of Chinese Proverbs* 53; trans. into Chinese of B. Franklin's *Autobiography* 23, of Barrie's and Shaw's plays, and Hardy's novels 26-33.
41 Buckland Crescent, London, N.W.3, England; Tsing Hua College, Kowloon, Hong Kong.

Hsu Ching-chung, DR.AGRIC.; Chinese politician; b. 19 July 1907, Taipei; ed. Taihoku Imperial Univ.
Professor, Nat. Taiwan Univ. 45-47; Dir. Agricultural and Forestry Admin., Taiwan Provincial Govt. 47-49; Commr. Dept. of Agriculture and Forestry, Taiwan Provincial Govt. 49-54, Commr. 54-57; mem. Cen. Planning and Evaluation Cttee., China Nationalist Party 55-61, Deputy Sec.-Gen. Cen. Cttee. 61-66; Minister of the Interior 66-72; Vice-Premier of Exec. Yuan June 72-; mem. Standing Cttee., Taiwan Land Bank 46-67, China Farmers' Bank 67-72; Medal of Clouds and Banner.
Publs. several studies on agricultural problems in Taiwan.
30, Lane 63, Liang Ning Street, Taipei, Taiwan.
Telephone: 772957.

Hsu Hsiang-ch'ien; politician and fmr. army officer, People's Repub. of China; b. 1902, Wu-tai, Shansi; ed. Taiyuan Normal School, Whampoa Mil. Acad.
Director Political Dept.. Student Army 26; joined CCP 27;

Workers' Leader in Canton Uprising 27; Commdr.-in-Chief 4th Front Army 31; Deputy Commdr. 129th Div. 39; mem. 7th Cen. Cttee. of CCP 45; Commdr., Political Commissar 1st Army Corps 48; Deputy Commdr. N. China Region, People's Liberation Army 49-54; Chief of Staff PLA 49-54; Vice-Chair. Nat. Defence Council 54-; Marshall PLA 55; mem. 8th Cen. Cttee. of CCP 56; Vice-Chair. Standing Cttee., Nat. People's Congress 65-; mem. 9th Cen. Cttee. of CCP 69, 10th Cen. Cttee. 73; Vice-Chair. Mil. Affairs Cttee., CCP Cen. Cttee. 75-.

Hsu Peh-yuan; Chinese banker and economist; b. 1903; ed. National Southeastern Univ. and Univs. of Chicago, Illinois and California.
Assistant Gen. Man. China Electric Corpn. 33; Deputy Dir.-Gen. Postal Remittances and Savings Bank, Shanghai 34-35; Man. Bank of Communications, Peking, Tientsin, Kunming 35-39; mem. People's Political Council 38-40; Deputy Sec.-Gen., Sec.-Gen. Joint Board Four Govt. Banks 39-48; Vice-Minister of Finance 46-48; Deputy Gov. Central Bank of China 49-50, Gov. 60-69; Chair. Bank of China 49-61, Bank of Taiwan 51-52; Commr. of Finance, Taiwan Provincial Govt. 53-54; Minister of Finance 54-58; Chair. Foreign Exchange and Trade Comm., Exec. Yuan 50-51, 53-54, 55-58, 63-69; Chair. Finance Cttee., China Kuomintang Party 54-70; Dean, Econs. Dept. Nat. War Coll. 58-70; Gov. for China (Taiwan) IBRD 54-58, IMF 64-69; Exec. Dir. Int. Monetary Fund (IMF) 70-72; Chair. Board CUTICO 73-; Order of Brilliant Star, First Class.
150 Nanking East Road, 2nd Section, Taipei, Taiwan.

Hsu Shih-yu; army officer, People's Repub. of China; b. 1906, Honan.
Commander 9th Army 33; Chief Commdr. of Cavalry 35; Brigade Commdr. 40; Commdr. Chinglo Mil. District 42, Ponai Mil. District 44; Commdr. 11th Army Corps, 3rd Field Army 48; Commdr. Shantung Mil. District, People's Liberation Army 50; Deputy Commdr. 3rd Field Army, PLA 54; mem. Nat. Defence Council 54-; Col.-Gen. 55; Alt. mem. 8th Cen. Cttee. of CCP 56; Commdr. Nanking Mil. Region, PLA 57-73; Vice-Minister of Nat. Defence 59-; Sec. E. China Bureau, CCP 66; Chair. Kiangsu Revolutionary Cttee. 68; mem. Politburo, 9th Cen. Cttee. of CCP 69; First Sec. CCP Kiangsu 71; mem. Politburo, 10th Cen. Cttee. of CCP 73, 75; Commdr. Canton Mil. Region, PLA 74-.

Hsueh Shao-ch'ing; army officer, People's Repub. of China.
Major-General Air Force; People's Liberation Army 55; Vice-Minister of Third Ministry of Machine Building 60-65; Deputy Commdr. PLA Air Force 71-.

Hu Nim; Cambodian politician; b. 1929.
Former deputy Nat. Assembly in Prince Sihanouk's party, *Sangkum Reastr Nyum* (Popular Socialist Community); left *Sangkum* party, went underground and became active in *Khmers Rouges* 67; Minister of Information and Propaganda Royal Govt. of Nat. Union of Cambodia (GRUNC) 70-76 (in exile 70-75, in Phnom-Penh 75-76), Democratic Cambodia 76-; mem. Politburo Nat. United Front of Cambodia (FUNC) 70-, rep. in S.W. Cambodia 70-75; mem. People's Representative Assembly March 76-.
Ministry of Information and Propaganda, Phnom-Penh, Cambodia.

Hu Wei; People's Repub. of China.
Deputy Commdr., Shansi People's Liberation Army 67; Vice-Chair. Shensi Provincial Revolutionary Cttee. 68; Alt. mem. 9th Central Cttee. of CCP 69, 10th Cen. Cttee. of CCP 73; Deputy Chief of Gen. Staff, PLA 74.

Hua Kuo-feng; People's Repub. of China.
Vice-Governor of Hunan 58-67; Sec. CCP Hunan 59; Vice-Chair. Hunan Revolutionary Cttee. 68, Chair. 70; mem. 9th Cen. Cttee. of CCP 69; First Sec. CCP Hunan 70; Political Commissar Canton Mil. Region, People's Liberation Army 72; First Political Commissar Hunan Mil. District, PLA 73; mem. Politburo, 10th Cen. Cttee. of CCP 73, 75, First Vice-Chair. Cen. Cttee. April 76-; Minister of Public Security 75-; Vice-Premier, State Council 75-76, Acting Premier Feb.-April 76, Premier April 76-.
Office of the Premier, State Council, Peking, People's Republic of China.

Huang Chen; Chinese diplomatist.
Deputy Dir. 18th Div., Shansi-Hopei-Shantung Border Region Army 44; after war Deputy Political Dir. in mil. admin. areas; Amb. to People's Republic of Hungary 50-54; Amb. to Republic of Indonesia 54-61; Deputy Foreign Minister 61-64; Amb. to France 64-73; Head Liaison Office, Washington, D.C. 73-; rep. at the Afro-Asian Conference 55.
Liaison Office of the People's Republic of China, Washington, D.C., U.S.A.

Huang Chieh; Chinese civil servant; b. 2 Nov. 1903, Hunan Province; ed. Mil. Acad., Army War Coll. and Nat. Defence Coll.
Commandant, Cen. Training Corps 45-48; Vice-Minister of Nat. Defence 48-49; Gov. of Hunan, concurrently Commdg. Gen. 1st Army 49; Commdg. Gen. Chinese Troops stationed in Indo-China 49-53; Taipei Garrison Command 53-54; C.-in-C. Chinese Army 54-57; Personal Chief of Staff to the Pres. 57-58; C.-in-C. Taiwan Garrison Gen. H.Q. 58-62; Gov. Taiwan Province 62-69; Minister of Nat. Defence 69-72; Gen. Special Adviser to Pres. on Mil. Strategy 72-; numerous decorations from China, U.S.A., Thailand, Philippines, Spain, Iran, Iraq, Korea and Venezuela.
213 Antung Street, Taipei, Taiwan.

Huang Ching-yao; army officer, People's Repub. of China.
Deputy Commdr. Heilungkiang Mil. District, People's Liberation Army 59; Commdr. Shensi Mil. District, PLA 67-; Vice-Chair. Shensi Revolutionary Cttee. 68; Sec. CCP Shensi 71.

Huang Hua; Chinese diplomatist, People's Repub. of China; b. 1910; ed. Yench'ing Univ., Peking.
Student leader in Peking, active in December 9th Movt. 35; Councillor, Ministry of Foreign Affairs 53; Chief Chinese del. at Panmunjon 53; Amb. to Ghana 60-66, to Egypt 66-70, to Canada April-Nov. 71; Perm. Rep. to UN Nov. 71-.
Permanent Mission of People's Republic of China to UN, 155 West 66th Street, New York, N.Y. 10023, U.S.A.

Huang Ou-tung; People's Repub. of China; b. *circa* 1907, Ping-hsiang, Kiangsi.
Regimental Commdr. 129th Div. 39, Brigade Commdr. 45; Gov. of Liaoning 49-55, 58-68; Mayor of Shenyang 52-54; Sec. CCP Liaoning 54-57, First Sec. 57-58, Second Sec. 58-68; Alt. mem. 8th Cen. Cttee. of CCP 56; Sec. N.E. Bureau, CCP 62-68; criticized and removed from office during Cultural Revolution 68; Vice-Chair. Liaoning Revolutionary Cttee. 73; Sec. CCP Liaoning 73-.

Huang Shao-ku; Chinese politician; b. 9 June 1901; ed. National Peking Normal Univ.
Secretary-General of Exec. Yuan 49-54; Vice-Prime Minister, Exec. Yuan 54-58, 66-69; Minister of Foreign Affairs 58-60; Amb. to Spain 60-62; Sec.-Gen. Nat. Security Council 67-.
10, Lane 85, Sungkiang Road, Taipei, Taiwan.

Hudson, Sir William, K.B.E., F.R.S., B.SC.(Eng.); British engineer; b. 27 April 1896; ed. Nelson Coll., New Zealand, Univs. of London and Grenoble.
Former Engineer, Sir W. G. Armstrong-Whitworth & Co. Ltd., Public Works Dept., New Zealand, Sir Alexander Gibb & Partners, Metropolitan Water, Sewerage and

Drainage Board, Sydney; Commr. Snowy Mountains Hydro-Electric Authority, Cooma, N.S.W. 49-67; Australasian Engineer Award 57, Kernot Memorial Medal 59; Fellow, Univ. Coll. London 61-; Hon. mem. Australasian Inst. of Mining and Metallurgy 61-; Hon. mem. of the Inst. of Engineers, Australia; LL.D. h.c. (Australian Nat. Univ.) 62; Hon. D.Eng. (Monash) 68; Hon. Fellow the Royal Australian Inst. of Architects 68; Hon. Member the Inst. of Royal Engineers 68.
39 Flanagan Street, Garran, A.C.T., Australia.
Telephone: 815137.

Hulme, Hon. Sir Alan Shallcross, K.B.E., F.C.A.; Australian politician; b. 14 Feb. 1907; ed. North Sydney Boys' High School.
Honorary Treas. King's Univ. Coll. 44-49; Pres. Queensland Div. Liberal Party of Australia 46-49, 62-63; mem. House of Reps. 49-61, 63-72; Minister for Supply 58-61; mem. Commonwealth Parl. Public Accounts Cttee. 52-58; Chair. Special Commonwealth Cttee. investigating Depreciation under Income Tax Acts 54-55, Commonwealth Immigration Planning Council 55-58; Dir. Chandlers (Aust.) Ltd., J. B. Chandler Investment Co. Ltd. 52-58, 62-63; Postmaster-Gen. 63-72; Vice-Pres. of Exec. Council 66-72.
Alcheringa Droughtmaster Stud, Eudlo, Queensland 4554, Australia.

Hunt, Ralph James Dunnet; Australian politician; b. 31 March 1928, Narrabri, N.S.W.; ed. Scots Coll., Sydney.
Grazier, C. J. S. Hunt and Sons 46-; mem. House of Reps. 69-; Minister of the Interior 71-72; Acting Minister of Shipping and Transport 71; opposition spokesman on the environment 75; Minister of Health Dec. 75-; Nat. Country Party.
Australian Parliament Offices, Chifley Square, Sydney, N.S.W.; Home: Merindah Avenue, Moree, N.S.W., Australia.

Husain, Akhter, O.B.E.; Pakistani administrator; b. 1902; ed. Hakimia High School, Burhanpur, M.A.O. Coll., Aligarh, and St. John's Coll., Cambridge.
Appointed to Indian civil service in Punjab 26; various admin. posts 30-43; Sec. Post-War Reconstruction Dept. 44; Chief Sec. Govt. Punjab 46-47; Financial Commr. and Sec. to Govt., West Punjab 47-53; mem. Tenancy Inquiry Cttee. 51, Liaquat Ali Assassination Inquiry Cttee. 51; special duty at Karachi for reorganization of Karachi Admin. 51; Chair. Lord Boyd Orr's Expert Cttee. 53; Sec. Ministry of Defence, Govt. Pakistan 53-57; Chair. Karachi Admin. Cttee. 55; Gov. West Pakistan 57-60; Minister of Information, Nat. Reconstruction and Kashmir Affairs 60, of Kashmir Affairs 60-61, of Education and Scientific Research, Minority Affairs 61-62; Chair. Land Reforms Comm. 58, Land Comm. and Provincial Admin. Comm. 59; Chief Election Commr. (Pakistan) 62-64; Chair. Nat. Press Trust 65, Investment Corpn. of Pakistan 66; mem. Advisory Council of Islamic Ideology; Dir. Agric. Devt. Bank of Pakistan 67-70; Chair. Water Allocation and Rate Cttee. of W. Pakistan 68-70, Burmah Shell Ltd. (Pakistan) 69-; Pres. Soc. for Promotion of Urdu Language 62-, Diabetic Asscn. of Pakistan 71-; Hilale-e-Pakistan 58; Hon. LL.D. (Punjab Univ.) 61.
29a Sunset Boulevard, Defence Housing Society, Karachi, Pakistan.

Husain, Maqbool Fida; Indian painter; b. 17 Sept. 1915.
Joined Progressive Artists Group, Bombay 48; first one-man exhbn., Bombay 50, later at Rome, Frankfurt, London, Zürich, Prague, Tokyo, New York, New Delhi, Calcutta, Kabul and Baghdad; mem. Lalit Kala Akademi, New Delhi 54; mem. Gen. Council Nat. Academy of Art, New Delhi 55; First Nat. Award for Painting 55; Int. Award, Biennale Tokyo 59.
Major works: Murals for Air India Int. at Hong Kong, Bangkok, Zürich and Prague 57, and WHO Building, New Delhi 63; Mural in Mosaic for Lever Bros. and Aligarh Univ. 64; working on High Ceramic Mural for Indian Govt. Building, New Delhi; Exhibitor "Art now in India" exhbn., London 67.
Film: *Through the Eyes of the Painter* 67 (Golden Bear Award, Berlin 67).
6 Zeenat Manzil L. Jamshedji Road, Mahim, Bombay 16, India.

Hussein bin Onn, Datuk, BARR.-AT-LAW; Malaysian lawyer and politician; b. 12 Feb. 1922; ed. Cambridge School, Indian Mil. Acad., Dehra Dun, Lincoln's Inn, England.
Commissioned in Indian Army 42, served in Middle East and India; Mil. Gen. H.Q., New Delhi; with British Liberation Forces, Malaya 45; served Malay Admin. Service, Kuala Selangor and Klang 46-47; Nat. Youth Leader and Sec. Gen. United Malays Nat. Org. (UMNO) 47; mem. Fed. Legislative Council, Johore Council of State and State Exec. Council 48-57; qualified as Barr.-at-Law, England, legal practice 60; re-joined UMNO 68, Deputy Pres. until 76, Pres. 76-; mem. of Parl. 70-; Minister of Educ. 70-73; Deputy Prime Minister 73-75, Prime Minister Jan. 76-; Minister of Trade and Industry 73-74, of Finance and Public Corpns. 74-75, of Defence Jan. 76-; Seri Paduka Mahkota Johor.
Prime Minister's Office, Kuala Lumpur 11-01; Home: 3 Jalan Kenny, Kuala Lumpur, Malaysia.

Hutasingh, Prakob, LL.B., D.JUR.; Thai jurist; b. 5 Feb. 1912; ed. Vajiravuth Coll., Univ. of Jena and Thammasat Univ., Bangkok.
Joined the judiciary 37; Asst. Judge Court of Appeal 41; Sec. Supreme Court 48; Asst. Judge Supreme Court 50; Judge, Appeal Court 53; Judge, Supreme Court 60; Pres. Supreme Court 67-72; Minister of Justice 73-74; Deputy Prime Minister June 74-75; Pres. Thai Bar and Inst. of Legal Educ., Thai Bar; Hon. D.C.L.
Publs. various legal textbooks.
2029/1 Banmai, Bangkok, Thailand.

Huxley, Sir Leonard George Holden, K.B.E., M.A., D.PHIL., PH.D., F.A.A.; Australian public official; b. 29 May 1902; ed. The Hutchins School, Hobart, Tasmania Univ. and New Coll., Oxford.
On scientific staff, C.S.I.R., Sydney 29-30; Lecturer, Univ. Coll., Nottingham, England 30-32; Head, Physics Dept., Univ. Coll., Leicester, England 32-40; Principal Scientific Officer, Telecommunications Research Establishment M.A.P. 40-46; Reader in Electromagnetism, Birmingham Univ., England 46-49; Elder Prof. of Physics, Adelaide Univ. 49-60; Vice-Chancellor, Australian Nat. Univ. 60-67; Pres. Australian Inst. of Physics 62-65; Fellow, Australian Acad. of Science 54-; Chair. Radio Research Board of Australia 58-63, Radio Frequency Allocation Cttee. 60-64, Australian Nat. Standards Comm. 53-65; mem. U.S. Educ. Foundation in Australia 60-64; mem. Nat. Library Council 60-72, Exec. Commonwealth Scientific and Industrial Research Org. (CSIRO) 60; mem. Australian-American Educ. Foundation 65-69; Chair. Gen. Council Australia-Britannica Awards Scheme 64-68; Trustee, Australian Humanities Research Council 68-70; mem. Council Canberra Coll. of Advanced Educ. 68-74.
Publs. *Wave Guides* (with R. W. Crompton) 49, *The Diffusion and Drift of Electrons in Gases* 74, numerous papers on gaseous electronics, electromagnetism, ionosphere and upper atmosphere.
19 Glasgow Place, Hughes, Canberra, A.C.T. 2605, Australia.
Telephone: Canberra 815560.

Huynh Tan Phat; Vietnamese politician; b. 1913.
Member Vanguard Youth 45; Editor *Thanh-nien* during anti-French struggle; remained in S. Viet-Nam after Geneva Agreement 54; Sec.-Gen. Democratic Party; mem.

Cen. Cttee. Nat. Liberation Front (N.L.F.) 64-; Pres. Provisional Revolutionary Govt. of S. Viet-Nam 69-76 (in Saigon 75-76); Vice-Premier Council of Ministers, Socialist Republic of Viet-Nam July 76-.
Council of Ministers, Hanoi, Viet-Nam.

Hyder, Sajjad, B.A.; Pakistani diplomatist; b. 1920; ed. Govt. High School, Jullundur, D.A.V. Coll., Jullundur, and Indian Mil. Acad., Dehra Dun.
War service; Third Sec., Indian Foreign Service, New Delhi 47, Second Sec., U.S.A. 48; Second Sec., First Sec. and Counsellor, U.K. 52; Dir. Pakistan Foreign Office, Karachi 55; Deputy High Commr., New Delhi 57-59, London 59-61; Amb. to Iraq 61-65, to United Arab Republic 65-68; High Commr. in India 68-71; Amb. to Fed. Repub. of Germany 72-74, to U.S.S.R. (also accred. to Finland) 75-.
Pakistan Embassy, 17 Sadova Kudrinskaya, Moscow, U.S.S.R.

Hyuga, Hosai; Japanese industrialist; b. 1906; ed. Univ. of Tokyo.
Head Office, Sumitomo Group 31-41; Govt. Service 41; Sumitomo Group 41-, Dir. Sumitomo Metal Industries Ltd. 49-, Man. Dir. 52-58, Senior Man. Dir. 58-60, Exec. Vice-Pres. 60-62, Pres. 62-74, Chair. 74-.
177-2 Higashiyama-cho, Ashiya-shi, Hyago-ken, 659 Japan.
Telephone: 0797-22-3249.

I

Ibe, Kyonosuke; Japanese banker; b. July 1908, Tokyo; ed. Tokyo High School, Tokyo Imperial Univ.
Joined Sumitomo Bank 33, Dir. 57-60, Man. Dir. 60-64, Senior Man. Dir. 64-71, Deputy Pres. 71-73, Pres. 73-; Chair. Board of Trustees Kansai Cttee. for Econ. Devt. 67-69, Trustee 69-; Trustee Japan Cttee. for Econ. Devt. 71-72, 73-; Exec. Dir. Japan Fed. of Econ. Orgs. 73-; Vice-Chair. Fed. of Bankers' Asscns. of Japan 73-74; Chair. Osaka Bankers' Asscn. 73-74, Vice-Chair. 74-.
The Sumitomo Bank, 22, 5-chome, Kitahama, Higashi-ku, Osaka; 31 Higahi Ashiya-machi, Ashiya City, Hyogo Prefecture, Japan.

Ibuka, Masaru; Japanese industrialist; b. 11 April 1908; ed. Waseda Senior High School and Waseda Univ.
Research Engineer, Photo-Chemical Laboratory 33-37; Man. Radio Telegraphy Dept., Japan Audio Optical Industrial Corpn. 37-40; Man. Dir. Japan Measuring Apparatus Co. Ltd. 40-45; Organizer, Tokyo Telecommunications Engineering Corpn. 45- (Sony Corpn. since 58), Pres., Man. Dir. 50-71, Chair. 71-; Chair. Japan Cttee. for Econ. Devt.; mem. Econ. Council; dir. several industrial asscns.; Blue Ribbon Medal 60; Founders Medal, IEEE 72; Hon. D.Sc. (Plano Univ.) 74.
7-35 Kitashinagawa 6-chome, Shinagawuku, Tokyo; and 7-1-702 Mita 2-chome, Minato-ku, Tokyo, Japan.

Ichikawa, Kon; Japanese film director; b. 1915; ed. Ichioka Commercial School, Osaka.
Films include: *Poo-San* 53, *A Billionaire* 54, *The Heart* 54, *Punishment Room* 55, *The Burmese Harp* 56, *The Men of Tohoku* 56, *Conflagration* 58, *Fires on the Plain* 59, *The Key* 59, *Bonchi* 60, *Her Brother* 60, *The Sin* 61, *Being Two Isn't Easy* 62, *The Revenge of Yuki-No-Jo* 63, *Alone on the Pacific* 63, *Tokyo Olympiad* 64, *Seishun* 70, *To Love Again* 71, *The Wanderers* 73, *Visions of Eight* (co-dir.) 73.

Ide, Ichitaro; Japanese politician; b. 1911; ed. Kyoto Univ.
Member, House of Reps.; Chair. House of Reps. Agriculture, Forestry and Fishery Affairs Cttee., also Budget Cttee.; fmr. Minister of Agriculture and Forestry; Vice-Chair. Liberal-Democratic Party Foreign Affairs Research Council; Minister for Posts and Telecommunications 70-71; Minister of State, Chief Cabinet Sec. Dec. 74-.
House of Representatives, Tokyo, Japan.

Idemitsu, Keisuke; Japanese business executive; b. 1900; ed. Tokyo Commercial Coll.
Managing Dir. Idemitsu Kosan Co. Ltd. 47, Senior Man. Dir. 50, Pres. 66, Chair. 72-.
Idemitsu Kosan Co. Ltd., 1-1, 3-chome, Marunouchi, Chiyoda-ku, Tokyo, Japan.

Idham Chalid, Dr. Kyai Haji; Indonesian politician; b. 27 Aug. 1922, Amuntai, Kalimantan; ed. Islamic Teachers' Coll., Ponorogo, E. Java.
Teacher 43-47; mem. Parl. of Repub. of United States of Indonesia 48; mem. House of Reps. 50; mem. Constituent Assembly 56; Second Deputy Prime Minister 56-59; mem. Supreme Advisory Council 59; mem. Exec. Board of Nat. Front 60, Deputy Chair. 61; mem. and Deputy Chair. Provisional People's Consultative Assembly (MPRS) 60-65, now Chair. and Speaker of the House; First Minister of People's Welfare 67-71; Chair. Nahdlatul-'Ulama (Moslem Scholars' Party) and Pres. Partai Persatuan Pembangunan (Devt. Unity Party); Star of Yugoslav Flag, Medal of Honour (Egypt).
51 Mangunsarkoro, Jakarta, Indonesia.

Ieng Sary; Cambodian politician; ed. Paris.
Former teacher; active in left-wing movements and forced to flee Phnom-Penh 63; prominent in *Khmers Rouges* insurgent movement 63-75; *Khmers Rouges* liaison officer to Royal Govt. of Nat. Union of Cambodia (GRUNC) in exile 71-75; mem. Politburo Nat. United Front of Cambodia (FUNC) 70-; Second Deputy Prime Minister with special responsibility for Foreign Affairs Aug. 75-.
Office of the Deputy Prime Minister, Phnom-Penh, Cambodia.

Ikeda, Daisaku; Japanese religious leader; b. 2 Jan. 1928; ed. Fuji Junior Coll.
President of Soka Gakkai 60-; founder, Min-on Concert Asscn. 63; founder, Soka Univ. 71, Soka Junior and Senior High Schools 73; founder, Oriental Inst. of Academic Research; Pres. Nichiren Shoshu Soka Gakkai Int. 75-.
Publs. *Science and Religion* 65, *The Human Revolution* (novel) Vols. I-III 73-76, *My Thought and Opinion* (essay) 69, *New Life* (poems) 70, *Essays on Life* 70, *Essay for Women* 71, *Ode to Youth* 72, *East and West: Dialogue with Richard E. Coudenhove-Kalergi* 72, *Dialogue on Life* (Vols. 1-3) 73-74, *My Views on Buddhism* 74, *The Living Buddha* 76, *The Toynbee-Ikeda Dialogue—Man Himself Must Choose* 76, *Buddhism: the Living Philosophy* 76.
c/o The Soka Gakkai, 32 Shinano-machi, Shinjuku-ku, Tokyo 160, Japan.

Ikeura, Kisaburo, LL.B.; Japanese banker; b. 21 April 1916, Wakayama Prefecture; ed. Tokyo Univ.
Industrial Bank of Japan Ltd. 39-, Dir. 64, Man. Dir. 65, Deputy Pres. 73, Pres. 75-.
3-3 Marunouchi 1-chome, Chiyoda-ku, Tokyo; Home: 22-12, 4-chome Numabukuro, Nakano-ku, Tokyo, Japan.
Telephone: 214-1111 (Office); 386-1443 (Home).

Ilangaratne, Tikiri Bandara; Ceylonese politician, writer, playwright, novelist; b. 27 Feb. 1913; ed. St. Anthony's Coll., Kandy.
Clerical Servant until 47; mem. of Parl. for Kandy 48, for Galaha 52; Gen. Sec. Sri Lanka Freedom Party 54-; mem. of Parl. for Hewaheta 56; Minister for Social Services and Housing 56-59, of Home Affairs 59, of Trade, Commerce, Food and Shipping 61-63, of Finance 63-64, of Trade and Supplies 64-65; Vice-Pres. Sri Lanka Freedom Party 66; mem. of Parl. for Kolonnawa 67, responsible for nationalizing foreign oil companies in Ceylon; Pres. Peace Council

of Ceylon; Minister of Foreign and Internal Trade 70-, of Public Admin. and Home Affairs Dept. 75-.
Publs. (in Sinhalese). Novels: *Wilambeeta, Denuwara, Kathava, Thilaka, Lasanda, Thilaka and Thilaka, Nedeyo*; Plays: *Häramitiya, Manthri Hamuduruwo, Jataka Natyaya, Rangamandala, Handahana, Ambaryaluwo*; Short stories: *Onchillawa*.
B-20 Government Bungalow, Stanmore Crescent, Colombo 7, Sri Lanka.

Imai, Kenji; Japanese architect; b. 11 Jan. 1895, Tokyo; ed. Architectural Dept., Waseda Univ., Tokyo.
Assistant Prof. Waseda Univ. 20-37, Prof. 37-65, Hon. Prof. 65-; Prof. Kantō Gakuin Univ., Yokohama 66-; Hon. Counsellor Tama Fine Arts Univ., Tokyo 65-; studied in Europe and America 26-27; mem. Catholic Art Soc. 49-; Rep. of Japan Branch of Gaudi Friends' Circle 56, participated in 10th Anniversary of Antonio Gaudi Friends' Circle, Barcelona 63; Hon. mem. Rudolf Steiner Goetheanum 63; one-man exhbn. of European sketches 64; Prize of Architectural Inst. of Japan 59, 62; Marquis Ohkuma Academic Prize, Waseda Univ. 62; Japan Art Acad. Prize 66.
Major works include: Waseda Univ. Library 25, Waseda Univ. Museum of Drama 28, Aeroplane Monument, Tokyo 41, Ohtakimachi Town Office, Chiba Prefecture 59, Memorial Centre for Japanese 26 Martyrs 62, Chapel for Sisters of the Visitation Convent (Kamakura) 65, *Toka Gakudo*—The Empress' Memorial Music Hall, Imperial Palace 66, Marquis Ohkuma Memorial Hall, Saga Prefecture 66, Toyama Memorial, Fine Arts Museum, Kawagoe Prefecture 70.
Publs. *Gunnar Asplund* 30, *Das Vorbild der Katholischen Gattin—Architecture and Humanity* 54, *Öryo Sobyö* (Sketch of Travel through Europe) 63, *Tabiji* (Voyage) 67; collection of artistic works in commemoration of 70th birthday 68.
4-12-28, Kitazawa, Setagaya-ku, Tokyo, Japan.
Telephone: 03-468-2708.

Inagaki, Hiroshi; Japanese film director; b. 1905.
Began career in films as actor, script-writer, etc. 14; Asst. to Teinosuke Kinugasa 27; Dir. 28-; at present under contract to Toho Film Co.; mem. Board Motion Picture Directors' Assen. of Japan; Ministry of Educ. Awards for *Edo Saigo No Hi* 42 and *Te O Tsunagu Kora* 48; Ministry of Welfare Award for *Wasurerareta Kora* 50; American Motion Picture Acad. Award for *Samurai* (a different film from *The Seven Samurai*) 56; Venice Film Festival Grand Prix, Tokyo Gold Prize and Sankei Silver Star Prize for *Muhomatsu No Issho* 57; Ministry of Educ. Awards for *Fu Rin Ka Zan* 70.
Films include *Tenka Taiheiki, Edo Saigo No Hi* (The Last Days of Edo), *Te O Tsunagu Kora* (Children Holding Hands Together), *Wasurerareta Kora* (Neglected Children), *Samurai, Muhomatsu No Issho* (The Rickshaw Man).
No. 7-10-5, Seijyo, Setagaya-ku, Tokyo, Japan.
Telephone: Tokyo 483-0845.

Inayama, Yoshihiro; Japanese industrialist; b. 2 Jan. 1904, Chuo-ku, Tokyo; ed. Tokyo Univ.
Yawata Iron and Steel Co. Ltd. 28-, Man. Dir. 50-60, Vice-Pres. 60-62, Pres. 62-70, also Chair. Japan Iron and Steel Federation 65-; Pres. Nippon Steel Corpn. 70-73, Chair. 73-; Chair. Int. Iron and Steel Inst. 71-73, Vice-Chair. 73-.
Nippon Steel Corporation, 6-3, Otemachi 2-chome, Tokyo, Japan.

Inche Othman Wok (*see* Othman bin Wok, Enche).

Inglés, José D.; Philippine lawyer and diplomatist; b. 24 Aug. 1910; ed. Univ. of the Philippines, Santo Tomás Univ., Manila, and Columbia Univ., New York.
Attorney 32-36; Legal Asst., Pres. of the Philippines 36-39; Asst. Solicitor-Gen. 40; Judge First Instance 41-43; Prof. Philippine Law School 45-46; Chair. Trusteeship Cttee., Paris 51; mem. Philippine del. to UN 46-56, 62-68, 74, Chair. Credentials Cttee.; Vice-Pres. Gen. Assembly 74; rep. to Security Council, Trusteeship Council, ECOSOC, numerous UN cttees.; Deputy Perm. Rep. to UN 55-56; Minister to Fed. Repub. of Germany 56-58, Amb. 58-62; Amb. to Thailand 62-66; rep. South-East Asia Treaty Org. (SEATO) 62-66, Council of Ministers 68; mem. Standing Cttee. Asscn. of South-East Asia (ASA) 63-66, Chair. Standing Cttee. ASEAN and ASPAC 70-71; Under-Sec. of Foreign Affairs 66-, Acting Sec. of Foreign Affairs intermittently 66-76; Sec.-Gen. Nat. Secr. (ASEAN) 66-69; Acting Perm. Rep. to UN Aug. 74-; Grosskreuz des Verdienstordens der Bundesrepublik Deutschland, Most Noble Order of the Crown of Thailand, Most Exalted Order of the White Elephant, Gran Cruz del Orden de Mayo, Grand-Croix de l'Ordre de Leopold II, Nat. Order of Viet-Nam; Gold Grotius Medal.
Publs. numerous papers on economics and int. affairs.
21 Vinzons Street, Heroes' Hill, Quezon City, Philippines.
Telephone: 99-3808.

Inoue, Shiro; Japanese banker; b. 1915, Tokyo; ed Tokyo Imperial Univ.
Joined Bank of Japan 38, Chief Rep., New York Office 60, Adviser to Gov. for Int. Finance 64, Exec. Dir. 67-; Head of Nagoya Branch 67, Rep. for Int. Affairs 68-72; Pres. Asian Devt. Bank 72-76.
c/o Asian Development Bank, P.O.B. 789, Manila, Philippines.
Telephone: 80-72-51.

Inoue, Yoshimi, LL.B.; Japanese business executive; b. 26 March 1908, Hiroshima Pref.; ed. Tokyo Univ.
Manager Printing Bureau, Ministry of Finance 54-56; Dir. Kobe Steel Ltd. 58-65, Dir. and Exec. Officer 65-69, Dir. and Senior Exec. Officer 69-71, Dir. and Vice-Pres. 71-72, Dir. and Pres. 72-74, Chair. Board of Dirs. 74-.
4-20-14, Miyamae, Suginami-ku, Tokyo, Japan.
Telephone: Tokyo 333-6751.

Inoue, Yuichi; Japanese artist; b. 1916, Tokyo.
Co-founder "Bokujin-kai" group of calligraphers 52-; rep. travelling exhbn. of Japanese Calligraphy, Europe 55, São Paulo Bienal 57, Brussels Int. Exhbn. 58, Kassel Int. Exhbn. 59, Pittsburgh Int. Exhbn. 61, São Paulo Bienal 61, one-man show at Ichibankan Gallery, Tokyo 71.
Ohkamiyashiki, 2475-2 Kurami, Samukawa-machi 253-01, Koza-gun, Kanagawa-ken, Japan.
Telephone: 0467-74-4721.

Inouye, Kaoru; Japanese banker; b. 13 May 1906, Chiba Pref.; ed. Tokyo Univ.
Joined The Dai-Ichi Bank Ltd. 29, Dir. 54, Deputy Pres. 61, Pres. 62-66, 69-71, Chair. 66-69; Chair. The Dai-Ichi Kangyo Bank 71-; Dir. Asahi Mutual Life Insurance Co., Taisei Fire and Marine Insurance Co. Ltd., K. Hattori and Co. Ltd.; auditor, Furukawa Electric Co.; adviser, Kawasaki Heavy Industries Ltd.; Exec. Dir. Fed. of Econ. Orgs.; Exec. Councillor, Tokyo Chamber of Commerce and Industry.
The Dai-Ichi Kangyo Bank, 6-2, 1-chome, Marunouchi, Chiyoda-ku, Tokyo 100, Japan.

Insisienmay, Thao Leuam; Laotian politician; b. 1917.
War service in Indochina; mem. Govt. 48-75; Deputy to Nat. Assembly 50-75; Minister of Nat. Educ., Fine Arts, Sport and Youth 62-74, concurrently of Religion 72-74; Vice-Premier and Minister of Educ. and the Arts 74-Dec. 75; Vice-Pres. of the Council 65-74; Officer Légion d'Honneur, and Grand Croix, Million d'Eléphants et du Parasol Blanc.

Irobe, Yoshiaki; Japanese banker; b. 18 July 1911, Tokyo; ed. Tokyo Imperial Univ.
Manager, Matsuyama Branch, The Bank of Japan 54, Deputy Chief, Personnel Dept. 56, Chief Sec. and Chief,

Foreign Relations Dept. 59, Chief, Personnel Dept. 62, Man. Nagoya Branch 63; Senior Man. Dir. The Kyowa Bank Ltd. 66, Deputy Pres. 68, Pres. 71-.
The Kyowa Bank Ltd., 5-1, 1-chome, Marunouchi, Chiyoda-ku, Tokyo; Home: 26-6, Saginomiya 6-chome, Nakano-ku, Tokyo, Japan.
Telephone: 999-0321 (Home).

Isarangkun Na Ayuthaya, Charunphan; Thai politician; b. 14 March 1914; ed. Chulalongkorn and Thammasat Univs., Bangkok, Nat. Defence Coll.
Served in Ministry of Interior 34-43; joined Ministry of Foreign Affairs 43; posted to Berne 47-51, London 56-60; Deputy Under-Sec. of State for Foreign Affairs 60; Amb. to Laos 61-65, to Spain, concurrently to Tunisia 65-70, to Austria, concurrently to Turkey 70-71; Under-Sec. of State for Foreign Affairs 71-73; Minister of Foreign Affairs 73-75.
c/o Ministry of Foreign Affairs, Bangkok, Thailand.

Ishibashi, Kanichiro; Japanese business executive; b. 1 March 1920; ed. Faculty of Law, Univ. of Tokyo.
Naval service 43-45; joined Bridgestone Tire Co. Ltd. 45, Dir. 49-, Vice-Pres. 50-63, Pres. 63-73, Chair. 73-; Dir. and Adviser Bridgestone Cycle Industry Co. Ltd., Bridgestone LPG Co. Ltd.; Man. Dir. Fed. of Econ. Orgs.
1 Napasaka-cho, Azabu, Minato-ku, Tokyo, Japan.
Telephone: 03-583-0150.

Ishida, Kazuto, LL.B.; Japanese judge; b. 1903; ed. Tokyo Imperial Univ.
Judge, Tokyo District Court 28-41; Dir. Personnel Affairs Bureau, Gen. Sec. Supreme Court 47-50; Deputy Sec.-Gen. Supreme Court 50-56; Chief Judge, Tokyo District Court 56-60; Sec.-Gen. Supreme Court 60-62; Pres. Tokyo High Court 62-63; Assoc. Justice, Supreme Court 63-67, Chief Justice 67-73; Vice-Pres. Int. Legal Soc. in Japan 60-62; Dir. Japan Bar Asscn.; Vice-Chair. World Asscn. of Judges 69-73.
3-9-22, Komachi, Kamakura-shi, Kanagawa-ken 248, Japan.

Ishida, Taizo; Japanese automobile executive; b. 16 Nov. 1888; ed. Shiga Prefectural Daiichi Junior High School.
President, Toyota Automatic Loom Works Ltd. 48-69, Chair. 69-, Adviser 73-; Pres. Toyota Motor Co. Ltd. 50-61, Chair. 61-71, Adviser 71-; Dir. Toyota Motor Sales U.S.A. Inc. 57-, Japan Automobile Mfrs. Asscn. Inc. 51-71; Textile Machinery Manufacturers Asscn. 51-71, Japan Industrial Vehicles Asscn. 68-71; Adviser, Japan Fed. of Employers' Asscns. 69; Hon. Consul of Portugal 70-; First Class Order of the Sacred Treasure; Blue Ribbon Medal 57, 2nd Order of the Sacred Treasure 64, 1st Order of the Sacred Treasure 70.
Toyota Motor Co. Ltd., 1 Toyota-cho, Toyota-shi, Aichi-ken 471; and 6-78 Hachiman-cho, Kariya-shi, Aichi, Japan.

Ishii, Mitsujiro, B.A.; Japanese politician; b. 1889; ed. Kobe Higher Commercial School and Tokyo Higher Commercial School.
Entered Higher Civil Service 13; Sec. to Gov.-Gen. of Formosa, concurrently Councillor to Gov.-Gen. of Formosa 15; Dir. *Asahi* (Newspaper Publishing Co.) 25, Man. Dir. 40-45; Pres. Asahi Movie Manufacturing Co. 37-41; joined Japan Liberal Party 46; elected to House of Reps. 46; Minister of Commerce and Industry, Yoshida Cabinet 47; Pres. Asahi Broadcasting Co. 51-52; Dir. Nishi Nippon Railroad Co. Ltd. 51-; Minister of Transportation Nov. 52-54; Chief Sec. of Liberal Party 54-55, Chair. Exec. Board of Liberal-Democratic Party 55-56, 60-; Deputy Prime Minister 57-58; Minister of Trade and Industry 60, of Justice 65-66; Speaker, House of Reps. 67-.
House of Representatives, Tokyo, Japan.

Ishikawa, Shigeru, D.ECON.; Japanese economist; b. 7 April 1918; ed. Tokyo Univ. of Commerce (now Hitotsubashi Univ.).
Attached to Jiji News Agency 45-56, Hong Kong Corresp. 51-53; Asst. Prof., Inst. of Econ. Research, Hitotsubashi Univ. 56-63, Prof. 63, Dir. 72-74.
Publs. *National Income and Capital Formation in Mainland China* 65, *Economic Development in Asian Perspective* 67, *Agricultural Development Strategies in Asia* 70.
19-9, 4-chome Kugayama, Suginami-ku, Tokyo, Japan.
Telephone: 332-8376.

Isles, Keith Sydney, C.M.G., B.COM., M.A., M.SC.; Australian economist; b. 4 Aug. 1902; ed. Univs. of Tasmania and Cambridge.
Lecturer in Political Economy, Univ. of Edinburgh 31-37; Prof. of Econs., Univ. Coll., Swansea 37-39; Prof. of Econs., Univ. of Adelaide 39-45; Prof. of Econs., Queen's Univ., Belfast 45-57, and Dean Faculty of Econs. 45-53; Vice-Chancellor, Univ. of Tasmania 57-67; Visiting Prof. of Econ., Ulster Univ. 68-69; Army service 44-45; Joint Local Sec. of British Asscn. for the Advancement of Science 52; mem. Board of Dirs., Charles Davis Ltd. (Tas.), Co-operative Motors Ltd. (Tas.); Hon. LL.D. (St. Andrews and Queens Univ. of Belfast), Hon. D.Litt. (Tasmania).
Publs. *Wages Policy and the Price Level* 34, *Money and Trade* 35, *Compulsory Saving* (with B. R. Williams) 42, chapters in *Ulster under Home Rule* (ed. Wilson) 55, *An Economic Survey of Northern Ireland* (with Norman Cuthbert) 57.
91 Esplanade, Rose Bay, Hobart, Tasmania 7015, Australia.
Telephone: 438580.

Ismail, Mohamed Ali, M.A.; Malaysian bank official and barrister-at-law; b. 16 Sept. 1918, Port Swettenham, Selangor; ed. Univ. of Cambridge and Middle Temple, London.
Controller, Trade Div., Ministry of Commerce and Industry 55-57; Minister Malaysian Embassy, Washington 57-58, Econ. Minister 58-60; Exec. Dir. IBRD, Int. Finance Corpn., Int. Devt. Asscn. 58-60; Deputy Gov. Central Bank of Malaysia 60-62, Gov. 62-; Chair. Capital Issues Cttee. 68-, Malaysian Industrial Devt. Finance Ltd. Aug. 69; Pres. Malaysian Inst. of Management 66-68; mem. Nat. Devt. Planning Cttee. 62-, Council of Univ. of Malaya 62-72, Board of Govs., Asian Inst. of Management 70-, Urban Devt. Authority 71-75; Adviser Nat. Corpn. 71-; Order of Panglima Mangku Negara 64; Hon. LL.D. (Univ. of Malaya) 73.
Central Bank of Malaysia, P.O.B. 922, Kuala Lumpur; Home: 23 Jalan Natesa, off Cangkat Tunku, Kuala Lumpur, Malaysia.
Telephone: 89931 (Office); 24185 (Home).

Itakura, Joji; Japanese banker; b. 3 June 1912, Kanagawa; ed. Keio Univ.
Managing Director, Mitsui Bank Ltd. 68-71, Senior Man. Dir. 71-72, Deputy Pres. 72-74, Pres. 74-.
The Mitsui Bank Ltd., 1-2 Yurakucho 1-chome, Chiyoda-ku, Tokyo 100; Home: 6-8 Kita 2-chome Shinohara, Kohuko-ku, Yokohama City, Kanagawa Prefecture, Japan.
Telephone: 501-1111 (Office); 045-401-5155 (Home).

Ito, Shinsui; Japanese painter; b. 1898; ed. Kiyokata Art School, Tokyo.
Has exhibited many pictures of women incl. *A Mirror* (Nat. Acad. of Art Prize 46); organizer of Jitsugetsu Sha, and art league of young painters of promise; has about 100 disciples; mem. Council of the Nat. Art Exhbn.; Sec. Japan Fed. of Art Socs.
Kita-Kamakura, Kanagawa Prefecture, Japan.

Itoh, Junji; Japanese business executive; b. 10 July 1922, Tsingtao, China; ed. Keio Univ.
With Kanegafuchi Spinning Co. Ltd. (now Kanebo Ltd.) 48-60; Dir. Kanebo Ltd. 61, Man. Dir. 64, Exec. Dir. 66, Vice-Pres. 68, Pres. 68-; Pres. Kanebo Cosmetics Inc. 69-, Kanebo Acryl Co. Ltd. 70-, Kanebo Foods Ltd. 71-,

Kanebo Textile Ltd. 75-, Kanebo Polyester Ltd. 72-, Kanebo Pharmaceutical Co. Ltd. 72-; Rep. Dir. Nippon Ester Co. Ltd. 68-; Dir. Matsuyama Petro-chemical Co. Ltd. 68-, Chair. 70-; Dir. Nippon Kynol Inc. 72-; Man. Dir. Japan Fed. of Econ. Orgs. 68-, Japan Spinners' Asscn. 68- (Chair. 71-72), Japan Chemical Fibres Asscn. 68-; Dir. Maruzen Oil Co. Ltd. 70-; Vice-Chair. Japan Textile Fed. 71-72; Trustee, Keio Univ. 70; Graõ Cruz Orden Academico São Francisco (Brazil) 72.
Kanebo Ltd., 3-80, Tomobuchi-cho 1-chome, Miyakojima-ku, Osaka 534; Home: 59, Yamate-cho, Ashiya, Hyogo 659, Japan.
Telephone: (06) 921-1231 (Office); (0797) 31-3308 (Home).

Itoh, Kyoichi; Japanese industrialist; b. 27 May 1914; ed. Kobe Univ.
Director Kureha Spinning Co. Ltd. 56, Man. Dir. 56-63, Exec. Dir. 63, Pres. 63-66; Dir. Nippon Lactum Co. Ltd. 63-; Dir. Japan Fed. of Econ. Orgs. 64-66; Dir. Japan Fed. of Employers' Asscns. 64-67; Exec. Vice-Pres. Toyobo Co. Ltd. 66-73; Chair. 73-74, Gen. Adviser 74-, Chair. Nippei Sangyo Ltd. 69, Toyo Pulp Co. Ltd. 75; Hon. Consul-Gen. of El Salvador, Osaka 58-.
Toyobo Co. Ltd., 8 Dojima Hamadori 2-chome, Kita-ku, Osaka; and 1845 Kuegazaka, Sumiyoshi-cho, Higashinada-ku, Kobe, Japan.

Itokawa, Hideo; Japanese aeronautic engineer; b. 1912; ed. Tokyo Univ.
Engineer, Nakajima Aircraft Co. 39-41; Asst. Prof. of Engineering at Tokyo Univ. 41-48, Prof. 48-67; Exec. Dir. Space Engineering Dept., Inst. of Industrial Science 55-; Pres. Japanese Rocket Soc. 56-58; Convenor Nat. Cttee. on Space Research, Japan Science Council 56-; mem. Nat. Space Council 60-; Dep. Dir. Inst. of Space and Aeronautical Science 64-67; Dir. Systems Research Inst. 67.
34-15, 4-chome, Matsubara, Setagaya-ku, Tokyo, Japan.

Iue, Yuro; Japanese business executive; b. 24 Nov. 1908.
Former Pres. Sanyo Electric Co., now Chair.
Sanyo Electric Co., 2-18 Keihanhondori, Moriguchi City, Osaka Pref.; 2-134, Aza Nagaoyama, Kirihata, Takarazuka City, Hyogo Pref., Japan.

Iuye, Kaoru; Japanese business executive; b. 1911.
President, Sanyo Electric Co., Ltd.
Sanyo Electric Co. Ltd., 2-18 Keihanhondori, Moriguchi City, Osaka Pref., Japan.

Iwai, Akira; Japanese railwayman and trade unionist; b. 1922; ed. Matsumoto High Elementary School, Nagano Prefecture.
Kamisuwa Engine Section, Nat. Railway 37-42; Military Service 42-46; Engine Driver, Kamisuwa Engine Section, Nat. Railway 46; Chief Joint Struggle Dept., Nat. Railway Workers' Union 50-51, Chief of Planning Dept. 51-55; Gen. Sec. Gen. Council of Trade Unions of Japan (SOHYO) 55-; Lenin Prize 70.
Publs. *We, Born in Taisho Era, The Workers, Diary of a General Secretary*.
Sohyo Kaikan, 8-2 Shiba Park, Minato-ku, Tokyo, Japan.

Iwasa, Yoshizane; Japanese banker; b. 6 Feb. 1906, Tokyo; ed. Tokyo Univ.
Manager, Kanagawa Branch, Yasuda Bank 44-45, Man. Loan Dept. (Head Office) 45-46, Personnel Dept. 46-47, Chief Man. Personnel Dept. 47-48; Dir. Yasuda Bank 48; Man. Dir. Fuji Bank 48-57, Deputy Pres. 57-63, Chair. of Board and Pres. 63-71, Chair. Advisory Cttee. 71-.
1-5-5, Otemachi, Chiyoda-ku, Tokyo 100; Home: 5-2-4, Minami-Aoyame, Minato-ku, Tokyo 107, Japan.

Iwasaki, Nobuhiko; Japanese business executive; b. 7 Nov. 1909, Tokyo; ed. Tokyo Univ.
Joined Sumitomo Shipbuilding and Machinery Co. 33, Dir. 55, Man. Dir. 59, Exec. Man. Dir. 64, Exec. Vice-Pres. 69, Pres. 70-73, Chair. 73-; Dir. Fed. of Econ. Orgs., Shipbuilders' Asscn. of Japan.
Sumitomo Shipbuilding and Machinery Co., 2-1, Ohtemachi 2-chome, Chiyoda-ku, Tokyo; Home: 7-13-501, Roppongi 1-chome, Minato-ku, Tokyo, Japan.
Telephone (03) 211-1361 (Office); (03) 585-2892 (Home).

J

Jack, Hon. Sir Roy Emile, Kt., LL.B.; New Zealand politician; b. 1915, New Plymouth; ed. Wanganui Collegiate School and Victoria Univ. Wellington.
Judge's assoc. 37-39; R.N.Z.A.F. 39-45; barrister and solicitor at Wanganui 46-; elected to Wanganui City Council 46; Deputy Mayor of Wanganui 47-56; mem. Parl. for Patea 54-63, for Waimarino 63-72, for Rangitikei 72-; Deputy Speaker of House of Reps. 61-67, Speaker 67-72, Dec. 75-; Minister of Justice and Attorney-Gen. Feb.-Nov. 72; Nat. Party.
Parliament House, Wellington; Home: 49 College Street, Wanganui, New Zealand.
Telephone: 49090, 48274, 7640 (Home).

Jain, Shanti Prasad, B.SC.; Indian industrialist; b. 1912; ed. Banaras Hindu Univ. and Agra Univ.
Controls a chain of industries in Bihar, U.P., Rajasthan, West Bengal and Kashmir; Chair. and Dir. Sahu Jain Ltd., Rohtas Industries Ltd., The Jaipur Udyog Ltd., Shree Krishna Gyanoday Sugar Ltd.; Pres. Shri Ahimsa Prachar Samity, Calcutta, Bihar Industries Asscn., Patna; formerly Pres. Federation of Indian Chamber of Commerce and Industry in India, All-India Org. of Employers, New Delhi, Indian Chamber of Commerce, Calcutta, Indian Paper Mills Asscn., Calcutta, Indian Sugar Mills Asscn., Calcutta, Bihar Chamber of Commerce, Patna, Employers' Asscn., Calcutta, Rajasthan Chamber of Commerce and Industry, Jaipur, Eastern U.P. Chamber of Commerce, Allahabad, Marwari Relief Soc., Calcutta; Founder, Baharatiya Jnanpith (Acad.), Banaras.
11 Clive Row, Calcutta 700001; Times House, 7 Bahadur Shah Zaffer Marg, New Delhi 110001, India.

Jain, Surendra Kumar, M.A., LL.M.; Indian international official; b. 22 Dec. 1922, India; ed. High School, New Delhi, Punjab and Lucknow Univs.
Lecturer, Delhi School of Law, Delhi Univ. 46-47; Int. Labour Office, Geneva 47-, Chef de Cabinet to Dir.-Gen. 57-59, Dir. Office for Near and Middle East, Istanbul 59-62, Field Office for Asia, Colombo 62-65, Regional Dir. for Asia, Bangkok 66-75, Deputy Dir.-Gen. in charge of Technical Programmes June 75-; Gold Medal (Lucknow Univ.).
Publs. articles on labour and social problems in *International Labour Review* and other journals.
International Labour Office, 1211 Geneva 22; Residence: 34 rue Daubin, 1203 Geneva, Switzerland.
Telephone: 98-52-11 (Office); 45-80-82 (Residence).

James, Sir (John) Morrice Cairns, P.C., G.C.M.G., C.V.O., M.B.E.; British diplomatist; b. 30 April 1916; ed. Bradfield, Oxford Univ.
Joined Dominions Office 39; Royal Navy, Royal Marines Second World War; staff of United Kingdom High Comm. in South Africa 46-47; Commonwealth Relations Office, London 47-52; Deputy U.K. High Commr., Lahore 52-53; attended Imperial Defence Coll. 54; Deputy U.K. High Commr., Karachi 55-56; Asst. Under-Sec. of State, Commonwealth Relations Office 57-58; Deputy U.K. High Commr., India 58-61, U.K. High Commr., Pakistan 61-65; Deputy Under-Sec. of State, Commonwealth Office, London 66-68, Perm. Under-Sec. of State 68; U.K. High Commr., India 68-70, U.K. High Commr. Australia 71-76; King of Arms of the Most Distinguished Order of Saints Michael and George 75.
La Plotte, Cap Saint-Pierre, Saint-Tropez 83, Var, France.

Japan, Emperor of (*see* Hirohito).

Jatoi, Ghulam Mustafa; Pakistani politician; b. 14 Aug. 1931, New Jatoi (Sind); ed. Karachi Grammar School.
President, District Local Board, Nawabshah 54; mem. Provincial Assembly of W. Pakistan 56; mem. Nat. Assembly 62-73; mem. Pakistan People's Party 69-; Minister for Political Affairs, Communications and Natural Resources Dec. 71-73; Chief Minister of Sind Dec. 73-; mem. Sind Provincial Assembly 73-; del. to UN Gen. Assembly 62-65.
Chief Minister's House, Karachi, Pakistan.

Jatti, Basappa Danappa, B.A., LL.B.; Indian politician; b. 10 Sept. 1912, Savalgi, Bijapur District; ed. Bijapur Govt. High School, Rajaram Coll., Sykes Law Coll., Kolhapur.
Practised law at Jamkhandi; State Minister, Jamkhandi, later Chief Minister; mem. Legislative Assembly, Bombay, later Mysore; Deputy Minister of Health and Labour, Bombay 52; Chair. Land Reforms Cttee.; Chief Minister, Mysore 58-62; Minister of Finance 62-65, of Food 65-67; Lieut.-Gov. of Pondicherry 68; Gov. of Orissa 72-74, Vice-Pres. of India Aug. 74-; Chair. Rajya Sabha 74-; LL.D. h.c. (Karnatak Univ.).
Office of the Vice-President, 6 Maulana Azad Road, New Delhi, India.

Jayakumar, Shunmugam, LL.B.; Singapore professor of law; b. 12 Aug. 1939, Singapore; ed. Univ. of Singapore and Yale Univ.
Part-time teacher, Faculty of Law, Univ. of Singapore; Graduate Asst. Ford Foundation 63-64; Asst. Lecturer, Faculty of Law, Univ. of Singapore 64-67, Assoc. Prof. 67-71, now Dean; Asst. Human Rights Officer, UN Div. of Human Rights 67; Perm. Rep. to UN 71-74; mem. del. to UN Gen. Assembly 70, 71, 72; has attended many confs. on int. law.
Publs. *Constitutional Law Cases from Malaysia and Singapore* 71, *Public International Law Cases from Malaysia and Singapore* and articles in journals.
Faculty of Law, University of Singapore, Singapore.

Jayawardena, M. D. H., DIP.ECON., BARR.-AT-LAW; Ceylonese lawyer and politician; b. 29 March 1915; ed. Trinity Coll., Kandy and Ceylon Univ. Coll., Colombo.
Advocate, Colombo and Avissawella 41; called to Lincoln's Inn, London 49; mem. House of Reps., Ceylon (later Nat. State Assembly, Sri Lanka) 52-56, 65-; Parl. Sec. to Minister of Finance 52-54; Minister of Finance 54-56; Joint Gen. Sec. United Nat. Party 58-; Minister of Health 65-June 70; fmr. Pres. Buddhist Theosophical Soc.; helped to form many cos. including Mercantile Credit Ltd., Ceylon Bulbs and Electricals Ltd. and Mahajana Credit Ltd.
National State Assembly, Colombo, Sri Lanka.

Jayewardene, Junius Richard; Ceylonese lawyer and politician; b. 17 Sept. 1906; ed. Royal Coll., Univ. Coll., and Law Coll., Colombo.
Member Colombo Municipal Council 40-43; mem. State Council 43-47; mem. House of Representatives 47-56, 60-75; Minister of Finance 47-53; Hon. Sec. Ceylon Nat. Congress 40-47; Hon. Treasurer United Nat. Party 47-48 and Vice-Pres. 53, 58-72, Sec. 72, Leader 73-; co-author of Colombo Plan 50; Leader of the House of Reps., Minister of Agriculture and Food 53-56, of Finance, Information, Broadcasting, Local Govt. and Housing March-July 60; Deputy Leader of Opposition 60-65, Leader 70-June 75, July 75-; Minister of State, and Parl. Sec. to Minister of Defence, Foreign Affairs and Planning 65-70; Sec., United Party 72, Leader 73-June 75, July 75-.
Publs. *Some Sermons of the Buddha* 40, *Buddhist Essays* (English and Sinhalese) 42, *In Council* (speeches) 46, *Buddhism and Marxism* 50, 3rd ed. 57, *Selected Speeches*.
66 Ward Place, Colombo, Sri Lanka.
Telephone: Colombo 95028.

Jejeebhoy, Sir Jamsetjee, Bt., B.A.; Indian industrialist; b. 19 April 1913; ed. St. Xavier's School and Coll., Bombay.
Chairman Board of Trustees, Sir J. J. Parsi Benevolent Institution, Sir J. J. Charity Funds, Rustomjee Jamsetjee Jejeebhoy Gujrati Schools' Funds, Bombay Panjrapole, Wadiaji's Fire Temple, Parsi Charity Org. Soc., Iran League, etc.; Trustee, Sir J. J. School of Arts, Byramjee Jejeebhoy Parsi Charitable Institution, Iranee Charity Funds and Dharamshala, Zoroastrian Building Fund, Petit Parsee Gen. Hosp., K.R. Cama Oriental Inst., Petit and Ashburner Fire Temples, etc.; Dir. Enjay Estates (Pvte) Ltd.
Maneckji Wadia Building, Mahatma Gandhi Road, Fort, Bombay 400 001; Home: Beaulieu, 95 Worli Seaface, Bombay 25, India.
Telephone: 251549 (Office); 453955 (Home).

Jen Jung; People's Repub. of China.
Member Chinese People's Volunteers Korean Truce Comm., N. Korea 60; Deputy Political Commissar Tibet Mil. Region, People's Liberation Army 65, First Political Commissar 71-; Vice-Chair. Tibet Revolutionary Cttee. 68, Chair. 71; First Sec. CCP Tibet 71; Alt. mem. 10th Cen. Cttee. of CCP 73.

Jha, Chandra Shekhar, O.B.E., M.SC., LL.B., I.C.S.; Indian diplomatist; b. 20 Oct. 1909, Madhubani, Bihar; ed. Patna Univ. and London School of Oriental Studies.
Joined Indian Civil Service 33; Asst. Magistrate and Collector, Bihar and Orissa 33-36; Under-Sec. Finance Department, Bihar 36-39, Deputy Commr. 39; later Controller and Sec. Supply and Transport Department, Orissa; Deputy Sec. Commonwealth Relations Department, Govt. of India 46-47; Joint Sec. Ministry of External Affairs 47-50; Chargé d'Affaires, Ankara 50-51; Amb. to Turkey 51-54; Joint Sec. Ministry of External Affairs 54-57; Amb. to Japan 57-59; Perm. Rep. to UN 59-62, Chair. Cttee. on Contributions 59-62, Chair. Human Rights Comm. 61-62; High Commr. in Canada 62-64; Commonwealth Sec., Ministry of External Affairs 64-65, Foreign Sec. Feb. 65-67; Amb. to France 67-Jan. 69; mem. Joint Inspection Unit, UN and Specialized Agencies, Geneva 69-.
Palais des Nations, Geneva, Switzerland.

Jha, Lakshmi Kant, M.B.E., B.A., I.C.S.; Indian politician and retd. civil servant; b. 22 Nov. 1913, Bhagalpur; ed. Hindu Univ., Banaras and Trinity Coll., Cambridge.
Indian civil service 36-67; Under-Sec. Govt. of Bihar, Local Self-Govt. Dept. 41-42; Deputy Sec. Supply Dept., Govt. of India 42-46; del. to UN Maritime Conf.; Chief Controller of Imports and Exports 47-50; Sec. Ministry of Commerce and Industry 50-56, 57-60; Sec. Ministry of Heavy Industries 56-57; Chair. GATT 57-58, UN Cttee. on Int. Commodity Arrangements 59-61; Sec. Ministry of Finance, Dept. of Econ. Affairs 60-64; Dir. Reserve Bank of India and State Bank of India; Alt. Gov. Int. Bank for Reconstruction and Devt. 60-64; Sec. to Prime Minister 64-67, retd. 67; Gov. Reserve Bank of India 67-70, IMF 69-70; Amb. to U.S.A. 70-73; Gov., State of Jammu and Kashmir 73-; Chair. UN Group of Eminent Persons on Multinational Corpns. 73-74, Jammu and Kashmir Devt. Review Cttee. 75-76.
Publs. *India's Foreign Trade*, Parts I and II, *Price Policy in a Developing Economy, Economic Development—Ends and Means, The International Monetary Scene and the Human Factor in Economic Development.*
Raj Bhavan, Srinagar (Jammu and Kashmir), India.

Jogjakarta, Sultan of; (*see* Hamengkubuwono IX, H.R.H. Sultan Dorodjatun).

Johnson, Leslie Royston; Australian politician; b. 22 Nov. 1924, Sydney.
Member Parl. for Hughes, N.S.W. 55, 58, 61, 63, 69-;

Minister of Housing 72-73, of Housing and Construction 73-75, of Aboriginal Affairs June-Nov. 75.
Parliament House, Canberra, A.C.T.; Home: 24 Mitchell Avenue, Jannali, N.S.W., Australia.

Johnson, Leslie Wilson, M.A.; Australian public servant; b. 2 April 1916; ed. Perth Modern School, Univ. of Western Australia.
Became teacher, then lecturer, and later Inspector, Educ. Dept. Western Australia 36-61; Dir. Educ. Papua New Guinea 62-66; mem. House of Assembly, Papua New Guinea 64-70; Asst. Admin. (Services) Papua New Guinea 66-70, Administrator 70-73, High Commr. 73-74; Dir. Australian Devt. Assistance Agency 74-.
ADAA, P.O. Box 887, Canberra City; Home: 70 Empire Circuit, Canberra, Australia.

Johore, H.H. The Sultan of; Sultan Ismail ibni al-Marhum Sultan Ibrahim, D.K., D.M.N., S.M.N., S.P.M.J., S.P.M.K., D.K. (Brunei), K.B.E., C.M.G., D.K. (Pahang); Ruler of Johore, Malaysia; b. 28 Oct. 1894, Johore Bahru.
Colonel Commandant, Johore Military and Volunteer Services; succeeded his father, Sultan Ibrahim, May 59; several foreign decorations.
Istana Bukit Serene, Johore Bahru, Malaya, Malaysia.

Jones, Charles Keith; Australian politician; b. 12 Sept. 1917; ed. Tighe's Hill Public School, Cook's Hill High School.
Alderman, Newcastle City Council 47-59, Deputy Lord Mayor 53, Lord Mayor 57; Councillor, Shortland County Council 57-59; mem. House of Reps. for Newcastle 58-; Deputy Chair. of Cttees. 61-66; mem. several Parl. cttees. including Parl. Select Cttee. on Aircraft Noise 69-71; Minister for Transport and for Civil Aviation 72-73, for Transport 73-Nov. 75; exec. mem. Boilermaker's Soc. 43-58; has held several posts in Labor Party admin.
Parliament House, Canberra, A.C.T. 2600; Dangar House, 14 Brown Street, Newcastle, N.S.W. 2300; Home: 57 Seventh Street, North Lambton, N.S.W. 2299, Australia.

Jones, Sir Philip Frederick, Kt., A.C.A., A.A.S.A.; Australian company director; b. 14 Aug. 1912, Napier, New Zealand; ed. Barker's Coll., Hornsby, N.S.W.
General Man. The Herald & Weekly Times Ltd., 53-63, Dir. 57-, Vice-Chair. 66-70, Chair. 70-; Chair. W. Australian Newspapers Ltd. 72-, Herald-Sun TV Pty. 73-; Dir. Australian Newsprint Mills Ltd. 57-, Vice-Chair. 60-; Dir. Tasman Pulp and Paper Co. Ltd. 63-74, Queensland Press Ltd. 70-.
The Herald and Weekly Times Group, 44 Flinders Street, Melbourne, Vic.; Home: 99 Spring Street, Melbourne, Vic. 3000, Australia.

Jung, Nawab Mir Nawaz (M. Mir Khan), B.A., LL.B., M.SC.; Pakistani financier and diplomatist; b. 1914; ed. Nizam's Coll., Hyderabad and Univs. of London, Paris and Geneva.
In service of Hyderabad State, holding posts of Cabinet Sec., Sec. Railways and Civil Aviation, Sec. Finance, Official Dir. State Bank, Deccan Airways, Coal Mines Co., etc.; prior to partition was Hyderabad's Envoy in London; Minister of Pakistan to Sweden, Norway, Denmark and Finland 51-53; Amb. to the UN 54-57, Pres. Econ. and Social Council of the UN 57-58; Amb. to France and to the Vatican 57-59; Amb.-at-Large to African States 60; Regional Rep. of UN to N.W. Africa, Dakar 61-65; UN Rep., Tunis 65-68; Senior Consultant to UN Devt. Programme (UNDP); Grand Officier de la Légion d'Honneur; Grand Officier Ordre National, Senegal; Ordre National, Mauritania; Grand Cordon de l'Ordre National, Tunisia.
Publs. *Federal Finance* 36, *Central Banking* 45, *Five Year Appraisals* (1960-64) *of UN and Agencies* (co-author).
UNDP, Palais des Nations, Geneva; and 137 rue de Lausanne, Geneva, Switzerland.

Jung Bahadur, Nawab Ali Yavar, B.A.; Indian state governor; b. 1905; ed. Nizam Coll., Hyderabad, Queen's Coll., Oxford.
Professor of History and Political Science, Osmania Univ. 30-35; Dir. of Information and Sec. External Affairs Cttee., Hyderabad Govt. 35-37; Sec. for Constitutional Affairs, Information and Broadcasting 37-42, for Home and Judicial Affairs 42-45; Vice-Chancellor, Osmania Univ. 45-46 and 48-52; Minister for Constitutional Affairs, Local Self-Govt., Police and Public Health and later for Educ. and Home Affairs 46-47; resigned from Hyderabad Govt. 47; del. and Deputy Chair. to many UN sessions; Amb. to Argentina, Minister to Chile 52-54; Amb. to Egypt, Minister to Lebanon and Libya 54-58; Chair. UN Cttee. SUNFED 56-57; Amb. to Yugoslavia and Greece, Minister to Bulgaria 58-61; Amb. to France 61-65; Vice-Chancellor, Muslim Univ. Aligarh 65-68; Amb. to U.S.A. 68-70; Gov. Maharashtra State 70-; mem. Standing Cttee., Inter-Univ. Board, Acad. Cttee. and Gov. Board, School of Int. Studies 66-68; Chair. Study Team on Defence, Admin. Reforms Comm. 67-68; mem. Cttee. on Role of Govs. 71-72; Pres. Nat. Ameer Khusrau Soc. 74-76; Hon. LL.D. (Osmania Univ.) 56; awarded Padma Bhushan 59.
Publs. *Hyderabad in Retrospect, External Relations of Hyderabad.*
Raj Bhavan, Bombay, India.
Telephone: 366660.

Jungalwalla, Nowshir K., O.B.E., M.B.B.S., M.R.C.S., M.R.C.P., M.PH.; Indian public health official; b. 1 Dec. 1912, Rangoon, Burma; ed. Univ. of Rangoon and Johns Hopkins Univ., U.S.A.
Indian Army Medical Services 39-46; Deputy Public Health Commr., Minister of Health 46-50; Regional Adviser, Regional Office for S.E. Asia, World Health Org. (WHO) 50-52, Rep. in Indonesia 52-55, Dir. Public Health Services, Geneva April 67-72; Deputy Dir.-Gen. of Health Services, India 55-57, 60-65, Additional Dir.-Gen. 65-67; Dir. All-India Inst. of Hygiene and Public Health 57-60; Dir. Health Services, Regional Office for S.E. Asia, New Delhi 72-; Hon. Fellow, American Public Health Asscn.; Fellow, Acad. of Medical Sciences (India); Deputy Dir.-Gen. of Health Services 63-65.
A2/2 Safdarjang Enclave, New Delhi 110016, India.
Telephone: 70591.

Jusuf, Lieut.-Gen. Andi Mohamad; Indonesian army officer and politician; b. 23 June 1929, Sulawesi; ed. Dutch Secondary School, and Higher Secondary School.
Former Chief of Staff of Hasanuddin and Commdr. S.E. Mil. District; Minister of Light and Basic Industry 66, of Basic Industry and Power 66, of Trade and Commerce 67, of Industry 68-.
Ministry of Industry, Jakarta, Indonesia.

K

Kadoorie, Horace, O.B.E., J.P.; Hong Kong industrial financier; b. 1902; ed. Cathedral School, Shanghai, Ascham St. Vincents, Eastbourne, and Clifton Coll., Bristol.
Partner, Sir Elly Kadoorie and Sons, Hong Kong; Chair. and Dir. numerous public companies incl. Hong Kong & Shanghai Hotels Ltd., China Light and Power Co. Ltd., Amalgamated Rubber Estates, Hong Kong and Kowloon Wharf and Godown Co. Ltd., Hong Kong and Whampoa Dock Co. Ltd., Peak Tramways Co. Ltd.; Dir. Rubber Trust Ltd., Hong Kong Carpet Manufacturers Ltd.; mem. and official numerous Hong Kong civic orgs.; Chevalier de la Légion d'Honneur; Ramon Magsaysay Award 62, Order of Leopold 66, Solomon Schechter Award 59.

Publ. *The Art of Ivory Sculpture in Cathay* (7 vols.).
Sir Elly Kadoorie and Sons, St. George's Building, 24th Floor, 2 Ice House Street, Hong Kong.
Telephone: 249221.

Kadoorie, Sir Lawrence, K.B.E.; Hong Kong business executive; b. 2 June 1899; ed. Cathedral School, Shanghai, Ascham St. Vincents, Eastbourne, Clifton Coll., Bristol and Lincoln's Inn, London.
Partner, Sir Elly Kadoorie and Sons, Hong Kong, Chair. Sir Elly Kadoorie Successors Ltd., St. George's Bldg. Ltd., Dir. Sir Elly Kadoorie Continuation Ltd.; Chair. China Light and Power Co. Ltd., Franki Piling and Engineering Co. Ltd., Hong Kong Carpet Manufacturers Ltd., Schroders and Chartered Ltd., Major Contractors Ltd., Nanyang Cotton Mill Ltd.; Dir. Island Dyeing and Printing Co. Ltd. and numerous other public companies; mem. and official numerous Hong Kong civic orgs.; Solomon Schechter Award 59; Officier Légion d'Honneur 75, l'Ordre de Leopold 66; Ramon Magsaysay Award 62; Hon. LL.D. (Univ. of Hong Kong) 61.
Sir Elly Kadoorie and Sons, St. George's Building, 24th Floor, 2 Ice House Street, Hong Kong.
Telephone: 5-249221 (Office); 3-016129 (Home).

Kai, Fumihiko; Japanese businessman; b. 17 May 1912; ed. Tokyo Univ.
Consul-Gen., Jakarta 52-55; Deputy Rep. of Japan to 9th Session of ECAFE Conf., Bandung 53; Counsellor, The Hague 53-55; Consul-Gen., Berlin 55-57, Hamburg 57-58; Dir. Japan External Trade Org. 58-61; Counsellor, Ministry of Foreign Affairs 61, Dir. Econ. Co-operation Bureau, Ministry of Foreign Affairs 61; fmr. Amb. to Malaysia; Amb. to Australia until 70, to Fed. Repub. of Germany 70-73, retd. 73; Man. Dir. Nissin Sugar Manufacturing Co. 73-; Panglima Mangku Negara (Malaysia), Gran Official Al Merito (Argentina), Grosskreuz (Fed. Repub. of Germany).
Nissin Sugar Manufacturing Co., 3, 2 chome, Koami-cho, Nihonbashi, Chuoku, Tokyo; and 10-14 2-chome, Harano-dai, Shinagawa-ku, Tokyo, Japan.
Telephone: (03) 782-0175.

Kaiser, Khwaqa Muhammad; Bangladesh diplomatist; b. 13 Sept. 1918; ed. Dacca Univ.
Indian Police Service 41-50; Second Sec. Deputy High Comm. for Pakistan, Calcutta 50; Deputy Sec. Ministry of External Affairs, Dacca 50-51; Deputy Sec. Ministry of External Affairs, Karachi 51-55; Counsellor, Peking 55-57; Consul-Gen., New York 57-60; Minister, Washington 60-62; High Commr. in Australia and New Zealand 62-65; Dir.-Gen. Ministry of Foreign Affairs, Pakistan 65-66; Pakistan Amb. to Sweden, Norway, Denmark, Finland 66-68, to People's Repub. of China 68-73, also accred. to Mongolia; Bangladesh Amb. to Burma 73-, also accred. to Thailand and Singapore; Sitara-e-Quaid-e-Azam 62.
Embassy of Bangladesh, 106-108 Rhyu Street, Rangoon, Burma.

Kakharov, Abdulakhad; Soviet politician; b. 1913; ed. Leninabad Pedagogical Inst.
Trade Union, Komsomol, Soviet and party work, Tadzhikistan 33-47; mem. C.P.S.U. 39-; Second Sec. Leninabad Regional Cttee., C.P. of Tadzhikistan 47-54; Chair. Exec. Cttee. Leninabad Regional Soviet of Workers' Deputies 54-55; Deputy Chair. Council of Ministers, Tadzhikistan 56-58; Chair. *Gosplan*, Tadzhikistan 57-61; Chair. Council of Ministers, Tadzhikistan 61-76, Cand. mem. Central Cttee. of C.P.S.U. 61-; mem. Presidium of Central Cttee. of C.P. of Tadzhikistan.
Council of Ministers of Tadzhikistan, Dushanbe, Tadzhik S.S.R., U.S.S.R.

Kamaladevi, Chattopadhyay; Indian political and social worker; b. 3 April 1903, Mangalore; ed. Mangalore, Bedford Coll. and London School of Economics, London Univ.
Joined Congress; elected to A.I.C.C. 27; Organizing Sec. and Pres. All-India Women's Conf.; imprisoned 30, 32, 34 and 42; founded Indian Co-operative Union to rehabilitate refugees on a co-operative basis 48; Chair. All-India Handicrafts Board 52-; Vice-Chair. Sangeet Natak Akad.; Pres. Theatre Centre of India; helped to found World Crafts Council and is its Senior Vice-Pres.; Indian and foreign awards; Deshikotlama Award (Vishwa Bharati Univ. at Shantiniketan) 70.
Publs. *In War-torn China, Japan: Its Weakness and Strength, Socialism and Society, America, the Land of Superlatives, Uncle Sam's Empire, Indian Handicrafts, Carpets and Floor Coverings of India.*
20 Canning Place, New Delhi; and Flat No. 6, Château Marine, Marine Drive, Bombay, India.
Telephone: New Delhi 386408; Bombay 299676.

Kamath, Hari Vishnu, B.SC.; Indian politician; b. 13 July 1907; ed. Mangalore and Presidency Coll., Madras.
Joined Indian Civil Service in London 29; served I.C.S. 30-38; resigned for political reasons; joined Congress and then the Forward Bloc as Sec.-Gen.; in prison 40-41, 42-45; mem. Constituent Assembly 46-49, and mem. Nagpur Provincial Congress Cttee.; mem. Provisional Parl. 50-52; Praja Socialist Mem. of Lok Sabha 55-57, 62-67; Chair. Praja Socialist Party, Madhya Pradesh 58-60; mem. Nat. Exec. Praja Socialist Party 53-71, Nat. Cttee. Socialist Party 71-; Chair. Central Parl. Board, Praja Socialist Party 65-70; mem. Admin. Reforms Comm., Govt. of India 66-70; candidate for Vice-Pres. 69.
Publs. *Communist China colonises Tibet, invades India* 59, *Principles and Techniques of Administration* 71.
Dhantoli, Nagpur, India.
Telephone: 22359 (Nagpur).

Kamei, Masao; Japanese business executive; b. 20 April 1916, Kobe City, Hyogo Pref.; ed. Tokyo Univ.
Director Sumitomo Electric Industries Ltd. 64-66, Man. Dir. 66-69, Senior Man. Dir. 69-71, Exec. Vice-Pres. 71-73, Pres. Nov. 73-.
7-25, 1-chome Kamikoshien, Nishinomiya City, Hyogo Prefecture, Japan.
Telephone: 0798-47-3948.

Kameoka, Takao; Japanese politician; b. 27 Jan. 1920.
Served as Major in Japanese Army; Private Sec. to Minister of Health and Welfare; mem. House of Reps. 60-; Deputy Minister of Posts and Telecommunications 65; Deputy Chief Sec. of the Cabinet, Minister of State 67-68; Minister of Construction 73-74.
13-9, Asagaya-Kita, 2-Chome, Suginami-ku, Tokyo 166, Japan.

Kamimura, Eisuke, B.A.; Japanese industrialist; b. 11 March 1900; ed. Tokyo Imperial Univ.
Joined Nippon Oil Co. 25; with Japan Oil Transportation Co. 46-49; Dir. Nippon Oil Co. 49-50, Man. Dir. 50-58, Vice-Pres. 58-61, Pres. 61, now Chair.; Dir. Nippon Petroleum Refining Co. 51-61, Pres. 61-; Chair. Japan Oil Transportation Co. 58-; Dir. Nippon Petrochemicals Co. 61-, Nisseki Real Estate Co. 59-, Nippon Petroleum Gas Co. 61-, Nippon Hodo Co. 60-, Nippon Speciality Lubricants Co. 60-; Chair. and Pres. Nippon Oil (Delaware) Ltd. 61-; Exec. Dir. Fed. of Econ. Orgs. 61-, Japan Fed. of Employers' Asscns. 61-.
Nippon Oil Co. Ltd., 3-12, Nishishimbashi 1-chome, Minato-ku, Tokyo 105; and 5-2-2 Den-enchofu, Ohta-ku, Tokyo, Japan.

Kanakaratne, Neville, M.A., LL.B.; Ceylonese diplomatist; b. 19 July 1923, Colombo; ed. Royal Coll., Colombo, Univs. of Ceylon and Cambridge and Middle Temple.
Crown Counsel, Dept. of Attorney-Gen. 51-57; First Sec. and Legal Adviser, Perm. Mission of Ceylon at UN 57-61; Legal Adviser to Special Rep. of UN Sec.-Gen. in the

Congo 61-62; Legal and Political Adviser to Commdr., UN Emergency Force, Gaza 62-64; Legal Adviser to Commdr. UN Peace Keeping Force, Cyprus and to Special Rep. of UN Sec.-Gen. 64-65; Senior Fellow, Centre for Int. Studies, New York Univ. 65-66; Minister for Econ. Affairs, Ceylon High Comm., London 67-70; Amb. to U.S.A. Sept. 70-; del. to numerous int. confs. and several sessions of UN Gen. Assembly.
Embassy of Sri Lanka, 2148 Wyoming Avenue, N.W., Washington, D.C.; House: 2503 30th Street, N.W., Washington, D.C., U.S.A.
Telephone: 483-4025 (Office); 387-0601 (Home).

Kanayama, Masahide; Japanese diplomatist; b. 24 Jan. 1909; ed. Faculty of Law, Tokyo Univ.
Entered Ministry of Foreign Affairs 34; served France 34, Geneva 35, Ministry of Foreign Affairs, Tokyo 39-41; Third, later Second Sec. Italy 41-44; First Sec., Vatican 52; Counsellor, Philippines 52-54; Consul-Gen. Honolulu 54-57; Dir.-Gen. European and Oceanic Affairs Bureau 57-61; Consul-Gen. New York 61-63; Amb. to Chile 64-66, to Poland 66-68, to Repub. of Korea 68-72; Dir. Joint Research Centre of Int. Relations, Inst. of Korean Studies.
2-1, 7-chome, Minamiaoyama, Minato-ku, Tokyo 107; Office: Mita Building 5-3, 1-chome, Mita, Minato-ku, Tokyo; Home: 4-3, 1-chome, Akatsutsumimachi, Setagaya-ku, Tokyo 156, Japan.

Kaneko, Saichiro; Japanese business executive; b. 1 Feb. 1900; ed. Keio Univ.
Chairman, Jujo Paper Co. Ltd.
Jujo Paper Co. Ltd., 12-1 Yurakucho 1-chome, Chiyoda-ku, Tokyo, Japan.

Kaneshige, Kankuro; Japanese engineer; b. 5 April 1899; ed. Tokyo Imperial Univ.
Technician, Kanegafuchi Spinning Co. 23-25; Asst. Prof. of Mechanical Engineering, Tokyo Imperial Univ. 25-42; Prof. of Mechanical Engineering, Univ. of Tokyo 42-60; Dir. Inst. of Industrial Science, Univ. of Tokyo 51-54; Dir. Nat. Aeronautical Laboratory 55-57; Pres. Science Council of Japan 58-60; Full-time Commr. of Atomic Energy Comm. of Japan 60-65; Chair. Nat. Space Activities Council 60-67; mem. UN Advisory Cttee. on the Application of Science and Technology to Devt. 64-69; Full-time mem. Council for Science and Technology 65-74; Trustee, Asian Inst. of Technology, Bangkok 71-76; Hon. D.Tech. (Bangkok) 76.
5-46-25 Asagayakita, Suginami-ku, Tokyo, Japan.
Telephone: 03-337-4991.

K'ang Chien-min; People's Repub. of China.
Divisional Commdr. 1st Field Army 49; Deputy Political Commissar Lanchow Mil. Region, People's Liberation Army 67-; Chair. Ninghsia Revolutionary Cttee. 68; Alt. mem. 9th Cen. Cttee. of CCP 69; First Sec. CCP Ninghsia 71; Alt. mem. 10th Cen. Cttee. of CCP 73.

K'ang Shih-en; People's Repub. of China.
Assistant to Minister of Petroleum Industry 55-56; Vice-Minister of Petroleum Industry 56; criticized and removed from office during the Cultural Revolution 67; Minister of Petroleum and Chemical Industries 75-.

Kanno, Wataro, PH.D.; Japanese politician and economist; b. 20 June 1895, Ehime; ed. Kyoto Univ.
Professor, Hikone Commercial Coll. 24-33, Osaka Commercial Coll. 33-35; Osaka Econ. Coll. 35-; Dir. Depts. of Educ. and Planning, Osaka 36-42; mem. House of Reps. 42-; Pres. Osaka Chamber of Commerce 43-45; Minister of State in Charge of Econ. Planning Agency 59-60, 68-70; responsible for *Expo 70*; Minister of Int. Trade and Industry 66-67; Order of the Rising Sun, First Class 71; Liberal Democrat.
Room 732, Shugiin Daiichi Giin Kaikan, Chiyoda-ku, Tokyo; Home: 4-17 Tezukayama-Higashi, Suniyoshi-ku, Osaka, Japan.
Telephone: 03-581-5111 (Office).

Karakeyev, Kurman Karakeyevich; Soviet historian; b. 1913, Kurmenty Village, Kirghizia; ed. Higher Party School and Acad. of Social Sciences.
Member C.P.S.U. 38-; C.P. work 39-60; mem. and Pres. Kirghiz Acad. of Sciences 60-; Corresp. mem. U.S.S.R. Acad. of Sciences 68-; Deputy to U.S.S.R. Supreme Soviet 62-; mem. Comm. for Legislative Proposals; mem. Cen. Cttee. C.P. of Kirghizia; Orders and medals of U.S.S.R.
Publs. *The History of Kirghiz SSR* (co-author and editor) 63, 68, *The History of the Communist Organizations in Central Asia* 67.
Presidium of Kirghiz S.S.R. Academy of Sciences, Ul. XXII Partsyesda 265-a, Frunze, U.S.S.R.

Karunanidhi, Dr. Muthuvel; Indian politician and playwright; b. 3 June 1924; ed. Thiruvarur Board High School.
Started first student wing of Dravidian movement called Tamilnadu Tamil Manavar Mandram; Editor-in-Charge *Kudiarasu*; journalist and stage and screen playwright in Tamil, acting in his own plays staged to collect funds for the Party; has written over 35 film-plays including the screen version of the Tamil classic *Silappadhikaram*, stage plays and short stories; one of the founder mems. of Dravida Munnetra Kazhagam Legislative Party (D.M.K.) 49, Treas. of the Party 61-; founder-editor of the Tamil daily organ of the D.M.K. *Musaroli*; represented Kulittalai in State Assembly 57-62, Thanjavur 62-67, Saidapet 68, re-elected 71; Deputy Leader of D.M.K. 68; led the Kallakkudi Agitation and was imprisoned for six months; fmr. Minister of Public Works; elected Leader of D.M.K. Feb. 69, re-elected 71; Chief Minister of Tamil Nadu (Madras) 69-Jan. 76; Hon. D.Litt. (Annamalai Univ.) 71; and Thamizha Vell (Patron of Tamil), Asscn. of Research Scholars in Tamil, and several awards for literary contrib.
Dravida Munnetra Kazhagam, Arivagam, Royapuram, Madras 13, Tamil Nadu, India.

Karunaratne, Nuwarapaksa Hewayalage Asoka Mahaname; Ceylonese politician; b. 26 Jan. 1916; ed. St. Anthony's Coll., Kandy and Nalanda Vidyalaya. Colombo.
Member of Parl. 58-; Parl. Sec. to Minister of Justice 60; Junior Minister of Justice 63, removed from office because of critical attitude to Govt.; helped to form Sri Lanka Freedom Socialist Party 64; Minister of Social Services 65-70; Sri Lanka Freedom Party.
Sri Lanka Freedom Party, 407 Galle Road, Colombo, Sri Lanka.

Kasuri, Mian Mahmud Ali; Pakistani lawyer and politician; b. 31 Oct. 1910, Kasur; ed. Punjab and Bombay Univs. and King's Coll., London.
Called to the Bar, Gray's Inn, London 35; started legal practice, Lahore High Court 37; mem. All India Muslim League Council 42-49; founding mem. and Pres. Azad Pakistan Party 50-57; mem. Nat. Awami Party 57-70, Pres. W. Pakistan Nat. Awami Party 65-70; mem. Pakistan People's Party 70-72, later Vice-Chair. and mem. Cen. Cttee., expelled Feb. 73; mem. Nat. Assembly 71-; Minister of Law and Parl. Affairs 71-72, resigned; joined opposition party Tehrik-i-Istiqlal 73; founder, Pakistan Inst. of Int. Affairs; Pres. West Pakistan High Court Bar Asscn. 58-59, 65-66; mem. Pakistan Law Comm. 59-60; Chair. West Pakistan Bar Council 63-65, 65-66, Vice-Chair. 67-69; Pres. Pakistan Legal Centre 63-64, 64-65; Vice-Pres. Int. Asscn. of Democratic Lawyers, World Habeas Corpus Org.; mem. Int. War Crimes Tribunal 66-68.
National Assembly, Islamabad, Pakistan.

Kato, Ichiro, LL.D.; Japanese lawyer, professor and university administrator; b. 28 Sept. 1922, Tokyo; ed. Faculty of Law, Univ. of Tokyo.

Associate Prof. of Law, Univ. of Tokyo 48-57, Prof. of Law 57-68, 74-; Dean of Law and Acting Pres. Univ. of Tokyo 68-69, Pres. 69-73; Vice-Rector UN Univ. 75-76; mem. Admin. Board, Int. Assсn. of Univs. 70-; Pres. Nat. Univ. Assсn. (Japan) 69-73; Matsunaga Foundation Prize 66.
Publs. Several books on legal subjects.
University of Tokyo, Hongo, Bunkyo-ku, Tokyo; 10-30, Seijo 3-chome, Setagaya-ku, Tokyo, Japan.
Telephone: 03-416-2769.

Kato, Tadao; Japanese diplomatist; b. 13 May 1916; ed. Tokyo Univ. and Cambridge Univ.
Consul, Singapore 52; First Sec., London 53; Counsellor, Econ. Affairs Bureau, Foreign Office 56-59; Counsellor, Wash. 60-63; Deputy Dir. Econ. Affairs Bureau, Foreign Office 63-66, Dir. 66-67; Amb. to Org. for Econ. Co-operation and Devt. (OECD) 67-70; Amb. to Mexico 70-74, to U.K. July 75-.
Embassy of Japan, 43 Grosvenor Street, London, W.1, England.

Kaul, Prince Mohan, M.B., B.S., D.P.H., F.R.C.P., F.I.A.M.S.; Indian physician and health official; b. 1 March 1906; ed. Punjab Univ. and Guy's Hospital, London.
Teacher, Infectious Diseases, and Medical Officer, Campbell Medical School, Calcutta 33-34; commissioned Indian Medical Service 34; army service, rose to Acting Col. 34-45; Deputy, Public Comm. Govt. of India 46; Deputy Dir.-Gen. Health Services, Ministry of Health; Dir. WHO Epidemiological Intelligence Station, Singapore 47-49; Dir. WHO Liaison Office to UN, New York 50-52; Dir. Div. External Relations and Technical Assistance 53-56; Asst. Dir.-Gen. UN World Health Org. (WHO) 56-67; Special Consultant WHO 68, 69, Short-term Consultant 70-75.
17-G, Maharani Bagh, New Delhi, India.
Telephone: 631481.

Kaul, Triloki Nath; Indian diplomatist; b. 8 Feb. 1913; ed. Univs. of Punjab, Allahabad, London.
Joined Indian Civil Service 37; served in United Provinces as Joint Magistrate and Collector 37-47; Sec. Indian Council of Agricultural Research, New Delhi 47; First Sec. Indian Embassy, Moscow 47-49, Washington 49-50; Counsellor 50-52, and Minister 52-53, Peking; Joint Sec. Ministry of External Affairs, New Delhi 53-57; Chair. Int. Comm. for Supervision and Control, Viet-Nam 57-58; Amb. to Iran 58-60; Deputy High Commr., U.K. 60-61, Acting High Commr. 61-62; Amb. to U.S.S.R. and Mongolia 62-66; Sec. to Govt. of India, Ministry of Foreign Affairs, New Delhi, June 66-68; Sec.-Gen. Ministry of Foreign Affairs 68-73; Amb. to U.S.A. 73-.
Embassy of India, 2107 Massachusetts Avenue, N.W., Washington, D.C., 20008, U.S.A.

Kawaguchi, Kaichi; Japanese international financial official; b. 13 April 1922, Wakayama; ed. Tokyo Univ.
Entered Ministry of Finance 47; First Sec. Embassy in Belgium and France 61-65; Dir. Tokyo Customs House 69-70; Insurance Comm., Ministry of Finance 71-72; Exec. Dir. IMF 72-.
International Monetary Fund, 19th and H Streets, N.W., Washington, D.C. 20431; Home: 5322 Falmouth Road, Bethesda, Md. 20016, U.S.A.
Telephone: EXec. 3-6362 (Office); 229-8694 (Home).

Kawaguchi, Toshiro; Japanese business executive; b. 9 July 1909, Shizuoka Pref.; ed. Tokyo Univ.
Director, Honshu Paper Co. Ltd. 64-66, Man. Dir. 66-69, Exec. Dir. 69-70, Exec. Vice-Pres. 70-71, Pres. and Chief Exec. Dir. 71-74, now Chair. of Board.
Honshu Paper Co. Ltd., 12-8, 5-chome Ginza, Chuo-ku, Tokyo; Home: 15-3, 1-chome, Okamoto, Setagaya-ku, Tokyo, Japan.
Telephone: 03-700-8525.

Kawai, Ryoichi; Japanese business executive; b. 18 Jan. 1917; ed. Tokyo Univ.
President, Komatsu Ltd.
Komatsu Bldg., 3-6, 2-chome, Akasaka, Minato-ku, Tokyo, Japan.
Telephone: 584-7111.

Kawai, Takaharu; Japanese business executive; b. 1905; ed. Kyoto Univ.
President and Rep. Dir. Nippon Mining Co. Ltd.; Chair. of Board 74-.
Nippon Mining Co. Ltd. 3 Akasaka-Aoicho, Minato-ku, Tokyo; 3-4-13 Nishiohi, Shinagawa-ku, Tokyo, Japan.
Telephone: (03) 582-2111.

Kawakami, Kenjiro; Japanese business executive; b. 22 Dec. 1906, Osaka-fu; ed. Tokyo Imperial Univ.
Joined Sumitomo & Co. Ltd. (later Sumitomo Head Office Ltd.) April 29; transferred to Sumitomo Copper Rolling & Steel Tubing Co. Ltd. (now Sumitomo Metal Industry Co. Ltd.) Sept. 29; Sumitomo Head Office Ltd. 44; Seika Kogyo Co. Ltd. (now Sumitomo Coal Mining Co. Ltd.) 46, Dir. 46, Man. Dir. 48; Man. Dir. Sumitomo Metal Mining Co. Ltd. 50, Senior Man. Dir. 56, Pres. 63-; Dir. Sulawisi Nickel Devt. Corpn. Co. Ltd.; Standing Dir. Japan Fed. of Employers' Assсns., Fed. of Econ. Orgs.; mem. Japan Cttee. for Econ. Devt.; Pres. Indonesian Nickel Devt. Co. Ltd. 69-73, Chair. of Board 73-; Blue Ribbon Medal.
Sumitomo Metal Mining Co. Ltd., 11-3, 5-chome, Shimbashi, Minato-ku, Tokyo; 5-26-1 Katasegama, Fujisawashi, Kanagawa Pref., Japan.

Kawamata, Katsuji; Japanese business executive; b. 1 March 1905; ed. Tokyo Univ. of Commerce.
Japan Industrial Bank 29-47, Branch Man. Hiroshima 46-47; Man. Dir. Nissan Motor Co. 47-57, Pres. 57-73, Chair. 73-; Chair. Nissan Diesel, Nissan Shatai, Japan Automobile Mfrs. Assсn. 62-72; Vice-Pres. Fed. of Econ. Orgs. (Keidanren) 72-.
Nissan Motor Co. Ltd., 17-1, 6-chome, Ginza Chuo-ku, Tokyo 104, Japan.

Kawasaki, Kunio; Japanese business executive; b. 23 Sept. 1907; ed. Tokyo Univ.
Japan Woollen Yarn Spinning Co. Ltd. 32-42, Toyobo Co. Ltd. (after merger) 42-, Dir. 56-57, Man. Dir. 57-61, Senior Man. Dir. 61-63, Vice-Pres. 63-66, Pres. 66-74, Chair. of Board 74-; Auditor Japan Exlan Co. Ltd. (acrylic fibres) 66-; Exec. Dir., Kansai Econs. Fed. 66-68, Vice-Pres. 68-; Exec. Dir. Fed. of Econ. Org. 66-, Japan Fed. of Employers' Assсn. 67-; Pres. Toyobo Petcord Co. Ltd. 69-; Gen. Counsellor Toyo Rubber Industry Co. Ltd. 71-; Chair. Japan Spinners' Assсn. 72-73; Pres. Osaka-São Paulo Sister City Assсn. 70-74, Dir. 74; Exec. Dir. Japan Textile Fed. 73-; Pres. Kansai Int. Students Inst. 74-; Vice-Pres. Japan Overseas Enterprise Assсn. 74-; Pres. Osaka Int. Trade Fair Comm. 74-; Blue Ribbon Medal 69.
Toyobo Co. Ltd., 8 Dojima Hamadori 2-chome, Kita-ku, Osaka 530; Home: 1-28, 1-chome, Hibarigaoka Yamate, Takarazuka City, Hyogo Prefecture, 665, Japan.
Telephone: 06-344-1331 (Office); 0727-59-2556 (Home).

Kayum, Abdul; Afghan physicist and politician; b. 1923, Wardak province; ed. Mil. School, Kabul, Teacher Training High School, Kabul, George Town Univ., U.S.A., London Univ.
Third Lieutenant, Ministry of Defence 46-50; Prof. of Science at Coll. of Science, Kabul Univ. 71-73; Minister of Mines and Industries 73-74, of Educ. Dec. 74-; rep. of Afghanistan at Int. Atomic Energy Confs. 61, 62.
Publs. *New Lines in the Linear Spectrum of Titanium* and many articles.
Ministry of Education, Kabul, Afghanistan.

Kedah, H.R.H. The Sultan of; Tuanku Abdul Halim Mu'adzam Shah ibni Al-Marhum Sultan Badishah, D.K., D.K.M., D.M.N., D.U.K., S.P.M.K., D.K. (Kelantan), D.K. (Pahang), S.S.D.K.; Ruler of Kedah, Malaysia; b. 28 Nov. 1927, Alor Setar; ed. Sultan Abdul Hamid Coll., Alor Setar and Wadham Coll., Oxford.
Raja Muda (Heir to Throne of Kedah) 49-58, Regent of Kedah 57-58, Sultan 58-; Timbalan Yang di-Pertuan Agong (Deputy Supreme Head of State of Malaysia) 65-70, Yang di-Pertuan Agong (Supreme Head of State of Malaysia) 70-75; Col. Commdt. Malaysian Reconnaissance Corps 66; First Class Order of the Rising Sun, Japan 70, Bintang Maha Putera, Klas Satu, Indonesia 70, Knight Grand Cross of the Bath, U.K. 72, Knight of the Order of St. John 72, Most Auspicious Order of the Rajamitrathorn, Thailand 73.
Alor Setar, Kedah, Malaysia.

Kelantan, H.R.H. the Sultan of; Tuanku Yahya Petra ibni Al Marhum Sultan Ibrahim, D.K., D.M.N., S.M.N., S.P.M.K., S.J.M.K., S.P.S.K., D.K. (Trengganu), D.K. (Selangor), D.K. (Brunei); Ruler of Kelantan, Malaysia; b. 10 Dec. 1917, Kota Bharu; ed. Francis Light School, Penang, and U.K.
Tengku Temanggong 39; Private Sec. to His Late Highness Sultan Ismail 45; Asst. State Treas., District Officer of Kota Bharu until 48; Tengku Mahkota Kelantan 48; Pres. Council of Religion and Malay Custom 48-53; Regent 53, 58; installed as Sultan of Kelantan 60; Timbalan Yang di-Pertuan Agong (Deputy Supreme Head of State of Malaysia) 70-75, Yang di-Pertuan Agong (Supreme Head of State of Malaysia) Sept. 75-; Col.-in-Chief Malaysian Artillery.
Kota Bahru, Kelantan, Malaysia.

Kelly, Sir Theo (William Theodore), Kt., O.B.E., F.A.I.M.; Australian business executive; b. 27 June 1907; ed. Sydney.
Served World War II, Wing Commdr. R.A.A.F. 42-44, Chair. Canteen Services Board 46-59; Man. Dir. Woolworths Ltd. Aust. 45-70, Chair. 63-; Chair. Woolworths (N.Z.) Ltd. and Woolworths (Properties) Ltd.; mem. Board, Reserve Bank of Aust. 61-; Dir. Aust. Mutual Life Assurance Co.; Chair. Computer Services of Aust. Pty. Ltd.; Dir. A.M.P. Soc. 67-, A.N.T.A. 59-; mem. Board, Royal N. Shore Hosp., Sydney Trustee, Nat. Parks and Wildlife Foundation.
Woolworths Limited, 534 George Street, P.O. Box 4068, Sydney 2000, Australia.

Keng Piao; Chinese diplomatist, politician and fmr. army officer, People's Repub. of China; b. 1909, Li-ling, Hunan; ed. Chinese Worker-Peasant Red Army Coll.
Major-General 46; Chief of Staff, N. China Field Army 47; Amb. to Sweden 50-56, concurrently Minister to Denmark 50-55, to Finland 51-54; Amb. to Pakistan 56-59; Vice-Minister of Foreign Affairs 60-63; Amb. to Burma 63-67, to Albania 69-71; Dir., Int. Liaison Dept., CCP 71-; mem. 9th (1969), 10th (73) Cen. Cttees., CCP.

Kerr, Sir John Robert, K.C.M.G., LL.B., Q.C.; Australian lawyer and public official; b. 24 Sept. 1914, Sydney; ed. Fort St. Boys' High School, Sydney Univ.
Admitted to New South Wales Bar 38; army service 39-46; Principal, Australian School of Pacific Admin. 46; Organizing Sec. South Pacific Comm. 46-47; Q.C. (N.S.W.) 53; mem. N.S.W. Bar Council 60-64; Vice-Pres. N.S.W. Bar Asscn. 62-63, Pres. 64; Vice-Pres. Law Council of Australia 62-64, Pres. 64-66; Pres. N.S.W. Marriage Guidance Council 61-62, Industrial Relations Soc. of Australia 64-66, Law Assen. for Asia and Western Pacific 66-70; Deputy Pres. Trades Practices Tribunal 66-72, Copyright Tribunal 69-72; Pres. Third Commonwealth and Empire Law Conf., Sydney 65; mem. Medical Board of N.S.W. 63-66, Board of the Council on New Guinea Affairs 64-71; Judge of Commonwealth Industrial Court and Judge of Supreme Court of A.C.T. 66-72, Judge of Courts of Marine Inquiry 67-72; Chief Justice, Supreme Court, N.S.W. 72-74; Lieut.-Gov. N.S.W. 73-74; Gov.-Gen. of Australia 74-; Hon. Life mem. Law Soc. of England and Wales 65; Hon. mem. American Bar Asscn. 67; K.St.J. 74.
Publs. papers and articles on industrial relations, New Guinea affairs, organization of legal profession, etc.
Government House, Canberra, A.C.T. 2600, Australia.

Keuneman, Pieter Gerald Bartholomeus, M.A.; Ceylonese politician; b. 3 Oct. 1917, Colombo; ed. Royal Coll. Colombo, Univ. Coll. Colombo, Pembroke Coll. Cambridge, and Gray's Inn, London.
Worked briefly as journalist in London; Asst. Editor, *Ceylon Daily News* 40-; founder mem. and Gen. Sec. Ceylon Communist Party (now Communist Party of Sri Lanka) 43-73, Chair. 73-; mem. Parl. for Colombo Central 47-; Minister of Housing and Construction May 70-.
Publs. several books, pamphlets and articles on socialism and political and economic problems of Sri Lanka.
Ministry of Housing and Construction, Colombo 1; Central Headquarters, Communist Party of Sri Lanka, 91 Cotta Road, Colombo 8; Home: 8/2 27th Lane, Colombo 3, Sri Lanka.
Telephone: 31466 (Ministry); 93855 (Communist Party H.Q.); 23620 (Home).

Khammao, Prince; Laotian diplomatist; b. 23 Sept. 1911, Luang Prabang; ed. Lycée Albert Sarraut, Hanoi and Univ. of Montpellier.
Secretary-General of the Royal Palace 41-42; Chief, Luang Prabang Province 48-51; King's Attorney, French Union, Vientiane 51-52; High Rep. of King of Laos to Pres. of Union, Paris 52-56; Amb. to Japan 56-58; Amb. to U.K. 59-62, 67-71; Sec.-Gen. Royal Palace 62-67; Perm. Rep. to UN Sept. 71-72; Pres. King's Council.

Khan, Akbar Ali, B.A., LL.B.; lawyer and fmr. state governor; b. 20 Nov. 1899, Hyderabad; ed. Jamia Millia, New Delhi; Aligarh Muslim Univ., Osmania and London Univs.
Called to the Bar, London; joined Congress 49; mem. Rajya Sabha 54-; Senior Advocate Supreme Court; Gov. of Uttar Pradesh 72-74, of Orissa 74-76; Pres. Maulana Abul Kalam Azad Oriental Research Inst., Osmania Univ. Graduates Asscn., Econ. Soc., All India Exhbn. Soc., Hyderabad; Vice-Pres. Hyderabad Municipal Corpn., Cen. Co-operative Union, Food Relief Asscn; Gen. Sec. Hyderabad Lawyers' Conf.; mem. Exec. Cttee. All India Co-operative Unions, exec. councils of several orgs.; Padma Bhushan 65.
Stone House, Secretariat Road, Saifabad, Hyderabad, Andhra Pradesh, India.

Khan, Ali Akbar; Indian musician; b. 1922; father of Ashish Khan (*q.v.*).
Concert Recitals on Sarod, in India since 36, and all over the world since 55; Founder Ali Akbar Coll. of Music, Calcutta 56; Musical Dir. of many films and numerous contributions on All India Radio; Lecture Recitals at Montreal and McGill Univs., Canada; first long-playing gramophone record introduced by Yehudi Menuhin; Pres. of India Award 63.

Khan, Ashish; Indian musician; b. 1939; son of Ali Akbar Khan (*q.v.*); studied with his father and with Ravi Shankar (*q.v.*) his uncle.
Gave first public concert playing sarod duets with grandfather, the late Alauddin Khan; appeared with both his father and grandfather and has given many solo recitals, performing all over the world; was youngest Indian musician to tour U.S.; appeared in Festival of India at Hollywood Bowl 67; has taught Indian music at Univ. of Washington, Seattle and Calif. State Coll., Long Beach; now teaching at Ali Akbar Coll. of Music, San Rafael; has composed film scores.

Khan, Ghulam Ishaq; Pakistani civil servant; b. 1915; ed. Islamia Coll., Peshawar, and Punjab Univ.
North-West Frontier Province (N.W.F.P.) Civil Service (India) 40-47, Sub-Divisional Officer, Treasury Officer and Magistrate First Class 40-44, Bursar and Sec. to Council of Management of Islamia Coll., Peshawar; Sec. to Chief Minister, N.W.F.P. 47; Home Sec. Food and Dir. Civil Supplies to Govt. N.W.F.P. 48; Devt. and Admin. Sec. for Agriculture, Animal Husbandry, Forests, Industries, Co-operatives and Village Aid 49-52; Devt. Commr. and Sec. to Devt. Dept., N.W.F.P. 53-56; Sec. for Devt. and Irrigation, Govt. of W. Pakistan 56-58; mem. W. Pakistan Water and Power Devt. Authority 58-61, Chair. 61-66; mem. Land Reforms Comm. 58-59; Sec. Finance, Govt. of Pakistan 66-70; Cabinet Sec., Govt. of Pakistan 70; Gov. State Bank of Pakistan 72-75; Tamgha-i-Pakistan 59; Sitara-i-Pakistan 62; Hilal-i-Quaid-i-Azam 68.
c/o State Bank of Pakistan, Central Directorate, P.O. Box 4456, I.I. Chundrigar Road, Karachi, Pakistan.

Khan, Khan Abdul Qayyum; Pakistani lawyer and politician; b. 1901, Chitral; ed. Islamia Coll., Peshawar and London School of Econs.
Called to the Bar, Lincoln's Inn, London 26; practised law in Peshawar; joined All India Congress Party during Civil Disobedience Movt.; mem. Indian Central Legislative Assembly 37; Dep. Leader, Congress Party in Legislative Assembly; joined All-Indian Muslim League 45; mem. Frontier Legislative Assembly and Leader Muslim League Assembly Party 46; political imprisonment 47; Chief Minister, N.W. Frontier Province 47; mem. Provincial Legislative Assembly 51; Minister of Industries, Food and Agriculture, Govt. of Pakistan 53-54; Pres. Pakistan Muslim League 58; political imprisonment 60, 62; formed Quaid-i-Azama Muslim League March 69; Pres. Pakistan Muslim League Jan. 70; mem. Nat. Assembly Dec. 70-; Minister for Interior and States and Frontier Regions April 71-.
Ministry of the Interior, Islamabad, Pakistan.

Khan, Air Marshal Mohammad Asghar; Pakistani air force officer and politician; b. 17 Jan. 1921; ed. Imperial Defence Coll., U.K.
Commander-in-Chief Pakistan Air Force and Mil. Adviser SEATO 57-65; Pres. Pakistan Int. Airlines 65-68; entered politics Nov. 68; head and founder of Istiqlal Party March 70.
Lahore, Pakistan.

Khan, Rana Mohammad Hanif (*see* Hanif Khan, Rana Mohammad).

Khan, Sultan Mohammad, B.A.; Pakistani diplomatist; b. 1919; ed. Ewing Christian Coll. and Allahabad Univ.
Commissioned Indian Army 42; Indian Political Service 46; Pakistan Diplomatic Service 47-; Pakistan High Comm., New Delhi 47, Cairo and Rome 48-50; Ministry of External Affairs, Karachi 50-53; Embassy, Peking and Ankara 53-57; Deputy High Commr. London 57-59; Ministry of External Affairs, Karachi 59-61; High Commr. in Canada 61-66, concurrently accredited as High Commr. in Jamaica 63-66, Trinidad and Tobago 63-66, Amb. to Cuba 64-66; Amb. to People's Repub. of China 66-68; Foreign Sec. 69-72; Amb. to U.S.A. 72-73, concurrently accred. to Jamaica and Venezuela 72-73, Mexico 73; Amb. to Japan 74-.
Embassy of Pakistan, 14-9 Moto Azabu, 2-chome, Minato-ku, Tokyo, Japan.

Khan, Gen. Yahya (*see* under Yahya Khan, Gen. Agha Muhammad).

Khanh, Brig.-General Nguyen (*see* under Nguyen Khanh).

Khanna, Charan Das, M.A., C.A.I.I.B., A.I.B.; Indian financial official; b. 22 March 1915, Kangra; ed. Punjab Univ.
Worked in various supervisory capacities in Indian and English commercial banks in India 38-48; joined Industrial Finance Corpn. of India 48, Sec. 65-66, Gen. Man. 66-70, Chair. 70-74; Dir. Industrial Reconstruction Corpn. of India 71-; Trustee, Unit of India 73-; Fellow, Econ. Devt. Inst. of World Bank; Pochkanwala Prize, Indian Inst. of Bankers.
Publs. several papers on banking and industrial finance.
Industrial Finance Corporation of India, Bank of Baroda Building, 16 Parliament Street, New Delhi 1, India.
Telephone: 312440 (Office); 672832 (Home).

Kharmawan, Byanti; Indonesian international finance official; b. 1 June 1906, Tegal, Central Java; ed. School of Economics, Rotterdam.
Became civil servant 49; Econ. Adviser, Ministry of Econ. Affairs and Ministry of Finance; Chief Econ. Adviser and Deputy Gov., Central Bank of Indonesia; Exec. Dir. Asian Devt. Bank 66-68; Exec. Dir. Int. Monetary Fund (IMF) 68-.
Publs. *Willem Kloos en de Dichtkunst* and articles on literary and economic topics.
International Monetary Fund, 19th and H Streets, N.W., Washington, D.C., 20431, U.S.A.

Khatri, Maj. Gen. Padma Bahadur, K.C.V.O.; Nepalese diplomatist; b. Feb. 1915, Kathmandu; ed. in Calcutta and Tri-Chandra Coll., Kathmandu.
Joined Nepal Army 35; war service 40-46; Military attaché Nepalese Embassy London 47-49; Observer, UN Gen. Assembly 48; Nepalese Liaison Officer to British Brig. of Gurkhas, Malaya 50; Nepalese rep. to Non-Aligned Conf., Bandung 55, Cairo 64; Sec. Coronation Cttee. 56; Chair. Nepal-China Boundary Cttee. 60-62; Minister of Defence 62-63, of Foreign Affairs 63-64, 72-75; Amb. to U.S.A., Argentina, Canada and Chile 64-68; Perm. Rep. to UN 64-72; fmr. Vice-Pres. UN Gen. Assembly (twice), Pres. UN Security Council (twice); Chair. UN Special Del. to Security Council, Guinea 70; accompanied the late H.M. King Mahendra on several State visits, etc.; Orders of Gorkha Dakshin Bahu I, Nepal Sripad II, Sainik Dirgha Sewa Patta, Nepal Tara I, Trisaktipatta I, Grand Cross (Fed. Repub. of Germany), Officier Légion d'Honneur (France).
Ministry of Foreign Affairs, Singha Durbar, Kathmandu; Gyaneswore, Kathmandu, Nepal.
Telephone: 12211, Ext. 231 (Office).

Khattak, Mohammed Yusuf, M.A.; Pakistani politician; b. 18 Nov. 1917, Oghi, Hazara, North West Frontier Province; ed. Islamia Coll., Peshawar, Govt. Coll. Lahore, Oxford Univ., Lincoln's Inn, London.
Worked in Muslim League and participated in Freedom movement and movement for establishment of Pakistan; volunteer relief work in Bihar 46; organized Muslim League in North West Frontier Province (N.W.F.P.) 47; Gen. Sec. Sarhad, N.W.F.P. Provincial Muslim League 49, now Pres. of N.W.F.P. Provincial Muslim League; Sec.-Gen. Pakistan Muslim League 49, now Senior Vice-Pres.; mem. del. to UN 51-52; Leader of Opposition in Nat. Assembly 62; Fed. Minister of Fuel, Power and Natural Resources 75-.
Ministry of Fuel, Power and Natural Resources, Islamabad, Pakistan.

Khieu Samphan; Cambodian politician; b. 1932; ed. Paris Univ.
Founded French-language journal, Cambodia; Deputy Nat. Assembly in Prince Sihanouk's party, *Sangkum Reastr Nyum* (Popular Socialist Community); served as Sec. of State for Commerce; left Phnom-Penh to join *Khmers Rouges* 67; Minister of Defence in Royal Govt. of Nat. Union of Cambodia (GRUNC) 70-75, Deputy Prime Minister 70-76 (in exile 70-75, in Phnom-Penh 75-76); Pres. of State Presidium (Head of State) April 76-; mem.

Politburo Nat. United Front of Cambodia (FUNC) 70-; C.-in-C. *Khmers Rouges* High Command 73-. State Presidium, Phnom-Penh, Cambodia.

Khiem, Gen. Tran Thien (*see* Tran Thien Khiem).

Khir Johari, Mohamed; Malaysian politician and diplomatist; b. 29 Jan. 1923, Kedah; ed. Sultan Abdul Hamid Coll., Kedah.
Secretary-General Saberkas (political body affiliated to United Malays Nat. Org.) 46; Sec.-Gen. UMNO 54-55, 66-69; played leading role in founding of UMNO-MCA-MIC Alliance; mem. Parl. for Kedah Tengah 55-; fmr. Minister of Educ., of Agriculture, and Co-operatives, of Trade and Industry; Minister without Portfolio, Amb. to U.S.A. 73-; Pres. Afro-Asian Rural Reconstruction Org. Confs., New Delhi 64, Nairobi 66, Pacific Area Travel Asscn. 71-72; leader of del. to UNCTAD III, Santiago 72; Chair. Nat. Family Planning Board, Zoological Soc., Nat. Soc. for the Deaf and several other voluntary orgs.; has attended numerous int. economic confs.; Hon. LL.D. (Univ. of Malaya) 66, Hon. D.Sc. & Ed. (De la Salle Coll., Manila) 67.
Embassy of Malaysia, 2401 Massachusetts Avenue N.W., Washington, D.C. 20008; Home: 2701 Albermarle Street N.W., Washington, D.C. 20008, U.S.A.

Khorana, Har Gobind, PH.D.; American (born India) scientist; b. 1922; ed. Punjab Univ.
Began career as organic chemist; worked with Sir Alexander Todd on nucleotides, Cambridge 50-52; later worked at Nat. Research Inst., Canada until 60; Prof. Inst. of Enzyme Chemistry, Univ. of Wisconsin 60-70; Sloan Prof. of Biology and Chemistry, Mass. Inst. of Technology 70-; Nobel Prize for Medicine and Physiology (with Holley and Nirenberg) for their interpretation of the genetic code and its function in protein synthesis 68; Louisa Gross Horwitz Prize for Biochemistry 68, Lasker Foundation Award 68, American Chemical Soc. Award, American Acad. of Achievement Award 71; Hon. D.Sc. (Liverpool, Delhi, Chicago).
Department of Biology and Chemistry, Massachusetts Institute of Technology, Cambridge, Mass. 02139, U.S.A.

Khosla, Dr. Ajudhia Nath; Indian fmr. university administrator, state governor and engineer; b. 11 Dec. 1892; ed. D.A.V. Coll., Lahore and Thomason Coll. of Engineering, Roorkee.
Chairman Central Water and Power Comm. 45-53; Founder Pres. Int. Comm. on Drainage and Irrigation 50, Hon. Pres. 54-; Vice-Pres. World Power Conf., Int. Comm. on Dams, Int. Asscn. for Hydraulic Research; Vice-Chancellor Roorkee Univ. 54-59; mem. Rajya Sabha (Parl.) 58-59, Planning Comm. 59-62; Gov. of Orissa 62-68; Pres. Inst. of Engineers 49-50, Central Board of Irrigation and Power 46-48, 51-, of Geophysics (India) 50-53, Nat. Inst. of Science 61-62; Chair. Boards of Consultants for Bhakra, Beas, Sabarigiri, Ramganga, Yamuna and Maneri Bhali projects, Chair. Ramganga Board of Consultants; Vice-Pres. D.A.V. Coll. Man. Comm., New Delhi; Padma Bhushan, Govt. of India Award; Hon. Life mem. Inst. of Engineers (India); Fellow, Indian Nat. Science Acad.; Life mem. American Soc. of Civil Engineers; Hon. degrees from various Univs.
Publs. *Design of Weirs on Permeable Foundations, Silting of Reservoirs, Rainfall and Runoff, Pressure Observations under Dams.*
15 Jangpura-B, Mathura Road, New Delhi 14, India.
Telephone: 76651 New Delhi.

Kijima, Torazo, B.ECONS.; Japanese business executive; b. 18 Dec. 1901; ed. Tokyo Imperial Univ.
Director Japanese Nat. Railways 50-52; mem. House of Councillors 53-59; Pres. Hinomaru Ceramic Industry Co. Ltd. 53-, Aito Vehicles Industries Co. Ltd.; Chair. Board of Dirs. Nippon Express Co. Ltd. 68-; Second Grand Order of Sacred Treasure (Japan) 72, Commdr., Grand Order (Malagasy Republic) 73.
3-12-9, Soto-Kanda, Chiyoda-ku, Tokyo; Home: 3-42-17, Wakamiya, Nakano-ku, Tokyo, Japan.

Kiki, Sir Albert Maori, K.B.E.; Papua New Guinea politician; b. 21 Sept. 1931, Orokolo, Gulf Province; ed. Fiji School of Medicine, Papua New Guinea Admin. Coll.
Public Health Officer, Welfare Officer, Patrol Officer 54-64; founded first trade union in Papua New Guinea 62; Pres. Council of Trade Unions 62-; land claims work with Koiari people; foundation mem. Pangu Pati 65-, Gen. Sec. 65-72; mem. City Council, Port Moresby 71-73; mem. for Port Moresby Inland, House of Assembly 72-; Minister for Lands and Environment 72-73, for Defence, Foreign Affairs, Trade, Migration and Customs 74-; Deputy Prime Minister 75-; Chair. Interim Constitutional Comm. 76.
Publs. *Ten Thousand Years in a Lifetime* (autobiography) 70; co-author *Ho Hao* (arts and culture of the Orokolo people) 72.
Central Government Offices, Waigani; Home: Granville Farm, 8 Mile, Port Moresby, New Guinea.

Kikutake, Kiyonori, B.A., F.A.I.A.; Japanese architect; b. 1 April 1928, Kurame; ed. Waseda Univ.
Established Kiyonori Kikutake & Assocs. (Architects) 53, now Rep. Dir.; Prof. Dept. of Architecture, Waseda Univ. 59-; mem. Board, Architectural Inst. of Japan 62-; Visiting Prof. Univ. of Hawaii 71; del. to UNESCO Int. Conf., Zurich 70; Hon. Fellow, American Inst. of Architects 71; several awards including Ministry of Educ. Arts Award 64, Architectural Inst. of Japan Award 64, Geijutsu Sensho Prize 64, Cultural merits of Kurume City 75; Major works include: Shimane Prefectural Museum 58, Office Building for Izumo Shrine, Tatebayashi City Hall, 63, Hotel Tokoen, Yonago-City, Miyakonojo City Hall, Pacific Hotel, Chigasaki 66, Iwate Prefectural Library 67, Shimane Prefectural Library, Hagi City Hall 68, Kurame City Hall 69, Expo Tower for *Expo 70*, Osaka 70, Pasadena Heights (tiered mass housing) 74, Aquapolis (floating module for ocean) Ocean, *Expo 75* 75, Hagi City Hall 75, redevelopment of Yanapa city centre 75, Tsukuba Academic New Town, pedestrian deck network and the Symbol Tower 76, Otsu shopping centre 76.
Publs. *Metabolism 1960* 60, *Taisha Kenchi ku-ron* (Metabolic Architecture) 68, *Ningen-no-Kenchiku* (Human Architecture) 70, *Ningen-no-Toshi* (A Human City) 70.
1-11-15, Ohtsuka, Bunkyo-ku, Tokyo, Japan.

Killen, (Denis) James, LL.B.; Australian lawyer and politician; b. 23 Nov. 1925, Dalby, Queensland; ed. Brisbane Grammar School and Univ. of Queensland.
Foundation Pres. Young Liberal's Movement, Queensland 49; Vice-Pres. Liberal Party Queensland Div. 53-56; mem. House of Reps. for Moreton, Queensland 55-; Minister for the Navy 69-71; opposition spokesman for educ. 73-74, for defence 75; Minister for Defence Nov. 75-.
Parliament House, Canberra, A.C.T. 2600; Commonwealth Parliament Offices, Adelaide Street, Brisbane, Queensland 4000; 22 Cook Street, Yeronga, Queensland 4104; Australia.
Telephone: 733955 (Parl. House); 2293975 (Brisbane); 652843 (Russell Hill).

Kim Dong Jo; Korean diplomatist; b. 14 Aug. 1918; ed. Coll. of Commerce, Seoul, Kyushu Imperial Univ. Law School, Japan.
Secretary-General, Ministry of Communications 49-51, Dir. Political Affairs 51-52, 54-57; Counsellor, Korean Embassy, Taiwan 52-54; Vice-Minister of Foreign Affairs 57-59; Special Envoy to Repub. of China, Malaysia, Philippines, Thailand and Repub. of Viet-Nam 59; private law practice 60-63; Leader Korean Del. to Asian People's Anti-Communist League, Viet-Nam 63; Chair. Foreign Relations and Defence Cttee. 63; Pres. Korea Trade Promotion Corpn. 64; Amb. to Japan 64-65, 66-67 to U.S.A. 67-73;

Amb.-at-large 65-66; Minister of Foreign Affairs 73-75; Leader econ. co-operation mission to South-East Asia 67; Hon. LL.D. (Illinois Coll.) 69.
San 8-35, Hannam-dong, Yongsan-ku, Seoul, Republic of Korea.

Kim Il; Korean politician.
Member, Presidium of Central Cttee. of Workers' Party of Korea; Vice-Premier, Democratic People's Repub. of Korea 56-57, First Vice-Premier 57-72; Premier Admin. Council 72-76, First Vice-Pres. April 76-.
Office of the First Vice-President, Pyongyang, Democratic People's Republic of Korea.

Kim Il Sung, Marshal; Korean politician; b. 15 April 1912 (as Kim Song Ju), Mangyongdae, Pyongyang.
Formed Communist Youth League 27; imprisoned 29-30; joined Communist Party 31; organized and led Korean People's Revolutionary Army in struggle against Japanese 32-45; Founded Fatherland Restoration Asscn. 36, elected Chair. 36; Founded Workers' Party of Korea, elected Chair. 45; Founded Korean People's Army 48; Premier of the Democratic People's Repub. of Korea 48-72, Pres. Dec. 72-; C.-in-C. 50-53; Marshal and Twice Hero of the Democratic People's Repub. of Korea, Hero of Labour of Democratic People's Repub. of Korea.
Publs. *Selected Works of Kim Il Sung* (6 vols.), etc.
Office of the President, Pyongyang, Democratic People's Republic of Korea.

Kim Jong Pil, Brig.-Gen.; Korean army officer and politician; b. 7 Jan. 1926, Puyo; ed. High School, Konguj, Seoul Nat. Univ. and Korean Military Acad.
Served in Korean war; Dir. Korean Central Intelligence Agency 61-63; mem. Nat. Assembly 63-68, 71-; Chair. Democratic Republican Party 63-68; Senior Adviser to Pres. 70; Vice-Pres. Democratic Republican Party March 71; Prime Minister 71-Dec. 75; mem. Spanish Nat. Acad.; Korean Nat. Acad.; numerous awards from Korean and foreign govts.; Hon. LL.D. (Long Island Univ., N.Y. 64, Chungang Univ. Seoul 66, Fairleigh Dickinson Univ. 68); Hon. D.Hum.Litt. (Westminster Coll., Fulton, Mo. 66); Hon. Ph.D. (Hongik Univ., Seoul) 74.
340-38, Sindang 4-dong, Sundong-ku, Seoul, Republic of Korea.

Kim, H.E. Cardinal Stephen Sou Hwan; Korean ecclesiastic; b. 8 May 1922, Taegu; ed. Sophia Univ., Tokyo, Major Seminary, Seoul, and Sociology Dept., Univ. of Munster, Germany.
Ordained priest 51; Pastor of Andong, Archdiocese of Taegu 51-53; Sec. to Archbishop of Taegu 53-55; Pastor of Kimchon (Taegu) 55-56; Editor-in-Chief *Catholic Shibo* (weekly) 64-66; sociology studies, Univ. of Munster, Germany 56-64; Dir. Sung-Eui Schools, Kimchon 55-56; Bishop of Masan 66-68; Archbishop of Seoul 68-; cr. Cardinal 69.
Archbishop's House, 2-Ga 1, Myong-Dong, Chung-gu, Seoul, Republic of Korea.

Kim Yong Shik; Korean diplomatist; b. 11 Nov. 1913; ed. Chu-ou Univ., Tokyo.
Consul, Hong Kong 49; Consul-Gen., Honolulu 49; Minister, Korean Mission, Japan 51; Minister, Korean Legation, France 57; Minister, Korean Mission, Geneva 59; Perm. Vice-Minister, Ministry of Foreign Affairs 60; Amb. to U.K. (also accred. to Sweden, Denmark, and Norway) 61; Amb. to the Philippines 62; Minister of Foreign Affairs March 63; Minister without Portfolio Dec. 63; Perm. Observer of Repub. of Korea at UN, concurrently accred. as Amb. to Canada 64-70; Special Asst. to Pres. for Foreign Affairs Dec. 70; Minister of Foreign Affairs 71-73, of the Board of Nat. Unification 73-74; Amb. to U.K. 74-.
Embassy of the Republic of Korea, 4 Palace Gate, London, W8 5NF, England.

Kimny, Nong; Cambodian diplomatist; b. Jan. 1912; ed. Sisowath Coll., Phnom-Penh and Lycée Chasseloup-Laubat, Saigon.
Entered Cambodian Admin. 32, Gov. of Kompong-Speu Province 40; Chief of King's Cabinet and Sec.-Gen. of Govt. 41-45; studied in France 46-50; Minister to U.S.A. 51-52, Amb. 52-54, 56-64; mem. Cambodian Del. to Geneva Conf. on Indochina 54; Vice-Pres. Council of Ministers and Minister of Foreign Affairs March-Aug. 56; Perm. Rep. to UN 56-64; Amb. to India 64-75, concurrently to Thailand Feb. 71-75.

Kimura, Motoo, PH.D., D.SC.; Japanese geneticist; b. 13 Nov. 1924, Okazaki; ed. Kyoto Univ., Univ. of Wisconsin.
Assistant Kyoto Univ. 47-49; Researcher Nat. Inst. of Genetics 49-57, Laboratory Head 57-64, Head of Dept. of Population Genetics 64-; Visiting Prof. of Univ. of Pavia 63, 65, Univ. of Wisconsin 66, Princeton Univ. 69, Stanford Univ. 73; Foreign mem. Nat. Acad. of Sciences, U.S.A. 73; Japanese Genetics Soc. Prize, Weldon Memorial Prize, Japan Acad. Prize, Japan Soc. of Human Genetics Prize.
Publs. *Outline of Population Genetics* (Japanese) 60, *Diffusion Models in Population Genetics* 64, *An Introduction to Population Genetics Theory* (with J. F. Crow) 70, *Theoretical Aspects of Population Genetics* (with T. Ohta) 71, *Future of Man from the Standpoint of Genetics* (editor, Japanese) 74.
National Institute of Genetics, Yata 1, 111, Mishima 411; Home: 7-24 Kiyozumi-cho, Mishuma 411, Japan.
Telephone: 0559-75-0771 (Office); 0559-75-8635 (Home).

Kimura, Toshio; Japanese politician; b. 1909; ed. Tokyo Univ.
Member, House of Reps.; fmr. Parl. Vice-Minister of Transport and Chief Cabinet Sec.; Minister of State in charge of Econ. Planning Agency 71-72; Minister of Foreign Affairs July-Dec. 74; Liberal-Democrat.
Keizai Kikakucho, 3-1-1 Kasumigaseki, Chiyoda-ku, Tokyo, Japan.

Kinoshita, James Otoichi; Japanese author; b. 3 June 1889; ed. Univs. of California and Southern California.
Former Corresp. Washington Disarmament Conf.; Editor *Tsingtao Leader* (English daily), Sec.-Gen. Tokyo Press Asscn. and Dir. Liberal News Agency; Exec. Dir. Japan Trade Promotion Asscn. 30, Pres. 48; Founder The Friends of the UN 48 (now The Friends of the World), Man. Dir. 52-, Vice-Pres. 62-69, Pres. 69-; Pres. Nippon Mutual Devt. Co. Ltd. 63.
Publs. *Is the World Growing Better?, World: A Spiritual System, Religion of Love* (trans.), *The Child Welfare Movement, Thrice Around the World, Rationalisation of American Industry, Cherry Blossom Around the World: Donation of Japanese Schoolchildren.*
2056 Izumi, Komae-Shi, Tokyo 182, Japan.
Telephone: 489-1300.

Kinoshita, Keisuke; Japanese film director; b. 1912; ed. Hamamatsu Industrial Coll.
Began his career in Shochiku Studio, Kamata; directed first film *Hanasaku Minato* 43; Henrietta Award for *Nijushi no Hitomi* 55, Golden Globe Award of Hollywood Foreign Press for *Taiyo to Bara* 57.
Films include *Hanasaku Minato* (Port of Flowers) 43, *Yabure Daiko* (Torn Drum), *Carmen kokyo ni Kaeru* (Carmen Comes Home) 49, *Nippon no Higeki* (The Tragedy of Japan) 53, *Nijushi no Hitomi* (Twenty-Four Eyes) 54, *Nogiku no Gotoki Kimi Nariki* (My First Love Affair) 55, *Yuyakegumo* (Farewell to Dreams), *Taiyo to Bara* (The Rose of his Arm) 56, *Yorokobi-mo Kanashimimo Ikutoshitsuki* (The Lighthouse), *Fuzen no Tomoshibi* (Danger Stalks Near) 57, *Narayama-bushi Ko* (Ballad of the Narayama), *Kono ten no Niji* (The External Rainbow) 58, *Kazahana* 59,

Sekishuncho, The River Fuefuki 61, *Eien no Hito* (Bitter Spirit) 62.
1366 Tsujido, Fujisawa, Kanagawa Prefecture, Japan.

Kirkup, James, B.A.; British writer; b. 23 April 1918; ed. Durham Univ.
Gregory Fellow in Poetry, Leeds Univ. 50-52; Visiting Poet, Bath Acad. of Art 53-56; travelling lectureship from Swedish Ministry of Educ. 56-57; Prof. of English Language and Literature, Salamanca (Spain) 57-58; Prof. of English Literature, Tohoku Univ. 59-61; Visiting Prof. of English Literature, Japan Women's Univ., Tokyo 64-; Visiting Prof. and Poet in Residence, Amherst Coll., Mass. 68-; Prof. of English Literature, Univ. of Nagoya, Japan 69-72; BBC TV Open Univ. 74-75; Fellowship in Creative Writing, Univ. of Sheffield 74-75; Literary Editor *Orient-West Magazine*, Tokyo 63-65; Visiting Prof. in Int. Literature, Ohio Univ. 75-76; Atlantic Award in Literature (Rockefeller Foundation) 59, F.R.S.L. 62, First Prize, Japan P.E.N. literary contest 65, Mildred Batchelder Award, A.L.A. 68, Arts Council Award 72; Crowned Ollave of the Order of Bards, Ovates and Druids 74; Hon. Fellow (Inst. of Psycho-physical Research, Oxford) 70; Fellow in Creative Writing (Sheffield Univ.) 74-75.
Publs. *The Cosmic Shape* 47, *The Drowned Sailor* 48, *The Creation* 50, *The Submerged Village* 51, *A Correct Compassion* 52, *A Spring Journey* 54, *Upon This Rock, The Dark Child, The Triumph of Harmony* 55, *The True Mystery of the Nativity, Ancestral Voices, The Radiance of the King* 56, *The Descent into the Cave, The Only Child* (autobiography) 57; TV plays: *The Peach Garden, Two Pigeons Flying High, Sorrows, Passions and Alarms* (autobiography) 60, *The True Mystery of the Passion, The Prodigal Son* (poems) 56-60, *These Horned Islands* (travel) 62, *The Love of Others* (novel) 62, *Tropic Temper* (travel) 63, *Refusal to Conform, Last and First Poems* 63, *The Heavenly Mandate* 64, *Japan Industrial*, Vols. I and II 64-65, *Tokyo* (travel) 66, *Bangkok* (travel) 67, *Michael Kohlhaas* 67, *Paper Windows: Poems from Japan* 68, *Filipinescas* (travel) 68, *One Man's Russia* (travel) 68, *Hong Kong* (travel) 69, *Japan Physical* (poems) 69, *White Shadows, Black Shadows: Poems of Peace and War* 70, *Japan Behind the Fan* (travel) 71, *The Body Servant: Poems of Exile* 71, *A Bewick Bestiary* (ill. poems) 71, *Insect Summer* (novel) 71, *Transmental Vibrations* 72, *The Magic Drum* (novel) 73, *Zen Gardens* (ill. poems) 73, *Poems of Takagi Kyozo* (trans. and editor), *Heaven, Hell and Hara-kiri* 74, *The Physicists, The Meteor, Play Strindberg* (trans.) 73, *Cyrano de Bergerac* (trans.) 74, *The Conformer* (trans) 75, *Modern Japanese Poetry* (trans.) 76, and numerous trans. from French, German and Japanese.
BM-Box 2780, London WC1V 6XX, England.

Kirloskar, Shantanu Laxman, B.SC.; Indian industrialist; b. 28 May 1903; ed. Massachusetts Inst. of Technology, U.S.A.
Kirloskar Brothers 26-; Chair. and Man. Dir. Kirloskar Oil Engines Ltd., Kirloskar Brothers Ltd., Poona; Chair. Kirloskar Pneumatic Co. Ltd., Swastik Rubber Products Ltd., Central Pulp Mills Ltd., Kirloskar Tractors Ltd., Pudumjee Pulp and Paper Mills Ltd., Poona Industrial Hotels Ltd., Kirloskar Cummins Ltd., Kirloskar Consultants Ltd., G. G. Dandekar Machine Works Ltd., Bharat Forge Co. Ltd.; Dir. numerous other cos.; fmr. Chair. Indian Inst. of Management, Ahmedabad; Past Pres. Mahratta Chamber of Commerce and Industries, Poona, Fed. of Indian Chambers of Commerce and Industry, New Delhi 65-66; First Pres. Indo-American Chamber of Commerce; nominated Dir. Reserve Bank of India, Industrial Devt. Bank of India; mem. Exec. Cttee., Int. Chamber of Commerce 76-; Padma Bhushan 65; Chair. Cttee. for Econ. Devt. in India; Sir Walter Puckey Prize 68; Life mem. Inst. of Engineers (India) 70; Karma Viroltama, Eng. Asscn. of India 72.
Publ. *Jet Yugateel Marathi Manus* (A man from Maharashtra in the Jet Age).
Office: Kirloskar Oil Engines Ltd., Corporate Office, 11 Koregaon Road, Poona-411001; Home: "Lakaki", Poona 16, India.
Telephone: 20080 (Office); 56471 (Home).

Kishi, Nobusuke; Japanese politician; b. 1896; elder brother of the late Eisaku Sato (Prime Minister of Japan, 1964-72); ed. Tokyo Imperial Univ.
Clerk of Ministry of Agriculture and Commerce 20; Chief of Industrial Admin. Section, Industrial Affairs Bureau 32, concurrently Sec., Ministry of Foreign Affairs 33; Chief of Archives Section, Ministry of Commerce and Industry 33; Sec. of Temporary Industrial Rationalization Bureau and Dir. of Industrial Affairs Bureau 35-36; served in various admin. capacities in Govt. of Manchukuo 36-39; Vice-Minister of Commerce and Industry 39-41 and Oct.-Nov. 43; Minister of Commerce and Industry Oct. 41-April 42; elected mem. of House of Reps. 42; Minister of State without Portfolio Oct. 43-July 44; dismissed from public service Dec. 47; apptd. Chair. Board of Dirs. of Toyo Pulp Mfg. Co. Ltd. 49; re-elected mem. of House of Reps. 53 and 55; Chair. of Railway Construction Council 55; Minister of Foreign Affairs Dec. 56; Prime Minister 57-60; Pres. Liberal-Democratic Party 57-60 (re-elected 59).
c/o Jiyu-Minshuto, 7, 2-chome, Hirakawacho, Chiyoda-ku, Tokyo, Japan.

Kittikachorn, Field-Marshal Thanom; Thai army officer and politician; b. 11 Aug. 1911, Tak; ed. Wat Kokplu School (Tak) and Military Acad., Bangkok.
Entered Mil. Survey Dept. as student officer 31, assigned to Planning Section 34; Lieut. in Mil. Educ. Dept. 35, Instructor 36-38, 39-41, 44-46; Capt. 38, student officer in Infantry School, active service in Shan State 41; Major 43, Lieut.-Col. 44; Instructor Mil. Acad. technical branch 46-47; Commdr. 21st Infantry Regt. 47; Col., Commdr. 11th Infantry Regt. 48; Deputy Commdr. 1st Infantry Div. 49, Commdr. 50; Major-Gen., Deputy Commdr. 1st Army 51; Commdr. 1st Army 54; Lieut.-Gen., mem. Defence Coll. 55; Deputy Minister of Co-operatives 55; Asst. C.-in-C. of Army 57 Deputy Minister of Defence April 57, Minister Sept. 57; Prime Minister, Minister of Defence, Gen. 58; Deputy Prime Minister and Minister of Defence 59-63; Prime Minister 63-71, Dec. 72-Oct. 73, Minister of Defence and Foreign Affairs 73; Chair. Nat. Exec. Council 71-72; Special A.D.C. to King; Chair. United Thai People's Party 68-73; in U.S.A. 73-74; detained upon return to Bangkok Dec. 74; now in Singapore.

Klatt, Werner, O.B.E., D.AGR. (BERLIN); British economist; b. 22 May 1904; ed. Univ. of Berlin.
Worked in U.K. Civil Service 40-66; Econ. Adviser at the Foreign Office 51-66; Rockefeller Award 66; St. Antony's Coll., Oxford.
Publs. *The Chinese Model* (editor and contributor) 65, numerous articles on Soviet Russia, China and Asia.
Adon Mount, Overhill Road, London, S.E.22, England.
Telephone: 01-693-1365.

Klychev, Anna Muchamed; Soviet politician; b. 1912; ed. Higher Party School.
Soviet Army 41-45; mem. C.P. of Soviet Union 47-; managerial work 47-51; party and political work 53-63; Chair. Presidium of Supreme Soviet of Turkmenian S.S.R. 63-; mem. Presidium of Central Cttee. of C.P. of Turkmenian S.S.R.; Deputy Chair. Presidium of Supreme Soviet of U.S.S.R.; mem. Central Auditing Comm., C.P.S.U.; Deputy to Supreme Soviet of Turkmenian S.S.R.
Presidium of Supreme Soviet of Turkmenian S.S.R., Ashkhabad, Turkmenian S.S.R., U.S.S.R.

Knight, Harold Murray, D.S.C., M.COM.; Australian banker; b. 13 Aug. 1919, Melbourne; ed. Scotch Coll. Melbourne, Univ. of Melbourne.
Commonwealth Bank of Australia 36-40; A.I.F. 40-43; Royal Australian Naval Volunteer Reserve (Lieut.) 43-45; Commonwealth Bank of Australia 46-55; Statistics Div., Research and Statistics Dept. of IMF 55-59, Asst. Chief 57-59; research economist, Reserve Bank of Australia 60, Asst. Man. Investment Dept. 62-64, Man. 64-68, Deputy Gov. and Deputy Chair. of Board 68-75, Gov. and Chair. of Board 75-.
Publ. *Introduccion al Analisis Monetario* (Spanish) 59.
Reserve Bank of Australia, 65 Martin Place, Sydney, N.S.W. 2000; Home: 20 Malton Road, Beecroft, N.S.W. 2119, Australia.

Kobayashi, Koji, D.ENG.; Japanese business executive; b. 1907; ed. Tokyo Imperial Univ.
Senior Vice-Pres. and Dir. Nippon Electric Co. Ltd. 56-61, Exec. Vice-Pres. 61-62, Senior Exec. Vice-Pres. 62-64, Pres. 64-; Chair. of Board Nippon Electric Tohaku Ltd. 73-; Chair. of Board Nippon Aviotronics Co. Ltd. 69-; Pres. Japan Electronic Industry Devt. Asscn. 73-; Pres. Japan Inst. of Industrial Eng. 74-; Vice-Pres. Japan Telecommunication Industrial Fed. 74-; Dir. Japan Management Asscn. 53-, Prime Minister's Prize for Export Promotion 64; Blue Ribbon Medal 64; Grand Cross (Peru) 70; Jordan Star, Third Class 72.
Publs. *Carrier Transmission System* 37, *Challenge to the Computer Age* 68, *The Problem of Management in the 1970s* 71, *Quality-oriented Management* 76.
Nippon Electric Co. Ltd., 33-1 Shiba Gochome, Minato-ku, Tokyo 108; and 15-10 Denenchofu 5-chome, Ohta-ku, Tokyo 145, Japan.

Kobayashi, Setsutaro; Japanese business executive; b. 7 Nov. 1899, Hyogo; ed. Kwansei Gakuin Univ.
With Iwai & Co. 23-33, Daicel Ltd. 33-34; joined Fuji Photo Film Co. Ltd. 34, Dir. 37-43, Man. Dir. 43, Senior Man. Dir. 43-58, Exec. Vice-Pres. 58-60, Pres. 60-71, Chair. of Board 71-; Pres. Fuji Xerox Co. Ltd. 62-76, Chair. 76-; Blue Ribbon Medal, Order of the Sacred Treasure.
Fuji Photo Film Co. Ltd., 26-30 Nishiazabu 2-chome, Minato-ku, Tokyo; Home: 34-9, Shimouma 6-chome, Setagaya-ku, Tokyo, Japan.
Telephone: 03-406-2111 (Office); 03-421-0322 (Home).

Kobayashi, Taiyu; Japanese business executive; b. 13 June 1912; ed. Kyoto Univ.
Pres. and Dir. Fujitsu Ltd.
2-6-1, Marunouchi, Chiyoda-ku, Tokyo, Japan.

Kodama, Tadayasu; Japanese shipping executive; b. 29 July 1898; ed. Kyoto Imperial Univ.
Nippon Yusen Kabushiki Kaisha (Japan Mail Steamship Co.) 22-, Dir. 47-, Man. Dir. 51-58, Vice-Pres. 58-61, Pres. 61-64, Chair. 64-71, now Adviser to the Board.
Nippon Yusen Kabushiki Kaisha, 3-2, 2-chome, Marunouchi, Chiyoda-ku, Tokyo, Japan.

Koga, Issac, PH.D.; Japanese radio engineer; b. 5 Dec. 1899; ed. Univ. of Tokyo.
Assistant Prof. Tokyo Inst. of Technology 29-39, Prof. 39-58; Prof. Univ. of Tokyo 44-60, Dean of Engineering 58-60; Vice-Pres. Int. Scientific Radio Union, Brussels 57-63, Pres. 63-66; Pres. Inst. of Electrical Communication Engineers of Japan 47-48; Pres. Inst. of Electrical Engineers of Japan 57-58; mem. Technical Advisory Cttee. Nat. Broadcasting Corpn. 51-66; mem. Advisory Council for Nat. Language, Ministry of Educ. 61-; mem. Advisory Cttee. for Radio and Telecommunications, Ministry of Posts and Telecommunications 63-72; mem. Advisory Council for Educ. of Educators, and Central Advisory Council for Educ. (both in Ministry of Educ.) 67-72; Pres. ITU Asscn. of Japan 61-; Fellow, Inst. of Electrical and Electronics Engineers, New York 57; Hon. mem. Inst. of Electrical Communication Engineers of Japan 64; Inst. of Electrical Engineers of Japan 65; Order of Cultural Merit 63; First Class Order of the Sacred Treasure 70; C. B. Sawyer Memorial Award 70.
Major works include: invention of crystal plates of zero frequency-temperature coefficient, investigation on piezoelectric oscillating crystal and quartz crystal circuit (Japan Acad. of Sciences Prize) 48, frequency demultiplier by means of a vacuum tube circuit.
17-5, 2-chome Aobadai, Megoruku, Tokyo 153, Japan.
Telephone: (Tokyo) 461-3395.

Koh, T. T. B., LL.B., LL.M.; Singapore law teacher and diplomatist; b. 12 Nov. 1937; ed. Univ. of Singapore and Harvard and Cambridge Univs.
Assistant Lecturer, Univ. of Singapore 62-64, Lecturer 64-; Sub-Dean, Faculty of Law, Univ. of Singapore 65-67, Vice-Dean 67-68; Visiting Lecturer, State Univ. of New York at Buffalo 67; fmr. Legal Adviser to trade unions in Singapore and fmr. Sec. Inst. of Int. Affairs, Singapore; Amb. and Perm. Rep. to UN 68-71, July 74-, concurrently High Commr. of Singapore in Canada 68-71; Assoc. Prof. of Law and Dean, Faculty of Law, Univ. of Singapore 71-74; Adrian Clarke Memorial Medal, Leow Chia Heng Prize, Public Service Star.
Faculty of Law, University of Singapore, Bukit Timah Road, Singapore 10, Singapore.
Telephone: 50451.

Kohra, Yoshimitsu; Japanese business executive; b. 4 March 1902; ed. Keio Univ.
Former Pres., Fujitsu Ltd., now Counsellor.
Fujitsu Ltd., Marunouchi, Chiyoda-ku, Tokyo, Japan.

Koirala, Bisweswar Prasad (half-brother of M. P. Koirala, *q.v.*); Nepalese politician; b. 1915; ed. Banaras and Calcutta Univs.
President Nepali Congress Party (*banned* 60); Minister for Home Affairs 51; Prime Minister May 59-60; imprisoned 60-68.
Now living in India.

Koirala, Matrika Prasad (half-brother of B. P. Koirala, *q.v.*); Nepalese politician and diplomatist; b. 1 Jan. 1912; ed. Benares and Patna, India.
Former Pres. Nepali Congress Party, Prime Minister and Minister of Gen. Admin. and Foreign Affairs 51-52, 53-55; nominated to Upper House of Parl.; Amb. to U.S. 62-64; Perm. Rep. to UN 62-64.
c/o Ministry of Foreign Affairs, Kathmandu, Nepal.

Koizumi, Tetsuzo; Japanese business executive; b. 11 March 1903; ed. Meiji Univ.
President, Honshu Paper Manufacturing Co. Ltd.
Honshu Paper Manufacturing Co. Ltd., 5-12-8 Ginza, Chuo-ku, Tokyo, Japan.

Kojima, Kiyoshi, PH.D.; Japanese economist; b. 22 May 1920; ed. Tokyo Univ. of Commerce and Economics, Leeds Univ. (U.K.) and Princeton Univ. (U.S.A.).
Assistant Prof. of Int. Econs., Hitotsubashi Univ. 45-60, Prof. 60-; Secretariat (Dir.) for UN Conf. on Trade and Devt. 63; British Council Scholarship 52-53, Rockefeller Foundation Fellowship 53-55.
Publs. (in Japanese): *Theory of Foreign Trade* 50, *Japan's Economic Development and Trade* 58, *Japan in the World Economy* 62, *The Economics of EEC* 62, *Trade Expansion for Developing Countries* 64, *World Trade and Multinational Corporations* 73; Editor (in English): *Japan and a Pacific Free Trade Area* 71, *Papers and Proceedings of a Conference on Pacific Trade and Development* 68, 69, 73; also articles in English on int. trade.
3-24-10 Maehara-cho Koganei-shi, Tokyo, Japan.

Komai, Kenichiro; Japanese business executive; b. 17 Dec. 1900; ed. Coll. of Technology, Tokyo Imperial Univ.

Hitachi Ltd. 25-, Man. of Hitachi Works 46-50, Dir. 46-55, Man. Dir. 55-57, Senior Man. Dir. 57-61, Pres. 61-71, Chair. of Board 71-; fmr. Chair. Tokyo Atomic Industrial Consortium; Exec. Dir. Japan Fed. of Econ. Orgs. 62-; Gov. Dir. Japan Fed. of Employers' Asscns. 62-; Pres. Electronic Machinery Industry Asscns. 65-68; Chair. Japan Consulting Inst. 65-.
2-3-2 Taiheidai, Tsujido, Fujisawa, Kanagawa-Ken, Tokyo, Japan.

Komoto, Toshio; Japanese politician; b. 1911, Aioi City Hyogo Prefecture; ed. Nihon Univ.
Former Parl. Vice-Minister for Econ. Planning Agency; fmr. Chair. of Justice Cttee., House of Reps.; fmr. Chair. Cabinet Cttee., House of Reps.; Minister of Posts and Telecommunications 68-70, of Int. Trade and Industry Dec. 74-; Pres. Sanko Steamship Co.; Liberal-Democrat.
Ministry of International Trade and Industry, 3-1, Kasumigaseki 1-chome, Chiyoda-ku, Tokyo, Japan.

Kono, Fumihiko, B.ENG.; Japanese business executive; b. 22 Nov. 1896; ed. Tokyo Univ.
Aircraft Designer, Mitsubishi Internal Combustion Engine Mfg. Co. Ltd. 21-45; Gen. Man. First Engineering Works, Mitsubishi Heavy Industries Ltd. 45, Kawasaki Engineering Works 45-50; Dir. and Gen. Man. Kawasaki Engineering Works, Mitsubishi Nippon Heavy Industries Ltd. 50-52, Man. Dir. 52-56, Vice-Pres. 56-61, Pres. 61-64; Exec. Vice-Pres. Mitsubishi Heavy Industries Ltd. 64-65, Pres. 65-70, Chair. 70-73; Dir. Mitsubishi Shoji Kaisha Ltd., Mitsubishi Steel Co. Ltd., Mitsubishi Atomic Power Industries Inc.; Vice-Pres. Fed. of Econ. Orgs.; Governing Dir. Japan Fed. of Employers' Asscns., The Shipbuilders' Asscn. of Japan; Vice-Pres. The Machinery Fed.; Blue Ribbon Medal.
Mitsubishi Heavy Industries Ltd., 5-1, Marunouchi 2-chome, Chiyoda-ku, Tokyo, Japan.

Koo, Vi Kyuin Wellington, B.A., M.A., PH.D.; Chinese diplomatist and judge; b. 29 Jan. 1888; ed. Columbia Univ.
Secretary to Pres. of China; Councillor in Foreign Office; Minister to U.S.A. 15; China's plenipotentiary, later head of del. to Versailles Peace Conf. 19; del. to the Assembly and China's rep. on Council of League of Nations (LN) 20-22; Minister to U.K. 21; plenipotentiary to Washington Conf. 31-22; Minister of Foreign Affairs, Peking 22-24; Finance Minister 26; Prime Minister and Minister of Foreign Affairs 26-27; mem. of the Int. Court of Arbitration at The Hague 27 and 33; Minister of Foreign Affairs 31; Chinese Assessor to LN Comm. of Inquiry 32; Minister to France 32-35; Amb. to France 36-41; Chinese Rep. on LN Council 32-34; chief del. to LN Assemblies 32-33, 35-36, 38; del. to World Monetary and Econ. Conf., London 33; del. to Conf. for Reduction and Limitation of Armaments, Geneva 33; Pres. of the 96th Session of League Council 37; del. to Sessions of League Council 37-39; chief del. to Brussels Conf. Nov. 37; Special Amb. to Belgium 38, the Vatican 39, Portugal 40; Amb. to U.K. 41-46, to U.S.A. 46-49, Chinese (Taiwan) Amb. to U.S.A. 49-56; del. to the Dumbarton Oaks Conf. 44; Acting Chair. Chinese del. to the San Francisco Conf.; Chair. Chinese del. to the Preparatory Comm., and the First Session of the UN Gen. Assembly 45-46; Acting Chair. Chinese del. to UN Assembly 47; Judge, Int. Court of Justice 57-66, Vice-Pres. 64-66; currently Senior Adviser to the Pres. of the Repub. of China (Taiwan); decorations from, China, Belgium, Brazil, Chile, France, Greece, Mexico, Portugal, Vatican; Hon. LL.D. from Colombia and Yale Univs., and Univs. of St. John's, Aberdeen, Birmingham, Manchester; L.H.D. (Rollins).
1185 Park Avenue, Apartment 10B, New York, N.Y. 10028, U.S.A.

Kosaka, Tokusaburo; Japanese politician; b. 20 Jan. 1916, Nagano Pref.; ed. Tokyo Univ.
Joined Asahi Newspaper Co.; Man. Shinetsu Chemical Industry Co. 49, Vice-Pres. 51, later Pres.; Dir. Japan Chemical Industry Asscn., Coal Industry Asscn., Shinano Mainichi Newspaper Co., Shinano Broadcasting Co.; mem. of House of Reps. 69-; Dir.-Gen. Prime Minister's Office 73-74.
21-28, Fukazawa-cho, 7-chome, Setagaya-ku, Tokyo 158, Japan.

Kotelawela, Col. the Rt. Hon. Sir John Lionel, K.B.E., C.H., P.C., J.P.; Ceylonese politician; b. 4 April 1897; ed. Christ's Coll., Cambridge, and Royal Coll., Colombo.
Member State Council 31; helped in foundation of United National Party, Pres. until 58; Minister for Agriculture and Lands 33; Minister for Communications and Works 35; Minister for Transport and Works 47-53; Leader of the House, Parl. of Ceylon 50-56; Prime Minister and Minister of Defence 53-56; Privy Councillor 54; Grand Cross Legion of Honour and numerous other decorations; Hon. LL.D. (Univ. of Ceylon).
Publ. *An Asian Prime Minister's Story* 56.
Kandawala, Kotelawalapura, Ratmalana, Sri Lanka; Brogues Wood, Biddenden, Kent, England.

Koyama, Goro; Japanese banker; b. 25 March 1909; ed. Tokyo Imperial Univ.
Managing Dir. The Mitsui Bank Ltd. 63-65, Deputy Pres. 65-68, Pres. 68-74, Chair. 74-.
The Mitsui Bank Ltd., 12 Yurakucho 1-chome, Chiyodaku, Tokyo; Home: 3-15-10, Takaido-Higashi, Suginami-ku, Tokyo, Japan.
Telephone: 501-1111 (Office); 333-0843 (Home).

Kripalani, Acharaya Jiwatram Bhagwandas, M.A.; Indian politician; b. 1888.
Professor in Bihar under Calcutta Univ. 12-17; worked with Gandhi 17-18, with Pandit Madan Mohan Malaviya 18; Prof. of Politics, Benares Hindu Univ. 19-20; active in Khadi and village work and Dir. Gandhi Ashram, U.P. 20-; Principal of Gujarat Vidyapith 22-27; imprisoned 30, 32, 34, 42-45; Pres. Indian Nat. Congress 46-47; mem. Constituent Assembly 46-51; formed Congress Democratic Front 51; founded *Vigil*, political weekly 50; formed Kisan Mazdoor Praja Party 51; Chair. Praja Socialist Party 53-57; mem. Lok Sabha (Parl.) 52-70.
Publs. *The Gandhian Way, The Non-Violent Revolution, The Indian National Congress, The Politics of Charkha, The Future of the Congress, The Fateful Year, Gandhi the Statesman, Basic Education, Gandhi—Life and Thought.*
A4 Sarvodaya Enclave, New Delhi 17; and Shri Gandhi Ashram, Lucknow, Uttar Pradesh, India.

Krishna Moorthi, C. S.; Indian civil servant and administrator; b. 1921; ed. Madras Univ.
Ordnance Officer, Indian Army 43-46; Asst. Commr. Refugees, Punjab 47; Sub-Collector and Joint Magistrate, Madras State 47-52; Board of Revenue, Madras 52-53; Ministry of Finance 54-58; Counsellor, Indian Comm.-Gen. for Econ. Affairs, Washington 58; Alt. Exec. Dir. Int. Bank for Reconstruction and Devt. and Int. Finance Corpn. 58; Minister (Econ.) Indian Embassy, Washington 61-63, Exec. Dir. for India, Int. Bank for Reconstruction and Devt., Int. Finance Corpn. and Int. Devt. Asscn. 62-63; Joint Sec. Dept. of Econ. Affairs, Ministry of Finance, New Delhi 63-66; Vice-Pres. Asian Devt. Bank, Manila, Philippines 66-.
Asian Development Bank, P.O.B. 789, Manila, Philippines.
Telephone: 80-72-51/143 (Office); 87-64-40 (Home).

Krishnan, Rappal Sangameswara, D.SC., PH.D.; Indian physicist; b. 1911; ed. Univ. of Madras, St. Joseph's Coll., Trichy, Indian Inst. of Science, and Trinity Coll., Cambridge.

Research Asst. Indian Inst. of Science 35-38; 1851 Exhbn. Overseas Scholar, Univ. of Cambridge 38-41; Lecturer in Physics, Inst. of Science 42-45, Asst. Prof. 45-48, Prof. and Head, Dept. of Physics 48-72, Emer. 72-73; Vice-Chancellor, Kerala Univ. July 73-; Visiting Prof. North Texas State Univ. 71-72; Fellow of Inst. of Physics, London, of American Physical Soc., of Indian Acad. of Sciences, and of Nat. Inst. of Sciences; Pres. Physics Section, Indian Science Congress 49; specialist in colloid optics, Raman effect in crystals, crystal physics and nuclear physics.
Publs. *Progress in Crystal Physics*, Vol. I, 58, *Two Chapters in Raman Effect*, Vol. I, 71.
Office of the Vice-Chancellor, Kerala University, Trivandrum 695001, South India.
Telephone: Trivandrum 60058; 60858 (Residence).

Krishnaswamy, K. S., PH.D.; Indian economist and banker; b. 1920; ed. Univ. of Mysore and London School of Economics.
Lecturer in Econs., Univ. of Bombay 46-47; Research Officer, Planning Comm., New Delhi; Research Officer, Research Dept., Reserve Bank of India, Bombay 52-54, Deputy Dir. of Research, Research Dept. 54-56; Staff mem. Econ. Devt. Inst. (World Bank), Washington 56-59; Deputy Chief, Industrial Finance Dept., Reserve Bank of India 59-61; Chief, Econ. Policy Section, Planning Comm. 61-64; Economic Adviser, Planning Commission 64-67; Dir. Econ. Devt. Inst., Int. Bank for Reconstruction and Devt. 67-71, Principal Adviser, Reserve Bank of India 72, Exec. Dir. 73-75, Deputy Gov. 75-; Chair. Oil Prices Cttee.; Pres. Indian Econ. Asscn. 76.
Reserve Bank of India, Central Office, Bombay 400001, India.

Ku Mu; politician, People's Repub. of China.
Mayor of Tsinan 50-52; Deputy Sec. CCP Shanghai 53-54; Vice-Chair. State Construction Comm. 54-56, State Econ. Comm. 56-65; Chair. State Capital Construction Comm. 65-67; criticized and removed from office during Cultural Revolution 67; Minister of State Capital Construction Comm. 73-; Vice Premier, State Council 75-.

Kubota, Yutaka, DR. ENG.; Japanese engineer and company director; b. 1890; ed. Tokyo Univ.
Chairman and Dir. Nippon Koei Co. Ltd.; Chair. Engineering Consulting Firms Asscn. of Japan Inc.; Chair. Japan Industrial Rehabilitation Engineering Asscn.; Dir. Yaku Island Electric Industrial Co. Ltd.; mem. Cttee. for Econ. Co-operation, Japanese Govt.; planned, design and supervised Balu Chaung Hydro-electric Projects for Burmese Govt. 54-, Da Nhim Hydro-electric Project for Vietnamese Govt. 56-, Kali Brantas Multipurpose Project for Indonesian Govt. 61-, Nam Ngum Multipurpose Project for UN 58-, Upper Se San Multipurpose Project in Viet-Nam for UN 62-, Karnali Hydro-electric Project in Nepal for UN 58-, Phang Rang Irrigation Project, Viet-Nam 63-, Sun Kosi Terai Plain Project, Nepal for UNDP/FAO 67-, Sempor Irrigation Project for ADB and Indonesian Govt. 69, 72-, Tiep Nhut Irrigation Project (Mekong) for IBRD 72-, Andong Dam Project for Korean Govt. 72-; Consultant to ECAFE (Econ. Comm. for Asia and the Far East) for devt. of Mekong River 51; Hon. mem. Japan Soc. of Civil Engineers; mem. Japan Consulting Engineers Asscn.; several decorations including First Order of Sacred Treasure 74, and orders from Cambodia, Laos and Repub. of Viet-Nam.
Publs. *The Fusenko Hydroelectric Power Plant* (Tokyo World Power Conf.) 29, *Water Power Generation and Dam Building* (in *An Outline of Civil Engineering*) 40-45.
Nippon Koei Co. Ltd., 1-11 Uchisaiwaicho 2-chome, Chiyoda-ku, Tokyo, Japan.

Kularatnam, Karthigesapillai, M.A., PH.D., DR.SC.; Ceylonese educationist, geographer and geologist; b. 28 May 1911.
Professor Emer. and Dean, Univ. of Sri Lanka; taught in Univs. of Edinburgh, Sheffield, Birmingham, London, Madras, New York, Kansas City and Sir George Williams (Montreal); Pres. Inst. of Environmental Sciences; Pres. Ceylon Geographical Soc., Gemmologists' Asscn. of Ceylon, Soil Conservation Soc.; Dir. Commonwealth Geographical Bureau; Senior Consultant, Population Div., UN/ESCAP.
Publs. several essays on Sri Lanka.
61 Abdul Caffoor Mawatha, Colombo 3, Sri Lanka.

Kulatov, Turabay; Soviet politician; b. 1908; ed. Kyzyl-Kiysk Soviet-Party School and Higher Party School.
Trade union official 34; mem. Bureau of the Central Cttee. of the C.P. of Kirghizia 38; Chair. of the Council of People's Commissars of Kirghizia 38-45; Chair. of the Presidium of the Supreme Soviet of Kirghizia 45-; Vice-Chair. of the Presidium of the Supreme Soviet of the U.S.S.R. 46-; mem. Central Auditing Comm., C.P.S.U.; Deputy to U.S.S.R. and Kirghizian S.S.R. Supreme Soviets; mem. Central Cttee. C.P. Kirghizian S.S.R., and mem. Politburo; awarded Order of Lenin (four times).
Supreme Soviet of Kirghizia, Frunze, Kirghizia, U.S.S.R.

Kumarasuriar, Chelliah, B.S.(ENG.), D.I.C., M.I.C.E., M.I.E.C. (Sri Lanka); Ceylonese engineer and politician; b. 8 Aug. 1926, Taiping, Malaya; ed. Univ. of Colombo and Imperial Coll., London.
Lecturer, Univ. of Ceylon 50; Research and Devt. Engineer, Health Dept., Ceylon until 60; Factory Dir. Glaxo-Allenbury's (Ceylon) Ltd. 70-71; Visiting Lecturer, Univ. of Ceylon; mem. Senate; Minister of Posts and Telecommunications 70-; Founder, Partner Ganeshan & Kumarasuriar 70-; mem. Parl. 72-; numerous honours and awards; Sri Lanka Freedom Party.
Publs. articles in specialist journals.
Ministry of Posts and Telecommunications, New O.T.S. Bldg., 4th Floor, Colombo; Home: 4/1 Ramakrishna Road, Colombo 6, Sri Lanka.
Telephone: 29567, 29112 (Office); 83310 (Home).

Kunaev, Askar Minliakhmedovich; Soviet metallurgist and politician; b. 1929; ed. Moscow Inst. of Steel and Alloys 51.
Steel founder, Kazakh Metallurgical Works, Temir-Tau, foreman, shift foreman, 51-53; laboratory asst., Inst. of Metallurgy and Ore-Dressing, Kazakh S.S.R. Acad. of Sciences 53, then junior research worker, senior research worker, head of Inst.; then Dir. Lab. of Physical Chem. of Alloying Metals; Vice-Pres. Kazakh S.S.R. Acad. of Sciences 72-74, Pres. 74-; Deputy to U.S.S.R. Supreme Soviet 74-; mem. Cttee. for Foreign Affairs, Soviet of Nationalities; mem. C.P.S.U. 71-; mem. C.P. of Khazakstan, Alma-Ata Regional Cttee.; mem. U.S.S.R. Acad. of Sciences; Kazakh S.S.R. State Prize 72; Order of the Red Banner of Labour.
Presidium of the Kazakh S.S.R. Academy of Sciences, 28 Ul. Shevchenko, Alma-Ata, U.S.S.R.

Kunayev, Dinmohammed Akhmedovich; Soviet (Kazakh) politician and mining engineer; b. 1912; ed. Moscow Inst. of Non-Ferrous Metals.
Former Dir. Kounrad Mine, Kazakh S.S.R.; Vice-Chair. Council of Ministers Kazakh S.S.R. 45-52, Chair. 52-60, 62-; First Sec. Kazakh C.P. 60-62, 64-; Alt. mem. Politburo, Central Cttee. of C.P.S.U. April 66- April 71, mem. April 71-; Deputy to Supreme Soviet of the U.S.S.R. and Supreme Soviet of the Kazakh S.S.R.; mem. Presidium of Supreme Soviet of the U.S.S.R. 62-; mem. C.P.S.U. Central Cttee. 56-; mem. and fmr. Pres. Acad. of Sciences of the Kazakh S.S.R.; Hero of Socialist Labour, Order of Lenin, Hammer and Sickle Gold Medal etc.
Central Committee of Communist Party of the Kazakh S.S.R., Alma-Ata, Kazakh S.S.R., U.S.S.R.

Kunihiko, Sasaki; Japanese banker; b. 20 Dec. 1908; ed. Tokyo Univ.
Manager, Business Devt. Dept., Yasuda Bank 47-48; Man. Business Devt. Dept., Fuji Bank 48-49, Man. Credit Dept. 49-50, Deputy Man. Osaka Branch 50-51, Chief Man. Foreign Div. 51-54, Dir. 54-57, Man. Dir. 57-63, Deputy Pres. 63-71, Chair. of the Board and Pres. 71-75, Hon. Chair. 75-.
The Fuji Bank Ltd., 5-5, 1-chome, Ohtemachi, Chiyoda-ku, Tokyo, Japan.

Kunzru, Pandit Hriday Nath, B.A., B.SC., D.LITT.; Indian politician; b. 1887; ed. Allahabad Univ. and London School of Economics and Political Science.
Joined Servants of Indian Soc. (national missionaries pledged to devote their lives to the service of India) 09, Life Pres. 36-; mem. Indian Legislative Assembly 27-30, Council of State 37-46, Constituent Assembly 46-50, Provisional Parl. 50-52, Upper House, Indian Parl. 52-62; Leader Indian Del. Inter-Parliamentary Union 56-61; Pres. East African Nat. Congress 29; Pres. Nat. Liberal Fed. 34; mem. Defence Consultative Cttee. 42-46; Leader, Govt. of India's Del. to South Africa 50; visited numerous countries to study condition of Indians settled in these places; mem. of Govt. of India's Del. to Malaya 46; Gen. Sec. All India Seva Samiti, Allahabad; Chair. Nat. Cadet Corps Cttee. 46-47, mem. Armed Forces Reorganization Cttee. 46-47, of State Reorganization Comm. 53-55, Univ. Grants Comm. 53-66; Pres. Indian Council of World Affairs 48-; Nat. Commr. Bharat Scouts and Guides 50-57, 61-63; Chair. Indian School of Int. Studies 55-70, of Railway Accidents Inquiry Cttee. 61-63; Pres. Indian Asscn. for Advancement of Urdu 62-72; Chair. Railways Study Team of Admin. Reform Comm. 67-69; mem. Exec. Council Agra Univ. 72-; Pres. Cen. Cttee., Convention on Nat. Consensus 71-74; Trustee, India Int. Centre; Vice-Pres. Indian Council for Cultural Relations; mem. Board of Govs., Inst. of Econ. Growth; Pres. Nat. Asscn. for the Blind (Delhi Branch); Vice-Pres. Bharatiya Adimjati Sevak Sangh; mem. Gov. Council Indian Law Inst.
Indian Council of World Affairs, Sapru House, Barakhamba Road, New Delhi 110001, India.
Telephone: 384943.

Kuo Mo-jo; historian and poet, People's Repub. of China; b. 1891, Loshan, Szechuan; ed. Tokyo No. 1 Higher School, Okayama No. 6 Higher School, Japan, Kyushu Imperial Univ. Medical School, Japan.
Founded Creation Soc. (publishing house) 20; involved in Nanchang Uprising 27; lived in Japan studying history and writing 28-37; founded *Salvation Daily* 37; Vice-Chair. Standing Cttee., Nat. People's Congress 54-; Vice-Chair. State Scientific Comm. 56-58; joined CCP 58; mem. 9th Cen. Cttee. of CCP 69, 10th Cen. Cttee. 73.
Publs. include *Fallen Leaves* 24, *Research on Ancient Chinese Society, The Bronze Age, Ten Critiques* 45, *Starry Canopy*, and translations of numerous books into Chinese including Goethe, Nietzsche, Marx, Turgenev, Galsworthy.

Kuraishi, Tadao; Japanese politician; b. 1900; ed. Hosei Univ.
Member, House of Reps.; Chair. House of Reps. Labour Affairs Cttee., Budget Cttee.; Minister of Labour 55-56, 58-59; Minister of Agriculture and Forestry 67-68, 70-71, 73-Dec. 74; Chair. Liberal-Democratic Party Nat. Org. Cttee.
House of Representatives, Tokyo, Japan.

Kurata, Motoharu, B.ENG.; Japanese business executive; b. 22 July 1901, Fukushima; ed. Tokyo Inst. of Technology.
Joined Asahi Glass Co. Ltd. 25, Man. Dir. 50-63, Exec. Vice-Pres. 63-67, Pres. 67-73, Chair. 73-; Pres. Iwaki Glass Co. Ltd.; Chair. of Board, Asahi Fiber Glass Co. Ltd.; Dir. Nippon Kogaku K.K.; Exec. Dir. Fed. of Econ. Orgs.; Medal of Hon. with Purple Ribbon and with Blue Ribbon.
4-23-12, Nishigotanda, Meguro-ku, Tokyo, Japan.
Telephone: 03-218-5555 (Office); 03-491-6230 (Home).

Kurokawa, (Noriaki) Kisho, M.TECH.; Japanese architect; b. 8 April 1934; ed. Kyoto and Tokyo Univs.
President, Kisho N. Kurokawa Architect & Assocs., Urban Design Consultants Co. Ltd.; Dir. Inst. of Social Engineering; Adviser, Japan Nat. Railways, Ministry of Public Welfare, Ministry of Educ., Japan Broadcasting Asscn.; mem. Architectural Inst. of Japan, Japan Soc. of Futurology, City Planning Inst. of Japan, etc.; awarded Takamura Kotaro Design Prize and prizes in int. competitions in Peru, France and Tanzania, prize for conference city, Abu Dhabi, United Arab Emirates 76.
Works include: Nitto Food Co. 63, Cen. Lodge in Nat. Children's Land 64, Hans Christian Andersen Memorial Lodge 64, Handicapped People's Town 66, Sagae City Hall 67, Odakyu Rest House 69, Sakura City Hall 69, Takara, Toshiba and Theme Pavilions, *Expo* 70, Sapporo Prince Hotel 71, Nakagin Business Capsule 71, Karuizawa Prince Hotel 73, Shirahama Prince Hotel 73, Bank of Fukuoka 74, Sony Building 74, Nat. Museum of Folklore 74, Hotel New Ohtani, Bulgaria 75.
Publs. include: *Concrete Prefabricated House, Metabolism* 60, *Urban Design* 64, *Action Architecture* 67, *Homo-Movens* 69, *Works of Kisho N. Kurokawa* 69, *Kisho N. Kurokawa* 69, *Creation of Contemporary Architecture* 71, *Complete Work Series of Existing Architects of Japan, Conception of Metabolism, Future of Life, Development of Post-Industrial Society, Entry into Urbanism.*
1-2-3 Kita Aoyama, Minato-Ku, Tokyo, Japan.

Kurosawa, Akira; Japanese film director; b. 1910; ed. Keika Middle School.
Joined Toho Film Co. as asst. dir. 36; dir. his first film *Sugata Sanshiro* 43; First Prize, Venice Film Festival for *Rashomon*, Silver Lion for *The Seven Samurai*, American Motion Picture Acad. Award for *Rashomon.*
Films: *Sugata Sanshiro, Ichiban Utsukushiku, Torano Owofumu Otokotachi, Waga Seishun ni Kuinashi, Subarashiki Nichiyobi, Yoidore Tenshi, Shizukanaru Ketto, Norainu, Rashomon, Hakuchi, Ikiru, The Seven Samurai, Ikimono no Kiroku, Kumonosu Jio, Donzoko, Kakushi Toride no San Akunin, The Hidden Fortress, Throne of Blood, Yojimbo, The Bad Sleep Well, Sanjuro, High and Low, Akahige, Redbeard, Dodes'ka-den.*

Kuwabara, Takeo, B.A.; Japanese writer; b. 10 May 1904; ed. Kyoto Univ.
Lecturer, Kyoto Univ. 31-42; Asst. Prof., Tohoku Univ. 43-48; Prof. Kyoto Univ. 48-68, Emer. Prof. 68-; Dir. Univ. Inst. of Humanistic Studies 59-63; mem. Science Council of Japan 50-70, Vice-Pres 60-70; Vice-Pres. Japan PEN Club 74-75.
Publs. *Fiction and Reality* 43, *Reflections on Contemporary Japanese Culture* 47, *Some Aspects of Contemporary French Literature* 49, *Introduction to Literature* 50, *Conquest of Mount Chogolisa* 59, *Studies on J.-J. Rousseau* 51, *Studies on the Encyclopédie* 54, *Studies on the French Revolution* 59, *Studies on Chomin Nakae* 66, *Selected Works* (in 7 vols. and 1 supplement) 68-72, *European Civilization and Japan* 74.
421, Tonodan-Yabunosita, Kamikyo-ku, Kyoto, 602 Japan.
Telephone: 231-0261.

Ky, Air Vice-Marshal Nguyen Cao (*see* Nguyen Cao Ky, Air Vice-Marshal).

Kyle, Air Chief Marshal Sir Wallace (Hart), G.C.B., C.B.E., D.S.O., D.F.C.; Australian air force officer and administrator; b. 22 Jan. 1910, Kalgoorlie, W.A.; ed. Guildford Grammar School, W.A., R.A.F. Coll., Cranwell, and R.A.F. Staff Coll., England.
17th Squadron 30-31, Fleet Air Arm 31-34; flying instructor 34-39; R.A.F. Bomber Command 40-45; R.A.F. Staff

Coll. 45-47; Middle East 48-50; ADC to King George VI 49; Asst. Commdt. R.A.F. Coll. Cranwell 50-52; Dir. of Operational Requirements, Air Ministry 52-54; Air. Officer Commanding, Malaya 55-57; Asst. Chief of Air Staff, Operational Requirements 57-59; Air Officer Commanding-in-Chief, Tech. Training Command 59-62; Vice-Chief of Air Staff 62-65; ADC to the Queen 66-68; Air Officer Commanding-in-Chief, Bomber Command 65-68, Strike Command 68; retd. 68; Gov. of Western Australia Oct. 75-.
Government House, Perth, Western Australia; and R.A.F. Club, 128 Picadilly, London, W.1, England.

Kyo, Machiko; Japanese actress; b. 1924.
Began her career as a dancer with the Shochiku Girls' Opera Co., Osaka; film début in *Saigo ni Warau Otoko* (Last Laughter) 49; later films: *Rashomon* 50, *Ugetsu Monogatari* 53, *Gate of Hell* 54, *Story of Shunkin* 55, *Akasen Chitai* (Street of Shame), *Teahouse of the August Moon* 56, *Yoru no Cho* (Night Butterflies) 57, *Odd Obsession* 59, *Floating Weeds* 59, *A Woman's Testament* 60; Best Actress Award for *Rashomon* 50; Jussie (Finland) Award 57.
Uni Japan Film, 9-13 Ginza 5-chome, Chuo-ku, Tokyo, Japan.

L

Laking, George Robert, C.M.G., LL.B.; New Zealand diplomatist and public servant; b. 15 Oct. 1912; ed. Auckland Grammar School, and Auckland and Victoria Univs.
Prime Minister's and External Affairs Depts. 40-49; Counsellor, New Zealand Embassy, Washington 49-54, Minister 54-56; Deputy Sec. of External Affairs, Wellington 56-58; Acting High Commr. for New Zealand in London 58-61; Amb. to European Economic Community (EEC) 60-61, to U.S.A. 61-67; Perm. Head, Prime Minister's Dept. and Sec. of Foreign Affairs 67-72; Parl. Commr. (Ombudsman) 75-.
3 Wesley Road, Wellington, New Zealand.

Lal, Bansi, LL.B.; Indian politician; b. 10 Oct. 1927, Golagarh, Bhiwani District; ed. privately and Law Coll., Jullundur.
Took part in Praja Mandal Movement, Loharu State; Sec. Loharu Praja Mandal 43-44; Pres. Mandal Congress Cttee., Kural 59-60; Gen. Sec. Tosham Mandal Congress Cttee. 55; mem. Punjab PCC 59-62, Rajya Sabha 60-66, Haryana Assembly 67-; Chief Minister Haryana 68-75; Minister without portfolio, Govt. of India, Nov.-Dec. 75, Minister of Defence Dec. 75-; Hon. LL.D. (Kurukshetra Univ.) 72, D.Sc. (Haryana Agric. Univ.) 72.
Ministry of Defence, New Delhi, India.

Lal, Bipen Behari, M.SC.; Indian state governor; b. 30 Jan. 1917, Allahabad, Uttar Pradesh; ed. St. Stephens Coll. Delhi, Allahabad Univ., Harvard Univ.
Indian Civil Service 41-; magistrate successively in Gorakhpur, Varanasi and district of Hardoi and Dehra Dun 42-51; successively Joint Sec. for Finance, Sec. for Finance, Commr. and Sec. for Irrigation and Power, Govt. of Uttar Pradesh (U.P.), Chair. U.P. State Electricity Board, mem. U.P. Univs. Comm. and U.P. Pay Rationalization Comm., Fellow, Harvard Univ. 51-66; Chief Sec. Govt. of U.P. 67-69; Additional Sec. Ministry of Finance, Govt. of India 69-70, Sec. Dept. of Personnel 70-71, Sec. Ministry of Industrial Devt. 71-73, Sec. Ministry of Commerce 73; Adviser to Gov. of Uttar Pradesh 73; Sec. of Planning Comm., Govt. of India 73-74; Chief Exec. of Sikkim 74-75, Gov. of Sikkim June 75-.
Raj Bhavan, Gangtok-737 101, Sikkim, India.

Lalbhai, Kasturbhai; Indian industrialist; b. 19 Dec. 1894; ed. Gujarat Coll., Ahmedabad.
Vice-President Ahmedabad Millowners' Asscn. 23-26, Pres. 33-35; mem. Central Legislative Assembly 23-26; Del. Int. Labour Conf. Geneva 29 and 34; Pres. Fed. of Indian Chamber of Commerce 34-35; Consultative mem. British Indian Trade Del. to U.K. 37; fmr. Dir. Reserve Bank of India; Adviser to Govt. of India in Indo-Burman Trade Negotiations 40; mem. Scientific and Industrial Research Board 40; mem. Textile Control Board 43; mem. Indian Del. to Cairo Cotton Conf. 43; Rep. of Govt. of India on Textile Cttee. of Combined Production and Resources Board, Washington 46; Head Indian Del. to Int. Cotton Textile Industry Conf. Manchester 52; Head Indian Del. to U.S.S.R. 54; Leader and Pres. of Jain Community in India; now Dir. in twenty concerns: textiles, insurance, electricity, steamship and motor companies, etc.; mem. Central Advisory Council, Govt. of India 53-; Chair. Nat. Research and Development Corpn. 54-; Chair. Western Regional Cttee., All India Council for Technical Educ. 55-; Chair. Inst. of Technology, Bombay 55-65; mem. Senate Gujarat Univ.; Chair. Indian Cotton Mills Fed. 56; Padma Bhushan 68.
Pankore's Naka, Ahmedabad; Home: Lalbag, Shahibag, Ahmedabad, India.

Lall, Arthur; Indian teacher and diplomatist; b. 14 July 1911; ed. Punjab and Oxford Univs.
Appointed to Indian Civil Service and served in the Punjab and with Central Govt.; Commercial Counsellor, High Comm., London 47-51; Consul-Gen., with rank of Minister, New York 51-54; Perm. Rep. to UN 54-59; Chair. UN Mission to Samoa 59; Amb. to Austria and Gov. Int. Atomic Agency 59-63; Prof., Cornell Univ. 63-; Prof. of International Relations, Columbia Univ., New York 65-; Consultant, UN Inst. for Training and Research, New York; Del. to UN Econ. and Social Council and Trusteeship Council; Del. to numerous int. confs.
Publs. *Modern International Negotiation* 66, *How Communist China Negotiates* 68, *The UN and the Middle East Crisis* 68, *The United Nations Security Council in the 1970s*; Novels: *The House at Adampur, Seasons of Jupiter.*
230 East 81st Street, New York, N.Y. 10028, U.S.A.

Laos, fmr. King of (*see* Savang Vatthana).

Lattimore, Owen; American teacher and writer; b. 29 July 1900; ed. Coll. Classique Cantonal, Lausanne, St. Bees School, Cumberland, and Harvard Univ.
Business and journalism China 19-25; travelled overland Peking to India 26-27; research work for Social Science Research Council in Manchuria 29-30, for Harvard-Yenching Inst., Peking 30-31, for Guggenheim Foundation 31-33; research, China and Mongolia 34-47; Editor *Pacific Affairs* 34-41; special political adviser to Gen. Chiang Kai-shek 41-42; Dir. of Pacific Operations, Office of War Information 43-44; mem. Vice-Pres. Wallace's Mission in Siberia and China 44; Econ. Adviser, U.S. reparations missions, Japan 45-46; chief of UN tech. aid exploratory mission, Afghanistan 50; travelled in Mongolia 61, 64, 66, 69, 70, 71, 72, 73; Prof. of Chinese Studies, Leeds Univ. 63-70; Pres. U.S. Mongolian Soc.; Hon. Pres. Soc. Franco-Mongole; Hon. Life Pres. Anglo-Mongolian Soc.; Hon. mem. Kőrösi Csoma Soc. (Hungary), American Geographical Soc., Foreign mem. Mongolian Acad. of Sciences 68-, mem. American Philosophical Soc., Royal Cen. Asian Soc.; Cuthbert Peek Grant 30 and Patron's Medal 42 of Royal Geographical Soc. (U.K.), Gold Medal of Geographical Soc. of Philadelphia 33; Hon. D.Litt. (Glasgow) 42, Hon. Ph.D. (Copenhagen) 71.
Publs. *The Desert Road to Turkestan* 28, *High Tartary* 30, *Manchuria: Cradle of Conflict* 32, *The Mongols of Manchuria* 34, *Inner Asian Frontiers of China* 40, *Mongol Journeys* 41, *America and China* 43, *The Making of Modern China* (with Eleanor Lattimore) 44, *Solution in Asia* 45, *China, A Short History* (with Eleanor Lattimore) 47, *The Situation in Asia* 49, *Pivot of Asia* 50, *Ordeal by Slander* 50, *Nationalism and Revolution in Mongolia* 55, *Nomads and Commissars* 62,

Studies in Asian Frontier History 62, *Silks, Spices, and Empire* (with Eleanor Lattimore) 68.
26 rue de Picpus, 75012 Paris, France.

Law, Phillip Garth, A.O., C.B.E., M.SC., D.APP.SC., F.A.I.P. Australian scientist, Antarctic explorer and educationist; b. 21 April 1912; ed. Ballarat Teachers' Coll., and Univ. of Melbourne.
Science master in secondary schools 33-38; Tutor in Physics, Newman Coll., Melbourne Univ. 40-47 and Lecturer in Physics 43-47; Research Physicist and Asst. Sec. Scientific Instrument and Optical Panel, Ministry of Munitions 40-45; Scientific Mission to New Guinea battle areas for the Australian Army 44; Senior Scientific Officer Australian Nat. Antarctic Research Expeditions 47-49, Leader 49-66; Dir. Antarctic Div., Dept. of External Affairs 49-66; Australian Observer Norwegian-British-Swedish Antarctic Expedition 50; led expeditions to establish first perm. Australian research station at Mawson, MacRobertson Land 54 and at Davis, Princess Elizabeth Land 57; exploration of coast of Australian Antarctica 54-66; mem. gov. council Melbourne Univ. 59-, La Trobe Univ. 64-74; Exec. Vice-Pres. Victoria Inst. of Colleges 66-; Chair. Australian Nat. Cttee. on Antarctic Research 66-; Pres. Royal Soc. of Victoria 67-68; Trustee of Science Museum of Victoria 68-; Pres. Melbourne Univ. Graduate Union 71-; Fellow, Tech. Soc.; Founder's Medal (Royal Geographical Soc.) 60, also medals of Royal Geographical Soc., Australia, and Royal Soc. of Tasmania.
Publs. *ANARE* (with Bechervaise) 57, also numerous articles on antarctic exploration and research and papers on cosmic rays, thermal conductivity, optics and education.
16 Stanley Grove, Canterbury, Victoria, Australia.
Telephone: 82-5630.

Le Duan; Vietnamese politician; b. 1908, Quang Tri Province, Central Viet-Nam.
Secretary with local railways, Hanoi; imprisoned for political activity 31, released 36, and again 40, released 45 when Viet Minh came to power; active mem. Communist Party of Indochina; prominent in Viet Minh resistance 46; Commr. Mil. Headquarters, S. Viet-Nam 52; Sec. Lao Dong Cen. Cttee. for Southern Region 56, Sec.-Gen. Lao Dong Party April 59, First Sec. Sept. 59-; mem. Nat. Defence Council, Socialist Repub. of Viet-Nam July 76-, Lao Dong Politburo, Cen. Cttee. and Secr.; accompanied Ho Chi Minh on official visits; led dels. to 23rd Soviet Party Congress 67, to Celebrations for 50th Anniversary of October Revolution 67, to Centenary of Lenin's birth 70.
Publs. major articles in *Nhan Dan* (party organ).
Central Committee, Lao Dong Party, Hanoi, Viet-Nam.

Le Duc Tho; Vietnamese politician; b. 14 Oct. 1911 (as Phan Dinh Khai).
Founder mem. Communist Party of Indochina 30; imprisoned, escaped to China 40; founder mem. Viet Minh, returned to Hanoi 45; Viet Minh del. for S. Viet-Nam 49; Sec.-Gen. Viet Minh Exec. Cttee., S. Viet-Nam, then mem. Cen. Cttee. Lao Dong Party; mem. Politburo, Lao Dong Party 55, Dir. Party Training School 59; mem. Lao Dong Secr. 60; Special Adviser to N. Vietnamese del. at Paris peace talks 68-72; led dels. to U.S.S.R. 61, France 65, 70, German Democratic Repub. 71, has attended several Communist Party congresses abroad; Nobel Peace Prize 73.
Central Committee, Lao Dong Party, Hanoi, Viet-Nam.

Lealofi IV, Hon. Tupua Tamasese; Samoan politician and doctor; b. 8 May 1922; ed. Apia Marist Brothers School, Malifa School and Fiji School of Medicine.
Medical practitioner with Western Samoa Health Dept. 40-69; succeeded to Paramount Chief (Tama-a-Aiga) of Tupua Tamasese 65; mem. Council of Deputies 68-69; mem. Parl. 70-; Prime Minister 70-73, May 75-March 76; Minister of Internal and External District Affairs, Labour and Audit, Police and Prisons 75-March 76.
c/o Office of the Prime Minister, Apia, Western Samoa.

Lee, General Honkon; Korean army officer and diplomatist; b. 7 Dec. 1920; ed. Japanese Imperial Mil. Acad.
Superintendent, Korean Mil. Acad. 46-48; Mil. Attaché, Washington 49; Commdg. Gen., Eighth Republic of Korea Army Division 49-50, Third Army Corps. 50-51, First Army Corps 52-54; UN Command Del. to Korean Armistice 51-52; Chair. Joint Chiefs of Staff 54-56, Chief of Staff 56-58; Nat. Pres. Korean Veterans Asscn. 58-61; Amb. to Philippines 61-62, to U.K. 62-67 (also to Scandinavian countries, Iceland, Malta and African countries concurrently); Amb. at Large 67-69; Chair. President's Advisory Comm. on Govt. Admin. 69; numerous decorations.
115-17, Taeshin-Dong, Sudaemoon-ku, Seoul, Republic of Korea.
Telephone: 33-3333.

Lee Kuan Yew, M.A.; Singapore politician and barrister; b. 16 Sept. 1923, Singapore; ed. Raffles Coll., Singapore, Fitzwilliam Coll., Cambridge, and Middle Temple, London.
One of the founders of the Socialist People's Action Party 54, Sec.-Gen. 54-; mem. Legislative Assembly 55-; (first) Prime Minister 59-; mem. Bureau of the Socialist Int. 67; Fellow, Inst. of Politics, Harvard Univ. 68; Hoyt Fellow, Berkeley Coll., Yale Univ. 70; Hon. Bencher of Middle Temple 69; Hon. Fellow, Fitzwilliam Coll., Cambridge 69, Royal Australasian Coll. of Surgeons 73, Royal Australasian Coll. of Physicians 74; Grand Cordon of Order of The Nile 62, Grand Cross of Royal Order, Cambodia 66, First Class Order of the Rising Sun, Japan 67, Bintang Republik Indonesia Adi Pradana 73, Order of Sikatuna, The Philippines 74; Hon. LL.D. (Royal Univ. of Cambodia 65, Hong Kong 70, Liverpool 71, Sheffield 71); Hon. C.H. 70; Hon. G.C.M.G. 72.
Prime Minister's Office, St. Andrew's Road, Singapore 6.
Telephone: 31155.

Lee Yong Leng; Singapore diplomatist; b. 26 March 1930, Singapore; ed. Univ. of Singapore and St. Antony's Coll., Oxford.
Lecturer and Prof., Univ. of Singapore 56-70; High Commr. to U.K. 71-75.
Publs. *North Borneo* 65, *Population and Settlement in Sarawak* 70.
c/o Ministry of Foreign Affairs, Singapore.

Lemberg, (Max) Rudolf, PH.D., DR.HABIL., F.A.A., F.R.S.; Australian research biochemist; b. 19 Oct. 1896, Breslau, Silesia; ed. Johannes Gymnasium, Breslau, Univs. of Breslau and Heidelberg.
Research Asst., Chem. Dept., Breslau Univ. 21-24; Chemist, C. F. Boehringer, Sons, Mannheim 24-26; mem. Staff, Chem. Dept., Heidelberg Univ. 26-33; Rockefeller Foundation Fellow, Dept. of Biochem., Cambridge (U.K.) 30-32, Fellow Academic Assistance Council, Cambridge 33-35; Head of Biochem. Dept., Inst. of Medical Research, Royal North Shore Hosp. of Sydney 35-72, Asst. Dir. of Inst. 53-72; Visiting Prof. Univ. of Pennsylvania 66; Prof. Emer. (Heidelberg) 56; Fellow of Royal Soc. 52-; Foundation Fellow, Australian Acad. of Sciences; Foreign mem. Accad. Anatomico-Chirurgica, Perugia; Corresp. mem. Heidelberg Acad. of Sciences; Hon. mem. Soc. of American Biol. Chemists; H. G. Smith Medal, Royal Australian Chem. Inst. 49; James Cook Medal, Royal Soc. of N.S.W. 65; Britannica-Australia Award in Science 65; Hon. D.Sc. (Sydney Univ.) 70, Walter Burfit Prize and Medal 71.
Publs. *Haematin Compounds and Bile Pigments* (with J. W. Legge) 49; Editor (with others) *Haematin Enzymes*

(2 vols.) 61; *Cytochromes* (with J. Barrett) 73; reviews on cytochrome oxidase, and numerous other reviews.
"The Sanctuary", 57 Boundary Road, Wahroonga, N.S.W., Australia.
Telephone: 48-3714.

Lesser, Most Rev. Norman Alfred, C.M.G., M.A., TH.D., D.D.; British ecclesiastic; b. 16 March 1902; ed. Liverpool Collegiate School, Fitzwilliam House and Ridley Hall, Cambridge.
Curate, Anfield 25-26, Formby 26-29; Curate-in-Charge, Norris Green 29-30; Chaplain of Cathedral, Liverpool 30-31; Vicar, Barrow-in-Furness 31-39; Hon. Canon, Rector and Sub-Dean, All Saints Cathedral, Nairobi 39-47; Provost of Nairobi 42-47; Bishop of Waiapu 47-; Primate and Archbishop of New Zealand 61-71, retd.
4 Sealy Road, Napier, New Zealand.

Lewis, Thomas Lancelot; Australian politician; b. 23 Jan. 1922, Adelaide; ed. St. Peter's Coll., Adelaide.
Member of N.S.W. Legislative Assembly for Wollondilly 57-; Minister for Lands, N.S.W. 65-75, for Mines 65-67, for Tourism 72-75; Premier and Treas. N.S.W. Jan. 75-Jan. 76; established Nat. Parks and Wildlife Service.
Redbraes, 17 Valetta Street, Moss Vale, N.S.W. 2577, Australia.
Telephone: (048) 911617 (Home).

Li Chen; politician, People's Repub. of China.
Brigade Political Commissar 47; Political Commissar Shenyang Mil. Region, People's Liberation Army 58; Maj.-Gen. PLA 63; Deputy Dir. Political Dept., Ministry of Railroads 63; mem. 9th Cen. Cttee. of CCP 69; Minister of Public Security 72-75; mem. 10th Cen. Cttee. of CCP 73.

Li Ch'iang; politician and telecommunications specialist, People's Repub. of China.
Member 6th Exec. Cttee., Nat. Fed. of Trade Unions 48-53; Dir. Radio Bureau, Ministry of Post and Telecommunications 50; Commercial Attaché, Embassy in Moscow 52-54; mem. Scientific Planning Comm., State Council 57; Deputy Dir. Bureau for Econ. Relations with Foreign Countries, State Council 61; Vice-Chair. Comm. for Econ. Relations with Foreign Countries 65-67; Vice-Minister of Foreign Trade 68-73; mem. 9th Cen. Cttee. of CCP 69; Minister of Foreign Trade 73-; mem. 10th Cen. Cttee. of CCP 73.

Li Chih-min; People's Repub. of China; b. 1908, Hunan.
Political Commissar, Chinese People's Volunteers in Korea 53; Col.-Gen. 56; Dir. Political Dept., People's Liberation Army Mil. Acad. 63; First Political Commissar Foochow Mil. Region, PLA 74.

Li Ching-ch'uan; People's Repub. of China; b. Huichang, Kiangsi.
Political Commissar 1st Front Army 31; guerrilla leader in Sikang 34; Political Commissar Suiyan-Mongolian Mil. Region 37, Shansi-Suiyuan Mil. Region 47; Dir. W. Szechuan Admin. Office 50; Gov. of Szechuan 52-55; Sec. CCP Szechuan 52-55, First Sec. 55-65; Political Commissar Szechuan Mil. District, People's Liberation Army 52, Chengtu Mil. Region, PLA 54-67; mem. 8th Cen. Cttee. of CCP 56; mem. of Politburo, CCP 58-67; First Sec. S.W. Bureau, CCP 61-67; Vice-Chair. Nat. People's Congress 65; criticized and removed from office during Cultural Revolution 67; mem. 10th Cen. Cttee. of CCP 73.

Li Choh-ming, K.B.E. (HON.), C.B.E., M.A., PH.D.; American (b. Chinese) educator and university professor; b. 17 Feb. 1912; ed. Univ. of Nanking, China, and Univ. of California (Berkeley).
Professor of Economics, Nankai, Southwest Associated and Nat. Central Univs., China 37-43; mem. special mission to U.S.A., Canada and U.K. 43-45; Deputy Dir.-Gen. Chinese Nat. Relief and Rehabilitation Admin. (CNRRA) 45-47; Chief Del. of Repub. of China to UN Econ. Comm. for Asia and the Far East 47-49; Chair. Board of Trustees for Rehabilitation Affairs, Nat. Govt. of China 49-50; Expert on the UN Population Comm. and Statistical Comm. 52-57; Lecturer, Assoc. Prof. and Prof. of Business Admin, sometime Dir. Centre for Chinese Studies, Univ. of Calif. (Berkeley) 51-63; Vice-Chancellor Chinese Univ. of Hong Kong 63-; Pres. Asscn. of Southeast Asian Insts. of Higher Learning 68-70; Dir. Asian Workshop on Higher Educ. 69; mem. Editorial Boards *Asian Economic Review, Asian Survey, Modern Asian Studies, China Quarterly, Tsing Hua Journal of Chinese Studies, Readers Digest (Chinese Edition)*: Life Fellow, Royal Econ. Soc., Royal Soc. of Arts, London; mem. American Econ. Asscn., Asscn. for Asian Studies (U.S.A.) and other socs.; Dr. of Law h.c. Univs. of Hong Kong, Michigan, Marquette, W. Ontario; D.Sc.S. (Pittsburgh); Elise and Walter A. Haas Int. Award (Univ. of Calif.) 74.
Publs. *Economic Development of Communist China* 59, *Statistical System of Communist China* 62; Editor: *Industrial Development in Communist China* 64, *Asian Workshop on Higher Education—Proceedings* 69, *The First Six Years 1963-69*.
Office of the Vice-Chancellor, Chinese University of Hong Kong, Shatin, New Territories, Kowloon, Hong Kong.
Telephone: NT-61-2581.

Li Hsien-nien; politician, People's Repub. of China; b. 1905, Huang-an, Hupeh.
Joined CCP 27; Political Commissar 30th Army, 4th Front Red Army 35; Commdr. 5th Column, New 4th Army 38; mem. 7th Cen. Cttee. of CCP 45; Gov. of Hupeh 49; Commdr., Political Commissar Hupeh Mil. District, People's Liberation Army 49; Vice-Premier, State Council 54-; Minister of Finance 54-75; mem. Poliburo, 8th Cen. Cttee. of CCP 56; Sec., Secr. of Cen. Cttee., CCP 58-66; Vice-Chair. State Planning Comm. 62; mem. Politburo, 9th Cen. Cttee. of CCP 69, Politburo, 10th Cen. Cttee. 73, 75.

Li Jui-shan; People's Repub. of China.
Secretary CCP Hunan 58-68; First Sec. CCP Changsha 59; Chair. Shensi Revolutionary Cttee. 68; Political Commissar Lanchow Mil. Region, People's Liberation Army 68; mem. 9th Cen. Cttee. of CCP 69; First Sec. CCP Shensi 71-; mem. 10th Cen. Cttee. of CCP 73.

Li Kuang-hsiang; People's Repub. of China.
Deputy Head, Propaganda Dept., Gen. Political Dept., People's Liberation Army 72-.

Li Kwoh-ting, B.S.; Chinese government official; b. 28 Jan. 1910; ed. Nat. Central Univ., China, and Cambridge Univ., England.
Superintendent of Tze Yu Iron Works, Chungking 42-45; Pres. Taiwan Shipbuilding Corpn. 51-53; mem. Industrial Devt. Comm., Econ. Stabilization Board 53-58; Sec.-Gen. Council for U.S. Aid, Convenor of Industrial Planning and Co-ordination Group of Ministry of Econ. Affairs, Head of Industrial Devt. and Investment Center 58-63; Vice-Chair. Council for Int. Econ. Co-operation and Devt. 63-73; Minister of Econ. Affairs 65-69, of Finance 69-76, without Portfolio June 76-; mem. Nat. Security Council 67-; Vice-Chair. Nat. Reconstruction Planning Cttee. 67-72; Ramon Magsaysay Award for Govt. Service 68 and decorations from Repub. of Korea, Spain, Repub. of Viet-Nam, Jordan, Madagascar, Thailand and Gabon.
Publs. *Symposium on Nuclear Physics, British Industries, Japanese Shipbuilding Industry, The Growth of Private Industry in Free China, Economic Policy and Economic Development.*
3 Lane 2, Tai-an Street, Taipei, Taiwan.
Telephone: 28525.

Li Pao-hua; People's Repub. of China; b. 1908, Lo-t'ing, Hopei; *s.* of Li Ta-chao.
Alternate mem. 7th Cen. Cttee. of CCP 45; Vice-Minister

of Water Conservancy 49-63 and of Electric Power 58-63; mem. 8th Cen. Cttee. of CCP 56; First Sec. CCP Anhwei 63-67; Third Sec. E. China Bureau, CCP 65; First Political Commissar Anhwei Mil. District, People's Liberation Army 66; criticized and removed from office during Cultural Revolution 67; mem. 10th Cen. Cttee. of CCP 73; Second Sec. CCP Kweichow 73.

Li Shui-ch'ing; politician, People's Repub. of China. Divisional Commdr., People's Liberation Army 49; Maj.-Gen. PLA 57; Chief of Staff Tsinan Mil. Region, PLA 68; mem. 9th Cen. Cttee. of CCP 69; Minister of First Ministry of Machine Building 72-75, First Minister of Mechanical Industry 75-; mem. 10th Cen. Cttee. of CCP 73.

Li Ta; army officer, People's Repub. of China; b. 1905, Shensi; ed. Moscow Mil. Acad., U.S.S.R.
Staff Officer, Red 6th Army, on Long March 34-36; Staff Officer, 129th Div. 37-45; Chief of Staff, Cen. Plains Field Army 47, Chinese People's Volunteers in Korea 53-54; Vice-Minister of Nat. Defence 54-59; Gen. 55; Chair. Nat. Defence Sports Asscn. 58-67; criticized and removed from office during Cultural Revolution 67; Deputy Chief of Cen. Staff, People's Liberation Army 72-; mem. 10th Cen. Cttee. of CCP 73.

Li Ta-chang; People's Repub. of China; b. 1910, Szechuan.
Director, Propaganda Dept., Taihang Sub-Bureau of N. China Bureau, CCP 44; Chief of Staff Shansi-Chahar-Honan Mil. Region 46; Mayor of Mutankiang 46; Political Commissar Mongolia-Ninghsia Mil. Region 46; Dir. S. Szechuan Admin. Office 50; Gov. of Szechuan 55-68; Sec. CCP Szechuan 54-; Alt. mem. 8th Cen. Cttee. of CCP 56; Sec. S.W. Bureau, CCP 64-67; First Sec. CCP Kweichow 65; Vice-Chair. Szechuan Revolutionary Cttee. 68; mem. 9th Cen. Cttee. of CCP 69, 10th Cen. Cttee. 73.

Li Teh-sheng, Gen.; army officer, People's Repub. of China. Company Commdr. Red 4th Front Army on Long March 34-36; Div. Commdr. 2nd Field Army, People's Liberation Army 49; Gen. PLA 64; Commdr. Anhwei Mil. District, PLA 67; Chair. Anhwei Revolutionary Cttee. 68; Alt. mem. Politburo, 9th Cen. Cttee. of CCP 69; Dir., Gen. Political Dept., People's Liberation Army 69-74; First Sec. CCP Anhwei 71-73; mem. Standing Cttee. of Politburo and Vice-Chair. 10th Cen. Cttee. of CCP 73; Commdr. Shenyang Mil. Region, PLA 74-75.

Liang Yuen-li (Liang Yun-li), LL.B., DR.JUR.; Chinese lawyer; b. 1904; ed. Nanyang Univ. Comparative Law School, Harvard and Geneva Univs.
Editor *China Law Review* 24-26; Lecturer Comparative Law School and Legal Editor *Commercial Press* 26-27; Sec. to Minister of Foreign Affairs 27 and Minister of Justice 28; Judge Shanghai Provisional Court 28; Prof. of Law, Comparative Law School 28-29; Sec. Washington Legation 29-33; Carnegie Teachers Fellow in Int. Law Harvard 30-31; Counsellor of Exec. Yuan 33; Senior Sec. of Ministry of Foreign Affairs 34; senior mem. Treaty Comm. of Ministry of Foreign Affairs and Prof. Central Univ. 36-37; contrib. Editor *China Critic*; First Sec. Embassy, London 39-42; Counsellor 43-46; mem. Chinese del. to Dumbarton Oaks and San Francisco Confs. 44-45; Chair. Cttee. of Experts, Security Council 46; Visiting Prof., Univ. of Michigan, Summer 47; Prof. Hague Acad. of Int. Law 48; Lecturer, N.Y. Univ. Law School 47-48, 49-50, Adjunct Assoc. Prof. 51-60, Adjunct Prof. 60-; Dir. Legal Dept. UN 46-64; Adviser, Chinese Del. to UN Gen. Assembly 64, 65, 68; Prof. Postgraduate Inst. of Int. Law and Diplomacy, Nat. Cheng-chi Univ., Taipei 68; elected Assoc. Inst. of Int. Law 50, elected titular mem. 65; Adviser, Ministry of Foreign Affairs, Dir. Treaty Dept. 69; mem. Perm. Court of Arbitration, The Hague 70-.
Publs. *The First Year of the Far Eastern Crisis, International Government, Sociology of Law, China* 46, *Le Développement et la Codification du Droit international* 48.
Graduate School of Int. and Comparative Legal Studies, Soochow University, Taipei, Taiwan.

Liao Ch'eng-chih; Chinese party official; b. 1908, Tokyo, Japan; ed. Lingnan Univ., Canton, Waseda Univ., Japan and Berlin and Hamburg Univs., Germany.
Joined CCP 25; studied Political Econ., Germany 28; Chair. Seaman's Union 33; participated in Long March 34-36; Dir. New China News Agency 38; prisoner of Kuomintang 42-46; Alt. mem. 7th Cen. Cttee. of CCP 45; Chair. Nat. Fed. of Democratic Youth 49; Dir. Inst. of Foreign Affairs 49-54; mem. 8th Cen. Cttee. of CCP 56; Chair. Comm. for Overseas Chinese Affairs 59-67; Pres. Overseas Chinese Univ., Fukien 61-67, China-Japan Friendship Asscn. 63-; criticized and removed from office during Cultural Revolution 67; rehabilitated and returned to previous positions 72; mem. 10th Cen. Cttee. of CCP 73.
People's Republic of China.

Liao Chih-kao; People's Repub. of China; b. *circa* 1908, Chien-ning, Szechuan; ed. Tsinghua Univ. Peking.
Director Political Dept., N. Shensi 47; Political Commissar Sikang Mil. District, People's Liberation Army 50-55; Gov. of Sikang Provisional Govt. 50-55; Vice-Gov. of Szechuan 55-68; Sec. CCP Szechuan 56-65, First Sec. 65-68; Alt. mem. 8th Cen. Cttee. of CCP 56; Sec. S.W. Bureau, CCP 64-68; criticized and removed from office during Cultural Revolution 68; Alt. mem. 10th Cen. Cttee. of CCP 73; First Sec. CCP Fukien 75-.

Licaros, Gregario S., LL.B., B.SC.; Philippine lawyer and banker; b. 12 March 1909; ed. Far Eastern Univ.
Chairman Board of Trustees, Govt. Service Insurance System 54-61; Chair. Board of Govs., Devt. Bank of the Philippines and mem. Central Bank Monetary Board 58-61; Chair. Board of Dirs., CCP Securities Corpn. 63-65; Gov. Central Bank of the Philippines Jan. 70-, concurrently Gov. Int. Monetary Fund for the Philippines; mem. Council of Central Bank Govs. of S.E. Asia, N.Z., Australia (SEANZA) 70-, Nat. Econ. Council, Financial and Fiscal Policy Council, Foreign Trade Council, Surigao Mineral Reservation Board 70-; mem. Board of Dirs., Philippine Deposit Insurance Corpn. 70-; Chair. Gold Mining Industry Assistance Board 70-; Outstanding CPA, Philippine Asscn. of Board of Examiners 58, and many other awards.
Central Bank of the Philippines, A. Mabini Street, Manila; Home: 802 Harvard Street, Mandaluyong, Rizal, Philippines.

Lim Chong Eu, Dr.; Malaysian politician; b. 28 May 1919, Penang; ed. Penang Free School, Edinburgh Univ.
Medical Officer (Flight Lieut.) Malayan Auxiliary Air Force 51-54; private medical practice; mem. Penang State Settlement Council 51; Radical Party 52-58; mem. Fed. Council for Penang 55-57, Alliance Chief Whip; Pres. Malayan Chinese Asscn. (M.C.A.) 58-59, resigned as Pres. 59, left M.C.A. 60; Chair. pro tem. Cttee. of United Democratic Party 62-63, Gen. Sec. 63-66, Pres. 66-68; Deputy Chair. Gerakan Rakyat Malaysia 68-71, Pres. 71-, Chair. Tanjong Branch 69-; mem. for Kota, Penang State Assembly, mem. for Tanjong, House of Reps. 64-; Chief Minister of Penang 69-; Chair. Penang State Goodwill Cttee. 69-, State Operations Cttee. 69-; mem. Malayan Medical Council 64; Pres. Northern Branch of Malayan Medical Asscn. 68-69, fmr. mem. Exec. Council; fmr. Pres. Penang Medical Practitioners' Soc., Hon. mem. 69-.
Pejabat Ketua Menteri, Bangunan Tuanku Syed Putra, Peti Surat 3006, Penang, Malaysia.

Lim Kim San; Singapore politician; b. 1916, Singapore; ed. Raffles Coll., Singapore.
Director United Chinese Bank Ltd., Chair. Batu Pahat Bank Ltd., and Pacific Bank Ltd. 40-; mem., Deputy Chair. Public Service Comm., Singapore 59-63; Chair.

Housing Devt. Board; Deputy Chair. Econ. Devt. Board; Minister for Nat. Devt. 63-65, for Finance 65-67, for the Interior and Defence 67-70, for Educ. 70-72; Minister of the Environment Sept. 72-75, for Nat. Devt. and Communications 76; mem. Dewan Ra'ayat; Darjah Utama Temasek (Order of Temasek) 62, Ramon Magsaysay Award for community leadership 65.
Ministry of National Development and Communications, Singapore.

Lim, Manuel, A.B., LL.B., LL.M., D.C.L.; Philippine lawyer and politician; b. 6 Aug. 1899; ed. Ateneo de Manila Univ., Univ. of Philippines and Univ. of Santo Tomás.
Lawyer 21-41, 45-47, 48-57, 58-60, 62-; Dean and Prof. Coll. of Law, Ateneo de Manila 36-41, 47-59; Prof. of Law, Univ. of Santo Tomás 38-41; judicial posts 41-46; Assoc. Justice Court of Appeals 46-47; Under-Sec. of Justice and Solicitor-Gen. 47-48; Vice-Pres. A. Soriano y Cia. 48-59, Dir. 54-59; Pres. and Dir. Realty Investments Inc. 50-; Chair. Mindanao Mother Lode Mines Inc. 49-60; Pres. Tax Service of Philippines Inc. 57-59; Sec. of Educ., Govt. of Philippines 57-59; Sec. of Commerce and Industry 60-62; Vice-Pres. and Gen. Counsel Philippine American Life Insurance Co. 62-70; Chair. Corporate Promotions Inc. 65-, Shrimp Processing Corpn. of the Philippines 68-, Pentagon Mines Inc. 70-, Pacific Richfield Corpn. 75-; Chair. Comm. on Asian and Far Eastern Affairs, Int. Chamber of Commerce 67-69; mem. Labour-Management Advisory Council 63-; Chair. Philippine Council, Int. Chamber of Commerce 63-; Pres. Philippine Motor Asscn. 73- (Dir. 65-); Chair. Consumers Union of the Philippines 73-; Vice-Chair. Energy Conservation Movement 75-; Pres. Philippine Constitution Asscn. 75-; mem. numerous legal and other asscns. and official of numerous industrial companies; many nat. and foreign hons., several mil. decorations.
103 Magallanes Avenue, Magallanes Village, Makati, Rizal D-708, Philippines.

Lin Chin-sheng, B.L.; Chinese politician; b. 4 Aug. 1916; ed. Law Coll., Tokyo Imperial Univ.
Magistrate, Chiayi Co. Govt. 52-55; Chair. Yunlin Co. H.Q., Kuomintang 55-58; Magistrate, Yunlin Co. Govt. 58-65; Dir. Cheng-Ching Lake Industrial Waterworks 65-67; Commr., Taiwan Provincial Govt. 66-69; Sec.-Gen. Taiwan Provincial H.Q., Kuomintang 67-68, Chair. Taipei Municipal H.Q. 69-70, Deputy Sec.-Gen. Cen. Cttee. 70-72; Minister of the Interior 72-76, of Communications June 76-; Order of the Brilliant Star.
Ministry of Communications, Taipei; Home: 40 Alley 14, Lane 15, Chung Shih Road, Section 1, Shin Lin, Taipei, Taiwan.

Lin Pin; army officer, People's Repub. of China.
Commander 43rd Brigade, 15th Column, Army Corps of Hsu Hsiang-chi'ien (*q.v.*) 48; Maj.-Gen. 60; Deputy Chief of Staff People's Liberation Army Armoured Force 51; Deputy Commdr. PLA Armoured Forces 72-.

Liu Chieh; Chinese diplomatist; b. 16 April 1906; ed. Oxford and Columbia Univs.
Foreign Service 31-; Chinese Del. to League of Nations 32-39; Counsellor, Chinese Embassy, London 33-40, Minister, Washington 40-45; Vice-Minister for Foreign Affairs 45-47; Amb. to Canada 47-63; Pres. UN Trusteeship Council 48; mem. Int. Law Comm. 61-66; Perm. Rep. of Repub. of China to UN 62-71; Amb. to the Philippines 72-76.
c/o Ministry of Foreign Affairs, Taipei, Taiwan.

Liu Chien-hsun; People's Repub. of China; b. 1907, Hopei.
Second Sec. CCP Hupeh 52-54, Sec. 54-55; Political Commissar Hupeh Mil. District, People's Liberation Army 52; Deputy Dir. Rural Dept., CCP 56; First Sec. CCP Kwangsi 57-61; Alt. mem. 8th Cen. Cttee. of CCP 56; First Sec. CCP Honan 61-66; Political Commissar Honan Mil. District, PLA 64; Sec. Cen.-South Bureau, CCP 65-66; Sec. CCP Peking 66; Second Sec. N. China Bureau, CCP 66; Vice-Chair. Peking Revolutionary Cttee. 67; First Political Commissar Honan Mil. District, PLA 67; Deputy Political Commissar Wuhan Mil. Region, PLA 67, Political Commissar 71-; Chair. Honan Revolutionary Cttee. 68; mem. 9th Cen. Cttee. of CCP 69; First Sec. CCP Honan 71; mem. 10th Cen. Cttee. of CCP 73.

Liu Hsi-yao; People's Repub. of China.
Deputy Sec. CCP Hupeh 53-54; Vice-Chair. State Technological Comm. 57-59, State Scientific and Technological Comm. 59-67; Alt. mem. 9th Cen. Cttee. of CCP 69; Dir. Scientific and Educ. Group, State Council 72-; Alt. mem. 10th Cen. Cttee. of CCP 73; Minister, Second Ministry of Machine Bldg. 75.

Liu Hsien-ch'uan; army officer, People's Repub. of China; b. 1914, Chiating, Fukien.
Joined Red Army 30; Maj.-Gen. Shenyang Mil. Region, People's Liberation Army 60; Commdr. Tsinghai Mil. District, PLA 66-, Inner Mongolia Mil. District, PLA 67; Chair. Tsinghai Revolutionary Cttee. 67; Deputy Commdr. Lanchow Mil. Region, PLA 68; mem. 9th Cen. Cttee. of CCP 69; First Sec. CCP Tsinghai 71; mem. 10th Cen. Cttee. of CCP 73.

Liu Hsing-yuan; People's Repub. of China; b. 1914, Hunan.
Deputy Political Commissar, Canton Mil. Region, People's Liberation Army 55, Second Political Commissar 63; Lieut.-Gen. 57; mem. Nat. Defence Council 65; Chair. Kwangtung Revolutionary Cttee. 69; mem. 9th Cen. Cttee. of CCP 69; First Sec. CCP Kwangtung 71; Chair. Szechuan Revolutionary Cttee. 72; First Sec. CCP Szechuan 72; First Political Commissar Chengtu Mil. Region, PLA 73-; mem. 10th Cen. Cttee. of CCP 73.

Liu Po-ch'eng; fmr. army officer, People's Repub. of China; b. 1892, Kai-hsien, Szechuan; ed. Chengtu Mil. School and Moscow Mil. Inst.,
Joined CCP 26; Head Chief of Staff Nanchang Uprising 27; Chief of Gen. Staff, Red Army 32; on Long March 34-35; Pres. Red. Army Univ., Kansu 36; Commdr. 129th Div., 8th Route Army 37-40; mem. 7th Cen. Cttee. of CCP 45; Commdr. 2nd Field Army 49-54; Second Sec. S.W. Bureau, CCP 50; Pres. Nanking Mil. Acad. 51-58; Vice-Chair. Nat. Defence Council 54-; Dir., Gen. Training Dept., People's Liberation Army 54-57; Marshal PLA 55; mem. Politburo, 8th Cen. Cttee. of CCP 56; Vice-Chair. Nat. People's Congress 59-; mem. Politburo, 9th Cen. Cttee. of CCP 69, Politburo, 10th Cen. Cttee. 73, 75.

Liu Tao-sheng; army officer, People's Repub. of China; b. 1916; ed. Red Army Coll.
Joined CCP 33; Political Commissar 22nd Div., Red Army 34; Vice-Adm. of Navy, People's Liberation Army 55; Deputy Commdr. PLA Navy 58-.

Liu Tzu-hou; People's Repub. of China; b. *circa* 1910, Hopei.
Joined CCP 37; Deputy Gov. of Hupeh 52-54, Gov. 54-56; Second Sec. CCP Hupeh 53-56; Dir. Sanmen Gorge Construction Bureau 56-58; Gov. of Hopei 58-68; Sec. CCP Hopei 58-64; Alt. mem. 8th Cen. Cttee. of CCP 56; Sec. N. China Bureau, CCP 63-68; Second Sec. CCP Hopei Revolutionary Cttee. 64-68; First Vice-Chair. Hopei Revolutionary Cttee. 68, Chair. 70; mem. 9th Cen. Cttee. of CCP 69; First Sec. CCP Hopei 71; mem. 10th Cen. Cttee. of CCP 73.

Lo Su Yin (Peter Lo), M.P., LL.B.; Malaysian lawyer and politician; b. 19 May 1923; ed. Sabah, Singapore and Victoria Univ., Wellington.

Member Sandakan Town Board 59-64, 1st Deputy Chair. 60-62; first local mem. P.S.C. 61; mem. Legislative Council, North Borneo 62-63; mem. I.G.C. for entry of Sabah into Malaysia 62-63; mem. Parl. 63-; Fed. Minister without Portfolio 64; Chief Minister Sabah 65-67; Chair. Sabah Chinese Asscn. of the State Alliance Party 65-; Malaysian Medal.
P.O. Box 1475, Kota Kinabalu, Sabah, Malaysia.

Loane, Most Rev. Sir Marcus Lawrence, K.B.E., M.A., D.D.; Australian ecclesiastic; b. 14 Oct. 1911; ed. The King's School, Parramatta, Univ. of Sydney, and Moore Theological Coll., Sydney.
Resident Tutor and Chaplain, Moore Theological Coll., Sydney 35-38, Vice-Principal 39-53, Principal 54-58; Canon, St. Andrew's Cathedral 49-58; Bishop Co-adjutor, Diocese of Sydney 58-66; Archbishop of Sydney and Metropolitan of New South Wales 66-.
Publs. *Oxford and the Evangelical Succession* 51, *Cambridge and the Evangelical Succession* 52, *Masters of the English Reformation* 55, *History of Moore Theological College* 55, *Life of Archbishop Mowll* 59, *Pioneers of the Reformation in England* 63, *The History of the China Inland Mission in Australia and New Zealand* 65, *Makers of Our Heritage* 67, *Do You Now Believe* 67, *The Hope of Glory* 68, *This Surpassing Excellence* 69, *They Were Pilgrims* 70, *By Faith We Stand* 71, *They Overcame* 71, *This Amazing Grace* 72, *The King is Here* 73, *Good News to Tell* 75.
70 Bathurst Street, Sydney, New South Wales, Australia.

Loc, Nguyen Van (*see* Nguyen Van Loc).

Lokanathan, Palamadai Samu, M.A., D.SC.; Indian economist; b. 10 Oct. 1894; ed. Univ. of Madras and London School of Economics and Political Science.
Professor of Econs., Univ. of Madras 41-42; Editor *Eastern Economist*, New Delhi 43-47; Exec. Sec. UN Econ. Comm. for Asia and the Far East (ECAFE), Bangkok 47-56; Dir.-Gen. Nat. Council of Applied Econ. Research, New Delhi 56-; Chair. Nat. Productivity Council 58-63, 64-66, Asian Productivity Org., Tokyo 63 (Dir. for India 62-66), Mettur Chemical and Industrial Corpn. Ltd., Mettur Dam, S. India and Int. Perspective Planning Team (for devt. of small industries) 63; Vice-Chair. Exec. Council of Central Inst. of Research and Training in Public Co-operation; Vice-Pres. Indian Council of World Affairs; Consultant to Inst. of Nat. Planning, Cairo 60; mem. Governing Council of Asian Inst. of Econ. Devt. and Planning, Bangkok, Nat. Savings Central Advisory Board at Ministry of Finance, Board of Trade, Export-Import Advisory Council of Industries, Panel of Economists on Planning Comm.; Visiting Prof., Dept. of Business Man. and Industrial Admin., Univ. of Delhi; Hon. Fellow London School of Econs. and Political Science; Most Noble Order of the Crown of Thailand First Class.
Publs. *Industrial Welfare in India, Industrial Organization in India, Indian Industry, Indian Economic System*, and many other economic and industrial surveys and reports.
5B Pusa Road, New Delhi 5, India.

Lon Nol, Marshal; Cambodian fmr. military commander and politician; b. 13 Nov. 1913, Kampong Leav; ed. Chasseloup Laubat High School, S. Viet-Nam, and Royal Mil. Acad., Cambodia.
Government official 37-52; Gov. of Kratie province 45, later Chief of Nat. Police; Army Area Commdr. 52; Gov. of Battambang province 54; Minister of Nat. Defence and Chief of Gen. Staff 55-66; C.-in-C. of the Khmer Royal Armed Forces 60; Deputy Prime Minister of Cambodia 63, Prime Minister 66-67, First Vice-Pres. in Charge of Nat. Defence 67-69; Prime Minister and Minister of Nat. Defence 69-71; led *coup* to overthrow Prince Norodom Sihanouk (*q.v.*) March 70; Titular Prime Minister 71-72; Pres. of Khmer Repub. 72-75; Supreme Commdr. of Armed Forces 72-74; Chair. Supreme State Council 73-74, High Exec. Council 74-75; left the country April 75.
Hawaii, U.S.A.

Lopez, Fernando; Philippine agriculturalist and politician; b. 13 April 1904, Jaro, Iloilo; ed. San Juan de Letrán Coll., Univ. of Santo Tomás.
Member, Philippine Bar 26; Mayor, Iloilo City 45; Senator of Philippines 47, Vice-Pres. 49, Sec. Agriculture and Natural Resources 50-71, Pres. Pro-Tempore 58, 60; Vice-Pres. of Philippines 65-69, 69-71; Sec. Agriculture and Natural Resources 70-71; Special Grand Cordon of Most Noble Order of Crown of Thailand; Officer of Nat. Order of Vietnam; Hon. LL.D., Manhattan Coll., New York City; Gran Cruz of Order of Isabel la Católica; Mil. Order of Christ, and many other awards.
706 Quirino Avenue, Tambo, Parañaque Rizal; 6 Flametree Place, Forbes Park, Makati Rizal, Philippines.

López, Salvador P.; Philippine journalist, diplomatist and university president; b. 27 May 1911; ed. Univ. of the Philippines.
With *Philippines Herald* 33-41; Radio Commentator 40-41; Army Service 42-46; Diplomatic Service 46-; Adviser on Political Affairs, Philippine Mission to UN 46-48, Senior Adviser 48-49, Chargé d'Affaires a.i. 50-52, Acting Perm. Rep. to UN 53-54; Minister to France 55-56, concurrently Minister to Belgium and Netherlands 55-59, to Switzerland 57-58; Amb. to France 56-62, concurrently Perm. Rep. to UNESCO 58-62, Minister to Portugal 59-62; Under-Sec. of Foreign Affairs, Philippines 62-63; Sec. of Foreign Affairs 63-64; Perm. Rep. to UN 64-68, concurrently Amb. to U.S.A., Dominican Repub., Haiti, Cuba 68-69; Pres. Univ. of the Philippines 69-75; numerous decorations.
Publs. *Literature and Society* 51, *Freedom of Information* 53, *English for World Use* 54, *The United States—Philippines Colonial Relationship* 66, *Human Rights and the Constitution* 70.
c/o University of the Philippines, Quezon City, Philippines.

Low, Alan Roberts, M.A.; New Zealand banker; b. 11 Jan. 1916; ed. Canterbury Univ. Coll.
Joined Reserve Bank of New Zealand 38; Mil. Service 42-44; Econ. Adviser, Reserve Bank of New Zealand 51, Asst. Gov. 60-62, Deputy Gov. 62-67, Gov. 67-.
Reserve Bank of New Zealand, P.O. Box 2498, 2 The Terrace, Wellington, New Zealand.

Lu Jui-lin; army officer, People's Repub. of China; b. 1908, Wuhsiang, Shansi.
Commander Tungchin Front Army, Shansi 46; Vice-Gov. of Sikang 50-54; Vice-Commdr. Yunnan Mil. District, People's Liberation Army 57; Deputy Commdr. Kunning Mil. Region, PLA 59-; Vice-Chair. Yunnan Revolutionary Cttee. 68; mem. 9th Cen. Cttee. of CCP 69; Sec. CCP Yunnan 71; First Sec. CCP Kweichow 73-; mem. 10th Cen. Cttee. of CCP 73.

Lu Nan-chiao; People's Repub. of China.
Deputy Political Commissar, Gen. Logistics Dept., People's Liberation Army 73-.

Lubis, Mochtar; Indonesian journalist; b. 1922.
Joined Indonesian Antara News Agency 45; Co-publisher daily *Indonesian Raya* 49-61, Editor 56-61, 66- (*Raya* banned Jan. 74); published and edited *The Times of Indonesia* 52; Nat. Literary Award 53; Pres. Magsaysay Award for the Press 58, Golden Pen of Freedom, Int. Fed. of Publishers 67.
Publs. *Pers and Wartawan, Tak Ada Esok, Si Djamal* (short stories), *Djalan Ada Udjung, Korean Notebook, Perkenalan Di Asia Tenggara, Melawat Ke Amerika, Stories from Europe, Indonesia Dimata Dunia, Stories from China, Twilight in Djakarta, Road with No End* 68.
17 Jalan Bonang, Jakarta III/20, Indonesia.

Luong Bang, Nguyen (*see* Nguyen Luong Bang).

Luvsanchültem, Nyamyn; Mongolian diplomatist.
Former Sec. of Presidium of People's Great Hural; Amb. to U.S.S.R. 64-75, also accred. to Sweden and Finland.
c/o Ministry of Foreign Affairs, Ulan Bator, Mongolia.

Lwin, U; Burmese diplomatist; b. 10 Dec. 1912.
Former officer, Burma army; Mil. Adviser, Burma Del. to UN Gen. Assembly 53; Amb. to Fed. Germany 66-71, also to Netherlands 69-71; Perm. Rep. to UN 71-72; Minister for Planning and Finance 72-75, for Information Oct. 75-; Deputy Prime Minister 74-.
Ministry of Information, Rangoon, Burma.

Lynch, Phillip Reginald, B.A., DIP.ED.; Australian politician; b. 27 July 1933, Melbourne; ed. Maris Bros. Coll., Hawthorn, Xavier Coll., Melbourne, Univ. of Melbourne.
Former school teacher; management consultant; fmr. co. dir.; fmr. Pres. Victorian Young Liberal Movement; mem. House of Reps. 66-; Minister for the Army 68-69, for Immigration and assisting the Treasurer 69-71, for Labour and Nat. Service 71-72; Deputy Leader of the Opposition, House of Reps. 72-75; Fed. Treas. Nov. 75-; del. to numerous confs., incl. Ministerial Council of OECD, Paris 70; Fellow, Inst. of Dirs., Australian Inst. of Management, Inst. of Sales and Marketing Execs.; Liberal.
House of Representatives, Canberra, A.C.T.; Home: "The Moorings", Denistoun Avenue, Mt. Eliza, Victoria 3930, Australia.

Lyons, Dame Enid Muriel, G.B.E., M.P. (widow of Joseph Aloysius Lyons, P.C., former Prime Minister of Australia); Australian politician; b. 9 July 1897; ed. State School, and Hobart Teachers' Training Coll.
M.P. (first woman mem. of House of Reps.) for Darwin 43-51; Int. Vice-Pres. St. Joan's Int. Social and Political Alliance 47-; Vice-Pres. of Exec. Council Dec. 49-51; newspaper columnist 51-54; mem. Australian Broadcasting Comm. 51-62; mem. Liberal Party; Hon. Fellow Australian Coll. of Nursing.
Publ. *So We Take Comfort* 65, 66 (autobiog.), *The Old Haggis* 69, *Among the Carrion Crows* 72.
Home Hill, Middle Road, Devonport, Tasmania, Australia.
Telephone: Devonport 24-2250.

M

Ma Hui; army officer, People's Repub. of China; b. 1910.
Divisional Commdr. 51; Maj.-Gen. People's Liberation Army 60; Deputy Commdr. Hopei Mil. District, PLA 64, Commdr. 65-; Vice-Chair. Hopei Revolutionary Cttee. 68; Sec. CCP Hopei 71.

Ma Ning; People's Repub. of China; b. Chinyang, Honan.
Regimental Commdr. 46; Deputy Dir., Org. Dept., People's Liberation Army Gen. Political Dept. 56; Commdr. Air Force Unit 7311, Kirin 68; mem. 10th Cen. Cttee. of CCP 73; Commdr. of Air Force, PLA 74.

Macapagal, Diosdado; Philippine politician; b. 28 Sept. 1910; ed. Santo Tomás Univ.
Diplomatic Service 46-49, Second Sec., Washington, D.C. 48; mem. House of Reps. 49-57; Vice-Pres. of the Philippines 57-61, Pres. 61-65; Chair. Liberal Party 57-61; Pres. Constitutional Convention 71.
92 Cambridge Circle, North Forbes Park, Makati, Rizal, The Philippines.

McClelland, Douglas; Australian politician; b. 5 Aug. 1926; ed. Parramatha Commercial Boys' High School, Metropolitan Business Coll.
Joined Australian Imperial Forces 44; Court Reporter 49-61; mem. N.S.W. Labor Party Exec. 57-61; mem. Senate 67-; Minister for the Media 72-75; Man. of Govt. Business in the Senate 72-75; Special Minister of State June-Nov. 75; mem. Senate Select Cttee. on the Encouragement of Australian Production for Television 62-63, Joint Cttee. on Broadcasting of Parl. Proceedings 65-, Joint Select Cttee. on the New and Perm. Parl. House 67-, Senate Select Cttee. on Medical and Hospital Costs 68-, Senate Standing Cttee. on Health and Welfare 70-; Labor Party.
Parliament House, Canberra, A.C.T.; Home: 1 Amy Street, Blakehurst, N.S.W. 2221, Australia.

McCombs, Sir Terence Henderson, Kt., O.B.E.; New Zealand diplomatist and politician; b. 5 Sept. 1905; ed. Canterbury Univ.
Member of Parl. for Lyttelton 35-51; Parl. Under-Sec. to the Minister of Finance 45-47; Minister of Educ. and in charge of Dept. of Scientific and Industrial Research 47-49; teacher and later Headmaster of Cashmere High School, Christchurch 51-72; mem. Council, Canterbury Univ. 57-68, Chancellor 69-73; High Commr. in U.K. and Amb. to Ireland 73-75; Head of enquiry into secondary educ., N.Z. 75-76; mem. Lyttelton Harbour Board, Lincoln Coll. Board of Govs., Christchurch Domains Board; Efficiency Decoration 43; Labour.
7 Freeman Street, Christchurch 8, New Zealand.

McCready, Allan; New Zealand politician; b. 1 Sept. 1916, Kawakawa; ed. Kawakawa.
Army service 39-45; worked in Post Office Dept.; Dir. Wellington Dairy Farmers' Co-operative; fmr. Dir. Hutt Valley Milk Treatment Corpn., Featherston Co-operative Dairy Co. Ltd.; M.P. for Otaki 60-; Postmaster-Gen., Minister of Marine and Fisheries 69-72, Minister in Charge of Govt. Printing Office 72; Minister of Defence, War Pensions and Rehabilitation Feb.-Dec. 72; Minister of Defence and Police Dec. 75-; National Party.
Parliament Buildings, Wellington; Home: South Road, Box 85, Manakau, New Zealand.

Macdonald, Sir Thomas Lachlan, K.C.M.G.; New Zealand politician and diplomatist; b. 14 Dec. 1898; ed. Southland Boys School, Invercargill, New Zealand.
Union Steamship Co. of New Zealand 15-18; N.Z. Army, Palestine and Egypt 18-19; farming 19-37; M.P. for Mataura 38-46, for Wallace 46-57; N.Z. Army, N. Africa 40-43; Minister of Defence 50-57, of Civil Aviation 50-54, of External Affairs 54-57, of Island Territories 54-57; High Commr. for New Zealand in U.K. 61-68; Amb. to European Econ. Community 61-67, concurrently Amb. to Ireland 66-68; New Zealand National Party.
1 Camellia Grove, Parklands, Waikanae, New Zealand.

McEwen, Rt. Hon. Sir John, P.C., G.C.M.G., C.H.; Australian fmr. politician and farmer; b. 29 March 1900, Chiltern, Victoria.
Enlisted Australian Imperial Force 18; farmer Stanhope, Victoria 19-; mem. House of Reps. for Echuca Div. 34-37, for Indi Div. 37-49, for Murray 49-71; Minister for the Interior 37-39, for External Affairs 40, and for Air and Civil Aviation 40-41; mem. Australian Advisory War Council 41-45, del. to UN Conf. on Int. Org. 45; Deputy Leader Country Party 43-58, Leader 58-71; Minister for Commerce and Agriculture 49-56, for Trade 56-71, for Trade and Industry 63-71; Deputy Prime Minister 58-71, interim Prime Minister Dec. 67-Jan. 68; Order of the Rising Sun, First Class (Japan) 73.
AMP Tower, 535 Bourke Street, Melbourne, Vic. 3000; Home: 679 Orrong Road, Toorak, Vic. 3142, Australia.
Telephone: Melbourne 62-1734.

McGuigan, Thomas Malcolm, J.P.; New Zealand politician; b. 20 Feb. 1921; ed. Christchurch Boys' High School, Christchurch Technical Evening School.
Served in Navy 41-45; secretarial and accountancy posts in manufacturing and retailing field 46-54; admin. posts,

Christchurch Hospital 55-57; Senior Admin. Officer, Princess Margaret Hosp., Christchurch 58-69; mem. Parl. 69-Nov. 75; Minister of Railways, Electricity and Civil Defence 72-74; Minister of Health and Minister in Charge of Public Trust Office Sept. 74-Nov. 75.
71 Main Road, Redcliffs, Christchurch 8, New Zealand.

McGuire, Dominic Paul, C.B.E.; Australian diplomatist and writer; b. 3 April 1903; ed. Christian Brothers' Coll., Adelaide, and Univ. of Adelaide.
Former Lecturer in History, Univ. of Adelaide, served Royal Australian Navy 39-45; Adviser, Commonwealth Prime Ministers' Conf., London 51; Del. to UN 53; Minister to Italy 53-58, Amb. 58-59; Knight Grand Cross of St. Sylvester 59, Commdr., Order of Merit of Italy 67.
Publs. *The Two Men* 32, *The Poetry of Gerald Manley Hopkins* 35, *7.30 Victoria* 35, *Prologue to the Gallows* 35, *Cry Aloud for Murder* 36, *Born to be Hanged* 36, *Burial Service* 37, *W.1* 37, *Restoring All Things* (with J. Fitzsimmons) 38, *Australian Journey* 39, *Spanish Steps* 40, *Westward the Course* 42, *Price of Admiralty* (with F. M. McGuire) 45, *The Three Corners of the World* 48, *Experiment in World Order* 48, *The Australian Theatre* (with B. P. Arnott and F. M. McGuire) 48, *Freedom for the Brave* 49, *Inns of Austria* 52, etc.
136 Mills Terrace, North Adelaide, South Australia 5006, Australia.
Telephone: 67-2214.

Machimura, Kungo; Japanese politician; b. 16 Aug. 1900, Sapporo City; ed. Tokyo Univ.
Entered Ministry of Home Affairs; Gov. Toyama and Niigata Prefs.; Dir. Police Bureau, Ministry of Home Affairs; Supt.-Gen. Metropolitan Police Bureau 45; mem. House of Reps.; affiliated to conservative group of fmr. Kaishinto (Progressive) Party, left when KP reformed to become Democratic Party, later helped to form Shinto Doshikai Party; Minister of Home Affairs 73-74; Independent.
28-18, Higashi-ga-oka, 1-chome, Meguro-ku, Tokyo, Japan.

MacIntyre, Duncan, D.S.O., O.B.E., E.D.; New Zealand farmer and politician; b. 1915, Hastings; ed. Larchfield School, Scotland, Christ's Coll., Cambridge.
Farming 33-39, 47-; army service 39-45; Territorial Army 49-60; Territorial mem. of N.Z. Army Board 60-; M.P. for Hastings 60-; Minister of Lands, Minister of Forests, Minister in Charge of the Valuation Dept. 66-72, of Maori and Island Affairs 69-72, of the Environment Feb.-Dec. 72, of Agriculture and Fisheries, of Maori Affairs, in Charge of the Rural Banking and Finance Corpn. Dec. 75-; National Party.
Parliament Buildings, Wellington, New Zealand.

McIntyre, Sir Laurence Rupert, Kt., C.B.E., M.A.; Australian specialist in international affairs and fmr. diplomatist; b. 22 June 1912; ed. Tasmania Univ. and Exeter Coll., Oxford.
Served in London 36, Canberra 40, Washington 42, Canberra (Head of Pacific Div.) 47, Singapore 50, Canberra (Asst. Sec.) 51, Singapore (Commr.) 52, London (Minister) 54; Amb. to Indonesia 57-60, to Japan 60-65; Deputy Sec. of External Affairs 65-70; Perm. Rep. to UN 70-75; Dir. Australian Inst. of Int. Affairs 75-.
Australian Institute of International Affairs, Box E 181, Post Office, Canberra, A.C.T. 2600; 44 Dominion Circuit, A.C.T. 2603, Australia.

McKay, Donald Norman; New Zealand politician; b. 1908; ed. Whangarei High School, Auckland Univ. Coll.
Led N.Z. del. to first Commonwealth Medical Conf., Edinburgh 65; M.P. for Marsden 54-72; Minister of Health, Minister of Social Security, Minister in Charge of the Child Welfare Div., Minister for the Welfare of Women and Children 62-72; Chair. Northland Harbour Board 74-; National Party.
Rosyth Road, Waipu, New Zealand.

Mackay, Ian Keith, C.M.G.; New Zealand broadcasting executive; b. 19 Oct. 1909; ed. Nelson Coll., New Zealand.
Broadcasting Station Man., New Zealand 39-43; Senior Exec., Commercial Div., New Zealand Broadcasting Comm. 44-50; Production Man., Macquarie Network, Australia 50-61; Dir.-Gen. Nigerian Broadcasting Corpn. 61-64, Adviser Board of Govs. 64-65; Public Relations Officer, Dept. of Information, Papua New Guinea 66-67, Broadcasts Supervisor (Management) 68-73; Asst. to Chair. Papua New Guinea Broadcasting Comm. 73-75, Consultant 75-; mem. Royal Soc. of Literature, Soc. of Authors.
Publs. *Broadcasting in New Zealand* 53, *Broadcasting in Australia* 57, *Macquarie—the Story of a Network* 60, *Broadcasting in Nigeria* 64, *Broadcasting in Papua New Guinea* 76, *Presenting Papua and New Guinea* (compiler), *Directory of Papua and New Guinea* (compiler), and other articles on broadcasting.
405A Main Road, Karori, Wellington, New Zealand.

Mackay, Malcolm George, PH.D; Australian politician; b. 29 Dec. 1919, Brighton, S. Australia; ed. Univs. of Adelaide, Melbourne and Edinburgh.
Served R.A.N.V.R. 41-44; fmr. Gen. Sec. Australian Council, World Council of Churches (WCC); Minister of Scots Church in Sydney 56-59; Master of Basser Coll., Univ. of N.S.W. 59-63; mem. Parl. for Evans (N.S.W.) 63-; Minister for the Navy 71-72; Liberal.
Parliament House, Canberra, A.C.T., Australia.

McKenzie, Lyndon L.; Australian airline executive; b. Cowell, S. Australia; ed. accountancy.
Served R.A.A.F., rose to rank of Flight Lieut. 40-46; joined Trans-Australia Airlines (TAA) 46; posts in finance, admin. and airport management depts. 46-55; Man. for Victoria, subsequently for Queensland 55-57; Commercial Dir. 57-71; Asst. Gen. Man. 71-73, Acting Gen. Man. Oct. 73, Gen. Man. Oct. 73-.
Trans-Australia Airlines, 50 Franklin Street, Melbourne 3000, Australia.

MacLehose, Sir (Crawford) Murray, K.C.M.G., K.C.V.O., M.B.E.; British diplomatist and administrator; b. 16 Oct. 1917, Glasgow; ed. Rugby School and Balliol Coll., Oxford.
Served with R.N.V.R. 39-45; entered diplomatic service 47; Acting Consul, Hankow 47, Acting Consul-Gen. 48; Foreign Office 50; First Sec., Prague 51; seconded to Commonwealth Relations Office for service in Wellington 54; returned to Foreign Office and transferred to Paris 56; Counsellor 59; Political Adviser, Hong Kong; Counsellor, Foreign Office 63; Principal Private Sec. to Sec. of State 65-67; Amb. to Repub. of Viet-Nam 67-69, to Denmark 69-71; Gov. of Hong Kong 71-.
Government House, Hong Kong; Beoch, Maybole, Ayrshire, Scotland.

McLennan, Sir Ian Munro, K.B.E., B.E.E.; Australian engineer; b. 30 Nov. 1909; ed. Scotch Coll., Melbourne and Melbourne Univ.
Assistant Gen. Man. Broken Hill Pty. Co. Ltd. 47-50, Gen. Man. 50-56, Dir. 53-, Senior Gen. Man. 56-59, Chief Gen. Man. 59-67, Man. Dir. 67-71, Chair. and Dir. of Admin. 71-; Chair. Joint War Production Cttee. 56-69, Defence Industrial Cttee. 69-; Councillor, Australian Mineral Devt. Laboratories (Chair. 59-67), Australian Inst. of Mining and Metallurgy (Pres. 51, 57, 72); Chair. BHP-GKN Holdings Ltd. 70-, Tubemakers of Australia Ltd. 73-; mem. Int. Council, Morgan Guarantee Trust Co. of N.Y. 73-; Dir. ICI Australia Ltd. 76-; mem., Deputy Chair. Immigration Planning Council 49-67; Australasian Inst. of Mining and Metallurgy Medal 59, Inst. of Production Engineers' James

N. Kirby Award 64, Australian Inst. of Engineers Medal 68. Office: 140 William Street, Melbourne; Home: Apartment 3, 112 Walsh Street, South Yarra 3141, Victoria, Australia. Telephone: 60-0701 (Office); 263651 (Home).

McMahon, Rt. Hon. William, P.C., C.H., LL.B., B.ECONS., Australian lawyer and politician; b. 23 Feb. 1908; ed. Sydney Univ.
Practised as solicitor until 39; served 39-45 war; mem. House of Reps. 49-; Minister for Navy and Air 51-54, for Social Services 54-56, for Primary Industry 56-58, for Labour and Nat. Service 58-66, Treas. 66-69; Acting Minister for Trade 56 (in charge C.S.I.R.O. 56), for Labour and Nat. Service 57, Nat. Devt. 59; Acting Attorney-Gen. 60, 61; Acting Minister for Territories 62; Vice-Pres. Executive Council 64-66; Deputy Leader Liberal Party 66-71, Leader 71-72; Minister for Foreign Affairs 69-71; Prime Minister 71-72; Leader Australian Del. Commonwealth Parl. Conf. New Delhi 57; Pres. ILO Regional Conf., Melbourne 62; Gov. Asian Devt. Bank 68-69, Chair. 68-69.
Parliament House, Canberra, A.C.T.; and Westfield Tower, 100 William Street, Sydney, N.S.W. 2010, Australia.
Telephone: 731023 (Canberra); 358-1433 (Sydney).

McMullin, Sir Alister Maxwell, K.C.M.G.; Australian politician; b. 14 July 1900.
Member of the Senate 51-71, Pres. 53-71; Chair. Gen. Council of Commonwealth Parl. Asscn. 59-60, 69-; Deputy Chair. Nat. Library of Australia; Chair. Parl. Library Cttee., Parl. Joint Select Cttee. on new and permanent Parliament House, Australian Advisory Council on Bibliographical Services; Chancellor Univ. of Newcastle, N.S.W.; mem. Liberal Party.
St. Aubin's, Scone, N.S.W. 2337, Australia.
Telephone: Scone 153.

McNeill, James Charles, C.B.E., F.A.S.A., F.A.I.M.; Australian accountant and business executive; b. 29 July 1916, Hamilton, N.S.W.; ed. Newcastle High School, N.S.W.
Accountant, The Broken Hill Pty. Co. Ltd. 47-54, Asst. Sec. 54-56, Asst. Gen. Man. (Commercial) 56-59, Gen. Man. (Commercial) 59-67, Exec. Gen. Man. (Finance) 67-71, Man. Dir. April 71-; Chair. Queensland Coal Mining Co. Ltd.; Pres. Dir. PT BHP Indonesia; Man. Dir. Australian Iron and Steel Pty. Ltd., Australian Wire Industries Pty. Ltd., Dampier Mining Co. Ltd., Groote Eylandt Mining Co. Ltd., Hermatite Petroleum Pty. Ltd., Tasmanian Electro Metallurgical Co. Ltd.; Dir. BHP-GKN Holdings Ltd. BHP Nominees Pty. Ltd., Hematite Petroleum (N.Z.) Ltd., Mount Newman Mining Co. Pty. Ltd.; Pres. Australian Mining Industry Council; mem. Mfg. Industries Advisory Council, Monash Univ. Council.
The Broken Hill Proprietary Co. Ltd., BHP House, 140 William Street, Melbourne 3000; 104 Mont Albert Road, Canterbury, Victoria, Australia.
Telephone: 600701 (Melbourne).

McNicol, David Williamson, C.B.E.; Australian diplomatist; b. 20 June 1913; ed. Carey Grammar School, Melbourne Kings Coll., Adelaide and Adelaide Univ.
Pilot, R.A.A.F. 40-45; Minister to Cambodia, Laos and Viet-Nam 55-56, Commr. to Singapore 58-60, High Commr. in Pakistan 62-65, in New Zealand 65-68; Amb. to Thailand and Rep. to SEATO 68-69; High Commr. in Canada 69-73; Deputy High Commr. in U.K. 73-75; Amb. to South Africa and High Commr. in Lesotho, Botswana and Swaziland 75-.
Australian Embassy, P.O. Box 4749, Cape Town 8000, South Africa.

Madan, Bal Krishna, PH.D.; Indian banker and economist; b. 13 July 1911; ed. Univ. of Punjab, Lahore.
Lecturer in Econs., Univ. of Punjab 36-37; Officer for Enquiry into Resources, Punjab Govt. 37-38; mem. Punjab Board for Econ. Enquiry 38-40, Sec. 38; Econ. Adviser to Punjab Govt. 40-41; Dir. of Research, Reserve Bank of India, Bombay 41-45, Econ. Adviser 50, Principal Adviser 57, Exec. Dir. 59, Deputy Gov. 64-67; Sec. Indian del. to Bretton Woods 44; Deputy Sec. Indian Tariff Board 45; mem. Indian Legislative Assembly and Assembly Cttee. on Bretton Woods Agreement 46; Alt. Exec. Dir. IMF 46-48, IBRD 47-48, Exec. Dir. IMF 48-50, 67-71; mem. Indian del., First Commonwealth Finance Ministers' Conf. London 49; adviser Indian del. to UN ECOSOC 49; mem. UN Cttee. on Domestic Financing of Econ. Devt. 49; mem. Finance Comm., Indian Govt. 52; mem. Taxation Enquiry Comm. 53-54; mem. Experts Group on UN Special Fund for Econ. Devt. 55; mem. Governing Body Indian Investment Centre 60-67. Board of Dirs., Industrial Finance Corpn. 62-64, Life Insurance Corpn. of India 64-66, Board of Trustees, Unit Trust of India 64, Nat. Council of Applied Econ. Research 74-, Risk Capital Foundation, New Delhi 75-, Nat. Inst. of Public Finance and Policy 76-; Pres. Indian Econ. Asscn. 61; Vice-Chair. Industrial Devt. Bank of India 64-67; Chair. Bonus Review Cttee., Govt. of India 72-74; Chair. Management Devt. Inst. 72-.
Publs. *India and Imperial Preference—A Study in Commercial Policy* 39, *Aspects of Economic Development and Policy* 64.
A-21, Palam Marg, Vasant Vihar, New Delhi 110 057, India.
Telephone: 670991, 670224.

Madgwick, Sir Robert Bowden, O.B.E., M.EC., D.PHIL. F.A.C.E.; Australian cultural administrator; b. 10 May 1905, North Sydney, N.S.W.; ed. N. Sydney Boys' High School, Univ. of Sydney and Balliol Coll., Oxford.
Lecturer in Econ. History, Univ. of Sydney 36-40, Sec. of Extension Board 37; Dir. Australian Army Educ. 41-46; Warden, New England Univ. Coll. 47-54; Vice-Chancellor, Univ. of New England 54-66; Chair. Australian Broadcasting Comm. 67-73; Chair. N.S.W. Advisory Cttee. on Cultural Grants 68-, Australian Frontier 74-; Chair. Board of Dirs., Nat. Inst. of Dramatic Art 68-72; Hon. D.Litt. (Sydney, Newcastle (N.S.W.), New England); Hon. LL.D. (Queensland).
Publs. *Immigration into Eastern Australia 1788–1851, Outline of Australian Economics* (with E. R. Walker).
3 Collins Road, St. Ives, N.S.W. 2000, Australia.

Madia, Chunilal Kalidas; Indian writer; b. 12 Aug. 1922; ed. Bhagwatsinjhi High School, Dhoraji, Gujarat, and H.L. Coll. of Commerce, Ahmedabad.
Writes mainly in Gujarati; Editorial Staff *Prabhat* and *Navsaurashtra* 42-44; Editor *Varta* (short story monthly) 43; Editorial Staff, Janmabhoomi Group of Newspapers, Bombay 45-50; Language Editor, U.S. Information Service, Bombay 50-62; now Editor *Ruchi* (literary and cultural magazine); Literary Editor *Sandesh* (Gujarati daily); Narmad Gold Medal for Best Play Writing 51; Ranajitram Gold Medal for Outstanding Creative Writing 57, numerous other prizes; del. Int. PEN Congress Ivory Coast 67.
Publs. (in Gujarati): novels: *Vyajano Varas, Velavelani Chhanyadi, Liludi Dharati, Kumkum Ane Ashaka;* short stories: *Ghooghavatan Pur, Padmaja, Champo Ane Kel, Tej Ane Timie, Roop-Aroop, Antasrota;* plays; *Rangada, Vishavimochan, Raktatilak, Shoonyashesh;* poems: *Sonnet* (collected sonnets); criticism: *Granthagarima, Shahamrig, Suvarnamrig;* in Malayalam: *Gujarati Kathakal.*
B-213, Chandralok, Manav Mandir Road, Malabar Hill, Bombay 6, India.
Telephone: 36-8245.

Madigan, Russel Tullie, O.B.E., LL.B.; Australian business executive; b. 22 Nov. 1920; ed. Univ. of Adelaide.
Joined Zinc Corpn. 46; travelling scholarship in Canada and U.S.A. 47-49, Underground Man. Zinc Corpn. Ltd.,

NBHC Ltd. 56-59; Gen. Man., Gen. Mining Div., Conzinc Riotinto Australia Ltd. 60-64, Dir. 68-; Man. Dir. Hamersley Iron 65-71, Chair. 71-; Chair. Blair Athol Coal Pty. Ltd. 71-, IOL Petroleum Ltd. 72-, Hamersley Holdings, Atlas Steels (Australia) Pty. Ltd. 76-; Dir. Rio Tinto Zinc Corpn. Ltd. 71-, Rio Tinto Zinc (Japan) Ltd., Commercial Union Assurance Co. 69-, Australian Mines and Metals Asscn. 71-; mem. Australia-Japan Business Cooperation Cttee., Pacific Basin Econ. Council, Trade Devt. Council; Fellow, S. Australian School of Mines.
Hamersley Holdings, 95 Collins Street, Melbourne, Victoria; Home: 60 Broadway, East Camberwell, Victoria, Australia.

Maeda, Shichinoshin; Japanese business executive; b. 1901; ed. Tokyo Univ.
President, Fuji Electric Co. Ltd. until 74, Chair. Nov. 74-.
Fuji Electric Co. Ltd., 1-1, Tanabeshinden, Kawasaki City, Kanagawa Prefecture, Japan.

Maegraith, Brian Gilmore, C.M.G., T.D., M.B., B.S., F.R.C.P. (L. & E.), F.R.A.C.P., B.SC., M.A., D.PHIL.; Australian professor of tropical medicine; b. 26 Aug. 1907; ed. St. Peter's and St. Mark's Colls., Univ. of Adelaide, Magdalen and Exeter Coll., Univ. of Oxford, Rhodes scholar.
Medical Fellow and Tutor in Physiology, Exeter Coll., Oxford 34-40; Univ. Lecturer and Demonstrator in Pathology, Oxford 37-44, Dean of Medical School 38-44; Lieut.-Col. R.A.M.C., O.C. Malaria Research Unit, War Office 39-45; mem. Medical Research Council Malaria Cttee. 43-46; Tropical Medicine Research Board (Medical Research Council) 59-69, Council Royal Society of Tropical Medicine 47-51 (Vice-Pres. 49-51, 57-59, Pres. 69-71); Dean, Liverpool School of Tropical Medicine 44-75, Prof. Tropical Medicine 44-72, Emer. 72-; Hon. Consulting Physician in Tropical Medicine, Royal Infirmary, Liverpool; Nuffield Consultant in Tropical Medicine, West Africa 49; Consultant, Faculty of Tropical Medicine, Bangkok 59-, and S.E. Asian Int. Centre for Tropical Medicine (SEAMES) 65-72; Chair. Council of European Insts. of Tropical Medicine 69-72, Pres. and Life mem. 75-; Hon. mem. Belgian, American, German and Canadian Socs. of Tropical Medicine; Chalmers Gold Medal, Royal Soc. of Tropical Medicine 51, Le Prince Medal, American Soc. of Tropical Medicine 55, Bernhard Nocht Medal (Hamburg) 57, Mary Kingsley Medal (Liverpool School of Tropical Medicine) 73; Hon. D.Sc. (Bangkok), Hon. M.D. (Athens) 72.
Publs. *Pathological Processes in Malaria* 48, *Clinical Tropical Diseases* (sixth edn.) 76, *Tropical Medicine for Nurses* (fourth edn.) 75, *Clinical Methods in Tropical Medicine* 62, *Exotic Diseases in Practice* 65.
School of Tropical Medicine, Pembroke Place, Liverpool 3, and 23 Eaton Road, Cressington Park, Liverpool 19, England.
Telephone: 051-427-1133.

Maekawa, Kunio, B.ENG.; Japanese architect; b. 14 May 1905; ed. Tokyo Imperial Univ.
Worked in Le Corbusier's office, Paris 28-30, Antonin Raymond's office, Tokyo 30-35; Pres., Kunio Maekawa Architect's Office 35-; Pres. Japan Architects Asscn. 59-62; mem. Japanese Del., Exec. Cttee. of Int. Union of Architects 59-69; numerous prizes and decorations.
Buildings include: Taiyo Bank (Nihon Sogo Bank) 52, Kanagawa Prefectural Library and Concert Hall 54, Japanese Pavilion, Brussels World Fair 58, Kyoto Cultural Centre 59, Gakushuin Univ. 60, Tokyo Metropolitan Festival Hall 61, Saitama Cultural Centre 66, Saitama Prefectural Museum 71.
Office: 8 Honshio-cho, Shinjuku-ku, Tokyo; Home: Kami-Osaki 3-10-59, Shinagawa-ku, Tokyo, Japan.
Telephone: Tokyo 351-7101 (Office).

Maeo, Shigesaburo; Japanese politician; b. 10 Dec. 1905; ed. Faculty of Law, Tokyo Imperial Univ.
Former Dir. of Taxation Bureau, Pres. Mint Agency of Finance Ministry, Minister of Int. Trade and Industry, Vice-Chair. Policy Affairs Research Council of Liberal Party, Chair. Local Admin. Cttee., Chair. Foreign Affairs Cttee., House of Reps.; mem. House of Reps.; fmr. Sec.-Gen. Liberal-Democratic Party; Minister of State, Dir.-Gen. Hokkaido Devt. Agency; Minister of Justice 71-72; Speaker House of Reps. 73-74.
Publs. *Zei no zuihitsu shu* (Essays on Taxation), *Seijika no saijiki* (Memoirs of a Statesman), *Seijika no tsurezuregusa* (Gleanings from my Leisure Hours as a Statesman), *Shin Keizai Seichoron to shin heiwashugi* (The New Economic Growth Doctrine and the New Pacifism), *Matsurigoto no Kokoro* (The Essence of Politics).
1-10-22, Shoto, Shibuya-ki, Tokyo, Japan.
Telephone: 467-7597.

Mafatlal, Arvind N.; Indian industrialist; b. 27 Oct. 1923, Ahmedabad; ed. St. Xavier's High School and Sydenham Coll. of Commerce and Econs., Bombay.
Chairman Mafatlal Group of Cos., Nat. Organic Chem. Industries Ltd., Polyolefins Industries Ltd., Hoechst Dyes and Chemicals Ltd., Nat. Machinery Mfrs. Ltd.; Dir. Tata Engineering and Locomotive Co. Ltd., Bombay Burmah Trading Corpn. Ltd., Industrial Investment Trust Ltd. and others; Trustee Bharatiya Agro-Industries Foundation, Uruli Kanchan; Chair. and Man. Trustee, Shri Sadguru Seva Singh Trust; employers' del. to 43rd ILO Conf.; mem. Maharashtra and Gujarat State Advisory Councils of Industries; Chair. Western Regional Cttee. of All-India Council of Tech. Educ.; Durga Prasad Khaitan Memorial Gold Medal 66, Business Leadership Award (Madras Man. Asscn.) 71.
Mafatlal House, Backbay Reclamation, Bombay 400 020; and 10 Altamount Road, Bombay 400 026, India.
Telephone: 29-11-99 (Office).

Mahathir bin Mohamed, Dr.; Malaysian politician; b. 20 Dec. 1925, Alor Star; ed. Sultan Abdul Hamid Coll. and Univ. of Malaya in Singapore.
Medical Officer, Kedah and Perlis 53-57; private practice 57-64; mem. UMNO to 69, 72-, mem. Supreme Council 72-; mem. House of Reps. for Kota Star Selatan 64-69, for Kubang Pasu 74-; mem. Senate 73; Chair. Food Industries of Malaysia Sdn. Bhd. 73; Minister of Educ. 74-; Deputy Prime Minister March 76-.
Publ. *The Malay Dilemma* 69.
Office of the Deputy Prime Minister, Kuala Lumpur, Malaysia.

Mahindra, Keshub, B.SC.; Indian business executive; b. 9 Oct. 1923, Simla; ed. Univ. of Pennsylvania, U.S.A.
President, Asscn. of Indian Automobile Mfrs. 64-65, Bombay Chamber of Commerce and Industry 66-67, Assoc. Chamber of Commerce and Industry 69-70, Maharashtra Econ. Devt. Council 69-70; Chair. Indian Council of Trade Fairs and Exhbns. 64-69, Indian Soc. of Advertisers 68-71; Chair. Mahindra and Mahindra Ltd., Union Carbide India Ltd., Remington Rand of India Ltd., Indian Aluminium Co. Ltd., Housing and Urban Devt. Corpn. Ltd., Int. Tractor Co. of India Ltd., Otis Elevator Co. (India) Ltd., Vickers Sperry of India Ltd., Machinery Mfrs. Corpn. Ltd.; Chair. Board of Govs., Indian Inst. of Management, Ahmedabad; dir. several cos.
Mahindra and Mahindra Ltd., Gateway Building, Apollo Bunder, Bombay 1; Home: St. Helen's Court, Pedder Road, Bombay 26, India.

Mahmud Husain, Abul Basher; Bangladesh judge; b. 1 Feb. 1916; ed. Shaistagonj High School, M.C. Coll., Sylhet, Dacca Univ.

Pleader, Judge's Court, Dacca 40-42; Additional Govt. Pleader, Habiganj 43-48; Advocate, Dacca High Court Bar 48-51; Attorney, Fed. Court of Pakistan 51-53, Advocate 53-58; Senior Advocate of Supreme Court of Pakistan 58-65; Asst. Govt. Pleader, High Court of East Pakistan 52-56, Senior Govt. Pleader and later acting Advocate-Gen. of East Pakistan 56-65; Judge, High Court of East Pakistan 65-72, of Bangladesh 72, of Appellate Div. of High Court 72, of Appellate Div. of Supreme Court 72-75; Chief Justice Nov. 75-; Councillor, Assam Provincial Muslim League 44-47, All-India Muslim League 45-47, All-Pakistan Muslim League 47-55; mem. Constituent Assembly of Pakistan 49-54, Commonwealth Parl. Assen. 50-54, Interparl. Union 50-54, Pakistan Tea Board 51-54, Exec. Council of Dacca Univ. 52-54, Bar Council of Dacca High Court 58-66.
Chief Justice's House, 19 Hare Road, Dacca 2, Bangladesh.
Telephone: 243334 and 281849.

Mahtab, Harekrushna, D.LITT., LL.D.; Indian politician and journalist; b. Nov. 1899; ed. Ravenshaw Coll., Cuttack.
Joined non-co-operation movement 21; worker for Indian Nat. Congress 21-; mem. Bihar & Orissa Legislative Council 24; Editor, *Prajatantra* and *Jhankar*; civil disobedience movements 30, 32; Pres. Utkal Provincial Congress Cttee. 30, 37; organized Inchudi Salt Satyagraha, imprisoned 30-31, 32, 42; mem. Congress Working Cttee. 38-46; Leader, Congress Assembly Party, Orissa; Chief Minister, Orissa State 46-50, 56-61; Minister for Commerce and Industry, Govt. of India 50-52; Sec.-Gen. Congress Parl. Party 52-55, Deputy Leader 62-63; Gov. of Bombay 55-56; mem. Lok Sabha 62-67, Orissa Legislative Assembly 67-.
Publs. *History of Orissa*; three novels, one play.
Ekrama Nivas, Bhuvaneshwar-2, Orissa, India.
Telephone: 51946.

Maiden, Alfred Clement Borthwick, B.A., C.B.E.; Australian business executive; b. 21 Aug. 1922; ed. Taree High School, New England Univ. Coll., Univ. of Sydney.
Agricultural Attaché, Washington, D.C. 51-53; Asst. Dir. Bureau of Agricultural Econs. 53-56, Dir. 59-62; Asst. Sec. Dept. of Trade 56-57; Commercial Counsellor, Washington, D.C. 57-59; Sec. Dept. of Primary Industry 62-68; Man Dir. Int. Wool Secr. 69-73; Chair. Australian Wool Corpn. 73-.
Australian Wool Corporation, Wool House, 578 Bourke Street, Melbourne 3000, Australia.

Maiti, Abha, B.A., LL.B.; Indian social worker and politician; b. 23 May 1925; ed. Univ. Law Coll., Calcutta.
Joined Quit India Movement 42; Sec. Women's subcttee. of West Bengal Pradesh Congress 48-54; mem. West Bengal Pradesh Congress Cttee. 54-59; Pres. Midnapore Congress Cttee. 59; mem. West Bengal Legislative Ass. 52-57; mem. All India Congress Cttee. 52-, Congress Working Cttee. 60-, Gen. Sec. Indian Nat. Congress 60-64; fmr. mem. Rajya Sabha; Joint Sec. Paschim Banga Khadi Kendra 57-; Minister of Refugee Relief and Rehabilitation, Relief and Social Welfare and Home (Constitution and Elections) for West Bengal 62-69.
P-14 Durga Charran Mitra Street, Calcutta 6, West Bengal; and 97 South Avenue, New Delhi, India.

Majid, Abdul, PH.D.; Afghan diplomatist and politician; b. 14 July 1914; ed. Cornell Univ. and Univ. of California, U.S.A.
Member Afghan Inst. of Bacteriology 41, Dir. 41-42; Prof. of Biology and Physiology, Kabul Univ. 40-46, Pres. of Univ. 46-48; Minister of Public Health 48-50; Minister of Education 50-56; Amb. to Japan 56-63, to U.S.A. 63-67, to U.K. 67-70; Minister of Justice and Attorney-Gen. 73-; Leader of Afghan del. to UN 66; Order of Educ. First Class 56, Sardar-i Ali 59, A. Haas Award (Univ. of Calif.) 66.
Ministry of Justice, Kabul, Afghanistan.

Maki, Fumihiko, B.ARCH., M.ARCH.; Japanese architect; b. 6 Sept. 1928; ed. Univ. of Tokyo, Cranbrook School of Art, Mich. and Harvard Univ.
Associate Prof. Washington Univ. 56-62, Harvard Univ. 62-66; Lecturer, Dept. of Urban Engineering, Univ. of Tokyo 64-; Principal Partner, Maki and Associates (architectural firm) 64-; Visiting Lecturer and Critic to various univs. and insts. in Canada and U.S. 60-; awards include Gold Medal of Japan Inst. of Architects 64; major works include Steinberg Hall, Washington Univ. 60, Toyoda Memorial Hall, Nagoya Univ. 60, Lecture Hall, Chiba Univ. 64, and Rissho Univ. Campus 66-; art award from Mainichi Press 69.
Publs. *Investigations in Collective Form* 64, *Movement Systems in the City* 65, *Metabolism* 60, *Structure in Art and Science* (contrib.) 65.
16-22, 5-chome Higashi-Gotanda, Shinagawa-ku, Tokyo, Japan.

Makita, Hisao, B.A.; Japanese industrialist; b. 13 Dec. 1909, Saga Pref.; ed. Tokyo Univ. of Commerce.
Joined Nippon Kokan K.K. 34, Dir. 57, Man. Dir. 65, Senior Man. Dir. 67, Exec. Vice-Pres. 68, Pres. 71-; Pres. Kokan Mining Co. (subsidiary of Nippon Kokan) Nov. 61-June 66; Dir. Int. Iron and Steel Inst.; Exec. Dir. and Industrial Relations Conf. Chair., The Japan Iron and Steel Fed.; Vice-Chair. The Japan Iron and Steel Exporters Assen.; Man. Dir. The Shipbuilders' Assen. of Japan; Dir. Fed. of Econ. Orgs. (Keidanren); Trustee, Japan Cttee. for Econ. Devt. (Keizai Doyukai); Exec. Dir. Japan Fed. of Employers' Assens.
Nippon Kokan K.K., 1-1-2, Marunouchi, Chiyodaku, Tokyo; Home: 2-4-1, Omiya, Suginami-ku, Tokyo 166, Japan.
Telephone: 03-311-0298.

Malakul, Mom Luang Peekdhip; Thai diplomatist; b. 1906; ed. Debsirindr School and Assumption Coll., Bangkok, the Inner Temple, London.
Attached to Office of Royal Households 32, to Protocol Div., Ministry of Foreign Affairs 35, Chief of Section 39, Chief of Div. 42; Sec., Rangoon 49, Chargé d'Affaires 50; Dir. Gen. Dept. of Econ. Affairs, Ministry of Foreign Affairs 53, Dir. Gen. Protocol Dept. 54; Deputy Under-Sec. of State for Foreign Affairs 57, Under-Sec. 57; Amb. to United Kingdom 58-62, to Pakistan 64-74; rep. of Ministry of Foreign Affairs, Thai Special Goodwill Mission to British Commonwealth in Far East 40; del. Franco-Thai Peace Convention, Tokyo 41, Official Mission to Tokyo 43; Deputy Chief Del. Burma Independence Celebrations 47; Knight Grand Cross of the Orders of the Crown of Thailand and White Elephant; Knight Grand Cross of Royal Victorian Order, Grand Officer Orders of Million Elephants and White Parasol, Hon. C.B.E. (U.K.), Spanish, Netherlands, Danish, Italian, Federal German, French, Belgian and Greek decorations.
c/o Ministry of Foreign Affairs, Bangkok, Thailand.

Malietoa Tanumafili II, H.H., C.B.E.; Samoan politician. b. 4 Jan. 1913; ed. Wesley Coll., Auckland, New Zealand; Adviser, Samoan Govt. 40; mem. New Zealand del. to UN 58; fmr. mem. Council of State; Joint Head of State of Western Samoa 61-63, Sole Head 63-; Fautua of Maliena.
Government House, Vailima, Apia, Western Samoa, South Pacific.

Malik, Abdul Mutaleb, M.D.; Pakistani physician and politician; b. 1905; ed. Calcutta Univ., Santiniketan, Bengal and Vienna Univ.
Practised medicine in Calcutta; joined All-India Muslim

League 36; former mem. Executive of All-India Trades Union Congress, Sec. of All-India Seafarers' Fed., Pres. Indian Quartermasters' Union and Indian Sailors' Union, Calcutta; Pres. of All-Pakistan Trades Union Fed. 47; former Minister of Agriculture, Co-operation, Forests, Fisheries and Labour, East Bengal; Minister in charge of Minorities Affairs 50-51; Minister of Labour and Works and Health 49-55; Chair. of Governing Body of ILO 53-54; Amb. to Switzerland 55-58, to Chinese People's Repub. 58-61, to Philippines 61-65; High Commr. in Australia 65-67; Minister of Health, Labour, Social Welfare and Family Planning 70-71; Gov. of East Pakistan (now Bangladesh) 71; arrested Dec. 71, sentenced to life imprisonment Nov. 72, released Dec. 73.
Rawalpindi, Pakistan.

Malik, Adam; Indonesian politician and diplomatist; b. 22 July 1917, Pematang Siantar, N. Sumatra; ed. Dutch primary school and a religious school.
Chairman, Partai Indonesia in Pematang Siantar and Medan, N. Sumatra 34; founded *Antara* Press Bureau (later *Antara* News Agency), Java 37; mem. Exec. Board Gerindo Party 40-41; later mem. Persatuan Perdjoeangan (Struggle Front) (a movt. to maintain independence); a founder of Partai Rakjat (People's Party) 46; Exec. mem. Murba Party 48-64 (when party was banned); elected to House of Reps. 56, mem. Provisional Supreme Advisory Council 59; Amb. to U.S.S.R. and Poland 59-62; mem. Exec. Board *Antara* 62; Minister of Commerce 63-65; Minister-Co-ordinator for the Implementation of Guided Economy 65; Minister of Foreign Affairs March 66-; Pres. UN Gen. Assembly 71-72; rep. of Indonesia at various int. confs. and has led Indonesian del. to sessions of UN Gen. Assembly since 66.
Ministry of Foreign Affairs, Jalan Sisinganangara 73, Kebayoran Baru, Jakarta; Jalan Diponegoro 17, Jakarta, Indonesia.

Malik, Bidhubhusan, M.A., LL.D., Barrister-at-Law; Indian lawyer; b. 11 Jan. 1895.
Advocate, Allahabad High Court 19; called to Bar, Lincoln's Inn 23; mem. Judicial Cttee. Banaras State 41-44; Special Counsel, Income Tax Dept. 43-44; Puisne Judge, High Court, Allahabad 44-47, Chief Justice High Court of Uttar Pradesh, Allahabad Dec. 47-Jan. 55 (acting Gov. U.P. March-April 49); Indian Rep. to Fed. of Malaya Constitutional Comm. 56-57; mem. Indian Airlines Corpn. 55-62; Commr. for Linguistic Minorities 57-62; Senior Advocate, Supreme Court of India; UN Constitutional Adviser for Congo 62; Constitutional Adviser, Kenya Conf., London 62; Adviser to Mauritius Govt. at Mauritius Conf. 65; Vice-Chancellor, Calcutta Univ. 62-68; Vice-Pres. Vishwa Hindu Dharm Sammelan; mem. Calcutta Univ. Senate, Exec. Council of Allahabad Univ. 71; Pres. Ishwar Saran Degree Coll., Allahabad; Pres. Jagat Saran Girls' Degree Coll.; Dir. Swadeshi Cotton Mills, Kanpur.
Publs. books on various branches of law.
23 Muir Road, Allahabad 1, India.

Malik, Gunwantsingh Jaswantsingh, B.SC., M.A.; Indian diplomatist; b. 29 May 1921, Karachi, Pakistan; ed. Bombay and Cambridge Univs.
Physicist, British Industrial Plastics 41-42; Tech. Officer R.A.F. 43-46; Indian Foreign Service 47-; Second Sec. Indian Embassy Belgium 48-50; in Ethiopia 50; Under-Sec. Ministry of External Affairs 50-52; First Sec. and Chargé d'Affaires Argentina 52-56; in Japan 56-59; Commercial Counsellor and Asst. Commr. Singapore 59-63; Dir. Ministry of Commerce 63-64; Joint Sec. Ministry of External Affairs 64-65; Amb. to the Philippines 65-68, to Senegal, concurrently to the Gambia, the Ivory Coast, Mauritania and Upper Volta 68-70, to Chile, concurrently to Ecuador, Colombia and Peru 70-74, to Thailand 74-; leader trade del. to S. America 64; mem. del. to ECAFE 65, to Group of 77 in Lima 71, to Gov. Body of UNDP 71, to UNCTAD III 72, to ESCAP 75; Chair. Tech. and Drafting Cttee., ESCAP 76.
Embassy of India, 139 Pan Road, Bangkok, Thailand; 21A Nizamuddin West, New Delhi, India.
Telephone: 35062 (Bangkok); 619785 (New Delhi).

Malikyar, Abdullah; Afghan diplomatist; b. 16 April 1909; ed. Istiklal Coll., Kabul, and Franco-Persian Coll., Teheran.
Secretary and Gen. Dir. Prime Minister's Office 31-35; Head, Govt. Purchasing Office, Europe 36-40; Vice-Pres. Central Bank and Deputy Minister of Commerce 41-42; Gov. of Herat 42-47, 51-52; Minister of Communications 48-50; Pres. Helmand Valley Authority Projects 53-62; Minister of Commerce 55-57, of Finance 57-June 64, Deputy Prime Minister 63-Feb. 64; Amb. to U.K. 64-67, to U.S.A. 67-, also accred. to Argentina, Brazil, Canada, Chile and Mexico; Sardar Ali and Reshteen Decoration.
Embassy of Afghanistan, 2341 Wyoming Avenue, N.W., Washington, D.C., U.S.A.

Mandloi, Bhagwantrao Annabhau, B.A., LL.B.; Indian politician; b. 15 Dec. 1892; ed. Govt. Coll., Jabalpur, and Univ. School of Allahabad.
Lawyer, Khandwa; Pres. Municipal Cttee., Khandwa (15 years); mem. Legislative Assembly of Cen. Provinces and Berar 35-37, of Madhya Pradesh 37-; imprisoned for political activities 40, 42; mem. Constituent Assembly and Parl.; Chief Whip, Madhya Pradesh Assembly Party; mem. Congress Parl. Board 51-52; Minister for Revenue, Survey and Settlement, Land Records, Land Reforms and Local Self Govt., Madhya Pradesh, later for Revenue and Educ. 52-56; Minister for Revenue and Local Govt. 56-61, for Revenue and Industries 61-62; Chief Minister, Madhya Pradesh 62-August 63; Pres. Madhya Pradesh Congress Cttee. Nov. 63-; Padma-Bhushan Award 70.
Ramkrishna Mandloi Road, Khandwa, Madhya Pradesh, India.

Manekshaw, Field Marshal Sam Hormuzji Franji Jamshedji, M.C.; Indian army officer; b. 3 April 1914, Amritsar; ed. Sherwood Coll., Nainital, Indian Military Acad., Dehra Dun and Imperial Defence Coll.
Commissioned 34; took part in Burma campaign, Second World War, wounded; later attended Staff Coll., Quetta; later returned to Burma campaign; Staff Officer, Indo-China 45; lecture tour, Australia 46; Staff Officer, Grade I, Mil. Operations Directorate, Army H.Q. 46-48, Dir. 48; later commanded infantry brigade for two years; Col. 8th Gurkha Rifles 53; then Dir. Mil. Training, Army H.Q.; then Commandant, Infantry School, Mhow; Div. Commdr. Jammu and Kashmir; Commandant, Defence Services Coll., Wellington 59-62; Corps Commdr. Eastern Frontier 62; later Gen. Officer C.-in-C. W. Command until 64; G.O.C.-in-C. Eastern Command 64-69; Chief of Army Staff 69-73; commanded operations in Indo-Pakistan war 71; promoted to rank of Field Marshal Jan. 73; Col. 8th Gurkha Rifles; awarded Padma Bhushan 68, Padma Vibhushan 72.
c/o Army Headquarters, DHQ P.O., New Delhi 110011, India.

Manickavasagar, Balasegaram, M.B., F.R.C.S., F.R.C.S.E., F.R.A.C.S., F.A.C.S., F.R.S.M.; Malaysian surgeon; b. 15 April 1929, Selangor; ed. King Edward VII Medical Coll., Singapore and Univ. of Malaya.
Medical Officer and later Registrar, Surgical Unit, Gen. Hosp., Kuala Lumpur 57-59, Consultant Surgeon Surgical Unit II 69-, Prof. and Head of Second Surgical Div. 72-; Consultant Surgeon, Kota Bharu, Kelantan 60-61; Consultant Surgeon and Head Dept. of Surgery, Gen. Hosp., Seremban 61-69; Examiner, Primary Fellowship Examination, Royal Coll. of Surgeons, Edinburgh 72, 74; mem.

Pan Pacific Surgical Asscn., Int. Fed. of Surgical Colls. Malaysian Medical Asscn. and many other orgs.; mem. Malaysian Acad. of Medicine, Singapore Acad. of Medicine; Hon. Fellow, Polish Asscn. of Surgeons, Philippine Coll. of Surgeons; Fellow, Asscn. of Surgeons of Great Britain and Ireland, American Soc. for the Advancement of Surgery of Trauma; mem. editorial cttee. *British Journal of Surgery, Journal of Medical Progress, Journal of Modern Medicine, Journal of Int. Surgery*, Editorial Board *Asian Journal of Medicine*, Editorial Advisory Cttee. *Clinical Oncology*, Editor-in-Chief *Malaysian Journal of Surgery*; Visiting Prof. Marburg Univ., Fed. Repub. of Germany 72, Madras Univ., India 75-76; Jacksonian Prize and Medal, Royal Coll. of Surgeons (U.K.) 70, and many other awards. Publs. more than 100 articles on the liver, pancreas, oesophagus, stomach, bone and joint surgery.
Department of Surgery, General Hospital, Kuala Lumpur; Home: 5 Jalan Liew Weng Chee, Off Jalan Yap Kwan Seng, Kuala Lumpur, Malaysia.
Telephone: 290421 Ext. 686 (Office); 84053 (Home).

Mansfield, Hon. Sir Alan James, K.C.M.G., K.C.V.O., K.ST.J., LL.B.; Australian judge; b. 30 Sept. 1902; ed. Univ. of Sydney.
Admitted to Bar of N.S.W. 24, Queensland 24; Lecturer in Bankruptcy and Company Laws Univ. of Queensland 39; practised as barrister-at-law Queensland 25-40; Judge of Supreme Court of Queensland 40-47; mem. Australian War Crimes Board of Enquiry 45; Australian rep. UN War Crimes Comm. London 45; Chief Australian Prosecutor Int. Mil. Tribunal for the Far East Jan. 46-Jan. 47; Chair. of Land Appeal Court Queensland 42-45; Chair. Aliens Tribunal 42-45; Chair. Royal Comms. on Queensland Sugar Industry 42, 50; Senior Puisne Judge of Queensland 47-55; Acting Chief Justice of Queensland 50, Chief Justice 56-66; Administrator of Govt. of Queensland 57-58; Chair. Central Sugar Cane Prices Board 55; Warden, Queensland Univ. 56-66, Chancellor, Queensland Univ. 66-; Gov. of Queensland 66-72; Hon. LL.D.
81 Monaco Street, Florida Gardens, Surfers Paradise, Queensland 4217, Australia.

Mao Tse-tung; Chinese party leader; b. 26 Dec. 1893, Shaoshan, Hunan; *m.* 1st Yang K'asi-hui 1920, 2nd Chiang Ch'ing (*q.v.*) 1939; ed. Hunan Prov. No. 1 Middle School, Hunan Prov. No. 1 Normal School.
Leader of Chinese Communist Revolution; organized New People's Soc. 17; Library Asst. Peking Univ. Library 18; edited, published *The Hsiang River Review* 19; Principal, Elementary School, Hunan 20-22; CCP activist in Hunan 22-23; mem. Politburo, 3rd Cen. Cttee. of CCP 23; Dir. Kuomintang Propaganda Dept. 25; organized Autumn Harvest Uprising, Hunan 27; Political Commissar Red Army 28; mem. 6th Cen. Cttee. of CCP 28; Chair. Cen. Chinese Soviet Repub. 31-34; led Long March to Yenan 34-36; Political Commissar, Chinese Worker-Peasant Red Army Coll. 36; Principal, Yenan Party School 42; Chair. Politburo, 7th Cen. Cttee. of CCP 45; attended Chungking Conf. between CCP and Kuomintang 45; assumed name of Li Te-sheng while heading CCP org., North Shensi 47; directed mil. operation with Chou En-lai from Hsiaoho 47; led forces to Shensi-Chalae-Hopei Border Region 48; Chair. Standing Cttee., Preparatory Cttee. for 1st Chinese People's Political Consultative Conf. 49; Chair. Cen. People's Govt. 49-54; Chair. People's Repub. of China 54-59; Chair. 8th Cen. Cttee. of CCP 56, mem. Standing Cttee. of Politburo 56; Chair. 9th Cen. Cttee. of CCP 69, mem. Standing Cttee. of Politburo 69; Chair. 10th Cen. Cttee. of CCP and mem. Standing Cttee. of Politburo 73, 75.
Publs. articles and pamphlets collected in 4 vols. of *Selected Works*.
(Died September, 1976.)

Mara, Ratu the Rt. Hon. Sir Kamisese Kapaiwai Tuimacilau, P.C., K.B.E., M.A.; Fiji politician; b. 13 May 1920; ed. Sacred Heart Coll. and Central Medical School, Suva, Fiji, Otago Univ., Oxford Univ., and London School of Economics.
Cadet, District Officer and Commissioner, Overseas Colonial Service, Fiji 51-61; mem. Legis. Council, Fiji 53-; mem. Exec. Council, Fiji 59-61; Founder of Alliance Party 62; Minister for Natural Resources 64-67; Leader, Fiji Delegation, Constitutional Conf., London 65; Chief Minister 67-70; Prime Minister 70-; Hon. Fellow Wadham Coll. 71; Grand Master of the Order of the Nat. Lion, Senegal 75; Hon. LL.D. (Guam, Otago, New Delhi).
The Office of the Prime Minister, Suva, Fiji.

Maramis, J. B. P.; Indonesian United Nations official; b. 23 Jan. 1922, Limbung, Celebes Island, Indonesia; ed. Univ. of Leyden.
Served in Directorate of Econ. Affairs, Ministry of Foreign Affairs 51-54; First Sec., Teheran 54-58; Deputy Head, Directorate of UN Affairs, Ministry of Foreign Affairs 58-60; Counsellor, Indonesian Mission to UN 60-65; Head, Directorate of Int. Orgs., Ministry of Foreign Affairs 65-68; del. to UN Gen. Assembly 66-68; Deputy Perm. Rep. to UN Oct. 69-71, Acting Perm. Rep. 71-72; Vice-Pres. UN Econ. and Social Council (ECOSOC) 69, Pres. 70; Amb. to Belgium and Luxembourg, Head Indonesian Mission to EEC 72-73; Exec. Sec. UN Econ. Comm. for Asia and the Far East (ECAFE) now Econ. and Social Comm. for Asia and the Pacific (ESCAP) 73-.
ESCAP, Sala Santitham, Bangkok 2, Thailand.

Marcos, Ferdinand Edralin; Philippine lawyer and politician; b. 11 Sept. 1917; ed. Univ. of the Philippines.
Lieutenant, later Major, in Philippines Army; took part in anti-Japanese resistance; Special Asst. to Pres. Manuel Roxas 46-47; mem. House of Reps. 49-59, Senate 59-66; Pres. of Senate 63-65; Pres. of Philippines 66- (re-elected Nov. 69), Prime Minister 73-; mem. Liberal Party until 64, Nat. Party 64-; Dag Hammarskjöld Award 68; numerous war decorations.
Malacañan Palace, Manila, Philippines.

Marsh, Dame Ngaio, D.B.E.; New Zealand novelist and theatrical producer; b. 23 April 1899, Ferdalton, Christchurch; ed. St. Margaret's Coll., New Zealand, and Canterbury Univ. Coll. School of Art, Christchurch, New Zealand.
Joined English theatrical company touring New Zealand; on stage for two years; Red Cross Transport Unit, Second World War; Producer, D. D. O'Connor Theatre Management, N.Z. 44; Hon. D.Litt. (Canterbury, N.Z.).
Publs. *A Man Lay Dead* 34, *Enter a Murderer* 35, *Nursing Home Murder* (with H. Jellett) 36, *Death in Ecstasy* 37, *Vintage Murder* 37, *Artists in Crime* 38, *Death in a White Tie* 38, *Overture to Death* 39, *Death at the Bar* 40, *Surfeit of Lampreys* 41, *Death and the Dancing Footman* 42, *Colour Scheme* 43, *Died in the Wool* 45, *Final Curtain* 47, *Swing Brother Swing* 48, *Opening Night* 51, *Spinsters in Jeopardy* 53, *Scales of Justice* 55, *Off With His Head* 57, *Singing in the Shrouds* 59, *False Scent* 60, *Hand in Glove* 62, *Dead Water* 64, *Black Beech and Honey Dew* (autobiography) 66, *Death at the Dolphin* 67, *Clutch of Constables* 68, *When in Rome* 69, *Tied Up in Tinsel* 72, *Black as He's Painted* 74; Television: *Evil Liver* (for ITV in Britain).
37 Valley Road, Christchurch 2, New Zealand; 69 Great Russell Street, London, WC1B 3DH, England.

Marshall, David Saul, LL.B.; Singapore lawyer and fmr. politician; b. 1908; ed. Raffles Institution, Middle Temple and Univ. of London.
Worked in Singapore as sharebroker, salesman and sec. to a shipping co. 24-32; then studied law in England and began legal career in Singapore 37-; joined Singapore Volunteer Corps 38; imprisoned by Japanese 42-45; founder Sec. War Prisoners' Asscn.; fmr. mem. Labour

Front; Chief Minister of Singapore 55-56; mem. Singapore Legislative Assembly 61-63; Chair. Singapore Inst. of S.E. Asian Studies 70-74; Del. to UN 23rd Gen. Assembly 68.
8/10 Bank of China, Chambers, Singapore 1.

Marshall, Rt. Hon. Sir John Ross, P.C., G.B.E., C.H., B.A., LL.M.; New Zealand lawyer and politician; b. 5 March 1912, Wellington; ed. Victoria Univ. Coll., Univ. of N.Z.
Admitted barrister and solicitor of Supreme Court of N.Z. 36; army service 41-46; M.P. 46-75; lecturer in law, Victoria Univ. Coll. 48-51; Minister Assisting the Prime Minister and Minister for State Advances Corpn., Public Trust Office and Census and Statistics 49-54; also Minister of Health 51-54, of Information and Publicity 51-57; Minister of Justice and Attorney-Gen. 54-57; Deputy Prime Minister 57, 60-72; Deputy Leader of Opposition 57-60, Leader 72-74; Minister of Industry and Commerce 60-69, and of Overseas Trade 60-72; Minister of Customs 60-61; Attorney-Gen. 69-71; Minister of Labour and Immigration 69-72; Prime Minister Feb.-Dec. 72; N.Z. rep. at Colombo Plan Conf., New Delhi 53; rep. N.Z. at GATT Ministerial Conf. 61, 63, 66, ECAFE Conf. 62, 64, 66, 68 and 70, Chair. ECAFE 65; N.Z. rep. at Commonwealth Prime Ministers' Conf. 62, Commonwealth Trade Ministers' Conf. 63, 66, Commonwealth Parl. Conf. 65; Privy Councillor 66; Chair. Nat. Devt. Council 69-72, N.Z. Comm. for Expo 70; Visiting Fellow, Victoria Univ. of Wellington; mem. Advisory Council, World Peace Through Law; Chair. Nat. Bank of N.Z. Ltd., Phillips Electrical Industries (N.Z.) Ltd., Contractors Bonding and Discount Corpn. Ltd.; Dir. Philips Electrical Industries, Norwich Union Insurance Soc., Hallenstein Bros. Ltd.; Hon. Bencher Gray's Inn 72; Consultant Partner Buddle, Anderson, Kent & Co., Wellington 75-, Fletcher Holdings Ltd., DRG (N.Z.) Ltd.; mem. Nat. Party, Leader 72-74.
Publ. *Law Relating to Watercourses.*
22 Fitzroy Street, Wellington 1, New Zealand.
Telephone: 736631.

Martodihardjo, Lt.-Gen. Sarbini; Indonesian army officer and politician b. 10 June 1914; ed. Kebumen, Cen. Java; ed. elementary and secondary schools and various military schools and courses.
Former public health service employee; subsequently served as commissioned officer in Indonesian army; Minister of Veterans and Demobilization 64-66, 66-68, of Defence Feb.-Mar. 66, of Transmigration and Co-operatives 68-71; mem. Supreme Advisory Council of Indonesia 71-, now Vice-Chair.; Chair. Nat. H.Q. of Indonesian Scout Movement, Cen. Council H.Q. of Veterans Legion of Indonesia; Chair. Univ. of Islamic Devt.
Graha Purna Yudha, Jalan Jenderal Soedirman, Sermanggi, Jakarta; Home: Jalan Imam Bonjol 48, Jakarta, Indonesia.

Masamune, Isao, B.ECON.; Japanese banker; b. 30 March 1912, Tokyo; ed. Tokyo Univ.
Joined Industrial Bank of Japan Ltd. 33, Dir. 57, Man. Dir. 59, Deputy Pres. 64, Pres. 68-75, Chair. 75-.
Office: 1-3-3 Marunouchi, Chiyoda-ku, Tokyo; Home: 2-21-5 Uehara, Shibuya-ku, Tokyo, Japan.
Telephone: 214-1111 (Office); 467-1843 (Home).

Masani, Minoo; Indian writer and business consultant; b. 20 Nov. 1905; ed. Elphinstone Coll., Bombay, and London School of Economics.
Barrister of Lincoln's Inn; one of the founders of Congress Socialist Party and Sec. till 39; Mayor of Bombay 43-44; mem. Constituent Assembly and Provisional Parl. of India 47-52; Amb. to Brazil 48-49; mem. UN Sub-Comm. on Discrimination and Minorities 47-52; mem. Lok Sabha 49-52, 57-62, 63-71, Chair. Public Accounts Cttee. 67-69; Pres. Swatantra Party 70-71.
Publs. *Our India, Socialism Reconsidered, Your Food, Picture of a Plan, Plea for the Mixed Economy, Our Growing Human Family, Communist Party of India—a Short History, Congress Misrule and the Swatantra Alternative, Is J.P. the Answer?*
Personnel and Productivity Services, 148 Mahatma Gandhi Road, Bombay 1, India.
Telephone: 254005.

Mashuri Saleh, Dr. Kangmas; Indonesian politician; b. 19 July 1925, Pati, Central Java; ed. Faculty of Law, Gadjah Mada Univ., Jogjakarta.
Teacher in schools in Jogjakarta and Dir. Army Secondary School 53-56; Chair. Team of Experts attached to Cen. War Admin. 57-60; mem. Advisory Board of Nat. Front for Liberation of W. Irian; in private employment 60-65; Deputy Minister of Higher Learning 66; Dir.-Gen. of Higher Learning 67; Minister of Educ. and Culture 68-74, of Information 74-.
Ministry of Information, Jakarta, Indonesia.

Matane, Paulias Nguna; Papua New Guinea diplomatist; b. 5 July 1932.
Senior positions in Dept. of Educ. 57-59; mem. Public Service Board 69; Head, Dept. of Lands, Surveys and Mines 69, of Business Devt. 70-75; Amb. to U.S.A. Sept. 75-, Perm. Rep. to UN Oct. 75-.
Permanent Mission of Papua New Guinea to the United Nations, 801 Second Avenue, 12th Floor, New York, N.Y. 10017, U.S.A.

Matheson, James Adam Louis, C.M.G., M.B.E., PH.D., F.I.C.E., F.I.STRUCT.E., F.I.E.AUST.; British engineer; b. 11 Feb. 1912; ed. Bootham School, York and Manchester Univ.
Lecturer, Birmingham Univ. 38-46; Prof. Civil Eng., Univ. of Melbourne 46-50; Beyer Prof. of Eng., Manchester Univ. 51-59; Vice-Chancellor, Monash Univ., Melbourne 59-76; Chancellor Papua New Guinea Univ. of Technology 73-75; mem. Mission on Technical Educ. to the W. Indies 57, Ramsey Cttee. on Devt. of Tertiary Educ. in Victoria 61-63, Commonwealth Scientific and Industrial Research Org. Advisory Council 62-67, Royal Comm. into Failure of Kings Bridge 62-63; Trustee Science Museum of Victoria 64-, Chair. 69-; mem. Council, Inst. of Engineers, Australia 65-, Senior Vice-Pres. 71-74, Pres. 75-; mem. Council, Inst. of Civil Engineers 66-68; Interim Council Univ. of Papua and New Guinea 65-68; Chair. Papua New Guinea Inst. of Higher Technical Educ. 66-72, Australian Vice-Chancellors Cttee. 67-68, Asscn. of Commonwealth Universities 67-69; Vice-Pres. Inst. of Structural Engineers 67-68; Hon. D.Sc., (Hong Kong) Hon. LL.D. (Manchester, Melbourne and Monash Univs.); Kernot Medal 70.
Publs. Papers on technical and educational subjects.
3 Koornalla Crescent, Mount Eliza, 3930 Victoria, Australia.
Telephone: 787-1931.

Matsubara, Yosomatsu; Japanese shipbuilding executive; b. 15 Dec. 1895; ed. Nagasaki Univ.
Kuhara Mining Co. until 34; Hitachi Seisaku (Mfg.) Co. 34-; Dir. Hitachi Shipbuilding and Eng. Co. 44-, Vice-Pres. 49-50, Pres. 50-62, Chair. 62-; Perm. Dir. Japan Fed. of Employers' Asscns.
Hitachi Shipbuilding and Engineering Co., 47 Edobori 1-chome, Nishi-ku, Osaka 550, Japan.

Matsuda, Kohei; Japanese business executive; b. 28 Jan. 1922, Osaka; ed. Law Dept., Keio Univ.
Director, Hiroshima Mazda Co. Ltd. 46, Pres. 56; Pres. Mazda Auto Hiroshima Co. Ltd. 59; Exec. Vice-Pres. Toyo Kogyo Co. Ltd. 61, Pres. 70-; Chair. Japan Automatic Transmission Co. Ltd.
10-31, Kaminobori-cho, Hiroshima, Japan.
Telephone: 0822-21-1438.

Matsui, Akira; Japanese atomic energy commissioner; b. 6 Jan. 1908; ed. Tokyo Imperial Univ.
Ministry of Foreign Affairs 31-70, Dir. Research Bureau

50, Deputy Vice-Minister for Admin. 53; Minister to France 55-57; Perm. Rep. to UNESCO 55-57, mem. Exec. Board 56-62; Amb. to Ceylon 57-59, to Sweden 59-62, concurrently to Iceland; Deputy Perm. Rep. to UN 62-63, Perm. Rep. 63-67; Amb. to France 67-70; Commr. Atomic Energy Comm. of Japan 70-76; Dr. h.c. (Seton Hall Univ.) 66; Hon. LL.D. (Grenoble) 70.
1207, 34-3-2-chome Mita, Minato-ku, Tokyo, Japan.

Matsukata, Masanobu; Japanese business executive; b. 13 Aug. 1907; ed. Keio Univ.
With Tokyo Gas, Electric and Engineering Co. Ltd. 32; Head of Gen. Affairs Dept., Tokyo Automobile Industry Co. Ltd., Hino Plant 40; Head of Sales Dept., Hino Heavy Industry Co. Ltd. 42, Head of Supply Div. 43, Dir. and Gen. Man. 45; Man. Dir. Hino Industry Co. Ltd. 46; Senior Man.-Dir. Hino Diesel Industry Co. Inc. 50, Vice-Pres. 54; Pres. Hino Motors Ltd. 61-74, Chair. 74-; now also Chair. Hino Motor Sales Ltd., Sitsui Seiki Kogyo Co. Ltd., Teikoku Auto Industry Co. Ltd.; Dir. Sawafuji Electrical Co. Ltd., Auto Industry Employers' Asscn., Japan Automobile Mfrs. Asscn. Inc., Japan Ordinance Asscn., Japan Automobile Chamber of Commerce; Financial Dir. Japan Fed. of Employers' Asscns.; Blue Ribbon Medal.
Hino Motors Ltd., Hinodai 3-1-1, Hino City, Tokyo, Japan.
Telephone: 03-272-4811 (Office).

Matsumoto, Shigeharu, B.A.; Japanese writer and business executive; b. 2 Oct. 1899, Osaka; ed. Faculty of Law, Univ. of Tokyo, Yale Univ., Univs. of Wisconsin, Geneva and Vienna.
Assistant, Faculty of Law, Univ. of Tokyo 28-30; Lecturer Chuo Univ., Hosei Univ., Japan Women's Univ. 29-33; Rep. Shanghai Branch Rengo News Service 33-34, Domei (now Kyodo) News Service 35-39; Editor-in-Chief Domei News Service 40-44, and Man. Dir. 44-45; mem. U.S. Educ. Comm. (Fulbright), Tokyo 54-57; Columnist Asahi Newspaper 56; Gen. Partner Matsumoto, Kojima and Masukata (law office) 47-; Man. Dir. Int. House of Japan, Inc. 52-65, Chair. Board of Dirs. Int. House of Japan, Inc. 65-; Pres. Japanese Asscn. for American Studies 52-67, Man. Dir. 68-; Pres. Inst. of Nat. Econ. (Kokumin Keizai Kenkyu Kyokai) 51-61; Dir. Nippon Light Metal Co. 57-75, Dentsu Advertising Ltd. 61-; Vice-Pres. Nat. Comm. of Japan for UNESCO 57-63; Counsellor, Inst. of Asian Econ. Affairs 60-; mem. Board of Govs. Japan Broadcasting Corpn. 61-65; Chair. Grew Foundation 71-, Bancroft Educational Aid Fund 71-; Hon. LL.D. (Rutgers Univ.) 66, Lit.D. (Sophia Univ.) 76; First Class Order of the Sacred Treasure 69.
Publs. edited *Memoirs of Aisuke Kabayama* (in Japanese) 56; co-edited *A Documentary History of American People* 6 vols. (in Japanese) 50-58; translated: Albert Thomas's *Histoire Anecdotique du Travail* 28, Dr. S. Johnson's *Beikoku San-ijin no Shogai to sono Shiteki Haikei* (with Y. Takagi) 29, C. A. Beard's *The Republic* 2 vols. 48-49, *A Basic History of the United States* 2 vols. (with K. Kishimura) 54-56, *American Spirit* (with Y. Takagi) 54; edited: Arnold Toynbee's *Lessons of History* (lectures in Japan) 57, *A History of the World* 45-61 (in Japanese) 62, *The Mind of India* (lectures in Japan by J. Nehru and others) 61, *Lectures on Aspects of American Culture* (lectures in Japan by David Riesman) 62, *Basic Problems of U.S. Foreign Policy* (lectures in Japan by George Kennan) 65; author: *Shanghai Jidai* (My Shanghai Days).
The International House of Japan, Inc., 11-16, 5-chome, Roppongi, Minato-ku, Tokyo, Japan.

Matsushita, Konosuke; Japanese businessman; b. 27 Nov. 1894, Wasa Village.
Founded Matsushita Electric Housewares Mfg. Works Co. 18, incorporated into Matsushita Electrical Industrial Co. Ltd. 35, fmr. Pres., Chair. 61-73, Adviser, mem. of the Board 73-; Pres. Matsushita Communication Industrial Co. Ltd. 58-66, Chair. 66-70; Pres. Matsushita Real Estate Co. Ltd. 52-; Pres. Matsushita Electronics Corpn. 52-66, Chair. 66-71, Dir. 71-; Chair. Kyushu Matsushita Electric Co. Ltd. 55-73, Auditor 74-; Chair. Nakagawa Electric Co. Ltd. (now Matsushita Reiki Co. Ltd.) 53-73, Matsushita Electric Works Ltd. 51-; Adviser Matsushita Electric Trading Co. Ltd. 52-; Chair. Matsushita Electric Corpn. of America 59-74; Chair. Victor Co. of Japan Ltd. 62-70; Man. Dir. Fed. of Econ. Orgs. of Japan 56-70; mem. Advisory Cttee. Japan Nat. Railway 62-71; Chair. Invention Asscn. of Japan 68-71, Adviser 71-; Blue Ribbon Medal 56; Commdr., Order of Orange Nassau (Netherlands) 58, Rising Sun 65; First Class Order of the Sacred Treasure 70; Commdr. Ordre de la Couronne (Belgium) 72; Hon. LL.D. (Waseda, Keio and Doshisha Univs.).
Publs. *What I do, and What I think, The Dream of My Work and the Dream of Our Life, The Words of Peace and Happiness through Prosperity, My View Towards Prosperity, Why?, Thoughts on Man, Looking Back on the Past and Forward to Tomorrow, Reflections on Business, Reflections on Management, A Way to Look at and Think About Things.*
Matsushita Electric Industrial Co. Ltd., 571 1006 Kadoma, Kadoma City, Osaka, Japan.
Telephone: Osaka (908)-1121.

Matsushita, Masaharu, B.IUR.; Japanese businessman; b. 17 Sept. 1912, Tokyo; ed. Tokyo Imperial Univ.
Mitsui Bank 35-40; Matsushita Electric Industrial Co. Ltd. 40-, Auditor 44-47, Dir. 47-49, Vice-Pres. 49-61, Pres. 61-; Auditor, Matsushita Real Estate Co. Ltd. 52-68, Dir. 68-; Dir. Matsushita Electronics Corpn. 52-72, Chair. 72-; Dir. Matsushita Communication Industrial Co. Ltd. 58-70, Chair. 70-; Dir. Matsushita Electric Corpn. of America 59-74, Chair. 74-; Dir. Kyushu Matsushita Electric Co. Ltd. 55-, Matsushita Seiko Co. Ltd. 58-, Matsushita Reiki Co. Ltd. 61-, Matsushita Electric Works Ltd. 61-, Matsushita Electric Trading Co. Ltd. 62-, Quasar Electronics Corpn. 74-; Pres. Electronic Industries of Japan 68-70; Commdr. Order of Orange Nassau (Netherlands).
Matsushita Electric Industrial Co. Ltd., 1006 Kadoma Kadoma City, Osaka, Japan.
Telephone: Osaka 908-1121.

Matsuzawa, Takuji; Japanese banker; b. 17 July 1913, Tokyo; ed. Tokyo Imperial Univ.
The Yasuda Bank Ltd. 38- (name changed to The Fuji Bank Ltd. 48), Chief Man. Planning and Co-ordination Div. 59-61, Dir. and Chief Man. Planning and Co-ordination Div. 61-63, Man. Dir. 63-71, Deputy Pres. 71-75, Chair. of Board and Pres. The Fuji Bank Ltd. 75-; Chair. of Research and Policy Cttee., Japan Cttee. for Econ. Devt. (Keizai Doyukai) 73-; Man. Dir. Japan Fed. of Econ. Orgs. (Keidanren) 75-.
The Fuji Bank Ltd., 5-5, 1-chome Otemachi, Chiyodaku, Tokyo; Home: 8-7, 2-chome Shoto, Shibuya-ku, Tokyo, Japan.
Telephone: 467-8838.

Maung, Maung, LL.D., J.S.D.; Burmese jurist; b. 31 Jan. 1925, Mandalay; ed. Rangoon, Utrecht and Yale Univs., and Lincoln's Inn, London.
Served in Burma Nat. Army and Resistance during Second World War; practised law; Lecturer in Internat. Law, Univ. of Rangoon; Deputy Attorney-Gen. of Burma 58-60; visiting lecturer Yale; Judge, Supreme Court 62; Chief Justice 65-72; Minister of Judicial Affairs 72-74; mem. State Council March 74-; Pres. Burma Red Cross Soc. 67-72.
Publs. *Burma in the Family of Nations* 56, *Burma's Constitution* 59, *A Trial in Burma* 62, *Aung San of Burma* 62, *Law and Custom in Burma* 63, *Burma and General Ne Win* 69, *To a Soldier Son* 74.
State Council, Rangoon, Burma.

May, Henry Leonard James; New Zealand politician; b. 13 April 1912, Petone; ed. Petone Convent, Petone and Wellington Technical Schools.
Member Parl. for Onslow 54-57, for Porirua 57-69, for Western Hutt 69-75; Minister of Local Govt., of Internal Affairs, of Civil Defence, Minister in charge of Valuation Dept. 72-75; Chair. Hutt Valley Electric Power Board 50-54.
16 Dowse Drive, Lower Hutt, New Zealand.

Meer, Khurshid Hasan; Pakistani lawyer and politician; b. 14 July 1925, Srinagar; ed. Aligarh Muslim Univ. and Law Coll., Lahore.
Practising lawyer, Rawalpindi 52-; joined Azad Pakistan Party 52; Sec. Combined Opposition Parties, Rawalpindi 64; founding mem. Pakistan People's Party; mem. Nat. Assembly 70-; Minister of Presidential Cabinet May 72-74, of Labour, Health, Social Welfare and Population Planning Oct.-Dec. 74.
National Assembly Secretariat, State Bank Building, Islamabad, Pakistan.

Mehta, Asoka, B.A.; Indian politician; b. 24 Oct. 1911; ed. Wilson Coll., Bombay, and Bombay Univ. School of Economics.
Founder-mem. of fmr. Socialist Party; imprisoned five times; Editor of official organ of former Socialist party 35-39; mem. Nat. Exec. of Socialist Party for 25 years; fmr. Chair. Praja Socialist Party; mem. Lok Sabha 54-57, 58-61, 67-; Deputy Chair. Indian Planning Comm. 63-66; Minister of Planning 66-67, of Petroleum, Chemicals and Social Welfare 67-68; detained July 75-May 76.
Publs. *The Communal Triangle in India, Who Owns India, Political Mind of India, Democratic Socialism, Politics of Planned Economy, Socialism and Peasantry, Indian Shipping and The Plan: Perspective and Problems.*
5 Dadysett Road, Bombay, India.
Telephone: 35-77-36.

Mehta, Hansa; Indian educationist and social reformer; b. 3 July 1897, Surat, Gujarat; ed. Baroda Coll. and Bombay Univ.
President Gujarat Women's Co-operative Soc. Bombay 29-49, The Bhagini Samej, Bombay 44-52; Parl. Sec. Govt. of Bombay (Educ. and Health) 37-39; mem. Bombay Legislative Council 37-39, 41-52; Vice-Chancellor Indian Women's Univ. 46-48; Pres. All Indian Women's Conf. 45-46; mem. Human Rights Comm., UN 47-50, Vice-Chair. 50-52; mem. Constituent Assembly 47-50; Secondary Educ. Comm. Govt. of India 52-; Vice-Chancellor, Maharaja Sayajirao Univ. of Baroda 49-58; mem. Gen. Advisory Board of Educ., Govt. of India; mem. Exec. Board UNESCO 58-60; Padma Bhushan 59; Hon. LL.D. (Leeds 64), Hon. D.Litt. (Allahabad 58, Baroda 59).
Publs. (Gujarati) *Balwartavali* 26, *Kishorvatavali* 28, *Tran Natako* 28, *Rukmini* 32, *Bavalana Parakrano* 34, *Golibarni Musafri* 34, *Arun nu Adbhut Swapnu* 34, *Himalaya Swarup ne Bija Natako* 41, Gujarati trans. *Hamlet, Merchant of Venice* 42, 44, *Tartuffe, Bourgoise Gentilhomme;* (English) *Women under the Hindu Law of Marriage and Succession* 44, *Tract on Post-War Educational Reconstruction* 45, *Civil Liberties* 45, *Adventures of King Vikram* 48.
Everest House, 14 Carmichael Road, Bombay 26, India.
Telephone: 364159.

Mehta, Jivraj Narayan, L.M.S., F.C.P.S. (Bombay), M.D., M.R.C.P. (London); Indian politician, physician and diplomatist; b. 29 Aug. 1887, Amreli, Gujarat; ed. Amreli High School, Grant Medical Coll., Bombay and The London Hospital, London.
Chief Medical Officer, State of Baroda 23-25; Dean, Seth G.S. Medical Coll. and K.E.M. Hospital 25-42; Pres. India Medical Conf. 30-44, 47; imprisoned for activities in "Quit India" Movt. 32-34, 42-44; Chair. Advisory Medical Board, Kasturba Gandhi Nat. Memorial Fund 44-50; mem. Board of Scientific and Industrial Research India 44-63; Sec. and Dir.-Gen. Health Services Govt. of India 47-48; Dewan State of Baroda 48-49; mem. Constituent Assembly for drafting the Constitution of Independent India 48-49; Minister for Public Works, Govt. of Bombay 49-51, Minister for Finance 52-60; Pres. Indian Conf. of Social Work 50, 52-54; mem. Atomic Research Cttee. 51-60; Vice-Chair. Gandhi Memorial Leprosy Foundation 52-72; mem. Gov. Body, All India Inst. of Medical Sciences 57-63, 71-; Chair. Exec. Council Cen. Drug Research Inst., Lucknow 48-60; Chair. Amreli Jilla Vidya Fund 59-, Exec. Council, Central Salt and Marine Chemicals Res. Inst. 61-63, 67-, Bombay Gandhi Smarak Nidhi 67-71; Vice-Pres. All-India Prohibition Council 67-72; Chief Minister Gujarat 60-63; Indian High Commr. in U.K. 63-66; mem. Lok Sabha 71-.
Publs. *Presence of Glycogen in Suprarenal Bodies, The Height, Weight & Chest Measurements Enquiry Relating to Some School Children in Bombay.*
Everest House, 14 Carmichael Road, Bombay 26, India.

Melville, Sir Leslie Galfreid, K.B.E., B.EC.; Australian economist; b. 26 March 1902, Marsfield; ed. Church of England Grammar School, Sydney, and Univ. of Sydney.
Public Actuary of South Australia 24-28; Prof. of Econs., Univ. of Adelaide 29-31; mem. of Cttees. on S. Australian Finances 27-30; mem. of Cttees. on Australian Finances and Unemployment 31 and 32; Financial Adviser to Australian Dels. at Imperial Econ. Conf. 32, and to Australian Del. at World Econ. Conf. 33; mem. Australian Financial and Econ. Advisory Cttee. 39; Chair. Australian Del. to UN Monetary Conf., Bretton Woods 44; mem. Advisory Council of Commonwealth Bank 45-50; Chair. UN Sub-Comm. on Employment and Econ. Stability 47-50; Asst. Gov. (Central Banking) Commonwealth Bank of Australia; Exec. Dir. Int. Monetary Fund and Int. Bank for Reconstruction and Devt. Nov. 50-53; Vice-Chancellor, Australian Nat. Univ. Canberra 53-60; mem. Board, Reserve Bank 59-63, 65-75; Chair. Commonwealth Grants Comm. 66-74; Chair. Tariff Board 60-63; Devt. Advisory Service, Int. Bank for Reconstruction and Devt. 63-65.
71 Stonehaven Crescent, Canberra, Australia.
Telephone: 811838.

Menon, Chelat Achutha, B.A., B.L.; Indian politician; b. 27 Jan. 1913, Trichur.
District Court Pleader, Trichur; took part in congress and trade union activities; restricted for one year for anti-war speech 40; joined Communist Party and detained for communist activities 42; Sec. District Cttee. of Communist Party 43-47; underground 48-52; elected to Travancore-Cochin Legislative Assembly 52; mem. Kerala Legislative Assembly 57, later Finance Minister; mem. Rajya Sabha 68-; Chief Minister of Kerala Nov. 69-.
Publs. Translation of *Short History of the World* by H. G. Wells, *Soviet Nadu, A Kissan Text Book, Kerala State—Possibilities and Problems,* translation of *Man Makes Himself* by Gordon Child, *Sheafs from Memory.*
Office of the Chief Minister of Kerala, Trivandrum, Kerala State, India.
Telephone: 4259 (Office); 5060 (Residence).

Menon, Lakshmi N., M.A., L.T., T.DIP., LL.B.; Indian politician; b. 1899, Trivandrum; ed. H.H. Maharaja's School and Coll. for Women, H.H. Maharaja's Arts Coll., Trivandrum, Lady Willingdon Training Coll., New Delhi, and Maria Grey Training Coll., London, Lucknow Univ.
Lecturer, Queen Mary's Coll., Madras 22-25, Gokhale Girls Schools, Calcutta 28-30, Isabella Theburn Coll., Lucknow 30-33; Alt. Del. to UN Gen. Ass. 48, 50, 53, 54, to UN Comm. on Status of Women, Beirut 49; Chief, Section on Status of Women, Human Rights Div., UN Secr., Lake Success 49-50; Principal, Women's Training Coll., Patna 51-53; Rep. Cttee. on Information from

Non-Self Governing Territories 53; Parl. Sec. to the Prime Minister 52-57; Deputy Minister of External Affairs 57-62; Minister of State, Ministry of External Affairs 62-66; State Commr. for Guides, Bihar 52-; Pres. All India Women's Conf. 55-59; Pres. Indian Fed. of Univ. Women 61-67; mem. Rajya Sabha 52-66; Chair. Kasturba Gandhi Nat. Memorial Trust 72-; Life mem. Cochin Univ. Senate 73-.
Publ. *The Position of Women.*
Plain View, Trivandrum, India.

Menon, Mambillikalathil Govind Kumar, M.SC., PH.D., F.R.S.; Indian physicist; b. 28 Aug. 1928, Mangalore; ed. Jaswant Coll., Jodhpur, Royal Inst. of Science, Bombay, and H. H. Wills Physics Laboratory, Univ. of Bristol.
Research Assoc., Univ. of Bristol 52-53; Senior Award of Royal Comm. for Exhbn. of 1851, Univ. of Bristol 53-55; Reader Tata Inst. of Fundamental Research, Bombay 55-58; Assoc. Prof. 58-60, Prof. and Dean of Physics Faculty 60-64, Senior Prof. and Deputy Dir. (Physics) 64-66, Dir. Tata Inst. of Fundamental Research 66-75; Chair. Electronics Comm. and Sec. to Govt. of India Dept. of Electronics; Scientific Adviser to Minister of Defence, Dir.-Gen. Defence Research and Devt. Org., Sec. for Defence Research; Chair. Electronics Trade and Tech. Devt. Corpn. Ltd., Bharat Dynamics Ltd.; mem. UN Advisory Cttee. on Application of Science and Tech. to Devt., Nat. Cttee. on Science and Tech.; Foreign Hon. mem. American Acad. of Arts and Sciences; Fellow Indian Acad. of Sciences (Pres. 74-76), Indian Nat. Science Acad.; Shanti Swarup Bhatnagar Award 60, Padma Shri 61, Padma Bhushan 68; Hon. D.Sc. (Delhi, Jodhpur, Sardar Patel Univs.).
Publs. 65 papers on cosmic ray and elementary particle physics.
Department of Electronics, Vigyan Bhavan Annexe, Maulana Azad Road, New Delhi 110011; Home: 81 Lodi Estate, New Delhi 11003, India.
Telephone: 38130 (Office); 611533 (Home).

Menon, Nedyam Balachandra, B.A.; Indian diplomatist; b. 18 March 1921, South India; ed. Allahabad Univ.
Indian Navy 43-46; Indian Embassy, The Hague 49; Indian Mil. Mission, Berlin 51; Indian Embassy, Kathmandu 54; High Comm. of India, Ottawa 57; Indian Embassy, Washington 59; Ministry of External Affairs Dir. (China Div.) 61; Nat. Defence Coll. 64; Indian Embassy, Bangkok and Perm. Del. to ECAFE 65; Deputy High Commr., Kuala Lumpur 66; Political Officer for Sikkim and Bhutan 67-70; Amb. to Indonesia 70-73; Joint Sec. Ministry of External Affairs 73-75; Amb. to Turkey Aug. 75-.
Embassy of India, 24 Sibris Kokak, Cankaya, Ankara, Turkey.
Telephone: 272420.

Menon, Parakat Achutha, B.A.; Indian diplomatist; b. 2 Jan. 1905, Palghat; ed. Presidency Coll., Madras, and New Coll., Oxford.
Joined I.C.S. 29; Under-Sec., Public Works Dept., Govt. of Madras 34-37; Under-Sec., Home Dept., Govt. of India 38-41; mem. Indian Legislative Assembly 38-39; Collector and District Magistrate, Guntur, Madras 41-43; Deputy Sec. and Sec., India Supply Mission, Washington, D.C. 43-47; Adviser, Indian del. to UN, San Francisco 45, N.Y. 46; served on Far East Comm., Washington, D.C. 46-47; del. UNRRA Conf., Atlantic City 46; Joint Sec. Ministry of External Affairs, Govt. of India 47-49; Minister to Portugal 49-51; Amb. to Belgium and concurrently Minister to Luxembourg 51-54; Amb. to Thailand 54-56, High Commr. to Australia and New Zealand 56-59; Amb. to Argentina 59-60, to Fed. Repub. of Germany 61-64; Hon. Chair. FACT, Kerala 65-70; Dir. State Bank of India 65-73, Cochin Refineries Ltd., Mysore Tools Ltd., Premier Breweries Ltd.; Chair. Madras Industrial Linings Ltd., Southern Regional Council of Indo-German Chamber of Commerce, Madras Literary Soc., Madras Kerala Samaj Educ. Soc.; Pres. Madras Musical Asscn., Fed. of Indo-German Socs. in India; Vice-Pres. Indian Council of World Affairs, Indian Inst. of Public Admin. (Madras Branch); mem. Exec. Council Indian Inst. of Public Admin., New Delhi.
Padmaja, 4A Tank Bund Road, Nungambakkam, Madras 34, India.
Telephone: 82832 (Home).

Menon, Vatakke Kurupath Narayana, M.A., PH.D.; Indian arts centre director; b. 27 June 1911, Trichur, Kerala; ed. Univ. of Madras and Edinburgh Univ.
Script Writer, Producer and Adviser for E. Services of B.B.C. during Second World War; returned to India 47; Dir. of Broadcasting, Baroda State 47-48; joined All-India Radio as Dir. of Staff Training 48, became Dir. of Delhi, Madras and Calcutta Stations, Dir. of External Services and Deputy Dir.-Gen.; Sec. Nat. Acad. of Music, Dance and Drama, India 63-65; Dir.-Gen. All-India Radio 65-68; Pres. Int. Music Council (UNESCO) 66-68, 76-78; mem. Faculty of Music, Delhi Univ.; Exec. Dir. Nat. Centre for the Performing Arts, Bombay 68-; Vice-Chair. Int. Inst. for Comparative Music Studies, Berlin; Dir. Film Finance Corpn. of India; Hon. Exec. Dir. Homi Bhabha Fellowships Council 68-; Scholar-in-Residence, Aspen Inst. for Humanistic Studies 73; Padma Bhushan 69; Trustee, Int. Broadcast Inst.
Publs. *Development of William Butler Yeats* 42, 60, *Kerala, a Profile* 61, *Balasaraswathi* 63, *The Communications Revolution* 76.
National Centre for the Performing Arts, Nariman Point, Bombay 400021, India.
Telephone: 310011 (Office); 316364 (Home).

Menzies, Rt. Hon. Sir Robert Gordon, K.T., C.H., P.C., F.R.S., Q.C., LL.M.; Australian politician; b. 20 Dec. 1894, Jeparit, Victoria; ed. Melbourne Univ.
Member Victoria Legislative Council 28-29; mem. Victoria Legislative Assembly 29-34; Hon. Minister Victorian Govt. 28-29, Attorney-Gen. and Minister for Railways 32 and Deputy Premier 32-34; mem. Federal House of Representatives for Kooyong 34-66; Commonwealth Attorney-Gen. and Minister for Industry 34-39; Prime Minister 39-41; Treas. 39-40; Minister for Defence Coordination Nov. 39-41, for Trade and Customs Feb.-March 40, for Information March-Dec. 40, for Munitions June-Nov. 40; mem. United Australia Party, Deputy Leader 36-39, Leader 39-41 and 43; Opposition mem. Advisory War Council 41-44; Leader Fed. Opposition 43-49; Prime Minister 49-66; Lord Warden of Cinque Ports 65-; Chancellor, Univ. of Melbourne 67-72; Leader of Mission to Pres. Nasser in Cairo on Suez Canal Aug./Sept. 56; numerous honorary degrees.
Publs. *The Rule of Law During War* 17, *Studies in the Australian Constitution* (joint author) 33, *To the People of Britain at War* (speeches) 41, *The Forgotten People* 43, *Speech is of Time* 58, *The Changing Commonwealth* 60, *Afternoon Light* (memoirs) 67, *Central Power in the Australian Commonwealth* 67, *The Measure of the Years* (memoirs, Vol. II) 70.
Office: 95 Collins Street, Melbourne, 3000 Victoria; Home: 2 Haverbrack Avenue, Malvern, 3144 Victoria, Australia.
Telephone: 639463 (Office); 205111 (Home).

Mifune, Toshiro; Japanese actor; b. 1 April 1920, Chintago, China.
First screen appearance in *Shin Baka Jidai* (These Foolish Times) 47; played leading role in *Rashomon* 50; other films in which he has played important roles include *Yoidore Tenshi* (Drunken Angel), *Shichinin no Samurai* (The Seven Samurai), *Miyamoto Musashi* (The Legend of Musashi) 54, *Kumonosu-Jo*, *Muhomatsu no Issho* (The

Rickshawman) 58, *Kakushitoride no San Akunin* (The Hidden Fortress) 58, *Sengoku Guntoden* (Saga of the Vagabonds) 59, *Nippon Tanjo* (The Three Treasures) 59, *Ankokugai no Taiketsu* (The Last Gunfight) 60, *Taiheiyo no Arashi* (The Storm of the Pacific), *Yosimbo, Tsubaki Sanjuro, Osakajo Monogatari* (Daredevil in the Castle), *Akahige* 65, *Grand Prix* 66, *Rebellion, Admiral Yamamoto* 68, *Hell in the Pacific* 68, *Furinkazan* 69, *Red Sun* 71, *Paper Tiger* 74.
Mifune Productions Co. Ltd., 9-30-7 Seijyo, Setagaya-ku, Tokyo; Home: 6-25-18 Seijo, Setagaya-ku, Tokyo, Japan. Telephone: (484) 1111 (Office); 484-2231 (Home).

Miki, Takeo, LL.M.; Japanese politician; b. 17 March 1907, Tokushima-ken; ed. Meiji Univ., Tokyo.
Member House of Reps. 37-; Minister of Communications 47-48, of Transport 54-55; Sec.-Gen. Liberal-Democratic Party 56, 64; State Minister, Dir.-Gen. of Econ. Planning Agency 58-59, of Science and Technology, Chair. of Atomic Energy Comm. 61-62; Minister of International Trade and Industry 65-66; Minister of Foreign Affairs 66-68; Deputy Prime Minister, Minister of State, Dir.-Gen. Environment Agency 72-74, resigned; Prime Minister Dec. 74-; Pres. Japanese Liberal-Democratic Party Dec. 74-; Hon. LL.D. (Univ. of Southern Calif., Columbia Univ.).
Office of the Prime Minister, Tokyo; and 18-20, Nanpeidai-machi, Shibuya-ku, Tokyo 180, Japan.

Mima, Yasuichi, B.COM.; Japanese industrialist; b. 3 Aug. 1903; ed. Tokyo Univ. of Commerce.
Kuhara Mining Co. (now Nippon Mining Co.) 28-, Dir. Nippon Mining Co. Ltd. 46-, Man. Dir. 47-57, Pres. 57, Chair. 69-74; Pres. Toho Titanium Co. 59, now Chair.; Pres. Abu Dhabi Oil Co. Ltd.; Chair. Kyodo Sekiyu K.K.; Dir. Teikoku Oil Co. Ltd. 57-, Japan Petroleum Fed. 57-; Governing Dir., Japan Fed. of Employers' Asscns. 59-, Exec. Dir., Japan Fed. of Econ. Orgs. 59-, Dir. Japan Management Asscn. 59-, Pres. Japan Mining Industry Asscn. 62-; Order of Merit, Chile 62.
Nippon Mining Co., 9 Aoi-cho, Akasaka, Minato-ku, Tokyo; Home: 108 Sekinecho, Suginamiku, Tokyo, Japan.

Minh, Dang Quang (*see* Dang Quang Minh).

Minh, Lt.-Gen. Duong Van (*see* Duong Van Minh, Lt.-Gen.).

Mintaredja, Hadji Mohamad Sjafa'at, M.LL.; Indonesian lawyer; b. 17 Feb. 1921, Bogor, Java; ed. Gadjahmada Univ., Leiden Univ., Netherlands, and Univ. of Indonesia, Jakarta.
Mem. of Board of many nat. youth movements 36-44; Judge, Court in Bandung 44-46; Chief, Legal Dept., Foreign Exchange Control 50-55; in private business (import, export, banking and industry) 57-65; Asst. to the Minister of Social Affairs 65-66; Chair. Board of Dirs. of two state construction companies 66-68; Minister of State 68-71; Minister of Social Affairs Sept. 71-; Chair. Partai Muslimin Indonesia 70; Gen. Chair. Partai Persatuan Pembangunan (grouping of the fmr. Islamic parties) Feb. 73-; Founder Islamic Indonesia Students Org., Chair. 47-; mem. Board of Muslim Social Org.
Publs. (in Indonesian): *A Reflection and Revision of Ideas: Islam and Politics, Islam and State in Indonesia* (also transl. in English, Dutch and Arabic) 71, *Rationalism versus Religious Belief, Family Life and the Haj Pilgrimage;* many articles in Indonesian magazines and journals.
Jalan K.H.A. Dahlan 21, Kebajoran Baru, Jakarta, Indonesia.
Telephone: 46717, 41329, 45042 ext. 10 (Office); 71216 (Home); 582089 (Official Residence).

Misra, Sirdar Iswary Raj, M.A., B.L.; Nepalese diplomatist; b. 29 Oct. 1917, Kathmandu; ed. St. Xavier's Coll., The Scottish Church Coll. and Univ. Law Coll., Calcutta, and Calcutta Univ.
Sectional Head, Dept. of Law, Kathmandu 42; Head of Buying Agency to Govt. of Nepal, Calcutta 43-45; Dept. of Law, Kathmandu 45-47; First Sec. Nepalese Embassy, London 47, later Counsellor; Deputy Sec. Ministry of Foreign Affairs 56-59; Registrar of Supreme Court, Kathmandu 59-60; Judge of Western High Court 60-61; Judge of Supreme Court 61-65; Amb. to France 65-67, to U.K. 65-69, and concurrently to Italy and Greece 68-69; Amb. to Pakistan 69-74, concurrently to Iran and Turkey 70-74; Suprasidha Prabala Gorakga Dakshina Bahu (Nepal); Knight Commdr. Order of Orange Nassau (Netherlands); Grand Officer of Merit (France); Officier Légion d'Honneur.
c/o Ministry of Foreign Affairs, Kathmandu, Nepal.

Mitra, Sombhu; Indian actor and stage director; b. 22 Aug. 1915; ed. Ballygunge Govt. High School and St. Xavier's Coll., Calcutta.
Public Stage, Bengal 39-42; Producer-Dir.-Actor, Indian People's Theatre Asscn. 43-46; Producer-Dir.-Actor Bohurupee (non-commercial theatre) 48-; Prof. and Head of Dept. of Drama, Rabindra Bharati Univ., Calcutta; Fellow Sangeet Natak Akademi, New Delhi; Grand Prix Karlovy Vary Film Festival 57; Padma Bhusan 69.
Productions include: *Four Chapters* (Tagore) 51, *An Enemy of the People* (Ibsen) 52, *Red Oleanders* (Tagore) 54, *The Doll's House* (Ibsen) 58, *Sacrifice* (Tagore) 61, *The King of the Dark Chamber* (Tagore) 64, *Oedipus Rex* (Sophocles) 64, *Baki Itihas* 67, *Pagla Ghora* 71.
Publs. *Abhinay-Natak-Mancha* 57, *Putul Khela* 58, *Kanchanranga* 61, *Ghurnee* 67, *Raja Oidipous* 69, *Prasanga Natya* 73.
Bohurupee, 11A Nasiruddin Road, Park Circus, Calcutta 700017; Home: 96 Park Street, Calcutta 700017, India.

Mitsui, Shingo, DR.AGR.SC.; Japanese agricultural scientist; b. 1 Jan. 1910, Tokyo; ed. Univ. of Tokyo.
Senior Chemist, Dept. of Agricultural Chem. Nat. Agricultural Experiment Station of Ministry of Agriculture and Forestry 32-45; Dir. of Dept. of Soil and Fertilizer 45-48; Asst. Prof. (Fertilizer and Plant Nutrition) Faculty of Agriculture, Univ. of Tokyo 48-52, Prof. (Fertilizer and Plant Nutrition) 52-63, Dean of Dept. of Chemical Sciences of Graduate School 63-65, Prof. Emer. 70-; mem. Scientific Advisory Cttee. of Int. Atomic Energy Agency (IAEA) 65-; Dir. Fertilizer Research Inst. 69-; Lecturer, FAO Int. Training Centre on Fertilizer and Soil for Rice, India 52; Councillor, Japan Radio Isotope Asscn. and Scientific Expert to Atomic Energy Comm., Japan 55-; Del. to numerous int. confs. on rice cultivation and peaceful uses of atomic energy; Prize of Japan Acad. and others.
Publs. *Dynamic Studies on the Nutrients Uptake by Crop Plants* (with others) Parts 1-45, 51-64, *Inorganic Nutrition Fertilization and Soil Amelioration for Lowland Rice* 54, *Efficient Use of Urea Fertilizer in Japan* 65.
Higashi Fushimi 2-2-25, Hoya-shi, Tokyo, Japan.
Telephone: 0424-63-1453.

Mitter, Gopendra Krishna; Indian judge; b. 24 Sept. 1906, Muzaffarpur, Bihar; ed. Zilla School, Muzaffarpur, Patna Coll., Bihar and Univ. Coll., London.
Called to the Bar, Lincoln's Inn, London; practised at the Bar, Calcutta High Court 35-52; Judge, Calcutta High Court 52-66; Judge, Supreme Court of India 66-74.
No. 10 Tees January Marg, New Delhi; 36/4 South End Park, Calcutta 29, India.

Miyake, Shigemitsu; Japanese banker; b. 27 Feb. 1911, Osaka; ed. Tokyo Imperial Univ.
Bank of Japan 33-67, Dir. 62-67; Deputy Pres. Tokai Bank Ltd. 67-68, Pres. 68-69, Chair. and Pres. 69-75, Chair. 75-; Exec. Dir. Japan Man. Orgs. 70, Japan Fed. of Econ. Orgs. 71; Pres. Nagoya Chamber of Commerce and Industry 74; Vice-Pres. Japan Chamber of Commerce and Industry 74; Blue Ribbon Medal 74.

Tokai Bank Ltd., 3-21-24, Nishiki, Naka-ku, Nagoya; Home: 2-24-3, Shimoyama-cho, Mizuho-ku, Nagoya, Japan.

Miyamoto, Kenji; Japanese writer and politician; b. 17 Oct. 1908; ed. Tokyo Imperial Univ.
Member C.P. of Japan 31-, mem. Cen. Cttee. 33-, Gen. Sec. of Cen. Cttee. 58-, Chair. of Presidium of Cen. Cttee. 70-; imprisoned 33-45.
Publs. *Problems of Democratic Revolution* 47, *Advance Towards Freedom and Independence* 49, *Twelve Years' Letters* 52, *World of Yuriko Miyamoto* 54, *Prospects of Japanese Revolution* 61, *The Path of Our Party's Struggle* 61, *Actual Tasks and the Communist Party of Japan* 66, *Selections from Literal Critiques of Kenji Miyamoto* 68, *The Road to a New Japan* 70, *Standpoint of the Communist Party of Japan* 72, *Dialogues with Kenji Miyamoto* 72, *Kenji Miyamoto with Pressmen* 73, *Abashiri Note* 75, *Interviews with Kenji Miyamoto* 75, *Kenji Miyamoto on Our Time* 75, *The Defeated Literature* 75.
Central Committee of the Communist Party of Japan, Sendagaya 4-chome 26, Shibuya-ku, Tokyo, Japan.

Miyazaki, Kagayaki; Japanese chemical executive; b. 19 April 1909, Nagasaki Prefecture; ed. Tokyo Univ.
Governing Dir. Japan Fed. of Employers' Asscns. 49-; Man. Dir. Japan Chemical Industry Asscn. 50-; with Asahi-Dow Ltd. 52; mem. Employers Cttee. of Central Labour Relations Board 53-62; Pres. Asahi Chemical Industry Co. Ltd. 61-; Exec. Dir. Fed. of Econ. Orgs. 61-; mem. Export and Import Trading Council, Ministry of Int. Trade and Industry 69-; Vice-Pres. Japan Textile Fed. 69-; mem. Tariff Council of Ministry of Finance 70-; Counsel, Japan Chemical Fibres Asscn. 71-; mem. Japan External Trade Operational Council 71-.
Asahi Chemical Industry Co. Ltd., 12, 1-chome, Yurakucho, Chiyoda-ku, Tokyo; 144 Funabashi-cho, Setagaya-ku, Tokyo, Japan.
Telephone: 429-2027.

Miyazaki, Kazuo; Japanese banker; b. 17 Feb. 1904, Tokyo; ed. Tokyo Commercial Coll.
Managing Director, The Long-Term Credit Bank of Japan Ltd. 52-58, Sen. Man. Dir. 58-63, Deputy Pres. 63-66, Pres. 66-71, Chair. of Board 71-; Medal with Blue Ribbon.
The Long-Term Credit Bank of Japan Ltd., 2-4 Otemachi 1-chome Chiyoda-ku, Tokyo 100; Home: 10-15 Nakamura 1-chome, Nerima-ku, Tokyo 176, Japan.
Telephone: Tokyo 211-5111 (Office); Tokyo 990-0854 (Home).

Miyazawa, Kiichi; Japanese politician; b. 8 Oct. 1919; ed. Tokyo Univ.
Ministry of Finance 41-49; Private Sec. to Minister of Finance 49-51, to Minister of Int. Trade and Industry 51-52; mem. House of Councillors 53-65, Chair. Steering Cttee. 61-62; Minister of State in charge of Econ. Planning Agency 62-64, 66-68; mem. House of Reps. 67-; Minister of Int. Trade and Industry (in charge of *Expo 70*) 70-71, of Foreign Affairs Dec. 74-.
Ministry of Foreign Affairs, Tokyo; 1-34, 6-chome, Jingu-mae, Shibuya-ku, Tokyo, Japan.

Mizukami, Tatsuzo, M.A.; Japanese business executive; b. 15 Oct. 1903, Kitakoma-gun; ed. Tokyo Commercial Coll.
Mitsui Bussan Kaisha 28-47; Exec. Man. Dir. Daiichi Bussan Kaisha Ltd. 47-57, Exec. Vice-Pres. 57-59; Exec. Vice-Pres. Mitsui and Co. 59-61, Pres. 61-69, Chair. 69-71, Dir. and Senior Adviser 71-73, Senior Adviser 73-; Chair. Int. Cttee., Industrial Structure Council 61-, Foreign Trade Cttee., Supreme Foreign Trade Council 62-, Int. Econ. Cttee., Econ. Council 64-; Exec. Dir. Fed. of Econ. Orgs. (Keidanren) 64-; Pres. Japan Foreign Trade Council Inc. 68-; Medal of Honour with Blue Ribbon, Gran Cruz de Mayo (Argentina), Gran Cruz (Peru).
Office: 2-9 Nishi Shimbashi It-chome, Minato-ku, Tokyo; Home: 30-2, 2-chome, Kakinokizaka, Meguro-ku, Tokyo, Japan.

Mizushima, Sanichiro, D.SC.; Japanese physical chemist; b. 21 March 1899, Tokyo; ed. Univ. of Tokyo.
Professor of Physical Chem., Univ. of Tokyo 38-59, Prof. Emer. 59-; mem. Japan Science Council 50-62; Dir. Tokyo Research Inst. of Yawata 59-69, Hon. Dir. 69-73; mem. Japan Acad.; Bureau mem. Int. Union of Pure and Applied Chem. 55-67; mem. Pontifical Acad. of Sciences, Nat. Acad. of Sciences (U.S.A.); Hon. mem. Royal Spanish Soc. of Physics and Chem., Higher Science Council of Spain, Indian Acad. of Sciences, American Acad. of Arts and Sciences, Chemical Soc. of Japan (Pres. 60-61); Chemical Soc. Prize 29, Imperial Acad. Prize 38, Decoration of Emperor for Cultural Merits 61, Decoration of Emperor of the First Class 70.
Publs. *Quantum Chemistry* 40, *Electric Waves and Matter* 46, *Structure of Molecules and Internal Rotation* 54, *Raman Effect* 58, *Collection of Scientific Papers* 59, *A History of Physical Chemistry in Japan* 72, *Ancient Tokaido Roads* 73.
2-10-6, Tamagawa-Denenchofu, Setagayaku, Tokyo 158, Japan.
Telephone: Tokyo 721-4045.

Mizuta, Mikio; Japanese politician; b. 1905; ed. Kyoto Univ.
Elected eight times as member of House of Reps. 46-; Parliamentary Vice-Minister of Finance 49-50; Dir. Economic Deliberation Board 53; Minister of International Trade and Industry 56-57; Minister of Finance 60-62, Dec. 66-68, 71-72; fmr. teacher, Senshu Univ., fmr. Dir. Tokyo Kohan Kogyo Co.; Liberal-Democratic Party.
2027, Hojo, Tateyama City, Chiba Prefecture, Japan.

Mody, Piloo, M.A.; Indian architect and politician; b. 14 Nov. 1926, Bombay; ed. Dun School, Dehra Dun, and Univ. of California.
Worked with Le Corbusier on Chandigarh project 51-53, practising architect 53-; mem. Lok Sabha 67-; fmr. Pres. Swatantra Party; now Gen. Sec. Bharatiya Lok Dal; Man. Trustee, March of the Nation Trust; Editor *The Nation Weekly*; detained June 75-.
Publs. *Zulfi my Friend* 73.
Mody and Colgan, Stadium House, 81-83 Vir Nariman Road, Bombay 20; Home: 20C Prithviraj Road, New Delhi, India.

Moertopo, Maj.-Gen. Ali; Indonesian army officer; b. 23 Sept. 1924; ed. Dutch Secondary School, Army Gen. Staff Coll.
Several army posts as 2nd Lieut., active in guerrilla war for nat. independence, 1st Lieut., Capt. active in putting down rebellion in West Sumatra 58, Maj. with Special Operational Command for the liberation of West Irian and Mandala Operational Command "Trikora" (People's Threefold Command) 61; promoted Lieut.-Col.; Asst. for Intelligence for army operations in West Irian 63, in confrontation with Malaysia and Singapore 64, later as Strategic Intelligence Officer of Special Operations prominent in settlement with Malaysia and Singapore; promoted Col.; Head Foreign Intelligence, Dept. of Chair. of Cabinet Presidium 67, Personal Asst. to the Pres. for Special Affairs 68-; promoted Brig.-Gen. 69, Maj.-Gen. 71; Deputy Head of State Intelligence for Operations; mem. People's Consultative Assembly 72-; several awards for distinguished army service including War for Independence Medal I, II, Medal of Loyalty, Medal of Defender.
Publ. *The Acceleration of Modernization during 25 Years of Development.*
52 Jalan Raden Saleh, Jakarta; Home: 18 Jalan Matraman Raya, Jakarta, Indonesia.

Mohamed, Azmi Bin Haji, S.S.M., P.M.N., D.P.M.K., P.S.B.; Malaysian company executive and fmr. judge; b. 26 June 1909; ed. Sultan Ibrahim School, Kedah and Inner Temple, London.
Joined Kedah Civil Service 33; appointed into Colonial Legal Service 48; returned to Kedah Civil Service 51; State Sec. 58; Judge of High Court of Fed. of Malaya 58; Chief Justice of Malaya 66-68; Lord Pres. of Fed. Court of Malaysia 68-74; Chair. UNITATA Sdn. Bhd. 75, British American Insurance (Malaysia) Sdn. Bhd. 76.
Oriental Plaza, Jalan Parry, Kuala Lumpur; Lorong Batai, Damansara Height, Kuala Lumpur, Malaysia.

Mohammed Zahir Shah; ex-King of Afghanistan; b. 15 Oct. 1914; ed. Habibia High School, Istiqlal Coll. (both in Kabul), Lycée Janson-de-Sailly and Univ. of Montpellier, France.
Graduated with highest honours; attended Infantry Officers' School, Kabul 32; married Lady Homira, November 4th 1931; children, Princess Bilqis, Prince Ahmad Shah Khan, Princess Maryam, Prince Mohammed Nadir Khan, Prince Shah Mahmoud Khan, Prince Mohammed Daoud Jan, Prince Mirvis Jan; Asst. Minister in Ministry of National Defence 32-33; acting Minister of Education 33; crowned King 8 Nov. 33, deposed 17 July 73, abdicated 24 Aug. 73.
c/o Afghan Embassy, Via Nomentana 120, Rome, Italy.

Mookerjee, Sir Birendra Nath, Kt., M.A., M.I.E.; Indian businessman; b. 14 Feb. 1899; ed. Hastings House and Sibpur Engineering Coll., Calcutta, and Trinity Coll., Cambridge.
Assistant Martin & Co. 24; Partner, Burn & Co. 31- and Martin & Co. 34-, Governing Dir. Martin Burn Ltd. 58-; mem. Munitions Board and Defence Council, Second World War; Sheriff, Calcutta 40; Chair. Board of Govs., Indian Inst. of Technology, Khasappur; Pres. Calcutta Board, fmr. Imperial Bank of India; Chair. Steel Corpn. of Bengal Ltd., Indian Iron and Steel Co. Ltd., Calcutta-72; mem. Governing Body, Sibpur Engineering Coll.; fmr. Fellow Faculty of Engineering, Calcutta Univ.; Chair. Indian Iron and Steel Co. Ltd. until 72; Dir. Darjeeling Himalayan Railway Co., and many others.
7 Harrington Street, Calcutta 16, India.

Moorehead, Alan, C.B.E.; Australian writer; b. 22 July 1910, Melbourne; ed. Scotch Coll. and Melbourne Univ.
Sunday Times Gold Medal 56; Duff Cooper Award (for *Gallipoli*) 56.
Publs. *Mediterranean Front* 41, *A Year of Battle* 43, *The End in Africa* 43, *African Trilogy* 44, *Eclipse* 45, *Montgomery* 46, *The Rage of the Vulture* 48, *The Villa Diana* 51, *The Traitors* 52, *Rum Jungle* 53, *A Summer Night* 54, *Gallipoli* 56, *The Russian Revolution* 58, *No Room in the Ark* 59, *The White Nile* 60, *The Blue Nile* 62, *Coopers Creek* (Royal Soc. of Literature Award) 63, *The Desert War* 65, *The Fatal Impact* 66, *Darwin and the Beagle* 69, *A Late Education* 70.
c/o National Bank of Australia, Australia House, Strand, London, W.C.2, England.

Moraes, Dominic; Indian writer and poet; b. 19 July 1938; ed. St. Mary's High School, Bombay, and Jesus Coll., Oxford.
Consultant UN Fund for Population Activities 73; Man. Editor *The Asia Magazine*, Hong Kong 72-; Hawthornden Prize for *A Beginning* 57.
Publs. include: *A Beginning* 57, *Gone Away* 60, *My Son's Father* (autobiog.) 68, *The Tempest Within* 72-73, *The People Time Forgot* 72, *A Matter of People* 74; books of poems and travel books on India.
31 Queen's Road Central, Hong Kong.

Mori, Haruki; Japanese diplomatist; b. 1911; ed. Univ. of Tokyo.
Ministry of Foreign Affairs, served U.S.A. and Philippines 35-41; Head of Econ. Section Dept. of Political Affairs 50-53; Counsellor Rome 53-55; Counsellor Asian Affairs Bureau, Tokyo 55-56; Private Sec. to Prime Minister 56-57; Counsellor Int. Co-operation 57; Dir.-Gen. of American Affairs Bureau 57-60; Minister to U.K. 60-63, to France 63-64; Perm. Rep. to OECD 64-67; Deputy Vice-Minister at Ministry of Foreign Affairs 67-70, Vice-Minister 70-72; Amb. to U.K. 72-75.
c/o Ministry of Foreign Affairs, Tokyo, Japan.

Morimoto, Kanzaburo; Japanese business executive; b. 13 Dec. 1892; ed. Kyoto Univ.
Takeda Chemical Industries Ltd. 19-, Statutory Auditor 25-33, Dir. 33-38, Managing Dir. 38-47, Senior Managing Dir. 47-60, Vice-Pres. 60-63, Chair. of Board of Dirs. 63-73, Advisory Councillor 73-; Pres. Daiwa Real Estate Co. Ltd. 57-; Yellow Ribbon Medal 63.
Takeda Chemical Industries, 2-27 Doshomachi, Higashi-ku, Osaka 541, Japan.

Morinaga, Teiichiro; Japanese banker; b. 9 Sept. 1910, Miyazaki Prefecture; ed. The Fifth Higher School, Kumamoto and Tokyo Imperial Univ.
Ministry of Finance 32-59, Deputy Vice-Minister of Finance 49-53, Dir. Budget Bureau 53-57, Vice-Minister of Finance 57-59; Pres. Small Business Finance Corpn. 61-62; Gov. The Export-Import Bank of Japan 62-67; Pres. The Tokyo Stock Exchange 67-74; Gov. Bank of Japan 74-.
Bank of Japan, 2-2-1 Hongoku-cho, Nihonbashi, Chuo-ku, Tokyo; Home: 6-23-18 Honkomagome, Bunkyo-ku, Tokyo, Japan.

Morita, Akio; Japanese business executive; b. 26 Jan. 1921, Nagoya; ed. Osaka Imperial Univ.
Co-founder SONY Corpn., Tokyo 46, Exec. Man. Dir. 58-59, Exec. Vice-Pres. 59-71, Pres. 71-76, Chair. of Board and Chief Exec. Officer 76-; Pres. SONY Corpn., America 60-66, Chair. of Board 66-72, also Pres. 68-71, Chair. Finance Cttee. 72-74, of Exec. Cttee. 74-; Dir. IBM World Trade Americas (Far East Corpn.); mem. Int. Council, Morgan Guaranty Trust Co.; mem. Rockefeller Univ. Council; Edwardo Rihan Award for Int. Marketing 69.
Publs. *Gakureki Muyouron* 66, *Shin Zitsuryoku Shugi* 69.
SONY Corporation, 7-35, Kitashinagawa 6-chome, Shinagawa-ku, Tokyo, Japan.
Telephone: 03-448-2002.

Moriyama, Kinji; Japanese politician; b. 10 Jan. 1917, Tochigi Pref.; ed. Tokyo Univ.
Served in Ministry of Foreign Affairs; mem. House of Reps. 49-, Chair. Labour and Welfare Cttee. 58-71, Construction Cttee. 65-; Pres. Japan Camera Inspection Unit 54-; Parl. Vice-Minister of Posts and Telecommunications 60-; Chair. of Labour and Welfare Cttee. 58-, 71-; Chair. Construction Cttee. of House of Reps. 65-; Minister of State, in charge of Science and Technology Agency 73-75.
13-2, Haneki-cho, 1-chome, Setagaya-ku, Tokyo 156, Japan.

Morrison, William Lawrence, B.ECONS.; Australian politician; b. 3 Nov. 1928; ed. North Sydney Technical High School, Univ. of Sydney, London School of Slavonic and East European Studies.
Joined Australian Diplomatic Service 50; Australian Embassy, Moscow 52-54; Econ. Relations Branch, Dept. of External Affairs 54-57; Australian Embassy, Bangkok, concurrently Liaison Officer UN Econ. Comm. for Asia, Chair. SEATO Cttee. on Soviet Econ. Penetration in Asia and Far East 57-59; Australian Embassy, Washington 59-61, Moscow 61-63; Head Information and Cultural Relations Branch, Dept. of External Affairs 63-66; Deputy High Commr. to Malaysia 67-68; mem. Parl. for St. George, N.S.W. 69-75; Deputy Chair. Joint Parl. Foreign Affairs Cttee. 69-72; Minister for Science 72-75, and External Territories 72-73; Asst. Minister for Foreign Affairs,

with special responsibility for Papua New Guinea 73-75, Asst. Minister for Defence 74-75, Minister for Defence June-Nov. 75; Labor Party.
20A Cripps Street, Arncliffe, New South Wales 2205, Australia.

Moses, Sir Charles Joseph Alfred, Kt., C.B.E.; Australian broadcasting official; b. 21 Jan. 1900, Little Hulton, Lancashire, England; ed. Oswestry Grammar School, and Royal Mil. Coll., Sandhurst.
Lieut. in 2nd Border Regt. (British Regular Army) 18-22; fruit-grower, Bendigo, Australia 23-24; motor salesman and sales manager 24-30; announcer, Nat. Broadcasting Service 30-32; N.S.W. Sporting and Talks Ed., Australian Broadcasting Comm. 33-34; Fed. Talks Controller, A.B.C. 35; Gen. Manager A.B.C. 35-65; Sec.-Gen. Asian Broadcasting Union 65-; joined A.I.F. 40; rose to rank of Lt.-Col. 42; served in Malaya Feb. 41-Feb. 42, New Guinea Sept. 42-Feb. 43; mentioned in despatches Sept. 43; Commdr., Order of Merit (Austria); Trustee and mem. Exec. Cttee., Australian Elizabethan Theatre Trust; Vice-Pres. Royal Agricultural Soc.; Pres. Austrian-Australian Cultural Soc.; mem. Council of Int. Broadcasting Inst., Council of Royal Inst. for Deaf/Blind Children (N.S.W.); mem. Australian-American Asscn., Int. Advisory Cttee. of Prix Jeunesse Foundation (Munich); Hon. Dir. Post-graduate Medical Foundation of Australia.
Home: 78 New Beach Road, Darling Point, Sydney; Office: c/o Asian Broadcasting Union, 203 Castlereagh Street, Sydney, N.S.W., Australia.
Telephone: 617406 (Office); 324224 (Home).

Moses, David Gnanapragasam, M.A., PH.D.; Indian philosopher; b. 22 Jan. 1902; ed. Madras Christian Coll. Madras Univ., Union Theological Seminary, Columbia Univ.
Philosophy Lecturer, Noble Coll., Madras Univ. 24-26; Prof. Hislop Coll., Nagpur 26-40, Principal 40-61, Dean Faculty of Arts 58-61; Vice-Pres., Int. Missionary Council 47-61; Pres. Nat. Christian Council of India 59-63; mem. Presidium, World Council of Churches 61-69.
Publ. *Religious Truth and the Relation Between Religions.*
Hislop College, Nagpur, India.

Mountford, Charles Pearcy, O.B.E., M.A., DIP.ANTHRO.; British ethnologist and student of Australian primitive art; b. 9 May 1890, Hallett, S. Australia; ed. Univs. of Adelaide and Cambridge.
Accompanied Univ. of Adelaide Expeditions as Ethnologist to Warburton Ranges, Western Australia 35, Granites, Central Australia 36, Nepabunna, South Australia 37, Yuendumu, Central Australia 51; and as Leader to Nepabunna, South Australia 38 and 39, Mann and Musgrave Ranges, Central Australia 40, Haaste Bluff, Central Australia 42, Western Arnhem Land 49, North-Eastern Arnhem Land 51, Ayers Rock, Central Australia 52, Central Mount Wedge, Central Australia 56, North-Western Central Australia 60, Ayers Rock 60, North-Western Australia 63, North-Eastern Australia 64; leader of Nat. Geographic Society of America Expeditions to Arnhem Land, Northern Australia 48, Melville Island, Northern Australia 54, North-Western Australia 63, Cape York, N.E. Australia; Hon. Life Fellow Nat. Geographic Soc. of America, John Lewis Gold Medal, Royal Geographic Soc. (South Australian Branch), Founder's Gold Medal, Royal Geographical Soc. of Australia (Queensland Branch), Franklin Burr Award, Nat. Geographic Soc. of America; Nuffield Research Scholar 57-59; Natural History Medallion of Australia 49; Sir Joseph Verco Award, Royal Soc. of S. Australia 71; Hon. Assoc. in Ethnology, S. Australia; Hon. D.Litt. (Melbourne).
Publs. *The Art of Albert Namatjira* 44, *Brown Men and Red Sand* 48, *The Art, Myth and Symbolism of Arnhem Land* 56, *Australian Tree Portraits* 56, *The Tiwi, Their Art, Myth and Ceremony* 58, *Australian Aboriginal Art* 61, *The Dreamtime: Aboriginal Mythology in the Art of Ainslie Roberts* 64, *Aboriginal Paintings from Australia* 65, *Ayers Rock—its People, their Beliefs and their Art* 65, *The Dawn of Time: Aboriginal Mythology in the Art of Ainslie Roberts* 66, *Australian Aboriginal Portraits* 67, *Wimbaraku and the Myth of Jarapiri* 67, *The Aborigines and their Country* 69, *Nomads of the Australian Deserts: their Beliefs and their Art* 72, *The Rainbow Serpent, Myths of Australia* 72, *Aboriginal Spirit, Children, the Mythical Beliefs* 73, *The Dreamtime Book* 73, *Sacred Engraved Objects of the Australian Aborigines* 76, *Cave Paintings of Northern Queensland* 76.
748 Beulah Rood, Norwood, S.A. 5067, Australia.
Telephone: 31-1806.

Moyle, Colin James; New Zealand politician; b. 18 July 1929; ed. Auckland Grammar School, Auckland Teachers' Training Coll., Auckland Univ.
Schoolteacher and dairy farmer 50-60; Dominion Organizer, N.Z. Labour Party 60-63; mem. Parl. 63-; Minister of Agriculture, Fisheries, Forests and Science 72-75.
Parliament Buildings, Wellington; Home: 125 Coronation Road, Papatoetor, Auckland, New Zealand.

Mudholkar, Janardan Ranganath, B.A., LL.B.; Indian judge; b. 1902; ed. Elphinstone Coll., Bombay, Sidney Sussex Coll., Cambridge, and Lincoln's Inn, London.
Legal practice (barrister) Amraoti 25-29, Nagpur 30-41; Dist. and Sessions Judge 41-48; Judge Nagpur High Court 48-56; Act. Chief Justice, Bombay High Court Aug.-Sept. 60; Judge Supreme Court of India 60-66; Chair. Press Council of India 66-70.
Press Council of India, 10 Janpatti, New Delhi 11, India.

Muhammadullah; Bangladesh lawyer and politician; b. 1921, Saicha; ed. Dacca and Calcutta Univs.
Joined Dacca Bar 50; Lawyer, High Court 64; mem. Awami League 50-; Sec. E. Pakistan Awami League 52-72; mem. E. Pakistan Provincial Assembly 70; Political Adviser to Acting Pres. Syed Nazrul Islam 71; Deputy Speaker Bangladesh Constituent Assembly April-Nov. 72, Speaker 72-73; Speaker Bangladesh Parl. 73-74; Acting Pres. of Bangladesh Dec. 73-Jan. 74, Pres. 74-75; Minister of Land Admin. and Land Reforms Jan.-Aug. 75; Vice-Pres. of Bangladesh Aug.-Nov. 75.

Muir, Sir David John, Kt., C.M.G., F.C.I.S., F.A.S.A., F.A.I.M., A.A.U.Q., J.P.; Australian civil servant; b. 20 June 1916, Brisbane; ed. Commercial High School, Brisbane.
Clerk, Lands Dept. 33; Private Sec. to Queensland Premier 39; Investigations Officer, Sugar Cane Prices Board 43; Official Sec. to Premier 46; Permanent Under-Sec., Premier and Chief Sec.'s Dept., and Clerk, Exec. Council of Queensland 48; Agent-Gen. for Queensland in London 51-64; Dir. of Industrial Development, Queensland, and Chair. Industries Assistance Board 64-; Australian rep. on Int. Sugar Council 51-64 (Chair. 58); Pres. Chartered Inst. of Secs. 64; Chair. Queensland Theatre Co.; mem. Brisbane Town Planning Advisory Cttee.; James N. Kirby Medal of Inst. of Production Engineers 69.
Home: 28 Buena Vista Avenue, Coorparoo, Brisbane; Office: M.I.M. Building, Ann Street, Brisbane, Queensland, Australia.
Telephone: 398-3012 (Home); 221-7765 (Office).

Mujeeb, Muhammad, B.A.; Indian educationist; b. 1902; ed. Oxford Univ.
Joined Jamia Millia 26; Vice-Chancellor Jamia Millia 48-.
Publs. *History of Russian Literature, History of European Political Thought, Story of the World* (in Urdu), *A Glimpse of New China, World History—Our Heritage, Kimiyagar* (Urdu short stories), *Ordeal, The Indian Muslims, Education and Traditional Values, Ghalib, Akhbar* (*The Great*),

Islamic Influence on Indian Society, Dr. Zakir Husain—A Biography.
Jamia Millia, Jamianagar, New Delhi, India.

Mukherjee, J. N., C.B.E., D.SC., F.N.I.; Indian chemist and soil scientist; b. 1893, Mahadebpur, Rajshahi; ed. Univs. of Calcutta and London.
Assistant to Palit Prof. of Chemistry, Calcutta Univ. 15-19; Guruprasad Prof. of Chemistry 21-37, Ghose Prof. of Chemistry 37-45; fmr. Dir. Indian Agricultural Research Inst., New Delhi and Cen. Building Research Inst. Roorkee; fmr. Chair. sub-cttee. Nat. Planning Cttee. of Indian Nat. Congress; leader Indian del. 3rd Int. Congress of Soil Science 35; Convener and Pres. Indian Soc. of Soil Science 35; mem. India Scientific Mission to U.K. and U.S.A. 45; mem. Royal Society Empire Scientific Conf. and British Commonwealth Official Scientific Conf. 46; Leader, Indian Del. to Conf. on Tropical and Sub-Tropical Soil, U.K. 48; mem. UN Scientific Conf. on Conservation and Utilisation of Resources and Pres. of its Land Section Meeting U.S.A. 49; mem. Gen. Assembly Int. Council of Scientific Unions, London 46, Copenhagen 49; mem. Exec. Cttee. and Board Int. Council of Scientific Unions 47-52; Vice-Pres. Int. Soil Science Congress, Netherlands 50; Foreign Sec. Nat. Inst. of Sciences of India 52; Pres. Indian Science Congress Asscn. 52; Pres. Trustees, Surendraneth Teaching Insts. 52-; mem. Central Tea Board 54; Scientific Adviser, Dept. of Agriculture and Forests, West Bengal 52-56; Administrator, Board of Secondary Education, West Bengal 55-56; mem. Union Public Service Comm. 56-58; Chair. Land Utilization Board, West Bengal 59-66; Padma Bhushan 64; Hon. D.Sc. (Calcutta Univ.) 75, (Burdwan Univ.) 76.
Publs. Over 250 papers on physical chemistry, electrochemistry, colloids, soil science, etc.
10 Puran Chand Nahar Avenue, Calcutta 13, India.
Telephone: 24-3845.

Mukherji, Ajoy Kumar; Indian politician; b. April 1901; ed. Hamilton School, Tamluk, Uttarpara Coll., Hooghly, and Presidency Coll., Calcutta.
Joined Non-Co-operation Movement 21; imprisoned several times during Civil Disobedience and Quit India Movements; mem. W. Bengal Legislative Assembly 52-; Minister of Irrigation, W. Bengal 52-63; Pres. W. Bengal Pradesh Cttee. 64-66; Founder-Pres. Bangla Congress 66-; Chief Minister of W. Bengal March 67-Nov. 67, Feb. 69-March 70, also Minister of Finance, etc.
Writers' Building, Calcutta. India.

Muldoon, Rt. Hon. Robert David, P.C., M.P., F.C.A.N.Z., C.M.A.N.Z., F.C.M.A., F.C.I.S., A.I.N.Z.; New Zealand politician and public accountant; b. 21 Sept. 1921, Auckland; ed. Mount Albert Grammar School.
Senior Partner, Kendon Mills Muldoon and Browne, Auckland; Lecturer in Auditing 48-54; Pres. New Zealand Inst. of Cost Accountants 56, Auckland Horticultural Council 59-60; M.P. for Tamaki 60-; Parl. Under-Sec. to Minister of Finance 63-66; Minister of Tourism and Publicity 67, of Finance 67-72; Deputy Prime Minister Feb.-Dec. 72; Dominion Councillor, New Zealand Nat. Party 60-, Deputy Parl. Leader 72-74, Leader of Opposition 74-75; Prime Minister and Minister of Finance Dec. 75-; mem. Select Cttees., on Fishing Industry 63, Road Safety 65, Parl. Procedure 67; mem. Public Expenditure Cttee. 61-66, Chair. 63-66; Lever Hulme Prize, Inst. of Cost and Works Accountants 47, Maxwell Award, New Zealand Inst. of Cost Accountants 56.
290 Kohimarama Road, Auckland, New Zealand.
Telephone: 583-788.

Munekata, Eiji, DR.ENG.SC.; Japanese industrialist; b. 24 Jan. 1908, Tokyo; ed. Tokyo Imperial Univ.
Section Chief, Nippon Bemberg Silk Co. 31; Chief Engineer, Chosen Artificial Petroleum Manufacturing Co. 39; Head of Dept., Nippon Chisso Fertilizer Co. 44; Dir., subsequently Man. Dir. Asahi Chemical Industry Co. 47; Dir. Japan Atomic Energy Research Inst. 62, Pres. 68-.
Publs. *Separation* 50, *Man-made Fibre* 55, *Researches on Chemistry and Industrialization* 65.
31 1-chome, Zenpukuji-machi, Suginami-ku, Tokyo, Japan.
Telephone: 03-390-6364.

Muradov, Nuritdin Muradovich; Soviet politician; b. 1915; ed. Central Planning-Economic Inst.
Member C.P.S.U. 46-; Chair. District Planning Cttee., then Economist, Uzbek S.S.R. State Planning Cttee., later Chief of Section, Republican People's Commissariat for Trade, then Vice-Chair. Exec. Cttee. Regional Soviet of Working People's Deputies 33-51; First Sec. Namangansky District Cttee. of C.P. Uzbekistan, later Chair. Exec. Cttee. of Namangan, then of Khorezm, Regional Soviet of Working People's Deputies 51-65; First Sec. Surkhandaryinsk Regional Cttee. of C.P. Uzbekistan 65-; mem. Central Cttee. of C.P. Uzbekistan; Deputy to U.S.S.R. Supreme Soviet; Hero of Socialist Labour.
Surkhandaryinsk Regional Committee of Communist Party of Uzbekistan, Termez, U.S.S.R.

Muramaya, Nagataka; Japanese newspaper proprietor; b. 1894; ed. Kyoto Imperial Univ.
Director *Asahi Shimbun* 20-; Managing Dir. Asahi Welfare and Cultural Asscn. 52; Chair. of Board *Asahi Evening News* 53-; Dir. Asahi Broadcasting Corpn., Osaka 55; Pres. Japan Newspaper Publishers' and Editors' Asscn. 55; Vice-Pres. Féd. Int. des Editeurs de Journaux et Publications 58-; Pres. *Asahi Shimbun* 60-64; numerous decorations.
16 1-chome, Ichibeicho, Azabu, Minato-ku, Tokyo, Japan.

Murano, Tatsuo, B.A.; Japanese banker; b. 18 May 1907, Gase City, Nara Pref.; ed. Faculty of Econs., Tokyo Univ.
Joined Yamaguchi Bank 32, Dir. 57, Man. Dir. 59, Senior Man. Dir. 61, Deputy Pres. 64; Pres. Sanwa Bank Ltd. 71-; Vice-Chair. Fed. of Bankers' Asscn. of Japan.
601, 5-12-24 Minamiaoyama Minato-ku, Tokyo 107; and 5-3-24 Nigawa-cho Nishinomiya, Hyogo 662, Japan.
Telephone: (03) 406-3366 (Tokyo); (0798) 52-8226 (Osaka).

Murata, Masachika; Japanese architect; b. 6 Sept. 1906, Yokkaichi Mie Pref.; ed. Tokyo Acad. of Fine Arts.
Designer, Shinichiro Okada Architect Office, Tokyo 29-30, Building Dept. of Ministry of Imperial Household, Tokyo 31-36; Researcher of facilities of Museums of Europe and America at request of Ministry of Educ. 37-39; Architect, Kameki Tuchiura Architect Office 40-46; Vice-Chief of Architectural Div., Conf. of Devt. of Kainan-tow (Hainan Island, China) 43; Pres. Masachika Murata Architect Office 46-; Dir. Board, Japan Architects' Asscn. 54-; Dir. Sports and Recreation Facilities, Unicn of Int. Architects 59-; Prize of Ministry of Construction 70; Nat. Medal for Merit 73; Architecture Prize, Middle Area of Japan 73.
Works include: Yokohama building of Yokohama Trading Building Co. Ltd. (Kanagawa Prefecture Architectural Prize) 51; Tokyo Metropolitan Indoor Pool, Tokyo 57; Exhbn. Halls of Tokyo Int. Trading Center, Tokyo 59; Tokyo Olympic Komazawa Stadium (Special Prize of Architectural Inst. of Japan and Building Contractors' Soc. of Japan) 62; Italian Embassy, Tokyo 63; Netherlands Pavilion for 1970 World Expo (with Prof. Bakema and Dr. Webber), Osaka 69; Yokohama Technical High School 70; Kanebo Cosmetics Inc. Buildings 75; Nagano Athletic Stadium 75; Dentsu Kobe Building 75.
Office: Jingugaien Building, 2-7-25 Kita Aoyama, Minato-ku, Tokyo 107; Home: 2-14-4 Moto-Azubu, Minato-ku, Tokyo 106, Japan.
Telephone: 403-1451 (Office); 451-1672 (Home).

Murdoch, Keith Rupert; Australian newspaper publisher; b. 11 March 1931, Melbourne, Victoria.
Managing Dir., News Ltd., and assoc. Companies, publishers

of *The Australian, The News* (Adelaide), *The Daily Mirror* (Sydney), *The Daily Telegraph* (Sydney), *Sunday Mirror* (Sydney), *The Sunday Telegraph* (Sydney), *Sunday Truth* (Brisbane), *Sunday Mail* (Adelaide), *Sunday Times* (Perth), *The News* (Darwin), *The New Idea*, etc.; Chair. Southern Television Corpn. Adelaide; Chair. News Int. Ltd., publishers of *The Sun* (London) 69-, *The News of the World* (London), *San Antonio Express* (Texas), *San Antonio News* (Texas), *National Star* (Washington).
News International Ltd., 30 Bouverie Street, London, E.C.4, England.

Murphy, Lionel Keith, LL.B., B.SC.; Australian lawyer and politician; b. 31 Aug. 1922, Sydney; ed. Sydney High School and Univ. of Sydney.
Admitted to N.S.W. Bar 47, Victoria 58; Q.C., N.S.W. 60-, Victoria 61-; mem. Senate 62-75, Leader of the Opposition 67-72; Attorney-Gen., Minister for Customs and Excise and Leader of Govt. in Senate 72-75; Judge, Australian High Court 75-; mem. Exec. Int. Comm. of Jurists Australian Section 63-; del. to UN Conf. on Human Rights, Teheran 68; mem. Exec. Council of Australian Nat. Univ.
High Court of Australia, Taylor Square, Darlinghurst, N.S.W. 2010, Australia.
Telephone: 31-5720.

Murray, Jack Keith, O.B.E., E.D., B.A., B.SC.AGR., N.D.D., F.A.I.A.S.; Australian agriculturalist; b. 8 Feb. 1889; ed. Univ. of Sydney.
Served in A.I.F. in both World Wars; retired with rank of Colonel; Lecturer in Bacteriology and Dairy Technology, Hawkesbury Agric. Coll., N.S.W. 20-23; Principal, Queensland Agric. Coll. 23-45; Prof. of Agric., Univ. of Queensland 27-45; Admin. of Territory of Papua and New Guinea Oct. 45-52; Pres. Exec. and Legislative Councils of the Territory; Macrossan Lecturer, Univ. of Queensland 46; Australian Del., S. Pacific Region Conf. 47; Fellow Australian Nat. Research Council; Pres. Section K (Agric. and Forestry), Australian and New Zealand Asscn. for the Advancement of Science 35; Pres. Queensland Royal Soc. 36, Hon. Life mem. 68; mem. Senate, Univ. of Queensland 53-55, 57-68, Gov. Cromwell Coll., Univ. of Queensland 53-55, 57-68; mem. Council of Univ. Women's Coll. 53-55, 57-68; Colombo Plan Adviser on Agricultural Educ. 56-57; Acting Warden Int. House, Univ. of Melbourne 60; D.Sc. h.c. (Queensland) 68.
49 Dell Road, St. Lucia, Brisbane, 4067, Queensland, Australia.
Telephone: Brisbane 70-2382.

Murtazayev, Kayum Murtazayevich; Soviet politician; b. 1926; ed. Fergana Pedagogical Inst.
Member C.P.S.U. 48-; industrial worker 42-48; Sec. of City Cttee., then of Regional Cttee., later First Sec. Central Cttee. of Young Communist League, Uzbekistan 48-58; Sec. Central Cttee. of Y.C.L., U.S.S.R. 58-60; First Sec. Tashkent City Cttee. of C.P. Uzbekistan 60-65; First Sec. Bokhara Regional Cttee. of C.P. Uzbekistan 65-; mem. Central Cttee. C.P. Uzbekistan; Deputy to U.S.S.R. Supreme Soviet; mem. Cttee. U.S.S.R. Parliamentary Group.
Bokhara Regional Committee of Communist Party of Uzbekistan, Bokhara, U.S.S.R.

Murthy, B. S., B.A., B.ED.; Indian politician; b. 1907; ed. Government Arts Coll. Rajahmundry, Training Coll. Rajahmundry, Madras Christian Coll. and Law Coll.
Parliamentary Sec. for Labour and Industry, Madras 37-39, 46-47; Chief Whip, Madras Legislative Congress Party 46-47; Pres. Andhra Pradesh Agricultural Labour Congress 46-, Andhra Provincial Harijan Sewak Sangh 40-49; fmr. Editor *Navjiwan* (Telugu weekly); mem. Lok Sabha 52-; Deputy Minister of Community Devt. and Co-operation April 62-67; Deputy Minister of Health and Family Planning 67, of Health, Family Planning and Urban Devt. Nov. 67-69; Min. of State for Health, Family Planning, Works, Housing and Urban Devt. Feb. 69; mem. Exec. Cttee. Gandhi Smarak Nidhi.
Publs. *Revolt of Six Cross, Agony, Andhra Virakumar, The Glimmer in Darkness, Depressed and Oppressed* 72.
5 Ashoka Road, New Delhi, India.

Musafir, Giani Gurmukh Singh; Indian writer and politician; b. 15 Jan. 1899, Udhwal, Pakistan; ed. Rawalpindi and Training Coll., Lahore.
Joined Congress 23; mem. All-India Congress Cttee. 30; mem. Constituent Assembly 47-52; mem. Parl. 52-66; mem. Exec. Congress Party in Parl. 52-66; mem. Working Cttee. of All-India Congress Cttee. 52-57; Pres. Punjab Pradesh Congress Cttee. 47-59; Chief Minister of Punjab 66-67; mem. Legislative Council, Punjab 66-; mem. Rajya Sabha 68-; Chair. Jallianwala Bag Memorial Trust Management Cttee.; took active part in Akali movement; Gen. Sec. Shri Gurudwara Prabandhak Cttee. and Shiromani Akali Dal; Leader and Del. to numerous int. conferences.
Publs. Short stories: *Vakhri Duniya, Sasta Tamasha, Alne de Bot, Kandhan Bol Pahiyan, 27 January, Sab Achha, Gutar, Allah Wale, Urwar Par;* Poetry: *Sabar de Ban, Prem Ban, Jivan Pandh, Toote Khamb, Musafirian, Kav Saneh, Sahaj Seti*; General: *Gandhi Gita, Anand Marg, Bagi Jernel, Vinvi Sadi de Shahid, Vekhia Suniya Gandhi, Vekhia Suniya Jawaharlal.*
21 Feroze Shah Road, New Delhi, India.
Telephone: 48191.

Mustapha bin datu Harun, Tun Datu Haji (*see* Harun, Tun Datu Haji Mustapha bin Datu).

Myint Maung, U.; Burmese diplomatist; b. 10 March 1921, Magwe; ed. Univ. of Rangoon.
Joined Army 42; has held the following positions: Head of Co-operative Dept.; Chief of Admin. Div. of Burma Socialist Programme Party, also mem. Party Inspection Cttee.; mem. Pyithu Hluttaw (People's Congress) for Magwe Constituency; mem. Board of Dirs. of People's Bank of the Union of Burma, Exec. Cttee. of Burma Sports and Physical Fitness Cttee., Cen. Cttee. of Burma Red Cross Soc.; Chair. Resettlement Cttee. of Cen. Security and Admin. Cttee., Independence Award Cttee.; Perm. Rep. to UN Aug. 75-.
Permanent Mission of Burma to the United Nations, 10 East 77th Street, New York, N.Y. 10021, U.S.A.

N

Na Champassak, Sisouk; Laotian government official and diplomatist; b. 1928; ed. Univ. of Paris and Acad. of Int. Law, The Hague.
Former Head, Political Dept., Board of Council of Ministers, later Head, Perm. Sec. of Political Affairs, Board of Council of Ministers; Dir. Secr.-Gen. of Council of Ministers 53-56; Deputy Perm. Rep. to UN 56-58; Sec. of State for Information and Youth 58-61; Perm. Rep. to UN 61-63; Amb. to India 63-64; Minister of Finance 64-74, of Defence and War Veterans 74-75.
Vientiane, Laos.

Nadao, Hirokichi; Japanese politician; b. 1899; ed. Tokyo Univ.
Entered Home Ministry 24; Gov. Oita Prefecture 41; Chief, Livelihood Bureau and Sanitation Bureau, Home Ministry 44; Vice-Minister of Home Affairs 45; mem. House of Reps. 45-; Minister of Educ. 56-57, 58-59, 63-64, Nov. 67-68; fmr. mem. House of Reps. Standing Cttees. for the Budget and Local Education; fmr. Vice-Chair. Political Affairs Investigation Cttee. of Liberal Democratic Party, Chair. Exec. Council Dec. 74-; mem. Local Admin. System Re-

search Council; Dir. Paper Bag Mfg. Co.; Liberal-Democratic Party.
House of Representatives, Tokyo, Japan.

Nagai, Michio; Japanese politician; ed. Kyoto Univ., Ohio State Univ.
Assistant Prof. Kyoto Univ.; later taught at Tokyo Inst. of Technology; editorial writer *Asahi Shimbun* 70; Dir. Communications Inst. of East-West Center, Hawaii 72-73; Minister of Educ. Dec. 74-.
Ministry of Education, Tokyo, Japan.

Nagano, Shigeo; Japanese business executive; b. 15 July 1900; ed. Tokyo Imperial Univ.
General Man. Fuji Steel Works, Japan Iron Steel Co. Ltd. 34-40; Gen. Man. Japan Iron and Steel Co. Ltd. 40-46; Man. Dir. Japan Iron and Steel Co. Ltd. 46-47, 48-50; First Deputy Dir. Japan Govt. Econ. Restabilization Board 47-48; Pres. Fuji Iron and Steel Co. Ltd. 50-70; Chair. Nippon Steel Corpn. 70-73, Dir. and Hon. Chair. 73-; Pres. Japan Chamber of Commerce and Industry 69-; Pres. Tokyo Chamber of Commerce and Industry 69-; Hon. Pres. Japan Iron and Steel Fed. 65-; Counsellor, Ministry of Foreign Affairs 62-; Vice-Pres. Pacific Basin Econ. Council 70-; Chair. Japan-Australia Business Co-operation Cttee. 61-; Japan-India Business Co-operation Cttee. 66-; Adviser, Fed. of Employers' Asscns. 70-, Fed. of Econ. Orgs. 70-; Counsellor, Bank of Japan 70-; Chair. Prime Minister's Council for Foreign Econ. Co-operation 69-; Order of Sacred Treasure, First Class 70; Hon. K.B.E.
Nippon Steel Corporation, 6-3, Otemachi 2-chome, Chiyoda-ku, Tokyo; Home: 34-4, Matsubara 4-chome, Setagaya-ku, Tokyo, Japan.
Telephone: 242-4111 (Office); 321-0141 (Home).

Nagata, Takao; Japanese business executive; b. 1 Sept. 1911; ed. Nagasaki Commercial High School.
With Hitachi Shipbuilding & Eng. Co. 34-, Dir. 51-60, Vice-Pres. 60-62, Pres. 62-; Chair. Japan Shipbuilders Asscn.
Hitachi Shipbuilding & Engineering Co. Ltd., 47, Edobori, 1-chome, Nishi-ku, Osaka, Japan.

Nagata, Takesi; Japanese geophysicist; b. 24 June 1913, Tokyo.
Director Nat. Inst. of Polar Research; Prof. Emer. Tokyo Univ.; recipient of lunar samples from U.S. *Apollo* missions; Foreign mem. Nat. Acad. of Sciences (U.S.A.).
National Institute of Polar Research, 9-10, Kaga-1, Itabashi-ku, Tokyo 173, Japan.

Naik, Vasantrao Phulsing; Indian politician; b. 1 July 1913; ed. Neil City High School, Nagpur, Morris Coll., and Univ. Coll. of Law, Nagpur.
Director Madhya Pradesh Co-operative Central Bank 51-52; mem. Legislative Assembly, Madhya Pradesh 52; Minister for Revenue, Madhya Pradesh; Minister for Co-operation, Bombay 56-57, for Agriculture and Aarey Milk Colony, Bombay 57-60; Minister for Revenue, Maharashtra 60-63, Chief Minister, Minister of Gen. Admin., Home Planning and Information 63-76.
c/o Office of the Chief Minister, Bombay, Maharashtra, India.

Nair, Raman Narayan, C.B.E.; Fijian diplomatist; b. 17 June 1922.
Clerk, Fiji Civil Service 40-62, District Officer and Commr. 62-70; High Commr. to Australia 70-76, to Papua New Guinea 75-.
Fiji High Commission, Port Moresby, Papua New Guinea.

Nair, Vallillath Madhathil Madhavan, M.A., BAR.-AT-LAW; Indian diplomatist; b. 8 Oct. 1919; ed. Presidency Coll., Madras, Brasenose Coll., Oxford, Gonville and Caius Coll., Cambridge, and Inner Temple, London.
Entered Indian Civil Service 42; Sub-Divisional Officer, Sitamarhi (Bihar) 44-46; Under Sec. Ministry of External Affairs, New Delhi 46-49; First Sec. Cairo 50-53; Deputy Sec. Ministry of External Affairs 53-55; Deputy High Commr. in Ceylon 55-56, Acting High Commr. 56-57; Commr. in Malaya and Singapore 57, High Commr. in Malaya 57-58; Amb. to Cambodia 58-60, to Norway 60-63; Joint Sec. Ministry of External Affairs 64-67; Amb. to Poland 67-70, to Morocco and Tunisia 70-74, to Spain 74-.
Embassy of India, Velázquez 93, Madrid 6, Spain.
Telephone: 276-7643.

Nakabe, Kenkichi; Japanese business executive; b. 25 March 1896, Akashi, Hyogo.
President Taiyo Fishery Co. 53-; Medal of Honour with Blue Ribbon, 2nd Class Order of the Rising Sun.
Taiyo Fishery Co. Ltd., 5-1 1-chome, Marunouchi, Chiyoda-ku-, Tokyo; Home: 2-14 1-chome, Ichigaya, Sadohara-cho, Shinjuku-ku, Tokyo, Japan.

Nakagawa, Toru; Japanese diplomatist; b. 30 March 1911, Tokyo; ed. Tokyo Univ.
Foreign Sevice 33-, served New York, and Ministry of Foreign Affairs 33-39; Sec. to Premier 39; Sec. China, concurrently Consul, Shanghai 42; Dir. Japanese Overseas Office, Philippines 52-53; Head, Asia Bureau, Ministry of Foreign Affairs 53-57; Minister, U.K. 57-60; Head, Treaty Dept., Ministry of Foreign Affairs 60-64; Amb. to Italy 64-65, to U.S.S.R. 65-71; Perm. Rep. to UN 71-73.
c/o Ministry of Foreign Affairs, 2-1 Kasumigaseki 2-chome, Chiyoda-ku, Tokyo 100; and 1-14 Nishiogiminami, Suginamiku, Tokyo, Japan.

Nakai, Haruo; Japanese business executive; b. 18 May 1911, Mie-ken; ed. Nagoya Univ.
Joined Nippon Suisan Kaisha Ltd. 33, Man. Accounting Dept. 51-57, Dir. 52-55, Man. Dir. 55-58, Senior Man. Dir. 58-61, Exec. Vice-Pres. 61-63, Exec. Pres. 63-73, Exec. Chair. 73-75, Dir. and Adviser Dec. 75-; Dir. Japan Fed. of Econ. Orgs.; mem. Nat. Fisheries Co-ordination Council, Nat. Marine Devt. Council; Blue Ribbon Medal.
Nippon Suisan Kaisha Ltd., 6-2 Otemachi 2-chome, Chiyoda-ku, Tokyo; Home: 3-6, 1-chome, Hikari-cho, Kokubunji-shi, Tokyo, Japan.
Telephone: 244-7000 (Office); 0425-72-0333 (Home).

Nakamura, Toshio; Japanese banker; b. 7 Jan. 1910, Ibaraki Pref.; ed. Law Dept., Tokyo Univ.
Joined the Mitsubishi Bank Ltd. 32, Dir. 60-, Man. Dir. 62, Deputy Pres. 65, Pres. 70-75, Chair. 75-; Dir. Mitsubishi Warehouse Co. Ltd., Fed. of Bankers' Asscn. of Japan; Auditor Mitsubishi Petroleum Devt. Co. Ltd. and Mitsubishi Petrochemical Co. Ltd.; Counsellor, Japan Fed. of Employers' Asscn.; Trustee, Japan Cttee. for Econ. Devt.
Office: 7-1, Marunouchi 2-chome, Chiyoda-ku, Tokyo; Home: 17-8, Mejirodai 1-chome, Bunkyo-ku, Tokyo, Japan.

Nakamura, Umekichi; Japanese lawyer and politician; b. 1902, Tokyo; ed. Hosei Univ.
Entered law practice 40; mem. House of Reps. 36-; joined Japan Liberal Party; Minister of Justice 56, 73-74.
5-26, Meijiro, 2-chome, Toshima-ku, Tokyo 171, Japan.

Nakasone, Yasuhiro; Japanese politician; b. 27 May 1918; ed. Tokyo Imperial Univ.
Member House of Reps.; fmr. Minister of State, Dir.-Gen. of Science & Technology Agency; Chair. Nat. Org. Liberal-Democratic Party, Joint Cttee. on Atomic Energy, Special Cttee. on Scientific Technology; Pres. Takushoku Univ.; Minister of Transport Nov. 67-Dec. 68; Minister of State, Dir.-Gen. Defence Agency Jan. 70-71; Chair. Exec. Council Liberal-Democratic Party 71-72, Sec.-Gen. 74-75; Minister of Int. Trade and Industry 72-74.
Publs. *Ideal of Youth, South Pole—Human & Science, Frontier in Japan.*
2-18-6, Takada, Toshima-ku, Tokyo, Japan.
Telephone: (03) 501-1511 (Office); 982-7896 (Home).

Nakayama, Komei; Japanese surgeon; b. 25 Sept. 1910, Tokyo; ed. Chiba Univ.
Assistant Prof. of Surgery, Chiba Univ. 41-47, Prof. of Surgery 47-63; Prof. of Surgery, Tokyo Women's Medical Coll. 64-, Pres. of Inst. of Gastroenterology; Visiting Prof. St. Vincent Hospital, Sydney, Australia 61; Vice-Pres. Medical Div., Japanese Science Council; Pres. Int. Coll. of Surgeons; numerous Japanese and foreign awards.
2-3-18-704 Hirakawa-cho, Chiyoda-ku, Tokyo, Japan.
Telephone: 261-0661.

Nakayama, Sohei, M.COM.; Japanese banker; b. 5 March 1906, Tokyo; ed. Tokyo Coll. of Commerce.
Nippon Kogyo Ginko (Industrial Bank of Japan Ltd.) 29-, Dir. 47-50, Man. Dir. 50-51; Dir. Japan Devt. Bank 51-54; Deputy Pres. Industrial Bank of Japan 54-61, Pres. 61-68, Chair. 68-70, Counsellor 70-; mem. Exec. Cttee. Japan Cttee. for Econ. Devt. 59-; Exec. Dir. Fed. of Econ. Orgs. 62-; Pres. Overseas Technical Co-operation Agency 68-; Dir. Matsushita Electric Industrial Co. Ltd. 71-; Chair. Cttee. for Energy Policy Promotion 73-.
3-3, Marunouchi 1-chome, Chiyoda-ku, Tokyo 100; Home: No. 10, 10, 6-chome, Zushi, Zushi-City, Kanagawa Prefecture, Japan.

Nakayasu, Kanichi; Japanese industrialist; b. 5 April 1895; ed. Mechanical Department, Tokyo Higher Engineering School.
Kobe Shipyard, Mitsubishi Shipbuilding Co. 18-23; Ube Cement Mfg. Co. 23, later Dir., Eng. Dept., Chief Engineer, Dir. 34, Vice-Pres. Ube Industries Ltd. 52-58, Pres. 58-; Dir. Korea Cement Mfg. Co.; Dir. Fed. of Japanese Employers' Asscns.
Ube Industries Ltd., 7-2, Kasumigaseki 3-chome, Chiyoda-ku, Tokyo 100, Japan.

Nam Duk Woo, PH.D.; Korean economist and politician; b. 10 Oct. 1924; ed. Kook Min Coll., Seoul, Seoul Nat. Univ., Okla. and Stanford Univs.
With Bank of Korea 52-54; Asst. Prof., Assoc. Prof., Prof., Dean of Econ. Dept., Kook Min Coll. 54-64; Prof. Sogang Univ. and Dir. Research Inst. for Econ. and Business 64-69; Minister of Finance 69; Gov. for Korea, IMF, IBRD, ADB 69-72, Chair. Board of Govs. ADB 69-72; Deputy Prime Minister and Chair. Econ. Planning Board 74-75; mem. Advisory Cttee. on Evaluation of Econ. Devt. Plan, Nat. Mobilization Board 64-69; Adviser to Korea Devt. Bank 64-69; Assoc. mem. Econ. and Scientific Council 67-69.
Publs. *History of Economic Theory* 58, *Price Theory* 65, *History of Economic Theory* (co-author) 62, *The Determinants of Money Supply and Monetary Policy: in the case of Korea 1954-64* 66.
82 Sejong-Ro, Jongro-Ku, Seoul; Home: 395-101 Seokyo-Dong, Mapo-Ku, Seoul, Republic of Korea.

Namgyal, Miwang Chogyal Chenpo Palden Thondup; fmr. Denzong Chogyal of Sikkim; b. 22 May 1923; ed. St. Joseph's Coll., Darjeeling and Bishop Cotton School, Simla.
Attended Indian Civil Service Training Course, Dehradun; Pres. Sikkim State Council 44-49; Pres. Maha Bodhi Soc. of India 53; Founder-Pres. Namgyal Inst. of Tibetology, Gangtok, Sikkim; succeeded his father as Chogyal of Sikkim Dec. 63, deposed April 75; married Sangey Deki (died 57), daughter of Theiji Tsewang Rinzing Namgyal of Lhasa 50; two sons and a daughter; married Miss Hope Cooke 63; one son and a daughter; O.B.E. 47; Padma Vibhushan 54; Commdr. Ordre de l'Etoile Noire 56; Order of Drak Jong Thusay, First Class 74; Hon. Maj.-Gen. of Indian Army 65; fmr. Col.-in-Chief Sikkim Guards.
c/o The Palace, Gangtok, Sikkim, India.

Narasimhan, Chakravarthi Vijayaraghava, M.B.E., M.A.; Indian civil servant; b. 21 May 1915, Srirangam, S. India; ed. Madras and Oxford Univs.
Entered Indian Civil Service 36, appointed to Madras Cadre 37, District Officer Madras 37-42, Madras Govt. Secr. (successively Under Sec., Deputy Sec. and Sec., Food Dept. and Board of Revenue) 42-50; successively Deputy Sec. and Joint Sec. Ministry of Food and Agriculture, Ministry of Finance, Govt. of India 50-56; Exec. Sec. UN Econ. Comm. for Asia and the Far East 56-59; Under Sec. for Special Political Affairs, UN 59-61, Chef de Cabinet 61-73; Under Sec. for Gen. Assembly Affairs 62-69; Deputy Administrator UN Devt. Programme 69-72; Under Sec.-Gen. for Inter-Agency Affairs and Co-ordination 73-; Hon. D.L. (Williams Coll., Mass.); Hon. D.Hum.Litt. (Colgate Univ., Hamilton, N.Y.).
300 East 33rd St., Apt. 11-M, New York, N.Y. 10016, U.S.A.
Telephone: 212-686-2398.

Narayan, Jaya Prakash; Indian politician; b. 11 Oct. 1902; ed. Bihar and U.S.A.
Member Working Cttee. Indian Nat. Congress 31, Act. Sec.-Gen. 31-32; founded Congress Socialist Party 34, Sec.-Gen. 34-50; founded Socialist Party 48; merged with Kisan Mazdoor Sabha Praja Party to form Praja Socialist Party, leader 52-57; a leader of Quit India Movement 42-43; imprisoned several times; Pres. Indian Railwaymen's Fed., All India Post and Telegraph Employees Union and Defence Employees Fed. 46-52; engaged in Bhoodan (Land Gift Movement) 57-; Pres. All India Panchayat Parishad, All India Asscn. of Voluntary Agencies for Rural Devt. 59-63; Chair. All India Peace Brigade, Afro-Asian Council, India-Pakistan Reconciliation Group, Co-Chair. World Peace Brigade; detained June 75, released on parole Nov. 75; participated in formation of a united opposition group of four parties 76.
Kadam Kuan, Patna 800003, Bihar, India.

Narayan, Rasipuram Krishnaswamy; Indian writer; b. 10 Oct. 1906.
Publs. (all in English), novels: *Swami and Friends* 35, *The Bachelor of Arts, The Dark Room, The English Teacher, Mr. Sampath, The Financial Expert, Waiting for the Mahatma, The Guide* 58, *The Man-Eater of Malgudi* 61, *Gods, Demons and Others* 64, *The Sweet-Vendor* 67; short stories: *An Astrologer's Day, The Lawley Road, A Horse and Two Goats*; non-fiction: *The Ramayana* (prose trans.) 72, *My Days* (autobio.) 74; Belles Lettres Award, English Speaking Union 75.
Yadavagiri, Mysore 2, India; c/o David Higham Associates, 5/8 Lower John Street, Golden Square, London, W1R 4HA, England.

Narayan, Shriman, M.A., M.A.(ECONS.); Indian administrator and diplomatist; b. 13 July 1912; ed. A. P. Mission High School, Mainpuri, Allahabad Univ., Calcutta Univ.
M.P. 52-57; General Sec. Indian Nat. Congress and Chief Editor All-India Congress Cttee. Econ. Review 52-58; mem. Indian Planning Comm. 58-64; Chair. Indian Planning Comm. Prohibition Enquiry Cttee. 54-55, Standing Cttee. on Basic Educ. 57-60; Amb. to Nepal 64-67; Gov. of Gujarat 67-73; Chancellor, Rajasthan Vidyapith, Udaipur Kashi Vidyapith 74, Kanpur Univ. 75-; Trustee Gujarat Vidyapith; Hon. D.Litt. (Karnatak Univ.) 72.
Publs. *Gandhian Plan for Economic Development, Gandhian Constitution for Free India, Fountain of Life, Socialism in Indian Planning, The Two Worlds, Towards a Socialist Economy, The Tragedy of a Wall, Trends in Indian Planning, Medium of Instruction, One Week with Vinoba, Principles of Gandhian Planning, Letters from Gandhi Nehru Vinoba, Gandhi: The Man and His Thought, Towards Better Education, India and Nepal, Vinoba: His Life and Work, Relevance of Gandhian Economics, Mahatma Gandhi: The Atomic Man, Memoirs: Window on Gandhi and Nehru, Those Ten Months: President's Rule in Gujarat;* several poems and essays in Hindi.
Jeevan Kutir, Wardha, India.
Telephone: Wardha 196.

Narita, Tomomi; Japanese politician; b. 21 April 1912; ed. Tokyo Univ.
Former Pres. Kagawa Prefectural Fed. of Socialist Party; mem. House of Reps.; successively, mem. Central Exec. Cttee. of Socialist Party, Chair., Control Cttee., Left Wing Socialist Party; Chair., Policy Board, Socialist Party 61-62, Sec.-Gen. 62-67, Chair. 68-.
2-1-12, Barcho, Takamatsu City, Kapawa Prefecture, Japan.

Narlikar, Jayant Vishnu, F.R.A.S., M.A., PH.D., SC.D.; Indian physicist; b. 19 July 1938, Kolhapur; ed. Banaras Hindu Univ. and Fitzwilliam Coll., Cambridge.
Berry Ramsey Fellow, King's Coll. Cambridge 63-69; Graduate Staff Mem., Inst. of Theoretical Astronomy, Cambridge 66-72; Senior Research Fellow, King's Coll. 69-72; Prof. Tata Inst. of Fundamental Research 72-; Jawaharlal Nehru Fellow 73-75; Fellow, Indian Acad. of Sciences; Padma Bhushan 65.
Publs. Articles on cosmology, general relativity and gravitation, quantum theory, astrophysics, etc., in the *Proceedings of the Royal Society, The Monthly Notices of the Royal Astronomical Society, The Astrophysical Journal, Nature, Observatory, The Annals of Physics,* and scientific articles in various magazines; (with Sir F. Hoyle): *Action at a Distance in Physics and Cosmology* 74.
Tata Institute of Fundamental Research, Bombay 400005; Home: Flat 701, Colaba Housing Colony, Homi Bhabha Road, Bombay, India.

Nasir, Ibrahim, K.C.M.G.; Maldivian politician; b. 2 Sept. 1926, Malé; ed. Ceylon (now Sri Lanka).
Under-Sec. of State to Minister of Finance and to Minister of Public Safety, Republic of Maldives 54; Minister of Public Safety 56, of Home Affairs Aug. 57; Prime Minister (1st term) Dec. 57, Prime Minister (2nd term) and Minister of Home Affairs, Finance, Educ., Trade, External Affairs and Public Safety 59, Prime Minister (3rd term), Minister of Finance, Educ., External Affairs and Public Safety 64; Pres. of the Maldives 68- (re-elected 73); Awards of Nishaan Gazeegege Izaiteri Veriya, Ranna Bandeiri Kilegefaanu; Hon. K.C.M.G.
Office of the President, Malé; Home: Velaanaage, Henvaru, Malé, Maldives.
Telephone: 822/270, 641 (Office); 546, 594 (Home).

Naskar, Purnendu Sekhar, M.A.; Indian politician and diplomatist; b. March 1921; ed. Calcutta Univ.
Member Lok Sabha 52-67, mem. Indian Del. to UN Gen. Assembly 54, 55 and 67; Parl. Sec. in Ministry of Works, Housing and Supply 56, later Deputy Minister in Ministry of Rehabilitation 58-64; Deputy Minister in Ministry of Health 64-66; Deputy Minister in Ministry of Home Affairs 66-67; High Commr. of India in New Zealand 69-74.
c/o Ministry of Foreign Affairs, New Delhi, India.

Nasriddinova, Yadgar Sadikovna; Soviet civil engineer and politician; b. 1920; ed. Inst. of Railway Transport Engineering, Tashkent.
Works Supt. Great Ferghana Canal, and the Construction of the Railway Line at "Angrenugol" Coalmines; later Sec. for School affairs Cen. Cttee. Young Communist League of Uzbekistan 42-50; mem. C.P.S.U. 42-; Party work 50-52; Minister of Building Materials, Uzbek S.S.R. 52-55, Vice-Chair. Council of Ministers 55-59; Chair. Presidium, Supreme Soviet of the Uzbek S.S.R. 59-70; Vice-Chair. Presidium of Supreme Soviet of U.S.S.R. 59-70; mem. Cen. Cttee. of C.P.S.U. 52-; mem. Cen. Cttee. of C.P. of Uzbekistan 52-; Chair. Soviet of Nationalities, U.S.S.R. Supreme Soviet 70-74; first Vice-Chair. Cttee. of U.S.S.R. Parl. Group.
Central Committee of the Communist Party of Uzbek S.S.R., Tashkent, Uzbek S.S.R., U.S.S.R.

Nasution, Gen. Abdul Haris; Indonesian retd. army officer; b. 3 Dec. 1918, Kotanopari, N. Sumatra; ed. Netherlands Military Acad., Bandung.
Sub-Lieut. Netherlands Indies Army 41; Col. 45; Commanding Gen. First Siliwangi Div. West Java; commanded guerilla warfare in West Java against Dutch Military Action 46-48; Dep. C.-in-C. of Armed Forces of Indonesia 48; Commanding Gen. Java Military and Territorial Command in defence of Java against Dutch second Military Action 48-49; suppressed Indonesian Communist Party's rebellion (Madiun revolt) 48; Army Chief of Staff 50-52, re-appointed 55-62; mem. Constituent Assembly 55; Chair. of Joint Chiefs of Staff and mem. Nat. Council 57; Lieut.-Gen. 58; planned campaign against rebellion in Sumatra and Sulawesi 58; Minister of Defence and People's Security 59-66; Chair. People's Consultative Congress 66-72; rank of Gen. 60; Deputy C.-in-C. West Irian (W. New Guinea) Liberation Command 62; retd. 62; numerous Indonesian and foreign awards.
Publs. *Principles of Guerilla Warfare, The Indonesian National Army, Notes on the Army Policy of the Republic of Indonesia, Truth and Justice, Dual Function of the Indonesian National Army, Towards a People's Army, To Safeguard the Banner of the Revolution, War for Freedom.*
40 Teuku Umar, Jakarta, Indonesia.

Nayar, Sushila, M.B., B.S., M.D., DR.P.H.; Indian physician; b. 26 Dec. 1914, Kunjah District, Gujrat, Pakistan; ed. Lahore Coll. for Women, Lady Hardinge Medical Coll., Delhi, Johns Hopkins Univ., U.S.A.
Medical attendant to Mahatma Gandhi and his Ashram; medical work at Sevagram and Noakhali, W. Punjab and Delhi; Chief Medical Officer Faridabad; Sec. Medical Board of Kasturba Trust; Sec. Leprosy Board of Gandhi Memorial Trust; participated in independence movement, imprisoned 42-44; mem. Lok Sabha 57-71; fmr. Minister of Health, Rehabilitation and Transport, Delhi State; Speaker Delhi Legislative Assembly 52-56; Minister of Health, Govt. of India 62-67; Pres. S.P.C.A. 52-62; Chair. Indian Red Cross; Pres. All-India Inst. of Medical Sciences, Tuberculosis Asscn. of India 64-67; Pres. Kasturba Health Soc. 64-; Dir. M.G. Inst. of Medical Sciences, Prof. of Preventive and Social Medicine 69-.
Publs. *Kasturba, Karavas ki Kahani,* etc.
Kasturba Hospital, Sevagram, Wardha A.2. Soami Napar, New Delhi 17, India.
Telephone: 022-R33; 74147 (New Delhi).

Nazarshoyev, Moyensho Nazarshoyevich; Soviet politician; b. 1929; ed. Dushanbe Pedagogical Inst.
Member C.P.S.U. 53-; Teacher, Tadzhik Univ., later Deputy Chief of Section; mem. Central Cttee. of C.P. of Tadzhikstan 63-; First Sec. Gorno-Badakhshansky Regional Cttee. of C.P. of Tadzhikstan 63-; Deputy to U.S.S.R. Supreme Soviet.
Gorno-Badakhshansky Regional Committee of Communist Party of Tadzhikstan, Khorog, U.S.S.R.

Ne Win, U (Maung Shu Maung); Burmese fmr. army officer and politician; b. 24 May 1911; ed. Govt. High School, Prome and Rangoon Univ.
Joined Allied Forces 45; Vice-Chief of Gen. Staff and Major-Gen. 48; Deputy Prime Minister 49-50; Gen. 56; Prime Minister and Minister of Defence Oct. 58-60; Chief of Gen. Staff 62-72; Prime Minister, Minister of Defence, Finance and Revenue, Nat. Planning and Justice 62-63; Prime Minister, Minister of Nat. Planning and Defence 63; Prime Minister and Minister of Defence, also Chair. of Revolutionary Council 65-74; Chair. Exec. Cttee. Burma Socialist Prog. Party 73-; Pres. of Burma March 74-; Legion of Merit (U.S.A.).
Office of the President, Rangoon, Burma.

Needham, Joseph, SC.D., F.R.S., F.B.A.; British biochemist, historian of science and orientalist; b. 1900, London; ed. Oundle School and Cambridge Univ.
Fellow Caius Coll., Cambridge 24-, Pres. 59-66, Master 66-; Head of Sino-British Science Co-operation Office and Counsellor British Embassy, Chungking 42-46; Head of Div. of Natural Sciences UNESCO 46-48; now Hon. Counsellor to UNESCO; numerous visiting professorships, etc. latest at British Columbia 75; foreign mem. Nat. Acad. of China, Royal Danish Acad.; mem. Int. Acads. of the History of Science, of the Philosophy of Science and the History of Medicine; Order of Brilliant Star (Repub. of China); Hon. D.Sc. (Brussels, E. Anglia, London), Hon. LL.D. (Toronto), Hon. D.Litt (Hong Kong, Salford); Sir Wm. Jones Medal, Asiatic Soc. of Bengal, George Sarton Medal, History of Science Soc., Leonardo da Vinci Medal, History of Technology Soc.
Publs. *Chemical Embryology* (3 vols.) 31, *Biochemistry and Morphogenesis* 42, *Science and Civilisation in China* (7 vols. in 12 or more parts) 54-, *Heavenly Clockwork* 60, *Development of Iron and Steel Technology in China* 64, *Within the Four Seas* 69, *The Grand Titration* 69, *Clerks and Craftsmen in China and the West* 70, *Moulds of Experience, a Pattern of Natural Philosophy* 76.
Master's Lodge, Gonville and Caius College, Cambridge, England.

Nehru, Braj Kumar, B.SC., B.SC.(ECON.); Indian civil servant and Barrister-at-Law; b. 4 Sept. 1909, Allahabad; ed. Allahabad Univ., London School of Economics, Balliol Coll., Oxford, Inner Temple, London.
Joined Indian Civil Service 34; Asst. Commr. 34-39; Under Sec., Dept. of Educ., Health and Lands, Govt. of India 39; Officer on special duty, Reserve Bank of India, Under Sec., Finance Dept., Govt. of India 40, Joint Sec. 47; Exec. Dir. World Bank 49-54, 58-62; Minister, Indian Embassy, U.S.A. 49-54; Joint Sec., Dept. of Econ. Affairs 54-57, Sec. 57-58, Commr. Gen. for Econ. Affairs 58-61; Amb. to U.S.A. 61-68; Gov. of Assam and Nagaland 68-73, of Meghalaya, Manipur and Tripura 72-73; High Commr. to U.K. 73-; rep. Reparations Conf. 45, Commonwealth Finance Ministers Conf., UN Gen. Assembly 49-52, 60, FAO Confs. 49-50, Sterling Balances Confs. 47-49, Bandung Conf. 55; deputed to enquire into Australian Fed. Finance 46; mem. UN Advisory Cttee. on Admin. and Budgetary Questions 51-53; mem. UN Investments Cttee. 61-; Fellow, London School of Econs.; Hon. LL.D. (Missouri Valley Coll.), Hon. Litt.D. (Jacksonville Univ.).
Publs. *Speaking of India, Australian Federal Finance.*
India House, Aldwych, London, WC2 4NA; Home: 9 Kensington Palace Gardens, London, W.8, England.
Telephone: 01-836-8484 (Office); 01-229-7241 (Home).

Nehru, Ratan Kumar; Indian fmr. civil servant, diplomatist and university administrator; b. 10 Oct. 1902; ed. Allahabad and Oxford Univs.
Joined Indian Civil Service 25; served Madhya Pradesh 25-33; joined Central Govt. Admin., successively held posts of Collector of Customs, Bombay and later Madras, Commr. of Northern India Salt Revenue, Deputy and Joint Sec. in various Govt. depts. and Chair. Central Board of Revenue; Sec. to Ministry of Communications 47; Minister in Washington 48; Minister to Sweden, Denmark and Finland 49-51; Special Sec. for UN Affairs and later Commonwealth Sec. in Ministry of External Affairs 51-52; Foreign Sec. in Ministry of External Affairs 52-55; Amb. to China 55-58; Amb. to U.A.R. concurrently accred. to Lebanon and Libya 58-60; Sec.-Gen. Ministry of External Affairs 60-65, Chair. Preparatory Cttees. of Govt. of India for Conf. on Disarmament, and the UN Trade and Devt. Conf. 63-65; mem. Board of Trade and Nat. Defence Council; Vice-Chancellor, Allahabad Univ. 65-70.
c/o Senate House, Allahabad, India.

Neilson, Hon. William Arthur; Australian politician; b. 27 Aug. 1925, Hobart, Tasmania; ed. Ogilvie Commercial High School.
Elected to Tasmanian House of Assembly 46; Labor Party Whip 46-55; Minister for Tourism, Immigration and Forests 56-58; Attorney-Gen. 58; Treasurer 59; Minister of Educ. 58, 59, 59-69, 72-74; Attorney-Gen. 74-75; Deputy Premier, Minister for the Environment, administering Police Dept. and the Licensing Act 74-75; Premier and Treasurer March 75-; Pres. Tasmanian Section of Australian Labor Party 68-69.
Parliament House, Hobart, Tasmania 7000; Home: 40 Cornwall Street, Rose Bay, Tasmania 7015, Australia.

Neklyudov, Alexei Ivanovich; Soviet politician; b. 1906; ed. Higher Party School.
Member C.P.S.U. 29-; Soviet Army 28-32; Deputy Chief, Section of Research Inst. 32-39; official, Central Cttee. of C.P. of Kazakhstan, later First Sec., City Cttee., then Sec. Regional Cttee. of C.P. of Uzbekistan 39-59; First Sec. East Kazakhstan Regional Cttee. of C.P. 59-; mem. Central Cttee. of C.P. of Kazakhstan; Deputy to U.S.S.R. Supreme Soviet.
East Kazakhstan Regional Committee of Communist Party of Kazakhstan, Ust-Kamenogorsk, U.S.S.R.

Nepal, King of (*see* Birendra Bir Bikram Shah Dev).

Newsom, David Dunlop, A.B., M.S.; American diplomatist; b. 6 Jan. 1918; ed. Richmond Union High School and Calif. and Columbia Univs.
Reporter, *San Francisco Chronicle* 40-41; U.S. Navy 41-45; Newspaper publisher 45-47; Information Officer, U.S. Embassy, Karachi 47-50; Consul, Oslo 50-51; Public Affairs Officer, U.S. Embassy, Baghdad 51-55; Dept. of State 55-59; U.S. Nat. War Coll. 59-60; First Sec. U.S. Embassy, London 60-62; Dir. Office of Northern African Affairs, State Dept. 62-65; Amb. to Libya 65-69; Asst. Sec. of State for African Affairs 69-74; Amb. to Indonesia 74-; Dept. of State Meritorious Service Award 58; Nat. Civil Service League Career Service Award 71; Rockefeller Public Service Award 73.
U.S. Embassy, 5 Jalan Merdeka Selatan, Jakarta, Indonesia.

Ngapo Ngawang-Jigme; Tibetan leader; b. 1909
Leader Tibetan Army resisting Chinese invasion 50; First Deputy Commdr. Tibet Mil. Region, People's Liberation Army 52; Vice-Chair. Preparatory Cttee. for Tibet Autonomous Region 59-65; Vice-Chair. Standing Cttee., Nat. People's Congress 65; Chair. Tibet Autonomous Region People's Govt. 65-68; Vice-Chair. Tibet Revolutionary Cttee. 68.

Ngo Dinh Nhu, Madame; Vietnamese politician.
Widow of Ngo Dinh Nhu, brother and Adviser to the late President Ngo Diem; arrested by Viet-Minh, later escaped 46; organized first popular demonstration in support of Govt. of Prime Minister Ngo Dinh Diem 54; Official Hostess for Pres. Ngo Dinh Diem 55-63; fmr. Deputy, Nat. Assembly, author of "Family Bill"; founder of programme of paramilitary service for women Oct. 61; Founder-Pres. Vietnamese Women's Solidarity Movement.

Nguyen Cao Ky, Air Vice-Marshal; Vietnamese air force officer and politician; b. 8 Sept. 1930; ed. High School, Hanoi, and Officers' Training School, Hanoi.
Flight Training, Marrakech until 54; commanded Transport Squadron 54, later commdr. Tan Son Nhât Air Force Base, Repub. of Viet-Nam; spent six months at U.S. Air Command and Staff Coll., Maxwell Field, Alabama, U.S.A.; later, Commdr. Air Force, Repub. of Viet-Nam; Prime Minister 65-67; Vice-Pres. Repub. of Viet-Nam 67-71.
Now in the U.S.A.

Nguyen Huu Tho; Vietnamese politician b. 10 July 1910, Cholon.
Participated in liberation war against French colonialists; organized mass demonstration, Saigon-Cholon area March 50 against U.S. interference; imprisoned 50-52; opposed 1954 Geneva agreements on Indo-China; founded Saigon-Cholon Peace Movement; subsequently arrested, escaped 61; Chair. of Cen. Cttee. of Nat. Liberation Front (NLF) 62-, of NLF Presidium 64-, of Consultative Council, Provisional Revolutionary Govt. of Repub. of South Viet-Nam 69-76 (in Saigon 75-76); Vice-Pres. Socialist Repub. of Viet-Nam July 76-.
Office of the Vice-President, Hanoi, Viet-Nam.

Nguyen Khanh, Brig.-Gen.; Vietnamese army officer and politician; b. 1927; ed. Viet-Nam Military Acad., Dalat, Army Staff Schools, Hanoi and France, and U.S. Command and General Staff Coll., Fort Leavenworth.
French Colonial Army 54, Vietnamese Army 54-; Chief of Staff to Gen. Duong Van Minh 55; took part in coup against Pres. Diem Nov. 63; Prime Minister Jan.-Oct. 64; Chair. Armed Forces Council Dec. 64-Feb. 65; led coup Jan. 65; roving Amb. 65.

Nguyen Luong Bang; North Vietnamese politician; b. 1904, Hai Duong.
Frequently arrested for political activities; sentenced to twenty years imprisonment 31, escaped 32, recaptured 33, escaped again 43; mem. Cen. Cttee. Working People's Party, Democratic Repub. of Viet-Nam 45; fmr. Dir. of State Bank and Govt. Gen. Inspector; fmr. Head Party Control Cttee.; Amb. to U.S.S.R. 52-57; Vice-Pres. of Democratic Repub. of Viet-Nam 69-76, of Socialist Repub. of Viet-Nam July 76-.
Office of the Vice-President, Hanoi, Viet-Nam.

Nguyen Thi Binh; Vietnamese politician; b. 1927; ed. Saigon.
Student political leader in Saigon; organized (with Nguyen Huu Tho) first anti-American demonstration 50; imprisoned by French authorities 51-54; Vice-Pres. South Vietnamese Cttee. for Solidarity with the American People; Council mem. Union of Women for the Liberation of South Viet-Nam; mem. Cen. Cttee. Nat. Liberation Front (NLF); appointed NLF spokesman to peace talks, Paris, Nov. 68; Minister of Foreign Affairs in Provisional Revolutionary Govt. of S. Viet-Nam 69-76 (in Saigon 75-76); Minister of Educ., Socialist Repub. of Viet-Nam June 76-.
Ministry of Education, Hanoi, Viet-Nam.

Nguyen Van Binh, Most Rev. Paul, LIC.TH.; Vietnamese ecclesiastic; b. 1 Sept. 1910; ed. Seminary of Saigon and Propaganda Fide Univ., Rome.
Ordained 37; Parish Priest, Duc-Hoa and Can-Dat; Prof., Major Seminary of Saigon 37-55; Bishop 55; Apostolic Vicar of Can-Tho 55-61; Archbishop of Saigon 61-; Pres. Episcopal Conf. of Viet-Nam 65.
Archevêché de Saigon, 180 rue Phan Dinh Phung, B.P. 2371, Viet-Nam.

Nguyen Van Loc, LL.M.; Vietnamese lawyer, writer and politician; b. 24 Aug. 1922; ed. Montpellier and Paris Univs.
Lawyer, Saigon Court of Appeal 55; Lecturer, Nat. Inst. of Admin. 65; Chair. People and Armed Forces Council 66, People and Armed Forces Council Political Cttee. 66; Vice-Chair. Constituent Assembly Electoral Law Preparation Cttee.; mem. Barristers Fraternity 61-67; Del. in charge of campaigning, Cttee. for Aid to War Victims, Red Cross; Counsellor Viet-Nam Asscn. for Protection of Human and People's Rights; Sec.-Gen., Inter-Schools Asscn. 65-67; Prime Minister of Repub. of Viet-Nam Nov. 67-May 68; Prof. Univ. of Hoa Hao 70; Founder, Rector Univ. Cao Dai 71-75.
Publs. *Rank* 48, *New Recruits* (novel) 48, *Uprising* (novel) 46, *Poems on Liberation* (collection) 49, *Recollections of the Green Years* 60, *Free Tribune* (collection) 66, *Poisonous Water* (novel) 71.
162 Gia Long, Saigon, Viet-Nam.

Nguyen Van Thieu, Lt.-Gen.; Vietnamese army officer and politician; b. 5 April 1923; ed. Catholic Pellerin School, Hué, and Nat. Military Acad., Hué.
Viet-Nam Nat. Army 48-54; Republic of Viet-Nam Army 54-75; Commdr. First Infantry Div. 60-62, Fifth Infantry Div. 62-64; Deputy Premier and Minister of Defence 64-65; Chair. Nat. Leadership Cttee. and Head of State 65-67; Pres. of Republic of Viet-Nam 67-April 75; founded Dan Chu Party 73; went to Taiwan April 75.
Taipei, Taiwan, China.

Nhu, Madame Ngo Dinh (*see* Ngo Dinh Nhu, Madame).

Ni Chih-fu; People's Repub. of China.
Engineer worker; invented Ni Chih-fu drillhead 53; Eng. Peking No. 1 Machine Tool Plant 64; mem. 9th Cen. Cttee. of CCP 69; active in Labour Union's activities 70-; alt. mem. Politburo, 10th Cen. Cttee. of CCP 73.

Niazi, Maulana Kausar; Pakistani journalist and politician; b. 21 April 1934; ed. Punjab Univ.
Former editor *Tasneem* (daily), Lahore and later *Kausar;* founded *Shahab* (weekly) 60; mem. Pakistan People's Party 70-; political imprisonment 70; Minister of Information and Broadcasting 72-74, of Religious Affairs 74, also of Minority Affairs Overseas 76-.
Publs. several books on religious and literary topics.
Ministry of Religious Affairs, Islamabad, Pakistan.

Nichols, Leslie Edwin, B.SC.(AGR); Australian dairy executive; b. 4 July 1912; ed. Univ. of Sydney.
Assistant Dir. of Dairying, Senior Dairy Technologist and Dir. of Research Queensland Dept. of Primary Industries 37-65; Commonwealth Dairy Expert 65-.
Department of Primary Industry, 10-16 Queen Street, Melbourne, Victoria, Australia.
Telephone: 620341.

Nieh Jung-chen, Marshal; politician and fmr. army officer, People's Repub. of China; b. 1899, Chiang-tsin, Szechuan; ed. Univ. de Travail, France, Far Eastern and Red Army Univs., Moscow.
Joined CCP 23; Political Instructor, Whampoa Mil. Acad. 25; participated in Nanchang and Canton Uprisings 27; Political Commissar 10th Army Corps 31-36; Commdr. Shansi-Chaha-Hopei Field Army 37-48; mem. 7th Cen. Cttee. of CCP 45; Mayor of Peking 49-51; Vice-Chair. Nat. Defence Council 54-; Marshal 55; mem. 8th Cen. Cttee. of CCP 56; Vice-Premier, State Council 56-74; Chair. Scientific and Technological Comm. 58-; mem. 9th Cen. Cttee. of CCP 69, 10th Cen. Cttee. 73.

Nijalingappa, Siddavanahalli; Indian lawyer and politician; b. 10 Dec. 1902, Haluvagula, Bellary District; ed. Bangalore and Poona Univ.
Advocate in Mysore High Court 26-39; convicted for political reasons 39, disbarred 40, imprisoned 42-44, 47; mem. Mysore Congress Working Cttee. 39-51; Pres. State Congress 45-46, Karnatak Provincial Congress Cttee. 46-54; mem. Indian Constituent Ass. 46-50, of Lok Sabha 52-56; Chief Minister of Mysore and leader Mysore Congress Legislative Party 56-58, 62-68; Pres. Indian Nat. Congress 68-71, Treas. 71-72 (of Congress Opposition Group 69-); Chair. Indian Oil Co. 60-62; mem. Lal Bahaddur Shastri Memorial Trust; Hon. LL.D. (Karnataka Univ.) 64.
Venkateshpur, Chitraduga, Mysore, India.

Nikaido, Susumu; Japanese politician; b. 1910; ed. Univ. of Southern Calif.
Member, House of Reps.; Deputy Sec.-Gen. Liberal-Democratic Party; former Dir.-Gen. Science and Technology Agency; Dir.-Gen. Hokkaido Devt. Agency;

Minister of State, Chief Cabinet Sec. July 72-74, Sec.-Gen. Liberal Democratic Party Nov.-Dec. 74.
House of Representatives, Tokyo, Japan.

Nimmanhaemin, Bisudhi, B.COMM.; Thai banker; b. 23 May 1915, Chiangmai; ed. Suan Kularb Coll., Bangkok, Henry Thornton School, London, London School of Economics.
Worked in the Office of Comptroller-Gen., Ministry of Finance 40; Head of Public Debt Div., Thai Nat. Banking Bureau 41-42; Head of Public Debt Div., Bank of Thailand 43-47, Head of Exchequer Dept. 48-53, Dir.-Asst. to the Gov. 54-64, Deputy Gov. 65-71, later Gov.; Man. Exchange Equalization Fund of Thailand 59-64; Alt. Gov. of IMF 59-64, later Gov.; Alt. Gov. IBRD 65-71; Assoc. mem. Cttee. of Twenty; Knight Grand Cross (First Class) Most Noble Order of the Crown of Thailand.
Bank of Thailand, P.O. Box 154, Bangkok; Home: 19 Intamra 3 Lane, Sudhisarn Road, Bangkok 4, Thailand.
Telephone: 818-890 (Office); 74-800 (Home).

Nishio, Suehiro; Japanese politician; b. 1891; ed. Primary School.
Factory apprentice 05; mem. Yuaikai (Workers' Friendship Soc., first Japanese trade union) 15, Sec. 19; founded Preparatory Cttee. for Trade Unions 16; arrested 20, 21, 22; del. to ILO Confs. 24, 32; Sec.-Gen. Sodomei (Gen. Fed. of Trade Unions) 25-40 (suppressed); founder mem. Exec. Shakai Minshu (Socialist People's) Party 25; mem. House of Reps. 28-38 (expelled) 39-; formed mems. of Shakai Taishu (Socialist Mass) Party 40, party banned; founded Social Democratic Party of Japan 45; re-established Sodomei 46; Deputy Prime Minister May 47-Feb. 48; resigned from Social Democratic Party 59; Founder Chair. Japan Democratic Socialist Party 61-67.
Publs. *With People* (autobiography) 50, *Road to the New Party* 59.
1 Shiba Sakuragawa-cho, Minato-ku, Tokyo, Japan.

Nitisastro, Widjojo, PH.D.; Indonesian politician; b. 23 Sept. 1927, Malang; ed. Univ. of Indonesia and Univ. of Calif., Berkeley, U.S.A.
Dean, Faculty of Econs., Univ. of Indonesia 65-67; seconded to UN as expert engaged in drawing up plan for 2nd UN Econ. Devt. Decade and mem. Gov. Council, UN Asian Inst. of Devt. and Planning 67-71; Minister of State for National Planning and Construction Sept. 71-74, for Economic, Financial and Industrial Affairs 74-.
Publs. include: *Population Trends in Indonesia, The Relevance of Growth Models for Less Developed Economies, The Role of Research in a University, Public Policies, Land Tenure and Population Movements, Population Problems and Indonesia's Economic Development.*
Ministry for National Planning and Construction, Jakarta, Indonesia.

Niwa, Kyoshiro; Japanese politician; b. 1904; ed. Tokyo Univ.
Member, House of Reps.; fmr. Parl. Vice-Minister of Home Affairs; Deputy Sec.-Gen. Liberal-Democratic Party; Minister of Transport 71-72.
House of Representatives, Tokyo, Japan.

Nixon, Peter James; Australian politician and farmer; b. 22 March 1928, Orbost, Victoria; ed. Wesley Coll. Melbourne.
Member, House of Representatives 61-; mem. Joint Cttee. Public Accounts 64; mem. Joint Cttee. Foreign Affairs 67; Minister for the Interior 67-71, for Shipping and Transport 71-72, for Transport Nov. 75-; Postmaster Gen. Nov.-Dec. 75; Country Party.
Parliament House, Canberra, Australia.
Telephone: Canberra 721211.

Nohara, Masakatsu; Japanese politician; b. 1906; ed. Utsonomiya Agricultural High School.
Member, House of Reps.; fmr. Dir. of a district forestry office; Parl. Vice-Minister for Agriculture; Chair. House of Reps., Agriculture, Forestry and Fishery Affairs Cttee.; Vice-Chair. Liberal-Democratic Party Exec. Board; Minister of Labour 70-71.
House of Representatives, Tokyo, Japan.

Nolan, Sidney Robert, C.B.E.; British (Australian) artist; b. 22 April 1917; ed. Melbourne State and Technical schools, Melbourne Nat. Gallery.
One-Man Shows Paris, London, New York, Rome, Venice, Zurich and capital cities of Australia; Arts Council Travelling Exhbns., Great Britain; also exhibited at Pittsburgh Int. Exhbn. 53, 54, 55, 64, 67, 71, New Delhi Int. Exhbn. 53, Pacific Loan Exhbn. Australia and U.S.A. 56, Brussels Int. Exhbn. 58, Documenta II, Kassel 59, Dunn Int. Exhbn. London 63, Edinburgh Festival 64, Retrospective Exhbn. 1937-67 Sydney, Melbourne 67, Perth 68, Aldeburgh Festival 64, 68, 71, Peking 75; retrospective exhbn. Darmstadt 71, Dublin 73, Stockholm 76; set designs for *Icare*, Sydney 49, *The Guide*, Oxford 61, the *Rite of Spring*, Covent Garden 62, *The Display*, Adelaide Festival 64, Canberra 65; Commr. for Australia and del. for Australian documentary films, Venice Biennale 54; Italian Govt. Scholarship 56; Commonwealth Fund Fellowship for travel in U.S.A. 59-61; Nat. Univ., Canberra Fellowship 65; made a number of films including *Toehold in History* 65, *Kelly Country, The Paintings of Sidney Nolan* 70; Hon. LL.D. (Australian Nat. Univ., Canberra) 71; Hon. Dr. Lit. (London) 71; Fellow, Bavarian Acad., York Univ. 71.
Principal works in Tate Gallery (London), Museum of Modern Art (New York), Nat. Galleries of Australia, Tom Collins Memorial (Perth Univ.), Contemporary Art Soc. and Arts Council of Great Britain (London), Power Bequest, Sydney Univ.
Publs. (illustrated) *Hear the Ocean* (Robert Lowell) 68, *Children's Crusade* (Bertold Brecht and Benjamin Britten) 73.
c/o Bank of New South Wales, 9 Sackville Street, London, W.1, England.

Norindr, Phagna Pheng; Laotian diplomatist; b. 17 May 1919, Luang Prabang; ed. in France.
Professor, Pavie School, Vientiane 41-46; Personal Sec. to Prime Minister Xieng Mao 46; Dir. Savannakhet School 47-51; Dir. of Customs 54-58; Dir. of Cabinets of Prime Ministers Phoui Sananikone and Kon Abhay 58-60; Deputy to Nat. Assembly 60-65; Sec.-Gen. Govt. of Laos 65-72; Amb. to U.S.A. and Perm. Rep. to UN 72-74.
c/o Ministry of Foreign Affairs, Vientiane, Laos.

Norodom Phurissara, Prince (*see* Phurissara, Prince Norodom).

Norodom Sihanouk, Prince Samdech Preah; fmr. Head of State of Cambodia; b. 31 Oct. 1922; ed. in Saigon and Saumur (France).
Elected King April 41; abdicated March 55; Founder Pres. Popular Socialist Community 55-70; Prime Minister and Minister of Foreign Affairs Oct. 55, March 56, Sept. 56, April 57; Perm. Rep. to UN Feb.-Sept. 56; elected Head of State after death of his father 60, deposed March 70; lived in Peking 70-75, founded Royal Govt. of Nat. Union of Cambodia (GRUNC) May 70; restored as Head of State when GRUNC forces overthrew Khmer Republic April 75, resigned April 76; adviser to the Govt. Nov. 75-; mem. People's Representative Assembly March 76-; journalist, musician, film maker (*Le Petit Prince*).
Publ. *My War with the C.I.A.* (with Wilfred Burchett) 73.
Phnom-Penh, Cambodia.

Norris, Sir Eric George, K.C.M.G.; British diplomatist; b. 14 March 1918, Hertford; ed. Hertford Grammar School and St. Catharine's Coll., Cambridge.
Military service 40-46; Dominions Office 46; First Sec., Dublin 48-50, Pakistan 52-55; Counsellor, Delhi 55-57;

Deputy High Commr., Bombay 57-60, Calcutta 62-65; Asst. Under Sec. of State, Commonwealth Office 66-68; High Commr. to Kenya 68-72; Deputy Under Sec. of State, Foreign and Commonwealth Office 72-73; High Commr. to Malaysia Jan. 74-.
British High Commission, Wisma Damansara, Jalan Samantan, Kuala Lumpur, Malaysia.

Nosaka, Sanzo; Japanese politician; b. 1892, Hagi, Yamaguchi Pref.; ed. Keio Univ.
Secretary Brotherhood Asscn. (later called Japanese Fed. of Labour) 17; visited U.K., Europe and U.S.S.R. 19-22, joined C.P. of Great Britain; founder mem. C.P. of Japan 22; arrested for first time 23; mem. Cen. Cttee. C.P. of Japan 31; in Moscow as mem. Presidium Exec. Cttee. Communist Int. 35-43; anti-war activities in U.S.A. 34-38 and in Yenan (China) 40-45; returned to Japan and elected mem. Cen. Cttee. and Politburo C.P. of Japan 46; mem. House of Reps. and Chair. Communist Group in Diet 46-50; underground activity 50-55; First Sec. Cen. Cttee. C.P. of Japan 55-58, Chair. 58-; mem. House of Councillors 56-.
Publs. *Selected Works*, 2 vols., *My Stormy Path* (autobiography).
26, 4-chome, Sendagaya, Shibuya-ku, Tokyo, Japan.
Telephone: 03-403-6111.

Nosavan, General Phoumi; Laotian army officer and politician.
Secretary of State for Defence 59; promoted to Gen. 60; Minister of Defence 60, and Sports, Youth and Ex-Servicemen 60; Deputy Premier, Minister of the Interior, Culture and Social Welfare 60; Deputy Premier and Minister of Defence 61; Vice-Premier and Minister of Finance July 62-65; exiled 65; Leader of Social Democratic Party.

Nu, U (formerly **Thakin Nu**), B.A.; Burmese politician and writer; b. 1907; ed. Rangoon Univ.
For some years headmaster Nat. High School, Pantanaw; joined Dobhama Asiayone (Our Burma) Organization; detained by British 40, released after Japanese occupation 43, worked for Dobhama Asiayone; Minister of Foreign Affairs 43-44; Minister for Publicity and Propaganda 44-45; Vice-Pres. Anti-Facist People's Freedom League (AFPFL) after Allied re-occupation; elected Speaker Constituent Assembly 47; Deputy Chair. Gov.'s Exec. Council 47; signatory Anglo-Burmese Treaty, London; Prime Minister 48-56, 57-58, worked on AFPFL re-organization 56-57; Prime Minister, Minister of Home Affairs, Relief and Resettlement, Democratization of Local Administration, Information, Transport, Posts and Telegraphs, Shipping and Aviation, Housing and Rehabilitation 60-62; in custody 62-Oct. 66; organizer and leader of opposition movement 69- (in Thailand 69-70).
Publs. Plays and stories.

Nur Khan, Air Marshal M.; Pakistani airline executive; b. 1923, Tamman; ed. Col. Brown's Cambridge School and Prince of Wales Royal Indian Mil. Coll.
Commissioned Royal Indian Air Force 41; Man. Dir. Pakistan Int. Airlines 59-65; C.-in-C. Pakistan Air Force 65-68; Gov. W. Pakistan 69; Chair. PIA Nov. 73-; Pres. Pakistan Hockey Federation 67-69; Hilal-e-Jurat 65.
Pakistan International Airlines Corporation, PIA Building, Karachi Airport, Pakistan.
Telephone: 412011-96.

Nurjadin, Air Chief Marshal Roesmin; Indonesian diplomatist; b. 31 May 1930, Malang; ed. Gadjah Mada Univ., R.A.F. Flight Instructor School, England, D.C. Staff Coll., Wellington, India.
Squadron Commdr. 53-62; Deputy C.-in-C. Operational Command, later C.-in-C. Air Defence Command 62-64; Air Attaché, Bangkok and Moscow 64-65; Minister, C.-in-C., Chief of Staff, Air Force 66-70; Amb. to U.K. 70-74, to U.S.A. 74-; various mil. and foreign decorations.
Embassy of Indonesia, 2020 Massachusetts Avenue, N.W., Washington, D.C. 20036, U.S.A.

Nyun, U; Burmese civil servant; b. 1911; ed. Rangoon Univ., London School of Economics, London Univ. School of Oriental Studies.
Joined Indian Civil Service 31; after Burmese independence Under-Sec. and later Sec., Ministry of Commerce and Industry 48-50; Chief, Industry and Trade Div., UN Econ. Comm. for Asia and the Far East (ECAFE) 51-57, Deputy Exec. Sec. ECAFE 57-59, Exec. Sec. Feb. 59-Aug. 73.
c/o Ministry of Foreign Affairs, Rangoon, Burma.

O

O'Brien, Terence John, M.C., C.M.G., M.A. (OXON.); British diplomatist; b. 13 Oct. 1921, Ranchi, India; ed. Greshams School, Merton Coll. Oxford.
Ayrshire Yeomanry, later Air Liaison Office with 83 Group R.A.F. 42-45; Dominions Office, Commonwealth Relations Office 47-49, 52-54; Second Sec. British High Comm. Ceylon 49-52; Principal, Treasury 54-56; Financial Sec. High Comm. Australia 56-58; Planning Officer, Commonwealth Relations Office 58-60; First Sec., High Comm. Malaya 60-63 (Sec. to Inter-Gov. Cttee. on Malaysia); Counsellor, High Comm. India 63-66; Imperial Defence Coll. 67; Counsellor, Foreign Office, F.C.O. 68-70; Amb. to Nepal 70-74, to Burma May 74-.
British Embassy, Rangoon, Burma; Home: Beaufort House, Woodcutts, Salisbury, Wiltshire, England.

O'Byrne, Justin; Australian politician; b. 1 June 1912, Launceston, Tasmania; ed. St. Patricks Coll., Launceston, Tasmania.
Engaged in pastoral industry, S.W. Queensland 30-39; R.A.A.F. 41-46, prisoner of war 41-44; mem. Senate 46-, Pres. 74-75; Opposition Whip, Govt. Whip 72-74; Treas. Fed. Exec. Australian Labor Party; Del. (Parl. Adviser) UN Gen. Assembly 71.
The Senate, Canberra, A.C.T.; Home: 11 Ramsay Street, Launceston, Tasmania, Australia.
Telephone: 31-5506 (Home).

Ochiai, Eiichi, B.SC.; Japanese trade unionist; b. 15 Jan. 1916; ed. Yokohama Nat. Univ.
Mitsui Metal Mine Co. Ltd. 36-41, Toshiba Electric Co. 43-46; Adviser, Japan Asscn. of Science and Technology 44-47; Pres. All-Japan Electric Industry Workers Unions 46-48; mem. Exec. Board Congress of Industrial Labour Union 46-49; Gen. Sec. Nat. Fed. of Industrial Orgs. 49-64; mem. Labour Problems Cttee. 61-64, Small and Medium Enterprise Retirement Countermeasure Cttee. 60-64; Dir. Tokyo Office, Int. Confederation of Free Trade Unions (ICFTU) and Special Rep. in Japan 64-; Trustee, Japan ILO Asscn. 62-.
Publs. *Import of Foreign Capital and Production Struggle* 49, *Directory of Trade Union Administration* 49, *Earth of North America and Blood of Great Britain* 59.
ICFTU Tokyo Office, Kaware Building, 1-5-8, Nishi-Shimbashi, Minato-ku, Tokyo 105; Home: 38-302 Keyakidai, 4-chome, Nishimachi, Kokubunji-Shi, Tokyo, Japan.
Telephone: 0425-03-503 (Office); 36-8306 (Home).

Oda, Shigeru, LL.D.; Japanese Lawyer; b. 22 Oct. 1924; ed. Univ. of Tokyo, Yale Univ.
Research Fellow, Univ. of Tokyo 47-49; lecturer, Univ. of Tôhoku 50-53, Asst. Prof. 53-59, Prof. 59-76; Tech. Adviser, Atomic Energy Comm. 61-64; Special Asst. to Minister of Foreign Affairs 73-76; mem. Science Council of Ministry of Educ. 69-76, of Council for Ocean Devt. in

Prime Minister's Office 71-76, Advisory Cttee. for Co-operation with UN Univ. 71-76; Judge, Int. Court of Justice Feb. 76-; del. to UN Confs. on Law of the Sea 58, 60, 73-75; Rep. at 6th Gen. Conf. of Inter-Governmental Oceanographic Comm. 69; consultative positions with bodies concerned with marine questions; Counsel for Fed. Repub. of Germany before Int. Court of Justice 68; Editor-in-Chief, *Japanese Annual of International Law* 73-.
Publs. in Japanese: *International Law of the Sea* 56-69, *International Law and Marine Resources* 71-75; in English: *International Control of Sea Resources* 62, *The International Law of Ocean Development* 72-74; various articles.
International Court of Justice, Peace Palace, The Hague 2102, The Netherlands.

Oda, Takio; Japanese diplomatist; b. 16 March 1907; ed. Tokyo Univ.
Successively Sec., Japanese Embassy, Wash.; Chief Econs. Dept., Cen. Post-War Liaison Office 46; Dir. Gen. Affairs, Commercial and Research Depts.; Dir. Int. Trade and Industry Bureau 50-52; Dir. Econs. Bureau of Foreign Ministry 52-54; Minister Plenipotentiary in Britain 54-57, Minister to Denmark 57-58, Amb. to Indonesia 58-62; Vice Foreign Minister 63-64; Chair. Board Int. Public Relations Co. 66-; Pres. Japan-Denmark Soc. 66.
Central Co-operative House, Apt. 410, 15 Ageba-cho, Shinjuku-ku, Tokyo, Japan.
Telephone: 260-5041 (Home); 501-7571 (Office).

Oë, Kenzaburo; Japanese author; b. 1935.
First stories published 57; Akutagawa prize for novella *The Catch* 58; first full-length novel *Pluck The Flowers, Gun The Kids* 58; represented young Japanese writers at Peking 60; travelled to Russia and Western Europe writing a series of essays on Youth in the West 61; Shinchosha Literary Prize 64; Tanizaki Prize 67.
Publs. *The Catch* 58, *Pluck The Flowers, Gun The Kids* 58, *Our Age* 59, *Screams* 62, *The Perverts* 63, *Hiroshima Notes* 63, *Adventures in Daily Life* 64, *A Personal Matter* 64, (English 69), *Football in The First Year of Mannen* 67.
585 Seijo-machi, Setagaya-Ku, Tokyo, Japan.
Telephone: 482-7192.

Oemar-Senoadji; Indonesian lawyer and politician; b. 5 Dec. 1915; Surukarta, Central Java; ed. Rechts Hoge School, Gadjah Mada Univ., Jogjakarta.
Worked for Ministry of Justice 45-50; Judge, Jogjakarta Regional Court 50; Chief Public Prosecutor, Regional Court of Justice, Semarang 50-53; Public Prosecutor, Jakarta 53-55; Head, Investigation Section, Attorney-Gen.'s Office 55-59; Deputy Attorney-Gen. of Supreme Court 59-60 Prof. Faculty of Law and Social Sciences, Univ. of Indonesia 60-, Dean 66; Minister of Justice 66-74; Chief Justice, Supreme Court 74-; mem. working cttee. Inst. for Devt. of Nat. Law 62; various awards.
Supreme Court of Indonesia, Jakarta, Indonesia.

Ogawa, Heishiro, B.A.; Japanese diplomatist; b. 17 March 1916; ed. Tokyo Univ. Law Dept.
Joined Ministry of Foreign Affairs 38; Consul, Hong Kong 52; Chief, China Div., Ministry of Foreign Affairs 54-57; Counsellor, Japanese Embassy, Washington 57-60; Consul-Gen., Hong Kong 60-66; Dir.-Gen. Asian Affairs Bureau 66-68; Amb. to Denmark 68-72; Pres. Foreign Service Inst. 72-73; Amb. to People's Republic of China Feb. 73-.
Embassy of Japan, Peking, People's Republic of China.

Ogawa, Masaru, B.A., M.A.; Japanese journalist; b. 22 March 1915; ed. Univ. of California at Los Angeles, Tokyo Imperial, Columbia Univs.
Domei News Agency 41-46; Kyodo News Service 46-48; *The Japan Times* 48-, Chief, political section 49, Asst. Man. Editor 50, Chief Writer 52, Man. Editor 58-64, Dir. 59-, Exec. Editor 64-68, Senior Editor 68-71, Chief Editorial Writer 69-71, Editor 71-; mem. Yoshida Int. Educ. Foundation 68-, Exec. Dir. 72-; mem. Japan Broadcasting Corpn. Overseas Programme Consultative Council 74-, Editorial Board *Media* Magazine, Hong Kong 74; Life Mem. Foreign Corresp. Club of Japan 73-; Pres. Pacific News Agency 73-; Lecturer, Tokyo Univ. 54-58.
2, 14-banchi, 5-chome, Mejiro, Toshima-ku, Tokyo, Japan.
Telephone: 951-5082.

Ogura, Takakazu; Japanese agriculturalist; b. 2 Oct. 1910, Fukui Prefecture; ed. Tokyo Imperial Univ.
Posts with Ministry of Agriculture and Forestry 34-56; Lecturer, Faculty of Agriculture, Univ. of Tokyo 47-61; Dir.-Gen. Food Agency 56-58; Sec.-Gen. Research Council on Agriculture, Forestry and Fisheries 58-60; Vice-Minister of Agriculture and Forestry 60-61; Chair. Research Council on Agriculture, Forestry and Fisheries 63-; Dir. Research Inst. on Mechanisation of Agric. 65-; Pres. Inst. of Developing Economies 67-72, Chair. 72-.
Publs. *Agricultural Policy of Japan* 65 (in Japanese), *Agricultural Development in Modern Japan* 66, *Agrarian Problems and Agricultural Policy in Japan* 67 (in English); articles in English and Japanese.
Institute of Developing Economies, 42 Ichigaya-Hommura-cho, Shinjuko-ku, Tokyo 162; Home: 29 Tokiwadai 1-chome, Itabashi-ku, Tokyo 174, Japan.
Telephone: Tokyo 960-1764 (Home).

Ohara, Eiichi; Japanese business executive; b. 2 Dec. 1912, Hiroshima; ed. Tokyo Univ.
With the Industrial Bank of Japan 36-63; Exec. Vice-Pres. Fuji Heavy Industries Ltd. 63-70, Pres. 70-; Chair. Fuji Robin Industries Ltd.; Pres. Transport Machine Industries Ltd.; mem. Japan Fed. of Econ. Orgs., Aircraft Industry Council; Dir. Japan Automobile Mfrs. Asscn.; Trustee, Japan Cttee. for Econ. Devt.
Fuji Heavy Industries Ltd., Subaru Buildings, 7, 1-chome, Nishishinjuku, Shinjuku-ku, Tokyo, Japan.

Ohira, Masayoshi; Japanese politician; b. 12 March 1910; ed. Tokyo Commercial Coll.
Ministry of Finance 36, Supt. Yokohama Revenue Office 37-38, Private Sec. to Minister of Finance 49; mem. House of Reps. 52-; Chief Cabinet Sec. 60-62; Minister of Int. Trade and Industry 68-70, of Foreign Affairs 62-64, 72-74, of Finance July 74-; Chair. Policy Board, Liberal-Democratic Party Nov. 67-68.
Publs. Essays: *Sugao no Daigishi* (A Parliamentarian as He Is) 54, *Random Thoughts on Public Finance* 56.
Ministry of Finance, Tokyo; and 105 Komagome Hayashi-cho, Bunkyo-ku, Tokyo, Japan.

Ohtaka, Masato, B.ARCH.; Japanese architect; b. 8 Sept. 1923; ed. Tokyo Univ.
At Maekawa-Kunio Architecture Design Office 49-61, established Ohtaka Architecture Design Office 62; also Lecturer Tokyo and Waseda Univs,; Art Award, Ministry of Educ. 70.
Works include Plan for new town at Tama, Tokyo, Chiba Public Hall and Agricultural Co-operative Asscns., Tochici Govt. Building.
Yoyogi Building, 5-18 Sendagaya, Shibuya-ku, Tokyo, Japan.

Ohtani, Ichiji; Japanese textile executive; b. 31 Aug. 1912, Kobe; ed. Kobe Univ.
Director Toyobo Co. Ltd. 64-68, Man. Dir. 68-72, Senior Man. Dir. 72-74, Deputy Pres. 74, Pres. 74-; Dir. Toyoba Petcord Co. Ltd. 69-; Vice-Pres. Industries Unidas, S.A. 73-.
Toyobo Co. Ltd., 8 Dojima Hamadori 2-chome, Kita-ku, Osaka 530; Home: 69 Yamate-cho, Ashiya-shi 659, Japan.
Telephone: (06) 344-1331 (Office); (0797) 22-2057 (Home).

Ohya, Kazuo, LL.B.; Japanese business executive; b. 8 Sept. 1902; ed. Kyoto Univ.
Sumitomo Ltd. Partnership Co. 28; Man. Dir. Nissin

Chemical Co. Ltd. (later Sumitomo Chemical Co. Ltd.) 47-56, Senior Man. Dir. Sumitomo Chemical Co. 56-63, Pres. 63-65, Counsellor 65-; Dir. Japan Exlan Co. Ltd. 63-, Chair. of Board 65-; Pres. Osaka Labour Standard Asscn. 63-; Perm. Dir. Japan Fed. of Employers' Asscn. 63-; Blue Ribbon Medal; 2nd Order of Merit (Sacred Treasure).
Japan Exlan Co. Ltd., 1-25 Dojima Hamadori 1-chome, Kita-ku, Osaka; Home: 2-27-6, Fujishirodai, Suita, Japan.
Telephone: Osaka (06)-344-1451 (Office); Senri (068) 32-7013 (Home).

Ohya, Shinzo; Japanese politician and business executive; b. 5 July 1894; ed. Tokyo Coll. of Commerce.
President Teikoku Rayon Co. Ltd. 45-48, 56-, name changed to Teijin Ltd. 62-; Pres. Teikin Petrochemical Industries Ltd., Teijin Chemicals Ltd., Teijin Hercules Chemical Co. Ltd., Teijin Agrochemicals Ltd., KK. Paris Nippon Kan, Iranian Petroleum Corpn. 71-; mem. House of Councillors 47-56; Minister of Int. Trade and Industry 48-49; Minister of Finance 48-49; Minister of Transportation 49-50; Pres. Japan Chemical Fibres Asscn. 47-48 and 71-73; Pres. of Japan Textile Federation 71-; Counsellor Osaka Chamber of Commerce and Industry 57-; Dir. of Fed. of Econ. Orgs. 58-, Japan Fed. of Employers' Asscns. 58-; Chair. Japanese Nat. Cttee. of Int. Chamber of Commerce 73-; Vice-Chair. Int. Protection Cttee. of Industrial Property, Int. Chamber of Commerce (ICC) 61-, now mem. Exec. Board of ICC; Counsellor Italy-Japan Soc. 63-, Japan-Singapore Asscn. 71-; Vice-Pres. France-Japan Soc. 64-; Pres. Germany-Japan Soc. 67-, Japan-Belgium Soc. 69, Madagascar-Japan Soc. 70-, Japan-Turkey Soc. 71-, Japan-Hungarian Econ. Club 71-, Japan-Thailand Trade Asscn. 72-, Tokyo Philharmonic Orchestra 72-, Kansai Kiin (Inst. of "Go") 75-; several decorations.
14-5 Kitabatake, 3-chome, Abeno-ku, Osaka; 16-22, 1-chome Todoroki, Setagaya-ku, Tokyo, Japan.

Okada, Kanjiro; Japanese business executive; b. 24 Oct. 1891; ed. Hitotsubashi Univ.
Chairman, Fujitsu Ltd.
Fujitsu Ltd., Marunouchi, Chiyoda-ku, Tokyo, Japan.

Okada, Kenzo; Japanese artist; b. 28 Sept. 1902; ed. Tokyo Fine Arts Univ.
Works in Guggenheim Museum, Museum of Modern Art (both in New York City); in Dunn Int. Exhbn., Tate Gallery, London 63; Campana Memorial Prize, Art Inst. of Chicago 54, Logan Prize 55.
51 West 11th Street, New York City 11, N.Y., U.S.A.

Okauchi, Hideo; Japanese business executive; b. 19 Nov. 1908, Ayauta-gun, Kagawa-ken; ed. Takamatsu Commercial High School (now Kagawa Univ.).
Joined Shiseido Co. Ltd. 29, Dir. 47, Man. Dir. 60, Senior Man. Dir. 66, Pres. 67-; Dir. Fed. of Econ. Orgs. 67-75, Chair. 75-; Exec. Counsellor, Tokyo Chamber of Commerce and Industry 67-; Rep. Dir. Tokyo Cosmetic Industry Asscn. 72-, Cosmetic Fair Trade Council 72-; Dir. Japan Cosmetic Industry Asscn. 72-, Japan Cosmetic Asscn. 71-.
Shiseido Company Ltd., 5-5 Ginza 7-chome, Chuo-ku, Tokyo; Home: 5-16-7 Nishikoiwa, Edogawa-ku, Tokyo, Japan.
Telephone: 572-5111 (Office); 657-0958 (Home).

Okazaki, Chu; Japanese banker; b. 1 Oct. 1904, Tokyo; ed. Tokyo Univ.
Joined The Bank of Kobe Ltd. (now the Taiyo Kobe Bank) 33, Man. Dir. 45-47, Pres. 47-67, Chair. 67-73, Dir. and Counsellor 73-; Blue Ribbon Medal 69; Order of the Rising Sun, Second Class 75.
1-3, Nishi-Suma, Suma-ku, Kobe City, Japan.
Telephone: 078-731-1004.

Okita, Saburo; Japanese economist; b. 3 Nov. 1914; ed. Engineering Faculty, Tokyo Univ.
Served in Ministry of Posts 37-39, Ministry of Greater East Asia 39-45, Ministry of Foreign Affairs 45-47, Econ. Stabilization Board, Chief Research Section 47; UN Econ. Comm. for Asia and the Far East 52; Chief, Econ. Co-op. Unit Econ. Planning Agency 53, Dir.-Gen. Planning Bureau 57-, Devt. Bureau 62-63; Pres. Japan Econ. Research Center 63-73, Chair. of the Board 73-; Pres. Overseas Econ. Co-operation Fund 73-; Int. Devt. Centre of Japan 73-; mem. UN Devt. Planning Cttee. 66-; mem. Pearson Comm. on Int. Devt. of World Bank 69; mem. OECD High Level Expert Group on Science Policy for the 1970s 70-71; mem. Board of Govs. of NHK (Japan Broadcasting Corpn.); Hon. Dr. Econ. (Nagoya Univ.).
Publs. *The Future of Japan's Economy* 60, *Japan's Post-War Economic Policy* 61, *Economic Planning* 62, *Conditions for a Developed Nation* 65, *Japanese Economy in the Asian Setting* 66, *Future Vision for Japanese Economy* 68, *Role of the Economist* 73, *The position of Japan, a Country of Poor Resources, in the World Economy* 75.
5-13-12 Koishikawa, Bunkyo-ku, Tokyo, Japan.
Telephone: 03-811-0742 and 03-814-3030.

Okudaira, Sen-ichi; Japanese banker; b. 20 Dec. 1910, Oita Pref.; ed. Kyoto Univ.
Director of Sumitomo Trust & Banking Co. Ltd. 57, Man. Dir. 60, Senior Man. Dir. 65, Deputy Pres. 69, Pres. 72-; Chair. Trust Co. Asscn. of Japan; Blue Ribbon Medal.
Sumitomo Trust & Banking Co. Ltd., 15, Kitahama 5-chome, Higashi-ku, Osaka; Home: 5-16, Chigusa 1-chome, Takarazuka City, Hyogo Pref., Japan.

Okuno, Seisuke; Japanese politician; b. 12 July 1913; ed. First High School, Univ. of Tokyo.
Chief, Gen. Affairs Section, Yamanashi Pref. Govt. and Kagoshima Pref. Govt. 38; Officer Dept. of Local Govt., Ministry of Home Affairs, 43; Head of Police Dept., Kochi Prefectural Govt. 47; Chief, Finance and Research Divs., Local Autonomy Agency 49; Dir. Bureau of Taxation, Ministry of Autonomy 53, Bureau of Finance 58; Perm. Vice-Minister, Ministry of Autonomy 63; mem. House of Reps. 63-; Minister of Educ. 72-74; Liberal Democratic Party.
Publs. Several articles on aspects of local government.
5-7-10 Jingumae, Shibuya-ku, Tokyo, Japan.

Oliphant, Sir Mark Laurence Elwin, K.B.E., F.R.S., KT. ST. J., PH.D., F.A.A.; British physicist; b. Australia 8 Oct. 1901; ed. Adelaide Univ., and Trinity Coll., Cambridge.
Messel Research Fellow, Royal Soc. 31; Lecturer and Fellow, St. John's Coll. 34; Asst. Dir. Research, Cavendish Lab., Cambridge 35; Prof. and Dir. of Dept. of Physics, Birmingham Univ. 37-50; Vice-Principal Sept. 48-49; Dir. of Postgraduate Research School of Physical Sciences, Australian Nat. Univ. 50-63; Prof. of Particle Physics 50-64; Pres. Australian Acad. of Sciences 54-57; Gov. of S. Australia 71-(Nov. 76); Hon. Fellow, St. John's Coll., Cambridge 52, Australian Nat. Univ. 68-71; several hon. degrees.
Government House, Adelaide, South Australia; (from Dec. 1976) 37 Colvin Street, Hughes, A.C.T. 2605, Australia.

Omar Ali Saifuddin, Sa'adul Khairi Waddin, H. H. Sultan, D.K., P.S.P.N.B., P.S.N.B., S.P.M.B., D.M.N., D.K. (Kel.), D.K. (J), D.K. (Sel.), K.C.M.G.; former ruler of Brunei; b. 1916; ed. Malay Coll., Kuala Kangsar, Perak, Malaya.
Served as a Govt. official in various depts. in Brunei; Grand Vizier (First Minister), mem. State Council 57-60; Sultan of Brunei 50-67; abdicated Oct. 67; visited U.K. and Europe 52, 53, 57, 59, 63, U.K. and America 65, U.K. 68; pilgrimage to Mecca 53-62, travelled round the world 65.
Istana Darul Hana, Brunei.

Omoto, Shimpei; Japanese business executive; b. 1908; ed. Hitotsubashi Univ.
President, Mitsui Mining & Smelting Co. Ltd.
Mitsui Mining & Smelting Co. Ltd., 2-1 Muromachi, Nihonbashi, Chuo-ku, Tokyo, Japan.

Ong, Tan Sri Haji Omar Yoke-Lin, P.M.N.; Malaysian politician, diplomatist, banker, industrialist and company director; b. 1917.
Member Kuala Lumpur Municipal Council 52-; co-founder Alliance Party; mem. Fed. Legislative Council 54-; Malayan Minister of Posts and Telecommunications 55-56, of Transport 56-57, of Labour and Social Welfare 57-59, of Health and Social Welfare 59-64; M.P. 59-62; Vice-Pres. Commonwealth Parl. Asscn. 61; Amb. to U.S.A. and UN 62-64; Amb. to U.S.A. 64-72; Minister without Portfolio, Malaysia 64-73; Pres. of Senate 73-; Chair. Asian Int. Merchant Bankers Bhd., Maju Jaya Industries Sdn. Bhd., Kemuncak Enterprises Sdn. Bhd., Syarikat Ong Yoke-Lin Sdn. Bhd., OYL Industries Sdn. Bhd., Raza Sdn. Bhd.; Dir. Esso Malaysia Berhad, Hume Industries (Malaysia) Berhad; Chair. Malaysian Red Cross Soc. 59-62; Hon. Order of the Crown of Selangor, First and Second Class, Most Illustrious Order of Kinabalu, First Class.
Dewan Ra'ayat, Kuala Lumpur, Malaysia.

Onn, Datuk Hussein bin (*see* Hussein bin Onn).

Ooka, Shohei; Japanese writer; b. 1909; ed. Univ. of Kyoto.
Translator of French literature, especially Stendhal; soldier and prisoner of war in the Philippines 44-45; novelist and critic 48-; Teacher at Meiji Univ. 52-55; visited U.S.A., England and France as Creative Fellow, Rockefeller Foundation 53-54; Yokomitsu Prize 49, Yomiuru Prize 52, Mainichi Shincho Prize 61, Mainichi Geijitsu Prize 72, Noma Prize 74, Asahi Prize 76.
Publs. Translated Alain's *Stendhal* 40, Stendhal's *Chartreuse de Parme* 49, etc.; novels: *Furyoki* (Memories of a Prisoner of War) 49, *Musashino Fujin* (A Woman of Musashino Plain) 50, *Nobi* (Fires of the Plain) 51, *Sanso* (Oxygen) 53, *Hamlet Nikki* (Diary of Hamlet) 55, *Kaei* (Under the Shadow of Cherry-blossom) 61, *Reite Senki* (Battle on Leyte) 71 *Nakahara Chuya* (biography) 74, etc.
7-15-12 Seijo, Satagaya-ku, Tokyo, Japan.

Ople, Blas F.; Philippine politician; b. 3 Feb. 1927, Hagonoy, Bulacan; ed. Philippine public and private schools, Far Eastern Univ. and Manuel L. Quezon Univ., Manila.
Copy editor and columnist *The Daily Mirror*, Manila 50-53; Asst. to Pres. Ramon Magsaysay on labour and agrarian affairs 54-57; writer and labour leader 58-64; Head, Propaganda Div., Ferdinand E. Marcos' presidential campaign 65; Special Asst. to Pres. Marcos and Commr., Social Security System 66; Sec. of Labour 67-; Chair. Nat. Manpower and Youth Council 67-71; mem. Board of Trustees, Land Bank 68-; Chair. Govt. Group, Int. Labour Conf. 69-, Pres. June 75-76; Chair. Asian Labour Ministers' Conf. 67; various govt. and civic awards.
61 Visayas Avenue, Project 6, Quezon City, Philippines.
Telephone: 99-67-56; 98-20-56.

Orazmukhamedov, Oraz Nazarovich; Soviet politician; b. 1928; ed. Tashkent Railway Engineering Inst. Mem. C.P.S.U. 48-, cand. mem. Cen. Cttee. 71-; railway engineer 45-59; party and state work 59-61; Dep. Chair. Council of Ministers, Turkmen S.S.R. 61-66; Sec. Cen. Cttee. C.P. of Turkmen S.S.R. 66-69; Chair. Council of Ministers and Minister of Foreign Affairs, Turkmen S.S.R. 69-75; Deputy U.S.S.R. Supreme Soviet 70-; mem. Bureau of Cen. Cttee. Turkmenistan C.P.; alt. mem. C.P.S.U. Cen. Cttee. 71-.
c/o Council of Ministers of the Turkmen S.S.R., Ashkhabad, U.S.S.R.

Oshima, Nagisa; Japanese film director; b. 1932, Kyoto; ed. Kyoto Univ.
With Shochiku Co. 54-59; formed own film company 59; has also directed television films.
Films: *Ai To Kibo No Machi* (A Town of Love and Hope) 59, *Seishun Zankoku Monogatari* (Cruel Story of Youth) 60, *Taiyo No Hakaba* (The Sun's Burial) 60, *Nihon No Yoru To Kiri* (Night and Fog in Japan) 60, *Shiiku* (The Catch) 61, *Amakusa Shiro Tokisada* (The Rebel) 62, *Etsuraku* (The Pleasures of the Flesh) 65, *Yunbogi No Nikki* (The Diary of Yunbogi) 65, *Hakuchu No Torima* (Violence at Noon) 66, *Ninja Bugeicho* (Band of Ninja) 67, *Nihon Shunka-ko* (A Treatise on Japanese Bawdy Songs) 67, *Muri Shinju Nihon No Natsu* (Japanese Summer: Double Suicide) 67, *Koshikei* (Death By Hanging) 68, *Kaettekita Yopparai* (Three Resurrected Drunkards) 68, *Shinjuku Dorobo Nikki* (Diary of a Shinjuku Thief) 68, *Shonen* (Boy) 69, *Tokyo Senso Sengo Hiwa* (He Died after the War) 70, *Gishiki* (The Ceremony) 71, *Tokyo Senso Sengo Hiwa* (The Story of a Young Man who left his Will on Film) 72, *Natsu No Imooto* (Dear Summer Sister) 72.
Sozosha, Daini Sanshu Building, 2-15-7 Akasaka, Minato-ku, Tokyo, Japan.

Otani, Sachio, B.ARCH.; Japanese architect; b. 20 Feb. 1924; ed. Univ. of Tokyo.
Architectural designer under Dr. Kenzo Tange 46-60; Lecturer in Architecture, Univ. of Tokyo 55-64, Assoc. Prof. of Urban Engineering 64-71, Prof. 71-; works include Kojimachi area (of Tokyo) redevelopment plan 60-64, Tokyo children's cultural centre 61-63 and Kyoto Int. Conf. Hall 63-66.
Department of Urban Engineering, Faculty of Engineering, University of Tokyo, 1-3-7 Hongo, Bunkyo-ku, Tokyo; Home: 111 Shoan Kita-machi, Suginami-ku, Tokyo, Japan.

Othman bin Wok; Singapore politician; b. 8 Oct. 1924; ed. Telok Saga Malay School, Raffles Inst. and London School of Journalism.
Worked on *Utusan Melayu* as reporter and Deputy Editor 46-63; mem. People's Action Party 54-; mem. Parl. for Pasir Panjang Constituency 63-; Minister for Social Affairs 63-65; Minister for Culture and Social Affairs, 65-68; Minister for Social Affairs 68-; Capt. in People's Defence Force.
Ministry for Social Affairs, Singapore.

Ovezov, Balysh; Soviet politician; b. 1915; ed. Teachers' Training School, Tashauz, Ashkhabad Pedagogical Inst.
Held Exec. posts in the Young Communist League 31-39; Sec. Central Cttee. of the Turkmenian Young Communist League 39; Deputy People's Commissar of Educ. of Turkmenia 40; Sec. Central Cttee. of the Turkmenian C.P. 45-50; mem. Central Auditing Cttee. of the Central Cttee. of the C.P.S.U. 52-61, mem. C.P.S.U. Central Cttee. 61-; Chair. of the Council of Ministers of Turkmen S.S.R. 51-60; 1st Sec. Central Cttee. C.P. of Turkmen S.S.R. 60-; Deputy to U.S.S.R. and Turkmen S.S.R. Supreme Soviets; awarded two Orders of Lenin, Order of the Red Banner of Labour, Badge of Honour (twice).
Central Committee of Communist Party of Turkmen S.S.R., Ashkhabad, Turkmen S.S.R., U.S.S.R.

P

Pahang, H.R.H. The Sultan of; Sultan Haji Ahmad Shah Ibni Almarhum Sultan Sir Abu Bakar Riyatuddin Almuadzam Shah, D.K., S.P.C.M., S.P.M.J.; Malaysian ruler; b. Oct. 1930, Pekan; ed. Malay Coll., Clifford School, Worcester Coll. Oxford and Univ. Coll. Exeter, England.
Secretariat, Kuala Lipis, mem. State Council and Chair. Council of Supporters until 55; Married H.R.H. the Tengku Ampuan, then Tengku Hajjah Afzan binti Tengku

Muhammad 54; Captain in Royal Malay Regt. 54, Commdr. then Lieut.-Col.; appointed Regent during his Father's absence 56, 59, 65; succeeded his late father as Ruler of Pahang 74; Timbalan Yang di-Pertuan Agong (Deputy Supreme Head of State) Sept. 75-.
Pekan Lama, Kuantan, Pahang, Malaysia.

Pai, Ei Whan, B.S., M.B.A.; Korean diplomatist and economist; b. 1907; ed. in Korea and Business Admin. Colleges in U.S.A.
With Brokerage Co., U.S.A. 38-42; Department of Justice, U.S.A. 42; Far Eastern Div., Office of Censorship, Wash., D.C. 43; Far Eastern Div., Foreign Econ. Admin., Wash., D.C. 44; Financial Adviser to Mil. Govt. Coll., Virginia; Asst. Dir. Dept. of Finance, Mil. Govt., Korea 46-49, Pres. of Fed. of Financial Asscns., Korea, Financial Adviser to Nat. Econ. Board, Mil. Govt. Korea; Pres. of Korean Chamber of Commerce, Hawaii, and Pres. of Far Eastern Trading Co., Hawaii 50; Gov. of Bank of Korea 60; Amb. to Japan 61, to Argentina, Chile, Paraguay, Uruguay and Bolivia 65, to U.K. 67-71; Amb.-at-Large 71-73; Pres. Overseas Econ. Research Inst. 73-; mem. Pres. Council of Econ. and Scientific Advisers 73-; Hon. Ph.D.
C.P.O. Box 5795, Seoul; Overseas Economic Research Institute, C.P.O. Box 5864, Seoul, Republic of Korea.

Pai Hsiang-kuo; politician, People's Repub. of China; b. Kwangtung.
People's Liberation Army Canton Units 69-70; Vice-Chair. Kwangtung Provincial Revolutionary Cttee. 70; Minister of Foreign Trade 70-73; numerous official journeys abroad, to U.S.A., France, Egypt, Pakistan, Peru, Chile, Canada and England.

Pai Ju-ping; People's Repub. of China; b. 1906, Shensi.
Director, Cen. Admin. of Handicraft Industry, State Council 54-58; Sec. CCP Shantung 58-67; Vice-Gov. of Shantung 58-63, Gov. 63-67; criticized and removed from office during Cultural Revolution 67; Vice-Chair. Shantung Revolutionary Cttee. 71; Deputy Sec. CCP Shantung 71; First Political Commissar Tsinan Mil. Region, PLA 74-; Second Sec. CCP Shantung 74-.

Pai, Tonse Ananth, B.COM.; Indian financial official and politician; b. 17 Jan. 1922; ed. Sydneham Coll., Bombay, Int. Summer School of Banking, Fed. Repub. of Germany.
Deputy Man. Syndicate Bank 43-44, Gen. Man. 44-61, Man. Dir. 62-64, 66-67, Chair. 67-70; Chair. Food Corpn. of India 65-66, Life Insurance Corpn. of India 70-72; mem. Madras and later Mysore Legislative Assembly, served various Cttees.; mem. Rajya Sabha 72-; Minister of Railways 72-73, of Heavy Industry 73-74, of Steel and Mines 73-74, of Industry and Civil Supplies 74-; Chair. Study Team of Reserve Bank of India; mem. Agricultural Study Team of Admin. Reforms Comm.; Padma Bhushan 72; Hon. LL.D. (Karnatak Univ.) 72; Hon. D.Litt. (Andhra Univ.).
Ministry of Industry and Civil Supplies, New Delhi; Home: 2 Hastings Road, New Delhi 11, India.
Telephone: 372555 (Home).

Paik, General Sun Yup; Korean army officer and diplomatist; b. 1920; ed. Pyongyang Normal School and Mukden Mil. Acad., Manchuria.
Korean Constabulary 46-48; Repub. of Korea Army 48-60, Chief of Staff 52-54, 57-59, Gen. 53, Chair. Joint Chiefs of Staff 59-60; Amb. to Repub. of China 60-61, to France 61-65, to Canada 65-69; Minister of Transportation 69-70; Pres. Korea Gen. Chemical Industry Corpn. 71-; decorations from Korea, France, U.S.A. and many other countries.
68 Kyunchi-dong, Chongro-ku, Seoul; Home: 339 Huam-Dong, Yong San-ku, Seoul, Republic of Korea.

Pak Chung Hi, General (see Park Chung Hee, General).

Pal, Benjamin Peary, M.SC., PH.D., F.R.S.; Indian agricultural scientist; b. 26 May 1906; ed. Rangoon and Cambridge Univs. Second Econ. Botanist, Imperial Agricultural Research Inst., 33-37, Imperial Econ. Botanist 37-50; Head of Botany Div., Indian Agricultural Research Inst., then Dir. 50-65; Dir.-Gen. Indian Council of Agricultural Research 65-71; fmr. Pres. of Botany and Agriculture sections, Indian Science Congress, Dir.-Gen. 70-71; fmr. Chair. Special Advisory Cttee. on Food and Agriculture, Dept. of Atomic Energy; has served on govt. educ. comm., heading task force on agricultural educ.; Vice-Pres. All India Fine Arts and Crafts Soc.; helped to establish Post-graduate School at Indian Agricultural Research Inst.; research in wheat breeding and genetics; revision work on Int. Code of Nomenclature of Agricultural and Horticultural Plants; Pres. Indian Nat. Science Acad.; mem. Royal Nat. Rose Soc.; mem. Indian Botanical Soc., Royal Horticultural Soc. of London, All Union Lenin Acad. of Agricultural Sciences, Japan Academy; Awards include Padma Shri 58, Rafi Ahmed Kidwai Memorial Prize of the Indian Council of Agricultural Research 57, Birbal Sahni Medal, Indian Botanical Soc. 62, Srinivasa Ramanujan Medal, Nat. Inst. of Sciences of India 64, Gold Medal, Rose Soc. of India 68; Padma Bhushan 68; hon. D.Sc.
Publs. *Beautiful Climbers of India, Charophyta, The Rose in India, Wheat, Flowering Shrubs* 68, *Bougainvilleas* 74; over 160 scientific papers.
P-11 Hauz Khas Enclave, New Delhi, India.

Panchen Lama (Panchen Erdeni); Tibetan religious and political leader; b. 1938 in Chinghai, China.
Installed as Panchen Lama at Tashilumpo Monastery 44, not accepted in Tibet, installed as Panchen Lama in new ceremony at Kumbun Monastery, Chinghai 49; first visited Tibet 52, in charge of Shigatse sub-region; mem. Nat. People's Congress 54-64, mem. Standing Cttee. 61-64; Vice-Chair. Preparatory Cttee. for Tibetan Autonomous Region 56-59, Provisional Chair. after flight of Dalai Lama to India 59-65; Hon. Chair. Chinese Buddhist Asscn. 53-; mem. Sino-Soviet Friendship Asscn. 54-; Chair. Tashilumpo Monastery Democratic Admin. Cttee. 61; denounced as reactionary by Chou En-lai 64.
Shigatse, Autonomous Region of Tibet, China.

Pandit, Vijaya Lakshmi; Indian politician and diplomatist; b. 18 Aug. 1900; sister of late Pandit Nehru; ed. privately.
Joined Non-Co-operation Movement, imprisoned for one year 31; mem. Allahabad Municipal Board 36, Chair. Education Cttee. Municipal Board; Minister of Local Self-Govt. and Public Health, Uttar Pradesh Govt. 37-39, 46-47 (1st woman minister); mem. Congress Party; sentenced to three terms of imprisonment 32, 41 and 42; detained under Defence Regulations 42-43; leader of Indian del. to UN 46-51, 63; Amb. to U.S.S.R. 47-49, to U.S.A. 49-51; mem. Lok Sabha 52-54; Pres. UN Gen. Assembly 53-54; High Commr. in U.K. and Amb. to Ireland 55-61, concurrently Amb. to Spain 58-61; Gov. of Maharashtra 62-64; mem. Lok Sabha 64-68; Hon. D.C.L. (Oxford).
181B Rajpur Road, Dehra Dun, Uttar Pradesh, India.

Pant, Apasaheb Balasaheb, M.A.; Indian politician and diplomatist; b. 11 Sept. 1912; ed. Univs. of Bombay and Oxford, and Lincoln's Inn, London.
Former Minister of Educ., Aundh State, Prime Minister 38-44, Minister 44-48; mem. All-India Congress Cttee. 48; Commr. for Govt. of India, British East Africa 48-54, concurrently Consul-Gen. in Belgian Congo and Ruanda-Urundi 48-54, concurrently Commr. in Central Africa and Nyasaland 50-54; Ministry of External Affairs, New Delhi 54-55; Political Officer, Sikkim and Bhutan 55-61; Amb. to Indonesia 61-64, to Norway 64-66, to U.A.R. 66, also accred. to Libya and Yemen; High Commr. to U.K. 69-72;

Amb. to Italy 72-, concurrently High Commr. to Malta 72-; Del. to UN Gen. Assembly 51, 52, 65; Padma Shri 54.
Publs. *Yoga* 68, *Surya Namaskar* 69, *Aggression and Violence: Gandhian Experiments to Fight Them* 68, *A Moment in Time*.
Indian Embassy, Lungotevere Mellini 17, Rome, Italy; Home: 893-895 Bhandarkar Inst. Road, Deccan Gymkhana, Poona 4, India.

Pant, Krishna Chandra, M.SC. Indian politician; b. 10 Aug. 1931, Bhowali, Nainital Dist.; ed. St. Joseph's Coll., Nainital, Univ. of Lucknow.
Member Parl. for Nainital 62-; Minister of Finance 67, of Steel and Heavy Engineering 69, of Home Affairs and Head Depts. of Electronics, Atomic Energy, Science and Technology 70; Minister of Irrigation and Power 73-74; Minister of State for Energy, Parl. Asst. to Prime Minister for Depts. of Atomic Energy, Electronics and Space Oct. 74; First Vice-Pres. Human Rights Comm. 66; leader del. to Int. Conf. on Human Rights, Teheran 68; del. to various other int. confs.; Hon. D.Sc. (Udaipur Univ.).
1 Teen Murti Marg, New Delhi, India.
Telephone: 374911, 372507.

Pant, Sumitranandan; Indian writer; b. 1900.
Member Sahitya Acad.; Padmabhushan 61; Sahitya Akademi Award; Bhartiya Jnanpith Award 69.
Publs. *Pallav* 26, *Vina-Gramthi* 30, *Birth of Poetry*, *Jyotsna* (drama) 34, *Panch Kahaniyan* (short stories) 36, *Uppara* (poetry) 49, *Gradya-Path* (essays) 53, *Chidambara* (poetry) 58, *Kala Aur Boodhachand* 59, *Lokayatan* (epic, Soviet Nehru Award), etc.
18-B7 K. G. Marg, Allahabad, Uttar Pradesh, India.

Panyarachun, Anand; Thai diplomatist; b. 9 Aug. 1932; ed. Bangkok Christian Coll., Dulwich Coll., London and Univ. of Cambridge.
Joined Ministry of Foreign Affairs 55; Sec. to Foreign Minister 58; First Sec. Perm. Mission to UN 64, Counsellor 66, Acting Perm. Rep. 67-72, concurrently Amb. to Canada; Perm. Rep. 72-75, also Amb. to U.S.A. 72-75; recalled May 75; Perm. Under-Sec. of State for Foreign Affairs Sept. 75-; Chair., Group of 77 on Law of the Sea 73; Rep. to UN ECOSOC 74-75; Chair., Thai Del. to 7th Special Session of UN Gen. Assembly, Vice-Chair. of *ad hoc* cttee. Sept. 75.
c/o Ministry of Foreign Affairs, Saranrom Palace, Bangkok, Thailand.

Parbo, Arvi Hillar, B.ENG.; British mining engineer; b. 10 Feb. 1926, Tallinn, Estonia; ed. Estonia, Germany and Univ. of Adelaide.
Western Mining Corpn. Ltd. 56-, mining eng. 56, Underground Man. Nevoria Mine 58, Technical Asst. to Man. Dir. Western Mining Corpn. 60, Deputy Gen. Supt. W. Australia 64, Gen. Man. Western Mining Corpn. Ltd. 68, Deputy Man. Dir. 70, Man. Dir. 71-, Vice-Chair. 73, Chair. 74-.
Western Mining Corporation Ltd., 459 Collins Street, P.O.B. 860K, Melbourne, Vic. 3001; Home: Longwood, Highbury Road, Vermont South, Vic. 3133, Australia.
Telephone: 67-7556 (Office); 232-8264 (Home).

Parecattil, H. E. Cardinal Joseph; Indian ecclesiastic; b. 1 April 1912, Kidangoor; ed. Papal Seminary, Candy, Sri Lanka.
Ordained 39; Titular Bishop of Aretusa (Syria) 53; Archbishop of Ernakulam 56-; mem. Pontifical Comm.; Vice-Pres. Catholic Bishops' Conf. on India 66, Pres. 72, 74; mem. Sacred Congregation for the Oriental Churches; cr. Cardinal 69; mem. Secr., Christian Unity, Rome 70, Secr. for non-Christians 74-; Pres. Pontifical Comm. for revision of Oriental Canon Law 72; Pres. Syro-Malabar Bishops' Conf., Kerala Catholic Bishops' Conf.; Chancellor, Pontifical Inst. of Philosophy and Theology, Alwaye.
Archbishop's House, Post Bag 1209, Cochin 682011, Kerala, India.

Parekh, Hasmukh, B.A., B.SC.; Indian investment broker; b. 10 March 1911, Surat; ed. Bombay Univ., London School of Econs.
Worked as stockbroker with leading Bombay firm 36-56; Deputy Gen. Man. Industrial Credit and Investment Corpn. of India 58-68, Deputy Chair. and Man. Dir. 68-71, Chair. and Man. Dir. 72-73, Exec. Chair. 73-.
Publs. *The Bombay Money Market* 53, *The Future of Joint Stock Enterprise in India* 58, *India and Regional Development* 69, *Management of Industry in India*.
Industrial Credit and Investment Corporation of India Ltd., 163 Backbay Reclamation, Bombay 400 020; Home: Kastur Nivas No. 1, French Road, Chowpatty, Bombay 400 007, India.
Telephone: 257351 (Office); 357949 (Home).

Park Chung Hee, General; Korean army officer and politician; b. 30 Sept. 1917; ed. Taegu Normal School, Japanese Military Acad., Artillery School (U.S.A.) and Military Command and General Staff Coll., Korea.
Teacher 37-40; Japanese Army 40-45; Korean Army 45-63; Deputy Chair. Supreme Council for Nat. Reconstruction May-July 61, Chair. July 61-Nov. 63; Acting Pres. of Repub. of Korea March 61-Nov. 63, Pres. Dec. 63-, re-elected 67, 71 and 72.
Publs. *Leadership: In the Midst of the Revolutionary Process* 61, *People's Path to the Fulfilment of Revolutionary Tasks: Direction for National Movement* 61, *Our Nation's Path* 62, *The State, the Revolution and I* 63, *To Build a Nation* 71.
Ch'ong Wa Dae (Presidential Mansion), Seoul, Republic of Korea.

Park Kyung Won, M.A.; Korean civil servant; b. 3 Jan. 1923, Julanam-Do; ed. U.S. Army Artillery School, Republic of Korea Commandant and Gen. Staff Coll., Nat. Defence Coll. and Dankuk Univ.
Minister of Home Affairs 62-63, 68-71; Dir. of Joint Staff, Rep. of Korea Army 63-65, Commdg. Gen. 2nd Army 65-66; Minister of Communication 66-67; Minister of Transport 67-68; Sec.-Gen. People's Council for Nat. Unification 72-74; Minister of Home Affairs 74-Dec. 75; various military and civil awards.
Gea-Dong, Jongro-Gu, Seoul, Republic of Korea.
Telephone: 73-0010, 75-5538.

Parmar, Y. S., B.A., M.A., LL.B., PH.D.; Indian lawyer, agriculturalist and politician; b. 4 Aug. 1906; ed. Shamsher High School, Nahan, Forman Christian Coll. (Punjab Univ.), Lahore, Canning Coll. (Lucknow Univ.), Lucknow.
Sub-judge and Magistrate, Sirmur State 30-37, District and Sessions Judge 37-41; Pres. Himalayan Hill States Regional Council 47; mem. Chief Commr.'s Advisory Council, Himachal Pradesh 48-50; mem. Constituent Assembly of India 49, Provincial Parl. 50-51; Pres. Himachal Pradesh Congress Cttee. 48-50, 60-64; Standing Council for Himachal Pradesh in Supreme Court of India 60-63; mem. Legislative Assembly and Chief Minister of Himachal Pradesh 52-56, 63-67, 67-.
Publs. *Social and Economic Background of Himalayan Polyandry*, *Himachal Pradesh—Its Proper Shape and Status*, *Case for Statehood and Strategy for the Development of Hill Areas*.
Office of the Chief Minister, Simla; and Village Bharyog, P.O. Bagthan, District Sirmur, Himachal Pradesh, India.

Parthasarathi, Gopalaswami, B.A., M.A.; Indian diplomatist; b. 7 July 1912; ed. Univ. of Madras and Oxford Univ.
Assistant Editor *The Hindu* 36-49; Chief Rep. Press Trust of India, London 49-52, Chief Ed. Press Trust of India 51-53; Chair. Int. Comm. for Cambodia 54-55; Int.

Supervisory Comm. for Viet-Nam 55-56; Amb. to Indonesia 57-58, to People's Republic of China 58-61; Chair. Int. Comm. for Supervision and Control, Viet-Nam 61-62; High Commr. in Pakistan 62-65, Perm. Rep. of India to UN Aug. 65-69; Chair. Policy Planning Cttee., Ministry of Foreign Affairs 75-; Vice-Chancellor of Jawaharlal Nehru Univ. 69-74; mem. Board of Trustees, UN Inst. for Training and Research 70-72.
Home: 31 Aurangzeb Road, New Delhi, India.

Patel, Baburao; Indian writer, editor, film producer and politician; b. 4 April 1904.
Began free-lance journalism 22; wrote, directed and produced motion pictures, founder and Editor *Filmindia* 35-; lectured in U.S. and Europe on India's ancient culture and civilization; set up a production code and fought for revision of film censorship; Ed. *Mother India*; Man. Dir. Sumati Publications Pvt. Ltd. 58; mem. Parl. 67-.
Publs. *Grey Dust, Burning Words, The Sermon of the Lord, Prayer Book, Rosary and the Lamp, Homœopathic Lifesavers for Home and Community;* Films: (wrote and produced) *Kismet, Mahananda, Bala Joban, My Darling, Maharanee, Draupadi, Gvalan.*
Girnar, Pali Hill, Bombay 50, India.
Telephone: 533414.

Patel, Hirubhai, C.I.E., B.A., B.COM.; Indian politician; b. 26 Aug. 1904, Bombay; ed. Oxford and London Univs.
Separation Officer, Sing 35; Finance Dept., Bombay 36; Sec. to Stock Exchange Cttee. 36-37; Trade Commr., for N. Europe, Hamburg 37-39; Deputy Trade Commr., London 39-40; Deputy Sec. Eastern Group Supply Council 41-42; Deputy Dir.-Gen. Supply Dept. 42-43; Joint Sec. and Sec. Industries and Civil Supplies Dept. 43-46, Cabinet Secr. 46-47; Defence and Partition Sec. 47-53; Sec. Food and Agriculture 53-54, Dept. of Econ. Affairs, Ministry of Finance 57; Principal Finance Sec. 57-59; Chair. Life Insurance Corpn. of India 56-57; Chair. Gujarat Electricity Board 60-66; mem. Gujarat Legislative Assembly 67-71; Chair. Charutar Vidyamandal, Vallal Vidyanagar 59-; Pres. Gujarat Swatantra Party 67-, All India Swatantra Party 71-; mem. Lok Sabha March 71-; Hon. LL.D. (Sardar Patel Univ.).
Charutar Vidyamandal, Vallabh Vidyanagar, W. Railway, India.
Telephone: 175.

Patel, Indraprasad Gordhanbhai, B.A., PH.D.; Indian economist; b. 1924; ed. Baroda Coll., Bombay Univ., King's Coll., Cambridge and Harvard Univ.
Professor of Econs., Maharaja Sayajirao Univ., Baroda 49-50; Economist and Asst. Chief, Financial Problems and Policies Div., Int. Monetary Fund 50-54; Deputy Econ. Adviser, Indian Ministry of Finance 54-58; Alt. Exec. Dir. for India, Int. Monetary Fund 58-61; Chief Econ. Adviser, Ministry of Finance, India 61-63, 65-67, Special Sec., Min. of Finance 68-69, Sec. 70-; Econ. Adviser Planning Comm. 61-63; visiting Prof., Delhi School of Econs., Delhi Univ. 64.
Ministry of Finance, Department of Economic Affairs, North Block, New Delhi 1, India.
Telephone: 372611.

Patel, Jeram; Indian painter and graphic designer; b. 20 June 1930; ed. Sir J. J. School of Art, Bombay, Central School of Arts and Crafts, London.
Reader in Applied Arts, M.S. Univ., Baroda 60-61; Reader in Visual Design, School of Architecture, Ahmedabad 61-62; Deputy Dir. All India Handloom Board 63-66; Reader in Applied Arts, M.S. Univ. Baroda 66-; mem. *Group 1890* (avant-garde group of Indian artists), Lalit Kala Akademi; one man exhbns. in London 59, New Delhi 60, 62-65, in Calcutta 66; in Tokyo Biennale 57-63, São Paulo Biennale 63; represented in Nat. Gallery of Modern Art, New Delhi, Art Soc. of India, Bombay, Sir J. J. Inst. of Applied Arts, Bombay, and in private collections in U.S.A., London, Paris and Tokyo; Lalit Kala Akademi Nat. Awards 57, 64; Bombay State Award 57; Silver Medal, Bombay Art Soc. 61, Gold Medal Rajkot Exhbn.
Faculty of Fine Arts, M.S. University, Baroda 2, India.

Pathak, Gopal Swarup, M.A., LL.B.; Indian lawyer and politician; b. 26 Feb. 1896.
Member Lok Sabha for Uttar Pradesh; fmr. Judge, Allahabad High Court; Pres. Indian Soc. of Int. Law, mem. Indian Comm. of Jurists; Minister of Law 66-67; Gov. of Mysore 67-69; Vice-Pres. of India 69-74, also Chair. Rajya Sabha 69-74.
c/o Rajya Sabha, New Delhi, India.

Patil, Sadashiv Kanoji; Indian politician; b. 14 Aug. 1900; ed. St. Xavier's Coll., Bombay, London School of Economics and Univ. Coll., London Univ.
Joined the Indian Nat. Congress 20 and was imprisoned eight times for a total of ten years; Gen. Sec. Bombay Provincial Congress Cttee. 29-45 and Pres. 46-57; mem. A.I.C.C. 30- and mem. of its Working Cttee. 45-51, 56-57, 60-, Treas. 60-64, 68-71; mem. Bombay Legislative Assembly 37-46; mem. of the Bombay Municipal Corpn. 35-52; Mayor of Bombay three terms 49-52; mem. Constituent Assembly 47-50; mem. Provincial Parl. 50-52; mem. of Lok Sabha 52-67, 69-70; Minister for Irrigation and Power 57-58; Minister for Transport and Communications 58-59, for Food and Agriculture 59-Aug. 63; mem. Congress Party Parl. Board Aug. 63-; Minister of Railways June 64-67.
Publs. *Indian National Congress: A Case for Reorganization.*
Home: Shanti Kuteer, Marine Drive, Bombay 20, India.

Patil, Veerendra, B.A., LL.B.; Indian politician and lawyer; b. 28 Feb. 1924, Chincholi, Gulbarga District; ed. Osmania Univ., Hyderabad.
Practised law 47, 50-55; mem. Hyderabad State Assembly 52, 57, 62-; Deputy Minister for Home and Industries, Mysore till 58; Minister for Excise and Rural Industries 61-62, for Public Works 62-; Chief Minister of Mysore May 68-72; mem. Rajya Sabha 72-; Pres. Karnataka Pradesh Congress Cttee. on Organization 71-; mem. del. to U.S.S.R. 65, Japan and S.E. Asia 70, Australia 72, U.K. and Europe 73.
23 Lower Palace Orchards, Bangalore 3, India.

Patterson, Rex Alan, B.COM., M.SC., PH.D.; Australian politician; b. 8 Jan. 1927, Bundaberg, Queensland; ed. Univ. of Queensland, Australian Nat. Univ., Univs. of Illinois and Chicago, U.S.A.
With Royal Australian Air Force Feb.-Sept. 45; mem. Research Staff, Bureau of Agricultural Econs. 49, Deputy Dir. 60-64; Dir. Northern Devt. Div., Dept. of Nat. Devt. until 66; mem. House of Reps. for Dawson, Queensland 66-75; Minister for Northern Devt. 72-75, for the Northern Territory 73-75, for N. Australia June-Nov. 75; Fulbright Scholar 58; Labor Party.
c/o Parliament House, Canberra, A.C.T., Australia.

Private, Dadasaheb Chintamani; Indian mathematician and fmr. state governor; b. 2 Aug. 1899; ed. Karnatak Coll. Dharwar, and Sidney Sussex Coll., Cambridge.
Professor of Mathematics, Banaras Hindu Univ. 28-30; entered Bombay Educ. Service 30; Dir. of Public Instruction, Bombay State 47-54; Vice-Chancellor Karnatak Univ. 54-67; Gov. of Punjab 67-74; mem. Official Language Comm. 55-56; Leader Indian Del. to 19th Int. Educ. Conf., Geneva 56; Padma Bhushan 67.
Publs. include *Elements of Calculus, Modern College Algebra, Memoirs of an Educational Administrator, Modern College Calculus.*
c/o Governor of Punjab, Chandigarh, Punjab, India.

Pazhwak, Abdurrahman; Afghan civil servant and diplomatist; b. 7 March 1919.
Has been successively mem. Historical Section of Afghan Acad.; Dir. Foreign Publications Section of Afghan Press

Dept.; Editor daily *Islah* and acting Dir.-Gen. of Bakhtar News Agency; Pashtu-Tolana, Afghan Acad.; Dir.-Gen. Publs. Section, Afghan Press Dept.; Sec. and Press and Cultural Attaché, Afghan Embassy, London; mem. of Section of Information Dept. of ILO.; Press and Cultural Attaché, Afghan Embassy, Wash.; Dir. Section for East Asia and Dir. a.i., Section for UN and Int. Confs., Afghan Ministry of Foreign Affairs, Dir.-Gen. Political Affairs in Ministry of Foreign Affairs 56; Perm. Rep. to UN 58-73; Amb. to Fed. Repub. of Germany 73, to India 73, also accred. to Burma; Pres. UN Human Rights Comm. 63, 21st Session of UN Gen. Assembly 66, 5th Special Session 66 and of Emergency Session of Gen. Assembly on Middle East 66; Special Envoy, Fourth Summit Conf. of Non-aligned Countries, Algiers 73 and Summit Conf. of Islamic Countries, Lahore 74; Special Envoy to Pres. of Bangladesh.
Publs. *Aryana or Ancient Afghanistan, Pakhtunistan* (both in English), *Tales of the People* 58 (in Persian), and many other works.
Embassy of Afghanistan, A-9 Ring Road, Lajrat Nagar 3, New Delhi, India.

Peacock, Hon. Andrew Sharp, LL.B., M.P.; Australian politician; b. 13 Feb. 1939, Melbourne; ed. Scotch Coll., Univ. of Melbourne.
President, Victorian Liberal Party 65-66; mem. House of Reps. for Kooyong, Vic. 66-; partner Rigby & Fielding & Holt, Newman & Holt, solicitors; Chair. Peacock & Smith Pty. Ltd., engineers 62-69; Minister for the Army 69-72; Assisting the Prime Minister 69-71, Assisting the Treasurer 71-72; Minister for External Territories Feb.-Dec. 72; mem. Opposition Exec. 73-75, Spokesman on Foreign Affairs 73-75; Minister for Foreign Affairs Nov. 75-, for the Environment Nov.-Dec. 75.
4 Treasury Place, Melbourne, Vic. 3000; Home: 30 Monomeath Avenue, Canterbury, Vic. 3126, Australia.

P'eng Ch'ung; People's Repub. of China; b. Fukien.
Mayor, Nanking 55-59; Deputy Sec., CCP Kiangsu 60-65, Sec. 65-68; Vice-Chair. Kiangsu Provincial Revolutionary Cttee. 68; Alt. mem. 9th Cen. Cttee. of CCP 69; Deputy Sec., CCP Kiangsu 71; Alt. mem. 10th Cen. Cttee. of CCP 73; First Sec., CCP Kiangsu 74.

Peng Shao-hui; army officer, People's Repub. of China; b. 1910, Hunan.
Company Commdr. Red Army 28, Div. Commdr. 33, Brigade Commdr. 38; Chief of Staff 1st Field Army 52; Deputy Commdr. N.W. Mil. Region, People's Liberation Army 54; Deputy Chief of Staff PLA 55-; Gen. 55; Deputy Dir., Gen. Training Dept., PLA 56; mem. 9th Cen. Cttee. of CCP 69, 10th Cen. Cttee. 73.

Penjor, Lyonpo Sangye; Bhutan diplomatist; b. 13 Feb. 1928, Bamthang; ed. local school.
Entered govt. service 45; Officer-in-charge of Royal Household of Tashichholing; Chief District Officer, Bamthang District, Deputy Chief Sec. 60; Minister for Communications 70-71; Perm. Rep. to UN Sept. 71-75; Amb. to India 75-.
Embassy of Bhutan, Chandra Gupta Marg, Chanakyapuri, New Delhi-21, India.

Penn-Nouth, Samdech; Cambodian politician; b. 1906; ed. Cambodian School of Administration.
Ministry of Colonies, Paris 38; Assistant to Minister of Palace 40; Acting Minister of Finance 45; Gov. of Phnom-Penh 46-48; Minister of State 46; Minister of State without Portfolio 47; Prime Minister Sept. 48-Jan. 49, 52-55, 58; Amb. to France 58-60; Prime Minister, Minister of the Interior and Minister of Religious Affairs Jan.-Nov. 61; Prime Minister and Minister of Religious Affairs 61-62; Adviser to the Govt. 67; Prime Minister 68-69; Prime Minister of Royal Govt. of Nat. Union of Cambodia (GRUNC) 70-76 (in Phnom-Penh 75-76); High Counsellor, State Presidium April 76-; numerous decorations.
State Presidium, Phnom-Penh, Cambodia.

Perera, Liyanagé Henry Horace, B.A.; Ceylonese international official; b. 9 May 1915; ed. St. Benedict's Coll., Colombo, Univ. Coll. London, Univ. of Ceylon.
Senior Master in Govt. and History, Ceylon 36-59; Asst. Registrar, Aquinas Univ. Coll., Colombo 60-61; Educ. Dir. World Fed. of UN Asscns. 61-63, Deputy Sec.-Gen. and Educ. Dir. 63-66, Sec.-Gen. 66-; mem. Int. Cttee. on Adult Educ. (UNESCO) 63; Pres. Conf. of Int. Non-Governmental Orgs. in Consultative Status with UN ECOSOC 69-72; William Russel Award 74; Award of Int. Asscn. of Educ. for World Peace 74; Gold Medal, Czechoslovak Soc. for Int. Relations.
Publs. *Ceylon and Indian History (Early Times to 1500), Ceylon Under Western Rule (1500-1948), Groundwork of Ceylon and World History (Early Times to 1500).*
World Federation of United Nations Associations, Centre International, P.O. Box 54, 1211 Geneva 20; Home: 22 avenue Luserna, 1203 Geneva, Switzerland.
Telephone: 34-49-60 (Office); 34-07-37 (Home).

Perera, Nanayakkarapathiraga Martin, PH.D., D.SC.; Ceylonese politician; b. 6 June 1905; ed. St. Thomas' and Ananda Colls., Ceylon, Ceylon Univ. Coll., and London School of Economics.
Lecturer, Ceylon Univ. 35-36, 45-46; Founder-mem. Lanka Sama Samaj Party 35, now Pres.; mem. State Council 36; imprisoned 40-41, 43-45; mem. House of Reps. (now Nat. State Assembly) 47-, Leader of the Opposition 47-52, 59-60; Minister of Finance June 64-65, 70-75; Mayor of Colombo 55; Pres. Ceylon Fed. of Labour; mem. Sri Lanka Branch and Exec. Cttee., Commonwealth Parl. Asscn.; Hon. D.Sc.
106 Cotta Road, Colombo, Sri Lanka.
Telephone: 91891 (Home).

Perlis, H.R.H. The Raja of; Tuanku, Syed Putra Ibni al-Marhum Syed Hassan Jamalullail, D.K., S.P.M.P., D.K.(M), D.M.N., S.M.N., D.K.(SEL), S.P.D.K.(SABAH), K.C.M.G.; ruler of Perlis, Malaysia.
Appointed Bakal Raja (Heir-Presumptive) of Perlis April 38; attached to Courts in Kangar 40; worked for a year in the Land Office, Kuala Lumpur, and for a year in the Magistrates' Court, Kuala Lumpur; in private business during Japanese occupation; Timbalan Yang di-Pertuan Agong (Deputy Supreme Head of State) of Malaya April-Sept. 60, Yang di-Pertuan Agong (Supreme Head of State) Sept. 60-Sept. 63, of Malaysia 63-65.
Istana Arau, Perlis; Home: Istana Kerangar Indah, Repoh, Perlis, Malaysia.

Pham Hung; Vietnamese politician; b. 1912, Vinh Long Province.
Joined Revolutionary Youth League under Ho Chi Minh in 1920s; founding mem. Indochinese Communist Party 30, later mem. of Lao Dong Party; imprisoned for 15 years by French and sentenced to death, later reprieved; mem. Cen. Cttee. Lao Dong Party 51-; Deputy Sec. Cen. Office of South Viet-Nam (COSVN) with responsibility for mil. operations in S. Viet-Nam 51-57; Minister at Office of Premier, Hanoi 57-67 (acting Premier during 61); Sec. of COSVN (in S. Viet-Nam) and Political Commissar of People's Liberation Armed Forces 67-June 76; Vice-Premier, Council of Ministers, Socialist Repub. of Viet-Nam June 76-; mem. Nat. Defence Council June 76-.
Council of Ministers, Hanoi, Viet-Nam.

Pham Van Dong; Vietnamese politician; b. 1 March 1906, Quang Nam Province (S. Viet-Nam).
Close collaborator of Ho Chi Minh; underground communist worker since 25; imprisoned by French authorities for seven years; upon release in 36, resumed revolutionary activities; a founder of the Revolutionary League for the

Independence of Viet-Nam (the *Viet-Minh*) 41; mem. *Lao Dong* (Viet-Nam Workers') Party 51-; Minister for Foreign Affairs, Democratic Repub. of Viet-Nam 54-61, Prime Minister 55-76; Prime Minister, Socialist Repub. of Viet-Nam July 76-; Vice-Chair. Nat. Defence Council July 76-.
Office of the Prime Minister, Hanoi, Viet-Nam.

Pham Van Ky; Vietnamese writer; b. 1916; ed. Secondary School, Hanoi, and Univ. of Paris.
Went to France 39; prepared thesis on religion for the Institut des Hautes Etudes Chinoises; Grand Prix du Roman, Académie Française 61.
Publs. *Fleurs de jade* (poems), *L'homme de nulle part* (short stories) 46, *Frères de sang* (novel) 47, *Celui qui régnera* (novel) 54, *Les yeux courroucés* (novel) 58, *Les contemporains* (novel) 59, *Perdre la demeure* (novel) 61, *Poème sur Soie* (poems) 61, *Des Femmes Assises Çà et Là* (novel) 64, *Mémoires d'un Eunuque* (novel) 66, *Le Rideau de Pluie* (play) 74.
62/2 avenue du Général de Gaulle, Maisons-Alfort 94700, France.
Telephone: 368-22-94.

Phan Huy Quat; Vietnamese physician and politician; b. 1 July 1909, Ha Tinh, Central Viet-Nam; ed. Hanoi Medical School and Univ. de Paris.
Associate Prof. of Biology, Hanoi Medical School 38-43; founder mem. and 1st Pres. Hanoi Univ. Student Asscn. 34; Cabinet Dir. Prime Minister's Office 45, Minister of Educ. 49; Minister of Nat. Defence 50, 53-54; Sec.-Gen. Nat. Popular Front 52; Acting Premier 54; imprisoned 60-63; Minister of Foreign Affairs, Repub. of Viet-Nam Feb.-Oct. 64; Prime Minister Feb.-June 65; mem. Viet-Nam Anti-Tuberculosis Asscn. 56, Chair. 69; Vice-Chair. Medical Asscn. 60-63; mem. Advisory Cttee., Int. League for the Rights of Man 65.
179 Hien Vaong Street, Saigon, Viet-Nam.
Telephone: 25674.

Phat, Huynh Tan (*see* Huynh Tan Phat).

Phillips, Sir John Grant, K.B.E., B.ECONS.; Australian banker (rtd.); b. 13 March 1911; ed. Univ. of Sydney.
Research Officer, N.S.W. Retail Traders' Asscn. 32-35; Econ. Asst., Royal Comm. on Monetary & Banking Systems 36-37; Econ. Dept., Commonwealth Bank of Australia 37-51, Investment Adviser 54-60; Deputy Gov. & Deputy Chair. of Board, Reserve Bank of Australia 60-68, Gov. & Chair. 68-75; leader del. to 6th conf. GATT 51; mem. Board Howard Florey Inst. of Experimental Physiology and Medicine 71-, Advisory Cttee. Australian Birthright Movement, Sydney 71-, Council Macquarie Univ. 67-.
Home: 3 Cyprian Street, Mosman, N.S.W. 2088, Australia.

Phomvihan, Kaysone; Laotian politician, b. 1920, Savannakhet Province; ed. Univ. of Hanoi.
Helped anti-French forces in Viet-Nam after 45; joined *Neo Lao Issara* (Free Lao Front) nationalist movement in exile in Bankok 45; attended first resistance congress; Minister of Defence in Free Lao Front resistance Govt. 50; C.-in-C. of *Pathet Lao* forces 54-57; mem. People's Party of Laos 55; mem. *Neo Lao Hak Sat* (Lao Patriotic Front) 56, Vice-Chair. 59, Vice-Chair. of Central Cttee. 64; Prime Minister of Laos Dec.75-; Gen. Sec. Central Cttee. Lao People's Revolutionary Party.
Office of the Prime Minister, Vientiane, Laos.

Phongsavan, Phagna Phéng; Laotian fmr. politician; b. 19 July 1910, Ban Pakham Luang-Prabang; ed. Pavie Coll., Vientiane.
Joined admin. service 29; Dir. Govt. Printing Office, Vientiane 43-44; Chaomuong (District Officer) of Tourakhom, Ban Keun 44-46; Rep. for Luang-Prabang, Nat. Assembly 47-51, re-elected 51, 55, 65; Vice-Minister of Interior and Sports and Youth 52-54; Minister of Nat. Econ. and Public Works 54-56; Pres. Nat. Assembly 56-59; Minister of Interior and Social Welfare 62-75, of Defence 75; Vice-Pres. Neutralist Party; many nat. and foreign decorations, including Grand Cross Royal Order of Thailand 56, Civil Merit Order 69, Public Instruction Medal 72.

Phoumsavan, Nouhak; Laotian politician; ed. primary school.
Owner of bus and truck business; mem. *Viet-Minh* del. for Conf. of Asian and Pacific Region in Peking 52; rep. of *Pathet Lao* at Geneva Conf. on Indochina with *Viet-Minh* del. 54; Minister of Foreign Affairs in *Neo Lao Issara* (Free Lao Front) resistance Govt.; Deputy for Sam Neua to Nat. Assembly 57; arrested 59, escaped 60; led *Neo Lao Hak Sat* (Lao Patriotic Front) del. to Ban Namone peace talks 61; mem. People's Party of Laos 55; mem. Lao Patriotic Front, mem. Standing Cttee. 64, of Central Cttee.; Deputy Prime Minister and Minister of Finance Dec. 75-.
Ministry of Finance, Vientiane, Laos.

Phuoc Van Cung; Vietnamese politician; b. 1908, Vinh Long Province; ed. Faculty of Medicine, Hanoi Univ.
Held admin. medical posts in the provinces and Saigon; joined army and rose to rank of Col. under Diem; joined resistance 60; Vice-Pres. Cen. Cttee. Nat. Liberation Front; Pres. S. Vietnamese Peace Cttee., NLF Red Cross Soc.; Vice-Pres. Revolutionary Govt. of S. Viet-Nam May 75-June 76; Minister of the Interior May 75-June 76.
c/o Ministry of the Interior, Hanoi, Viet-Nam.

Phurissara, Prince Norodom; Cambodian lawyer and politician; b. 1919.
Government Service 44-70; Deputy Provincial Gov., later in Ministry of Foreign Affairs and Ministry of Planning; Deputy State Sec. of Interior 61, State Sec. 62-64; Dir. of Admin. of Council of Ministers 64-66; Dean of Faculty of Law, Royal Univ., Phnom Penh 64-66; Minister of Foreign Affairs 66-70; joined Nat. United Front of Cambodia (FUNC) 72; Minister of Justice and Judicial Reforms, Royal Govt. of Nat. Union of Cambodia (GRUNC) 73-76 (in Phnom-Penh 75-76).
c/o Ministry of Justice, Phnom-Penh, Cambodia.

P'i Ting-chun; army officer, People's Repub. of China; b. 1914, Anhwei.
Lieutenant-General, People's Liberation Army 61; Deputy Commdr. Foochow Mil. Region, PLA 61; Vice-Chair. Fukien Revolutionary Cttee. 68; mem. 9th Cen. Cttee. of CCP 69; Commdr. Lanchow Mil. Region, PLA 70-73; Vice-Chair. Kansu Revolutionary Cttee. 70; Sec. CCP Kansu 71; mem. 10th Cen. Cttee. of CCP 73; Commdr. Foochow Mil. Region, PLA 74-.

Piampongsarn, Sawet; Thai politician.
Minister without portfolio 48; Deputy Minister of Finance 49-51; Deputy Prime Minister, Minister of Finance April 76-.
Ministry of Finance, Bangkok, Thailand.

Pirzada, Abdul Hafiz; Pakistani lawyer and politician; b. 24 Feb. 1935, Sukkur; ed. D. J. Sindh Govt. Science Coll. and in U.K.
Called to the Bar, Lincoln's Inn, London 57; commenced legal practice in High Court of W. Pakistan, Karachi 57 and joined Chambers of Zulfikar Ali Bhutto 57-58; Advocate, W. Pakistan High Court and Supreme Court of Pakistan; mem. Cen. Cttee. Pakistan People's Party; mem. Nat. Assembly 70-; Minister of Law and Parl. Affairs, Educ. and Provincial Co-ordination 71-74, of Educ. and Science, Technology and Provincial Co-ordination 74-76, of Educ. and Provincial Co-ordination Feb. 76-.
Ministry of Education and Provincial Co-ordination, Rawalpindi, Pakistan.

Pirzada, Sharifuddin, LL.B., S.PK.; Pakistani lawyer and politician; b. 12 June 1923; ed. Univ. of Bombay.
Secretary Muslim Students' Fed. 43-45; Sec. Provincial

Muslim League 46; Man. Editor *Morning Herald* 46; Prof., Sind Muslim Law Coll., Karachi 47-55; Adviser to Constitution Comm. of Pakistan 60; Chair. Pakistan Company Law Comm. and mem. Int. Rivers Cttee. 60; Pres. Pakistan Branch Int. Law Asscn. and Pres. Legal Aid Soc.; Pres. Karachi Bar Asscn.; Senior Advocate, Supreme Court of Pakistan; Attorney-Gen. of Pakistan 64-66, 68-71; Minister of Foreign Affairs 66-68.
Publs. include: *Evolution of Pakistan, Fundamental Rights and Constitutional Remedies in Pakistan, Foundations of Pakistan* Vol. I 69, Vol. II 70.
C-37, K.D.A. Scheme No. 1, Habib Ibrahim Rahimtoola Road, Karachi, Pakistan.

Plimsoll, Sir James, C.B.E.; Australian diplomatist; b. 25 April 1917; ed. Sydney High School and Univ. of Sydney.
With Econ. Dept., Bank of New South Wales, Sydney 38-42; served in Australian Army 42-47; mem. Australian Del., Far Eastern Comm. 45-48; Rep. UN Comm. for Unification and Rehabilitation of Korea 50-52; Asst. Sec., Dept. of External Affairs 53-59; Perm. Rep. to UN 59-63; High Commr. in India and Amb. to Nepal 63-65; Sec. Dept. of External Affairs 65-70; Amb. to U.S.A. 70-74, to U.S.S.R. March 74-.
Australian Embassy, 13 Kropotkinsky Pereulok, Moscow, U.S.S.R.

Pol Pot (*see Tol Sant*).

Polyansky, Dmitri Stepanovich; Soviet politician and diplomatist; b. 7 Nov. 1917, Slavyanoserbskoe, Ukraine;; ed. Kharkov Inst. of Agriculture and Higher Party School of Central Cttee. of C.P.S.U.
Exec. work in Young Communist League, service in Soviet army and study at Higher Party School 39-42; Party work in Siberia 42-45; exec. in Central Cttee. of Party 45-49; Second Sec. Crimea regional Cttee. of Party, and Chair. Exec. Cttee. Crimea regional Soviet of Working People's Deputies 49-52; First Sec. Crimea regional Cttee. of Party 54-55; First Sec. of Chkalovsk (now Orenburg) regional Cttee. then First Sec. of Krasnodar territorial Party Cttee. 55-58; Chair. Council of Ministers of R.S.F.S.R. 58-62; Dep. Premier U.S.S.R. 62-65, First Deputy Premier 65-74; Deputy Supreme Soviet of the U.S.S.R. 64-; mem. C.P.S.U. Cen. Cttee. 56-; alt. mem. Presidium of Central Cttee. of C.P.S.U. 58-60, mem. 60-66; mem. Political Bureau 66-76; Minister of Agriculture 73-76; Amb. to Japan 76-; Order of Lenin (twice), etc.
Publs. *Pearl of Russia* 58, *Great Plans for the Economic and Cultural Progress of the Russian Federation* 59.
Embassy of the U.S.S.R., 2-1-1 Azabudai, Minato-ku, Tokyo, Japan.

Ponce Enrile, Juan, LL.M.; Philippine lawyer and professor of taxation; b. 14 Feb. 1924, Gonzaga, Cagayan; ed. Ateneo de Manila, Univ. of the Philippines and Harvard Law School.
Under-Secretary of Finance 66-68; Acting Sec. of Finance; Acting Insurance Commr.; Acting Commr. of Customs; Sec. of Justice 68-70, of Nat. Defence 70-71 (resigned), 72-; Chair. Board of Dirs., Philippine Nat. Bank, Nat. Investment and Devt. Corpn., Philippine Veterans Bank, Philippine Coconut Authority; Chair. Exec. Cttee. of Nat. Security Council; Dir. Philippine Communication Satellite Corpn., Private Devt. Corpn. of the Philippines, Philippine Nat. Oil Co.; Trustee, Cultural Centre of the Philippines, Devt. Acad. of the Philippines; mem. Nat. Econ. and Devt. Authority, Energy Devt. Board, numerous law and commercial asscns.; Commdr. Philippine Legion of Honour.
Publs. *A Proposal on Capital Gains Tax* 60, *Income Tax Treatment of Corporate Merger and Consolidation Revisited* 62, *Tax Treatment of Real Estate Transactions* 64.
Office of the Secretary of National Defence, Camp General Emilio Aguinaldo, Quezon City; Home: Urdaneta Village, Makati, Rizal, Philippines.

Ponnamperuma, Lakshman George, PH.D., D.I.C., F.R.I.C., M.I.CHEM.E., C.ENG.; Ceylonese chemical engineer and administrator; b. 10 Oct. 1916; ed. Ceylon Univ. Coll. & Imperial Coll. of Science & Technology, London Univ.
Research Officer, Dept. of Industries 41-54; Man. Ceylon Govt. Cement Works 54-58; Gen. Man. Ceylon Cement Corpn. 58-65; Chair. Petro Chemicals Planning Cttee. 60; Pres. Chemical Soc. of Ceylon 64; Chair. & Man. Dir. Ceylon Cement Corpn. 65-67; Dir. & Vice-Chair. Ceylon Inst. of Scientific & Industrial Research 67; Consultant to UNESCO on Conf. on the Application of Science & Technology to the Devt. of Asia (CASTASIA) 67; Special Asst. to Asst. Dir.-Gen. for Science, UNESCO, Paris 70; Dir. ECAFE/UNESCO Science and Technology Unit, Bangkok 71; mem. Industrial Cttee. of Nat. Planning 59, ECAFE Advisory Council on Industrial Research 66; Dir. Devt. Finance Corpn. of Ceylon 65, of State Fertilizer Mfg. Corpn. 66; Vice-Chair. Nat. Science Council of Ceylon; mem. Board of Regents, Univ. of Ceylon; Dir. Regional Science Co-operation UNESCO 71.
Publs. miscellaneous works on technical and managerial subjects.
UNESCO Regional Office, P.O. Box 1425, Bangkok, Thailand.

Poonacha, Cheppudira Mathana; Indian politician; b. 1910; ed. St. Aloysius Coll., Mangalore.
Joined Satyagraha Movement 30, imprisoned for Satyagraha activities; Sec. District Congress Cttee., Coorg 33; mem. Exec. Cttees., Karnatak and All India Congress Cttees. and Coorg District Board 38, Pres., Coorg District Board 41; mem. Exec. Cttee. Coorg Legislative Council and Leader, Congress Legislative Party in the Council 45-46; mem. Constituent Assembly and Provisional Parl. 47-51; Chief Minister of Coorg 52-56; Minister for Industries and Commerce 57, and later for Home and Industries at Mysore; Chair. State Trading Corpn. of India 59-63; Leader of Trade Dels. to various countries 61, 63; mem. Rajya Sabha 64; Minister for Revenue and Expenditure 64-66; Minister of State in Ministry of Transport and Aviation 66-67; Minister of Railways 67-69; Minister of Steel and Heavy Engineering 69; Chair. Malabar Chemicals and Fertilizers Ltd. 70-71.
Home Estate, Athur Post via Pollibetta, Coorg, Karnataka State, India.
Telephone: Gonicopal 85.

Popal, Ali Ahmad, PH.D.; Afghan educationist and diplomatist; b. 22 Feb. 1916; ed. Nedjat Secondary School, Kabul, and Univ. of Jena.
Teacher and Dir., Nedjat School, Kabul 42-46; Dir. of Teachers Training Coll. 46-47; Head of Primary Educ. Dept., Ministry of Educ. 47-49, also Teacher and Dean in Faculty of Women, Kabul Univ. 47-49; Head of Gen. Educ. Dept., Ministry of Educ. 49-51, Deputy Minister of Educ. 52-56, Minister of Educ. 56-64, Second Vice-Premier 62-64; Amb. to German Fed. Repub., also accred. to Sweden and Switzerland 64-66; Amb. to Turkey 66-67; First Deputy Prime Minister and Minister of Educ. 67-68; Amb. to Pakistan, also accred. to Sri Lanka and Thailand 69-74, to Japan 74-; Order of Maaref, 3rd Class 46, 1st Class 64; Order of Sardar-e-Ali 58, and orders from Egypt, Yugoslavia and Fed. Repub. of Germany.
Embassy of Afghanistan, 31-21, Jingumae 6-chome, Shibuya-ku, Tokyo, Japan.

Porritt, Baron (Life Peer), cr. 73; **Arthur Porritt,** G.C.M.G., G.C.V.O., C.B.E.; British (b. New Zealand) surgeon and administrator; b. 10 Aug. 1900; ed. Wanganui Collegiate School and Otago Univ., New Zealand, Oxford Univ. and St. Mary's Hosp. Medical School, London.
St. Mary's Hospital Surgical Staff 36-65; War service with R.A.M.C. Second World War; mem. Royal medical Household 36-67; Surgeon to Duke of York 36, to House-

hold 37-46, to King George VI 46-52, Sergeant-Surgeon to Queen Elizabeth 53-67; Consulting Surgeon to the Army; Pres. Royal Coll. of Surgeons of England 60-63; Pres. B.M.A. 60-61; mem. Int. Olympic Cttee. 34-73; Chair. British Empire and Commonwealth Games 48-67, Vice-Pres. 68-; Pres. Royal Soc. of Medicine 66-67; Gov.-Gen. of New Zealand 67-72; Hon. Pres. Medical Comm. on Accident Prevention, Co. of Veteran Motorists, Medical Council on Alcoholism, British Assen. of Sport and Medicine; Chair. Arthritis and Rheumatism Council 74-, Royal Masonic Hospital, African Medical Research Foundation; Vice-Pres. Royal Commonwealth Soc., English-Speaking Union; mem. Chapter, Gen. Order of St. John; Dir. Sterling Winthrop Pharmaceuticals Ltd., Sterling Europa; Hon. Fellow, Royal Coll. of Surgeons of Edinburgh, Glasgow, Ireland, Australasia and Canada, and American and South African Coll. of Surgeons; Hon. Fellow, Royal Coll. of Physicians (London), Royal Australian Coll. of Physicians, Royal Coll. of Obstetricians and Gynaecologists; Gold Medal B.M.A., bronze medal, 100 metres, Olympic Games 24; Hon. LL.D. St. Andrews, Birmingham, Otago and New Zealand, Hon. D.Sc. Oxford, Hon. M.D. Bristol.
Publs. *Athletics* (with D. G. A. Lowe) 29, *Essentials of Modern Surgery* (with R. M. Handfield-Jones) 39, and numerous articles in medical journals.
57 Hamilton Terrace, London, N.W.8, England.

Powles, Sir Guy Richardson, K.B.E., C.M.G., E.D., LL.B.; New Zealand public servant; b. 5 April 1905; ed. Wellington Coll., Victoria Univ. Coll.
Barrister, Supreme Court of New Zealand 27-40; War Service, to rank of Col. 40-46; Counsellor, Wash.; High Commr., Western Samoa 49-60; High Commr. India 60-62, Ceylon 60-62, Amb. to Nepal 61-62; Ombudsman, New Zealand 62-75, Chief Ombudsman 75-; Race Relations Conciliator 71-73; Pres. N.Z. Inst. of Int. Affairs 67-71; Commr., Churches Comm. on Int. Affairs 73, Int. Comm. of Jurists 75; Hon. LL.D.
Office of the Ombudsman, Wellington; Home: 34A Wesley Road, Wellington C.1, New Zealand.
Telephone: 738-068.

Prabhjot Kaur; Indian poet and politician; b. 6 July 1927; ed. Khalsa Coll. for Women, Lahore and Punjab Univ.
First collected poems published 43 (aged sixteen); rep. India at numerous int. literary confs.; mem. Legislative Council, Punjab 66-; mem. Central Comm. of UN Educational, Scientific and Cultural Org. (UNESCO); Editor *Vikendrit*; Assoc. Editor *Byword*; received honours of Sahitya Sharomani 64 and Padma Shri 67; title of Rajya Kavi (Poet Laureate) by Punjab Govt. 64 and the Sahitya Akademi Award 65; Grand Prix de la Rose de France 68; Most Distinguished Order of Poetry, World Poetry Society Intercontinental, U.S.A. 74.
Publs. 35 books, including: Poems: *Supne Sadhran* 49, *Do Rang* 51, *Pankheru* 56, *Lala* (in Persian) 58, *Benkapani* 58, *Pabbi* 62, *Plateau* (English) 66, *Khari* 67, *Wad-Darshi Sheesha* 72, *Madhiantr* 74; Short stories: *Kinke* 52, *Aman de Na* 56.
D-203, Defence Colony, New Delhi 24, India.

Prakasa, Sri, B.A., LL.B.; Indian barrister and politician; b. 3 Aug. 1890; ed. Allahabad and Cambridge Univs.
Connected with *Leader*, Allahabad 17-18, *Independent*, Allahabad 19, *Aj*, Banaras 20-43, *National Herald*, Lucknow 38-48, *Sansar*, Banaras 43-49; mem. A.I.C.C. 18-45; founder mem. Kashi Vidyapith 21; Chancellor 69; mem. Banaras Municipal Board 21-25; Gen. Sec. United Provinces Congress Cttee. 28-34, and Indian Nat. Congress 29-31; Pres. U.P. Political Conf. 34 and Pres. United Provinces Congress Cttee. 34-35; mem. Legislative Assembly 34-35; Chair. Reception Cttee. Indian Nat. Congress 36; imprisoned for Congress activities 30, 32, 41 and 42; mem. Constituent Assembly for Uttar Pradesh 46; High Commr. in Pakistan 47-49; Gov. of Assam 49-50; Union Minister of Commerce 50-51, for Natural Resources and Scientific Research 51-52; Gov. of Madras 52-56, of Bombay 56-60, of Maharashtra 60-62; mem. of Lok Sabha 50-51 (resigned); Padma Vibushan 57.
Publs. *Annie Besant: As Woman and as Leader, Pakistan: Birth and Early Days* (in English), *Grihast Gita, Sphut Vichar, Hamari antarik Gatha, Nagarik Shastra* (in Hindi), *Dr. Bhagandas as Philosopher and Man* (in English and Hindi), *Education in a Democracy, State Governors in India.*

Pramoj, Mom Rachawongse Kukrit; Thai politician; b. 20 April 1911; brother of M. R. Seni Pramoj (*q.v.*); ed. Suan Kularb Coll., Trent Coll., U.K., Queen's Coll., Oxford.
With Revenue Dept., Ministry of Finance; Siam Commercial Bank; Head of Gov.'s Office, Bank of Thailand, later Head of Issue Dept.; mem. Parl. 46-76; Deputy Minister of Finance 47-48, later of Commerce; Founded *Siam Rath* newspaper 50; Leader Social Action Party; Speaker Nat. Assembly 73-74; Prime Minister March 75-April 76, also Minister of the Interior Jan.-April 76; Dir. of Thai Studies, Thammasat Univ.; Pres. Exec. Cttee., Foundation for the Assistance of Needy Schoolchildren; appeared in film *The Ugly American* 63.
Social Action Party, Bangkok, Thailand.

Pramoj, Mom Rachawongse Seni; Thai lawyer and politician; b. 26 May 1905, Nakhon Sawan Province; brother of M. R. Kukrit Pramoj (*q.v.*); ed. Trent Coll., U.K. and Worcester Coll., Oxford.
Called to English Bar and later to Thai Bar; Judge, Appeal Court, Bangkok; Minister, Thai Legation, Washington, D.C.; Prime Minister 45-46; law practice 46-; successively Minister of Foreign Affairs, of Justice, of Educ. 46-47; lectured at Chulalongkorn Univ. 47; Deputy Leader Prachatipat Party (Democratic Party), Leader 68-; mem. Nat. Assembly 69-71; Prime Minister Feb.-March 75, April 76-; Minister of the Interior April 76-.
Publs. several law books and English translations of Thai poetry.
Office of the Prime Minister, Bangkok, Thailand.

Prapas Charusathiara, Field-Marshal (*see* Charusathiara, Field-Marshal Prapas).

Prasad, Baleshwar, I.A.S., M.A.; Indian civil servant; b. 1 Jan. 1914; ed. Patna Univ.
Assistant Magistrate 50; Deputy Commr. 52; Political Adviser to Indian del. to Viet-Nam Int. Supervision and Control Comm. 56-59; Dewan (Prime Minister) of Sikkim 59-63; Chief Commr., Manipur 63-69, Lt.-Gov. 69-70; Amb. to Burma 70-71; Lt.-Gov., Tripura 71, New Delhi 72-.
Raj Niwas, New Delhi 6, India.

Prasad, P. S. Narayan; Indian economist; b. 24 Sept. 1910; ed. Andhra, Banaras Univs.
Lecturer Andhra Univ. 34-36; Prof. of Econs., Wadia Coll., Poona 37-40; Head, Econs. Dept., Maharajah's Coll., Jaipur 40-45; Reserve Bank of India 46-53; Exec. Dir. for India on Int. Monetary Fund 53-57, 71-75; Asst. Dir. Econ. Staff, IBRD 57-; Chair. World Bank's Mission to Libya 58-60; Econ. Adviser to Nigeria 61-63; Dir. Asian Inst. of Econ. Devt. and Planning, Bangkok 63-70; mem. Advisory Board of the Mekong Co-ordination Cttee.; Hon.D.Litt. (Andhra Univ.).
42-Pitakande, Kandy, Sri Lanka.
Telephone: 4490.

Prawiro, Radius, M.A.; Indonesian economist and banker; b. 29 June 1928; ed. Senior High School, Yogjakarta, Nederlandsche Economische Hoogeschool, Rotterdam, Econ. Univ. of Indonesia.
Secretary Defence Cttee., Yogjakarta during revolution

45; with Army High Command, Yogjakarta 46-47; Angauta Tentara Pelajar (Army) 48-51; Officer in Govt. Audit Office, Ministry of Finance 53-65; Vice-Minister, Deputy Supreme Auditor, mem. Supreme Audit Office 65-66; Gov. Bank Indonesia 66-73; Gov. for Indonesia, IMF 67-72; Chair. Board of Govs., IBRD 71-72; Alt. Gov. Asian Devt. Bank 67-72; Minister of Trade 73-; Chair. Indonesian Asscn. of Accountants 65-; mem. Econ. Council of the Pres. 68-, Nat. Econ. Stabilization Council 68-, Gov. Board Christian Univ. of Indonesia, Supervisory Board Trisakti Univ.
Ministry of Trade, Jakarta; Home: Jalan Imam Bonjol 4, Jakarta, Indonesia.

Price, James Robert, D.PHIL., D.SC., F.A.A.; Australian organic chemist; b. 25 March 1912, Kadina, S. Australia; ed. St. Peter's Coll., Adelaide and Univs. of Adelaide and Oxford.
Head, Chemistry Section, John Innes Horticultural Inst., U.K. 37; Minister of Supply (U.K.) 39; Council for Scientific and Industrial Research (C.S.I.R.) Div. of Industrial Chem., Australia 45; Officer in charge, Organic Chem. Section, Commonwealth Scientific and Industrial Research Org. (CSIRO) 60, subsequently Chief Organic Chem. Div.; mem. Exec. CSIRO 66; Chair. CSIRO May 70-; Fellow, Australian Acad. of Science, Chair. Nat. Cttee. for Chem. 66-69; Pres. Royal Australian Chem. Inst. (R.A.C.I.) 63-64; H. G. Smith Memorial Medal (R.A.C.I.) 56, Leighton Memorial Medal (R.A.C.I.) 69.
Publs. Numerous scientific papers and articles.
CSIRO, Canberra, A.C.T., Australia.

Pringle, John Martin Douglas, M.A.; British journalist; b. 28 June 1912; ed. Shrewsbury School, and Lincoln Coll., Oxford.
Member staff of *Manchester Guardian* 34-39; served in Army 40-44; Asst. Editor *Manchester Guardian* 44; joined staff *The Times* 48; Editor *Sydney Morning Herald* 52-57, 65-70; Deputy Editor *The Observer* 58-63; Man. Editor *Canberra Times* 64-65.
Publs. *China Struggles for Unity* 38, *Australian Accent* 58, *Australian Painting Today* 63, *On Second Thoughts* 71, *Have pen: will travel* 73.
27 Bayview Street, McMahon's Point, North Sydney, N.S.W., Australia.
Telephone 92-7560.

Pumphrey, Sir John Laurence, K.C.M.G.; British diplomatist; b. 22 July 1916; ed. Winchester and New Coll., Oxford.
Foreign Office 45-47; Asst. Private Sec. to Prime Minister 47-50; Berlin 50-53; Foreign Office 53-60, Head of Establishment and Organization Dept. 55-60; Counsellor and Head of Chancery, Singapore 60-63, Belgrade 63-65; Deputy High Commr., Kenya 65-67; High Commr. to Zambia 67-71; High Commr. to Pakistan 71-72, Amb. Jan. 72-76; retd.
c/o Foreign and Commonwealth Office, London S.W.1, England.

Puntsagnorov, Tsevegzhauyn; Mongolian diplomatist; b. 11 Aug. 1924, Ulan Bator; ed. Moscow Univ.
Former lecturer, Mongolian State Univ.; served on Cen. Cttee. of Mongolian People's Revolutionary Party until 62; Editor-in-Chief *Unen* (official Govt. and Party newspaper) 62; Deputy to Great People's Khural (Parliament); Chair. Mongolian Inter-Parl. Group; Deputy Chair. Council of Ministers 63-72; Minister of Culture 71-72; Perm. Rep. to UN Sept. 72-; corresp. mem. Acad. of Sciences of Mongolia.
Publs. a book on Mongolian history and numerous articles.
Permanent Mission of Mongolia to United Nations, 6 East 77th Street, New York, N.Y. 10021, U.S.A.

Puri, Kanwal Raj, B.A., LL.B.; Indian banker; b. 25 Feb. 1920, Lahore (now in Pakistan); Managing Dir. Sunlight of India; Div. Man. Life Insurance Corpn. of India 56-61, Zonal Man. 61-60, Exec. Dir. 70-72, Man. Dir. 72, Chair. 72-75; Gov. Reserve Bank of India Aug. 75-.
Reserve Bank of India, Central Office, Bombay; Residence: Reserve Bank House, 5 Carmichael Road, Bombay 26, India.
Telephone: 268634 (Office); 361634 (Home).

Puri, Yogendra Krishna; Indian diplomatist; b. 25 July 1916; ed. Government Coll., Lahore, and Univ. Coll., London.
Indian Civil Service, Assam 38-46; Deputy Sec., Ministry of Finance 47; Minister without Portfolio 47; Dir.-Gen. Ministry of Rehabilitation 48; Deputy High Commr. in Pakistan 48-51; Deputy Sec. Ministry of External Affairs 51-53; Indian Embassy, Paris 53-55; Counsellor Indian High Comm., London 55; Joint Sec. Ministry of External Affairs 55-60; High Commr. in Malaya 60-63, in Malaysia 63-64; Amb. to Morocco and Tunisia 64-67, to Sweden 68-69; High Commr. in Ceylon 70-72; Amb. to Fed. Repub. of Germany 72-75; Pres. Colombo Plan Council for Technical Co-operation in S. and S.E. Asia. 72; del. to Afro-Asian Conf., Algiers 65, 66.
c/o Ministry of External Affairs, New Delhi 110011, India.

Q

Quat, Phan Huy (*see* Phan Huy Quat).

Qureshi, Anwar Iqbal, B.A., M.A., M.SC., PH.D.; Pakistani economist; b. 10 April 1910; ed. Forman Christian Coll., Lahore, London School of Economics, Trinity Coll., Dublin.
Professor, Head Econs. Dept., Osmania Univ. 37-47; Econ. Adviser, Govt. of Hyderabad 44-47; Deputy Econ. Adviser Govt. of Pakistan 47-51; Adviser, IMF 51-55; Financial and Econ. Adviser, Saudi Arabia 55-59; Econ. Adviser and Sec. Govt. of Pakistan 61-68, Additional Sec. 68-70, rtd.; Chief Economist, Sabasun Tech. Services, Lahore 74-; mem. Council for Econ. Advisory Affairs 75-; Pres. Pakistan Econ. Asscn. Sitara-i-Quaid-i-Azam 65.
Publs. *The Farmer and His Debt* 34, *Agricultural Credit* 36, *The State and Economic Life* 37, *State Banks for India* 39, *Islam and the Theory of Interest* 46, *The Future of Co-operative Movement in India* 47, *Economic Development of Hyderabad* 48, *Development in Pakistan's Economy since the Revolution* 60, *Pakistan's March on Road to Prosperity* 65, *Mr. Mujib's Six Points: An Economic Appraisal* 70, *Economic Problems Facing Pakistan* 71.
Al-Haniyah, 295/3 Sarwar Road, Lahore Cantt, Pakistan.
Telephone: 70431.

Qureshi, Ishtiaq Husain, M.A., PH.D.; Pakistani scholar and politician; b. 20 Nov. 1903; ed. St. Stephen's Coll. (Univ. of Delhi), and Sidney Sussex Coll., Cambridge.
Lecturer in History, St. Stephens Coll. 28; Reader in History Univ. of Delhi 40, Prof. and Head of Dept. of History 44, Dean of Faculty of Arts 45; mem. for Bengal, Constituent Assembly of Pakistan 47; Prof. of History and Head of Dept. of History, Punjab Univ. 48; Deputy Minister of the Interior, Information and Broadcasting, Refugees and Rehabilitation, Govt. of Pakistan 49, Minister of State 50, Minister for Refugees and Rehabilitation, Information and Broadcasting 51-53; Minister of Educ. 53-55; mem. Advisory Council of Islamic Ideology 62-63, Nat. Comm. on Educ. and Manpower 68-69; Visiting Prof. Columbia Univ., New York 55-60; Dir. Central Inst. of Islamic Research, Karachi 60-62; Vice-Chancellor Univ. of Karachi 61-71; Star of Pakistan 64.
Publs. *The Administration of the Sultanate of Delhi* 41, *The Pakistani Way of Life* 56, *The Muslim Community in the Indo-Pakistan Sub-Continent* 62, *The Struggle for Pakistan*

65, *The Administration of the Mughul Empire* 67, *Ulema in Politics* 72, *Education in Pakistan* 75.
Zeba Manzar, 1 Sharafabad, Shahid-i-Millat Road, Karachi 5, Pakistan.
Telephone: 411339.

R

Rabukawaqa, Josua Rasilau, C.B.E., M.V.O.; Fijian diplomatist; b. 2 Dec. 1917; ed. Queen Victoria School, Fiji, Teachers' Training Coll., Auckland, N.Z.
Teacher, Fiji 38-52; Platoon Officer 1st Battalion Fiji Infantry Regt. Malayan Campaign 54-55; Adjutant Fiji Mil. Forces 55-56; Co-operatives Inspector 53-57; Asst. Econ. Devt. Officer 57-61; Asst. Roko 59-62; District Officer, Overseas Colonial Service 62-68; Clerk to Council; First Protocol Officer in Fiji; Commr. Central 69-70; High Commr. to U.K. 70-, accred. to EEC 71-.
Fiji High Commission, 25 Upper Brook Street, London, W1Y 1PD; Residence: 41 Campden Hill Court, Campden Hill Road, London, W.8, England.

Raghavan, Venkatarama, M.A., PH.D.; Indian Sanskrit scholar; b. 22 Aug. 1908; ed. Tiruvarur High School and Madras Univ.
Superintendent Sarasvati Mahal Manuscript Library. Tanjore 30; successively Research Scholar, Research Asst., Lecturer, Reader, Prof. and Head of Dept., Madras Univ. Dept. of Sanskrit 31-69; Editor *Journal of Oriental Research, Madras Music Academy Journal, Sanskrita-Pratibha, Sanskrit Ranga Annual, Malayamaruta*; mem. Govt. of India Sanskrit Comm. and Cen. Sanskrit Board, Indian Acad. of Letters; Fellow, Acad. of Music, Dance and Drama; Hon. corresp. mem. Ecole Française d'Extrême Orient, Austrian Acad. of Sciences; Pres. All-India Oriental Conf., Int. Asscn. of Sanskrit Studies 73; Kane Gold Medal (Bombay Asiatic Soc.) 53; awarded titles of Kavikokila and Sakalakala-Kalapa by Sankaracharya 53; Padma Bhushan by Govt. of India 63; Indian Acad. of Letters, Award for best book on Sanskrit research 66; Jawaharlal Nehru Fellowship 69; Gold Medal and Membership of Noble Order of St. Martin (Austria) 67; Kalidas Award (Uttar Pradesh) 74, (Madhya Pradesh) 75; Hon. D.Litt. (Sanskrit Univ. Varanasi).
Publs. include: English: *Some Concepts of Alankara Sastra* 42, 73, *New Catalogus Catalogorum* 49-68, *The Indian Heritage, Sanskrit and Allied Indological Studies in Europe, Yantras or Mechanical Contrivances in Ancient India* 56, *Concept of Culture* 71, *Seasons in Sanskrit Literature* 72; Tamil: *Varalakshmivratam* (short stories) 50, *Bharata Natya* 59, *Kadaikkadal* 59, *Nataka Lakshanaratnakosa* 61, *Bhoja's Sringara Prakasa* 63; Patel Lectures: *The Great Integrators—Saint-Singers of India* 66, *Nrttaratnavali* 68, *The Greater Ramayana* 73, *Sanskrit in Allied Indian Studies in N.S.* 75, *Ramayana in Greater India* 75; Sanskrit: *Rasalila, Kamasuddhi, Manunitichola, Davabandi Varadaraia, Prekshanakatrayi, Vimukti, Valmiki pratibha, Natirpuja, Vidyanathavidambana, Anarkali* 74 (poems and plays).
7 Srikrishanpuram Street, Royapettah, Madras 14, India.
Telephone: 85091 (Home).

Raghuramaiah, Kotha, M.A., LL.B., BAR-AT-LAW; Indian lawyer and politician; b. 1912; ed. Lucknow Univ. and the Middle Temple.
Legal practice 37-41; Provincial Judicial Service 41-51; mem. Lok Sabha 52-; Deputy Minister of Defence 57-62; Minister of State in the Ministry of Defence 62-63; Minister of Defence Production 62-64, of Supply 64-65, of Technical Devt., Supply and Social Security 65-67; Minister of State for Law 67, Minister of State in Ministry of Petroleum and Chemicals and of Social Welfare 67, Minister 68-69; Minister of State for Parl. Affairs, Shipping and Transport 69-71 (with cabinet status 70-71); Minister for Parl. Affairs 73-, and for Works and Housing 74-; mem. Railway Corruption Enquiry Cttee. 54; Chair. Petitions Cttee., Lok Sabha 55-57; Congress Party.
14 Asoka Road, New Delhi, India.

Rahim, Jalaluddin Abdur; Pakistani diplomatist and politician; b. 27 July 1906, Calcutta; ed. Trinity Coll., Cambridge and Univ. of Munich.
Entered Indian Civil Service and served in Madras Presidency 31; transferred to Finance Dept., Govt. of India 36; Indian Trade Commr. for Egypt and other Middle Eastern Countries 45; Chargé d'Affaires, Pakistan Embassy, Cairo 47; Joint Sec. Ministry of Foreign Affairs and Commonwealth Relations 50; Amb. to Belgium 52-53; Sec. Ministry of Foreign Affairs and Commonwealth Relations 53-55; subsequently Amb. to Fed. Repub. of Germany, to Spain and to France; retd. from Govt. Service 67; founder mem. Pakistan People's Party, Sec.-Gen. 69; Minister for Production and Presidential Affairs and also for Commerce 72-74.
c/o Pakistan People's Party, Islamabad, Pakistan.

Rahimtoola, Sir Fazal Ibrahim, Kt., B.A., C.I.E., J.P.; Indian industrialist; b. 21 Oct. 1895; ed. St. Xavier's High School and Coll., Bombay, and Poona Law Coll.
Director, Dhrangadhra Chemicals Ltd., Ahmedabad Advance Mills Ltd., Tata Power Co. Ltd., Tata Iron and Steel Co. Ltd., Swadeshi Mills Ltd., Overseas Communications Service (Government of India), New Swadeshi Sugar Mills Ltd., Sultania Cotton Mfg. Co. Ltd., Fazalbhai Ibrahim and Co. Pvt. Ltd.; mem. Central Legislative Assembly 25-30, Legislative Assembly 37, Bombay Legislative Council 48, Indian Tariff Board 30, Acting Pres. 32, Pres. 35; Sheriff of Bombay 50; Chair. Indian Fisheries Cttee. and Deep-Sea Fisheries Station, Govt. of India; Dir. Nat. War Front; mem. War Risk Insurance Claims Cttee. of Govt. of India, Central Food Council and its Standing Cttee., Post-War Reconstruction Cttee. for Agricultural Research, Govt. Price-Fixation Cttee. (Planning Dept.), All-Indian Council for Technical Educ., UNESCO Nat. Comm. for India and its Science Sub-Comm., East India Asscn., London, etc.; Del. to UNESCO Conf., Florence 50; Econ. Adviser to Junagadh State (Saurashtra); Pres. Urdu Newspapers Asscn.; Hon. Consul-Gen. for Thailand in Bombay; F.R.S.A.; Chair. Cttee. of hosts 38th Int. Eucharistic Congress.
Ismail Building, 381 Dr. Dadabhoy Naoroji Road, Fort, Bombay 1, B.R., India.
Telephone: 255046 (Office); 364031 (Home).

Rahimtoola, Habib Ibrahim, B.A., LL.B., F.R.P.S., F.R.S.A.; Pakistani diplomatist and politician; b. 10 March 1912; ed. St. Xavier's School and Coll., and Government Law Coll., Bombay.
Was Dir. over 15 joint stock companies in India; Pres. Fed. of Muslim Chambers of Commerce and Industry, New Delhi 47-48; Bombay Provincial Muslim Chamber of Commerce 44-47; Bombay Provincial Muslim League Parl. Board for Local Bodies 45-47; Del. Prime Ministers' Confs. London 48, 49, 51, Commonwealth Conf., S.E. Asia, London 50, Afro-Asian Conf. Bandung 55; Leader Pakistan Trade Del. to British East Africa 56; High Commr. for Pakistan in Great Britain 47-52; Amb. to France 52-53; Gov. Sind 53, Punjab 54; Minister for Commerce, Central Govt. 54-55, for Commerce and Industries 55-56; Chair. Karachi Development Authority 58-60, Water Co-ordination Council 58-60, Pakistan Govt. Shipping Rates Advisory Board 59-, Pakistan Red Cross 71-, Bandenawaz Ltd., Pakistan Oxygen Ltd., United Bank Ltd., Pakistan Chemicals Ltd., Int. Industries Ltd., Pakistan Cables Ltd., Chambon (Pakistan) Ltd., Pakistan-Japan Cultural

Asscn., Royal Commonwealth Soc., Pakistan; Pakistan-Ceylon Asscn., Photographic Soc. of Pakistan.
"Kulib", B/59, K.D.A. No. 1, Habib I. Rahimtoola Road, Karachi 8, Pakistan.

Rahma Brahmam, Muluktla, B.E.; Indian oil executive; b. 24 Aug. 1912, Paddapuram, Andrha; ed. Madras Univ.
Superintendent Engineer and Engineer-in-Charge, Kandla Port Trust 50-59; Chief Engineer and Gen. Man., Gauhati Refinery, Assam 59-65; Man. Dir. Madras Refineries Ltd. 65-69, Chair. and Man. Dir. 69-71; Chair. Indian Oil Corpn. Ltd. 71-73, Madras Refineries Ltd., Bongaigaon Refinery and Petrochemicals Ltd.; Fellow, Inst. of Engineers (India); Padma Bhushan 70.
Publs. technical papers in engineering journals in India and abroad.
c/o Madras Refineries Ltd., Manali, Madras 600068; Home: 4837 Anna Nagar, Madras 600040, India.
Telephone: 44749 (Office); 666818 (Home).

Rahman, Sheikh Abdur, B.A., M.A.; Pakistani judge; b. 4 June 1903; ed. Islamia Coll. Lahore, Govt. Coll. Lahore, and Exeter Coll., Oxford.
Joined Indian Civil Service as Asst. Commr. 28, later District and Sessions Judge and Legal Remembrancer, Punjab; Acting Judge, Lahore High Court 46; mem. Bengal Boundary Comm. 47; Custodian Evacuee Property 48; Additional Judge, Lahore High Court 48, Permanent Judge 48; Vice-Chancellor Punjab Univ. 50; Acting Chief Justice, Lahore High Court 54, Chief Justice 54-55; Permanent Chief Justice of Western Pakistan High Court 55-58; Judge, Supreme Court of Pakistan 58, Chief Justice until 68; Chair. Board for Advancement of Literature, Lahore; Vice-Chair. Bazm-i-Iqlal, Lahore; Dir. Inst. of Islamic Culture; Hon. LL.D. (Cairo, Punjab Univs.).
Publs. *Tarjuman-i-Asrar* (Urdu translation), *Hadis-i Dil* (Speeches, lectures in Urdu) 63, *Safar* (Urdu poetry) 64, *Punishment of Apostasy in Islam* 72.
65 Main Gulberg, Lahore, Pakistan.
Telephone: 80109.

Raisani, Sardar Ghaus; Pakistani politician; b. 6 Sept. 1924, Kanak, Baluchistan; ed. Col. Brown Public School, Dehra Dun.
Commissioned, Indian Army 45, served 45-48; Tribal Chief, Baluchistan 49-; active in politics 49-; Convener, Baluchistan State Muslim League; mem. W. Pakistan Assembly 56; founder and Convener, Baluchistan United Front 70; President, Baluchistan Assembly 70-72, Leader of the Opposition 72-74; Gov. of Baluchistan 71-72; Fed. Minister of Food and Agriculture 72-74; Senior Minister Baluchistan Prov. Cabinet 74-; Pres. Pakistan People's Party Baluchistan 74-.
Baluchistan Assembly, Baluchistan; 47 Lytton Road, Quetta, Pakistan.
Telephone: 73357 (Office); 70661 and 75357 (Home).

Rajah, Arumugam Ponnu; Singapore lawyer and diplomatist; b. 23 July 1911; ed. St. Paul's Inst., Seremban, Raffles Inst. and Coll., Singapore, and Oxford Univ., England.
Singapore City Councillor 47-57; mem. Singapore Legislative Assembly 59-63, Speaker 64-66; High Commr. in U.K. 66-71; High Commr. to Commonwealth of Australia 71-73; practising lawyer in Singapore 73-; mem. Board of Trustees, Singapore Improvement Trust 49-57; mem. of Council, Raffles Coll., Univ. of Malaya 55-63; Chair. Public Accounts Cttee., Legislative Assembly 59-63.
c/o Ministry of Foreign Affairs, Singapore.

Rajaratnam, Sinnathamby; Singapore politician; b. 23 Feb. 1915, Ceylon (now Sri Lanka); ed. Raffles Inst., Singapore, King's Coll., London.
Assoc. Editor *Singapore Standard* 50-54; Editorial Staff *Straits Times* 54-59; mem. Malayanization Cttee. 55; mem. Minimum Standards of Livelihood Cttee. 56; Convenor and Founder-mem. of People's Action Party; mem. Legislative Assembly for Kampong Glam constituency 59-; Minister for Culture 59-65, for Foreign Affairs 65-, concurrently for Labour 68-71.
Ministry for Foreign Affairs, 1st Floor, Government Offices, St. Andrew's Road, Singapore 6.
Telephone: 322142.

Ram, Dr. Bharat, B.A.; Indian industrialist, b. 5 Oct. 1914; ed. privately and at St. Stephen's Coll., Delhi.
Joined Delhi Cloth and General Mills Co. 35, Joint Man. Dir. 48, Chair. Board of Dirs. 58-; also Chair. Bengal Potteries, Shriram Bearings; Chair. Coromandel Fertilisers 67-; Chair. Indian Airlines 67-69; Chair. Indian Cotton Mills Federation 61-63; Pres. Fed. of Indian Chambers of Commerce & Industry 63-64; Pres. Int. Chamber of Commerce 69-71; mem. Board of Govs., Delhi and Pilani Insts. of Technology; Dir. New India Assurance Co., Escorts, Bajaj Electricals.
25 Sarder Patel Road, New Delhi, India.

Ram, Jagjivan, B.SC.; Indian politician; b. 5 April 1908, Arrar, Bihar; ed. Benares Hindu Univ. and Calcutta Univ.
General Sec. All-India Depressed Classes League until 36, Pres. 36-46; mem. Legislative Council, Bihar 36, Parl. Sec. 37-39; formed Bihar Provincial *Khet Mazdoor Sabha* (Agricultural Labourers' Org.) 37; Sec. Bihar Provincial Congress Cttee. 40-46; Vice-Pres. Bihar Branch All-India T.U.C. 40-46; imprisoned 40, 42, released 43; Chair. Preparatory Conf. of ILO Asian Region 47, leader del. to ILO Conf., Chair. Conf. 50; Minister for Labour 56-52 (Interim Govt. and first Fed. Govt.), for Communications 52-56, 62-63, for Railways and Transport 56-57, for Railways 57-62, for Transport 63-64, for Labour and Employment 66-67, for Food, Agriculture, Community Devt. and Co-operation 67-70, for Defence 70-74, for Agriculture and Irrigation Oct. 74-; Pres. Indian Nat. Congress 69-74; leader Indian del. to FAO Conf. Italy 67, 74, 75, the Netherlands 70; mem. Working Cttee. and Central Parl. Board All-India Congress Cttee. 48-; Chair. Indian Inst. of Public Admin. 74-; Hon. D.Sc. (Vickram Univ.).
Ministry of Agriculture and Irrigation, New Delhi; Home: 6 Krishna Menon Marg, New Delhi 110011, India.
Telephone: 381129 (Office); 376555 (Home).

Ramachandran, Gopalasamudram Narayana, D.SC., PH.D., F.R.S.A.; Indian scientist and university professor; b. 8 Oct. 1922; ed. Maharaja's Coll., Ernakulam (Cochin), Indian Inst. of Science, Univs. of Madras and Cambridge.
Lecturer in Physics, Indian Inst. of Science 46-49, Asst. Prof. 49-52; 1851 Exhbn. Scholar, Univ. of Cambridge 47-49; Prof. and Head of Dept. Univ. of Madras 52-70, Dean of Faculty 63-70; Prof. of Biophysics, Indian Inst. of Science 70-; ed. *Journal of the Indian Inst. of Science* 73-; mem. 6 editorial boards; Fellow, Indian Acad. of Sciences 50 (Vice-Pres. 62-66); mem. Nat. Cttee. for Biophysics 61-; Fellow Indian Nat. Science Acad. 63-; part-time Prof., Univ. of Chicago 67-; Hon. mem. American Soc. of Biological Chemists 65-; Hon. Foreign mem. American Acad. of Arts and Sciences 70-; Bhatnagar Memorial Prize 68, Ramanujam Medal 72, Meghnad Saha Medal 71, J.C. Bose Award (U.G.C.) 74, Gold Medal and Prize (Bose Inst.) 75.
Publs. contributions to books and journals, ed. four books on optics, crystal physics, X-ray crystallography and biophysics.
Indian Institute of Science, Bangalore 560 012; Home: 41 16th Cross, Malleswaram, Bangalore 560 005, India.

Ramachandran, T. N.; Indian archaeologist; b. 16 March 1903; ed. Presidency Coll., Madras Univ. and London Univ. Inst. of Archaeology.

Curator Archaeological Section, Madras Govt. Museum 25-35; Asst. Suprintendent Archaeological Survey of India, Calcutta 35-38, Superintendent 38-52, Deputy Dir. Gen. Delhi 52-53, Joint Dir. Gen. 53-58; Special Officer Nagarjunakonda Excavations, Govt. of India Dept. of Archaeology 58-61; Special Officer for Archaeology, Govt. of Madras 61-, for Publications, H.R. & C.E. Dept. 66-68; Tagore Prof. for Humanities, Univ. of Madras 69-70; mem. Central Film Censor Board 67-; Pres. Asiatic Section, I.C.O.M.; Fellow Asiatic Soc. (Narasimhacharya Prize), Bysany Madhava Gold Medal (Madras Univ.), Lokavedasamanvayakalpataru 63, Padma Bhushan 64.
Publs. 200 including *Buddhist Sculptures from Goli* 29, *South Indian Metal Images* 32, *The Golden Age of Indo-Javanese Art* 33, *The Royal Artist Mahendra Varman I* 33, *Three Styles of Temple Architecture* 34, *Tiruparuttikuwram and its temples* 34, *Nagarjunakonda* 38, *Jaina Monuments of India* 44, *Khandagiri and Udayagiri Caves* 50, *Nagapattinam Buddhist Bronzes* 54, *Archaeological Reconnaissance in Afghanistan* 56, *New Light on Indus Culture* 58, *Historic India and her temples* 58, *Preservation of Monuments* 55, *The Great Temple of Tanjore, The Sittannavasal Cave* 62, *Is the World Morally Progressing?, Radhakrishna Sataka, Kusumaksharamala, Rama Sataka, Buddhist India and the World, Homage to Vaisali, Asvamedha Sites Near Kalsi, Kiratarjuniya in Indian Art, Temple Inscriptions and Music* 68, *Indian Wood Carving* 68, *Ramasatakam* 68, *Thiruvanaikka Temple* 70, *Hymn To Mahabalipuram* 70.
2 Third Main Road, Nehrunagar, Adayar, Madras 20, India.

Ramaiah, Kotha Raghu (*see* Raghuramaiah, Kotha).

Ramalingaswami, Vulimiri, M.D., D.SC., F.R.C.P.; Indian medical scientist; b. 8 Aug. 1921, Srikakulum, Andhra Pradesh; ed. Univ. of Oxford.
Pathologist for Indian Council of Medical Research at Nutrition Research Laboratories, Coonor 47-54; Asst. Sec. and Deputy Dir. Indian Council of Medical Research 54-57; Prof. of Pathology and Head of Dept., All-India Inst. of Medical Sciences 57-69, Dir. and Prof. of Pathology 69-; Pres. Indian Asscn. for Advancement of Medical Educ. 74-; Fellow Indian Acad. of Medical Science 61-, Indian Nat. Science Acad. 71; Hon. Fellow, American Coll. of Physicians 70-; Foreign Assoc., Nat. Acad. of Sciences, U.S.A. 73-; Dr. Sc. h.c. (Andhra Univ.) 67, Hon. Dr. Med. (Karolinska Inst.) 74; Silver Jubilee Research Award, Medical Council of India 74; Padma Bhushan 71; Bernard Prize, WHO 76.
Publs. author and co-author of many papers, articles, lectures, monographs and books.
Director's Bungalow, All-India Institute of Medical Sciences, 78123 Ansari Nagar, New Delhi 110016, India.
Telephone: 78361-619481/311 (Office).

Raman, Papanasam Setlur, M.A.; Singapore diplomatist; b. 5 Oct. 1920, India; ed. Madras Christian Coll. and Univ. of Madras.
Former teacher; Supervisor, Pan-Malayan Indian Programme 58-59; Asst. Controller of Programmes 60-63; Deputy Dir. Broadcasting 63-65, Dir. 65-68; Amb. to Indonesia 68-69, to Australia 69-71, to U.S.S.R. 71-; Meritorious Service Medal.
Embassy of Singapore, Moscow, U.S.S.R.; Home: 47 Hillside Drive, Singapore.

Ramanathan, Kalpathi Ramakrishna, M.A., D.SC.; Indian scientist; b. 1893; ed. Victoria Coll., Palghat and Presidency Coll., Madras.
Demonstrator in Physics, Trivandrum Coll. 14-21; Hon. Dir. Trivandrum Observatory; Madras Univ. Research Scholar under Prof. C. V. Raman 21-22; Lecturer in Physics, Univ. Coll., Rangoon 22-25; joined Indian Meteorological Dept. 25-48; Dir. Kodaikanal and Bombay Observatories; Superintending Meteorologist, Poona 39; Deputy Dir.-Gen. of Observatories until 48; Dir. Physical Research Laboratory Ahmedabad 48-66, Prof. 66-; Pres. Indian Science Congress, Mathematics and Physics Section, Lahore 39; Founder Fellow of Indian Acad. of Sciences and of Nat. Inst. of Sciences of India; Pres. Int. Asscn. of Meteorology 51-54, Int. Union of Geodesy and Geophysics 54-57; Chair. Radio Research Cttee., India 66-71, Cloud and Rain Physics and Cosmic Ray Research Cttee. 56-66; Chair. Cen. Board of Geophysics 57-; Pres. Int. Ozone Comm. 59-60, Chair. 60-67, now hon. mem; Pres. Indian Nat. Cttee. for IQSY (Int. Year of the Quiet Sun); Chair. Indian Nat. Cttee. for Int. Hydrological Decade 66-74, for Int. Hydrological Programme 74-; main fields of research: problems of molecular scattering of light in fluids, anisotropy of molecules, atmospheric and solar radiation, study of the Indian monsoon, general circulation of the atmosphere, atmospheric ozone, physics of the ionosphere and aeronomy; Hon. Fellow, Royal Meteorological Soc., London 60; Award of Int. Meteorological Org. 61; Padma Bhushan 65, Padma Vibhushan 76.
Physical Research Laboratory, Navrangpura, Ahmedabad 9, Gujarat, India.
Telephone: 40242-46.

Ramanujam, G.; Indian trade unionist; b. 2 Feb. 1916.
Founder-Sec. Tamilnad Indian Nat. Trade Union Congress; Pres. Indian Nat. Plantation Workers Fed. 60; Pres. Indian Nat. Trade Union Congress 58, 59, Gen. Sec. 65-75; Man. Editor *Indian Worker* 65-75.
Publs. *From the Babul Tree, Industrial Relations—A Point of View, The Payment of Bonus Act, Payment of Gratuity Act.*
c/o Indian National Trade Union Congress, 17 Janpath, New Delhi, India.

Ramkumar, Ramkumar, M.A.; Indian artist; b. 23 Sept. 1924; ed. Delhi Univ., Académie André Lhote, Paris, and Acad. Montmartre, Paris (with Fernand Léger).
Worked in bank for one year; French Govt. scholarship, Paris 50-52; returned to India 52; exhbns. in Europe 55, 58; travelled in Europe, Afghanistan, Ceylon, Turkey and Egypt; mem. Lalit Kala Akademi, Sahitya Akademi; Nat. Award, Nat. Art Exhbn., India 56, 58; one-man exhbns. in Delhi, Bombay, Calcutta, Paris, Prague, Warsaw, Colombo 50-65; Group exhbns. with other Indian artists in London, New York, Tokyo, etc.; exhibited at Int. exhbns., Venice, São Paulo (Hon. mention 59), Tokyo.
Publs. two novels, two story collections and a travel book.
14 A/20 W.E. Area, New Delhi 5, India.

Rana, Damodar Shumshere Jung Bahadur, B.A.; Nepalese social worker and politician; b. 1928; ed. Missionary School Darjeeling, Central Hindu School, Banaras and Banaras Hindu Univ.
Executive mem. social orgs. in Nepal 54-60; Chief Admin. Morang District 61; Chair. Special Comm. Kosi Zone 61, Commr. 62-64; mem. Nat. Panchayat, mem. Exec. Cttee. and Foreign Affairs Cttee.; Amb. to the U.S.S.R. 64-70, concurrently to Poland, Hungary and Czechoslovakia; Zonal Commr., Janakpur 70-71; awarded Prabala Gorkha Dakchina Bahu and Subikhyat Trisakti Patt.
Phora Darbar, Kathmandu, Nepal.

Ranga, N. G.; Indian politician; b. 7 Nov. 1900; ed. Oxford Univ., England.
College Prof. of Econs., Madras Univ., India; Founder Indian Peasant Movement 30; mem. Lok Sabha 34-; mem. Congress Working Cttee. 47-51; founder Bharat Krishikar Lok (Peasant Peoples) Party 51; mem. Congress 55, Gen. Sec. Congress Parl. Party 59; leader Swatantra Group, Lok Sabha 59-71; Hon. Principal Indian Peasants' Inst., Nidubrolu, A.P.

Publs. About 43 books, including *Credo of World Peasantry* 57, *Towards World Peace* 57, *Fight for Freedom* (autobiog.) 68, *Bapu Blesses* (talks with Gandhi) 70, *Kakatiya Nayaks* (14th Century Story of South Indian Freedom Fighters) 71.
Ponnur, Andhra Pradesh, India.
Telephone: Ponnur 106.

Rankin, Hon. Dame Annabelle, D.B.E.; Australian fmr. politician and diplomatist; b. 28 July 1908, Brisbane; ed. Childers, Howard and Glennie Memorial School, Toowoomba.
State Sec. Queensland Girl Guides Assn.; served in Second World War in Voluntary Aid Detachment and as Y.W.C.A. Asst. Commr. for Queensland attached to the Army; Organizer Jr. Red Cross in Queensland 46; mem. Senate 46; mem. Parl. Standing Cttee. on Broadcasting 47, Parl. Public Works Cttee. 50; Opposition Chief Whip in Senate 47-49, Govt. Whip 51-66; Vice-Pres. Liberal Party Queensland 49; Minister for Housing Jan. 66-March 71; High Commr. in New Zealand 71-74; mem. Commonwealth Parl. Del. to Canada 52; Vice-Pres. Multiple Handicapped Children's Assn.; Patron Cystic Fibrosis Assn., mem. Fed. Cttee. of Outward Bound Assn., Advisory Cttee. of Australian Broadcasting, Queensland; Liberal.
c/o Ministry of Foreign Affairs, Canberra, A.C.T., Australia.

Rao, Calyampudi Radhakrishna, M.A., SC.D., F.N.A., F.R.S.; Indian statistician; b. 10 Sept. 1920; ed. Andhra and Calcutta Univs.
Research at Indian Statistical Inst. 43-46, Cambridge Univ. 46-48; Prof. and Head of Div. of Theoretical Research and Training 49-64; Dir. Research and Training School, Indian Statistical Inst. 64-72, Sec. and Dir. 72-76, Jawaharhal Nehru Prof. 76-; Fellow Inst. of Math. Statistics Pres.-elect 75-76, Pres. 76-77; Fellow American Statistical Assn., Econometric Soc., Indian Acad. of Sciences; Foreign Hon. Fellow, King's Coll. Cambridge, Royal Statistical Soc.; Hon. Foreign mem. American Acad. of Arts and Science; Treas. Int. Statistical Inst. 61-65, Pres.-elect 75-77, Pres. 77-79; Editor of *Sankhya* (Indian Journal of Statistics); Bhatnagar Memorial Award for Scientific Research; Padma Bhushan; Guy Silver Medal, Royal Statistical Soc.; Hon. D.Sc. (Andhra, Leningrad), Hon. D.Litt. (Delhi); Meghnad Saha Gold Medal, Indian Nat. Science Acad.
Publs. include: *Advanced Statistical Methods in Biometric Research, Linear Statistical Inference and its Application, Generalized Inverse of Matrices and its Applications, Characterization Problems of Mathematical Statistics*; over 150 research papers in mathematical statistics.
Indian Statistical Institute, T.S.J.S. Sansanwal Marg, New Delhi-110029, India.
Telephone: 678287 and 70172.

Rao, Chandra Rajeswar; Indian politician; b. 6 June 1914; ed. Hindu High School, Masulipatam, and Banaras Hindu Univ.
At Vizagapatam Medical Coll. 36-37; joined Communist Party, Andhra 36; mem. Central Cttee. Communist Party of India 48, Gen. Sec. 50-51, 64-75; Order of Lenin, U.S.S.R. 74.
"Ajoy Bhavan", Kotla Road, New Delhi, India.

Rao, Chintamani Nagesa Ramachandra, M.SC., D.SC., PH.D., F.R.I.C.; Indian chemist; b. 30 June 1934, Bangalore; ed. Mysore, Banaras, Purdue and California Univs.
Lecturer, Indian Inst. of Science, Bangalore 59-63; Prof., later Senior Prof., Indian Inst. of Technology, Kanpur 63-, Dean of Research and Devt. 69-72; Visiting Prof. Purdue Univ., U.S.A. 67-68, Oxford Univ. 74-75; Chair. IUPAC Cttee. on Teaching of Chem.; mem. Nat Cttee. on Science and Tech. 70-74, editorial boards of seven int. journals; Fellow, Indian Acad. of Sciences, Indian Nat. Science Acad., St. Catherine's Coll., Oxford 74-75; Jawarhalal Nehru Fellow, Indian Inst. of Tech.; Marlow Medal, Faraday Soc. 67; Bhatnagar Award 68; Padma Shri 74.
Publs. *Ultraviolet Visible Spectroscopy* 60, *Chemical Applications of Infrared Spectroscopy* 63, *Spectroscopy in Inorganic Chemistry* 70, *Modern Aspects of Solid State Chemistry* 70, *Solid State Chemistry* 74; *nearly* 200 original research papers.
Indian Institute of Technology, Kanpur 208016, India.

Rao, Kanuru Lakshmana, PH.D., F.I.C.E., F.I.STRUCT.E., F.I.E.; Indian engineer and politician; b. 15 July 1902; ed. Univ. of Madras and Univ. of Birmingham.
Former Chief Engineer (Floods), Indian Central Govt.; fmr. mem. (Design and Research), Central Water and Power Comm. and Pres. Central Board of Irrigation and Power; mem. Lok Sabha 62-; Minister of State for Irrigation and Power 63-73; Pres. Int. Soc. of Soil Mechanics and Foundation Engineering; Pres. Inst. of Engineers 59-61; Padma Bhushan 63; D.Sc. (Andhra Univ.).
Publ. *Calculations, Designs and Testing of Reinforced Concrete, India's Water Wealth.*
7 Lodi Estate, New Delhi 3, India.
Telephone: 611073.

Rao, K. N., M.B., B.S., M.D.; Indian medical official and administrator; b. 31 Jan. 1907; ed. Univ. of Madras.
Entered Indian Medical Service 35; Prof. of Medical Jurisprudence, Christian Medical Coll., Vellore 48-49; Tuberculosis Advisor to Govt. of Madras 51-54; Dir. of Medical Services, Andhra Pradesh 54-63; Dir.-Gen. of Health Services, Govt. of India 64-68; Chair. Exec. Board, WHO 67-68; Pres. World Fed. of Public Health Assns. 67-68; Pan American Health Org. and WHO Consultant on Medical Educ. in Latin America 68; WHO Visiting Prof. of Int. Health, School of Hygiene, Toronto Univ. 68; Exec. Dir., Indian Assn. for Advancement of Medical Educ. 68-70; WHO Consultant, Medical Educ. in Africa 70; Sec.-Gen. Population Council of India 70-73; Visiting Prof. of Medicine, Sri Ventiateswara Univ. 70-71; Editor-in-Chief *Journal of Medical Education* 70-74; Exec. Dir. Indian Acad. of Medical Sciences 75-; consultant, Pan American Health Org. and WHO on Health and Population Dynamics 73-74; Sec. Nat. Board of Examinations 75-; official on numerous Indian and int. health orgs.; numerous awards.
Publs. *Recent Development in the Field of Health and Medical Education* 66, *India and World Health* 68; *Philosophy of Medicine* 68; Gen. Ed. *Text Book of Tuberculosis* 72.
Indian Academy of Medical Sciences, CII/16, Ansari Nagar, New Delhi 16; Home: D-57 Naraina, New Delhi 110028, India.

Rao, Raja; Indian writer; b. 21 July 1909; ed. Nizam Coll., Hyderabad, Univs. of Montpellier and Paris.
Professor of Philosophy, Univ. of Texas.
Publs. *Kanthapura, Cow of the Barricades, The Serpent and the Rope*; short stories in French and English, *The Cat and Shakespeare*, a novel.
c/o Department of Philosophy, University of Texas, Austin, Tex., U.S.A.

Rao, Vijayendra Kasturi Ranga Varadaraja, M.A., B.A., PH.D., PH.D., D.C.L.; Indian economist and educationist; b. 8 July 1908; ed. Wilson Coll., Bombay, and Gonville and Caius Coll., Cambridge.
Principal and Prof. of Econs., L.D. Arts Coll., Ahmedabad 37-42; Prof. and Head of Dept. of Econs., Delhi Univ. 42-57; Dir. of Statistics, Govt. of India 44-45; Planning Adviser, Govt. of India 45-46; Food and Econ. Adviser, Embassy of India, Washington 46-47; Founder and Dir. Delhi School of Econs., Delhi Univ. 49-57, Vice-Chancellor, 57-60, Prof. emer. 66-; Founder and Dir. Inst. of Econ. Growth 60-63; mem. Indian Planning Comm. 63-66; Chair. UN Sub-Comm. on Econ. Devt. 47-50; mem. Lok Sabha

37-; Union Minister for Transport and Shipping 67-69, for Education and Youth Services 69-71; founder and Dir. Inst. for Social and Econ. Change, Bangalore 72; Hon. D.C.L. (Oxford) 69; Hon. Fellow Gonville and Caius Coll., Cambridge 71; Padma Vibhushan Award 74.
Publs. *Taxation of Income in India* 31, *An Essay on India's National Income, 1925-29* 39, *The National Income of British India, 1931-32* 40, *War and Indian Economy* 43, *India and International Currency Plans* 46, *Post-war Rupee* 48, *Foreign Aid and India's Economic Development* 62, *Essays on Economic Development* 63, *Greater Delhi—A Study in Urbanisation 1947-57* 65, *Education and Human Resource Development* 66, *Gandhian Alternative to Western Socialism* 70, *The Nehru Legacy* 71, *Values and Economic Development, The Indian Challenge* 71, *Growth with Justice in Asian Agriculture, Inflation and India's Economic Crisis* (co-author) 73, *Iran's Fifth Plan—An Attempted Economic Leap* 75, *The Indian Road to Democratic Socialism—An Indian View* 76.
Post Bag No. 4003, Bangalore 560040; Home: "Dayanidi", 1170-A, 26-A Main Road, 4th "T" block Jayanagar, Bangalore 560011, India.
Telephone: 66224 (Office); 41515 (Home).

Rashid, Sheikh Mohammad, B.A., LL.B.; Pakistani lawyer and politician; b. 24 May 1915, Kalawala, Sheikhupura District.
Joined Muslim League 40; imprisoned for political activities 47; mem. Pakistan Muslim League Council 48-50; organized Azad Pakistan Party (later re-named Nat. Awami Party), Sec.-Gen. 52; launched Kisan Morcha Movt. Lahore 56; founder mem. Pakistan People's Party; Advocate, Supreme Court of Pakistan; mem. Nat. Assembly; Minister of Social Welfare, Health and Family Planning 71-74, of Food, Agriculture, Co-operatives, Works, Underdeveloped Areas and Land Reforms Oct. 74-, concurrently of Works Oct. 74-Feb. 76.
8 Zaldar Road, Ichhra, Lahore; 59-9F/6-3 Islamabad, Pakistan.
Telephone: 22633 (Office); 21550 (Home).

Rashidov, Sharaf Rashidovich; Soviet politician; b. 1917; ed. Zhizak Teachers' Training Coll., Uzbek State Univ.
Teacher 36-37; Sec. and Asst. Ed. 38-41, Ed. of the newspaper *Lenin-Yuly* 41, 43; School Dir. 42; cadres Sec. of the Samarkand Regional Cttee. of the Party 44-47; Chief Ed. of the republican newspaper *Kzyl Uzbekistan*, Pres. of the Presidium of the Uzbek Union of Soviet Writers 47-50; Pres. of the Presidium of the Supreme Soviet of Uzbekistan, Vice-Pres. of the Presidium of the Supreme Soviet of the U.S.S.R. 50-59; one of the chief organisers of the Afro-Asian Solidarity Cttee., Cairo 57; 1st Sec. Uzbek Communist Party 59-; Candidate mem. Presidium of Cen. Cttee. of C.P.S.U. 61-66, Alt. mem. Politburo 66-; awarded Order of Lenin, Order of the Red Banner of Labour, Order of the Red Star, Badge of Honour.
Central Committee of Communist Party of Uzbekistan, Tashkent, Uzbek S.S.R., U.S.S.R.

Rasulov, Jabar; Soviet politician; b. 1913; ed. Mid-Asian Cotton Inst.
Member of Communist Party 39-; People's Commissar for Agriculture, Tadzhik 45; Chair. Tadzhik Council of Ministers 46-55; Deputy U.S.S.R. Supreme Soviet 46, 50, 54, 58, 62, 66; Deputy Chair. Soviet of Union; mem. Cen. Revision Comm., C.P.S.U. 52-56; mem. Bureau Cen. Cttee. C.P., Tadzhik S.S.R. 54; mem. Econ. Comm., Council of Nationalities, U.S.S.R. Supreme Soviet 54-58; Deputy Minister of Agriculture U.S.S.R. 55; Sec. Gen. Cttee. Tadzhik C.P. 58-60; Amb. to Togo 60-61; First Sec. Cen. Cttee. of C.P. of Tadzhik S.S.R. 61-; mem. Cen. Cttee. C.P.S.U. 56-; Order of Lenin (five times); Order of the Red Banner of Labour.
Central Committee of Communist Party of Tadzhik S.S.R., Dushanbe, Tadzhik S.S.R., U.S.S.R.

Rau, Chalapathi M., M.A., B.L.; Indian newspaper editor.
Assistant Editor *National Herald*, Lucknow 38-42; Asst. Editor *Hindustan Times*, New Delhi 43-45; Asst. Editor *National Herald* 45-46, and Editor 46-; Alt. rep. UNESCO Gen. Conf. New Delhi 56, Paris 60; Rep. UN Gen. Assembly 58; Vice-Pres. UNESCO Conf. on Journalism Training 56; Rep. UN Gen. Assembly 58; Pres. Indian Fed. of Working Journalists; mem. Indian Press Comm., Exec. Cttee. Jawaharlal Nehru Memorial Trust, Exec. Council Nehru University; Chair. Nehru Fund, Nehru Memorial Museum and Library; Nehru Award; Hon. D.Litt. (Agra, Andhra Univs.), Hon. LL.D. (Sri Venkateswara Univ.).
Publ. *Fragments of a Revolution, Gandhi and Nehru* 67, *The Press in India* 68, *All in All* 72, *Jawaharlal Nehru* 73.
National Herald, Herald House, Bahadushah, Zafar, Marg, New Delhi; and 13 Shahjahan Road, New Delhi, India.
Telephone: 271547 (Office); 383855 (Home).

Rau, Lady Dhanvanthi Rama, M.A.; Indian social worker; b. 10 May 1893; ed. St. Mary's High School, Hubli, and Presidency Coll., Univ. of Madras.
Lecturer in English, Queen Mary's Coll., Univ. of Madras 17-19; Sec. All India Child Marriage Abolition League, Simla 27-28; mem. Board, Int. Alliance of Women for Suffrage and Equal Citizenship 32-38; Pres. Bombay Branch, All India Women's Conf. (A.I.W.C.) 46, Pres. A.I.W.C. 46-47; Pres. Family Planning Asscn. of India 49-63; mem. Family Planning Programmes and Research Cttee., Ministry of Health, Govt. of India 53, Chair. Social and Moral Hygiene Enquiry Cttee. 55; mem. Central Social Welfare Board 56-61; mem. Consultative Cttee. of Planning Comm. for Third Five Year Plan (Health) 61; Pres. Int. Planned Parenthood Fed. 63-71; Kaiser-I-Hind Gold Medal (U.K.) 38; Lasker Award (U.S.A.) 55; Padma Bhushan 59.
D/10, Mafatlal Park, Bhulabhai Desai Road, Bombay 26, India.

Rau, Santha Rama (daughter of Lady Rama Rau, *q.v.*); Indian writer; b. 24 Jan. 1923; ed. St. Paul's Girls' School, London, and Wellesley Coll., U.S.A.
Numerous journeys in Europe, India, America, South-East Asia, Japan and Russia; fmr. teacher Hani Freedom School, Tokyo; English teacher at Sarah Lawrence Coll. 71-; Hon. doctorates from Bates, Brandeis and Roosevelt Colls.
Publs. *Home to India, East of Home, Remember the House, View to the South-East, My Russian Journey, The Cooking of India* 69, *The Adventuress* 71; dramatised version of E. M. Forster's *A Passage to India*; *Gifts of Passage* (autobiog.).
10/D Mafatlal Park, Bhulabhai Desai Road, Bombay, India; and 522 East 89th Street, New York, N.Y. 10028, U.S.A.

Ray, Ajit Nath, M.A.; Indian judge; b. 29 Jan. 1912, Calcutta; ed. Presidency Coll., Calcutta, Oriel Coll., Oxford and Gray's Inn, London.
Formerly practised as a barrister, Calcutta High Court; Judge, Calcutta High Court 57; Judge, Supreme Court of India 69-73, Chief Justice 73-; Hon. Fellow, Oriel Coll. Oxford; Pres. Int. Law Asscn.
15 Panditia Place, Calcutta 29; 5 Krishna Menon Marg, New Delhi 11, India.
Telephone: 47-5213 (Calcutta); 372922 and 375439 (New Delhi).

Ray, Satyajit; Indian film director; b. 2 May 1921; ed. Ballygunge Govt. School, Presidency Coll., Calcutta.
Commerical artist in Calcutta before beginning his career

in films; directed *Pather Panchali* 54 (Cannes Int. Film Festival Award for "the most human document" 56, Golden Laurel Award, Edinburgh Film Festival 57), *Aparajito* 56 (sequel to *Pather Panchali*, Grand Prix, Venice Film Festival 57), *The Philosopher's Stone*, *Jalsaghar* (The Music Room), *Apur Sansar* (The World of Apu), *The Goddess* 61, *Three Daughters* 61, *Abhijan* 62, *Kanchanjangha* 62, *Mahanagar* 64, *Charulata* 65, *Kapurush-o-Mahapurush* 65, *Nayak* 66, *Chiriakhana* 68, *The Adventures of Goopy and Bagha* 69, *Days and Nights in the Forest* 69, *Seemabaddha* (Company Limited) 70, *Pratidwandi* 71, *The Adversary* 71, *Company Limited* 72, *Distant Thunder* 73 (Golden Bear Award, Berlin Film Festival 73), *Golden Fortress* 74, *The Middleman* 75; composed the music for all his films since *Three Daughters*; Editor *Sande*, children's magazine; Magsaysay Award for Journalism and Literature 67; Order of the Yugoslav Flag 71; Hon. D.Litt. (Royal Coll. of Art, London) 74.
Flat No. 8, 1/1 Bishop Lefroy Road, Calcutta 20, India.
Telephone: 44-8747.

Ray, Siddhartha Sankar; Indian politician; b. 20 Oct. 1920, Calcutta; ed. Mitra Inst., Calcutta, Presidency Coll., Calcutta, Univ. Law Coll., Calcutta, London Univ.
Called to the Bar, Inner Temple, London; joined Calcutta Bar 47; mem. Legislative Assem. 57, re-elected 58, 62, 67, 69; fmr. Minister of Law and Tribal Welfare, Govt. of West Bengal; Leader of Opposition, West Bengal Govt. 67; mem. Lok Sabha 70, West Bengal Legislative Assembly 72-, Minister of Educ., Culture and Social Welfare, Govt. of India 71-72; Chief Minister of W. Bengal 72-; Congress Party.
Writers' Buildings, Calcutta; and 2 Beltola Road, Calcutta 700026, India.

Raza, Nawabzada Agha Mohammad; Pakistani diplomatist; ed. Bishop Cotton's School, Simla and Royal Mil. Acad., Sandhurst.
Worked in Foreign and Political Dept., Govt. of India 30-34; served in World War II; on establishment of Pakistan was appointed Adjutant-Gen. responsible for reorganization of Pakistan Army; Amb. to People's Repub. of China 51-54, 62-66, to Iran 55-59, to France 60-62, to Italy 66-69, to U.S.A. (also accred. to Mexico, Venezuela and Jamaica) 71-72; Sec. Ministry of Foreign Affairs 72-; Hilal-i-Quaid-i-Azam, Hilal-i-Khidmat, Sitara-i-Pakistan, and decorations from France, Iran and The Vatican.
Ministry of Foreign Affairs, Islamabad, Pakistan.

Read, Air Marshal Charles Frederick, C.B., C.B.E., D.F.C., A.F.C.; retd. Australian air force officer; b. 9 Nov. 1918, Sydney; ed. Sydney Grammar School and Imperial Defence Coll.
Director Operations, Royal Australian Air Force 60-64, Commdt., R.A.A.F. Acad., Point Cook, Vic. 66-68, O.C. R.A.A.F. Richmond, N.S.W. 68-69, Deputy Chief of Staff 69-72, Chief of Staff 72-75.
2007 Pittwater Road, Bayview, New South Wales 2104, Australia.
Telephone: 997-1686.

Reddi, Bezwada Gopala; Indian politician; b. 5 Aug. 1907; ed. Visva Bharathi, Santiniketan.
Served in Govt. of Madras successively as Minister of Local Administration, Leader of House and Minister for Finance, Commercial Taxes, Elections, Agencies, Motor Transport and Registration; Pro-Chancellor of Andhra Pradesh Univ. 51-57; head of United Congress Legislative Party, Andhra Pradesh Assembly 55-; Chief Minister and Minister of Finance, Education, Press, Stationery and Home Dept., Andhra Pradesh 55-56, Home Minister 56-57, Finance Minister 57-58; Minister for Economic Affairs Govt. of India April-May 58, Minister Revenue and Civil Expenditure May 58-61, of Housing, Works and Supply 61-62; Minister of Information and Broadcasting 62-63; Gov. of Uttar Pradesh 67-72; mem. Rajya Sabha 58-60, Lok Sabha 62; mem. Indian Congress Party, Pres. Andhra Pradesh Congress Cttee. 53; Deputy Leader Congress Party 65-67; Hon. D.Litt.
Publs. Eight books including *Chitranguda*.
c/o Governor's Camp, Raj Bhavan, Lucknow, Uttar Pradesh, Naini Tal, India.

Reddy, Kasu Brahmananda, B.A., B.L.; Indian politician b. 1909.
President Guntur District Board 36; mem. Madras Assembly 46-52; Gen. Sec. Andhra Pradesh Congress Cttee. 55; Minister of Finance and Planning, Andhra Pradesh 60-62, of Finance and Co-operation 62-64, Chief Minister 64-71; Union Minister of Communications Jan.-Oct. 74; Minister of Home Affairs Oct. 74-.
Ministry of Home Affairs, New Delhi, India.

Reddy, Kolli Venkata Raghunatha, M.A., LL.B.; Indian lawyer and politician; b. 4 Sept. 1924; ed. V. R. Coll., Nellore, and Annamalai Univ. and Lucknow Univ.
Member Senate Annamalai Univ. 47-59; Advocate, Madras High Court 50, Supreme Court 58, also Andhra Pradesh High Court; mem. Rajya Sabha 62-; Union Minister of State for Industrial Devt. and Company Affairs 67-70, of Company Affairs 70-72, of Labour and Rehabilitation 73-.
Publ. *Criminal Law—Procedural and Substantial.*
Ministry of Labour and Rehabilitation, New Delhi; and c/o Rajya Sabha, New Delhi, India.

Reddy, Marri Channa, M.B., B.S.; Indian agriculturalist and politician; b. 13 Jan. 1919; ed. Chadarghat High School and Osmania Univ.
Left medical practice to devote himself to politics in Hyderabad; held organizational posts in Indian Nat. Congress Party; leader in Hyderabad Congress; mem. Rajya Sabha 50-51; Minister of Agriculture, Andhra Pradesh 52, later Minister of Planning, Rehabilitation, Panchyat Raj, Industry and Commerce, Commercial Taxes, Education and Finance, Andhra Pradesh; Union Minister of Steel, Mines and Metals 67-68; now Gov. of Uttar Pradesh.
Raj Bhavan, Lucknow, Uttar Pradesh, India.

Reddy, Neelam Sanjiva; Indian politician; b. 1913; ed. Adyar Arts Coll., Anantapur.
Sec. Andhra P.C.C. 36-46; active in Satyagraha movement; mem. and Sec. Madras Legislative Assembly 46; mem. Indian Constituent Assembly 47; Minister for Prohibition, Housing and Forests, Madras Govt. 49-51; Pres. Andhra Pradesh Congress Cttee. 51-; mem. Rajya Sabha 52-53; mem. Andhra Pradesh Legislative Assembly 53-; Deputy Chief Minister, Andhra Pradesh 53-56, Chief Minister 56-57; Leader, Andhra Congress Legislature Party 53-; Pres. All-India Congress Party 60-62; Chief Minister, Andhra Pradesh 62-64; Minister of Steel and Mines, India 64-65, of Transport, Aviation, Shipping and Tourism 65-67; Speaker of Lok Sabha 67-69; candidate in presidential election 69.
c/o Lok Sabha, New Delhi, India.

Reddy, Pingle Jaganmohan, B.COM., B.A., LL.B. (CANTAB.), BARR.-AT-LAW; Indian judge; b. 23 Jan. 1910, Hyderabad; ed. Univs. of Leeds and Cambridge.
Legal practice 37-46; Legal dept. Govt. of Hyderabad 46-48; District and Sessions Judge, Secunderabad 48; Puisne Judge, High Court, Hyderabad 52-56; Judge, High Court, Andhra Pradesh 56-66, Chief Justice 66-69; Judge Supreme Court of India 69-; mem. Syndicate and Dean, Faculty of Law, Osmania Univ. 52-59.
Publs. *The Hyderabad Excess Profits Tax Act*, *Quest of Justice*.
11 Motilal Nehru Marg, New Delhi 11; also Lumbini Gardens, Saifabad, Hyderabad 22, India.

Reece, Eric Elliott; Australian trade unionist and fmr. politician; b. 6 July 1909, Mathinna, Tasmania.
Former organizer, Australian Workers' Party; Fed. Pres. Australian Labor Party 52-55; mem. for Braddon, Tasmanian House of Assembly 46-75; State Minister of Housing and Building Supplies, Tasmania 46-47, of Lands and Works 47-58, of Mines 47-69, 72-75; Treas. 59-69, 72-75; Deputy Premier of Tasmania 58, Premier 58-69, 72-75; Leader of Opposition 69-72.
59 Howard Road, Glenorchy, Tasmania 7010, Australia.

Rees, Albert Lloyd George, D.SC., PH.D., D.I.C., F.R.A.C.I., F.A.A.; Australian scientist; b. 15 Jan. 1916, Melbourne; ed. Univs. of Melbourne and London.
Lecturer in Chem., Univ. of W. Australia 39; Beit Scientific Research Fellow, Imperial Coll., London 39-41; Extra-Mural Research in Chem. Defence, Ministry of Supply, U.K., 39-41; Research and Devt. Philips Electrical Industries, U.K. 41-44; with Commonwealth Scientific and Industrial Research Org. (CSIRO) 44-, Chief Div. of Chemical Physics 58-; Chair. Chem. Research Labs 61-70; mem. Bureau and Exec. Cttee., Int. Union of Pure and Applied Chem. 63-73, Vice-Pres. 67-69, Pres. 69-71; mem. Exec. Cttee. ICSU 69-72, Gen. Cttee. 72-; mem. Board of Studies, Victoria Inst. of Colls. 68-; Pres. Royal Australian Chem. Inst. (R.A.C.I.) 67-68; mem. Council Australian Acad. of Science 63-68, 69-73; Liversidge Lecturer, Royal Soc. of N.S.W. 52; Einstein Memorial Lecturer, Australian Inst. of Physics 70; Rennie Medal 46, H. G. Smith Medal (R.A.C.I.) 51, Leighton Memorial Medal (R.A.C.I.) 70.
Publs. *Chemistry of the Defect Solid State* 54, and many articles in learned journals.
CSIRO, Division of Chemical Physics, P.O.B. 160, Clayton, Victoria 3168; Home: 9 Ajana Street, North Balwyn, Victoria 3104, Australia.
Telephone: 544-0633 (Office); 857-9358 (Home).

Refshauge, Major-Gen. Sir William Dudley, C.B.E., E.D., M.B., B.S., F.R.C.O.G., F.R.A.C.S., F.R.A.C.P., F.A.C.M.A.; Australian medical administrator; b. 3 April 1913, Melbourne; ed. Hampton High School and Scotch Coll., Melbourne and Melbourne Univ.
Resident Medical Officer, Alfred Hosp., Melbourne 39, Women's Hosp. Melbourne 46; Registrar, Women's Hosp. 46-47, Medical Supt. 48-51; Deputy Dir.-Gen. Army Medical Services 51-55, Dir.-Gen. 55-60; Commonwealth of Australia Dir.-Gen. of Health 60-73; Chair. Nat. Health and Medical Research Council 60-73, Commonwealth Council for Nat. Fitness 60-73, Commonwealth Health Insurance Council 60-73, etc.; mem. Exec. Board, WHO 67-70, Chair. 69-70; Pres. World Health Assembly 71; Sec.-Gen. World Medical Asscn. 73-76; Fellow, Royal Soc. of Medicine; Hon. Life mem. Australian Dental Asscn.; Hon. Fellow, Royal Soc. of Health; patron Australian Sports Medicine Asscn.
Publs. various publications in *Medical Journal of Australia* and *New Zealand Medical Journal.*
102 Dalley Crescent, Latham, A.C.T. 2601, Australia.
Telephone: 544573 (Home).

Renshaw, John Brophy; Australian politician; b. 8 Aug. 1909, Wellington, N.S.W.; ed. Binnaway School and Holy Cross Coll., Ryde, Sydney.
Farmer; mem. Binnaway-Coonabarabran Shire Council 37; Shire Press. 39; mem. New South Wales legislature 41-, Minister for Lands, N.S.W. Govt. 50-52, for Public Works and Local Govt. 52-59, Deputy Premier and Treas. 59-64, Minister for Industrial Development and Decentralization 62-64, Premier, Treas., Minister for Industrial Devt. and Decentralization 64-65, Treas. May 76-; Leader of Opposition in Legislative Assembly 65-68; Labor Party.
Parliament House, Sydney, New South Wales, Australia.
Telephone: 2032111.

Reyes, Narciso G., A.B.; Philippine journalist and diplomatist; b. 6 Feb. 1914; ed. Univ. of Santo Tomás.
Associate Editor *Philippines Commonweal,* Manila 35-41; mem. Nat. Language Faculty, Ateneo de Manila 39-41; Assoc. Editor *Manila Post* 45-47; Assoc. News Editor *Evening News,* Manila 47-48; Man. Dir. Philippine Newspaper Guild's organ 47-48; Adviser to Philippine Mission to UN and Rep. of the Philippines to numerous ECOSOC sessions and UN Gen. Assemblies, and many other UN activities 48-54; Philippine Amb. to Burma 58-62, to Indonesia 62-67, to U.K. 67-70; Perm. Rep. to UN 70-; Chair. 19th Session UN Social Development Comm. 68, Social Panel, Int. Non-Governmental Organizations Conf. on Human Rights 68, 26th UN Gen. Assembly Econ. and Financial Cttee., UNICEF Exec. Board 72-74; Pres. UNDP Governing Council 74-.
Permanent Mission of the Philippines to the United Nations, 556 Fifth Avenue, New York, N.Y. 10036, U.S.A.

Riches, Edward John, M.A.; New Zealand international civil servant (retd.); b. 30 July 1905; ed. Univ. of New Zealand and Univ. of Michigan, U.S.A.
Joined Research Div. of Int. Labour Office 27, Asst. Econ. Adviser 41, Acting Chief, Econ. and Statistical Section 41-46, Econ. Adviser 46-60, Treasurer and Financial Comptroller (Asst. Dir.-Gen.) 61-70, Special Adviser (part-time, in charge of planning and construction of new headquarters) 70-75.
22 Avenue Krieg, 1208 Geneva, Switzerland.
Telephone: 47-86-69 (Home).

Ride, Sir Lindsay Tasman, Kt., C.B.E.; British (b. Australian) physiologist and specialist in Asian studies; b. 10 Oct. 1898; ed. Scotch Coll., Melbourne, Melbourne Univ., New Coll., Oxford, and Guy's Hospital Medical School, London.
Former Demonstrator in Physiology and Pharmacology, Guy's Hospital, London; Prof. of Physiology, Univ. of Hong Kong 28-52, Dean of Medical Faculty and Vice-Chancellor 49-64, Dir. of Inst. of Modern Asian Studies 60-64, Prof. Emer. 65-; Chair. Asscn. of Univs. of British Commonwealth 60-61; Vice-Pres. Asscn. of S.E. Asian Institutions of Higher Learning 63-64; Research Assoc., Inst. of Social Studies, Chinese Univ. of Hong Kong 65-68; Hon. LL.D. (Toronto, Melbourne, London and Hong Kong); Hon. R.A.M.
Publs. *Genetics and the Clinician* 40, *Morrison, The Scholar and the Man* 58, *Biographical Note on James Legge* 61, *The Old Protestant Cemetery, Macao* 63 and various papers on human genetics.
Villa Monte Rosa, E2/11, 41A Stubbs Road, Hong Kong.

Rigby, Sir Ivo Charles Clayton, Kt.; British judge; b. 2 June 1911; ed. Magdalen Coll. School, Oxford and Inner Temple.
Called to the Bar 32; Magistrate, Gambia 35-38; Chief Magistrate, Crown Counsel and Pres. of District Court, Palestine 38-48; Asst. Judge, Nyasaland 48-54; Pres. of Sessions Court, Malaya 54-55; Puisne Judge, Malaya 52-61; Senior Puisne Judge, Hong Kong 61-70, Chief Justice of Hong Kong and Brunei 70-73; Pres. Court of Appeal, Brunei June 73-; Recorder of the Crown Court (U.K.) 75-.
Publs. *The Law Reports of Nyasaland* 34-52.
8 More's Garden, Cheyne Walk, London, SW3 5BB, England.
Telephone: 01-352 0120.

Rinchin, Lodongiyn; Mongolian agronomist and politician; b. 25 July 1929, Gobi Altai; ed. Agricultural Inst., U.S.S.R.
Agronomist, Chief of Dept., Chief Agronomist, Ministry of Livestock Husbandry 55-60; Deputy Minister, First Deputy Minister, Ministry of Agriculture 60-67; Chair. Supreme Council, Agricultural Co-operative Board 67-70; Minister of Foreign Affairs 70-; mem. Cen. Cttee. Mongolian People's Revolutionary Party 61-; Deputy to the Great People's Hural; various state orders and medals.
Ministry of Foreign Affairs, Ulan Bator, Mongolia.

Rishtya, Kassim; Afghan civil servant and diplomatist; b. 1913; ed. Istiqlal High School, Kabul.
Clerk in Press Section, Ministry of Foreign Affairs 31; Chief Clerk Foreign Relations Section, Ministry of Communications 32; trans. at Afghan Acad. of Literature 33, mem. 34, Dir. Publs. Div. 36, Vice-Pres. 38; Dir.-Gen. of Publs. Press Dept. 40-44, Pres. 48; Pres. Govt. Econ. Planning Board 49, Govt. Co-operative Org. 52, Bakhtar News Agency 54; Minister of Information 56-60; Afghan Del. to UN 10th Gen. Assembly; headed Press Del. to U.S.S.R. 56; Amb. to Czechoslovakia, Poland and Hungary 60-62, to United Arab Republic 62-63; Minister of Information 63-64, of Finance 64-65; mem. Constituent Assembly 64; Amb. to Japan 70-73 (retd.), concurrently accred. to the Philippines; Editor *Kabul Almanack* and *Kabul Magazine* 36-38; mem. Drafting Cttee. for the New Constitution 63-64.
Publs. *Afghanistan in the 19th Century*, *Jawani Afghan*, and several novels.
c/o Ministry of Foreign Affairs, Kabul, Afghanistan.

Ritchie, Robert James, C.B.E.; Australian airline executive; b. 5 Nov. 1915; ed. Cleveland Street High School, Sydney.
Joined Amalgamated Wireless Australia Ltd. 29, later flew with Kingsford Smith Aerial Services Ltd., Sydney, and Mandated Airlines Ltd., New Guinea; Pilot, W. R. Carpenter & Co. 38; First Officer, Qantas Empire Airways Ltd. 43, Captain 44, Flight Captain 46; Flight Captain (Constellations) 47-48; Flight Superintendent, Kangaroo Service 47-49; Asst. Operations Manager, Qantas 49-55, Technical Manager 55-59, Dir. of Technical Services 59-61, Deputy Chief Exec. and Deputy General Manager 61-67, General Manager 67-, Dir. 70-; Vice-Chair. Air Niugini 73-; Dir. Qantas Wentworth Holdings Ltd. 67-.
Qantas House, 70 Hunter Street, Sydney, New South Wales; Home: 12 Graham Avenue, Pymble, New South Wales 2073, Australia.

Rithaudeen al-Haj bin Tengku Ismail, Y.M. Tengku Ahmad; Malaysian lawyer and politician; b. 1933; mem. of Royal family of Kelantan; ed. Nottingham Univ.
Member of Kelantan State Parl. for Kota Bharu; fmr. legal adviser to Kelantan State Govt., resigned to enter private practice; Minister with Special Functions Assisting Prime Minister on Foreign Affairs 73-75; mem. Supreme Council, United Malays' Nat. Org. June 75-; Minister for Foreign Affairs Aug. 75-; Chair. Farmers' Org. Authority.
Ministry of Foreign Affairs, Kuala Lumpur, Malaysia.

Rivett, Rohan Deakin, B.A.; Australian journalist; b. 1917; ed. Wesley Coll., Melbourne, Queen's Coll., Melbourne Univ. and Balliol Coll., Oxford.
Reporter, *Melbourne Argus* 39-40; War Corresp. Radio Singapore 41-42; Prisoner of War 42-45; Reporter, *Melbourne Herald* 46-48, Corresp. in China 47; Reporter Melbourne Herald Cable Service, Britain and Europe 48-51; Editor-in-Chief *Adelaide News* 51-60; Dir. News Ltd. of Australia 52-60; News Commentator, BBC and ABC 46-; Chair. Australian Cttee., Int. Press Inst. (IPI) 54-62, Dir. IPI 62-64, Hon. Life mem. 64-; Commentator on int. affairs (TV and radio) 64-; Columnist, *Canberra Times* 64-; Pres. Melbourne Press Club 74-76; mem. Council Soc. of Authors 65-, Monash Univ. 74-; Coronation Medal; Commonwealth Literary Award 67; Fellow, Queen's Coll., Univ. of Melbourne 67; Fellow, Royal Soc. of Arts (U.K.) 72.
Publs. *Behind Bamboo* 46, *Near North* 48, Three Cricket Booklets 47-51, *The Migrant and the Community* 58, *Australia Looks Ahead* (Co-Author) 61, *Australia and the Monarchy* (Co-Author) 64, *Australian Citizen: Herbert Brookes 1867-1963* 65, *The Journalist's Craft* (Co-Author) 65, *Australia* 68, *Writing About Australia* 69, *David Rivett—Fighter for Australian Science* 72.
147 Wattle Valley Road, Camberwell, Victoria, 3124, Australia.
Telephone: Melbourne 29-39-13.

Roberts, Sir Denys Tudor Emil, K.B.E., Q.C., M.A., B.C.L.; British barrister and administrator; b. 19 Jan. 1923, London; ed. Aldenham School, Wadham Coll., Oxford and Lincoln's Inn.
Royal Artillery (Captain) 43-46; English Bar 50-53; Crown Counsel, Nyasaland (now Malawi) 53-59; Attorney-Gen. Gibraltar 60-62; Solicitor-Gen. Hong Kong 62-66, Attorney-Gen. 66-73; Colonial Sec. Hong Kong 73-.
Publs. five novels 55-65.
Colonial Secretariat, Hong Kong; Home: Victoria House, 15 Barker Road, Hong Kong.

Robertson, Sir Rutherford Ness, Kt., C.M.G., D.SC., PH.D., F.R.S.; Australian botanist; b. 29 Sept. 1913; ed. St. Andrew's Coll., Christchurch, New Zealand, Sydney Univ., and St. John's Coll., Cambridge.
Assistant Lecturer, later Lecturer in Botany, Sydney Univ. 39-46; Senior Research Officer, later Chief Research Officer, Commonwealth Scientific and Industrial Research Org. (C.S.I.R.O.), Div. of Food Preservation 46-59, mem. Exec. of C.S.I.R.O. 59-62; Visiting Prof. Univ. of California 58-59; Prof. of Botany, Univ. of Adelaide 62-69; Chair. Australian Research Grants Cttee. 65-69, Australian Nat. Univ.; Master, Univ. House 70-72; Dir. Research School Biological Sciences, Australian Nat. Univ. 73-; Fellow Australian Acad. of Science 54, Pres. 70-74; Foreign Assoc. U.S. Acad. of Sciences 62; Pres. Australian and New Zealand Assen. for the Advancement of Science 65; Foreign mem. American Philosophical Soc. 71; Hon. mem. Royal Soc. of New Zealand 71; Foreign Hon. mem. American Acad. of Arts and Sciences 72; Hon. Fellow St. John's Coll., Cambridge 73-; Clarke Memorial Medal, Royal Soc. of New South Wales 54, Farrer Memorial Medal 63, A.N.Z.A.A.S. Medal 68, Mueller Medal 70, Burnet Medal 75.
Publs. *Electrolytes in Plant Cells* (co-author) 61, *Protons, Electrons, Phosphorylation and Active Transport* 68.
Research School of Biological Science, Australian National University, Canberra, Australia.
Telephone: 49-2469.

Robinson, Kenneth Ernest, C.B.E., M.A., D.LITT., F.R.HIST.S.; British university teacher; b. 9 March 1914; de. Monoux Grammar School, Walthamstow, and Hertford Coll., Oxford, and London School of Economics.
Entered Colonial Office 36; Asst. Sec. 46-48, resgnd.; Fellow of Nuffield Coll. 48-57, Librarian 51-57; Reader in Commonwealth Govt., Oxford 48-57; Leverhulme Research Fellow 52-53; Visiting Lecturer, School of Advanced Int. Studies, Johns Hopkins Univ. 54, Duke Univ. 63, Acadia Univ. 63; part-time mem., Directing Staff, Civil Service Selection Board 51-56; Prof. of Commonwealth Affairs and Dir. of Inst. of Commonwealth Studies, Univ. of London 57-65; mem. Colonial Econ. Research Cttee. 49-62, Colonial Social Science Research Council 58-62, Council of Overseas Devt. Inst. 60-65, Royal Inst. of Int. Affairs 62-65, Int. African Inst. 60-65, African Studies Assen. of U.K. 63-65, Association of Commonwealth Universities 67-69, Hong Kong Management Assen. 66-72, World Health Foundation Hong Kong 71-72, Admin. Board, S.E. Asia Inst. of Higher Learning 71-72, Inter-Univ. Council for Higher Educ. Overseas 73-; Gov. London School of Econs. 59-65; Vice-Chancellor, Univ. of Hong Kong 65-72; Hallsworth Res. Fellow, Manchester Univ. 72-74; Dir. Commonwealth Studies Resources Survey, Univ. of London 74-76; corresp. mem. Acad. des Sciences d'Outre-Mer, Paris, Editor *Journal of Commonwealth Political Studies* 61-65; Special Commonwealth Award, Ministry of

Overseas Devt. 65; Hon. LL.D. (Chinese Univ. of Hong Kong) 69, Hon. D.Litt. (Univ. of Hong Kong) 72.
Publs. *Africa Today* (co-author) 55, *Africa in the Modern World* (co-author) 55, *Five Elections in Africa* (with W. J. M. Mackenzie) 60, *Essays in Imperial Government* (with A. F. Madden) 63, *The Dilemmas of Trusteeship* 65, *A Decade of the Commonwealth* (with W. B. Hamilton and C. Goodwin) 66, *University Co-operation and Asian Development* (co-author) 67, *L'Europe au XIXe et XXe siècles*, Vol. VII (co-author) 68.
10c St. Augustine's Road, London, NW1 9RN; The Old Rectory, Church Westcote, Oxfordshire, England.
Telephone: 01-485-1198; and Shipton-under-Wychwood 830586.

Roem, Mohammad; Indonesian politician; b. 1908; ed. Law School, Jakarta.
Solicitor in private practice, Jakarta 39-45; fmr. leader of Islamic Youth Movement; Indonesian Minister of the Interior 46-48; Del. to Round Table Conf. with Netherlands Govt. 49; first High Commr. of Indonesia to the Netherlands 50; Minister of Foreign Affairs 50-51, of Home Affairs 52-53; First Vice-Premier 56-57; mem. Exec. Cttee. Masjumi Party 57-59, 3rd Deputy Chair. 59; Pres. Islamic Univ., Medan; detained early 60s; founder mem. Partai Muslimin Indonesia 67, Chair. 68-72.
c/o Jalan Tjhik Ditiro 58, Jakarta, Indonesia.

Romero, José E., A.B., LL.B.; Philippine diplomatist and attorney-at-law; b. 1897; ed. Univ. of the Philippines.
Elected mem. of Provincial Board of Oriental Negroes 25-31; House of Reps. and Nat. Assembly 31-46; Chair. of Cttee. on Public Instruction, House of Reps., and *ex-officio* mem. Board of Regents, Univ. of the Philippines 34-36; elected to Constitutional Convention and Chair. of Cttee. on Rules and Floor Leader 34-35; Floor Leader of Nat. Assembly 36-38; Chair. Cttee. on Economic Readjustment 38-41; Chair. Cttee. on Foreign Relations and of Joint Congressional Cttee. on Rehabilitation and Reconstruction 45-46; elected to Philippine Senate 46; Minister to Great Britain and concurrently to Norway, Sweden and Denmark 49-54; Rep. Philippines Sugar Asscn., Washington, D.C. 54-57; Sec.-Treas. Philippine Sugar Asscn. 57-59, 61-74, Senior Consultant 75-; Sec. of Educ. 59-61; Vice-Pres. Philippine Asscn.; Pres. Asscn. of Surviving Delegates to the First Constitutional Convention 60-, Philippine Constitution Asscn. 63-64; mem. Board of Regents, Univ. of the Philippines 59-69, Bar of U.S. Supreme Court, American Soc. of Int. Law; Patron Int. Bar Asscn.; Pres. Philippine Ambs. Asscn. 75.
Philippine Sugar Association, R-809 Sikatuna Building, Ayala Avenue, Makati, Rizal; 15 Galaxy Street, Bel-Air III, Makati, Rizal, Philippines.
Telephone: 88-60-62 (Office); 87-72-96 (Home).

Romualdez, Eduardo Z.; Philippine banker and politician; b. 22 Nov. 1909, Tolosa, Leyte; ed. Univs. of the Philippines and Santo Thomas, and Georgetown Univ., Washington, D.C.
President, Bankers Asscn. of the Philippines 50-53; Dir. Chamber of Commerce of the Philippines 50-52; Vice-Pres. American Bankers' Asscn. 51-56; Chair. Board of Dirs., Philippine Air Lines (PAL) 54-62, Pres. 61-62; Gov. IMF 56-61, IBRD 56-61, IFC 57-61; Chair. Rehabilitation Finance Corpn., Devt. Bank of the Philippines; Pres. Philippines Nat. Bank; Pres. Philippine Trust Co. 47-54, 62-65, Fidelity and Surety Co. of the Philippines Inc. 47-54, 62-65; Sec. of Finance, Repub. of the Philippines 65-70; Chair. Asian Devt. Bank 67-68; Amb. to U.S.A. 71-; mem. numerous cttees., etc., and del. to many int. confs.
Embassy of the Philippines, 1617 Massachusetts Ave., N.W., Washington, D.C. 20036, U.S.A.

Romulo, Brig.-Gen. Carlos Peña; Philippine writer, educator and diplomatist; b. 14 Jan. 1899; ed. Univ. of the Philippines and Columbia Univ.
Associate Prof. of English, Univ. of the Philippines 26-30, mem. Board of Regents 31-41; Editor-in-Chief TVT Publications 31, Publisher DMHM Newspapers 37-41; Staff of Gen. MacArthur and Sec. of Information and Public Relations, Philippine War Cabinet in U.S.A. 43-44, Brigadier-Gen. 44; Acting-Sec. of Public Instruction 44-45, Chief Del. to UN 45-55, Pres. 49-50, Security Council 57; Sec. of Foreign Affairs 50-52; Amb. to the U.S.A. 52-53, 55-62, Special Envoy 54-55, concurrently Minister to Cuba 59; Pres. Univ. of the Philippines 62-68, Philippine Acad. of Sciences and Humanities; Presidential Adviser on Foreign Affairs; Sec. Dept. of Educ. 66 68; Sec. for Foreign Affairs 68-; numerous decorations, honours, hon. degrees and awards.
Publs. *I saw the Fall of the Philippines* 42, *Mother America* 43, *My Brother Americans* 45, *Crusade in Asia* 55, *The Meaning of Bandung* 56, *The Magsaysay Story* 56, *Friend to Friend* 58, *I Walked with Heroes* (*An Autobiography*) 61, *Contemporary Nationalism and World Order* 64, *Mission to Asia* 64, *Identity and Change* 65, *Evasions and Response* 66, *Clarifying The Asian Mystique* 69.
Department of Foreign Affairs, Padre Faura, Manila; and 74 McKinley Road, Forbes Park, Makati, Rizal, Philippines.

Rosales, H. E. Cardinal Julio; Philippine ecclesiastic; b. 18 Sept. 1906.
Ordained 29; Bishop of Tagbiliran 46-49; Archbishop of Cebu 49-; cr. Cardinal 69; Pres. Catholic Bishops' Conf. of the Philippines 61-65, 74-76; mem. Sacred Congregation of the Clergy, Rome, Sacred Congregation of Catholic Educ., Rome, Secr. for Non-Christians, Rome; Grand Cross, Order of St. Raymundo de Pennafort, Knight Order of Corpus Christi in Toledo; Grand Cross of Isabel la Católica, Spain; LL.D. (Univ. of San Carlos); D.H. (De La Salle Coll.).
Archbishop's Residence, P.O.B. 52, Cebu City, Philippines.

Rowland, Air Marshal James Anthony, D.F.C., A.F.C., B.E., C.ENG., F.R.AE.S.; Australian air force officer; b. 1 Nov. 1922, Armidale, N.S.W.; ed. Univ. of Sydney.
Master Bomber, Pathfinder, Bomber Command R.A.F. 44; with R.A.A.F.: Chief Test Pilot, Aircraft Research and Devt. Unit 51-54, C.O. 58-60; Officer Commanding Research and Devt. 58-60; Chief Tech. Officer, No. 82 Wing 57, Mirage Mission, Paris 61-64; Commanding No. 3 Aircraft Depot, Amberley 67-68; Senior Tech. Staff Officer, HQ Operational Command 69-70; with Dept. of Air: Dir.-Gen. of Aircraft Eng. 72, Air. Mem. for Tech. Services 73-74; Chief of Air Staff, R.A.A.F. 75-; Councillor, Royal Aeronautical Soc., Australian Branch 73-75.
Publs. official reports, contributions to journals.
Department of Defence, Russell Offices, Canberra, A.C.T.; Home: 4 Galway Place, Deakin, A.C.T. 2600, Australia.
Telephone: 65-5474 (Office); 813483 (Home).

Rowland, John Russell; Australian diplomatist; b. 10 Feb. 1925; ed. Cranbrook School, Sydney, and Univ. of Sydney.
Department of External Affairs 44-, served Moscow 46-48, Saigon 52, 54-55, Washington 55-56, London 57-59; Asst. Sec., Dept. of External Affairs 61-65; Amb. to U.S.S.R. 65-68; First Asst. Sec. Dept. of External Affairs 69; High Commr. to Malaysia 69-72; Amb. to Austria 73-74, concurrently accred. to Czechoslovakia, Hungary and Switzerland; Deputy Sec., Dept. of Foreign Affairs 75-.
Publs. *The Feast of Ancestors, Snow* (poetry).
c/o Department of External Affairs, Canberra, A.C.T., Australia.

Rowling, Wallace Edward, M.A.; New Zealand politician; b. 15 Nov. 1927; ed. Nelson Coll. and Canterbury Univ.
Former Educ. Officer, New Zealand Army; mem. Parl. for Buller 62-72, Tasman 72-; Pres. Labour Party 70-73, 74-; Minister of Finance, in charge of Dept. of Statistics, Friendly Socs. 72-74; Prime Minister 74-Nov. 75; also

Minister of Foreign Affairs and Minister in Charge of Audit Dept., Legislative Dept. and N.Z. Security Intelligence Service 74-Nov. 75; Leader of the Opposition Dec. 75-.
Office of the Leader of the Opposition, Parliament Buildings, Wellington, New Zealand.

Roy, Bhabesh Chandra, D.I.C., M.SC., DR.ING.; Indian geologist; b. 1 Aug. 1907; ed. Imperial Coll., London, Univ. of Nancy, and Univ. of Freiberg, Germany.
Joined Geological Survey of India 37, Dir. 58-61, Dir.-Gen. 61-65; UN Fellow in U.S.A. and Canada 57; mem. Oil and Natural Gas Comm. 64; Del. to ECAFE Mineral Confs. in Tokyo 55, Kuala Lumpur 58, U.S.S.R., U.K., France and Germany 55, Rome and Bandung 63, Vienna 64, Antwerp 66, Mexico City 67, New Zealand 70; Leader Del. Int. Geological Congress, Copenhagen 60; and numerous other int. geological meetings; Pres. Geological, Mining and Metallurgical Inst. of India 58-59, Indian Asscn. of Geohydrologists 70-71; Co-ordinator Geological Map for Asia and Far East 58-68; Vice-Pres. Int. Union of Geological Sciences 61-68; Sec.-Gen. Int. Geol. Congress, New Delhi 64; Chair. Dept. of Geology, Univ. of Nigeria 66-67, U.G.C. Prof., Presidency Coll., Calcutta 68-; Editor *Journal of Mines, Metals and Fuels* 68-; Vice-Pres. IGC Comm., History of Geol. Sciences 68-; Fellow, Nat. Inst. of Sciences of India; Medal of Czechoslovak Acad. of Sciences 69.
Publs. include: *Mineral Resources of Bombay* 51, *Economic Geology and Mineral Resources of Saurashtra* 53, *The Nellore Mica Belt* 56, *The Economic Geology and Mineral Resources of Rajasthan and Ajmer* 57; numerous articles on Geology and Mineral Resources.
37/3, Southend Park, Calcutta 29, India.
Telephone: 46-3189.

Roy, Raja Tridiv; Pakistani politician; b. 14 May 1933.
Called to the Bar, Lincoln's Inn, London 51; Chief Chakma Community 53; mem. E. Pakistan Provincial Assembly 62-70; mem. Nat. Assembly 70-; Minister of Minority Affairs and of Tourism 71-74; rep. of Pakistan to 6th World Buddhist Council, Rangoon and 2,500th Buddha Jayanti celebrations, New Delhi 56, 10th conf. of World Fellowship of Buddhists, Colombo 72; del. to World Food Conference 63, to UN Gen. Assembly 64, 72; Special Envoy to S. Asian countries 71, to Latin America, U.S.A. and Caribbean 74-75; Adviser to Prime Minister on Tourism 75-.
248-BF 6/2, Margalla Road, Islamabad, Pakistan.

Roy Chowdhury, Devi Prasad, M.B.E.; Indian sculptor and painter; b. 15 June 1899.
Principal Govt. Coll. of Arts and Crafts, Madras 29-57; fmr. Chair. Lalita Kala Akad., New Delhi; Dir. and Pres. Art Seminar of UNESCO, Tokyo 55; Hon. Fellow Lalit Kala Acad., New Delhi; many prizes in Nat. Modern Sculpture exhbns., Govt. of India; Hon. D.Litt. (Rabindra Bharati Univ., Calcutta) 68; Padma Bhushan 58.
Sculptures include: *Martyrs Memorial* group composition of eleven double life size figures, New Delhi (work in progress 75), *Triumph of Labour* at Madras and New Delhi, *Mahatma Gandhi* at Madras and Calcutta, *Rhythm*, Nat. Museum, New Delhi, *Moti Lal Nehru* at Parliament House, New Delhi.
Publs. Twelve books of short stories and novels, and articles on art.
63 Shambhu Nath Pandit Street, Calcutta 25, India.
Telephone: 47-2921.

Rujirawongse, Gen. Prasert; Thai army officer and politician; b. 4 Dec. 1911, Chadaburi; ed. Royal Mil. Cadet Acad., Artillery School for Officers and Nat. Defence Coll.
Commissioned 32; Dep. Dir.-Gen. of Police 57, Dir.-Gen. 63, also Dep. Minister of Interior 63; Minister of Public Health 69, 72-73; Dir. of Civil Admin. 70; Dir. of Public Health and Educ. of Nat. Exec. Council 71-72; Chair. Bank of Ayudhya; Knight Grand Cordon, Order of Crown of Thailand, Order of White Elephant; Victory Medal, Chakra Mala Medal and other decorations.
Bank of Ayudhya Ltd., P.O. Box 491, Bangkok, Thailand.
Telephone: 49254 (Home).

Rukmini, Devi; Indian dancer and arts patron; b. 1904, Madurai.
Started dancing under Anna Pavlova; extensive tours throughout India and Europe with dance recitals and lectures; lecture visits to U.S.A.; also lectures and writes on Theosophy, Religion, Art, Culture, Educ., etc.; Dir. Arundale Training Centre, Madras, Int. Soc. for the Prevention of Cruelty to Animals, London for India, Dr. V. Swaminatha Iyer Tamil Library; Head Int. Theosophical Centre, Huizen, Holland; Pres. The Bharata Samaj, Indian Vegetarian Congress, Kalakshetra (Int. Art Centre), Besant Centenary Trust, Young Men's Indian Asscn.; Chair. Animal Welfare Board and mem. various int. animal welfare orgs.; fmr. mem. Rajya Sabha (Parl.); decorations: Padma Bhushan 56, Sangit Natak Akademi Award 57, Queen Victoria Silver Medal of R.S.P.C.A. 58, Prani Mitra (Animal Welfare Board) 68; D.H. (Wayne Univ.) 60; Fellowship, Sangit Natak Akademi 68; D.h.c. (Rabindra Bharathi Univ.), Calcutta 70; Desikothama, Viswabharati Univ., Shantiniketan 72.
Productions: *The Light of Asia, Incidents from the Life of Bishma, Karaikal Ammayar* (Tamil), *Rukmini Swayamwaram* (Kathakali), *Kutrala Kuravanji* (temple drama), *Kumara Sambhavam, Usha Parinayam* (Telegu), *Sita Swayamwaram, Rama Vanagamanam, Paduka Pattabhi shekham, Sabari Moksham, Choodamani Pradanam, Maha Pattabhishekkam, Gita Govinham, Andal Charitram, Kannapar Kuravanji, Rukmini Kalyanam, Dhruva Charitram, Krishnamari Kuravanji, Shakuntalam, Shyama, Kuchelopakhyanam.*
Publs. *Yoga: Art or Science, Message of Beauty to Civilisation, Women as Artists, Dance and Music, The Creative Spirit, Art and Education.*
Animal Welfare Board of India, Gandhinagar, Madras-20; Kalakshetra, Madras-41, India.
Telephone: 74307 (Office); 74836 (Home).

Rustomji, Nari Kaikhosru, M.A.; Indian civil servant; b. 16 May 1919; ed. Bedford School and Christ's Coll., Cambridge, England.
Joined Indian Civil Service 41; Under-Sec. Assam Home and Political Dept. 44; Adviser to Gov. of Assam 48; Dewan (Prime Minister) of Sikkim, Speaker, Sikkim Council, Pres. Sikkim Exec. Council 54-59; Adviser to Governor of Assam for North East Frontier Agency and Nagaland 59; Adviser to King of Bhutan 63-66; Chief Sec. to Govt. of Assam 66, and Meghalaya 71; Ford Foundation Fellowship 64.
Publs. Editor *Nagas in the Nineteenth Century* (Verrier Elwin); *Enchanted Frontiers: Sikkim, Bhutan and India's North-Eastern Borderlands.*
"Lumpyngad", Bivar Road, Shillong, India.
Telephone: Shillong 3083.

Ryan, Peter Allen, B.A., M.M.; Australian publisher; b. 4 Sept. 1923; ed. Malvern Grammar School, Melbourne and Univ. of Melbourne.
Military Service 42-45; Dir. United Service Publicity Pty. Ltd. 53-57; Public Relations Manager, Imperial Chemical Industries of Australia and New Zealand Ltd. 57-61; Asst. to Vice-Chancellor, Univ. of Melbourne 62; Dir. Melbourne Univ. Press 62-.
Publs. *Fear Drive My Feet* 59, *The Preparation of Manuscripts* 66, *The Encyclopaedia of Papua and New Guinea* (Gen. Editor) 72, *Redmond Barry* 72.
932 Swanston Street, Carlton, Victoria 3053, Australia.

S

Sadli, Mohammad, M.SC., PH.D.; Indonesian politician; b. 10 June 1922; ed. Univs. of Gadjah Mada and Indonesia, Mass. Inst. of Technology, Univ. of Calif. (Berkeley) and Harvard Univ.
Lecturer, Univ. of Indonesia 57, Army Staff Coll. 58, Navy Staff Coll. 58; Dir. Inst. of Econ. and Social Research, Faculty of Econs., Univ. of Indonesia 57-63; Asst. to Pres., Univ. of Indonesia 63-64; mem. Gov. Council, UN Asian Inst. of Devt. and Planning 63-64; Fellow, Harvard Univ. Centre for Int. Affairs 63-64; Chair. Indonesian Economists Asscn. 66-67; Chair. Technical Cttee. for Foreign Investment 67; Minister of Manpower 71-73, of Mining Affairs 73-; mem. UN Group on Multinational Cos. 73-74.
Ministry of Mines, Merdeka Selatan 18, Jakarta; Home: Brawijaya IV, 24 Kebayoran Baru, Jakarta-Selatan, Indonesia.
Telephone: 50232 (Office); 72599 (Home).

Sadykov, Abid Sadykovich; Soviet chemist; b. 1913; ed. Central Asia State Univ.
Teacher, Uzbek State Univ. 39-41, Central Asia State Univ. 41-46; Dir. Inst. of Chemistry, Uzbek Acad. of Sciences 46-50; Rector, Tashkent State Univ. 58-66; mem. Uzbek Acad. of Sciences 47-, Pres. 66-; Corresp. mem. U.S.S.R. Acad. of Sciences 66-73, mem. 73-; mem. C.P.S.U. 46-; orders and medals of U.S.S.R.
Publs. *The Chemistry of Alkaloids, Cotton Leaves as Valuable Chemical Raw Material.*
Presidium of Uzbek Academy of Sciences, Ul. Kuibysheva 15, Tashkent, U.S.S.R.

Sahay, Bhagwan, B.SC.; Indian civil servant and diplomatist; b. 15 Feb. 1905; ed. Univ. of Allahabad and School of Oriental Studies, London.
Joined Indian Civil Service 29; District Magistrate 35-37; Deputy Sec. Industries Dept., United Provinces 37-39, Commr. Census Operations 39-41; Sec. Indian Council of Agricultural Research, New Delhi 41-43; Joint Sec. Dept. of Agriculture, Govt. of India 44-45; Commr. of Food and Civil Supplies 46-49; Chief Sec. United Provinces 49-51; Chief Commr. of Himachal Pradesh 51-52, of Bhopal State 52-54; Amb. to Nepal 54-59; Chief Commr. of Delhi 59-63; Lieut.-Gov. of Himachal Pradesh 63, then Kerala; Gov. of Jammu and Kashmir 67-73; Padma Bhushan 61.
c/o Office of the Governor, Srinagar, Jammu and Kashmir, India.

Saheki, Isamu, LL.B.; Japanese business and transport executive; b. 25 March 1903; ed. Tokyo Imperial Univ.
Kinki Nippon Railway Co. 25-, Vice-Pres. 47-51, Pres. 51-73, Chair. 73-; Chair. Kintetsu Business Group; Pres. Osaka Chamber of Commerce and Industry; Vice-Pres. Fed. of Econ. Orgs.; Adviser Japan Air Lines; Founder Yamato Bunka-kan Museum, History Class on Nara; Exec. of many orgs. and asscns.; Blue Ribbon Medal.
6-1-1 Uehommachi, Tennoji-ku, Osaka; Home: 2-1-4 Tomigaoka, Nara City, Japan.
Telephone: 06 (771) 3331, 0742 (45) 4550 (Home).

Sahgal, Nayantara; Indian writer; b. 10 May 1927, Allahabad; ed. Wellesley Coll., U.S.A.
Scholar-in-residence, holding creative writing seminar, Southern Methodist Univ. Dallas, Texas 73; adviser English Language Board, Sahitya Akademi (Nat. Acad. of Letters), New Delhi.
Publs. *Prison and Chocolate Cake, A Time to be Happy, From Fear Set Free* 62, *This Time of Morning, Storm in Chandigarh* 69, *History of the Freedom Movement* 70, *The Day in Shadow* 72.
10 Massey Hall Jai Singh Road, New Delhi 110001, India.

Said, Hakim Mohammed; Pakistani physician; b. 9 Jan. 1920; ed. Ayurvedic and Unani Tibbia (Medical) Coll., Delhi.
Founder, Sec.-Gen. Soc. for Promotion of Eastern Medicine 56; Founder, Pres. Coll. of Eastern Medicine, Karachi 58; Pres. Inst. of Health and Medical Research; Pres. Hamdard Nat. Foundation; Pres. Soc. for the Promotion and Improvement of Libraries; mem. Cen. Advisory Cttee. Pakistan Broadcasting Corpn.; organized Health of the Nation Conf., Karachi 71, formed Nat. Health Cttee.; Consultant mem. Technical Devt. Board, Union Int. d'Education pour la Santé, Paris until 76; participant, organizer many int. confs. and congresses; Sitara-i-Imtiaz (Award for Social and Educ. Service, Govt. of Pakistan) 66.
Publs. *Medicine of China, Europe Nama, Germany Nama, Wonders of the Human Body, Health of the Nation, The Employer and Employee, Tazkara-i-Muhammad, Pharmacopoeia of Eastern Medicine, Main Currents of Contemporary Thought in Pakistan* (2 vols.).
Hamdard National Foundation, Hamdard Centre, Nazimabad, Karachi 18; Home: Hamdard Manzil, 58/1 Shikarpur Colony, New Town, Karachi 5, Pakistan.

Saifudin; Uighur Moslem, People's Republic of China; b. 1916, Artush, Sinkiang; ed. Cen. Asia Univ., Moscow.
Leader of Uighur Uprisings 33, 44; Minister of Educ., E. Turkistan Repub. 45; Deputy Chair. Sinkiang People's Govt. 49-54, Chair. 55-68; Deputy Commdr. Sinkiang Mil. Region, People's Liberation Army 49, 55-; Second Sec. CCP Sinkiang 56-58; Alt. mem. 8th Cen. Cttee. of CCP 56; Pres. Sinkiang Univ. 64; Vice-Chair. Sinkiang Revolutionary Cttee. 68, Chair. 72; mem. 9th Cen. Cttee. of CCP 69; Second Sec. CCP Sinkiang 71, First Sec. 73-; Alt. mem. Politburo, 10th Cen. Cttee. of CCP 73, 75; First Political Commissar Sinkiang Mil. Region, PLA 74-; Chair. Presidium Nat. People's Congress 75-.

Saigol, Mohammed Rafique; Pakistani business executive; b. 1933, Calcutta; ed. Aitchison Coll., Lahore and Clemson Coll., S.C., U.S.A.
Formerly Man. Dir. Kohinoor Textile Mills, Lyallpur and Chair. Cen. Board of Management of the Saigol Group; Chair. Lyallpur Improvement Trust 58; mem. Nat. Assembly, Parl. Sec. to Govt. of Pakistan 65-69; Chair. All Pakistan Textile Mills Asscn. 67-68; Pres. Lahore Chamber of Commerce and Industry 68-69, Lahore Stock Exchange Ltd. 71; Man. Dir. Progressive Papers Ltd. 71, Pakistan Int. Airlines Corpn. 72-73; Chair. Saigol Brothers Ltd., Nat. Construction Co. (Pakistan) Ltd.; Man. Trustee Saigol Foundation; Dir. State Bank of Pakistan, Sui Northern Gas Pipelines Ltd.; mem. Advisory Council on Econ. Affairs, and other advisory bodies.
6 Egerton Road, Lahore; Home: 91-E-1 Gulberg 3, Lahore, Pakistan.

Saito, Eiichi; Japanese newspaper executive; b. 3 Dec. 1910, Osaka; ed. Osaka Higher Commercial School.
Reporter, *Mainichi Shimbun*, Osaka 31; Overseas correspondent, London 41; Asst. City News Editor, Osaka 42; Chief, Kyoto Branch Office 45; City News Editor, Osaka 47; Editorial Writer 50; overseas correspondent, U.S.A. 51; Asst. Man. Editor 54; Chief, London Office 56; Gen. Man., European Office 57; Man. Editor, Osaka 61, Tokyo 63; mem. Board of Dirs. 64; Man. Dir. and Exec. Editor 68-.
Mainichi Shimbun, 1-1-1, Hitotsubashi, Chiyoda-ku, Tokyo; New Akasaka Corporas, 12-4, Akasaka 8-chome, Minato-ku, Tokyo, Japan.

Saito, Kiyoshi; Japanese wood print artist; b. 1907, Fukushima Pref.
First specialized in oil painting and held many exhbns. in Japan; later turned to wood printing, often using Haniwa (Ancient Clay Image) as material; one-man exhbn. Corcoran Gallery of Art, Washington, D.C. 57; numerous

exhbns. throughout U.S.A. 57-59; took part in Asia and Africa Art exhbn. sponsored by Egyptian Govt. and won prize 57; one-man exhbns. at Nordness Gallery, New York 62, Sydney and Melbourne 65, Fine Arts Gallery of San Diego 69; two-man exhbn. Hawaii Museum 64; awarded the Int. Biennial Exhbn. of Prints in Yugoslavia; awarded Prize for Japanese Artists at Int. Arts Exhbn., Brazil.
1-23-14, Nishimikado Kamakura City, Kanagawa Pref., Japan.
Telephone: 956-6695.

Saito, Kunikichi; Japanese politician; b. 1909.
Specialized in welfare and medical affairs, Labour Ministry; mem. for Fukushima Pref., House of Reps.; Deputy Sec.-Gen. Liberal Democratic Party (LDP); Chair. House of Reps. Finance Cttee.; Deputy Chief Cabinet Sec., Parl. Vice-Minister of Finance; Minister of Health and Welfare 72-74.
House of Representatives, Tokyo, Japan.

Saito, Nobufusa, D.SC.; Japanese atomic scientist; b. 28 Sept. 1916; ed. Tokyo Imperial Univ.
Former Asst. Prof., Kyushu and Seoul Univs., Prof. of Inorganic Chemistry, Tokyo Univ. 56-; fmr. Consultant to Int. Atomic Energy Agency (I.A.E.A.), Dir. of Isotopes Div. 63-65; Prof. Inorganic and Nuclear Chemistry, Tokyo Univ. 65-, Dir. Radioisotope Centre 70-; Dir. Japan Radioisotopes Assen. 67-; Technical Adviser, Japan Atomic Energy Research Inst. 66-; mem. Chemical Soc. of Japan, American Chemical Soc., Atomic Energy Soc. of Japan, Japan Soc. for Analytical Chem.; Co-Editor *Int. Journal of Applied Radiation & Isotopes*; Chem. Soc. of Japan Award 74.
Department of Chemistry, Faculty of Science, University of Tokyo, Bunkyo-ku, Tokyo; 5-12-9, Koshigoe, Kamakura, Japan.

Saito, Shizuo; Japanese diplomatist; b. 1914; ed. Tokyo Imperial Univ.
Counsellor, London 59-62; Minister in Bangkok 62-63; Dir. UN Bureau 63-64; Amb. to Indonesia 64-66; Deputy Vice-Minister for Admin., Ministry of Foreign Affairs 66-69; Amb. to Australia 70-74, concurrently to Fiji, Nauru 72-74; Perm. Rep. to UN 74-.
Permanent Mission of Japan to the United Nations, 886 UN Plaza, New York, N.Y. 10017, U.S.A.

Saito, Shoichi; Japanese business executive; b. June 1908, Nagoya; ed. Tohoku Univ.
With Toyoda Automatic Loom Works 35-37; joined Toyota Motor Co. 37, mem. Board of Dirs. 46-50, Man. Dir. 50-60, Exec. Vice-Pres. 67-73, Chair. 73-; Dir. Toyota Motor Sales U.S.A. Inc. 67-; Dir. Toyota Central Research and Devt. Laboratories Inc. 68-; Pres. Soc. of Automotive Engineers of Japan 68-72; Auditor Toyota Automatic Loom Works Ltd., Aisin Seiki Co. Ltd., Towa Real Estate Co. Ltd. 73-; Hon. Blue Ribbon Medal 70.
Publs. *The Earth is Round, America: the Country of Automobiles.*
Toyota Motor Co. Ltd., 1 Toyota-cho, Toyota-shi, Aichi-ken; Home: 26 Takamine-cho, Showa-ku, Nagoya-shi, Aichi-ken 471, Japan.
Telephone: 0565-28-2121 (Office).

Sakaguchi, Jiro; Japanese business executive; b. 19 Jan. 1895; ed. Hitotsubashi Univ.
President Nippon Rayon Co.
Nippon Rayon Co., 1-2 Nakatsuhondori, Oyoduku, Osaka, Japan.

Sakamoto, Isamu; Japanese business executive; b. 23 Oct. 1911; ed. Kyoto Univ.
Director and Man. Engineering Div. and Research and Devt. Labs., Sumitomo Electric Industries Ltd. (SEI) 58; Man. Dir. SEI 61, Exec. Vice-Pres. 69, Pres. 69-73, Chair. of Board Nov. 73-; Chair. Nuclear Fuel Industries Ltd.; Dir. Meidensha Ltd., Sumitomo-3M Co. Ltd.; Vice-Chair. Japan-U.S. Soc. of Osaka; Chair. Int. Wrought Copper Council.
5-3, 2-chome, Fujishirodai, Suita City, Osaka, Japan.
Telephone: 06-872-2837.

Sakata, Michita; Japanese politician; b. 1916; ed. Tokyo Imperial Univ.
Former Private Sec. to Minister of Commerce and Industry; fmr. Parl. Vice-Minister for Transport; fmr. Minister of Health and Welfare; Minister of Education 68-71; Minister of State, Dir.-Gen. of Defence Agency Dec. 74-; mem. House of Reps.; Liberal Democrat.
Dai-ichi Gi-in-kaikan, 2-2-1, Nagato-cho, Chiyoda-ku Tokyo, Japan.
Telephone: Tokyo 581-4877.

Sakurada, Takeshi; Japanese industrialist; b. 17 March 1904; ed. Tokyo Univ.
Nisshin Spinning Co. Ltd. 43-, Man. Dir. 44-45, Pres. 45-64, Chair. of Board 64-70, Adviser 70-; Dir. The Industry Club of Japan 49-; Adviser to Board, Japan Radio Co. Ltd. 56, New Japan Radio Co. Ltd. 59; Auditor Fuji Television Broadcasting Co. Ltd. 67-; Chair. Toho Rayon Co. Ltd. 66-; Promoter and Auditor Arabian Oil Co. Ltd. 58-; mem. Public Security Comm. 64-; Deputy Chair. Fiscal System Council 65-75, Chair. 75-; fmr. Pres. Japan Fed. of Employers' Asscns.
8, 22-Kamiyamacho, Shibuyaku, Tokyo, Japan.

Salam, Abdus, M.A., PH.D., D.SC., F.R.S.; Pakistani physicist; b. 29 Jan. 1926; ed. St. John's Coll., Cambridge and Government Coll., Lahore.
Professor of Mathematics, Govt. Coll., Lahore 51-54; Head, Mathematics Dept., Panjab Univ., Lahore 52-54; Lecturer, Univ. of Cambridge 54-56; Prof. of Theoretical Physics, Imperial Coll. of Science and Technology, Univ. of London 57; mem. Pakistan Atomic Energy Comm. 59-, Pakistan Science Council 62-; Chief Scientific Adviser to Pres. 61-74; Gov., Int. Atomic Energy Agency 62-63; Dir. Int. Centre for Theoretical Physics 64-; mem. UN Advisory Cttee. on Science and Technology 64-, Chair. 71; mem. scientific Council Stockholm Int. Peace Research Inst. (SIPRI) 70-; Vice-Pres. Int. Union of Pure and Applied Physics 72-; mem. London and American Physical Socs.; Fellow, Royal Swedish Acad. of Sciences; Foreign mem. U.S.S.R. Acad. of Sciences, American Acad. of Arts and Sciences; Oppenheimer Prize and Medal; Atoms for Peace Award 68 and many others.
Department of Physics, Imperial College of Science and Technology, London, S.W.7, England; and International Centre for Theoretical Physics, Prosecco-Miramare 21, Trieste, Italy.
Telephone: 01-589-5111, ext. 2513; Trieste 22 42 81/6.

Salas, Rafael M.; Philippine United Nations official; b. 7 Aug. 1928, Bago, Negros Occidental; ed. Univ. of the Philippines and Harvard Univ. Littauer Centre of Public Admin.
Chair. Pres. Consultative Council of Students 54; Asst. to Exec. Sec., Office of the Pres. 54-55; Technical Adviser to the Pres. 56-57; Supervising Economist, Nat. Econ. Council 57-60, Exec. Dir. with Cabinet rank 60-61, Acting Chair. 66, 68; Special Asst. to Sec. of Agriculture and Natural Resources 61, to the Pres. for Local Govts. 61; Lecturer in Political Science and Econ., Univ. of the Philippines 55-59, in Econs., Graduate School of Far Eastern Univ. 60-61, in Law, Univ. of Philippines 63-66, mem. Board of Regents 66-69, Asst. to Vice-Pres. 62-63; Gen. Man. *Manila Chronicle* 63-65; Chair. of Board Govt. Service Insurance System 66; Action Officer, Nat. Rice and Corn Sufficiency Programme 66-69; Overall Co-ordinator and Action Officer for Nat. Projects 66-69; Chair. Govt. Re-org. Comm. 68-69; Exec. Sec. of the Philippines 66-69; Exec. Dir. UN Fund for Population Activities 69-; Asst.

Sec.-Gen. UNDP 71-72; UN Official in charge of World Population Year 74; del. UNESCO conf. on Media and Youth 52; Exec.-Sec. UNESCO Nat. Comm. for the Philippines 57; Asst. Sec.-Gen. 2nd Asian Productivity Conf. 60; mem. del. to ECAFE 61, adviser 62, 68; Amb. to Indonesia on Merdeka Day 67; Vice-Pres. UN Int. Conf. on Human Rights 68, mem. del. UN Gen. Assembly 68; Vice-Pres. Pledging Cttee. UNDP 68; Ph.D. (h.c.), DHL (h.c.); U.S. Agency for Int. Devt. Fellowship in Local Govt. Planning.
Publs. fmr. Ed. *Philippine Law Journal*; articles in Philippine magazines and newspapers.
United Nations Fund for Population Activities, United Nations, New York, N.Y. 10017, U.S.A.

Salato, Esika Macu, C.B.E.; Fijian civil servant and international official; b. 1 May 1915; ed. Queen Victoria School and Central Medical School.
Medical practice 35-74; Fiji Royal Naval Reserve Force 43-46; Deputy Dir. Medical Services 65-68, Dir. 68-74; Mayor of Suva 70; Acting High Commr. in U.K. and Rep. to EEC 74; Sec.-Gen. South Pacific Comm. Oct. 75-.
Secretariat, South Pacific Commission, Post Box D 5, Nouméa New Caledonia.

Sambasivan, Dr. G.; Indian malariologist.
Malariologist, Travancore 35; Indian Medical Service 40; Asst. Dir. Malaria Inst. of India 47; World Health Organization 49-, Senior Malaria Adviser, South East Asia Regional Office of WHO, New Delhi 61-64; Dir. WHO Malaria Eradication Activities 64-.
WHO, Avenue Appia, Geneva, Switzerland.

Samphan, Khieu (*see* Khieu Samphan).

San Yu, Brig.-Gen.; Burmese army officer and politician; b. 1919, Prome; ed. Univ. of Rangoon and an American military coll.
Commissioned 42, served in Second World War; Mil. Sec. to Chief of Gen. Staff 56-59; Officer commanding the North and North-West mil. areas; mem. Revolutionary Council, Deputy Chief of Gen. Staff, Commdr. of Land Forces and Minister of Finance and Revenue 63; Gen. Sec. Cen. Organizing Cttee., Burmese Socialist Programme Party 65-73; Gen. Sec. Burma Socialist Prog. Party 73-; Minister of Nat. Planning, Finance and Revenue 69-72; Deputy Prime Minister 71-74; Minister of Defence 72-74; Chief of Gen. Staff April 72-74; Sec. Council of State March 74-.
Council of State, Rangoon, Burma.

Sananikone, Phoui; Laotian politician; b. 1903.
Head of Province 41-46; Pres. Chamber of Deputies 48-50, 60-74 (Nat. Assembly dissolved); Prime Minister and Pres. of the Council of Ministers Feb. 50-Nov. 51, 58-Dec. 59; Minister of Foreign Affairs 53-54, 54-56, 57-58, 59; Vice-Pres. Council of Ministers 53-56; numerous other cabinet posts; Pres. Nat. Assembly; Pres. Nationalist group and Speaker, Rassemblement du Peuple Lao 62-74; Minister of Finance 74-75; Grand Croix Ordre Royal du Million d'Eléphants et du Parasol Blanc; Commdr. Légion d'Honneur; Croix de Guerre avec palme.
c/o Ministry of Finance, Vientiane, Laos.

Sarasin, Pote; Thai politician and barrister-at-law; b. 25 March 1907, Bangkok; ed. Wilbraham Acad., Mass. and Middle Temple, London.
Practised law in Thailand 33-45; Senator and Minister of Foreign Affairs 48-50; Amb. to U.S.A. and Chair. Fifth Cttee. UN Asscn. 52-57; Prime Minister 57-58; Sec.-Gen. SEATO 57-63; Minister of Econ. Affairs and Nat. Devt. 63-68; Minister of Econ. Affairs 68-69; Chair. Board of Investment 68-; Vice-Chair. United Thai People's Party (now merged with Social Nat. Party) 68-; Deputy Prime Minister and Minister of Nat. Devt. 69-71; mem. Nat. Exec. Council and Dir. Econ., Finance and Industry Affairs 71-72; mem. Thai Bar Assсn.
Saha-Pracha-Thai, 1/226, Sri Ayudhya, Dusit, Bangkok, Thailand.

Sarin Chhak, Dr.; Cambodian politician.
Minister of Foreign Affairs in Royal Govt. of Nat. Union 70-75.
c/o Ministry of Foreign Affairs, Phnom-Penh, Cambodia.

Sasaki, Tadashi; Japanese banker; b. 19 May 1907, Sendai City; ed. Dept. of Econs., Tokyo Imperial Univ. (now Tokyo Univ.).
Joined the Bank of Japan 30, Chief Personnel, Dept. 46-47, Chief, Co-ordination Dept. 47-51, Chief, Business Dept. 51-54, Exec. Dir. 54-62, Vice.Gov. 62-69, Gov. Dec. 69-74; Chair. Keizai Doyukai (Japan Cttee. for Econ. Devt.) 75-.
4-6 Marunouchi 1-chome, Chiyoda-ku, Tokyo; Home: 5-34-10 Yoyogi, Shibuya-ku, Tokyo 151, Japan.

Sasaki, Yoshitake; Japanese politician.
Director, Atomic Energy Comm. 56; mem. Liberal Democratic Party, fmr. Head of LDP Cttee. on Science and Technology; mem. House of Reps. (five times); Dir. Science and Technology Agency Dec. 74-.
House of Representatives, Tokyo, Japan.

Sathe, Ramchandra, M.D., F.R.C.P., M.R.C.P.; Indian physician; b. 28 Nov. 1905; ed. Elphinstone High School, Elphinstone Coll., Grant Medical Coll., Bombay, and St. Bartholomew's Hospital, London.
Emeritus Prof. of Medicine and Hon. Dir. of Postgraduate Studies in Medicine, Grant Medical Coll., Bombay; Pres. Assсn. of Physicians of India 60, Indian Medical Assсn. 62, World Medical Assсn. 62-63; Vice-Chancellor Bombay Univ. 63-66; Deputy Pres. World Conf. on Medical Educ. 66; Pres. Diabetic Assсn. of India; mem. Health Survey and Planning Cttee., Drugs and Equipment Standards Cttee., Indian Pharmacopeia Cttee., Nat. Formulary Cttee., Govt. of India; J. J. Gold Medal for Clinical Medicine; Hewlett Prize for Hygiene.
Publs. include: articles on nutritional oedema, cirrhosis of liver, treatment of hypertension, diabetes, jaundice, etc.
Nagindas Mansion, Girgaum Road, near Opera House, Bombay 400 004, India.
Telephone: 356465.

Sato, Mitsugi, B.SC., M.SC.; Japanese dairy executive; b. 14 Feb. 1898; ed. Colls. of Agriculture, Hokkaido Imperial Univ. and Ohio State Univ.
Managed dairy plant, Dept. of Dairying, Ohio State Univ. 22; Plant Man. and Technical Chief, Fed. of Hokkaido Co-op. Creamery Asscns. 25-37, Senior Exec. Dir. Hokkaido Kono-Kosha 41-45; Staff mem. and Adviser Econ. Stabilization Board 46-49; Area Dir. Dairy Soc. Int. 49-57, Vice-Pres. 58-; Pres. Hokkaido Co-op. Dairy Co. 49; Pres. Snow Brand Milk Products Co. 50-63, Chair. 63-71, Dir. and Councillor 71-73, Adviser 73-; Dir. Hokkaido Broadcasting Co. 51-70, Sapporo Co-op Bank 51-, Chair. 57-58; mem. Exec. Cttee. Fed. of Japan Employers' Assсn.; Pres. Hokkaido Employers' Assсn. 62-; Pres. Rakuno Gakuen Coll. of Dairying 66-69, Chair. Board of Trustees 66-; Del. int. dairy asscns.; awards include Ranju Decoration 60 and Dairy Soc. Int. Certificate of Honour as "Herald" 65; Third Class Order of the Sacred Treasure 68; Commdr. Royal Order of St. Olav (Norway); Centennial Achievement Award (Ohio State Univ.) 70; Chair. Hokkaido Sangro Club 74-.
Publs. *What We Should Eat* 29, *Dairy Industry in New Zealand and Australia* 42, *Zenshichi Sato and Self Help* 67, *Study on Food Problems and Promotion of Dairying* 70.
Snow Brand Milk Products Co. Ltd., 36 Naebo-cho,

Sapporo; Home: 580 Nishi 8, Minami 16, Sapporo, Japan.

Satpathy, Nandini; Indian politician and social worker; b. 9 June 1931, Cuttack; ed. Ravenshaw Coll., Cuttack.
Leader of the student movements in Orissa and Sec. Girls Students' Asscn. 48-49; took part in many welfare activities, organized and became Sec. of the Orissa Women's Relief Cttee.; organized Orissa branch, Asscn. of Social and Moral Hygiene in India 58; associated with numerous nat. welfare, literary and other orgs.; mem. Rajya Sabha (Upper House) 62-71; Deputy Minister for Information and Broadcasting 66-69; Deputy Minister attached to Prime Minister 69-70; Minister of State for Information and Broadcasting 70-72; Leader Indian film del. to Moscow 66, 68 and Tashkent 72; del. Gen. Conf. UNESCO, Paris 72; mem. Indian del. to Commemorative Session UN, N.Y.C. 70; Chief Minister of Orissa 72-73, 74-; Pres. Orissa Pradesh Congress Cttee. 73-76; mem. Working Cttee. of the All India Congress Cttee.; Chair. Orissa Flood and Cyclone Relief Cttee.; mem. Board of Dirs. Int. Centre of Films for Children and Young People, Paris 68-; Editor *Dharitri* (Mother Earth) and *Kalana* (Assessment), monthly magazines; received many literary prizes; popular short story writer.
Publs. *Ketoti Katha*, collection of short stories.
Office of the Chief Minister, Bhubaneswar, Orissa, India.
Telephone: 51100 (Office); 50200, 51200 (Residence); 234 and 235 (Home).

Savang Vathana, Boroma-setha Khatya Sourya Vongsa Phra Maha Sri, L. EN D.; fmr. King of Laos; b. 13 Nov. 1907; ed. Paris Univ.
Took active part in politics during the lifetime of his father; Chief Del. Arbitration Comm. Washington 47, Japanese Peace Treaty Conf. San Francisco 51; appointed Regent Aug. 59; succeeded his father King Sisavang Vong Oct. 59; abdicated Nov. 75 (monarchy abolished Dec. 75); Supreme Adviser to Pres. of Laos Dec. 75-.
c/o Office of the President, Vientiane, Laos.

Saw, U Ba (*see* Ba Saw, U).

Sawada, Setsuzo, LL.B.; Japanese diplomatist and administrator; b. 1884; ed. Tokyo Imperial Univ.
Foreign Service 09-; Sec. Japanese Embassy, London 11-18; Counsellor, Washington 24-29; Consul Gen. N.Y. 29-30; Minister to League of Nations 30-33; Amb. to Brazil 34-38; Diplomatic Adviser to Prime Minister Suzuki 45; Pres. Tokyo Univ. for Foreign Studies 49-55; Vice-Pres. Nat. Comm. for UNESCO 52-59; Pres. Govt. Council for Overseas Emigration 59-62, Inst. of World Economy 39-, Nippon Brazilian Central Asscn. 45-75; Adviser, Japan Red Cross Soc. 60-; Grand Cordon of Cruzero do Sul, Brazil 38, First Class of Sacred Treasure, Japan 37, Grand Cordon, First Class of Rising Sun, Japan 40.
Inamuragasaki, 3-chome 10-25, Kamakura, Japan.

Sawamura, Takayoshi, B.COM. SC.; Japanese business executive; b. 6 Feb. 1913; ed. Kobe Univ.
Joined Nippon Express Co. Ltd., Dir. 64, Man. Dir. 66, Senior Man. Dir. 66, Pres. 68-; Ministry of Transport Award 72.
3-12-9, Soto-Kanda, Chiyoda-ku; Home: 5-15-5, Shimoigusa, Suginami-ku, Tokyo, Japan.

Saxbe, William B., LL.B.; American politician and diplomatist; b. 25 June 1916, Mechanicsburg, Ohio; ed. Mechanicsburg High Schools and Ohio State Univ.
Member Ohio House of Reps. 47-54 (Majority Leader 51-52, Speaker of the House 53-54); Chair. Ohio Program Comm. 53; Ohio Attorney-Gen. 57-58, 63-68; Chair. Ohio Crime Comm. 69-70; U.S. Senator 69-73; Attorney-Gen. 73-74; Amb. to India 75-; mem. Cttee. on Armed Services, Govt. Operations, Post Office, Civil Service and Special Cttee. on Ageing; Republican.
American Embassy, Shantipath, Chanakyapuri, New Delhi, India.

Saxena, Surrendra Kumar, M.A., M.SOC.SC., PH.D.; Indian International Co-operative official; b. 3 April 1926; ed. Univ. of Agra, Inst. of Social Studies, The Hague, Municipal Univ., Amsterdam.
Assistant Prof., Dept. of Econs., Birla Coll., Pilani 49-52; Research Fellow, Inst. of Social Studies, The Hague 55-56; with ICA Regional Office and Educ. Centre for S.E. Asia 59-61, Regional Officer 61-68; Dir. Int. Co-operative Alliance (ICA) 68-; Dr. h.c. (Univ. of Sherbrooke, Canada).
Publs. *Nationalisation and Industrial Conflict: Example of British Coal Mining* 55, *Agricultural Co-operation in S.E. Asia* 61, *Role of Foreign Aid in Development of Co-operative Processing* 65, *Activities and Role of the International Co-operative Alliance in S.E. Asia* 66, *The International Co-operative Alliance and Co-operative Trade* 67, etc.
International Co-operative Alliance, 11 Upper Grosvenor Street, London, W1X 9PA; Home: 6 Hoe Meadow, Seelys Estate, Beaconsfield, Bucks., England.
Telephone: 01-499-5991. (Office)

Sayem, Abusadat Mohammad, B.A., B.L.; Bangladesh lawyer and politician; b. 1 March 1916; ed. Rangpur Zilla School, Presidency Coll., Calcutta, Carmichael Coll., Rangpur, Univ. Law Coll., Calcutta.
Advocate, Calcutta High Court 44; joined Dacca High Court Bar 47; Examiner in Law, Dacca Univ.; mem. Local Board, State Bank of Pakistan until 56; Sponsor, Gen. Sec. and Vice-Pres. East Pakistan Lawyers Asscn.; fmr. Sec. and Vice-Pres. High Court Bar Asscn.; Advocate, Fed. Court of Pakistan 51-59; Senior Advocate, Supreme Court of Pakistan 59-62; mem. Bar Council until 62; Judge High Court, Dacca 62; mem. of various legal comms. of inquiry; mem. Pakistan Election Comm. for nat. and provincial assemblies 70-71; first Chief Justice, High Court of Bangladesh 72; Chief Justice, Supreme Court 72-75; Pres. of Bangladesh, Chief Martial Law Admin., Minister of Defence, of Law, of Parl. Affairs and Justice, of Foreign Affairs and of Agriculture Nov. 75-.
Office of the President, Dacca, Bangladesh.

Sayer, Guy Mowbray, J.P.; British banker; b. 18 June 1924; ed. Hong Kong, Shrewsbury School, England.
With The Hongkong and Shanghai Banking Corpn. 61-, Accountant, Rangoon Branch 61, Man. 63, Man. Osaka Branch 64, Monkok Branch 65, Staff Controller, Head Office 68, Gen. Man. 69, Dir. 70, Deputy Chair. 71, Chair. 72-; Chair. Mercantile Bank Ltd., Hong Kong, The Hong Kong Bank of California, San Francisco, Hong Kong Finance Ltd., Sydney; mem. Exec. Council, Hong Kong Govt., Exchange Fund Advisory Cttee.; Treas. Univ. of Hong Kong; Fellow, Inst. of Bankers, London; Liveryman, Worshipful Company of Innholders, Freeman of the City of London.
The Hongkong and Shanghai Banking Corpn., 1 Queen's Road Central; Home: Skyhigh, 10 Pollocks Path, Hong Kong.

Schaaf, C(arl) Hart, A.B., PH.D.; American United Nations official; b. 14 Jan. 1912; ed. Univ. of Michigan, Montpellier, Stockholm.
Associate Professor of Administration, Coll. of William and Mary (Richmond Div.) 40-42; State Rationing Admin., Virginia 42-43; Asst. Dep. Dir.-Gen. and Chief, Supply for Europe, UN Relief and Rehabilitation Admin. 44-47; Assoc. Prof. of Admin., School of Business and Public Admin., Cornell Univ. 47-49; Exec. Dir., United World Federalists 49; Deputy Exec. Sec. UN ECAFE 49-54; Resident Rep. in Israel for UN TAB 54-57, in the Philippines 57-59; Exec. Agent, Cttee. for Coordination of Investigations of the Lower Mekong Basin 59-70; Dir. Career Secr. of UN; resident rep. in Sri Lanka and the

Maldives and mem. Advisory Board of Cttee. for Co-ordination of Investigations of Lower Mekong Basin 70-: Ramon Magsaysay Foundation Award for Int. Understanding (awarded to Mekong Cttee.) 66, Outstanding Achievement Award (Univ. of Michigan) 66.
Publs. *Fiscal Planning at the State Level* 41, *Economic Co-operation in Asia* 50, *The United Nations Economic Commission for Asia and the Far East* 53, *The Lower Mekong* (with Russell Fifield) 62, *Burke's Idea, Partition* (plays) 48.
United Nations, P.O. Box 1505, Colombo, Sri Lanka.

Scott, John Vivian, LL.B.; New Zealand diplomatist; b. 19 Nov. 1920; ed. Victoria Univ., Wellington.
Joined New Zealand Dept. of External Affairs 47; has served in Canberra, New York and London; mem. New Zealand Perm. Mission at UN 51-55; Amb. to Japan 65-69; Perm. Rep. to UN 69-73; Deputy Sec. of Foreign Affairs, Wellington 73-.
Ministry of Foreign Affairs, Wellington, New Zealand.

Sculthorpe, Peter Joshua, M.B.E.; Australian composer; b. 29 April 1929; ed. Launceston Grammar School, Univ. of Melbourne and Wadham Coll., Oxford.
Reader in Music, University of Sydney 68-; Visiting Fellow, Yale Univ. 65-67; Visiting Prof. Univ. of Sussex 71-72; commissions from Australian Broadcasting Comm., Birmingham Chamber Music Soc., Australian Elizabethan Theatre Trust and Australian Ballet, etc; Encyclopaedia Britannica Award for the Arts 68.
Compositions published include: *The Loneliness of Bunjil* 54, *Sonatina* 54, *Variations* 54, *Irkanda I* 55, *Sonata for Viola and Percussion* 60, *Irkanda IV* 61, *The Fifth Continent* 63, *String Quartet No. 6* 65, *Sun Music I* 65, *Canto 1520* 66, *Night Piece* 66, *Red Landscape* 66, *Morning Song* 66, *Sun Music III* 67, *Three Haiku* 67, *Sun Music IV* 67, *Tabuh Tabuhan* 68, *Autumn Song* 68, *Sun Music II* 68, *Interlude* 68, *Sun Music Ballet* 68, *From Tabuh Tabuhan* 68, *Sea Chant* 68, *Ketjak* 69, *String Quartet Music* 69, *Love 200* 70, *The Stars Turn* 70, *Music for Japan* 70, *Rain* 70, *Overture for a Happy Occasion* 70, *Dream* 70, *Night* 71, *Snow, Moon and Flowers* 71, *Stars* 71, *Landscape* 71, *How the Stars were Made* 71, *Ketjak* 72, *Koto Music* 72, *Rites of Passage* 73, *Music of Early Morning* 74, documentary and feature film scores, music for theatre, radio and television.
147B Queen Street, Woollahra, Sydney, New South Wales 2025, Australia.
Telephone: 32-4701.

Seda, Frans; Indonesian politician and economist; b. 4 Oct. 1926, Lekebai, Island of Flores; ed. elementary and secondary schools and Catholic Univ. of Econs., Tilburg, Netherlands.
Secretary-General Indonesian Nat. Cttee. of Int. Chamber of Commerce (ICC), Jakarta; mem. Gotong-Royong House of Reps.; Gen. Chair. Exec. Board, Indonesian Catholic Party, Head Econ. Section of the Party in Jakarta; Minister of Plantation 64, of Agriculture 66, of Finance 67, of Transport, Communications and Tourism 68-74.
c/o Ministry of Communications, Jakarta, Indonesia.

Segawa, Minoru; Japanese investment executive; b. 31 March 1906; ed. Osaka Commercial Univ.
Nomura Securities Ltd. 29-, Dir. 46-, Man. Dir. 48-52, Senior Man. Dir. 52-56, Exec. Vice-Pres. 56-59, Pres. 59-68, Chair. 68-; Dir. Tokyo Securities Dealers Asscn. 62-, Tokyo Stock Exchange 62- (now Chair.), Mainichi Broadcasting Co. Ltd. 53-, Nippon Koka Railway Co. Ltd. 61-; Auditor, Toho Distiller Co. Ltd. 53-, Tokyo Koku Precision Instrument Co. 57-.
Nomura Securities Co. Ltd., 1, Nihonbashi 1-chome, Chuo-ku, Tokyo 103; and 15-14, Minami-Aoyama 1-chome, Minato-ku, Tokyo, Japan.

Sehgal, Amar Nath, B.SC., M.A.; Indian sculptor; b. 5 Feb. 1922, Campbellpur, West Pakistan; ed. Punjab Univ., Govt. Coll., Lahore, and New York Univ.
One-man exhbns. New York 50-51, Paris 52, East Africa and India; Hon. Art Consultant to Ministry of Community Devt., Govt. of India 55-66; organized sculpture exhbn., Belgrade 64, Musée d'Art Moderne, Paris 65, Paulskirche, Frankfurt 65, Haus am Lutzoplatz Berlin 66, Musées Royaux D'Art et Histoire, Brussels 66, Musée de l'Etat, Luxembourg 66, Wiener Secession, Vienna 66, Flemish Acad. Arts 67, 25th Independence Celebration, Retrospective exhbn. (1947–72), Nat. Gallery, New Delhi 72, City Hall Ottawa 73, 10th Tokyo Int. Fair 73, Aerogolf Luxembourg 75, etc.; participated in Sculpture Biennale, Musée Rodin, Paris 66 and UNESCO Conf. on role of art in contemporary soc. 74; Sculpture Award, Lalit Kala Akademy 57; President's Award, Lalit Kala Akademy 58 (donated to Prime Minister Nehru during Chinese invasion).
Major works: *Voice of Africa* (Ghana) 59, *A Cricketer* 61, Mahatma Gandhi, Amritsar, *To Space Unknown* (bronze, Moscow) 63; commissioned to decorate Vigyan Bhawan (India's Int. Conferences Building) with bronze sculptural mural depicting rural life of India; bronze work *Conquest of the Moon* in White House Collection 69; bronze work *Rising Tide*, Ford Foundation Collection 69; bronze work *Anguished Cries*, West Berlin 71; Gandhi Monument, Luxembourg 72; Monument to Aviation, New Delhi Airport 72; works in Jerusalem, Vienna, Paris, West Berlin, Wiesbaden, Antwerp, New Delhi.
Publs. *Arts and Aesthetics, Organising Exhibitions in Rural Areas.*
J-23 Jangpura Extension, New Delhi 110014, India.
Telephone: 79206.

Seidler, Harry, O.B.E., M.ARCH.; Australian (b. Austrian) architect; b. 25 June 1923; ed. Wasagymnasium, Vienna, Austria, Cambridge Technical School, U.K., Univ. of Manitoba, Canada, Harvard Univ., U.S.A., and Black Mountain Coll., U.S.A.
Postgraduate work under Walter Gropius, Harvard Univ. 46; study with painter Joseph Albers, Black Mountain Coll. 46; Chief Asst. with Marcel Breuer, New York 46-48; Principal Architect, Harry Seidler and Assocs., Sydney, Australia 48-; Hon. Fellow American Inst. of Architects 66, Hon. F.A.I.A., M.R.A.I.C., F.R.A.I.A.; Wilkinson Award 65, 66, 67; Amer. Inst. of Architects Pan Pacific Citation 68; Sir John Sulman Medal 51, 67; Architecture and Arts Building of the Year Award 60, Civic Design Award 67; major works: city centre redevelopment "Australia Square", Sydney 62-66; office complex, Dept. of Trade, Canberra 70; M.L.C. Center, Martin Place, Sydney 72-75; Australian Embassy, France 74-77.
Publs. *Houses, Interiors and Projects 1949-1954, Harry Seidler 1955-63, Australia Square, Sydney* 69, *Architecture in the New World, The Work of Harry Seidler by Peter Blake* 73.
Office: 2 Glen Street, Milsons Point, New South Wales 2061; Home: 13 Kalang Avenue, Killara, N.S.W. 2071, Australia.
Telephone: 9221388 (Office); 4985986 (Home).

Sema, Hokishe, B.A.; Indian politician; b. March 1921, Sutemi; ed. Mokokchung High School, Serampur Coll., W. Bengal, and St. Anthony's Coll., Shillong.
Founder-Leader of Youth orgs. for unity and understanding among the various Naga tribes 42-48; opponent of secessionist policy and movement 48-52; Educ. Service 52-55; Admin. Service 56-58; mem. Sema Public Orgs. and mem. Naga People's Convention 58-60; mem. Select and Drafting Cttees. of Naga People's Convention 60-61; Exec. Councillor, Finance (Nagaland) 61-63; elected to Nagaland Legislative Assembly, Minister of Finance and Health 64-68; re-elected for Legislative Assembly as

Leader of Nagaland Nationalist Org. 69; Chief Minister of Nagaland 69-74.
Nagaland Nationalist Organization, P.O. Kohima, India.

Sen, Amartya Kumar, M.A., PH.D.; Indian economist; b. 3 Nov. 1933, Santiniketan, Bengal; ed. Presidency Coll., Calcutta and Trinity Coll., Cambridge.
Professor of Econs., Jadavpur Univ., Calcutta 56-58; Fellow, Trinity Coll., Cambridge 57-63; Prof. of Econs., Univ. of Delhi 63-71, Chair. Dept. of Econs. 66-68; Hon. Dir. Agricultural Econs. Research Centre, Delhi 66-68, 69-71; Prof. of Econs. London School of Econs. 71-; Visiting Prof., Univ. of Calif., Berkeley 64-65, Harvard Univ. 68-69; Fellow, Econometric Soc.
Publs. *Choice of Techniques: An Aspect of Planned Economic Development* 60, *Growth Economics* 70, *Collective Choice and Social Welfare* 70, *On Economic Inequality* 73, *Employment, Technology and Development* 75; articles in various journals in economics, philosophy and political science.
London School of Economics and Political Science, Houghton Street, Aldwych, London, W.C.2, England.
Telephone: 01-405-7686.

Sen, Asoke-Kumar, M.A., M.SC.; Indian lawyer and politician; b. 10 Oct. 1913; ed. Jagannath Intermediate Coll., Dacca, Presidency Coll., Calcutta, Dacca Univ. and London School of Economics.
Called to Calcutta Bar 41; Prof. City Coll. 41-43; Junior Standing Counsel, West Bengal Govt. 50-56; Law Minister and mem. of the Indian Cabinet 57-66, of Social Security 64-66, and of Posts and Telegraphs 63-64; fmr. Editor *Calcutta Law Journal*; Senior Advocate, Supreme Court of India; mem. Parl.
Publ. *Handbook of Commercial Law.*
9 Raisina Road, New Delhi, India.
Telephone: New Delhi 381429.

Sen, S. R., PH.D.; Indian international bank official; b. 2 July 1916; ed. Calcutta Univ., Univ. of Dacca and London School of Econs.
Taught economics, Univ. of Dacca 40-48; Deputy Econ. Adviser, Govt. of India 48-51; Econ. and Statistical Adviser, Ministry of Food and Agric., Govt. of India 51-58; Joint Sec. (Plan Co-ordination and Admin.), Planning Comm. 59-63; Adviser (Programme Admin.) and Additional Sec., Govt. of India 63-69; Vice-Chair. Irrigation Comm., Govt. of India 69-70; Exec. Dir. IBRD, IFC and IDA 70-; has taken part in and led numerous Indian and int. agric. and devt. Comms., and Delegations; Pres. Int. Asscn. of Agric. Economists 70-76.
Publs. *Strategy for Agricultural Development, Economics of Sir James Steuart, Population and Food Supply, Planning Machinery in India, Growth and Instability in Indian Agriculture, Politics of Indian Economy.*
International Bank for Reconstruction and Development, 1818 H Street, N.W., Washington, D.C. 20433, U.S.A.

Sen, Samar, B.A., B.SC.; Indian diplomatist; b. 10 Aug. 1914; ed. Univs. of Calcutta, London and Oxford.
Joined Indian Civil Service 38; Liaison Officer to UN 46-48; later Under-Sec. and Deputy Sec. in Indian Govt.; Consul-Gen., Geneva 53; Chair. Int. Supervision and Control Comm., Laos 55-57, 61; Joint Sec. Ministry of External Affairs 57-59; High Commr. in Australia and New Zealand 59-62; special duty, Morocco 62; Amb. to Algeria 62-64, to Lebanon (also accred. to Jordan and Kuwait and as High Commr. to Cyprus) 65-66; High Commr. in Pakistan 66-68, in Bangladesh July 74-; Perm. Rep. to UN 69-74; Kaiser-i-Hind 43, Padma Sri 57.
Indian High Commission, 120 Road 2, Dhanmondi, Dacca, Bangladesh.

Sen, Satyendra Nath, M.A., PH.D.; Indian university administrator; b. April 1907; ed. London Univ.
Former Dean of Faculties of Arts and Commerce, Univ. of Calcutta, Prof. of Econs. 58-, Vice-Chancellor 68-; Visiting Prof. Princeton and Stanford Univs. 62-63; mem. Gov. Body, Research and Training School, Indian Statistical Inst., Calcutta; mem. Board of Trustees, Indian Museum, Victoria Memorial, Mahajati Sadan (all in Calcutta); mem. various govt. advisory bodies, etc.
Publs. *Central Banking in Underdeveloped Money Markets* 52, *The City of Calcutta: A Socio-economic survey 1954-55 to 1957-58* 60, *The Co-operative Movement in West Bengal* 66, *Industrial Relations in the Jute Industry in West Bengal* (with T. Piplai) 68.
Office of the Vice-Chancellor, University of Calcutta, Calcutta, India.

Sen, Sukumar, M.A., PH.D.; Indian philologist; b. 4 March 1900; ed. Raj Coll. Burdwan, Sanskrit Coll. and Univ. of Calcutta.
Research Student Univ. of Calcutta 24-26, Khaira Research Scholar 27-29, Lecturer 30-54, Khaira Prof. of Indian Linguistics and Phonetics and Head of Dept. of Comparative Philology 54-64; Pres. Linguistic Soc. of India 54; Fellow, Asiatic Soc.; Fellow, Sahitya Acad.; Chair. Paribhaska Samsad, Govt. of W. Bengal.
Publs. English: *History of Brajabuli Literature* 35, *Old Persian Inscriptions of the Achaemenian Emperors* 41, *History and Prehistory of Sanskrit* 57, *History of Bengali Literature* 59, *Etymological Dictionary of Bengali*, etc.; Bengali: *History of Bengali Literature*, 4 vols. 41-58, *History of Indian Literature.*
403 Grand Trunk Road, Burdwan, India.

Sen, Triguna, D.ING.; Indian educationist and technologist; b. 24 Dec. 1905; ed. Calcutta and Germany.
Administrative Officer, Coll. of Eng. and Technology, Bengal 43-44, Principal 44-55; Rector, Jadavpur Univ. 55-64; Vice-Chancellor 64-66; Vice-Chancellor Banaras Hindu Univ. 66-67; Mayor of Calcutta 58, 59; Pres. Asscn. of Principals of Technical Insts. in India 61, 62, Inter-Univ. Board of India and Ceylon 63, Inst. of Engineers (India) 62-63, 63-64; Dir. Central Board of State Bank of India 59-62; Dir. Reserve Bank of India 64-66; mem. Educ. Comm. 64-66, Inst. of Mech. Engineers (London); Minister of Educ. 67-69; Minister of Petroleum and Chemicals and Mines and Metals Feb. 69-71; Padma Bhushan 65.
c/o Ministry of Petroleum and Chemicals and Mines and Metals, New Delhi, India.

Senanayake, E. L., B.SC.; Ceylonese politician; b. Aug. 1920; ed. Trinity Coll., Kandy.
Member of Kandy Municipal Council 43-; Mayor of Kandy; M.P. for Kandy 52-; represented Ceylon in Econ. Cttee. at 20th Gen. Session of UN 65; mem. Exec. Cttee. Inter-Parl. Asscn.; represented Ceylon at Inter-Parl. Confs., Belgrade 63, Dublin 65, Canberra 66; represented Ceylon at World Mayors' Conf., Bangkok and Paris 67; Founder mem. United Nat. Party; Minister of Health 68-70.
House of Representatives, Colombo, Sri Lanka.

Senanayeke, Maithripala; Ceylonese politician; b. 1916; ed. St. Joseph's Coll., Anuradhapura, St. John's Coll., Jaffna, and Nalanda Vidyalaya, Colombo.
Joined Govt. Service 40, Cultivation Officer 40-47; mem. Parl. 47-; Deputy Minister of Home Affairs 52; Minister of Transport and Works 56-Dec. 59; Minister of Industries, Home Affairs and Cultural Affairs July 60-July 63; Minister of Commerce and Industries July 63-June 64, of Rural and Industrial Development 64-65; Minister of Irrigation, Power and Highways 70-; Leader, House of Reps. 70-; Sri Lanka Freedom Party.
121 MacCarthy Road, Colombo 7, Sri Lanka.

Sengoku, Jo, LL.B.; Japanese business executive; b. 26 Jan. 1904, Osaka; ed. Tokyo Univ.
Director, Kuraray Co. Ltd. 42, Man. Dir. 45, Senior Man.

Dir. 48, Vice-Pres. 61, Pres. 68-75, Chair. 75; Pres. Kyowa Gas Chemical Industry Co. 61-; Dir. Keihanshin Real Estate Co. 52-, Kurashiki Cen. Hosp. 68, Sanyo Broadcasting Co., Hotel Plaza 69; Blue Ribbon Medal; Second Order of Merit, Order of Sacred Treasure.
Kuraray Co. Ltd., 8, Umeda, Kita-ku, Osaka City; Home 1-37, Kumoicho, Nishinomiya, Hyogo Pref., Japan.

Serisawa, Kojiro; Japanese author; b. 1897; ed. Tokyo and Paris Univs.
Administrative Official Ministry of Agriculture 22-25; Prof. at Chuo Univ. 30-32; Pres. Japanese PEN Club 48-; mem. Japanese Acad.; awarded Prix des Amitiés Françaises 59, Prize of Japanese Govt. 70, of Japanese Acad. 72.
Publs. *Death in Paris* 40, *One World* 54, *Mrs. Aida* 57, *Under the Shadow of Love and Death* 53, *House on the Hill* 59, *Parting* 61, *Love, Intelligence and Sadness* 62, *Fate of Man* (14 vols.) 62-71.
5-8-3 Higashinakano, Nagano-ku, Tokyo, Japan.

Setalvad, Motilal Chimanlal, B.A., LL.B.; Indian lawyer; b. 12 Nov. 1884; ed. Elphinstone Coll., and Government Law Coll.
Advocate Bombay High Court 11; Advocate-Gen., Bombay 37; resigned 42; mem. Indian del. to the Gen. Assembly of the UN 47, 48, 49 (Leader); Principal Rep. of India for the Kashmir question at the Security Council Session 52; Attorney-Gen. of India 50-62; Chair. Law Comm. 55; mem. All-India Bar Cttee.; Vice-Pres. Indian Branch Int. Law Asscn.; Pres. Bar Asscn. of India, India Comm. of Jurists; Leader Indian Del. Asian-African Legal Consultative Cttee. 57, 58, 60, 61, 62; Presented Indian case (*v.* Portugal) Int. Court of Justice 58-60; mem. Rajya Sabha 66-72; Hon. LL.D. Banaras Hindu Univ. 67; Padma Vibhushan.
Publs. *Civil Liberties, Common Law in India* (Hamlyn Lectures) 60, *Law and Culture* 63, *Role of English Law in India* 66, *Secularism* 66, *The Indian Constitution 1950–65* 67, *United Nations and World Peace* 67, *Bhulabhai Desai* 68, *My Life, Law and Other Things* 70, *Tagore Law Lectures* 73.
Nirant, Juhu, Bombay 54, India.
Telephone: 532119 (Bombay).

Sethi, Prakash Chandra, B.A., LL.B.; Indian politician; b. 19 Oct. 1920, Jhalrapatan, Rajasthan; ed. Madhav Coll., Ujjain and Holkar Coll., Indore.
President Madhav Nagar Ward Congress 47, Ujjain District Congress 51, 54, 57, Textile Clerks Asscn. 48-49; Vice-Pres. Madhya Bharat Employees Asscn. 42, 49, 52; Treas. Madhya Bharat Congress 54-55; mem. Ujjain District and Madhya Bharat Congress Cttee. Exec. 53-57; Dir. Ujjain District Co-operative Bank 57-59; A.I.C.C. Zonal Rep. for Karnatak, Maharashtra, Bombay and Gujarat 55-56; observer for Bihar 66; mem. Rajya Sabha 61-67, Lok Sabha 67-; Deputy Minister for Steel, Heavy Industries and Mines, Cen. Govt. 62-67, Minister of State 67-69; Minister of Revenue and Expenditure 69-70, of Defence Production 70-71, of Petroleum and Chemicals 71-72; Chief Minister Madhya Pradesh 72-75; Minister of Fertilizers and Chemicals Dec. 75-; rep. Govt. of India at Commonwealth Finance Ministers' Conf., Barbados 69; leader del. to Colombo Plan Conf., Victoria 69; Gov. for India, Asian Devt. Bank, Manila, and IBRD 69.
Ministry of Fertilizers and Chemicals, New Delhi, India.

Sethna, Homi Nusserwanji, B.SC., M.S.E., D.SC.; Indian engineer; b. 24 Aug. 1923; ed. St. Xavier's School and Coll., Bombay, Bombay and Michigan Univs.
Works Man. Indian Rare Earths Ltd. (Govt. co.) 49-59; Joined Atomic Energy Establishment, Trombay (now Bhabha Atomic Research Centre) 59, Dir. 66-; constructed Monazite Plant, Alwaye, Kerala, Thorium and Uranium Metal Plants and Plutonium Plant, Trombay, Bombay and Uranium Mill, Jagugoda, Bihar; Deputy Sec.-Gen. of UN Conf. on Peaceful Uses of Atomic Energy, Geneva 58; Chair. Fertilizer Corpn. of India Ltd. until 73, Madras and Rajasthan Atomic Power Project Boards, Atomic Energy Comm. 72; mem. Board of Govs. Indian Inst. of Technology, Powai 71-74, Tata Memorial Centre, Indian Rare Earths Ltd., Electronic Corpn. of India Ltd.; mem. Gov. Council Tata Inst. of Fundamental Research; mem. Int. Atomic Energy Agency 66, UN Cttee. of Specialists on Nuclear Technology and the Developing Countries; Sec. Govt. Dept. of Atomic Energy, Chair. Atomic Energy Comm. 72; mem. Cttee. on Scientific Research, Planning Comm., Indian Inst. of Chemical Eng., Inst. of Eng., UN and IAEA Scientific Advisory Cttees.; Life mem. Indian Acad. of Science; Fellow Indian Nat. Science Acad.; Padma Shri Award 59; Shanti Swarup Bhatnagar Memorial Award 60, Padma Bhushan 66; Padma Vibushan 75; Sesquicentennial Award, Univ. of Michigan 67; Sir Walter Puckey Award 71; Sir William Jones Memorial Medal, Asiatic Soc. of Calcutta 74, Padma Vibhushan 75; Dr. h.c. (Marathwada) 73, (Jawaharlal Nehru Technological Univ.) 74, (Roorkee) 75, Hon. LL.D. (Bombay) 74.
12th Floor, Department of Atomic Energy Officers' Apartments, Little Gibbs Road No. 2, Malabar Hill, Bombay 400 006, India.

Sha Feng; politician, People's Repub. of China.
Minister of Agriculture and Forestry 69-.

Shafiq, Mohammad Musa, M.A.; Afghan politician; b. 1924, Kabul; ed. Ghazi High School, Al Azhar Univ., Cairo and Columbia Univ., U.S.A.
Joined Ministry of Justice 57, later became Dir. Legislative Dept.; also taught at Faculty of Law and Political Science, Kabul Univ.; Partner, private law firm, Kabul 61; Deputy Minister of Justice 63-66; Adviser, Ministry of Foreign Affairs 66-68; Amb. to Egypt (also accred. to Lebanon, Sudan and Ghana) 68-71; Minister of Foreign Affairs 71-73, Prime Minister 72-73.

Shah, Kodardas Kalidas, B.A., LL.B.; Indian lawyer and politician; b. 15 Oct. 1908; ed. Gujarat Coll. and New Poona Coll.
Joined Nat. Movement 30, in custody 32, detained for participation in "Quit India" Campaign 42; Fellow S.P. Coll., Poona; Teacher, Poddar High School, Santa Cruz, Bombay; started legal practice, Bombay 34; Legal Adviser to Maharajah of Baroda 48-67; mem. Bombay Legislative Assembly 52, Rajya Sabha (Upper House of Parl.) 60-; Gen. Sec. Bombay Pradesh Cttee., Vice-Pres. 55-57, Pres. 57-60; Gen. Sec. All-India Congress Cttee. 62-63; Union Minister of Information and Broadcasting 67-69; Minister of Health, Family Planning, Works, Housing and Urban Devt. 69-71; Gov. of Tamil Nadu 71-June 76; Sec. Bombay Famine Relief Cttee.; Leader Indian Del. to Apartheid Conf. London 64; Count Bernadotte Medal, Red Cross 70.
8 Dr. R. Prasad Road, New Delhi, India.

Shah, Rishikesh; Nepalese politician and diplomatist; b. 1925; ed. Patna Univ. and Allahabad Univ., India.
Lecturer in English and Nepali Literature, Tri-Chandra Coll. 45-48; Opposition Leader, First Advisory Ass. 52; Gen. Sec., Nepali Congress 53-55; Permanent Rep. (with rank of Ambassador) to United Nations 56-61, Ambassador to U.S.A. 58-61; Minister of Finance, Planning and Econ; Affairs 61-62; Minister of Foreign Affairs July-Sept. 62. Ambassador-at-Large 62-63; Visiting Prof. East-West Center, Hawaii 65-66; mem. Parl. 67-; arrest reported Dec. 74.
Shri Nivas, Kamal Pokhari, Kathmandu, Nepal.
Telephone: 11766.

Shahi, Agha, M.A., LL.B.; Pakistani diplomatist; b. 25 Aug. 1920; ed. Madras Univ. and Allahabad Univ.
Indian Civil Service 43; Pakistan Foreign Service 51-; Deputy Sec., Ministry of Foreign Affairs, in charge of

UN and Int. Confs. Branch 51-55; First Counsellor and Minister, Wash. 55-58; Deputy Perm. Rep. to UN 58-61; Dir.-Gen. in charge Divs. of UN and Int. Conf. Affairs, Soviet, Chinese and Arab Affairs, Ministry of Foreign Affairs 61-64; Additional Foreign Sec. 64-67; Perm. Rep. to UN 67-72; Chair. Pakistan Del. UN Gen. Assembly; Pakistan Rep. to Security Council 68-69; Pres. UN Security Council Jan. 68; Pres. Governing Council for UN Devt. Programme 69; Pakistan Rep. to Conf. of the Cttee. on Disarmament 69; Foreign Sec. 72-.
Ministry of Foreign Affairs, Islamabad, Pakistan.

Shankar (Shankar Pillai, K.); Indian newspaper cartoonist; b. 31 July 1902.
Former cartoonist for *Hindustan Times*, New Delhi; founded *Indian News Chronicle*, Delhi 47; Founder and Editor *Shankar's Weekly* 48-; initiated Shankar's Int. Children's Art Competition 49; founded Children's Book Trust 57 of which he is now Exec. Trustee; Dir. Int. Dolls Museum 65; Founder and Editor *Children's World Magazine* 68; founder and Dir. Children's Library and Reading Room.
9 Purana Kila Road, New Delhi 1, India.

Shankar, Ravi; Indian sitar player and composer; b. 7 April 1920; ed. under Ustad Allauddin Khan of Maihar.
Trained in the *Guru-Shishya* tradition; pupil of Ustad Allauddin Khan 38; solo sitar player; fmr. Dir. of Music All-India Radio and founder of the Nat. Orchestra; Founder-Dir. Kinnara School of Music, Bombay 62-; many recordings of traditional and experimental variety in India, U.K. and the U.S.A.; Concert tours in Europe, U.S.A. and the East; Visiting Lecturer Univ. of Calif 65; appeared in film *Raga* 74; Silver Bear of Berlin; Award of Indian Nat. Acad. for Music, Dance and Drama 62; award of Padma Bhushan 67.
Film Scores: *Pather Panchali, The Flute and the Arrow, Nava Rasa Ranga, Charly*, etc. and many musical compositions.
Publ. *My Music, My Life* 69.
c/o K. C. Vajifdar, 17 Warden Court, Second Floor, Gowalia Tank Road, Bombay-36, India.
Telephone: 350586.

Shankar, Uday, A.R.C.A. (known as **Udayshankar**); Indian dancer and artist.
Joined Anna Pavlova's Company, London 22, touring America, Canada and Mexico; formed own troupe, numerous tours of America and Europe; founded Uday Shankar India Culture Centre for dance, drama and music, Almora, closed during Second World War, reopened Calcutta 65; composed ballets; produced and directed film *Kalpana* (Imagination); created innumerable dance dramas and two shadow plays, *Ramleela* and *Lord Buddha*; Fellow, Sangeet Natak Akad.; Nat. Award as Creative Artist; Hon. D.Litt., Rabindra Bharati Univ.; Padma Vibushan 71.
82/9 Ballygunge Place, Flat 20, Floor 10, Calcutta 19, India.

Shann, Keith Charles Owen, C.B.E., B.A.; Australian diplomatist; b. 22 Nov. 1917; ed. Trinity Grammar School, Kew, and Trinity Coll., Melbourne Univ., Australia.
United Nations Div., Dept. of External Affairs 46-49; Australian Mission to UN, New York 49-52; Head, UN Branch, Dept. of External Affairs 52-55; Australian Minister to the Philippines 55-56; Amb. 56-59; Australian External Affairs Officer, London 59-62; Amb. to Indonesia 62-66; First Asst. Sec. Dept. of External Affairs 66-70, Deputy Sec. 70-74, Amb. to Japan 74-.
Embassy of Australia, 1-14 Mita 2-chome, Minato-ku, Tokyo, Japan; Home: 11 Grey Street, Deakin, Canberra 2600, Australia.

Shantaram, V(ankudre); Indian film director, producer and actor; b. 18 Nov. 1901; ed. Kolhapur High School.
Worked in film industry 20-; Fouder mem. Prabhat Film Co., Poona: fmr. Chief Producer Govt. of India Films Div., mem. Censor Board, Film Advisory Board, Film Enquiry Cttee.; has directed and produced over 60 films 26-, including *King of Ayodhya, Chandrasena, Duniya-na-mane, Shakuntala* (first Indian film released in U.S.A.), *Ramjoshi, Amar Bhoopali, Jhanak Jhanak Payal Baaje* and *Do Ankhen Barah Haath* (11 awards incl. Berlin Gold Bear, Int. Catholic Award and Hollywood Foreign Press Award).
Rajkamal Kalamandir Private Ltd. Parel, Bombay 12, India.

Sharma, Shanker Dayal, M.A., LL.M., PH.D.; Indian lawyer and politician; b. 19 Aug. 1918; ed. Lucknow Univ., Cambridge Univ. and Lincoln's Inn.
Taught law at Cambridge Univ. 46-47; Brandeis Fellow, Harvard Law School; detained during merger of Bhopal State with Indian Union; mem. All India Congress Cttee. 50-, Gen. Sec. 68-72, Pres. 72-74; Pres. Bhopal State Congress Cttee. 50-52, Madhya Pradesh 67-68; Chief Minister of Bhopal State 52-56; Minister in Madhya Pradesh Govt. 56-67; mem. Lok Sabha 71-; Union Minister of Communications Oct. 74-; led Indian del. to UNESCO Conf. of Asian Nations on elementary educ. 58-59; D.P.A. (London), Hon. LL.D. (Vikram and Bhopal Univs.).
Publ. *Congress Approach to International Affairs.*
Sardar Patel Bhavan, Parliament Street, New Delhi 110001; Residence: 2 Jantar Mantar Road, New Delhi 110001; Home: 135/1 Professor's Colony, Bhopal, Madhya Pradesh, India.

Sheares, Benjamin Henry, M.D., M.S., F.R.C.O.G., F.A.C.S.; Singapore physician and Head of State; b. 12 Aug. 1907, Singapore; ed. St. Andrew's School, Raffles Inst., and King Edward VII Coll. of Medicine, Singapore.
Assistant Medical Officer, Outram Road Gen. Hospital 29-31; Head Dept. of Obstetrics and Gynaecology, Kandang Kerbau Hosp., also Medical Supt. 42-45; Acting Prof. King Edward VII Coll. of Medicine and Gynaecology 45; Hon. Consultant, British Military Hosp. 48; Prof. of Obstetrics and Gynaecology, Univ. of Malaya in Singapore 50-60; private practice 60-; Hon. Consultant Kandang Kerbau Hosp. 60-; Pres. of Singapore Jan. 71-; Hon. Fellow, Royal Soc. of Medicine 75, Royal Coll. of Obstetricians and Gynaecologists 76; Dato of Kedah and Kelantan (Malaysia); Litt.D. h.c.; G.C.B. (U.K.); Star of the Repub. of Indonesia Adipurna 74; Ancient Order of Sikatuna (Raja) (Philippines) 76.
Publs. About 20 articles on obstetrics and gynaecology in professional journals.
The Istana, Singapore 9, Singapore.
Telephone: 375522.

Shelat, Jayendra Manilal, M.A.; Indian judge; b. 16 July 1908, Umreth, Gujarat; ed. Elphinstone Coll., Bombay, Univ. of London and Inner Temple, London.
Started practice, Bombay High Court 33; Judge, City Civil Court and Additional Sessions Judge, Greater Bombay 48-54; Principal Judge and Sessions Judge 54-57; Additional Judge, Bombay High Court Jan.-Nov. 57, Judge 57-60; Judge, Gujarat High Court 60-63; Chief Justice, Gujarat State 63-66; Judge, Supreme Court of India 66-73.
Publs. *Akbar, The Trial of Gandhi, The Spirit of the Constitution.*
2 Motilal Nehru Marg, New Delhi, India.
Telephone: 38-1620.

Shen, James, C.H., M.A.; Chinese diplomatist; b. 15 June 1909; ed. Yenching Univ., Peiping (Peking), Univ. of Missouri, Columbia, U.S.A.
Editor Cen. News Agency, Nanking 36-37; Chief Editorial Section, Int. Dept., Ministry of Information, Chungking

38-43; Dir. Pacific Coast Bureau, Ministry of Information 43-47; Dir. of Int. Dept., Govt. Information Office 47-48, Dir.-Gen. 61-66; Sec. to Pres. of Repub. of China, Taipei, 56-59; Dir. of Information Dept., Ministry of Foreign Affairs, Taipei 59-61; Amb. to Australia 66-68; Vice-Minister of Foreign Affairs 68-71; Amb. to U.S.A. April 71-; Faculty-Alumni Gold Medal (Univ. of Missouri) 72.
Chinese Embassy, 2311 Massachusetts Avenue, N.W., Washington, D.C. 20008; Home: 3225 Woodley Road, N.W., Washington, D.C. 20008, U.S.A.

Shibata, Yuji; Japanese inorganic chemist; b. 28 Jan. 1882; ed. Imperial Univ. of Tokyo, Univs. of Leipzig, Zürich and Paris.
Professor of Inorganic Chemistry, Univ. of Tokyo 13-42; Prof. Univ. of Nagoya 42-48; Rector Tokyo Metropolitan Univ. 49-57; mem. Japan. Acad. 44, Pres. 62-70; Hon. mem. Rumanian Acad.; Sakurai Medal, Japan Chemical Soc. 19, Imperial Medal of Japan Acad. 27.
Major works include: study of colour change of salt solutions, study of absorption spectra of the metal complex, works on spectrochemistry, co-ordination chemistry and geochemistry.
Publs. *Spectrochemistry I, II, Inorganic Chemistry I,II, III.*
1-30-8 Ookayama, Meguro-ku, Tokyo, Japan.

Shiga, Yoshio; Japanese journalist; b. 8 Jan. 1901; ed. Imperial Univ., Tokyo.
Joined Communist Party 23, becoming editor of *Marxism;* elected mem. of Central Cttee. of Communist Party 27; imprisoned for political reasons 28-45; re-elected mem. of Central Cttee. 45; mem. of House of Representatives 46-47 and 49-50; removed from public office by Gen. MacArthur, June 50; underground activity 50-54; re-elected mem. House of Reps. 55-; mem. Presidium Central Cttee. Japanese Communist Party, expelled from Party 64; founded the Voice of Japan Soc.; edited internationalist newspaper *Nihon-no-Koe*, Chair. 69; mem. editorial Cttee. Moscow Peace Manifesto 57.
Publs. *Eighteen Years of Imprisonment* 47, *On the State* 49, *Japanese Revolutionaries* 56, *On Japan* 60, *My Appeal against Atomic Bomb* 64, *Kuril and Security in Asia* 71, *World Currency Crisis and Labour* 72, *The Japanese Imperialism* 72, *Collective Security of Asia and Kuril Problem* 74, *Problems of the Communist Movement in Japan* 74, *Kuril Problems* (2 vols.) 75.
Minamicho 3-26-15, Kichijoji, Musashino City, Tokyo 180, Japan.

Shiina, Etsusaburo, LL.D.; Japanese politician; b. 1898; ed. Tokyo Univ.
Former Pres. Tohoku Wool Manufacturing Co. and Dir. Toho Bussan Trading Co.; mem. House of Reps.; Sec.-Gen. of Cabinet 59-60; Minister of Int. Trade and Industry 60-61, Nov. 67-68; Minister of Foreign Affairs 64-Dec. 66; Chair. Liberal-Dem. Party Exec. Board Dec. 66-; Liberal-Democrat; Order of the Rising Sun, First Class 68.
14 Hanezawa-cho, Shibuya-ku, Tokyo, Japan.

Shimizu, Kisaburo; Japanese business executive; b. 18 Oct. 1903; ed. Tokyo Univ.
President, Mitsubishi Rayon Co. Ltd. and Nitto Chemical Co. Ltd.
Mitsubishi Rayon Co. Ltd., 8, 2-chome, Kyobashi, Chuo-ku, Tokyo, Japan.

Shimoda, Takeso; Japanese diplomatist; b. 3 April 1907; ed. Tokyo Imperial Univ.
Entered Japanese Diplomatic Service 31, served Nanking, Moscow, The Hague; Dir. Treaties Bureau Ministry of Foreign Affairs 52-57; Minister to U.S.A. 57-60; Adviser to Minister of Foreign Affairs 60-61; Amb. to Belgium and Chief of Japanese Del. to European Communities 60-63; Amb. to U.S.S.R. 63-65; Vice-Minister of Foreign Affairs 65-67; Amb. to U.S.A. 67-70; Justice of the Supreme Court 70-; Judge, Perm. Court of Arbitration 72-; Dir. Japanese Asscn. of Int. Law, Japanese Asscn. of Maritime Law; Hon. mem. American Bar Asscn.; Hon. LL.D. (Univ. of Nebraska); numerous foreign decorations.
1-4-16, Nishikata, Bunkyo-ku, Tokyo, Japan.

Shinde, Annasaheb P., LL.B.; Indian lawyer and agriculturist; b. 21 Jan. 1922; ed. Law Colls., Poona and Ahmedabad.
Political imprisonment 42; organized landowning farmers who had leased land to private sugar factories for nominal rents; Chair. Maharashtra State Co-operative Sugar Factories Fed., Poona; Vice-Chair. Pravara Co-operative Sugar Factory, Pravaranagar, Pravara Agricultural and Industrial Devt. Co-operative Soc. Ltd.; mem. Management Cttees., All India Co-operative Sugar Factories Fed., New Delhi, Maharashtra State Co-operative Union; Dir. Land Mortgage Bank, Ahmednagar; mem. All India Congress Cttee. and Maharashtra Pradesh Congress Cttee.; mem. Lok Sabha 62-67; Parl. Sec. to Minister of Food and Agriculture 62-63, to Minister for Community Devt. and Co-operation 64-65; Deputy Minister for Food, Agriculture, Community Devt. and Co-operation 66-67; Minister of State for Food, Agriculture, Community Devt. and Co-operation 67-71, for Agriculture and Irrigation 71-.
Publs. *Problems of Indian Agriculture and Food*, *The Indo-Pakistan Conflict.*
1 Motilal Nehru Marg, New Delhi, India.

Shindo, Sadakazu; Japanese business executive; b. 4 March 1910; ed. Kyushu Univ.
President, Mitsubishi Electric Corpn.
Mitsubishi Electric Corpn., 2-2-3 Marunouchi, Chiyoda-ku, Tokyo; 1-12-8 Gotokuji, Setagayaku, Tokyo, Japan.
Telephone: 03-425-2500 (Home).

Shinohara, Shuichi; Japanese banker; b. 13 Oct. 1906, Nagano-shi, Nagano Pref.; ed. Faculty of Law, Univ. of Tokyo.
Joined The Bank of Japan 30, Chief, Statistics Dept. 46, Man. Sendai Branch 47, Deputy Chief, Personnel Dept. 52, Chief, Business Dept. 54, Chief, Bank Relations and Supervision Dept. 57-58; Deputy Pres. The Kyowa Bank Ltd. 58-62, Pres. 62-71, Chair. 71-.
The Kyowa Bank Ltd., 5-1, Marunouchi 1-chome, Chiyoda-ku, Tokyo; 7-13, Nishiogi Kita 1-chome, Suginami-ku, Tokyo, Japan.
Telephone: 390-4080.

Shinto, Hisashi; Japanese business executive; b. 2 July 1910; ed. Kyushu Imperial Univ.
Pres. Ishikawajima-Harima Heavy Industries Co. Ltd.
Ishikawajima-Harima Heavy Industries Co. Ltd., New Otemachi Building, 2-2-1 Otemachi, Chiyoda-ku, Tokyo; Home: 1-9-15 Zenpukuji, Suginami-ku, Tokyo, Japan.

Shirayanagi, Mgr. Peter Seiichi; Japanese ecclesiastic; b. 17 June 1928; ed. Faculty of Theology, Sophia Univ., Tokyo and Urban Coll., Rome.
Ordained Priest 54, subsequently at Tokyo Chancery Office; Procurator, Archdiocese of Tokyo 60; Auxiliary Bishop of Tokyo and Titular Bishop of Atenia in Pisidia 66; Coadjutor-Archbishop "cum jure successionis" Dec. 69-Feb. 70; Archbishop of Tokyo Feb. 70-.
Sekiguchi, 3-chome, 16-15 Bunkyo-ku, Tokyo 112, Japan.

Shoaib, Mohamed, M.B.E., M.A., LL.B.; Pakistan economist and banker; b. 5 Sept. 1905; ed. Allahabad Univ.
Appointed to Provincial Admin. Service 26, to Indian Mil. Accounts Dept. 29; Chief Controller Army Factory Accounts, Govt. of India 42; after Partition appointed Adviser on Mil. Finance; Special Del. Sterling Accounts Settlement Confs.; Exec. Dir. Int. Bank for Reconstruction and Devt. representing Pakistan, Egypt, Ethiopia, Iran, and Middle Eastern countries 52-58; Minister of Finance, Govt. of Pakistan 58-62, of Econ. Co-ordination 62; Exec. Dir. IBRD 62-63, Vice-Pres. 66-Dec. 75; Minister of

Finance (Pakistan) 62-66; Fellow, Inst. of Cost and Management Accountants (London), Inst. of Costs and Works Accountants (India), Inst. of Industrial Accountants (Pakistan); mem. Nat. Asscn. of Accountants, New York.
International Bank for Reconstruction and Development, Washington; Home: 5825 Tanglewood Drive, Bethesda, Md. 20034, U.S.A.
Telephone: (301) 320-3275.

Shono, Senkichi, LL.B.; Japanese banker; b. 22 Sept. 1913, Tokyo; ed. Tokyo Univ.
Joined The Mitsui Trust Co. Ltd. 37; Dir. The Mitsui Trust & Banking Co. Ltd. 59, Man. Dir. 65, Senior Man. Dir. 68, Pres. 71-; Dir. Mitsui Devt. Co. 72-, Mitsui Kanko Devt. Co. Ltd. 73-, Mitsui Memorial Hosp. 74-; Trustee, Japan Cttee. for Econ. Devt. 68-; Exec. Dir. Fed. of Econ. Org. 71-; Dir. Japan Fed. of Employers' Asscns. 71-; Chair. The Trust Companies Asscn. of Japan 72.
The Mitsui Trust & Banking Co. Ltd., 1-1, Nihonbashi-Muromachi 2-chome, Chuo-ku, Tokyo; 1605 Fueta, Kamakura-shi, Japan.
Telephone: (0467) 31-1647.

Shrimali, Kalu Lal, M.A., PH.D.; Indian educationist and politician; b. 30 Dec. 1909; ed. Banaras Hindu Univ., Calcutta Univ. and Columbia Univ., New York.
Life mem. Vidya Bhavan Soc. 31-; Parl. Sec. Ministry of Educ. New Delhi 53-55, Deputy Minister for Educ. 55-57, Minister of State in Ministry of Educ. and Scientific Research 57-58, Minister of Education 58-63; Vice-Chancellor Univ. of Mysore 64-69; Vice-Chancellor Banaras Hindu Univ. 69-; Chair. Asscn. of Commonwealth Univs., Inter-Univ. Board of India 72-73; mem. Admin Board, Int. Asscn. of Univs. 70-74, Vice-Pres. 75-80; D.Litt. h.c. (Banaras Hindu Univ.), LL.D. h.c. (Mysore Univ.), Hon. D.Sc. (Kiev, U.S.S.R.), Padma Vibhushan 76.
Publs. *Bachon Ki Kuch Samasyayen* (Hindi), *Shiksha aur Bhartiya Loktantra* (Hindi), *The Wardha Scheme*, *Adventures in Education*, *Problems of Education in India*, *Education in Changing India*, *The Prospects of Democracy in India*, *A Search for Values in Indian Education*.
Banaras Hindu University, Varanasi 5, India.

Shukla, Shyama Charan; Indian politician; b. 27 Feb. 1925, Raipur; ed. Raipur, Banaras and Nagpur.
Member of Parl. for Vidhan Sabha 57-; Minister for Irrigation 67; Chief Minister, Madhya Pradesh 69-72, Dec. 75-; Chief Editor, Founder *Mahakoshal*.
Chief Minister's Residence, Shamla Road, Bhopal, Madhya Pradesh, India.

Shukla, Vidya Charan, B.A.; Indian politician; b. 2 Aug. 1929, Raipur; ed. Morris Coll., and Univ. Coll. of Law, Nagpur.
Member, Lok Sabha 57-62, 62-67, 67-70; Deputy Minister, Communications and Parl. Affairs 24 Jan.-14 Feb. 66; Deputy Minister for Home Affairs 66-67; Minister of State in Ministry of Home Affairs 67-70; Minister of Revenue and Expenditure in Ministry of Finance 70-71, Minister of Defence Production 71-74, Minister of State for Planning 74-75, for Information and Broadcasting June 75-.
Ministry of Information and Broadcasting, New Delhi; Shukla Bhavan, Budhapara, Raipur, Madhya Pradesh, India.

Sicat, Gerardo P., M.A., PH.D.; Philippine professor of economics and government official; b. 7 Oct. 1935; ed. Univ. of the Philippines and Massachusetts Inst. of Technology.
Professor of Economics, Univ. of the Philippines 69-, Regent 72-; Chair. Nat. Econ. Council and Cen. Planning Agency, Govt. of the Philippines 70-72; Dir.-Gen. Nat. Econ. and Devt. Authority 72-; mem. Monetary Board of the Philippines, Gov. Council of Asian Devt. Inst.
Publs. *Production Functions in Philippine Manufacturing* 64, *Regional Economic Development in the Philippines* 70, *Philippine Development and Economic Policy* 72, *Taxation and Progress* 72, *New Economic Developments in the Philippines* 74, and several other works.
National Economic and Development Authority, Padre Faura Street, Manila, Philippines.
Telephone: 58-56-14, 59-48-75, 50-39-71.

Siddiqi, M. Raziuddin, M.A., PH.D., D.SC.; Pakistani educationist; b. 7 April 1905; ed. Osmania, Cambridge, Berlin, Göttingen, Leipzig, Paris Univs.
Professor of Mathematics, Dir. of Research and Vice-Chancellor, Osmania Univ. 31-50; Dir. of Research and Vice-Chancellor, Peshawar Univ. 50-58; Vice-Chancellor, Univ. of Sind 59-64; Pres. Pakistan Acad. of Sciences 61-73, Sec. 73-; Vice-Chancellor, Univ. of Islamabad 65-73; Joint Sec. (in charge) Scientific and Technological Research Div., President's Secretariat.
Publs. *Lectures on Quantum Mechanics* 37, *Boundary Problems in Non-linear Partial Differential Equations* 38, *Theory of Relativity* 40, *Problems of Education* 43.
University of Islamabad, 77-E, Satellite Town, Rawalpindi, Pakistan.

Siddiqui, Salimuzzaman, M.B.E., D.PHIL., F.R.S.; Pakistani scientist; b. 19 Oct. 1897, Subeha, U.P., India; ed. Muslim Univ., Aligarh, India, Univ. Coll. London and Univ. of Frankfurt-am-Main.
Director Research Inst., Ayurvedic and Unani Tibbi Coll., Delhi 28-40; Organic Chemist, Council of Scientific and Industrial Research (India) 40-44, Acting Dir. 44-47; Dir. Nat. Chemical Lab. (India) 47-51; Dir. Dept. Scientific and Industrial Research (Pakistan) 51-66; Dir. and Chair. Pakistan Council of Scientific and Industrial Research 53-66; Chair. Nat. Science Council 61-66; Dir. Postgraduate Inst. of Chem., Univ. of Karachi, Pakistan 66-; Pres. Pakistan Acad. of Sciences 67; mem. Vatican Acad. of Sciences and Pontifical Acad.; Gold Medal, U.S.S.R. Acad. of Sciences; President's Pride of Performance Medal (Pakistan) 66; Hon. D.Sc. (Karachi and Leeds); D.Med. h.c. (Frankfurt).
Publs. Over a hundred research papers and memoirs on chemical studies relating to alkaloids, also studies on natural resins, plant bitters and plant colouring matters. Granted over 50 patents to processes concerned with utilization of natural products.
Postgraduate Institute of Chemistry, University of Karachi, Karachi; 8 A, Karachi University Campus, Country Club Road, Karachi 32, Pakistan.
Telephone: 413414 (Office); 416993 (Home).

Sihanouk, Prince Samdech Preah Norodom (*see* Norodom Sihanouk, Prince Samdech Preah).

Sikivou, Semesa Koroikilai, C.B.E., M.A.; Fijian diplomatist; b. 13 Feb. 1917, Vutia, Rewa; ed. Rewa Central School, Suva Methodist Boys' School and Teachers' Training Inst., Davuilevu, Auckland Univ. Coll. and Inst. of Educ., Univ. of London.
Served as Asst. Master Suva Methodist Boys' School 35-42; war service as Lieut., Fiji Military Forces 42-46; Asst. Master Queen Victoria School 49, 51-59; mem. Fiji Legis. Council 56-66; Educ. Officer 60-62; Asst. Dir. of Educ. 63-66, Deputy Dir. 66-70; Perm. Rep. of Fiji to UN 70-, concurrently High Commr. in Canada May 71-, Amb. to U.S.A. July 71-; Vice-Pres. of 28th Session of UN Gen. Assembly 73; mem. Fiji Broadcasting Comm. 55-62, 66-70; mem. Fijian Affairs Board 55-66, 69-70, Fijian Devt. Fund Board 56-66, Native Land Trust Board 65-70; mem. Advisory Council on Educ. 54-70; mem. Council of Chiefs 52-70; mem. many other govt. and civic bodies.
c/o Permanent Mission of Fiji to the United Nations, 1 United Nations Plaza, 26th Floor, New York, N.Y. 10017, U.S.A.

Sikri, Sarv Mittra; Indian judge; b. 26 April 1908, Lahore (Pakistan); ed. Trinity Hall, Cambridge and Lincoln's Inn, London.
Started practice, Lahore High Court 30; Asst. Advocate-Gen., Punjab 49, Advocate-Gen. 51-64; Judge, Supreme Court of India 64-71; Chief Justice of India 71-73; Pres. Indian Law Inst., Indian Branch, Int. Law Asscn.; Hon. Pres. Indian Soc. of Int. Law; mem. Indian Comm. of Jurists; del. to various int. confs.
B-18 Maharani Bagh, New Delhi, India.

Simagin, Nikolai Alexeyevich; Soviet foreign trade official; b. 1907; ed. Inst. of Foreign Trade.
Member C.P.S.U. 30-; Dir. *Sovmongoltorg* 40-47; Chair. *Dalingtorg* 47-50; Office Dir. *Vostokintorg* 50-52; Chief, *Avtovneshtrans* Office 52-55; Deputy Commercial Rep., later Commercial Rep., of U.S.S.R. in Mongolia 55-60; Official, Ministry of Foreign Trade 60-65; U.S.S.R. Commercial Rep. in Mongolia 65-; Order of Red Banner of Labour (twice) and Honour Badge.
U.S.S.R. Trade Representation, Ulan Bator, Mongolia.

Simakov, Kayum Mukhamedzhanovich; Soviet politician; b. 1904; ed. Sverdlovsk Inst. of Non-Ferrous Metals.
Member C.P.S.U. 41-; Chief Engineer, Leningrad and Chimkent; Chair. East Kazakhstan Econ. Council 34-61; Vice-Chair. Council of Ministers of Kazakh S.S.R. 61-; Chair. State Planning Cttee. Kazakh S.S.R. 65-; mem. Central Cttee. of C.P., Kazakh S.S.R.; Deputy to U.S.S.R. Supreme Soviet; mem. Cttee. for Planning and Budget, Soviet of Union.
Council of Ministers of Kazakh S.S.R., Alma-Ata, U.S.S.R.

Simatupang, Lieut.-Gen. Tahi Bonar; Indonesian international church official and retd. army officer; b. 28 Jan. 1920, Sidikalang; ed. Mil. Acad.
Director of Org., Gen. Staff of Indonesian Nat. Army 45-48; Deputy Chief of Staff, Armed Forces 48-49, Acting Chief of Staff 49-51, Chief of Staff 51-54; Mil. Adviser to Govt. 54-59; retd. from mil. service 59; Pres. Council of Churches in Indonesia 71-, Christian Conf. in Asia 72-, World Council of Churches 75-; mem. Supreme Advisory Council, Repub. of Indonesia 73-; D.Hum.Litt. (Tulsa Univ.) 69.
Publs. *Pioneer in War, Pioneer in Peace* (Role of the Armed Forces in Indonesia) 54, *Report from Banaran—Experiences during the People's War* 59, *Christian Task in Revolution* 66.
Jalan Diponegoro 55, Jakarta, Indonesia.
Telephone: 48234.

Sinclair, Ernest Keith, C.M.G., O.B.E., D.F.C., F.R.G.S.; Australian journalist; b. 13 Nov. 1914; ed. Melbourne High School.
Served R.A.F., Second World War; C.O. 97 Pathfinder Sqdn. 44-45, mentioned in dispatches; Foreign Corresp., Europe 38, 46; Editor *The Age* 59-66; Chair. Australian Assoc. Press 65-66; Dir. Gen. Television Corpn. 59-66; Consultant to Prime Minister of Australia 67-72, and to Dept. of Prime Minister and Cabinet 67-74; Assoc. Commr. Industries Assistance Comm. 74-; Dir. Australian Paper Manufacturers and Hecla-Rowe Ltd.; Deputy Chair. Australian Tourist Comm. 69-75; Dir. Hecron Ltd.; mem. Pacific Basin Econ. Council, Australia-Japan Business Co-operation Cttee.; Vice-Pres. Library Council of Victoria; Chair. Humanities Board, Victoria Inst. of Colls. 67-72; Observer, Nat. Capital Planning Cttee. 67-73.
138 Toorak Road, South Yarra, Victoria 3141, Australia.
Telephone: 26-4331 (Melbourne).

Sinclair, Ian McCahon, B.A., LL.B.; Australian barrister, grazier and politician; b. 10 June 1929; ed. Knox Grammar School, Wahroonga and Sydney Univ.
Barrister 52-; mem. House of Representatives for New England 63-; Minister of State for Social Services, Canberra 65-68; Minister assisting Minister for Trade and Industry 66-71; Minister of State for Shipping and Transport 68-71; Minister for Primary Industry 71-72; Deputy Leader Country Party 71-; opposition spokesman on agriculture 74-75; Minister of Agriculture and for N. Australia Nov.-Dec. 75; Minister for Primary Industry and Leader of the House Dec. 75-; Grazier and Man. Dir. Sinclair Pastoral Co. 53-; Dir. Farmers and Graziers' Co-operative Co. Ltd. 62-65; mem. Legislative Council, N.S.W. 61-63; Country Party.
Office: Parliament House, Canberra, A.C.T.; Home: Glenclair, Bendemeer, N.S.W., Australia.

Singh, Air Chief Marshal Arjan, D.F.C.; Indian air force officer; b. 15 April 1919; ed. Government Coll., Lahore, R.A.F. Coll., Cranwell, and Imperial Defence Coll., London.
Wing Commdr. 45, Group Capt. 47, Air Commodore 50, Air Vice-Marshal 59, Air Marshal 64, Air Chief Marshal 66; Chief of Air Staff 64-69; Amb. to Switzerland 71-74; High Commr. to Kenya 74-; Patron, All India Fed. of the Deaf; Padma Vibhushan.
Indian High Commission, P.O. Box 30074, Nairobi, Kenya.

Singh, Dinesh, B.A.; Indian politician; b. 19 July 1925, Kalakankar, Uttar Pradesh; ed. Doon School, Dehra Dun, Colvin Coll. and Lucknow Univ.
Member of Parl. 57-; fmr. Sec. to the High Comm. for India in London, to the Embassy in Paris; led Indian Dels. to FAO, ECAFE and UN; Deputy Minister for External Affairs 62-Jan. 66; Minister of State for External Affairs 66-67; Minister of Commerce 67-69, of External Affairs 69-70, of Industry and Internal Trade 70-71; Pres. UNCTAD II 68-72.
1 Thyagraj Marg, New Delhi 110011; Home: Rajbhwan, P.O. Kalakankar (U.P.), India.
Telephone: 371766 (New Delhi); 40 (Kalakankar).

Singh, Gurmukh Nihal, M.SC.; Indian fmr. barrister, political scientist and state governor; b. 14 March 1895; ed. London School of Economics and Middle Temple, London.
Prof. of Economics and Political Science, later Rama Varma Prof. of Political Science, Banaras Hindu Univ. 20-39, Dean of Faculty of Arts 20-39; Principal of H.L. Coll. of Commerce, Ahmedabad, India 39-43; Principal, Ramjas Coll., Delhi 43-50, S.R. Coll. of Commerce, Delhi 50-52; mem. Delhi State Legislative Assembly 52-56, Speaker 52-55, Chief Minister 55-56; Gov. of Rajasthan 56-62; Founder mem., Sec. and Treas. 39-41 and Pres. 42, Indian Political Science Asscn.; Founder mem., Exec. mem. and Vice-Pres. Indian Council of World Affairs and Indian Inst. of Public Admin., Delhi; mem. Indian Inst. Constitutional and Parl. Studies, Delhi; Founder mem. Guru Nanak Foundation, Delhi 65-.
C-193, Defence Colony, New Delhi 3, India.
Telephone: 626855.

Singh, Hukam; Indian politician; b. 30 Aug. 1895; ed. Govt. High School, Montgomery, Khalsa Coll., Amritsar and Law Coll., Lahore.
Lawyer; fmr. Pres., Singh Sabha, Montgomery; Man. Khalsa High School, Montgomery 41, 43-45; Pres. Shiromani Akali Dal, District Bar Asscn.; imprisoned 23-25, 55; Puisne Judge, State High Court, Kapurthala 47-48; mem. Constituent Ass. 48-50, Provisional Parl. 50-52, Lok Sabha (Parl.) 52-57, 57-; Dep. Speaker, Lok Sabha 56-62, Speaker 62-67; Gov. of Rajasthan 67-72; Del. to Commonwealth Parl. Confs. 59, 61, 62; Hon. Litt.D.
Publs. *Russia as I Saw It, Russia Today, Some Reflections.*
Lok Sabha, New Delhi, India.

Singh, Dr. Jogendra; Indian politician; b. 30 Oct. 1903, Rai Bareli, Uttar Pradesh; ed. Colvin Talukedar Coll., Royal Indian Mil. Coll., Dehra Dun.

Member Cen. Legislative Assembly 34-46, Constituent Assembly 46-49, Provisional Parl. 49-52, Lok Sabha 52-62, Rayja Sabha 65-71; Chair. Indian Refineries 63-64; mem. Indian Agricultural Comm. 70-71; Chair. Delhi Sikh Gurdwara Board 71-April 75; Gov. of Orissa 71-72, of Rajasthan 72-.
Office of the Governor, Raj Bhavan, Jaipur, Rajasthan, India.

Singh, Karan, M.A., PH.D.; Indian politician; b. 9 March 1931; ed. Doon School, Univ. of Jammu and Kashmir and Delhi Univ.
Appointed Regent of Jammu and Kashmir 49; elected Sadar-i-Riyasat (Head of State) by Jammu and Kashmir Legislative Assembly Nov. 52; recognized by Pres. of India and assumed office 17 Nov. 1952, re-elected 57 and 62, Gov. 65-67; Union Minister for Tourism and Civil Aviation 67-73, for Health and Family Planning 73-; Vice-Pres. World Health Assembly 75-76; fmr. Chancellor Jammu and Kashmir Univ. and Banaras Hindu Univ.; Sabhapati, Ramcharit Manas Chatuhshati Rashtriya Samiti; Sec. Jawaharlal Nehru Memorial Fund; Chair. Indian Board for Wild Life and of Project Tiger; Hon. Major-Gen. Indian Army.
Publs. *The Political Thought of Sri Aurobindo Ghosh*, essays, poems.
3 Nyaya Marg, Chanakyapuri, New Delhi, India.

Singh, Kewal; Indian diplomatist; b. 1 June 1915; ed. Forman Christian Coll., Lahore, Law Coll., Lahore, and Balliol Coll., Oxford.
Joined Indian Civil Service 38; Indian Civil Service appointments 40-48; First Sec. Indian Embassy, Ankara 48-49; Indian Military Mission, Berlin 49-51; Chargé d'Affaires, Lisbon 51-53; Consul-General, Pondicherry 53-54; Chief Commr., State of Pondicherry, Karaikal, Mahe and Yanan 54-57; awarded Padma Shri for distinguished services leading to merger of French Possessions with India; Amb. to Cambodia 57-58, to Sweden, Denmark and Finland 59-62; Deputy High Commr. in U.K. 62-65; High Commr. in Pakistan 65-66; Amb. to U.S.S.R. and Mongolia 66-69; Sec. in Ministry of External Affairs 68-70; Amb. to Fed. Repub. of Germany 70-72; Foreign Sec. 72-.
Ministry of External Affairs, New Delhi, India.

Singh, Khushwant, LL.B.; Indian author; b. 1915; ed. Government Coll., Lahore, King's Coll. and Inner Temple, London.
Practised, High Court, Lahore 39-47; joined Indian Ministry of External Affairs 47; Press Attaché, Canada and then Public Relations Officer, London 48-51; Ministry of Information and Broadcasting; edited *Yojana*; Dept. of Mass Communication, UNESCO 54-56; commissioned by Rockefeller Foundation and Muslim Univ.. Aligarh to write a history of the Sikhs 58; Editor *The Illustrated Weekly of India*; Grove Press Award; Padma Bhushan 74.
Publs. *Mark of Vishnu* 49, *The Sikhs* 51, *Train to Pakistan* 54, *Sacred Writings of the Sikhs* 60, *I shall not hear the Nightingale* 61, *Umrao Jan Ada—Courtesan of Lucknow* (trans.) 61, *Historv of the Sikhs (1769-1839)* Vol. I 62, *Ranjit Singh: Maharaja of the Punjab* 62, *Fall of the Sikh Kingdom* 62, *The Skeleton* (trans.) 63, *Land of the Five Rivers* (trans.) 64, *History of the Sikhs (1839-Present Day)* 65, *Khushwant Singh's India* 69.
Times of India Building, Dr. D. Naoroji Road, Bombay 1, India.
Telephone: 268271.

Singh, Nagendra, M.A., LL.D., D.LITT., D.PHIL., D.SC., D.C.L.; Indian civil servant and international lawyer; b. 18 March 1914, Dungarpur, Rajasthan; ed. Agra and Cambridge Univs. and Gray's Inn, London.
Entered Indian Civil Service 38; recent posts include: Special Sec. Ministry of Information and Broadcasting 64, Ministry of Transport Aug. 64; Sec. Ministry of Transport and Dir.-Gen. of Shipping 66; Sec. to Pres. of India 66-; Constitutional Adviser to Govt. of Bhutan 70-; Chair. Govt. Shipping Corpn. 62, The Mogul Line Ltd. 60-61, 63-67, The Hindustan Shipyard Ltd. 62-67 (Dir. 56-67); mem. Indian Constituent Assembly 47-48; Justice of the Peace, Bombay 48-; Nehru Prof. of Int. Law and Co-operation, Graduate Inst. of Int. Studies, Univ. of Geneva; Prof. of Human Rights and Int. Co-operation, Univ. of Tribhuban, Nepal; Prof. of Int. Law and Maritime Law, Univ. of Madras; mem. Perm. Court of Arbitration, The Hague 67; mem. Int. Law Comm. 66-, Vice-Chair. 69; Vice-Chair. UN Comm. on Int. Trade Law 69, Chair. 71; Judge Int. Court of Justice 73-, Vice-Pres. Feb. 76-(79); mem. Panel of Legal Experts, IAEA; founder mem. Int. Council for Environmental Law 69; Assoc. Inst. de Droit International; Pres. Maritime Law Asscn. of India; mem. American Soc. of Int. Law, Indian Inst. of Public Admin., India Int. Centre, etc.; Visiting Prof., Univs. of Delhi, Udaipur, Bombay and Banaras; Pres. IMCO Assembly 63-65; Pres. ILO Maritime Session 70; Pres. Afro-Asian Legal Consultative Cttee. 73; Chair. or mem. many other int. cttees. and leader, Indian del. to numerous confs., etc.; Padma Vibhushan Award 73.
Publs. *Termination of Membership of International Organizations* 58, *Nuclear Weapons and International Law, Defence Mechanism of the Modern State* 63, *The Concept of Force and Organization of Defence in the Constitutional History of India* 69, *Achievements of UNCTAD I and II in the field of Invisibles* 69, *India and International Law* 69, *Bhutan* 71; several vols. of lectures and numerous articles on questions of int. law, etc.
International Court of Justice, Peace Palace, The Hague 2012, Netherlands; 6 Akbar Road, New Delhi, India.

Singh, Raja Roy; Indian educationist; b. 5 April 1918; ed. Univ. of Allahabad.
Entered Indian Admin. Service 43; fmr. Dir. of Educ., Uttar Pradesh; fmr. Joint Sec., Fed. Ministry of Educ., New Delhi; fmr. Joint Dir. Indian Council of Educational Research and Training, Nat. Inst. of Educ.; at Office of Educational Planning, UNESCO Headquarters, Paris 64-65; Dir. UNESCO Regional Office for Educ. in Asia 65-.
UNESCO Regional Office for Education in Asia, Darakarn Building, 920 Sukhumvit Road, Bangkok, Thailand.

Singh, Ram Subhag, M.A., PH.D.; Indian politician; b. 7 July 1917; ed. Missouri Univ.
Joined Congress Party 35; mem. of Parl. 50-; Sec. Parl. Congress Party 55-62; Minister of State in the Ministry of Agriculture 62-64, in Ministry of Social Security and Cottage Industries 64-66; Minister of State for Railways 66-67; Chief Whip, Parl. Congress Party 67-69; Minister of Parl. Affairs and Communications 67-69, of Railways 69; Parl. Leader Congress Party—Opposition 69-71.
Khajuriah, Arrah, Bihar, India.

Singh, Sher, M.A.; Indian agriculturalist and politician; b. 18 Sept. 1917; ed. Delhi Univ.
Former Lecturer, M.S.J. Coll., Bharatpur, and Lecturer in Mathematics, Jat Coll., Rohtak; elected to Punjab Legislative Assembly 46, 52, 57, Punjab Legislative Council 62; Parl. Sec., Punjab 48-51; Deputy Leader of Congress Legislative Party in Punjab 56-57; Minister of Irrigation and Power, Punjab 56-57; now mem. Lok Sabha; Minister of State in Ministry of Educ. 67-69; Minister of State for Communications 69-71; Minister of State, Ministry of Agriculture 71-74, Ministry of Communications 74-75; Chancellor of Gurukul (system of teaching based on ancient Indian culture), Jhajjar; mem. Syndicate of Gurukul, Kangri Univ.; fmr. Founder-Pres. Haryana Lok Samiti; del. to several int. confs.
c/o Ministry of Communications, New Delhi, India.

Singh, Swaran, M.SC., LL.B.; Indian politician; b. 19 Aug. 1907; ed. Govt. Coll., Lahore, and Lahore Law Coll.

Elected Punjab Legislative Assembly 46; Minister of Development, Food, Civil Supplies 46-47; mem. Gov.'s Security Council, then Partition Cttee. 47; Minister of Home, Gen. Admin., Revenue, Irrigation and Electricity in first Punjab Congress Ministry 47-49; resigned to resume legal practice; Minister of Capital Projects and Electricity 52; Minister for Works, Housing and Supply (Central Govt.) 52-57; elected to Rajya Sabha; initiated Subsidized Industrial Housing Scheme; led Indian del. to ECOSOC in 54 and 55; Lok Sabha (Parl.) 57-; Minister for Steel, Mines and Fuel 57-62; Minister for Railways 62-63, of Food and Agriculture 63-64, of Industry, Engineering and Technical Development 64, of External Affairs 64-66, 70-74, of Defence 66-70, 74-Nov. 75; led Indian del. to UN Gen. Assembly 64-66, 70-73, ECOSOC 54, 55; Rep. to Commonwealth Prime Ministers' Conf. 71, 73.
7 Hastings Road, New Delhi, India.

Singh, Tarlok, B.A., B.SC.; Indian economist; b. 26 Feb. 1913; ed. St. Vincent's School and Deccan Coll., Poona, Gujarat Coll., Ahmedabad and London School of Economics.
Indian Civil Service 37-62; Colonization Officer, Nili Bar Colony, Punjab 43; Finance Dept. Govt. of India 44-46; Private Sec. to Vice-Pres. Interim Govt. and to Prime Minister 46-47; Dir.-Gen. of Rehabilitation 47-49; with Planning Comm. 50-67, Additional Sec. 58-62, mem. 62-67; Hon. Fellow, London School of Econs.; Fellow, Inst. for Int. Econ. Studies, Univ. of Stockholm 67, 69-70; Visiting Senior Research Economist, Woodrow Wilson School, Princeton Univ. 68; Deputy Exec. Dir. (Planning) UNICEF 70-74; Hon. Fellow, London School of Econs.; Padma Shri 54, Padma Bhushan 62; Söderström Medal, Swedish Royal Acad. of Sciences 70.
Publs. *Poverty and Social Change* 45, 69, *Resettlement Manual for Displaced Persons* 52, *Towards an Integrated Society* 69, *India's Development Experience* 74.
74 Paschimi Marg, New Delhi 57; and 110 Sundar Nagar, New Delhi, India.
Telephone: 67-13-42.

Singh, Ujjal, M.A.; Indian fmr. state governor and politician; b. 27 Dec. 1895; ed. Khalsa High School, Amritsar, Govt. Coll., Lahore.
Member Punjab Legislature 26-56; Del. to first and second Round Table Confs., London 30, 31; mem. Cons. Cttee. 32; Parl. Sec. (Home) 37-42; mem. Central Advisory Board of Educ. in India, All India Council ot Technical Educ. 45-49; Minister, Industries and Civil Supplies, E. Punjab Govt. 49; Minister, Finance and Industries 52-56; mem. Second Finance Comm. 57; Governor of Punjab 65-66, of Madras (now Tamil Nadu) 66-71.
12 Kasturba Gandhi Marg, New Delhi 1, India.
Telephone: 48861.

Singh Deo, Rajendra Narayan; Indian politician, fmr. Maharaja of Patna; b. 31 March 1912; ed. Mayo Coll., Ajmer and St. Columba's Coll. Hazaribagh.
Ruler of Patna State 33, later becoming the first ruler to sign the merger agreement with the Indian Union; formed political party Ganatantra Parishad 49 (merged with Swatantra Party 62); elected to Lok Sabha 52; Leader of Opposition, Orissa Legislative Assembly 57-59; Dep. Leader, Coalition Govt. and Finance Minister 59-61; re-elected to Orissa Legislative Assembly as Leader of Opposition 61-66, 72-; Chief Minister of Orissa 67-70; Deputy Chief Minister, Minister of Industries 71-72; fmr. Chair. Eastern States Board of Forestry and Agriculture, Vice-Pres. Council of Rulers of Eastern States Agency, mem. Standing Cttee. Eastern States Union; Pres. Orissa Unit of Swatantra Party and mem. of its Gen. Council, Nat. Exec. and Cen. Parl. Board.
Bhuvaneshwar, Orissa, India.

Singhania, Lakshmipat (brother of Sir Padampat Singhania, *q.v.*); Indian businessman; b. 23 Feb. 1910.
Entered business 29; Dir.-in-charge Aluminium Corpn. of India Ltd.; former Pres. Merchants' Chamber of U.P., Kanpur 46 and 47, and Bharat Chamber of Commerce, Calcutta 48-49; mem. Coal Control Board, Bharat Chamber of Commerce, Indian Central Jute Cttee., Joint Consultative Board of Industry and Labour, Indian Inst. of Social Welfare and Business Management, All-India Board of Technical Studies in Commerce and Business Admin., etc.; Underwriter, Lloyd's Society of London; fmr. Pres. Fed. Indian Chamber of Commerce and Industry, Indian Nat. Cttee. of the Int. Chamber of Commerce (58); President All-India Organization of Industrial Employers.
Home: J. K. House, 12 Alipore Road, Calcutta 700027; Office: 7 Council House Street, Calcutta 70001, India.

Singhania, Sir Padampat, Kt. (brother of Lakshmipat Singhania, *q.v.*); Indian industrialist; b. 1905; ed. privately.
President J.K. Org. (Juggilal Kamlapat Group of Mills), Kanpur; a pioneer of cotton and woollen textiles, rayon, nylon, jute, sugar, hosiery, iron and steel, aluminium, plastic, strawboard, paper, chemical, mining, electronics and television, dry-cell battery, agricultural equipment, cement, tyre and oil industries; Founder Merchants' Chamber of U.P.; fmr. Pres. Federation of Indian Chambers of Commerce and Industries; mem. 1st Indian Parl.; fmr. Chair. Board of Governors, Indian Inst. of Technology, Kanpur; Hon. D.Lit. (Kanpur Univ.).
Kamla Tower, Kanpur, India.
Telephone: 62532.

Sinha, Mahamaya Prasad; Indian social worker and politician; b. 1 May 1910; ed. Punjab, Calcutta, Patna, Banares Hindu Univs.
Joined Indian Nat. Congress 25; imprisoned several times; District Congress Pres. for eighteen years; mem. A.I.C.C. for twenty-two years; Pres. Gandhi Memorial Cttee. Bihar 48; Pres. K.M.P.P.; Pres. Praja Socialist Party (P.S.P.) Bihar 53; mem. Bihar Asscn. 46-47; mem. of Parl. 50-52; Pres. United Front 67-68; Pres. All-India Bharatiya Kranti Dal (B.K.D.); fmr. Chief Minister, Bihar.
Publs. articles on various subjects.
1 Strand Road, Patna, Bihar, India.

Sinha, Satya Narayana; Indian politician; b. 1900; ed. Patna.
Joined Non-Violence Movement and imprisoned 20; mem. Bihar Legislature 26-30; mem. Indian Constituent Assembly 26-47, of Lok Sabha 47-; Minister of State for Parl. Affairs 49-52; Minister for Parl. Affairs 52-67, of Information and Broadcasting Sept. 63-June 64, of Civil Aviation June 64, of Communications 64-67; Minister without Portfolio March-Nov. 67; Minister of Health, Family Planning and Urban Devt. 67-69, of Information, Broadcasting and Communications 69-71; Gov. of Madhya Pradesh 71-; Pres. Indian Council of Medical Research; Chief Whip Congress Party in Central Assembly and Constituent Assembly.
Raj Bhavan, Bhopal, Madhya Pradesh, India.

Siregar, Melanchton; Indonesian teacher and politician; b. 7 Aug. 1912, Pea-Arung Humbang, N. Tapanuli; ed. Christian Teachers' Training Coll. (H.I.K.), Solo and Coll. for Headmasters' Degree, Bandung.
Teacher and Headmaster in various schools 38-45; Dir. Higher Technical School, Pematang Siantar 45-47; Head of Gen. and Vocational Training Divs. of Service of Education, Instruction and Culture, Pematang Siantar, Sumatra Representative Council 48-50; mem. Parl. 56-71; Inspector of Secondary Schools in N. Sumatra 47-51; Co-ordinator of Office for Inspection of Education of N. Sumatra Region, Medan 52-56; mem. of Exec., North Sumatra Representative Council 48-50; Gen. Chair. in N. Sumatra and Co-ordinator in Sumatra, PARKINDO

(Protestant political party) 50-60, Vice-Chair. Man. Board 60-64, Gen. Chair. of Exec. Board 64-67, Gen. Chair. 67-; Vice-Chair. People's Congress (MPRS) 66-72; mem. of Indonesian dels. to UN 57, 67.
59 H.O.S. Tjokroaminto Street, Jakarta, Indonesia.
Telephone: 45322-3.

Siriwardane, Codippilliarachchige Don Stanislaus; Ceylonese diplomatist; b. 26 March 1911; ed. Ananda Coll., Colombo and London Univ.
Advocate of Supreme Court, Ceylon; Major, Ceylon Light Infantry; mem. Royal Comm. on Educ. 61; mem. Royal Comm. on Buddhist Affairs 57; mem. Ceylon Senate 61-67; Amb. to U.S.S.R., Czechoslovakia, Poland, Hungary, Romania and German Democratic Repub. 73-74, to Pakistan, also accred. to Iran, 74-.
Embassy of Sri Lanka, 468-F, Sector G-6/4, Islamabad, Pakistan; Home: Longdon Place, Colombo 7, Sri Lanka.

Siwabessy, Gerrit Agustinus; Indonesian radiologist and politician; b. 19 Aug. 1914, Saparua, Moluccas; ed. Medical schools, Surabaya, Univ. of Jakarta and Univ. of London.
Radiologist, Cen. Hosp., Surabaja 42-45, Cen. Hosp., Malang 45-47, Cen. Hosp., Jakarta 48; Chief Doctor, Cen. Hosp., Jakarta, concurrently Doctor at Mil. Hosp. 53; Head Indonesian Inst. of Radiology 54; Dir.-Gen. Indonesian Inst. of Atomic Energy 58-73; lecturer, Univ. of Indonesia 56; mem. Nat. Council 57; mem. Indonesian Nat. Planning Council 59; Minister of Health 66-; del. to several int. radiology and atomic energy confs.
Ministry of Health, Jakarta, Indonesia.

Smedley, Harold, C.M.G., M.B.E.; British diplomatist; b. 19 June 1920, Hove, Sussex; ed. Aldenham School and Pembroke Coll., Cambridge.
Royal Marine Commandos, Second World War; Dominions Office 46, British High Comm., New Zealand 48-50, S. Rhodesia 51-53, India 57-60; Private Sec. to Commonwealth Sec. 54-57; later Head of News Dept., Commonwealth Relations Office; High Commr. to Ghana 64-65, 66-67; Amb. to Laos 67-70; Asst. Under-Sec. of State, Foreign and Commonwealth Office 70-72; Sec.-Gen. Comm. on Rhodesian Opinion 71-72; High Commr. to Sri Lanka and Amb. (non-resident) to the Maldives 73-75; High Commr. in New Zealand and Gov. of Pitcairn Island 76-.
British High Commission, P.O. Box 1812, Wellington, New Zealand; Home: Sherwood, Oak End Way, Woodham, Weybridge, Surrey, England.

Snedden, Rt. Hon. Billy Mackie, P.C., Q.C., M.P.; Australian lawyer and politician; b. 31 Dec. 1926.
Admitted to Supreme Court, W.A. 51, Victoria 55, Victorian Bar 55; Migration Officer Italy, England 52-54; mem. House of Reps. Bruce, Victoria 55-; Commonwealth Attorney-Gen. 63-66; appointed Q.C. 64; Chair. First Commonwealth Law Ministers Conf., Canberra 65; Australian Rep. Second Commonwealth Law Ministers Conf. London 66; Fed. Minister of Immigration Dec. 66-69, of Labour and Nat. Service 69-71; Treasurer 71-72; Leader House of Reps. 66-71; Deputy Leader of the Liberal Party 71-72, Party Leader and Leader of Opposition 72-75; Speaker of House of Reps. Feb. 76-.
Office of the Speaker, Parliament House, Canberra, A.C.T. 2600; Home: 22 Pine Crescent, Ringwood, Victoria, Australia.

Somare, Michael Thomas; Papua New Guinea politician; b. 9 April 1936; ed. Sogeri Secondary School, Admin. Coll.
Teacher 56-62; Asst. Area Educ. Officer, Madang 62-63; Broadcasts Officer, Dept. of Information and Extension Services, Wewak 63-66, journalist 66-68; mem. House of Assembly for E. Sepik Region 68-72; Parl. Leader of Pangu Pati and of Coalition Govt. 72-76; Deputy Chair. Admin.'s Exec. Council 72-73, Chair. Exec. Council (Cabinet) 73-75; Chief Minister 72-75, Prime Minister Sept. 75-; Minister of Information and Extension Services 74-75; Sana (Chief) of Saet clan, Murik Lakes area 74-; Chair. Board of Trustees, P.N.G. Museum; mem. Second Select Cttee, on Constitutional Devt. 68-72, Advisory Cttee. of Australian Broadcasting Comm.
Office of the Prime Minister, Waigani; Home: Karan, Murik Lakes, East Sepik, Papua New Guinea.
Telephone: 44501 (Office).

Son Sann; Cambodian fmr. politician; b. 1911, Phnom-Penh; ed. Ecole des Hautes Etudes Commerciales de Paris.
Deputy Gov. Provinces of Battambang and Prey-Veng 35-39; Head of Yuvan Kampuchearath (Youth Movement); Minister of Finance 46-47; Vice-Pres. Council of Ministers 49; Minister of Foreign Affairs 50; Mem. of Parl. for Phnom-Penh and Pres. Cambodian Nat. Assembly 51-52; Gov. of Nat. Bank of Cambodia 55-68; Minister of State (Finance and Nat. Economy) 61-62; Vice-Pres. in charge of Economy, Finance and Planning 65-67; Prime Minister 67; First Vice-Pres. in charge of Econ. and Financial Affairs 68; Grand Cordon de l'Ordre Royal du Cambodge, Commdr. du Sowathara (Mérite économique), Légion d'Honneur, Commdr. du Monisaraphon, Médaille d'Or du Règne, Grand Officier du Million d'Eléphants (Laos), etc.

Son Sen; Cambodian politician; b. *c.* 1930; ed. Univ. in France.
Exile in Hanoi 63; mem. Cen. Cttee. *Pracheachan* (Cambodian Communist Party); liaison officer between *Khmers Rouges* and exiled Royal Govt. of Nat. Union in Peking 70; Chief of Gen. Staff, *Khmer Rouge* armed forces 71-; Third Deputy Prime Minister, Minister of Defence Aug. 75-.
Ministry of Defence, Phnom-Penh, Cambodia.

Souphanouvong; Laotian politician; b. 1902; ed. Lycée Saint-Louis (Paris), Ecole Nationale des Ponts et Chaussées.
Studied engineering in France; returned to Laos 38 and became active in the Nationalist Movement; joined Pathet Lao and fought against the French; formed nationalist party (Neo Leo Haksat) in Bangkok 50; Leader of the Patriotic Front; Minister of Planning, Reconstruction and Urbanism 58; arrested 59, escaped May 60 and rejoined Pathet Lao Forces; Pathet Lao del. Geneva Conf. on Laos 61-62; Vice-Premier and Minister of Econ. Planning 62-74; Chair. Joint Nat. Political Council 74-75, Pres. of Laos Dec. 75-.
Office of the President, Vientiane, Laos.

Souvanlasy, Khamking, L. en D.; Laotian government official and diplomatist; b. 14 Sept 1926; ed. Collège Pavie, Vientiane, and Univ. of Paris.
Head of Dept., Ministry of Foreign Affairs 53-54, Ministry of Nat Educ. 54-55; Under-Sec. to Pres. of Council of Ministers 55-56; Counsellor, Laotian Embassy, Tokyo 56-58, Chargé d'Affaires a.i. 58-59; Sec. of State in Presidency of Council of Ministers (in charge of Foreign Affairs and Nat. Information) 59; Sec. of State for Foreign Affairs 60; Adviser, Ministry of Foreign Affairs 61-62; Amb. to People's Republic of China 63-65, to U.S.A. 66-70; Perm. Rep. to UN 66-70; Act. Minister of Justice 70-74, Minister 74-75; Grand Officer Order of Million Elephants and White Parasol 70; Hon. Phagna Kittikhoun Sounthone 71.
c/o Ministry of Justice, Vientiane, Laos.

Souvanna Phouma, Prince; Laotian engineer and politician; b. 7 Oct. 1901; ed. Coll. Paul Bert and Lycée Albert Sarraut, Hanoi, Univs. of Paris and Grenoble.
Entered Public Works Service of Indo-China 31; Engineer at Phoukhoun 40-41, at Luang Prabang 41-44; Chief Engineer, Bureau à la Circonscription Territoriale des Travaux Publics du Laos 44-45; Principal Engineer (1st Class) of the Public Works Service of Indochina; Minister of Public Works 50-51; Prime Minister, Pres. of the

Council, Minister of Public Works and of Planning 51-54; Vice-Pres. of the Council and Minister of Nat. Defence and Ex-Servicemen 54-56; Prime Minister, Pres. of the Council, Minister of Nat. Defence and Ex-Servicemen, of Foreign Affairs and of Information 56-57, Prime Minister 57-58; Amb. to France 58-59; Pres. National Assembly 60; Prime Minister, Minister of Defence and Foreign Affairs Aug.-Dec. 60; Leader of Neutralist Govt. 60-62; Prime Minister 62-75; Minister of Defence and Veterans and Social Affairs 62-74, of Foreign Affairs 64-74, of Rural Devt. 71-74; Adviser to the Govt. Dec. 75-; Grand Cross Order of Million Elephants, Commdr. Légion d'Honneur, etc.
c/o Office of the Prime Minister, Vientiane, Laos.

Souza, Francis Newton; Indian painter; b. 12 April 1924, ed. St. Xavier's Coll. and Sir J. J. School of Art, Bombay, Central School of Art, London, Ecole des Beaux Arts; Paris.
In London 49-; one-man exhbns. London and major English cities, Paris, Stockholm, Frankfurt, Stuttgart, Bombay, New Delhi, Copenhagen, Johannesburg and in U.S.A.; represented in Baroda Museum, Nat. Gallery, New Delhi, Tate Gallery, London, Wakefield Gallery, Haifa Museum, Nat. Gallery, Melbourne, Museum of Modern Art, N.Y., Musée d'Art Moderne, Paris, etc.; retrospective exhbns. in London 51, New Delhi 65, Leicester 67, Detroit 68, Minneapolis Int. Art Festival 72; Guest Lecturer, Cooper Union, Asia Soc., N.Y.; represented in hundreds of private collections throughout the world; several awards.
Publ. *Words and Lines* (autobiography) 59.
148 W. 67th Street, New York, N.Y. 10023, U.S.A.
Telephone: 212-874-2181.

Spender, Sir Percy Claude, K.C.V.O., K.B.E., KT.ST.J., Q.C., B.A., LL.B.; retd. Australian diplomatist and international judge; b. 5 Oct. 1897; ed. Sydney Univ.
Entered public service as Clerk, Sydney Town Hall 15; enlisted A.I.F. 18; called to N.S.W. Bar 23; K.C. 35; mem. House of Reps. for Warringah, N.S.W. 37-51; mem. Fed. Exec. Council 39, Vice-Pres. Exec. Council 40; Minister without Portfolio 39; Acting Treas. 39, Treas. 40; Minister for Army 40-41; mem. Australian War Cabinet 40-41; mem. of Govt. and later Opposition mem. Australian Advisory War Council 41-45; Lieut.-Col. Active List, Australian Mil. Forces 42-45; Minister for External Affairs 49-51; Amb. to U.S.A. 51-58; Chair. Australian del. to British Commonwealth Foreign Ministers Conf., Colombo 50, and to UN 50: Vice-Pres. Fifth Gen. Assembly 50-51; Vice-Chair. Australian del. to Gen. Assemblies, later Chair. 52-56; Vice-Pres. Japanese Peace Treaty Conf. San Francisco 51; Chair. Australian del. to Twelve Power Conf. to settle draft statute for Int. Atomic Energy Agency 56 and to several other int. confs.; Australian Gov. IMF, IBRD 51-53, 56, Alt. Gov. IMF 54-55; Judge of Int. Court of Justice 58-67, Pres. 64-67; Dir. of a number of public cos.; Chair. of Trustees apptd. by Australian Museum to establish a nat. index of Australian birds in colour; mem. Council of Assicurazioni Generali, Italy; Grande Ufficiale, Ordine al Merito (Italy) 76; Hon. LL.D., D.C.L., Litt.D.
Publs. *Company Law and Practice* 39, *Foreign Policy—the Next Phase* 44, *Exercises in Diplomacy* 69, *Politics and A Man* 72.
Headingley House, 11 Wellington Street, Woollahra, Sydney, N.S.W. 2025, Australia.
Telephone: 32-32-52; 328-71-71.

Spicer, Sir John Armstrong, Kt., Q.C.; Australian lawyer; b. 5 March 1899; ed. in Torquay (England) and Melbourne.
Admitted Barrister and Solicitor 21; K.C. 48; Senator Commonwealth Parl. 40-44, and 49-56; Attorney-Gen. 49-56; Chief Judge, Australian Industrial Court 56- (fmrly. Commonwealth Industrial Court).
153 Glen Iris Road, Glen Iris, Melbourne, Victoria, Australia.
Telephone: 25-2882.

Sridharmadhibes, Chao Phya; Thai politician and jurist; b. 30 Oct. 1885.
President Supreme Court 27-28; Minister of Justice 28-32, 37-38, 44-45, and 46; mem. Assembly of People's Reps. 33-44, and 46; Minister of Finance 33-34; Pres. Assembly of People's Reps. 34-36; mem. Perm. Court of Arbitration, The Hague 35-41, 48-66; Minister of Foreign Affairs 38-39; Minister of Public Health 44-45; Senator and Pres. of Senate 47-51, mem. and Pres. Constituent Assembly 48-49; Privy Councillor 52-; Exec. Vice-Pres. Thai Red Cross 60-64.
Villa Chittasukh, Silom Road, Bangkok, Thailand.

Srivastava, Chandrika Prasad, LL.B., M.A.; Indian international civil servant; b. 8 July 1920, Unnao; ed. Univ. of Lucknow.
Deputy Dir.-Gen. of Shipping, Govt. of India 54-57; Joint Sec. to Prime Minister 64-66; Chair. State Shipping Corpn. of India 66-73; Pres. Indian Nat. Shipowners' Asscn. 71-73; Dir. Reserve Bank of India 73-74; Pres. UN Diplomatic Conf. on a Code of Conduct for Liner Confs. 73-74; Sec.-Gen. Inter-Governmental Maritime Consultative Org. (IMCO) Jan. 74-; Gold Medal for English (Univ. of Lucknow); Padma Bhushan 72.
Publs. contributions to maritime journals.
Inter-Governmental Maritime Consultative Organization, 101-104 Piccadilly, London, W1V 0AE; 2 Parklands, Ice House Wood, Oxted, Surrey, England.

Stewart, D. S., O.B.E.; Australian mechanical and electrical engineer; b. 18 Dec. 1919, Brisbane; ed. Queensland Univ.
Former Man. Britannia Production and Devt., Bristol Aircraft Co.; Dir., Gen. Man. Hestair Group; Dir. of Eng., Clyde Eng. Pty. Ltd., Chief Exec., Hadfields-Goodwin-Scotts Group; Man. Dir. Hamersley Holdings Ltd. and Hamersley Iron Pty. Ltd. March 73-; Fellow, Inst. of Engs., Australia; Assoc. Fellow, Royal Aeronautical Soc.
Hamersley Iron Pty. Ltd., 95 Collins Street, Melbourne 3000, Australia.

Stewart, Francis Eugene; Australian politician; b. 20 Feb. 1923; ed. Christian Brothers Coll., St. Mary's Cathedral, Sydney.
Clerk, Transport Dept., N.S.W. Govt. 39; Army Service 41-45; Transport Dept. 46-53; mem. House of Reps. for Lang 53-; mem. Fed. Parl. Labor Party Exec. 69-75; Minister of Tourism and Recreation Dec. 72-75, concurrently Minister Assisting the Treasurer 73-75; Minister Assisting Minister for Repatriation, Compensation and Social Security 75; Pres. Pacific Area Travel Asscn. (PATA) until 73, Vice-Pres. and Life Member Exec. Council Nov. 73-75.
2A Wilson Avenue, Belmore, N.S.W.; and Shop 2, The Boulevarde, Lakemba, N.S.W., Australia.

Stewart, Stanley Toft; Singapore administrator and fmr. diplomatist; b. 13 June 1910; ed. St. Xavier's Inst. and Raffles Coll., Singapore.
Teacher, Malay Coll., Kuala Kangsar, Perak 33-34; joined Straits Settlements Civil Service 34; Asst. District Officer, Butterworth 36-39, Balik Pulau 39; District Officer, Balik Pulau 46, Butterworth 47, Chair. Rural Board, Province Wellesley 47, also mem. Penang State Legis. Council; later Chair. Province Wellesley War Exec. Cttee., mem. State War Exec. Cttee.; in Singapore 52-; Deputy Chair. Rural Board, Singapore 52-54, Chair. 54-55; Deputy Sec. Ministry of Local Govt. Lands and Housing 55-57; Deputy Chief Sec. 57-59; Perm. Sec. Ministry of Home Affairs 59-63, Perm. Sec. to Prime Minister 61-66, later also Perm. Sec. to Deputy Prime Minister and Head of Civil Service; Singapore High Commr. in Australia 66-69; Perm. Sec.

Ministry of Foreign Affairs 69-72; mem. Presidential Council; Exec. Sec. Singapore Nat. Stadium 73, Chair., Dir. 74; Singapore State Meritorious Service Medal 62.
103 Holland Road, Singapore 10, Singapore.

Stone, John O., B.SC., B.A.; Australian financial executive; b. 31 Jan. 1929; ed. Univ. of Western Australia and New Coll., Oxford.
Assistant to Australian Treasury Rep. in London 54-56, Australian Treasury Rep. in London 58-61; in Research and Information Div., Gen. Financial and Econ. Policy Branch, Dept. of Treasury, Canberra 56-57, in Home Finance Div. 61-62, Asst. Sec. Econ. and Financial Surveys Div. 62-66; Exec. Dir. for Australia, New Zealand and South Africa, IMF, IBRD 67-70; First Asst. Sec., Revenue, Loans and Investment Div., Dept. of Treasury, Canberra 71; Sec. Australian Loan Council and Nat. Debt Comm. 71; Deputy Sec. (Econ.), Dept. of Treasury 71-; mem. Australian dels. to GATT, IMF and IBRD annual meetings, OECD, etc.
Department of the Treasury, Canberra, A.C.T. 2600, Australia.
Telephone: 63-3740.

Street, Anthony Austin; Australian politician; b. 8 Feb. 1926, Victoria; ed. Melbourne Grammar School.
Royal Australian Navy; primary producer; mem. House of Reps. for Corangamite 66; Sec. Govt. Mems. Defence and Wool Cttees. 67-71; mem. Joint Parl. Ctee. on Foreign Affairs 69; Chair. Fed. Rural Cttee. of Liberal Party 70-74; mem. Fed. Exec. Council 71; Asst. Minister of Labour and Nat. Service 72; mem. Liberal Party shadow cabinet for social security, health and welfare 73, for primary industry, shipping and transport 73, for science and tech. and A.C.T. 74, for labour 75; Minister for Labour and Immigration Nov.-Dec. 75; Minister for Employment and Industrial Relations, and Minister Assisting the Prime Minister in Public Service Matters Dec. 75-; Liberal.
Department of Employment and Industrial Relations, 239 Bourke Street, Melbourne, Victoria; and Parliament House, Canberra, A.C.T.; Home: Eildon, Lismore, Victoria, Australia.

Su Chen-hua; People's Repub. of China; b. 1909, Hunan; ed. Red Army Acad.
Joined Red Army 29; on Long March 34-35; Political Commissar 7th Army Corps, 2nd Field Army 49; Sec. CCP Kweichow 50; Deputy Political Commissar of Navy, People's Liberation Army 53, Political Commissar 57-; Adm. 56; Alt. mem. 8th Cen. Cttee. of CCP 56; Alt. mem. Politburo, 10th Cen. Cttee. of CCP 73, 75.

Su Yu; politician and army officer, People's Repub. of China; b. 1909, Fukien; ed. Hunan Prov. No. 2 Normal School, Changte.
Commander Training Battalion, Red Army Coll. 31; Deputy Commdr. N. Kiangsu Command, New 4th Army 39; Alt. mem. 7th Cen. Cttee. of CCP 45; Deputy Commdr. 3rd Field Army 48; Acting Mayor of Nanking 49; Chief of Staff People's Liberation Army 54-58; Gen. 55; mem. 8th Cen. Cttee. of CCP 56; Vice-Minister of Nat. Defence 59-; mem. 9th Cen. Cttee. of CCP 69, 10th Cen. Cttee. 73.

Subandrio, Dr.; Indonesian politician, diplomatist and surgeon; b. 1914; ed. Medical Univ., Jakarta.
Active in Nat. Movement as student and gen. practitioner; worked with underground anti-Japanese Forces during Second World War; forced to leave post at Jakarta Cen. Hosp. and then established a private practice at Semarang; following Declaration of Independence abandoned practice to become Sec.-Gen., Ministry of Information and was later sent by Indonesian Govt. as special envoy to Europe; established Information Office, London 47; Chargé d'Affaires, London 49, Amb. to U.K. 50-54, to U.S.S.R. 54-56; Foreign Minister 57-66; Second Deputy First Minister 60-66, concurrently Minister for Foreign Econ. Relations 62-66; sentenced to death Oct. 66; sentence commuted to life imprisonment April 70.
Jakarta, Indonesia.

Subbulakshmi, Madurai Shanmugavadivu; Indian singer; b. 1916; ed. privately.
Recitals with mother Veena Shanmugavadivu 28-32, independent concerts and recitals in India 32-, and at Edinburgh Int. Festival; in London, Frankfurt, Geneva and Cairo; concert tour U.S.A. 66; numerous recordings and film appearances; Padma Bhushan decoration (Govt. of India) 54; Pres. Award for Classical Carnatic Music 56; Ramon Magsaysay Award 74; Padma Vibhushan 75; Hon. D.Litt. (Shri Venkateswara Univ.) 71; Hon. D.Mus. (Delhi) 73.
Kalki Buildings, Chetput, Madras 600031, India.
Telephone: 61324.

Subramaniam, Chidambaram, B.A., B.L.; Indian politician; b. 30 Jan. 1910; ed. Madras Univ.
Joined Satyagraha Movement and imprisoned 32; started law practice in Coimbatore 36, imprisoned 41, 43; Pres. Coimbatore District Congress, mem. All India Congress Cttee.; mem. Constituent Assembly of India 46-51, Madras Legislative Assembly 52-62; Minister of Finance, Educ. and Law, Madras State 52-62; mem. Lok Sabha 62-67, Minister of Steel and Heavy Industry, Cen. Govt. 62-63, of Steel, Mines and Heavy Eng. 63-64, of Food and Agriculture 64-67, Aug.-Oct. 74, also of Community Devt. and Co-operation 66-67; Pres. Tamil Nadu Congress Cttee. 68-69; Chair. Cttee. on Aeronautics, Govt. of India 67-68; mem. Nat. Exec. Indian Nat. Congress 68-; Minister of Planning, Science and Technology 71-72, of Industrial Devt., Science and Technology 72-74, of Finance Oct. 74-.
Publs. Travelogues in Tamil: *Countries I Visited, Around the World, India of My Dreams.*
Ministry of Finance, New Delhi; and River View, Guindy, Madras 25, India.

Subroto, Prof., M.A., PH.D.; Indonesian politician; b. 19 Sept. 1928, Surakarta; ed. Univ. of Indonesia, McGill, Stanford and Harvard Univs.
Former Dir.-Gen. of Research and Devt., Ministry of Trade; Prof. in Int. Econs., Univ. of Indonesia; Minister of Manpower, Transmigration and Co-operatives Sept. 71-.
Publs. numerous books on economic topics.
Ministry of Manpower, Transmigration and Co-operatives, Jakarta, Indonesia.

Sucharitkul, Sompong, M.A., D.PHIL., LL.M.; Thai diplomatist and international lawyer; b. 4 Dec. 1931, Bangkok; ed. Univs. of Oxford and Paris, Harvard Law School, Middle Temple. London and Int. Law Acad., The Hague.
Lecturer in Int. Law and Relations, Chulalongkorn Univ. 56, also lecturer in Int. Econ. Law, Thammasat Univ.; mem. Nat. Research Council 59-70; joined Ministry of Foreign Affairs 59, Sec. to Minister 64-67, Dir.-Gen. Econ. Dept. 68-70; Amb. to Netherlands (also accred. to Belgium and Luxembourg) April 70-73, to Japan 74-; Rep. of Thailand, UN Comm. on Int. Trade Law (UNCITRAL) 67; mem. Civil Aviation Board of Thailand; del. to various int. confs., etc.
Publs. various books and articles on int. law and int. trade law.
Royal Thai Embassy, 14-6, Kami-Osaki, 3-chome, Shinagawa-ku, Tokyo, Japan.

Sueyoshi, Toshio, B.A.(ECON.); Japanese business executive; b. 13 Feb. 1907, Tokyo; ed. Tokyo Univ. of Commerce.
Mitsui Mining Co. 30-31; Miike Nitrogen Industries Co. 31-37; Toyo Koatsu Industries Inc. 37-68, Dir. 47-55; Man. Dir. 55-57, Vice-Pres. 57-68; Vice-Pres. Mitsui Toatsu Chemicals Inc. 68-70, Pres. 70-; Pres. Japan Phosphatic and Compound Fertilizers Mfrs. Assen. 71; Blue Ribbon Medal 68.

Mitsui Toatsu Chemicals Inc., 2-5, Kasuimgaseki 3-chome, Chiyoda-ku, Tokyo; Home: 45-7, Kitasenzoku 2-chome, Ohta-ku, Tokyo, Japan.
Telephone: 581-6111 (Office); 729-2270 (Home).

Suganami, Shoji; Japanese business executive; b. 27 Feb. 1902; ed. Tokyo Imperial Univ.
Civil Servant, Ministry of Commerce and Industry and Munitions Ministry 26-46; Man. Dir. Hino Diesel Industry Co. Inc. 48; Pres. Hino Diesel Sales Co. Inc. 51; Pres. Hino Renault Sales Co. Inc. 54; Pres. Hino Motor Sales Ltd. 59; Vice-Pres. Hino Motors Ltd., Chair. 65-; now also Pres. Japan Electronic Computer Co. Ltd., Hino Motor Sales Ltd., Kobikikan Bldg. Co. Ltd., Japan Automobile Mfrs. Asscn. Inc.; Man. Dir. Japan Automobile Chamber of Commerce; Blue Ribbon Medal.
Hino Motors Ltd., Hinodai 3-1-1, Hino City, Tokyo, Japan.
Telephone: 03-272-4811.

Sugitani, Takeo, B.L.; Japanese banker; b. 7 Aug. 1903, Miyagi Pref.; ed. Tokyo Imperial Univ.
Joined the Mitsui Trust Co. Ltd. 26; Dir. The Tokyo Trust & Banking Co. Ltd. 48; Man. Dir. The Mitsui Trust & Banking Co. Ltd. 53, Pres. 60-68, Chair. 68-71, Counsellor 71-; Auditor, Mitsui Petrochemical Industries Ltd. 67-; Counsellor, Mitsui Real Estate Co. Ltd. 61-, Mitsui Mining Co. Ltd. 64-; Counsellor and Auditor, Japan Women's Univ. 73-.
The Mitsui Trust & Banking Co. Ltd., 1-1 Nihonbashi Muromachi 2-chome, Chuo-ku, Tokyo; 14-5 Meguro 3-chome, Meguro-ku, Tokyo, Japan.
Telephone: 03-712-1600.

Sugiura, Binsuke; Japanese banker; b. 13 Nov. 1911, Tokyo; ed. Tokyo Univ.
Director, Long-Term Credit Bank of Japan Ltd. 58-61, Man. Dir. 61-68, Senior Man. Dir. 68-69, Deputy Pres. 69-71, Pres. 71-.
The Long-Term Credit Bank of Japan Ltd., 2-4, Otemachi 1-chome, Chiyoda-ku, Tokyo 100; Home: 31-5, Kami-Meguro 3-chome, Meguro-ku, Tokyo 153, Japan.
Telephone: 211-5111 (Office); 719-5505 (Home).

Suharto, Gen., T.N.I.; Indonesian army officer and politician; b. 8 June 1921; ed. Indonesian Army Staff and Command Coll.
Officer in Japanese-sponsored Indonesian Army 43; Battalion, later Regimental, Commdr. Jogjakarta 45-50; Regimental Commdr., Central Java 53; Brig.-Gen. 60; Deputy Chief of Army Staff 60-65; Chief of Army Staff 65-68, Supreme Commdr. 68-73; Minister of Army 65; Deputy Prime Minister for Defence and Security 66; Chair. of Presidium of Cabinet 66-67, in charge of Defence and Security, also Minister of Army July 66; Full Gen. 66; Acting Pres. of Indonesia 67-68; Prime Minister 67-, concurrently Minister for Defence and Security 67-73; Pres. of Indonesia March 68-.
Office of the President, 15 Jalan Merdeka Utara; Home: 8 Jalan Tjendana, Jakarta, Indonesia.

Sukhadia, Mohan Lal, L.E.E.; Indian politician; b. 1916; ed. Nathdwara (Udaipur) and Bombay Univ.
Active mem. Praja Mandal organization in former Mewar State 39-; interned during "Quit India" movement 42; fmr. Minister for Civil Supplies, Post-War Development, Relief and Rehabilitation, Mewar State 46; Minister of Development when State of Rajasthan was first formed; mem. Rajasthan Legislative Asscn.; Minister for Civil Supplies, Agriculture and Irrigation 51-52, Minister for Revenue (except Forests and Co-operation) and Famine Relief 52-54; Chief Minister, Rajasthan 54-71; Gov. of Karnataka 72-75, of Andhra Pradesh 75-76, of Tamil Nadu June 76-; Hon. LL.D., Univ. of Udaipur 74; Congress Party.
Raj Bhavan, Madras, Tamil Nadu, India.

Sukhedev; Indian film maker; b. 1933; ed. Bombay.
Has directed, produced, edited and acted in films since 60; has produced documentaries and short films; Padma Shree Award 68.
Works: *And Miles to Go, After the Eclipse, An Indian Day* (fmrly. *India '67*), *Thoughts on a Museum, Khilonewalla, Nine Months to Freedom* 72.
c/o Film Niryat, 6/33-37, Tardeo AC Market Building, P.O. Box 7928, Tardeo Road, Bombay 34, India.

Sullivan, William Healy; American diplomatist; b. 12 Oct. 1922; ed. Brown Univ. and Fletcher School of Law and Diplomacy.
United States Navy 43-46; Foreign Service 47-, served Bangkok 47-49, Calcutta 49-50, Tokyo 50-52, Rome 52-55, The Hague 55-58; Officer-in-Charge, Burma Affairs, Dept. of State 58-59; Foreign Affairs Officer 59; UN Adviser, Bureau of Far Eastern Affairs 60-63; Special Asst. to Under-Sec. for Political Affairs 63-64; Amb. to Laos 64-69; Deputy Asst. Sec. of State for E. Asia (with special responsibility for Viet-Nam); Amb. to the Philippines 73-.
American Embassy, Roxas Boulevard, Manila, Philippines.

Sun Chien; Chinese government official.
Vice-Premier, State Council 75-.
People's Republic of China.

Sunario, Dr.; Indonesian diplomatist and university principal; b. 28 Aug. 1902; ed. Univ. of Leiden, Netherlands.
Judicial Officer, District Court, Madiun and Ponorogo 23-24; Solicitor and barrister in Jakarta, Makasar and Medan 27-41; Chief Ed. *Sedya-Tama*, Jogjakarta 41-42; Senior Official, Dept. of Justice, Jakarta 42-45; co-founder, later Dean of Law Faculty and Lecturer in Political Sciences, Gadjah Mada Univ., Jogjakarta 46-47; Political Sec. Del. of Republic of Indonesia for Indonesia-Dutch negotiations 47-48; Deputy Chief Ed. *Pemandangan*, Jakarta 49-50; mem. Provisional Parl., Jakarta 50-53; Chair. Parl. Mission to U.K. 51; Chair. Indonesian UN Asscn., Jakarta 51-53; Chair. Indonesian Nat. Group of the Interparl. Union 51-53; Foreign Minister 53-55 and leader of Indonesian del. to UN Gen. Assembly 53, 54; Chair. Indonesian del. Colombo Plan Conf., Ottawa 54; Deputy Chair. Indonesian del. Asian-African Conf., Bandung 55; Extraordinary Prof. in Constitutional and Diplomatic History, Univ. of Indonesia 55-56; Amb. to U.K. 56-61; Prof. of Political Science and Int. Law and Relations, President of Diponegoro State Univ., Semarang 63-; founder mem. Nationalist Party (P.N.I.).
Universitas Diponegoro, Jalan Hajam Wuruk, Semarang, Java, Indonesia.

Sunderland, Sir Sydney, Kt., C.M.G., D.SC., M.D., B.S., F.R.A.C.P., F.R.A.C.S., F.A.A.; Australian anatomist; b. 31 Dec. 1910; ed. Melbourne Univ.
Senior Lecturer in Anatomy Melbourne Univ. 36-37; Asst. Neurologist Alfred Hospital Melbourne 36-37; Demonstrator Dept. of Human Anatomy Oxford 38, Prof. of Anatomy and Histology Melbourne Univ. 38-61, of Experimental Neurology 61-75, Emer. 76-, Dean Medical Faculty 53-71; Visiting Specialist, injuries of the peripheral nervous system, Australian Gen. Mil. Hospital 41-45; Visiting Prof. of Anatomy, Johns Hopkins Univ. 53-54; mem. Nat. Health and Medical Research Council of Australia 53-69; Foundation Fellow and Sec. for Biol. Sciences, Australian Acad. of Sciences 55-58; Trustee Nat. Museum of Victoria 54-; mem. Zool. Board of Victoria 44-65; Deputy Chair. Advisory Cttee. of Victorian Mental Hygiene Authority 52-63; rep. Pacific Science Council 57-69; mem. Defence Research and Development Policy Cttee. 57-75, Medical Services Cttee. 57-, Commonwealth Dept. of Defence; Nat. Radiation Advisory Cttee. 57-64, Chair. 59-64; Chair. Safety Review Cttee. 61-74-Australian Atomic Energy Comm.; Medical Research

Advisory Cttee. of Nat. Health and Medical Research Council 53-69, Chair. 64-69; Chair. Protective Chemistry Research Advisory Cttee., Dept. of Supply 64-73; mem. Scientific Advisory Cttee. Australian Atomic Energy Comm. 62-63; Australian Univs. Comm. 62-, Cttee. of Management Royal Melbourne Hospital 63-71, Victorian Medical Advisory Cttee. 62-71, Advisory Medical Council of Australia 70-71; Gov. Ian Potter Foundation 64-; mem. Victorian Branch Council, Australian Medical Asscn. 69-68; mem. Board, Walter & Eliza Hall Inst. of Medical Research 68-75; Trustee, The Van Cleef Foundation 71-; Fogarty Scholar-in-Residence, Nat. Insts. of Health, U.S.A. 72-73; Hon. M.D. (Univ. of Tasmania) 70, (Univ. of Queensland) 75, Hon. LL.D. (Univ. of Melbourne) 75.
Publ. *Nerves and Nerve Injuries* 68.
c/o Department of Experimental Neurology, University of Melbourne, Parkville 3052, Victoria, Australia.
Telephone: 340484.

Sung Chih-kuang; Chinese diplomatist; b. April 1916, Kwangtung Province; ed. univ.
Counsellor, embassy to German Democratic Repub.; Deputy Dir. Dept. of W. European Affairs, Ministry of Foreign Affairs; Counsellor, embassy to France; Amb. to German Democratic Repub. 70-72, to U.K. 72-.
Embassy of the People's Republic of China, 31 Portland Place, London, W1N 3AG, England.

Sung Ch'ing-ling; former government official, People's Repub. of China; b. 1894, Shanghai; ed. Wesleyan Coll., U.S.A.
Secretary to Sun Yat-sen 15; led Left Kuomintang after Kuomintang-CCP Split 27; in Moscow 27-29; Vice-Chair. Cen. People's Govt. 49-54; Vice-Chair. People's Repub. of China 59-74; Chair. China Welfare Inst.; Publisher of *China Reconstructs*; Stalin Peace Prize 51.
Publ. *The Struggle for New China* 52.

Sung Pei-chang; Chinese party official.
Deputy Political Commissar, Anhwei Mil. District, People's Liberation Army 68; Vice-Chair. Anhwei Revolutionary Cttee. 68, Chair. 75-; Sec. CCP Anhwei 71, First Sec. 75-.
People's Republic of China.

Suphamongkhon, Konthi, G.C.V.O., LL.B.; Thai lawyer and diplomatist; b. 3 Aug. 1916; ed. Univs. of Bangkok and Paris.
Chief of Section, Political Div., Ministry of Foreign Affairs 40-42; Second Sec., Tokyo 42-44; Chief of Political Div., Western Affairs Dept., Ministry of Foreign Affairs 44-48, Dir.-Gen. Western Affairs Dept. 48-50, Dir.-Gen. UN Dept. 50-52; Minister to Australia 52-56, Amb. to Australia, concurrently to New Zealand 56-59; Dir.-Gen. Dept. of Int. Orgs., Ministry of Foreign Affairs 59-63; Adviser on Foreign Affairs to Prime Minister 62-64; Sec.-Gen. South East Asia Treaty Organization (SEATO) 64-65; Amb. to Fed. Repub. of Germany 65-70, concurrently to Finland 67-70, to U.K. May 70-; numerous decorations.
Publ. *Thailand and Her Relations with France* 40.
Royal Thai Embassy, 30 Queen's Gate, London, SW7 5JB, England.
Telephone: 01-589-0173.

Suromihardjo, Maj.-Gen. Suadi; Indonesian army officer and diplomatist; b. 1921; ed. Staff Coll., Quetta, Pakistan, Fort Bliss, U.S.A.
Department of Interior 39; 1st Lieutenant Indonesian Army 42; C.O. (Lt.-Col.) 1st Regiment 10th Div. 45; mem. UN Comm. for Indonesia 47; Deputy Chief of Staff Diponegoro Div, Central Java 50; C.O. 21st Regiment VI Div., South Kalimantan 51; C.O. 23rd Regiment VII Div. South Sulawesi 54; C.O. Indonesian Contingent UNEF, Egypt 57; Commandant Indonesian Command and General Staff Coll., Bandung 59; Amb. to Australia 61-64, to Ethiopia 64-69; Gov. Indonesia Nat. Defence Council 68-.
Lembaga Pertahanan Nasional, Jalan Kebon Sirih 28, Jakarta, Indonesia.

Suryadhay, Phagna Prasith Inpeng; Laotian diplomatist; b. 13 Feb. 1923; ed. Pavie Coll. Vientiane, Lycée Sisowath, Phnom-Penh, Inst. d'Etudes Politiques, Paris.
First Sec., Embassy of Laos, Washington 53-55; Sec.-Gen. Council of Ministers 55-58; Sec. of State for Justice 58-59, for Educ. 59-60; mem. of Parl. 60-71; Minister of Finance and Nat. Econ. 60-62, of Finance 62; Editor of *The Nation*, daily newspaper 62-71; Vice-Pres. Nat. Assembly 62-63; Minister of Justice and in charge of Planning and Devt. Co-operation 64-71; Amb. to U.K. 71-75; Order of the Reign of Sisavang Vong-Sisavang Vatthana, Officer Mérite Civique, Grand Officer Million Elephants and Order of the Great Friendship (Cambodia).
Ministry of Foreign Affairs, Vientiane, Laos.

Sutami, Dr.; Indonesian engineer and politician; b. 19 Oct. 1928, Surakarta, Cen. Java; ed. Inst. of Technology, Bandung.
Employee Hollandse Beton Maatschappij N.V. 56-58; Dir. Hutama Karya Co. 59; mem. Indonesian Nat. Research Inst.; Asst. Dean, Technical Faculty, Univ. of Indonesia 64; Minister without Portfolio 65, of Public Works 66-, also of Energy 68-; mem. Indonesian Council of Science 68.
Ministry of Public Works, Jakarta, Indonesia.

Sutowo, Lieut.-Gen. Dr. Ibnu; Indonesian industrialist.
President-Director, Pertamina -March 76.
P. N. Pertamina, 2-4-6 Perwira, Jakarta, Indonesia.

Suzuki, Gengo; Japanese financial executive; b. 11 Feb. 1904; ed. Government College of Commerce, Taiho-ku and Univ. of Wisconsin.
Lecturer and Professor in Econ. Govt. Coll. of Commerce, Taiho-ku, Taiwan 31-49, concurrently Civil Administration Official, Govt.-Gen. Taiwan 44-45, Prof. of Econs., Taiwan Province School of Law and Commerce 45-47, Prof. of Econ. Nat. Univ. of Taiwan 47-48; Deputy Financial Commr., Ministry of Finance, Japanese Govt. 49-51, Financial Commr. 51-57; Financial Minister, Embassy in U.S.A. 57-60; Special Asst. to Minister for Foreign Affairs, and to Minister of Finance 60-66; Auditor, Bank of Japan, Tokyo 66-70; Exec. Dir. for Burma, Japan, Nepal, Sri Lanka and Thailand, IMF, IBRD 60-66; mem. Advisory Board, Cttee. for Co-ordination of Investigations of the Lower Mekong Basin 68-; mem. World Bank's Investment Dispute Conciliation Panel 68-74; Chair. Board Assoc. Japanese Bank (Int.) Ltd., London 70-; Rep. Dir. Int. Devt. Journal 70-; Gov. and steering cttee. mem., Atlantic Inst. for Int. Affairs (Paris) 71-; mem. European Atlantic Group 71-; mem. Council of Int. Chamber of Commerce (Paris) 74-.
29-30 Cornhill, London, E.C.3.; Home: Flat 38, London House, 7-9 Avenue Road, London, N.W.8, England; 2-5-13 Nukuikita-machi, Koganeishi, Tokyo, Japan; and 1508 The Olympus, 6301 Stevenson Avenue, Alexandria, Virginia, U.S.A.
Telephone: 01-623-5661 (London Office); 01-586-2721 (London Home); 0423-83-5751 (Tokyo Home).

Suzuki, Haruo, LL.B.; Japanese business executive; b. 31 March 1913, Hayama, Kanagawa Pref.; ed. Tokyo Univ.
With Nomura Securities Co. Ltd. 36-39; joined Showa-Denko K.K. 39, Exec. Vice-Pres. 59-71, Pres. 71-; Chair. AA Chemical Co., Showa Neoprene K.K., Showa Yuka K.K. 71-, Showa Unox K.K. 75-; Pres. Tokuyama Petrochem. Co. 71-; Dir. N.Z. Aluminium Smelters Ltd. 72-, Industria Venezolana de Aluminio C.A. 73-; Chair. Japan Carbon Asscn., Abrasive Industry Asscn.; Vice-Chair. Japan Light Metal Smelters' Asscn.; Dir. Int. Primary

Aluminium Inst.; Chair. Industrial Policy Cttee. Keidanren (Japan Fed. of Econ Orgs.); Vice-Chair. Japan-German Dem. Repub. Econ. Cttee., Japan-Southern U.S. Asscn.; mem. Council for Industrial Policy (Japan), Industrial Structure Council and Electric Utility Industry Council of Ministry of Int. Trade and Industry, Cttee. on Financial Systems Research of Ministry of Finance.
Publ. *Chemical Industry* 68.
Showa Denko K.K., 13-9, Shiba Daimon 1-chome, Minato-ku, Tokyo; Home: 2-7-1-810 Mita, Minato-ku, Tokyo, Japan.
Telephone: 432-5111 (Office).

Suzuki, Hideo; Japanese investment banker; b. 4 June 1917, Hayama, Kanagawa Pref.; ed. Univ. of Tokyo.
Entered Ministry of Finance 40; Deputy Supt. of Kobe Customs, Ministry of Finance 53-55; Head, Treasury Div., Financial Bureau, Ministry of Finance 55-57; Head Govt., Investment Div., Financial Bureau, Ministry of Finance 57-58, Co-ordinating Div., Foreign Exchange Bureau 58-59; Financial Counsellor, Japanese Embassy, Consul in New York and Rep. of Ministry of Finance in New York 59-62; Deputy Dir. Int. Finance Bureau Ministry of Finance 62-64; mem. Policy Board, Bank of Japan, concurrently Deputy Dir. Int. Finance Bureau, Ministry of Finance 64-65; Dir. Int. Finance Bureau 65-66; Special Adviser to Minister of Finance and Special Asst. to Minister of Foreign Affairs 66-74; Exec. Dir. IMF 66-72; Vice-Chair., Deputies of Cttee. of 20, IMF 72-74; Adviser, Nomura Securities Co.; Chair., Nomura Securities Int. Inc., Nomura Europe, N.V. 74-.
The Nomura Securities Co., 1-9-1, Nihoubashi, Chuo-ku, Tokyo 103, Japan.

Suzuki, Hiroaki, LL.B.; Japanese business executive; b. 15 Feb. 1916, Kyoto; ed. Kyoto Univ.
Kobe Steel Ltd. 43-, Dir. 69-70, Dir. and Exec. Officer 70-72, Dir. and Senior Exec. Officer 72-74, Dir. and Vice-Pres. 74, Dir. and Pres. 74-.
5-17-603, 6-chome, Okamoto, Higashinada-ku, Kobe, Japan.
Telephone: Kobe 452-1800.

Suzuki, Kyoji, M.A.; Japanese business executive; b. 18 March 1909, Kyoto; ed. Tokyo Imperial Univ.
With Dai-Ichi Bank Ltd. 31-48; Dir. Ajinomoto Co. Inc. 48, Exec. Vice-Pres. 59, Exec. Dir. Ajinomoto-Insud S.p.A., Rome 63; Pres. Ajinomoto Inc. 65-73, Chair. 73-75; Auditor May 75-; Chair. Knorr Food Products (Japan) Ltd.; Blue Ribbon Medal.
Ajinomoto Co. Inc., 1-6 Kyobashi, Chuo-ku; Home: 3-8-2 chome Shoto, Shibuya-ku, Tokyo, Japan.
Telephone: 03-272-1111.

Suzuki, Shunzo; Japanese business executive; b. 24 May 1903; ed. Shizuoka Univ.
President, Suzuki Motor Co. Ltd. until 73, Chair. 73-.
Suzuki Motor Co. Ltd., 300 Takatsuka, Kamimura, Hamaganun, Shizuoka Prefecture, Japan.

Suzuki, Ziro; Japanese business executive; b. 8 Nov. 1912; ed. Tokyo Inst. of Tech.
Chairman, The Furukawa Electric Co. Ltd. 74-.
Furukawa Electric Co. Ltd., 6-1, Marunouchi 2-chome, Chiyoda-ku, Tokyo; 13-5 Higashiterao-Nakadai, Tsurumi-ku, Yokohama, Japan.
Telephone: 03-213-0811 (Office); 045-581-6285.

Swaminathan, Jagdish; Indian painter; b. 21 June 1928; ed. Delhi Polytechnic and Acad. of Fine Arts, Warsaw.
Early career of freedom fighter, trade unionist, journalist, and writer of children's books; mem. Delhi State Cttee. of Congress Socialist Party and Editor of its weekly organ, *Mazdoor Awaz;* Senior Art Teacher, Cambridge School, New Delhi; Founder-mem. *Group 1890* (avant-garde group of Indian artists); mem. Nat. Cttee., Int. Asscn. of the Arts 67-, Exec. Cttee. Delhi Slipi Chakra 67, also Founder-Editor monthly journal, *Contra 66* and full-time painter; one-man exhbns. in New Delhi 62, 63, 64, 65, 66, in Bombay 66; in group shows Warsaw 61, Saigon 63, Tokyo Biennale 65, *Art Now in India*, London, New-castle and Brussels 65-66, *Seven Indian Painters*, London 67; mem. Int. Jury, São Paulo Bienal 69; Jawaharlal Nehru Fellow for thesis *The Significance of the Traditional Numen to Contemporary Art* 69; represented in various public and private collections in India and abroad.
c/o Gallery Chemould, Jahangir Art Gallery, Mahatma Gandhi Road, Bombay 1; and 6/17 W.E.A.. New Delhi 5, India.

Swe, Ba (*see* Ba Swe, U).

Syed Putra bin Syed Hassan Jamalullail (*see* Perlis).

Syme, Sir Colin York, Kt., LL.B.; Australian businessman; b. 22 April 1903; ed. Perth and Melbourne Univs.
Partner firm of Hedderwick, Fookes and Alston 28-66; Dir. Broken Hill Pty. Co. Ltd. 37-71, Chair. 52-71, Dir. of Admin. 66-71; Chair. Tubemakers of Australia Ltd. 66-73; Pres. Walter and Eliza Hall Inst. of Medical Research; Dir. Australian Industry Devt. Corpn.; Chair. inquiry into hospital and health services in Victoria; Hon. D.Sc.
22 Stonnington Place, Toorak, Victoria 3142, Australia.
Telephone: 20-5254.

T

Tajitsu, Wataru; Japanese banker; b. 25 March 1902; ed. Tokyo Univ.
Joined Mitsubishi Bank 26, Pres. and Chair. of the Board 64-70, Chair. 70-; Chair. The Mitsubishi Foundation; Exec. Dir. Japan Fed. of Employers' Asscns., Fed. of Econ. Orgs.; Blue Ribbon medal.
Mitsubishi Bank, 7-1, 2-chome, Marunouchi, Chiyoda-ku, Tokyo; Home: 6-41, 7-chome, Akasaka, Minato-ku, Tokyo, Japan.

Takeda, Chobei; Japanese business executive; b. 29 April 1905; ed. Keio Gijuku Univ.
President, Takeda Chemical Industries Ltd. until 74, Chair. 74-.
Takeda Chemical Industries, 27 Doshomachi 2-chome, Higashi-ku, Osaka, Japan.

Takeiri, Yoshikatsu; Japanese politician; b. 10 Jan. 1926, Nagano Prefecture; ed. Inst. of Politics (Seiji Daigakko).
With Japan Nat. Railways 48-59; Bunkyo Ward Ass. Tokyo 59; Tokyo Metropolitan Ass. 63-67; Vice Sec.-Gen. Komeito (Clean Govt.) Party Nov. 64-67, Chair. 67-; mem. House of Reps. 67-.
17 Minamimoto-machi, Shinjuku-ku, Tokyo 160, Japan.
Telephone: 353-0111.

Takeshita, Noburu; Japanese politician; b. 1929; ed. Waseda Univ.
Member, House of Reps.; fmr. Vice-Minister of Int. Trade and Industry; Deputy Chief Cabinet Sec. until 74, Chief Cabinet Sec. Nov. 74-; Vice-Chair. Diet Policy Cttee. of Liberal-Democratic Party; State Minister and Chief Cabinet Sec. 71-72.
House of Representatives, Tokyo, Japan.

Takeuchi, Shunichi; Japanese oil executive; b. 17 Jan. 1896; ed. Tokyo Higher Commercial School.
Mitsubishi Holding Co. 17; Mitsubishi Trading Co. Ltd. 18-40, Manager, Produce Dept., London Branch 21-29, Asst. Gen. Manager, New York Branch 34-35, Gen. Manager, San Francisco and Seattle Branches 35-40; Gen. Manager, Mitsubishi Oil Co. Ltd. 41, Dir. and Pres. 46-61, Chair. of Board 61-66, Senior Adviser 66-; Dir. Japan Productivity Centre 58-; Pres. Japan Management School 58-; Chair. of Board of Dirs. The English Language

Educ. Council Inc. 63-; Vice-Pres. The Japan-British Soc., Tokyo 64-; Blue Ribbon Award 59, Order of the Rising Sun (Third Class) 66.
5-31, Matsugaoka 2-chome, Kugenuma, Fujisawa, Kanagawa Prefecture, Japan.

Talboys, Brian Edward, M.P.; New Zealand farmer and politician; b. 7 June 1921, Wanganui; ed. Wanganui Collegiate School, and Victoria Univ., Wellington.
R.N.Z.A.F. 39-45; joined *New Zealand Dairy Exporter* 50, later Asst. Editor; M.P. 57-, Parl. Under-Sec. 60-62; Minister of Agriculture 62-69, of Educ. 69-72, of Science 64-72, of Industries and Commerce and of Overseas Trade 72; Deputy Prime Minister, Minister of Foreign Affairs, Overseas Trade and Nat. Devt. Dec. 75-; National Party.
Parliament House, Wellington; and 134 Park Street, Winton, Southland, New Zealand.
Telephone: 44-595 (Home).

Talwar, Raj Kumar, M.A., C.A.I.I.B.; Indian banker; b. 3 June 1922, Gujrat (West Punjab).
Joined State Bank of India 43, Sec. and Treas. Hyderabad Circle 65-66, Bombay Circle 66-68, Man. Dir. 68-69, Chair. 69-; *ex-officio* Chair. seven subsidiary banks; Vice-Pres. Indian Inst. of Bankers 69-; Dir. Industrial Reconstruction Corpn. of India Ltd., Calcutta; mem. Small Scale Industries Board, Gov. Board of Nat. Inst. of Bank Management, Board of Govs. Indian Inst. of Management.
State Bank of India, Central Office, New Administrative Building, Madame Cama Road, Bombay 400 021; and Dunedin, 5 J. M. Mehta Road, Bombay 400006, India.

Tambunan, A. M.; Indonesian politician; b. 25 Sept. 1911, Djandjiangkola, N. Sumatra; ed. Dutch elementary and secondary schools and Univ. of Law, Jakarta.
Worked at Law Court, Jakarta; Judge at Tjirebon Law Court; mem. Indonesian Nat. Cen. Cttee.; Deputy Chair. House of Reps. 50-56; mem. House of Reps. 56; mem. Supreme Advisory Council 59; Minister of Social Affairs 66-71; Vice-Pres. and Hon. mem. PARKINDO (Indonesian Protestant Party); mem. Exec. Board, Indonesian Council of Churches; Hon. Chair. Indonesian Council of Churches; Satya Lantjana award; Hon. LL.D. (St. Olaf Coll., Northfield, Minn. and Tennessee Temple Coll., Chattanooga, Tenn., U.S.A.).
c/o Ministry of Social Affairs, Jakarta, Indonesia.

Tan Chee Khoon, L.M.S.; Malaysian politician and medical practitioner; b. 4 March 1919; ed. High School, Kajang, Victoria Inst., King Edward VII Coll. of Medicine, Singapore.
Served at Gen. Hospital, Kuala Lumpur 50-51; private practice 52-; Chair. Kuala Lumpur Branch, Labour Party of Malaya 56-68, Selangor Div. 59-61; Nat. Vice-Chair. Labour Party 59-62; Nat. Treas. Labour Party of Malaya 63-68; mem. Dewan Raayat for the constituency of Batu 64, Selangor State Assembly, constituency of Kepong 64-; Sec.-Gen. Parti Gerakan Rakyat; Pres. Malayan Medical Asscn. 67; mem. Malayan Medical Council 61-; mem. Nik Kamil Cabinet Cttee. to make recommendations on medical legislation in Malaysia; mem. Singapore Medical Council, Vice-Chair. 67, Chair. 71; mem. Council, Univ. of Malaya 59-76, Board of Management, Univ. Hosp. 68-76, Higher Educ. Council 73-76, Tariff Advisory Board 66-68, 68-70.
316 Jalan Tuanku Abdul Rahman, Kuala Lumpur, Malaysia.

T'an Chen-lin; politician, People's Repub. of China; b. 1902, Yu-hsien, Hunan; ed. Juichen Red Army Univ. and Moscow Red Army Univ.
Joined CCP 26; participated in Autumn Harvest Uprising 27; Political Commissar in Red Army during Civil and Sino-Japanese Wars; mem. 7th Cen. Cttee. of CCP 45; Gov. of Chekiang 49-50; Sec. CCP Chekiang 49-52; Gov. of Kiangsu 52-55; mem., Sec. of Secr., Deputy Sec.-Gen. 8th Cen. Cttee. of CCP 56; mem. Politburo, CCP 58-67; Vice-Premier, State Council 59-; Dir. Office of Agriculture and Forestry, State Council 62-67; Vice-Chair. State Planning Comm. 62-67; criticized and removed from office during Cultural Revolution 68; mem. 10th Cen. Cttee. of CCP 73.

T'an Ch'i-lung; People's Repub. of China; b. 1912, Kiangsi.
Director Political Dept., Hunan-Hupeh-Kiangsi Border Region 37; Political Commissar, Guerrilla Force 43, People's Liberation Army 44-49; Deputy Sec. CCP Chekiang 49-52, Sec. 52-55; Political Commissar Chekiang Mil. District, PLA 52-55; Gov. of Chekiang 52-55; Acting Gov. of Shantung 54; Alt. mem. 8th Cen. Cttee. of CCP 56; Sec. CCP Shantung 55-56, Second Sec. 56-61, First Sec. 61-67; Gov. of Shantung 58-63; First Political Commissar Tsinan Mil. Region, PLA 63; Sec. E. China Bureau, CCP 65-67; criticized and removed from office during Cultural Revolution 67; Alt. mem. 9th Cen. Cttee. of CCP 69; Vice-Chair. Fukien Revolutionary Cttee. 70; Sec. CCP Fukien 71; Sec. CCP Chekiang 72, First Sec. 73-; Vice-Chair. Chekiang Revolutionary Cttee. 73; mem. 10th Cen. Cttee. of CCP 73.

Tan Chin Tuan, Tan Sri, P.S.M., C.B.E., J.P.; Singapore banker and company director; b. 21 Nov. 1908, Singapore; ed. Anglo-Chinese School.
Member Singapore Municipal Comm. 39-41; Deputy Pres. Singapore Legislative Council 51-55; mem. Singapore Exec. Council 48-55; Chair. Kinta Ellas Tin Dredging Ltd. 69-74, Oversea-Chinese Banking Corpn. Ltd. 66-, Fraser & Neave Ltd. 57-, Great Eastern Life Assurance Co. Ltd. 69-, Int. Bank of Singapore 74-, Malayan Breweries Ltd. 57-, Wearne Bros. Ltd. 74-, Overseas Assurance Corpn. Ltd. 69-, Robinson & Co. Ltd. 57-, Sime Darby Holdings Ltd. 73-, The Straits Trading Co. Ltd. 65-; Dir. Gopeng Consolidated Ltd. 67-, Petaling Tin Berhad 67-, Tronoh Mines Ltd. 67-, United Malacca Rubber Estates Berhad 69-; Dir. Tanjong Tin Dredging Ltd. 69-75; Pres. Raffles Hotel Ltd. 69-; Fellow, Inst. of Bankers (London) 65, Australian Inst. of Man. 62.
Oversea-Chinese Banking Corporation Ltd., OCBC Centre, Chulia Street, Singapore 1; Home: 42 Cairnhill Road, Singapore 9, Singapore.

Tan Siew Sin, Hon. Tun, S.S.M., J.P.; Malaysian businessman and politician; b. 1916; ed. Malacca and Raffles Coll. Singapore.
Malacca Municipal Commr. 46-49; mem. Fed. Legislative Council 48-, mem. Standing Cttee. on Finance 49-55; mem. Rubber Producers' Council 51-57, Vice-Chair. 57; mem. Rubber Industry Replanting Board 52-57, Vice-Chair. 57; Treas.-Gen. Alliance Party 59-69, Vice-Chair. 61-; Pres. Malayan Estate Owners' Asscn. 56, 57; mem. Malacca Chinese Advisory Board 50-55; Hon Sec. Malacca Branch, Malayan Chinese Asscn. 49-57, Chair. Malacca Branch 57-61; Vice-Pres. Malayan Chinese Asscn. 57-61, Pres. 61-74, Hon. Pres. 74-; Fed. Minister of Commerce and Industry 57-59, Minister of Finance, Malaya 59-63, Malaysia 63-69; Minister with Special Functions 69-70; Minister of Finance 70-74; Pro-Chancellor Malaysia Nat. Univ. 71-; Assoc. mem. IMF Cttee. of Twenty 73-; Treas.-Gen. Alliance Party 59-69, Vice-Chair. 61-; Chair. Commonwealth Parl. Asscn.; Dir. Unitac Ltd. 51-57, Malaka Pinda Rubber Estates Ltd., United Malacca Rubber Estate Ltd., Leong Hin San Ltd. 41-57, Sime Darby Holdings U.K. 74, Siemens Components Sdn. Bhd. 74, Highlands and Lowlands Para Rubber Co. Ltd. 74; Hon. LL.D. (Univ. of Malaya) 65; several decorations including Seri Setia Mahkota 67; Order of Sikatuna (Class Data) of the Philippines 68; Bintang Mahaputera Kelas Dua of Indonesia 70.
Universiti Kebangsaan Malaysia, P.O.B. 1124, Jalan

Pantai, Kuala Lumpur 22-12; Home: 8 Jalan Clifford, Kuala Lumpur, Malaya, Malaysia.
Telephone: 27171.

Tanaka, Fumio; Japanese business executive; b. 29 July 1910; ed. Kyushu Univ.
President, Oji Paper Co. Ltd.
Oji Paper Co. Ltd., 4-7-5 Ginza, Chuo-ku, Tokyo, Japan.

Tanaka, Kakuei; Japanese politician; b. 4 May 1918, Niigata Prefecture; ed. Chuo Technical School.
Member, House of Reps. 47-; Minister of Posts and Telecommunications (Kishi Cabinet) 57; Chair. Policy Board of Liberal-Dem. Party 61-65, Sec.-Gen. Liberal-Dem. Party 65-66, 68-70, Pres. 72-July 76; Minister of Finance 62-65, of Int. Trade and Industry 71-72; Prime Minister 72-74; Chair. Board of Dirs., Echigo Traffic Co. Ltd. 60-; arrested on corruption charges July 76, resgnd. from party leadership July 76.
Publ. *Building a New Japan* 72.
12-19-12, Mezirodai, Bunkyo-ku, Tokyo, Japan.

Tanaka, Kyubei, B.ECON.; Japanese banker; b. 8 March 1903, Wakayama Pref.; ed. Econ. Dept., Tokyo Imperial Univ.
Managing Director, The Mitsui Bank Ltd. 55-58, Senior Man. Dir. 58-61, Deputy Pres. 61-65, Pres. 65-68, Chair. 68-74, Dir., Counsellor 74-; Blue Ribbon Medal.
The Mitsui Bank Ltd., 12, Yurakucho 1-chome, Chiyoda-ku, Tokyo 100; Home: 35-20, Sanno 1-chome, Ota-ku, Tokyo 143, Japan.
Telephone: 501-1111 (Office); 774-2777 (Home).

Tanaka, Masami; Japanese politician; ed. Tokyo Univ.
Member House of Reps. (seven times); Chair. Social Cttee. of Liberal Democratic Party Policy Affairs Research Council; Parl. Vice-Minister of Health and Welfare; Minister of Health and Welfare Dec. 74-.
Ministry of Health and Welfare, Tokyo, Japan.

Tanaka, Shigematsu; Japanese business executive; b. 31 March 1898; ed. Osaka Higher Technical School.
Entered Mitsui & Co. 18; later joined Mitsui Shipbuilding & Engineering Co. Ltd., Man. Dir. 46, Senior Man. Dir. 47, Vice-Pres. 58-60, Pres. 60; Commander's Cross of the Order of the Dannebrog (Denmark) 67, Order of the Sacred Treasure, Second Class 68.
2-3, 2-chome, Hiroo, Shibuyaku, Tokyo, Japan.

Tanco, Arturo R., Jr., D.B.A., M.I.L.R.; Philippine government executive; b. 22 Aug. 1933, Manila; ed. De la Salle Coll., Manila, Ateneo de Manila Univ., Union Coll. of New York, Cornell and Harvard Univs.
General Man. and mem. Board, Philippine Investment Management Inc. (PHINMA) 56; Pres. and Gen. Man., Management and Investment Devt. Associates Inc., (MIDA) 64; Vice-Chair. Asian Vegetable Research and Devt. Centre (Taipei), Int. Rice Research Inst. (Manila); Under-Sec. for Agriculture, Dept. of Agriculture and Natural Resources 70-71; Sec. of Agriculture and Natural Resources 71-75, of Agriculture 75-.
Publs. articles in magazines and newspapers including the *Financial Times* (London) and *The Sunday Times Magazine* (London).
Department of Agriculture, Diliman, Quezon City; Home: No. 3 Second Street, Villamar Court, Paranaque, Rizal, Philippines.
Telephone: 99-89-46, 99-87-41 (Office).

Tang Ming-chao; Chinese United Nations official; b. 1910, Kwangtung Province; ed. Tsinghua Univ. and Univ. of California, U.S.A.
Former mem. Council, Chinese People's Inst. on Foreign Affairs, Chinese People's Asscn. for Friendship with Foreign Countries; Deputy to Nat. Congress, People's Repub. of China; Under-Sec.-Gen. for Political Affairs, Trusteeship and Decolonization, UN April 72-; mem. del. to UN Gen. Assembly 71.
United Nations, First Avenue, New York, N.Y. 10017, U.S.A.

Tange, Sir Arthur Harold, Kt., C.B.E., B.A.; Australian diplomatist; b. 18 Aug. 1914; ed. Univ. of W. Australia.
Economist, various Australian Govt. Depts., Canberra 42-45; First Sec., Dept. of External Affairs 45; First Sec., Australian Mission to UN, N.Y. 46-48; Counsellor, UN Div., Canberra 48-50; Asst. Sec. Dept. of External Affairs 51-53; Minister, Australian Embassy, Washington, D.C. 53-54; Sec. External Affairs 54-65; High Commr. to India and Amb. to Nepal 65-70; Sec., Dept. of Defence, Canberra March 70-; mem. Australian del. Bretton Woods Monetary Conf., UN Preparatory Conf. UN Gen. Assembly 46, 47, 50, 51 and Econ. and Social Council, Reparations Conf., Paris; ILO, Paris, Montreal and San Francisco; British Commonwealth Confs., London, Colombo, Sydney 49-63, etc.
32 La Perouse Street, Canberra, A.C.T. 2603, Australia.
Telephone: 958879.

Tange, Kenzo, DR. ENG.; Japanese architect; b. 4 Sept. 1913; ed. Tokyo Univ.
Member Japanese Architects Asscn., Hon. mem. American Acad. of Arts and Letters, Akad. der Künste, Germany; Hon. Fellow American Inst. of Architects; Royal Gold Medal, Royal Inst. of British Architects 65; A.I.A. Gold Medal, American Inst. of Architects 66; Hon. Dr. Fine Arts, Univ. of Buffalo, N.Y.; Hon. Dr.-Ing., Technische Hochschule, Stuttgart; Hon. Dr. Arch., Politecnico di Milano, Italy; Hon. Dr. Arts, Harvard Univ.; Grande Médaille d'Or, French Acad. of Architecture 73.
Buildings include: Peace Memorial Park and Buildings, Hiroshima, Tokyo City Hall, Tokyo, Kurashiki City Hall, Kurashiki, Kagawa Prefectural Govt. Office, Takamatsu, Roman Catholic Cathedral, Tokyo, Nat. Gymnasiums for 1964 Olympic Games, Tokyo, Skopje City Centre Reconstruction Project, Skopje, Yugoslavia, Yamanashi Press and Broadcasting Centre, Yamanashi, Master Plan for *Expo 70*, Osaka, Fiera District Centre, Bologna, Italy.
1702, 34-3-2, Mita, Minato-ku, Tokyo, Japan.
Telephone: Tokyo 455-2787.

Taniguchi, Toyosaburo; Japanese textile executive; b. 29 July 1901; ed. Tokyo Univ.
Director Osaka Godo Spinning Co. Ltd. 29-31; Dir. Toyobo Co. Ltd. 31-42, Exec. Vice-Pres. 51-59, Pres. 59-66, Chair. of Board 66-72, Gen. Adviser 72-; Auditor Japan Exlan Co. Ltd. 56-66; Rep. Dir. Kansai Cttee. for Econ. Devt. 59-60; Pres. Toyobo-Howa Textile Eng. Co. Ltd. 61-; Junior Vice-Pres. IFCATI 64-66, Senior Vice-Pres. 66-68, Pres. 68-70; Chair. Japan Spinners Asscns. 66-68; Vice-Pres. Japan Tax Asscn. 67-; Pres. Expo Textile Asscn. 67-71, Japan Textile Color Design Center 68-72; Pres. Japan Textile Fed. 70-71, Supreme Adviser 71-; Blue Ribbon Medal 65, First Class Order of the Sacred Treasure 73.
Toyobo Co. Ltd., 8 Dojima Hamadori 2-chome, Kita-ku, Osaka 530; Home: 283 Gunge Kakiuchi, Mikage-cho, Higashinada-ku, Kobe 658, Japan.
Telephone: 06-344-1331 (Office); 078-851-2327 (Home).

Taniguchi, Yoshiro, D.ENG.; Japanese architect; b. 24 June 1904, Kanazawa; ed. Tokyo Imperial Univ.
Assistant Prof., Tokyo Univ. of Engineering 31-43, Prof. 43-45, Prof. Emer. 65-; Dir. Museum Meiji-mura, Inuyama 65-; mem. Cultural Properties Specialists Council of Japan 52-; mem. Japan Acad. of Arts; Prizes of Japan Inst. of Architecture 42, 49, 56; Award of Japan Acad. of Arts 61.
Works include: Nat. monument for the unknown war-dead, Tokyo 59, Palace for Crown Prince of Japan 60, Hotel Okura, Tokyo 62, Imperial Theatre 66, Gallery of

Eastern Antiquities at Tokyo Nat. Museum 68, Tokyo Nat. Museum of Modern Art 69, Hotel Okura Amsterdam, Amsterdam (in collaboration) 71.
7-11-7, Koyama, Shinagawa-ku, Tokyo, Japan.
Telephone: 03-781-1990.

Tashiro, Kikuo; Japanese newspaper executive; b. 22 April 1917; ed. Waseda Univ.
Joined *Asahi Shimbun* 40; City Editor 59, Man. Editor 66; Exec. Dir. in charge of Editorial Affairs 69-.
Asahi Shimbun, 3, 2-chome, Yuraku-cho, Chiyoda-ku, Tokyo, Japan.

Tata, Jehangir Ratanji Dadabhoy; Indian industrialist; b. 29 July 1904.
Joined Tata Sons Ltd. 26; Chair. Tata Sons Ltd., Tata Industries Ltd., The Tata Iron and Steel Co. Ltd., The Tata Oil Mills Co. Ltd., Tata Chemicals Ltd., Tata Ltd., London, Tata Inc., New York, Tata Inst. of Fundamental Research, Indian Hotels Co. Ltd., Sir Dorabji Tata Trust, Lady Tata Memorial Trust, J. N. Tata Endowment, Nat. Centre for the Performing Arts, Homi Bhabha Fellowships Council, Air-India, Family Planning Foundations; Pres. Court of Indian Inst. of Science, Bangalore; Dir. Tata Engineering and Locomotive Co. Ltd., Investment Corpn. of India Ltd.; mem. Indian Airlines, Atomic Energy Comm.; Trustee Gandhi Smarak Nidhi, Kasturba Gandhi Nat. Memorial Trust, Jawaharlal Nehru Memorial Fund; first pilot to qualify in India 29, solo flight to U.K. 30; founded Tata Airlines 32; Hon. Air Vice Marshal, Indian Air Force; Officeri Légion d'Honneur 54, Padma Bhushan 55; Hon. D.Sc. (Allahabad) 47.
Bombay House, Homi Modi Street, Bombay 400 023; Home: The Cairn, Altamount Road, Bombay 400 026, India.

Tatad, Francisco, LITT.B.; Philippine writer and politician; b. 4 Oct. 1939; ed. Univ. of Santo Tomas, Manila.
Former Corresp., Agence France-Presse; fmr. Columnist *Manila Daily Bulletin*; Press Sec. and Presidential Spokesman 69-; Sec. of Public Information 72-.
Department of Public Information, Malacañang, Manila; Home: 2 Arfel Homes, Diliman, Quezon City, Philippines.

Taufa'ahau Tupou IV, G.C.V.O., K.C.M.G., K.B.E., B.A., LL.B.; H.M. King of Tonga; b. 4 July 1918; eldest son of the late Queen Salote Tupou III of Tonga and the late Hon. Uiliame Tungi, C.B.E., Premier of Tonga; ed. Tupou Coll. Tonga, Newington Coll. and Sydney Univ., N.S.W.; married H.R.H. Princess Mata'aho 47; four children, of whom the eldest, Crown Prince Tupoutoa, is heir to the throne.
Premier of Tonga 49-65; King of Tonga 65-; Chancellor of the University of the South Pacific 70-73; Hon. LL.D.
The Palace, Nuku'alofa, Tonga.

Tebbit, Sir Donald Claude, K.C.M.G., M.A.; British diplomatist; b. 4 May 1920, Cambridge; ed. Perse School, Cambridge, Cambridge Univ.
Royal Naval Voluntary Reserve 41-46; Foreign Office 46-48; Second Sec., British Embassy, U.S.A. 48-51; Foreign Office 51-54; First Sec. (Commercial), Federal Repub. of Germany 54-58; Private Sec. to Minister of State, Foreign Office 58-61, Counsellor 62, Sec. Cttee. on Representational Services Overseas 62-64; Counsellor and Head of Chancery, Denmark 64-67; Head of W. and Gen. Africa Dept. Commonwealth Office 67; Asst. Under-Sec. of State, FCO 68; Commercial Minister, U.S.A. 70-71, Minister 71-72; Deputy Under-Sec. of State, FCO 73-76; High Commr. to Australia 76-.
British High Commission, Commonwealth Avenue, Canberra, A.C.T., Australia; Home: Hill Cottage, Hill Close, Harrow on the Hill, Middx., England.

Templeton, Malcolm J. C.; New Zealand diplomatist; b. 12 May 1924, Dunedin; ed. Otago Univ.
Joined Ministry of Foreign Affairs 46; held diplomatic posts in U.S.A. 51-57; Head UN Div., later Defence Div., Ministry of Foreign Affairs 57; Counsellor, London 62, Minister 64-67; Imperial Defence Coll., London 63; Asst. Sec. of Foreign Affairs 67-72; seconded to Prime Minister's Dept. as Deputy Perm. Head 72; Acting Deputy Sec. of Foreign Affairs Jan.-May 73; Perm. Rep. to UN Aug. 73-; rep. to several int. confs., including meeting of Colombo Plan, SEATO Council, Commonwealth Prime Ministers, UN Gen. Assemblies, Third UN Conf. on Law of the Sea, and other UN confs.
Permanent Mission of New Zealand to United Nations, 1 United Nations Plaza, 25th Floor, New York, N.Y. 10017, U.S.A.

Teng Hsiao-p'ing; politician, People's Repub. of China; b. 1904, Kuang-an, Szechuan; ed. French School, Chungking, in France and Far Eastern Univ., Moscow.
Dean of Educ., Chungshan Mil. Acad., Shensi 26; Chief of Staff Red Army 30; Dir. Propaganda Dept., Gen. Political Dept., Red Army 32; on long March 34-36; Political Commissar during Sino-Japanese War; mem. 7th Cen. Cttee. of CCP 45; Political Commissar 2nd Field Army, People's Liberation Army 48-54; First Sec. E. China Bureau, CCP 49; Sec.-Gen. Cen. Cttee. of CCP 53-56; Minister of Finance 53; Vice-Chair. Nat. Defence Council 54-67; Vice-Premier, State Council 54-67; mem. Politburo, CCP 55-57; Sec., Secr. of Cen. Cttee., CCP 56-67; Gen. Sec. 8th Cen. Cttee. of CCP 56; criticized and removed from office during cultural revolution 67; mem. 10th Cen. Cttee., CCP 73, Vice-Chair. Jan. 75-April 76; mem. Politburo of CCP 74-April 76, of Standing Cttee. of Politburo 75-April 76; Vice-Chair. Mil. Affairs Cttee. of Cen. Cttee. 75; Chief of Gen. Staff, PLA Jan. 75-April 76; First Vice-Premier, State Council Jan. 75-April 76.

Teng Ying-ch'ao; Chinese party official; b. 1903, Hsinyang, Honan; *m.* late Chou En-lai 1925 (died 1976); ed. Tientsin No. 1 Girls Nat. School.
Arrested for involvement in May 4th Movt. 19; studied in France 20; participated in Long March 34-36; Dir. Women's Work Dept., Cen. Cttee. of CCP 37; Alt. mem. 7th Cen. Cttee. of CCP 45; Vice-Chair. Nat. Women's Federation of China 53-; mem. 8th Cen. Cttee. of CCP 56, 9th Cen. Cttee. 69, 10th Cen. Cttee. 73.

Tennekoon, Herbert Ernest, M.B.E., B.A., F.R.S.A., F.I.B.A.; Ceylonese administrator; b. 30 Sept. 1911, Kandy; ed. St. Anthony's Coll., Kandy and Univs. of Colombo, London and Oxford.
Entered Ceylon Civil Service 35, held various judicial and admin. appointments 36-52; Commr. of Lands 53; Commr. for Registration of Indian and Pakistani Residents 54; Controller of Immigration and Emigration 57; Acting Perm. Sec. to Ministry of Defence and External Affairs 58, Perm. Sec. 60; Acting Perm. Sec. to Ministry of Commerce, Trade, Food and Shipping 61; Perm. Sec. to Ministry of Agriculture, Lands, Irrigation and Power 63; Sec. to Treasury and Perm. Sec. to Ministry of Finance 63; Special Adviser to GATT, Geneva 65; Amb. to Japan 66; Gov. Central Bank of Ceylon 71-; Vice-Pres. (Sri Lanka Chapter), Soc. for Int. Devt.; Fellow, Int. Bankers' Asscn.
Central Bank of Ceylon, Colombo; Home: Bank House, 206 Bauddhaloka Mawatha, Colombo 7, Sri Lanka.
Telephone: 27486 (Office); 81506 (Home).

Tennekoon, William; Ceylonese banker; b. 1 June 1912; ed. St. Anthony's Coll. Kandy, Trinity Coll., Kandy, and Univ. Coll. of Ceylon.
First Agent (Kandy Branch), Bank of Ceylon 41-43, Deputy Accountant 43-47, Accountant 47-49, Head Office Man. 49-50; Chief Accountant, Cen. Bank of Ceylon 50-55, Dir. of Bank Supervision 51-57, Dep. Gov. 57-67, Gov. 67-71; Alt. Exec. Dir. Int. Monetary Fund 53-54, 62-

64, Int. Bank for Reconstruction and Devt. 54-55; Exec. Dir. Asian Devt. Bank 71-74.
14 Real Street, Urdaneta Village, Makati, Rizal, Philippines.

Tenzing Norgay, G.M.; Nepalese climber; b. about 1914 in eastern Nepal, migrated to Bengal 32.
Took part (as porter) in expedition under Shipton 35, Ruttledge 36 and Tilman 38; joined small expedition to Karakoram 50, and French expedition to Nanda Devi 51, when he and one Frenchman climbed the east peak; Sirdar to both Swiss expeditions 52, joining assault parties and reaching about 28,000 feet; Sirdar to British Everest expedition 53, when he and Hillary reached the summit on 29 May; Dir. of Field Training, Himalayan Mountaineering Inst., Darjeeling 54-.
1 Tonga Road, Ghang-La, Darjeeling, West Bengal, India.

Terao, Takeo; Japanese banker; b. 5 April 1905; ed. Tokyo Univ.
Nomura (now Daiwa) Bank 29-, Dir. 47-, later Managing Dir., Pres. 50-73, Chair. 73-; Vice-Pres. Fed. of Bankers' Asscns. of Japan; Pres. Osaka Bankers' Asscn.; Vice-Pres. Osaka Chamber of Commerce and Industry.
Daiwa Bank Ltd., 21, Bingomachi 2-chome, Higashi-ku, Osaka, Japan.

Thailand, King of (*see* Bhumibol Adulyadej).

Thajeb, Sjarif, M.D.; Indonesian diplomatist; b. 7 Aug. 1920, Peureula, Aceh; ed. Jakarta Medical Coll., Harvard Medical School, Temple Univ. School of Medicine, Philadelphia, Pa. and Army Staff and Command School, Jakarta.
Former army doctor; Lecturer, Children's Div., Dept. of Medicine, Univ. of Indonesia; Pres. Univ. of Indonesia; Minister of Higher Educ. and Sciences; Vice-Chair. of Parl.; Amb. to U.S.A. 71-74; Minister of Educ. and Culture 74-; participant in several int. paediatric confs.; Hon doctorate, Univ. of Mindanao (Philippines); several medals and decorations.
Publs. papers and articles on various subjects published in numerous paediatric magazines and journals.
Ministry of Education and Culture, Jakarta, Indonesia.

Thammasak, Sanya; Thai lawyer and politician; b. 5 April 1907, Bangkok; ed. Bangkok and London.
Former Chief Justice, Supreme Court; fmr. Rector, Thammasat Univ.; Pres. Privy Council 69-73; Prime Minister 73-75; Vice-Pres. World Buddhist Fed., Buddhist Asscn. of Thailand.
Buddhist Association of Thailand, 41 Phra Aditya Street, Bangkok, Thailand.

Thapa, Surya Bahadur; Nepalese politician; b. 20 March 1928; ed. Allahabad Univ., India.
House Speaker, Advisory Assembly to King of Nepal 58; mem. Upper House of Parl. 59; Minister of Forests, Agriculture, Commerce and Industry 60; Minister of Finance and Econ. Affairs 62; Vice-Chair. Council of Ministers, Minister of Finance, Econ. Planning, Law and Justice 63; Vice-Chair. Council of Ministers, Minister of Finance, Law and Gen. Admin. 64-65; Chair. Council of Ministers, Minister of Palace Affairs, Gen. Admin. and Panchayat Affairs 65-69; mem. Royal Advisory Cttee. 69-72; arrested Aug. 72; Tri-Shakti-Patta 63, Gorkha Dakshinbahu I 65.
Naxal, Kathmandu, Nepal.

Thapa, Vishwa Bandhu, B.A.; Nepalese agronomist and politician; b. 1927; ed. Adaisha, Vidyalaya, Biratnagar, Nepal; Central Hindu Coll., Banaras Hindu Univ. India.
Executive Cttee. Nepali Congress Party 51-, Gen. Sec. 58; mem. Lower House of Parl. 59-, Chief Govt. Whip 59-60; mem. Council of Ministers 60-69; mem. Royal Advisory Cttee. 69-; Minister of Nat. Guidance, Home and Panchayats 60-64; Vice-Chief, Council of Ministers, Minister of Home and Panchayat Devt. 64-65.
Bharatpur, Chitwan, Nepal.

Thi Binh, Nguyen (*see* Nguyen Thi Binh).

Thi Han, Thiri Pyanchi U; Burmese politician; b. 1912; ed. Rangoon Univ.
General Sec. Rangoon Univ. Students' Union 36; Asst. Quarter-Master Gen., War Office (Burma); Deputy Controller of Civil Supplies 49, later Dir. of Procurement and Dir. of Defence Industries, Ministry of Defence; Minister of Trade Devt., Commodity Distribution and Co-operatives 59; Minister of Foreign Affairs 62-69, also of Public Works and Housing, Mines and Labour 62-64, also of Nat. Planning 64-69, Vice-Chair. Socialist Economy Planning Cttee. 67-69.
c/o Ministry of Foreign Affairs, Rangoon, Burma.

Thieu, Lt.-Gen. Nguyen Van (*see* Nguyen Van Thieu, Lt.-Gen.).

Tho, Le Duc (*see* Le Duc Tho).

Thomson, David Spence, M.C., M.P.; New Zealand dairy farmer and politician; b. 14 Nov. 1915; ed. Stratford Primary and High School.
Territorial Army 31-59, served Middle East 39-45, Prisoner of war 42, Brigadier (Reserve of Officers); Chair. Fed. Farmers Sub-provincial Exec. 59-63; M.P. for Stratford 63-; Minister of Defence, Minister in charge of Tourism, Minister in charge of Publicity 66-67; Minister of Defence, Minister in charge of War Pensions, Minister in charge of Rehabilitation 67-72, also of Police 69; Assoc. Minister in charge of Labour and Immigration 71-72, Minister Feb.-Dec. 72; Minister of Justice Dec. 75-; National Party.
Parliament Buildings, Wellington; Home: Bird Road, Stratford, New Zealand.

Thondaman, Savumiamoorthy; Ceylonese agriculturist; b. 30 Aug. 1913; ed. St. Andrew's Coll., Gampola.
Member Ceylon Parl. 47-51, 60-70; mem. ILO Asian Advisory Cttee.; Substitute Deputy mem. Governing Body of ILO; mem. Exec. Board ICFTU; Vice-Pres. ICFTU-ARO; Pres. Ceylon Worker's Congress; Leader of movement for political and econ. rights of Tamil community in Sri Lanka.
Wavendon Group, Ramboda, Sri Lanka.

Tin Pe, Brigadier; Burmese army officer and politician.
Member Burmese Revolutionary Council 62-74; Minister of Agriculture and Forests, Co-operatives, Commodity Distribution, and Land Nationalization 62-64, of Supplies, Co-operatives, Agriculture and Trade 64-72.
Burma Socialist Programme Party, Rangoon, Burma.

Ting Sheng; army officer, People's Repub. of China; b. 1912, Kiangsi; ed. Red Army School and Mil. Coll.
Participated in Long March 34-35; Battalion Commdr. 37; Div. Commdr. 4th Field Army 49; Commdr. 54th Army, People's Liberation Army, Tibet 54-55; Deputy Commdr. Sinkiang Mil. Region, PLA 63-68; Canton Mil. Region, PLA 68; mem. 9th Cen. Cttee. of CCP 69; Sec. CCP Kwangtung 71; Commdr. Canton Mil. Region, PLA 72-73; Chair. Kwangtung Revolutionary Cttee. 72-; First Sec. CCP Kwangtung 72-73; mem. 10th Cen. Cttee. of CCP 73; Commdr. Nanking Mil. Region, PLA 74-.

Tirikatene-Sullivan, Tini Whetu Marama, B.A.; New Zealand politician; b. 1932; ed. Rangiora High School, Victoria Univ. of Wellington, Nat. Univ. of Australia.
Secretary, Royal Tour Staff for visit of H.M. Queen Elizabeth II and H.R.H. The Duke of Edinburgh 53-54; fmr. Social Worker, Depts. of Maori Affairs, Social Security and Child Welfare; mem. for Southern Maori Electorate, N.Z. House of Reps. 67-; Minister of Tourism 72-, Minister for the Environment 74-75.
Parliament Buildings, Wellington; Home: 260A Tinakori Road, Wellington, New Zealand.

Tizard, Robert James, M.A.; New Zealand teacher and politician; b. 7 June 1924; ed. Auckland Grammar School, Auckland Univ.
Served in R.N.Z.A.F., Canada, U.K. 42-46; Junior Lecturer in History, Auckland Univ. 49-53, teaching posts 55-57, 61-62; mem. Parl. 57-60, 63-; Minister of Health and State Services 72-74, in charge of State Advances Corpn. 72-73; Deputy Prime Minister, Minister of Finance, Minister in Charge of Friendly Socs. 74-75; Chair. Board of Govs. Asian Devt. Bank 74-75; Deputy Leader of the Opposition 75-.
Parliament Buildings, Wellington; Home: 84A Beresford Street, Auckland 1, New Zealand.

Toh Chin Chye, PH.D.; Singapore physiologist and politician; b. 10 Dec. 1921; ed. Raffles Coll., Singapore, Univ. Coll., London Univ., and National Inst. for Medical Research, London.
Chair. People's Action Party 54-; Reader in Physiology, Univ. of Singapore 58-64; Deputy Prime Minister of Singapore 59-68; Minister for Science and Technology 68-75, for Health 75-; founder mem. of People's Action Party, now Chair.; mem. Parl. Singapore 59-75; Chair., Board of Govs., Singapore Polytechnic 59-; Vice-Chancellor, Univ. of Singapore 68-75; Chair., Board Regional Inst., for Higher Educ. and Devt. 70-75.
Ministry of Health, Palmer Road, Singapore 2; Home: 23 Greenview Crescent, Singapore 11, Singapore.

Tokunaga, Masatoshi; Japanese politician; b. Aug. 25 1913.
Director Japan Bereaved Asscn.; mem. House of Councillors 59-; Deputy Minister of Health and Welfare; Standing Chair. Ministry of Finance; Minister of Transport 73-74
12-17, Sasuke, 2-chome, Kamakura City, Kanagawa Prefecture 248, Japan.

Tol Saut; Cambodian politician; b. Memot, Eastern Cambodia.
Worked on rubber plantation; joined resistance under Ho Chi Minh in 40s; mem. Indo-Chinese Communist Party until 46, *Pracheachon* (Cambodian Communist Party) 46-; mem. People's Representative Assembly representing rubber plantation workers March 76-; Prime Minister April 76-.
Office of the Prime Minister, Phnom-Penh, Cambodia.

Tolstikov, Vasili Sergeyevich; Soviet politician; b. 1917; ed. Leningrad Inst. of Railway Engineering.
Soviet Army 41-46; construction orgs., Leningrad 46-52; mem. C.P.S.U. 48-; party and Soviet work 52-57; First Deputy Chair. Exec. Cttee. Leningrad Soviet of Workers' Deputies 57-60; Sec., later Second Sec. Leningrad Regional Cttee., C.P.S.U. 60-62, First Sec. 62- 70; Amb. to People's Republic of China 70-; mem. Presidium of U.S.S.R. Supreme Soviet 62-71; mem. Central Cttee. of C.P.S.U. 61-; Deputy to U.S.S.R. and R.S.F.S.R. Supreme Soviets.
Soviet Embassy, Peking, People's Republic of China.

Tomii, Kazuo; Japanese business executive; b. 14 Aug. 1908; ed. Toyama Univ.
President, Unitika Ltd.
Unitika Ltd., 68 Kitakyutaro-machi, 4-chome, Higash-ku, Osaka; Home: 1-21-2, Hamayashiki, Kawanishi City, Hyogo Pres., Japan.

Tomonaga, Sin-itiro, D.SC.; Japanese physicist; b. 31 March 1906; ed. Third High School, Kyoto, and Kyoto Imperial Univ.
Research student, Inst. of Physical and Chemical Research 32-39; studies, Univ. of Leipzig 37-39; Asst., Inst. of Physical and Chemical Research 39-40; Lecturer, Tokyo Bunrika Univ. (absorbed into Tokyo Univ. of Educ. 49) 40, Prof. of Physics 41-; Dir. of Inst. of Optical Research, Kyoiku Univ. (Tokyo Univ. of Educ.) 63-69; Pres. Tokyo Univ. of Educ. 56-62; Pres. Science Council of Japan 63-69; Japan Academy Prize 48, Order of Culture 52, Lomonosov Medal (U.S.S.R.) 64; Nobel Prize for Physics 65.
Publs. *On the photo-electric production of positive and negative electrons* 34, *Innere Reibung und Wärmeleitfähigkeit der Kernmaterie* 38, *On a Relativistically Invariant Formulation of the Quantum Theory of Wave Fields* 46, *On the Effect of the Field Reactions on the Interaction of Mesotrons and Nuclear Particles I, II III IV* 46-47, *A Self-Consistent Subtraction Method in Quantum Field Theory I, II* 48, *Remarks on Bloch's Method of Sound Waves to Many-Fermion Problems* 50.
3-17-12, Kyonan-cho, Musashino City, Tokyo, Japan.
Telephone: 0422-32-2410.

Ton Duc Thang; Vietnamese politician; b. 20 Aug. 1888, Long Xuyen Province.
Went to France and joined French Navy 12; returned to Saigon 20; joined Viet-Nam Revolutionary Youth Soc. 25; imprisoned by French 29-45; mem. Communist Party of Indo-China 30; held exec. Party and Govt. posts 45-, including Deputy Chair., then Chair. of Standing Cttee. of Democratic Repub. of Viet-Nam (D.R.V.) Nat. Assembly; Chair. of Central Cttee. Presidium of Viet-Nam Fatherland Front; mem. Central Cttee. of Working People's Party of Viet-Nam; Vice-Pres. D.R.V. 60-69, Pres. 69-76; Pres. Socialist Repub. of Viet-Nam July 76-; Chair. Nat. Defence Council July 76-, Central Board of Vietnamese-Soviet Friendship Soc.; at Congress of Working People's Party of Viet-Nam 51, 60; Leader Nat. Assembly del. to U.S.S.R. 56; Lenin Int. Prize for Promotion of Peace Among Nations, Order of Lenin of U.S.S.R. 67.
Office of the President, Hanoi, Viet-Nam.

Tonga, H.M. King of (*see* Taufa'ahau Tupou IV).

Tonkin, Hon. John Trezise, M.L.A.; Australian politician; b. 2 Feb. 1902, Boulder.
Member W. Australia Legislative Ass. 33-; Minister of Educ. and Social Services 43; Deputy Leader of Opposition 47; Minister for Educ., Works and Water Supplies 53; Deputy Premier 55-59; Deputy Leader of Opposition 59-67, Leader 67-71, 74-; Premier of W. Australia, Treas. and Minister of Cultural Affairs 71-74; Leader of the Opposition 74-76; Labor Party; Fellow, Australian Soc. of Accountants.
Parliament House, Perth, Western Australia.

Tope, Trimbak Krishna, M.A., LL.B.; Indian lawyer and teacher; b. 28 Feb. 1914, Yeola, Nasik District; de. Bombay Univ.
Professor of Sanskrit, Ramnarain Ruia Coll. 39-47; Advocate, Bombay High Court 46; Prof. of Law, Govt. Law Coll. 47, Principal and Perry Prof. of Jurisprudence 58-; Vice-Chancellor, Univ. of Bombay 71-; Pres. Maharashtra Samajik Parishad.
Publs. *Why Hindu Code?, Indian Constitution, A Modern Sage.*
University of Bombay, Bombay 32, India.
Telephone: 255726 (Office); 291750 (Home).

Toshima, Kenkichi, B.S.; Japanese metallurgical engineer and business executive; b. 30 June 1902; ed. Kyoto Univ.
Kobe Steel Ltd., Kobe 32-, Dir. 49-53, Man. Dir. 53-56, Senior Man. Dir. 56-58, Pres. 58-, Chair. 72-74, Adviser 74-; Blue Ribbon Medal, Kien Itto Zuihosho.
Office: Kobe Steel Ltd., 3-18, 1-chome, Wakinohama-cho, Fukiai-ku, Kobe; Home: 15-16 Rokurokuso-cho, Ashiya City, Hyogo Prefecture, Japan.
Telephone: Kobe 251-1551 (Office); Ashiya 22-4561 (Home).

Toyoda, Eiji; Japanese motor executive; b. 1913, Nagoya; ed. Tokyo Univ.
Joined Toyoda Motor Co. Ltd. 38, Dir. 45-50, Man. Dir. 50-60, Vice-Pres. 60-67, Pres. 67-; Dir. Aishin Seiko Co. Ltd., Toyoda Automatic Loom Works Ltd., Toyoda Machine Works Ltd., Toyota Cen. Research and Devt. Laboratories Inc., Toyota Motor Sales Co. Ltd., Toyota

Motor Thailand Co. Ltd., Toyota Motor Sales U.S.A. Inc., Aichi Steel Works Ltd., Towa Real Estate Co. Ltd.; Chair. Japan Automobile Asscn.; Pres. Japan Automotive Industry Asscn.; Auditor Toyoda Tsusho Kaisha Ltd.; Blue Ribbon Medal and many other hons.
Office: 1 Toyota-cho, Toyota-shi, Aichi; Home: 12 Yagen, Takernachi, Toyota-shi, Aichi, Japan.

Toyv, Luvsandorjiyn; Mongolian diplomatist and politician; b. 1915; ed. Pedagogical Coll. and Mongolian State Univ., Ulan Bator.
Chief of Educ. Dept., Mongolian Ministry of Educ. 35-36; Editor *Youth* (newspaper) 36-37, *Ulaan Od* (army newspaper) 37-47; Pres. Mongolian Writers' Union 47-50; Counsellor, Mongolian Embassy, Moscow 53-57; Head of Dept., Ministry of Foreign Affairs, Ulan Bator 57-60; Counsellor, Peking 60-62; Perm. Rep. to UN 64-66; First Deputy Foreign Ministry 66-68; Minister of Foreign Affairs 68-70; mem. Central Cttee. Mongolian People's Revolutionary Party 66-.
Mongolian People's Revolutionary Party, Ulan Bator, Mongolia.

Tran Buu Kiem; Vietnamese politician; b. 1921, Can Tho; ed. Faculty of Law, Hanoi Univ.
Member of Indo-Chinese Student Org.; organized a popular uprising in Saigon 45; Sec.-Gen. Admin. and Resistance Cttee. for Southern Region of Viet-Nam, Indo-Chinese Student Org., Deputy Dir. for Econ. Services in Southern Region 50; Deputy Sec.-Gen., Cen. Cttee. of Democratic Party 60; mem. Cen. Cttee. Nat. Liberation Front; Pres. Student Union of S. Viet-Nam; head of NLF Del. to Paris Conf. on Viet-Nam; Minister to Presidency, Provisional Revolutionary Govt. of S. Viet-Nam May 75-June 76.
Office of the President, Hanoi, Viet-Nam.

Tran Nam Trung (*see* Tran Van Tra, Gen.).

Tran Thien Khiem, Gen.; Vietnamese army officer and politician; b. 15 Dec. 1925.
Army Service 47-75; held off attempted coup against President Diem 60, took part in coup against him 63; with Gen. Nguyen Khan led coup removing Gen. Duong Van Minh 64; Defence Minister and C.-in-C. 64; Amb. to U.S. Oct. 64-Oct. 65, to Taiwan Oct. 65-May 68; Minister of the Interior 68-73, Deputy Prime Minister March-Aug. 69, Prime Minister 69-75, Minister of Defence 72-75; flew to Taiwan April 75.

Tran Van Chuong, S.J.D.; Vietnamese lawyer and diplomatist; b. 1898; ed. Univ. of Paris.
Lawyer, South and North Viet-Nam 25-47; Vice-Pres. Grand Council for Econ. and Financial Interests of Indochina 38; mem. Fed. Council of Indochina 40; Minister of Foreign Affairs and Vice-Premier 45; Judge, Franco-Vietnamese Court of Cassation and Council of State 53-54; Minister of State, Republic of Viet-Nam 54; Amb. to United States 54-63, to Brazil 59-63, to Mexico 62-63; Minister to Argentina 60-63.
Publ. *Essai sur l'Esprit du Droit Sino-Annamite* 22.
5601 Western Avenue, N.W., Washington D.C. 20015, U.S.A.

Tran Van Huong; Vietnamese politician; b. 1 Dec. 1903, Former school-teacher; participated in Viet-Minh resistance against French; Mayor of Saigon 54; political imprisonment 60, Prime Minister, Repub. of Viet-Nam 64-65, 68-69; Vice-Pres. 71-75, Pres. 21-28 April 75; Hon. Corporal Repub. of Viet-Nam Armed Forces 74.

Tran Van Lam; Vietnamese politician and pharmacist; b. 30 July 1913, Cho Lon; ed. Hanoi Univ.
Charter Sec.-Gen. Viet-Nam Pharmacists Asscn. 51-52; elected Saigon City Council 52; mem. Cttee. for Protection of Econ. Interests of the South Vietnamese People 52-54; Speaker, Constituent Assembly; First Legis. Assembly 56-57; Majority Leader in Assembly 57-61; Amb. to Australia and New Zealand 61-64; Chair., Board Viet-Nam Commercial and Industrial Bank 64-67; Chair. Cong Thuong Dia Oc Cong Ty 66-67; Man. Dir. Saigon Duoc Cuoc 64-67; Minister of Foreign Affairs 68-73; Speaker of Senate 73-75.

Tran Van Tra, Gen.; Vietnamese army officer and politician (also known as Tu Chi and Tran Nam Trung); b. 1918, Quang Ngai Province, S. Viet-Nam.
Alternate mem. Cen. Cttee. Lao Dong party; Deputy Chief of Staff, N. Vietnamese Army; Chair. Mil. Affairs Cttee., Cen. Office of S. Viet-Nam (COSVN) 64-76; Minister of Defence, Provisional Revolutionary Govt. of S. Viet-Nam 69-76 (in Saigon 75-76); rose to rank of General May 75; head of mil. cttee. controlling Saigon and district May 75-Jan. 76; Chair. Inspectorate, Council of Ministers, Socialist Repub. of Viet-Nam July 76-.
Council of Ministers, Hanoi, Viet-Nam.

Trengganu, H.H. The Sultan of; Tuanku Ismail Nasiruddin Shah ibni Almarhum Sultan Zainal Abidin, D.K., D.M.N., S.P.M.T., K.C.M.G.; Ruler of Trengganu, Malaysia; b. 24 Jan. 1907.
Joined Trengganu Civil Service 29, later served as High Court Registrar and Chief Magistrate; acceded to throne of Trengganu 45, installed 49; Timbalan Yang di-Pertuan Agong (Deputy Head of State) of Malaya, later Malaysia 60-65, Yang di-Pertuan Agong (Head of State) 65-70.
Istana Badariah, Kuala Trengganu, Trengganu, West Malaysia.

Tripathi, Kamalapati; Indian politician.
Member, Legislative Assembly of Uttar Pradesh 36-; Minister for Irrigation and Information and later for Home Affairs, Educ. and Information, U.P.; Deputy Chief Minister of Uttar Pradesh 69-71, Chief Minister 71-73; Minister of Shipping and Transport 73-75, of Railways Feb. 75-; mem. Rajya Sabha 73-.
Ministry of Railways, New Delhi, India.

Tripp, John Peter, C.M.G.; British diplomatist; b. 27 March 1921; ed. Sutton Valence School, Institut de Touraine.
Royal Marines 41-46; Sudan Political Service 46-54; with Foreign Service (later Diplomatic Service) 54-, Amb. to Libya 70-74; High Commr. in Singapore 74-.
British High Commission, Tanglin Circus, Singapore 10, Singapore.

Truong Nhu Tang; Vietnamese lawyer and politician; b. 1923, Cholon; ed. Univ. of Paris.
Controller-General, Vietnamese Bank for Trade and Industry; Dir.-Gen. of a sugar co., Saigon; Sec.-Gen. Org. for Nat. Self-Determination; mem. Cttee. for Peace; joined Nat. Liberation Front 68; Minister of Justice, Provisional Revolutionary Govt. of S. Viet-Nam May 75-June 76.
c/o Council of Ministers, Hanoi, Viet-Nam.

Ts'ao Li-huai; army officer, People's Repub. of China; b. Fukien.
Chief of Staff Garrison Command H.Q., Yenan 42; Commdr. 49th Army, 4th Field Army 49; Commdr. 4th Field Army 53; Commdr. of Air Force, People's Liberation Army 56; Lieut.-Gen. 56, Deputy Commdr. 56-; mem. 9th Cen. Cttee. of CCP 69, 10th Cen. Cttee. 73.

Ts'ao Ssu-ming; army officer, People's Repub. of China. Secretary CCP Sinkiang 71; Commdr. Sinkiang Mil. Region, People's Liberation Army 73-.

Tsedenbal, Yumjaagiyn; Mongolian politician; b. 17 Sept. 1916; ed. in Mongolia and U.S.S.R.
Teacher at Ulan Bator Financial Coll.; then Dep. Minister, later Minister of Finance 39-40; Sec.-Gen. Central Cttee. Mongolian People's Revolutionary Party 40-54, First Sec.

58-; Deputy C.-in-C. of Mongolian Army 41-45; Chair. State Planning Comm. 45-48; Deputy Chair. Council of Ministers 48-52, Chair. 52-74; Chair. Presidium, the People's Great Hural June 74-; Mongolian and foreign decorations including Order of Sühbaatar, Order of Lenin, Hero of Mongolian People's Republic and Labour Hero of Mongolian People's Republic; Hon. mem. Acad. of Sciences.
Government Palace, Ulan Bator, Mongolia.

Tseng Shao-shan; People's Repub. of China; b. 1910, Hunan.
On Long March 34-35; Regimental Commdr. 38; Brigade Commdr. 41; Deputy Commdr. E. Szechuan Mil. District, People's Liberation Army 50-52; Lieut.-Gen. PLA 57; Commdr. Tsinan Mil. Region, PLA 57; Political Commissar Shenyang Mil. Region, PLA 60; mem. 9th Cen. Cttee. of CCP 69; Second Sec. CCP Liaoning 71, First Sec. 75-; Vice-Chair. Liaoning Revolutionary Cttee. 73, Chair. 75-; mem. 10th Cen. Cttee. of CCP 73.

Tseng Ssu-yu; army officer, People's Repub. of China; b. 1907.
Staff Officer Red 1st Front Army 35; Commdr. 4th Column, N. China PLA 48; Lieut.-Gen. Shenyang Mil. Region, PLA 60, Deputy Commdr. 65-67; Commdr. Wuhan Mil. Region, PLA 67-73; mem. 9th Cen. Cttee. of CCP 69; First Sec. CCP Hupeh 71; mem. 10th Cen. Cttee. of CCP 73; Commdr. Tsinan Mil. Region, PLA 74-.

Tsevegmid, Dondogiin; Mongolian biologist and diplomatist; b. 26 March 1915; ed. Moscow Univ.
Teacher 30-45; Chancellor Ulan Bator Univ., and Chair. Cttee. of Sciences 59-60; Deputy Minister of Foreign Affairs 60-62; Amb. to People's Republic of China 62; Chancellor, Ulan Bator Univ. 67-; Chair. People's Great Hural of Mongolia 69-72; Deputy Prime Minister 72-; Del. to UN 61; Corresp. mem. Mongolian Acad. of Sciences; Dr. h.c. Moscow Lomonosov and Berlin Humboldt Univs.
Publs. *The Ecological and Morphological Analysis of the Duplicidentate* 50, *Fauna of the Transaltai* 63, *Selected Works* 46, 56, 74.
Government Palace, Ulan Bator, Mongolia.

Tsukasa, Tadashi; Japanese publisher and book executive; b. 5 Oct. 1893.
With Maruzen Co. 06, Dir. 40-, Pres. 47-71, Chair. 71-; Vice-Pres. Tokyo Chamber of Commerce and Industry; Chair. Tokyo Stationery Industrial Asscn., Japan Book Importers' Asscn.; mem. Board of Trustees and Dir. Japanese Nat. Cttee. of Int. Chamber of Commerce; Pres. Tokyo Distribution Center Co.; Vice-Pres., Tokyo Trade Fair Asscn.; Dir. Tokyo Foreign Trade Asscn.; 2nd Class Order Rising Sun 64, Ordre des Arts et Lettres 63, 1st Class Order of the Sacred Treasure 71.
3-10, Nihombashi 2-chome, Chuo-ku, Tokyo; and 5-15, 1-chome, Kitazawa, Setagaya-ku, Tokyo, Japan.
Dir. Tokyo Foreign Trade Asscn.
Maruzen Co. Ltd., 6 Tori-Nichome, Nihonbashi, Tokyo; and 5-15, 1-chome, Kitazawa, Setagaya-ku, Tokyo, Japan.

Tsuruoka, Senjin; Japanese diplomatist; b. 2 June 1907; ed. Tokyo Imperial Univ.
Attaché, Paris 32; Sec. of Office of Japanese Govt. for Int. Confs., Geneva 39; First Sec., Switzerland 45; Chief of Legal Section, Ministry of Foreign Affairs 46; Deputy Dir. of Immigration Bureau, Ministry of Justice 52; Chief Japanese Del. to numerous int. confs. 55-58; Amb. to Vatican 58-59; Dir. UN Bureau, Ministry of Foreign Affairs 59-62; Amb. to Vatican 56-59, to Sweden 62-66, to Switzerland 66-67; Perm. Rep. to UN 67-71, Amb. at Large 71-; mem. UN Int. Law Comm. 62-.
Ministry of Foreign Affairs, Tokyo, Japan.

Tu Chi (*see* Tran Van Tra, Gen.).

Tu'ipelahake, H.R.H. Prince Fatafehi, C.B.E.; Tongan politician; b. 7 Jan. 1922, second son of the late Queen Salote Tupou III and the late Hon. Uilami Tungi, C.B.E., Premier of Tonga; ed. Newington Coll., Sydney, N.S.W., and Gatton Agricultural Coll., Queensland; married H.R.H. Princess Melenaite 47; six children.
Governor of Vava'u 52-65; Prime Minister of Tonga 65-, also Minister for Foreign Affairs, Agriculture, Tourism, Telegraphs and Telephones; Chair. Tonga Copra Board and Tonga Produce Board.
Office of the Prime Minister, Nuku'alofa, Tonga.

Tupou IV, Taufa'ahau (*see* Taufa'ahau Tupou IV).

Tze-chung Li; Chinese librarian; b. 1927, Kiangsu; ed. Soochow Univ., Southern Methodist Univ., Harvard Univ., Columbia Univ., New School for Social Research.
District Judge 49-51; Section Chief, Ministry of Nat. Defence 51-56; Vice-Pres. Atlantic Fiscal Corpn., New York 62-64; Asst. Prof. of Library Science, Asst. Librarian Illinois Normal Univ. 65-66; Asst. Prof. of Political Science and Library Science Rosary Coll. 66-70, Assoc. Prof. of Library Science 70-74, Prof. 75-; Visiting Assoc. Prof. Nat. Taiwan Univ., Soochow Univ. 69; Dir. Nat. Cen. Library 70-72, Consultant 74-; Consultant Dr. Sun Yat-sen Memorial Library, Taipei 71; mem. Nat. Council of Culture Renaissance 70-; Chair. Graduate Inst. of Library Science, Nat. Cen. Library 71-72; mem. of Board, Center for American Studies, Academia Sinica 71-73; mem. Editorial Board, Journal of Library and Information Science 75-; Pres. Chinese-American Educ. Foundation, Chicago 69-70; Chair. Cttee. on High School Library Standards, Ministry of Educ. 72; Convenor, Board of Dirs., Chinese Library Asscn. 70-71; Regional Rep. Int. Asscn. of Orientalist Librarians 71-; Pres. Mid-West Chinese-American Librarians Asscn. 73-; Sec.-Treas., Int. Relations Round Table, American Library Asscn. 75-; Elsie O. and Philip D. Sang Award for Excellence in Teaching (Rosary Coll.) 71.
Publs. seven books, and many articles.
Graduate School of Library Science, Rosary College, River Forest, Ill. 60305, U.S.A.

U

Uchida, Tsuneo; Japanese politician; b. 1907; ed. Tokyo Univ.
Member, House of Reps.; Dir. Property Custodian Bureau of Ministry of Finance; Parl. Vice-Minister for Int. Trade and Industry, subsequently for Science and Technology; Chair. House of Reps. Commerce and Industry Cttee.; Chair. Liberal-Democratic Party Tax System Research Council; Minister of Health and Welfare 70-71; Dir. Econ. Planning Agency 73-74.
House of Representatives, Tokyo, Japan.

Ulanfu, Gen.; Chinese (Mongolian) politician; b. 1906, Suiyuan; ed. Mongolian-Tibetan School, Peking, Far Eastern Univ., Moscow.
Joined CCP 25; Alt. mem. 7th Cen. Cttee. of CCP 45; Chair. Inner Mongolia People's Govt. 47-67; Commdr., Political Commissar Inner Mongolia Mil. Region, People's Liberation Army 47-67; Vice-Premier, State Council 54-; Chair. Nationalities Comm. 54-67; First Sec. CCP Inner Mongolia 54-67; Gen. 55; Alt. mem. Politburo, CCP 56-67; criticized and removed from office during Cultural Revolution 67; mem. 10th Cen. Cttee. of CCP 73; Perm. Chair. Presidium, Nat. People's Congress 75-.

Ulfat, Gul Pacha; Afghan poet and writer; b. 1909; ed. private studies.
Staff writer *Anis* (daily) 35-36; Writers' Soc. 36; later mem. staff *Islah* (daily); Editor *Kabul Magazine* 46; Editor *Nangrahar* (weekly) 48; Chief of Tribal Affairs in Nangrahar Province; mem. House of Reps. from Jalalabad

(Nangrahar), and Second Deputy to Pres. of House 49, mem. from Karghaie 52; Pres. of Afghan Acad. 56; Pres. of Tribal Affairs (mem. Central Cabinet) 63; Rep. in Shura-i-Milli (formerly House of Reps.) from Jalalabad 65-69; Pres. Afghan-U.S.S.R. Friendship Soc. 59-63.
Publs. Twenty-five books on literary, social and political subjects and numerous essays.
Sher Shah Maina, Kabul, Afghanistan.

Underwood, Eric John, A.O., C.B.E., PH.D., F.R.S.; Australian agronomist; b. 7 Sept. 1905, London, England; ed. Univs. of Western Australia, Cambridge, England, and Wisconsin, U.S.A.
Research Officer in Animal Nutrition, Dept. of Agriculture, Western Australia 32-45; Hackett Prof. of Agriculture and Dir. Inst. of Agriculture, Univ. of W. Australia 46-70; mem. of Exec. Commonwealth Scientific and Industrial Org. 66-75; Centennial Prof. of Nutrition, Univ. of Calif. 68; Harkness Fellow, Commonwealth Fund of New York 36-38; F.A.A., F.A.I.A.S.; Hon. mem. American Inst. of Nutrition, Hon. Resident Fellow, Univ. of W.A.; Hon. D.Rur.Sci. (Univ. of New England); Hon. D.Sc.Agric. (Univ. of W. Australia, Univ. of Melbourne); Medal of Australian Inst. of Agricultural Science 51, Kelvin Medal of Royal Soc. of W. Australia 59, Farrer Memorial Medal 67, Burnet Medal of Australian Acad. of Science 73.
Publs. *Principles of Animal Production* 46, *Trace Elements in Human and Animal Nutrition* 56 (3rd edn. 71), *The Mineral Nutrition of Livestock* (F.A.O./C.A.B.) 66; and approx. 100 research papers and reviews.
CSIRO, Floreat Park; Home: 3 Cooper Street, Nedlands, Western Australia.
Telephone: 80-3838 (Office); 86-2620 (Home).

Unger, Leonard, A.B.; American diplomatist; b. 17 Dec. 1917, San Diego, Calif.; ed. Harvard Univ.
National Resources Planning Board 39-41; Dept. of State 41-, served Trieste, Naples; Officer in Charge of Politico-Military Affairs, European Regional Affairs Div., State Dept. 53-57; Deputy Chief of Mission, American Embassy, Bangkok, Thailand 58-62; Amb. to Laos 62-64; Deputy Asst. Sec. of State for Far Eastern Affairs 65-67; Amb. to Thailand 67-74, to Taiwan 74-.
American Embassy, 2 Chung Hsiao Road, Sec. 2, Taipei, Taiwan; Home: 12701 Circle Drive, Rockville, Md. 20850, U.S.A.

Upadhyay, Shailendra Kumar; Nepalese diplomatist; b. 13 Sept. 1929; ed. Benares Hindu Univ.
Assistant Minister for Forest and Food and Agriculture 62-64; Minister in charge of Panchayat 64-65; mem. Rashtriya Panchayat 62-71; Vice-Chair. Nat. Planning Comm. 68-70; Minister for Home and Panchayat and Minister for Land Reforms and Information 70-71; Perm. Rep. to UN June 72-; leader of del. to meeting of Board of Govs. of IBRD 65.
Permanent Mission of Nepal to United Nations, 711 Third Avenue, Room 1806, New York, N.Y. 10017, U.S.A.

Uquaili, Nabi Baksh Mohammed Sidiq, F.C.A.; Pakistani accountant and banker; b. 11 Aug. 1913, Karachi.
Experience of agricultural banking, commercial banking, central banking, exchange control and industrial and investment banking for over thirty years; Minister of Finance 66-69; has represented Pakistan on many int. confs. on banking, finance and econs.; dir. of several financial, commercial and industrial enterprises in Pakistan; awards from Pakistan and Fed. Repub. of Germany.
22F Dawood Colony, Stadium Road, Karachi-5, Pakistan.
Telephone: 225432, 516001/272 (Office); 411013 (Home).

Urabe, Shizutaro; Japanese architect; b. 31 March 1909; ed. Kyoto Univ.
Kurashiki Rayon Co. Ltd. 34-64; Lecturer (part-time) in Architecture, Osaka Univ. Technical Course 54-55; Lecturer (part-time) in Architecture, Kyoto Univ. Technical Course 62-66; Pres. K.K., S. Urabe & Assoc. Architects 62-; Prize of *Mainichi Shuppan Bunka Sho* (publication) 61; Osaka Prefecture Architectural Contest Prize 62; *Annual of Architecture* Prize 63; Architectural Inst. of Japan Prize 64; Osaka Prefecture Order of Merit 65.
Buildings include: Ohara Museum (Annex) 61, Suita Service Area 63 and other offices of Japan Road Corpn. 65, Kurashiki Int. Hotel 63, Aizenbashi Hospital and Nursery School, etc. 65, Asahi Broadcasting Co. Ltd. (consultant) 66, Tokyo Zokei Univ. 66, Tokyo Women's Christian Coll., Research Inst. 67.
Offices: S. Urabe and Assoc. Architects, 7th Floor, New Hankyu Building, 8, Umeda, Kita-ku, Osaka; Z-4 Muromachi Nihonbashi, Chuo-ku, Tokyo; Home: 1-181, Kotoen, Nishinomiya Hyogo, Japan.

Uren, Thomas; Australian politician; b. 28 May 1921, Balmain, Sydney.
Army service 39-45; mem. Parl. for Reid 58-; mem. Fed. Parl. Labor Party Exec. 69-, Deputy Leader Jan. 76-; First Minister of Urban and Regional Devt. 72-75; del. to Australian Area Conf. of Commonwealth Parl. Assen., Darwin 68, to Australian Parl. Mission to Europe 68, to Commonwealth Parl. Assen., Conf. Canberra 70; Labor Party.
Parliament House, Canberra, A.C.T. 2600, Australia.

Usami, Makoto; Japanese banker; b. 5 Feb. 1901; ed. Keio Univ.
Entered Mitsubishi Bank, Ltd. 24, Manager Econ. Research Dept. 47, Manager General Affairs Dept. 49, Dir. 50, Dir. and Manager Head Office 51-54, Managing Dir. 54-59, Deputy Pres. 59-61, Pres. 61-64; Governor Bank of Japan 64-69; Chair. Board of Counsellors, Keio Univ. 66-; Chair. Fed. of the Bankers' Assen. of Japan 62-63.
Room 524, Marunouchi Yaesi Building, 6-2, 2 Marunouchi, Chiyoda-ku, Tokyo; Home: 24-15, 1 Minami-Aoyama, Minato-ku, Tokyo, Japan.
Telephone: 211-2670 (Office); 401-8675 (Home).

Usmani, Ishrat Husain, PH.D.; Pakistani scientist and administrator; b. 15 April 1917; ed. Aligarh Univ., Bombay Univ. and Imperial Coll. of Science and Technology, London.
Joined Madras Cadre of Indian Civil Service 42; fmr. Chief Controller of Imports and Exports, Pakistan; fmr. Chair. W. Pakistan Mineral Development Corpn.; Chair. Pakistan Atomic Energy Comm. 60-72; Sec., Ministry of Education 69-, Ministry of Science and Technology 72-; Chair. Pakistan Power Comm. 61-62; Chair. Board of Govs., IAEA, Vienna 62-63; mem.-Sec. Scientific Comm., Pakistan 59-61; mem. Nat. Science Council, Pakistan; Hon. Consultant to UN Sec.-Gen. on Nuclear Non-proliferation Treaty; Hon. Vice-Pres. Inst. of Nuclear Engineers, U.K.
Ministry of Science and Technology, Islamabad, Pakistan.

Usmanov, Saidmakhmud Nogmanovich, M.SC.; Soviet politician; b. 1929; ed. Tashkent Agricultural Inst. and Cotton Research Inst.
Member C.P.S.U. 55-; Technician, post-graduate student 51-55; scientific worker 55-56; Teacher, Tashkent Higher Party School 56-58; Official, Central Cttee. of C.P. Uzbekistan 58-59; Sec. Surkhandaryinsk Regional Cttee. of C.P. Uzbekistan 59-61; Chair. Exec. Cttee. Surkhandaryinsk Regional Soviet of Working People's Deputies 61-62; Sec. Central Cttee. of C.P. Uzbekistan 62-63; First Deputy Minister of Production and Provision of Agricultural Produce Uzbekistan 63-64; First Sec. Samarkand Regional Cttee. of C.P. Uzbek S.S.R. 64-; mem. Central Revision Comm. of C.P.S.U. 66-71; mem. C.P.S.U. Cen. Cttee. 71-; Deputy to U.S.S.R. Supreme Soviet; mem. Cttee. for Agriculture, Soviet of Union.
Samarkand Regional Committee of Communist Party of Uzbekistan, Samarkand, U.S.S.R.

V

Va'ea of Houma, Baron; Tongan diplomatist; b. 1921; ed. Wesley Coll., Auckland, N.Z.
Served R.N.Z.A.F. 42-44; Tonga Civil Service 45-53; A.D.C. to Queen Salote of Tonga 53-58; Gov. of Ha'apai 59-67; Acting Minister of Police 68-69; Commr., Consul in the U.K. 69-70, High Commr. 70-72; Minister of Commerce, Labour and Industry 73-, Deputy Minister of Finance 72-74; Minister of Tourism and Co-op. Soc. 73-; mem. Privy Council of Tonga 59-67, 73-.
Ministry of Commerce, Nuku'alofa, Tonga.

Vaidialingam, C. A., B.A., B.L.; Indian judge; b. 30 June 1907; ed. Presidency Coll. and Law Coll., Madras.
Advocate, High Court, Madras 31; Govt. Pleader, Madras 53-57; Judge, High Court, Kerala 57-66; Judge, Supreme Court of India 66-74.
c/o Supreme Court of India, New Delhi, India.

Vajpayee, Atal Bihari, M.A.; Indian politician; b. 25 Dec. 1926; ed. Victoria Coll. Gwalior, D.A.V. Coll., Kanpur.
Member, Indian Nat. Congress 42-46; mem. Lok Sabha 57-62, 67-, Rajya Sabha 62; mem. Rashtriya Swayamsewak Sangh 41; founder mem. Bharatiya Jana Sangh, Pres. 68-74, Parl. Leader 74-; Chair. Public Accounts Cttee. 69-70.
Publs. *Amar Balidan, Mrityuya Hatya, Jana Sangh our Musalman.*
1 Ferozeshah Road, New Delhi 1, India.
Telephone: 387-446.

Van Praagh, Dame Margaret (Peggy), D.B.E.; British ballet director; b. 1 Sept. 1910; ed. King Alfred School, London.
Dancer with Dame Marie Rambert 33; examiner for Cecchetti Soc. 35-; dancer, Sadler's Wells Ballet 41-46, ballet mistress Sadler's Wells Theatre Ballet 46-51; Asst. Dir. to Dame Ninette de Valois 51-56; Artistic Dir., Borovansky Ballet, Australia 60-61; Artistic Dir., The Australian Ballet 62-74; Hon. D.Litt. (Univ. of New England) 74.
Publs. *How I became a Ballet Dancer, The Choreographic Art* (with Peter Brisnon).
24/248 The Avenue, Parkville, Victoria 3052, Australia.
Telephone: 38-5773 (Victoria).

Vanprapar, Kamol, BARR.-AT-LAW; Thai lawyer; b. 7 Dec. 1908; ed. Ministry of Justice Law School, Nat. Defence Coll.
Public Prosecutor 30-68; Dir.-Gen., Public Prosecutor's Dept. 68-72; Minister of Justice 72-73, of the Interior 73-74; Kt. Grand Cordon, Order of the Crown of Thailand; Kt. Grand Cross, Order of the White Elephant.
644/3 Samsen Road, Bangkok 3, Thailand.
Telephone: 211888 (Office); 815601 (Home).

Vargas, Lieut.-Gen. Jesús Miranda; Philippine army officer and int. official; b. 22 March 1905; ed. Manila North High School and Philippine Constabulary Acad.
Philippine Constabulary 30-36; Philippine Army 37-51; Artillery training U.S.A. 39-40; U.S. Army 41-45, in Japanese P.O.W. Camp; Command and Gen. Staff Coll., Fort Leavenworth, U.S.A. 46-47; C.O. 5th Battalion Combat Team 50-51; Vice-Chief of Staff 51-53, Chief of Staff 54-56; Mil. Adviser to SEATO 54-56; retired from armed forces 56; Sec. of Nat. Defence 57-59; Chair. Board of Dirs. Nat. Waterworks and Sewerage Authority 57-59; Vice-Pres. Philippine-American Life Assurance Co. 59-; Pres. Philippine-American Management and Financing Co. 60-; Chair. Board of Trustees Ramon Magsaysay Award Foundation 62-65; Sec.-Gen. South East Asia Treaty Org. (SEATO) 65-72; many decorations.
Philippine American Life Assurance Co., Philamlife Bldg., UN Avenue, Ermita, Manila, Philippines.

Vasan, S. S.; Indian editor and film producer; b. 1903.
Entered journalism; founded *Ananda Vikatan*, a Tamil journal 28; entered film business 39; founded Gemini Studios 41; Editor *Ananda Vikatan*; Chair. Gemini Pictures Circuit Ltd.; elected to Parliament; mem. Indian and Eastern Newspaper Soc.
Gemini House, Edward Elliot Road, Mylapore, Madras 4, India.

Verghese, Boobli George; Indian journalist; b. 21 June 1927, Maymyo; ed. The Doon School, Dehra Dun, St. Stephen's Coll., Delhi and Trinity Coll., Cambridge.
Assistant editor, *The Times of India* Bombay 49, transferred to New Delhi Bureau 51; Chief, New Delhi News Bureau, *Times of India* 56-62; Asst. Editor, *Times of India*, Bombay 62-66; Information Adviser to Prime Minister of India 66-68; Editor, *Hindustan Times* 69-Sept. 75; Magsaysay Award for Journalism 75.
Publs. *Himalayan Endeavour* 62, *Our Neighbour Pakistan* 64, *Design for Tomorrow* 65, *Beyond the Famine* 67, *An End to Confrontation* 72.

Vernon, Sir James, C.B.E., PH.D.; Australian business executive; b. 13 June 1910, Tamworth; ed. Sydney Univ., Univ. Coll. London.
Chief Chemist, Colonial Sugar Refining Co. Ltd. (C.S.R.) 38-51, Senior Exec. Officer 51-56, Asst. Gen. Man. 56-57, Gen. Man. 58-72, Dir. 58-; Dir. United Telecasters Sydney Ltd., MLC Ltd., Commercial Banking Co. of Sydney Ltd., Westham Dredging Australia Party Ltd.; Chair. Martin Corpn. Ltd., Commonwealth Cttee. of Econ. Inquiry 63-65; Vice-Pres. Australian Industries Devt. Assen.; Vice-Pres. Australian-Japan Business Co-op. Cttee., Pres. 72-; Pres. Australian Cttee. of the Pacific Basin Econ. Council 72-; Chair. Comm. of Inquiry, Australian Post Office 73-74, Manufacturing Industries Advisory Council; mem. Chase Manhattan Bank Int. Advisory Cttee.; Hon. D.Sc. (Sydney and Newcastle); A. E. Leighton Memorial Medal, Royal Australian Chemical Inst. 65, John Storey Medal, Australian Inst. of Management.
16 O'Connell Street, Sydney, New South Wales 2000, Australia; Home: 27 Manning Road, Double Bay, N.S.W. 2028, Australia.

Villa, José Garcia, A.B.; Philippine poet and critic; b. 5 Aug. 1914; ed. Univs. of the Philippines and New Mexico and Columbia Univ.
Associate Editor New Directions Books 49; Cultural Attaché Philippine Mission to UN 53-63; Dir. N.Y. City Coll. Poetry Workshop 52-63, Prof. of Poetry, New School for Social Research 64-74; Philippines Presidential Adviser on Cultural Affairs 68-; Guggenheim Fellowship 43, Bollingen Fellowship 51, Rockefeller Grant 64; American Acad. of Arts and Letters Award 42, Shelley Memorial Award 59, Pro Patria Award 61, Philippines Cultural Heritage Award 62; Nat. Artist in Literature 73; Hon. D.Litt. (Far Eastern Univ.) 59, L.H.D. (Univ. of the Philippines) 73.
Publs. *Footnote to Youth* (stories) 33, *Many Voices* 39, *Poems by Doveglion* 41, *Have Come, Am Here* 42, *Volume Two* 49, *Selected Poems and New* 58, *Poems Fifty-five* 62, *Poems in Praise of Love* 62, *Selected Stories* 62, *The Portable Villa* 63, *The Essential Villa* 65; Editor: *E. E. Cummings, Marianne Moore*, *A Celebration for Edith Sitwell*, *A Doveglion Book of Philippine Poetry.*
780 Greenwich Street, New York City 14, N.Y., U.S.A.

Vines, William Joshua, C.M.G.; Australian business executive and grazier; b. 27 May 1916; ed. Haileybury Coll., Victoria.
Army service, Middle East, New Guinea and Borneo 39-45; Sec. Alexander Fergusson Pty. Ltd. 38-47; Dir. Goodlass Wall and Co. Pty. Ltd. 47-49. Lewis Berger and Sons (Australia) Pty. Ltd. and Sherwin Williams Co. (Aust.) Pty. Ltd. 52-55; Man. Dir. Lewis Berger and Sons (Victoria)

Pty. Ltd. 49-55; Man. Dir. Lewis Berger & Sons Ltd. 55-60; Man. Dir. Berger, Jenson & Nicholson Ltd. 60-61; Man. Dir. Int. Wool Secretariat 61-69, mem. Board 69-; Chair. and Man. Dir. Dalgety Australia Ltd.; Chair. Carbonless Papers (Wiggins Teape); Dir. Commercial Union of Aust. Ltd., Assoc. Pulp and Paper Mills Ltd., Tubemakers of Australia Ltd., Port Phillip Mills Pty. Ltd.; mem., Exec. of CSIRO; Chair. of Council, Hawkerbury Agricultural Coll.
73 Yarranabbe Road, Darling Point 2027; "Old Southwood", Tara 4421, Queensland, Australia.
Telephone: 328-7970.

Vinicchayakul, Serm, D.en. D.; Thai politician and lawyer, b. 2 June 1908; ed. Assumption Coll. and Faculté de Droit; Univ. of Paris.
Appointed Sec. Gen. of Judicial Council 46; Gov. Bank of Thailand 46-47, 52-54; Prof. of Law Thammasat Univ. 54; Under-Sec. for Finance 54-65; Gov. IBRD, IFC and IDA 65; Minister of Finance 65-71, 72-73; Chair. Exec. Board of Econ. and Social Devt. Council 72; Senator 74-; Knight Grand Cross (1st Class), Order of Chula Chom Klao; Knight Grand Cordon (Special Class), Order of the White Elephant; Knight Grand Cordon, Order of the Crown of Thailand.
159 Asoke Road, Bangkok, Thailand.

Vira, Dharma; Indian civil servant and diplomatist; b. 20 Jan. 1906; ed. Lucknow and Allahabad Univs., and London School of Economics and Political Science.
Joined Civil Service 30; Joint Magistrate Aligarh 30-34, Almora 34-36, Bareilly 36; Joint Sec. Industries and Agricultural Exhibition, Lucknow 36-37; Officiating District Magistrate, Bareilly 37; District Magistrate, Etah 37-38, Almora 38-41; with Commerce Dept., Govt. of India 41-44, Deputy Sec. Industries and Civil Supplies Dept. 44-45, Textile Commr. 45-47, Joint Sec. to Cabinet 47-50; Principal Private Sec. to Prime Minister 50-51; Commercial Adviser, High Comm. London 51-53; Amb. to Czechoslovakia 54-56; Sec. Ministry of Works, Housing and Rehabilitation 56-63; Chief Commr. for Delhi 63-64; Cabinet Sec. and Sec. to the Council of Ministers 64-66; Chair. Atomic Energy Comm. and Sec. Dept. of Atomic Energy 66; Gov., Punjab and Haryana 66-67; Gov. of W. Bengal 67-69, of Mysore 69-72; Chair. Admin. Staff Coll. of India; Pres. Bharat Scouts and Guides.
A53 Vasant Vihar, New Delhi, India.

Virata, Cesar Enrique, B.S.B.A., B.S.M.E., M.B.A.; Philippine financial executive; b. 12 Dec. 1930; ed. Univs. of the Philippines and Pennsylvania.
Instructor and lecturer, Graduate School, Univ. of the Philippines 53-61, Dean Coll. of Business Admin. 61-69; Principal and Head, Management Services Div., Sycip, Gorres, Velayo & Co. (accountants) 56-67; Chair. Board of Investments 67-70; Deputy Dir.-Gen. Presidential Econ. Staff 67-68; Under-Sec. of Industry, Dept. of Commerce and Industry 67-69; Chair. and Dir. Philippine Nat. Bank 67-69; Minister of Finance and mem., Monetary Board, Cen. Bank of the Philippines 70-; Chair. Land Bank of the Philippines 73-; mem. Nat. Econ. and Devt. Authority 72-; Diploma of Merit, Univ. of the Philippines 69, Hon. LL.D. 76; Hon. D.H.L. (Ateneo Univ.) 74, Hon. D.P.A. (St. Louis) 75.
Publs. Articles in work simplification, industrial engineering, business policy, monetary and fiscal policies.
Department of Finance, Manila; Home: 63 East Maya Drive, Quezon City, Philippines.
Telephone: 59-52-62 and 59-71-39 (Office); 99-74-19 (Home).

Viswanathan, Kambanthodath Kunhan, B.A., B.L.; Indian administrator; b. 4 Nov. 1914, Mattancheri, Kerala.
Law practice in Cochin 38; mem. Cochin Assembly, later mem. Travancore-Cochin Assembly 48-50; mem. Kerala Assembly 57, re-elected 60; Sec. Congress Legislature Party 57-59, 60-64; Gen. Sec. Kerala Pradesh Congress Cttee. 66-69, Convener ad hoc 69, Pres. 70-73; editor *The Republic*, Malayalam weekly 67-69; Gov. of Gujarat 73-.
Raj Bhavan, Shahibag, Ahmedabad-380004, Gujarat, India.
Telephone: 66477.

Viswanathan, Venkata; Indian civil servant; b. 25 Jan. 1909; ed. Central Coll., Bangalore, Univ. Coll., London, and Balliol Coll., Oxford.
Indian Civil Service 30-; Asst. and Joint Magistrate, Agra, Azamgarth, Banaras 31-36; District Magistrate, Banaras 36; Asst. Settlement Officer and Settlement Officer, Bahraich, Kheri 36-40; Under-Sec., Govt. of India 40, Deputy Sec. 42; Sec. to Rep. of Govt. of India in Ceylon 43; Additional Deputy Sec. and Sec. to Rep. of Govt. of India with Govt. of Burma 44; Registrar of Co-operative Socs. U.P. 46; District Magistrate, Dehra Dun 47; Indian Alt. Del. on UN Comm., Palestine 47; Deputy High Commr. in Pakistan 47-48; Chief Sec. and Adviser Madhya Bharat 48-50; Chief Commr., Bhopal 50-52; Joint Sec. Ministry of States and Ministry of Home Affairs 52-58; Special Sec. Ministry of Home Affairs 58, Sec. 61-64; Chief Commr., Delhi 64-67; Gov. of Kerala 67-74.
c/o Office of the Governor, Trivandrum, Kerala, India.

Vo Nguyen Giap, General; Vietnamese army officer; b. 1912; ed. French lycée in Hue, and law studies at Univ. of Hanoi.
History teacher, Thang Long School, Hanoi; joined Viet-Nam C.P. in early 1930s; fled to China 39; helped organize Viet-Minh Front, Viet-Nam 41; Minister of Interior 45, became Commdr.-in-Chief of Viet-Minh Army 46; defeated French at Dien-Bien-Phu 54; Deputy Prime Minister, Minister of Defence and Commdr.-in-Chief, Democratic Repub. of Viet-Nam until 76; mem. Nat. Defence Council, Vice-Premier, Council of Ministers and Minister of Nat. Defence, Socialist Repub. of Viet-Nam July 76-; mem. Politburo Lao-Dong Party.
Publs. *People's War, People's Army, Big Victory, Great Task* 68.
Ministry of National Defence, Hanoi, Viet-Nam.

Vu Van Mau, LL.B., LL.D.; Vietnamese lawyer, diplomatist and politician; b. 25 July 1914; ed. Univ. of Hanoi and Univ. of Paris.
Lawyer, Hanoi 49; Dean, Faculty of Law, Univ. of Saigon 55-58; First Pres. Vietnamese Supreme Court of Appeal 55; Min. of Foreign Affairs, Repub. of Viet-Nam 55; Sec. of State for Foreign Affairs 56-63 (resgnd.); Pres. Vietnamese Nat. Asscn. of Comparative Law; Amb. to United Kingdom, Belgium and Netherlands 64-65; Prof. of Law, Univ. of Saigon 65-; Senator 70-75; Prime Minister 28-30 April 75.
Publs. Legal Works in French and Vietnamese.
132 Suong Nguyet Anh, Saigon, Viet-Nam.

Vuong Van Bac; Vietnamese diplomatist; b. 1927, Bac Ninh, N. Viet-Nam; ed. Hanoi Univ., Michigan State Univ., Vanderbilt Univ., U.S.A.
Admitted to Hanoi Bar Asscn. 52, Saigon Bar Asscn. 54; Prof. of Constitutional and Political Science, Nat. Inst. of Admin. 55; Chair. Dalat Univ. 65; Sec.-Gen. Viet-Nam Lawyer's Fed. 61; mem. Council of Lawyers, Saigon High Court 62-68, Board of Dirs., Viet-Nam Council on Foreign Relations 68; Legal Adviser to Repub. of Viet-Nam Liaison and Observation Del. at Paris talks 68; Amb. to U.K. 72-73; Minister of Foreign Affairs 73-75; has attended numerous int. confs. on legal and econ. affairs.

W

Wada, Haruo; Japanese trade unionist; b. 15 March 1919; ed. Toba Mercantile Marine School.
Joined Yamashita Shipping Co. 39, Navigator with Yamashita Coastal Shipping Co. 45, resigned to become full-time mem. All Japan Seamen's Union 46; founder-mem. SOHYO (General Council of Japanese Trade Unions) 49-52; Gen. Sec. Japanese T.U.C. 54-64; mem. Exec. Board ICFTU 62-65; Vice-Pres. All Japanese Seamen's Union 64-68; Vice-Pres. Japanese Confederation of Labour (DOMEI) 64-67; Pres. ICFTU-ARO 65-68.
Publs. *Introduction to the Trade Union Movement* 58, *Tomorrow in the Trade Union Movement* 67.
12-12, Minamicho 2-chome, Kichishoji, Musachino City, Japan.
Telephone: 47-5248.

Wada, Tsunesuke; Japanese business executive; b. 3 Nov. 1887; ed. Kobe Univ.
Furukawa Mining Co.; later with Furukawa Trading Co.; fmr. Man. Dir. and Pres. Fujitsu Ltd., Chair. 58-; fmr. Man. Dir., Pres., Chair., Adviser Fuji Electric Co. Ltd.
Fuji Electric Co. Ltd., 11, Yurakucho 1-chome, Chiyoda-ku, Tokyo; and Kami-osaki 2-8-12, Shinagawa-ku, Tokyo, Japan.

Wadati, Kiyoo; Japanese meteorologist; b. 8 Sept. 1902, Nagoya; ed. Tokyo Univ.
Entered Meteorological Observatory; has conducted research into earthquakes, tidal waves, etc.; fmr. Dir. of Gen. Meteorological Observatory; fmr. Pres. Science Council of Japan; Pres. Saitama Univ. 66-; Pres. Japan Acad.
Publs. *Earthquakes, Meteorological Glossary, Oceanographic Glossary.*
Saitama University, 255 Shimo-Okubo, Urawa City, Saitama, Japan.

Wadia, Sophia; Indian editor; b. 13 Sept. 1901; ed. Lycée Molière, Paris, Columbia Univ., New York, School of Oriental and African Studies, London.
Lecturer; founder-organizer P.E.N. All-India Centre; Pres. Indian Inst. of World Culture, Bangalore, Asian Book Trust, Bombay, Balkan-ji-Bari (The Child Welfare Asscn. of India); Assoc. United Lodge of Theosophists; Editor *Aryan Path* 29- and *The Indian P.E.N.* 34-, Bombay; Vice-Pres. All-India Animal Welfare Asscn.; also worker in women's social, educational and cultural movements.
Publs. *The Brotherhood of Religions, Preparation for Citizenship.*
Theosophy Hall, 40 New Marine Lines, Bombay 400-020, India.
Telephone: 292173.

Wahi, Prem Nath, M.D., F.R.C.P.; Indian physician; b. 10 April 1908; ed. K.G. Medical Coll., Lucknow, London Hospital Medical School, London, and New England Deaconess Hospital, Boston, U.S.A.
Professor of Pathology, S.N. Medical Coll., Agra 41-; Principal, S.N. Medical Coll., Agra 60-; Dean, Faculty of Medicine, Agra Univ. 61-64; Dir. WHO Int. Reference Centre and Cancer Registry 63-; mem. Expert Panel of WHO on Cancer, Lyon, France 65-; has attended numerous int. conferences on cancer; Lady Brahamachari Readership, Calcutta Univ. 65; Fellow, Nat. Inst. of Sciences, India; Founder Fellow, Coll. of Pathologists, London 63; Founder Fellow, Indian Acad. of Medical Sciences 64.
S.N. Medical College, Agra (U.P.), India.

Walding, Joseph A.; New Zealand politician; b. 1926, Christchurch; ed. Wellington and Dunedin.
Served in Merchant Navy, World War II, France, Atlantic and Pacific; City Councillor, Palmerston North; mem. Parl. for Palmerston North 67-75; founder, Man. Dir. Export Co.; Minister of Overseas Trade 72-75, of the Environment 72-74, of Recreation and Sport 72-75, also Assoc. Minister of Foreign Affairs 72-75; fmr. Pres., Sec. Palmerston North Workers' Educ. Asscn.
Parliament Buildings, Wellington, New Zealand.

Walker, Sir (Charles) Michael, G.C.M.G.; British diplomatist; b. 22 Nov. 1916, Simla, India; ed. Charterhouse, and New Coll., Oxford.
Army service 39-45; Dominions Office 47-49; First Sec. British Embassy, Washington 49-51; Office of High Commr., Calcutta and New Delhi 52-55; Establishment Officer Commonwealth Relations Office 55-58; Imperial Defence Coll. 58-59; Asst. Under-Sec. of State and Dir. of Establishments and Org., Commonwealth Relations Office 59-62; High Commr. to Ceylon 62-65, to Malaysia 66-71; Sec. to Overseas Devt. Admin., Foreign and Commonwealth Office 71-73; High Commr. to India 73-.
British High Commission, Shantipath, Chanakyapuri, New Delhi, India; 40 Bourne, Street, London, S.W.1, England.

Walker, Sir (Edward) Ronald, C.B.E., M.A., PH.D., LITT.D., D.SC. ECON.; Australian economist and diplomatist; b. 26 Jan. 1907; ed. Univ. of Sydney, and Cambridge Univ.
Lecturer in Economics, Univ. of Sydney 27-38; Prof. of Economics, Univ. of Tasmania 39-46; Economic Adviser, N.S.W. Treasury 38-39, Govt. of Tasmania 39-42; Deputy Dir.-Gen. Australian Dept. of War Organization of Industry 42-45; Economic Counsellor for Europe and Counsellor, Australian Embassy, Paris 45-50; Exec. mem. Australian Nat. Security Resources Board 50-52; Amb. to Japan 52-55, to UN 56-59, and Australian Rep. on the Security Council 56-57; Chair. UNESCO Exec. Board 47-48, Pres. UNESCO Gen. Conf. 49; Chair. UN Experts on Full Employment 49; Australian Rep. on Disarmament Comm. 56-58, on Econ. and Social Council 62-64 (Pres. 64), Advisory Cttee. on Application of Science and Technology 64-74; leader UN technical assistance missions to Tunisia 65, to Pakistan 68; Amb. to France 59-68, to Fed. Repub. of Germany 68-71, to OECD ,Paris 71-73; Special Adviser to Govt. on Multi-national Corpns. 73-74.
Publs. *An Outline of Australian Economics* 31, *Australia in the World Depression* 33, *Money* (co-author) 35, *Unemployment Policy* 36, *War-time Economics* 39, *From Economic Theory to Policy* 42, *The Australian Economy in War and Reconstruction* 47, *National and International Measures for Full Employment* (in collab.) 50.
1 Rue de Longchamp, Paris, France.

Walker, Herbert John, F.C.A.; New Zealand chartered accountant and politician; b. 2 June 1919, Rangiora.
Accountant, Lincoln Agricultural Coll. 54-60; Lincoln Coll. Board of Govs. 60-70; Pres. Canterbury Trustee Savings Bank 69; mem. Parl. 60-; Minister of Tourism, Minister in charge of Publicity, Minister of Broadcasting 69-72, Postmaster-Gen. Feb.-Dec. 72; Minister of Social Welfare Dec. 75-; Order of St. Lazarus of Jerusalem.
Ministry of Social Welfare, Wellington; 36 Jennifer Street, Christchurch, New Zealand.
Telephone: 49-090 (Wellington); 515703 (Christchurch).

Walsh, Alan, M.SC.TECH., D.SC., F.INST.P., F.A.I.P., F.A.A., F.R.S.; British physicist; b. 19 Dec. 1918, Darwen, Lancs.; ed. Darwen Grammar School and Manchester Univ.
At British Non-Ferrous Metals Research Asscn. 39-46; seconded to Ministry of Aircraft Production 43; with Commonwealth Scientific and Industrial Research Org. (C.S.I.R.O.), Australia 46-, Asst. Chief of Div. of Chemical Physics, C.S.I.R.O. 61-; Pres. Australian Inst. of Physics 67-68; Hon. Fellow Chemical Soc. of London 72, Hon. mem., Soc. for Analytical Chemistry, Royal Soc. of New Zealand 75; foreign mem. Royal Acad. of Sciences, Stockholm; Hon. D.Sc. Monash Univ.; Britannica Australia Science Award 66, Royal Soc. of Victoria Medal 69,

Talanta Gold Medal 69, Maurice Hasler Award of Soc. of Applied Spectroscopy, U.S.A. 72, James Cook Medal, Royal Soc. of New South Wales 76, Torbern Bergman Medal (Swedish Chemical Soc.) 76.
Publs. numerous papers in scientific journals.
Division of Chemical Physics, Commonwealth Scientific and Industrial Research Organisation, P.O.B. 160, Clayton, Victoria, 3168; Home: 11 Dendy Street, Brighton, Victoria 3186, Australia.
Telephone: 544-0633 (Office); 92-4897 (Home).

Wan Waithayakon, Prince Krommun Naradhip Bongsprabandh, M.A.; Thai fmr. diplomatist and politician; b. 25 Aug. 1891; ed. Marlborough Coll., Balliol Coll., Oxford, and Ecole des Sciences Politiques, Paris.
Secretary Thai Legation, Paris 17-19; Private Sec. to Minister of Foreign Affairs 19-24; Under-Sec. of State for Foreign Affairs 24-26; Minister to London 26-30; Adviser to Premier's Office and Foreign Office, Bangkok 33-46; Amb. to U.S.A. 47-52; Permanent Del. to UN 47-59; Pres. UN Gen. Assembly 56-57, Conf. on Law of the Sea 58, 60; Minister of Foreign Affairs 52-58; Deputy Prime Minister 59-68; Rector, Thammasat Univ. 63-71; Rapporteur, Asian-African Conf., Bandung 55; Hon. D.Litt. (Chulalongkorn), Hon. D.Pol.Sc. (Thammasat), Hon. D.Law (Columbia, New York, Fairleigh Dickinson), Hon. D.C.L. (Oxford); Knight of the Most Illustrious Order of the Royal House of Chakri.
[*Died* 6 September, 1976].

Wanchoo, Kailas Nath; Indian judge; b. 25 Feb. 1903; ed. Pandit Pirthi Nath High School, Kanpur, Muir Central Coll., Allahabad, and Wadham Coll., Oxford.
Magistrate and Judge, United Provinces (later Uttar Pradesh) 26-51; Judge, Allahabad High Court 47-51; Chief Justice, Rajasthan High Court 51-58; Judge, Supreme Court of India 58-67; Chief Justice of India 67, retired 68; Chair. Railway Accidents Inquiry Cttee. 68-69, Board of Arbitration (JCM), Ministry of Labour & Employment July 68-75; Chair. Direct Taxes Inquiry Cttee., Ministry of Finance 70-71; Comm. on charges of corruption in West Bengal 74-75; Chair. Kashmir Pandit Benefit Trust, New Delhi; LL.D. (Agra Univ.) 67.
6 Friends Colony, New Delhi, India.
Telephone: 630504.

Wanchoo, Niranjan Nath, O.B.E., M.A.; Indian state governor and fmr. civil servant; b. 1 May 1910, Satna; ed. Punjab Univ., Lahore, Cambridge Univ., Imperial Defence Coll., London.
Director-General of Ordnance Factories 48; Controller-Gen. of Defence Production 56-57; mem. Univ. Grants Comm. 58-61; Chair. Nat. Productivity Council 67-72; mem. Planning Board, Govt. of Madhya Pradesh 72-73; Gov. of Kerala April 73-.
Raj Bhavan, Trivandrum, Kerala; Home: 43 Anand Lok, New Delhi, India.

Wan Li; Chinese government official; b. Szechuan.
Vice-Minister of Building Construction 52-56; Minister of Urban Construction 56-58; Sec. CCP, Peking 58-66; Vice-Mayor of Peking 58-66; criticized and removed from office during Cultural Revolution 67; Minister of Railways 75-.
People's Republic of China.

Wang Chen; People's Repub. of China; b. 1909, Liuyang, Hunan.
Regimental Political Commissar 30; Alt. mem. 7th Cen. Cttee. of CCP 45; Commdr. of 1st Army Corps, 1st Field Army, People's Liberation Army 49; Commdr. Sinkiang Mil. Region, PLA 50; Minister of State Farms and Land Reclaimation 56; mem. 8th Cen. Cttee. of CCP 56, 9th Cen. Cttee. 69, 10th Cen. Cttee. 73; Vice-Premier of State Council 75-.

Wang Chia-tao; People's Repub. of China.
Major-General, Commdr. Heilungkiang Mil. District, People's Liberation Army 64-; Vice-Chair. Heilungkiang Revolutionary Cttee. 67, Chair. 70; Alt. mem. 9th Cen. Cttee. of CCP 69; First Sec. CCP Heilungkiang 71; Alt. mem. 10th Cen. Cttee. of CCP 73.

Wang Chien; Chinese party official.
Deputy Sec.-Gen. Rural Work Dept., CCP Cen. Cttee. 55; visited Eastern Europe 55; Sec. CCP Shansi 57, Second Sec. 66-67, Sec. 73, First Sec. 75-; Gov. of Shansi 65-67; alt. mem. 10th Cen. Cttee. CCP 73; Vice-Chair. Shansi Revolutionary Cttee. 73, Chair. 75-.
People's Republic of China.

Wang Huai-hsiang; People's Repub. of China.
Political Commissar 3rd Field Army 49; Deputy Political Commissar Kirin Mil. District, People's Liberation Army 64; Chair. Kirin Revolutionary Cttee. 68; mem. 9th Cen. Cttee. of CCP 69; First Sec. CCP Kirin 71; mem. 10th Cen. Cttee. of CCP 73.

Wang Hung-wen; party leader, People's Repub. of China; b. 1937.
Worker Shanghai No. 17 Cotton Textile Mill; founded Shanghai Workers Revolutionary Rebel Gen. H.Q. during Cultural Revolution 67; Vice-Chair. Shanghai Revolutionary Cttee. 68; Sec. CCP Shanghai 71; Political Commissar Shanghai Garrison District, PLA 72; First Vice-Chair. CCP 73-76, Vice-Chair. April 76-; mem. Standing Cttee. of Politburo, CCP 73.

Wang Kuo-chuan; Chinese diplomatist; b. 1911.
Ambassador to German Democratic Republic 57-64, to Poland 64-69; Pres. Chinese People's Asscn. for Friendship with Foreign Countries June 72-; Amb. to Australia 73-.
Embassy of the People's Republic of China, Canberra, Australia.

Wang Ling, M.A., PH.D.; Chinese historian; b. 23 Dec. 1918, Nangtung, Kiang Su Province; ed. National Central Univ., China and Trinity Coll., Cambridge.
Junior Research Fellow, Inst. of History and Philology, Academia Sinica 41-44; Senior Lecturer, Nat. Fu-tan Univ. 44-45, Assoc. Prof. 45-46; Collaborator to J. Needham, F.R.S., Cambridge Univ. 46-57; Visiting Lecturer, Cambridge Univ. 53, Canberra Univ. Coll., Melbourne Univ. 57-59; Assoc. Fellow, Nat. Acad. of Science, Academia Sinica 55-57; Senior Lecturer Univ. Coll., Australian Nat. Univ., Canberra 60-61, Assoc. Prof. 61-63; Professorial Fellow, Inst. of Advanced Studies, Australian Nat. Univ. 63-; Visiting Prof. of Chinese Literature, Cornell Univ. 66; Visiting Prof. of Chinese Classics, Wisconsin Univ. 66; mem. Comm. for History of the Social Relations of Science of Int. Union for the History of Science 48-56; corresp. mem. Int. Acad. of History of Science, Paris 64-.
Publs. *Science and Civilisation in China* (assisted Dr. J. Needham, F.R.S.) Vol. I 54, Vol. II 56, Vol. III 59, Vol. IVa 62, Vol. IVb 64, Vol. IVc 71, *Heavenly Clockwork* (assisted Dr. J. Needham, F.R.S.) 60, *A Study on the Chiu Chang Suan Shu* 62.
Institute of Advanced Studies, Australian National University, Canberra, A.C.T. 2600, Australia.

Wang Liu-sheng; People's Repub. of China.
Major-General People's Liberation Army, Shanghai 64; Deputy Political Commissar Nanking Mil. Region, PLA 66; Alt. mem. 9th Cen. Cttee. of CCP 69; First Political Commissar Wuhan Mil. Region, PLA 72; Second Sec. CCP Hupeh 72; Alt. mem. 10th Cen. Cttee. of CCP 73.

Wang Pi-ch'eng; army officer, People's Repub. of China; b. 1912, Hunan.
Deputy Commdr. Chekiang Mil. District, People's Liberation Army 49, Commdr. 51; Maj.-Gen. PLA 55; Commdr. Shanghai Garrison District, PLA 55-61; Deputy Commdr. Nanking Mil. Region, PLA 61; Deputy Commdr. Kunming

Mil. Region, PLA 69, Commdr. 72-; Second Sec. CCP Yunnan 71; First Vice-Chair. Yunnan Revolutionary Cttee. 72; mem. 10th Cen. Cttee. of CCP 73.

Wang Shang-jung; People's Repub. of China; b. 1906, Shansi; ed. Sun Yat-sen Univ., Moscow.
On Long March 34; Div. Commdr., Red Army 36; Commdr. Tsinghai Mil. District 49; Lt.-Gen. 55; Alt. mem. 8th Cen. Cttee. of CCP 58; Dir. Combat Dept., People's Liberation Army Gen. Staff H.Q. 59-66; criticized and removed from office during Cultural Revolution 67; Deputy Chief of Gen. Staff, PLA 74.

Wang Shou-tao; communications specialist, People's Repub. of China; b. 1907, Liu-yang, Hunan; ed. State Agriculture School, Changsha, Peasant Movt. Training Inst.
Joined CCP 25; Sec. CCP Hunan-Hopei-Kiangsu Special Cttee. 28; revolutionary work in Shanghai 30-32; Political Commissar on Long March 34; Alt. mem. 7th Cen. Cttee. of CCP 45; Gov. of Hunan 50-52; Vice-Minister of Communications 52-54; Dir. Sixth Staff Office, State Council 54-58; mem. 8th Cen. Cttee. of CCP 56; Minister of Communications 58-64; Sec. Cen.-South Bureau, CCP 64-67; Vice-Chair. Kwangtung Revolutionary Cttee. 68-; mem. 9th Cen. Cttee. of CCP 69; Sec. CCP Kwangtung 71-; mem. 10th Cen. Cttee. of CCP 73.

Wang Tung-hsing; People's Repub. of China.
Bodyguard of Mao Tse tung 47; Capt. of Guards of Cen. Cttee., CCP 47-49; Capt. of Guards, Gen. Admin. Council 49-54; Vice-Minister of Public Security 55-58, 62-; Vice-Gov. of Kiangsi 58-60; Sec. CCP Kiangsi 58-60; mem. Cen. Cultural Revolution Group 67; Dir. Admin. Office of Cen. Cttee., CCP 69; Alt. mem. Politburo, 9th Cen. Cttee. of CCP 69; mem. Politburo, 10th Cen. Cttee. of CCP 73.

Wang Yi; army officer, People's Repub. of China.
Major-General People's Liberation Army 64; Commdr. Tientsin Garrison District, PLA 69-; Vice-Chair. Tientsin Revolutionary Cttee. 70; Sec. CCP Tientsin 71.

Wang Yun-wu; Chinese writer, editor and government official; b. 1888; ed. privately.
Managing Director and Editor-in-Chief Commercial Press Shanghai 21-36; mem. Presidium People's Political Council 38-46; Minister of Econ. Affairs 46-47; Vice-Pres. Exec. Yuan 47-48 and 58-63; Vice-Pres. Examination Yuan 54-58; Minister of Finance 48; Chair. Presidential Comm. on Admin. Reform 58-59; Prof. Nat. Cheng-chi Univ., Taiwan 54-; Senior Adviser to Pres. of the Republic 64-; Chair. Sun Yat-sen Cultural Foundation; inventor of the Wang System of Chinese Lexicography; Hon. LL.D. (Seoul).
Publs. Works on education, scientific management, international relations, political theories, etc.
8 Lane 19, Sec. IV, South Hsin Hseng Road, Taipei, Taiwan.

Wangchuk, Jigme Singhye; Druk Gyalpo (King) of Bhutan; b. 11 Nov. 1955; ed. North Point, Darjeeling, Ugyuen Wangchuk Acad., Paro, also in England.
Crown Prince March 72; succeeded to throne 24 July 72, crowned 2 June 74; Chair. Planning Comm. of Bhutan March 72-; Commdr.-in-Chief of Armed Forces.
Royal Palace, Thimphu, Bhutan.

Wardhana, Ali, M.A., PH.D.; Indonesian economist and politician; b. 6 May 1928, Surakarta, Central Java; ed. Univ. of Indonesia, Jakarta and Univ. of California (Berkeley), U.S.A.
Director Research Inst. of Econ. and Social Studies 62-67; Prof. of Econs. and Dean, Faculty of Econs., Univ. of Indonesia 67-; Econ. Adviser to Gov. of Cen. Bank 64-68; mem. team of experts of Presidential Staff 66-68; Minister of Finance 68-; Chair. Board of Govs. Cttee. on Reform of the Int. Monetary System and Related Issues, IMF 72-74; Grand Cross Order of Leopold II (Belgium) 70, Order of Oranje Nassau (Netherlands) 71.
Ministry of Finance, Jakarta, Indonesia.

Wark, Sir Ian (William), Kt., C.M.G., C.B.E., D.SC., PH.D.; Australian physical chemist; b. 8 May 1899; ed. Scotch Coll., Melbourne, and Univs. of Melbourne, London and Calif. (Berkeley).
Exhibition of 1851 Science Research Scholarship 21-24; Lecturer in Chemistry, Univ. of Sydney 25; Research Chemist, Electrolytic Zinc Co. of Australasia Ltd. 26-39; Commonwealth Scientific and Industrial Research Organization, Chief, Div. of Industrial Chemistry 40-58, Dir. Chemical Research Laboratories 58-60, mem. of Exec. 61-65, Consultant, CSIRO Minerals Research Laboratories 71-; Gov. Ian Potter Foundation 64-; Chair. Commonwealth Advisory Cttee. on Advanced Educ. 65-71; Gen. Pres. Royal Australian Chemical Inst. 57-58; Fellow, Australian Acad. of Science 54; Treas. 59-63; hon. mem. Australasian Inst. Mining and Metallurgy 60-; Fellow Univ. Coll. London 65, Australian Acad. of Technological Sciences; Australia and New Zealand Asscn. for the Advancement of Science Medal 73.
Publs. *Principles of Flotation* (monograph) 38, (revised with K. L. Sutherland 55), *Why Research?* 68.
31 Linum Street, Blackburn, 3130 Victoria, Australia.

Watanabe, Tadao; Japanese banker; b. 3 Sept. 1898, Hokkaido; ed. Tokyo Univ.
Joined Bank of Japan 24; transferred to Sanwa Bank 45, Managing Dir. 45-46, Senior Managing Dir. 46-47, Pres. 47-60, Chair. 60-; Man. Dir. Kansai Econ. Fed.; Dir. Ohbayashi Road Construction Co., Fujita Tourist Enterprise Co., Mainichi Broadcasting Co., Osaka UNESCO Asscn. and numerous other socs.; Auditor, Osaka Gas Co.; Adviser Teijin Ltd., Kansai Electric Power Co., Takashimaya Co., Toyo Trust and Banking Co., Fed. of Econ. Org., Japan Fed. of Employers' Asscn.; Pres. Sandwa Midori Fund.
4-10 Fushimimachi, Higashi-ku, Osaka; 1-18 Kawanishicho, Ashiyashi, Hyogo Prefecture; 5-16-35, Roppongi, Minato-ku, Tokyo, Japan.
Telephone: 0797-22-2910 (Ashiya); 03-583-2715 (Tokyo).

Watanabe, Takeshi; Japanese banker and financial consultant; b. 15 Feb. 1906; ed. Law School of Tokyo Imperial Univ.
Ministry of Finance, Japan 30, serving as Chief Liaison Officer, Chief of the Minister's Secr. and Financial Commr.; Minister, Japanese Embassy in Washington 52-56; Exec. Dir. IBRD and IMF for Japan 56-60; int. financial consultant 60-65; Adviser to Minister of Finance, Japan 65; Pres. Asian Devt. Bank, Manila 66-72; Adviser to Pres. Bank of Tokyo 73-; Chair. Trident Int. Finance Ltd., Hong Kong; Japanese Chair. Trilateral Comm.
Publ. *Japanese Finance in Early Post-War Years* 66, *Diary of ADB President* (in Japanese).
35-19 Oyamacho, Shibuyaku, Tokyo, Japan.

Watt, Rt. Hon. Hugh, P.C.; New Zealand politician and diplomatist; b. 1912; ed. Seddon Technical Coll.
Former Dir. in sheetmetal and eng. company; mem. Parl. for Onehunga 53-75; Minister of Works and Electricity 57-60; Deputy Prime Minister 72-74, Acting Prime Minister Aug.-Sept. 74; Minister of Labour 72-74, of Works and Devt. 72-75, in charge of Publicity 72-74, in charge of Earthquake and War Damage Comm. 74-75; High Commr. to U.K. and Amb. to Ireland 75-76; Hon. Freeman, Butchers' Co. 75.
c/o New Zealand High Commission, New Zealand House, Haymarket, London S.W.1, England.
Telephone: 01-930 8422.

Webster, James Joseph, A.A.S.A.; Australian politician; b. 14 June 1925, Flinders Island, Tasmania; ed. Caulfield Grammar School, Royal Melbourne Tech. Coll.

Member of Senate 64-, Deputy Pres. and Chair. of Cttees. 74-75; leader of Nat. Country Party in Senate 76-; Minister for Science Dec. 75-.
Parliament House, Canberra, A.C.T. 2600; Home: Mickleham Road, Yuroke, Victoria, Australia.

Weerasinghe, Oliver, O.B.E., F.R.I.B.A., M.T.P.I.; Ceylonese city planner and diplomatist; b. 29 Sept. 1907; ed. Royal Coll., Colombo, Sri Lanka, and Univ. of Liverpool, England.
Directed planning and development of new city of Anuradhapura, Ceylon 40-56; Head, Town and Country Planning Dept., Ceylon 47-56; Chair. Board of Improvement Commrs., Colombo 53-56; Chief, Planning and Urbanization Section, Dept. of Econ. and Social Affairs, UN, New York 56-64; Exec. Sec. UN Seminar on Regional Planning, Tokyo 58, UN Expert Group on Metropolitan Planning, Stockholm 61, UN Symposium on New Towns, Moscow 64; Deputy Dir. Centre for Housing, Building and Planning, UN, New York 65; Amb. of Ceylon to the U.S.A. 65-71, and to Mexico 67-71; Distinction in Town Planning, Royal Inst. of British Architects 46.
Publ. *Town Planning in Ceylon* 47.
c/o Ministry of Foreign Affairs, Colombo, Sri Lanka.

Wei Kuo-ch'ing; Chinese party official; b. 1914, Tunglan. Kwangsi.
Regimental Commdr. 33; on Long March 34-35; Deputy Political Commissar 10th Army Corps, 3rd Field Army, People's Liberation Army 49; Mayor of Foochow 49; Gov. of Kwangsi 55-58; Alt. mem. 8th Cen. Cttee. of CCP 56; Sec. CCP Kwangsi 57-61, First Sec. 61-68; Chair. Kwangsi People's Govt. 58-68; First Political Commissar Kwangsi Mil. District, PLA 64-73; Sec. Cen.-South Bureau, CCP 66; Political Commissar Canton Mil. Region, PLA 67-; Chair. Kwangsi Revolutionary Cttee. 68; mem. 9th Cen. Cttee. of CCP 69; First Sec. CCP Kwangsi 71-75; First Sec. Kwangtung CCP Cttee. 75-; mem. Politburo, 10th Cen. Cttee. of CCP 73.

Wei Tao-ming, LL.D.; Chinese diplomatist and politician; b. 1899; ed. Univ. of Paris.
Minister of Justice 28-29; Mayor of Nanking 30-32; Sec.-Gen. Executive Yuan 37-41; Amb. to France 41-42, to U.S.A. 42-46; Vice-Pres. Legislative Yuan 46-47; Gov. Taiwan Province 47-49; Adviser to Pres. 49-64; Amb. to Japan 64-66; Minister of Foreign Affairs 66-71.
Publ. *Le Chèque en Chine.*
No. 10, Lane 119, Roosevelt Road, Sec I, Taipei, Taiwan.

Wells, Rear Adm. David Charles, C.B.E.; Australian naval officer; b. 19 Nov. 1918, Inverell, N.S.W.; ed. St. Peter's Coll., Adelaide, Royal Australian Naval Coll.
Communications Officer, Royal Naval Air Station, Culdrose 50-51; attended RN Staff Course, Greenwich 52; In Command, HMAS *Queenborough* 54-55; Dir. of Plans, Navy Officer 59-60; In Command, HMAS *Voyager* 61-62; Deputy Dir. RN Staff Coll., Greenwich 62-64; attended Imperial Defence Coll. 65; In Command, HMAS *Melbourne* 65-66; Commdg. Officer Royal Australian Navy Air Station, Nowra (HMAS *Albatross*) 67; Flag Officer-in-Charge, East Australia Area 68-69; Deputy Chief of Naval Staff 70-71; Commdr. Australia, New Zealand and U.K. Forces (ANZUK) in Malaysia and Singapore 72-73; Flag Officer Commanding H.M. Australian Fleet 74-.
Dept. of Defence, Navy Office, Canberra, A.C.T.; Home: Morundah, Sackville North, N.S.W. 2756, Australia.

West, Morris (Langlo); Australian author; b. 26 April 1916; ed. Univ. of Melbourne.
Teacher of Modern Languages and Mathematics, New South Wales and Tasmania 33-39; Army service 39-43; Nat. Brotherhood Award, Nat. Council of Christians and Jews 60, James Tait Black Memorial Prize 60, Royal Soc. of Literature Heinemann Award 60 (All prizes for *The Devil's Advocate*); Fellow. Royal Soc. of Literature, World Acad. of Arts and Sciences; Hon. D.Litt. (Santa Clara Univ., Calif.).
Publs. *Gallows on the Sand* 55, *Kundu* 56, *Children of the Sun* 57, *The Crooked Road* (English title *The Big Story*) 57, *Backlash* (English title *Second Victory*) 58, *The Devil's Advocate* 59, *Daughter of Silence* 61, *The Shoes of the Fisherman* 63, *The Ambassador* 65, *The Tower of Babel* 68, *The Heretic* (play) 70, *Scandal in the Assembly* (with Robert Francis) 70, *Summer of the Red Wolf* 71, *The Salamander* 73, *Harlequin* 74.
c/o Paul R. Reynolds Inc., 12 East 41st Street, New York, N.Y. 10017, U.S.A.

White, Sir Frederick William George, K.B.E., M.SC., PH.D., F.A.A., F.R.S.; Australian physicist; b. 1905; ed. Victorian Univ. Coll., New Zealand, and Cambridge Univ.
Post-graduate work at Cavendish Laboratory, Cambridge 29-31; Demonstrator in Physics, Lecturer in Physics, King's Coll., London 31-37; Prof. of Physics, Canterbury Univ. Coll., New Zealand 37; seconded to Council for Scientific and Inductrial Research as Chair. Radiophysics Advisory Board 41; Chief Div. of Radiophysics 42; Exec. Officer CSIR 45, mem. Exec. Cttee. 46, Chief Exec. Officer Commonwealth Scientific and Industrial Research Organization (CSIRO) 49-56; Deputy Chair. CSIRO 57-59, Chair. 59-70; Hon. D.Sc. (Monash Univ., Australian Nat. Univ., Univ. of Papua New Guinea).
Publ. *Electromagnetic Waves* 34.
57 Investigator Street, Red Hill, Canberra 2603, A.C.T., Australia.

White, George David Lloyd, M A., M.V.O.; New Zealand diplomatist; b. 21 March 1918; ed. Timaru Boys' High School, Canterbury College, Univ. of New Zealand.
Served N.Z. Army, Middle East 41-45; with N.Z. Public Service 45-49; joined Ministry of Foreign Affairs 49; Econ. Counsellor, N.Z. Embassy, London 54-55, Wash. 56-61; Deputy High Commr., London 61-64; Deputy Sec. of Foreign Affairs 64-32; Amb. to U.S.A. 72-.
Embassy of New Zealand, 19 Observatory Circle, N.W., Washington, D.C. 20008, U.S.A.

White, Sir Harold Leslie, Kt., C.B.E., M.A., F.L.A.A., Australian librarian; b. 14 June 1905; ed. Wesley Coll., Melbourne, and Queen's Coll. of Melbourne Univ.
Commonwealth Parl. Library 23-67, Commonwealth Parl. Librarian and Nat. Librarian 47-67; Nat. Librarian, Nat. Library of Australia 47-70; Chair. Standing Cttee. Australian Advisory Council on Bibliographical Services 60-70; Gov. Australian Film Inst.; Chair. Advisory Cttee. *Australian Encyclopaedia*, mem. Nat. Memorials Cttee. 75-; mem. Australian Cttees. for UNESCO, Australian Nat. Film Board; mem. UNESCO Int. Cttee. on Bibliography, Documentation and Terminology 61-65; Hon. Fellow, Aust. Acad. of the Humanities; Fellow, Acad of Social Sciences in Australia.
Publ. (ed.) *Canberra: A Nation's Capital.*
Home: 27 Mugga Way, Red Hill, Canberra, A.C.T. 2603, Australia.

White, Patrick, B.A.; Australian writer; b. 28 May 1912, London, England; ed. Cheltenham Coll., and King's Coll., Cambridge.
Intelligence officer, R.A.F., World War II; W. H. Smith & Son Award 59; Nobel Prize for Literature 73; Australian of the Year 74; A.C. 75; resgnd. from Order of Australia June 76.
Publs. *Happy Valley* 39, *The Living and the Dead* 41, *The Aunt's Story* 48, *The Tree of Man* 55, *Voss* 57, *Riders in the Chariot* 61, *The Burnt Ones* 64, *Four Plays* 65, *The Solid Mandala* 66, *The Vivisector* 70, *The Eye of The Storm* 73, *The Cockatoos* 74, *A Fringe of Leaves* 76.
20 Martin Road, Centennial Park, Sydney, N.S.W., Australia.

Whitehouse, Charles S.; American diplomatist; b. 5 Nov. 1921, Paris, France; ed. Yale Univ.
Marine Corps 43-46; research analyst, Dept. of Defense 47-48; Dept. of State 48-; Political Officer U.S. mission, Istanbul, Turkey 52-54, embassy Cambodia 54-56; Special Asst. to Under-Sec. of State for Econ. Affairs 56-69; Political Officer, S. Africa 59-62; Int. Relations Officer, Washington, D.C. 62-65; Nat. War Coll. 65-66; Deputy Chief of Mission and Counsellor, Guinea 66-69; Regional Dir. AID, S. Viet-Nam 69-70; Acting Deputy Asst. Sec. of State for E. Asian-Pacific Affairs 70-71; Deputy Chief of Mission and Counsellor, S. Viet-Nam 72-73; Amb. to Laos 73-75, to Thailand 75-; State Dept. Superior Honor Award 68, AID Distinguished Honor Award 71, State Dept. Distinguished Honor Award 73.
American Embassy in Bangkok, c/o APO San Francisco, Calif. 96346, U.S.A.

Whitlam, (Edward) Gough, Q.C., B.A., LL.B., M.P.; Australian barrister and politician; b. 11 July 1916; ed. Knox Grammar School, Sydney, Canberra High School, Canberra Grammar School and Univ. of Sydney.
Royal Australian Air Force 41-45; admitted to New South Wales Bar 47; mem. House of Representatives 52-; mem. Parl. Cttee. on Constitutional Review 56-59; mem. Federal Parl. Exec. of Australian Labor Party 59-; Deputy Leader of Australian Labor Party in Fed. Parliament 60-67, Leader 67-; Prime Minister 72-75, concurrently Minister of Foreign Affairs 72-73.
Publs. *The Constitution v. Labor* 57, *Australian Foreign Policy* 63, *Socialist Policies within the Constitution* 65, *Australia—Base or Bridge* (Evatt Memorial Lecture) 66, *Beyond Viet-Nam—Australia's Regional Responsibility* 68, *Australia: An Urban Nation* 70, *The New Federation* 71, *Towards a New Australia—Australia and her Region* 72, *Labor in Power* 72.
Parliament House, Canberra, A.C.T. 2600, Australia.

Wickramanayake, Ratnasiri; Ceylonese politician; b. 5 May 1933, Millewa; ed. Ananda Coll. Colombo, Lincoln's Inn, London.
President, Ceylonese Student Asscn. in U.K. 55, Ceylonese and African Student Congress, London 55; leader del. of Ceylon to World Youth Congress, Poland 55; mem. for Horana, Nat. State Assembly 60-; Deputy Minister of Justice 70-; Minister of Plantation Industries 75-.
Ministry of Plantation Industries, P.O.B. 1652, Colombo; Home: 36/2 Kuruppu Road, Colombo 8, Sri Lanka.

Wild, John Paul, F.R.S., F.A.A., M.A., SC.D.; Australian radio astronomer; b. 1923, Sheffield, England; ed. Whitgift School, Croydon, England and Peterhouse, Cambridge.
Radar Officer, Royal Navy 43-47; Researcher in Radio Astronomy, especially of the Sun, Radiophysics Div. of Commonwealth Scientific and Industrial Research Org. (C.S.I.R.O.), N.S.W., Australia 47-, Dir. C.S.I.R.O. Solar Radio Observatory, Culgoora, N.S.W. 66-, Chief of Radiophysics Div. 71-; Pres. Radio Astronomy Comm. of Int. Astronomical Union 67-70; Foreign mem. American Philosophical Soc.; Foreign Hon. mem. American Acad. of Arts and Sciences; Corresp. mem. Royal Soc. of Sciences, Liège; Edgeworth David Medal, Hendryk Arctowski Gold Medal of Nat. Acad. of Sciences, U.S., Balthasar van der Pol Gold Medal of Int. Union of Radio Science, Herschel Medal of Royal Astronomical Soc.
Publs. Various papers on radio astronomy in scientific journals.
Division of Radiophysics, Commonwealth Scientific and Industrial Research Organization, P.O.B. 76, Epping, N.S.W. 2121, Australia.
Telephone: Sydney 869-1111.

Wild, Rt. Hon. Chief Justice Sir Richard, P.C., K.C.M.G., Q.C; New Zealand judge; b. 1912, Blenheim; ed. Feilding High School, Victoria Univ., Wellington.
Solicitor-General 57-65; Chief Justice of New Zealand 66-; Hon. LL.D. (Victoria); Hon. Bencher, Inner Temple, London.
Supreme Court, Wellington, New Zealand.

Wilford, Sir (Kenneth) Michael, K.C.M.G.; British diplomatist; b. 31 Jan. 1922, Wellington, New Zealand; ed. Wrekin Coll. and Cambridge Univ.
Army service 40-46 (mentioned in despatches); Foreign (later Diplomatic) Service 47-; Third Sec., British Embassy Germany 47; Asst. Private Sec. to Sec. of State, FO 49; served France 52, Singapore 55; Asst. Private Sec. to Sec. of State, FO 59; Private Sec. to Lord Privy Seal 60; served Morocco 62; Counsellor, Office of British Chargé d'Affaires, also Consul-Gen., People's Repub. of China 64-66; Visiting Fellow, All Souls Coll., Oxford 66-67; Counsellor, U.S.A. 67-69; Asst. Under-Sec. of State, F.C.O. 69-73, Deputy Under-Sec. of State 73-75; Amb. to Japan 75-.
British Embassy, 1, Ichiban-cho, Chiyoda-ku, Tokyo, Japan; Home: Brook Cottage, Abbotts Ann, Andover, Hants., England.

Willesee, Donald Robert; Australian politician; b. 14 April 1916, Derby, W. Australia; ed. State schools.
Member of Senate 49-, Leader of Opposition in Senate 66-67, Deputy Leader 69-72; Special Minister of State 72; Minister Assisting the Prime Minister 72-73, for Foreign Affairs 73-75; Vice-Pres. Exec. Council 72-75; mem. Joint Cttee. on Foreign Affairs 67-, Privileges Cttee. 69-; mem. several Parl. dels. abroad; Labor.
c/o Parliament House, Canberra, A.C.T., Australia.

Willis, Sir Eric Archibald, K.B.E., C.M.G.; Australian politician; b. 15 Jan. 1922, Murwillumbah, N.S.W.; ed. Murwillumbah High School, Univ. of Sydney.
Member N.S.W. Legislative Assembly 50-, Deputy Leader of Opposition 59-65; Minister for Labour and Industry 65-71, Chief Sec. 65-72, Minister for Tourism 65-72, for Sport 71-72, for Educ. 72-76, Premier and Treas. Jan.-May 76.
16 Crewe Street, Bardwell Park, N.S.W. 2207, Australia.

Wilson, Ralph Frederick, O.B.E., M.COM.; British (New Zealand) economist and politician; b. 21 Sept. 1912; ed. Otago Boys' High School and Univ. of Otago.
Assistant Sec. Bureau of Industry 38; Private Sec. Minister of Supply and Industries and Commerce 41-47; Sec. N.Z. Board of Trade 50-54; Sec. N.Z. Retailers' Fed. 54-59; Gen. Dir. N.Z. Nat. Party 59-73; Economist M. Y. Walls and Assocs. 73-.
88 Cecil Road, Wadestown, Wellington; and Bowring Building, 69-71 Boulcott Street, Wellington 1, New Zealand.

Win Maung, U, B.A.; Burmese politician; b. 1916; ed. Judson Coll., Rangoon.
Joined Burmah Oil Co. after leaving coll.; then entered govt. dept.; joined Army as 2nd Lieut. 40; during Second World War took active part in resistance movement of Anti-Fascist Organization; went to India, where he received training in tactics of military and guerrilla warfare at Mil. Coll., Calcutta and Mil. Camp, Colombo 44; re-joined guerrilla forces in Burma 45; Vice-Pres. Karen Youth Organization and Ed. *Taing Yin Tha* 45; mem. Constituent Assembly 47; Minister for Industry and Labour 47, of Transport and Communications 49; later Minister for Port, Marine, Civil Aviation and Coastal Shipping; mem. Burmese Parl. for Maubin South (Karen) 51-55 and 56-57; Pres. of the Union of Burma 57-62; detained after *coup d'état* 67.
Rangoon, Burma.

Winneke, Sir Henry Arthur, K.C.M.G., O.B.E., KT.ST.J., Q.C.; Australian state governor; b. 29 Oct. 1908, Melbourne; ed. Ballarat Grammar School, Melbourne and Melbourne Univ.

Admitted to Bar 31; war service in R.A.A.F., Group Captain, Dir. Personnel Services 39-46; returned to bar 46; mem. Victorian Bar Council 48-50; Appointed King's Counsel for Victoria 49; Senior Counsel to Attorney-Gen., Victoria and Crown Prosecutor 49-51; Solicitor-Gen. Victoria 51-64; Chief Justice of Supreme Court of Victoria 64-74; Lieut. Gov. of Victoria 72-74, Gov. May 74-.
Government House, Melbourne, Victoria 3004, Australia.
Telephone: 63-9971.

Withers, Reginald Grieve, LL.B.; Australian politician; b. 26 Oct. 1924, Bunbury, W.A.; ed. Bunbury and Univ. of Western Australia.
Royal Australian Navy 42-46; mem. Bunbury Municipal Council 54-56, Bunbury Diocesan Council 58-59, Treas. 61-68; State Vice-Pres., Liberal and Country League of W.A. 58-61, State Pres. 61-65; mem. Fed. Exec. of Liberal Party 61-65, Fed. Vice-Pres. 62-65; mem. Senate for W.A. Feb.-Nov. 66, Nov. 67-, Govt. Whip in Senate 69-71, Leader of Opposition in Senate 72-75; Special Minister of State, Minister for A.C.T., Minister for the Media and Minister for Tourism and Recreation Nov.-Dec. 75, Leader of Govt. in Senate and Minister for Admin. Services Dec. 75-; fmr. Chair. Joint Cttee. on A.C.T., Select Cttee. on Foreign Ownership and Control of Australian Resources, Senate Standing Cttee. on Constitutional and Legal Affairs; mem. del to Conf. of Commonwealth Parl. Asscn., Trinidad 69; Liberal.
Parliament House, Canberra, A.C.T. 2600; and Australian Parliament Offices, Hamersley House, 191 St. George's Terrace, Perth, W.A. 6000, Australia.
Telephone: 72-6650 (Canberra); 222-991 (Perth).

Woolcott, Richard, B.A.; Australian diplomatist; b. 11 June 1928; ed. Frankston High School, Geelong Grammar School, Univ. of Melbourne and London Univ. School of Slavonic and East European Studies.
Joined Australian Foreign Service 51; served in Australian missions in London, Moscow (twice), S. Africa, Malaya, Singapore and Accra; attended UN Gen. Assembly 62; Acting High Commr. to Singapore 63-64; High Commr. to Ghana 67-70; accompanied Prime Ministers Menzies 65, Holt 66, McMahon 71, 72 and Whitlam 73, 74 on visits to Asia, Europe, the Americas and the Pacific; Head, South Asia Div., Dept. of Foreign Affairs 73; Deputy Sec., Dept. of Foreign Affairs 74; Amb. to Indonesia March 75-.
Australian Embassy, 15 Jalan Thamrin, Gambir, Jakarta, Indonesia.

Wriedt, Kenneth Shaw; Australian politician; b. 11 July 1927; ed. Univ. High School, Melbourne.
Served in the Merchant Navy 44-58; State Insurance Office, Tasmania 58-68; mem. Senate 68-, Leader of Govt. in Senate Feb.-Nov. 75; Minister of Primary Industry Dec. 72-73, for Agriculture 74-75, for Minerals and Energy Oct.-Nov. 75; Leader of Opposition in the Senate Jan. 76-; Labor Party.
Parliament House, Canberra, A.C.T. 2600; Marine Board Building, Hobart, Tasmania 7000; Home: 25 Corinth Street, Howrah, Hobart, Tasmania 7018, Australia.

Wright, Judith Arundell; Australian writer; b. 31 May 1915, Armidale, N.S.W.; ed. New England Girls' School, Armidale, N.S.W., and Sydney Univ.
Commonwealth Literary Fund Scholarship 49, 62; Lecturer in Australian literature at various Australian univs.; Encyclopedia Britannica Writers' Award 64; Hon. D.Litt., Univs. of Old and New England; F.A.H.A. 71.
Publs. Poetry: *The Moving Image* 46, *Woman to Man* 49, *The Gateway* 53, *The Two Fires* 55, *A Book of Birds* 62, *Five Senses* 63, *The Other Half* 66, *Collected Poems* 71, *Alive* 73; criticism: *Charles Harpur* 63, *Preoccupations in Australian Poetry* 64; anthologies: *A Book of Australian Verse* 56, *New Land, New Language* 57; biography: *The Generations of Man* 58; short stories: *The Nature of Love* 66; Prose: *Because I was Invited* 75; also books for children.
c/o Post Office, Braidwood, New South Wales 2622, Australia.

Wright, Reginald Charles, B.A., LL.B.; Australian politician; b. 10 July 1905, Tasmania; ed. Univ. of Tasmania.
Called to the Bar 28; Lecturer in Law Univ. of Tasmania 31-41, 44-45; Pres. Tasmanian Liberal Party 45-46; mem. State House of Assembly, becoming Deputy Leader of the Opposition 46-49; mem. Senate 49-; Govt. Whip 50-51; sat on numerous Parl. cttees.; Fed. Minister for Works and in Charge of Tourist Activities 68-72; War service in Australian Imperial Force 41-44; Liberal.
The Senate, Canberra, A.C.T., Australia.

Wu Kuei-hsien; People's Repub. of China; b. 1935.
Woman worker in textile mill at N.W. State Cotton Mill No. 1, Sian; mem. Shensi Revolutionary Cttee. 68; mem. 9th Cen. Cttee. of CCP 69; Deputy Sec. CCP Shensi 71; Alt. mem. Politburo, CCP 73; Vice-Premier, State Council 75-.

Wu Te; People's Repub. of China; b. 1914, Fengjun, Hopei; ed. China Univ., Peking.
Workers leader in Tangshan 35; Regimental Political Commissar 42; Vice-Minister of Fuel Industry 49-50; Sec. CCP Pingyuan 50-52; Deputy Sec. CCP Tientsin 52-55; Deputy Mayor of Tientsin 52-53, Mayor 53-55; Pres. Tientsin Univ. 52-57; Alt. mem. 8th Cen. Cttee. of CCP 56; First Sec. CCP Kirin 56-66; Political Commissar Kirin Mil. District, People's Liberation Army 58; Sec. N.E. Bureau, CCP 61; Second Sec. CCP Peking 66; Acting Mayor of Peking 66; Vice-Chair. Peking Revolutionary Cttee. 67-72, Chair. 72; mem. 9th Cen. Cttee. of CCP 69; Head of Cultural Group, State Council 71; Second Sec. CCP Peking 71, First Sec. 72; mem. 10th Politburo, CCP 73, Second Political Commissar, Peking Mil. Region, PLA.

X

Xuan Thuy; Vietnamese politician; b. 2 Sept. 1912.
In numerous nat. liberation movements until 45; later Editor *Cuu Quoc* (National Salvation—organ of the Viet-Minh); Pres. Asscn. of Journalists of Democratic Repub. of Viet-Nam; Deputy Vice-Speaker and Sec.-Gen. of Nat. Assembly, Democratic Repub. of Viet-Nam; mem. Presidium Fatherland Front Cen. Cttee.; Deputy Chair. Democratic Repub. of Viet-Nam Del. to Geneva Conf. on Laos 61; Minister of Foreign Affairs 63-65; Minister without Portfolio to head Democratic Repub. of Viet-Nam's negotiating team, Paris 68-73; Vice-Chair. Standing Cttee., Nat. Assembly of Socialist Repub. of Viet-Nam July 76-; mem. Secr. Cen. Cttee. Lao Dong Party.
National Assembly, Hanoi, Viet-Nam.

Y

Ya'acob, Tunku, D.K., P.M.N., S.P.M.S., C.M.G.; Malaysian diplomatist; b. 27 Dec. 1899; ed. Malay Coll., Kuala Kangsar, Queen's Coll., Cambridge, and Imperial Coll. of Agriculture, Trinidad.
Entered Dept. of Agriculture, Kedah State 30, Dir. 46; mem. Kedah State Legislature 31-49; fmr. Deputy Dir. Fed. Dept. of Agriculture; Keeper of the Rulers' Seal 50-51; Regent of State of Kedah in Sultan's absence 51; joined Fed. Exec. Council with Portfolio of Agriculture 51-54; Keeper of Rulers' Seal 54; mem. Public Service Appointments and Promotions Board 54, Deputy Chair. 56 and

Chair. (reconstituted as Public Services Comm.) 57-; High Commr. for the Fed. of Malaya in the U.K. 58-63, High Commr. for Malaysia 63-65; Amb. to Belgium 66-68; Amb. to France, Switzerland 66-70; awarded Insignia Commdr. of St. Michael and St. George 47, of Panglima Mangku Negara 59; Chair. Univ. Council and Pro-Chancellor, Univ. of Singapore 56-58; title of Tunku Panglima Besar conferred by Sultan of Kedah 50; Insignia of Derjat Kerabat (D.K.) 61; Grand Cross Order of Homayoun (Iran); Hon. LL.D., Univ. of Malaya.
Johore Bahru, Malaysia.

Yahya Khan, Gen. Agha Muhammad H.PK., H.J.; Pakistani former army officer; b. 4 Feb. 1917; ed. Punjab Univ. and Indian Military Acad.
Service on N.W. Frontier before Second World War; service in Middle East and Italy, Second World War; set up Pakistan Staff Coll. 47, later Chief of Staff, Pakistan Army; Chair. Capital Comm. 59; G.O.C. East Pakistan 62; Commdr. Infantry Div. 65; C.-in-C. Pakistan Army Sept. 66-69; imposed Martial Law and became Pres. of Pakistan March 69-Dec. 71; detained Dec. 71; house arrest; released July 74.
Rawalpindi, Pakistan.

Yamagata, Shiro, B.ENG.; Japanese business executive; b. 26 Dec. 1902, Iwakuni City; ed. Tokyo Univ.
Osaka Refinery, Mitsubishi Metal Corpn. 27-, Man. Osaka Refinery 47-48, Dir. 50-, Man. Dir. 56-60, Pres. 60-67, Chair. 67-71; Pres. Mitsubishi Nuclear Fuel Co. Ltd. 71-, Cordon of the Rising Sun, Second Class 73.
Mitsubishi Nuclear Fuel Company Limited, Tokyo, Japan.

Yamamura, Shinjio; Japanese politician; b. 1908; ed. Sawara Middle School.
Entered fertilizer and rice business; fmr. Dir.-Gen. Prefectural Food Corpn., and Exec. of other food orgs.; fmr. mem. Japanese Prefectural Asscn.; mem. House of Reps. 45-, fmr. Vice-Minister of Labour; Head of Admin. Agency July 63-July 64; Pres. Yamamura Shipbuilding Co., Sawara Shipbuilding Co.; Liberal-Dem. Party.
House of Representatives, Tokyo, Japan.

Yamanaka, Sadanori; Japanese politician; b. 1921; ed. in Taipei.
Member, House of Reps.; fmr. Parl. Vice-Minister for Finance; Chair. House of Reps. Finance Cttee.; Deputy Sec.-Gen. Liberal-Democratic Party (LDP); Vice-Chair. LDP Policy Board; Minister of State and Dir.-Gen. of Prime Minister's Office 70-72; Minister of State, Dir.-Gen. Defence Agency 73-74.
9-7-45 Akasaka, Minato-ku, Tokyo, Japan.

Yamashita, Isamu; Japanese business executive; b. 15 Feb. 1911; ed. Tokyo Imperial Univ.
Joined shipbuilding dept., Mitsui & Co. 33; entered Tamano Shipyard Ltd. (predecessor of Mitsui Shipbuilding & Engineering Co. Ltd.) 37; Man. Dir. Mitsui Shipbuilding & Engineering Co. Ltd. 62, Senior Man. Dir. 66, Vice-Pres. 68, Pres. 70-.
Mitsui Shipbuilding & Engineering Co. Ltd., 6-4, Tsukiji 5-chome, Chuo-ku, Tokyo, Japan.
Telephone: 544-3001.

Yanagi, Masuo; Japanese banker; b. 22 June 1900; ed. Keio Univ., Tokyo.
Mitsui Bank 21-, branches in U.S.A. and Great Britain 31-33, Branch Man., Osaka 52, Man. Dir. 57, Pres. 59-64, Adviser 65-; Auditor Mitsui Mutual Life Insurance Co. 65-, Fujikura Cable Works Ltd., Fuji Xerox Corpn. 71-.
1-2 Yurakucho 1-chome, Chiyoda-ku, Tokyo, Japan.

Yang Ta-yi; army officer, People's Repub. of China.
Major-General People's Liberation Army 63; Deputy Commdr. Hunan Mil. District, PLA 67, Commdr. 69-; Vice-Chair. Hunan Revolutionary Cttee. 68; Deputy Sec. CCP Hunan 70.

Yang Te-chih; army officer, People's Repub. of China; b. 1910, Li-ling, Hunan; ed. Red Army Acad. and Nanking Mil. Acad.
Joined CCP 27; on Long March 34-35; Regimental Commdr., Red Army 35; Commdr. Ninghsia Mil. Region, People's Liberation Army 49; Chief of Staff Chinese People's Volunteers in Korea 51, Deputy Commdr. Chinese People's Volunteers 53-54, Commdr. 54-55; mem. Nat. Defence Council 54; Gen. 55; Alt. mem. 8th Cen. Cttee. of CCP 56; Commdr. Tsinan Mil. Region, PLA 58-73; First Vice-Chair. Shantung Revolutionary Cttee. 67, Chair. 71; mem. 9th Cen. Cttee. of CCP 69; First Sec. CCP Shantung 71; mem. 10th Cen. Cttee. of CCP 73; Commdr. Wuhan Mil. Region, PLA 74-.

Yang Yung; army officer, People's Repub. of China; b. 1906, Liuyang, Hunan; ed. Red Army Coll.
Joined CCP 26; Regimental Deputy Commdr., Red Army 37; Commdr. 5th Army Group, 2nd Field Army, People's Liberation Army 48; Deputy Commdr. 2nd Field Army, PLA 49; Gov. of Kweichow 49-55; Deputy Commdr. Chinese People's Volunteers, Korea 54, Commdr. Chinese People's Volunteers 55-58; Alt. mem. 8th Cen. Cttee. CCP 56; Commdr. Peking Mil. Region, PLA 60-67; criticized and removed from office during Cultural Revolution 67; Commdr. Sinkiang Mil. Region, PLA 73-; Vice-Chair. Sinkiang Revolutionary Cttee. 73; Second Sec. CCP Sinkiang 73.

Yano, Jun'ya; Japanese politician; b. 27 April 1932, Osaka; ed. Kyoto Univ.
With Ohbayashi-gumi Ltd. 56-; mem. Osaka Prefectural Assembly 63; mem. House of Reps. 67-; Sec.-Gen. Komeito (Clean Govt.) Party 67-.
Komeito Party, 17 Minamimotomachi, Shinjuku-ku, Tokyo; 536 Mikuriya, Higashi-Osaka-shi, Osaka, Japan.
Telephone: 06-788-0443.

Yao Wen-yuan; journalist, People's Repub. of China; b. 1924.
Journalist and youth activist before Cultural Revolution; leading pro-Maoist journalist during Cultural Revolution 65-68; Editor *Wen Hui Bao* 66, *Liberation Daily* 66; mem. Cen. Cultural Revolution Group, CCP 66; Vice-Chair. Shanghai Revolutionary Cttee. 67-; Editor *People's Daily* 67-; mem. Politburo, CCP 69; Second Sec. CCP Shanghai 71; mem. Politburo, 10th Cen. Cttee. of CCP 73, 75-.

Yara, Chobyo; Japanese teacher and government official; b. 13 Dec., Okinawa; ed. Okinawa Normal School and Hiroshima Univ.
Teacher in various secondary schools 30-43, Taiwan Univ. 43-46; Principal, Chinen Senior High School 47-50; Dir. of Educ. Dept., Govt. of Ryukyu 50-68; Pres. Okinawa Teachers' Asscn. 52; elected Chief Exec. Govt. of Ryukyu Islands 62-72; Gov. Okinawa Pref. 72-.
Publs. *My Past Time* 68, *My Personal History* 70.
260 Daido Naha City, Okinawa, Japan.
Telephone: 32-4380.

Yashiro, Yukio; Japanese art historian and fmr. museum director; b. 5 Nov. 1890; ed. Tokyo Imperial Univ.
Studied art in Tokyo, Florence, London, Paris and Berlin; Prof. Imperial School of Fine Arts, Tokyo 17-42; Dir. Inst. of Art Research, Tokyo 30-42; Lecturer Harvard Univ., U.S.A. 33; Dir. The Museum Yamato Bunkakan, Nara 60-70; Commdr. Ordine al Merito (Italy).
Publs. *Sandro Botticelli* (3 vols.) 25; *Japanische Malerei der Gegenwart* 31, *Characteristics of Japanese Art* 43, *Masterpieces of Far Eastern Arts in European and American Collections* (2 vols.) 42, *2000 Years of Japanese Art* 58, *Art Treasures of Japan* (2 vols.) 61, *Characteristics of Japanese Art* (revised edn., 2 vols.) 65.
1013 Kitahonmachi, Oiso-chō, Nakagun, Kanagawa-ken, Japan.

Yasui, Kaoru, LL.D.; Japanese jurist; b. 25 April 1907, Osaka; ed. Tokyo Univ.
Assistant Prof. Tokyo Univ. 32-42, Prof. 42-48; Prof. Hosei Univ. 52-, Dean Faculty of Jurisprudence 57-63, Dir. 63-66; Leader (Chair. etc.) Japan Council Against Atomic and Hydrogen Bombs 54-65; Pres. Japanese Inst. for World Peace 65-; Pres. Maruki Gallery for Hiroshima Panels 68-; Lenin Peace Prize 58; Peace Medal (Fed. Repub. of Germany) 60; Gold Medal (Czechoslovakia) 65; Hon. Dr. Law (San Gabriel Coll. U.S.A.).
Publs. *Outline of International Law* 39, *Banning Weapons of Mass Destruction* 55, *People and Peace* 55, *Collection of Treaties* 60, *My Way* 67, *The Dialectical Method and the Science of International Law* 70.
Minami-Ogikubo 3-13-11, Suginamiku, Tokyo, Japan.

Yasui, Kizo; Japanese business executive; b. 2 Dec. 1899, Shiga; ed. Tokyo Univ. of Commerce.
Joined the Mitsui Bank Ltd. 26, Dir. 51, Man. Dir. 54, Senior Man. Dir. 57, Deputy Pres. 59; President Mitsui Petrochemicals Co., Ltd. 61; Exec. Vice-Pres. Toray Industries Inc. 63, Chair. 71-; Pres. Japan Chemical Fibers Assen. 73-; Order of the Rising Sun 70.
Toray Industries Inc., Toray Building, 2 Nihonbashi, Muromachi, 2-chome, Chuo-ku, Tokyo; No. 5-36, 4-chome Minamiazabu, Minato-ku, Tokyo 106, Japan.
Telephone: 03-473-0520.

Yasukawa, Takeshi, B.A.; Japanese diplomatist; b. 16 Feb. 1914, Tokyo; ed. Tokyo Imperial Univ.
Entered diplomatic service 39; Counsellor, Washington, D.C. 57-61; Asst. Deputy Vice-Minister for Admin., Ministry of Foreign Affairs 61-65; Dir.-Gen. American Affairs Bureau, Ministry of Foreign Affairs 65-67; Amb. to Philippines 67-69; Deputy Vice-Minister of Foreign Affairs 70-72; Amb. to U.S.A. July 73-.
Embassy of Japan, 2516 Massachusetts Avenue, N.W., Washington, D.C. 20008, U.S.A.
Telephone: 234-2266.

Yeh Chien-ying, Marshal; party leader and fmr. army officer, People's Repub. of China; b. 1899, Mei-hsien, Kwangtung; ed. Yunnan Mil. Inst., Sun Yat-sen Univ., Moscow, in France and Germany.
Instructor Whampoa Mil. Acad. 24; joined CCP 24; participated in Nanchang Uprising 27, Canton Uprising 27; Principal Red Army Coll. 31; Deputy Chief of Staff on Long March 34-36; mem. 7th Cen. Cttee. of CCP 45; Mayor of Peking 49; First Political Commissar Canton Mil. District, People's Liberation Army 49; Gov. of Kwangtung 49-55; Vice-Chair. Nat. Defence Council 54-; Dir. Inspectorate of Armed Forces, PLA 54-58; Marshal PLA 55; mem. 8th Cen. Cttee. of CCP 56; Pres. PLA Mil. Acad. 58; Sec., Secr. of Cen. Cttee., CCP 66; presumed Acting Minister of Nat. Defence 71-75, Minister 75-; Vice-Chair. CCP 73; mem. Standing Cttee. of Politburo, 10th Cen. Cttee. of CCP 73, Vice-Chair. 75-.

Yeh Fei; People's Repub. of China; b. 1909, Fu-an, Fukien.
Guerrilla leader in Fukien 26-29; joined CCP 27; Div. Commdr. New 4th Army 41; Corps Commdr. 3rd Field Army 49; Vice-Gov. of Fukien 49-54, Gov. 55-59; Mayor of Amoy 49; First Sec. CCP Fukien 55-68; Gen. 55; Alt. mem. 8th Cen. Cttee. of CCP 56; Political Commissar Foochow Mil. Region, People's Liberation Army 57-67; Sec. E. China Bureau, CCP 63-68; criticized and removed from office during Cultural Revolution 67; Alt. mem. 10th Cen. Cttee. of CCP 73; Minister of Communications 75-.

Yeh, George Kung-chao, B.A., M.A.; Chinese politician and diplomatist; b. 1904; ed. Amherst Coll., Mass., U.S.A., and Cambridge Univ.
Professor of English, Nat. Peking Univ. 26-27; Asst. Prof. Nat. Chinan Univ. 27-29; Prof. Tsing Hua Univ. 29-35; Prof. and Chair. Dept. Western Languages and Literature, Nat. Peking Univ. 35-39; Research Fellowship, China Foundation 37-39; Dir. British Malaya Office, Chinese Ministry of Information 40-41, Dir. U.K. Office 42-46; Counsellor and concurrently Dir. of European Affairs Dept., Ministry of Foreign Affairs 46-47; Admin. Vice-Minister of Foreign Affairs 47-49; Ambassador Extraordinary on Special Mission to Burma 47; Vice-Minister 49, Minister of Foreign Affairs (Taiwan) 49-58; Chair. Chinese Del., Seventh, Ninth and later Sessions UN Gen. Assembly; Amb. to U.S.A. 58-61; Minister without Portfolio 61-; Special Grand Cordon, Order of Brilliant Star, Order of Propitious Clouds, many foreign decorations; Hon. LL.D. (Seoul, Amherst).
Publs. *Social Forces in English Literature, Introducing China, The Concept of Jen, Cultural Life in Ancient China* (Royal Soc. of Arts Medal 43), *On Ancient Chinese Poetry*.
The Executive Yuan, Taipei, Taiwan.

Yen Chia-kan, Dr., B.SC.; Chinese politician; b. 23 Oct. 1905, Soochow, Kiangsu; ed. St. John's Univ., Shanghai.
Various government posts including Commr. of Reconstruction, Fukien Provincial Govt. 38-39, Finance Commr. Fukien Province, Chair. Fukien Provincial Bank 39-45; Dir. of Procurement, War Production Board 45; Communications Commr., Taiwan Provincial Govt. 45-46, Finance Commr. 46-49; Chair. Bank of Taiwan 46-49; Minister of Econ. Affairs, Republic of China (Taiwan) 50, of Finance 50-54, 58-63; Vice-Chair. Council for U.S. Aid 50, 63; Gov. of Taiwan 54-57; Minister without Portfolio 57-58; Chair. Council for U.S. Aid 57-58; Pres. Exec. Yuan (Prime Minister) 63-72; Chair. Council for Int. Econ. Co-operation and Devt. 63-69; Vice-Pres. Repub. of China (Taiwan) 66-75, Pres. April 75-; Hon. LL.D. (Nat. Seoul Univ., Korea) 64, Hon. D.Pol. (Nat. Chulalongkorn Univ., Thailand) 68; numerous awards.
Office of the President, Taipei, Taiwan; 4 Section II, Chungking Road, South Taipei, Taiwan.

Yendo, Masayoshi, B.ENG.; Japanese architect; b. 30 Nov. 1920, Yokohama; ed. Waseda Univ.
Murano architect office 45-49; Pres. M. Yendo Associated Architects and Engineers 52-; Vice-Pres., Fed. of Japanese Architectural Design Supervisory Assen. 75-; Dir. Board, Japan Architects Assen. 71-, Tokyo Architectural Design Supervisory Assen. 75-; Geijutsu Sensyo (Art Commendation Award) 65; Architectural Inst. of Japan Award 65.
Buildings include: 77th Bank Head Office 57, Hieizan Int. Sightseers' Hotel 59, Keio Terminal and Dept. Store Building 60, Resort Hotel Kasyoen 62, Yamaguchi Bank Head Office 62, 77th Building (77th Bank, Tokyo Branch) 63, Japan Coca-Cola Concentrating Plant 64, Coca-Cola (Japan) Head Office 68, Yakult Honsha Co. Ltd. Head Office 70, Tokyo American Club 71, Heibon-sha Co. Ltd. Head Office 72, Taiyo Fishery Co. Ltd. Head Office 73, Seiyu Store Kasugai Shopping Centre 75.
M. Yendo Associated Architects and Engineers, 5-6, 8-chome, Ginza, Chuo-ku, Tokyo, Japan.
Telephone: 572-8321 (Tokyo).

Yokota, Takashi; Japanese banker; b. 31 Jan. 1909, Tokyo; ed. Keio Univ.
Joined The Nippon Kangyo Bank Ltd. 33, Dir. 58, Deputy Pres. 66, Pres. 69; Pres. The Dai-Ichi Kangyo Bank Ltd. 71-; Exec. Dir., Fed. Econ. Org. Japanese Fed. of Employers Assen.; Dir., Fukoku Mutual Life Insurance Co.
The Dai-Ichi Kangyo Bank Ltd., 6-2, Marunouchi 1-chome, Chiyoda-ku, Tokyo; 5-35 Nishi-Azabu 3-chome, Minato-ku, Tokyo, Japan.
Telephone: 03-216-1111 (Office); 03-405-0510 (Home).

Yokoyama, Soichi; Japanese banker; b. 30 Nov. 1914, Tokyo; ed. Hitotsubashi Univ.
Yokohama Specie Bank 38-47; Bank of Tokyo Ltd. 47-, Dir., Agent of New York Agency 63, Resident Dir. for

Europe, London 65, Man. Dir. 65, Senior Man. Dir. 69, Deputy Pres. 72, Pres. 73-; Chair. Bank of Tokyo (Holland) NV 73-, Bank of Tokyo (Luxembourg) SA 74-; Dir. UBAN—Arab Japanese Finance Ltd., Hong Kong 74-, Banque Européene de Tokyo SA, Paris 73-, Western American Bank (Europe) Ltd., London 73-; Fed. of Bankers' Asscns. of Japan 73-; Exec. Dir. Japan Fed. of Employers' Asscns. 73-; Trustee Japan Cttee. for Econ. Devt. 73-; mem. Operational Council of Japan External Trade Org. (JETRO) 73-; Chair. Cttee. on Int. Finance, Fed. of Econ. Org. 74-.
Bank of Tokyo Ltd., 2-1-1, Muromachi, Nihombashi, Chuo-ku, Tokyo 103; Home 14-25, Sugamo 3-chome, Toshima-ku, Tokyo 170, Japan.
Telephone: 03-270-8111 (Office); 03-918-1894 (Home).

Yong Nyuk Lin; Singapore politician and diplomatist; b. 24 June 1918, Seremban, Malaya; ed. Raffles Coll.
Teacher in Malaya 38-41; Overseas Assurance Corpn., Singapore, rising to Gen. Man. 41-58, resigned; Minister for Educ. 59-63; Chair. Singapore Harbour Board 61-62; Minister for Health 63-68, for Communications 68-75, without Portfolio 75-76; High Commr. to U.K. Sept. 75-.
Singapore High Commission, 2 Wilton Crescent, London, SW1X 8RW; Residence: 2 Broadwalk House, 51 Hyde Park Gate, London, S.W.7, England.
Telephone: 01-235-8315 (Office); 01-589-8451 (Residence).

Yoshida, Kenzuo; Japanese diplomatist; b. 19 Sept. 1917, Toyama; ed. Tokyo Univ.
Consul-General in Honolulu, U.S.A. 61-63; Counsellor in U.K., concurrently Consul-Gen. in London 63-65, Minister in U.K. 65; Minister in Republic of Korea 65-67; Amb. to Tanzania 67-69, concurrently to Zambia 68-69; Dir.-Gen. Immigration Bureau, Ministry of Justice, Tokyo 69-72; Dir.-Gen. Asian Affairs Bureau, Ministry of Foreign Affairs 72-73; Amb. to Australia 73-76, concurrently to Nauru 74-76 and to Fiji 74-76.
Ministry of Foreign Affairs, Tokyo, Japan.

Yoshida, Taroichi; Japanese international banker; ed. Tokyo Imperial Univ.
Served Ministry of Finance, Dir. of Banking Bureau, later Vice-Minister for Int. Affairs and Special Adviser to Minister 44-76; Pres. Asian Devt. Bank 76-.
Asian Development Bank, 2330 Roxas Boulevard, Pasay City, P.O.B. 789, Manila, Philippines.

Yoshiki, Masao, DR. ENG.; Japanese engineer; b. 20 Jan. 1908, Nagasaki; ed. Univ. of Tokyo.
Lecturer, School of Engineering, Univ. of Tokyo 30-32; Asst. Prof., Univ. of Tokyo 32-44, Prof. of Naval Architecture 44-68; Pres. Soc. of Naval Architects of Japan 61-63; Dean, School of Engineering, Univ. of Tokyo 62-64; Chair. Int. Ships Structures Congress 67-70; Chief Dir., Japan Soc. for the Promotion of Science 68-; Prof. Emer. Univ. of Tokyo; Commr. Space Activities Comm. 68-74, 76-; Vice-Pres. Science Council of Japan 69-71; mem. Council for Science and Technology 74-; Prize of Japan Acad. 66, Purple Ribbon Decoration 68.
Publs. Articles in journals.
c/o Science and Technology Agencies, 2-2 Kasumigaseki 3-chome, Chiyoda-ku, Tokyo; Home: 43-14, Izumi 2-chome, Suginami-ku, Tokyo, Japan.
Telephone: 03-581-1559 (Office); 03-328-0210 (Home).

Yoshikuni, Ichiro; Japanese civil servant; b. 2 Sept. 1916, Yokohama; ed. Tokyo Imperial Univ.
With Ministry of Commerce and Industry 40-47; mem. Board of Trade 47-48; Attorney-Gen.'s Office, Legislative Bureau 48-52; Cabinet Legislative Bureau 52-, Dir. of Third Div. 59-64, Dir. First Div. 64, Asst. Dir.-Gen. 64-72, Dir.-Gen. 72-74.
Publs. (co-author) *Manual on the Drafting, Application and Interpretation of Law* 49, *Legislative Drafting* 52, *Dictionary of Public Finance and Accounting* 74.
5-35-17 Jingumae, Shibuya-ku, Tokyo, Japan.
Telephone: 03-581-1491 (Office); 03-409-0285 (Home).

Yoshimura, Junzo; Japanese architect; b. 7 Sept. 1908; ed. Tokyo Acad. of Fine Arts.
At architectural office of Antonin Raymond 31-42; own architectural practice 43-; Asst. Prof. in Architecture, Tokyo Univ. of Arts 44-61, Prof. 62-70, Emer. Prof. 70-; mem. Architectural Inst. of Japan, Japan Architects' Asscn.; Hon. Fellow, American Insts. of America 75; Architectural Inst. Prize 56, Parsons Medal (New York) 56; Award from Japanese Acad. of Arts 75.
Works include: Int. House of Japan, Tokyo 55, Public Kambara Hospital 56, The Motel on the Mountain, New York 56, Hotel Kowakien, Hakone, 59, Mountain House for Yawata Iron and Steel Co., Kujyu 60, N.C.R. H.Q., Tokyo 62, Americana Building, Osaka 65, Prefectural Aichi Univ. of Arts, Aichi 65-, Hotel Fujita, Kyoto 70, Japan House, New York 71, Nara Nat. Museum 73, and many residences.
2-38 Akasaka 5-chome, Minato-ku, Tokyo; Home: 5-30-24 Minamidai, Nakano-ku, Tokyo, Japan.

Yoshiyama, Hirokichi; Japanese business executive; b. 1 Dec. 1911; ed. Faculty of Engineering, Univ. of Tokyo.
Joined Hitachi Ltd. 35, Dir. 61, Exec. Man. Dir. 64, Senior Exec. Man. Dir. 68, Exec. Vice-Pres. 69, Pres. Nov. 71-; Chair. Tokyo Atomic Industrial Consortium.
Hitachi Ltd., New Marunouchi Building, No. 5-1, 1-chome, Marunouchi, Chiyoda-ku, Tokyo 100, Japan.
Telephone: 03-212-1111.

Yosizaka, Takamasa; Japanese architect and town planner; b. 13 Feb. 1917; ed. Waseda Univ., Tokyo.
Lecturer, Japan Women's Coll. 42-50, Tokyo Agricultural School 45-48, Yamanasi Univ. 56-57, Tucumán Nat. Univ., Argentina 61-62; Asst. Prof. Waseda Univ. 50, Prof. 59, Head of Dept. of Architecture 64-66, Dean of School of Science and Engineering, Waseda Univ. 69-72; Manager Waseda Univ. Expedition to Equatorial Africa 58, and Leader of its MacKinley Alaska Expedition 60; Vice-Pres. Architectural Inst. of Japan 66-68, Pres 73.-74; Dir. Japanese Asscn. of Architects 66-68.
Principal works: Japanese Pavilion, Venice Biennale 56, Maison Franco-Japonais 59, Athénée Français 62, Gotu City Hall 62, Univ. Seminar House 65; Projects: Redevelopment Plans for Takada-no Baba District and Izu, Oosima; Space Museum 69; Future of Sendai City 73.
Publs. *Form and Environment* 55, *Primitive Country to Civilized Country* 61, *Study on Dwelling* 65, *A Study for 21st Century Japan* 70, *Directives* 73; trans. into Japanese *Le Modulor*, *Modulor II*, *Vers une Architecture* (Le Corbusier), *Erreurs Monumentales* (M. Ragon), *Moi, j'aime pas la mer* (Xénakis).
2-17-24 Hyakunintyo, Sinziku-ku, Tokyo 160, Japan.

Yotsumoto, Kiyoshi; Japanese business executive; b. 29 Sept. 1908; ed. Kyoto Univ.
President, Kawasaki Heavy Industries Ltd.
Kawasaki Heavy Industries Ltd., Nissei-Kawasaki Building, 16-1, Nakamachi-dori 2-chome, Ikuta-ku, Kobe, P.O. Box 1140 Kobe Central; Home: 2-22-15, Minami Senzoku, Ohtaku, Tokyo, Japan.
Telephone: 726-0585.

Youde, Edward, C.M.G., M.B.E.; British diplomatist; b. 19 June 1924, Penarth, Glam.; ed. School of Oriental and African Studies, London Univ.
Served in various diplomatic posts in China, U.S.A. and U.K. 47-65; Counsellor, Perm. Mission to UN 65-69; Private Sec. to Prime Minister 69-70; Imperial Defence Coll. 70-71; Head Personnel Services Dept., Foreign and

Commonwealth Office 71-73; Asst. Under-Sec. of State, FCO 73-74; Amb. to People's Repub. of China 74-.
c/o Foreign and Commonwealth Office, London, S.W.1, England.
Telephone: 01-930-8440.

Yousuf, Lt.-Gen. Mohammed; Pakistani diplomatist; b. 14 Oct. 1908, Quetta; ed. Royal Mil. Coll. Sandhurst.
Lieutenant-General 54, retired from army 56; High Commr. in Australia and New Zealand 56-59, in U.K. 59-63; Amb. to Afghanistan 63-68; High Commr. in U.K. 71-72, Amb. 72; Amb. to Switzerland 72-; Sitara-i-Pakistan, Nishani Liagat (Iran), Legion d'Honneur (France).
Embassy of Pakistan, Bernastrasse 47, Berne, Switzerland.

Yu Ch'iu-li; politician, People's Repub. of China; b. 1914, Szechuan.
Political Commissar of Detachment, 120th Div. 34; Deputy Political Commissar Tsinghai Mil. District, People's Liberation Army 49; Lieut.-Gen. PLA 55; Dir. Finance Dept., PLA 56-57; Political Commissar Gen. Logistics Dept., PLA 57-58; Minister of Petroleum Industry 58; Vice-Chair. State Planning Comm. 65, Chair. 72-; mem. 9th Cen. Cttee. of CCP 69, 10th Cen. Cttee. 73, Vice-Premier, State Council Jan. 75-.

Yu Kuo-hua; Chinese banker; b. 1914; ed. Tsinghua Univ., Harvard Univ. Graduate School, U.S.A., London School of Econs.
Secretary to Pres. of Nat. Mil. Council 36-44; Alt. Exec. Dir. Int. Bank for Reconstruction and Devt. 47-50; Pres. Cen. Trust of China 55-61; Man. Dir. China Devt. Corpn. 59-67; Chair. Board of Dirs., Bank of China 61-67, China Insurance Co. Ltd. 61-67; Alt. Gov. IBRD 64-67, Gov. for Repub. of China 67-69; Minister of Finance 67-69; Gov. Cen. Bank of China 69-; Minister without Portfolio 69-; Gov. Int. Monetary Fund 69-, Asian Devt. Bank 69-; Dr. h.c. (St. John's Univ., Jamaica, N.Y.).
Central Bank of China, Paoching Road, Taipei, Taiwan.

Yu Pin, H.E. Cardinal Paul; Chinese ecclesiastic; b. 13 April 1901.
Ordained 28; Titular Bishop of Sozusa di Palestrina 36; Archbishop of Nanking 46-, (now in Taiwan); cr. Cardinal 69.
Cardinal Archbishop of Nanking, Taipei, Taiwan.

Yu Tai-chung; People's Repub. of China.
Commander People's Liberation Army Unit 6410, Kiangsu 68; Alt. mem. 9th Cen. Cttee. of CCP 69; Chair. Inner Mongolia Revolutionary Cttee. 70; First Sec. CCP Inner Mongolia 71; mem. 10th Cen. Cttee. of CCP 73.

Yukawa, Hideki, D.SC.; Japanese physicist; b. 23 Jan. 1907; ed. Kyoto Univ.
Lecturer, Kyoto Univ. 32, Osaka Univ. 33; Asst. Prof. Osaka Univ. 36; Prof. of Physics, Kyoto Univ. 39-70 (on leave of absence 48-52), Prof. Emeritus 70-; Visiting Prof., Inst. for Advanced Study, Princeton 48-49; Prof. of Physics, Columbia Univ. 51-; Imperial Prize, Japan Acad. 40; Order of Decoration of Japan 43; mem. Japan Acad. 46; Foreign Assoc., Nat. Acad. of Sciences, U.S. 49; Nobel Prize for Physics 49; Prof. Emeritus (Osaka Univ.); Dir. Research Inst. for Fundamental Physics, Kyoto Univ. 53-70; Hon. Citizen of Kyoto; Hon. Dr. (Univs., of Paris and Moscow); Hon. mem. Royal Soc. of Edinburgh, Indian Acad. of Sciences, Accademia Nazionale dei Lincei; mem. Pontificia Academia Scientiarum; foreign mem. Royal Soc. London.
Yukawa Hall, Kyoto University, Kyoto; Izumigawa, Shimogamo, Sakyo-ku, Kyoto, Japan.

Yukawa, Morio; Japanese diplomatist (retd.) and government official; b. 23 Feb. 1908; ed. Tokyo Univ.
Entered Foreign Service 33; served U.K., Geneva; Dir. Econ. Stabilization Board, Cabinet 50-51; Dir. Econ. Affairs Bureau, Foreign Office 51-52; Minister-Counsellor to France 52-54; Dir. Int. Co-operation Bureau, Foreign Office 54-55; Dir. Econ. Affairs Bureau, Foreign Office 55-57; Amb. to Philippines 57-61; Deputy Vice-Minister, Foreign Office 61-63; Amb. to Belgium, Luxembourg and European Econ. Community 63-68, to U.K. 68-72; Grand Master of Ceremonies, Imperial Household 73-.
Hilltop, 5-10 Sanbancho, Chiyoda-ku, Tokyo 102, Japan.

Yusuf bin Sheikh Abdul Rahman, Tan Sri Datuk Chik Mohamed, P.M.N., S.P.M.P., J.P., O.B.E.; Malaysian politician; b. 3 March 1907; ed. Anderson School, Ipoh, Malaysia, Newton Coll. School, Devon, Exeter Coll., Oxford Univ., Inner Temple, London.
Founder mem. Perak Malay League, elected Pres. 47; founder mem. UMNO, Vice-Pres. 48-50, Vice-Pres. UMNO, Malaya 51-54; Dato Bendahara, Perak; mem. Perak State Council 48-54, Fed. Legislative Council 48-54; Speaker House of Reps., Malaysia 64-; Asst. Food Controller, Perak; mem. several cttees. of civic orgs. and dir. numerous companies.
Parliament House, Lake Gardens, Kuala Lumpur; Home: No. 1, Jalan Clifford, Kuala Lumpur, Malaysia.

Z

Zafrulla Khan, Sir Muhammad, K.C.S.I., B.A., LL.B., HON.LL.D. (Cantab); Pakistani politician; b. 6 Feb. 1893; ed. Govt. Coll., Lahore, and King's Coll., London.
Barrister-at-Law (Lincoln's Inn); Advocate, Sialkot, Punjab 14-16; practised Lahore High Court 16-35; mem. Punjab Legislative Council 26-35; del. Indian Round Table Confs. 30, 31, 32; del. Joint Select Cttee. of Parl. on Indian Reforms 33; Pres. All-India Muslim League 31; mem. Gov.-Gen.'s Exec. Council 35-41; leader Indian del. to Assembly of LN. 39; Agent-Gen. of Govt. of India in China 42; Judge Fed. Court of India 41-June 47; Constitutional Adviser to H.H. Ruler of Bhopal June-Dec. 47; Leader Pakistan Del. to Annual Session of UN Gen. Assembly Sept.-Nov. 47; Minister of Foreign Affairs and Commonwealth Relations, Govt. of Pakistan Dec. 47; Leader Pakistan Del. to UN Security Council on India-Pakistan dispute 48-54, and to sessions of UN Gen. Assembly 47-54; Leader Pakistan del. to San Francisco Conf. on Japanese Peace Treaty 51; Leader Pakistan Del. to SEATO Conf. Manila 54; Judge at the Int. Court of Justice, The Hague 54-61, Vice-Pres. 58-61; Perm. Rep. of Pakistan to UN 61-64; Judge, Int. Court of Justice 64-73, Pres. 70-73; Pres. 17th session UN General Assembly 62-63.
Publ. *Islam: Its Meaning for Modern Man* 62.
16 Gressenhall Road, London, S.W.18, England.

Zahir, Abdul; Afghan politician; b. 3 May 1910, Lagham; ed. Habibia High School, Kabul and Columbia and Johns Hopkins Univs., U.S.A.
Practised medicine in U.S.A. before returning to Kabul 43; Chief Doctor, Municipal Hospitals, Kabul 43-50; Deputy Minister of Health 50-55, Minister 55-58; Amb. to Pakistan 58-61; Chair. House of the People 61-64, 65-69; Deputy Prime Minister and Minister of Health 64-65; Amb. to Italy 69-71; Prime Minister June 71-Dec. 72.
c/o Office of the Prime Minister, Kabul, Afghanistan.

Zakaria, Haji Mohamed Ali; Malaysian diplomatist; b. 8 Oct. 1929, Kuala Lumpur; ed. Univ. of Malaya, Singapore, and London School of Econs.
Served in various capacities in Malaysian Civil Service; entered foreign service 56; Second Sec., later Information Officer, London 57-59; First Sec., later Counsellor, Perm. Mission of Malaya at UN 59-65; Deputy Sec. (Gen. Affairs), Ministry of Foreign Affairs 65-67; Deputy High Commr. to U.K. 67-68; High Commr. to Canada 68; Perm. Rep. to UN May 70-75.
c/o Ministry of Foreign Affairs, Kuala Lumpur, Malaysia.

Zeidler, D. R., C.B.E., M.SC., F.R.A.C.I., M.I.CHEM.E., F.A.I.M.; Australian business executive; b. 18 March 1918; ed. Scotch Coll., Univ. of Melbourne.
With CSIRO 42-52; joined ICI Australia Research Dept. 52, Research Man. 53-59, Devt. Man. 59-62, Controller Dyes and Fabrics Group 62-63, Dir. 63-71, Man. Dir. 71-72, Deputy Chair. 72-73; Chair. ICI Australia Ltd. May 73-; Chair. Dulux Australia Ltd., Nobel (Australasia) Pty. Ltd.; Dir. Commercial Bank of Australia Ltd., ICI N.Z. Ltd.; mem. Commonwealth Immigration Cttee. on Overseas Professional Qualifications.
ICI Australia Ltd., ICI House, 1, Nicholson Street, Melbourne; Home: 2A Grange Avenue, Canterbury, Vic. 3126, Australia.

Zobel de Ayala, Jaime, B.A.; Philippine industrialist and diplomatist; b. 18 July 1934; ed. La Salle, Madrid, Harvard Univ.
Chairman of Board, Ayala Corpn.; Attorney-in-Fact, Ayala Corpn. and subsidiaries; Dir. Shell Refining Co., Shell Co. of the Philippines, Central Azucarera Don Pedro, San Miguel Corpn.; Amb. to U.K. 71-74; Pres. Cultural Centre of the Philippines 69-70; Comendador de la Orden del Merito Civil (Spain).
c/o Ministry of Foreign Affairs, Manila, Philippines.

Weights and Measures

Principal weights and units of measurement in common use as alternatives to the Metric and Imperial systems.

WEIGHT

Unit	Country	Imperial Equivalent	Metric Equivalent
Acheintaya	Burma	360.1 lb.	163.33 kg.
Arroba	Philippines	25.35 lb.	11.5 kg.
Baht, Bat, Kyat or Tical	Burma, Thailand (Old Chinese System)	0.266 oz.	7.56 gm.
	Siamese system	0.529 oz.	14.11 gm.
Beittha or Viss	Burma	3.601 lb.	1.63 kg.
Candareen or Fen	China (Old system)	0.0133 oz.	0.378 gm.
	China (New system)	0.010 oz.	0.283 gm.
	Hong Kong	0.0133 oz.	0.378 gm.
Candy	Sri Lanka	560 lb.	254 kg.
	India—Bombay	560 lb.	254 kg.
	India—Madras	500 lb.	226.8 kg.
	Burma	80 tons	81 metric tons
Catty, Chang, Chin, Gin, Kan, Kati, Katti, Kin or Kon	China (Old system)	1.333 lb.	0.603 kg.
	China (New system)	1.102 lb.	0.5 kg.
	Hong Kong	1.333 lb.	0.603 kg.
	Indonesia	1.362 lb.	0.617 kg.
	Japan	1.323 lb.	0.6 kg.
	Malaysia and Singapore	1.333 lb.	0.603 kg.
	Thailand (Old Chinese system)	1.333 lb.	0.603 kg.
	Siamese	1.333 lb.	0.603 kg.
Charak	Afghanistan	3.894 lb.	17.278 kg.
Chittack	India	2.057 oz.	57.5 gm.
Fan	China (Old system)	0.0133 oz.	0.378 gm.
	China (New system)	0.011 oz.	0.311 gm.
	Hong Kong	0.0133 oz.	0.378 gm.
Hyaku-mé	Japan	13.226 oz.	374.85 gm.
Kharwar	Afghanistan	1,246.2 lb.	564.528 kg.
Khord	Afghanistan	3.89 oz.	110.28 gm.
Koyan	Malaysia and Singapore	5,333.3 lb.	2,419 kg.
Kwan or Kan	Japan	8.267 lb.	3.749 kg.
Liang, Leung or Tael	China (Old system)	1.333 oz.	37.8 gm.
	China (New system)	1.102 oz.	31.18 gm.
	Hong Kong	1.333 oz.	37.8 gm.
Mace	China (Old system)	0.133 oz.	3.78 gm.
	China (New system)	0.110 oz.	3.11 gm.
	Hong Kong	0.133 oz.	3.78 gm.
Maund	Bangladesh	82.28 lb.	37.29 kg.
	India—Government	82.28 lb.	37.29 kg.
	India—Bombay	28 lb.	12.7 kg.
	India—Madras	25 lb.	11.34 kg.
	Pakistan	82.28 lb.	37.29 kg.
Me	Japan	0.133 oz.	3.78 gm.
Momme	Japan	0.133 oz.	3.78 gm.
Neal	Cambodia	1.323 lb.	0.6 kg.
Ngamus	Burma	0.288 oz.	8.2 gm.
Nijo	Japan	0.529 oz.	15.02 gm.
Pa	India	8.288 oz.	235 gm.

[*continued*

WEIGHT—*continued*]

UNIT	COUNTRY	IMPERIAL EQUIVALENT	METRIC EQUIVALENT
Picul, Pikul, Picol, Taam or Tam	China (Old system)	133.33 lb.	60.48 kg.
	China (New system)	110.23 lb.	50 kg.
	Hong Kong	133.33 lb.	60.48 kg.
	India	133.33 lb.	60.48 kg.
	Indo-China (Old Chinese system)	133.33 lb.	60.48 kg.
	Indo-China (Siamese system)	132.277 lb.	60 kg.
	Indonesia	136.16 lb.	61.76 kg.
	Japan	132.276 lb.	60 kg.
	Malaysia and Singapore	133.33 lb.	60.48 kg.
	Sabah and Sarawak	135.64 lb.	61.53 kg.
	Philippines	139.44 lb.	63.25 kg.
	Thailand (Old Chinese system)	133.33 lb.	60.48 kg.
	Thailand (Siamese system)	133.5 lb.	60.55 kg.
Pood or Poud	U.S.S.R.	36.113 lb.	16.38 kg.
Pyi	Burma	4.69 lb.	2.13 kg.
Quintal	Indonesia	220.462 lb.	100 kg.
	Philippines	101.4 lb.	46 kg.
Seer	Afghanistan	15.58 lb.	7.07 kg.
	India—Government	2.057 lb.	0.93 kg.
	India—Madras	0.617 lb.	0.28 kg.
	India—Bombay	0.72 lb.	0.33 kg.
	Pakistan	2.057 lb.	0.93 kg.
Tahil	Malaysia and Singapore	1⅓ oz.	37.8 gm.
Tan	China (Old system)	133.3 lb.	60.48 kg.
	China (New system)	110.23 lb.	50 kg.
Tola	India and Pakistan	180 grains	11.66 gm.
Visham	India	3 lb.	1.36 kg.
Viss	Burma	3.601 lb.	1.63 kg.

LENGTH

UNIT	COUNTRY	IMPERIAL EQUIVALENT	METRIC EQUIVALENT
Archinne	U.S.S.R.	27.996 in.	71.1 cm.
Ch am am	Cambodia	9.84 in.	24.9 cm.
Chang	China	3.45 yd.	3.34 m.
Ch'ek or Foot	Hong Kong—by statute	14⅝ in.	37.16 cm.
	Hong Kong—in practice	14.14 in.	35.82 cm.
Cheung	Hong Kong	4.063 yd.	3.698 m.
Ch'ih	China (Old system)	35.814 in.	91 cm.
	China (New system)	13.123 in.	33.27 cm.
Cho	Japan (length)	119.302 yd	109.12 cm.
Chung	South Korea		
Coss	India—Bengal, Pakistan and Bangladesh	2,000 yd.	1920.2 m.
Cubit	Burma	18 in.	45.72 cm.
Danda	India, Pakistan and Bangladesh	2 yd.	1.83 m.
El, Ell or Ella	Indonesia	27.08 in.	68.8 cm.
	Malaysia and Singapore	1 yd.	0.914 m.
	Sabah	1 yd.	0.914 m.
Fen	China	0.13 in.	0.33 cm.

[*continued*

LENGTH—*continued*]

UNIT	COUNTRY	IMPERIAL EQUIVALENT	METRIC EQUIVALENT
Garwode	Burma	12.727 miles	20.44 km.
Gereh-gaz-sha	Afghanistan	2.6 in.	6.6 cm.
Girah	Pakistan	2.25 in.	5.7 cm.
Gudge, Gueza, Guz or Ver	India—Bengal	36 in.	91.44 cm.
	India—Bombay	27 in.	68.58 cm.
	India—Madras	33 in.	83.82 cm.
	Pakistan and Bangladesh	36 in.	91.44 cm.
Hat	Cambodia	19.68 in.	50 cm.
Hath	India, Pakistan and Bangladesh	18 in.	45.72 cm.
Hiro	Japan	1.657 yd.	1.516 m.
Jareeb	Pakistan—Punjab	22 yd.	20.117 m.
Jo	Japan	3.314 yd.	3.032 m.
Kawtha	Burma	3.182 miles	5.116 km.
Ken	Japan South Korea	1.988 yd.	1.82 m.
Keup	Thailand	9.07 in.	23.04 cm.
Koss	India—Bengal	2,000 yd.	1,828.8 m.
Lan	Burma	2 yd.	1.83 m.
Li or Lei	China (Old system)	706–745 yd.	645–681 m.
	China (New system)	546.8 yd.	500 m.
	Hong Kong	706–745 yd.	645–681 m.
	South Korea	2.44 miles	3.926 km.
Niew	Thailand	0.820 in.	2.09 cm.
Oke thapa	Burma	70 yd.	64 m.
Paal	Java	1,647 yd.	1,506 m.
	Sumatra	2,025 yd.	1,851.7 m.
Palgate	Burma	1 in.	2.54 cm.
Pulgada	Philippines	0.914 in.	2.31 cm.
Ri	Japan—length	2.44 miles	3.926 km.
	Japan—marine measure	1 nautical mile	1.85 km.
Sawk	Burma	19.8 in.	50.29 cm.
Sen	Thailand	43.74 yd.	40 m.
Shaku	Japan	11.93 in.	30.3 cm.
Sun	Japan	1.193 in.	3.02 cm.
Taing	Burma	2.43 miles	3.911 km.
Tar	Burma	3.5 yd.	3.2 m.
Taung	Burma	18 in.	45.72 cm.
Tjengkal	Indonesia	4 yd.	3.66 m.
Ts'un	China (Old system)	1.41 in.	3.58 cm.
	China (New system)	1.312 in.	3.33 cm.
	Hong Kong	1.41 in.	3.58 cm.
Ungul	India, Pakistan and Bangladesh	0.75 in.	1.9 cm.
Verst or Versta	U.S.S.R.	0.6629 miles	1.067 km.
Wah	Thailand	2.19 yd.	2 m.
Yote	Thailand	9.942 miles	16 km.
Yuzamar	Burma	47.121 miles	75.83 km.

CAPACITY

Unit	Country	Imperial Equivalent	Metric Equivalent
Bag	Burma	27 galls.	122.75 lit.
Bottle	Sri Lanka	0.16 galls.	0.73 lit.
Cavan	Philippines	16.5 galls.	75 lit.
Chupa	Philippines	0.0825 galls.	0.37 lit.
Chupak	Malaysia and Singapore	0.25 galls.	1.14 lit.
Ganta	Philippines	0.660 galls.	3 lit.
Gantang	Malaysia and Singapore	1 gall.	4.55 lit.
	Indonesia (used mainly for rice)	1.887 galls.	8.58 lit.
Go	Japan	1.27 gills	0.17 lit.
Gwe	Burma	4.5 galls.	20.45 lit.
Koku	Japan	39.682 galls.	180.38 lit.
Kwe	Burma	4.5 galls.	20.45 lit.
Kwien	Thailand	439.95 galls.	2,000 lit.
Pau	Singapore	½ pint	0.28 lit.
Pyi	Burma	0.56 galls.	2.56 lit.
Sale	Burma	0.14 galls.	0.64 lit.
Sat	Thailand	4.40 galls.	20 lit.
Sayut	Burma	1.12 galls.	5.12 lit.
Seik	Burma	2.250 galls.	10.24 lit.
Ser	India	1.76 pints	1 lit.
Shaku	Japan	0.127 gill	0.017 lit.
Sho	Japan	0.397 galls.	1.8 lit.
Suk	South Korea	38.682 galls.	175.8 lit.
Tanan	Thailand	0.22 galls.	1 lit.
Tin, Tunn, Tin-han or basket	Burma (Thamardi)	9 galls.	40.91 lit.
Tinaja	Philippines	10.56 galls.	48 lit.
To	Japan	3.97 galls.	17.76 lit.

AREA

Unit	Country	Imperial Equivalent	Metric Equivalent
Bahoe or Bouw	Indonesia	1.7536 acres	.709 ha.
Bigha	India	0.625 acres	.253 ha.
	Pakistan—Punjab	1,620 sq. yds.	1354.5 m.^{2}
	Bangladesh	1,600 sq. yds.	1337.8 m.^{2}
Bu	Japan	3.95 sq. yds.	3.3 m.^{2}
Cawny or Cawnie	India—Madras	1.322 acres	.534 ha.
Chattak	Bangladesh	5 sq. yds.	4.18 m.^{2}
Ch'ing	China (New system)	16.47 acres	6.66 ha.
Cho	Japan (square measure)	2.45 acres	1 ha.
Chungbo or Jongbo	Korea	2.45 acres	1 ha.
Cottah	Bangladesh	80 sq. yds.	66.89 m.^{2}
Jemba	Malaysia and Singapore	16 sq. yds.	13.38 m.^{2}
Marabba	Pakistan	25 acres	10.12 ha.
Maw	China	0.165 acres	0.65 ha.
Morabba	Pakistan—Punjab	25 acres	10.12 ha.
Mou or Mow	China	0.165 acres	0.065 ha.
Ngan	Thailand	478.4 sq. yds.	400 m.^{2}
Paal	Indonesia	561.16 acres	227.08 ha.
Rai	Thailand	0.395 acres	0.16 ha.
Se	Japan	118.61 sq. yds.	48 m.^{2}
Square	Sri Lanka	100 sq. yds.	40.47 m.^{2}
Tan	Japan	0.245 acres	0.1 ha.
Tsubo	Japan	3.95 sq. yds.	3.3 m.^{2}

DEPTH

Unit	Country	Imperial Equivalent	Metric Equivalent
Sazhene	U.S.S.R.	1 fathom	1.83 m.

QUANTITY

Unit	Country	Quantity
Crore	India, Pakistan, Bangladesh	10,000,000 (1,00,00,000)
Lakh	India, Pakistan, Bangladesh	100,000 (1,00,000)

METRIC TO IMPERIAL CONVERSIONS

Metric Units	Imperial Units	To Convert Metric into Imperial Units Multiply by:	To Convert Imperial into Metric Units Multiply by:
Weight			
Gramme (gm.)	Ounce (Avoirdupois)	0.035274	28.3495
Kilogramme (kg.)	Pound (lb.)	2.204622	0.453592
Metric ton ('000 kg.)	Short ton (2,000 lb.)	1.102311	0.907185
	Long ton (2,240 lb.)	0.984207	1.016047
	(The short ton is in general use in the U.S.A., while the long ton is normally used in Britain and the Commonwealth.)		
Length			
Centimetre (cm.)	Inch	0.393701	2.54
Metre (m.)	Yard (=3 feet)	1.09361	0.9144
Kilometre (km.)	Mile	0.62137	1.609344
Capacity			
Litre (lit.)	Gallon (=8 pints)	0.219969	4.54609
	Gallon (U.S.)	0.264172	3.78541
Area			
Square metre ($m.^2$)	Square yard	1.19599	0.836127
Hectare (ha.)	Acre	2.47105	0.404686
Square kilometre ($km.^2$)	Square mile	0.386102	2.589988

SYSTEMS OF MEASUREMENT

WEIGHT

Afghanistan	Kharwar = 80 Seer
	Seer = 4 Charak
	Charak = 16 Khord
Burma	Candy = 500 Acheintaya
	Acheintaya = 10 Beittha or Viss
	Beittha or Viss = 200 Ngamus
China	Picul = 100 Catty
	Catty = 16 Liang
	Liang = 10 Mace
	Mace = 10 Fan or Candareen
India, Pakistan and Bangladesh	Maund = 40 Seer
	Seer = 16 Chittack
	Pa = 20 Tola
Japan	Picul = 16 Kwan (Kan)
	Kwan = 16 Hyaku-mé
	Hyaku-mé = 20 Nijo
	Nijo = 5 Me or Mommé
Malaysia	Koyan = 40 Picul
Philippines	Quintal = 4 Arroba
Thailand	Picul = 100 Catty or Kon
	Catty = 40 Baht or Kyat

LENGTH

Burma	Garwoke = 4 Kawtha
	Oke thapa = 20 Tar
	Tar = 7 Cubit or Taung
	Lan = 4 Cubit or Taung
	Cubit = 18 Palgate
Cambodia	Hat = 2 Chamam
China	Li = 1,500 Ch'
	Ch'ih = 10 Ts u
	Ts'un = 10 Fen
Hong Kong	Cheung = 10 Chek
	Chek Ch='ih (see China)
India, Pakistan and Bangladesh	Coss = 1,000 Danda
	Danda = 2 Gudge
	Gudge = 2 Hath
	Hath = 24 Ungul
Japan	Jo = 2 Hiro
	Hiro = 5 Shaku
	Shaku = 10 Sun
Thailand	Sen = 20 Wah
	Wah = 8 Keup

CAPACITY

Burma	Bag = 3 Tin
	Tin = 2 Kwe
	Kwe = 2 Seik
	Seik = 2 Sayut
	Sayut = 2 Pyi
Japan	To = 10 Sho
	Sho = 10 Go
	Go = 10 Shaku
Philippines	Cavan = 25 Ganta
	Tinaja = 15 Ganta
	Ganta = 8 Chupa
Thailand	Kwien = 100 Sat
	Sat = 20 Tanan

AREA

China	Ch'ing = 100 Mou (Mow)
Indonesia	Paal = 320 Bahoe or Bouw
Japan	Cho = 10 Bu or Tan
	Bu = 2 Se
	Se = 30 Tsubo
Pakistan	Bigha = 20 Cottah
	Cottah = 16 Chattah
Thailand	Ngan = 2½ Rai

Calendars and Time Reckoning

THE MUSLIM CALENDAR

The Muslim era dates from July 16th, A.D. 622, which was the beginning of the Arab year in which the *Hijra*, Muhammad's flight from Mecca to Medina, took place. The Muslim or Hijra Calendar is lunar, each year having 354 or 355 days, the extra day being intercalated eleven times every thirty years. Accordingly the beginning of the Hijra year occurs earlier in the Gregorian Calendar by a few days each year. The Muslim year 1395 A.H. began on January 14th, 1975.

The year is divided into the following months:

1. Muharram	30 days	7. Rajab	30 days
2. Safar	29 ,,	8. Shaaban	29 ,,
3. Rabia I	30 ,,	9. Ramadan	30 ,,
4. Rabia II	29 ,,	10. Shawwal	29 ,,
5. Jumada I	30 ,,	11. Dhu'l-Qa'da	30 ,,
6. Jumada II	29 ,,	12. Dhu'l-Hijja	29 or 30 days

The Hijra Calendar is used for religious purposes throughout the Islamic world and is the official calendar in Saudi Arabia and the Yemen. In most Arab countries it is used side by side with the Gregorian Calendar for official purposes, but in Indonesia, Malaysia and Pakistan the Gregorian Calendar has replaced it.

PRINCIPAL MUSLIM FESTIVALS

New Year: 1st Muharram. The first ten days of the year are regarded as holy, especially the tenth.

Ashoura: 10th Muharram. Celebrates the first meeting of Adam and Eve after leaving Paradise, also the ending of the Flood and the death of Hussain, grandson of Muhammad. The feast is celebrated with fairs and processions.

Mouloud (*Birth of Muhammad*): 12th Rabia I.

Leilat al Meiraj (*Ascension of Muhammad*): 27th Rajab.

Ramadan (*Month of Fasting*): Begins 1st Ramadan.

Id ul Fitr or **Id ul Saghir** or **Küçük Bayram** (*The Small Feast*): Three days beginning 1st Shawwal. This celebration follows the constraint of the Ramadan fast.

Id ul Adha or **Id al Kabir** or **Büyük Bayram** (*The Great Feast, Feast of the Sacrifice*): Four days beginning on 10th Dhu'l-Hijja. The principal Muslim festival, commemorating Abraham's sacrifice and coinciding with the pilgrimage to Mecca. Celebrated by the sacrifice of a sheep, by feasting and by donations to the poor.

Hijra Year	1395		1396		1397	
New Year . . .	Jan. 14th,	1975	Jan. 3rd,	1976	Dec. 23rd,	1976
Ashoura . . .	Jan. 23rd,	,,	Jan. 12th,	,,	Jan. 1st,	1977
Mouloud . . .	March 25th,	,,	March 13th,	,,	March 3rd,	,,
Leilat al Meiraj .	Aug. 5th,	,,	July 24th,	,,	July 14th,	,,
Ramadan begins .	Sept. 7th,	,,	Aug. 26th,	,,	Aug. 16th,	,,
Id ul Fitr . .	Oct. 7th,	,,	Sept. 25th,	,,	Sept. 15th,	,,
Id ul Adha . .	Dec. 14th,	,,	Dec. 2nd,	,,	Nov. 22nd,	,,

Note: Local determinations may vary by one day from those given here.

HINDU CALENDARS

In India there are two principal Hindu calendars, the Vikrama and the Saka.

The Vikrama or Samvat era is dated from a victory of King Vikramaditya in 58 B.C. The year 1977 of the Christian era therefore corresponds to 2034 in the Vikrama era. The New Year begins in March or April in eastern India, but in October or November in the western States.

The Saka era, beginning in A.D. 78, is attributed to the Saka King Kanishka. 1976 of the Christian era corresponds with 1898 of the Saka era.

The Official Calendar in India, adopted in 1957, is based on the Saka year but has been fixed in relation to the Gregorian calendar so that New Year (Chaitra 1) falls always on March 22nd, except in Leap Years when it falls on March 21st. This calendar is used for dating official documents, for All-India Radio broadcasts, and other official purposes; however, the Gregorian calendar is still widely used in India.

FESTIVALS

Holi: Spring Festival in honour of Krishna, usually held in March.

Mahendra Jatra: Nepalese festival to ensure the monsoon rains; June.

Dussera: Ten-day festival of Durga; early October.

Diwali: Festival of lights, dedicated to Lakshmi; late October.

There is also a large number of local agricultural and commemorative festivals.

BUDDHIST AND THE SOUTH INDIAN CALENDARS

The Buddhist era is attributed to the death of Buddha, historically dated at about 483 B.C. The era in use in fact dates from 544 B.C., making the year 1976 of the Christian era equal to 2519 of the Buddhist era. The Jain era, based on the death of Mahavira, starts in 528 B.C., making A.D. 1976 equal to 2503.

In south and south-east Asia there is widespread use of a lunar year of 354 days, with months of alternately 29 or 30 days, and with extra (intercalary) months approximately every third year. Under this system New Year may fall in either April or March. In Burma, New Year is regularly on April 13th. The Burmese era, the *Khaccapancha*, is ascribed to the ruler Popa Sawrahan, and begins in A.D. 638. 1976 of the Gregorian calendar is equivalent to 1338 B.E.

Sri Lanka adopted the Buddhist calendar as its official and commercial calendar in 1966. Sunday is treated as a normal working day, while the lunar quarter days (Poya days) are public holidays; some of these are two-day holidays. New Year in on April 13th or 14th.

Thailand used the Burmese calendar until 1889, when a new civil era was introduced commemorating the centenary of the first king of Bangkok. Since 1909 a calendar based on the year 543 B.C. (traditionally the year of Gautama Buddha's attainment of nirvana) has been in official use. The months have been adapted to correspond with those of the Gregorian calendar, but New Year is on April 1st every year. In this calendar, the *Pra Putta Sakarat*, A.D. 1977 is equivalent to 2519.

FESTIVALS

The principal festivals in the Buddhist calendars are the New Year and the spring and autumn equinox, and local festivals connected with important pagodas.

THE CHINESE CALENDAR

China has both lunar and solar systems of dividing the year. The lunar calendar contains twelve months of 29 or 30 days, and in each period of 19 years 7 intercalary months are inserted at appropriate intervals. In order not to disturb the twelve-month cycle these extra months bear the same title as that which has preceded them. The intercalary months may not be introduced after the first, eleventh or twelfth month of any year.

The solar year used by the peasant community of China begins regularly on February 5th of the Gregorian calendar, and is divided into 24 sections of 14, 15 or 16 days. This calendar is not upset by the discrepant cycle of the moon, and is therefore suitable for the regulation of agriculture.

Until the Revolution of 1911 years were named according to a sixty-year cycle, made up of ten stems (*Ban*) and twelve branches (*Jy*). Each year of the cycle has a composite name composed of a different combination of stem and branch. Similar sixty-year cycles of year-names have been in use in Thailand and Japan at various times.

Since 1911 years have been dated from the Revolution as Years of the Republic; A.D. 1977 is the 66th year of the Republican era. In the People's Republic of China the Gregorian system is used.

Japan has used the Gregorian system since 1873, but a National Calendar has also been introduced, derived from the traditional date of accession of the first Emperor, Zinmu, in 660 B.C. The year A.D. 1977 corresponds to 2636 of this era.

STANDARD TIME

The following table gives the standard time adopted in the various countries and territories covered in this book, in relation to Greenwich Mean Time (G.M.T.). For the U.S.S.R., figures refer to Zone time, one hour behind Standard time.

+4
- U.S.S.R. (Ashkhabad)

+4½
- Afghanistan

+5
- Maldives
- Pakistan
- U.S.S.R. (Alma-Ata, Karaganda, Frunze)

+5½
- Bhutan
- India
- Nepal
- Sri Lanka

+6
- Bangladesh
- China (Tibet A.R.)
- U.S.S.R. (Novosibirsk, Krasnoyarsk)

+6½
- Burma
- Cocos (Keeling) Is.

+7
- Cambodia
- China (Chungking, Lanchow)
- Indonesia (Sumatra, Java, Bali, Madura)
- Laos
- Mongolia (Western)
- Thailand
- U.S.S.R. (Irkutsk)
- Viet-Nam

+7½
- Peninsular Malaysia
- Singapore

+8
- Australia (W. Australia)
- Brunei
- China (Peking, Shanghai)
- East Timor
- Hong Kong
- Indonesia (Kalimantan, Celebes)
- Macao
- Malaysia (East)
- Mongolia (Eastern)
- Philippines
- Taiwan
- U.S.S.R. (Yakutsk)

+8½
- China (Harbin)

+9
- Indonesia (Moluccas, W. Irian)
- Japan
- Korea
- U.S.S.R. (Khabarovsk, Vladivostok)

+9½
- Australia (Northern Territory, South Australia)

+10
- Australia (Vic., N.S.W., Qld., Tas.)
- Caroline Is.
- Guam
- Mariana Is.
- Papua New Guinea (excl. Solomon Is.)
- U.S.S.R. (Magadan, Sakhalin)

+11
- New Caledonia
- New Hebrides
- Solomon Is.
- Truk Is.
- U.S.S.R. (Petropavlovsk, Kamchatskii)

+11½
- Nauru
- Norfolk Is.

+12
- Fiji
- Gilbert Is.
- Marshall Is.
- New Zealand (Chatham Is. +12¼)
- Tuvalu
- U.S.S.R. (Anadyr)
- Wallis and Futuna Is.

+13
- Tonga

−11
- American Samoa
- Niue
- Tokelau Is.
- Western Samoa

−10½
- Cook Is.

−10
- French Polynesia
- Hawaii

−9
- Pitcairn Is.

Research Institutes

Associations and institutions studying the Far East and Australasia

(*See also* Regional Organizations—Education *in Part I.*)

AFGHANISTAN

Anjumani Tarikh (*Historical Society*): Kabul; f. 1931; to study and promote international knowledge of the history of Afghanistan; Head Dr. M. Yakub Wahidi; publs. *Aryana* (quarterly, in Pashtu and Dari) and *Afghanistan* (English and French, quarterly).

AUSTRALIA

Australian Institute of International Affairs: Box E 181, Post Office, Canberra; f. 1932; 2,177 mems.; brs. in all States; Pres. Rt. Hon. Sir Garfield Barwick; Dir. Sir Laurence McIntyre; publs. *The Australian Outlook* (3 times yearly), *World Review* (3 times yearly), *Dyason House Papers* (5 times yearly).

Centre of South-East Asian Studies: Monash University, Clayton, Vic. 3168; Dir. J. A. C. Mackie, M.A.

Faculty of Asian Studies: Australian National University, Box 4, P.O., Canberra, A.C.T. 2600; Dean Prof. A. H. Johns.

Research School of Pacific Studies: Australian National University, Box 4, G.P.O. Canberra, A.C.T. 2601; Dir. Prof. Wang Gungwu; publs. *Journal of Pacific History, Bulletin of Indonesian Economic Studies, Papers in Far Eastern History.*

AUSTRIA

Afro-Asiatisches Institut in Wien: A-1090 Vienna, Türkenstrasse 3; f. 1959; cultural and other exchanges between Austria and African and Asian countries, lectures, economic and social research, seminars; library of 1,000 vols.; Gen. Sec. A. Grünfelder.

Institut für Japanologie der Universität Wien (*Inst. for Japanese Studies*): A-1010 Vienna, Universitätsstrasse 7; f. 1965; Chair. Prof. Dr. Josef Kreiner; publ. *Beiträge zur Japanologie* (irregular).

Institut für Sinologie der Universität Wien: Rathausstrasse 19/9 A-1010 Vienna; Dir. Prof. Dr. Otto Ladstätter.

BANGLADESH

Bangladesh Economic Association: c/o Economics Dept., Dacca University, Dacca; f. 1958 to promote economic research; Pres. Dr. Mazharul Huq; Sec. Dr. S. R. Bose.

Bangladesh Institute of Development Studies: Adamjee Court, Motijheel Commercial Area, Dacca 2; f. 1957; basic research on development; training in socio-economic analysis and research methodology for its professional mems. and for mems. of other organizations; library of 35,000 vols.; Member-in-charge Dr. Mosharaff Hussain; publ. *Bangladesh Development Studies* (quarterly).

Varendra Research Museum: Rajshahi; f. 1910, under control of University of Rajshahi since 1964; investigation and encouragement of history, archaeology, anthropology, literature, and art; collection and preservation of archaeological and other relics, ancient MSS., etc., and publication of original works on these subjects; library of about 10,000 vols.; 7,570 items in museum, including 4,500 ancient MSS.; Dir. Dr. M. Rahman, M.A., PH.D., F.R.A.S.; publ. *Journal of the Varendra Research Museum* (annually).

BELGIUM

Hoger Instituut voor Oosterse, Oosteuropese en Afrikaanse Taalkunde en Geschiedenis (*Institute of Oriental, East European and African Philology and History*): Universiteitstraat 16, Ghent; attached to the State University of Ghent; f. 1957; Pres. W. Couvreur.

Institut Orientaliste: Faculté de Philosophie et Lettres de l'Université Catholique de Louvain, Redingenstr. 16, 3000-Louvain; f. 1936; Pres. Prof. J. Ries; publs. *Le Muséon* (periodical), *Bibliothèque du Muséon, Publications de l'Institut Orientaliste de Louvain* (*P.I.O.L.*).

BULGARIA

Research Centre for Asia and Africa: Dept. of Philosophy, Economics and Law, Bulgarian Academy of Sciences, "7 Noemvri" 1, Sofia; f. 1957; Dir. Acad. E. Kamenov; publ. *Afrikano-Aziatski Problemi.*

BURMA

Burma Council of World Affairs: Rangoon; objects: to promote the study of Burmese and international questions so as to develop a body of informed opinion on world affairs and Burma's position in the international scene; organizes discussions, lectures, etc.; functions as the UN Association for Burma; Patron U Aung Tha Gyaw; Pres. U San Maung; Sec. U Khant.

Burma Research Society: Universities' Central Library, University Post Office, Rangoon; f. 1910 to promote cultural and scientific studies and research relating to Burma and neighbouring countries; 1,040 mems.; 855 vols.; Pres. U Tha Myat; Hon. Sec. Dr. Shein; publ. *Journal* (twice yearly).

International Institute of Advanced Buddhistic Studies: Kaba-aye Pagoda Compound, Rangoon; a government-supported centre for research and studies in Buddhist and allied subjects; library of 17,000 vols.; Dir. U Hpe Aung.

CAMBODIA

Institut Bouddhique: Phnom-Penh; f. 1930; Buddhist studies and the Khmer culture; publs. *Dictionnaire Cambodgien* and numerous bulletins; Dir. Leang Hap An.

CANADA

Department of Asian Studies, University of British Columbia: Vancouver V6T 1W5, British Columbia; Head Prof. E. G. Pulleyblank.

CZECHOSLOVAKIA

Department of Oriental Studies: Slovak Academy of Sciences, Klemensova 27, Bratislava; f. 1970; 10 mems.; Pres. Dr. I. Doležal, Dr. V. Krupa; publ. *Asian and African Studies* (annual).

Oriental Institute: Czechoslovak Academy of Sciences, Prague I, Lázeňská 4; f. 1922; publs. *Archiv orientální* (quarterly), *Nový Orient* (monthly).

FRANCE

Association pour une meilleure connaissance de l'Asie (A.M.C.A.): 54 rue de Varenne, 75007 Paris; Dir. François Joyaux; publ. *Mondes Asiatiques* (quarterly).

Centre d'Etudes de l'Orient Contemporain: 13 rue du Four 75006 Paris; f. 1945; publ. *Cahiers de l'Orient Contemporain* (bi-monthly).

Centre de Hautes Etudes sur l'Afrique et l'Asie Modernes: 13 rue du Four, 75006 Paris; f. 1936; library of 9,000 vols.; Dir. G. R. MALÉCOT; publs. *L'Afrique et L'Asie Modernes* (quarterly), *Cahiers de l'Afrique et l'Asie* (irregular), *Langues et Dialectes d'Outre-Mer* (irregular), *Recherches et Documents du CHEAM* (irregular).

Ecole des Langues Orientales Anciennes: U.E.R. de Théologie et de Sciences Religieuses, 21 Rue d'Assas, 75006 Paris; Dir. Rev. P. D'AUDIBERT-CAILLE DU BOURGUET.

Institut National des Langues et Civilisations Orientales: 2 rue de Lille, Paris 7e.

Musée Cernuschi: 7 ave. Velasquez, Paris 8e; f. 1896; ancient and contemporary Chinese art; Dir. VADIME ELISSEEFF.

Musée Guimet (*Asiatic Dept. of National Museum*): 6 Place d'Iéna, 75116 Paris; f. 1889; library of 100,000 vols.; art, archaeology, religions, history, literature and music of India, Central Asia, Tibet, Afghanistan, China, Korea, Japan, Cambodia, Thailand, Laos, Burma and Indonesia; Chief Curator Mlle J. AUBOYER; Librarian Mlle A. HAUCHECORNE; publ. *Annales du Musée Guimet.*

Société Asiatique: 3 rue Mazarine, Paris 6e; f. 1822; library of 80,000 vols.; 500 mems.; Pres. C. CAHEN; Secs. Y. HERVOUET, M. SOYMIÉ, L. BAZIN; publs. *Journal Asiatique, Cahiers.*

Unité d'Enseignement et de Recherche (U.E.R.) Asie Orientale: Université Paris VII, 2 place Jussieu, 75221 Paris Cedex 05; f. 1971; Principal Officers H. MAËS (Japanese studies); Y. HERVOUËT; L. VANDERMEERSCH (Chinese studies); LI OGG (Korean studies); NGUYEN PHU PHONG (Vietnamese studies).

U.E.R. Etudes Slaves, Orientales, et Asiatiques: Université Paris-Vincennes, route de la Tourelle, 75571 Paris Cedex 12; Dir. Y HERVOUET.

U.E.R. Langues et Civilisations de l'Orient et de l'Afrique du Nord: Université de Paris III, 17 rue de la Sorbonne, 75230 Paris Cedex 05.

GERMAN DEMOCRATIC REPUBLIC

Arbeitsgruppe Geschichte Chinas, Zentralinstitut für Geschichte (Wissenschaftsbereich Allgemeine Geschichte): 108 Berlin, Clara-Zetkin-Str. 26; publ. *Orientalische Literaturzeitung* (monthly), *Mitteilungen* (annual).

Ostasiatische Sammlung des Staatliche Museen zu Berlin: Berlin, 102 Bodestrasse 1/3; Dir. BRUNO VOIGT.

Vorderasiatisches Museum: Berlin, 102 Bodestrasse 1/3; Dir. Prof. GERHARD RUDOLF MEYER.

FEDERAL REPUBLIC OF GERMANY

China-Institut: Johann Wolfgang von Goethe-Universität, D6 Frankfurt/Main, Dantestr. 4-6; Dir. Prof. Dr. TSUNG-TUNG CHANG.

Deutsch-Indische Gesellschaft e.V.: D-7000 Stuttgart 1, Charlottenplatz 17; Sec.-Gen. Dr. N. KLEIN; publ. *Indo-Asia* (quarterly).

Deutsche Orient-Gesellschaft: Museum für Vor- und Frühgeschichte, 1 Berlin 19, Schloss Charlottenburg, Langhansbau; f. 1898; 450 mems.; Pres. Dr. EVA NAGEL-STROMMENGER; Sec. Prof. Dr. VOLKMAR FRITZ; publs. *Mitteilungen, Wissenschaftliche Veröffentlichungen, Abhandlungen.*

Deutsches Orient-Institut: 2000 Hamburg 13, Mittelweg 150; f. 1960 to study modern Near and Middle East; library of 18,000 vols.; Dir. Dr. U. STEINBACH; publs. *Orient* (quarterly), *Mitteilungen* (irregular).

Institut für Asienkunde: 2000 Hamburg 13, Rothenbaumchaussee 32; f. 1956; research and documentation into all aspects of contemporary South, South-East and East Asia; Pres. Dr. W. RÖHL; Dir. Dr. W. DRAGUHN.

Museum für Islamische Kunst: Stiftung Preussischer Kulturbesitz, 1000 Berlin 33 (Dahlem), Takustrasse 40; f. 1904; Dir. Prof. Dr. KLAUS BRISCH.

Museum für Ostasiatische Kunst (*Museum of Far Eastern Art*): Berlin-Dahlem, Lansstr. 8; Dir. Prof. Dr. B. VON RAGUÉ.

Südasien-Institut der Universität Heidelberg: Heidelberg, Im Neuenheimer Feld 330; Dir. Prof. Dr. B. KNALL; Exec. Sec. Dr. D. HALCOUR.

HONG KONG

Centre of Asian Studies: University of Hong Kong; f. 1967; East and South-East Asia; Dir. Prof. FRANK H. H. KING, M.A., D.PHIL.; Research Officer STEVE S. K. CHIN; publs. monographs and occasional papers series, research guides and bibliographies (ISSN: HKO 441-1900); *Journal of Oriental Studies.*

Institute of Chinese Studies: Chinese University of Hong Kong, Shatin, New Territories; f. 1967; Dir. CHO-MING LI, K.B.E., PH.D., LL.D.

New Asia Institute of Advanced Chinese Studies and Research: New Asia College of the Chinese University of Hong Kong, Shatin, New Territories; Chinese history, philosophy and literature; section on South-East Asian studies; Dir. C. I. TANG, B.A.

Research Institute of Far Eastern Studies: Chung Chi College of the Chinese University of Hong Kong, Shatin, New Territories; publ. *Journal.*

HUNGARY

Institute for World Economics of the Hungarian Academy of Sciences (fmrly. Afro-Asian Research Centre): H-1531 Budapest, P.O. Box 36; f. 1965; library of 28,000 vols.; Dir. JÓZSEF BOGNÁR, C.M.; publs. *Studies on Developing Countries, Trends in World Economy, Abstracts of Hungarian Economic Literature.*

INDIA

Abul Kalam Azad Oriental Research Institute: Public Gardens, Hyderabad 4, Andhra Pradesh; f. 1959; research in history, philosophy, culture and languages; Pres. PADMA BHUSHAN MIR AKBAR ALI KHAN, M.P.; Hon. Gen. Sec. and Dir. KHWAJA MUHAMMAD AHMAD; publs. various.

All-India Oriental Conference: Bhandarkar Oriental Research Institute, Poona 4; f. 1919; 1,000 mems.; Pres. Prof. C. SIVARAMAMURTI; Sec. Prof. R. N. DANDEKAR; publs. *Proceedings of its Sessions, Index of Papers* (in 3 vols.).

Ancient Indian History and Kannada Research Institute: Karnatak University, Dharwar, Karnataka; Dir. Dr. S. H. RITTI, M.A., PH.D.

Anjuman-i-Islam Urdu Research Institute: 92 D. Nayoroji Rd., Bombay 1; f. 1947; graduate and postgraduate research in Urdu language and literature; library of 15,000 vols.; Dir. Z. H. MADANI; publs. *Nawa-e-Adab* (quarterly) and research books (in Urdu).

Asian Relations Organization: Sapru House, Barakhambra Rd., New Delhi; f. 1947 by the first Asian Relations Conference; objectives: (*a*) to promote the study and understanding of Asian problems and relations in their Asian and world aspects; (*b*) to foster friendly relations and co-operation among the peoples of Asia and between them and the rest of the world; and (*c*) to further their progress and well-being; Hon. Sec. B. SHIVA RAO; Joint Gen. Sec. A. APPADORAI.

Asian Research Centre, Institute of Economic Growth (fmrly. *Research Centre on Social and Economic Development in Asia*): University Enclave, Delhi 7; Dir. P. B. DESAI; Head Dr. T. N. MADAN; publs. *Studies in Asian Social Development* (occasional), *Contributions to Indian Sociology: New Series* (twice a year), *Asian Social Science Bibliography* (annual).

Asiatic Society of Bengal, The: 1 Park St., Calcutta; f. 1784; 696 mems.; Pres. Dr. B. MUKERJI, D.SC., M.D., F.N.A., F.A.S., F.A.A.S.; Gen. Sec. Dr. S. K. MITRA, M.A., LL.B., D.PHIL., F.A.S.; publs. *Journal* (4 issues a year), *Year Book, Bibliotheca Indica, Monographs,* etc.

Asiatic Society of Bombay: Town Hall, Bombay; f. 1804; 1,511 mems.; library of 225,013 vols.; Pres. Shri K. T. DESAI, B.A., LL.B.; Hon. Sec. Shri RUSI J. DARUWALA, B.COM., A.C.A.; publs. *Journal, Monographs, Annual reports,* quarterly lists of new accessions.

Bhandarkar Oriental Research Institute: Poona 411004; f. 1917; Sec. Dr. R. N. DANDEKAR, M.A., PH.D.; Curator Dr. G. K. BHAT, M.A., PH.D.; 580 mems.; library of 40,000 vols., 30,000 MSS.; publs. *Annals of the Bhandarkar Oriental Research Institute* (Parts I-IV published annually), *Bhandarkar Oriental Series, Bombay Sanskrit and Prakrit Series, Government Oriental Series,* Critical Editions of the *Mahabharata* and *Harivamisa.*

Bharatiya Vidya Bhavan: Chaupatty Rd., Bombay 7; f. 1938; objects are to conserve, develop and diffuse Indian culture; post-graduate courses in Indology; colleges of arts, science, commerce and engineering; college of journalism, advertisement and printing; schools of music, dancing, dramatic art; 1,000 mems.; library of 70,000 vols.; Pres. DHARAMSEY M. KHATAU; Vice-Pres. GIRDHARILAL MEHTA; Hon. Dir. Prof. J. H. DAVE, M.A., LL.B.; Joint Dir. and Exec. Sec. S. RAMAKRISHNAN; publs. *Bharatiya Vidya* (quarterly), *Samvid* (Sanskrit quarterly), *Bhavan's Journal* (fortnightly), *Samarpan* (Gujarati fortnightly), 10 vols. out of 11 of the *History and Culture of the Indian People,* and 53 research works under the *Singhi Jain Series,* 32 vols. of *Bharatiya Vidya Series,* 290 vols. of *Book University Series,* 25 vols. of *Pocket Gandhi Series* and 250 vols. of *General Series.*

K. R. Cama Oriental Institute and Library: 136 Bombay Samachar Marg, Fort, Bombay-23; f. 1916; 150 mems.; library of 15,000 vols. 1,750 MSS., 4,500 journals; Pres. ADI N. CHINOY; Secs. Dr. K. M. JAMASP-ASA, N. D. MINOCHEHR-HOMJI and Dr. H. E. EDULJEE; Librarian Miss H. B. TARAPOREWALA, B.A.; publ. *Journal* (annually).

Faculty of Oriental Learning and Theology (*Sanskri-Mahavidyalaya*): Banaras Hindu University, Varanasi 5, U.P.; Dean A. N. RAMNATH DIXIT.

G.N.J. Kendriya Sanskrit Vidyapeetha (*fmrly. Ganganatha Jha Research Institute*): Allahabad 211002, U.P.; f. 1943; research into Sanskrit and other Oriental languages; library of 13,700 vols., 16,000 MSS.; Chair. Dr. B. R. SAKSENA, M.A., D.LITT.; publ. *Quarterly Research Journal* and other texts and treatises.

Gujarat Research Society: Sasodhan Samdan, South Ave., Khar, Bombay 400052; f. 1936; to organize and co-ordinate research in social and cultural activities; library of 10,000 vols.; Pres. Dr. M. R. SHAH; publ. *Journal of the Gujarat Research Society* (quarterly).

Heras Institute of Indian History and Culture: St. Xavier's College, Bombay 400001; f. 1926; Dir. J. VELINKAR; publ. *Indica* (twice yearly).

Indian Council for Cultural Relations: Azad Bhavan, Indraprastha Estate, New Delhi 1; f. 1950 to strengthen cultural relations between India and other countries; br. offices in Bombay, Calcutta, Madras and Bangalore; cultural centres in Suva (Fiji), Georgetown (Guyana) and San Francisco (U.S.A.); activities include exchange visits, publications, exhibitions and lectures including the Azad Memorial Lectures; establishment of chairs and centres of Indian studies abroad and welfare of overseas students in India; administration of Jawaharlal Nehru Award for International Understanding; library of over 25,000 vols. on India and other countries; publs. interpretations of Indian Art and Culture and translations of Indian works into foreign languages; Pres. Sardar SWARAN SINGH; Sec. Mrs. S. KOCHAR; publs. *Indian Horizons* (in English, quarterly), *Cultural News from India* (in English, quarterly), *Thaqafatul-Hind* (in Arabic, quarterly), *Papeles de la India* (in Spanish, quarterly), *Rencontre avec l'Inde* (in French, quarterly), *ICCR Newsletter* (English quarterly for foreign students).

Indian Council of World Affairs: Sapru House, Barakhamba Rd., New Delhi 1; f. 1943; non-governmental institution for the study of Indian and International questions; 1,000 mems.; library of 74,000 vols., 800 periodicals; Pres. Dr. H. N. KUNZRU; Hon. Sec.-Gen. S. L. POPLAI; publs. *India Quarterly, Foreign Affairs Reports* (monthly), *Documentation on Asia, India in World Affairs.*

Indian Economic Association: Delhi School of Economics, Delhi 9; f. 1918; Pres. Prof. V. M. DANDEKAR; Hon Sec. Prof. K. A. NAQVI; publ. *Indian Economic Journal.*

International Academy of Indian Culture: J 22 Hauz Khas Enclave, New Delhi 16; f. 1935; to study India's artistic and historic relations with other Asian countries; library of 12,000 vols.; Hon. Dir. Dr. LOKESH CHANDRA; Hon. Sec. Dr. SHARADA RANI; publs. *Satapitaka Series* (irregular).

Islamic Research Association: 8 Shepherd Rd., Bombay 8; f. 1933; Pres. Prof. S. S. DESNAVI; publs. 12 vols. of research work on *Islamic Studies.*

Ismaili Society: P.O.B. 6052, Bombay 5; f. 1946; Pres. G. H. BUNDALLY; Hon. Editor W. IVANOW; publ. translations and texts of Ismaili works, monographs on Ismailism.

K. M. Institute of Hindi Studies and Linguistics: Agra Univ., Agra 4, U.P.; Dir. Dr. R. B. SHARMA.

Kuppuswami Sastri Research Institute, The: Sanskrit College, Madras 4; f. 1944; promotion of Oriental learning; 300 mems.; library of 20,000 vols. (including palm-leaf MSS.); Sec. and Dir. Dr. V. RAGHAVAN; publs. *Journal of Oriental Research* (quarterly) and numerous research publs.

Maha Bodhi Society: 4A Bankim Chatterjee St., Calcutta 12; f. 1891; 11 brs. in other cities; 1,800 mems.; Gen. Sec. Ven. N. JINARATANA NAYAKA THERA, M.A.; publs. *Mahabodhi Journal* (English monthly). *Dharmaduta* (Hindi monthly), books on Buddhism.

Mumbai Marathi Granth Sangrahalaya: Bombay; f. 1898; research in Marathi language and literature; Pres. S. K. PATIL.

Nalanda Pali Institute: P.O. Nalanda, District Nalanda, Bihar; f. 1951; studies and research in Pali language and literature; library of 70,000 vols.; Dir. B. J. KASHYAP; publ. *Nava Nalanda Mahavihara Research* (annual).

Oriental Institute: Tilak Rd., Baroda; f. 1915; library of 36,400 vols. on Indology and Sanskrit, MSS. library of 25,783 MSS.; 7 mems.; Dir. Prof. Dr. A. N. JANI; Deputy Dir. Shri J. P. THAKER; publs. *Gaekwad's Oriental Series, M.S. Lecture Series, M.S. University Oriental Series, Critical Edition of Vishnupurana Project, Svadhyaya* (Gujarati research quarterly), *Journal of the Oriental Institute, Sayaji Sahityamala* (Gujarati, 352 vols.), *Baljnanamala* (Gujarati, 203 vols.), etc.

Oriental Research Institute: Mysore; library of 30,000 vols.; collection of 20,000 ancient MSS.; Dir. G. MARULASIDDAIAH, M.A., PH.D.

Sikkim Research Institute of Tibetology (fmrly. the *Namgyal Institute of Tibetology*): Gangtok, Sikkim; f. 1958; research centre for study of Mahayana (Northern Buddhism); library of Tibetan literature (canonical of all sects and secular) in MSS. and xylographs; museum of icons and art objects; Dir. NIRMAL C. SINHA; publs. in Tibetan, Sanskrit and English, including *Bulletin of Tibetology* (3 times a year).

Sri Venkateswara University Oriental Research Institute: Tirupati, Andhra Pradesh; f. 1939; research in language and literature, philosophy and religion, arts and archaeology, history and social sciences; publs. *Institute Journal* and other treatises.

Tamil Nadu Tamil Development and Research Council: Directorate of Tamil Development "Kuralagam", Madras-600001; f. 1959; development of Tamil in all its aspects, especially as a modern language; Chair. Chief Minister; Vice-Chair. Minister for Education and Tourism; Sec.-Dir. of Tamil Development; publ. *Tamil Nadu Tamil Bibliography*.

Vishveshvaranand Vishva Bandhu Institute of Sanskrit and Indological Studies: Sadhu Ashram P.O., Hoshiarpur; f. 1965; postgraduate teaching, research and study in Indology and Sanskrit, including language, literature and religion; 3,200 mems.; library of 80,000 vols.; Dirs. S. BHASKARAN NAIR, K. V. SARMA; publs. *Panjab University Indological Series, Vishveshvaranand Indological Journal* (6 monthly).

INDONESIA

Indonesian Institute of World Affairs: c/o University of Indonesia, Jakarta; Chair. Prof. SUPOMO; Sec. Mr. SUDJATMOKO.

Lembaga Kebudajaan Indonesia (*Institute for Indonesian Culture*): Medan Merdeka Barat 12, Jakarta; f. 1778; Pres. Prof. Dr. P. A. HOESEIN DJAJADININGRAT; Vice-Pres. Prof. Dr. R. PRIJONO WINDUWINOTO; publs. *Modjalah untuk Ilmu Bahasa, Ilmu Bumidan Kebudajan Indonesia* (Journal for Indonesian Language, Geography and Culture), *Yearbook*, and other monographs.

National Economic and Social Research Institute: Dept. of Social Sciences and Humanities, Indonesian Institute of Sciences, Gondangdia Lama 39, Jakarta; f. 1963; Dir. TAUFIK ABDULLAH.

National Institute for Cultural Studies: Dept. of Social Sciences and Humanities, Indonesian Institute of Sciences, Jalan Pejambon 3, P.O. Box 165, Jakarta.

Pusat Pengembangan dan Pembinaan Bahasa (*National Centre for Language Development*): Jalan Diponegoro 82, P.O. Box 2625, Jakarta; f. 1975; attached to the Ministry of Education and Culture; scientific research on languages and foreign language teaching; library of 30,000 vols.; Dir. Dr. AMRAN HALIM; Librarian Miss IPON PURAWIDJAJA; publs. *Bahasa dan Sastra* (bi-monthly), *Pengajaran Bahasa dan Sastra* (bi-monthly).

IRAN

Asia Institute: Pahlavi University, Shiraz; Dir. Dr. M. NAVABI; publs. *Bulletin, Monographs.*

ISRAEL

Department of East Asian Studies: Institute of Asian and African Studies, The Hebrew University of Jerusalem; provides degree courses, covering history, social sciences and language, in Chinese studies, Japanese studies and South-East Asian studies; Chair. Prof. ELLIS JOFFE.

Asia Research Unit: Harry S. Truman Research Institute, The Hebrew University of Jerusalem: affiliated to the above; sponsors research, organizes conferences and helps publish work relating to China, Japan and South-East Asia; Unit Co-ordinator Dr. MARTIN RUDNER; publs. *Jerusalem Studies on Asia* (series) and *Asia Reprint Series.*

ITALY

Istituto Italiano per il Medio e l'Estremo Oriente (ISMEO): Palazzo Brancaccio, via Merulana 248, Rome; f. 1933; a library and museum of oriental art are attached to the Institute; Pres. Prof. GIUSEPPE TUCCI; Cultural Dir. Prof. ANTONIO GARGANO; publs. *East and West* (quarterly), *Rome Oriental Series, Nuovo Ramusio, Archaeological Reports, Restorations.*

Istituto Universitario Orientale (*Oriental Institute*): Piazza San Giovanni Maggiore 30, 80100 Naples; f. 1732; library of 100,000 vols.; Dir. Prof. R. RUBINACCI; publ. *Annali.*

Museo d'Arte Orientale "Edoardo Chiossone": Villetta di Negro, Genoa; f. 1905; paintings from 11th to 19th century; Chinese and Japanese works of art.

JAPAN

Ajia Seikei Gakkai: (*Society for Asian Political and Economic Studies*): Keio University, Mita, Minatoku, Tokyo; f. 1953; 450 mems.; Pres. N. YAMAMOTO; publ. *Asiatic Studies* (quarterly).

Asiatic Society of Japan: C.P.O. Box 592, Tokyo; f. 1872; Hon. Pres. NICK SCHENK; Hon. Sec. H. BINS; publs. *Transactions, Kojiki.*

Centre for East Asian Cultural Studies: c/o The Toyo Bunko, Honkomagome 2-chome, 28-21, Bunkyo-ku, Tokyo, 113, f. 1961; Dir. KAZUO ENOKI; publs. *East Asian Cultural Studies, Directories, East Asian Cultural Studies Series, bibliographies,* translations of historical documents.

Centre for Southeast Asian Studies: Shimoadachi-cho 46, Yohsida, Sakyoku, Kyoto; attached to Kyoto University; Dir. Prof. S. ICHIMURA; publs. *Southeast Asian Studies* (quarterly), *Monographs* (English and Japanese, irregular), *Discussion Papers* and *Reprint Series* (irregular).

China Research Institute: 4-1-34 Kudan-kita, Chiyoda-ku, Tokyo; f. 1946; Dir. T. ITO; publs. *China Research Monthly, Asia Economic Bulletin* (36 issues yearly) and *New China Year Book.*

Foreign Affairs Association of Japan: Togyo Kaikan, 7, 1-chome, Yuraku-cho, Chiyoda-ku, Tokyo; f. 1932; Rep. HELEN M. UNO; publs. *Contemporary Japan* (quarterly), *Japan Year Book*.

Institute for Humanistic Studies (*Zinbun Kagaku Kenkyusho*): 47 Kitashirakawa, Sakyo-ku, Kyoto; f. 1939; attached to Kyoto University; Dir. Prof. Dr. TATSUSABURO HAYASHIYA; the Institute is divided into three sections, dealing with Japanese, Oriental, and Western Culture; publs. *Journal of Oriental Studies* (annual), *Journal of Humanistic Studies* (annual), *Memoirs* (annual), *Annual Bibliography of Oriental Studies*, *Social Survey Reports*.

Institute for the Study of Languages and Cultures of Asia and Africa: Tokyo University of Foreign Studies, 51 Nishigawara, 4-chome, Kita-ku, Tokyo; f. 1964; 30 researchers, 34 administrators, 16,532 vols.; Dir. M. OKA; publs. *Journal of Asian and African Studies* (annually), *Newsletter* (thrice yearly).

Institute of Developing Economies (*Ajia Keizai Kenkyusho*): 42 Ichigaya-Hommura-cho, Shinjuku-ku, Tokyo 162, Japan; f. 1958; 273 mems.; Chair. TAKEKAZU OGURA; Pres. NOBORU KANOKOGI; Dirs. ETSURO OIZUMI, TAKEHARU SASAMOTO, BUNJI MUROYA; library of 116,147 vols.; publs. *Ajia Keizai* (monthly), *The Developing Economies* (quarterly, in English), *Library Bulletin* (monthly), *Ajia Doko Nempo* (annual); Occasional Papers Series (irregular, in English), Trade Statistics, Union Catalogues, Asian Economic Studies Series, Research Materials, Translation Series, Bibliography Series, etc.

The Institute of Oriental Culture: University of Tokyo, 7-3-1 Hongo, Bunkyo-ku, Tokyo; f. 1941; Dir. Y. SAEKI; publs. *Memoirs* (3 issues a year), *Oriental Culture* (2 issues a year).

Japan Economic Research Center (*Nihon Keizai Kenkyu* (*Center*): Nikkei Building, 9-5, Otemachi, 1-chome, Chiyoda-ku, Tokyo; f. 1964; 270 mems.; library of 30,000 vols.; Chair. S. OKITA; Pres. H. KANAMORI; publs. *Nihon Keizai Kenkyu Center Kaiho* (fortnightly), *Quarterly Forecast of Japan's Economy* (quarterly, English), *English Reprint Series* (irregular).

Manyo Gakkai (*Society for Manyo Studies*): Kansai University, Senriyama Suita-shi, Osaka; f. 1951; 810 mems.; publ. *The Manyo* (quarterly).

Nihon-Indogaku-Bukkyôgakukai (*Japanese Association of Indian and Buddhist Studies*): c/o Department of Indian Philosophy and Sanskrit Philology, Faculty of Letters, The University of Tokyo, Bunkyo-ku, Tokyo; f. 1951; 1,512 mems.; Pres. SHOSON MIYAMOTO; publ. *Journal of Indian and Buddhist Studies* (Indogaku Bukkyôgaku Kenkyû).

Oriental Library (*Tôyô Bunko*): Honkomagome 2-chome, 28-21, Bunkyo-ku, Tokyo 113; f. 1924; 512,168 vols.; Librarian NAOSHIRO TSUJI; publs. *Tôyô Gakuho* (quarterly), *Memoirs of the Research Department*, Monographs Series A, Miscellaneous Series C.

Tokyo Shina Gakkai (*Tokyo Sinological Society*): Faculty of Letters, The University of Tokyo, Bunkyo-ku, Tokyo; f. 1897; Pres. SEIICHI UNO; publ. *Tokyo Shinagaku-ho*.

Toyo Ongaku Gakkai (*The Society for Research in Asiatic Music*): c/o Tokyo National Research Institute of Cultural Properties, Ueno Park, Tokyo; f. 1936; aims to promote research in Asian music and ethnomusicology; 500 mems.; Pres. Prof. KÁSHÓ MATIDA; publ. *Journal* (quarterly).

Toyoshi Kenkyukai (*The Society for Oriental Research*): Kyoto University, Kyoto City; f. 1935; 1,300 mems.; Pres. I. MIYAZAKI; publ. *Journal* (quarterly).

REPUBLIC OF KOREA

Asiatic Research Center: Korea University, Anam-Dong, Seoul; Dir. Prof. JUN-YOP KIM; publ. *Journal of Asiatic Studies*.

Institute of Far Eastern Studies: Yonsei University, Sodaemoon-ku, Seoul; f. 1949; Dir. Dr. YI-SUP HONG; publ. *Journal of Far Eastern Studies* (annual).

MALAYSIA

Language and Literary Agency (*Dewan Bahasa dan Pustaka*): P.O.B. 803, Kuala Lumpur; f. 1959; to develop and enrich the Malay language; to develop literary talent particularly in Malay; to print, publish or assist in the printing or publication of publications in Malay and other languages; to standardize spelling and pronunciation and devise appropriate technical terms in Malay; library of 65,000 vols., in Malay, English, Indonesian, Arabic and others; Chair. TAN SRI HAJI HAMDAN BIN SHEIKH TAHIR; Dir.-Gen. (Ag.) HAJI HASSAN BIN AHMAD; publs. *Dewan Bahasa*, *Dewan Masyarakat*, *Dewan Pelajar*, *Dewan Sastra* (monthly), *Nusantara*, *Journal Kementerian Pelajaran Malaysia* (quarterly), *Buletin Pendidikan* (every 2 months), *Malaysia in History*, *Rintisains* (every 6 months), *Jernal* (annually).

MEXICO

Centre for Asian and North African Studies: El Colegio de Mexico, Guanajuato 125, Mexico 7, D.F.; publ. *Estudios de Asia y Africa* (3 times a year); Dir. Prof. OMAR MARTÍNEZ LEGORRETA.

NETHERLANDS

Koninklijk Instituut voor Taal-, Land- en Volkenkunde: Stationsplein 10, Leiden; f. 1851 to promote the study of linguistics, geography, anthropology and history of South-East Asia (especially Indonesia), the South Pacific area and the Caribbean region (in particular Surinam and the Dutch Antilles); 1,010 mems.; library of over 90,000 vols.; Pres. Dr. A. J. PIEKAAR; Gen. Sec. Dr. J. NOORDUYN; publs. *Bijdragen* (quarterly), *F Verhandelingen*, *Bibliotheca Indonesica*, F Bibliographical series, translation series.

NEW CALEDONIA

Société des Etudes Mélanésiennes: Nouméa.

NEW ZEALAND

New Zealand Geographical Society: Department of Geography, University of Canterbury, Christchurch; f. 1944 to promote and stimulate the study of geography; branches in Auckland, Christchurch, Dunedin, Hamilton, Palmerston North and Wellington; 1,100 mems. in New Zealand, 630 overseas mems.; Pres. A. E. MCQUEEN, M.A., M.CIT.; Sec. R. G. CANT, M.A., PH.D.; publs. *New Zealand Geographer* (twice yearly) and the *New Zealand Journal of Geography* (twice yearly), *Proceedings of the New Zealand Geography Conference*.

New Zealand Institute of Economic Research: P.O.B. 3479, Wellington; f. 1958; research into New Zealand economic development; quarterly analysis and forecast of economic conditions; Dir. J. K. MCDONALD; Chair. Dr. G. A. LAU; Sec. A. J. MCDONALD.

Polynesian Society: P.O.B. 10323, The Terrace, Wellington 1; f. 1892; to promote studies and publications dealing with native peoples of Polynesia, Melanesia and Micronesia; library; 1,500 mems.; Pres. J. M. MCEWEN; Hon. Sec. P. RANBY; publs. *Memoirs*, *Journal* (quarterly), *Maori Monographs*, *Maori Texts*.

Ross Dependency Research Committee: Department of Scientific and Industrial Research, Private Bag. Wellington; responsible to the Minister of Science for co-ordinating all New Zealand activity in the Ross Dependency; Chair. J. H. MILLER; Sec. T. D. REYNOLDS.

PAKISTAN

Anjuman Taraqqi-e-Urdu Pakistan: Urdu Rd., Karachi 1; f. 1902; for promotion of Urdu language and literature; administers the Urdu college; research library of 50,000 vols. and MSS.; Pres. AKHTAR HUSAIN, C.S.P.; Sec. JAMILUDDIN A'ALI; publs. *Urdu* (quarterly), *Quami Zaban* (monthly).

Institute of Islamic Culture: Club Rd., Lahore; f. 1950; about 150 publications on Islamic subjects in English and Urdu; monthly magazine *Al-Maarif*; Dir. Prof. M. SAEED SHEIKH; Sec. M. ASHRAF DARR.

Islamic Research Institute: P.O.B. 1035, Islamabad; f. 1960; to conduct and co-ordinate research in Islamic studies; library of 23,201 vols., 419 microfilms, 96 MSS.; Dir. ZAHID MULLICK; publs. *Islamic Studies* (English, quarterly), *Al-Dirasat al-Islamiyya* (Arabic, (quarterly), *Fikr-o-Nazar* (Urdu, monthly).

Oriental College: University of the Punjab, Lahore; f. 1870; Principal E. BRELVI, M.A., PH.D.

Pakistan Economic Research Institute (P.E.R.I.): 9 Jan. Mohammad Rd., Anarkali, Lahore; f. 1955 to undertake socio-economic investigations and co-ordinate research in economic problems of Pakistan; to collect, compile and interpret statistical data; to publish the results and findings of investigations; Dir. AZIZ A. ANWAR; Sec. RASHID A. ARSHAD; publs. *Economics and Commerce* (fortnightly), Research Papers.

Pakistan Historical Society: 30 New Karachi Co-operative Housing Society, Karachi 5; f. 1950; historical studies and research; particularly history of Islam and the Indo-Pakistan Sub-Continent; Pres. FAZLUR RAHMAN; Gen. Sec. Dr. S. MOINUL HAQ; publs. *Journal* (quarterly), Monographs, Research Studies.

Pakistan Institute of Development Economics: P.O. Box 1091, Islamabad; f. 1956; library of 11,000 vols., 325 current periodicals; to train post-graduate scholars on methods of economic research, planning and administration; Dir. M. L. QURESHI; Deputy Sec. M. A. HAFEEZ; publ. *Pakistan Development Review* (quarterly).

Pakistan Institute of International Affairs: Strachen Rd., Karachi; f. 1947 to study international affairs and to promote the scientific study of international politics, economics and jurisprudence; library of 15,000 vols.; 400 mems.; Pres. The Minister of Foreign Affairs; Sec. KH. SARWAR HASAN; publs. *Pakistan Horizon* (quarterly); books and monographs.

PHILIPPINES

Institute of Philippine Culture: Ateneo de Manila University, Loyola Heights, Quezon City, P.O. Box 154, Manila; f. 1960 to study local problems of development including poverty; Dir. Ms. MARY R. HOLLNSTEINER; publs. (irregular) *IPC Papers, IPC Monographs, IPC Poverty Research Series, IPC Reprints,* and final reports of IPC projects (mimeo).

Institute of Research for Filipino Culture: Mindanao State University, Marawi City M-206; f. 1962 to study the folk culture of the Philippines; Dir. Dr. MAMITUA SABER (acting).

Philippine Centre for Advanced Studies: University of the Philippines, Quezon City; publs. *Asian Studies* (3 times a year), *Occasional Papers, Monograph* series, *Bibliography* series; Chancellor R. SANTOS-CUYUGAN.

Philippine Institute of Filipino Culture and Foreign Languages: The Philippine Women's University, Taft Ave., Manila; Dir. Mrs. Y. VELOSO.

Research Institute for Mindanao Culture: Xavier University, Cagayan de Oro City; f. 1957; to study and assist the development of north Mindanao and its peoples; Dir. FRANCIS C. MADIGAN, PH.D.; publs. *Xavier University Studies* (irregular), *Bulletin of APRIAS—Asian Population and Information Society* (quarterly).

POLAND

Komitet Nauk Orientalistycznych PAN (*The Committee for Oriental Studies of the Polish Academy of Sciences*): Grójecka 17 pok. 111 02-021 Warsaw, Poland; Pres. Prof. Dr. TADEVSZ LEWICKI; publs. *Rocznik Orientalistyczny*, series *Prace orientalistyczne*.

Polskie Towarzystwo Orientalistyczne (*Polish Oriental Society*): Warsaw, ul. Śniadeckich 8,; f. 1922; Pres. TADEUSZ LEWICKI Sec. LESZEK CYRZYK; publ. *Przegląd Orientalistyczny* (quarterly).

SINGAPORE

Art Museum and Exhibition Gallery: University of Singapore, Singapore 10; f. 1955; Asian art, including classical Chinese ceramics, painting and sculpture, Chinese export wares, Islamic pottery, classical Indian sculptures, Indian Moghul miniature painting, Indian historical and traditional textiles, Thai, Khmer and Annamese ceramics, Khmer sculptures, contemporary Indian painting, contemporary Malaysian and Indonesian painting and traditional textiles; Curator WILLIAM WILLETTS, M.A., B.A., B.SC.

The China Society: 190 Keng Lee Rd., Singapore 11; f. 1948 to promote Chinese culture and to introduce Chinese culture to the non-Chinese; 250 mems.; Pres. LEE SIOW MONG; publ. *Annual of China Society*.

Economic Research Centre: University of Singapore, Bukit Timah Rd., Singapore 10; Dir. Dr. PANG ENG FONG.

Institute of Asian Studies: Nanyang Univ., Upper Jurong Rd., Singapore 22; f. 1957 to collect material on South-East Asia for research and reference, and to publish academic research papers and reference books; Dir. GWEE YEE HEAN, M.A.; publ. *Bulletin* (annual).

Institute of South-east Asian Studies: Cluny Rd., Singapore 10; f. 1968 to undertake research on the contemporary problems of South-East Asia and its recent history especially in sociology, anthropology, economics, history, geography and political science; library of 23,000 vols.; Dir. Prof. KERNIAL SINGH SANDHU; Exec. Sec. C. P. CHIN; Librarian P. LIM PUI HUEN.

Royal Asiatic Society, Malaysian Branch: National Museum, Stamford Rd.; Pres. Tan Sri NIK A. KAMIL Bin Haji NIK MAHMUD; publs. *Journal* (annual) and occasional monographs.

Singapore Indian Fine Arts Society: P.O.B. 2812, 71 Bournemouth Rd., Singapore 15; f. 1949; Pres. M. KARTHIGESU; Hon. Gen. Sec. I. S. MENON.

SPAIN

Asociación Española de Orientalistas: Limite 5, Madrid 3; publ. *Boletin* (annual).

SRI LANKA

Buddhist Academy of Sri Lanka: 109 Rosmead Place, Colombo.

Department of Buddhist Studies, University of Sri Lanka: Vidyalankara Campus, Kelaniya, Colombo; Dir. Prof. W. S. KARUNARATNE, PH.D.

Maha Bodhi Society of Sri Lanka: 130 Maligakande Road, Maradana, Colombo 10; f. 1891 for propagation of Buddhism throughout the world; 12,000 mems.; Pres. Sir CYRIL DE ZOYSA, Kt., J.P.; Hon. Sec. LALITH HEWAVIRARANE; publs. *Sinhala Bauddhaya* (weekly), *Sinhala Bauddhaya* (Wesak number; annual).

Royal Asiatic Society: 1st Floor, Grandstand Bldg., Reid Ave., Colombo 7; f. 1845 and incorporated with the Royal Asiatic Society of Great Britain and Ireland; institutes and promotes inquiries into the history, religions, languages, literature, arts, sciences and social conditions of the present and former inhabitants of Ceylon and connected cultures; Pres. Dr. H. W. TAMBIAH, Q.C., B.SC., LL.B.; Hon. Secs. P. R. SITTAMPALAM, K. M. W. KURUPPU; library contains one of the largest existing collections of books on Ceylon, and others on Indian and Eastern culture in general; publ. *Journal.*

SWEDEN

Swedish Oriental Society: Stockholm.

SWITZERLAND

Schweizerische Gesellschaft für Asienkunde—Société suisse d'études asiatiques: Sekretariat, Ostasiatisches Seminar, Universität, Mühlegasse 21, 8001 Zürich; f. 1947; 300 mems.; Pres. R. P. KRAMERS; publ. *Asiatische Studien/Etudes Asiatiques* (twice yearly).

TAIWAN

Academia Historica: 2 Peiping Rd., Taipei; contains national archives, library, documents; engaged in preparing history of China since the establishment of the Republic of China; Pres. HUANG CHI-LU.

The China Society: Roosevelt Road 3-202-2, P.O. Box 1637, Taipei; f. 1960 as a centre for Chinese studies; about 100 mems.; Pres. Dr. ALBERT R. O'HARA, S.J.: Vice-Pres. Dr. CHEN CHI-LU; publ. *Journal of the China Society.*

College of Chinese Culture: Huakang, Yang Ming Shan; f. 1962; Pres. PAUL S. Y. HSIAO; 150 teachers; 1,019 students; library of 210,488 vols.

THAILAND

Buddhist Research Centre: Wat Benchamabopitr, Bangkok; f. 1961; sponsored by Department of Religious Affairs, Ministry of Education; publ. *Pali-Thai-English Dictionary*, vol. 1.

Siam Society (*formerly* the Thailand Society): 131 Asoke Rd., Bangkapi, P.O.B. 65, Bangkok; f. 1904; approx. 1,500 mems.; for the investigation and encouragement of art, science and literature of Thailand and neighbouring countries; library of 20,000 vols.; Pres. H.R.H. Prince WAN WAITHAYAKORN; Hon. Sec. MOM RACHAWONG PIMSAI AMRANAND; publs. *Journals, Index to the Journal, Natural History Bulletins, Florae Siamensis Enumeratio*, occasional books.

U.S.S.R.

Biruni Institute of Oriental Studies: Uzbek S.S.R. Academy of Sciences, Ul. Navoi 55-a, Tashkent; Dir. S. A. AZIMDZHANOVA.

Institute of Oriental Studies of the Department of History, U.S.S.R. Academy of Sciences: Armyansky per. 2, Moscow; Dir. Acad. B. G. GAFUROV; publ. *Asia and Africa Today* (monthly).

Institute of the Far East: Department of Economics, U.S.S.R. Academy of Sciences, 2nd Yaroslavskaya ul. 3, Moscow; Dir. M. I. SLADKOVSKY.

Institute of Oriental Languages of the Academy of Sciences of the Armenian S.S.R.: Ul. Abovyana 15, Erevan 1; Dir. G. K. SARKISYAN.

Institute of Oriental Studies of the Academy of Sciences of the Georgian S.S.R.: Ul. Tskhakaya 10, Tbilisi; Dir. G. V. TSERETELI.

Institute of Peoples of the Near and Middle East of the Academy of Sciences of the Azerbaijan S.S.R.: Prospekt Narimanova 31, Baku; Dir. G. M. ARAZLY.

Scientific Council for Oriental Studies: Department of History, U.S.S.R. Academy of Sciences, Ul. D. Ulyanova 19, Moscow; Chair. Acad. B. G. GAFUROV.

Section of Oriental Studies of the Academy of Sciences of the Armenian S.S.R.: Ul. Abovyana 15, Erevan; Dir. O.G. INJIKYAN.

Section of Oriental Studies and Ancient Scriptures of the Academy of Sciences of the Tajik S.S.R.: Parvin ul. 8, Dushanbe; Dir. A. M. MIRZOEV.

UNITED KINGDOM

British Association of Orientalists: c/o Dept. of Persian, University of Edinburgh, 8 Buccleuch Place, Edinburgh, EH8 9LW; f. 1950; Chair. Dr. A. TAHERI; Sec. Dr. G. R. SABRI-TABRIZI; publ. *Bulletin.*

Central Asian Research Centre: 1B Parkfield Street, London, N.1; f. 1952; Dir. DAVID L. MORISON; publs. *Soviet and Chinese Reports on South and South-East Asia, Central Asian Review.*

Centre of Japanese Studies: University of Sheffield, Sheffield S10 2TN; Dir. Prof. G. BOWNAS, M.A.

Centre of South Asian Studies: University of Cambridge, Laundress Lane, Cambridge, CB2 1SD; Dir. B. H. FARMER, M.A.

Centre for South-East Asian Studies: The University of Hull, Cottingham Rd., Hull; Dir. Prof. M. A. JASPAN, PH.D.; publs. *Hull Monographs on South-East Asia; Reprints of Publications by Staff Members.*

China Society: 31B Torrington Square, London, W.C.1; f. 1906 to encourage the study of the Chinese language, literature, history, folk-lore, art, etc.; *c.* 150 mems.; Pres. Col. KENNETH CANTLIE; Chair. H. C. COLLAR, C.B.E.; Sec. Vice-Adm. Sir JOHN GRAY, K.B.E., C.B.

Contemporary China Institute: School of Oriental and African Studies, Malet Street, London, WC1E 7HP; f. 1968; Head Dr. CHRISTOPHER HOWE; publs. *The China Quarterly, Modern China Studies International Bulletin.*

Department of Chinese Studies: University of Leeds, Leeds 2; Dir. Prof. G. B. DOWNER, B.A.

European Association for Japanese Studies: c/o The Hon. Sec. Prof. P. G. O'NEILL, S.O.A.S., University of London, Malet St., London, WC1E 7HP; f. 1973; Hon. Pres. Prof. Dr. JOSEF KREINER; publs. *Newsletter of the European Association for Japanese Studies* (twice yearly).

India Office Library (Foreign and Commonwealth Office): 197 Blackfriars Rd., London, S.E.1; f. 1801; about 300,000 European and Oriental printed books, 20,500 oriental MSS., 12,000 British paintings and drawings relating principally to India and the East, 12,000 oriental drawings and miniatures and 120,000 photographs; Dir. Miss J. C. LANCASTER, F.S.A., F.R.HIST.S.; publs. *Annual Report, Guide* and catalogues of the collections.

India Office Records (Foreign and Commonwealth Office): 197 Blackfriars Rd., London, S.E.1; official archives of the London administration (200,000 vols. and files), official publications (100,000 vols., 20,000 maps) and private papers (20,000 vols. and boxes) relating to pre-Independence India (1600–1947); some post-1947 private papers; Dir. Miss J. C. LANCASTER, F.S.A., F.R.HIST.S.; publs. *Annual Report*, Catalogues, Lists and Guides.

Institute of Development Studies at The University of Sussex: Falmer, Brighton, Sussex, BN1 9RE; f. 1966; Dir. RICHARD JOLLY; publs. *IDS Bulletin* (quarterly), *IDS Discussion Papers, IDS Communications Series, Annual Report*, books, library of occasional guides and Research reports.

Oriental Ceramic Society: 31B Torrington Square, London, W.C.1; f. 1921 to increase knowledge and appreciation of Eastern ceramic and other arts; Pres. Sir JOHN ADDIS, K.C.M.G.; Sec. Vice-Adm. Sir JOHN GRAY, K.B.E., C.B.; Hon. Sec. Lt.-Col. W. B. R. NEAVE-HILL.

Oriental Institute: University of Oxford, Pusey Lane, Oxford; f. 1960; Sec. Mrs. A. M. LONSDALE.

Royal Asiatic Society of Great Britain and Ireland: 56 Queen Anne St., London, W1M 9LA; f. 1823 for the study of the history, sociology, institutions, customs, languages and art of Asia; approx. 800 mems.; approx. 500 subscribing libraries; branches in various Eastern cities; Sec. Miss D. CRAWFORD; publs. *Journal* and monographs on Oriental subjects; library of 100,000 vols. and 1,500 MSS.

Royal Society for Asian Affairs: 42 Devonshire Street, London, W.1; f. 1901; 1,500 mems. with knowledge of, and interest in, Central Asia, Middle and Far East; library of about 5,000 vols.; Pres. The Lord GREENHILL of HARROW, G.C.M.G., O.B.E.; Chair. Sir STANLEY TOMLINSON, K.C.M.G., LL.D.; Sec. Miss M. FITZSIMONS; publ. *Journal* (3 issues per annum).

St. Antony's College: Oxford; f. 1950; Far East Centre devoted to the study of the modern Far East; Warden A. R. M. CARR, M.A.

School of African and Asian Studies: University of Sussex, Falmer, Brighton, BN1 9QN; Dean Dr. I. LL. GRIFFITHS, B.SC.(ECON.), PH.D.

School of Oriental and African Studies: University of London, W.C.1; f. 1916; library of over 400,000 vols. and 1,700 MSS.; Dir. Prof. C. D. COWAN, M.A., PH.D.; publs. *The Bulletin, Calendar, Annual Report.*

UNITED STATES OF AMERICA

American Asiatic Association: India House, 1 Hanover Square, New York 4, N.Y.; f. 1898; 46 mems.; Pres. M. ZUCKERMAN; Sec. D. G. ALLEN, c/o Manufacturers Hanover Trust Co., 44 Wall St., New York 4, N.Y.

American Oriental Society: 329 Sterling Memorial Library, Yale Station, New Haven, Conn.; f. 1842; 1,700 mems.; library of 19,560 vols.; Pres. EDWARD SCHAFER; Sec. HUGH M. STIMSON; publ. *Journal of the American Oriental Society* (quarterly).

The Asia Foundation: P.O.B. 3223, San Francisco, Calif. 94108 (Main Office); offices in Washington and 12 Asian countries; f. 1954; 3,770 vols. on current Asian and world affairs; to strengthen Asian educational, cultural and civic activities with private American assistance; fields of interest include law, urban and rural development, communications and regional organizations, nutrition, family planning, health delivery systems; Chair. Board of Trustees RUSSELL G. SMITH; Pres. HADYN WILLIAMS; Sec. TURNER H. MCBAINE; publs. *The Asian Student* (every 2 weeks), *The Asian Student Orientation Handbook, Program Quarterly, President's Review* (annual).

Asian Language and Area Council: University of Hawaii, 2444 Dole Street, Honolulu, Hawaii 96822; Presides over three Language and Area Centres: East Asia, Southeast Asia, and South Asia; Chair. Prof. D. W. Y. KWOK; Exec. Sec. W. G. HACKLER.

Asian Studies Program: University of Hawaii, 2444 Dole Street, Honolulu, Hawaii 96822; Dir. Prof. D. W. Y. KWOK.

Association for Asian Studies Inc.: One Lane Hall, University of Michigan, Ann Arbor, Mich. 48109; f. 1941; Sec.-Treas. RICHARD L. PARK; publs. *Asian Studies Newsletter, Asian Studies Professional Review, Bibliography of Asian Studies, Journal of Asian Studies*, doctoral dissertations on Asia.

Boston Museum of Fine Arts: Boston, Mass. 02115; a private corporation; incorp. 1870; department of Asiatic art with outstanding collection of Chinese and Japanese sculpture, painting, and ceramics; Indian and Mohammadan art; library of 105,000 books and periodicals; 60,000 pamphlets; Acting Dir. JAN FONTEIN; publs. *Calendar of Events* (monthly), *Bulletin* (quarterly), catalogues, handbooks.

Columbia University East Asian Institute: 507 Kent Hall, New York, N.Y. 10027; library of 230,000 vols.; Dir. J. W. MORLEY.

Columbia University Southern Asian Institute: c/o Columbia University, Morningside Heights, New York, N.Y. 10027; Dir. HOWARD WRIGGINS.

Cornell University China-Japan Program: Ithaca, N.Y.; Dir. Dr. MARTIE W. YOUNG.

Cornell University South Asia Program: 221 Morrill Hall, Ithaca, N.Y.; Dir. Dr. GERALD B. KELLEY.

Cornell University Southeast Asia Language and Area Center: Ithaca, N.Y. 14853; f. 1950 for the development of instruction and research on South-East Asia; library of 100,000 vols.; 71 graduate students; Dir. Prof. FRANK H. GOLAY.

M. H. De Young Memorial Museum: Golden Gate Park, San Francisco, Calif. 94118; f. 1895; art displays from Indonesia and Islands of South Pacific; Dir. IAN MCKIBBIN WHITE.

Duke University Program in Comparative Studies on Southeast Asia: Duke University, Durham, N.C. 27706; Chair. Dr. RICHARD L. FOX; publs. monographs.

East-West Center—Center for Cultural and Technical Interchange between East and West: Honolulu, Hawaii; f. 1960; to promote understanding among the peoples of Asia, the Pacific area, and the United States through cultural and technical interchange. Six divisions: Population Institute, Communication Institute, Technology and Development Institute, Food Institute, Culture Learning Institute and Open Grants; Pres. EVERETT KLEINJANS.

Freer Gallery of Art: 12th St. and Jefferson Drive, S.W., Washington, D.C. 20560; established 1906; opened 1923; devoted to research on the outstanding collections of Chinese, Japanese, Indian and Islamic art; gift of the late Charles L. Freer, of Detroit; library of 41,000 vols.; Dir. HAROLD P. STERN, M.A., PH.D.; Asst. Dir. THOMAS LAWTON, M.F.A., PH.D.; Head Cons. WILLIAM THOMAS CHASE, M.F.A.; publs. *Annual Report, Occasional Papers, Oriental Studies, Ars Orientalis*, etc.

George Washington University Institute for Sino-Soviet Studies: 2130 H Street, N.W., Suite 601, Washington, D.C. 20052; Dir. Dr. GASTON J. SIGUR.

Harvard University East Asian Research Center: 1737 Cambridge Street, Cambridge, Mass. 02138; Dir. Prof. EZRA F. VOGEL; publs. *Harvard East Asian Monographs, Harvard, East Asian Series* (Harvard Univ. Press).

Harvard-Yenching Institute: 2 Divinity Ave., Cambridge, Mass. 02138; f. 1928 to promote the growth and advancement of higher education in East Asia, especially with regard to the history and culture of that area; publs. *Harvard Journal of Asiatic Studies, Harvard-Yenching Institute Monographs, Harvard-Yenching Institute Studies, Scripta Mongolica;* Dir. ALBERT M. CRAIG.

Indiana University Asian Studies Research Institute: Goodbody Hall, Bloomington, Ind. 47401; research into social sciences and humanities of (primarily) Inner Asia; Dir. DENIS SINOR.

Pacific Sociological Association: Dept. of Sociology, Arizona State University, Tempe, Arizona 85281; 1,000 mems.; Pres. DAVID GOLD; Sec./Treas. RON HARDERT; publ. *Pacific Sociological Review.*

Research Institute on International Change: School of International Affairs Building, 420 West 118th St., New York, N.Y. 10027; Dir. Prof. ZBIGNIEW BRZEZINSKI.

St. John's University Center of Asian Studies: Grand Central and Utopia Parkways, Jamaica, N.Y. 11439; Dir. Dr. PAUL K. T. SIH.

Seton Hall University Institute of Far Eastern Studies: South Orange, N.J.; library of 30,000 vols.; Dir. JOHN B. TSU; Librarian WILLIAM FIELD.

Stanford University—University of California, Berkeley, Joint NDEA East Asia Language and Area Center: Bldg. 600-T, Stanford University, and 12 Barrows Hall, University of California, Berkeley; f. 1973; Co-Dirs. Prof. ALBERT E. DIEN (Stanford), Prof. JOHN C. JAMIESON (Berkeley); publs. bi-weekly newsletter, library brochure, Joint Center brochure, Bay Area directory of East Asian scholars.

State University of Iowa Far Eastern Language and Area Center: Dept. of E. Asian Languages and Literature, University of Iowa, Iowa City, Iowa; Chair. Prof. M. RYAN.

University of Arizona Department of Oriental Studies: Tucson, Ariz.; Head. Dr. ANDRES D. ONATE.

University of California Department of Oriental Languages: 104 Durant Hall, Berkeley, Calif. 94720; Chair. Prof. L. R. LANCASTER, PH.D.

University of California Department of South and Southeast Asia Studies: Berkeley, Calif. 94720; Adviser: B. A. VAN NOUTEN.

University of Chicago Oriental Institute: Chicago, Ill. 60637; Dir. Prof. J. A. BRINKMAN, PH.D.

University of Kansas Center for East Asian Studies: Lawrence, Kansas; Dir. Prof. GRANT K. GOODMAN.

University of Michigan Center for Chinese Studies: 104 Lane Hall, Ann Arbor, Mich.; library of 100,000 vols.; Dir. ALBERT FEUERWERKER.

University of Michigan Center for Japanese Studies: 108 Lane Hall, Ann Arbor, Mich.; f. 1947; library of 140,000 vols.; Dir. Dr. ROBERT E. COLE; publs. occasional papers, bibliographic series.

University of Michigan Center for South and Southeast Asian Studies: Lane Hall, Ann Arbor, Mich. 48107; Dir. THOMAS R. TRAUTMANN.

University of Oklahoma Asian Studies Committee: Norman, Okla.; Chair. Dr. SIDNEY BROWN.

University of Oregon Museum of Art: Eugene, Ore.; Oriental and Greater Pacific Basin collections and the works of contemporary American artists and craftsmen; over 8,000 works; Dir. RICHARD C. PAULIN.

University of Pennsylvania, Department of South Asia Regional Studies: 34th and Walnut Streets, Philadelphia, Pa. 19174; library of 100,000 vols.; Librarian KANTA BHATIA.

University of Pittsburgh Department of East Asian Languages and Literatures: Pittsburgh, Pa. 15260; Chair. Dr. WILLIAM F. DORRILL.

University of Southern California East Asian Studies Center: University Park, Los Angeles, Calif. 90007; f. 1962; Dir. Dr. GEORGE OAKLEY TOTTEN III; publs. occasional papers.

University of Southern California Research Institute on Communist Strategy and Propaganda: University Park, Los Angeles, Calif. 90007; library of 50,000 vols.; Librarian Mrs. I. O. HABERLY.

University of Wisconsin East Asian Studies Program: 1440 Van Hise Hall, Madison, Wis. 53706; Chair. Prof. SOLOMON B. LEVINE.

Wake Forest University Asian Studies Program: P.O.B. 7547, Reynolda Station, Winston-Salem, N.C. 27109; library of 25,000 vols.; Dir. Dr. B. G. GOKHALE; publ. *Asian Studies*, Vols. I and II.

Yale University South East Asia Studies Center: 77 Prospect St., New Haven, Conn. 06520; library of *c.* 75,000 vols.

VATICAN

Pontificium Institutum Orientalium Studiorum (*Pontifical Institute of Oriental Studies*): 7 Piazza Santa Maria Maggiore, 00185 Rome; f. 1917; library of 107,000 vols.; Rector Rev. EDUARD HUBER, S.J.; Sec. Rev. J. ŘEZÁČ, S.J.; publs. *Orientalia Christiana Periodica, Orientalia Christiana Analecta, Concilium Florentinum* (*Documenta et Scriptores*), *Anaphorae Syriacae.*

VIET-NAM

Hoi Phôt Hoc Nam Viet (*Association for Buddhist Studies*): Xa-Loi Pagoda, 89 Ba Huyen Thanh Quan, Saigon; f. 1950; study and practice of Buddhism 26,000 mems.; 5,000 vols.; meditation room; Pres. Dr. CAO VAN TRI (acting); publ. *Tu Quang.*

Vietnamese Association for Asian Cultural Studies and Relations: 34 Pham Dang Hung, Saigon; 175 mems. in Viet-Nam, 92 abroad; Pres. NGUYEN DANG THUC.

Vietnamese Association for Confucianist Studies (*Hoi Khong-Hoc Viet-Nam*): 137-139 Phan Thanh Gian, Saigon; 14,000 mems.; Pres. HOANG NAM HUNG.

SELECT BIBLIOGRAPHY (PERIODICALS)

Acta Orientalia. Publ. Munksgaard, Norre Spgad 35, DK 1370 Copenhagen K, Denmark, by the Oriental Societies of Denmark, Norway, and Sweden; history and language of the Near and Far East; once or twice yearly; Editor Prof. Spren Egerod; Editorial Sec. Lise Sode Mogensen, Institute of Assyriology, Kejsergade 2, DK 1150 Copenhagen K, Denmark.

Acta Orientalia Academiae Scientiarum Hungaricae. Magyar Tudományos Akadémia Orientalisztikai Közleményei, Budapest V, Roosevelt-tér 9, Hungary; three times a year.

Africasia. 32 rue Washington, Paris 8, France; f. 1969; fortnightly; information, analysis and opinion.

L'Afrique et L'Asie Modernes. Centre de Hautes Etudes sur l'Afrique et l'Asie Modernes, 13 rue du Four, 75006 Paris, France; quarterly.

Afro-Asian and World Affairs. Institute of Afro-Asian and World Affairs, 17 Theatre Communication Building, Connaught Circus, New Delhi 1, India.

Afro-Asian Economic Review. Afro-Asian Organization for Economic Co-operation, Chamber of Commerce Building, Mindan El Falakry, Special P.O. Bag, Cairo, Egypt.

Annals of the Bhandarkar Oriental Research Institute. Bhandarkar Oriental Research Institute, Poona 411004, India; annually.

Annual Bibliography of Oriental Studies. Research Institute for Humanistic Studies, Kyoto University, 47 Kitashirakawa, Sakyo-ku, Kyoto, Japan.

Archaeology and Physical Anthropology in Oceania. The University, Sydney, N.S.W., Australia; f. 1966; 3 issues a year; Editor A. P. Elkin.

Archiv für Orientforschung. Graz, Austria; f. 1923; Editors Dr. Ernst Weidner and Prof. Hans Hirsch (Vienna); Publisher Ferdinand Berger and Sohne, A-3580 Horu, Nö. Austria; irregular, vol. 24—1974, vol. 25—1977.

Archív Orientální. Journal of African, Asian and Latin American Studies of the Czechoslovak Academy of Sciences; Lázeňská 4, 118 37 Prague I, Czechoslovakia; contributions in English or French, German, Russian and Spanish with English résumé; f. 1929; book reviews and notes; quarterly.

Asia and Africa Today. Institute of Asian Peoples and Institute of Africa, U.S.S.R. Academy of Sciences, Moscow, U.S.S.R.; scientific, social and political; monthly.

Asian Affairs. Journal of the Royal Society for Asian Affairs, 42 Devonshire St., London, W.1, England; covers economic and political problems affecting the Near East, Far East and the Orient; quarterly; Editor P. Robertson.

Asian and African Studies. Israel Oriental Society, The Hebrew University, Jerusalem, Israel; f. 1965; annual; Editor Gabriel Baer.

Asian Institute Newsletter. Asian Development Institute, ESCAP, Sala Santitham, Bangkok, Thailand.

Asian Recorder. C-1/9 Tilak Marg, P.O.B. 595, New Delhi-1, India; f. 1955; record of Asian events; weekly; Editor M. Henry Samuel.

Asian Studies. Philippine Centre for Advanced Studies, University of the Philippines, Quezon City, Philippines; 3 times a year; Editor Luis V. Teodoro, Jr.

Asian Survey. Periodicals Dept., University of California Press, 2223 Fulton St., Berkeley, Calif. 94720, U.S.A.; f. 1961; monthly; Editors Robert A. Scalapino and Leo E. Rose; circ. 3,500.

Asiatic Studies. Ajia Seikei Gakkai, Keio University, Mita, Minato-ku, Tokyo, Japan; quarterly.

Asiatische Forschungen. Otto Harrassowitz, Wiesbaden, Taunusstr. 5, Federal Republic of Germany; f. 1959; irregular; Editor Walther Heissig, Univ. Bonn, Regina Pacisureg 7.

Asiatische Studien/Etudes Asiatiques. Publ. A. Francke A.G. Verlag, Berne, Switzerland; for the Swiss Society for Asian Studies; Editor Paul Horsch, Regensdorferstrasse 153, 8049 Zürich, Switzerland; semi-annual.

L'Asie Nouvelle. 97 rue St. Lazare, 75009 Paris, France; bi-monthly; Dir. René Finkelstein.

Asien-Bibliographie. Asien Bucherei, D-359 Bad Wildungen, Federal Republic of Germany; quarterly.

Australian Book Review. 27 Park Rd., Kensington Park, S. Aust.; f. 1962; monthly; Editors Max Harris, Rosemary Wighton.

Australian Geographer. Geographical Society of New South Wales, Science House, Gloucester St., Sydney, N.S.W. 2000, Australia; f. 1928; Editor Dr. Philip Tilley.

Australian Outlook. Australian Institute of International Affairs, Box E 181, Post Office, Canberra, Australia; 3 times a year.

Australian Quarterly. Australian Institute of Political Science, 84½ Pitt St., Sydney, N.S.W. 2000, Australia; f. 1929; quarterly; Editor G. G. Masterman.

Bibliotheca Orientalis. Published by Netherlands Institute for the Near East, Noordeindsplein 4-6, Leiden, Netherlands; f. 1943; Editors E. van Donzel, H. J. A. de Meulanaere, C. Nijiland; bi-monthly.

Bulletin of Indonesian Economic Studies. Dept. of Economics, Research School of Pacific Studies, Australian National University, Box 4, P.O., Canberra, A.C.T. 2600, Australia; 3 times yearly.

Bulletin of the School of Oriental and African Studies. School of Oriental and African Studies, University of London, Malet St., London, WC1E 7HP, England; f. 1917; 3 issues annually.

Central Asiatic Journal. Otto Harrassowitz, Wiesbaden, Taunusstr. 5, Federal Republic of Germany, and N.V. Uitgeverij Mouton & Co., The Hague, Herderstraat 5, Netherlands; English language; languages, literature, history and archaeology; annual; Editor-in-Chief K. Jahn.

China Quarterly. Contemporary China Institute, School of Oriental and African Studies, Malet St., London, WC1E 7HP, England; f. 1959; all aspects of 20th.-century China, including Taiwan and the overseas Chinese; quarterly; Editor Dick Wilson.

China Reconstructs. China Welfare Institute, Peking, People's Republic of China; economic, social and cultural affairs; illustrated; English, Spanish, French, Russian and Arabic editions; monthly.

China Report. Centre for the Study of Developing Societies, 29 Rajpur Rd., Delhi 110054, India; topical notes and research articles, book reviews, and documentation; bi-monthly; Editor C. R. M. Rao.

CHINESE CULTURE. Institute for Advanced Chinese Studies, Box 12, Yang Ming Shan, Taiwan; f. 1957; English language; quarterly; Editor Dr. CHANG CHI-YUN.

CHUNG CHI JOURNAL. Research Institute of Far Eastern Studies, Chung Chi College, Chinese University of Hong Kong, Shatin, N.T., Hong Kong; f. 1961; semi-annual; Editor Dr. A. T. ROY.

CONTEMPORARY CHINA. University of Hong Kong, Hong Kong.

CONTEMPORARY JAPAN. Foreign Affairs Association of Japan, Togyo Kaikan, 7, 1-chome, Yuraku-cho, Tokyo, Japan; English language; quarterly.

EAST AND WEST. Istituto Italiano per il Medio e l'Estremo Oriente (ISMEO), Palazzo Brancaccio, via Merulana 248, Rome, Italy; f. 1950; quarterly.

EAST ASIAN CULTURAL STUDIES. Centre for East Asian Cultural Studies, c/o The Toyo Bunko, Honkomagome 2-chome, 28-21, Bunkyo-ku, Tokyo, 113 Japan; f. 1961; quarterly; Editor Prof. K. ENOKI.

EASTERN CULTURE RESEARCH JOURNAL. Sung Kyun Kwan University, Seoul, Republic of Korea.

EASTERN ECONOMIST. United Commercial Bank Building, Parliament St., New Delhi, India; f. 1943; economic and financial weekly in English; Editor V. BALASUBRAMANIAN; printer and publisher R. P. AGARUALA.

ECONOMIST. 1-11 Yuraku-cho, Chiyoda-ku, Tokyo, Japan; f. 1923; economic weekly; Editorial Chief S. YAMAMOTO.

ESTUDIOS DE ASIA Y AFRICA. Centre for Asian and North African Studies, El Colegio de Mexico, Guanajuato 125, Mexico 7, D.F., Mexico; 3 times annually.

FAR EAST REPORTER. Box 1536, New York, N.Y. 10017, U.S.A.; f. 1952; 4 to 6 issues annually; Publisher MAUD RUSSELL.

FAR EAST TRADE AND DEVELOPMENT. Laurence French Publications Ltd., 3 Belsize Crescent, London, N.W.3, England; monthly; Editor LAURENCE FRENCH.

FAR EASTERN ECONOMIC REVIEW. Marina House, P.O.B. 160, Hong Kong; f. 1946; weekly; Editor DEREK DAVIES.

HARVARD EAST ASIAN MONOGRAPH. Harvard Univ. Press; published by Harvard Univ. E. Asian Research Center, 1737 Cambridge St., Cambridge, Mass. 02138, U.S.A.

HARVARD JOURNAL OF ASIATIC STUDIES. Harvard-Yen-ching Institute, 2 Divinity Ave., Mass. 02138, U.S.A.; f. 1936.

INDIA QUARTERLY. c/o Asia Publishing House, Calicut St., Ballard Estate, Bombay 1, India; f. 1953; journal of the Indian Council of World Affairs; English language; quarterly; Editor S. L. POPLAI.

INDIAN AND FOREIGN REVIEW. India Ministry of Information and Broadcasting, Publications Division, Government of India, Old Secretariat, New Delhi 6, India.

INDIAN ECONOMIC JOURNAL. Department of Economics, University of Bombay, Bombay 1, India; English language; quarterly.

INDIAN LITERATURE. Sahitya Akademi, Rabindra Bhavan, 35 Ferozeshah Rd., New Delhi, India; English language; bi-monthly.

INDIAN STUDIES. 3 Sanbhunath Pandit St., Calcutta 20, India; English language; quarterly; Editor DEBIPRASAD CHATTOPADHYAYA.

INDICA. Heras Institute of Indian History and Culture, St. Xavier's College, Bombay 400001, India; English language; twice yearly; Editor A. D'COSTA.

INDO-ASIA. Publ. Kohlhammer G.m.b.H., Stuttgart, for Deutsch-Indische Gesellschaft, D-7000 Stuttgart 1, Charlottenplatz 17, Federal Republic of Germany; political, cultural and economic studies; German language, quarterly; Editor Dr. GISELHER WIRSING.

INTERNATIONAL GUIDE TO INDIC STUDIES. American Bibliographic Service, Darien, Conn., 06820 U.S.A.; f. 1961; a continuous index to periodical literature.

INTERNATIONAL STUDIES. Publ. by Vikas Publishing House Pvt. Ltd., New Delhi 110002, India; for the School of International Studies, Jawaharlal Nehru University, New Delhi 110057, India; English language; quarterly; Editor M .S. AGWANI.

ISLAMIC CULTURE. Islamic Culture Board, Post Box 171, opp. Osmania University Post Office, Hyderabad 7, India; f. 1927; quarterly.

JAIN JOURNAL. P 25 Kalakar St., Calcutta 7, India; English language; quarterly; Editor GANESH LALWANI.

JAPAN QUARTERLY. Asahi Shimbun Kaikan, Yuraku-cho, Chiyoda-ku, Tokyo, Japan; English language; quarterly; Editor EBATA KIYOSHI.

JOURNAL ASIATIQUE. Journal de la Société Asiatique, 3 rue Mazarine, Paris 6e, France; f. 1822; covers all phases of Oriental research; quarterly.

JOURNAL OF ASIAN AND AFRICAN STUDIES. Department of Sociology, York University, Toronto 12, Canada.

JOURNAL OF ASIAN HISTORY. Otto Harrassowitz, Wiesbaden, Taunusstr. 5, Federal Republic of Germany; f. 1967; bi-annual; Editor DENIS SINOR, Goodbody Hall, Indiana Univ., Bloomington, Ind. 47401, U.S.A.

JOURNAL OF ASIAN STUDIES. Association for Asian Studies, One Lane Hall, Ann Arbor, Mich. 48109, U.S.A.; f. 1941, formerly *Far Eastern Quarterly*; English language; quarterly.

JOURNAL OF ASIATIC STUDIES. Asiatic Research Center, Korea University, Anam-Dong, Seoul, Republic of Korea; f. 1958; quarterly; Editor LEE SANG-EUEN.

JOURNAL OF FAR EASTERN STUDIES. Institute of Far Eastern Studies, Yonsei University, Sodaemoon-ku, Seoul, Republic of Korea; f. 1954; annual.

JOURNAL OF CONTEMPORARY ASIA. P.O. 49010, Stockholm 49, Sweden; Editors Dr. MALCOLM CALDWELL, JONATHAN FAST, PETER LIMQUECO; f. 1970; English language; quarterly.

JOURNAL OF ORIENTAL RESEARCH. Kuppaswami Sastri Research Institute, Sanskrit College, Madras 4, India; quarterly (now issued in one consolidated annual volume).

JOURNAL OF ORIENTAL STUDIES. Centre of Asian Studies, University of Hong Kong, Hong Kong; Editors Dr. K. C. CHAN, Mr. CHUANG SHEN, Dr. WONG SIU KIT.

JOURNAL OF ORIENTAL STUDIES. Research Institute for Humanistic Studies, Kyoto University, 47 Kitashirakawa Sakyo-ku, Kyoto, Japan; annual.

JOURNAL OF PACIFIC HISTORY. Research School of Pacific Studies, Australian National University, Box 4, G.P.O., Canberra, A.C.T. 2601, Australia; f. 1966; twice yearly.

JOURNAL OF THE MALAYSIAN BRANCH OF THE ROYAL ASIATIC SOCIETY. c/o Arkib Negara Malaysia, 4th Floor, Government Offices Jalan Sultan, Petaling Jaya, Malaysia; f. 1877; Pres. Tan Sri NIK AHMED KAMIL; Hon. Sec. and Editor Tan Sri MUBIN SHEPPARD; twice yearly; monographs, reprints; membership 660.

JOURNAL OF THE SIAM SOCIETY. Central P.O.B. 65, Bangkok, Thailand; f. 1904; English language; semi-annual; Editor Mrs. NISA SHEANAKUL.

ASIA QUARTERLY. Centre Sud-Est Asiatique et de l'Extreme-Orient, 44 Av. Jeanne, 1050 Brussels; Dir. DANIEL ELLEGIERS; English language; quarterly.

JOURNAL OF SOUTH-EAST ASIAN STUDIES. Department of History, University of Singapore; f. 1970; published and distributed by FEP International Ltd.; Editor Dr. ERNEST CHEW; twice yearly; circ. 1,000.

JOURNAL OF THE AMERICAN ORIENTAL SOCIETY. American Oriental Society, 329 Sterling Memorial Library, New Haven, Conn., U.S.A.; f. 1842; Biblical studies, Ancient Near East, South Asia and Far East; quarterly.

JOURNAL OF THE ASIATIC SOCIETY. 1 Park St., Calcutta 16, India; English language; irregular.

JOURNAL OF THE BURMA RESEARCH SOCIETY. c/o University Library, University of Arts and Science, Rangoon, Burma; f. 1911; bi-annual.

JOURNAL OF THE ECONOMIC AND SOCIAL HISTORY OF THE ORIENT. Publ. E. J. Brill, Oude Rijn 33a, Leiden, Netherlands; f. 1957; three times a year; English, French and German text.

JOURNAL OF THE ORIENTAL SOCIETY OF AUSTRALIA. Morgan's Book Shop, 104 Bathurst Rd., Sydney, N.S.W., Australia; f. 1961; semi-annual; Editor Prof. A. R. DAVIS.

JOURNAL OF TROPICAL GEOGRAPHY. Departments of Geography, University of Singapore and University of Malaya, Singapore and Kuala Lumpur, Malaysia; f. 1953; bi-annual; Editor OOI JIN-BEE.

AL-MAARIF. Institute of Islamic Culture, Club Rd., Lahore, Pakistan; f. 1955/68; monthly; Editor S. H. RAZZAQI; Chair. Prof. M. SAEED SHEIKH; Sec. M. ASHRAF DARR.

MIZAN SUPPLEMENT B: SOVIET AND CHINESE REPORTS ON SOUTH AND SOUTH-EAST ASIA. Publ. Central Asian Research Centre, 1B Parkfield St., London, N.W.1, England; f. 1966; bi-monthly.

MODERN ASIA. P.O.B. 770, Hong Kong; f. 1967; bi-monthly; Editor DAVID J. ROADS.

MODERN ASIAN STUDIES. Cambridge University Press, Bentley House, 200 Euston Rd., London, N.W.1, England; f. 1967; quarterly; Editor Dr. GORDON JOHNSON.

MONDES ASIATIQUES. 54 rue de Varenne, 75007 Paris, France; French quarterly; Editor FRANCOIS JOYAUX.

MONGOLIAN STUDIES. Journal of the Mongolia Society. P.O.B. 606, Bloomington, Ind. 47401, U.S.A.; f. 1962; annual; Orientalist periodical emphasizing Mongolia and Inner Asia of all periods; Dir. Prof. Dr. JOHN R. KRUEGER.

LE MUSÉON. B.P. 41, Louvain, Belgium; f. 1882; review of Oriental studies; two double vols. a year; Editor Prof. G. GARITTE, Beukenlaan 9, Héverlé-Louvain.

NARODY ASII I AFRIKI (Istoriya, Ekonomika, Kultura). 13 Khohlovsky per., Moscow 2 , U.S.S.R.; Akad. Nauk S.S.S.R., Institut Vostokovedeniya, Institut Afriki, Moscow, U.S.S.R.; f. 1955; bi-monthly; Editor-in-Chief Prof. I. S. BRAGINSKY.

NEW GUINEA RESEARCH BULLETIN. Australian National University Press, P.O.B. 4, Canberra, A.C.T. 2600, Australia; at least 5 times a year.

OCEANIA. The University, Sydney, N.S.W., Australia; f. 1930; anthropology; quarterly; Editor A. P. ELIKN.

ORIENS. International Society for Oriental Research, Frankfurt/Main, Federal Republic of Germany; f. 1948; articles in German, French and English, on the history and archaeology of the Near and Far East; annual; Editor Prof. Dr. R. SELLHEIM.

ORIENS. Milletlerarası Sark Tetkikleri Cemiyeti, Türkiyat Enstitüsü, Istanbul University, Bayezit, Istanbul, Turkey; f. 1948; Editor F. KÖPRÜLÜ.

ORIENS EXTREMUS. Publ. Otto Harrassowitz, Wiesbaden, Taunusstr. 5, Federal Republic of Germany; f. 1954; German and English language; semi-annual; Editors O. BENL, W. FRANKE, W. FUCHS.

ORIENTAL ECONOMIST. Hongoku-cho, Nihonbashi, Chuo-ku, Tokyo, Japan; f. 1934; economics and politics; monthly; Editor K. UKAJI.

ORIENTALISTISCHE LITERATURZEITUNG. Akademie der Wissenschaften des DDR, 108 Berlin, Leipzigerstr. 3-4, German Democratic Republic; f. 1898; bibliography of Oriental studies; monthly; Editor Prof. Dr. F. HINTZE.

OSTASIATISCHE FORSCHUNGEN. Papers produced by the Sinology Section of the Deutsche Akademie der Wissenschaften, Akademei-Verlag, 108 Berlin, Leipziger Str. 3-4; f. 1960.

PACIFIC AFFAIRS. Publishers University of British Columbia, Vancouver B.C., V6T IW5 Canada; f. 1928; covers political, economic, social and diplomatic problems of eastern and southern Asia and Australasia; quarterly; Editor WILLIAM L. HOLLAND.

PACIFIC COMMUNITY. P.O.B. 2043S, G.P.O., Melbourne 3001, Australia; f. 1969; quarterly; Asian and Pacific Affairs; Journal of the Pacific Institute; circ. 600; Published by Hawthorn Press; Editor CHRISTOPHER CLARK.

PACIFIC COMMUNITY. Jiji Press Ltd., Central P.O.B. 1007, Tokyo, Japan; f. April 1969; political, economic, diplomatic, cultural, military, etc.; quarterly (Jan., April, July, Oct.); Editor KIKUO SATO; Managing Editor NORIO IGUCHI.

PACIFIC HISTORICAL REVIEW. Pacific Coast Branch, American Historical Society, c/o University of California Press, Berkeley, Calif. 94720, U.S.A.; f. 1932; quarterly; Editor NORRIS HUNDLEY; circ. 1,870.

PACIFIC ISLANDS MONTHLY. Pacific Publications (Aust.) Pty. Ltd., 76 Clarence St., Sydney 2000, N.S.W., Australia; f. 1930; news magazine of the South Pacific; monthly; Editor JOHN CARTER.

PACIFIC SOCIOLOGICAL REVIEW. Pacific Sociological Association, Dept. of Sociology, Arizona State University, U.S.A.

PACIFIC VIEWPOINT. Victoria University, Private Bag, P.O. Wellington, New Zealand; f. 1960; semi-annual; Editors Prof. R. F. WATTERS, Dr. J. M. KIRBY.

PAKISTAN DEVELOPMENT REVIEW. Pakistan Institute of Development Economics, P.O. Box 1091, Islamabad, Pakistan; f. 1961, fmrly. *The Economic Digest*; quarterly; Editor M. L. QURESHI.

PAKISTAN HORIZON. Pakistan Institute of International Affairs; Strachen Rd., Karachi, Pakistan; f. 1948; English language; quarterly; Editor K. SARWAR HASSAN.

POPULATION REVIEW. P.O.B. 3030, New Delhi 1, India; f. 1956; English language; quarterly; Editor Dr. S. CHANDRASEKHAR.

PROBLEMS IN THE EASTERN WORLD. Institute for Foreign Studies, P.O.B. 1538, Tokyo, Japan; f. 1961; occasional; Editor TAIJIRO ICHIKAWA.

PRZEGLĄD ORIENTALISTYCZNY. Polish Oriental Society, Warsaw, ul. Śniadeckich 8, Poland; quarterly.

QUARTERLY CHECK-LIST OF ORIENTAL STUDIES. American Bibliographic Service, Darien, Conn. 06820, U.S.A.; f. 1959; international index of current books, monographs, brochures and separates.

RESEARCH PAPERS IN GEOGRAPHY. Published twice-yearly by the Dept. of Geography, Sydney University and the Geographical Society of New South Wales, Science House, Gloucester St., Sydney, N.S.W. 2000, Australia.

RIVISTA DEGLI STUDI ORIENTALI. Scuola Orientale, University of Rome, Rome, Italy; f. 1907; quarterly; Publisher GIOVANNI BARDI.

ROCZNIK ORIENTALISTYCZNY. Grójecka 17, Warsaw, Poland; f. 1915; Editor-in-Chief EDWARD TRYJARSKI; Sec. JANUSZ DANECKI; semi-annual.

ROYAL ASIATIC SOCIETY OF GREAT BRITAIN AND IRELAND JOURNAL. 56 Queen Anne St., London, W1M 9LA, England; f. 1834; covers all phases of Oriental research.

SHANKAR'S WEEKLY. Odeon Top, Connaught Place, New Delhi, India; f. 1948; English language; comment and news; weekly; Editor K. S. PILLAI.

SOUTH EAST ASIA QUARTERLY. Central Philippine University, Iloilo City, Philippines; English language; quarterly.

SOUTH PACIFIC BULLETIN. South Pacific Commission, Box 306 Haymarket, N.S.W., Australia 2000; f. 1951; quarterly; English and French editions; Editor C. E. BIRCHMEIER.

STATESMAN. Chowringhee Square, New Delhi, India; f. 1875; overseas weekly; English language.

STUDIA ORIENTALIA. Societas Orientalis Fennica,Helsinki 17, Snellmaninkatu 9-11, Finland; f. 1925; Editor Dr. HEIKKI PALVA.

SURVEY OF PEOPLE'S REPUBLIC OF CHINA PRESS. U.S. Consulate-General, Hong Kong.

T'OUNG PAO. Publ. E. J. Brill, Oude Rijn 33a, Leiden, Netherlands, for C.N.R.S., Paris and Netherlands Organization for the Advancement of Pure Research, The Hague; f. 1890; irregular; a leading journal of Far Eastern studies; Editors PAUL DEMIÉVILLE, A. F. P. HULSEWE.

UNITED ASIA. 12 Rampart Row, Bombay 1, India; f. 1948; English language; bi-monthly; Editor-in-Chief G. S. POHEKAR.

UNIVERSITY OF MANILA JOURNAL OF EAST ASIATIC STUDIES. 546 Dr. M. V. de los Santos St., Manila, Philippines; f. 1951; quarterly; Editor CHARLES O. HOUSTON.

WALKABOUT. 18 Collins St., Melbourne, Vic., Australia; f. 1934; magazine of the Australian way of life; monthly; Editor J. Ross.

WIENER ZEITSCHRIFT FÜR DIE KUNDE DES MORGENLÄNDES. Oriental Institute of the University of Vienna, A-1010 Wien 1, Universitätstrasse 7/V, Austria; annual.

WORLD FEATURE SERVICES LTD. (Asia-F) -8, Bhagat Singh Marg, New Delhi-110001, India; f. 1971; news features; and at 134 Lower Marsh, Westminster Bridge Rd., London, S.E.1; daily.

ZEITSCHRIFT DER DEUTSCHE MORGENLÄNDISCHE GESELLSCHAFT. Deutsche Morgenländische Gesellschaft, 355 Marburg/Lahn, Postfach 642, Federal Republic of Germany; f. 1948; covers the history, languages and literature of the Orient; semi-annual.

ZEITSCHRIFT DER DEUTSCHEN MORGENLÄNDISCHEN GESELLSCHAFT. Deutsche Morgenländische Gesellschaft, 355 Marburg/Lahn, Postfach 642, Federal Republic of Germany; f. 1948; covers the history, languages and literature of the Orient; semi-annual.

ZENTRALASIATISCHE STUDIEN. Publ. Otto Harrassowitz, Wiesbaden, Taunusstr. 5, Federal Republic of Germany for the Seminar für Sprache und Kulturwissenschaft Zentralasiens der Universität Bonn; f. 1967; annual.